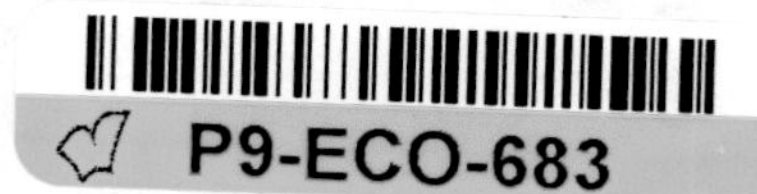

COMICS VALUES ANNUAL

2001 EDITION

THE COMIC BOOK PRICE GUIDE

by Alex G. Malloy

edited by Stuart W. Wells III

features editor: Robert J. Sodaro

Published by

Antique Trader Books, a division of

Please call or write for your free catalog of publications.
Our toll-free number to place an order or obtain a free catalog is 800-258-0929 or please use our regular business telephone 715-445-2214 for editorial comment and further information.

Designed by Stuart W. Wells III

ISBN: 0-87349-260-9

Printed in the United States of America

CONTENTS

Welcome to the 21st Century

By Alex G. Malloy

If ever in the history of the comic industry, the industry itself was in need of a drastic overhaul this is it. Just as Stan Lee, Jack Kirby, Steve Ditko, and the rest of the fledgling Marvel Comics revitalized the industry back in the early 1960s; the direct sales market revitalized it in the 1970s, and the radical approach of Image, Malibu, and the concept of creator/owner comics revitalized it in the 1980s, the industry once more needs a serious shot in the arm. Sure, sure, the industry is still limping along, and there are still many bright spots, but overall, we need a major revitalization. No longer can we simply go along the way we've been going for the past several years. Mike Gold, the subject of our feature interview discusses that at length in this volume.

Yes, we understand that last year (2000) gave us the huge smash hit *X-Men* movie, which set new standards for comic book movies, and we further understand that 2001 and beyond promises us not only the long-awaited *Spider-Man* movie (although sans James "*Terminator*, *Titanic*" Cameron in the director's chair and with Tobey Maguire as Peter Parker/Spider-Man), but also *Batman Year 1*. We also know that Mirimax has optioned numerous Marvel characters, including another *Blade* flick once again starring Wesley Snipes.)

Of course we know all of those things. But we still insist that comic books themselves are desperately in need of salvation. As we close out the 20th century, word on the street is that Marvel Comics will run out of money before the end of the year. (As we go to press well before that, Marvel just might be out of business before we hit the shelves. A darn shame if it occurs). Feature editor Robert J. Sodaro indicated to us that in a previous conversation with Mike Gold they discussed the very real possibility of a world without Spider-Man, a concept that Sodaro, by his own admission, a major Spider-fan, had trouble accepting. Gold countered that an earlier generation could have made the same comment about Zorro, The Lone Ranger, Doc Savage, Tarzan, Sherlock Holmes or a number of other literary icons.

Well, perhaps it is time that we all get our heads around that concept. Part of this is because of what the disastrous gold-foil alternate covers of the last decade have done to this industry. We spent far too much time, energy, and effort paying more attention to the packaging of comics than to the substance. This resulted in the former powerhouse of Marvel Comics being so desperate for a movie franchise that it virtually signed away all licensing rights to the *X-Men* movie, in order to cut a deal to get the film made. According to all reliable sources, none (or very little) of the profits resulting from the licensing rights to the movie went back into the house of ideas itself. Thus, while the film itself made a metric ton of dough, Marvel Comics' publishing division made nil.

As for the rest of the field; it consists of DC (which has a couple of Batman films in the works), Image, Dark Horse, and a pileup of small publishers. We personally believe that the industry will survive (with or without Marvel), and that there will always be comic books to sit down, read, and enjoy. While we are not certain who the players will be, or what genre will emerge or remain, or even what form the comics themselves will take, we know that comic books themselves are still a viable form of entertainment, and will continue well into this new century.

As always, we'd like to thank those people who have helped us get this far, the various publishers, creators, and fans who publish, create, and read comics; our own publishers at Krause; editor Stuart Wells, III (who laid the entire thing out and is the keeper of our archives), feature editor Robert J. Sodaro, featured guest Mike Gold, and everyone else who had a hand in getting this latest volume of CVA into your hands.

To Infinity and Beyond... the Future of Comics

An interview with Mike Gold

By Robert J. Sodaro

There are probably many people reading this who have no idea who Mike Gold is, or why he rates either a feature interview in CVA or at the very least an interview of this length. Then there are people who may know who he is, and his contribution to the field, but are still fuzzy about some of his background. Did you know that not only does he have a deep commitment to youth education, and social services, but that he co-created the National Runaway Switchboard? How about that he once helped smuggle letters from POWs in 1969 out of Vietnam and to the U.S. press? Or even that he worked for Abbie Hoffman and the infamous Chicago Seven? (Even this interviewer, who has known him for several years, and has interviewed him a number of times didn't know that last one.)

Still, it has been his many accomplishments to the field of comics that has landed him this slot. These include helping to found and establish the direct sales market, co-founding First Comics with its innovative approach to publishing, his work as a senior editor at DC, and as a retailer working with the ill-fated Dream Factory chain of comic shops. But rather than us expounding at length about his many accomplishments, we're going to let him do that.

****

Bob Sodaro: Let's start off with something easy. How did you get into comics?

Mike Gold: That's an interesting question. I actually started out doing some consulting work for some of the retailers in the Midwest, primarily in Chicago, and in the general Midwest area. This was at the very outset of the direct sales business. It was when Phil Seuling started up his distribution company, but he only had DC. Marvel hadn't jumped in on it yet, and I was helping to promote some of theses stores and comics as a hobby throughout the media primarily in the Midwest, but also nationally.

Bob: You hail from Chicago, don't you?

Mike: Oh yeah, sure. Really, at the time, I was both a writer — as in writing for publications that would ostensibly pay me — and broadcaster where I did get paid. I was on radio in Chicago for seven years, and I was doing a lot of work in the youth social services field. I had worked in doing communication and education work for drug-abuse prevention program. I co-created the National Runaway Switchboard program. That was sort of the day job. Back in those days I didn't like sleeping, I think. The comic book thing happened sort of organically. By helping some of these guys promote their stores and helping the hobby be promoted both locally and nationally, that sort of got me into the early days of the direct sales market, as my sort of coercing retailers into getting involved. I thought that it was a good thing, and thought it would help establish the hobby. From there I, and a number of other people, worked on creating the Chicago ComiCon.

Bob: What year was this?

Mike: The first ComicCon was in '76. So, I started working on that in '75. I had already been working with these retailers for several years before that. I can point out that I had also done some freelance work for newspaper syndicates before that as well, for newspaper comic strips, as opposed to comic books. My actual real start was in 1965 (five or six — I think it was '65), working as sort of an intern for the old National Newspaper Syndicate working on *Buck Rogers*, among other thing. That's how I really got my start. So it all kind of grew organically from there. But again, we started up the Chicago ComicCon in '75, very early '76, like Feb. '76, we were looking around for guests of honor. We had Harvey Kurtzman and Stan Lee lined up for our first Chicago ComicCon, and Jenette Kahn was just made Publisher at DC. I knew Jenette from my work in the Social Services field — because one of the magazines that she was publishing for Scholastic Press really jumped on the National Runway Switchboard program that I had co-created. She gave us a lot of promotion and publicity. I worked very closely with one of their editor/writers, and Jenette and I got to know each other through that. So when she became publisher at DC I was first astonished. Wow, this woman I know from Scholastic is the publisher at DC. So I called her up, and I congratulated her, and I invited her to become our third guest of honor at the first Chicago ComicCon. She and I just started talking, and within about three or four weeks of conversation — taking time out for meals and naps and stuff — she had me come out to New York because Neal Adams was looking for somebody to be sort of a manager of Continuity Associates. I was really ambivalent about that. I had known Neal from the Organic Theater Days (from Stuart Gordon's Organic Theater, which is a theater company that had produced the play *Warp*).

Warp #2, © First Comics

Bob: Yeah, I was going to say, didn't you work on *Warp*?

Mike: Yeah I did work on the Organic Theater, but I didn't work on *Warp*. I was a fanboy with *Warp*.

Bob: I still have a *Warp* poster.

Mike: I had a number of friends who were actors, and a number of friends of mine were involved in the Organic Theater, and a couple of them were in *Warp*. This is around 1971, and that's where I met Neal. It's not that I didn't like Neal, of course like most comic fans at the time, I worshiped Neal.

Bob: Of course, who didn't? (*Neal Adams was the subject of* CVA*'s 1996 cover feature interview* — ed.) Neal was our Eric Clapton, as it were.

Mike: Yeah, I think that's true. I think that's very true.

Bob: It's probably still true.

Mike: I wasn't really keen on the idea of moving to New York and working in a business capacity for Continuity Associates, but I figured, "What the Hell?" Jenette was nice enough to invite me out, and the fanboy in me wanted to take the tour of DC Comics, and physically meet Jenette. Our entire relationship at that point was over the telephone. I flew out to New York, and Neal didn't show up for the lunch. So Jenette and I wound up having a three-or four-hour conversation at Charley O's. (At that time there was only one Charley O's, in New York.) We were sort of scaring people around us because, for four hours, we were talking passionately about comics — where it should be and where it's been — what it means, and how to fix it all, you know. I had a swell time and I flew back to Chicago having had a swell day. The next day Jenette calls up and says, "You know, I don't think I want you to work for Neal." And I'm thinking, OK (laughter), I mean, I wasn't really keen on the idea anyway. She says, "I want you to work for me." Ah, whole other thing, now. Now I'm all of a sudden offered a job at DC Comics. So, I was, as they say in the business, "between radio jobs."

(General laughter)

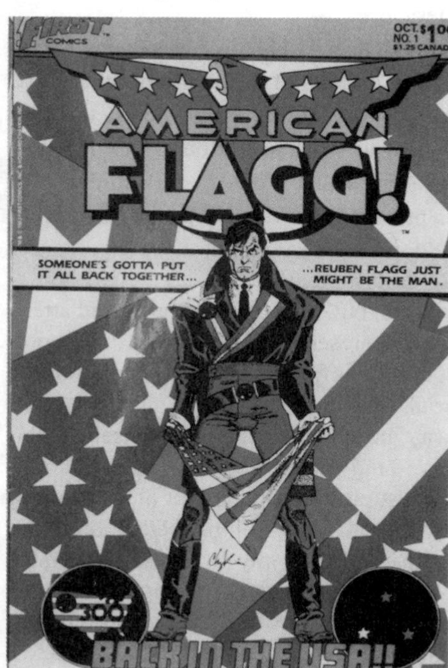

American Flagg #1, © Howard Chaykin

Bob: I know a guy in radio who says he was "de-hired" from a radio station.

Mike: Oh yeah, when it happens it's the best thing in the world. (Laughter) It's not a job that carries a lot of security.

Bob: Having sometimes worked in radio, or rather having not worked in radio sometimes myself, I know exactly what you mean by that.

Mike: Sure. But, since this was a period of time when I was really lucky to have still been able to do free-form radio as long as I had. I started in 1969, this is now 1976. I had pretty much left my own free will the radio station I had been working for because they went into rigid play lists, and I didn't want to do that. So I didn't have a radio job to keep me in Chicago, I was still doing work with the Runaway program with a few social services agencies, and freelance writing you can do anywhere; if you can do it at all (laughter).

Bob: Which we've proven that you

Badger #16, © First Comics

can't.

Mike: Well, there are good days and bad days. So I figured, what the heck, maybe I should try this thing. It fulfills a fanboy dream and working for Warner Communications was kind of a cool idea, or seemed like a cool idea at the time.

Bob: I'm sure that in the mid-1970s it **was** a cool idea.

Mike: So in '76 I went out there, and pretty much my job at that time was to increase DC's presence in the direct sales market. Which was obvious because I knew a lot about it having increased the retailer's presence in the direct sales market over the past several years. And Jenette had really liked that first Chicago ComicCon and all that. I had already taken this job at that point. That's really how I got into the comic book business. Oh, incidentally, 10 years earlier, I sort of had that brush with the comic strip business.

Bob: Was it then that you worked in an editorial capacity at DC or was that later on?

Mike: That was later on. My job, in addition to doing sort of the promotions stuff, you do — really Marketing 101 stuff — I created the first newsletter that would go to the retailers, to advise them of what would be in that month's comic books. Previously, it was just a list. But I would write little articles about each comic book that DC was publishing. Nobody else had done that in the direct-sales market before. We did that every month.

Bob: Well, there was no direct sales market prior to that.

Mike: Well, it had been going on for a few years, but, nobody had really paid attention to it, and then, I'd also manage DC's presence at the major comic book shows. In turn I would take the input that I got from fans and — more important — from retailers, back to editorial, back to Joe Orlando, primarily, and around '77 that started working its way into the comicbooks themselves. We started to pay attention to what was going on in the direct sales market. Previously DC's attitude was fans are just pimples on the butt of the reading public. One could argue that that was, and — if they still paid attention to the general public — that would still be true. During my two years I literally quadrupled DC's sales in the direct sales market, just by paying attention to it. Both ways, by representing the needs and desires of the fans and retailers to editorial and by representing the company to the fans and the retailers.

Bob: Not to skip over any of the important stuff you did, but eventually you left DC and returned to Chicago to found First Comics.

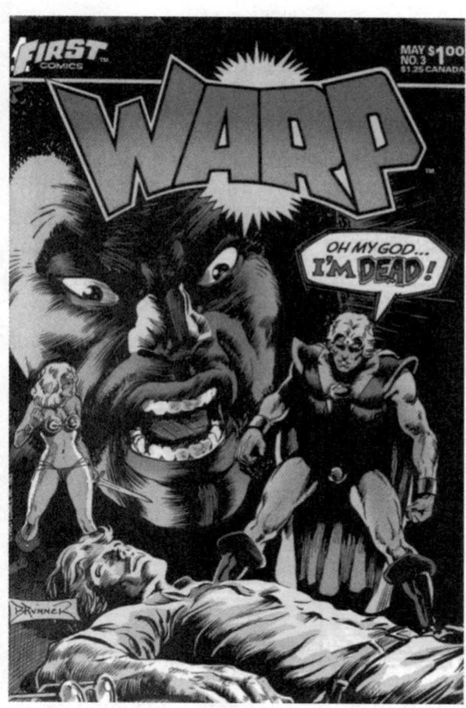

Warp #3, © First Comics

Mike: Well, there's a little bit of time between them. I had taken the job with the intention of staying either one or two years; certainly no more than two years. I had other things that I had wanted to accomplish. I had also made some promises to some people, particularly back in the social services field. Quite literally, a lawyer friend of mine, who was on the board of directors of one of this social service organizations, had called me to remind me that I was due back. That was fine, I went back. Remember the lawyer, because he's going to pop up in my life story in a minute.

Bob: I think I know part of this story already, but go on.

Mike: So I did that, and we created a few other social service programs. I have a real dedication to the youth social services field, political issues and all that as well. But, I'm still a fanboy and I really enjoyed my time at DC. Then Jim Steranko, of all people, had recommended to Rick Obidiah — who was the producer of the Organic Theater at that point — that Rick get a hold of me to help promote the re-launch of *Warp*. *Warp* had been tied up in litigation. Rick called me up, and explained who he was and that they were bringing *Warp* back. I already knew that part because, again, I have friends who were in the cast of the Organic Theater. The Organic Theater, by the way is a place where guys like Joe Mantegna and Denis Franz came from. It's really a major theater company. It was a hell of a blast working with Stuart Gordon and those people. So, I meet with Rick. He explained to the their plans for the revival of *Warp* and his main goal is to get the comic book fans and science fiction fans into the theater to be really excited about it. Because that could provide the framework that would keep the play alive in order to find its own audience. I agreed with that and we did that. Keeping in mind that *Warp* is really three plays, not just one. It's a major commitment to mount that production. So we did all of that, and somewhere along the way I turned to Obidiah, and said, "You know, this is such a solid, traditional comic book story, you could probably make a comic book out of this. He said, "OK, great, let's do that." I said, fine, and I became his consultant in terms of how to market that to DC or Marvel. We arranged for a premiere of *Warp 2*, which most New Yorkers hadn't seen because when it played on Broadway five or ten years earlier, it bombed after a week or two. People just didn't understand it. This was five years before *Star Wars*. People didn't understand what this stuff was all about. (Laughter) *People* were just dumbfounded. But the fans, who were now in the comic book business, were fascinated by it, so we held a special performance, a Saturday evening performance, during the Chicago ComicCon of *Warp 2*, which none of these people had seen. We knew full well, that if we played our cards right, we would get the interest of both DC and Marvel. I explained to Rick exactly how that would come out. Exactly how Paul Levitz (DC), would treat him, Exactly how Jim Shooter (Marvel), would treat him. Which essentially was that Paul would make all of these sort of offers — and I explained what those offers meant — and then that Jim would say, "Oh, Marvel's bigger and better, we'll beat DC." And that's exactly how it came down. But, before Rick actually went to New York to have those business meetings, for the licensing end of things, I told Rick, "There's something you should know. This is what the direct sales business is all about, and we could publish our own comics for the direct sales business." Essentially I was just talking about *Warp* at that time. "You know if you put the mechanics together, you should put some money into it and have a distribution system you can advertise your costs and do more books." Rick said, "No, no. That isn't what I want to do. I just want to license this stuff and sign the paychecks." I said, "Oh, you want money for this?"

(General laughter)

Bob: Oh, well that's different!

Mike: That's different. If you want to make money then this is what's going to happen; and I gave him sort of a hit list of the top 25 things that are going to happen during this negotiations. Rick looked at me and said, "Oh, you're an idiot. This is never going to happen. These people are professional business people they would never act like this." I said that the comic books business is a cottage industry. DC might be owned by Warner Communications, but it's certainly not in the driver's seat of Warner Communications. There's a movie studio and a record industry and the book publishers and somewhere way down on the list, there is DC Comics. It's really a cottage industry. So Rick went to New York and had the conversations. In the middle of the day that he got there, he calls me and said, "You're absolutely right. Every single thing on your list of the things that you predicted happened. Let's do it ourselves." He didn't totally throw in the towel, he continued negotiating with them in case we couldn't raise the money or we couldn't get off the ground. He didn't want to screw up the property, which was the right thing to do. He flew back from New York the following day, which was a lot, considering he's a New Yorker, and I came up with the name First Comics that next day and, boom, That's how First Comics started.

Bob: At first you came out with a number of very cool comics including, *American Flagg* by Howard Chaykin…

Mike: I had a marketing plan which was editorial driven. Which was, we would start off with *Warp*, because that was the property that everybody was interested in seeing, because the play was so hot and the industry was so hot on it. I really didn't have any plans or any belief that *Warp* was going to be a perennial title. Part of that overall plan was to take an artist who was pissed off at the comic book industry and bring him back into the fold and say, "Look, First Comics is so great, that we got, 'Blank' back. 'Blank' being Frank Brunner.

American Flagg #3, © Howard Chaykin

Next I wanted to bring back a comic by the people who created it. In this case it was *E-Man* with Joe Staton, who I wanted as my art director. By this point I had already done a comic book with Joe Staton. We had done a promotional comic book, called *Weird Organic Tales* for the Organic Theater. By this point Rick was no longer involved with the Organic Theater, but Joe Staton and Bruce Paterson were the artists on that 16-page promotional comic. So I offered Joe the art director job, now Joe's a swell guy and an enormously creative talent and I really wanted him as one of the founding fathers of First Comics. So he was already involved, let's see if we can get the rights to *E-Man* from Charlton. Which we did, we bought them out from Charlton under a plan that eventually Joe would reimburse us for our expenses, and then he would own it. Nick Cuti couldn't write it because he was editing over at DC and DC wouldn't give him dispensation to write for another publisher. Which is understandable. The third thing was a brand new, completely original comic from an established talent, which was *Jon Sable Freelance*, from Mike Grell. (*Mike Grell was the* CVA *feature interview in 1997*—ed.) The fourth book was *Starslayer*, which was an established book, but I wanted to put new talent on it, brand new talent. That's where John Ostrander came in. I'd know John Ostrander since about '71. He had co-written a play for the Organic Theater. He was an actor as well. While he didn't perform with the Organic Theater, he had performed at the Goodwin Theater, which is a more prestigious theater. I shouldn't say more prestigious, but an extremely prestigious theater. We brought in Lenin Deisol and Tim Truman to draw it. New talent — the public never heard of John Ostrander or Tim Truman. The fourth title proved that we could create new talent. The fifth comic was an extreme title. Something that DC or Marvel would not handle at that point in time, by an established guy. That's how we got to *American Flagg* by Howard Chaykin. Howard had quit the comics business. I had actually talked him back in. I'm not sure he's ever forgiven me for that.

(General Laughter)

Bob: I've spoken to Howard a number of times, and you're probably right.

Mike: The biggest problem that has always faced the comic book industry — is it a creative force where the creativity leads, or is it a commercial force? That's true for all commercial media, except for television. In comics, it's a little different. If you're an extremely successful comic book, you're still only going to make a certain amount of money. Hopefully, the creators will share fairly

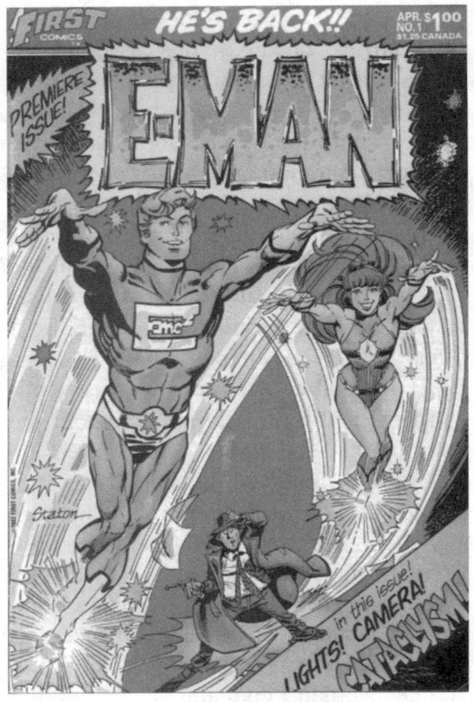

E-Man #1, © *First Comics*

in that money. The publisher, at best, is only going to make a certain amount. But the merchandising has potential that can be very serious. As we've learned from everything since the *Batman* movie, and arguably the *Batman* TV show. (The licensing potential) is extraordinary. So, are you in the comic book licensing business, where you get the toys and TV, and the movie and the Underoos? Or are you in the comic book story telling business and you let that be the horse. What's the horse, what's the cart? Howard, who has spent most of the last 10 years or so in Hollywood, writing TV shows and that sort of thing, knows that. It's funny, he has worked for, really, the licensee end of things but, as a comic book creator, he wants to be a story teller. He's right that comic book stories are going to come when you are trying to write comic book stories, and not when you are trying to invent licensing deals. It's just that simple. Anyway, there was a sixth book that I had in the marketing plan that created First Comics. The sixth book was a title that was very extreme, like *American Flagg* — something that people like Marvel or DC wouldn't have published, and also done by people that nobody had heard of. That's where *Mars* by Mark Wheatley and Marc Hempel came in.

Bob: That was an amazing book.

Mike: Right. It really lost First Comics a lot of money in terms of the first print publishing itself. But in terms of prestige, in terms of getting people to see First Comics as a creative force. You'd expect something as creative as *American Flagg* from Howard Chaykin, but you had never heard or Wheatley and Hempel at that point. To see that we could develop something like that; that really made people take notice of us.

Bob: The thing that I loved about *American Flagg* was that, at that point, I was a young man. I was probably in my early 20s I believe, and it was the first comic I ever remember reading — or at least the first comic in a very, very long time — that assumed I got the joke. It assumed I understood what was going on. It didn't paint me a picture from the ground up with every single detail in it. Howard left stuff out, because he meant for you to get it.

Mike: We didn't footnote the book to death.

Bob: Right. And *Mars* was amazing because there were no captions in that first couple of books. It was just the story. There was nothing beyond that.

Mike: I have such enormous respect for Mark Wheatley and Marc Hempel. We did *Breathtaker* together at DC several years later — same thing. I have such

Jon Sable Freelance #14, © First Comics

respect for them. They have such a unique and original view, and still there 'til this day. Anyway, that's the First Comic story, and I could go on, and on and on.

Bob: I recall a storyline in *Sable* that revolved in part around smuggling information out of Vietnam, that peripherally involved you. I remember because as I read the story I recalled having read about the incident when I was younger. Some time after that I spoke to Mike Grell about it in an interview. I told him that I recalled the incident, or at least the factual elements of the incident. Which is when he told me that you were involved in the incident. Could you talk about that?

Mike: In 1969, 1970 — I spent three years working for Abbie Hoffman, in addition to all this other crap that I was doing

Bob: (Laughter) Oh my God!

Mike: One of those years was spent on the conspiracy trial, the Chicago Seven trial, which was really the Chicago Eight, but we were high, we couldn't count.

(General Laughter)

Mike: Part of that was in 1969, I think it was August — don't hold me to that — it was very clear, that the North Vietnamese were interested, as a gesture, in releasing some POWs. They wouldn't release them to the U.S. government; they wanted to release them to the peace movement. Rennie Davis was one of the defendants, went out with Bill Kunstler, to ultimately Vietnam and brought back those first POWs. I was involved in that, and mind you I was 19 at the time. I was involved in that in terms of first making the arrangements and all that other stuff. I was also handling a lot of the political activities around that, including in assisting in smuggling out of letters from other POWs towards being released. Smuggling those letters out of Hanoi through Germany to New York where I was waiting — well I wasn't waiting, I was an intimate part of that — but it was my responsibility to get those letters out after that. So that was kind of cool. Now all of a sudden I'm James Bond. We're smuggling these letters out, and doing the right thing, because I'm involved in getting the first POWs ever out of the Vietnam War. At the same time behind the Hanoi government's back and as well as behind the U.S. government's back smuggling out all of these letters of POWs who weren't being released. Yeah, I'm real proud of that one.

Bob: Hey, I'm just happy that I know you and that you did it.

Mike: (Laughter)

Bob: I swear I was reading that comic and saying, "Damn! I remember reading about this." Then when I spoke to Grell, he said, "Yeah that was Mike Gold

Starslayer #7, © First Comics

that was doing that." Which blew my mind because at that time you were just this guy I knew who was doing funny books.

Mike: Yeah, there's a lot of stuff in my background that didn't make it into my 30-second resume, and that's part of it. Obviously, if there's one thing that I'm most proud of in my life, it is this. It's right up there with working with early childhood education, which I'm really proud of as well.

Bob: Then you eventually left First Comics and went back to DC.

Mike: Yeah, for two good reasons. I disagreed with the way the company was being run. Now there were five board members. I was one, our business manager was another. Our business manager and I were out voted on almost everything, three to two. My problem was, we'd be having this cash-flow problem, or in some cases we'd be having some real money problems. Instead of getting better terms from the printer or from the engravers, or what have you, they just wanted to not pay the writers and artists.

Bob: Oh sure, instead of trying to get better deals, let's screw the creative staff. That's pretty typical.

Mike: Right. Which is a time-honored tradition.

Bob: One that still goes on today.

Mike: Not one that I care to be a part of. The business manager had quit the company for a variety of reasons. The other three people on the board were Rick Obidiah, who was the publisher, and a lawyer who was the lawyer from the social services agency that wanted me to leave DC back in 1978 to go back and work in the social services field. And a business man. We just disagreed and those disagreements became very emotional because these guys, the writers and artists that were talking about were — almost all of them — friends of mine. Those that hadn't been friends of mine, pretty much become friends of mine, and most of them are friends of mine to this day. And they were getting screwed.

Bob: It's funny, a few years ago I did an interview with Jeff Rovin on the rise and fall of Atlas/Seaboard comics (*which ran in the 1998 edition of* **CVA** — ed.), and the story he told is the story you're telling today.

Bob: Yeah, it's a time-honored tradition. Paul Levitz and I made that comparison once, comparing Rick Obidiah to other publishers in the history of comics. I don't think that that's necessarily fair, I should point out, but it was just the starting point of that conversation. I have no ill will towards Rick. I don't think we've seen each other for five or six years, but we had a very pleasant time. So what happened was, I was very disenfranchised from First because my friends weren't getting paid, and also from a business perspective, if you don't produce good comics, you're not going to sell, and if you're not paying people, you not going to produce good comics. It was a bad business decision, it was a bad personal decision. I went on a leave of absence with the full belief and understanding that the minute that it was announced that I was on a leave of absence that I would get job offers. I just wanted to see what would happen and see what options I would have in my life, including outside of comics. Well, I go on a leave of absence I take drive up to Upper Peninsula, Michigan. In the beginning of October it's really beautiful, it's just gorgeous, and spent a week just chilling out literally, because it's pretty cold up at Lake Superior. It was great, just beautiful. I let go of a lot of bad energy, came back, turned on the answering machine, and I had seven job offers. I had 25 messages, and seven of them were job offers. The first message and the last message on that tape were from Dick Giordano. "Let's talk." So I'm thinking how much of the stuff that I pulled off at First Comics which I was very proud of could I actually accomplish over at DC. So I flew out there and we cut ourselves a deal, and I went off to work at DC. Where I was hired — at that time — a senior editor, then became director of development, and then added group editor to that so I was director of development/group editor.

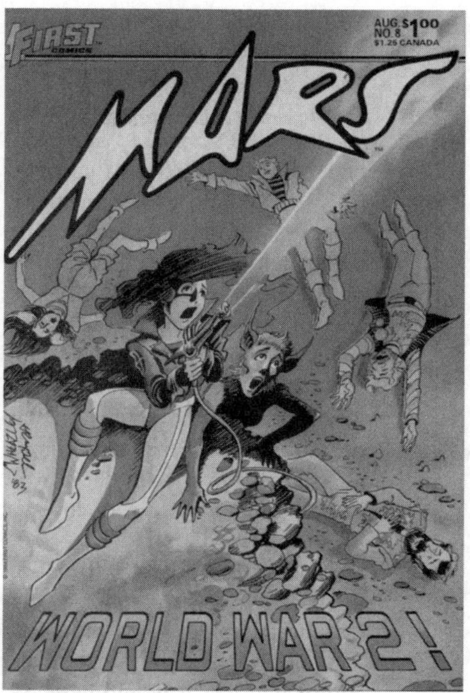

Mars #8, © First Comics

Bob: So you were back at DC for a number of years where you brought Mike Grell back in…

Mike: Oh, a lot, Mike Baron — almost everybody I had worked with at First Comics I had worked with at DC, and many, many other people, as well. So it was the best of both worlds for me, I was in hog heaven; I worked with all of these wonderfully creative people, including my old buddies from First Comics. I was thrilled.

Bob: Ultimately you left DC…

Mike: …After seven years…

Bob: …After seven years, and went back into the retail end of comics with Mike

Raub. (*Mike Raub was interviewed in the 2000 edition of* CVA, *offering his view of the retail end of the business*—ed.)

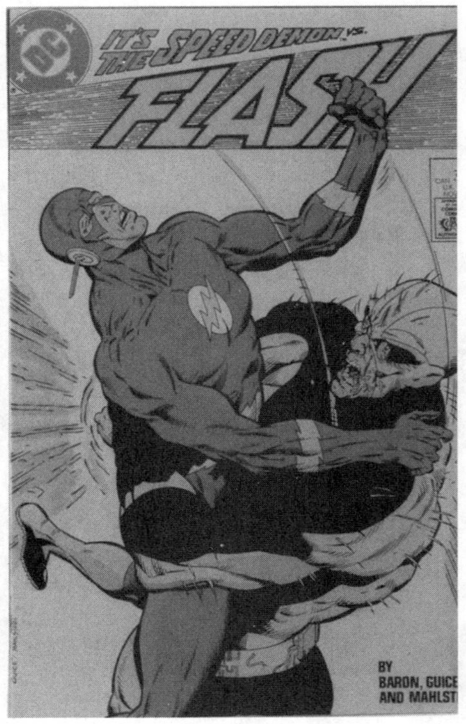

Flash, 2nd Series, #6, © DC Comics, Inc.

Mike: Well, there's some stuff in between. The last year I spent at DC, I knew and I had told them — both Giordano and the head of personnel at Warner Bros. that my intention was to leave at the end of my seventh year. So I spent that last year pretty much closing out the projects that I was involved in. I did a few special new things, some as a favor to Giordano, some because it was my job, and some out of loyalty to the writers and artists that worked with me, not to leave them hanging. So, I spent a year of time winding all that up, with the full understanding that at the end of that year I would be leaving the company and limiting my work in comics. At that time Image Comics was starting up and I knew that Todd McFarlane had made an offer to Mike Grell. Mike had made me part of that package, although, as long as I was working at DC, I wasn't working on any of that stuff. The minute I was gone from DC, I did work on it. So, essentially, I went, although not full-time, from DC to working with Grell at Image Comics (*Jim Valentino, Image co-founder and current publisher, and Whilce Portacio, Image co-founder, were both interviewed in 1999 for* **CVA**—ed.) Now, at that same time, I also was working with Mike Raub on this retailing venture. At the very same time, my career went back to the marketing end of comics, but with one foot in marketing and one foot in editorial. So I was doing both. After the Image stuff we packaged some books for Acclaim — what is now Acclaim Comics, but was Valiant at the time, and a couple of other publishers. I worked with some other talent, but almost all of it was with Grell. Out of friendship, really. It wasn't my main gig, by any stretch of the imagination. I was doing a lot of media consulting work at that time, too, that was completely outside of comics. I was having a good time.

Bob: Could you talk a little bit about some of the stuff that you're doing right now. I know that you're doing the "how-to-do comics" books with Frank McLaughlin.

Mike: That's right. Our first one came out earlier this year (2000), *How to Draw those Bodacious Bad Babes of Comics*.

Bob: Yeah, I've seen that on the stands.

Wasteland #6, © DC Comics, Inc.

Mike: It's great fun, and our publisher is very happy with the sales, and we just finished our second one, which *is How to Draw those Mad Malevolent Monsters of Comics* (the title may change). These are obviously very market driven. I don't know if we'll do a third one or not. The relationship with the publisher — well with a couple of people on the publisher's staff — is not what I would like. I'm not trying to speak for Frank here, but comics is a very unique business. It doesn't go by any of the other business models they teach you at the Harvard School of Business. That's one of the reasons that comics has had so much problems in the last 10 years. All these outsiders have come in and said, "Wow, look how much money is being made. If we just applied real business standards to comics, then the world would be a better place." Invariably, those people — each and every one of them — will fail. Our relationship with our publisher is that they are not thinking of comics as any other business. We should be presenting things a certain way, and the book should look like any other book. They shouldn't. They should have a certain type of energy you get out of comics. I write to that energy — and they don't have any problem with that; Frank draws to that energy — and they he don't have any problem with that. But, when you package it all together, and you lay it out right and all this other stuff, Mark Wheatley is the colorist; they didn't understand it.

Bob: It doesn't look like it's supposed to look.

Mike: I have an art director who is fighting it very, very aggressively. Luckily that's Frank's job to deal with that, because she (the art director) just doesn't understand comics, and you can tell she doesn't like it. The obvious visual sexism of comics offended her, and I understand that and I'm sympathetic to her.

Bob: Where do you see comics going in the next century; or at the very least over the next decade? I've just been reading how Marvel is probably going to run out of money before the end of the year (2000). Is that like a real thing, or are people just panicking?

Mike: Well, maybe. It's really possible.

Bob: What would happen if that happened? I mean, if they really did run out of money? Do they simply stop publishing? Do the Marvel characters just go away? Does somebody else step in and buy them for pennies?

Mike: Any of those things could happen. Most likely the latter, and probably not for pennies, probably for real money. They own thousands and thousands of characters. I think that we got so caught up in selling to a fail-safe audience, selling to the fans, that we forgot that comics is inherently at the entry point of children's medium. It doesn't have to be up and down the stream, but as an entry level point you have to be producing comics for kids, and right now only Archie Comics is doing that.

Bob: It's kind of funny that you should say that because I've been having this conversation for the past several weeks with people, and it's not so much a comic book discussion, it's a sports discussion. I'm very angry with Major League Baseball (and that includes the owners and the networks) over the fact that the World Series started at 8 at night here on the East Coast. Now I understand that part of that reason was to make it accessible to the West Coast. First of all, this year (2000), it happened to be strictly a New York City game, so my feeling was, screw the West Coast.

Mike: Yeah, but the networks can't change the schedule…

Bob: Yeah, I understand that…

Mike: …And by the way, you happen to be 100 percent right because nobody outside the New York area happened to watch the damn thing. It was the lowest ratings ever.

Bob: **…**By putting it that late, they took a very short-term stance, and determined to make a bunch of money this year with prime-time sponsorships. However, what they are doing, and I don't think they understand this. My 9-year-old son got to watch a total of three innings of the entire series.

Mike: Think about who you're talking to. I grew up on the North side of Chicago, to me—playing baseball at night is sacrilegious.

Bob: This is true! Right! Exactly! (Laughter)

Mike: It's supposed to be out in real grass, in a real stadium…

Bob: …In the middle of the afternoon!

Mike: …In real air…

Bob: So unless I make a concerted effort to expose my son to baseball, take him to games, and let him stay up past his bedtime to watch games, let him stay up to watch the World Series — and there are people like myself who are not going to do that — you're going to wind up with an entire generation of young kids who are going to grow up not being used to watching baseball. By the time they get to be my age, with children my son's age, not only will they not be watching baseball; their children will not be watching baseball either. Nobody is going to be sitting in the stands. It won't matter if the clubs are giving away bricks of gold; nobody is going to be watching baseball anymore, because they simply got out

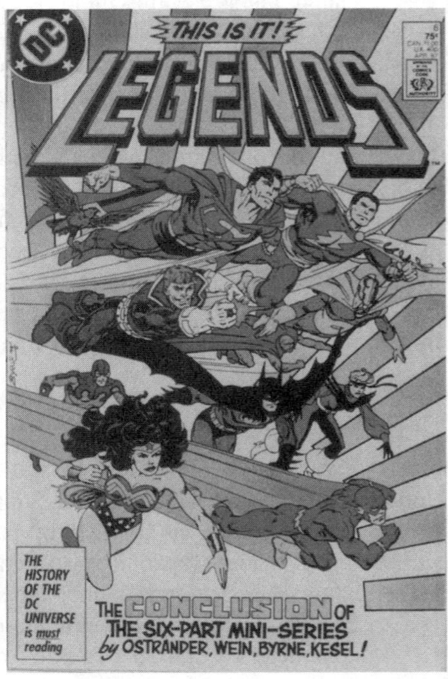

Legends #6, © DC Comics, Inc.

of the habit. This is exactly what comics has done. I started reading comics in the early '60s. Spider-Man was in high school, and I was in grade school. I grew up and he didn't. I wound up graduating college before he did. Eventually I was reading comics staring characters that were younger than me. Meanwhile the entire industry grew up at the same time, and there were no more kid comics. When they then discovered this, they had to go back and try to create comicbooks for kids. They wound up doing *Power Pack*.

Mike: *Power Pack* was a comic about kids, not for kids.

Bob: Right, exactly; and they were doing it wrong.

Mike: I liked the original *Power Pack*. I'm not putting the book down, but the concept was not—"The Comicbook Industry, the Next Generation," and that's what we need, and we still need that now, and now we need it damn fast. The idea here is, not just to have comics for kids. You need superhero comics, that kids can understand, that 9-year-olds, 10-year-olds, 11-year-olds can understand. Then, as they grow older, they get fed along into the comics that are for teenagers, and for young adults.

Bob: I went from Archie, Charlton, and Dell, to Marvel and DC, and ultimately to First, and Image and others. The problem is that I grew up, and all of a sudden, I'm older than comics, and the audience is younger. I remember being at a comicbook convention in the 1980s, and someone asked Chris Claremont how long he had been writing *X-Men*. Chris asked how old the kid was, and the answer was 18. Chris responded, "A year longer than you've been alive."

Mike: And that's okay, I guess, but if the object is for the X-Men to become icons, which they finally have, then the X-Men should never leave those 11-year-olds in the dust. Never. I think that what the comic industry needs from this point forward — what's it's needed for the last five or six years — is a new philosophy. It has needed one desperately the day everybody decided that publishing alternate covers and foil covers was more important than publishing good comics. What we've needed ever since that point in time is a philosophy that reaches both audiences; that reaches the traditional comic book fan market, which is a broad market, but thin. It reaches a wide range of age, but very few people. And also an entry-level audience, that provides superhero comics that heroic adventure, that heroic fantasy. You don't have to have a cape and a costume to be a superhero comic — *Jon Sable* was a superhero comic, so was *American Flagg*, so was *The Question*. I mean, *The Question* was a great book and so was *American Flagg,* but those were not books, for 10- and 11-year-olds. You need to have heroic characters for that market; and kids had to

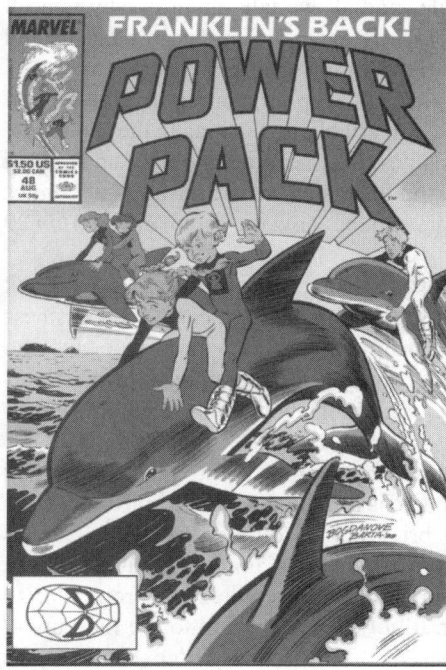

Power Pack #48, © DC Comics, Inc.

be able to afford it. By afford it, I'm not referring to the price of comics; $2.00, $3.00; whatever. I'm talking about the price of entry. If you're a Batman fan, and you like watching Batman on TV; if you're an X-Men fan, you like the movie, and you find a comic book store - which is hard enough - and you look at all this X-Men stuff, and you look at all this Batman stuff, and you realize that if you want it all, if you want to stay on top of it, if you want to get enough of it so that you understand the story, you're making a commitment that 12-year-olds, maybe even 15-year-olds, cannot afford every month.

Bob: That's because the publishers think that if one Spider-Man title is selling 100,000 copies a month, and they publish 10 Spider-Man titles they are going to sell 1,000,000 copies. No! They are going to sell 10,000 of each title, and the total number of Spider-Man books will be just a little over 100,000.

Mike: I know of ways of doing that, of creating an industry that goes along those lines. It partially embraces everything that's great about comics today, with everything that was great about comics 10 year ago, and 20 years ago, all three of those points in time. Therefore, I'm certain that other people who have that same type of history of the business end of comics know that as well. I don't understand why it's not being done. I understand why I'm not doing it. I'm not in that line of work right now, but I don't understand why others are not doing it. Every once in a while I ask them — most of, a lot of my friends are in the comic business — these conversations come up incessantly. You go to the National Cartoonist Society dinners here in Connecticut, and there always Mort Walker (*Beetle Bailey*), and those guys, but all the comic book guys sit at like two tables and all we talk about is why is it all going to hell in a hand basket? Everybody agrees what the problem is, and they sort of agree what the solution is. Why it is not being implemented? I don't know. My best guess is that outsiders keep on coming in, and they all go, "Oh, I know how to save comics." Invariably they all make the same mistakes and it winds up going up in flames. You need people who understand the business of comics, who understand the history of the business of comics — not who drew *Spider-Man* 20 years ago, but how they sold *Spider-Man* 20 years ago.

Bob: I remember that when Mike Raub was starting to expand his comic book store business (Dream Factory) into the beginnings of a chain. His business model was that he wanted to hire two people to run every store. One guy who was a comic book fan and knew what comics were about and a business person at an equal level who knew little or nothing about comics, but knew how to run a small business.

Mike: The reason that Mike, as long as he was running his comic book stores, had run successful comic book stores, and he is running his own comic book store to this day. There was only the brief period during the CIE (Comics International Entertainment) period when he wasn't running it, but if you take that out of the mix, when he was running the stores which was from 1985 to the year 2000 and counting. He ran it not only according to the fan knowledge that he had, but also according to the business knowledge that he had as a broadcaster. Mike and I are similar in that regard. Although Mike was in the

Jon Sable Freelance #30,
© First Comics

broadcasting business longer than I. That's a very hardcore business. By bringing those — I don't want to say traditional business values, but nobody is better at promotion than people who succeed in radio. You know promotion and marketing backwards and forwards. He brought those types of values to his comic book stores, and that's why, as long as he was running it - again, to this very day - he's been successful. You have to bring that type of philosophy, that type of knowledge, knowing both the business of comics, the history of the business of comics, and real-world attributes into the industry and the trick is, the history of the business of comics is the horse. It's what's going to get you down that road. You need the other two things there too, but what's going to get you down that road is an understanding of how it's worked before and how you can update and apply those types of techniques.

Bob: It's not so much about selling, but about marketing. How do you best position this thing? How do you see the growing interactivity of electronic entertainment affecting comics? There are so many people who have cited video games as the death knell of comics…

Mike: Oh crap. I don't believe it. Let me tell you why. They used to say the death knell of comics was television, remember it was the 1950s. You weren't born.

Bob: Yes I was.

Mike: Well, you were a small child. Well. In 1950 you weren't, and I was.

Bob: Okay, fine. Be that way.

Mike: I was born in 1950. In the mid-50s. When you were born, comic sales were tanking. Of course today, we'd give our left nut to get those types of sales.

Bob: Right!

Mike: But in those days, we were doing very, very poorly, a lot of publishers were going out of business. Yes, there were all these problems with Wertham (Fredric Wertham, author of *Seduction of the Innocent*)—and all this other stuff, but Wertham wasn't the death knell of comics, Wertham was just the death knell of the creativity of comics, for a short period of time. What had been selling comics was the distribution system, the fact that there were corner grocery stores, each small town had their own little newsstand that was reached by every magazine ever published. Those mom and pop operations were going out of business, and being replaced by big supermarkets, big drug stores, and mostly big shopping malls. They made that transition. It wasn't television that was hurting comic sales; it was the failure of the distribution system that we had in the 1950s. Now we had a big collapse of the comics industry or the comics distribution in the early 70s. Same thing. We were making the transition from the last vestige of those mom and pop stores into the big shopping malls. In the big shopping malls you couldn't buy a comic book. Walden Books didn't start carrying comics until much later than that. The big bookstores in the shopping malls didn't carry comics in most of their outlets in the 1970s. There weren't enough bookstores in shopping malls in those days to carry that weight anyway. Ultimately, what saved the business was the direct sales end of things. Now, for 20 years we've had the direct sales thing sailing. That collapsed because of greed, speculation, and the publishers just trying to play it safe, and believing that alternate covers were more important than the story. Of course I'm oversimplifying here. The people in the industry at that time knew the problems with that philosophy. The newcomers were creating a lot of pressure along those same ways to compete. And all the air went out of the business, and still hasn't returned. Our best argument is that it's leveled off where less than a dozen regular ongoing monthly titles are selling more than 50,000 copies in direct sales. That's a crime. What you have to do is adjust to the 21st century marketing philosophy and retailing concept the way that we adjusted to the direct sales market in the late 70s and with the loss of the mom and pop stores in the 1950s. Every time we blamed it on something else. We're blaming it on video games today and on computers. We were blaming it on movies and *Star Wars* and that sort of stuff in the 70s. There was this big implosion at DC in '78, and we were blaming it on television before that — now you're getting it all for free. For crying out loud, during the Depression, when nobody had any money, and radio was free, you took whatever little money you had and went out and bought a radio because it was an ongoing source of free entertainment in the house, that's when the comics industry was created. That's when it got off the ground. That's when I'm not sure we've ever had such great days as we had during that period of time, when during the Depression and World War II. Nobody had any money. Hell, during the Depression we didn't even have any paper! And everything that you had, sold. If comics could sell in the 1930s with reprint of newspaper strips and sell like nobody's business, and nobody had any money, then comics can sell in the 21st century. Blaming it on video games is a copout. (Laughter)

Bob: Fine, I totally believe you. I can buy that. I'll use Spider-Man as an example because I'm a Spider-Man fan. Stan wrote the most amazing stuff in Spider-Man. He spent over 100 issues with essentially the same cast. He'd introduce new villains every once in a while, but for all intents and purposes it was the same core cast of characters, and you really and truly got to know who these people were. Then he left and Roy Thomas, Gerry Conway, and others followed him, and you wound up with writers doing what Stan did, without understanding why Stan was doing what he was doing it. Then it was just a shadow of what Stan had been doing. I honestly believe that the first person to come along who was really able to write Stan Lee's Spider-Man after Stan was Roger Stern. Sterno was writing stuff that I remember reading, and going "Who is this guy? He's great!"

Mike: I agree with you, I believe that Roger's contribution to Spider-Man in particular was one of the most under-rated achievements in comics. Although I have to tell you that Brian Bendis, not just because of The *Ultimate Spider-*

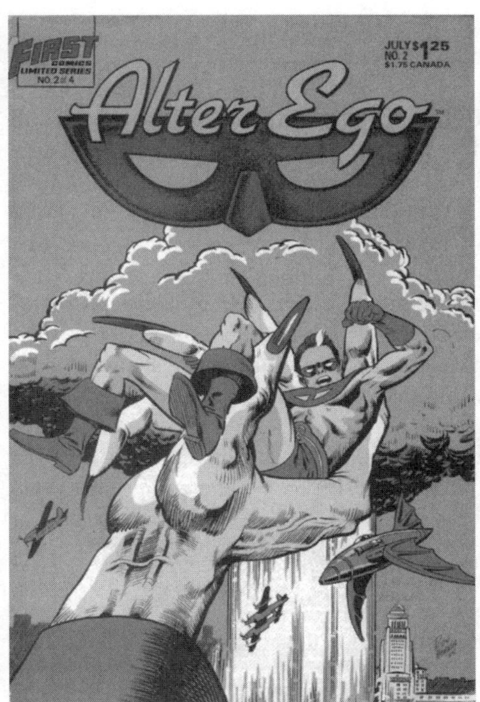

Alter Ego #2, © First Comics

Man, but many, many of his other books, is one of the best writers I've seen come down the pike ever.

Bob: Could you talk a little more about the future of the industry?

Mike: The real crises in comics right now is the profitability is so negative right now that it is very hard to attract the type of money its going to take in order to save it. My response to that is that the original comic publishers in the 1930s and the successful comic book publishers, many of the successful comic book publishers since that point in time didn't have a hell of a lot of money either. They weren't destitute, but they didn't have a hell of a lot of money either. What it takes is to get people out of their damn suits...and get them into real-world publishing. There are magazines that are profitable, that have lower budgets than comicbooks — it's very expensive to produce comic books — and higher cover prices that can make it. You can save this industry, but it takes saving now. We can make it to the 21st century, but it's going to take, if not the things that I've talked about, then something else to make it work. It needs saving.

Bob: Do you think that the success of the X-Men movie will help recussitate comics? Or could we wind up with no comics, but just movies about comics?

Mike: Absolutely. Well, sure, because comic characters are not unique to comics. We had the Scarlet Pimpernel long before we had comics. We had Zorro long before we had comics. These are superheroes. The *X-Men* movie could create comicbook readers except that if you're 12-years-old and dig the *X-Men* movie and you want to read the *X-Men* comic book, you'd have to find a comic book store. Then if you found a comic book store you'd have to figure out what amongst all those 18,000 different *X-Men* titles that are on the wall are the ones that you could understand. Chances are that you're going to walk away bewildered, assuming that you can find a store in the first place, without reading any of them. But if you do, you are not going to get a satisfying experience because it takes 400 issues to understand the story. Not even 400 issues of the same book, but a total 400 issues across a dozen different books, and you don't know which dozen books.

Bob: When John Byrne went over to **Superman** in 1986 I tried to read those titles, but you had to read all four titles and John wasn't writing and drawing all four of them. I read the first couple that John did and loved them, but when I got to the first non-John Byrne book the art was so different than John's that it was jarring. I couldn't read it, so I decided to only read John's books and screw the continuity, because John was doing the best stuff.

Mike: My daughter is a big X-Man fan, and she became an assistant manager of a comic book store. Then she went off to college and had a life. Now, she still reads comics, she reads *Wonder Woman* and five or six other titles. She'd love to be able to read the *X-Men*. She'd love to be able to go back. At the time she stopped reading *X-Men* I think that there were only three or four X-Men books being published or at least three or four that were tied together. She could handle that although that's quite a commitment in and of itself. A 12-year-old couldn't handle a four-book-a-month commitment in order to understand the X-Men but she was like 16 or 18 at the time. She had a job, so she could do it. She was working in a comic book store; of course she was doing it. Once she had college expenses and that sort of stuff it really wasn't worth not only her time, but her money as well. So now, she's got the time, she's pretty much got the money — to the extent that any of us do — and she would like to read the X-Men. And she can't! Because there isn't an *X-Men* title for her to follow; where she would only have to read one or two or maybe three. She doesn't really want to read more than that. Therefore, the *X-Men*, which she always enjoyed, is something that is denied to her. There are thousands of potential readers who are like her.

Bob: I would love to read *Spider-Man* again. Hell, I'd love to read all the Marvel titles that I used to read, but I'll never again be able to afford to buy all of those titles anymore. What I may end up doing, if I'm lucky enough, is go back and read *Spider-Man*, and I probably won't even be able to read all of *Spider-Man* titles, but perhaps the core books.

Mike: This is the philosophy behind *The Ultimate Marvel* line. This re-do of Spider-Man where you only have to read that one book. *Ultimate X-Men* comes out next month (December 2000), the same thing. Then they have an *Ultimate Team-Up* book. Ah-ha! Which means that there are a million other characters, which means that *The Ultimate Marvel Universe* can instantly expand to a million different characters. You can see, unless they're extremely careful *The Ultimate Marvel* line is just going to wind up being the same as the regular Marvel line, with too many interrelated titles.

Bob: It's going to be *Marvel 2099, The New Universe*…

Mike: Right, but they do have the opportunity to avoid that sand trap, and I hope they do. That doesn't quite meet what I was talking about earlier, but it's very close, and the first book that they have, *The Ultimate Spider-Man*, is extremely well done, and that's really the most important thing.

CVA GRADING GUIDE

In David Brins science fiction–fantasy novel, *The Practice Effect*, things improve with use. You start with a crudely made tool and keep using it until it becomes a fine instrument. If our world worked that way, you could read your golden age comics as often as you liked and they would just get better looking each time. Unfortunately, our world does not work that way, and reading your comics (along with just about everything else) causes comics to deteriorate.

Even if you could protect your comics from external light, heat, cold, moisture, pressure and everything else, you couldn't protect them from their own paper. Most comic books were printed on pulp paper, which has a high acid content. This means that the paper slowly turns brittle with age, no matter what you do to it, short of special museum-style preservation.

Very old, well-preserved comics are coveted collectors items. In most cases, people did not save their comic books for future generations. They read them and discarded them. Comic books were considered harmless ephemera for children. When these children outgrew their comics, their parents often threw them away. If everybody kept all of their comics, comics would not be valuable because everybody would have them scattered about the house!

The value of any comic depends on scarcity, popularity and condition. Scarcity increases with age and popularity depends on the whim of the public — only condition automatically decreases with age. Newer comics are generally available in near-mint condition, so newer comics in lesser condition have little collector potential. However, older comics are scarce, so they are still collectible in less than near-mint condition, but the value is obviously less. This is a basic tenet of all collectibles. A car is more valuable with its original paint. A baseball card is more valuable if it has not been marred by bicycle spokes. Coke bottles, stamps, coins, and toys in good condition are all more valuable than their abused counterparts. Comic books are no exception.

New comic book collectors should learn how to assess the prospective value of a comic in order to protect themselves from being fleeced by unscrupulous dealers or hucksters. Yet, a majority of dealers, especially store owners, can be considered reliable judges of comic grade. Because comic retail may be their primary source of income, certain dealers are particularly adept at noticing comic book imperfections, especially in issues they intend to purchase. As such, hobbyists and collectors must understand that dealers need to make a minimum profit on their investments. Buying collectible comics entails certain risks. Therefore, dealers must scrutinize a comic to determine if the particular book will stand a chance of resale. Well-preserved comics are invariably more desirable to dealers because they are more desirable to collectors.

There are eight standard comic grades: mint, near mint, very fine, fine, very good, good, fair, and poor. Clearly, these eight grades could be split into even finer categories when haggling over an exceptionally rare or coveted Golden Age comic. In most cases, however, comic books can be evaluated using these eight standard grades. The values listed in *Comics Values Annual* are all for comics in "near mint" condition. The grading/price chart given at the back of this book should be used to adjust this price for comics in different grades.

Mint

Finding new comics in true mint condition can be difficult. Finding old comics in mint condition is almost impossible. Mint condition comics usually fetch prices higher than price guide listings. Mint comics can sell for 120 percent or more of *Comics Values Annual* listed prices. The reason for this is the strict criteria reserved for mint comics.

Mint comics are perfect comics and allow no room for imperfections. Pages and covers must be free of discoloration, wear, and wrinkles. A mint comic is one that looks like it just rolled off the press. Staples and spine must meet perfectly without cover "rollover." The cover must be crisp, bright, and trimmed perfectly. The staples must not be rusted and the cover should not have any visible creases.

The interior pages of a mint comic are equally crisp and new. A mint comic must not show any signs of age or decay. Because of the paper stock used on many older comics, acid and oxygen cause interior pages to yellow and flake. It is much harder to find pre-1970 mint comics because of inferior storage techniques and materials. In the early days of collecting, few people anticipated that the very boxes and bags in which they stored their comics were contributing to decay. Acid from bags, backing boards, and boxes ate away at many comics.

Near Mint

A near mint comic and a mint comic are close siblings, with their differences slight, even to an experienced eye. Most of the new comics on the shelf of the local comic shop are in near mint condition. These are comics that have been handled gingerly to preserve the original luster of the book.

Near mint comics are bright, clean copies with no major or minor defects. Slight stress lines near the staples and perhaps a very minor printing defect are permissible. Corners must still be sharp and devoid of creases. Interior pages of newsprint stock should show almost no discernible yellowing. Near mint comics usually trade for 100 percent of the suggested *Comics Values Annual* listed prices.

Very Fine

A very fine comic is one that is routinely found on the shelves and back issue bins of most good direct market comic shops. This grade comic has few defects, none of them major. Stress around the staples of a very fine comic are visible but not yet radical enough to create wrinkles. Both the cover and interior pages should still be crisp and sharp, devoid of flaking and creases. Interior pages may be slightly yellowed from age.

Most high-quality older comics graded as very fine can obtain 80-90 percent of *Comics Values Annual* listed prices. Newer comics graded as very fine get about 70-85 percent because many near mint copies probably exist. Despite that, very fine comics are desirable for most collectors.

Fine

Fine comics are often issues that may have been stored carefully under a bed or on a shelf by a meticulous collector. This grade of comic is also very desirable because it shows little wear and retains much of its original sharpness. The cover may be slightly off center from rollover. The cover retains less of its original gloss and may even possess a chip or wrinkle. The comers should be sharp but may also have a slight crease. Yellowing begins to creep into the interior pages of a comic graded as fine.

Fine comics are respectable additions to collections and sell for about 40-60 percent of the listed prices.

Very Good

A very good comic may have been an issue passed around or read frequently. This grade is the common condition of older books. Its cover will probably have lost some luster and may have two or three creases around the staples or edges. The corners of the book may begin to show the beginnings of minor rounding and chipping, but it is by no means a damaged or defaced comic. Comics in very good condition sell for about 30-40 percent of *Comics Values Annual* listed prices.

Good

A good comic is one that has been well read and is beginning to show its age. Although both front and back covers are still attached, a good grade comic may have a number of serious wrinkles and chips. The corners and edges of this grade comic may show clear signs of rounding and flaking. There should be no major tears in a good comic nor should any pages be clipped out or missing. Interior pages may be fairly yellowed and brittle. Good comics sell for about 15-25 percent of the *Comics Values Annual* listed prices.

Fair

A fair comic is one that has definitely seen better days and has considerably limited resale value for most collectors. This comic may be soiled and damaged on the cover and interior. Fair comics should be completely intact and may only be useful as a comic to lend to friends. Fair comics sell for about 10-20 percent of the *Comics Values Annual* listed prices.

Poor

Comics in poor condition are generally unsuitable for collecting or reading because they range from damaged to unrecognizable. Poor comics may have been water damaged, attacked by a small child, or worse, perhaps, gnawed on by the family pet! Interior and exterior pages may be cut apart or missing entirely. A poor comic sells for about 5-15 percent of the *Comics Values Annual* listed price.

Sniffing Out Grades

Despite everything that is mentioned about comic grading, the process remains relative to the situation. A comic that seems to be in very good condition may actually be a restored copy. A restored copy is generally considered to be in between the grade it was previous to restoration and the grade it has become. Many collectors avoid restored comics entirely.

Each collector builds his collection around what he believes is important. Some want every issue of a particular series or company. Others want every issue of a favorite artist or writer. Because of this, many collectors will purchase lower-grade comics to fill out a series or to try out a new series. Mint and near mint comics are usually much more desirable to hard-core collectors. Hobbyists and readers may find the effort and cost of collecting only high-grade comics financially prohibitive.

Getting artists or writers to autograph comics has also become a source of major dispute. Some collectors enjoy signed comics and others consider those very comics defaced! The current trends indicate that most collectors do enjoy signed comics. A signature does not usually change the grade of the comic.

As mentioned, comic grading is a subjective process that must be agreed upon by the buyer and seller. Buyers will often be quick to note minor defects in order to negotiate a better price. Sellers are sometimes selectively blind to their comic's defects. *Comics Values Annual:2001* provides this grading guide as a protection for both parties.

Name	Abbreviation
Abel, Jack	**JA**
Abell, Dusty	DAb
Abnett, Dan	DAn
Abrams, Paul	PIA
Adams, Art	AAd
Adams, Neal	NA
Addeo, Stephen	StA
Adkins, Dan	DA
Adlard, Charlie	CAd
Albano, John	JAo
Albrecht, Jeff	JAl
Alcala, Alfredo	AA
Alcazar, Vincent	VAz
Alexander, Chris	CAx
Alibaster, Jo	JoA
Allred, Michael	MiA
Alstaetter, Karl	KIA
Althorp, Brian	BAp
Amaro, Gary	GyA
Amendola, Sal	Sal
Ammerman, David	DvA
Anderson, Bill	BAn
Anderson, Brent	BA
Anderson, Murphy	MA
Andriola, Alfred	AlA
Andru, Ross	RA
Aparo, Jim	JAp
Aragones, Sergio	SA
Arcudi, John	JAr
Artis, Tom	TAr
Ashe, Edd	EA
Augustyn, Brian	BAu
Austin, Terry	TA
Avison, Al	AAv
Ayers, Dick	DAy
Bachalo, Chris	**CBa**
Badger, Mark	MBg
Bagley, Mark	MBa
Baikie, Jim	JBa
Bailey, Bernard	BBa
Bair, Michael	MIB
Baker, Kyle	KB
Baker, Matt	MB
Balent, Jim	JBa
Banks, Darryl	DBk
Barks, Carl	CB
Baron, Mike	MBn
Barr, Mike	MiB
Barras, John	DBs
Barreiro, Mike	MkB
Barreto, Ed	EB
Barry, Dan	DBa
Batista, Chris	CsB
Battlefield, D.	DB
Beatty, John	JhB
Beatty, Terry	TBe
Beauvais, Denis	DB
Beeston, John	JBe
Belardinelli, M.	MBe
Bell, Bob Boze	BBB
Bell, George	GBl
Bell, Julie	JuB
Benefiel, Scott	ScB
Benes, Ed	EBe
Benitez, Joe	JBz
Benjamin, Ryan	RBn
Bennett, Joe	JoB
Bennett, Richard	RiB
Benson, Scott	StB
Berger, Charles	ChB
Bernado, Ramon	RBe
Bernstein, Robert	RbB
Bierbaum, Mary	MBm
Bierbaum, Tom	TBm
Biggs, Geoffrey	GB
Binder, Jack	JaB
Bingham, Jerry	JBi
Birch, JJ	JJB
Biro, Charles	CBi
Bisley, Simon	SBs
Bissette, Stephen	SBi
Blaisdell, Tex	TeB
Blasco, Jesus	JBl
Blevins, Bret	BBl
Blum, Alex	AB
Bode, Vaughn	VB
Bogdanove, Jon	JBg
Bolland, Brian	BB
Bolle, Frank	FBe
Boller, David	DdB
Bolton, John	JBo
Bond, Philip	PBd
Booth, Brett	BBh
Boring, Wayne	WB
Bossart, William	WmB
Boxell, Tim	TB
Bradstreet, Tim	TBd
Braithwaite, Doug	DBw
Brasfield, Craig	CrB
Braun, Russell	RsB
Breeding, Brett	BBr
Brereton, Daniel	DlB
Brewster, Ann	ABr
Breyfogle, Norm	NBy
Bridwell, E. Nelson	ENB
Briefer, Dick	DBr
Bright, Mark	MBr
Brigman, June	JBr
Broderick, Pat	PB
Brodsky, Allyn	AyB
Broom, John	JBm
Broome, Matt	MtB
Brothers, Hernandez	HB
Brown, Bob	BbB
Browne, Dick	DkB
Brunner, Frank	FB
Bryant, Rick	RkB
Buckingham, Mark	MBu
Buckler, Rich	RB
Budget, Greg	GBu
Bugro, Carl	CBu
Bulanadi, Danny	DBl
Burchett, Rick	RBr
Burgard, Tim	TmB
Burke, Fred	FBk
Burns, John	JBn
Burns, Robert	RBu
Burroughs, W.	WBu
Buscema, John	JB
Buscema, Sal	SB
Busiek, Kurt	KBk
Butler, Jeff	JBt
Butler, Steve	SBt
Buzz	Buzz
Byrd, Mitch	MBy
Byrne, John	JBy
Calafiore, Jim	**JCf**
Caldes, Charles	CCa
Callahan, Jim	JiC
Calnan, John	JCa
Cameron, Don	DCn
Cameron, Lou	LC
Campbell, Eddie	ECa
Campbell, J. Scott	JSC
Campbell, Stan	StC
Campenella, Robert	RbC
Campos, Marc	MCa
Capullo, Greg	GCa
Cardy, Nick	NC
Carey, Mike	MCy
Cariello, Sergio	SCi
Carlin, Mike	MCr
Carpenter, Brent D.	BDC
Carralero, Ricky	RCl
Carrasco, Dario	DoC
Carter, Joe	JCt
Case, Richard	RCa
Casey, Joe	JoC
Castellaneta, Dan	DaC
Castellini, Claudio	CCt
Castrillo, Anthony	ACa
Chadwick, Paul	PC
Chan, Ernie	ECh
Chang, Bernard	BCh
Charest, Travis	TC
Chase, Bobbie	BCe
Chaykin, Howard	HC
Check, Sid	SC
Chen, Mike	MCh
Chen, Sean	SCh
Chestney, Lillian	LCh
Chiarello, Mark	MCo
Chichester, D.G.	DGC
Chiodo, Joe	JCh
Choi, Brandon	BCi
Chriscross	Ccs
Christopher, Tom	TmC
Chua, Ernie	Chu
Chun, Anthony	ACh
Churchhill, Ian	IaC
Cirocco, Frank	FC
Citron, Sam	SmC
Claremont, Chris	CCl
Clark, Mike	MCl
Clark, Scott	ScC
Cockrum, Dave	DC
Cohn, Gary	GCh
Coker, Tomm	TCk
Colan, Gene	GC
Colby, Simon	SCy
Cole, Jack	JCo
Cole, Leonard B.	LbC
Colletta, Vince	ViC
Collins, Max Allan	MCn
Collins, Mike	MC
Collins, Nancy	NyC
Colon, Ernie	EC
Conner, Amanda	ACo
Conway, Gerry	GyC
Cooper, Dave	DvC
Cooper, John	JCp
Corben, Richard	RCo
Costanza, Peter	PrC
Cowan, Denys	DCw
Cox, Jeromy	JCx
Craig, Johnny	JCr
Crandall, Reed	RC
Crespo, Steve	SCr
Crilley, Mark	MCi
Crumb, Robert	RCr
Cruz, E. R.	ERC
Cruz, Jerry	JCz
Cruz, Roger	RCz
Culdera, Chuck	CCu
Cullins, Paris	PCu
Currie, Andrew	ACe
Damaggio, Rodolfo	**RDm**
Daniel, Tony	TnD
Danner, Paul	PuD
Darrow, Geof	GfD
David, Peter	PDd
Davis, Alan	AD
Davis, Dan	DDv
Davis, Guy	GyD
Davis, Jack	JDa
Davis, Malcolm	MDa
Davison, Al	ADv
Day, Dan	Day
Day, Gene	GD
DeFalco, Tom	TDF
Deitch, Kim	KDe
Delano, Jamie	JaD
DeLaRosa, Sam	SDR
Delgado, Richard	RdD
Dell, John	JhD
DeMatteis, J. M.	JMD
DeMulder, Kim	KDM
Deodato, Jr., Mike	MD2
Derenick, Tom	TDr
DeZago, Todd	TDz
DeZuniga, M.	MDb
DeZuniga, Tony	TD
Diaz, Paco	PaD
Dillin, Dick	DD
Dillon, Glyn	GlD
Dillon, Steve	SDi
Dini, Paul	PDi
Ditko, Steve	SD
Dixon, Chuck	CDi
Dixon, John	JDx
Dobbyn, Nigel	ND
Dodson, Terry	TyD
Doherty, Peter	PD
Dominguez, Luis	LDz
Doran, Colleen	CDo
Dorey, Mike	MDo
Dorkin, Evan	EDo
Dorman, Dave	DvD
Doucet, Julie	JDo
Drake, Stan	SDr
Dresser, Larry	LDr
Dringenberg, Mike	MDr
Drucker, Mort	MD
DuBerkr, Randy	RDB
Duffy, Jo	JDy
Dumm, Gary	GDu
Dunn, Ben	BDn
Duranona, Leo	LDu
Duursema, Jan	JD
Dwyer, Kieron	KD
Eastman, Kevin	**KEa**
Eaton, Scott	SEa
Edginton, Ian	IEd
Edlund, Ben	BEd
Egeland, Marty	MEg
Eisner, Will	WE

Name	Abbreviation
Elder, Bill	BE
Eldred, Tim	TEl
Elias, Lee	LE
Elliot, D.	DE
Ellis, Warren	WEl
Ellison, Harlan	HaE
Emberlin, Randy	RyE
Englehart, Steve	SEt
Ennis, Garth	GEn
Epting, Steve	SEp
Erskine, Gary	GEr
Erwin, Steve	StE
Esposito, Mike	ME
Estes, John	JEs
Estrada, Ric	RE
Evans, George	GE
Everett, Bill	BEv
Ewins, Brett	BEw
Ezquerra, Carlos	CE
Fabry, Glenn	**GF**
Fago, Al	AFa
Farmer, Mark	MFm
Fegredo, Duncan	DFg
Feldstein, Al	AF
Ferry, Pascual	PFe
Fine, Lou	LF
Fingeroth, Danny	DFr
Finnocchiaro, Sal	SF
Fleisher, Michael	MFl
Fleming, Robert	RFl
Flemming, Homer	HFl
Foreman, Dick	DiF
Forte, John	JF
Forton, Gerald	GFo
Fosco, Frank	FFo
Foster, Alan Dean	ADF
Fox, Gardner	GaF
Fox, Gill	GFx
Fox, Matt	MF
Fraga, Dan	DaF
Franchesco	Fso
Frank, Gary	GFr
Frazetta, Frank	FF
Freeman, John	JFr
Freeman, Simon	SFr
Frenz, Ron	RF
Friedman, Michael Jan	MFr
Friedrich, Mike	MkF
Frolechlich, A.	AgF
Fry III, James	JFy
Fujitani(Fuje), Bob	BF
Furman, Simon	SFu
Gaiman, Neil	**NGa**
Galan, Manny	MaG
Gallant, Shannon	ShG
Gammill, Kerry	KGa
Garcia, Dave	DaG
Garner, Alex	AGo
Garney, Ron	RG
Garzon, Carlos	CG
Gascoine, Phil	PGa
Gaughan, Jack	JGa
Gecko, Gabe	GG
Geggan	Ggn
Gerard, Ruben	RGd
Gerber, Steve	SvG
Giacoia, Frank	FrG
Giarrano, Vince	VGi
Gibbons, Dave	DGb
Gibson, Ian	IG
Giella, Joe	JoG
Giffen, Keith	KG
Gilbert, Michael T.	MGi
Giordano, Dick	DG
Glanzman, Sam	SG
Golden, Michael	MGo
Gonzalez, Jorge	JGz
Goodman, Till	TGo
Goodwin, Archie	AGw
Gordon, Al	AG
Gottfredson, Floyd	FG
Gould, Chester	ChG
Grant, Alan	AlG
Grant, Steve	StG
Grau, Peter	PGr
Gray, Mick	MGy
Green, Dan	DGr
Green, Randy	RGr
Greene, Sid	SGe
Grell, Mike	MGr
Griffith, Bill	BG
Griffiths, Martin	MGs
Grindberg, Tom	TGb
Gross, Daerick	DkG
Gross, Peter	PrG
Grossman, R.	RGs
Gruenwald, Mark	MGu
Grummett, Tom	TG
Guardineer, Frank	FG
Guay, Rebecca	RGu
Guice, Jackson	JG
Guichet, Yvel	YG
Guinan, Paul	PGn
Gulacy, Paul	PG
Gustovich, Mike	MG
Ha, Gene	**GeH**
Haley, Matt	MHy
Hall, Bob	BH
Halsted, Ted	TeH
Hama, Larry	LHa
Hamilton, Tim	TH
Hamner, Cully	CHm
Hampton, Bo	BHa
Hampton, Scott	SHp
Hanna, Scott	SHa
Hannigan, Ed	EH
Hanson, Neil	NHa
Harras, Bob	BHs
Harris, N. Steven	NSH
Harris, Tim	THa
Harris, Tony	TyH
Harrison, Lou	LuH
Harrison, Simon	SHn
Hart, Ernest	EhH
Hartsoe, Everette	EHr
Hathaway, Kurt	KtH
Hawkins, Matt	MHw
Hayes, Drew	DHa
Haynes, Hugh	HH
Hazlewood, Douglas	DHz
Heath, Russ	RH
Hebbard, Robert	RtH
Heck, Don	DH
Heisler, Mike	MHs
Hempel, Mark	MaH
Henry, Flint	FH
Herman, Jack	JH
Hernandez, Gilbert	GHe
Hernandez, Jaime	JHr
Herrera,Ben	BHr
Hester, Phil	PhH
Hewlett, Jamie	JHw
Hibbard, E.E.	EHi
Hicklenton, John	JHk
Higgins, Graham	GHi
Higgins, John	JHi
Higgins, Michael	MHi
Hitch, Bryan	BHi
Hobbs, Bill	BlH
Hoberg, Rick	RHo
Hoffer, Mike	MkH
Hogarth, Burne	BHg
Holcomb, Art	AHo
Holdredge, John	JHo
Hoover, Dave	DHv
Hopgood, Kevin	KHd
Horie, Richard	RHe
Hotz, Kyle	KHt
Howarth, Matt	MHo
Howell, Rich	RHo
Hudnall, James	JHl
Hughes, Adam	AH
Hund, Dave	DeH
Hunt, Chad	CH
Immonen, Stuart	**SI**
Infantino, Carmine	CI
Ingles, Graham	GrI
Iorio, Medio	MI
Isherwood, Geoff	GI
Ivie, Larry	LI
Ivy, Chris	CIv
Jackson, Julius	**JJn**
Janke, Dennis	DJa
Janson, Klaus	KJ
Javinen, Kirk	KJa
Jenkins, Paul	PJe
Jenney, Robert	RJ
Jensen, Dennis	DJ
Jimenez, Leonardo	LJi
Jimminiz, Phil	PJ
Johnson, Dave	DvJ
Johnson, Jeff	JJ
Johnson, Paul	PuJ
Johnson, Todd	TJn
Jones, Casey	CJ
Jones, Gerard	GJ
Jones, J.B.	JJo
Jones, Jeff	JeJ
Jones, Kelley	KJo
Jones, Malcolm	MJ
Jones, R.A.	RAJ
Jones, Robert	RJn
Jurgens, Dan	DJu
Jusko, Joe	JJu
Kaluta, Mike	**MK**
Kamen, Jack	JKa
Kaminski, Len	LKa
Kane & Romita	K&R
Kane, Bob	Bka
Kane, Gil	GK
Kanigher, Bob	BbK
Kaniuga, Trent	TKn
Karounos, Paris T.	PaK
Katz, Jack	JKz
Kavanagh, Terry	TKa
Kelly, Walt	WK
Kennedy, Cam	CK
Keown, Dale	DK
Kerschl, Karl	KlK
Kesel, Babara	BKs
Kesel, Karl	KK
Kieth, Sam	SK
King, Hannibal	HbK
Kinsler, Everett R.	EK
Kirby, Jack	JK
Kisniro, Yukito	YuK
Kitson, Barry	BKi
Kobasic, Kevin	KoK
Kolins, Scott	ScK
Krause, Peter	PKr
Krenkel, Roy	RKu
Krigstein, Bernie	BK
Kristiansen, Teddy H.	TKr
Kruse, Brandon	BKr
Kubert, Adam	AKu
Kubert, Andy	NKu
Kubert, Joe	JKu
Kupperberg, Paul	PuK
Kurtzman, Harvey	HK
Kwitney, Alisa	AaK
LaBan, Terry	**TLa**
Lago, Ray	RyL
Laird, Peter	PLa
Lanning, Andy	ALa
Lansdale, Joe	JLd
Lapham, Dave	DL
Lark, Michael	MLr
Larkin, Bob	BLr
LaRocque, Greg	GrL
Larroca, Salvador	SvL
Larsen, Erik	EL
Lash, Batton	BLs
Lashley, Ken	KeL
Lavery, Jim	JLv
Lawlis, Dan	DLw
Lawrence, Terral	TLw
Lawson, Jim	JmL
Layton, Bob	BL
Leach, Garry	GL
Leach, Rick	RkL
Lee, Elaine	ELe
Lee, Jae	JaL
Lee, Jim	JLe
Lee, Patrick	PtL
Lee, Scott	ScL
Lee, Stan	StL
Leeke, Mike	MLe
Leialoha, Steve	SL
Leon, John Paul	JPL
Leonardi, Rick	RL
Levins, Rik	RLe
Lieber, Larry	LLi
Liefeld, Rob	RLd
Lightle, Steve	SLi
Lim, Ron	RLm
Linsner, Joseph M.	JLi
Livingstone, R.	RLv
Lloyd, David	DvL
Lobdell, Scott	SLo
Locke, Vince	VcL
Loeb, Jeph	JLb
Lopez, Jose	JL
Lopresti, Aaron	AaL
Louapre, Dave	DLp
Lowe, John	Low
Lubbers, Bob	BLb

Lustbader, Eric Van. . . ELu
Luzniak, Greg. . . . . . . GLz
Lyle, Tom . . . . TL
Macchio, Ralph . . . . RMc
Mack, David. . . . . DMk
Mackie, Howard. . . . . HMe
Madan, Dev. . . . . DeM
Madureira, Joe . . . . . . JMd
Maggin, Elliot S. . . . . ESM
Maguire, Kevin. . . . . . . KM
Magyar, Rick . . . . RM
Mahlstedt, Larry . . . . . LMa
Mahnke, Doug . . . . . . DoM
Mandrake, Tom . . . . . TMd
Maneely, Joe . . . . JMn
Manley, Mike. . . . . MM
Mann, Roland . . . . . . RMn
Mann, Roland. . . . . . . Man
Manning, Russ. . . . . . RsM
Marais, Raymond . . . RdM
Mariotte, Jeff . . . . JMi
Maroto, Esteban . . . . . EM
Marrinan, Chris . . . . . ChM
Marrs, Lee . . . . LMr
Martin, Gary . . . . GyM
Martin, Joe . . . . JMt
Martinbrough, Shawn. SMa
Martinez, Henry . . . . . HMz
Martinez, Roy Allan . . RMr
Marz, Ron . . . . RMz
Marzan, Jose . . . . JMz
Mason, Tom . . . . TMs
Massengill, Nathan . . NMa
Matsuda, Jeff . . . . JMs
Mattsson, Steve . . . . . SMt
Maus, Bill. . . . . BMs
Mayer, Sheldon . . . . . ShM
Mayerik, Val . . . . VMk
Mazzucchelli, David . . . DM
McCarthy, Brendon . . BMy
McCloud, Scott . . . . . . SMl
McCorkindale, B . . . . BMC
McCraw, Tom . . . . . . TMw
McCrea, John . . . . . . JMC
McDaniel, Scott . . . . . SMc
McDaniel, Walter. . . . WMc
McDonnell, Luke. . . . . LMc
McDuffie, Dwayne. . . DMD
McFarlane, Todd . . . . . TM
McGregor, Don . . . . . DMG
McKean, Dave . . . . . . DMc
McKeever, Ted. . . . . . TMK
McKenna, Mike . . . . . MkK
McKie, Angus . . . . . . AMK
McKone, Mike. . . . . . MMK
McLaughlin, Frank . . . FMc
McLaughlin, Sean . . . SML
McLeod, Bob . . . . BMc
McMahon, M. . . . . . . MMc
McManus, Shawn . . . SwM
McWilliams, Al . . . . . . AMc
Medina, Angel . . . . . . AMe
Medley, Linda . . . . LiM
Mercadoocasio, Harvey . . . . HMo
Meskin, Mort . . . . MMe
Messner-Loebs, Bill . . BML
Michelinie, David . . . . DvM
Miehm, Grant . . . . GtM
Mighten, Duke . . . . . . DMn
Mignola, Michael . . . . MMi
Miki, Danny . . . . DaM
Milgrom, Al . . . . AM
Millar, Mark . . . . MMr
Miller, Frank. . . . . FM
Miller, Mike S. . . . . . . MsM
Miller, Steve. . . . . SM
Milligan, Peter. . . . . . . PrM
Mills, Pat . . . . PMs
Minor, Jason. . . . . JnM
Mitchel, Barry . . . . BM
Moder, Lee. . . . . LMd
Moebius . . . . Moe
Moeller, Chris. . . . . . . CsM
Moench, Doug . . . . . . DgM
Montano, Steve . . . . . SeM
Mooney, Jim. . . . . JM
Moore, Alan . . . . AMo
Moore, Jeff . . . . JMr
Moore, Jerome . . . . . . JeM
Moore, John Francis. . JFM
Moore, Terry . . . . TMr
Morales, Rags . . . . . . RgM
Moretti, Mark . . . . MMo
Morgan, Tom . . . . TMo
Morisi, Pete . . . . PMo
Morosco, Vincent . . . . VMo
Morrison, Grant . . . . . GMo
Morrow, Gray . . . . GM
Mortimer, Win . . . . . . WMo
Motter, Dean. . . . . DMt
Moy, Jeffrey . . . . JMy
Murray, Brian . . . . BrM
Musial, Joe. . . . . JoM
Muth, Jon J. . . . . JMu
Mychaels, Marat . . . . MMy
Naifeh, Ted . . . . TNa
Napolitano, Nick. . . . . NNa
Napton, Bob. . . . . BNa
Nauck, Todd . . . . TNu
Neary, Paul . . . . PNe
Nebres, Rudy. . . . . RN
Nelson. . . . . Nel
Netzer, Mike . . . . MN
Newton, Don . . . . DN
Nguyen, Hoang . . . . . HNg
Nichols, Art . . . . ANi
Nicieza, Fabian . . . . . FaN
Nino, Alex . . . . AN
Nocenti, Ann . . . . ANo
Nocon, Cedric . . . . . . CNn
Nodell, Martin . . . . . . MnN
Nolan, Graham . . . . . . GN
Nord, Cary . . . . CNr
Norem, Earl . . . . EN
Nostrand, Howard . . . . HN
Novick, Irv . . . . IN
Nowlan, Kevin . . . . KN
Nutman, Philip . . . . . . PNu
O'Barr, James . . . . . . JOb
O'Neil, Denny . . . . . . DON
O'Neill, Kevin. . . . . . . KON
Olbrich, Dave. . . . . DO
Olivetti, Ariel . . . . AOl
Olliffe, Patrick. . . . . PO
One, Dark . . . . DOe
Ordway, Jerry . . . . JOy
Orlando, Joe. . . . . JO
Ortiz, Jose. . . . . JOt
Oskner, Bob. . . . . BO
Ostrander, John . . . . . JOs
Owen, James . . . . JOn
Ozkan, Tayyar . . . . . . TOz
Pace, Richard . . . . . . RPc
Pacella, Mark. . . . . . . MPa
Pacheco, Carlos. . . . . CPa
Palais, Rudy. . . . . RP
Palmer, Tom . . . . TP
Palmiotti, Jimmy . . . . . . JP
Pamai, Gene. . . . . GPi
Panalign, Noly . . . . NPl
Paniccia, Mark . . . . . . MPc
Panosian, Dan . . . . . . DPs
Parkhouse, Annie . . . . APh
Parkhouse, Steve . . . . SvP
Parobeck, Mike . . . . . MeP
Pascoe, James . . . . . JmP
Pasko, Martin. . . . . . . MPk
Patterson, Bruce . . . . . BrP
Pearson, Jason. . . . . . JPn
Pelletier, Paul . . . . PaP
Pence, Eric . . . . ErP
Pennington, Mark. . . . MPn
Pensa, Shea Anton . . SAP
Perez, George . . . . GP
Perham, James. . . . . . JPh
Perlin, Don. . . . . DP
Perryman, Edmund . . . EP
Peterson, Brandon . . . BPe
Peterson, Jonathan. . . JPe
Petrucha, Stefan . . . . . SPr
Peyer, Tom . . . . TPe
Phillips, Joe . . . . JoP
Phillips, Scott. . . . . SPl
Phillips, Sean . . . . SeP
Pini, Richard . . . . RPi
Pini, Wendy. . . . . WP
Platt, Stephen. . . . . . . SPa
Pleece, Warren . . . . . WaP
Ploog, Mike . . . . MP
Plunkett, Kilian. . . . . . . KPl
Pollack, Rachel . . . . . RaP
Pollard, Keith . . . . KP
Pollina, Adam. . . . . . . AdP
Pope, Paul . . . . PPo
Porch, David . . . . DPo
Portacio, Whilce . . . . WPo
Porter, Howard . . . . . . HPo
Post, Howard. . . . . . . HwP
Potts, Carl . . . . CP
Powell, Bob . . . . BP
Power, Dermot. . . . . . DPw
Pratt, George . . . . GgP
Priest, Christopher . . . CPr
Prosser, Jerry . . . . JeP
Pugh, Steve . . . . StP
Pulido, Brian. . . . . BnP
Queen, Randy . . . . . RQu
Quesada, Joe. . . . . JQ
Quinn, David . . . . DQ
Quinones, Peter. . . . . . PQ
Raab, Ben. . . . . BRa
Raboy, Mac . . . . MRa
Ramos, Humberto . . . HuR
Ramos, Rodney . . . . . RyR
Randall, Ron . . . . RoR
Raney, Tom . . . . TR
Rankin, Rich . . . . RRa
Rapmund, Norm. . . . . NRd
Raymond, Alex. . . . . . . AR
Redondo, Nestor . . . . . NR
Reed, David . . . . DvR
Reeves-Stevens, Judith . . . . JRv
Reinhold, Bill . . . . BR
Richards, Ted . . . . TR
Richardson, Mike . . . . MRi
Ricketts, Mark . . . . . . MRc
Rico, Don . . . . DRi
Ridgeway, John. . . . . . JRy
Rieber, John Ney . . . . JNR
Riley, John . . . . JnR
Riply . . . . Rip
Robbins, Frank. . . . . . . FR
Robbins, Trina. . . . . . . TrR
Robertson, Darrick . . . DaR
Robinson, James . . . . JeR
Rodier, Denis . . . . DRo
Rogers, Marshall . . . . . MR
Romita, John . . . . JR
Romita, John Jr. JR2
Rosenberger, J. . . . . . JRo
Ross, Alex . . . . AxR
Ross, David . . . . DR
Ross, John . . . . JRs
Ross, Luke . . . . LRs
Roth, Werner. . . . . WR
Royle, Jim . . . . JRl
Royle, John . . . . JRe
Rozum, John . . . . JRz
Rubi, Melvin. . . . . MvR
Rubinstein, Joe. . . . . . JRu
Rude, Steve. . . . . SR
Ruffner, Sean . . . . SRf
Russell, P. Craig . . . . . CR
Russell, Vince . . . . . . VRu
Ryan, Matt. . . . . MRy
Ryan, Paul. . . . . PR
Ryder, Tom . . . . TmR
Sakai, Stan . . . . SS
Sale, Tim . . . . TSe
Salmons, Tony . . . . . . TSa
Saltares, Javier. . . . . . . JS
Sanders, Jim III. JS3
Sasso, Mark . . . . MSo
Saviuk, Alex. . . . . AS
Schaffenberger, Kurt. . . KS
Schane, Tristan . . . . . TnS
Schiller, Fred . . . . FdS
Schmitz, Mark . . . . . . MaS
Schultz, Mark. . . . . . . MSh
Scoffield, Sean . . . . . . SSc
Scott, Jeffery. . . . . JSc
Scott, Trevor. . . . . TvS
Seagle, Steven T. . . . . SSe
Sears, Bart. . . . . BS
Sekowsky, Mike . . . . . MSy
Semeiks, Val . . . . VS
Senior, Geoff. . . . . GSr
Serpe, Jerry . . . . JyS
Severin, John . . . . JSe
Shamray, Gerry . . . . . GSh
Shanower, Eric . . . . . . EiS
Sharp, Liam . . . . LSh
Shaw, Sean . . . . SSh
Sherman, Jim . . . . JSh

Name	Abbreviation
Shoemaker, Terry	TSr
Shooter, Jim	JiS
Shum, Howard	HSm
Shuster, Joe	JoS
Sibal, Jonathan	JSb
Siegel & Shuster	S&S
Sienkiewicz, Bill	BSz
Silvestri, Eric	EcS
Silvestri, Mark	MS
Sim, Dave	DS
Simon & Kirby	S&K
Simon, Joe	JSm
Simonson, Louise	LSi
Simonson, Walt	WS
Simpson, Don	DSs
Simpson, Howard	HSn
Simpson, Will	WSm
Sinnott, Joe	JSt
Skroce, Steve	SSr
Smith, Andy	ASm
Smith, Barry W.	BWS
Smith, Beau	BSt
Smith, Cam	CaS
Smith, Jeff	JSi
Smith, John	JnS
Smith, Malcolm	MSt
Smith, Paul	PS
Smith, Robin	RSm
Smith, Ron	RS
Snejbjerg, Peter	PSj
Sniegoski, Tom	TSg
Spark	Spk
Sparling, Jack	JkS
Spiegelman, Art	ASp
Spiegle, Dan	DSp
Spinks, Frank	FrS
Springer, Frank	FS
Sprouse, Chris	CSp
St.Pierre, Joe	JPi
Starlin, Jim	JSn
Starr, Leonard	LSt
Staton, Joe	JSon
Steacy, Ken	KSy
Steffan, Dan	DnS
Stelfreeze, Brian	BSf
Stephenson, Eric	ErS
Steranko, Jim	JSo
Stern, Roger	RSt
Stern, Steve	SSt
Stevens, Dave	DSt
Stiles, Steve	SvS
Story, Karl	KIS
Stout, William	WiS
Stradley, Randy	RSd
Strazewski, Len	LeS
Stroman, Larry	LSn
Sullivan, Lee	LS
Sutton, Tom	TS
Swan, Curt	CS
Sweetman, Dan	DSw
Taggart, Tom	**TTg**
Takenaga, Francis	FTa
Takezaki, Tony	ToT
Talbot, Bryan	BT
Tallarico, Tony	TyT
Tan, Billy	BTn
Tanaka, Masashi	MTk
Tanghal, Romeo	RT
Tappin, Steve	SeT
Taylor, David	DTy
Taylor, R.G.	RGT
Templeton, Ty	TTn
Teney, Tom	TmT
Tenney, Mark	MaT
Texeira, Mark	MT
Thibert, Art	ATi
Thomas, Dann	DTs
Thomas, Roy	RTs
Thomason, Derek	DeT
Thompson, Jill	JIT
Thorne, Frank	FT
Tinker, Ron	RnT
Torres, Angelo	AT
Toth, Alex	ATh
Totleben, John	JTo
Trimpe, Herb	HT
Truman, Timothy	TT
Truog, Chas	ChT
Tucci, Bill	BiT
Turner, Dwayne	DT
Tuska, George	GT
Ulm, Chris	**CU**
Vachss, Andrew	**AVs**
Vado, Dan	DVa
Valentino, Jim	JV
Vallejo, Boris	BV
Van Fleet, John	JVF
Vancata, Brad	BVa
Vance, Steve	SVa
VanHook, Kevin	KVH
Vargas, Vagner	VV
Veitch, Rick	RV
Velez, Ivan, Jr.	IV
Velluto, Sal	SaV
Vess, Charles	CV
Vey, Al	AV
Vigil, Tim	TV
Vokes, Neil	NV
Von Eeden, Trevor	TVE
Vosburg, Mike	MV
Wagner, Matt	**MWg**
Wagner,Ron	RoW
Waid, Mark	MWa
Walker, Kevin	KeW
Waltrip, Jason	JWp
Waltrip, John	JWt
Ward, Bill	BWa
Warner, Chris	CW
Warren, Adam	AWa
Washington 3, Robert	3RW
Watkiss, John	JWk
Weeks, Lee	LW
Wein, Len	LWn
Weinstein, Howard	HWe
Welch, Larry	LyW
Wendel, Andrew	AdW
Wenzel, David	DWe
Weringo, Mike	MeW
West, Kevin	KWe
Weston, Chris	CWn
Wheatley, Mark	MkW
Whitney, Ogden	OW
Wiacek, Bob	BWi
Wiesenfeld, Aron	AWs
Wildey, Doug	DW
Wildman, Andrew	Wld
Williams, Anthony	AWi
Williams, David	DdW
Williams, J.H.	JWi
Williams, Keith	KWi
Williams, Kent	KW
Williams, Scott	SW
Williamson, Al	AW
Williamson, Skip	SWi
Willingham, Bill	BWg
Willis, Damon	DaW
Wilshire, Mary	MW
Wilson, Colin	CWi
Wilson, Gahan	GW
Wilson, Keith S.	KSW
Woch, Stan	SnW
Woggin, Bill	BWo
Wojtkiewicz, Chuck	Woj
Wolf, Chance	CWf
Wolfe, Joseph	JWf
Wolfman, Marv	MWn
Wolverton, Basil	BW
Wood, Bob	BoW
Wood, Teri Sue	TWo
Wood, Wally	WW
Woodring, Jim	JWo
Wormer, Kirk Van	KWo
Wright, Greg	GWt
Wrightson, Berni	BWr
Wyman, M.C.	MCW
Yaep, Chap	**CYp**
Yeates, Tom	TY
Yeowell, Steve	SY
Zabel, Joe	**JZe**
Zachary, Dean	DZ
Zaffino, Jorge	JZ
Zeck, Mike	MZ
Zick, Bruce	BZ
Zulli, Michael	MZi
Zyskowski, Joseph	JZy
Zyskowski, Steven	SZ

GENERAL ABBREVIATIONS FOR COMICS LISTINGS

Adaptation	Adapt.
Appearance of	A:
Anniversary	Anniv.
Annual	Ann.#
Art & Plot	(a&pl)
Art & Script	(a&s)
Artist	(a)
Back-Up Story	BU:
Beginning of	B:
Birth of	b:
Cameo Appearance	C:
Cover	(c)
Cover and Script	(c&s)
Crossover with	x-over
Death/Destruction of	D:
Edition	Ed.
Ending of	E:
Features	F:
Giant Size	G-Size
Golden Age	G.A.
Graphic Album	GAm
Graphic Novel	GN or GNv
Hardcover	HC
Identity Revealed	IR:
Inks by	(i)
Introduction of	I:
Joins of	J:
King Size	K-Size
Leaving of	L:
New Costume	N:
No Issue Number	N#
Origin of	O:
Painted Cover	P(c)
Part	pt. or Pt.
Pencils by	(p)
Photographic cover	Ph(c)
Plotted by	(pl)
Prestige Format	PF
Preview	Prev.
Reprinted issue	rep.
Retold	rtd.
Return/Revival of	R:
Scripted/Written by	(s)
Scripts & inks	(s&i)
Silver Age	S.A.
Softcover	SC
Special	Spec.
Team-up	T.U.
Trade Paperback	TPB
Versus	V: or vs.
Wedding of	W:
With	w/
Without	w/o

3RW. Robert Washington 3
AA. . . . . . . Alfredo Alcala
AAd . . . . Art Adams
AaK . . . . Alisa Kwitney
AaL . . . . . . Aaron Lopresti
AAv . . . . Al Avison
AB. . . . . Alex Blum
ABr . . . . Ann Brewster
ACa . . . . Anthony Castrillo
ACe . . . . . . Andrew Currie
ACh . . . . . . Anthony Chun
ACo. . . . . Amanda Conner
AD . . . . Alan Davis
ADF. . . . Alan Dean Foster
AdP . . . . Adam Pollina
ADv . . . . Al Davison
AdW. . . . . Andrew Wendel
AF . . . . Al Feldstein
AFa . . . . Al Fago
AG . . . . Al Gordon
AgF . . . . A. Frolechlich
AGo . . . . Alex Garner
AGw. . . . . Archie Goodwin
AH . . . . Adam Hughes
AHo. . . . . Art Holcomb
AIA. . . . . . . Alfred Andriola
AKu . . . . Adam Kubert
ALa . . . . Andy Lanning
AlG . . . . Alan Grant
AM . . . . Al Milgrom
AMc . . . . . . Al McWilliams
AMe. . . . . . . Angel Medina
AMK. . . . . . . Angus McKie
AMo . . . . Alan Moore
AN . . . . Alex Nino
ANi . . . . Art Nichols
ANo . . . . Ann Nocenti
AOl. . . . . Ariel Olivetti
APh . . . . Annie Parkhouse
AR . . . . Alex Raymond
AS . . . . Alex Saviuk
ASm . . . . Andy Smith
ASp. . . . . . Art Spiegelman
AT . . . . Angelo Torres
ATh . . . . Alex Toth
ATi . . . . Art Thibert
AV. . . . . Al Vey
AVs. . . . . . Andrew Vachss
AW. . . . . Al Williamson
AWa . . . . . . Adam Warren
AWi . . . . Anthony Williams
AWs . . . . Aron Wiesenfeld
AxR. . . . . Alex Ross
AyB . . . . Allyn Brodsky
BA . . . . . Brent Anderson
BAn . . . . Bill Anderson
BAp . . . . Brian Althorp
BAu. . . . . . Brian Augustyn
BB . . . . Brian Bolland
BBa . . . . . . Bernard Bailey
BbB . . . . Bob Brown
BBB . . . . . . Bob Boze Bell
BBh. . . . . Brett Booth
BbK . . . . Bob Kanigher
BBl. . . . . Bret Blevins
BBr. . . . . . . Brett Breeding
BCe . . . . . . Bobbie Chase
BCh. . . . . . Bernard Chang
BCi . . . . Brandon Choi
BDC . . . Brent D Carpenter
BDn. . . . . Ben Dunn
BE . . . . Bill Elder
BEd . . . . Ben Edlund
BEv . . . . Bill Everett
BEw . . . . Brett Ewins
BF . . . . . Bob Fujitani(Fuje)
BG . . . . Bill Griffith
BH. . . . . Bob Hall
BHa. . . . . Bo Hampton
BHg . . . . . . Burne Hogarth
BHi . . . . Bryan Hitch
BHr . . . . Ben Herrera
BHs. . . . . Bob Harras
BiT . . . . Bill Tucci
BK . . . . . . Bernie Krigstein
Bka . . . . Bob Kane
BKi. . . . . Barry Kitson
BKr . . . . . . Brandon Kruse
BKs . . . . Babara Kesel
BL. . . . . Bob Layton
BLb. . . . . Bob Lubbers
BlH . . . . Bill Hobbs
BLr. . . . . Bob Larkin
BLs . . . . Batton Lash
BM . . . . Barry Mitchel
BMc . . . . Bob McLeod
BMC . . . . B. McCorkindale
BML . . Bill Messner-Loebs
BMs . . . . Bill Maus
BMy . . . Brendon McCarthy
BNa . . . . Bob Napton
BnP . . . . Brian Pulido
BO . . . . Bob Oskner
BoW . . . . Bob Wood
BP. . . . . Bob Powell
BPe . . . Brandon Peterson
BR. . . . . Bill Reinhold
BRa. . . . . Ben Raab
BrM. . . . . Brian Murray
BrP . . . . . Bruce Patterson
BS . . . . Bart Sears
BSf. . . . . . Brian Stelfreeze
BSt . . . . Beau Smith
BSz. . . . . . Bill Sienkiewicz
BT . . . . Bryan Talbot
BTn . . . . Billy Tan
Buzz . . . . Buzz
BV . . . . Boris Vallejo
BVa . . . . Brad Vancata
BW . . . . . . Basil Wolverton
BWa . . . . Bill Ward
BWg. . . . . . Bill Willingham
BWi . . . . Bob Wiacek
BWo . . . . Bill Woggin
BWr . . . . . . Berni Wrightson
BWS . Barry Windsor-Smith
BZ . . . . Bruce Zick
CAd . . . . . Charlie Adlard
CaS. . . . . Cam Smith
CAx . . . . . Chris Alexander
CB . . . . Carl Barks
CBa. . . . . . . Chris Bachalo
CBi . . . . Charles Biro
CBu . . . . Carl Bugro
CCa . . . . . Charles Caldes
CCl . . . . . Chris Claremont
Ccs. . . . . Chriscross
CCt . . . . Claudio Castellini
CCu. . . . . . Chuck Culdera
CDi . . . . Chuck Dixon
CDo . . . . . . Colleen Doran
CE. . . . . . Carlos Ezquerra
CG . . . . Carlos Garzon
CH . . . . Chad Hunt
ChB. . . . . . Charles Berger
ChG . . . . . . Chester Gould
ChM. . . . . . Chris Marrinan
CHm . . . . . . Cully Hamner
ChT . . . . Chas Truog
Chu . . . . Ernie Chua
CI . . . . . Carmine Infantino
Clv . . . . Chris Ivy
CJ. . . . . Casey Jones
CK . . . . Cam Kennedy
CNn. . . . . . . Cedric Nocon
CNr. . . . . Cary Nord
CP. . . . . Carl Potts
CPa . . . . . Carlos Pacheco
CPr . . . . Christopher Priest
CR . . . . . . P. Craig Russell
CrB . . . . . . Craig Brasfield
CS . . . . Curt Swan
CsB. . . . . Chris Batista
CsM . . . . Chris Moeller
CSp . . . . . . Chris Sprouse
CU. . . . . Chris Ulm
CV . . . . Charles Vess
CW. . . . . Chris Warner
CWf . . . . Chance Wolf
CWi. . . . . Colin Wilson
CWn . . . . . . Chris Weston
CYp . . . . Chap Yaep
DA. . . . . Dan Adkins
DAb. . . . . Dusty Abell
DaC . . . . Dan Castellaneta
DaF . . . . Dan Fraga
DaG . . . . Dave Garcia
DaM . . . . Danny Miki
DAn. . . . . Dan Abnett
DaR . . . Darrick Robertson
DaW. . . . . . . Damon Willis
Day . . . . Dan Day
DAy . . . . Dick Ayers
DB . . . . D. Battlefield
DB . . . . . . Denis Beauvais
DBa . . . . Dan Barry
DBk . . . . Darryl Banks
DBl. . . . . . . Danny Bulanadi
DBr. . . . . Dick Briefer
DBs . . . . John Barras
DBw . . . . Doug Braithwaite
DC . . . . Dave Cockrum
DCn . . . . . . Don Cameron
DCw . . . . . . Denys Cowan
DD. . . . . Dick Dillin
DdB . . . . David Boller
DDv . . . . Dan Davis
DdW . . . . . David Williams
DE . . . . D. Elliot
DeH. . . . . Dave Hund
DeM . . . . Dev Madan
DeT . . . . Derek Thomason
DFg. . . . . Duncan Fegredo
DFr . . . . . Danny Fingeroth
DG . . . . Dick Giordano
DGb . . . . . . Dave Gibbons
DGC. . . . . . D.G. Chichester
DgM . . . . . . Doug Moench
DGr . . . . Dan Green
DH. . . . . Don Heck
DHa . . . . Drew Hayes
DHv . . . . Dave Hoover
DHz . . Douglas Hazlewood
DiF . . . . Dick Foreman
DJ . . . . Dennis Jensen
DJa . . . . Dennis Janke
DJu . . . . Dan Jurgens
DK . . . . Dale Keown
DkB. . . . . Dick Browne
DkG . . . . . . Daerick Gross
DL. . . . . Dave Lapham
DlB . . . . . . Daniel Brereton
DLp. . . . . . . Dave Louapre
DLw . . . . Dan Lawlis
DM . . . David Mazzucchelli
DMc . . . . Dave McKean
DMD . . . Dwayne McDuffie
DMG . . . . . Don McGregor
DMk . . . . David Mack
DMn . . . . . . Duke Mighten
DMt . . . . Dean Motter
DN. . . . . Don Newton
DnS . . . . Dan Steffan
DO . . . . Dave Olbrich
DoC. . . . . . Dario Carrasco
DOe. . . . . Dark One
DoM . . . . . . Doug Mahnke
DON . . . . . . O'Neil, Denny
DP . . . . Don Perlin
DPo . . . . Porch, David
DPs. . . . . . . Dan Panosian
DPw. . . . . . Power, Dermot
DQ. . . . . David Quinn
DR . . . . Ross, David
Rd. . . . . . Richard Delgado
DRi. . . . . Don Rico
DRo . . . . Denis Rodier
DS. . . . . Dave Sim
DSp . . . . Dan Spiegle
DSs . . . . Don Simpson
DSt . . . . Dave Stevens
DSw . . . . . Dan Sweetman
DT. . . . . . . Dwayne Turner
DTs . . . . Dann Thomas
DTy . . . . David Taylor
DvA. . . . David Ammerman
DVa . . . . Dan Vado
DvC . . . . Dave Cooper
DvD. . . . . . . Dave Dorman
DvJ. . . . . . . Dave Johnson
DvL. . . . . David Lloyd
DvM. . . . . David Michelinie
DvR . . . . David Reed
DW . . . . Doug Wildey
DWe . . . . . . David Wenzel
DZ . . . . Dean Zachary
EA . . . . Edd Ashe
EB . . . . Ed Barreto
EBe. . . . . Ed Benes
EC . . . . Ernie Colon
ECa . . . . . Eddie Campbell
ECh. . . . . Ernie Chan
EcS . . . . Eric Silvestri
EDo . . . . Evan Dorkin
EH . . . . Ed Hannigan
EhH. . . . . Ernest Hart

EHi . . . . E.E. Hibbard
EHr. . . . . Everette Hartsoe
EiS. . . . . . . Eric Shanower
EK . . . . . Everett R. Kinsler
EL. . . . . Erik Larsen
ELe . . . . Elaine Lee
ELu . . . Eric Van Lustbader
EM . . . . . . Esteban Maroto
EN . . . . Earl Norem
ENB . . . E. Nelson Bridwell
EP . . . . Edmund Perryman
ERC . . . . E.R. Cruz
ErP . . . . Eric Pence
ErS . . . . . Eric Stephenson
ESM . . . . Elliot S. Maggin
FaN . . . . . Fabian Nicieza
FB . . . . Frank Brunner
FBe. . . . . Frank Bolle
FBk . . . . Fred Burke
FC. . . . . Frank Cirocco
FdS. . . . . Fred Schiller
FF . . . . Frank Frazetta
FFo . . . . Frank Fosco
FG. . . . . Frank Guardineer
FG. . . . . Floyd Gottfredson
FH . . . . Flint Henry
FM . . . . Frank Miller
FMc. . . . Frank McLaughlin
FR . . . . Frank Robbins
FrG . . . . Frank Giacoia
FrS. . . . . Frank Spinks
FS . . . . Frank Springer
Fso. . . . . Franchesco
FT . . . . Frank Thorne
FTa . . . . Francis Takenaga
GaF . . . . Gardner Fox
GB. . . . . . . Geoffrey Biggs
GBl. . . . . George Bell
GBu . . . . Greg Budget
GC. . . . . Gene Colan
GCa . . . . Greg Capullo
GCh. . . . . Gary Cohn
GD . . . . Gene Day
GDu. . . . . Gary Dumm
GE . . . . George Evans
GeH . . . . Gene Ha
GEn . . . . Garth Ennis
GEr. . . . . Gary Erskine
GF. . . . . Glenn Fabry
GfD . . . . Geof Darrow
GFo. . . . . . . Gerald Forton
GFr . . . . Gary Frank
GFx . . . . Gill Fox
GG . . . . Gabe Gecko
Ggn . . . . Geggan
GgP . . . . George Pratt
GHe . . . Gilbert Hernandez
GHi . . . . . Graham Higgins
GI . . . . . . Geoff Isherwood
GJ. . . . . Gerard Jones
GK . . . . Gil Kane
GL. . . . . Garry Leach
GlD . . . . Glyn Dillon
GLz . . . . Greg Luzniak
GM. . . . . Gray Morrow
GMo . . . . . Grant Morrison
GN. . . . . . . Graham Nolan
GP . . . . George Perez
GPi . . . . Gene Pamai

Grl . . . . Graham Ingles
GrL. . . . . . Greg LaRocque
GSh . . . . . Gerry Shamray
GSr . . . . Geoff Senior
GT . . . . George Tuska
GtM . . . . Grant Miehm
GW. . . . . . . Gahan Wilson
GWt . . . . Greg Wright
GyA . . . . Gary Amaro
GyC . . . . . . Gerry Conway
GyD . . . . Guy Davis
GyM . . . . Gary Martin
HaE. . . . . . Harlan Ellison
HB . . . Hernandez Brothers
HbK. . . . . . . Hannibal King
HC . . . . . Howard Chaykin
HFl. . . . . Homer Flemming
HH. . . . . Hugh Haynes
HK . . . . . Harvey Kurtzman
HMe . . . . . Howard Mackie
HMo . . . .
Harvey Mercadoocasio
HMz . . . . . Henry Martinez
HN. . . . . Howard Nostrand
HNg. . . . . . Hoang Nguyen
HPo . . . . . . Howard Porter
HSm . . . . . . Howard Shum
HSn . . . . Howard Simpson
HT. . . . . Herb Trimpe
HuR. . . . Humberto Ramos
HWe . . . Howard Weinstein
HwP . . . . Howard Post
IaC . . . . . . Ian Churchhill
IEd . . . . Ian Edginton
IG . . . . Ian Gibson
IN . . . . Irv Novick
IV . . . . Ivan Velez, Jr.
JA . . . . Jack Abel
JaB. . . . . Jack Binder
JaD . . . . Jamie Delano
JaL. . . . . Jae Lee
JAl. . . . . Jeff Albrecht
JAo . . . . John Albano
JAp . . . . Jim Aparo
JAr . . . . John Arcudi
JB . . . . John Buscema
JBa. . . . . Jim Baikie
JBa. . . . . Jim Balent
JBe . . . . John Beeston
JBg. . . . . . Jon Bogdanove
JBi . . . . Jerry Bingham
JBl . . . . Jesus Blasco
JBm . . . . John Broom
JBn . . . . John Burns
JBo. . . . . John Bolton
JBr . . . . June Brigman
JBt . . . . Jeff Butler
JBy . . . . John Byrne
JBz. . . . . Joe Benitez
JCa . . . . John Calnan
JCf . . . . Jim Calafiore
JCh. . . . . Joe Chiodo
JCo . . . . Jack Cole
JCp. . . . . John Cooper
JCr . . . . Johnny Craig
JCt . . . . Joe Carter
JCx . . . . Jeromy Cox
JCz. . . . . Jerry Cruz
JD . . . . Jan Duursema

JDa . . . . Jack Davis
JDo . . . . Julie Doucet
JDx . . . . John Dixon
JDy . . . . Jo Duffy
JeJ . . . . Jeff Jones
JeM . . . . . . Jerome Moore
JeP . . . . Jerry Prosser
JeR. . . . . James Robinson
JEs . . . . John Estes
JF . . . . John Forte
JFM . . John Francis Moore
JFr . . . . John Freeman
JFy . . . . James Fry III
JG . . . . Jackson Guice
JGa . . . . . . Jack Gaughan
JGz . . . . . Jorge Gonzalez
JH . . . . Jack Herman
JhB. . . . . John Beatty
JhD . . . . John Dell
JHi . . . . John Higgins
JHk . . . . . John Hicklenton
JHl. . . . . . . James Hudnall
JHo . . . . . John Holdredge
JHr . . . . Jaime Hernandez
JHw . . . . . . Jamie Hewlett
JiC . . . . Jim Callahan
JiS . . . . Jim Shooter
JJ . . . . Jeff Johnson
JJB. . . . . JJ Birch
JJn . . . . Julius Jackson
JJo . . . . J.B. Jones
JJu . . . . Joe Jusko
JK. . . . . Jack Kirby
JKa . . . . Jack Kamen
JkS . . . . Jack Sparling
JKu . . . . Joe Kubert
JKz . . . . Jack Katz
JL . . . . Jose Lopez
JLb . . . . Jeph Loeb
JLd. . . . . Joe Lansdale
JLe . . . . Jim Lee
JLi . . . . Joseph M. Linsner
JlT. . . . . Jill Thompson
JLv. . . . . Jim Lavery
JM . . . . Jim Mooney
JMC . . . . John McCrea
JMd . . . . . . Joe Madureira
JMD. . . . . . J.M. DeMatteis
JMi . . . . Jeff Mariotte
JmL . . . . Jim Lawson
JMn. . . . . Joe Maneely
JmP . . . . . . James Pascoe
JMr. . . . . Jeff Moore
JMs. . . . . Jeff Matsuda
JMt . . . . Joe Martin
JMu . . . . Jon J. Muth
JMy. . . . . Jeffrey Moy
JMz. . . . . Jose Marzan
JnM . . . . Jason Minor
JnR . . . . John Riley
JNR . . . . John Ney Rieber
JnS . . . . John Smith
JO . . . . Joe Orlando
JoA. . . . . Jo Alibaster
JoB . . . . Joe Bennett
JoC . . . . Joe Casey
JOb . . . . James O'Barr
JoG. . . . . Joe Giella
JoM . . . . Joe Musial

JOn . . . . James Owen
JoP . . . . Joe Phillips
JoS . . . . Joe Shuster
JOs. . . . . . John Ostrander
JOt . . . . Jose Ortiz
JOy . . . . Jerry Ordway
JP. . . . . . . Jimmy Palmiotti
JPe . . . Jonathan Peterson
JPh . . . . James Perham
JPi . . . . Joe St.Pierre
JPL. . . . . . John Paul Leon
JPn . . . . Jason Pearson
JQ . . . . Joe Quesada
JR . . . . John Romita
JR2 . . . . . John Romita, Jr.
JRe . . . . John Royle
JRl. . . . . Jim Royle
JRo . . . . J. Rosenberger
JRs . . . . John Ross
JRu . . . . Joe Rubinstein
JRv Judith Reeves-Stevens
JRy . . . . . . John Ridgeway
JRz . . . . John Rozum
JS . . . . Javier Saltares
JS3 . . . . . . Jim Sanders III
JSb . . . . . . Jonathan Sibal
JSc . . . . Jeffery Scott
JSC. . . . J. Scott Campbell
JSe. . . . . John Severin
JSh . . . . Jim Sherman
JSi. . . . . Jeff Smith
JSm . . . . Joe Simon
JSn . . . . Jim Starlin
JSo. . . . . Jim Steranko
JSon . . . . Joe Staton
JSt . . . . Joe Sinnott
JTo . . . . John Totleben
JuB. . . . . Julie Bell
JV . . . . Jim Valentino
JVF . . . . . . John Van Fleet
JWf . . . . Joseph Wolfe
JWi . . . . J.H. Williams
JWk . . . . John Watkiss
JWo. . . . . Jim Woodring
JWp . . . . Jason Waltrip
JWt . . . . John Waltrip
JyS . . . . Jerry Serpe
JZ. . . . . Jorge Zaffino
JZe . . . . Joe Zabel
JZy . . . . Joseph Zyskowski
K&R. . . . . Kane & Romita
KB . . . . Kyle Baker
KBk. . . . . Kurt Busiek
KD . . . . Kieron Dwyer
KDe . . . . Kim Deitch
KDM . . . . . . Kim DeMulder
KEa. . . . . . . Kevin Eastman
KeL . . . . Ken Lashley
KeW. . . . . Kevin Walker
KG . . . . Keith Giffen
KGa . . . . Kerry Gammill
KHd . . . . . Kevin Hopgood
KHt . . . . Kyle Hotz
KJ . . . . Klaus Janson
KJa . . . . Kirk Javinen
KJo . . . . Kelley Jones
KK . . . . Karl Kesel
KlA . . . . Karl Alstaetter
KlK. . . . . Karl Kerschl

Abbreviation	Name
KIS	Karl Story
KM	Kevin Maguire
KN	Kevin Nowlan
KoK	Kevin Kobasic
KON	Kevin O'Neill
KP	Keith Pollard
KPl	Kilian Plunkett
KS	Kurt Schaffenberger
KSW	Keith S. Wilson
KSy	Ken Steacy
KtH	Kurt Hathaway
KVH	Kevin VanHook
KW	Kent Williams
KWe	Kevin West
KWi	Keith Williams
KWo	Kirk Van Wormer
LbC	**Leonard B. Cole**
LC	Lou Cameron
LCh	Lillian Chestney
LDr	Larry Dresser
LDu	Leo Duranona
LDz	Luis Dominguez
LE	Lee Elias
LeS	Len Strazewski
LF	Lou Fine
LHa	Larry Hama
LI	Larry Ivie
LiM	Linda Medley
LJi	Leonardo Jimenez
LKa	Len Kaminski
LLi	Larry Lieber
LMa	Larry Mahlstedt
LMc	Luke McDonnell
LMd	Lee Moder
LMr	Lee Marrs
Low	John Lowe
LRs	Luke Ross
LS	Lee Sullivan
LSh	Liam Sharp
LSi	Louise Simonson
LSn	Larry Stroman
LSt	Leonard Starr
LuH	Lou Harrison
LW	Lee Weeks
LWn	Len Wein
LyW	Larry Welch
MA	**Murphy Anderson**
MaG	Manny Galan
MaH	Mark Hempel
Man	Roland Mann
MaS	Mark Schmitz
MaT	Mark Tenney
MB	Matt Baker
MBa	Mark Bagley
MBe	M. Belardinelli
MBg	Mark Badger
MBm	Mary Bierbaum
MBn	Mike Baron
MBr	Mark Bright
MBu	Mark Buckingham
MBy	Mitch Byrd
MC	Mike Collins
MCa	Marc Campos
MCh	Mike Chen
MCi	Mark Crilley
MCl	Mike Clark
MCn	Max Allan Collins
MCo	Mark Chiarello
MCr	Mike Carlin
MCW	M.C. Wyman
MCy	Mike Carey
MD	Mort Drucker
MD2	Mike Deodato, Jr.
MDa	Malcolm Davis
MDb	M. DeZuniga
MDo	Mike Dorey
MDr	Mike Dringenberg
ME	Mike Esposito
MEg	Marty Egeland
MeP	Mike Parobeck
MeW	Mike Weringo
MF	Matt Fox
MFl	Michael Fleisher
MFm	Mark Farmer
MFr	Michael Jan Friedman
MG	Mike Gustovich
MGi	Michael T. Gilbert
MGo	Michael Golden
MGr	Mike Grell
MGs	Martin Griffiths
MGu	Mark Gruenwald
MGy	Mick Gray
MHi	Michael Higgins
MHo	Matt Howarth
MHs	Mike Heisler
MHw	Matt Hawkins
MHy	Matt Haley
MI	Medio Iorio
MiA	Michael Allred
MiB	Mike Barr
MJ	Malcolm Jones
MK	Mike Kaluta
MkB	Mike Barreiro
MkF	Mike Friedrich
MkH	Mike Hoffer
MkK	Mike McKenna
MkW	Mark Wheatley
MlB	Michael Bair
MLe	Mike Leeke
MLr	Michael Lark
MM	Mike Manley
MMc	M. McMahon
MMe	Mort Meskin
MMi	Michael Mignola
MMK	Mike McKone
MMo	Mark Moretti
MMr	Mark Millar
MMy	Marat Mychaels
MN	Mike Netzer
MnN	Martin Nodell
Moe	Moebius
MP	Mike Ploog
MPa	Mark Pacella
MPc	Mark Paniccia
MPk	Martin Pasko
MPn	Mark Pennington
MR	Marshall Rogers
MRa	Mac Raboy
MRc	Mark Ricketts
MRi	Mike Richardson
MRy	Matt Ryan
MS	Mark Silvestri
MSh	Mark Schultz
MsM	Mike S. Miller
MSo	Mark Sasso
MSt	Malcolm Smith
MSy	Mike Sekowsky
MT	Mark Texeira
MtB	Matt Broome
MTk	Masashi Tanaka
MV	Mike Vosburg
MvR	Melvin Rubi
MW	Mary Wilshire
MWa	Mark Waid
MWg	Matt Wagner
MWn	Marv Wolfman
MZ	Mike Zeck
MZi	Michael Zulli
NA	**Neal Adams**
NBy	Norm Breyfogle
NC	Nick Cardy
ND	Nigel Dobbyn
Nel	Nelson
NGa	Neil Gaiman
NHa	Neil Hanson
NKu	Andy Kubert
NMa	Nathan Massengill
NNa	Nick Napolitano
NPl	Noly Panalign
NR	Nestor Redondo
NRd	Norm Rapmund
NSH	N. Steven Harris
NV	Neil Vokes
NyC	Nancy Collins
OW	**Ogden Whitney**
PaD	**Paco Diaz**
PaK	Paris T. Karounos
PaP	Paul Pelletier
PB	Pat Broderick
PBd	Philip Bond
PC	Paul Chadwick
PCu	Paris Cullins
PD	Peter Doherty
PDd	Peter David
PDi	Paul Dini
PFe	Pascual Ferry
PG	Paul Gulacy
PGa	Phil Gascoine
PGn	Paul Guinan
PGr	Peter Grau
PhH	Phil Hester
PJ	Phil Jimminiz
PJe	Paul Jenkins
PKr	Peter Krause
PlA	Paul Abrams
PLa	Peter Laird
PMo	Pete Morisi
PMs	Pat Mills
PNe	Paul Neary
PNu	Philip Nutman
PO	Patrick Olliffe
PPo	Paul Pope
PQ	Peter Quinones
PR	Paul Ryan
PrC	Peter Costanza
PrG	Peter Gross
PrM	Peter Milligan
PS	Paul Smith
PSj	Peter Snejbjerg
PtL	Patrick Lee
PuD	Paul Danner
PuJ	Paul Johnson
PuK	Paul Kupperberg
RA	**Ross Andru**
RAJ	R.A. Jones
RaP	Rachel Pollack
RB	Rich Buckler
RbB	Robert Bernstein
RbC	Robert Campenella
RBe	Ramon Bernado
RBn	Ryan Benjamin
RBr	Rick Burchett
RBu	Robert Burns
RC	Reed Crandall
RCa	Richard Case
RCl	Ricky Carralero
RCo	Richard Corben
RCr	Robert Crumb
RCz	Roger Cruz
RDB	Randy DuBerkr
RdM	Raymond Marais
RDm	Rodolfo Damaggio
RdD	Richard Delgado
RE	Ric Estrada
RF	Ron Frenz
RFl	Robert Fleming
RG	Ron Garney
RGd	Ruben Gerard
RgM	Rags Morales
RGr	Randy Green
RGs	R. Grossman
RGT	R.G. Taylor
RGu	Rebecca Guay
RH	Russ Heath
RHe	Richard Horie
RHo	Rick Hoberg
RHo	Rich Howell
RiB	Richard Bennett
Rip	Riply
RJ	Robert Jenney
RJn	Robert Jones
RkB	Rick Bryant
RkL	Rick Leach
RKu	Roy Krenkel
RL	Rick Leonardi
RLd	Rob Liefeld
RLe	Rik Levins
RLm	Ron Lim
RLv	R. Livingstone
RM	Rick Magyar
RMc	Ralph Macchio
RMn	Roland Mann
RMr	Roy Allan Martinez
RMz	Ron Marz
RN	Rudy Nebres
RnT	Ron Tinker
RoR	Ron Randall
RoW	on Wagner
RP	Rudy Palais
RPc	Richard Pace
RPi	Richard Pini
RQu	Randy Queen
RRa	Rich Rankin
RS	Ron Smith
RsB	Russell Braun
RSd	Randy Stradley
RsM	Russ Manning
RSm	Robin Smith
RSt	Roger Stern
RT	Romeo Tanghal
RtH	Robert Hebbard
RTs	Roy Thomas
RV	Rick Veitch
RyE	Randy Emberlin
RyL	Ray Lago
RyR	Rodney Ramos

Abbreviation	Name
S&K	**Simon & Kirby**
S&S	Siegel & Shuster
SA	Sergio Aragones
Sal	Sal Amendola
SAP	Shea Anton Pensa
SaV	Sal Velluto
SB	Sal Buscema
SBi	Stephen Bissette
SBs	Simon Bisley
SBt	Steve Butler
SC	Sid Check
ScB	Scott Benefiel
ScC	Scott Clark
SCh	Sean Chen
SCi	Sergio Cariello
ScK	Scott Kolins
ScL	Scott Lee
SCr	Steve Crespo
SCy	Simon Colby
SD	Steve Ditko
SDi	Steve Dillon
SDr	Stan Drake
SDR	Sam DeLaRosa
SEa	Scott Eaton
SeM	Steve Montano
SeP	Sean Phillips
SEp	Steve Epting
SeT	Steve Tappin
SEt	Steve Englehart
SF	Sal Finnocchiaro
SFr	Simon Freeman
SFu	Simon Furman
SG	Sam Glanzman
SGe	Sid Greene
SHa	Scott Hanna
ShG	Shannon Gallant
ShM	Sheldon Mayer
SHn	Simon Harrison
SHp	Scott Hampton
SI	Stuart Immonen
SK	Sam Kieth
SL	Steve Leialoha
SLi	Steve Lightle
SLo	Scott Lobdell
SM	Steve Miller
SMa	Shawn Martinbrough
SmC	Sam Citron
SMc	Scott McDaniel
SMI	Scott McCloud
SML	Sean McLaughlin
SMt	Steve Mattsson
SnW	Stan Woch
SPa	Stephen Platt
Spk	Spark
SPI	Scott Phillips
SPr	Stefan Petrucha
SR	Steve Rude
SRf	Sean Ruffner
SS	Stan Sakai
SSc	Sean Scoffield
SSe	Steven T. Seagle
SSh	Sean Shaw
SSr	Steve Skroce
SSt	Steve Stern
StA	Stephen Addeo
StB	Scott Benson
StC	Stan Campbell
StE	Steve Erwin
StG	Steve Grant
StL	Stan Lee
StP	Steve Pugh
SVa	Steve Vance
SvG	Steve Gerber
SvL	Salvador Larroca
SvP	Steve Parkhouse
SvS	Steve Stiles
SW	Scott Williams
SWi	Skip Williamson
SwM	Shawn McManus
SY	Steve Yeowell
SZ	Steven Zyskowski
TA	**Terry Austin**
TAr	Tom Artis
TB	Tim Boxell
TBd	Tim Bradstreet
TBe	Terry Beatty
TBm	Tom Bierbaum
TC	Travis Charest
TCk	Tomm Coker
TD	Tony DeZuniga
TDF	Tom DeFalco
TDr	Tom Derenick
TDz	Todd DeZago
TeB	Tex Blaisdell
TeH	Ted Halsted
TEI	Tim Eldred
TG	Tom Grummett
TGb	Tom Grindberg
TGo	Till Goodman
TH	Tim Hamilton
THa	Tim Harris
TJn	Todd Johnson
TKa	Terry Kavanagh
TKn	Trent Kaniuga
TKr	Teddy H. Kristiansen
TL	Tom Lyle
TLa	Terry LaBan
TLw	Terral Lawrence
TM	Todd McFarlane
TmB	Tim Burgard
TmC	Tom Christopher
TMd	Tom Mandrake
TMK	Ted McKeever
TMo	Tom Morgan
TmR	Tom Ryder
TMr	Terry Moore
TMs	Tom Mason
TmT	Tom Teney
TMw	Tom McCraw
TNa	Ted Naifeh
TnD	Tony Daniel
TnS	Tristan Schane
TNu	Todd Nauck
ToT	Tony Takezaki
TOz	Tayyar Ozkan
TP	Tom Palmer
TPe	Tom Peyer
TR	Tom Raney
TR	Ted Richards
TrR	Trina Robbins
TS	Tom Sutton
TSa	Tony Salmons
TSe	Tim Sale
TSg	Tom Sniegoski
TSr	Terry Shoemaker
TT	Timothy Truman
TTg	Tom Taggart
TTn	Ty Templeton
TV	Tim Vigil
TVE	Trevor Von Eeden
TvS	Trevor Scott
TWo	Teri Sue Wood
TY	Tom Yeates
TyD	Terry Dodson
TyH	Tony Harris
TyT	Tony Tallarico
VAz	**Vincent Alcazar**
VB	Vaughn Bode
VcL	Vince Locke
VGi	Vince Giarrano
ViC	Vince Colletta
VMk	Val Mayerik
VMo	Vincent Morosco
VRu	Vince Russell
VS	Val Semeiks
VV	Vagner Vargas
WaP	**Warren Pleece**
WB	Wayne Boring
WBu	W. Burroughs
WE	Will Eisner
WEI	Warren Ellis
WiS	William Stout
WK	Walt Kelly
Wld	Andrew Wildman
WmB	William Bossart
WMc	Walter McDaniel
WMo	Win Mortimer
Woj	Chuck Wojtkiewicz
WP	Wendy Pini
WPo	Whilce Portacio
WR	Werner Roth
WS	Walt Simonson
WSm	Will Simpson
WW	Wally Wood
YG	**Yvel Guichet**
YuK	Yukito Kisniro

GENERAL ABBREVIATIONS FOR COMICS LISTINGS

A:	Appearance of
(a)	Artist
Adapt.	Adaptation
Anniv.	Anniversary
Ann.#	Annual
(a&pl)	Art & Plot
(a&s)	Art & Script
B:	Beginning of
b:	Birth of
BU:	Back-Up Story
C:	Cameo Appearance
(c)	Cover
(c&s)	Cover and Script
D:	Death/Destruction of
Ed.	Edition
E:	Ending of
F:	Features
G.A.	Golden Age
GAm.	Graphic Album
GN or GNv	Graphic Novel
G-Size	Giant Size
HC	Hardcover
I:	Introduction of
(i)	Inks by
IR:	Identity Revealed
J:	Joins of
K-Size	King Size
L:	Leaving of
N:	New Costume
N#	No Issue Number
O:	Origin of
P(c)	Painted Cover
(p)	Pencils by
PF	Prestige Format
Ph(c)	Photographic cover
(pl)	Plotted by
Prev.	Preview
pt. or Pt.	Part
rep.	Reprinted issue
R:	Return/Revival of
rtd.	Retold
(s)	Scripted/Written by
S.A.	Silver Age
SC	Softcover
(s&i)	Scripts & inks
Spec.	Special
TPB	Trade Paperback
T.U.	Team-up
V: or vs.	Versus
W:	Wedding of
w/	With
w/o	Without
x-over	Crossover with

DC COMICS

A. BIZARRO

1999

1 (of 4) SvG,MBr,F:Al Bizarro 2.50
2 SvG,MBr,A:Superman. 2.50
3 SvG,MBr, ... 2.50
4 SvG,MBr, Viva Bizarro 2.50

ABSOLUTE VERTIGO

1995

Ashcan: Invisibles, other samples . . 6.00

ACCELERATE

DC/Vertigo June, 2000

1 (of 4) Great Escape 2.95
2 Great Escape,pt.2. . . . . 2.95
3 Great Escape,pt.3. . . . . 2.95
4 Great Escape,pt.4,concl.. . . . . . . 2.95

Action #30 © DC Comics, Inc.

ACTION

June, 1938

1 JoS,I&O:Superman;Rescues Evelyn Curry from electric chair. 200,000.00
2 JoS,V:Emil Norvell 22,000.00
3 JoS,V:Thorton Blakely 15,000.00
4 JoS,V:Coach Randall. 8,600.00
5 JoS,Emergency of Vallegho Dam 8,500.00
6 JoS,I:Jimmy Olsen, V:Nick Williams 8,400.00
7 JoS,V:Derek Niles 15,000.00
8 JoS,V:Gimpy 6,500.00
9 JoS,A:Det.Captain Reilly . . . 6,200.00
10 JoS,Superman fights for prison reform 10,000.00
11 JoS,Disguised as Homer Ramsey 3,300.00
12 JoS,Crusade against reckless drivers 3,500.00
13 JoS,I:Ultra Humanite. 5,700.00
14 JoS,BKa,V:Ultra Humanite, B:Clip Carson 3,300.00
15 JoS,BKa,Superman in Kidtown 4,700.00
16 JoS,BKa,Crusade against Gambling. 2,500.00
17 JoS,BKa,V:Ultra Humanite . 3,700.00
18 JoS,BKa,V:Mr.Hamilton O:Three Aces 2,400.00
19 JoS,BKa,V:Ultra Humanite B:Superman (c) 3,300.00
20 JoS,BKa,V:Ultra Humanite . 3,200.00
21 JoS,BKa,V:Ultra Humanite . 2,200.00
22 JoS,BKa,War between Toran and Galonia. 2,000.00
23 JoS,BKa,SMo,I:Lex Luthor . 6,000.00
24 JoS,BKa,BBa,SMo,FG,Meets Peter Carnahan 2,000.00
25 JoS,BKa,BBa,SMo,V:Medini 2,000.00
26 JoS,BKa,V:Clarence Cobalt. 2,000.00
27 JoS,BKa,V:Mr & Mrs.Tweed 1,600.00
28 JoS,BKa,JBu,V:Strongarm Bandit 1,600.00
29 JoS,BKa,V:Martin 2,000.00
30 JoS,BKa,V:Zolar 1,600.00
31 JoS,BKa,JBu,V:Baron Munsdorf 1,100.00
32 JoS,BKa,JBu,I:Krypto Ray Gun V:Mr.Preston 1,200.00
33 JoS,BKa,JBu,V:Brett Hall, O:Mr. America 1,200.00
34 JoS,BKa,V:Jim Laurg 1,100.00
35 JoS,BKa,V:Brock Walter . . . 1,100.00
36 JoS,BKa,V:StuartPemberton 1,100.00
37 JoS,BKa,V:Commissioner Kennedy, O:Congo Bill. . . . 1,200.00
38 JoS,BKa,V:Harold Morton . . 1,100.00
39 JoS,BKa,Meets Britt Bryson 1,100.00
40 JoS,BKa,Meets Nancy Thorgenson 1,100.00
41 JoS,BKa,V:Ralph Cowan, E:Clip Carson 1,000.00
42 V:Lex Luthor,I&O:Vigilante. . 1,400.00
43 V:Dutch O'Leary,Nazi(c) . . . 1,000.00
44 V:Prof. Steffens,Nazi(c). . . . 1,000.00
45 V:Count Von Henzel, I:Stuff,Nazi(c). 1,000.00
46 V:The Domino. 1,000.00
47 V:Lex Luthor—1st app. w/super powers,I:Powerstone 1,400.00
48 V:The Top 1,000.00
49 I:Puzzler 1,050.00
50 Meets Stan Doborak 1,000.00
51 I:Prankster 1,050.00
52 V:Emperor of America. 1,100.00
53 JBu,V:Night-Owl. 700.00
54 JBu,Meets Stanley Finchcomb 625.00
55 JBu,V:Cartoonist Al Hatt. 625.00
56 V:Emil Loring 625.00
57 V:Prankster 625.00
58 JBu,V:Adonis 625.00
59 I:Susie Thompkins,Lois Lane's niece. 600.00
60 JBu,Lois Lane-Superwoman! . 650.00
61 JBu,Meets Craig Shaw. 600.00
62 JBu,V:Admiral Von Storff 600.00
63 JBu,V:Professor Praline 600.00
64 I:Toyman 700.00
65 JBu,V:Truman Treadwell 575.00
66 JBu,V:Mr.Annister 575.00
67 JBu,Superman School for Officer's Training 575.00
68 A:Susie Thompkins 575.00
69 V:Prankster 575.00
70 JBu,V:Thinker 575.00
71 Superman Valentine's Day Special 550.00
72 V:Mr. Sniggle 550.00
73 V:Lucius Spruce. 550.00
74 Meets Adelbert Dribble. 550.00
75 V:Johnny Aesop. 550.00
76 A Voyage with Destiny 550.00
77 V:Prankster 550.00
78 The Chef of Bohemia. 550.00
79 JBu,A:J. Wilbur Wolfingham . . 550.00
80 A:Mr. Mxyzptlk (2nd App). . . . 800.00
81 Meets John Nicholas 575.00
82 JBu,V:Water Sprite. 525.00
83 I:Hocus and Pocus. 525.00
84 JBu,V:Dapper Gang 525.00
85 JBu,V:Toyman 525.00
86 JBu,V:Wizard of Wokit 525.00
87 V:Truck Hijackers. 525.00
88 A:Hocus and Pocus 525.00
89 V:Slippery Andy 525.00
90 JBu,V:Horace Rikker and the Amphi-Bandits 525.00
91 JBu,V:Davey Jones 500.00
92 JBu,V:Nowmie Norman 500.00
93 Superman Christmas story. . . 500.00
94 JBu,V:Bullwer `Bull' Rylie. . . . 500.00
95 V:Prankster 500.00
96 V:Mr. Twister 500.00
97 A:Hocus and Pocus 500.00
98 V:Mr. Mxyzptlk, A:Susie Thompkins 500.00
99 V:Keith Langwell 500.00
100 I:InspectorErskineHawkins 1,100.00
101 V:Specs Dour,A-Bomb(c). . 1,050.00
102 V:Mr. Mxyzptlk 500.00
103 V:Emperor Quexo 500.00
104 V:Prankster 500.00
105 Superman Christmas story. . 500.00
106 Clark Kent becomes Baron Edgestream 500.00
107 JBu,A:J.Wilbur Wolfingham . 500.00
108 JBu,V:Vince Vincent. 500.00
109 V:Prankster 500.00
110 A:Susie Thompkins 500.00
111 Cameras in the Clouds. 500.00
112 V:Mr. Mxyzptlk 500.00
113 Just an Ordinary Guy 500.00
114 V:Mike Chesney. 500.00
115 Meets Arthur Parrish 500.00
116 A:J. Wilbur Wolfingham 500.00
117 Superman Christmas story . . 500.00
118 The Execution of Clark Kent. 500.00
119 Meets Jim Banning. 500.00
120 V:Mike Foss. 500.00
121 V:William Sharp 500.00
122 V:Charley Carson. 500.00
123 V:Skid Russell 500.00
124 Superman becomes radioactive 525.00

Action #31 © DC Comics, Inc.

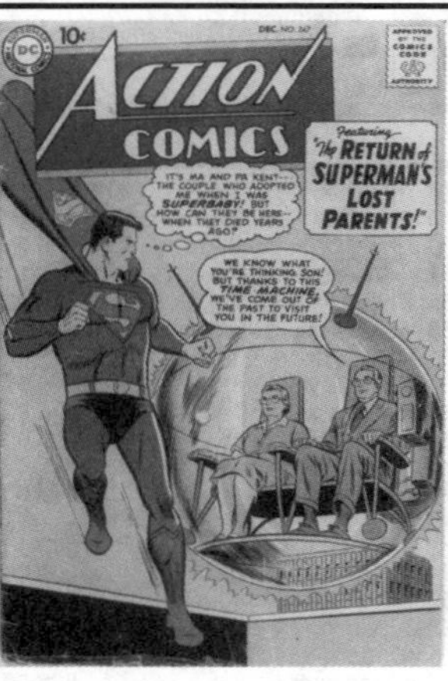

Action #250 © DC Comics, Inc.

Action #271 © DC Comics, Inc.

125 V:Lex Luthor 525.00
126 V:Chameleon 475.00
127 JKu,Superman on Truth or Consequences 525.00
128 V:`Aces' Deucey 450.00
129 Meets Gob-Gob 450.00
130 V:Captain Kidder 450.00
131 V:Lex Luthor 450.00
132 Superman meets George Washington 450.00
133 V:Emma Blotz 450.00
134 V:Paul Strong. 450.00
135 V:John Morton 450.00
136 Superman Show-Off! 450.00
137 Meets Percival Winter 450.00
138 Meets Herbert Hinkle 450.00
139 Clark Kent...Daredevil! 450.00
140 Superman becomes Hermit . 450.00
141 V:Lex Luthor 450.00
142 V:Dan the Dip 450.00
143 Dates Nikki Larve. 450.00
144 O:Clark Kent reporting for Daily Planet 450.00
145 Meets Merton Gloop 425.00
146 V:Luthor. 425.00
147 V:`Cheeks' Ross 425.00
148 Superman, Indian Chief 425.00
149 The Courtship on Krypton! . . 425.00
150 V:Morko 425.00
151 V:Mr.Mxyzptlk,Lex Luthor and Prankster. 425.00
152 I:Metropolis Shutterbug Society 425.00
153 V:Kingpin 425.00
154 V:Harry Reed 425.00
155 V:Andrew Arvin 425.00
156 Lois Lane becomes Super-woman,V:Lex Luthor. 425.00
157 V:Joe Striker 425.00
158 V:Kane Korrell O:Superman (retold) 1,000.00
159 Meets Oswald Whimple 400.00
160 I:Minerva Kent 400.00
161 Meets Antara 400.00
162 V:`IT!'. 350.00
163 Meets Susan Semple. 350.00
164 Meets Stefan Andriessen . . . 350.00
165 V:Crime Czar 350.00
166 V:Lex Luthor 350.00
167 V:Prof. Nero. 350.00
168 O:Olaf 350.00
169 Caveman Clark Kent!. 350.00
170 V:Mad Artist of Metropolis . . 350.00
171 The Secrets of Superman . . 350.00
172 Lois Lane..Witch! 350.00
173 V:Dragon Lang. 350.00
174 V:Miracle Twine Gang 350.00
175 V:John Vinden 350.00
176 V:Billion Dollar Marvin Gang 350.00
177 V:General 350.00
178 V:Prof. Sands. 350.00
179 Superman in Mapleville 350.00
180 V:Syndicate of Five 350.00
181 V:Diamond Dave Delaney . . 325.00
182 The Return from Planet Krypton 325.00
183 V:Lex Luthor 325.00
184 Meets Donald Whitmore. . . . 325.00
185 V:Issah Pendleton 325.00
186 The Haunted Superman. . . . 325.00
187 V:Silver 325.00
188 V:Cushions Raymond gang . 325.00
189 Meets Mr.&Mrs. John Vandeveir 325.00
190 V:Mr. Mxyzptlk 325.00
191 V:Vic Vordan 325.00
192 Meets Vic Vordan. 325.00
193 V:Beetles Brogan 325.00
194 V:Maln 325.00
195 V:Tiger Woman 325.00
196 Superman becomes Mental Man 325.00
197 V:Stanley Stark 325.00
198 The Six Lives of Lois Lane . . 325.00
199 V:Lex Luthor 325.00
200 V:Morwatha 325.00
201 V:Benny the Brute 325.00
202 Lois Lane's X-Ray Vision . . . 325.00
203 Meets Pietro Paresca. 325.00
204 Meets Sam Spulby. 325.00
205 Sergeant Superman. 325.00
206 Imaginary story featuring Lois Lane 325.00
207 Four Superman Medals!. . . . 325.00
208 V:Mr. Mxyzptlk 325.00
209 V:`Doc' Winters 325.00
210 V:Lex Luthor,I:Superman Land. 325.00
211 Superman Spectaculars 300.00
212 V:Thorne Varden 300.00
213 V:Paul Paxton 300.00
214 Superman,Sup.Destroyer! . . 300.00
215 I:Superman of 2956 . . . . 300.00
216 A:Jor-El 300.00
217 Meets Mr&Mrs.Roger Bliss. . 300.00
218 I:Super-Ape from Krypton. . . 300.00
219 V:Art Shaler 300.00
220 The Interplanetary Olympics 300.00
221 V:Jay Vorrell 275.00
222 The Duplicate Superman . . . 275.00
223 A:Jor-El 275.00
224 I:Superman Island 275.00
225 The Death of Superman. . . . 275.00
226 V:Lex Luthor 250.00
227 The Man with the Triple X-Ray Eyes 250.00
228 A:Superman Museum 250.00
229 V:Dr. John Haley 250.00
230 V:Bart Wellins 250.00
231 Sir Jimmy Olsen, Knight of Metropolis 250.00
232 Meets Johnny Kirk 250.00
233 V:Torm 250.00
234 Meets Golto 250.00
235 B:Congo Bill, B:Tommy Tomorrow 250.00
236 A:Lex Luthor 250.00
237 V:Nebula Gang 250.00
238 I:King Krypton,the Gorilla . . . 250.00
239 `Superman's New Face'. . . . 250.00
240 V:Superman Sphinx 250.00
241 WB,A:Batman,Fortress of Solitude (Fort Superman) . . . 200.00
242 I&O:Brainiac 1,500.00
243 Lady and the Lion 200.00
244 CS,A:Vul-Kor,Lya-La 200.00
245 WB,V:Kak-Kul 200.00
246 WB,A:Krypton Island 200.00
247 WB,Superman Lost Parents. 200.00
248 B&I:Congorilla 200.00
249 AP,A:Lex Luthor. 200.00
250 WB,`The Eye of Metropolis' . 200.00
251 AP,E:Tommy Tomorrow 200.00
252 I&O:Supergirl 1,500.00
253 B:Supergirl. 400.00
254 I:Adult Bizarro 300.00
255 I:Bizarro Lois 200.00
256 `Superman of the Future' . . . 135.00
257 WB,JM,V:Lex Luthor 135.00
258 A:Cosmic Man 135.00
259 A:Lex Luthor,Superboy. 135.00
260 A:Mighty Maid 135.00
261 I:Streaky,E:Congorilla. 135.00
262 A:Bizarro 135.00
263 O:Bizarro World 150.00
264 V:Bizarro 125.00
265 A:Hyper-Man 125.00
266 A:Streaky,Krypto 125.00
267 JM,3rd A:Legion,I:Invisible Kid 400.00
268 WB,A:Hercules 125.00
269 A:Jerro. 125.00
270 CS,JM,A:Batman 135.00
271 A:Lex Luthor 125.00
272 A:Aquaman 125.00
273 A:Mr.Mxyzptlk 125.00
274 A:Superwoman 125.00
275 WB,JM,V:Braimiac 125.00
276 JM,6th A:Legion,I:Brainiac 5, Triplicate Girl,Bouncing Boy . 175.00
277 CS,JM,V:Lex Luthor. 100.00
278 CS,Perry White Becomes Master Man 100.00
279 JM,V:Hercules,Samson 100.00
280 CS,JM,V:Braniac, A:Congorilla 100.00
281 JM,A:Krypto. 100.00
282 JM,V:Mxyzptlk 100.00
283 CS,JM,A:Legion of Super Outlaws 125.00
284 A:Krypto,Jerro 100.00
285 JM,Supergirl Existence Revealed, C:Legion (12th app.). 125.00
286 CS,JM,V:Lex Luthor. 75.00
287 JM,A:Legion. 75.00
288 JM,A:Mon-El 75.00
289 JM,A:Adult Legion 75.00
290 JM,C:Phantom Girl. 75.00
291 JM,V:Mxyzptlk 75.00

Action #280 © DC Comics, Inc.

292 JM,I:Superhorse 75.00
293 JM,O:Comet-Superhorse . . . 125.00
294 JM,V:Lex Luthor. 75.00
295 CS,JM,O:Lex Luthor 75.00
296 V:Super Ants 75.00
297 CS,JM,A:Mon-El 75.00
298 CS,JM,V:Lex Luthor. 75.00
299 O:Superman Robots 75.00
300 JM,A:Mxyzptlk 75.00
301 CS(c),JM,O:Superhorse. 40.00
302 CS(c),JM,O:Superhorse. 40.00
303 CS(c),Red Kryptonite story. . . 40.00
304 CS,JM,I&O:Black Flame. 50.00
305 CS(c),O:Supergirl. 40.00
306 JM,C:Mon-El,Brainiac 5 . . . . . 40.00
307 CS,JM,A:Saturn Girl. 40.00
308 CS(c),V:Hercules 40.00
309 CS,A:Batman,JFK,Legion. . . . 50.00
310 CS,JM,I:Jewel Kryptonite 35.00
311 CS,JM,O:Superhorse 35.00
312 CS,JM,V:Metallo-Superman . . 35.00
313 JM,A:Supergirl,Lex Luthor, Batman 35.00
314 JM,A:Justice League 35.00
315 JM,V:Zigi,Zag. 35.00
316 JM,A:Zigi,Zag,Zyra. 35.00
317 JM,V:Lex Luthor. 35.00
318 CS,JM,A:Brainiac. 35.00
319 CS,JM,A:Legion,V:L.Luthor . . 35.00
320 CS,JM,V:Atlas,Hercules 35.00
321 CS,JM,A:Superhorse 35.00
322 JM,`Coward of Steel' 35.00
323 JM,A:Superhorse. 35.00
324 JM,A:Abdul 35.00
325 CS,JM,SkyscraperSuperman . 35.00
326 CS,JM,V:Legion of Super Creatures 35.00
327 CS,JM,C:Brainiac. 35.00
328 JM,Hands of Doom 35.00
329 JM,V:Drang 35.00
330 CS,JM,Krypto 35.00
331 CS,V:Dr.Supernatural. 35.00
332 CS,A:Brainiac 35.00
333 CS(c),A:Lex Luthor 35.00
334 JM(c),A:Lex Luthor,80pgs . . . 60.00
335 CS,V:Lex Luthor 30.00
336 CS,O:Akvar 30.00
337 CS,V:Tiger Gang 30.00
338 CS,JM,V:Muto 30.00
339 CS,V:Muto,Brainiac 30.00
340 JM,I:Parasite 30.00
341 CS,V:Vakox,A:Batman 20.00
342 WB,JM,V:Brainiac 20.00
343 WB,V:Eterno 20.00
344 WB,JM,A:Batman. 20.00
345 CS(c),A:Allen Funt. 20.00
346 WB,JM. 20.00
347 CS(c),A:Supergirl, 80pgs.. . . . 50.00
348 WB,JM,V:Acid Master 20.00
349 WB,JM,V:Dr.Kryptonite. 20.00
350 A:JLA 20.00
351 WB,I:Zha-Vam 20.00
352 WB,V:Zha-Vam 20.00
353 WB,JM,V:Zha-Vam. 20.00
354 JM,A:Captain Incredible 20.00
355 WB,JM,V:Lex Luthor 20.00
356 WB,JM,V:Jr. Annihilitor. 20.00
357 WB,JM,V:Annihilitor 20.00
358 NA(c),CS,JM,A:Superboy. . . . 20.00
359 NA(c),CS,KS,C:Batman 20.00
360 CS(c),A:Supergirl, 80pgs.. . . . 45.00
361 NA(c),A:Parasite 18.00
362 RA,KS,V:Lex Luthor. 18.00
363 RA,KS,V:Lex Luthor. 18.00
364 RA,KS,V:Lex Luthor. 18.00
365 A:Legion & J.L.A.. . . . . 18.00
366 RA,KS,A:J.L.A. 18.00
367 NA(c),CS,KS,A:Supergirl 18.00
368 CS,KS,V:Mxyzptlk 18.00
369 CS,KS,Superman's Greatest Blunder 18.00
370 NA(c),CS,KS 18.00
371 NA(c),CS,KS 18.00
372 NA(c),CS,KS 18.00
373 A:Supergirl,(giant size). 35.00
374 NA(c),CS,KS,V:Super Thief . . 17.00
375 CS,KS,The Big Forget 17.00
376 CS,KS,E:Supergirl 17.00
377 CS,KS,B:Legion. 17.00
378 CS,KS,V:Marauder. 17.00
379 CS,JA,MA,V:Eliminator 17.00
380 KS,Confessions of Superman 17.00
381 CS,Dictators of Earth 17.00
382 CS,Clark Kent-Magician. 15.00
383 CS,The Killer Costume. 15.00
384 CS,The Forbidden Costume. . 15.00
385 CS,The Mortal Superman. . . . 15.00
386 CS,Home For Old Supermen . 15.00
387 CS,A:Legion,Even Supermen Die 15.00
388 CS,A:Legion,Puzzle of The Wild Word 15.00
389 A:Legion,The Kid Who Struck Out Superman. 15.00
390 CS,`Self-Destruct Superman'. 15.00
391 CS,Punishment of Superman's Son. 15.00
392 CS,E:Legion 15.00
393 CS,MA,RA,A:Super Houdini . . 15.00
394 CS,MA. 15.00
395 CS,MA,A:Althera 15.00
396 CS,MA. 15.00
397 CS,MA,Imaginary Story 15.00
398 NA(c),CS,MA,I:Morgan Edge . 15.00
399 NA(c),CS,MA,A:Superbaby . . 15.00
400 NA(c),CS,MA,Kandor Story . . 25.00
401 CS,MA,V:Indians 12.00
402 NA(c),CS,MA,V:Indians 20.00
403 CS,MA,Vigilante rep. 20.00
404 CS,MA,Aquaman rep 20.00
405 CS,MA,Vigilante rep. 20.00
406 CS,MA,Atom & Flash rep. . . . 20.00
407 CS,MA,V:Lex Luthor 20.00
408 CS,MA,Atom rep.. . . . . 20.00
409 CS,MA,T.Tommorrow rep. . . . 20.00
410 CS,MA,T.Tommorrow rep. . . . 20.00
411 CS,MA,O:Eclipso rep. 20.00
412 CS,MA,Eclipso rep. 20.00
413 CS,MA,V:Brainiac 20.00
414 CS,MA,B:Metamorpho 10.00
415 CS,MA,V:Metroplis Monster . . 10.00
416 CS,MA. 10.00
417 CS,MA,V:Luthor. 10.00
418 CS,MA,V:Luthor, E:Metamorpho 10.00
419 CS,MA,CI,DG,I:HumanTarget. 11.00
420 CS,MA,DG,V:Towbee. 9.00
421 CS,MA,B:Green Arrow. 10.00
422 CS,DG,O:Human Target 9.00
423 CS,MA,DG,A:Lex Luthor 9.00
424 CS,MA,Green Arrow 10.00
425 CS,DD,NA,DG,B:Atom. 20.00
426 CS,MA,Green Arrow 7.00
427 CS,MA,DD,DG,Atom 7.00
428 CS,MA,DG,Luthor 7.00
429 CS,BO,DG,C:JLA 7.00
430 CS,MA,DD,DG,Atom 7.00
431 CS,MA,Green Arrow 7.00
432 CS,MA,DG,Toyman 7.00
433 CS,BO,DD,DG,A:Atom. 7.00
434 CS,DD,Green Arrow 7.00
435 FM(c),CS,DD,DG,Atom 7.00
436 CS,DD,Green Arrow 7.00
437 CS,DG,Green Arrow (100 page giant). 25.00
438 CS,BO,DD,Atom 7.00
439 CS,BO,DD,Atom 7.00
440 1st MGr Green Arrow. 15.00
441 CS,BO,MGr,A:Green Arrow, Flash,R:Krypto 7.00
442 CS,MS,MGr,Atom 7.00
443 CS,A:JLA(100 pg.giant) 15.00
444 MGr,Green Arrow. 7.00
445 MGr,Green Arrow. 7.00
446 MGr,Green Arrow. 7.00
447 CS,BO,RB,KJ,Atom 7.00
448 CS,BO,DD,JL,Atom 7.00
449 CS,BO. 10.00
450 MGr,Green Arrow. 7.00
451 MGr,Green Arrow. 5.50
452 CS,MGr,Green Arrow. 5.50
453 CS,Atom 5.00
454 CS,E:Atom. 5.00
455 CS,Green Arrow 5.50
456 CS,MGr,Green Arrow. 5.50
457 CS,MGr,Green Arrow. 5.50
458 CS,MGr,I:Black Rock 5.50
459 CS,BO,Blackrock 5.00
460 CS,I:Karb-Brak 5.00
461 CS,V:Karb-Brak 5.00
462 CS,V:Karb-Brak 5.00
463 CS,V:Karb-Brak 5.00
464 CS,KS,V:Pile-Driver 5.00
465 CS,FMc,Luthor 5.00
466 NA(c),CS,V:Luthor 5.00
467 CS,V:Mzyzptlk 5.00
468 NA(c),CS,FMc,V:Terra-Man . . . 5.00
469 CS,TerraMan 5.00
470 CS,Flash Green Lantern 5.00
471 CS,V:Phantom Zone Female . . 5.00
472 CS,V:Faora Hu-Ul 5.00
473 NA(c),CS,Phantom Zone

Action #394 © DC Comics Inc.

Action #423 © DC Comics, Inc.

Villains 5.00
474 KS,V:Doctor Light 5.00
475 KS,V:Karb-Brak,A:Vartox 5.00
476 KS,V:Vartox 5.00
477 CS,DD,Land Lords of Earth . . . 5.00
478 CS,Earth's Last 5.00
479 CS. 5.00
480 CS,A:JLA,V:Amazo 5.00
481 CS,A:JLA,V:Amazo 5.00
482 CS,Amazo. 5.00
483 CS,Amazo,JLA 5.00
484 CS,W:Earth 2 Superman
& Lois Lane 7.00
485 NA(c),CS,rep.Superman#233. . 6.00
486 GT,KS,V:Lex Luthor 5.00
487 CS,AS,O:Atom. 5.50
488 CS,AS,A:Air Wave 5.00
489 CS,AS,A:JLA,Atom 5.00
490 CS,Brainiac 5.00
491 CS,A:Hawkman 5.00
492 CS,`Superman's After Life'. . . . 5.00
493 CS,A:UFO 5.00
494 CS. 5.00
495 CS. 5.00
496 CS,A:Kandor 5.00
497 CS. 5.00
498 CS,Vartox 5.00
499 CS,Vartox 5.00
500 CS,Superman's Life Story
A:Legion. 7.00
501 KS. 3.00
502 CS,A:Supergirl,Gal.Golem 3.00
503 CS,`A Save in Time' 3.00
504 CS,`The Power and Choice'. . . 3.00
505 CS. 3.00
506 CS. 3.00
507 CS,A:Jonathan Kent 3.00
508 CS,A:Jonathan Kent 3.00
509 CS,JSn,DG 3.50
510 CS,Luthor 3.00
511 CS,AS,V:Terraman,
A:Air Wave. 3.00
512 CS,RT,V:Luthor,A:Air Wave . . . 3.00
513 CS,RT,V:Krell,A:Air Wave. 3.00
514 CS,RT,V:Brainiac,A:Atom. 3.00
515 CS,AS,A:Atom. 3.00
516 CS,AS,V:Luthor,A:Atom 3.00
517 CS,DH,A:Aquaman 3.00
518 CS,DH,A:Aquaman 3.00
519 CS,DH,A:Aquaman 3.00
520 CS,DH,A:Aquaman 3.00
521 CS,AS,I:Vixen,A:Atom 3.00
522 CS,AS,A:Atom. 3.00
523 CS,AS,A:Atom. 3.00
524 CS,AS,A:Atom. 3.00
525 JSon,FMc,AS,I:Neutron
A:Air Wave. 3.00
526 JSon,AS,V:Neutron 3.00
527 CS,AS,I:Satanis,A:Aquaman . . 3.25
528 CS,AS,V:Brainiac,A:Aq'man . . . 3.00
529 GP(c),CS,DA,AS,A:Aquaman,
V:Brainiac. 3.00
530 CS,DA,Brainiac 3.00
531 JSon,FMc,AS,A:Atom 3.00
532 CS,C:New Teen Titans. 3.00
533 CS,V:The. 3.00
534 CS,AS,V:Satanis,A:Air Wave . . 3.00
535 GK(c),JSon,AS,
A:Omega Men 3.00
536 JSon,AS,FMc,A:Omega Men . . 3.00
537 IN,CS,AS,V:Satanis
A:Aquaman 3.00
538 IN,AS,FMc,V:Satanis,
A:Aquaman 3.00
539 KG(c),GK,AS,DA,A:Flash,
Atom,Aquaman 3.00
540 GK,AS,V:Satanis 3.00
541 GK,V:Satanis. 3.00
542 AS,V:Vandal Savage 3.00
543 CS,V:Vandal Savage 3.00
544 CS,MA,GK,GP,45th Anniv.
D:Ardora,Lexor. 4.00
545 GK,Brainiac 3.00
546 GK,A:JLA,New Teen Titans . . . 3.00
547 GK(c),CS. 3.00
548 GK(c),AS,Phantom Zone 3.00
549 GK(c),AS. 3.00
550 AS(c),GT. 3.00
551 GK,Starfire becomes
Red Star 3.00
552 GK,Forgotten Heroes
(inc.Animal Man) 6.00
553 GK,Forgotten Heroes(inc.
Animal Man). 6.00
554 GK(a&c) 2.75
555 CS,A:Parasite (X-over
Supergirl #20) 2.75
556 CS,KS,C:Batman. 2.75
557 CS,Terra-man 2.75
558 KS. 2.75
559 KS,AS 2.75
560 AS,KG,BO,A:Ambush Bug 2.75
561 KS,WB,Toyman 2.75
562 KS,Queen Bee. 2.75
563 AS,KG,BO,A:Ambush Bug 2.75
564 AS,V:Master Jailer. 2.75
565 KG,KS,BO,A:Ambush Bug 2.75
566 BO(i),MR 2.75
567 KS,AS,PB 2.75
568 CS,AW,AN. 2.75
569 IN 2.75
570 KS. 2.75
571 BB(c),AS,A:Thresh 222 . . . . . . 2.75
572 WB,BO 2.75
573 KS,BO,AS 2.75
574 KS. 2.75
575 KS,V:Intellax 2.75
576 KS,Earth's Sister Planet. 2.75
577 KG,BO,V:Caitiff 2.75
578 KS,Parasite 2.75
579 KG,BO,Asterix Parody 2.75
580 GK(c),KS,Superman's Failure . 2.75
581 DCw(c),KS,Superman
Requires Legal aid 2.75
582 AS,KS,Superman's Parents
Alive. 2.75
583 CS,KS,AMo(s),Last Pre
Crisis Superman. 7.00
584 JBy,DG,A:NewTeenTitans,
I:Modern Age Superman. 4.00
585 JBy,DG,Phantom Stranger. . . . 3.50
586 JBy,DG,Legends,V:New
Gods,Darkseid 3.50
587 JBy,DG,Demon 3.50
588 JBy,DG,Hawkman 3.50
589 JBy,DG,Gr.Lant.Corp. 3.50

Action #662 © DC Comics, Inc.

590 JBy,DG,Metal Men. 3.50
591 JBy,V:Superboy,A:Legion. 3.50
592 JBy,Big Barda 3.50
593 JBy,Mr. Miracle 3.50
594 JBy,A:Booster Gold 3.50
595 JBy,A:M.Manhunter,
I:Silver Banshee. 3.50
596 JBy,A:Spectre,Millenium. 3.50
597 JBy,L.Starr(i),Lois V:Lana. 3.50
598 JBy,TyT,I:Checkmate 4.00
599 RA,JBy(i),A:MetalMen,
BonusBook. 3.50
600 JBy,GP,KS,JOy,DG,CS,MA,
MMi,A:Wonder Woman;
Man-Bat,V:Darkseid 7.00

Becomes:

ACTION WEEKLY

1988–89

601 GK,DSp,CS,DJu,TD,
B:Superman,Gr.Lantern,
Blackhawk,Deadman,Secret
Six,Wilddog 2.50
602 GP(c),GK,DSp,CS,DJu,TD. . . . 2.50
603 GK,CS,DsP,DJu,TD 2.50
604 GK,DSp,CS,DJu,TD. 2.50
605 NKu/AKu(c),GK,DSp,CS,
DJu,TD 2.50
606 DSp,CS,DJu,TD. 2.50
607 SLi(c),TD,DSp,CS,DJu. 2.50
608 DSp,CS,DJu,TD,E:Blackhawk . 2.50
609 BB(c),DSp,DJu,TD,CS,
E:Wild Dog,B:Black Canary . . . 2.50
610 KB,DJu,CS,DSp,TD,CS
A:Phantom Stranger. 2.50
611 AN(c),DJu,DSp,CS,BKi,TD,
BKi,B:Catwoman 3.00
612 PG(c),DSp,CS,BKi,TD,
E:Secret Six,Deadman 2.75
613 MK(c),BKi,CS,MA,TGr,
Nightwing,B:Phantom Stranger. 2.75
614 TG,CS,Phantom Stranger
E:Catwoman 2.75
615 MMi(c),CS,MA,BKi,TGr,
Blackhawk,B:Wild Dog 2.50
616 ATh(c),CS,MA,E:Bl.Canary . . . 2.50
617 CS,MA,JO,A:Ph.Stranger. 2.50
618 JBg(c),CS,MA,JKo,TD,
B:Deadman,E:Nightwing. 2.50
619 CS,MA,FS,FMc,KJo,TD,FMc,
B:Sinister Six.. . . . . 2.50
620 CS,MA,FS,FMc,KJo,TD 2.50
621 JO(c),CS,MA,FS,FMc,KJo,
TD,MBr,E:Deadman 2.50
622 RF(c),MBr,TL,CS,MA,FS,

FMc,A:Starman,E:Wild Dog,Blackhawk 2.50
623 MBr,TD,CS,MA,FS,FMc,JL, JKo,A:Ph.Stranger, B:Deadman,Shazam 2.50
624 AD(c),MBr,FS,FMc,CS,MA, TD,B:Black Canary. 2.50
625 MBr,FS,FMc,CS,MA, TD,FMc 2.50
626 MBr,FS,FMc,CS,MA,JKo,TD, E:Shazam,Deadman 2.50
627 GK(c),MBr,RT,FS,FMc,CS, MA,TMd,B:Nightwing,Speedy . . 2.50
628 TY(c),MBr,RT,TMd,CS,MA, FS,FMc,B:Blackhawk 2.50
629 CS,MA,MBr,RT,FS,FMc,TMd . . 2.50
630 CS,MA,MBr,RT,FS,FMc,TMd, E:Secret Six. 2.50
631 JS(c),CS,MA,MBr,RT,TMd, B:Phantom Stranger. 2.50
632 TGr(c),CS,MA,MBr,RT,TMd . . . 2.50
633 CS,MA,MBr,RT,TMd. 2.50
634 CS,MA,MBr,RT,TMd,E:Ph.Strangr, Nightwing/Speedy,Bl.hawk 2.50
635 CS,MA,MBr,RT,EB,E:Black Canary,Green Lantern 2.50
636 DG(c),CS,MA,NKu,MPa,FMc, B:Demon,Wild Dog,Ph.Lady, Speedy,A:Phantom Stranger. . . 2.50
637 CS,MA,KS,FMc,MPa, B:Hero Hotline 2.50
638 JK(c),CS,MA,KS,FMc,MPa. . . . 2.50
639 CS,MA,KS,FMc,MPa 2.50
640 CS,KS,MA,FS,FMc,MPa, E:Speedy,Hero Hotline 2.50
641 CS,MA,JL,DG,MPa,E:Demon, Phant.Lady,Superman,Wild Dog, A:Ph.Stranger,Hum.Target 2.50
642 GK,SD,ATi,CS,JAp,JM,CI,KN, Green Lantern,Superman 2.50

Becomes:

ACTION COMICS

1989–97

643 B:RSt(s),GP,BBr,V:Intergang . . 3.50
644 GP,BBr,V:Matrix. 2.75
645 GP,BBr,I:Maxima 2.75
646 KG,V:Alien Creature, A:Brainiac 3.00
647 GP,KGa,BBr,V:Brainiac 2.75
648 GP,KGa,BBr,V:Brainiac 2.75
649 GP,KGa,BBr,V:Brainiac 2.75
650 JOy,BBr,CS,BMc,GP,KGa, ATi,DJu,A:JLA,C:Lobo 4.50
651 GP,KGa,BBr,Day of Krypton Man #3,V:Maxima 3.00
652 GP,KGa,BBr,Day of Krypton Man #6,V:Eradicator. 3.00
653 BMc,BBr,D:Amanda. 2.75
654 BMc,BBr,A:Batman Pt.3. . . . . . 3.00
655 BMc,BBr,V:Morrisson,Ma Kent's Photo Album 2.75
656 BMc,BBr,Soul Search #1, V:Blaze 2.75
657 KGa,BBr,V:Toyman 2.75
658 CS,Sinbad Contract #3 . . . . . . 2.75
659 BMc,BBr,K.Krimson Kryptonite #3 . . . . 4.00
660 BMc,BBr,D:Lex Luthor 3.50
661 BMc,BBr,A:Plastic Man 2.75
662 JOy,JM,TG,BMc,V:Silver Banshee,Clark tells Lois his identity 4.50
662a 2nd printing 2.75
663 BMc,Time & Time Again,pt.2, A:JSA,Legion 2.75
664 BMc,Time & Time Again,pt.5 . . 2.75
665 TG,V:Baron Sunday. 2.75
666 EH,Red Glass Trilogy,pt.3 . . . . 2.75
667 JOy,JM,TG,ATi,DJu,Revenge of the Krypton Man,pt.4 . . . . . . 3.00
668 BMc,Luthor confirmed dead . . . 2.75
669 BMc,V:Intergang,A:Thorn. 2.75
670 BMc,A:Waverider,JLA,JLE 2.75
671 KD,Blackout,pt.2 . . . . 2.75
672 BMc,Superman Meets Lex Luthor II 2.75
673 BMc,V:Hellgramite 2.75
674 BMc,Panic in the Sky (Prologue) R:Supergirl(Matrix) 6.00
675 BMc,Panic in the Sky #4, V:Brainiac. 3.00
676 B:KK(s),JG,A:Supergirl,Lex Luthor II 2.75
677 JG,Supergirl V:Superman 2.75
678 JG,O:Lex Luthor II 2.75
679 JG,I:Shellshock 2.75
680 JG,Blaze/Satanus War,pt.2 . . . 2.75
681 JG,V:Hellgramite 2.75
682 DAb,TA,V:Hi-Tech 2.75
683 JG,I:Jackal,C:Doomsday 3.00
683a 2nd printing 2.00
684 JG,Doomsday Pt.4. . . . . 4.00
684a 2nd printing 2.00
685 JG,Funeral for a Friend#2 . . . . 3.00
686 JG,Funeral for a Friend#6 . . . . 3.00
687 JG,Reign of Superman #1,Direct Sales,Die-Cut(c),Mini-Poster, F:Last Son of Krypton. 2.50
687a newsstand Ed. 2.00
688 JG,V:Guy Gardner 3.00
689 JG,V:Man of Steel,A:Superboy, Supergirl,R:Real Superman . . . 3.50
690 JG,Cyborg Vs. Superboy 2.50
691 JG,A:All Supermen,V:Cyborg Superman,Mongul 3.00
692 JG,A:Superboy,Man of Steel . . 2.25
693 JG,A:Last Son of Krypton. 2.25
694 JG,Spilled Blood#2,V:Hi-Tech. . 2.25
695 JG,Foil(c),I:Cauldron,A:Lobo . . 3.00
695a Newsstand Ed. 2.00
696 JG,V:Alien,C:Doomsday. 2.50
697 JG,Bizarro's World#3, V:Bizarro 2.25
698 JG,A:Lex Luthor. 2.25
699 JG,A:Project Cadmus 2.25
700 JG,Fall of Metropolis#1 . . . . . . 3.00
700a Platinum Edition. 15.00
701 JG,Fall of Metropolis#5, V:Luthor 2.25
702 JG,DvM,B:DyM(s),R:Bloodsport 2.25
703 JG,DvM,Zero Hour. 2.25
704 JG,DvM,Eradicator. 2.25
705 JG,DvM,Supes real? 2.25
706 JG,DvM,A:Supergirl 2.25

Action #687 (die-cut) © DC Comics Inc.

707 JG,DvM,V:Shado Dragon. 2.25
708 JG,DvM,R:Deathtrap 2.25
709 JG,DvM,A:Guy Gardner, Warrior. 2.25
710 JG,DvM,Death of Clark Kent,pt.3 [new Miraweb format begins] . . 2.25
711 JG,DvM,Death of Clark Kent,pt.7 . . . . 2.25
712 Rescue Jimmy Olsen. 2.25
713. . . . . 2.25
714 R:The Joker. 2.25
715 DvM,DaR,V:Parasite 2.25
716 DvM,DaR,Trial of Superman . . 2.25
717 DvM,DaR,Trial of Superman . . 2.25
718 DvM,DRo,mystery of Demolitia 2.25
719 DvM,DRo. 2.25
720 DvM,DRo,Lois ends engagement. 3.50
721 DvM,DRo,lottery fever 2.25
722 DvM,DaR,Tornados in Smallville 2.25
723 V:Brainiac 2.25
724 V:S.T.A.R.labs monster 2.25
725 Tolos 2.25
726 DvM(s),TMo,DRo,Krisis of the Krimson Kryptonite follow-up . . 2.25
727 DvM(s),TMo,DRo,brutal weather in Metropolis, Final Night tie-in . 2.50
728 DvM(s),TG,DRo, Some Honeymoon!. 2.50
729 DvM(s),TG,DRo, in Fortress of Solitude 2.50
730 DvM(s),TG,Ro, ... 2.50
731 DvM(s),TG,DRo, R:Cauldron . . 2.50
732 DvM(s),TG,DRo, Atomic Skull rampages through Metropolis . . 2.25
733 DvM(s),TG,DRo, V:Matallo, A:Ray. 2.25
734 DvM(s),TG,DRo, Superman & Atom in Kandor 2.25
735 DvM(s),TG,DRo, V:Savior 2.25
736 DvM(s),TG,DRo. 2.25
737 MWa(s),TG,DRo, Luthor gets day in court 2.00
738 SI,JMz,Lois sent to Australia . . 2.00
739 SI,JMz,Superman imprisoned . 2.00
740 SI,JMz,Lucy Lane disappears . 2.00
741 SI,JMz,V:C.O.M.P.U.T.O. 2.00
742 SI,JMz. 2.00
743 SI,JMz,F:Slam Bradley. 2.00
744 SI,JMz,Millennium Giants x-over. 2.00
745 SI,JMz,The Prankster 2.00
746 SI,JMz,The Prankster,pt.2 . . . . 2.00
747 SI,JMz,The Prankster,pt.3 . . . . 2.00
748 SI,JMz,Dominus Theory. 2.00
749 RMz(s),TGb,TP,City of the Future, pt.1 x-over 2.00
750 SI,JMz,I:Crazytop, 48-page . . . 3.50
751 SI,JMz,A:Geo-Force 2.00
752 SI,JMz,Supermen of America x-over. 2.00
753 SI,JMz,A:JLA. 2.00
754 SI,JMz,R:Dominus, A:Wonder Woman 2.00
755 SI&MMr(s),King of the World aftermath 2.00
756 VGi,old villain is back. 2.00
757 TPe(s),TGb,Hawkworld,pt.3 . . . 2.00
758 SI,JMz,V:Boss Moxie 2.00
759 RF,SB,Strange Visitor,pt.3 . . . . 2.00
760 JRu,F:Encantadora 2.00
761 JRu 2.00
762 JRu,V:Demon Etrigan 2.00
763 JRu,V:Brainiac 13 . . . . 2.00
764 JRu,marital troubles. 2.00
765 JRu,V:Joker & Harley Quinn . . 2.00
766 F:Batman. 2.00
767 CriticalCondition,pt.4,x-over . . . 2.00
768 F:Marvel Family. 2.25
769 Superman:Arkham,concl. 2.25

Action #759 © DC Comics, Inc.

770 Superman:Emperor,48-pg. 4.00
771 CDi(s),F:Nightwing. 2.25
772 V:Ra's al Ghul,pt.1 . . . . 2.25
Ann.#1 AAd,DG,A:Batman 8.00
Ann.#2 MMi,CS,GP,JOy,DJu,BBr, V:Mongul 4.00
Ann.#3 TG,Armageddon X-over . . . 3.00
Ann.#4 Eclipso,A:Captain Marvel 3.00
Ann.#5 MZ(c),Bloodlines, I:Loose Cannon 3.00
Ann.#6 Elseworlds,JBy(a&S) 3.00
Ann.#7 Year One Annual 4.00
Ann.#8 DvM,"Legends of the Dead Earth". 3.00
Ann.#9 DvM,VGi,BBr,Pulp Heroes . 4.00
Archives, Vol. 1 S&S rep. 50.00
Archives, Vol. 2 S&S rep. 50.00
Gold.Ann.rep.#1 . . . . 1.50
#0 Peer Pressure,pt.4 (1994) 2.00
Spec.#1,000,000 MSh(s),RLm,JMz. 2.00

ADAM STRANGE
1990

1 NKu,A.Strange on Rann 5.00
2 NKu,Wanted:Adam Strange 4.50
3 NKu,final issue 4.50

ADVANCED DUNGEONS & DRAGONS
1988–91

1 JD,I:Onyx,Priam,Timoth, Cybriana,Vajra,Luna 5.00
2 JD,V:Imgig Zu,I:Conner 4.00
3 JD,V:Imgig Zu. 4.00
4 JD,V:Imgig Zu,I:Kyriani 3.00
5 JD,Spirit of Myrrth I. 3.00
6 JD,Spirit of Myrrth II 3.00
7 JD,Spirit of Myrrth III. 2.50
8 JD,Spirit of Myrrth IV 2.50
9 JD,Catspawn Quartet I 2.50
10 JD,Catspawn Quartet II 2.50
11 JD,Catspawn Quartet III. 2.50
12 JD,Catspawn Quartet IV 2.50
13 JD,Spell Games I. 2.50
14 JD,Spell Games II 2.50
15 JD,Spell Games III. 2.50
16 JD,Spell Games IV 2.50
17 JD,RM,Kyriani's Story I 2.50
18 JD,RM,Kyriani's Story II. 2.50
19 JD,RM,Luna I 2.50
20 JD,RM,Luna II 2.50

Advanced Dungeons & Dragons #1 © DC Comics, Inc.

21 JD,RM,Luna III 2.50
22 JD,RM,Luna IV 2.50
23 TMd,RM,Siege Dragons I. 2.50
24 Scavengers 2.50
25 JD,RM,Centaur Village 2.00
26 JD,Timoth the Centaur. 2.00
27 JD,Kyriani,Dragons Eye #1 . . . . 2.00
28 JD,Dragons Eye #2 . . . . 2.00
29 JD,RM,Dragons Eye #3 . . . . 2.00
30 JD,RM,Carril's Killer Revealed 2.00
31 TMd,Onyx'Father,pt.1 . . . . 2.00
32 TMd,Onyx'Father,pt.2 . . . . 2.00
33 JD,Waterdeep,pt.1. . . . . 2.00
34 JD,Waterdeep,pt.2. . . . . 2.00
35 JD,RM,Waterdeep,pt.3. . . . . 2.00
36 JD,RM,final issue. 2.00
Ann.#1 JD,RM,Tmd 4.00

ADVENTURE COMICS
Nov., 1938–83
[Prev: New Comics]

32 CF(c) 3,400.00
33 . . . . 1,600.00
34 FG(c) 1,600.00
35 FG(c) 1,600.00
36 Giant Snake(c) 1,600.00
37 Rampaging Elephant(c). . . . 1,600.00
38 Tiger(c). 1,600.00
39 Male Bondage(c). 1,700.00
40 CF(c),1st app. Sandman . . 35,000.00
41 Killer Shark(c). 4,500.00
42 CF,Sandman(c). 5,500.00
43 CF(c) 2,500.00
44 CF,Sandman(c). 5,500.00
45 FG(c) 2,500.00
46 CF,Sandman(c). 3,800.00
47 Sandman (c) 3,600.00
48 1st app.& B:Hourman 22,000.00
49 . . . . 2,000.00
50 Hourman(c). 1,900.00
51 BBa(c),Sandman(c). 2,500.00
52 BBa(c),Hourman(c) 1,800.00
53 BBa(c),1st app. Minuteman. 1,700.00
54 BBa(c),Hourman(c) 1,700.00
55 BBa(c),same. 1,700.00
56 BBa(c),same. 1,700.00
57 BBa(c),same. 1,700.00
58 BBa(c),same. 1,700.00
59 BBa(c),same. 1,700.00
60 Sandman(c) 2,500.00
61 CF(c),JBu,Starman(c) 12,000.00
62 JBu(c),JBu,Starman(c) 1,400.00
63 JBu(c),JBu,same. 1,400.00
64 JBu(c),JBu,same. 1,400.00
65 JBu(c),JBu,same. 1,400.00
66 JBu(c),JBu,O:Shining Knight, Starman(c) 2,000.00
67 JBu(c),JBu,O:Mist 1,500.00
68 JBu(c),JBu,same. 1,500.00
69 JBu(c),JBu,1st app. Sandy, Starman(c) 1,600.00
70 JBu(c),JBu,Starman(c) 1,500.00
71 JBu(c),JBu,same. 1,400.00
72 JBu(c),S&K,JBu,Sandman. 11,000.00
73 S&K(c),S&K,I:Manhunter . . 12,000.00
74 S&K(c),S&K,You can't Escape your Fate-The Sandman . . 1,500.00
75 S&K(c),S&K,Sandman and Sandy Battle Thor in `Villian from Valhalla' 1,500.00
76 S&K(c),Sandman(c),S&K . . 1,500.00
77 S&K,(c),S&K,same 1,500.00
78 S&K(c),S&K,same. 1,500.00
79 S&K(c),S&K,Manhunter in `Cobras of the Deep' 1,600.00
80 S&K(c),Sandman(c),S&K . . 1,500.00
81 S&K(c),MMe,S&K,same . . . 1,000.00
82 S&K(c),S&K,Sandman X-Mas story 1,000.00
83 S&K(c),S&K,Sandman Boxing(c),E:Hourman. 1,000.00
84 S&K(c),S&K 1,000.00
85 S&K(c),S&K,Sandman in `The Amazing Dreams of Gentleman Jack' 1,000.00
86 S&K(c),Sandman(c) 1,000.00
87 S&K(c),same. 1,000.00
88 S&K(c),same. 1,000.00
89 S&K(c),same. 1,000.00
90 S&K(c),same. 1,000.00
91 S&K(c),JK 850.00
92 S&K(c). 750.00
93 S&K(c),Sandman in `Sleep for Sale' 750.00
94 S&K(c),Sandman(c). 750.00
95 S&K(c),same 750.00
96 S&K(c),same 750.00
97 S&K(c),same 750.00
98 JK(c),Sandman in `Hero of Dreams' 750.00
99 JK(c) 750.00
100 . . . . 1,000.00
101 S&K(c). 750.00
102 S&K(c). 750.00
103 B:Superboy stories,(c),BU: Johnny Quick,Aquaman,Shining Knight,Green Arrow 2,500.00
104 S&S,ToyTown USA 800.00
105 S&S,Palace of Fantasy 550.00
106 S&S,Weather Hurricane 550.00
107 S&S,The Sky is the Limit . . . 550.00
108 S&S,Proof of the Proverbs . . 550.00
109 S&S,You Can't Lose. 550.00
110 S&S,The Farmer Takes it Easy 550.00
111 S&S,The Whiz Quiz Club . . . 550.00
112 S&S,Super Safety First 550.00
113 S&S,The 33rd Christmas . . . 500.00
114 S&S,Superboy Spells Danger 500.00
115 S&S,The Adventure of Jaguar Boy. 500.00
116 S&S,JBu,Superboy Toy Tester. 500.00
117 S&S,JBu,Miracle Plane 500.00
118 S&S,JBu,The Quiz Biz Broadcast. 500.00
119 WMo,JBu,Superboy Meets Girls. 500.00
120 S&S,JBu,A:Perry White; I:Ringmaster. 525.00
121 S&S,Great Hobby Contest . . 450.00

122 S&S,Superboy-Super-Magician 450.00
123 S&S,Lesson For a Bully 450.00
124 S&S,Barbed Wire Boys Town 450.00
125 S&S,The Weight Before Christmas 450.00
126 S&S,Superboy:Crime Fighting Poet 450.00
127 MMe,O:Shining Knight; Super Bellboy 450.00
128 WMo,How Clark Kent Met Lois Lane' 450.00
129 WMo,Pupils of the Past 450.00
130 WMo,Superboy Super Salesman 450.00
131 WMo,The Million Dollar Athlete 400.00
132 WMo,Superboy Super Cowboy 400.00
133 WMo,Superboy's Report Card 400.00
134 WMo,Silver Gloves Sellout . . 400.00
135 WMo,The Most Amazing of All Boys 400.00
136 WMo,My Pal Superboy 400.00
137 WMo,Treasure of Tondimo . . 400.00
138 WMo,Around the World in Eighty Minutes 400.00
139 WMo,Telegraph Boy 400.00
140 Journey to the Moon 400.00
141 WMo,When Superboy Lost His Powers 400.00
142 WMo,The Man Who Walked With Trouble 450.00
143 WMo,The Superboy Savings Bank,A:Wooden Head Jones 450.00
144 WMo,The Way to Stop Superboy 450.00
145 WMo,Holiday Hijackers 450.00
146 The Substitute Superboy . . . 450.00
147 Clark Kent,Orphan 450.00
148 Superboy Meets Mummies . . 450.00
149 Fake Superboys 450.00
150 FF,Superboy's Initiation 500.00
151 FF,No Hunting(c) 500.00
152 Superboy Hunts For a Job . . 425.00
153 FF,Clark Kent,Boy Hobo 500.00
154 The Carnival Boat Crimes . . 350.00
155 FF,Superboy-Hollywood Actor 425.00
156 The Flying Peril 350.00
157 FF,The Worst Boy in Smallville 400.00
158 The Impossible Task 350.00
159 FF,Superboy Millionaire? . . . 400.00

Adventure #40 © DC Comics Inc.

160 Superboy's Phoney Father . . 350.00
161 FF 400.00
162 `The Super-Coach of Smallville High!' 350.00
163 FF,`Superboy's Phoney Father' 400.00
164 Discovers the Secret of a Lost Indian Tribe! 350.00
165 `Superboy's School for Stunt Men!' 350.00
166 `The Town That Stole Superboy' 350.00
167 `Lana Lang, Super-Girl!' 350.00
168 `The Boy Who Out Smarted Superboy' 350.00
169 `Clark Kent's Private Butler' 350.00
170 `Lana Lang's Big Crush' 325.00
171 `Superboy's Toughest Tasks!' 325.00
172 `Laws that Backfired' 325.00
173 `Superboy's School of Hard Knocks' 325.00
174 `The New Lana Lang!' 325.00
175 `Duel of the Superboys' 325.00
176 `Superboy's New Parents!' . . 325.00
177 `Hot-Rod Chariot Race!' 325.00
178 `Boy in the Lead Mask' 325.00
179 `The World's Whackiest Inventors' 325.00
180 Grand Prize o/t Underworld . 325.00
181 `Mask for a Hero' 325.00
182 The Super Hick from Smallville' 300.00
183 `Superboy and Cleopatra' . . 300.00
184 `The Shutterbugs of Smallville' 300.00
185 `The Mythical Monster' 300.00
186 . . . . . 300.00
187 `25th Century Superboy' . . . 300.00
188 `The Bull Fighter from Smallville' 300.00
189 Girl of Steel(Lana Lang) 300.00
190 The Two Clark Kents 300.00
191 . . . . . 300.00
192 `The Coronation of Queen Lana Lang' 300.00
193 `Superboy's Lost Costume' . 300.00
194 `Super-Charged Superboy' . . 300.00
195 `Lana Lang's Romance on Mars!' 300.00
196 `Superboy vs. King Gorilla' . . 300.00
197 V:Juvenile Gangs 300.00
198 `The Super-Carnival from Space' 300.00
199 `Superboy meets Superlad' . 300.00
200 `Superboy and the Apes!' . . . 450.00
201 `Safari in Smallville!' 300.00
202 `Superboy City, U.S.A.' 300.00
203 `Uncle Superboy!' 325.00
204 `The Super-Brat of Smallville' 300.00
205 `The Journey of the Second Superboy!' 300.00
206 `The Impossible Creatures' . 300.00
207 `Smallville's Worst Athlete' 300.00
208 `Rip Van Winkle of Smallville?' 300.00
209 `Superboy Week!' 300.00
210 I:Krypto,`The Superdog from Krypton' 3,200.00
211 `Superboy's Most Amazing Dream!' 275.00
212 `Superboy's Robot Twin' . . . 275.00
213 `The Junior Jury of Smallville!' 275.00
214 A:Krypto 500.00
215 `The Super-Hobby of Superboy' 275.00
216 `The Wizard City' 275.00

217 `Superboy's Farewell to Smallville' 275.00
218 `The Two World's of Superboy' 275.00
219 The Rip Van Wrinkle of Smallville 275.00
220 The Greatest Show on Earth A:Krypto 275.00
221 `The Babe of Steel' 250.00
222 `Superboy's Repeat Performance' 250.00
223 `Hercules Junior' 250.00
224 `Pa Kent Superman' 250.00
225 `The Bird with Super-Powers' 250.00
226 `Superboy's Super Rival!' . . . 250.00
227 `Good Samaritan of Smallville' 250.00
228 `Clark Kent's Body Guard' . . 250.00
229 . . . . . 250.00
230 `The Secret of the Flying Horse' 225.00
231 `The Super-Feats of Super-Baby!' 225.00
232 `The House where Superboy was Born' 225.00
233 `Joe Smith, Man of Steel!' . . 225.00
234 `The 1,001 Rides of Superboy!' 225.00
235 `The Confessions of Superboy!' 225.00
236 `Clark Kent's Super-Dad!' . . . 225.00
237 Robot War of Smallville! 225.00
238 `The Secret Past of Superboy's Father' 225.00
239 `The Super-Tricks of the Dog of Steel' 225.00
240 `The Super Teacher From Krypton' 225.00
241 `The Super-Outlaw of Smallville' 225.00
242 `The Kid From Krypton' 225.00
243 `The Super Toys From Krypton' 225.00
244 `The Poorest Family in Smallville' 225.00
245 `The Mystery of Monster X' . 225.00
246 `The Girl Who Trapped Superboy!' 225.00
247 I&O:Legion 5,000.00
248 Green Arrow 175.00
249 CS,Green Arrow 175.00
250 JK,Green Arrow 175.00
251 JK,Green Arrow 175.00
252 JK,Green Arrow 175.00
253 JK,1st Superboy &

Adventure #293 © DC Comics Inc.

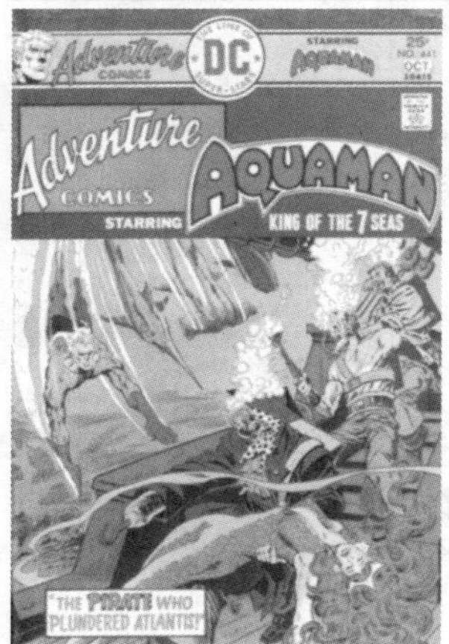

Adventure #441 © DC Comics, Inc.

Robin T.U. 250.00
254 JK,Green Arrow 185.00
255 JK,Green Arrow 185.00
256 JK,O:Green Arrow 600.00
257 CS,LE,A:Hercules,Samson. . 150.00
258 LE,Aquaman,Superboy 150.00
259 I:Crimson Archer 150.00
260 1st S.A. O:Aquaman 650.00
261 GA,A:Lois Lane 135.00
262 O:Speedy 135.00
263 GA,Aquaman,Superboy 135.00
264 GA,A:Robin Hood 135.00
265 GA,Aquaman,Superboy 135.00
266 GA,I:Aquagirl 135.00
267 N:Legion(2nd app.) 850.00
268 I:Aquaboy 135.00
269 I:Aqualad,E:Green Arrow . . . 225.00
270 2nd A:Aqualad,B:Congorilla . 135.00
271 O:Lex Luthor rtd. 250.00
272 I:Human Flying Fish 135.00
273 Aquaman,Superboy 135.00
274 Aquaman,Superboy 135.00
275 O:Superman/Batman
T.U. rtd 200.00
276 Superboy,3rd A:Metallo 125.00
277 Aquaman,Superboy 125.00
278 Aquaman,Superboy 125.00
279 CS,Aquaman,Superboy 125.00
280 CS,A:Lori Lemaris 125.00
281 Aquaman,Superboy
E:Congorilla 125.00
282 5th A:Legion,I:Starboy 200.00
283 I:Phantom Zone 175.00
284 CS,JM,Aquaman,Superboy . 125.00
285 WB,B:Bizarro World 150.00
286 I:Bizarro Mxyzptlk. 150.00
287 I:Dev-Em,Bizarro Perry White,
Jimmy Olsen 100.00
288 A:Dev-Em 100.00
289 Superboy. 100.00
290 8th A:Legion,O&J:Sunboy,
I:Brainiac 5 . . . . 175.00
291 A:Lex Luthor 85.00
292 Superboy,I:Bizarro Lucy Lane,
Lana Lang 85.00
293 CS,O&I:Marv-El,I:Bizarro
Luthor. 125.00
294 I:Bizarro M.Monroe,JFK 125.00
295 I:Bizarro Titano 85.00
296 A:Ben Franklin,George
Washington 85.00
297 Lana Lang Superboy Sister . . 85.00
298 The Fat Superboy 85.00
299 I:Gold Kryptonite 85.00
300 B:Legion,J:Mon-El,
E:Bizarro World 400.00
301 CS,O:Bouncing Boy 125.00
302 CS,Legion 100.00
303 I:Matter Eater Lad 100.00
304 D:Lightning Lad 100.00
305 A:Chameleon Boy 100.00
306 I:Legion of Sub.Heroes 100.00
307 I:Element Lad 100.00
308 I:Light Lass 100.00
309 I:Legion of Super Monsters . . 80.00
310 A:Mxyzptlk. 80.00
311 CS,V:Legion of Substitue
Heroes 70.00
312 R:Lightning Lad 80.00
313 CS,J:Supergirl 70.00
314 A:Hitler 70.00
315 A:Legion of Substitute
Heroes 70.00
316 O:Legion 60.00
317 I&J:Dreamgirl. 60.00
318 Legion 60.00
319 Legion 60.00
320 A:Dev-Em 60.00
321 I:Time Trapper 75.00
322 JF,A:Legion of Super Pets . . . 50.00
323 JF,BU:Kypto. 50.00
324 JF,I:Legion of
Super Outlaws 50.00
325 JF,V:Lex Luthor 50.00
326 BU:Superboy 50.00
327 I&J:Timber Wolf 50.00
328 Legion 50.00
329 I:Legion of Super Bizarros . . . 50.00
330 Legion 50.00
331 Legion 35.00
332 Legion 35.00
333 Legion 35.00
334 Legion 35.00
335 Legion 35.00
336 Legion 35.00
337 Legion 35.00
338 Legion 35.00
339 Legion 35.00
340 I:Computo 35.00
341 CS,D:Triplicate Girl (becomes
Duo Damsel) 28.00
342 CS,Star Boy expelled. 25.00
343 CS,V:Lords of Luck 25.00
344 CS,Super Stalag,pt.1. . . . . . . 25.00
345 CS,Super Stalag,pt.2 . . . . 25.00
346 CS,I&J:Karate Kid,Princess
Projectra,I:Nemesis Kid 30.00
347 CS,Legion 22.00
348 I:Dr.Regulus. 25.00
349 CS,I:Rond Vidar. 20.00
350 CS,I:White Witch 25.00
351 CS,R:Star Boy 20.00
352 CS,I:Fatal Fire 20.00
353 CS,D:Ferro Lad 25.00
354 CS,Adult Legion. 20.00
355 CS,J:Insect Queen. 18.00
356 CS,Five Legion Orphans 18.00
357 CS,I:Controller 18.00
358 I:Hunter 18.00
359 CS,Outlawed Legion,pt.1 . . . . 18.00
360 CS,Outlawed Legion,pt.2 . . . . 18.00
361 I:Dominators (30th century) . . 18.00
362 I:Dr.Mantis Morto 18.00
363 V:Dr.Mantis Morlo 18.00
364 A:Legion of Super Pets 18.00
365 CS,I:Shadow Lass,
V:Fatal Five 18.00
366 CS,J:Shadow Lass. 18.00
367 N:Legion H.Q.,I:Dark Circle . . 18.00
368 CS. 18.00
369 CS,JAb,I:Mordru 18.00
370 CS,JAb,V:Mordru 18.00
371 CS,JAb,I:Chemical King. 20.00
372 CS,JAb,J:Timber Wolf,
Chemical King 20.00
373 I:Tornado Twins 16.00

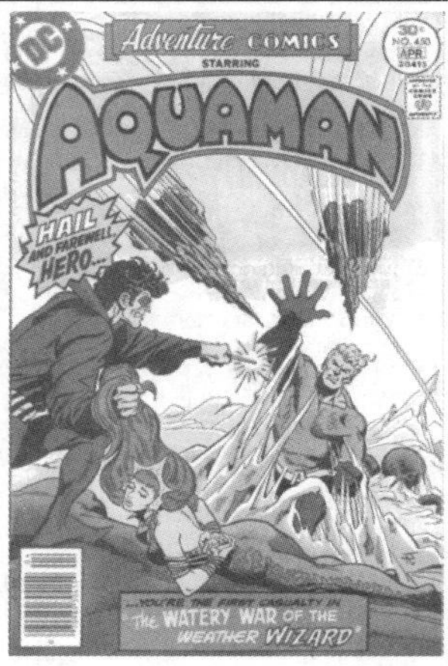

Adventure #450 © DC Comics, Inc.

374 WM,I:Black Mace. 16.00
375 I:Wanderers. 16.00
376 Execution of Cham.Boy 16.00
377 Heroes for Hire 16.00
378 Twelve Hours to Live 16.00
379 Burial In Space 16.00
380 The Amazing Space Odyssey
of the Legion,E:Legion 16.00
381 The Supergirl Gang
C:Batgirl,B:Supergirl 70.00
382 NA(c),The Superteams Split
Up,A:Superman 17.00
383 NA(c),Please Stop my Funeral,
A:Superman,Comet,Streaky . . 17.00
384 KS,The Heroine Haters,
A:Superman. 17.00
385 Supergirl's Big Sister 17.00
386 The Beast That Loved
Supergirl 17.00
387 Wolfgirl of Stanhope;
A:Superman;V:Lex Luthor. . . . 17.00
388 Kindergarten Criminal;
V:Luthor,Brainiac 17.00
389 A:Supergirl's Parents,
V:Brainiac. 17.00
390 Linda Danvers Superstar
(80 page giant). 35.00
391 The Super Cheat;A:Comet. . . 17.00
392 Supergirls Lost Costume 17.00
393 KS,Unwanted Supergirl 17.00
394 KS,Heartbreak Prison 17.00
395 Heroine in Haunted House. . . 17.00
396 Mystery o/t Super Orphan . . . 17.00
397 Now Comes Zod,N:Supergirl,
V:Luthor 17.00
398 Maid of Doom,A:Superman,
Streaky,Krypto,Comet. 17.00
399 CI,Johnny Dee,Hero Bum . . . 30.00
400 MSy,35th Anniv.,Return of the
Black Flame 25.00
401 MSy,JAb,The Frightened
Supergirl,V:Lex Luthor 15.00
402 MSy,JAb,TD,I:Starfire,
Dr.Kangle 17.00
403 68 page giant. 35.00
404 MSy,JAb,V:Starfire. 15.00
405 V:Starfire,Dr.Kangle 15.00
406 MSy,JAb,Suspicion 15.00
407 MSy,JAb,Suspicion Confirmed
N:Supergirl. 15.00
408 The Face at the Window 15.00
409 MSy,DG,Legion rep.. . . . . 17.00
410 N:Supergirl 17.00
411 CI,N:Supergirl 17.00
412 rep.Strange Adventures #180

 All comics prices listed are for *Near Mint* condition.

(I:Animal Man). 120.00
413 GM,JKu,rep.Hawkman 17.00
414 Animal Man rep. 17.00
415 BO,GM,CI,Animal Man rep. . . 17.00
416 CI,All women issue,giantsize . 17.00
417 GM,inc.rep.Adventure #161, Frazetta art. 18.00
418 ATh,Black Canary 35.00
419 ATh,Black Canary 17.00
420 Animal Man rep. 18.00
421 MSy,Supergirl 10.00
422 MSy,Supergirl 10.00
423 MSy,Supergirl 10.00
424 MSy,E:Supergirl,A:JLA. 10.00
425 AN,ATh,I:Captain Fear. 20.00
426 MSy,DG,JAp,Vigilante 10.00
427 TD. 10.00
428 TD,I:Black Orchid. 35.00
429 TD,AN,Black Orchid. 20.00
430 A:Black Orchid. 20.00
431 JAp,ATh,B:Spectre. 40.00
432 JAp,AN,A:Spectre,Capt.Fear . 20.00
433 JAp,AN 20.00
434 JAp 20.00
435 MGr(1st work),JAp,Aquaman . 20.00
436 JAp,MGr,Aquaman. 20.00
437 JAp,MGr,Aquaman. 20.00
438 JAp,HC,DD,7 Soldiers 20.00
439 JAp 20.00
440 JAp,O:New Spectre 25.00
441 JAp,B:Aquaman. 5.00
442 JAp,A:Aquaman. 5.00
443 JAp 8.00
444 JAp 5.00
445 JAp,RE,JSon,Creeper 5.00
446 JAp,RE,JSon,Creeper 8.00
447 JAp,RE,JSon,Creeper 8.00
448 JAp,Aquaman 5.00
449 JAp,MN,TA,Jonn J'onz. 5.00
450 JAp,MN,TA,Supergirl 5.00
451 JAp,MN,TA,Hawkman 5.00
452 JAp,Aquaman 5.00
453 MA,CP,JRu,B:Superboy & Aqualad 5.00
454 CP,DG,A:Kryptonite Kid 5.00
455 CP,DG,A:Kryptonite Kid E:Aqualad 5.00
456 JSon,JA. 5.00
457 JSon,JA,JO,B:Eclipso 6.00
458 JSon,JAp,JO,BL,E:Superboy & Eclipso 5.00
459 IN,FMc,JAp,JSon,DN,JA,A:Wond. Woman,New Gods,Green Lantern, Flash,Deadman,(giant size) . . 15.00
460 IN,FMc,JAp,DN,DA,JSon,JA, D:Darkseid 15.00
461 IN,FMc,JAp,JSon,DN,JA, B:JSA & Aquaman 15.00
462 IN,FMc,DH,JL,DG,JA, D:Earth 2,Batman. 15.00
463 DH,JL,JSon,FMc 10.00
464 DH,JAp,JSon,DN,DA, Deadman 10.00
465 DN,JSon,DG,JL 10.00
466 MN,JL,JSon,DN,DA 10.00
467 JSon,SD,RT,I:Starman B:Plastic Man. 12.00
468 SD,JSon 4.00
469 SD,JSon,O:Starman 4.00
470 SD,JSon,O:Starman 4.00
471 SD,JSon,I:Brickface. 4.00
472 SD,RT,JSon. 4.00
473 SD,RT,JSon. 4.00
474 SD,RT,JSon. 4.00
475 BB(c),SD,RT,JSon,DG, B:Aquaman 4.00
476 SD,RT,JSon,DG. 4.00
477 SD,RT,JSon,DG. 4.00
478 SD,RT,JSon,DG. 4.00
479 CI,DG,JSon,Dial H For Hero, E:Starman and Aquaman 4.00
480 CI,DJ,B:Dial H for Hero 4.00
481 CI,DJ 4.00
482 CI,DJ,DH 4.00
483 CI,DJ,DH 4.00
484 GP(c),CI,DJ,DH 4.00
485 GP(c),CI,DJ. 4.00
486 GP(c),DH,RT,TVE 4.00
487 CI,DJ,DH 4.00
488 CI,DJ,TVE 4.00
489 CI,FMc,TVE. 4.00
490 GP(c),CI,E:Dial H for Hero. . . . 4.00
491 KG(c),DigestSize,DN, Shazam,rep.other material . . . 15.00
492 KG(c),DN,E:Shazam 15.00
493 KG(c),GT,B:Challengers of the Unknown,reprints 15.00
494 KG(c),GT,Challengers, reprints. 15.00
495 ATh,reprints,Challengers 15.00
496 GK(c),ATh,reprints, Challengers 15.00
497 ATh,DA,reps.,E:Challengers. . 15.00
498 GK(c),reprints,Rep.Legion . . . 15.00
499 GK(c),reprints,Rep 15.00
500 KG(c),Legion reprints,Rep . . . 15.00
501 reprints,Rep. 15.00
502 reprints,Rep. 15.00
503 reprints,final issue 15.00
Giant #1, 80 page, 7 tales (1998) . . 6.00

ADVENTURE COMICS
1999

1 JeR,PSj,F:Starman & The Atom . 2.00

ADVENTURES IN THE DC UNIVERSE
1997–98

1 F:New JLA 4.00
2 F:The Flash,Catwoman. 2.00
3 Wonder Woman vs. Cheetah; Poison Ivy vs. Batman 2.00
4 F:Green Lantern vs. Glorious Godfrey; Mister Miracle 2.00
5 F:Martian Manhunter, all alien issue 2.00
6 F:Ocean Master, Power Girl 2.00
7 SVa(s),F:Shazam Family 2.00
8 SVa(s),F:Blue Beetle & Booster Gold 2.00
9 SVa(s),F:Flash,V:Grodd,Cipher. . 2.00

Adventures in the DC Universe #15
© DC Comics Inc.

10 SVa(s),Legion month 2.00
11 SVa(s),F:Green Lantern & Wonder Woman 2.00
12 SVa(s). 2.75
13 SVa(s),A:Martian Manhunter . . . 2.00
14 SVa(s),Flash races Superboy. . . 2.00
15 SVa(s),Shazam,Aquaman 2.00
16 SVa(s),F:Green Lantern. 2.00
17 SVa(s),F:Batman, Creeper. 2.00
18 SVa(s),F:JLA 2.75
19 F:Catwoman, Wonder Woman . . 2.00
Ann.#1 magic amulets,5 stories . . . 4.00

ADVENTURES IN THE RIFLE BRIGADE
DC/Vertigo August 2000

1 (of 3) GEn,. 2.50
2 F:Gerta Gash 2.50
3 GEn,Up Yours Fritz, concl. 2.50

ADVENTURES OF ALAN LADD
1949–51

1 Ph(c) 750.00
2 Ph(c) 400.00
3 Ph(c) 300.00
4 Ph(c) 300.00
5 Ph(c),inc.Destination Danger. . 225.00
6 Ph(c) 225.00
7 . . . . 225.00
8 Grand Duchess takes over . . . 225.00
9 Deadlien in Rapula 225.00

ADVENTURES OF BOB HOPE
1951–68

1 Ph(c). 1,300.00
2 Ph(c) 600.00
3 Ph(c) 350.00
4 Ph(c) 325.00
5 thru 10 . . . . @300.00
11 thru 20 . . . . @150.00
21 thru 40 . . . . @100.00
41 thru 90 . . . . @75.00
91 thru 93 . . . . @30.00
94 C:Aquaman 35.00
95 thru 105 . . . . @30.00
106 thru 109 NA . . . . @45.00

ADVENTURES OF DEAN MARTIN AND JERRY LEWIS
1952–57

1 . . . . 700.00
2 . . . . 325.00
3 thru 10 . . . . @150.00
11 thru 20 . . . . @100.00
21 thru 40 . . . . @75.00

Becomes:

ADVENTURES OF JERRY LEWIS
1957–71

41 thru 55 . . . . @65.00
56 thru 69 . . . . @50.00
70 thru 87 . . . . @40.00
88 A:Bob Hope. 45.00
89 thru 91 . . . . @30.00
92 C:Superman 40.00
93 thru 96 . . . . @25.00
97 A:Batman & Joker 48.00
98 thru 100 . . . . @35.00
101 NA. 45.00
102 NA, A:Beatles 50.00
103 and 104 NA . . . . @45.00

105 A:Superman. 40.00
106 thru 111 . . . . @20.00
112 A:Flash 35.00
113 thru 116 . . . . @20.00
117 A:Wonder Woman 30.00
118 thru 124 . . . . @15.00

ADVENTURES OF FORD FAIRLANE

1990

1 DH,DG 2.00
2 thru 4 DH . . . . @2.00

ADVENTURES OF THE OUTSIDERS

(see BATMAN & THE OUTSIDERS)

ADVENTURES OF OZZIE AND HARRIET

1949–50

1 Ph(c) 750.00
2 . . . . 375.00
3 thru 5 . . . . @300.00

ADVENTURES OF REX, THE WONDERDOG

1952–59

1 ATh 850.00
2 ATh 400.00
3 ATh 325.00
4 . . . . 250.00
5 . . . . 250.00
6 thru 11 . . . . @150.00
12 thru 20 . . . . @100.00
21 thru 46 . . . . @75.00

ADVENTURES OF SUPERBOY (See: SUPERBOY)

ADVENTURES OF SUPERMAN (See: SUPERMAN)

AGENT LIBERTY SPECIAL

1992

1 DAb,O:Agent Liberty. 2.00

ALIEN NATION

1988

1 JBi,movie adaption 2.50

ALL-AMERICAN COMICS

1939–48

1 B:Hop Harrigan,Scribbly,Mutt&Jeff, Red,White&Blue,Bobby Thatcher, Skippy,Daiseybelle,Mystery Men of Mars,Toonerville. 6,000.00
2 B:Ripley's Believe It or Not. . 1,700.00
3 Hop Harrigan (c) 1,200.00
4 Flag(c). 1,200.00
5 B:The American Way 1,200.00
6 ShM(c),Fredric Marchin in `The American Way' 1,000.00
7 E:Bobby Thatcher,C.H.

All-American #30 © DC Comics, Inc.

Claudy's `A Thousand Years in a Minute' 1,000.00
8 B:Ultra Man 1,500.00
9 . . . . 1,000.00
10 ShM(c),E:The American Way, Santa-X-Mas(c) 950.00
11 Ultra Man(c). 900.00
12 E:Toonerville Folks. 900.00
13 `The Infra Red Des'Royers' . . 900.00
14. . . . . 900.00
15 E:Tippie and Reg'lar Fellars . . 900.00
16 O&1st App:Green Lantern, B:Lantern(c). 75,000.00
17 SMo(c) 13,500.00
18 SMo(c) 8,500.00
19 SMo(c),O&I: Atom, E:Ultra Man. 13,000.00
20 I:Atom's costume,Hunkle becomes Red Tornado. . . . 3,800.00
21 E:Wiley of West Point & Skippy 2,400.00
22 . . . . 2,200.00
23 E:Daieybelle 2,200.00
24 E:Ripley's Believe It or Not . 2,700.00
25 O&I:Dr. Mid-Nite 8,400.00
26 O&I:Sargon the Sorcerer. . . 3,200.00
27 I:Doiby Dickles 3,500.00
28 . . . . 1,300.00
29 ShM(c) 1,300.00
30 ShM(c) 1,300.00
31 Adventures of the underfed orphans. 1,300.00
32 . . . . 1,000.00
33 . . . . 1,000.00
34 . . . . 1,000.00
35 Doiby discovers Lantern's ID 1,000.00
36 . . . . 1,000.00
37 . . . . 1,000.00
38 . . . . 1,000.00
39 . . . . 1,000.00
40 . . . . 1,000.00
41 . . . . 800.00
42 . . . . 800.00
43 . . . . 800.00
44 `I Accuse the Green Lantern! . 800.00
45 . . . . 800.00
46 . . . . 800.00
47 Hop Harrigan meets the Enemy,(c). 800.00
48 . . . . 800.00
49 . . . . 800.00
50 E:Sargon 800.00
51 `Murder Under the Stars' 700.00
52 . . . . 700.00
53 Green Lantern delivers

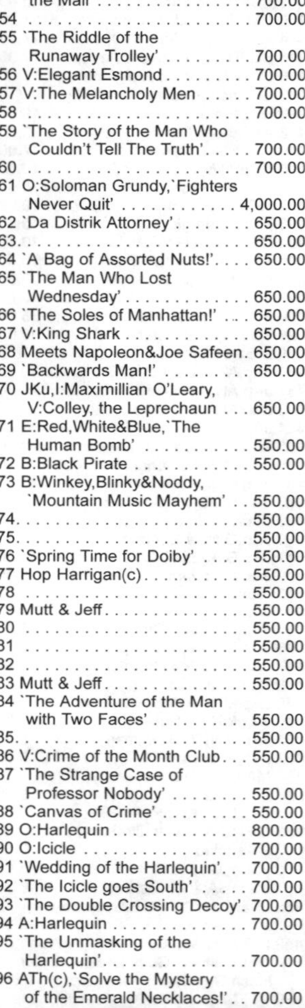

the Mail 700.00
54 . . . . 700.00
55 `The Riddle of the Runaway Trolley' 700.00
56 V:Elegant Esmond 700.00
57 V:The Melancholy Men 700.00
58 . . . . 700.00
59 `The Story of the Man Who Couldn't Tell The Truth'. 700.00
60 . . . . 700.00
61 O:Soloman Grundy,`Fighters Never Quit' 4,000.00
62 `Da Distrik Attorney'. 650.00
63. . . . . 650.00
64 `A Bag of Assorted Nuts!'. . . . 650.00
65 `The Man Who Lost Wednesday' 650.00
66 `The Soles of Manhattan!' . . . 650.00
67 V:King Shark 650.00
68 Meets Napoleon&Joe Safeen. 650.00
69 `Backwards Man!' 650.00
70 JKu,I:Maximillian O'Leary, V:Colley, the Leprechaun . . . 650.00
71 E:Red,White&Blue,`The Human Bomb' 550.00
72 B:Black Pirate 550.00
73 B:Winkey,Blinky&Noddy, `Mountain Music Mayhem' . . 550.00
74. . . . . 550.00
75. . . . . 550.00
76 `Spring Time for Doiby' 550.00
77 Hop Harrigan(c). 550.00
78 . . . . 550.00
79 Mutt & Jeff. 550.00
80 . . . . 550.00
81 . . . . 550.00
82 . . . . 550.00
83 Mutt & Jeff. 550.00
84 `The Adventure of the Man with Two Faces' 550.00
85. . . . . 550.00
86 V:Crime of the Month Club. . . 550.00
87 `The Strange Case of Professor Nobody' 550.00
88 `Canvas of Crime' 550.00
89 O:Harlequin 800.00
90 O:Icicle 700.00
91 `Wedding of the Harlequin'. . . 700.00
92 `The Icicle goes South' 700.00
93 `The Double Crossing Decoy'. 700.00
94 A:Harlequin 700.00
95 `The Unmasking of the Harlequin'. 700.00
96 ATh(c),`Solve the Mystery of the Emerald Necklaces!' . . 700.00

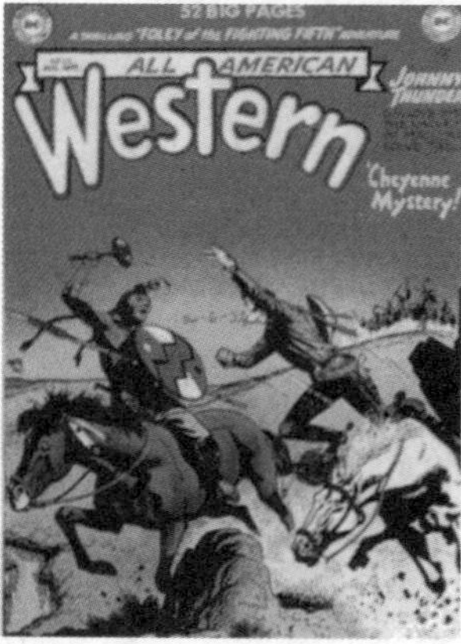

All-American Western #115 © DC Comics, Inc.

97 ATh(c),`The Country Fair Crimes'. 700.00
98 ATh,ATh(c),`End of Sports!' . . 700.00
99 ATh,ATh(c),E:Hop Harrigan . . 700.00
100 ATh,I:Johnny Thunder. . . . 1,500.00
101 ATh,ATh(c),E:Mutt & Jeff. . 1,000.00
102 ATh,ATh(c),E:GrnLantern . 2,000.00
Becomes:

ALL-AMERICAN WESTERN

1948–52

103 A:Johnny Thunder,`The City Without Guns,'All Johnny Thunder stories 400.00
104 ATh(c),`Unseen Allies' 275.00
105 ATh(c),`Hidden Guns'. 225.00
106 ATh(c),`Snow Mountain Ambush'. 175.00
107 ATh(c),`Cheyenne Justice' . . 225.00
108 ATh(c),`Vengeance of the Silver Bullet' 175.00
109 ATh(c),`Secret of Crazy River' 175.00
110 ATh(c),`Ambush at Scarecrow Hills' 175.00
111 ATh(c),`Gun-Shy Sheriff'. . . . 175.00
112 ATh(c),`Double Danger' 175.00
113 ATh(c),`Johnny Thunder Indian Chief' 200.00
114 ATh(c),`The End of Johnny Thunder'. 175.00
115 ATh(c),`Cheyenne Mystery' . 175.00
116 ATh(c),`Buffalo Raiders of the Mesa' 175.00
117 ATh(c),V:Black Lightnin 150.00
118 ATh(c),`Challenge of the Aztecs' 150.00
119 GK(c),`The Vanishing Gold Mine' 150.00
120 GK(c),`Ambush at Painted Mountain'. 150.00
121 ATh(c),`The Unmasking of Johnny Thunder'. 150.00
122 ATh(c),`The Real Johnny Thunder'. 150.00
123 GK(c),`Johnny Thunder's Strange Rival'. 150.00
124 ATh(c),`The Iron Horse's Last Run' 150.00
125 ATh(c),`Johnny Thunder's Last Roundup' 150.00
126 ATh(c),`Phantoms of the Desert' 150.00
Becomes:

ALL-AMERICAN MEN OF WAR

1952–66

127 (0) 850.00
128 (1) 600.00
2 JGr(c),Killer Bait 450.00
3 Pied Piper of Pyong-Yang 450.00
4 JGr(c),The Hills of Hate 450.00
5 One Second to Zero 325.00
6 IN(c),Jungle Killers 325.00
7 IN(c),Beach to Hold 325.00
8 IN(c),Sgt. Storm Cloud 325.00
9 . . . . 325.00
10. . . . . 325.00
11 JGr(c),Dragon's Teeth 325.00
12. . . . . 300.00
13 JGr(c),Lost Patrol. 300.00
14 IN(c),Pigeon Boss 300.00
15 JGr(c),Flying Roadblock. 300.00
16 JGr(c),The Flying Jeep. 300.00
17 JGr(c),Booby Trap Ridge 300.00
18 JKu(c),The Ballad of Battling Bells 300.00
19 JGr(c),IN,Torpedo Track. 225.00
20 JGr(c),JKu,Lifenet to Beach Road 225.00
21 JGr(c),IN,RH,The Coldest War 225.00
22 JGr(c),IN,JKu,Snipers Nest . . 225.00
23 JGr(c),The Silent War 225.00
24 JGr(c),The Thin Line 225.00
25 JGr(c),IN,For Rent-One Foxhole 225.00
26. . . . . 225.00
27 JGr(c),RH,Fighting Pigeon . . . 225.00
28 JGr(c),RA,JKu,Medal for A Dog 225.00
29 IN(c),JKu,Battle Bridges. 250.00
30 JGr(c),RH,Frogman Hunt 200.00
31 JGr(c),Battle Seat 225.00
32 JGr(c),RH,Battle Station. 225.00
33 JGr(c),IN,Sky Ambush 225.00
34 JGr(c),JKu,No Man's Alley . . . 200.00
35 JGr(c),IN, Battle Call 200.00
36 JGr(c),JKu,Battle Window . . . 175.00
37 JGr(c),JKu,The Big Stretch . . 175.00
38 JGr(c),RH,JKu,The Floating Sentinel. 175.00
39 JGr(c),JKu,The Four Faces of Sgt. Fay 175.00
40 JGr(c),IN,Walking Helmet. . . . 175.00
41 JKu(c),RH,JKu,The 50-50 War 150.00
42 JGr(c),JKu,Battle Arm 150.00
43 JGr(c),JKu,Command Post. . . 150.00
44 JKu(c),The Flying Frogman . . 150.00
45 JGr(c),RH,Combat Waterboy . 150.00
46 JGr(c),IN,RH,Tank Busters. . . 150.00
47 JGr(c),JKu,MD,Battle Freight . 150.00
48 JGr(c),JKu,MD,Roadblock . . . 150.00
49 JGr(c),Walking Target 150.00
50 IN,RH,Bodyguard For A Sub . 150.00
51 JGr(c),RH,Bomber's Moon. . . 125.00
52 JKu(c),RH,MD,Back Seat Driver. 125.00
53 JKu(c),JKu,Night Attack 125.00
54 JKu(c),IN,Diary of a Fighter Pilot 125.00
55 JKu(c),RH,Split-Second Target 125.00
56 JKu,IN,RH,Frogman Jinx 125.00
57 Pick-Up for Easy Co. 125.00
58 JKu(c),RH,MD,A Piece of Sky 125.00
59 JGr(c),JKu,The Hand of War . 125.00
60 JGr(c),The Time Table 125.00
61 JGr(c),IN,MD,Blind Target . . . 125.00
62 JGr(c),RH,RA,No(c) 125.00
63 JGr(c),JKu,Frogman Carrier. . 125.00
64 JKu(c),JKu,RH,The Other Man's War 125.00
65 JGr(c),JKu,MD,Same Old Sarge. 125.00
66 JGr(c),The Walking Fort. 125.00
67 JGr(c),RH,A:Gunner&Sarge, The Cover Man 300.00
68 JKu(c),Gunner&Sarge, The Man & The Gun. 150.00
69 JKu(c),A:Tank Killer, Bazooka Hill 150.00
70 JKu(c),IN,Pigeon Without Wings 125.00
71 JGr(c),A:Tank Killer,Target For An Ammo Boy 75.00
72 JGr(c),A:Tank Killer,T.N.T. Broom 75.00
73 JGr(c),JKu,No Detour 75.00
74 The Minute Commandos 75.00
75 JKu(c),Sink That Flattop. 75.00
76 JKu(c),A:Tank Killer, Just One More Tank 75.00
77 JKu(c),IN,MD,Big Fish-little Fish. 75.00
78 JGr(c),Tin Hat for an Iron Man. 75.00
79 JKu(c),RA,Showdown Soldier . 75.00
80 JGr(c),RA,The Medal Men 75.00
81 JGr(c),IN,Ghost Ship of Two Wars. 70.00
82 IN(c),B:Johnny Cloud, The Flying Chief. 100.00
83 IN(c),Fighting Blind 70.00
84 IN(c),Death Dive 65.00
85 RH(c),Battle Eagle. 65.00
86 JGr(c),Top-Gun Ace. 65.00
87 JGr(c),Broken Ace 65.00
88 JGr(c),The Ace of Vengeance . 65.00
89 JGr(c),The Star Jockey 65.00
90 JGr(c),Wingmate of Doom 50.00
91 RH(c),Two Missions To Doom . 50.00
92 JGr(c),The Battle Hawk 50.00
93 RH(c),The Silent Rider. 50.00
94 RH(c),Be Brave-Be Silent 50.00
95 RH(c),Second Sight For a Pilot 50.00
96 RH(c),The Last Flight of Lt. Moon. 50.00
97 IN(c),A 'Target' Called Johnny. 50.00
98 The Time-Bomb Ace 50.00
99 IN(c),The Empty Cockpit 50.00
100 RH(c),Battle o/t Sky Chiefs. . . 50.00
101 RH(c),Death Ship of Three Wars 35.00
102 JKu(c),Blind Eagle-Hungry Hawk 35.00
103 IN(c),Battle Ship-Battle Heart 35.00
104 JKu(c),The Last Target. 35.00
105 IN(c),Killer Horse-Ship 35.00
106 IN(c),Death Song For A Battle Hawk 35.00
107 IN(c),Flame in the Sky 35.00
108 IN(c),Death-Dive of the Aces . 35.00
109 IN(c),The Killer Slot 35.00
110 RH(c),The Co-Pilot was Death. 35.00
111 RH(c),E:Johnny Cloud, Tag–You're Dead 35.00
112 RH(c),B:Balloon Buster,Lt. Steve Savage-Balloon Buster . 35.00
113 JKu(c),The Ace of Sudden Death 35.00
114 JKu(c),The Ace Who Died Twice 35.00
115 IN(c),A:Johnny Cloud, Deliver One Enemy Ace-Handle With Care. 35.00
116 JKu(c),A:Baloon Buster, Circle of Death 35.00
117 Sept.–Oct., 1966 . . . . 35.00

All-American Western #117
© DC Comics Inc.

DC COMICS

ALL-AMERICAN COMICS
1999

1 RMz(s),F:Green Lantern & Johnny Thunder 2.00

ALL-FLASH
1941–47

1 EHi,O:Flash,I:The Monocle 14,000.00

All-Flash #2 © DC Comics, Inc.

2 EHi,The Adventure of Roy Revenge 2,700.00
3 EHi,The Adventure of Misplaced Faces 1,400.00
4 EHi,Tale of the Time Capsule. 1,300.00
5 EHi,The Case of the Patsy Colt! Last Quarterly 1,000.00
6 EHi,The Ray that Changed Men's Souls 800.00
7 EHi,Adventures of a Writers Fantasy, House of Horrors . . 800.00
8 EHi,Formula to Fairyland! 800.00
9 EHi,Adventure of the Stolen Telescope. 800.00
10 EHi,Case of the Curious Cat . 800.00
11 EHi,Troubles come in Doubles 700.00
12 EHi,Tumble INN to Trouble, Becomes Quarterly on orders from War Production Board O:The Thinker 700.00
13 EHi,I:The King 700.00
14 EHi,I:Winky,Blinky & Noddy Green Lantern (c). 800.00
15 EHi,Secrets of a Stranger . . . 600.00
16 EHi,A:The Sinister 600.00
17 Tales of the Three Wishes . . . 550.00
18 A:Winlky,Blinky&Noddy B:Mutt & Jeff reprints 550.00
19 No Rest at the Rest Home . . . 550.00
20 A:Winky, Blinky & Noddy 550.00
21 I:Turtle. 500.00
22 The Money Doubler,E:Mutt & Jeff reprints. 500.00
23 The Bad Men of Bar Nothing . 500.00
24 I:Worry Wart,3 Court Clowns Get Caught 500.00
25 I:Slapsy Simmons, Flash Jitterbugs 500.00
26 I:The Chef,The Boss,Shrimp Coogan,A:Winky, Blinky & Noddy 550.00
27 A:The Thinker,Gangplank Gus story 500.00
28 A:Shrimp Coogan,Winky, Blinky & Noddy. 500.00
29 The Thousand-Year Old Terror, A:Winky,Blinky & Noddy 500.00
30 The Vanishing Snowman 500.00
31 A:Black Hat,The Planet of Sport 500.00
32 I:Fiddler,A:Thinker 800.00

ALL FUNNY COMICS
1943–48

1 Genius Jones 400.00
2 same 150.00
3 same 100.00
4 same 100.00
5 thru 10 . . . . @100.00
11 Genius Jones. 75.00
12 same 50.00
13 same 75.00
14. . . . . 60.00
15. . . . . 75.00
16 A:DC Superheroes. 250.00
17 thru 23 . . . . @75.00

ALL-STAR COMICS
Summer, 1940–51

1 B:Flash,Hawkman,Hourman, Sandman,Spectre,Red White & Blue 13,000.00
2 B:Green Lantern and Johnny Thunder. 5,000.00
3 First meeting of Justice Society with Flash as Chairman . . 35,000.00
4 First mission of JSA 5,000.00
5 V:Mr. X,I:Hawkgirl 4,000.00
6 Flash leaves 2,900.00
7 Green Lantern becomes Chairman, L:Hourman, C:Superman, Batman & Flash. 3,000.00
8 I:Wonder Women;Starman and Dr. Mid-Nite join,Hawkman becomes chairman 26,000.00
9 JSA in Latin America 2,400.00
10 C:Flash & Green Lantern, JSA Time Travel story 2,400.00
11 Wonder Women joins; I:Justice Battalion 2,200.00
12 V:Black Dragon society 2,200.00
13 V:Hitler 2,000.00
14 JSA in occupied Europe . . . 2,000.00
15 I:Brain Wave,A:JSA's Girl Friends 2,000.00
16 Propaganda/relevance issue 1,600.00
17 V:Brain Wave 1,600.00
18 I:King Bee. 1,700.00
19 Hunt for Hawkman 1,600.00
20 I:Monster 1,600.00
21 Time travel story 1,500.00
22 Sandman and Dr. Fate leave, I:Conscience, Good Fairy. . 1,500.00
23 I:Psycho-Pirate 1,500.00
24 Propaganda/relevance issue, A:Conscience&Wildcat,Mr.Terrific; L:Starman & Spectre; Flash & Green Lantern return . . . 1,500.00
25 JSA whodunit issue. 1,300.00
26 V:Metal Men from Jupiter . . 1,300.00
27 Handicap issue,A:Wildcat . . 1,300.00
28 Ancient curse comes to life . 1,100.00
29 I:Landor from 25th century . 1,100.00
30 V:Brain Wave 1,100.00
31 V:Zor 1,100.00
32 V:Psycho-Pirate 1,100.00
33 V:Soloman Grundy,A:Doiby Dickles, Last appearance Thunderbolt. 2,400.00
34 I:Wizard 1,000.00
35 I:Per Degaton 1,000.00
36 A:Superman and Batman . . 2,300.00
37 I:Injustice Society of the World. 1,300.00
38 V:Villians of History, A:Black Canary 1,500.00
39 JSA in magic world, Johnny Thunder leaves . . . 1,000.00
40 A:Black Canary,Junior Justice Society of America. 1,000.00
41 Black Canary joins,A:Harlequin, V:Injustice Society of the World. 1,000.00
42 I:Alchemist. 950.00
43 V:Interdimensional gold men . 950.00
44 I:Evil Star. 950.00
45 Crooks develop stellar JSA powers 900.00
46 Comedy issue 900.00
47 V:Billy the Kid 900.00
48 Time Travel story 900.00
49 V:Comet-being invaders. 900.00
50 V:College classmate of Flash . 950.00
51 V:Diamond men from center of the Earth 900.00
52 JSA disappears from Earth for years 900.00
53 Time Travel issue. 900.00
54 Circus issue. 900.00
55 JSA fly to Jupiter 900.00
56 V:Chameleons from 31st Century. 900.00
57 I:Key. 1,300.00

Becomes:

ALL STAR WESTERN
April–May, 1951

58 Trigger Twins. 325.00
59 . . . . 150.00
60 . . . . 150.00
61 thru 64 ATh 125.00
65 & 66. . . . . @125.00
67 GK,B:Johnny Thunder 150.00
68 thru 81 . . . . @75.00
82 thru 98 . . . . @60.00
99 FF 75.00
100 . . . . 60.00
101 thru 104 . . . . @45.00
105 O:JSA, March, 1987. . . . . 45.00
106 and 107 . . . . @45.00
108 O:Johnny Thunder 125.00
109 thru 116 . . . . @45.00
117 CI,O:Super-Chief 60.00
118 . . . . 45.00
119 . . . . 40.00

All-Star Comics #41 © DC Comics, Inc.

ALL-STAR COMICS
1976–78
58 RE,WW,R:JSA,I:Power Girl . . . 17.00
59 RE,WW,Brain Wave. 10.00
60 KG,WW,I:Vulcan 10.00
61 KG,WW,V:Vulcan. 10.00
62 KG,WW,A:E-2 Superman. 10.00
63 KG,WW,A:E-2 Superman, Solomon Grundy 10.00
64 WW,Shining Knight 10.00
65 KG,WW,E-2 Superman, Vandal Savage. 10.00
66 JSon,BL,Injustice Society. 10.00
67 JSon,BL. 10.00
68 JSon,BL. 10.00
69 JSon,BL,A:E-2 Superman, Starman,Dr.Mid-Nite 15.00
70 JSon,BL,Huntress 9.00
71 JSon,BL 9.00
72 JSon,A:Golden.Age Huntress. . . 9.00
73 JSon 9.00
74 JSon 9.00

ALL STAR COMICS
1999
1 JeR(s),F:Justice Society of America, V:Stalker's Seven. . 3.00
2 JeR(s) conclusion. 3.00
Giant #1 80-page 5.00

ALL STAR SQUADRON
1981–87
1 RB,JOy,JSa,I:Degaton 3.50
2 RB,JOy,Robotman 2.00
3 RB,JOy,Robotman 2.00
4 RB,JOy,Robotman 2.00
5 RB/JOy,I:Firebrand(Dannette). . . 2.00
6 JOy,Hawkgirl 2.00
7 JOy,Hawkgirl 2.00
8 DH/JOy,A:Steel 2.00
9 DH/JOy,A:Steel 2.00
10 JOy,V:Binary Brotherhood 2.00
11 JOy,V:Binary Brotherhood 2.00
12 JOy,R:Dr.Hastor O:Hawkman. . . 2.00
13 JOy,photo(c) 2.00
14 JOy,JLA crossover. 2.00
15 JOy,JLA crossover. 2.00
16 I&D:Nuclear. 2.00
17 Trial of Robotman 2.00
18 V:Thor 2.00
19 V:Brainwave 2.00
20 JOy,V:Brainwave 2.00
21 JOy,I:Cyclotron (1st JOy Superman). 2.50
22 JOy,V:Deathbolt,Cyclotron 2.00
23 JOy,I:Amazing-Man 2.00
24 JOy,I:Brainwave,Jr.. . . . . 2.50
25 JOy,I:Infinity Inc. 2.50
26 JOy,Infinity Inc. 2.50
27 Spectre 2.00
28 JOy,Spectre. 2.00
29 JOy,retold story 2.00
30 V:Black Dragons 2.00
31 All-Star gathering. 2.00
32 O:Freedom Fighters. 2.00
33 Freedom Fighters,I:Tsunami. . . . 2.00
34 Freedom Fighters 2.00
35 RB,Shazam family. 2.00
36 Shazam family. 2.00
37 A:Shazam Family 2.00
38 V:The Real American. 2.00
39 V:The Real American. 2.00
40 D:The Real American 2.00
41 O:Starman. 2.00
42 V:Tsunami,Kung. 2.00
43 V:Tsunami,Kung. 2.00
44 I:Night & Fog 2.00
45 I:Zyklon 2.00
46 V:Baron Blitzkrieg 2.00

All Star Squadron #58
© DC Comics,Inc.

47 TM,O:Dr.Fate. 4.00
48 A:Blackhawk 2.00
49 A:Dr.Occult 2.00
50 Crisis. 2.50
51 AA,Crisis 2.00
52 Crisis. 2.00
53 Crisis,A:The Dummy 2.00
54 Crisis,V:The Dummy 2.00
55 Crisis,V:Anti-Monitor 2.00
56 Crisis. 2.00
57 A:Dr.Occult 2.00
58 I:Mekanique. 2.00
59 A:Mekanique,Spectre. 2.00
60 Crisis 1942, conclusion 2.00
61 O:Liberty Belle. 2.00
62 O:The Shining Knight. 2.00
63 O:Robotman 2.00
64 WB/TD,V:Funny Face 2.00
65 DH/TD,O:Johnny Quick 2.00
66 TD,O:Tarantula 2.00
67 TD,Last Issue,O:JSA 2.00
Ann.#1 JOy,O:G.A.,Atom 2.00
Ann.#2 JOy,Infinity Inc. 2.00
Ann.#3 WB,JOy,KG,GP,DN. 2.00

ALL STAR WESTERN
(see WEIRD WESTERN TALES)

ALPHA CENTURION
1996
Spec.#1 . . . . 3.00

AMBER: THE GUNS OF AVALON
Aug., 1996
1 (of 3) adapt. of Roger Zelazny classic 6.95
2 and 3 conclusion. . . . . @6.95

AMBUSH BUG
1985
1 KG,I:Cheeks. 2.00
2 KG thru 4 . . . . @2.00

AMBUSH BUG: STOCKING STUFFER 1986
1 KG,R:Cheeks 2.00

AMBUSH BUG: NOTHING SPECIAL 1992
1 KG,A:Sandman,Death 2.50

AMERICA vs. JUSTICE SOCIETY
Jan.,–April, 1985
1 AA,R,Thomas Script. 2.50
2 AA 2.00
3 AA 2.00
4 AA,. 2.00

AMERICAN FREAK: A TALE OF THE UN-MEN
Vertigo 1994
1 B:DLp,(s),VcL,R:Un-Men 2.25
2 VcL,A:Crassus 2.25
3 VcL,A:Scylla. 2.25
4 VcL,A:Scylla. 2.25
5 VcL,Final Issue. 2.25

AMETHYST
[Limited Series] 1983–84
[PRINCESS OF GEMWORLD]
1 Origin 2.00
2 thru 7 EC . . . . @2.00
8 EC,O:Gemworld 2.00
9 thru 12 EC . . . . @2.00
Spec.#1 KG 2.00

[Regular Series]
1985–86
1 thru 12 EC . . . . @2.00
13 EC,Crisis,A:Dr.Fate 2.00
14 EC. 2.00
15 EC,Castle Amethyst Destroyed . 2.00
16 EC. 2.00
Spec.#1 EM 2.00

[Mini-Series]
1987–88
1 EM 2.00
2 & 3 EM . . . . @2.00
4 EM,O:Mordru 2.00

ANARKY
March, 1997
1 AIG(s),NBy,JRu,Anarky vs. Etrigan 2.50
2 AIG(s),NBy,JRu,V:Darkseid. 2.50
3 AIG(s),NBy,JRu,A:Batman 2.50
4 AIG(s),NBy,JRu,A:Batman,concl. 2.50

ANARKY
1999
1 AIG(s),NBy,JRu,F:JLA 2.50
2 AIG(s),NBy,JRu,F:GreenLantern . 2.50
3 AIG(s),NBy,JRu,F:GreenLantern . 2.50
4 AIG(s),NBy,JRu,V:Ra's al Ghul . . 2.50
5 AIG(s),NBy,JRu,V:Ra's al Ghul,pt.2 . . . . 2.50
6 AIG(s),NBy,JRu,F:Ra's al Ghul,pt.3 . . . . 2.50
7 AIG,NBy,JRu,Day of Judgment . . 2.50
8 AIG(s),NBy,JRu, final issue 2.50

ANGEL & THE APE
1991
1 Apes of Wrath,pt.1 . . . . 2.00
2 Apes of Wrath,pt.2, A:G.Gardner. 2.00
3 Apes of Wrath,pt.3, A: Inferior Five 2.00
4 Apes of Wrath,pt.4, A: Inferior Five, final issue 2.00

Anima #12 © DC Comics, Inc.

ANIMA
Vertigo 1994–95

1 R:Anima 2.00
2 V:Scarecrow. 2.00
3 V:Scarecrow. 2.00
4 A:Nameless one 2.00
5 CI,V:Arkana 2.00
6 CI,V:Arkana 2.00
7 Zero Hour. 2.00
8 Nameless One 2.00
9 Superboy & Nameless One 2.00
10 A:Superboy 2.00
11 V:Nameless One 2.00
12 A:Hawkman,V:Shrike 2.00
13 A:Hawkman,Shrike 2.00
14 Return to Gotham City. 2.00
15 V:Psychic Vampire, final issue . . 2.25

ANIMAL ANTICS
1946–49

1 . . . . 350.00
2 . . . . 165.00
3 thru 10 . . . . @100.00
11 thru 23 . . . . @65.00

ANIMAL-MAN
1988–95

1 BB(c),B:GMo(s),ChT,DHz, B:Animal Rights,I:Dr.Myers 5.00
2 BB(c),ChT,DHz,A:Superman 4.00
3 BB(c),ChT,DHz,A:B'wana Beast . 3.00
4 BB(c),ChT,DHz,V:B'wana Beast, E:Animal Rights 3.00
5 BB(c),ChT,DHz, I&D:Crafty Coyote 3.50
6 BB(c),ChT,DHz,A:Hawkman 3.00
7 BB(c),ChT,DHz,D:Red Mask 3.00
8 BB(c),ChT,DHz,V:Mirror Master . 3.00
9 BB(c),DHz,TG,A:Martian Manhunter 3.00
10 BB(c),ChT,DHz,A:Vixen, B:O:Animal Man 3.00
11 BB(c),ChT,DHz,I:Hamed Ali, Tabu,A:Vixen 3.00
12 BB(c),D:Hamed Ali,A:Vixen, B'wanaBeast 3.00
13 BB(c),I:Dominic Mndawe,R:B'wana Beast,Apartheid 3.00
14 BB(c),TG,SeM,A:Future Animal Man,I:Lennox 3.00
15 BB(c),ChT,DHz,A:Dolphin 3.00
16 BB(c),ChT,DHz,A:JLA. 3.00
17 BB(c),ChT,DHz,A:Mirr.Master . . . 3.00
18 BB(c),ChT,DHz,A:Lennox. 3.00
19 BB(c),ChT,DHz,D:Ellen, Cliff,Maxine 3.00
20 BB(c),ChT,DHz,I:Bug-Man 3.00
21 BB(c),ChT,DHz,N&V:Bug-Man . . 3.00
22 BB(c),PCu,SeM,A:Rip Hunter. . . 3.00
23 BB(c),A:Phantom Stranger. 2.50
24 BB(c),V:Psycho Pirate 2.50
25 BB(c),ChT,MFm,I:Comic Book Limbo 2.50
26 BB(c),E:GMo(s),ChT,MFm, A:Grant Morrison 2.50
27 BB(c),B:PMi(s),ChT,MFm. 2.50
28 BB(c),ChT,MFm,I:Nowhere Man, I&D:Front Page 2.50
29 ChT,SDi,V:National Man 2.50
30 BB(c),ChT,MFm,V:Angel Mob . . 2.50
31 BB(c),ChT,MFm. 2.50
32 BB(c),E:PMi(s),ChT,MFm. 2.50
33 BB(c),B:TV(s),SDi,A:Travis Cody 2.50
34 BB(c),SDi,Requiem 2.50
35 BB(c),SDi,V:Radioactive Dogs . . 2.50
36 BB(c),SDi,A:Mr.Rainbow 2.50
37 BB(c),SDi,Animal/Lizard Man. . . 2.50
38 BB(c),SDi,A:Mr.Rainbow 2.00
39 BB(c),TMd,SDi,Wolfpack in San Diego 2.00
40 BB(c),SDi,War of the Gods x-over. 2.00
41 BB(c),SDi,V:Star Labs Renegades,I:Winky 2.00
42 BB(c),SDi,V:Star Labs Renegades. 2.00
43 BB(c),SDi,I:Tristess,A:Vixen 2.00
44 BB(c),SDi,A:Vixen 2.00
45 BB(c),StP,SDi,I:L.Decker 2.00
46 BB(c),SDi,I:Frank Baker. 2.00
47 BB(c),SDi,I:Shining Man, (B'wana Beast). 2.00
48 BB(c),SDi,V:Antagon 2.00
49 BB(c),SDi,V:Antagon 2.00
50 BB(c),E:TV(s),SDi,I:Metaman. . . 3.50
51 BB(c),B:JaD(s),StP,B:Flesh and Blood. 2.50
52 BB(c),StP,Homecoming 2.50
53 BB(c),StP,Flesh and Blood. 2.50
54 BB(c),StP,Flesh and Blood. 2.50
55 BB(c),StP,Flesh and Blood. 2.50
56 BB(c),StP,E:Flesh and Blood, Double-sized 3.50

Vertigo

57 BB(c),StP,B:Recreation, Ellen in NY. 3.00
58 BB(c),StP,Wild Side 2.50
59 BB(c),RsB,GHi(i),Wild Town. . . . 2.50
60 RsB,GHi(i),Wild life 2.50
61 BB(c),StP,Tooth and Claw#1 . . . 2.50
62 BB(c),StP,Tooth and Claw#2 . . . 2.50
63 BB(c),V:Leviathan 2.50
64 DIB(c),WSm,DnS(i), Breath of God. 2.50
65 RDB(c),WSm, Perfumed Garden. 2.25
66 A:Kindred Spirit 2.25
67 StP,Mysterious Ways #1 . . . . . . 2.25
68 StP,Mysterious Ways #2 . . . . . . 2.25
69 Animal Man's Family 2.25
70 GgP(c),StP 2.25
71 GgP(c),StP,Maxine Alive? 2.25
72 StP 2.25
73 StP,Power Life Church. 2.25
74 StP,Power Life Church. 2.25
75 StP,Power Life Church. 2.25
76 StP,Pilgrimage problems 2.00
77 Cliff shot 2.00
78 StP,Animal Man poisoned 2.00
79 New Direction 2.00
80 New Direction 2.00
81 Wild Type,pt.1 . . . . 2.00

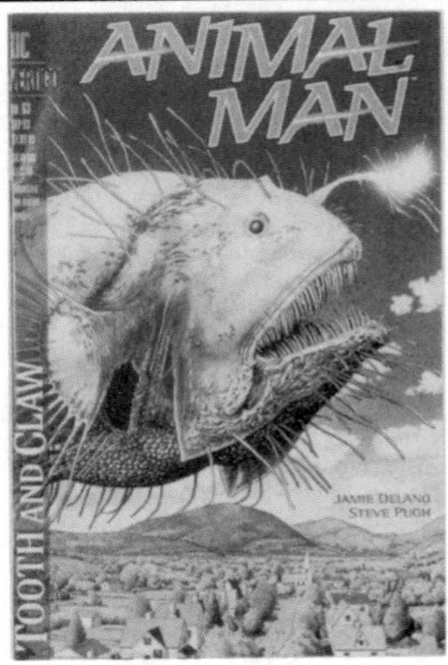

Animal Man #63 © DC Comics, Inc.

82 Wild Type,pt.2 . . . . 2.00
83 Wild Type,pt.3 . . . . 2.00
84 F:Maxine,SupernaturalDreams. . 2.00
85 Animal Mundi,pt.1 . . . . 2.25
86 Animal Mundi,pt.2 . . . . 2.25
87 Animal Mundi,pt.3 . . . . 2.25
88 Morphogenetic Fields. 2.25
89 final issue 2.25
Ann.#1 BB(c),JaD,TS(i),RIB(i), Children Crusade,F:Maxine . . . 4.25
TPB Rep.#1 thru #10 . . . . 19.95

ANIMANIACS
Warner Bros./DC May, 1995

1 F:Yakko,Wakko,Dot 1.50
2 Health Spa 1.50
3 Travel back in time 1.50
4 . . . . 1.50
5 . . . . 1.50
6 V:Cleopatra 1.50
7 Scratchinsniff Replaced 1.50
8 Disputin win Newton. 1.50
9 thru 12 . . . . @1.50
13 thru 17. . . . . @1.75
18 visit to France 1.75
19 "The Y Files" 1.75
20 "Rebels Just Because". 1.75
21 x-mas issue,A:Santa 1.75
22 . . . . 1.75
23 F:Hellow Nurse 1.75
24 F:The Goodfeathers,A:Pinky and the Brain 1.75
25 F:Slappy Squirrel. 1.75
26 "Haunted House of Pancakes" . . 1.75
27 "Plane for Keeps". 1.75
28 "Science Issue" 1.75
29 "The Return of Hello Nurse, Agent of H.U.B.B.A." 1.75
30 "Electro-Walter and Dyna-Squirrel" 1.75
31 Nastina LeCreep 2.00
32 "Lifestiles of the Old & Cranky" . 2.00
33 "The Long Lost Warner". 2.00
34 Minerxa, Warrior Princess 2.00
35 . . . . 2.00
36 Generation Gap. 2.00
37 F:Brain 2.00
38 special all-cute issue 2.00
39 Arnold Nobel 2.00
40 Slappy Squirrel 2.00
41 Slappy's Mother Goose 2.00
42 Stepford Warner 2.00
43 F:Pinky & The Brain. 2.00
44 F:Pinky & The Brain. 2.00

45 Brain Loses his Mind 2.00
46 F:Lobel Ebrain 2.00
47 Brainita 2.00
48 Brain Takes over world 2.00
49 Shakespeare, Jane Austen 2.00
50 Hello Nurse 2.00
51 Away With Wurds 2.00
52 I Never Promised You a Kindergarten 2.00
53 F:Pinky and the Brain 2.00
54 F:Pinky and the Brain 2.00
55 F:Pinky and the Brain 2.00
56 F:Pinky and the Brain 2.00
57 F:Pinky and the Brain 2.00
58 F:Pinky and the Brain 2.00
59 F:Pinky and the Brain,concl. . . . 2.00
Christmas Spec. 1.50

ANTHRO

1968–69

1 HwP 40.00
2 HwP 28.00
3 thru 5 HwP . . . . @28.00
6 HwP,WW(c&a) 28.00

AQUAMAN

[1st Regular Series] 1962–78

1 NC,I:Quisp 700.00
2 NC,V:Captain Sykes 300.00
3 NC,Aquaman from Atlantis . . . 175.00
4 NC,A:Quisp 150.00
5 NC,The Haunted Sea 150.00
6 NC,A:Quisp 125.00
7 NC,Sea Beasts of Atlantis. . . . 125.00
8 NC,Plot to Steal the Seas 125.00
9 NC,V:King Neptune. 125.00
10 NC,A:Quisp 125.00
11 I: Mera 100.00
12 NC,The Cosmic Gladiators. . . 100.00
13 NC,Invasion of the Giant Reptiles 100.00
14 NC,AquamanSecretPowers . . 100.00
15 NC,Menace of the Man-Fish . 100.00
16 NC,Duel of the Sea Queens. . 100.00
17 NC,Man Who Vanquished Aquaman 100.00
18 W:Aquaman & Mera. 100.00
19 NC,Atlanteans for Sale. 100.00
20 NC,Sea King's DoubleDoom . 100.00
21 NC,I:Fisherman 60.00
22 NC,The Trap of the Sinister Sea Nymphs 60.00
23 NC,I:Aquababy 60.00
24 NC,O:Black Manta 60.00
25 NC,Revolt of Aquaboy 60.00
26 NC,I:O.G.R.E. 60.00
27 NC,Battle of the Rival Aquamen'. 60.00
28 NC,Hail Aquababy,King of Atlantis. 60.00
29 I:Ocean Master 50.00
30 NC,C:JLA 50.00
31 NC,V:O.G.R.E.. . . . . 50.00
32 NC,V:Tryton. 50.00
33 NC,I:Aquagirl 60.00
34 NC,I:Aquabeast 35.00
35 I:Black Manta. 35.00
36 NC,What Seeks the Awesome Threesome?. 35.00
37 I:Scavenger 35.00
38 NC,I:Liquidator. 35.00
39 NC,How to Kill a Sea King 35.00
40 JAp,Sorcerers from the Sea . . . 35.00
41 JAp,Quest for Mera,pt.1 . . . . . . 20.00
42 JAp,Quest for Mera,pt.2. . . . . . 20.00
43 JAp,Quest for Mera,pt.3. . . . . . 20.00
44 JAp,Quest for Mera,pt.4. . . . . . 20.00
45 JAp,Quest for Mera,pt.5. . . . . . 20.00
46 JAp,Quest for Mera concl. 20.00
47 JAp,Revolution in Atlantis #1 rep.Adventure #268 . . . . 20.00
48 JAp,Revolution in Atlantis #2 rep.Adventure #260 . . . . 25.00
49 JAp,As the Seas Die 20.00
50 JAp,NA,A:Deadman. 50.00
51 JAp,NA,A:Deadman. 50.00
52 JAp,NA,A:Deadman. 50.00
53 JAp,Is California Sinking? 8.00
54 JAp,Crime Wave 8.00
55 JAp,Return of the Alien 8.00
56 JAp,I&O:Crusader (1970). 8.00
57 JAp,V:Black Manta (1977) 8.00
58 JAp,O:Aquaman rtd 9.00
59 JAp,V:Scavenger. 8.00
60 DN,V:Scavenger 8.00
61 DN,BMc,A:Batman. 8.00
62 DN,A:Ocean Master. 7.00
63 DN,V:Ocean Master, final issue. 7.00

[2nd Regular Series] 1991–92

1 Poseidonis Under Attack, C:J'onn J'onzz,Blue Beetle 2.25
2 V:Oumland 2.00
3 I:Iqula. 2.00
4 V:Iqula,A:Queequeg 2.00
5 A:Aqualad,Titans,M.Manhunter, R:Manta 2.00
6 V: Manta. 2.00
7 R:Mera 2.00
8 A:Batman,V:NKV Demon 2.00
9 Eco-Wars#1,A:Sea Devils. 2.00
10 Eco-Wars#2,A:Sea Devils 2.00
11 V:Gigantic Dinosaur 2.00
12 A:Iaula. 2.00
13 V:The Scavenger. 2.00
14 V:The Scavenger. 2.00

[3rd Regular Series] 1994–97

0 B:PDd(s),Paternal secret 7.50
1 PDd(s),R:Aqualad,I:Charybdis . . 7.00
2 V:Charybdis 8.00
3 B:PDd(s),Superboy. 4.00
4 B:PDd(s),Lobo 4.00
5 New Costume. 4.00
6 V:The Deep Six 3.00
7 Kako's Metamorphosis 3.00
8 V:Corona and Naiad 3.00
9 JPi(c&a),V:Deadline,A:Koryak. . . 2.00
10 A:Green Lantern,Koryak 2.00
11 R:Mera 2.00
12 F:Mera. 2.00
13 V:Thanatos 2.00
14 PDd,V:Major Disaster,Underworld Unleashed tie-in 2.00
15 PDd,V:Tiamat 2.00
16 PDd,A:Justice League 2.00
17 PDd,V:underwater gargoyles . . . 2.00
18 . . . . 2.00
19 PDd,V:Ocean Master. 2.00
20 PDd,V:Ocean Master. 2.00
21 PDd,JCf,A:Dolphin, V:ThiernaNaOge 2.00
22 PDd(s). 2.00
23 PDd(s),I:Deep Blue (Neptune Perkins) 2.00
24 PDd(s),A:Neptune Perkins 2.00
25 PDd(s),MEg,HSm,Atlantis united, Aquaman king? 2.00
26 PDd(s),MEg,HSm,Oceans threatened, Final Night tie-in. . . 2.00
27 PDd(s),MEg,HSm,V:Demon Gate, dolphin killer 2.00
28 PDd(s),JCf,JP,A:J'Onn J'Onzz . . 2.00
29 PDd(s),MEg,HSm,. 2.00
30 PDd(s),MEg,HSm,"The Pit" 2.00
31 PDd(s),V:The Shark, mind-controlled aquatic army 2.00
32 PDd(s),A:Swamp Thing 2.00
33 PDd(s),Aquaman's dark powers affect him physically 2.00
34 PDd(s),V:Triton 2.00
35 PDd(s),JCf,I:Gamesman, A:Animal Man. 2.00
36 PDd(s),JCf,R:Poseidonis, Tempest,Vulko 2.00
37 PDd,JCf,Genesis,V:Darkseid . . . 2.00
38 PDd,JCf,capitalism 2.00
39 PDd,JCf,Perkins Family Reunion 2.00
40 PDd,JCf,Dr. Polaris 2.00
41 PDd,JCf,BSf,F:Power Girl 2.00
42 PDd,JCf. 2.00
43 PDd,JCf,Millennium Giants, pt.2 x-over, A:Superman Red . . 2.00
44 PDd,JCf,F:Golden Age Flash, Sentinel 2.00
45 PDd,JCf,V:Triton 2.00
46 PDd,JCf,news of Mera. 2.00
47 DAn,Shadows on Water,pt.1 . . . 2.00
48 DAn,Shadows on Water,pt.2 . . . 2.00
49 DAn,ALa,JCf,V:Tempest. 2.00
50 EL,NRd,New Costume. 2.00
51 EL,NRd,V:King Noble 2.00
52 EL,V:Fire Trolls 2.00
53 EL,A:Superman 2.00
54 EL,A:Landlovers 2.00
55 EL,wooing Mera. 2.00
56 EL,V:Piranha Man,pt.1. . . . . 2.00
57 EL,V:Piranha Man,pt.2. . . . . 2.00
58 EL,V:DemonGate & BlackManta 2.00
59 EL,drugs in Atlantis 2.00
60 NRd,W:Tempest & Dolphin 2.00
61 NRd,Day of Judgment x-over. . . 2.00
62 EL(s),NRd 2.00
63 NRd. 2.00
64 DJu,SEp,NRd 2.00
65 DJu,SEp,NRd 2.00
66 DJu,PR,NRd,F:JLA 2.00
67 DJu,SEp,NRd 2.00
68 DJu,SEp,NRd,V:Cerdia 2.00
69 DJu,SEp,NRd,. 2.00
70 DJu,new alliance 2.50
71 DJu,SEp,NRd,A:Warlord 2.50
72 DJu,SEp,NRd,V:Ch'Rinn 2.50
73 DJu,SEp,NRd,V:Valgos 2.50
74 DJu,SEp,NRd,death of friend. . . 2.50
Ann.#1 Year One Annual, V:Triton, A:Superman,Mera 4.00
Ann.#2 Legends o/t Dead Earth . . . 3.50
Ann.#3 Pulp Heroes (Hard Boiled) . 4.50
Ann.#4 PDa, Ghosts. 3.50
Ann.#5 JOs(s),MBr,DG, JLApe Gorilla Warfare 3.00
Spec.#1,000,000 DAn&ALa(s),TGb, BAn, King of Waterworld. 2.00

Aquaman 3rd Series #7
© DC Comics Inc.

DC COMICS

Secret Files #1 EL 5.00
TPB Time and Tide. 10.00

AQUAMAN

[1st Limited Series] 1986

1 V:Ocean Master 5.00
2 V:Ocean Master 3.00
3 V:Ocean Master 3.00
4 V:Ocean Master 3.00

[2nd Limited Series] 1989

1 CS,Atlantis Under Siege 3.00
2 CS,V:Invaders 2.00
3 CS,Mera turned Psychotic 2.00
4 CS,Poseidonis Under Siege 2.00
5 CS,Last Stand,final issue 2.00
Spec#1 MPa,Legend o/Aquaman . . 2.00

AQUAMAN: TIME & TIDE

1993–94

1 PDd(s),O:Aquaman 3.00
2 and 3 PDd(s),O:Aquaman
contd. . . . . @2.00
4 PDd(s),O:Aquaman,final issue. . . 2.00
TPB rep.#1–4 . . . . 10.00

ARAK

1981–85

1 EC,O:Ara 3.00
2 EC 2.00
3 EC,I:Valda 2.00
4 thru 10 EC . . . . @2.00
11 EC,AA 2.00
12 EC,AA,I:Satyricus 2.00
13 thru 19 AA . . . . @2.00
20 AA,O:Angelica 2.00
21 thru 23 AA. 2.00
24 Double size 2.00
25 thru 30. . . . . @2.00
31 D Arak,becomes shaman. 2.00
32 thru 48 . . . . @2.00
49 CI/TD 2.00
50 TD. 2.00
Ann.#1 . . . . 2.00

ARCANA: THE BOOKS OF MAGIC

Vertigo 1994

Ann.#1 JBo(c),JNR(s),PrG,Children's
Crusade,R:Tim Hunter,
A:Free Country. 5.00

Argus #1 © DC Comics, Inc.

ARGUS

[Mini-Series] 1995

1 R:Argus,I:Raver 2.00
2 Blinded by metahuman hitmen . . 2.00
3 Spy Satellite 2.00
4 The Watcher. 2.00
5 Data Highways 2.00
6 Restored Sight 2.00

ARION, LORD OF ATLANTIS

1982–85

1 JDu 2.00
2 JDu 2.00
3 JDu 2.00
4 JDu,O:Arion 2.00
5 JDu 2.00
6 JDu 2.00
7 thru 12 . . . . @2.00
13 JDu 2.00
14 JDu 2.00
15 JDu 2.00
16 thru 35 . . . . @2.00
Spec. 2.00

ARION THE IMMORTAL

1 RWi,R:Arion 2.00
2 RWi,V:Garffon 2.00
3 RWi,V:Garn Daanuth 2.00
4 RWi,V:Garn Daanuth 2.00
5 RWi,Darkworlet. 2.00
6 RWi,MG,A:Power Girl 2.00

ARMAGEDDON 2001

May, 1991

1 DJu,DG,I&O:Waverider. 4.00
1a 2nd printing 2.00
1b 3rd printing (silver) 2.00
2 DJu,ATi,Monarch revealed as Hawk,
D:Dove,L:Capt Atom(JLE) 2.00
Spec.#1 MR 2.00

ARMAGEDDON 2001 ARMAGEDDON: THE ALIEN AGENDA

1991–92

1 DJu,JOy,A:Monarch,Capt.Atom. . 2.00
2 V:Ancient Romans 2.00
3 JRu(i),The Old West. 2.00
4 DG,GP,V:Nazi's,last issue 2.00

ARMAGEDDON: INFERNO

1992

1 TMd,LMc,A:Creeper,Batman,
Firestorm 2.00
2 AAd,LMc,WS,I:Abraxis,A:Lobo . . 2.00
3 AAd,WS,LMc,TMd,MN,R:Justice
Society. 2.00
4 AAd,WS,LMc,TMd,MN,DG,
V:Abraxis,A:Justice Society . . . 2.00

ARSENAL

Aug., 1998

1 (of 4) F:Black Canary 2.50
2 F:Green Arrow 2.50
3 F:Vandal Savage 2.50
4 conclusion 2.50

ARTEMIS: REQUIEM

1996

1 BML(s) (of 6). 2.00
2 thru 6 BML(s),EBe, ... @2.00

Artemis: Requiem #3 © DC Comics, Inc.

ATARI FORCE

1984–85

1 JL,I:TempestDart 2.00
2 JL. 2.00
3 JL. 2.00
4 RA/JL/JO 2.00
5 RA/JL/JO 2.00
6 thru 12 JL . . . . @2.00
13 KG 2.00
14 thru 21 EB . . . . @2.00

ATLANTIS CHRONICLES

1990

1 EM,Atlantis 50,000 years ago . . . 3.50
2 EM,Atlantis Sunk 3.25
3 EM,Twin Cities of Poseidonis
& Tritonis 3.25
4 EM,King Orin's Daughter
Cora Assumes Throne 3.25
5 EM,Orin vs. Shalako. 3.25
6 EM,Contact with Surface
Dwellers. 3.25
7 EM,Queen Atlanna gives Birth to
son(Aquaman)48 pg.final issue. 3.25

ATOM, THE

1962–68

1 MA,GK,I:Plant Master 775.00
2 MA,GK,V:Plant Master 325.00
3 MA,GK,I:Chronos 225.00
4 MA,GK,Snapper Carr 150.00
5 MA,GK 150.00
6 MA,GK 150.00
7 MA,GK,1st Atom & Hawkman
team-up 250.00
8 MA,GK,A:JLA,V:Doctor Light. . 125.00
9 MA,GK 125.00
10 MA,GK. 125.00
11 MA,GK. 100.00
12 MA,GK. 100.00
13 MA,GK. 100.00
14 MA,GK. 100.00
15 MA,GK. 100.00
16 MA,GK 75.00
17 MA,GK 75.00
18 MA,GK 75.00
19 MA,GK,A:Zatanna 75.00
20 MA,GK 75.00
21 MA,GK 50.00
22 MA,GK 50.00
23 MA,GK 50.00

24 MA,GK,V:Jason Woodrue 50.00
25 MA,GK 50.00
26 GK. 45.00
27 GK. 45.00
28 GK. 45.00
29 GK,A:E-2 Atom,Thinker. 150.00
30 GK. 50.00
31 GK,A:Hawkman 45.00
32 GK. 45.00
33 GK. 45.00
34 GK,V:Big Head 45.00
35 GK. 45.00
36 GK,A:Golden Age Atom 65.00
37 GK,I:Major Mynah 45.00
38 "Sinister stopover Earth" 45.00
Becomes:

ATOM & HAWKMAN
1968–69

39 MA, V:Tekla 50.00
40 DD,JKu,MA 40.00
41 DD,JKu,MA 40.00
42 MA,V:Brama 40.00
43 MA,I:Gentleman Ghost. 40.00
44 DD. 40.00
45 DD. 40.00

ATOM SPECIAL

1 SDi,V:Chronos (1993). 3.00
2 Zero Hour Atom (1994). 3.00

AVATAR
1991

1 A:Midnight & Allies 8.00
2 Search for Tablets 6.00
3 V:Cyric, Myrkul, final issue 6.00

AZRAEL
1994

1 I:New Azreal,Brian Bryan 6.00
2 A:Batman,New Azreal. 4.50
3 V:Order of St. Dumas 3.50
4 The System 3.00
5 BKi(c&a),R:Ra's al Ghul,Talia [new Miraweb format begins] . . 3.00
6 BKi(c&a),Ra's al Ghul,Talia 2.50
7 Sister Lily's Transformation 2.50
8 System Secret 2.25
9 Jean Paul Vanishes 2.25
10 DON,BKi,JmP,F:Neron, Underworld Unleashed tie-in. . . 2.00
11 DON,BKi,JmP,A:Batman 2.00
12 DON,BKi,JmP,Azrael looks for Shondra 2.00
13 DON,BKi,Demon Time,pt.1 . . . . 2.00
14 DON,BKi,Demon Time,pt.2 . . . . 2.00
15 DON,BKi,Contagion,pt.5 . . . . . . 2.50
16 DON,BKi,Contagion,pt.10 . . . . . 2.00
17 DON,BKi,JmP,A:Dr.Orchid 2.00
18 DON,BKi,JmP,A:Dr.Orchid 2.00
19 DON(s) 2.00
20 DON(s) 2.00
21 DON(s) 2.00
22 DON(s),BKi,JmP,"Angel in Hiding," pt.2 (of 3) 2.00
23 DON(s),BKi,JmP,"Angel in Hiding," pt.3 . . . . 2.00
24 DON(s),BKi,JmP,The Order's return 2.00
25 DON(s),BKi,JmP,V:Brother Rollo 2.00
26 . . . . 2.00
27 DON(s),BKi,JmP,"Angel Insane, "pt.1 . . . . 2.00
28 DON(s),BKi,JmP,Joker, Riddler & Two-Face escape from Arkham Asylum 2.00
29 DON(s),DBw,JmP, F:Ra's Al Ghul, pt.1 . . . . 2.00
30 DON(s),DBw,JmP, F:Ra's Al Ghul, pt.2 . . . . 2.00
31 DON(s),JmP "Angel and the Monster Maker" pt.1 (of 3) 2.00
32 DON(s),JmP "Angel and the Monster Maker" pt.2 . . . . 2.00
33 DON(s),JmP "Angel and the Monster Maker" pt.3 concl. 2.00
34 DON(s),JmP,Genesis, a parademon 2.00
35 DON(s),JmP,F:Hitman 2.00
36 DON,JmP,Return of Bane,pt.1 . . 2.00
37 DON,JmP,Return of Bane,pt.2 . . 2.00
38 DON,JmP,Return of Bane,pt.3 . . 2.00
39 DON,JmP 2.00
40 DON,JmP,Cataclysm,pt.4,x-over 4.50
41 DON,JmP,A:Devil Latour 2.00
42 DON,JmP,Madame Kalypso 2.00
43 DON,JmP,Lilhy,Brian Bryan 2.00
44 DON,JmP,Luc & Lilhy disappear 2.00
45 DON,JmP,V:Deathstroke, A:Calibax 2.00
46 DON(s),JmP,V:Calibax. 2.25
47 Road to No Man's Land, flip-book Batman:Shadow of the Bat 4.00
48 DON(s),JmP,No Man's Land . . . 2.25
49 DON(s),JmP,New Costume 2.25
50 DON(s),JmP,New Costume 2.25
51 DON(s),JmP,V:Demonic Trio . . . 2.25
52 DON(s),JmP,No Man's Land . . . 2.25
53 DON(s),JmP,V:Joker 2.25
54 DON(s),JmP,V:Death Dancer. . . 2.25
55 DON(s),JmP,V:Death Dancer. . . 2.25
56 DON(s),JmP,A:Batgirl 2.25
57 DON(s),JmP,No Man's Land . . . 2.25
58 DON(s),JmP,Day of Judgment x-over 2.25
59 DON(s),JmP,F:Catwoman 2.25
60 DON(s) 2.25
61 DON(s),F:Batgirl,V:Joker 2.25
62 DON(s) 2.25
63 DON(s),F:Huntress 2.25
64 DON(s),F:Huntress 2.25
65 DON(s),Nicholas Scratch 2.50
66 DON(s),F:Lilhi 2.50
67 DON(s),JmP,to Africa. 2.50
68 DON(s),JmP, ... 2.50
69 DON(s),JmP,stranded 2.50
70 DON(s),SCi,JmP,Prophet,pt.1 . . 2.50
71 DON(s),SCi,JmP,Prophet,pt.2 . . 2.50
Ann.#1 Year One Annual 4.00
Ann.#2 Legends o/t Dead Earth . . . 3.00
Ann.#3 Pulp Heroes (Hard Boiled) . 4.00
Spec.#1,000,000 DON(s),VGi,JmP F:Green Arrow,Robin,Hawkman 2.00
GN Azrael/Ash 5.00

Azrael #20 © DC Comics Inc.

AZRAEL/ASH
March, 1997

1 one-shot DON(s),JQ,V:Surtr, A:Batman, x-over 5.00

AZRAEL PLUS
Oct., 1996

1 one-shot, DON(s),VGi,F:Vic Sage, The Question 3.00

AZTEK: THE ULTIMATE MAN
1996–97

1 GMo&MMr(s),NSH,I:Aztek & Synth 4.00
2 GMo&MMr(s),NSH,A:Green Lantern 2.00
3 GMo&MMr(s),NSH,V:Doll-Face. . 2.00
4 GMo&MMr(s),NSH,I:Lizard King, Vanity. 2.00
5 GMo&MMr(s),NSH,O:Aztek, V:Lizard King 2.00
6 GMo&MMr(s),NSH,V:Vanity, A: Joker 2.00
7 GMo&MMr(s),NSH,A:Batman . . . 2.00
8 GMo&MMr(s),NSH,return to Brotherhood of Zuetzatcoatl,A:Raptor . 2.00
9 GMo&MMr(s),NSH,V:Parasite, A:Superman. 2.00
10 GMo&MMr(s),NSH,A:Justice League, final issue 5.00

BABYLON 5
1995

1 From TV series. 16.00
2 From TV series. 11.00
3 Mysterious Assassin 8.00
4 V:Mysterious Assassin 8.00
5 Shadows of the Present,pt.1. . . . 8.00
6 Shadows of the Present,pt.2. . . . 8.00
7 Shadows of the Present,pt.3. . . . 7.00
8 Laser-Mirror Starweb,pt.1 . . . . . . 7.00
9 Laser-Mirror Starweb,pt.2 . . . . . . 7.00
10 Laser-Mirror-Starweb,pt.3 . . . . . 7.00
11 final issue 7.00
TPB The Price of Peace 10.00

BABYLON 5: IN VALEN'S NAME
Jan., 1998

1 (of 3) PDd, from TV series 3.00
2 PDd 3.00
3 PDd 3.00

BATGIRL
1988

Spec.#1 V: Cormorant,I:Slash. 8.00

BATGIRL
Feb., 2000

1 No Man's Land follow-up 2.50
2 saves dying man 2.50
3 A:Batman 2.50
4 A:Batman 2.50
5 V:Ezra 2.50
6 A:Batman 2.50
7 A:Batman, ... 2.50
8 V:Lady Shiva 2.50
9 Batgirl questions her motives . . . 2.50
Ann.#1 Planet DC,A:Batman. 3.50

Batman #40 © DC Comics, Inc.

BATGIRL ADVENTURES

Dec., 1997

1-shot RBr,V:Poison Ivy,A:Harley Quinn 4.00

BATMAN

Spring, 1940

1 I:Joker,Cat(Catwoman), V:Hugo Strange 65,000.00
2 V:Joker/Catwoman team . . 12,000.00
3 V:Catwoman 7,500.00
4 V:Joker 6,000.00
5 V:Joker 4,500.00
6 V:`Clock Maker' 3,800.00
7 V:Joker 3,700.00
8 V:Joker 3,500.00
9 V:Joker 3,500.00
10 V:Catwoman 3,500.00
11 V:Joker,Penguin 5,500.00
12 V:Joker 2,300.00
13 V:Joker 2,600.00
14 V:Penguin;Propaganda sty . 2,500.00
15 V:Catwoman 2,300.00
16 I:Alfred,V:Joker 4,500.00
17 V:Penguin 1,600.00
18 V:Tweedledum & Tweedledee 2,000.00
19 V:Joker 1,600.00
20 V:Joker 1,600.00
21 V:Penguin 1,100.00
22 V:Catwoman,Cavalier 1,100.00
23 V:Joker 1,700.00
24 I:Carter Nichols, V:Tweedledum & Tweedledee 1,200.00
25 V:Joker/Penguin team 1,800.00
26 V:Cavalier 1,100.00
27 V:Penguin 1,500.00
28 V:Joker 1,200.00
29 V:Scuttler 1,100.00
30 V:Penguin,I:Ally Babble 1,100.00
31 I:Punch and Judy 900.00
32 O:Robin,V:Joker 950.00
33 V:Penguin,Jackall 1,000.00
34 A:Ally Babble 900.00
35 V:Catwoman 900.00
36 V:Penguin,A:King Arthur 900.00
37 V:Joker 1,200.00
38 V:Penguin 900.00
39 V:Catwoman,Christmas Story. 900.00
40 V:Joker 1,200.00
41 V:Penguin 700.00
42 V:Catwoman 700.00
43 V:Penguin 700.00
44 V:Joker,A:Carter Nichols,Meets ancester Silas Wayne 1,200.00
45 V:Catwoman 700.00
46 V:Joker,A:Carter Nichols, Leonardo Da Vinci 650.00
47 O:Batman,V:Catwoman 2,800.00
48 V:Penguin, Bat-Cave story . . . 800.00
49 I:Mad Hatter & Vicki Vale. . . 1,400.00
50 V:Two-Face,A:Vicki Vale 750.00
51 V:Penguin 650.00
52 V:Joker 800.00
53 V:Joker 800.00
54 V:`The Treasure Hunter' 650.00
55 V:Joker 800.00
56 V:Penguin 650.00
57 V:Joker 700.00
58 V:Penguin 650.00
59 I:Deadshot 650.00
60 V:`Shark' Marlin 700.00
61 V:Penguin 800.00
62 O:Catwoman,I:Knight & Squire 1,000.00
63 V:Joker 650.00
64 V:Killer Moth 600.00
65 I:Wingman,V:Catwoman 625.00
66 V:Joker 625.00
67 V:Joker 625.00
68 V:Two-Face,Alfred story 550.00
69 I:King of the Cats, A:Catwoman 600.00
70 V:Penguin 550.00
71 V:Mr. Cipher 550.00
72 `The Jungle Batman' 550.00
73 V:Joker,A:Vicki Vale 650.00
74 V:Joker 550.00
75 I:The Gorilla Boss 550.00
76 V:Penguin 550.00
77 `The Crime Predictor' 550.00
78 `The Manhunter from Mars' . . 650.00
79 A:Vicki Vale 550.00
80 V:Joker 550.00
81 V:Two-Face 550.00
82 `The Flying Batman' 500.00
83 V:`Fish' Frye 500.00
84 V:Catwoman 600.00
85 V:Joker 500.00
86 V:Joker 500.00
87 V:Joker 500.00
88 V:Mr. Mystery 500.00
89 I:Aunt Agatha 500.00
90 I:Batboy 400.00
91 V:Blinky Grosset 400.00
92 I:Ace, the Bat-Hound 400.00
93 `The Caveman Batman' 500.00
94 Alfred has Amnesia 400.00
95 `The Bat-Train' 400.00
96 `Batman's College Days' 400.00
97 V:Joker 400.00
98 A:Carter Nichols,Jules Verne . 400.00
99 V:Penguin,A:Carter Nichols, Bat Masterson 400.00
100 `Great Batman Contest' . . . 2,200.00
101 `The Great Bat-Cape Hunt' . 450.00
102 V:Mayne Mallok 400.00
103 A:Ace, the Bat-Hound 400.00
104 V:Devoe 400.00
105 A:Batwoman 450.00
106 V:Keene Harper gang 375.00
107 V:Daredevils 375.00
108 Bat-cave story 375.00
109 `The 1,000 Inventions of Batman' 375.00
110 V:Joker 375.00
111 . . . . 325.00
112 I:Signalman 325.00
113 I:Fatman 325.00
114 . . . . 325.00
115 . . . . 325.00
116 . . . . 325.00
117 . . . . 325.00
118 . . . . 325.00
119 . . . . 325.00
120 . . . . 325.00

Batman #41 © DC Comics, Inc.

121 I:Mr.Freeze 400.00
122 . . . . 235.00
123 A:Joker 225.00
124 “Mystery Seed from Space” . 225.00
125 . . . . 225.00
126 . . . . 225.00
127 A:Superman & Joker 235.00
128 . . . . 225.00
129 O:Robin(Retold) 265.00
130 . . . . 225.00
131 I:2nd Batman 175.00
132 `Lair of the Sea-Fox' 175.00
133 . . . . 175.00
134 . . . . 175.00
135 . . . . 175.00
136 A:Joker,Bat-Mite 200.00
137 V:Mr.Marvel,The Brand 175.00
138 A:Bat-Mite 175.00
139 I:Old Batgirl 200.00
140 A:Joker 200.00
141 V:Clockmaster 175.00
142 Batman robot story 175.00
143 A:Bathound 175.00
144 A:Joker,Bat-Mite,Bat-Girl . . . 175.00
145 V:Mr.50,Joker 185.00
146 A:Bat-Mite,Joker 125.00
147 Batman becomes Bat-Baby . 125.00
148 A:Joker 150.00
149 V:Maestro 125.00
150 V:Biff Warner,Jack Pine 125.00
151 V:Harris Boys 100.00
152 A:Joker 110.00
153 Other Dimension story 100.00
154 V:Dr. Dorn 100.00
155 1st S.A. Penguin 450.00
156 V:Gorilla Gang 110.00
157 V:Mirror Man 110.00
158 A:Bathound,Bat-Mite 110.00
159 A:Joker,Clayface 125.00
160 V:Bart Cullen 110.00
161 A:Bat-Mite 110.00
162 F:Robin 110.00
163 A:Joker 110.00
164 CI,A:Mystery Analysts,new Batmobile 100.00
165 V:The Mutated Man 100.00
166 Escape story 100.00
167 V:Karabi & Hydra, the Crime Cartel 100.00
168 V:Mr. Mammoth 100.00
169 A:Penguin 125.00
170 V:Getaway Genius 100.00
171 CI,1st S.A. Riddler 450.00
172 V:Flower Gang 65.00
173 V:Elwood Pearson 65.00
174 V:Big Game Hunter 65.00

All comics prices listed are for *Near Mint* condition.

175 V:Eddie Repp 65.00
176 Giant rep.A:Joker,Catwom.. . . 75.00
177 BK,A:Elongated Man,Atom. . . 65.00
178 CI 65.00
179 CI,2nd Riddler(Silver). 135.00
180 BK,A:Death-Man 65.00
181 CI,I:Poison Ivy 150.00
182 A:Joker,(giant size rep). 70.00
183 CI,A:Poison Ivy 100.00
184 CI,Mystery of the Missing Manhunters 60.00
185 Giant rep. 65.00
186 A:Joker 50.00
187 Giant rep.A:Joker. 65.00
188 CI,A:Eraser 35.00
189 CI,A:Scarecrow 55.00
190 CI,A:Penguin 45.00
191 CI,The Day Batman Soldout. . 35.00
192 CI,The Crystal ball that betrayed Batman 35.00
193 Giant rep. 45.00
194 MSy,BK,A:Blockbuster,Mystery Analysts of Gotham City 35.00
195 CI 35.00
196 BK,Psychic Super-Sleuth 35.00
197 MSy,A:Bat Girl,Catwoman . . . 75.00
198 A:Joker,Penguin,Catwoman, O:Batman rtd,(G-Size rep) . . . 75.00
199 CI,`Peril o/t Poison Rings' . . . 35.00
200 NA(c),O:rtd,A:Joker,Pengiun, Scarecrow 150.00
201 A:Batman Villians. 40.00
202 BU:Robin. 25.00
203 NA(c),(giant size). 45.00
204 FR(s),IN,JG 25.00
205 FR(s),IN,JG 25.00
206 FR(s),IN,JG 25.00
207 FR(s),IN,JG 25.00
208 GK,new O:Batman, A:Catwoman. 50.00
209 FR(s),IN,JG 25.00
210 A:Catwoman 27.00
211 FR(s),IN,JG 22.00
212 FR(s),IN,JG 22.00
213 RA,30th Anniv.Batman,new O: Robin,rep.O:Alfred,Joker 70.00
214 IN,A:Batgirl 22.00
215 IN,DG 22.00
216 IN,DG,I:DaphnePennyworth . . 22.00
217 NA(c). 24.00
218 NA(c),giant 50.00
219 NA,IN,DG,Batman Xmas 45.00
220 NA(c),IN 22.00
221 IN,DG 22.00
222 IN,Rock'n Roll story 40.00
223 NA(c),giant 40.00
224 NA(c). 22.00
225 NA(c),IN,DG 22.00
226 IN,DG I:10-Eyed Man. 22.00
227 IN,DG,A:Daphne Pennyworth 22.00
228 giant Deadly Traps rep. 40.00
229 IN 22.00
230 NA(c),Robin. 22.00
231 F:Ten-Eyed Man 22.00
232 DON(s),NA,DG, I:Ras al Ghul 100.00
233 giant Bruce Wayne iss. 35.00
234 NA,DG,IN,1stS.A.Two-Face . 125.00
235 CI,V:Spook 25.00
236 NA. 30.00
237 NA. 55.00
238 NA,JC,JKu,giant 40.00
239 NA,RB 22.00
240 NA(c),RB,giant,R-Ghul. 22.00
241 IN,DG,RB,A:Kid Flash 22.00
242 RB,MK. 22.00
243 NA,DG,Ras al Ghul 40.00
244 NA,Ras al Ghul 40.00
245 NA,IN,DG,FMc,Ras al Ghul . . 40.00
246. . . . . 22.00
247 Deadly New Year. 22.00
248. . . . . 22.00
249 `Citidel of Crime' 22.00
250 IN,DG 22.00
251 NA,V:Joker 60.00
252. . . . . 22.00
253 AN,DG,A:Shadow 22.00
254 NA,GK,B:100 page issues . . . 30.00
255 GK,CI,NA,DG,I:CrazyQuilt . . . 45.00
256 Catwoman 25.00
257 IN,DG,V:Penguin 25.00
258 IN,DG 25.00
259 GK,IN,DG,A:Shadow 25.00
260 IN,DG,Joker. 45.00
261 CI,GK,E:100 page issues. . . . 25.00
262 A:Scarecrow 22.00
263 DG(i),A:Riddler 15.00
264 DON(s),DG,A:Devil Dayre . . . 13.00
265 RB,BWr 13.00
266 DG,Catwoman(old Costume) . 15.00
267 DG 13.00
268 DON(s),IN,TeB,V:Sheikh 13.00
269 A:Riddler 13.00
270 B:DvR(s) 13.00
271 IN,FMc. 13.00
272 JL 13.00
273 V:Underworld Olympics/76 . . . 13.00
274 . . . . 13.00
275 . . . . 13.00
276 . . . . 13.00
277 . . . . 13.00
278 . . . . 13.00
279 A:Riddler 14.00
280 . . . . 12.00
281 . . . . 12.00
282 . . . . 12.00
283 V:Camouflage 12.00
284 JA,R:Dr.Tzin Tzin. 12.00
285 . . . . 12.00
286 V:Joker 15.00
287 BWi,MGr,Penguin 12.00
288 BWi,MGr,Penguin 12.00
289 MGr, V:Skull. 12.00
290 MGr,V:Skull Dagger 12.00
291 B:Underworld Olympics #1, A:Catwoman. 12.00
292 A:Riddler 12.00
293 A:Superman & Luthor 12.00
294 E:DvR(s),E:Underworld Olympics,A:Joker 14.00
295 GyC(s),MGo,JyS,V:Hamton . . 12.00
296 B:DvR(s),V:Scarecrow 12.00
297 RB,Mad Hatter. 12.00
298 JCA,DG,V:Baxter Bains 12.00

Batman #476 © DC Comics Inc.

299 DG 12.00
300 WS,DG,A:Batman E-2, Robin E-2. . . . . 22.00
301 JCa,TeB. 10.00
302 JCa,DG,V:Human Dynamo . . 10.00
303 JCa,DG 10.00
304 E:DvR(s),V:Spook 10.00
305 GyC,JCa,DeH,V:Thanatos . . . 11.00
306 JCa,DeH,DN,V:Black Spider. . 11.00
307 B:LWn(s),JCa,DG, I:Limehouse Jack 11.00
308 JCa,DG,V:Mr.Freeze 11.00
309 E:LWn(s),JCa,FMc, V:Blockbuster 11.00
310 IN,DG,A:Gentleman Ghost . . . 11.00
311 SEt,FMc,IN,Batgirl, V:Dr.Phosphorus. 11.00
312 WS,DG,Calenderman. 11.00
313 IN,FMc,VTwo-Face 11.00
314 IN,FMc,V:Two-Face 11.00
315 IN,FMc,V:Kiteman 11.00
316 IN,FMc,F:Robin, V:Crazy Quilt 11.00
317 IN,FMc,V:Riddler 12.00
318 IN,I:Fire Bug 11.00
319 JKu(c),IN,DG,A:Gentleman Ghost,E:Catwoman. 11.00
320 BWr(c) 11.00
321 DG,WS,A:Joker,Catwoman . . 12.00
322 V:Cap.Boomerang,Catwoman 11.00
323 IN,A:Catwoman 11.00
324 IN,A:Catwoman 11.00
325. . . . . 11.00
326 A:Catwoman 11.00
327 IN,A:Proffessor.Milo 11.00
328 A:Two-Face 11.00
329 IN,A:Two-Face 11.00
330. . . . . 11.00
331 DN,FMc,V:Electrocutioner . . . 11.00
332 IN,DN,Ras al Ghul.1st solo Catwoman story 12.00
333 IN,DN,A:Catwoman, Ras al Ghul 10.00
334 FMc,Ras al Ghul,Catwoman. . 10.00
335 IN,FMc,Catwoman,Ras al Ghul 10.00
336 JL,FMc,Loser Villains 10.00
337 DN,V:Snow Man 10.00
338 DN,Deathsport. 10.00
339 A:Poison Ivy 10.00
340 GC,A:Mole. 10.00
341 A:Man Bat 10.00
342 V:Man Bat 10.00
343 GC,KJ,I:The Dagger 10.00
344 GC,KJ,Poison Ivy. 10.00
345 I:New Dr.Death,A:Catwoman . 10.00
346 DN,V:Two Face 10.00
347 A:Alfred 10.00
348 GC,KJ,Man-Bat,A:Catwoman. 10.00
349 GC,AA,A:Catwoman 10.00
350 GC,TD,A:Catwoman 10.00
351 GC,TD,A:Catwoman 10.00
352 Col Blimp. 10.00
353 JL,DN,DA,A:Joker 11.00
354 DN,AA,V:HugoStrange,A: Catwoman 10.00
355 DN,AA:A:Catwoman. 10.00
356 DG,DN,Hugo Strange 10.00
357 DN,AA,I:Jason Todd. 11.00
358 A:King Croc 10.00
359 DG,O:King Croc,Joker 11.00
360 I:Savage Skull 10.00
361 DN,Man-Bat,I:Harvey Bullock. 10.00
362 V:Riddler 10.00
363 V:Nocturna. 10.00
364 DN,AA,J.Todd 1st full solo story (cont'd Detective #531) . 10.00
365 DN,AA,C:Joker 10.00
366 DN,AA,Joker,J.Todd in Robin Costume 15.00
367 DN,AA,PoisonIvy 9.00

DC COMICS

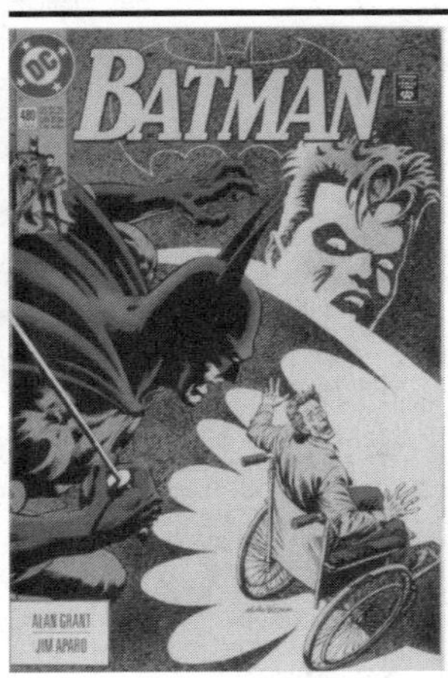

Batman #480 © DC Comics, Inc.

368 DN,AA,I:2nd Robin (Jason Todd) 12.00
369 DN,AA,I:Dr.Fang,V:Deadshot . . 7.00
370 DN,AA 7.00
371 DN,AA,V:Catman 5.00
372 DN,AA,A:Dr.Fang 4.50
373 DN,AA,V:Scarecrow 4.50
374 GC,AA,V:Penguin 5.00
375 GC,AA,V:Dr.Freeze 4.50
376 DN,Halloween issue 4.50
377 DN,AA,V:Nocturna 4.50
378 V:Mad Hatter 4.50
379 V:Mad Hatter 4.50
380 AA,V:Nocturna 4.50
381 V:Batman 4.50
382 A:Catwoman 5.00
383 GC 4.50
384 V:Calender Man 4.50
385 V:Calender Man 4.50
386 I:Black Mask 4.50
387 V:Black Mask 4.50
388 V:Capt.Boomerang & Mirror Master 4.50
389 V:Nocturna,Catwoman 5.00
390 V:Nocturna,Catwoman 5.00
391 V:Nocturna,Catwoman 5.00
392 A:Catwoman 5.00
393 PG,V:Cossack 4.00
394 PG,V:Cossack 4.00
395 V:Film Freak 4.00
396 V:Film Freak 4.00
397 V:Two-Face,Catwoman 4.50
398 V:Two-Face,Catwoman 4.50
399 HaE(s),Two-Face 4.00
400 BSz,AAd,GP,BB,A:Joker 20.00
401 JBy(c),TVE,Legends, A:Magpie 4.00
402 JSn,Fake Batman 4.00
403 DCw,Batcave discovered 4.00
404 DM,FM(s),B:Year 1,I:Modern Age Catwoman 12.00
405 FM,DM,Year 1 . . . . 7.00
406 FM,DM,Year 1 . . . . 7.00
407 FM,DM,E:Year 1 . . . . 7.00
408 CW,V:Joker, new O:Jason Todd 5.00
408a 2nd printing 2.00
409 DG,RA,V:Crime School 5.00
409a 2nd printing 2.00
410 DC,Jason Todd 5.00
411 DC,DH,V:Two Face 4.00
412 DC,DH,I:Mime 4.00
413 DC,DH 4.00
414 JAp,Slasher 4.00
415 JAp,Millenium Week #2 . . . . . . 4.00
416 JAp,1st Batman/Nightwing T.U. 4.00
417 JAp,B:10 Nights,I:KGBeast . . . 9.00
418 JAp,V:KGBeast 7.00
419 JAp,V:KGBeast 7.00
420 JAp,E:10 Nights,D:KGBeast . . . 7.00
421 DG 4.50
422 MBr,V:Dumpster Slayer 4.00
423 TM(c),DC,Who is Batman 5.00
424 MBr,Robin 4.00
425 MBr,Gordon Kidnapped 4.00
426 JAp,B:Death in the Family, V:Joker 11.00
427 JAp,V:Joker 9.00
428 JAp,D:2nd Robin 7.00
429 JAp,A:Superman, E:Death in the Family 5.00
430 JAp,JSn,V:Madman 4.00
431 JAp,Murder Investigation 3.25
432 JAp 3.25
433 JBy,JAp,Many Deaths of the Batman #1 . . . . 4.00
434 JBy,JAp,Many Deaths #2 . . . . . 3.50
435 JBy,Many Deaths #3 . . . . 3.50
436 PB,B:Year#3,A:Nightwing,I:Tim Drake as child 5.00
436a 2ndPrint(green DC logo) 2.00
437 PB,year#3 . . . . 3.50
438 PB,year#3 . . . . 3.00
439 PB,year#3 . . . . 3.00
440 JAp,Lonely Place of Dying #1, A:Tim Drake (face not shown) . 3.50
441 JAp,Lonely Place Dying 3.50
442 JAp,I:3rd Robin(Tim Drake) . . . 5.00
443 JAp,I:Crimesmith 2.50
444 JAp,V:Crimesmith 2.50
445 JAp,I:K.G.Beast Demon 2.50
446 JAp,V:K.G.Beast Demon 2.50
447 JAp,D:K.G.Beast Demon 2.50
448 JAp,A:Penguin#1 . . . . 2.75
449 MBr,A:Penguin#3 . . . . 2.75
450 JAp,I:Joker II 2.50
451 JAp,V:Joker II 2.50
452 KD,Dark Knight Dark City#1 . . . 2.50
453 KD,Dark Knight Dark City#2 . . . 2.50
454 KD,Dark Knight Dark City#3 . . . 2.50
455 Identity Crisis#1, A:Scarecrow 2.50
456 IdentityCrisis#2 . . . . 3.00
457 V:Scarecrow,A:Robin, New Costume 5.00
457a 2nd printing 2.50
458 R:Sarah Essen 2.50
459 A:Sarah Essen 2.50
460 Sisters in Arms,pt.1 A:Catwoman 3.00
461 Sisters in Arms,pt.2 Catwoman V:Sarah.Essen 3.00
462 Batman in San Francisco 2.50
463 Death Valley 2.50
464 V:Two-Hearts 2.50
465 Batman/Robin T.U. 3.00
466 Robin Trapped 2.50
467 Shadowbox #1(sequel to Robin Mini-Series) 3.00
468 Shadowbox #2 . . . . 2.50
469 Shadowbox #3 . . . . 2.50
470 War of the Gods x-over 2.50
471 V:Killer Croc 2.50
472 The Idiot Root,pt.1 . . . . 2.50
473 The Idiot Root,pt.3 . . . . 2.50
474 Destroyer,pt.1 (LOTDK#27) . . . 3.00
475 R:Scarface,A:VickiVale 2.50
476 A:Scarface 2.50
477 Ph(c),Gotham Tale,pt.1 . . . . . . 2.50
478 Ph(c),Gotham Tale,pt.2 . . . . . . 2.50
479 TMd,I:Pagan 2.50
480 JAp,To the father I never knew 2.50
481 JAp,V:Maxie Zeus 2.50
482 JAp,V:Maxie Zeus 2.50

Batman #500 © DC Comics, Inc.

483 JAp,I:Crash & Burn 2.50
484 JAp,R:Black Mask 2.50
485 TGr,V:Black Mask 2.50
486 JAp,I:Metalhead 2.50
487 JAp,V:Headhunter 2.50
488 JAp,N:Azrael 8.00
489 JAp,Bane vs Killer Croc, I:Azrael as Batman 6.00
489a 2nd Printing 2.00
490 JAp,Bane vs.Riddler 7.00
490a 2nd Printing 1.75
490b 3rd Printing 1.50
491 JAp,V:Joker,A:Bane 4.50
491a 2nd Printing 1.50
492 B:DgM(s),NB,Knightfall#1, V:Mad Hatter,A:Bane 5.00
492a Platinum Ed. 9.00
492b 2nd Printing 1.50
493 NB,Knightfall,#3,Mr.Zsasz 3.50
494 JAp,TMd,Knightfall #5,A:Bane, V:Cornelius,Stirk,Joker 3.00
495 NB,Knightfall#7,V:Poison Ivy,A:Bane 3.00
496 JAp,JRu,Knightfall#9,V:Joker, Scarecrow,A:Bane 3.00
497 JAp,DG,Knightfall#11,V:Bane, Batman gets back broken 4.50
497a 2nd Printing 2.00
498 JAp,JRu,Knightfall#15,A:Bane, Catwoman,Azrael Becomes Batman 2.50
499 JAp,SHa,Knightfall#17, A:Bane,Catwoman 2.50
500 JQ(c),JAp,MM,Die Cut(c), Direct Market,Knightfall#19, V:Bane,N:Batman 3.00
500a KJo(c),Newstand Ed. 2.50
501 MM,I:Mekros 2.50
502 MM,V:Mekros 2.50
503 MM,V:Catwoman 2.50
504 MM,V:Catwoman 2.50
505 MM,V:Canibal 2.50
506 KJo(c),MM,A:Ballistic 2.50
507 KJo(c),MM,A:Ballistic 2.50
508 KJo(c),MM,V:Abattior 2.50
509 KJo(c),MM,KnightsEnd#1, A:Shiva 3.00
510 KJo(c),MM,Knights End #7, V:Azrael 2.50
511 Zero Hour, A:Batgirl 2.50
512 Killer Croc sewer battles 2.50
513 Two-Face and convicts 2.50
514 Identity Crisis 2.50
515 KJo,Return of Bruce Wayne, Troika,pt.1 . . . . 2.50

515 Collector's Edition 3.50
516 V:The Sleeper 2.50
517 V:The Sleeper 2.50
518 V:The Black Spider 2.50
519 KJo,V:The Black Spider
[new Miraweb format begins] . . 2.50
520 EB,A:James Gordon 2.50
521 R:Killer Croc 2.50
522 R:Scarecrow 2.50
523 V:Scarecrow 2.50
524 DgM,KJo,V:Scarecrow 2.50
525 DgM,KJo,Underworld
Unleashed tie-in 2.50
526 DgM,A:Alfred,Nightwing,Robin . 2.50
527 DgM,V:Two-Face,I:Schism 2.50
528 . . . . 2.50
529 DgM,KJo,Contagion,pt.6 . . . . . 2.75
530 DgM,KJo,The Aztec
Connection,pt.1 . . . . 2.75
530a collector's edition 2.75
531 DgM,KJo,The Aztec
Connection,pt.2 . . . . 2.50
531a collectors edition 3.00
532 DgM(s),KJo,"The Aztec Connection," pt.3, A:Deadman 2.50
532a card stock cover 3.00
533 DgM(s),KJo,Legacy prelude . . . 2.50
534 DgM(s),KJo,Legacy, pt.5 . . . . . 2.50
535 DgM(s),KJo,JhB,I:The Ogre,
double size. 3.50
535a Collector's edition,
gatefold cover 4.00
536 DgM(s),KJo,JhB,V:Man-Bat,
Final Night tie-in 2.50
537 DgM(s),KJo,JhB,A:Man-Bat,
pt.2 . . . . 2.50
538 DgM(s),KJo,JhB,A:Man-Bat,
pt.3 . . . . 2.50
539 . . . . 2.50
540 DgM(s),KJo,JhB,Spectre,pt.1 . . 2.50
541 DgM(s),KJo,JhB,Spectre,pt.2 . . 2.50
542 DgM(s),KJo,JhB,V:Faceless,
pt. 1 . . . . 2.50
543 DgM(s),KJo,JhB,pt. 2. . . . . 2.50
544 DgM(s),KJo,JhB, F:Joker,pt.1. . 2.50
545 DgM(s),KJo, F:Joker, Demon,
pt.2 . . . . 2.50
546 DgM(s),KJo,JhB,F:Joker,
Demon, pt.3 concl. 2.50
547 DgM,KJo,JhB,Genesis tie-in. . . 2.50
548 DgM,KJo,JhB,V:Penguin, pt.1 . 2.50
549 DgM,KJo,JhB,V:Penguin, pt.2 . 2.50
550 DgM,KJo,JhB,I:Chase 3.50
550a deluxe, with file card inserts . . 3.50
551 DgM,KJo,JhB,F:Ragman 2.25
552 DgM, ... 2.25
553 DgM,KJo,SB,Cataclysm
x-over, pt.3. . . . . 3.00
554 DgM,KJo,SB,Cataclysm, ... 3.00
555 DGm,JhB,SB,BSf,Aftershock . . 2.25
556 DGm,NBy,BSf,Aftershock. 2.25
557 DGm,VGi,SB,BSf,F:Ballistic . . . 2.25
558 DGm,JAp,SB,doubts 2.25
559 DgM(s),BH,SB,Aftershock 2.25
560 CDi,SB,A:Nightwing & Robin . . 2.25
561 CDi(s),JAp, No Man's Land . . . 2.25
562 CDi(s),JAp, No Man's Land . . . 2.25
563 No Law and A New Order, pt.3 2.25
564 F:Batgirl, Mosaic,pt.1 . . . . 2.25
565 F:Batgirl, Mosaic,pt.3 . . . . 2.25
566 JBg,A:Superman 2.25
567 SCi,F:Batgirl, pt.1,x-over 2.25
568 DJu,BSz,Fruit of the
Earth, pt.2 . . . . 2.25
569 F:Batgirl. 2.25
570 MD2,No Man's Land, The
Code, pt.1 . . . . 2.25
571 CDi,MtB,Goin'Downtown,pt.1 . . 2.25
572 Jurisprudence,pt.1 . . . . 2.25
573 . . . . 2.25
574 Endgame, pt.2 x-over 2.25
575 LHa,SMc,KIS 2.25
576 LHa,SMc,KIS,kidnapping 2.25
577 LHa,SMc,KIS,rodents. 2.25
578 LHa,SMc,MPn,serial killer 2.25
579 LHa,SMc,KIS,V:Orca,pt.1 . . . . . 2.25
580 LHa,SMc,KIS,V:Orca,pt.2. . . . . 2.25
581 LHa,SMc,KIS,V:Orca,pt.3. . . . . 2.25
582 SMc,KIS,Fearless,pt.1 . . . . 2.25
583 SMc,Kls,Fearless,pt.2 . . . . 2.25
584 SMc,KIS,A:Penguin 2.25
Ann.#1 CS 700.00
Ann.#2 . . . . 300.00
Ann.#3 A:Joker. 300.00
Ann.#4 . . . . 150.00
Ann.#5 . . . . 150.00
Ann.#6 . . . . 125.00
Ann.#7 . . . . 125.00
Ann.#8 TVE,A:Ras al Ghul 8.00
Ann.#9 JOy,AN,PS 7.00
Ann.#10 DCw,DG,V:HugoStrange. . 7.00
Ann.#11 JBy(c),AMo(s),V:Penguin . 8.00
Ann.#12 RA,V:Killer 5.00
Ann.#13 A:Two-Face 6.00
Ann.#14 O:Two-Face 4.00
Ann.#15 Armageddon,pt.3 . . . . 6.00
Ann.#15a 2nd printing(silver) 2.50
Ann.#16 SK(c),Eclipso,V:Joker 3.00
Ann.#17 EB,Bloodline#8,
I:Decimator. 3.00
Ann.#18 Elseworld Story. 3.50
Ann.#19 Year One, O:Scarecrow . . 5.00
Ann.#20 Legends o/t Dead Earth . . 3.50
Ann.#21 Pulp Heroes (Weird
Mystery) DgM(s). 4.50
Ann.#22 BWr(c) Ghosts 3.50
Ann.#23 CDi(s),GN,MPn, JLApe
Gorilla Warfare 3.50
Ann.#24 Planet DC. 3.50

Specials & 1-shots

Giant Ann.#1 Facsimile edition 5.00
Spec.#0 (1994). 3.00
Spec.#1 MGo,I:Wrath 4.00
Spec.#1,000,000 DgM(s),SB,
F:Toy Wonder. 2.00
Giant #1, 7 tales, 80-page (1998) . . 5.00
Giant #2, 80-page (1999) 4.95
Giant #3 CDi(s) 80-page (2000) . . . 5.95
Batman: Arkham Asylum — Tales
of Madness, AIG, Cataclysm
tie-in (1998) 3.00
Batman: Batgirl, JBa,RBr,
Girlfrenzy (1998) 2.00
Batman: Blackgate, CDi(s), JSon,
in Blackgate prison (1996) 4.50

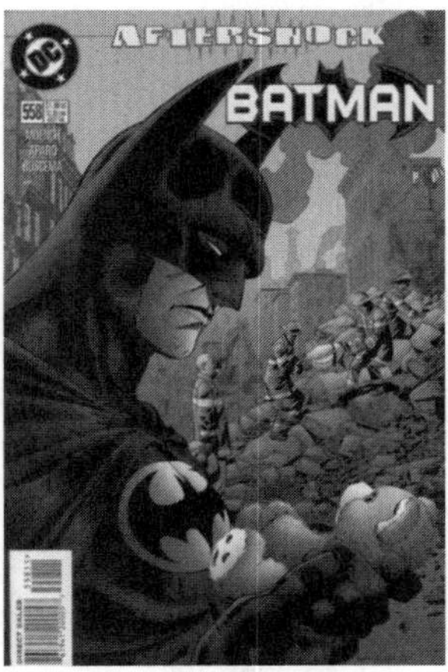

Batman #558 © DC Comics Inc.

Batman: Blackgate — Isle of Men,
DgM, JAp,BSf,BSz,
Cataclysm (1998) 3.00
Batman Dark Knight Gallery (1995). 3.50
Batman: Day of Judgment 3.95
Batman: Death of Innocents, DON(s),
JSt, BSz, Land mine victims
(1996) 4.00
Batman Gallery,collection of past
(c),posters,pin-ups,JQ(c) (1992) 4.00
Batman: Gotham By Gaslight,MMi,
V:Jack the Ripper. 6.00
Gotham City Secret Files #1. . . . . . 4.95
Batman: The Hill (2000) 2.95
Batman: Joker's Apprentice 4.00
Batman: The Killing Joke,BB,AMo(s),
O:Joker,Batgirl paralyzed
(1988) 15.00
2nd thru 6th Printings . . . . . . @5.00
Batman: Mitefall, V:Bane
Mite (1995). 4.95
Batman: Penguin Triumphant
(1992) 5.00
Batman: Plus (1997). 3.00
Batman Record Comic (1996) 1.00
Batman/Riddler: The Riddle
Factory (1995) 4.95
Secret Files #1 SMc(c) inc.
O:Batman (1997) 6.00
Batman: Seduction of the Gun,
V:Illegal Gun Control (1992) . . . 3.00
3-D Batman:Scarecrow. 4.00
Batman/Two-Face: Crime and
Punishment (1995). 4.95
2nd printing (1998). 5.00
Two-Face Strikes Twice #1. . . . . . . 5.25
Two-Face Strikes Twice #2. . . . . . . 5.25
Batman: Vengeance of Bane,
GN,I:Bane (1992). 30.00
2nd Printing 5.00
Batman: Vengeance of Bane II
(1995) 3.95
Batman Villains Secret Files,
AIG,CDi,RMz,BB,F:Greatest Foes
(1998) 5.00

Elseworld 1-shots

Batman of Arkham (2000). 5.95
Batman: The Blue, The Grey, and
The Bat, JL (1992) 5.95
Batman: Brotherhood of the Bat
(1995) 5.95
Batman: Castle of the Bat. 5.95
Batman: Dark Allegiances (1996) . . 5.95
Batman: Holy Terror (1991). 6.50
Batman: I, Joker, BH, in
2083 (1998) 4.95
Batman: In Darkest Knight
MiB(s),JBi (1994) 5.50
Batman Knightgallery (1995). 3.50
Batman: Masque, MGr, in turn of
the century Gotham 7.00
Batman: Master of the Future,EB,
Sequel to Goth.by Gaslight
(1991) 6.00
Batman: Scar of the Bat (1996). . . . 5.00
Batman: Two Faces (1998). 4.95
Batman: Master of the Future(1998) 5.95

Graphic Novels

The Abduction 6.00
Batman A Lonely Place of Dying
(1990) rep. Batman #440–442
& New Titans #60–61 . . . . 4.00
Batman: Blind Justice, rep. Detective
Comics #598–#600 (1992) 7.50
Batman: Bloodstorm 13.00
Batman: Bullock's Law 5.00
The Book of Shadows 6.00
Batman: Dark Joker, KJo 12.00
Many Deaths of the Batman;
rep. #433-#435 (1992) 3.95
Batman: Dreamland (2000). 5.95

Batman/Harley Quinn Graphic Novel
© DC Comics Inc.

Batman: Ego (2000) 6.95
Batman: Full Circle AD, A:Reaper (1992). 7.00
Batman: Harley Quinn (1998) 5.95
Batman: Mr. Freeze 5.00
No Man's Land, 48-page No Law and a New Order, pt.1 . . . . 3.00
No Man's Land, lenticular (c) 4.00
No Man's Land Gallery 4.00
Nosferatu 6.00
Batman: Poison Ivy. 5.00
Reign of Terror 5.00
Batman: Scar of the Bat 5.00
The Scottish Connection. 6.00
Batman: Ten Knights of the Beast, rep. #417–#420 (1994). 5.95
Batman: Two Faces 5.00
Batman: The Ultimate Evil:
1 Novel adaptation (of 2) 5.95
2 Novel adaptation, finale 5.95

Hard Covers & Trade Paperbacks

The Batman Adventures 8.00
HC Batman Archives Vol.3 . . . . . . 39.95
HC Archives, Vol. 4, rep.. . . . . 50.00
Batman: Anarky 13.00
Batman: Arkham Asylum,DMc
HC (1989) 28.00
TPB 15.00
Birth of the Demon, O:Ras al Ghul (1992)
HC 25.00
TPB (1993). 13.00
Batman: Black and White 19.95
Batman: Bloodstorm,KJo,V:Joker, Vampires, (sequel to Red Rain)
HC 24.95
TPB 12.95
Bride of the Demon, TGr, V:Ra's al Ghul
HC 21.00
TPB 13.00
Batman: Cataclysm
TPB 18.00
Batman: The Chalice (2000)
TPB 14.95
Contagion. 13.00
Crimson Mist
HC 25.00
The Dark Knight Adventures. 8.00
The Dark Knight Archives Vol.3
HC 49.95
Batman: Dark Knight Dynasty, three elseworlds stories
HC (1998) 25.00
TPB (1999). 14.95
Batman: A Death in the Family, rep. Batman #426-429 (1988)
TPB 8.00
2nd printing 5.00
3rd printing. 4.00
Batman: Digital Justice (1990)
HC 26.00
Batman: Faces (1995)
TPB 10.00
Batman: Fortunate Son (1999)
TPB 14.95
Batman: Gothic, rept. Legends of the Dark Knight #6–#10 (1992)
TPB 13.00
New printing. 13.00
Greatest Batman Stories
HC 35.00
TPB 16.00
Greatest Batman Stories, Vol. 2
TPB 17.00
Batman in the Sixties
TPB 19.95
Batman in the Seventies
TPB 19.95
Greatest Joker Stories
HC 20.00
TPB 15.00
Batman: Knight's End, rep. Batman #509–#510, Shadow of the Bat #29–#30, Detective #676–#677, Legends #62–#63, Catwoman #12, Robin #8–#9
TPB 14.95
Knightfall rep. #1-#11
TPB 12.95
Knightfall rep. #12-#19
TPB 12.95
Batman: The Last Angel, F:Catwoman V:Aztec bat-god (1994)
TPB 12.95
Batman: The Last Arkham
TPB 12.95
Legacy, seq.to Contagion, rep.(1996)
TPB 18.00
Batman: Night Cries,SHa 30.00
TPB 13.00
Batman: Prodigal, rep,
TPB 15.00
Batman: Son of the Demon,JBi (1987)
HC 55.00
TPB 17.00
2nd thru 4th printings . . . . . . @8.95
Batman: Strange Apparitions (1999)
TPB 12.95
Batman: Tales of the Demon (1991)
TPB 20.00
TPB (1999). 17.95
Batman: Thrillkiller 13.00
Batman: Year One Rep. Batman #404-#407 (1998)
HC 16.00
TPB 14.00
2nd Printing 10.00
3rd Printing. 10.00
Batman: Four of a Kind, from Year One annuals (1998)
TPB 15.00
Year Two (1990) rep. Detective Comics #575–#578
TPB 10.00

Movies

TPB The Movies, (all 4) (1997) . . . 20.00
Batman, JOy, Movie adaptation . . . 3.00
Perfect Bound 6.00
Batman Returns, SE,JL Movie Adaption, ... 6.00
Newsstand Format 4.00
Batman: Mask of the Phantasm, animated movie adapt. 5.25
Newstand Ed.. . . . . 3.25
Batman Forever, Movie Adaptation . 5.95
Newsstand version 3.95
Batman and Robin, DON(s), Movie Adaptation (1997). 3.95
Collector's edition, ... 5.95
GN Batman: Bane, BSz(c) movie tie-in (1997) 4.95
GN Batman: Batgirl, BSz(c) movie tie-in (1997) 4.95
GN Batman: Mr. Freeze, BSz(c) movie tie-in (1997) 4.95
GN Batman: Poison Ivy, BSz(c) movie tie-in (1997) 4.95

X-overs

Batman & Superman Adventures: World's Finest (1997) adaptation of animated adventures, 64pg . 7.00
Batman/Captain America (DC/Marvel 1996) Elseworlds 6.00
Batman/Deadman, Death and Glory, JeR(s),JEs (1996)
HC 25.00
TPB 12.95
Batman/Demon (1996) 5.00
Batman/Demon: A Tragedy (2000) . 5.95
Batman/Dracula: Red Rain KJo,MJ, Batman becomes Vampire,
HC Elseworlds Story (1991) . . 35.00
SC (1992) 12.00
TPB Elseworlds (1999). 12.95
Batman/Green Arrow: The Poison Tomorrow,MN,JRu,V:Poison Ivy (1992). 6.25
GN rep. (2000). 5.95
Batman/Houdini: The Devil's Workshop (1993) 6.50
Batman: Huntress/Spoiler—Blunt Trauma, CDi,Cataclysm (1988). 3.00
Batman/Judge Dredd: Judgement on Gotham,SBs,V:Scarecrow, Judge Death (1991) 9.00
Batman/Judge Dredd: Vendetta in Gotham, AIG(s),V:Ventriliquist (1993) 5.25
Batman/Judge Dredd: The Ultimate Riddle (1995) 5.00
Batman/Lobo, Elseworlds (2000) . . 5.95
Batman/Phantom Stranger, AIG(s), Lemurian artifact (1997) 5.00
Batman/Punisher: Lake of Fire, DON(s),BKi,A:Punisher,V:Jigsaw (DC/Marvel 1994). 5.25
Batman/Spawn: War Devil, DgM,CDi, AIG(s), KJ,V:Croatoan (1994) . . 6.00
Batman/Spawn: War Devil (1999) . . 4.95
Batman/Spider-Man JMD,GN,KK, V:Kingpin&Ra's al Ghul(1997). . 5.00
Batman vs. The Incredible Hulk (DC/Marvel 1995). 4.00

BATMAN ADVENTURES
1992–95
(Based on TV cartoon series)

1 MeP,V:Penguin. 5.00
2 MeP,V:Catwoman 4.00
3 MeP,V:Joker 3.00
4 MeP,V:Scarecrow 3.00
5 MeP,V:Scarecrow 3.00
6 MeP,A:Robin 3.00
7 MeP,V:Killer Croc,w/card. 6.00
8 MeP,Larceny my Sweet 2.50
9 MeP,V:Two Face. 2.50
10 MeP,V:Riddler 3.00
11 MeP,V:Man-Bat 2.00
12 MeP,F:Batgirl. 2.00
13 MeP,V:Talia 2.00
14 MeP,F:Robin 2.00
15 MeP,F:Commissioner Gordon . . 2.00
16 MeP,V:Joker 2.00
17 MeP,V:Talia 2.00

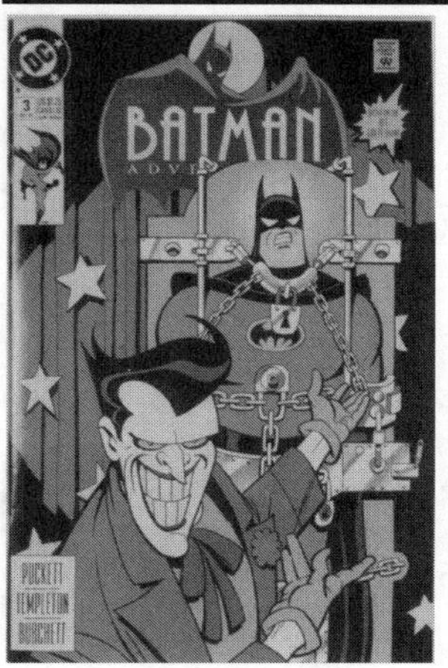

Batman Adventures #3
© DC Comics, Inc.

18 MeP,R:Batgirl. 2.00
19 MeP,V:Scarecrow. 2.00
20 MeP,V:Mastermind,Mr.Nice, Perfessor 2.00
21 MeP,V:Man-Bat,Tygrus. 2.00
22 MeP,V:Two-Face 2.00
23 MEP,V:Poison Ivy 2.00
24 MeP,I:Kyodi Ken 2.00
25 MeP,dbl.size,Superman 2.50
26 MeP,A:Robin,Batgirl. 2.00
27 MeP,I:Doppleganger 2.00
28 Joker. 2.00
29 A:Talia 2.00
30 O:Mastermind, Mr. Nice 2.00
31 I:Anarcky 2.00
32 Criminals dressed as Napoleonic Soldiers 2.00
33 Bruce and date mugged. 2.00
34 V:Dr. Hugo Strange 2.00
35 A:Catwoman 2.00
36 V:Joker, Final issue 2.00
Ann.#1 Roxy Rocket. 3.00
Ann.#2 JBa,BBl,DG,TG,SHa,BKi,MM, GN,JRu,V:Demon,Ra's al Ghul,Etrigan 3.50
Holiday Special. 2.95
Spec. Mad Love 3.95
TPB Collected Adventures #1 . . . . . 6.00
TPB Collected Adventures #2 . . . . . 6.00

BATMAN ADVENTURES: THE LOST YEARS
Nov., 1997

1 (of 5) BHa,TBe,Batgirl. 2.00
2 BHa,TBe,Dick Grayson quits . . . 2.00
3 . . . . 2.00
4 BHa,TBe,F:Tim Drake. 2.00
5 BHa,TBe,Tim Drake new Robin . 2.00

BATMAN ADVENTURES: THE LOST YEARS
1999

1 (of 6) TBe. 2.00
2 . . . . 2.00
3 . . . . 2.00
4 . . . . 2.00
5 . . . . 2.00
6 . . . . 2.00
TPB series rep. 5.95

BATMAN AND THE OUTSIDERS
Aug., 1983

1 B:MiB(s),JAp,O:Outsiders, O:Geo Force 3.00
2 JAp,V:Baron Bedlam 2.50
3 JAp,V:Agent Orange. 2.00
4 JAp,V:Fearsome Five 2.00
5 JAp,A:New Teen Titans. 2.50
6 JAp,V:Cryonic Man. 2.00
7 JAp,V:Cryonic Man. 2.00
8 JAp,A:Phantom Stranger 2.00
9 JAp,I:Master of Disaster 2.00
10 JAp,A:Master of Disaster 2.00
11 JAp,V:Takeo. 2.00
12 JAp,DG,O:Katana 2.00
13 JAp,Day,O:Batman 2.00
14 BWg,Olympics,V:Maxi Zeus. . . . 2.00
15 TVE,Olympics,V:Maxi Zeus 2.00
16 JAp,L:Halo. 2.00
17 JAp,V:Ahk-Ton. 2.00
18 JAp,V:Ahk-Ton. 2.00
19 JAp,A:Superman 2.00
20 JAp,V:Syonide,R:Halo 2.00
21 TVE,JeM,Solo Stories 2.00
22 AD,O:Halo,I:Aurakles. 2.00
23 AD,O:Halo,V:Aurakles 2.00
24 AD,C:Kobra 2.00
25 AD,V:Kobra 2.00
26 AD. 2.00
27 AD,V:Kobra 2.00
28 AD,I:Lia Briggs(Looker) 2.00
29 AD,V:Metamorpho 2.00
30 AD,C:Looker 2.00
31 AD,I&J:Looker 2.00
32 AD,L:Batman. 2.00
Ann.#1 JA N:Geo-Force, I:Force of July 2.00
Ann.#2 V:Tremayne,W:Metamorpho & Sapphire Stagg 2.00
Becomes:

ADVENTURES OF THE OUTSIDERS
May, 1986

33 AD,V:Baron Bedlam. 2.00
34 AD,Masters of Disaster 2.00
35 AD,V:Adolph Hitler. 2.00
36 AD,A:Masters of Disaster. 2.00
37 . . . . 2.00
38 . . . . 2.00
39 thru 47 JAp,reprints

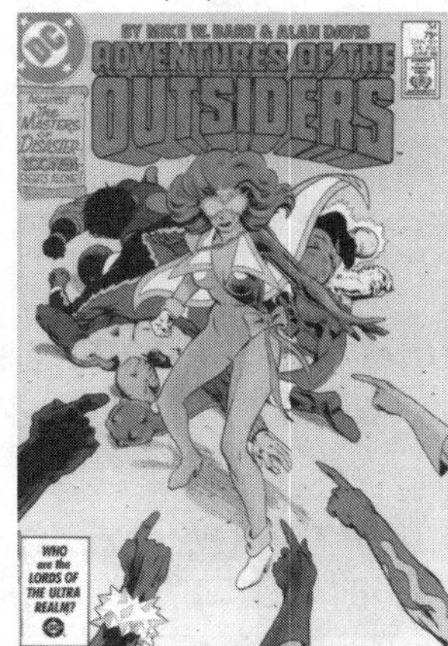

Adventures of the Outsiders #34
© DC Comics Inc.

Outsiders #1-#9 . . . . @2.00

BATMAN AND ROBIN ADVENTURES, THE
Nov., 1995

1 TTn 3.00
2 TTn,V:Two-Face. 2.50
3 TTn,V:The Riddler 2.50
4 TTn,V:The Penguin. 2.50
5 TTn 2.50
6 TTn,Robin Fired? 2.00
7 TTn,V:Scarface. 2.00
8 TTn(s) 2.00
9 TTn(s),F:Batgirl & Talia. 2.00
10 TTn(s),F:Ra's Al Ghul 2.00
11 TTn(s),Alfred & Robin look for monster in Batcave 2.00
12 TTn(s),BKr,RBr, sequel to "Bane" TV episode 2.00
13 TTn(s),BKr,RBr,V:Scarecrow . . . 2.00
14 TTn(s),BKr,RBr,young criminal turns to Batman for help 2.00
15 TTn(s) 2.00
16 TTn(s),V:Catman,A:Catwoman. . 2.00
17 PDi&TTn(s),JSon,RBr,Mad Hatter dies in Arkham. 2.00
18 TTn(s),BKr,TBe,A:Joker, Harley Quinn 2.00
19 TTn(s),BKr,TBe,The Huntress . . 2.00
20 TTn(s),BKr,TBe, office pool 2.00
21 TTn(s),JSon,Riddler kidnaps Commissioner Gordon 2.00
22 TTn(s),BKr,TBe,V:Two-Face . . . 2.00
23 TTn(s),TBe,V:Killer Croc 2.00
24 TTn(c),F:Poison Ivy 2.00
25 TTn,TBe,final issue, 48pg 3.00
Ann.#1 PDi(s),TTn, sequel to Batman: Mask of the Phantasm 3.00
Ann.#2 JSon,TBe,V:Hypnotist. 4.00
Sub-Zero one-shot, F:Mr. Freeze, Nora, 64pg. 3.95

BATMAN & SUPERMAN: WORLD'S FINEST
1999

1 (of 10) KK(s),DTy,RbC,48-page . 6.00
2 KK(s),DTy,RbC 3.50
3 KK(s),DTy,RbC,Arkham Asylum . 3.00
4 KK(s),DTy,RbC,Metropolis 3.00
5 KK(s),DTy,RbC,Batgirl 3.00
6 KK(s),DTy,RbC,trade identities . . 3.00
7 KK(s),PD,RbC 3.00
8 KK(s),PD,RbC 3.00
9 KK(s),RbC,split issue 2.50
10 concl. 2.50
GN 6.95

BATMAN: BANE OF THE DEMON
Feb., 1998

1 (of 4) CDi,GN,TP, Bane & Ra's al Ghul 2.00
2 CDi,GN,TP,Talia 2.00
3 CDi,GN,TP,the Lazarus Pit 2.00
4 CDi,GN,TP,Bane imprisoned. . . . 2.00

BATMAN BEYOND
Mini-series 1999

1 (of 6) RBr,TBe,Rebirth 2.00
2 RBr,TBe,Rebirth,pt.2. . . . . 2.00
3 RBr,TBe,V:Blight. 2.00
4 JSon,TBe,F:Demon Etrigan 2.00
5 JSon,TBe,V:Mummy. 2.00
6 JSon,TBe,V:Inque. 2.00
TPB rep. mini-series 10.00

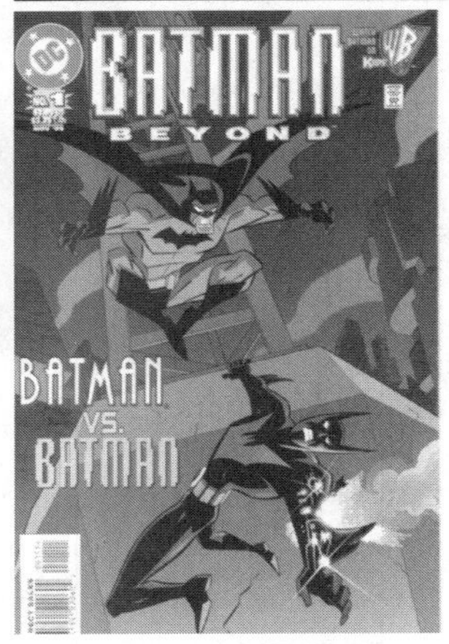

Batman Beyond #1 © DC Comics, Inc.

BATMAN BEYOND
1999

1 Batman: Classic vs. Future 2.00
2 V:Inque. 2.00
3 . . . . 2.00
4 V:Royal Flush Gang 2.00
5 V:Shriek 2.00
6 V:Stalker 2.00
7 V:Jokerz. 2.00
8 V:Vendetta 2.00
9 V:Curare. 2.00
10 V:Golem 2.00
11 nanotechnology 2.00
12 F:Terminal 2.00
13 Commissioner Barbara Gordon . 2.00
14 F:Etrigan the Demon 2.00
Spec. Return of the Joker. 3.00

BATMAN BLACK & WHITE
1996

1 JLe(c) numerous artists (of 4) . . . 6.00
2 thru 4 . . . . @5.00
HC 40.00

BATMAN: BOOK OF THE DEAD
1999

1 (of 2) DgM(s),BKi,Elseworlds . . . 5.00
2 DgM(s),BKi,Conclusion. 5.00

BATMAN CHRONICLES
1995

1 CDi,LW,BSz, multiple stories. . . . 4.00
2 V:Feedback 3.50
3 All villains issue 3.50
4 F:Hitman 10.00
5 Oracle, Year One story 3.00
6 Ra's Al Ghul 3.00
7 JOy,LW, woman on death row. . . 3.00
8 Talia goes to Gotham to eliminate Batman 3.00
9 CDi(s),F:Batgirl, Mr. Freeze, Poison Ivy 3.00
10 BSn, anthology 3.00
11 CDi,JFM, Elseworlds stories. . . . 3.00
12 Cataclysm x-over. 3.00
13 F:GCPD 3.00
14 SB(c),F:Alfred,Huntress 3.00
15 Road to No Man's Land 3.00
16 F:Batgirl,No Man's Land tie-in . . 3.00
17 V:Penguin,No Man's Land 3.00
18 No Man's Land 3.00
19 . . . . 3.00
20 SBe(s)&IEd(s),48-pg. 3.00
21 DG,JRu,3 Elsewords tales 3.00
22 F:Lady Shiva,48-pg.. . . . . 3.00
Gallery #1, Pin-ups. 3.50
GN The Gauntlet 4.95

BATMAN: THE CULT
1988

1 JSn,BWr,V:Deacon Blackfire. . . . 9.00
2 JSn,BWr,V:Deacon Blackfire. . . . 7.00
3 JSn,BWr,V:Deacon Blackfire. . . . 7.00
4 JSn,BWr,V:Deacon Blackfire. . . . 6.00
TPB Rep.#1-#4. . . . . 14.95

BATMAN: DARK KNIGHT OF THE ROUND TABLE
1998

1 (of 2) BL,DG,Elseworlds,48pg. . . 5.00
2 BL,DG, conclusion 5.00

BATMAN: THE DARK KNIGHT RETURNS
1986

1 FM,KJ,V:Two-Face 20.00
1a 2nd printing 5.00
1b 3rd printing. 3.00
2 FM,KJ,V:Sons of the Batman . . 10.00
2a 2nd printing 3.00
2b 3rd printing. 2.50
3 FM,KJ,D:Joker 7.00
3a 2nd printing 3.00
4 FM,KJ,Batman vs.Superman, A:Green Arrow,D:Alfred 5.00
HC 50.00
Paperback book 20.00
Warner paperback 17.00
HC,sign/num. 270.00
2nd-8th printing 12.95
TPB 10th Anniv. Spec, 224 pg. . . . 14.95

BATMAN: DARK VICTORY
Oct., 1999

1 (of 13) JLb,TSe,48-pg. 7.00
2 JLb,TSe 5.00
3 JLb,TSe,V:Scarecrow 3.00
4 JLb,TSe,V:Two-Face 3.00
5 JLb,TSe,F:Catwoman 3.00
6 JLb,TSe,F:Penguin. 3.00
7 JLb,TSe,V:Calendar Man 3.00
8 JLb,TSe,V:Hang Man 3.00
9 JLb,TSe,F:Bruce & Dick 3.00
10 JLb,TSe,V:Two-Face 3.00
11 JLb,TSe,V:Poison Ivy. 3.00
12 JLb,TSe,Revenge 3.00
13 JLb,TSe, conclusion 5.00

BATMAN: THE DOOM THAT CAME TO GOTHAM
Sept., 2000

1 (of 3) Elseworlds. 4.95
2 MMi,DJa, return from the Arctic . 4.95
3 conclusion 4.95

BATMAN FAMILY
Sept.,–Oct., 1975

1 MGr,NA(rep.) Batgirl & Robin begins,giant 15.00
2 V:Clue Master. 10.00
3 Batgirl & Robin reveal ID 10.00
4 . . . . 10.00
5 . . . . 10.00

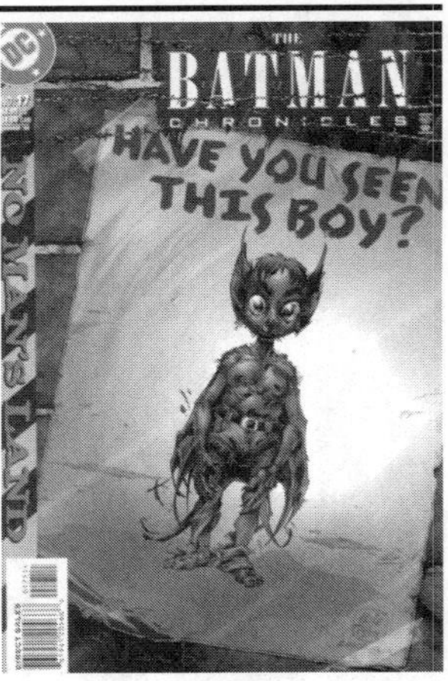

Batman Chronicles #17 © DC Comics, Inc.

6 Joker Daughter. 15.00
7 CS,A:Sportsmaster, G.A.Huntress 9.00
8 First solo Robin story, C:Joker's Daughter. 9.00
9 Joker's Daughter 15.00
10 R:B'woman,1st solo Batgirl sty. 15.00
11 MR,Man-Bat begins 12.00
12 MR 12.00
13 MR,DN,BWi 12.00
14 HC/JRu,Man-Bat 9.00
15 MGo,Man-Bat 9.00
16 MGo,Man-Bat 9.00
17 JA,DH,MG,Batman, B:Huntress A:Demon,MK(c),A:Catwoman . 12.00
18 MGo,JSon,BL,Huntress,BM . . . 12.00
19 MGo,JSon,BL,Huntress,BM . . . 12.00
20 MGo,JSon,DH,A:Ragman, ElongatedMan, Oct.–Nov.,1978 . . . . .12.00

BATMAN: GCPD
[Mini-Series] Aug., 1996

1 CDi(s),JAp,BSz 2.25
2 CDi(s),JAp,BSz 2.25
3 CDi(s), JAp,BSz,F:Montoya, Kitch & Bullock. 2.25
4 CDi(s), JAp,BSz, finale 2.25

BATMAN: GORDON'S LAW
October, 1996

1 CDi(s),KJ,Gordon looks for bad cops 2.00
2 CDi(s),KJ,Gordon combats corruption. 2.00
3 CDi(s),KJ,. 2.00
4 (of 4) CDi(s),KJ, concl. 2.00

BATMAN: GORDON OF GOTHAM
April, 1998

1 (of 4) DON,DG,KJ,F:Jim Gordon. 2.00
2 DON,DG,KJ,Cuchulain 2.00
3 DON,DG,KJ,break-in 2.00
4 DON,DG,KJ,past revealed 2.00

BATMAN: GOTHAM ADVENTURES
April, 1998

1 TTn,RBr,TBe,F:Joker 3.00
2 TTn,RBr,TBe,F:Two-Face 2.00
3 TTn,RBr,TBe,V:Scarecrow 2.00
4 TTn,RBr,TBe,A:Catwoman 2.00
5 RBr,TBe,TTn,A:Mr.Freeze 2.00
6 TTn,RBr,TBe,O:Deadman 2.00
7 TTn,RBe,TBe,V:Danger Dixon 2.00
8 TTn,RBe,TBe,Batgirl 2.00
9 TTn,RBe,TBe,V:League of Assassins 2.00
10 TTn,RBe,TBe,F:Nightwing & Robin, A:Harley Quinn 2.00
11 TTn,RBe,TBe,V:Riddler 2.00
12 TTn,RBe,TBe,V:Two-Face 2.00
13 RBe,TBe,V:Mastermind 2.00
14 TTn(s),TBe,V:Harley Quinn 2.00
15 V:Bane 2.00
16 TBe,Alfred Kidnapped 2.00
17 TBe 2.00
18 TBe,R:Man-Bat 2.00
19 TBe,Eden's Own,Poison Ivy 2.00
20 TBe, 2.00
21 TBe, 2.00
22 TBe,F:Comm.Gordon & Batgirl 2.00
23 TBe,V:Ra's al Ghul 2.00
24 TBe,F:Killer Croc 2.00
25 TBe,A:Flash 2.00
26 TBe,F:Kristov 2.00
27 TBe, 2.00
28 TBe,V:Riddler 2.00
29 CDi(s),TBe,Batman poisoned 2.00
30 TBe,F:Clayface 2.00
31 TTn,TBe,Blackout in Gotham 2.00
TPB Batman: Gotham Adventures 9.95

BATMAN: GOTHAM KNIGHTS
Feb., 2000

1 WEl,JLe 2.50
2 JBy,BB(c),F:Batgirl 2.50
3 PPo,PR,BB(c),Samsara,pt.1 2.50
4 PR,BB(c),Samsara,pt.2 2.50
5 BB(c)V:The Key 2.50
6 WS,PR,JPL,F:Oracle 2.50
7 SD,PR, 2.50
8 Transference,pt.1 2.50
9 Transference,pt.2 2.50
10 Transference,pt.3, 2.50

BATMAN: GOTHAM NIGHTS

1 Gotham City Mini-series 2.00
2 Lives of Gotham Citizens 2.00
3 Lives of Gotham Citizens 2.00
4 Lives of Gotham Citizens 2.00

BATMAN: GOTHAM NIGHTS II
1995

1 Sequel to Gotham Nights 2.00
2 F:Carmine Sansone 2.00
3 Fire 2.00
4 JQ(c) Decisions 2.00

BATMAN: HAUNTED GOTHAM
December, 1999

1 (of 4) DgM,KJo,JhB,Elseworlds 4.95
2 DgM,KJo,JhB 4.95
3 DgM,KJo,JhB,V:Ophidus 4.95
4 DgM,KJo,JhB,concl. 4.95

BATMAN/HELLBOY/ STARMAN
DC/Dark Horse 1998

1 JeR(s),MMi, x-over 2.50
2 JeR(s),MMi, conclusion 2.50

BATMAN/HUNTRESS: CRY FOR BLOOD
April, 2000

1 (of 6) RBr,O:Huntress 2.50
2 RBr,A:Question 2.50
3 RBr,A:Richard Dragon 2.50
4 RBr, 2.50
5 RBr, 2.50
6 RBr,Claudio's killer,concl. 2.50

BATMAN: IT'S JOKER TIME
May, 2000

1 (of 3) BH 4.95
2 BH 4.95
3 BH, concl. 4.95

BATMAN: JAZZ
[Mini-Series] 1995

1 I:Blue Byrd 2.50
2 V:Brotherhood of Bop 2.50
3 F:Blue Byrd 2.50

BATMAN/JUDGE DREDD: DIE LAUGHING
1998

1 (of 2) AIG(s),GF 48-pg. 5.00
2 AIG(s),GF conclusion 5.00

BATMAN: LEGENDS OF THE DARK KNIGHT
1989

1 EH,Shaman of Gotham,pt.1, Yellow(c) 4.00
1a Blue,Orange or Pink(c) 4.00
2 EH,Shaman of Gotham,pt.2 3.00
3 EH,Shaman of Gotham,pt.3 3.00
4 EH,Shaman of Gotham,pt.4 3.00
5 EH,Shaman of Gotham,pt.5 3.00
6 KJ,Gothic,pt.1 3.00
7 KJ,Gothic,pt.2 2.50

Batman GCPD #4 © DC Comics Inc.

8 KJ,Gothic,pt.3 2.50
9 KJ,Gothic,pt.4 2.50
10 KJ,Gothic,pt.5 2.50
11 PG,TA,Prey,pt.1 6.00
12 PG,TA,Prey,pt.2 5.00
13 PG,TA,Prey,pt.3 5.00
14 PG,TA,Prey,pt.4 5.00
15 PG,TA,Prey,pt.5 4.00
16 TVE,Venom,pt.1 5.00
17 TVE,JL,Venom,pt.2 5.00
18 TVE,JL,Venom,pt.3 5.00
19 TVE,JL,Venom,pt.4 5.00
20 TVE,JL,Venom,pt.5 5.00
21 BS,Faith,pt.1 2.50
22 BS,Faith,pt.2 2.50
23 BS,Faith,pt.3 2.50
24 GK,Flyer,pt.1 2.50
25 GK,Flyer,pt.2 2.50
26 GK,Flyer,pt.3 2.50
27 Destroyer,pt.2 (Batman#474) 3.00
28 MWg,Faces,pt.1,V:Two-Face 4.00
29 MWg,Faces,pt.2,V:Two-Face 4.00
30 MWg,Faces,pt.3,V:Two-Face 4.00
31 BA,Family 2.50
32 Blades,pt.1 2.50
33 Blades,pt.2 2.50
34 Blades,pt.3 2.50
35 BHa,Destiny Pt.1 2.50
36 BHa,Destiny Pt.2 2.50
37 I:Mercy,V:The Cossack 2.50
38 KON,R:Bat-Mite 2.50
39 BT,Mask#1 2.50
40 BT,Mask#2 2.50
41 Sunset 2.25
42 CR,Hothouse #1 2.25
43 CR,Hothouse #2,V:Poison Ivy 2.25
44 SMc,Turf #1 2.25
45 Turf#2 2.25
46 RH,A:Catwoman,V:Catman 2.50
47 RH,A:Catwoman,V:Catman 2.50
48 RH,A:Catwoman,V:Catman 2.50
49 RH,A:Catwoman,V:Catman 2.50
50 BBl,JLe,KN,KM,WS,MZ,BB, V:Joker 6.00
51 JKu,A:Ragman 2.50
52 Tao #1,V:Dragon 2.50
53 Tao #2,V:Dragon 2.50
54 MMi 2.50
55 B:Watchtower 2.50
56 CDi(s),V:Battle Guards 2.50
57 CDi(s),E:Watchtower 2.50
58 Storm 2.75
59 DON(s),RoW,B:Qarry 2.75
60 RoW,V:Asp 2.75
61 RoW,V:Asp 2.75
62 RoW,KnightsEnd#4,A:Shiva, Nightwing 3.50
63 Knights End #10,V:Azrael 2.50
64 CBa 2.50
65 Joker 2.50
66 Joker 2.50
67 Going Sane,pt.3 2.50
68 Going Sane,pt.4 2.50
69 Criminals,pt.1 2.50
70 Criminals,pt.2 2.50
71 Werewolf,pt.1 2.50
72 JWk(c&a),Werewolf,pt.2 [new Miraweb format begins] 2.50
73 JWk(c&a),Werewolf,pt.3 2.50
74 Engins,pt.1 2.50
75 Engins,pt.2 2.50
76 The Sleeping,pt.1 2.50
77 The Sleeping,pt.2 2.50
78 The Sleeping,pt.3 2.50
79 Favorite Things 2.50
80 Idols,pt.1 2.50
81 Idols,pt.2 2.50
82 Idols, climax 2.50
83 new villain 2.50
84 WEl(s) 2.50
85 JeR(s) 2.50

Batman Legends of the Dark Knight #113 © DC Comics, Inc.

86 DgM,JWi,MGy,Conspiracy,pt.1 . . 2.50
87 DgM,JWi,MGy,Conspiracy,pt.2 . . 2.50
88 DgM,JWi,MGy,Conspiracy,pt.3 . . 2.50
89 AlG(s),"Clay," pt. 1 . . . . 2.50
90 AlG(s),"Clay," pt. 2 . . . . 2.50
91 "Freakout," pt.1 . . . . 2.50
92 GEn(s),WSm,"Freakout," pt.2. . . 2.50
93 GEn(s),WSm,"Freakout," pt.3. . . 2.50
94 MGi(s),Saul Fisher's story 2.50
95 DAn&ALa(s),AWi,ALa,"Dirtty Tricks" pt.1 . . . . 2.50
96 DAn&ALa(s),AWi,ALa,"Dirty Tricks" pt.2 . . . . 2.50
97 DAn&ALa(s),AWi,ALa,"Dirty Tricks" concl. 2.50
98 PJe(s),SeP,"Steps," pt.1. . . . . . . 2.50
99 PJe(s),SeP,"Steps," pt.2. . . . . . . 2.50
100 DON,JRo,F:Robin, 64pg. 4.00
101 CE,KN(c)100 years in future . . 2.50
102 JRo,PuJ,"Spook," pt.1 . . . . 2.50
103 JRo,PuJ,"Spook," pt.2 . . . . 2.50
104 JRo,PuJ,"Spook," pt.3 . . . . 2.50
105 TVE,JRu,"Duty," pt.1 . . . . 2.50
106 TVE,JRu,"Duty," pt.2 . . . . 2.50
107 LMr,"Stalking," pt.1. . . . . 2.50
108 LMr,"Stalking," pt.2. . . . . 2.50
109 SEt,DAb,Primal Riddle,pt.1 . . . 2.50
110 SEt,DAb,Primal Riddle,pt.2 . . . 2.50
111 SEt,DAb,Primal Riddle,pt.3. . . . 2.50
112 DVa,FC,V:Lord Demise,pt.1 . . . 2.50
113 DVa,FC,V:Lord Demise,pt.2 . . . 2.50
114 JeR(s),DIB,TBd 2.50
115 LMc,DIB(c). 2.50
116 IEd,Bread and Circuses,pt.1. . . 2.50
117 IEd,Bread and Circuses,pt.2. . . 2.50
118 JPn,Alfred in No Man's Land . . 2.50
119 MD2,Claim Jumping,pt.1 . . . . . 2.50
120 MD2,Assembly 2.50
121 RBr,V:Mr.Freeze 2.50
122 LHa(s),PG, Low Road to Golden Mountain,pt.1 . . . . 2.50
123 PR,ALa,Underground Railroad,pt.1. . . . . 2.50
124 CDi(s),MkK,No Man's Land . . . 2.50
125 No Man's Land 2.50
126 Endgame, pt.1 x-over. 2.50
127 MRy,F:Green Arrow,pt.1. . . . . . 2.50
128 MRy,F:Green Arrow,pt.2. . . . . . 2.50
129 MRy,F:Green Arrow,pt.3. . . . . . 2.50
130 MRy,F:Green Arrow,pt.4. . . . . . 2.50
131 MRy,F:Green Arrow,pt.5. . . . . . 2.50
132 AGw,JeR,MR,BWi,Siege,pt.1 . . 2.25
133 AGw,JeR,MR,BWi,Siege,pt.2 . . 2.25
134 AGw,JeR,MR,BWi,Siege,pt.3 . . 2.25
135 AGw,JeR,MR,BWi,Siege,pt.4 . . 2.25
136 AGw,JeR,MR,BWi,Siege,pt.5 . . 2.25
Ann.#1 JAp,KG,DSp,TL,JRu, MGo,JQ,`Duel',C:Joker. 5.50
Ann.#2 MN,LMc,W:Gordn&Essen . . 4.00
Ann.#3 MM,I:Cardinal Sin 3.75
Ann.#4 JSon(c),Elseworlds Story . . 3.75
Ann.#5 CDi(s)Year One Annuals, O:Man-Bat 3.95
Ann.#6 Legends o/t Dead Earth . . . 2.95
Ann.#7 Pulp Heroes (War) 3.95
Halloween Spec.I 6.95
Halloween Spec.II. 4.95
Ghosts, Halloween Special 4.95
TPB Shaman rep.#1-#5 (1993) . . . 12.95
TPB Batman: Gothic, rep. #6-#10 (1992) 12.95
TPB Prey, rep.Legends of the Dark Knight #11–#15 (1992) 12.95
TPB Batman: Venom, TVE, rep. #16–#20 (1993) 9.95
TPB Collected Legends of the Dark Knight,BB(c),rep.#32-#34,#38, #42-#43 (1994). 12.95
TPB Other Realms 13.00

BATMAN: THE LONG HALLOWEEN

October, 1996

1 (of 13) JLb,TSe,Who is Holiday? F: usual suspects 11.00
2 JLb(s),TSe,V:Holiday,A:Solomon Grundy. 8.00
3 JLb,TSe,. 9.00
4 JLb(s),TSe,"New Year's Eve" . . . 9.00
5 JLb(s),TSe,F:Poison Ivy, Search for Holiday 5.00
6 JLb(s),TSe,F:Poison Ivy, Catwoman 5.00
7 JLb(s),TSe,V:The Riddler 4.00
8 JLb(s),TSe,V:Scarecrow 4.00
9 JLb(s),TSe,A:Holiday,Scarecrow . 4.00
10 JLb(s),TSe,V:Scarecrow,Mad Hatter. 4.00
11 JLb(s),TSe,V:Holiday 4.00
12 JLb(s),TSe,Harvey Dent. 4.00
13 JLb(s),TSe,concl.,48pg. 7.00
TPB Haunted Knight, rep. Fears, Madness & Ghosts 12.95
TPB The Long Halloween 19.95

BATMAN: MAN-BAT

1995

1 R:Man-Bat, painted series 5.00
2 F:Marilyn Muno. 5.00
3 JBo,Elseworlds story, concl. 5.00
TPB rep. mini-series 14.95

BATMAN: NO MAN'S LAND

Sept., 1999

0 F:Huntress 4.95
Secret Files #1 . . . . 4.95
TPB Vol. 1, x-over rep. 12.95
TPB Vol. 2, x-over rep. 12.95
TPB Vol. 3, x-over rep. 12.95

BATMAN: OUTLAWS

July, 2000

1 (of 3) DgM,PG 4.95
2 DgM,PG,V:Bloodhawks. 4.95
3 DgM,PG,concl. 4.95

BATMAN: RUN, RIDDLER RUN

1992

1 MBg,Batman V:Riddler 5.50
2 MBg,Batman V:Riddler 5.25
3 MBg,V:Perfect Securities 5.25

BATMAN: SHADOW OF THE BAT

1992–97

1 NB,Last Arkham Pt.1 . . . . 3.50
1a Collector set,w/posters,pop-up . 5.50
2 NB,Last Arkham Pt.2 . . . . 3.00
3 NB,Last Arkham Pt.3 . . . . 3.00
4 NB,Last Arkham Pt.4 . . . . 3.00
5 NB,A:Black Spider 2.50
6 NB,I:Chancer 2.50
7 Misfits Pt.1 . . . . 2.50
8 Misfits Pt.2 . . . . 2.50
9 Misfits Pt.3 . . . . 2.50
10 MC,V:Mad Thane of Gotham . . . 2.50
11 V:Kadaver 2.50
12 V:Kadaver,A:Human Flea. 2.50
13 NB,`The Nobody' 2.50
14 NB,Gotham Freaks#1 . . . . 2.50
15 NB,Gotham Freaks#2 . . . . 2.50
16 BBl,MM,A:Anarchy,Scarecrow . . 2.50
17 BBl,V:Scarecrow 2.50
18 BBl,A:Anarchy,Scarecrow 2.50
19 BBl,Knightquest:The Crusade,pt.2, V:Gotham criminals 2.50
20 VGi,Knightquest:The Crusade, V:Tally Man 2.50
21 BBl,Knightquest:The Search, V:Mr.Asp 2.50
22 BBl,Knightquest:The Search, In London. 2.50
23 BBl,Knightquest:The Search . . . 2.50
24 BBl,Knightquest:The Crusade . . 2.50
25 BSf(c),BBl,Knightquest: Crusade, A:Joe Public,V:Corrosive Man . 2.50
26 BSf(c),BBl,Knightquest: Crusade, V:Clayface 2.50
27 BSf(c),BBl,Knightquest: Crusade, I:Clayface Baby 2.50
28 BSf(c),BBl 2.50
29 BSf(c),BBl,KnightsEnd#2, A:Nightwing 3.50
30 BSf(c),BBl,KnightsEnd#8, V:Azrael 2.50
31 Zero Hour, V:Butler 2.50

Batman Shadow of the Bat #51 © DC Comics, Inc.

32 Ventriloquist,Two-Face. 2.50
33 Two-Face 2.50
34 V:Tally Man 2.50
35 BKi,Return of Bruce Wayne, Troika,pt.2 . . . . 2.50
35a Collectors Edition. 3.00
36 Black Canary 2.50
37 Joker Hunt. 2.50
38 V:The Joker. 2.50
39 BSf(c),R:Solomon Grundy [new Miraweb format begins] . . 2.50
40 BSf(c), F:Anarky 2.50
41 Explosive Dirigible 2.50
42 . . . . 2.50
43 Secret of the Universe,pt1 . . . . . 2.50
44 AlG,BSz(c) Secret of the Universe,pt.3 . . . . 2.50
45 AlG,BSz(c) 100 year old corpse . 2.50
46 AlG,BSz(c) V:Cornelius Stirk . . . 2.50
47 AlG,BSz(c) V:Cornelius Stirk . . . 2.50
48 AlG 2.50
49 AlG,Contagion,pt.7 . . . . 2.50
50 AlG,Nightmare on Gotham,pt.1 . 2.50
51 AlG,DTy, Nightmare on Gotham,pt.2 (of 3) 2.50
52 AlG(s),"Nightmare on Gotham," pt.3 . . . . 2.50
53 AlG(s),Legacy, prelude 2.50
54 AlG(s),Legacy, pt. 4, x-over 2.50
55 AlG(s),RBr,KJ,Bruce Wayne a murderer? A:Nightwing. 2.50
56 AlG(s),DTy,SnW,"Leaves of Grass,pt.1,V:Poison Ivy 2.50
57 AlG(s),DTy,SnW,"Leaves of Grass,pt.2 . . . . 2.50
58 AlG(s),DTy,SnW,"Leaves of Grass,pt.3 . . . . 2.50
59 AlG(s),DTy,SnW,"Killer, Killer," pt.1 . . . . 2.50
60 AlG(s),DTy,SnW,"Killer, Killer," pt.2 . . . . 2.50
61 AlG(s),JAp,SnW,night of second chances 2.50
62 AlG(s),DTy,SnW,Two-Face,pt.1 . 2.50
63 AlG(s),DTy,SnW,Two-Face,pt.2 . 2.50
64 AlG(s),DTy,SnW,A:Jason Blood . 2.50
65 AlG(s),NBy,JRu, A:Oracle, pt.1 . 2.50
66 AlG(s),NBy,JRu, V:Thinker, Cheat, pt.2 . . . . 2.50
67 AlG(s),NBy,SnW,CsM,V:Thinker, Cheat, pt.3, concl. 2.50
68 AlG(s),JAp,SnW,annual killer . . . 2.50
69 AlG(s),MBu,WF,CsM, The Spirit of 2000, pt. 1 . . . . . . 2.50
70 AlG(s),MBu,WF,CsM, pt.2 . . . . . 2.50
71 AlG(s),MBu,WF,CsM,detective . . 2.50
72 AlG(s),MBu,WF 2.50
73 AlG(s),MBu,WF,Cataclysm x-over,pt.1 . . . . 3.00
74 AlG(s),MBu,WF,Cataclysm cont. 2.50
75 AlG(s),MBu,WF,Aftershock. 3.00
76 AlG(s),MBu,WF,Aftershock. 2.50
77 AlG(s),MBu,WF,quake-torn 2.50
78 AlG(s),MBu,Aftershock. 2.50
79 AlG(s),MBu,V:Mad Hatter, Narcosis. 2.50
80 Road to No Man's Land, flip-book Azrael:Agent of the Bat #47 . . . 4.00
81 AlG(s),MBu,No Man's Land 2.50
82 AlG(s),MBu,No Man's Land 2.50
83 No Law and a New Order, pt.2. . 2.50
84 IEd,Bread and Circuses, pt.2 . . . 2.50
85 IEd(s),Bread & Circuses,concl. . . 2.50
86 GyD,No Man's Land 2.50
87 MD2, Claim Jumping, pt.2 . . . . . 2.50
88 DJu,BSz,Fruit of the Earth,pt.1 . . . . 2.50
89 IEd(s),SB,No Man's Land. 2.50
90 LHa(s),PG,No Man's Land 2.50
91 PR,ALa,Underground Railroad,pt.2. . . . . 2.50
92 No Man's Land,A:Superman . . . 2.50
93 No Man's Land 2.50
94 final issue 2.50
Ann.#1 TVE,DG,Bloodlines#3, I:Joe Public 4.00
Ann.#2 Elseworlds story 4.00
Ann.#3 Year One Annual 4.00
Ann.#4 Legends of the Dead Earth 3.00
Ann.#5 AlG(s), Pulp Heroes 4.00
Spec.#1,000,000 AlG(s),MBu, Origin of 853rd-century Dark Knight 2.00

BATMAN: SWORD OF AZRAEL
1992–93

1 JQ,KN,I:Azrael 10.00
2 JQ,KN,A:Azrael 7.00
3 JQ,KN,V:Biis,A:Azrael. 5.00
4 JQ,KN,V:Biis,A:Azrael. 5.00
TPB rep.#1-#4 . . . . 11.00
TPB Platinum 25.00

BATMAN/GRENDEL: DEVIL'S MASQUE & DEVIL'S RIDDLE

1 MWg,Batman meets Grendel . . . 5.25
2 MWg,Batman Vs. Grendel 5.25

BATMAN: TOYMAN
1998

1 (of 4) LHa(s),AWi,KJ. 2.25
2 LHa(s),AWi,KJ 2.25
3 LHa(s),AWi,KJ 2.25
4 LHa(s),AWi,KJ conclusion. 2.25

BATMAN vs. PREDATOR
DC/Dark Horse 1991–92

1 NKu,AKu,inc.8 trading cards bound in (Prestige). 5.00
1a Newsstand 4.00
2 NKu,AKu,Inc. pinups (prestige) . . 4.00
2a Newsstand 3.00
3 NKu,AKu,conclusion,inc. 8 trading cards (Prestige) 4.00
3a Newsstand 3.00
TPB,rep.#1-#3 . . . . 5.95

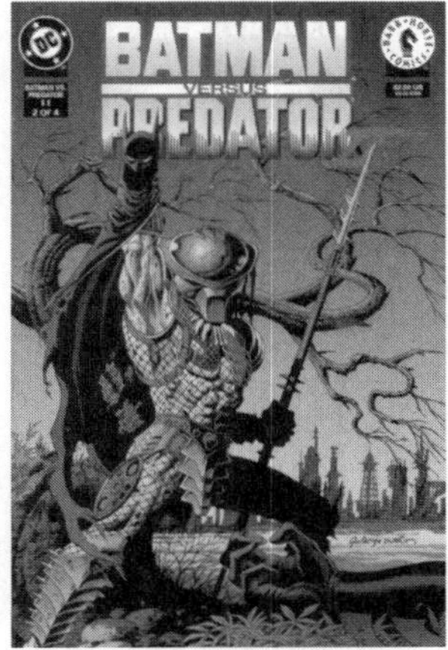

Batman Versus Predator II Bloodmatch #2 © DC Comics Inc.

BATMAN vs. PREDATOR II BLOODMATCH
1994–95

1 R:Predators 2.75
2 A:Huntress 2.50
3 Assassins. 2.50
4 V:Head Hunters 2.50
TPB Rep.#1-#4. . . . . 6.95

BATMAN/PREDATOR III: BLOOD TIES
DC/Dark Horse 1997

1 (of 4) CDi,RDm,RbC, vs. pair of Predators 2.00
2 CDi,RDm,RbC, pt.2 . . . . 2.00
3 CDi,RDm,RbC, pt.3 . . . . 2.00
4 CDi,RDm,RbC, concl. 2.00
TPB rep.. . . . . 8.00

BATMAN/WILDCAT
Feb., 1997

1 (of 3) CDi&BSt(s),SCi,ATi, Batman and Robin discover Secret Ring of combat 2.25
2 CDi&BSt(s),SCi,V:KGBeast, Willis Danko 2.25
3 CDi&BSt(s),SCi, Batman vs. Wildcat, concl. 2.25

BEAST BOY
Nov., 1999

1 (of 4)BRa,Clv 2.95
2 BRa,Clv,A:Nightwing 2.95
3 BRa,Clv,V:Nightwing. 2.95
4 BRa,Clv,F:Flamebird 2.95

BATTLEAXES
DC Vertigo March, 2000

1 (of 4) female sword & sorcery . . . 2.50
2 . . . . 2.50
3 . . . . 2.50
4 conclusion 2.50

BATTLE CLASSICS
Sept.,–Oct., 1978

1 JKu, reprints. 2.00

BEAUTIFUL STORIES FOR UGLY CHILDREN
Piranha Press 1989–91

1 thru 11 . . . . @2.00
12 thru 14. . . . . @2.50
15 Blood Day 2.50
16 thru 23. . . . . @2.50

BEOWOLF
April-May, 1975

1 thru 5 . . . . @1.00
6 Feb.–March, 1976 . . . . 1.00

BEST OF THE BRAVE & THE BOLD

1 JL(c),NA,rep.B&B #85. . . . . 2.50
2 JL(c),NA,rep.B&B #81 . . . . 2.50
3 JL(c),NA,rep.B&B #82 . . . . 2.50
4 JL(c),NA,rep.B&B #80 . . . . 2.50
5 JL(c),NA,rep.B&B #93 . . . . 2.50
6 JL(c),NA,rep.B&B #83 . . . . 2.50

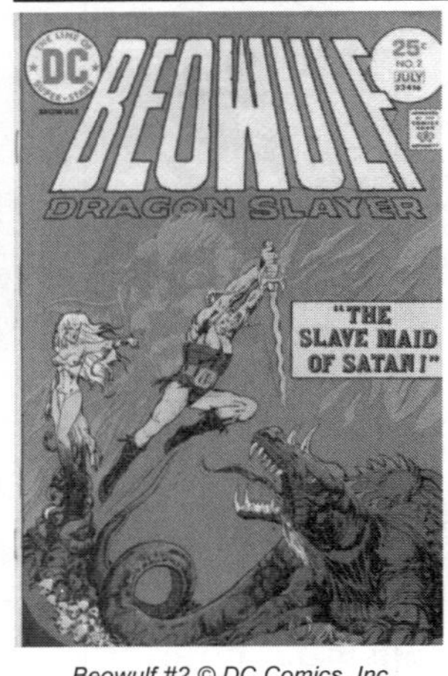

Beowulf #2 © DC Comics, Inc.

BEWARE THE CREEPER

1968–69

1 . . . . 12.00
2 thru 6 . . . . @7.50

BIG ALL-AMERICAN COMIC BOOK

Dec., 1944

1 JKu 11,000.00

BIG BOOK OF FUN COMICS

Spring, 1936

1 . . . . 13,000.00

THE BIG BOOK OF ...:

DC/Paradox Press B&W 1994–98

TPB Conspiracies (1995) 12.95
TPB Death (1994). 12.95
TPB Hoaxes (1996) 14.95
TPB Little Criminals (1996) 14.95
TPB Losers 14.95
TPB Martyrs (1997) 15.00
TPB Scandal (1997) 15.00
TPB Thugs (1996) 14.95
TPB Unexplained DgM(s) (1997) . 14.95
TPB Urban Legends (1994) 12.95
TPB Weirdos (1995) 12.95
TPB Weird Wild West (1998) 15.00
TPB Big Book of the '70s (2000). . 14.95

BIRDS OF PREY: MANHUNT

1996

1 CDi(s),MHy,F:Black Canary, Oracle 5.00
2 CDi(s),MHy,V,Archer Braun, A:Catwoman 4.00
3 CDi(s),MHy,V:Catwoman, Huntress 4.00
4 CDi(s),MHy,V:Lady Shiva 4.00
1-shot Birds of Prey: Batgirl CDi, Batgirl & Black Canary (1997). . 3.00
1-shot Birds of Prey: Revolution CDi(s),BMc. 3.00
1-shot Birds of Prey: The Ravens, CDi, Girlfrenzy (1998). 2.00
1-shot Birds of Prey: Wolves CDi,DG (1997) 3.00

BIRDS OF PREY

1998

1 CDi(s),Black Canary & Oracle. . . 3.00
2 CDi(s),V:Jackie Pajamas 2.50
3 CDi(s),V:Hellbound 2.50
4 CDi(s),V:Ravens. 2.50
5 CDi(s),V:Ravens,pt.2 . . . . 2.50
6 CDi(s),V:Ravens,pt.3 . . . . 2.50
7 CDi(s),PKr, ... 2.50
8 CDi(s),F:Nightwing 2.50
9 CDi(s),V:Iron Brigade 2.50
10 CDi(s),DG,V:Dr.Pop 2.50
11 CDi(s),DG 2.50
12 CDi(s),DG,F:Catwoman 2.50
13 CDi(s),DG 2.50
14 CDi(s),DG,V:Lashina 2.50
15 CDi(s),JG 2.50
16 CDi(s),JG,V:maniac 2.50
17 CDi(s),JG,V:Joker 2.50
18 CDi(s),JG,Transbelvia 2.50
19 CDi(s),JG,A:Nightwing,Robin . . . 2.50
20 CDi(s),Hunt for Oracle,pt.2. . . . . 2.50
21 CDi(s),Hunt for Oracle,concl. . . . 2.50
22 CDi(s),Gorilla City 2.50
23 CDi(s),Gorilla City 2.50
24 CDi,search for heart donor. 3.00
TPB Birds of Prey. 18.00

BLACK CANARY

[Limited Series] 1991–92

1 TVE/DG,New Wings,pt.1 . . . . . . 2.25
2 TVE/DG,New Wings,pt.2 . . . . . . 2.00
3 TVE/DG,New Wings,pt.3 . . . . . . 2.00
4 TVE/DG,New Wings,pt.4,Conc . . 2.00

[Regular Series] 1993

1 TVE,Hero Worship,pt.1 . . . . 2.25
2 TVE,Hero Worship,pt.2. . . . . 2.00
3 TVE,Hero Worship,pt.3. . . . . 2.00
4 TVE,V:Whorrsman 2.00
5 . . . . 2.00
6 Blynde Woman's Bluff. 2.00
7 TVE,V:Maniacal Killer 2.00
8 . . . . 1.75
9 A:Huntress 1.75
10 TVE,A:Nightwing,Huntress. 1.75
11 TVE,A:Nightwing 1.75
12 final issue 1.75

BLACK CANARY/ORACLE: BIRDS OF PREY

1996

1-shot DDi, double size. 3.95

BLACK CONDOR

1992–93

1 I&O:Black Condor. 2.00
2 V:Sky Pirate 2.00
3 V:Sky Pirate 2.00
4 V:The Shark 2.00
5 V:Mind Force 2.00
6 V:Mind Force 2.00
7 Forest Fire 2.00
8 MG,In Jail. 2.00
9 A:The Ray 2.00
10 . . . . 2.00
11 O:Black Condor 2.00

BLACKHAWK

Prev: Golden Age

1957–1984

108 DD,CCu,DD&CCu(c),The Threat from the Abyss A:Blaisie 450.00

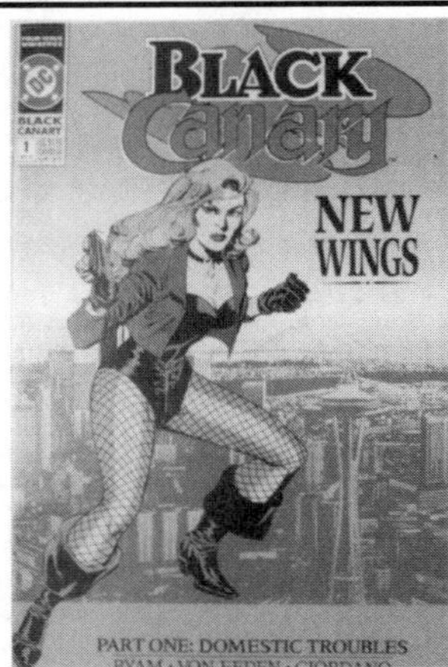

Black Canary #1 © DC Comics, Inc.

109 DD,CCu,DD&CCu(c),The Avalance Kid 150.00
110 DD,CCu,DD&CCu(c),Mystery of Tigress Island 150.00
111 DD,CCu,DD&CCu(c),Menace of the Machines 150.00
112 DD,CCu,DD(c),The Doomed Dog Fight 150.00
113 DD,CCu,CCu(c),Volunteers of Doom 150.00
114 DD,CCu,DD&CCu(c),Gladiators of Blackhawk Island 150.00
115 DD,CCu,DD&CCu(c),The Tyrant's Return 150.00
116 DD,CCu,DD&CCu(c),Prisoners of the Black Island 175.00
117 DD,CCu,DD&CCu(c),Menace of the Dragon Boat 140.00
118 DD,CCu,DD&SMo(c),FF,The Bandit With 1,000 Nets. 150.00
119 DD,CCu,DD&SMo(c), V:Chief Blackhawk 125.00
120 DD,CCu,DD&SMo(c),The Challenge of the Wizard 125.00
121 DD,CCu,DD&CCu(c),Secret Weapon of the Archer. 125.00
122 DD,CCu,DD&CCu(c),The Movie That Backfired 125.00
123 DD,CCu,DD&CCu(c),The Underseas Gold Fort 125.00
124 DD,CCu,DD&CCu(c),Thieves With A Thousand Faces 125.00
125 DD,CCu,DD&CCu(c),Secrets o/t Blackhawk Time Capsule. 125.00
126 DD,CCu,DD&CCu(c),Secret of the Glass Fort. 125.00
127 DD,CCu,DD&CCu(c),Blackie-The Winged Sky Fighter 125.00
128 DD,CCu,DD&CCu(c),The Vengeful Bowman. 125.00
129 DD,CCu,DD&CCu(c),The Cavemen From 3,000 B.C. . . 125.00
130 DD,CCu,DD&SMo(c),The Mystery Missle From Space . 125.00
131 DD,CCu,DD&CCu(c),The Return of the Rocketeers 85.00
132 DD,CCu,DD&CCu(c),Raid of the Rocketeers 85.00
133 DD,CCu,DD&CCu(c),Human Dynamo 85.00
134 DD,CC,DD&CC(c),The Sinister Snowman 85.00
135 DD,CCu,DD&CCu(c),The Underworld Supermarket 85.00
136 DD,CCu,DD&CCu(c),The

Menace of the Smoke-Master. 85.00
137 DD,CCu,DD&CCu(c),The Weapons That Backfired. 85.00
138 DD,CCu,DD&SMo(c),The Menace of the Blob 85.00
139 DD,CCu,DD&CCu(c),The Secret Blackhawk. 85.00
140 DD,CCu,DD&CCu(c),The Space Age Marauders 85.00
141 DD,CCu,DD&CCu(c),Crimes of the Captive Masterminds . . 60.00
142 DD,CCu,DD&CCu(c),Alien Blackhawk Chief. 60.00
143 DD,SMo,DD&CCu(c),Lady Blackhawk's Rival. 60.00
144 DD,CCu,DD&CCu(c),The Underworld Sportsmen 60.00
145 DD,CCu,DD&CCu(c),The Deadly Lensman 60.00
146 DD,CCu,DD&CCu(c),The Fantastic Fables of Blackhawk 60.00
147 DD,SMo,DD&CCu(c),The Blackhawk Movie Queen 60.00
148 DD,CCu,DD&CCu(c),Four Dooms For The Blackhawks . . 60.00
149 DD,CCu,DD&CCu(c),Masks of Doom 60.00
150 DD,CCu,DD&SMo(c), Blackhawk Mascot from Space 50.00
151 DD,CCu,Lost City 75.00
152 DD,CCu,DD&SMo(c),Noah's Ark From Space 50.00
153 DD,CCu,DD&SMo(c), Boomerang Master. 50.00
154 DD,CCu,DD&SMo(c),The Beast Time Forgot 50.00
155 DD,CCu,DD&CCu(c),Killer Shark's Land Armada 50.00
156 DD,CCu,DD&SMo(c),Peril of the Plutonian Raider. 50.00
157 DD,CCu,DD&SMo(c),Secret of the Blackhawk Sphinx. 50.00
158 DD,CCu,DD&SMo(c),Bandit Birds From Space. 50.00
159 DD,CCu,DD&SMo(c),Master of the Puppet Men 50.00
160 DD,CCu,DD&CCu(c),The Phantom Spy 50.00
161 DD,SMo,DD&SMo(c),Lady Blackhawk's Crime Chief 50.00
162 DD,CCu,DD&CCu(c),The Invisible Blackhawk 50.00
163 DD,CCu,DD&SMo(c), Fisherman of Crime 50.00
164 DD,O:Blackhawk retold 75.00
165 DD,V:League of Anti Blackhawks 35.00
166 DD,A:Lady Blackhawk 35.00
167 DD,The Blackhawk Bandits . . 35.00
168 DD,Blackhawk Time Travelers 32.00
169 DD,Sinister Hunts of Mr. Safari 32.00
170 DD,A:Lady Blackhawk,V:Killer Shark 32.00
171 DD,Secret of Alien Island 32.00
172 DD,Challenge of the GasMaster 32.00
173 DD,The Super Jungle Man. . . 32.00
174 DD,Andre's Impossible World 32.00
175 DD,The Creature with Blackhawk's Brain 32.00
176 DD,Stone Age Blackhawks . . 30.00
177 DD,Town that time Forgot . . . 30.00
178 DD,Return of the Scorpions . . 30.00
179 DD,Invisible Dr.Dunbar. 30.00
180 DD,Son of Blackhawk 30.00
181 DD,I:Tom Thumb Blackhawk . 32.00
182 DD,A:Lady Blackhawk 32.00
183 DD,V:Killer Shark. 32.00
184 DD,Island of Super Monkeys 32.00
185 DD,Last 7 days of the Blackhawks 32.00
186 DD,A:Lady Blackhawk 32.00
187 DD,V:Porcupine 32.00
188 DD,A:Lady Blackhawk 32.00
189 DD:O:rtd 32.00
190 DD,FantasticHumanStarfish . . 32.00
191 DD,A:Lady Blackhawk 32.00
192 DD,V:King Condor 20.00
193 DD,The Jailer's Revenge 20.00
194 DD,The Outlaw Blackhawk. . . 20.00
195 DD,A:Tom Thumb Blackhawk. 20.00
196 DD,Blackhawk WWII Combat Diary story 20.00
197 DD:new look 20.00
198 DD:O:rtd 22.00
199 DD,Attack with the Mummy Insects 22.00
200 DD,A:Lady Blackhawk, I:Queen Killer Shark 22.00
201 DD,Blackhawk Detached Diary Story,F:Hendrickson 22.00
202 DD,Combat Diary,F:Andre . . . 22.00
203 DD:O:Chop-Chop. 22.00
204 DD,A:Queen Killer Shark 22.00
205 DD,Combat Diary story 22.00
206 DD,Combat Diary, F:Olaf 22.00
207 DD,Blackhawk Devil Dolls . . . 22.00
208 DD,Detached service diary F:Chuck 22.00
209 DD,V:King Condor 22.00
210 DD,Danger..Blackhawk Bait rep.Blackhawk #139. . . . . 15.00
211 DD,GC,Detached service diary. 15.00
212 DD,Combat Diary, F:Chop-Chop 15.00
213 DD,Blackhawk goes Hollywood 15.00
214 DD,Team of Traitors. 15.00
215 DD,Detached service diary F:Olaf. 15.00
216 DD,A:Queen Killer Shark 15.00
217 DD,Detached service diary F:Stanislaus 15.00
218 DD,7 against Planet Peril. . . . 15.00
219 DD,El Blackhawk Peligroso . . 15.00
220 DD,The Revolt of the Assembled Man 15.00
221 DD,Detach service diary F:Hendrickson 15.00
222 DD,The Man from E=MC2 . . . 15.00
223 DD,V:Mr.Quick CHange 15.00

Blackhawk #225 © DC Comics Inc.

224 DD,Combat Diary, F:Stanislaus 15.00
225 DD,A:Queen Killer Shark 15.00
226 DD,Secret Monster of Blackhawk Island 15.00
227 DD,Detached Service diary F:Chop-Chop 15.00
228 DD (1st art on JLA characters) Blackhawks become super-heroes, Junk-Heap heroes #1(C:JLA) . 18.00
229 DD,Junk-Heap Heroes #2 (C:JLA). 15.00
230 DD,Junk-Heap Heroes concl. (C:JLA). 15.00
231 DD,A:Lady Blackhawk 15.00
232 DD,A:Lady Blackhawk 15.00
233 DD,Too Late,The Leaper 15.00
234 DD,The Terrible Twins 15.00
235 DD,A Coffin for a Blackhawk. 15.00
236 DD,Melt,Mutant, Melt 15.00
237 DD,Magnificent 7 Assassins. . 15.00
238 DD,Walking Booby-Traps 15.00
239 DD,The Killer That Time Forgot 15.00
240 DD,He Who Must Die. 15.00
241 DD,A Blackhawk a Day 15.00
242 Blackhawks back in blue & black costumes 15.00
243 Mission Incredible (1968) 15.00
244 GE,new costumes,Blackhawks become mercenaries (1976) . . . 4.50
245 GE,Death's Double Deal 3.00
246 RE,GE,Death's Deadly Dawn. . 3.00
247 RE,AM,Operation:Over Kill. . . . 3.00
248 JSh,Vengeance is Mine!.. Sayeth the Cyborg 3.00
249 RE,GE,V:Sky-Skull 3.00
250 RE,GE,FS,D:Chuck(1977) 3.00
251 DSp,Back to WWII(1982). 3.00
252 thru 258 DSp . . . . @3.00
259 . . . . 3.00
260 HC,ATh 3.00
261 thru 271 DSp . . . . @3.00
272. . . . . 3.00
273 DSp. 3.00
274 DSp. 3.00

[2nd Series]

1 HC Mini-series,Blackhawk accused of communism 3.50
2 HC,visits Soviet Union 3.00
3 HC,Atom Bomb threat to N.Y. . . . 3.00

[3rd Series]

1 All in color for a Crime,pt.1 I:The Real Lady Blackhawk . . . 2.00
2 All in color for a Crime,pt.2 . . . . . 2.00
3 Agent Rescue Attempt in Rome . 2.00
4 Blackhawk's girlfriend murdered . 2.00
5 I:Circus Organization 2.00
6 Blackhawks on false mission . . . 2.00
7 V:Circus,A:Suicide Squad, rep. 1st Blackhawk story 2.50
8 Project: Assimilation 2.00
9 V:Grundfest 2.00
10 Blackhawks Attacked. 2.00
11 Master plan revealed 2.00
12 Raid on BlackhawkAirwaysHQ. . 2.00
13 Team Member Accused of 2.00
14 Blackhawk test pilots 2.00
15 Plans for independence 2.00
16 Independence, final issue 2.00
Ann.#1 Hawks in Albania 2.95
Spec.#1 Assassination of JFK to Saigon,1975. . . . . 3.50

BLACK HOOD

Impact 1991–92

1 O:Black Hood. 2.00
2 Nick Cray becomes Black Hood . 1.50
3 New Year's Eve,A:Creeptures. . . 1.50

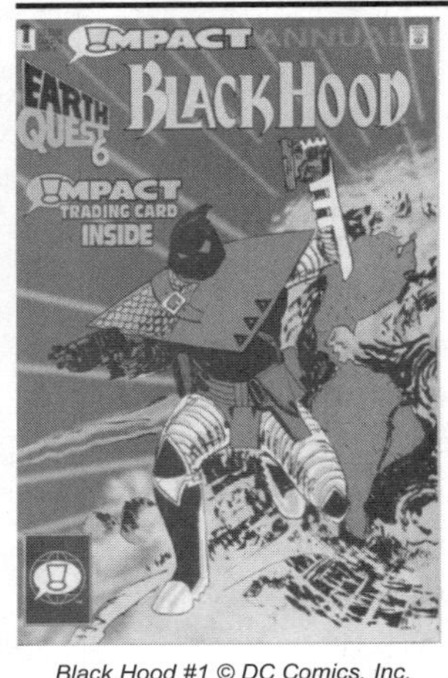

Black Hood #1 © DC Comics, Inc.

4 Nate Cray become Black Hood, Dr.M.Harvey becomes Ozone. . 1.50
5 E:Nate Cray as Black Hood V:Ozone. 1.50
6 New Black Hood. 1.50
7 History of Seaside City 1.75
8 V:Hit Coffee 1.75
9 V:Hit Coffee 1.75
10 Slime of Your Life #1 . . . . . 1.75
11 Slime of Your Life #2 . . . . . 1.75
12 Final Issue. 1.75
Ann#1 Earthquest,w/trading card . . 2.50

BLACK LAMB, THE
DC/Helix Sept., 1996

1 TT,Vampire saga 2.50
2 TT,war between werewolf clans . 2.50
3 TT,O:Black Lamb,V:Lykaon. 2.50
4 TT thru 6. . . . . @2.50

BLACK LIGHTNING
1977–78

1 TVE/FS,I&O:Black Lightning 4.50
2 TVE/FS,A:Talia. 3.00
3 TVE,I:Tobias Whale 3.00
4 TVE,A:Jimmy Olsen 3.00
5 TVE,A:Superman 3.00
6 TVE,I:Syonide 3.00
7 TVE,V:Syonide. 3.00
8 TVE,V:Tobias Whale. 3.00
9 TVE,V:Annihilist 3.00
10 TVE,V:Trickster 3.00
11 TVE,BU:The Ray 3.50

[2nd Series] 1995–96

1 He's Back. 2.50
2 V:Painkiller 2.50
3 V:Painkiller 2.50
4 V:Painkiller,Royal Family. 2.50
5 Flashbacks of Past 2.50
6 V:Gangbuster 3.00
7 V:Gangbuster 3.00
8 V:Tobias Whale 3.00
9 I&V:Demolition 3.00
10 Jefferson Pierce becomes Black Lightning full time 3.00
11 Hunt for Sick Nick 3.00
12 V:Sick Nick's death squad 3.00
13 final issue 3.00

BLACK MASK
1993–94

1 I:Black Mask. 5.00
2 V:Underworld 5.00
3 V:Valentine 5.00

BLACK ORCHID
1993–95

1 DMc,O:Black Orchid, A:Batman,Luthor,Poison Ivy . . . 6.00
2 DMc,O:cont,Arkham Asylum 7.00
3 DMc,A:SwampThing,conc. 6.00
TPB rep. #1 thru #3 . . . . . 20.00

Vertigo

1 DMc(c),B:DiF(s),JIT,SnW,I:Sherilyn Somers,I:Logos,F:Walt Brody . . 2.50
1a Platinum Ed. 12.00
2 JIT,SnW,Uprooting,V:Logos. 2.25
3 JIT,SnW,Tainted Zone, V:Fungus 2.25
4 JIT,SnW,I:Nick & Orthia. 2.25
5 DMc(c),JIT,SnW, A:Swamp Thing 2.25
6 JIT,BMc(i),God in the Cage 2.25
7 JIT,RGu,SnW, Upon the Threshold 2.25
8 DMc(c),RGu,A:Silent People. . . . 2.25
9 DMc(c),RGu 2.25
10 DMc(c),RGu 2.25
11 DMc(c),RGu,In Tennessee 2.25
12 DMc(c),RGu 2.25
13 DMc(c),RGu,F:Walt Brody 2.25
14 DMc(c),RGu,Black Annis 2.25
15 DMc(c),RGu,Kobolds 2.25
16 DMc(c),RGu,Suzy,Junkin 2.25
17 Twisted Season,pt.1 . . . . . 2.25
18 Twisted Season,pt.2 . . . . . 2.25
19 Twisted Season,pt.3 . . . . . 2.25
20 Twisted Season,pt.4 . . . . . 2.25
21 Twisted Season,pt.5 . . . . . 2.25
22 Twisted Season,pt.6, final iss. . . 2.25
Ann.#1 DMc(c),DiF(s),GyA,JnM,F:Suzy, Childrens Crusade,BU:retells Adventure Comics#430 . . . . . 4.25

BLASTERS SPECIAL
1989

1 A:Snapper Carr, Spider Guild . . . 2.00

BLOOD: A TALE
DC/Vertigo Sept., 1996
[Mini-series, re-release of Marvel Epic]

1 JMD(s),KW, quest for truth begins 3.00
2 JMD(s),KW, Blood falls in love . . 3.00
3 JMD(s),KW, companion dies. . . . 3.00
4 JMD(s),KW, finale. 3.00

BLOOD & SHADOWS
(Vertigo) 1996

1 . . . . . 6.00
2 Journal of Justice Jones 6.00
3 Chet Daley flung into 21st century 6.00
4 V:God of the Razor, finale. 6.00

BLOODBATH
1993

1 A:Superman 3.75
2 A:New Heroes 3.75

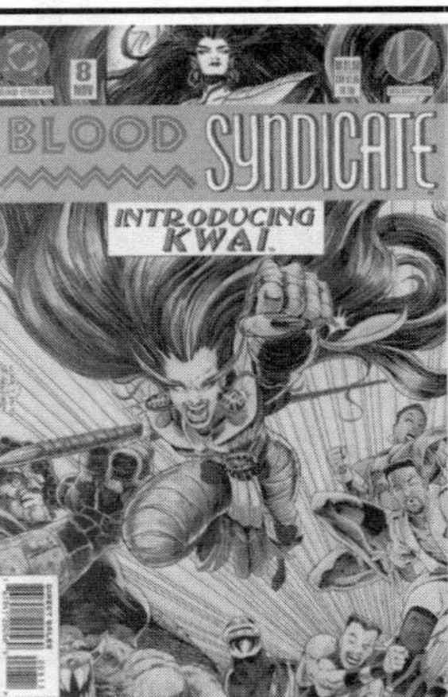

Blood Syndicate #8 © DC Comics, Inc.

BLOODPACK
[Mini-Series] 1995

1 I:Blood Pack, V:Demolition 2.00
2 A:Superboy 2.00
3 Loira's Corpse 2.00
4 Real Heroes Final Issue 2.00

BLOOD SYNDICATE
(Milestone) 1993–96

1 I:Blood Syndicate,Rob Chaplick, Dir.Mark.Ed.,w/B puzzle piece, Skybox card,Poster 3.50
1a Newstand Ed. 2.00
2 I:Boogieman,Tech-9 Vs. Holocaust. 2.00
3 V:S.Y.S.T.E.M.,I:Mom,D:Tech-9. . 2.00
4 V:S.Y.S.T.E.M. 2.00
5 I:John Wing,Kwai,Demon Fox. . . 2.00
6 V:John Wing. 2.00
7 I:Edmund,Cornelia 2.00
8 V:Demon Fox 2.00
9 O:Blood Syndicate,I:Templo 2.00
10 WS(c),Ccs,Shadow War,I:Iota, Sideshow,Rainsaw,Slag,Ash, Bad Betty,Oro. 2.25
11 IV(s),Ccs,A:Aquamaria. 2.00
12 IV(s),Ccs,V:Dinosaur 2.00
13 IV(s),Ccs,B:Roach War 2.00
14 IV(s),Ccs,V:Roaches 2.00
15 IV(s),Ccs,E:Roach War 2.00
16 IV(s),Ccs,Worlds Collide#6, A:Superman. 2.00
17 Ccs,Worlds Collide#13,V:Rift . . . 2.00
18 Ccs,V:S.Y.S.T.E.M. 2.00
19 . . . . . 2.00
20 . . . . . 2.00
21 . . . . . 2.00
22 . . . . . 2.00
23 F:Boogieman. 2.00
24 L:Third Rail,Brickhouse 2.00
25 R:Tech-9 . . . . . 3.50
26 Return of the Dead 2.00
27 R:Masquerade. 2.00
28 Tech-9 takes control. 2.50
29 Reader's Choice 2.00
30 Long Hot Summer 2.50
31 V:New Threat 2.50
32 MC(c),V:Soulbreaker 2.50
33 Kwai returns to paris Island 2.00
34 Visit to Kwen Lun 2.50
35 final issue 3.50

BLOODY MARY

DC/Helix Aug., 1996

1 (of 4) GEn(s),CE, near-future war 3.00
2 thru 4 GEn(s),CE, near-future war, concl. . . . . @3.00

BLOODY MARY: LADY LIBERTY

DC/Helix July, 1996

1 (of 4) GEn(s),CE, ... 2.75
2 GEn(s),CE,V:Achilles Seagal . . . 2.75
3 GEn(s),CE,V:Vatman 2.75
4 GEn(s),CE,V:Vatman, concl. 2.75

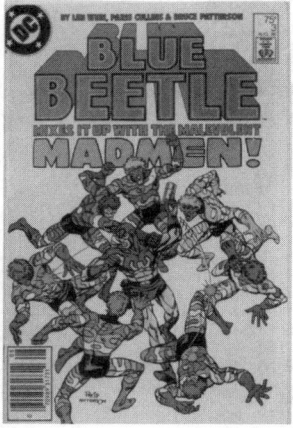

Blue Beetle #3 © DC Comics Inc.

BLUE BEETLE

1986–88

1 O:Blue Beetle 3.00
2 V:Fire Fist. 2.00
3 V:Madmen 2.00
4 V:Doctor Alchemy. 2.00
5 A:Question 2.00
6 V:Question 2.00
7 A:Question 2.00
8 A:Chronos 2.00
9 A:Chronos 2.00
10 Legends, V:Chronos 2.00
11 A:New Teen Titans. 2.00
12 A:New Teen Titans. 2.00
13 A:New Teen Titans. 2.00
14 Pago Island,I:Catalyst 2.00
15 RA:V:Carapax 2.00
16 RA,Chicago Murders 2.00
17 R:Dan Garrett/Blue Beetle 2.00
18 D:Dan Garrett 2.00
19 RA,R:Dr. Cyber 2.00
20 RA,Millennium,A:JLI. 2.00
21 RA,A:Mr.Miracle, Millennium tie in 2.00
22 RA,Prehistoric Chicago 2.00
23 DH,V:The Madmen 2.00
24 DH,final issue 2.00

BLUE DEVIL

1984–86

1 O:Blue Devil. 3.00
2 . . . . 2.00
3 A:Superman. 2.00
4 A:JLA. 2.00
5 . . . . 2.00
6 EC,I:Bolt. 2.00
7 KG 2.00
8 GV 2.00
9 thru 16 . . . . @2.00
17 Crisis. 1.75
18 Crisis. 1.75
19 . . . . 1.75
20 RM,Halloween 1.75
21 RM,I:Roadmaster. 1.75
22 RM,A:Jorj & Lehni 1.75
23 A:Jorj & Lehni 1.75
24 V:Blue Devil Toys. 1.75
25 Mary Frances Cassidy 1.75
26 Special Baseball issue. 1.75
27 Godfrey Goose 1.75
28 real live fan guest star 1.75
29 . . . . 1.75
30 Double sized 1.75
31 BSz,V:Seraph 1.75
Ann.#1 . . . . 2.00

BOB, THE GALACTIC BUM

[Mini-Series] 1995

1 A:Lobo 2.50
2 Planet Gnulp,A:Lobo. 2.50
3 V:Khunds 2.50
4 Rando's Coronation 2.50

BODY DOUBLES

Aug., 1999

1 (of 4) DAn,ALa,JoP. 2.50
2 DAn,ALa,JoP 2.50
3 DAn,ALa,JoP 2.50

BOGIE MAN, THE

DC/Paradox/Pocket 1998

TPB 6"x8" AIG,b&w 14.00

BOMBA, THE JUNGLE BOY

1967–68

1 CI,MA,I:Bomba 15.00
2 thru 7 . . . . @10.00

BOOK OF FATE, THE

1 KG(s),RoW,BR, ... 3.00
2 KG(s),RoW,BR,"The Chaos-Order War," pt.1 (of 4) 3.00
3 KG(s),RoW,BR,"The Chaos-Order War," pt.2 . . . . 3.00
4 KG(s),RoW,BR,"The Chaos-Order War," pt.3, A:Two-Face . . 3.00
5 KG(s),RoW,BR,"The Chaos-Order War," pt.4 . . . . 3.00
6 KG(s),RoW,BR,Convergence," pt.1 x-over 3.00
7 KG(s),RoW,BR, Signs, pt.1 . . . . . 3.00
8 KG(s),RoW,BR, Signs, pt.2. . . . . 3.00
9 KG,AIG,BR,Signs, pt.3 . . . . 3.00
10 KG,AIG,BR,Signs,pt.4 . . . . 3.00
11 KG,AIG, in a Swiss Jail 3.00
12 AIG,KG,F:Lobo, final issue. 3.00

BOOKS OF FAERIE, THE

DC/Vertigo Jan., 1997

1 PrG,F:Titania and Auberon 2.50
2 PrG, ... 2.50
3 (of 3) PrG. 2.50
TPB 15.00

BOOKS OF FAERIE, THE: AUBERON'S TALE

DC/Vertigo June, 1998

1 (of 3) PrG,VcL,F:Early life of King Auberon 3.00
2 PrG,VcL, early life 3.00
3 PrG,VcL, early life, concl. 3.00
TPB Books of Faerie 15.00

BOOKS OF FAERIE, THE: MOLLY'S STORY

DC/Vertigo 1999

1 (of 4) JNR(s) 3.00
2 CV(c) 3.00
3 CV(c) 3.00
4 CV(c) conclusion 3.00

BOOKS OF MAGIC

[Limited Series] 1990–91

1 B:NGa(s),JBo,F:Phantom Stranger, A:J.Constantine,Tim Hunter, Doctor Occult,Mister E 10.00
2 SHp,F:J.Constantine,A:Spectre, Dr.Fate,Demon,Zatanna 10.00
3 CV,F:Doctor Occult, A:Sandman 9.00
4 E:NGa(s),PuJ,F:Mr.E,A:Death. . . 9.00
TPB rep.#1-#4 . . . . 20.00

[Regular Series] Vertigo 1994–97

1 MkB,B:Bindings,R:Tim Hunter. . . 5.00
1a Platinum Edition 9.00
2 CV(c),MkB,V:Manticore. 4.00
3 CV(c),MkB,E:Bindings 4.00
4 CV(c),MkB,A:Death 5.00
5 CV(c),I:Khara 3.00
6 Sacrifices,pt.I 3.00
7 Sacrifices,pt.II. 3.00
8 Tim vs. evil Tim 3.00
9 Artificial Heart,pt.1 . . . . 3.00
10 Artificial Heart,pt.2 . . . . 3.00
11 Artificial Heart,pt.3 . . . . 3.00
12 Small Glass Worlds,pt.1. . . . . . . 3.00
13 Small Glass Worlds,pt.2. . . . . . . 3.00
14 CV(c),A:The Wobbly 3.00
15 Hell and Back,pt.1 . . . . 3.00
16 Hall and Back,pt.2 . . . . 3.00
17 Playgrounds,pt.1 . . . . 3.00
18 JNR,PrG,Playgrounds,cont. 3.00
19 JNR,PrG,Playgrounds,concl. . . . 3.00
20 Barabatos gives the orders 3.00
21 JNR,PrG,Molly seeks Mayra . . . 3.00
22 . . . . 3.00
23 JNR,V:Margraves Strafenkinder. 3.00
24 JNR,PrG,F:Molly vs. Amadan . . 3.00
25 JNR,PrG,Death and the Endless 3.00
26 JNR,PrG,Rites of Passage, pt.1. 3.00
27 JNR,PrG,Rites of Passage, pt.2. 3.00
28 JNR,PrG,Rites of Passage, pt.3, Cupid & Psyche 3.00
29 JNR,PrG,"Rite of Passage" 3.00
30 JNR,PrG,"Rite of Passage" 3.00
31 JNR,PrG,"Rite of Passage" 3.00
32 JNR(s),PSj,"Rites of Passage". . 3.00
33 JNR(s),PSj,"Rites of Passage". . 3.00
34 JNR(s),PSj,"Rites of Passage". . 3.00
35 JNR(s),PrG,"Rites of Passage" . 3.00
36 JNR,"Rites of Passage" cont . . . 3.00
37 JNR,"Rites of Passage" cont. . . . 3.00
38 JNR,"Rites of Passage" concl. . . 3.00
39 PrG, at Sphinx casino 3.00
40 JNR(s),F:Tim & Molly. 3.00
41 JNR(s),V:Gargoyles. 3.00
42 JNR(s),JIT,magical havok. 3.00
43 JNR(s),PrG,F:The Wobbly 3.00
44 JNR(s),goodbye to Zatanna 3.00
45 JNR(s) Slave of Heavens, pt.1. . 3.00
46 JNR(s) Slave of Heavens, pt.2. . 3.00
47 JNR(s) Slave of Heavens, pt.3. . 3.00
48 JNR(s) Slave of Heavens, pt.4. . 3.00
49 JNR(s) Slave of Heavens, pt.5. . 3.00
50 JNR(s) Slave of Heavens, pt.6. . 3.00
51 PrG,MK,an Opener 2.50

52 PrG,MK,Homecoming 2.50
54 PrG,MK,V:Thomas. 2.50
55 PrG,MK,Coming of the Other . . . 2.50
56 PrG,MK,Last Molly Story 2.50
57 PrG,MK,after car crash 2.50
58 PrG,MK,The Other. 2.50
59 PrG,MK,The Other. 2.50
60 PrG,MK,The Other. 2.50
61 PrG,MK(c),The Other, concl. . . . 2.50
62 PrG,MK(c),crossroads 2.50
63 GyA,MK(c), ... 2.50
64 PrG,MK(c),Wild Hunt 2.50
65 PrG,MK,new life cont. 2.50
66 PrG,A Day,A Night &
A Dream,pt.1 . . . . 2.50
67 PrG,A Day, A Night &
A Dream,concl.. . . . . 2.50
68 PrG 2.50
69 PrG 2.50
70 PrG 2.50
71 PrG,MK(c) 2.50
72 PrG,MK(c),F:Timothy Hunter . . . 2.50
73 PrG,MK(c),V:Other self 2.50
74 PrG,MK(c),V:Other self 2.50
75 PrG,MK(c), final issue 2.50
Ann.#2 JNR(s) Minotaur 4.00
Ann.#3 PrG 4.00
TPB Rep. #5-#13 & Rave #1 . . . . 12.95
TPB Reckonings, 192pg.
rep. #14–#20 . . . . 12.95
TPB rep mini-series 20.00
TPB Bindings, GyA,PrG,WK 13.00
TPB Transformations PrG,MK. . . . 13.00
TPB The Books of Magic 20.00
TPB Girl in the Box. 15.00
TPB The Burning Girl 17.95

BOOSTER GOLD

1986–88

1 DJ,V:Blackguard. 3.00
2 DJ,V:Minddancer 2.00
3 DJ,V:Minddancer 2.00
4 DJ,V:Minddancer 2.00
5 DJ,V:Fascinator 2.00
6 DJ,A:Superman 2.00
7 DJ,A:Superman 2.00
8 DJ,A:Braniac 5,Cham.Boy,
Ultra Boy,pt.1 . . . . 2.00
9 DJ,A:Braniac 5,Cham.Boy,
Ultra Boy,pt.2 . . . . 2.00
10 DJ,V:1000 . . . . 2.00
11 DJ,V:Shockwave 2.00
12 DJ,Booster Weakening 2.00

Booster Gold #24 © DC Comics, Inc.

13 DJ,I:Rip Hunter(modern) 2.00
14 DJ,Rip Hunter 2.00
15 DJ,Rip Hunter 2.00
16 DJ,Boosters new company 2.00
17 DJ,A:Cheshire & Hawk 2.00
18 DJ,V:Broderick. 2.00
19 DJ,V:Rainbow Raider. 2.00
20 DJ,V:Rainbow Raider. 2.00
21 DJ,Goldstar captured by aliens . 2.00
22 DJ,A:J.L.I.,D:Goldstar 2.00
23 DJ,A:Superman & Luthor 2.00
24 DJ,Millenium 2.00
25 DJ,last issue 2.00

BOY COMMANDOS

Winter, 1942–43

1 S&K,O:Liberty Belle;Sandman
& Newsboy Legion. 5,000.00
2 S&K. 1,300.00
3 S&K 850.00
4 . . . . 600.00
5 . . . . 600.00
6 S&K 575.00
7 S&K 400.00
8 S&K 400.00
9 . . . . 400.00
10 S&K. 400.00
11 Infinity(c) 400.00
12 thru 16 . . . . @200.00
17 Science Fiction(c) 225.00
18 . . . . 200.00
19 . . . . 200.00
20. . . . . 225.00
21. . . . . 150.00
22 . . . . 150.00
23 S&K,S&K,(c) 200.00
24 . . . . 175.00
25 . . . . 175.00
26 Science Fiction(c) 200.00
27 . . . . 150.00
28 . . . . 150.00
29 S&K story 160.00
30 Baseball Storm 160.00
31 . . . . 150.00
32 A:Dale Evans(c). 160.00
33 . . . . 150.00
34 I:Wolf. 150.00
35 . . . . 150.00
36 Nov.–Dec., 1949 . . . . 225.00

BRAVE AND THE BOLD

Aug.–Sept., 1955

1 JKu,RH,IN,I:VikingPrince,Golden
Gladiator,Silent Knight 3,000.00
2 F:Viking Prince 1,300.00
3 F:Viking Prince 650.00
4 F:Viking Prince 650.00
5 B:Robin Hood 700.00
6 JKu,F:Robin Hood,E:Golden
Gladiator 500.00
7 JKu,F:Robin Hood 500.00
8 JKu,F:Robin Hood 500.00
9 JKu,F:Robin Hood 500.00
10 JKu,F:Robin Hood 500.00
11 JKu,F:Viking Prince 400.00
12 JKu,F:Viking Prince 400.00
13 JKu,F:Viking Prince 400.00
14 JKu,F:Viking Prince 375.00
15 JKu,F:Viking Prince 375.00
16 JKu,F:Viking Prince 375.00
17 JKu,F:Viking Prince 375.00
18 JKu,F:Viking Prince 375.00
19 JKu,F:Viking Prince 375.00
20 JKu,F:Viking Prince 375.00
21 JKu,F:Viking Prince 375.00
22 JKu,F:Viking Prince 375.00
23 JKu,O:Viking Prince 400.00
24 JKu,E:Viking Prince,Silent
Knight. 375.00

Brave and the Bold #129
© DC Comics, Inc.

25 RA,I&B:Suicide Squad 400.00
26 F:Suicide Squad 350.00
27 Creature of Ghost Lake 325.00
28 I:Justice League of
America,O:Snapper Carr . . 5,500.00
29 F:Justice League. 2,400.00
30 F:Justice League. 2,000.00
31 F:Cave Carson 350.00
32 F:Cave Carson 250.00
33 F:Cave Carson 250.00
34 JKu,I&O:S.A. Hawkman . . . 2,000.00
35 JKu:F:Hawkman 500.00
36 JKu:F:Hawkman 500.00
37 F:Suicide Squad 400.00
38 F:Suicide Squad 225.00
39 F:Suicide Squad 225.00
40 JKu,F:Cave Carson 150.00
41 F:Cave Carson 150.00
42 JKu,F:Hawkman 300.00
43 JKu,O:Hawkman 350.00
44 JKu,F:Hawkman 250.00
45 CI,F:Strange Sports 75.00
46 CI,F:Strange Sports 75.00
47 CI,F:Strange Sports 75.00
48 CI,F:Strange Sports 75.00
49 CI,F:Strange Sports 75.00
50 F:GreenArrow & JonnJ'onzz. . 175.00
51 F:Aquaman & Hawkman 250.00
52 JKu,F:Sgt.Rock 150.00
53 ATh,F:Atom & Flash. 75.00
54 I&O:Teen Titans 275.00
55 F:Metal Man & Atom 65.00
56 F:Flash & J'onn J'onzz. 65.00
57 I&O:Metamorpho 150.00
58 F:Metamorpho 75.00
59 F:Batman & Green Lantern . . 100.00
60 A:Teen Titans,I:Wonder Girl . . 100.00
61 MA,O:Starman,BlackCanary. . 125.00
62 MA,O:Starman,BlackCanary. . 125.00
63 F:Supergirl&WonderWoman. . . 55.00
64 F:Batman,V:Eclipso 70.00
65 DG,FMc,F:Flash & Doom
Patrol 30.00
66 F:Metamorpho & Metal Men. . . 30.00
67 CI,F:Batman & Flash 50.00
68 F:Batman,Metamorpho,Joker,
Riddler,Penguin 65.00
69 F:Batman & Green Lantern . . . 35.00
70 F:Batman & Hawkman. 35.00
71 F:Batman & Green Arrow. 35.00
72 CI,F:Spectre & Flash 40.00
73 F:Aquaman & Atom 32.00
74 B:Batman T.U.,A:Metal Men. . . 32.00
75 F:Spectre. 32.00

76 F:Plastic Man 32.00
77 F:Atom 32.00
78 F:Wonder Woman 32.00
79 NA,F:Deadman 60.00
80 NA,DG,F:Creeper 45.00
81 NA,F:Flash 45.00
82 NA,F:Aquaman,O:Ocean
Master 45.00
83 NA,F:Teen Titans 50.00
84 NA,F:Sgt.Rock 45.00
85 NA,F:Green Arrow 45.00
86 NA,F:Deadman 45.00
87 F:Wonder Woman 30.00
88 F:Wildcat 30.00
89 RA,F:Phantom Stranger 30.00
90 F:Adam Strange 30.00
91 F:Black Canary 30.00
92 F:Bat Squad 30.00
93 NA,House of Mystery 45.00
94 NC,F:Teen Titans 25.00
95 F:Plastic Man 22.00
96 F:Sgt.Rock 22.00
97 NC(i),F:Wildcat 22.00
98 JAp,F:Phantom Stranger 22.00
99 NC,F:Flash 22.00
100 NA,F:Green Arrow 40.00
101 JA,F:Metamorpho 20.00
102 NA,JA,F:Teen Titans 20.00
103 FMc,F:Metal Men 10.00
104 JAp,F:Deadman 10.00
105 JAp,F:Wonder Woman 10.00
106 JAp,F:Green Arrow 10.00
107 JAp,F:Black Canary 10.00
108 JAp,F:Sgt.Rock 10.00
109 JAp,F:Demon 10.00
110 JAp,F:Wildcat 10.00
111 JAp,F:Joker 15.00
112 JAp,F:Mr.Miracle 18.00
113 JAp,F:Metal Men 18.00
114 JAp,F:Aquaman 18.00
115 JAp,O:Viking Prince 18.00
116 JAp,F:Spectre 18.00
117 JAp,F:Sgt.Rock 18.00
118 JAp,F:Wildcat,V:Joker 20.00
119 JAp,F:Man-Bat 8.00
120 JAp,F:Kamandi 8.00
121 JAp,F:Metal Men 8.00
122 JAp,F:Swamp Thing 8.00
123 JAp,F:Plastic Man 8.00
124 JAp,F:Sgt.Rock 8.00
125 JAp,F:Flash 8.00
126 JAp,F:Aquaman 8.00
127 JAp,F:Wildcat 8.00
128 JAp,F:Mr.Miracle 8.00
129 F:Green Arrow,V:Joker 13.00
130 F:Green Arrow,V:Joker 13.00
131 JAp,F:WonderWoman,
A:Catwoman 10.00
132 JAp,F:King Fu Foom 8.00
133 JAp,F:Deadman 8.00
134 JAp,F:Green Lantern 8.00
135 JAp,F:Metal Men 8.00
136 JAp,F:Metal Men,Green Arr.. . . 8.00
137 F:Demon 8.00
138 JAp,F:Mr.Miracle 8.00
139 JAp,F:Hawkman 8.00
140 JAp,F:Wonder Woman. 8.00
141 JAp,F:Bl.Canary,A:Joker 15.00
142 JAp,F:Aquaman 7.00
143 O:Human Target 7.00
144 JAp,F:Green Arrow 7.00
145 JAp,F:Phantom Stranger 7.00
146 JAp,F:E-2 Batman 7.00
147 JAp,A:Supergirl 7.00
148 JSon,JAp,F:Plastic Man 7.00
149 JAp,F:Teen Titans 7.50
150 JAp,F:Superman 7.00
151 JAp,F:Flash 7.50
152 JAp,F:Atom 7.00
153 DN,F:Red Tornado 7.00
154 JAp,F:Metamorpho 7.00
155 JAp,F:Green Lantern 7.00
156 DN,F:Dr.Fate 7.00
157 JAp,F:Kamandi 7.00
158 JAp,F:Wonder Woman 7.00
159 JAp,A:Ras al Ghul 7.00
160 JAp,F:Supergirl 7.00
161 JAp,F:Adam Strange 7.00
162 JAp,F:Sgt.Rock 7.00
163 DG,F:Black Lightning 7.00
164 JL,F:Hawkman 7.00
165 DN,F:Man-bat 7.00
166 DG,TA,DSp,F:Black Canary
A:Penguin,I:Nemesis 7.00
167 DC,DA,F:Blackhawk 7.00
168 JAp,DSp,F:Green Arrow 5.25
169 JAp,DSp,F:Zatanna 5.00
170 JA,F:Nemesis 5.00
171 JL,DSp,V:Scalphunter 5.00
172 CI,F:Firestorm 5.00
173 JAp,F:Guardians 5.00
174 JAp,F:Green Lantern 5.00
175 JAp,A:Lois Lane 5.00
176 JAp,F:Swamp Thing 5.00
177 JAp,F:Elongated Man 5.00
178 JAp,F:Creeper 5.00
179 EC,F:Legion o/Superheroes . . . 5.00
180 JAp,F:Spectre,Nemesis 5.00
181 JAp,F:Hawk & Dove 5.00
182 JAp,F:E-2 Robin 5.00
183 CI,V:Riddler 6.00
184 JAp,A:Catwoman 6.00
185 F:Green Arrow 5.00
186 JAp,F:Hawkman 5.00
187 JAp,F:Metal Men 5.00
188 JAp,F:Rose & Thorn 5.00
189 JAp,A:Thorn 5.00
190 JAp,F:Adam Strange 5.00
191 JAp,V:Joker,Penguin 9.00
192 JAp,F:Superboy 5.00
193 JAp,D:Nemesis 5.00
194 CI,F:Flash 5.00
195 JA,I:Vampire 5.00
196 JAp,F:Ragman 5.00
197 JSon,W:Earth II Batman &
Catwoman 5.00
198 F:Karate Kid 5.00
199 RA,F:Spectre 5.00
200 DGb,JAp,A:Earth-2 Batman,I:
Outsiders (GeoForce,Katana,Halo),
E:Batman T.U.,final issue 12.00

[Limited Series]

1 SAP,Green Arrow/Butcher T.U. . . 2.00
2 SAP,A:Black Canary,Question. . . 2.00
3 SAP,Green Arrow/Butcher. 2.00
4 SAP,GA on Trial;A:Black
Canary 2.00
5 SAP,V:Native Canadians,I.R.A. . . 2.00

BREATHTAKER

1990

1 I:Breathtaker(Chase Darrow) . . . 6.00
2 Chase Darrow captured 6.00
3 O:Breathtaker 6.00
4 V:The Man, final issue 4.95
TPB Breathtaker 15.00

BRAINBANX

DC/Helix Jan., 1997

1 ELe(s),"Down Upon the
Darkness" 2.50
2 ELe(s),Anna flees to the Sheol . . 2.50
3 Ele(s),Anna stranded 2.50
4 ELe(s),Anna & Logan 2.50
5 ELe(s),"To Enter the Kingdom" . . 2.50
6 (of 6) 2.50

BRAVE OLD WORLD

DC/Vertigo Dec., 1999

1 (of 4) BML,GyD,PhH,Y2K story. . 2.50
2 BML,GyD,PhH 2.50
3 BML,GyD,PhH 2.50
4 BML,GyD,PhH 2.50

BROTHER POWER, THE GEEK

Sept.–Oct., 1968

1 . . . . 45.00
2 Nov.–Dec., 1968 . . . . 25.00

Bugs Bunny #2 © DC Comics Inc.

BUGS BUNNY

1990

1 A:Bugs,Daffy,Search for Fudd
Statues 2.00
2 Search for Statues cont.
V:WitchHazel 2.00
3 Bugs&Co.in outer space, final. . . 2.00

BUGS BUNNY & FRIENDS: A COMIC CELEBRATION

Warner Bros./DC May, 2000

TPB 14.95

BUTCHER, THE

[Limited Series] 1990

1 MB,I:John Butcher 3.50
2 MB,in San Francisco 3.00
3 MB,V:Corporation 3.00
4 MB,A:Green Arrow 2.50
5 MB,A:Corvus,final issue 2.25

BUZZY

1944–58

1 . . . . 175.00
2 . . . . 80.00
3 thru 5 . . . . @45.00
6 thru 10 . . . . @40.00
11 thru 15 . . . . @30.00
16 thru 25 . . . . @30.00
26 thru 35 . . . . @25.00
36 thru 45 . . . . @20.00
46 thru 77 . . . . @20.00

CAMELOT 3000

Dec., 1982

1 BB,O:Arthur,Merlin 3.50
2 BB,A:Morgan LeFay 3.00
3 BB,J:New Knights. 3.00
4 BB,V:McAllister. 3.00
5 BB,O:Morgan Le Fay 3.00
6 BB,TA,W:Arthur 3.00
7 BB,TA,R:Isolde 3.00
8 BB,TA,D:Sir Kay 3.00
9 BB,TA,L:Sir Percival 3.00
10 BB,TA,V:Morgan Le Fay 3.00
11 BB,TA,V:Morgan Le Fay. 3.00
12 BB,TA,D:Arthur 3.00

CAPTAIN ACTION

[Based on toy] Oct.–Nov., 1968

1 WW,I:Captain Action,Action Boy,A:Superman. 100.00
2 GK,WW, V:Krellik 50.00
3 GK,I:Dr.Evil. 50.00
4 GK,A:Dr.Evil 50.00
5 GK,WW,A:Matthew Blackwell, last issue 50.00

Captain Atom #43 © DC Comics, Inc.

CAPTAIN ATOM

March, 1987

1 PB,O:Captain Atom 3.00
2 PB,C:Batman 2.00
3 PB,O:Captain Atom 2.00
4 PB,A:Firestorm 2.00
5 PB,A:Firestorm 2.00
6 PB,Dr.Spectro. 2.00
7 R:Plastique. 2.00
8 PB,Capt.Atom/Plastique 2.00
9 V:Bolt 2.00
10 PB,A:JLI 2.50
11 PB,A:Firestorm 2.00
12 PB,I:Major Force 2.00
13 PB,Christmas issue 2.00
14 PB,A:Nightshade 2.00
15 PB,Dr.Spectro, Major Force 2.00
16 PB,A:JLI,V:Red Tornado 2.00
17 V:Red Tornado;A:Swamp Thing,JLI 2.00
18 PB,A:Major Force 2.00
19 PB,Drug War 2.00
20 FMc,BlueBeetle 2.00
21 PB,A:Plastique,Nightshade 2.00
22 PB,A:MaxLord,Nightshade, Plastique 2.00
23 PB,V:The Ghost. 2.00
24 PB,Invasion X-over 2.00
25 PB,Invvasion X-over 2.00
26 A:JLA,Top Secret,pt.1 . . . . 2.00
27 A:JLA,Top Secret,pt.2 . . . . 2.00
28 V:Ghost, Top Secret,pt.3 . . . . . . 2.00
29 RT,Captain Atom cleared (new direction) 2.00
30 Janus Directive #11,V:Black Manta. 2.00
31 RT,Capt.Atom's Powers, A:Rocket Red. 2.00
32 Loses Powers 2.00
33 A:Batman 2.50
34 C:JLE 2.00
35 RT,Secret o/t Silver Shield, A:Major Force 2.00
36 RT,Las Vegas Battle,A:Major Force 2.00
37 I:New Atomic Skull. 2.00
38 RT,A:Red Tornado, Black Racer 2.00
39 RT,A:Red Tornado 2.00
40 RT,V:Kobra 2.00
41 RT,A:Black Racer, Red Tornado 2.00
42 RT,A:Phantom Stranger,Red Tornado,Black Racer, Death from Sandman 2.00
43 RT,V:Nekron 2.00
44 RT,V:Plastique 2.00
45 RT,A:The Ghost,I:Ironfire 2.00
46 RT,A:Superman 2.00
47 RT,A:SupermanV:Ghost. 2.00
48 RT,R:Red Tornado 2.00
49 RT,Plastique on trial. 2.00
50 RT,V:The Ghost,DoubleSize. . . . 3.00
51 RT. 2.00
52 RT,Terror on RTE.91' 2.00
53 RT,A:Aquaman 2.00
54 RT,A:Rasputin,Shadowstorm . . . 2.00
55 RT,Inside Quantum Field 2.00
56 RT,Quantum Field cont. 2.00
57 RT,V:ShadowStorm, Quantum.Field 2.00
Ann.#1 I:Maj.Force 2.00
Ann.#2 A:RocketRed,Maj.Force . . . 2.00

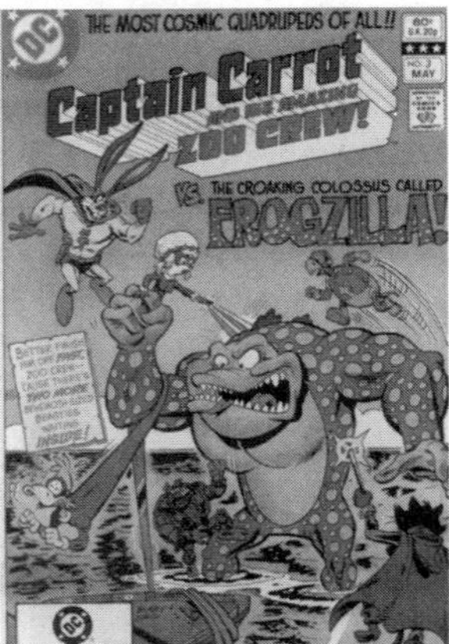

Captain Carrot #3 © DC Comics, Inc.

CAPTAIN CARROT

March, 1982

1 RA,A:Superman,Starro 2.00
2 AA 2.00
3 thru 19 . . . . @2.00
20 A:Changeling,Nov., 1983 . . . . . . 2.00

CAPTAIN STORM

May–June, 1964

1 IN(c),Killer Hunt 40.00
2 IN(c),First Shot-Last Shot 25.00
3 JKu,Death of a PT Boat 25.00
4 IN(c),First Command-Last Command 25.00
5 IN(c), Killer Torpedo 25.00
6 JKu,IN(c),Medals for an Ocean. 25.00
7 IN(c),A Bullet For The General . 25.00
8 IN(c),Death of A Sub 25.00
9 IN(c),Sink That Flattop 25.00
10 IN(c),Only The Last Man Lives. 25.00
11 IN(c),Ride a Hot Torpedo 25.00
12 JKu(c),T.N.T. Tea Party Abroad PT 47. . . . . 25.00
13 JKu,Yankee Banzai 25.00
14 RH(c),Sink Capt. Storm 25.00
15 IN(c),My Enemy-My Friend . . . 25.00
16 IN(c),Battle of the Stinging Mosquito 25.00
17 IN(c),First Shot for a Dead Man 25.00
18 March-April, 1967 . . . . 25.00

CARTOON NETWORK PRESENTS

Warner Bros./DC June, 1997

1: Dexter's Laboratory 2.00
2: Space Ghost coast-to-coast. . . . 2.00
3 Cartoon All-Stars 2.00
4 Dial `M' for Monkey 2.00
5 Birdman 2.00
6 Cow and Chicken 2.00
7 Wacky Racers 2.00
8 . . . . 2.00
9 Toonami 2.00
10 Cow and Chicken 2.00
11 Wacky Races. 2.00
12 Cartoon All-Stars 2.00
13 Toonami 2.00
14 Cow and Chicken 2.00
15 Wacky Races 2.00
16 Top Cat 2.00
17 Toonami 2.00
18 Cartoon All-Stars 2.00
19 Cow & Chicken 2.00
20 Secret Squirrel, Atom Ant 2.00
21 Toonami 2.00
22 Quick Draw McGraw 2.00
23 Jabberjaws 2.00
24 Scrappy Doo, final issue 2.00

CARTOON NETWORK STARRING

Warner Bros./DC 1999

1 F:Powerpuff Girls 2.00
2 F:Jonny Bravo 2.00
3 F:Cow & Chicken 2.00
4 F:Space Ghost 2.00
5 . . . . 2.00
6 F:Johnny Bravo 2.00
7 F:Cow & Chicken 2.00
8 F:Johnny Bravo 2.00
9 F:Space Ghost: Coast-to-Coast . 2.00
10 F:Cow & Chicken. 2.00
11 F:Johnny Bravo 2.00
12 F:Space Ghost: Coast-to-Coast . 2.00
13 F:Cow & Chicken. 2.00
14 F:Johnny Bravo 2.00
15 F:Space Ghost: Coast-to-Coast . 2.00
16 F:Cow & Chicken. 2.00

CATWOMAN

[Limited Series] 1989

1 O:Catwoman 8.00
2 Catwoman'sSister kidnapped . . . 6.00

3 Battle . . . 5.00
4 Final,V:Batman . . . 5.00

[Regular Series] 1993

0 JBa,O:Catwoman . . . 3.50
1 B:JDy(s),JBa,DG,A:Bane . . . 5.00
2 JBa,DG,A:Bane . . . 3.50
3 JBa,DG,at Santa Prisca . . . 3.50
4 JBa,DG,Bane's Secret . . . 3.00
5 JBa,V:Ninjas . . . 3.00
6 JBa,A:Batman . . . 3.00
7 JBa,A:Batman . . . 3.00
8 JBa,V:Zephyr . . . 3.00
9 JBa,V:Zephyr . . . 3.00
10 JBa,V:Arms Dealer . . . 3.00
11 JBa . . . 3.00
12 JBa,Knights End #6,A:Batman . . 5.00
13 JBa,Knights End,Aftermath#2 . . 3.00
14 JBa,Zero Hour . . . 3.00
15 JBa,new path . . . 3.00
16 JBa,Island forterss . . . 3.00
17 . . . 3.00
18 . . . 3.00
19 Amazonia . . . 3.00
20 Hollywood . . . 3.00
21 JBa(c&a)V:Movie Monster [new Miraweb format begins] . . 2.00
22 JBa(c&a) Family Ties,pt.1 . . . 2.00
23 Family Ties,pt.2 . . . 2.00
24 . . . 2.00
25 A:Robin,Psyba-Rats . . . 2.50
26 AlG,JBa,The Secret of the Universe,pt.2 (of 3) . . . 2.00
27 CDi,Underworld Unleashed tie-in 2.00
28 CDi,Catwoman enlists help . . . 2.00
29 CDi,A:Penguin . . . 2.00
30 . . . 2.00
31 . . . 3.00
32 CDi,JBa,Contagion,pt.9 . . . 3.00
33 CDi,JBa,Hellhound,pt.1 . . . 2.00
34 CDi,JBa,Hellbound,pt.2 (of 3) . . . 2.00
35 CDi,JBa . . . 2.50
36 CDi,JBa, Legacy, pt.2 x-over . . . 2.00
37 CDi,JBa, Panara, the Leopard Woman . . . 2.00
38 DgM(s),JBa,MPn,"Catwoman, Year One," pt.1 (of 3) . . . 2.00
39 DgM(s),JBa,MPn,"Catwoman, Year One," pt. 2 . . . 2.00
40 DgM(s),JBa,MPn,"Catwoman, Year One," pt. 3 . . . 2.00
41 DgM(s),JBa,I:MorelandMcShane 2.00
42 DgM(s),JBa,"Red Fang and Claw," pt.1 . . . 2.00
43 DgM(s),JBa,"Red Fang and Claw," pt.2 . . . 2.00
44 DgM(s),JBa,"Red Fang and Claw," pt.3 . . . 2.00
45 DgM(s),JBa,"Nine Deaths of the Cat" . . . 2.00
46 DgM(s),JBa,F:Two Face, pt.1 . . . 2.00
47 DgM(s),JBa,F:Two Face, pt.2 . . . 2.00
48 DgM(s),JBa,V:Morella, pt.1 . . . 2.00
49 DgM(s),JBa,V:Morella, pt. 2 . . . 2.00
50 DgM(s),JBa,V:Cybercat . . . 3.00
50a metallic cover, collectors ed. . . . 3.00
51 DgM(s),JBa,F:Huntress,pt.1 . . . 2.00
52 DgM(s),JBa,F:Huntress,pt.2 . . . 2.00
53 DgM(s),JBa,F:identity learned . . 2.00
54 JBa,improving security . . . 2.00
55 JBa, . . . 2.00
56 JBa,Cataclysm x-over,pt.6 . . . 2.00
57 JBa,Cataclysm, V:Poison Ivy . . . 2.00
58 JBa,F:Scarecrow, pt.1 . . . 2.00
59 JBa,F:Scarecrow, pt.2 . . . 2.00
60 JBa,F:Scarecrow, pt.3 . . . 2.00
61 JBa,Bank robbery . . . 2.00
62 JBa,A:Nemesis . . . 2.00
63 JBa,A:Batman & Joker, pt.1 . . . 2.00
64 JBa,A:Batman & Joker, pt.2 . . . 2.00
65 JBa,A:Batman & Joker, pt.3 . . . 2.00
66 JBa,I'll Take Manhattan,pt.1 . . . 2.00
67 JBa,I'll Take Manhattan,pt.2 . . . 2.00
68 JBa,I'll Take Manhattan,pt.3 . . . 2.00
69 JBa,I'll Take Manhattan,pt.4 . . . 2.00
70 JBa,I'll Take Manhattan,pt.5 . . . 2.00
71 JBa,I'll Take Manhattan,pt.6 . . . 2.00
72 JOs(s),JBa,A:Batman . . . 2.00
73 JOs(s),JBa,No Man's Land . . . 2.00
74 JOs(s),JBa,No Man's Land . . . 2.00
75 JOs(s),JBa,No Man's Land . . . 2.00
76 JOs(s),JBa,No Man's Land . . . 2.00
77 JOs(s),JBa,No Man's Land . . . 2.00
78 . . . 2.00
79 A:Batman . . . 2.00
80 going to jail . . . 2.00
81 solitary confinement . . . 2.00
82 payback time . . . 2.00
83 A:Batman,CommissionerGordon 2.25
84 F:Harley Quinn . . . 2.25
85 anger & revenge . . . 2.25
86 V:Banner . . . 2.25
87 NSH, from Catwoman's past . . . 2.25
Ann.#1 Elseworlds Story,A:Ra's Al Ghul . . . 2.95
Ann.#2 JBa(c&a) Year One Annuals, Young Selina Kyle . . . 3.95
Ann.#3 Legends of the Dead Earth . 2.95
Ann.#4 Pulp Heroes (Macabre) . . . 3.95
Spec. Catwoman Defiant,TGr,DG, V:Mr.Handsome . . . 6.00
Spec. Catwoman Plus, LKa,AWi, ALa, F:Screamqueen (1997) . . . 3.00
Spec.#1,000,000 JBa, on prison planet of Pluto . . . 2.00
TPB The Catfile, rep.#15–#19 . . . 10.00

CATWOMAN: GUARDIAN OF GOTHAM

1999

1 (of 2) Elseworlds,V:Bat-Man . . . 6.00
2 DgM,JBa . . . 6.00

CATWOMAN/WILDCAT

June, 1998

1 (of 4) CDi,TP,SCi,BSf, V:Claw Hammer . . . 2.50
2 CDi,BSt,TP,SCi,BSf . . . 2.50
3 CDi,BSt,TP,SCi,BSf, . . . 2.50
4 CDi,BSt,TP,SCi,BSf . . . 2.50

CENTURIONS

June, 1987

1 DH,V:Doc Terror . . . 2.00

Chain Gang War #1 © DC Comics Inc.

2 DH,O:Centurions . . . 2.00
3 DH,V:Doc Terror . . . 2.00
4 DH,Sept., 1987 . . . 2.00

CHAIN GANG WAR

1993–94

1 I:Chain Gang . . . 2.50
2 V:8-Ball . . . 2.00
3 C:Deathstroke . . . 2.00
4 C:Deathstroke . . . 2.00
5 Embossed(c),A:Deathstroke . . . 2.50
6 A:Deathstroke,Batman . . . 2.00
7 V:Crooked Man . . . 2.00
8 B:Crooked Man . . . 2.00
9 V:Crooked Man . . . 2.00
10 A:Deathstroke,C:Batman . . . 2.00
11 A:Batman . . . 2.00
12 E:Crooked Man,D:Chain Gang, Final Issue . . . 2.00

CHALLENGERS OF THE UNKNOWN

1958–78

1 JK&JK(c),The Man Who Tampered With Infinity . . . 2,200.00
2 JK&JK(c),The Monster Maker . 800.00
3 JK&JK(c),The Secret of the Sorcerer's Mirror . . . 700.00
4 JK,WW,JK(c),The Wizard of Time . . . 550.00
5 JK,WW&JK(c),The Riddle of the Star-Stone . . . 550.00
6 JK,WW,JK(c),Captives of the Space Circus . . . 550.00
7 JK,WW,JK(c),The Isle of No Return . . . 550.00
8 JK,WW,JK&WW(c),The Prisoners of the Robot Planet 550.00
9 The Plot To Destroy Earth . . . 250.00
10 The Four Faces of Doom . . . 250.00
11 The Creatures From The Forbidden World . . . 175.00
12 The Three Clues To Sorcery . 175.00
13 The Prisoner of the Tiny Space Ball . . . 175.00
14 O: Multi Man . . . 175.00
15 Lady Giant and the Beast . . . 175.00
16 Prisoners of the Mirage World 150.00
17 The Secret of the Space Capsules . . . 150.00
18 Menace of Mystery Island . . . 150.00
19 The Alien Who Stole a Planet 150.00
20 Multi-Man Strikes Back . . . 150.00
21 Weird World That Didn't Exist. 150.00
22 The Thing In Challenger Mountain . . . 150.00
23 The Island In The Sky . . . 90.00
24 The Challengers Die At Dawn . 90.00
25 Captives of the Alien Hunter . . 90.00
26 Death Crowns The Challenge King . . . 90.00
27 Master of the Volcano Men . . . 90.00
28 The Riddle of the Faceless Man . . . 90.00
29 Four Roads to Doomsday . . . 90.00
30 Multi-Man...Villain Turned Hero . . . 90.00
31 O:Challengers . . . 90.00
32 One Challenger Must Die . . . 40.00
33 Challengers Meet Their Master 40.00
34 Beachhead, USA . . . 40.00
35 War Against The Moon Beast . 40.00
36 Giant In Challenger Mountain . . 40.00
37 Triple Terror of Mr. Dimension . 40.00
38 Menace the Challengers Made. 40.00
39 Phantom of the Fair . . . 40.00
40 Super-Powers of the Challengers . . . 40.00
41 The Challenger Who Quit . . . 20.00

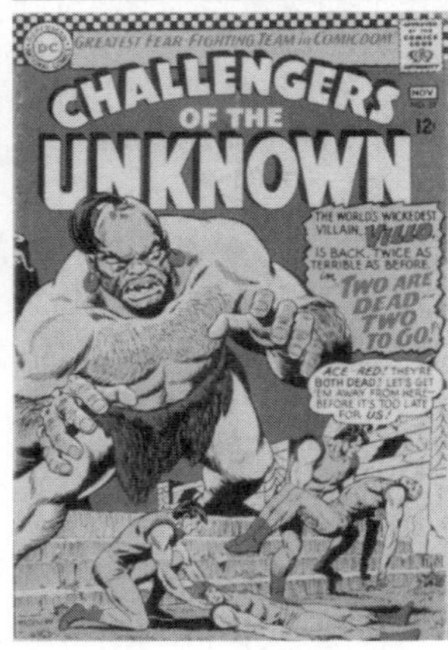

Challengers of the Unknown #52
© DC Comics, Inc.

42 The League of Challenger-Haters 20.00
43 New look begins 20.00
44 The Curse of the Evil Eye 20.00
45 Queen of the Challenger-Haters 20.00
46 Strange Schemes of the Gargoyle 20.00
47 The Sinister Sponge 20.00
48 A:Doom Patrol 20.00
49 Tyrant Who Owned the World . 20.00
50 Final Hours for the Challengers 20.00
51 A:Sea Devil 20.00
52 Two Are Dead - Two To Go . . . 20.00
53 Who is the Traitor Among Us? . 20.00
54 War of the Sub-Humans. 20.00
55 D:Red Ryan. 20.00
56 License To Kill 20.00
57 Kook And The Kilowatt Killer . . 20.00
58 Live Till Tomorrow 20.00
59 Seekeenakee - The Petrified Giant 20.00
60 R:Red Ryan. 20.00
61 Robot Hounds of Chang 20.00
62 Legion of the Weird 20.00
63 None Shall Escape the Walking Evil 20.00
64 JKu(c),Invitation to a Hanging . 20.00
65 The Devil's Circus 10.00
66 JKu(c),Rendezvous With Revenge 10.00
67 NA(c),The Dream Killers 10.00
68 NA(c),One of Us is a Madman . 10.00
69 JKu(c),I:Corinna. 10.00
70 NA(c),Scream of Yesterdays . . 10.00
71 NC(c),When Evil Calls 10.00
72 NA(c),A Plague of Darkness . . 10.00
73 NC(c),Curse of the Killer Time Forgot 10.00
74 GT&NA(c),A:Deadman. 20.00
75 JK(c),Ultivac Is Loose 7.00
76 JKu(c),The Traitorous Challenger 7.00
77 JK(c),Menace of the Ancient Vials 7.00
78 JK(c),The Island of No Return . . 5.00
79 JKu(c),The Monster Maker. 5.00
80 NC(c),The Day The Earth Blew Up 5.00
81 MN&NA(c),Multi-Man's Master Plan 5.00
82 MN&NA(c),Swamp Thing. 5.00
83 Seven Doorways to Destiny. . . . 5.00
84 To Save A Monster 5.00
85 The Creature From The End Of Time 5.00
86 The War At Time's End 5.00
87 final issue, July, 1978. . . . . 5.00

CHALLENGERS OF THE UNKNOWN

1991

1 BB(c) In The Spotlight 2.00
2 . . . . 2.00
3 Challengers `Split Up'. 2.00
4 `Separate Ways'. 2.00
5 Moffet. 2.00
6 GK(c),Challengers reunited. 2.00
7 AAd(c),June pregnant. 2.00
8 final issue. 2.00

CHALLENGERS OF THE UNKNOWN

1 StG(s),JPL 3.00
2 StG(s),LKa,JPL,SMa,Zombies . . 2.50
3 StG(s),JPL,death of Challenger . 2.50
4 StG&LKa(s),JPL,SMa, O:Challengers 2.50
5 StG&LKa(s)JPL,SMa, V:The Fearslayer 2.50
6 StG(s),JPL,SMa,"Convergence" pt. 3 x-over. 2.50
7 StG(s),JPL,"Past Perfect" pt.1 (of 3) 2.50
8 StG(s),JPL,"Past Perfect" pt.2. . . 2.50
9 StG(s),JPL,"Past Perfect"pt.3 . . . 2.50
10 StG(s),JIT,F:Brenda Ruskin 2.50
11 StG(s),JPL,in Gothan, pt.1 . . . . . 2.50
12 StG(s),JPL,in Gothan, pt.2. . . . . 2.50
13 StG(s),F:Marlon Corbett. 2.50
14 . . . . 2.50
15 StG(s),JPL,Millennium Giants pt. 3, x-over 2.75
16 StG(s),JPL,MZ, original Chalis . . 2.75
17 StG(s),JPL,disappearances 2.75
18 StG(s),DRo,MZ, final issue 2.75

CHASE

Dec., 1997

1 JWi,MGy,from Batman #550 . . . . 2.50
2 JWi,MGy 2.50
3 JWi,MGy,Rocket Reds 2.50
4 JWi,MGy,F:Teen Titans. 2.50
5 JWi,MGy,flashback story. 2.50
6 JWi,MGy,Chase's past 2.50
7 JWi,Shadowing the Bat,pt.1 . . . . 2.50
8 JWi,Shadowing the Bat,pt.2 . . . . 2.50
9 JWi,MBr,MGy,A:Green Lantern . . 2.50
Spec.#1,000,000 Final Issue. 2.50

CHECKMATE

April, 1988

1 From Vigilante & Action Comics . 3.00
2 Chicago Bombings cont. 2.00
3 V:Terrorist Right 2.00
4 V:Crime Lords Abroad,B.U.Story `Training of a Knight' begins . . . 2.00
5 Renegade nation of Quarac 2.00
6 Secret Arms Deal 2.00
7 Checkmate Invades Quarac 2.00
8 Consequences-Quarac Invasion . 2.00
9 Checkmate's security in doubt . . 2.00
10 V:Counterfeiting Ring. 2.00
11 Invasion X-over 2.00
12 Invasion Aftermath extra 2.00
13 CommanderH.Stein's vacation . . 2.00
14 R:Blackthorn 2.00
15 Janus Directive #1. . . . . 2.00
16 Janus Directive #3. . . . . 2.00
17 Janus Directive #6. . . . . 2.00
18 Janus Directive #9. . . . . 2.00
19 Reorganization of Group 2.00
20 `Shadow of Bishop' A:Peacemaker,pt.1 . . . . 2.00
21 Peacemaker behind Iron Curtain,pt.2 . . . . 2.00
22 Mystery of Bishop Cont.,pt.3 . . . 2.00
23 European Scientists Suicides,pt.4 . . . . 2.00
24 Bishop Mystery cont.,pt.5. . . . . . 2.00
25 Bishop's Identity Revealed. 2.00
26 Mazarin kidnaps H.Stein's kids . 2.00
27 Stein rescue attempt,I:Cypher . . 2.00
28 A:Cypher, Bishop-Robots. 2.00
29 A:Cypher,Blackthorn 2.00
30 Irish Knight W.O'Donnell/British Knight L.Hawkins team-up 2.00
31 V:Cypher International 2.00
32 V:Cypher International 2.00
33 final issue (32 pages). 2.00

CHIAROSCURO: THE PRIVATE LIVES OF LEONARDO DaVINCI

Vertigo 1995–96

1 Biographical, Adult 2.50
2 Two of Da Vinci Sisters. 2.50
3 . . . . 2.50
4 F:Salari 2.95
5 Crazy Leonardo 2.95
6 Salai schemes,O:Mona Lisa 2.95
7 V:Borgia & Machiavelli 2.95
8 daVinci returns to Florence 2.95
9 . . . . 2.95
10 finale 2.95

CHILDREN'S CRUSADE

Vertigo 1993–94

1 NGa(s),CBa,MkB(i),F:Rowland, Payne (From Sandman) 4.75
2 NGa(s),AaK(s),JaD(s),PSj,A:Tim Hunter,Suzy,Maxine,final issue . 4.50

CHRISTMAS WITH THE SUPER-HEROES

1988–89

1 JBy(c). 2.95
2 PC,GM,JBy,NKu,DG A:Batman Superman,Deadman,(last Supergirl appearance) 2.95

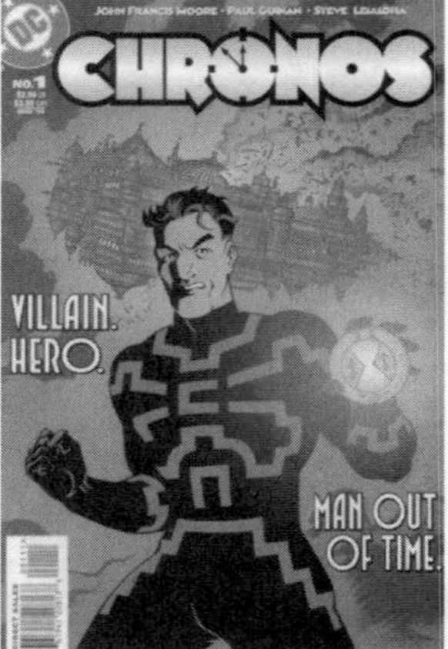

Chronos #1 © DC Comics, Inc.

CHRONOS

Jan., 1998

1 JFM,PGn,SL,Time Travel 2.50
2 JFM,PGn,SL. 2.50
3 JFM,PGn,SL, in 1873 . . . . 2.50
4 JFM,PGn,SL,in Chronopolis 2.50
5 JFM,PGn,DHz,SL,WalkerGabriel 2.50
6 JFM,PGn,Tattooed man 2.50
7 JFM,PGn,DRo,SL,Star City. 2.50
8 JFM,PGn,DRo,SL,
V:Metrognomes 2.50
9 JFM(s),PGn,SL, The Man
Who Chose Not to Exist 2.50
10 JFM(s),PGn,SL,Forever Engin . . 2.50
11 JFM(s),PGn,SL final issue 2.50
Spec.#1,000,000 JFM(s) Steals
time gauntlets. 2.50

CINDER & ASHE

March, 1988

1 JL,I:Cinder & Ashe 2.00
2 JL,Viet Nam Flashbacks 2.00
3 JL,Truth About Lacey revealed . . 2.00
4 JL,final issue, June, 1988 . . . . . . 2.00

CLASH

1991

1 AKu,I:Joe McLash(b/w). 4.95
2 AKu,Panja-Rise to Power 4.95
3 AKu,V:Archons,conclusion 4.95

CLAW THE UNCONQUERED

May–June, 1975

1 . . . . 3.50
2 . . . . 2.50
3 Nudity panel 2.50
4 . . . . 3.00
5 . . . . 2.50
6 . . . . 2.50
7 . . . . 2.50
8 KG 2.50
9 KG/BL,Origin 2.50
10 KG 2.50
11 KG 2.50
12 KG/BL,Aug.–Sept., 1978. . . . . . 2.50

COMET, THE

Impact 1991–92

1 TL,I&O:Comet I:Applejack, Victoria
Johnson, Ben Lee 3.00
2 TL,A:Applejack,Lance Perry 2.00
3 TL,V:Anti-nuclear terrorists 2.00
4 TL,I&V:Black Hood,I:Inferno 2.00
5 V:Cyborg Soldier 2.00
6 TL,I:The Hangman 2.00
7 `Press Problems' 2.00
8 TL,Comet ID discovered 2.00
9 TL,`Bad Judgment' 2.00
10 Fly/Comet T.U.,V:Dolphus 2.00
11 V:Inferno 2.00
12 V:Inferno 2.00
13 O:Comet's Powers. 2.00
14 O:Comet's Powers Pt.2 . . . . 2.00
15 Rob finds his mother 2.00
16 V:Aliens. 2.00
17 "Shocking Truth" 2.00
18 Last Issue 2.00
Ann.#1 Earthquest,w/trading card . . 2.50

COMIC CAVALCADE

1942–43

1 Green Lantern, Flash,
Wildcat, Wonder Woman,
Black Pirate 8,500.00
2 ShM,B:Mutt & Jeff 2,000.00
3 ShM,B:HotHarrigan,Sorcerer 1,300.00
4 Gay Ghost, A:Scribby,
A:Red Tornado 1,200.00
5 Green Lantern, Flash
Wonder Woman. 1,100.00
6 Flash, Wonder Woman
Green Lantern 900.00
7 A:Red Tornado, E:Scribby. . . . 900.00
8 Flash, Wonder Woman
Green Lantern. 900.00
9 Flash, Wonder Woman
Green Lantern 900.00
10 Flash, Wonder Woman
Green Lantern 900.00
11 Flash, Wonder Woman
Green Lantern. 750.00
12 E:Red, White & Blue 750.00
13 A:Solomon Grundy 1,200.00
14 Flash, Wonder Woman,
Green Lantern 750.00
15 B:Johnny Peril 800.00
16 Flash, Wonder Woman,
Green Lantern 750.00
17 Flash, Wonder Woman,
Green Lantern 750.00
18 Flash, Wonder Woman,
Green Lantern 750.00
19 Flash, Wonder Woman,
Green Lantern 750.00
20 Flash, Wonder Woman,
Green Lantern 750.00
21 Flash, Wonder Woman,
Green Lantern 750.00
22 A:Atom 750.00
23 A:Atom 750.00
24 A:Solomon Grundy. 850.00
25 A:Black Canary 600.00
26 ATh, E:Mutt & Jeff 600.00
27 ATh,ATh(c). 600.00
28 ATh E:Flash, Wonder Woman
Green Lantern 600.00
29 E:Johnny Peril 700.00
30 RG,B:Fox & Crow 350.00
31 thru 39 RG . . . . @175.00
40 RG,ShM 150.00
41 thru 49 RG,ShM . . . . @125.00
50 thru 62 RG,ShM . . . . @150.00
63 RG,ShM, July 1954 . . . . 250.00

CONGO BILL

Aug.–Sept., 1954

1 . . . . 750.00
2 . . . . 600.00
3 thru 6 . . . . 500.00
7 Aug.–Sept.,1955 . . . . @500.00

Congorilla #2 © DC Comics Inc.

CONGO BILL

Vertigo 1999

1 (of 4) RCo(c) 3.00
2 RCo(c) 3.00
3 RCo(c) 3.00
4 . . . . 3.00

CONGORILLA

1992–93

1 R:Congo Bill. 2.00
2 BB(c),V:Congo Bill 2.00
3 BB(c),V:Congo Bill 2.00
4 BB(c),V:Congo Bill 2.00

CONJURORS

1999

1 (of 3) CDi(s),EB, Elseworlds 3.00
2 CDi(s),EB, ... 3.00
3 CDi(s),EB, concl. 3.00

CONQUEROR OF THE BARREN EARTH

1985

1 thru 4 . . . . @2.00

COOL WORLD

1992

1 Prequel to Movie 2.00
2 Movie Adapt. 2.00
3 Movie Adapt. 2.00
4 . . . . 2.00

COPS

1988–89

1 PB,O:Cops,double-size. 2.00
2 PB,V:Big Boss 2.00
3 PB,RT,V:Dr.Bad Vibes 2.00
4 BS,A:Sheriff Sundown 2.00
5 PB,Blitz the Robo-Dog 2.00
6 PB,A:Ms.Demeaner 2.00
7 PB,A:Tramplor 2.00
8 PB,V:BigBoss & Ally 2.00
9 PB,Cops Trapped 2.00
10 PB,Dr.Bad Vibes becomes
Dr.Goodvibes 2.00
11 PB,V:Big Boss 2.00
12 PB,V:Dr.Badvibe's T.H.U.G.S . . . 2.00
13 Berserko/Ms.Demeanor
marriage proposal 2.00
14 A:Buttons McBoom-Boom 2.00
15 Cops vs. Crooks, final issue. . . . 2.00

COSMIC BOY

Dec., 1986

1 KG,EC,Legends tie-in 2.00
2 KG,EC,`Is History Destiny' 2.00
3 KG,EC,`Past,Present,Future' . . . 2.00
4 KG,EC,Legends 2.00

COSMIC ODYSSEY

1988

1 MMi,A:Superman,Batman,John
Stewart,Starfire,J'onnJ'onzz,
NewGods,Demon,JSn story . . . 4.00
2 MMi,`Disaster'(low dist) 5.00
3 MMi,Return to New Genesis 3.00
4 MMi,A:Dr.Fate, final 3.00

Crusaders #1 © DC Comics, Inc.

CREATURE COMMANDOS
March, 2000

1 (of 8) TT,SEa, ... 2.50
2 TT,SEa,V:Saturna 2.50
3 TT,SEa, ... 2.50
4 TT,SEa, ... 2.50
5 TT,SEa,F:Claw 2.50
6 TT,SEa,V:Saturna 2.50
7 TT,SEa,V:Claw 2.50
8 TT,SEa,War Movie, concl. 2.50

CREEPER, THE
Oct., 1997

1 LKa,SMa,SB,R:Creeper 2.50
2 LKa,SMa,SB,A:Dr. Skolos 2.50
3 LKa,SMa,SB,V:Proteus 2.50
4 LKa,SMa,SB 2.50
5 LKa,SMa,SB, new job 2.50
6 LKa,SMa,SB, strange meals 2.50
7 LKa,SMa,SB,F:Joker, pt.1 . . . . . . 2.50
8 LKa,SMa,SB,F:Joker, pt.2 . . . . . . 2.50
9 DAn,ALa,All-star issue 2.50
10 LKa,SB,Jack Ryder 2.50
11 LKa,SB,SMa,Creeper splits again 2.50
Spec.#1,000,000 LKa,SB,final issue 2.50

CRIMSON AVENGER
1988

1 Mini-series 2.00
2 V:Black Cross 2.00
3 `V:Killers of the Dark Cross' 2.00
4 `V:Dark Cross,final issue 2.00

CRISIS ON INFINITE EARTHS
April, 1985

1 B:MWn(s),GP,DG,I:Pariah,I&O:Alex Luthor,D:Crime Syndicate 7.00
2 GP,DG,V:Psycho Pirate, A:Joker,Batman 6.00
3 GP,DG,D:Losers 5.00
4 GP,D:Monitor,I:2nd Dr.Light 5.00
5 GP,JOy,I:Anti-Monitor 5.00
6 GP,JOy,I:2nd Wildcat,A:Fawcett, Quality & Charlton heroes 5.00
7 GP,JOy,DG,D:Supergirl 7.00
8 GP,JOy,D:1st Flash 9.00
9 GP,JOy,D:Aquagirl 4.00
10 GP,JOy,D:Psimon,A:Spectre . . . 4.00
11 GP,JOy,D:Angle Man 5.00
12 E:MWn(s),GP,JOy,D:Huntress,Kole, Kid Flash becomes 2nd Flash, D:Earth 2 . . . . 5.00

CRUCIBLE
Impact 1993

1 JQ,F:The Comet 2.00
2 JQ,A:Black Hood,Comet 2.00
3 JQ,Comet Vs.Black Hood 2.00
4 JQ,V:Tomorrow Men 2.00
5 JQ,Black Hod vs Shield 2.00
6 JQ,V:The Crucible 2.00

CRUEL AND UNUSUAL
Vertigo 1999

1 (of 4) JaD&TPe(s),JMC,satire . . . 3.00
2 thru 4 JaD&TPe(s),JMC . . . . . @3.00

CRUSADERS
Impact May, 1992

1 DJu(c),I:Crusaders,inc Trading cards 2.00
2 V:Kalathar 2.00
3 V:Kalathar 2.00
4 Crusaders form as group 2.00
5 V:Cyber-Punks 2.00
6 V:Cyborg Villains 2.00
7 Woj,Low,F:Fireball 2.00
8 Last Issue 2.00

CYBERELLA
DC/Helix Sept., 1996

1 HC(s),DCn, ... 2.25
2 HC(s),DCn,Secret history revealed 2.25
3 HC(s),DCn,Sunny goes on rampage 2.25
4 HC(s),DCn,Attack on MacroCorp 2.25
5 HC(s),DCn,V:Army of Necronauts 2.25
6 HC(s),DCn, ... 2.25
7 HC(s),DCn,Trip to Hell 2.25
8 HC(s),DCn,V:BTIII, concl. 2.50
9 DCn, The Informers 2.25
10 HC(s),DCn,Wuvzums, Digitina,pt.1 . . . . 2.25
11 HC(s),DCn,Wuvzums,pt.2 . . . . . 2.25
12 HC(s),final issue 2.50

DALE EVANS COMICS
1948–52

1 Ph(c),ATh,B:Sierra Smith 800.00
2 Ph(c),ATh 400.00
3 ATh 225.00
4 thru 11 . . . . @225.00
12 thru 24 . . . . @125.00

DAMAGE
1994–96

1 I:Damage,V:Metallo 2.00
2 V:Symbolix 2.00
3 V:Troll 2.00
4 V:Troll 2.00
5 A:New Titans,V:Baron 2.25
6 Zero Hour,A:New Titans 2.25
7 Trial 2.00
8 Fragments,pt.1 . . . . 2.00
9 Fragments,pt.2 . . . . 2.00
10 Fragments,pt.3 . . . . 2.00
11 Fragments,pt.4 . . . . 2.00
12 Fragments,pt.5 . . . . 2.00
13 Picking Up The Pieces,pt.1 . . . . 2.25
14 Picking Up The Pieces,pt.2 A:The Ray 2.25
15 Picking Up the Pieces,pt.3 . . . . . 2.25
16 . . . . 2.25
17 V:Bounty 2.25
18 Underworld Unleashed tie-in . . . 2.25
19 Underworld Unleashed tie-in . . . 2.25
20 final issue 2.25

DANGER TRAIL
July–Aug., 1950

1 CI,Ath,I:King For A Day 950.00
2 ATh 700.00
3 ATh 1,000.00
4 ATh 600.00
5 March-April, 1951 . . . . 600.00

DANGER TRAIL

1 thru 4 CI,FMc,F:King Faraday V:Cobra 2.00

DARK MANSION OF FORBIDDEN LOVE, THE
Sept.–Oct., 1971

1 . . . . 6.00
2 and 4 March-April, 1972 . . . . . @3.50

DARKSEID VS. GALACTUS: THE HUNGER

1 Orion vs. Silver Surfer 4.95
GN JBy,in Apokolips 6.00

DARKSTARS
1992–96

0 History 2.00
1 TC(c),LSn,I:Darkstars 3.50
2 TC(c),LSn,F:Ferin Colos 2.50
3 LSn,J:Mo,Flint,V:Evil Star 2.00
4 TC,V:Evilstar 3.00
5 TC,A:Hawkman,Hawkwoman . . . 3.00
6 TC,A:Hawkman 2.50
7 TC,V:K'llash 2.00
8 F:Ferris Colos 2.00
9 Colos vs K'lassh 2.00
10 V:Con Artists 2.00
11 TC,Trinity#4,A:Green Lantern, L.E.G.I.O.N. 2.00
12 TC(c),Trinity#7,A:Green Lantern, L.E.G.I.O.N. 2.00
13 TC(c),V:Alien Underworld 2.00
14 I:Annihilator 2.00
15 V:Annihilator 2.00
16 V:Annihilator 2.00

Darkstars #7 © DC Comics, Inc.

All comics prices listed are for *Near Mint* condition.

17 Murders 2.00
18 B:Eve of Destruction 2.00
19 A:Flash 2.00
20 E:Eve of Destruction 2.00
21 A:John Stewart,Donna Troy 2.00
22 A:Controllers 2.25
23 Donna Troy is new Darkstar. . . . 2.25
24 Zero Hour,V:HalJordan,Entropy . 2.25
25 Stewart 2.25
26 Alien criminals 2.25
27 and 28 . . . . @2.00
29 V:Alien Syndicate. 2.00
30 A:Green Lantern 2.00
31 V:Darkseid. 2.25
32 Crimelord/Syndicate War,pt.3, A:New Titans,Supergirl, Deathstroke 2.25
33 V:Jeddigan 2.25
34 . . . . 2.25
35 A:Flash 2.25
36 MkF,MC,A:Flash 2.25
37 MkF,MC,Colos vs. Warrior 2.25
38 final issue 2.25

DAY OF JUDGMENT

Sept., 1999

1 (of 5) Spectre x-over. 2.95
2 F:Wonder Woman, Supergirl. . . . 2.50
3 F:Superman & Green Lantern. . . 2.50
4 F:Superman's team 2.50
5 conclusion 2.50
Spec. Secret Files #1 . . . . 4.95

DC CHALLENGE

Nov., 1985

1 GC,Batman 2.50
2 Superman 2.00
3 CI,Adam Strange 2.00
4 GK/KJ,Aquaman. 2.00
5 DGb,Dr.Fate,Capt.Marvel 2.00
6 Dr. 13. . . . . 2.00
7 Gorilla Grodd 2.00
8 DG,Outsiders, New Gods 2.00
9 New Teen Titans,JLA 2.00
10 CS,New Teen Titans,JLA 2.00
11 KG,Outsiders. 2.00
12 DCw,TMd,DSp,New Teen Titans, Oct., 1986 . . . . 2.50

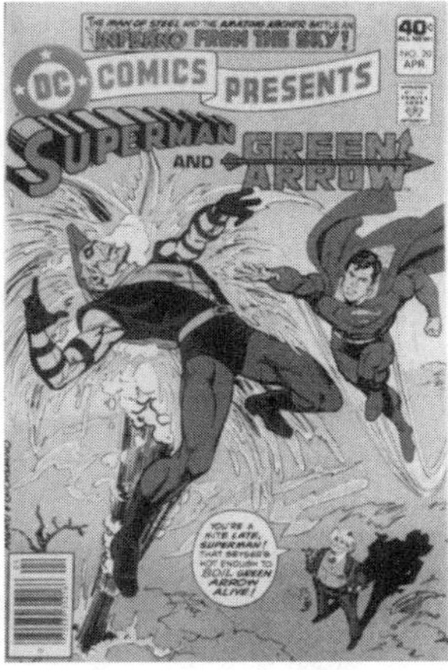

DC Comics Presents #20
© DC Comics Inc.

DC COMICS PRESENTS

July–Aug., 1978

[all have Superman]

1 JL,DA,F:Flash. 7.00
2 JL,DA,F:Flash. 4.00
3 JL,F:Adam Strange. 4.00
4 JL,F:Metal Men,A:Mr.IQ 4.00
5 MA,F:Aquaman 4.00
6 CS,F:Green Lantern 4.00
7 DD,F:Red Tornado 4.00
8 MA,F:Swamp Thing 4.00
9 JSon,JA,RH,F:Wonder Woman. . 4.00
10 JSon,JA,F:Sgt.Rock. 4.00
11 JSon,F:Hawkman. 3.00
12 RB,DG,F:Mr.Miracle. 3.00
13 DD,DG,F:Legion 4.00
14 DD,DG,F:Superboy 3.00
15 JSon,F:Atom,C:Batman 3.00
16 JSon,F:Black Lightning 3.00
17 JL,F:Firestorm 3.00
18 DD,F:Zatanna 3.00
19 JSon,F:Batgirl 3.50
20 JL,F:Green Arrow 2.50
21 JSon,JSa,F:Elongated Man 2.50
22 DD,FMc,F:Captain Comet 2.50
23 JSon,F:Dr.Fate 2.50
24 JL,F:Deadman. 2.50
25 DD,FMc,F:Phantom Stranger. . . 2.50
26 GP,DG,JSn,I:New Teen Titans, Cyborg,Raven,Starfire A:Green Lantern. 15.00
27 JSn,RT,I:Mongul 4.00
28 JSn,RT,GK,F:Mongul 3.50
29 JSn,RT,AS,F:Spectre 3.50
30 CS,AS,F:Black Canary. 3.00
31 JL,DG,AS,F:Robin 3.00
32 KS,AS,F:Wonder Woman. 3.00
33 RB,DG,AS,F:Captain Marvel . . . 3.00
34 RB,DG,F:Marvel Family 3.00
35 CS,GK,F:Man-bat 3.00
36 JSn,F:Starman. 3.50
37 JSn,AS,F:Hawkgirl. 3.00
38 GP(c),DH,AS,DG,D:Crimson Avenger,F:Flash 3.00
39 JSon,AS,F:PlasticMan,Toyman . 3.00
40 IN,FMc,AS,F:Metamorpho 3.00
41 JL,FMc,GC,RT,I:New Wonder Woman,A:Joker 8.00
42 IN,FMc,F:Unknown Soldier 3.00
43 BB(c),CS,F:Legion. 3.00
44 IN,FMc,F:Dial H for Hero 3.50
45 RB,F:Firestorm 3.00
46 AS,I:Global Guardians 3.00
47 CS,I:Masters of Universe. 3.00
48 GK(c),AA,IN,FMc,F:Aquaman . . 3.00
49 RB,F:Shazam!,V:Black Adam. . . 3.00
50 KS,CS,F:Clark Kent. 3.00
51 AS,FMc,CS,F:Atom,Masters of the Universe. 3.00
52 KG,F:Doom Patrol, I:Ambush Bug 3.00
53 CS,TD,RA,DG,I:Atari Force 3.00
54 DN,DA,F:Gr.Arrow,Bl.Canary . . . 3.00
55 AS,F:Air Wave,A:Superboy 3.00
56 GK(c),F:Power Girl 3.00
57 AS,FMc,F:Atomic Knights 3.00
58 GK(c),AS,F:Robin,Elongated Man 3.00
59 KG,KS,F:Ambush Bug 3.00
60 GK(c),IN,TD,F:Guardians. 3.00
61 GP,F:Omac 3.00
62 GK(c),IN,F:Freedom Fighters. . . 3.00
63 AS,EC,F:Amethyst. 3.00
64 GK(c),AS,FMc,F:Kamandi 3.00
65 GM,F:Madame Xanadu 3.00
66 JKu,F:Demon 3.00
67 CS,MA,F:Santa Claus 3.00
68 GK(c),CS,MA,F:Vixen 3.00
69 IN,DJ,F:Blackhawk 3.00
70 AS,TD,F:Metal Men 3.00

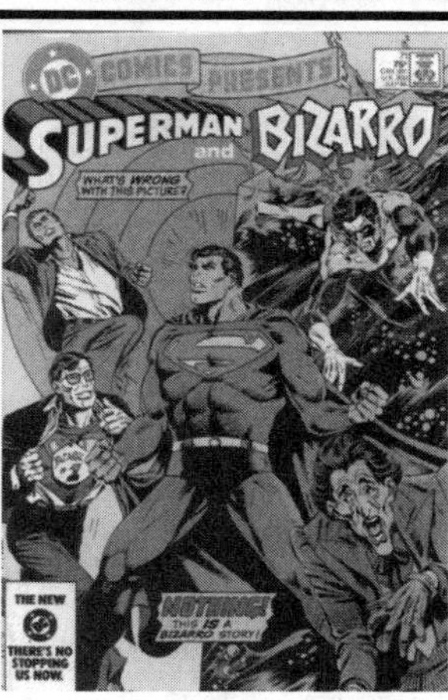

DC Comics Presents #71
© DC Comics, Inc.

71 CS,F:Bizarro 3.00
72 AS,DG,F:Phant.Stranger,Joker. . 5.00
73 CI,F:Flash 3.00
74 AS,RT,F:Hawkman 3.00
75 TMd,F:Arion. 3.00
76 EB,F:Wonder Woman 3.00
77 CS,F:Forgotten Heroes 5.00
78 CS,F:Forgotten Villains 5.00
79 CS,AW,F:Legion 3.00
80 CS,F:Clark Kent. 3.00
81 KG,BO,F:Ambush Bug. 3.00
82 KJ,F:Adam Strange 3.00
83 IN,F:Batman/Outsiders. 3.00
84 JK,ATh,MA,F:Challengers 3.00
85 RV,AW,AMo(s), F:Swamp Thing 7.00
86 Crisis,F:Supergirl 3.00
87 CS,AW,Crisis,I:Earth Prime Superboy 3.00
88 KG,Crisis,F:Creeper. 3.00
89 MMi(c),AS,F:Omega Men 3.00
90 DCw,F:Firestorm,Capt.Atom. . . . 3.00
91 CS,F:Captain Comet 3.00
92 CS,F:Vigilante 3.00
93 JSn(c),AS,KS,F:Elastic Four . . . 3.00
94 GP(c),TMd,DH,Crisis,F:Lady Quark,Pariah,Harbinger 3.00
95 MA(i),F:Hawkman 3.00
96 JSon,KS,F:Blue Devil. 3.00
97 RV,F:Phantom Zone Villians, final issue,double-sized 3.00
Ann.#1,RB,F:Earth 2 Superman . . . 3.00
Ann.#2 GK(c),KP,I:Superwoman . . . 2.00
Ann.#3 GK,F:Captain Marvel 2.00
Ann.#4 EB,JOy,F:Superwoman. . . . 2.00

DC/MARVEL: ALL ACCESS

October, 1996

sequel to DC Versus Marvel

1 (of 4) RMz(s),JG,JRu, crossover crisis again, 48pg 4.00
2 RMz(s),JG,JRu,F:Jubilee,Robin, Daredevil,Two-Face 3.00
3 RMz(s),JG,JRu,F:Doctor Strange, X-Men 3.00
4 RMz(s),JG,JRu,48pg 3.50

DC/MARVEL CROSSOVER CLASSICS

TPB, rep. all x-overs 17.95

DC GRAPHIC NOVEL
Nov., 1983

1 JL,Star Raiders 8.00
2 Warlords 8.00
3 EC,Medusa Chain 8.00
4 JK,Hunger Dogs 15.00
5 Me and Joe Priest 8.00
6 Space Clusters 8.00

DC MILLENNIUM EDITIONS
Dec., 1999–2000

Action Comics #1 3.95
Action Comics #252 2.50
Adventure Comics #247 2.50
Adventure Comics #761 3.95
All-Star Comics #3 3.95
All-Star Comics #3, chromium
All-Star Western #10 2.95
Batman: Dark Knight Returns #1 5.95
The Brave and the Bold #28 2.50
The Brave and the Bold #85 2.50
Crisis on Infinte Earths #1 2.50
Detective Comics #27 3.95
Detective Comics #38 3.95
Detective Comics #327 2.50
Detective Comics #359 2.50
Detective Comics #395 2.50
Flash Comics #1 3.95
Flash #123 2.50
Gen 13 #1 2.50
Green Lantern/Green Arrow #76 2.50
Hellblazer #1 2.95
House of Mystery #1 2.50
House of Secrets #92 2.50
JLA #1 2.50
Justice League #1 2.50
Justice League #1, chromium
Kingdom Come #1 5.95
The Man of Steel #1 2.50
Military Comics #1 3.95
More Fun Comics #101 2.95
Mysterious Suspense #1 2.50
New Gods #1 2.50
New Teen Titans #1 2.50
Our Army at War #81 2.50
Plop! #1 2.50
Police Comics #1 3.95
Preacher #1 2.95
Saga of the Swamp Thing #21 2.50
Sandman #1 2.95
Sensation Comics #1 3.95
Showcase #22 2.50
Showcase #4 2.50
Spirit #1 3.95
Superman #1 3.95
Superman #1 Chromium edition
Superman #76 2.95
Superman #75 Death of Superman 2.50
Superman's Pal Jimmy Olsen #1 2.50
Watchmen #1 2.50
Whiz Comics #2 3.95
WildC.A.T.S #1 2.50
Wonder Woman 1st.Series #1 3.95
Wonder Woman #1 2.50
World's Finest Comics #71 2.50
Young Romance #1 2.95

DC ONE MILLION
1998

1 GMo(s),VS,in 853rd-century 3.00
2 GMo(s),VS,V:Hourman Virus 2.00
3 GMo(s),VS,V:Solaris 2.00
4 GMo(s),VS,finale 2.00
TPB series rep. 14.95

DC REPLICA EDITIONS
1999–2000

Justice Society of America 100-page Super Spectacular #1 6.95
Teen Titans Annual #1 (1967) 4.95
Sgt. Rock's Prize Battle Tales 80-pg. Giant 5.95

DC SCIENCE FICTION GRAPHIC NOVEL
1985–87

1 KG,Hell on Earth 7.00
2 Nightwings 7.00
3 Frost and Fire 7.00
4 Merchants of Venus 7.00
5 Metalzoic 7.00
6 MR,Demon-Glass Hand 7.00
7 Sandkings 7.00

DC SPECIAL
Oct.–Dec., 1968
[All reprint]

1 CI,F:Flash,Batman,Adam Strange, (#1 thru #21 reps) 40.00
2 F:Teen Titans 75.00
3 GA,F:Black Canary 45.00
4 Mystery 28.00
5 JKu,F:Viking Prince/Sgt.Rock 28.00
6 Wild Frontier 28.00
7 F:Strange Sports 28.00
8 Wanted 28.00
9 28.00
10 LAW 28.00
11 NA,BWr,F:Monsters 28.00
12 JKu,F:Viking Prince 28.00
13 F:Strange Sports 28.00
14 Wanted,F:Penguin/Joker 30.00
15 GA,F:Plastic Man 30.00
16 F:Super Heroes & Gorillas 12.00
17 F:Green Lantern 12.00
18 Earth Shaking Stories 12.00
19 F:War Against Gianta 12.00
20 Green Lantern 12.00
21 F:War Against Monsters 12.00
22 Three Musketeers 12.00
23 Three Musketeers 12.00
24 Three Musketeers 12.00
25 Three Musketeers 12.00
26 F:Enemy Ace(rep) 12.00
27 RB,JR,F:Captain Comet 12.00
28 DN,DA,Earth disasters 12.00
29 JSon,BL,O:JSA 12.00

DC SPECIAL SERIES
Sept., 1977

1 MN,DD,IN,FMc,JSon,JA,BMc, JRu,F:Batman,Flash,Green Lantern,Atom,Aquaman 11.00
2 BWr(c),BWr,F:Swamp Thing rep. 6.00
3 JKu(c),F:Sgt.Rock 8.00
4 AN,RT,Unexpected Annual 8.00
5 CS,F:Superman 8.00
6 BMc(i),Secret Society Vs.JLA 8.00
7 AN,F:Ghosts 8.00
8 RE,DG,F:Brave&Bold,Deadman 8.00
9 SD,RH,DAy,F:Wonder Woman 8.00
10 JSon,MN,DN,TA,Secret Origins, O:Dr.Fate 8.00
11 JL,KS,MA,IN,WW,AS,F:Flash 8.00
12 MK(c),RT,RH,TS,Secrets of Haunted House 8.00
13 JKu(c),RT,SBi,RE,F:Sgt.Rock 8.00
14 BWr(c),F:Swamp Thing rep. 8.00
15 MN,JRu,MR,DG,MGo, F:Batman 10.00
16 RH,D:Jonah Hex 35.00
17 F:Swamp Thing rep. 8.00
18 JK(c),digest,F:Sgt.Rock rep. 8.00
19 digest,Secret Origins O:Wonder Woman 8.00
20 BWr(c),F:Swamp Thing rep. 8.00
21 FM,JL,DG,RT,DA,F:Batman, Legion 18.00
22 JKu(c),F:G.I.Combat 8.00
23 digest size,F:Flash 8.00
24 F:Worlds Finest 8.00
25 F:Superman II,Photo Album 8.00
26 RA,F:Superman's Fortress 11.00
27 JL,DG,F:Batman vs.Hulk 22.00

DC Super-Stars #2 © DC Comics, Inc.

DC SUPER-STARS
1976–78

1 F:Teen Titans rep. 15.00
2 F:DC Super-Stars of Space 10.00
3 CS,F:Superman,Legion 10.00
4 DC,MA,F:Super-Stars of Space 10.00
5 CI,F:Flash rep. 10.00
6 MA,F:Super-Stars of Space 10.00
7 F:Aquaman rep. 10.00
8 CI,MA,F:Adam Strange 12.00
9 F:Superman rep. 10.00
10 DD,FMc,F:Superhero Baseball Special,A:Joker 12.00
11 GM,Super-Stars of Magic 10.00
12 CS,MA,F:Superboy 10.00
13 SA 18.00
14 RB,BL,JA,JRu,Secret Origins 10.00
15 JKu(c),RB,RT(i),War Heroes 10.00
16 DN,BL,I:Star Hunters 10.00
17 JSon,MGr,BL,I&O:Huntress,O:Gr. Arrow,D:EarthII Catwoman 15.00
18 RT,DG,BL,F:Deadman,Phantom Stranger 15.00

DC TWO THOUSAND
July, 2000

1 (of 2) TPe,VS 6.95
2 TPe,VS,JLA & Golden age JSA 6.95

DC UNIVERSE HEROES
1998

Secret Files #1 5.00

DC UNIVERSE HOLIDAY BASH

1-shot, yuletide tales 3.95
3 64-pg 5.00
Holiday Bash II, GN stories, 64pg. 4.00

DC UNIVERSE: TRINITY
1993
1 TC,GeH,BKi,F:Darkstars,Green Lantern,L.E.G.I.O.N.,V:Triarch . 3.50
2 BKi,SHa,F:Darkstars,Green Lantern, L.E.G.I.O.N.,V:Triarch. 3.50

DC UNIVERSE VILLAINS
1999
Secret Files #1 . . . . 5.00

DC VS. MARVEL
1996
1 RMz 5.50
1 2nd printing 4.00
2 & 3 see Marvel
4 PDa 5.00

DEAD CORPS(e)
DC/Helix (July, 1998)
1 StP, C.J.Rataan 2.50
2 StP, CJ becomes an expired 2.50
3 StP,Death is not the end 2.50
4 StP, conclusion 2.50

DEADENDERS
DC/Vertigo Jan., 2000
1 WaP,Stealing the Sun,pt.1 . . . . . 2.50
2 WaP,Stealing the Sun,pt.2 . . . . . 2.50
3 WaP,Stealing the Sun,pt.3 . . . . . 2.50
4 WaP,Stealing the Sun,pt.4 . . . . . 2.50
5 WaP,Now and Then,pt.1 . . . . 2.50
6 WaP,Now and Then,pt.2 . . . . 2.50
7 WaP,Now and Then,pt.3 . . . . 2.50
8 WaP,scooter races 2.50
9 More Fun in New World,pt.1 . . . . 2.50
10 More Fun in New World,pt.2 . . . 2.50
TPB Stealing the Sun, rep. 9.95

DEADMAN
May, 1985
1 CI,NA,rep 3.00
2 NA,rep. 3.00
3 NA,rep. 2.50
4 NA,rep. 2.50
5 NA,rep. 2.50
6 NA,rep. 2.50
7 NA,rep.Nov., 1985. . . . . 2.50

[Mini-Series] 1986
1 JL,A:Batman. 2.50
2 JL,V:Sensei,A:Batman 2.00
3 JL,D:Sensei 2.00
4 JL,V:Jonah, final issue 2.00

DEADMAN: EXORCISM
[Limited-Series] 1992
1 KJo,A:Phantom Stranger 5.25
2 KJo,A:Phantom Stranger 5.25

DEADMAN: LOST SOULS
TPB Mike Baron, Kelly Jones 19.95

DEADMAN: LOVE AFTER DEATH
1989–90
1 KJo,Circus of Monsters. 4.25
2 KJo,Circus of Monsters. 4.25

DEADSHOT
1988–89
1 LMc,From Suicide Squad 2.00
2 LMc,Search for Son 2.00
3 LMc,V:Pantha. 2.00
4 LMc,final issue 2.00

DEATH GALLERY
Vertigo
1 DMc(c),NGa Death Sketch Various Pinups 3.50

DEATH: THE HIGH COST OF LIVING
Vertigo 1993
1 B:NGa(s),CBa,MBu(i),Death becomes Human,A:Hettie 9.00
1a Platinum Ed. 18.00
2 CBa,MBu(i),V:Eremite,A:Hettie . . 4.50
3 E:NGa(s),CBa,MBu(i),V:Eremite, A:Hettie 3.50
3a Error Copy 7.00
HC 19.95
TPB w/Tori Amos Intro 12.95

DEATH: THE TIME OF YOUR LIFE
Vertigo 1995
1 NGa,MBu,four-issue miniseries. . 2.95
2 NGa,MBu,F:Foxglove 2.95
3 NGa,MBu,conclusion 2.95
HC NGa(s),rep. #1–#4 . . . . 19.95
TPB NGa(s),rep.. . . . . 12.95

DEATHSTROKE: THE TERMINATOR
1991–94
1 MZ(c),(from New Teen Titans) SE,I:2nd Ravager. 4.00
1a Second Printing,Gold 3.00
2 MZ(c),SE,Quraci Agents 3.50
3 SE,V:Ravager. 3.00
4 SE,D:2ndRavager(Jackel). 3.00
5 Winter Green Rescue Attempt . . 3.00
6 MZ(c),SE,B:City of Assassins, A:Batman 3.00
7 MZ(c),SE,A:Batman 2.50
8 MZ(c),SE,A:Batman 2.00
9 MZ(c),SE,E:City of Assassins, A:Batman;I:2nd Vigilante 2.00
10 MZ(c),ANi,GP,A:2nd Vigilante . . 2.00
11 MZ(c),ANi,GP,A:2nd Vigilante. . . 2.00

Deathstroke the Terminator #17
© DC Comics Inc.

12 MGo,Short Stories re:Slade 2.00
13 SE,V:Gr.Lant.,Flash,Aquaman . . 2.00
14 ANi,Total Chaos#1,A:New Titans, Team Titans,V:Nightwing 2.00
15 ANi,Total Chaos#4,A:New Titans, Team Titans,I:Sweet Lili 2.00
16 ANi,Total Chaos#7. . . . . 2.00
17 SE,Titans Sell-Out #2 A:Brotherhood of Evil 2.00
18 SE,V:Cheshire,R:Speedy. 2.00
19 SE,V:Broth.of Evil,A:Speedy . . . 2.00
20 SE,MZ(c),V:Checkmate 2.00
21 SE,MZ(c),A:Checkmate 2.00
22 MZ(c),Quality of Mercy#1. . . . . . 2.00
23 MZ(c),Quality of Mercy#2. . . . . . 2.00
24 MZ(c),V:The Black Dome. 2.00
25 MZ(c),V:The Black Dome. 2.00
26 MZ(c),SE,in Kenya. 2.00
27 MZ(c),SE,B:World Tour, in Germany 2.00
28 MZ(c),SE,in France 2.00
29 KM(c),SE,in Hong Kong. 2.00
30 SE,A:Vigilante 2.00
31 SE,in Milwaukie 2.00
32 SE,in Africa 2.00
33 SE,I:Fleur de Lis 2.00
34 SE,E:World Tour 2.00
35 V:Mercenaries 2.00
36 V:British General 2.00
37 V:Assassin. 2.00
38 A:Vigilante. 2.25
39 A:Vigilante. 2.25
40 Wedding in Red. 2.25
Ann.#1 Eclipso,A:Vigilante 3.75
Ann.#2 SE,I:Gunfire 4.00
Ann.#3 Elseworlds Story. 4.25
TPB Full Circle rep#1-#4, New Titans#70 . . . . 12.95
Becomes:

DEATHSTROKE: THE HUNTED
1994–95
0 Slade 2.50
41 Bronze Tiger 2.25
42 Wounded. 2.25
43 . . . . 2.00
44 . . . . 2.00
45 A:New Titans. 2.00
Becomes:

DEATHSTROKE
1995–96
46 Checkmate,Wintergreen 2.00
47 I:New Vigilante 2.00
48 Crimelord/Syndicate War,pt.1 . . . 2.25
49 Crimelord/Syndicate War,pt.4 A:Supergirl, New Titans, Hawkman Blood Pack. 2.25
50 A:Titans,Outsiders,Steel. 3.50
51 No Fate or Future,pt.1 . . . . 2.25
52 No Fate or Future,pt.2 . . . . 2.25
53 The Borgia Plague,pt.1 . . . . 2.25
54 The Borgia Plague,pt.2 . . . . 2.25
55 MWn,Rebirth? 2.25
56 MWn,Night of the Karrion,pt.2 . . 2.25
57 . . . . 2.25
58 MWn,V:The Joker 2.25
59 MWn,F:Hellriders. 2.25
60 MWn,final issue 2.25

DEATHWISH
1994–95
1 New mini-series 2.50
2 F:Rahme 2.50
3 . . . . 2.50
4 V:Boots 2.50

Demon 2nd Series #15
© DC Comics, Inc.

DEMOLITION MAN

1993–94

1 thru 4 Movie Adapt 2.00

DEMON

[1st Regular Series] 1972–74

1 JK,I:Demon 15.00
2 JK 7.00
3 JK 6.00
4 JK 6.00
5 JK 6.00
6 JK 5.00
7 JK 5.00
8 JK 5.00
9 JK 5.00
10 JK 5.00
11 JK 5.00
12 JK 5.00
13 JK 5.00
14 JK 5.00
15 JK 5.00
16 JK 5.00

[Limited Series] 1987

1 MWg,B:Jason Blood's Case 2.00
2 MWg,Fight to Save Gotham 2.00
3 MWg,Fight to Save Gotham 2.00
4 MWg,final issue 2.00

[2nd Regular Series] 1990–95

0 Relationships 2.00
1 VS,A:Etrigan (32 pages) 3.00
2 VS,V:TheCrone 2.50
3 VS,A:Batman 2.25
4 VS,A:Batman 2.25
5 VS,ThePit 2.25
6 VS,In Hell 2.25
7 VS,Etrigan-King of Hell 2.25
8 VS,Klarion the Witch Boy 2.25
9 VS,Jason Leaves Gotham 2.25
10 VS,A:PhantomStranger 2.25
11 VS,A:Klarion,C:Lobo 2.50
12 VS,Etrigan Vs. Lobo 2.50
13 VS,Etrigan Vs. Lobo 2.50
14 VS,V:Odd Squad,A:Lobo 2.50
15 VS,Etrigan Vs.Lobo 2.50
16 VS,Etrigan & Jason Blood switch bodies 2.00
17 VS, War of the Gods x-over 2.00
18 VS,V:Wotan,A:Scape Goat. 2.00
19 VS,O:Demon,Demon/Lobo pin-up. 3.00
20 VS,V:Golden Knight 2.00
21 VS,Etrigan/Jason, A:Lobo,Glenda 2.00
22 MWg,V:Mojo & Hayden 2.25
23 VS,A:Robin 2.00
24 VS,A:Robin 2.00
25 VS,V:Gideon Ryme 2.00
26 VS,B:America Rules 2.00
27 VS,A:Superman. 2.00
28 VS,A:Superman. 2.00
29 VS,E:America Rules 2.00
30 R:Asteroth 2.00
31 VS(c),A:Lobo 2.00
32 VS(c),A:Lobo,W.Woman 2.00
33 VS(c),A:Lobo,V:Asteroth 2.00
34 A:Lobo. 2.00
35 A:Lobo,V:Belial 2.00
36 A:Lobo,V:Belial 2.00
37 A:Lobo,Morax 2.00
38 A:Lobo,Morax 2.00
39 A:Lobo. 2.00
40 New Direction,B:GEn(s). 3.50
41 V:Mad Bishop 2.50
42 V:Demons 2.25
43 A:Hitman 10.00
44 V:Gotho-Demon,A:Hitman 15.00
45 V:Gotho-Demon,A:Hitman 15.00
46 R:Haunted Tank. 2.50
47 V:Zombie Nazis 2.00
48 A:Haunted Tank,V:Zombie Nazis 2.00
49 b:Demon's Son,A:Joe Gun. 2.00
50 GEn(s). 3.00
51 GEn(s),Son & Lovers. 2.25
52 Etrigan & son–Hitman 4.00
53 Glenda & child–Hitman 4.00
54 Suffer the Children. 2.00
55 Rebellion 2.00
56 F:Etrigan 2.00
57 Last Stand. 2.00
58 Last issue 2.00
Ann.#1 Eclipso,V:Klarion. 3.25
Ann.#2 I:Hitman 15.00

DESTINY: A CHRONICLE OF DEATHS FORETOLD

DC/Vertigo (Sept., 1997)

1 (of 3) F:Destiny of the Endless . . 6.00
2 Destiny of the Endless, pt.2 . . . . 6.00
3 Destiny of the Endless, pt.3 . . . . 6.00
TPB series rep.. . . . . 14.95

DETECTIVE COMICS

March, 1937

1 I:Slam Bradley 65,000.00
2 JoS 15,000.00
3 JoS 10,000.00
4 JoS 6,500.00
5 JoS 6,000.00
6 JoS 4,500.00
7 JoS 4,500.00
8 JoS,Mr. Chang(c). 7,000.00
9 JoS 4,500.00
10 . . . . 4,500.00
11 . . . . 3,500.00
12 . . . . 3,500.00
13 . . . . 3,500.00
14 . . . . 3,500.00
15 . . . . 3,500.00
16 . . . . 3,500.00
17 I:Fu Manchu 3,500.00
18 Fu Manchu(c) 5,000.00
19 . . . . 3,000.00
20 I:Crimson Avenger 5,500.00
21 . . . . 3,000.00
22 . . . . 3,500.00
23 . . . . 3,000.00
24 . . . . 3,000.00
25 . . . . 3,000.00
26 . . . . 3,000.00

Detective #43 © DC Comics, Inc.

27 BK,I:Batman 180,000.00
28 BK,V:Frenchy Blake 16,000.00
29 BK,I:Doctor Death 28,000.00
30 BK,V:Dr. Death 6,000.00
31 BK,I:Monk 28,000.00
32 BK,V:Monk 5,500.00
33 O:Batman,V:Scarlet Horde 38,000.00
34 V:Due D'Orterre 4,500.00
35 V:Sheldon Lenox. 8,200.00
36 I:Hugo Strange 5,800.00
37 V:Count Grutt, last Batman solo 6,000.00
38 I:Robin, the Boy Wonder . . 33,000.00
39 V:Green Dragon 5,500.00
40 I:Clayface (Basil Karlo) 6,500.00
41 V:Graves. 3,000.00
42 V:Pierre Antal 2,000.00
43 V:Harliss Greer 2,000.00
44 Robin Dream Story 2,000.00
45 V:Joker 3,000.00
46 V:Hugo Strange 1,800.00
47 Meets Harvey Midas 1,800.00
48 Meets Henry Lewis 1,800.00
49 V:Clayface 1,800.00
50 V:Three Devils 1,800.00
51 V:Mindy Gang 1,200.00
52 V:Loo Chung. 1,200.00
53 V:Toothy Hare gang 1,200.00
54 V:Hook Morgan. 1,200.00
55 V:Dr. Death 1,200.00
56 V:Mad Mack 1,200.00
57 Meet Richard Sneed 1,200.00
58 I:Penguin 3,500.00
59 V:Penguin 1,500.00
60 V:Joker,I:Air Wave. 1,500.00
61 The Three Racketeers 1,200.00
62 V:Joker 2,000.00
63 I:Mr. Baffle 1,200.00
64 I:Boy Commandos,V:Joker . 3,800.00
65 Meet Tom Bolton. 2,500.00
66 I:Two-Face 3,000.00
67 V:Penguin 1,800.00
68 V:Two-Face. 1,500.00
69 V:Joker 1,500.00
70 Meet the Amazing Carlo . . . 1,000.00
71 V:Joker 1,200.00
72 V:Larry the Judge 900.00
73 V:Scarecrow 1,100.00
74 I:Tweedledum & Tweedledee . 900.00
75 V:Robber Baron 900.00
76 V:Joker 1,500.00
77 V:Dr. Matthew Thorne 900.00
78 V:Baron Von Luger. 900.00
79 `Destiny's' Auction 900.00
80 V:Two-Face. 1,000.00
81 I:Cavalier 750.00
82 V:Blackee Blondeen. 750.00

 All comics prices listed are for *Near Mint* condition.

83 V:Dr. Goodwin 775.00
84 V:Ivan Krafft. 750.00
85 V:Joker 1,000.00
86 V:Gentleman Jim Jewell. 700.00
87 V:Penguin 750.00
88 V:Big Hearted John 700.00
89 V:Cavalier 700.00
90 V:Capt. Ben 700.00
91 V:Joker 900.00
92 V:Braing Bulow 600.00
93 V:`Tiger' Ragland. 600.00
94 V:Lefty Goran 600.00
95 V:The Blaze. 600.00
96 F:Alfred 600.00
97 V:Nick Petri 600.00
98 Meets Casper Thurbridge. . . . 600.00
99 V:Penguin 900.00
100 V:Digger 1,000.00
101 V:Joe Bart 600.00
102 V:Joker 850.00
103 Meet Dean Gray 600.00
104 V:Fat Frank gang 600.00
105 V:Simon Gurlan 600.00
106 V:Todd Torrey. 600.00
107 V:Bugs Scarpis 600.00
108 Meet Ed Gregory 600.00
109 V:Joker 800.00
110 V:Prof. Moriarty 600.00
111 `Coaltown, USA' 600.00
112 `Case Without A Crime' 600.00
113 V:Blackhand. 600.00
114 V:Joker 800.00
115 V:Basil Grimes 600.00
116 A:Carter Nichols, Robin Hood 600.00
117 `Steeplejack's Slowdown' . . . 600.00
118 V:Joker 800.00
119 V:Wiley Derek 600.00
120 V:Penguin 1,600.00
121 F:Commissioner Gordon . . . 600.00
122 V:Catwoman 1,100.00
123 V:Shiner. 600.00
124 V:Joker 750.00
125 V:Thinker 575.00
126 V:Penguin 575.00
127 V:Dr. Agar 575.00
128 V:Joker 750.00
129 V:Diamond Dan mob 575.00
130. . . . . 575.00
131 V:`Trigger Joe' 475.00
132 V:Human Key. 475.00
133 Meets Arthur Loom 475.00
134 V:Penguin 500.00
135 A:Baron Frankenstein, Carter Nichols 500.00
136 A:Carter Nichols. 500.00
137 V:Joker 650.00
138 V:Joker,O:Robotman 900.00
139 V:Nick Bailey 500.00
140 I:Riddler 4,400.00
141 V:`Blackie' Nason. 500.00
142 V:Riddler 950.00
143 V:Pied Piper. 525.00
144 A:Kay Kyser (radio personality). 525.00
145 V:Yellow Mask mob 525.00
146 V:J.J. Jason 525.00
147 V:Tiger Shark. 525.00
148 V:Prof. Zero 525.00
149 V:Joker 800.00
150 V:Dr. Paul Visio 525.00
151 I&O:Pow Wow Smith 550.00
152 V:Goblin. 550.00
153 V:Slits Danton 650.00
154 V:Hatch Marlin 550.00
155 A:Vicki Vale 550.00
156 `The Batmobile of 1950' 550.00
157 V:Bart Gillis 500.00
158 V:Dr. Doom 500.00
159 V:T. Worthington Chubb 500.00
160 V:Globe-Trotter 500.00
161 V:Bill Waters 525.00
162 Batman on railroad. 525.00
163 V:Slippery Jim Elgin 525.00
164 Bat-signal story 525.00
165 `The Strange Costumes of Batman' 525.00
166 Meets John Gillen 525.00
167 A:Carter Nichols, Cleopatra . 525.00
168 O:Joker. 3,500.00
169 V:`Squint' Tolmar 525.00
170 Batman teams with Navy and Coast Guard 525.00
171 V:Penguin 700.00
172 V:Paul Gregorian 500.00
173 V:Killer Moth 500.00
174 V:Dagger. 500.00
175 V:Kangaroo Kiley 500.00
176 V:Mr. Velvet 500.00
177 Bat-Cave story. 400.00
178 V:Baron Swane 400.00
179 `Mayor Bruce Wayne'. 400.00
180 V:Joker 425.00
181 V:Human Magnet. 400.00
182 V:Maestro Dorn 400.00
183 V:John Cook 400.00
184 I:Firefly(Garfield Lynns) 400.00
185 `Secret's of Batman's Utility Belt' 400.00
186 `The Flying Bat-Cave' 400.00
187 V:Two-Face 425.00
188 V:William Milden 400.00
189 V:Styx 400.00
190 Meets Dr. Sampson, O:Batman. 575.00
191 V:Executioner 400.00
192 V: Nails Riley 400.00
193 V:Joker 425.00
194 V:Sammy Sabre. 400.00
195 Meets Hugo Marmon 400.00
196 V:Frank Lumardi 400.00
197 V:Wrecker 400.00
198 Batman in Scotland 400.00
199 V:Jack Baker 400.00
200 V:Brand Keldon 550.00
201 Meet Human Target 400.00
202 V:Jolly Roger 400.00
203 V:Catwoman 425.00
204 V:Odo Neral. 400.00
205 O:Bat-Cave 525.00
206 V:Trapper. 400.00
207 Meets Merko the Great 400.00
208 V:Groff. 400.00
209 V:Inventor 400.00
210 V:`Brain' Hobson 400.00
211 V:Catwoman 400.00
212 Meets Jonathan Bard. 400.00

Detective #99 © DC Comics Inc.

213 V:Mirror-Man 450.00
214 'The Batman Encyclopedia' . 400.00
215 I:Ranger, Legionairy, Gaucho & Musketeer,A:Knight & Squire (See World's Finest 89) 350.00
216 A:Brane Taylor 350.00
217 Meets Barney Barrows. 350.00
218 V:Dr. Richard Marston 350.00
219 V:Marty Mantee 350.00
220 A:Roger Bacon, historical scientist/philosopher 350.00
221 V:Paul King 350.00
222 V:`Big Jim' Jarrell. 350.00
223 V:`Blast' Varner 350.00
224. . . . . 350.00
225 I&O:Martian Manhunter (J'onn J'onzz) 6,000.00
226 O:Robin's costume, A:J'onn J'onzz 1,400.00
227 A:Roy Raymond, J'onn J'onzz 500.00
228 A:Roy Raymond, J'onnJ'onz 500.00
229 A:Roy Raymond, J'onnJ'onz 500.00
230 A:Martian Manhunter,I:Mad Hatter. 525.00
231 A:Batman,Jr.,Roy Raymond J'onn J'onzz 350.00
232 A:J'onn J'onzz 325.00
233 I&O:Batwoman 1,300.00
234 V:Jay Caird 325.00
235 O:Batman's Costume 600.00
236 V:Wallace Walby 400.00
237 F:Robin 325.00
238 V:Checkmate(villain) 325.00
239 Batman robot story. 325.00
240 V:Burt Weaver 325.00
241 The Rainbow Batman. 325.00
242 Batcave story. 275.00
243 V:Jay Vanney. 275.00
244 O:Batarang 275.00
245 F:Comm.Gordon 275.00
246. . . . . 275.00
247 I:Professor Milo 275.00
248. . . . . 275.00
249 V:Collector. 275.00
250 V:John Stannor 275.00
251 V:Brand Ballard 250.00
252 Batman in a movie 250.00
253 I:Terrible Trio 250.00
254 A:Bathound 250.00
255 V:Fingers Nolan 250.00
256 Batman outer-space story . . 250.00
257 Batman sci-fi story 250.00
258 Batman robot story. 250.00
259 I:Calendar Man 250.00
260 Batman outer space story . . 250.00
261 I:Dr. Double X 200.00
262 V:Jackal-Head 200.00
263 V:The Professor. 200.00
264. . . . . 200.00
265 O:Batman retold. 300.00
266 V:Astro. 200.00
267 I&O:Bat-Mite 250.00
268 V:"Big Joe" Foster 200.00
269 V:Director. 200.00
270 Batman sci-fi story 210.00
271 V:Crimson Knight,O:Martian Manhunter(retold) 210.00
272 V:Crystal Creature 210.00
273 A:Dragon Society 150.00
274 V:Nails Lewin. 150.00
275 A:Zebra-Man 150.00
276 A:Batmite. 150.00
277 Batman Monster story 150.00
278 A:Professor Simms 150.00
279 Batman robot story. 150.00
280 A:Atomic Man 150.00
281 Batman robot story. 125.00
282 Batman sci-fi story 125.00

Detective #258 © DC Comics, Inc.

283 V:Phantom of Gotham City. . 125.00
284 V:Hal Durgan 125.00
285 V:Harbin 125.00
286 A:Batwoman 125.00
287 A:Bathound 125.00
288 V:Multicreature. 125.00
289 A:Bat-Mite 125.00
290 Batman's robot story 125.00
291 Batman sci-fi story 125.00
292 Last Roy Raymond 125.00
293 A:Aquaman,J'onnJ'onzz. . . . 125.00
294 V:Elemental Men,
A:Aquaman 125.00
295 A:Aquaman 125.00
296 A:Aquaman 125.00
297 A:Aquaman 125.00
298 I:Clayface(Matt Hagen) . . . 250.00
299 Batman sci-fi stories. 100.00
300 I:Mr.Polka-dot,E:Aquaman . . 125.00
301 A:J'onnJ'onzz. 100.00
302 A:J'onnJ'onnz 80.00
303 A:J'onnJ'onnz 80.00
304 A:Clayface,J'onnJ'onz 80.00
305 Batman sci-fi story 80.00
306 A:J'onnJ'onnz 80.00
307 A:J'onnJ'onnz 80.00
308 A:J'onnJ'onnz 80.00
309 A:J'onnJ'onnz 80.00
310 A:Bat-Mite,J'onnJ'onnz. 80.00
311 I:Cat-Man,Zook 90.00
312 A:Clayface,J'onnJ'onnz 70.00
313 A:J'onnJ'onnz 70.00
314 A:J'onnJ'onnz 70.00
315 I:Jungle Man 70.00
316 A:Dr.DoubleX,J'onnJ'onz 70.00
317 A:J'onnJ'onnz 70.00
318 A:Cat-Man,J'onnJ'onnz 70.00
319 A:J'onnJ'onnz 70.00
320 A:Vicki Vale 70.00
321 I:Terrible Trio 75.00
322 A:J'onnJ'onnz 65.00
323 I:Zodiac Master,
A:J'onn J'onnz 65.00
324 A:Mad Hatter,J'onnJ'onnz . . . 65.00
325 A:Cat-Man,J'onnJ'onnz 65.00
326 Batman sci-fi story 65.00
327 CI,25th ann,symbol change . 125.00
328 D:Alfred,I:WayneFoundation. 125.00
329 A:Elongated Man 65.00
330 "Fallen Idol of Gotham" 65.00
331 A:Elongated Man 65.00
332 A:Joker 50.00
333 A:Gorla 50.00
334 . . . . 50.00
335 . . . . 50.00
336 . . . . 50.00

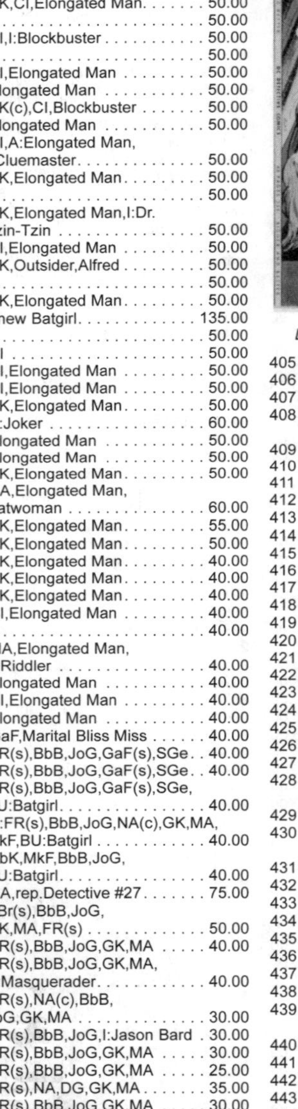

337 "Deep Freeze Menace 50.00
338 . . . . 50.00
339 . . . . 50.00
340 . . . . 50.00
341 A:Joker 60.00
342. . . . . 50.00
343 BK,CI,Elongated Man. 50.00
344. . . . . 50.00
345 CI,I:Blockbuster 50.00
346. . . . . 50.00
347 CI,Elongated Man 50.00
348 Elongated Man 50.00
349 BK(c),CI,Blockbuster 50.00
350 Elongated Man 50.00
351 CI,A:Elongated Man,
I:Cluemaster. 50.00
352 BK,Elongated Man. 50.00
353. . . . . 50.00
354 BK,Elongated Man,I:Dr.
Tzin-Tzin 50.00
355 CI,Elongated Man 50.00
356 BK,Outsider,Alfred 50.00
357. . . . . 50.00
358 BK,Elongated Man. 50.00
359 I:new Batgirl. 135.00
360. . . . . 50.00
361 CI 50.00
362 CI,Elongated Man 50.00
363 CI,Elongated Man 50.00
364 BK,Elongated Man. 50.00
365 A:Joker 60.00
366 Elongated Man 50.00
367 Elongated Man 50.00
368 BK,Elongated Man. 50.00
369 CA,Elongated Man,
Catwoman 60.00
370 BK,Elongated Man. 55.00
371 BK,Elongated Man. 50.00
372 BK,Elongated Man. 40.00
373 BK,Elongated Man. 40.00
374 BK,Elongated Man. 40.00
375 CI,Elongated Man 40.00
376. . . . . 40.00
377 MA,Elongated Man,
V:Riddler 40.00
378 Elongated Man 40.00
379 CI,Elongated Man 40.00
380 Elongated Man 40.00
381 GaF,Marital Bliss Miss 40.00
382 FR(s),BbB,JoG,GaF(s),SGe . 40.00
383 FR(s),BbB,JoG,GaF(s),SGe. . 40.00
384 FR(s),BbB,JoG,GaF(s),SGe,
BU:Batgirl. 40.00
385 E:FR(s),BbB,JoG,NA(c),GK,MA,
MkF,BU:Batgirl 40.00
386 BbK,MkF,BbB,JoG,
BU:Batgirl. 40.00
387 RA,rep.Detective #27 . . . . . . 75.00
388 JBr(s),BbB,JoG,
GK,MA,FR(s) 50.00
389 FR(s),BbB,JoG,GK,MA 40.00
390 FR(s),BbB,JoG,GK,MA,
A:Masquerader. 40.00

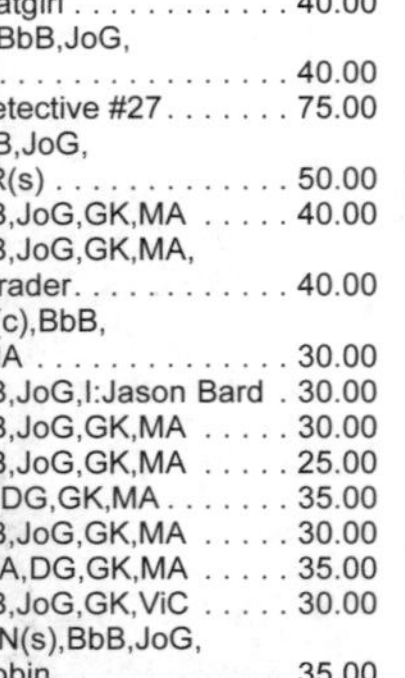

391 FR(s),NA(c),BbB,
JoG,GK,MA 30.00
392 FR(s),BbB,JoG,I:Jason Bard . 30.00
393 FR(s),BbB,JoG,GK,MA 30.00
394 FR(s),BbB,JoG,GK,MA 25.00
395 FR(s),NA,DG,GK,MA 35.00
396 FR(s),BbB,JoG,GK,MA 30.00
397 DON(s),NA,DG,GK,MA 35.00
398 FR(s),BbB,JoG,GK,ViC 30.00
399 NA(c),DON(s),BbB,JoG,
GK,ViC,Robin 35.00
400 FR(s),NA,DG,GK,I:Man-Bat . . 60.00
401 NA(c),FR(s),JoG,
BbB,JoG,GK,ViC 30.00
402 FR(s),NA,DG,V:Man-Bat 35.00
403 FR(s),BbB,JoG,NA(c),GK,ViC,
BU:Robin 35.00
404 NA,GC,GK,A:Enemy Ace 37.00

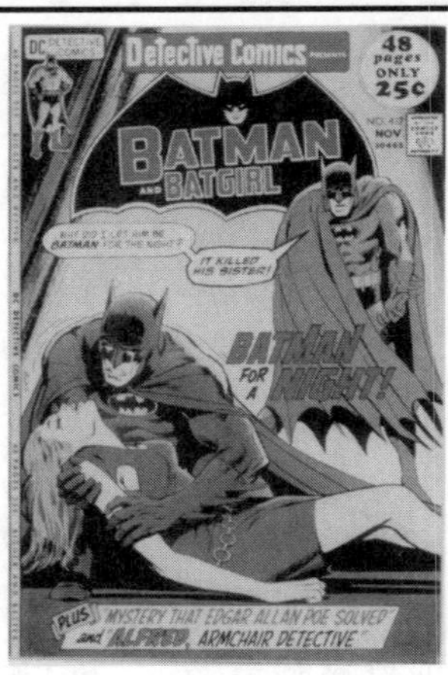

Detective #417 © DC Comics, Inc.

405 IN,GK,I:League of Assassins . 35.00
406 DON(s),BbB,FrG 35.00
407 FR(s),NA,DG,V:Man-bat. 37.00
408 MWn(s),LWn(s),NA,DG,
V:DrTzin Tzin 37.00
409 B:FR(s),BbB,FrG,DH,DG 32.00
410 DON(s),FR(s),NA,DG,DH. . . . 32.00
411 NA(c),DON(s),BbB,DG,DH . . . 22.00
412 NA(c),BbB,DG,DH 22.00
413 NA(c),BbB,DG,DH 22.00
414 DON(s),IN,DG,DH 25.00
415 BbB,DG,DH 25.00
416 DH. 25.00
417 BbB,DG,DH,BU:Batgirl. 25.00
418 DON(s),DH,IN,DG,A:Creeper. 25.00
419 DON(s),DH 25.00
420 DH. 25.00
421 DON(s),BbB,DG,DH,A:Batgirl. 22.00
422 BbB,DG,DH,Batgirl 22.00
423 BbB,DG,DH 22.00
424 BbB,DG,DH,Batgirl 22.00
425 BWr(c),DON(s),IN,DG,DH . . . 22.00
426 LWn(s),DG,A:Elongated Man . 15.00
427 IN,DG,DH,BU:Batgirl 15.00
428 BbB,DG,ENB(s),DD,JoG,
BU:Hawkman 15.00
429 DG,JoG,V:Man-Bat 15.00
430 BbB,NC,ENS(s),DG,
A:Elongated Man 15.00
431 DON(s),IN,MA 15.00
432 MA,A:Atom 15.00
433 DD,DG,MA 15.00
434 IN,DG,ENB(s),RB,DG 15.00
435 E:FR(s),DG,IN 15.00
436 MA,(i),DG,A:Elongated Man . . 15.00
437 JA,WS,I:Manhunter 27.00
438 JA,WS,Manhunter 36.00
439 DG,WS,O:Manhunter,Kid
Eternity rep. 36.00
440 JAp,WS 36.00
441 HC,WS 36.00
442 ATh,WS. 36.00
443 WS,D:Manhunter 36.00
444 JAp,B:Bat-Murderer,
A:Ra's Al Ghul 36.00
445 JAp,MGr,A:Talia 36.00
446 JAp,last giant. 14.00
447 DG(i),A:Creeper. 14.00
448 DG(i),E:Bat-Murderer,
A:Creeper,Ra's Al Ghul. 14.00
449 'Midnight Rustler in Gotham' . 14.00
450 WS 15.00
451. . . . . 14.00
452. . . . . 14.00
453. . . . . 14.00

454 . . . 14.00
455 MGr,A:Hawkman,V:Vampire . . 14.00
456 V:Ulysses Vulcan . . . 14.00
457 O:Batman rtd . . . 15.00
458 A:Man Bat . . . 14.00
459 A:Man Bat . . . 14.00
460 . . . 14.00
461 V:Capt.Stingaree . . . 12.00
462 V:Capt.Stingaree,A:Flash . . . 12.00
463 MGr,Atom,I:Calc.,Bl.Spider . . . 12.00
464 MGr,TA,BlackCanary . . . 12.00
465 TA,Elongated Man . . . 12.00
466 MR,TA,V:Signalman . . . 20.00
467 MR,TA . . . 20.00
468 MR,TA,A:JLA . . . 20.00
469 WS,I:Dr.Phosphorus . . . 12.00
470 WS,AM,V:Dr.Phosphorus . . . 12.00
471 MR,TA,A:Hugo Strange . . . 20.00
472 MR,TA,A:Hugo Strange . . . 20.00
473 MR,TA,R:Deadshot . . . 20.00
474 MR,TA,A:Penguin, N:Deadshot . . . 22.00
475 MR,TA,A:Joker . . . 32.00
476 MR,TA,A:Joker . . . 32.00
477 MR,DG,rep.NA . . . 22.00
478 MR,DG,I:3rd Clayface . . . 20.00
479 MR,DG,A:3rd Clayface . . . 20.00
480 DN,MA . . . 12.00
481 JSt,CR,DN,DA,MR, A:ManBat . . . 20.00
482 HC,MGo,DG,A:Demon . . . 10.00
483 DN,DA,SD,A:Demon, 40 Anniv. . . . 15.00
484 DN,DA,Demon,O:1st Robin . . . 8.00
485 DN,DA,D:Batwoman,A:Demon A:Ras al Ghul . . . 7.00
486 DN,DA,DG,I:Odd Man, V:Scarecrow . . . 7.00
487 DN,DA,A:Ras Al Ghul . . . 7.00
488 DN,V:Spook,Catwoman . . . 8.00
489 IN,DH,DN,DA,Ras Al Ghul . . . 8.00
490 DN,DA,PB,FMc,A:Black Lightning;A:Ras Al Ghul . . . 8.00
491 DN,DA,PB,FMc,A:Black Lightning;V:Maxie Zeus . . . 8.00
492 DN,DA,A:Penguin . . . 8.00
493 DN,DA,A:Riddler . . . 8.00
494 DN,DA,V:Crime Doctor . . . 8.00
495 DN,DA,V:Crime Doctor . . . 8.00
496 DN,DA,A:Clayface I . . . 7.00
497 DN,DA . . . 7.00
498 DN,DA,V:Blockbuster . . . 7.00
499 DN,DA,V:Blockbuster . . . 7.00
500 DG,CI,WS,TY,JKu,Dead-man,Hawkman,Robin . . . 12.00
501 DN,DA . . . 7.00
502 DN,DA . . . 7.00
503 DN,DA,Batgirl,Robin, V:Scarecrow . . . 7.00
504 DN,DA,Joker . . . 9.00
505 DN,DA . . . 7.00
506 DN,DA . . . 7.00
507 DN,DA . . . 7.00
508 DN,DA,V:Catwoman . . . 8.00
509 DN,DA,V:Catman,Catwoman . . 8.00
510 DN,DA,V:Madhatter . . . 7.00
511 DN,DA,I:Mirage . . . 7.00
512 GC,45th Anniv. . . . 7.00
513 V:Two-Face . . . 8.00
514 . . . 7.00
515 . . . 7.00
516 . . . 7.00
517 . . . 7.00
518 V:Deadshot . . . 7.00
519 . . . 7.00
520 A:Hugo Strange,Catwoman . . . 8.00
521 IN,TVE,A:Catwoman,B:BU:Green Arrow . . . 8.50
522 D:Snowman . . . 7.00
523 V:Solomon Grundy . . . 7.00
524 2nd A:J.Todd . . . 8.00
525 J.Todd . . . 7.00
526 DN,AA,A:Joker,Catwoman 500th A:Batman . . . 15.00
527 V:Man Bat . . . 4.00
528 Green Arrow,Ozone . . . 4.00
529 I:Night Slayer,Nocturna . . . 4.00
530 V:Nocturna . . . 4.00
531 GC,AA,Chimera,J.Todd (see Batman #364) . . . 4.00
532 GC,Joker . . . 7.00
533 . . . 4.00
534 GC,A:Gr.Arrow,V:PoisonIvy . . . 4.00
535 GC,A:Gr.Arrow,V:Crazy Quitt 2nd A:New Robin . . . 6.00
536 GC,A:Gr.Arrow,V:Deadshot . . . 4.00
537 GC,A:Gr.Arrow . . . 4.00
538 GC,A:Gr.Arrow,V:Catman . . . 4.00
539 GC,A:Gr.Arrow . . . 4.00
540 GC,A:Gr.Arrow,V:Scarecrow . . . 4.00
541 GC,A:Gr.Arrow,V:Penguin . . . 5.50
542 GC,A:Gr.Arrow . . . 4.00
543 GC,A:Gr.Arrow,V:Nightslayer . . 4.00
544 GC,A:Gr.Arrow,V:Nightslayer Nocturna . . . 4.00
545 . . . 4.00
546 . . . 4.00
547 . . . 4.00
548 PB . . . 4.00
549 PB,KJ,AMo(s),Gr.Arrow . . . 4.50
550 KJ,AMo(s),Gr.Arrow . . . 4.50
551 PB,V:Calendar Man . . . 4.00
552 V:Black Mask . . . 4.00
553 V:Black Mask . . . 4.00
554 KJ,N:Black Canary . . . 4.00
555 GC,DD,GreenArrow . . . 4.00
556 GC,Gr.Arrow,V:Nightslayer . . . 4.00
557 V:Nightslayer . . . 4.00
558 GC,Green Arrow . . . 4.00
559 GC,Green Arrow . . . 4.00
560 GC,A:Green Arrow . . . 4.00
561 . . . 4.00
562 GC,V:Film Freak . . . 4.00
563 V:Two Face . . . 4.00
564 V:Two Face . . . 4.00
565 GC,A:Catwoman . . . 5.50
566 GC,Joker . . . 6.00
567 GC,HarlanEllison . . . 5.00
568 KJ,Legends tie-in,A:Penguin . . 5.50
569 AD,V:Joker . . . 7.00
570 AD,EvilCatwoman,A:Joker . . . 7.00
571 AD,V:Scarecrow . . . 4.00
572 AD,CI,A:Elongated Man,Sherlock Holmes,SlamBradley,50thAnn. . 4.00
573 AD,V:Mad Hatter . . . 4.00

Detective #572 © DC Comics Inc.

574 AD,End old J.Todd/Robin sty . . 4.00
575 AD,Year 2,pt.1,I:Reaper . . . 8.00
576 TM,AA,Year 2,pt.2, R:Joe Chill . . . 6.00
577 TM,AA,Year 2,pt.3,V:Reaper . . 6.00
578 TM,AA,Year 2,pt.4, D:Joe Chill . . . 6.00
579 I:NewCrimeDoctor . . . 3.00
580 V:Two Face . . . 3.00
581 V:Two Face . . . 3.00
582 Millenium X-over . . . 3.00
583 I:Ventriloquist . . . 3.00
584 V:Ventriloquist . . . 3.00
585 I:Rat Catcher . . . 3.00
586 V:Rat Catcher . . . 3.00
587 NB,V:Corrosive Man . . . 3.00
588 NB,V:Corrosive Man . . . 3.00
589 Bonus Book #5 . . . 4.00
590 NB,V:Hassan . . . 3.00
591 NB,V:Rollo . . . 3.00
592 V:Psychic Vampire . . . 3.00
593 NB,V:Stirh . . . 3.00
594 NB,A:Mr.Potato . . . 3.00
595 IN,bonus book #11 . . . 3.00
596 V:Sladek . . . 3.00
597 V:Sladek . . . 3.00
598 DCw,BSz,Blind Justice #1 . . . 5.00
599 DCw,BSz,Blind Justice #2 . . . 4.00
600 DCw,BSz,Blind Justice #3, 50th Anniv.(double size) . . . 5.00
601 NB,I:Tulpa . . . 3.00
602 NB,A:Jason Blood . . . 2.50
603 NB,A:Demon . . . 2.50
604 NB,MudPack #1,V:Clayface, poster insert . . . 2.50
605 NB,MudPack #2,V:Clayface . . . 2.50
606 NB,MudPack #3,V:Clayface . . . 2.50
607 NB,MudPack #4,V:Clayface, poster insert . . . 2.50
608 NB,I:Anarky . . . 2.00
609 NB,V:Anarky . . . 2.00
610 NB,V:Penguin . . . 3.00
611 NB,V:Catwoman,Catman . . . 3.00
612 NB,A:Vicki Vale . . . 2.00
613 Search for Poisoner . . . 2.00
614 V:Street Demons . . . 2.00
615 NB,Return Penguin #2 (see Batman #448-#449) . . . 3.00
616 NB . . . 2.00
617 A:Joker . . . 2.00
618 NB,DG,A:Tim Drake . . . 2.00
619 NB,V:Moneyspider . . . 2.00
620 NB,V:Obeah,Man . . . 2.00
621 NB,SM,Obeah,Man . . . 2.00
622 Demon Within,pt.1 . . . 2.25
623 Demon Within,pt.2 . . . 2.25
624 Demon Within,pt.3 . . . 2.25
625 JAp,I:Abattior . . . 2.00
626 JAp,A:Electrocutioner . . . 2.00
627 600th issue w/Batman,rep. Detective #27 . . . 4.00
628 JAp,A:Abattoir . . . 2.00
629 JAp,`The Hungry Grass' . . . 2.00
630 JAp,I:Stiletto . . . 2.00
631 JAp,V:Neo-Nazi Gangs . . . 2.00
632 JAp,V:Creature . . . 2.00
633 TMd,Fake Batman? . . . 2.00
634 `The Third Man' . . . 2.00
635 Video Game,pt.1 . . . 2.00
636 Video Game,pt.2 . . . 2.00
637 Video Game,pt.3 . . . 2.00
638 JAp,Walking Time Bomb . . . 2.00
639 JAp,The Idiot Root,pt.2 . . . 2.00
640 JAp,The Idiot Root,pt.4 . . . 2.00
641 JAp,Destroyer,pt.3 (see LOTDK#27) . . . 2.00
642 JAp,Faces,pt.2 . . . 2.00
643 JAp,`Librarian of Souls' . . . 2.00
644 TL,Electric City,pt.1 A:Electrocutioner . . . 2.00
645 TL,Electric City,pt.2 . . . 2.00

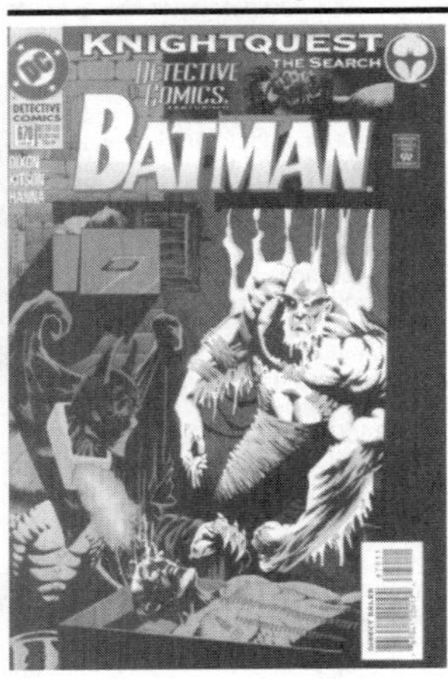

Dective #670 © DC Comics, Inc.

646 TL,Electric City,pt.3 . . . . 2.00
647 TL,V:Cluemaster 2.00
648 MWg(c),TL,V:Cluemaster. 2.00
649 MWg(c),TL,V:Cluemaster. 2.00
650 TL,A:Harold,Ace 2.00
651 TL,`A Bullet for Bullock' 2.00
652 GN,R:Huntress 2.00
653 GN,A:Huntress 2.00
654 MN,The General,pt.1 . . . . 2.00
655 MN,The General,pt.2 . . . . 2.00
656 MN,The General,pt.3,C:Bane. . 4.00
657 MN,A:Azrael,I:Cypher 5.00
658 MN,A:Azrael 3.00
659 MN,Knightfall#2, V:Ventriloquist,A:Bane 3.00
660 Knightfall#4,Bane Vs. Killer Croc 2.50
661 GN,Knightfall#6,V:Firefly, Joker,A:Bane 2.50
662 GN,Knightfall#8,V:Firefly, Joker,A:Huntress,Bane. 2.50
663 GN,Knightfall#10,V:Trogg, Zombie,Bird,A:Bane 2.50
664 GN,Knightfall#12,A:Azrael 2.50
665 GN,Knightfall#16,A:Azrael 2.50
666 GN,SHa,A:Azrael,Trogg, Zombie,Bird 2.25
667 GN,SHa,Knightquest:Crusade, V:Trigger Twins 2.00
668 GN,SHa,Knightquest:Crusade, Robin locked out of Batcave . . . 2.00
669 GN,SHa,Knightquest:Crusade, V:Trigger Twins 2.00
670 GN,SHa,Knightquest:Crusade, F:Rene Montoya. 2.00
671 GN,SHa,V:Joker 2.00
672 KJ(c),GN,SHa,Knightquest: Crusade,V:Joker. 2.00
673 KJ(c),GN,SHa,Knightquest: Crusade,V:Joker. 2.00
674 KJ(c),GN,SHa,Knightquest: Crusade 2.00
675 Foil(c),KJ(c),GN,SHa,Knightquest: Crusade,V:Gunhawk,foil(c) 3.50
675a Newsstand ed. 2.00
675b Platinum edition 5.00
676 KJ(c),GN,SHa,Knights End #3, A:Nightwing 3.00
677 KJ(c),GN,SHa,Knights End #9 V:Azrael 3.00
678 GN,SHa,Zero Hour 2.00
679 Ratcatcher. 2.00
680 Batman,Two-Face 2.00
681 CDi,GN,KJ,Jean-Paul Valley . . 2.00
682 CDi,GN,SHa,Return of Bruce Wayne,Troika,pt.3. . . . . 2.00
682a Collector's Edition 2.50
683 R:Penguin,I:Actuary 2.00
684 Daylight Heist 2.00
685 Chinatown War 2.00
686 V:King Snake,Lynx. 2.00
687 CDi,SHa,V:River Pirate 2.00
688 V:Captian Fear 2.00
689 F:Black Mask,Firefly. 2.00
690 F:Black Mask,Firefly. 2.00
691 V:Spellbinder 2.00
692 CDi,SHa,Underworld Unleashed tie-in 2.00
693 CDi,SHa,V:Poison Ivy & Agent Orange 2.00
694 CDi,find plant-killer. 2.00
695 CDi 3.00
696 CDi,GN,SHa,Contagion,pt.8. . . 3.00
697 CDi,GN,SHa,pt.1 (of 3) V:Lock-up. 2.00
698 CDi(s),A:Two-Face. 2.00
699 CDi(s),. 2.00
700 double size, Legacy, pt.1 x-over, R:Bane 3.50
700a cardstock cover 5.00
701 Legacy, pt. 6 x-over, V:Bane . . 2.00
702 CDi(s),GN,SHa,Legacy aftermath 2.00
703 CDi(s),GN,SHa, riots in Gotham City, Final Night tie-in 2.00
704 CDi(s),GN,TP,V:Al Gabone . . . 2.00
705 CDi(s),GN,Riddler & Cluemaster clash 2.00
706 CDi(s),GN 2.00
707 CDi(s),GN,Riddler/Cluemaster concl. 2.00
708 CDi(s),GN,BSz,F:Deathstroke, R:Gunhawk, pt.1 (of 3) 2.00
709 CDi(s),GN,BSz,F:Deathstroke, Gunhawk,pt.2. . . . . 2.00
710 CDi(s),GN,BSz,F:Deathstroke, Gunhawk,pt.3. . . . . 2.00
711 CDi(s),GN,CaS,Bruce Wayne fights crime 2.00
712 CDi(s),GN,I:Gearhead 2.00
713 CDi(s),GN,V:Gearhead,pt.2 . . . 2.00
714 CDi(s),GN,F:Martian Manhunter 2.00
715 CDi(s),GN,F:Martian Manhunter pt.2 . . . . 2.00
716 CDi,JAp,SNw,BSf, ... 2.00
717 CDi,GN,BSf,V:Gearhead,pt.1 . . 2.00
718 CDi,GN,BSf,V:Gearhead,pt.2 . . 2.00
719 . . . . 2.00
720 CDi,GN,KJ,Cataclysm x-over,pt.5 . . . . 2.00
721 CDi,GN,KJ,Cataclysm 2.00
722 CDi,JAp,BSf,Aftershock 2.00
723 CDi,BSz,Brotherhood of the Fist x-over, pt.2. . . . . 2.00
724 CDi,JAp,BSf,F:Nightwing 2.00
725 CDi,TP,BSf,Aftershock 2.00
726 CDi(s),BSf,V:Joker. 2.00
727 . . . . 2.00
728 CDi(s),BSf,SB,No Man's Land . 2.00
729 CDi(s),SB,No Man's Land 2.00
730 No Law and a New Order, concl. 2.00
731 F:Batgirl, Mosaic, pt.2 . . . . 2.00
732 F:Batgirl, Mosaic, pt.4 . . . . 2.00
733 SB,Alfreds advice 2.00
734 F:Batgirl,pt.2 x-over 2.00
735 DJu,BSz,Fruit of the Earth,pt.3 . . . . 2.00
736 LHa(s),MD2,V:Bane. 2.00
737 TMo, No Man's Land, The Code, concl. 2.00
738 CDi,MtB,Goin'Downtown,pt.2 . . 2.00
739 Jurisprudence,concl. 2.00
740 . . . . 2.00
741 Endgame, pt.3,40-pg.x-over. . . 2.50
742 SMa,40-pg. 2.50

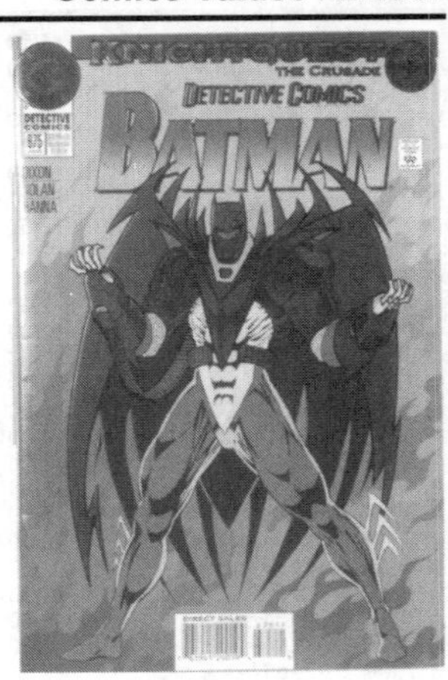

Dective #675 © DC Comics, Inc.

743 SMa,40-pg,new logo 2.50
744 SMa,40-pg. 2.50
745 SMa,V:Whisperer. 2.50
746 SMa,B.U.:The Jacobian 2.50
747 JJ,F:Renee Montoya 2.50
748 JJ,Urban Renewal,pt.1. . . . . . . 2.50
749 JJ,PhH,Urban Renewal,pt.2 . . . 2.50
750 V:Ra's Al Ghul,64-pg.. . . . . 4.95
751 SMa,JJ,DPS,F:Poison Ivy 2.50
Ann.#1 KJ,TD,A:Question,Talia, V:Penguin 6.00
Ann.#2 VS,A:Harvey Harris. 6.00
Ann.#3 DJu,DG,Batman in Japan . . 2.50
Ann.#4 Armageddon,pt.10 . . . . 3.00
Ann.#5 SK(c),TMd,Eclipso,V:The Ventriloquist,Joker 3.00
Ann.#6 JBa,I:Geist 2.75
Ann.#7 CDi,Elseworlds Story 3.25
Ann.#8 CDi,KD(c) Year One Annual O:The Riddler. 3.95
Ann.#9 Legends o/t Dead Earth . . . 2.95
Ann.#10 Pulp Heroes (War) CDi(s), SB,KJ. 3.95
Spec.#1,000,000 CDi(s) 2.00
TPB Manhunter AGw,WS 10.00

DETENTION COMICS
Aug., 1996

one-shot DON(s) 64pg, 3 stories. . . 3.50

DEXTER'S LABORATORY
Warner Bros./DC 1999

1 Kirbytron 6000 . . . . 2.00
2 Let's Save the World, You Jerk . . 2.00
3 Habi-Travails 2.00
4 Dexter impersonates mom 2.00
5 . . . . 2.00
6 Chicken pox 2.00
7 Beast Master 2.00
8 giant Dee-Dee 2.00
9 Doreen 2.00
10 blue hole 2.00
11 Mom's rubber gloves 2.00
12 Protoplasm Man 2.00
13 Forget Me Not 2.00
14 brown-nosing. 2.00
15 Totally Tanked 2.00
16 Dee Dee's Pony Tale 2.00

DHAMPIRE: STILLBORN
DC/Vertigo Sept., 1996

GN Nancy A. Collins adaptation . . . 5.95

 All comics prices listed are for *Near Mint* condition.

DOC SAVAGE

1987–88

1 AKu/NKu,D:Orig. Doc Savage. . . 2.50
2 AKu/NKu,V:Nazi's. 2.50
3 AKu/NKu,V:Nazi's. 2.50
4 AKu/NKu,V:Heinz 2.50

[2nd Series] 1988–90

1 `Five in the Sky'(painted cov.). . . 3.00
2 Chip Lost in Himalayas. 2.25
3 Doc declares war on USSR 2.25
4 DocSavage/Russian team-up . . . 2.25
5 V:The Erisians 2.25
6 U.S.,USSR,China Alliance
vs. Erisians 2.25
7 Mind Molder,pt.1, I:Pat Savage . . 2.25
8 . . . . 2.25
9 In Hidalgo. 2.25
10 V:Forces of the Golden God . . . 2.25
11 Sunlight Rising,pt.1 . . . . 2.25
12 Sunlight Rising,pt.2 . . . . 2.25
13 Sunlight Rising,pt.3 . . . . 2.25
14 Sunlight Rising,pt.4 . . . . 2.25
15 SeaBaron #1 . . . . 2.25
16 EB,Shadow & Doc Savage 2.25
17 EB,Shadow & Doc Savage 2.25
18 EB,Shadow/DocSavage conc. . . 2.25
19 All new 1930's story. 2.25
20 V:Airlord & his Black Zepplin . . . 2.25
21 Airlord (30's story conc.) 2.25
22 Doc Savages Past,pt.1 . . . . 2.25
23 Doc Savages Past,pt.2 . . . . 2.25
24 Doc Savages Past,pt.3 (final). . . 2.25
Ann.#1 1956 Olympic Games 4.50

DOCTOR FATE

July, 1987

1 KG,V:Lords of Chaos 2.50
2 KG,New Dr. Fate 2.50
3 KG,A:JLI. 2.50
4 KG,V:Lords of Chaos Champion . 2.50

[2nd Series] 1988–92

1 New Dr.Fate,V:Demons 2.50
2 A:Andrew Bennett(I,Vampire) . . . 2.00
3 A:Andrew Bennett(I,Vampire) . . . 2.00
4 V:I,Vampire. 2.00
5 Dr.Fate & I,Vampire in Europe . . 2.00
6 A:Petey 2.00
7 Petey returns home dimension . . 2.00
8 Linda become Dr.Fate again. . . . 2.00
9 Eric's Mother's Ghost,
A:Deadman 2.00
10 Death of Innocence,pt.1. . . . . . . 2.00
11 Return of Darkseid, Death of
Innocence,pt.2 . . . . 2.00
12 Two Dr.Fates Vs.Darkseid,
Death of Innocence,pt.3 . . . . . . 2.00
13 Linda in the Astral Realm,
Death of Innocence,pt.4 . . . . . . 2.00
14 Kent & Petey vs. Wotan. 2.00
15 V:Wotan,A:JLI 2.00
16 Flashback-novice Dr.Fate 2.00
17 Eric's Journey thru afterlife. 2.00
18 Search for Eric. 2.00
19 A:Dr.Benjamine Stoner, Lords of
Chaos, Phantom Stranger,
Search for Eric continued 2.00
20 V:Lords of Chaos,Dr.Stoner,
A:Phantom Stranger. 2.00
21 V:Chaos,A:PhantomStranger . . . 2.00
22 A:Chaos and Order 2.00
23 Spirits of Kent & Inza Nelson . . . 2.00
24 L:Dr.Fate Characters 2.00
25 I:New Dr. Fate 2.00
26 Dr.Fate vs. Orig.Dr.Fate. 2.00
27 New York Crime. 2.00
28 `Diabolism' 2.00
29 Kent Nelson. 2.00
30 `Resurrection' 2.00
31 `Resurrection' contd. 2.00
32 War of the Gods x-over 2.00
33 War of the Gods x-over 2.00
34 A:T'Gilian. 2.00
35 Kent Nelson in N.Y. 2.00
36 Search For Inza,A:Shat-Ru 2.00
37 Fate Helmet Powers revealed . . 2.00
38 `The Spirit Motor,'Flashback. . . . 2.00
39 U.S.Senate Hearing. 2.00
40 A:Wonder Woman 2.00
41 O:Chaos and Order,last issue . . 2.00
Ann.#1 TS,R:Eric's dead mother. . . 3.00

DOCTOR MID-NITE

1999

1 (of 3) MWg,F:Dr. Piter Cross. . . . 6.00
2 MWg 6.00
3 MWg, conclusion 6.00
TPB 19.95

DOME, THE: GROUND ZERO

DC/Helix (July, 1998)

1-shot DGb,AMK 8.00

DOOM FORCE

Spec.#1 MMi(c),RCa,WS,PCu,KSy,
I:Doom Force 2.75

DOOM PATROL

[1st series]

(see MY GREATEST ADVENTURE)

DOOM PATROL

[2nd Regular Series]

Oct., 1987

1 SLi,R:Doom Patrol,plus Who's Who
background of team, I:Kalki . . . 4.50
2 SLi,V:Kalki 3.50
3 SLi,I:Lodestone 3.50
4 SLi,I:Karma 3.50
5 SLi,R:Chief. 3.50
6 B:PuK(s),EL,GyM(i),
I:Scott Fischer 4.50
7 EL,GyM(i),V:Shrapnel. 3.50
8 EL,GyM(i),V:Shrapnel. 3.50
9 E:PuK(s),EL,GyM(i),V:Garguax,
& Bonus Book 3.50

Doom Patrol #14 © DC Comics Inc.

10 EL,A:Superman. 3.50
11 EL,R:Garguax 3.00
12 EL,A:Garguax 3.00
13 EL,A:Power Girl. 3.00
14 EL,A:Power Girl. 3.00
15 EL,Animal-Veg-.Mineral Man . . . 3.00
16 V:GenImmotus,Animal-Veg.-
Mineral Man. 3.00
17 D:Celsius,A:Aquaman & Sea
Devils, Invasion tie-in 4.00
18 Invasion. 3.00
19 B:GMo(s),New Direction,
I:Crazy Jane. 7.00
20 I:Rebis(new Negative-Being),
A:CrazyJane,Scissormen 4.00
21 V:Scissormen 3.50
22 City of Bone,V:Scissormen. 3.50
23 A:RedJack,Lodestone kidnap. . . 3.50
24 V:Red Jack 3.50
25 Secrets of New Doom Patrol . . . 3.50
26 I:Brotherhood of Dada 3.00
27 V:Brotherhood of Dada 3.00
28 Trapped in nightmare,V:Dada . . 3.00
29 Trapped in painting,
A:Superman. 3.00
30 SBs(c),V:Brotherhood of Dada. . 3.00
31 SBs(c),A:The Pale Police. 3.00
32 SBs(c),V:Cult of
Unwritten Book. 3.00
33 SBs(c),V:Cult,A:Anti-God
the DeCreator 3.00
34 SBs(c),Robotman vs. his brain,
R:The Brain & Mr.Mallah 3.00
35 SBs(c),A:Men from
N.O.W.H.E.R.E. 3.00
36 SBs(c),V:Men from
N.O.W.H.E.R.E. 3.25
37 SBs(c),Rhea Jones Story. 2.50
38 SBs(c),V:Aliens 2.50
39 SBs(c),V:Aliens 2.50
40 SBs(c),Aliens. 2.50
41 SBS(c),Aliens 2.50
42 O:Flex Mentallo 2.50
43 SBs(c),V:N.O.W.H.E.R.E.. . . . . . 2.50
44 SBs(c),V:N.O.W.H.E.R.E.. . . . . . 2.50
45 . . . . 2.50
46 SBs(c),RCa,MkK,A:Crazy Jane,
Dr.Silence 2.50
47 Scarlet Harlot (Crazy Jane) 2.50
48 V:Mr.Evans 2.50
49 TTg(c),RCa,MGb,I:Mr.Nobody . . 2.50
50 SBs(c),V:Brotherhood of Dada
& bonus artists portfolio 3.00
51 SBs(c),Mr.Nobody Runs for
President 2.50
52 SBs(c),Mr.Nobody saga conc. . . 2.50
53 SBs(c),Parody Issue,A:Phantom
Stranger,Hellblazer,Mr.E 2.50
54 Rebis'Transformation. 2.50
55 SBs(c),V:Crazy Jane,
Candle Maker. 2.50
56 SBs(c),RCa,V:Candle Maker . . . 2.50
57 SBs(c),RCa,V:Candle Maker,
O:Team,Double-sized 3.00
58 SBs(c),V:Candle Maker 2.25
59 TTg(c),RCa,SnW(i),A:Candlemaker
D:Larry Trainor. 2.25
60 JHw(c),RCa,SnW(i),
V:Candlemaker,A:Magnus 2.25
61 TTg(c),RCa,SnW(i),A:Magnus
D:Candlemaker 2.25
62 DFg(c),RCa,SnW(i),
V:Nanomachines 2.25
63 E:GMo(s),RCa,R:Crazy Jane,
V:Keysmiths,BU:Sliding from the
Wreckage. 2.25

Vertigo 1993

64 BB(c),B:RaP(s),RCa,SnW(i),
B:Sliding from the Wreckage,
R:Niles Caulder 2.25
65 TTg(c),RCa,SnW(i),Nannos 2.25

66 RCa,E:Sliding from the Wreckage 2.25
67 TTg(c),LiM,GHi(i),New HQ,I:Charlie, George,Marion,V:Wild Girl 2.25
68 TTg(c),LiM,GHi(i),I:Indentity Addict 2.25
69 TTg(c),LiM,GHi(i),V:Identity Addict 2.25
70 TTg(c),SEa,TS(i),I:Coagula, V:Codpiece 2.25
71 TTg(c),LiM,TS(i),Fox & Crow . . . 2.25
72 TTg(c),LiM,TS(i),Fox vs Crow . . 2.25
73 LiM,GPi(i),Head's Nightmare . . . 2.25
74 LiM,TS(i),Bootleg Steele 2.25
75 BB(c),TMK,Teiresias Wars#1, Double size 2.25
76 Teiresias Wars#2 . . . . 2.25
77 BB(c),TMK,N:Cliff 2.25
78 BB(c),V:Tower of Babel 2.25
79 BB(c),E:Teiresias Wars 2.25
80 V:Yapping Dogs 2.25
81 B:Masquerade 2.25
82 E:Masquerade 2.25
83 False Memory 2.00
84 The Healers 2.00
85 Charlie the Doll 2.00
86 Imagine Ari's Friends 2.00
87 KB(c),Imagine Ari's Friends,pt.4,final issue 2.00
Ann.#1 A:Lex Luthor 2.00
Ann.#2 RaP(s),MkW,Children's Crusade,F:Dorothy,A:Maxine . . 4.25
Doom Patrol/Suicide Squad #1 EL, D:Mr.104,Thinker,Psi,Weasel . . 2.50
TPB Crawling From the Wreckage, SBs(c),rep.#19-#25 . . . . 19.95

DOOMSDAY

Ann.#1 Year One annuals 3.95

DOORWAY TO NIGHTMARE

1978

1 I:Madame Xanadu 6.00
2 thru 5 . . . . @6.00

DOUBLE ACTION COMICS

Jan., 1940

2 Pre-Hero DC 12,500.00

DRAGONLANCE

1988–91

1 Krynn's Companion's advent. . . . 3.50
2 Vandar&Riva vs.Riba's brother . . 3.50
3 V:Takhesis,Queen of Darkness . . 3.00
4 V:Lord Soth & Kitiara 3.00
5 V:Queen of Darkness 3.00
6 Gnatch vs. Kalthanan 3.00
7 Raistlin's Evil contd. 3.00
8 Raistlin's Evil concl. 2.00
9 Journey to land o/t Minotaurs A:Tanis, Kitiara 2.00
10 Blood Sea,`Arena of Istar' 2.00
11 Cataclysm of Krynn Revealed `Arena of Istar' contd. 2.00
12 Horak vs.Koraf, Arena contd. . . . 2.00
13 Test of High Sorcery #1 . . . . 2.00
14 Test of High Sorcery #2 . . . . 2.00
15 Test of High Sorcery #3 . . . . 2.00
16 Test of High Sorcery #4 . . . . 2.00
17 Winter'sKnight:DragonkillPt.1 . . . 2.00
18 Winter'sKnight:DragonkillPt.1 . . . 2.00
19 Winter'sKnight:DragonkillPt.1 . . . 2.00
20 Winter'sKnight:DragonkillPt.1 . . . 2.00
21 Move to New World 2.00
22 Taladas,pt.1,A:Myrella 2.00

DragonLance #28 © DC Comics, Inc.

23 Taladas,pt.2,Riva vs. Dragon . . . 2.00
24 Taladas,pt.3,V:Minotaur Lord . . . 2.00
25 Taladas,pt.4,V:Axantheas. 2.00
26 Rune Discovery,V:Agents of Eristem 2.00
27 V:Agents of Eristem 2.00
28 Riva continued. 2.00
29 Riva continued. 2.00
30 Dwarf War,pt.1 . . . . 2.00
31 Dwarf War,pt.2 . . . . 2.00
32 Dwarf War,pt.3 . . . . 2.00
33 Dwarf War,pt.4 . . . . 2.00
34 conc., last issue 2.00
Ann.#1 Myrella of the Robed Wizards 2.95

DREAMING, THE

DC/Vertigo June, 1996

1 TLa(s),PSj,"The Goldie Factor,"pt.1 . . . . 4.50
2 TLa(s),PSj,"The Goldie Factor,"pt.2 . . . . 4.00
3 TLa(s),PSj,"The Goldie Factor,"pt.3 . . . . 4.00
4 SvP,"The Lost Boy," pt.1 (of 4) . . 3.50
5 SvP,"The Lost Boy," pt.2 . . . . 2.50
6 SvP,"The Lost Boy," pt.3 . . . . 2.50
7 SvP,"The Lost Boy," pt.4 . . . . 2.50
8 AaK(s),MZi, visitor from Cain's past 2.50
9 BT(s),PD,TOz,"Weird Romance," pt.1 (of 4) 2.50
10 BT(s),PD,TOz,"Weird Romance," pt.2 . . . . 2.50
11 BT(s),PD,TOz,"Weird Romance," pt.3 . . . . 2.50
12 BT(s),PD,TOz,"Weird Romance," pt.4 . . . . 2.50
13 TLa,JIT,"Coyote's Kiss," pt. 1 . . . 2.50
14 TLa,JIT,"Coyote's Kiss," pt. 2 . . . 2.50
15 . . . . 2.50
16 GyA,F:Nuala 2.50
17 PD,DMc,Souvenirs, pt.1. . . . . . . 2.50
18 PD,DMc,Souvenirs, pt.2. . . . . . . 2.50
19 PD,DMc,Souvenirs, pt.3. . . . . . . 2.50
20 ADv, The Dark Rose, pt.1 . . . . . 2.50
21 ADv, The Dark Rose, pt.2 . . . . . 2.50
22 The Unkindness of One, pt.1 . . . 2.50
23 The Unkindness of One, pt.2 . . . 2.50
24 The Unkindness of One, pt.3 . . . 2.50
25 My Life as a Man 2.50
26 Restitution 2.50
27 Caretaker Cain 2.50
28 victims of famous fires 2.50
29 PSj,DMc,Abel'sHouse ofSecrets 2.50
30 DMc(c),Lucien's mysteries 2.50
31 House of Secrets, 48-pg. 4.00
32 DG,SvP 2.50
33 The Little Mermaid 2.50
34 MaH, Cave of Nightmares 2.50
35 DMc(c),Kaleidoscope 2.50
36 DMc(c),The Gyres, pt.1 . . . . 2.50
37 DMc(c),The Gyres, pt.2 . . . . 2.50
38 DMc(c),The Gyres, pt.3 . . . . 2.50
39 DMc(c),Lost Language of Flowers 2.50
40 DMc(c),Foxes & Hounds,pt.1 . . . 2.50
41 DMc(c),Foxes & Hounds,pt.2 . . . 2.50
42 DMc(c),Foxes & Hounds,pt.3 . . . 2.50
43 DMc(c),Foxes & Hounds,pt.4 . . . 2.50
44 Trinket,pt.1 . . . . 2.50
45 Trinket,pt.2 . . . . 2.50
46 Trinket,pt.3 . . . . 2.50
47 CV,RoR 2.50
48 . . . . 2.50
49 DMc(c),The Dawn Stone 2.50
50 DMc(c),rebuilding. 2.50
51 DMc(c),in Manhattan 2.50
52 Exiles,pt.1 . . . . 2.50
53 Exiles,pt.2 . . . . 2.50
54 Exiles,pt.3 . . . . 2.50
55 F:Danny Nod 2.50
TPB Beyond the Shores of Night . 20.00
TPB Through the Gates of Horn & Ivory 20.00
GN Trial and Error 6.00

DYNAMIC CLASSICS

Sept-Oct., 1978

1 Rep. Detective 395 & 438. . . . . . 3.00

ECLIPSO

1992–94

1 BS,MPn,V:South American Drug Dealers 2.50
2 BS,MPn,A:Bruce Gordon 2.00
3 BS,MPn,R:Amanda Waller 2.00
4 BS,A:Creeper,Cave Carson 2.00
5 A:Creeper,Cave Carson 2.00
6 LMc,V:Bruce Gordon 2.00
7 London,1891 . . . . 2.00
8 A:Sherlock Holmes 2.00
9 I:Johnny Peril 2.00
10 CDo,V:Darkseid. 2.00
11 A:Creeper,Peacemaker,Steel . . . 2.00

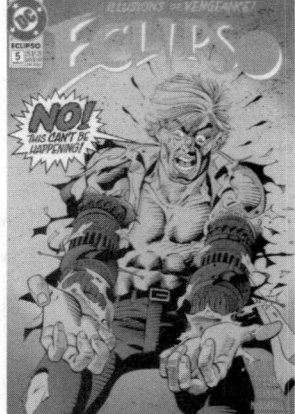

Eclipso #5 © DC Comics, Inc.

12 V:Shadow Fighters 2.00
13 D:Manhunter,Commander Steel, Major Victory,Peacemaker, Wildcat,Dr.Midnight,Creeper . . . 2.00
14 A:JLA 2.00
15 A:Amanda Waller. 2.00
16 V:US Army 2.00
17 A:Amanda Waller,Martian Manhunter,Wonder Woman,Flash, Bloodwynd,Booster Gold 2.00
18 A:Spectre,JLA,final issue 2.00
Ann.#1 I:Prism 2.50

ECLIPSO: THE DARKNESS WITHIN

1992

1 BS,Direct w/purple diamond, A:Superman,Creeper 4.00
1a BS,Newstand w/out diamond . . 3.00
2 BS,MPn,DC heroes V:Eclipso, D:Starman 3.00

EGYPT

1995–96

1 College Experiments. 3.50
2 College Experiments. 3.00
3 New York Haunt 3.00
4 V:Seth,Isis 3.00
5 V: The Priests. 3.00
6 . . . . 3.00
7 finale 3.00

80 PAGE GIANTS

Aug., 1964

1 Superman. 500.00
2 Jimmy Olsen. 300.00
3 Lois Lane 250.00
4 Golden Age-Flash. 250.00
5 Batman. 250.00
6 Superman. 200.00
7 JKu&JKu(c),Sgt. Rock's Prize Battle Tales 200.00
8 Secret Origins,O:JLA,Aquaman, Robin,Atom, Superman 450.00
9 Flash 175.00
10 Superboy. 175.00
11 Superman,A:Lex Luthor 175.00
12 Batman 175.00
13 Jimmy Olsen 175.00
14 Lois Lane. 175.00
15 Superman & Batman 175.00
16 JLA #39. . . . . 75.00
17 Batman #176. . . . . 40.00
18 Superman #183. . . . . 18.00
19 Our Army at War #164. . . . . . . 10.00
20 Action #334 . . . . 16.00
21 Flash #160 . . . . 30.00
22 Superboy #129 . . . . 7.00
23 Superman #187. . . . . 13.00
24 Batman #182. . . . . 26.00
25 Jimmy Olsen #95. . . . . 10.00
26 Lois Lane #68. . . . . 10.00
27 Batman #185. . . . . 35.00
28 World's Finest #161 . . . . 11.00
29 JLA #48. . . . . 16.00
30 Batman #187. . . . . 35.00
31 Superman #193. . . . . 13.00
32 Our Army at War #177. . . . . 8.00
33 Action #347 . . . . 11.00
34 Flash #169 . . . . 30.00
35 Superboy #138 . . . . 6.00
36 Superman #197. . . . . 12.00
37 Batman #193. . . . . 16.00
38 Jimmy Olsen #104. . . . . 5.00
39 Lois Lane #77 . . . . 6.00
40 World's Finest #170. . . . . 10.00
41 JLA #58. . . . . 12.00
42 Superman #202. . . . . 12.00
43 Batman #198. . . . . 24.00
44 Our Army at War #190. . . . . 5.00
45 Action #360 . . . . 8.00
46 Flash #178 . . . . 18.00
47 Superboy #147 . . . . 7.00
48 Superman #207. . . . . 12.00
49 Batman #203. . . . . 14.00
50 Jimmy Olsen #113. . . . . 5.00
51 Lois Lane #86 . . . . 6.00
52 World's Finest #179. . . . . 6.00
53 JLA #67. . . . . 8.00
54 Superman #212. . . . . 12.00
55 Batman #208. . . . . 13.00
56 Our Army at War #203. . . . . 5.00
57 Action #373 . . . . 8.00
58 Flash #187 . . . . 13.00
59 Superboy #156 . . . . 6.00
60 Superman #217. . . . . 10.00
61 Batman #213. . . . . 35.00
62 Jimmy Olsen #122. . . . . 5.00
63 Lois Lane #95 . . . . 5.00
64 World's Finest #188. . . . . 6.00
65 JLA #76. . . . . 7.00
66 Superman #222. . . . . 10.00
67 Batman #218. . . . . 13.00
68 Our Army at War #216. . . . . 5.00
69 Adventure #390 . . . . 6.00
70 Flash #196 . . . . 12.00
71 Superboy #165 . . . . 6.00
72 Superman #227. . . . . 10.00
73 Batman #223. . . . . 14.00
74 Jimmy Olsen #131. . . . . 5.00
75 Lois Lane #104 . . . . 4.00
76 World's Finest #197. . . . . 5.00
77 JLA #85. . . . . 6.00
78 Superman #232. . . . . 10.00
79 Batman #228. . . . . 12.00
80 Our Army at War #229. . . . . 5.00
81 Adventure #403 . . . . 6.00
82 Flash #205 . . . . 9.00
83 Superboy #174 . . . . 5.00
84 Superman #239. . . . . 10.00
85 Batman #233. . . . . 12.00
86 Jimmy Olsen #140. . . . . 5.00
87 Lois Lane #113 . . . . 4.00
88 World's Finest #206. . . . . 5.00
89 JLA #93. . . . . 6.00

EL DIABLO

1989–91

1 I:El Diablo, double-size. 2.50
2 V:Crime Lord Benny Contreras . . 2.00
3 'Day of the Dead' Celebration. . . 2.00

Elongated Man #1 © DC Comics Inc.

4 Storm #1 . . . . 2.25
5 Storm #2 . . . . 2.25
6 Storm #3 . . . . 2.25
7 Storm #4 . . . . 2.25
8 V:Car-Theft Ring. 2.00
9 V:Crime Lord of Dos Rios 2.00
10 The Franchise #1. . . . . 2.00
11 The Franchise #2. . . . . 2.00
12 A:Greg Sanders (golden age) . . 2.00
13 The River #1 . . . . 2.00
14 The River #2 . . . . 2.00
15 The River #3 . . . . 2.00
16 Final Issue. 2.00

ELECTRIC WARRIOR

1986–87

1 SF series,I:Electric Warriors 2.50
2 'Bloodstalker Mode' 2.00
3 Rogue Warrior vs. Z-Primes 2.00
4 Primmies vs. Electric Warriors . . 2.00
5 Lek 0-03 Rebels 2.00
6 Lek 0-03 vs. Masters 2.00
7 Lek'sFate,Derek Two-Shadows. . 2.00
8 Derek Two-Shadows Betrayed . . 2.00
9 Fate of Derek Two-Shadows. . . . 2.00
10 Two-Shadows as one 2.00
11 Rebellion 2.00
12 Rebellion continued 2.00
13 V:Prime One 2.00
14 Mutants Join Rebellion. 2.00
15 Invaders Arrival 2.00
16 Unified Warriors vs. Invaders . . . 2.00
17 V:Terrans, O:Electric Warriors . . 2.00
18 Origin continued, final issue. . . . 2.00

ELONGATED MAN

1992

1 A:Copperhead 2.00
2 Modora,A:Flash,I:Sonar 2.00
3 A:Flash,V:Wurst Gang 2.00

ELSEWORLD'S FINEST

DC/Elseworlds 1998

1 (of 2) JFM,KD,F:Bruce Wayne and Clark Kent, ... 5.00
2 JFM,KD,concl. 5.00
GN Supergirl & Batgirl 6.00

ELVIRA

1986–87

1 DSp,BB(c) 3.25
2 thru 10 . . . . @2.00
11 DSt(c)Find Cain 2.50

ENIGMA

Vertigo 1993

1 B:PrM(s),DFg,I:Enigma,Michael Smith,V:The Head 3.00
2 DFg,I:The Truth 3.00
3 DFg,V:The Truth,I:Envelope Girl, Titus Bird 3.00
4 DFg,D:The Truth,I:Interior League. 3.00
5 DFg,I:Enigma's Mother 3.00
6 DFg,V:Envelope Girl 3.00
7 DFg,V:Enigma's Mother,D:Envelope Girl,O:Enigma. 3.00
8 E:PrM(s),DFg,final issue 3.00
TPB Rep. #1-#8 . . . . 19.95

ERADICATOR

1996

1 IV,Low, ... 2.00
2 IV,Low, ... 2.00
3 IV,Low,"Reign of the Superman" concl.A:Superboy 2.00

ESSENTIAL VERTIGO: SWAMP THING

DC/Vertigo Sept., 1996

B&W reprints

1 AMo(s), rep. Saga of the Swamp Thing #21. . . . . . . 2.50
2 thru 11 AMo(s), rep. Saga of the Swamp Thing #22–#31. . @2.00
12 AMo(s) rep. Saga Ann. #2 . . . . . 2.00
13 AMo(s) rep. Saga #32–#42 . . @2.00
24 AMo,Windfall, final issue 2.25

ESSENTIAL VERTIGO: THE SANDMAN

DC/Vertigo 1996

3 NGa(s),SK,MDr,rep. 2.00
4 NGa(s),SK,MDr,rep. F:Etrigan the Demon 2.00
5 NGa(s),SK,MJ,F:Morpheus, John Dee 2.00
6 NGa(s),SK,MJ,V:Dr. Destiny 2.00
7 . . . . 2.00
8 NGa(s),MDr,MJ,"The Sound of Her Wings" 2.00
9 NGa(s),MDr,MJ,"The Doll's House" F:Nada. 2.00
10 NGa(s),MDr,MJ,"The Doll's House". 2.00
11 NGa(s),MDr,RT 2.00
12 NGa(s),CBa,MJ,"The Doll's House," pt.3 . . . . 2.00
13 NGa,rep. "Doll's House," pt.4 . . . 2.00
14 NGa,rep. "Doll's House," pt.5 . . . 2.00
15 NGa,rep. "Doll's House," pt.6 . . . 2.00
16 NGa,rep. "Lost Hearts". 2.00
17 NGa,rep. "Dream Country". 2.00
18 NGa,"Dream of a Thousand Cats" 2.00
19 NGa,rep.Sandman #19 . . . . 2.00
20 NGa,rep.Sandman #20 . . . . 2.00
21 NGa,rep.Sandman #21 . . . . 2.00
22 NGa,rep.Season of Mists pt.1 . . 2.00
23 NGa,rep.Season of Mists pt.2 . . 2.00
24 NGa,rep.Season of Mists pt.3 . . 2.00
25 NGa,rep.Season of Mists pt.4 . . 2.00
26 NGa,rep.Season of Mists pt.5 . . 2.00
27 NGa,rep.Season of Mists,pt.6 . . 2.25
28 NGa,rep.Season of Mists,epilog. 2.25
29 NGa,rep.Thermidor 2.25
30 NGa,rep.August. 2.25
31 NGa,rep.Three Septembers and a January 2.25
32 NGa,rep. Sandman Special #1 final issue. 4.50

Fate #0 © DC Comics, Inc.

EXTREME JUSTICE

1995–96

O New Group 3.00
1 V:Captain Atom 2.00
2 V:War Cyborgs 2.00
3 V:Synge 2.00
4 R:Firestorm the Nuclear Man . . . 2.00
5 Firestorm & Elementals 2.00
6 Monarch,Captain Atom, Booster Gold, Maxima. 2.00
7 F:Monarch,Captain Atom 2.00
8 . . . . 2.00
9 F:Firestorm. 2.00
10 Underworld Unleashed tie-in . . . 2.00
11 Underworld Unleashed tie-in . . . 2.00
12 Monarch's scheme revealed . . . 2.00
13 Monarch vs. Captain Atom. 2.00
14 . . . . 2.00
15 TMo,V:The Slavemaster from the Stars 2.00
16 TMo,V:Legion of Doom 2.00
17 TMo,V:Legion of Doom 2.00

EXTREMIST

Vertigo 1993

1 B:PrM(s),TMK,I:The Order, Extremist(Judy Tanner). 2.50
1a Platinum Ed. 8.00
2 TMK,D:Extremist(Jack Tanner) . . 2.25
3 TMK,V:Patrick 2.25
4 E:PrM(s),TMK,D:Tony Murphy . . 2.25

FACE, THE

GN DFg,PrM 5.50

FAITH

DC/Vertigo Sept., 1999

1 (of 5) TMK 2.50
2 TMK. 2.50
3 TMK. 2.50
4 TMK. 2.50
5 TMK. 2.50

FAMILY MAN

Paradox 1995

1 I:Family Man. 5.50
2 V:Brother Charles. 5.50
3 Escape. 5.50

FANBOY

1999

1 (of 6) SA, various artists 2.50
2 . . . . 2.50
3 A:JLA 2.50
4 SA, A:Sgt. Rock 2.50
5 SA, A:Batman. 2.50
6 SA, A:Wonder Woman, concl. . . . 2.50

FAREWELL MOONSHADOW

DC/Vertigo

GN JMD(s),JMu, prose & pictures. . 8.50

FATE

1994–96

1 Dr. Fate 2.50
2 Nabu,Astral plane. 2.25
3 Bloodstain 2.00
4 Decisions 2.00
5 Judged by Enclave 2.00
6 V:Grimoire 2.00
7 V:Dark Agent 2.00
8 V:Dark Agent 2.25
9 Tries to change his destiny 2.25
10 A:Zatanna 2.25
11 . . . . 2.25
12 A:Sentinel 2.25
13 V:Blaze 2.25
14 LKa,ALa,AWi,Underworld Unleashed tie-in 2.25
15 LKa,ALa,AWi,V:Charnelle 2.25
16 LKa,ALa,AWi,canibal drug-cult. . 2.25
17 LKa,ALa,AWi 2.25
18 LKa,ALa,AWi,V:Charnelle 2.25
19 LKa,ALa,AWi,V:men in black . . . 2.25

FAULT LINES

DC/Vertigo March, 1997

Mini-series

1 LMr(s),F:Tracey Farrand. 2.50
2 LMr(s) 2.50
3 LMr(s) 2.50
4 LMr(s) 2.50
5 (of 6) LMr(s) 2.50
6 LMrs(s) concl.. . . . . 2.00

FIGHTING AMERICAN

1994

1 GrL,R:Fighting American 2.00
2 GrL,Media Circus 2.00
3 GrL,I&V:Gross Nation Product, Def Iffit 2.00
4 GrL,V:Gross Nation Product, Def Iffit. 2.00
5 GrL,PhorOptor 2.00
6 Final Issue 2.00

FINAL NIGHT, THE

Sept., 1996

[Cross-Over Series]

1 KK(s),SI,JMz, Alien crash lands on Earth. 2.00
2 KK(s),SI,JMz, Earth's sun extinguished. 2.00
3 KK(s),SI,JMz, Attempts to stave off inevitable. 2.00
4 KK(s),SI,JMz, Can they save the world, and at what price? 2.00
TPB rep.. . . . . 13.00

FIghting American #6 © DC Comics, Inc.

FINALS
DC/Vertigo 1999
1 (of 4) College satire 3.00
2 JIT,pt.2 . . . . 3.00
3 JIT,pt.3 . . . . 3.00
4 JIT,conclusion 3.00

FIREBRAND
1995
1 SaV,Alex Sanchez becomes Firebrand 2.00
2 SaV 2.00
3 SaV,Generation Prime case climax 2.00
4 SaV,Young gang member 2.00
5 SaV,V;serial killer(s) 2.00
6 BAu,SaV 2.00
7 . . . . 2.00
8 . . . . 2.00
9 final issue 2.00

FIRESTORM
March, 1978
1 AM,JRu,I&O:Firestorm 4.00
2 AM,BMc,A:Superman 3.00
3 AM,I:Killer Froat 3.00
4 AM,BMc,I:Hyena. 3.00
5 AM,BMc,Hyena 3.00

FIRESTORM, THE NUCLEAR MAN
(see FURY OF FIRESTORM)

First Issue Special #4
© DC Comics Inc.

FIRST ISSUE SPECIAL
April, 1975
1 JK,Atlas 6.00
2 Green Team 7.00
3 Metamorpho 5.00
4 Lady Cop 5.00
5 JK,Manhunter 6.00
6 JK,Dingbats 5.00
7 SD,Creeper 5.00
8 MGr,Warlord 15.00
9 WS,Dr.Fate. 7.00
10 Outsiders(not Batman team) . . . 5.00
11 NR,AM Code:Assassin. 5.00
12 new Starman 5.00
13 return of New Gods 8.00

FLASH COMICS
Jan., 1940
1 SMo,SMo(c),O:Flash,Hawkman,The Whip & Johnny Thunder,B:Cliff Cornwall,Minute Movies . . 60,000.00
2 B:Rod Rain 6,500.00
3 SMo,SMo(c),B:The King. . . . 5,000.00
4 SMo,SMo(c),F:The Whip . . . 4,000.00
5 SMo,SMo(c),F:The King. . . . 3,200.00
6 F:Flash 4,500.00
7 Hawkman(c) 3,800.00
8 Male bondage(c) 2,500.00
9 Hawkman(c) 3,000.00
10 SMo,SMo(c),Flash(c) 3,000.00
11 SMo,SMo(c) 1,600.00
12 SMo,SMo(c),B:Les Watts . . 1,600.00
13 SMo,SMo(c) 1,600.00
14 SMo,SMo(c) 1,600.00
15 SMo,SMo(c) 1,600.00
16 SMo,SMo(c) 1,600.00
17 SMo,SMo(c),E:CliffCornwall 1,600.00
18 SMo,SMo(c) 1,600.00
19 SMo,SMo(c) 1,600.00
20 SMo,SMo(c) 1,600.00
21 SMo(c) 1,400.00
22 SMo,SMo(c) 1,400.00
23 SMo,SMo(c) 1,400.00
24 SMo,SMo(c),Flash V:Spider-Men of Mars,A:Hawkgirl. . . 1,500.00
25 SMo,SMo(c). 950.00
26 SMo,SMo(c). 950.00
27 SMo,SMo(c). 950.00
28 SMo,SMo(c),Flash goes to Hollywood. 950.00
29 SMo,SMo(c) 1,000.00
30 SMo,SMo(c),Flash in`Adventure of the Curiosity Ray!' 950.00
31 SMo,SMo(c),Hawkman(c) . . . 900.00
32 SMo,SM(c),Flash in`Adventure of the Fictious Villians' 900.00
33 SMo,SMo(c). 900.00
34 SMo,SMo(c),Flash in `The Robbers of the Round Table' 900.00
35 SMo,SMo(c). 900.00
36 SMo,SMo(c),F:Flash, The Mystery of the Doll Who Walks Like a Man' 900.00
37 SMo,SMo(c). 900.00
38 SMo,SMo(c). 900.00
39 SMo,SMo(c). 900.00
40 SMo,SMo(c),F:Flash, Man Who Could Read Man's Souls! . . . 900.00
41 SMo,SMo(c). 800.00
42 SMo,SMo(c),Flash V:The Gangsters Baby!. 800.00
43 SMo,SMo(c). 800.00
44 SMo,SMo(c),Flash V:The Liars Club. 800.00
45 SMo,SMo(c),F:Hawkman,Big Butch Makes Hall of Fame . . 800.00
46 SMo,SMo(c). 800.00
47 SMo,SMo(c),Hawkman in Crime Canned for the Duration 800.00
48 SMo,SMo(c). 800.00
49 SMo,SMo(c). 800.00
50 SMo,SMo(c),Hawkman, Tale of the 1,000 Dollar Bill 800.00
51 SMo,SMo(c). 700.00
52 SMo,SMo(c),Flash, Machine that Thinks Like a Man 700.00
53 SMo,SMo(c),Hawkman, Simple Simon Met the Hawkman . . . 700.00
54 SMo,SMo(c),Flash, Mysterious Bottle from the Sea. 700.00
55 SMo,SMo(c),Hawkman, Riddle of the Stolen Statuette! 700.00
56 SMo,SMo(c). 700.00
57 SMo,SMo(c),Hawkman, Adventure of the Gangster & the Ghost . 700.00
58 SMo,SMo(c),`Merman meets the Flash' 700.00
59 SMo,SMo(c),Hawkman V:Pied Piper 700.00
60 SMo,SMo(c),Flash V:The Wind Master. 700.00
61 SMo,SMo(c),Hawkman V:The Beanstalk 700.00
62 JKu,Flash in `High Jinks on the Rinks' 800.00
63 JKu(c),Hawkman in `The Tale of the Mystic Urn' 600.00
64 . . . . 600.00
65 JKu(c),Hawkman in `Return of the Simple Simon'. 600.00
66 . . . . 600.00
67 JKu(c) 600.00
68 Flash in `The Radio that Ran Wild' 600.00
69 . . . . 600.00
70 JKu(c) 600.00
71 JKu(c),Hawkman in `Battle of the Birdmen'. 600.00
72 JKu 600.00
73 JKu(c) 600.00
74 JKu(c) 600.00
75 JKu(c),Hawkman in `Magic at the Mardi Gras'. 600.00
76 A:Worry Wart 600.00
77 Hawkman in `The Case of the Curious Casket' 600.00
78 . . . . 600.00
79 Hawkman in `The Battle of the Birds' 600.00
80 Flash in `The Story of the Boy Genius' 600.00
81 JKu(c),Hawkman's Voyage to Venus. 600.00
82 A:Walter Jordan 600.00
83 JKu,JKu(c),Hawkman in `Destined for Disaster' 600.00
84 Flash V:`The Changeling'. . . . 600.00
85 JKu,JKu(c),Hawkman in Hollywood 600.00
86 JKu,1st Black Canary,Flash V:Stone Age Menace 2,200.00
87 Hawkman meets the Foil. . . 1,000.00
88 JKu,Flash in `The Case of the Vanished Year!' 1,000.00
89 I:The Thorn. 1,000.00
90 Flash in `Nine Empty Uniforms'. 1,000.00
91 Hawkman V:The Phantom Menace 1,100.00
92 1st full-length Black Canary story 3,000.00
93 Flash V:Violin of Villainy . . . 1,200.00
94 JKu(c). 1,200.00
95 . . . . 1,200.00
96 . . . . 1,200.00
97 Flash in `The Dream that Didn't Vanish' 1,200.00
98 JKu(c),Hawkman in `Crime Costume!'. 1,200.00
99 Flash in `The Star Prize of the Year' 1,200.00
100 Hawkman in `The Human -Fly Bandits!' 2,700.00
101 . . . . 2,000.00
102 Hawkman in `The Flying Darkness' 2,000.00
103 . . . . 2,400.00
104 JKu,Hawkman in `Flaming Darkness' Feb., 1949. . . . . 6,400.00

FLASH
Feb.–March, 1959
105 CI,O:Flash,I:Mirror Master. 5,800.00

DC COMICS

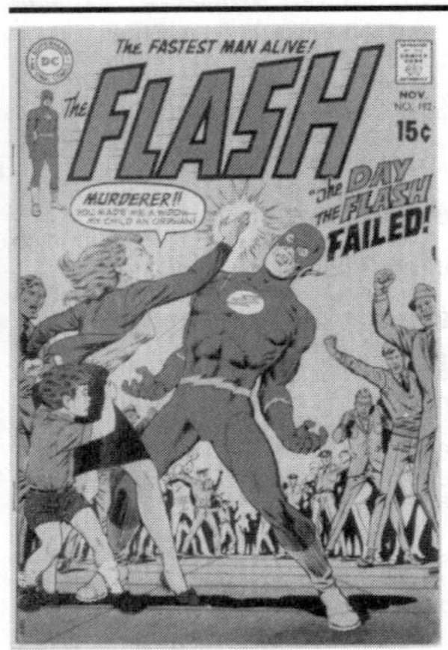

Flash #192 © DC Comics, Inc.

106 CI,I&O:Gorilla Grodd,
O:Pied Piper 1,600.00
107 CI,A:Grodd. 900.00
108 CI,A:Grodd. 700.00
109 CI,A:Mirror Master 550.00
110 CI,MA,I:Kid Flash,
Weather Wizard. 1,350.00
111 CI,A:Kid Flash,The Invasion
Of the Cloud Creatures. 400.00
112 CI,I&O:Elongated Man,
A:Kid Flash. 450.00
113 CI,I&O:Trickster 375.00
114 CI,A:Captain Cold 300.00
115 CI,A:Grodd. 250.00
116 CI,A:Kid Flash,The Man
Who Stole Central City 250.00
117 CI,MA,I:Capt.Boomerang . . . 300.00
118 CI,MA 225.00
119 CI,W:Elongated Man 225.00
120 CI,A:Kid Flash,Land of
Golden Giants 225.00
121 CI,A:Trickster. 175.00
122 CI,I&O:The Top 175.00
123 I:Earth 2,R:G.A.Flash 1,300.00
124 CI,A:Capt.Boomerang 150.00
125 CI,A:Kid Flash,The
Conquerors of Time 135.00
126 CI,A:Mirror Master 135.00
127 CI,A:Grodd. 135.00
128 CI,O:Abra Kadabra 135.00
129 CI,A:Capt.Cold,Trickster,A:Gold.
Age Flash,C:JLA (flashback). 300.00
130 CI,A:Mirror Master,
Weather Wizard 135.00
131 CI,A:Green Lantern 125.00
132 CI,A:Daphne Dean. 125.00
133 CI,A:Abra Kadabra. 125.00
134 CI,A:Captain Cold 125.00
135 CI,N:Kid Flash 125.00
136 CI,A:Mirror Master 125.00
137 CI,Vandal Savage,R:JSA,
A:G.A.Flash 450.00
138 CI,A:Pied Piper 125.00
139 CI,I&O:Prof.Zoom(Reverse
Flash). 150.00
140 CI,O:Heat Wave. 120.00
141 CI,A:Top. 100.00
142 CI,A:Trickster. 100.00
143 CI,A:Green Lantern 100.00
144 CI,A:Man Missile,Kid Flash. . 100.00
145 CI,A:Weather Wizard 100.00
146 CI,A:Mirror Master 100.00
147 CI,A:Mr.Element,A:Reverse
Flash 100.00
148 CI,A:Capt.Boomerang 100.00

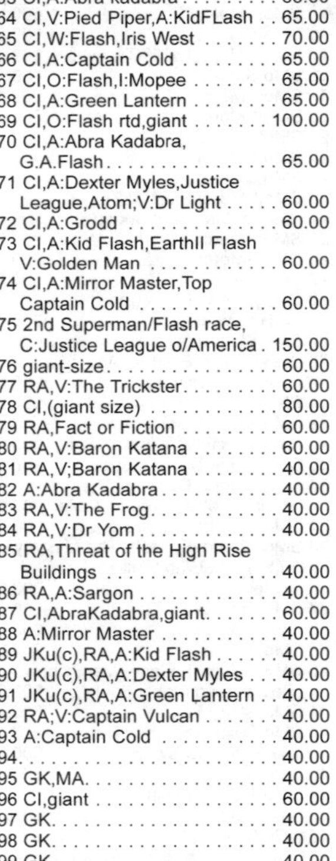
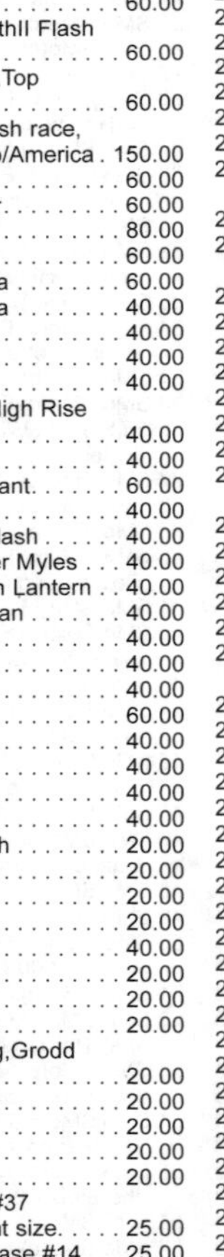

149 CI,A:Abra Kadabra. 100.00
150 CI,A:Captain Cold 100.00
151 CI,A:Earth II Flash,
The Shade 125.00
152 CI,V:Trickster 75.00
153 CI,A:Mr.Element,Rev.Flash . . 75.00
154 CI,The Day Flash Ran Away
with Himself 75.00
155 CI,A:MirrorMaster,Capt.Cold,Top
Capt. Boomerang,Grodd. 75.00
156 CI,A:Kid Flash,The Super Hero
who Betrayed the World 75.00
157 CI,A:Doralla Kon,The Top. . . . 75.00
158 CI,V:The Breakaway Bandit
A:The Justice League. 75.00
159 CI,A:Kid Flash 75.00
160 CI,giant 100.00
161 CI,A:Mirror Master 65.00
162 CI,Who Haunts the Corridor
of Chills 65.00
163 CI,A:Abra kadabra 65.00
164 CI,V:Pied Piper,A:KidFLash . . 65.00
165 CI,W:Flash,Iris West 70.00
166 CI,A:Captain Cold 65.00
167 CI,O:Flash,I:Mopee 65.00
168 CI,A:Green Lantern 65.00
169 CI,O:Flash rtd,giant 100.00
170 CI,A:Abra Kadabra,
G.A.Flash. 65.00
171 CI,A:Dexter Myles,Justice
League,Atom;V:Dr Light 60.00
172 CI,A:Grodd 60.00
173 CI,A:Kid Flash,EarthII Flash
V:Golden Man 60.00
174 CI,A:Mirror Master,Top
Captain Cold 60.00
175 2nd Superman/Flash race,
C:Justice League o/America . 150.00
176 giant-size 60.00
177 RA,V:The Trickster. 60.00
178 CI,(giant size) 80.00
179 RA,Fact or Fiction 60.00
180 RA,V:Baron Katana 60.00
181 RA,V;Baron Katana 40.00
182 A:Abra Kadabra 40.00
183 RA,V:The Frog. 40.00
184 RA,V:Dr Yom 40.00
185 RA,Threat of the High Rise
Buildings 40.00
186 RA,A:Sargon 40.00
187 CI,AbraKadabra,giant. 60.00
188 A:Mirror Master 40.00
189 JKu(c),RA,A:Kid Flash 40.00
190 JKu(c),RA,A:Dexter Myles . . . 40.00
191 JKu(c),RA,A:Green Lantern . . 40.00
192 RA;V:Captain Vulcan 40.00
193 A:Captain Cold 40.00
194. . . . . 40.00
195 GK,MA. 40.00
196 CI,giant 60.00
197 GK. 40.00
198 GK. 40.00
199 GK. 40.00
200 IN,MA 40.00
201 IN,MA,A:G.A. Flash 20.00
202 IN,MA,A:Kid Flash 20.00
203 IN 20.00
204. . . . . 20.00
205 giant 40.00
206 A:Mirror Master 20.00
207. . . . . 20.00
208. . . . . 20.00
209 A:Capt.Boomerang,Grodd
Trickster 20.00
210 CI 20.00
211 O:Flash 20.00
212 A:Abra Kadabra 20.00
213 CI 20.00
214 CI,rep.Showcase #37
(O:Metal Men),giant size. . . . 25.00
215 IN,FMc,rep.Showcase #14 . . . 25.00

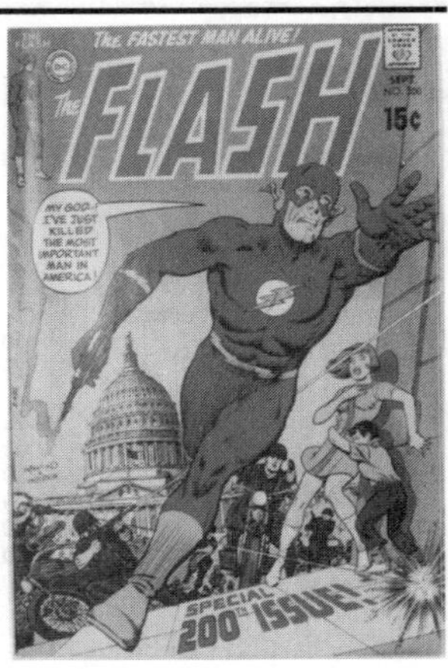

Flash #200 © DC Comics, Inc.

216 A:Mr.Element. 20.00
217 NA,A:Gr.Lant,Gr.Arrow. 22.00
218 NA,A:Gr.Lant,Gr.Arrow. 22.00
219 NA,L:Greeen Arrow 22.00
220 IN,DG,A:KidFlash,Gr.Lantern . 20.00
221 IN 15.00
222 IN 15.00
223 DG,Green Lantern 15.00
224 IN,DG,A:Green Lantern 15.00
225 IN,DG,A:Gr.Lant,Rev.Flash . . 12.00
226 NA,A:Capt. Cold 15.00
227 IN,FMc,DG,Capt.Boomerang,
Green Lantern 12.00
228 IN 12.00
229 IN,FMc,A:Green Arrow,
V:Rag Doll (giant size) 20.00
230 A:VandalSavage,Dr.Alchemy . 12.00
231 FMc. 12.00
232 giant 35.00
233 giant 35.00
234 V:Reverse Flash 10.00
235. . . . . 8.00
236 MGr. 8.00
237 IN,FMc,MGr,A:Prof Zoom,
Green Lantern 10.00
238 MGr. 8.00
239 . . . . 8.00
240 MGr. 8.00
241 A:Mirror Master 8.00
242 MGr,D:Top 8.00
243 IN,FMc,MGr,TA,O:Top,
A:Green Lantern. 8.00
244 IN,FMc,A:Rogue's Gallery 8.00
245 IN,FMc,DD,TA,I:PlantMaster . . 8.00
246 IN,FMc,DD,TA,I:PlantMaster . . 8.00
247. . . . . 8.00
248 FMc,IN,I:Master 8.00
249 FMc,IN,V:Master 8.00
250 IN,FMc,I:Golden Glider 8.00
251 FMc,IN,V:Golden Glider. 6.00
252 FMc,IN,I:Molder 6.00
253 FMc,IN,V:Molder 6.00
254 FMc. 6.00
255 FMc,A:MirrorMaster 6.00
256 FMc,V:Top 6.00
257 FMc,A:Green Glider. 6.00
258 FMc,A:Black Hand 6.00
259 FMc,IN 6.00
260 FMc,IN 6.00
261 FMc,IN,V:Golden Glider. 6.00
262 FMc,IN,V:Golden Glider. 6.00
263 FMc,IN,V:Golden Glider. 6.00
264 FMc,IN,V:Golden Glider. 6.00
265 FMc,IN 6.00
266 FMc,IN,V:Heat Wave 6.00

 All comics prices listed are for *Near Mint* condition.

267 FMc,IN,V:Heat Wave . . . 6.00
268 FMc,IN,A:E2 Flash . . . 6.00
269 FMc,IN,A:Kid Flash . . . 6.00
270 FMc,IN,V:Clown . . . 6.00
271 RB,V:Clown . . . 6.00
272 RB,V:Clown . . . 6.00
273 RB . . . 6.00
274 RB . . . 6.00
275 AS,D:Iris West,PCP story . . . 7.00
276 AS,A:JLA . . . 6.00
277 AS,FMc,A:JLA, V:MirrorMaster . . . 6.00
278 A:Captain.Boomerang & Heatwave . . . 6.00
279 A:Captain.Boomerang & Heatwave . . . 6.00
280 DH . . . 6.00
281 DH,V:Reverse Flash . . . 7.00
282 DH,V:Reverse Flash . . . 7.00
283 DH,V:Reverse Flash . . . 7.00
284 DH,Flash's life story I:Limbo Lord . . . 6.00
285 DH,V:Trickster . . . 6.00
286 DH,I:Rainbow Raider . . . 6.00
287 DH,V:Dr.Alchemy . . . 6.00
288 DH,V:Dr.Alchemy . . . 6.00
289 DH,GP,1st GP DC art; V:Dr. Alchemy;B:B.U.Firestorm . . . 8.00
290 GP . . . 5.00
291 GP,DH,V:Sabretooth . . . 5.00
292 GP,DH,V:Mirror Master . . . 5.00
293 GP,DH,V:Pied Piper . . . 5.00
294 GP,DH,V:Grodd . . . 5.00
295 CI,JSn,V:Grodd . . . 5.00
296 JSn,A:Elongated Man . . . 5.00
297 CI,A:Captain Cold . . . 5.00
298 CI,V:Shade,Rainbowraider . . . 5.00
299 CI,V:Shade,Rainbowraider . . . 5.00
300 A:New Teen Titans . . . 6.00
301 CI,A:Firestorm . . . 5.00
302 CI,V:Golden Glider . . . 5.00
303 CI,V:Golden Glider . . . 5.00
304 CI,PB,I:Col.Computron;E:B.U. Firestorm . . . 5.00
305 KG,CI,A:G.A.Flash,B:Dr.Fate . . . 4.00
306 CI,KG,V:Mirror Master . . . 4.00
307 CI,KG,V:Pied Piper . . . 3.00
308 CI,KG . . . 3.00
309 CI,KG . . . 4.00
310 CI,KG,V:Capt.Boomerang . . . 3.00
311 CI,KG,V:Capt.Boomerang . . . 3.00
312 CI,A:Heatwave . . . 3.00
313 KG,A:Psylon,E:Dr.Fate . . . 3.00
314 CI,I:Eradicator . . . 3.00
315 CI,V:Gold Face . . . 3.00
316 CI,V:Gold Face . . . 3.00
317 CI,V:Gold Face . . . 3.00
318 CI,DGb,V:Eradicator;B: B.U.Creeper . . . 3.00
319 CI,DGb,V:Eradicator . . . 3.00
320 CI,V:Eradicator . . . 3.00
321 CI,D:Eradicator . . . 3.00
322 CI,V:Reverse Flash . . . 3.00
323 CI,V:Reverse Flash;E: B.U.Creeper . . . 3.00
324 CI,D:Reverse Flash . . . 4.00
325 CI,A:Rogues Gallery . . . 3.00
326 CI,A:Weather Wizard . . . 3.00
327 CI,A:JLA,G.Grodd . . . 3.00
328 CI . . . 3.00
329 CI,A:J.L.A.,G.Grodd . . . 3.00
330 CI,FMc,V:G.Grodd . . . 3.00
331 CI,FMc,V:G.Grodd . . . 3.00
332 CI,FMc,V:Rainbow Raider . . . 3.00
333 CI,FMc,V:Pied Piper . . . 3.00
334 CI,FMc,V:Pied Piper . . . 3.00
335 CI,FMc,V:Pied Piper . . . 3.00
336 CI,FMc,V:Pied Piper . . . 3.00
337 CI,FMc,V:Pied Piper . . . 3.00
338 CI,FMc,I:Big Sir . . . 3.00
339 CI,FMc,A:Big Sir . . . 3.00
340 CI,FMc,Trial,A:Big Sir . . . 3.00
341 CI,FMc,Trial,A:Big Sir . . . 3.00
342 CI,FMc,Trial,V:RogueGallery . . . 3.00
343 CI,FMc,Trial,A:GoldFace . . . 3.00
344 CI,O:Kid Flash,Trial . . . 3.00
345 CI,A:Kid Flash,Trial . . . 3.00
346 CI,FMc,Trial,V:AbraKadabra . . . 3.00
347 CI,FMc,Trial,V:AbraKadabra . . . 3.00
348 CI,FMc,Trial,V:AbraKadabra . . . 3.00
349 CI,FMc,Trial,V:AbraKadabra . . . 3.00
350 CI,FMc,Trial,V:AbraKadabra . . . 7.00
Ann.#1 O:ElongatedMan, G.Grodd . . . 325.00

FLASH

[2nd Series] Oct., 1985

1 JG,Legends,C:Vandal Savage . . . 8.00
2 JG,V:Vandal Savage . . . 4.00
3 JG,I:Kilgore . . . 3.00
4 JG,A:Cyborg . . . 3.00
5 JG,V:Speed Demon . . . 3.00
6 JG,V:Speed Demon . . . 3.00
7 JG,V:Red Trinity . . . 3.00
8 JG,V:BlueTrinity,Millenium . . . 3.00
9 JG,I:Chunk,Millenium . . . 3.00
10 V:Chunk,Chunks World . . . 2.50
11 Return to Earth . . . 2.50
12 Velocity 9 . . . 2.50
13 Vandal Savage,V:Velocity 9 Adicts . . . 2.50
14 V:Vandal Savage . . . 2.50
15 A:Velocity 9 Junkies . . . 2.50
16 C:V.Savage,SpeedMcGeePt.1 . . . 2.50
17 GLa,Speed McGee,pt.2 . . . 2.50
18 GLa,SpeedMcGeePt.3, V:V.Savage . . . 2.25
19 JM:+bonus book,R:Rogue Gallery,O:Blue/Red Trinity . . . 2.25
20 A:Durlan . . . 2.25
21 A:Manhunter,Invasion x-over . . . 2.25
22 A:Manhunter,Invasion x-over . . . 2.25
23 V:Abrakadabra . . . 2.25
24 GLa,FlashRegainsSpeed, A:L.Lane . . . 2.25
25 GLa,Search for Flash . . . 2.25
26 GLa,I:Porcupine Man . . . 2.25
27 GLa,Porcupine Man as Flash . . . 2.25
28 GLa,A:Golden Glider, Capt.Cold . . . 2.25
29 A:New Phantom Lady . . . 2.25
30 GLa,Turtle Saga,pt.1 . . . 2.25
31 GLa,Turtle Saga,pt.2 . . . 2.00
32 GLa,Turtle Saga,pt.3, R:G.A.Turtle . . . 2.00

Flash 2nd Series #6 © DC Comics Inc.

33 GLa,Turtle Saga,pt.4 . . . 2.00
34 GLa,Turtle Saga,pt.5 . . . 2.00
35 GLa,Turtle Saga,pt.6, D:G.A.Turtle . . . 2.00
36 GLa,V:Cult . . . 2.00
37 GLa,V:Cult . . . 2.00
38 GLa,V:Cult . . . 2.00
39 GLa,V:Cult . . . 2.00
40 GLa,A:Dr.Alchemy . . . 2.00
41 GLa,A:Dr.Alchemy . . . 2.00
42 GLa,MechanicalTroubles . . . 2.00
43 GLa,V:Kilgore . . . 2.00
44 GLa,V:Velocity . . . 2.00
45 V:Gorilla Grod . . . 2.00
46 V:Gorilla Grod . . . 2.00
47 V:Gorilla Grod . . . 2.00
48 . . . 2.00
49 A:Vandal Savage . . . 2.00
50 N:Flash (double sz)V:Savage . . . 5.00
51 I:Proletariat . . . 2.00
52 I.R.S. Mission . . . 2.00
53 A:Superman,Race to Save Jimmy Olsen . . . 2.00
54 Terrorist Airline Attack . . . 2.00
55 War of the Gods x-over . . . 2.00
56 The Way of a Will,pt.1 . . . 2.00
57 The Way of a Will,pt.2 . . . 2.00
58 Meta Gene-activated Homeless . 2.00
59 The Last Resort . . . 2.00
60 Love Song of the Chunk . . . 2.00
61 Wally's Mother's Wedding Day . . . 2.00
62 GLa,Year 1,pt.1 . . . 2.25
63 GLa,Year 1,pt.2 . . . 2.00
64 GLa,Year 1,pt.3 . . . 2.00
65 GLa,Year 1,pt.4 . . . 2.00
66 A:Aq'man,V:Marine Marauder . . . 2.00
67 GLa,V:Abra Kadabra . . . 2.00
68 GLa,V:Abra Kadabra . . . 2.00
69 GLa,Gorilla Warfare#2 . . . 2.00
70 Gorilla Warfare#4 . . . 2.00
71 GLa,V:Dr.Alchemy . . . 2.00
72 GLa,V:Dr.Alchemy,C:Barry Allen . . . 2.50
73 GLa,Xmas Issue,R:Barry Allen . . . 4.50
74 GLa,A:Barry Allen? . . . 3.00
75 GLa,A:Reverse Flash,V:Mob Violence . . . 3.50
76 GLa,A:Reverse Flash . . . 2.25
77 GLa,G.A.Flash vs Reverse Flash . . . 2.25
78 GLa,V:Reverse Flash . . . 2.25
79 GLa,V:Reverse Flash,48 pgs. . . 3.25
80 AD(c),V:Frances Kane . . . 3.00
80a Newstand Ed . . . 2.00
81 AD(c) . . . 2.00
82 AD(c),A:Nightwing . . . 2.00
83 AD(c),A:Nightwing,Starfire . . . 2.00
84 AD(c),I:Razer . . . 2.00
85 AD(c),V:Razer . . . 2.00
86 AD(c),A:Argus . . . 2.00
86 V:Santa Claus . . . 2.00
87 Chrismas issue . . . 2.00
88 . . . 2.00
89 On Trial . . . 2.00
90 On Trial#2 . . . 2.00
91 Out of Time . . . 5.00
92 I:3rd Flash . . . 12.00
93 A:Impulse . . . 5.00
94 Zero Hour . . . 5.00
95 Terminal Velocity,pt.1 . . . 4.00
96 Terminal Velocity,pt.2 . . . 4.00
97 Terminal Velocity,pt.3 . . . 2.00
98 Terminal Velocity,pt.4 . . . 2.00
99 Terminal Velocity,pt.5 . . . 2.00
100 I:New Flash . . . 5.00
100a Collector's Edition . . . 2.50
101 Velocity Aftermath . . . 2.00
102 V:Mongul . . . 2.00
103 Supernatural threat from Linda's Past Secret . . . 2.00

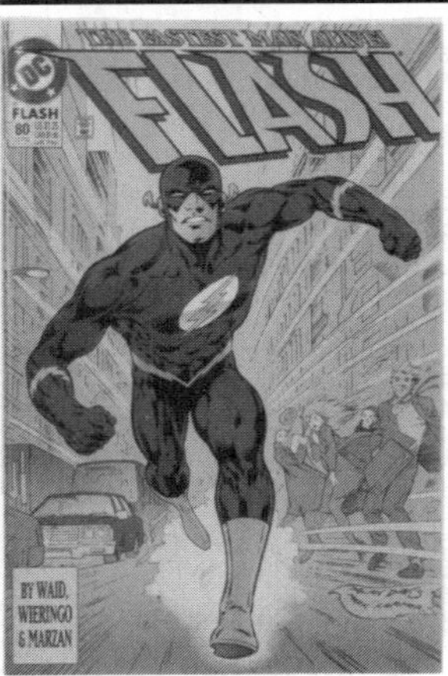

Flash 2nd Series #80
© DC Comics, Inc.

104 Exorcise Demons. 2.00
105 . . . . 2.00
106 R:Magenta. 2.00
107 MWa,Underworld Unleashed tie-in. 2.00
108 MWa,Dead Heat,pt.1 . . . . 2.00
109 MWa,Dead Heat,pt.2 . . . . 2.00
110 MWa,Dead Heat,pt.4 . . . . 2.00
111 MWa,Dead Heat,pt.6 . . . . 2.00
112 MWa,New Flash in town. 2.00
113 MWa,F:Linda 2.00
114 MWa,V:Chillblaine 2.00
115 thru 117 . . . . @2.00
118 MWa&BAu(s),Flash returns from the future 2.00
119 MWa&BAu(s),PR,Final Night tie-in. 2.00
120 MWa&BAu(s),PR,"Presidential Race," pt.1 . . . . 2.00
121 MWa&BAu(s),PR,"Presidential Race," pt.2 . . . . 2.00
122 MWa&BAu(s),PR, ... 2.00
123 MWa&BAu(s),PR,Flash moves to Santa Marta 2.00
124 MWa&BAu(s),PR,Wally doesn't know reality from illusion 2.00
125 MWa&BAu(s),PR,California, V:Major Disaster. 2.00
126 MWa&BAu(s),PR,V:Major Disaster 2.00
127 MWa&Bau(s),PR,"Hell to Pay," pt. 1 (of 3) 2.00
128 MWa&BAu(s),PR,"Hell to Pay" pt. 2, A:JLA 2.00
129 MWa&BAu(s),PR,"Hell to Pay" pt. 3, concl. 2.00
130 GMo&MMr(s),PR,new menace. 2.00
131 GMo&MMr(s),PR,V:The Suit . . 2.50
132 GMo&MMr(s),PR,V:The Suit . . 2.50
133 GMo&MMr(s),PR,V:Mirror Master 2.00
134 GMo&MMr(s),PR,V:Weather Wizard & Captain Cold 2.00
135 GMo&MMr(s), ... 2.00
136 GMo&MMr(s),PR,Human Race,pt.1 . . . . 2.00
137 GMo&MMr(s),PR,Human Race,pt.2 . . . . 2.00
138 GMo&MMr(s),PR,Human Race,pt.3 . . . . 2.00
139 MMr(s),Clv,Black Flash,pt.1 . . . 2.00
140 MMr(s),Clv,Black Flash,pt.2 . . . 2.00
141 MMr(s),Clv,Black Flash,pt.3 . . . 2.00
142 MWa&BAu(s),Clv,SLi,wedding of Wally West & Linda Park 2.00
143 MWa&BAu(s),Clv,V:CobaltBlue 2.00
144 MWa&BAu(s),Clv,O:CobaltBlue 2.00
145 MWa&BAu(s),PaP,VRu, Chain Lightning, pt.1 . . . . 2.00
146 MWa&BAu(s),PaP,VRu, Chain Lightning, pt.2 . . . . 2.00
147 MWa&BAu(s),PaP,VRu, Chain Lightning, pt.3 . . . . 2.00
148 MWa&BAu(s),PaP,VRu, Chain Lightning, pt.4 . . . . 2.00
149 MWa&BAu(s),PaP,VRu, Chain Lightning, pt.5 . . . . 2.00
150 MWa&BAu(s),PaP,VRu, Chain Lightning, pt.6, 48-page 3.00
151 MWa&BAu(s),PaP,A:Robin & Aqualad, flashback issue. . . . 2.00
152 MWa&BAu(s),PaP,VRu, new costume 2.00
153 MWa&BAu(s),PaP,JMz, V:Folded Man. 2.00
154 MWa&BAu(s),PaP,JMz, ... 2.00
155 MWa&BAu(s),PaP,JMz, V:Replicant. 2.00
156 MWa&BAu(s),PaP,JMz. 2.00
157 MWa&BAu(s),PaP,JMz,fate of Linda Park 2.00
158 MWa&BAu(s),PaP,DHz 2.00
159 MWa&BAu(s),PaP,Dark Flash . 2.00
160 BAu(s),Honeymoon on the Run 2.00
161 PaP,DHz,F:Original JSA. 2.00
162 PaP,DHz,R:Felix Faust. 2.00
163 RLm,DHz,A:JLA. 2.25
164 DHz,BBo(c),Wonderland,pt.1 . . 2.25
165 DHz,Wonderland,pt.2. . . . . 2.25
166 DHz,Wonderland,pt.3. . . . . 2.25
167 DHz,Wonderland,pt.4. . . . . 2.25
Ann.#1 JG,The Deathtouch. 4.00
Ann.#2 A:Wally's Father 3.00
Ann.#3 Roots 2.50
Ann.#4 Armageddon,pt7 . . . . 2.50
Ann.#5 TC(1st Full Work),Eclipso, V:Rogue's Gallery. 8.00
Ann.#6 Bloodlines#4,I:Argus. 2.75
Ann.#7 Elseworlds story 2.95
Ann.#8 Year One story 3.00
Ann.#9 Legends o/t Dead Earth . . . 2.95
Ann.#10 Pulp Heroes (Romance) . . 3.95
Ann.#11 BAu,BWr, Ghosts 3.00
Ann.#12 DBw,AAd(c),JLApe: Gorilla Warfare 2.95
Ann.#13 Planet DC. 3.50
Spec #1,IN,DG,CI,50th Anniv., Three Flash's 4.50
Spec.#1,000,000 MWa(s),JMz, A:Capt.Marvel of 853rd-cent. . . 2.00
T.V. Spec.#1,JS,w/episode guide . . 4.25
TPB Terminal Velocity. 12.95
TPB The Life Story of the Flash . . 13.00
TPB The Return of Barry Allen . . . 13.00
TPB Born to Run 13.00
TPB Dead Heat 14.95
Secret Files #1 MWa,BAu,PRy, O:Flash family 5.00
Secret Files #2 (1999) 4.95
HC Flash Archives,Vol.#1 . . . . . . 50.00
HC Flash Archives,Vol.#2 . . . . 49.95
Giant #1 MWa,80-page (1998) 5.00
Giant #2 80-page 5.00

FLASH & GREEN LANTERN: THE BRAVE & THE BOLD

1999

1 (of 6) MWa&TPe(s),BKi 2.50
2 MWa&TPe(s),BKi 2.50
3 MWa&TPe(s),BKi 2.50
4 MWa&TPe(s),BKi 2.50

Flash Gordon #1 © DC Comics, Inc.

5 MWa&TPe(s),BKi 2.50
6 MWa&TPe(s),BKi,concl. 2.50

THE FLASH PLUS

Nov., 1996

1 MWa(s),F:Wally West, Dick Grayson 3.50

FLASH GORDON

1988

1 DJu,I:New Flash Gordon. 2.00
2 DJu,A:Lion-Men,Shark-Men 2.00
3 DJu,V:Shark-Men 2.00
4 DJu,Dale Kidnapped by Voltan . . 2.00
5 DJu,Alliance Against Ming 2.00
6 DJu,Arctic City 2.00
7 DJu,Alliance vs. Ming 2.00
8 DJu,Alliance vs. Ming 2.00
9 DJu,V:Ming, final issue 2.00

FLASHPOINT

Oct., 1999

1 (of 3) NBy,Elseworlds 2.95
2 NBy,Flash in wheelchair 2.95
3 NBy 2.95

FLINCH

DC/Vertigo 1999

1 JLe,RCo,horror anthology. 2.50
2 BSz,RCo(c),3 horror tales. 2.50
3 KJo,3 horror tales. 2.50
4 TTn,PGu,3 horror tales. 2.50
5 JLd(s),RBr,3 horror tales. 2.50
6 WML(s) 2.50
7 WML(s) 2.50
8 . . . . 2.50
9 3 tales ofhorror. 2.50
10 . . . . 2.50
11 JLd(s) 2.50
12 . . . . 2.50
13 hubris & dark whimsy. 2.50
14 . . . . 2.50
15 3 grim tales 2.50

FLINTSTONES AND THE JETSONS, THE

Warner Bros./DC

1 Ancestors & Descendents meet . 2.00
2 Dino wins a contest, Bay

Watchdog 2.00
3 Mr. Spacely a baby 2.00
4 cavewomen 2.00
5 21st century house party 2.00
6 Thanksgiving Feast 2.00
7 CDi, Spy Who Grounded Me . . . 2.00
8 . . . . 2.00
9 I, Rosey 2.00
10 Beast of Bedrock 2.00
11 Mr. Spacely, time travel 2.00
12 Animal appliances on strike 2.00
13 F:Astro 2.00
14 Flintstone Files, UFOs 2.00
15 Mr. Spacely, most powerful being in the universe 2.00
16 The Yelling Man 2.00
17 Scooba Dabba Doo 2.00
18 holiday special 2.00
19 bizarre world 2.00
20 Sherock Holmes 2.00
21 final issue 2.00

FLY, THE

Impact 1991–92

1 I&O:Fly I:Arachnus,Chromium . . . 2.50
2 V:Chromium 2.00
3 O:Arachnus, I:Lt.Walker Odell . . . 2.00
4 A:Black Hood, V:Arachnus 2.00
5 V:Arachnus 2.00
6 I:Blackjack 2.00
7 Oceanworld,V:Dolphus 2.00
8 A:Comet,Dolphus 2.00
9 F:Fireball, with trading card 2.00
10 V:General Mechanix 2.00
11 Suicide Issue 2.00
12 V:Agent from WEB 2.00
13 I:Tremor 2.00
14 and 15 V:Domino . . . . @2.00
16 V:Arachnus 2.00
17 Final Issue 2.00
Ann.#1 Earthquest,pt.4,w/card 2.50

FORBIDDEN TALES OF DARK MANSION

May–June, 1972

5 thru 15 Feb.–March, 1974 . . . . @2.00

FOREVER PEOPLE, THE

1971–72

1 I:Forever People,A:Superman, A:Darkseid 50.00
2 A:Darkseid 30.00
3 A:Darkseid 30.00
4 A:Darkseid 30.00
5 . . . . 25.00
6 thru 11 . . . . @12.50

FOREVER PEOPLE

1988

1 Return of Forever People 2.00
2 'Return of Earth of Yesterday' . . . 2.00
3 A:Mark Moonrider 2.00
4 The Dark controlls M.Moonrider . 2.00
5 R:MotherBox,Infinity Man 2.00
6 Donny's Fate, final issue 2.00

FORGOTTEN REALMS

1989–91

1 A:RealmsMaster,PriamAgrivar . . 4.00
2 Mystic Hand of Vaprak, A:Ogre Mage 3.00
3 Mystic Hand of Vaprak contd. . . . 2.75
4 Ogre Mage vs.Omen the Wizard. 2.75
5 Dragon Reach #1 . . . . 2.75
6 Dragon Reach #2 . . . . 2.50
7 Dragon Reach #3 . . . . 2.50
8 Dragon Reach #4 . . . . 2.50
9 V:Giant Squid 2.50
10 'Head Cheese' 2.50
11 Triangles #1 . . . . 2.50
12 Triangles #2 . . . . 2.50
13 Triangles #3 . . . . 2.50
14 A:Lich Viranton the Mage 2.00
15 Avatar Comics tie-in 2.00
16 Mad Gods and Paladins,pt.1 . . . 2.00
17 Mad Gods and Paladins,pt.2 . . . 2.00
18 Mad Gods and Paladins,pt.3 . . . 2.00
19 Mad Gods and Paladins,pt.4 . . . 2.00
20 Realms Master Crew captured . . 2.00
21 Catewere Tribe 2.00
22 V:The Akri 2.00
23 A:Sandusk the Leprechaun 2.00
24 'Everybody wants to rule the realms' 2.00
25 The Wake, final issue 2.00
Ann.#1 V:Advanced D&D crew 3.50

FOUR STAR BATTLE TALES

1973

1 thru 5 . . . . @2.00

FOUR HORSEMEN

DC/Vertigo Dec. 1999

1 (of 4) F:Famine 2.50
2 F:War 2.50
3 F:Pestilence 2.50
4 F:Death, concl. 2.50

FOUR STAR SPECTACULAR

March–April, 1976

1 . . . . 2.00
2 thru 6 . . . . @2.00

FOURTH WORLD GALLERY

1-shot pin-up collection (1996) 3.50

FOX AND THE CROW

Dec.–Jan., 1951

1 . . . . 850.00
2 . . . . 400.00
3 . . . . 250.00
4 . . . . 250.00
5 . . . . 250.00
6 thru 10 . . . . @175.00
11 thru 20 . . . . @125.00
21 thru 40 . . . . @125.00
41 thru 60 . . . . @60.00
61 thru 80 . . . . @35.00
81 thru 94 . . . . @30.00
95 . . . . 35.00
96 thru 99 . . . . @15.00
100 . . . . 18.00
101 thru 108 . . . . @15.00

From Beyond The Unknown #10
© DC Comics Inc.

Becomes:

STANLEY & HIS MONSTER

109 thru 112 Oct.Nov.,1968 . . . . @10.00

FREEDOM FIGHTERS

March–April, 1976

1 Freedom Fighters go to Earth 1 . 2.00
2 . . . . 2.00
3 . . . . 2.00
4 . . . . 2.00
5 A:Wonder Woman 2.00
6 . . . . 2.00
7 . . . . 2.00
8 . . . . 2.00
9 . . . . 2.00
10 O:Doll Man 2.00
11 O:Ray 2.00
12 O:Firebrand 2.00
13 O:Black Condor 2.00
14 A:Batgirl 2.00
15 O:Phantom Lady 2.00

FROM BEYOND THE UNKNOWN

Oct.–Nov., 1969

1 JKu,CI 50.00
2 MA(c),CI,ATh 20.00
3 NA(c),CI 18.00
4 MA(c),CI 18.00
5 MA(c),CI 18.00
6 NA(c),I:Glen Merrit 20.00
7 CI,JKu(c) 25.00
8 NA(c),CI 25.00
9 NA(c),CI 25.00
10 MA(c),CI 25.00
11 MA(c),CI 25.00
12 JKu(c),CI 25.00
13 JKu(c),CI,WW 25.00
14 JKu(c),CI 25.00
15 MA(c),CI 25.00
16 MA(c),CI 25.00
17 MA(c),CI 25.00
18 MK(c),CI 12.00
19 MK(c),CI 12.00
20. . . . . 12.00
21. . . . . 12.00
22 MA(c) 15.00
23 CI,Space Museum 12.00
24 CI 12.00

FUNNY STOCKING STUFFER

March, 1985

1 . . . . 2.00

FUNNY STUFF

Summer, 1944

1 B:3 Mousketeer Terrific Whatzit 650.00
2 . . . . 350.00
3 . . . . 200.00
4 . . . . 175.00
5 . . . . 175.00

DC COMICS

6 thru 10 . . . . @150.00
11 thru 20 . . . . @125.00
21 . . . . 75.00
22 C:Superman 300.00
23 thru 30 . . . . @75.00
31 thru 78 . . . . @50.00
79 July-Aug., 1954 . . . . 50.00

Fury of Firestorm #22
© DC Comics, Inc.

FURY OF FIRESTORM

June, 1982

1 PB,I:Black Bison 3.00
2 PB,V:Black Bison 2.00
3 PB,V:Pied Piper, Killer Frost 2.00
4 PB,A:JLA,Killer Frost 2.00
5 PB,V:Pied Piper 2.00
6 V:Pied Piper 2.00
7 I:Plastique 2.00
8 V:Typhoon 2.00
9 V:Typhoon 2.00
10 V:Hyena 2.00
11 V:Hyena 2.00
12 PB,V:Hyena 2.00
13 . . . . 2.00
14 PB,I:Enforcer,A:Multiplex 2.00
15 V:Multiplex 2.00
16 V:Multiplex 2.00
17 I:2000 Committee,Firehawk 2.00
18 I:Tokamak,A:Multiplex 2.00
19 GC,V:Goldenrod 2.00
20 A:Killer Frost 2.00
21 D:Killer Frost 2.50
22 O:Firestorm 2.50
23 I:Bug & Byte 2.00
24 I:Blue Devil,Bug & Byte 2.50
25 I:Silver Deer 2.00
26 V:Black Bison 2.00
27 V:Black Bison 2.00
28 I:Slipknot 2.00
29 I:2000 C'tee,I:Breathtaker 2.00
30 V:2000 Committee 2.00
31 V:2000 Committee 2.00
32 Phantom Stranger 2.00
33 A:Plastique 2.00
34 I:Killer Frost 2 . . . . 2.00
35 V:K.Frost/Plastique,I:Weasel . . . 2.00
36 V:Killer Frost & Plastique 2.00
37 . . . . 2.00
38 V:Weasel 2.00
39 V:Weasel 2.00
40 . . . . 2.00
41 Crisis 2.00
42 Crisis,A:Firehawk 2.00
43 V:Typhoon 2.00
44 V:Typhoon 2.00
45 V:Multiplex 2.00
46 A:Blue Devil 2.00
47 A:Blue Devil 2.00
48 I:Moonbow 2.00
49 V:Moonbow 2.00
50 W:Ed Raymond 2.00
51 A:King Crusher 2.00
52 A:King Crusher 2.00
53 V:Steel Shadow 2.00
54 I:Lava 2.00
55 Legends,V:World's Luckiest Man 2.00
56 Legends,A:Hawk 2.00
57 . . . . 2.00
58 I:Parasite II 2.00
59 . . . . 2.00
60 Secret behind Hugo's accident . . 2.00
61 V:Typhoon 2.00
61a Superman Logo 55.00
62 A:Russian 'Firestorm' 2.00
63 A:Capt.Atom 2.00
64 A:Suicide Squad 2.00
Ann.#1 EC,A:Firehawk, V:Tokamak 2.25
Ann.#2 . . . . 2.25
Ann.#3 . . . . 2.25
Ann.#4 KG,CS,GC,DG 2.25
Becomes:

FIRESTORM, THE NUCLEAR MAN

Nov., 1987

65 A:New Firestorm 2.00
66 A:Green Lantern 2.00
67 Millenium, Week 1 . . . . 2.00
68 Millenium 2.00
69 V:Zuggernaut,Stalnivolk USA . . . 2.00
70 V:Flying Dutchman 2.00
71 Trapped in the Timestream 2.00
72 V:Zuggernaut 2.00
73 V:Stalnivolk & Zuggernaut 2.00
74 Quest for Martin Stein 2.00
75 Return of Martin Stein 2.00
76 Firestorm & Firehawk vs Brimstone 2.00
77 Firestorm & Firehawk in Africa . . 2.00
78 'Exile From Eden',pt.1 . . . . 2.00
79 'Exile From Eden',pt.2 . . . . 2.00
80 A:Power Girl,Starman,Invasion x-over 2.00
81 A:Soyuz,Invasion aftermath 2.00

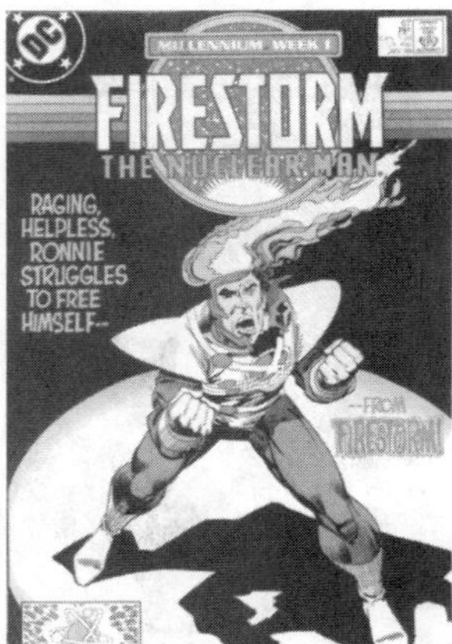

Firestorm The Nuclear Man #67
© DC Comics, Inc.

82 Invasion Aftermath 2.00
83 V:Svarozhich 2.00
84 . . . . 2.00
85 Soul of Fire,N:Firestorm 2.00
86 TMd,Janus Directive #7 . . . . 2.00
87 TMd 2.00
88 TMd,E:Air Wave B:Maser 2.00
89 TMd,V:Firehawk,Vandermeer Steel 2.00
90 TMd,Elemental War #1 . . . . 2.00
91 TMd,Elemental War #2 . . . . 2.00
92 TMd,Elemental War #3 . . . . 2.00
93 TMd,Elemental War concl. 2.00
94 TMd,A:Killer Frost 2.00
95 TMd,V:Captains of Industry 2.00
96 TMd,A:Shango,African God & Obatala,Lord o/t White Cloth. . . 2.00
97 TMd,A:Obatala,V:Shango 2.00
98 TMd,A:Masar 2.00
99 TMd,A:Brimstone,PlasmaGiant . 2.00
100 TMd,AM,V:Brimstone (Firestorm back-up story) final issue 3.00
Ann.#5 JLI,Suicide Squad I:New Firestorm 2.50

GAMMARAUDERS

1989

1 I:Animal-Warrior Bioborgs 2.00
2 V:The Slugnoids 2.00
3 V:Slugnoids,I:Squawk the Penguinoid 2.00
4 V:Slugnoids 2.00
5 V:Bioborg/Podnoid 2.00
6 Slash vs.Sassin,A:RadicalDebs . 2.00
7 Jok findsSword that was broken . 2.00
8 Jok's search for KirkwardDerby. . 2.00
9 Jok the Congressman 2.00
10 The Big Nada, final issue 2.00

GANG BUSTERS

1947–58

1 . . . . 700.00
2 . . . . 300.00
3 . . . . 225.00
4 . . . . 225.00
5 . . . . 225.00
6 . . . . 225.00
7 . . . . 225.00
8 . . . . 225.00
9 Ph(c) 175.00
10 Ph(c) 175.00
11 Ph(c) 150.00
12 Ph(c) 150.00
13 Ph(c) 150.00
14 Ph(c),FF 300.00
15 . . . . 125.00
16 . . . . 125.00
17 . . . . 300.00
18 . . . . 125.00
19 . . . . 125.00
20 . . . . 125.00
21 thru 25 . . . . @100.00
26 JK 100.00
27 thru 40 . . . . @90.00
41 thru 44 . . . . @75.00
45 Comics Code 75.00
46 thru 50 . . . . 75.00
51 MD 75.00
52 thru 67 . . . . @75.00

GANGLAND

April, 1998

1 (of 4) crime anthology 3.00
2 Platinum Nights 3.00
3 Gang Buff 3.00
4 conclusion 3.00
TPB series rep. 12.95

GEMINI BLOOD

DC/Helix

1 . . . . 2.25
2 . . . . 2.25
3 Royal Caste 2.50
4 V:Shraddhan 2.25
5 WSi(c),V:Rolk 2.25
6 . . . . 2.50
7 BSz, Gillian's secret revealed . . . 2.50
8 Loothka 2.50
9 Nick captured by Loothka, final issue 2.50

GENESIS

Aug., 1997

1 (of 4) JBy,RoW,JRu,AD,MFm, Marvel x-over 2.00
2 JBy,RoW,JRu,AD,MFm,x-over . . 2.00
3 JBy,RoW,JRu,AD,MFm,x-over . . 2.00
4 JBy,RoW,JRu,AD,MFm,concl. . . . 2.00

GHOSTDANCING

Vertigo 1995

[Mini-Series]

1 I:Snake,Ghost Dancing 2.00
2 Secrets 2.00
3 I:Father Craft 2.50
4 Coyote prisoner 2.50
5 F:Snot Boy 2.50

GHOSTS

Sept.–Oct., 1971

1 JAp,NC(c),Death's Bride-groom! 100.00
2 WW,NC(c),Mission Supernatural 50.00
3 TD,NC(c),Death is my Mother . . 40.00
4 GT,NC(c),The Crimson Claw . . . 40.00
5 NC(c),Death, The Pale Horseman 40.00
6 NC(c),A Specter Poured The Potion 20.00
7 MK(c),Death's Finger Points . . . 20.00
8 NC(c),The Cadaver In The Clock 20.00
9 AA,NC(c),The Last Ride Of Rosie The Wrecker 20.00
10 NC(c),A Specter Stalks Saigon 20.00
11 NC(c),The Devils Lake 15.00
12 NC(c),The Macabre Mummy Of Takhem-Ahtem 15.00
13 NC(c),Hell Is One Mile High . . . 15.00
14 NC(c),The Bride Wore A Shroud 15.00
15 AA,NC(c),The Ghost That Wouldn't Die 15.00
16 NC(c),Death's Grinning Face . . 15.00
17 NC(c),Death Held the Lantern High 15.00
18 AA,NC(c),Graveyard of Vengeance 15.00
19 AA,NC(c),The Dead Live On . . 15.00
20 NC(c),The Haunting Hussar Of West Point 15.00
21 NC(c),The Ghost In The Devil's Chair 10.00
22 NC(c),The Haunted Horns Of Death 10.00
23 NC(c),Dead Is My Darling! 10.00
24 AA,NC(c),You Too, Will Die . . . 10.00
25 AA,NC(c),Three Skulls On The Zambezi 10.00
26 DP,NC(c),The Freaky Phantom Of Watkins Glen 10.00
27 NC(c),Conversation With A Corpse 10.00
28 DP,NC(c),Flight Of The Lost Phantom 10.00
29 NC(c),The Haunted Lady Of Death 10.00
30 NC(c),The Fangs of the Phantom 10.00
31 NC(c),Blood On The Moon 10.00
32 NC(c),Phantom Laughed Last . 10.00
33 NC(c),The Hangman of Haunted Island 10.00
34 NC(c),Wrath of the Ghost Apes 10.00
35 NC(c),Feud with a Phantom . . . 10.00
36 NC(c),The Boy Who Returned From The Gave 10.00
37 LD(c),Fear On Ice 10.00
38 LD(c),Specter In The Surf 10.00
39 LD(c),The Haunting Hitchhicker 10.00
40 LD(c),The Nightmare That Haunted The World 18.00
41 LD(c),Ship of Specters 15.00
42 LD(c),The Spectral Sentries . . . 15.00
43 LD(c),3 Corpses On A Rope . . 15.00
44 LD(c),The Case of the Murdering Specters 15.00
45 LD(c),Bray of the Phantom Beast 15.00
46 LD(c),The World's Most Famous Phantom 15.00
47 LD(c),Wrath of the Restless Specters 15.00
48 DP,LD(c),The Phantom Head . . 15.00
49 The Ghost in the Cellar 15.00
50 Home Is Where The Grave Is . 15.00
51 The Ghost Who Would Not Die 15.00
52 LD(c),The Thunderhead Phantom 15.00
53 LD(c),Whose Spirit Invades Me 15.00
54 LD(c),The Deadly Dreams Of Ernie Caruso 15.00
55 LD(c),The House That Was Built For Haunting 15.00
56 LD(c),The Triumph Of The Teen-Age Phantom 15.00
57 LD(c),The Flaming Phantoms of Oradour 15.00
58 LD(c),The Corpse in the Closet 15.00
59 LD(c),That Demon Within Me . . 15.00
60 LD(c),The Spectral Smile of Death 8.00
61 LD(c),When Will I Die Again 8.00
62 LD(c),The Phantom Hoaxer! . . . 8.00
63 LD(c),The Burning Bride 8.00
64 LD(c),Dead Men Do Tell Tales . . 8.00
65 LD(c),The Imprisoned Phantom . 8.00
66 LD(c),Conversation With A Corpse 8.00
67 LD(c),The Spectral Sword 8.00
68 LD(c),The Phantom of the Class of '76 . . . . 5.00
69 LD(c),The Haunted Gondola . . . 5.00
70 LD(c),Haunted Honeymoon 5.00
71 LD(c),The Ghost Nobody Knew . 5.00
72 LD(c),The Ghost of Washington Monument 5.00
73 LD(c),The Specter Of The Haunted Highway 5.00
74 LD(c),The Gem That Haunted the World! 5.00
75 LD(c),The Legend Of The Lottie Lowry 5.00
76 LD(c),Two Ghosts of Death Row 5.00
77 LD(c),Ghost, Where Do You Hide? 5.00
78 LD(c),The World's Most Famous Phantom 5.00
79 LD(c),Lure of the Specter 5.00
80 JO(c),The Winged Specter 5.00
81 LD(c),Unburied Phantom 5.00
82 LD(c),The Ghost Who Wouldn't Die 5.00
83 LD(c),Escape From the Haunt of the Amazon Specter 5.00
84 LD(c),Torment of the Phantom Face 5.00
85 LD(c),The Fiery Phantom of Faracutin 5.00
86 LD(c),The Ghostly Garden 5.00
87 LD(c),The Phantom Freak 5.00
88 LD(c),Harem In Hell 5.00
89 JKu(c),Came The Specter Shrouded In Seaweed 5.00
90 The Ghost Galleon 5.00
91 LD(c),The Haunted Wheelchair . 5.00
92 DH(c),Double Vision 5.00
93 MK(c),The Flaming Phantoms of Nightmare Alley 5.00
94 LD(c),Great Caesar's Ghost 5.00
95 All The Stage Is A Haunt 5.00
96 DH(c),Dread of the Deadly Domestic 5.00
97 JAp(c),A Very Special Spirit A:Spectre 10.00
98 JAp(c),The Death of a Ghost A:Spectre 10.00
99 EC(c),Till Death Do Us Join A:Spectre 10.00
100 EC&DG(c),The Phantom's Final Debt 5.00
101 MK(c),The Haunted Hospital . . 3.00
102 RB&DG(c),The Fine Art Of Haunting 3.00
103 RB&DG(c),Visions and Vengeance 3.00
104 LD(c),The First Ghost 3.00
105 JKu(c) 3.00
106 JKu(c) 3.00
107 JKu(c) 3.00
108 JKu(c) 3.00
109 EC(c) 3.00
110 EC&DG(c) 3.00
111 JKu(c) 3.00
112 May, 1982 . . . . 3.00

Ghosts #75 © DC Comics Inc.

GIANTKILLER

1999

1 (of 6) 2.50
2 DIB 2.50
3 DIB 2.50
4 DIB,O:Jill 2.50
5 DIB,V:Nox 2.50
6 . . . . 2.50

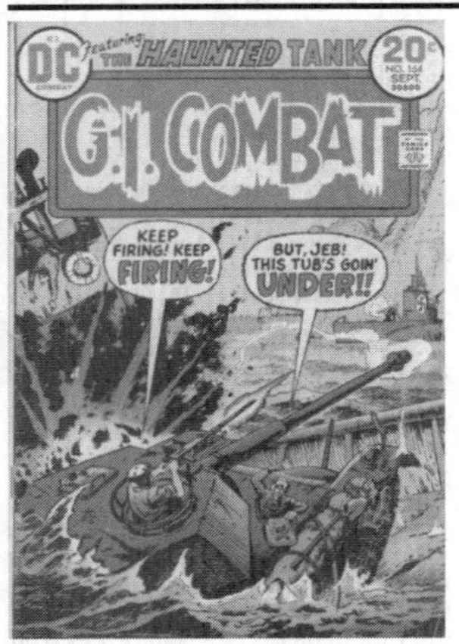

G. I Combat #164 © DC Comics, Inc.

G.I. COMBAT
Jan., 1957
Prev: Golden Age

44 RH,JKu,The Eagle and the Wolves . . . 500.00
45 RH,JKu,Fireworks Hill . . . 275.00
46 JKu,The Long Walk To Wansan . . . 200.00
47 RH, The Walking Weapon . . . 200.00
48 No Fence For A Jet . . . 200.00
49 Frying Pan Seat . . . 200.00
50 Foxhole Pilot . . . 200.00
51 RH,The Walking Grenade . . . 175.00
52 Jku,JKu(c),Call For A Tank. . . 175.00
53 JKu,The Paper Trap . . . 175.00
54 RH,JKu,Sky Tank . . . 175.00
55 Call For A Gunner . . . 150.00
56 JKu,JKu(c),The D.I.-And the Sand Fleas . . . 150.00
57 RH,Live Wire For Easy . . . 150.00
58 JKu(c),Flying Saddle . . . 150.00
59 JKu,Hot Corner . . . 175.00
60 RH,Bazooka Crossroads . . . 175.00
61 JKu(c),The Big Run . . . 125.00
62 RH,JKu,Drop An Inch . . . 125.00
63 MD,JKu(c),Last Stand . . . 125.00
64 MD,RH,JKu,JKu(c),The Silent Jet . . . 125.00
65 JKu,Battle Parade . . . 125.00
66 MD,The Eagle of Easy Company . . . 150.00
67 JKu(c),I:Tank Killer . . . 150.00
68 JKu,RH,The Rock . . . 300.00
69 JKu,RH,The Steel Ribbon . . . 125.00
70 JKu,Bull's-Eye Bridge . . . 125.00
71 MD,JKu(c),Last Stand . . . 100.00
72 MD,JKu(c),Ground Fire . . . 100.00
73 RH,JKu(c),Window War . . . 100.00
74 RH,A Flag For Joey . . . 100.00
75 RH,Dogtag Hill . . . 125.00
76 MD,RH,JKu,Bazooka For A Mouse . . . 125.00
77 RH,JKu,H-Hour For A Gunner 125.00
78 MD,RH,JKu(c),Who Cares About The Infantry . . . 125.00
79 JKu,RH,Big Gun-Little Gun . . 125.00
80 JKu,RH(c),Flying Horsemen. . 125.00
81 Jump For Glory . . . 90.00
82 IN,Get Off My Back . . . 90.00
83 Too Tired To Fight . . . 90.00
84 JKu(c),Dog Company Is Holding . . . 80.00
85 IN,JKu(c),The T.N.T. Trio . . . 80.00
86 JKu,RH(c),Not Return . . . 80.00
87 RH(c),I:Haunted Tank . . . 500.00
88 RH,JKu(c),Haunted Tank Vs. Ghost Tank . . . 90.00
89 JA,RH,IN,Tank With Wings . . . 90.00
90 JA,IN,RH,Tank Raiders . . . 90.00
91 IN,RH,The Tank and the Turtle. 90.00
92 JA,IN,The Tank of Doom . . . 90.00
93 RH(c),JA,No-Return Mission . . 90.00
94 IN,RH(c),Haunted Tank Vs. The Killer Tank . . . 90.00
95 JA,RH(c),The Ghost of the Haunted Tank . . . 90.00
96 JA,RH(c),The Lonesome Tank . 90.00
97 IN,RH(c),The Decoy Tank . . . 90.00
98 JA,RH(c),Trap of Dragon's Teeth . . . 90.00
99 JA,JKu,RH(c),Battle of the Thirsty Tanks . . . 90.00
100 JA,JKu,Return of the Ghost Tank . . . 90.00
101 JA,The Haunted Tank Vs. Attila's Battle Tiger . . . 75.00
102 JKu(c),Haunted Tank Battle Window . . . 75.00
103 JKu,JA,RH(c),Rabbit Punch For A Tiger . . . 75.00
104 JA,JKu,RH(c),Blind Man's Radar . . . 75.00
105 JA,JKu(c),Time Bomb Tank . . 75.00
106 JA,JKu(c),Two-Sided War . . . 75.00
107 JKu(c),The Ghost Pipers . . . 75.00
108 JKu(c),The Wounded Won't Wait,I:Sgt.Rock . . . 75.00
109 JKu(c),Battle of the Tank Graveyard . . . 75.00
110 IN,JKu(c),Choose Your War . . 75.00
111 JA,JKu(c),Death Trap . . . 75.00
112 JA,JKu(c),Ghost Ace . . . 50.00
113 JKu,RH(c),Tank Fight In Death Town . . . 50.00
114 JA,RH(c),O:Haunted Tank . . 125.00
115 JA,RH(c),MedalsForMayhem . 50.00
116 IN,JA,JKu(c),Battle Cry For A Dead Man . . . 50.00
117 JA,RH,JKu(c),Tank In The Ice Box . . . 50.00
118 IN,JA,RH(c),My Buddy-My Enemy . . . 50.00
119 IN,RH(c),Target For A Firing Squad . . . 50.00
120 IN,JA,RH(c),Pull ATiger'sTail . 50.00
121 RH(c),Battle of Two Wars . . . 35.00
122 JA,JKu(c),Who Dies Next? . . . 35.00
123 IN,RH(c),The Target of Terro . 35.00
124 IN,RH(c),Scratch That Tank . . 35.00
125 RH(c),Stay Alive-Until Dark . . 35.00
126 JA,RH(c),Tank Umbrella . . . 35.00
127 JA,JKu(c),Mission-Sudden Death . . . 35.00
128 RH(c),The Ghost of the Haunted Tank . . . 35.00
129 JA,RH(c),Hold That Town For A Dead Man . . . 35.00
130 RH(c),Battle of the Generals . 35.00
131 JKu&RH(c),Devil For Dinner. . 35.00
132 JA,JKu(c),The Executioner. . . 35.00
133 JKu(c),Operation:Death Trap . 35.00
134 MD,JKu(c),Desert Holocaust . 35.00
135 GE,JKu(c),Death is the Joker. 35.00
136 JKu(c),Kill Now-Pay Later . . . 35.00
137 JKu(c),We Can't See . . . 35.00
138 JKu(c),I:The Losers . . . 75.00
139 JKu(c),Corner of Hell . . . 30.00
140 RH,MD,JKu(c),The LastTank . 30.00
141 MD,JKu(c),Let Me Live.. Let Me Die . . . 15.00
142 RH,JKu(c),Checkpoint-Death . 15.00
143 RH,JKu(c),The Iron Horseman 15.00
144 RH,MD,JKu(c),Every Man A Fort . . . 25.00
145 MD,JKu(c),Sand,Sun and Death . . . 25.00
146 JKu(c),Move the World . . . 25.00
147 JKu(c),Rebel Tank . . . 25.00
148 IN,JKu(c),The Gold-Plated General . . . 25.00
149 JKu(c),Leave The Fighting To Us . . . 15.00
150 JKu(c),The Death of the Haunted Tank . . . 15.00
151 JKu(c),A Strong Right Arm . . . 15.00
152 JKu(c),Decoy Tank . . . 15.00
153 JKu(c),The Armored Ark . . . 15.00
154 JKu(c),Battle Prize . . . 15.00
155 JKu(c),The Long Journey . . . 10.00
156 JKu(c),Beyond Hell . . . 10.00
157 JKu(c),The Fountain . . . 10.00
158 What Price War . . . 10.00
159 JKu(c),Mission Dead End . . . 10.00
160 JKu(c),Battle Ghost . . . 10.00
161 JKu(c),The Day of the Goth . . 10.00
162 JKu(c),The Final Victor . . . 10.00
163 A Crew Divided . . . 10.00
164 Siren Song . . . 10.00
165 JKu(c),Truce,Pathfinder . . . 10.00
166 Enemy From Yesterday . . . 10.00
167 JKu(c),The Finish Line . . . 10.00
168 NA(c),The Breaking Point . . . 10.00
169 WS(c),The Death of the Haunted Tank . . . 10.00
170 Chain of Vengeance . . . 10.00
171 JKu(c),The Man Who Killed Jeb Stuart . . . 9.00
172 RH(c),At The Mercy of My Foes . . . 9.00
173 JKu(c),The Final Crash . . . 9.00
174 JKu(c),Vow To A Dead Foe . . . 9.00
175 JKu(c),The Captive Tank . . . 9.00
176 JKu(c),A Star Can Cry . . . 9.00
177 JKu(c),The Tank That Missed D-Day . . . 9.00
178 JKu(c),A Tank Is Born . . . 9.00
179 JKu(c),One Last Charge . . . 9.00
180 JKu(c),The Saints Go Riding On . . . 9.00
181 JKu(c),The Kidnapped Tank . . . 9.00
182 JKu(c),Combat Clock . . . 9.00
183 JKu(c),6 Stallions To Hell- And Back . . . 9.00
184 JKu(c),Battlefield Bundle . . . 9.00
185 JKu(c),No Taps For A Tank . . . 9.00
186 JKu(c),Souvenir From A Headhunter . . . 9.00
187 JKu(c),The General Died Twice . . . 9.00
188 The Devil's Pipers . . . 9.00

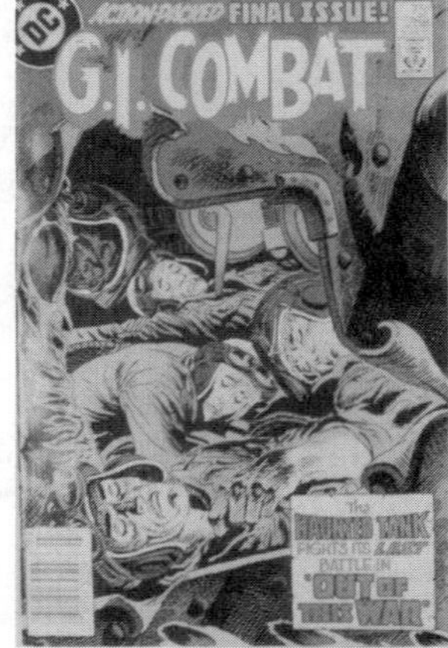

G.I. Combat #288 © DC Comics, Inc.

189 The Gunner is a Gorilla 9.00
190 The Tiger and The Terrier 9.00
191 Decoy For Death 9.00
192 The General Has Two Faces . . 9.00
193 JKu(c),The War That Had To Wait 9.00
194 GE(c),Blitzkrieg Brain. 9.00
195 JKu(c),The War That Time Forgot 9.00
196 JKu(c),Dead Men Patrol. 9.00
197 JKu(c),Battle Ark 9.00
198 JKu(c),The Devil Rides A Panzer 9.00
199 JKu(c),A Medal From A Ghost . 9.00
200 JKu(c),The Tank That Died. . . 10.00
201 NA&RH(c),The Rocking Chair Soldiers. 10.00
202 NA&RH(c),Walking Wounded Don't Cry 10.00
203 JKu(c),To Trap A Tiger. 10.00
204 JKu(c),A Winter In Hell. 10.00
205 JKu(c),A Gift From The Emperor 10.00
206 JKu(c),A Tomb For A Tank . . . 10.00
207 JKu(c),Foxhole for a Sherman 10.00
208 JKu(c),Sink That Tank 10.00
209 JKu(c),Ring Of Blood 10.00
210 JKu(c),Tankers Also Bleed . . . 10.00
211 JKu(c),A Nice Day For Killing . . 7.00
212 JKu(c),Clay Pigeon Crew 7.00
213 JKu(c),Back Door To War. 7.00
214 JKu(c),The Tanker Who Couldn't Die 7.00
215 JKu(c),Last Stand For Losers. . 7.00
216 JKu(c),Ghost Squadron 7.00
217 JKu(c), The Pigeon Spies 7.00
218 JKu(c), 48 Hours to Die 7.00
219 thru 230 . . . . @7.00
231 thru 288 . . . . @6.00

GIFTS OF THE NIGHT

DC/Vertigo 1999

1 (of 4) PC,JBo 3.00
2 PC,JBo. 3.00
3 PC,JBo. 3.00
4 PC,JBo, conclusion 3.00

GILGAMESH II

1989

1 JSn,O:Gilgamesh 5.00
2 JSn,V:Nightshadow 4.50
3 JSn,V:Robotic Ninja 4.50
4 JSn,final issue 4.00

GIRL WHO WOULD BE DEATH, THE

DC/Vertigo 1998

1 (of 4) F:Plath 2.50
2 . . . . 2.50
3 . . . . 2.50
4 . . . . 2.50

GODDESS

Vertigo 1995–96

[Mini-Series]

1 I:Rosie Nolan 4.00
2 Rosie arrested 4.00
3 I:Jenny 4.00
4 CIA Chase 4.00
5 V:Agent Hooks 4.00
6 V:Harry Hooks 4.00
7 Mudhawks Past 4.00
8 finale 4.00

GOLDEN AGE

Elseworld 1993–94

1 PS,F:JSA,All-Star Squadron 8.00
2 PS,I:Dynaman 7.00
3 PS,IR:Mr. Terrific is Ultra-Humanite. 7.00
4 PS,D:Dynaman,Mr. Terrific 6.00

GON

DC/Paradox 1996

Book 1 . . . . 6.00
Book 2 Gon Again! 6.00
Book 3 Here Today,Gon Tomorrow . 6.00
Book 4 Going, Going, Gon 6.00
TPB Gon Swimmin' 7.00
TPB Color Spectacular 6.00
TPB Gon Wild rep. books 3 & 4 . . 10.00

GREATEST STORIES EVER TOLD

Greatest Superman Stories Ever Told:
HC 75.00
SC 15.95
Greatest Batman Stories Ever Told:
HC 60.00
SC 16.00
Vol.#2 Catwoman & Penguin 16.95
Greatest Joker Stories Ever Told:
HC 45.00
SC BBo(c) 15.00
Greatest Flash Stories Ever Told:
HC 30.00
SC 15.00
Greatest Golden Age Stories Ever Told:
HC 25.00
SC 15.00
Greatest Fifties Stories Ever Told:
HC 30.00
SC 15.00
Greatest Team-Up Stories Ever Told:
HC 25.00
SC 15.00

GREEN ARROW

[Limited Series] 1983

1 TVE,DG,O:Green Arrow 5.00
2 TVE,DG,A:Vertigo. 3.50
3 TVE,DG,A:Vertigo. 3.50
4 TVE,DG,A:Black Canary. 3.50

Green Arrow #73 © DC Comics Inc.

[Regular Series] 1988–97

1 EH,DG,V:Muncie 5.00
2 EH,DG,V:Muncie 4.00
3 EH,DG,FMc,V:Fyres 4.00
4 EH,DG,FMc,V:Fryes 4.00
5 EH,DG,FMc,Gauntlet 4.00
6 EH,DG,FMc,Gauntlet 4.00
7 EB,DG,A:Black Canary. 4.00
8 DG,Alaska 3.50
9 EH,DG,FMc,R:Shado 3.50
10 EH,DG,FMc,A:Shado. 3.50
11 EH,DG,FMc,A:Shado. 3.50
12 EH,DG,FMc,A:Shado. 3.00
13 DJu,DG,FMc,Moving Target. . . . 3.00
14 EH,DG,FMc. 3.00
15 EH,DG,FMc,Seattle And Die . . . 3.00
16 EH,DG,FMc,Seattle And Die . . . 3.00
17 DJu,DG,FMc,The Horse Man. . . 2.50
18 DJu,DG,FMc,The Horse Man. . . 2.50
19 EH,DG,FMc,A:Hal Jordan 2.50
20 EH,DG,FMc,A:Hal Jordan 2.50
21 DJu,DG,B:Blood of Dragon, A:Shado. 2.50
22 DJu,DG,A:Shado 2.50
23 DJu,DG,A:Shado 2.50
24 DJu,DG,E:Blood of Dragon 2.50
25 TVE,Witch Hunt #1 . . . . 2.25
26 Witch Hunt #2 . . . . 2.25
27 DJu,DG,FMc,R:Warlord 2.25
28 DJu,DG,FMc,A:Warlord 2.25
29 DJu,DG,FMc,Coyote Tears 2.25
30 DJu,DG,FMc,Coyote Tears 2.25
31 FMc,V:Drug Dealers 2.25
32 FMc,V:Drug Dealers 2.25
33 DJu,FMc,Psychology Issue 2.25
34 DJu,DG,A:Fryes,Arrested. 2.25
35 B:Black Arrow Saga,A:Shade. . . 2.25
36 Black Arrow Saga,A:Shade 2.25
37 Black Arrow Saga,A:Shade 2.25
38 E:Black Arrow Saga,A:Shade. . . 2.25
39 DCw,Leaves Seattle 2.25
40 MGr,Spirit Quest,A: Indian Shaman. 2.25
41 DCw,I.R.A.. . . . . 2.25
42 DCw,I.R.A 2.25
43 DCw,I.R.A.. . . . . 2.25
44 DCw,Rock'n'Runes,pt.1 . . . . 2.25
45 Rock'n'Runes,pt.2 . . . . 2.25
46 DCw,Africa 2.25
47 DCw,V:Trappers 2.25
48 DCw,V:Trappers 2.25
49 V:Trappers. 2.25
50 MGr(c),50th Anniv.,R:Seattle . . . 3.00
51 Tanetti's Murder,pt.1 . . . . 2.25
52 Tanetti's Murder,pt.2 . . . . 2.25
53 The List,pt.1,A:Fyres 2.25
54 The List,pt.2,A:Fyres 2.25
55 Longbow Hunters tie-in 2.25
56 A:Lt. Cameron 2.25
57 And Not A Drop to Drink,pt.1 . . . 2.25
58 And Not A Drop to Drink,pt.2 . . . 2.25
59 Predator,pt.1 . . . . 2.25
60 Predator,pt.2 . . . . 4.00
61 FS,F:Draft Dodgers 2.25
62 FS 2.25
63 FS,B:Hunt for Red Dragon. 2.25
64 FS,Hunt for Red Dragon 2.25
65 MGr(c),Hunt for Red Dragon . . . 2.25
66 MGr(c),E:Hunt for Red Dragon. . 2.25
67 MGr(c),FS,V:Rockband Killer. . . 2.25
68 MGr(c),FS,BumRap. 2.25
69 MGr(c),Reunion Tour #1 . . . . . . 2.25
70 Reunion Tour #2 . . . . 2.25
71 Wild in the Streets #1 . . . . 2.25
72 MGr(c),Wild in the Streets#2 . . . 2.25
73 MGr(c),F:Vietnam Vet 2.25
74 SAP,MGr(c),V:Sniper 2.25
75 MGr(c),A:Speedy Shado, Black Canary 3.00
76 MGr(c),R:Eddie Fyers 2.25
77 MGr(c),A:Eddie Fyers 2.25

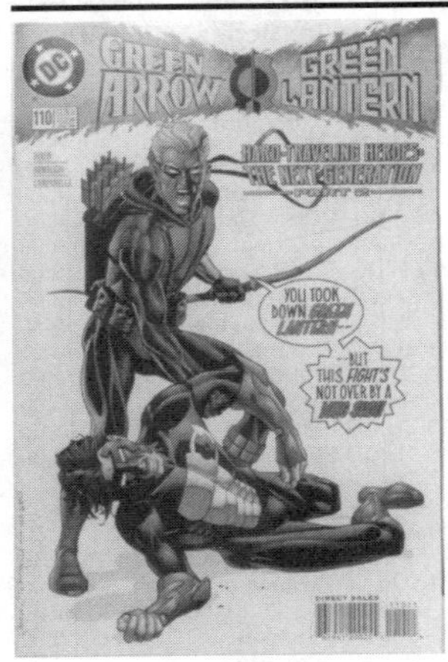

Green Arrow #110 © DC Comics, Inc.

78 MGr(c),V:CIA 2.25
79 MGr(c),V:CIA 2.25
80 MGr(c),E:MGr(s),V:CIA 2.25
81 B:CDi(s),JAp,V:Shrapnel,
Nuklon 2.25
82 JAp,I:Rival 2.25
83 JAp,V:Yakuza 2.25
84 E:CDi(s),JAp,In Las Vegas 2.25
85 AIG(s),JAp,A:Deathstroke 2.25
86 DgM(s),JAp,A:Catwoman 2.25
87 JAp,V:Factory Owner 2.25
88 JAp,A:M.Manhunter,Bl.Beetle . . . 2.25
89 JAp,A:Anarky 2.50
90 Zero Hour 2.50
91 Hitman 2.50
92 Partner attacked 2.50
93 Secrets of Red File 2.50
94 I:Camo Rouge 2.50
95 V:Camo Rouge 2.50
96 I:Slyfox,A:Hal Jordan 2.25
97 Where Angels Fear to
Tread,pt.2 . . . . 2.50
98 Where Angels Fear to
Tread,pt.3, A:Arsenal 2.50
99 Where Angels Fear to Tread . . . 2.50
100 . . . . 7.00
101 A:Superman,Black Canary . . . 20.00
102 CDi,RbC,Underworld
Unleashed tie-in 3.00
103 CDi,RbC,Underworld
Unleashed tie-in 3.00
104 CDi,RbC,A:Green Lantern 3.00
105 CDi,RbC,A:Robin 3.00
106 . . . . 2.25
107 CDi,RbC,protects child-king . . . 2.25
108 CDi,A:Thorn 2.25
109 CDi,JAp,BSz,in Metropolis 2.25
110 CDi(s),RbC,I:Hatchet, Green
Lantern x-over 3.50
111 CDi(s),RbC,I:Hatchet, Green
Lantern x-over 3.50
112 CDi(s),RbC, ... 2.25
113 CDi(s),RbC,In the Mongolian
wastes 2.25
114 CDi(s) RbC,airplane downed,
Final Night tie-in 2.25
115 CDi(s),RbC,"The Iron Death,"
pt.1 . . . . 2.25
116 CDi(s),RbC,"The Iron Death,"
pt.2 . . . . 2.25
117 CDi(s),RbC,"The Iron Death,"
pt.3, concl. 2.25
118 CDi(s),DBw,RbC,"Endangered
Species" pt.1 . . . . 2.25
119 CDi(s),DBw,RbC,"Endangered
Species" pt.2 . . . . 2.25
120 CDi(s),RbC,at grandfather's
ranch 2.25
121 CDi(s),RbC,V:The Silver
Monkey 2.25
122 CDi(s),RbC, at Idaho ranch . . . 2.25
123 CDi(s),JAp,KJ,"The
Stormbringers" concl. 2.25
124 CDi(s),RbC,V:Milo Armitage . . . 2.25
125 CDi(s),DBw,Green Lantern
x-over,pt.1, 48pg 3.50
126 CDi(s),DBw,x-over, pt.3 . . . . . . 2.50
127 CDi(s),DBw,to San Francisco . . 2.50
128 CDi(s),DWb,Russian Mob 2.50
129 CDi,DBw,Jansen prisoner,pt.2 . 2.50
130 CDi,DBw, ... 2.50
131 CDi,DBw,F:Crackshot 2.50
132 CDi,DBw,Eddie Fyers returns . . 2.50
133 CDi,DBw,Eddie Fyers pt.2 . . . . 2.50
134 CDi,DBw,Brotherhood of
the Fist x-over,pt.1 . . . . 2.50
135 CDi,DBw,Brotherhood of the
Fist x-over, concl. 2.50
136 CDi,DBw,Green Pastures,pt.1 . 2.50
137 CDi(s),A:Superman 2.50
Ann.#1 A:Question,FablesII 3.50
Ann.#2 EH,DG,FMc,A:Question . . . 3.00
Ann.#3 A:Question 2.50
Ann.#4 `The Black Alchemist' 3.25
Ann.#5 TVE,FS,Eclipso,Batman . . . 3.25
Ann.#6 JBa(c),I:Hook 3.50
Ann.#7 CDi, Year One 3.95
Spec. #0 Return 2.00
Spec.#1,000,000 CDi(s), A:Superman
final issue 2.00

GREEN ARROW LONGBOW HUNTERS

Aug., 1987

1 MGr,N:GreenArrow,I:Shado 4.00
1a 2nd printing 2.50
2 MGr,`Shadow' Revealed 4.00
2a 2nd printing 2.50
3 MGr,Tracking Snow 4.00
TPB, rep. #1-#3 . . . . 12.95

GREEN ARROW: THE WONDER YEARS

1993

1 MGr,GM,B:New O:Green Arrow . 2.50
2 MGr,GM,I:Brianna Stone 2.00
3 MGr,GM,A:Brianna Stone 2.00
4 MGr,GM,Conclusion 2.00

GREEN CANDLES

1995

1 Paradox Mystery,F:John Halting 5.95
2 F:John Halting 5.95
3 finale 5.95
TPB B&W rep. #1–#3 . . . . 9.95

GREEN LANTERN

Autumn, 1941

1 O:Green Lantern, V:Master of
Light, Arson in the Slums . 28,000.00
2 V:Baldy,Tycoon's Legacy . . . 6,200.00
3 War cover 4,400.00
4 Doiby and Green Lantern
join the Army 3,300.00
5 V:Nazis and Black
Prophet,A:General Prophet 2,200.00
6 V:Nordo & Hordes of War Hungy
Henchmen,Exhile of Exiles,
A:Shiloh 1,700.00
7 The Wizard of Odds 2,000.00
8 The Lady and Her Jewels,

Green Lantern #25 © DC Comics, Inc.

A:Hop Harrigan 1,700.00
9 V:The Whistler, The School
for Vandals 1,500.00
10 V:Vandal Savage,The Man Who
Wanted the World,O:Vandal
Savage 1,500.00
11 The Distardly Designs of
Doiby Dickles' Pals 1,100.00
12 O:The Gambler 1,100.00
13 A:Angela Van Enters 1,100.00
14 Case of the Crooked Cook . 1,100.00
15 V:Albert Zero, One...Two...
Three...Stop Thinking 1,100.00
16 V:The Lizard 1,100.00
17 V:Kid Triangle, Reward for
Green Lantern 1,100.00
18 V:The Dandy,The Connoisseur of
crime,X-mas(c) 1,200.00
19 V:Harpies, Sing a Song of
Disaster A:Fate 1,100.00
20 A:Gambler 1,100.00
21 V:The Woodman,The Good
Humor Man 1,000.00
22 A:Dapper Dan Crocker 1,000.00
23 Doiby Dickles Movie
Ajax Pictures 1,000.00
24 A:Mike Mattson,OnceA Cop 1,000.00
25 The Diamond Magnet 1,000.00
26 The Scourge of the Sea . . . 1,000.00
27 V:Sky Pirate 1,100.00
28 The Tricks of the
Sports Master 1,000.00
29 Meets the Challange of
the Harlequin 1,000.00
30 I:Streak the Wonder Dog . . . 1,000.00
31 The Terror of the Talismans . . 900.00
32 The Case of the
Astonishing Juggler 900.00
33 Crime goes West 900.00
34 Streak meets the Princess . . . 900.00
35 V:The Three-in-One Criminal . 900.00
36 The Mystery of the
Missing Messanger 1,000.00
37 A:Sargon 1,000.00
38 DoublePlay,May-June,1949 . 1,000.00

GREEN LANTERN

1960–72, 1976–86

1 GK,O:Green Lantern 3,000.00
2 GK,I:Qward,Pieface 800.00
3 GK,V:Qward 450.00
4 GK,Secret of GL Mask 350.00
5 GK,I:Hector Hammond 350.00
6 GK,I:Tomar-Re 350.00
7 GK,I&O:Sinestro 300.00

8 GK,1st Story in 5700 A.D.. . . . 300.00
9 GK,A:Sinestro. 300.00
10 GK,O:Green Lantern's Oath . . 300.00
11 GK,V:Sinestro 200.00
12 GK,Sinestro,I:Dr.Polaris 200.00
13 GK,A:Flash,Sinestro. 225.00
14 GK,I&O:Sonar,1st Jordan
Brothers story. 175.00
15 GK,Zero Hour story 165.00
16 GK,MA,I:Star Saphire,
O:Abin Sur 175.00
17 GK,V:Sinestro 165.00
18 GK. 165.00
19 GK,A:Sonar 165.00
20 GK,A:Flash 175.00
21 GK,O:Dr.Polaris 150.00
22 GK,A:Hector Hammond,Jordan
Brothers story. 150.00
23 GK,I:Tattooed Man. 150.00
24 GK,O:Shark 150.00
25 GK,V:Sonar,HectorHammond. 150.00
26 GK,A:Star Sapphire 150.00
27 GK. 150.00
28 GK,I:Goldface 150.00
29 GK,I:Black Hand 160.00
30 GK,I:Katma Tui 150.00
31 GK,Jordan brothers story. . . . 120.00
32 GK. 120.00
33 GK,V:Dr. Light 120.00
34 GK,V:Hector Hammond 120.00
35 GK,I:Aerialist 120.00
36 GK. 120.00
37 GK,I:Evil Star. 120.00
38 GK,A:Tomar-Re 120.00
39 GK,V:Black Hand. 120.00
40 GK,O:Guardians,A:Golden
Age Green Lantern. 550.00
41 GK,A:Star Sapphire 75.00
42 GK,A:Zatanna 75.00
43 GK,A:Major Disaster 75.00
44 GK,A:Evil Star. 75.00
45 GK,I:Prince Peril,A:Golden
Age Green Lantern. 125.00
46 GK,V:Dr.Polaris 75.00
47 GK,5700 A.D. V:Dr.Polaris 75.00
48 GK,I:Goldface 75.00
49 GK,I:Dazzler 75.00
50 GK,V:Thraxon the Powerful . . . 75.00
51 GK,Green Lantern's Evil
Alter-ego 55.00
52 GK,A:Golden Age Green
Lantern Sinestro. 100.00
53 GK,Cl,Jordon brothers story. . . 55.00
54 GK,Menace in the Iron Lung . . 55.00
55 GK,Cosmic Enemy #1 . . . . 55.00
56 GK. 55.00
57 GK,V:Major Disaster 55.00
58 GK,Perils of the Powerless
Green Lantern 55.00
59 GK,I:Guy Gardner(imaginary
story) 225.00
60 GK,I:Lamplighter 50.00
61 GK,A:Gold.Age Gr.Lantern. . . . 55.00
62 Steel Small,Rob Big. 50.00
63 NA(c),This is the Way the
World Ends 50.00
64 MSy,We Vow Death to Green
Lantern. 50.00
65 MSy,Dry up and Die. 50.00
66 MSy,5700 AD story 50.00
67 DD,The First Green Lantern. . . 50.00
68 GK,I Wonder where the
Yellow Went? 50.00
69 GK,WW,If Earth Fails the
Test.. It Means War 50.00
70 GK,A Funny Thing Happened
on the way to Earth 50.00
71 GK,DD,MA,Jordan brothers . . . 25.00
72 GK,Phantom o/t SpaceOpera. . 25.00
73 GK,MA,A:Star Sapphire,
Sinestro 25.00
74 GK,MA,A:Star Sapphire,
Sinestro 25.00
75 GK,Qward 25.00
76 NA,Gr.Lantern & Gr.Arrow
team-up begins. 200.00
77 NA,Journey to Desolation 60.00
78 NA,A:Black Canary,A Kind of
Loving..A Way to Death 60.00
79 NA,DA,A:Black Canary,Ulysses
Star is Still Alive 50.00
80 NA,DG,Even an Immortal
can die 50.00
81 NA,DG,A:Black Canary,Death
be my Destiny 40.00
82 NA,DG,A:Black Canary,
V:Sinestro,(BWr 1 page). 40.00
83 NA,DG,A:BlackCanary,Gr.Lantern
reveals I.D. to Carol Ferris . . . 40.00
84 NA,BWr,V:Black Hand 40.00
85 NA,Speedy on Drugs,pt.1,
rep.Green Lantern #1 . . . . 60.00
86 NA,DG,Speedy on Drugs,pt.2,
ATh(rep)Golden Age G.L.. . . . 60.00
87 NA,DG,I:John Stewart,
2nd Guy Gardner app. 35.00
88 all reprints.. . . . . 15.00
89 NA,And Through Him Save
the World 27.00
90 MGr,New Gr.Lantern rings 12.00
91 MGr,V:Sinestro 7.00
92 MGr,V:Sinestro 7.00
93 MGr,TA,War Against the
World Builders 7.00
94 MGr,TA,DG,Green Arrow
Assassin,pt.1 . . . . 7.00
95 MGr,Gr.Arrow Assassin,pt.2 . . . . 7.00
96 MGr,A:Katma Tui 7.00
97 MGr,V:Mocker 7.00
98 MGr,V:Mocker 7.00
99 MGr,V:Mocker 7.00
100 MGr,AS,I:Air Wave. 15.00
101 MGr,A:Green Arrow 7.00
102 AS,A:Green Arrow 6.00
103 AS,Earth-Asylum for an Alien. . 6.00
104 AS,A:Air Wave. 6.00
105 AS,Thunder Doom. 6.00
106 MGr,Panic..In High Places
& Low 6.00
107 AS,Green Lantern Corp.story. . 6.00
108 MGr,BU:G.A.Green Lantern,
V:Replikon 7.00
109 MGr,Replicon#2,GA.GL.#2. . . . 6.00
110 MGr,GA.GL.#3 . . . . 6.00
111 AS,O:Green Lantern,
A:G.A.Green Lantern 7.00

Green Lantern #12 © DC Comics Inc.

112 AS,O&A:G.A. Green Lantern . 12.00
113 AS,Christmas story 5.00
114 AS,I:Crumbler 5.00
115 AS,V:Crumbler 5.00
116 Guy Gardner as Gr.Lantern . . 30.00
117 JSon,I:KariLimbo,V:Prof.Ojo . . . 5.00
118 AS,V:Prof.Ojo. 5.00
119 AS,G.L.& G.A.solo storys 5.00
120 DH,A:Kari,V:El Espectro. 3.50
121 DH,V:El Espectro. 3.50
122 DH,A:Guy Gardner,Superman . 6.00
123 JSon,DG,E:Green Lantern/Green
Arrow T.U.,A:G.Gardner,
V:Sinestro 7.00
124 JSon,V:Sinestro 3.50
125 JSon,FMc,V:Sinestro 3.50
126 JSon,FMc,V:Shark. 3.50
127 JSon,FMc,V:Goldface 3.50
128 JSon,V:Goldface 3.50
129 JSon,V:Star Sapphire. 3.50
130 JSon,FMc,A:Sonar,B:Tales of the
Green Lantern Corps 3.00
131 JSon,AS,V:Evil Star 3.00
132 JSon,AS,E:Tales of GL Corps
B:B.U.Adam Strange 3.00
133 JSon,V:Dr.Polaris. 2.50
134 JSon,V:Dr.Polaris. 2.50
135 JSon,V:Dr.Polaris. 2.50
136 JSon,A:Space Ranger,
Adam Strange 2.50
137 JSon,Cl,MA,I:Citadel,A:Space
Ranger,A.Strange. 2.50
138 JSon,A&O:Eclipso 4.00
139 JSon,V:Eclipso. 3.00
140 JSon,I:Congressman Block
Adam Strange 2.50
141 JSon,I:OmegaMen. 6.00
142 JSon,A:OmegaMen 4.00
143 JSon,A:OmegaMen 4.00
144 JSon,D:Tattooed Man,Adam
Strange 2.50
145 JSon,V:Goldface 2.50
146 JSon,Cl,V:Goldface
E:B.U.Adam Strange 2.50
147 JSon,Cl,V:Goldface 2.50
148 JSon,DN,DA,V:Quardians 2.50
149 JSon,A:GL.Corps. 2.50
150 JSon,anniversary. 3.50
151 JSon,GL.Exiled in space 2.50
152 JSon,Cl,GL Exile #2 . . . . 2.50
153 JSon,Cl,Gr.Lantern Exile #3. . . 2.50
154 JSon,Gr.Lantern Exile #4 . . . . . 2.50
155 JSon,Gr.Lantern Exile #5 . . . . . 2.50
156 GK,Gr.Lantern Exile #6 . . . . . . 2.50
157 KP,IN,Gr.Lantern Exile #7 . . . . 2.50
158 KP,IN,Gr.Lantern Exile #8 . . . . 2.50
159 KP,Gr.Lantern Exile #9. . . . . . . 2.50
160 KP,Gr.Lantern Exile #10. . . . . . 2.50
161 KP,A:Omega Men,Exile #11 . . . 2.50
162 KP,Gr.Lantern Exile #12. . . . . . 2.50
163 KP,Gr.Lantern Exile #13. . . . . . 2.50
164 KP,A:Myrwhidden,Exile #14 . . . 2.50
165 KP,A:John Stewart & Gr.Arrow
Green Lantern Exile #15. . . . . . 2.00
166 GT,FMc,DGi,Exile #16 . . . . 2.00
167 GT,FMc,G.L.Exile #17 . . . . 2.00
168 GT,FMc,G.L. Exile #18. . . . . . . 2.00
169 Green Lantern Exile #19 . . . . . 2.00
170 GT,MSy,GreenLanternCorps . . 2.00
171 ATh,TA,DGb,Green Lantern
Exile #20 . . . . 2.00
172 DGb,E:Gr.Lant.Exile. 2.00
173 DGb,I:Javelin,A:Congressman
Bloch 2.00
174 DGb,V:Javelin 2.00
175 DGb,A:Flash 2.25
176 DGb,V:The Shark 2.00
177 DGb,rep. Gr.Lant #128. . . . . . . 2.00
178 DGb,A:Monitor,V:Demolition
Team 2.00
179 DGb,I:Predator 2.00

180 DGb,A:JLA 2.00
181 DGi,Hal Jordan quits as GL . . . 2.75
182 DGi,John Stewart taks over V:Major Disaster. 2.50
183 DGi,V:Major Disaster 2.50
184 DGb,Rep. Gr.Lant. #59 . . . . . . 3.50
185 DGi,DH,V:Eclipso. 4.00
186 DGi,V:Eclipso 4.00
187 BWi,John Stewart meets Katma Tui 2.25
188 JSon,C:GrArrow,V:Sonar,John Stewart reveals I.D. to world. . . 3.50
189 JSon,V:Sonar 2.00
190 JSon,A:Green Arrow/Black Canary,Guy Gardner 2.00
191 JSon,IR:Predator is Star Sapphire 2.00
192 JSon,O:Star Sapphire 2.00
193 JSon,V:Replikon, A:G.Gardner. 2.50
194 JSon,Crisis,R:G.Gardner 5.00
195 JSon,Guy Gardner as Green Lantern,develops attitude 9.00
196 JSon,V:Shark,Hal Jordan regains ring 3.00
197 JSon,V:Shark,Sonar, Goldface 3.00
198 JSon,D:Tomar-Re,Hal returns as Green Lantern,(double size) . . . 3.00
199 JSon,V:Star Sapphire. 2.00
200 JSon,final Gr.Lantern issue . . . 2.50
Becomes:

GREEN LANTERN CORPS
1986–88

201 JSon,I:NewGr.LantCorps,V:Star Sapphire, Sonar, Dr.Polaris. . . . 2.00
202 JSon,set up headquarters 2.00
203 JSon,tribute to Disney 2.00
204 JSon,Arisia reaches puberty . . 2.00
205 JSon,V:Black Hand 2.00
206 JSon,V:Black Hand 2.00
207 JSon, Legneds crossover. 2.00
208 JSon,I:Rocket Red Brigade, Green Lanterns in Russia#1 . . . 2.00
209 JSon,In Russia #2 . . . . 2.00
210 JSon,In Russia #3 . . . . 2.00
211 JSon,John Stewart proposes to Katma Tui. 2.00
212 JSon,W:J.Stewart&KatmaTui . . 2.00
213 Json,For Want of a Male 2.00
214 IG,5700 A.D. Story. 2.00

Green Lantern Corps #220
© DC Comics, Inc.

215 IG,Salaak and Chip quit. 2.00
216 IG,V:Carl 2.00
217 JSon,V:Sinestro. 2.00
218 BWg,V:Sinestro. 2.00
219 BWg,V:Sinestro 2.00
220 JSon,Millenium,pt.3 . . . . 2.00
221 JSon,Millenium 2.00
222 JSon,V:Sinestro. 2.00
223 GK,V:Sinestro 2.00
224 GK,V:Sinestro 2.00
Ann.#1 GK 2.00
Ann.#2 JSa,BWg,S:AnM. 2.50
Ann.#3 JBy,JL,JR 2.00
Spec.#1 A:Superman 2.00
Spec.#2 MBr,RT,V:Seeker. 2.00
TPB rep.#84-#87,#89,Flash #217-#219 . . . . 12.95
TPB rep. reprints of #1-#7 . . . . 8.95

GREEN LANTERN
[2nd Regular Series] 1990

1 PB,A:Hal Jordan,John Stuart, Guy Gardner 5.00
2 PB,A:Tattooed Man. 3.00
3 PB,Jordan vs.Gardner 4.00
4 PB,Vanishing Cities 2.00
5 PB Return to OA 2.00
6 PB 3GL'sCaptive 2.00
7 PB R:Guardians 2.00
8 PB R:Guardians 2.00
9 JSon,G.Gardner,pt.1. . . . . 3.00
10 JSon,G.Gardner,pt.2 . . . . 3.00
11 JSon,G.Gardner,pt.3 . . . . 3.00
12 JSon,G.Gardner,pt.4 . . . . 3.00
13 Jordan,Gardner,Stuart(giant) . . . 2.50
14 PB,Mosaic,pt.1 . . . . 2.00
15 RT,Mosaic,pt.2. . . . . 2.00
16 MBr,RT,Mosaic,pt.3 . . . . 2.00
17 MBr,RT,Mosaic,pt.4 . . . . 2.00
18 JSon,JRu,G.Gardner, A:Goldface 2.00
19 MBr,PB,JSon,A:All Four G.L.'s, O:Alan Scott,A:Doiby Dickles (D.Size-50th Ann.Iss.) 3.00
20 PB,RT,Hal Jordan G.L. Corp story begins, A:Flicker 2.00
21 PB,RT,G.L. Corp.,pt.2, V:Flicker. 2.00
22 PB,RT,G.L. Corp.,pt.3, R:Star Sapphire 2.00
23 PB,RT,V:Star Sapphire, A:John Stuart 2.00
24 PB,RT,V:Star Sapphire. 2.00
25 MBr,JSon,RT,Hal Vs.Guy, A:JLA. 2.75
26 MBr,V:Evil Star,Starlings 2.00
27 MBr,V:Evil Star,Starlings 2.00
28 MBr,V:Evil Star,Starlings 2.00
29 MBr,RT,R:Olivia Reynolds 2.00
30 MBr,RT,Gorilla Warfare#1 . . . . . 2.00
31 MBr,RT,Gorilla Warfare#3 . . . . . 2.00
32 RT(i),A:Floro,Arisia 2.00
33 MBr,RT,Third Law#1, A;New Guardians. 2.00
34 MBr,RT,Third Law#2,I:Entropy . . 2.00
35 MBr,RT,Third Law#3,V;Entropy . 2.00
36 V:Dr.Light 2.00
37 MBg,RT,A:Guy Gardner 2.00
38 MBr,RT,A:Adam Strange 2.00
39 MBr,RT,A:Adam Strange 2.00
40 RT(i),A:Darkstar, V:Reverse Flash. 2.00
41 MBr,RT,V:Predator, C:Deathstroke 2.00
42 MBr,RT,V:Predator, Deathstroke 2.00
43 RT(i),A:Itty 2.00
44 RT(i),Trinity#2,A:L.E.G.I.O.N . . . 2.00
45 GeH,Trinity#5,A:L.E.G.I.O.N., Darkstars 2.00

Green Lantern 2nd Series #53
© DC Comics, Inc.

46 MBr,A:All Supermen, V:Mongul 8.00
47 A:Green Arrow. 6.00
48 KM(c),B:Emerald Twilight,I:Kyle Rayner (Last Green Lantern) . . 7.00
49 KM(c),GJ(s),A:Sinestro 6.00
50 KM(c),GJ(s),D:Sinestro,Kiliwog, Guardians,I:Last Green Lantern (in Costume) 8.00
51 V:Ohm,A:Mongul 4.00
52 V:Mongul 2.00
53 A:Superman,V:Mongul 2.00
54 D:Alex,V:Major Force. 2.00
55 Zero Hour,A:Alan Scott, V:Major Force. 2.25
56 Green Lantern and ring 2.00
57 Psimon 2.00
58 Donna Troy,Felix Faust 2.00
59 V:Dr. Polaris 2.00
60 Capital Punishment,pt.3. . . . . . . 2.00
61 V:Kalibak,A:Darkstar 2.00
62 V:Duality,R:Ganthet 2.00
63 Parallax View: The Resurrection of Hal Jordan,pt.1. . . . . 2.00
64 Parallax View,pt.2,A:Superman, Flash,V:Parallax 2.00
65 Siege of ZiCharan,pt.2. . . . . 2.00
66 V:Sonar 2.00
67 A:Flash,V:Sonar. 2.00
68 RMz,RT,Underworld Unleashed tie-in 2.00
69 RMz,RT,Underworld Unleashed tie-in 2.00
70 RMz,RT,A:Supergirl 2.00
71 RMz,RT,Hero Quest,pt.1 . . . . . . 2.00
72 RMz,RT,Hero Quest,pt.2 . . . . . . 2.00
73 RMz,RT,Hero Quest,pt.3 . . . . . . 2.00
74 RMz,RT,A:Adam Strange, V:Grayven 2.00
75 A:Adam Strange 2.00
76 Green Arrow x-over 2.00
77 Green Arrow x-over 2.00
78 . . . . 2.00
79 V:Sonar 2.00
80 RMz(s),JWi,MGy,V:Dr. Light, Final Night tie-in 2.00
81 RMz(s),DBk,RT,Memorial for Hal Jordan 4.00
81a deluxe edition + extra stories, foil cover on cardstock 6.00
82 RMz(s),TGb,RT,F:Kyle Rayner, Alan Scott, Guy Gardner & John Stewart 2.00

83 . . . . 2.00
84 "Retribution," pt.2. . . . . 2.00
85 "Retribution," concl. 2.00
86 RMz,JJ,RT,A:Jade, V:Obsidian. . 2.00
87 RMz,TGb,RT,A:Martian Manhunter, vs. alien invasion . . 2.00
88 RMz(s),DBk,TA,A:Donna Troy, visit Kyle's mom 2.00
89 RM(s),TA,V:Machine Messiah . . 2.00
90 RM(s),Why did Kyle Rayner become Green Lantern. 2.00
91 RMz(s),DBk,TA,V:Desaad 2.00
92 RMz(s),DBk,TA,A:Green Arrow, x-over. 2.00
93 RMz(s),DBk,TA,F:Deadman. . . . 2.00
94 RMz(s),PaP,TA,F:Superboy 2.00
95 RMz(s),JSn,TA, deep space. . . . 2.00
96 RMz(s) 2.00
97 RMz(s),MMK,TA,V:Grayven 2.00
98 RMz,DBk,TA,Future Shock,pt.1 . 2.00
99 RMz,DBk,TA,Future Shock,pt.2 . 2.00
100 RMz,DBk,AT,Kyle Rayner and Hal Jordan,V:Sinestro, 48pg . . . 3.00
100a deluxe edition 3.00
101 RMz(s),JJ,BWi,Emerald Knights,pt.1, bi-weekly 2.00
102 RMz(s),PaP,TA,Emerald Knights,pt.2, bi-weekly 2.00
103 RMz(s),JJ,BWi,Emerald Knights,pt.3, bi-weekly 2.00
104 RMz(s),JJ,BWi,Greener Pastures x-over, concl., Emerald Knights,pt.4, bi-weekly 2.00
105 RMz(s),JJ,SEa,BWi,Emerald Knights,pt.5, bi-weekly 2.00
106 RMz(s),PaP,TA,Emerald Knights,concl.. . . . . 2.00
107 RMz(s),TA,Emerald Knights aftermath 2.00
108 DBk,TA,A:Wonder Woman. . . . 2.00
109 RMz(s),PaP,TA 2.00
110 RMz(s),TA,A:Green Arrow 2.00
111 RMz(s),TA,DBk,V:Fatality 2.00
112 RMz(s),TA,DBk,back to Earth. . 2.00
113 RMz(s),TA,DBk,Burning in Effigy,pt.1 . . . . 2.00
114 RMz(s),TA,DBk,Burning in Effigy,pt.2 . . . . 2.00
115 DJu(s),A:Plastic Man & Booster Gold, pt.1 . . . . 2.00
116 DJu(s),A:Plastic Man & Booster Gold, pt.1 . . . . 2.00
117 RMz(s),DBk,TA,R:Donna Troy . 2.00
118 RMz(s),DBk,TA,Day of Judgment x-over 2.00
119 RMz,DBk,CaS,Day of Judgment aftermath 2.00
120 RMz,DBk,CaS 2.00
121 RMz,DBk,CaS 2.00
122 RMz,DBk,CaS 2.00
123 RMz,DBk,V:Controllers 2.00
124 RMz,DBk,V:Controllers 2.00
125 RMz,unmooning secrets 2.00
126 goes undercover 2.00
127 F:Effigy & Killer Frost 2.25
128 F:Arsenal. 2.25
129 DBk,ASm,V:Manhuters 2.25
130 DBk,ASm,V:Manhunters 2.25
131 DBk,ASm,V:Manhunters 2.25
Ann.#1 Eclipso,V:Star Sapphire . . . 2.75
Ann.#1 80pg, rep.. . . . . 5.00
Ann.#2 Bloodlines#7,I:Nightblade . . 2.50
Ann.#3 Elseworlds Story. 3.00
Ann.#4 Year One story 3.00
Ann.#5 Legends o/t Dead Earth . . . 3.00
Ann.#6 RMz(s),JJ,Low,Pulp Heroes, 64pg. 4.00
Ann.#7 SV,RLm,CIv,BWr,Ghosts. . . 3.00
Ann.#8 MCa,AAd(c),JLApe:Gorilla Warfare 3.00
Ann.#9 Planet DC. 3.50
Spec.#1,000,000 RMz(s),BHi,PNe . 2.00
Spec. 3-D #1 V:Dr. Light. 4.00
Secret Files #1. . . . . 5.00
Secret Files Spec.#2 . . . . 5.00
Green Lantern Plus, 1-shot RMz(s), F:The Ray,V:Dr. Polaris 3.00
Green Lantern/Silver Surfer, 1-shot DC/Marvel RMz,TA A:Thanos vs. Parallax 5.00
Green Lantern Gallery, 1 one-shot life in pictures 3.50
Green Lantern: Ganthet's Tale, 1-shot, JBy,O:Guardians. 7.00
Giant #1 80-page 5.00
Giant #2 80-page 5.00
Giant #3 80-page 5.95
GN Ganthet's Tale, JBy 6.00
HC Archives, Vol.1, 2nd print 50.00
HC Green Lantern Archive,Vol.2 . . 50.00
HC Green Lantern/Green Arrow Collection 75.00
TPB A New Dawn. 10.00
TPB Emerald Twilight 6.25
TPB Emerald Knights 13.00
TPB A New Dawn. 10.00
TPB Baptism of Fire 13.00
TPB Fear Itself 14.95
TPB Emerald Allies, rep.. . . . . 14.95

GREEN LANTERN & SENTINEL: HEART OF DARKNESS

Feb., 1998

1 (of 3) RMz(s),PaP,DDv 3.00
2 RMz(s),PaP,DDv. 3.00
3 RMz(s),PaP,DDv. 3.00

GREEN LANTERN: CIRCLE OF FIRE

Aug., 2000

1 (of 2) NBy,64-pg. x-over 4.95
2 48-pg.x-over concl.. . . . . 3.75
Spec.Gr.Lant.: Adam Strange #1 . . 2.50
Spec.Gr.Lant.: The Atom #1 . . . . . . 2.50
Spec.Gr.Lant.: Firestorm #1 . . . . . . 2.50
Spec.Gr.Lant.: Green Lantern #1 . . 2.50
Spec.Gr.Lant.: Power Girl #1 . . . . . 2.50

Green Lantern Corps Quarterly #5
© DC Comics Inc.

GREEN LANTERN CORPS QUARTERLY

1992–94

1 DAb,JSon,FH,PG,MBr,F:Alan Scott G'nort 3.00
2 DAb,JSon,PG,AG,Alan Scott . . . 2.75
3 DAb,RT,F:Alan Scott,G'Nort 2.75
4 TA,AG(i),F:H.Jordan,G'Nort 2.75
5 F:Alan Scott,I:Adam 2.75
6 JBa,TC,F:Alan Scott 3.25
7 Halloween Issue 3.25
8 GeH,SHa,final issue 3.25

GREEN LANTERN: EMERALD DAWN

[1st Limited Series] 1989–90

1 MBr,RT,I:Mod.Age.Gr.Lantern . . . 5.00
2 MBr,RT,I:Legion (not group) 4.00
3 MBr,RT,V:Legion. 3.00
4 MBr,RT,A:Green Lantern Corps . 3.00
5 MBr,RT,V:Legion. 3.00
6 MBr,RT,V:Legion. 3.00
TPB rep#1-#6. . . . . 5.50

[2nd Limited Series] 1991

1 MBr,A:Sinestro,Guy Gardner. . . . 2.00
2 MBr,RT,V:Alien Aliance 2.00
3 MBr,RT,Sinestro's Home Planet 2.00
4 MBr,RT,Korugar Revolt 2.00
5 MBr,RT,A:G.Gardner. 2.00
6 MBr,RT,Trial of Sinestro 2.00

GREEN LANTERN/ GREEN ARROW

1983–84

1 NA rep.. 5.00
2 NA,DG rep. 4.00
3 NA,DG rep. 4.00
4 NA,DG rep. 4.00
5 NA,DG rep. 4.00
6 NA,DG rep. 4.00
7 NA,DG rep. 4.00
TPB Roadback 8.95
TPB Traveling Heroes, Vol.1. . . . . 12.95
TPB Traveling Heroes, Vol.2. . . . . 12.95

GREEN LANTERN: MOSAIC

1992–93

1 F:John Stewart 2.00
2 D:Ch'p 2.00
3 V:Sinestro. 2.00
4 F:The Children on Oa 2.00
5 V:Hal Jordan 2.00
6 A:Kilowog 2.00
7 V:Alien Faction 2.00
8 V:Ethereal Creatures 2.00
9 Christmas issue 2.00
10 V:Guardians 2.00
11 R:Ch'p 2.00
12 V:KKK 2.00
13 V:KKK,Racism. 2.00
14 A:Salaak,Ch'p 2.00
15 A:Katma Tui,Ch'p. 2.00
16 LMc,A:JLA,Green Lantern 2.00
17 A:JLA 2.00
18 final issue 2.00

GREEN LANTERN: THE NEW CORPS

1999

1 (of 2) CDi(s),SEa 5.00
2 CDi(s),SEa, concl. 5.00

GREGORY III

Bookshelf Ed. 5.00
Platinum Ed. 8.00

GRIFFIN
1991–92

1 I:Matt Williams as Griffin 5.50

Gross Point #2 © DC Comics, Inc.

2 V:Carson 5.25
3 A:Mary Wayne 5.25
4 A:Mary Wayne 5.25
5 Face to Face with Himself 5.25
6 Final Issue 5.25

GROSS POINT
July 1997

1 MWa&BAu(s) parody 2.50
2 Independence Day picnic 2.50
3 Ed Gein High School 2.50
4 paranoid driving instructor 2.50
5 Halloween 2.50
6 trip to Chicago 2.50
7 stuck in Gross Point 2.50
8 Dru Hardly & Nancy Boys 2.50
9 2.50
10 Businessman of the Year 2.50
11 Mystery Meat 2.50
12 Cold Hands, Still Heart 2.50
13 terminal illness 2.50
14 The Aisle of Doctor Morose 2.50

GUARDIANS OF METROPOLIS
Nov., 1994

1 Kirby characters 2.00
2 Donovan's creations 2.00
3 2.00
4 Female Furies 2.00

GUNFIRE
1994–95

1 B:LWn(s),StE,I:Ricochet 2.00
2 StE,V:Ricochet 2.00
3 StE,I:Purge 2.00
4 StE,V:Maraud 3 2.00
5 StE,I:Exomorphic Man 2.00
6 New costume 2.00
7 Ragnarok 2.00
8 V:Tattoo 2.00
9 V:Ragnarock 2.00
10 V:Yakuza 2.00
11 V:Yakuza 2.00
12 I:New Weapon 2.00
13 A:JLA,V:Ragnarok, final issue 2.25

GUNS OF THE DRAGON
Aug., 1998

1 (of 4) TT, set in 1920s 2.50
2 TT 2.50
3 TT 2.50
4 TT conclusion 2.50

GUY GARDNER
1992–94

1 JSon,A:JLA,JLE 2.00
2 JSon,A:Kilowog 2.00
3 JSon,V:Big,Ugly Alien 2.00
4 JSon,G.Gardner vs Ice 2.00
5 JSon,A:Hal Jordan,V:Goldface 2.00
6 JSon,A:Hal Jordan,V:Goldface 2.00
7 JSon,V:Goldface 2.00
8 JSon,V:Lobo 2.00
9 JSon,Boodikka 2.00
10 JSon,V:Boodikka 2.00
11 JSon,B:Year One 2.00
12 JSon,V:Batman,Flash,Green Lantern 2.00
13 JSon,Year One#3 2.00
14 JSon,E:Year One 2.00
15 V:Bad Guy Gardner 2.00
16 B:CDi(s),MaT,V:Guy's Brother 2.00
Becomes:

GUY GARDNER: WARRIOR
1994–96

17 V:Militia 2.00
18 B:Emerald Fallout,N:Guy Gardner, V:Militia 4.00
19 A:G.A.Green Lantern,V:Militia 4.00
20 A:JLA,Darkstars 2.00
21 E:Emerald Fallout,V:H.Jordan 2.00
22 I:Dementor 2.00
23 A:Buck Wargo 2.00
24 Zero Hour 2.00
25 A:Buck Wargo 2.50
26 Zero Hour 2.00
27 Capital Punishment 2.00
28 Capital Punishment,pt.2 2.00
29 I:Warriors Bar 2.00
29a Collector's Edition 3.25

Guy Guardner Warrior #38
© DC Comics, Inc.

30 V:Superman,Supergirl 2.00
31 A:Sentinel,Supergirl, V:Dementor 2.00
32 Way of the Warrior,pt.1,A:JLA 2.00
33 Way of the Warrior,pt.4 2.00
34 2.00
35 Return of an Old Foe 2.00
36 Underworld Unleashed tie-in 2.00
37 Underworld Unleashed tie-in 2.00
38 A new woman 2.00
39 guest stars galore 2.00
40 2.00
41 V:Dungeon 2.00
42 Martika revealed as Seductress 2.00
43 V:5 foes 2.00
Ann.#1 Year One Annual, Leechun vs. Vuldarians 3.50

GUY GARDNER: REBORN
1992

1 JSon,JRu,V:Goldface,C:Lobo 6.00
2 JSon,JRu,A:Lobo,V:Weaponers of Qward 5.50
3 JSon,JRu,A:Lobo,N:G.Gardner V:Qwardians 5.50

HACKER FILES
1992–93

1 TS,Soft Wars#1,I:Jack Marshall 2.25
2 TS,Soft Wars#2 2.00
3 TS,Soft Wars#3 2.00
4 TS,Soft Wars#4 2.00
5 TS,A:Oracle(Batgirl) 2.00
6 TS,A:Oracle,Green Lantern 2.00
7 TS,V:Digitronix 2.00
8 TS,V:Digitronix 2.00
9 TS,V:Digitronix 2.00
10 V:Digitronix 2.00
11 TS,A:JLE 2.00
12 TS,V:Digitronix,final issue 2.00

HAMMER LOCKE
1992–93

1 I:Hammerlocke 2.50
2 V:Tharn the Iron Spider 2.00
3 V:Tharn the Iron Spider 2.00
4 O:Hammerlocke 2.00
5 V:Sahara Skyhawk 2.00
6 V:Tharn the Iron Spider 2.00
7 V:Tharn 2.00
8 CSp,V:Iron Spider 2.00

HARDCORE STATION
May, 1998

1 (of 6) JSn,JRu,F:Maximillian 2.50
2 JSn,JRu,V:Synnar 2.50
3 JSn,JRu,F:Kyle Rayner 2.50
4 JSn,JRu,V:Synnar 2.50
5 JSn,JRu,F:JLA 2.50
6 JSn,JRu,conclusion 2.50

HARDWARE
(Milestone) 1993–96

1 DCw,I:Hardware,Edwin Alva,Reprise, Dir.Mark.Ed.,w/A puzzle piece, Skybox Card,Poster 4.00
1a NewsstandEd. 2.00
1b Platinum Ed. 6.00
2 DCw,V:Repirise,I:Barraki Young 2.00
3 DCw,O:EDwin Alva, I:S.Y.S.T.E.M. 2.00
4 DCw,V:S.Y.S.T.E.M. 2.00
5 DCw,I:Deathwish 2.00
6 DCw,V:Deathwish 2.00
7 DCw,O:Deathwish 2.00
8 DCw(c),O:Hardware 2.00
9 DCw(c),I:Technique 2.00

10 DCw(c),I:Harm,Transit 2.00
11 WS(c),DCw,Shadow War, I:Iron Butterfly,Dharma 2.00
12 RB,V:Harm 2.00
13 DCw,A:Reprise 2.00
14 DCw 2.00
15 DCw(c),HuR,V:Alva 2.00
16 Die-Cut(c),JBy(c),DCw, N:Hardware 4.25
16a Newsstand ED. 2.25
17 Worlds Collide,pt.2,A:Steel. 2.00
18 Worlds Collide,pt.9,V:Rift 2.00
19 I:Evan,Tetras 2.00
20 . . . . 2.00
21 Arcana,Helga. 2.00
22 Curt & Assistant. 2.00
23 . . . . 2.00
24 . . . . 2.00
25 V:Death Row, Sanction 2.95
26 Hunt For Deathwish,pt.1 . . . . . . 2.00
27 Hunt For Deathwish,pt.2 . . . . . . 2.00
28 Hunt For Deathwish,pt.3 . . . . . . 2.00
29 Long Hot Summer, A:The Blood Syndicate, spec.low price 2.00
30 Long Hot Summer 2.50
31 . . . . 2.50
32 Control of Alva 2.50
33 HC(c), Cyborg 2.50
34 V:Huaca Aires 2.50
35 A:Sanction. 2.50
36 A:Sanction. 2.50
37 . . . . 2.50
38 V:Malleus, without armor 2.50
39 F:Sabrina Alva. 2.50
40 V:Top Dog 2.50
41 . . . . 2.50
42 . . . . 2.50
43 . . . . 2.50
44 A:Heroes 2.50
45 DGC(s),Hardware & Hard Company go back to basics . . . 2.50
46 DGC(s),discovery of Edwin Alva's artificial intelligence 2.50
47 DGC(s),the truth behind a brutal murder 2.50
48 . . . . 2.50
49 DGC(s),Moe(c),V:Tyrant. 2.50
50 DGC(s), 48pg. anniversary issue 3.95
51 DMc(s) final issue 2.50

HARLEY QUINN
October, 2000

1 KK,TyD,A:Batman,48 pg. 2.95

HAWK & DOVE
[1st Regular Series] 1968–69

1 SD 55.00
2 SD 45.00
3 GK 40.00
4 GK 40.00
5 GK,C:Teen Titans 45.00
6 GK 40.00

[Limited Series] 1988–89

1 RLd,I:New Dove 4.00
2 RLd,V:Kestrel 3.50
3 RLd,V:Kestrel 3.50
4 RLd,V:Kestrel 3.50
5 RLd,V:Kestrel,O:New Dove. 3.50
TPB rep. #1-#5. . . . . 9.95

[2nd Regular Series] 1989–91

1 A:Superman,Green Lantern Hawkman. 2.00
2 V:Aztec Goddess 2.00
3 V:Aztec Goddess 2.00
4 I:The Untouchables 2.00
5 I:Sudden Death, A:1st Dove's Ghost. 2.00
6 A:Barter,Secrets o/Hawk&Dove. . 2.00
7 A:Barter,V:Count St.Germain . . . 2.00
8 V:Count St.Germain 2.00
9 A:Copperhead 2.00
10 V:Gauntlet & Andromeda 2.00
11 A:New Titans,V:M.A.C., Andromeda Gauntlet 2.00
12 A:New Titans,V:Scarab 2.00
13 1960's,I:Shellshock 2.00
14 Prelue to O:Hawk & Dove, V:Kestrel 2.00
15 O:Hawk & Dove begins 2.00
16 HawkV:Dove,V:Lord of Chaos . . 2.00
17 V:Lords-Order & Chaos 2.00
18 The Creeper #1 . . . . 2.00
19 The Creeper #2 . . . . 2.00
20 KM,DG,Christmas Story. 2.00
21 Dove 2.00
22 V:Sudden Death 2.00
23 A:Velv.Tiger,SuddenDeath 2.00
24 A:Velv.Tiger,SuddenDeath 2.00
25 Recap 1st 2 yrs.(48 pg) 2.50
26 Dove's past 2.00
27 The Hunt for Hawk. 2.00
28 War of the Gods,A:Wildebeest A:Uncle Sam,final issue, double size. 2.50
Ann.#1 In Hell. 2.00
Ann.#2 CS,KGa,ArmageddonPt.5 . . 2.00
TPB RLd 9.95

HAWK & DOVE
Sept., 1997

1 (of 5) MBn,DZ,DG,Sasha Martens & Wiley Wolverman 2.50
2 MBn,DZ,DG,Vixen & Vigilante. . . 2.50
3 MBn,DZ,DG,grave desecrations . 2.50
4 MBn,DZ,DG,V:Suicide Squad . . . 2.50

HAWKMAN
[1st Regular Series]1964–68

1 MA,V:Chac. 550.00
2 MA,V:Tralls. 200.00
3 MA,V:Sky Raiders. 135.00
4 MA,I&O:Zatanna. 150.00
5 MA 135.00
6 MA 125.00
7 MA,V:I.Q. 125.00
8 MA 125.00
9 MA,V:Matter Master 125.00
10 MA,V:Caw 125.00
11 MA. 75.00
12 MA 75.00

Hawkman 2nd Series #15
© DC Comics Inc.

13 MA 75.00
14 GaF,MA,V:Caw 75.00
15 GaF,MA,V:Makkar 75.00
16 GaF,MA,V:Ruthvol 75.00
17 GaF,MA,V:Raven 75.00
18 GaF,MA,A:Adam Strange. 50.00
19 GaF,MA,A:Adam Strange. 50.00
20 GaF,MA,V:Lionmane 45.00
21 GaF,MA,V:Lionmane 45.00
22 V:Falcon 45.00
23 V:Dr.Malevolo 45.00
24 Robot Raiders from Planet Midnight 45.00
25 DD,V:Medusa,G.A.Hawkman . . 45.00
26 RdM,CCu,DD. 45.00
27 DD,JKu(c),V:Yeti 45.00

[2nd Regular Series] 1986–87

1 DH,A:Shadow Thief 3.00
2 DH,V:Shadow Thief 2.00
3 DH,V:Shadow Thief 2.00
4 DH A:Zatanna 2.00
5 DH,V:Lionmane 2.00
6 DH,V:Gentleman Ghost, Lionmane 2.00
7 DH,Honor Wings 2.00
8 DH,Shadow War contd. 2.00
9 DH,Shadow War contd. 2.00
10 JBy(c),D:Hyatis Corp 2.00
11 End of Shadow War. 2.00
12 Hawks on Thanagar. 2.00
13 DH,Murder Case 2.00
14 DH,Mystery o/Haunted Masks . . 2.00
15 DH,Murderer Revealed 2.00
16 DH,Hawkwoman lost 2.00
17 EH,DH,final issue 2.00
TPB rep.Brave & Bold apps. 19.95

[3rd Regular Series] 1993–96

1 B:JOs(s),JD,R:Hawkman, V:Deadline 4.00
2 JD,A:Gr.Lantern,V:Meta-Tech . . . 2.50
3 JD,I:Airstryke 2.25
4 JD,RM 2.00
5 JD(c),V:Count Viper 2.00
6 JD(c),A:Eradicator 2.00
7 JD(c),PuK(s),LMc,B:King of the Netherworld 2.00
8 LMc,E:King of the Netherworld . . 2.00
9 BML(s) 2.00
10 I:Badblood 2.00
11 V:Badblood 2.00
12 V:Hawkgod 2.25
13 V:Hawkgod 2.25
14 New abilities,pt.1 . . . . 2.00
15 New abilities,pt.2 . . . . 2.00
16 Eyes of the Hawk,pt.3 . . . . 2.00
17 Eyes of the Hawk,pt.4 . . . . 2.00
18 Seagle,Ellis, Pepoy 2.00
19 F:Hawkman 2.00
21 RLm,V:Shadow Thief, Gentleman Ghost 2.25
22 Way of the Warrior,pt.3 A:Warrior,JLA 2.25
23 Way of the Warrior,pt.6 . . . . 2.25
24 . . . . 2.25
25 V:Lionmane,painted(c) 2.25
26 WML,Underworld Unleashed tie-in 2.25
27 WML,Underworld Unleashed tie-in 2.25
28 WML,V:Doctor Polaris 2.25
29 HC(c),V:Vandal Savage 2.25
30 . . . . 2.25
31 serial killer has Tangarian technology 2.25
32 MC,Search for serial killer 2.25
Ann.#1 JD,I:Mongrel 3.75
Ann.#2 Year One Annual 3.95
HC Hawkman Archives, Vol.1 . . . . 49.95

Hawkworld #19 © DC Comics, Inc.

HAWKWORLD

1989

1 TT,Hawkman, Origin retold 5.00
2 TT,Katar tried for treason 4.00
3 TT,Hawkgirl's debut 4.00

[1st Regular Series] 1990–93

1 GN,Byth on Earth,R:Kanjar Ro . . 3.00
2 GN,Katar & Shayera in Chicago . 2.50
3 GN,V:Chicago Crime 2.00
4 GN,Byth's Control Tightens. 2.00
5 GN,Return of Shadow Thief 2.00
6 GN,Stolen Thanagarian Ship . . . 2.00
7 GN,V:Byth 2.00
8 GN,Hawkman vs. Hawkwoman. . 2.00
9 GN,Hawkwoman in Prison 2.00
10 Shayera returns to Thanagar . . . 2.00
11 GN,Blackhawk,Express 2.00
12 GN,Princess Treska. 2.00
13 TMd,A:Firehawk,V:Marauder . . . 2.00
14 GN,Shayera's Father 2.00
15 GN,War of the Gods X-over. . . . 2.00
16 GN War of the Gods X-over. . . . 2.00
17 GN,Train Terrorists 2.00
18 GN,V:Atilla. 2.00
19 GN,V:Atilla. 2.00
20 V:Smir'Beau 2.00
21 GN,Thanagar Pt.1,
A:J.S.A. Hawkman 2.00
22 GN,Thanagar Pt.2 . . . . 2.00
23 GN,Thanagar Pt.3 . . . . 2.00
24 GN,Thanagar Pt.4 . . . . 2.00
25 GN,Thanagar Pt.5 . . . . 2.00
26 GN,V:Attilla battle armor 2.00
27 JD,B:Flight's End 2.00
28 JD,Flight's End #2 . . . . 2.00
29 TT(c),JDu,Flight's End #3 . . . . . 2.00
30 TT,Flight's End #4 . . . . 2.00
31 TT,Flight's End #5 . . . . 2.00
32 TT,V:Count Viper,final issue 2.50
Ann.#1 A:Flash. 4.50
Ann.#2 Armageddon,pt.6 . . . . 4.00
Ann.#2a reprint (Silver). 3.50
Ann.#3 Eclipso tie-in. 3.25

HAYWIRE

1988–89

1 . . . . 2.00
2 . . . . 2.00
3 thru 13 . . . . 2.00

HEARTLAND

DC/Vertigo Jan., 1997

1 GEn(s),SDi,Kit faces childhood
memories. 4.95

HEART OF THE BEAST

GNv SeP 19.95

HEART THROBS

DC/Vertigo 1998

1 (of 4) anthology 3.00
2 modern romance 3.00
3 . . . . 3.00
4 . . . . 3.00

Heckler #6 © DC Comics, Inc.

HEAVY LIQUID

DC/Vertigo 1999

1 PPo,pt 1 of 5 . . . . 6.00
2 PPo,pt.2. . . . . 6.00
3 PPo,pt.3. . . . . 6.00
4 PPo,pt.4. . . . . 6.00
5 PPo,pt.5. . . . . 6.00

HECKLER, THE

1992–93

1 KG,MJ,I:The Heckler 2.00
2 KG,MJ,V:The Generic Man 2.00
3 KG,MJ,V:Cosmic Clown 2.00
4 KG,V:Bushwacker. 2.00
5 KG,Theater Date 2.00
6 KG,I:Lex Concord. 2.00
7 KG,V:Cuttin'Edge 2.00

HELLBLAZER

Jan., 1988

1 B:JaD(s),JRy,F:John
Constantine 18.00
2 JRy,I:Papa Midnight 10.00
3 JRy,I:Blathoxi 9.00
4 JRy,I:Resurrection Crusade,
Gemma 9.00
5 JRy,F:Pyramid of Fear 9.00
6 JRy,V:Resurrection Crusade,
I:Nergal 6.00
7 JRy,V:Resurrection Crusade,
I:Richie Simpson 6.00
8 JRy,AA,Constantine receives
demon blood,V:Nergal 6.00
9 JRy,A:Swamp Thing 6.00
10 JRy,V:Nergal 6.00
11 MBu,Newcastle Incident,pt.1 . . . 5.00
12 JRy,D:Nergal 5.00
13 JRy,John has a Nightmare. 4.00
14 JRy,B:The Fear Machine,
I:Mercury,Marj,Eddie. 4.00
15 JRy,Shepard's Warning. 4.00
16 JRy,Rough Justice 4.00
17 MkH,I:Mr. Wester. 4.00
18 JRy,R:Zed 4.00
19 JRy,I:Simon Hughes 7.00
20 JRy,F:Mr.Webster 5.00
21 JRy,I:Jallakuntilliokan. 5.00
22 JRy,E:The Fear Machine.. . . . . . 5.00
23 I&D:Jerry O'Flynn 4.00
24 E:JaD(s),I:Sammy Morris 4.00
25 GMo(s),DvL,Early Warning 4.00
26 GMo(s) 4.00
27 NGa(s),DMc,Hold Me. 10.00
28 B:JaD(s),RnT,KeW,F:S.Morris . . 4.00
29 RnT,KeW,V:Sammy Morris. 4.00
30 RnT,KeW,D:Sammy Morris. 4.00
31 E:JaD(s),SeP,Constantine's
Father's Funeral. 4.00
32 DiF(s),StP,I&D:Drummond 3.50
33 B:JaD(s),MPn,I:Pat McDonell. . . 3.50
34 SeP,R:Mercury,Marj 3.50
35 SeP,Constantine's Past 3.50
36 Future Death,(preview of
World Without End) 3.50
37 Journey to England's Secret
Mystics. 3.50
38 Constantine's Journey contd. . . . 3.50
39 Journey to Discovery 3.50
40 DMc,I:2nd Kid Eternity 4.00
41 B:GEn(s),WSm,MPn,Dangerous
Habits 6.00
42 Dangerous Habits 4.50
43 I:Chantinelle 4.50
44 Dangerous Habits 4.50
45 Dangerous Habits 4.50
46 Dangerous Habits epilogue,
I:Kit(John's girlfriend) 4.50
47 SnW(i),Pub Where I Was Born. . 4.00
48 Love Kills. 4.00
49 X-mas issue,Lord o/t Dance. . . . 4.00
50 WSm,Remarkable Lives,A:Lord
of Vampires (48pgs) 6.00
51 JnS,SeP,Laundromat-
Possession. 5.00
52 GF(c),WSm, Royal Blood. 5.00
53 GF(c),WSm, Royal Blood. 5.00
54 GF(c),WSm, Royal Blood. 5.00
55 GF(c),WSm, Royal Blood. 5.00
56 GF(c),B:GEn(s),DvL,
V:Danny Drake. 5.00
57 GF(c),SDi,Mortal Clay#1,
V:Dr. Amis 5.00
58 GF(c),SDi,Mortal Clay#2,
V:Dr. Amis 5.00
59 GF(c),WSm,MkB(i),KDM,B:Guys
& Dolls 5.00
60 GF(c),WSm,MkB(i),F:Tali,
Chantinelle. 5.00
61 GF(c),WSm,MkB(i),E:Guys &
Dolls, V:First of the Fallen. 5.00
62 GF(c),SDi,End of the Line,I:Gemma,
AIDS storyline insert w/Death . . 5.00

Vertigo

63 GF(c),SDi,C:Swamp Thing,Zatanna
Phantom Stranger 5.00
64 GF(c),SDi,B:Fear & Loathing,
A:Gabriel (Racism). 4.00
65 GF(c),SDi,D:Dez 4.00
66 GF(c),SDi,E:Fear and Loathing . 4.00
67 GF(c),SDi,Kit leaves John 4.00
68 GF(c),SDi,F:Lord of Vampires,
Darius,Mary 4.00
69 GF(c),SDi,D:Lord of Vampires . . 4.00
70 GF(c),SDi,Kit in Ireland 4.00
71 GF(c),SDi,A:WWII Fighter Pilot . 4.00
72 GF(c),SDi,B:Damnation's

Flame,A:Papa Midnight 4.00
73 GF(c),SDi,Nightmare NY, A:JFK. 4.00
74 GF(c),SDi,I:Cedella,A:JFK 4.00
75 GF(c),SDi,E:Damnation'sFlame . 4.00
76 GF(c),SDi,R:Brendan. 4.00
77 Returns to England 4.00
78 GF(c),SDi,B:Rake at the Gates of Hell 4.00
79 GF(c),SDi,In Hell 4.00
80 GF(c),SDi,In London 4.00
81 GF(c),SDi 4.00
82 Kit 4.00
83 Rake,Gates of Hell 4.00
84 John's past 4.00
85 Warped Notions,pt.1 . . . . 4.00
86 Warped Notions,pt.2 . . . . 4.00
87 Warped Notions,pt.3 . . . . 4.00
88 Warped Notions,pt.4 . . . . 4.00
89 Dreamtime. 4.00
90 Dreamtime,pt.2 . . . . 4.00
91 Visits Battlefield 4.00
92 Critical Mass,pt.1 . . . . 4.00
93 Critical Mass,pt.2. . . . . 4.00
94 Critical Mass,pt.3. . . . . 4.00
95 SeP,Critical Mass,pt.4 . . . . 4.00
96 SeP,Critical Mass,pt.5 . . . . 4.00
97 SeP,Critical Mass epilogue. 4.00
98 SeP, helps neighbor. 4.00
99 SeP. 4.00
100 SeP, In a coma 5.00
101 SeP,deal with a demon 3.50
102 SeP,Difficult Beginnings, pt.1 (of 3) 3.50
103 SeP,"Difficult Beginnings, pt.2" . 3.50
104 SeP,"Difficult Beginnings, pt.3" . 3.50
105 . . . . 3.50
106 PJe(s),SEp,"In the Line of Fire," pt.1 (of 2) 3.50
107 PJe(s),SEp,"In the Line of Fire," pt. 2 . . . . 3.50
108 PJe(s),SeP,a Bacchic celebration 3.50
109 PJe(s),SeP,cattle mutilations in Northern England 3.50
110 PJe(s),SeP,"Last Man Standing," pt.1 . . . . 3.50
111 PJe(s),SeP,"Last Man Standing," pt.2 . . . . 3.50
112 PJe(s),SeP,"Last Man Standing," pt.3 . . . . 3.50
113 PJe(s),SeP,"Last Man Standing," pt.4 . . . . 3.50
114 PJe(s),SeP,"Last Man Standing," pt.5 . . . . 3.50
115 PJe(s),SeP(s),Dani's ex-boyfriend 3.50
116 SeP, "Widdershins" pt.1 (of 2). . 3.50
117 SeP, "Widdershins" pt.2 . . . . . . 3.50
118 PJe(s),SeP,John's a Godfather. 4.00
119 PJe(s),SeP,disasters 3.50
120 PJe(s),SeP,10th anniv. 48pg . . 3.00
121 PJe(s),SeP, Up the Down Staircase pt.1 . . . . 3.00
122 PJe(s),SeP, Up the Down Staircase pt.2. . . . . 3.00
123 PJe(s),SeP, Up the Down Staircase pt.3. . . . . 3.00
124 PJe(s),SeP, Up the Down Staircase pt.4. . . . . 3.00
125 PJe(s),SeP, How to Play with Fire, pt.1 . . . . 3.00
126 PJe(s),SeP,Play/Fire,pt.2 . . . . . 3.00
127 PJe(s),SeP,Play/Fire,pt.3 . . . . . 3.00
128 PJe(s),SeP,Play/Fire,pt.4 . . . . . 3.00
129 . . . . 3.00
130 GEn,JHi,GF,Son of Man,pt.2 . . 3.00
131 GEn,JHi,GF,Son of Man,pt.3 . . 2.50
132 GEn,JHi,GF,Son of Man,pt.4 . . 2.50
133 GEn,JHi,GF,Son of Man,pt.5 . . 2.50
134 WEl(s),JHi,Haunted,pt.1. . . . . . 2.50

Hellblazer #4 © DC Comics Inc.

135 WEl(s),JHi,Haunted,pt.2. . . . . . 2.50
136 WEl(s),JHi,Haunted,pt.3. . . . . . 2.50
137 WEl(s),JHi,Haunted,pt.4. . . . . . 2.50
138 WEl(s),JHi,Haunted,pt.5. . . . . . 2.50
139 WEl(s),JHi,Haunted,pt.6. . . . . . 2.50
140 WEl(s),Locked 2.50
141 WEl(s),ALa 2.50
142 WEl,TBd,Setting Sun 2.50
143 WEl,TBd,Telling Tales 2.50
144 GEr,ALa,Ashes & Honey,pt.1 . . 2.50
145 GEr,ALa,Ashes & Honey,pt.2 . . 2.50
146 RC,Hard Time 2.50
147 RC,Hard Time,pt.2 . . . . 2.50
148 RC,Hard Time,pt.3 . . . . 2.50
149 RC,Hard Time,pt.4 . . . . 2.50
150 RC,Hard Time,concl. 2.50
151 Good Intentions,pt.1. . . . . 2.50
152 Good Intentions,pt.2. . . . . 2.50
153 Good Intentions,pt.3. . . . . 2.50
154 Good Intentions,pt.4. . . . . 2.50
155 Good Intentions,pt.5. . . . . 2.50
Ann.#1 JaD(s),BT,Raven Scar 7.00
Spec.#1 GF(c),GEn(s),SDi,John Constantine's teenage years . . 4.50
Secret Files #1 . . . . 4.95
TPB Original Sins,rep.#1–#9. . . . . 19.95
TPB Dangerous Habits, rep.#41-#46 . . . . 14.95
TPB Fear and Loathing. 14.95
TPB Damnation's Flame 17.00

HELLBLAZER/ THE BOOKS OF MAGIC

Oct., 1997

1 (of 2) PJe,JNR 2.50
2 PJe,JNR. 2.50

HELLBLAZER SPECIAL: BAD BLOOD

DC/Vertigo July, 2000

1 (of 4) JaD,PBd 3.50
2 JaD,PBd, ... 3.50
3 JaD,PBd. 3.50
4 JaD,PBd,concl. 3.50

HERCULES UNBOUND

Oct.–Nov., 1975

1 thru 11 . . . . @2.00
12 Aug.–Sept., 1977. . . . . 2.00

HEROES

Milestone 1996

1 Six heroes join 2.50
2 battle royale 2.50
3 . . . . 2.50
4 . . . . 2.50
5 . . . . 2.50
6 final issue. 2.50

HEROES AGAINST HUNGER

1 NA,DG,JBy,CS,AA,BWr,BS, Superman,Batman 3.50

HERO HOTLINE

1 thru 6, Mini-series . . . . @2.00

HEX

Sept., 1985

1 MT,I:Hex. 2.50
2 MT 2.00
3 MT,V:Conglomerate 2.00
4 MT,V:Conglomerate 2.00
5 MT,A:Chainsaw Killer 2.00
6 MT,V:Conglomerate 2.00
7 MT,Tries to Return to own era. . . 2.00
8 MT,The Future 2.50
9 MT,Future Killer Cyborgs 2.00
10 MT,V:Death Cult 2.00
11 MT,V:The Batman 3.00
12 MT,A:Batman,V:Terminators. . . . 3.00
13 MT,I:New Supergroup 2.50
14 MT,A:The Dogs of War. 2.00
15 KG,V:Chainsaw Killer. 2.00
16 KG,V:Dogs of War 2.00
17 KG,Hex/Dogs of War T.U. V:XXGG. 2.00
18 KGr,Confronting the Past,final Issue 2.00

HISTORY OF DC UNIVERSE

Sept., 1986

1 GP, From start to WWII. 5.00
2 GP, From WWII to present 5.00

A HISTORY OF VIOLENCE

DC/Paradox Press March 1997

GN B&W 9.95

HITCHHIKER'S GUIDE TO THE GALAXY

1 Based on the book 7.00
2 Based on the book 6.50
3 Based on the book 6.50
GN from Douglas Adams book . . . 14.95

HITMAN

1996–97

1 GEn, F:Tommy Monaghan 11.00
2 GEn, Attempt to kill Joker 8.00
3 GEn(s),JMC, Mawzin & The Arkanonne 4.50
4 GEn(s),JMC, ... 3.00
5 GEn(s),JMC, ... 3.00
6 GEn(s),JMC,A:Johnny Navarone, Natt the Hatt. 3.00
7 GEn(s),JMC, Pat's dead, Hitman wants revenge 3.00
8 GEn(s),JMC,barricaded in Noonan's Bar, Final Night tie-in. 3.00
9 GEn(s),JMC,A:Six-Pack 3.00
10 GEn(s),JMC,A:Green Lantern . . 3.00
11 . . . . 2.25

DC COMICS

12 GEn(s),JMC,"Local Heroes, "A:Green Lantern 2.25
13 . . . . 2.25
14 GEn(s),JMC, "Zombie Night at the Aquarium," concl. 2.25
15 GEn(s),JMC, "Ace of Killers," pt.1, V:Mawzir 2.25
16 GEn(s),JMC, "Ace of Killers," pt.2 . . . . 2.25
17 GEn(s),JMC, "Ace of Killers," pt.3,A:Catwoman, Demon Etrigan 2.25
18 GEn(s),JMC, "Ace of Killers," pt.4,A:Demon Etrigan, Baytor . 2.25
19 GEn(s),JMC,Ace/Killers,pt.5, . . . 2.25
20 GEn(s),JMC,Ace/Killers,concl. . . 2.50
21 GEn(s),JMC,Romeo & Juliet . . . 2.50
22 GEn(s),JMC,holiday special 2.25
23 GEn(s),JMc,"Who Dares Wins," pt.1 . . . . 2.50
24 GEn(s),JMc,Dares/Wins,pt.2 . . . 2.50
25 GEn(s),JMc,Dares/Wins,pt.3 . . . 2.50
26 GEn(s),JMc,Dares/Wins,pt.4 . . . 2.50
27 GEn(s),JMc,Dares/Wins,pt.5 . . . 2.50
28 GEn(s),JMC,aftermath 2.50
29 GEn(s),JMC,Tommy's Heroes, pt.1 . . . . 2.50
30 GEn(s),JMC,Heroes, pt.2 . . . . . . 2.50
31 GEn(s),JMC,Heroes, pt.3 . . . . . . 2.50
32 GEn(s),JMC,Heroes, pt.4 . . . . . . 2.50
33 GEn(s),JMC,Heroes, pt.5 . . . . . . 2.50
34 GEn(s),A:Superman 2.50
35 GEn(s),Frances Monaghan 2.50
36 GEn(s), ... 2.50
37 GEn(s). 2.50
38 GEn(s),Dead Man's Land, concl. 2.50
39 GEn(s),JMC,A:RingoChen,pt.1. . 2.50
40 GEn(s),JMC,A:RingoChen,pt.2. . 2.50
41 GEn(s),JMC,A:RingoChen,pt.3. . 2.50
42 GEn(s),JMC,A:RingoChen,pt.4. . 2.50
43 GEn(s),JMC, ... 2.50
44 GEn(s),JMC. 2.50
45 GEn(s),JMC. 2.50
46 GEn(s),JMC. 2.50
47 GEn(s),JMC,Old Dog 2.50
48 GEn(s),JMC,Old Dog,pt.2 . . . . . 2.50
49 GEn(s),JMC,Old Dog,pt.3 . . . . . 2.50
50 GEn(s),JMC,Hitman's future . . . 2.50
51 GEn(s),JMC,Superguy,pt.1 . . . . 2.50
52 GEn(s),JMc,Superguy,pt.2 . . . . 2.50
53 GEn(s),JMc,ClosingTime,pt.1. . . 2.50
54 GEn(s),JMc,ClosingTime,pt.2. . . 2.50
55 GEn(s),JMc,ClosingTime,pt.3. . . 2.50
56 GEn,JMC,GL,O:Tommy Monaghan 2.50
Ann.#1 Pulp Heroes (Western) 3.95
Spec.#1,000,000 GEn(s),JMC 2.50
Spec. Hitman/Lobo: That Stupid Bastich! 3.95
TPB rep. Demon Annual #2, Batman Chronicles #4, Hitman #1–#3 . 10.00
TPB Ten Thousand Bullets, rep. #4–#8 . . . . 10.00
TPB Hitman: Ten Thousand Bullets 10.00
TPB Hitman: Local Heroes 18.00
TPB Hitman GEn(s),JMC 9.95
TPB Ace of Killers 17.95

HOPALONG CASSIDY
Feb., 1954

86 GC,Ph(c):William Boyd & Topper, `The Secret of the Tattooed Burro' 275.00
87 GC,Ph(c),`The Tenderfoot Outlaw' 160.00
88 Ph(c),GC,`15 Robbers of Rimfire Ridge' 100.00
89 GC,Ph(c),`One-Day Boom Town' 100.00
90 GC,Ph(c),`Cowboy Clown Robberies' 85.00

Hopalong Cassidy #108
© DC Comics, Inc.

91 GC,Ph(c),`The Riddle of the Roaring R Ranch' 100.00
92 GC,Ph(c),`The Sky-Riding Outlaws' 100.00
93 GC,Ph(c),`The Silver Badge of Courage' 100.00
94 GC,Ph(c),`Mystery of the Masquerading Lion' 100.00
95 GC,Ph(c),`Showdown at the Post-Hole Bank' 100.00
96 GC,Ph(c),`Knights of the Range' 100.00
97 GC,Ph(c),`The Mystery of the Three-Eyed Cowboy' . . . 100.00
98 GC,Ph(c),`Hopalong's Unlucky Day' 100.00
99 GC,Ph(c),`Partners in Peril' . . 100.00
100 GC,Ph(c),`The Secrets of a Sheriff' 120.00
101 GC,Ph(c),`Way Out West Where The East Begins' 75.00
102 GC,Ph(c),`Secret of the Buffalo Hat' 75.00
103 GC,Ph(c),`The Train-Rustlers of Avalance Valley' 75.00
104 GC,Ph(c),`Secret of the Surrendering Outlaws' 75.00
105 GC,Ph(c),`Three Signs to Danger' 75.00
106 GC,Ph(c),`The Secret of the Stolen Signature' 75.00
107 GC,Ph(c),`The Mystery Trail to Stagecoach Town' 75.00
108 GC,Ph(c),`The Mystery Stage From Burro Bend' 75.00
109 GC,`The Big Gun on Saddletop Mountain' 75.00
110 GC,`The Dangerous Stunts of Hopalong Cassidy' 65.00
111 GC,`Sheriff Cassidy's Mystery Clue' 65.00
112 GC,`Treasure Trail to Thunderbolt Ridge 65.00
113 GC,`The Shadow of the Toy Soldier 65.00
114 GC,`Ambush at Natural Bridge' 65.00
115 GC,`The Empty-Handed Robberies' 65.00
116 GC,`Mystery of the Vanishing Cabin' 65.00
117 GC,`School for Sheriffs' 65.00
118 GC,`The Hero of Comanche Ridge' 65.00
119 GC,`The Dream Sheriff of Twin Rivers' 65.00
120 GC,`Salute to a Star-Wearer' . 65.00
121 GC,`The Secret of the Golden Caravan' 65.00
122 GC,`The Rocking Horse Bandits' 65.00
123 GK,`Mystery of the One-Dollar Bank Robbery' . . . 65.00
124 GK,`Mystery of the Double-X Brand' 65.00
125 GK,`Hopalong Cassidy's Secret Brother' 65.00
126 GK,`Trail of the Telltale Clues' 65.00
127 GK,`Hopalong Cassidy's Golden Riddle' 65.00
128 GK,`The House That Hated Outlaws' 65.00
129 GK,`Hopalong Cassidy's Indian Sign' 65.00
130 GK,`The Return of the Canine Sheriff' 65.00
131 GK&GK(c),`The Amazing Sheriff of Double Creek' 65.00
132 GK,`Track of the Invisible Indians' 65.00
133 GK,`The Golden Trail to Danger' 65.00
134 GK,`Case of the Three Crack-Shots' 65.00
135 GK,May-June, 1959 . . . . 65.00

HORRORIST
(Vertigo) 1995

1 I:Horrorist 6.50
2 conclusion 6.50

HOT WHEELS
March–April, 1970

1 ATh 25.00
2 thru 5 ATh . . . . @20.00
6 NA 30.00

HOURMAN
1999

1 TPe,RgM,A:JLA 2.50
2 TPe(s),RgM,F:Tomorrow Woman 2.50
3 TPe(s),RgM,Timepoint,pt.1 . . . . . 2.50
4 TPe(s),RgM,Timepoint,pt.2 . . . . . 2.50
5 TPe(s),RgM,Rex Tyler's life 2.50
6 TPe,RgM,JLAndroids,pt.1 . . . . . . 2.50
7 TPe,RgM,JLAndroids,pt.2 . . . . . . 2.50
8 TPe,RgM,Day of Judgment x-over 2.50
9 TPe,RgM,F:Rick Tyler 2.50
10 TPe,RgM 2.50
11 TPe,RgM,One Million,pt.1 . . . . . 2.50
12 TPe,RgM,One Million,pt.2 . . . . . 2.50
13 TPe,RgM,One Million,pt.3 . . . . . 2.50
14 TPe,RgM,V:Undersoul 2.50
15 TPe,RgM,human secrets 2.50
16 TPe,RgM,F:Snapper 2.50
17 TPe,100 Years of Solitude 2.50
18 TPe,RgM,High Society,pt.1 . . . . 2.50
19 TPe,RgM,High Society,pt.2 . . . . 2.50
20 TPe,RgM,F:Snapper 2.50
21 TPe,RgM,reduced to nothing . . . 2.50

HOUSE OF MYSTERY
Dec.–Jan., 1952

1 I Fell In LoveWithA Monster . 1,800.00
2 The Mark of X. 800.00
3 . . . . 600.00
4 The Man With the Evil Eye . . . 450.00
5 The Man With the Strangler Hands! 450.00

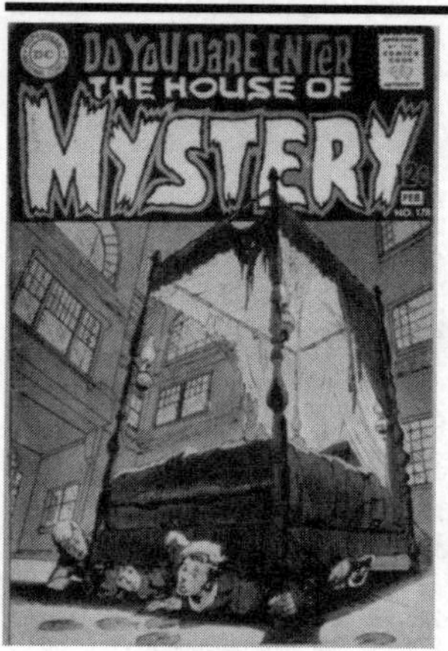

House of Mystery #178
© DC Comics, Inc.

6 The Monster in Clay! 350.00
7 Nine Lives of Alger Denham! . 350.00
8 . . . . 350.00
9 . . . . 350.00
10 The Wishes of Doom 350.00
11 Deadly Game of G-H-O-S-T . 275.00
12 The Devil's Chessboard 275.00
13 The Theater Of A Thousand Thrills! 275.00
14 . . . . 275.00
15 The Man Who Could Change the World 275.00
16 Dead Men Tell No Tales! 225.00
17 . . . . 200.00
18 . . . . 200.00
19 . . . . 200.00
20 The Beast Of Bristol. 200.00
21 Man Who Could See Death . . 200.00
22 The Phantom's Return 200.00
23 . . . . 200.00
24 Kill The Black Cat 200.00
25 The Man With Three Eyes! . . 200.00
26 . . . . 175.00
27 Fate Held Four Aces! 175.00
28 The Wings Of Mr. Milo! 175.00
29 . . . . 175.00
30 . . . . 175.00
31 The Incredible Illusions! 175.00
32 Pied Piper of the Sea. 175.00
33 Mr. Misfortune! 175.00
34 The Hundred Year Duel 175.00
35 . . . . 175.00
36 The Treasure of Montezuma! . 150.00
37 MD,The Statue That Came to Life. 150.00
38 The Voyage Of No Return . . . 150.00
39 . . . . 150.00
40 The Coins That Came To Life. 150.00
41 The Impossible Tricks! 150.00
42 The Stranger From Out There 150.00
43 . . . . 150.00
44 The Secret Of Hill 14 . . . . 150.00
45 . . . . 150.00
46 The Bird of Fate. 150.00
47 The Robot Named Think 150.00
48 The Man Marooned On Earth. 150.00
49 The Mysterious Mr. Omen . . . 150.00
50 . . . . 160.00
51 Man Who Stole Teardrops . . . 125.00
52 The Man With The Golden Shoes. 125.00
53 The Man Who Hated Mirrors . 125.00
54 The Woman Who Lived Twice 125.00
55 I Turned Back Time 125.00
56 The Thing In The Black Box. . 125.00
57 The Untamed. 125.00
58 . . . . 125.00
59 The Tomb Of Ramfis 125.00
60 The Prisoner On Canvas 125.00
61 JK,Superstition Day 125.00
62 The Haunting Scarecrow 90.00
63 JK,The Lady & The Creature . 125.00
64 The Golden Doom 90.00
65 JK,The Magic Lantern 125.00
66 JK,Sinister Shadow 125.00
67 The Wizard of Water 90.00
68 The Book That Bewitched 90.00
69 The Miniature Disasters 90.00
70 JK,The Man With Nine Lives . 100.00
71 Menace of the Mole Man 100.00
72 JK,Dark Journey 100.00
73 Museum That Came to Life . . . 90.00
74 Museum That Came To Life. . . 90.00
75 Assignment Unknown! 90.00
76 JK,Prisoners Of The Tiny Universe. 90.00
77 The Eyes That Went Berserk . . 85.00
78 JK(c),The 13th Hour 90.00
79 JK(c),The Fantastic Sky Puzzle 90.00
80 Man With Countless Faces! . . . 85.00
81 The Man Who Made Utopia . . . 85.00
82 The Riddle of the Earth's Second Moon. 85.00
83 The Mystery of the Martian Eye 85.00
84 JK,BK,The 100-Century Doom 135.00
85 JK(c),Earth's Strangest Salesman. 85.00
86 The Baffling Bargains. 80.00
87 The Human Diamond. 80.00
88 Return of the Animal Man . . . 85.00
89 The Cosmic Plant! 85.00
90 The Invasion Of the Energy Creatures! 85.00
91 DD&SMo(c),The Riddle of the Alien Satellite 85.00
92 DD(c),Menace of the Golden Globule 85.00
93 NC(c),I Fought The Molten Monster 85.00
94 DD&SMo(c),The Creature In Echo Lake 85.00
95 The Wizard's Gift. 85.00
96 The Amazing 70-Ton Man 85.00
97 The Alien Who Change History 85.00
98 DD&SMo(c),The Midnight Creature. 85.00
99 The Secret of the Leopard God 85.00
100 The Beast Beneath Earth. . . 100.00
101 The Magnificent Monster 80.00
102 Cellmate to a Monster 80.00
103 Hail the Conquering Aliens. . . 80.00
104 I was the Seeing-Eye Man . . . 80.00
105 Case of the Creature X-14 . . . 80.00
106 Invaders from the Doomed Dimension 80.00
107 Captives o/t Alien Fisherman 80.00
108 RMo,Four Faces of Frank Forbes 80.00
109 ATh,JKu,Secret of the Hybrid Creatures 80.00
110 Beast Who Stalked Through Time. 80.00
111 Operation Beast Slayer 80.00
112 Menace of Craven's Creatures 80.00
113 RMo,Prisoners of Beast Asteroid 80.00
114 The Movies from Nowhere . . . 80.00
115 Prisoner o/t Golden Mask. . . . 80.00
116 RMo,Return of the Barsfo Beast 80.00
117 Menace of the Fire Furies . . . 75.00
118 RMo,Secret o/SuperGorillas . . 75.00
119 Deadly Gift from the Stars . . . 75.00
120 ATh,Catman of KarynPeale . . 75.00
121 RMo,Beam that Transformed Men 75.00
122 Menace fo the Alien Hero. . . . 75.00
123 RMo,Lure o/t Decoy Creature. 75.00
124 Secret of Mr. Doom 75.00
125 Fantastic Camera Creature . . 75.00
126 The Human Totem Poles 75.00
127 RMo,Cosmic Game o/Doom. . 75.00
128 NC,The Sorcerer's Snares . . . 75.00
129 Man in the Nuclear Trap. 75.00
130 The Alien Creature Hunt 75.00
131 Vengeance o/t GeyserGod . . . 60.00
132 MMe,Beware My Invisible Master 60.00
133 MMe,Captive Queen of Beast Island 60.00
134 MMe,Secret Prisoner of Darkmore Dungeon 60.00
135 MMe,Alien Body Thief 60.00
136 MMe,Secret o/t StolenFace . . 60.00
137 MMe,Tunnel to Disaster 60.00
138 MMe,Creature Must Die 60.00
139 MMe,Creatures of Vengeful Eye 60.00
140 I&Only app.:Astro. 60.00
141 MMe,The Alien Gladiator 60.00
142 MMe,The Wax Demons 60.00
143 J'onn J'onzz begins 250.00
144 J'onn J'onzz on Weird World of Gilgana. 150.00
145 J'onn J'onzz app 100.00
146 BP,J'onn J'onzz 100.00
147 J'onn J'onzz. 100.00
148 J'onn J'onzz. 100.00
149 ATh,J'onn J'onzz 100.00
150 MMe,J'onn J'onzz 100.00
151 J'onn J'onzz. 100.00
152 MMe,J'onn J'onzz 100.00
153 J'onn J'onzz. 100.00
154 J'onn J'onzz. 100.00
155 J'onn J'onzz. 100.00
156 JM,I:Dial H for Hero (Giantboy Cometeer,Mole)J.J'onzz sty . 125.00
157 JM,Dial H for Hero (Human Bullet,Super Charge,Radar Sonar Man) J'onn J'onnzz sty 100.00
158 JM,Dial H for Hero (Quake

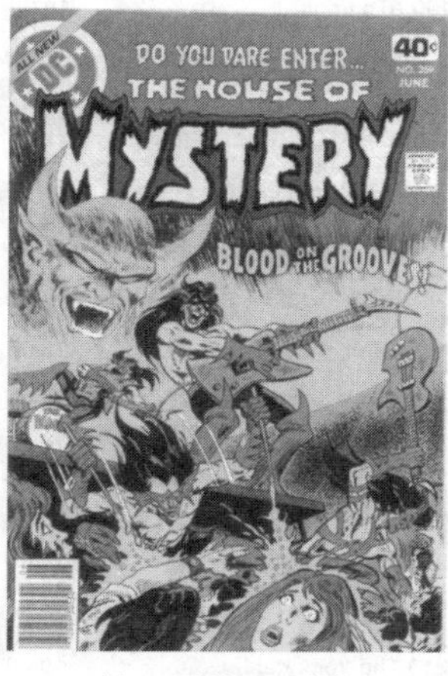

House of Mystery #269
© DC Comics Inc.

MasterSquid)J'onn J'onzz sty . 90.00
159 JM,Dial H for Hero (Human Starfish,Hypno Man,Mighty Moppet) J'onn J'onzz sty 90.00
160 JM,Dial H for Hero (King Kandy A:Plastic Man,I:Marco Xavier (J'onn J'onzz new secret I.D.) 150.00
161 JM,Dial H for Hero (Magneto, Hornet Man,Shadow Man) . . . 75.00
162 JM,Dial H for Hero (Mr.Echo, Future Man) J'onnJ'onzz sty . . 75.00
163 JM,Dial H for Hero(Castor&Pollux, King Coil) J'onnJ'onzz sty. . . . 75.00
164 JM,Dial H for Hero (Super Nova Zip Tide) J'onnJ'onzz sty 75.00
165 JM,Dial H for Hero (Whoozis, Whatsis,Howzis) J'onn J'onzz story. 75.00
166 JM,Dial H for Hero (Yankee Doodle Kid,Chief Mighty Arrow) J'onn J'onzz sty 75.00
167 JM,Dial H for Hero (Balloon Boy, Muscle Man,Radar Sonar Man) J'onn J'onzz sty 75.00
168 JM,Dial H for Hero (Thunderbolt, Mole,Cometeer,Hoopster) J'onn J'onzz sty 75.00
169 JM,I:Gem Girl in Dial H for Hero,J'onnJ'onzz sty 75.00
170 JM,Dial H for Hero (Baron BuzzSaw,Don Juan,Sphinx Man) J'onn J'onzz sty. 75.00
171 JM,Dial H for Hero (King Viking Whirl-I-Gig) J'onnJ'onzz sty . . 65.00
172 JM,Dial H for Hero 65.00
173 E:Dial H for Hero,F:J'onn Jonzz 65.00
174 New direction,SA pg.13 . . . . . 50.00
175 I:Cain. 30.00
176 SA,Cain's Game Room 30.00
177 Curse of the Car 30.00
178 NA,The Game 40.00
179 BWr,NA,JO,Widow'sWalk 75.00
180 GK,WW,BWr,SA,Room 13 . . . 30.00
181 BWr,The Siren of Satan 30.00
182 ATh,The Devil's Doorway 30.00
183 BWr,WW(i),DeadCanKill. 30.00
184 ATh,GK,WW,Eye o/Basilisk . . 25.00
185 AW,The Beautiful Beast 30.00
186 BWr,NA,Nightmare. 35.00
187 ATh,Mask of the Red Fox. 18.00
188 TD,BWr,House of Madness . . 30.00
189 WW(i),Eyes of the Cat 18.00
190 ATh,Fright 18.00
191 BWr,TD,Christmas Story,. 18.00
192 JAp,GM,DH,Garnener of Eden 18.00
193 BWr. 20.00
194 ATh,NR,RH(rep),JK(rep) Born Loser 25.00
195 NR,BWr,ThingsOld..Things Forgotten 30.00
196 GM,GK,ATh(rep)A Girl & Her Dog 20.00
197 DD,NR,House of Horrors 18.00
198 MSy,NC,Day of the Demon . . 20.00
199 WW,RB,Sno'Fun 25.00
200 MK,TD,The Beast's Revenge . 25.00
201 JAp,The Demon Within 18.00
202 MSy,GC(rep),SA,The Poster Plague,John Prentice? 18.00
203 NR,Tower of Prey. 18.00
204 BWr,AN,All in the Family 20.00
205 The Coffin Creature 10.00
206 MSy,TP,The Burning 10.00
207 JSn,The Spell 15.00
208 Creator of Evil 10.00
209 AA,JAp,Tomorrow I Hang. . . . 15.00
210 The Immortal 10.00
211 NR,Deliver Us From Evil 15.00
212 MA,AN,Ever After 10.00

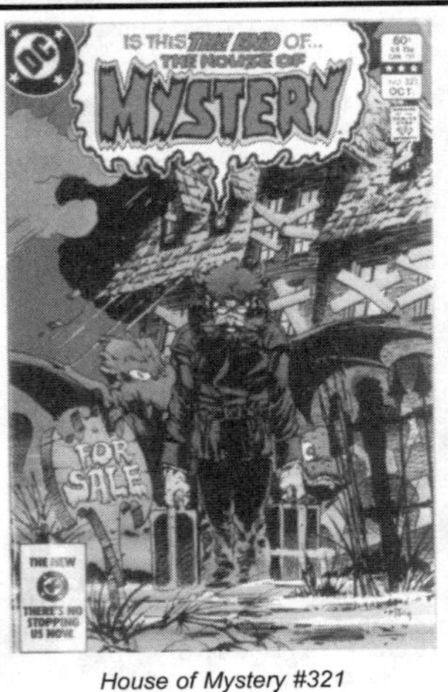

House of Mystery #321
© DC Comics, Inc.

213 AN,Back from the Realm of 15e Damned 15.00
214 NR,The Shaggy Dog 15.00
215 The Man Who Wanted Power over Women. 10.00
216 TD,Look into My Eyes & Kill. . 10.00
217 NR,AA,Swamp God 15.00
218 FT,An Ice Place to Visit 10.00
219 AA,NR,Pledge to Satan 10.00
220 AA,AN,They Hunt Butterflies Don't They? 10.00
221 FT,BWr,MK,He Who Laughs Last 15.00
222 AA,Night of the Teddy Bear . . 10.00
223 Demon From the Deep 10.00
224 FR,AA,SheerFear,B:100pg. . . 35.00
225 AA,FT,AN,See No Evil 35.00
226 AA,FR,NR,SA,Monster in House Tour of House of Mystery 35.00
227 NR,AA,The Carriage Man . . . 35.00
228 FR,NA(i),The Rebel 35.00
229 NR,Nightmare Castle, last 100 page 35.00
230 Experiment In Fear 8.00
231 Cold,Cold Heart. 8.00
232 Last Tango in Hell 8.00
233 FR,Cake! 8.00
234 AM,Lafferty's Luck 8.00
235 NR,Wings of Black Death. 8.00
236 SD,NA(i)Death Played a Sideshow 10.00
237 FT,Night of the Chameleon . . . 8.00
238. . . . . 8.00
239 Day of the Witch 8.00
240 The Murderer. 8.00
241 FR,NR,DeathPulls theStrings . . 8.00
242 FR,The Balloon Vendor 8.00
243 Brother Bear 8.00
244 FT,Kronos..Zagros-Eborak 8.00
245 AN,Check the J.C.Demon Catalogue Under...Death 8.00
246 DeathVault of Eskimo Kings . . . 8.00
247 SD,Death Rides the Waves . . . 8.00
248 NightJamieGaveUp theGhost. . 8.00
249 Hit Parade of Death 8.00
250 AN,Voyage to Hell 8.00
251 WW,AA,theCollector,68 pgs . . 10.00
252 DP,RT,AA,FR,AN,ManKillers . 10.00
253 TD,AN,GK,KJ,Beware the Demon Child 7.00
254 SD,AN,MR,TheDevil's Place . . 8.00
255 RE,GM,SometimesLeopards . 10.00
256 DAy,AN,Museum of Murders . 10.00
257 RE,MGo,TD(i),MBr,Xmas iss. . . 8.00
258 SD,RB,BMc,DG(i),The Demon and His Boy 8.00
259 RE,RT,MGo,DN,BL,`Hair Today, Gone Tomorrow,last giant. 9.00
260 Go to Hades 8.00
261 The Husker 8.00
262 FreedFrom Infernos of Hell . . . 8.00
263 JCr,Is There Vengeance After Death?. 8.00
264 Halloween Issue 8.00
265 The Perfect Host 8.00
266 The Demon Blade 8.00
267 A Strange Way to Die 8.00
269 Blood on the Grooves 8.00
270 JSh,JRu,JBi,Black Moss 8.00
271 TS,HellHound of Brackenmoor 8.00
272 DN,DA,theSorcerer's Castle. . . 8.00
273 The Rites of Inheritance. 8.00
274 MR,JBi,Hell Park 8.00
275 JCr,`Final Installment' 8.00
276 SD,MN,`Epode' 8.00
277 HC,AMi,`LimitedEngagement' . 8.00
278 `TV or Not TV' 8.00
279 AS,Trial by Fury. 8.00
280 VMK,DAy,Hungry Jaws of Death 8.00
281 Now Dying in this Corner 8.00
282 JSw,DG,Superman/Radio Shack ins 8.00
283 RT,AN`Kill Me Gently' 8.00
284 KG,King and the Dragon 8.00
285 Cold Storage 8.00
286 Long Arm of the Law 8.00
287 NR,AS,BL,Legend o/t Lost. . . . 8.00
288 DSp,Piper at Gates of Hell. . . . 8.00
289 Brother Bobby's Home for Wayward Girls & Boys 8.00
290 TS,I:I..Vampire. 8.00
291 TS,DAy,I..Vampire #2. . . . . 8.00
292 TS,MS,TD,RE,DSp,Wendigo . . 8.00
293 GT,TS,A:I..Vampire #3 . . . . 8.00
294 CI,TY,GT,TD,The Darkness . . . 8.00
295 TS,TVE,JCr,I..Vampire #4 . . . . 8.00
296 CI,BH,Night Women. 8.00
297 TS,DCw,TD,I..Vampire #5 . . . . 8.00
298 TS,`Stalker on a Starless Night' 8.00
299 TS,DSp,I..Vampire #6 . . . . 8.00
300 GK,DA,JSon,JCr,DSp,Anniv. . . 8.00
301 JDu,TVE,KG,TY `...Virginia' . . . 8.00
302 TS,NR,DSp,I..Vampire #7 . . . . 8.00
303 TS,DSp,I..Vampire #8 . . . . 8.00
304 EC,RE,I..Vampire #9 . . . . 8.00
305 TVE,EC,I..Vampire #10 . . . . . . 8.00
306 TS,TD,I..Vampire #11, A:Jack the Ripper. 8.00
307 TS,I..Vampire #12 . . . . 8.00
308 TS,MT,NR,I..Vampire #13. . . . . 8.00
309 TS,I..Vampire #14 . . . . 8.00
310 TS(i),I..Vampire #15. . . . . 8.00
311 I..Vampire #16 . . . . 8.00
312 TS(i),I..Vampire #17. . . . . 8.00
313 TS(i),CI,I..Vampire #18. . . . . . . 8.00
314 TS,I..Vampire #19 . . . . 8.00
315 TS(i),TY,I..Vampire #20 . . . . . . 8.00
316 TS(i),GT,TVE,I..Vampire #21 . . 8.00
317 TS(i),I..Vampire #22. . . . . 8.00
318 TS(i),I..Vampire #23. . . . . 8.00
319 TS,JOy,I..Vampire conc.. . . . . . 8.00
320 GM,Project: Inferior 8.00
321 final issue 8.00
Welcome Back to the House of Mystery GN BWr(c) horror stories rep. . . 6.00

HOUSE OF SECRETS

Nov.–Dec., 1956

1 MD,JM,The Hand of Doom. . 1,300.00
2 JPr,RMo,NC,Mask of Fear . . . 500.00

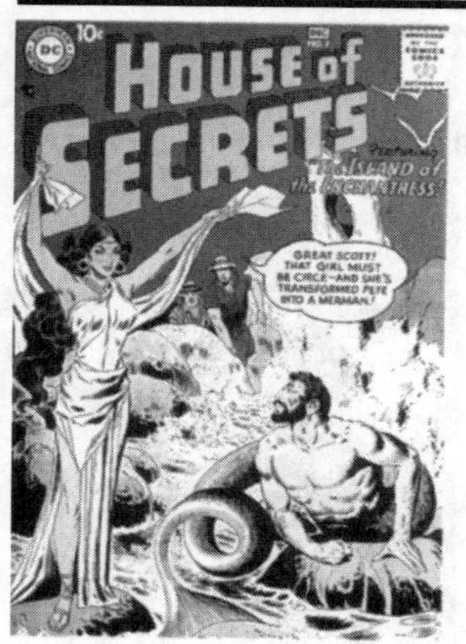

House of Secrets #7
© DC Comics, Inc.

3 JM,JK,MMe,The Three Prophecies 375.00
4 JM,JK,MMe,Master of Unknown 300.00
5 MMe,The Man Who Hated Fear 200.00
6 NC,MMe,Experiment 1000 . . . 200.00
7 RMo,Island o/t Enchantress . . 200.00
8 JK,RMo,The Electrified Man . . 225.00
9 JM,JSt,The Jigsaw Creatures . 175.00
10 JSt,NC,I was a Prisoner of the Sea 175.00
11 KJ(c),NC,The Man who couldn't stop growing 175.00
12 JK,The Hole in the Sky 200.00
13 The Face in the Mist 150.00
14 MMe,The Man who Stole Air . 150.00
15 The Creature in the Camera. . 150.00
16 NC,We matched wits with a Gorilla genius 125.00
17 DW,Lady in the Moon. 125.00
18 MMe,The Fantastic Typewriter 125.00
19 MMe,NC,Lair of the Dragonfly 125.00
20 Incredible FireballCreatures . . 125.00
21 Girl from 50,000 Fathoms . . . 125.00
22 MMe,Thing from Beyond 125.00
23 MMe,I&O:Mark Merlin 135.00
24 NC,Mark Merlin story 125.00
25 MMe,Mark Merlin story. 100.00
26 NC,MMe, Mark Merlin story . . 100.00
27 MMe,Mark Merlin 100.00
28 MME,Mark Merlin. 100.00
29 NC,MMe,Mark Merlin 100.00
30 JKu,MMe,Mark Merlin 100.00
31 DD,MMe,RH,Mark Merlin 80.00
32 MMe,Mark Merlin 80.00
33 MMe,Mark Merlin 80.00
34 MMe,Mark Merlin 80.00
35 MMe,Mark Merlin 80.00
36 MMe,Mark Merlin 80.00
37 MMe,Mark Merlin 80.00
38 MMe,Mark Merlin 80.00
39 JKu,MMe,Mark Merlin 80.00
40 NC,MMe,Mark Merlin 80.00
41 MMe,Mark Merlin 80.00
42 MMe,Mark Merlin 80.00
43 RMo,MMe,CI,Mark Merlin 80.00
44 MMe,Mark Merlin 80.00
45 MMe,Mark Merlin 80.00
46 MMe,Mark Merlin 80.00
47 MMe,Mark Merlin 80.00
48 ATh,MMe,Mark Merlin 80.00
49 MMe,Mark Merlin 80.00
50 MMe,Mark Merlin 80.00
51 MMe,Mark Merlin 75.00
52 MMe,Mark Merlin 75.00
53 CI,Mark Merlin 75.00
54 RMo,MMe,Mark Merlin 75.00
55 MMe,Mark Merlin 75.00
56 MMe,Mark Merlin 75.00
57 MMe,Mark Merlin 75.00
58 MMe,O:Mark Merlin 75.00
59 MMe,Mark Merlin 75.00
60 MMe,Mark Merlin 75.00
61 I:Eclipso,A:Mark Merlin 175.00
62 MMe,Eclipso,Mark Merlin 100.00
63 GC,ATh,Eclipso,Mark Merlin . . 75.00
64 MMe,ATh,M Merlin,Eclipso. . . . 75.00
65 MMe,ATh,M Merlin,Eclipso. . . . 75.00
66 MMe,ATh,M Merlin,Eclipso . . . 110.00
67 MMe,ATh,M Merlin,Eclipso. . . . 75.00
68 MMe,Mark Merlin,Eclipso 70.00
69 MMe,Mark Merlin,Eclipso 70.00
70 MMe,Mark Merlin,Eclipso 70.00
71 MMe,Mark Merlin,Eclipso 70.00
72 MMe,Mark Merlin,Eclipso 70.00
73 MMe,D:Mark Merlin,I:Prince Ra-Man; Eclipso 70.00
74 MMe,Prince Ra-Man,Eclipso . . 70.00
75 MMe,Prince Ra-Man,Eclipso . . 70.00
76 MMe,Prince Ra-Man,Eclipso . . 70.00
77 MMe,Prince Ra-Man,Eclipso . . 70.00
78 MMe,Prince Ra-Man,Eclipso . . 70.00
79 MMe,Prince Ra-Man,Eclipso . . 70.00
80 MMe,Prince Ra-Man,Eclipso . . 70.00
81 I:Abel, new mystery format Don't Move It 50.00
82 DD,NA,One & only, fully guaranteed super-permanent 100%. . 30.00
83 ATh,The Stuff that Dreams are Made of 30.00
84 DD,If I had but world enough and time. 30.00
85 DH,GK,NA,Second Chance . . . 40.00
86 GT,GM,Strain. 20.00
87 DD,DG,RA,MK,The Coming of Ghaglan 40.00
88 DD,The Morning Ghost 30.00
89 GM,DH,Where Dead MenWalk. 30.00
90 GT,RB,NA,GM,The Symbionts . 35.00
91 WW,MA,The Eagle's Talon. . . . 35.00
92 BWr,TD(i),I:Swamp Thing (Alex Olson) 500.00
93 JAp,TD,ATh(rep.)Lonely in Death 20.00
94 TD,ATh(rep.)Hyde.and go Seek 20.00
95 DH,NR,The Bride of Death. . . . 18.00
96 DD,JAb,WW, the Monster 22.00
97 JAp,Divide and Murder 20.00
98 MK,ATh(rep),Born Losers. 20.00
99 NR,TD(i),Beyond His Imagination 20.00
100 TP,TD,AA,Rest in Peace 25.00
101 AN,Small Invasion 20.00
102 NR,A Lonely Monstrosity 20.00
103 AN,Village on Edge o/Forever 15.00
104 NR,AA,GT,Ghosts Don't Bother Me...But... . . . . 12.00
105 JAp,AA,An Axe to Grind. 12.00
106 AN,AA,This Will Kill You. 15.00
107 AA,The Night of the Nebbish . 15.00
108 A New Kid on the Block 12.00
109 AA,AN...And in Death, there is no Escape 12.00
110 Safes Have Secrets, Too 10.00
111 TD,Hair-I-Kari. 10.00
112 Case of the Demon Spawn . . 10.00
113 MSy,NC,NR,Spawns of Satan 10.00
114 FBe,Night Game 10.00
115 AA,AN,Nobody Hurts My Brother. 10.00

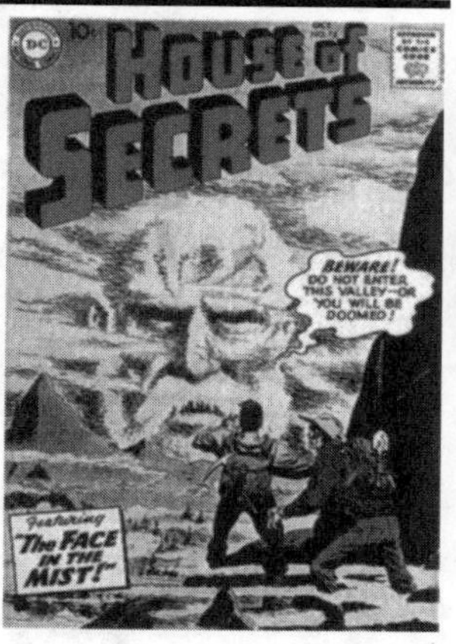

House of Secrets #13
© DC Comics Inc.

116 NR,Like Father,Like Son 10.00
117 AA,AN,Revenge for the Deadly Dummy 10.00
118 GE,Very Last Picture Show . . 10.00
119 A Carnival of Dwarves 10.00
120 TD,AA,The Lion's Share 10.00
121 Ms.Vampire Killer. 10.00
122 AA,Requiem for Igor 7.00
123 ATh,A Connecticut Ice Cream Man in King Arthur's Court 8.00
124 Last of the Frankensteins. 7.00
125 AA,FR,Instant Re-Kill 7.00
126 AN,On Borrowed Time. 7.00
127 MSy,A Test of Innocence 7.00
128 AN,Freak Out! 7.00
129 Almost Human 7.00
130 All Dolled Up!. 7.00
131 AN,Point of No Return 7.00
132 Killer Instinct 7.00
133 Portraits of Death. 7.00
134 NR,Inheritance of Blood 7.00
135 The Vegitable Garden 7.00
136 Last Voyage of Lady Luck 7.00
137 The Harder They Fall. 7.00
138 Where Dreams are Born 10.00
139 SD,NR,A Real Crazy Kid 10.00
140 NR,O:Patchwork Man 20.00
141 You Can't Beat the Devil 6.00
142 Playmate 6.00
143 The Evil Side 6.00
144 The Vampire of Broadway 6.00
145 Operation wasSuccessful,But. . 6.00
146 Snake's Alive. 6.00
147 AN,The See-Through Thief . . . 6.00
148 SD,Sorcerer's Apprentice. 6.00
149 The Evil One 6.00
150 A:PhantomStranger & Dr.13. . . 6.00
151 MGo,Nightmare 6.00
152 Sister Witch 6.00
153 VM,AN,Don't Look Now 6.00
154 JL,Last issue 6.00

HOUSE OF SECRETS

DC/Vertigo Aug., 1996

1 SSe(s),TKr, judgments on your darkest secrets. 4.00
2 SSe(s),TKr, F:Rain 3.00
3 SSe(s),TKr,Seattle's citizens secrets. 3.00
4 SSe(s),TKr,Eric's secrets exposed 3.00
5 . . . . 3.00
6 SSe(s),DFg,Other rooms: "Meeting" 3.00

7 SSe(s),TKr,"Blueprint: Elevation A" 3.00
8 SSe(s),TKr,"The Road to You," pt.1 . . . . 3.00
9 SSe(s),TKr,"The Road to You," pt.2 . . . . 3.00
10 SSe(s),TKr,"The Road to You," pt.3, concl 3.00
11 "The Book of Law" pt.1 (of 5) . . . 3.00
12 "The Book of Law" pt.2 . . . . 3.00
13 SSe,The Book of Law, pt.3 . . . . 3.00
14 SSe,The Book of Law, pt.4 . . . . 3.00
15 SSe,The Book of Law, pt.5 . . . . 3.00
16 SSe,Book of Law, epilogue 3.00
17 SSe,The Road to You, pt.1 . . . . 3.00
18 SSe,The Road to You, pt.2 . . . . 3.00
19 SSe,The Road to You, pt.3 . . . . 3.00
20 SSe,Other Rooms story 3.00
21 SSe,Basement, pt.1 . . . . 3.00

Human Target #1 © DC Comics, Inc.

22 SSe,Basement, pt.2 . . . . 3.00
23 SSe,Basement, pt.3 . . . . 3.00
24 SSe,TKr,"Attic" 3.00
25 SSe,TKr, final issue 3.00
TPB Foundation, rep.#1–#5 . . . . . 14.95

HUMAN TARGET SPECIAL

1 DG(i),Prequel to T.V. Series 2.00

HUMAN TARGET

DC/Vertigo 1999

1 (of 4) PrM(s) 3.00
2 PrM(s) 3.00
3 PrM(s) 3.00
4 PrM(s), concl. 3.00
TPB 12.95

HUNTER'S HEART

1995

1 Cops vs. Serial Killer 4.95
2 . . . . 4.95
3 F:Lieutenant Slidell 4.95

HUNTRESS, THE

1989–90

1 JSon/DG 2.00
2 JSon,Search for Family's Murderer 2.00
3 JSon,A:La Bruja 2.00
4 JSon,Little Italy/Chinatown Gangs 2.00
5 JSon,V:Doctor Mandragora 2.00
6 JSon,Huntress'secrets revealed . 2.00
7 JSon,V:Serial Killer 2.00
8 JSon,V:Serial Killer 2.00
9 JSon,V:Serial Killer 2.00
10 JSon,Nuclear Terrorists in NY . . 2.00
11 JSon,V:Wyvern,Nuclear Terrorists contd. 2.00
12 JSon,V:Nuclear Terrorists cont . . 2.00
13 JSon,Violence in NY 2.00
14 JSon,Violence contd.,New Mob boss 2.00
15 JSon,I:Waterfront Warrior 2.00
16 JSon,Secret of Waterfront Warrior revealed 2.00
17 JSon,Batman+Huntress#1 . . . . . 2.00
18 JSon,Batman+Huntress#2 . . . . . 2.00
19 JSon,Batman+Huntress#3,final issue 2.00

HUNTRESS

[Limited Series] 1994

1 CDi(s),MN,V:Redzone 2.00
2 MN,V:Redzone 2.00
3 MN,V:Redzone 2.00
4 MN,V:Spano,Redzone 2.00

ICON

Milestone 1993–96

1 Direct Market Ed.,MBr,MG,I:Icon, Rocket,S.H.R.E.D.,w/poster, card,C puzzle piece 3.50
1a Newsstand Ed. 2.00
2 MBr,MG,I:Payback 2.00
3 MBr,MG,V:Payback 2.00
4 MBr,MG,Teen Pregnancy Issue . . 2.00
5 MBr,MG,V:Blood Syndicate 2.00
6 MBr,MG,V:Blood Syndicate 2.00
7 MBr,MG 2.00
8 MBr,MG,O:Icon 2.00
9 WS(c),MBr,MG,Shadow War, I:Donner,Blitzen1.75
10 MBr,MG,V:Holocaust 2.00
11 MBr,Hero Worship 2.00
12 Sanctimony 2.00
13 MBr,Rocket & Static T.U. 2.00
14 JBy(c) 2.00
15 Worlds Collide,pt.4,A:Superboy . 2.00
16 Worlds Collide,pt.11, V:Superman,Rift 2.00
17 Mothership Connection 2.00
18 Mothership Connection,pt.2 . . . . 2.00
19 Mothership Connection,pt.3 . . . . 2.00
20 Rocket 2.00
21 . . . . 2.00
22 . . . . 2.00
23 New Rocket 2.00
24 F:Buck Wild 2.00
25 V:Oblivion 3.00
26 V:Oblivion 2.00
27 Move to Paris Island projects . . . 2.50
28 Long Hot Summer 2.50
29 Long Hot Summer 2.50
30 Icon Leaves Earth 2.50
31 HC(c) Readers Choice comic . . . 2.00
32 Rocket, Galactic Corporate 2.50
33 V:Rocket 2.50
34 V:Cooperative 2.50
35 . . . . 2.50
36 Rocket returns to Earth 2.50
37 MBr,RT,F:Rocket 2.50
38 DMD(s),RT 2.50
39 DMD(s),RT,V:Holocaust & Blood Syndicate 2.50
40 DMD(s),RT, V:Holocaust 2.50
41 DMD(s),RT, V:Blood Syndicate. . 2.50
42 DMD(s),RT 2.50

Immortal Doctor Fate #1
© DC Comics, Inc.

43 DMD(s),RT,"Blood Reign" concl. 2.50
44 DMD(s),RT,V:Smurphs 2.50
45 DMD(s),RT, final issue 2.50
TPB A Hero's Welcome 12.95

I DIE AT MIDNIGHT

DC/Vertigo Dec., 1999

GN 64-pg. 6.95

IMMORTAL DR. FATE

1995

1 WS,KG,rep. 2.00
2 and 3 KG,rep. . . . . @2.00

IMPACT WINTER SPECIAL

Impact 1991

1 CI/MR/TL,A:All Impact Heros, President Kidnapped 2.50

IMPULSE

1995–98

1 Young Flash Adventures 11.00
2 V:Terrorists 3.50
3 In School 3.00
4 V:White Lightning 3.00
5 V:White Lightning 2.00
6 . . . . 2.00
7 V:Gridlock 2.00
8 MWa,Underworld Unleashed tie-in 2.00
9 MWa,F:XS, ... 2.00
10 MWa,Dead Heat,pt.3 . . . . 2.00
11 MWa,Dead Heat,pt.5 . . . . 2.00
12 . . . . 2.00
13 MWa,new daredevil in town 2.00
14 AWi,A:White Lightning 2.00
15 . . . . 2.00
16 . . . . 2.00
17 . . . . 2.00
18 MPk(s),AWi,Virtual reality nightmare 2.00
19 MWa(s),HuR, Bart's dreams. . . . 2.00
20 MWa(s),HuR, baseball 2.00
21 MWa(s),F:Legion of Super-Heroes 2.00
22 MWa(s) 2.00
23 MWa(s),HuR,Mercury at a crossroads 2.00

24 MWa(s),HuR,Impulse's mother comes from the future 2.00
25 MWa(s),HuR,Impulse & his mom in 30th century 2.00
26 MWa(s),Bart Allen back in the 20th century 2.00
27 MWa(s) 2.00
28 . . . . 2.00
29 BML,Bart searches for Max Mercury 2.00
30 BML, pt.2, Genesis tie-in 2.00
31 BML, pt.3,V:Dr. Morlo. 2.00
32 BML,Max is home 2.00
33 BML,White Lightning 2.00
34 BML,Devonian Age, pt.1 . . . . . . 2.00
35 BML 2.00
36 BML,Court Dates 2.00
37 BML,Dr. Morlo 2.00
38 BML,freak snow storm 2.00
39 BML,V:Trickster 2.00
40 BML,WF, kid picnic 2.00
41 Return of Arrowette 2.00
42 BML(s),virtual monsters 2.25
43 BML(s),F:Jamal 2.25
44 BML(s),V:Evil Eye 2.25
45 BML(s),Christmas 2.25
46 BML(s),Chain Lightning x-over. . 2.25
47 BML(s),A:Superman 2.25
48 BML(s),A:Riddler 2.25
49 BML(s),C:Flash 2.25
50 TDz(s),A:Batman, Joker. 2.25
51 TDz(s),V:Frog Prince 2.25
52 TDz(s),WS,F:Kalibak,pt.1. . . . . . 2.25
53 TDz(s),WS,F:Kalibak,pt.2. . . . . . 2.25
54 TDz(s),Day of Judgment x-over . 2.25
55 V:Sir Real 2.25
56 . . . . 2.25
57 TDz(s),F:Plastic Man 2.25
58 TDz(s),F:Max Mercury 2.25
59 TDz(s),F:Arrowette 2.25
60 DMD(s),V:Alabama 2.25
61 F:Max Mercury,S.T.R.I.P.E. 2.25
62 TDz(s),Mercury Falling,pt.1 . . . . 2.25
63 TDz(s),Mercury Falling,pt.2 . . . . 2.50
64 TDz(s),Mercury Falling,pt.3 . . . . 2.50
65 TDz(s),Mercury Falling,pt.4 . . . . 2.50
66 TDz(s),Mercury Falling,pt.5 . . . . 2.50
67 TDz,RyR,Mercury Falling epilogue 2.50
Ann.#2 Pulp Heroes (Western) 3.95
Spec.#1,000,000 BML(s) 2.25
GN Bart Saves the Universe. 6.00
TPB Reckless Youth MWa(s) rep. Flash #92–#94 . . . . 14.95
Spec. Impulse/Atom Double-Shot DJu, x-over concl. (1997) 3.00
Spec. Impulse Plus 48pg. with Grossout (1997) 2.95

INDUSTRIAL GOTHIC

Vertigo 1995

1 Jail Break Plans 2.50
2 thru 5 Jail Break Plans . . . . . . @2.50

INFERIOR FIVE

March–April, 1967

1 MSy 40.00
2 MSy,A:Plastic Man 25.00
3 . . . . 18.00
4 . . . . 18.00
5 . . . . 18.00
6 . . . . 18.00
7 . . . . 18.00
8 . . . . 18.00
9 . . . . 18.00
10 A:Superman 18.00
11 JO(c&a). 18.00
12 JO(c&a). 18.00

INFERNO

Aug., 1997

1 (of 4) SI, from Legion 4.00
2 SI,mall grrls 2.50
3 SI,Legion Month tie-in. 2.50
4 SI, concl. 2.50

INFINITY, INC.

March, 1984

1 JOy,O:Infinity Inc. 3.00
2 JOy,End of Origin 2.50
3 JOy,O:Jade 2.25
4 JOy,V:JSA 2.25
5 JOy,V:JSA 2.25
6 JOy,V:JSA 2.25
7 JOy,V:JSA 2.25
8 JOy,V:Ultra Humanite 2.25
9 JOy,V:Ultra Humanite 2.25
10 JOy,V:Ultra Humanite. 2.00
11 DN,GT,O:Infinity Inc. 2.00
12 Infinity Unmasks,I:Yolanda Montez (New Wildcat) 2.00
13 DN,V:Rose & Thorn 2.00
14 1st TM DC art,V:Chroma 9.00
15 TM,V:Chroma 3.00
16 TM,I:Helix (Mr. Bones) 3.00
17 TM,V:Helix. 3.00
18 TM,Crisis. 3.00
19 TM,JSA,JLA x-over, I:Mekanique 3.00
20 TM,Crisis. 3.00
21 TM,Crisis,I:HourmanII, Dr.Midnight. 3.00
22 TM,Crisis. 3.00
23 TM,Crisis. 3.00
24 TM,Crisis. 3.00
25 TM,Crisis,JSA 3.00
26 TM,V:Carcharo 3.00
27 TM,V:Carcharo 3.00
28 TM,V:Carcharo 3.00
29 TM,V:Helix. 3.00
30 TM,Mourning of JSA 3.00
31 TM,V:Psycho Pirate 3.00
32 TM,V:Psycho Pirate 3.00
33 TM,O:Obsidian 3.00
34 TM,A: Global Guardians 3.00
35 TM,V:Infinitors 3.00
36 TM,V:Injustice Unl.. . . . . 3.00
37 TM,TD,O:Northwind. 3.00
38 Helix on Trial 2.00
39 O:Solomon Grundy 2.00
40 V:Thunderbolt 2.00
41 Jonni Thunder 2.00

Infinity Inc. #26 © DC Comics Inc.

42 TD,V:Hastor,L:Fury 2.00
43 TD,V:Hastor,Silver Scarab 2.00
44 TD,D:Silver Scarab 2.00
45 MGu,A:New Teen Titans, V:Ultra-Humanite 2.00
46 TD,Millenium,V:Floronic Man . . . 2.00
47 TD,Millenium,V:Harlequin. 2.00
48 TD,O:Nuklon 2.00
49 Silver Scarab becomes Sandman 2.00
50 TD,V:The Wizard,O:Sandman . . 2.50
51 W:Fury & Sandman,D:Skyman. . 2.00
52 V:Helix. 2.00
53 V:Justice Unlimited,last issue . . . 2.00
Ann.#1 TM,V:Thorn 4.00
Ann.#2 V:Degaton,x-over Young All-Stars Annual #1. . . . . 2.00
Spec.#1 TD,A:Outsiders,V:Psycho Pirate 2.00

INVASION!

1988–89

1 TM,I:Vril Dox,Dominators (20th century). 4.00
2 TM,KG,DG,I:L.E.G.I.O.N. 3.00
3 BS,DG,I:Blasters 3.00
Daily Planet-Invasion! 16p 2.00

INVISIBLES

Vertigo 1994–96

1 GMo(s). 3.50
2 GMo(s),Down & Out,pt.1. . . . . . . 2.50
3 GMo(s),Down & Out,pt.2. . . . . . . 2.50
4 GMo(s),Down & Out,pt.3. . . . . . . 2.50
5 Arcadia,pt.1 . . . . 2.25
6 Arcadia,pt.2 . . . . 2.25
7 Arcadia,pt.3 . . . . 2.25
8 Arcadia,pt.4 . . . . 2.25
9 SeP(c),L:Dane 2.50
10 SeP(c),CWn,Jim Crow v. Zombies 2.50
11 V:New Breed of Hunter 2.50
12 . . . . 2.50
13 GMO,Sheman,pt.1. . . . . 2.50
14 GMo,SeP,Sheman,pt.2. . . . . 2.50
15 GMo,Sheman,pt.3 . . . . 2.50
16 GMo,An offer from Sir Miles. . . . 4.00
17 GMo,Entropy in the U.K.,pt.1 . . . 4.00
18 GMo,Entropy in the U.K.,pt.2 . . . 4.00
19 GMo,Entropy in the U.K.,pt.3 . . . 5.00
20 GMo,F:RaggedRobin,Dane,Boy . 7.50
21 GMo,PuJ,F:Dane. 7.50
22 GMo(s),MBu,MPn 7.50
23 GMo(s),MBu,MPn 7.50
24 GMo(s),MBu,MPn 7.50
25 GMo(s),MBu,MPn,final issue Aug. 1996. . . . . 11.00

[Volume 2]

DC/Vertigo 1996

1 GMo(s),PJ,"Black Science," pt.1 . 6.00
2 GMo(s),PJ,"Black Science," pt.2 . 5.00
3 GMo(s),PJ,"Black Science," pt.3 . 5.00
4 GMo(s),PJ,"Black Science," pt.4 . 4.00
5 GMo(s),PJ,In SanFrancisco,pt.1 . 4.00
6 GMo(s),PJ,In SanFrancisco,pt.2 . 3.00
7 GMo(s),PJ,BB(c) "Time Machine Go" concl. 3.00
8 GMo(s),PJ,BB(c) "Sensitive Criminals," pt.1. . . . . 3.00
9 GMo(s),PJ,BB(c) "Sensitive Criminals," pt.2. . . . . 3.00
10 GMo(s),PJ,Sensitive Criminals pt.3, concl. 3.00
11 GMo(s),PJ,BB(c),Hand of Glory pt.1 . . . . 3.00
12 GMo(s),PJ,BB(c),Glory, pt.2. . . . 3.00
13 GMo(s),PJ,BB(c),Glory concl. . . 3.00
14 GMo(s),BB(c),Archons aftermath 3.00
15 GMo(s),BB(c), The Philadelphia

Experiment, pt.1 . . . . 3.00
16 GMo(s),BB(c),Experiment,pt.2 . . 3.00
17 GMo,CWn,BB,Black Science II pt.1 . . . . 3.00
18 GMo,CWn,BB,Science,pt.2 . . . . 3.00
19 GMo,CWn,BB,Science,pt.3 . . . . 3.00
20 GMo,CWn,BB(c),Science,pt.4 . . 2.50
21 GMo,CWn,BB(c),King Mob 2.50
22 GMo,CWn,BB(c) The Tower. . . . 2.50
TPB Counting to None 20.00
TPB Say You Want a Revolution. . 20.00
TPB Bloody Hell in America 13.00

VOLUME 3
DC/Vertigo 1999

12 GMo,Satanstorm,pt.1. . . . . 3.00
11 GMo,Satanstorm,pt.2. . . . . 3.00
10 GMo,Satanstorm,pt.3. . . . . 3.00
9 GMo,Satanstorm,pt.4 . . . . 3.00
8 GMo,Karmageddon,pt.1 . . . . 3.00
7 GMo,Karmageddon,pt.2 . . . . 3.00
6 GMo,Karmageddon,pt.3 . . . . 3.00
5 GMo. 2.95
4 GMo,Invisible Kingdom,pt.1 . . . . 2.95
3 GMo,Invisible Kingdom,pt.2 . . . . 2.95
2 GMo,Invisible Kingdom,pt.3 . . . . 2.95
1 GMo,conclusion 2.95
TPB Kissing Mister 19.95
TPB Say You Want a Revolution. . 19.95
TPB Counting to None 19.95
GN The Mystery Play 9.95

IRONWOLF
1986

1 HC,rep. 2.00

Isis #1 © DC Comics, Inc.

IRONWOLF: FIRES OF THE REVOLUTION
1992

Hardcov.GN MMi,CR,R:Ironwolf . . 29.95
TPB Fires of the Revolution 15.00

ISIS
Oct.–Nov., 1976

1 RE/WW 5.00
2 MN. 2.00
3 . . . . 2.00
4 . . . . 2.00
5 . . . . 2.00
6 . . . . 2.00
7 O:Isis 2.00
8 Dec.–Jan., 1977–78 . . . . 2.00

IT'S GAMETIME
Sept.,–Oct., 1955

1 . . . . 600.00
2 . . . . 500.00
3 . . . . 500.00
4 March-April, 1956 . . . . 500.00

JACKIE GLEASON AND THE HONEYMOONERS
June–July, 1956

1 Based on TV show 650.00
2 . . . . 450.00
3 . . . . 350.00
4 . . . . 350.00
5 . . . . 350.00
6 . . . . 350.00
7 . . . . 350.00
8 . . . . 350.00
9 . . . . 350.00
10 . . . . 350.00
11 . . . . 350.00
12 April-May, 1958 . . . . 400.00

JACK KIRBY'S FOURTH WORLD
Jan., 1997

1 JBy,Worlds of New Genesis & Apokolips become one 2.00
2 JBy,F:Big Barda vs. Thor 2.00
3 JBy,at Wall of the Source 2.00
4 JBy,Can Highfather save his son 2.00
5 JBy,conflict between the gods. . . 2.00
6 JBy,Cause of Orion's transformation 2.00
7 JBy,Orion taught lesson 2.00
8 JBy,WS,Genesis tie-in 2.00
9 JBy,WS(c),Genesis aftermath . . . 2.00
10 JBy,WS, ... 2.00
11 JBy,WS,F:Orion 2.00
12 JBy,WS,F:Mister Miracle 2.00
13 JBy,WS 2.00
14 JBy,WS,Promethean Giant. 2.00
15 JBy,WS,Armaghetto. 2.00
16 JBy,WS,Kalibak vs. Darkseid . . . 2.00
17 JBy,WS,Darkseid 2.00
18 JBy,WS,Darkseid freed 2.00
19 JBy,WS,two stories 2.00
20 JBy,WS,A:Superman,final issue . 2.25

Jaguar #6 © DC Comics, Inc.

JAGUAR
Impact

1 I&O:Jaguar I: Timon De Guzman, Maxx 13,Prof.Ruiz, Luiza Timmerman 2.00
2 Development of Powers 2.00
3 A:Maxx-13 . . . . 2.00
4 A:Black Hood 2.00
5 V:Void,The Living Black Hole . . . 2.00
6 `The Doomster,'A:Maxx-13 . . . . . 2.00
7 Jaguar Secret Discovered, V:Void 2.00
8 V:Aryan League 2.00
9 I:Moonlighter(w/trading cards). . . 2.00
10 V:Invisible Terror 2.00
11 Defending Comedienne 2.00
12 V:The Bodyguard. 2.00
13 V:Purge 2.00
14 'Frightmare in Rio',last iss. 2.00
Ann.#1 Earthquest,w/trading card . . 2.50

JEMM, SON OF SATURN
Sept., 1984

1 GC/KJ mini-series. 2.00
2 GC. 2.00
3 GC,Origin 2.00
4 A:Superman 2.00
5 Kin 2.00
6 thru 12 GC, Aug. 1985 . . . . . . @2.00

JIMMY WAKELY
Sept.,–Oct., 1949

1 Ph(c),ATh,The Cowboy Swordsman 900.00
2 Ph(c),ATh,The Prize Pony. . . . 400.00
3 Ph(c),ATh,The Return of Tulsa Tom 400.00
4 Ph(c),ATh,FF,HK,Where's There's Smoke There's Gunfire. 425.00
5 ATh,The Return of the Conquistadores 300.00
6 ATh,Two Lives of Jimmy Wakely 300.00
7 The Secret of Hairpin Canyon. 300.00
8 ATh,The Lost City of Blue Valley 300.00
9 ATh,The Return of the Western Firebrands 250.00
10 ATh,Secret of Lantikin's Light. 250.00
11 ATh,Trail o/a Thousand Hoofs 250.00
12 ATh,JKU,The King of Sierra Valley 250.00
13 ATh,The Raiders of Treasure Mountain 250.00
14 ATh(c),JKu,The Badmen of Roaring Flame Valley 250.00
15 GK(c),Tommyguns on the Range 250.00
16 GK(c),The Bad Luck Boots. . . 225.00
17 GK(c),Terror at Thunder Basin 225.00
18 July-Aug., 1952 . . . . 250.00

JLA
Nov., 1996

1 GMo(s),HPo,JhD,V:Hyperclan. . 18.00
2 . . . . 15.00
3 GMo(s),HPo,JhD,"War of the Worlds" 10.00
4 GMo(s),HPo,JhD,battle of the super-heroes, conc. 10.00
5 GMo(s),HPo,JhD "Woman of Tomorrow" 6.00
6 GMo(s),HPo,JhD,"Fire in theSky" 5.00
7 GMo(s),HPo,JhD,"Heaven on Earth". 5.00
8 GMo(s),HPo,JhD,"Imaginary

Stories" F:Green Arrow. 5.00
9 GMo(s),V:The Key 5.00
10 GMo(s),HPo,JhD,R:Injustice Gang, pt.1 (of 6). 3.00
11 GMo(s),HPo,JhD,Rock of Ages, pt.2 . . . . 3.00
12 GMo(s),HPo,JhD,Rock of Ages, pt.3, A:Hourman 3.00
13 GMo(s),HPo,JhD,Rock of Ages, pt.4 . . . . 3.00
14 GMo(s),HPo,JhD,Rock of Ages, pt.5 . . . . 3.00
15 GMo(s),HPo,JhD,Rock of Ages pt.6, concl, 48 pg. 3.00
16 GMo(s),HPo,JhD, new member . 2.00
17 GMo(s),HPo,JhD, V:Prometheus 2.00
18 MWa,Engine of Chance, pt.1 . . . 2.00
19 MWa,Engine of Chance, pt.2 . . . 2.00
20 MWa,F:Adam Strange,pt.1. . . . . 2.00
21 MWa,F:Adam Strange,pt.2. . . . . 2.00
22 GMo(s),The Star Conqueror. . . . 2.00
23 GMo,V:Star Conqueror, A:Sandman 2.00
24 GMo,HPo,Ultra-Marines,pt.1 . . . 2.00
25 GMo,HPo,Ultra-Marines,pt.2 . . . 2.00
26 GMo,HPo,Ultra-Marines,pt.3 . . . 2.00
27 GMo,HPo,CrisisTimesFive,pt.1 . 2.00
28 GMo,HPo,CrisisTimesFive,pt.2 . 2.00
29 GMo,HPo,CrisisTimesFive,pt.3 . 2.00
30 GMo,HPo,CrisisTimesFive,pt.4 . 2.00
31 GMo,HPo,CrisisTimes Five,concl. 2.00
32 MWa(s),No Man's Land 2.00
33 MWa(s),No Man's Land 2.00
34 GMo,Super-villains riot. 2.00
35 JMD(s),F:New Spectre. 2.00
36 GMo,HPo,World War 3,pt.1 . . . . 2.00
37 GMo,HPo,World War 3,pt.2 . . . . 2.00
38 GMo,HPo,World War 3,pt.3 . . . . 2.00
39 GMo,HPo,World War 3,pt.4 . . . . 2.00
40 GMo,HPo,World War 3,pt.5 . . . . 2.00
41 GMo,HPo,World War 3, concl.48-pg. 3.00
42 miniscule civilization 2.00
43 MWa(s),HPo,V:Ra's al Ghul 2.25
44 HPo,Tower of Babel,pt.2 . . . . . . 2.25
45 HPo,Tower of Babel,pt.3 . . . . . . 2.25
46 HPo,Tower of Babel,concl. 2.25
47 MWa,BHi,PNe,Queen ofFables . 2.25
48 MWa,BHi,PNe,Queen ofFables. . 2.25
Ann.#1 Pulp Heroes (Hard Boiled) . 3.95
Ann.#2 TTn,BWr,Ghosts 3.00
Ann.#3 JLApe Gorilla Warfare. 3.00
Ann.#4 Planet DC. 3.50
Spec.#1,000,000 GMo(s),HPo, V:Justice Legion A 2.00
SuperSpec.#1 Justice League of America 6.00
Giant #1, 7 new stories, 80-pg. 5.00
Giant #2, 80-page. 4.95
Giant #3, 80-page. 5.95
JLA: Tomorrow Woman, 1-shot TPe,Girlfrenzy (1998) 2.00
GN New World Order GMo(s),HPo, JhD, rep. #1–#4 . . . . 5.95
GN American Dreams rep.#5–#9 . . 8.00
GN Secret Files 4.00
GN Secret Files deluxe. 5.00
GN Secret Files #2. . . . . 4.00
GN Secret Files #3 How Talia stole Batman's Secret Files. 4.95
GN Foreign Bodies. 6.00
GN JLA/WildC.A.T.S, GMo(s), VS,x-over. 6.00
TPB Heaven's Ladder. 9.95
TPB JLA:Rock of Ages 10.00
TPB Strength in Numbers 13.00
TPB Justice League of America: The Nail, Elseworlds. 13.00
TPB Secret Origins Featuring JLA 15.00
GN JLA: Superpower 5.95
GN JLA Primeval 5.95
JLA/Witchblade, x-over. 6.00
HC JLA: Earth 2 . . . . 24.95
HC Justice League of America Archives Vol. 4 . . . . 50.00
HC Justice League of America Archives Vol. 6 . . . . 50.00
JLA Showcase 80-pg Giant #1 . . . . 4.95

JLA: CREATED EQUAL

Feb., 2000

1 FaN,KM,JRu,Elseworlds 5.95
2 FaN,KM,JRu. 5.95

JLA: PARADISE LOST

Nov., 1997

1 (of 3) MMr,AOI,F:Zauriel 2.00
2 MMr,AOI,F:Zauriel,Martian Manhunter 2.00

JLA/TITANS

1998

1 (of 3) JLA vs. Teen Titans 3.00
2 . . . . 3.00
3 conclusion, New Titans. 3.00
TPB The Technis Imperative 12.95

JLA: WORLD WITHOUT GROWN-UPS

June, 1998

1 (of 2) I:Young Justice 48pg 5.00
2 Young Justice, concl. 5.00
TPB World Without Grown-Ups. . . 10.00

JLA: YEAR ONE

Nov., 1997

1 (of 12) MWa,BAu,BKi,48pg. 3.00
2 MWa,BAu,BKi,V:Vandal Savage . 2.00
3 MWa,BAu,BKi. 2.00
4 MWa,BAu,BKi,V:Locus 2.00
5 MWa,BAu,BKi,F:Doom Patrol . . . 2.00
6 MWa,BAu,BKi,V:Doom Patrol . . . 2.00
7 MWa,BAu,BKi,V:Weapon Master 2.00
8 MWa,BAu,BKi,MIB,V:Locus. 2.00
9 MWa,BAu,BKi,MIB,V:Locus. 2.00
10 MWa,BAu,BKi,MIB,V:Locus 2.00
11 MWa,BAu,BKi,MIB 2.00
12 MWa,BAu,BKi,MIB, concl. 3.00
TPB Year One 20.00

The Joker #1 © DC Comics, Inc.

JOHNNY THUNDER

Feb.–March, 1973

1 ATh 5.00
2 GK,MD 4.00
3 ATh,GK,MD,July-Aug., 1973 . . . . 4.00

JOKER, THE

1975–76

1 IN,DG,A:TwoFace. 25.00
2 IN,JL WillieTheWeeper 13.00
3 JL,A:Creeper 12.00
4 JL,A:GreenArrow 10.00
5 . . . . 10.00
6 V:Sherlock Holmes 10.00
7 IN,A:Luthor. 10.00
8 . . . . 10.00
9 A:Catwoman. 12.00
Greatest Joker Stories Ever Told:
1 HC 45.00
1a SC 16.00
The Devil's Advocate HC GN 24.95
GN. 12.95

JONAH HEX

1977–85

1 'Vengeance For A Fallen Gladiator' 45.00
2 'The Lair of the Parrot' 20.00
3 'The Fugitive' 14.00
4 'The Day of Chameleon'. 14.00
5 'Welcome to Paradise' 14.00
6 'The Lawman'. 10.00
7 'Son of the Apache' 10.00
8 O:Jonah Hex 9.00
9 BWr(c) 9.00
10 GM(c),'Violence at Vera Cruz' . . 9.00
11 'The Holdout'. 7.00
12 JS(c) 7.00
13 'The Railroad Blaster' 7.00
14 'The Sin Killer'. 7.00
15 'Saw Dust and Slow Death' 7.00
16 'The Wyandott Verdict!' 5.00
17 . . . . 5.00
18 . . . . 5.00
19 'The Duke of Zarkania!' 5.00
20 'Phantom Stage to William Bend' 5.00
21 'The Buryin!' 5.00
22 'Requiem For A Pack Rat' 5.00
23 'The Massacre of the Celestials!' 5.00
24 'Minister of the Lord' 5.00
25 'The Widow Maker' 5.00
26 'Death Race to Cholera Bend!' . 4.00
27 'The Wooden Six Gun!' 4.00
28 'Night of the Savage'. 4.00
29 'The Innocent' 4.00
30 O:Jonah Hex 4.50
31 A:Arbee Stoneham 4.00
32 A:Arbee Stoneham 4.00
33 'The Crusador' 4.00
34 'Christmas in an Outlaw Town'. . 4.00
35 'The Fort Charlotte Brigade'. . . . 4.00
36 'Return to Fort Charlotte' 4.00
37 DAy,A:Stonewall Jackson. 4.00
38 . . . . 4.00
39 'The Vow of a Samurai!' 4.00
40 DAy. 4.00
41 DAy,'Two for the Hangman!' . . . 4.00
42 'Wanted for Murder'. 4.00
43 JKu(c) 4.00
44 JKu(c),DAy 4.00
45 DAy,Jonah gets married. 4.00
46 JKu(c),DAy 4.00
47 DAy,'Doom Rides the Sundown Town' 4.00
48 DAy,A:El Diablo 4.00
49 DAy. 4.00
50 DAy,'The Hunter'. 4.00

51 DAy,`The Comforter' 3.50
52 DAy,`Rescue!' 3.50
53 DAy 3.50
54 . . . . 3.50
55 `Trail of Blood' 3.50
56 DAy,`The Asylum' 3.50
57 B:El Diablo backup story 3.50
58 DAy,`The Treasure of Catfish Pond' 3.50
59 DAy,`Night of the White Lotus' . . 3.50
60 DAy,`Domain of the Warlord' . . . 3.50
61 DAy,`In the Lair of the Manchus!' 3.50
62 DAy,`The Belly of the Malay Tiger!' 3.50
63 DAy 3.50
64 DAy,`The Pearl!' 3.50
65 DAy,`The Vendetta!' 3.50
66 DAy`Requiem for a Coward' . . . 3.50
67 DAy,`Deadman's Hand!' 3.50
68 DAy,`Gunfight at Gravesboro!' . . 3.50
69 DAy,`The Gauntlet!' 3.50
70 DAy 3.50
71 DAy,`The Masquerades' 3.50
72 DAy,`Tarantula' 3.50
73 DAy,Jonah in a wheel chair 3.50
74 DAy,A:Railroad Bill 3.50
75 DAy,JAp,A:Railroad Bill 3.50
76 DAy,Jonah goes to Jail 3.00
77 DAy,`Over the Wall' 3.00
78 DAy,Me Ling returns 3.00
79 DAy,`Duel in the Sand' 3.00
80 A:Turnbull 3.00
81 thru 89 DAy . . . . @3.00
90 thru 92 . . . . @3.00

JONAH HEX AND OTHER WESTERN TALES

Sept.–Oct., 1979

1 . . . . 2.00
2 NA,ATh,SA,GK 3.00
3 Jan.–Feb., 1980 . . . . 2.00

JONAH HEX: RIDERS OF THE WORM AND SUCH

Vertigo 1995

[Mini-Series]

1 R:Ronah Hex 3.25
2 At Wildes West Ranch 3.00
3 History Lesson 3.00
4 I:Autumn Brothers 3.00

Jonah Hex: Riders of the Worm and Such #4 © DC Comics, Inc.

5 V:Big worm, final issue 3.00

JONAH HEX: SHADOWS WEST

Vertigo 1998

1 (of 3) JLd(s),TTn. 3.00
2 JLd(s),TTn 3.00
3 JLd(s),TTn concl. 3.00

JONAH HEX: TWO-GUN MOJO

Vertigo 1993

1 B:JLd(s),TT,SG(i),R:Jonah Hex, I:Slow Go Smith 8.00
1a Platinum Ed. 20.00
2 TT,SG(i),D:Slow Go Smith,I:Doc Williams,Wild Bill Hickok 6.00
3 TT,SG(i),Jonah captured 5.00
4 TT,SG(i),O:Doc Williams 5.00
5 TT,SG(i),V::Doc Williams. 5.00

JONNI THUNDER

Feb., 1985

1 DG,origin issue. 2.00
2 DG 2.00
3 DG 2.00

JONNY DOUBLE

DC/Vertigo (July, 1998)

1 . . . . 3.00
2 MCo(c) detective 3.00
3 . . . . 3.00
4 . . . . 3.00

JSA

1999

1 JeR,V:Dark Lord. 2.50
2 JeR,AD&Mfm(c),A:Hawkgirl 2.50
3 JeR,AD&MFm(c),V:Dark Lord . . . 2.50
4 JeR,AD&MFm(c),V:Mordru 2.50
5 JeR,AD&MFm(c), ... 2.50
6 . . . . 2.50
7 Darkness Falls, pt.1 . . . . 2.50
8 Darkness Falls, pt.2 . . . . 2.50
9 Darkness Falls, pt.3 . . . . 2.50
10 V:Injustice Society 2.50
11 V:Kobra 2.50
12 V:Kobra,Whitehorse project 2.50
13 Hunt for Extant,pt.1 . . . . 2.50
14 Hunt for Extant,pt.2 . . . . 2.50
15 Hunt for Extant,concl. 2.50
16 Injustice be Done, pt.1 . . . . 2.50
17 Injustice be Done, pt.2 . . . . 2.50
Ann.#1 Planet DC. 3.50
Secret Files #1 . . . . 5.00
TPB Justice be Done 14.95

JSA: THE LIBERTY FILES

Dec., 1999

1 (of 2) Elseworlds. 7.00
2 TyH, concl. 7.00

JUDGE DREDD

1994–96

1 R:Judge Dredd 2.50
2 Silicon Dreams 2.25
3 Terrorists 2.50
4 Mega-City One crisis 2.25
5 Solitary Dredd 2.25
6 V:Richard Magg 2.25
7 . . . . 2.25
8 V:Ministry of Fear 2.25
9 V:Mister Synn 2.25
10 D:Judge Dredd 2.25
11 Mega-City One Chaos 2.25
12 V:Wally Squad 2.25
13 Block Wars,pt.1 . . . . 2.25
14 Block Wars,pt.2 . . . . 2.25
15 Block Wars,pt.3 . . . . 2.25
16 R:Judge with a Grudge 2.25
17 F:Judge Cadet Lewis, Nova Scotia 2.25
18 final issue 2.25
Movie Adaptation 5.95

JUDGE DREDD: LEGENDS OF THE LAW

1994–95

1 Organ Donor,pt.1 . . . . 2.50
2 Organ Donor,pt.2 . . . . 2.25
3 Organ Donor,pt.3 . . . . 2.25
4 Organ Donor,pt.4 . . . . 2.25
5 Trial By Gunfire,pt.1 . . . . 2.25
6 Trial By Gunfire,pt.2 . . . . 2.25
7 JHi(c),Trial By Gunfire,pt.3 . . . . . 2.25
8 JBy(s),Fall From Grace,pt.1 . . . . 2.25
9 Fall From Grace,pt.2. . . . . 2.25
10 Fall From Grace,pt.3 . . . . 2.25
11 Dredd of Night,pt.1. . . . . 2.25
12 Dredd of Night,pt.2 . . . . 2.25
13 Dredd of Night,pt.3,final issue . . 2.25

JUNK CULTURE

DC/Vertigo May, 1997

1 (of 2) TMK 2.50
2 (of 2) TMK "Deuces Wild" 2.50

Justice, Inc. #1 © DC Comics, Inc.

JUSTICE, INC.

May–June, 1975

1 AMc,JKu(c),O:Avenger 3.00
2 JK 2.00
3 JK 2.00
4 JK,JKu(c),Nov.–Dec., 1975 . . . . 2.00

[Mini-Series] 1989

1 PerfectBound `Trust & Betrayal' . 4.00
2 PerfectBound 4.00

JUSTICE LEAGUE AMERICA

(see JUSTICE LEAGUE INTERNATIONAL)

 All comics prices listed are for *Near Mint* condition.

JUSTICE LEAGUE EUROPE
1989–93

1 BS,A:Wonder Woman. 4.00
2 BS,Search for Nazi-Killer 3.00
3 BS,A:Jack O'Lantern, Queen Bee. 2.50
4 BS,V:Queen Bee 2.50
5 JRu,BS,Metamorpho's Baby, A:Sapphire Starr. 2.50
6 BS,V:Injustice League. 2.00
7 BS,Teasdale Imperative#2, A:JLA. 2.00
8 BS,Teasdale Imperative#4, A:JLA. 2.00
9 BS,ANi,A:Superman 2.00
10 BS,V:Crimson Fox 2.00
11 BS,C:DocMagnus&Metal Men . . 2.00
12 BS,A:Metal Men. 2.00
13 BS,V:One-Eyed Cat, contd from JLA #37 . . . . 2.00
14 I:VCR 2.00
15 BS,B:Extremists Vector saga, V:One-Eyed Cat,A:BlueJay. . . . 2.00
16 BS,A:Rocket Reds, Blue Jay . . . 2.25
17 BS,JLI in Another Dimension . . . 2.25
18 BS,Extremists Homeworld 2.25
19 BS,E:Extremist Vector Saga. . . . 2.25
20 MR,I:Beefeater,V:Kilowog 2.00
21 MR,JRu,New JLE embassy in London,A:Kilowog 2.00
22 MR,JLE's Cat stolen 2.00
23 BS,O:Crimson Fox. 2.00
24 BS,Worms in London. 2.00
25 BS,V:Worms 2.00
26 BS,V:Starro 2.00
27 BS,JLE V:JLE,A:JLA,V:Starro . . 2.00
28 BS, JLE V:JLE,A:J'onnJ'onzz, V:Starro 2.00
29 BS,Breakdowns #2,V:Global Guardians 2.00
30 Breakdowns#4,V:J.O'Lantern. . . 2.00
31 Breakdowns #6,War of the Gods tie-in 2.00
32 Breakdowns #8,A:Chief(Doom Patrol) 2.00
33 Breakdowns #10,Lobo vs. Despero. 2.00
34 Breakdowns #12,Lobo vs.Despero. 2.00
35 Breakdowns #14,V:Extremists, D:Silver Sorceress 2.00
36 Breakdowns #16,All Quit 2.00
37 B:New JLE,I:Deconstructo 2.00
38 V:Deconstructo,A:Batman 2.00
39 V:Deconstructo,A:Batman 2.00
40 J:Hal Jordan,A:Metamorpho. . . . 2.00
41 A:Metamorpho,Wond.Woman . . 2.00
42 A:Wonder Woman,V:Echidna . . . 2.00
43 V:Amos Fortune. 2.00
44 V:Amos Fortune. 2.00
45 Red Winter#1,V:Rocket Reds. . . 2.00
46 Red Winter#2 . . . . 2.00
47 Red Winter#3,V:Sonar. 2.00
48 Red Winter#4,V:Sonar. 2.00
49 Red Winter #5,V:Sonar 2.00
50 Red Winter#6,Double-sized, V:Sonar,J:Metamorpho 3.50
Ann.#1 A:Global Guardians 2.00
Ann.#2 MR,CS,ArmageddonPt.7. . . 3.00
Ann.#3 RT(i),Eclipso tie-in 2.75
Justice League Spectacular JLE(c) New Direction. 2.00
Becomes:

Justice League International [2nd Series]

Justice League Europe #11
© DC Comics, Inc.

JUSTICE LEAGUE [INTERNATIONAL]
[1st Series] 1987

1 KM,TA,New Team,I:Max. Lord. . . 6.00
2 KM,AG,A:BlueJay & Silver Sorceress. 4.00
3 KM,AG,J:Booster Gold, V:Rocket Lords 3.00
3a Superman Logo 60.00
4 KM,AG,V:Royal Flush. 3.00
5 KM,AG,A:The Creeper 3.00
6 KM,AG,A:The Creeper 3.00
Becomes:

JUSTICE LEAGUE INTERNATIONAL
1988–89

7 KM,AG,L:Dr.Fate,Capt.Marvel, J:Rocket Red,Capt.Atom (Double size) 3.00
8 KM,AG,KG,Move to Paris Embassy, I:C.Cobert,B.U.Glob.Guardians. 2.50
9 KM,AG,KG,Millennium,Rocket Red-Traitor. 2.50
10 KG,KM,AG,A:G.L.Corps, Superman,I:G'Nort 2.50
11 KM,AG,V:Construct,C:Metron. . . 2.50
12 KG,KM,AG,O:Max Lord 2.50
13 KG,AG,A:Suicide Squad 2.50
14 SL,AG,J:Fire&Ice,L:Ron, I:Manga Kahn. 2.50
15 SL,AG,V:Magna Kahn 2.00
16 KM,AG,I:Queen Bee 2.00
17 KM,AG,V:Queen Bee. 2.00
18 KM,AG,MPn,A:Lobo,Guy Gardner (bonus book) 3.00
19 KM,JRu,A:Lobo vs.Guy Gardner, J:Hawkman & Hawkwoman . . . 3.00
20 KM,JRu(i),A:Lobo,G.Gardner . . . 2.00
21 KM,JRu(i),A:Lobo vs.Guy Gardner 2.00
22 KM,JRu,Imskian Soldiers 2.00
23 KM,JRu,I:Injustice League 2.00
24 KM,JRu,DoubleSize + Bonus Bk#13,I:JusticeLeagueEurope . 4.00
25 KM(c),JRu(i),Vampire story 2.00
Ann.#1 BWg,DG,CR. 2.00
Ann.#2 BWg,JRu,A:Joker 3.00
Ann.#3 KM(c),JRu,JLI Embassies. . 2.50
Spec.#1 Mr.Miracle. 2.00
Spec.#2,The Huntress 2.95
TPB new beginning,rep.#1-#7. . . . 12.95
TPB The Secret Gospel of Maxwell Lord Rep. #8-#12, Ann.#1 . . . 12.95
Becomes:

JUSTICE LEAGUE AMERICA
1989–96

26 KM(c),JRu(i),Possessed Blue Beetle 2.50
27 KM(c),JRu,DG(i),'Exorcist', (c)tribute. 2.00
28 KM(c),JRu(i), A:Black Hand 2.00
29 KM(c),JRu(i),V:Mega-Death 2.00
30 KM(c),BWg,JRu,J:Huntress, D:Mega-Death 2.00
31 ANi,AH,JRu,Teasdale Imperative #1,N:Fire,Ice,A:JLE. 3.00
32 ANi,AH,Teasdale Imperative #3, A:JLE. 3.00
33 ANi,AH,GuyGardner vs.Kilowog. 2.50
34 ANi,AH,`Club JLI,'A:Aquaman . . 2.50
35 ANi,JRu,AH,A:Aquaman 2.50
36 Gnort vs. Scarlet Skier. 2.00
37 ANi,AH,L:Booster Gold 2.00
38 JRu,AH,R:Desparo,D:Steel 2.00
39 JRu,AH,V:Desparo,D:Mr.Miracle, Robot. 2.00
40 AH,Mr.Miracle Funeral. 2.00
41 MMc,MaxForce 2.00
42 MMc,J:L-Ron 2.00
43 AH,KG,The Man Who Knew Too Much #1. . . . . 2.00
44 AH,Man Knew Too Much #2. . . . 2.00
45 AH,MJ,JRu,Guy & Ice's 2nd date 2.00
46 Glory Bound #1,I:Gen.Glory. . . . 2.00
47 Glory Bound #2,J:Gen.Glory . . . 2.00
48 Glory Bound #3,V:DosUberbot . . 2.00
49 Glory Bound #4 . . . . 2.00
50 Glory Bound #5 (double size). . . 2.50
51 JRu,AH,V:BlackHand, R:Booster Gold. 2.00
52 TVE,Blue Beetle Vs. Guy Gardner A:Batman. 2.00
53 Breakdowns #1, A:JLE. 2.00
54 Breakdowns #3, A:JLE. 2.00
55 Breakdowns #5,V:Global Guardians 2.00
56 Breakdowns #7, U.N. revokes JLA charter 2.00
57 Breakdowns #9,A:Lobo, V:Despero 2.00
58 BS,Breakdowns #11,Lobo Vs.Despero 2.00
59 BS,Breakdowns #13, V:Extremists. 2.00
60 KM,TA,Breakdowns #15, End of J.L.A.. . . . . 2.00
61 DJu,I:Weapons Master,B:New JLA Line-up,I:Bloodwynd 3.00
62 DJu,V:Weapons Master 2.00
63 DJu,V:Starbreaker 2.00
64 DJu,V:Starbreaker 2.00
65 DJu,V:Starbreaker 2.00
66 DJu,Superman V:Guy Gardner . 2.00
67 DJu,Bloodwynd mystery. 2.00
68 DJu,V:Alien Land Baron. 2.00
69 DJu, Doomsday Pt.1-A 10.00
69a 2nd printing 2.00
70 DJu,Funeral for a Friend#1 . . . . 6.00
70a 2nd printing 2.00
71 DJu,J:Agent Liberty,Black Condor, The Ray,Wonder Woman 5.00
71a Newsstand ed.. . . . . 2.00
71b 2nd Printing. 1.50
72 DJu,A:Green Arrow,Black Canary,Atom,B:Destiny's Hand . 4.00
73 DJu,Destiny's Hand #2 . . . . 3.00
74 DJu,Destiny's Hand #3 . . . . 2.00
75 DJu,E:Destiny's Hand #4,Martian Manhunter as Bloodwynd 2.00

DC COMICS

Justice League America #65
© DC Comics, Inc.

76 DJu,Blood Secrets#1, V:Weaponmaster 2.00
77 DJu,Blood Secrets#2, V:Weaponmaster 2.00
78 MC,V:The Extremists 2.00
79 MC,V:The Extremists 2.00
80 KWe,N:Booster Gold 2.00
81 KWe,A:Captain Atom 2.00
82 KWe,A:Captain Atom 2.00
83 KWe,V:Guy Gardner 2.00
84 KWe,A:Ice 2.00
85 KWe,V:Frost Giants 2.00
86 B:Cults of the Machine 2.00
87 N:Booster Gold 2.00
88 E:Cults of the Machine 2.00
89 Judgement Day#1, V:Overmaster 2.00
90 Judgement Day#4 . . . . 2.00
91 Aftershocks #1 . . . . 2.00
92 Zero Hour,I:Triumph 2.00
93 Power Girl and child 2.00
94 Scarabus 2.00
95 . . . . 2.00
96 Funeral 2.00
97 I:Judgment 2.00
98 J:Blue Devil, Ice Maiden 2.00
99 V:New Metahumes 2.00
100 GJ,Woj,V:Lord Havok,dbl.size . 3.00
100a Collector's Edition 4.00
101 GJ,Woj,Way of the Warrior,pt.2 . . . . 2.00
102 Way of the Warrior,pt.5 . . . . . . 2.00
103 . . . . 2.00
104 F:Metamorpho 2.00
105 GJ,Woj,Underworld Unleashed tie-in 2.00
106 GJ,Woj,Underworld Unleashed tie-in 2.00
107 GJ,Woj,secret of Power Girl's son 2.00
108 GJ,Woj,The Arcana revealed . . 2.00
109 . . . . 2.00
110 GJ,Woj,V:El Diablo 2.00
111 GJ,Woj,The Purge,pt.1 (of 3) . . 2.00
112 GJ,Woj,The Purge,pt.2 (of 3) . . 2.00
113 GJ,Woj,The Purge,pt.3 (of 3) . . 2.00
Ann.#4 KM(c),I:JL Antartica 3.00
Ann.#5 MR,KM,DJu,Armageddon . 3.00
Ann.#5a 2nd Printing,silver 2.00
Ann.#6 DC,Eclipso 2.75
Ann.#7 I:Terrorsmith 2.75
Ann.#8 Elseworlds Story 3.25
Ann.#9 Year One Annual 3.50
Ann.#10 CPr(s),SCi,NNa,"Legends of the Dead Earth" 2.95
Justice League Spectacular DJu, JLA(c) New Direction 2.00
Archives Vol. 4 . . . . 50.00

JUSTICE LEAGUE OF AMERICA: THE NAIL

June, 1998

Elseworlds

1 World without a Superman 5.00
2 AlD,MFm,Robin & Batgirl dead . . 5.00
3 AlD,MFm,concl. 5.00

JUSTICE LEAGUE INTERNATIONAL

[2nd Regular Series] 1993–94

Prev: Justice League Europe

51 Aztec Cult 2.00
52 V:Aztec Cult 2.00
53 R:Fox's Husband 2.00
54 RoR,I:Creator 2.00
55 RoR,A:Creator 2.00
56 RoR,V:Terrorists 2.00
57 RoR,V:Terrorists 2.00
58 RoR,V:Aliens 2.00
59 RoR,A:Guy Gardner 2.00
60 GJ(s),RoR 2.00
61 GJ(s),V:Godfrey 2.00
62 GJ(s),N:Metamorpho,V:Godfrey . 2.00
63 GJ(s),In Africa 2.00
64 GJ(s),V:Cadre 2.00
65 JudgmentDay#3,V:Overmaster . 2.00
66 JudgmentDay#6,V:Overmaster . 2.00
67 Aftershock #3 . . . . 2.00
68 Zero Hour, Final Issue 2.00
Ann.#4 Bloodlines#9,I:Lionheart . . . 2.75
Ann.#5 . . . . 3.25
Ann.#5 Elseworlds Story 2.95

JUSTICE LEAGUE [INTERNATIONAL] QUARTERLY

1990–94

1 I:Conglomerate 4.00
2 MJ(i),R:Mr.Nebula 3.50
3 V:Extremists,C:Original JLA 3.50
4 KM(c),MR,CR,A:Injustice League 3.00
5 KM(c),Superhero Attacks 3.00
6 EB,Elongated Man,B.U.Global Guardians,Powergirl,B.Beetle . . 3.00
7 EB,DH,MR.Global Guardians . . . 3.00
8 . . . . 3.00
9 DC,F:Power Girl,Booster Gold . . 3.50
10 F:Flash,Fire & Ice 3.50
11 F:JL Women 3.50
12 F:Conglomerate 3.50
13 V:Ultraa 7.00
14 MMi(c),PuK(s),F:Captain Atom,Blue Beetle,Nightshade,Thunderbolt . 3.75
15 F:Praxis 3.50
16 F:Gen Glory 3.50
17 Final Issue 3.50

JUSTICE LEAGUE: A MIDSUMMER'S NIGHTMARE

1996

1 (of 3) MWa(s),FaN,JJ,DaR, ... 5.00
2 MWa(s),FaN,JJ,DaR,Batman & Superman attempt to free other heroes 4.00
3 MWa&FaN(s), Know-Man's plot revealed, finale . . . . @4.00
TPB Rep. 3 issues 8.95

Justice League of America #35
© DC Comics, Inc.

JUSTICE LEAGUE OF AMERICA

Oct.–Nov., 1960

1 MSy,I&O:Despero 3,800.00
2 MSy,A:Merlin 750.00
3 MSy,I&O:Kanjar Ro 650.00
4 MSy,J:Green Arrow 450.00
5 MSy,I&O:Dr.Destiny 400.00
6 MSy,Prof. Fortune 350.00
7 MSy,Cosmic Fun-House 350.00
8 MSy,For Sale-Justice League . 350.00
9 MSy,O:JLA 450.00
10 MSy,I:Felix Faust 300.00
11 MSy,A:Felix Faust 225.00
12 MSy,I&O:Dr Light 225.00
13 MSy,A:Speedy 225.00
14 MSy,J:Atom 225.00
15 MSy,V:Untouchable Aliens . . . 200.00
16 MSy,I:Maestro 175.00
17 MSy,A:Tornado Tyrant 175.00
18 MSy,V:Terrane,Ocana 175.00
19 MSy,A:Dr.Destiny 175.00
20 MSy,V:Metal Being 175.00
21 MSy,R:JSA,1st S.A Hourman, Dr.Fate 350.00
22 MSy,R:JSA 325.00
23 MSy,I:Queen Bee 100.00
24 MSy,A:Adam Strange 100.00
25 MSy,I:Draad,the Conqueror . . 100.00
26 MSy,A:Despero 100.00
27 MSy,V:I,A:Amazo 100.00
28 MSy,I:Headmaster Mind, A:Robin 100.00
29 MSy,I:Crime Syndicate,A:JSA, 1st S.A. Starman 150.00
30 MSy,V:Crime Syndicate, A:JSA 125.00
31 MSy,J:Hawkman 100.00
32 MSy,I&O:Brain Storm 75.00
33 MSy,I:Endless One 60.00
34 MSy,A:Dr.Destiny,Joker 65.00
35 MSy,A:Three Demons 60.00
36 MSy,A:Brain Storm, Handicap story 60.00
37 MSy,A:JSA,x-over, 1st S.A.Mr.Terrific 100.00
38 MSy,A:JSA,Mr.Terrific 100.00
39 Giant 110.00
40 MSy,A:Shark,Penguin 60.00
41 MSy,I:Key 60.00

All comics prices listed are for *Near Mint* condition.

42 MSy,A:Metamorpho 50.00
43 MSy,I:Royal Flush Gang 50.00
44 MSy,A:Unimaginable 50.00
45 MSy,I:Shaggy Man. 50.00
46 MSy,A:JSA,Blockbuster,Solomon Grundy,1st S.A.Sandman . . . 110.00
47 MSy,A:JSA,Blockbuster, Solomon Grundy 50.00
48 Giant 60.00
49 MSy,A:Felix Faust 40.00
50 MSy,A:Robin 40.00
51 MSy,A:Zatanna,Elong.Man. . . . 40.00
52 MSy,A:Robin,Lord of Time 40.00
53 MSy,A:Hawkgirl 40.00
54 MSy,A:Royal Flush Gang 40.00
55 MSy,A:JSA,E-2 Robin 60.00
56 MSy,A:JSA,E-2 Robin 45.00
57 MSy,Brotherhood 40.00
58 Reprint(giant size).. . . . . 45.00
59 MSy,V:Impossibles. 40.00
60 MSy,A:Queen Bee,Batgirl. 40.00
61 MSy,A:Lex Luthor,Penguin 40.00
62 MSy,V:Bulleters 30.00
63 MSy,A:Key. 30.00
64 DD,I:Red Tornado,A:JSA 32.00
65 DD,A:JSA 32.00
66 DD,A:Demmy Gog 30.00
67 MSy,Giant reprints 45.00
68 DD,V:Choas Maker 30.00
69 DD,L:Wonder Woman 28.00
70 DD,A:Creeper 25.00
71 DD,L:J'onn J'onnz 25.00
72 DD,A:Hawkgirl 25.00
73 DD,A:JSA 25.00
74 DD,D:Larry Lance,A:JSA 25.00
75 DD,J:Black Canary 25.00
76 Giant,MA,two page pin-up 25.00
77 DD,A:Joker,L:Snapper Carr . . . 22.00
78 DD,R:Vigilante 22.00
79 DD,A:Vigilante 22.00
80 DD,A:Tomar-Re,Guardians. . . . 22.00
81 DD,V:Jest-Master. 22.00
82 DD,A:JSA 20.00
83 DD,A:JSA,Spectre 20.00
84 DD,Devil in Paradise 20.00
85 Giant reprint. 30.00
86 DD,V:Zapper 20.00
87 DD,A:Zatanna,I:Silver Sorceress,Blue Jay. 22.00
88 DD,A:Mera. 22.00
89 DD,A:Harlequin Ellis, (i.e. Harlan Ellison) 22.00
90 CI(c),MA(ci),DD,V:Pale People. 22.00
91 DD,A:JSA,V:Solomon Grundy . 22.00
92 DD,A:JSA,V:Solomon Grundy . 20.00
93 DD:A:JSA,(giant size) 25.00
94 DD,NA,O:Sandman,rep. Adventure #40 . . . . 90.00
95 DD,rep.More Fun Comics #67, All American Comics #25 . . . . 30.00
96 DD,I:Starbreaker 28.00
97 DD,MS,O:JLA 25.00
98 DD,A:Sargon,Gold.Age reps . . 22.00
99 DD,G.A. reps.. . . . . 22.00
100 DD,A:JSA,Metamorpho, R:7 Soldiers of Victory 35.00
101 DD,A:JSA,7 Soldiers 17.00
102 DD,DG,A:JSA,7 Soldiers D:Red Tornado 17.00
103 DD,DG,Halloween issue, A:Phantom Stranger. 14.00
104 DD,DG,A:Shaggy Man, Hector Hammond 14.00
105 DD,DG,J:ElongatedMan 14.00
106 DD,DG,J:RedTornado 14.00
107 DD,DG,I:Freedom Fighters, A:JSA. 15.00
108 DD,DG,A:JSA, Freedom Fighters 15.00
109 DD,DG,L:Hawkman 14.00
110 DD,DG,A:John Stew4rt, Phantom Stranger 25.00
111 DD,DG,I:Injustice Gang 25.00
112 DD,DG,A:Amazo 25.00
113 DD,DG,A:JSA 25.00
114 DD,DG,A:SnapperCarr 25.00
115 DD,FMc,A:J'onnJ'onnz 25.00
116 DD,FMc,I:Golden Eagle 25.00
117 DD,FMc,R:Hawkman 9.00
118 DD,FMc 9.00
119 DD,FMc,A:Hawkgirl 9.00
120 DD,FMc,A:Adam Strange. 9.00
121 DD,FMc,W:Adam Strange 9.00
122 DD,FMc,JLA casebook story V:Dr.Light 9.00
123 DD,FMc,A:JSA. 10.00
124 DD,FMc,A: JSA 10.00
125 DD,FMc,A:Two-Face 9.00
126 DD,FMc,A:Two-Face 9.00
127 DD,FMc,V:Anarchist. 9.00
128 DD,FMc,J:W.Woman 9.00
129 DD,FMC,D:RedTornado 9.00
130 DD,FMc,O:JLASatellite 9.00
131 DD,FMc,V:Queen Bee,Sonar . . 9.00
132 DD,FMc,A:Supergirl. 9.00
133 DD,FMc,A:Supergirl. 9.00
134 DD,FMc,A:Supergirl. 9.00
135 DD,FMc,A:Squad.of Justice . . . 9.00
136 DD,FMc,A:E-2Joker. 12.00
137 DD,FMc,Superman vs. Capt. Marvel. 15.00
138 NA(c),DD,FMc,A:Adam Strange 9.00
139 NA(c),DD,FMc,A:AdamStrange, Phantom Stranger,doub.size. . 10.00
140 DD,FMc,Manhunters 10.00
141 DD,FMc,Manhunters 10.00
142 DD,FMc,F:Aquaman,Atom, Elongated Man 10.00
143 DD,FMc,V:Injustice Gang . . . 10.00
144 DD,FMc,O:JLA. 10.00
145 DD,FMc,A:Phant.Stranger . . . 10.00
146 J:Red Tornado,Hawkgirl 10.00
147 DD,FMc,A:Legion. 10.00
148 DD,FMc,A:Legion. 10.00
149 DD,FMc,A:Dr.Light. 10.00
150 DD,FMc,A:Dr.Light. 10.00
151 DD,FMc,A:Amos Fortune 9.00
152 DD,FMc. 9.00
153 GT,FMc,I:Ultraa 9.00
154 MK(c),DD,FMc. 9.00
155 DD,FMc. 9.00
156 DD,FMc. 9.00
157 DD,FMc,W:Atom 9.00

Justice League of America #206
© DC Comics, Inc.

158 DD,FMc,A:Ultraa 9.00
159 DD,FMc,A:JSA,Jonah Hex, Enemy Ace 5.00
160 DD,FMc,A:JSA,Jonah Hex, Enemy Ace 5.00
161 DD,FMc,J:Zatanna. 5.00
162 DD,FMc. 5.00
163 DD,FMc,V:Mad Maestro. 5.00
164 DD,FMc,V:Mad Maestro. 5.00
165 DD,FMc. 5.00
166 DD,FMc,V:Secret Society. 5.00
167 DD,FMc,V:Secret Society. 5.00
168 DD,FMc,V:Secret Society. 5.00
169 DD,FMc,A:Ultraa 5.00
170 DD,FMc,A:Ultraa 5.00
171 DD,FMc,A:JSA,D:Mr.Terrific . . . 5.00
172 DD,FMc,A:JSA,D:Mr.Terrific . . . 5.00
173 DD,FMc,A:Black Lightning 5.00
174 DD,FMc,A:Black Lightning 5.00
175 DD,FMc,V:Dr.Destiny 5.00
176 DD,FMc,V:Dr.Destiny 4.00
177 DD,FMc,V:Desparo 4.00
178 JSn(c),DD,FMc,V:Desparo 4.00
179 JSn(c),DD,FMc,J:Firestorm . . . 4.00
180 JSn(c),DD,FMc,V:Satin Satan . 4.00
181 DD,FMc,L:Gr.Arrow,V:Star 5.00
182 DD,FMc,A:Green Arrow, V:Felix Faust 5.00
183 JSn(c),DD,FMc,A:JSA, NewGods. 5.00
184 GP,FMc,A:JSA,NewGods. 5.00
185 JSn(c),GP,FMc,A:JSA, New Gods 5.00
186 FMc,GP,V:Shaggy Man 4.00
187 DH,FMc,N:Zatanna 4.00
188 DH,FMc,V:Proteus 4.00
189 BB(c),RB,FMc,V:Starro 4.00
190 BB(c),RB,LMa,V:Starro 4.00
191 RB,V:Amazo 4.00
192 GP,O:Red Tornado. 4.00
193 GP,RB,JOy,I:AllStarSquad 4.00
194 GP,V:Amos Fortune 3.00
195 GP,A:JSA,V:Secret Society . . . 3.00
196 GP,RT,A:JSA,V:Secret Soc. . . . 3.00
197 GP,RT,KP,A:JSA,V:Secret Society. 3.00
198 DH,BBr,A:J.Hex,BatLash 3.00
199 GP(c),DH,BBr,A:Jonah Hex, BatLash 3.00
200 GP,DG,BB (1st Batman),PB,TA, BBr,GK,CI,JAp,JKu,Anniv.,A:Adam Strange,Phantom Stranger, J:Green Arrow 5.00
201 GP(c),DH,A:Ultraa 2.00
202 GP(c),DH,BBr,JLA in Space. . . 2.00
203 GP(c),DH,RT,V:Royal Flush Gang 2.00
204 GP(c),DH,RT,V:R.FlushGang . . 2.00
205 GP(c),DH,RT,V:R.FlushGang . . 2.00
206 DH,RT,A:Demons 3 . . . . 2.00
207 GP(c),DH,RT,A:All Star Squadron,JSA 2.50
208 GP(c),DH,RT,A:All Star Squadron,JSA 2.50
209 GP(c),DH,RT,A:All Star Squadron,JSA 2.50
210 RB,RT,JLA casebook #1 . . . . . 2.00
211 RB,RT,JLA casebook #2 . . . . . 2.00
212 GP(c),RB,PCu,RT,c.book #3 . . 2.00
213 GP(c),DH,RT 2.00
214 GP(c),DH,RT,I:Siren Sist.h'd . . 2.00
215 GP(c),DH,RT 2.00
216 DH. 2.00
217 GP(c),RT(i) 2.00
218 RT(i),A:Prof.Ivo 2.00
219 GP(c),RT(i),A:JSA 2.25
220 GP(c),RT,O:Bl.Canary,A:JSA . . 2.25
221 Beasts #1 . . . . 2.00
222 RT(i),Beasts #2 . . . . 2.00
223 RT(i),Beasts #3 . . . . 2.00
224 DG(i),V:Paragon 2.00

DC COMICS

225 V:Hellrazor. 2.00
226 FMc(i),V:Hellrazor 2.00
227 V:Hellrazor,I:Lord Claw 2.00
228 GT,AN,R:J'onnJonzz,War of the Worlds,pt.1 . . . . 2.00
229 War of the Worlds,pt.2 . . . . 2.00
230 War of the Worlds conc. 2.00
231 RB(i),A:JSA,Supergirl. 2.25
232 A:JSA Supergirl 2.25
233 New JLA takes over book, B:Rebirth,F:Vibe 2.00
234 F:Vixen 2.00
235 F:Steel. 2.00
236 E:Rebirth,F:Gypsy 2.00
237 A:Superman,Flash,WWoman . . 2.00
238 A:Superman,Flash,WWoman . . 2.00
239 V:Ox 2.00
240 MSy,TMd 2.00
241 GT,V:Amazo 2.00
242 GT,V:Amazo,Mask(Toy tie-in) insert 2.00
243 GT,L:Aquaman,V:Amazo 2.00
244 JSon,Crisis,A:InfinityInc,JSA . . 2.00
245 LMc,Crisis,N:Steel 2.00
246 LMc,JLA leaves Detroit 2.00
247 LMc,JLA returns to old HQ. . . . 2.00
248 LMc,F:J'onn J'onzz 2.00
249 LMc,Lead-in to Anniv. 2.00
250 LMc,Anniv.,A:Superman, Green Lantern,Green Arrow, Black Canary,R:Batman 2.75
251 LMc,V:Despero 2.00
252 LMc,V:Despero,N:Elongated Man 2.00
253 LMc,V:Despero 2.00
254 LMc,V:Despero 2.00
255 LMc,O:Gypsy. 2.00
256 LMc,Gypsy 2.00
257 LMc,A:Adam,L:Zatanna 2.00
258 LMc,Legends x-over,D:Vibe . . . 2.00
259 LMc,Legends x-over 2.00
260 LMc,Legends x-over,D:Steel . . 2.00
261 LMc,Legends,final issue. 4.00
Ann.#1 DG(i),A:Sandman 3.00
Ann.#2 I:NewJLA 2.00
Ann.#3 MG(i),Crisis 2.00

JUSTICE LEAGUE TASK FORCE

1993–96

1 F:Mart.Manhunter,Nightwing, Aquaman,Flash,Gr.Lantern 2.00

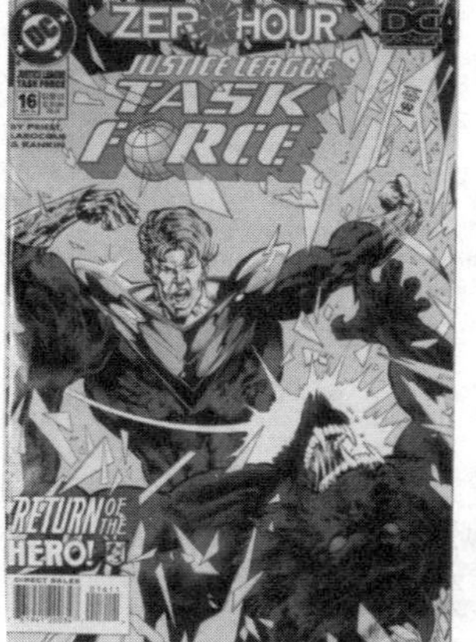

Justice League Task Force #16
© DC Comics, Inc.

2 V:Count Glass,Blitz. 2.00
3 V:Blitz,Count Glass. 2.00
4 DG,F:Gypsy,A:Lady Shiva 2.00
5 JAl,Knightquest:Crusade,F:Bronze Tiger,Green Arrow,Gypsy 2.00
6 JAl,Knightquest:Search,F:Bronze Tiger,Green Arrow,Gypsy 2.00
7 PDd(s),F:Maxima,Wonder Woman, Dolphin,Gypsy,Vixen,V:Luta . . . 2.00
8 PDd(s),SaV,V:Amazons 2.00
9 GrL,V:Wildman 2.00
10 Purification Plague#1. . . . . 2.00
11 Purification Plague#2. . . . . 2.00
12 Purification Plague#3. . . . . 2.00
13 Jugdement Day#2, V:Overmaster 2.00
14 Jugdement Day#5, V:Overmaster. 2.00
15 Aftershocks #2. . . . . 2.00
16 Zero Hour,A:Triumph 2.00
17 Savage 2.00
18 Savage 2.00
19 Martian Manhunter. 2.00
20 Savage Legacy,pt.4 . . . . 2.00
21 F:Martian Manhunter 2.00
22 F:Triumph 2.00
23 V:Vampire 2.00
24 F:Von Mauler, Gypsy 2.00
25 A:Impulse & Damage, V:Mystek. 2.00
26 Cut Day. 2.00
27 F:L-Ron 2.00
28 Triumph vs. Manhunter 2.00
29 A:Glenn Gammeron. 2.00
30 Underworld Unleashed tie-in . . . 2.00
31 Despero on trial. 2.00
32 Despero vs. terrorists. 2.00
33 . . . . 2.00
34 On Earth, or Skartaris? 2.00
35 A:Warlord Travis Morgan 2.00

JUSTICE RIDERS

1999

1-shot, Elseworlds 6.00

JUSTICE SOCIETY OF AMERICA

[Limited Series]

April–Nov., 1991

1 B:Veng.From Stars,A:Flash. 2.00
2 A:BlackCanary,V:Solomon Grundy, C:G.A.Green Lantern. 2.00
3 A:G.A.Green Lantern,Black Canary, V:Sol.Grundy 2.00
4 A:G.A.Hawkman,C:G.A.Flash . . . 2.00
5 A:G.A.Hawkman,Flash 2.00
6 FMc(i),A:Bl.Canary,G.A.Gr.Lantern, V:Sol.Grundy,V.Savage. 2.00
7 JSA united,V:Vandal Savage . . . 2.00
8 E:Veng.FromStar,V:V.Savage, Solomon Grundy 2.00
Spec.#1 DR,MG,End of JSA. 2.00

[Regular Series] 1992–93

1 V:The New Order 2.00
2 V:Ultra Gen 2.00
3 R:Ultra-Humanite 2.00
4 V:Ultra-Humanite 2.00
5 V:Ultra-Humanite 2.00
6 F:Johnny Thunderbolt. 2.00
7 ..Or give me Liberty 2.00
8 Pyramid Scheme 2.00
9 V:Kulak. 2.00
10 V:Kulak,final issue 2.00

KAMANDI, THE LAST BOY ON EARTH

Oct.–Nov., 1972

1 JK,O:Kamandi 34.00

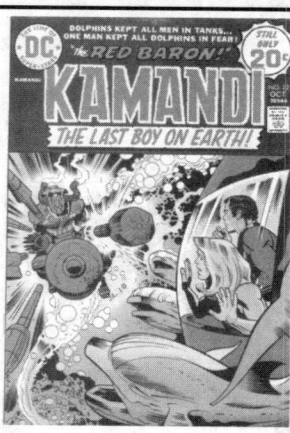

Kamandi The Last Boy on Earth #22
© DC Comics, Inc.

2 JK 20.00
3 JK 9.00
4 JK,I:Prince Tuftan 9.00
5 JK 9.00
6 JK 9.00
7 JK 7.00
8 JK 7.00
9 JK 7.00
10 JK. 7.00
11 JK. 7.00
12 JK. 7.00
13 thru 24 JK . . . . @6.00
25 thru 28 JK . . . . @4.00
29 A:Superman 4.00
30 JK. 3.00
31 . . . . 3.00
32 Double size 4.00
33 thru 57. . . . . @3.00
58 A:Karate Kid 3.00
59 JSn,A:Omac, Sept.–Oct,1978 . . 5.00

KAMANDI: AT EARTH'S END

[Mini-Series] 1993

1 R:Kamandi 2.00
2 V:Kingpin,Big Q 2.00
3 A:Sleeper Zom,Saphira. 2.00
4 A:Superman 2.00
5 A:Superman,V:Ben Boxer. 2.00
6 final issue. 2.00

KARATE KID

March–April, 1976

1 I:Iris Jacobs,A:Legion 4.00
2 A:Major Disaster. 3.00
3 thru 10 . . . . @3.00
11 A:Superboy/Legion 3.00
12 A:Superboy/Legion 3.00
13 A:Superboy/Legion 3.00
14 A:Robin 3.00
15 July-Aug., 1978 . . . . 3.00

KENTS, THE

1997

1 (of 12) JOs(s),TT,MiB 2.50
2 JOs(s),TT,MiB, tragedy strikes . . 2.50
3 JOs,TT,MiB,Jed & Nate Kent . . . 2.50
4 JOs,TT,MiB,Bleeding Kansas, concl. 2.50
5 JOs,TT,Brother vs.Brother pt.1 . . 2.50
6 JOs,TT,Brother vs.Brother pt.2 . . 2.50

 All comics prices listed are for *Near Mint* condition.

7 JOs,TT,MiB,Quantrill, Wild Bill Hickcock. 2.50
8 JOs, ... 2.50
9 JOs,TMd,To the Stars by Hard Ways,pt.1 . . . . 2.50
10 JOs,TMd,To the Stars,pt.2 . . . . . 2.50
11 JOs,TMd,To the Stars,pt.3 . . . . . 2.50
12 JOs,TMd,To the Stars,pt.4 . . . . . 2.50
TPB The Kents, rep. 19.95

KID ETERNITY
1991

1 GMo(s),DFg,O:Kid Eternity 5.50
2 GMo(s),DFg,A:Mr.Keeper 5.50
3 GMo(s),DFg,True Origin revealed, final issue. 5.50

KID ETERNITY
Vertigo 1993–94

1 B:ANo(s),SeP,R:Kid Eternity, A:Mdm.Blavatsky,Hemlock 2.75
2 SeP,A:Sigmund Freud,Carl Jung, A:Malocchio 2.50
3 SeP,A:Malocchio,I:Dr.Pathos. . . . 2.25
4 SeP,A:Neal Cassady. 2.25
5 SeP,In Cyberspace 2.25
6 SeP,A:Dr.Pathos,Marilyn Monroe 2.25
7 SeP,I:Infinity 2.25
8 SeP,In Insane Asylum. 2.25
9 SeP,Asylum,A:Dr.Pathos. 2.25
10 SeP,Small Wages 2.25
11 ANi(s),I:Slap 2.25
12 SeP,A:Slap 2.25
13 SeP,Date in Hell,pt.1 . . . . 2.25
14 SeP,Date in Hell,pt.2 . . . . 2.25
15 SeP,Date in Hell,pt.3 . . . . 2.25
16 SeP,The Zone 2.25

KILL YOUR BOYFRIEND
Vertigo 1995, 1999

GNv PBd(c) (1995). 4.95
1-shot GMo (1999) 6.00

KINGDOM, THE
1998

1 (of 2) MWa,AOl. 3.00
2 MWa,MZ,JhB,V:Gog 3.00
Spec.#1 Kid Flash 2.00
Spec.#1 Offspring. 2.00
Spec.#1 Nightstar. 2.00
Spec.#1 Planet Krypton 2.00
Spec.#1 Son of the Bat. 2.00
DirectCurrents Spec. . . . . free
TPB 14.95

KINGDOM COME
Elseworlds 1996

1 MWa,AxR. 9.00
2 MWa,AxR,R:JLA. 8.00
3 MWa,AxR,A:Capt. Marvel 8.00
4 MWa,AxR, final issue 8.00
HC Elseworlds rep. 29.95
TPB MWa,AxR, rep. 15.00

KISSYFUR
1989

1 . . . . 2.00

KOBALT
Milestone 1994–95

1 JBy(c),I:Kobalt,Richard Page . . . 2.25
2 . . . . 2.00
3 I:Slick,Volt,Red Light. 2.00
4 I:Slick,Volt,Red Light. 2.00
5 Richard Page 2.00
6 Volt. 2.00
7 Static 2.00
8 A:Hardward 2.00
9 . . . . 2.00
10 A:Harvest 2.00
11 V:St.Cloud 2.00
12 V:Rabid 2.00
13 V:Harvester. 2.00
14 Long Hot Summer, V:Harvester . 2.50
15 Long Hot Summer 2.50

KOBRA
1976–77

1 JK,I:Kobra & Jason Burr 4.00
2 I:Solaris 2.50
3 KG/DG,TA,V:Solaris 2.50
4 V:Servitor 2.50
5 RB/FMc,A:Jonny Double. 2.50
6 MN/JRu,A:Jonny Double. 2.50
7 MN/JRu,A:Jonny Double last iss. 2.50

KONG THE UNTAMED
June–July, 1975

1 thru 4 . . . . @7.00

Korak Son of Tarzan #46
© DC Comics, Inc.

5 Feb.–March, 1976 . . . . 5.00

KORAK, SON OF TARZAN
1975
(Prev. published by Gold Key)

46 B:Carson of Venus, 1972 . . . . . . 4.00
47 . . . . 3.50
48 thru 59, 1975. . . . . 3.00
Becomes:

TARZAN FAMILY

KRYPTON CHRONICLES
1981

1 CS,A:Superman 3.00
2 CS,A:Black Flame 2.00
3 CS,O:Name of Kal-El 2.00

LAST DAYS OF THE JUSTICE SOCIETY
1986

1 . . . . 3.00

LAST ONE
Vertigo 1993

1 B:JMD(s),DSw,I:Myrwann,Patrick Maguire's Story 3.25
2 DSw,Pat's Addiction to Drugs . . . 3.00
3 DSw,Pat goes into Coma 3.00
4 DSw,In Victorian age 3.00
5 DSw,Myrwann Memories 3.00
6 E:JMD(s),DSw,final Issue 3.00

L.A.W.
1999

1 (of 6) BL,DG,Living Assault Weapons 2.50
2 BL,DG 2.50
3 BL,DG 2.50
4 BL,DG,rescue JLA 2.50
5 BL,DG 2.50
6 BL,DG,conclusion. 2.50

LAZARUS FIVE
May, 2000

1 (of 5) THy,F:Inquisitors 2.50
2 THy,F:Hank the Swede. 2.50
3 THy,The Decayed Ones,Digit . . . 2.50
4 THy,The Decayed Ones 2.50
5 THy,conclusion. 2.50

LEADING COMICS
Winter, 1941–42

1 O:Seven Soldiers of Victory, B:Crimson Avenger,Green Arrow & Speedy,Shining Knight, A:The Dummy 3,700.00
2 MMe,V:Black Star 1,300.00
3 V:Dr. Doome 1,000.00
4 `Seven Steps to Conquest', V:The Sixth Sense 750.00
5 `The Miracles that Money Couldn't Buy' 750.00
6 `The Treasure that Time Forgot' 650.00
7 The Wizard of Wisstark. 650.00
8 Seven Soldiers Go back through the Centuries 650.00
9 V:Mr. X,`Chameleon of Crime'. 650.00
10 King of the Hundred Isles. . . . 650.00
11 `The Hard Luck Hat!' 450.00
12 `The Million Dollar Challenge!' 450.00
13 `The Trophies of Crime' 450.00
14 Bandits from the Book' 450.00
15 (fa) 200.00
16 thru 22 (fa) . . . . @80.00
23 (fa),I:Peter Porkchops 200.00
24 thru 30 (fa) . . . . @65.00
31 (fa) 60.00
32 (fa) 60.00
33 (fa) 65.00
34 thru 40 (fa) . . . . @60.00
41 (fa),Feb.–March, 1950 . . . . 60.00

LEAGUE OF JUSTICE
1996

1 (of 2) Elseworlds. 5.95
2 (of 2) Elseworlds. 5.95

LEAVE IT TO BINKY
Feb.–March, 1948

1 . . . . 225.00
2 . . . . 100.00
3 & 4 . . . . @60.00
5 thru 14 . . . . @30.00
15 SM,Scribbly 40.00
16 thru 60 . . . . @25.00
61 thru 71 . . . . @22.00

LEGEND OF THE HAWKMAN

July, 2000

1 BRa,Hawkman & Hawkgirl 4.95
2 BRa,V:Thanagarian zealots 4.95
3 BRa,concl. 4.95

LEGEND OF THE SHIELD

Impact 1991–92

1 I:Shield,V:Mann-X,I:Big Daddy, Lt.Devon Hall,Arvell Hauser,Mary Masterson-Higgins 2.00
2 Shield in Middle East 2.00
3 Shield Goes A.W.O.L. 2.00
4 Hunt for Shield 2.00
5 A:Shield's Partner Dusty 2.00
6 O:Shield, V:The Jewels. 2.00
7 Shield/Fly team-up 2.00
8 V:Weapon 2.00
9 Father Vs. Son 2.00
10 Arvell Hauser. 2.00
11 inc,Trading cards 2.00
12 . . . . 2.00
13 Shield court martialed 2.00
14 Mike Barnes becomes Shield. . . 2.00
15 Shield becomes a Crusader. . . . 2.00
16 V:Soviets,final issue. 2.00
Ann.#1 Earthquest,w/trading card . . 2.25

LEGEND OF WONDER WOMAN

1986

1 Return of Atomia 3.00
2 A:Queens Solalia & Leila 3.00
3 Escape from Atomia 3.00
4 conclusion 3.00

LEGENDS

1986–87

1 JBy,V:Darkseid 3.00
2 JBy,A:Superman. 2.00
3 JBy,I:Suicide Squad 2.00
4 JBy,V:Darkseid 2.00
5 JBy,A:Dr. Fate 2.00
6 JBy,I:Justice League. 5.00
TPB rep.#1-#6 JBy(c) 9.95

LEGENDS OF

Legends #3 © DC Comics, Inc.

DANIEL BOONE, THE

Oct., 1955–Jan., 1957

1 . . . . 500.00
2 . . . . 350.00
3 thru 8 . . . . 300.00

LEGENDS OF THE DARK KNIGHT

(see BATMAN)

LEGENDS OF THE DC UNIVERSE

Dec., 1997

1 JeR,VS,PNe,A:Superman, pt.1 . . 3.50
2 JeR,VS,PNe,A:Superman, pt.2 . . 4.00
3 JeR,VS,PNe,A:Superman, pt.3 . . 2.00
4 BML,MD2,VRu,Moments, pt.1. . . 2.00
5 BML,MD2,VRu,Moments, pt.2. . . 2.00
6 DTy,KN,Robin meets Superman . 2.00
7 DON,DG,Peacemakers, pt.1 . . . . 2.00
8 DON,DG,Peacemakers, pt.2. . . . 2.00
9 DON,DG,Peacemakers, pt.3. . . . 2.00
10 TyD,KN,F:Batman & Batgirl,pt.1 . 2.00
11 KN,TyD,F:Batman & Batgirl,pt.2 . 2.00
12 CPr(s),Critical Mass,pt.1 . . . . . . 2.00
13 CPr(s),Critical Mass,pt.2 . . . . . . 2.00
14 JK,BR,SR,64-page 4.00
15 RCa,Dark Matters, pt.1 . . . . 2.00
16 RCa,Dark Matters, pt.2 . . . . 2.00
17 RCa,Dark Matters, pt.3 . . . . 2.00
18 MWn(s),JG,F:New Teen Titans . 2.00
19 RT,F:Impulse 2.00
20 StG(s),MZ,KJ,Trail of the Traitor, pt.1. . . . . 2.00
21 StG(s),MZ,KJ,Trail of the Traitor, pt.2. . . . . 2.00
22 Transilvane,pt.1 . . . . 2.00
23 Transilvane,pt.2 . . . . 2.00
24 StP,The Jump,pt.1 . . . . 2.00
25 StP,The Jump,pt.2 . . . . 2.00
26 TVE,JRu,Aquaman&Joker,pt.1 . . 2.00
27 TVE,JRu,Aquaman&Joker,pt.2 . . 2.00
28 GK,KJ,pt.1. . . . . 2.00
29 GK,KJ,pt.2,F:Traitor 2.00
30 CPr(s),Wonder Woman,pt.1 . . . . 2.00
31 CPr(s),Wonder Woman,pt.2 . . . . 2.50
32 CPr(s),Wonder Woman,pt.3 . . . . 2.50
33 JMD,MZi,VcL,F:Spectre,pt.1 . . . 2.50
34 JMD,MZi,VcL,F:Spectre,pt.2 . . . 2.50
35 JMD,MZi,VcL,F:Spectre,pt.3 . . . 2.50
Giant #1 JKu(c), 80 pg.. . . . . 5.00
Spec 3-D Gallery #1 . . . . 3.00
GN Crisis on Infinite Earths. 5.00

LEGENDS OF THE LEGION

Dec., 1997

1 (of 4) BKi,TPe,TNu,O:Ultra Boy . 2.75
2 . . . . 2.50
3 BKi,TPe,O:Umbra. 2.50
4 BKi,TPe,O:Star Boy 2.50

LEGENDS OF THE WORLD FINEST

1994

1 WS(s),DIB,V:Silver Banshee, Blaze,Tullus,Foil(c). 6.00
2 WS(s),DIB,V:Silver Banshee, Blaze,Tullus,Foil(c). 6.00
3 WS(s),DIB,V:Silver Banshee, Blaze,Tullus,Foil(c). 6.00
TPB 14.95

L.E.G.I.O.N. '89 #6 © DC Comics, Inc.

L.E.G.I.O.N. '89-94

1989–94

1 BKi,V:Computer Tyrants 4.50
2 BKi,V:Computer Tyrants 3.00
3 BKi,V:Computer Tyrants, A:Lobo 3.00
4 BKi,V: Lobo 3.00
5 BKi,J:Lobo(in the rest of the series),V:Konis-Biz 3.00
6 BKi,V:Konis-Biz 3.00
7 BKi,Stealth vs. Dox. 3.00
8 BKi,R:Dox 3.00
9 BKi,J:Phase (Phantom Girl) 2.50
10 BKi,Stealth vs Lobo 2.50
11 BKi,V:Mr.Stoorr 2.50
12 BKi,V:Emerald Eye 2.50
13 BKi,V:Emerald Eye 2.50
14 BKi,V:Pirates 2.50
15 BKi,V:Emerald Eye 2.50
16 BKi,J:LarGand 2.50
17 BKi,V:Dragon-Ro 2.50
18 BKi,V:Dragon-Ro 2.50
19 V:Lydea,L:Stealth. 2.50
20 Aftermath. 2.50
21 D:Lyrissa Mallor,V:Mr.Starr. 2.50
22 V:Mr.Starr 2.50
23 O:R.J.Brande(double sized) 3.50
24 BKi,V:Khunds 2.50
25 BKi,V:Khunds 2.50
26 BKi,V:Khunds 2.50
27 BKi,J:Lydea Mallor. 2.50
28 KG,Birth of Stealth's Babies. . . . 2.50
29 BKi,J:Capt.Comet,Marij'n Bek . . 2.50
30 BKi,R:Stealth. 2.50
31 Lobo vs.Capt.Marvel 3.50
32 V:Space Biker Gang 2.00
33 A:Ice-Man 2.00
34 MPn,V:Ice Man 2.00
35 Legion Disbanded 2.00
36 Dox proposes to Ignea. 2.00
37 V:Intergalactic Ninjas 2.00
38 BKi,Lobo V:Ice Man. 2.00
39 BKi,D:G'odd,V:G'oddSquad 2.00
40 BKi,V:Kyaltic Space Station 2.00
41 BKi,A:Stealth'sBaby. 2.00
42 BKi,V:Yeltsin-Beta 2.00
43 BKi,V:Yeltsin-Beta 2.00
44 V:Yeltsin-Beta,C:Gr.Lantern 2.00
45 . . . . 2.00
46 BKi,A:Hal Jordan 2.00
47 BKi,Lobo vs Hal Jordan 2.00
48 BKi,R:Ig'nea 2.00
49 BKi,V:Ig'nea. 2.00
50 BKi,V:Ig'nea,A:Legion'67 . . . . . . 3.75

51 F:Lobo,Telepath 2.00
52 BKi,V:Cyborg Skull of Darius . . . 2.00
53 BKi,V:Shadow Creature 2.00
54 BKi,V:Shadow Creature 2.00
55 BKi,V:Shadow Beast 2.00
56 BKi,A:Masked Avenger 2.00
57 BKi,Trinity,V:Green Lantern 2.00
58 BKi,Trinity#6,A:Green Lantern, Darkstar 2.00
59 F:Phase. 2.00
60 V:Phantom Riders 2.00
61 Little Party 2.00
62 A:R.E.C.R.U.I.T.S. 2.00
63 A:Superman 2.00
64 BKi(c),V:Mr.B. 2.00
65 BKi(c),V:Brain Bandit 2.00
66 Stealth and Dox name child 2.00
67 F:Telepath 2.00
68 . . . . 2.00
69 . . . . 2.00
70 Zero Hour, last issue 2.50
Ann.#1 A:Superman,V:Brainiac. . . . 5.50
Ann.#2 Armageddon 2001 . . . . 3.50
Ann.#3 Eclipso tie-in. 3.25
Ann.#4 SHa(i),I:Pax 3.75
Ann.#5 Elseworlds story 3.50

LEGION OF SUBSTITUTE HEROES

1985

Spec.#1 KG 1.50

LEGION OF SUPER-HEROES

[Reprint Series] 1973

1 rep. Tommy Tomorrow 20.00
2 rep. Tommy Tomorrow 12.00
3 rep. Tommy Tomorrow 10.00
4 rep. Tommy Tomorrow 10.00

[1st Regular Series] 1980–84

Prev: SUPERBOY (& LEGION)

259 JSon,L:Superboy 7.00
260 RE,I:Circus of Death 4.50
261 RE,V:Circus of Death. 3.50
262 JSh,V:Engineer 3.50
263 V:Dagon the Avenger. 3.50
264 V:Dagon the Avenger. 3.50
265 JSn,DG,Superman/Radio Shack insert 3.50
266 R:Bouncing Boy,Duo Damsel . . 3.00
267 SD,V:Kantuu 3.00
268 SD,BWi,V:Dr.Mayavale 3.00
269 V:Fatal Five 3.00
270 V:Fatal Five 3.00
271 V:Tharok (Dark Man) 2.50
272 CI,SD,O:J:Blok, I:New Dial `H' for Hero 2.50
273 V:Stargrave 2.50
274 SD,V:Captain Frake 2.50
275 V:Captain Frake. 2.50
276 SD,V:Mordru 2.50
277 A:Reflecto(Superboy). 2.50
278 A:Reflecto(Superboy). 2.50
279 A:Reflecto(Superboy). 2.50
280 R:Superboy 2.50
281 SD,V:Time Trapper 2.50
282 V:Time Trapper 2.50
283 O:Wildfire 2.50
284 PB,V:Organleggor 2.50
285 PB,KG(1st Legion)V:Khunds . . 3.00
286 PB,KG,V:Khunds 3.00
287 KG,V:Kharlak. 4.00
288 KG,V:Kharlak. 3.00
289 KG,Stranded 3.00
290 KG,B:Great Darkness Saga, J:Invisible Kid II 3.00
291 KG,V:Darkseid's Minions 2.00
292 KG,V:Darkseid's Minions 2.00
293 KG,Daxam destroyed. 2.00
294 KG,E:Great Darkness Saga, V:Darkseid,A:Auron,Superboy . 2.00
295 KG,A:Green Lantern Corps . . . 2.00
296 KG,D:Cosmic Boys family 2.00
297 KG,O:Legion,A:Cosmic Boy . . . 2.00
298 KG,EC,I:Amethyst 2.00
299 KG,R:Invisible Kid I 2.00
300 KG,CS,JSon,DC,KS,DG. 4.00
301 KG,R:Chameleon Boy 2.00
302 KG,A:Chameleon Boy 2.00
303 KG,V:Fatal Five 2.00
304 KG,V:Fatal Five 2.00
305 KG,V:Micro Lad 2.00
306 KG,CS,RT,O:Star Boy 2.00
307 KG,GT,Omen. 2.00
308 KG,V:Omen 2.00
309 KG,V:Omen 2.00
310 KG,V:Omen 2.00
311 KG,GC,New Headquarters 2.00
312 KG,V:Khunds. 2.00
313 KG,V:Khunds. 2.00
Ann.#1 IT,KG,I:Invisible Kid. 3.50
Ann.#2 DGb,W:Karate Kid and Princess Projectra 2.00
Ann.#3 CS,RT,A:Darkseid. 2.00
Ann.#4 reprint. 2.00
Ann.#5 reprint. 2.00
Legion Archives Vol 1 HC 39.95
Legion Archives Vol 2 HC 39.95
Legion Archives Vol 3 HC 39.95
Legion Archives Vol 4 HC 39.95
Becomes:

TALES OF LEGION OF SUPER HEROES

Legion of Super-Heroes 3rd Series #11
© DC Comics, Inc.

LEGION OF SUPER-HEROES

[3rd Regular Series] 1984–89

1 KG,V:Legion of Super-Villains. . . 4.00
2 KG,V:Legion of Super-Villains. . . 3.00
3 KG,V:Legion of Super-Villains. . . 3.00
4 KG,D:Karate Kid. 3.00
5 KG,D:Nemesis Kid 3.00
6 JO,F:Lightning Lass 2.50
7 SLi,A:Controller 2.50
8 SLi,V:Controller 2.50
9 Sli,V:Sklarians 2.50
10 V:Khunds. 2.50
11 EC,KG,L:Orig 3 members 2.50
12 SLi,EC,A:Superboy 2.50
13 SLi,V:Lythyls,F:TimberWolf 2.50
14 SLi,J:Sensor Girl (Princess Projectra),Quislet,Tellus,Polar Boy,Magnetic Kid 2.50
15 GLa,V:Dr. Regulus. 2.50
16 SLi,Crisis tie-in,F:Braniac5. . . . . 2.50
17 GLa,O:Legion 2.50
18 GLa,Crisis tie-in,V:InfiniteMan . . 2.50
19 GLa,V:Controller 2.50
20 GLa,V:Tyr 2.50
21 GLa,V:Emerald Empress 2.00
22 GLa,V:Restorer,A:Universo 2.00
23 SLi,GLa,A:Superboy, Jonah Hex 2.00
24 GLa,NBi,A:Fatal Five 2.00
25 GLa,V:FatalFive. 2.00
26 GLa,V:FatalFive,O:SensorGirl . . 2.00
27 GLa,GC,A:Mordru 2.00
28 GLa,L:StarBoy. 2.00
29 GLa,V:Starfinger 2.00
30 GLa,A:Universo. 2.00
31 GLa,A:Ferro Lad,Karate Kid. . . . 2.00
32 GLa,V:Universo,I:Atmos. 2.00
33 GLa,V:Universo 2.00
34 GLa,V:Universo 2.00
35 GLa,V:Universo,R:Saturn Girl . . 2.00
36 GLa,R:Cosmic Boy 2.00
37 GLa,V:Universo,I:Superboy (Earth Prime) 12.00
38 GLa,V:TimeTrapper, D:Superboy 14.00
39 CS,RT,O:Colossal Boy. 2.00
40 GLa,I:New Starfinger 2.00
41 GLa,V:Starfinger 2.00
42 GLa,Millenium,V:Laurel Kent . . . 2.00
43 GLa,Millenium,V:Laurel Kent . . . 2.00
44 GLa,O:Quislet 2.00
45 GLa,CS,MGr,DC,30th Ann. 3.00
46 GLa,Conspiracy. 2.00
47 GLa,PB,V:Starfinger 2.00
48 GLa,Conspiracy,A:Starfinger . . . 2.00
49 PB,Conspiracy,A:Starfinger 2.00
50 KG,V:Time Trapper,A:Infinite Man,E:Conspiracy 3.00
51 KG,V:Gorak,L:Brainiac5 . . . . 2.00
52 KG,V:Gil'Dishpan. 2.00
53 KG,V:Gil'Dishpan. 2.00
54 KG,V:Gorak. 2.00
55 KG,EC,JL,EL,N:Legion 2.00
56 EB,V:Inquisitor. 2.00
57 KG,V:Emerald Empress 2.00
58 KG,V:Emerald Empress. 2.00
59 KG,MBr,F:Invisible Kid. 2.00
60 KG,B:Magic Wars 2.00
61 KG,Magic Wars 2.00
62 KG,D:Magnetic Lad 2.00
63 KG,E:Magic Wars #4,final iss. . . 2.00
Ann.#1 KG,Murder Mystery. 2.50
Ann.#2 KG,CS,O:Validus, A:Darkseid 3.00
Ann.#3 GLa,I:2nd Karate Kid 2.50
Ann.#4 BKi,V:Starfinger 2.50
Ann #5 I:2nd Legion Sub.Heroes . . 2.50

[4th Regular Series] 1989–97

1 KG,R:Cosmic Boy, Chameleon . . 5.00
2 KG,R:Ultra Boy,I:Kono 3.50
3 KG,D:Block,V:Roxxas. 3.50
4 KG,V:Time Trapper. 3.50
5 KG,V:Mordru,A:Glorith 3.50
6 KG,I:Laurel Gand 3.50
7 KG,V:Mordru 3.00
8 KG,O:Legion 3.00
9 KG,O:Laurel Gand 3.00
10 KG,V:Roxxas. 3.00
11 KG,V:Roxxas. 3.00
12 KG,I:Kent Shakespeare 3.00
13 KG,V:Dominators,posters. 3.00
14 KG,J:Tenzil Kem 3.00
15 KG,Khund Invasion 3.00
16 KG,V:Khunds. 3.00

Legion of Super Heroes, 4th Series, #110 © DC Comics, Inc.

17 KG,V:Khunds. 3.00
18 KG,V:Khunds. 3.00
19 KG,cont.from Adv.of Superman #478,A:Original Dr. Fate 3.00
20 KG,V:Dominators. 3.00
21 KG,B:Quiet Darkness, A:Lobo,Darkseid. 3.50
22 KG,A:Lobo,Darkseid 3.00
23 KG,A:Lobo,Darkseid 3.00
24 KG,E:Quiet Darkness,A:Lobo, Darkseid,C:Legionairres 3.00
25 DAb,I:Legionairres. 3.50
26 JPn,B:Terra Mosaic,V:B.I.O.N . . 2.50
27 JPn,V:B.I.O.N. 2.50
28 JPn,O:Sun Boy 2.50
29 JPn,I:Monica Sade. 2.50
30 JPn,V:Dominators 2.50
31 CS,AG,F:Shvaughn as man. . . . 2.50
32 JPn,D:Karate Kid,Prin.Projectra, Chameleon Boy(Legionaires) . . 2.50
33 R:Kid Quantum 2.50
34 R:Sun Boy 2.50
35 JPN,V:Dominators 2.50
36 JPn,E:Terra Mosaic 2.50
37 JBr,R:Star Boy,Dream Girl 2.50
38 JPn,Earth is destroyed. 5.00
39 SI,A:Legionnaires 2.50
40 SI,Legion meets Legionnaires . . 2.50
41 SI,F:The Legionnaires 2.50
42 SI,V:Glorith 2.50
43 SI,B:Mordru Arises. 2.50
44 SI,R:Karate Kid 2.50
45 SI,R:Roxxas 2.50
46 SI,. 2.50
47 SI,. 2.50
48 SI,E:Mordru Arises. 2.50
49 F:Matter Eater Lad. 2.50
50 W:Tenzil & Saturn Queen, R:Wlidfire,V:B.I.O.N 4.00
51 R:Kent,Celeste,Ivy,V:Grimbor. . . 2.50
52 F:Timber Wolf 2.50
53 SI,V:Glorith 2.50
54 SI,Foil,Die-Cut(c), N:L.E.G.I.O.N. 5.00
55 SI,On Rimbor. 2.50
56 SI,R:Espionage Squad. 2.50
57 SI,R:Khund Legionnaires 2.50
58 SI,D:Laurel Gand. 2.50
59 SI,R:Valor,Dawnstar. 2.25
60 SI,End of an Era#3 . . . . 2.25
61 SI,End of an Era#6 . . . . 2.25
62 I:New Team. 2.25
63 Alien Attack 2.25
64 . . . . 2.25
65 . . . . 2.25
66 I:New Team Members 2.25
67 F:Leviathan 2.25
68 F:Leviathan 2.25
69 V:Durlan 2.25
70 A:Andromeda, Brainiac 5 . . . . . . 2.25
71 Planet Trom. 2.25
72 . . . . 2.25
73 Sibling Rivalry,pt.1 . . . . 2.25
74 Future Tense,pt2 . . . . 2.25
75 Two Timer,pt.1 (of 2) 2.25
76 F:Valor & Triad. 2.25
77 F:Brainiac 5. . . . . 2.25
78 . . . . 2.25
79 Fatal Five attacks 2.25
80 V:Fatal Five 2.25
81 R:Dirk Morgna 2.25
82 . . . . 2.25
83 . . . . 2.25
84 . . . . 2.25
85 TPe&TMw(s),LMd,A:Superman, back in 20th century 2.25
86 TPe&TMw(s),LMd,Final Night tie-in. 2.25
87 TPe&TMw(s),LMd,F:Deadman . . 2.25
88 TPe&TMw(s),LMd,A:Impulse . . . 2.25
89 TPe&TMw(s),LMd,. 2.25
90 TPe&TMw(s),LMd,V:Dr. Psycho . 2.25
91 TPe&TMw(s),LMd,Legion back together, but trapped in timestream 2.25
92 TPe&TMs(s),LMd,"Displaced in Time" 2.25
93 TPe&TMw(s),MC, All-tragedy issue 2.25
94 TPe&TMw(s),LMd,"22 short pages about the Legion of Super-Heroes" 2.25
95 MFm,F:Brainiac 5 . . . . 2.25
96 MFm,wedding 2.25
97 TPe,LMd,Genesis tie-in 2.50
98 TPe&TMC,LMd,C.O.M.P.U.T.O. the Conqueror, pt.1. . . . . 2.50
99 TPe&TMw,LMd,Computo, pt.2 . . 2.50
100 TPe&TMw,LMd,Computo, pt.3 . 7.50
101 TPe&TMw(s),AD&MFm(c), F:Sparks 2.50
102 . . . . 2.50
103 TPe&TMw,AD&MFm(c),Star Boy 2.50
104 TPe&TMw,AD&MFm(c), changes 2.50
105 TPe&TMw,AD&MFm(c), Adventures in Action x-over . . . 2.50
106 TPe&TMw,AD&MFm(c),Dark Circle Rising, x-over pt.2 . . . . . 2.50
107 TPe&TMw,AD&MFm(c),Dark Circle Rising, x-over pt.4 . . . . . 2.50
108 TPe&TMw,AD&MFm(c),Dark Circle Rising, x-over pt.6 . . . . . 2.50
109 DDv,AD,MFm,F:Violet 2.50
110 TPe,V:Thunder. 2.50
111 TPe&TMw(s),V:Daxamite 2.50
112 TPe&TMw(s),In Space 2.50
113 TPe&TMw(s),Kinetix 2.50
114 TPe&TMw(s),Bizarro Legion,pt.1 . . . . 2.50
115 TPe&TMw(s),Bizarro Legion, pt.2 . . . . 2.50
116 TPe&TMw(s),V:Pernisius,pt.1 . . 2.50
117 TPe&TMw(s),V:Pernisius,pt.2 . . 2.50
118 TPe&TMw(s),V:Pernisius,pt.3 . . 2.50
119 TPe&TMw(s),A:Valor & Phase . 2.50
120 TPe,TMw,V:Fatal Four,pt.1. . . . 2.50
121 TPe,TMw,V:Fatal Five,pt.2 . . . . 2.50
122 DAn,ALa,Legion of the Damned,pt.1. . . . . 2.50
123 DAn,ALa,Legion of the Damned,pt.3. . . . . 2.50
124 DAn,ALa,Legion of the Damned, aftermath 2.50
125 DAn,ALa,final issue 2.50
Ann.#1 O:Ultra Boy,V:Glorith. 3.50
Ann.#2 O:Valor. 3.50
Ann.#3 N:Timberwolf 4.00
Ann.#4 I:Jamm 3.50
Ann.#5 SI(c),CDo,MFm,TMc, Elseworlds Story 3.75
Ann.#6 Year One Annual + pin-ups. 3.95
Ann.#7 TPe(s),MC,MFm,"Legends of the Dead Earth" 3.50
Spec.#1,000,000 TPe(s),KG,AG . . . 2.50
TPB Great Darkness Saga 17.95
TPB Legion Archives, rep.#1-#3 . . 39.95
TPB Legion Archives, rep.#4 . . . . . 49.95
TPB The Beginnings of Tomorrow. 17.95
HC Archives, Vol. 1. . . . . 49.95
HC Archives, Vol. 6 rep.Adventure #350–358. . . . . 49.95
HC Archives, Vol. 7. . . . . 49.95
HC Archives, Vol. 9. . . . . 49.95
HC Archives, Vol. 10. . . . . 49.95
GN Secret Files, inc.O:Legion. 5.00
GN Secret Files #2. . . . . 4.95

LEGIONNAIRES

1992

1 CSp,V:Mano and the Hand,Bagged w/SkyBox promo card. 4.00
1a w/out card 3.00
2 CSp,V:Mano. 3.00
3 CSp,I:2nd Emerald Empress. . . . 3.00
4 CSp,R:Fatal Five 3.00
5 CSp,V:Fatal Five 3.00
6 CSp,V:Fatal Five 2.50
7 AH,V:Devil Fish 2.50
8 CDo,F:Brainiac 5 . . . . 2.50
9 CSp,A:Kid Quantum 2.50
10 CSp,A:Kono,I:2nd Kid Pyscho . . 2.50
11 CSp,J:2nd Kid Pyscho 2.50
12 CSp,A:2nd Kid Pyscho. 2.50
13 FFo,V:Grimbor. 2.50
14 V:Grimbor 2.50
15 V:Grimbor 2.50
16 In Time 2.50
17 End of An Era #1. . . . . 2.50
18 Zero Hour, LSH 2.50
19 Problems. 2.50
20 Moon Battle 2.50
21 and 22 . . . . @2.50
23 Saturday Night. 2.50
24 F:Triad. 2.50
25 F:Chameleon. 2.50

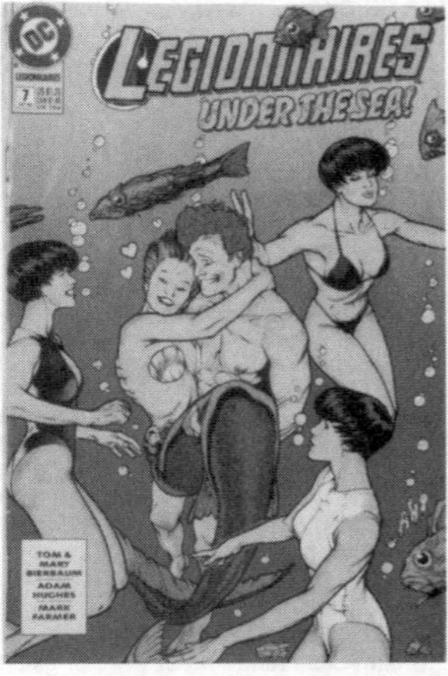

Legionnaires #7 © DC Comics, Inc.

26 F:Apparition, Ultra Boy. 2.50
27 V:The Daxamites 2.25
28 V:Daxamites 2.25
29 . . . . 2.25
30 Silbing Rivalry,pt.2 . . . . 2.25
31 Future Tense,pt.3. . . . . 2.25
32 Two Timer, pt.2 . . . . 2.25
33 deadly new villain 2.25
34 Shrinking Violet killed?. 2.25
35 . . . . 2.25
36 RSt,V:Fatal Five 2.25
37 RSt,A:Kinetix,The Empress 2.25
38 . . . . 2.25
39 . . . . 2.25
40 . . . . 2.25
41 RSt&TMw(s),JMy,Legion of Super-Heroes #84 aftermath . . 2.25
42 RSt&TMw(s),JMy,Mysa vs. Kinetix 2.25
43 RSt&TMw(s),JMy,Legionnaire try-outs. 2.25
44 TPe&TMw(s),JMy,revenge by rejected applicants 2.25
45 . . . . 2.25
46 RSt&TMw(s),JMy,M'Onel's life hangs by a thread 2.25
47 TPe&TMw(s),JMy,Brainiac 5 has plan to return Legionnaires to the future 2.25
48 RSt&TMw(s),JMy,"Dawn of the Dark Lord," pt.1 . . . . 2.25
49 RSt&TMw(s),JMy,"Dawn of the Dark Lord," pt.2 . . . . 2.25
50 RSt&TMw(s),JMy,"The Bride of Mordru" 48pg, with poster. 4.50
51 "Picking Up the Pieces" 2.25
52 RSt&TMw(s),JMy,"LeVlathan" . . 2.25
53 RSt&TMw(s),JMy,F:Monstress . . 2.25
54 TPe&TMw(s),JMy,F:G.A. Legion 2.25
55 RSt&TMw(s),JMy,V:Composite Man 2.25
56 RSt&TMw(s),JMy,F:M'Onel 2.25
57 RSt&TMw(s),JMy,V:Khunds 2.25
58 . . . . 2.25
59 RSt&TMw(s),JMy,date night. . . . 2.50
60 RSt&TMw(s),JMy,2 join, 2 leave. 2.50
61 RSt&TMw(s),JMy,Adventures in Action x-over 2.50
62 RSt&TMw(s),JMy,Dark Circle Rising x-over, pt.1. . . . . . 2.50
63 RSt&TMw(s),JMy,Dark Circle Rising, x-over, pt.3 . . . . 2.50
64 RSt&TMw(s),JMy, Dark Circle Rising, x-over pt.5 . . . . 2.50
65 RSt&TMw(s),JMy,aftermath 2.50
66 F:Invisible Kid 2.50
67 RSt&TMw(s),JMy,Star Boy. 2.50
68 RSt&TMw(s),JMy,Cosmic Boy . . 2.50
69 RSt&TMw(s),JMy,Lori Morning. . 2.50
70 RSt&TMw(s),JMy,Alux Cuspin . . 2.50
71 RSt&TMw(s),JMy,Dragonmage . 2.50
72 RSt&TMw(s),JMy,V:Mordru 2.50
73 RSt&TMw(s),JMy,V:Mordru 2.50
74 RSt&TMw(s),JMy,V:Elements of Disaster 2.50
75 TPe(s),JMy, ... 2.50
76 RSt&TMw(s),JMy. 2.50
77 RSt,TMw(s),JMy 2.50
78 DAn&ALa(s),rescue mission . . . 2.50
79 ALa,Legion of the Damned,pt.2 . 2.50
80 ALa,Legion of the Damned,pt.4 . 2.50
81 DAn&ALa(s),final issue 2.50
Ann.#1 Elseworlds Story. 2.95
Ann.#2 Year One Story. 3.00
Ann.#3 RSt&TMw(s) Legends of the Dead Earth. 3.50
Spec.#1,000,000 TPe(s),SeP, Justice Legion L. 2.50

LEGIONNAIRES THREE

1986

1 EC,Saturn Girl,Cosmic Boy. 4.00
2 EC,V:Time Trapper,pt.1. . . . . 3.00
3 EC,V:Time Trapper,pt.2. . . . . 3.00
4 EC,V:Time Trapper,pt.3. . . . . 2.75

LEGION LOST

March, 2000

1 (of 12) DAn,ALa 2.50
2 DAn,ALa,V:Progeny 2.50
3 DAn,ALa,V:Progeny 2.50
4 DAn,ALa, ... 2.50
5 DAn,ALa,Brainiac 5.1 . . . . 2.50
6 DAn,ALa,F:Umbra 2.50
7 DAn,ALa,F:Ultra Boy 2.50
8 DAn,ALa, ... 2.50

LEGION: SCIENCE POLICE

June, 1998

1 (of 4) DvM,PR,JRu,set in 30th century 2.50
2 DvM,PR,JRu,Jarik Shadder 2.50
3 DvM,PR,JRu, ... 2.50
4 DvM,PR,JRu 2.25

Life, The Universe and Everything #1
© DC Comics, Inc.

LIFE, THE UNIVERSE AND EVERYTHING

1996

1 thru 3 Doug Adams adapt. . . . @6.95

LIMITED COLLECTORS EDITION

Summer, 1973

21 Shazam. 30.00
22 Tarzan 25.00
23 House of Mystery. 35.00
24 Rudolph, the Red-nosed Reindeer 50.00
25 NA,NA(c),Batman 40.00
27 Shazam. 25.00
29 Tarzan 25.00
31 NA,O:Superman 25.00
32 Ghosts. 35.00
33 Rudolph. 45.00
34 X-Mas with Superheroes 22.00
35 Shazam. 20.00
36 The Bible. 22.00
37 Batman 25.00
38 Superman 20.00
39 Secret Origins 20.00
40 Dick Tracy 20.00
41 ATh,Super Friends. 20.00
42 Rudolph 20.00
43 X-mas with Super-Heroes 20.00
44 NA,Batman 20.00
45 Secret Origins-Super Villains . . 20.00
46 ATh,JLA. 20.00
47 Superman 20.00
48 Superman-Flash Race 20.00
49 Superboy & Legion of Super-Heroes. 20.00
50 Rudolph. 25.00
51 NA,NA(c),Batman 20.00
52 NA,NA(c),The Best of DC 20.00
57 Welcome Back Kotter 20.00
59 NA,BWr,Batman,1978 . . . . 25.00

LITTLE SHOP OF HORRORS

1 GC. 2.50

LOBO

[1st Limited Series] 1990–91

1 SBs,Last Czarnian #1. . . . . 4.00
1a 2nd Printing 2.00
2 SBs,Last Czarnian #2. . . . . 3.00
3 SBs,Last Czarnian #3. . . . . 3.00
4 SBs,Last Czarnian #4. . . . . 3.00
Ann.#1 Bloodlines#1,I:Layla 3.75
Lobo Paramilitary X-Mas SBs 5.50
Lobo:Blazing Chain of Love,DCw . . 1.50
TPB Last Czarnian,rep.#1-#4 . . . . . 9.95
TPB Lobo's Greatest Hits 12.95

[Regular Series] 1993–97

1 VS,Foil(c),V:Dead Boys 3.25
2 VS 3.00
3 VS 2.75
4 VS,Quigly Affair 2.75
5 V:Bludhound. 2.50
6 I:Bim Simms. 2.50
7 A:Losers. 2.50
8 A:Losers. 2.50
9 V:Lobo 2.50
10 Preacher 2.50
11 Goldstar vs. Rev.Bo 2.50
12 . . . . 2.50
13 . . . . 2.50
14 Lobo, P.I.. . . . . 2.50
15 Lobo, P.I.,pt.2 . . . . 2.50
16 Lobo, P.I.,pt.3 . . . . 2.50
17 Lobo, P.I.,pt.4 . . . . 2.50
18 Lobo, P.I.,pt.5 . . . . 2.50
19 . . . . 2.50
20 Toilot Fight. 2.50
21 AIG,KON,R:Space Cabby 2.50
22 AIG,UnderworldUnleashed tie-in 2.50
23 AIG,Stargaze Rally,pt.1 . . . . . . 2.50
24 AIG,Stargaze Rally,pt.2 . . . . . . 2.50
25 AIG 2.50
26 AIG,V:Erik the Khund. 2.50
27 AIG,V:Billy Krono. 2.50
28 AIG,A:Great Big Fat Bastiches. . 2.50
29 . . . . 2.50
30 . . . . 2.50
31 . . . . 2.50
32 AIG(s),Lobo attends a seance, frags himself. 2.50
33 AIG(s),Lobo returns from spirit world 2.50
34 AIG(s),vs. Japan, whaling, ... 2.50
35 AIG(s) "Deathtrek" 2.50
36 . . . . 2.50
37 AIG(s),BKi,Lobo's Guide to Girls 2.50
38 AIG(s),Bomandi The Last Boy

Lobo #0 © DC Comics, Inc.

on Earth 2.50
39 AIG(s),"In the Belly of the Behemoth,"pt. 1 . . . . 2.50
40 AIG(s),"In the Belly of the Behemoth,"pt. 2 . . . . 2.50
41 AIG(s),roommates 2.50
42 AIG(s),A:Perfidia 2.50
43 AIG(s),A:Jonas 2.50
44 AIG(s),Genesis tie-in 2.50
45 AIG(s),battle royale 2.50
46 AIG(s),Jackie Chin 2.50
47 AIG(s),V:Kiljoy Riggs 2.50
48 AIG(s),F:the penguins 2.50
49 AIG(s) 2.50
50 AIG(s),war on DC universe 2.50
51 AIG(s),Slater and Candy 2.50
52 AIG(s),Goldstar funeral 2.50
53 AIG(s),disrupted ceremony. 2.50
54 AIG(s),Good Vibes machine. . . . 2.50
55 AIG(s),Sheepworld. 2.50
56 AIG(s),MPn,GLz,the wedding . . . 2.50
57 AIG(s),MPn,GLz, Intergalactic Police convention 2.50
58 KG&AIG(s) 2.50
59 AIG(s),V:Bad Wee Bastards. . . . 2.50
60 AIG(s),All-New, Nonviolent Adventures of Superbo, pt.1 . . . 2.50
61 AIG(s),Superbo, pt.2 . . . . 2.50
62 AIG(s),Superbo, pt.3 . . . . 2.50
63 AIG(s),Soul Brothers,pt.1 . . . . . . 2.50
64 AIG(s),Soul Brothers,pt.2 final issue. 2.50
Ann.#1 Bloodlines. 4.00
Ann.#2 Elseworlds Story. 3.50
Ann.#3 AIG Year One 4.95
Spec.#1,000,000 AIG(s),GLz 2.50
Spec. Lobo's Big Babe Spring Break, Miss Voluptuous Contest 2.50
Spec. Blazing Chains of Love 2.00
Spec. Bounty Hunting for Fun and Profit, F:Fanboy. 4.95
Spec. Lobo: Chained AIG(s), Lobo in prison 2.50
Spec. Lobo/Demon: Hellowe'en, AIG(s),VGi 2.25
Spec. Lobo In the Chair, AIG(s) . . . 2.25
Spec. Lobo:I Quit,AIG, nicotine withdrawal 2.25
Spec. Lobo/Judge Dredd: Psycho Bikers vs. Mutants From Hell . . 4.95
Spec. Lobo: Portrait of a Victim VS,I:John Doe 2.00
GN Fragtastic Voyage AGr, miniaturized 6.00
TPB Lobo's Back's Back. 10.00
TPB Lobo's Greatest Hits 13.00
Convention Special, comic con 2.00

LOBO: A CONTRACT ON GAWD

1994

1 AIG(s),KD. 2.00
2 AIG(s),KD,A:Dave. 2.00
3 AIG(s),KD. 2.00
4 AIG(s),KD,Final Issue 2.00

LOBO'S BACK

1992

1 SBs,w/3(c) inside,V:Loo 2.50
1a 2nd printing 2.00
2 SBs,Lobo becomes a woman . . . 2.50
3 SBs,V:Heaven 2.50
4 SBs,V:Heaven 2.50
TPB GF(c),rep.#1-#4 . . . . 9.95

LOBO: DEATH & TAXES

Aug., 1996

[Mini-series]

1 (of 4) KG&AIG(s) 2.25
2 KG&AIG(s),Interstellar Revenue learns Lobo doesn't pay taxes . 2.25
3 KG&AIG(s),Lobo walks into IRS trap 2.25
4 KG&AIG(s),Lobo destroys IRS . . 2.25

LOBO: INFANTICIDE

1992–93

1 KG,V:Su,Lobo Bastards 2.00
2 Lobo at Boot Camp 2.00
3 KG,Lobo Vs.his offspring 2.00
4 KG,V:Lobo Bastards. 2.00

LOBO/MASK

1 AIG&JAr(s),DoM,Kwi, humorous x-over. 5.95
2 AIG&JAr(s),DoM,Kwi, concl. 5.95

LOBO: UNAMERICAN GLADIATORS

1993

1 CK,V:Satan's Brothers 2.00
2 CK,V:Jonny Caesar 2.00
3 CK,MMi(c),V:Satan Brothers 2.00
4 CK,MMi(c),V:Jonny Caeser. 2.00

LOBOCOP

1 StG(s) 2.25

LOIS AND CLARK: THE NEW ADVENTURES OF SUPERMAN

TPB 9.95
TPB stories that became episodes 10.00

LOIS LANE

Aug., 1986

1 and 2 GM . . . . @3.00

LONG HOT SUMMER, THE

Milestone 1995

[Mini-Series]

1 Blood Syndicate v. G.R.I.N.D. . . . 2.95
2 A:Icon,Xombi,Hardware 2.50

Looney Tunes #33 © DC Comics, Inc.

LOONEY TUNES MAG.

1 thru 6 . . . . @2.00

LOONEY TUNES

1994

1 thru 6 Warner Bros. cartoons. . @2.00
7 thru 11 Warner Bros. . . . . @2.00
12 The Cotton Tail Club 2.00
13 F:Tasmanian Devil 2.00
14 Football Season. 2.00
15 Jewel Thief 2.00
16 F:Yosemite Sam,Speedy Gonzales 2.00
17 F:Sylvester 2.00
18 . . . . 2.00
19 Ben Hur Spoof. 2.00
20 F:Sylvester 2.00
21 thru 23 . . . . @2.00
24 thru 32 . . . . @2.00
33 F:Tasmanian Devil 2.00
34 F:Daffy 2.00
35 F:Daffy DangerDuck 2.00
36 F:Tweety 2.00
37 F:Crusher, Bugs. 2.00
38 . . . . 2.00
39 F:Miss Prissy, Foghorn 2.00
40 F:Sylvester and Tweety 2.00
41 F:Porky, Sylvester 2.00
42 F:Sylvester,Pepe 2.00
43 F:Bugs, Sylvester 2.00
44 Frankentweety. 2.00
45 Bad Hare Day 2.00
46 Le Cage Aux Pew 2.00
47 Snow Way Out 2.00
48 Rocky Road. 2.00
49 F:Pepe Le Pew 2.00
50 The Gangs all here 2.00
51 Daffy 2.00
52 Bugs, Sam. 2.00
53 Postman Always Brings Mice. . . 2.00
54 Marvin & Taz 2.00
55 Twuce or Consequences 2.00
56 Foghorn & Henry Hawk 2.00
57 Claws & Effect. 2.00
58 . . . . 2.00
59 . . . . 2.00
60 . . . . 2.00
61 . . . . 2.00
62 . . . . 2.00
63 . . . . 2.00
64 Marvin the Martian. 2.00
65 Roadrunner 2.00
66 Duck Tracy vs. Bugs Bunny. . . . 2.00

67 Bugs & Foghorn 2.00
68 MacDuck 2.00
69 Yosemite Sam 2.00
70 Daffy 2.00
71 Hare-a 51 . . . . 2.00

LOOSE CANNON

[Mini-Series] 1995

1 AdP,V:Bounty Hunters 2.00
2 V:Bounty Hunters & The Eradicator 2.00
3 A:Eradicator 2.00

LORDS OF THE ULTRAREALM

1986

1 PB 3.50
2 PB 2.00
3 thru 6 PB . . . . @2.00
Spec.#1 PB,DG,Oneshot 2.25

LOSERS SPECIAL

1985

1 Crisis,D:Losers 2.00

LUCIFER

DC/Vertigo Apr., 2000

1 Lucifer strugles to regain power . 2.50
2 Living Tarot Deck 2.50
3 V:Jill Presto 2.50
4 WaP,F:Elaine Belloc 2.50
5 PrG,House of Windowless Rooms,pt.1 . . . . 2.50
6 PrG,Windowless Rooms,pt.2 . . . 2.50
7 PrG,Windowless Rooms,pt.3 . . . 2.50

MADAME XANADU

1981

1 MR/BB 2.00

MAJOR BUMMER

June, 1997

1 JAr(s),DoM,I:Major Bummer 2.50
2 JAr(s),DoM,Major Bummer gets new costume 2.50
3 JAr(s),DoM,bad guys arrive 2.50
4 JAr(s),DoM,alien germs 2.50
5 JAr(s),DoM,dinosaurs, Nazis. . . . 2.50
6 JAr(s),DoM,Mutant bully 2.50
7 JAr(s),DoM 2.50
8 . . . . 2.50
9 JAr(s),DoM,epic fight 2.50
10 JAr(s),DoM,Nunzio dead? 2.50
11 JAr(s),DoM,everyone dies? 2.50
12 JAr(s),DoM,Lou Martin dead . . . 2.50
13 JAr(s),DoM,Lauren 2.50
14 JAr(s),DoM,tells the future off. . . 2.50
15 JAr(s),DoM, final issue. 2.50

MAN-BAT

1975–76

1 SD,AM,A:Batman 20.00
2 V:The Ten-Eyed Man 15.00
Reprint NA(c) 10.00

MAN-BAT

1996

1 CDi,terrorizes city 2.25
2 . . . . 2.25
3 CDi,V:Steeljacket, finale 2.25

MAN-BAT vs. BATMAN

1 NA,DG,reprint. 4.00

A MAN CALLED AX

Aug. 1997

1 MWn(s),SwM, part rep. 2.50
2 MWn(s),SwM, ... 2.50
3 MWn(s),SwM, vs. DC universe . . 2.50
4 MWn(s),SwM,killer cyborg 2.50
5 MWn(s),SwM,R-Mor 2.50
6 MWn(s),SwM, ... 2.50
7 MWn(s),SwM,battle in Bedlam . . 2.50
8 MWn(s),SwM,final issue 2.50

Manhunter #13 © DC Comics, Inc.

MANHUNTER

1988–90

1 from Millenium-Suicide Squad. . . 2.50
2 in Tokyo,A:Dumas. 2.00
3 The Yakuza,V:Dumas 2.00
4 Secrets Revealed-Manhunter, Dumas & Olivia 2.00
5 A:Silvia Kandery 2.00
6 A:Argent,contd.Suicide Squad Annual #1. . . . . 2.00
7 Vlatavia, V:Count Vertigo 2.00
8 FS,A:Flash,Invasion x-over 2.00
9 FS,Invasion Aftermath extra (contd from Flash #22) 2.00
10 Salvage,pt.1 . . . . 2.00
11 Salvage,pt.2. . . . . 2.00
12 . . . . 2.00
13 V:Catman 2.00
14 Janus Directive #5 . . . . 2.00
15 I:Mirage 2.00
16 V:Outlaw 2.00
17 In Gotham,A:Batman 2.00
18 Saints & Sinners,pt.1,R:Dumas . 2.00
19 Saints & Sinners,pt.2,V:Dumas . 2.00
20 Saints & Sinners,pt.3,V:Dumas . 2.00
21 Saints & Sinners,pt.4, A:Manhunter Grandmaster 2.00
22 Saints & Sinners,pt.5, A:Manhunter Grandmaster 2.00
23 Saints & Sinners,pt.6,V:Dumas . 2.00
24 DG,Showdown, final issue 2.00

[2nd Series] 1994–95

0 . . . . 2.50
1 . . . . 2.50
2 N:Wild Huntsman 2.50
3 V:Malig 2.50
4 Necrodyne 2.50
5 V:Skin Walker 2.50
6 V:Barbarian,Incarnate 2.50
7 V:Incarnate,A:White Lotus & Capt. Atom 2.25
8 V:Butcher Boys. 2.25
9 V:Butcher Boys. 2.25
10 V:Necrodyne 2.25
11 Return of Old Enemy 2.25
12 Underworld Unleashed, finale . . 2.25

MAN OF STEEL

1986

1 JBy,DG,I:Modern Superman 5.00
1a 2nd edition 3.00
2 JBy,DG,R:Lois Lane 3.50
3 JBy,DG,A:Batman. 3.00
4 JBy,DG,V:Lex Luther 3.00
5 JBy,DG,I:Modern Bizarro 3.00
6 JBy,DG,A:Lana Lang 3.00
TPB rep. Man of Steel #1–#6 . . . . 12.95
TPBa 2nd printing. 7.95

MANY LOVES OF DOBIE GILLIS

May–June, 1960

1 . . . . 200.00
2 . . . . 100.00
3 . . . . 75.00
4 . . . . 75.00
5 thru 9 . . . . @50.00
10 thru 25 . . . . @45.00
26 Oct., 1964 . . . . 45.00

MARTIAN MANHUNTER

1988

1 A:JLI 2.50
2 A:JLI,V:Death God 2.50
3 V:Death God,A:Dr.Erdel 2.50
4 A:JLI,final issue 2.50

[Mini-Series]

1 EB,American Secrets #1. . . . . . . 5.25
2 EB,American Secrets #2. . . . . . . 4.95
3 EB,American Secrets #3. . . . . . . 4.95

MARTIAN MANHUNTER

Aug., 1998

0 JOs,TMd,A:Batman,Superman . . 2.00
1 JOs,TMd,V:Headman 2.00
2 JOs,TMd,V:Antares 2.00
3 JOs,TMd,V:Bette Noir. 2.00
4 JOs,TMd,J'emm, Son of Saturn . 2.00
5 JAr,JD,A:Chase 2.00
6 JOs,TMd,A:JLA,pt.1 . . . . 2.00
7 JOs(s),TMd,A:JLA,pt.2 . . . . 2.00
8 JOs(s),TMd,A:JLA,pt.3 . . . . 2.00
9 JOs(s),TMd,A:JLA,pt.4 . . . . 2.00
10 JOs(s),A:Fire 2.00
11 JOs,PNe,BHi, ... 2.00
12 JOs,TMd,Day of Judgment x-over. 2.00
13 JOs,TMd,Rings of Saturn,pt.1 . . 2.00
14 JOs,TMd,Rings of Saturn,pt.2 . . 2.00
15 JOs,TMd,Rings of Saturn,pt.3 . . 2.00
16 JOs,TMd,Rings of Saturn,pt.4 . . 2.00
17 JOs,TMd,Rings of Saturn,pt.5 . . 2.00
18 JOs,TMd,V:Kanto 2.50
19 JOs,TMd,defeated, captured . . . 2.50
20 JOs,TMd,year one on earth 2.50
21 JOs,TT,A:Abin Sur 2.50
22 JOs,TMd,A:Batman 2.50
23 JOs,TMd,F:Spectre 2.50
24 JOs,TMd,F:Just.Leag.Int. 2.50
25 JOs,TMd,F:Gypsy 2.50
Ann.#1 TT,AOI,BWr,Ghosts x-over . 3.00
Ann.#2 AAd(c),JLApe:Gorilla Warfare 2.95
Spec.#1,000,000 JOs,TMd 2.00

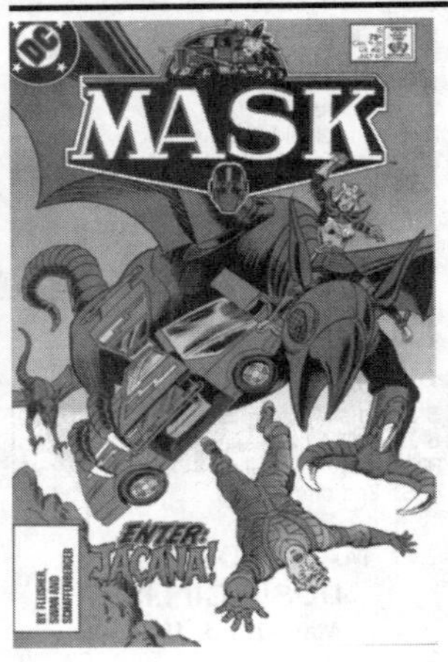

Mask #6 © DC Comics, Inc.

MASK

Dec., 1985

1 HC(c),TV tie-in,I:Mask Team 2.00
2 HC(c),In Egypt,V:Venom 2.00
3 HC(c),`Anarchy in the U.K.' 2.00
4 HC(c),V:Venom, final issue, March, 1986 . . . . 2.00

[2nd Series] Feb.–Oct., 1987

1 CS/KS,reg.series 2.00
2 CS/KS,V:Venom 2.00
3 CS/KS,V:Venom 2.00
4 CS/KS,V:Venom 2.00
5 CS/KS,Mask operatives hostage. 2.00
6 CS/KS,I:Jacana 2.00
7 CS/KS,Mask gone bad? 2.00
8 CS/KS,Matt Trakker,V:Venom . . . 2.00
9 CS/KS,V:Venom, last issue 2.00

MASTERS OF THE UNIVERSE

May, 1986

1 GT,AA,O:He-Man 2.50
2 GT,AA,V:Skeletor 2.50
3 GT,V:Skeletor 2.50

MASTERWORKS SERIES OF GREAT COMIC BOOK ARTISTS

May, 1983

1 . . . . 2.50
2 . . . . 2.50
3 Dec., 1983 . . . . 2.50

'MAZING MAN

Jan., 1986

1 I:Maze 2.00
2 . . . . 2.00
3 . . . . 2.00
4 . . . . 2.00
5 . . . . 2.00
6 Shea Stadium. 2.00
7 Shea Stadium. 2.00
8 Cat-Sitting 2.00
9 Bank Hold-up 2.00
10 . . . . 2.00
11 Jones Beach 2.00
12 FM(c),last issue, Dec., 1986 . . . 2.00
Spec.#1 . . . . 2.25
Spec.#2 . . . . 2.25
Spec.#3 KB/TM 2.25

MEN OF WAR

Aug., 1977

1 I:Gravedigger,Code Name: Gravedigger,I:Enemy Ace 9.00
2 JKu(c),The Five-Walled War 6.00
3 JKu(c),The Suicide Strategem . . 5.00
4 JKu(c),Trail by Fire 5.00
5 JKu(c),Valley of the Shadow 5.00
6 JKu(c),A Choice of Deaths 5.00
7 JKu(c),Milkrun 5.00
8 JKu(c),Death-Stroke 5.00
9 JKu(c),Gravedigger-R.I.P. 5.00
10 JKu(c),Crossroads 5.00
11 JKu(c),Berkstaten 4.00
12 JKu(c),Where Is Gravedigger? . . 4.00
13 JKu(c),Project Gravedigger - Plus One 4.00
14 JKu(c),The Swirling Sands of Death 4.00
15 JKu(c),The Man With the Opened Eye 4.00
16 JKu(c),Hide and Seek The Spy . 4.00
17 JKu(c),The River of Death 4.00
18 JKu(c),The Amiens Assault 4.00
19 JKu(c),An Angel Named Marie. . 4.00
20 JKu(c),Cry:Jerico 4.00
21 JKu(c),Home-Is Where The Hell Is 4.00
22 JKu(c),Blackout On The Boardwalk 4.00
23 JKu(c),Mission: Six Feet Under . 4.00
24 JKu&DG(c),The Presidential Peril 4.00
25 GE(c),Save the President 4.00
26 March, 1980 . . . . 4.00

MENZ INSANA

DC/Vertigo 1998

GN JBo 7.95

MERCY

Vertigo

Graphic Novel I:Mercy 8.00

METAL MEN

1965–78

[1st Regular Series]

1 RA,I:Missile Men. 500.00
2 RA,Robot of Terror 185.00
3 RA,Moon's Invisible Army 100.00
4 RA,Bracelet of Doomed Hero . 100.00
5 RA,Menace of the Mammoth Robots 100.00
6 RA,I:Gas Gang 85.00
7 RA,V:Solar Brain 55.00
8 RA,Playground of Terror 55.00
9 RA,A:Billy 55.00
10 RA,A:Gas Gang. 55.00
11 RA,The Floating Furies 55.00
12 RA,A:Missle Men 50.00
13 RA,I:Nameless. 50.00
14 RA,A:Chemo 50.00
15 RA,V:B.O.L.T.S. 50.00
16 RA,Robots for Sale 50.00
17 JKu(c),RA,V:Bl.Widow Robot . . 50.00
18 JKu(c),RA 50.00
19 RA,V:Man-Horse of Hades. . . . 50.00
20 RA,V:Dr.Yes. 50.00
21 RA,C:Batman & Robin,Flash Wonder Woman 35.00
22 RA,A:Chemo 35.00
23 RA,A:Sizzler 35.00
24 RA,V:Balloonman. 35.00
25 RA,V:Chemo 35.00
26 RA,V:Metal Mods. 35.00

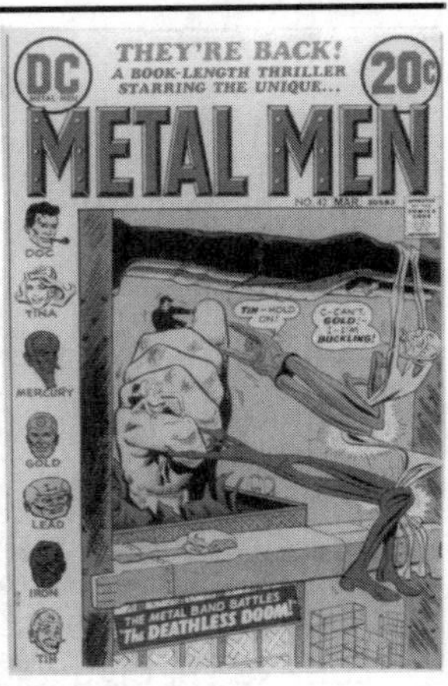

Metal Men #42 © DC Comics, Inc.

27 RA,O:Metal Men,rtd 50.00
28 RA. 35.00
29 RA,V:Robot Eater 35.00
30 RA,GK,in the Forbidden Zone . 35.00
31 RA,GK. 25.00
32 RA,Robot Amazon Blues 20.00
33 MS,The Hunted Metal Men . . . 20.00
34 MS 20.00
35 MS 20.00
36 MS,The Cruel Clowns 20.00
37 MS,To walk among Men. 20.00
38 MS 20.00
39 MS,Beauty of the Beast 20.00
40 MS 20.00
41 MS 20.00
42 RA,reprint 12.00
43 RA,reprint 12.00
44 RA,reprint,V:Missile Men 12.00
45 WS 12.00
46 WS,V:Chemo. 12.00
47 WS,V:Plutonium Man. 12.00
48 WS,A:Eclipso. 15.00
49 WS,A:Eclipso. 15.00
50 WS,JSa 10.00
51 JSn,V:Vox 10.00
52 JSn,V:Brain Children 10.00
53 JA(c),V:Brain Children 10.00
54 JSn,A:Green Lantern 10.00
55 JSn,A:Green Lantern 10.00
56 JSn,V:Inheritor. 10.00

[Limited Series] 1993–94

1 DJu,BBr,Foil(c) 5.00
2 DJu,BBr,O:Metal Men 3.00
3 DJu,BBr,V:Missile Men 3.00
4 DJu,BBr,final issue 3.00

METAMORPHO

July–Aug., 1965

[Regular Series]

1 A:Kurt Vornok 100.00
2 Terror from the Telstar. 60.00
3 Who stole the USA 60.00
4 V:Cha-Cha Chaves. 40.00
5 V:Bulark 40.00
6 . . . . 40.00
7 thru 9 . . . . @35.00
10 I:Element Girl. 45.00
11 thru 17 March-April, 1968 . . . @20.00

[Limited Series]

1 GN,V:The Orb of Ra 2.00
2 GN,A:Metamorpho's Son 2.00
3 GN,V:Elemental Man 2.00
4 GN,final Issue. 2.00

 All comics prices listed are for *Near Mint* condition.

METROPOLIS S.C.U.
Nov., 1994
1 Special Police unit 2.00
2 Eco-terror in Metropolis 2.00
3 Superman 2.00
4 final issue 2.00

MICHAEL MOORCOCK'S MULTIVERSE
DC/Helix (Sept., 1997)
1 WS,three stories, inc. Eternal Champion adapt. 2.50
2 WS,Eternal Champion 2.50
3 WS,Moonbeams & Roses 2.50
4 WS,Moonbeams & Roses 2.50
5 . . . . 2.50
6 Duke Elric. 2.50
7 Metatemporal Detective 2.50
8 Castle Silverskin 2.50
9 Duke Elric. 2.50
10 Eternal Champion 2.50
11 WS, Silverskin 2.50
12 WS, concl. 2.50
TPB rep. #1–#12 . . . . 19.95

MILLENNIUM
Jan., 1988
1 JSa,SEt, The Plan 2.00
2 JSa,SEt, The Chosen 2.00
3 JSa,SEt, Reagen/Manhunters . . . 2.00
4 JSa,SEt, Mark Shaw/Batman . . . 2.00
5 JSa,SEt, The CHosen. 2.00
6 JSa,SEt, Superman 2.00
7 JSa,SEt, Boster Gold 2.00
8 JSa,SEt,I:New Guardians 2.00

MILLENNIUM FEVER
1995–96
1 Young Love 2.50
2 Nightmares Worsen 2.50
3 Worst Nightmare 2.50
4 . . . . 2.50

MINX, THE
DC/Vertigo (Aug., 1998)
1 PrM,SeP,The Chosen, pt.1 . . . . . 2.50
2 PrM,SeP,The Chosen, pt.2 . . . . . 2.50
3 PrM,SeP,The Chosen, pt.3 . . . . . 2.50
4 PrM,SeP,Monkey Quartet,pt.1 . . . 2.50
5 PrM,SeP,Monkey Quartet,pt.2 . . . 2.50
6 PrM,SeP,Monkey Quartet,pt.3 . . . 2.50
7 PrM,SeP,Monkey Quartet,pt.4 . . . 2.50
8 PrM,SeP,final issue. 2.50

MISTER E
1991
1 (From Books of Magic) 2.00
2 A:The Shadower. 2.00
3 A:The Shadower. 2.00
4 A:Tim Hunter, Dr. Fate, Phantom Stranger, final issue 2.00

MISTER MIRACLE
1971–78
1 JK,I:Mr.Miracle 38.00
2 JK,I:Granny Goodness 20.00
3 JK,`Paraniod Pill' 20.00
4 JK,I:Barda 25.00
5 JK,I:Vermin Vundabar 25.00
6 JK,I:Female Furies 25.00
7 JK,V:Kanto 25.00
8 JK,V:Lump 25.00
9 JK,O:Mr.Miracle,C:Darkseid . . . 15.00
10 JK,A:Female Furies 15.00
11 JK,V:Doctor Bedlum. 15.00

Mister Miracle #18 © DC Comics, Inc.

12 JK 15.00
13 JK 15.00
14 JK 15.00
15 JK,O:Shilo Norman 15.00
16 JK 15.00
17 JK 15.00
18 JK,W:Mr.Miracle & Barda 15.00
19 MR,NA,DG,TA,JRu,AM 15.00
20 MR 7.00
21 MR 7.00
22 MR 7.00
23 MG 7.00
24 MG,RH 7.00
25 MG,RH 7.00
Spec.#1 SR 3.50

[2nd Series] 1989–91
1 IG. 2.50
2 IG. 2.00
3 IG,A:Highfather,Forever People . 2.00
4 IG,A:The Dark,Forever People . . 2.00
5 IG,V:TheDark,A:ForeverPeople. . 2.00
6 A:G.L. Gnort. 2.00
7 A:Blue Beetle,Booster Gold 2.00
8 RM,A:Blue Beetle,Booster Gold . 2.00
9 I:Maxi-Man 2.00
10 V:Maxi-Man 2.00
11. . . . . 2.00
12 . . . . 2.00
13 Manga Khan Saga begins, A:L-Ron,A:Lobo 3.00
14 A:Lobo. 2.50
15 Manga Khan contd 2.00
16 MangaKhan cont.,JLA#39tie-in . 2.00
17 On Apokolips,A:Darkseid 2.00
18 On Apokolips 2.00
19 Return to Earth, contd from JLA#42. . . . . 2.00
20 IG,Oberon 2.00
21 Return of Shilo. 2.00
22 New Mr.Miracle revealed 2.00
23 Secrets of the 2 Mr. Miracles revealed, A:Mother Box 2.00
24 . . . . 2.00
25 . . . . 2.00
26 Monster Party,pt.1 . . . . 2.00
27 Monster Party,pt.2, A:Justice League 2.00
28 final issue 2.00

MISTER MIRACLE
1996
1 JK, new mythology 2.00
2 V:Justice League 2.00
2 How can Scott Free save Big Barda. 2.00
3 accepts his powers 2.00
4 corruption throughout the cosmos 2.00
5 SCr 2.00
6 SCr 2.00
7 final issue. 2.00
TPB Jack Kirby's Mister Miracle . . 13.00

MR. DISTRICT ATTORNEY
Jan.–Feb., 1948
1 The Innocent Forger 850.00
2 The Richest Man In Prison . . . 350.00
3 The Honest Convicts 250.00
4 The Merchant of Death 250.00
5 The Booby-Trap Killer 250.00
6 The D.A. Meets Scotland Yard 200.00
7 The People vs. Killer Kane . . . 200.00
8 The Rise and Fall of 'Lucky' Lynn 200.00
9 The Case of the Living Counterfeit 200.00
10 The D.A. Takes a Vacation. . . 150.00
11 The Game That Has No Winners 150.00
12 Fake Accident Racket 150.00
13 The Execution of Caesar Larsen 150.00
14 The Innocent Man In Murderers' Row 150.00
15 Prison Train 150.00
16 The Wire Tap Crimes 150.00
17 The Bachelor of Crime 150.00
18 The Case of the Twelve O'Clock Killer 150.00
19 The Four King's Of Crime . . . 150.00
20 You Catch a Killer 150.00
21 I Was A Killer's Bodyguard. . . 100.00
22 The Marksman of Crime. 100.00
23 Diary of a Criminal 100.00
24 The Killer In The Iron Mask . . 100.00
25 I Hired My Killer 100.00
26 The Case of the Wanted Criminals 100.00
27 The Case of the Secret Six . . 100.00
28 Beware the Bogus Beggars . . 100.00
29 The Crimes of Mr. Jumbo. . . . 100.00
30 Man of a Thousand Faces . . . 100.00
31 The Hot Money Gang. 100.00
32 The Case o/t Bad Luck Clues. 100.00
33 A Crime Is Born 100.00
34 The Amazing Crimes of Mr. X 100.00
35 This Crime For Hire 100.00
36 The Chameleon of Crime. . . . 100.00
37 Miss Miller's Big Case 100.00
38 The Puzzle Shop For Crime. . 100.00
39 Man Who Killed Daredevils . . 100.00
40 The Human Vultures 100.00
41 The Great Token Take 100.00
42 Super-Market Sleuth 100.00
43 Hotel Detective 100.00
44 S.S. Justice,B:Comics Code . . 75.00
45 Miss Miller, Widow 75.00
46 Mr. District Attorney, Public Defender 75.00
47 The Missing Persons Racket . . 75.00
48 Manhunt With the Mounties . . . 75.00
49 The TV Dragnet. 75.00
50 The Case of Frank Bragan, Little Shot. 75.00
51 The Big Heist. 75.00
52 Crooked Wheels of Fortune . . . 75.00
53 The Courtroom Patrol 75.00
54 The Underworld Spy Squad . . . 75.00
55 The Flying Saucer Mystery . . . 75.00
56 The Underworld Oracle 75.00
57 The Underworld Employment Agency. 75.00
58 The Great Bomb Scare 75.00

DC COMICS

59 Great Underworld Spy Plot . . . 75.00
60 The D.A.'s TV Rival 75.00
61 SMo(c),Architect of Crime 75.00
62 A-Bombs For Sale 75.00
63 The Flying Prison. 75.00
64 SMo(c),The Underworld Treasure Hunt 75.00
65 SMo(c),World Wide Dragnet . . 75.00
66 SMo(c),The Secret of the D.A.'s Diary 75.00
67 Jan.–Feb., 1959. . . . . 75.00

MR. PUNCH

HC DMc,NGa,Nightmarish tale, 1994 . . . . 24.95

MOBFIRE
1994–95

1 WaP,Gangsters in London 2.50
2 WaP, ... 2.50
3 WaP,The Bocor. 2.50
4 WaP,V:Bocor 2.50
5 WaP,Voice in My Head 2.50
6 WaP,Genetic Babies, final issue . 2.50

MODESTY BLAISE

1 DG,V:Gabriel 4.95
2 DG,V:Gabriel 4.95
GN Spy Thriller. 19.95

MOONSHADOW
Vertigo 1994–95

1 JMD(s),JMu,rep. 2.25
2 thru 4 JMD . . . . @2.25
5 fully painted 2.25
6 . . . . 2.25
7 F:Shady Lady. 2.25
8 Rep. Search for Ira 2.25
9 JMD,JMu,A:Tittletat Twins. 2.25
10 JMD,JMu,Interplanetary Prostitutes 2.25
11 JMu,Ira's life story 2.25
12 Rep. w/6pg new material 2.95

MORE FUN COMICS
(See: NEW FUN COMICS)

Ms. Tree Quarterly #2
© DC Comics, Inc.

MOVIE COMICS
April, 1939

1 'Gunga Din' 3,000.00
2 Stagecoach 1,800.00
3 East Side of Heaven 1,400.00
4 Captain Fury,B:Oregon Trail. 1,100.00
5 Man in the Iron Mask 1,100.00
6 Sept., 1939 . . . . 1,500.00

MS. TREE QUARTERLY

1 MGr,A:Batman 3.50
2 A:Butcher 2.95
3 A:Butcher 2.95
4 'Paper Midnight' 3.95
5 Murder/Rape Investigation 3.95
6 Gothic House 3.95
7 . . . . 3.95
8 CI,FMc,Ms Tree Pregnant(c), B.U. King Faraday 3.95
9 Child Kidnapped 3.95
10 V:International Mob 3.50

MUKTUK WOLFSBREATH: HARD-BOILED SHAMAN
DC/Vertigo (June, 1998)

1 (of 3) TLa,SvP,lady shaman 2.50
2 . . . . 2.50
3 TLa,SvP, concl.. . . . . 2.50

MUTT AND JEFF
1939

1 . . . . 1,200.00
2 . . . . 650.00
3 Bucking Broncos. 500.00
4 and 5 . . . . @450.00
6 thru 10 . . . . @200.00
11 thru 20 . . . . @125.00
21 thru 30 . . . . @100.00
31 thru 50 . . . . @70.00
51 thru 70 . . . . @50.00
71 thru 80 . . . . @40.00
81 thru 99 . . . . @35.00
100 . . . . 40.00
101 thru 103 . . . . @35.00
104 thru 148 . . . . @25.00

MY GREATEST ADVENTURE
Jan.–Feb., 1955

1 LSt,I Was King Of Danger Island 1,300.00
2 My Million Dollar Dive 600.00
3 I Found Captain Kidd's Treasure 375.00
4 I Had A Date With Doom 375.00
5 I Escaped From Castle Morte . 350.00
6 I Had To Spend A Million 350.00
7 I Was A Prisoner On Island X . 325.00
8 The Day They Stole My Face . 325.00
9 I Walked Through The Doors of Destiny. 325.00
10 We Found A World Of Tiny Cavemen 325.00
11 LSt(c),My Friend, Madcap Manning. 250.00
12 MMe(c),I Hunted Big Game in Outer Space 250.00
13 LSt(c),I Hunted Goliath The Robot 250.00
14 LSt,I Had the Midas Touch of Gold. 250.00
15 JK, I Hunted the Worlds Wildest Animals 250.00
16 JK,I Died a Thousand Times . 250.00
17 JK,I Doomed the World 250.00
18 JK(c),We Discovered The Edge of the World. 250.00

My Greatest Adventure #40
© DC Comics, Inc.

19 I Caught Earth's Strangest Criminal 250.00
20 JK,I Was Big-Game on Neptune 250.00
21 JK,We Were Doomed By The Metal-Eating Monster. . . 250.00
22 I Was Trapped In The Magic Mountains 200.00
23 I Was A Captive In Space Prison 200.00
24 NC(c),I Was The Robinson Crusoe of Space. 200.00
25 I Led Earth's Strangest Safari! 200.00
26 NC(c),We Battled The Sand Creature 200.00
27 I Was the Earth's First Exile . . 200.00
28 I Stalked the Camouflage Creatures 250.00
29 I Tracked the Forbidden Powers 150.00
30 We Cruised Into the Supernatural! 150.00
31 I Was A Modern Hercules . . . 125.00
32 We Were Trapped In A Freak Valley! 125.00
33 I Was Pursued by the Elements 125.00
34 DD,We Unleashed The Cloud Creatures 125.00
35 I Solved the Mystery of Volcano Valley 125.00
36 I Was Bewitched By Lady Doom 125.00
37 DD&SMo(c),I Hunted the Legendary Creatures! 125.00
38 DD&SMo(c),I Was the Slave of the Dream-Master. 125.00
39 DD&SMo(c),We were Trapped in the Valley of no Return . . . 125.00
40 WeBattled the StormCreature 125.00
41 DD&SMo(c),I Was Tried by a Robot Court 100.00
42 DD&SMo(c),My Brother Was a Robot 100.00
43 DD&SMo(c),I Fought the Sonar Creatures 100.00
44 DD&SMo(c),We Fought the Beasts of Petrified Island . . . 100.00
45 DD&SMo(c),We Battled the Black Narwahl 100.00
46 DD&SMo(c),We Were Prisoners of the Sundial of Doom 100.00
47 We Became Partners of the

 All comics prices listed are for *Near Mint* condition.

Beast Brigade. 100.00
48 DD&SMo(c),I Was Marooned
On Earth 100.00
49 DD&SMo(c),I Was An Ally
Of A Criminal Creature 100.00
50 DD&SMo(c),I Fought the
Idol King. 100.00
51 DD&SMo(c),We Unleashed
the Demon of the Dungeon. . . 85.00
52 DD&SMo(c),I Was A
Stand-In For an Alien 85.00
53 DD&SMo(c),I, Creature Slayer . 85.00
54 I Was Cursed With
an Alien Pal 85.00
55 DD&SMo(c),I Beacame The
Wonder-Man of Space 85.00
56 DD&SMo(c),My Brother-The
Alien. 85.00
57 DD&SMo(c),Don't Touch Me
Or You'll Die 85.00
58 DD&SMo(c),ATh,I was Trapped
in the Land of L'Oz 100.00
59 DD&SMo(c),Listen Earth-I
Am Still Alive 100.00
60 DD&SMo(c),ATh,I Lived in
Two Worlds 100.00
61 DD&SMo(c),ATh,I Battled For
the Doom-Stone 100.00
62 DD&SMo(c),I Fought For
An Alien Enemy 50.00
63 DD&SMo(c),We Braved the
Trail of the Ancient Warrior . . . 50.00
64 DD&SMo(c),They Crowned My
Fiance Their King! 50.00
65 DD&SMo(c),I Lost the Life
or Death Secret 50.00
66 DD&SMo(c),I Dueled with
the Super Spirits. 50.00
67 I Protected the Idols
of Idoro! 50.00
68 DD&SMo(c),My Deadly Island
of Space. 50.00
69 DD&SMo(c),I Was A Courier
From the Past 50.00
70 DD&SMo(c),We Tracked the
Fabled Fish-Man! 50.00
71 We Dared to open the Door
of Danger Dungeon 50.00
72 The Haunted Beach. 50.00
73 I Defeiller Mountain 50.00
74 GC(c),We Were Challenged
By The River Spirit 50.00
75 GC(c),Castaway Cave-Men
of 1950. . . . . 50.00
76 MMe(c),We Battled the
Micro-Monster 50.00
77 ATh,We Found the Super-
Tribes of Tomorrow. 55.00
78 Destination-'Dead Man's Alley'. 50.00
79 Countdown in Dinosaur Valley . 50.00
80 BP,I:Doom Patrol 400.00
81 BP,ATh,I:Dr. Janus 160.00
82 BP,F:Doom Patrol 150.00
83 BP,F:Doom Patrol 150.00
84 BP,V:General Immortus 150.00
85 BP,ATh,F:Doom Patrol 150.00
Becomes:

DOOM PATROL

March, 1964

86 BP,I:Brogherhood of Evil 100.00
87 BP,O:Negative Man 80.00
88 BP,O:Chief. 75.00
89 BP,I:Animal-Veg.-MineralMan. . 75.00
90 BP,A:Brotherhood of Evil 75.00
91 BP,I:Manto, Gargvax 75.00
92 BP,I:Dr.Tyme, A:Mento 75.00
93 BP,A:Brotherhood of Evil 75.00
94 BP,I:Dr.Radich, The Claw. 75.00
95 BP,A:Animal-Vegetable
-Mineral Man 75.00
96 BP,A:General Immortus,
Brotherhood of Evil. 70.00
97 BP,A:General Immortus,
Brotherhood of Evil. 70.00
98 BP,I:Mr.103 . . . . 70.00
99 I:Beast Boy 80.00
100 BP,O:Beast Boy,Robotman. . 100.00
101 BP,A:Beast Boy 50.00
102 BP,A:Beast Boy,Challengers
of the Unknown 45.00
103 BP,A:Beast Boy 45.00
104 BP,W:Elasti-Girl,Mento,
C:JLA,Teen Titans 45.00
105 BP,A:Beast Boy 45.00
106 BP,O:Negative Man 45.00
107 BP,A:Beast Boy, I:Dr.Death . . 45.00
108 BP,A:Brotherhood of Evil 45.00
109 BP,I:Mandred 45.00
110 BP,A:Garguax,Mandred,
Brotherhood of Evil. 40.00
111 BP,I:Zarox-13,A:Brotherhood
of Evil. 40.00
112 BP,O:Beast Boy,Madame
Rouge 40.00
113 BP,A:Beast Boy,Mento 40.00
114 BP,A:Beast Boy 40.00
115 BP,A:Beast Boy 40.00
116 BP,A:Madame Rouge 40.00
117 BP,I:Black Vulture. 40.00
118 BP,A:Beast Boy 40.00
119 BP,A:Madam Rouge. 40.00
120 I:Wrecker. 40.00
121 JO,D:Doom Patrol 100.00
122 rep.Doom Patrol #89 . . . . 5.00
123 rep.Doom Patrol #95 . . . . 5.00
124 rep.Doom Patrol #90 . . . . 5.00

[2nd Series]
See: DOOM PATROL

MY NAME IS CHAOS

1992

1 JRy,Song Laid Waste to Earth . . 4.95
2 JRy,Colonization of Mars 4.95
3 JRy,Search for Eternal Beings . . 4.95
4 JRy,final issue 4.95

MY NAME IS HOLOCAUST

Milestone 1995

[Mini-Series]

1 F:Holocaust (Blood Syndicate) . . 2.00
2 V:Cantano 2.00
3 A:Blood Syndicate 2.00

MYSTERY IN SPACE

April–May, 1951

1 CI&FrG(c),FF,B:Knights of the
Galaxy,Nine Worlds to
Conquer 2,800.00
2 CI(c),MA,A:Knights of the
Galaxy, Jesse James-
Highwayman of Space. . . . 1,100.00
3 CI(c),A:Knights of the
Galaxy, Duel of the Planets. . 850.00
4 CI(c),S&K,MA,A:Knights of the
Galaxy, Master of Doom 750.00
5 CI(c),A:Knights of the Galaxy,
Outcast of the Lost World . . . 750.00
6 CI(c),A:Knights of the Galaxy,
The Day the World Melted . . 550.00
7 GK(c),ATh,A:Knights of the Galaxy,
Challenge o/t Robot Knight. . 550.00
8 MA,It's a Women's World 550.00
9 MA(c),The Seven Wonders
of Space. 550.00
10 MA(c),The Last Time I
Saw Earth 550.00
11 GK(c),Unknown Spaceman . . 400.00
12 MA,The Sword in the Sky. . . . 400.00
13 MA(c),MD,Signboard
in Space. 400.00
14 MA,GK(c),Hollywood
in Space. 400.00
15 MA(c),Doom from Station X . . 400.00
16 MA(c),Honeymoon in Space. . 400.00
17 MA(c),The Last Mile of Space 400.00
18 MA(c),GK,Chain Gang
of Space. 400.00
19 MA(c),The Great
Space-Train Robbery 375.00
20 MA(c),The Man in the
Martian Mask 350.00
21 MA(c),Interplanetary
Merry- Go-Round 350.00
22 MA(c),The Square Earth 350.00
23 MA(c),Monkey-Rocket
to Mars. 350.00
24 MA(c),A:Space Cabby,
Hitchhiker of Space 350.00
25 MA(c),Station Mars on the Air 325.00
26 GK(c),Earth is the Target 325.00
27 The Human Fishbowl. 325.00
28 The Radio Planet. 325.00
29 GK(c),Space-Enemy
Number One. 325.00
30 GK(c),The Impossible
World Named Earth 325.00
31 GK(c),The Day the Earth
Split in Two. 300.00
32 GK(c),Riddle of the
Vanishing Earthmen 300.00
33 The Wooden World War. 300.00
34 GK(c),The Man Who
Moved the World 300.00
35 The Counterfeit Earth. 300.00
36 GK(c),Secret of the
Moon Sphinx 300.00
37 GK(c),Secret of the
Masked Martians 300.00
38 GK(c),The Canals of Earth. . . 300.00
39 GK(c),Sorcerers of Space . . . 300.00
40 GK(c),Riddle of the
Runaway Earth. 300.00
41 GK(c),The Miser of Space . . . 250.00
42 GK(c),The Secret of the
Skyscraper Spaceship 250.00
43 GK(c),Invaders From the
Space Satellites 250.00
44 GK(c),Amazing Space Flight
of North America 250.00
45 GK(c),MA,Flying Saucers
Over Mars 250.00

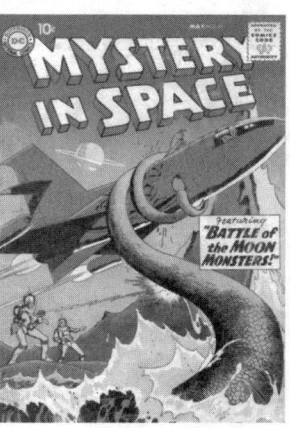

Mystery in Space #51
© DC Comics, Inc.

Mystery in Space #107
© DC Comics, Inc.

46 GK(c),MA,Mystery of the Moon Sniper. 250.00
47 GK(c),MA,Interplanetary Tug of War 250.00
48 GK(c),MA,Secret of the Scarecrow World 250.00
49 GK(c),The Sky-High Man 250.00
50 GK(c),The Runaway Space-Train 250.00
51 GK(c),MA,Battle of the Moon Monsters. 250.00
52 GK(c),MSy,Mirror Menace of Mars. 250.00
53 GK(c),B:Adam Strange stories, Menace o/t Robot Raiders . 1,700.00
54 GK(c),Invaders of the Underground World 400.00
55 GK(c),The Beast From the Runaway World 300.00
56 GK(c),The Menace of the Super-Atom 200.00
57 GK(c),Mystery of the Giant Footsteps 200.00
58 GK(c),Chariot in in the Sky. . . 200.00
59 GK(c),The Duel of the Two Adam Stranges 200.00
60 GK(c),The Attack of the Tentacle World 200.00
61 CI&MA(c),Threat of the Tornado Tyrant 175.00
62 CI&MA(c),The Beast with the Sizzling Blue Eyes 175.00
63 The Weapon that Swallowed Men 175.00
64 The Radioactive Menace 175.00
65 Mechanical Masters of Rann . 175.00
66 Space-Island of Peril 175.00
67 Challenge of the Giant Fireflies. 175.00
68 CI&MA(c),Fadeaway Doom . . 175.00
69 CI&MA(c),Menace of the Aqua-Ray Weapon 175.00
70 CI&MA(c),Vengeance of the Dust Devil. 175.00
71 CI&MA(c),The Challenge of the Crystal Conquerors. 175.00
72 The Multiple Menace Weapon 125.00
73 CI&MA(c),The Invisible Invaders of Rann 125.00
74 CI&MA(c),The Spaceman Who Fought Himself. 125.00
75 CI&MA(c),The Planet That Came to a Standstill 250.00
76 CI&MA(c),Challenge of the Rival Starman. 125.00
77 CI&MA(c),Ray-Gun in the Sky 125.00
78 CI&MA(c),Shadow People of the Eclipse 125.00
79 CI&MA(c),The Metal Conqueror of Rann. 125.00
80 CI&MA(c),The Deadly Shadows of Adam Strange . . 125.00
81 CI&MA(c),The Cloud-Creature That Menaced Two Worlds . . . 90.00
82 CI&MA(c),World War on Earth and Rann 90.00
83 CI&MA(c),The Emotion-Master of Space. 90.00
84 CI&MA(c),The Powerless Weapons of Adam Strange. . . 90.00
85 CI&MA(c),Riddle of the Runaway Rockets 90.00
86 CI&MA(c),Attack of the Underworld Giants 90.00
87 MA(c),The Super-Brain of Adam Strange,B:Hawkman. . 200.00
88 CI&MA(c),The Robot Wraith of Rann 175.00
89 MA(c),Siren o/t Space Ark . . . 175.00
90 CI&MA(c),Planets and Peril, E:Hawkman. 175.00
91 CI&MA(c),Puzzle of the Perilous Prisons 40.00
92 DD&SMo(c),The Alien Invasion From Earth,B:Space Ranger. . 45.00
93 DD&SMo(c),The Convict Twins of Space. 45.00
94 DD&SMo(c),The Adam Strange Story 45.00
95 The Hydra-Head From Outer Space. 45.00
96 The Coins That Doomed Two Planets 45.00
97 The Day Adam Strange Vanished 45.00
98 The Wizard of the Cosmos. . . . 45.00
99 DD&SMo(c),The World-Destroyer From Space 45.00
100 DD&SMo(c),GK,The Death of Alanna 45.00
101 GK(c),The Valley of 1,000 Dooms 45.00
102 GK,The Robot World of Rann 45.00
103 The Billion-Dollar Time-Capsule(Space Ranger),I:Ultra the Multi-Agent. 45.00
104 thru 109 . . . . @25.00
110 Sept. 1966 . . . . 25.00
111 JAp,SD,MR,DSp,Sept. 1980 . . 25.00
112 JAp,TS,JKu(c) 25.00
113 JKu(c),MGo 25.00
114 JKu(c),JCr,SD,DSp 25.00
115 JKu(c),SD,GT,BB 25.00
116 JSn(c),JCr,SD 25.00
117 DN,GT,March, 1981 . . . . 25.00

MYSTERY PLAY
Vertigo

HC GMo(s),JMu 19.95

MYTHOS: THE FINAL TOUR
DC/Vertigo Oct., 1996

1 JNR(s),GyA,PrG,F:Rock Star Adam Case 5.95
2 JNR(s),PSj,F:Rock Star Adam Case 5.95
3 JNR(s), finale 5.95

NATHANIEL DUSK
Feb., 1984

1 GC(p). 2.00
2 GC(p). 2.00
3 GC(p). 2.00
4 GC(p), May 1984 . . . . 2.00

NATHANIEL DUSK II
Oct., 1985

1 thru 4 GC,Jan., 1986. . . . . @2.00

NATIONAL COMICS
1999

1 MWa(s),AAl,F:Flash & Mr. Terrific 2.00

NAZZ, THE
1990–91

1 Michael'sBook 5.50
2 Johnny'sBook. 5.00
3 Search for Michael Nazareth. . . . 5.00
4 V:Retaliators,final issue 5.00

NEVADA
DC/Vertigo (March, 1998)

1 (of 6) SvG,SL,show girl. 2.50
2 SvG,SL,dismembered corpse . . . 2.50
3 SvG,SL,stabbed an inhuman . . . 2.50
4 SvG,SL,another dimension 2.50
5 SvG,SL 2.50
6 SvG,SL,Big Bang, concl.. . . . . . . 2.50
TPB Nevada, rep.. . . . . 15.00

NEW ADVENTURES OF SUPERBOY
(See: SUPERBOY)

NEW BOOK OF COMICS
1937

1 Dr.Occult 15,000.00
2 Dr.Occult 7,000.00

NEW COMICS
1935

1 . . . . 18,000.00
2 . . . . 7,000.00
3 thru 6 . . . . @5,000.00
7 thru 11 . . . . @4,000.00
Becomes:

NEW ADVENTURE COMICS
Jan., 1937

12 S&S 4,000.00
13 thru 20 . . . . @3,000.00
21 . . . . 2,600.00
22 thru 31 . . . . @2,200.00
Becomes:

ADVENTURE COMICS

NEW FUN COMICS
Feb., 1935

1 B:Oswald the Rabbit, Jack Woods. 40,000.00
2 . . . . 18,000.00
3 . . . . 8,500.00
4 . . . . 8,500.00
5 . . . . 8,500.00
6 S&S,B:Dr.Occult, Henri Duval 20,000.00
Becomes:

MORE FUN COMICS

7 S&S,WK 5,200.00
8 S&S,WK 5,000.00
9 S&S,E:Henri Duval. 6,000.00

More Fun #40 © DC Comics, Inc.

10 S&S 3,500.00
11 S&S,B:Calling all Girls 3,200.00
12 S&S 2,800.00
13 S&S 2,800.00
14 S&S,Color,Dr.Occult 13,000.00
15 S&S 4,800.00
16 S&S,Christmas(c) 4,800.00
17 S&S 4,500.00
18 S&S 2,000.00
19 S&S 2,000.00
20 HcK,S&S 2,000.00
21 S&S 1,900.00
22 S&S 1,900.00
23 S&S 1,900.00
24 S&S 1,900.00
25 S&S 1,700.00
26 S&S 1,700.00
27 S&S 1,700.00
28 S&S 1,700.00
29 S&S 1,700.00
30 S&S 1,700.00
31 S&S 1,700.00
32 S&S,E:Dr. Occult. 1,700.00
33 . . . . 1,700.00
34 . . . . 1,700.00
35 . . . . 1,700.00
36 B:Masked Ranger 1,700.00
37 thru 40 . . . . @1,700.00
41 E:Masked Ranger 1,300.00
42 thru 50 . . . . @1,300.00
51 I:The Spectre 5,000.00
52 O:The Spectre,pt.1,
E:Wing Brady 55,000.00
53 O:The Spectre,pt.2,
B:Capt.Desmo 35,000.00
54 E:King Carter,Spectre(c) . . . 9,000.00
55 I:Dr.Fate,E:Bulldog Martin,
Spectre(c) 12,000.00
56 B:Congo Bill,Dr.Fate(c) 4,500.00
57 Spectre(c). 3,000.00
58 Spectre(c). 3,000.00
59 A:Spectre 2,800.00
60 Spectre(c). 3,000.00
61 Spectre(c). 2,800.00
62 Spectre(c). 2,700.00
63 Spectre(c),E:St.Bob Neal . . 2,700.00
64 Spectre(c),B:Lance Larkin . . 2,700.00
65 Spectre(c). 2,700.00
66 Spectre(c). 2,700.00
67 Spectre(c),O:Dr. Fate,
E:Congo Bill,Biff Bronson . . 6,500.00
68 Dr.Fate(c),B:Clip Carson . . . 2,000.00
69 Dr.Fate(c) 2,000.00
70 Dr.Fate(c),E:Lance Larkin . . 2,000.00
71 Dr.Fate(c),I:Johnny Quick . . 5,000.00
72 Dr. Fate has Smaller Helmet,
E:Sgt. Carey,Sgt.O'Malley . 1,800.00
73 Dr.Fate(c),I:Aquaman,Green
Arrow,Speedy 12,000.00
74 Dr.Fate(c),A:Aquaman. 2,000.00
75 Dr.Fate(c) 1,800.00
76 Dr.Fate(c),MMe,E:Clip Carson,
B:Johnny Quick 1,800.00
77 MMe,Green Arrow(c). 1,800.00
78 MMe,Green Arrow(c). 1,800.00
79 MMe,Green Arrow(c). 1,800.00
80 MMe,Green Arrow(c). 1,800.00
81 MMe,Green Arrow(c). 1,000.00
82 MMe,Green Arrow(c). 1,000.00
83 MMe,Green Arrow(c). 1,000.00
84 MMe,Green Arrow(c). 1,100.00
85 MMe,Green Arrow(c). 1,000.00
86 MMe 1,000.00
87 MMe,E:Radio Squad 1,000.00
88 MMe,Green Arrow(c). 1,000.00
89 MMe,O:Gr.Arrow&Speedy . . 1,200.00
90 MMe,Green Arrow(c). 1,000.00
91 MMe,Green Arrow(c) 750.00
92 MMe,Green Arrow(c) 750.00
93 MMe,B:Dover & Clover 750.00
94 MMe,Green Arrow(c) 750.00
95 MMe,Green Arrow(c) 750.00
96 MMe,Green Arrow(c) 750.00
97 MMe,JKu,E:Johnny Quick . . . 750.00
98 E:Dr. Fate 750.00
99 Green Arrow(c) 750.00
100 Anniversary Issue 1,000.00
101 O&I:Superboy,
E:The Spectre 7,500.00
102 A:Superboy. 1,000.00
103 A:Superboy 800.00
104 Superboy(c). 650.00
105 Superboy(c). 650.00
106 . . . . 650.00
107 E:Superboy 650.00
108 A:Genius Jones,`Genius
Meets Genius' 150.00
109 A:Genius Jones, The
Disappearing Deposits 150.00
110 A:Genius Jones, Birds,
Brains and Burglary 150.00
111 A:Genius Jones, Jeepers
Creepers 150.00
112 A:Genius Jones, The
Tell-Tale Tornado 150.00
113 A:Genius Jones, Clocks
and Shocks 150.00
114 A:Genius Jones, The
Milky Way. 150.00
115 A:Genius Jones,Foolish
Questions. 150.00
116 A:Genius Jones,Palette
For Plunder 150.00
117 A:Genius Jones,Battle of
the Pretzel Benders 150.00
118 A:Genius Jones,The
Sinister Siren 150.00
119 A:Genius Jones,A
Perpetual Jackpot. 150.00
120 A:Genius Jones,The Man
in the Moon 150.00
121 A:Genius Jones,The
Mayor Goes Haywire 125.00
122 A:Genius Jones,When Thug-
Hood Was In Floor 125.00
123 A:Genius Jones,Hi Diddle
Diddle, the Cat and the Fiddle. . . . .
. . . . 125.00
124 A:Genius Jones,
The Zany Zoo. 125.00
125 Genius Jones,
Impossible But True 575.00
126 A:Genius Jones,The Case
of the Gravy Spots 125.00
127 Nov.–Dec., 1947 . . . . 225.00

NEW GODS, THE
Feb.–March, 1971

1 JK,I:Orion 60.00
2 JK 30.00
3 JK 25.00
4 JK,O:Manhunter, rep. 16.00
5 JK,I:Fastbak & Black Racer . . . 16.00
6 JK 16.00
7 JK,O:Orion 16.00
8 JK 16.00
9 JK,I:Forager 16.00
10 JK 16.00
11 JK 16.00
12 DN,DA,R:New Gods 6.00
13 DN,DA. 6.00
14 DN,DA. 6.00
15 RB,BMc. 6.00
16 DN,DA. 6.00
17 DN,DA. 6.00
18 DN,DA. 6.00
19 DN,DA. 6.00

NEW GODS
(Reprints) 1984

1 JK reprint 2.25
2 JK reprint 2.00
3 JK reprint 2.00
4 JK reprint 2.00
5 JK reprint 2.00
6 JK rep.+NewMaterial 2.00

NEW GODS
[2nd Series] 1989

1 From Cosmic Odyssey 2.00
2 A:Orion of New Genesis 2.00
3 A:Orion. 2.00
4 Renegade Apokolyptian Insect
Colony 2.00
5 Orion vs. Forager 2.00
6 A:Eve Donner, Darkseid 2.00
7 Bloodline #1 . . . . 2.00
8 Bloodline #2 . . . . 2.00
9 Bloodline #3 . . . . 2.00
10 Bloodline #4 . . . . 2.00
11 Bloodline #5. . . . . 2.00
12 Bloodlines #6. . . . . 2.00
13 Back on Earth 2.00
14 I:Reflektor 2.00
15 V:Serial Killer. 2.00
16 A:Fastbak & Metron 2.00
17 A:Darkseid, Metron 2.00

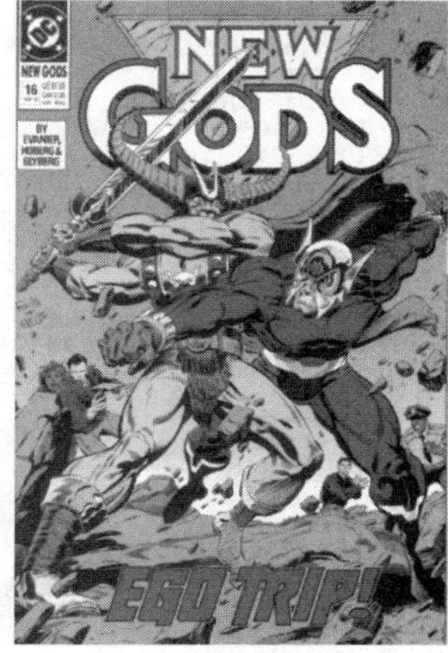

New Gods, 2nd Series #16
© DC Comics, Inc.

18 A:YugaKhan,Darkseid,
Moniters 2.00
19 V:Yuga Khan 2.00
20 Darkseid Dethroned,
V:Yuga Khan 2.00
21 A:Orion 2.00
22 A:Metron 2.00
23 A:Forever People 2.00
24 A:Forever People 2.00
25 The Pact #1,R:Infinity Man 2.00
26 The Pact #2 . . . . 2.00
27 Asault on Apokolips,Pact#3 . . . . 2.00
28 Pact #4, final issue 2.00

[3rd Series] 1995–97

1 F:Orion vs. Darkseid 2.00
2 RaP,UnderworldUnleashed tie-in. 2.00
3 RaP,Darkseid destroyed 2.00
4 RaP,F:Lightray 2.00
5 RaP,F:Orion 2.00
6 . . . . 2.00
7 RaP,R:Darkseid 2.00
8 RaP,DZ,F:Highfather,Darkseid . . 2.00
9 thru 11 . . . . @2.00
12 JBy,BWi,F:Metron 2.00
13 JBy,BWi,Orion reappears
on Earth 2.00
14 JBy,BWi,A:Forever People,
Lightray 2.00
TPB rep. #1–#11,b&w 12.00
Secret Files #1 KK,JBy 5.00

NEW GUARDIANS

1988–89

1 JSon,from Millenium series 3.00
2 JSon,Colombian Drug Cartel . . . 2.00
3 JSon,in South Africa,
V:Janwillem's Army 2.00
4 JSon,V:Neo-Nazi Skinheads
in California 2.00
5 JSon,Tegra Kidnapped 2.00
6 JSon, In China, Invasion x-over . 2.00
7 JSon, Guardians Return Home . . 2.00
8 JSon, V:Janwillem 2.00
9 JSon, A:Tome Kalmaku,
V:Janwillem 2.00
10 JSon, A:Tome Kalmaku 2.00
11 PB,Janwillem's secret 2.00
12 PB,New Guardians Future
revealed, final issue 2.00

NEW TEEN TITANS

Nov., 1980

1 GP,RT,V:Gordanians (see DC
Comics Presents #26 . . . . 12.00
2 GP,RT,I:Deathstroke the
Terminator, I&D:Ravager 12.00
3 GP,I:Fearsome Five 4.00
4 GP,RT,A:JLA,O:Starfire 5.00
5 CS,RT,O:Raven,I:Trigon 5.00
6 GP,V:Trigon,O:Raven 3.00
7 GP,RT,O:Cyborg 4.00
8 GP,RT,A Day in the Life 3.00
9 GP,RT,A:Terminator,
V:Puppeteer 4.00
10 GP,RT,A:Terminator 5.00
11 GP,RT,V:Hyperion 3.00
12 GP,RT,V:Titans of Myth 3.00
13 GP,RT,R:Robotman 3.00
14 GP,RT,I:New Brotherhood of
Evil,V:Zahl and Rouge 3.00
15 GP,RT,D:Madame Rouge 3.00
16 GP,RT,I:Captain Carrot 3.00
17 GP,RT,I:Frances Kane 3.00
18 GP,RT,A:Orig.Starfire 3.00
19 GP,RT,A:Hawkman 3.00
20 GP,RT,V:Disruptor 3.00
21 GP,RT,GC,I:Brother Blood,
Night Force 3.00
22 GP,RT,V:Brother Blood 2.50

New Teen Titans #19
© DC Comics, Inc.

23 GP,RT,I:Blackfire 2.50
24 GP,RT,A:Omega Men,I:X-hal . . . 2.50
25 GP,RT,A:Omega Men 2.50
26 GP,RT,I:Terra,Runaway #1 . . . . . 2.50
27 GP,RT,A:Speedy,Runaway #2 . . 2.50
28 GP,RT,V:Terra 3.00
29 GP,RT,V:Broth.of Evil 2.00
30 GP,RT,V:Broth.of Evil,J:Terra . . . 2.00
31 GP,RT,V:Broth.of Evil 2.00
32 GP,RT,I:Thunder & Lightning . . . 2.00
33 GP,I:Trident 2.00
34 GP,V:The Terminator 3.00
35 KP,RT,V:Mark Wright 2.00
36 KP,RT,A:Thunder & Lightning . . . 2.00
37 GP,RT,A:Batman/Outsiders(x-over
BATO#5),V:Fearsome Five 2.00
38 GP,O:Wonder Girl 2.00
39 GP,Grayson quits as Robin 5.00
40 GP,A:Brother Blood 2.00
Ann.#1 GP,RT,Blackfire 3.50
Ann.#2 GP,I:Vigilante 3.00
Ann.#3 GP,DG,D:Terra,A:Deathstroke
V:The H.I.V.E.. . . . . 3.50
Ann.#4 rep.Direct Ann.#1 . . . . 2.00
TPB Judas Contract rep.#39-#44,
Ann.#3,new GP(c) 14.95

[Special Issues]

Keebler:GP,DG,Drugs 2.50
Beverage:Drugs,RA 2.50
IBM:Drugs 3.00
Becomes:

TALES OF THE TEEN TITANS

1984–88

41 GP,A:Brother Blood 2.00
42 GP,DG,V:Deathstroke 5.00
43 GP,DG,V:Deathstroke 5.00
44 GP,DG,I:Nightwing,O:Deathstroke
Joe Wilson becomes Jericho . 10.00
45 GP,A:Aqualad,V:The H.I.V.E. . . . 2.00
46 GP,A:Aqualad,V:The H.I.V.E. . . . 2.00
47 GP,A:Aqualad,V:The H.I.V.E. . . . 2.00
48 SR,V:The Recombatants 2.00
49 GP,CI,V:Dr.Light,A:Flash 2.00
50 GP/DG W:Wonder Girl & Terry
Long,C:Batman, Wonder
Woman 2.50
51 RB,A:Cheshire 2.00
52 RB,A:Cheshire 2.00
53 RB,I:Ariel,A:Terminator 2.50
54 RB,A:Terminator 2.50
55 A:Terminator 2.50
56 A:Fearsome Five 2.00
57 A:Fearsome Five 2.00
58 E:MWn(s),A:Fearsome Five 2.00
59 rep. DC presennts #26 . . . . 2.00
60 thru 91 rep. . . . . @2.00

[Limited Series]

1 GP,O:Cyborg 2.00
2 GP,O:Raven 2.00
3 GD,O:Changling 2.00
4 GP/EC,O:Starfire 2.00

NEW TEEN TITANS

[Direct sales series]

Aug., 1984

1 B:MWn(s),GP,L:Raven 4.00
2 GP,D:Azareth,A:Trigon 3.00
3 GP,V:Raven 3.00
4 GP,V:Trigon,Raven 3.00
5 GP,D:Trigon,Raven disappears . . 3.00
6 GP,A:Superman,Batman 2.50
7 JL,V:Titans of Myth 2.50
8 JL,V:Titans of Myth 2.50
9 JL,V:Titans of Myth,I:Kole 2.50
10 JL,O:Kole 2.50
11 JL,O:Kole 2.50
12 JL,Ghost story 2.50
13 EB,Crisis 2.25
14 EB,Crisis 2.25
15 EB,A:Raven 2.25
16 EB,A:OmegaMen 2.25
17 EB,V:Blackfire 2.25
18 E:MWn(s),EB,V:Blackfire 2.25
19 EB,V:Mento 2.25
20 GP(c),EB,V:Cheshire,J.Todd . . . 2.25
21 GP(c),EB,V:Cheshire,J.Todd . . . 2.25
22 GP(c),EB,V:Blackfire,Mento,
Brother Blood 2.25
23 GP(c),V:Blackfire 2.25
24 CB,V:Hybrid 2.25
25 EB,RT,V:Hybrid,Mento,A:Flash . . 2.25
26 KGa,V:Mento 2.25
27 KGa,Church of Br.Blood 2.00
28 EB,RT,V:BrotherBlood,A:Flash . . 2.00
29 EB,RT,V:Brother Blood,
A:Flash,Robin 2.00
30 EB,Batman,Superman 2.25
31 EB,RT,V:Brother Blood,A:Flash
Batman,Robin,Gr.Lantern Corps
Superman 2.00
32 EB,RT,Murder Weekend 2.00
33 EB,V:Terrorists 2.00
34 EB,RT,V:Mento,Hybird 2.00
35 PB,RT,V:Arthur & Eve 2.00
36 EB,RT,I:Wildebeest 2.50
37 EB,RT,V:Wildebeest 2.00
38 EB,RT,A:Infinity 2.00
39 EB,RT,F:Raven 2.00
40 EB,RT,V:Gentleman Ghost 2.00
41 EB,V:Wildebeest,A:Puppeteer,
Trident,Wildebeest 2.00
42 EB,RT,V:Puppeteer,Gizmo,
Trident,Wildebeest 2.00
43 CS,RT,V:Phobia 2.00
44 RT,V:Godiva 2.00
45 EB,RT,A:Dial H for Hero 2.00
46 EB,RT,A:Dial H for Hero 2.00
47 O:Titans,C:Wildebeest 2.00
48 EB,RT,A:Red Star 2.00
49 EB,RT,A:Red Star 2.00
Ann.#1 A:Superman,V:Brainiac 2.50
Ann.#2 JBy,JL,O:Brother Blood 3.00
Ann.#3 I:Danny Chase 2.50
Ann.#4 V:Godiva 2.50
Becomes:

NEW TITANS

1988–96

50 B:MWn(s),GP,BMc,B:Who is
Wonder Girl? 4.00
51 GP,BMc 3.00

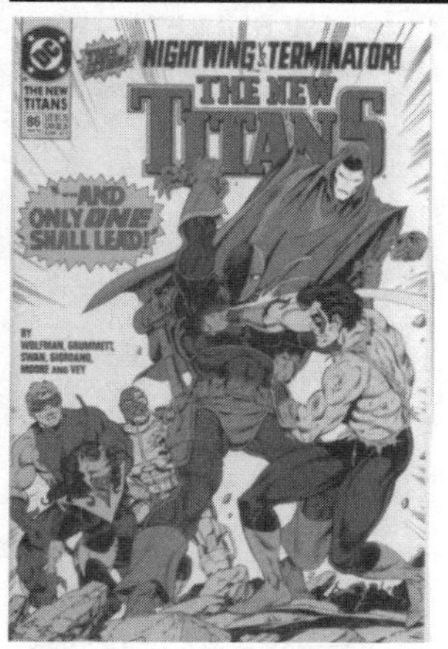

New Titans #86 © DC Comics, Inc.

52 GP,BMc 3.00
53 GP,RT 3.00
54 GP,RT,E:Who is Wonder Girl? . . 3.00
55 GP,RT,I:Troia 3.00
56 MBr,RT,Tale of Middle Titans . . . 2.50
57 GP,BMc,V:Wildebeast 2.50
58 GP,TG,BMc,V:Wildebeast 2.50
59 GP,TG,BMc,V:Wildebeast 2.50
60 GP,TG,BMc,3rd A:Tim Drake (Face Revealed),Batman 5.00
61 GP,TG,BMc,A:Tim Drake, Batman 5.00
62 TG,AV,A:Deathstroke 3.00
63 TG,AV,A:Deathstroke 3.00
64 TG,AV,A:Deathstroke 3.00
65 TG,AV,A:Deathstroke,Tim Drake, Batman 3.00
66 TG,AV,V:Eric Forrester 2.50
67 TG,AV,V:Eric Forrester 2.50
68 SE,V:Royal Flush Gang 2.50
69 SE,V:Royal Flush Gang 2.50
70 SE,A:Deathstroke 3.00
71 TG,AV,B:Deathstroke, B:Titans Hunt 5.00
72 TG,AV,D:Golden Eagle 4.00
73 TG,AV,I:Phantasm 4.00
74 TG,AV,I:Pantha 3.00
75 TG,AV,IR:Jericho/Wildebeest . . . 3.00
76 TG,AV,V:Wildebeests 2.50
77 TG,AV,A:Red Star,N:Cyborg 2.50
78 TG,AV,V:Cyborg 2.50
79 TG,AV,I:Team Titans 3.00
80 KGa,PC,A:Team Titans 2.50
81 CS,AV,War of the Gods 2.50
82 TG,AV,V:Wildebeests 2.50
83 TG,AV,D:Jericho 3.00
84 TG,AV,E:Titans Hunt 2.50
85 TG,AV,I:Baby Wildebeest 2.50
86 CS,AV,E:Deathstroke. 2.50
87 TG,AV,A:Team Titans 2.50
88 TG,AV,CS,V:Team Titans 2.50
89 JBr,I:Lord Chaos 2.50
90 TG,AV,Total Chaos#2,A:Team Titans,D'stroke,V:Lord Chaos . . 2.00
91 TG,AV,Total Chaos#5,A:Team Titans,D'stroke,V:Lord Chaos . . 2.00
92 E:MWn(s),TG,AV,Total Chaos#8, A:Team Titans,V:Lord Chaos . . 2.00
93 TG,AV,Titans Sell-Out#3 . . . . . . 2.00
94 PJ,F:Red Star & Cyborg 2.00
95 PJ,Red Star gains new powers . 2.00
96 PJ,I:Solar Flare, V:Konstantine 2.00
97 TG,AV,B:The Darkening,R:Speedy V:Brotherhood of Evil 2.00
98 TG,AV,V:Brotherhood of Evil . . . 2.00
99 TG,AV,I:Arsenal (Speedy) 2.00
100 TG,AV,W:Nightwing&Starfire, V:Deathwing,Raven,A:Flash,Team Titans,Hologram(c) 4.00
101 AV(i),L:Nightwing 2.00
102 AV(i),A:Prester John 2.00
103 AV(i),V:Bro. of Evil 2.00
104 Terminus #1. . . . . 2.00
105 Terminus #2. . . . . 2.00
106 Terminus #3. . . . . 2.00
107 Terminus #4. . . . . 2.00
108 A:Supergirl,Flash 2.00
109 F:Starfire 2.00
110 A:Flash,Serg.Steele 2.00
111 A:Checkmate 2.00
112 A:Checkmate 2.00
113 F:Nightwing 2.25
114 L:Starfire, Nightwing,Panthra, Wildebeest 2.00
115 A:Trigon 2.00
116 Changling 2.00
117 V:Psimon 2.00
118 V:Raven + Brotherhood 2.00
119 Suffer the Children,pt.1 . . . . . . 2.00
120 Forever Evil,pt.2 . . . . 2.00
121 Forever Evil,pt.3 . . . . 2.00
122 Crimelord/Syndicate War,pt.2 J:Supergirl 2.25
123 MWn(s),RRa,O:Minion 2.25
124 The Siege of Zi Charan 2.25
125 The Siege of Zi Charan 3.00
126 Meltdown,pt.1 . . . . 2.25
127 MWn,Meltdown, cont. 2.25
128 MWn,Meltdown, cont. 2.25
129 MWn,Meltdown, cont. 2.25
130 MWn,Meltdown,final issue 2.25
Ann.#5 V:Children of the Sun 3.00
Ann.#6 CS,F:Starfire. 3.00
Ann.#7 Armageddon 2001,I:Future Teen Titans 4.00
Ann.#8 PJ,Eclipso,V:Deathstroke . . 3.75
Ann.#9 Bloodlines#5,I:Anima 3.75
Ann.#10 Elseworlds story 3.75
Ann.#11 Year One Annual. 3.95
#0 Spec. Zero Hour,new team 2.00

NEW TITANS SELL-OUT SPECIAL

1 SE,AV,AH,I:Teeny Titans, w/Nightwing poster 3.75

NEW YEAR'S EVIL:

Dec., 1997

Body Doubles #1 DAn,ALa,JoP, JPn(c) 2.00
Dark Nemesis #1 DJu,Ccs,JPn(c). . 2.00
Darkseid #1 JBy,SB,JPn(c) 2.00
Gog #1 MWa,JOy,DJa,JPn(c) 2.00
Mr. Mxyzptlk #1 AlG,TMo,JPn(c). . . 2.00
Prometheus #1 GMo,JPn(c) 2.00
Scarecrow #1 PrM,DFg,JPn(c) 2.00
The Rogues #1 BAu,RoW,JPn(c) . . 2.00

NEW YORK WORLD'S FAIR

1 1939 . . . . 25,000.00
2 1940 . . . . 14,000.00

NIGHT FORCE

Aug., 1982

1 GC,1:Night Force 2.00
2 thru 13 GC . . . . @2.50
14 GC,Sept.,1983. . . . . 2.50

Night Force #2 © DC Comics Inc.

NIGHT FORCE

Oct., 1996

1 MWn(s),BA,Baron Winters leads. 2.25
2 MWn(s) 2.25
3 MWn(s) 2.25
4 MWn(s),EB,"Hell Seems a Heaven" 2.25
5 MWn(s),Low,SMa,"Dreamers of Dreams" pt.1 . . . . 2.25
6 MWn(s),Low,SMa,"Dreamers of Dreams" pt.2 . . . . 2.25
7 MWn(s),Low,SMa,"Dreamers of Dreams" pt.3 . . . . 2.25
8 MWn(s),"Convergence," x-over . . 2.25
9 MWn(s),Low,Sma,"The Eleventh Man" pt.1 (of 3) 2.25
10 MWn(s),"Eleventh Man" pt.2 . . . 2.50
11 MWn(s),"Eleventh Man" pt.3. . . . 2.50
12 MWn(s),Lady of the Leopard final issue,Sept. 1997 . . . . 2.50

NIGHTWING

1995

1 R:Nightwing 3.50
2 N:Nightwing 3.00
3 visit to Kravia (of 4). 3.00
4 conclusion 3.00

NIGHTWING

Aug., 1996

1 CDi(s),SMc,KIS,Nightwing goes to Bl□haven 4.00
2 CDi(s),SMc,KIS,V:smugglers. . . . 2.50
3 CDi(s),SMc,KIS,run-down bank "held up" 2.25
4 CDi(s),SMc,KIS,V:Lady Vick 2.25
5 CDi(s),SMc,KIS, ... 2.25
6 CDi(s),SMc,KIS,A:Tim Drake . . . 2.25
7 CDi(s),SMc,KIS,"Rough Justice" . 2.25
8 CDi(s),SMc,KIS,V: the kingpin of Bl□haven 2.00
9 CDi(s),SMc,KIS,kidnapping, pt.1 . 2.00
10 CDi(s),SMc,KIS,nightmare or dream? 2.00
11 CDi(s),SMc,V:Soames, Blockbuster 2.00
12 CDi(s),SMc,Mutt 2.00
13 CDi(s),SMc,KIS,A:Batman 2.00
14 CDi(s),SMc,KIS,A:Batman,pt.2. . 2.00
15 CDi(s),SMc,KIS,A:Batman,pt.3. . 2.00
16 CDi(s),SMc,KIS,Nightwingmobile 2.00
17 CDi(s),SMc,KIS,V:Man-Bat. 2.00

18 CDi(s),SMc,KIS 2.00
19 CDi(s),SMc,KIS,Cataclysm x-over, pt.2 . . . . 2.00
20 CDi(s),SMc,KIS,Cataclysm. 2.00
21 CDi(s),SMc,KIS,post Cataclysm 2.00
22 CDi(s),SMc,KIS,V:Lady Vic 2.00
23 Brotherhood of the Fist x-over, pt.4. . . . . 2.00
24 CDi(s),SMc,KIS,cop story. 2.00
25 CDi(s),SMc,KIS,A:Robin 2.00
26 CDi(s),SMc,KIS,A;Huntress 2.00
27 CDi(s),SMc,KIS,V:Torque 2.00
28 CDi(s),SMc,KIS,V:Torque 2.00
29 CDi(s),SMc,KIS,A:Huntress 2.00
30 CDi(s),SMc,KIS,A:Superman . . . 2.00
31 CDi(s),SMc,KIS,A:Nite-Wing . . . 2.00
32 CDi(s),SMc,KIS,V:DoubleDare . . 2.00
33 CDi(s),SMc,KIS, V:Electrocutioner 2.00
34 CDi(s),SMc,KIS,x-over 2.00
35 CDi(s),SMc,KIS,No Man's Land,pt.1 . . . . 2.00
36 CDi(s),SMc,No Man's Land,pt.2 . . . . 2.00
37 CDi(s),SMc,KIS,No Man's Land, concl. 2.00
38 CDi(s),SMc,KIS,F:Oracle 2.00
39 CDi(s),SMc,KIS 2.00
40 CDi(s),SMc,KIS,R:Tarantula 2.00
41 CDi(s),Police Academy grad . . . 2.00
42 CDi(s),V:Nite-wing 2.00
43 CDi(s),V:Torque 2.00
44 CDi(s),F:Nite-wing 2.00
45 CDi(s),Hunt for Oracle,pt.1. . . . . 2.00
46 CDi(s),Hunt for Oracle,pt.3. . . . . 2.50
47 CDi(s),showdown. 2.50
48 CDi(s),JMz,F:Slyph 2.50
49 CDi(s),JMz,F:Torque 2.50
50 CDi,JMz,at crossroads,48-pg. . . 3.50
Ann.#1 Pulp Heroes (Romance) . . 3.95
Spec.#1,000,000 CDi(s),SMc,KIS . . 2.00
Secret Files #1 64-page 4.95
Giant #1 80-pg.CDi,I:Hella 5.95
TPB A Knight in Bludhaven,CDi, SMc,KIS, rep. #1–#8. . . . . 15.00
TPB Ties That Bind, DON,AIG, DG,KIS,rep. 13.00
TPB Rough Justice. 18.00
TPB Love and Bullets,rep. 17.95

NIGHTWING: ALFRED'S RETURN

1 . . . . 3.50

NIGHTWING AND HUNTRESS

March, 1998

1 (of 4) BSz,conflict 2.00
2 BSz,good cop, bad cop. 2.00
3 BSz,Malfatti 2.00
4 BSz,concl. 2.00

NUTSY SQUIRREL

Sept.–Oct., 1954

61 SM 40.00
62 thru 71 . . . . @25.00
72 Nov., 1957. . . . . 25.00

OMAC

Sept.–Oct., 1974

1 JK,I&O:Omac 10.00
2 JK,I:Mr.Big 6.00
3 JK,100,000 foes 6.00
4 JK,V:Kafka 6.00
5 JK,New Bodies for Old 6.00
6 JK,The Body Bank 6.00
7 JK,The Ocean Stealers. 6.00
8 JK,Last issue 6.00

[2nd Series] 1991

1 JBy,B&W prestige. 5.00
2 JBy,The Great Depression era . . 4.50
3 JBy,`To Kill Adolf Hitler'. 4.50
4 JBy,D:Mr.Big. 4.50

Omega Men #4 © DC Comics, Inc.

OMEGA MEN

Dec., 1982

1 KG,V:Citadel. 3.50
2 KG,O:Broot. 2.00
3 KG,I:Lobo. 4.00
4 KG,D:Demonia,I:Felicity 2.00
5 KG,V:Lobo 3.00
6 KG,V:Citadel,D:Gepsen 2.00
7 O:Citadel,L:Auron 2.00
8 R:Nimbus,I:H.Hokum 2.00
9 V:HarryHokum,A:Lobo 2.00
10 A:Lobo (First Full Story). 3.00
11 V:Blackfire 2.00
12 R:Broots Wife 2.00
13 A:Broots Wife 2.00
14 Karna 2.00
15 Primus Goes Mad 2.00
16 Spotlight Issue. 2.00
17 V:Psions 2.00
18 V:Psions 2.00
19 V:Psions,C:Lobo 2.00
20 V:Psions,A:Lobo 2.00
21 Spotlight Issue. 2.00
22 Nimbus 2.00
23 Nimbus 2.00
24 Okaara 2.00
25 Kalista 2.00
26 V:Spiderguild 2.00
27 V:Psions 2.00
28 V:Psions 2.00
29 V:Psions 2.00
30 R:Primus,I:Artin 2.00
31 Crisis tie-in 2.00
32 Felicity. 2.00
33 Regufe World 2.00
34 A:New Teen Titans. 2.00
35 A:New Teen Titans. 2.00
36 Last Days of Broot. 2.00
37 V:Spiderguild,A:Lobo 2.00
38 A:Tweener Network 1.75
Ann.#1 KG,R:Harpis. 2.25
Ann.#2 KG,O:Primus 2.25

100 BULLETS

DC/Vertigo 1999

1 F:Dizzy Cordova & Agent Graves 2.50
2 . . . . 2.50
3 F:Mr.Shepard 2.50
4 Shot, Water Back,pt.1. . . . . 2.50
5 Shot, Water Back,pt.2. . . . . 2.50
6 Short Con, Long Odds,pt.1 . . . . . 2.50
7 Short Con, Long Odds,pt.2 . . . . . 2.50
8 F:Agent Graves 2.50
9 Right Ear,Left in the Cold,pt.1 . . . 2.50
10 Right Ear,Left in the Cold,pt.2 . . 2.50
11 F:Lilly Roach 2.50
12 Parlez Kung Vous,pt.1 . . . . 2.50
13 Parlez Kung Vous,pt.2 . . . . 2.50
14 Parlez Kung Vous,concl. 2.50
15 Hang Up on Hang Low,pt.1 . . . . 2.50
16 Hang Up on Hang Low,pt.2 . . . . 2.50
17 Hang Up on Hang Low,pt.3 . . . . 2.50
TPB First Shot,Last Call 9.95

100% TRUE?

DC/Paradox Press B&W 1996

1 rep. from Paradox Press books. . 3.50

ORION

April, 2000

1 WS,Darkseid 2.50
2 WS,V:Darkseid 2.50
3 WS,FM,V:Suicide Jockeys 2.50
4 WS,DGb,V:Darkseid 2.50
5 WS,V:Darkseid 2.50
6 WS,EL,AG,F:Mortalla 2.50
7 WS,HC,V:Kalibak 2.50

OUR ARMY AT WAR

Aug., 1952

1 CI(c),Dig Your FoxholeDeep. 1,500.00
2 CI(c),Champ 700.00
3 GK(c),No Exit 500.00
4 IN(c),Last Man 450.00
5 IN(c),T.N.T. Bouquet 425.00
6 IN(c),Battle Flag 425.00
7 IN(c),Dive Bomber 425.00
8 IN(c),One Man Army. 425.00
9 GC(c),Undersea Raider 425.00
10 IN(c),Soldiers on the High Wire 425.00
11 IN(c),Scratch One Meatball . . 425.00
12 IN(c),The Big Drop. 300.00
13 BK(c),Ghost Ace 400.00

Our Army at War #7
© DC Comics, Inc.

14 BK(c),Drummer of Waterloo . . 350.00
15 IN(c),Thunder in the Skies . . . 300.00
16 IN(c),A Million To One Shot . . 300.00
17 IN(c),The White Death 300.00
18 IN(c),Frontier Fighter 300.00
19 IN(c),The Big Ditch 300.00
20 IN(c),Abandon Ship 300.00
21 IN(c),Dairy of a Flattop. 200.00
22 JGr(c),Ranger Raid 200.00
23 IN(c),Jungle Navy 200.00
24 IN(c),Suprise Landing 200.00
25 JGr(c),Take 'Er Down. 200.00
26 JGr(c),Sky Duel 200.00
27 IN(c),Diary of a Frogman 200.00
28 JGr(c),Detour-War 200.00
29 IN(c),Grounded Fighter 200.00
30 JGr(c),Torpedo Raft 200.00
31 IN(c),Howitzer Hill 200.00
32 JGr(c),Battle Mirror 175.00
33 JGr(c),Fighting Gunner 175.00
34 JGr(c),Point-Blank War 175.00
35 JGr(c),Frontline Tackle 175.00
36 JGr(c),Foxhole Mascot. 175.00
37 JGr(c),Walking Battle Pin 175.00
38 JGr(c),Floating Pillbox 175.00
39 JGr(c),Trench Trap. 175.00
40 RH(c),Tank Hunter 175.00
41 JGr(c),Jungle Target 175.00
42 IN(c),Shadow Targets. 150.00
43 JGr(c),A Bridge For Billy 150.00
44 JGr(c),Thunder In The Desert 150.00
45 JGr(c),Diary of a Fighter Pilot. 150.00
46 JGr(c),Prize Package 150.00
47 JGr(c),Flying Jeep 150.00
48 JGr(c),Front Seat. 150.00
49 JKu(c),Landing Postponed . . . 150.00
50 JGr(c),Mop-Up Squad 150.00
51 JGr(c),Battle Tag 125.00
52 JGr(c),Pony Express Pilot . . . 125.00
53 JGr(c),One Ringside-For War. 125.00
54 JKu(c),No-Man Secret 125.00
55 JGr(c),No Rest For A Raider . 125.00
56 JKu(c),You're Next. 125.00
57 JGr(c),Ten-Minute Break 125.00
58 JKu(c),The Fighting SnowBird 125.00
59 JGr(c),The Mustang Had
My Number 125.00
60 JGr(c),Ranger Raid 125.00
61 JGr(c),A Pigeon For Easy Co. 110.00
62 JKu(c),Trigger Man. 110.00
63 JGr(c),The Big Toss 110.00
64 JKu(c),Tank Rider 110.00
65 JGr(c),Scramble-War Upstairs 110.00
66 RH(c),Gunner Wanted 110.00
67 JKu(c),Boiling Point 110.00
68 JKu(c),End of the Line 110.00
69 JGr(c),Combat Cage 110.00
70 JGr(c),Torpedo Tank. 110.00
71 JGr(c),Flying Mosquitoes 110.00
72 JGr(c),No. 1 Pigeon 110.00
73 JKu(c),Shooting Gallery 110.00
74 JGr(c),Ace Without Guns 110.00
75 JGr(c),Blind Night Fighter. . . . 110.00
76 JKu(c),Clipped Hellcat 110.00
77 JGr(c),Jets Don't Dream. 110.00
78 IN(c),Battle Nurse 110.00
79 JGr(c),What's the Price
of a B-17?. 110.00
80 JGr(c),The Sparrow And
The...Hawk 110.00
81 JGr(c),Sgt. Rock in The
Rock of Easy Co.. . . . . 2,400.00
82 JGr(c),Gun Jockey. 550.00
83 JGr(c),B:Sgt.Rock Stories,
The Rock and the Wall . . . 1,500.00
84 JKu(c),Laughter On
Snakehead Hill. 250.00
85 JGr(c),Ice Cream Soldier 300.00
86 RH(c),Tank 711 . . . . 200.00
87 RH(c),Calling Easy Co. 200.00
88 JKu(c),The Hard Way. 200.00
89 RH(c),No Shoot From Easy . . 200.00
90 JKu(c),3 Stripes Hill 200.00
91 JGr(c),No Answer from Sarge 200.00
92 JGr(c),Luck of Easy 150.00
93 JGr(c),Deliver One Airfield . . . 150.00
94 JKu(c),Target-Easy Company. 150.00
95 JKu(c),Battle Of The Stripes. . 150.00
96 JGr(c),Last Stand For Easy . . 150.00
97 JKu(c),What Makes A
Sergeant Run? 150.00
98 JKu(c),Soldiers Never Die . . . 150.00
99 JKu(c),Easy's Hardest Battle . 150.00
100 JKu(c),No Exit For Easy. . . . 150.00
101 JKu(c),End Of Easy 125.00
102 JKu(c),The Big Star 125.00
103 RH(c),Easy's Had It 125.00
104 JKu(c),A New Kind Of War. . 125.00
105 JKu(c),T.N.T. Birthday 125.00
106 JKu(c),Meet Lt. Rock 125.00
107 JKu(c),Doom Over Easy. . . . 125.00
108 JGr(c),Unknown Sergeant . . 125.00
109 JKu(c),Roll Call For Heroes . 125.00
110 JKu(c),That's An Order. 125.00
111 JKu(c),What's The Price
Of A Dog Tag 125.00
112 JKu(c),Battle Shadow 125.00
113 JKu(c),Eyes Of A
Blind Gunner 125.00
114 JKu(c),Killer Sergeant 125.00
115 JKu(c),Rock's Battle Family . 125.00
116 JKu(c),S.O.S. Sgt. Rock 125.00
117 JKu(c),Snafu Squad 100.00
118 RH(c),The Tank Vs. The
Tin Soldier 100.00
119 JKu(c),A Bazooka For
Babyface 100.00
120 JGr(c),Battle Tags
For Easy Co. 75.00
121 JKu(c),New Boy In Easy 75.00
122 JKu(c),Battle of the
Pajama Commandoes 75.00
123 JGr(c),Battle Brass Ring 75.00
124 JKu(c),Target-Sgt. Rock 75.00
125 JKu(c),Hold-At All Costs. 75.00
126 RH(c),The End Of
Easy Company. 75.00
127 JKu(c),4 Faces of Sgt. Rock. . 75.00
128 JKu(c),O:Sgt. Rock 225.00
129 JKu(c),Heroes Need Cowards 75.00
130 JKu(c),No Hill For Easy 75.00
131 JKu(c),One Pair of
Dogtags For Sale 75.00
132 JKu(c),Young Soldiers
Never Cry. 75.00

Our Army at War #9
© DC Comics, Inc.

133 JKu(c),Yesterday's Hero. 75.00
134 JKu(c),The T.N.T. Book 75.00
135 JKu(c),Battlefield Double 75.00
136 JKu(c),Make Me A Hero. 75.00
137 JKu(c),Too Many Sergeants . . 75.00
138 JKu(c),Easy's Lost Sparrow . . 75.00
139 JKu(c),A Firing Squad
For Easy 75.00
140 JKu(c),Brass Sergeant 75.00
141 JKu(c),Dead Man's Trigger. . . 75.00
142 JKu(c),Easy's New Topkick . . 75.00
143 JKu(c),Easy's T.N.T. Crop . . . 75.00
144 JKu(c),The Sparrow And
The Tiger 75.00
145 JKu(c),A Feather For
Little Sure Shot. 75.00
146 JKu(c),The Fighting Guns
For Easy 75.00
147 JKu(c),Book One:Generals
Don't Die 75.00
148 JKu(c),Book Two:Generals
Don't Die:Generals Are
Sergeants With Stars 75.00
149 JKu(c),Surrender Ticket 75.00
150 JKu(c),Flytrap Hill 75.00
151 JKu(c),War Party,
I:Enemy Ace. 350.00
152 Jku(c),Last Man-Last Shot . . 100.00
153 JKu(c),Easy's Last Stand . . . 150.00
154 JKu(c),Boobytrap Mascot 60.00
155 JKu(c),No Stripes For Me. . . 125.00
156 JKu(c),The Human Tank Trap 60.00
157 JKu(c),Nothin's Ever
Lost In War. 60.00
158 JKu(c),Iron Major-Rock
Sergeant 60.00
159 JKu(c),The Blind Gun. 60.00
160 JKu(c),What's The Color
Of Your Blood. 60.00
161 JKu(c),Dead End
For A Dogface 60.00
162 JKu(c),The Price and
The Sergeant 60.00
163 JKu(c),Kill Me-Kill Me. 60.00
164 JKu(c),No Exit For Easy,
reprint from #100 . . . . 100.00
165 JKu(c),The Return of the
Iron Major. 50.00
166 JKu(c),Half A Sergeant 50.00
167 JKu(c),Kill One-Save One . . . 50.00
168 JKu(c),I Knew The
Unknown Soldier 100.00
169 JKu(c),Nazi On My Back 50.00
170 JKu(c),Buzzard Bait Hill 50.00
171 JKu(c),The Sergeant Must Die 40.00
172 JKu(c),A Slug for a Sergeant . 40.00
173 JKu(c),Easy's Hardest Battle,
reprint from #99 . . . . 40.00
174 JKu(c),One Kill Too Many. . . . 40.00
175 JKu(c),T.N.T. Letter 40.00
176 JKu(c),Give Me Your Stripes . 40.00
177 JKu(c),Target-Easy Company,
reprint from #94 . . . . 40.00
178 JKu(c),Only One Medal
For Easy 40.00
179 JKu(c),A Penny Jackie
Johnson 40.00
180 JKu(c),You Can't
Kill A General. 40.00
181 RH(c),Monday's Coward-
Tuesday's Hero 40.00
182 NA,RH(c),The Desert Rats
of Easy. 50.00
183 NA,JKu(c),Sergeants Don't
Stay Dead 50.00
184 JKu(c),Candidate For A
Firing Squad. 35.00
185 JKu(c),Battle Flag For A G.I. . 35.00
186 NA,JKu(c),3 Stripes Hill
reprint from #90 . . . . 50.00
187 JKu(c),Shadow of a Sergeant. 35.00

188 JKu(c),Death Comes for Easy 35.00
189 JKu(c),The Mission Was Murder 35.00
190 JKu(c),What Make's A Sergeant Run?, reprint from #97. . . . . 35.00
191 JKu(c),Death Flies High, A:Johnny Cloud 35.00
192 JKu(c),A Firing Squad For A Sergeant. 35.00
193 JKu(c),Blood In the Desert . . . 35.00
194 JKu(c),Time For Vengeance . . 35.00
195 JKu(c),Dead Town 35.00
196 JKu(c),Stop The War-I Want To Get Off 35.00
197 JKu(c),Last Exit For Easy. . . . 35.00
198 JKu(c),Plugged Nickel 35.00
199 JKu(c),Nazi Ghost Wolf 35.00
200 JKu(c),The Troubadour 40.00
201 JKu(c),The Graffiti Writer 25.00
202 JKu(c),The Sarge Is Dead . . . 25.00
203 JKu(c),Easy's Had It, reprint from # 103. . . . . 25.00
204 JKu(c) 25.00
205 JKu(c) 25.00
206 JKu(c),There's A War On 25.00
207 JKu(c),A Sparrow's Prayer . . . 25.00
208 JKu(c),A Piece of Rag...And A Hank of Hair 25.00
209 JKu(c),I'm Still Alive 25.00
210 JKu(c),I'm Kilroy. 25.00
211 JKu(c),The Treasure of St. Daniel 25.00
212 JKu(c),The Quiet War 25.00
213 JKu(c),A Letter For Bulldozer . 25.00
214 JKu(c),Where Are You? 25.00
215 JKu(c),Pied Piper of Peril 25.00
216 JKu(c),Doom Over Easy, reprint from # 107. . . . . 25.00
217 JKu(c),Surprise Party. 15.00
218 JKu(c),Medic!. 15.00
219 JKu(c),Yesterday's Hero. 15.00
220 JKu(c),Stone-Age War 15.00
221 JKu(c),Hang-Up 15.00
222 JKu(c),Dig In, Easy 15.00
223 JKu(c),On Time 15.00
224 JKu(c),One For The Money . . 15.00
225 JKu(c),Face Front 15.00
226 JKu(c),Death Stop 15.00
227 JKu(c),Traitor's Blood. 15.00
228 JKu(c),It's A Dirty War 15.00
229 JKu(c),The Battle of the Sergeants, reprint from #128 . 35.00
230 JKu(c),Home Is The Hunter . . 15.00
231 JKu(c),My Brother's Keeper . . 15.00
232 JKu(c),3 Men In A Tub 15.00
233 JKu(c),Head Count 15.00
234 JKu(c),Summer In Salerno . . . 15.00
235 JKu(c),Pressure Point 15.00
236 JKu(c),Face The Devil 15.00
237 JKu(c),Nobody Cares. 15.00
238 JKu(c),I Kid You Not. 15.00
239 JKu(c),The Soldier 15.00
240 JKu(c),NA 30.00
241 JKu(c),War Story 20.00
242 JKu(c),Infantry 20.00
243 JKu(c),24 Hour Pass 15.00
244 JKu(c),Easy's First Tiger 15.00
245 JKu(c),The Prisoner. 15.00
246 JKu(c),Naked Combat 15.00
247 JKu(c),The Vision 14.00
248 JKu(c),The Firing Squad 14.00
249 JKu(c),The Luck of Easy,WW. 15.00
250 JKu(c),90 Day Wonder. 14.00
251 JKu(c),The Iron Major 14.00
252 JKu(c),The Iron Hand. 14.00
253 JKu(c),Rock and Iron 14.00
254 JKu(c),The Town 14.00
255 JKu(c),What's It Like 14.00
256 JKu(c),School For Sergeants . 14.00
257 JKu(c),The Castaway. 14.00
258 JKu(c),The Survivors 14.00
259 JKu(c),Lost Paradise 14.00
260 JKu(c),Hell's Island 14.00
261 JKu(c),The Medal That Nobody Wanted 12.00
262 JKu(c),The Return 12.00
263 JKu(c),The Cage 12.00
264 JKu(c),The Hunt. 12.00
265 JKu(c),The Brother. 12.00
266 JKu(c),The Evacuees. 12.00
267 JKu(c),A Bakers Dozen 12.00
268 JKu(c),The Elite 12.00
269 JKu(c) 12.00
270 JKu(c),Spawn of the Devil . . . 12.00
271 JKu(c),Brittle Harvest 12.00
272 JKu(c),The Bloody Flag 12.00
273 JKu(c),The Arena. 12.00
274 JKu(c),Home Is The Hero . . . 12.00
275 JKu(c),Graveyard Battlefield. . 12.00
276 JKu(c),A Bullet For Rock 12.00
277 JKu(c),Gashouse Gang 12.00
278 JKu(c),Rearguard Action 12.00
279 JKu(c),Mined City 12.00
280 JKu(c),Mercy Mission. 12.00
281 JKu(c),Dead Man's Eyes 12.00
282 JKu(c),Pieces of Time 12.00
283 JKu(c),Dropouts. 12.00
284 JKu(c),Linkup. 12.00
285 JKu(c),Bring Him Back. 12.00
286 JKu(c),Firebird 12.00
287 JKu(c),The Fifth Dimension . . 12.00
288 JKu(c),Defend-Or Destroy . . . 12.00
289 JKu(c),The Line 12.00
290 JKu(c),Super-Soldiers 12.00
291 JKu(c),Death Squad. 12.00
292 JKu(c),A Lesson In Blood. . . . 12.00
293 JKu(c),It Fiqures 12.00
294 JKu(c),Coffin For Easy. 12.00
295 JKu(c),The Devil in Paradise . 12.00
296 JKu(c),Combat Soldier 12.00
297 JKu(c),Percentages 12.00
298 JKu(c),Return to Chartres . . . 12.00
299 JKu(c),Three Soldiers 12.00
300 JKu(c),300th Hill 12.00
301 JKu(c),The Farm 12.00

Becomes:

SGT. ROCK

1977–88

302 JKu(c),Anzio-The Bloodbath, part I 8.00
303 JKu(c),Anzio, part II 6.00
304 JKu(c),Anzio, part III 6.00
305 JKu(c),Dead Man's Trigger, reprint from #141 . . . . 6.00
306 JKu(c),The Last Soldier 6.00
307 JKu(c),I'm Easy 6.00
308 JKu(c),One Short Step. 6.00
309 JKu(c),Battle Clowns 6.00
310 JKu(c),Hitler's Wolf Children . . . 6.00
311 JKu(c),The Sergeant and the Lady. 6.00
312 JKu(c),No Name Hill 6.00
313 JKu(c),A Jeep For Joey 6.00
314 JKu(c),Gimme Sky. 6.00
315 JKu(c),Combat Antenna. 6.00
316 JKu(c),Another Hill. 6.00
317 JKu(c),Hell's Oven 6.00
318 JKu(c),Stone-Age War 6.00
319 JKu(c),To Kill a Sergeant 6.00
320 JKu(c),Never Salute a Sergeant 6.00
321 JKu(c),It's Murder Out Here . . . 5.00
322 JKu(c),The Killer 5.00
323 JKu(c),Monday's Hero 5.00
324 JKu(c),Ghost of a Tank 5.00
325 JKu(c),Future Kill, part I 5.00
326 JKu(c),Future Kill, part II 5.00
327 JKu(c),Death Express 5.00
328 JKu(c),Waiting For Rock 5.00
329 JKu(c),Dead Heat 5.00
330 JKu(c),G.I. Trophy 5.00
331 JKu(c),The Sons of War. 5.00
332 JKu(c),Pyramid of Death 5.00
333 JKu(c),Ask The Dead. 5.00
334 JKu(c),What's Holding Up The War. 5.00
335 JKu(c),Killer Compass 5.00
336 JKu(c),The Red Maple Leaf . . . 5.00
337 JKu(c),A Bridge Called Charlie. 5.00
338 JKu(c),No Escape From the Front 5.00
339 JKu(c),I Was Here Before 5.00
340 JKu(c),How To Win A War 5.00
341 JKu(c),High-Flyer. 5.00
342 JKu(c),The 6 sides of Sgt. Rock 5.00
343 thru 350 . . . . @5.00
351 thru 422 . . . . @3.00

Our Fighting Fources #7
© DC Comics, Inc.

OUR FIGHTING FORCES

Oct.–Nov., 1954

1 IN,JGr(c),Human Booby Trap . 850.00
2 RH,IN,IN(c),Mile-Long Step. . . 400.00
3 RA,JKu(c),Winter Ambush . . . 350.00
4 RA,JGr(c),The Hot Seat 250.00
5 IN,RA,JGr(c),The Iron Punch . 250.00
6 IN,RA,JGr(c),The Sitting Tank . 225.00
7 RA,JKu,JGr(c),Battle Fist 225.00
8 IN,RA,JGr(c),No War For A Gunner 225.00
9 JKu,RH,JGr(c),Crash-Landing At Dawn 225.00
10 WW,RA,JGr(c),Grenade Pitcher 225.00
11 JKu,JGr(c),Diary of a Sub . . . 175.00
12 IN,JKu,JGr(c),Jump Seat 175.00
13 RA,JGr(c),Beach Party. 175.00
14 JA,RA,IN,JGr(c),Unseen War . 175.00
15 RH,JKu,JGr(c),Target For A Lame Duck 175.00
16 RH,JGr(c),Night Fighter 175.00
17 RA,JGr(c),Anchored Frogman 175.00
18 RH,JKu,JGr(c),Cockpit Seat. . 175.00
19 RA,JKu(c),StraightenThat Line 175.00
20 RA,MD,JGr(c),The Floating Pilot 175.00
21 RA,JKu(c),The Bouncing Baby of Company B 125.00
22 JKu,RA,JGr(c),3 Doorways To War 125.00
23 RA,IN,JA,JGr(c),Tin Fish Pilot 125.00
24 RA,RH,JGr(c),Frogman Duel . 125.00
25 RA,JKu(c),Dead End 125.00
26 IN,RH,JKu(c),Tag Day 125.00

27 MD,RA,JKu(c),TNT Escort . . . 125.00
28 RH,MD,JKu(c),AllQuiet atC.P. 125.00
29 JKu,JKu(c),Listen To A Jet . . . 125.00
30 IN,RA,JKu(c),Fort
For A Gunner 125.00
31 MD,RA,JKu(c),Silent Sub 125.00
32 RH,MD,RH(c),Paper Work War. 125.00
33 RH,JKu,JKu(c),Frogman
In A Net 125.00
34 JA,JGr,JKu(c),Calling U-217. . 125.00
35 JA,JGr,JKu(c),Mask of
a Frogman 125.00
36 MD,JA,JKu(c),Steel Soldier . . 125.00
37 JA,JGr,JGr(c),Frogman
In A Bottle 125.00
38 RH,RA,JA,JGr(c),Sub Sinker . 125.00
39 JA,RH,RH(c),Last Torpedo . . . 125.00
40 JGr,JA,JKu,JKu(c),The
Silent Ones 125.00
41 JGr,RH,JA,JKu(c),Battle
Mustang 150.00
42 RH,MD,JGr(c),Sorry-
Wrong Hill 100.00
43 MD,JKu,JGr(c),Inside Battle . . 100.00
44 MD,RH,RA,JGr(c),Big Job
For Baker 100.00
45 RH,RA,JGr(c),B:Gunner and
Sarge, Mop-Up Squad 350.00
46 RH,RA,JGr(c),Gunner's Squad 150.00
47 RH,JKu(c),TNT Birthday. 100.00
48 JA,RH,JGr(c),A Statue
For Sarge 100.00
49 MD,RH,JGr(c),Blind Gunner. . 125.00
50 JA,RH,JGr(c),I:Pooch,My
Pal, The Pooch. 100.00
51 RA,JA,RH(c),Underwater
Gunner. 75.00
52 MD,JKu,JKu(c),The Gunner
and the Nurse 75.00
53 JA,RA,JGr(c),An Egg
For Sarge. 75.00
54 . . . . 75.00
55 MD,RH,JGr(c),The Last Patrol . 75.00
56 RH,RA,JGr(c),Bridge of Bullets 75.00
57 JA,IN,JGr(c),A Tank For Sarge. 75.00
58 JA,JGr(c),Return of the Pooch . 75.00
59 RH,JA,JGr(c),Pooch-Patrol
Leader 75.00
60 RH,JA,JGr(c),Tank Target 75.00
61 JA,JGr(c),Pass to Peril. 75.00
62 JA,JGr(c),The Flying Pooch . . . 75.00
63 JA,RH,JGr(c),Pooch-Tank
Hunter 75.00
64 JK,RH,JGr(c),A Lifeline
For Sarge. 75.00
65 IN,JA,JGr(c),Dogtag Patrol. . . . 75.00
66 JKu,JA,JGr(c),Trail of the
Ghost Bomber 75.00
67 IN,JA,JGr(c),Purple Heart
For Pooch 75.00
68 JA,JGr(c),Col. Hakawa's
Birthday Party. 75.00
69 JA,JKu,JGr(c),
Destination Doom. 75.00
70 JA,JKu(c),The Last Holdout . . . 75.00
71 JA,JGr(c),End of the Marines . . 35.00
72 JA,JGr(c),Four-Footed Spy . . . 35.00
73 IN,JGr(c),The Hero Maker 35.00
74 IN,JGr(c),Three On A T.N.T.
Bull's-Eye. 35.00
75 JKu(c),Purple Heart Patrol 35.00
76 JKu(c),The T.N.T. Seat. 35.00
77 JKu(c),No Foxhole-No Home . . 35.00
78 JGr(c),The Last Medal 35.00
79 JA,JGr(c),Backs to the Sea . . . 35.00
80 JA,JGr(c),Don't Come Back . . . 35.00
81 JA,JGr(c),Battle of
the Mud Marines 30.00
82 JA,JGr(c),Battle of the
Empty Helmets. 30.00
83 RA,JKu(c),Any Marine
Can Do It 30.00
84 JA,JKu(c),The Gun of Shame . 30.00
85 Ja,JKu(c),The TNT Pin-Points . 30.00
86 JKu(c),3 Faces of Combat 30.00
87 JKu(c),Battle o/t Boobytraps. . . 30.00
88 GC,JKu(c),Devil Dog Patrol . . . 30.00
89 JKu(c),TNT Toothache 30.00
90 JKu(c),Stop the War. 30.00
91 JKu(c),The Human Shooting
Gallery 20.00
92 JA,JKu(c),The Bomb That
Stopped The War 20.00
93 IN,JKu(c),The Human Sharks. . 20.00
94 RH(c),E:Gunner,Sarge & Pooch,
The Human Blockbusters 20.00
95 GC,RH(c),B:The Fighting Devil
Dog, Lt. Rock, The
Fighting Devil Dog 20.00
96 JA,RH(c),Battle of Fire 20.00
97 IN(c),Invitation To A
Firing Squad. 20.00
98 IN(c),E:The Fighting Devil
Dog, Death Wore A Grin. 20.00

Our Fighting Fources #8
© DC Comics, Inc.

99 JA,JKu(c),B:Capt. Hunter,
No Mercy in Vietnam 25.00
100 GC,IN(c),Death Also
Stalks the Hunter 20.00
101 JA,RH(c),Killer of Vietnam . . . 20.00
102 RH,JKu(c),Cold Steel
For A Hot War 20.00
103 JKu(c),The Tunnels of Death . 20.00
104 JKu(c),Night Raid In Vietnam . 20.00
105 JKu(c),Blood Loyality 20.00
106 IN(c),Trail By Fury 20.00
107 IN(c),Raid Of The Hellcats . . . 20.00
108 IN(c),Kill The Wolf Pack 20.00
109 IN(c),Burn, Raiders, Burn. . . . 20.00
110 IN(c),Mountains Full of Death. 20.00
111 IN(c),Train of Terror 20.00
112 IN(c),What's In It For
The Hellcats?. 20.00
113 IN(c),Operation-Survival 20.00
114 JKu(c),No Loot For The
Hellcats 20.00
115 JKu(c),Death In The Desert . . 20.00
116 JKu(c),Peril From the Casbah 20.00
117 JKu(c),Colder Than Death . . . 20.00
118 JKu(c),Hell Underwater 20.00
119 JKu(c),Bedlam In Berlin 20.00
120 JKu(c),Devil In The Dark 20.00
121 JKu(c),Take My Place 20.00
122 JKu(c),24 Hours To Die 20.00
123 JKu(c),B:Born Losers,No
Medals No Graves 40.00
124 JKu(c),Losers Take All 18.00
125 Daughters of Death 18.00
126 JKu(c),Lost Town 18.00
127 JKu(c),Angels Over Hell's
Corner 18.00
128 JKu(c),7 11 War. 18.00
129 JKu(c),Ride The Nightmare . . 18.00
130 JKu(c),Nameless Target. 18.00
131 JKu(c),Half A Man 18.00
132 JKu(c),Pooch, The Winner . . . 18.00
133 JKu(c),Heads or Tails. 18.00
134 JKu(c),The Real Losers 18.00
135 JKu(c),Death Picks A Loser . . 18.00
136 JKu(c),Decoy For Death. 18.00
137 JKu(c),God Of The Losers . . . 18.00
138 JKu(c),The Targets. 18.00
139 JKu(c),The Pirate. 18.00
140 JKu(c),Lost...One Loser 18.00
141 JKu(c),Bad Penny, The 18.00
142 JKu(c), 1/2 A Man 18.00
143 JKu(c),Diamonds Are
For Never. 18.00
144 JKu(c),The Lost Mission. 18.00
145 JKu(c),A Flag For Losers 18.00
146 JKu(c),The Forever Walk 18.00
147 NA(c),The Glory Road 18.00
148 JKu(c),The Last Charge 18.00
149 FT(c),A Bullet For
A Traitor. 18.00
150 JKu(c),Mark Our Graves 18.00
151 JKu(c),Kill Me With Wagner . . 18.00
152 JK(c),A Small Place In Hell . . 18.00
153 JK(c),Big Max 18.00
154 JK(c),Bushido,Live By The
Code, Die By The Code 18.00
155 JK(c),The Partisans 18.00
156 JK(c),Good-Bye Broadway. . . 18.00
157 JK(c),Panama Fattie 18.00
158 JK(c),Bombing Out On
The Panama Canal 18.00
159 JK(c),Mile-A-Minute Jones . . . 18.00
160 JKu(c),Ivan 18.00
161 JKu(c),The Major's Dream . . . 18.00
162 Gung-Ho 18.00
163 JKu(c),The Unmarked Graves 18.00
164 JKu(c),A Town Full Of Losers. 18.00
165 LD(c),The Rowboat Fleet. . . . 18.00
166 LD(c),Sword of Flame 18.00
167 LD(c),A Front Seat In Hell . . . 18.00
168 LD(c),A Cold Day To Die 18.00
169 JKu(c),Welcome Home-And
Die. 18.00
170 JKu(c),A Bullet For
The General. 18.00
171 JKu(c),A Long Day...
A Long War 18.00
172 JKu(c),The Two-Headed Spy . 18.00
173 JKu(c),An Appointment
With A Direct Hit. 18.00
174 JKu(c),Winner Takes-Death . . 18.00
175 JKu(c),Death Warrant 18.00
176 JKu(c),The Loser Is A
Teen-Ager 18.00
177 JKu(c),This Loser Must Die . . 18.00
178 JKu(c),Last Drop For Losers . 18.00
179 JKu(c),The Last Loser 18.00
180 JKu(c),Hot Seat In A
Cold War 18.00
181 JKu(c),Sept.–Oct., 1978. . . . . 18.00

OUTCASTS
Oct., 1987

1 . . . . 2.00
2 thru 11 . . . . @2.00

OUTLAW NATION
DC/Vertigo August, 2000

1 JaD(s),F:pulp-fiction writer 2.50
2 JaD(s),Southern bayou 2.50

DC COMICS

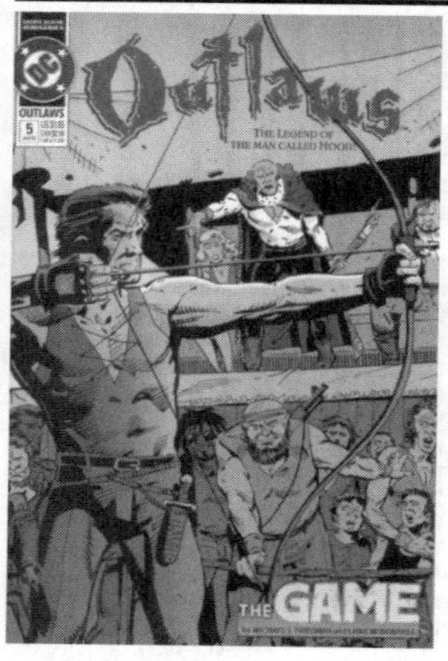

Outlaws #5 © DC Comics, Inc.

OUTLAWS
1991

1 LMc,I:Hood 2.00
2 LMc,O:Hood 2.00
3 LMc,V:Evil King 2.00
4 LMc,V:Lord Conductor 2.00
5 LMc,Archery contest 2.00
6 LMc,Raid on King's Castle 2.00
7 LMc,Refuge, V:Lord Conductor . . 2.00

OUTSIDERS, THE
Nov., 1985
[1st Regular Series]

1 JAp,I:Looker 3.00
2 JAp,V:Nuclear Family 2.50
3 JAp,V:Force of July 2.00
4 JAp,V:Force of July 2.00
5 JAp,Christmas Issue 2.00
6 JAp,V:Duke of Oil 2.00
7 JAp,V:Duke of Oil 2.00
8 JAp,Japan 2.00
9 JAp/SD/JOp,Bik Lightning 2.00
10 JAp,I:Peoples Heroes 2.00
11 JAp,Imprisoned in death camp . . 2.00
12 JAp,Imprisoned in death camp . . 2.00
13 JAp,desert island 2.00
14 JAp,Looker/murder story 2.00
15 DJu,V:Bio-hazard 2.00
16 Halo vs.Firefly 2.00
17 JAp,J:Batman 2.00
18 JAp,BB,V:Eclipso 2.00
19 JAp,V:Windfall 2.00
20 JAp,Masters of Disaster 2.00
21 JAp,V:Kobra,I:Clayface IV 2.00
22 JAp,V:Strike Force Kobra 2.00
23 Return of People's Heroes 2.00
24 TVE,JAp,V:Skull,A:Duke of Oil . . 2.00
25 JAp,V:Skull 2.00
26 JAp,in Markovia 2.00
27 EL,Millenium 2.00
28 EL,Millenium,final issue 2.00
Ann.#1,KN,V:Skull,A:Batman 2.50
Spec.#1,A:Infinity,Inc 2.00

[2nd Regular Series] 1993–95

1 Alpha,TC(c),B:MiB(s),PaP,
I:Technocrat,Faust,Wylde 3.00
1a Omega,TC(c),PaP,V:Vampires . 3.00
2 PaP,V:Sanction 2.00
3 PaP,V:Eradicator 2.00
4 PaP,A:Eradicator 2.00
5 PaP,V:Atomic Knight,A:Jihad 2.00
6 PaP,V:Jihad 2.00
7 PaP,C:Batman 2.00
8 PaP,V:Batman,I:Halo 2.00
9 PaP,V:Batman 2.00
10 PaP,B:Final Blood, R:Looker . . . 2.25
11 PaP,Zero Hour,E:Final Blood . . . 2.00
12 PaP 2.00
13 New base 2.00
14 Martial Arts Spectacular 2.00
15 V:New Year's Evil 2.00
16 R:Windfall 2.00
17 A:Green Lantern 2.00
18 Sins of the Father 2.00
19 Sins of the Father, pt.2. . . . . 2.25
20 DvA,V:Metamorpho 2.25
21 A:Apokolips 2.25
22 Alien Assassin 2.25
23 V:Defilers 2.25
24 finale 2.25

PARALLAX: EMERALD NIGHT

1 RMz(s),MMK,MkK, pivotal tie-in
to Final Night 4.50

PEACEMAKER
Jan., 1988

1 A:Dr.Tzin-Tzin 2.00
2 The Wages of Tzin 2.00
3 and 4 . . . . @2.00

PENGUIN TRIUMPHANT

1 JSon,A:Batman,Wall Street 6.00

PETER CANNON: THUNDERBOLT
1992–93

1 thru 6 MC . . . . @2.00
7 MC,`Battleground' 2.00
8 MC,Cairo Kidnapped 2.00
9 MC 2.00
10 MC,A:JLA 2.00
11 MC,V:Havoc,A:Checkmate 2.00
12 MC,final Issue 2.00

PETER PANDA
Aug.–Sept., 1953

1 . . . . 165.00
2 . . . . 95.00
3 thru 9 . . . . @60.00
10 Aug.–Sept., 1958 . . . . 60.00

PETER PORKCHOPS
Nov.–Dec., 1949

1 . . . . 250.00
2 . . . . 125.00
3 thru 10 . . . . @100.00
11 thru 30 . . . . @75.00
31 thru 61 . . . . @50.00
62 Oct.–Dec., 1960 . . . . 50.00

PHANTOM, THE
Oct., 1987

1 JO,A:Modern Phantom,13th
Phantom 2.00
2 JO,Murder Trial in Manhattan . . . 2.00
3 JO,A:Chessman 2.00
4 JO,V:Chessman,final issue 2.00

PHANTOM, THE
1989–90

1 LMc,V:Gun Runners 2.50
2 LMc,V:Gun Runners 2.00
3 LMc,V:Drug Smugglers 2.00
4 LMc,In America,A:Diana Palner . 2.00
5 LMc,Racial Riots 2.00
6 LMc,in Africa,Toxic Waste
Problem 2.00
7 LMc,`Gold Rush' 2.00
8 LMc,`Train Surfing' 2.00
9 LMc,`The Slave Trade' 2.00
10 LMc,Famine in Khagana 2.00
11 LMc,Phantom/Diana Wedding
proposal 2.00
12 LMc,Phantom framed for
murder 2.00
13 W:Phantom & Diana Palner
C:Mandrake last issue 2.00

PHANTOM STRANGER
Aug.–Sept., 1952

1 . . . . 1,500.00
2 . . . . 900.00
3 . . . . 750.00
4 . . . . 750.00
5 . . . . 750.00
6, June-July, 1953 . . . . 750.00

PHANTOM STRANGER
May–June, 1969

1 Cl rep.&new material 85.00
2 Cl rep.&new material 35.00
3 Cl rep.&new material 35.00
4 NA,I:Tala,1st All-new issue 40.00
5 MSy,MA,A:Dr.13 . . . . 25.00
6 MSy,A:Dr.13 . . . . 25.00
7 JAp,V:Tala 25.00
8 JAp,A:Dr.13 . . . . 25.00
9 JAp,A:Dr.13 . . . . 25.00
10 JAp,I:Tannarak 25.00
11 JAp,V:Tannarak 20.00
12 JAp,TD,Dr.13 solo story 20.00
13 JAp,TD,Dr.13 solo 20.00
14 JAp,TD,Dr.13 solo 20.00
15 JAp,ATh(rep),TD,Iron Messiah . 15.00
16 JAp,TD,MMes(rep)Dr.13 solo . . 15.00
17 JAp,I:Cassandra Craft 15.00
18 TD,Dr.13 solo 15.00
19 JAp,TD,Dr.13 solo 15.00
20 JAp,`And A Child
Shall Lead Them' 15.00
21 JAp,TD,Dr.13 solo 12.00
22 JAp,TD,I:Dark Circle 12.00
23 JAp,MK,I:Spawn-Frankenstein . 12.00

Phantom Stranger #36
© DC Comics, Inc.

24 JAp,MA,Spawn Frankenstein . . 20.00
25 JAp,MA,Spawn Frankenstein . . 20.00
26 JAp,A:Frankenstein 20.00
27 V:Dr. Zorn 20.00
28 BU:Spawn of Frankenstein. . . . 20.00
29 V:Dr.Zorn,BU:Frankenstein . . . 20.00
30 E:Spawn of Frankenstein 20.00
31 B:BU:Black Orchid 20.00
32 NR,BU:Black Orchid 20.00
33 MGr,A:Deadman 12.00
34 BU:Black Orchid 20.00
35 BU:Black Orchid 20.00
36 BU:Black Orchid 20.00
37 "Crimson Gold,"BU:Black Orchid. 20.00
38 "Images of the Dead". 20.00
39 A:Deadman 15.00
40 A:Deadman 15.00
41 A:Deadman 15.00

PHANTOM STRANGER
Oct., 1987–Jan., 1988

1 MMi,CR,V:Eclipso. 3.00
2 and 4 MMi,CR,V:Eclipso . . . . . @2.25

PHANTOM ZONE, THE
Jan., 1982

1 GD/TD,A:Jax-Ur 2.00
2 GC/TD,A:JLA 2.00
3 GC/TD,A:Mon-El. 2.00
4 GC/TD 2.00

PICTURE STORIES FROM THE BIBLE
Autumn, 1942–43

1 thru 4 Old Testament. . . . . . @160.00
1 thru 3 New Testament . . . . . @175.00

Pinky and the Brain #14
© DC Comics, Inc.

PINKY AND THE BRAIN
Warner Bros./DC

1 thru 4 . . . . @2.00
5 Oklahoma crud. 2.00
6 "Plan Brain From Outer Space". . 2.00
7 Yuletide tale 2.00
8 . . . . 2.00
9 SML(s) back to school 2.00
10 V:Melmouse 2.00
11 "Narftasia" 2.00
12 "Beach Blanket Brain" 2.00
13 "Ali Brain and the Forty Thieves" 2.00
14 "Brainlet" 2.00
15 "Biker Mamas from Heck" 2.00
16 "Verminator II:Judgment Night". . 2.00
17 Halloween 2.00
18 "Braintech," Manga-style issue. . 2.00
19 "Anti-Claus" 2.00
20 "The Mice in Pink" 2.00
21 . . . . 2.00
22 "The Mouse in the Iron Mask" . . 2.00
23 King of the Sea Monkeys. 2.00
24 Love with Cupcake 2.00
25 Dark Pinky. 2.00
26 G.I. Brain. 2.00
27 Final Issue. 2.00

PLASTIC MAN
[1st Series]
Nov.,–Dec., 1966

1 GK,I:Dr.Drome (1966 series begins). 75.00
2 V:The Spider 35.00
3 V:Whed 35.00
4 V:Dr.Dome 35.00
5 1,001 Plassassins. 35.00
6 V:Dr.Dome 35.00
7 O:Plastic Man Jr.,A:Original Plastic Man,Woozy Winks. . . . 35.00
8 V:The Weasel. 25.00
9 V:Joe the Killer Pro. 25.00
10 V:Doll Maker(series ends) 25.00
11 (1976 series begins) 7.00
12 I:Carrot-Man 7.00
13 A:Robby Reed. 7.00
14 V:Meat By-Product & Sludge . . . 7.00
15 I:Snuffer,V:Carrot-Man 7.00
16 V:Kolonel Kool. 7.00
17 O:Plastic Man 7.00
18 V:Professor Klean 7.00
19 I&Only App.Marty Meeker 7.00
20 V:Snooping Sneetches Oct.–Nov., 1977 . . . . 7.00
HC Archives, Vol.1 . . . . 50.00

PLASTIC MAN
1988–89

1 Mini-series,Origin retold 2.00
2 V:The Ooze Brothers 2.00
3 In Los Angeles 2.00
4 End-series,A:Superman 2.00

PLASTIC MAN
1999

Spec.#1 TTn(s),ALo,RBr,48-page . . 4.00

PLOP!
Sept.,–Oct., 1973

1 SA-AA,GE,ShM 35.00
2 AA,SA 15.00
3 AA,SA 15.00
4 BW,SA 15.00
5 MA,MSy,SA 15.00
6 MSy,SA 15.00
7 SA 15.00
8 SA 15.00
9 SA 15.00
10 SA. 15.00
11 ATh,SA 15.00
12 SA. 15.00
13 WW(c),SA 15.00
14 WW,SA 15.00
15 WW(c),SA 15.00
16 SD,WW,SA 15.00
17 SA. 15.00
18 SD,WW,SA 15.00
19 WW,SA 15.00
20 SA,WW 15.00
21 JO,WW 20.00
22 JO,WW,BW 20.00
23 BW,WW. 20.00
24 SA,WW,Nov.–Dec., 1976 . . . . . 20.00

POWER GIRL
[Mini-Series] 1988

1 . . . . 2.00
2 A:The Weaver, mongo Krebs . . . 2.00
3 V:The Weaver 2.00
4 V:Weaver, final issue 2.00

POWER OF SHAZAM!
1995–97

1 R:Captain Marvel 2.00
2 V:Arson Fiend. 2.00
3 V:Ibac. 2.00
4 JOy,R:Mary Marvel,Tawky, Tawny 2.00
5 JOy(c&a),F:Mary Marvel, V:Black Adam. 2.00
6 R:Captain Marvel 2.00
7 V:Captain Nazi 2.00
8 R:Captain Marvel,Jr. 2.00
9 JOy,MM,V:Black Adam 2.00
10 JOy,MM,V:Seven Deadly Enemies of Man 2.00
11 JOy,MM,R:Ibis as Capt.Marvel . . 2.00
12 JOy,MM,How Billy Batson's father met Shazam. 2.00
13 JOy,MM. 2.00
14 JOy,GK,MM,F:CaptainMarvelJr . 2.00
15 JOy,MM,V:Mr.Mind. 2.00
16 thru 18 . . . . @2.00
19 JOy(s),GK,MM,Captain Marvel Jr. V:Captain Nazi. 2.00
20 JOy(s),PKr,MM,A:Superman . . . 2.00
21 JOy(s),PKr,MM,V:Liquidator 2.00
22 JOy(s),PKr,MM,A:Batman 2.00
23 JOy(s),PKr,MM, ... 2.00
24 JOy(s),PKr,MM,V:Baron Blitz-krieg, prelude to new family . . . 2.00
25 JOy(s),PKr,MM,The Marvel Family '97 . . . . 2.00
26 JOy(s),PKr,MM,new Capt. Marvel framed for murder 2.00
27 JOy(s),PKr,MM,D:Captain Marvel 2.00
28 JOy(s),DG, V:Patty Patty Bang Bang. 2.00
29 JOy(c),DG,F:Hoppy 2.00
30 JOy(c),PKr,DG,V:Mr. Finish 2.00
31 JOy,PKr,DG,Genesis x-over. . . . 2.00
32 JOy,PKr,DG,Genesis aftermath . 2.00
33 JOy,PKr,DG,Madam M, Sin 2.00
34 JOy,PKr,DG,F:Gangbuster 2.00
35 JOy,PKr,DG,Lightning & Stars, pt.2 x-over 2.00
36 JOy 2.00
37 JOy,MM,DG,F:Capt.Marvel Jr. . . 2.00
38 JOy,PKr,DG,Monster Society of Evil, pt.1. . . . . 2.00
39 JOy,PKr,DG,Monster, pt.2 . . . . . 2.00
40 JOy,PKr,DG,Monster, pt.3 . . . . . 2.00
41 JOy,PKr,DG,Monster, pt.4 . . . . . 2.00
42 JOy,DG,new logo & design 2.00
43 JOy,DG,I:Bulletgirl 2.50
44 JOy,DG,V:Chain Lightning 2.50
45 JOy,DG,A:JLA 2.50
46 JOy,DG,A:Superman 2.50
47 JOy,V:Black Adam, final issue . . 2.50
Ann.#1 JOy(s),MM,"Legends of the Dead Earth" 2.95
Spec.#1,000,000 JOy,DG 2.50
GN Power of Shazam. 7.50
HC JOy(a&s),O:Captain Marvel . . 22.00
GNv JOy(a&s),O:Captain Marvel . . 9.95
TPB JOy, reoffer. 7.50

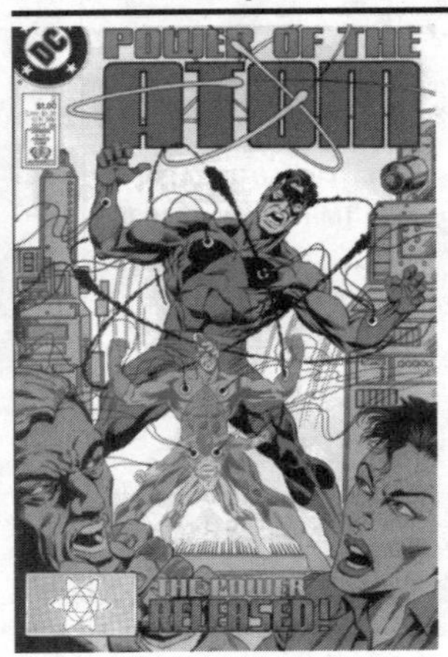

Power of the Atom #2
© DC Comics, Inc.

POWER OF THE ATOM

1988–89

1 1st Issue, Origin retold 2.00
2 Return of Powers 2.00
3 I:Strobe 2.00
4 A:Hawkman+bonus book #8 . . . . 2.00
5 DT,A:Elongated Man. 2.00
6 JBy,V:Chronos 2.00
7 GN,Invasion,V:Khunds,Chronos . 2.00
8 GN,Invasion,V:Chronos 2.00
9 GN,A:Justice League 2.00
10 GN,I:Humbug 2.00
11 GN,V:Paul Hoben 2.00
12 GN,V:Edg the Destroyer 2.00
13 GN,Blood Stream Journey 2.00
14 GN,V:Humbug 2.00
15 GN,V:Humbug 2.00
16 GN,V:The CIA 2.00
17 GN,V:The Sting 2.00
18 GN,V:The CIA, last issue 2.00

POWERPUFF GIRLS

Warner Bros./DC March, 2000

1 . . . . 2.00
2 DaF, ... 2.00
3 mysterious meteor 2.00
4 video game 2.00
5 Tooth Fairy 2.00
6 Dial M for Mojo. 2.00
7 Remote Controlled 2.00
8 Mayor, May 1 . . . . 2.00
Double Whammy, rep. #1 & #2 . . . . 3.95

PREACHER

Vertigo 1995

1 I:Jesse Custer, Genesis 25.00
2 Saint of Killers 18.00
3 GF(c),I:Angels 15.00
4 GF(c),V:Saint of Killers 10.00
5 Naked City,pt.1 . . . . 10.00
6 Naked City,pt.2. . . . . 10.00
7 Naked City,pt.3. . . . . 8.00
8 GEn,SDi,All in the Family,pt.1 . . . 5.00
9 GEn,SDi,All in the Family,pt.2 . . . 5.00
10 GEn,SDi,All in the Family,pt.3 . . 5.00
11 GEn,SDi,All in the Family,pt.4 . . 5.00
12 GEn,SDi,All in the Family,pt.5 . . 6.00
13 GEn,SDi,Hunters,pt.1 . . . . 5.00
14 GEn,SDi,Hunters,pt.2 (of 4) 4.00
15 and 16 . . . . @4.00
17 Star captures Cassidy 3.00
18 GEn(s),SDi,secret of Jesse Custer's cigarette lighter. 3.00
19 GEn(s),SDi,"Crusaders," pt.1 . . . 3.00
20 GEn(s),SDi,"Crusaders," pt.2 . . . 3.00
21 GEn(s),SDi,"Crusaders," pt.3 . . . 3.00
22 GEn(s),SDi,"Crusaders," pt.4 . . . 3.00
23 GEn(s),SDi,"Crusaders," pt.5 . . . 3.00
24 GEn(s),SDi,"Crusaders" concl. . . 3.00
25 GEn(s),SDi,"Cry Blood, Cry Erin". 3.00
26 GEn(s),SDi,"To the Streets of Manhattan I Wandered Away". . 2.50
27 GEn(s),SDi, Jessie & Tulip in New York, pt.1 . . . . 2.50
28 GEn(s),SDi, Jessie & Tulip in New York, pt.2 . . . . 2.50
29 GEn(s),SDi, south to New Orleans 2.50
30 GEn,SDi,in New Orleans 2.50
31 GEn,SDi,in New Orleans 2.50
32 GEn,SDi,in New Orleans 2.50
33 GEn,SDi,in New Orleans,concl. . 2.50
34 GEn,SDi,War in the Sun,pt.1 . . . 2.50
35 GEn,SDi,War in the Sun,pt.2 . . . 2.50
36 GEn,SDi,War in the Sun,pt.3 . . . 2.50
37 GEn,SDi,War in the Sun,pt.4 . . . 2.50
38 GEn,SDi,GF,Utah radioactive . . . 2.50
39 GEn,SDi,GF,out of the desert. . . 2.50
40 GEn,SDi,GF,Arsefaced World . . 2.50
41 . . . . 2.50
42 GEn(s),SDi,GF,V:Meatman 2.50
43 GEn(s),SDi,GF,V:Meat Man 2.50
44 GEn(s),SDi,GF,Gunther Hahn . . 2.50
45 GEn(s),SDi,GF,V:Meat Man 2.50
46 GEn(s),SDi,GF,Miss Oatlash . . . 2.50
47 GEn(s),SDi,GF,Salvation 2.50
48 GEn(s),SDi,GF,Salvation 2.50
49 GEn(s),SDi,GF,First Contact . . . 2.50
50 GEn(s),SDi,GF,48-page 3.75
51 GEn(s),SDi,GF,Tulip's past,pt.1 . 2.50
52 GEn(s),SDi,GF,Tulip's past,pt.2 . 2.50
53 GEn(s),SDi,GF,road trip story. . . 2.50
54 GEn(s),SDi,GF,Jesse & Tulip . . . 2.50
55 GEn(s),SKi,GF. 2.50
56 GEn(s),GF. 2.50
57 GEn(s), ... 2.50
58 GEn(s),SDi, ... 2.50
59 GEn(s),SDi,Alamo,pt.1. . . . . 2.50
60 GEn(s),SDi,Alamo,pt.2. . . . . 2.50
61 GEn(s),SDi,Alamo,pt.3. . . . . 2.50
62 GEn(s),SDi,Alamo,pt.4. . . . . 2.50
63 GEn(s),SDi,Alamo,pt.5. . . . . 2.50
64 GEn(s),SDi,Alamo,pt.6. . . . . 2.50
65 GEn(s),SDi,Alamo,pt.7. . . . . 2.50
66 GEn(s),SDi,Alamo,pt.8, final issue. 2.50
TPB Gone to Texas, rep.#1–#7. . . 15.00
TPB Proud Americans GEn(s) . . . 15.00
TPB Until the End of the World . . . 15.00
TPB Ancient History 15.00
TPB War in the Sun 15.00
TPB All Hell's A-Coming 17.95
HC Preacher: Dead or Alive – The Collected Covers, GF 30.00
GN Preacher Spec. Cassidy: Blood and Whisky, GEn(s) (1997). . . . 6.00
GN Tall in the Saddle 5.95
Spec. The Good Old Boys, parody . 5.50
Spec. The Story of You-Know-Who GEn(s),RCa,O:Arseface (1996) 5.00
Spec. One Man's War. 4.95

PREACHER SPECIAL: SAINT OF KILLERS

DC/Vertigo 1996

1 GEn(s),StP. 6.00
2 GEn(s),StP. 4.50
3 GEn(s),StP. 3.50
4 GEn(s),StP. 3.00

PREZ

Aug.,–Sept., 1973

1 I:Prez (from Sandman #54). . . . 12.00
2 thru 4 F:Prez 8.00

PRIDE & JOY

DC/Vertigo May, 1997

[Mini-series]

1 (of 4) GEn(s),JHi, ... 2.50
2 GEn(s),JHi 2.50
3 GEn(s),JHi 2.50
4 GEn(s),JHi,concl. 2.50

Primal Force #0 © DC Comics, Inc.

PRIMAL FORCE

1994–95

O New Team 2.00
1 Claw. 2.00
2 Cataclysm 2.00
3 . . . . 2.00
4 Claw. 2.00
5 V:Demons 2.00
6 V:The Four Beasts 2.00
7 Trip to the Past. 2.00
8 N.Choles(p),I:New Team. 2.25
9 Maltis worsens, Tornado speaks . 2.25
10 V:August 2.25
11 . . . . 2.25
12 Black Condor vs. August 2.25
13 Underworld Unleashed tie-in . . . 2.25
14 final issue 2.25

PRINCE

Piranha Press

1 DCw,KW,based on rock star . . . 10.00
1a Second printing 2.50
1b 3rd printing 2.00

PRISONER, THE

1988–89

1 Based on TV series 5.00
2 `By Hook or by Crook' 5.00
3 `Confrontation' 5.00
4 `Departure' final issue. 5.00

PROPOSITION PLAYER

DC/Vertigo Oct., 2000

1 (of 6) PGn,BWg,. 2.50
2 PGn,BWg, ... 2.50
3 PGn,BWg, ... 2.50

 All comics prices listed are for *Near Mint* condition.

4 PGn,BWg, ... 2.50
5 PGn,BWg 2.50
6 PGn,BWg, poker game ends . . . 2.50

PSYBA-RATS, THE
[Mini-Series] 1995

1 CDi,A:Robin 2.50
2 CDi,A:Robin 2.00
3 CDi,F:Razorsharp,final issue. . . . 2.00

PSYCHO

1 I:Psycho 12.00
2 Sonya Rescue 10.00
3 `Psycho against the World' 7.00

PULP FANTASTIC
DC/Vertigo Dec., 1999

1 (of 3) HC,RBr,detective. 2.50
2 HC,RBr 2.50
3 HC,RBr,conclusion 2.50

QUEST FOR CAMELOT
June, 1998

1-shot movie adaptation 5.00

QUESTION, THE
Feb., 1987

1 DCw,R:Question,I:Myra,A:Shiva . 3.00
2 DCw,A:Batman,Shiva 2.00
3 DCw,I:Mayor Firman. 2.00
4 DCw,V:Hatch 2.00
5 DCw,Hub City fall Apart 2.00
6 DCw,Abuse story 2.00
7 DCw,V:Mr.Volk 2.00
8 DCw,I:Mikado 2.00
9 DCw,O:Rodor 2.00
10 DCw,O:Rodor cont. 2.00
11 DCw,Transformation. 2.00
12 DCw,Poisoned Ground 2.00
13 DCw,V:The Spartans 2.00
14 DCw,V:The Spartans 2.00
15 DCw,The Klan in Hub City 2.00
16 DCw,`Butch Cassidy & Sundance Kid' 2.00
17 DCw,A:Green Arrow 2.50
18 DCw,A:Green Arrow 2.50
19 DCw,V:Terrorists 2.00
20 DCw,Travelling Circus 2.00
21 DCw,V:Junior Musto 2.00
22 DCw,Election Night 2.00
23 DCw,Election Night contd. 2.00
24 DCw,Election Night contd. 2.00
25 DCw,Myra Critically Ill 2.00
26 A:Riddler 2.00
27 DCw 2.00
28 DCw,A:Lady Shiva. 2.00
29 DCw,V:Lady Shiva. 2.00
30 DCw,A:Lady Shiva. 2.00
31 DCw,Hub City Chaos contd 2.00
32 DCw,Identity Crisis. 2.00
33 DCw,Identity Crisis contd 2.00
34 DCw,Identity Crisis contd 2.00
35 DCw,Fate of Hub City 2.00
36 DCw,final issue (contd.G.A.Ann#3 Question Quarterly #1) 2.00
Ann.#1 DCw,A:Batman,G.A. 3.00
Ann.#2 A:Green Arrow 4.00

QUESTION QUARTERLY

1 DCw. 4.50
2 DCw. 3.95
3 DCw(c) Film 2.95
4 DCw,MM,`Waiting for Phil' 2.95
5 DCw,MMi,MM,last issue 2.95

RAGMAN
[1st Limited Series] 1976–77

1 I&O:Ragman. 10.00
2 I:Opal 6.00
3 V:Mr. Big 5.00
4 JKu(1st interior on character) . . . 5.00
5 JKu,O:Ragman,final issue. 5.00

[2nd Limited Series] 1991–92

1 PB,O:Ragman 3.00
2 PB,O:Ragman Powers 3.00
3 PB,Original Ragman 2.75
4 PB,Gang War 2.75
5 PB,V:Golem 2.75
6 PB,V:Golem,A:Batman 2.75
7 PB,V:Golem,A:Batman 2.75
8 PB,V:Golem,A:Batman 2.75

RAGMAN: CRY OF THE DEAD
1993–94

1 JKu(c),R:Ragman. 2.00
2 JKu(c),A:Marinette 2.00
3 JKu(c),V:Marinette 2.00
4 JKu(c),Exorcism 2.00
5 JKu(c),V:Marinette 2.00
6 JKu(c),final issue 2.00

THE RAY
[Limited Series] 1992

1 JQ,ANi,I&O:Ray(Ray Torril). 5.00
2 JQ,ANi,I:G.A. Ray. 4.00
3 JQ,ANi,A:G.A. Ray 3.00
4 JQ,ANi,V:Dr.Polaris 4.00
5 JQ,ANi,V:Dr.Polaris 3.00
6 JQ,ANi,C:Lobo,final issue 3.00
TPB In A Blaze of Power 9.95

[Regular Series] 1994–96

1 JQ(c),RPr,V:Brinestone, A:Superboy 3.00
1a Newsstand Ed. 2.00
2 RPr,V:Brinestone,A:Superboy . . . 2.00
3 RPr,I:Death Masque 2.00
4 JQ(c),RPr,I:Death Masque, Dr. Polarus. 2.00
5 JQ(c),RPr,V:G.A.Ray 2.00
6 JQ(c),RPr,V:Black Canary. 2.00
7 JQ(c),RPr,V:Canary/Ray 2.00
8 V:Lobo,Black Canary 2.00
9 Ray Undoes the past 2.00
10 F:Happy Terril 2.00
11 30 years in future. 2.00

The Ray #1 © DC Comics, Inc.

12 V:Mystech 2.00
13 V:Death Masque 2.25
14 The Ray needs help, V:Death Masque 2.25
15 F:Vandal Savage 2.25
16 D:Happy Terrill. 2.25
17 I:Josh Terrill,V:Atomic Skull 2.25
18 Underworld Unleashed tie-in . . . 2.25
19 Underworld Unleashed tie-in . . . 2.25
20 F:Black Condor 2.25
21 Black Condor captured 2.25
22 . . . . 2.25
23 V:Death Masque 2.25
24 . . . . 2.25
25 double size 3.50
26 . . . . 2.25
27 . . . . 2.25
28 CPr,final issue 2.25
Ann.#1 Year One Annual 3.95

REAL FACT COMICS
March–April, 1946

1 S&K,Harry Houdini story 500.00
2 S&K, Rin-Tin-Tin story 350.00
3 H.G. Wells story 300.00
4 Jimmy Stewart story,B:Just Imagine 350.00
5 Batman & Robin(c) 1,500.00
6 O:Tommy Tomorrow. 1,000.00
7 `The Flying White House' 150.00
8 VF,A:Tommy Tomorrow 500.00
9 S&K,Glen Miller story 250.00
10 `The Vigilante' by MMe 250.00
11 EK,`How the G-Men Capture Public Enemies!' 150.00
12 `How G-Men are Trained'. . . . 150.00
13 Dale Evans story 450.00
14 Will Rogers story,`Diary of Death' 125.00
15 A:The Master Magician- Thurston. 125.00
16 A:Four Reno Brothers, T.Tommorrow 400.00
17`I Guard an Armored Car' 125.00
18 `The Mystery Man of Tombstone'. 125.00
19 `The Weapon that Won the West'. 125.00
20 JKu 150.00
21 JKu,July-Aug., 1949. . . . . 125.00

REAL SCREEN COMICS
Spring, 1945

1 B:Fox & the Crow,Flippity & Flop 850.00
2 (fa) 400.00
3 (fa) 200.00
4 thru 7 (fa) . . . . @150.00
8 thru 11 (fa) . . . . @125.00
12 thru 20 (fa) . . . . @90.00
21 thru 30 (fa) . . . . @75.00
31 thru 40 (fa) . . . . @50.00
41 thru 128 (fa) . . . . @40.00
Becomes:

TV SCREEN CARTOONS

129 thru 137 . . . . @40.00
138 Jan.–Feb., 1961. . . . . 40.00

REALWORLDS
March, 2000

GN Batman, 48-pg.. . . . . 6.00
GN Wonder Woman, 48-pg. 6.00
GN JLA, 48-pg. 6.00
GN Superman 6.00

R.E.B.E.L.S '94

0 New team. 2.00

R.E.B.E.L.S. '94 #0 © DC Comics, Inc.

1 L.E.G.I.O.N.,Green Lantern 2.00
2 Dissent. 2.00
3 . . . . 2.00
4 Ship goes Insane 2.00

R.E.B.E.L.S '95

5 F:Dox. 2.00
6 Dox Defeated 2.00
7 John Sin. 2.00
8 V:Galactic Bank 2.25
9 F:Dox,Ignea,Garv,Strata 2.25
10 V:World Bank. 2.25
11 . . . . 2.25
12 F:Iceman Assassin 2.25
13 Underworld Unleashed tie-in . . . 2.25
14 F:Lyrl Dox 2.25

R.E.B.E.L.S. '96

15 V:Lyrl Dox 2.25
16 V:Lyrl Dox's satellite. 2.25

RED TORNADO

1985

1 CI/FMc 2.00
2 CI/FMc,A:Superman 2.00
3 CI/FMc 2.00
4 CI/FMc 2.00

RELATIVE HEROES

Feb., 2000

1 (of 6) Olympian super-teens 2.50
2 Things to Do in Olympus
When Your're Dead 2.50
3 F:Impulse 2.50
4 F:Blindside 2.50
5 O:Omni 2.50
6 Concl.. 2.50

REMARKABLE WORLDS OF PHINEAS B. FUDDLE

DC/Paradox 1999

1 (of 4) F:Angus & McKee 6.00
2 . . . . 6.00
3 ancient India. 6.00
4 concl. 6.00

RESTAURANT AT THE END OF THE UNIVERSE

1994

1 Adapt. 2nd book in Hitchhikers'
Guide to the Galaxy,
I:The Restaurant 7.00
2 V:The Meal. 7.00
3 Final issue 7.00

RESURRECTION MAN

March, 1997

1 DAn(s),JG,lenticular death's
head cover. 7.00
2 DAn(s),JG,V:Amazo 5.00
3 DAn(s),JG,"Scorpion Memories"
pt.1 (of 3) 2.50
4 DAn(s),JG,"Scorpion Memories"
pt.2 . . . . 2.50
5 DAn(s),JG,"Scorpion Memories"
pt.3 concl. 2.50
6 DAn&ALa(s),JoP,Genesis tie-in. . 2.50
7 DAn&ALa(s),TGb,BG,A:Batman . 2.50
8 DAn&ALa(s),BG,Big Howler 2.50
9 DAn&ALa(s),F:Hitman, pt.1. . . . . 2.50
10 DAn&ALa(s),F:Hitman, pt.2 . . . . 2.50
11 DAn&ALa(s), Origin of the
Species, pt.1 . . . . 2.50
12 DAn&ALa(s), Origin of the
Species, pt.2 . . . . 2.50
13 DAn&ALa(s),Candy Man 2.50
14 DAn&ALa(s),really dead?. 2.50
15 DAn&ALa(s),JG,V:Rider. 2.50
16 DAn&ALa(s),BG,Avenging
Angels x-over pt.1 . . . . 2.50
17 DAn&ALa(s),BG,Avenging
Angels x-over pt.3 . . . . 2.50
18 DAn&ALa(s),A:Phantom Stranger,
Deadman 2.50
19 DAn&ALa(s),Cape Fear, pt.1 . . . 2.50
20 DAn&ALa(s),Cape Fear, pt.2 . . . 2.50
21 DAn&ALa(s),Cape Fear, pt.3 . . . 2.50
22 DAn&ALa(s) 2.50
23 DAn&ALa(s),Resurrection
Woman 2.50
24 DAn&ALa(s) 2.50
25 DAn&ALa(s)Millennium
Meteor,pt.1 . . . . 2.50
26 DAn&ALa(s)Millennium Meteor,
pt.2,A:Superman, Titans 2.50
27 DAn&ALa(s)Millennium Meteor,
pt.3,final issue 2.50
Spec.#1,000,000 DAn&ALa(s) 2.50

RICHARD DRAGON, KUNG FU FIGHTER

April–May, 1975

1 O:Richard Dragon. 10.00
2 JSn/AM 9.00
3 JK 8.00
4 RE/WW 6.00
5 RE/WW 6.00
6 RE/WW 6.00
7 RE/WW 6.00
8 RE/WW 6.00
9 RE 5.00
10 RE. 5.00
11 RE. 5.00
12 RE. 5.00
13 thru 17 RE . . . . @5.00
18 Nov.–Dec., 1977 . . . . 5.00

RIMA, THE JUNGLE GIRL

April–May, 1974

1 NR,I:Rima,O:Pt. 1. . . . . 10.00
2 NR,O:Pt.2. . . . . 5.00

Rima, The Jungle Girl #1
© DC Comics, Inc.

3 NR,O:Pt.3. . . . . 5.00
4 NR,O:Pt.4. . . . . 5.00
5 NR 5.00
6 NR 5.00
7 April-May, 1975 . . . . 5.00

RING, THE

1 GK,Opera Adaption 12.00
2 GK,Sigfried's Father's Sword . . . 7.00
3 GK,to save Brunhilde 6.00
4 GK, final issue 6.00
TPB rep.#1 thru #4 . . . . 19.95

RIP HUNTER, TIME MASTER

March–April, 1961

1 . . . . 500.00
2 . . . . 250.00
3 thru 5 . . . . @150.00
6 and 7 Ath . . . . @125.00
8 thru 15 . . . . @75.00
16 thru 20 . . . . @75.00
21 thru 28 . . . . @75.00
29 Nov.–Dec., 1965 . . . . 75.00

ROAD TO PERDITION

DC/Paradox/Pocket (April, 1998)

TPB 6"x8" 304pg., b&w. 14.00

ROBIN

[1st Limited Series] 1991

1 TL,BB(c),Trial,pt.1(&Poster) 5.00
1a 2nd printing 2.50
1b 3rd printing 2.00
2 TL,BB(c) Trial,pt.2 . . . . 2.50
2a 2nd printing 2.00
3 TL,BB(c) Trial,pt.3 . . . . 2.00
4 TL,Trial,pt.4 . . . . 2.00
5 TL,Final issue,A:Batman. 2.00
TPB BB(c),rep.#1–#5,Batman
#455–#457 . . . . 7.95

[2nd Limited Series] 1991
[ROBIN II: THE JOKER'S WILD]

1 Direct,Hologram(c)Joker face . . . 2.00
1a (c)Joker straightjacket. 2.00
1b (c)Joker standing 2.00
1c (c)Batman. 2.00
1d Newsstand(no hologram) 1.50

 All comics prices listed are for *Near Mint* condition.

1e collectors set,extra holo. 5.00
2 Direct,Hologram(c) Robin/Joker Knife 2.00
2a (c)Joker/Robin-Dartboard 2.00
2b (c)Robin/Joker-Hammer 2.00
2c Newsstand(no hologram) 1.50
2d collectors set,extra holo. 5.00
3 Direct,Holo(c)Robin standing . . . 2.00
3a (c)Robin swinging 1.50
3b Newsstand(no hologram) 1.50
3c collectors set,extra holo. 3.00
4 Direct,Hologram 2.00
4a Newsstand (no hologram). 1.50
4b collectors set,extra holo. 2.00
Collectors set (#1 thru #4). 30.00

[3rd Limited Series] 1992–93

[ROBIN III: CRY OF THE HUNTRESS]

1 TL,A:Huntress,Collector's Ed. movable(c),poster. 3.00
1a MZ(c),Newsstand Ed. 2.00
2 TL,V:KGBeast,A:Huntress. 2.75
2a MZ(c),Newsstand Ed 2.00
3 TL,V:KGBeast,A:Huntress. 2.75
3a MZ(c),newsstand Ed. 2.00
4 TL,V:KGBeast,A:Huntress. 2.75
4a MZ(c),newsstand Ed. 2.00
5 TL,V:KGBeast,A:Huntress. 2.75
5a MZ(c),newsstand Ed. 2.00
6 TL,V:KGBeast,King Snake, A:Huntress. 2.75
6a MZ(c),Newsstand Ed. 2.00

[Regular Series] 1993–99

1 B:CDi(s),TG,SHa,V:Speedboyz. . 4.00
1a Newstand Ed. 2.00
2 TG,V:Speedboyz 2.00
3 TG,V:Cluemaster, Electrocutioner 2.00
4 TG,V:Cluemaster,Czonk, Electrocutioner 2.00
5 TG,V:Cluemaster,Czonk, Electrocutioner 2.00
6 TG,A:Huntress 2.00
7 TG,R:Robin's Father. 2.00
8 TG,KnightsEnd#5,A:Shiva 3.00
9 TG,Knights End:Aftermath 2.25
10 TG,Zero Hour,V:Weasel. 2.00
11 New Batman 2.00
12 Robin vs. thugs 2.00
13 V:Steeljacket 2.00
14 CDi(s),TG,Return of Bruce Wayne,Troika,pt.4. . . . . 2.00
14a Collector's edition 2.50
15 Cluemaster Mystery. 2.00
16 F:Spoiler 2.00
17 I:Silver Monkey,V:King Snake,Lynx [New Miraweb format begins] . . 2.00
18 Gotham City sabotaged 2.00
19 V:The General 2.00
20 F:Robin 2.00
21 Ninja Camp,pt.1. . . . . 2.00
22 CDi,TG,Ninja Camp,pt.2 . . . . . . 2.00
23 CDi,Underworld Unleashed tie-in 2.00
24 CDi,V:Charaxes. 2.00
25 CDi,F:Green Arrow 2.00
26 . . . . 2.00
27 . . . . 2.00
28 CDi,Contagion: conclusion. 2.00
29 CDi,FFo,SnW,A:Maxie Zeus . . . 2.00
30 CDi,FFo,SnW,A:Maxie Zeus . . . 2.00
31 CDi(s),A:Wildcat 2.00
32 CDi(s),Legacy, pt. 3 x-over. 2.00
33 CDi(s),Legacy, pt. 7 x-over. 2.00
34 CDi(s),JhD,action at a Shakespear play 2.00
35 CDi(s),Robin & Spoiler, Final Night tie-in 2.00
36 CDi(s),V:Toyman, The General . 2.00
37 CDi(s),V:The General, Toyman . 2.00
38 CDi(s),. 2.00
39 CDi(s), pt.2 . . . . 2.00
40 CDi(s),. 2.00
41 CDi(s),F:Tim and Ariana 2.00
42 CDi(s),F:Crocky the Crocodile . . 2.00
43 CDi(s),A:Spoiler. 2.00
44 CDi(s) Pt.2 (of 2) 2.00
45 CDi(s) Tim Drake grounded 2.00
46 CDi(s) Genesis tie-in 2.00
47 CDi,V:General, pt.1 . . . . 2.00
48 CDi,V:General, pt.2 . . . . 2.00
49 CDi,to Paris 2.00
50 CDi(s),F:Lady Shiva & King Snake, 48pg. 3.00
51 CDi(s) 2.00
52 CDi(s) Cataclysm x-over,pt.7 . . . 2.00
53 CDi(s),SnW,Cataclysm concl.. . . 2.00
54 CDi(s),SnW,Aftershock 2.00
55 CDi(s),SnW, Brotherhood of the Fist x-over, pt.3. . . . . 2.00
56 CDi(s),SnW,tearful turning point. 2.00
57 CDi(s),SnW,A:Spoiler. 2.00
58 CDi(s),SnW,A:Spoiler. 2.00
59 CDi(s),SnW,V:Steeljacket. 2.00
60 CDi(s),SnW,Alvin Draper 2.00
61 CDi(s),SnW,V:Phil Delinger 2.00
62 CDi(s),SnW,A:Flash, pt.1 . . . . . . 2.00
63 CDi(s),SnW,A:Flash, pt.2 . . . . . . 2.00
64 CDi(s),SnW,A:Flash, pt.3 . . . . . . 2.00
65 CDi(s),SnW,A:Spoiler. 2.00
66 CDi(s),SnW,V:demons 2.00
67 CDi(s),SnW,No Man's Land 2.00
68 CDi(s),No Man's Land 2.00
69 CDi(s),No Man's Land 2.00
70 CDi(s),No Man's Land 2.00
71 CDi(s),V:Killer Croc 2.00
72 CDi(s) 2.00
73 CDi(s),F:Batgirl 2.00
74 CDi(s),F:Batman & Nightwing . . 2.00
75 CDi(s),48-pg. 3.00
76 CDi(s),R:Man-Bat 2.00
77 CDi(s),I:Jaeger 2.00
78 CDi(s),V:Arrakhat. 2.00
79 CDi(s),F:Green Arrow 2.25
80 CDi(s),A:Star 2.25
81 CDi(s),MPn,. 2.25
82 CDi(s),Spoiler,Star. 2.25
83 CDi,Vacation time 2.25
Ann.#1 TL,Eclipso tie-in,V:Anarky . . 3.00
Ann.#2 KD,JL,Bloodlines#10, I:Razorsharp 2.75
Ann.#3 Elseworlds Story. 3.25
Ann.#4 Year One Annual 2.95
Ann.#5 CDi,Legends of the Dead Earth 2.95

Robin #12 © DC Comics, Inc.

Ann.#5 Legends o/t Dead Earth . . . 2.95
Ann.#6 Pulp Heroes (Western), CDi(s) 3.95
Spec.#1,000,000 CDi(s),SnW 2.00
Spec. Robin/Argent Double Shot DJu,CDi,V:Spoiler x-over (1997) 2.00
TPB A Hero Reborn,JAp,TL 4.95
TPB Tragedy and Triumph, TL,NBy. 9.95
TPB Robin: Flying Solo. 12.95
80-page Giant #1 CDi. 5.95

ROBIN PLUS

1 MWa&BAu(s), F:Bart Allen, skiing rips, V:Mystral 2.95
2 LKa,CDi,AWi,ALa,F:Fang 3.00

ROBIN 3000

1 CR,Elseworlds,V:Skulpt 5.25
2 CR,Elseworlds,V:Skulpt 5.25

ROBIN: YEAR ONE

October, 2000

1 CDi,SBe,F:Dick Grayson 4.95

ROBIN HOOD TALES

Jan.–Feb., 1957–Mar.–Apr., 1958

7 . . . . 250.00
8 thru 14 . . . . @200.00

ROBOTECH DEFENDERS

1 MA,mini-series 3.50
2 MA 3.00

ROGAN GOSH

Vertigo 1994

1 PF PrM(s) (From Revolver). 7.25

RONIN

July, 1983

1 FM,1:Billy 6.00
2 FM,I:Casey. 5.00
3 FM,V:Agat 5.00
4 FM,V:Agat 5.00
5 FM,V:Agat 6.00
6 FM,D:Billy. 8.00
Paperback, FM inc. Gatefold. 12.00

ROOTS OF THE SWAMP THING

July, 1986

1 BWr,rep.SwampThing#1 . . . . 3.00
2 BWr,rep.SwampThing#3 . . . . 3.00
3 BWr,rep.SwampThing#5 . . . . 3.00
4 BWr,rep.SwampThing#7 . . . . 3.00
5 BWr,rep.SwampThing#9
, H.O.S. #92, final issue 3.00

RUDOLPH THE RED–NOSED REINDEER

Dec., 1950

1950 . . . . 100.00
1951 thru 1954. . . . . @60.00
1955 thru 1962 Winter . . . . @40.00

RUSSIAN ROULETTE

Vertigo 1999

1 (of 3) 3.00

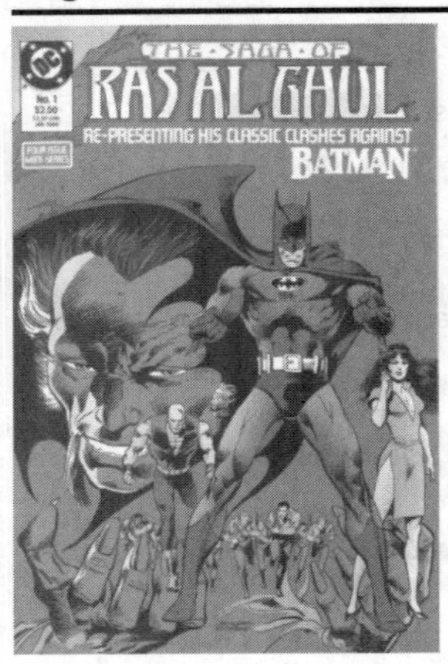

Saga of Ras Al Ghul #1
© DC Comics, Inc.

SAGA OF RAS AL GHUL

1988

1 NA,DG,reprints 5.00
2 rep. 4.00
3 rep.Batman #242ó 4.00
4 rep.Batman #244õ,
Detective #410 . . . . 4.00
TPB reps. 17.95

SAGA OF THE SWAMP THING

1982–85

1 JmP(s),TY,DSp,O:Swamp Thing,
BU:PhantomStranger 4.00
2 Ph(c),TY,DSp,I:Grasp 2.00
3 TY,DSp,V:Vampires 2.00
4 TY,TD,V:Demon 2.00
5 TY 2.00
6 TY,I:General Sunderland. 2.00
7 TY 2.00
8 TY 2.00
9 TY 2.00
10 TY. 2.00
11 TY,I:Golem. 2.00
12 LWn(s),TY 2.00
13 TY,D:Grasp 2.00
14 A:Phantom Stranger 2.00
15 . . . . 2.00
16 SBi,JTo 2.00
17 I:Matthew Cable. 4.00
18 JmP(s),LWn(s),SBi,JTo,BWr,
R:Arcane 2.00
19 JmP(s),SBi,JTo,V:Arcane 2.00
20 B:AMo(s),Day,JTo(i),D:Arcane
(Original incarnation) 15.00
21 SBi,JTo,O:Swamp Thing,I:Floronic
Man,D:General Sunderland . . 13.00
22 SBi,JTo,O:Floronic Man 10.00
23 SBi,JTo,V:Floronic Man 10.00
24 SBi,JTo,V:Floronic Man,A:JLA,
In Arkham 10.00
25 SBi,A:Jason Blood,I:Kamara . . . 8.00
26 SBi,A:Demon,
D:Matthew Cable 8.00
27 SBi,D:Kamara,A:Demon 7.00
28 SwM,Burial of Alec Holland 7.00
29 SBi,JTo,R:Arcane. 7.00
30 SBi,AA,D:Abby,C:Joker,
V:Arcane 9.00
31 RV,JTo,D:Arcane 6.00
32 SwM,Tribute to WK Pogo strip . . 6.00
33 rep.H.O.S.#92,A:Cain & Abel . . . 6.00
34 SBi,JTo,Swamp Thing & Abby
Fall in Love 8.00
35 SBi,JTo,Nukeface,pt.1 . . . . 5.00
36 SBi,JTo,Nukeface,pt.2 . . . . 5.00
37 RV,JTo,I:John Constantine,
American Gothic,pt.1 . . . . 17.00
38 SnW,JTo,V:Water-Vampires
(Pt.1) A:J.Constantine 6.00
39 SBi,JTo,V:Water-Vampires
(Pt.2) A:J.Constantine 5.00
40 SBi,JTo,C:J.Constantine,
The Curse 5.00
41 SBi,AA,Voodoo Zombies #1. . . . 3.00
42 SBi,JTo,RoR,
Voodoo Zombies #2 . . . . 3.00
43 SnW,RoR,Windfall,
I:Chester Williams 3.00
44 SBi,JTo,RoR,V:Serial Killer,
C:Batman,Constantine,Mento . . 5.00
45 SnW,AA,Ghost Dance 3.00
Ann.#1 MT,TD,Movie Adaption 2.00
Ann.#2 AMo(s),E:Arcane,A:Deadman,
Phantom Stranger,Spectre,
Demon,Resurrection of Abby . . 7.00
Ann.#3 AMo(s),Ape issue 4.00
TPB rep.#21-#27 . . . . 12.95
TPB rep.#28-#34,Ann.#2 . . . . 14.95
TPB Love and Death 19.95
Becomes:

SWAMP THING

SANDMAN

[1st Regular Series] 1974–75

1 JK,I&O:Sandman,I:General
Electric. 22.00
2 V:Dr.Spider. 10.00
3 Brain that Blanked
out the Bronx 10.00
4 JK,Panic in the Dream Stream . 10.00
5 JK,Invasion of the Frog Men . . . 10.00
6 JK,WW,V:Dr.Spider. 10.00

[2nd Regular Series] 1989–93

1 B:NGa(s),SK,I:2nd Sandman . . 50.00
2 SK,A:Cain,Abel. 20.00
3 SK,A:John Constantine. 18.00
4 SK,A:Demon. 15.00
5 SK,A:Mr.Miracle,J'onnJ'onzz . . . 15.00
6 V:Doctor Destiny. 10.00
7 V:Doctor Destiny. 9.00
8 Sound of her wings,F:Death . . . 30.00
8a Guest Ed.Pin-Up Cover 75.00
9 Tales in the Sand,Doll's House
prologue. 9.00
10 B:Doll's House,A:Desire
& Despair,I:Brut & Glob 9.00
11 MovingIn,A:2ndS-man 9.00
12 Play House,D;2ndS'man 9.00
13 Men of Good Fortune,A:Death,
Lady Constantine 9.00
14 Collectors,D:Corinthian 8.00
15 Into' Night,DreamVortex. 7.00
16 E:Doll's House,Lost Hearts 7.00
17 Calliope. 7.00
18 Dream of a 1000 Cats 7.00
18a error pg.1. . . . . 20.00
19 Midsummer Nights Dream 6.00
19a error copy 15.00
20 Strange Death Element Girl,
A:Death 7.00
21 Family Reunion,B:Season
of Mists 8.00
22 Season of Mists,I:Daniel Hall . . 13.00
23 Season of Mists. 7.00
24 Season of Mists. 7.00
25 Season of Mists. 7.00
26 Season of Mists. 6.00
27 E:Season of Mists 6.00

Sandman #1 © DC Comics, Inc.

28 Ownership of Hell 6.00
29 A:Lady J.Constantine. 5.00
30 Ancient Rome;A:Death,Desire . . 5.00
31 Ancient Rome,pt.2 . . . . 5.00
32 B:The Game of You 5.00
33 The Game of You 5.00
34 The Game of You 4.00
35 The Game of You 4.00
36 The Game of You,48pgs 5.00
37 The Game of You,Epilogue 4.00
38 Convergence. 4.00
39 Convergence,A:Marco Polo 4.00
40 Convergence,A:Cain,Abel,Eve,
Matthew the Raven 4.00
41 JIT,VcL,(i),B:Brief Lives,
F:Endless. 4.00
42 JIT,VcL,(i),F:Delirium,Dream. . . . 4.00
43 JIT,VcL,(i),A:Death,Etain 4.00
44 JIT,VcL,(i),R:Corinthian,
Destruction. 4.00
45 JIT,VcL,(i),F:Tiffany,
Ishtar(Belli). 4.00
46 JIT,VcL,(i),F:Morpheus/Bast,
A:Aids insert story,F:Death . . . 4.00

Vertigo 1994–96

47 JIT,VcL,(i),A:Endless 4.00
48 JIT,VcL,(i),L:Destruction 4.00
49 JIT,VcL,(i),E:Brief Lives,
F:Orpheus 4.00
50 DMc(c),CR,Tales of Baghdad,
pin-upsby TM,DMc,MK 5.00
50a Gold Ed. 25.00
51 BT,MBu(i),B:Inn at the end of
the World,Gaheris' tale 4.00
52 BT,MBu(i),JWk,Cluracan's
Story 4.00
53 BT,DG,MBu(i),MZi,Hob's
Leviathan 4.00
54 BT,MiA,MBu(i),R:Prez 4.00
55 SAp,VcL,BT,MBu(i),F:Klaproth
Cerements's Story 4.00
56 BT,MBu(i),DG(i),SLi(i),GyA,TyH(i),
E:Inn at the end of the World,
C:Endless 4.00
57 MaH,B:Kindly Ones,Inc.American
Freak Preview 5.00
58 MaH,Kindly Ones,pt.2,
A:Lucifer. 3.50
59 MaH,Kindly Ones,pt.3,R:Fury. . . 3.50
60 MaH,Kindly Ones,pt.4 . . . . 3.50
61 MaH,Kindly Ones,pt.5 . . . . 3.50
62 Kindly Ones,pt.6,Murder 3.50
63 MaH,Kindly Ones,pt.7,
A:Rose Walker 3.50
64 Kindly Ones,pt.8 . . . . 3.50

 All comics prices listed are for *Near Mint* condition.

65 MaH,Kindly Ones,pt.9,Dream Kingdom . . . 3.50
66 MaH,Kindly Ones,pt.10 . . . 3.50
67 MaH,Kindly Ones,pt.11 . . . 3.50
68 MaH,Kindly Ones,pt.12 . . . 3.50
69 MaH,Kindly Ones finale . . . 3.50
70 The Wake,pt.1 . . . 3.50
71 The Wake,pt.2 . . . 3.50
72 NGa,DMc,The Wake,pt.3 . . . 3.50
73 NGa,Sunday Mourning . . . 3.50
74 NGa,V:Lord of Dreams . . . 3.50
TPB Preludes & Nocturnes, rep. #1–#8 . . . 20.00
TPB Doll's House, rep #8–#16 . . . 18.00
HC The Doll's House . . . 30.00
TPB Dream Country,Rep.#17-#20. 15.00
TPB Fables & Reflections,rep. . . . 20.00
HC Fables and Reflections . . . 30.00
TPB Season of Mists,rep.#21-#28. 20.00
HC Season of Mists . . . 40.00
TPB A Game of You,rep.#32–#37 . 20.00
HC A Game of You,rep.#32-#37 . . 32.00
TPB Brief Lives. . . . 20.00
HC Brief Lives . . . 30.00
TPB The Wake, rep. #70–#75. . . . 20.00
HC The Wake. . . . 30.00
TPB World's End DMc(c) . . . 20.00
Sandman Covers, 1989–96 . . . 40.00
Spec.BT,Glow in the Dark(c),The Legend of Orpheus, (inc. Portrait Gallery) . . . 6.00

SANDMAN MYSTERY THEATRE

Vertigo 1993–99

1 B:MWg(s),GyD,R:G.A.Sandman, B:Tarantula,I:Mr.Belmont, Dian Belmont . . . 5.00
2 GyD,V:Tarantula . . . 3.00
3 GyD,V:Tarantula . . . 3.00
4 GyD,E:Tarantula . . . 3.00
5 JWk,B:The Face. . . . 3.00
6 JWk,The Face #2 . . . 3.00
7 JWk,The Face #3 . . . 3.00
8 JWk,E:The Face. . . . 3.00
9 RGT,B:The Brute,I:Rocket Ramsey . . . 3.00
10 RGT,The Brute#2. . . . 3.00
11 RGT,The Brute#3. . . . 3.00
12 RGT,E:The Brute . . . 3.00
13 GyD,B:The Vamp. . . . 3.00
14 GyD,The Vamp#2 . . . 3.00
15 GyD,The Vamp#3 . . . 3.00
16 GyD,E:The Vamp. . . . 3.00
17 GyD,B:The Scorpion . . . 3.00
18 GyD,The Scorpion,pt.2 . . . 3.00
19 GyD,The Scorpion,pt.3 . . . 3.00
20 GyD,The Scorpion,pt.4 . . . 3.00
21 Dr. Death. . . . 3.00
22 Dr. Death,pt.2 . . . 3.00
23 Dr. Death,pt.3 . . . 3.00
24 Dr. Death,pt.4 . . . 3.00
25 The Butcher,pt.1 . . . 3.00
26 The Butcher,pt.2 . . . 3.00
27 The Butcher,pt.3 . . . 3.00
28 The Butcher,pt.4 . . . 3.00
29 The Hourman,pt.1 . . . 3.00
30 The Hourman,pt.2 . . . 3.00
31 The Hourman,pt.3 . . . 3.00
32 The Hourman,pt.4 . . . 3.00
33 The Python,pt.1 . . . 3.00
34 The Python,pt.2 . . . 3.00
35 The Python,pt.3. . . . 3.00
36 The Python,pt.4 . . . 3.00
37 The Mist,pt.1 . . . 3.00
38 The Mist,pt.2 . . . 3.00
39 The Mist,pt.3 . . . 3.00
40 The Mist,pt.4 . . . 3.00
41 MWg&SSe(s),GyD, Phantom of the Fair pt. 1. . . . 2.50
42 MWg&SSe(s),GyD, Phantom of the Fair pt. 2. . . . 2.50
43 MWg&SSe(s),GyD, Phantom of the Fair pt. 3. . . . 2.50
44 MWg&SSe(s),GyD, Phantom of the Fair pt. 4. . . . 2.50
45 MWg&SSe(s),"The Blackhawk," pt.1 . . . 2.50
46 MWg&SSe(s),"The Blackhawk," pt.2 . . . 2.50
47 MWg&SSe(s),"The Blackhawk," pt.3 . . . 2.50
48 MWg&SSe(s),RCa,"The Blackhawk" concl.. . . . 2.50
49 MWg&SSe(s),"The Scarlet Ghost," pt.1 . . . 2.50
50 MWg&SSe(s),"The Scarlet Ghost," pt.2, 48pg . . . 4.50
51 MWg&SSe(s),"The Scarlet Ghost," pt.3 . . . 2.50
52 MWg&SSe(s),"The Scarlet Ghost," pt.4 . . . 2.50
53 MWg&SSe(s),The Crone,pt.1. . . 2.50
53 MWg&SSe(s),The Crone,pt.2. . . 2.50
54 SSe&MWg(s),The Crone,pt.3. . . 2.50
55 SSe&MWg(s),The Crone,pt.4. . . 2.50
56 SSe&MWg(s),The Crone, concl. 2.50
57 SSe&MWg(s),The Cannon,pt.1 . 2.50
58 SSe&MWg(s),The Cannon,pt.2 . 2.50
59 SSe&MWg(s),The Cannon,pt.3 . 2.50
60 SSe&MWg(s),The Cannon,pt.4 . 2.50
61 SSe(s),GyD,The City, pt.1 . . . 2.50
62 SSe(s),GyD,The City, pt.2 . . . 2.50
63 SSe(s),GyD,The City, pt.3 . . . 2.50
64 SSe(s),GyD,The City, pt.4 . . . 2.50
65 SSe,GyD,The Goblin, pt.1 . . . 2.50
66 SSe,GyD,The Goblin, pt.2 . . . 2.50
67 SSe,GyD,The Goblin, pt.3 . . . 2.50
68 SSe,GyD,The Goblin, pt.4 . . . 2.50
69 SSe,GyD . . . 2.50
70 SSe,GyD,final issue. . . . 2.50
Ann.#1 . . . 3.95
TPB The Tarantula . . . 14.95
TPB The Dream Hunters . . . 19.95
HC The Dream Hunters . . . 29.95
HC The Wake, rep.. . . . 29.95
TPB Season of the Mists . . . 19.95
TPB Sandman Companion . . . 14.95

SANDMAN PRESENTS: LOVE STREET

Vertigo 1999

1 (of 3) MZi,VcL, . . . 3.00
2 MZi,VcL,F:John Constantine. . . . 3.00
3 MZi,VcL,Concl. . . . 3.00

SANDMAN PRESENTS: LUCIFER

Vertigo 1999

1 (of 3) SHp, Morningstar Option . . 3.00
2 SHp . . . 3.00
3 SHp, conclusion . . . 3.00

SANDMAN PRESENTS: MERV PUMPKINHEAD — AGENT OF DREAM

DC/Vertigo 1999

1 One-Shot, MBu. . . . 6.00

SANDMAN PRESENTS: PETREFAX

DC/Vertigo Jan., 2000

1 (of 4) SL. . . . 2.95
2 SL, . . . 2.95
3 SL, . . . 2.95
4 SL,concl. . . . 2.95

SCARAB

Vertigo 1993–94

1 GF(c),B:JnS(s),SEa,MkB(i), R&O:Scarab,V:Halaku-umid . . . 2.25
2 GF(c),SEa,MkB(i),A:Phantom Stranger. . . . 2.25
3 GF(c),SEa,MkB(i),in North Carolina . . . 2.25
4 GF(c),SEa,MkB(i),V:Rathoroch . . 2.25
5 GF(c),SEa,MkB(i) . . . 2.25
6 GF(c),SEa,MkB(i),V:Gloryboys . . 2.25
7 GF(c),SEa,MkB(i),V:Scientists . . 2.25
8 GF(c),SEa,MkB(i),Final Issue . . . 2.25

SCARE TACTICS

Oct., 1996

1 LKa(s),AWi,ALa,monsters of the MTV age . . . 2.25
2 LKa(s),AWi,ALa,I:Scaremobile . . 2.25
3 LKa(s),AWi,ALa, . . . 2.25
4 LKa(s),AWi,ALa, "Big For His Age," O:Grossout . . . 2.25
5 LKa(s),AWi,ALa, Valentine's Day issue . . . 2.25
6 LKa(s),AWi,Ala, F:Fang . . . 2.25
7 LKa(s),AWi,ALa, F:The Children of the Beast . . . 2.25
8 LKa(s),AWi,ALa, Convergence, x-over, concl. . . . 2.25
9 LKa(s),AWi,ALa,"Snake Oil" concl. . . . 2.25
10 LKa(s),AWi,ALa,in Gotham . . . 2.25
11 LKa(s),AWi,ALa,A:Batman . . . 2.25

Scarlett #3 © DC Comics, Inc.

SCARLETT

1993–94

1 I:Scarlett,Blood of the Innocent . . 3.50
2 Blood of the Innocent cont. . . . 2.00
3 Blood of the Innocent cont. . . . 2.00
4 V:The Nomads . . . 2.00
5 GM,O:Nomads . . . 2.00
6 thru 8 GM,Blood of the Damned . 2.00
9 GM,V:Undead. . . . 2.00
10 B:Blood of the City. . . . 2.00
11 I:Afterburn . . . 2.00
12 V:Sligoth . . . 2.00
13 V:Gearsman . . . 2.00
14 final issue . . . 2.00

SCENE OF THE CRIME

Vertigo 1999

1 (of 4) 2.50
2 thru 4 . . . . @2.50
TPB A Little Piece of Goodnight . . 12.95

SCRIBBLY

Aug., 1948–Dec.,–Jan., 1951–52

1 SM 800.00
2 . . . . 500.00
3 . . . . 400.00
4 . . . . 400.00
5 . . . . 400.00
6 thru 10 . . . . @275.00
11 thru 15 . . . . @250.00

SCOOBY-DOO

Warner Bros./DC June, 1997

1 . . . . 2.00
2 . . . . 2.00
3 A wedding 2.00
4 Mad Hounds of the Hunt. 2.00
5 Freddy's Grampa Ted 2.00
6 Ghost Riders in Disguise 2.00
7 Mystery of the Missing Cargo . . . 2.00
8 . . . . 2.00
9 Mardi Gras 2.00
10 mystery convention 2.00
11 evil genie 2.00
12 comic book con. 2.00
13 real monster 2.00
14 beneath New York City 2.00
15 Big Puce 2.00
16 . . . . 2.00
17 . . . . 2.00
18 . . . . 2.00
19 Ghost of Holiday Presents 2.00
20 Wraithcar Driver. 2.00
21 . . . . 2.00
22 Curse of Wrangler Field 2.00
23 two fish stories. 2.00
24 Surf's up 2.00
25 Phantom of the Mosh Pit 2.00
26 One Night in Roswell, pt.1 . . . . . 2.00
27 One Night in Roswell, pt.2 . . . . . 2.00
28 . . . . 2.00
29 Barber shop. 2.00
30 . . . . 2.00
31 . . . . 2.00
32 DAn,JSon 2.00
33 JSon,Return of the Star Dog . . . 2.00
34 JSon,Hound of the Basketcases 2.00
35 JSon,Pizza in a Cup 2.00
36 JSon,Double Trouble 2.00
37 Bee Ball. 2.00
38 on vacation 2.00
39 2 Heads are Better than None . . 2.00
40 Roc Around the Clock 2.00
41 Electric monster haunts trolly . . 2.00
Spooky Spectacular 2000. . . . . 3.95

SEA DEVILS

Sept.–Oct., 1961

1 RH 550.00
2 RH 300.00
3 RH 175.00
4 RH 150.00
5 RH 150.00
6 thru 10 RH . . . . @85.00
11 . . . . 65.00
12 . . . . 65.00
13 JKu,GC,RA 65.00
14 thru 20. . . . . @65.00
21 I:Capt X,Man Fish 40.00
22 thru 35, May-June, 1967. . . . @40.00

SEBASTIAN O

Vertigo 1993

1 GMo(s),SY,I:Sebastian O,A:Lord Lavender,Roaring Boys 2.50
2 GMo(s),SY,V:Roaring Boys, Assassins,A:Abbe 2.50
3 GMo(s),SY,D:Lord Lavender 2.50

SECRET FILES & ORIGINS: DCU

2000

TPB DAn,ALa,guide to DCU 6.95

SECRET HEARTS

Sept.,–Oct., 1949–July, 1971

1 `Make Believe Sweetheart' . . . 400.00
2 ATh,`Love Is Not A Dream' . . . 200.00
3 `Sing Me A Love Song' 175.00
4 ATh 175.00
5 ATh 175.00
6 . . . . 175.00
7 . . . . 300.00
8 . . . . 125.00
9 . . . . 125.00
10 thru 20 . . . . @125.00
21 thru 26. . . . . @75.00
27 B:Comics Code 50.00
28 thru 30 . . . . @50.00
31 thru 70 . . . . @45.00
71 thru 110 . . . . @25.00
111 thru 120 . . . . @20.00
121 thru 150 . . . . @12.00
151 thru 153 . . . . @10.00

SECRET ORIGINS

Feb., 1973–Oct., 1974

1 O:Superman,Batman,Ghost, Flash 20.00
2 O:Green Lantern,Atom, Supergirl 10.00
3 O:Wonder Woman,Wildcat 10.00
4 O:Vigilante by MMe 10.00
5 O:The Spectre 10.00
6 O:Blackhawk,Legion of Super Heroes 10.00
7 O:Robin, Aquaman 10.00

SECRET ORIGINS

April, 1986

1 JOy,WB,F:Superman 4.00

Secret Origins #17 © DC Comics, Inc.

Secret Origins #37 © DC Comics, Inc.

2 GK,F:Blue Beetle 3.50
3 JBi,F:Captain Marvel 3.00
4 GT,F:Firestorm 2.75
5 GC,F:Crimson Aventer 3.00
6 DG,MR,F:Batman. 5.00
7 F:Sandman,Guy Gardner 3.50
8 MA,F:Shadow Lass,Dollman. . . . 2.50
9 GT,F:Skyman,Flash 2.50
10 JL,JO,JA,F:Phantom Stranger . . 2.25
11 LMc,TD,F:Hawkman,Powergirl . . 2.00
12 F:Challengers of the Unknown I:G.A. Fury 2.00
13 EL,F:Nightwing 3.00
14 F:Suicide Squad 2.25
15 KMo,DG,F:Deadman,Spectre. . . 2.25
16 AKu,F:Hourman,Warlord 2.00
17 KGi,F:Green Lantern 2.25
18 . . . . 2.00
19 JM(c),MA. 2.00
20 RL,DG,F:Batgirl 3.00
21 GM,MA,F:Jonah Hex 2.00
22 F:Manhunter,Millennium tie-in . . 2.00
23 F:Manhunter,Millennium tie-in . . 2.00
24 F:Dr.Fate,Blue Devil. 2.00
25 F:The Legion 2.00
26 F:Black Lightning 2.00
27 F:Zatanna,Zatara 2.00
28 RLd,GK,F:Nightshade,Midnight . 2.00
29 F:Atom,Red Tornado 2.00
30 F:Elongated Man 2.00
31 F:Justice Society of America. . . . 2.00
32 F:Justice League America.. . . . . 3.00
33 F:Justice League Inter.. . . . . 2.00
34 F:Justice League Inter.. . . . . 2.00
35 KSu,F:Justice League Inter. 2.00
36 F:Green Lantern 3.00
37 F:Legion of Subst. Heroes 2.00
38 F:Green Arrow,Speedy 2.00
39 F:Batman,Animal Man 3.50
40 F:Gorilla City 2.00
41 F:Flash Villains 2.50
42 DC,F:Phantom Girl 2.00
43 TVE,TT,F:Hawk & Dove. 2.00
44 F:Batman,Clayface tie-in 3.00
45 F:Blackhawk,El Diablo 2.00
46 CS,F:All Headquarters 2.00
47 CS,F:The Legion 2.00
48 KG,F:Ambush Bug. 2.00
49 F: The Cadmus Project 2.50
50 GP,CI,DG,F:Batman,Robin, Flash,Black Canary 4.00
Ann.#1 JBy,F:Doom Patrol 3.00
Ann.#2 CI,MA,F:Flash 2.00
Ann.#3 F:The Teen Titans. 3.00
Spec.#1 SK,PB,DG,F:Batman's worst

Villains,A:Penguin. 4.00
TPB DG,New Origin Batman. 4.50
GN rep of 1961 Annual. 5.00
Replica Edition 80-page 5.00

SECRET ORIGINS OF SUPER-VILLAINS
DC 2000

1 80-pg. Giant 4.95

SECRET SOCIETY OF SUPER-HEROES
August, 2000

1 (of 2) HC,MMK,JP,Elseworlds . . . 5.95
2 HC,MMK,JP,concl. 5.95

SECRET SOCIETY OF SUPER-VILLAINS
May–June, 1976

1 A:Capt.Boomerang, Grodd, Sinestro 2.50
2 R:Capt.Comet,A:Green Lantern . 2.50
3 A:Mantis, Darkseid 2.00
4 A:Kalibak,Darkseid,Gr.Lantern . . 2.00
5 RB,D:Manhunter,A:JLA. 2.00
6 RB/BL,A:Black Canary 2.00
7 RB/BL,A:Hawkgirl,Lex Luthor . . . 2.00
8 RB/BL,A:Kid Flash 2.00
9 RB/BMc,A:Kid Flash, Creeper. . . 2.00
10 DAy/JAb,A:Creeper 2.00
11 JO,N:Wizard 2.00
12 BMc,A:Blockbuster 2.00
13 A:Crime Syndicate of America . . 2.00
14 A:Crime Syndicate of America . . 2.00
15 A:G.A.Atom, Dr. Mid Nite 2.00

SECRETS OF HAUNTED HOUSE
April–May, 1975

1 LD(c),Dead Heat. 25.00
2 ECh(c),A Dead Man 15.00
3 ECh(c),Pathway To Purgatory . . 15.00
4 LD(c),The Face of Death 15.00
5 BWr(c),Gunslinger! 17.00
6 JAp(c),Deadly Allegiance 10.00
7 JAp(c),It'll Grow On You 10.00
8 MK(c),Raising The Devil 10.00
9 LD(c),The Man Who Didn't Believe in Ghosts 10.00
10 MK(c),Ask Me No Questions . . 10.00
11 MK(c),Picasso Fever! 10.00
12 JO&DG(c),Yorick's Skull. 10.00
13 JO&DG(c),The Cry of the Warewolf 10.00
14 MK(c),Selina 10.00
15 LD(c),Over Your Own Dead Body 7.00
16 MK(c),Water, Water Every Fear . 7.00
17 LD(c),Papa Don. 7.00
18 LD(c),No Sleep For The Dying. . 7.00
19 LD(c),The Manner of Execution . 7.00
20 JO(c),The Talisman of the Serpent 7.00
21 LD(c),The Death's Head Scorpion. 7.00
22 LD(c),See How They Die 7.00
23 LD(c),The Creeping Red Death . 7.00
24 LD(c),Second Chance To Die. . . 7.00
25 LD(c),The Man Who Cheated Destiny. 7.00
26 MR(c),Elevator to Eternity 7.00
27 DH(c),Souls For the Master 7.00
28 DH(c),Demon Rum 7.00
29 MK(c),Duel of Darkness. 7.00
30 JO(c),For the Love of Arlo 7.00
31 I:Mister E. 8.00
32 The Legend of the Tiger's Paw . 4.00
33 In The Attic Dwells Dark Seth . . 4.00
34 Double Your Pleasure 4.00
35 Deathwing, Lord of Darkness. . . 4.00
36 RB&DG(c),Sister Sinister 4.00
37 RB&DG(c),The Third Wish Is Death. 4.00
38 RB&DG(c),Slaves of Satan 4.00
39 RB&DG(c),The Witch-Hounds of Salem 4.00
40 RB&DG(c),The Were-Witch of Boston 4.00
41 JKu(c),House at Devil's Tail 4.00
42 JKu(c),Mystic Murder. 4.00
43 JO(c),Mother of Invention. 4.00
44 BWr(c),Halloween God 4.00
45 EC&JO(c),Star-Trakker 4.00
46 March, 1982 . . . . 4.00

SINISTER HOUSE OF SECRET LOVE
Oct.–Nov., 1971

1 . . . . 35.00
2 JJ(c). 15.00
3 ATh 14.00
4 April-May, 1972 . . . . 12.00
Becomes:

SECRETS OF SINISTER HOUSE
June–July, 1972

5 . . . . 35.00
6 . . . . 20.00
7 NR 20.00
8 . . . . 20.00
9 . . . . 20.00
10 NA(i) 25.00
11 . . . . 12.00
12 . . . . 12.00
13 . . . . 12.00
14 . . . . 12.00
15 . . . . 12.00
16 . . . . 12.00
17 DBa. 12.00
18 June-July, 1974 . . . . 12.00

SECRETS OF THE LEGION OF SUPER-HEROES
Jan., 1981

1 O:Legion 3.50
2 O:Brainaic 5 . . . . 3.50
3 March, 1981,O:Karate Kid 3.50

SEEKERS
Vertigo

1 & 2 . . . . @2.50

SEEKERS INTO THE MYSTERY

1 . . . . 2.50
2 . . . . 2.50
3 . . . . 2.50
4 JMD,Lucas Hart spirit resurrected. 2.50
5 JMD,JMu, ... 2.50
6 . . . . 2.50
7 . . . . 2.50
8 . . . . 2.50
9 JMD(s),MZi,"Falling Down from Heaven," pt.4 concl. 2.50
10 JMD(s),JMu,F:Charlie Limbo . . . 2.50
11 JMD(s),JIT,"God's Shadow" pt.1 . 2.50
12 JMD(s),JIT,"God's Shadow" pt.2. 2.50
13 JMD(s),JIT,"God's Shadow" pt.3. 2.50
14 JMD(s),JIT,"In God's Shadow," concl. 2.50
15 JMD(s),JMu,Hart meets Magician, final issue 3.00

SENSATION COMICS
1942–52

1 I:Wonder Woman,Wildcat. . 23,000.00
2 I:Etta Candy & the Holiday Girls, Dr. Poison 3,800.00
3 Diana Price joins Military Intelligence 2,000.00
4 I:Baroness PaulaVon Gunther 1,500.00
5 V:Axis Spies 1,200.00
6 Wonder Woman receives magic lasso,V:Baroness Gunther . 1,200.00
7 V:Baroness Gunther 850.00
8 Meets Gloria Bullfinch 850.00
9 A:The Real Diana Prince 850.00
10 V:Ishti 850.00
11 I:Queen Desira. 850.00
12 V:Baroness Gunther. 750.00
13 V:Olga,Hitler(c) 1,000.00
14 . . . . 800.00
15 V:Simon Slikery 800.00
16 V:Karl Schultz 800.00
17 V:Princess Yasmini 800.00
18 V:Quito 800.00
19 Wonder Woman goes berserk. 800.00
20 V:Stoffer 800.00
21 V:American Adolf 600.00
22 V:Cheetah 600.00
23 'War Laugh Mania'. 600.00
24 I:Wonder Woman's mental radio 600.00
25 . . . . 600.00
26 A:Queen Hippolyte. 600.00
27 V:Ely Close 600.00
28 V:Mayor Prude. 600.00
29 V:Mimi Mendez 600.00
30 V:Anton Unreal 600.00
31 `Grow Down Land'. 450.00
32 V:Crime Chief 450.00
33 Meets Percy Pringle. 450.00
34 I:Sargon. 500.00
35 V:Sontag Henya in Atlantis. . . 400.00
36 V:Bedwin Footh 400.00
37 A:Mala((1st app. All-Star #8) . 400.00
38 V:The Gyp 400.00
39 V:Nero. 400.00
40 I:Countess Draska Nishki. . . . 400.00
41 V:Creeper Jackson 350.00
42 V:Countess Nishki 350.00
43 Meets Joel Heyday 350.00
44 V:Lt. Sturm 350.00

Sensation #22 © DC Comics, Inc.

DC COMICS

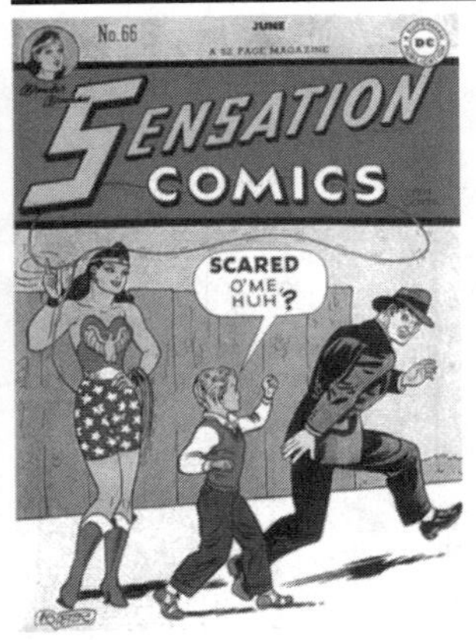

Sensation #66 © DC Comics, Inc.

45 V:Jose Perez 350.00
46 V:Lawbreakers Protective League 350.00
47 V:Unknown 350.00
48 V:Topso and Teena 350.00
49 V:Zavia 350.00
50 V:`Ears' Fellock 350.00
51 V:Boss Brekel 300.00
52 Meets Prof. Toxino 300.00
53 V:Wanta Wynn 300.00
54 V:Dr. Fiendo 300.00
55 V:Bughumans 300.00
56 V:Dr. Novel 300.00
57 V:Syonide 300.00
58 Meets Olive Norton 300.00
59 V:Snow Man 300.00
60 V:Bifton Jones 300.00
61 V:Bluff Robust 300.00
62 V:Black Robert of Dogwood . . 300.00
63 V:Prof. Vibrate 300.00
64 V:Cloudmen 300.00
65 V:Lim Slait 300.00
66 V:Slick Skeener 300.00
67 V:Daredevil Dix 300.00
68 `Secret of the Menacing Octopus' 325.00
69 V:Darcy Wells 275.00
70 Unconquerable Woman of Cocha Bamba 275.00
71 V:Queen Flaming 275.00
72 V:Blue Seal Gang 275.00
73 Wonder Woman time travel story. 275.00
74 V:Spug Spangle 275.00
75 V:Shark 275.00
76 V:King Diamond 275.00
77 V:Boss Brekel 275.00
78 V:Furiosa 275.00
79 Meets Leila and Solala 275.00
80 V:Don Enrago 275.00
81 V:Dr. Frenzi 300.00
82 V:King Lunar 225.00
83 V:Prowd 225.00
84 V:Duke Daxo 225.00
85 Meets Leslie M. Gresham . . . 225.00
86 `Secret of the Amazing Bracelets' 225.00
87 In Twin Peaks(in Old West) . . 225.00
88 Wonder Woman in Holywood . 225.00
89 V:Abacus Rackeett gang 225.00
90 `The Secret of the Modern Sphinx' 225.00
91 . . . . 225.00
92 V:Duke of Deceptions 225.00
93 V:Talbot 225.00
94 Girl Issue 325.00
95 . . . . 300.00
96 . . . . 300.00
97 . . . . 300.00
98 `Strange Mission' 300.00
99 I:Astra 300.00
100 . . . . 450.00
101 `Battle for the Atom World' . . 300.00
102 `Queen of the South Seas' . . 300.00
103 V:Robot Archers 300.00
104 `The End of Paradise Island' 300.00
105 `Secret of the Giant Forest' . 300.00
106 E:Wonder Woman 300.00
107 ATh,Mystery issue 550.00
108 ATh,I:Johnny Peril 450.00
109 Ath,A:Johnny Peril 550.00

Becomes:

SENSATION MYSTERY

1952–53

110 B:Johnny Peril 300.00
111 `Spectre in the Flame' 275.00
112 `Death has 5 Guesses' 275.00
113 . . . . 275.00
114 GC,`The Haunted Diamond' . 275.00
115 `The Phantom Castle' 275.00
116 `The Toy Assassins', July-Aug., 1953 . . . . 275.00

SENSATION COMICS

1999

1 JeR(s),ScB, F:Wonder Woman & Hawkgirl 2.00

SERGEANT BILKO

May–June, 1957

1 Based on TV show 600.00
2 . . . . 300.00
3 . . . . 250.00
4 . . . . 200.00
5 . . . . 200.00
6 thru 17 . . . . @175.00
18 March-April, 1960 . . . . 175.00

SERGEANT BILKO'S PVT. DOBERMAN

June–July, 1958

1 . . . . 350.00
2 . . . . 200.00
3 . . . . 150.00
4 . . . . 150.00
5 . . . . 150.00
6 thru 10 . . . . @100.00
11 Feb.–March, 1960 . . . . 100.00

SGT. ROCK (See: OUR ARMY AT WAR)

SGT. ROCK SPECIAL

Oct., 1988

#1 rep.Our Army at War#162-#63 . . 2.00
#2 rep.Brave & Bold #52 . . . . 2.00
#3 rep.Showcase #45 . . . . 2.00
#4 rep.Our Army at War#147-#48 . . 2.00
#5 rep.Our Army at War#81g . 2.00
#6 rep.Our Army at War #160 . . . . . 2.00
#7 rep.Our Army at War #85 . . . . . . 2.00
#8 rep. 2.00
#9 thru #20 reprints . . . . @2.00
Spec. #1 TT,MGo,JKu,CR,(new stories) 2.95

SGT. ROCK'S PRIZE BATTLE TALES

Winter, 1964

1 . . . . 325.00

SHADE

June–July, 1977

[1st Regular Series]

1 SD,I&O: Shade 4.00
2 SD,V:Form 3.25
3 SD,V:The Cloak 2.75
4 SD,Return to Meta-Zone 2.75
5 SD,V:Supreme Decider 2.75
6 SD,V:Khaos 2.75
7 SD,V:Dr.Z.Z. 2.75
8 SD,last issue 2.75

SHADE, THE

Feb., 1997

1 (of 4) JeR(s),GeH,A:Ludlows . . . 2.25
2 JeR(s),JWi,MGy,poisoned by love of his life 2.25
3 JeR(s),BBl,Golden Age Flash Jay Garrick retiring 2.25
4 JeR(s),MZi,V:last of the Ludlows . 2.25

SHADE, THE CHANGING MAN

July, 1990

1 B:PrM(s),CBa,MPn,I:Kathy George, I&D:Troy Grezer 5.00
2 CBa,MPn,Who Shot JFK#1 . . . . . 4.00
3 CBa,MPn,Who Shot JFK#2 . . . . . 3.00
4 CBa,MPn,V:American Scream . . 3.00
5 CBa,MPn,V:Hollywood Monsters 3.00
6 CBa,MPn,V:Ed Loot 3.00
7 CBa,MPn,I:Arnold Major 3.00
8 CBa,Mpn,I:Lenny 3.00
9 CBa,MPn,V:Arnold Major 3.00
10 CBa,MPn,Paranioa 2.75
11 CBa,MPn,R:Troy Grezer 2.50
12 CBa,MPn,V:Troy Grezer 2.50
13 CBa,MPn,I:Fish Priest 2.50
14 CBa,MPn,V:Godfather of Guilt . . 2.50
15 CBa,MPn,I:Spirit 2.50
16 CBa,MPn,V:American Scream . . 2.50
17 RkB(i),V:Rohug 2.50

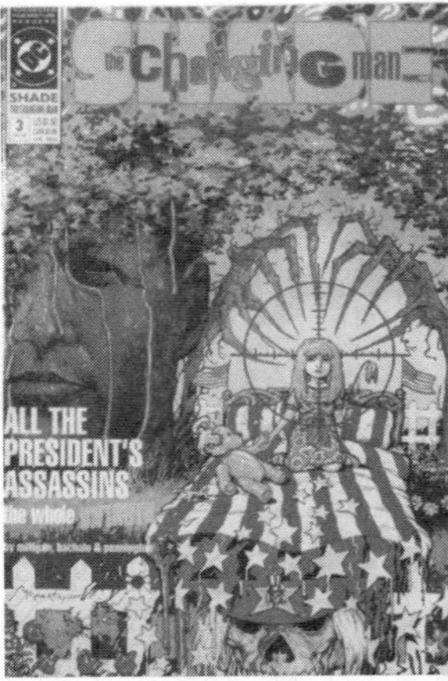

Shade, The Changing Man #3 © DC Comics, Inc.

18 MPn,E:American Scream. 2.50
19 MPn,V:Dave Messiah Seeker. . . 2.50
20 JD,CBa,MPn,RkB,R:Roger 2.50
21 MPn,The Road,A:Stringer 2.25
22 The Road,Childhood 2.25
23 The Road 2.25
24 The Road 2.25
25 The Road 2.25
26 MPn(i),F:Lenny 2.25
27 MPn(i),Shade becomes female . 2.25
28 MPn(i),Changing Woman#2. . . . 2.25
29 MPn(i),Changing Woman#3. . . . 2.25
30 Another Life. 2.25
31 Ernest & Jim#1 . . . . 2.25
32 Ernest & Jim#2 . . . . 2.25

Vertigo

33 CBa,B:Birth Pains 2.25
34 CBa,RkB(i),GID(i),A:Brian Juno, Garden of Pain. 2.25
35 CBa,RkB(i),E:Birth Pains, V:Juno 2.25
36 CBa,PrG(i),RkB(i),B:Passion child, I:Miles Laimling 2.25
37 CBa,RkB(i),Shade/Kathy 2.25
38 CBa,RkB(i),Great American Novel 2.25
39 CBa,SEa,RkB(i),Pond Life 2.25
40 PBd,at Hotel Shade 2.25
41 GID,Pandora's Story,Kathy is pregnant. 2.25
42 CBa,RkB(i),SY,B:History Lesson, A:John Constantine 2.50
43 CBa,RkB(i),PBd,Trial of William Matthieson,A:J.Constantine . . . 2.50
44 CBa,RkB(i),E:History Lesson, D:William Matthieson,A:John Constantine 2.50
45 CBa,B:A Season in Hell. 2.25
46 CBa(c),GID,Season in Hell#2. . . 2.25
47 CBa(c),GID,A:Lenny 2.25
48 CBa(c),GID 2.25
49 CBa(c),GID,Kathy's Past 2.25
50 GID,BBl,MiA,pin-up gallery. 3.25
51 GID,BBl,MiA,Masks,pt.1. . . . . . . 2.00
52 GID,BBl,MiA,Masks,pt.2. . . . . . . 2.00
53 GID,BBl,MiA,Masks,pt.3. . . . . . . 2.00
54 Meeting 2.00
55 . . . . 2.00
56 . . . . 2.00
57 MBu,PrM,F:George 2.00
58 PrM,Michael Lark. 2.00
59 MBu,PrM,Nasty Infections,pt.1 . . 2.25
60 MBu,PrM,Nasty Infections,pt.2 . . 2.25
61 MBu,PrM,Nasty Infections,pt.3 . . 2.25
62 Nasty Infections,pt.4 . . . . 2.25
63 Nasty Infections,finale 2.25
64 The Madness. 2.25
65 The Roots of Madness,pt.1 . . . . 2.25
66 The Roots of Madness,pt.2 . . . . 2.25
67 The Roots of Madness,pt.3 . . . . 2.25
68 After Kathy,pt.1 . . . . 2.25
69 After Kathy,pt.2 . . . . 2.25
70 After Kathy,pt.3, final issue. 2.25

SHADO: SONG OF THE DRAGON

1992

1 GM(i),From G.A. Longbow Hunters 5.50
2 GM(i),V:Yakuza 5.00
3 GM(i),V:Yakuza 5.00
4 GM(i),V:Yakuza 5.00

SHADOW, THE

[1st Regular Series] 1973–75

1 MK,The Doom Puzzle. 28.00
2 MK,V:Freak Show Killer 18.00
3 MK,BWr 20.00
4 MK,Ninja Story 18.00
5 FR 10.00
6 MK 18.00
7 FR 9.00
8 FR 9.00
9 FR 9.00
10 . . . . 9.00
11 A:Avenger 9.00
12 . . . . 9.00

[Limited Series] 1986

1 HC,R:Shadow. 6.00
2 HC,O:Shadow 4.00
3 HC,V:Preston Mayrock 3.00
4 HC,V:Preston Mayrock 3.00
TPB rep. #1 thru #4 . . . . 12.95

[2nd Regular Series] 1987–89

1 BSz,Shadows & Light,pt.1 . . . . . 3.50
2 BSz,Shadows & Light,pt.2 . . . . . 3.50
3 BSz,Shadows & Light,pt.3 . . . . . 3.50
4 BSz,Shadows & Light,pt.4 . . . . . 3.50
5 BSz,Shadows & Light,pt.5 . . . . . 3.50
6 BSz,Shadows & Light,pt.6 . . . . . 3.50
7 MR,KB,Harold Goes to Washington 2.50
8 KB,Seven Deadly Finns,pt.1 . . . . 2.50
9 KB,Seven Deadly Finns,pt.2 . . . . 2.50
10 KB,Seven Deadly Finns,pt.3 . . . 2.50
11 KB,Seven Deadly Finns,pt.4. . . . 2.50
12 KB,Seven Deadly Finns,pt.5 . . . 2.50
13 KB,Seven Deadly Finns,pt.6 . . . 2.50
14 KB,Body And Soul,pt.1 . . . . 2.50
15 KB,Body And Soul,pt.2 . . . . 2.50
16 KB,Body And Soul,pt.3 . . . . 2.50
17 KB,Body And Soul,pt.4 . . . . 2.50
18 KB,Body And Soul,pt.5 . . . . 2.50
19 KB,Body And Soul,pt.6 . . . . 2.50
Ann.#1 JO,AA,Shadows & Light prologue. 3.00
Ann.#2 KB,Agents 2.50

SHADOW CABINET

Milestone 1994–95

0 WS(c),3RL,Shadow War,Foil(c),A:All Milestone characters 3.00
1 JBy(c),3RW,I&D:Corpsickle. 2.00
2 3RW,V:Arcadian League 2.00
3 3RW,F:Sideshow 2.00
4 3RW,F:Sideshow 2.00
5 . . . . 2.00
6 . . . . 2.00
7 . . . . 2.00
8 New Cabinet. 2.00
9 R:Old Cabinet. 2.00

Shadow Cabinet #6 © DC Comics, Inc.

10 V:Red Dog. 2.00
11 Death Issue 2.00
12 SYSTEM 2.00
13 A:Hardware,Starlight 2.00
14 Long Hot Summer, Iron Butterfly Starlight 2.50
15 Long Hot Summer 2.50
16 Changing of the Guard 2.50
17 V:Dharma,final issue 2.50

SHADOWDRAGON ANNUAL

1995

Ann.#1 Year One Annual 3.50

SHADOW OF BATMAN

1 reprints of Detective Comics . . . 10.00
2 thru 4 . . . . @7.50

SHADOW OF THE BATMAN

1985–86

1 WS,AM,MR,rep. 7.00
2 MR,TA,rep.A:Hugo Strange 5.00
3 MR,TA,rep.A:Penguin 5.00
4 MR,TA,rep.A:Joker 6.00
5 MR,DG,rep. 5.00

SHADOW'S FALL

1994–95

1 JVF,Voyage of self-discovery . . . 3.00
2 JVF,More of tale 3.00
3 JVF,Shen confronts shadow 3.00
4 JVF,Gale wounded 3.00
5 JVF,Shadow goes Berserk 3.00
6 JVF,F:Warren Gale,final issue. . . 3.00

SHADOW STRIKES!, THE

1989–92

1 EB,Death's Head 3.00
2 EB,EB,PoliticalKiller,V:Rasputin . 2.50
3 EB,V:Mad Monk,V:Rasputin 2.50
4 EB,D:Mad Monk,V:Rasputin 2.50
5 EB,Shadow & Doc Savage#1 . . . 2.50
6 Shadow & Doc Savage #3 . . . . . 2.50
7 RM,A:Wunderkind,O:Shadow's Radio Show 2.50
8 EB,A:Shiwan Khan 2.50
9 Fireworks#2 . . . . 2.50
10 EB,Fireworks#3 . . . . 2.50
11 EB,O:Margo Lane 2.50
12 EB,V:Chicago Mob 2.50
13 EB,V:Chicago Mob 2.50
14 EB,V:Chicago Mob 2.50
15 EB,V:Chicago Mob 2.50
16 Assassins,pt.1 . . . . 2.50
17 Assassins,pt.2 . . . . 2.50
18 Shrevvie 2.50
19 NY,NJ Tunnel. 2.50
20 Shadow+Margo Vs.Nazis. 2.50
21 V:Shiwan Khan 2.50
22 V:Shiwan Khan 2.50
23 V:Shiwan Khan 2.50
24 Search for Margo Lane 2.50
25 In China. 2.50
26 V:Shiwan Khan 2.50
27 V:Shiwan Khan,Margo Rescued. 2.50
28 SL,In Hawaii 2.50
29 DSp,`Valhalla',V:Nazis 2.50
30 The Shadow Year One,pt.1 . . . . 2.50
31 The Shadow Year One,pt.2 . . . . 2.50
Ann.#1 DSp `Crimson Dreams'. . . . 4.00

DC COMICS

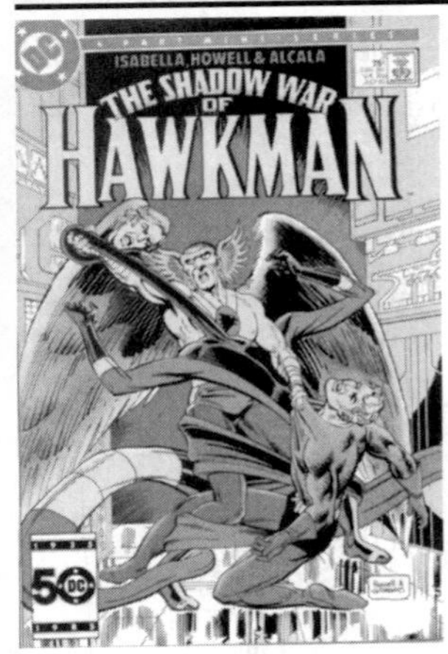
Shadow War of Hawkman #3
© DC Comics, Inc.

SHADOW WAR OF HAWKMAN
May, 1985

1 AA,V:Thangarians. 2.00
2 AA,V:Thangarians. 2.00
3 AA,V:Thangarians,A:Aquaman, Elong.Man 2.00
4 AA,V:Thangarians. 2.00
Spec.#1 V:Thangarians 2.00

SHAZAM!
1973–78
[1st Regular Series]

1 B:DON(s),CCB,O:Capt.Marvel . 10.00
2 CCB,A:Mr.Mind. 5.00
3 CCB,V:Shagg Naste 4.00
4 E:DON(s),CCB,V:Ibac. 4.00
5 B:ESM(s),CCB,A:Leprechaun . . . 4.00
6 B:DON(s),CCB,Dr,Sivana 4.00
7 CCB,A:Capt Marvel Jr. 4.00
8 CCB,O:Marvel Family. 25.00
9 E:DON(S)DC,CCB,A:Mr.Mind, Captain Marvel Jr. 4.00
10 ESM(s)CCB,BO. 4.00
11 ViCKS,BO,rep.. . . . . 4.00
12 BO,DG 15.00
13 BO,KS,A:Luthor. 15.00
14 KS,A:Monster Society 15.00
15 KS,BO,Luther 15.00
16 KS,BO. 15.00
17 KS,BO. 15.00
18 KS,BO. 4.00
19 KS,BO,Mary Marvel. 4.00
20 KS,A:Marvel Family 4.00
21 reprint 4.00
22 reprint 4.00
23 reprint 4.00
24 reprint 4.00
25 KS,DG,I&O:Isis 5.00
26 KS. 4.00
27 KS,A:Kid Eternity. 5.00
28 KS. 4.00
29 KS. 4.00
30 KS. 4.00
31 KS,A:Minute Man. 4.00
32 KS. 4.00
33 KS. 4.00
34 O:Capt.Marvel Jr.. . . . . 4.00
35 DN,KS,A:Marvel Family 4.00

SHAZAM ARCHIVES

1 Rep.Whiz Comics#2-#15 . . . . . 49.95

SHAZAM, THE NEW BEGINNING
April, 1987

1 O:Shazam & Capt.Marvel 2.00
2 V:Black Adam. 2.00
3 V:Black Adam. 2.00
4 V:Black Adam. 2.00

SHERLOCK HOLMES
Sept.–Oct., 1975

1 . . . . 25.00

SHEVA'S WAR
DC/Helix (Aug., 1998)

1 (of 5) CsM,Iron Empires 3.00
2 CsM,Iron Empires. 3.00
3 CsM,Iron Empires. 3.00
4 CsM, ... 3.00
5 CsM 3.00

SHOWCASE
1956–70, 1977–78

1 F:Fire Fighters 3,200.00
2 JKu,F:Kings of Wild 900.00
3 F:Frogmen 850.00
4 CI,JKu,I&O:S.A. Flash (Barry Allen) 26,000.00
5 F:Manhunters 1,000.00
6 JK,I&O:Challengers of the Unknown 3,600.00
7 JK,F:Challengers 1,800.00
8 CI,F:Flash,I:Capt.Cold 13,000.00
9 F:Lois Lane 7,000.00
10 F:Lois Lane. 2,500.00
11 JK(c),F:Challengers. 1,600.00
12 JK(c),F:Challengers 1,600.00
13 CI,F:Flash,Mr.Element. 4,200.00
14 CI,F:Flash,Mr.Element. 5,000.00
15 I:Space Ranger. 1,800.00
16 F:Space Ranger 1,000.00
17 GK(c),I:Adam Strange. 2,200.00
18 GK(c),F:Adam Strange 1,200.00
19 GK(c),F:Adam Strange 1,300.00
20 I:Rip Hunter 900.00
21 F:Rip Hunter 500.00
22 GK,I&O:S.A. Green Lantern (Hal Jordan) 4,800.00
23 GK,F:Green Lantern 1,600.00
24 GK,F:Green Lantern 1,600.00
25 JKu,F:Rip Hunter 300.00
26 JKu,F:Rip Hunter 300.00
27 RH,I:Sea Devils 800.00
28 RH,F:Sea Devils 400.00
29 RH,F:Sea Devils 400.00
30 O:Aquaman 750.00
31 GK(c),F:Aquaman 400.00
32 F:Aquaman 400.00
33 F:Aquaman 450.00
34 GK,MA,I&O:S.A. Atom 1,400.00
35 GK,MA,F:Atom. 800.00
36 GK,MA,F:Atom. 600.00
37 RA,I:Metal Man 550.00
38 RA,F:Metal Man. 500.00
39 RA,F:Metal Man. 350.00
40 RA,F:Metal Man. 325.00
41 F:Tommy Tomorrow 175.00
42 F:Tommy Tomorrow 175.00
43 F:Dr.No(James Bond 007) . . . 500.00
44 F:Tommy Tomorrow 125.00
45 JKu,O:Sgt.Rock 250.00
46 F:Tommy Tomorrow 100.00
47 F:Tommy Tomorrow 100.00
48 F:Cave Carson 75.00
49 F:Cave Carson 75.00

Showcase #60 © DC Comics, Inc.

50 MA,CI,F:I Spy 75.00
51 MA,CI,F:I Spy 75.00
52 F:Cave Carson 75.00
53 JKu(c),RH,F:G.I.Joe. 75.00
54 JKu(c),RH,F:G.I.Joe. 75.00
55 MA,F:Dr.Fate,Spectre,1st S.A. Green Lantern,Solomon Grundy 260.00
56 MA,F:Dr.Fate 75.00
57 JKu,F:Enemy Ace 150.00
58 JKu,F:Enemy Ace 125.00
59 F:Teen Titans 100.00
60 MA,F:Spectre. 250.00
61 MA,F:Spectre. 150.00
62 JO,I:Inferior 5. . . . . 75.00
63 JO,F:Inferior 5 . . . . 50.00
64 MA,F:Spectre. 150.00
65 F:Inferior 5. . . . . 50.00
66 I:B'wana Beast. 30.00
67 F:B'wana Beast 30.00
68 I:Maniaks. 30.00
69 F:Maniaks 30.00
70 I:Binky 30.00
71 F:Maniaks 30.00
72 JKu,ATh,F:Top Gun 30.00
73 SD,I&O:Creeper. 125.00
74 I:Anthro 75.00
75 SD,I:Hawk & Dove 100.00
76 NC,I:Bat Lash 50.00
77 BO,I:Angel & Ape 50.00
78 I:Jonny Double. 30.00
79 I:Dolphin 50.00
80 NA(c),F:Phantom Stranger. . . . 65.00
81 I:Windy & Willy 25.00
82 I:Nightmaster 60.00
83 BWr,MK,F:Nightmaster 50.00
84 BWr,MK,F:Nightmaster 50.00
85 JKu,F:Firehair 18.00
86 JKu,F:Firehair 18.00
87 JKu,F:Firehair 18.00
88 F:Jason's Quest. 10.00
89 F:Jason's Quest. 10.00
90 F:Manhunter 9.00
91 F:Manhunter 9.00
92 F:Manhunter 9.00
93 F:Manhunter 9.00
94 JA,JSon,I&O:2nd Doom Patrol 12.00
95 JA,JSon,F:2nd Doom Patrol. . . . 9.00
96 JA,JSon,F:2nd Doom Patrol. . . . 9.00
97 JO,JSon,O:Power Girl 6.00
98 JSon,DG,Power Girl 6.00
99 JSon,DG,Power Girl 6.00
100 JSon,all star issue 7.00
101 JKu(c),AM,MA,Hawkman 6.00

102 JKu(c),AM,MA,Hawkman 6.00
103 JKu(c),AM,MA,Hawkman 6.00
104 RE,OSS Spies 6.00
TPB Rep.1956–59 . . . . 20.00

Shawcase '93 #3 © DC Comics, Inc.

SHOWCASE '93

1 AAd(c),EH,AV,F:Catwoman, Blue Devil,Cyborg. 4.00
2 KM(c),EH,AV,F:Catwoman, Blue Devil,Cyborg. 3.50
3 KM(c),EH,TC,F:Catwoman, Blue Devil,Flash 3.00
4 F:Catwoman,Blue Devil, Geo-Force 3.00
5 F:KD,DG,BHi,F:Robin,Blue Devil,Geo-Force 3.00
6 MZ(c),KD,DG,F:Robin,Blue Devil,Deathstroke 3.00
7 BSz(c),KJ,Knightfall#13,F:Two-Face,Jade&Obsidian 5.00
8 KJ,Knightfall#14,F:Two-Face, Peacemaker,Fire and Ice 4.00
9 F:Huntress,Peacemaker,Shining Knight 3.00
10 BWg,SI,F:Huntress,Batman, Dr.Light,Peacemaker,Deathstroke, Katana,M.Manhunter 3.00
11 GP(c),F:Robin,Nightwing, Peacemaker,Deathstroke,Deadshot, Katana,Dr.Light,Won.Woman . . 3.00
12 AD(c),BMc,F:Robin,Nightwing, Green Lantern,Creeper. 3.00

SHOWCASE '94

1 KN,F:Joker,Gunfire,Orion,Metro . 2.50
2 KON(c),E:Joker,B:Blue Beetle. . . 2.50
3 MMi(c),B:Razorsharpe 2.50
4 AIG(s),DG,F:Arkham Asylum inmates E:Razorsharpe,Blue Bettle 2.50
5 WS(c),CDi(s),PJ,B:Robin&Huntress, F:Bloodwynd,Loose Cannon. . . 2.50
6 PJ,KK(s),F:Robin & Huntress . . . 2.50
7 JaL(c),PDd(s),F:Comm. Gordon . 2.50
8 AIG(s),O:Scarface,Ventriloquist, F:Monarch,1st Wildcat 3.00
9 AIG(s),DJ,O:Scarface,Ventriloquist, F:Monarch,Waverider 2.75
10 JQ(c),AIG(s),F:Azrael,Zero Hour, B:Black Condor 3.00
11 Black Condor, Man-Bat 2.25
12 Barbara Gordon. 2.50

SHOWCASE '95

1 Supergirl. 3.00
2 . . . . 3.00
3 F:Eradicator,Claw 3.00
4 A:Catwoman,Hawke 3.00
5 F:Thorne,Firehawk 3.00
6 DRo(c&a),F:Lobo,Bibbo 3.00
7 F:Mongul 3.00
8 . . . . 3.00
9 F:Lois Lane 3.00
10 F:Gangbuster 3.00
11 F:Agent Liberty 3.00
12 F:Supergirl,Maitresse. 3.00

SHOWCASE '96

1 F:Steel & Warrior 3.00
2 F:Steel and Warrior 3.00
3 . . . . 3.00
4 F:Firebrand. 3.00
5 F:Green Arrow & Thorn 3.00
6 F:Superboy, Animated Series . . . 3.00
7 F:Mary Marvel 3.00
8 F:Superman, Superboy & Supergirl 4.00
9 F:Lady Shiva & Shadowdragon, Martian Manhunter 3.00
10 F:Ultra Boy, Captain Comet 3.00
11 Legion of Super-Heroes 3.00
12 "10,000 Brainiacs" 3.00

SILVER AGE DC CLASSICS

Action #252(rep). 2.00
Adventure #247(rep). 2.00
Brave and Bold #28 (rep) 2.00
Detective #225 (rep). 2.00
Detective #327 (rep). 2.00
Green Lantern #76 (rep). 2.00
House of Secrets #92 (rep). 2.00
Showcase #4 (rep) 2.00
Showcase #22 (rep) 2.00
Sugar & Spike #99(1st printing) . . . 2.00

SILVER AGE
May, 2000

Secret Files #1 . . . . 4.95
Justice League of America #1. . . . . 2.50
Challengers of the Unknown #1 . . . 2.50
Teen Titans #1 . . . . 2.50
Doom Patrol #1 . . . . 2.50
Dial "H" For Hero #1. . . . . 2.50
The Flash #1 . . . . 2.50
Green Lantern #1 . . . . 2.50
The Brave and the Bold #1. . . . . . . 2.50
Showcase #1 . . . . 2.50
80-Page Giant #1, 80-pg 5.95
Silver Age #1, 48-pg. 3.95

SILVER BLADE
Sept., 1987

1 KJ,GC,maxi-series 2.00
2 thru 12 GC . . . . @2.00

SINS OF YOUTH
March, 2000

Aquaboy/Lagoon Man #1 x-over . . . 2.50
Batboy & Robin #1 x-over. 2.50
JLA/Jr. #1 x-over 2.50
Kid Flash/Impulse #1 x-over 2.50
Secret/Deadboy #1 x-over 2.50
Starwoman & JSA #1 x-over. 2.50
Superman,Jr./Superboy,Sr.#1 x-over. 2.50
Wonder Girls #1 x-over. 2.50

SKIN GRAFT
Vertigo 1993

1 B:JeP(s),WaP,I:John Oakes, A:Tattooed Man(Tarrant). 3.25
2 WaP,V:Assassins 3.00
3 WaP,In Kyoto,I:Mizoguchi Kenji. . 3.00
4 E:JeP(s),WaP,V:Tarrant,Kenji . . . 3.00

SKREEMER
May, 1989

1 . . . . 2.00
2 thru 6 . . . . @2.00

SKULL AND BONES
1992

1 EH,I&O:Skull & Bones 4.95
2 EH,V:KGB 4.95
3 EH,V:KGB 4.95

SLASH MARAUD
Nov., 1987

1 PG 2.25
2 PG 2.00
3 thru 10 PG . . . . @2.00

SMASH COMICS
1999

1 TPe(s),F:Doctor Mid-Nite & Hourman. 2.00

SONIC DISRUPTORS
1987–88

1 thru 10 . . . . @2.00

SON OF AMBUSH BUG
July, 1986

1 . . . . 2.00
2 thru 6 KG . . . . @2.00

SOVEREIGN SEVEN
1995–98

1 CCl(s),DT,I:Sovereign Seven, V:Female Furies,A:Darkseid . . . 3.00
2 I:Nike,Kratos,Zelus,Bia 2.50
3 V:Nike,Kratos,Zelus,Bia 2.50
4 I:Skin Dance. 2.50
5 CCl,DT,V:Skin Dance 2.50
6 CCl,DT,V:Force Majeure 2.50
7 CCl,DT,Wild Hunt,pt.2. . . . . 2.50
8 CCl,DT,Clv,Wild Hunt,pt.3. . . . . . 2.50
9 CCl,DT,Clv 2.50
10 CCl,DT,Clv,Road Trip,pt.1 . . . . . 2.50
11 CCl,DT,Clv,Road Trip,pt.2 (of 3). 2.50
12 CCl(s) 2.25
13 CCl(s) 2.25
14 CCl(s) 2.25
15 CCl,DT,Clv,Sovereign team betrayed. 2.25
16 CCl,DT,Clv,Network betrays Sovereigns, Final Night tie-in . . 2.25
17 CCl(s),RLm,Clv,V:Network. 2.25
18 CCl(s),RLm,Clv,V:Network and Kim 2.25
19 CCl(s) 2.25
20 CCl(s),VGi,Finale trapped in Forest Fire 2.25
21 CCl(s),RLm,DC,Clv,Danae's secret 2.25
22 CCl(s),RLm,DC,Clv,Indigo & Rampart fall 2.25
23 CCl(s),RLm,DC,Clv,Finale hallucinates 2.25
24 CCl(s),RLm,Clv,A:Superman . . . 2.25
25 CCl(s),RLm,Clv,V:Power Girl . . . 2.25

Sovereign Seven #18
© DC Comics, Inc.

26 CCl(s),RLm,Clv,A:Hitman. 2.25
27 CCl(s),RLm,Clv,Genesis tie-in . . 2.25
28 CCl(s),RLm,Clv,A:Impulse 2.25
29 CCl(s),RLm,Clv,Sovereign dies . 2.25
30 CCl(s),RLm,Clv,revenge 2.25
31 CCl(s),RLm,Clv,F:Power Girl . . . 2.25
32 CCl(s),RLm,Clv,F:Power Girl . . . 2.25
33 CCl(s),RLm,Clv,F:Power Girl . . . 2.25
34 CCl(s),RLm,Clv,in Kuristan 2.25
35 CCl(s),RLm,Clv,The Rapture . . . 2.25
36 CCl(s),RLm,Clv,final issue 2.25
Ann.#1 CCl, Year One Annual 4.00
Ann.#2 CCl(s),RL,KJ,Legends of the Dead Earth. 3.00
TPB CCl(s),DT, rep.#1–#5 . . . . . . 12.95

SOVEREIGN SEVEN PLUS

1 one-shot. 2.95

SPACE JAM

Warner Bros./DC Oct., 1996

one-shot comic adaptation of movie 5.95

SPANNER'S GALAXY

Dec., 1984

1 mini-series 2.00
2 thru 6 . . . . @2.00

SPECTRE, THE

1967–69

1 MA,V:Captain Skull. 100.00
2 NA,V:Dirk Rawley 75.00
3 NA,A:Wildcat 75.00
4 NA 75.00
5 NA 75.00
6 MA 45.00
7 MA,BU:Hourman 45.00
8 MA,Parchment of Power Perilous 45.00
9 BWr(2nd BWr Art). 50.00
10 MA 45.00

[2nd Regular Series] 1987–89

1 GC,O:Spectre. 3.00
2 GC,Cult of BRM 3.00
3 GC,Fashion Model Murders 2.50
4 GC 2.50
5 GC,Spectre's Murderer. 2.50
6 GC,Spectre/Corrigan separated . 2.50
7 A:Zatanna,Wotan 2.50
8 A:Zatanna,Wotan 2.50
9 GM,Spectre's Revenge. 2.50
10 GM,A:Batman,Millenium 2.50
11 GM,Millenium. 2.50
12 GM,The Talisman,pt.1 . . . . 2.50
13 GM,The Talisman,pt.2 . . . . 2.50
14 GM,The Talisman,pt.3 . . . . 2.50
15 GM,The Talisman,pt.4 . . . . 2.50
16 Jim Corrigan Accused 2.50
17 New Direction,`Final Destiny' . . . 2.50
18 Search for Host Body. 2.50
19 `Dead Again' 2.50
20 Corrigan Detective Agency 2.50
21 A:Zoran 2.00
22 BS,Sea of Darkness,A:Zoran . . . 2.00
23 A:Lords of Order, Invasion x-over. 2.00
24 BWg,Ghosts i/t Machine#1. . . . . 2.00
25 Ghosts in the Machine #2 . . . . . 2.00
26 Ghosts in the Machine #3 . . . . . 2.00
27 Ghosts in the Machine #4 . . . . . 2.00
28 Ghosts in the Machine #5 . . . . . 2.00
29 Ghosts in the Machine #6 . . . . . 2.00
30 Possession 2.00
31 Spectre possessed, final issue. . 2.00
Ann.#1, A:Deadman 2.75

[3rd Regular Series] 1992–97

1 B:JOs(s),TMd,R:Spectre, Glow in the dark(c). 7.00
2 TMd,Murder Mystery. 6.00
3 TMd,O:Spectre. 4.00
4 TMd,O:Spectre. 4.00
5 TMd,BB(c),V:Kidnappers 3.50
6 TMd,Spectre prevents evil 3.50
7 TMd 3.50
8 TMd,Glow in the dark(c) 5.00
9 TMd,MWg(c),V:The Reaver 3.00
10 TMd,V:Michael. 3.00
11 TMd,V:Azmodeus. 3.00
12 V:Reaver 3.00
13 TMd,V:Count Vertigo, Glow in the Dark(c) 4.00
14 JoP,A:Phantom Stranger 2.50
15 TMd,A:Phantom Stranger,Demon, Doctor Fate,John Constantine . 2.50
16 JAp,V:I.R.A. 2.50
17 TT(c),TMd,V:Eclipso 2.50
18 TMd,D:Eclipso 2.50
19 TMd,V:Hate 2.50
20 A:Lucien 2.50
21 V:Naiad,C:Superman 3.00
22 A:Superman 2.50
23 Book of Judgment, pt.1 . . . . 2.50
24 Book of Judgment, pt.2 . . . . 2.50
25 Book of Judgment, pt.3 . . . . 2.50
26 . . . . 2.50
27 R:Azmodus 2.50
28 V:Azmodus 2.50
29 V:Azmodus 2.50
30 V:Azmodus 2.50
31 Descent into Pandemonium 2.25
32 V:Killo 2.25
33 . . . . 2.25
34 Power of the Undead. 2.25
35 JOs,TMd,Underworld Unleashed tie-in 2.25
36 JOs,TMd,Underworld Unleashed tie-in 2.25
37 JOs,TMd,The Haunting of America,pt.1. . . . . 2.25
38 JOs,TMd,The Haunting of America,pt.2. . . . . 2.25
39 JOs,TMd,The Haunting of America,pt.3. . . . . 2.25
40 JOs,TMd,The Haunting of America,pt.4. . . . . 2.25
41 JOs,TMd,The Haunting of America,pt.5. . . . . 2.25
42 JOs,TMd,The Haunting of America,pt.6. . . . . 2.25
43 Witchcraft 2.25
44 Madame Xanadu 2.25

Spectre Annual #1 © DC Comics, Inc.

45 . . . . 2.25
46 JOs(s),TMd,discovery of the Spear of Destiny. 2.25
47 JOs(s),TMd,"The Haunting of America" Final Night tie-in 2.25
48 JOs(s),TMd,"The Haunting of America" 2.25
49 JOs(s),TMd,"The Haunting of America" 2.25
50 JOs(s),TMd,. 2.25
51 JOs(s),TMd,A:Batman,Joker . . . 2.25
52 JOs(s),TMd,Nate Kane discovers murder evidence 2.25
53 JOs(s),TMd,"Haunting of Jim Corrigan" cont. 2.25
54 JOs(s),TMd,hunt for murderer of Mister Terrific 2.25
55 JOs(s),TMd,Corrigan implicated in murder 2.25
56 JOs(s),TMd,JTo "Haunting if Jim Corrigan" 2.50
57 JOs(s),TMd,Spectre & Jim Corrigan in Heaven 2.50
58 JOs,TMd,Genesis tie-in 2.50
59 JOs,TMd,BWr(c), alien pod 2.50
60 JOs,TMd,Quest for God, cont. . . 2.50
61 JOs,TMd,Quest for God, concl. . 2.50
62 JOs,TMd,final issue 2.50
Ann.#1 JOs,TMd,Year One. 4.00
TPB Punishment and Crimes 10.00
TPB Crimes & Punishments, JOs,TMd 10.00

SPEED FORCE

Sept., 1997

1 MWa,BAu,JBy,BML,JAp,BSn, Flash stories, 64pg. 4.00

SPELLJAMMER

Sept., 1990

1 RogueShip#1 . . . . 3.00
2 RogueShip#2 . . . . 2.50
3 RogueShip#3 . . . . 2.00
4 RogueShip#4 . . . . 2.00
5 New Planet. 2.00
6 Tember, Planet contd 2.00
7 Planet contd 2.00
8 conclusion 2.00
9 Meredith Possessed 2.00
10 Tie-in w/Dragonlance #33&34 . . 2.00
11 Dwarf Citidel 2.00
12 Kirstig Vs. Meredith 2.00
13 Tember to the Rescue 2.00

14 Meredith's Son #1 . . . 2.00
15 Meredith's Son #2 . . . 2.00

STALKER
1975–1976

1 O&I:Stalker . . . 5.00
2 thru 4 . . . @2.50

STANLEY & HIS MONSTER
(see FOX AND THE CROW)

STANLEY & HIS MONSTER

1 R:Stanley . . . 2.00
2 I:Demon Hunter . . . 2.00
3 A:Ambrose Bierce . . . 2.00
4 final issue . . . 2.00

S.T.A.R. CORPS

1 A:Superman . . . 2.00
2 I:Fusion,A:Rampage . . . 2.00
3 I:Brainstorm . . . 2.00
4 I:Ndoki . . . 2.00
5 I:Trauma . . . 2.00
6 I:Mindgame . . . 2.00

STAR CROSSED
DC/Helix April, 1997

1 (of 3) MHo,Dyltah's romance with Saa . . . 2.50
2 MHo,"Love During Wartime" . . . 2.50
3 (of 3) . . . 2.50

[NEIL GAIMAN & CHARLES VESS'] STARDUST
DC/Vertigo Oct., 1997

1 (of 4) NGa(s),CV . . . 6.00
2 NGa(s),CV adult faerie tale . . . 6.00
3 NGa(s),CV . . . 6.00
4 NGa(s),CV . . . 6.00

STARFIRE
1976–77

1 . . . 2.00
2 thru 8 . . . @2.00

STAR HUNTERS
Oct.–Nov., 1977

1 DN&BL . . . 10.00
2 LH&BL . . . 5.00
3 MN&BL,D:Donovan Flint . . . 5.00
4 thru 7 . . . @5.00

STARMAN
1988–92

1 TL,I&O:New Starman . . . 4.00
2 TL,V:Serial Killer,C:Bolt . . . 3.00
3 TL,V:Bolt . . . 3.00
4 TL,V:Power Elite . . . 2.50
5 TL,Invasion,A:PowerGirl, Firestorm . . . 2.50
6 TL,Invasion,A:G.L.,Atom . . . 2.50
7 TL,Soul Searching Issue . . . 2.50
8 TL,V:LadyQuark . . . 2.50
9 TL,A:Batman,V:Blockbuster . . . 2.50
10 TL,A:Batman,V:Blockbuster . . . 2.50
11 TL,V:Power Elite . . . 2.50
12 TL,V:Power Elite,A:Superman . . . 2.50
13 TL,V:Rampage . . . 2.50
14 TL,A:A:Superman,V:Parasite . . . 2.50
15 TL,V:Deadline . . . 2.50
16 TL,O:Starman . . . 2.50
17 TL,V:Dr.Polaris,A:PowerGirl . . . 2.50
18 TL,V:Dr.Polaris,A:PowerGirl . . . 2.50
19 TL,V:Artillery . . . 2.50
20 TL,FireFighting . . . 2.50
21 TL,Starman Quits . . . 2.50
22 TL,V:Khunds . . . 2.50
23 TL,A:Deadline . . . 2.50
24 TL,A:Deadline . . . 2.50
25 TL,V:Deadline . . . 2.50
26 V:The Mist . . . 2.50
27 V:The Mist . . . 2.50
28 A:Superman . . . 7.00
29 V:Plasmax . . . 2.50
30 Seduction of Starman #1 . . . 2.50
31 Seduction of Starman #2 . . . 2.50
32 Seduction of Starman #3 . . . 2.50
33 Seduction of Starman #4 . . . 2.50
34 A:Batman . . . 2.50
35 A:Valor,Mr.Nebula,ScarletSkier . . . 2.50
36 A:Les Mille Yeux . . . 2.50
37 A:Les Mille Yeux . . . 2.50
38 War of the Gods X-over . . . 2.50
39 V:Plasmax . . . 2.50
40 V:Las Vegas . . . 2.50
41 V:Maaldor . . . 2.50
42 Star Shadows,pt.1,A:Eclipso . . . 3.00
43 Star Shadows,pt.2,A:Lobo, Eclipso . . . 2.50
44 Star Shadows,pt.3,A:Eclipso V:Lobo . . . 2.50
45 Star Shadows,pt.4, V:Eclipso . . . 2.50

2nd Series 1994

0 New Starman . . . 10.00
1 Threat of the Mist . . . 10.00
2 . . . 8.00
3 V:Son of the Mist . . . 7.00
4 . . . 7.00
5 V:Starman . . . 7.00
6 Times Past Features . . . 7.00
7 Sinister Circus . . . 5.00
8 TyH(c),Sinister Circus . . . 5.00
9 TyH(c),Mist's daughter breaks out of prison . . . 5.00
10 Sins of the Chile,prelude . . . 5.00
11 . . . 5.00
12 JeR,TyH,Sins of the Child,pt.1 . . . 5.00
13 JeR,TyH,Sins of the Child,pt.2 . . . 5.00
14 JeR,TyH,Sins of the Child,pt.3 . . . 5.00
15 JeR,TyH,Sins of the Child,pt.4 . . . 5.00
16 JeR,TyH,Sins of the Child,pt.5 . . . 4.00
17 JeR,TyH . . . 4.00
18 JeR,TyH,Orig.Starman vs.The Mist . . . 4.00

Starman #2 © DC Comics, Inc.

19 JeR,TyH,Talking with David 2 . . . 4.00
20 JeR(s),TyH,GyD,"Sand and Stars," pt.1 . . . 4.00
21 JeR(s),TyH,GyD,"Sand and Stars," pt.2 . . . 3.00
22 JeR(s),TyH,GyD,"Sand and Stars," pt.3 . . . 3.00
23 JeR(s),TyH,GyD,"Sand and Stars," pt.4 concl . . . 3.00
24 JeR(s),TyH,"Hell & Back," pt.1 . . . 3.00
25 JeR(s),TyH,"Hell & Back," pt.2 . . . 3.00
26 JeR(s),TyH,"Hell & Back," pt.3 . . . 3.00
27 . . . 3.00
28 JeR(s)Superfreaks and Backstabbers . . . 3.00
29 JeR(s),TyH,GyD,V:The Shade, Starman history . . . 3.00
30 JeR(s),TyH,"Infernal Devices" pt.1 (of 6) . . . 3.00
31 JeR(s),TyH,"Infernal Devices" pt.2 . . . 3.00
32 JeR(s),TyH,"Infernal Devices" pt.3 . . . 3.00
33 JeR(s),TyH,"Infernal Devices" pt.4,A:Batman, Sentinel . . . 3.00
34 JeR(s),TyH,A:Batman, Sentinel, Floronic Man . . . 3.00
35 JeR(s),TyH,A:Batman, Floronic Man, Sentinel . . . 3.00
36 JeR(s),TyH,F:Will Payton . . . 3.00
37 JeR(s),TyH,F:Golden Age Heroes . . . 2.50
38 JeR(s),TyH,new JLE . . . 2.50
39 JeR(s),TyH,Lightning & Stars, pt.1 x-over . . . 2.50
40 JeR(s),TyH . . . 2.50
41 JeR(s),GEr,TyH . . . 2.50
42 JeR(s),MS,Nazis,Demon . . . 2.50
43 JeR(s),TyH,help from JLA . . . 2.50
44 JeR(s),times past story . . . 2.50
45 JeR(s),search for Will Payton . . . 2.50
46 JeR(s),TyH,Bobo . . . 2.50
47 JeR,SY,TyH, . . . 2.50
48 JeR,SY,A:Swamp Thing . . . 2.50
49 JeR,SY,Talking with David . . . 2.50
50 JeR(s),PSj,48-page . . . 4.00
51 JeR(s),PSj,to Krypton . . . 2.50
52 JeR(s),PSj,A:Adam Strange . . . 2.50
53 JeR(s),PSj,A:Adam Strange . . . 2.50
54 JeR(s),Times Past tale . . . 2.50
55 JeR(s),PSj,A:Space Cabby . . . 2.50
56 JeR(s),PSj,A:ElongatedMan . . . 2.50
57 JeR(s),PSj,TyH,AxR,A:Tigorr & Fastbak, pt.1 . . . 2.50
58 JeR,TyH,AxR, pt.2 . . . 2.50
59 JeR,TyH,AxR, pt.3 . . . 2.50
60 JeR,TyH,AxR, concl. . . . 2.50
61 JeR,TyH,AxR . . . 2.50
62 JeR,PSj,Grand Guignol,pt.1 . . . 2.50
63 JeR,PSj,Grand Guignol,pt.2 . . . 2.50
64 JeR,PSj,Grand Guignol,pt.3 . . . 2.50
65 JeR,PSj,Grand Guignol,pt.4 . . . 2.50
66 JeR,PSj,Grand Guignol,pt.5 . . . 2.50
67 JeR,PSj,Grand Guignol,pt.6 . . . 2.50
68 JeR,PSj,Grand Guignol,pt.7 . . . 2.50
69 JeR,PSj,flashback . . . 2.50
70 JeR,PSj,Grand Guignol,pt.8 . . . 2.50
71 JeR,PSj,Grand Guignol,pt.9 . . . 2.50
72 JeR,PSj,Grand Guignol, concl. . . 2.50
Ann.#1 Legends o/t Dead Earth . . . 3.50
Ann.#2 Pulp Heroes (Romance) . . . 3.95
Spec.#1,000,000 JeR(s),PSj . . . 2.50
Secret Files #1,O:Starmen . . . 5.00
Giant #1 80-page . . . 5.00
Spec. Starman: The Mist, F:Mary Marvel, Girlfrenzy (1998) . . . 2.00
TPB Sins of the Father,rep.#0–#5 . 12.95
TPB Night and Day, rep. stories from #7–#16 . . . 14.95
TPB A Wicked Inclination, rep. . . . 18.00
TPB Times Past . . . 18.00

TPB Infernal Devices 17.95
HC Starman Archives 49.95

STARS AND S.T.R.I.P.E.

1999

0 LMd,DDv,I:Courtney Whitman . . . 3.00
1 LMd,DDv,O:Star-Spangled Kid . . 2.50
2 LMd,DDv,V:Paintball 2.50
3 LMd,DDv,V:Skeeter 2.50
4 LMd,DDv,Day of Judgment x-over. 2.50
5 LMd,DDv,F:Young Justice,pt.1 . . 2.50
6 . . . . 2.50
7 LMd,DDv,F:Mike Dugan 2.50
8 LMd,DDv 2.50
9 LMd,DDv,R:Nebula Man 2.50
10 LMd,DDv,cheating 2.50
11 DDv,V:Dr. Graft 2.50
12 DDv,V:Dragon King 2.50
13 DDv,V:Dragon King 2.50
14 LMd,DDv,final issue 2.50

STAR SPANGLED COMICS

Oct., 1941

1 O:Tarantula,B:Captain X of the R.A.F.,Star Spangled Kid, Armstrong of the Army. . . . 4,300.00
2 V:Dr. Weerd. 1,400.00
3 . . . . 850.00
4 V:The Needle 850.00
5 V:Dr. Weerd 850.00
6 E:Armstrong 550.00
7 S&K,O&1st app:The Guardian, B:Robotman,The Newsboy Legion, TNT 6,500.00
8 O:TNT & Dan the Dyna-Mite 1,800.00
9 . . . . 1,400.00
10 . . . . 1,400.00
11 . . . . 1,100.00
12 Newsboy Legion stories, `Prevue of Peril!' 1,100.00
13 `Kill Dat Story!' 1,100.00
14 `Meanest Man on Earth' . . . 1,100.00
15 `Playmates of Peril' 1,100.00
16 `Playboy of Suicide Slum!' . . 1,100.00
17 V:Rafferty Mob 1,100.00
18 O:Star Spangled Kid 1,300.00
19 E:Tarantula 1,000.00
20 B:Liberty Belle. 1,000.00
21 . . . . 800.00
22 `Brains for Sale' 800.00
23 `Art for Scrapper's Sake' 800.00
24 . . . . 800.00

Star Spangled #10 © DC Comics, Inc.

25 `Victuals for Victory' 800.00
26 `Louie the Lug goes Literary' . 800.00
27 `Turn on the Heat!' 800.00
28 `Poor Man's Rich Man' 800.00
29 `Cabbages and Comics' 800.00
30 . . . . 450.00
31 `Questions Please!' 450.00
32 . . . . 450.00
33. . . . . 450.00
34 `From Rags to Run!' 450.00
35 `The Proud Poppas' 450.00
36 `Cowboy of Suicide Slum' . . . 450.00
37 . . . . 450.00
38 . . . . 450.00
39 `Two Guardians are a Crowd'. 450.00
40 . . . . 450.00
41 Back the 6th War Loan(c) . . . 375.00
42 . . . . 375.00
43 American Red Cross(c) 375.00
44 . . . . 375.00
45 7th War Loan (c) 375.00
46 . . . . 375.00
47 . . . . 375.00
48 . . . . 375.00
49 . . . . 375.00
50 . . . . 375.00
51 A:Robot Robber. 375.00
52 `Rehearsal for Crime' 375.00
53 `The Poet of Suicide Slum' . . . 375.00
54 `Dead-Shot Dade's Revenge'. 375.00
55 `Gabby Strikes a Gusher' 375.00
56 `The Treasuer of Araby' 375.00
57 `Recruit for the Legion' 375.00
58 `Matadors of Suicide Slum' . . 375.00
59 . . . . 375.00
60 . . . . 375.00
61 . . . . 375.00
62 `Prevue of Tomorrow' 375.00
63 . . . . 375.00
64 `Criminal Cruise' 375.00
65 B:Robin,(c) & stories 1,200.00
66 V:No Face 700.00
67 `The Castle of Doom 550.00
68 . . . . 550.00
69 `The Stolen Atom Bomb' 850.00
70 V:The Clock. 550.00
71 `Perils of the Stone Age' 550.00
72 `Robin Crusoe'. 550.00
73 V:The Black Magician 550.00
74 V:The Clock 550.00
75 The State vs. Robin 550.00
76 V:The Fence 550.00
77 `The Boy who Wanted Robin for Christmas' 550.00
78 ``Rajah Robin' 550.00
79 `V:The Clock,`The Tick-Tock Crimes'. 550.00
80 `The Boy Disc Jockey' 550.00
81 `The Seeing-Eye Dog Crimes' 450.00
82 `The Boy who Hated Robin' . . 450.00
83 `Who is Mr. Mystery',B:Captain Compass backup story 450.00
84 How can we Fight Juvenile Delinquency? 650.00
85 `Peril at the Pole' 450.00
86 . . . . 475.00
87 V:Sinister Knight 650.00
88 Robin Declares War on Batman, B:Batman app. 525.00
89 `Batman's Utility Belt?' 525.00
90 `Rancho Fear!' 525.00
91 `Cops 'n' Robbers?' 525.00
92 `Movie Hero No. 1?' 525.00
93 . . . . 525.00
94 `Underworld Playhouse' 525.00
95 `The Man with the Midas Touch', E:Robin(c),Batman story 525.00
96 B:Tomahawk(c) & stories 350.00
97 `The 4 Bold Warriors' 300.00
98 . . . . 300.00
99 `The Second Pocahontas' . . . 300.00
100 `The Frontier Phantom' 300.00
101 Peril on the High Seas 250.00
102 . . . . 250.00
103 `Tomahawk's Death Duel!' . . 250.00
104 `Race with Death!' 250.00
105 `The Unhappy Hunting Grounds' 250.00
106 `Traitor in the War Paint' . . . 250.00
107 `The Brave who Hunted Tomahawk' 250.00
108 `The Ghost called Moccasin Foot!' 250.00
109 `The Land Pirates of Jolly Roger Hill!' 250.00
110 `Sally Raines Frontier Girl' . . 275.00
111 `The Death Map of Thunder Hill'. 275.00
112 . . . . 300.00
113 FF,V:`The Black Cougar' . . . 325.00
114 `Return of the Black Cougar' 350.00
115 `Journey of a Thousand Deaths'. 300.00
116 `The Battle of Junction Fort' . 300.00
117 `Siege?' 300.00
118 V:Outlaw Indians 250.00
119 `The Doomed Stockade?' . . . 225.00
120 `Revenge of Raven Heart!' . . 225.00
121 `Adventure in New York!' . . . 225.00
122 `I:Ghost Breaker,(c)& stories 250.00
123 `The Dolls of Doom' 200.00
124 `Suicide Tower' 200.00
125 The Hermit's Ghost Dog!' . . . 200.00
126 `The Phantom of Paris!' 200.00
127 `The Supernatural Alibi!' 200.00
128 C:Batman,`The Girl who lived 5,000 Years!' 200.00
129 `The Human Orchids' 250.00
130 `The Haunted Town', July, 1952. . . . . 275.00

Becomes:

STAR SPANGLED WAR STORIES

Aug., 1952

131 CS&StK(c),I Was A Jap Prisoner of War 900.00
132 CS&StK(c),The G.I. With The Million-Dollar Arm 600.00
133 CS&StK(c),Mission-San Marino 500.00
3 CS&StK(c),Hundred-Mission Mitchell. 275.00
4 CS&StK(c),The Hot Rod Tank . 275.00
5 LSt(c),Jet Pilot 275.00
6 CS(c),Operation Davy Jones. . 275.00
7 CS(c),Rookie Ranger,The. . . . 200.00
8 CS(c),I Was A Holywood Soldier 200.00
9 CS&StK(c),Sad Sack Squad . . 200.00
10 CS,The G.I. & The Gambler. . 200.00
11 LSt(c),The Lucky Squad. 200.00
12 CS(c),The Four Horseman of Barricade Hill 200.00
13 No Escape. 200.00
14 LSt(c),Pitchfork Army 200.00
15 The Big Fish 200.00
16 The Yellow Ribbon 200.00
17 IN(c),Prize Target. 200.00
18 IN(c),The Gladiator 200.00
19 IN(c),The Big Lift 200.00
20 JGr(c),The Battle of the Frogmen. 200.00
21 JGr(c),Dead Man's Bridge . . . 150.00
22 JGr(c),Death Hurdle 150.00
23 JGr(c),The Silent Frogman. . . 150.00
24 JGr(c),Death Slide 150.00
25 JGr(c),S.S. Liferaft 150.00
26 JGr(c),Bazooka Man 150.00
27 JGr(c),Taps for a Tail Gunner . 150.00
28 JGr(c),Tank Duel 150.00
29 JGr(c),A Gun Called Slugger . 150.00

30 JGr(c),The Thunderbolt Tank . 150.00
31 IN(c),Tank Block. 100.00
32 JGr(c),Bridge to Battle 100.00
33 JGr(c),Pocket War 100.00
34 JGr(c),Fighting...Snowbirds . . 100.00
35 JGr(c),Zero Hour 100.00
36 JGr(c),A G.I. Passed Here . . . 100.00
37 JGr(c),A Handful of T.N.T. . . . 100.00
38 RH(c),One-Man Army 100.00
39 JGr(c),Flying Cowboy. 100.00
40 JGr(c),Desert Duel. 100.00
41 IN(c),A Gunner's Hands. 85.00
42 JGr(c),Sniper Alley. 85.00
43 JGr(c),Top Kick Brother 85.00
44 JGr(c),Tank 711
Doesn't Answer 85.00
45 JGr(c),Flying Heels 85.00
46 JGr(c),Gunner's Seat. 85.00
47 JGr(c),Sidekick 85.00
48 JGr(c),Battle Hills. 85.00
49 JGr(c),Payload. 85.00
50 JGr(c),Combat Dust. 85.00
51 JGr(c),Battle Pigeon. 70.00
52 JGr(c),Cannon-Man 70.00
53 JGr(c),Combat Close-Ups 70.00
54 JGr(c),Flying Exit 70.00
55 JKu(c),The Burning Desert. . . . 70.00
56 JKu(c),The Walking Sub 70.00
57 JGr(c),Call For a Frogman 70.00
58 JGr(c),MD,Waist Punch 70.00
59 JGr(c),Kick In The Door 70.00
60 JGr(c),Hotbox 70.00
61 JGr(c),MD,Tow Pilot. 70.00
62 JGr(c),The Three GIs. 70.00
63 JGr(c),Flying Range Rider 70.00
64 JGr(c),MD,Frogman Ambush . . 70.00
65 JGr(c),JSe,Frogman Block. . . . 70.00
66 JGr(c),Flattop Pigeon. 70.00
67 RH(c),MD,Ashcan Alley 70.00
68 JGr(c),The Long Step 70.00
69 JKu(c),Floating Tank, The' 70.00
70 JKu(c),No Medal For
Frogman 65.00
71 JKu(c),Shooting Star 65.00
72 JGr(c),Silent Fish. 65.00
73 JGr(c),MD,The Mouse &
the Tiger. 65.00
74 JGr(c),MD,Frogman Bait 65.00
75 JGr(c),MD,Paratroop
Mousketeers. 65.00
76 MD,JKu(c),Odd Man 65.00
77 MD,JKu(c),Room to Fight. 65.00
78 MD,JGr(c),Fighting Wingman . . 65.00
79 MD,JKu(c),Zero Box 65.00
80 MD,JGr(c),Top Gunner. 65.00
81 MD,RH(c),Khaki Mosquito 65.00
82 MD,JKu(c),Ground Flier 65.00
83 MD,JGr(c),Jet On
My Shoulder. 65.00
84 MD,IN(c),O:Mademoiselle
Marie 150.00
85 IN(c),A Medal For Marie. 80.00
86 JGr(c),A Medal For Marie. 80.00
87 JGr(c),T.N.T. Spotlight 75.00
88 JGr(c),The Steel Trap 75.00
89 IN(c),Trail of the Terror. 75.00
90 RA(c),Island of
Armored Giants 350.00
91 JGr(c),The Train of Terror 55.00
92 Last Battle of the
Dinosaur Age 125.00
93 Goliath of the Western Front . . 55.00
94 JKu(c),The Frogman and
the Dinosaur. 125.00
95 Guinea Pig Patrol,Dinosaurs . 125.00
96 Mission X,Dinosaur 125.00
97 The Sub-Crusher, Dinosaur . . 125.00
98 Island of Thunder, Dinosaur . . 125.00
99 The Circus of Monsters,
Dinosaur. 125.00
100 The Volcano of Monsters,
Dinosaur. 150.00
101 The Robot and the Dinosaur
. . . . 125.00
102 Punchboard War, Dinosaur . 125.00
103 Doom at Dinosaur Island,
Dinosaur. 125.00
104 The Tree of Terror,
Dinosaurs. 125.00
105 The War of Dinosaur Island . 125.00
106 The Nightmare War,
Dinosaurs. 125.00
107 Battle of the Dinosaur
Aquarium 125.00
108 Dinosaur D-Day 125.00
109 The Last Soldiers. 125.00
110 thru 133 . . . . @125.00
134 NA. 100.00
135 . . . . 75.00
136. . . . . 75.00
137 Dinosaur 75.00
138 Enemy Ace 100.00
139 O:Enemy Ace 90.00
140 . . . . 65.00
141 . . . . 65.00
142 . . . . 50.00
143 . . . . 50.00
144 NA,JKu 60.00
145 . . . . 50.00
146 . . . . 50.00
147 . . . . 50.00
148 . . . . 50.00
149 . . . . 50.00
150 JKu,Viking Prince. 50.00
151 I:Unknown Soldier 50.00
152 . . . . 15.00
153 . . . . 15.00
154 O:Unknown Soldier 40.00
155. . . . . 10.00
156 I:Battle Album 8.00
157 thru 160. . . . . 6.00
161 E:Enemy Ace. 6.00
162 thru 170 . . . . @10.00
171 thru 200 . . . . @8.00
201 thru 204 . . . . @3.00
Becomes:

UNKNOWN SOLDIER
April–May, 1977

205 thru 247 . . . . @10.00
248 and 249 O:Unknown Soldier. @5.00
250 . . . . 5.00
251 B:Enemy Ace. 5.00
252 thru 268 . . . . @5.00

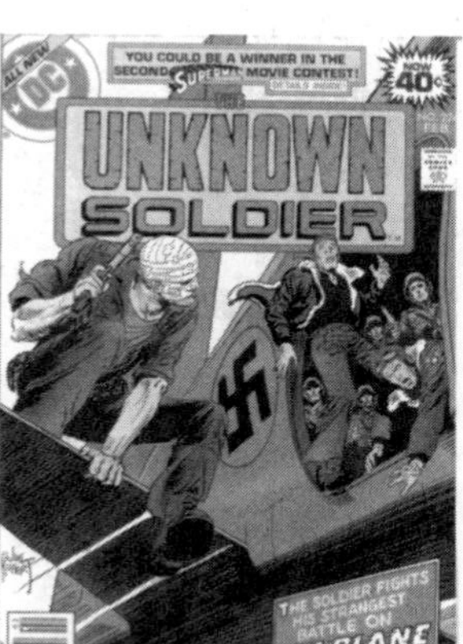

Unknown Soldier #224
© DC Comics, Inc.

STAR SPANGLED COMICS
1999

1 CWn, F:Sandman & Star
Spangled Kid 2.00

Star Trek #45 © DC Comics, Inc.

STAR TREK
1984–88
[1st Regular Series]

1 TS,The Wormhole Connection . 15.00
2 TS,The Only Good Klingon 8.00
3 TS,Errand of War 7.00
4 TS,Deadly Allies 7.00
5 TS,Mortal Gods 7.00
6 TS,Who is Enigma? 6.00
7 EB,O:Saavik. 6.00
8 TS,Blood Fever 6.00
9 TS,Mirror Universe Saga #1 . . . . 6.00
10 TS,Mirror Universe Saga #2. . . . 6.00
11 TS,Mirror Universe Saga #3. . . . 6.00
12 TS,Mirror Universe Saga #4. . . . 6.00
13 TS,Mirror Universe Saga #5. . . . 5.00
14 TS,Mirror Universe Saga #6. . . . 5.00
15 TS,Mirror Universe Saga #7. . . . 5.00
16 TS,Mirror Universe Saga end. . . 5.00
17 TS,The D'Artagnan Three 5.00
18 TS,Rest & Recreation 5.00
19 DSp,W.Koenig story. 5.00
20 TS,Girl. 5.00
21 TS,Dreamworld 5.00
22 TS,The Wolf #1 . . . . 5.00
23 TS,The Wolf #2 . . . . 4.00
24 TS,Double Blind #1 . . . . 4.00
25 TS,Double Blind #2. . . . . 4.00
26 TSV:Romulans 4.00
27 TS,Day in the Life 4.00
28 GM,The Last Word 4.00
29 Trouble with Bearclaw 4.00
30 CI,F:Uhura. 4.00
31 TS,Maggie's World 4.00
32 TS,Judgment Day 4.00
33 TS,20th Anniv. 5.00
34 V:Romulans. 3.00
35 GM,Excelsior. 3.00
36 GM,StarTrek IV tie-in 3.00
37 StarTrek IV tie-in 3.00
38 AKu,The Argon Affair. 3.00
39 TS,A:Harry Mudd. 3.00
40 TS,A:Harry Mudd. 3.00
41 TS,V:Orions 3.00
42 TS,The Corbomite Effect 3.00
43 TS,Paradise Lost #1 . . . . 3.00
44 TS,Paradise Lost #2 . . . . 3.00
45 TS,Paradise Lost #3 . . . . 3.00

46 TS,Getaway. 3.00
47 TS,Idol Threats 3.00
48 TS,The Stars in Secret Influence 3.00
49 TS,Aspiring to be Angels 3.00
50 TS,Anniv.. . . . . 4.00
51 TS,Haunted Honeymoon 3.00
52 TS,'Hell in a Hand Basket' 3.00
53 `You're Dead,Jim' 3.00
54 Old Loyalties 3.00
55 TS,Finnegan's Wake 3.00
56 GM,Took place during 5 year Mission 3.00
Ann.#1 All Those Years Ago 4.00
Ann.#2 DJw,The Final Voyage 3.00
Ann.#3 CS,F:Scotty 3.00
Star Trek III Adapt.TS. 2.50
Star Trek IV Adapt. TS 2.50
StarTrek V Adapt. 2.50

[2nd Regular Series] 1989–96

1 The Return. 9.00
2 The Sentence. 5.00
3 Death Before Dishonor 4.00
4 Reprocussions 4.00
5 Fast Friends 4.00
6 Cure All 4.00
7 Not Sweeney! 4.00
8 Going,Going 3.50
9 ...Gone 3.50
10 Trial of James Kirk #1 . . . . 3.50
11 Trial of James Kirk #2 . . . . 3.50
12 Trial of James Kirk #3 . . . . 3.50
13 Return of Worthy #1 . . . . 3.50
14 Return of Worthy #2 . . . . 3.50
15 Return of Worthy #3 . . . . 3.50
16 Worldsinger 3.00
17 Partners? #1 . . . . 3.00
18 Partners? #2 . . . . 3.00
19 Once A Hero 3.00
20 . . . . 3.00
21 Kirk Trapped 3.00
22 A:Harry Mudd 3.00
23 The Nasgul,A:Harry Mudd 3.00
24 25th Anniv.,A:Harry Mudd 3.50
25 Starfleet Officers Reunion 2.50
26 Pilkor 3 . . . . 2.50
27 Kirk Betrayed. 2.50
28 V:Romulans. 2.50
29 Mediators 2.50
30 Veritas #1 . . . . 2.50
31 Veritas #2 . . . . 2.50

Star Trek, 2nd Series #56
© DC Comics, Inc.

32 Veritas #3 . . . . 2.50
33 Veritas #4 . . . . 2.50
34 JD,F:Kirk,Spock,McCoy 2.50
35 Tabukan Syndrome#1 . . . . 2.50
36 Tabukan Syndrome#2 . . . . 2.50
37 Tabukan Syndrome#3 . . . . 2.50
38 Tabukan Syndrome#4 . . . . 2.50
39 Tabukan Syndrome#5 . . . . 2.50
40 Tabukan Syndrome#6 . . . . 2.50
41 Runaway 2.50
42 Helping Hand. 2.50
43 V:Binzalans 2.50
44 Acceptable Risk. 2.50
45 V:Trelane. 2.50
46 V:Captain Klaa. 2.50
47 F:Spock & Saavik 2.50
48 The Neutral Zone. 2.50
49 weapon from Genesis 2.50
50 "The Peacemaker". 4.00
51 "The Price" 2.50
52 V:Klingons 2.50
53 Timecrime #1. . . . . 2.50
54 Timecrime #2. . . . . 2.50
55 Timecrime #3. . . . . 2.50
56 Timecrime #4. . . . . 2.50
57 Timecrime #5. . . . . 2.50
58 F:Chekov. 2.50
59 Uprising 2.50
60 Hostages 2.50
61 On Talos IV 2.50
62 Alone,pt.1, V:aliens 2.50
63 Alone,pt.2 . . . . 2.50
64 Kirk 2.50
65 Kirk in Space 2.50
66 Spock 2.50
67 Ambassador Stonn 2.50
68 . . . . 2.50
69 Wolf in Cheap Clothing,pt.1 . . . . 2.50
70 Wolf in Cheap Clothing,pt.2 . . . . 2.50
71 Wolf in Cheap Clothing,pt.3 . . . . 2.75
72 Wolf in Cheap Clothing,pt.4 . . . . 2.75
73 Star-crossed,pt.1 . . . . 2.75
74 Star-crossed,pt.2 . . . . 2.50
75 Star-crossed,pt.3 . . . . 4.00
76 Tendar. 2.50
77 to the Romulan Neutral Zone . . . 2.50
78 The Chosen,pt.1 (of 3). 2.50
79 The Chosen,pt.2 . . . . 2.50
80 The Chosen,pt.3 . . . . 2.50
Ann.#1 GM,sty by G.Takei(Sulu) . . . 4.00
Ann.#2 Kirks 1st Yr At Star Fleet Academy 4.00
Ann #3 KD,F:Ambassador Sarek . . 3.50
Ann.#4 F:Spock on Pike's ship 3.50
Ann.#6 Convergence,pt.1 . . . . 3.95
Spec.#1 PDd(s),BSz. 3.75
Spec.#2 The Defiant. 3.95
Spec.#3 V:Orion pirates 3.95
Debt of Honor,AH,CCI(s),HC. 27.00
Debt of Honor SC 14.95
Spec. 25th Anniv.. . . . . 6.95
Star Trek VI,movie adapt(direct) . . . 5.95
Star Trek VI,movie(newsstand) 2.95
TPB Best of Star Trek reps. 19.95
TPB Star Trek: Revisitations rep. #22–#24,F:Gary Seven, #49–#50,F:Harry Mudd, 176-pg. 19.95
TPB Who Killed Captain Kirk?, rep.Star Trek#49-#55 . . . . 16.95
TPB The Ashes of Eden, Shatner novel adapt. 14.95

STAR TREK: THE MODALA IMPERATIVE

1991

1 Planet Modula 6.00
2 Modula's Rebels. 4.50
3 Spock/McCoy rescue Attempt. . . 4.00
4 Rebel Victory 4.00
TPB reprints both minis 19.95

Star Trek The Next Generation #63
© DC Comics, Inc.

STAR TREK: THE NEXT GENERATION

Feb., 1988

[1st Regular Series]

1 based on TV series,Where No Man Has Gone Before 10.00
2 Spirit in the Sky 8.00
3 Factor Q. 5.00
4 Q's Day 5.00
5 Q's Effects 5.00
6 Here Today. 5.00

[2nd Regular Series] 1989–95

1 Return to Raimon 15.00
2 Murder Most Foul 9.00
3 Derelict. 7.50
4 The Hero Factor 7.50
5 Serafin's Survivors 6.00
6 Shadows in the Garden 6.00
7 The Pilot. 5.00
8 The Battle Within 5.00
9 The Pay Off 5.00
10 The Noise of Justice 5.00
11 The Imposter 4.00
12 Whoever Fights Monsters 4.00
13 The Hand of the Assassin 4.00
14 Holiday on Ice 4.00
15 Prisoners of the Ferengi. 3.50
16 I Have Heard the Mermaids Singing. 3.50
17 The Weapon 3.50
18 MM,Forbidden Fruit 3.50
19 The Lesson 3.50
20 Lost Shuttle 3.50
21 Lost Shuttle cont.. . . . . 3.50
22 Lost Shuttle cont.. . . . . 3.50
23 Lost Shuttle cont.. . . . . 3.50
24 Lost Shuttle conc. 3.50
25 Okona S.O.S. 3.50
26 Search for Okona 3.50
27 Worf,Data,Troi,Okona trapped on world 3.50
28 Worf/K'Ehleyr story 3.50
29 Rift,pt.1 . . . . 3.50
30 Rift,pt.2 . . . . 3.50
31 Rift conclusion 3.50
32 . . . . 3.50
33 R:Mischievous Q 3.50
34 V:Aliens,F:Mischievous Q 3.50
35 Way of the Warrior. 3.50
36 Shore Leave in Shanzibar#1 . . . 3.25
37 Shore Leave in Shanzibar#2 . . . 3.25
38 Shore Leave in Shanzibar#3 . . . 3.25

39 Divergence #1 . . . 3.25
40 Divergence #2 . . . 3.25
41 V:Strazzan Warships . . . 3.25
42 V:Strazzans . . . 3.25
43 V:Strazzans . . . 3.25
44 Disrupted Lives . . . 3.25
45 F:Enterprise Surgical Team . . . 3.25
46 Deadly Labyrinth . . . 3.25
47 Worst of Both World's#1 . . . 3.00
48 Worst of Both World's#2 . . . 3.00
49 Worst of Both World's#3 . . . 3.00
50 Double Sized,V:Borg . . . 4.00
51 V:Energy Beings . . . 3.00
52 in the 1940's . . . 3.00
53 F:Picard . . . 3.00
54 F:Picard . . . 3.00
55 Data on Trial . . . 3.00
56 Abduction . . . 3.00
57 Body Switch . . . 3.00
58 Body Switch . . . 3.00
59 B:Children in Chaos . . . 3.00
60 Children in Chaos#2 . . . 3.00
61 E:Children in Chaos . . . 3.00
62 V:Stalker . . . 3.00
63 A:Romulans . . . 3.00
64 Geordie . . . 3.00
65 Geordie . . . 3.00
66 . . . 3.00
67 Friends/Strangers . . . 3.00
68 Friends/Strangers,pt.2 . . . 3.00
69 Friends/Strangers,pt.3 . . . 3.00
70 Friends/Strangers,pt.4 . . . 3.00
71 War of Madness,pt.1 . . . 2.50
72 War of Madness,pt.2 . . . 2.50
73 War of Madness,pt.3 . . . 2.50
74 War of Madness,pt.4 . . . 2.50
75 War of Madness,pt.5 . . . 4.00
76 F:Geordi . . . 2.50
77 Gateway, pt.1 . . . 2.50
78 Gateway, pt.2 . . . 2.50
79 Crew transformed into androids . 2.50
80 Mysterious illness . . . 2.50
Ann.#1 A:Mischievous Q. . . . 4.50
Ann.#2 BP,V:Parasitic Creatures . . . 4.00
Ann.#3 . . . 2.50
Ann.#4 MiB(s),F:Dr.Crusher . . . 4.00
Ann.#6 Convergence,pt.2 . . . 3.95
Series Finale . . . 4.25
Spec.#1 . . . 3.75
Spec.#2 CCI(s) . . . 4.00
Star Trek N.G.:Sparticus . . . 5.00
TPB Beginnings, BSz(c) rep. . . . 19.95

STAR TREK: THE NEXT GENERATION DEEP SPACE NINE

1994–95

1 Crossover with Malibu . . . 2.50
2 . . . 2.50

STAR TREK: THE NEXT GENERATION ILL WIND

1995–96

1 Solar-sailing race . . . 2.50
2 Explosion Investigated . . . 2.50
3 A bomb aboard ship . . . 2.50
4 finale . . . 2.50

STAR TREK THE NEXT GENERATION MODALA IMPERATIVE

1991

1 A:Spock,McCoy . . . 6.00
2 Modula Overrun by Ferengi . . . 5.00
3 Picard,Spock,McCoy & Troi trapped . . . 4.00
4 final issue . . . 4.00

STAR TREK THE NEXT GENERATION SHADOWHEART

1994–95

1 thru 3 . . . @2.25
4 Worf Confront Nikolai . . . 2.25

STATIC

Milestone 1993–96

1 JPL,I:Static,Hotstreak,Frieda Goren, w/poster,card,D puzzle piece . . 4.00
1a Newstand Ed. . . . 2.00
1b Platinum Ed. . . . 8.00
2 JPL,V:Hotstreak,I:Tarmack . . . 2.00
3 JPL,V:Tarmack . . . 2.00
4 JPL,A:Holocaust,I:Don Cornelius . . . 2.00
5 JPL,I:Commando X . . . 2.00
6 JPL,V:Commando X . . . 2.00
7 3RW,V:Commando X . . . 2.00
8 WS(c),3RW,Shadow War,I:Plus. . 2.00
9 3RW,I:Virus . . . 2.00
10 3RW,I:Puff,Coil . . . 2.00
11 3RW,V:Puff,Coil . . . 2.00
12 3RW,I:Joyride . . . 2.00
13 I:Shape Changer . . . 2.00
14 Worlds Collide,V:Rift . . . 2.75
15 V:Paris Bloods . . . 2.00
16 Revelations . . . 2.00
17 Palisade . . . 2.00
18 Princess Nightmare . . . 2.00
19 . . . 2.00
20 . . . 2.00
21 A:Blood Syndicate . . . 2.00
22 V:Rabis . . . 2.00
23 A:Boogieman . . . 2.00
24 A:Dusk . . . 2.00
25 Long Hot Summer, V:Dusk, 48pgs . . . 3.95
26 Long Hot Summer . . . 2.50
27 . . . 2.50
28 Drug Raid . . . 2.50
29 HC(c), Friend Drug Dealer . . . 2.50
30 Deals with Friend's Death . . . 2.50
31 GK . . . 2.50
32 V:Swarm . . . 2.50
33 . . . 2.50
34 V:Ruberband Man . . . 2.50

Static #13 © DC Comics, Inc.

35 new Prometheus . . . 2.50
36 JP,V:Sinister Botanist . . . 2.50
37 . . . 2.50
38 . . . 2.50
39 . . . 2.50
40 JMr . . . 2.50
41 Virgil's relationship with Daisy . . 2.50
42 V:six enemies . . . 2.50
43 A:Brickhouse, V:Frieda Goren . . 2.50
44 . . . 2.50
45 MBr(s),JMr,Static lays a trap for Laserjet . . . 2.50
46 MBr(s),JMr . . . 2.50
47 DMD(s),JMr, final issue . . . 2.50

STATIC SHOCK

1999

TPB Static Shock: Trial by Fire . . . 10.00

STEEL

1994–98

1 JBg(c),B:LSi(s),CsB,N:Steel . . . 3.00
2 JBg(c),CsB,V:Toastmaster . . . 2.00
3 JBg(c),CsB,V:Amertek . . . 2.00
4 JBg(c),CsB . . . 2.00
5 JBg(c),CsB,V:Sister's Attacker . . 2.00
6 JBg(c),CsB,Worlds Collide,pt.5 . . 2.00
7 Worlds Collide,pt.6 . . . 2.00
8 Zero Hour,I:Hazard . . . 2.00
9 F:Steel . . . 2.00
10 F:Steel . . . 2.00
11 . . . 2.00
12 . . . 2.00
13 A:Maxima . . . 2.00
14 A:Superman . . . 2.00
15 R:White Rabbit . . . 2.00
16 V:White Rabbit [new Miraweb format begins] . . 2.00
17 Steel controls armor powers . . . 2.00
18 Abduction . . . 2.00
19 . . . 2.00
20 Body Rejects Armor . . . 2.00
21 LSi,Underworld Unleashed tie-in . . . 2.00
22 Steel separated from Superboy . 2.00
23 Steel attacked . . . 2.00
24 V:Hazard's . . . 2.00
25 . . . 2.00
26 Natasha gains superpowers . . . 2.00
27 LSi,V:Hazard . . . 2.00
28 . . . 2.00
29 . . . 2.00
30 . . . 2.00
31 LSi(s),V:Armorbeast . . . 2.00
32 V:Blockbuster . . . 2.00
33 JAp,DG,Natasha's drug abuse . . 2.00
34 CPr(s),DCw,TP,A:Natasha, in Jersey City . . . 2.00
35 CPr(s),DCw,TP, . . . 2.00
36 CPr(s),DCw,TP,Combing the sewers of Jersey City . . . 2.00
37 CPr(s),DCw,TP,John Irons, Amanda Quick & Skorpio a romantic triangle . . . 2.00
38 CPr(s),DCw,TP,A:The Question . 2.00
39 CPr(s),DCw,TP,V:Crash . . . 2.00
40 CPr(s),VGi,Steel tries out new hammer . . . 2.00
41 CPr(s),DCw,TMo, John Irons guilty of murder? . . . 2.00
42 CPr(s),DCw,TP,Irons and Amanda assaulted . . . 2.00
43 CPr(s),DCw,TP,to Metropolis . . . 2.00
44 CPr(s),DCw,TP,Genesis tie-in . . 2.50
45 CPr(s),DCw,TP,seek policeman . 2.50
46 CPr(s),DCw,TP,F:Superboy . . . 2.50
47 CPr(s),DCw,TP,F:Amanda . . . 2.50
48 . . . 2.50
49 CPr(s),DCw,TP,V:Deadline . . . 2.50
50 CPr(s),DCw,TP,Millennium

Giants 2.50
51 CPr(s),DCw,TP,bounty hunter . . 2.50
52 CPr(s),final issue 2.50
1-shot, movie adaptation. 5.00
Ann.#1 Elseworlds story 2.95
TPB THe Forging of a Hero LSi(s) 19.95

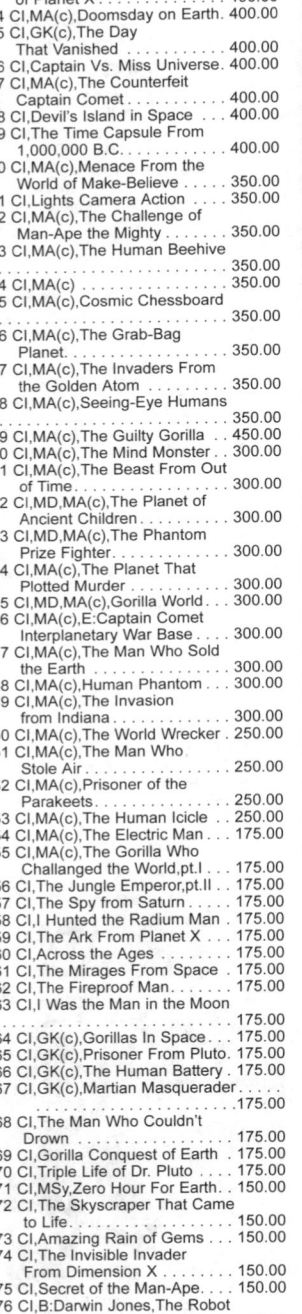

Steel, The Indestructible Man #3
© DC Comics, Inc.

STEEL, THE INDESTRUCTIBLE MAN

March, 1978

1 DH,I:Steel. 5.00
2 DH 3.00
3 DH 3.00
4 DH 3.00
5 Oct.–Nov., 1978 . . . . 5.00

STRANGE ADVENTURES

1950–74

1 The Menace of the Green Nebula. 2,800.00
2 S&K,JM(c),Doom From Planet X 1,400.00
3 The Metal World 900.00
4 BP,The Invaders From the Nth Dimension 900.00
5 The World Inside the Atom . . . 700.00
6 The Confessions of a Martian . 700.00
7 The World of Giant Ants 700.00
8 MA,ATh,Evolution Plus 700.00
9 MA,B:Captain Comet,The Origin of Captain Comet . . 1,700.00
10 MA,CI,The Air Bandits From Space 700.00
11 MA,CI,Day the Past Came Back 500.00
12 MA,CI,GK(c),The Girl From the Diamond Planet 500.00
13 MA,CI,GK(c),When the Earth was Kidnapped. 500.00
14 MA,CI,GK(c),Destination Doom 500.00
15 MA,CI,GK(c),Captain Comet-Enemy of Earth 450.00
16 MA,CI,GK(c),The Ghost of Captain Comet 450.00
17 MA,CI,GK(c),Beware the Synthetic Men 450.00
18 CI,MA(c),World of Flying Men 450.00
19 CI,MA(c),Secret of the Twelve Eternals 450.00
20 CI,Slaves of the Sea Master. . 450.00
21 CI,MA(c),Eyes of the Other Worlds 400.00
22 CI,The Guardians of the Clockwork Universe 400.00
23 CI,MA(c),The Brain Pirates of Planet X 400.00
24 CI,MA(c),Doomsday on Earth. 400.00
25 CI,GK(c),The Day That Vanished 400.00
26 CI,Captain Vs. Miss Universe. 400.00
27 CI,MA(c),The Counterfeit Captain Comet. 400.00
28 CI,Devil's Island in Space . . . 400.00
29 CI,The Time Capsule From 1,000,000 B.C. 400.00
30 CI,MA(c),Menace From the World of Make-Believe 350.00
31 CI,Lights Camera Action 350.00
32 CI,MA(c),The Challenge of Man-Ape the Mighty 350.00
33 CI,MA(c),The Human Beehive 350.00
34 CI,MA(c) 350.00
35 CI,MA(c),Cosmic Chessboard 350.00
36 CI,MA(c),The Grab-Bag Planet. 350.00
37 CI,MA(c),The Invaders From the Golden Atom 350.00
38 CI,MA(c),Seeing-Eye Humans 350.00
39 CI,MA(c),The Guilty Gorilla . . 450.00
40 CI,MA(c),The Mind Monster . . 300.00
41 CI,MA(c),The Beast From Out of Time. 300.00
42 CI,MD,MA(c),The Planet of Ancient Children 300.00
43 CI,MD,MA(c),The Phantom Prize Fighter. 300.00
44 CI,MA(c),The Planet That Plotted Murder 300.00
45 CI,MD,MA(c),Gorilla World . . . 300.00
46 CI,MA(c),E:Captain Comet Interplanetary War Base 300.00
47 CI,MA(c),The Man Who Sold the Earth 300.00
48 CI,MA(c),Human Phantom . . . 300.00
49 CI,MA(c),The Invasion from Indiana 300.00
50 CI,MA(c),The World Wrecker . 250.00
51 CI,MA(c),The Man Who Stole Air 250.00
52 CI,MA(c),Prisoner of the Parakeets. 250.00
53 CI,MA(c),The Human Icicle . . 250.00
54 CI,MA(c),The Electric Man . . . 175.00
55 CI,MA(c),The Gorilla Who Challanged the World,pt.I . . . 175.00
56 CI,The Jungle Emperor,pt.II . . 175.00
57 CI,The Spy from Saturn 175.00
58 CI,I Hunted the Radium Man . 175.00
59 CI,The Ark From Planet X . . . 175.00
60 CI,Across the Ages 175.00
61 CI,The Mirages From Space . 175.00
62 CI,The Fireproof Man. 175.00
63 CI,I Was the Man in the Moon 175.00
64 CI,GK(c),Gorillas In Space . . . 175.00
65 CI,GK(c),Prisoner From Pluto. 175.00
66 CI,GK(c),The Human Battery . 175.00
67 CI,GK(c),Martian Masquerader. 175.00
68 CI,The Man Who Couldn't Drown 175.00
69 CI,Gorilla Conquest of Earth . 175.00
70 CI,Triple Life of Dr. Pluto 175.00
71 CI,MSy,Zero Hour For Earth. . 150.00
72 CI,The Skyscraper That Came to Life. 150.00
73 CI,Amazing Rain of Gems . . . 150.00
74 CI,The Invisible Invader From Dimension X 150.00
75 CI,Secret of the Man-Ape. . . . 150.00
76 CI,B:Darwin Jones,The Robot From Atlantis 150.00

Strange Adventures #231
© DC Comics, Inc.

77 CI,A:Darwin Jones,The World That Slipped Out of Space . . 150.00
78 CI,The Secret of the Tom Thumb Spaceman 150.00
79 CI,A:Darwin Jones,Invaders from the Ice World 150.00
80 CI,Mind Robbers of Venus . . . 150.00
81 CI,The Secret of the Shrinking Twins 150.00
82 CI,Giants of the Cosmic Ray . 135.00
83 CI,Assignment in Eternity. . . . 135.00
84 CI,Prisoners of the Atom Universe. 135.00
85 CI,The Amazing Human Race 135.00
86 CI,The Dog That Saved the Earth 135.00
87 CI,New Faces For Old 135.00
88 CI,A:Darwin Jones,The Gorilla War Against Earth 135.00
89 CI,Earth For Sale. 135.00
90 CI,The Day I Became a Martian 135.00
91 CI,Midget Earthmen of Jupiter 135.00
92 CI,GK(c),The Amazing Ray of Knowledge 135.00
93 CI,GK(c),A:Darwin Jones, Space-Rescue By Proxy. . . . 135.00
94 MA,CI,GK(c),Fisherman of Space. 135.00
95 CI,The World at my Doorstep. 135.00
96 CI,MA(c),The Menace of Saturn's Rings 135.00
97 CI,MA(c),MSy,Secret of the Space-Giant 135.00
98 CI,GK(c),MSy,Attack on Fort Satellite 135.00
99 CI,MSy,GK(c),Big Jump Into Space. 135.00
100 CI,MSy,The Amazing Trial of John (Gorilla) Doe 150.00
101 CI,MSy,GK(c),Giant From Beyond. 100.00
102 MSy,GK(c),The Three Faces of Barry Morrell. 100.00
103 GK(c),The Man Who Harpooned Worlds 100.00
104 MSy,GK(c),World of Doomed Spacemen 100.00
105 MSy,GK(c),Fisherman From the Sea 100.00
106 MSy,CI,GK(c),Genie in the Flying Saucer 100.00
107 MSy,CI,GK(c),War of the Jovian Bubble-Men. 100.00

108 MSy,CI,GK(c),The Human Pet of Gorilla Land 100.00
109 MSy,CI,GK(c),The Man Who Weighted 100 Tons. 100.00
110 MSy,CI,GK(c),Hand From Beyond. 100.00
111 MSy,CI,GK(c),Secret of the Last Earth-Man. 100.00
112 MSy,CI,GK(c),Menace of the Size-Changing Spaceman 100.00
113 MSy,CI,GK(c),Deluge From Space. 100.00
114 MSy,CI,GK(c),Secret of the Flying Buzz Saw. 100.00
115 MSy,CI,GK(c),The Great Space-Tiger Hunt 100.00
116 MSy,CI,RH,GK(c),Invasion of the Water Warriors 100.00
117 MSy,CI,GK(c),I:Atomic Knights. 600.00
118 MSy,CI,The Turtle-Men of Space. 125.00
119 MSy,CI,MA(c),Raiders From the Giant World 100.00
120 MSy,CI,MA,Attack of the Oil Demons 250.00
121 MSy,CI,MA(c),Invasion of the Flying Reptiles 75.00
122 MSy,CI,MA(c),David and the Space-Goliath 75.00
123 MSy,CI,MA(c),Secret of the Rocket-Destroyer 150.00
124 MSy,CI,MA(c),The Face-Hunter From Saturn. 85.00
125 MSy,CI,The Flying Gorilla Menace 75.00
126 MSy,CI,MA(c),Return of the Neanderthal Man 150.00
127 MSy,CI,MA(c),Menace From the Earth-Globe. 75.00
128 MSy,CI,MA(c),The Man With the Electronic Brain 75.00
129 MSy,CI,MA(c),The Giant Who Stole Mountains 80.00
130 MSy,CI,MA.War With the Giant Frogs 75.00
131 MSy,CI,MA(c),Emperor of the Earth 75.00
132 MSy,CI,MA(c),The Dreams of Doom. 80.00
133 MSy,CI,MA(c),The Invisible Dinosaur 75.00
134 MSy,CI,MA(c), The Aliens Who Raided New York 80.00
135 MSy,CI,MA(c),Fishing Hole in the Sky. 75.00
136 MSy,CI,MA(c),The Robot Who Lost Its Head 50.00
137 MSy,CI,MA(c),Parade of the Space-Toys 50.00
138 MSy,CI,MA(c),Secret of the Dinosaur Skeleton 80.00
139 MSy,CI,MA(c),Space-Roots of Evil. 50.00
140 MSy,CI,MA(c),Prisoner of the Space-Patch. 50.00
141 MSy,CI,MA(c),Battle Between the Two Earths. 75.00
142 MSy,CI,MA(c),The Return of the Faceless Creature 50.00
143 MSy,CI,MA(c),The Face in the Atom-Bomb Cloud 50.00
144 MSy,CI,MA(c),A:Atomic Knights, When the Earth Blacked Out 100.00
145 MSy,CI,MA,The Man Who Lived Forever. 50.00
146 MSy,CI,MA(c),Perilous Pet of Space. 50.00
147 MSy,CI,MA(c),The Dawn-World Menace 70.00
148 MSy,CI,MA(c),Earth Hero, Number One 50.00
149 MSy,CI,MA(c),Raid of the Rogue Star. 50.00
150 MSy,CI,MA(c),When Earth Turned into a Comet. 70.00
151 MSy,CI,MA(c),Invasion Via Radio-Telescope. 50.00
152 MSy,MA(c),The Martian Emperor of Earth 50.00
153 MSy,MA(c),Threat of the Faceless Creature 50.00
154 CI,MSy,MA,GK(c),Earth's Friendly Invaders 50.00
155 MSy,MA,GK(c),Prisoner of the Undersea World 50.00
156 MSy,CI,MA(c),The Man With the Head of Saturn 50.00
157 MSy,CI,MA(c),Plight of the Human Cocoons. 50.00
158 MSy,CI,MA(c),The Mind Masters of Space 50.00
159 MSy,CI,MA(c),The Maze of Time. 50.00
160 MSy,CI,MA(c),A:Atomic Knights, Here Comes the Wild Ones 50.00
161 MSy,CI,MA(c),Earth's Frozen Heat Wave,E:Space Museum . 40.00
162 CI,MA(c),Mystery of the 12 O'Clock Man 40.00
163 MA(c),The Creature in the Black Light 40.00
164 DD&SMo(c),I Became a Robot 40.00
165 DD&SMo(c),I Broke the Supernatural Barrier 40.00
166 DD&SMo(c),I Lived in Two Bodies 40.00
167 JkS(c),The Team That Conqured Time. 40.00
168 JkS(c),I Hunted Toki the Terrible. 40.00
169 DD&SMo(c),The Prisoner of the Hour Glass 40.00
170 DD&SMo(c),The Creature From Strange Adventures. . . . 40.00
171 The Diary of the 9-Planet Man? 40.00
172 DD&SMo(c),I Became the Juggernaut Man 40.00
173 The Secret of the Fantasy Films. 40.00
174 JkS(c),The Ten Ton Man 40.00

Strange Adventures #243
© DC Comics, Inc.

175 Danger: This Town is Shrinking 40.00
176 DD&SMo(c),The Case of the Cosmonik Quartet. 40.00
177 I Lived a Hundred Lives, O:Immortal Man 40.00
178 JkS(c),The Runaway Comet. . 40.00
179 JkS(c),I Buried Myself Alive . . 40.00
180 CI,I:Animal Man,`I Was the Man With Animal Powers . . . 225.00
181 The Man of Two Worlds 25.00
182 JkS(c),The Case of the Blonde Bombshell 25.00
183 JM(c),The Plot to Destroy the Earth 25.00
184 GK(c),A:Animal Man,The Return of the Man With Animal Powers 150.00
185 JkS(c),Ilda-Gangsters Inc. . . . 25.00
186 Beware the Gorilla Witch 25.00
187 JkS(c),O:The Enchantress . . . 28.00
188 SD,JkS(c),I Was the Four Seasons. 25.00
189 SD,JkS(c),The Way-Out Worlds of Bertram Tilley 25.00
190 CI,A:Animal Man,A-Man-the Hero with Animal Powers . . . 150.00
191 JkS(c),Beauty vs. the Beast . . 25.00
192 Freak Island. 25.00
193 The Villian Maker 25.00
194 JkS(c),The Menace of the Super- Gloves 25.00
195 JkS(c),Secret of the Three Earth Dooms,A:Animal Man . 100.00
196 JkS(c),Mystery of the Orbit Creatures. 25.00
197 The Hostile Hamlet 22.00
198 JkS(c),Danger! Earth is Doomed 22.00
199 Robots of the Round Table. . . 22.00
200 . . . . 22.00
201 JkS,Animal Man. 50.00
202. . . . . 22.00
203. . . . . 22.00
204. . . . . 22.00
205 CI,I&O:Deadman 100.00
206 NA,MSy. 75.00
207 NA. 50.00
208 NA. 50.00
209 NA. 50.00
210 NA. 50.00
211 NA. 50.00
212 NA. 50.00
213 NA. 50.00
214 NA. 50.00
215 NA. 50.00
216 NA. 50.00
217 MA,MSy,A:Adam Strange. . . . 15.00
218 MA,CI,MSy 15.00
219 CI,JKu 15.00
220 CI,JKu 15.00
221 CI 15.00
222 MA,New Adam Strange 30.00
223 MA,CI 15.00
224 MA,CI 15.00
225 MA,JKu 15.00
226 MA,JKu,New Adam Strange. . 25.00
227 JKu 15.00
228 NA(c). 30.00
229 . . . . 15.00
230 GM(c) 15.00
231 E:Atomic Knights 15.00
232 JKu 15.00
233 JKu 15.00
234 JKu 15.00
235 NA(c). 20.00
236. . . . . 15.00
237. . . . . 12.00
238 MK(c) 12.00
239 . . . . 12.00
240 MK(c) 12.00

241 . . . . 12.00
242 MA 12.00
243 F:Adam Strange. 12.00
244 Oct.–Nov., 1974 . . . . 12.00

STRANGE ADVENTURES
DC Vertigo Sept., 1999

1 (of 4) BB,DGb. 2.50
2 KJ,Expiration Date 2.50
3 . . . . 2.50
4 concl. 2.50

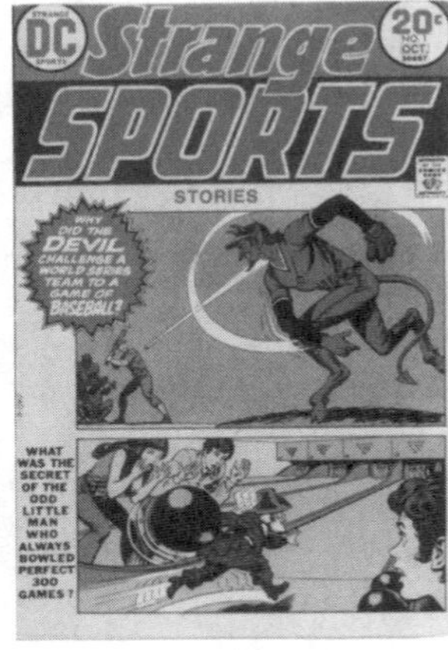

Strange Sports Stories #1
© DC Comics, Inc.

STRANGE SPORTS STORIES
Sept.–Oct., 1973

1 CS,DG 25.00
2 thru 6 . . . . @15.00

STREETS
1993

1 Tenderloin 5.00
2 Procurement. 5.00
3 . . . . 5.00

SUGAR & SPIKE
April–May, 1956

1 SM 1,600.00
2 SM 600.00
3 SM 450.00
4 SM 350.00
5 SM 350.00
6 thru 10 SM . . . . @250.00
11 thru 20 SM . . . . @200.00
21 thru 29 SM . . . . @100.00
30 SM,A:Scribbly 125.00
31 thru 50 SM . . . . @100.00
51 thru 70 SM . . . . @70.00
71 thru 79 SM . . . . @50.00
80 SM,I:Bernie the Brain. 50.00
81 thru 97 SM . . . . @40.00
98 SM,Oct.–Nov., 1971. . . . . 40.00

STUCK RUBBER BABY SOFTCOVER
DC/Paradox Press

GN by Howard Cruise. 14.00

SUICIDE SQUAD
1987–91

1 LMc,Legends,I:Jihad. 2.50
2 LMc,V:The Jihad. 2.00
3 LMc,V:Female Furies 2.00
4 LMc,V:William Hell 2.00
5 LM,A:Penguin. 2.50
6 LM,A:Penguin. 2.50
7 LMc,V:Peoples Hero. 2.00
8 LMc,O:SquadMembers. 2.00
9 LMc,Millenium 2.00
10 LMc,A:Batman. 2.00
11 LMc,A:Vixen,Speedy 2.00
12 LMc,Enchantress,
V:Nightshade 2.00
13 LMc,X-over,JLI#13. . . . . 2.00
14 Nightshade Odyssey #1. . . . . . . 2.00
15 Nightshade Odyssey #2. . . . . . . 2.00
16 R:Shade 3.00
17 LMc,V:The Jihad 2.00
18 LMc,V:Jihad. 2.00
19 LMc,Personal Files 1988 . . . . . . 2.00
20 LMc,V:Mirror Master 2.00
21 LMc,bonus book #10 . . . . 2.00
22 LMc,D:Senator Cray 2.00
23 LMc,Invasion 2.00
24 LMc,V:Guerillas 2.00
25 L:Nightshade 2.00
26 D:Rick Flag,Jihad 2.00
27 Janus Directive #2. . . . . 2.00
28 Janus Directive #4. . . . . 2.00
29 Janus Directive #8. . . . . 2.00
30 Janus Directive #10. . . . . 2.00
31 Personal Files 1989. . . . . 2.00
32 V:Female Furies 2.00
33 GI,V:Female Furies 2.00
34 GI,V:Granny Goodness 2.00
35 LMc,GI,V:Female Furies 2.00
36 GI,D:Original Dr.Light. 2.00
37 GI,A:Shade,The Changing
Man,V:Loa 2.00
38 LMc,GI,O:Bronze Tiger 2.00
39 GI,D:Loa 2.00
40 Phoenix Gambit #1,A:Batman
Int. Poster 2.00
41 Phoenix Gambit #2 . . . . 2.00
42 Phoenix Gambit,A:Batman. 2.00
43 Phoenix Gambit,A:Batman. 2.00
44 I:New Atom,O:Captain
Boomerang 2.00
45 A:Kobra. 2.00
46 A:Kobra. 2.00
47 GI,A:Kobra,D:Ravan 2.00
48 GI,New Thinker 2.00
49 GI,New Thinker 2.00
50 GI,50 Years of S.Squad 2.00
51 A:Deadshot 2.00
52 R:Docter Light 2.00
53 GI,The Dragon's Horde #1. . . . . 2.00
54 GI,The Dragon's Horde #2. . . . . 2.00
55 GI,The Dragon's Horde #3. . . . . 2.00
56 GI,The Dragon's Horde #4. . . . . 2.00
57 GI,The Dragon's Horde conc.. . . 2.00
58 GI,War of the Gods x-over 2.00
59 GI,A:Superman, Batman,
Aquaman,A:Jihad, Hayoth 2.00
60 GI,A:Superman,Batman,
Aquaman,Jihad,The Hayoth . . . 2.00
61 GI,A:Superman,Batman,
Aquaman,V:Jihad 2.00
62 GI,R:Ray Palmer,A:Batman
Superman,Aquaman. 2.00
63 GI,I:Gvede, Lord of Death 2.00
64 GI,A:Task Force X 2.00
65 GI,Bronze Tiger 2.00
66 GI,Final Iss.E:Suicide Squad . . . 2.00
Ann.#1 GN,V:Argent,A:Manhunter . 2.00

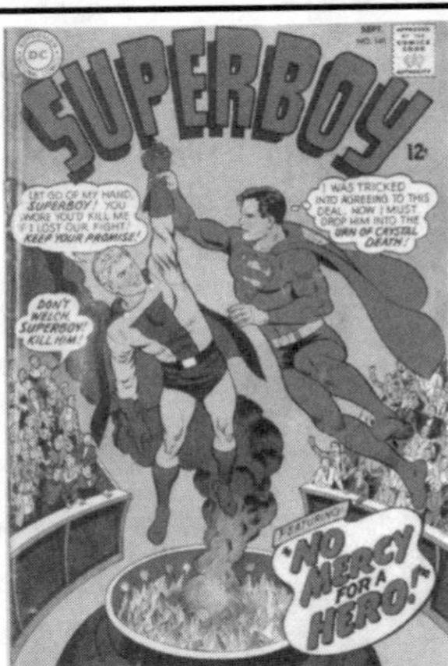

Superboy #141 © DC Comics, Inc.

SUPERBOY
1949–76

1 Superman (c). 7,000.00
2 `Superboy Day' 1,600.00
3 . . . . 1,200.00
4 The Oracle of Smallville 800.00
5 Superboy meets Supergirl,
Pre-Adventure #252 . . . . 750.00
6 I:Humpty Dumpty,the Hobby
Robber. 700.00
7 WB,V:Humpty Dumpty 700.00
8 CS,I:Superbaby,V:Humpty
Dumpty 650.00
9 V:Humpty Dumpty. 650.00
10 CS,I:Lana Lang 650.00
11 CS,2nd Lang,V:Humpty
Dumpty 550.00
12 CS,The Heroes Club 550.00
13 CS,Scout of Smallville 550.00
14 CS,I:Marsboy. 550.00
15 CS,A:Superman. 550.00
16 CS,A:Marsboy 375.00
17 CS,Superboy's Double. 375.00
18 CS,Lana Lang-Hollywood
Star. 375.00
19 CS,The Death of Young
Clark Kent 375.00
20 CS,The Ghost that Haunted
Smallville 375.00
21 CS,Lana Lang-Magician. 275.00
22 CS,The New Clark Kent. 275.00
23 CS,The Super Superboy 275.00
24 CS,The Super Fat Boy of
Steel 275.00
25 CS,Cinderella of Smallville . . . 275.00
26 CS,A:Superbaby 275.00
27 CS,Clark Kent-Runaway. 275.00
28 CS,The Man Who Defeated
Superboy 275.00
29 CS,The Puppet Superboy . . . 275.00
30 CS,I:Tommy Tuttle 200.00
31 CS,The Amazing Elephant
Boy From Smallville 200.00
32 CS,His Majesty King
Superboy 200.00
33 CS,The Crazy Costumes of
the Boy of Steel. 200.00
34 CS,Hep Cats o/Smallville. . . . 200.00
35 CS,The Five Superboys 200.00
36 . . . . 200.00
37 CS,I:Thaddeus Lang 200.00
38 CS,Public Chimp #1. . . . . 200.00
39 CS,Boy w/Superboy Powers . 200.00
40 CS,The Magic Necklace. 225.00
41 CS,Superboy Meets

Superbrave. 225.00
42 CS,Gaucho of Smallville 225.00
43 CS,Super-Farmer o/Smallville
. . . . 225.00
44 The Amazing Adventure of
Superboy's Costume 225.00
45 A Trap For Superboy 225.00
46 The Battle of Fort Smallville . . 225.00
47 CS,A:Superman. 225.00
48 CS,Boy Without Super-Suit . . 225.00
49 I:Metallo (Jor-El's Robot) 225.00
50 The Super-Giant of Smallville. 125.00
51 I:Krypto 150.00
52 CS,The Powerboy from Earth. 150.00
53 CS,A:Superman. 150.00
54 CS,The Silent Superboy. 150.00
55 CS,A:Jimmy Olson. 150.00
56 CS,A:Krypto. 150.00
57 CS,One-Man Baseball Team . 150.00
58 CS,The Great Kryptonite
Mystery 150.00
59 CS,A:Superbaby 150.00
60 The 100,000 Cowboy. 150.00
61 The School For Superboys. . . 125.00
62 I:Gloria Kent 125.00
63 CS,The Two Boys of Steel . . . 125.00
64 CS,A:Krypto. 125.00
65 Superboy's Moonlight Spell . . 125.00
66 The Family with X-Ray Eyes . 125.00
67 I:Klax-Ar 125.00
68 O&I:Bizarro 500.00
69 How Superboy Learned
To Fly. 100.00
70 O:Superboy's Glasses 100.00
71 A:Superbaby 100.00
72 The Flying Girl of Smallville . . 100.00
73 CS,A:Superbaby 100.00
74 A:Jor-El & Lara 100.00
75 A:Superbaby 100.00
76 I:Super Monkey 100.00
77 Superboy's Best Friend 100.00
78 O:Mr.Mzyzptik 175.00
79 A:Jar-El & Lara 100.00
80 Superboy meets Supergirl . . . 125.00
81 The Weakling From Earth 75.00
82 A:Bizarro Krypto 75.00
83 I:Kryptonite Kid 75.00
84 A:William Tell. 75.00
85 Secret of Mighty Boy 75.00
86 I:PeteRoss,A:Legion 150.00
87 I:Scarlet Jungle of Krypton. . . . 80.00
88 The Invader from Earth 80.00
89 I:Mon-El. 250.00
90 A:Pete Ross 75.00
91 CS,Superboy in Civil War. 75.00
92 CS,I:Destructo,A:Lex Luthor. . . 75.00
93 A:Legion 65.00
94 I:Superboy Revenge Squad,
A:Pete Ross. 60.00
95 Imaginary Story,The Super
Family From Krypton 60.00
96 A:Pete Ross,Lex Luther. 60.00
97 Krypto Story. 60.00
98 Legion,I&O:Ultraboy. 60.00
99 O: The Kryptonite Kid 60.00
100 I:Phantom Zone. 175.00
101 The Handsome Hound
of Steel 50.00
102 O:Scarlet Jungle of Krypton . . 50.00
103 CS,A:King Arthur,Jesse James
Red Kryptonite 50.00
104 O:Phantom Zone 50.00
105 CS,`The Simpleton of Steel'. . 50.00
106 CS,A:Brainiac 50.00
107 CS,I:Superboy Club of
Smallville 55.00
108 The Kent's First Super Son . . 50.00
109 The Super Youth of Bronze . . 50.00
110 A:Jor-El 50.00
111 Red Kryptonite Story 50.00
112 CS,A:Superbaby 50.00
113 `The Boyhood of Dad Kent' . . 50.00
114 A:Phantom Zone,
Mr.Mxyzptlk 50.00
115 A:Phantom Zone,Lex Luthor. . 50.00
116 `The Wolfboy of Smallville' . . . 50.00
117 A:Legion 50.00
118 CS,`The War Between
Superboy and Krypto'. 50.00
119 V:Android Double. 40.00
120 A:Mr.Mxyzptlk 40.00
121 CS,A:Jor-El,Lex Luthor 40.00
122 Red Kryptonite Story 40.00
123 CS,The Curse of the
Superboy Mummy 40.00
124 I:Insect Queen 40.00
125 O:Kid Psycho. 40.00
126 O:Krypto 40.00
127 A:Insect Queen 45.00
128 A:Phantom Zone,Kryptonite
Kid,Dev En 45.00
129 rep.A:Mon-El,SuperBaby 45.00
130. . . . . 25.00
131 A;Lex Luthor,Mr.Mxyzptlk,I:
Space Canine Patrol Agents. . 25.00
132, CS,A:Space Canine
Patrol Agents 25.00
133 A:Robin, repr.. . . . . 25.00
134 `The Scoundrel of Steel'. 25.00
135 A:Lex Luthor 25.00
136 A:Space Canine Agents 25.00
137 Mysterious Mighty Mites. 25.00
138 giant, Superboy's Most
Terrific Battles. 45.00
139 `The Samson of Smallville'. . . 25.00
140 V:The Gambler 25.00
141 No Mercy for a Hero 25.00
142 A:Super Monkey 25.00
143 NA(c),`The Big Fall' 25.00
144 `Superboy's Stolen Identity' . . 25.00
145 NA(c)Kents become young . . 25.00
146 NA(c),CS,`The Runaway'. . . . 25.00
147 giant O:Legion. 30.00
148 NA(c),CS,C:PolarBoy. 20.00
149 NA(c),A:Bonnie & Clyde. 20.00
150 JAb,V:Mr.Cipher. 20.00
151 NA(c),A:Kryptonite Kid 20.00
152 NA(c),WW. 20.00
153 NA(c),WW,A;Prof Mesmer . . . 20.00
154 WW(i),A:Jor-El & Lara
`Blackout For Superboy' 20.00
155 NA(c),WW,`Revolt of the
Teenage Robots' 20.00
156 giant 20.00
157 WW 20.00
158 WW,A:Jor-El & Lara. 20.00

Superboy #173 © DC Comics, Inc.

159 WW(i),A:Lex Luthor 20.00
160 WW,`I Chose Eternal Exile' . . 20.00
161 WW,`The Strange Death of
Superboy'. 20.00
162 A:Phantom Zone 20.00
163 NA(c),`Reform School Rebel'. 20.00
164 NA(c),`Your Death Will
Destroy Me' 20.00
165 giant 25.00
166 NA(c),A:Lex Luthor 15.00
167 NA(c),MA,A:Superbaby 15.00
168 NA(c),MA,Hitler 15.00
169 MA,A:Lex Luthor 15.00
170 MA,A:Genghis Khan 15.00
171 MA,A:Aquaboy. 15.00
172 MA(i),GT,A:Legion,
O:Lightning Lad,Yango 16.00
173 NA(c),GT,DG,O:CosmicBoy . . 15.00
174 giant 20.00
175 NA(c),MA,Rejuvenation of
Ma & Pa Kent. 15.00
176 NA(c),MA,GT,WW,A:Legion . . 15.00
177 MA,A:Lex Luthor 15.00
178 NA(c),MA,Legion Reprint 15.00
179 MA,A:Lex Luthor 15.00
180 MA,O:Bouncing Boy. 15.00
181 MA 15.00
182 MA,A:Bruce Wayne 15.00
183 MA,GT,CS(rep),A:Legion 15.00
184 MA,WW,O:Dial H rep. 15.00
185 A:Legion 12.00
186 MA 7.00
187 MA 7.00
188 MA,DC,O:Karkan,A:Legn 7.00
189 MA 7.00
190 MA,WW. 7.00
191 MA,DC O:SunBoy retold 7.00
192 MA 7.00
193 MA,WW,N:Chameleon Boy,
Shrinking Violet 7.00
194 MA 7.00
195 MA,WW,I:Wildfire,
N:Phantom Girl. 7.00
196 last Superboy solo. 8.00
197 DC,Legion begins, New
Costumes,I:Tyr 12.00
198 DC N:Element Lad,
Princess Projects 7.00
199 DC,A:Tyr, Otto Orion 7.00
200 DC,M:Bouncing Boy
& Duo Damsel 12.00
201 DC,Wildfire returns 7.00
202 N:Light Lass 30.00
203 MGr,D:Invisible Kid 18.00
204 MGr,A:Supergirl 12.00
205 MGr,CG,100 pages 30.00
206 MGr,A:Ferro Lad 12.00
207 MGr,O:Lightning Lad 12.00
208 MGr,CS,68pp,Legion of
Super Villains 14.00
209 MGr,N:Karate Kid. 12.00
210 MGr,O:Karate Kid 14.00
211 MGr. 7.00
212 MGr,L:Matter Eater Lad 7.00
213 MGr,V:Benn Pares. 7.00
214 MGr,V:Overseer. 7.00
215 MGr,A:Emerald Empress 7.00
216 MGr,I:Tyroc 7.00
217 MGr,I:Laurel Kent. 7.00
218 J:Tyroc,A:Fatal Five 7.00
219 MGr,A:Fatal Five 7.00
220 MGi,BWi 7.00
221 MGr,BWi,I:Grimbor. 5.00
222 MGr,BWi,MN,BL,A:Tyroc 5.00
223 MGr,BWi 5.00
224 MGr,BWi,V:Pulsar Stargrave . . 5.00
225 MGr(c),BWi,JSh,MN 5.00
226 MGr(c),MN,JSh,JA,
I:Dawnstar 5.00
227 MGr(c),JSon,JA,V:Stargrave . . 5.00
228 MGr(c),JSh,JA,

D:Chemical King 5.00
229 MGr(c),JSh,JA,V:Deregon 5.00
230 MGr(c),JSh,V:Sden 5.00
Becomes:

SUPERBOY & THE LEGION OF SUPER-HEROES

1976–79

231 MGr(c),JSh,MN,JA,doub.size begins,V:Fatal Five. 8.00
232 MGr(c),JSh,RE,JA,V: Dr.Regulus 8.00
233 MGr(c),JSh,BWi,MN,BL, I:Infinite Man 8.00
234 MGr(c),RE,JA,V:Composite Creature. 8.00
235 MGr,GT 8.00
236 MGr(c),BMc,JSh,MN,JRu, V:Khunds 8.00
237 MGr(c),WS,JA 8.00
238 JSn(c),reprint. 8.00
239 MGR(c),JSn,JRu,Ultra Boy accused 8.00
240 MGr(c),HC,BWi,JSh,BMc, O:Dawnstar;V:Grimbor 8.00
241 JSh,BMc,A:Ontir 8.00
242 JSh,BMc,E:Double Size 8.00
243 MGr(c),JA,JSon 8.00
244 JSon,V:Dark Circle. 8.00
245 MA,JSon,V:Mordu 8.00
246 MGr(c),JSon,DG,MA, V:Fatal Five 6.00
247 JSon,JA,anniv.issue. 6.00
248 JSon 6.00
249 JSon,JA. 6.00
250 JSn,V:Omega 6.00
251 JSn,Brainiac 5 goes insane . . . 6.00
252 JSon,V:Starburst bandits 5.00
253 JSon,I:Blok,League of Super Assassins 5.00
254 JSon,V:League of Super Assassins. 5.00
255 JSon,A:Jor-El. 5.00
256 JSon 5.00
257 SD,JSon,DA,V:Psycho Warrior 5.00
258 JSon,V:Psycho Warrior 5.00
Becomes:

LEGION OF SUPER HEROES

[2nd Series]

[NEW ADVENTURES OF] SUPERBOY

Jan., 1980

1 KS 2.00
2 KS 2.00
3 KS 2.00
4 KS 2.00
5 KS 2.00
6 KS 2.00
7 KS,JSa. 2.00
8 thru 33 KS . . . . @2.00
34 KS,I:Yellow Peri 2.00
35 thru 44 KS . . . . @2.00
45 KS,I:Sunburst 2.00
46 KS,A:Sunburst. 2.00
47 KS,A:Sunburst. 2.00
48 KS. 2.00
49 KS,A:Zatara. 2.00
50 KS,KG,A:Legion 2.00
51 KS,FM(c)In Between Years 2.00
52 KS. 2.00
53 KS. 2.00
54 KS. 2.00

New Adventures of Superboy #8
© DC Comics, Inc.

SUPERBOY

1990–91

1 TV Tie-in,JM,photo(c) 2.00
2 JM,T.J.White Abducted 2.00
3 JM,`Fountain of Youth' 2.00
4 JM,`Big Man on Campus' 2.00
5 JM,Legion Homage 2.00
6 JM,Luthor. 2.00
7 JM,Super Boy Arrested. 2.00
8 JM,AAd(i),Bizarro 2.00
9 JM/CS,PhantomZone#1 . . . . 2.00
10 JM/CS,PhantomZone#2. . . . . . . 2.00
11 CS. 2.00
12 CS,X-Mas in Smallville. 2.00
Becomes:

ADVENTURES OF SUPERBOY

1991

13 A:Mr.Mxyzptlk 2.50
14 CS,A:Brimstone. 2.00
15 CS,Legion Homage 2.00
16 CS,Into the Future 2.00
17 CS,A:Luthor. 2.00
18 JM,`At the Movies'. 2.00
19 JM,Blood Transfusion 2.00
20 JM,O:Nicknack,(G.Gottfried script). 2.00
21 V:Frost Monster 2.00
22 . . . . 2.00
Spec.#1 CS,A:Ma Kent. 2.50

SUPERBOY

[2nd Series]

1994

1 B:KK(s),TG,DHz,V:Sidearm 3.00
2 TG,DHz,I:Knockout. 2.50
3 TG,DHz,I:Scavenger. 2.00
4 TG,DHz,MeP,I:Lock n' Load 2.00
5 TG,DHz,I:Silver Sword 2.00
6 TG,DHz,Worlds Collide,pt.3 C:Rocket 2.00
7 Worlds Collide, pt.8,V:Rift 2.00
8 Zero Hour,A:Superboy 2.00
9 Silican Dragon 2.00
10 Monster. 2.00
11 Techno. 2.00
12 Copperhead. 2.00
13 Watery Grave,pt.1 . . . . 2.00
14 Watery Grave,pt.2 . . . . 2.00
15 Watery Grave,pt.3 . . . . 2.00
16 TG,DHz,KK,V:Loose Cannon [New Miraweb format begins] . . 2.00
17 TG,DHz,KK Looking for Roxy Leech 2.00
18 V:Valor. 2.00
19 . . . . 2.00
20 R:Scavenger 2.00
21 KK,TG,DHz,Future Tense,Pt.1 . . 2.00
22 KK,TG,DHz,Underworld Unleashed x-over 2.00
23 KK,TG,DHz,V:Technician 2.00
24 KK,TG,DHz,V:Silversword 2.00
25 New Gods 3.00
26 KK,DHz,Losin'it,pt.2. . . . . 2.00
27 KK,DHz,Losin'it,pt.3. . . . . 2.00
28 KK,DHz,Losin'it,pt.4 (of 6) 2.00
29 . . . . 2.00
30 . . . . 2.00
31 . . . . 2.00
32 RMz(s),RBe,DHz,V:King Shark . 2.00
33 RMz(s),RBe,DHz, survivors flee to Hawaii, Final Night tie-in. . . . 2.00
34 RMz(s),RBe,DHz, V:Dubbilex. . . 2.00
35 RMz(s),RBe,DHz, Superboy abducted 2.00
36 RMz(s),RBe,DHz,V:King SHark . 2.00
37 RMz(s),SB,V:Sledge 2.00
38 RMz(s),RBe,DHz,"Meltdown," pt.1 (of 3). 2.00
39 RMz(s),RBe,DHz,"Meltdown," pt.2 . . . . 2.00
40 RMz(s),RBe,DHz,"Meltdown," pt.2 x-over 2.00
41 RMz(s),RBe,DHz,"Meltdown," pt.3 concl. 2.00
42 SB, ... 2.00
43 SB,Lanie & Ken. 2.00
44 SB,island of teenagers. 2.00
45 RMz,DHz,TGu,A:Legion. 2.00
46 RMz,DHz,TGu,V:Silver Sword . . 2.00
47 RMz,DHz,TGu,F:Green Lantern. 2.00
48 BKs,DHz,TGu,theme park 2.00
49 DHz. 2.00
50 KK,TGu,Last Boy on Earth pt.1 . 2.00
51 KK,TGu,Last Boy on Earth pt.2 . 2.00
52 KK,TGu,Last Boy on Earth pt.3 . 2.00
53 KK,TGu,Last Boy on Earth pt.4 . 2.00
54 KK,TGu,A:Wild Men. 2.00
55 KK,TGu,V:Grokk, Hex 2.00
56 KK,TGu,Project Cadmus 2.00
57 KK,TGu,Demolition Run,pt.1 . . . 2.00
58 KK,TGu,Demolition Run,pt.2 . . . 2.00
59 KK,DAb,A:Superman 2.00

Superboy 2nd Series #9
© DC Comics, Inc.

60 KK,TGu,A:JLA,Hyper-Tension,pt.1 . . . . 2.00
61 KK,TGu,Hyper-Tension,pt.2 . . . . 2.00
62 KK,TGu,Hyper-Tension,pt.3 . . . . 2.00
63 KK,TGu,Hyper-Tension,pt.4 . . . . 2.00
64 KK,TGu,Hyper-Tension,pt.5 . . . . 2.00
65 KK,TGu,guest-star packed. 2.00
66 KK,TGu,Wild Lands 2.00
67 KK,AaL, in Wild Lands. 2.00
68 KK,TG,MM,Day of Judgment x-over, F:Demon. 2.00
69 KK,TG,return to Hawaii 2.00
70 KK,TG,Evil Factory,pt.1 . . . . 2.00
71 KK,TG,Evil Factory,pt.2 . . . . 2.00
72 KK,TG,Evil Factory,pt.3 . . . . 2.00
73 KK,TG,Evil Factory,pt.4 . . . . 2.00
74 KK,TG,Sins of Youth 2.00
75 KK,TG,as normal teenager 2.00
76 KK,TG,still Superboy 2.00
77 KK,TG,MBa,V:Kossak 2.25
78 KK,TG,prisoners 2.25
79 KK,TG,V:Kossak the Slaver 2.25
80 BHr,F:The Titans,pt.1. . . . . 2.25
81 BHr,F:The Titans,pt.2. . . . . 2.25
Ann.#1 Elseworlds Story. 3.50
Ann.#2 KK,BKs, Year One 4.00
Ann.#3 Legends o/t Dead Earth . . . 3.00
Ann.#4 Pulp Heroes (High-Adventure) 4.00
Spec.#1,000,000 KK,TGu 2.00

SUPERBOY & THE RAVERS

1 KK&SMt(s),PaP,DDv, ... 2.00
2 KK&SMt(s),PaP,DDv,InterC.E.P.T. pursues Superboy and Kaliber . 2.00
3 KK&SMT(s),PaP,DDv,teleported to Rann,V:Half-Life 2.00
4 KK&SMt(s),PaP,DDv,A:Adam Strange 2.00
5 KK&SMt(s),PaP,DDv,O:Hero. . . . 2.00
6 KK&SMt(s),PaP,DDv, ... 2.00
7 KK&SMt(s),PaP,DDv, "Road Trip," pt.1,A:Impulse 2.00
8 KK&SMt(s),PaP,DDv, "Road Trip," pt.2,A:Guy Gardner 2.00
9 KK&SMt(s),PaP,DDv, "Road Trip," pt.3,A:Aura. 2.00
10 KK&SMt(s),DDv, "Meltdown," pt. 4 . . . . 2.00
11 KK&SMt(s),PaP,DDv, Superboy presumed dead 2.00
12 KK(s),AaL,. 2.00
13 KK(s),SMt,F:Hero,Sparx 2.00
14 KK&SMt(s),Genesis tie-in 2.00
15 KK&SMt(s),new Rave 2.00
16 KK&SMt(s),Half-Life. 2.00
17 KK&SMt(s),Kaliber. 2.00
18 KK&SMt(s),V:Qward 2.00
19 . . . . 2.00

SUPERBOY PLUS

Nov., 1996

1 RMz(s),ASm,F:Captain Marvel Jr.. . . . . 2.95
2 LKa,AWi,ALa,F:Slither 3.00

SUPERBOY/RISK DOUBLE-SHOT

Dec., 1997

1 DJu,JoP,x-over 2.00

SUPER DC GIANT

1970–71, 1976

S-13 Binky 100.00
S-14 Top Guns of the West. 35.00
S-15 Western Comics. 30.00

Super DC Giant, S-15
© DC Comics, Inc.

S-16 Best of the Brave & the Bold 30.00
S-17 Love 1970 . . . . 100.00
S-18 Three Mouseketeers. 60.00
S-19 Jerry Lewis. 70.00
S-20 House of Mystery 50.00
S-21 Love 1971 . . . . 100.00
S-22 Top Guns of the West. 25.00
S-23 The Unexpected. 30.00
S-24 Supergirl 30.00
S-25 Challengers of the Unknown. 40.00
S-26 Aquaman 25.00
S-27 Strange Flying Saucer Advengures (1976). 20.00

SUPER FRIENDS

Nov., 1976

1 ECh(c),JO,RE,`Fury of the Superfoes',A:Penguin. 20.00
2 RE,A:Penguin. 10.00
3 RF(c),RF,A:JLA 8.00
4 RF,V:Riddler,I:Skyrocket 8.00
5 RF(c),RF,V:Greenback 8.00
6 RF(c),RF,A:Atom 7.00
7 RF(c),RF,I:Zan & Jana, A:Seraph 7.00
8 RF(c),RF,A:JLA 7.00
9 RF(c),RF,A:JLA,I:Iron Maiden . . . 7.00
10 RF(c),RF`TheMonkeyMenace' . . 7.00
11 RF(c),RF 6.00
12 RF(c),RF,A:TNT. 6.00
13 RF(c),RF 6.00
14 RF(c),RF 6.00
15 RF(c),RF, A:The Elementals. . . . 6.00
16 RF(c),RF,V:The Cvags. 6.00
17 RF(c),RF,A:Queen Hippolyte . . . 6.00
18 KS(c),V:Tuantra,Time Trapper . . 6.00
19 RF(c),RF,V:Menagerie Man 6.00
20 KS(c),KS,V:Frownin' Fritz. 6.00
21 RF(c),RF,V:Evil Superfriends Doubles 5.00
22 RF(c),RF,V:Matador Mob 5.00
23 FR(c),RF,V:Mirror Master. 5.00
24 RF(c),RF,V:Exorians 5.00
25 RF(c),RF,V:Overlord, A:Green Lantern, Mera. 5.00
26 RF(c),RF,A:Johnny Jones 5.00
27 RF(c),RF,`The Spaceman Who Stole the Stars 5.00
28 RF(c),RF,A:Felix Faust. 5.00
29 RF(c),RF,B.U.KS,`Scholar From the Stars 5.00
30 RF(c),RF,V:Grodd & Giganta . . . 5.00
31 RF(c),RF,A:Black Orchid 6.00
32 KS(c),KS,A:Scarecrow. 4.00
33 RF(c),RF,V:Menagerie Man 4.00
34 RF(c)RF,`The Creature That Slept a Million Years'. 4.00
35 RT,`Circus o/t Super Stars 4.00
36 RF(c),RF,A:Plastic Man & Woozy 4.00
37 RF(c),RF,A:Supergirl; B.U. A:Jack O'Lantern 4.00
38 RF(c),RF,V:Grax; B.U. A:Serpah 4.00
39 RF(c),RF,A:Overlord; B.U. A:Wonder Twins 4.00
40 RF(c),RF,V:The Monacle; B.U. Jack O'Lantern 4.00
41 RF(c),RF,V:Toyman; B.U. A:Seraph 4.00
42 RT,A:Flora,V:Flame; B.U.Wonder Twins' Christmas Special 4.00
43 KS(c),RT,V:Futuro; B.U.JSon A:Plastic Man. 4.00
44 KS(c),RT,`Peril o/t Forgotten Identities'; B.U.Jack O'Lantern . 4.00
45 KS(c),RT,A:Bushmaster, Godiva, Rising Sun, Olympian, Little Mermaid, Wild Huntsman; B.U. Plastic Man,V: Sinestro. . . 4.00
46 RT,V:The Conqueror; B.U. BO,Seraph 4.00
47 KS(c),RT,A:Green Fury Aug. 1981 . . . . 5.00

SUPERGIRL

[1st Regular Series]

Nov., 1972—Sept., 1974

1 `Trail of the Madman'; Superfashions From Fans; B:B.U. DG,Zatanna 30.00
2 BO(c)A:Prof.Allan,Bottle City of Kandor 15.00
3 BO(c),`The Garden of Death' . . 10.00
4 V:Super Scavanger. 15.00
5 BO(c),A:Superman,V:Dax; B.U. MA:Rep.Hawkman #4. . . . . . . 18.00
6 BO(c),`Love & War' 15.00
7 BO(c),A:Zatanna. 15.00
8 BO(c),A:Superman,Green Lantern, Hawkman 18.00
9 BO(c),V:Sharkman 15.00
10 A:Prey,V:Master Killer 15.00

[DARING NEW ADVENTURES OF] SUPERGIRL

[2nd Regular Series]

Nov., 1982

1 CI,BO,I:Psi; B:B.U.Lois Lane . . . 2.00
2 CI,BO,C:Decay. 2.00
3 CI,BO,V:Decay,`Decay Day' 2.00
4 CI,BO,V:The Gang 2.00
5 CI,BO,V:The Gang 2.00
6 CI,BO,V:The Gang 2.00
7 CI,BO,V:The Gang 2.00
8 CI,BO,A:Doom Patrol 2.00
9 CI,BO,V:Reactron A:Doom Patrol 2.00
10 CI,BO,`Radiation Fever'. 2.00
11 CI,BO,V:Chairman 2.00
12 CI,BO,V:Chairmann 2.00
13 CI,BO,N:Supergirl,A:Superman V:Blackstarr 2.00

Becomes:

SUPERGIRL

Dec., 1983–Sept., 1984

14 GK(c),CI,BO,V:Blackstarr A:Rabbi Nathan Zuber 2.00
15 CI,BO,V:Blackstarr,

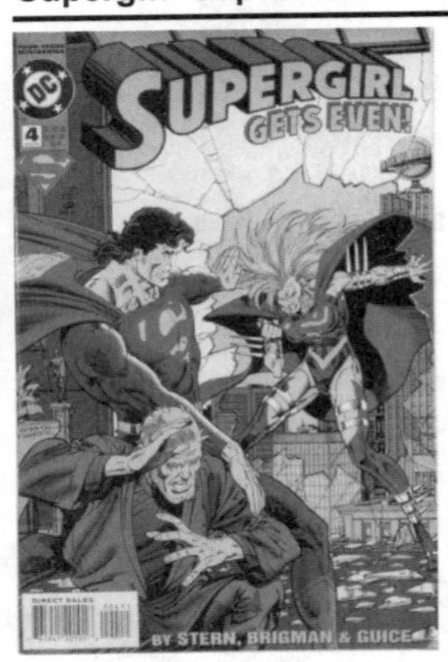

Supergirl Limited Series #4
© DC Comics, Inc.

A:Blackstarr's Mom 2.00
16 KG/BO(c),CI,BO, A:Ambush Bug 2.00
17 CI/DG(c),CI,BO,V:Matrix Prime 2.00
18 DG(c),CI,BO, V:Kraken 2.00
19 EB/BO(c),CI,BO,`Who Stole Supergirl's Life'. 2.00
20 CI,BO,C:JLA,Teen Titans: Teh Parasite 2.00
21 EB/BO(c),EB,Kryptonite Man . . . 2.00
22 EB(c),CI,BO,`I Have Seen the Future & it is Me' 2.00
23 EB(c),CI,BO,`The Future Begins Today 2.00
Spec.#1 JL/DG(c),GM,MovieAdapt . 2.00
Spec.#1 AT,Honda give-away 2.00

[Limited Series] 1994

1 KGa(c),B:RSt(s),JBr,O:Supergirl . 5.00
2 KGa(c),JBr 4.00
3 KGa(c),JBr,D:Clones 3.00
4 KGa(c),RSt(s),JBr,final Issue . . . 3.00

SUPERGIRL
Sept., 1996

1 PDd(s),GFr,CaS,. 11.00
2 PDd(s),GFr,CaS,V:Chakat 5.00
3 PDd(s),GFr,CaS,V:Grodd, Final Night tie-in 4.00
4 PDd(s),GFr,CaS,transformed into savage 3.00
5 PDd(s),GFr,CaS,Supergirl visits the Kents,V:Chemo 3.00
6 PDd(s),GFr,CaS, ... 3.00
7 PDd(s),GFr,CaS,Supergirl learns about Linda Danvers 3.00
8 PDd(s),GFr,CaS,Buzz gets date with Supergirl 3.00
9 PDd(s),GFr,CaS,V:Tempus 3.00
10 PDd(s),Linda tries to relax 3.00
11 PDd(s),CaS,V:Silver Banshee . . 3.00
12 PDd(s),Mattie possessed by Silver Banshee. 3.00
13 CaS, 3 girls dreams invaded by incubus 2.50
14 PDa,CaS,Genesis tie-in 2.00
15 PDa,CaS,V:Extremists 2.00
16 PDa,CaS,F:Power Girl. 2.00
17 PDa,CaS,L-Ron, Despero 2.00
18 PDa,CaS,V:Despero 2.00
19 . . . . 2.00
20 PDa,CaS,Millennium Giants. . . . 2.00
21 PDa,CaS,Comet 2.00
22 PDa, ... 2.00
23 PDa,A:Steel. 2.00
24 PDa,Avenging Angels x-over . . . 2.00
25 PDa,truth about Comet 2.00
26 PDd,truth discovered 2.00
27 PDd(s),V:Female Furies,pt.1 . . . 2.00
28 PDd(s),V:Female Furies,pt.2 . . . 2.00
29 PDd(s),V:Female Furies,pt.3 . . . 2.00
30 PDd(s),V:Matrix 2.00
31 PDd(s),A:Superman. 2.00
32 PDd(s),SeP,V:Mr.Carnivean 2.00
33 PDd(s),V:Mr.Carnivean 2.00
34 PDd(s),V:Parasite 2.00
35 PDd(s),V:Parasite, concl. 2.00
36 PDd(s),Young Justice x-over,Hell's Angel's,pt.2. . . . . . 2.00
37 PDd(s),Hell's Angels,pt.4 . . . . . . 2.00
38 PDd(s),Day of Judgment x-over . 2.00
39 PDd(s),F:Comet. 2.00
40 PDd(s). 2.00
41 PDd(s),F:Ember,V:Satan Girl . . . 2.00
42 PDd(s),dates Dick Malverne. . . . 2.00
43 PDd(s),date become nightmare . 2.00
44 PDd(s),F:Dick Malverne,dying . . 2.00
45 PDd(s),F:Comet,V:Carnivore . . . 2.00
46 PDd(s),V:Comet,Carnivore. 2.00
47 PDd(s),V:Carnivore 2.25
48 PDd(s), ... 2.25
49 PDd(s),V:Carnivore 2.25
50 PDd(s),48-pg. 4.00
51 PDd(s),to Metropolis, minus powers 2.25
Ann.#1 Legends o/t Dead Earth . . . 3.00
Ann.#2 TPe,CDi,ACa, Pulp Heroes. 4.00
Spec.#1,000,000 PDd(s),DAb 2.00
TPB rep. Supergirl #1–#9 . . . . 15.00
Spec. Supergirl/Lex Luthor JBr, F:Lex Luthor (1993) 4.00
Spec. Supergirl/Prism Double-Shot DJu,TGb,CIv, x-over (1997) . . . 2.00

SUPER HEROES BATTLE SUPER GORILLA
Winter, 1976

1 Superman Flash rep. 1.00

SUPERMAN
1939–86

1 JoS,O:Superman,reprints Action Comics #1-#4 . . . . 150,000.00
2 JoS,I:George Taylor 12,000.00
3 JoS,V:Superintendent Lyman 7,000.00
4 JoS,V:Lex Luthor 5,200.00
5 JoS,V:Lex Luthor 3,800.00
6 JoS,V:`Brute' Bashby 2,700.00
7 JoS,I:Perry White. 2,500.00
8 JoS,V:Jackal 2,400.00
9 JoS,V:Joe Gatson 2,400.00
10 JoS,V:Lex Luthor 2,200.00
11 JoS,V:Rolf Zimba 1,700.00
12 JoS,V:Lex Luthor 1,700.00
13 JoS,I:Jimmy Olsen,V:Lex Luthor,`The Archer' 1,700.00
14 JoS,I:Lightning Master. 2,800.00
15 JoS,V:The Evolution King . . 1,700.00
16 JoS,V:Mr. Sinus 1,600.00
17 JoS,V:Lex Luthor,Lois Lane first suspects Clark is Superman 1,600.00
18 JoS,V:Lex Luthor 1,400.00
19 JoS,V:Funnyface, 1st Imaginary story 1,400.00
20 JoS,V:Puzzler,Leopard 1,400.00
21 JoS,V:Sir Gauntlet. 1,000.00
22 JoS,V:Prankster 1,000.00
23 JoS,Propaganda story. 1,000.00
24 V:Cobra King 1,400.00

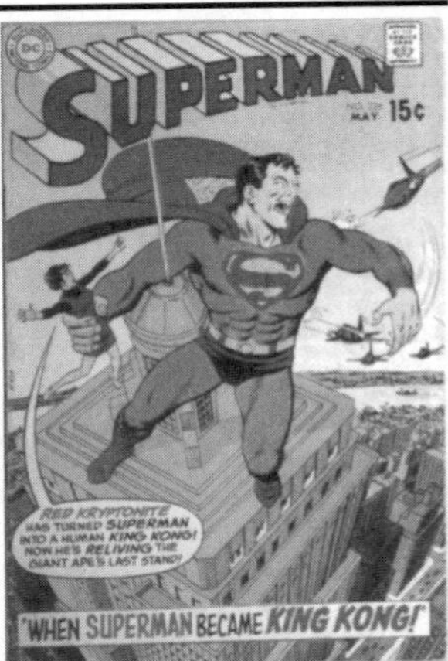

Superman #226 © DC Comics, Inc.

25 Propaganda story 1,000.00
26 I:J.Wilbur Wolfingham, A:Mercury 1,000.00
27 V:Toyman 1,000.00
28 V:J.Wilbur Wolfingham, A:Hercules. 1,000.00
29 V:Prankster. 1,000.00
30 I&O:Mr. Mxyztplk. 1,500.00
31 V:Lex Luthor 900.00
32 V:Toyman 900.00
33 V:Mr. Mxyztptlk 900.00
34 V:Lex Luthor 900.00
35 V:J.Wilbur Wolfingham 900.00
36 V:Mr. Mxyztptlk 900.00
37 V:Prankster,A:Sinbad 900.00
38 V:Lex Luthor 900.00
39 V:J.Wilbur Wolfingham 900.00
40 V:Mr. Mxyzptlk,A:Susie Thompkins 900.00
41 V:Prankster 650.00
42 V:J.Wilbur Wolfingham 650.00
43 V:Lex Luthor 650.00
44 V:Toyman,A:Shakespeare . . . 650.00
45 A:Hocus & Pocus,Lois Lane as Superwoman 650.00
46 V:Mr. Mxyzptlk,Lex Luthor, Superboy flashback 650.00
47 V:Toyman 650.00
48 V:Lex Luthor 650.00
49 V:Toyman 650.00
50 V:Prankster 650.00
51 V:Mr. Mxyzptlk 500.00
52 V:Prankster 500.00
53 WB,O:Superman. 2,200.00
54 V:Wrecker 500.00
55 V:Prankster 500.00
56 V:Prankster 500.00
57 V:Lex Luthor 500.00
58 V:Tiny Trix 500.00
59 V:Mr.Mxyzptlk 500.00
60 V:Toyman 500.00
61 I:Kryptonite,V:Prankster. . . . 1,000.00
62 V:Mr.Mxyzptlk,A:Orson Welles 500.00
63 V:Toyman 500.00
64 V:Prankster 500.00
65 V:Mala,Kizo and U-Ban 500.00
66 V:Prankster 500.00
67 A:Perry Como,I:Brane Taylor. 500.00
68 V:Lex Luthor 500.00
69 V:Prankster,A:Inspector Erskine Hawkins. 500.00
70 V:Prankster 500.00
71 V:Lex Luthor 475.00

72 V:Prankster 475.00
72a giveaway 750.00
73 Flashback story 475.00
74 V:Lex Luthor 475.00
75 V:Prankster 475.00
76 A:Batman (Superman & Batman revel each other's identities). 1,400.00
77 A:Pocahontas 450.00
78 V:Kryptonian snagriff, A:Lana Lang. 450.00
79 V:Lex Luthor,A:Inspector Erskine Hawkins. 450.00
80 A:Halk Kar. 450.00
81 V:Lex Luthor 450.00
82 V:Mr. Mxyzptlk 425.00
83 V:`The Brain' 425.00
84 Time-travel story 425.00
85 V:Lex Luthor 425.00
86 V:Mr.Mxyzptlk 425.00
87 WB,V:The Thing from 40,000 AD' 425.00
88 WB,V:Lex Luthor,Toyman, Prankster team. 450.00
89 V:Lex Luthor 425.00
90 V:Lex Luthor 450.00
91 `The Superman Stamp' 425.00
92 Goes back to 12th Century England 425.00
93 V:`The Thinker' 425.00
94 `Clark Kent's Hillbilly Bride' . . 425.00
95 A:Susie Thompkins 425.00
96 V:Mr. Mxyzptlk 350.00
97 `Superboy's Last Day In Smallville'. 350.00
98 `Clark Kent, Outlaw!' 350.00
99 V:Midnite gang. 350.00
100 F:Superman-Substitute Schoolteacher 1,700.00
101 A:Lex Luthor 300.00
102 I:Superman Stock Company 300.00
103 A:Mr.Mxyzptlk 300.00
104 F:Clark Kent,Jailbird. 300.00
105 A:Mr.Mxyzptlk 300.00
106 A:Lex Luthor 325.00
107 F:Superman In 30th century (pre-Legion) 300.00
108 I:Perry White Jr. 300.00
109 I:Abner Hokum. 300.00
110 A:Lex Luthor 300.00
111 Becomes Mysto the Great . . 250.00
112 A:Lex Luthor 250.00
113 A:Jor-El 250.00
114 V:The Great Mento. 250.00
115 V:The Organizer. 250.00
116 Return to Smallville 250.00
117 A:Lex Luthor 250.00
118 F:Jimmy Olsen. 250.00
119 A:Zoll Orr 250.00
120 V:Gadget Grim. 250.00
121 I:XL-49 (Futureman). 225.00
122 In the White House 225.00
123 CS,pre-Supergirl tryout A:Jor-El & Lara. 250.00
124 F:Lois Lane 225.00
125 F:Superman College Story . . 225.00
126 F:Lois Lane 225.00
127 WB,I&O:Titano. 250.00
128 V:Vard & Boka 225.00
129 WB,I&O:Lori Lemaris 250.00
130 A:Krypto,the Superdog 225.00
131 A:Mr. Mxyzptlk 175.00
132 A:Batman & Robin 175.00
133 F:Superman Joins Army. . . . 175.00
134 A:Supergirl & Krypto 175.00
135 A:Lori Lemaris,Mr.Mxyzptlk . 175.00
136 O:Discovery Kryptonite. 175.00
137 CS,I:Super-Menace 175.00
138 A:Titano,Lori Lemaris 175.00
139 CS,O:Red Kryptonite 175.00
140 WB,I:Bizarro Jr,Bizarro Supergirl,Blue Kryptonite. . . . 200.00
141 I:Lyla Lerrol,A:Jor-EL & Lara 150.00
142 WB,CS,A:Al Capone 150.00
143 WB,F:Bizarro meets Frankenstein 150.00
144 O:Superboy's 1st Public Appearance 150.00
145 F:April Fool's Issue 150.00
146 F:Superman's life story 175.00
147 CS,I:Adult Legion. 175.00
148 CS,V:Mxyzptlk 150.00
149 CS:A:Luthor,C:JLA. 150.00
150 CS,KS,V:Mxyzptlk 75.00
151 CS. 75.00
152 A:Legion 75.00
153 CS. 75.00
154 CS,V:Mzyzptlk 75.00
155 WB,CS,V:Cosmic Man 75.00
156 CS,A:Legion,Batman 75.00
157 CS,I:Gold kryptonite. 90.00
158 CS,I:Nightwing&Flamebird . . . 75.00
159 CS,Imaginary Tale F:Lois Lane 75.00
160 CS,F:Perry White. 75.00
161 D:Ma & Pa Kent. 90.00
162 A:Legion 90.00
163 CS. 75.00
164 CS,Luthor,I:Lexor. 75.00
165 CS,A:Saturn Woman 75.00
166 CS. 75.00
167 CS,I:Ardora,Brainiac 100.00
168 CS. 75.00
169 Great DC Contest 75.00
170 CS,A:J.F.Kennedy,Luthor 75.00
171 CS,Mxyzptlk. 75.00
172 CS,Luthor,Brainiac 75.00
173 CS,A:Batman. 75.00
174 Mxyzptlk 75.00
175 CS,Luthor 75.00
176 CS,Green Kryptonite 75.00
177 Fortress of Solitude 75.00
178 CS, Red Kryptonite 75.00
179 CS,Clark Kent in Marines. . . . 75.00
180 CS. 75.00
181 Superman 2965. . . . . 75.00
182 CS,Toyman 75.00
183 giant 75.00
184 Secrets of the Fortress. 60.00
185 JM,Superman's Achilles Heel. 60.00
186 CS,The Two Ghosts of Superman 60.00
187 giant 60.00

Superman #227 © DC Comics, Inc.

188 V:Zunial,The Murder Man. . . . 65.00
189 WB,The Mystery of Krypton's Second Doom 60.00
190 WB,I:Amalak 60.00
191 The Prisoner of Demon 60.00
192 CS,Imaginary Story, I:Superman Jr. 60.00
193 giant 60.00
194 CS,Imaginary,A:Supes Jr. . . . 60.00
195 CS,V:Amalak 60.00
196 WB,reprint 60.00
197 giant 60.00
198 CS,F:The Real Clark Kent . . . 60.00
199 CS,F:Superman/Flash race, A:JLA 250.00
200 WB,A:Brainiac 60.00
201 CS,F:Clark Kent Abandons Superman 45.00
202 A:Bizarro,(giant size) 50.00
203 F:When Superman Killed His Friends 40.00
204 NA(c),RA,A:Lori Lemaris 40.00
205 NA(c),I:Black Zero 40.00
206 NA(c),F:The Day Superman Became An Assistant 40.00
207 CS,F:The Case Of the Collared Crimefighter 45.00
208 NA(c),CS 40.00
209 CS,F:The Clark Kent Monster 40.00
210 CS,F:Clark Kent's Last Rites . 40.00
211 CS,RA 40.00
212 giant 50.00
213 CS,JA,V:Luthor,C:Brainiac 5. . 40.00
214 NA(c),CS,JA,F:The Ghosts That Haunted Superman 35.00
215 NA(c),CS,JA,V:Luthor, Imaginary Story 35.00
216 JKu(c),RA,Superman in Nam . 35.00
217 CS,A:Mr.Mxyzptlk. 40.00
218 CS,JA,A:Mr.Mxyzptlk 35.00
219 CS,F:Clark Kent-Hero, Superman Public Enemy 35.00
220 CS,A:Flash 35.00
221 CS,F:The Two Ton Superman 35.00
222 giant 50.00
223 CS,A:Supergirl. 35.00
224 CS,Imaginary Story 35.00
225 CS,F:The Secret of the Super Imposter. 35.00
226 CS,F:When Superman Became King Kong 35.00
227 Krypton,(giant) 40.00
228 CS,DA 35.00
229 WB,CS 35.00
230 CS,DA,Luthor 35.00
231 CS,DA,Luthor 35.00
232 F:Krypton,(giant) 40.00
233 CS,MA,I:Quarrum 35.00
234 NA(c),CS,MA. 35.00
235 CS,MA. 35.00
236 CS,MA,DG,A:Green Arrow. . . 35.00
237 NA(c),CS,MA. 35.00
238 CS,MA,GM 35.00
239 giant 45.00
240 CS,DG,MK,A:I-Ching 15.00
241 CS,MA,A:Wonder Woman . . . 20.00
242 CS,MA,A:Wonder Woman . . . 20.00
243 CS,MA. 20.00
244 CS,MA. 20.00
245 100 pg reprints. 25.00
246 CS,MA,RB,I:S.T.A.R. Labs . . . 20.00
247 CS,MA,Guardians o/Universe. 20.00
248 CS,MA,A:Luthor,I:Galactic Golem 20.00
249 CS,MA,DD,NA,I:Terra-Man. . . 25.00
250 CS,MA,Terraman 20.00
251 CS,MA,RB 20.00
252 NA(c),rep.100pgs. 30.00
253 CS,MA. 20.00
254 CS,MA,NA 25.00
255 CS,MA,DG. 10.00

Superman #237 © DC Comics, Inc.

256 CS,MA. 10.00
257 CS,MA,DD,DG,A:Tomar-Re . . 10.00
258 CS,MA,DC. 10.00
259 CS,MA,A:Terra-Man. 10.00
260 CS,DC,I:Valdemar 10.00
261 CS,MA,V:Star Sapphire 10.00
262 CS,MA. 10.00
263 CS,MA,DD,FMc 10.00
264 DC,CS,I:SteveLombard 10.00
265 CS,MA. 10.00
266 CS,MA,DD,V:Snowman 10.00
267 CS,MA,BO 10.00
268 CS,BO,DD,MA,A:Batgirl 10.00
269 CS,MA. 10.00
270 CS,MA,V:Valdemar 10.00
271 CS,BO,DG,V:Brainiac 10.00
272 100pg.reprints 30.00
273 CS,DG. 10.00
274 CS. 10.00
275 CS,DG,FMc. 10.00
276 CS,BO,I&O:Captain Thunder . 10.00
277 CS. 10.00
278 CS,BO,Terraman,100page . . . 30.00
279 CS,Batgirl,Batman 10.00
280 CS,BO. 10.00
281 CS,BO,I:Vartox 10.00
282 CS,KS,N:Luthor 10.00
283 CS,BO,Mxyzptlk. 10.00
284 CS,BO,100p reprint 30.00
285 CS,BO. 10.00
286 CS,BO. 10.00
287 CS,BO,R:Krypto. 10.00
288 CS,BO. 10.00
289 CS,BO,JL 10.00
290 CS,V:Mxyzptlk 10.00
291 CS,BO. 10.00
292 CS,BO,AM,O:Luthor. 10.00
293 CS,BO. 10.00
294 CS,JL,A:Brain Storm 10.00
295 CS,BO. 10.00
296 CS,BO,Identity Crisis #1 . . . . 10.00
297 CS,BO,Identity Crisis #2 . . . . 10.00
298 CS,BO,Identity Crisis #3 . . . . 10.00
299 CS,BO,Identity Crisis #4
A:Luthor,Brainiac,Bizarro 10.00
300 CS,BO,2001,anniversary 25.00
301 BO,JL,V:Solomon Grundy 5.00
302 JL,BO,V:Luthor,A:Atom 5.00
303 CS,BO,I:Thunder&Lightning . . . 5.00
304 CS,BO,V:Parasite 5.00
305 CS,BO,V:Toyman. 5.00
306 CS,BO,V:Bizarro 5.00
307 NA(c),JL,FS,A:Supergirl. 5.00
308 NA(c),JL,FS,A:Supergirl. 5.00
309 JL,FS,A:Supergirl. 5.00
310 CS,V:Metallo 5.00
311 CS,FS,A:Flash 5.00
312 CS,FS,A:Supergirl 5.00
313 NA(c),CS,DA,A:Supergirl 5.00
314 NA(c),CS,DA,A:Gr.Lantern. . . . 5.00
315 CS,DA,V:Blackrock 5.00
316 CS,DA,V:Metallo 5.00
317 NA(c),CS,DA,V:Metallo 5.00
318 CS. 5.00
319 CS,V:Solomon Grundy. 5.00
320 CS,V:Solomon Grundy. 5.00
321 CS,V:Parasite 5.00
322 CS,V:Solomon Grundy. 5.00
323 CS,DA,I:Atomic Skull 5.00
324 CS,A:Atomic Skull 5.00
325 CS. 5.00
326 CS,V:Blackrock 5.00
327 CS,KS,V:Kobra,C:JLA 5.00
328 CS,KS,V:Kobra 5.00
329 KS,CS. 5.00
330 CS,F:glasses explained 5.00
331 CS,I:Master Jailer 5.00
332 CS,V:Master Jailer. 5.00
333 CS,V:Bizarro 5.00
334 CS. 5.00
335 CS,W:Mxyzptlk 5.00
336 CS,V:Rose And Thorn 5.00
337 CS,A:Brainiac,Bizarro 5.00
338 CS,F:Kandor enlarged 5.00
339 CS,I:N.R.G.X. 5.00
340 CS,V:N.R.G.X 5.00
341 CS,F:Major Disaster. 5.00
342 CS,V:Chemo 5.00
343 CS. 5.00
344 CS,A:Phantom Stranger. 5.00
345 CS,`When time ran backward' . 5.00
346 CS,`Streak of Bad Luck'. 5.00
347 JL 5.00
348 CS. 5.00
349 CS,V:Mxyzptlk 5.00
350 CS,`Clark Kent's Vanishing
Classmate' 4.00
351 CS,JL,A:Mxyzptlk. 4.00
352 CS,RB 4.00
353 CS,origin 4.00
354 CS,JSon,I:Superman 2020. . . . 4.00
355 CS,JSon,F:Superman 2020 . . . 4.00
356 CS,V:Vartox. 4.00
357 CS,DCw,F:Superman 2020 . . . 4.00
358 CS,DG,DCw 4.00
359 CS. 4.00
360 CS,AS,F:World of Krypton 4.00
361 CS,AS 4.00
362 CS,KS,DA 4.00
363 CS,RB,C:Luthor. 4.00
364 GP(c),RB,AS 4.00
365 CS,KS 4.00
366 CS,KS 4.00
367 CS,GK,F:World of Krypton 4.00
368 CS,AS 4.00
369 RB,FMc,V:Parasite 4.00
370 CS,KS,FMc,A:Chemo 4.00
371 CS. 4.00
372 CS,GK,F:Superman 2021 . . . . 4.00
373 CS,V:Vartox. 4.00
374 GK(c),CS,DA,KS,V:Vartox 4.00
375 CS,DA,GK,V:Vartox 4.00
376 CS,DA,CI,BO,SupergirlPrev. . . 3.00
377 GK(c),CS,V:Terra-Man 3.00
378 CS. 3.00
379 CS,V:Bizarro 3.00
380 CS. 3.00
381 GK(c),CS. 3.00
382 GK(c),CS. 3.00
383 CS. 3.00
384 GK(c),CS. 3.00
385 GK(c),CS,V:Luthor 3.00
386 GK(c),CS,V:Luthor 3.00
387 GK(c),CS. 3.00
388 GK(c),CS. 3.00
389 GK(c),CS. 3.00
390 GK(c),CS,V:Vartox 3.00

Superman #299 © DC Comics, Inc.

391 GK(c),CS,V:Vartox. 3.00
392 GK(c),CS,V:Vartox. 3.00
393 IN,DG,V:Master Jailer 3.00
394 CS,V:Valdemar 3.00
395 CS,V:Valdemar 3.00
396 CS. 3.00
397 EB,V:Kryptonite Man 3.00
398 CS,AS,DJ 3.00
399 CS,BO,EB 3.00
400 HC(c),FM,AW,JO,JSo,MR,
TA,WP,MK,KJ,giant 8.00
401 CS,BO,V:Luthor. 3.00
402 CS,BO,WB 3.00
403 CS,BO,AS 3.00
404 CI,BO,V:Luthor 3.00
405 KS,KK,AS,F:Super-Batman . . . 3.00
406 IN,AS,KK. 3.00
407 IN,V:Mxyzptlk. 3.00
408 CS,AW,JRu,F:Nuclear
Holocaust. 3.00
409 CS,AW,KS 3.00
410 CS,AW,V:Luthor. 3.00
411 CS,MA,F:End Earth-Prime 3.00
412 CS,AW,V:Luthor. 3.00
413 CS,AW,V:Luthor. 3.00
414 CS,AW,Crisis tie-in. 3.50
415 CS,AW,Crisis,W:Super Girl . . . 3.50
416 CS,AW,Luthor 3.00
417 CS,V:Martians 3.00
418 CS,V:Metallo 3.00
419 CS,V:Iago 3.00
420 CS,F:Nightmares 3.00
421 CS,V:Mxyzptlk 3.00
422 BB(c),CS,TY,LMa,V:Werewolf . 3.00
423 AMo(s),CS,GP,F:Last
Superman 9.00
Ann.#1 I:Supergirl Rep. 1,000.00
Ann.#2 I&O:Titano 450.00
Ann.#3 I:Legion 300.00
Ann.#4 O:Legion. 250.00
Ann.#5 A:Krypton 200.00
Ann.#6 A:Legion. 200.00
Ann.#7 O:Superman,Silver Anniv. . . . . .
. . . . .150.00
Ann.#8 F:Secret origins 125.00
Ann.#9 GK(c),ATh,TA,CS,
A:Batman 6.00
Ann.#10 CS,MA,F:Sword of
Superman 5.00
Ann.#11 AMo(s),DGb,A:Batman,
Robin,Wonder Woman 6.00
Ann.#12 BB(c),AS,A:Lex Luthor,
Last War Suit 3.00
Game Give-away 10.00
Giveaway CS,AT 2.00
Pizza Hut 1977. . . . . 6.00

Radio Shack 1980 JSw,DG. 5.00
Radio Shack 1981 CS 5.00
Radio Shack 1982 CS 5.00
Spec.#1 GK 3.50
Spec.#2 GK,V:Brainiac 3.50
Spec.#3 IN,V:Amazo 3.50
Superman III Movie,CS. 2.00
Superman IV Movie,DH,DG,FMc . . 2.00
Becomes:

ADVENTURES OF SUPERMAN

1987

424 JOy,I:Man O'War 2.50
425 JOy,Man O'War 2.25
426 JOy,Legends,V:Apokolips. 2.25
427 JOy,V:Qurac 2.25
428 JOy,V:Qurac,I:JerryWhite 2.25
429 JOy,V:Concussion 2.25
430 JOy,V:Fearsome Five. 2.25
431 JOy,A:Combattor 2.00
432 JOy,I:Jose Delgado 2.00
433 JOy,V:Lex Luthor 2.00
434 JOy,I:Gang Buster 2.50
435 JOy,A:Charger. 2.00
436 JOy,Millenium x-over 2.00
437 JOy,Millenium X-over. 2.00
438 JOy,N:Brainiac. 2.50
439 JOy,R:Superman Robot 2.00
440 JOy,A:Batman,Wond.Woman . . 2.00
441 JOy,V:Mr.Mxyzptlk 2.00
442 JOy,V:Dreadnaught,A:JLI 2.00
443 JOy,DHz,I:Husque 2.00
444 JOy,Supergirl SagaPt.2 . . . . . . 2.00
445 JOy,V:Brainiac. 2.00
446 JOy,A:Gangbuster,
A:Luthor's Old Costume 2.00
447 JOy,A:Gangbuster 2.00
448 JOy,I:Dubbilex,A:Gangbuster . . 2.00
449 JOy,Invasion X-over. 2.00
450 JOy,Invasion X-over. 2.00
451 JOy,`Superman in Space' 2.00
452 DJu,V:Wordbringer. 2.00
453 JOy,DJu,A:Gangbuster 2.00
454 JOy,DJu,I:New Mongul. 2.50
455 DJu,ATb,A:Eradicator. 3.50
456 DJu,ATb,V:Turmoil 2.00
457 DJu,V:Intergang. 2.00
458 DJu,KJ,R:Elastic Lad
(Jimmy Olsen) 2.00
459 DJu,V:Eradicator 3.00
460 DJu,NKu,V:Eradicator 3.00
461 DJu,GP,V:Eradicator 3.00
462 DJu,ATb,Homeless
Christmas Story 2.00
463 DJu,ATb,Superman Races
Flash 3.00
464 DJu,ATb,Day of Krypton
Man #2,A:Lobo. 3.50
465 DJu,ATb,Day of Krypton
Man #5,V:Draaga 3.00
466 DJu,DG,V:Team Excalibur
Astronauts,I:Hank Henshaw
(becomes Cyborg Superman). . 4.50
467 DJu,ATb,A:Batman 2.50
468 DJu,ATb,Man Of Steel's
Journal,V:Hank Henshaw 3.00
469 DJu,ATb,V:Dreadnaught. 2.00
470 DJu,ATb,Soul Search #3,
D:Jerry White 2.00
471 CS,Sinbad Contract #2 . . . . . . 2.00
472 DJu,ATb,Krisis of Krimson
Kryptonite #2 . . . . 3.00
473 DJu,ATb,A:Green Lantern,
Guy Gardner 2.00
474 DJu,ATb,Drunk Driving issue . . 2.00
475 DJu,ATb,V:Kilgrave,Sleez 2.00
476 DJu,BBr,Time & Time Again,pt.1,
A:Booster Gold,Legion 2.00
477 DJu,BBr,T & T Again,pt.4,
A:Legion. 2.00
478 DJu,BBr,T & T Again,pt.7,
A:Legion,Linear Man 2.00
479 EH,Red Glass Trilogy#2. . . . . . 2.00
480 JOy,DJu,BMc,TG,BBr,CS,
Revenge of the Krypton
Man,pt.3. . . . . 3.00
481 1st TG Supes,DHz,V:Parasite . 2.00
482 TG,DHz,V:Parasite 2.00
483 TG,DHz,V:Blindspot. 2.00
484 TG,Blackout #1,V:Mr.Z. 2.00
485 TG,DHz,Blackout #5,A:Mr.Z . . . 2.00
486 TG,V:Purge 2.00
487 TG,DHz,X-mas,A:Agent
Liberty 2.00
488 TG,Panic in the Sky,pt.3,
V:Brainiac. 3.00
489 TG,Panic in the Sky,Epiloge. . . 2.50
490 TG,A:Agent Liberty,Husque . . . 2.00
491 TG,DHz,V:Cerberus,Metallo. . . 2.00
492 WS(c),V:Sons of Liberty,
A:Agent Liberty. 2.00
493 TG,Blaze/Satanus War,pt.1 . . . 2.00
494 TG,DHz,I:Kismet 2.00
495 TG,DHz,A:Forever People,
Darkseid. 2.00
496 V:Mr.Mxyzptlk,C:Doomsday . . . 2.00
496a 2nd printing 2.00
497 TG,Doomsday Pt.3,A:Maxima,
Bloodwynd 5.00
497a 2nd printing 2.00
498 TG,Funeral for a Friend#1 . . . . 4.00
498a 2nd Printing 2.00
499 TG,DHz,Funeral for a
Friend#5. . . . . 3.50
500 JOy(c),B:KK(s),TG,DJu,JBg,JG,
BBr,Bagged,Superman in limbo,
I:Four Supermen,Direct Sales. . 3.50
500a Newsstand Ed. 3.00
500b Platinum Ed. 15.00
501 TG,Reign of Supermen#2,Direct
Sales,Die-Cut(c),Mini-poster
F:Superboy 3.00
501a Newstand Ed. 2.00
502 TG,A:Supergirl,V:Stinger 2.00
503 TG,Cyborg Superman Vs.
Superboy 2.50
504 TG,DHz,A:All Supermen,
V:Mongul 2.50
505 TG,DHz,Superman returns to
Metropolis,Holografx(c). 2.50
505a Newstand Ed. 2.00
506 TG,DHz,A:Guardian. 2.00
507 Spilled Blood#1,V:Bloodsport . . 2.00

Adventures of Superman #502
© DC Comics, Inc.

508 BKi,A:Challengers of the
Unknown 2.00
509 BKi,A:Auron. 2.00
510 BKi,Bizarro's World#2,
V:Bizarro 2.00
511 BKi,A:Guardian 2.00
512 BKi,V:Parasite 2.00
513 BKi,Battle for Metropolis #4 . . . 2.00
514 BKi,Fall of Metropolis #4 . . . . . 2.00
515 BKi,Massacre in Metropolis . . . 2.00
516 BKi,Zero Hour,I:Alpha
Centurion 2.00
517 BKi,deathtrap. 2.00
518 BKi 2.00
519 KK,BKi,Secret of Superman's
Tomb 2.00
520 SI,KK,JMz,100 crimes at
midnight. 2.00
521 SI,KK,R:Thorn 2.00
522 SI,KKIdentity known. 2.00
523 SI,KK,Death of C.Kent,pt.2. . . . 2.00
524 SI,KK,Death of C.Kent,pt.6
[New Miraweb format begins] . . 2.00
525 SI,KK. 2.00
526 Bloodsport vs. Bloodsport 2.00
527 . . . . 2.00
528 Trial of Superman,prelude 2.00
529 Trial of Superman 2.00
530 KK,SI,JMz,Trial of Superman . . 2.00
531 KK,SI,JMz,Trial of Superman,
concl. 2.00
532 KK,SI,JMz, return of Lori
Lemaris 2.00
533 KK,SI,JMz 2.00
534 KK,SI,JMz,V:Lord Satannus. . . 2.00
535 KK,SI,JMz,Lois & LoriLemaris . 2.00
536. . . . . 2.00
537. . . . . 2.00
538. . . . . 2.00
539 F:Guardian and the Newsboy
Legion 2.00
540 KK(s),TyD,KIS,A:Ferro, Final
Night tie-in 2.00
541 KK(s),SI,JMz,on Honeymoon,
A:Superboy,Tana Moon, Kekona . . .
. . . . .2.00
542 KK&JOy(s),PR,JMz,V:Misa . . . 2.00
543 . . . . 2.00
544 KK(s),SI,JMz,"Who Killed Clark
Kent in braod daylight?. 2.00
545 KK(s),SEa,JMz,Return of the
Atomic Skull,new blue costume 2.00
546 KK(s),SI,JMz,V:Metallo, uses
new powers 2.00
547 KK(s),SI,JMz,Superman goes
to Kandor,A:The Atom 2.00
548 KK(s),SI,JMz,V:Lex Luthor. . . . 2.00
549 KK(s),SI,JMz,F:Jimmy Olsen . . 2.00
550 KK(s),SI,TGu,JMz,DRo, 48pg . 3.50
551 DJu,TGu,DRo,Genesis,
V:Cyborg 2.00
552 KK,TGu,DRo,V:Parasite. 2.00
553 KK,TGu,DRo,disappearances . 2.00
554 KK,TGu,DRo,disappearances . 2.00
555 KK,TRu,DRo,Red/Blue x-over . 2.00
556 KK,TRu,DRo,Red & Blue. 2.00
557 KK,VS,DRo,Millennium Giants
x-over. 2.00
558 KK,JOy,DRo,silver age?,pt.1 . . 2.00
559 KK,JOy,DRo,silver age?,pt.2 . . 2.00
560 KK,JOy,DRo,silver age?,pt.3 . . 2.00
561 KK,JOy,TGu,DRo,Waverider . . 2.00
562 KK(s),JOy,TGu,DRo,Lexcom . . 2.00
563 RMz,TGb,TP,City of the
Future, pt.4 x-over 2.00
564 KK&JOy(s),TGu,DRo,
A:Geo-Force 2.00
565 KK&JOy(s),TGu,DRo,A:JLA . . . 2.00
566 KK&JOy(s),TGu,DRo,V:Lex
Luthor 2.00
567 KK&JOy(s),DRo,PR, ... 2.00
568 LSi(s),TMo,DRo,V:Metallo 2.00

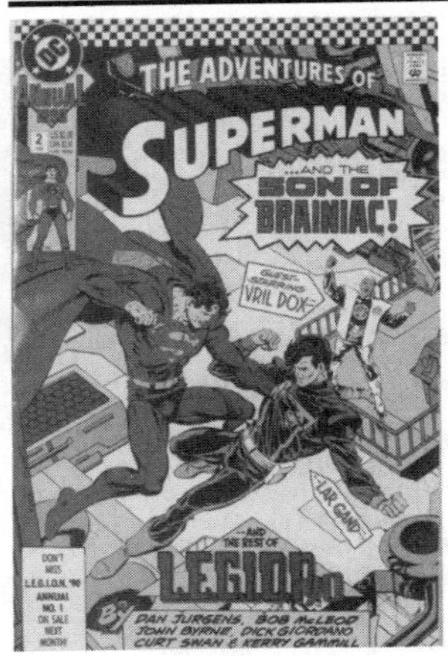

Adventures of Superman Annual #2
© DC Comics, Inc.

569 LSi(s),TMo,DRo,V:S.C.U. 2.00
570 RMz&TPe(s),TGb,TP,
A:JLA,pt.2 x-over 2.00
571 LSi(s),DRo,V:Atomic Skull 2.00
572 RF,SB,Strange Visitor,pt.2 . . . . 2.00
573 SI,SEp,DRo,flashbacks 2.00
574 SI 2.00
575 SI,F:Lex Luthor 2.00
576 SI,V:Brainiac 13. . . . . 2.00
577 SI,JMz,A:Luthor 2.00
578 JMD(s),JMz,alien utopia. 2.00
579 JMD(s),Lois has vanished 2.00
580 JMD(s),CriticalCondition,pt.2 . . 2.00
581 JMD(s),V:Adversary,Lex Luthor
. . . . 2.25
582 JMD(s),Arkham,pt.2. . . . . 2.25
583 JMD,JMz,Superman:Emperor . 2.25
584 JMD(s),JMz,V:Devouris 2.25
585 JMD,JMz,V:LexLuthor,Satanus. 2.25
Ann.#1 JSn(c),DJu,I:Word Bringer . 3.00
Ann.#2 CS/JBy,KGa/DG,BMc,
A:L.E.G.I.O.N.'90 (Lobo). 4.00
Ann.#3 BHi,JRu,DG,
Armageddon 2001. . . . . 3.00
Ann.#4 BMc,A:Lobo,Guy Gardner,
Eclipso tie-in. 3.00
Ann.#5 TG,I:Sparx 2.75
Ann.#6 MMi(c),Elseworlds Story . . . 3.00
Ann.#7 Year One Story. 4.00
Ann.#8 Legends o/t Dead Earth . . . 2.95
Ann.#9 Pulp Heroes (Western) 3.95
Spec.#1,000,000 ALa&DAn(s)LMa,
A:Teen Titans, V:Solaris 2.00

SUPERMAN'S BUDDY
1954

1 w/costume 1,200.00
1 w/out costume 400.00

SUPERMAN'S CHRISTMAS ADVENTURE

1 (1940) 4,200.00
2 (1944). 950.00

SUPERMAN AND THE GREAT CLEVELAND FIRE
1948

1 for Hospital Fund 550.00

SUPERMAN (miniature)
1942

1 Py-Co-Pay Tooth Powder
Give- Away. 700.00
2 CS,Superman Time Capsule. . 500.00
3 CS,Duel in Space 450.00
4 CS,Super Show in Metropolis . 450.00

SUPERMAN RECORD COMIC
1966

1 w/record 150.00
1 w/out record 75.00

SUPERMAN SPECTACULAR
1982

1 A:Luthor & Terra-Man 2.50

SUPERMAN-TIM STORE PAMPHLETS
1942

Superman-Tim store Monthly
Membership Pamphlet, 16
pages of stories, games,
puzzles (1942), each 800.00
Superman-Tim store Monthly
Membership Pamphlet, 16
pages of stories, games,
puzzles (1943), each 400.00
Superman-Tim store Monthly
Membership Pamphlet, 16
pages of stories, games,
puzzles (1944), each 300.00
Superman-Tim store Monthly
Membership Pamphlet, 16
pages of stories, games,
puzzles (1945), each 250.00
Superman-Tim store Monthly
Membership Pamphlet, 14-16
pages of stories, games,
puzzles, 5"x8" color(c),
(1946), each. 400.00
Superman-Tim stamp
album, 1946 . . . . 300.00
Superman-Tim store Monthly
Membership Pamphlet, 14-16
pages of stories, games,
puzzles, 5"x8" color(c),
(1947), each. 250.00
Superman-Tim stamp album,
Superman story, 1947. . . . . . 325.00
Superman-Tim store Monthly
Membership Pamphlet, 14-16
pages of stories, games,
puzzles, 5"x8" color(c),(1948),
each 200.00
Superman-Tim stamp
album, 1948 . . . . 225.00
Superman-Tim store Monthly
Membership Pamphlet, 14-16
pages of stories, games,
puzzles, 5"x8" color(c),
(1949), each. 200.00
Superman-Tim store Monthly
Membership Pamphlet, 14-16
pages of stories, games,
puzzles, 5"x8" color(c)
(1950), each. 250.00

SUPERMAN WORKBOOK
1945

1 rep. Superman #14 . . . . 1,100.00

Superman 2nd Series #1
© DC Comics, Inc.

SUPERMAN
[2nd Regular Series] 1987

1 JBy,TA,I:Metallo 5.00
2 JBy,TA,V:Luthor 3.00
3 JBy,TA,Legends tie-in 2.50
4 JBy,KK,V:Bloodsport. 2.25
5 JBy,KK,V:Host 2.00
6 JBy,KK,V:Host 2.00
7 JBy,KK,V:Rampage 2.00
8 JBy,KK,A:Superboy,Legion 2.00
9 JBy,KK,V:Joker. 4.00
10 JBy,KK,V:Rampage 2.00
11 JBy,KK,V:Mr.Mxyzptlk 2.00
12 JBy,KK,A:Lori Lemerias 2.00
13 JBy,KK,Millenium. 2.00
14 JBy,KK,A:Green Lantern 2.00
15 JBy,KK,I:New Prankster. 2.00
16 JBy,KK,A:Prankster 2.00
17 JBy,KK,O:Silver Banshee. 2.00
18 MMi,KK,A:Hawkman 2.00
19 JBy,V:Skyhook. 2.00
20 JBy,KK,A:Doom Patrol 2.50
21 JBy,A:Supergirl 2.00
22 JBy,A:Supergirl 2.00
23 MMi,CR,O:Silver Banshee 2.00
24 KGa,V:Rampage 2.00
25 KGa,V:Brainiac 2.00
26 KGa,BBr,V:Baron Sunday 2.00
27 KGa,BBr,V:Guardian 2.00
28 KGa,BBr,Supes Leaves Earth . . 2.00
29 DJu,BBr,V:Word Bringer. 2.00
30 KGa,DJu,A:Lex Luthor. 2.00
31 DJu,PCu,V:Mxyzptlk 2.00
32 KGa,V:Mongul 2.00
33 KGa,A:Cleric 2.00
34 KGa,V:Skyhook 2.00
35 CS,KGa,A:Brainiac 2.00
36 JOy,V:Prankster. 2.00
37 JOy,A:Guardian 2.00
38 JOy,Jimmy Olsen Vanished 2.00
39 JOy,KGa,V:Husque 2.00
40 JOy,V:Four Armed Terror 2.00
41 JOy,Day of Krypton Man #1,
A:Lobo 3.50
42 JOy,Day of Krypton Man #4,
V:Draaga 3.50
43 JOy,V:Krypton Man 2.00
44 JOy,A:Batman 2.00
45 JOy,F:Jimmy Olsen's Dairy 2.00
46 DJu,JOy,A:Jade,Obsidian,
I:New Terra-Man. 2.00
47 JOy,Soul Search #2,V:Blaze . . . 2.00
48 CS,Sinbad Contract #1 . . . . 2.00

49 JOy,Krisis of K.Kryptonite#1. . . . 3.00
50 JBy,KGa,DJu,JOy,BBr,CS,Krisis of Krimson Kryptonite #4, Clark Proposes To Lois. 6.00
50a 2nd printing 2.00
51 JOy,I:Mr.Z 2.00
52 KGa,V:Terra-Man. 2.00
53 JOy,Superman reveals i.d.. . . . . 3.50
53a 2nd Printing 2.00
54 JOy,KK,Time & Time Again#3 . . 2.00
55 JOy,KK,Time & Time Again#6 . . 2.00
56 EH,KK,Red Glass Trilogy#1 . . . . 2.00
57 JOy,DJu,BBr,ATi,JBg,BMc,TG, Revenge o/t Krypton Man #2 . . 3.50
58 DJu,BBr,I:Bloodhounds 2.00
59 DJu,BBr,A:Linear Men 2.00
60 DJu,EB,I:Agent Liberty, V:Intergang 2.00
61 DJu,BBr,A:Waverider, V:Linear Men 2.00
62 DJu,BBr,Blackout #4,A:Mr.Z. . . . 2.00
63 DJu,A:Aquaman 2.00
64 JG,Christmas issue 2.00
65 DJu,Panic in the Sky#2, I:New Justice League 3.50
66 DJu,Panic in the Sky#6, V:Brainiac. 8.00
67 DJu,Aftermath 2.00
68 DJu,V:Deathstroke. 2.00
69 WS(c),DJu,A:Agent Liberty 2.00
70 DJu,BBr,A:Robin,V:Vampires . . . 2.00
71 DJu,Blaze/Satanus War. 2.00
72 DJu,Crisis at Hand#2. . . . . 2.00
73 DJu,A:Waverider,V:Linear Men,C:Doomsday. 4.00
73a 2nd printing 2.00
74 DJu,V:Doomsday,A:JLA 7.00
74a 2nd printing 2.00
75 DJu,V:Doomsday,D:Superman, Collectors Ed.. . . . . 15.00
75a newstand Ed.. . . . . 9.00
75b 2nd printing 4.00
75c 3rd printing 2.00
75d 4th Printing 2.00
75e Platinum Ed. 60.00
76 DJu,BBr,Funeral for Friend#4. . . 3.00
77 DJu,BBr,Funeral for Friend#8. . . 3.00
78 DJu,BBr,Reign of Supermen#3, Die-Cut(c),Mini poster,F:Cyborg Supes,A:Doomsday 2.50
78a Newsstand Ed. 2.00
79 DJu,BBr,Memorial Service for Clark 2.00
80 DJu,BBr,Coast City Blows up, V:Mongul 4.00
81 DJu,O:Cyborg Superman. 3.50
82 DJu,Chromium(c),A:All Supermen, V:Cyborg Superman 5.00
82a Newstand Ed. 2.25
83 DJu,A:Batman 2.00
84 DJu,V:Toyman 2.00
85 DJu,V:Toyman 2.00
86 DJu,A:Sun Devils. 2.00
87 DJu(c&s),SI,JRu,Bizzaro's World#1, R:Bizarro. 2.00
88 DJu(c&s),SI,JRu,Bizzaro's World#5, D:Bizarro. 2.00
89 DJu(c&s),V:Cadmus Project. . . . 2.00
90 DJu(c&s),Battle for Metropolis#3 . . . . 2.00
91 DJu(c&s),Fall of Metropolis#3 . . 2.00
92 Massacre in Metropolis 2.00
93 Zero Hour,A:Batman 2.00
94 Conduit 2.00
95 Brainiac. 2.00
96 Virtual Reality 2.00
97 Shadow Dragon. 2.00
98 R:Shadow Strike 2.00
99 R:Agent Liberty 2.00
100 BBr,DJu,Death of C.Kent,pt.1. . 2.95
100a Collectors Edition. 3.95

101 Death of Clark Kent,pt.5 [New Miraweb format begins] . . 2.00
102 DJu,A:Captain Marvel 2.00
103 O:Arclight 2.00
104 . . . . 2.00
105 A:Green Lantern 2.00
106 DJu,RF,The Trial of Superman . 2.00
107 DJu,RF,The Trial of Superman . 2.00
108 DJu,RF,The Trial of Superman . 2.00
109 DJu,RF,V:Kill Fee. 2.00
110 . . . . 2.00
111 DJu,RF,Cat Grant in charge . . . 2.00
112 DJu,RF,Lois & Clark. 2.00
113 DJu(s),RF,JRu, ... 2.00
114 DJu(s),RF,JRu,A:Brainiac. 2.00
115 DJu(s),RF,JRu,Lois leaves Metropolis 2.00
116 DJu(s),RF,JRu,battle city siga concl., V:Daxamite,B.U. Teen Titans preview 2.00
117 DJu(s),RF,JRu,V: his own robots, Final Night tie-in 2.00
118 DJu(s),RF,JRu,F:time-lost Legion of Super Heroes 2.00
119 DJu(s),RF,JRu,A:Legion of Super Heroes. 2.00
120 DJu(s),RF,JRu, ... 2.00
121 DJu(s),RF,JRu,"They Call it Suicide Slum". 2.00
122 DJu(s),RF,JRu,Lois visits Fortress of Solitude 2.00
123 DJu(s),RF,Jru,Superman gets New Costume 2.00
123a collector's edition, glow-in-the-dark cover, ... 2.00
124 DJu(s),RF,JRu,A:Scorn, prince of Kandor 2.00
125 DJu(s),RF,JRu,Kandor and Metropolis,A:Atom 2.00
126 DJu(s),RF,JRu,A:Batman 2.00
127 DJu(s),RF,JRu,F:Jimmy Olsen . 2.00
128 DJu(s),RF,JRu, Genesis tie-in . 2.00
129 DJu(s),PR,JRu,A:Scorn 2.00
130 DJu(s),RF,JRu,dragon's tooth . 2.00
131 DJu(s),RF,JRu,Luthor & Contessa's kid 2.00
132 DJu,RF,JRu,Red/Blue x-over . . 2.00
133 . . . . 2.00
134 DJu,RF,JRu,Millennium Giants. 2.00
135 DJu,RF,JRu,aftermath 2.00
136 DJu,PR,JRu,The Superman of 2999 A.D., pt.1 . . . . 2.00
137 DJu,PR,JRu,2999 AD,pt.2 . . . . 2.00

Superman 2nd Series #91
© DC Comics, Inc.

138 DJu,PR,JRu,2999 AD,pt.3 . . . . 2.00
139 DJu(s),JSn,JRu,V:Dominus . . . 2.00
140 RMz(s),TGb,TP,City of the Future, pt.3 x-over 2.00
141 DJu(s),SEa,JRu,I:Outburst. . . . 2.00
142 DJu(s),JRu,F:Outburst 2.00
143 DJu(s),SEp,JRu, ... 2.00
144 DJu(s),SEp,JRu,V:Lex Luthor. . 2.00
145 DJu(s),SEp,JRu,hate mail 2.00
146 DJu(s),SEp,JRu,V:Toyman. . . . 2.00
147 RMz(s),TGb,BAn,A:JLA,pt.1. . . 2.00
148 DJu(s),SEp,JRu, ... 2.00
149 RF,SB,Strange Visitor,pt.1 . . . . 2.00
150 DJu(s),SEp,JRu,48-pg. 2.95
150a foil cover 3.95
151 JLb,MMK,Faster than a speeding bullet. 2.00
152 JLb,MMK. 2.00
153 JLb,MMK,V:Imperiex 2.00
154 JLb,CaS,V:Brainiac 13. . . . . . . 2.00
155 JLb,CaS,F:Superboy 2.00
156 JLb,CaS,V:Parasite 2.00
157 JLb,CaS,Lois vs. Superman?. . 2.00
158 JLb,CaS,CriticalCondition,pt.1 . 2.00
159 JLb,CaS,F:Green Lantern 2.25
160 JLb,CaS,Arkham,pt.1 . . . . 2.25
161 JLb,CaS,Superman:Emperor? . 2.25
162 JLb,CaS,A:Aquaman,pt.1. . . . . 2.25
163 JLb,PaP,CaS,F:Aquaman,pt.2 . 2.25
Ann.#1 RF,BBr,A:Titano 2.00
Ann.#2 RF,BBr,R:Newsboy Legion & Guardian. 3.00
Ann.#3 DAb(1st Work),TA,DG, Armageddon 2001. . . . . 9.00
Ann.#3a 2nd printing(silver) 2.00
Ann.#4 Eclipso 2.75
Ann.#5 Bloodlines#6,DL,I:Myriad . . 2.75
Ann.#6 Elseworlds Story. 2.95
Ann.#7 WS(c),Year One Annual A:Dr. Occult 3.95
Ann.#8 Legends o/t Dead Earth . . . 2.95
Ann.#9 Pulp Heroes (High-Adventure) DJu 3.95
Ann.#10 DJu(s),PR,CIv,BWr, Ghosts 3.00
Ann.#11 JoP,AAd(c),JLApe:Gorilla Warfare 2.95
Ann.#12 Planet DC. 3.50
Spec.#1,000,000 DAn&ALa(s),NBy. 2.00
Giant Ann.#1 Replica edition. 5.00
Giant #1 80-page 5.00
Giant #2 80-page 5.00
Giant #3 80-page 5.95
Spec.#0 PeerPressure,pt.3 (1994) . 2.00
Spec.King of the World, foil. 5.00
Spec.King of the World, reg. 4.00
Spec. Superman: Lois Lane, Girlfrenzy (1998) 2.00
Spec.#1 WS,V:L.Luthor,`Sandman' . 6.00
Spec. Superman Plus One (1997) . 3.00
Spec.#1 Superman: The Earth Stealers, JBy,CS,JOy (1988) . . 3.50
2nd printing 3.00
Spec. Superman:Emperor?(2000). . 3.50
Spec. Superman Forever, KK,DJu,LSi, JBy,SI,DG, Luthor's kidnapped daughter (1998) 5.00
Deluxe ed.,AxR(c), lenticular . . 6.00
Spec.#1 Superman: The Legacy of Superman,WS,JG,F:Guardian, Waverider,Sinbad (1993) 4.00
Spec. Superman & Savage Dragon: Metropolis, KK,JBg,x-over 4.95
Spec. Superman/Toyman (1996). . . 2.00
Spec. Team Superman, MMr(s), DHz,48-page,F:Superboy, Supergirl & Steel 3.00
Spec. 3-D #1 LSi,V:Mainframe 4.00
Spec. Whatever Happened to the Man of Tomorrow 6.00
Spec. Superman Y2K,JBg (1999). . 4.95

Superman Special #1
© DC Comics, Inc.

Newstime-The Life and Death of the Man of Steel-Magazine, DJu,BBr,JOy,JG,JBg. 3.25
Spec.#1 Superman Gallery (1993) . 2.95
Superman Secret Files, DJu,JOy, etc.,inc. O:Superman (1997). . . 5.00
Secret Files #2 . . . . 5.00
Secret Files #1 Superman Villains . 5.00
Spec. Metropolis Secret Files #1. . . 4.95
Spec. Team Superman Secret Files 5.00
GN Death of Superman rep.(1993) . 6.00
Later printings 5.95
Platinum Edition 15.00
GN Superman At Earth's End (Elseworlds 1995). 4.95
GN Superman: Distant Fires, HC,GK, nuclear winter (1997) 6.00
GN Superman: Earth Day 1991, KGa Metropolis `Clean-Up'. 5.50
GN Superman For Earth (1991) . . . 4.95
GN Superman: Kal, Medieval Superman (Elseworlds 1995) . . 5.95
GN Superman: Last God of Krypton 5.00
GN Superman's Metropolis, RLo & RTs(s),TMK, in Fritz Lang's Metropolis (Elseworlds 1996) . . 5.95
GN The Superman Monster 7.00
GN A Nation Divided 5.00
GN Superman: The Odyssey 5.00
GN Peace on Earth, oversized . . . 10.00
GN Superman Red/Superman Blue, V:Toyman, Cyborg, Superman split into two entities (1997) . . . 4.00
Deluxe, 3-D cover 5.00
GN Superman: Silver Banshee, 48-pg., prestige format (1998) 5.00
GN Superman: Speeding Bullets, EB (Elseworlds 1993). 6.00
GN Superman, Under a Yellow Sun by Clark Kent,KGa,EB (1994). . 5.95
GN Superman: The Wedding Album, collector's edition, 96-pg., cardstock cover 4.95
GN War of the Worlds,Elseworlds. . 6.00
GN Superman, Inc.. . . . . 6.95
GN Superman: Mann & Superman . 5.95
TPB Superman: Bizarro's World . . 10.00
TPB Tales of the Bizarro World . . . 14.95
TPB Superman: The Death of Clark Kent, rep. (1997) 20.00
TPB Eradication 13.00
TPB Exile 15.00
TPB Superman/Fantastic Four . . . 10.00
TPB Krisis of the Krimson Kryptonite rep. 12.95
TPB Panic in the Sky rep.. . . . . 9.95
TPB Return of Superman rep. Reign of Superman 14.95
TPB The Revenge Squad (2000) . 12.95
TPB Son of Superman (2000). . . . 14.95
HC Son of Superman,Elseworlds . 24.95
TPB Superman Vs. Revenge Squad 13.00
TPB They Saved Luthor's Brain . . 14.95
TPB Time and Time Again (1994). . 7.50
TPB The Wedding and Beyond rep. 15.00
TPB World Without Superman 7.50
TPB Superman in the sixties. 20.00
TPB Superman in the seventies . . 20.00
TPB Sunday Classics 1939–1943. 19.95
TPB The Dailies,Vol.1. . . . . 14.95
TPB The Dailies,Vol.2. . . . . 14.95
TPB The Dailies,Vol.3. . . . . 14.95
HC Superman: End of the Century 24.95
Archives, Vol. 1 S&S rep. 50.00
Archives, Vol. 2 S&S rep. 50.00
Archives, Vol. 3 S&S rep. 50.00
Archives, Vol. 4 S&S rep. 50.00
Archives, Vol. 5 S&S rep. 49.95
Superman Archives HC rep 39.95
Greatest Superman Stories Ever Told:
HC 75.00
TPB 15.95

SUPERMAN ADVENTURES
Sept., 1996

1 PDi(s),RBr,TA, from animated TV show. 3.00
2 SMI,RBr,TA,V:Metallo 2.50
3 SMI(s),RBr,TA,V:Brainiac 2.50
4 SMI(s), ... 2.50
5 SMI(s),BBI,TA,V:Livewire 2.50
6 SMI(s),RBr,TA,Metropolis in ruins. 2.50
7 SMI(s),RBr,TA,V:Jax-Ur, Mala . . . 2.50
8 SMI(s),RBr,TA,V:Jax-Ur 2.50
9 SMI(s),MM,TA,"Return of the Hero" 2.50
10 SMI(s),RBr,TA,V:Toyman 2.50
11 SMI(s),RBr,TA,struck down by strange malady 2.50
12 SMI(s),RBr,TA,BB, Kryptonian virus, concl. 2.50
13 SMI(s),RBr,TA,BB, alien races . . 2.50
14 TA,Angela Chen 2.00
15 RBr,TA,Superman's pal Bibbo . . 2.00
16 MMr(s),TA, meets Man of Steel . 2.00
17 . . . . 2.00
18 TA,should Clark quit?. 2.00
19 TA,V:Multi-Face 2.00
20 RBr,TA,V:MasterTrax 2.00
21 Supergirl Adventures, 64pg.. . . . 5.50
22 MMr,TA,RBr,War Games, pt.1 . . 2.00
23 MMr,TA,RBr,War Games, pt.2 . . 2.00
24 MMr,TA,RBr,V:Parasite 2.00
25 MMr,TA,RBr,F:Batgirl,C:Batman, Robin, Nightwing 2.00
26 MMr,TA,V:Mr.Mxyzptlk 2.00
27 MMr,TA,F:Lex Luthor 2.00
28 MMr,MM,TA,F:Jimmy Olsen 2.00
29 MMr,TA,A:Lobo, Bizarro 2.00
30 MMr,TA,A:Lara, pt.1. . . . . 2.00
31 MMr,TA,A:Lara, pt.2. . . . . 2.00
32 DvM(s),Lois Hypnotized. 2.00
33 DvM(s),TA,Secret Identity 2.00
34 MMr(s),TA,MM,A:Dr.Fate 2.00
35 MMr(s),TA,A:Toyman 2.00
36 MMr(s),TA, many emergencies . 2.00
37 MMr(s),TA,Clark Kent,Public Enemy Number One. 2.00
38 MMr(s),TA,V:Parasite. 2.00
39 TA 2.00
40 TTn(s),TA,F:Mxyzptlk. 2.00
41 TTn,RBr,22 stories. 2.00
42 TA,F:Mr. Miracle 2.00
43 TA,MM(c),Mother Box 2.00
44 TA,MM(c),F:The Commander. . . 2.00
45 TA,MM(c),Three young sisters . . 2.00
46 TA,MM(c),Smallville 2.00
47 TA,MM(c),shrinking ray 2.00
48 TA,MM(c),alien abduction 2.00
49 TA,MM(c),powers lost 2.00
50 TA,MM(c),accused of murder. . . 2.00
Ann.#1 JoS,DDv,V:Akamin 4.00
TPB rep.#1–#6. . . . . 8.00
Spec. #1 Superman vs. Lobo – Misery in Space, DvM,MM, A:Man of Tomorrow 3.00

SUPERMAN & BATMAN: GENERATIONS — AN IMAGINARY TALE
1998

1 (of 4) JBy, Elseworlds. 5.00
2 JBy,V:Bat-Mite 5.00
3 JBy. 5.00
4 JBy, conclusion. 5.00
TPB, rep. 14.95

SUPERMAN & BUGS BUNNY
1999

1 (of 4) JSon,TP 2.50
2 TP 2.50
3 TP,JSon 2.50

SUPERMAN: THE DARK SIDE
Elseworlds, Aug., 1998

1 JFM,KD,First Son of Apokolips . . 5.00
2 . . . . 5.00
3 KD, conclusion 5.00
TPB Superman: The Dark Side. . . 13.00

SUPERMAN/DOOMSDAY: HUNTER/PREY
1994

1 DJu(a&s),BBr,R:Doomsday,R:Cyborg

Superman Doomsday Hunter Prey #3
© DC Comics, Inc.

 All comics prices listed are for *Near Mint* condition.

Superman,A:Darkseid. 5.50
2 DJu(a&s),BBr,V:Doomsday,Cyborg Superman,A:Darkseid. 5.25
3 DJu(a&s),BBr,V:Doomsday 5.25
TPB Rep. #1-#3 . . . . 14.95

SUPERMAN: THE DOOMSDAY WARS
1998

1 (of 3) DJu,BBr,R:Doomsday 5.00
2 DJu,V:Doomsday 5.00
3 DJu, conclusion 5.00

SUPERMAN FAMILY
Prev: Superman's Pal, Jimmy Olsen
1974–82

164 KS,NC(c),Jimmy Olsen:`Death Bites with Fangs of Stone' . . . 35.00
165 KS,NC(c),Supergirl:`Princess of the Golden Sun' 22.00
166 KS,NC(c),Lois Lane:`The Murdering Arm of Metropolis' . 20.00
167 KS,NC(c),Jimmy Olsen:`A Deep Death for Mr. Action' . . . 20.00
168 NC(c),Supergirl:`The Girl with the See-Through Mind' . . 20.00
169 NC(c),Lois Lane:`Target of the Tarantula' 20.00
170 KS(c),Jimmy Olsen:`The Kid Who Adopted Jimmy Olsen' . . 15.00
171 ECh(c),Supergirl:`Cleopatra-Queen of America' 15.00
172 KS(c),Lois Lane:`The Cheat the Whole World Cheered' . . . 15.00
173 KS(c),Jimmy Olsen:`Menace of the Micro-Monster' 15.00
174 KS(c),Supergirl:`Eyes of the Serpent' 15.00
175 KS(c),Lois Lane:`Fadeout For Lois'. 15.00
176 KS(c),Jimmy Olsen:`Nashville, Super-Star' . 15.00
177 KS(c),Supergirl:`Bride of the Stars' 10.00
178 KS(c),Lois Lane:`The Girl With the Heart of Steel'. 10.00
179 KS(c),Jimmy Olsen:`I Scared Superman to Death' 10.00
180 KS,Supergirl:`The Secret of the Spell-Bound Supergirl' . . . 10.00
181 ECh(c),Lois Lane:`The Secret Lois Lane Could Never Tell' . . 10.00
182 CS&NA(c),Jimmy Olsen: `Death on Ice' 10.00
183 NA(c),Supergirl:`Shadows of Phantoms' 10.00
184 NA(c),Supergirl:`The Visitors From The Void'. 10.00
185 NA(c),Jimmy Olsen: The Fantastic Fists and Fury Feet of Jimmy Olsen' 10.00
186 JL&DG(c),Jimmy Olsen: `The Bug Lady'. 10.00
187 JL(c),Jimmy Olsen:`The Dealers of Death' 10.00
188 JL&DG(c),Jimmy Olsen: `Crisis in Kandor' 10.00
189 JL(c),Jimmy Olsen:`The Night of the Looter'. 10.00
190 Jimmy Olsen:`Somebody Stole My Town'. 10.00
191 Superboy:`The Incredible Shrinking Town' 10.00
192 RA&DG(c),Superboy:`This Town For Plunder' 10.00
193 RA&DG(c),Superboy:`Menace of the Mechanical Monster'. . . 10.00
194 MR,Superboy:`When the Sorcerer Strikes'. 10.00
195 RA&DG(c),Superboy:`The Curse of the Un-Secret Identity' 10.00
196 JL&DG(c),Superboy:`The Shadow of Jor-El' 10.00
197 JL(c),Superboy:`Superboy's Split Personality'. 10.00
198 JL(c),Superboy:`Challenge of the Green K-Tastrophe'. . . . 10.00
199 RA&DG(c),Supergirl:`The Case of Cape Caper' 10.00
200 RA&DG(c),Lois Lane: `Unhappy Anniversary' 11.00
201 RA&DG(c),Supergirl:`The Face on Cloud 9' 7.00
202 RA&DG(c),Supergirl:`The Dynamic Duel' 7.00
203 RA&DG(c),Supergirl:`The Supergirl From Planet Earth'. . . 7.00
204 RA&DG(c),Supergirl:`The Earth-quake Enchantment' 7.00
205 RA&DG(c),Supergirl:`Magic Over Miami' 7.00
206 RA&DG(c),Supergirl:`Strangers at the Heart's Core' 7.00
207 RA&DG(c),Supergirl:`Look Homeward, Argonian' 7.00
208 RA&DG(c),Supergirl:`The Super-Switch to New York' 7.00
209 Supergirl:`Strike Three-You're Out' 7.00
210 Supergirl:`The Spoil Sport of New York'. 7.00
211 RA&DG(c):Supergirl:`The Man With the Explosive Mind' 7.00
212 RA&DG(c):Supergirl:`Payment on Demand' 7.00
213 . . . . 7.00
214 . . . . 7.00
215 . . . . 7.00
216 thru 222 . . . . @7.00

SUPERMAN FOR ALL SEASONS
June, 1998

1 (of 4) JLb,TSe, from farmboy to superhero. 5.00
2 JLb,TSe,V:Lex Luthor 5.00
3 JLb,TSe,V:Lex Luthor 5.00
4 JLb,TSe, conclusion 5.00
HC Superman for All Seasons . . . 24.95

SUPERMAN/GEN13
DC/Wildstorm April, 2000

1 (of 3) AH, x-over. 2.50
1a variant cover (1:4). 2.50
2 AH,x-over. 2.50
2a variant cover (1:4). 2.50
3 AH, 40-pg. 3.50

SUPERMAN: LAST SON OF EARTH
July, 2000

1 (of 2) Elseworlds. 5.95
2 Green Lantern's powers 5.95

SUPERMAN: THE MAN OF STEEL
1991–97

1 B:LSi(s),DJu,BMc,JOy,BBr,TG, Revenge o/t Krypton Man#1 . . . 5.00
2 JBg,V:Cerberus 3.00
3 JBg,War of the Gods X-over. . . . 2.50
4 JBg,V:Angstrom 2.50
5 JBg,CS,V:Atomic Skull 2.50
6 JBg,Blackout#3,A:Mr.Z 2.50
7 JBg,V:Cerberus 2.50
8 KD,V:Jolt,Blockhouse 2.50
9 JBg,Panic in the Sky#1, V:Brainiac. 3.00
10 JBg,Panic in the Sky#5, D:Draaga 2.50
11 JBg,V:Flashpoint 2.50
12 JBg,V:Warwolves. 2.50
13 JBg,V:Cerberus 2.50
14 JBg,A:Robin,V:Vampires 2.50
15 KG,KGa,Blaze/Satanus War . . . 2.50
16 JBg,Crisis at Hand#1 . . . . 2.50
17 JBg,V:Underworld, C:Doomsday 8.00
17a 2nd printing 2.50
18 JBg,I:Doomsday,V:Underworld. 10.00
18a 2nd printing 4.00
18b 3rd printing 2.50
19 JBg,Doomsday,pt.5 . . . . 5.00
19a 2nd printing 2.50
20 JBg,Funeral for a Friend#3 . . . . 3.00
21 JBg,Funeral for a Friend#7 . . . . 3.00
22 JBg,Reign of Supermen#4,Direct Sales,Die-Cut(c),mini-poster, F:Man of Steel 2.50
22a Newsstand Ed. 2.00
23 JBg,V:Superboy. 2.00
24 JBg,V:White Rabbit,A:Mongul . . 2.00
25 JBg,A:Real Superman 3.00
26 JBg,A:All Supermen,V:Mongul, Cyborg Superman 2.50
27 JBg,A:Superboy,Lex Luthor 2.00
28 JBg(c),A:Steel 2.00
29 LSi(s),JBg,Spilled Blood#3, V:Hi-Tech,Blood Thirst 2.00
30 LSi(s),JBg,V:Lobo,Vinyl(c) 2.50
30a Newstand Ed. 2.00
31 MBr,A:Guardian. 2.00
32 MBr,Bizarro's World#4, V:Bizarro 2.00
33 MBr,V:Parasite. 2.00
34 JBg,A:Lex Men,Dubbile Men . . . 2.00
35 JBg,Worlds Collide#1, I:Fred Bentson 2.00
36 JBf,Worlds Collide,pt.10,V:Rift A:Icon 2.00
37 JBg,Zero Hour,A:Batman 2.00
38 Mystery 2.00
39 JBg,Luthor. 2.00
40 . . . . 2.00
41 Locke 2.00
42 F:Locke 2.00

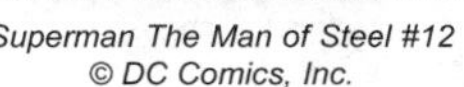

Superman The Man of Steel #12
© DC Comics, Inc.

43 V:Deathtrap 2.00
44 Prologue to Death 2.00
45 JGb,DJa,Death of Clark Kent,pt.4
[New Miraweb format begins] . . 2.00
46 JBg,DJa,A:Shadowdragon 2.00
47 O:Bloodsport 2.00
48 . . . . 2.00
49 Skyhook 2.00
50 JBg,DJa,The Trial of
Superman, 48pg. 2.95
51 JBg,DJa,The Trial of Superman . 2.00
52 JBg,The Trial of Superman 2.00
53 JBg,DRo,A:Lex Luthor,Contessa
. . . . 2.00
54 JBg 2.00
55 JBg,DJa, Clark dates Lori
Lemaris 2.00
56 JBg,DJa, manipulator revealed . 2.00
57 RSt,JBg,DJa, more twisters 2.00
58 LSi(s),JBg,DJa,A:Supergirl. 2.00
59 LSi(s),JBg,DJa,Parasite, Steel . . 2.00
60 LSi(s),JBg,DJa,R:Bottled City
of Kandor 2.00
61 LSi(s),JBg,DJa,V:Riot 2.00
62 LSi(s),JBg,DJa, Superman
looses powers, Final Night tie-in . . .
. . . . .2.00
63 LSi(s),JBg,DJa,Clark is
kidnapped & revealed identity. . 2.00
64 LSi(s),JBg,DJa,Superman tries to
restore his powers 2.00
65 LSi(s),SB,DJa,V:Superman
Revenge Squad 2.00
66 LSi(s),JBg,DJa,V:Rajiv. 2.00
67 LSi(s),JBg,DJa,New powers
prequel. 2.00
68 LSi(s),JBg,DJa,V:Metallo 2.00
69 KK&LSi(s),SEa,DJa,A:Atom,
in Kandor 2.00
70 LSi(s),SEa,DJa,V:Saviour 2.00
71 LSi(s),SEa,DJa,V:Mainframe,
Superman Revenge Squad. . . . 2.00
72 LSi(s),SEa,JP,DJa,JBg,Genesis
V:Mainframe. 2.00
73 LSi&MWa(s),SEa,DJa,V:Revenge
Squad 2.00
74 LSi(s),SEa,DJa,dragon's tooth . . 2.00
75 LSi(s),DJa,JBg,Mr.Mxyzptlk dies
parody of Superman #75 . . . . . 2.00
76 LSi(s),JBb,DJa,V:Mokkari 2.00
77 . . . . 2.00
78 JBg, Millennium Giants, pt.1
x-over. 2.00
79 JBg, Millennium Giants 2.00
80 LSi,JBg,DJa,golden age?,pt.1 . . 2.00
81 LSi,JBg,DJa,golden age?,pt.2 . . 2.00
82 LSi,JBg,DJa,golden age?,pt.3 . . 2.00
83 LSi,SEa,DJa,Dominus 2.00
84 RMz(s),TGb,TP,City of the
Future, pt.2 x-over 2.00
85 JBg,DJa,V:Simyan & Mokkari. . . 2.00
86 LSi(s),SEa,DJa,dreams
of disasters 2.00
87 MSh(s),DoM,DJa,A:Steel,
Superboy, Supergirl 2.00
88 MSh(s),DoM,DJa 2.00
89 MSh(s),DoM,V:Dominus. 2.00
90 MSh(s),V:Superman's Robot . . . 2.00
91 MSh(s),DoM,paranoia 2.00
92 TPe(s),TGb,TP,Secret
origins,concl. 2.00
93 MSh,DoM 2.00
94 RF,SB,Strange Visitor,concl. . . . 2.00
95 MSh,DoM,Fortress of Solitude . . 2.00
96 MSh,DoM, ... 2.00
97 MSh,DoM,F:Eradicator. 2.00
98 MSh,DoM,V:Brainiac 13. . . . . . . 2.00
99 MSh,DoM,new armor. 2.00
100 MSh,DoM,new Fortress of
Solitude, 48-pg. 3.00
100a Collectors edition 4.00
101 MSh,DoM,growing sicker 2.00
102 MSh,DoM,Crit.Condition,pt.3 . . 2.00
103 MSh,DoM,A:Supergirl 2.25
104 MSh,DoM,Arkham,pt.3. . . . . . . 2.25
105 MSh,DoM,Superman:Emperor . 2.25
106 MSh,HuR,V:Kosnor,Netkon . . . 2.25
107 MSh,DoM, to Phantom Zone . . 2.25
Ann.#1 Eclipso tie-in,A:Starman . . . 2.75
Ann.#2 Bloodlines#2,I:Edge 2.75
Ann.#3 MBr,Elseworlds Story 2.95
Ann.#4 Year One Annual 2.95
Ann.#5 Legends o/t Dead Earth . . . 2.95
Ann.#6 Pulp Heroes (Hard Boiled)
LSi(s),DJa 3.95
Spec.#1,000,000 KK&JOy(s),
AWi,DJa. 2.00
Gallery 1 . . . . 3.50
TPB 7.50

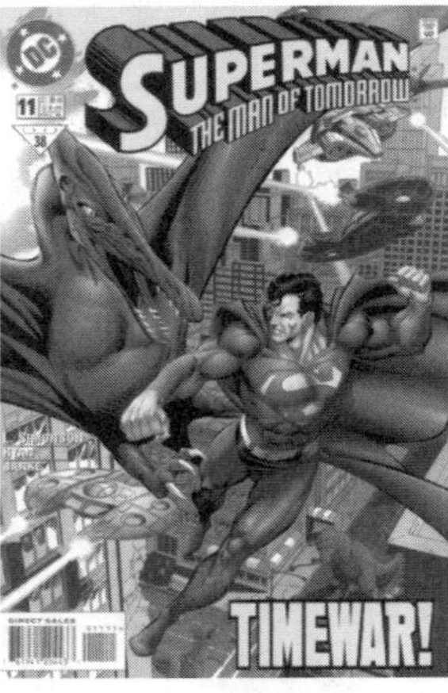

Superman: The Man of Tomorrow #11 © DC Comics, Inc.

SUPERMAN: THE MAN OF TOMORROW
1995–96

1 TGu,BBr,RSt(s),V:Lex Luthor . . . 2.00
2 v:Parasite. 2.00
3 TG,BBr, The Trial of Superman. . 2.00
4 RSt(s),PR,BBr,A:Shazam 2.00
5 RSt(s),PR,BBr,Wedding of Lex
Luthor 2.00
6 RSt(s),PR,BBr,Superman V:
Jackal again. 2.00
7 RSt(s),PR,BBr, ... 2.00
8 RSt(s),PR,BBr,V:Carbide 2.00
9 RSt(s),PR,BBr,Ma and Pa Kent
open their album 2.00
10 . . . . 2.00
11 LSi(s),PR,DJa,BBr 2.00
12 LSi(s),PR,DJa,. 2.00
13 LSi(s),PR,DJa,A:JLA 2.00
14 LSi(s),PR,DJa,V:Riot 2.00
15 Day of Judgment x-over,48-pg. . 2.95
Spec.#1,000,000 MSh(s),DRo 2.00

SUPERMAN'S GIRL FRIEND, LOIS LANE
1958–74

1 CS,KS 3,500.00
2 CS,KS 900.00
3 CS,KS,spanking panel shown . 550.00
4 CS,KS 450.00
5 CS,KS 425.00
6 CS,KS 350.00
7 CS,KS 350.00
8 CS,KS 300.00
9 CS,KS, A:Pat Boone. 300.00
10 CS,KS 300.00
11 CS,KS 200.00
12 CS,KS 200.00
13 CS,KS 175.00
14 KS,`Three Nights in the
Fortress of Solitude' 165.00
15 KS,I:Van-Zee 165.00
16 KS, Lois' Signal-Watch. 165.00
17 KS,CS,A:Brainiac. 165.00
18 KS,A:Astounding Man 165.00
19 KS,`Superman of the Past'. . . 150.00
20 KS,A:Superman. 150.00
21 KS,A:Van-Zee 150.00
22 KS,A:Robin Hood. 150.00
23 KS,A:Elastic Lass, Supergirl. . 150.00
24 KS,A:Van-Zee, Bizarro 150.00
25 KS,`Lois Lane's
Darkest Secret'. 125.00
26 KS,A:Jor-El 125.00
27 KS,CS,A:Bizarro 125.00
28 KS,A:Luthor 125.00
29 CS,A:Aquaman,Batman,Green
Arrow 125.00
30 KS,A:Krypto,Aquaman 75.00
31 KS,A:Lori Lemaris 70.00
32 KS,CS,A:Bizarro 70.00
33 KS,CS,A:Phantom Zone,Lori
Lemaris, Mon-El 75.00
34 KS,A:Luthor,Supergirl. 70.00
35 KS,CS,A:Supergirl 70.00
36 KS,CS,Red Kryptonite Story . . 70.00
37 KS,CS,`The Forbidden Box' . . . 70.00
38 KS,CS,A:Prof.Potter,
Supergirl 70.00
39 KS,CS,A:Supergirl,Jor-El,
Krypto, Lori Lemaris 70.00
40 KS,`Lois Lane, Hag!' 70.00
41 KS,CS,`The Devil and
Lois Lane' 70.00
42 KS,A:Lori Lemaris 70.00
43 KS,A:Luthor. 70.00
44 KS,A:Lori Lemaris,Braniac,
Prof. Potter. 70.00
45 KS,CS,`The Superman-Lois
Hit Record' 70.00
46 KS,A:Luthor. 70.00
47 KS,`The Incredible Delusion' . . 70.00
48 KS,A:Mr. Mxyzptlk 70.00
49 KS,The Unknown Superman . . 70.00
50 KS,A:Legion 60.00
51 KS,A:Van-Zee & Lori Lemaris . 50.00
52 KS,`Truce Between Lois

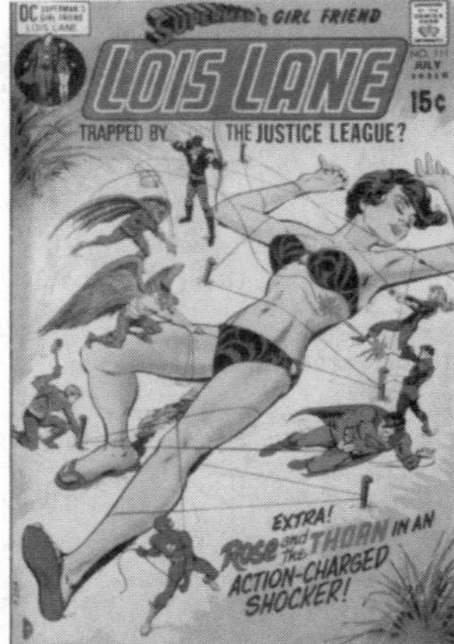

Superman's Girl Friend Lois Lane #111 © DC Comics, Inc.

 All comics prices listed are for *Near Mint* condition.

Lane and Lana Lang' 50.00
53 KS,A:Lydia Lawrence. 50.00
54 KS,CS,`The Monster That Loved Lois Lane' 50.00
55 KS,A:Superigrl 50.00
56 KS,`Lois Lane's Super-Gamble!' 55.00
57 KS,`The Camera From Outer Space' 50.00
58 KS,`The Captive Princess' 50.00
59 KS,CS,A:Jor-El & Batman 50.00
60 KS,`Get Lost,Superman!' 50.00
61 KS,A:Mxyzptlk 50.00
62 KS,A:Mxyzptlk 50.00
63 KS,`The Satanic Schemes of S.K.U.L.'. 50.00
64 KS,A:Luthor 50.00
65 KS,A:Luthor 50.00
66 KS,`They Call Me the Cat!'. . . . 50.00
67 KS,`The Bombshell of the Boulevards' 50.00
68 giant size 60.00
69 KS,Lois Lane's Last Chance . . 50.00
70 KS,I:Silver Age Catwoman, A:Batman,Robin,Penguin . . . 250.00
71 KS,A:Catwoman,Batman, Robin,Penguin 150.00
72 KS,CS,A:Ina Lemaris. 25.00
73 KS,`The Dummy and the Damsel!'. 25.00
74 KS,A:Justice League & Bizarro World,I:Bizarro Flash 35.00
75 KS,`The Lady Dictator'. 25.00
76 KS,A:Hap-El 25.00
77 giant size. 50.00
78 KS,Courtship,Kryptonian Style . 25.00
79 KS,B:NA(c) 20.00
80 KS,`Get Out of My Life, Superman' 20.00
81 KS,`No Witnessesin Outerspace' 20.00
82 GT,A:Brainiac&Justice League . 20.00
83 GT,`Witch on Wheels' 20.00
84 GT,KS,`Who is Lois Lane?' . . . 20.00
85 GT,KS,A:Kandorians 20.00
86 giant size. 40.00
87 GT,KS,A:Cor-Lar 20.00
88 GT,KS,`Through a Murderer's Eyes' 20.00
89 CS,A:Batman & Batman Jr. . . . 25.00
90 GT,A:Dahr-nel 20.00
91 GT,A:Superlass 20.00
92 GT,A:Superhorse 20.00
93 GT,A:Wonder Woman 20.00
94 GT,KS,A:Jor. 20.00
95 giant size. 40.00
96 GT,A:Jor 15.00
97 GT,KS,A:Lori Lemaris, Luma Lynai,Lyla Lerrol 15.00
98 GT,A:Phantom Zone 15.00
99 GT,KS,A:Batman 15.00
100 GT,A:Batman 15.00
101 GT,KS,`The Super-Reckless Lois Lane' 15.00
102 GT,KS,When You're Dead, You're Dead 15.00
103 GT,KS,A:Supergirl 15.00
104 giant size. 40.00
105 RA,I&O:Rose & Thorn 40.00
106 WR,`I am Curious Black!'. . . . 15.00
107 WR,The Snow-Woman Wept . 15.00
108 WR,The Spectre Suitor 15.00
109 WR,`I'll Never Fall in Love Again' 15.00
110 WR,`Indian Death Charge!' . . 15.00
111 WR,A:Justice League. 15.00
112 WR,KS,A:Lori Lemaris 15.00
113 giant size 40.00
114 WR,KS,A:Rose & Thorn 15.00
115 WR,A:The Black Racer 15.00
116 WR,A:Darkseid & Desaad . . . 15.00
117 WR,`S.O.S From Tomorrow!' . 15.00
118 WR,A:Darkseid & Desaad . . . 15.00
119 WR,A:Darkseid & Lucy Lane . 15.00
120 WR,`Who Killed Lucy Lane?' . 15.00
121 WR,A:The Thorn 15.00
122 WR,A:The Thorn 15.00
123 JRo,`Ten Deadly Division of the 100' 15.00
124 JRo,`The Hunters' 10.00
125 JRo,`Death Rides Wheels!' . . 10.00
126 JRo,`The Brain Busters'. 10.00
127 JRo,`Curse of the Flame' 10.00
128 JRo,A:Batman & Aquaman . . 10.00
129 JRo,`Serpent in Paradise' . . . 10.00
130 JRo,`The Mental Murster'. . . . 10.00
131 JRo,Superman–Marry Me!'. . . 10.00
132 JRo,Zatanna B.U. 10.00
133 JRo,`The Lady is a Bomb' . . . 10.00
134 JRo,A:Kandor 10.00
135 JRo,`Amazing After-Life of Lois Lane'. 10.00
136 JRo,A:Wonder Woman. 10.00
137 JRo,`The Stolen Subway'. . . . 12.00
Ann.#1 . . . . 175.00
Ann.#2 . . . . 125.00

SUPERMAN: SILVER BANSHEE

1998

1 (of 2) DIB(s),ALa. 2.25
2 DIB(s),ALa, conclusion 2.25

SUPERMAN'S NEMESIS, LEX LUTHOR

1999

1 (of 4) VS,DJa,. 2.50
2 VS,DJa. 2.50
3 VS,DJa. 2.50
4 VS,DJa, conclusion 2.50

SUPERMAN'S PAL, JIMMY OLSEN

1954–74

1 CS,`The Boy of 100 Faces!'. 4,500.00
2 CS,The Flying Jimmy Olsen. 1,500.00
3 CS,`The Man Who Collected Excitement 750.00
4 CS,`King For A Day!' 550.00
5 CS,`The Story of Superman's Souvenirs. 500.00

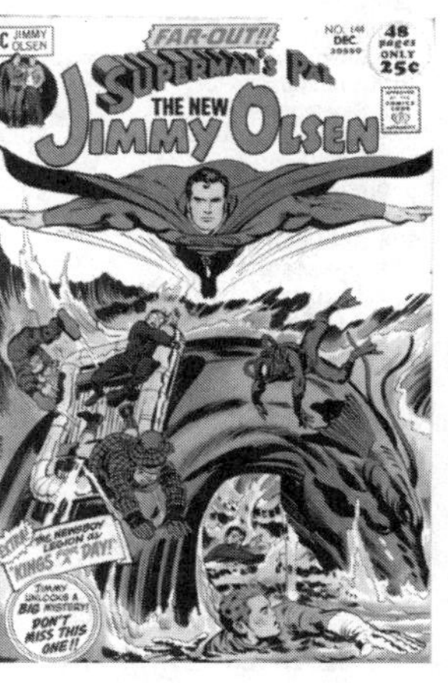

Superman's Pal Jimmy Olsen #144
© DC Comics, Inc.

6 CS,Kryptonite story. 375.00
7 CS,`The King of Marbles' 375.00
8 CS,`Jimmy Olsen, Crooner' . . 350.00
9 CS,`The Missile of Steel'. 350.00
10 CS,`Jungle Jimmy Olsen'. . . . 350.00
11 CS,`TNT.Olsen,The Champ'. . 250.00
12 CS,`Invisible Jimmy Olsen'. . . 250.00
13 CS,`Jimmy Olsen's Super Issue' 225.00
14 CS,`The Boy Superman' 225.00
15 CS,`Jimmy Olsen,Speed Demon' 225.00
16 CS,`The Boy Superman' 225.00
17 CS,J.Olsen as cartoonist 225.00
18 CS,A:Superboy 225.00
19 CS,`Supermam's Kid Brother . 200.00
20 CS,`Merman of Metropolis'. . . 200.00
21 CS,`The Wedding of Jimmy Olsen'. 175.00
22 CS,`The Super Brain of Jimmy Olsen' 175.00
23 CS,`The Adventure of Private Olsen'. 175.00
24 CS,`The Gorilla Reporter'. . . . 175.00
25 CS,`The Day There Was No Jimmy Olsen. 175.00
26 CS,`Bird Boy of Metropolis' . . 150.00
27 CS,`The Outlaw Jimmy Olsen' 150.00
28 CS,`The Boy Who Killed Superman' 150.00
29 CS,A:Krypto. 150.00
30 CS,`The Son of Superman' . . 150.00
31 CS,I:Elastic Lad 125.00
32 CS,A:Prof.Potter 125.00
33 CS,`Human Flame Thrower'. . 125.00
34 CS,`Superman's Pal of Steel'. 125.00
35 CS,`Superman's Enemy' 125.00
36 CS,I:Lois Lane,O:Jimmy Olsen as Superman's Pal 125.00
37 CS,O:Jimmy Olsen's SignalWatch, A:Elastic Lad(Jimmy Olsen) . 125.00
38 CS,`Olsen's Super-Supper' . . 125.00
39 CS,`The Super-Lad of Space' 125.00
40 CS,A:Supergirl,Hank White (Perry White's son) 125.00
41 CS,`The Human Octopus' 90.00
42 CS,`Jimmy The Genie'. 90.00
43 WB,CS,`Jimmy Olsen's Private Monster'. 90.00
44 CS,`Miss Jimmy Olsen' 90.00
45 CS,A:Kandor 90.00
46 CS,A:Supergirl,Elastic Lad 90.00
47 CS,`Monsters From Earth!'. . . . 90.00
48 CS,I:Superman Emergency Squad 90.00
49 CS,A:Congorilla & Congo Bill. . 90.00
50 CS,A:Supergirl,Krypto,Bizarro . 90.00
51 CS,A:Supergirl. 75.00
52 CS,A:Mr. Mxyzptlk, Miss Gzptlsnz. 75.00
53 CS,A:Kandor,Lori Lemaris, Mr.Mxyztlk 75.00
54 CS,A:Elastic Lad 75.00
55 CS,A:Aquaman,Thor 75.00
56 KS,Imaginary story 75.00
57 KS,A:Supergirl,Imaginary story. 40.00
58 CS,C:Batman. 40.00
59 CS,A:Titano 40.00
60 CS,`The Fantastic Army of General Olsen'. 40.00
61 CS,Prof. Potter 40.00
62 CS,A:Elastic Lad,Phantom Zone 40.00
63 CS,A:Supergirl,Kandor 45.00
64 CS,`Jimmy Olsen's Super-Romance 35.00
65 CS,A:Miss Gzptlsnz 35.00
66 CS,KS,A:Mr. Mxyzptlk 35.00
67 CS,`The Dummy That Haunted Jimmy Olsen' 35.00

DC COMICS

Superman's Pal Jimmy Olsen #148
© DC Comics, Inc.

68 CS,'The Helmet of Hate' 35.00
69 CS,A:Nightwing,Flamebird 35.00
70 A:Supergirl,Lori Lemaris, Element Lad 35.00
71 CS,A:Mr. Mxyzptlk 30.00
72 CS,A:Legion of Super-Heroes, Jimmy Olsen becomes honorary member. 35.00
73 A:Kandor 35.00
74 CS,A:Mr. Mxyzptlk,Lex Luthor . 32.00
75 CS,A:Supergirl. 32.00
76 CS,A:Legion of Super-Heroes . 32.00
77 CS,Jimmy Olsen becomes Colossal Boy, A:Titano 32.00
78 CS,A:Aqualad 32.00
79 CS,'The Red-Headed Beetle of 1,000 B.C.' 32.00
80 CS,A:Bizarro 32.00
81 CS,KS,A:Lori Lemaris,I&O only A:Mighty Eagle 32.00
82 CS,'The Unbeatable Jimmy Olsen' 32.00
83 CS,A:Kandor 32.00
84 CS,A:Titano. 32.00
85 CS,C:Legion of Super-Heroes . 35.00
86 CS,A:Congorilla,Braniac. 32.00
87 A:Lex Luthor,Brainiac,Legion of Super-Villians 35.00
88 C:Legion of Super-Heroes 32.00
89 I:Agent Double-Five,C:John F. Kennedy. 32.00
90 CS,A:Mr. Mxyzptlk 32.00
91 CS,C:Batman & Robin 32.00
92 JM,A:Batman,Robin,Supergirl . 32.00
93 'The Batman-Superman of Earth-X!' 32.00
94 O:Insect Queen retold 32.00
95 Giant. 35.00
96 I:Tempus 25.00
97 A:Fortress of Solitude 25.00
98 'The Bride of Jungle Jimmy'. . . 25.00
99 A:Legion of Super-Heroes 25.00
100 A:Legion of Super-Heroes . . . 35.00
101 A:Jor-El and Lara. 20.00
102 'Superman's Greatest Double Cross!' 20.00
103 'The Murder of Clark Kent!' . . 18.00
104 Giant 30.00
105 V:Tempus 18.00
106 CS,A:Legion of Super-Heroes 18.00
107 A:Krypto 18.00
108 CS,'The Midas of Metropolis'. 18.00
109 A:Lex Luthor 18.00

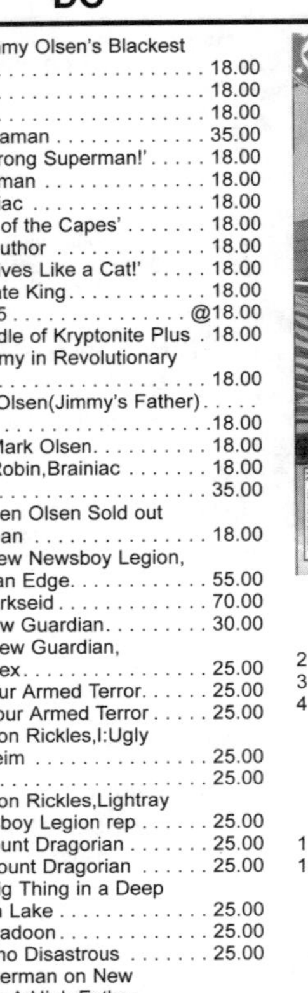

110 CS,'Jimmy Olsen's Blackest Deeds!'. 18.00
111 . . . . 18.00
112 . . . . 18.00
113 V:Magnaman 35.00
114 'The Wrong Superman!' 18.00
115 A:Aquaman 18.00
116 A:Brainiac 18.00
117 'Planet of the Capes' 18.00
118 A:Lex Luthor 18.00
119 'Nine Lives Like a Cat!' 18.00
120 V:Climate King. 18.00
121 thru 125 . . . . @18.00
126 CS,Riddle of Kryptonite Plus . 18.00
127 CS,Jimmy in Revolutionary War. 18.00
128 I:Mark Olsen(Jimmy's Father). 18.00
129 MA,A:Mark Olsen. 18.00
130 MA,A:Robin,Brainiac 18.00
131 . . . . 35.00
132 MA,When Olsen Sold out Superman 18.00
133 JK,B:New Newsboy Legion, I:Morgan Edge. 55.00
134 JK,I:Darkseid 70.00
135 JK,I:New Guardian. 30.00
136 JK,O:New Guardian, I:Dubbilex. 25.00
137 JK,I:Four Armed Terror. 25.00
138 JK,V:Four Armed Terror 25.00
139 JK,A:Don Rickles,I:Ugly Mannheim 25.00
140 . . . . 25.00
141 JK,A:Don Rickles,Lightray B:Newsboy Legion rep 25.00
142 JK,I:Count Dragorian 25.00
143 JK,V:Count Dragorian 25.00
144 JK,A Big Thing in a Deep Scottish Lake 25.00
145 JK,Brigadoon. 25.00
146 JK,Homo Disastrous 25.00
147 JK,Superman on New Genesis,A:High Father, I:Victor Volcanium. 25.00
148 JK,V:Victor Volcanium, E:Newsboy Legion rep 25.00
149 BO(i),The Unseen Enemy, B:Plastic Man rep 20.00
150 BO(i) A Bad Act to Follow . . . 20.00
151 BO(i),A:Green Lantern 20.00
152 MSy,BO,I:Real Morgan Edge . 20.00
153 MSy,Murder in Metropolis. . . . 20.00
154 KS,The Girl Who Was Made of Money 20.00
155 KS,Downfall of Judas Olsen. . 20.00
156 KS,Last Jump for a Skyjacker 20.00
157 KS,Jimmy as Marco Polo 20.00
158 KS,A:Lena Lawrence (Lucy Lane) 20.00
159 KS,Jimmy as Spartacus. 20.00
160 KS,A:Lena Lawrence (Lucy Lane) 20.00
161 KS,V:Lucy Lane. 20.00
162 KS,A:Lex Luthor. 20.00
163 KS,Jimmy as Marco Polo 20.00

SUPERMAN: SAVE THE PLANET

Aug., 1998

1 LSi,SEa,DRo,JP,KN, last front page. 3.00
1 collector's edition 4.00

SUPERMAN, THE SECRET YEARS

Feb., 1985

1 CS,KS,FM(c) 2.50

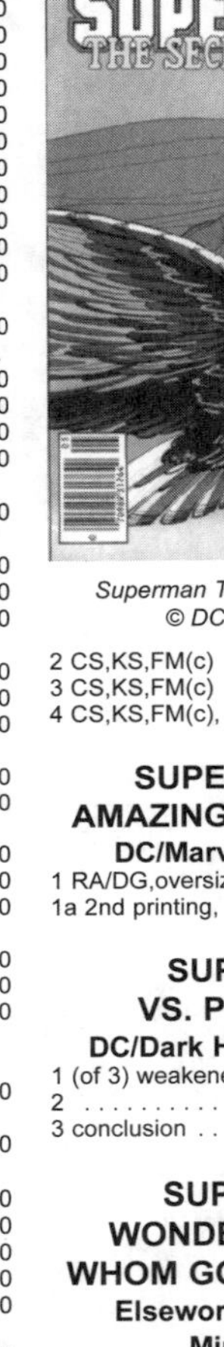

Superman The Secret Years #4
© DC Comics, Inc.

2 CS,KS,FM(c) 2.00
3 CS,KS,FM(c) 2.00
4 CS,KS,FM(c), May 1985. . . . . . . 2.00

SUPERMAN VS. AMAZING SPIDER-MAN

DC/Marvel April, 1976

1 RA/DG,oversized 75.00
1a 2nd printing, signed 125.00

SUPERMAN VS. PREDATOR

DC/Dark Horse May, 2000

1 (of 3) weakened by virus. 5.00
2 . . . . 5.00
3 conclusion 5.00

SUPERMAN/ WONDER WOMAN: WHOM GODS DESTROY

Elseworlds Oct., 1996

Mini-series

1 CCl(s),DAb, Lois becomes the immortal Wonder Woman 5.00
2 CCl(s),DAb, search for Lana Lang 5.00
3 . . . . 5.00
4 CCl(s),DAb, romance of the century, concl. 5.00

SUPERMEN OF AMERICA

1999

GN with membership kit 5.00
GN standard edition 4.00
1 (of 6) FaN,DBw, ... 2.50
2 FaN,DBw,V:Lex Luthor 2.50
3 FaN,DBw,F:Brahma 2.50
4 FaN,DBw,F:White Lotus 2.50
5 FaN,F:The Loser 2.50
6 FaN,A:Superman,concl. 2.50

SUPER POWERS

1984

[Kenner Action Figures]

1 A:Batman & Joker 4.00
2 A:Batman & Joker 4.00

3 A:Batman & Joker 4.00
4 A:Batman & Joker 4.00
5 JK(c),JK,A:Batman & Joker. 4.00

[2nd Series] 1985–86

1 JK,'Seeds of Doom' 3.50
2 JK,'When Past & Present Meet' . 3.50
3 JK,'Time Upon Time' 3.50
4 JK,There's No Place Like Rome . 3.50
5 JK,'Once Upon a Tomorrow'. . . . 3.50
6 JK,'Darkkseid o/t Moon' 3.50

[3rd Series] 1986

1 CI,'Threshold'. 2.50
2 CI,'Escape'. 2.50
3 CI,'Machinations' 2.50
4 CI,'A World Divided'. 2.50

SUPER-TEAM FAMILY

1975–78

1 rep. 15.00
2 Creeper/Wildcat 9.00
3 RE/WW,Flash & Hawkman 9.00
4 . . . . 10.00
5 . . . . 10.00
6 . . . . 10.00
7 . . . . 10.00
8 JSh,Challengers 10.00
9 JSh,Challengers 10.00
10 JSh,Challengers 10.00
11 Supergirl,Flash,Atom 10.00
12 Green Lantern,Hawkman 10.00
13 Aquaman, Capt. Comet 10.00
14 Wonder Woman,Atom 10.00
15 Flash & New Gods. 11.00

SWAMP THING

[1st Regular Series]

Oct.–Nov., 1972

1 B:LWn(s),BWr,O:Swamp Thing . 85.00
2 BWr,I:Arcane 40.00
3 BWr,I:Patchwork Man 30.00
4 BWr 25.00
5 BWr 25.00
6 BWr 25.00
7 BWr,A:Batman 30.00
8 BWr,Lurker in Tunnel 13 . . . . . . 20.00
9 BWr 20.00
10 E:BWr,A;Arcane. 20.00
11 thru 22 NR . . . . @8.00
23 NR,reverts to Dr.Holland 8.00
24 NR 8.00
TPB rep.#1-#10,House of Secrets
#92, Dark Genesis Saga. 19.95

SWAMP THING

1986–96

Previously:

SAGA OF THE SWAMP THING

46 B:AMo(s) cont'd,SBi,JTo,Crisis,
A:John Constantine,Phantom
Stranger. 4.00
47 SBi,Parliment of Trees,Full
origin,A:Constantine 3.00
48 SBi,JTo,V:Brujeria,
A:Constantine. 3.00
49 SBi,AA,A:Constantine,Demon,Ph.
Stranger,Spectre,Deadman. . . . 3.00
50 SBi,RV,JTo,concl.American
Gothic,D:Zatara&Sargon,
Double Size 6.00
51 RV,AA,L:Constantine 3.00
52 RV,AA,Arkham Asylum,A:Flor.
Man,Lex Luthor,C:Joker,
2-Face,Batman. 4.00
53 JTo,V:Batman,Swamp Thing
Banished to Space 4.00
54 JTo script,RV,AA,C:Batman 3.00
55 RV,AA,JTo,A:Batman,. 3.00
56 RV,AA,My Blue Heaven 3.00
57 RV,AA,A:Adam Strange 3.00
58 RV,AA,A:Adam Strange,GC,
Spectre preview 3.00
59 JTo,RV,AA,D:Patchwork Man . . . 3.00

Direct Sales Only

60 JTo,Loving the Alien. 3.00
61 RV,AA,All Flesh is Grass
G.L.Corps X-over 3.00
62 RV(&script),AA,Wavelength,
A:Metron,Darkseid 3.00
63 RV,AA,Loose Ends(reprise) 3.00
64 E:AMo(s),SBi,TY,RV,AA,
Return of the Good Gumbo . . . 3.00
65 RV,JTo,A:Constantine 3.50
66 RV,Elemental Energy. 2.50
67 RV,V:Solomon Grundy,
Hellblazer preview 4.00
68 RV,O:Swamp Thing 2.50
69 RV,O:Swamp Thing 2.50
70 RV,AA,Quest for SwampThing . . 2.50
71 RV,AA,Fear of Flying 2.50
72 RV,AA,Creation 2.50
73 RV,AA,A:John Constantine. 3.00
74 RV,AA,Abbys Secret 2.50
75 RV,AA,Plant Elementals. 2.50
76 RV,AA,A:John Constantine. 3.00
77 TMd,AA,A:John Constantine . . . 3.00
78 TMd,AA,Phantom Pregnancy. . . 2.50
79 RV,AA,A:Superman,Luthor. 2.50
80 RV,AA,V:Aliends 2.50
81 RV,AA,Invasion x-over 2.50
82 RV,AA,A:Sgt.Rock & Easy Co. . . 2.50
83 RV,AA,A:Enemy Ace 2.50
84 RV,AA,A:Sandman. 8.00
85 RV,TY,Time Travel contd. 2.50
86 RV,TY,A:Tomahawk 2.50
87 RV,TY,Camelot,A:Demon 2.50
88 RV,TY,A:Demon,Golden
Gladiator 2.50
89 MM,AA,The Dinosaur Age 2.50
90 BP,AA,Birth of Abbys Child
(Tefe) 2.75
91 PB,AA,Abbys Child (New
Elemental) 2.50
92 PB,AA,Ghosts of the Bayou 2.50
93 PB,AA,New Power. 2.50
94 PB,AA,Ax-Murderer 2.50
95 PB,AA,Toxic Waste Dumpers. . . 2.50
96 PB,AA,Tefes Powers 2.50
97 PB,AA,Tefe,V:Nergal,
A:Arcane 2.50
98 PB,AA,Tefe,in Hell 2.50
99 PB,AA,Tefe,A:Mantago,

Swamp Thing #86 © DC Comics. Inc.

John Constantine 3.00
100 PB,AA,V:Angels of Eden,
(48 pages) 3.50
101 AA,A:Tefe 2.50
102 V:Mantagos Zombies,inc. prev.
of Worlds Without End 2.50
103 Green vs. Grey 2.50
104 Quest for Elementals,pt.1. . . . . 2.50
105 Quest for Elementals,pt.2. . . . . 2.50
106 Quest for Elementals,pt.3. . . . . 2.50
107 Quest for Elementals,pt.4. . . . . 2.50
108 Quest for Elementals,pt.5. . . . . 2.50
109 Quest for Elementals,pt.6. . . . . 2.50
110 TMd,A:Father Tocsin 2.50
111 V:Ghostly Zydeco Musician . . . 2.50
112 TMd,B:Swamp Thing
for Governor. 2.50
113 E:Swamp Thing for Governor. . 2.50
114 TMd,Hellblazer. 2.75
115 TMd,A:Hellblazer,V:Dark
Conrad. 2.75
116 From Body of Swamp Thing. . . 2.25
117 JD,The Lord of Misrule,
Mardi Gras 2.25
118 A Childs Garden,A:Matthew
the Raven 2.25
119 A:Les Perdu. 2.25
120 F:Lady Jane. 2.25
121 V:Sunderland Corporation 2.25
122 I:The Needleman 2.25
123 V:The Needleman 2.25
124 In Central America. 2.25
125 V:Anton Arcane,20th Anniv. . . . 3.75
126 Mescalito 2.25
127 Project Proteus #1 . . . . 2.25
128 Project proteus #2 . . . . 2.25

Vertigo

129 CV(c),B:NyC(s),SEa,KDM(i),
Sw.Thing's Deterioration. 2.25
130 CV(c),SEa,KDM(i),A:John
Constantine,V:Doctor Polygon . 2.25
131 CV(c),SEa,KDM(i),I:Swamp
Thing's,Doppleganger,
F:The Folk 3.00
132 CV(c),SEa,KDM(i),
V:Doppleganger 3.00
133 CV(c),SEa,KDM(i),R:General
Sunderland,V:Thunder Petal. . . 3.00
134 CV(c),SEa,KDM(i),Abby Leaves,
C:John Constantine 3.00
135 CV(c),SEa,KDM(i),A:J.Constantine,
Swamp Thing Lady Jane meld . 3.00
136 CV(c),RsB,KDM(i),A:Lady Jane,
Dr.Polygon,John Constantine . . 3.00
137 CV(c),E:NyC(s),RsB,KDM(i),
IR:Sunderland is Anton Arcane,
A:J.Constantine 3.00
138 CV(c),DiF(s),RGu,KDM,B:Mind
Fields 3.00
139 CV(c),DiF(s),RGu,KDM,A:Black
Orchid,In Swamp Thing's mind,
cont'd. fr.Black Orchid #5 . . . . . 3.00
140 B:Bad Gumbo 3.00
140a Platinum Ed. 10.00
141 A:Abigail Arcane 3.00
142 Bad Gumbo#3 . . . . 3.00
143 E:Bad Gumbo 3.00
144 In New York City 3.00
145 In Amsterdam 3.00
146 V:Nelson Strong. 3.00
147 Hunter 3.00
148 Sargon 3.00
149 Sargon 3.00
150 V:Sargon 3.50
151 . . . . 2.25
152 River Run,pt.1 . . . . 2.25
153 River Run 2.25
154 River Run 2.25
155 River Run 2.25
156 PJ,River Run. 2.25
157 . . . . 2.25

158 . . . 2.25
159 Swamp Dog. . . 2.25
160 PhH,KDM,Atmospheres . . . 2.25
161 Atmospheres . . . 2.25
162 Atmospheres . . . 2.25
163 Atmospheres . . . 2.25
164 . . . 2.25
165 CS,KDM,F:Chester Williams . . 2.25
166 PhH,KDM,Trial by Fire,pt.1 . . . 2.25
167 PhH,KDM,Trial by Fire,pt.2 . . . 2.25
168 MMr(s),PhH,KDM,Trial by Fire, pt.3 . . . 2.25
169 MMr(s),PhH,KDM,Trial by Fire, pt.4 . . . 2.25
170 MMr(s),PhH,KDM,Trial by Fire, pt.5 . . . 2.25
171 MMr(s),PhH,KDM,"Trial by Fire," pt.6 last issue . . . 2.25
Ann.#4 PB/AA,A:Batman . . . 2.75
Ann.#5 A:BrotherPower Geek. . . 3.25
Ann.#6 Houma . . . 3.50
Ann.#7 CV(c),NyC(s),MBu(i),Childrens Crusade,F:Tefe,A:Maxine,BU: Beauty and the Beast . . . 4.25

SWAMP THING
DC/Vertigo March, 2000

1 JRu,F:Tefe Holland . . . 2.50
2 JRu,new secrets. . . 2.50
3 JRu, . . . 2.50
4 Killing Time,pt.1 . . . 2.50
5 Killing Time,pt.2 . . . 2.50
6 Killing Time,pt.3 . . . 2.50
7 RM . . . 2.50
8 RM . . . 2.50
Secret Files #1, 64-pg. . . . 4.95

SWORD OF SORCERY
Feb.–March, 1973

1 MK(c),HC . . . 25.00
2 BWv,NA,Hc. . . . 30.00
3 BWv,HC,MK,WS. . . . 25.00
4 HC,WS. . . . 10.00
5 Nov.–Dec., 1973. . . . 10.50

SWORD OF THE ATOM
Sept., 1983

1 GK . . . 2.00
2 thru 4 GK . . . @2.00
Spec.#1 GK . . . 2.00
Spec.#2 GK . . . 2.00
Spec.#3 PB . . . 2.00

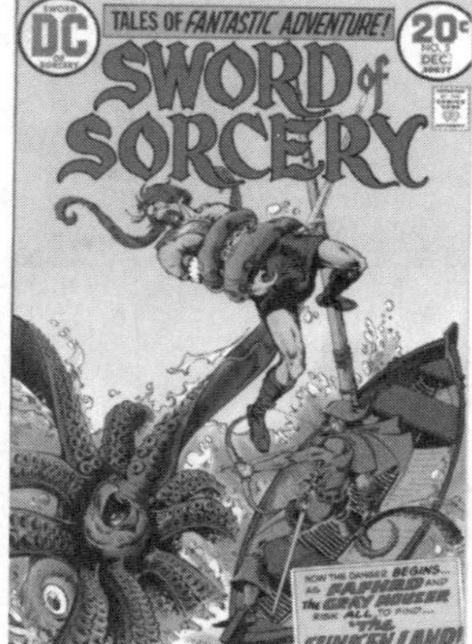

Sword of Sorcery #5
© DC Comics, Inc.

SYSTEM, THE
DC/Vertigo 1996

TPB by Peter Kuper . . . 12.95

Tailgunner Jo #4 © DC Comics, Inc.

TAILGUNNER JO
Sept., 1988

1 . . . 2.00
2 . . . 2.00
3 . . . 2.00
4 . . . 2.00
5 . . . 2.00
6 . . . 2.00

TAKION
1996

1 PuK,AaL,Josh Sanders becomes Takion . . . 2.00
2 thru 4 . . . @2.00
5 PuK,AaL,Adventures of Source Elemental" cont. . . . 2.00
6 PuK,AaL,Final Night tie-in. . . . 2.00
7 PuK,AaL,Arzaz trains Takion, final issue. . . . 2.00

TALES OF THE GREEN LANTERN CORPS
May, 1981

1 JSon,FMc,O:Green Lantern . . . 2.00
2 JSon,FMc. . . . 2.00
3 JSon,FMc. . . . 2.00

TALES OF THE LEGION OF SUPER HEROES
Aug., 1984
(Previously: Legion of Super Heroes)

314 KG,V:Ontiir . . . 2.00
315 KG(i),V:Dark Circle . . . 2.00
316 KG(i),O:White Witch. . . . 2.00
317 KG(i),V:Dream Demon . . . 2.00
318 KG(i),V:Persuader . . . 2.00
319 KG(i),V:Persuader, A:Superboy . . . 2.00
320 DJu,V:Magpie . . . 2.00
321 DJu,Exile,V:Kol . . . 2.00
322 DJu,Exile,V:Kol . . . 2.00
323 DJu,Exile,V:Kol . . . 2.00
324 DJu,EC,V:Dev-Em . . . 2.00
325 DJu,V:Dark Circle . . . 2.00
326 reprint of Baxter #1 . . . 2.00
327 reprint of Baxter #2 . . . 2.00
328 reprint of Baxter #3 . . . 2.00
329 reprint of Baxter #4 . . . 2.00
330 reprint of Baxter #5 . . . 2.00
331 reprint of Baxter #6 . . . 2.00
332 reprint of Baxter #7 . . . 2.00
333 reprint of Baxter #8 . . . 2.00
334 reprint of Baxter #9 . . . 2.00
335 reprint of Baxter #10 . . . 2.00
336 reprint of Baxter #11 . . . 2.00
337 reprint of Baxter #12 . . . 2.00
338 reprint of Baxter #13 . . . 2.00
339 reprint of Baxter #14 . . . 2.00
340 reprint of Baxter #15 . . . 2.00
341 reprint of Baxter #16 . . . 2.00
342 reprint of Baxter #17 . . . 2.00
343 reprint of Baxter #18 . . . 2.00
344 reprint of Baxter #19 . . . 2.00
345 reprint of Baxter #20 . . . 2.00
346 reprint of Baxter #21 . . . 2.00
347 reprint of Baxter #22 . . . 2.00
348 reprint of Baxter #23 . . . 2.00
349 reprint of Baxter #24 . . . 2.00
350 reprint of Baxter #25 . . . 2.00
351 reprint of Baxter #26 . . . 2.00
352 reprint of Baxter #27 . . . 2.00
353 reprint of Baxter #28 . . . 2.00
354 reprint of Baxter #29 . . . 2.00
Ann.#4 rep. Baxter Ann.#1 . . . 2.00
Ann.#5 rep. Baxter Ann.#2 . . . 2.00

TALES OF THE NEW TEEN TITANS
June, 1982

1 GP, O:Cyborg . . . 2.00
2 GP, O:Raven . . . 2.00
3 GD, O:Changling . . . 2.00
4 GP/EC,O:Starfire . . . 2.00

TALES OF THE TEEN TITANS
(see NEW TEEN TITANS)

TALES OF THE UNEXPECTED
1956–68

1 The Out-Of-The-World Club . 1,100.00
2 . . . 550.00
3 . . . 375.00
4 Seven Steps to the Unknown . 375.00
5 . . . 375.00
6 'The Girl in the Bottle'. . . . 275.00
7 NC(c),Pen That Never Lied. . . 275.00
8 . . . 275.00
9 LSt(c),The Amazing Cube. . . . 275.00
10 MMe(c),The Strangest Show On Earth . . . 275.00
11 LSt(c),Who Am I?. . . . 175.00
12 JK,Four Threads of Doom . . . 200.00
13 JK(c),Weapons of Destiny . . . 200.00
14 SMo(c),The Forbidden Game. 175.00
15 JK,MMe,Three Wishes to Doom . . . 200.00
16 JK,The Magic Hammer . . . 200.00
17 JK,Who Is Mr. Ashtar? . . . 200.00
18 JK(c),MMe,A Man Without A World . . . 200.00
19 NC,Man From Two Worlds. . . 150.00
20 NC(c),The Earth Gladiator . . . 150.00
21 JK,The Living Phantoms . . . 200.00
22 JK(c),The Man From Robot

Island 200.00
23 JK,The Invitation From Mars! . 200.00
24 LC,The Secret Of Planetoid Zero! 175.00
25 The Sorcerer's Asteroid! 175.00
26 MMe,The Frozem City 175.00
27 MMe,The Prison In Space . . . 175.00
28 The Melting Planet. 175.00
29 The Phantom Raider 175.00
30 The Jinxed Planet 175.00
31 RH,Keep Off Our Planet. 125.00
32 Great Space Cruise Mystery . 125.00
33 The Man Of 1,000 Planets . . . 125.00
34 Ambush In Outer Space. 125.00
35 MMe,I was a Space Refugee . 125.00
36 The Curse Of The Galactic Goodess 125.00
37 The Secret Prisoners Of Planet 13. . . . . 125.00
38 The Stunt Man Of Space 125.00
39 The Creatures From The Space Globe 125.00
40 B:Space Ranger,The Last Days Of Planet Mars!. 1,000.00
41 SMo(c),The Destroyers From The Stars! 300.00
42 The Secret Of The Martian Helmet. 300.00
43 The Riddle Of The Burning Treasures,I:Space Ranger . . 750.00
44 DD&SMo(c),The Menace Of The Indian Aliens 225.00
45 DD&SMo(c),The Sheriff From Jupiter. 225.00
46 DD&SMo(c),The Duplicate Doom!. 225.00
47 DD(c),The Man Who Stole The Solar System. 175.00
48 Bring 'Em Back Alive- From Space 175.00
49 RH,The Fantastic Lunar-Land 175.00
50 MA,King Barney The Ape. . . . 175.00
51 Planet Earth For Sale. 150.00
52 Prisoner On Pluto 150.00
53 InterplanetaryTroubleShooter . 150.00
54 The Ugly Sleeper Of Klanth, Dinosaur. 160.00
55 The Interplanetary Creature Trainer 150.00
56 B:Spaceman At Work,Invaders From Earth 150.00
57 The Jungle Beasts Of Jupiter. 150.00
58 The Boss Of The Saturnian Legion 150.00
59 The Man Who Won A World. . 150.00
60 School For Space Sleuths . . . 150.00
61 The Mystery Of The Mythical Monsters. 125.00
62 The Menace Of The Red Snow Crystals 125.00
63 Death To Planet Earth 125.00
64 Boy Usurper Of Planet Zonn . 125.00
65 The Creature That Couldn't Exist 125.00
66 MMe,Trap Of The Space Convict. 125.00
67 The Giant That Devoured A Village. 125.00
68 Braggart From Planet Brax . . . 75.00
69 Doom On Holiday Asteroid. . . . 75.00
70 The Hermit Of Planetoid X 75.00
71 Manhunt In Galaxy G-2!. 75.00
72 The Creature Of 1,000 Dooms. 75.00
73 The Convict Defenders Of Space!. 75.00
74 Prison Camp On Asteroid X-3!. 75.00
75 The Hobo Jungle Of Space . . . 75.00
76 The Warrior Of Two Worlds!. . . 75.00
77 Dateline-Outer Space 75.00
78 The Siren Of Space. 75.00
79 Big Show On Planet Earth! . . . 75.00
80 The Creature Tamer! 75.00
81 His Alien Master! 75.00
82 Give Us Back Our Earth!, E:Space Ranger. 75.00
83 DD&SMo(c),The Anti-Hex Merchant!. 45.00
84 DD&SMo(c),The Menace Of The 50-Fathom Men. 45.00
85 JkS(c),The Man Who Stole My Powers,B:Green Glob. 45.00
86 DD&SMo(c),They'll Never Take Me Alive! 40.00
87 JkS(c),The Manhunt Through Two Worlds 40.00
88 DD&SMo(c),GK,The Fear Master 40.00
89 DD,SMo(c),Nightmare on Mars 40.00
90 JkS(c),The Hero Of 5,000 BC . 40.00
91 JkS(c),The Prophetic Mirages, I:Automan. 50.00
92 The Man Who Dared To Die! . . 40.00
93 JkS(c),Prisoners Of Hate Island 40.00
94 The Monster Mayor - USA 40.00
95 The Secret Of Chameleo-Man . 40.00
96 Wanted For Murder...1966... 6966. 40.00
97 One Month To Die 40.00
98 Half-Man/Half Machine. 40.00
99 JkS(c),Nuclear Super-Hero! . . . 40.00
100 Judy Blonde, Secret Agent! . . 50.00
101 The Man in The Liquid Mask!. 35.00
102 Bang!Bang! You're Dead 35.00
103 JA,ABC To Disaster 35.00
104 NA(c),Master Of The Voodoo Machine. 35.00

Becomes:

UNEXPECTED, THE
1968–82

105 The Night I Watched Myself Die 40.00
106 B:Johnny Peril,The Doorway Into Time 25.00
107 MD,JkS(c),The Whip Of Fear! 28.00
108 JkS(c),Journey To A Nightmare 25.00
109 JkS(c),Baptism By Starfire! . . 25.00
110 NA(c),Death Town, U.S.A.! . . . 30.00
111 NC(c),Mission Into Eternity . . . 25.00
112 NA(c),The Brain Robbers! . . . 30.00
113 NA(c),The Shriek Of Vengeance 30.00

Tales of the Unexpected #9
© DC Comics, Inc.

114 NA(c),My Self-My Enemy! . . . 30.00
115 BWr,NA(c),Diary Of A Madman 30.00
116 NC(c),Express Train To Nowhere!. 25.00
117 NC(c),Midnight Summons The Executioner! 20.00
118 NA(c),A:Judge Gallows,Play A Tune For Treachery. 20.00
119 BWr,NC(c),Mirror,Mirror On The Wall 25.00
120 NC(c),Rambeau's Revenge . . 20.00
121 BWr,NA(c),Daddy's Gone-A-Hunting 25.00
122 WW,DG(c),The Phantom Of The Woodstock Festival. . . 20.00
123 NC(c),Death Watch! 20.00
124 NA(c),These Walls Shall Be Your Grave 22.00
125 NC(c),Screech Of Guilt! 20.00
126 ATh,NC(c),You Are Cordially Invited To Die! 20.00
127 GT,JK,ATh,NC(c),Follow The Piper To Your Grave 20.00
128 DW,BWr,NC(c),Where Only The Dead Are Free! 30.00
129 NC(c),Farewell To A Fading Star 20.00
130 NC(c),One False Step 20.00
131 NC(c),Run For Your Death! . . 20.00
132 MD,GT,NC(c),The Edge Of Madness 20.00
133 WW,JkS(c),A:Judge Gallows, Agnes Doesn't Haunt Here Anymore! 22.00
134 GT,NC(c),The Restless Dead. 20.00
135 NC(c),Death, Come Walk With Me! 20.00
136 SMo,GT,NC(c),An Incident of Violence 20.00
137 WW,NC(c),Dark Vengeance! . 18.00
138 WW,NC(c),Strange Secret of the Huan Shan Idol. 18.00
139 GT,NC(c),The 2 Brains of Beast Bracken!. 15.00
140 JkS(c),The Anatomy of Hate . 15.00
141 NC(c),Just What Did Eric See? 15.00
142 NC(c),Let The Dead Sleep! . . 15.00
143 NC(c),Fear is a Nameless Voice 15.00
144 NC(c),The Dark Pit of Dr. Hanley 15.00
145 NC(c),Grave of Glass. 15.00
146 NC(c),The Monstrosity! 15.00
147 NC(c),The Daughter of Dr. Jekyll 15.00
148 NC(c),Baby Wants Me Dead! . 15.00
149 NC(c),To Wake the Dead 15.00
150 NC(c),No One Escapes From Gallows Island 15.00
151 NC(c),Sorry, I'm Not Ready To Die! 15.00
152 GT,NC(c),Death Wears Many Faces. 15.00
153 NC(c),Who's That Sleeping In My Grave? 15.00
154 NC(c),Murder By Madness. . . 15.00
155 NC(c),Non-Stop Journey Into Fear 15.00
156 NC(c),A Lunatic Is Loose Among Us! 15.00
157 NC(c),The House of the Executioner 15.00
158 NC(c),Reserved for Madmen Only. 15.00
159 NC(c),A Cry in the Night 15.00
160 NC(c),Death of an Exorcist. . . 15.00
161 BWr,NC(c),Has Anyone Seen My Killer 25.00
162 JK,NC(c),I'll Bug You To Your Grave 18.00

DC COMICS

163 DD,LD(c),Room For Dying 8.00
164 House of the Sinister Sands. . . 8.00
165 LD(c),Slayride in July. 8.00
166 LD(c),The Evil Eyes of Night . . 8.00
167 LD(c),Scared Stiff 8.00
168 LD(c),Freak Accident 8.00
169 LD(c),What Can Be Worse
Than Dying?. 8.00
170 LD(c),Flee To Your Grave 8.00
171 LD(c),I.O.U. One Corpse 8.00
172 LD(c),Strangler in Paradise . . . 8.00
173 LD(c),What Scared Sally? 8.00
174 LD(c),Gauntlet of Fear 8.00
175 LD(c),The Haunted Mountain . . 8.00
176 JkS(c),Having A
Wonderful Crime 8.00
177 ECh(c),Reward for the Wicked. 8.00
178 LD(c),Fit To Kill! 8.00
179 LD(c),My Son, The Mortician . . 8.00
180 GT,LD(c),The Loathsome
Lodger of Nightmare Inn 11.00
181 LD(c),Hum of the Haunted 8.00
182 LD(c),Sorry, This Coffin
is Occupied 8.00
183 LD(c),The Dead Don't
Always Die 8.00
184 LD(c),Wheel of Misfortune!. . . . 8.00
185 LD(c),Monsters from a
Thousand Fathoms 8.00
186 LD(c),To Catch a Corpse 8.00
187 LD(c),Mangled in Madness . . . 8.00
188 LD(c),Verdict From The Grave . 8.00
189 SD,LD(c),Escape From The
Grave. 10.00
190 LD(c),The Jigsaw Corpse. . . . 10.00
191 MR,JO(c),Night of the Voodoo
Curse 11.00
192 LD(c),A Killer Cold & Clammy 10.00
193 DW,LD(c),Don't Monkey the
Murder 10.00
194 LD(c),Have I Got a Ghoul
For You 10.00
195 JCr,LD(c),Whose Face is at
My Window 10.00
196 LD(c),The Fear of Number 13 . 6.00
197 LD(c),Last Laugh of a Corpse . 6.00
198 JSn(c),Rage of the
Phantom Brain 6.00
199 LD(c),Dracula's Daughter. 6.00
200 GT,RA&DG(c),A:Johnny Peril,
House on the Edge of Eternity . 7.00
201 Do Unto Others 6.00
202 JO,LD(c),Death Trap 6.00
203 MK(c),Hang Down Your
Head, Joe Mundy 6.00
204 DN,JKu(c),Twinkle, Twinkle
Little Star 6.00
205 JkS,A:Johnny Peril,The Second
Possession of Angela Lake . . . 6.00
206 JkS,A:Johnny Peril,The
Ultimate Assassin. 6.00
207 JkS,A:Johnny Peril,Secret of
the Second Star 6.00
208 JkS,A:Johnny Peril,Factory
of Fear 6.00
209 JkS,Game for the Ghastly 6.00
210 Vampire of the Apes,Time
Warp 6.00
211 A:Johnny Peril,The Temple
of the 7 Stars 6.00
212 JkS,MK(c),A:Johnny Peril,The
Adventure of the Angel's Smile. 6.00
213 A:Johnny Peril,The Woman
Who Died Forever 6.00
214 JKu(c),Slaughterhouse Arena . 6.00
215 JKu(c),Is Someone
Stalking Sandra 6.00
216 GP,JKu(c),Samurai Nightmare . 6.00
217 ShM,DSp,EC(c),Dear Senator . 6.00
218 KG,ECh&DG(c),I'll Remember
You Yesterday 6.00
219 JKu(c),A Wild Tale 6.00
220 ShM,JKu(c),The Strange
Guide. 6.00
221 SD,ShM,JKu(c),Em the
Energy Monster 6.00
222 KG,SD(c). 6.00

TALES OF THE WILDERNESS

1 GK,special 2.00

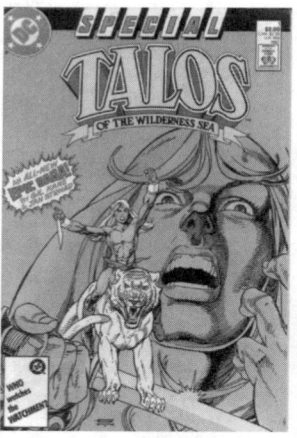

Talos of the Wilderness Sea #1
© DC Comics, Inc.

TALOS OF THE WILDERNESS SEA
Aug., 1987

1-shot GK 2.00

TANGENT COMICS
(All Oct., 1997)

The Atom #1 DJu,PR,V:Fatal Five . 3.00
The Flash #1, TDz,GFr,CaS 3.00
Doom Patrol #1 DJu,SCh,. 3.00
Green Lantern #1 JeR,JWi,MGy . . . 3.00
The Joker #1 KK,MHy, ... 3.00
Metal Men #1 MRz,MkK 3.00
Nightwing #1 JOs,JD 3.00
Sea Devils #1 KBk,VGi,TP 3.00
The Secret Six #1 CDi,TG, ... 3.00

TANGENT '98
(All June, 1998)

The Batman #1 DJu,KJ. 2.00
JLA #1 DJu,DBk,V:UltraHumanites . 2.00
Joker's Wild #1 KK. 2.00
Nightwing: Night Force #1 JOs 2.00
Powergirl #1 RMz 2.00
The Superman #1 Harvey Dent . . . 2.00
Tales of the Green Lantern #1 . . . . 2.00
The Trials of the Flash #1,
V:Plastic Man 2.00
Wonder Woman #1 PDa, ... 2.00

TANK GIRL
1995

1 Movie Adaptation 6.00

TANK GIRL: APOCALYPSE
1995–96

1 AIG,BBo(c). 2.25
2 AIG,BBo(c)Tank Girl Pregnant. . . 2.25
3 AIG,BBo(c). 2.25
4 AIG, finale 2.25

TANK GIRL: THE ODYSSEY
Vertigo 1995

1 New Limited Series. 2.25
2 BBo(c),Land of Milk & Honey . . . 2.25
3 I:The Sirens 2.25

Tarzan #213 © DC Comics, Inc.

TARZAN
April, 1972
(Prev. published by Gold Key)

207 JKu,O:Tarzan,pt.1 . . . . 30.00
208 thru 210 JKu,O:Tarzan,pt.2–4. 16.00
211 thru 258 Feb., 1977 . . . . . . @15.00

TARZAN FAMILY
Nov.–Dec., 1975
(Prev.: Korak, Son of Tarzan)

60 B:Korak 15.00
61 thru 66 Nov.–Dec.,1976 . . . . @10.00

TATTERED BANNERS
1998

1 (of 4) AIG(s),MMc. 3.00
2 AIG&KG(s),MMc. 3.00
3 AIG(s),MMc 3.00
4 AIG(s),MMc, conclusion 3.00

TEAM TITANS
1992–94

1 KM,Total Chaos#3,A:New Titans,
Deathstroke,V:Lord Chaos,
BU:KGa,Killowat. 2.50
1a BU:AV(i),Mirage 2.50
1b BU:MN,GP,Nightrider 2.50
1c BU:AH,Redwing 2.50
1d BU:GP(i),Terra 2.50
2 KM,Total Chaos#6,A:New
Titans, V:Chaos,C:Battalion . . . 2.00
3 KM,Total Chaos#9,V:Lord
Chaos, A:New Titans 2.00

4 KM,Titans Sell-Out#4, J:Battalion, Troia . . . 2.00
5 KM,A:Battalion . . . 2.00
6 ANi,A:Battalion . . . 2.00
7 PJ,I:Nightwing of 2001 . . . 2.00
8 PJ,A:Raven . . . 2.00
9 PJ,V:Bloodwing . . . 2.00
10 PJ,V:Vampiric Creatures . . . 2.00
11 PJ,F:Battalion . . . 2.00
12 PJ,F:Battalion . . . 2.00
13 PJ,New Direction . . . 2.00
14 PJ,V:Clock King,Chronos,Calendar Man,Time Commander . . . 2.00
15 PJ . . . 2.00
16 PJ,F:Nightrider . . . 2.00
17 PJ,A:Deathwing . . . 2.00
18 IR:Leader . . . 2.00
19 V:Leader . . . 2.00
20 PJ,V:Lazarium . . . 2.00
21 PJ,V:US Government . . . 2.00
22 PJ,A:Chimera . . . 2.25
23 PJ,I:Warhawk(Redwing) . . . 2.25
24 PJ,Zero Hour,R.Kole,last issue . . 2.25
Ann.#1 I:Chimera . . . 3.50
Ann.#2 PJ,Elseworlds Story . . . 3.75

TEEN BEAT

Nov.–Dec., 1967

1 Monkees photo . . . 25.00

Becomes:

TEEN BEAM

2 Monkees . . . 20.00

TEEN TITANS

[1st Series]

Jan., 1966

1 NC,Titans join Peace Corps . . 200.00
2 NC,I:Garn Akaru . . . 100.00
3 NC,I:Ding Dong Daddy . . . 60.00
4 NC,A:Speedy . . . 60.00
5 NC,I:Ant . . . 60.00
6 NC,A:Beast Boy . . . 45.00
7 NC,I:Mad Mod . . . 45.00
8 IN/JAb,I:Titans Copter . . . 45.00
9 NC,A:Teen Titan Sweatshirts . . 45.00
10 NC,I:Bat-Bike . . . 45.00
11 IN/NC A:Speedy . . . 40.00
12 NC,in Spaceville . . . 45.00
13 NC,Christmas story . . . 40.00
14 NC,I:Gargoyle . . . 40.00
15 NC,I:Capt. Rumble . . . 40.00
16 NC,I:Dimension X . . . 40.00
17 NC,A:Mad Mod . . . 40.00
18 NC,1:Starfire (Russian) . . . 40.00
19 GK,WW,J:Speedy . . . 40.00
20 NA,NC J:Joshua . . . 42.00
21 NA,NC,A:Hawk,Dove . . . 42.00
22 NA,NC,O:Wondergirl . . . 42.00
23 GK,NC,N:Wondergirl . . . 20.00
24 GK,NC . . . 20.00
25 NC,I:Lilith,A:J.L.A. . . . 20.00
26 NC,I:Mal . . . 20.00
27 NC . . . 20.00
28 NC,A:Ocean Master . . . 20.00
29 NC,A:Ocean Master . . . 20.00
30 NC,A:Aquagirl . . . 20.00
31 NC,GT,A:Hawk,Dove . . . 20.00
32 NC,I:Gnarrk . . . 15.00
33 GT,NS,A:Gnarrk . . . 15.00
34 GT,NC . . . 15.00
35 GT,NC,O:Mal . . . 15.00
36 GT,NC,JAp,V:Hunchback . . . 15.00
37 GT,NC . . . 15.00
38 GT,NC . . . 15.00
39 GT,NC,Rep.Hawk & Dove . . . 15.00
40 NC,A:Aqualad . . . 15.00
41 NC,DC,Lilith Mystery . . . 15.00
42 NC . . . 15.00
43 NC,Inherit the Howling Night . . 15.00
44 C:Flash . . . 15.00
45 IN,V:Fiddler . . . 15.00
46 IN,A:Fiddler . . . 15.00
47 C:Two-Face . . . 7.00
48 I:Bumblebee,Harlequin, A:Two-Face . . . 14.00
49 R:Mal As Guardian . . . 7.00
50 DH,I:Teen Titans West . . . 14.00
51 DH,A:Teen Titans West . . . 7.00
52 DH,A:Teen Titans West . . . 7.00
53 O:Teen Titans, A:JLA . . . 8.00

TEEN TITANS, THE

Aug., 1996

1 DJu(s),GP,"Titan's Children," pt.1 (of 3) . . . 5.00
2 DJu(s),GP,"Titan's Children," pt.2,V:Prysm . . . 4.00
3 DJu(s),GP,"Titan's Children," pt.3 . . . 3.50
4 DJu(s),GP,"Coming Out," pt.1, A:Robin . . . 3.00
5 DJu(s),GP,"Coming Out," pt.2 . . . 3.00
6 DJu(s),DJu,GP,F:Risk . . . 3.00
7 DJu(s),DJu,GP,The Atom quits team . . . 3.00
8 DJu(s),DJu,GP,J:Atom,V:Dark Nemesis . . . 3.00
9 DJu(s),DJu,GP,"Lost World of Skartaris," pt.1 . . . 3.00
10 DJu(s),DJu,GP,"Lost World of Skartaris," pt.2 . . . 3.00
11 DJu(s),DJu,GP,"Lost World of Skartaris" concl.,A:Warlord, . . . 3.00
12 DJu(s),DJu,GP,Original Titans, pt.1 (of 4) 48pg . . . 4.00
13 DJu,GP,Original Titans, pt.2 Genesis tie-in . . . 2.50
14 DJu,GP,Original Titans, pt.3 . . . 2.50
15 DJu,GP,Original Titans, pt.4 . . . 2.50
16 DJu,GP,aftermath . . . 2.50
17 DJu,PJ,team reunites . . . 2.50
18 DJu,PR . . . 2.50
19 DJu,PJ,Millennium Giants, A:Superman Red . . . 2.50
20 DJu, night with the Titans . . . 2.50
21 DJu,Titans Hunt,pt.1 . . . 2.50
22 DJu,Titans Hunt,pt.2 . . . 2.50
23 DJu,Titans Hunt,pt.3 . . . 2.50
24 DJu,Titans Hunt,pt.4, final issue . . . 2.50
Ann.#1 Pulp Heroes (High-Adventure) . . . 3.95

Teen Titans #45 © DC Comics, Inc.

Annual #1 (1967) 80-page, rep. . . . 5.00

TEEN TITANS SPOTLIGHT

Aug., 1986

1 DCw,DG,Starfire "Apartheid" . . . 2.50
2 DCw,DG,Starfire Apartheid#2 . . . 2.00
3 RA,Jericho . . . 2.00
4 RA,Jericho . . . 2.00
5 RA,Jericho . . . 2.00
6 RA,Jericho . . . 2.00
7 JG,Hawk . . . 2.50
8 JG,Hawk . . . 2.00
9 Changeling . . . 2.00
10 EL,Aqualad And Mento . . . 2.00
11 JO,Brotherhood of Evil . . . 2.00
12 EC,Wondergirl . . . 2.00
13 Cyborg . . . 2.00
14 1stNightwing/Batman Team-up . . . 2.50
15 EL,Omega Men . . . 2.00
16 Thunder And Lightning . . . 2.00
17 DH,Magennta . . . 2.00
18 ATi,Aqualad,A:Aquaman . . . 2.00
19 Starfire,A:Harbinger,Millennium X-over . . . 2.00
20 RT(i),Cyborg . . . 2.00
21 DSp,Flashback sty w/orig.Teen Titans . . . 1.00

TEMPEST

Mini-series Sept., 1996

1 (of 4) from Aquaman . . . 2.00
2 new costume . . . 2.00
3 O:Tempest . . . 2.00
4 finale . . . 2.00

TEMPUS FUGITIVE

1990

1 KSy,Time Travel,I:Ray 27 . . . 5.00
2 KSy,Viet Nam . . . 5.00
3 KSy,World War I . . . 5.00
4 KSy,final issue . . . 5.00

TERMINAL CITY

DC/Vertigo 1996–97

1 thru 3 DMt(s),MLr, . . . @2.50
4 DMt(s),MLr,I:Kid Gloves . . . 2.50
5 DMt(s),MLr,Missing link on the loose . . . 2.50
6 DMt(s),MLr, . . . 2.50
7 DMt(s),MLr,A:Lady in Red . . . 2.50
8 DMt(s),MLr, . . . 2.50
9 (of 9) DMt(s),MLr,finale . . . 2.50
TPB rep. mini-series . . . 20.00

TERMINAL CITY: AERIAL GRAFFITI

DC/Vertigo (Sept., 1997)

1 (of 5) DMt,MLr,MCo(c) . . . 2.50
2 DMt,MLr,MCo(c),F:Cosmo Quinn . . . 2.50
3 DMt,MLr,MCo(c), . . . 2.50
4 DMt,MLr,MCo(c) . . . 2.50

3-D BATMAN

1953, 1966

1 rep.Batman #42 & #48 . . . 900.00
1a A:Tommy Tomorrow (1966) . . 275.00

THRILLER

Nov., 1983

1 TVE . . . 2.00
2 TVE,O:Thriller . . . 2.00
3 TVE . . . 2.00

4 TVE 2.00
5 TVE,DG,Elvis satire 2.00
6 TVE,Elvis satire 2.00
7 TVE 2.00
8 TVE 2.00
9 TVE 2.00
10 TVE. 2.00
11 AN. 2.00
12 AN. 2.00

THRILLING COMICS
1999

1 CDi(s),RH,F:Hawkman & Wildcat. 2.00

THRILLKILLER
Elseworlds

1 HC(s),DIB,F:Robin and Batgirl . . 3.50
2 HC(s),DIB, ... 3.00
3 HC(s),DIB,conl.. . . . . 3.00

THRILLKILLERS '62
Feb., 1998

GN HC,DIB. 5.00

Timber Wolf #4 © DC Comics, Inc.

TIMBER WOLF
1992–93

1 AG(i),V:Thrust 2.00
2 V:Captain Flag 2.00
3 AG(i),V:Creeper 2.00
4 AG(i),V:Captain Flag. 2.00
5 AG(i),V:Dominators,Capt.Flag. . . 2.00

TIME BREAKERS
DC/Helix

1 (of 5) RaP(s),CWn,time paradoxes created 2.50
2 RaP(s),CWn, ... 2.50
3 RaP(s),CWn,expedition to 20th century England 2.50
4 RaP(s),CWn,Angela travels back in time 2.50
5 RaP(s),CWn,final issue. 2.50

TIME MASTERS
Feb., 1990

1 ATi,O:Rip Hunter,A:JLA. 2.50
2 ATi,A:Superman 2.00
3 ATi,A:Jonah Hex, Cave Carson. . 2.00
4 ATi,Animal Man #22 x-over 2.00
5 ATi,A:Viking Prince 2.00
6 ATi,A:Dr.Fate 2.00
7 ATi,A:GrLantern,Arion. 2.00
8 ATi,V:Vandal Savage 2.00

TIME WARP
Oct.–Nov., 1979

1 JAp,RB,SD,MK(c),DN,TS 15.00
2 DN,JO,TS,HC,SD,MK(c),GK . . . 10.00
3 DN,SD,MK(c),TS 10.00
4 MN,SD,MK(c),DN 10.00
5 DN,MK(c),July 1980 . . . . 8.00

TITANS
1999

1 MBu, new team, two covers 2.50
2 MBu,A:Superman 2.50
3 MBu 2.50
4 MBu,V:Goth 2.50
5 MBu,A:Siren 2.50
6 MBu,A:Green Lantern. 2.50
7 MBu,Velocity 10, pt.1 . . . . 2.50
8 MBu,Velocity 10, pt.2 . . . . 2.50
9 Day of Judgment x-over 2.50
10 MBu,F:Changeling & Deathstroke 2.50
11 MBu. 2.50
12 MBu,This Immortal Coil,pt.3. . . . 3.50
13 internal fight. 2.50
14 to Scotland 2.50
15 MBu,pt.1 . . . . 2.50
16 MBu,V:Gargoyle 2.50
17 ALa,into space. 2.50
18 ALa,into space,pt.2 . . . . 2.50
19 ALa,into space,pt.3 . . . . 2.50
20 ALa,end of Cyborg. 2.50
21 PaP,Hangmen 2.50
22 PaP,Arsenal vs. Deathstroke . . . 2.50
Ann.#1 Planet DC. 3.50
Spec. Secret Files #1 . . . . 5.00
Spec. Secret Files #2 . . . . 5.00
GN Scissors, Paper, Stone, manga style (1997) 5.00

TITANS SELL-OUT SPECIAL

1 SE,AV,I:Teeny Titans, w/Nightwing poster. 3.75

TITANS, THE/LEGION OF SUPER-HEROES: UNIVERSE ABLAZE
Jan. 2000

1 (of 4) DJu,PJ 5.00
2 DJu,PJ 5.00
3 DJu,PJ 5.00
4 DJu,PJ, concl. 5.00

TOMAHAWK
1950–72

1 Prisoner Called Tomahawk. . 1,400.00
2 FF(4pgs),Four Boys Against the Frontier 550.00
3 Warpath 325.00
4 Tomahawk Wanted: Dead or Alive. 325.00
5 The Girl Who Was Chief 325.00
6 Tomahawk-King of the Aztecs . 250.00
7 Punishment of Tomahawk 250.00
8 The King's Messenger 250.00
9 The Five Doomed Men 250.00
10 Frontied Sabotage 250.00
11 Girl Who Hated Tomahawk. . . 200.00
12 Man From Magic Mountain. . . 200.00
13 Dan Hunter's Rival. 200.00
14 The Frontier Tinker 200.00
15 The Wild Men of Wigwam Mountain 200.00
16 Treasure of the Angelique . . . 200.00
17 Short-Cut to Danger. 200.00
18 Bring In M'Sieur Pierre. 200.00
19 The Lafayette Volunteers 200.00
20 NC(c),The Retreat of Tomahawk 200.00
21 NC(c),The Terror of the Wrathful Spirit. 125.00
22 CS(c),Admiral Tomahawk. . . . 125.00
23 CS(c),The Indian Chief From Oxford. 125.00
24 NC(c),Adventure In the Everglades 125.00
25 NC(c),The Star-Gazer of Freemont 125.00
26 NC(c),Ten Wagons For Tomahawk 125.00
27 NC(c),Frontier Outcast. 125.00
28 I:Lord Shilling. 150.00
29 The Conspiracy of Wounded Bear. 175.00
30 The King of the Thieves 125.00
31 NC(c),The Buffalo Brave From Misty Mountain 125.00
32 NC(c),The Clocks That Went to War 125.00
33 The Paleface Tribe. 125.00
34 The Capture of General Washington 125.00
35 Frontier Feud. 125.00
36 NC(c),A Cannon for Fort Reckless 125.00
37 NC(c),Feathered Warriors . . . 125.00
38 The Frontier Zoo 125.00
39 The Redcoat Trickster 125.00
40 Fearless Fettle-Daredevil 125.00
41 The Captured Chieftain 125.00
42 The Prisoner Tribe 125.00
43 Tomahawk's Little Brother . . . 125.00
44 The Brave Named Tomahawk 125.00
45 The Last Days of Chief Tory. . 125.00
46 The Chief With 1,000 Faces. . . 75.00
47 The Frontier Rain-Maker 75.00
48 Indian Twin Trouble 75.00
49 The Unknown Warrior 75.00
50 The Brave Who Was Jinxed. . . 75.00
51 General Tomahawk 75.00
52 Tom Thumb of the Frontier. . . . 75.00
53 The Four-Footed Renegade. . . 75.00
54 Mystery of the 13th Arrows . . . 75.00
55 Prisoners of the Choctaw. 75.00
56 The Riddle of the Five Little Indians 75.00
57 The Strange Fight

Tomahawk #2 © DC Comics, Inc.

 All comics prices listed are for *Near Mint* condition.

at Fort Bravo 100.00
58 Track of the Mask 50.00
59 The Mystery Prisoner of
Lost Island 50.00
60 The Amazing Walking Fort. . . . 50.00
61 Tomahawk's Secret Weapons . 50.00
62 Strongest Man in the World . . . 50.00
63 The Frontier Super Men. 50.00
64 The Outcast Brave. 50.00
65 Boy Who Wouldn't Be Chief. . . 50.00
66 DD&SMo(c),A Trap For
Tomahawk 50.00
67 DD&SMo(c),Frontier Sorcerer . 50.00
68 DD&SMo(c),Tomahawk's
Strange Ally 50.00
69 DD&SMo(c),Tracker-King
of the Wolves 50.00
70 DD&SMo(c),Three Tasks
for Tomahawk. 50.00
71 DD&SMo(c),The Boy Who
Betrayed His Country 50.00
72 DD&SMo(c),The Frontier Pupil. 50.00
73 DD&SMo(c),The Secret of
the Indian Sorceress. 50.00
74 DD&SMo(c),The Great
Paleface Masquerade. 50.00
75 DD&SMo(c),The Ghost of
Lord Shilling 50.00
76 DD&SMo(c),The Totem-Pole
Trail 50.00
77 DD&SMo(c),The Raids of
the One-Man Tribe 50.00
78 DD&SMo(c),The Menace
of the Mask 50.00
79 DD&SMo(c),Eagle Eye's
Debt of Honor. 50.00
80 DD&SMo(c),The Adventures
of Tracker. 35.00
81 The Strange Omens of
the Indian Seer. 35.00
82 The Son of the Tracker 35.00
83 B:Tomahawk Rangers,
Against the Tribe 35.00
84 There's a Coward Among
the Rangers 35.00
85 The Wispering War 35.00
86 Rangers vs. King Colossus . . . 25.00
87 The Secrets of Sgt.
Witch Doctor 25.00
88 The Rangers Who Held
Back the Earth 25.00
89 The Terrible Tree-Man 25.00
90 The Prisoner In The Pit 25.00
91 The Tribe Below the Earth 25.00
92 The Petrified Sentry of
Peaceful Valley. 25.00
93 The Return of King Colosso . . . 25.00
94 Rip Van Ranger 25.00
95 The Tribe Beneath the Sea . . . 25.00
96 The Ranger Killers. 25.00
97 The Prisoner Behind the
Bull's-Eye. 25.00
98 The Pied Piper Rangers. 25.00
99 The Rangers vs.ChiefCobweb . 25.00
100 The Weird Water-Tomahawk . 30.00
101 Tomahawk, Enemy Spy 20.00
102 The Dragon Killers. 20.00
103 The Frontier Frankenstein . . . 20.00
104 The Fearful Freak of
Dunham's Dungeon 20.00
105 The Attack of the Gator God . 20.00
106 The Ghost of Tomahawk 20.00
107 Double-Cross of the
Gorilla Ranger 20.00
108 New Boss For the Rangers . . 20.00
109 The Caveman Ranger 20.00
110 Tomahawk Must Die. 20.00
111 Vengeance of the Devil-Dogs . 20.00
112 The Rangers vs. Tomahawk. . 20.00
113 The Mad Miser of
Carlisle Castle 20.00
114 The Terrible Power of
Chief Iron Hands 20.00
115 The Deadly Flaming Ranger. . 20.00
116 NA(c),The Last Mile of
Massacre Trail 20.00
117 NA(c),Rangers'Last Stand . . . 20.00
118 NA(c),Tomahawk, Guilty
of Murder 20.00
119 NA(c),Bait For a Buzzard 20.00
120 NC(c),The Coward Who
Lived Forever. 20.00
121 NA(c),To Kill a Ranger 20.00
122 IN(c),Must the Brave Die 20.00
123 NA(c),The Stallions of Death . 20.00
124 NA(c),The Valley of
No Return 20.00
125 NA(c),A Chief's Feather
For Little Bear 20.00
126 NA(c),The Baron of
Gallows Hill 20.00
127 NA(c),The Devil is Waiting . . . 20.00
128 NA(c),Rangers-Your 9
Lives For Mine 20.00
129 NA(c),Treachery at
Thunder Ridge 20.00
130 NA(c),Deathwatch at
Desolation Valley 20.00
131 JKu(c),B:Son of Tomahawk,
Hang Him High. 20.00
132 JKu(c),Small Eagle...Brother
Hawk 15.00
133 JKu(c),Scalp Hunter. 15.00
134 JKu(c),The Rusty Ranger. . . . 15.00
135 JKu(c),Death on Ghost
Mountain 15.00
136 JKu(c),A Piece of Sky 20.00
137 JKu(c),Night of the Knife 20.00
138 JKu(c),A Different Kind
of Christmas. 20.00
139 JKu(c),Death Council 25.00
140 Jku(c),The Rescue. 20.00

Tor #5 © DC Comics, Inc.

TOR

May–June, 1975

1 JKu,O:Tor. 15.00
2 thru 6, Tor reprints. . . . . @10.00

TOTAL JUSTICE

Sept., 1996

1 thru 3 CPr(s),RBe,DG, toy
line tie-in. . . . . @2.25

TOTAL RECALL

1990

1 Movie Adaption. 3.00

TOTEMS

DC/Vertigo Dec., 1999

GN TPe,DFg 5.95

TOXIC GUMBO

DC/Vertigo (March, 1998)

1-shot GN. 6.00

TRANSMETROPOLITAN

DC/Helix July, 1997

1 WEI,DaR,JeM, gonzo journalism
in 21st century 2.50
2 WEI,DaR,Angels 8 district. 2.50
3 WEI,DaR, riot in Angels 8 . . . . . . 2.50
4 WEI,DaR, Vs President of US. . . 2.50
5 WEI,DaR, Watches TV 2.50
6 WEI,DaR,evangelicals 2.50
7 WEI,DaR 2.50
8 WEI,DaR,AnotherColdMorning . . 2.50
9 WEI,DaR,Wild in the Country . . . 2.50
10 WEI,DaR,Freeze Me with
Your Kiss, pt.1 . . . . 2.50
11 WEI,DaR,Freeze Me, pt.2 . . . . . 2.50
12 WEI,DaR,Freeze Me, pt.3 . . . . . 2.50
13 WEI,DaR,JaL(c),Year of the
Bastard, pt.1. . . . . 2.50
14 WEI,DaR,JaL(c),Bastard,pt.2 . . . 2.50
15 WEI,DaR,JaL(c),Bastard,pt.3 . . . 2.50
16 WEI,DaR,Bastard,pt.4 . . . . 2.50
17 WEI,DaR,Bastard,pt.5 . . . . 2.50
18 WEI,DaR,Bastard, concl. 2.50
19 WEI,DaR,New Scum,pt.1 . . . . . . 2.50
20 WEI,DaR,New Scum,pt.2. . . . . . 2.50
21 WEI,DaR,New Scum,pt.3. . . . . . 2.50
22 WEI,DaR,New Scum,pt.4. . . . . . 2.50
23 WEI,DaR,New Scum,pt.5. . . . . . 2.50
24 WEI,DaR,New Scum,pt.6. . . . . . 2.50
25 WEI,DaR,JLe(c),Days in
the City #1 . . . . 2.50
26 WEI,DaR,RyR,JLe(c),Days in
the City #2 . . . . 2.50
27 WEI,DaR,RyR,JLe(c) 2.50
28 WEI,DaR,RyR,LonelyCity,pt.1 . . 2.50
29 WEI,DaR,RyR,LonelyCity,pt.2 . . 2.50
30 WEI,DaR,RyR,LonelyCity,pt.3 . . 2.50
31 WEI,DaR,RyR,F:Spider 2.50

Transmetropolitan #8
© DC Comics, Inc.

DC COMICS

32 WEI,DaR,RyR, ... 2.50
33 WEI,DaR,RyR 2.50
34 WEI,DaR,RyR,Gouge Away,pt.1. 2.50
35 WEI,DaR,RyR,Gouge Away,pt.2. 2.50
36 WEI,DaR,RyR,Gouge Away,pt.3. 2.50
37 WEI,DaR,Back to Basics,pt.1 . . . 2.50
38 WEI,DaR,Back to Basics,pt.2 . . . 2.50
39 WEI,DaR,Back to Basics,pt.3 . . . 2.50
TPB Lust For Life 15.00
TPB Year of the Bastard 12.95
TPB Back on the Street 7.95
TPB The New Scum, rep.#19–#24 . . . . 12.95
GN I Hate it Here 5.95

TRENCHCOAT BRIGADE
Vertigo 1999

1 (of 4) JNR(s),F:John Constantine, Mister E, Dr.Occult, Phantom Stranger 2.50
2 JNR 2.50
3 JNR 2.50
4 JNR, conclusion 2.50

TRIUMPH
[Mini-Series] 1995

1 From Zero Hour 2.00
2 Teamates Peril 2.00
3 V:Mind Readers 2.00

TROUBLE MAGNET
Dec., 1999

1 (of 4) KPl, F:robot whose mind has been stolen 2.50
2 KPl. 2.50
3 KPl 2.50
4 KPl,concl. 2.50

TRUE FAITH
DC/Vertigo (Aug., 1997)

TPB GEn,WaP, series rep. 13.00

TSR WORLDS
TSR 1990

1 I:SpellJammer 4.50

TV SCREEN CARTOONS
(see REAL SCREEN COMICS)

2020 VISIONS
DC/Vertigo April, 1997

1 (of 12) the Disunited States of America 2.25
2 JaD(s), ... 2.25
3 JaD(s), ... 2.25
4 JaD(s),WaP, "La Tormenta" pt.1 (of 3) 2.25
5 JaD(s),WaP, "La Tormenta" pt.2 . 2.25
6 JaD(s),WaP,"La Tormenta" pt.3 . . 2.25
7 JaD(s),"Renegade," pt.1 . . . . 2.25
8 JaD(s),"Renegade," pt.2 . . . . 2.25
9 JaD(s),"Renegade," pt.3 . . . . 2.25
10 JaD(s),Repro-Man,pt.1. . . . . 2.25
11 JaD(s),Repro-Man,pt.2. . . . . 2.25
12 JaD(s),Repro-Man,pt.3. . . . . 2.25

TWILIGHT
1990–91

1 JL,Last Frontier 5.50
2 JL,K.SorensenVs.T.Tomorrow . . . 5.00
3 JL,K.SorensenVs.T.Tomorrow . . . 5.00

UNAUTHORIZED BIO OF LEX LUTHOR

1 EB 4.00

UNCLE SAM
DC/Vertigo (Nov., 1997)

GN 1 (of 2) AxR 5.00
GN 2 AxR. 5.00
TPB 9.95

UNDERWORLD
Dec., 1987

1 EC,New Yorks Finest 2.00
2 EC,A:Black Racer. 2.00
3 EC,V:Black Racer. 2.00
4 EC,final issue 2.00

UNDERWORLD UNLEASHED
1995–96

1 PWa,F:Neron 5.00
2 PWa,Neron Vs.Green Lantern . . 4.00
3 PWa,conclusion 4.00
Abyss—Hell's Sentinel 1-shot 3.00
Apokolips-Dark Uprising 1-shot. . . . 3.00
Batman—Devil's Asylum 1-shot AIG,BSz 3.00
Patterns of Fear 1-shot 3.00

UNEXPECTED, THE
(see TALES OF THE UNEXPECTED)

UNKNOWN SOLDIER
(see STAR SPANGLED)

UNKNOWN SOLDIER
April, 1988

1 True Origin revealed,Viet Nam 1970 . . . . 4.00
2 Origin contd., Iran 1977 . . . . 3.00
3 Origin contd., Afghanistan1982 . . 3.00
4 Nicaragua. 3.00
5 Nicaragua contd. 3.00
6 . . . . 3.00
7 Libia 3.00
8 Siberia, U.S.S.R. 3.00
9 North Korea 1952 . . . . 3.00
10 C.I.A.. . . . . 3.00
11 C.I.A., Army Intelligence. 3.00
12 final issue,1989 . . . . 3.00

UNKNOWN SOLDIER
DC/Vertigo Feb. 1997

1 (of 4) GEn(s),KPl,F:maverick CIA agent. 7.00
2 GEn(s),KPl,search for Unknown Soldier continues 5.00
3 GEn(s),KPl,search for Unknown Soldier continues 5.00
4 GEn(s),KPl,intrigue, finale. 5.00
TPB series rep.. . . . . 13.00

UNTOLD LEGEND OF BATMAN
July, 1980

1 JA,JBy,(1st DC work)O:Batman . 6.00
2 JA,O:Joker&Robin 4.50
3 JA,O:Batgirl 4.50

V #13 © DC Comics, Inc.

V
(TV Adaptation)
Feb., 1985

1 CI/TD 3.00
2 thru 5 CI/TD . . . . @2.00
6 thru 16 CI/TD . . . . @2.00
17 & 18 DG. . . . . @2.00

VALOR
1992–94

1 N:Valor,A:Lex Luthor Jr. 2.50
2 MBr,AG,V:Supergirl 2.00
3 MBr,AG,V:Lobo. 2.00
4 MBr,AG,V:Lobo. 2.00
5 MBr,A:Blasters 2.00
6 A:Blasters,V:Kanjar Ru 2.00
7 A:Blasters. 2.00
8 AH(c),V:The Unimaginable 2.00
9 AH(c),PCu,A:Darkstar. 2.00
10 AH(c),V:Unimaginable 2.00
11 A:Legionnaires. 2.00
12 AH(c),B:D.O.A. 3.00
13 AH(c),D:Valor's Mom 3.00
14 AH(c),A:JLA,Legionnaires 2.50
15 SI(c),D.O.A #4. . . . . 2.00
16 CDo,D.O.A #5. . . . . 2.00
17 CDo,LMc,D:Valor 2.00
18 A:Legionnaires. 2.00
19 CDo,A:Legionnaires,V:Glorith. . . 2.00
20 CDo,A:Wave Rider 2.00
21 . . . . 2.00
22 End of an Era,pt.2 . . . . 2.00
23 Zero Hour 2.50

VAMPS
Vertigo 1994–95

1 BB(c) 3.00
2 BB(c) 3.00
3 thru 5 BB(c) . . . . @3.00
6 BB(c),last issue 3.00
TPB 10.00

VAMPS: HOLLYWOOD & VEIN
Vertigo 1996

1 F:Mink 2.50
2 . . . . 2.50
3 I:Maggot. 2.50
4 F:Mink,Screech 2.50
5 off to rescue Hugh Evans (of 6) . 2.50

6 . . . . 2.50

VAMPS: PUMPKIN TIME

Vertigo 1998

1 (of 3) Halloween mini-series 2.50
2 . . . . 2.50
3 . . . . 2.50

VERMILLION

DC/Helix Aug., 1996

1 ADv,MKu(c) Lucius Shepard story. 2.50
2 ADv,MKu(c) Jonathan Cave's cover blown 2.50
3 ADv,riot aboard space ship, Ildiko's tale 2.50
4 ADv,Starship's engines run wild . 2.50
5 ADv 2.50
6 ADv,Creation of Vermillion 2.50
7 ADv,Jonathan Cave discovers hiding place of enemy 2.50
8 ADv,"Joyland" 2.50
9 GEr, the library in Kaia Mortai . . . 2.50
10 GEr, "Lord Iron and Lady Manganese, pt.2 . . . . 2.50
11 GEr,"Lord Iron and Lady Manganese" concl. 2.50
12 final issue 2.50

V FOR VENDETTA

Sept., 1988

1 Reps.Warrior Mag(U.K.),I:V, A:M.Storm (Moore scripts) 5.00
2 Murder Spree 3.50
3 Govt. Investigators close in. 3.00
4 T.V. Broadcast take-over. 3.00
5 Govt.Corruption Expose 3.00
6 Evey in Prison 3.00
7 Evey released 2.50
8 Search for V,A:Finch. 2.50
9 V:Finch. 2.50
10 D:V 2.50
TPB 1990. . . . . 14.95

VERTIGO GALLERY: DREAMS AND NIGHTMARES

1995

1 Various artists. 3.50

VERTIGO JAM

1993

1 GF(c),NGa(s),ANo(s),PrM(s),GEn(s), JaD(s),KN,SDi,SEa,NyC(s),EiS,PhH, KDM(i),SeP,MiA,RaP(s),MPn(i), Vertigo Short Stories 4.50

VERTIGO PREVIEW

1992

Preview of new Vertigo titles, new Sandman story 2.00

VERTIGO VERITE: HELL ETERNAL

Feb, 1998

1-shot JaD,SeP 7.00

VERTIGO VERITE: THE SYSTEM

1 thru 3 . . . . @3.00
GN Seven Miles a Second 8.00

VERTIGO VERITE: THE UNSEEN HAND

DC/Vertigo 1996

1 thru 3 TLa. . . . . @2.50
4 TLa, final issue. 2.50

VERTIGO VISIONS: DR. OCCULT

1 F:Dr. Occult 4.00

VERTIGO VISIONS: DR. THIRTEEN

DC/Vertigo July, 1998

GN evil artificial intelligence 6.00

VERTIGO VISIONS: THE GEEK

1993

1 RaP(s),MiA,V:Dr.Abuse. 4.25

VERTIGO VISIONS: PHANTOM STRANGER

1993

1 AaK(s),GyD,The Infernal House . 3.75

VERTIGO VISIONS: THE EATERS

1995

1 I:The Quills. 5.00

VERTIGO VISIONS: TOMAHAWK

DC/Vertigo May, 1998

GN RaP,TY 5.00

VERTIGO: WINTER'S EDGE

DC/Vertigo 1998

TPB BB(c) rep. 8.00
GN Winter's Edge II 7.00
GN Winter's Edge III. 6.95

VEXT

1999

1 KG,MMK,MkM 2.50
2 KG,MMK,MkM 2.50
3 KG,MMK,MkM 2.50
4 KG,MMK,MkM 2.50
5 KG,MMK,MkM 2.50
6 KG,MMK,MkM, final issue. 2.50

VIGILANTE

Oct., 1983

1 KP,DG,F:Adrian Chase 3.50
2 KP 3.00
3 KP,Cyborg 2.50
4 DN,V:Exterminator 2.50
5 KP 2.50
6 O:Vigilante 3.00
7 O:Vigilante 3.00
8 RA,V:Electrocutioner. 2.50
9 RA,V:Electrocutioner. 2.50
10 RA,DG,avenges J.J. 2.50
11 RA,V:Controller 2.00
12 GK,"Journal" 2.00
13 GK,"Locke Room Murder" 2.00
14 RA,V:Hammer 2.00
15 RA,V:Electrocutioner 2.00
16 RA. 2.00
17 Moore 3.00
18 Moore 3.00
19 RA. 2.00
20 A:Nightwing 2.50
21 A:Nightwing 2.50
22 . . . . 2.00
23 V:Electrocutioner 2.00
24 "Mother's Day". 2.00
25 RM,V:Police Torturers 2.00
26 V:Electrocutioner 2.00
27 V:Electrocutioner 2.00
28 New Vigilante 2.00
29 RM,New Vigilante 2.00
30 RM,D:Glitz Jefferson 2.00
31 RM,New York Violence 2.00
32 RM,New York Violence 2.00

Vigilante #33 © DC Comics, Inc.

33 RM,V:Rapist 2.00
34 . . . . 2.00
35 JBy(c),O:MadBomber 2.00
36 MGr(c),V:Peacemaker 2.25
37 MGr,RM,V:Peacemaker 2.25
38 MGr,PeaceMaker. 2.25
39 White Slavery 2.00
40 HC(c),White Slavery 2.00
41 . . . . 2.00
42 A:Peacemaker,V:Terrorists. 2.00
43 V:PeaceMaker. 2.00
44 DC,V:Qurac. 2.00
45 I:Black Thorn. 2.00
46 Viigilante in Jail 2.00
47 A:Batman 2.50
48 I:Homeless Avenger 2.00
49 . . . . 2.00
50 KSy(c)D:Vigilante. 2.50
Ann.#1 . . . . 3.00
Ann.#2 V:Cannon 2.50

VIGILANTE: CITY LIGHTS, PRAIRIE JUSTICE

1995–96

1 JeR,MCo,(of 4). 2.50
2 JeR,V:Bugsy Siegel 2.50
3 JeR 2.50
4 finale 2.50

VIPER

1994

1 Based on the TV Show. 2.25
2 . . . . 2.00

3 . . . . 2.00
4 final issue 2.00

WANDERERS
June, 1988

1 I:New Team 3.00
2 V:The Performer 3.00
3 A:Legion of Superheroes 3.00
4 V:Controller Hunters 3.00
5 O:Wanderers 3.00
6 V:Terrorists 3.00
7 V:Medtorians 3.00
8 O:Psyche 3.00
9 O:Psyche 3.00
10 F:Quantum Queen 3.00
11 F:Quantum Queen 3.00
12 V:Aliens 3.00
13 V:Dinosaurs 3.00

WANTED: THE WORLD'S MOST DANGEROUS VILLAINS
July–Aug., 1972

1 rep. Batman,Green Lantern 4.00
2 Batman/Joker/Penguin 5.00
3 . . . . 3.00
4 . . . . 3.00
5 . . . . 3.00
6 . . . . 3.00
7 . . . . 3.00
8 . . . . 3.00
9 . . . . 3.00

WARLORD
Jan., 1976

1 MGr,O:Warlord 15.00
2 MGr,I:Machiste 10.00
3 MGr,`War Gods of Skartaris' 7.00
4 MGr,`Duel of the Titans' 7.00
5 MGr,`The Secret of Skartaris' . . . 7.00
6 MGr,I:Mariah,Stryker 5.00
7 MGr,O:Machiste 5.00
8 MGr,A:Skyra 5.00
9 MGr,N:Warlord 5.00
10 MGr,I:Ashiya 5.00
11 MGr,rep.1st Issue special #8 . . . 4.00
12 MGr,I:Aton 4.00
13 MGr,D:Stryker 4.00
14 MGr,V:Death 4.00

Warlord #87 © DC Comics, Inc.

15 MGr,I:Joshua 4.00
16 MGr,I:Saaba 4.00
17 MGr,`Citadel of Death' 4.00
18 MGr,I:Shadow 4.00
19 MGr,`Wolves of the Steppes' . . . 4.00
20 MGr,I:Joshua clone 5.00
21 MGr,D:Joshua clone,Shadow . . . 3.00
22 MGr`Beast in the Tower' 3.00
23 MGr,`Children of Ba'al' 3.00
24 MGr,I:ligia 3.00
25 MGr,I:Ahir 3.00
26 MGr,`The Challenge' 3.00
27 MGr,`Atlantis Dying' 3.00
28 MGr,I:Wizard World' 3.00
29 MGr,I:Mongo Ironhand' 3.00
30 MGr,C:Joshua 3.00
31 MGr,`Wing over Shamballah' . . . 3.00
32 MGr,I:Shakira 3.00
33 MGr,Birds of Prey,A:Shakira 3.00
34 MGr,Sword of the Sorceror, I:Hellfire 3.00
35 MGr,C:Mike Grell 3.00
36 MGr,`Interlude' 3.00
37 MGr,JSn,I:Firewing,B:Omac 6.00
38 MGr,I:Jennifer,A:Omac 3.00
39 MGr,JSn,`Feast of Agravar' 4.00
40 MGr,N:Warlord 3.00
41 MGr,A:Askir 2.50
42 MGr,JSn,A:Tara,Omac 3.50
43 MGr,JSn,`Berserk'A:Omac 3.50
44 MGr,`The Gamble' 3.00
45 MGr,`Nightmare in Vista Vision',A:Omac 3.00
46 MGr,D:Shakira 3.00
47 MGr,I:Mikola,E:Omac 3.00
48 MGr,EC,TY,I:Arak,Claw(B) 3.00
49 MGr,TY,A:Shakira,E:Claw 2.50
50 MGr,`By Fire and Ice' 2.50
51 MGr,TY,rep.#1, I(B):Dragonsword 2.00
52 MGr,TY,`Back in the U.S.S.R. . . 2.50
53 MT,TY,`Sorcerer's Apprentice' . . 2.00
54 MT,`Sorceress Supreme', E:Dragonsword 2.00
55 MT,`Have a Nice Day' 2.00
56 MT,JD,I:Gregmore,(B:)Arion 2.00
57 MT,`The Two Faces of Travis Morgan' 2.00
58 MT,O:Greamore 2.00
59 MGr,A:Joshua 2.00
60 JD,`Death Dual' 2.00
61 JD,A:Greamore 2.00
62 JD,TMd,A:Mikola,E:Arion 2.00
63 JD,RR,I(B):Barren Earth 2.00
64 DJu,RR`Elsewhere' 2.00
65 DJu,RR,A:Wizard World, No Barren Earth 2.00
66 DJu`Wizard World', No Barren Earth 2.00
67 DJu,RR,`The Mark' 2.00
68 DJu,RR 2.00
69 DJu,RR 2.00
70 DJu,`Outback' 2.00
71 DJu/DA,`The Journey Back' No Barren Earth 2.00
72 DJu,DA,I:Scarhart,No Barren Earth 2.00
73 DJ,DA,`Cry Plague' 2.00
74 DJu,No Barren Earth 2.00
75 DJu,`All Dreams Must Pass' No Barren Earth 2.00
76 DJu,DA,RR,A:Sarga 2.00
77 DJu,DA,RR,Let My People Go . . 2.00
78 DJu,RR,`Doom's Mouth' 2.00
79 PB,RM,`Paradox',No Barren Earth 2.00
80 DJu,DA,RR,`Future Trek' 2.00
81 DJu,DA,RR,`Thief's Magic' 2.00
82 DJu,DA,RR,`Revolution' 2.00
83 DJu,RR,`All the President's Men' 2.00

Warlord #124 © DC Comics, Inc.

84 DJu,DA,RR,`Hail to the Chief' . . 2.00
85 DJu,RR,`The Price of Change' . . 2.00
86 DJ,DA,No Barren Earth 2.00
87 DJu,RB,RR,I:Hawk 2.00
88 DJu,RB,RR,I:Patch,E:Barren Earth 2.00
89 RB,I:Sabertooth 2.00
90 RB,`Demon's of the Past' 2.00
91 DJu,DA,I:Maddox,O:Warlord O:Jennifer 2.00
92 NKu,`Evil in Ebony' 2.00
93 RR,A:Sabertooth 2.00
94 `Assassin's Prey' 2.00
95 AKu,`Dragon's Doom' 2.00
96 `Nightmare Prelude' 2.00
97 RB,A:Saaba,D:Scarhart 2.00
98 NKu,Crisis tie-in 2.00
99 NKu`Fire and Sword' 2.00
100 AKu,D:Greamore,Sabertooth . . 2.00
101 MGr,`Temple of Demi-god' 2.00
102 I:Zuppara,Error-Machiste with two hands 2.00
103 JBi,`Moon Beast' 2.00
104 RR,`Dragon Skinner' 2.00
105 RR,`Stalilers of Skinner' 2.00
106 RR,I:Daimon 2.00
107 RR,`Bride of Yano' 2.00
108 RR,I:Mortella 2.00
109 RR,A:Mortella 2.00
110 RR,A:Skyra III 2.00
111 RR,`Tearing o/t Island Sea' 2.00
112 RR,`Obsession' 2.00
113 RR,`Through Fiends Destroy Me' 2.00
114 RR,`Phenalegeno Dies' 2.00
115 RR,`Citadel of Fear' 2.00
116 RR,`Revenge of the Warlord' . . 2.00
117 RR,A:Power Girl 2.00
118 RR,A:Power Girl 2.00
119 RR,A:Power Girl 2.00
120 ATb,A:Power Girl 2.00
121 ATb,A:Power Girl 2.00
122 ATb,A:Power Girl 2.00
123 JD,TMd,N:Warlord 2.00
124 JD,TMd,I:Scavenger 2.00
125 JD,TMd,D:Tara 2.00
126 JD,TMd,A:Machiste 2.00
127 JD,`The Last Dragon' 2.00
128 JD,I:Agife 2.00
129 JD,Vision of Quest 2.00
130 JD,A:Maddox 2.00
131 JD,RLd,`Vengeful Legacies' . . . 3.00
132 `A New Beginning' 2.00
133 JD,final issue (44pg) 2.00
Ann.#1 MGr,A:Shakira 3.00

Ann.#2 I:Krystovar 2.00
Ann.#3 DJu,`Full Circle' 2.00
Ann.#4 A:New Gods, Legends tie-in 2.00
Ann.#5 AKu,Hellfire 2.00
Ann.#6 F:New Gods 2.00
TPB Warlord:Savage Empire, Rep.#1-#10,#12,Special #8. . . 19.95

[Limited Series]

1 Travis Morgan retrospective 2.00
2 Fate of T. Morgan revealed. 2.00
3 Return of Deimos 2.00
4 V:Deimos 2.00
5 MGr(c),Skartaros at War. 2.00
6 finale 2.00

WAR OF THE GODS

1 GP,A:Lobo,Misc.Heroes,Circe (direct) 2.00
2 GP,A:Misc.Heroes,V:Circe, w/poster 2.00
2a (Newsstand) 2.00
3 GP,A:Misc.Heroes,V:Circe, w/poster 2.00
3a Newsstand 2.00
4 GP,A:Misc.Heroes,V:Circe, w/poster 2.00
4a Newsstand 2.00

WASTELAND

Dec., 1987

1 Selection of Horror stories 2.00
2 . . . . 2.00
3 . . . . 2.00
4 . . . . 2.00
5 `The big crossover story' 2.00
6 . . . . 2.00
7 `Great St.Louis Electrical Giraffe Caper'. 2.00
8 `Dead Detective'. 2.00
9 . . . . 2.00
10 TT,African Folk Tale 2.00
11 `Revenge o/t Swamp Creature' . 2.00
12 JO,`After the Dead Detective'. . . 2.00
13 TT(c),JO 2.00
14 JO,RM,`Whistling Past the Graveyard' 2.00
15 JO,RM. 2.00
16 JO. 2.00
17 JO. 2.00
18 JO,RM,final issue 2.00

Watchman #9 © DC Comics, Inc.

WATCHMEN

Sept., 1986

1 B:AMo,DGb,D:Comedian 7.50
2 DGb,Funeral for Comedian. 5.00
3 DGb,F:Dr.Manhattan. 5.00
4 DGb,O:Dr.Manhattan 5.00
5 DGb,F:Rorschach. 5.00
6 DGb,O:Rorschach 5.00
7 DGb,F:Nite Owl 5.00
8 DGb,F:Silk Spectre. 5.00
9 DGb,O:Silk Spectre 5.00
10 DGb,A:Rorschach 5.00
11 DGb,O:Ozymandius. 5.00
12 DGb,D:Rorsharch 5.00
TPB rep.#1-#12 . . . . 14.95
TPB 20.00

WEB, THE

Impact 1991–92

1 I:Gunny, Bill Grady, Templar 2.00
2 O:The Web, I:Brew, Jump, Sunshine Kid 2.00
3 Minions of Meridian, I:St.James . 2.00
4 Agent Jump vs. UFO 2.00
5 Agent Buster/Fly team-up V:Meridian 2.00
6 I:Posse,A:Templar 2.00
7 V:Meridian's Forces 2.00
8 R: Studs. 2.00
9 Earthquest,pt.1. . . . . 2.50
10 V:Templar 2.00
11 V:Templar 2.00
12 “The Gauntlet”,A:Shield 2.00
13 Frenzy#1. . . . . 2.00
14 Frenzy#2. . . . . 2.00
Ann.#1 Earthquest,w/trading card . . 2.50

WEIRD, THE

April, 1988

1 BWr,A:JLI 4.00
2 BWr,A:JLI 3.00
3 BWr,V:Jason. 3.00
4 final issue. 2.50

WEIRD

DC/Paradox Press 1997

1 B&W magazine. 3.00
2 . . . . 3.00
3 . . . . 3.00

WEIRD WAR TALES

Sept.–Oct., 1971

1 JKu(c),JKu,RH,Fort which Did Not Return 175.00
2 JKu,MD,Military Madness 65.00
3 JKu(c),RA,The Pool 55.00
4 JKu(c),Ghost of Two Wars 50.00
5 JKu(c),RH,Slave 50.00
6 JKu(c),Pawns, The Sounds of War 30.00
7 JKu(c),JKu,RH,Flying Blind 30.00
8 NA(c),The Avenging Grave 45.00
9 NC(c),The Promise 30.00
10 NC(c),Who is Haunting the Haunted Chateau 30.00
11 NC(c),ShM,Oct. 30, 1918: The German Trenches, WWI . 20.00
12 MK(c),God of Vengeance. 20.00
13 LD(c),The Die-Hards 20.00
14 LD(c),ShM,The Ghost of McBride's Woman 20.00
15 LD(c),Ace King Just Flew In From Hell 20.00
16 LD(c),More Dead Than Alive . . 20.00
17 GE(c),Dead Man's Hands 20.00
18 GE(c),Captain Dracula 20.00
19 LD(c),The Platoon That Wouldn't Die. 20.00
20 LD(c),Operation Voodoo 20.00
21 LD(c),One Hour To Kill. 15.00
22 LD(c),Wings of Death. 15.00
23 LD(c),The Bird of Death 15.00
24 LD(c),The Invisible Enemy 15.00
25 LD(c),Black Magic...White Death 15.00
26 LD(c),Jump Into Hell 15.00
27 LD(c),Survival of the Fittest. 15.00
28 LD(c),Isle of Forgotten Warriors 15.00
29 LD(c),Breaking Point 15.00
30 LD(c),The Elements of Death. . 15.00
31 LD(c),Death Waits Twice 15.00
32 LD(c),The Enemy, The Stars . . 15.00
33 LD(c),Pride of the Master Race 15.00
34 LD(c),The Common Enemy . . . 15.00
35 LD(c),The Invaders 15.00
36 JKu(c),Escape 20.00
37 LD(c),The Three Wars of Don Q 7.00
38 JKu(c),Born To Die 7.00
39 JKu(c),The Spoils of War 7.00
40 ECh(c),Back From The Dead . . . 7.00
41 JL(c), The Dead Draftees of Regiment Six 7.00
42 JKu(c),Old Soldiers Never Die 7.00
43 ECh(c),Bulletproof 7.00
44 JKu(c),ShM,The Emperor Weehawken 7.00
45 JKu(c),The Battle of Bloody Valley. 7.00
46 Kill Or Be Killed 7.00
47 JKu(c),Bloodbath of the Toy Soldiers 7.00
48 JL(c),Ultimate Destiny 7.00
49 The Face Of The Enemy 7.00
50 ECh(c),-An Appointment With Destiny. 7.00
51 JKu(c),Secret Weapon. 7.00
52 JKu(c),The Devil Is A Souvenir Hunter 7.00
53 JAp(c), Deadly Dominoes 7.00
54 GM(c),Soldier of Satan 7.00
55 JKu(c),A Rebel Shall Rise From The Grave. 7.00
56 AM(c),The Headless Courier . . . 7.00
57 RT(c),Trial By Combat 7.00
58 JKu(c),Death Has A Hundred Eyes 7.00
59 The Old One 7.00
60 JKu(c),Night Flight. 7.00
61 HC(c),Mind War. 5.00
62 JKu(c),The Grubbers 5.00
63 JKu(c),Battleground 5.00
64 JKu(c),Deliver Me For D-Day . . . 5.00
65 JKu(c),The Last Cavalry Charge 5.00
66 JKu(c),The Iron Star 5.00
67 JKu(c),The Attack of the Undead 5.00
68 FM,JKu(c),The Life and Death of Charlie Golem 5.00
69 JKu(c),The Day After Doomsday 5.00
70 LD(c),The Blood Boat 5.00
71 LD(c),False Prophet. 5.00
72 JKu(c),Death Camp 5.00
73 GE(c),The Curse of Zopyrus . . . 5.00
74 GE(c),March of the Mammoth . . 5.00
75 JKu(c),The Forgery 5.00
76 JKu(c),The Fire Bug. 5.00
77 JKu(c),Triad. 5.00
78 JKu(c),Indian War In Space 5.00
79 JKu(c),The Gods Themselves . . 5.00
80 JKu(c),An Old Man's Profession. 5.00
81 JKu(c),It Takes Brains To Be A Killer 5.00

82 GE(c),Funeral Fire 5.00
83 GE(c),Prison of the Mind 5.00
84 JKu(c),Devil's Due 5.00
85 thru 124 June 1983 . . . . @5.00

WEIRD WAR TALES
DC/Vertigo April, 1997

1 (of 4) anthology 3.00
2 MK(c) 3.00
3 . . . . 3.00
4 final issue 3.00
Spec.#1 GEn (2000) 5.00

ALL-STAR WESTERN
Aug.–Sept., 1970

1 NA(c),CI 35.00
2 NA(c),GM,B:Outlaw 16.00
3 NA(c),GK,O:El Diablo 15.00
4 NA(c),GK,JKu,GM 15.00
5 NA(c),JAp,E:Outlaw 15.00
6 GK,B:Billy the Kid 15.00
7 . . . . 20.00
8 E:Billy the Kid 20.00
9 FF 20.00
10 GM,I:Jonah Hex 225.00
11 GM,A:Jonah Hex 125.00

Becomes:

WEIRD WESTERN TALES
June–July, 1972

12 NA,BWr,JKu 75.00
13 . . . . 50.00
14 ATh 25.00
15 NA(c),GK 25.00
16 thru 28 . . . . @15.00
29 O:Jonah Hex 25.00
30 . . . . 10.00
31 thru 38 . . . . @10.00
39 I&O:Scalphunter 10.00
40 thru 70 . . . . @7.00

Weird Western Tales #28
© DC Comics, Inc.

WEIRD WORLDS
Aug.–Sept., 1971

1 JO,MA,John Carter 35.00
2 NA,JO(c),MA,BWr 30.00
3 MA,NA 15.00
4 MK(c),MK 10.00
5 MK(c),MK 10.00
6 MK(c),MK 10.00
7 John Carter ends 10.00
8 HC,I:Iron Wolf 10.00
9 and 10 HC . . . . @10.00

WESTERN COMICS
Jan.–Feb., 1948

1 MMe,B:Vigilante,Podeo Rick, Wyoming Kid,Cowboy Marshal 650.00
2 MMe,Vigilante vs. Dirk Bigger . 325.00
3 MMe,Vigilante vs. Pecos Kid . . 275.00
4 MMe,Vigilante as Pecos Kid . . 275.00
5 I:Nighthawk 225.00
6 Wyoming Kid vs. `The Murder Mustang' 200.00
7 Wyoming Kid in `The Town That Was Never Robbed' . . . 200.00
8 O:Wyoming Kid 250.00
9 Wyoming Kid vs. Jack Slaughter 175.00
10 Nighthawk in `Tunnel of Terror' 175.00
11 Wyoming Kid vs. Mayor Brock 150.00
12 Wyoming Kid vs. Baldy Ryan . 150.00
13 I:Running Eagle 150.00
14 Wyoming Kid in `The Siege of Praire City 150.00
15 Nighthawk in `Silver, Salt and Pepper 150.00
16 Wyoming Kid vs. Smilin' Jim . 150.00
17 BP,Wyoming Kid vs. Prof. Penny 150.00
18 LSt on Nighthawk,WyomingKid in `Challenge of the Chiefs' . . 150.00
19 LSt,Nighthawk in `The Invisible Rustlers' 150.00
20 LSt,Nighthawk in `The Mystery Mail From Defender Dip' 100.00
21 LSt,Nighthawk in `Rattlesnake Hollow' 100.00
22 LSt,I:Jim Pegton 100.00
23 LSt,Nighthawk reveals ID to Jim 100.00
24 The $100,000 Impersonation . 100.00
25 V:Souix Invaders 100.00
26 The Storming of the Sante Fe Trail 100.00
27 The Looters of Lost Valley . . . 100.00
28 The Thunder Creek Rebellion 100.00
29 Six Guns of the Wyoming Kid. 100.00
30 V:Green Haired Killer 100.00
31 The Sky Riding Lawman 100.00
32 Death Rides the Stage Coach 100.00
33 . . . . 100.00
34 Prescription For Killers 100.00
35 The River of Rogues 100.00
36 Nighthawk(c),Duel in the Dark . 75.00
37 The Death Dancer 75.00
38 Warpath in the Sky 75.00
39 Death to Fort Danger 75.00
40 Blind Man's Bluff 75.00
41 thru 60 . . . . @75.00
61 thru 85 . . . . @50.00

WHERE IN THE WORLD IS CARMEN SANDIEGO?
DC/Helix 1996

1 thru 3 . . . . @2.00
4 . . . . 2.00

WHY I HATE SATURN
DC/Vertigo Dec., 1999

TPB 17.95

WILL EISNER LIBRARY
April, 2000

TPB The Building 9.95
TPB City People Notebook 9.95
TPB A Contract with God 12.95
GN The Dreamer 7.95
TPB Dropsie Avenue 15.95
TPB A Family Matter 15.95
TPB Invisible People 12.95
TPB Life on Another Planet 12.95
HC Minor Miracles,four tales 30.00
TPB Minor Miracles 13.00
TPB New York: The Big City 12.95
TPB To the Heart of the Storm . . . 14.95
TPB Will Eisner Reader 10.00
HC The Spirit Archives Vol.1 . . . . . 49.95
HC The Spirit Archives Vol.2 . . . . . 49.95

WHO'S WHO
1985–87

1 . . . . 3.50
2 thru 9 . . . . @3.00
10 inc. 3.00
11 inc. Infinity Inc. 3.00
12 inc. Kamandi 3.00
13 inc. Legion of Super Heroes/ Villains 3.00
14 inc. 3.00
15 inc. Metal Men 3.00
16 inc. New Gods 3.00
17 inc. Outsiders 3.00
18 inc. Power Girl 3.00
19 inc. Robin 3.00
20 inc. 3.00
21 inc. The Spectre 3.00
22 inc. Superman 3.00
23 inc. Teen Titans 3.00
24 inc. Unknown Soldier 3.00
25 inc. 3.00
26 inc. 3.00

WHO'S WHO
(PACKET)

1 inc. Superman 6.00
1a 2nd printing 5.50
2 inc. Flash 5.50
2a 2nd printing 5.00
3 inc. Green Lantern 5.50
4 inc. Wonder Woman 5.50
5 inc. Batman 5.50
6 inc. Hawkman 5.50
7 inc. Shade 5.50
8 inc. Lobo 6.00
9 inc. Legion of Super-Heroes 5.50
10 inc. Robin 5.50
11 inc. L.E.G.I.O.N. '91 . . . . 5.50
12 inc. Aquaman 5.50
13 Villains issue, inc. Joker 6.00
14 inc. New Titans 5.50
15 inc. Doom Patrol 5.50
16 inc. Catwoman,final issue 5.00

WHO'S WHO IN IMPACT

1 Shield 4.95
2 Black Hood 4.95

WHO'S WHO IN THE LEGION
1987–88

1 History/Bio of Legionnaires 3.00
2 inc. Dream Girl 3.00
3 inc. Karate Kid 3.00
4 inc. Lightning Lad 3.00
5 inc. Phantom Girl 3.00
6 inc. Timber Wolf 3.00
7 wraparound(c) 3.00

WHO'S WHO IN STAR TREK
1987

1 HC(c) 6.00
2 HC(c) 6.00

WHO'S WHO UPDATE '87

1 inc. Blue Beetle 3.00
2 inc. Catwoman 3.00
3 inc. Justice League. 3.00
4 . . . . 3.00
5 inc. Superboy 3.00

WHO'S WHO UPDATE '88

1 inc. Brainiac 3.00
2 inc. JusticeLeagueInternational. . 3.00
3 inc. Shado 3.00
4 inc. Zatanna 3.00

WHO'S WHO UPDATE '93

1 F:Eclipso,Azrael 5.25

WILD DOG

Sept., 1987

1 mini series DG(i),I:Wild Dog 3.00
2 DG(i),V:Terrorists 2.50
3 DG(i) 2.50
4 DG(i),O:Wild Dog, final issue . . . 2.50
Spec.#1 . . . . 2.50

WILD WILD WEST

1999

1-shot movie adaptation 5.00

WINDY & WILLY

May–June, 1969

1 thru 4 . . . . @20.00

WISE SON: THE WHITE WOLF

DC/Milestone Sept., 1996

1 by Ho Che Anderson 2.50
2 thru 4 . . . . @2.50

WITCHCRAFT

Vertigo 1994

1 CV(c),Three Witches from Sandman 4.00
2 F:Mildred 3.50
3 Final issue 3.25
TPB rep. mini-series. 14.95

WITCHCRAFT: LA TERREUR

Feb., 1998

1 (of 3) JeR, sequel. 2.50
2 JeR 2.50
3 JeR 2.50

WITCHING HOUR

1969–78

1 NA,ATh. 100.00
2 ATh 40.00
3 ATh,BWr. 50.00
4 ATh 25.00
5 ATh,BWr. 40.00
6 ATh 40.00
7 ATh 25.00
8 NA,ATh. 25.00
9 ATh 25.00
10 ATh 25.00
11 ATh 25.00
12 ATh 25.00
13 NA. 30.00
14 AW,CG,NA(c) 35.00
15 thru 20 . . . . @15.00
21 thru 30 . . . . @12.00

Witching Hour #14 © DC Comics, Inc.

31 thru 37 . . . . @12.00
38 100-pg. 40.00
39 thru 60 . . . . @10.00
61 thru 85 . . . . @8.00

THE WITCHING HOUR

DC/Vertigo Dec. 1999

1 (of 3) JLb,CBa,ATi 5.95
2 JLb,CBa,ATi 5.95
3 JLb,CBa,ATi, concl. 5.95
HC series rep. JLb, CBa 29.95

WONDER WOMAN

1942–86

1 O:Wonder Woman,A:Paula Von Gunther 19,000.00
2 I:Earl of Greed,Duke of Deception and Lord Conquest, A:Mars. 2,500.00
3 Paula Von Gunther reforms . 1,600.00
4 A:Paula Von Gunther 1,300.00
5 I:Dr. Psycho,A:Mars 1,300.00
6 I:Cheetah. 1,100.00
7 . . . . 1,100.00
8 I:Queen Clea 1,100.00
9 I:Giganto 1,100.00
10 I:Duke Mephisto Saturno. . . 1,100.00
11 I:Hypnoto 800.00
12 I:Queen Desira 800.00
13 V:King Rigor & the Seal Men . 800.00
14 I:Gentleman Killer 800.00
15 I:Solo. 800.00
16 I:King Pluto 800.00
17 Wonder Woman goes to Ancient Rome. 800.00
18 V:Dr. Psycho 800.00
19 V:Blitz 800.00
20 V:Nifty and the Air Pirates . . . 800.00
21 I:Queen Atomia 700.00
22 V:Saturno 700.00
23 V:Odin and the Valkyries 700.00
24 I:Mask 700.00
25 V:Purple Priestess 700.00
26 I:Queen Celerita. 700.00
27 V:Pik Socket 700.00
28 V:Cheetah,Clea,Dr. Poison, Giganta,Hypnata,Snowman, Zara (Villainy,Inc.). 550.00
29 V:Paddy Gypso 550.00
30 'The Secret of the Limestone Caves'. 550.00
31 V:Solo 500.00
32 V:Uvo 500.00
33 V:Inventa 500.00
34 V:Duke of Deception 500.00
35 'Jaxo,Master of Thoughts' . . . 500.00
36 V:Lord Cruello 500.00
37 A:Circe 500.00
38 V:Brutex. 500.00
39 'The Unmasking of Wonder Woman' 500.00
40 'Hollywood Goes To Paradise Island' 500.00
41 'Wonder Woman,Romance Editor' 375.00
42 V:General Vertigo. 375.00
43 'The Amazing Spy Ring Mystery' 375.00
44 V:Master Destroyer 375.00
45 'The Amazon and the Leprachaun' 750.00
46 V:Prof. Turgo 350.00
47 V:Duke of Deception 350.00
48 V:Robot Woman. 350.00
49 V:Boss 350.00
50 V:Gen. Voro 350.00
51 V:Garo. 250.00
52 V:Stroggo 250.00
53 V:Crime Master of Time 250.00
54 A:Merlin 250.00
55 'The Chessmen of Doom' . . . 250.00
56 V:Plotter Gang 250.00
57 V:Mole Men 250.00
58 V:Brain 250.00
59 V:Duke Dozan 250.00
60 A:Paula Von Gunther 250.00
61 'Earth's Last Hour'. 200.00
62 V:Angles Andrews 200.00
63 V:Duke of Deception 200.00
64 V:Thought Master 200.00
65 V:Duke of Deception 200.00
66 V:Duke of Deception 200.00
67 'Confessions of a Spy'. 200.00
68 'Landing of the Flying Saucers' 200.00
69 A:Johann Gutenberg,Chris. Columbus, Paul Revere and the Wright Brothers 200.00
70 I:Angle Man 200.00
71 'One-Woman Circus' 200.00
72 V:Mole Goldings 200.00
73 V:Prairie Pirates. 200.00
74 'The Carnival of Peril' 200.00
75 V:Angler. 200.00
76 . . . . 200.00
77 V:Smokescreen gang. 200.00
78 V:Angle Man 200.00

Wonder Woman #122 © DC Comics, Inc.

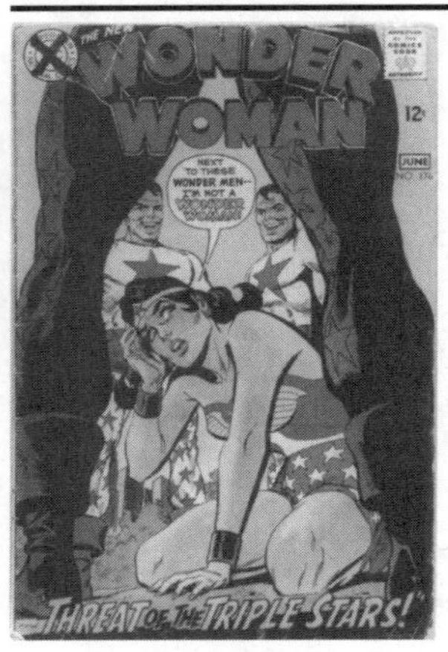

Wonder Woman #176
© DC Comics, Inc.

79 V:Spider. 200.00
80 V:Machino 200.00
81 V:Duke of Deception,
Angle Man 200.00
82 A:Robin Hood 200.00
83 `The Boy From Nowhere'. . . . 200.00
84 V:Duke of Deception,
Angle Man 200.00
85 V:Capt. Virago 200.00
86 V:Snatcher. 200.00
87 `The Day the Clocks Stopped'
. . . . 200.00
88 V:Duke of Deception 200.00
89 `The Triple Heroine' 200.00
90 Wonder Woman on Jupiter. . . 200.00
91 `The Interplanetary Olympics'. 150.00
92 V:Angle Man 150.00
93 V:Duke of Deception 150.00
94 V:Duke of Deception,
A:Robin Hood. 150.00
95 O:Wonder Woman's tiara 150.00
96 V:Angle Man 150.00
97 `The Runaway Time Express'
. . . . 150.00
98 . . . . 150.00
99 V:Silicons. 150.00
100 Anniversary Issue 175.00
101 V:Time Master 125.00
102 F:Steve Trevor. 125.00
103 V:Gadget-Maker. 125.00
104 A:Duke of Deception 125.00
105 O,I:Wonder Woman 700.00
106 W.Woman space adventure . 125.00
107 Battles space cowboys. 125.00
108 Honored by U.S. Post Off. . . 125.00
109 V:Slicker 125.00
110 I:Princess 1003 . . . . 125.00
111 I:Prof. Menace 125.00
112 V:Chest of Monsters. 100.00
113 A:Queen Mikra. 100.00
114 V:Flying Saucers 100.00
115 A:Angle Man 100.00
116 A:Professor Andro 100.00
117 A:Etta Candy 100.00
118 A:Merman 100.00
119 A:Mer Boy 100.00
120 A:Hot & Cold Alien. 100.00
121 A:Wonder Woman Family . . . 75.00
122 I:Wonder Tot 75.00
123 A:Wonder Girl,Wonder Tot . . . 75.00
124 A:Wonder Girl,Wonder Tot . . . 75.00
125 WW-Battle Prize 75.00
126 I:Mr.Genie 75.00
127 Suprise Honeymoon 60.00
128 O:InvisiblePlane. 50.00
129 A:WonderGirl,WonderTot 50.00
130 A:Angle Man 50.00
131 . . . . 50.00
132 V:Flying Saucer 50.00
133 A:Miss X 50.00
134 V:Image-Maker 50.00
135 V:Multiple Man. 50.00
136 V:Machine Men 50.00
137 V:Robot Wonder Woman 50.00
138 V:Multiple Man. 50.00
139 Amnesia revels Identity 50.00
140 A:Morpheus,Mr.Genie 50.00
141 A:Angle Man 50.00
142 A:Mirage Giants. 50.00
143 A:Queen Hippolyte. 50.00
144 I:Bird Boy. 50.00
145 V:Phantom Sea Beast 50.00
146 $1,000 Dollar Stories 50.00
147 Wonder Girl becomes Bird Girl
and Fish Girl. 50.00
148 A:Duke of Deception 50.00
149 Last Day of the Amazons. . . . 50.00
150 V:Phantome Fish Bird 50.00
151 F:1st Full Wonder Girl story . . 40.00
152 F:Wonder Girl 40.00
153 V:Duke of Deception 40.00
154 V:Boiling Man 40.00
155 I married a monster 40.00
156 V:Brain Pirate 40.00
157 A:Egg Fu,the First 40.00
158 A:Egg Fu,the First 40.00
159 Origin 40.00
160 A:Cheetah,Dr. Psycho 40.00
161 A:Angle Man 40.00
162 O:Diana Prince 40.00
163 A:Giganta 40.00
164 A:Angle Man 40.00
165 A:Paper Man,Dr.Psycho. 40.00
166 A:Egg Fu,The Fifth. 40.00
167 A:Crimson Centipede. 40.00
168 RA,ME,V:Giganta. 40.00
169 RA,ME,Crimson Centipede . . 40.00
170 RA,ME,V:Dr.Pyscho. 40.00
171 A:Mouse Man 25.00
172 IN,A:Android Wonder Woman
. . . . 25.00
173 A:Tonia 25.00
174 A:Angle Man 25.00
175 V:Evil Twin. 25.00
176 A:Star Brothers 25.00
177 A:Super Girl. 25.00
178 MSy,DG,I:New Wonder
Woman 35.00
179 D:Steve Trevor,I:Ching. 30.00
180 MSy,DG,wears no costume
I:Tim Trench. 22.00
181 MSy,DG,A:Dr.Cyber. 22.00
182 MSy,DG. 22.00
183 MSy,DG,V:War. 22.00
184 MSy,DG,A:Queen Hippolyte. . 22.00
185 MSy,DG,V:Them 22.00
186 MSy,DG,I:Morgana 22.00
187 MSy,DG,A:Dr.Cyber. 22.00
188 MSy,DG,A:Dr.Cyber. 22.00
189 MSy,DG. 22.00
190 MSy,DG. 22.00
191 MSy,DG. 22.00
192 MSy,DG. 22.00
193 MSy,DG. 22.00
194 MSy,DG. 22.00
195 MSy,WW 25.00
196 MSy,DG,giant,Origin rep. 22.00
197 MSy,DG. 22.00
198 MSy,DG. 22.00
199 JJ(c),DG 30.00
200 JJ(c),DG 20.00
201 DG,A:Catwoman 15.00
202 DG,A:Catwoman,I:Fafhrd
& the Gray Mouser. 15.00
203 DG,Womens lib 15.00
204 DH,BO,rewears costume 20.00
205 DH,BO. 15.00
206 DH,O:Wonder Woman 15.00

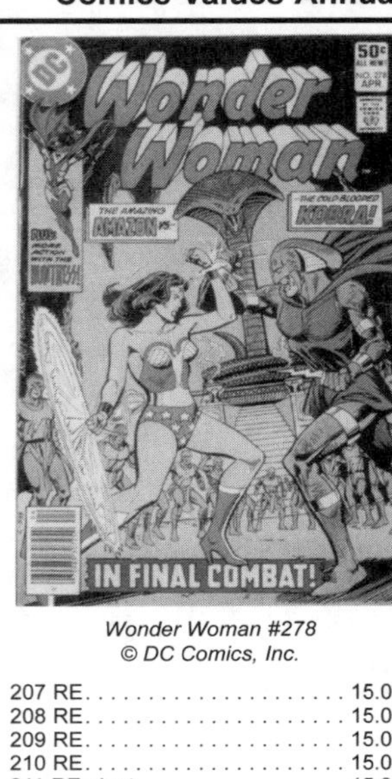

Wonder Woman #278
© DC Comics, Inc.

207 RE. 15.00
208 RE. 15.00
209 RE. 15.00
210 RE. 15.00
211 RE,giant. 15.00
212 CS,A:Superman,tries to
rejoin JLA. 15.00
213 IN,A:Flash 10.00
214 CS,giant,A:Green Lantern . . . 10.00
215 A:Aquaman 10.00
216 A:Black Canary 10.00
217 DD,A:Green Arrow,giant. 20.00
218 KS,Red Tornado 7.00
219 CS,A:Elongated Man 7.00
220 DG,NA,A:Atom 7.00
221 CS,A:Hawkman 7.00
222 A:Batman 7.00
223 R:Steve Trevor 7.00
224 thru 227 . . . . @7.00
228 B:War stories. 7.00
229 . . . . 7.00
230 V:Cheetah 7.00
231 . . . . 7.00
232 MN,A:JSA 7.00
233 GM 7.00
234 . . . . 7.00
235 . . . . 7.00
236. 7.00
237 RB(c),O:Wonder Woman 10.00
238 RB(c). 5.00
239 RB(c). 5.00
240. 5.00
241 JSon,DG,A:Spectre 5.00
242 thru 247 . . . . @5.00
248 D:Steve Trevor 5.00
249 A:Hawkgirl. 5.00
250 I:Orana 5.00
251 O:Orana 5.00
252 . . . . 5.00
253 . . . . 5.00
254 . . . . 5.00
255 V:Bushmaster 5.00
256 V:Royal Flush Gang. 5.00
257 thru 261 . . . . @5.00
262 RE,A:Bushmaster 5.00
263 thru 266 . . . . @5.00
267 R:Animal Man 12.00
268 A:Animal Man 10.00
269 WW(i),Rebirth of Wonder
Woman,pt.1 . . . . 3.00
270 Rebirth,pt.2 . . . . 3.00
271 JSon,B:Huntress,Rebirth,pt.3. . 3.00
272 JSon 3.00
273 JSon,A:Angle Man. 3.00

274 JSon,I:Cheetah II . . . 3.00
275 JSon,V:Cheetah II . . . 3.00
276 JSon,V:Kobra . . . 3.00
277 JSon,V:Kobra . . . 3.00
278 JSon,V:Kobra . . . 3.00
279 JSon,A:Demon,Catwoman . . . 3.50
280 JSon,A:Demon,Catwoman . . . 3.50
281 JSon,Earth 2 Joker . . . 4.00
282 JSon,Earth 2 Joker . . . 4.00
283 Earth 2 Joker . . . 4.00
284 . . . 3.00
285 JSon,V:Red Dragon . . . 3.00
286 . . . 3.00
287 DH,RT,JSon,Teen Titans . . . 3.00
288 GC,RT,New Wonder Woman . . 3.00
289 GC,RT,JSon,New W.Woman . . 3.00
290 GC,RT,JSon,New W.Woman . . 3.00
291 GC,FMc,A:Zatanna . . . 3.00
292 GC,FMc,RT,Supergirl . . . 3.00
293 GC,FMc,Starfire,Raven . . . 3.00
294 GC,FMc,JSon,V:Blockbuster . . 3.00
295 GC,FMc,JSon,Huntress . . . 3.00
296 GC,Fmc,JSon . . . 3.00
297 MK(c),GC,FMc,JSon . . . 3.00
298 GC,FMc,JSon . . . 3.00
299 GC,FMc,JSon . . . 3.00
300 GC,FMc,RA,DG,KP,RB,KG
C:New Teen Titans . . . 4.50
301 GC,FMc . . . 3.00
302 GC,FMc,V:Artemis . . . 3.00
303 GC,FMc,Huntress . . . 3.00
304 GC,FMc,Huntress . . . 3.00
305 GC,Huntress,I:Circe . . . 5.00
306 DH,Huntress . . . 3.00
307 DH,Huntress,Black Canary . . . 3.00
308 DH,Huntress,Black Canary . . . 3.00
309 DH,Huntress . . . 3.00
310 DH,Huntress . . . 3.00
311 DH,Huntress . . . 3.00
312 DH,DSp,A:Gremlins . . . 3.00
313 DH,V:Circe . . . 3.00
314 DH,Huntress . . . 3.00
315 DH,Huntress . . . 3.00
316 DH,Huntress . . . 3.00
317 DH,V:Cereberus . . . 3.00
318 DH,V:Space Aliens . . . 3.00
319 DH,V:Dr.Cyber . . . 3.00
320 DH . . . 3.00
321 DH,Huntress . . . 3.00
322 IN . . . 3.00
323 DH,A:Cheetah, Angle Man . . . 3.00
324 DH . . . 3.00
325 DH . . . 3.00
326 DH . . . 3.00
327 DH,Crisis . . . 3.00
328 DH,Crisis . . . 3.00
329 DH,Crisis, giant . . . 3.00

WONDER WOMAN

[2nd Regular Series] 1987

1 GP,O:Amazons,Wonder Woman . 7.00
2 GP,I:Steve Trevor . . . 4.00
3 GP,I:Julia Vanessa . . . 4.00
4 GP,V:Decay . . . 4.00
5 GP,V:Deimos,Phobos . . . 4.00
6 GP,V:Ares . . . 3.50
7 GP,I:Myndi Mayer . . . 3.50
8 GP,O:Legends,A:JLA,Flash . . . 3.50
9 GP,I:New Cheetah . . . 3.50
10 GP,V:Seven Headed Hydra,
Challenge of the Gods,pt.1,
gatefold(c) . . . 3.00
10a regular(c) . . . 3.00
11 GP,V:Echidna,Challenge
of the Gods,pt.3 . . . 3.00
12 GP,Millenium,V:Pan, Challenge
of the Gods,pt.3,
Millenium x-over . . . 3.00
13 GP,Millenium,A:Ares,Challenge
of the Gods,pt.4 . . . 3.00
14 GP,A:Hercules . . . 3.00
15 GP,I:New Silver Swan . . . 3.00
16 GP,V:Silver Swan . . . 3.00
17 GP,DG,V:Circe . . . 3.00
18 GP,DG,V:Circe,+Bonus bk#4 . . . 3.00
19 GP,FMc,V:Circe . . . 3.00
20 GP,BMc,D:Myndi Mayer . . . 3.00
21 GP,BMc,L:Greek Gods,
Destruction of Olympus . . . 2.50
22 GP,BMc,F:Julia, Vanessa . . . 2.50
23 GP,R:Hermes,V:Phobos,
Prelude to New Titans #50 . . . 2.50
24 GP,V:Ixion, Phobos . . . 2.50
25 CMa,Invasion,A:JLA . . . 2.50
26 CMa,Invasion,V:Capt.Atom . . . 2.50
27 CMa,V:Khunds,A:Cheetah . . . 2.50
28 CMa,V:Cheetah . . . 2.50
29 CMa,V:Cheetah . . . 2.50
30 CMa,V:Cheetah . . . 2.50
31 CMa,V:Cheetah . . . 2.50
32 TG,V:Amazons,A:Hermes . . . 2.50
33 CMa,V:Amazons,Cheetah . . . 2.50
34 CMa,I:Shim'Tar . . . 2.50
35 CMa,V:Shim'Tar . . . 2.50
36 CMa,A:Hermes . . . 2.50
37 CMa,V:Discord,A:Superman . . . 2.50
38 CMa,V:Eris . . . 2.50
39 CMa,V:Eris,A:Lois Lane . . . 2.50
40 CMa,V:Eris,A:Lois Lane . . . 2.50
41 CMa,RT,F:Julia,Ties that Bind . . 2.50
42 CMa,RT,V:Silver Swan . . . 2.50
43 CMA,RT,V:Silver Swan . . . 2.50
44 CMa,RT,V:SilverSwan . . . 2.50
45 CM,RT,Pandora's Box . . . 2.50
46 RT,Suicide Issue,D:Lucy . . . 2.50
47 RT,A:Troia . . . 2.50
48 RTP,A:Troia . . . 2.50
49 recap of 1st four years . . . 2.50
50 RT,SA,BB,AH,CM,KN,PCR,MW
A:JLA,Superman . . . 3.00
51 RT,V:Mercury . . . 2.50
52 CM,KN,Shards,V:Dr.Psycho . . . 2.50
53 RT,A:Pariah . . . 2.50
54 RT,V:Dr.Psycho . . . 2.50
55 RT,V:Dr.Psycho . . . 2.50
56 RT,A:Comm.Gordon . . . 2.50
57 RT,A:Clark Kent,Bruce Wayne . . 2.50
58 RT,War of the Gods,V:Atlas . . . 3.00
59 RT,War of the Gods,
A:Batman Robin . . . 3.00
60 RT,War of the Gods,
A:Batman, Lobo . . . 3.00
61 RT,War of the Gods,V:Circe . . . 3.00

Wonder Woman 2nd Series #57
© DC Comics, Inc.

62 War o/t Gods,Epilogue . . . 2.50
63 BB(c)A:Deathstroke,Cheetah . . . 2.00
64 BB(c),Kidnapped Child . . . 2.00
65 BB(c),PCu,V:Dr.Psycho . . . 2.00
66 BB(c),PCu,Exodus In Space#1 . 2.00
67 BB(c),PCu,Exodus In Space#2 . 2.00
68 BB(c),PCu,Exodus In Space#3 . 2.00
69 PCu, Exodus In Space#4 . . . 2.00
70 PCu,Exodus In Space#5 . . . 2.00
71 BB(c),DC,RT,Return fr.space . . . 2.00
72 BB(c),O:retold . . . 2.00
73 BB(c),Diana gets a job . . . 2.00
74 BB(c),V:White Magician . . . 2.00
75 BB(c),A:The White Magician . . . 2.00
76 BB(c),A:Doctor Fate . . . 2.00
77 BB(c) . . . 2.00
78 BB(c),A:Flash . . . 2.00
79 BB(c),V:Mayfly,A:Flash . . . 2.00
80 BB(c),V:Ares Buchanan . . . 2.00
81 BB(c),V:Ares Buchanan . . . 2.00
82 BB(c),V:Ares Buchanan . . . 2.00
83 BB(c),V:Ares Buchanan . . . 2.00
84 BB(c),V:Ares Buchanan . . . 2.00
85 BB(c) . . . 15.00
86 BB(c),Turning Point . . . 6.00
87 BB(c),No Quarter,NoSanctuary . 6.00
88 BB(c),A:Superman . . . 8.00
89 BB(c),A:Circle . . . 7.00
90 New Direction . . . 8.00
91 Choosing Wonder Woman . . . 5.00
92 New Wonder Woman . . . 5.00
93 New Wonder Woman . . . 4.00
94 . . . 6.00
95 V:Cheetah . . . 6.00
96 V:The Joker . . . 6.00
97 V:The Joker . . . 6.00
98 BB(c),F:Artemis . . . 3.00
99 BB(c),A:White Magician . . . 3.00
100 BB(c) White Magician defeats
Artemis . . . 6.00
100a Collector's ed., holo(c) . . . 3.95
101 V:White Magician . . . 3.00
102 V:Metron,Darkseid . . . 2.25
103 JBy,A:Darkseid . . . 2.00
104 JBy,Diana takes crown? . . . 2.00
105 JBy,Grecian artifact comes
to life . . . 2.00
106 JBy,A:The Demon,Phantom
Stranger . . . 2.00
107 . . . 2.00
108 JBy,F:The Demon,Arion,The
Phantom Stranger . . . 2.00
109 JBy,V:The Flash,I:Champion . . 2.00
110 JBy,V:Sinestro . . . 2.00
111 JBy,I:New Wonder Girl,
V:Doomsday . . . 2.00
112 JBy,V:Doomsday,A:Superman . 2.50
113 JBy,Wonder Girl vs. Decay . . . 2.00
114 JBy,V:Doctor Psycho . . . 2.00
115 JBy,beneath the Arctic ice . . . 2.00
116 JBy,beneath the Arctic ice . . . 2.00
117 JBy,V:Earth Moovers . . . 2.00
118 JBy . . . 2.00
119 JBy,fight to regain Cheetah's
humanity, cont. . . . 2.00
120 JBy,48pg., pin-ups . . . 3.00
121 JBy,Wonder Woman reverting
to clay . . . 2.00
122 JBy,Gods of Olympus are back
. . . 2.00
123 JBy,R:Artemis . . . 2.00
124 JBy,A:Demon . . . 2.00
125 JBy,A:Donna Troy & JLA . . . 2.00
126 JBy,JL,Genesis tie-in . . . 2.00
127 JBy,JL(c),new era . . . 2.00
128 JBy,JL,V:Egg Fu . . . 2.00
129 JBy,JL,Hippolyta debuts as
replacement Wonder Woman . . 2.00
130 JBy,JL,pt.1,A:Golden-age
Flash . . . 2.00
131 JBy,pt.2 . . . 2.00
132 JBy,pt.3,A:Justice Society . . . 2.00

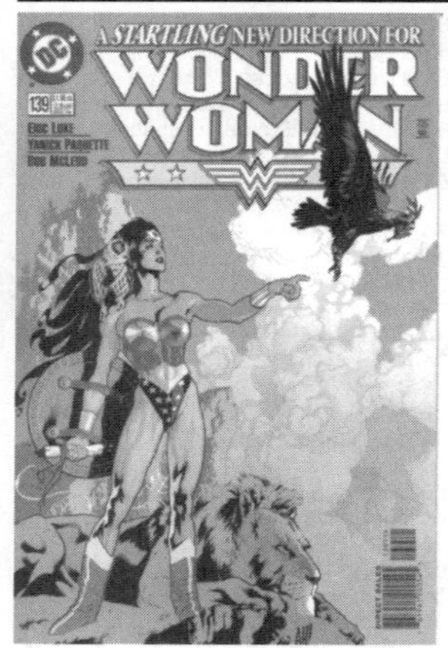

Wonder Woman 2nd Series #139
© DC Comics, Inc.

133 . . . . 2.00
134 JBy,Who is Donna Troy? 2.00
135 JBy,secret revealed 2.00
136 JBy,back to Earth. 2.00
137 CPr,V:Circe, pt.1 . . . . . . 2.00
138 MBr,F:Hippolyta,V:Circe,pt.2 . . 2.00
139 MBr, ... 2.00
140 BMc,A:Superman & Batman . . 2.00
141 BMc,A:Superman & Batman . . 2.00
142 BMc,The Wonder Dome. 2.00
143 BMc,Devastation,pt.1. . . . . 2.00
144 BMc,Devastation,pt.2. . . . . 2.00
145 BMc,Devastation,pt.3. . . . . 2.00
146 BMc,Devastation,pt.4. . . . . 2.00
147 BMc,GodWar begins 2.00
148 BMc,GodWar, pt.2 . . . . . . 2.00
149 RBr,BMc,GodWar,pt.3 . . . . 2.00
150 GodWar, 48-pg 2.95
151 AH(c),V:Dr. Poison. 2.00
152 . . . . 2.00
153 MMr,F:Wonder Girl 2.00
154 Three Hearts,pt.1. . . . . . 2.00
155 Three Hearts,pt.2. . . . . . 2.00
156 Devastation Returns,pt.1 . . . 2.00
157 Devastation Returns,pt.2 . . . 2.00
158 Devastation Returns,concl. . . 2.00
159 WonderDome comes to Earth . 2.25
160 A Piece of You,pt.1 . . . . . 2.25
161 A Piece of You,pt.2 . . . . . 2.25
162 GodComplex,pt.1,A:Aquaman . 2.25
163 GodComplex,pt.2,A:Aquaman . 2.25
Ann.#1,GP,AAd,RA,BB,JBo,JL,CS
Tales of Paradise Island 2.00
Ann.#2 CM,F:Mayer Agency. . . . 2.50
Ann.#3 Eclipso tie-in. 2.50
Ann.#4 Year One Annual 3.50
Ann.#5 JBy,DC,NBy,Legends of the
Dead Earth. 2.95
Ann.#6 Pulp Heroes (Macabre). . . 3.95
Ann.#7 Ghosts 3.00
Ann.#8 JLApe Gorilla Warfare. . . . 3.00
Spec.#1,000,000 CPr(s),MC,BMc . . 2.00
Spec #1 A:Deathstroke,Cheetah . . . 2.25
Spec.#0 History of Amazons. 7.00
TPB The Contest, rep. #90,#0
#91-#93 . . . . 9.95
TPB The Challenge of Artemas . . . 9.95
TPB Second Genesis JBy, rep.
#101–#105. . . . . 9.95
GN Amazonia, BML 8.00
GN The Once and Future Story . . . 5.00
GN Amazonia, Elseworlds 8.00
Archives, Vol. 1. . . . . 50.00

Secret Files #2. . . . . 5.00
Spec. Wonder Woman: Donna Troy
Girlfrenzy (1998) 2.00
Spec. Wonder Woman Plus CPr(s),MC,
TP,Jesse Quick & Wonder
Woman (1996). 2.95
HC Archives Vol.2. . . . . . . 49.95

WORLD OF KRYPTON
July, 1979

1 HC/MA.O:Jor-El 10.00
2 HC/MA,A:Superman 6.00
3 HC 6.00

[2nd Series] 1987–88

1 MMi,John Byrne script 3.00
2 MMi,John Byrne script 3.00
3 MMi,John Byrne script 3.00
4 MMi,A:Superman 3.00

WORLD OF METROPOLIS
1988

1 DG(i),O:Perry White 2.50
2 DG(i),O:Lois Lane. 2.50
3 DG(i),Clark Kent. 2.50
4 DG(i),O:Jimmy Olsen 2.50

WORLD OF SMALLVILLE
1988

1 KS/AA,Secrets of Ma&Pa Kent . . 2.00
2 KS/AA,`Stolen Moments' 2.00
3 KS/AA,Lana Lang/Manhunter . . . 2.00
4 KS/AA,final issue 2.00

WORLDS COLLIDE
1994

1 MBr(c),3RW,CsB,Ccs,DCw,
TG,A:Blood Syndicate,Icon,
Hardware,Static,Superboy,
Superman,Steel,Vinyl Cling(c) . 4.25
1a Newsstand Ed. 2.75

WORLD'S BEST COMICS
Spring, 1941

1 Superman vs. the Rainmaker,
Batman vs. Wright 15,000.00
Becomes:

WORLD'S FINEST COMICS
1941–86

2 Superman V:`The Unknown X',
Batman V:Ambrose Taylor . 4,500.00
3 I&O:Scarecrow. 3,000.00
4 Superman V:Dan Brandon,
Batman V:Ghost Gang. . . . 2,200.00
5 Superman V:Lemuel P.Potts,
Batman V:Brains Kelly 2,200.00
6 Superman V:Metalo,Batman
meets Scoop Scanlon 1,600.00
7 Superman V:Jenkins,Batman
V:Snow Man Bandits 1,600.00
8 Superman:`Talent Unlimited'
Batman V:Little Nap Boyd,
B:Boy Commandos 1,400.00
9 Superman:`One Second to
Live',Batman V:Bramwell B.
Bramwell 1,400.00
10 Superman V:The Insect Master,
Batman reforms Oliver Hunt
. . . . 1,300.00
11 Superman V:Charlie Frost,
Batman V:Rob Calendar . . 1,200.00
12 Superman V:Lynx,Batman:
`Alfred Gets His Man'. 1,200.00
13 Superman V:Dice Dimant,
Batman,V:Swami Pravhoz . 1,200.00

World's Finest Comics #144
© DC Comics, Inc.

14 Superman V:Al Bandar,Batman
V:Jib Buckler 1,200.00
15 Superman V:Derby Bowser,
Batman V:Mennekin. 1,200.00
16 Superman:`Music for the Masses,
Batman V:Nocky Johnson . 1,200.00
17 Superman:`The Great Godini',
Batman V:Dr.Dreemo. 1,100.00
18 Superman:`The Junior Reporters,
Batman V:Prof.Brane 1,000.00
19 A:The Joker 1,000.00
20 A:Toyman 1,000.00
21 Superman:`Swindle in
Sweethearts!' 700.00
22 Batman V:Nails Finney. 700.00
23 Superman:`The Colossus
of Metropolis' 700.00
24 . . . . 700.00
25 Superman V:Ed Rook,Batman:
`The Famous First Crimes' . . 700.00
26 `Confessions of Superman' . . 700.00
27 `The Man Who Out-Supered
Superman 700.00
28 A:Lex Luther,Batman V:Glass
Man 700.00
29 Superman:`The Books that
couldn't be Bound' 700.00
30 Superman:`Sheriff Clark Kent`,
Batman V:Joe Coyne 700.00
31 `Superman's Super-Rival`,Batman:
`Man with the X-Ray Eyes' . . 600.00
32 Superman visits
Ancient Egypt. 600.00
33 `Superman Press, Inc.',
Batman V:James Harmon . . . 600.00
34 `The Un-Super Superman' . . . 600.00
35 Daddy Superman,A:Penguin . 600.00
36 Lois Lane,Sleeping Beauty. . . 600.00
37 `The Superman Story`,Batman
V:T-Gun Jones 600.00
38 If There were No Superman . . 600.00
39 Superman V:Big Jim Martin,
Batman V:J.J.Jason 600.00
40 Superman V:Check,Batman:`4
Killers Against Fate!'. 600.00
41 I:Supermanium,
E:Boy Commandos. 450.00
42 Superman goes to Uranus,
A:Marco Polo & Kubla Khan . 450.00
43 A:J.Wilbur Wolfingham. 450.00
44 Superman:`The Revolt of the
Thought Machine'. 450.00
45 Superman:`Lois Lane and Clark
Kent,Private Detectives. . . . 450.00
46 Superman V:Mr. 7 . . . . . . 450.00
47 Superman:`The Girl Who

Hated Reporters 450.00
48 A:Joker 450.00
49 Superman meets the Metropolis Shutterbug Society, A:Penguin 450.00
50 `Superman Super Wrecker' . . 450.00
51 Superman:`The Amazing Talents of Lois Lane'. 450.00
52 A:J.Wilbur Wolfingham. 450.00
53 Superman V:Elias Toomey . . . 450.00
54 `The Superman Who Avoided Danger!' 450.00
55 A:Penguin 450.00
56 Superman V:Dr.Vallin,Batman V:Big Dan Hooker. 450.00
57 `The Artificial Superman' 450.00
58 Superman V:Mr.Fenton 450.00
59 A:Lex Luthor,Joker. 450.00
60 A:J.Wilbur Wolfingham. 450.00
61 A:Joker,`Superman's Blackout' 425.00
62 A:Lex Luthor 425.00
63 Superman:`Clark Kent, Gangster' 425.00
64 Superman:`The Death of Lois Lane,Batman:`Bruce Wayne... Amateur Detective' 425.00
65 `The Confessions of Superman', Batman V:The Blaster. 600.00
66 `Superman,Ex-Crimebuster; Batman V:Brass Haley 425.00
67 Superman:`Metropolis-Crime Center!' 425.00
68 Batman V:The Crimesmith . . . 425.00
69 A:Jor-El,Batman V:Tom Becket 425.00
70 `The Two Faces of Superman', Batman:`Crime Consultant' . . 425.00
71 B:Superman/Batman team-ups 850.00
72 V:Heavy Weapon gang 600.00
73 V:Fang. 600.00
74 `The Contest of Heroes'. 500.00
75 V:The Purple Mask Mob. 425.00
76 `When Gotham City Challenged Metropolis 325.00
77 V:Prof.Pender 325.00
78 V:Varrel mob 325.00
79 A:Aladdin. 325.00
80 V:Mole. 325.00
81 Meet Ka Thar from future. . . . 275.00
82 A:Three Musketeers. 275.00
83 `The Case of the Mother Goose Mystery' 275.00
84 V:Thad Linnis gang 275.00
85 Meet Princess Varina 275.00
86 V:Henry Bartle 275.00
87 V:Elton Craig 275.00
88 1st team-up Luthor & Joker . . 300.00
89 I:Club of Heroes. 275.00
90 A:Batwoman 275.00
91 V:Rohtul,descendent of Lex Luthor. 200.00
92 Ist & only A:Skyboy 175.00
93 V:Victor Danning 200.00
94 O:Superman/Batman team, A:Lex Luthor. 550.00
95 `Battle o/t Super Heroes' 175.00
96 `Super-Foes from Planet X' . . 175.00
97 V:Condor Gang 175.00
98 I:Moonman 175.00
99 JK,V:Carl Verril 175.00
100 A:Kandor, Lex Luthor 325.00
101 A:Atom Master. 150.00
102 V:Jo-Jo Groff gang, B:Tommy Tomorrow 150.00
103 `The Secrets of the Sorcerer's Treasure 150.00
104 A:Lex Luthor 150.00
105 V:Khalex 150.00
106 V:Duplicate Man. 150.00

World's Finest Comics #174
© DC Comics, Inc.

107 `The Secret of the Time Creature' 150.00
108 `The Star Creatures' 150.00
109 V:Fangan. 150.00
110 `The Alien Who Doomed Robin!' 150.00
111 V:Floyd Frisby 150.00
112 . . . . 150.00
113 1st Bat-Mite/Mr.Mxyzptlk team-up 150.00
114 `Captives o/t Space Globes' . 150.00
115 The Curse That Doomed Superman 125.00
116 V:Vance Collins 125.00
117 A:Batwoman,Lex Luthor 125.00
118 V:Vath-Gar 125.00
119 V:General Grambly. 125.00
120 V:Faceless Creature 125.00
121 I:Miss Arrowette. 125.00
122 V:Klor 60.00
123 A:Bat-Mite & Mr. Mxyzptlk . . . 60.00
124 V:Hroguth,E:Tommy Tomorrow. 60.00
125 V:Jundy,B:Aquaman. 60.00
126 A:Lex Luthor 60.00
127 V:Zerno 60.00
128 V:Moose Morans 60.00
129 Joker/Luthor T.U. 75.00
130 . . . . 60.00
131 V:Octopus 60.00
132 V:Denny Kale,Shorty Biggs . . 60.00
133 . . . . 60.00
134 V:Band of Super-Villians 60.00
135 V:The Future Man 60.00
136 The Batman Nobody Remembered 60.00
137 A:Lex Luthor 60.00
138 V:General Grote. 60.00
139 V:Sphinx Gang,E:Aquaman . . 60.00
140 CS,V:Clayface 60.00
141 CS,A:Jimmy Olsen. 60.00
142 CS,O:Composite Man 60.00
143 CS,A:Kandor,I:Mailbag. 50.00
144 CS,A:Clayface,Brainiac 50.00
145 CS,Prison for Heroes 50.00
146 CS,Batman,Son of Krypton . . 50.00
147 CS,A:Jimmy Olsen. 50.00
148 CS,A:Lex Luthor,Clayface . . . 50.00
149 CS,The Game of the Secret Identities 50.00
150 CS,V:Rokk and Sorban 35.00
151 CS,A:Krypto,BU:Congorilla. . . 35.00
152 CS,A:The Colossal Kids,Bat-mite,V:Mr.Mxyzptlk 35.00
153 CS,V:Lex Luthor 35.00
154 CS,The Sons of Batman & Superman(Imaginary) 35.00
155 CS,The 1000th Exploit of Batman & Superman 35.00
156 CS,I:BizarroBatman,V:Joker. 100.00
157 CS,The Abominable Brats (Imaginary story) 35.00
158 CS,V:Brainiac 35.00
159 CS,A:Many Major villians,I:Jim Gordon as Anti-Batman & Perry White as Anti-Superman 35.00
160 V:Dr Zodiac.. . . . . 35.00
161 CS,80 page giant. 40.00
162 V:The Jousting Master 30.00
163 CS,The Court of No Hope . . . 30.00
164 CS,I:Genia,V:Brainiac 30.00
165 CS,The Crown of Crime. 30.00
166 CS,V:Muto & Joker 32.00
167 CS,The New Superman & Batman(Imaginary) V:Luthor . . 30.00
168 CS,R:Composite Superman . . 30.00
169 The Supergirl/Batgirl Plot; V:Batmite,Mr.Mxyzptlk 30.00
170 80 page giant,reprint 30.00
171 CS,V:The Executioners 30.00
172 CS,Superman & Batman Brothers (Imaginary). 30.00
173 CS,The Jekyll-Hyde Heroes . . 75.00
174 CS,Secrets of the Double Death Wish 30.00
175 NA(1st Batman),C:Flash 30.00
176 NA,A:Supergirl & Batgirl. 30.00
177 V:Joker & Luthor 30.00
178 CS,The Has-Been Superman. 20.00
179 CS,giant 30.00
180 RA,ME,Supermans Perfect Crime. 20.00
181 RA,ME. 20.00
182 RA,ME,The Mad Manhunter. . 20.00
183 RA,ME,Supermans Crimes of the Ages. 20.00
184 RA,ME,A:JLA,Robin. 20.00
185 CS,The Galactic Gamblers. . . 20.00
186 RA,ME,The Bat Witch 20.00
187 RA,ME,Demon Superman . . . 20.00
188 giant,reprint 30.00
189 RA,ME,V:Lex Luthor 20.00
190 RA,V:Lex Luthor 18.00
191 RA,A:Jor-El,Lara 18.00
192 RA,The Prison of No Escape . 18.00
193 The Breaking of Batman and Superman 18.00
194 RA,ME,Inside the Mafia 18.00
195 RA,ME,Dig Now-Die Later . . . 18.00
196 CS,The Kryptonite Express, E:Batman 18.00
197 giant 35.00
198 DD,B:Superman T.U., A:Flash. 90.00
199 DD,Superman & Flash race . . 90.00
200 NA(c),DD,Prisoners of the Immortal World; A:Robin. 20.00
201 NA(c),DD,A Prize of Peril, A:Green Lantern,Dr. Fate. . . . 15.00
202 NA(c),DD,Vengeance of the Tomb Thing,A:Batman 15.00
203 NA(c),DD,Who's Minding the Earth,A:Quamar 15.00
204 NA(c),DD,Journey to the End of Hope,A:Wonder Woman . . . 15.00
205 NA(c),DD,The Computer that Captured a Town,Frazetta Ad, A:Teen Titans 20.00
206 DD,giant reprint 30.00
207 DD,Superman,A:Batman, V:Dr.Light 15.00
208 NA(c),DD,A:Dr Fate 15.00
209 NA(c),DD,A:Green Arrow, Hawkman,I&V:The Temper . . 15.00
210 NA(c),DD,A:Batman. 15.00

DC COMICS

DC COMICS

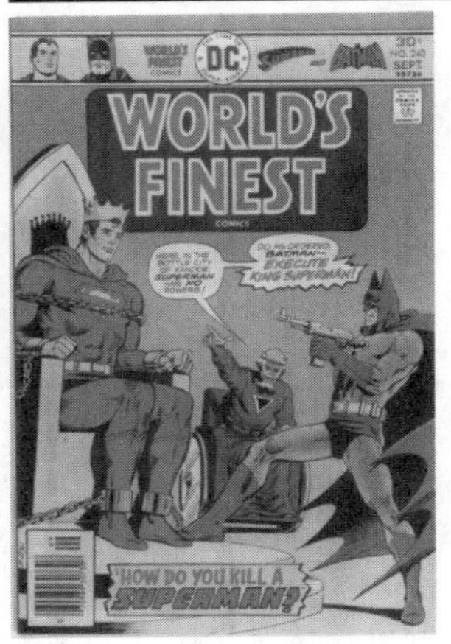

World's Finest Comics #240
© DC Comics, Inc.

211 NA(c),DD,A:Batman 15.00
212 CS(c),And So My World Begins,A:Martian Manhunter. . 15.00
213 DD,Peril in a Very Small Place,A:The Atom 15.00
214 DD,A:Vigilante 15.00
215 DD,Saga of the Super Sons (Imaginary story) 15.00
216 DD,R:Super Sons,Little Town with a Big Secret. 15.00
217 DD,MA,Heroes with Dirty Hands 15.00
218 DD,DC,A:Batman, BU:Metamorpho 15.00
219 DD,Prisoner of Rogues Rock; A:Batman 15.00
220 DD,MA,Let No Man Write My Epitaph,BU:Metamorpho. 15.00
221 DD,Cry Not For My Forsaken Son; R:Super Sons. 15.00
222 DD,Evil In Paradise 15.00
223 DD,giant,A:Deadman,Aquaman Robotman 20.00
224 DD,giant,A:Super Sons, Metamorpho,Johnny Quick . . . 20.00
225 giant,A:Rip Hunter,Vigilante, Black Canary,Robin 15.00
226 A:Sandman,Metamorpho, Deadman,Martian Manhunter . 20.00
227 MGr,BWi,A:The Demonic Duo, Vigilante,Rip Hunter,Deadman, I:Stargrave 20.00
228 ATh,A:Super Sons,Aquaman, Robin,Vigilante 20.00
229 I:Powerman,A:Metamorpho . . 15.00
230 A:Super-Sons,Deadman, Aquaman 15.00
231 A:Green Arrow,Flash 15.00
232 DD,The Dream Bomb 15.00
233 A:Super-Sons 15.00
234 CS,Family That Fled Earth. . . 15.00
235 DD,V:Sagitaurus 15.00
236 DD,A:The Atom 15.00
237 Intruder from a Dead World . . 15.00
238 DD,V:Luthor,A:Super-Sons. . . 15.00
239 CS,A:Gold(from Metal Men) . . 15.00
240 DD,A:Kandor 12.00
241 Make Way For a New World . 12.00
242 EC,A:Super-Sons. 12.00
243 CS,AM,A:Robin 12.00
244 NA(c),JL,MA,MN,TA,giant B:Green Arrow 12.00
245 NA(C),CS,MA,MN,TA, GM,JSh,BWi,giant 12.00
246 NA(c),KS,MA,MN,TA,GM, DH,A:JLA 12.00
247 KS,GM,giant 12.00
248 KS,GM,DG,TVE,A:Sgt.Rock. . 12.00
249 KS,SD,TVE,A:Phantom Stranger,B:Creeper. 12.00
250 GT,SD,Superman,Batman, Wonder Woman,Green Arrow, Black Canary,team-up 10.00
251 GT,SD,JBi,BL,TVE,RE, JA,A:Poison Ivy,Speedy, I:CountVertigo 10.00
252 GT,TVE,SD,JA,giant. 10.00
253 KS,DN,TVE,SD,B:Shazam. . . . 7.00
254 GT,DN,TVE,SD,giant 7.00
255 JL,DA,TVE,SD,DN,KS, E:Creeper 7.00
256 MA,DN,KS,DD,Hawkman,Black Lightning,giant 7.00
257 DD,FMc,DN,KS,GT,RB, RT,giant 7.00
258 NA(c),RB,JL,DG,DN,KS,RT, giant. 7.00
259 RB,DG,MR,MN,DN,KS. 7.00
260 RB,DG,MN,DN 7.00
261 RB,DG,AS,RT,EB,DN, A:Penguin, Terra Man. 7.00
262 DG,DN,DA,JSon,RT, Aquaman 7.00
263 RB,DG,DN,TVE,JSh,Aquaman, Adam Strange 7.00
264 RB,DG,TVE,DN,Aquaman 7.00
265 RB,DN,RE,TVE 7.00
266 RB,TVE,DN 7.00
267 RB,DG,TVE,AS,DN, A:Challengers of the Unknown . 7.00
268 DN,TVE,BBr,RT,AS 7.00
269 RB,FMc,TVE,BBr,AS,DN,DA . . 7.00
270 NA(c),RB,RT,TVE,AS, DN,LMa 7.00
271 GP(c),RB,FMc,O:Superman/ Batman T.U. 6.00
272 RB,DN,TVE,BBr,AS 5.00
273 TVE,LMa,JSon,AS,DN,DA, A:Plastic Man 5.00
274 TVE,LMa,BBr,GC,AS,DN, Green Arrow. 5.00
275 RB,FMc,TVE,LMa,DSp,AS, DN,DA,A:Mr.Freeze 5.00
276 GP(c),RB,TVE,LMa,DSp,CI, DN,DA 5.00
277 GP(c),RT,TVE,DSp,AS,DN, DH,V:Dr.Double X 5.00
278 GP(c),RB,TVE,LMa,DSp,DN . . 5.00
279 KP,TVE,LMa,AS,DN, B:Kid Eternity 5.00
280 RB,TVE,LMa,AS,DN 5.00
281 GK(c),IN,TVE,LMa,AS,DN 5.00
282 IN,FMc,GK,CI,last giant E:Kid Eternity 5.00
283 GT,FMc,GK 5.00
284 GT,DSp,A:Legion,E:G.Arrow . . 5.00
285 FM(c),RB,A:Zatanna 5.00
286 RB,A:Flash 5.00
287 TVE,A:Flash 5.00
288 A:JLA 5.00
289 GK(c),Kryll way of Dying 5.00
290 TD(i),I:Stalagron 5.00
291 WS(c),TD(i),V:Stalagron. 5.00
292 thru 294 . . . . @5.00
295 FMc(i) 5.00
296 RA. 5.00
297 GC,V:Pantheon 5.00
298 V:Pantheon 5.00
299 GC,V:Pantheon 5.00
300 RA,GP,KJ,MT,FMc,A:JLA 5.00
301 Rampage. 3.00
302 DM,NA(rep) 3.00
303 Plague 3.00
304 SLi,O:Null&Void 3.00

World's Finest Comics #303
© DC Comics, Inc.

305 TVE,V:Null&Void 3.00
306 SLi,I:Swordfish & Barracuda . . 3.00
307 TVE,V:Null&Void 3.00
308 GT,Night and Day 3.00
309 MT,AA,V:Quantum 3.00
310 I:Sonik. 3.00
311 A:Monitor 3.00
312 AA,I:Network 3.00
313 AA(i),V:Network 3.00
314 AA(i),V:Executrix 3.00
315 V:Cathode 3.00
316 LSn,I:Cheapjack 3.00
317 LSn,V:Cheapjack 3.00
318 AA(i),A:Sonik. 3.00
319 AA(i),I:REM 3.00
320 AA(i),V:REM 3.00
321 AA,V:Chronos 3.00
322 KG,The Search 3.00
323 AA(i),final issue 3.00

WORLD'S FINEST
[Limited Series] 1990

1 SR,KK,Worlds Apart 8.00
2 SR,KK,Worlds Collide 6.00
3 SR,KK,Worlds At War. 6.00
TPB rep.#1-#3 . . . . 19.95

WORLD'S FINEST: SUPERBOY/ROBIN
Oct., 1996

1 (of 2) CDi&KK(s),TG,SHa, V:Poison Ivy, Metallo 5.00
2 CDi&KK(s),TG,SHa, V:Poison Ivy, Metallo 5.00

WORLD'S GREATEST SUPER-HEROES
1977

1 A:Batman,Robin 2.50

WORLD WITHOUT END
1990

1 The Host, I:Brother Bones 5.00
2 A:Brother Bones. 3.50
3 . . . . 3.50
4 House of Fams. 2.50
5 Female Fury. 2.50
6 conclusion 2.50

WRATH OF THE SPECTRE
May, 1988
1 JAp,rep.Adventure #431-#433 . . 2.50
2 JAp,rep.Adventure #434-#436 . . 2.50
3 JAp,rep.Adventure #437-#440 . . 2.50
4 JAp,reps.,final issue 2.50

XENOBROOD
1994–95
0 New team. 2.00
1 Battles 2.00
2 Bestiary 2.00
3 A:Superman 2.00
4 V:Bestiary. 2.00
5 V:Vimian. 2.00
6 final issue. 2.00

XERO
March, 1997
1 Cpr(s),Ccs,Trane Walker/Xero . . 3.00
2 CPr(s),Ccs,"The Rookie". 2.50
3 Cpr(s),Ccs,"The Beast". 2.50
4 CPr(s) 2.50
6 CPr, Genesis tie-in 2.50
7 CPr(s),O:Zero, pt.1 . . . . 2.50
8 CPr,O:Zero 2.00
9 CPr(s), ... 2.00
10 CPr,a matter of ethics 2.00
11 . . . . 2.00
12 CPr, final issue, Xero dead 2.00

XOMBI
Milestone 1994–96
0 WS(c),DCw,Shadow War,Foil(c), I:Xombi,Twilight 2.50
1 JBy(c),B:Silent Cathedrals 2.00
1a Platinum ed. 12.00
2 I:Rabbi Simmowitz,Golms,Liam Knight of the Spoken Fire 2.50
3 A:Liam 2.00
4 Silent Cathedrals 2.00
5 Silent Cathedrals 2.50
6 Silent Cathedrals 2.50
7 School of Anguish 2.50
8 School of Anguish,pt.2 . . . . 2.50
9 School of Anguish,pt.3 . . . . 2.50
10 School of Anguish,pt.4. . . . . 2.50
11 School of Anguish,pt.5 . . . . 2.50
12 Truth and Surprises 2.50
13 V:Kinderessen 2.50
14 Long Hot Summer, A:Cheryl Saltz 2.50
15 Long Hot Summer 2.50
16 Long Hot Summer 2.50
17 Reader's Choice 2.50
18 Serpent's Tail. 2.50
19 Mister Missy, Bellhop 2.50
20 . . . . 2.50
21 final issue 3.50

YOUNG ALL-STARS
June, 1987
1 I:IronMunro&FlyingFox,D:TNT. . . 4.50
2 V:Axis Amerika 2.50
3 V:Axis Amerika 2.00
4 I:The Tigress 2.00
5 I:Dyna-mite,O:Iron Munro 2.00
6 . . . . 2.00
7 Baseball Game,A:Tigress 2.00
8 Millenium 2.00
9 Millenium 2.00
10 Hugo Danner. 2.00
11 'Birth of Iron Munro'. 2.00
12 'Secret of Hugo Danner' 2.00
13 'V:Deathbolt,Ultra-Humanite . . . 2.00
14 Fury+Ultra Humanite 2.00
15 IronMunro At high school. 2.00
16 Ozyan Inheritance 2.00
17 Ozyan Inheritance 2.00
18 Ozyan Inheritance 2.00
19 Ozyan 2.00
20 O:Flying Fox 2.00
21 Atom & Evil#1 . . . . 2.00
22 Atom & Evil#2 . . . . 2.00
23 Atom & Evil#3 . . . . 2.00
24 Atom & Evil#4 . . . . 2.00
25 . . . . 2.00
26 End of the All Stars? 2.00
27 'Sons of Dawn' begins. 2.00
28 Search for Hugo Danner 2.00
29 A:Hugo Danner 2.00
30 V:Sons of Dawn. 2.00
31 V:Sons of Dawn,last issue 2.00
Ann.#1 MG,V:Mekanique 2.50

YOUNG HEROES IN LOVE
April, 1997
1 DeM,F:Hard Drive. 3.00
2 DeM,sex, lies and superheroics . 2.50
3 A:Superman 2.50
4 F:Hard Drive. 2.50
5 Genesis tie-in 2.00
6 The Rat Pack 2.00
7 Secret Identity Issu. 2.00
8 V:Scarecrow 2.00
9 F:Frostbite & Bonfire. 2.00
10 V:Grundo'mu 2.00
11 V:Grundo'mu 2.00
12 Hard Drive dead? 2.00
13 New leader picked 2.00
14 Man of Inches vs. Man of Candles 2.00
15 Junior vs. Birthday Boy 2.00
16 DeM,Zip-Kid 2.00
17 DeM,Monstergirl's Uncle 2.50
Spec.#1,000,000 DeM final issue . . 2.50

YOUNG JUSTICE
July, 1998
1 PDd,TNu,Robin,Superboy, Impulse 4.50
2 PDd,TNu,V:Super-Cycle 3.00
3 PDd(s),TNu,V:Mr.Mxyzptlk 3.00
4 PDd(s),TNu,Girls join team 3.00
5 PDd(s),TNu,V:Harm 3.00
6 PDd(s),TNu,F:JLA 3.00
7 PDd(s),TNu,A:Nightwing 3.00
8 CDi(s),TNu,A:Razorsharp 3.00
9 PDd(s),V:Huggathugees 3.00
10 PDd(s),V:The Acolyte 3.00
11 PDd(s),Rescue Red Tornado . . . 3.00
12 PDd(s),TNu,Supergirl x-over Hell's Angels,pt.1 . . . . 3.00
13 PDd(s), Hell's Angels,pt.3 . . . . . 3.00
14 PDd(s),Day of Judgment x-over . 3.00
15 PDd(s),F:Arrowette 3.00
16 PDd(s). 2.50
17 PDd(s),A:A.P.E.S. 2.50
18 PDd(s),Young Injustice. 2.50
19 PDd(s),I:Empress 2.50
20 PDd(s),new team. 2.50
21 PDd(s),all new?. 2.50
22 Day in the life 2.50
23 PDd,TNu,AustraliaGames,pt.1 . . 2.50
24 PDd,TNu,AustraliaGames,pt.2 . . 2.50
25 PDd,TNu,Into space,pt.1 . . . . . . 2.50
26 PDd,TNu,Into space,pt.2 . . . . . . 2.50
Spec.#1,000,000 PDd(s),TNu 2.50

Young Justice Secret Files #1
© DC Comics, Inc.

Giant#1 Secret Origins, 80-page. . . 5.00
Giant#1 80-page. 5.00
Secret Files #1 . . . . 5.00
Spec.#1 Young Justice in No Man's Land, CDi(s) 4.00
Spec.#1 Young Justice: The Secret Impulse,Superboy,Robin (1998) 2.00
TPB A League of Their Own. 14.95

YOUNG JUSTICE: SINS OF YOUTH
March, 2000
1 (of 2) PDd,x-over 4.00
2 PDd,x-over 4.00
Secret Files #1 . . . . 5.00
TPB Sins of Youth 20.00

YOUNG LOVE
Sept.–Oct., 1963
39 . . . . 40.00
40 thru 50 . . . . @25.00
51 thru 70 . . . . @20.00
71 thru 80 . . . . @15.00
81 thru 126 . . . . @12.00

ZATANNA
1987
1 R:Zatanna 2.25
2 N:Zatanna 2.25
3 Come Together. 2.25
4 V:Xaos 2.25

ZERO HOUR: CRISIS IN TIME
1994
4 DJu(a&s),JOy,A:All DC Heroes, D;2nd Flash 3.50
3 DJu(a&S),JOy,D:G.A.Sandman, G:A.Atom,Dr.Fate,1st Wildcat IR:Time Trapper is Rokk Krinn, Hawkmen merged 2.00
2 DJu(a&s),Joy 2.00
1 DJu(a&s),JOy,b:Power Gir's Child 2.00
0 DJu(A&s),JOy,Gatefold(c),Extant vs. Spectre. 2.00

DC COMICS

Amazon #1 © DC/Marvel

Generation Hex #1 © DC/Marvel

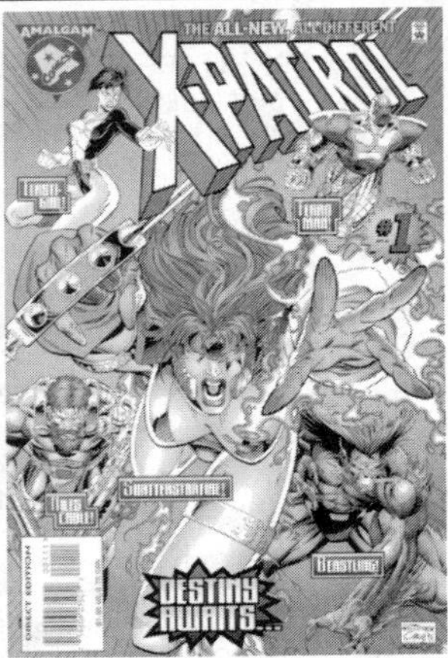

X-Patrol #1 © DC/Marvel

AMAZON
DC 1996–97

1 JBy,TA 3.00
1 one-shot JBy,Princess Ororo is Wonder Woman 2.00

ASSASSINS
DC 1996–97

1 DGC,SMc. 3.00
1 one-shot DGC(s),SMc,F:Dare and Catsai 2.00

BAT-THING
DC 1997

1 one-shot LHa(s),RDm,BSz, V:motorcycle gang 2.00

BRUCE WAYNE: AGENT OF S.H.I.E.L.D.
Marvel Comics 1996

1 CDi, ... 3.00

BULLETS & BRACELETS
Marvel Comics 1996

1 JOs,GFr,CaS 3.00

CHALLENGERS OF THE FANTASTIC
Marvel 1997

1 KK,TGu,AV. 2.00

DARK CLAW ADVENTURES, THE
DC 1997

1 one-shot TTy,RBr,V:Ladia Talia . . 2.00

DC VERSUS MARVEL MARVEL VERSUS DC

1 (DC)DJu. 6.00
1a 2nd printing 4.00
2 (Marvel)PDd,DJu 5.00
2a 2nd printing 4.00
3 (Marvel)DJu 4.00
4 (DC)PDd,DJu 4.00
TPB rep. mini series #1–#4. . . . . . 12.95

DOCTOR STRANGEFATE
DC Comics 1996–97

1 RMz,KN 3.00
1 one-shot RMz(s),JL,KN,Supreme Lord of Order 2.00

EXCITING X-PATROL
Marvel 1997

1 BKs,BHi 2.00

GENERATION HEX
DC 1997

1 one-shot,PrM(s),AdP,F:Jono Hex, Madam Banshee 2.00

IRON LANTERN
Marvel 1997

1 KB,PSm,AW. 2.00

JLX
DC Comics 1996–97

1 MWa,GJ, ... 3.00
1 one-shot,MWa(s),GJ,HPo,JhD . . 2.00

JLX UNLEASHED
DC 1997

1 one-shot, CPr,"The Inextinguishable Flame" 2.00

LEGENDS OF THE DARK CLAW
DC Comics 1996–97

1 LHa,JBa, ... 3.00
1 one-shot LHa(s),JBa, ... 2.00
1 2nd printing 2.00

LOBO THE DUCK
DC 1997

1 one-shot, AIG,VS,. 2.00

MAGNETO & THE MAGNETIC MEN
Marvel Comics 1996

1 MWa,GJ,JMs,ATi 3.00

MAGNETIC MEN FEATURING MAGNETO
Marvel 1997

1 TPe,BKi,DPs 2.00

SPEED DEMON
Marvel Comics 1996

1 HMe,SvL,AM 3.00

SPIDER-BOY
Marvel Comics 1996

1 KK,MeW. 3.00

SPIDER-BOY TEAM-UP
Marvel Comics 1997

1 KK,RSt. 2.00

SUPER-SOLDIER
DC Comics 1996–97

1 MWa,DGb 3.00
1-shot MWa(s),DGb,V:Ultra-Metallo, Green Skull, Hydra . . . 2.00

SUPER SOLDIER: MAN OF WAR
DC 1997

1 one-shot MWa(s),DGb,JP, V:Nazis 2.00

THORION OF THE NEW ASGODS
Marvel 1997

1 KG,JR2 . . . . 2.00

X-PATROL
Marvel Comics 1996

1 KK,BKs 3.00
The Amalgam Age of Comics: The DC Comics Collection TPBs 12.95
The Amalgam Age of Comics: The Marvel Comics Collection TPBs 12.95
Return to the Amalgam Age of Comics: The DC Comics Collection TPB . . 13.00

MARVEL

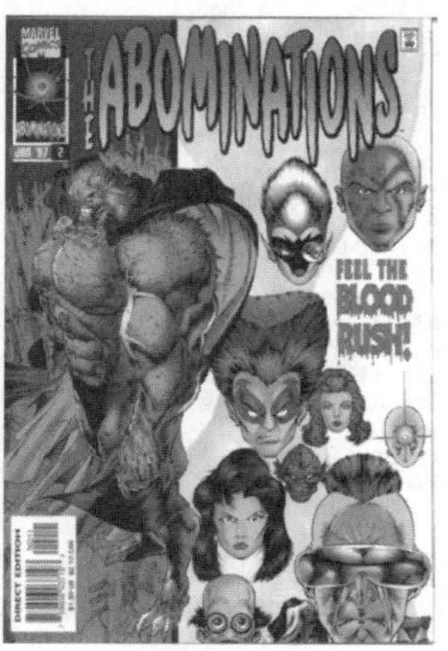

Abominations #2
© Marvel Entertainment Group

ABOMINATIONS
1996
1 (of 3) IV,AMe, Future Imperfect spin-off. 2.00
2 IV,AMe, ... 2.00
3 IV,AMe, ... 2.00

ABRAHAM STONE
1995
1 JKu, Early 20th century. 7.00
2 Wandering Man in the 20s 7.00

ACTION FORCE
March, 1987
1 U.K. G.I. Joe Series 2.00
2 thru 39 . . . . @2.00
40 1988 . . . . 2.00

ACTUAL CONFESSIONS
See: LOVE ADVENTURES

ACTUAL ROMANCES
Oct., 1949
1 . . . . 60.00
2 Photo Cover 40.00

ADVENTURE INTO FEAR
See: FEAR

ADVENTURE INTO MYSTERY
Atlas 1956–57
1 BEv(c),Future Tense 280.00
2 Man on the 13th Floor 160.00
3 Next Stop Eternity 135.00
4 AW, The Hex 150.00
5 BEv,The People Who Weren't. 140.00
6 The Wax Man. 140.00
7 . . . . 140.00

ADVENTURES INTO TERROR
See: JOKER COMICS

ADVENTURES INTO WEIRD WORLDS
Jan., 1952–June 1954
1 RH,GT,The Walking Death . . . 450.00
2 The Thing In the Bottle 250.00
3 The Thing That Waited 175.00
4 BEv,RH,TheVillage Graveyard 175.00
5 BEv,I Crawl Thru Graves 175.00
6 The Ghost Still Walks 175.00
7 Monsters In Disguise 175.00
8 Nightmares. 175.00
9 Do Not Feed. 175.00
10 BEv,Down In The Cellar. 175.00
11 Phantom 150.00
12 Lost In the Graveyard 150.00
13 Where Dead Men Walk 150.00
14 A Shriek In the Night 150.00
15 Terror In Our Town. 150.00
16 The Kiss of Death 150.00
17 RH,He Walks With A Ghost . . 150.00
18 Ivan & Petroff. 150.00
19 It Happened One Night 150.00
20 The Doubting Thomas 150.00
21 What Happened In the Cave . 150.00
22 RH,The Vampire's Partner . . . 150.00
23 The Kiss of Death 125.00
24 Halfway Home 125.00
25 BEv,JSt,The Mad Mamba. . . . 125.00
26 Good-Bye Earth. 150.00
27 The Dwarf of Horror Moor . . . 250.00
28 DW,Monsters From the Grave 150.00
29 Bone Dry 100.00
30 JSt,The Impatient Ghost 100.00

ADVENTURES OF CAPTAIN AMERICA
Sept., 1991
1 KM,JRu,O:Capt. America 5.75
2 KM,KWe,TA,O:Capt.America . . . 5.50
3 KM,KWe,JRu,D:Lt.Col.Fletcher . . 5.50
4 KWe,JRu,V:Red Skull. 5.50

ADVENTURES OF CYCLOPS & PHOENIX
1994
1 SLo(s),GeH,AV,O:Cable 4.00
2 SLo(s),GeH,AV,O:Cable 3.50
3 SLo(s),GeH,AV,O:Cable 3.50
4 SLo(s),GeH,AV,O:Cable 3.50
TPB Rep. #1-#4 . . . . 14.95

ADVENTURES OF HOMER GHOST
Atlas June–Aug., 1957
1 . . . . 45.00
2 . . . . 35.00

ADVENTURES OF PINKY LEE
Atlas July, 1955
1 . . . . 200.00
2 . . . . 125.00
3 thru 5 . . . . @100.00

ADVENTURES OF SNAKE PLISSKIN
1997
1-shot LKa, *Escape From L.A.* movie adapt. 3.00

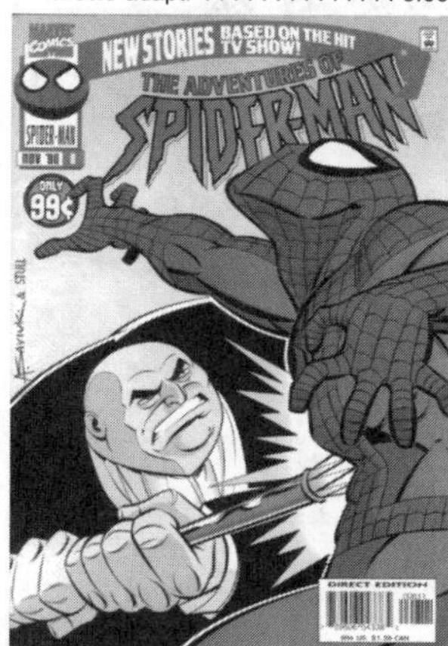

Adventures of Spider-Man #8
© Marvel Entertainment Group

ADVENTURES OF SPIDER-MAN
1996
1 from animated TV show 2.00
2 V:Hammerhead 2.00
3 thru 8 . . . . 2.00
8 AS,V:Kingpin 2.00
9 MHi,A:Dr. Strange, ... 2.00
10 AS,V:The Beetle 2.00
11 AS,V:Doctor Octopus, Venom . . 2.00
12 AS,V:Doctor Octopus, Venom . . 2.00

ADVENTURES OF THE UNCANNY X-MEN
1995
1 Rep. 2.50

ADVENTURES OF THE X-MEN
1996–97
1 from animated TV show 2.50
2 X-Factor vs. X-Men. 2.00
3 thru 7 . . . . 2.00
8 RMc,BHr,GyM,Gambit back in New Orleans 2.00
9 RMc,GyM,F:Storm 2.00
10 RMc,A:Vanisher. 2.00
11 RMc,V:Man-Thing 2.00
12 RMc,Age of Apocalypse. 2.00

ADVENTURES ON THE PLANET OF THE APES
Oct., 1975
1 GT,Planet of the Apes Movie Adaptation 2.50
2 GT,Humans Captured. 2.50

Adventures on the Planet of the Apes #1 © Marvel Entertainment Group

3 GT,Man Hunt 2.50
4 GT,Trial By Fear 2.50
5 GT, Fury in the
Forbidden Zone 2.50
6 GT,The Forbidden Zone,Cont'd. . 2.50
7 AA,Man Hunt Cont'd. 2.50
8 AA,Brent & Nova Enslaved 2.50
9 AA,Mankind's Demise. 2.50
10 AA,When Falls the Lawgiver . . . 2.50
11 AA,The Final Chapter;
Dec., 1976 . . . . 2.50

ADVENTURES OF THE THING

April–July, 1992

1 rep. Marvel 2 in 1 #50. . . . . 2.50
2 rep. Marvel 2 in 1 #80
B.U. Ghost Rider 2.00
3 rep. Marvel 2 in 1 #51. . . . . 2.00
4 rep. Marvel 2 in 1 #77. . . . . 2.00

AGE OF INNOCENCE

1995

1-shot Timeslid aftermath 2.50

AIRTIGHT GARAGE

Epic July–Oct. 1993

1 thru 4 rep.Moebius GNv . . . . . @2.50

AKIRA

Epic Sept., 1988

1 The Highway,I:Kaneda,Tetsuo,
Koy,Ryu,Colonel,Takaski. 17.00
1a 2nd printing 3.00
2 Pursuit,I:Number27,(Masaru) . . . 8.00
2a 2nd printing 3.50
3 Number 41,V:Clown Gang 8.00
4 King of Clowns,V:Colonel 8.00
5 Cycle Wars,V:Clown Gang 7.00
6 D:Yamagota 6.00
7 Prisoners and Players,I:Miyo . . . 6.00
8 Weapon of Vengeance 6.00
9 Stalkers 6.00
10 The Awakening 6.00
11 Akira Rising 5.50
12 Enter Sakaki 5.50
13 Desperation. 5.50
14 Caught in the Middle 5.50
15 Psychic Duel 5.50
16 Akira Unleashed 5.50
17 Emperor of Chaos 5.50
18 Amid the Ruins 5.00
19 To Save the Children 5.00
20 Revelations 5.00
21 . . . . 5.00
22 . . . . 5.00
23 . . . . 5.00
24 Clown Gang 5.00
25 Search For Kay 5.00
26 Juvenile A Project 5.00
27 Kay and Kaneda 5.00
28 Tetsuo 5.00
29 Tetsuo 5.00
30 Tetsuo,Kay,Kaneda 5.00
31 D:Kaori,Kaneda,Vs.Tetsuo 5.00
32 Tetsuo'sForces vs.U.S.Forces . . 5.00
33 Tetsuo V:Kaneda 5.00
34 64pt. R:Otomo 8.00
35 Leads toward final battle 8.00
36 Lady Miyako 8.00
37 ghost of Tetsuo 8.00
38 conclusion 8.00
TPB Akira:Reprints#1-#3 . . . . 13.95
TPB Akira:Reprints#4-#6 . . . . 13.95
TPB Akira:Reprints#7-#9 . . . . 13.95
TPB Akira:Reprints#10-#12. . . . . . 14.95
TPB Akira:Reprints#13-#15. . . . . . 14.95
TPB Akira:Reprints#16-#18. . . . . . 14.95
TPB Akira:Reprints#19-#21. . . . . . 16.95
TPB Akira:Reprints#22-#24. . . . . . 16.95
TPB Akira:Reprints#25-#27. . . . . . 16.95
TPB Akira:Reprints#28-#30. . . . . . 17.95

ALADDIN

1 . . . . 2.00
2 . . . . 2.00
3 . . . . 2.00
4 . . . . 2.00
5 A:Queen Tatiana. 2.00
6 A:Zena 2.00
7 Genie Convention. 2.00
8 Body Switch 2.00
9 Archery Contest 2.00
10 Genie winds back his powers. . . 2.00
11 Magic Carpet Grand Prix 2.00
12 F:Iago 2.00

ALF

Star March, 1988

1 Photo Cover 3.00
1a 2nd printing 2.00
2 Alf Causes trouble 2.00
3 More adventures 2.00
4 Willie on Melmac 2.00
5 I:Alf's evil twin. 2.00
6 Photo Cover 2.00
7 Pygm-Alien. 2.00
8 Ochmoneks' Garage. 2.00
9 Alf's Independence Day 2.00
10 Alf goes to College 2.00
11 Halloween special 2.00
12 Alf loses memory. 2.00
13 Racetrack of my Tears. 2.00
14 Night of the Living Bread 2.00
15 Alf on the Road 2.00
16 More Adventures. 2.00
17 Future vision 2.00
18 More Adventures 2.00
19 The Alf-strologer 2.00
20 Alf the Baby Sitter,pt.1 . . . . 2.00
21 Alf the Baby Sitter,pt.2 . . . . 2.00
22 X-Men parody 2.00
23 Alf visits Australia 2.00
24 Rhonda visits Earth 2.00
25 More Adventures. 2.00
26 Alf gets a job 2.00
27 Alf lost. 2.00
28 Alf's Amnesia. 2.00
29 Alf/Brian reporters 2.00
30 Shakespeare Baby 2.00
31 Alf's Summer Camp. 2.00
32 Arnold Schwarzemeimac 2.00
33 Dungeons & Dragons Spoof . . . 2.00
34 Alf-Red & Alf-Blue(2 Alfs). 2.00
35 Gone with the Wind 2.00
36 More Adventures 2.00
37 Melmacian Gothic 2.00
38 Boundtree Hunters. 2.00
39 Pizarro Alf 2.00
40 A:Zoreo 2.00
41 TV. 2.00
42 V:Alf 2.00
43 House Break-in 2.00
44 A:Fantastic Fur 2.00
45 Melmenopaus 2.00
46 Goes to Center of Earth. 2.00
47 Meteor Bye-Products,pt.1 . . . . . 2.00
48 Meteor Bye-Products,pt.2 . . . . . 2.00
49 1st Rhonda solo story 2.00
50 Final Issue, giant size 2.50
Ann.#1 Evol.War. 3.00
Ann.#2 . . . . 2.00
Spring Spec.#1. . . . . 2.00
Holiday Spec.#2 . . . . 2.00

ALIEN LEGION

Epic April, 1984

1 FC,TA,I:Sarigar,Montroc 4.00
2 FC,TA,CP,V:Harkilons. 3.50
3 FC,TA,CW,V:Kroyzo 3.00
4 FC,TA,CW,F:Skob 3.00
5 FC,CW,D:Skob. 3.00
6 FC,CW,WPo,V:Harkilons 3.00
7 CW,WPo,I:Lora. 2.50
8 CW,WPo,V:Harkilons 2.50
9 CW,V:Harkilons 2.50
10 CW,LSn,V:Harkilons 2.50
11 CW,LSn,V:Harkilons. 2.50
12 LSn,A:Aob-Sin. 2.50
13 LSn,F:Montroc. 2.50
14 LSn,V:Cordar. 2.50
15 LSn,V:Alphor,Betro,&Gamoid . . . 2.50
16 LSn,J:Tomaro 2.50
17 LSn,Durge on Drugs 2.50
18 LSn,V:Dun. 2.50
19 LSn,A:GalarcyScientist 2.50
20 LSn,L:Skilene 2.50

[2nd Series] Aug. 1987

1 LSn,I:Guy Montroc 3.00
2 LSn,V:Quallians 2.50
3 LSn,Hellscope 2.50
4 LSn,V:Harkillons. 2.50
5 LSn,F:JuggerGrimrod 2.50
6 LSn,F:JuggerGrimrod 2.50
7 LSn,A:Guy Montroc 2.50
8 LSn,I:Nakhira 2.50
9 LSn,V:Harkilons 2.50
10 LSn,V:Harkilons. 2.50
11 LSn,V:Harkilons 2.50
12 LSn,Tamara Pregnant 2.50
13 LSn,V:MomojianKndrel 2.50
14 LSn,J:Saravil 2.50
15 LSn,J:Spellik 2.50
16 LSn,D:Jugger's Father. 2.50
17 LSn,O:JuggerGrimrod 2.50
18 LSn,O:JuggerGrimrod 2.50
GN Grimrod 5.95

ALIEN LEGION: BINARY DEEP

Epic 1993

1-shot with trading card 3.50

MARVEL

ALIEN LEGION: JUGGER GRIMROD

Epic Aug., 1992

Book One 6.00

ALIEN LEGION: ONE PLANET AT A TIME

Epic Heavy Hitters May, 1993

1 HNg,CDi,One Planet at a Time . . 5.00
2 HNg,CDi. 5.00
3 HNg,CDi. 5.00

ALIEN LEGION: ON THE EDGE

Epic Nov., 1990

1 LSn,V:B'Be No N'ngth 5.00
2 LSn,V:B'Be No N'ngth 5.00
3 LSn,V:B'Be No N'ngth 5.00
4 LSn,V:B'Be No N'ngth 5.00

ALIEN LEGION: TENANTS OF HELL

Epic 1991

1 LSn,Nomad Squad On Combine IV 4.50
2 LSn,L:Torie Montroc,I:Stagg 4.50
TPB Alien Legion:Slaughterworld . 10.00

ALL-SELECT COMICS

Fall, 1943

Timely (Daring Comics)

1 B:Capt.America,Sub-Mariner, Human Torch;WWII 8,400.00
2 A:Red Skull,V:Axis Powers. . 2,700.00
3 B:Whizzer,V:Axis 1,600.00
4 V: Axis. 1,300.00
5 E:Sub-Mariner,V:Axis 1,200.00
6 A:The Destroyer,V:Axis 1,000.00
7 E:Whizzer,V:Axis 1,000.00
8 V:Axis Powers 1,000.00
9 V:Axis Powers 1,000.00
10 E:Capt.America,Human Torch; A:The Destroyer 1,000.00
11 I:Blonde Phantom,A:Miss America. 1,900.00
Becomes:

All-Select #4
© Marvel Entertainment Group

BLONDE PHANTOM

12 B:Miss America;The Devil's Playground 1,200.00
13 B:Sub-Mariner;Horror In Hollywood 700.00
14 E:Miss America;Horror At Haunetd Castle. 650.00
15 The Man Who Deserved To Die 650.00
16 A:Capt.America,Bucky; Modeled For Murder. 850.00
17 Torture & Rescue. 600.00
18 Jealously,Hate & Cruelty 600.00
19 Killer In the Hospital. 600.00
20 Blonde Phantom's Big Fall . . . 600.00
21 Murder At the Carnival. 600.00
22 V: Crime Bosses 600.00
Becomes:

LOVERS

23 Love Stories 150.00
24 My Dearly Beloved. 50.00
25 The Man I Love 60.00
26 thru 29. . . . . @40.00
30 MK 60.00
31 thru 36 . . . . @40.00
37 . . . . 60.00
38 BK. 60.00
39 . . . . 40.00
40. . . . . 40.00
41BEv 50.00
42 thru 65 . . . . @40.00
66 . . . . 35.00
67 ATh 50.00
68 thru 86 Aug. 1957 . . . . @35.00

ALL SURPRISE

Timely Fall, 1943

1 (fa),F:Super Rabbit,Gandy, Sourpuss 200.00
2 . . . . 100.00
3 . . . . 75.00
4 thru 10 . . . . @75.00
11 HK. 100.00
12 Winter, 1946 . . . . 75.00

ALL-TRUE CRIME

See: OFFICIAL TRUE CRIME CASES

ALL WINNERS COMICS

Summer, 1941

1 S&K,BEv,B:Capt.America & Bucky, Human Torch & Toro,Sub-Mariner A:The Angel,Black Marvel 15,000.00
2 S&K,B:Destroyer,Whizzer. . . 4,000.00
3 BEv,Bucky & Toro Captured . 2,400.00
4 BEv,Battle For Victory For America. 2,500.00
5 V:Nazi Invasion Fleet 1,500.00
6 V:Axis Powers,A: Black Avenger 1,600.00
7 V:Axis Powers 1,200.00
8 V:Axis Powers 1,100.00
9 V:Nazi Submarine Fleet 1,100.00
10 V:Nazi Submarine Fleet . . . 1,200.00
11 V: Nazis 1,000.00
12 A:Red Skull,E:Destroyer; Jap P.O.W. Camp 1,200.00
13 V:Japanese Fleet 1,000.00
14 V:Japanese Fleet 1,000.00
15 Japanese Supply Train 1,000.00
16 In Alaska V:Gangsters. 1,000.00
17 V:Gansters;Atomic Research Department 1,000.00
18 V:Robbers;Internal Revenue Department 1,100.00
19 I:All Winners Squad, Fall, 1946 . . . . 3,500.00
21 A:All-Winners Squad;Riddle of the Demented Dwarf . . . 3,000.00
Becomes:

ALL TEEN COMICS

20 F:Georgie,Willie, Mitzi,Patsy Walker 150.00
Becomes:

TEEN COMICS

21 HK,A:George,Willie,Mitzi, Patsy Walker, Hey Look 125.00
22 A:George,Willie,Margie, Patsy Walker 75.00
23 A:Patsy Walker,Cindy,George . 75.00
24 . . . . 85.00
25. . . . . 75.00
26. . . . . 75.00
27. . . . . 75.00
28. . . . . 80.00
29. . . . . 75.00
30 HK,Hey Look 100.00
31 thru 34 . . . . @75.00
35 May, 1950 . . . . 75.00
Becomes:

JOURNEY INTO UNKNOWN WORLDS

Atlas Sept., 1950

36(1) RH,End of the Earth. . . . 1,800.00
37(2) BEv,GC,When Worlds Collide 800.00
38(3) GT,Land of Missing Men . . 700.00
4 MS,RH,Train to Nowhere 450.00
5 MS,Trapped in Space 450.00
6 GC,RH,World Below the Atlantic. 450.00
7 BW,RH,House That Wasn't. . . 700.00
8 RH,The Stone Thing. 450.00
9 MS,JSt,The People Who Couldn't Exist 500.00
10 THe Undertaker 400.00
11 BEv,Frankie Was Afraid 300.00
12 BK,Last Voice You Hear. 300.00
13 The Witch Woman 250.00
14 BW,BEv,CondemnedBuilding . 550.00
15 They Crawl By Night 550.00
16 Scared to Death. 250.00
17 BEv,GC,RH,The Ice Monster Cometh. 250.00
18 The Broth Needs Somebody . 275.00
19 MF,GC,The Long Wait 275.00
20 GC,RH,The Race That Vanished 250.00
21 MF. 225.00

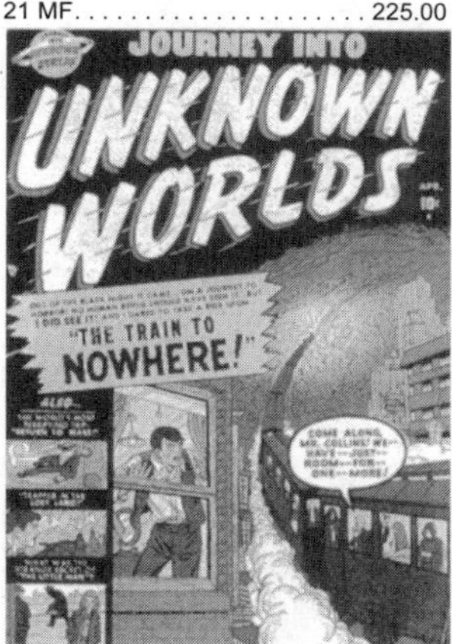

Journey Into Unknown Worlds #4
© Marvel Entertainment Group

22 thru 33 @225.00
34 MK,AT 200.00
35 AT 200.00
36 thru 44 @125.00
45 AW,SD 135.00
46 & 47 @125.00
48 GW 125.00
49 125.00
50 JDa,RC 125.00
51 WW,SD,JSe 135.00
52 125.00
53 RC,BP 125.00
54 AT,BP 125.00
55 AW,RC,BEv 125.00
56 BEv 125.00
57 JO 110.00
58 MO 110.00
59 AW,August, 1957 125.00

ALL WINNERS COMICS

[2nd Series] August, 1948

1 F:Blonde Phantom,A:Capt.America Sub-Mariner,Human Torch 2,000.00

Becomes:

ALL WESTERN WINNERS

2 B,I&O:Black Rider,B:Two-Gun Kid, Kid-Colt 650.00
3 Black Rider V: Satan 325.00
4 Black Rider Unmasked 300.00

Becomes:

WESTERN WINNERS

5 I Challenge the Army 250.00
6 The Mountain Mystery 200.00
7 Ph(c) Randolph Scott 200.00

Becomes:

BLACK RIDER

8 Ph(c),B:Black Rider;Valley of Giants 350.00
9 Wrath of the Redskin 175.00
10 O:Black Rider 200.00
11 Redmen on the Warpath 125.00
12 GT,The Town That Vanished 125.00
13 The Terrified Tribe 125.00
14 The Tyrant of Texas 125.00
15 Revolt of the Redskins 100.00
16 100.00
17 100.00
18 100.00
19 SSh,GT,A:Two-Gun Kid 100.00
20 GT 110.00
21 SSh,GT,A:Two-Gun Kid 100.00
22 SSh,A:Two-Gun Kid 100.00
23 SSh,A:Two-Gun Kid 100.00
24 SSh,JSt 100.00
25 SSh,JSt,A:Arrowhead 100.00
26 SSh,A:Kid-Colt 100.00
27 SSh,A:Kid-Colt 110.00

Becomes:

WESTERN TALES OF BLACK RIDER

28 JSe,D:Spider 125.00
29 90.00
30 90.00
31 90.00

Becomes:

GUNSMOKE WESTERN

32 MD,MB,F:Kid Colt,Billy Buckskin 125.00
33 MD 100.00
34 MB 75.00
35 100.00
36 AW 100.00
37 JDa 75.00
38 50.00
39 50.00
40 AW 75.00
41 35.00
42 35.00
43 40.00
44 AT 45.00
45 thru 55 @40.00
56 MB 45.00
57 thru 76 @40.00
77 July, 1963 35.00

TIMELY PRESENTS: ALL-WINNERS

Oct., 1999

Spec. 48-pg. 4.00

ALPHA FLIGHT

August, 1983

1 JBy,I:Puck,Marrina,Tundra 3.00
2 JBy,I:Master,Vindicator Becomes Guardian,B:O:Marrina 2.00
3 JBy,O:Master,A:Namor,Invisible Girl, 2.00
4 JBy,A:Namor,Invisible Girl, E:O:Marrina,A:Master 2.00
5 JBy,B:O:Shaman,F:Puck 2.00
6 JBy,E:O:Shaman,I:Kolomag 2.00
7 JBy,B:O:Snowbird,I:Delphine Courtney & Deadly Ernest 2.00
8 JBy,E:O:Snowbird,O:Deadly Ernest,I:Nemesis 2.00
9 JBy,O:Aurora,A:Wolverine, Super Skrull 2.00
10 JBy,O:Northstar,V:SuperSkrull 2.00
11 JBy,I:Omega Flight,Wild Child O:Sasquatch 2.00
12 JBy,D:Guardian,V:Omega Flight 2.00
13 JBy,C:Wolverine,Nightmare 3.00
14 JBy,V:Genocide 2.00
15 JBy,R:Master 2.00
16 JBy,BWi,V:Master,C:Wolverine I:Madison Jeffries 2.25
17 JBy,BWi,A:Wolverine,X-Men 3.00
18 JBy,BWi,J:Heather,I:Ranaq 2.00
19 JBy,I:Talisman,V:Ranaq 2.00
20 JBy,I:Gilded Lily,N:Aurora 2.00
21 JBy,BWi,O:Gilded Lily,Diablo 2.00
22 JBy,BWi,I:Pink Pearl 2.00
23 JBy,BWi,D:Sasquatch, I:Tanaraq 2.00
24 JBy,BWi,V:Great Beasts,J:Box 2.00
25 JBy,BWi,V:Omega Flight I:Dark Guardian 2.00

Alpha Flight #15
© Marvel Entertainment Group

26 JBy,BWi,A:Omega Flight,Dark Guardian 2.00
27 JBy,V:Omega Flight 2.00
28 JBy,Secret Wars II,V:Omega Flight,D:Dark Guardian 2.00
29 MMi,V:Hulk,A:Box 2.00
30 MMi,I&O:Scramble,R:Deadly Ernest 2.00
31 MMi,D:Deadly Ernest, O:Nemesis 2.00
32 MMi(c),JBg,O:Puck,I:2nd Vindicator 2.00
33 MMi(c),SB,X-Men,I:Deathstrike 3.00
34 MMi(c),SB,Wolverine,V: Deathstrike 3.00
35 DR,R:Shaman 2.00
36 MMi(c),DR,A:Dr.Strange 2.00
37 DR,O:Pestilence,N:Aurora 2.00
38 DR,A:Namor,V:Pestilence 2.00
39 MMi(c),DR,WPo,A:Avengers 2.25
40 DR,WPo,W:Namor & Marrina 2.25
41 DR,WPo,I:Purple Girl, J:Madison Jeffries 2.25
42 DR,WPo,I:Auctioneer,J:Purple Girl, A: Beta Flight 2.25
43 DR,WPo,V:Mesmero,Sentinels 2.25
44 DR,WPo,D:Snowbird, A:Pestilence 2.25
45 JBr,WPo,R:Sasquatch, L:Shaman 2.25
46 JBr,WPo,I:2nd Box 2.25
47 MMi,WPo,TA,Vindicator solo 2.25
48 SL(i),I:Omega 2.25
49 JBr,WPo,I:Manikin,D:Omega 2.25
50 WS(c),JBr,WPo,L:Northstar,Puck, Aurora,A:Loki,Double size 2.50
51 JLe(1st Marv),WPo(i),V:Cody 4.00
52 JBr,WPo(i),I:Bedlam, A:Wolverine 3.00
53 JLe,WPo(i),I:Derangers,Goblyn D&V:Bedlam,A:Wolverine 3.00
54 WPo(i),O&J:Goblyn 2.00
55 JLe,TD,V:Tundra 2.50
56 JLe,TD,V:Bedlamites 2.50
57 JLe,TD,V:Crystals, C:Dreamqueen 2.50
58 JLe,AM,V:Dreamqueen 2.50
59 JLe,AM,I:Jade Dragon,R:Puck 2.50
60 JLe,AM,V:J.Dragon,D.Queen 2.50
61 JLe,AM,on Trial (1st JLe X-Men) 2.50
62 JLe,AM,V:Purple Man 2.50
63 MG,V:U.S.Air Force 2.00
64 JLe,AM,V:Great Beasts 2.50
65 JLe(c),AM(i),Dream Issue 2.00
66 JLe(c),I:China Force 2.00
67 JLe(c),O:Dream Queen 2.00
68 JLe(c),V:Dream Queen 2.00
69 JLe(c),V:Dream Queen 2.00
70 MM(i),V:Dream Queen 2.00
71 MM(i),I:Sorcerer 2.00
72 V:Sorcerer 2.00
73 MM(i),V:Sorcerer 2.00
74 MM(i),Alternate Earth 2.00
75 JLe(c),MMi(i),Double Size 3.00
76 MM(i),V:Sorcerer 2.00
77 MM(i),V:Kingpin 2.00
78 MM(i),A:Dr.Strange,Master 2.00
79 MM(i),AofV,V:Scorpion,Nekra 2.00
80 MM(i),AofV,V:Scorpion,Nekra 2.00
81 JBy(c),MM(i),B:R:Northstar 2.00
82 JBy(c),MM(i),E:R:Northstar 2.00
83 JSh 2.00
84 MM(i),Northstar 2.00
85 MM(i) 2.00
86 MBa,MM,V:Sorcerer 2.00
87 JLe(c),MM(i),A:Wolverine 3.00
88 JLe(c),MM(i),A:Wolverine 3.00
89 JLe(c),MM(i),R:Guardian,A: Wolverine 3.00

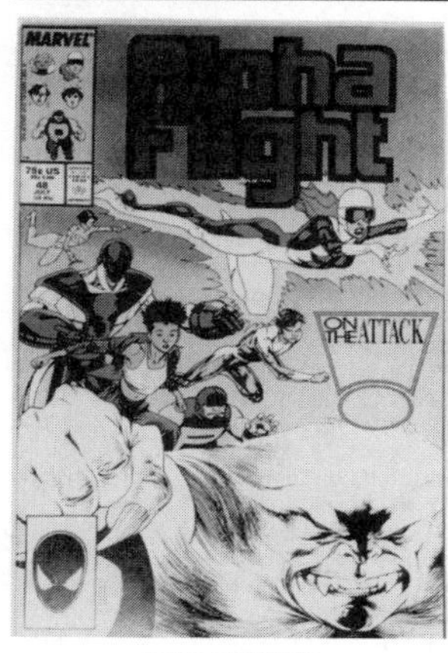

Alpha Flight #48
© Marvel Entertainment Group

90 JLe(c),MM(i),A:Wolverine. 3.00
91 MM(i),A:Dr.Doom. 2.00
92 Guardian vs.Vindicator. 2.00
93 MM(i),A:Fant.Four,I:Headlok . . . 2.00
94 MM(i),V:Fant.Four,Headlok 2.00
95 MM(i),Lifelines 2.00
96 MM(i),A:Master 2.00
97 B:Final Option,A:Her 2.00
98 A:Avengers 2.00
99 A:Avengers 2.00
100 JBr,TMo,DR,LMa,E:Final Option A:Galactus,Avengers,D: Guardian,G-Size. 2.50
101 TMo,Final Option Epilogue, A:Dr.Strange,Avengers 2.00
102 TMo,I:Weapon Omega, ... 2.00
103 TMo,V:Diablo,U.S.Agent 2.00
104 TMo,N:Alpha Flight,Weapon Omega is Wild Child. 2.00
105 TMo,V:Pink Pearl. 2.00
106 MPa,Aids issue,Northstar acknowledges homosexuality . . 2.50
106a 2nd printing 2.50
107 A:X-Factor,V:Autopsy. 2.00
108 A:Soviet Super Soldiers. 2.00
109 V:Peoples Protectorate 2.00
110 PB,Infinity War,I:2nd Omega Flight,A:Wolverine 2.00
111 PB,Infinity War,V:Omega Flight,A:Wolverine 2.00
112 PB,Infinity War,V:Master. 2.00
113 V:Mauler 2.00
114 A:Weapon X 2.00
115 PB,I:Wyre,A:Weapon X 2.00
116 PB,I:Rok,V:Wyre 2.00
117 PB,V:Wyre. 2.00
118 PB,V:Thunderball. 2.00
119 PB,V:Wrecking Crew 2.00
120 PB,10th Anniv.,V:Hardliners, w/poster. 2.50
121 PCu,V:Brass Bishop,A:Spider-Man,Wolverine,C:X-Men. 2.00
122 PB,BKi,Inf.Crusade 2.00
123 PB,BKi,Infinity Crusade 2.00
124 PB,BKi,Infinity Crusade 2.00
125 PB,V:Carcass 2.00
126 V:Carcass 2.00
127 SFu(s),Infinity Crusade 2.00
128 B:No Future. 2.00
129 C:Omega Flight 2.00
130 E:No Future,last issue, Double Sized 2.50
Ann.#1 LSn,V:Diablo,Gilded Lily . . . 3.00
Ann.#2 JBr,BMc 2.00

Spec.#1 PB,A:Wolverine, O:First Team,V:Egghead. 3.75
Spec.#1–#3 Newsstand versions of #97–#99 . . . . @1.50
Spec.#4 Newsstand ver.of #100 . . . 2.00

ALPHA FLIGHT
1997

1 SSe,ScC, former team kidnapped, I:Murmur, Radius,Flex, Guardian 5.00
2 SSe,ScC 3.00
2 variant cover. 3.00
3 SSe,ScC, ... 3.00
4 SSe,ScC,V:Mesmero 2.50
5 SSe,ScC,A:Mesmero 2.50
6 SSe,What's up with Sasquatch? . 2.50
7 SSe,Evils explode. 2.50
8 SSe,ScC,North & South prelude . 2.50
9 SSe,ScC,North & South pt.1, X-men x-over 2.50
10 SSe,Flung into Prometheus Pit . 2.50
11 SSe,race to save 2 worlds 2.50
12 SSe,Alphan dies,48pg. double size 3.00
13 SSe,F:Basil Killbrew 2.00
14 SSe,I:Brass Bishop 2.00
15 SSe. 2.00
16 SSe,V:Brass Bishop. 2.00
17 SSe,V:X the Unknown 2.00
18 SSe,Alpha:Omega,pt.1 . . . . 2.00
19 SSe,Alpha:Omega,pt.2 . . . . 2.00
20 SSe,Alpha:Omega,pt.3 . . . . 2.00
Spec. #1 SSe,"In the Beginning," Flashback, A:Wolverine 2.00
Ann.1998 Alpha Flight/Inhumans . . 3.50

ALPHA FLIGHT SPECIAL
1991

1 thru 4 reprints . . . . @2.00

AMAZING ADVENTURES
June, 1961

1 JK,SD,O&B:Dr.Droom;Torr . 1,300.00
2 JK,SD,This is Manoo 600.00
3 JK,SD,Trapped in the Twilight World 550.00
4 JK,SD, I Am X 500.00
5 JK,SD, Monsteroso 500.00
6 JK,SD,E:Dr.Droom; Sserpo . . . 500.00
Becomes:

Amazing Adult Fantasy #12
© Marvel Entertainment Group

AMAZING ADULT FANTASY
Dec., 1961

7 SD,Last Man on Earth 600.00
8 SD,The Coming of the Krills . . 500.00
9 SD,The Terror of Tim Boo Ba . 450.00
10 SD,Those Who Change 450.00
11 SD,In Human Form 450.00
12 SD,Living Statues 450.00
13 SD,At the Stroke of Midnight . 450.00
14 SD,Beware of the Giants 475.00
Becomes:

AMAZING FANTASY
August, 1962

15 JK(c),SD,I&O:Spider-Man,I:Aunt May, Flash Thompson, Burglar, I&D:Uncle Ben. 28,000.00
Marvel Milestone rep.#15 (1992). . . 3.00

[Second Series] 1995

15a gold Rep. (1995) 25.00
16 KBk, O:Spider-Man,painted 4.00
17 KBk, More early adventures. . . . 4.00
18 KBk,conclusion 4.00

AMAZING ADVENTURES
August, 1970
[1st Regular Series]

1 JK,JB,B:Inhumans,Bl.Widow. . . 50.00
2 JK,JB,A:Fantastic Four. 20.00
3 JK,GC,BEv,V:Mandarin. 20.00
4 JK,GC,BEv,V:Mandarin. 20.00
5 NA,TP,DH,BEv,V:Astrologer . . . 30.00
6 NA,DH,SB,V:Maximus 30.00
7 NA,DH,BEv 30.00
8 NA,DH,BEv,E:Black Widow, A:Thor,(see Avengers #95). . . 30.00
9 MSy,BEv,V:Magneto 15.00
10 GK(c),MSy,V:Magneto, E:Inhumans 15.00
11 GK(c),TS,B:O:New Beast, A:X-Men. 90.00
12 GK(c),TS,MP,A:Iron Man 25.00
13 JR(c),TS,V:New Br'hood Evil Mutants,I:Buzz Baxter (Mad Dog) 25.00
14 GK(c),TS,JM,V:Quasimodo . . . 25.00
15 JSn(c),TS,A:X-Men,V:Griffin. . . 25.00
16 JSn(c),FMc(i),V:Juggernaut . . . 25.00
17 JSn,A:X-Men,E:Beast 25.00
18 HC,NA,B:Killraven 25.00
19 HC,Sirens on 7th Avenues. 7.00
20 Coming of the Warlords 7.00
21 Cry Killraven 7.00
22 Killraven 7.00
23 Killraven 7.00
24 New Year Nightmare-2019AD . . 7.00
25 RB,V:Skar 7.00
26 GC,V:Ptson-Rage Vigilante 7.00
27 CR,JSn,V:Death Breeders 7.00
28 JSn,CR,V:Death Breeders 7.00
29 CR,Killraven 7.00
30 CR,Killraven 7.00
31 CR,Killraven 7.00
32 CR,Killraven 7.00
33 CR,Killraven 7.00
34 CR,D:Hawk 7.00
35 KG,Killraven Continued 7.00
36 CR,Killraven Continued 7.00
37 CR,O:Old Skull 7.00
38 CR,Killraven Continued. 7.00
39 CR,E:Killraven. 7.00

[2nd Regular Series]

1 rep.X-Men#1,38,Professor X. . . . 7.00
2 rep.X-Men#1,39,O:Cyclops. 6.00
3 rep.X-Men#2,40,O:Cyclops. 6.00
4 rep.X-Men#2,41,O:Cyclops. 6.00
5 rep.X-Men#3,42,O:Cyclops. 6.00

MARVEL

6 JBy(c),rep.X-Men#3,43,Cyclops . 6.00
7 rep.X-Men#4,44,O:Iceman 6.00
8 rep.X-Men#4,45,O:Iceman 6.00
9 JBy(c),X-Men#5,46,O:Iceman . . . 6.00
10 rep.X-Men#5,47,O:Iceman 6.00
11 rep.X-Men#6,48,Beast 6.00
12 rep.X-Men#6,Str.Tales#168 . . . . 6.00
13 rep.X-Men #7. . . . . 6.00
14 rep.X-Men #8. . . . . 6.00

AMAZING COMICS

Timely Comics Fall, 1944

1 F:Young Allies,Destroyer, Whizzer, Sergeant Dix . . . 1,500.00

Becomes:

COMPLETE COMICS

2 F:Young Allies,Destroyer,Whizzer Sergeant Dix; Winter '44-45 . . . . 1,100.00

AMAZING DETECTIVE CASES

Atlas Nov., 1950

3 Detective/Horror Stories 200.00
4 Death of a Big Shot 125.00
5 . . . . 125.00
6 Danger in the City 125.00
7 . . . . 100.00
8 . . . . 100.00
9 GC, The Man Who Wasn't . . . 100.00
10 GT. 100.00
11 The Black Shadow. 150.00
12 MS,BK, Harrigan's Wake 150.00
13 BEv,JSt,. 200.00
14 Hands Off; Sept., 1952 . . . . . 150.00

AMAZING HIGH ADVENTURE

August, 1984

1 BSz,JSo,JS 3.00
2 PS,AW,BSz,TA,MMi,BBI,CP,CW . 2.50
3 MMi,VM,JS. 2.50
4 JBo,JS,SBi 2.50
5 JBo; Oct., 1986 . . . . 2.50

AMAZING SCARLET SPIDER

1 MBa,LMa,VirtualMortality,pt.2 . . . 2.50
2 TDF,MBa,CyberWar,pt.2 . . . . 2.50

AMAZING SPIDER-MAN

March, 1963

1 JK(c),SED,I:Chameleon,J.Jonah & John Jameson,A:F.Four . . 20,000.00
2 SD,I:Vulture,Tinkerer C:Mysterio(disguised) 3,200.00
3 SD,I&O:Dr.Octopus 2,400.00
4 SD,I&O:Sandman,I:Betty Brant,Liz Allen 1,800.00
5 SD,V:Dr.Doom,C:Fant.Four . 1,500.00
6 SD,I&O:Lizard,The Connors. 1,300.00
7 SD,V:Vulture. 900.00
8 SD,JK,I:Big Brain,V:Human Torch,A:Fantastic Four 850.00
9 SD,I&O:Electro 900.00
10 SD,I:Enforcers,Big Man 850.00
11 SD,V:Dr.Octopus, D:Bennett Brant 500.00
12 SD,V:Dr.Octopus 500.00
13 SD,I:Mysterio. 700.00
14 SD,I:Green Goblin, V:Enforcers, Hulk. 1,700.00
15 SD,I:Kraven,A:Chameleon . . . 600.00
16 SD,A:Daredevil, V:Ringmaster 400.00
17 SD,2nd A:Green Goblin, A:Human Torch. 600.00
18 SD,V:Sandman,Enforcers, C:Avengers,F.F.,Daredevil. . . 400.00
19 SD,V:Sandman,I:Ned Leeds A:Human Torch. 350.00
20 SD,I&O:Scorpion 400.00
21 SD,A:Beetle,Human Torch . . . 275.00
22 SD,V:The Clown,Masters of Menace 350.00
23 SD,V:GreenGoblin(3rd App.) . 400.00
24 SD,V:Mysterio 225.00
25 SD,I:Spider Slayer,Spencer Smythe,C:Mary Jane 275.00
26 SD,I:CrimeMaster,V:Green Goblin 325.00
27 SD,V:CrimeMaster, Green Goblin 300.00
28 SD,I:Molten Man,Peter Parker Graduates High School,rare in near-mint condition 400.00
29 SD,V:Scorpion 175.00
30 SD,I:Cat Burglar. 175.00
31 SD,I:Gwen Stacy,Harry Osborn Prof.Warren,V:Dr.Octopus. . . 175.00
32 SD,V:Dr.Octopus 175.00
33 SD,V:Dr.Octopus 175.00
34 SD,V:Kraven 175.00
35 SD,V:Molten Man. 175.00
36 SD,I:The Looter. 175.00
37 SD,V:Professor Stromm, I:Norman Osborn 175.00
38 SD,V:Joe Smith(Boxer) 175.00
39 JR,IR:Green Goblin is Norman Osborn. 225.00
40 JR,O:Green Goblin 325.00
41 JR,I:Rhino,C:Mary Jane. 175.00
42 JR,V:John Jameson,I:Mary Jane (Face Revealed) 150.00
43 JR,O:Rhino 100.00
44 JR,V:Lizard(2nd App.) 100.00
45 JR,V:Lizard 100.00
46 JR,I&O:Shocker 110.00
47 JR,V:Kraven 100.00
48 JR,I:Fake Vulture,A:Vulture . . 100.00
49 JR,V:Fake Vulture,Kraven . . . 100.00
50 JR,I:Kingpin,Spidey Quits, C:Johnny Carson 400.00
51 JR,V:Kingpin 175.00
52 JR,V:Kingpin,I:Robbie Robertson,D:Fred Foswell . . . 85.00
53 JR,V:Dr.Octopus 75.00
54 JR,V:Dr.Octopus 75.00
55 JR,V:Dr.Octopus 75.00

Amazing Spider-Man #4
© Marvel Entertainment Group

56 JR,V:Dr.Octopus,I:Capt.Stacy . 75.00
57 JR,DH,A:Kazar 75.00
58 JR,DH,V:Spencer Smythe, Spider Slayer 75.00
59 JR,DH,V:Kingpin 75.00
60 JR,DH,V:Kingpin 75.00
61 JR,DH,V:Kingpin 75.00
62 JR,DH,V:Medusa 55.00
63 JR,DH,V:1st & 2nd Vulture 55.00
64 JR,DH,V:Vulture. 55.00
65 JR,JM,V:Prisoners 55.00
66 JR,DH,V:Mysterio 55.00
67 JR,JM,V:Mysterio,I:Randy Robertson 55.00
68 JR,JM,V:Kingpin 60.00
69 JR,JM,V:Kingpin 60.00
70 JR,JM,V:Kingpin 60.00
71 JR,JM,V:Quicksilver,C:Scarlet Witch,Toad,A:Kingpin 50.00
72 JR,JB,JM,V:Shocker 50.00
73 JR,JB,JM,I:Man Mountain Marko, Silvermane. 50.00
74 JR,JM,V:Silvermane. 45.00
75 JR,JM,V:Silvermane,A:Lizard . . 45.00
76 JR,JM,V:Lizard,A:H.Torch 45.00
77 JR,JM,V:Lizard,A:H.Torch 45.00
78 JR,JM,I&O:Prowler 50.00
79 JR,JM,V:Prowler 45.00
80 JR,JB,JM,V:Chameleon 45.00
81 JR,JB,JM,I:Kangaroo 45.00
82 JR,JM,V:Electro 45.00
83 JR,I:Richard Fisk(as Schemer), Vanessa(Kingpin's wife) V:Kingpin 50.00
84 JR,JB,JM,V:Schemer,Kingpin. . 45.00
85 JR,JB,JM,V:Schemer,Kingpin. . 45.00
86 JR,JM,V:Black Widow, C:Iron Man, Hawkeye 45.00
87 JR,JM,Reveals ID to his friends,changes mind 45.00
88 JR,JM,V:Dr.Octopus. 45.00
89 GK,JR,V:Dr.Octopus 45.00
90 GK,JR,V:Dr.Octopus D:Capt.Stacy 60.00
91 GK,JR,I:Bullit. 45.00
92 GK,JR,V:Bullit,A:Iceman 45.00
93 JR,V:Prowler 45.00
94 JR,SB,V:Beetle,O:Spider-Man . 70.00
95 JR,SB,London,V:Terrorists 45.00
96 GK,JR,A:Green Goblin,Drug Mention,No Comic Code. 90.00
97 GK,V:Green Goblin,Drugs 75.00
98 GK,V:Green Goblin,Drugs 75.00
99 GK,Prison Riot,A:Carson 50.00
100 JR(c),GK,Spidey gets four arms from serum 185.00
101 JR(c),GK,I:Morbius,the Living Vampire,A:Lizard 140.00
101a Reprint,Metallic ink. 2.50
102 JR(c),GK,O:Morbius, V:Lizard 135.00
103 GK,V:Kraven,A:Kazar. 35.00
104 GK,V:Kraven,A:Kazar. 35.00
105 GK,V:Spenser Smythe, Spider Slayer 35.00
106 JR,V:Spenser Smythe, Spider Slayer 35.00
107 JR,V:Spenser Smythe, Spider Slayer 35.00
108 JR,R:Flash Thompson, I:Sha-Shan,V:Vietnamese 35.00
109 JR,A:Dr.Strange, V:Vietnamese. 35.00
110 JR,I:The Gibbon. 35.00
111 JR,V:The Gibbon,Kraven 35.00
112 JR,Spidey gets an Ulcer. 35.00
113 JSn,JR,I:Hammerhead V:Dr.Octopus 35.00
114 JSn,JR,V:Hammerhead,Dr. Octopus,I:Jonas Harrow 35.00

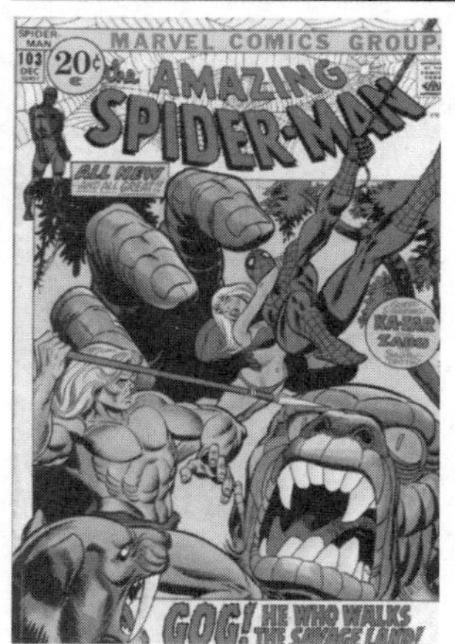

Amazing Spider-Man #103
© Marvel Entertainment Group

115 JR,V:Hammerhead, Dr.Octopus 35.00
116 JR,JM,V:The Smasher 35.00
117 JR,JM,V:Smasher,Disruptor . . 35.00
118 JR,JM,V:Smasher,Disruptor . . 35.00
119 JR,A:Hulk. 50.00
120 GK,JR,V:Hulk. 50.00
121 GK,JR,V:Green Goblin D:Gwen Stacy,Drugs 135.00
122 GK,JR,D:Green Goblin. 160.00
123 GK,JR,A:Powerman. 30.00
124 GK,JR,I:Man-Wolf 30.00
125 RA,JR,O:Man-Wolf 30.00
126 JM(c),RA,JM,V:Kangaroo, A: Human Torch 30.00
127 JR(c),RA,V:3rd Vulture, A:Human Torch 30.00
128 JR(c),RA,V:3rd Vulture. 30.00
129 K&R(c),RA,I:Punisher, Jackal. 175.00
130 JR(c),RA,V:Hammerhead, Dr.Octopus,I:Spider-Mobile . . . 22.00
131 GK(c),RA,V:Hammerhead, Dr.Octopus. 22.00
132 GK(c),JR,V:Molten Man 20.00
133 JR(c),RA,V:Molten Man 20.00
134 JR(c),RA,I:Tarantula,C: Punisher(2nd App.). 27.00
135 JR(c),RA,V:Tarantula, A:Punisher 55.00
136 JR(c),RA,I:2nd GreenGoblin. . 40.00
137 GK(c),RA,V:Green Goblin . . . 35.00
138 K&R(c),RA,I:Mindworm 25.00
139 K&R(c),RA,I:Grizzly,V:Jackal . 25.00
140 GK(c),RA,I:Gloria Grant, V:Grizzly,Jackal 25.00
141 JR(c),RA,V:Mysterio. 25.00
142 JR(c),RA,V:Mysterio. 25.00
143 K&R(c),RA,I:Cyclone 25.00
144 K&R(c),RA,V:Cyclone 25.00
145 K&R(c),RA,V:Scorpion 25.00
146 RA,JR,V:Scorpion 25.00
147 JR(c),RA,V:Tarantula 25.00
148 GK(c),RA,V:Tarantula,IR:Jackal is Prof.Warren 30.00
149 K&R(c),RA,D:Jackal. 45.00
150 GK(c),RA,V:Spenser Smythe . 20.00
151 RA,JR,V:Shocker. 17.00
152 K&R(c),RA,V:Shocker 17.00
153 K&R(c),RA,V:Paine 17.00
154 JR(c),SB,V:Sandman 17.00
155 JR(c),SB,V:Computer. 16.00
156 JR(c),RA,I:Mirage,W:Ned Leeds & Betty Brant 16.00
157 JR(c),RA,V:Dr.Octopus 16.00
158 JR(c),RA,V:Dr.Octopus 16.00
159 JR(c),RA,V:Dr.Octopus 16.00
160 K&R(c),RA,V:Tinkerer 16.00
161 K&R(c),RA,A:Nightcrawler, C:Punisher 16.00
162 JR(c),RA,Nightcrawler, Punisher,I:Jigsaw 16.00
163 JR(c),RA,Kingpin 10.00
164 JR(c),RA,Kingpin 10.00
165 JR(c),RA,Lizard 10.00
166 JR(c),RA,Lizard 10.00
167 JR(c),RA,V:Spiderslayer, I:Will-o-the Wisp 10.00
168 JR(c),KP,V:Will-o-the Wisp . . . 12.00
169 RA,V:Dr.Faustas 10.00
170 RA,V:Dr.Faustas 10.00
171 RA,A:Nova. 11.00
172 RA,V:Molten Man. 10.00
173 JR(c),RA,JM,V:Molten Man . . 10.00
174 RA,TD,JM,A:Punisher 15.00
175 RA,JM,A:Punisher,D:Hitman. . 15.00
176 RA,TD,V:Green Goblin. 12.00
177 RA,V:Green Goblin 12.00
178 RA,JM,V:Green Goblin. 12.00
179 RA,V:Green Goblin 12.00
180 RA,IR&V:Green Goblin is Bart Hamilton. 12.00
181 GK(c),SB,O:Spider-Man.. . . . . 8.00
182 RA,A:Rocket Racer 7.00
183 RA,BMc,V:Rocket Racer 7.00
184 RA,V:White Tiger 7.00
185 RA,V:White Tiger 7.00
186 KP,A:Chameleon,Spidey cleared by police of charges . . . 7.00
187 JSn,BMc,A:Captain America,V:Electro. 8.00
188 KP,A:Jigsaw. 7.00
189 JBy,JM,A:Man-Wolf 8.00
190 JBy,JM,A:Man-Wolf 8.00
191 KP,V:Spiderslayer 6.00
192 KP,JM,V:The Fly 6.00
193 KP,JM,V:The Fly 6.00
194 KP,I:Black Cat 16.00
195 KP,AM,JM,O:Black Cat 7.00
196 AM,JM,D:Aunt May,A:Kingpin . 6.00
197 KP,JM,V:Kingpin 6.00
198 SB,JM,V:Mysterio 6.00
199 SB,JM,V:Mysterio 6.00
200 JR(c),KP,JM,D:Burglar,Aunt May alive,O:Spider-Man. 25.00
201 KP,JM,A:Punisher 10.00
202 KP,JM,A:Punisher 10.00
203 FM(c),KP,A:Dazzler 7.00
204 JR2(c),KP,V:Black Cat 6.00
205 KP,JM,V:Black Cat. 6.00
206 JBy,GD,V:Jonas Harrow. 8.00
207 JM,V:Mesmero. 6.00
208 JR2,AM,BBr,V:Fusion(1stJR2 SpM art),I:Lance Bannon 7.00
209 KJ,BMc,JRu,BWi,AM, I:Calypso, V:Kraven 8.00
210 JR2,JSt,I:Madame Web 8.00
211 JR2,JM,A:Sub-mariner. 6.00
212 JR2,JM,I:Hydro-Man 6.00
213 JR2,JM,V:Wizard 6.00
214 JR2,JM,V:Frightful Four, A: Namor,Llyra 6.00
215 JR2,JM,V:Frightful Four, A: Namor,Llyra 6.00
216 JR2,JM,A:Madame Web 6.00
217 JR2,JM,V:Sandman, Hydro-Man 6.00
218 FM(c),JR2,JM,AM,V:Sandman Hydro-Man 6.00
219 FM(c),LMc,JM,V:Grey Gargoyle,A:Matt Murdock 6.00
220 BMc,A:Moon Knight 6.00
221 JM(i),A:Ramrod 5.00
222 WS(c),BH,JM,I:SpeedDemon . . 5.00

Amazing Spider-Man #252
© Marvel Entertainment Group

223 JR2,AM,A:Red Ghost. 5.00
224 JR2,V:Vulture. 5.00
225 JR2,BWi,V:Foolkiller 5.00
226 JR2,JM,A:Black Cat. 5.00
227 JR2,JM,A:Black Cat. 5.00
228 RL,Murder Mystery 5.00
229 JR2,JM,V:Juggernaut. 7.00
230 JR2,JM,V:Juggernaut. 7.00
231 JR2,AM,V:Cobra 5.00
232 JR2,JM,V:Mr.Hyde 5.00
233 JR2,JM,V:Tarantula 5.00
234 JR2,DGr,V:Tarantula 5.00
235 JR2,V:Tarantula,C:Deathlok O:Will-o-the-Wisp 5.00
236 JR2,D:Tarantula. 5.00
237 BH,A:Stilt Man. 5.00
238 JR2,JR,I:Hobgoblin (inc. Tattoo transfer). 65.00
238a w/out Tattoo 12.00
239 JR2,V:Hobgoblin 35.00
240 JR2,BL,Vulture. 5.00
241 JR2,O:Vulture 5.00
242 JR2,Mad Thinker 5.00
243 JR2,Peter Quits School 5.00
244 JR2,KJ,V:Hobgoblin. 9.00
245 JR2,V:Hobgoblin 12.00
246 JR2,DGr,Daydreams issue. . . . 5.00
247 JR2,JR,V:Thunderball 5.00
248 JR2,BBr,RF,TA,V:Thunderball, Kid who Collects Spider-Man . . 5.00
249 JR2,DGr,V:Hobgoblin, A:Kingpin 10.00
250 JR2,KJ,V:Hobgoblin. 10.00
251 RF,KJ,V:Hobgoblin,Spidey Leaves for Secret Wars 10.00
252 RF,BBr,returns from Secret Wars,N:Spider-Man 28.00
253 RL,I:Rose 8.00
254 RL,JRu,V:Jack O'Lantern. 5.00
255 RF,JRu,Red Ghost. 5.00
256 RF,JRu,I:Puma,A:Black Cat . . . 6.00
257 RF,JRu,V:Puma, A:Hobgoblin 8.00
258 RF,JRu,A:Black Cat,Fant.Four, Hobgoblin,V:Black Costume . . 11.00
259 RF,JRu,A:Hobgoblin,O: Mary Jane 12.00
260 RF,JRu,BBr,V:Hobgoblin 8.00
261 CV(c),RF,JRu,V:Hobgoblin. . . . 8.00
262 Ph(c),BL,Spidey Unmasked . . . 7.00
263 RF,BBr,I:Spider-Kid 4.00
264 Paty,V:Red Nine 4.00
265 RF,JRu,V:Black Fox,

MARVEL

I:Silver Sable 10.00
265a 2nd printing 2.00
266 RF,JRu,I:Misfits,Toad 4.00
267 BMc,PDd(s),A:Human Torch . . 4.00
268 JBy(c),RF,JRu,Secret WarsII . . 4.00
269 RF,JRu,V:Firelord. 4.00
270 RF,BMc,V:Firelord,
A:Avengers,I:Kate Cushing 4.00
271 RF,JRu,A:Crusher Hogan,
V:Manslaughter 4.00
272 SB,KB,I&O:Slyde 4.00
273 RF,JRu,Secret Wars II,
A:Puma 4.00
274 TMo,JR,Secret Wars II,
Beyonder V:Mephisto,A:1st
Ghost Rider 6.00
275 RF,JRu,V:Hobgoblin,O:Spidey
(From Amaz.Fantasy#15) 7.00
276 RF,BBr,V:Hobgoblin 6.00
277 RF,BL,CV,A:Daredevil,
Kingpin. 5.00
278 A:Hobgoblin,V:Scourge,
D:Wraith. 4.00
279 RL,A:Jack O'Lantern,
2nd A:Silver Sable 4.00
280 RF,BBr,V:Sinister Syndicate,
A:Silver Sable,Hobgoblin,
Jack O'Lantern 4.00
281 RF,BBr,V:Sinister Syndicate,
A:Silver Sable,Hobgoblin,
Jack O'Lantern 10.00
282 RL,BL,A:X-Factor. 4.00
283 RF,BL,V:Titania,Absorbing
Man,C:Mongoose 4.00
284 RF,BBr,JRu,B:Gang War,
A: Punisher,Hobgoblin 7.00
285 MZ(c),A:Punisher,Hobgoblin. . . 9.00
286 ANi(i),V:Hobgoblin,A:Rose 8.00
287 EL,ANi,A:Daredevl,Hobgoblin. . 6.00
288 E:Gang War,A:Punisher,
Falcon,Hobgoblin,Daredevil,
Black Cat, Kingpin 7.00
289 TMo,IR:Hobgoblin is Ned Leeds,
I:2nd Hobgoblin (Jack O'
Lantern) 20.00
290 JR2,Peter Proposes. 4.00
291 JR2,V:Spiderslayer 4.00
292 AS,V:Spiderslayer,Mary
Jane Accepts proposal 4.00
293 MZ,BMc,V:Kraven 10.00
294 MZ,BMc,D:Kraven 10.00
295 BSz(c),KB(i),Mad Dog,pt.#2 . . . 4.00
296 JBy(c),AS,V:Dr.Octopus 4.00
297 AS,V:Dr.Octopus 4.00
298 TM,BMc,V:Chance,C:Venom
(not in costume) 35.00
299 TM,BMc,V:Chance,I:Venom . . 20.00
300 TM,O:Venom 65.00
301 TM,A:Silver Sable 15.00
302 TM,V:Nero,A:Silver Sable. . . . 15.00
303 TM,A:Silver Sable,Sandman . . 15.00
304 TM,JRu,V:Black Fox,Prowler
I:Jonathan Caesar 12.00
305 TM,JRu,V:BlackFox,Prowler. . 12.00
306 TM,V:Humbug,Chameleon . . . 11.00
307 TM,O:Chameleon. 11.00
308 TM,V:Taskmaster,J.Caesar. . . 11.00
309 TM,I:Styx & Stone 11.00
310 TM,V:Killershrike 11.00
311 TM,Inferno,V:Mysterio 11.00
312 TM,Inferno,Hobgoblin V:
Green Goblin 15.00
313 TM,Inferno,V:Lizard 10.00
314 TM,X-mas issue,V:J.Caesar. . 10.00
315 TM,V:Venom,Hydro-Man 15.00
316 TM,V:Venom 15.00
317 TM,V:Venom,A:Thing 15.00
318 TM,V:Scorpion 8.00
319 TM,V:Scorpion,Rhino 8.00
320 TM,B:Assassin Nation Plot
A:Paladin,Silver Sable 8.00
321 TM,A:Paladin,Silver Sable 6.00
322 TM,A:Silver Sable,Paladin 6.00
323 TM,A:Silver Sable,Paladin,
Captain America. 6.00
324 TM(c),EL,AG,V:Sabretooth,A:
Capt.America,Silver Sable 9.00
325 TM,E:Assassin Nation Plot,
V:Red Skull,Captain America,
Silver Sable 6.00
326 V:Graviton,A of V. 4.00
327 EL,AG,V:Magneto,A of V. 5.00
328 TM,V:Hulk,A of V. 8.00
329 EL,V:Tri-Sentinel 6.00
330 EL,A:Punisher,Black Cat 6.00
331 EL,A:Punisher,C:Venom. 6.00
332 EL,V:Venom,Styx & Stone 7.00
333 EL,V:Venom,Styx & Stone 7.00
334 EL,B:Sinister Six,A:Iron Man . . 4.00
335 EL,TA,A:Captain America. 4.00
336 EL,D:Nathan Lubensky,
A:Dr.Strange,Chance 3.50
337 WS(c),EL,TA,A:Nova 3.50
338 EL,A:Jonathan Caesar. 3.50
339 EL,JR,E:Sinister Six,A:Thor
D:Jonathan Caesar 3.50
340 EL,V:Femme Fatales 3.00
341 EL,V:Tarantula,Powers Lost . . . 3.00
342 EL,A:Blackcat,V:Scorpion. 3.00
343 EL,Powers Restored,
C:Cardiac,V:Chameleon 3.00
344 EL,V:Rhino,I:Cardiac,Cletus
Kassady(Carnage),A:Venom. . . 8.00
345 MBa,V:Boomerang,C:Venom,
A:Cletus Kassady(infected
with Venom-Spawn) 9.00
346 EL,V:Venom. 6.00
347 EL,V:Venom. 6.00
348 EL,A:Avengers. 3.00
349 EL,A:Black Fox 3.00
350 EL,V:Doctor Doom,Black Fox. . 4.00
351 MBa,A:Nova,V:Tri-Sentinal. . . . 4.00
352 MBa,A:Nova,V:Tri-Sentinal. . . . 3.00
353 MBa,B:Round Robin:The Side
Kick's Revenge,A:Punisher,
Nova,Moon Knight,Darkhawk . . 3.00
354 MBa,A:Nova,Punisher,
Darkhawk,Moon Knight. 3.00
355 MBa,A:Nova,Punisher,
Darkhawk,Moon Knight. 3.00
356 MBa,A:Moon Knight,
Punisher,Nova 3.00
357 MBa,A:Moon Knight,
Punisher,Darkhawk,Nova 3.00

Amazing Spider-Man #228
© Marvel Entertainment Group

358 MBa,E:Round Robin:The Side
Kick's Revenge,A:Darkhawk,
Moon Knight,Punisher,Nova,
Gatefold(c) 3.00
359 CMa,A:Cardiac,C:Cletus
Kasady (Carnage) 4.00
360 CMa,V:Cardiac,C:Carnage. . . . 5.00
361 MBa,I:Carnage 9.00
361a 2nd printing 2.00
362 MBa,V:Carnage,Venom 6.00
362a 2nd printing 1.50
363 MBa,V:Carnage,Venom,. 5.00
364 MBa,V:Shocker 2.50
365 MBa,JR,V:Lizard,30th Anniv.,
Hologram(c),w/poster,Prev.of
Spider-Man 2099 by RL 6.00
366 JBi,A:Red Skull,Taskmaster . . . 2.50
367 JBi,A:Red Skull,Taskmaster . . . 2.50
368 MBa,B:Invasion of the Spider
Slayers #1,BU:Jonah Jameson. 2.00
369 MBa,V:Electro,BU:Green
Goblin 2.00
370 MBa,V:Scorpion,BU:A.May . . . 2.00
371 MBa,V:Spider-Slayer,
BU:Black Cat 2.00
372 MBa,V:Spider-Slayer 2.00
373 MBa,V:Sp.-Slayer,BU:Venom . . 3.00
374 MBa,V:Venom 4.00
375 MBa,V:Venom,30th Anniv.,Holo
graphx(c) 5.00
376 V:Styx&Stone,A:Cardiac 2.00
377 V:Cardiac,O:Styx&Stone 2.00
378 MBa,Total Carnage#3,V:Shriek,
Carnage,A:Venom,Cloak 2.00
379 MBa,Total Carnage#7,
V:Carnage,A:Venom. 2.00
380 MBa,Maximum Carnage#11 . . . 2.00
381 MBa,V:Dr.Samson,A:Hulk 2.00
382 MBa,V:Hulk,A:Dr.Samson 2.00
383 MBa,V:Jury 2.00
384 MBa,AM,V:Jury 2.00
385 B:DvM(s),MBa,RyE,V:Jury 2.00
386 MBa,RyE,B:Lifetheft,V:Vulture . 3.00
387 MBa,RyE,V:Vulture 3.00
388 Blue Foil(c),MBa,RyE,RLm,TP,
E:Lifetheft,D:Peter's Synthetic
Parents,BU:Venom,Cardiac,
Chance, ... 4.00
388a Newsstand Ed. 3.00
389 MBa,RyE,E:Pursuit,
V:Chameleon, ... 2.00
390 MBa,RyE,B:Shrieking,
A:Shriek,w/cel 3.25
390a Newsstand Ed. 2.00
391 MBa,RyE,V:Shriek,Carrion 2.00
392 MBa,RyE,V:Shriek,Carrion. . . . 2.00
393 MBa,RyE,E:Shrieking,
V:Shriek,Carrion 2.00
394 MBa,RyE,Power & Responsibility,
pt.2,V:Judas Traveller, ... 4.00
394a w/flip book,2 covers 2.00
395 MBa,RyE,R:Puma 2.00
396 MBa,RyE,A:Daredevil,
V:Vulture, Owl 2.00
397 MBa,Web of Death,pt.1,
V:Stunner,Doc Ock 2.50
398 MBa,Web of Death,pt.3 . . . . . . 2.00
399 MBa,Smoke and Mirrors,pt.2 . . 2.00
400 MBa,Death of a Parker 7.00
400a die-cut cover 3.00
401 MBa,The Mark of Kaine,pt.2. . . 2.00
402 MBa,R:Judas Travellor. 2.00
403 MBa,JMD,LMa The Trial of
Peter Parker, pt.2 . . . . 2.00
404 Maximum Clonage. 2.00
405 JMD,DaR,LMa,Exiled,pt.2, ... 2.00
406 I:New Doc Ock 2.00
407 TDF,MBa,LMa,Return of
Spider-Man,pt.2 . . . . 2.00
408 TDF,MBa,LMa,Media
Blizzard,pt.2 . . . . 2.00

Amazing Spider-Man #400
© Marvel Entertainment Group

409 . . . . 2.00
410 . . . . 2.00
411 TDF,MBa,LMa,Blood Brothers,pt.2 . . . . 2.00
412 . . . . 2.00
413 . . . . 2.00
414 A:The Rose 2.00
415 Onslaught saga,V:Sentinels . . . 2.50
416 Onslaught epilogue 3.00
417 TDF,RG,secrets of Scrier & Judas Traveler 2.00
418 Revelations,pt.3, R:Norman Osborn. 2.50
419 TDF,SSr,V:Black Tarantula 2.00
420 TDF,SSr,X-Man x-over,pt.1. . . . 2.00
421 TDF,SSr,I:Dragonfly; Electro Kidnapped 2.50
422 TDF,SSr,V:Electro,Tarantula . . . 2.50
423 TDF,V:Electro 2.00
424 TDF,JoB,V:Black Tarantula, The Hand, Dragonfly, Delilah, The Rose, Elektra 2.00
425 TDF,SSr, V:Electro,double size. 3.50
426 TDF,SSr,V:Doctor Octopus. . . . 2.00
427 TDF,SSr,JR gatefold cover, V:Doctor Octopus. 2.50
428 TDF,SSr,V:Doctor Octopus. . . . 2.00
429 TDF,A:Daredevil, X-Man, Absorbing Man, Titania. 2.00
430 TDF,SSr,V:Carnage,A:Silver Surfer. 2.00
431 TDF,SSr,V:Carnage (with Silver Surfer's powers). 2.00
432 SSr,JR2,Spider-Hunt,pt.2 x-over. 2.00
432a variant cover 3.50
433 TDF,TL,Identity Crisis prelude, good-bye to Joe Robertson . . . 2.00
434 TDF,JoB,Identity Crisis, as Ricochet vs. Black Tarantula. . . 2.00
435 TDF,MD2,Ricochet,A:Delilah . . 2.00
436 TDF,JoB,V:Black Tarantula. . . . 2.00
437 TDF,JoB,V:Plant Man. 2.00

Bi-weekly

438 TDF,V:Daredevil. 2.00
439 TDF,future history chronicle . . . 2.00
440 JBy,The Gathering of the Five, Pt.2 (of 5) x-over 2.00
441 JBy,V:Green Goblin, The Final Chapter, pt.1 . . . . 2.00
Minus 1 Spec., TDF,JBe, flashback, early Kingpin 2.00
Ann.#1 SD,I:Sinister Six 700.00
Ann.#2 SD,A:Dr.Strange 275.00
Ann.#3 JR,DH,A:Avengers 100.00
Ann.#4 A:H.Torch,V:Mysterio, Wizard 90.00
Ann.#5 JR(c),A:Red Skull,I:Peter Parker's Parents. 100.00
Ann.#6 JR(c),Rep.Ann.#1,Fant. Four Ann.#1,SpM #8 . . . . 40.00
Ann.#7 JR(c),Rep.#1,#2,#38. . . . . 35.00
Ann.#8 Rep.#46,#50. . . . . 35.00
Ann.#9 JR(c),Rep.Spec.SpM #2 . . 20.00
Ann.#10 JR(c),GK,V:Human Fly . . 15.00
Ann.#11 GK(c),DP,JM,JR2,AM,. . . 12.00
Ann.#12 JBy(c),KP,Rep.#119, #120. 12.00
Ann.#13 JBy,TA,V:Dr.Octopus. . . . 12.00
Ann.#14 FM,TP,A:Dr.Strange, V:Dr.Doom,Dormammu. 12.00
Ann.#15 FM,KJ,BL,Punisher 15.00
Ann.#16 JR2,JR,I:New Captain Marvel,A:Thing 7.00
Ann.#17 EH,JM,V:Kingpin. 7.00
Ann.#18 RF,BL,JG,V:Scorpion 7.00
Ann.#19 JR(c),MW,V:Spiderslayer . 7.00
Ann.#20 BWi(i),V:Iron Man 2020. . . 7.00
Ann.#21 JR(c),PR,W:SpM,direct . . 16.00
Ann.#21a W:SpM,news stand 12.00
Ann.#22 JR(c),MBa(1stSpM),SD, JG,RLm,TD,Evolutionary War, I:Speedball,New Men 7.00
Ann.#23 JBy(c),RLd,MBa,RF, AtlantisAttacks#4,A:She-Hulk . . 7.00
Ann.#24 GK,SD,MZ,DGr, A:Ant Man 4.00
Ann.#25 EL(c),SB,PCu,SD, Vibranium Vendetta#1,Venom. . 6.00
Ann.#26 Hero Killers#1,A:New Warriors,BU:Venom,Solo 5.00
Ann.#27 TL,I:Annex,w/card. 3.50
Ann.#28 SBt(s),V:Carnage,BU:Cloak & Dagger,Rhino 3.25
Ann. '96 two new stories, 48pg, . . . 3.00
Ann. '97 RSt,TL,RJn, 48pg, ... 3.00
Ann. '98 TL,TDF,F:Spider-Man & Devil Dinosaur, 48pg 3.00
G-Size Superheroes #1 GK, A:Morbius,Man-Wolf 30.00
G-Size #1 JR(c),RA,DH, A:Dracula 12.00
G-Size #2 K&R(c),RA,AM, A:Master of Kung Fu 10.00
G-Size #3 GK(c),RA,DocSavage. . 10.00
G-Size #4 GK(c),RA,Punisher. . . . 35.00
G-Size #5 GK(c),RA,V:Magnum . . . 8.00
G-Size #6 Rep.Ann.#4 . . . . 7.00
G-Size Spec.#1 O:Symbiotes 4.50
Marvel Milestone rep. #1 (1993) . . . 2.95
Marvel Milestone rep. #3 (1995) . . . 2.95
Marvel Milestone rep. #129 (1992) . 2.95
Marvel Milestone rep. #149 (1994) . 2.95
GNv Fear Itself RA,A:S.Sable 12.95
GNv Spirits of the Earth CV,Scotland, V:Hellfire Club 25.00
TPB Assassination Plot, rep.#320-325 . . . . 14.95
TPB Carnage,rep.#361-363 . . . . . . 6.95
TPB Cosmic Adventures rep. Amaz.SpM #327-329,Web #59 61,Spec.SpM #158-160 . . . . . 19.95
TPB Kraven's Last Hunt, Reps. AS #293,294,Web.#31,32,P.Parker #131,132,SC 15.95
HC 19.95
TPB Origin of the Hobgoblin rep.#238, 239,244,245,249-251 . . . . 14.95
TPB Saga of the Alien Costume,reps. #252-259 . . . . 9.95
TPB Spider-Man Vs. Venom,reps. A.SpM#298-300,315-317 . . . . 10.00
TPB Venom Returns rep.Amaz.SpM. #331-333,344-347 . . . . 12.95
TPB The Wedding,Reps.A.S. #290-292,Ann#21. . . . . 12.95
Nothing Can Stop the Juggernaut, reps.#229,230 . . . . 3.95
Sensational Spider-Man,reps. Ann.#14,15; 4.95
Skating on Thin Ice(Canadian) . . . 15.00
Skating on Thin Ice(US) 2.00
Soul of the Hunter MZ,BMc, R:Kraven 7.00
Unicef:Trial of Venom, A:Daredevil,V:Venom 50.00

See Also:
PETER PARKER;
SPECTACULAR SPIDER-MAN;
WEB OF SPIDER-MAN

AMAZING SPIDER-MAN

Nov., 1998

1 HMe,JBy,DHz,V:Scorpion,48-page prismatic etched (c) 3.00
2 HMe,JBy,DHz,I:Shadrac 2.00
2a variant BiT cover 2.00
3 HMe,JBy,DHz,V:Shadrac, A:Iceman 2.00
4 HMe,JBy,SHa,A:Fantastic Four. . 2.00
5 HMe,JBy,SHa,I:new Spider-Woman 2.00
6 JBy,HMe,SHa,F:Spider-Woman . 2.00
7 JBy,HMe,SHa,Reality Bent 2.00
8 JMy,HMe,SHa,JR2(c), Reality Bent x-over. 2.00
9 JMy,HMe,SHa,JR2(c),V:Scorpion 2.00
10 JMy,HMe,SHa,JR2(c),Mary Jane 2.00
11 HMe,SHa,JBy,marital problems . 2.00
12 HMe,SHa,JBy,48-pg. 3.00
13 HMe,JBy 2.00
14 HMe,JBy,A:Sp.-Woman,x-over . . 2.00
15 HMe,JBy,DGr,x-over 2.00
16 HMe,JBy,DGr,Mary Jane gone . . 2.00
17 HMe,JBy,DGr,A:Sandman 2.00
18 HMe,JBy,JR,V:Green Goblin . . . 2.25
19 HMe,EL,DGr,Eddie Brock 2.25
20 HMe,EL,JBy,100-pg 3.00
21 HMe,EL,JhB,AlistairSmythe 2.25
22 HMe,JR2,SHa,Senator Ward . . . 2.25
23 HMe,JR2,SHa,Ranger 2.25
24 HMe,JR2,SHa,Max.Security. . . . 2.25
Ann.1999 JB,HMe, 48-page 3.50
Ann.2000 HMe,48-pg.. . . . . 3.50
Giant Sized 80-pg. 4.50

Amazing Spider-Man Vol. 2 #1
© Marvel Entertainment Group

Coll.Classics rep. #300 . . . . 2.50
Coll.Classics rep. #300 signed . . . 30.00
Coll.Classics rep. Sp-M #1 . . . . 2.50
Coll.Classics rep. Sp-M #1 signed. 30.00

AMAZING SPIDER-MAN INDEX
See: OFFICIAL MARVEL INDEX TO THE AMAZING SPIDER-MAN

AMAZING SPIDER-MAN COLLECTION

1 Mark Bagley card set 3.00
2 and 3 MBa, from card set . . . . @3.00

AMAZING X-MEN, THE
March–June, 1995

1 X-Men after Xavier 4.00
2 Exodus,Dazzler,V:Abyss 3.00
3 F:Bishop 3.00
4 V:Apocalypse 2.50
TPB Rep. #1-#4 . . . . 9.00

AMERICAN TAIL II
Dec., 1991

1 movie adaption 2.00
2 movie adaption 2.00

A-NEXT
Aug., 1998

1 TDF,RF,BBr,Next Generation of Avengers 2.00
2 TDF,RF,BBr,V:Kree & Sentry. . . . 2.00
2a variant cover. 2.00
3 TDF,RF,BBr,Orig.Defenders vs. New Avengers 2.00
4 TDF,RF,BBr,turning points. 2.00
5 TDF,RF,BBr,SB,Ghosts of the Past 2.00
6 TDF,RF,BBr,Majority Rules 2.00
7 TDF,RF,BBr,Last Days of the Avengers 2.00
8 TDF,RF,BBr,A:Ant-Man,Uneasy Allies 2.00
9 TDF,RF,BBr,Critical Choices 2.00
10 TDF,RF,BBr,Incredible Journeys. 2.00
11 TDF,RF,BBr,A:Captain America & Doctor Doom 2.00
12 TDF,RF,BBr,I:Revengers 2.00

ANIMAX
Star Comics Dec., 1986–June 1987

1 Based on Toy Line 2.00
2 thru 4 . . . . @2.00

ANNEX
Aug.–Nov., 1994

1 WMc,I:Brace, Crucible of Power . 2.00
2 WMc,V:Brace, Crucible, pt.2 . . . . 2.00
3 Crucible of Power, pt.3 . . . . 2.00
4 Crucible of Power, pt.4 . . . . 2.00

ANNIE
(Treasury Edition)
Oct., 1982

1 Movie Adaptation 2.00
2 Nov., 1982 . . . . 2.00

ANNIE OAKLEY
Atlas Spring, 1948

1 A:Hedy Devine 350.00
2 CCB,I:Lana,A:Hedy Devine . . 200.00
3 . . . . 175.00
4 . . . . 175.00
5 . . . . 125.00
6 . . . . 100.00
7 . . . . 100.00
8 . . . . 100.00
9 AW, ... 110.00
10 . . . . 75.00
11 June, 1956. . . . . 80.00

ANT-MAN'S BIG CHRISTMAS
Dec., 1999

GN 48-pg. 6.00

A-1
1993

1 The Edge 6.00
2 Cheeky,Wee Budgie Boy 6.00
3 King Leon. 6.00
4 King Leon. 6.00

APOCALYPSE STRIKEFILES

1 After Xavier special. 2.50

ARCHANGEL
1996

1-shot B&W 2.50

ARIZONA KID
Atlas March, 1951

1 RH,Coming of the Arizona Kid 175.00
2 RH,Code of the Gunman 85.00
3 RH(c) 75.00
4 . . . . 75.00
5 . . . . 75.00
6 Jan., 1952 . . . . 75.00

ARRGH!
Dec., 1974
Satire

1 Vampire Rats 15.00
2 . . . . 10.00
3 Beauty And the Big Foot 10.00
4 The Night Gawker 10.00
5 Sept., 1975 . . . . 10.00

ARROWHEAD
April, 1954

1 Indian Warrior Stories 125.00
2 . . . . 75.00
3 . . . . 75.00
4 Nov., 1954 . . . . 75.00

ASTONISHING
See: MARVEL BOY

ASTONISHING TALES
August, 1970

1 BEv(c),JK,WW,KaZar,Dr.Doom . 40.00
2 JK,WW,Ka-Zar,Dr.Doom 20.00
3 BWS,WW,Ka-Zar,Dr.Doom 28.00
4 BWS,WW,Ka-Zar,Dr.Doom 28.00
5 BWS,GT,Ka-Zar,Dr.Doom 28.00
6 BWS,BEv,GT,I:Bobbi Morse . . . 28.00
7 HT,GC,Ka-Zar,Dr.Doom 15.00

Astonishing Tales #9
© Marvel Entertainment Group

8 HT,TS,GT,GC,TP,Ka-Zar 15.00
9 GK(c),JB,Ka-Zar,Dr.Doom. 12.00
10 GK(c),BWS,SB,Ka-Zar. 15.00
11 GK,O:Kazar 12.00
12 JB,DA,NA,V:Man Thing 12.00
13 JB,RB,DA,V:Man Thing 10.00
14 GK(c),rep. Kazar 7.00
15 GK,TS,Kazar 7.00
16 RB,AM,A:Kazar 7.00
17 DA,V:Gemini 7.00
18 JR(c),DA,A:Kazar 7.00
19 JR(c),DA,JSn,JA,I:Victorious . . . 7.00
20 JR(c),A:Kazar 7.00
21 RTs(s),DAy,B:It 7.00
22 RTs(s),DAy,V:Granitor 7.00
23 RTs(s),DAy,A:Fin Fang Foom. . . 7.00
24 RTs(s),DAy,E:It 7.00
25 RB(a&s),B:I&O:Deathlok, GP(1st art) 30.00
26 RB(a&s),I:Warwolf 7.00
27 RB(a&s),V:Warwolf 7.00
28 RB(a&s),V:Warwolf 7.00
29 rep.Marv.Super Heroes #18 . . . . 8.00
30 RB(a&s),KP, ... 7.00
31 RB(a&s),BW,KP,V:Ryker 7.00
32 RB(a&s),KP,V:Ryker 6.00
33 RB(a&s),KJ,I:Hellinger 6.00
34 RB(a&s),KJ,V:Ryker 6.00
35 RB(a&s),KJ,I:Doomsday-Mech. . 6.00
36 RB(a&s),KP,E:Deathlok, I:Godwulf 20.00

ASTONISHING X-MEN
March–June,1995

1 Uncanny X-Men 5.00
2 V:Holocaust 3.50
3 V:Abyss 3.00
4 V:Beast,Infinities. 2.50
TPB Rep. #1-#4 . . . . 8.95

ASTONISHING X-MEN
July, 1999

1 (of 3) BPe,HMe,new X-Men team 2.50
2 BPe,HMe,The Shattering x-over . 2.50
3 BPe,HMe,Shattering,concl 2.50
TPB 160-pg. 15.95

A-TEAM
March, 1984

1 . . . . 2.00
2 . . . . 2.00
3 May, 1984 . . . . 2.00

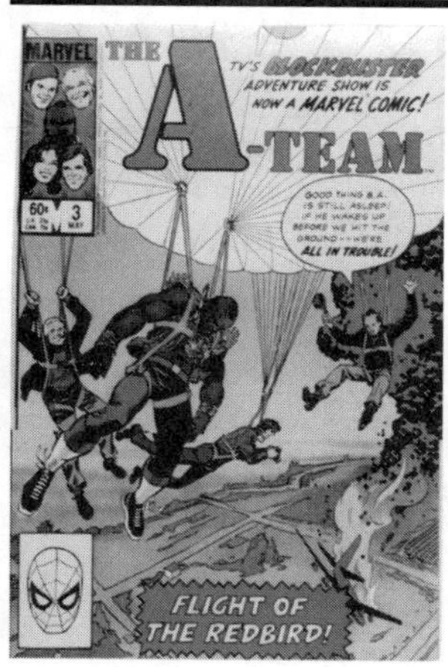

A-Team #3
© Marvel Entertainment Group

ATOMIC AGE

Epic Nov., 1990

1 AW 4.50
2 AW 4.50
3 AW,Feb., 1991 . . . . 4.50

AVATAARS: COVENANT OF THE SHIELD

July, 2000

1 (of 3) LKa,Capt.Avalon 3.00
2 LKa,Dreadlord 3.00

AVENGERS

Sept., 1963

1 JK,O:Avengers,V:Loki 2,500.00
2 JK,V:Space Phantom 650.00
3 JK,V:Hulk,Sub-Mariner 400.00
4 JK,R&J:Captain America . . . 1,600.00
5 JK,L:Hulk,V:Lava Men. 250.00
6 JK,I:Masters of Evil. 200.00
7 JK,V:Baron Zemo, Enchantress 200.00
8 JK,I:Kang 190.00
9 JK(c),DH,I&D:Wonder Man . . . 215.00
10 JK(c),DH,I:Immortus. 175.00
11 JK(c),DH,A:Spider-Man, V:Kang 200.00
12 JK(c),DH,V:Moleman, Red Ghost 125.00
13 JK(c),DH,I:Count Nefaria 125.00
14 JK,DH,V:Count Nefaria 125.00
15 JK,DH,D:Baron Zemo 100.00
16 JK,J:Hawkeye,Scarlet Witch, Quicksilver 135.00
17 JK(c),DH,V:Mole Man,A:Hulk . 100.00
18 JK(c),DH,V:The Commisar . . . 100.00
19 JK(c),DH,I&O:Swordsman, O:Hawkeye 90.00
20 JK(c),DH,WW,V:Swordsman, Mandarin 60.00
21 JK(c),DH,WW,V:Power Man (not L.Cage),Enchantress. . . . 60.00
22 JK(c),DH,WW,V:Power Man. . . 60.00
23 JK(c),DH,JR,V:Kang 45.00
24 JK(c),DH,JR,V:Kang 45.00
25 JK(c),DH,V:Dr.Doom 50.00
26 DH,V:Attuma 45.00
27 DH,V:Attuma,Beetle. 45.00
28 JK(c),DH,I:1st Goliath, I:Collector. 50.00
29 DH,V:Power Man,Swordsman . 45.00
30 JK(c),DH,V:Swordsman 45.00
31 DH,V:Keeper of the Flame. . . . 45.00
32 DH,I:Bill Foster 30.00
33 DH,V:Sons of the Serpent A:Bill Foster 30.00
34 DH,V:Living Laser 30.00
35 DH,V:Mandarin 30.00
36 DH,V:The Ultroids 30.00
37 GK(c),DH,V:Ultroids. 30.00
38 GK(c),DH,V:Enchantress, Ares,J:Hercules 30.00
39 DH,V:Mad Thinker 30.00
40 DH,V:Sub-Mariner 30.00
41 JB,V:Dragon Man,Diablo 25.00
42 JB,V:Dragon Man,Diablo 25.00
43 JB,V:Red Guardian 25.00
44 JB,V:Red Guardian, O:Black Widow. 25.00
45 JB,V:Super Adoptoid 25.00
46 JB,V:Whirlwind. 25.00
47 JB,GT,V:Magneto. 28.00
48 GT,I&O:New Black Knight 28.00
49 JB,V:Magneto 28.00
50 JB,V:Typhon 25.00
51 JB,GT,R:Iron Man,Thor V:Collector 25.00
52 JB,J:Black Panther, I:Grim Reaper. 30.00
53 JB,GT,A:X-Men; x-over X-Men #45 . . . . 40.00
54 JB,GT,V:Masters of Evil I:Crimson Cowl(Ultron) 25.00
55 JB,I:Ultron,V:Masters of Evil. . . 20.00
56 JB,D:Bucky retold, V:Baron Zemo 20.00
57 JB,I:Vision,V:Ultron 70.00
58 JB,O&J:Vision 45.00
59 JB,I:Yellowjacket 20.00
60 JB,W:Yellowjacket & Wasp. . . . 20.00
61 JB,A:Dr.Strange,x-over Dr. Strange #178 . . . . 20.00
62 JB,I:Man-Ape,A:Dr.Strange . . . 20.00
63 GC,I&O:2nd Goliath(Hawkeye) V:Egghead 20.00
64 GC,V:Egghead,O:Hawkeye . . . 20.00
65 GC,V:Swordsman,Egghead . . . 20.00
66 BWS,I:Ultron 6,Adamantium. . . 17.00
67 BWS,V:Ultron 6 . . . . 17.00
68 SB,V:Ultron 15.00
69 SB,I:Nighthawk,Grandmaster, Squadron Supreme, V:Kang . . 17.00
70 SB,O:Squadron Supreme V:Kang. 15.00
71 SB,I:Invaders,V:Kang. 35.00
72 SB,A:Captain Marvel, I:Zodiac 15.00
73 HT(i),V:Sons of Serpent. 15.00
74 JB,TP,V:Sons of Serpent, IR:Black Panther on TV 15.00
75 JB,TP,I:Arkon. 16.00
76 JB,TP,V:Arkon 15.00
77 JB,TP,V:Split-Second Squad . . 15.00
78 SB,TP,V:Lethal Legion 15.00
79 JB,TP,V:Lethal Legion 15.00
80 JB,TP,I&O:Red Wolf. 16.00
81 JB,TP,A:Red Wolf 15.00
82 JB,TP,V:Ares,A:Daredevil. 15.00
83 JB,TP,I:Valkyrie, V:Masters of Evil 25.00
84 JB,TP,V:Enchantress,Arkon . . . 15.00
85 JB,V:Squadron Supreme 15.00
86 JB,JM,A:Squad Supreme. 15.00
87 SB(i),O:Black Panther, V: A.I.M. 30.00
88 SB,JM,V:Psyklop,A:Hulk, Professor.X 15.00
89 SB,B:Kree/Skrull War. 15.00
90 SB,V:Sentry #459,Ronan, Skrulls 15.00
91 SB,V:Sentry #459,Ronan,

Avengers #10
© Marvel Entertainment Group

Skrulls 15.00
92 SB,V:Super Skrull,Ronan, ... 15.00
93 NA,TP,V:Super-Skrull,G-Size . . 60.00
94 NA,JB,TP,V:Super-Skrull, I:Mandroids 40.00
95 NA,TP,V:Maximus,Skrulls, A:Inhumans,O:Black Bolt 40.00
96 NA,TP,V:Skrulls,Ronan 40.00
97 GK&BEv(c),JB,TP,E:Kree-Skrull War,V:Annihilus,Ronan,Skrulls, A:Golden Age Heroes. 20.00
98 BWS,SB,V:Ares,R:Hercules, R&N:Hawkeye 25.00
99 BWS,TS,V:Ares 25.00
100 BWS,JSr,V:Ares & Kratos . . . 75.00
101 RB,DA,A:Watcher 15.00
102 RB,JSt,V:Grim Reaper, Sentinels 15.00
103 RB,JSt,V:Sentinels. 15.00
104 RB,JSt,V:Sentinels. 15.00
105 JB,JM,V:Savage Land Mutates; A:Black Panther 15.00
106 GT,DC,RB,V:Space Phantom . 15.00
107 GT,DC,JSn,V:Space Phantom, Grim Reaper. 18.00
108 DH,DC,JSt,V:Space Phantom,Grim Reaper 15.00
109 DH,FMc,V:Champion, L:Hawkeye 15.00
110 DH,V:Magneto,A:X-Men 25.00
111 DH,J:Bl.Widow,A:Daredevil, X-Men,V:Magneto. 25.00
112 DH,I:Mantis,V:Lion-God, L:Black Widow 20.00
113 FBe(i),V:The Living Bombs. . . 12.00
114 JR(c),V:Lion-God,J:Mantis, Swordsman 12.00
115 JR(c),A:Defenders,V:Loki, Dormammu 12.00
116 JR(c),A:Defenders,S.Surfer V:Loki,Dormammu 12.00
117 JR(c),FMc(i),A:Defenders,Silv. Surfer,V:Loki,Dormammu 12.00
118 JR(c),A:Defenders,S.Surfer V:Loki,Dormammu 12.00
119 JR(c),DH(i),V:Collector 12.00
120 JSn(c),DH(i),V:Zodiac 12.00
121 JR&JSn(c),JB,DH,V:Zodiac . . 12.00
122 K&R(c),V:Zodiac 12.00
123 JR(c),DH(i),O:Mantis 12.00
124 JR(c),JB,DC,V:Kree,O:Mantis. 12.00
125 JR(c),JB,DC,V:Thanos. 20.00
126 DC(i),V:Klaw,Solarr 12.00
127 GK(c),SB,JSon,A:Inhumans,

MARVEL

V:Ultron,Maximus 12.00
128 K&R(c),SB,JSon,V:Kang 12.00
129 SB,JSon,V:Kang 12.00
130 GK(c),SB,JSon,V:Slasher, Titanic Three 12.00
131 GK(c),SB,JSon,V:Kang, Legion of the Unliving 12.00
132 SB,JSon,Kang,Legion of the Unliving 12.00
133 GK(c),SB,JSon,O:Vision 12.00
134 K&R(c),SB,JSon,O:Vision . . . 12.00
135 JSn&JR(c),GT,O:Mantis, Vision,C:Thanos 13.00
136 K&R(c),rep Amazing Adv#12 . 12.00
137 JR(c),GT,J:Beast, Moondragon 12.00
138 GK(c),GT,V:Toad 12.00
139 K&R(c),GT,V:Whirlwind 10.00
140 K&R(c),GT,V:Whirlwind 10.00
141 GK(c),GP,V:Squad.Sinister. . . . 7.00
142 K&R(c),GP,V:Squadron Sinister,Kang 7.00
143 GK(c),GP,V:Squadron Sinister,Kang 7.00
144 GP,GK(c),V:Squad.Sinister, O&J:Hellcat,O:Buzz Baxter. . . . 7.00
145 GK(c),DH,V:Assassin 7.00
146 GK(c),DH,KP,V:Assassin 7.00
147 GP,V:Squadron Supreme 7.00
148 JK(c),GP,V:Squad.Supreme . . . 7.00
149 GP,V:Orka 8.00
150 GP,JK,rep.Avengers #16 . . . . . 7.00
151 GP,new line-up, R:Wonder Man 9.00
152 JB,JSt,I:New Black Talon 9.00
153 JB,JSt,V:L.Laser,Whizzer. 7.00
154 GP,V:Attuma 7.00
155 SB,V:Dr.Doom,Attuma 7.00
156 SB,I:Tyrak,V:Attuma 7.00
157 DH,V:Stone Black Knight 7.00
158 JK(c),SB,I&O:Graviton, ... 7.00
159 JK(c),SB,V:Graviton, ... 7.00
160 GP,V:Grim Reaper 7.00
161 GP,V:Ultron,A:Ant-Man. 7.00
162 GP,V:Ultron,I:Jocasta 7.00
163 GT,A:Champions,V:Typhon . . . 8.00
164 JBy,V:Lethal Legion 8.00
165 JBy,V:Count Nefario. 6.00
166 JBy,V:Count Nefario. 6.00
167 GP,A:Guardians,A:Nighthawk, Korvac,V:Porcupine 4.00
168 GP,A:Guardians,V:Korvac, I:Gyrich 4.00
169 SB,I:Eternity Man. 4.00
170 GP,R:Jocasta,C:Ultron, A:Guardians. 4.00
171 GP,V:Ultron,A:Guardians, Ms Marvel 4.00
172 SB,KJ,V:Tyrak 4.00
173 SB,V:Collector 4.00
174 GP(c),V:Collector 4.00
175 V&O:Korvac,A:Guardians. 4.00
176 V:Korvac,A:Guardians 4.00
177 DC(c),D:Korvac,A:Guardians . . 4.00
178 CI,V:Manipulator 4.00
179 JM,AG,V:Stinger,Bloodhawk. . . 4.00
180 JM,V:Monolith,Stinger, D:Bloodhawk 4.00
181 JBy,GD,I:Scott Lang. 6.00
182 JBy,KJ,V:Maximoff 6.00
183 JBy,KJ,J:Ms.Marvel 6.00
184 JBy,KJ,J:Falcon, V:Absorbing Man 6.00
185 JBy,DGr,O:Quicksilver & Scarlet Witch,I:Bova,V:Modred 6.00
186 JBy,DGr,V:Modred,Chthon 6.00
187 JBy,DGr,V:Chthon,Modred 6.00
188 JBy,DGr,V:The Elements 6.00
189 JBy,DGr,V:Deathbird 6.00
190 JBy,DGr,V:Grey Gargoyle, A:Daredevil 6.00
191 JBy,DGr,V:Grey Gargoyle, A:Daredevil 6.00
192 I:Inferno. 3.00
193 FM(c),SB,DGr,O:Inferno. 3.00
194 GP,JRu,J:Wonder Man. 3.00
195 GP,JRu,A:Antman, I&C:Taskmaster 5.00
196 GP,JA,A:Antman, V:Taskmaster,. 3.00
197 CI,JAb,V:Red Ronin 3.00
198 GP,DGr,V:Red Ronan 3.00
199 GP,DGr,V:Red Ronan 3.00
200 GP,DGr,V:Marcus, L:Ms.Marvel 5.00
201 GP,DGr,F:Jarvis. 3.00
202 GP,V:Ultron 3.00
203 CI,V:Crawlers,F:Wonderman . . 3.00
204 DN,DGr,V:Yellow Claw 3.00
205 DGr,V:Yellow Claw. 3.00
206 GC,DGr,V:Pyron 3.00
207 GC,DGr,V:Shadowlord 3.00
208 GC,DGr,V:Berserker 3.00
209 DGr,A:Mr.Fantastic,V:Skrull . . . 3.00
210 GC,DGr,V:Weathermen 3.00
211 GC,DGr,Moon Knight,J:Tigra . . 3.00
212 DGr,V:Elfqueen 3.00
213 BH,DGr,L:Yellowjacket 3.00
214 BH,DGr,V:Gh.Rider,A:Angel . . . 5.00
215 DGr,A:Silver Surfer, V:Molecule Man 2.50
216 DGr,A:Silver Surfer, V:Molecule Man 2.50
217 BH,DGr,V:Egghead, R:Yellowjacket,Wasp3 . . . . 2.50
218 DP,V:M.Hardy 2.50
219 BH,A:Moondragon,Drax 2.50
220 BH,DGr,D:Drax,V:MnDragon . . 2.50
221 J:She Hulk. 2.50
222 V:Masters of Evil 2.50
223 A:Antman 2.50
224 AM,A:Antman 2.50
225 A:Black Knight. 2.50
226 A:Black Knight. 2.50
227 J:2nd Captain Marvel, O:Avengers 2.50
228 V:Masters of Evil 2.50
229 JSt,V:Masters of Evil 2.50
230 A:Cap.Marvel,L:Yellowjacke . . . 2.50
231 AM,JSi,J:2nd Captain Marvel, Starfox 2.50
232 AM,JSi. 2.50
233 JBy,V:Annihilus 2.50
234 AM,JSi,O:ScarletWitch. 2.50
235 AM,JSi,V:Wizard 2.50

Avengers #133
© Marvel Entertainment Group

236 AM,JSi,A:SpM,V:Lava Men . . . 2.50
237 AM,JSi,A:SpM,V:Lava Men . . . 2.50
238 AM,JSi,V:Moonstone, O:Blackout 3.00
239 AM,JSi,A:David Letterman 3.50
240 AM,JSi,A:Dr.Strange 2.50
241 AM,JSi,V:Morgan LeFey 2.50
242 AM,JSi,Secret Wars. 2.50
243 AM,JSi,Secret Wars. 2.50
244 AM,JSi,V:Dire Wraiths 2.50
245 AM,JSi,V:Dire Wraiths 2.50
246 AM,JSi,V:Eternals 2.50
247 AM,JSi,A:Eternals,V:Deviants . 2.50
248 AM,JSi,A:Eternals,V:Deviants . 2.50
249 AM,JSi,A:Maelstrom 2.50
250 AM,JSi,A:W.C.A. V:Maelstrom. 3.50
251 BH,JSi,A:Paladin 2.50
252 BH,JSi,J:Hercules V:Blood Brothers 2.50
253 BH,JSi,J:Black Knight 2.50
254 BH,JSi,A:W.C.A. 2.50
255 TP,p(c),JB,Legacy of Thanos/Santuary II. 2.50
256 JB,TP,A:Kazar 2.50
257 JB,TP,D:Savage Land, I:Nebula 3.00
258 JB,TP,A:SpM,Firelord,Nebula. . 2.50
259 JB,TP,V:Nebula 2.50
260 JB,TP,SecretWarsII, IR:Nebula is Thanos' Granddaughter 2.50
261 JB,TP,Secret Wars II 2.50
262 JB,TP,J:Submariner 2.50
263 JB,TP,X-Factor tie-in, Rebirth,Marvel Girl,pt.1. . . . . . . 6.00
264 JB,TP,I:2nd Yellow Jacket 2.50
265 JB,TP,Secret Wars II 2.50
266 JB,TP,Secret Wars II,A: Silver Surfer 2.50
267 JB,TP,V:Kang. 2.50
268 JB,TP,V:Kang. 2.50
269 JB,TP,V:Kang,A:Immortus 2.50
270 JB,TP,V:Moonstone 2.50
271 JB,TP,V:Masters of Evil 2.50
272 JB,TP,A:Alpha Flight 2.50
273 JB,TP,V:Masters of Evil 2.50
274 JB,TP,V:Masters of Evil 2.50
275 JB,TP,V:Masters of Evil 2.50
276 JB,TP,V:Masters of Evil 2.50
277 JB,TP,V:Masters of Evil 2.50
278 JB,TP,V:Tyrok,J:Dr.Druid 2.50
279 JB,TP,new leader. 2.50
280 BH,KB,O:Jarvis 2.50
281 JB,TP,V:Olympian Gods. 2.50
282 JB,TP,V:Cerberus 2.50
283 JB,TP,V:Olympian Gods. 2.50
284 JB,TP,V:Olympian Gods. 2.50
285 JB,TP,V:Zeus. 2.50
286 JB,TP,V:Fixer. 2.50
287 JB,TP,V:Fixer. 2.50
288 JB,TP,V:Sentry 459 . . . . 2.50
289 JB,TP,J:Marrina 2.50
290 JB,TP,V:Adaptoid 2.50
291 JB,TP,V:Marrina. 2.50
292 JB,TP,V:Leviathon 2.50
293 JB,TP,V:Leviathon 2.50
294 JB,TP,V:Nebula 2.50
295 JB,TP,V:Nebula 2.50
296 JB,TP,V:Nebula 2.50
297 JB,TP,V:Nebula 2.50
298 JB,TP,Inferno,Edwin Jarvis. . . . 2.50
299 JB,TP,Inferno,V:Orphan Maker,R:Gilgemesh 2.50
300 JB,TP,WS,Inferno,V:Kang, O:Avengers,J:Gilgemesh, Mr.Fantastic,Invis.Woman. 4.00
301 BH,DH,A:SuperNova 2.00
302 RB,TP,V:SuperNova, A:Quasar 2.00
303 RB,TP,V:SuperNova,A:FF 2.00
304 RB,TP,V:U-Foes,Puma. 2.00

 All comics prices listed are for *Near Mint* condition.

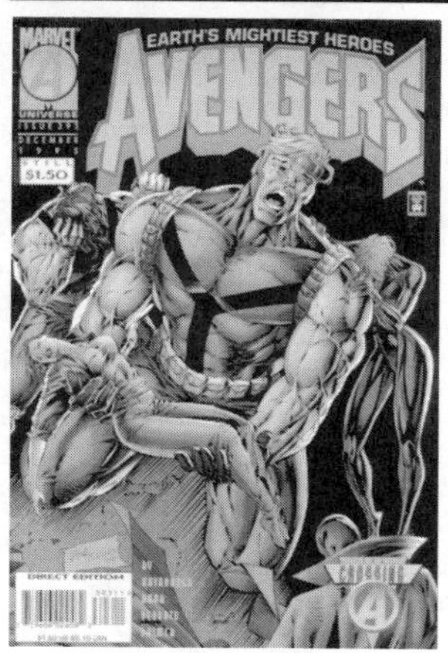

Avengers #393
© Marvel Entertainment Group

305 PR,TP,V:Lava Men. 2.00
306 PR,TP,O:Lava Men 2.00
307 PR,TP,V:Lava Men. 2.00
308 PR,TP,A:Eternals,J:Sersi 2.00
309 PR,TP,V:Blastaar 2.00
310 PR,TP,V:Blastaar 2.00
311 PR,TP,Acts of Veng.,V:Loki . . . 2.00
312 PR,TP,Acts of Vengeance, V:Freedom Force 2.00
313 PR,TP,Acts of Vengeance, V:Mandarin,Wizard 2.00
314 PR,TP,J:Sersi,A:Spider-Man, V:Nebula 2.00
315 PR,TP,A:SpM,V:Nebula 2.00
316 PR,TP,J:Spider-Man 2.00
317 PR,TP,A:SpM,V:Nebula 2.00
318 PR,TP,A:SpM,V:Nebula 2.00
319 PR,B:Crossing Line 2.00
320 PR,TP,A:Alpha Flight 2.00
321 PR,Crossing Line#3. . . . . 2.00
322 PR,TP,Crossing Line#4 . . . . . . 2.00
323 PR,TP,Crossing Line#5 . . . . . . 2.00
324 PR,TP,E:Crossing Line. 2.00
325 V:MotherSuperior, Machinesmith 2.00
326 TP,I:Rage 5.00
327 TP,V:Monsters 2.00
328 TP,O:Rage. 4.00
329 TP,J:Sandman,Rage 2.00
330 TP,V:Tetrarch of Entropy 2.00
331 TP,J:Rage,Sandman 2.00
332 TP,V:Dr.Doom 2.00
333 HT,V:Dr.Doom 2.00
334 NKu,TP,B:Collector, A:Inhumans 2.00
335 RLm(c),SEp,TP,V:Thane Ector,A:Collector, ... 2.00
336 RLm(c),SEp,TP 2.00
337 RLm(c),SEp,TP,V:ThaneEctor . 2.00
338 RLm(c),SEp,TP,A:Beast, ... 2.00
339 RLm(c),SEp,TP,E:Collector 2.00
340 RLm(c),F:Capt.Amer.,Wasp . . . 2.00
341 SEp,TP,A:New Warriors,V:Sons of Serpents 2.00
342 SEP,TP,A:New Warriors, V:Hatemonger 2.00
343 SEp,TP,J:Crystal,C&I:2nd Swordsman,Magdalene 2.00
344 SEp,TP,I:Proctor 2.00
345 SEp,TP,Oper. Galactic Storm Pt.5,V:Kree,Shiar 2.00
346 SEp,TP,Oper. Galactic Storm Pt.12,I:Star Force 2.00
347 SEp,TP,Oper. Galactic Storm Pt.19,D:Kree Race,Conclusion . 2.00
348 SEp,TP,F:Vision. 2.00
349 SEp,TP,V:Ares 2.00
350 SEp,TP,rep.Avengers#53,A:Prof. X,Cyclops,V:StarJammers 3.00
351 KWe,V:Star Jammers. 2.00
352 V:Grim Reaper. 2.00
353 V:Grim Reaper. 2.00
354 V:Grim Reaper. 2.00
355 BHs(s),SEp,I:Gatherers, Coal Tiger 2.00
356 B:BHs(s),SEp,TP,A:Bl.Panther D:Coal Tiger. 2.00
357 SEp,TP,A:Watcher 2.00
358 SEp,TP,V:Arkon 2.00
359 SEp,TP,A:Arkon 2.00
360 SEp,TP,V:Proctor,double-size, bronze foil(c) 4.00
361 SEp,I:Alternate Vision 2.00
362 SEp,TP,V:Proctor 2.00
363 SEp,TP,V:Proctor,D:Alternate Vision,C:Deathcry,Silver Foil(c), 30th Anniv., ... 3.00
364 SEp,TP,I:Deathcry,V:Kree 2.00
365 SEp,TP,V:Kree. 2.00
366 SEp,TP,V:Kree,N:Dr.Pym,Gold Foil(c). 4.50
367 F:Vision 2.00
368 SEp,TP,Bloodties#1, A:X-Men. 3.00
369 SEp,TP,E:BHs(s),Bloodties#5, D:Cortez,V:Exodus,Platinum Foil(c). 3.00
370 SEp(c),TP(c),GI,V:Deviants, A:Kro,I:Delta Force. 2.00
371 GM,TP,V:Deviants,A:Kro 2.00
372 B:BHs(s),SEp,TP,I:2nd Gatherers,A:Proctor 2.00
373 SEp,TP,I:Alternate Jocasta, V:Sersi 2.00
374 SEp,TP,O&IR:Proctor is Alternate Black Knight. 2.00
375 SEp,TP,Double Sized,D:Proctor, L:Sersi,Black Knight 3.25
376 F:Crystal,I:Terrigen. 2.00
377 F:Quicksilver 2.00
378 TP,I:Butcher 2.00
379 TP,Hercules,V:Hera 2.00
379a Avengers Double Feature #1 flip-book with Giant-Man #1 . . . 2.50
380 Hera 6.00
380a Avengers Double Feature #2 flip-book with Giant Man #2 . . . 5.00
381 Quicksilvr, Scarlet Witch. 4.00
381a Avengers Double Feature #3 flip-book with Giant Man #3 . . . 2.50
382 Wundagore 2.00
382a Avenders Double Feature #4 flip-book with Giant Man #4 . . . 2.50
383 A:Fantastic Force,V:Arides. . . . 3.00
384 Hercules Vs. Stepmom 4.00
385 V:Red Skull 3.00
386 F:Black Widow. 3.00
387 Taking A.I.M.,pt.2. . . . . 3.00
388 Taking A.I.M.,pt.4. . . . . 3.00
389 B:Mike Deodato 3.00
390 BHs,TP,The Crossing, prelude . 3.00
391 BHs,Cont. From Avg. Crossing 3.00
392 BHs,TP,The Crossing. 3.00
393 BHs,TP,The Crossing. 3.00
394 BHs,TP,The Crossing. 3.00
395 BHs,TP,Timeslide concludes . . 3.00
396 . . . . 3.00
397 TP,Incred.Hulk #440 x-over . . . 3.00
398 TP,V:Unknown foe 3.00
399 . . . . 3.00
400 MeW,MWa,double size 4.50
401 MeW,MWa,Onslaught saga . . . 3.00
402 MWa,MD2,Onslaught, finale. . . 3.00
Ann.#1 DH,V:Mandarin, Masters of Evil 75.00
Ann.#2 DH,JB,V:Scar.Centurion . . 40.00
Ann.#3 rep.#4,T.ofSusp.#66-68. . . 25.00
Ann.#4 rep.#5,#6 . . . . 17.00
Ann.#5 JK(c),rep.#8,#11 . . . . 17.00
Ann.#6 GP,HT,V:Laser,Nuklo, Whirlwind 10.00
Ann.#7 JSn,JRu,V:Thanos,A:Captain Marvel,D:Warlock(2nd) 20.00
Ann.#8 GP,V:Dr.Spectrum. 7.00
Ann.#9 DN,V:Arsenal 6.00
Ann.#10 MGo,A:X-Men,Spid.Woman, I:Rogue,V:Br.o/Evil Mutants . . 30.00
Ann.#11 DP,V:Defenders 5.00
Ann.#12 JG,V:Inhumans,Maximus . 4.00
Ann.#13 JBy,V:Armin Zola 4.00
Ann.#14 JBy,KB,V:Skrulls. 4.00
Ann.#15 SD,KJ,V:Freedom Force . . 4.00
Ann.#16 RF,BH,TP,JR2,BSz,KP,AW, MR,BL,BWi,JG,KN,A:Silver Surfer,Rebirth Grandmaster . . . 4.50
Ann.#17 MBr,MG,Evol.Wars,J:2nd Yellow Jacket 4.00
Ann.#18 MBa,MG,Atlan.Attack#8, J:Quasar 3.00
Ann.#19 HT,Terminus Factor. 2.50
Ann.#20 Subterran.Odyssey#1 . . . . 2.50
Ann.#21 Citizen Kang#4. . . . . 2.50
Ann.#22 I:Bloodwraith,w/card 3.25
Ann.#23 JB 3.25
G-Size#1 JR(c),RB,DA,I:Nuklo . . . 10.00
G-Size#2 JR(c),DC,O:Kang, D:Swordsman,O:Rama-Tut. . . . 7.00
G-Size#3 GK(c),DC,V:Kang,Legion of the Unliving 5.00
G-Size#4 K&R(c),DH,W:Scarlet Witch &Vision,O:Mantis,Moondragon . 7.00
G-Size#5 rep,Annual #1.. . . . . 3.00
GNv Death Trap:The Vault RLm, A:Venom 20.00
Marvel Milestone rep. #1 (1993) . . . 2.95
Marvel Milestone rep. #4 (1995) . . . 2.95
Marvel Milestone rep. #16 (1993) . . 2.95
TPB Greatest Battles of the Avengers 15.95
TPB Korvac Saga,rep.#167-177 . . 12.95
TPB Yesterday Quest,Rep.#181,182 185-187 . . . . 6.95

AVENGERS

Nov., 1996

1 RLd,JV,CYp,JSb,Heroes Reborn, F:Thor, Captain America,

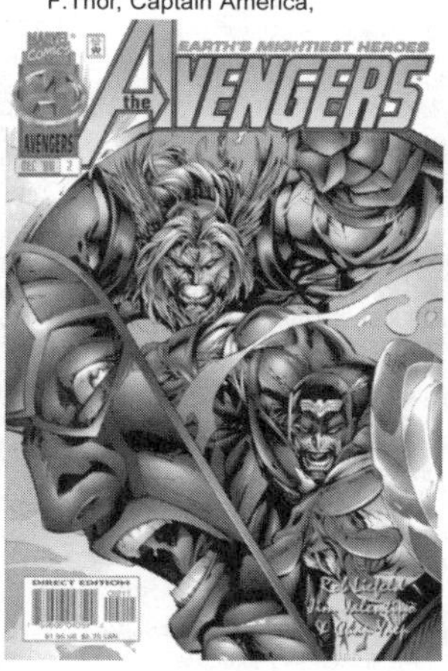

Avengers Vol. 2 #2
© Marvel Entertainment Group

V:Loki. 6.00
1A Variant cover 7.50
1 gold signature edition, bagged . 20.00
2 RLd,JV,CYp,JSb,V:Kang. 4.00
3 RLd,JV,CYp,JSb,V:Kang,A:Nick Fury 4.00
4 RLd,JLb,CYp,JSb, ... 4.00
4A variant cover 4.00
5 RLd,CYp,JSb,V:Hulk,concl. 3.50
6 RLd,JLb,CYp,JSb,"Industrial Revolution," pt.1 x-over 3.50
7 RLd,JLb,IaC,JSb, ... 3.50
8 RLd,JLb,IaC,JSb,F:Simon Williams (Wonder Man),V:Ultron, Lethal Legion 3.50
9 JLb,RLd,IaC,F:Vision, Wonder Man 3.50
10 WS,. 3.50
11 . . . . 3.50
12 WS,Galactus Saga, x-over. 3.50
13 JeR, Wildstorm x-over 3.50
Minus 1 Spec., JLb,RLd,IaC,JSb, flashback 2.50

AVENGERS

Dec., 1997

1 GP,KBk,AV,F:Everyone,48 pg. . . 5.00
2 KBk,GP,AV,A:Scarlet Witch 3.50
3 KBk,GP,AV,trapped in midieval present. 3.00
4 KBk,GP,AV,who makes the team?. 3.00
5 KBk,GP,AV,Squadron Supreme. . 2.00
6 KBk,GP,AV,V:SquadronSupreme. 2.00
7 KBk,GP,AV,Live Kree or Die, pt.4, concl 2.00
8 KBk,GP,AV,I:Triathlon 2.00
9 KBk,GP,AV,V:Moses Magnum . . . 2.00
10 KBk,GP,AV,V:Grim Reaper. 2.00
11 KBk,GP,AV,V:Grim Reaper. 2.00
12 KBk,GP,AV,V:Thunderbolts 48-page 40.00
13 KBk,GP,AV,R:New Warriors 2.00
14 KBk,GP,AV,R:Beast 2.00
15 KBk,GP,AV,A:Iron Man. 2.00
16 JOy,AG,R:Photon 2.00
16a variant JOy,GP cover. 2.00
17 JOy,AG,A:Warbird & Black Knight. 2.00
18 JOy,AG,V:Wrecking Crew 2.00
19 KBk,GP,AV,Ultron,pt.1 . . . . 2.00
19a signed 30.00
20 KBk,GP,AV,Ultron,pt.2 . . . . 2.00
21 KBk,GP,AV,Ultron,pt.3 . . . . 2.00
22 KBk,GP,AV,Ultron,pt.4 . . . . 2.00
23 KBk,GP,AV,V:Wonder Man. 2.00
24 KBk,GP,AV 2.00
25 KBk,GP,AV, 48-pg. 3.00
26 KBk,GP,AV,SI,V:Triune. 2.00
27 KBk,GP,AV,100-pg. 3.00
28 KBk,GP,AV,Kulan Gath,pt.1 . . . . 2.00
29 KBk,GP,AV,Kulan Gath,pt.2 . . . . 2.25
30 KBk,GP,AV,Kulan Gath,pt.3 . . . . 2.25
31 KBk,GP,AV,F:Vision 2.25
32 KBk,GP,AV,F:Black Widow. 2.25
33 KBk,GP,AV,Thunderbolts 2.25
34 KBk,GP,AV,Thunderbolts 2.25
35 KBk,JR2,AV,MaximumSecurity. . 2.25
Ann. '98 Avengers/Squadron Supreme KBk,CPa,GP, 48pg 2.50
Ann.1999 KBk,JFM, Why Avengers disbanded, 48-page 3.50
Ann.2000 KBk,NBy,48-pg 3.50
Rough Cut Edition KBk,GP, 48pg, original pencils of #1, b&w 3.00
Spec. 1-1/2, 32-pg.RSt 2.50
Spec. Avengers: Year in Review. . . 3.00
TPB Essential Avengers 14.95
TPB Essential Avengers, Vol.2 . . . 14.95
TPB Avengers: Under Siege. 16.95
TPB Avengers Visionaries: George Perez, 176-page 16.95
TPB The Morgan Conquest 14.95
TPB The Kree/Skrull War 24.95

Avengers Forever #1
© Marvel Entertainment Group

AVENGERS FOREVER

Oct., 1998

1 (of 12) GP,KBk,CPa,Rick Jones radiation poisoning 4.00
2 GP,KBk,CPa,new Avengers 3.00
3 GP,KBk,CPa,Kang/Immortus. . . . 3.00
4 KBk,different eras 3.00
4a, b & c variant covers . . . . @3.00
5 KBk,RSt,A:1950s Avengers 3.00
6 KBk,RSt,V:Immortus. 3.00
7 KBk,RSt,reunited 3.00
8 KBk,Immortus' plan 3.00
9 KBk,RSt,Kang the Conqueror . . . 3.00
10 KBk,RSt,V:Immortus 3.00
11 KBk,RSt,V:Avengers Battalion . . 3.00
12 KBk,RSt,concl.. . . . . 3.00

AVENGERS INDEX

See: OFFICIAL MARVEL INDEX TO THE AVENGERS

AVENGERS INFINITY

July, 2000

1 (of 4) RSt,SCh,SHa 3.00
2 RSt,SCh,SHa,Servitors. 3.00
3 RSt,SCh,SHa,Infinites. 3.00
4 RSt,SCh,SHa,concl 3.00

AVENGERS LOG

1994

1 GP(c),History of the Avengers . . 2.25

AVENGERS SPOTLIGHT

August, 1989

Formerly: Solo Avengers

21 AM,DH,TMo,JRu,Hawkeye, Starfox 2.00
22 AM,DH,Hawkeye,O:Swordsman. 2.00
23 AM,DH,KD,Hawkeye,Vision 2.00
24 AM,DH,Hawkeye,O:Espirita 2.00
25 AM,TMo,Hawkeye,Rick Jones . . 2.00
26 A of V,Hawkeye,Iron Man. 2.00
27 A of V,AM,DH,DT,Hawkeye, Avengers 2.00
28 A of V,AM,DH,DT,Hawkeye, Wonder Man,Wasp. 2.00
29 A of V,DT,Hawkeye,Iron Man . . . 2.00
30 AM,DH,Hawkeye,New Costume. 2.00
31 AM,DH,KW,Hawkeye,US.Agent . 2.00
32 AM,KW,Hawkeye,U.S.Agent . . . 2.00
33 AM,DH,KW,Hawkeye,US.Agent . 2.00
34 AM,DH,KW,SLi(c),Hawkeye U.S.Agent 2.00
35 JV,Gilgamesh 2.00
36 AM,DH,Hawkeye 2.00
37 BH,Dr.Druid 2.00
38 JBr,Tigra 2.00
39 GCo,Black Knight 2.00
40 Vision,Last Issue 2.00

AVENGERS STRIKEFILE

1994

1 BHa(s),Avengers Pin-ups 2.00

AVENGERS: THE CROSSING

1995

1 BHs,Death of an Avenger, chromium cover,48pg. 6.00

AVENGERS: THE TERMINATRIX OBJECTIVE

1993

1 B:MGu(s),MG,Holografx(c), V:Terminatrix 2.75
2 MG,V:Terminatrix,A:Kangs 2.00
3 MG,V:Terminatrix,A:Kangs 2.00
4 MG,Last issue 2.00

AVENGERS: TIMESLIDE

1996

1 BHs,TKa,End of the Crossing Megallic chrome cover 5.00

AVENGERS TWO: WONDER MAN & THE BEAST

Mar., 2000

1 (of 3) RSt,MBa, ... 3.00
2 RSt,MBa, ... 3.00
3 RSt,MBa,concl.. . . . . 3.00

AVENGERS/ULTRAFORCE

1995

1 V:Malibu's Ultraforce. 4.00

AVENGERS: UNITED THEY STAND

Sept., 1999

1 TTn,RCa, Cartoon tie-in 3.00
2 TTn, ... 2.00
3 TTn, ... 2.00
4 TTn, ... 2.00
5 TTn,Hawkeye&Black Widow 2.00
6 TTn,A:Capt.America 2.00
7 TTn,F:Devil Dinosaur,Moonboy. . 3.00

AVENGERS UNIVERSE

June, 2000

1 rep. 3 stories, 80-pg.. . . . . 5.00
2 rep. 3 stories, 80-pg.. . . . . 5.00
3 rep. 3 stories, 80-pg.. . . . . 5.00
4 rep. 3 stories, 80-pg.. . . . . 4.00

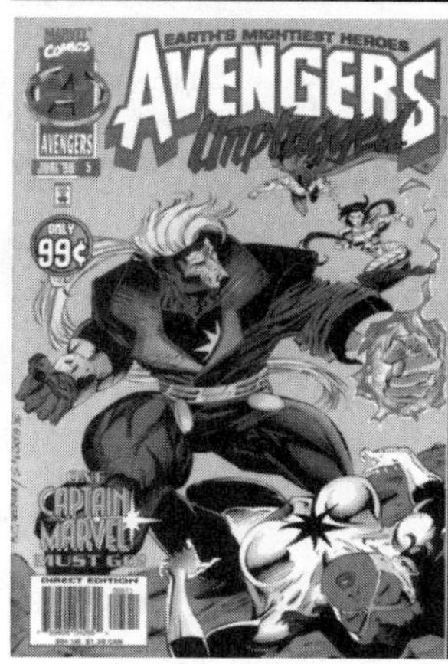

Avengers Unplugged #5
© Marvel Entertainment Group

5 rep. 3 stories, 80-pg. 4.00

AVENGERS UNLEASHED

1 V:Count Nefarious 2.00

Becomes:

AVENGERS UNPLUGGED

1996

2 Crushed by Graviton. 2.00
3 x-over with FF Unplugged. 2.00
4 . . . . 2.00
5 . . . . 2.00

AVENGERS WEST COAST

Sept., 1989

Prev: West Coast Avengers

47 JBy,V:J.Random 2.00
48 JBy,V:J.Random 2.00
49 JBy,V:J.Random,W.Man. 2.00
50 JBy,R:G.A.Human Torch 2.00
51 JBy,R:Iron Man 2.00
52 JBy,V:MasterPandmonum 2.00
53 JBy,Acts ofVeng.,V:U-Foes 2.00
54 JBy,Acts ofVeng.,V:MoleMan . . . 2.00
55 JBy,Acts ofVeng.finale,V:Loki
Magneto kidnaps Sc.Witch 2.50
56 JBy,V:Magneto. 2.50
57 JBy,V:Magneto. 2.50
58 V:Vibro, ... 2.00
59 TMo,V:Hydro-Man,A:Immortus . . 2.00
60 PR,V:Immortus, ... 2.00
61 PR,V:Immortus 2.00
62 V:Immortus 2.00
63 PR,I:Living Lightning 2.00
64 F:G.A.Human Torch 2.00
65 PR,V:Ultron,Grim Reaper. 2.00
66 PR,V:Ultron,Grim Reaper. 2.00
67 PR,V:Ultron,Grim Reaper. 2.00
68 PR,V:Ultron 2.00
69 PR,USAgent vs Hawkeye,
I:Pacific Overlords 2.50
70 DR,V:Pacific Overlords 2.00
71 DR,V:Pacific Overlords 2.00
72 DR,V:Pacific Overlords 2.00
73 DR,V:Pacific Overlords 2.00
74 DR,J:Living Lightning,Spider
Woman,V:Pacific Overlords. . . . 2.00
75 HT,A:F.F,V:Arkon,double 2.25
76 DR,Night Shift,I:Man-Demon 2.00
77 DR,A:Satannish & Nightshift . . . 2.00
78 DR,V:Satannish & Nightshift . . . 2.00
79 DR,A:Dr.Strange,V:Satannish. . . 2.00
80 DR,Galactic Storm,pt.2 . . . . 2.00
81 DR,Galactic Storm,pt.9 . . . . 2.00
82 DR,Galactic Storm,pt.16
A:Lilandra. 2.00
83 V:Hyena 2.00
84 DR,I:Deathweb,A:SpM,
O:Spider-Woman 2.00
85 DR,A:SpM,V:Death Web 2.00
86 DR,A:SpM,V:Death Web 2.00
87 DR,A:Wolverine,V:Bogatyri 2.00
88 DR,A:Wolverine,V:Bogatyri 2.00
89 DR,V:Ultron 2.00
90 DR,A:Vision,V:Ultron 2.00
91 DR,V:Ultron,I:War Toy 2.00
92 DR,V:Goliath(Power Man) 2.00
93 DR,V:Doctor Demonicus 2.00
94 DR,J:War Machine. 2.00
95 DR,A:Darkhawk,V:Doctor
Demonicus. 2.00
96 DR,Inf.Crusade x-over 2.00
97 ACe,Inf.Crusade,V:Power
Platoon 2.00
98 DR,I:4th Lethal Legion 2.00
99 DR,V:4th Lethal Legion 2.00
100 DR,D:Mockingbird,V:4th Lethal
Legion,Red Foil(c) 3.50
101 DR,Bloodties#3,V:Exodus 4.00
102 DR,L:Iron Man,Spider-Woman,
US Agent,Scarlet Witch,War
Machine,last issue 4.00
Ann.#4 JBy,TA,MBa,Atlan.Attacks
#12,V:Seven Brides of Set 4.00
Ann.#5 Terminus Factor 3.50
Ann.#6 Subterranean Odyssey#5 . . 2.50
Ann.#7 Assault on Armor City#4 . . . 2.25
Ann.#8 DR,I:Raptor w/card. 3.25

BACKPACK MARVELS:

Avengers 7.00
Spider-Man Vol. 1. . . . . 7.00
X-Men Vol.1 . . . . 7.00
X-Men Vol.2 . . . . 7.00

BALDER THE BRAVE

Nov., 1985

1 WS,SB,V:Frost Giants 2.00
2 WS,SB,V:Frost Giants 2.00
3 WS,SB,V:Frost Giants 2.00
4 WS,SB,V:Frost Giants;Feb,1986. 2.00

BARBIE

Jan., 1991

1 polybagged with Credit Card. . . 10.00
2 . . . . 6.00
3 . . . . 5.00
4 Ice Skating 5.00
5 Sea Cruise 5.00
6 Sun Runner Story. 5.00
7 Travel issue 5.00
8 TV Commercial. 5.00
9 Music Tour Van. 5.00
10 Barbie in Italy 5.00
11 Haunted Castles 5.00
12 Monkey Bandit. 5.00
13 MW,A:Skipper,Ken. 5.00
14 Country Fair 5.00
15 Barbie in Egypt,pt.1 . . . . 5.00
16 Barbie in Egypt,pt.2 . . . . 5.00
17 Weightwatchers/Art issue. 5.00
18 V:heavy Metal Band. 5.00
19 A:Surfer Pal. 5.00
20 Skipper at Special Olympics . . . 5.00
21 I:Whitney,female fire fighter 5.00
22 Barbie in Greece 5.00
23 thru 27 . . . . @5.00
28 Valentine's Day Issue. 5.00
29 Skipper babysits 5.00
30 Cowgirls on the Range 5.00
31 Rest and Relaxation 5.00

Barbie #61
© Marvel Entertainment Group

32 A:Dandy the Gorilla 5.00
33 thru 41 . . . . @5.00
42 thru 49 . . . . @5.00
50 Anniv. issue, Disney World(c). . . 6.00
51 Vet's assistant 4.00
52 Valentines Day Special 4.00
53 Marooned 4.00
54 Female Inventors. 4.00
55 in Nashville 4.00
56 Sherlock Barbie 4.00
57 Nashville 4.00
58 Barbie Teaches Skating 4.00
59 Famous Females. 4.00
60 Halloween Hero. 4.00
61 Alaska Gold Rush 4.00
62 Christmas/Nutcracker 4.00
63 . . . . 4.00
64 . . . . 4.00
65 Under Antarctica 4.00
66 . . . . 4.00

BARBIE FASHION

Jan., 1991

1 polybagged with doorknob
hanger 5.00
2 thru 63 . . . . @2.50

BATTLE

Atlas March, 1951

1 They called Him a Coward . . . 200.00
2 The War Department Secrets . 100.00
3 The Beast of the Bataan 75.00
4 I:Buck Private O'Toole 75.00
5 Death Trap Of Gen. Wu. 75.00
6 RH 75.00
7 Enemy Sniper 75.00
8 A Time to Die 75.00
9 RH 60.00
10 . . . . 60.00
11 thru 20 . . . . @55.00
21 . . . . 65.00
22 . . . . 45.00
23 . . . . 50.00
24 . . . . 45.00
25 . . . . 40.00
26 JR 40.00
27 . . . . 40.00
28 JSe 40.00
29 . . . . 40.00
30 . . . . 40.00
31 RH. 40.00
32 JSe,GT 40.00
33 GC,JSe,JSt 40.00

34 JSe 40.00
35 . . . . . 40.00
36 BEv. 40.00
37 RA,JSt. 45.00
38 . . . . . 35.00
39 . . . . . 35.00
40 . . . . . 35.00
41 . . . . . 35.00
42 thru 46 . . . . . @35.00
47 JO 35.00
48 . . . . . 35.00
49 JDa 45.00
50 BEv 35.00
51 . . . . . 35.00
52 GWb 35.00
53 BP. 35.00
54 . . . . . 35.00
55 GC,AS,BP 50.00
56 . . . . . 35.00
57 . . . . . 35.00
58 . . . . . 35.00
59 . . . . . 35.00
60 A:Combat Kelly 35.00
61 A:Combat Kelly 35.00
62 A:Combat Kelly 35.00
63 SD. 75.00
64 JK 75.00
65 JK 75.00
66 JSe,JK,JDa 75.00
67 JSe,JK,AS,JDa 75.00
68 JSe,JK,AW,SD. 75.00
69 RH,JSe,JK,SW 60.00
70 BEv,SD; June, 1960. . . . . 60.00

BATTLE ACTION
Atlas Feb., 1952

1 . . . . . 175.00
2 . . . . . 90.00
3 . . . . . 50.00
4 . . . . . 50.00
5 . . . . . 50.00
6 . . . . . 50.00
7 . . . . . 50.00
8 . . . . . 50.00
9 . . . . . 50.00
10 . . . . . 50.00
11 thru 15 . . . . . @40.00
16 thru 26. . . . . @35.00
27. . . . . 35.00
28. . . . . 30.00
29 . . . . . 30.00
30 August, 1957 . . . . . 35.00

BATTLEBOOKS
Nov., 1998

Captain America, BiT(c) 4.00
Citizen V, BiT(c) 4.00
Colossus, BiT(c). 4.00
Elektra, BiT(c) 4.00
Gambit, BiT(c) 4.00
Iron Man, BiT(c) 4.00
Rogue, BiT(c). 4.00
Spider-Girl, BiT(c). 4.00
Spider-Man, BiT(c) 4.00
Storm, BiT(c) 4.00
Thor, BiT(c) 4.00
Wolverine, BiT(c) 4.00

BATTLE BRADY
See: MEN IN ACTION

BATTLEFIELD
Atlas April, 1952

1 RH, Slaughter on Suicide Ridge 150.00
2 . . . . . 75.00
3 Ambush Patrol 75.00
4 . . . . . 75.00
5 Into the Jaws of Death 75.00
6 thru 10 . . . . . @40.00
11 GC,May, 1953 . . . . . 40.00

BATTLEFRONT
Atlas June, 1952

1 RH(c),Operation Killer 200.00
2 . . . . . 100.00
3 Spearhead 75.00
4 Death Trap of General Chun . . 75.00
5 Terror of the Tank Men 75.00
6 A:Combat Kelly. 75.00
7 A:Combat Kelly 75.00
8 A:Combat Kelly 75.00
9 A:Combat Kelly 75.00
10 A:Combat Kelly 75.00
11 thru 20 . . . . . @60.00
21 thru 39 . . . . . @40.00
40 AW 75.00
41 . . . . . 40.00
42 AW 60.00
43 thru 48 August,1957. . . . . @45.00

BATTLEGROUND
Atlas Sept., 1954

1 . . . . . 125.00
2 JKz. 65.00
3 thru 8 . . . . . @50.00
9 . . . . . 50.00
10 . . . . . 35.00
11 AW 60.00
12 . . . . . 30.00
13 AW 60.00
14 JD 35.00
15 . . . . . 30.00
16 . . . . . 30.00
17 . . . . . 30.00
18 AS. 60.00
19 . . . . . 30.00
20 August, 1957 . . . . . 30.00

BATTLESTAR GALACTICA
March, 1979

1 EC,B:TV Adaptation; Annihalation 6.00
2 EC,Exodus 5.00
3 EC,Deathtrap 5.00
4 WS,Dogfight 5.00

Battlestar Galactica #1
© Marvel Entertainment Group

5 WS,E:TV Adaptation;Ambush . . 5.00
6 Nightmare 4.00
7 Commander Adama Trapped . . . 4.00
8 Last Stand 4.00
9 Space Mimic 4.00
10 This Planet Hungers 4.00
11 WS,Starbbuck's Dilemma. 4.00
12 WS,Memory Ends 4.00
13 WS,All Out Attack 4.00
14 Radiation Threat 4.00
15 Ship of Crawling Death 4.00
16 . . . . . 4.00
17 Animal on the Loose 4.00
18 Battle For the Forbidden Fruit . . 4.00
19 Starbuck's Back. 4.00
20 Duel to the Death 4.00
21 To Slay a Monster...To Deatroy a World 4.00
22 WS,A Love Story?. 4.00
23 Dec., 1981. . . . . 4.00

BATTLETIDE
1990

1 thru 4 F: Death's Head II and Killpower. . . . . @2.00

BATTLETIDE II
1993

1 Foil embossed cover 2.95
2 thru 8 F: Death's Head II and Killpower. . . . . @2.00

BEAST
March, 1997

1 (of 3) KG,CNn,F:Karma, Cannonball, V:Viper & Spiral. 2.50
2 KG,CNn,V:Spiral. 2.50
3 KG,CNn, concl.. . . . . 2.50

BEAUTY AND THE BEAST
Jan., 1985

1 DP,Beast & Dazzler,direct. 3.00
1a DP,Beast & Dazzler,UPC 2.00
2 DP,Beast & Dazzler 2.00
3 DP,Beast & Dazzler 2.00
4 DP,Beast & Dazzler 2.00

BEAUTY AND THE BEAST
1992

1 . . . . . 2.00
2 Wardrobe's birthday party. 2.00
3 . . . . . 2.00
4 . . . . . 2.00
5 . . . . . 2.00
6 Lumiere takes Cogsworth's job . . 2.00
7 Belle & Chip caught in snow 2.00
8 . . . . . 2.00
9 Can Beast prove his love? 2.00
10 Chip & Belle have a snow ball . . 2.00
11 History of Beast's Castle 2.00
12 . . . . . 2.00
13 The Dessert Disaster. 2.00

BEAVIS & BUTT-HEAD
March, 1994

1 Based on the MTV Show 5.00
1a 2nd Printing 2.50
2 Dead from the Neck up. 3.50
3 Break out at Burger World 3.00
4 Tattoo Parlor. 2.25
5 Field Day 2.25
6 Revulsion 2.25
7 Oldies bot. 2.25
8 Be a clown 2.25
9 Makin' movies 2.25
10 Halloween 2.25

Beavis and Butt-Head #4
© Marvel Entertainment Group

11 . . . . 2.00
12 . . . . 2.00
13 . . . . 2.00
14 Join Biker Gang 2.00
15 Spring Break 2.00
16 Capture The Flag 2.00
17 with video camera 2.00
18 Woodsuck 2.00
19 break-up? 2.00
20 Solar Eclipse 2.00
21 Male Cheerleaders 2.00
22 Antics at theme park 2.00
23 Witless 2.00
24 Holiday suck-tacular 2.00
25 . . . . 2.00
26 . . . . 2.00
27 Easter spirit 2.00
28 . . . . 2.00
TPB Greatest Hits, rep.#1–#4 . . . . 12.95
TPB Holidazed and Confused 12.95

BEFORE THE FANTASTIC 4: GRIMM AND LOGAN
May, 2000

1 (of 3) LHa,Wolverine&Thing 3.00
2 LHa,A:Carol Danvers 3.00
3 LHa,concl. 3.00

BEFORE THE FANTASTIC 4: REED RICHARDS
July, 2000

1 (of 3) PDa,DFg,V:Dr.Doom 3.00
2 PDa,DFg, ... 3.00
3 PDa,DFg,concl 3.00

BEFORE THE FANTASTIC 4: THE STORMS
Oct., 2000

1 (of 3) TKa,CAd,F:Sue & Johnny Storm 3.00

BEST OF MARVEL '96

TPB 224pg. 20.00

BEST WESTERN
June, 1949

58 A:KidColt,BlackRider,Two-Gun Kid; Million Dollar Train Robbery 175.00
59 A:BlackRider,KidColt,Two-Gun Kid;The Black Rider Strikes . 150.00

Becomes:

WESTERN OUTLAWS & SHERIFFS

60 PH(c),Hawk Gaither 125.00
61 Ph(c),Pepper Lawson 90.00
62 Murder at Roaring House Bridge 90.00
63 thru 65 . . . . . @90.00
66. . . . . . 60.00
67. . . . . . 80.00
68 thru 72 . . . . . @60.00
73 June, 1952 . . . . . 50.00

BEWARE
March, 1973

1 Reprints 25.00
2 thru 8 . . . . . @20.00

Becomes:

TOMB OF DARKNESS

9 Reprints 20.00
10 thru 22 . . . . . @15.00
23 November, 1976 . . . . . 20.00

BIKER MICE FROM MARS
1993

1 I:Biker Mice 2.00
2 thru 3 . . . . . 2.00

BILL & TED'S BOGUS JOURNEY
Nov., 1991

1 Movie Adaption. 3.25

BILL & TED'S EXCELLENT COMICS
Dec., 1991

1 From Movie; Wedding Reception 2.00
2 Death Takes a Vacation 2.00
3 `Daze in the Lives' 2.00
4 Station Plague 2.00
5 Bill & Ted on Trial 2.00
6 Time Trial 2.00
7 Time Trial, Concl 2.00
8 History Final 2.00
9 I:Morty(new Death) 2.00
10 'Hyperworld' 2.00
11 Lincoln assassination 2.00
12 Last issue 2.00

BILLY BUCKSKIN WESTERN
Atlas Nov., 1955

1 MD,Tales of the Wild Frontier . 100.00
2 MD,Ambush 75.00
3 MD,AW, Thieves in the Night . . 75.00

Becomes:

2-GUN KID

4 SD,A: Apache Kid 75.00

Becomes:

TWO-GUN WESTERN

5 B:Apache Kid,Doc Holiday, Kid Colt Outlaw 75.00
6 . . . . . 40.00
7 . . . . . 40.00
8 RC 50.00
9 AW. 60.00
10 . . . . . 35.00
11 AW 60.00
12 Sept., 1957,RC 45.00

BISHOP
1994

1 Mountjoy, foil cover. 4.50
2 foil stamped cover 4.00
3 JOs 3.50
4 V:Mountjoy 3.50

BISHOP: THE LAST X-MAN
Aug., 1999

1 R:Bishop, 48-page debut 3.00
2A I:Nom,Link,Jinx & Scorch 2.00
2B variant (c). 2.00
3 V:Chronomancer 2.00
4 . . . . . 2.00
5 V:The Kith 2.00
6 V:Chronomancer 2.00
7 ATi,A:Hellfire Club. 2.00
8 ATi,V:GOL-19 . . . . . 2.00
9 ATi,A:Trevor Fitzroy 2.25
10 ATi,Morlocks 2.25
11 ATi,A:Trevor Fitzroy 2.25
12 ATi,Chronowar,pt.1 . . . . . 2.25
13 ATi,Chronowar,pt.2 . . . . . 2.25
14 ATi,Chronowar,pt.3 . . . . . 2.25
15 ATi,Maximum Security 2.25

BISHOP: XAVIER'S SECURITY ENFORCER
Nov., 1997

1 (of 3) JOs,SEp 2.50
2 JOs,SEp,hunted by X.S.E. 2.50
3 JOs,SEp,Bishop v. Rook, concl. . 2.50

BIZARRE ADVENTURES
See: MARVEL PREVIEW

BLACK AXE

1 JR2(c),A:Death's Head II 2.00
2 JR2(2),A:Sunfire,V:The Hand . . . 2.00
3 A:Death's Head II,V:Mesphisto . . 2.00
4 in ancient Egypt 2.00
5 KJ(c),In Wakanda 2.00
6 KJ(c),A:Black Panther. 2.00
7 KJ(c),A:Black Panther. 2.00
8 thru 13 . . . . . @2.00

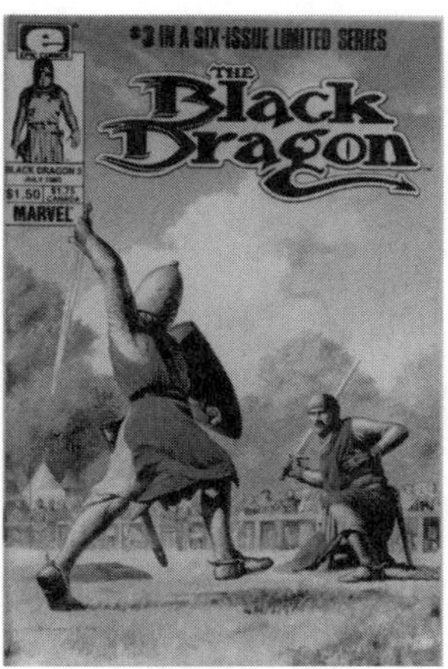

Black Dragon #3
© Marvel Entertainment Group

BLACK CAT
[Limited Series]
1 Wld,A:Spider-Man,V:Cardiac, I:Faze. 2.00
2 Wld,V:Faze. 2.00
3 Wld,Cardiac 2.00
4 Wld,V:Scar 2.00

BLACK DRAGON
Epic May, 1985
1 JBo 4.00
2 thru 6 JBo. . . . . @3.00

BLACK GOLIATH
Feb., 1976—Nov., 1976
1 GT,O:Black Goliath,Cont's From Powerman #24 . . . . . 15.00
2 GT,V:Warhawk 7.00
3 GT,D:Atom-Smasher. 7.00
4 KP,V:Stilt-Man 7.00
5 D:Mortag 7.00

BLACK KNIGHT, THE
Atlas May, 1955—April, 1956
1 O: Crusader;The Black Knight Rides 650.00
2 Siege on Camelot 500.00
3 Blacknight Unmasked 400.00
4 Betrayed 400.00
5 SSh,The Invincible Tartar 400.00

BLACK KNIGHT
June, 1990—Sept., 1990
1 TD,R:Original Black Knight 2.00
2 TD,A:Dreadknight. 2.00
3 RB,A:Dr.Strange. 2.00
4 RB,TD,A:Dr Strange, Valkyrie . . . 2.00

BLACK KNIGHT: EXODUS
1996
1-shot R:Black Knight,A:Sersi, O:Exodus. 2.50

BLACK PANTHER
[1st Series]
Jan., 1977—May, 1979
1 JK,V:Collectors. 25.00

Black Knight: Exodus #1
© Marvel Entertainment Group

2 JK,V:Six Million Year Man 10.00
3 JK,V:Ogar. 10.00
4 JK,V:Collectors 10.00
5 JK,V:Yeti. 10.00
6 JK,V:Ronin 10.00
7 JK,V:Mister Little. 10.00
8 JK,D:Black Panther. 10.00
9 JK,V:Jakarra. 10.00
10 JK,V:Jakarra 10.00
11 JK,V:Kilber the Cruel 10.00
12 JK,V:Kilber the Cruel 10.00
13 JK,V:Kilber the Cruel 10.00
14 JK,A:Avengers,V:Klaw 11.00
15 JK,A:Avengers,V:Klaw 11.00

BLACK PANTHER
July, 1988—Oct., 1988
[1st Mini-Series]
1 I:Panther Spirit 2.50
2 V:Supremacists 2.50
3 A:Malaika 2.50
4 V:Panther Spirit 2.50

[2nd Mini-Series]
PANTHER'S PREY
May, 1991
1 DT,A:W'Kabi,V:Solomon Prey . . . 4.95
2 thru 4 DT,V:Solomon Prey. . . . @4.95

BLACK PANTHER
Sept., 1998
1 CPr,MT,A:T'Challa 2.50
2 CPr,MT,A:Mephisto. 2.50
2a variant cover. 2.50
3 CPr,MT,JQ,I:Achebe 2.50
4 CPr,MT,JQ,V:Mephisto 2.50
5 CPr,V:Mephisto. 2.50
6 CPr,JJu,V:Kraven the Hunter . . . 2.50
7 CPr,JJu,V:Kraven, round 2 . . . . . 2.50
8 CPr,JJu,A:Avengers 2.50
9 CPr,MM,A:Avengers 2.50
10 CPr,MM,political counter-attack 2.50
11 CPR,MBr,Enemy of the State,pt.3 . . . . . 2.50
12 CPr,MBr,Enemy o/t State,pt.4 . . 2.50
13 CPr,A:T'Challa. 2.50
14 CPr,. 2.50
15 CPr,A:Hulk. 2.50
16 CPr,V:Killmonger 2.50
17 CPr,V:Killmonger 2.50
18 CPr,V:Killmonger,A:Nakia. 2.50
19 CPr,F:Queen Divine. 2.50
20 CPr,F:Moon Knight 2.50
21 CPr,F:Moon Knight 2.50
22 CPr,A:T'Challa. 2.50
23 CPr,Cat Trap,pt.2,x-over 2.50
24 CPr,MBr,Malice 2.50
25 CPr,Maximum Security 2.50

BLACK RIDER
See: ALL WINNERS COMICS

BLACK RIDER RIDES AGAIN
Atlas Sept., 1957
1 JK,Treachery at Hangman's Ridge 175.00

BLACKSTONE, THE MAGICIAN
May, 1948—Sept., 1948
2 B:Blonde Phantom 500.00
3 . . . . . 300.00
4 Bondage(c). 325.00

BLACK WIDOW
Apr., 1999
1 (of 3) Black Widow replaced? . . . 4.50
1a variant cover (1:4). 4.50
2 A:Daredevil. 3.00
3 conclusion 3.00
TPB Web of Intrigue, rep. Marvel Fanfare #10–#13 . . . . . 4.00

BLACKWULF
1994–95
1 AMe,Embossied(c),I:Mammoth, Touchstone,Toxin,D:Pelops, V:Tantalus, ... 2.75
2 AMe,I:Sparrow,Wildwind 2.00
3 AMe,I:Scratch. 2.00
4 AMe,I:Giant-man 2.00
5 AMe 2.00
6 AMe,Tantalus 2.00
7 AMe,V:Tantalus 2.00
8 AMe 2.00
9 Seven Worlds of Tantalus,pt.1 A:Daredevil 2.00
10 Seven Worlds of Tantalus,pt.2, last issue 2.00

BLADE, THE VAMPIRE HUNTER
1994–95
1 Foil(c),Clv(i),R:Dracula 3.00
2 Clv(i),V:Dracula 2.00
3 Clv(i) 2.00
4 Clv(i) 2.00
5 Clv(i) 2.00
6 Clv(i) 2.00
7 Clv(i) 2.00
8 Bible John, Morbius 2.00
9 . . . . . 2.00
10 R:Dracula 2.00
11 Dracula Untombed,pt.2 . . . . . 2.00

BLADE
Sept., 1998
1 (of 6) DMG,40-page, photo(c) . . 3.50
1a variant cover (1:4). 3.50
2 DMG,A:Morbius,Dominique. 3.00
2a variant cover. 3.00
3 DMG, ... 3.00
4 DMG,F:Morbius 3.00
1-shot Blade: Crescent City Blues, MPe,V:Deacon Frost (1-98) . . . 3.50
1-shot DMG, movie tie-in (2-98) . . . 3.00
1-shot movie adaptation,48 pg 6.00

BLADE: VAMPIRE HUNTER
Oct., 1999
1 (of 6) BS, 48-pg.. . . . . 3.50
2 BS 2.50
3 BS,V:Reaper 2.50
4 BS,V:Hrolf 2.50
5 BS,V:Reaper 2.50
6 BS,V:Reaper, concl. 2.50

BLADE RUNNER
Oct., 1982
1 AW, Movie Adaption 2.00
2 AW, ... 2.00

Blaze #8
© Marvel Entertainment Group

BLAZE
[Limited Series] 1993–94
1 HMe(s),RoW,A:Clara Menninger . 2.00
2 HMe(s),RoW,I:Initiate 2.00
3 HMe(s),RoW, ... 2.00
4 HMe(s),RoW,D:Initiate,Last issue 2.00

[Regular Series] Aug., 1994
1 HMz,LHa,foil (c) 3.25
2 HMz,LHa,I:Man-Thing. 2.00
3 HMz,LHa,V:Ice Box Bob 2.00
4 HMz,LHa,Apache Autumn,pt.1 . . 2.00
5 HMz,LHa,Apache Autumn,pt.2 . . 2.00
6 Apache Autumn,pt.3. . . . . 2.00
7 Carnivale Quintano. 2.00
8 A:Arcae 2.00
9 Clara's Eyeballs 2.00
10 Undead M.C.. . . . . 2.00
11 A:Punisher. 2.00
12 reunited with children, final iss. . 2.00

BLAZE CARSON
Sept., 1948
1 SSh(c),Fight,Lawman or Crawl 200.00
2 Guns Roar on Boot Hill 150.00
3 A:Tex Morgan 150.00
4 A:Two-Gun Kid 150.00
5 A:Tex Taylor 150.00
Becomes:

REX HART
6 CCB,Ph(c),B:Rex Hart, A:Black Rider 150.00
7 Ph(c),Mystery at Bar-2 Ranch 125.00
8 Ph(c),The Hombre Who Killed His Friends 125.00
Becomes:

WHIP WILSON
9 Ph(c),B:Whip Wilson,O:Bullet; Duel to the Death 500.00
10 Ph(c),Wanted for Murder 275.00
11 Ph(c) 275.00
Becomes:

GUNHAWK, THE
12 The Redskin's Revenge 150.00
13 GT,The Man Who Murdered Gunhawk 100.00
14 . . . . 100.00
15 . . . . 100.00
16 . . . . 100.00
17 . . . . 100.00
18 Dec., 1951 . . . . 100.00

BLAZE OF GLORY
Dec., 1999
1 (of 4) JOs,F:John Woo 3.00
2 JOs, ... 3.00
3 JOs, ... 3.00
4 JOs,concl. 3.00

BLAZE, THE WONDER COLLIE
Oct., 1949
2 Ph(c),Blaze-Son of Fury 175.00
3 Ph(c), Lonely Boy;Feb.,1950. . 150.00

BLONDE PHANTOM
See: ALL-SELECT COMICS

BLOOD
Feb., 1988—April, 1988
1 . . . . 6.00
2 thru 4 . . . . @5.00

BLOOD & GLORY
1993
1 KJ Cap & the Punisher 6.00
2 KJ Cap & the Punisher 6.00
3 KJ Cap & the Punisher 6.00

BLOODLINES
Epic 1992
1 F:Kathy Grant-Peace Corps 6.00

BLOODSEED
1993
1 LSh,I:Bloodseed 2.25
2 LSh,V:Female Bloodseed 2.25

BOOK OF THE DEAD
1993–94
1 thru 4 Horror rep . . . . @2.00
5 and 6 . . . . @2.00

BOZZ CHRONICLES, THE
Epic Dec., 1985
1 thru 5 . . . . @2.00
6 May, 1986 . . . . 2.00

BRATS BIZARRE
Epic *Heavy Hitters* 1994
1 with trading card. 3.25
2 thru 4 with trading card . . . . . . @2.50

BREAK THE CHAIN
1 KB,KRS-One,w/audio tape 7.00

BRUTE FORCE
August, 1990
1 JD/JSt 2.00
2 . . . . 2.00
3 . . . . 2.00
4 November, 1990 . . . . 2.00

BUCK DUCK
Atlas June, 1953
1 (fa)stories 60.00

Buckaroo Banzai #1
© Marvel Entertainment Group

2 and 3 . . . . @25.00
4 Dec., 1953 . . . . 25.00

BUCKAROO BANZAI
Dec., 1984
1 Movie Adaption. 3.00
2 Conclusion, Feb., 1985. . . . . 2.00

BUG
1997
1-shot 48pg 3.00

BULLWINKLE & ROCKY
Star Nov., 1987
1 EC&AM,Based on 1960's TV Series 3.00
2 EC&AM, ... 2.00
3 EC&AM,Rumpled Mudluck Thyme Mag 2.00
4 EC&AM,Boris and Natasha. 2.00
5 EC&AM, ... 2.00
6 EC&AM,Wassamatta Me 2.00
7 EC&AM,Politics,Moose V:Boris . . 2.00
8 EC&AM,Superhero, March,1989 . 2.00
9 EC 2.00
TPB, Bullwinkle & Rocky Collection AM,early stories 4.95

CABLE
[Limited Series] 1992
1 JR2,DGr,V:Mutant Liberation Front,A:Weapon X 4.00
2 JR2,DGr,V:Stryfe,O:Weapon X . . 3.00

[Regular Series] May 1993
1 B:FaN(s),ATi,O:Cable,V:New Canaanites,A:Stryfe,foil(c) 5.00
2 ATi,V:Stryfe 3.00
3 ATi,A:Six Pack 2.50
4 ATi,A:Six Pack 2.50
5 DaR,V:Sinsear 2.50
6 DT,A:Tyler,Zero,Askani, Mr.Sinister,C:X-Men 3.00
7 V:Tyler,A:Askani,X-Men,Domino . 3.00
8 O:Cable,V:Tyler,A:X-Men,Cable is Nathan Summers 3.00
9 MCW,B:Killing Field,A:Excalibur, V:Omega Red 2.50
10 MCW,A:Acolytes,Omega Red . . 2.50
11 MCW,E:Killing Field,D:Katu 2.50

MARVEL

12 SLo(s),B:Fear & Loathing,
V:Senyaka 2.50
13 V:D'Spayre 2.50
14 V:S'yM. 2.50
15 A:Thorn 2.50
16 Foil(c),Dbl-size,A:Jean,Scott
Logan,V:Phalanx 9.00
16a Newsstand ed. 3.00
17 Deluxe ed. 3.00
17a Newsstand ed. 2.00
18 Deluxe ed. 3.00
18a Newsstand ed. 2.00
19 Deluxe ed. 3.00
19a Newsstand ed. 3.00
20 V:Legion, Deluxe ed. w/card . . . 5.00
20a Newsstand ed. 2.00
21 Cable makes tough decisions,
A:Domino 2.50
22 V:Fortress 2.50
23 IaC,A:Domino 2.50
24 F:Blaquesmith 2.50
25 IaC,SHa,F:Cable's Wife,foil(c) . . 5.00
26 Tries to return to X-Mansion. . . . 2.25
27 IaC, A:Domino 2.25
28 IaC,SHa,concl. war in Genosha . 2.25
29 . . . . 2.25
30 . . . . 2.25
31 IaC, cont.X-Men/Cable war 2.25
32 Onslaught saga 3.00
33 Onslaught saga 3.00
34 Onslaught saga 3.00
35 Onslaught saga 2.25
36 . . . . 2.25
37 JLb,IaC,SHa,V:Askani'son,
Kane 2.25
38 JLb,IaC,SHa,V:PSycho-Man,
A:Kane. 2.25
39 JLb,IaC,SHa,V:Psycho-Man. . . . 2.25
40 TDz,IaC,SHa,A:Renee
Majcomb 2.25
41 TDz,SHa,F:Bishop 2.25
42 TDz,RGr,SHa,"The Prophecy
of the Twelve". 2.25
43 TDz,RGr,Images of Nathan's
past 2.25
44 TDz,RGr,SHa,A:Madelyne Pryor
(Cable's mom) 2.25
45 JeR,RGr,Zero Tolerance,
"No Escape,"pt.2 . . . . 2.25
46 JeR,RGr,SHa,Zero Tolerance,
"No Escape," pt.2 (of 3) 2.25
47 JeR,RGr,SHa, Operation Zero
Tolerance, V:Batsion. 2.25
48 JeR,SHa,V:Hellfire Club. 2.25
49 JeR,SHa,V:Hellfire Club. 2.25

Cable #20
© Marvel Entertainment Group

50 JeR,SHa,A:Cyclops, Phoenix,
Union Jack, 48pg 3.50
51 JeR,Hellfire Hunt 2.00
52 JeR,Hellfire Hunt, pt.5 . . . . 2.00
53 JoC,Hellfire Hunt, concl. 2.00
54 JoC,A:Black Panther,V:Klaw . . . 2.00
55 JoC,A:Irene Merryweather,
Domino 2.00
56 JoC,V:Stilt-Man & Hydro-Man . . 2.00
57 JoC,Cable powers altered by
EMP wave 2.00
58 JoC,Persecution, pt.1. . . . . 2.00
59 JoC,I:Agent 18,V:Zzaxx 2.00
60 JoC,Nemesis Contract,pt.2 . . . . 2.00
61 JoC,Nemesis Contract,pt.3 . . . . 2.00
62 JoC,Nemesis Contract,pt.4 . . . . 2.00
63 JoC,Blood Brothers,pt.2,x-over . 2.00
64 JoC,O:Cable 2.00
65 JoC,Millennium countdown 2.00
66 JoC,Sign of the End Times,pt.1 . 2.00
67 JoC,Sign of the End Times,pt.2 . 2.00
68 JoC,Sign of the End Times,pt.3 . 2.00
69 JoC,A:Blaquesmith,Archangel . . 2.00
70 JoC,A:Archangel 2.00
71 RLd,abandons his destiny,
with RLd poster 2.00
72 RLd,reunited with X-force. 2.00
73 RLd,reunited 2.00
74 V:Caliban. 2.00
75 . . . . 2.00
76 Apocalypse The 12:pt.6 . . . . 2.00
77 Ages of Apocalypse,pt.2 . . . . . . 2.00
78 mutant no more 2.00
79 X-Men: Revolution 2.00
79a variant (c) 2.00
80 Apocalypse gone. 2.25
81 The Undying 2.25
82 Nathan Summers, murderer?. . . 2.25
83 R:Domino 2.25
84 Phoenix & Beast 2.25
85 Mother Askani, Gaunt 2.25
86 Gaunt 2.25
Ann. '98 AOI(c) F:Cable vs. Machine
Man, O:Bastion 3.00
Ann.1999 48-page 3.50
Minus 1 Spec., TDz,JeR, flashback. 1.95
GN Cable/Wolverine Guts 'N'
Glory 6.00
Cable: Second Genesis 4.00
TPB Cable,rep.New Mutants
#87-94 . . . . 15.95

CABLE & X-FORCE

Cable & X-Force '95 Spec. 3.95
Cable & X-Force '96 Spec.48pg. . . . 3.00
Cable & X-Force '97 Spec.#1
JFM,CJ,V:Malekith,48pg. 3.00

CADILLACS & DINOSAURS

Epic Nov., 1990

1 Rep.Xenozoic Tales 3.00
2 Rep.Xenozoic Tales 2.50
3 Rep.Xenozoic Tales 2.50
4 Rep.Xenozoic Tales 2.50
5 Rep.Xenozoic Tales 2.50
6 Rep.Xenozoic Tales, April,1991 . 2.50

CAGE

1992–93

1 DT,R:Luke Cage,I:Hardcore,. . . . 2.50
2 DT,V:Hammer. 2.00
3 DT,A:Punisher,V:Untouchables . . 2.00
4 DT,A:Punisher,V:Untouchables . . 2.00
5 DT,I:New Power Man 2.00
6 DT,V:New Power Man. 2.00
7 DT,A:Avengers West Coast. 2.00
8 DT,V:Steele,Wonder Man 2.00
9 V:Rhino,A:Hulk 2.00
10 DT,V:Hulk,Rhino 2.00
11 DT,V:Rapidfire 2.00
12 A:Iron Fist,double size 2.50
13 V:The Thinker 2.00
14 PCu,I:Coldfire 2.00
15 DT,For Love Nor Money#2,
A:Silver Sable,Terror. 2.00
16 DT,For Love Nor Money#5,
A:Silver Sable,Terror. 2.00
17 DT,Infinty Crusade 2.00
18 A:Dred,V:Creed 2.00
19 A:Dakota North 2.00
20 Last issue 2.00

CAMP CANDY

May, 1990

1 thru 6, Oct. 1990 . . . . @2.00

CAPTAIN AMERICA COMICS

Timely/Atlas May, 1941

1 S&K,Hitler(c),I&O:Capt.America &
Bucky,A:Red Skull,B:Hurricane,
Tuk the Caveboy 60,000.00
2 S&K,RC,AAv,Hitler(c),
I:Circular Shield;Trapped
in the Nazi Stronghold . . 10,000.00
3 S&K,RC,AAv,Stan Lee's 1st Text,
A:Red Skull,Bondage(c) . . 8,500.00
4 S&K,AAv,Horror Hospital . . . 5,000.00
5 S&K,AAv,Ringmaster's
Wheel of Death 4,500.00
6 S&K,AAv,O:Father Time,
E:Tuk 4,000.00
7 S&K,A: Red Skull 4,500.00
8 S&K, The Tomb 4,000.00
9 S&K,RC,V:Black Talon 3,500.00
10 S&K,RC,Chamber
of Horrors 3,500.00
11 AAv,E:Hurricane;Feuding
Mountaneers 3,000.00
12 AAv,B:Imp,E:Father Time;
Pygmie's Terror 2,800.00
13 AAv,O:Secret Stamp;All Out
For America. 3,000.00
14 AAv,V:Japs;Pearl Harbor
Symbol cover. 2,800.00
15 AAv,Den of Doom 2,800.00
16 AAv,A:R.Skull;CapA
Unmasked. 3,500.00
17 AAv,I:Fighting Fool;
Graveyard 2,500.00
18 AAv,V:Japanese 2,200.00
19 AAv,V:Ghouls,
B:Human Torch 1,800.00
20 AAv,A:Sub-Mariner,V:Nazis . 1,800.00
21 SSh(c),Bucky Captured. . . . 1,700.00
22 SSh(c),V:Japanese 1,700.00
23 SSh(c),V:Nazis 1,700.00
24 SSh(c),V:Black
Dragon Society 1,700.00
25 SSh(c),V:Japs;Drug Story . . 1,700.00
26 ASh(c),V:Nazi Fleet. 1,600.00
27 ASh(c)CapA&Russians
V:Nazis, E:Secret Stamp . . 1,600.00
28 ASh(c),NaziTorture
Chamber 1,600.00
29 ASh(c),V:Nazis;French
Underground 1,600.00
30 SSh(c),Bucky Captured. . . . 1,600.00
31 ASh(c),Bondage(c) 1,500.00
32 SSh(c),V: Japanese
Airforce 1,500.00
33 ASh(c),V:Nazis;Brenner
Pass 1,500.00
34 SSh(c),Bondage(c) 1,500.00
35 SSh(c),CapA in Japan. 1,500.00
36 SSh(c),V:Nazis;Hitler(c). . . . 2,000.00
37 ASh(c),CapA in Berlin,
A:Red Skull 1,600.00
38 ASh(c),V:Japs;Bondage(c) . 1,400.00
39 ASh(c),V:Japs;Boulder Dam 1,400.00

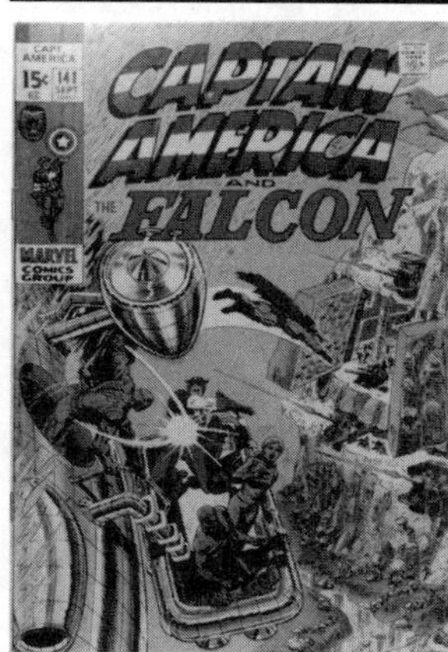

Captain America #141
© Marvel Entertainment Group

40 SSh(c),V:Japs;Ammo Depot . . . 1,400.00
41 ASh(c),Final Japanese War(c) . . . 1,300.00
42 ASh(c),V:Bank Robbers . . . 1,300.00
43 ASh(c),V:Gangsters . . . 1,300.00
44 ASh(c),V:Gangsters . . . 1,300.00
45 ASh(c),V:Bank Robbers . . . 1,300.00
46 ASh(c),Holocaust(c) . . . 1,300.00
47 ASh(c),Final Nazi War(c). . . 1,300.00
48 ASh(c),V:Robbers . . . 1,200.00
49 ASh(c),V:Sabatuers. . . 1,200.00
50 ASh(c),V:Gorilla Gang. . . 1,300.00
51 ASh(c),V:Gangsters . . . 1,200.00
52 ASh(c),V:Atom Bomb Thieves . . . 1,200.00
53 ASh(c),V:Burglars . . . 1,200.00
54 ASh(c),TV Studio, V:Gangsters . . . 1,200.00
55 V:Counterfeiters . . . 1,200.00
56 SSh(c),V:Art Theives. . . 1,200.00
57 Symbolic CapA(c) . . . 1,200.00
58 ASh(c),V:Bank Robbers . . . 1,200.00
59 SSh(c)O:CapA Retold;Private Life of Captain America . . . 2,500.00
60 V:The Human Fly . . . 1,200.00
61 SSh(c),V:Red Skull; Bondage(c) . . . 1,900.00
62 SSh(c),Kingdom of Terror . . 1,200.00
63 SSh(c),I&O:Asbestos Lady; The Parrot Strikes . . . 1,300.00
64 Diamonds Spell Doom . . . 1,200.00
65 When Friends Turn Foes. . . 1,200.00
66 O:Golden Girl;Bucky Shot . . 1,400.00
67 E:Toro(in Human Torch); Golden Girl Team-Up . . . 1,200.00
68 A:Golden Girl;Riddle of the Living Dolls . . . 1,200.00
69 Weird Tales of the Wee Males, A:Sun Girl. . . 1,200.00
70 A:Golden Girl,Sub-Mariner, Namora;Worlds at War. . . 1,200.00
71 A:Golden Girl; Trapped . . . 1,200.00
72 Murder in the Mind . . . 1,200.00
73 The Outcast of Time . . . 1,200.00
74 A:Red Skull;Capt.America's Weird Tales . . . 3,800.00
75 Thing in the Chest. . . 1,200.00
76 JR(c),Capt.America,Commie Smasher . . . 1,200.00
77 Capt.A,Commie Smasher. . . 800.00
78 JR(c),V:Communists; Sept.,1954 . . . 800.00
Marvel Milestone rep. #1 (1995) . . . 3.95

CAPTAIN AMERICA
Prev: Tales of Suspense
April, 1968

100 JK,A:Avengers . . . 300.00
101 JK,I:4th Sleeper . . . 75.00
102 JK,V:Red Skull,4th Sleeper . . 40.00
103 JK,V:Red Skull. . . 40.00
104 JK,DA,JSo,V:Red Skull . . . 40.00
105 JK,DA,A:Batroc . . . 40.00
106 JK,Cap.Goes Wild . . . 40.00
107 JK,Red Skull . . . 40.00
108 JK,Trapster . . . 40.00
109 JK,O:Captain America . . . 60.00
110 JSo,JSt,A:Hulk,Rick Jones in Bucky Costume . . . 55.00
111 JSo,JSt,I:Man Killer . . . 55.00
112 JK,GT,Album . . . 35.00
113 JSo,TP,Avengers, D:Madame Hydra . . . 55.00
114 JR,SB,C:Avengers . . . 20.00
115 JB,SB,A:Red Skull . . . 20.00
116 GC,JSt,A:Avengers . . . 20.00
117 JR(c),GC,JSt,I:Falcon . . . 50.00
118 JR(c),GC,JSt,A:Falcon . . . 20.00
119 GC,JSt,O:Falcon . . . 20.00
120 GC,JSt,A:Falcon . . . 20.00
121 GC,JSt,V:Man Brute. . . 15.00
122 GC,JSt,Scorpion . . . 12.00
123 GC,JSt,A:NickFury, V:Suprema . . . 12.00
124 GC,JSt,I:Cyborg. . . 12.00
125 GC,Mandarin . . . 12.00
126 JK&BEv(c),GC,A:Falcon . . . 12.00
127 GC,WW,A:Nick Fury . . . 12.00
128 GC,V:Satan's Angels . . . 12.00
129 GC,Red Skull. . . 12.00
130 GC,I:Batroc . . . 15.00
131 GC,V:Hood . . . 11.00
132 GC,A:Bucky Barnes . . . 11.00
133 GC,O:Modok,B:Capt.America/ Falcon Partnership . . . 11.00
134 GC,V:Stone Face. . . 11.00
135 JR(c),GC,TP,A:Nick Fury . . . 11.00
136 GC,BEv,V:Tyrannus . . . 11.00
137 GC,BEv,A:Spider-Man . . . 13.00
138 JR,A:Spider-Man . . . 12.00
139 JR,Falcon solo. . . 9.00
140 JR,O:Grey Gargoyle . . . 9.00
141 JR,JSt,V:Grey Gargoyle. . . 7.00
142 JR,JSt,Nick Fury . . . 7.00
143 JR,Red Skull . . . 10.00
144 GM,JR,N:Falcon,V:Hydra. . . 7.00
145 GK,JR,V:Hydra . . . 7.00
146 JR(c),SB,V:Hydra. . . 6.00
147 GK(c),SB,V:Hydra . . . 6.00
148 SB,JR,Red Skull . . . 6.00
149 GK(c),SB,JM,V:Batroc . . . 6.00
150 K&R(c),SB,V:The Stranger. . . 6.00
151 SB,V:Mr.Hyde . . . 6.00
152 SB,V:Scorpion,Mr.Hyde . . . 6.00
153 SB,JM,V:50's Cap . . . 6.00
154 SB,V:50's Cap . . . 6.00
155 SB,FMc,O:50's Cap . . . 6.00
156 SB,FMc,V:50's Cap . . . 6.00
157 SB,I:The Viper . . . 6.00
158 SB,V:The Viper . . . 6.00
159 SB,V:PlantMan,Porcupine . . . 6.00
160 SB,FMc,V:Solarr . . . 6.00
161 SB,V:Dr.Faustus . . . 6.00
162 JSn(c),SB,V:Dr.Faustus . . . 6.00
163 SB,I:Serpent Squad . . . 7.00
164 JR(c),I:Nightshade. . . 7.00
165 SB,FMc,V:Yellow Claw. . . 6.00
166 SB,FMc,V:Yellow Claw. . . 6.00
167 SB,V:Yellow Claw . . . 6.00
168 SB,I&O:Phoenix (2nd Baron Zemo) . . . 7.00
169 SB,FMc,C:Black Panther . . . 6.00
170 K&R(c),SB,C:Black Panther . . . 6.00
171 JR(c),SB,A:Black Panther . . . 6.00

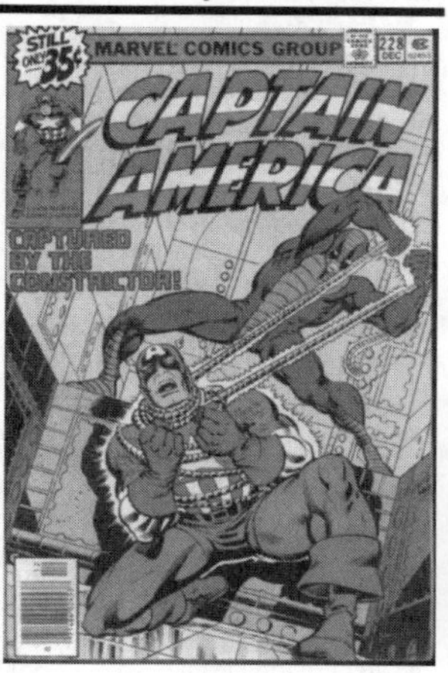

Captain America #228
© Marvel Entertainment Group

172 GK(c),SB,C:X-Men. . . 15.00
173 GK(c),SB,A:X-Men. . . 16.00
174 GK(c),SB,A:X-Men. . . 16.00
175 SB,A:X-Men. . . 16.00
176 JR(c),SB,O:Capt.America . . . 8.00
177 JR(c),SB,A:Lucifer,Beast . . . 6.00
178 SB,A:Lucifer . . . 6.00
179 SB,A:Hawkeye. . . 6.00
180 GK(c),SB,I:1st Nomad(Cap). . . 8.00
181 GK(c),SB,I&O:New Cap . . . 7.00
182 FR,Madam Hydra . . . 7.00
183 GK(c),FR,R:Cap,D:New Cap . . 8.00
184 K&R(c),HT,A:Red Skull . . . 5.00
185 GK(c),SB,FR,V:Red Skull. . . 5.00
186 GK(c),FR,O:Falcon . . . 6.00
187 K&R(c),FR,V:Druid. . . 5.00
188 GK(c),SB,V:Druid. . . 5.00
189 GK(c),FR,V:Nightshade . . . 5.00
190 GK(c),FR,A:Nightshade . . . 5.00
191 FR,A:Stilt Man,N.Fury . . . 5.00
192 JR(c),FR,A:Dr.Faustus . . . 5.00
193 JR(c),JK,`Mad Bomb'. . . 5.00
194 JK,I:Gen.Heshin. . . 5.00
195 JK,1984. . . 5.00
196 JK,Madbomb . . . 5.00
197 JK,Madbomb . . . 5.00
198 JK,Madbomb . . . 5.00
199 JK,Madbomb . . . 5.00
200 JK,Madbomb . . . 7.00
201 JK,Epilogue . . . 4.00
202 JK,Night People. . . 4.00
203 JK,Night People. . . 4.00
204 JK,I:Argon . . . 4.00
205 JK,V:Argon . . . 4.00
206 JK,I:Swine . . . 4.00
207 JK,V:Swine . . . 4.00
208 JK,I:Arnim Zola,D:Swine . . . 4.00
209 JK,O:Arnim Zola,I:Primus. . . 4.00
210 JK,A:Red Skull. . . 4.00
211 JK,A:Red Skull. . . 4.00
212 JK,A:Red Skull. . . 4.00
213 JK,I:Night Flyer . . . 4.00
214 JK,D:Night Flyer . . . 4.00
215 GT,Redwing. . . 4.00
216 Reprint,JK . . . 4.00
217 JB, I:Quasar(Marvel Boy) I:Vamp . . . 5.00
218 SB,A:Iron Man . . . 4.00
219 SB,JSt,V:TheCorporation . . . 4.00
220 SB,D:L.Dekker. . . 4.00
221 SB,Ameridroid . . . 4.00
222 SB,I:Animus(Vamp) . . . 4.00
223 SB,Animus. . . 4.00

MARVEL

224 MZ,V:Animus 4.00
225 SB,A:Nick Fury 4.00
226 SB,A:Nick Fury 4.00
227 SB,A:Nick Fury 4.00
228 SB,Constrictor 4.00
229 SB,R:SuperAgents of Shield . . 4.00
230 SB,A:Hulk 4.00
231 SB,DP,A:Grand Director 4.00
232 SB,DP,V:Grand Director 4.00
233 SB,DP,D:Sharon Carter 4.00
234 SB,DP,A:Daredevil 4.00
235 SB,FM,A:Daredevil 4.00
236 SB,V:Dr.Faustus 4.00
237 SB,`From the Ashes' 4.00
238 SB,V:Hawk Riders 4.00
239 JBy(c),SB,V:Hawk Riders 4.00
240 SB,V:A Guy Named Joe 4.00
241 A:Punisher 9.00
242 JSt,A:Avengers 3.50
243 GP(c),RB,V:Adonis 3.50
244 TS,`A Monster Berserk' 3.50
245 CI,JRn,Nazi Hunter 3.50
246 GP(c),JBi,V:Joe 3.50
247 JBy,V:BaronStrucker 4.00
248 JBy,JRu,Dragon Man 4.00
249 JBy,O:Machinesmith,
A:Air-Walker 4.00
250 JBy,Cap for Pres 4.00
251 JBy,V:Mr.Hyde 4.00
252 JBy,V:Batrok 4.00
253 JBy,V:Baron Blood 4.00
254 JBy,D:B.Blood,UnionJack,I:3rd
Union Jack 4.00
255 JBy,40th Anniv.,O:Cap 4.00
256 GC,V:Demon Druid 2.50
257 A:Hulk 2.50
258 MZ,V:Blockbuster 2.50
259 MZ,V:Dr. Octopus 2.50
260 AM,In Jail 2.50
261 MZ,A:Nomad 3.00
262 MZ,V:Ameridroid 2.50
263 MZ,V:Red Skull 2.50
264 MZ,X-Men 4.00
265 MZ,A:Spider-Man,N.Fury 3.00
266 MZ,A:Spider-Man 3.00
267 MZ,V:Everyman 2.50
268 MZ,A:Defenders(x-over from
Def.#106) 2.50
269 MZ,A:Team America 2.50
270 MZ,V:Tess-One 2.50
271 MZ,V:Mr.X 2.50
272 MZ,I:Vermin 3.00
273 MZ,A:Nick Fury 2.50
274 MZ,D:SamSawyer 2.50
275 MZ,V:Neo-Nazis 2.50
276 MZ,V:Baron Zemo 2.50
277 MZ,V:Baron Zemo 2.50
278 MZ,V:Baron Zemo 2.50
279 MZ,V:Primus 2.50
280 MZ,V:Scarecrow 2.50
281 MZ,A:Spider Woman,
R:'50's Bucky 2.50
282 MZ,I:2nd Nomad 4.00
282a (second primting) 2.00
283 MZ,A:Viper 4.00
284 SB,Nomad 3.00
285 MZ,V:Porcupine 3.00
286 MZ,V:Deathlok 5.00
287 MZ,V:Deathlok 5.00
288 MZ,V:Deathlok,D:Hellinger 5.00
289 MZ,A:Red Skull 2.50
290 JBy(c),RF,A:Falcon 2.50
291 JBy(c),HT,V:Tumbler 2.50
292 I&O:Black Crow 2.50
293 V:Mother Superior 2.50
294 R:Nomad 2.50
295 V:Sisters of Sin 2.50
296 V:Baron Zemo 2.50
297 O:Red Skull 2.50
298 V:Red Skull 2.50
299 V:Red Skull 2.50
300 D:Red Skull 4.00
301 PNe,A:Avengers 2.00
302 PNe,I:Machete,V:Batroc 2.00
303 PNe,V:Batroc 2.00
304 PNe,V:Stane Armor 2.00
305 PNe,A:Capt.Britain,V:Modred . . 2.00
306 PNe,A:Capt.Britain,V:Modred . . 2.00
307 PNe,I:Madcap 2.00
308 PNe,I:Armadillo,
Secret WarsII 2.00
309 PNe,V:Madcap 2.00
310 PNe,V:Serpent Society,I:Cotton
Mouth,Diamondback 2.50
311 PNe,V:Awesome Android 2.00
312 PNe,I:Flag Smasher 2.00
313 PNe,D:Modok 2.00
314 PNe,A:Nighthawk 2.00
315 PNe,V:Serpent Society 2.00
316 PNe,A:Hawkeye 2.00
317 PNe,I:Death-Throws 2.00
318 PNe,V&D:Blue Streak 2.00
319 PNe,V:Scourge,D:Vamp 2.00
320 PNe,V:Scourge 2.00
321 PNe,V:Flagsmasher,
I:Ultimatum 2.00
322 PNe,V:Flagsmasher 2.00
323 PNe,I:Super Patriot
(US Agent) 5.00
324 PNe,V:Whirlwind,Trapster 2.00
325 I:Slug,A:Nomad 2.00
326 V:Dr.Faustus 2.00
327 MZ(c)V:SuperPatriot 3.00
328 MZ(c),I:Demolition Man 2.00
329 MZ(c),A:Demolition Man 2.00
330 A:Night Shift,Shroud 2.00
331 A:Night Shift,Shroud 2.00
332 BMc,Rogers resigns 7.00
333 B:John Walker Becomes
6th Captain America 5.00
334 I:4th Bucky 4.00
335 V:Watchdogs 3.00
336 A:Falcon 2.50
337 TMo,I:The Captain 2.50
338 KD,AM,V:Professor Power 2.50
339 KD,TD,Fall of Mutants,
V:Famine 2.50
340 KD,AM,A:Iron Man, ... 2.00
341 KD,AM,I:Battlestar,A:Viper 2.00
342 KD,AM,A:D-Man,Falcon,
Nomad,Viper 2.00
343 KD,AM,A:D-Man,Falcon,
Nomad 2.00
344 KD,AM,A:D-Man,Nomad 2.50

Captain America #366
© Marvel Entertainment Group

345 KD,AM,V:Watchdogs 2.00
346 KD,AM,V:Resistants 2.00
347 KD,AM,V:RWinger&LWinger . . 2.00
348 KD,AM,V:Flag Smasher 2.00
349 KD,AM,V:Flag Smasher 2.00
350 KD,AM,doub-size,Rogers Ret.
as Captain Am,V:Red Skull,
E:6th Cap 4.00
351 KD,AM,A:Nick Fury 2.00
352 KD,AM,I:Supreme Soviets 2.00
353 KD,AM,V:Supreme Soviets . . . 2.00
354 KD,AM,I:USAgent,
V:Machinesmith 3.00
355 RB,AM,A:Falcon,Battlestar 2.00
356 AM,V:Sisters of Sin 2.00
357 KD,AM,V:Sisters of Sin
Baron Zemo,Batroc 2.00
358 KD,B:Blood Stone Hunt 2.00
359 KD,V:Zemo,C:Crossbones 2.00
360 KD,I:Crossbones 2.00
361 KD,V:Zemo,Batroc 2.00
362 KD,V:Zemo,Crossbones 2.00
363 KD,E:Blood Stone Hunt,
V:Crossbones,C:Wolverine 2.00
364 KD,V:Crossbones 2.00
365 KD,Acts of Vengeance,
V:SubMariner,Red Skull 2.00
366 1st RLm Capt.Amer.,Acts of
Vengeance,V:Controller 2.00
367 KD,Acts of Vengeance,
Magneto Vs. Red Skull 2.50
368 RLm,V:Machinesmith 2.00
369 RLm,I:Skeleton Crew 2.00
370 RLm,V:Skeleton Crew 2.00
371 RLm,V:Trump,Poundcakes 2.00
372 RLm,B:Streets of Poison,
Cap on Drugs,C:Bullseye 2.50
373 RLm,V:Bullseye,A:Bl.Widow . . . 2.00
374 RLm,V:Bullseye,A:Daredevil . . . 2.00
375 RLm,V:Daredevil 2.00
376 RLm,A:Daredevil 2.00
377 RLm,V:Crossbones,Bullseye . . 2.00
378 RLm,E:Streets of Poison,Red
Skull vs Kingpin,V:Crossbones . 2.00
379 RLm(c),V:Serpent Society 2.00
380 RLm,V:Serpent Society 2.00
381 RLm,V:Serpent Society 2.00
382 RLm,V:Serpent Society 2.00
383 RLm(c),RLm,50th Anniv.
64Pages 4.00
384 RLm,A:Jack Frost 2.00
385 RLm,A:USAgent 2.00
386 RLm,Cap./USAgent T.U. 2.00
387 B:Superia Strategem 2.00
388 A:Paladin 2.00
389 Superia Strategem #3 . . . . 2.00
390 Superia Strategem #4 . . . . 2.00
391 Superia Strategem #5 . . . . 2.00
392 E:Superia Strategem 2.00
393 V:Captain Germany 2.00
394 A:Red Skull,Diamondback 2.00
395 A:Red Skull,Crossbones 2.00
396 I:2nd Jack O'Lantern 2.00
397 V:Red Skull,X-Bones,Viper 2.00
398 Operation:Galactic Storm
Pt.1,V:Warstar 2.00
399 Operation Galactic Storm
Pt.8,V:Kree Empire 2.00
400 Operation Galactic Storm
Pt.15,BU:rep.Avengers #4 . . . . 4.00
401 R:D-Man,A:Avengers 2.00
402 RLe,B:Man & Wolf,
A:Wolverine 2.00
403 RLe,A:Wolverine 2.00
404 RLe,A:Wolverine 2.00
405 RLe,A:Wolverine 2.00
406 RLe,A:Wolverine 2.00
407 RLe,A:Wolverine,Cable 2.00
408 RLe,E:Man & Wolf 2.00
409 RLe,V:Skeleton Crew 2.00
410 RLe,V:Crossbones,Skel.Crew . 2.00

Captain America #436
© Marvel Entertainment Group

411 RLe,V:Snapdragon. 2.00
412 RLe,V:Batroc,A:Shang-Chi. . . . 2.00
413 A:Shang-Chi,V:Superia 2.00
414 RLe,A:Kazar,Black Panther . . . 2.00
415 Rle,A:Black Panther,Kazar. . . . 2.00
416 RLe,Savage Land Mutates, A:Black.Panther,Kazar 2.00
417 RLe,A:Black Panther,Kazar, V:AIM. 2.00
418 RLe,V:Night People 2.00
419 RLe,V:Viper 2.00
420 RLe,I:2nd Blazing Skull, A:Nightshift. 3.00
421 RLe,V:Nomad 2.00
422 RLe,I:Blistik 2.00
423 RTs(s),MCW,V:Namor 2.00
424 MGv(s),A:Sidewinder 2.00
425 B:MGu(s),DHv,Embossed(c), I:2nd Super Patriot,Dead Ringer 3.50
426 DHv,A:Super Patriot,Dead Ringer,V:Resistants 2.00
427 DHv,V:Super Patriot,Dead Ringer 2.00
428 DHv,I:Americop 2.00
429 DHv,V:Kono 2.00
430 Daemon Dran, Americop 2.00
431 DHv,I:Free Spirit 2.00
432 DHv,Fighting Chance 2.00
433 DHv,Baron Zemo 2.00
434 DHv,A:Fighting Spirit, V:King Cobra 2.00
435 DHv,Fighting Chance 2.00
436 V:King Cobra, Mister Hyde, Fighting Chance conclusion . . . 2.00
437 Cap in a Coma 2.00
438 I:New Body Armor 2.00
439 Dawn's Early Light,pt.2 . . . . . . 2.00
440 Taking A.I.M.,pt.1. . . . . 2.00
441 Taking A.I.M.,pt.3. . . . . 2.00
442 Batroc, Cap,V:Zeitgeist 2.00
443 MGu,24 hours to live 2.00
444 MWa,RG,President Kidnapped. 6.00
445 MWa,RG,R:Captain America . . 4.00
446 MWa,RG,Operation Rebirth,pt.2 . . . . 3.50
447 MWa,RG,Op.Rebirth,pt.3 . . . . . 3.50
448 MWa,RG,Operation Rebirth,pt.4,double size 6.00
449 MWa,RG,A:Thor 2.50
450 MWa,RG,Man Without a Country, pt,1. . . . . 2.50
450a alternate cover. 4.00
451 MWa,RG,DRo,Man Without A Country,pt.2,new costume . . . 2.00
452 MWa,RG,Man Without a Country, pt.3. . . . . 2.00
453 MWa,RG Man Without a Country, concl.,old costume . . . 2.00
454 MWa,RG,A:Avengers. 2.00
Ann.#1 rep.. . . . . 22.00
Ann.#2 rep.. . . . . 11.00
Ann.#3 JK, ... 5.00
Ann.#4 JK,V:Magneto,I:Mutant Force 10.00
Ann.#5 `Deathwatcher' 4.00
Ann.#6 A:Contemplator. 4.00
Ann.#7 O:Shaper of Worlds 4.00
Ann.#8 MZ,A:Wolverine 30.00
Ann.#9 MBa,SD,Terminus Factor #1,N:Nomad. 4.50
Ann.#10 MM,Baron Strucker,pt.3 (see Punisher Ann.#4) 2.50
Ann.#11 Citizen Kang#1 . . . . 2.50
Ann.#12 I:Bantam,w/card 3.25
Ann.#13 RTs(s),MCW, ... 3.25
Drug Wars PDd(s),SaV,A:New Warriors 2.00
G-Size#1 GK(c),rep.O:Cap.Amer. . . 7.00
HC vol.Slipcase Rep.#1 thru #10 (From 1940's) 75.00
Medusa Effect RTs(s),MCW,RB, V:Master Man. 2.95
Movie Adapt 2.00
Spec.#1 Rep.Cap.A #110,#111 . . . . 2.00
Spec.#2 Rep.Cap.A.#113 & Strange Tales #169. . . . . 2.00
TPB Bloodstone Hunt,rep. #357-364 . . . . 15.95
TPB Captain America: Man Without a Country, MWa,RG,SK, rep. (1998) 15.00
TPB Streets of Poison, rep. #372–#377
TPB War and Remembrance, rep. #247–#255 . . . . 12.95
Collector's Preview. 1.95
Ashcan. 75

[2nd Series] Nov., 1996

1 RLd,CDi,JSb, Heroes Reborn, I:Nick Fury,48pg. 5.00
1A Stars and stripes background variant cover 7.50
1b gold signature edition, cardstock cover 18.00
1c San Diego Con edition 25.00
2 RLd,JLb,JSb,Falcon & Red Skull. 3.00
3 RLd,JLb,JSb,A:Hulk,V:Red Skull & Master Man. 2.50
4 RLd,JLb,JSb,F:Prince Namor,. . . 2.50
5 RLd,JLb,JSb,V:Crossbones 2.50
6 RLd,JLb,JSb,"Industrial Revolution," epilogue,A:Cable. . 2.50
7 RLd,JLb,DaF, ... 2.00
8 RLd,JLb,SPa,A:Nick Fury, WWII story 2.00
9 JLb,RLd,SPa,WWII story. 2.00
10 JLb,RLd,SPa,WWII story, concl.. 2.00
11 JeR,JoB,Odyssey across America, pt.4, concl.. . . . . 2.00
12 JeR,JoB,Heroes Reborn, Galactus concl. 3.00
13 JeR,RLm,Wildstorm x-over 2.50
Ashcan, ComicCon. 5.00

[3rd Series] Nov., 1997

1 MWa,RG,BWi,A:Lady Deathstrike, Red Skull, Sharon Carter, 48-pg 4.00
1a variant cover. 15.00
2 MWa,RG,BWi,A devastating loss 5.00
2a variant cover. 4.00
3 MWa,RG,BWi,V:Hydra 4.00
4 MWa,RG,BWi,F:Batroc 3.00
5 MWa,RG,BWi,V:Hordes of Hydra. 3.00

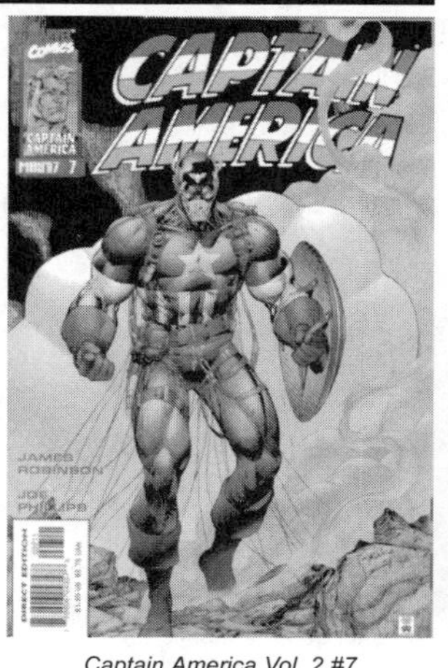

Captain America Vol. 2 #7
© Marvel Entertainment Group

6 MWa,RG,V:Skrulls 3.00
7 MWa,NKu,Power & Glory concl. . 2.00
8 MWa,Nku,Live Kree or Die, pt.2 x-over. 3.50
9 MWa,NKu,American Nightmare, pt.1 . . . . 3.00
10 MWa,NKu,American Nightmare, pt.2 . . . . 3.00
11 MWa,NKu,American Nightmare, pt.3. . . . . 3.00
12 MWa,NKu,American Nightmare, pt.4, 48-page 3.00
13 MWa,MFm,R:Red Skull 2.00
14 MWa,MFm,R:Red Skull 2.00
15 MWa,NKu,V:Red Skull. 2.00
16 MWa,NKu,V:Red Skull. 2.00
17 MWa,NKu,V:Red Skull. 2.00
18 MWa,LW,RbC,V:Cosmic Cube double sized. 3.00
19 MWa,NKu,V:2 foes 2.00
20 MWa,NKu,Shield secrets 2.00
21 MWa,NKu,A:Black Panther 2.00
22 MWa,NKu,A:Black Panther 2.00
23 MWa,Capt.America convict? . . . 2.00
24 TDF,RF,V:Hydra. 2.00
25 DJu,NKu,DGr,Twisted Tomorrows,pt.1. . . . . 2.00
26 DJu,NKu,DGr,Twisted,pt.2 . . . . . 2.00
27 DJu,NKu,DGr,Twisted,pt.3 . . . . . 2.00
28 DJu,NKu,DGr,V:CountNefaria . . 2.00
29 DJu,DGr,A:Ka-Zar 2.00
30 DJu,DGr,NKu,Savage Land 2.25
31 DJu,NKu,DGr,F:Sharon Carter. . 2.25
32 DJu,JO,kidnapped 2.25
33 DJu,ATi,Protocide 2.25
34 DJu,ATi,Cache. 2.25
35 DJu,ATi,Protocide 2.25
36 DJu,ATi,Maximum Security 2.25
Ann.1998 Captain America/ Citizen V,KBk,KK, 48-page 3.50
Ann. 1999 JoC,V:Flag Smasher, 48-page 3.50
Ann.2000 DJu,DGr,48-pg. 3.50
Spec.#1 Captain America (2000) . . 2.25
TPB The Classic Years,Vol.2 . . . . 24.95
TPB Essential Captain America . . 14.95

CAPTAIN AMERICA: SENTINEL OF LIBERTY

July, 1998

1 MWa,RG,new foe, in future. 2.00
1 signed by MWa & RG 5.00
2A MWa,RG(c&a) F:Invaders,

MARVEL

V:Nazis 2.00
2B variant JSm(c) 2.00
3 MWa,RG,DGr,A:Sub-Mariner . . . 2.00
4 MWa,RG,DGr,A:Human Torch. . . 2.00
5 MWa,RG,MFm,Tales of
Suspense pt.1 . . . . 2.00
6 MWa,RG,MFm,Tales of
Suspense pt.2 . . . . 3.50
7 RSt,RF,civil war tale concl. 2.00
8 MWa,R:Falcon 2.00
9 MWa,A:Falcon 2.00
10 psychedelic look back 2.00
11 MWa,A:Human Torch. 2.00
12 MWa,DGr,F:Bucky,48-page 3.50
Spec.RoughCut #1,MWa,RG,48-pg. 3.00

CAPTAIN BRITAIN CLASSICS

1 AD rep.. . . . . 2.50

CAPTAIN CONFEDERACY

Epic Nov., 1991

1 I:Capt.Confederacy,Kid Dixie . . . 2.25
2 Meeting of Superhero Reps 2.25
3 Framed for Murder 2.25
4 Superhero conference,final iss. . . 2.25

CAPTAIN JUSTICE

March, 1988

1 Based on TV Series 2.00
2 April, 1988 . . . . 2.00

CAPTAIN MARVEL

May, 1968

1 GC,O:retold,V:Sentry#459 . . . . 75.00
2 GC,V:Super Skrull 25.00
3 GC,V:Super Skrull 25.00
4 GC,Sub-Mariner 20.00
5 DH,I:Metazoid. 20.00
6 DH,I:Solam. 12.00
7 JR(c),DH,V:Quasimodo. 12.00
8 DH,I:Cuberex 12.00
9 DH,D:Cuberex 12.00
10 DH,V:Number 1 . . . . 12.00
11 BWS(c),I:Z0. . . . . 12.00
12 K&R(c),I:Man-Slayer 9.00
13 FS,V:Man-Slayer 9.00
14 FS,Iron Man 9.00
15 TS,DA,Z0 . . . . 8.00
16 DH,Ronan 8.00
17 GK,DA,O:R.Jones ret,N:Capt.
Marvel 9.00
18 GK,JB,DA,I:Mandroid. 8.00
19 GK,DA,Master.of.MM 8.00
20 GK,DA,I:Rat Pack 8.00
21 GK,DA,Hulk. 8.00
22 GK(c),WB,V:Megaton. 8.00
23 GK(c),WB,FMc,V:Megaton 8.00
24 GK(c),WB,ECh,I:L.Mynde 8.00
25 1st JSn,Cap.Marvel,Cosmic
Cube Saga Begins 15.00
26 JSn,DC,Thanos(2ndApp.)
A:Thing 20.00
27 JSn,V:Thanos,A:Mentor,
Starfox, I:Death 12.00
28 JSn,DGr,Thanos Vs.Drax,
A:Avengers 12.00
29 JSn,AM,O:Zeus,C:Thanos
I:Eon,O:Mentor. 9.00
30 JSn,AM,Controller,C:Thanos . . . 9.00
31 JSn,AM,Avengers,
Thanos,Drax,Mentor. 9.00
32 JSn,AM,DGr,O:Drax,
Moondragon,A:Thanos 9.00
33 JSn,KJ,E:Cosmic Cube Saga
1st D:Thanos. 12.00
34 JSn,JA,V:Nitro(leads to

Captain Marvel #62
© Marvel Entertainment Group

his Death) 7.00
35 GK(c),AA,Ant Man 5.00
36 AM,Watcher,Rep.CM#1 . . . . 5.00
37 AM,KJ,Nimrod 5.00
38 AM,KJ,Watcher 5.00
39 AM,KJ,Watcher 5.00
40 AM,AMc,Watcher. 5.00
41 AM,BWr,CR,BMc,TA,Kree 4.00
42 AM,V:Stranger,C:Drax 4.00
43 AM,V:Drax. 4.00
44 GK(c),AM,V:Drax. 4.00
45 AM,I:Rambu 4.00
46 AM,TA,D:Fawn 4.00
47 AM,TA,A:Human Torch 4.00
48 AM,TA,I:Chetah 4.00
49 AM,V:Ronan,A:Cheetah 4.00
50 AM,TA,Avengers,
V:Super Adaptiod 3.00
51 AM,TA,V:Mercurio,4-D Man 3.00
52 AM,TA,V:Phae-dor. 3.00
53 AM,TA,A:Inhumans 3.00
54 PB,V:Nitro 3.00
55 PB,V:Death-grip. 3.00
56 PB,V:Death-grip. 3.00
57 PB,V:Thor,A;Thanos 5.00
58 PB,Drax/Titan 3.00
59 PB,Drax/Titan,I:Stellarax 3.00
60 PB,Drax/Titan 3.00
61 PB,V:Chaos. 3.00
62 PB,V:Stellarax 3.00
G-Size #1 reprints 8.00

CAPTAIN MARVEL

1989

1 MBr,I:Powerkeg,V:Moonstone . . . 3.00
1 DyM(s),MBr,V:Skinhead(1993) . . 2.00
PF Death of Captain Marvel 7.95
TPB Life of Captain Marvel,JSn . . 14.95

CAPTAIN MARVEL

1995

1 FaN,R:Captain Marvel(son of). . . 3.00
2 FaN,V:X-Treme,Erik the Red . . . 3.00
3 FaN,V:X-treme 3.00
4 thru 6 FaN . . . . @3.00

CAPTAIN MARVEL

Dec., 1999

1A PDa,Ccs,A:Rick Jones 2.50
1B variant JOy (c) 2.50
2 PDa,Ccs. 2.50
3 PDa,Ccs,V:Wendigo 2.50
4 PDa,Ccs,A:Moondragon 2.50
5 PDa,Ccs,V:Drax 2.50
6 PDa,Ccs,V:Marlo 2.50
7 PDa,Ccs,A:Comet Man. 2.50
8 PDa,Ccs,V:Super-Skrull 2.50
9 PDa,Ccs,V:Hyssta 2.50
10 PDa,Ccs,V:Genis. 2.50
11 PDa,JSn 2.50
12 PDa,Ccs,Maximum Security. . . . 2.50

CAPTAIN PLANET

Oct., 1991

1 I&O:Captain Planet. 2.00
2 V:Dr.Blights' Smog Monster 2.00
3 V:Looten Plunder 2.00
4 `Pollutionland'. 2.00
5 V:Duke Nukem 2.00
6 A:Capt.Pollution,Eco-Villains. . . . 2.00
7 thru 9 . . . . @2.00
10 V:Litterbug 2.00
11 BHi,V:Greedly 2.00
12 V:Looten Plunder,last issue 2.00

CAPT. SAVAGE & HIS LEATHERNECK RAIDERS

Jan., 1968

1 SSh(c),C:Sgt Fury;The Last
Bansai 35.00
2 SSh(c),O:Hydra;Return of Baron
Strucker 20.00
3 SSh,Two Against Hydra 20.00
4 SSh,V:Hydra;The Fateful Finale 20.00
5 SSh,The Invincible Enemy 20.00
6 Mission;Save a Howler 20.00
7 SSh,Objective:Ben Grimm 22.00
8 Mission:Foul Ball 20.00
Becomes:

CAPT. SAVAGE & HIS BATTLEFIELD RAIDERS

9 . . . . 6.00
10 To the Last Man. 5.00
11 A:Sergeant Fury. 5.00
12 V:The Japanese 3.75
13 The Junk Heap Juggernauts . . . 5.00
14 Savage's First Mission. 5.00
15 Within the Temple Waits Death . 5.00
16 V:The Axis Powers 5.00
17 V:The Axis Powers 5.00
18 V:The Axis Powers 5.00
19 March, 1970 . . . . 5.00

CARE BEARS

Star Nov., 1985

1 . . . . 2.00
2 thru 14 . . . . @2.00

Marvel

15 thru 20 . . . . @2.00

CARNAGE

1-shot Carnage: Its a Wonderful
Life (1996) 2.00
1-shot Carnage: Mindbomb
foil cover (1996) 2.95

CARTOON KIDS

Atlas 1957

1 A:Dexter the Demon,Little
Zelda,Willie,Wise Guy. 50.00

CAR WARRIORS

Epic 1990

1 Based on Roll Playing Game . . . 2.25
2 Big Race Preparations 2.25

3 Ft.Delorean-Lansing Race begin. 2.25
4 Race End, Final issue. 2.25

CASEY–CRIME PHOTOGRAPHER
August, 1949
1 Ph(c),Girl on the Docks. 165.00
2 Ph(c),Staats Cotsworth 125.00
3 Ph(c),He Walked With Danger. 125.00
4 Ph(c),Lend Me Your Life 125.00
Becomes:

TWO GUN WESTERN
[1st Series]
5 JB,B,I&O:Apache Kid 150.00
6 The Outcast 100.00
7 Human Sacrifice 100.00
8 JR,DW,A:Kid Colt,Texas Kid, Doc Holiday 100.00
9 A:Kid Colt,Marshall"Frosty" Bennet Texas Kid 100.00
10. . . . . 100.00
11 thru 14 June, 1952 . . . . @75.00

CASPER
1996
1 From Animated TV show 2.00
2 visit to Harvey Castle 2.00
3 and 4 . . . . 2.00

CAT, THE
Nov., 1972—June 1973
1 JM,I&O:The Cat 25.00
2 JM,V:The Owl 17.00
3 BEv,V:Kraken 17.00
4 JSn,V:Man-Bull 17.00

CENTURY: DISTANT SONS
1996
1-shot DAn,48pg. 3.00

CHAMBER OF CHILLS
Nov., 1972
1 SSh,A Dragon Stalks By Night,(H.Ellison adapt.). 25.00
2 FB,BEv,SD,Monster From the Mound,(RE Howard adapt.) . . 15.00
3 FB,BEv,SD, Thing on the Roof . 15.00

Chamber of Darkness #5
© Marvel Entertainment Group

4 FB,BEv,SD, Opener of the Crypt,(J.Jakes,E.A.Poe adapt.) 15.00
5 FB,BEv,SD, Devils Dowry 15.00
6 FB,BEv,SD, Mud Monster 15.00
7 thru 24 FB,BEv,SD . . . . @15.00
25 FB,BEv,SD November, 1976 . . 15.00

CHAMBER OF DARKNESS
Oct., 1969
1 JB, Tales of Maddening Magic . 50.00
2 NA(script),Enter the Red Death. 25.00
3 JK,BWS,JB, Something Lurks on Shadow Mountain 30.00
4 JK Monster Man Came Walking, BU:BWS. 60.00
5 JCr,JK,SD, And Fear Shall Follow, plus Lovecraft adapt. . 20.00
6 SD 20.00
7 SD,JK,BWr, Night of the Gargoyle 35.00
8 DA,BEv, Beast that Walks Like a Man Special, 5 Tales of Maddening Magic,Jan. 1972. . 20.00
Becomes:

MONSTERS ON THE PROWL
9 SAD,BWS,Monster Stories Inc,Gorgilla. 25.00
10 JK,Roc 15.00
11 JK,A Titan Walks the Land 15.00
12 HT,JK,Gomdulla The Living Pharoah 15.00
13 HT,JK,Tragg. 15.00
14 JK,SD,Return of the Titan 15.00
15 FrG,JK,The Thing Called It . . . 15.00
16 JSe,SD,JK, Serpent God of Lost Swamp,A:King Kull 15.00
17 JK,SD,Coming of Colossus . . . 15.00
18 JK,SD,Bruttu 15.00
19 JK,SD,Creature From the Black Bog. 15.00
20 JK,SD,Oog Lives Again 15.00
21 JK,SD,A Martian Stalks the City 15.00
22 JK,SD,Monster Runs Amok . . . 12.00
23 JK,The Return of Grogg. 12.00
24 JK,SD, Magnetor 12.00
25 JK,Colossus Lives Again 12.00
26 JK,SD,The Two Headed Thing. 12.00
27 JK,Sserpo 12.00
28 JK,The Coming of Monsteroso. 12.00
29 JK,SD Monster at my Window . 12.00
30 JK,Diablo Demon from the 5th Dimension, Oct., 1974 . . . . . . 12.00

CHAMPIONS
June, 1986
1 GK(c),DH,I&O:Champions 20.00
2 DH,O:Champions 14.00
3 GT,Assault on Olympus 13.00
4 GT,`Murder at Malibu' 12.00
5 DH,I:Rampage 12.00
6 JK(c),GT,V:Rampage 12.00
7 GT,O:Black Widow,I:Darkstar . . 12.00
8 BH,O:Black Widow 12.00
9 BH,BL,V:Crimson Dynamo 12.00
10 BH,BL,V:Crimson Dynamo. . . . 12.00
11 JBy,A:Black Goliath,Hawkeye. . 13.00
12 JBy,BL,V:Stranger 13.00
13 JBy,BL,V:Kamo Tharn 13.00
14 JBy,I:Swarm 13.00
15 JBy,V:Swarm 13.00
16 BH,A:Magneto,Dr.Doom, Beast 12.00
17 GT,JBy,V:Sentinels,last issue . . 13.00

CHILDREN OF THE VOYAGE
Frontier 1993
1 F:Sam Wantling 3.25
2 Counterfeit Man 2.25
3 V:Voyager. 2.25
4 Last Issue. 2.25

Chili #8
© Marvel Entertainment Group

CHILI
May, 1969
1 Millie's Rival 50.00
2 . . . . 25.00
3 . . . . 15.00
4 . . . . 15.00
5 . . . . 15.00
6 thru 15 . . . . @12.00
16 thru 20 . . . . @10.00
21 thru 25 . . . . @8.00
26 Dec., 1973 . . . . 8.00
Spec.#1, 1971 . . . . 15.00

CHUCK NORRIS
Star Jan.–Sept., 1987
1 SD 2.00
2 thru 5 . . . . @2.00

CINDY COMICS
See: KRAZY COMICS

CLANDESTINE
Oct. 1994–Sept., 1995
Preview issue, Intro (1994) 2.00
1 MFm,AD,foil(c) 3.25
2 Wraparound (c),A:Silver Surfer . . 2.50
3 I:Argent,Kimera,A:SilverSurfer . . 2.50
4 R:Adam 2.50
5 MFm,AD,O:Adam Destine. 2.50
6 A:Spider-Man 2.50
7 A:Spider-Man 2.50
8 A:Dr.Strange. 2.50
9 Training Time 2.50
10 A:Britanic. 2.50
11 V:Modan 2.50
12 Aftermath. 2.50
13 Who Will Lead 2.50
14 Vincent Vs. Adam 2.50
TPB AD,MFm (1997) 12.00

CLASSIC CONAN
See: CONAN SAGA

CLASSIC X-MEN
See: X-MEN

CLIVE BARKER'S BOOK OF THE DAMNED
Epic Nov., 1991
1 JBo,Hellraiser companion 5.00
2 MPa,Hellraiser Companion 5.00

CLIVE BARKER'S HELLRAISER
Epic 1989–93
1 BWr,DSp 7.00
2 . . . . 6.00
3 . . . . 6.50
4 . . . . 4.50
5 . . . . 4.50
6 . . . . 7.00
7 The Devil's Brigade #1 . . . . 7.00
8 The Devil's Brigade #2&3 . . . . . . 7.00
9 The Devil's Brigade #4&5 . . . . . . 7.00
10 The Devil's Brigade #6&7
foil Cover 5.00
11 The Devil's Brigade #8&9. . . . . . 4.50
12 The Devil's Brigade #10-12 . . . . 4.50
13 MMi,RH,Devil's Brigade #13 . . . 4.50
14 The Devil's Brigade #14. . . . . . . 5.00
15 The Devil's Brigade #15. . . . . . . 5.00
16 E:Devil's Brigade 5.00
17 BHa,DR,The Harrowing 10.00
18 O:Harrowers 5.00
19 A:Harrowers 5.00
20 NGa(s),DMc,Last Laugh 9.00
Dark Holiday Spec.#1 (1992) 5.00
Spring Slaughter Spec.#1 (1994) . . 7.00
Summer Spec.#1 (1992 . . . . 6.00

CLOAK & DAGGER
[Limited Series] Oct., 1983
1 RL,TA,I:Det.O'Reilly,
Father Delgado 2.50
2 RL,TA,V:Duane Hellman. 2.00
3 RL,TA,V:Street Gang 2.00
4 RL,TA,O:Cloak & Dagger, ... 2.00

Cloak & Dagger #1
© Marvel Entertainment Group

CLOAK & DAGGER
[1st Regular Series] July 1985
1 RL,Pornography 2.50
2 RL,Dagger's mother 2.00
3 RL,A:Spider-Man 2.25
4 RL,Secret Wars II 2.00
5 RL,I:Mayhem 2.00
6 RL,A:Mayhem. 2.00
7 RL,A:Mayhem. 2.00
8 TA, Drugs 2.00
9 AAd,TA,A:Mayhem 2.75
10 BBI,TA,V:Dr. Doom 2.00
11 BBI,TA,Last Issue 2.00

[Mutant Misadventures of] CLOAK & DAGGER
[2nd Regular Series] Oct., 1988
1 CR(i),A:X-Factor 3.00
2 CR(i),C:X-Factor,V:Gromitz. 2.50
3 SW(i),JLe(c),A:Gromitz 2.00
4 TA(i),Inferno,R:Mayhem 2.00
5 TA(i),R:Mayhem 2.00
6 TA(i),A:Mayhem 2.00
7 A:Crimson Daffodil,V:Ecstacy . . . 2.00
8 Acts of Vengeance prelude. 2.00
9 Acts of Vengeance 2.00
10 Acts of Vengeance,"X-Force"
name used,Dr.Doom. 2.00
11 . . . . 2.00
12 A:Dr.Doom. 2.00
13 A:Dr.Doom. 2.00
14 & 15 RL . . . . @2.00
16 RL,A:Spider-Man 2.00
17 A:Spider-Man, ... 2.00
18 Inf.Gauntlet X-over,
A:Spider-Man, Ghost Rider. . . . 2.50
19 O:Cloak & Dagger,final issue . . . 2.50
GNv Predator and Prey 14.95

A CLUELESS VALENTINE
1 characters from movie, 48-pg. . . 2.50

CODENAME: GENETIX
1993
1 PGa,A:Wolverine 2.00
2 PGa,V:Prime EvilA:Wolverine . . . 2.00
3 . . . . 2.00
4 A:Wolverine,Kazar 2.00

CODE OF HONOR
1996
1 (of 4) CDi,TnS,I:Jeff Piper,
fully painted 5.95
2 thru 4 CDi, ... @5.95

CODE NAME: SPITFIRE
See: SPITFIRE AND THE TROUBLESHOOTERS

COLOSSUS
Aug., 1997
1-shot BRa,Colossus & Meggan
V:Arcade, 48pg 3.00

COLOSSUS: GOD'S COUNTRY
PF V:Cold Warriors. 7.00

COMBAT
Atlas June, 1952
1 War Stories, Bare Bayonets . . 175.00
2 RH, Break Thru,(Dedicated to
US Infantry) 85.00
3 . . . . 60.00
4 BK 75.00
5 thru 10 . . . . @50.00
11 April, 1953 . . . . 60.00

COMBAT CASEY
See: WAR COMBAT

COMBAT KELLY AND THE DEADLY DOZEN
Atlas Nov., 1951
1 RH,Korean war stories 175.00
2 Big Push. 75.00
3 The Volunteer. 60.00
4 V:Communists 60.00
5 OW,V:Communists 60.00
6 V:Communists 60.00
7 V: Communists 60.00
8 Death to the Reds 60.00
9 . . . . 60.00
10 . . . . 60.00
11 . . . . 50.00
12 thru 16 . . . . @50.00
17 A:Combat Casey 75.00
18 A:Battle Brady 35.00
19 V:Communists 35.00
20 V:Communists 35.00
21 Transvestite Cover. 40.00
22 thru 40 . . . . @30.00
41 thru 44 August, 1957 . . . . . . @30.00

COMBAT KELLY
June, 1972
1 JM, Stop the Luftwaffe 20.00
2 The Big Breakout 10.00
3 O:Combat Kelly 10.00
4 Mutiny,A:Sgt.Fury and the
Howling Commandoes 10.00
5 Escape or Die 10.00
6 The Fortress of Doom. 10.00
7 Nun Hostage,V:Nazis 10.00
8 V:Nazis. 10.00
9 Oct., 1973 . . . . 10.00

COMET MAN
Feb., 1987
1 BSz(c),I:Comet Man 2.00
2 BSz(c),A:Mr.Fantastic. 2.00
3 BSz(c),A:Hulk. 2.00
4 BSz(c),A:Fantistic Four. 2.00
5 BSz(c),A:Fantastic Four 2.00
6 BSz(c),Last issue, July,1987 . . . . 2.00

COMIX BOOK
(Black & White Magazine) 1974
1 . . . . 25.00
2 . . . . 20.00
3 . . . . 25.00
4 . . . . 12.00
5 1976 . . . . 12.00

COMIX ZONE
1 video game tie-in 2.50
2 video game tie-in 2.50

COMMANDO ADVENTURES
Atlas June, 1957
1 Seek, Find and Destroy 60.00
2 MD, Hit 'em and Hit 'em
Hard, August,1957 . . . . 60.00

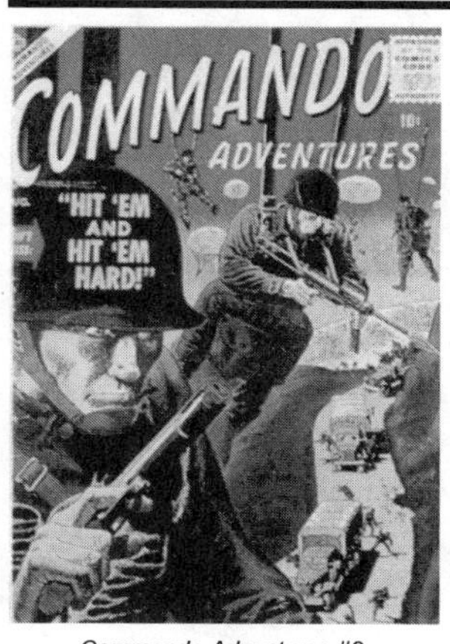

Commando Adventures #2
© Marvel Entertainment Group

COMPLETE COMICS
See: AMAZING COMICS

COMPLETE MYSTERY
August, 1948

1 Seven Dead Men 350.00
2 Jigsaw of Doom 300.00
3 Fear in the Night. 300.00
4 A Squealer Dies Fast 300.00
Becomes:

TRUE COMPLETE MYSTERY

5 Rice Mancini,
The Deadly Dude 200.00
6 Ph(c),Frame-up that Failed . . 150.00
7 Ph(c),Caught 150.00
8 Ph(c),The Downfall of Mr.
Anderson, Oct., 1949 . . . . . . 150.00

CONAN
1995–96

1 Pit Fighter. 3.00
2 LHa,Hyborean tortue factory 3.00
3 V:Cannibals 3.00
4 LHa,JP,Rune Conan Prelude . . . 3.00
5 LHa,V:yeti. 3.00
6 LHa, the plague 3.00
7 LHa,BBl,V:The Iron Man. 3.00
8 . . . . 3.00
9 . . . . 3.00
10 Conan kidnapped by Amazons . 3.00
11 . . . . 3.00

CONAN: DEATH COVERED IN GOLD
July, 1999

1 (of 3) RTs 3.00
2 RTs 3.00
3 RTs,JB,concl. 3.00

CONAN THE ADVENTURER
1994–95

1 RT(s),RK,Red Foil(c) 3.00
2 RT(s),RK 2.00
3 RT(s),RK 2.00
4 . . . . 2.00
5 . . . . 2.00
6 . . . . 2.00
7 . . . . 2.00
8 . . . . 2.00
9 . . . . 2.00
10 . . . . 2.00
11 Torture Chamber 2.00
12 Abominations of Yondo 2.00
13 Seven Warriors 2.00
14 RTs,Young Conan,last issue. . . . 2.00

CONAN THE BARBARIAN
Oct., 1970

1 BWS/DA,O:Conan,A:Kull 225.00
2 BWS/SB,Lair o/t Beast-Men . . . 80.00
3 BWS,SB,Grey God Passes. . . 135.00
4 BWS,SB,Tower o/t Elephant . . . 60.00
5 BWS,Zukala's Daughter 60.00
6 BWS,SB,Devil Wings Over
Shadizar. 35.00
7 BWS,SB,DA,C:Thoth-Amon,
I:Set 35.00
8 BWS,TS,TP,Keepers o/t Crypt . 35.00
9 BWS,SB,Garden of Fear. 35.00
10 BWS,SB,JSe,Beware Wrath of
Anu;BU:Kull 50.00
11 BWS,SB,Talons of Thak. 50.00
12 BWS,GK,Dweller in the Dark,
Blood of the Dragon B.U. 25.00
13 BWS,SB,Web o/t Spider-God. . 25.00
14 BWS,SB,Green Empress of
Melnibone 40.00
15 BWS,SB 40.00
16 BWS,Frost Giant's Daughter . . 25.00
17 GK,Gods of Bal-Sagoth,
A:Fafnir 11.00
18 GK,DA,Thing in the Temple,
A:Fafnir 11.00
19 BWS,DA,Hawks from
the Sea 22.00
20 BWS,DA,Black Hound of
Vengeance,A:Fafnir 22.00
21 BWS,CR,VM,DA,SB, Monster
of the Monoliths 20.00
22 BWS,DA,rep.Conan #1 . . . . . . 22.00
23 BWS,DA,Shadow of the
Vulture,I:Red Sonja 30.00
24 BWS,Song of Red Sonja 38.00
25 JB,SB,JSe,Mirrors of Kharam
Akkad,A:Kull. 8.00
26 JB,Hour of the Griffin 6.00
27 JB,Blood of Bel-Hissar. 5.00
28 JB,Moon of Zembabwei 5.00
29 JB,Two Against Turan 5.00
30 JB,The Hand of Nergal 5.00
31 JB,Shadow in the Tomb 4.00
32 JB,Flame Winds of Lost Khitai . . 4.00
33 JB,Death & 7 Wizards 4.00
34 JB,Temptress in the Tower
of Flame. 4.00
35 JB,Hell-Spawn of Kara-Shehr . . 4.00
36 JB,Beware of Hyrkanians
bearing Gifts. 4.00
37 NA,Curse of the Golden Skull . 10.00
38 JB,Warrior & Were-Woman 3.50
39 JB,Dragon from the
Inland Sea. 3.50
40 RB,Fiend from Forgotten City. . . 3.50
41 JB,Garden of Death & Life 5.00
42 JB,Night of the Gargoyle 5.00
43 JB,Tower o/Blood,A:RedSonja . . 5.00
44 JB,Flame&Fiend,A:RedSonja. . . 6.00
45 JB,Last Ballad of Laza-Lanti . . . 6.00
46 JB,JSt,Curse of the Conjurer . . . 4.00
47 JB,DA,Goblins in the
Moonlight 4.00
48 JB,DG,DA,Rats Dance at Raven
gard,BU:Red Sonja 4.00
49 JB,DG,Wolf-Woman. 4.00
50 JB,DG,Dweller in the Pool 4.00
51 JB,DG,Man Born of Demon 4.00

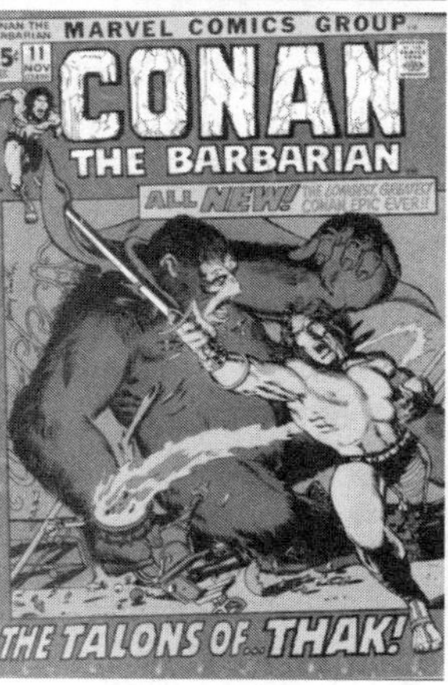

Conan The Barbarian #11
© Marvel Entertainment Group

52 JB,TP,Altar and the Scorpion . . . 4.00
53 JB,FS,Brothers of the Blade. . . . 4.00
54 JB,TP,Oracle of Ophir 4.00
55 JB,TP,Shadow on the Land 4.00
56 JB,High Tower in the Mist 4.00
57 MP,Incident in Argos 4.00
58 JB,Queen o/tBlackCoast,
2nd A:Belit 6.00
59 JB,Ballad of Belit,O:Belit 3.50
60 JB,Riders o/t River Dragons. . . . 3.50
61 JB,She-Pirate,I:Amra 3.50
62 JB,Lord of the Lions,O:Amra . . . 3.50
63 JB,Death Among Ruins,
V&D:Amra 3.50
64 JSon,AM,rep.Savage Tales#5 . . 3.50
65 JB,Fiend o/tFeatheredSerpent . . 3.50
66 JB,Daggers & Death Gods,
C:Red Sonja. 3.50
67 JB,Talons of the Man-Tiger,
A:Red Sonja. 3.50
68 JB,Of Once & Future Kings,
V:KingKull,A:Belit,Red Sonja . . 3.50
69 VM,Demon Out of the Deep. . . . 3.50
70 JB,City in the Storm. 3.50
71 JB,Secret of Ashtoreth 3.50
72 JB,Vengeance in Asgalun 3.50
73 JB,..In the Well of Skelos. 3.50
74 JB,Battle at the Black Walls
C:Thoth-Amon 3.50
75 JB,Hawk-Riders of Harakht 3.50
76 JB,Swordless in Stygia 3.50
77 JB,When Giants Walk
the Earth 3.50
78 JB,rep.Savage Sword #1,
A:Red Sonja. 3.50
79 HC,Lost Valley of Iskander. 3.50
80 HC,Trial By Combat. 3.50
81 HC,The Eye of the Serpent 3.00
82 HC,The Sorceress o/t Swamp . . 3.00
83 HC,The Dance of the Skull 3.00
84 JB,Two Against the Hawk-City,
I:Zula 3.00
85 JB,Of Swordsmen & Sorcerers,
O:Zulu 3.00
86 JB,Devourer of the Dead 3.00
87 TD, rep. Savage Sword #3. . . . . 3.00
88 JB,Queen and the Corsairs 3.00
89 JB,Sword & the Serpent,
A:Thoth-Amon 3.00
90 JB,Diadem of the Giant-Kings . . 3.00
91 JB,Savage Doings in Shem 3.00
92 JB,The Thing in the Crypt 3.00
93 JB,Of Rage & Revenge 3.00

MARVEL

94 JB,BeastKing ofAbombi,L:Zulu. . 3.00
95 JB,The Return of Amra 3.00
96 JB,Long Night of Fang
& Talon,pt.1 . . . . 3.00
97 JB,Long Night of Fang
& Talon,pt.2 . . . . 3.00
98 JB,Sea-Woman 3.00
99 JB,Devil Crabs o/t Dark Cliffs. . . 3.00
100 JB,Death on the Black Coast,
D:Belit (double size). 3.50
101 JB,The Devil has many Legs . . 2.00
102 JB,The Men Who
Drink Blood 2.00
103 JB,Bride of the Vampire 2.00
104 JB,The Vale of Lost Women. . . 2.00
105 JB,Whispering Shadows 2.00
106 JB,Chaos in Kush 2.00
107 JB,Demon of the Night. 2.00
108 JB,Moon-Eaters of Darfar 2.00
109 JB,Sons o/t Bear God 2.00
110 JB,Beward t/Bear o/Heaven . . . 2.00
111 JB,Cimmerian Against a City . . 2.00
112 JB,Buryat Besieged 2.00
113 JB,A Devil in the Family 2.00
114 JB,The Shadow of the Beast . . 2.00
115 JB,A War of Wizards, A:Red
Sonja Double size 10th Anniv.
(L:Roy Thomas script) 2.50
116 JB,NA,Crawler in the Mist 2.00
117 JB,Corridor of Mullah-Kajar . . . 2.00
118 JB,Valley of Forever Night 2.00
119 JB,Voice of One Long Gone. . . 2.00
120 JB,The Hand of Erlik 2.00
121 JB,BMc,Price of Perfection. . . . 2.00
122 JB,BMc,The City Where Time
Stood Still. 2.00
123 JB,BMc,Horror Beneath the
Hills 2.00
124 JB,BMc,the Eternity War 2.00
125 JB,BMc,the Witches ofNexxx . . 2.00
126 JB,BMc,Blood Red Eye
of Truth 2.00
127 GK,Snow Haired Woman
of the Wastes 2.00
128 GK,And Life Sprang Forth
From These 2.00
129 GK,The Creation Quest 2.00
130 GK,The Quest Ends. 2.00
131 GK,The Ring of Rhax. 2.00
132 GK,Games of Gharn 2.00
133 GK,The Witch of Widnsor. 2.00
134 GK,A Hitch in Time 2.00
135 MS,JRu,The Forest o/t Night . . 2.00
136 JB,The River of Death 2.00
137 AA,Titans Gambit. 2.00
138 VM,Isle of the Dead 2.00
139 VM,In the Lair of
the Damned 2.00
140 JB,Spider Isle 2.00
141 JB,The Web Tightens. 2.00
142 JB,The Maze,the Man,
the Monster 2.00
143 JB,Life Among the Dead 2.00
144 JB,The Blade & the Beast 2.00
145 Son of Cimmeria 2.00
146 JB,Night o/t Three Sisters 2.00
147 JB,Tower of Mitra. 2.00
148 JB,The Plague of Forlek 2.00
149 JB,Deathmark 2.00
150 JB,Tower of Flame. 2.00
151 JB,Vale of Death 2.00
152 JB,Dark Blade of
Jergal Zadh 2.00
153 JB,Bird Men of Akah Ma'at. . . . 2.00
154 JB,the Man-Bats of
Ur-Xanarrh 2.00
155 JB,SL,The Anger of Conan . . . 2.00
156 JB,The Curse 2.00
157 JB,The Wizard. 2.00
158 JB,Night of the Wolf. 2.00
159 JB,Cauldron of the Doomed. . . 2.00
160 Veil of Darkness. 2.00
161 JB,House of Skulls,A:Fafnir . . . 2.00
162 JB,Destroyer in the Flame,
A:Fafnir 2.00
163 JB,Cavern of the Vines of
Doom,A:Fafnir 2.00
164 The Jeweled Sword of Tem . . . 2.00
165 JB,V:Nadine. 2.00
166 JB,GI,Blood o/t Titan,A:Fafnir. . 2.00
167 JB,Creature From Time's
Dawn,A:Fafnir 2.00
168 JB,Bird Woman & the Beast. . . 2.00
169 JB,Tomb of the Scarlet Mage . . 2.00
170 JB,Dominion of the Dead,
A&D:Fafnir 2.00
171 JB,Barbarian Death Song 2.00
172 JB,Reavers in Borderland 2.00
173 JB,Honor Among Thieves 2.00
174 JB,V:Tetra 2.00
175 JB,V:Spectre ofDeath. 2.00
176 JB,Argos Rain 2.00
177 JB,V:Nostume 2.00
178 JB,A:Tetra,Well of Souls. 2.00
179 JB,End of all there is,A:Kiev. . . 2.00
180 JBV:AnitRenrut 2.00
181 JB,V:KingMaddoc II 2.00
182 JB,V:King of Shem. 2.00
183 JB,V:Imhotep 2.00
184 JB,V:Madoc. 2.00
185 JB,R:Tetra 2.00
186 JB,The Crimson Brotherhood. . 2.00
187 JB,V:Council of Seven 2.00
188 JB,V:Devourer-Souls 2.00
189 JB,V:Devourer-Souls 2.00
190 JB,Devourer-Souls. 2.00
191 Deliverance 2.00
192 JB,V:TheKeeper 2.00
193 Devourer-Souls 2.00
194 V:Devourer-Souls. 2.00
195 Blood of Ages 2.00
196 V:Beast 2.00
197 A:Red Sonja 2.00
198 A:Red Sonja 2.00
199 O:Kaleb 2.00
200 JB,D.sizeV:Dev-Souls 2.50
201 NKu,GI,Thulsa Doom. 2.00
202 . . . . 2.00
203 V:Thulsa Doom 2.00
204 VS,GI,A:Red Sonja,I:Strakkus . 2.00
205 A:Red Sonja 2.00
206 VS,GI,Heku trilogy,pt.1. . . . . . . 2.00
207 VS,GI,Heku,pt.2,O:Kote 2.00
208 VS,GI,Heku,pt.3. . . . . 2.00

Conan the Barbarian #169
© Marvel Entertainment Group

209 VS,GI,Heku epilogue 2.00
210 VS,GI,V:Sevante 2.00
211 VS,GI,V:Sevante 2.00
212 EC,GI 2.00
213 V:Ghamud Assassins. 2.00
214 AA. 2.00
215 VS,AA,Conan Enslaved 2.00
216 V:Blade of Zed. 2.00
217 JLe(c),V:Blade of Zed 2.00
218 JLe(c),V:Picts 2.00
219 JLe(c),V:Forgotten Beasts 2.00
220 Conan the Pirate 2.00
221 Conan the Pirate 2.00
222 AA,DP,Revenge. 2.00
223 AA,Religious Cult. 2.00
224 AA,Cannibalism 2.00
225 AA,Conan Blinded 2.00
226 AA,Quest for Mystic Jewel 2.00
227 AA,Mystic Jewel,pt.2 . . . . 2.00
228 AA,Cannibalism,pt.1 . . . . 2.00
229 AA,Cannibalism,pt.2 . . . . 2.00
230 FS,SDr,Citadel,pt.1 . . . . 2.00
231 FS,DP,Citadel,pt.2 . . . . 2.00
232 RLm,Birth of Conan 3.00
233 RLm,DA,B:Conan as youth . . . 2.00
234 RLm,DA 2.00
235 RLm,DA 2.00
236 RLm,DA 2.00
237 DA,V:Jormma 2.00
238 DA,D:Conan 2.00
239 Conan Possessed 2.00
240 Conan Possessed 2.00
241 TM(c),R:RoyThomasScript. . . . 3.50
242 JLe(c),A:Red Sonja 2.50
243 WPo(c),V:Zukala,. 2.00
244 A:Red Sonja,Zula. 2.00
245 A:Red Sonja,V:King
of Vampires 2.00
246 A:Red Sonja,V:MistMonster . . . 2.00
247 A:Red Sonja,Zula. 2.00
248 V:Zulu 2.00
249 A:Red Sonja,Zula. 2.00
250 A:RedSonja,Zula,V:Zug
double size. 2.00
251 Cimmeria,V:Shumu Gorath . . . 2.00
252 ECh. 2.00
253 ECh,V:Kulan-Goth(X-Men
Villain) 2.00
254 ECh,V:Shuma-Gorath (Dr.
Strange Villain). 2.00
255 ECh,V:Shuma-Gorath 2.00
256 ECh,D:Nemedia's King 2.00
257 ECh,V:Queen Vammator 2.00
258 AA(i),A:Kulan Gath 2.00
259 V:Shuma-Gorath 2.00
260 AA(i),V:Queen Vammatar. 2.00
261 V:Cult of the Death Goddess . . 2.00
262 V:The Panther 2.00
263 V:Malaq. 2.00
264 V:Kralic 2.00
265 V:Karlik 2.00
266 Conan the Renegade(adapt.). . 2.00
267 adaption of Tor. 2.00
268 adaption of Tor. 2.00
269 V:Agohoth,Prince Borin 2.00
270 Devourer of the Dead 2.00
271 V:Devourer of Souls. 2.00
272 V:Devourer 2.00
273 V:Purple Lotus. 2.00
274 V:She-Bat 2.00
275 RTs(s),Last Issue cont. in
Savage Sword of Conan. 5.00
G-Size#1 GK,TS,Hour of the
Dragon, inc.rep.Conan#3,
I:Belit 8.00
G-Size#2 GK,TS,Conan Bound,
inc. rep Conan #5. . . . . 5.00
G-Size#3 GK,TS,To Tarantia
& the Tower,inc.rep.Conan#6 . . 5.00
G-Size#4,GK,FS,Swords of the
South,inc.rep.Conan #7 . . . . . . 5.00

G-Size#5 rep.Conan #14,#15
& Back-up story #12 . . . . 5.00
KingSz.#1 rep.Conan #2,#4 . . . . . 13.00
Ann.#2 BWS,Phoenix on the Sword
A:Thoth-Amon 4.00
Ann.#3 JB,HC,Mountain of
the Moon God, B.U.Kull story . . 2.00
Ann.#4 JB,Return of the
Conqueror,A:Zenobia 2.00
Ann.#5 JB,W:Conan/Zenobia 2.00
Ann.#6 GK,King of the
Forgotten People 2.00
Ann.#7 JB,Red Shadows
& Black Kraken 1.50
Ann.#8 VM,Dark Night of the
White Queen 1.50
Ann.#9 . . . . 1.50
Ann.#10 Scorched Earth
(Conan #176 x-over) 1.50
Ann.#11 . . . . 1.50
Conan-Barbarian Movie Spec.#1 . . 1.25
Conan-Barbarian Movie Spec.#2 . . 1.25
Conan-Destroyer Movie Spec.#1 . . 1.25
Red Nails Special Ed.BWS 4.00
TPB Conan & Ravagers Out
of Time. 9.95
TPB Conan the Reaver. 9.95
TPB Conan the Rogue,JB,V:
Romm 9.95
TPB Horn of Azroth 9.95
TPB Skull of Set 9.95
TPB Essential Conan 14.95

CONAN: THE FLAME AND THE FIEND

June, 2000

1 (of 3) RTs,GI,V:Kulan Gath 3.00
2 RTs,GI,Bone Dragon. 3.00
3 RTs,GI,concl. 3.00

CLASSIC CONAN

June, 1987

1 BWS,rep. 2.00
2 BWS,rep. 2.00
3 BWS,rep. 2.00

Becomes:

CONAN SAGA

4 rep. 3.00
5 rep. 3.00
6 rep. 3.00
7 rep. 3.00
8 rep. 3.00
9 rep. 3.00
10 rep. 3.00
11 rep. 2.50
12 rep. 2.50
13 rep. 2.50
14 rep.Savage Sword #5 . . . . 2.50
15 rep.Savage Sword #7 . . . . 2.50
16 rep.Savage Sword #12 . . . . 2.50
17 rep.Savage Sword 2.50
18 rep.Savage Sword 2.50
19 rep.Savage Sword #28 . . . . 2.50
20 rep.Savage Sword #25 . . . . 2.50
21 rep.Savage Sword 2.50
22 rep.Giant Size Conan #1&2 . . . . 2.50
23 rep.Hour of the Dragon 2.50
24 rep.Hour of the Dragon 2.50
25 rep.Savage Sword 2.50
26 rep.Savage Sword #11. . . . . 2.50
27 rep.Savage Sword #15 . . . . 2.50
28 rep.Savage Sword #16 . . . . 2.25
29 rep.Savage Sword #17 . . . . 2.25
30 rep.Savage Sword #18 . . . . 2.25
31 rep.Savage Sword #19 . . . . 2.25
32 rep.Savage Sword #5 . . . . 2.25
33 rep.Savage Sword #5 . . . . 2.25
34 rep.Savage Sword # 2.25
35 rep.Savage Sword #32 . . . . 2.25
36 rep.Savage Sword #12 . . . . 2.25
37 rep.Savage Sword #34 . . . . 2.25
38 rep.Conan #94_. 2.25
39 rep.Conan #96a. 2.25
40 rep.Savage Sword #26 . . . . 2.25
41 rep.Savage Sword #27 . . . . 2.25
42 rep.Savage Sword #40 . . . . 2.25
43 rep.Savage Sword #41 . . . . 2.25
44 rep.Savage Sword #42 . . . . 2.25
45 rep.Savage Sword #43 . . . . 2.25
46 rep.Savage Sword #15 . . . . 2.25
47 rep.Savage Sword #22 . . . . 2.25
48 rep.Savage Sword #23 . . . . 2.25
49 rep.Sav.Sword Super Spec#2 . . 2.25
50 rep.Conan #58. . . . . 2.25
51 rep.Conan #59<. 2.25
52 rep.Conan #61. . . . . 2.25
53 thru 63 rep.Savage Sword . . . @2.25
64 thru 94 rep. . . . . @2.25
95 D:Belit 2.25
96 . . . . 2.25
97 Red Sonja rep. 2.25
98 rep. #106–#108 . . . . 2.25

Conan Classic #5
© Marvel Entertainment Group

CONAN CLASSICS

1994–95

1 rep. Conan #1 . . . . 2.00
2 rep. Conan #2 . . . . 2.00
3 rep. Conan #3 . . . . 2.00
4 thru 8 rep. Conan #4–#8. . . . . . . 2.00
9 Garden of Fear. 2.00
10 V:Anu 2.00
11 New Sword Manuever 2.00

CONAN/RUNE

1995

1 BWS,Conan Vs. Rune 3.50

CONAN

1 CCt, ... 2.00
2 CCt,V:Sorcerer 2.00
3 (of 3) CCt, ... 2.00

CONAN: RIVER OF BLOOD

April, 1998

1 (of 3) Valeria, vs. giant crocs. . . . 2.50
2 Caught in the middle of a war . . . 2.50
3 Lord of the Crocodiles, concl. . . . 2.50

CONAN THE BARBARIAN VS. THE LORD OF THE SPIDERS

Jan., 1998

1 (of 3) RTs,V:Harpagus 2.50
2 RTs, ... 2.50
3 RTs,V:Harpagus 2.50

CONAN: THE RETURN OF STYRM

Sept., 1998

1 (of 3) V:Mecora. 2.50
2 (of 3) V:Mecora. 3.00
3 conclusion 3.00

CONAN: THE SCARLET SWORD

Oct., 1998

1 (of 3) RTs,V:Thun'da. 3.00
2 RTs,A:Helliana 3.00
3 RTs,conclusion 3.00

CONAN: THE USURPER

Oct., 1997

1 (of 3) CDi,KJ,Conan attacks
Cimmeria? 2.50
2 CDi,KJ,. 2.50
3 CDi,KJ, concl.. . . . . 2.50

KING CONAN

March, 1980

1 JB/ECh,I:Conn,V:Thoth-Amon. . . 3.00
2 JB,Black Sphinx of Nebthu 2.50
3 JB,Dragon Wings Over
Zembabwei 2.50
4 JB,V:Thoth-Amon 2.50
5 JB,The Sorcerer in the Realm
of Madness 2.50
6 JB,The Lady's Name Is...Trouble 2.50
7 PS,JB. 2.75
8 A:Queen Reclaimed 2.75
9 JB,V:Medusa Monster. 2.25
10 V:Sea Monster. 2.25
11 V:Giant Totem Monster. 2.00
12 V:Monster 2.00
13 V:Monster 2.00
14 V:Demon 2.00

Conan The King #21
© Marvel Entertainment Group

MARVEL

15 V:Sea Monster. 2.00
16 Conan Into Battle. 2.00
17 A:Conn 2.00
18 King of the Freaks? 2.00
19 MK(c),Skull & X-Bones cover. . . 2.00
Becomes:

CONAN THE KING

20 MS,The Prince is Dead 2.00
21 MS,Shadows 2.00
22 GI/MS,The Black Dragons,Prince Conan II back-up story begins . 2.00
23 MS/GI,Ordeal 2.00
24 GI/MS,Fragments:AWitch'sTale . 2.00
25 MS/GI,Daggers 2.00
26 MS/GI,PrinceConanII B.U.ends . 2.00
27 MS/GI,A Death in Stygia 2.00
28 MS/GI,Call of the Wild, A:Red Sonja. 2.00
29 MS,The Sleeping Lion 2.00
30 GI,Revenge on the Black River . 2.00
31 GI,Force of Arms 2.00
32 GI,Juggernaut 2.00
33 . . . . 2.00
34 . . . . 2.00
35 . . . . 2.00
36 . . . . 2.00
37 AW,Sack of Belverus 2.00
38 MM,A:Taurus,Leora 2.00
39 The Tower 2.00
40 . . . . 2.00
41 V:Leora 2.00
42 Thee Armada,A:Conn 2.00
43 . . . . 2.00
44 . . . . 2.00
45 V:Caliastros 2.00
46 V:Caliastros 2.00
47 TD,V:Caliastros 2.00
48 . . . . 2.00
49 . . . . 2.00
50 GI,50th Anniversary issue 2.00
51 GI,Death of Prince Conn 2.00
52 GI,Prince Conn story contd 2.00
53 GI,A:Thoth-Amon. 2.00
54 GI,V:Thoth-Amon. 2.00
55 GI,Sorcerers Ring,final issue . . . 2.00

CONAN THE SAVAGE
1995–96
(Black & White Magazine)

1 New Series. 3.00
2 CDi,Conan a gladiator 3.00
3 V:Monster. 3.00

Coneheads #3
© Marvel Entertainment Group

4 CDi,Conan vs. Rune. 3.00
5 MBn,VMk,Ice age tale. 3.00
6 Bros.Hildebrandt(c),V:FallenIdol . 3.00
7 CDi,F:Iron Maidens. 3.00
8 & 9 . . . . @3.00
10 JB story, 48pg.. . . . . 3.00

CONEHEADS
1994

1 Based Saturday Night Live 2.00
2 There Goes the Neighborhood . . 2.00
3 In Paris. 2.00

CONSPIRACY
Dec., 1997

1 (of 2) DAn,Were the origins of Marvel's superheroes really a conspiracy, not an accident?. . . 3.00
2 DAn,concl. 3.00

CONTEST OF CHAMPIONS
June, 1982

1 JR2,Grandmaster vs. Mistress Death, A:Alpha Flight 7.00
2 JR2,Grandmaster vs. Mistress Death, A:X-Men 5.00
3 JR2,D:Grandmaster, Rebirth Collector, A:X-Men 5.00

CONTEST OF CHAMPIONS II
July, 1999

1 (of 5) CCl,Marvel vs. Marvel 2.50
2 CCl,Atlas vs. Storm 2.50
3 CCl,super hero slugfest 2.50
4 CCl. 2.50
5 CCl, conclusion 2.50
TPB Contest of Champions, 160-page, '70s rep. 17.95

COPS: THE JOB
1992

1 MGo(c),V:Serial killer 2.00
2 MGo(c). 2.00
3 MGo(c),V:Eviscerator 2.00
4 MGo(c),D:Eviscerator,Nick 2.00

COSMIC POWERS
1994

1 RMz(s),RLm,JP,F:Thanos. 2.75
2 RMz(s),JMr,F:Terrax 2.75
3 RMz(s),F:Jack of Hearts 2.75
4 RMz(s),RLm,F:Legacy 2.75
5 RMz(s),F&O:Morg 2.75
6 RMz(s),F&O:Tyrant. 2.75

COSMIC POWERS UNLIMITED
1995–96

1 Surfer vs. Thanos 3.95
2 Jack of Hearts vs. Jakar 3.95
3 GWt,JB,F:Lunatik,64pg. 3.95
4 GWt,SEa,cont.StarMasters#3 . . . 3.95
5 GWt,SEa,R:Captain Universe . . . 3.95

COUNT DUCKULA
Star Nov., 1988

1 O:Count Duckula,B:Dangermouse 4.00
2 A:Danger Mouse 3.00
3 thru 15 . . . . @3.00

COWBOY ACTION
See: WESTERN THRILLERS

COWBOY ROMANCES
Oct., 1949

1 Ph(c),Outlaw and the Lady . . . 175.00
2 Ph(c),William Holden/Mona Freeman,Streets of Laredo . . 125.00
3 Phc,Romance in Roaring Valley 100.00
Becomes:

YOUNG MEN

4 A Kid Names Shorty 135.00
5 Jaws of Death 90.00
6 Man-Size 90.00
7 The Last Laugh 90.00
8 Adventure stories continued . . . 90.00
9 Draft Dodging story. 90.00
10 US Draft Story 90.00
11 Adventure stories continued . . . 75.00
12 B:On the Battlefield, inc.Spearhead 75.00
13 RH,Break-through 75.00
14 RH,Fox Hole 75.00
15 Battlefield stories cont,. 75.00
16 Sniper Patrol 75.00
17 Battlefield stories cont,. 75.00
18 BEv,Warlord. 75.00
19 BEv 75.00
20 BEv,E:On the Battlefield 75.00
21 B:Flash Foster and his High Gear Hot Shots 75.00
22 Screaming Tires. 75.00
23 E:Flash Foster and his High Gear Hot Shots 75.00
24 BEv,B:Capt. America,Human Torch,Sub-Mariner,O:Capt. America,Red Skull 1,500.00
25 BEv,JR, Human Torch,Capt. America,Sub-Mariner 800.00
26 BEv,Human Torch, Capt. America,Sub Mariner 800.00
27 Bev, Human Torch/Toro V:Hypnotist 800.00
28 E:Human Torch, Capt.America, Sub Mariner,June, 1954 . . . . 800.00

COWGIRL ROMANCES
See: DARING MYSTERY

COYOTE
Epic June, 1983

1 SL,. 2.00
2 SL 2.00
3 BG 2.00
4 SL 2.00
5 SL 2.00
6 SL 2.00
7 SL,SD 2.00
8 SL 2.00
9 SL,SD 2.00
10 SL. 2.00
11 FS,1st TM art,O:Slash 4.00
12 TM 2.00
13 TM 2.00
14 FS,TM,A:Badger 2.00
15 SL. 2.00
16 SL,A:Reagan,Gorbachev 2.00

CRASH RYAN
Epic Oct., 1984

1 War Story 2.00
2 Doomsday 2.00
3 Fortress Japan 2.00

MARVEL

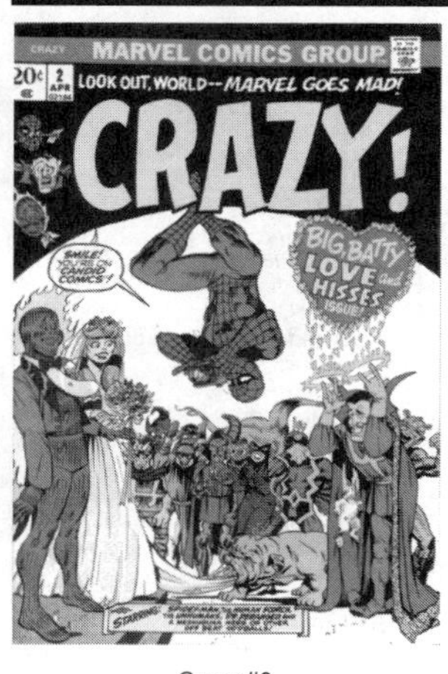

Crazy #2
© Marvel Entertainment Group

4 Jan., 1985 . . . . 2.00

CRAZY
Atlas Dec., 1953
1 BEv,satire, Frank N.Steins Castle. 200.00
2 BEv,Beast from 1000 Fathoms 150.00
3 Bev,Madame Knockwurst's Whacks Museum 125.00
4 BEv,I Love Lucy satire 125.00
5 BEv,Censorship satire. 125.00
6 BEv,satire 125.00
7 BEv,satire,July, 1954 . . . . 125.00

CRAZY
Feb., 1973–June, 1973
1 Not Brand Echh reps, Forbushman. 20.00
2 Big,Batty Love & Hisses issue . 15.00
3 Stupor-Man,A:FantasticalFour. . 15.00

CREATURES ON THE LOOSE
See: TOWER OF SHADOWS

CRIME CAN'T WIN
See: KRAZY COMICS

CRIME FIGHTERS
April, 1948—Nov., 1949
1 Police Stories 175.00
2 Jewelry robbery 75.00
3 The Nine who were Doomed. . . 75.00
4 Human Beast at Bay. 50.00
5 V:Gangsters 50.00
6 Pickpockets 50.00
7 True Cases, Crime Can't Win . . 50.00
8 True Cases, Crime Can't Win . . 50.00
9 Ph(c),It Happened at Night 50.00
10 Ph(c),Killer at Large 50.00
Atlas Sept., 1954—Jan., 1955
11 V:Gangsters. 75.00
12 V:Gangsters. 75.00
13 Clay Pidgeon 75.00

CRITICAL MASS
Epic Jan.–July, 1990
1 KS,GM,BSzF:ShadowlineSaga . . 4.95
2 . . . . 4.95
3 GM,SDr,JRy 4.95
4 . . . . 4.95
5 JZ 4.95
6 . . . . 4.95
7 July, 1990. . . . . 4.95

CROSSOVER CLASSICS
TPB Marvel and D.C. GP(c),reprints both Spider-Man/Superman,the Batman/Hulk and the X-Men/New Teen Titans Battles 18.00

CRYPT OF SHADOWS
Jan., 1973
1 BW,RH,Midnight on Black Mountain 20.00
2 Monster at the Door 15.00
3 Dead Man's Hand. 15.00
4 CI,Secret in the Vault 15.00
5 JM,The Graveyard Ghoul 15.00
6 BEv,Don't Bury Me Deep 15.00
7 JSt,The Haunting of Bluebeard . 15.00
8 How Deep my Grave 15.00
9 Beyond Death. 15.00
10 A Scream in the Dark. 15.00
11 The Ghouls in my Grave 10.00
12 Behind the Locked Door 10.00
13 SD,Back From the Dead 10.00
14 The Thing that Creeps 10.00
15 My Coffin is Crowded. 10.00
16 . . . . 10.00
17 In the Hands of Shandu 10.00
18 SD,Face of Fear 10.00
19 SD,Colossus that Challenged the World 10.00
20 A Monster walks Among Us . . . 10.00
21 SD,Death Will Be Mine, Nov. 1975. . . . . 10.00

CUPID
Dec., 1949
1 Ph(c),Cora Dod's Amazing Decision 100.00
2 Ph(c),Betty Page, Mar. 1950 . . 200.00

CURSE OF THE WEIRD
1993–94
1 thru 4 SD,rep. 50's Sci-Fi 2.00

CUTTING EDGE
1995
1 WML,F:Hulk,Ghosts of the Future tie-in 2.95

CYBERSPACE 3000
1 A:Dark Angel,Galactus,V:Badoon, Glow in the dark(c). 3.00
2 SeT,A:Galactus,Dark Angel. 2.00
3 SeT,A:Galactus,Keeper. 2.00
4 SeT,A:Keeper 2.00
5 SeT,A:Keeper 2.00
6 SeT,A:Warlock 2.00
7 SeT,I:Gamble 2.00
8 SeT,A:Warlock 2.00
9 SeT 2.00
10 SeT 2.00
11 SeT 2.00

DAILY BUGLE
B&W 1996
1 (of 3) KIK,GA 2.50
2 KIK,GA 2.50
3 KIK,GA 2.50

DAKOTA NORTH
1986
1 (Now in Cage) 2.00
2 . . . . 2.00
3 . . . . 2.00
4 . . . . 2.00
5 Feb., 1987 . . . . 2.00

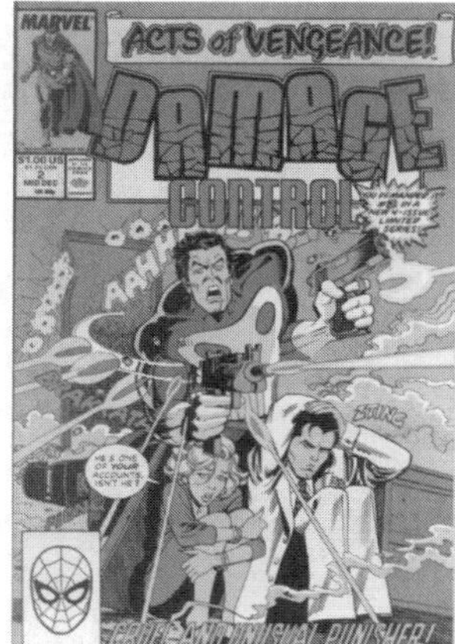

Damage Control #2
© Marvel Entertainment Group

DAMAGE CONTROL
May, 1989
1 EC/BWi;A:Spider-Man 2.50
2 EC/BWi;A:Fant.Four 2.00
3 EC/BWi;A:Iron Man 2.00
4 EC/BWi;A:X-Men 2.00
[2nd Series] 1989–90
1 EC,A:Capt.America&Thor 3.00
2 EC,A:Punisher 2.50
3 EC 2.00
4 EC,Punisher. 2.00
[3rd Series] 1991
1 Clean-up Crew Returns 2.00
2 A:Hulk,New Warriors 2.00
3 A:Avengers W.C.,Wonder Man, Silver Surfer. 2.00
4 A:SilverSurfer & others 2.00

DANCES WITH DEMONS
Frontier 1993
1 CAd 3.50
2 CAd,V:Manitou 2.50
3 CAd,V:Manitou 2.50
4 CAd,last issue 2.50
5 Okay, there's more! 2.50
6 . . . . 2.50

DAREDEVIL
April, 1964
1 B:StL(s),JK(c),BEv,I&O:Daredevil, I:Karen Page,Foggy Nelson. 2,000.00
2 JK(c),JO,V:Electro 550.00
3 JK(c),JO,I&O:The Owl 375.00
4 JK(c),JO,I&O:Killgrave 325.00
5 JK(c),WW,V:Masked Matador . 225.00
6 WW,I&O Original Mr. Fear. . . . 150.00
7 WW,I:Red Costume,V:Namor . 275.00
8 WW,I&O:Stiltman 150.00
9 WW(i),Killers Castle 150.00

10 WW(i),V:Catman 150.00
11 WW(i),R:Cat 125.00
12 JK,JR,2nd A:Kazar 125.00
13 JK,JR,O:Ka-Zar 75.00
14 JR,If This Be Justice 75.00
15 JR,A:Ox 75.00
16 JR,A:Spider-Man,
I:Masked Marauder 125.00
17 JR,A:Spider-Man 100.00
18 DON(s),JR,I:Gladiator 60.00
19 JR,V:Gladiator 60.00
20 JR(c),GC,V:Owl 50.00
21 GC,BEv,V:Owl 40.00
22 GC,V:Tri-man 40.00
23 GC,V:Tri-man 40.00
24 GC,A:Ka-Zar 40.00
25 GC,V:Leapfrog 40.00
26 GC,V:Stiltman 40.00
27 GC,Spider-Man 40.00
28 GC,V:Aliens 40.00
29 GC,V:The Boss 40.00
30 BEv(c),GC,A:Thor 40.00
31 GC,V:Cobra 30.00
32 GC,V:Cobra 30.00
33 GC,V:Beetle 30.00
34 BEv(c),GC,O:Beetle 30.00
35 BEv(c),GC,A:Susan Richards 30.00
36 GC,A:FF 30.00
37 GC,V:Dr.Doom 30.00
38 GC,A:FF 30.00
39 GC,GT,V:Unholy Three 30.00
40 GC,V:Unholy Three 30.00
41 GC,D:Mike Murdock 25.00
42 GC,DA,I:Jester 25.00
43 JK(c),GC,A:Capt.America 24.00
44 JSo(c),GC,V:Jester 20.00
45 GC,V:Jester 20.00
46 GC,V:Jester 20.00
47 GC,`Brother Take My Hand' 20.00
48 GC,V:Stiltman 20.00
49 GC,V:Robot,I:Starr Saxon 20.00
50 JR(c),BWS,JCr,V:Robot 25.00
51 B:RTs(s),BWS,V:Robot 25.00
52 BWS,JCr,A:Black Panther 25.00
53 GC,O:Daredevil 27.00
54 GC,V:Mr.Fear,A:Spidey 17.00
55 GC,V:Mr.Fear 15.00
56 GC,V:Death Head 15.00
57 GC,V:Death Head 15.00
58 GC,V:Stunt Master 15.00
59 GC,V:Torpedo 15.00
60 GC,V:Crime Wave 15.00
61 GC,V:Cobra 15.00
62 GC,O:Night Hawk 15.00
63 GC,V:Gladiator 15.00
64 GC,A:Stuntmaster 15.00
65 GC,V:BrotherBrimstone 15.00
66 GC,V:BrotherBrimstone 15.00
67 BEv(c),GC,Stiltman 15.00
68 AC,V:Kragg Blackmailer,
a:Bl.Panther,DD'sID Rev. 15.00
69 E:RTs(s),GC,V:Thunderbolts,
A:Bl.Panther(DD's ID Rev) 15.00
70 GC,V:Terrorists 15.00
71 RTs(s),GC,V:Terrorists 16.00
72 GyC(s),GC,Tagak,V:Quother 13.00
73 GC,V:Zodiac 13.00
74 B:GyC(s),GC,I:Smasher 13.00
75 GC,V:El Condor 13.00
76 GC,TP,V:El Condor 13.00
77 GC,TP,V:Manbull 13.00
78 GC,TP,V:Manbull 13.00
79 GC,TP,V:Manbull 13.00
80 GK(c),GC,TP,V:Owl 13.00
81 GK(c),GC,JA,A:Black Widow 22.00
82 GK(c),GC,JA,V:Scorpion 13.00
83 JR(c),BWS,BEv,V:Mr.Hyde 14.00
84 GK(c),GC,Assassin 13.00
85 GK(c),GC,A:Black Widow 13.00
86 GC,TP,V:Ox 13.00
87 GC,TP,V:Electro 13.00
88 GK(c),GC,TP,O:Black Widow 13.00
89 GC,TP,A:Black Widow 13.00
90 E:StL(s),GK(c),GC,TP,V:Ox 13.00
91 GK(c),GC,TP,I:Mr. Fear III 13.00
92 GK(c),GC,TP,A:BlackPanther 13.00
93 GK(c),GC,TP,A:Black Widow 13.00
94 GK(c),GC,TP,V:Damon Dran 13.00
95 GK(c),GC,TP,V:Manbull 13.00
96 GK(c),GC,ECh,V:Manbull 13.00
97 GK(c),V:Dark Messiah 13.00
98 E:GyC(s),GC,ECh,V:Dark
Messiah 13.00
99 B:SvG(s),JR(c),V:Hawkeye 13.00
100 GC,V:Angar the Screamer 25.00
101 RB,A:Angar the Screamer 9.00
102 A:Black Widow 9.00
103 JR(c),DH,A:Spider-Man 9.00
104 GK(c),DH,V:Kraven 9.00
105 DH,JSn,DP,C:Thanos 15.00
106 JR(c),DH,A:Black Widow 9.00
107 JSn(c),JB(i),A:Capt.Marvel 9.00
108 K&R(c),PG(i),V:Beetle 9.00
109 GK(c),DH(i),V:Beetle 9.00
110 JR(c),GC,A:Thing,O:Nekra 9.00
111 JM(i),I:Silver Samurai 10.00
112 GK(c),GC,V:Mandrill 9.00
113 JR(c),V:Gladiator 9.00
114 GK(c),I:Death Stalker 9.00
115 V:Death Stalker 8.00
116 GK(c),GC,V:Owl 8.00
117 E:SvG(s),K&R(c),V:Owl 8.00
118 JR(c),DH,I:Blackwing 8.00
119 GK(c),DH(i),V:Crusher 8.00
120 GK(c),V:Hydra,I:El Jaguar 8.00
121 GK(c),A:Shield 6.00
122 GK(c),V:Blackwing 6.00
123 V:Silvermane,I:Jackhammer 6.00
124 B:MWn(s),GK(c),GC,KJ,
I:Copperhead 6.00
125 GK(c),KJ(i),V:Copperhead 6.00
126 GK(c),KJ(i),D: 2nd Torpedo 6.00
127 GK(c),KJ(i),V:3rd Torpedo 6.00
128 GK(c),KJ(i),V:Death Stalker 6.00
129 KJ(i),V:Man Bull 6.00
130 KJ(i),V:Brother Zed 6.00
131 KJ(i),I&O:2nd Bullseye 20.00
132 KJ(i),V:Bullseye 7.00
133 JM(i),GK(c),V:Jester 7.00
134 JM(i),V:Chamelon 7.00
135 JM(i),V:Jester 7.00
136 JB,JM,V:Jester 7.00
137 JB,V:Jester 7.00
138 JBy,A:Ghost Rider 9.00

Daredevil #52
© Marvel Entertainment Group

139 SB,V:A Bomber 5.00
140 SB,V:Gladiator 5.00
141 GC,Bullseye 5.00
142 GC,V:Cobra 5.00
143 E:MWn(s),GC,V:Cobra 5.00
144 GT,V:Manbull 5.00
145 GT,V:Owl 5.00
146 GC,V:Bullseye 6.00
147 GC,V:Killgrave 5.00
148 GC,V:Deathstalker 5.00
149 KI,V:Smasher 5.00
150 GC,KJ,I:Paladin 5.00
151 GC,Daredevil Unmasked 5.00
152 KJ,V:Paladin 5.00
153 GC,V:Cobra 5.00
154 GC,V:Mr. Hyde 5.00
155 V:Avengers 5.00
156 GC,V:Death Stalker 5.00
157 GC,V:Death Stalker 5.00
158 FM,V:Death Stalker 40.00
159 FM,V:Bullseye 22.00
160 FM,Bullseye 14.00
161 FM,V:Bullseye 14.00
162 SD,JRu,`Requiem' 5.00
163 FM,V:Hulk,I:Ben Urich 14.00
164 FM,KJ,A:Avengers 14.00
165 FM,KJ,V:Dr.Octopus 14.00
166 FM,KJ,V:Gladiator 14.00
167 FM,KJ,V:Mauler 14.00
168 FM,KJ,I&O:Elektra 45.00
169 FM,KJ,V:Bullseye 15.00
170 FM,KJ,V:Bullseye 15.00
171 FM,KJ,V:Kingpin 7.00
172 FM,KJ,V:Bullseye 7.00
173 FM,KJ,V:Gliadator 7.00
174 FM,KJ,A:Gladiator 7.00
175 FM,KJ,A:Elektra,V:Hand 8.00
176 FM,KJ,A:Elektra 7.00
177 FM,KJ,A:Stick 8.00
178 FM,KJ,A:PowerMan&I.Fist 7.00
179 FM,KJ,V:Elektra 7.00
180 FM,KJ,V:Kingpin 7.00
181 FM,KJ,V:Bullseye,D:Elektra,
A:Punisher 12.00
182 FM,KJ,A:Punisher 7.00
183 FM,KJ,V:PunisherDrug 7.00
184 FM,KJ,V:PunisherDrug 7.00
185 FM,KJ,V:King Pin 5.00
186 FM,KJ,V:Stiltman 5.00
187 FM,KJ,A:Stick 5.00
188 FM,KJ,A:Black Widow 5.00
189 FM,KJ,A:Stick,A:BlackWidow 5.00
190 FM,KJ,R:Elektra 6.00
191 FM,TA,A:Bullseye 5.00
192 KJ,V:Kingpin 3.00
193 KJ,Betsy 3.00
194 KJ,V:Kingpin 3.00
195 KJ,Tarkington Brown 3.00
196 KJ,A:Wolverine 9.00
197 V:Bullseye 2.50
198 V:Dark Wind 2.50
199 V:Dark Wind 2.50
200 JBy(c),V:Bullseye 3.00
201 JBy(c),A:Black Widow 2.50
202 I:Micah Synn 2.50
203 JBy(c),I:Trump 2.50
204 BSz(c),V:Micah Synn 2.50
205 I:Gael 2.50
206 V:Micah Synn 2.50
207 BSz(c),A:Black Widow 2.50
208 Harlan Ellison 3.00
209 Harlan Ellison 3.00
210 DM,V:Micah Synn 2.50
211 DM,V:Micah Synn 2.50
212 DM,V:Micah Synn 2.50
213 DM,V:Micah Synn 2.50
214 DM,V:Micah Synn 2.50
215 DM,A:Two-Gun Kid 2.50
216 DM,V:Gael 2.50
217 BS(c),V:Gael 2.50
218 KP,V:Jester 2.50

Daredevil #225
© Marvel Entertainment Group

219 FM,JB 3.00
220 DM,D:Heather Glenn 2.50
221 DM,Venice. 2.50
222 DM,A:Black Widow 2.50
223 DM,Secret Wars II 2.50
224 DM,V:Sunturion 2.50
225 DM,V:Vulture 2.50
226 FM(plot),V:Gladiator. 3.00
227 FM,Kingpin,Kar.Page 6.00
228 FM,DM,V:Kingpin. 4.00
229 FM,Kingpin,Turk 4.00
230 R:Matt's Mother 4.00
231 FM,DM,V:Kingpin. 4.00
232 FM,V:Kingpin,Nuke 4.00
233 FM,Kingpin,Nuke,Capt.Am. . . . 4.00
234 SD,KJ,V:Madcap 2.00
235 SD,KJ,V:Mr. Hyde 2.00
236 BWS,A:Black Widow 4.00
237 AW(i),V:Klaw 2.00
238 SB,SL,AAd(c)V:Sabretooth . . . 6.00
239 AAd(c),AW,GI(i),V:Rotgut 2.00
240 AW,V:Rotgut 2.00
241 MZ(c),TM,V:Trixter. 3.00
242 KP,V:Caviar Killer. 2.00
243 AW,V:Nameless One 2.00
244 TD(i),V:Nameless One 2.00
245 TD(i),A:Black Panther 2.00
246 TD(i),V:Chance 2.00
247 KG,A:Black Widow. 2.00
248 RL,AW,A:Wolverine,
V:Bushwhacker 6.00
249 RL,AW,V:Wolverine,
Bushwhacker 6.00
250 JR2,AW,I:Bullet 3.50
251 JR2,AW,V:Bullet. 3.00
252 JR2,AW,Fall o/Mutants. 4.50
253 JR2,AW,V:Kingpin 3.00
254 JR2,AW,I:Typhoid Mary 7.00
255 JR2,AW,A:Kingpin,TMary. 5.00
256 JR2,AW,A:Kingpin,TMary. 5.00
257 JR2,AW,A:Punisher 5.00
258 RLm,V:Bengal 3.50
259 JR2,AW,V:TyphoidMary 4.00
260 JR2,AW,V:T.Mary,K.pin 4.00
261 JR2,AW,HumanTorch. 2.50
262 JR2,AW,Inferno 2.50
263 JR2,AW,Inferno 2.50
264 SD,AW,MM,V:The Owl. 2.50
265 JR2,AW,Inferno 2.50
266 JR2,AW,V:Mephisto 2.50
267 JR2,AW,V:Bullet. 2.50
268 JR2,AW,V:TheMob. 2.50
269 JR2,AW,V:Pyro&Blob 2.50
270 JR2,AW,A:Spider-Man,
I:Blackheart 3.00
271 JR2,AW,I:Number9 . . . . 2.50
272 JR2,AW,I:Shotgun 3.00
273 JR2,AW,V:Shotgun 2.50
274 JR2,AW,V:Inhumans 2.50
275 JR2,AW,ActsOfVen.,V:Ultron . . 2.50
276 JR2,AW,ActsOfVen.,V:Ultorn . . 2.50
277 RL,AW,Vivian's Story 2.00
278 JR2,AW,V:Blackheart,
A:Inhumans 2.50
279 JR2,AW,V:Mephisto,
A:Inhumans 2.50
280 JR2,AW,V:Mephisto,
A:Inhumans 2.50
281 JR2,AW,V:Mephisto,
A:Inhumans 2.50
282 JR2,AW,V:Mephisto,
A:Silver Surfer, Inhumans. 2.50
283 MBa,AW,A:Captain America . . 2.00
284 LW,AW,R:Bullseye 2.00
285 LW,AW,B:Bullseye
become DD#1 . . . . 2.00
286 LW,AW,GCa,Fake
Daredevil #2. . . . . 2.00
287 LW,AW,Fake Daredevil #3 . . . . 2.00
288 LW,AW,A:Kingpin 2.00
289 LW,AW,A:Kingpin 2.00
290 LW,AW,E:Fake Daredevil 2.00
291 LW,AW,V:Bullet 2.00
292 LW,A:Punisher,V:Tombstone . . 2.00
293 LW,A:Punisher,V:Tombstone . . 2.00
294 LW,V:The Hand.. . . . . 2.00
295 LW,V:The Hand,
A:GhostRider.. . . . . 2.00
296 LW,AW,V:The Hand 2.00
297 B:DGC(s),LW,AW,B:Last Rites,
V:Typhoid Mary,A:Kingpin 3.50
298 LW,AW,A:Nick Fury,Kingpin . . . 2.50
299 LW,AW,A:Nick Fury,Kingpin . . . 2.50
300 LW,AW,E:Last Rites, ... 4.00
301 V:The Owl 2.00
302 V:The Owl 2.00
303 V:The Owl. 2.00
304 AW,Non-action issue 2.00
305 AW,A:Spider-Man 2.00
306 AW,A:Spider-Man 2.00
307 1st SMc DD,Dead Man's Hand #1,
A:Nomad 3.00
308 SMc,Dead Man's Hand #5,
A:Punisher,V:Silvermane 2.00
309 SMc,Dead Man's Hand#7,
A:Nomad,Punisher 2.00
310 SMc,Inf.War,V:Calipso 2.00
311 SMc,V:Calypso 2.00
312 Firefighting issue 2.00
313 SMc,V:Pyromaniac 2.00
314 SMc,V:Mr.Fear,I:Shock. 2.00
315 SMc,V:Mr.Fear. 2.00
316 Goes Underground 2.00
317 SMc,Comedy Issue 2.00
318 SMc,V:Taskmaster. 2.00
319 SMc,Fall from Grace Prologue,
A:Silver Sable,Garrett,Hand . . . 5.00
319a 2nd Printing 2.00
320 SMc,B:Fall from Grace,
V:Crippler,S.Sable,A:Stone 5.00
321 SMc,N:Daredevil,A:Venom,
Garret, V:Hellspawn,Glow
in the Dark(c) 3.00
321a Newsstand Ed. 3.00
322 SMc,A:Venom,Garret,Siege . . . 3.00
323 SMc,V:Venom,A:Siege,Garret,
I:Erynys 2.50
324 SMc,A:Garret,R:Elektra,
A:Stone, Morbius 2.50
325 SMc,E:Fall from Grace, A:Garret,
Siege,Elektra,Morbius,V:Hand,
D:Hellspawn,Double size 3.00
326 SMc,B:Tree of Knowledge,
I:Killobyte,A:Capt.America 2.00

Daredevil #358
© Marvel Entertainment Group

327 E:DGC(s),SMc,A:Capt.Amer. . . 2.00
328 GtW(s),V:Wirehead,A:Captain
America,S.Sable,Wild Pack . . . 2.00
329 B:DGC(s),SMc,A:Captain
America, S.Sable,Iron Fist 2.00
330 SMc,A:Gambit 2.00
331 SMc,A:Captain America,
VLHydra. 2.00
332 A:Captain America,Gambit. . . . 2.00
333 TGb,GWt. 2.00
334 TGb,GWt. 2.00
335 . . . . 2.00
336 . . . . 2.00
337 V:Kingpin,A:Blackwulf 2.00
338 Wages of Sin,pt.1 . . . . 2.00
339 Wages of Sin,pt.2 . . . . 2.00
340 R:Kingpin. 2.00
341 Kingpin 2.00
342 DGc,KP,V:Kingpin 2.00
343 Without Costume 2.00
344 Identity Crisis,pt.1 . . . . 2.00
345 Identity Crisis,pt.2 . . . . 2.00
346 V:Sir 2.00
347 V:mystery man. 2.00
348 In NY City 2.00
349 Retreats to the Chaste. 2.00
350 Double size 3.50
351 . . . . 2.50
352 Return of Matt Murdock 2.50
353 KK,CNr,A:Mr. Hyde 2.00
354 KK,CNr,A:Spider-Man 2.00
355 KK,CNr,A:Pyro. 2.00
356 KK,CNr,. 2.00
357 KK,CNr,. 2.00
358 KK,CNr,MRy,A:Mysterio 2.00
359 KK,CNr,A:Absorbing Man. 2.00
360 KK,CNr,MRy,V:Onslaught. 2.00
361 KK,CNr,MRy,A:Black Widow . . 2.00
362 KK,CNr,Romance 2.00
363 KK,GC,CaS,V:Insomnia 2.00
364 KK,CNr,MRy,V:Insomnia 2.00
365 CNr,MRy,V:Mr. Fear,
A:Molten Man. 2.00
366 GC,V:Gladiator 2.00
367 GC,V:Gladiator, concl. 2.00
368 GC,A:Black Widow and Omega
Red 2.00
369 AOI,V:Soviet Super Soldiers. . . 2.00
370 GC,Black Widow, concl.. . . . . . 2.00
371 AOI,Matt Murdock & Karen
Page's relationship 2.00
372 AOI,Killers after Karen Page . . 2.00
373 AOI,V:The 3. . . . . 2.00

MARVEL

374 AOI,V:Mr. Fear. 2.00
375 AOI,RL,V:Mr. Fear,double size . 3.00
376 SLo,CHm,Daredevil deep undercover. 2.00
377 SLo,TMo,SHa,Flying Blind, pt.2 . . . . 2.00
378 SLo,TMo,SHa,Flying Blind, pt.3 . . . . 2.00
379 SLo,CHm,Flying Blind,concl. . . 2.00
380 DGC,LW,RbC, V:Bullseye,Bushwacker,Kingpin, double size . . . 3.00
Minus 1 Spec., GC, flashback. 2.50
Ann.#1 GC 30.00
Ann.#2 reprints. 8.00
Ann.#3 reprints. 8.00
Ann.#4 (1976)GT,A:Black Panther,Namor. 6.00
Ann.#5 (1989)MBa,JLe,JR2,KJ, WPo,AM,Atlantis Attacks, A:Spider-Man 5.00
Ann.#6 TS,Lifeform#2,A:Typhoid Mary 2.75
Ann.#7 JG,JBr,Von Strucker Gambit,pt.1,A:Nick Fury 2.50
Ann.#8 Sys.Bytes#2,A:Deathlok . . . 2.75
Ann.#9 MPa,I:Devourer,w/card,tie-in to "Fall From Grace". 5.00
Ann.#10 I:Ghostmaker,A:Shang Chi, Elektra 3.25
G-Size #1 GK(c),reprints. 12.00
TPB Born Again,rep.#227-#233 . . 10.95
TPB Fall of the Kingpin, rep.#297-300 . . . . 15.95
TPB Gangwar,Reprints #169-#172,#180 . . . . 12.95
TPB Marked for Death,reps#159-161,163,164. . . . . 9.95
Daredevil/Punisher:Child's Play reprints#182-#184 . . . . 7.00
TPB Daredevil: Man Without Fear. 15.95

DAREDEVIL

Sept., 1998

1 JP,JQ,F:Matt Murdock 4.00
1a Deluxe edition. 7.50
2 JP,JQ,blind faith dilemma 5.00
2a variant JSC cover. 5.00
3 JP,JQ,Guardian Devil,pt.3. . . . . . 2.50
4 JP,JQ,Guardian Devil,pt.4. . . . . . 2.50
5 JP,JQ,Guardian Devil,pt.5. . . . . . 2.50
6 JP,JQ,Guardian Devil,pt.6. . . . . . 2.50
7 JP,JQ,Guardian Devil,pt.7. . . . . . 2.50
8 JP,JQ,Guardian Devil,concl. 2.50
8a signed 30.00
9 JP,JQ,DMk,V:Kingpin 2.50
9a signed 30.00
10 JP,JQ,DMk,I:Echo 2.50
11 JP,JQ,DMk,A:Kingpin 2.50
12 JP,JQ,DMk,V:Kingpin 2.50
13 JP,JQ,DMk,V:Kingpin 2.50
14 JP,JQ,DMk,Wilson Fisk 3.00
15 JQ,DMk,KN,A:Black Widow 3.00
16 JQ,DMk,trial of Kingpin 3.00
17 JQ,DMk,Ben Urich. 3.00
18 JQ,DMk,Leap Frog 3.00
Spec.Daredevil vs. Punisher. 3.50
Spec.#1 Daredevil (2000). 2.25
TPB rep. #1–#3 . . . . 9.95
TPB Gang War,FM,KJ 15.95
TPB Visionaries, JP,JQ & Kevin Smith 192-pg. 20.00
TPB Visionaries, FM. 24.95

DAREDEVIL/BATMAN

1997

Spec. DGC,SMc, 48-pg. 6.00

DAREDEVIL/ DEADPOOL '97

Spec, BCh, JHo, Two annuals in one, 48-pg.. . . . . 5.00

DAREDEVIL: THE MAN WITHOUT FEAR

1993–94

1 B:FM(s),JR2,AW,O:Daredevil, A:Stick,D:Daredevil's Father . . . 7.00
2 JR2,AW,A:Stick,Stone,Elektra . . . 6.00
3 JR2,AW,A:Elektra,Kingpin. 5.00
4 JR2,AW,A:Kingpin,I:Mickey. 5.00
5 JR2,AW,A:Mickey,Last Issue. . . . 5.00
TPB rep.#1#5 . . . . 15.95

DAREDEVIL: NINJA

Oct., 2000

1 (of 3) Stick 3.00

DAREDEVIL/SHI SHI/DAREDEVIL

Marvel/Crusade 1996

1 (Daredevil/Shi) TSg,AW, x-over,pt.1 . . . . 3.00
1 (Shi/Daredevil)x-over, pt.2. . . . . . 3.00

DARING MYSTERY COMICS

Timely Jan., 1940

1 ASh(c),JSm,O:Fiery Mask, A:Monako John Steele,Doc Doyle, Flash FosterBarney Mullen, Sea Rover, Bondage (c). . 17,500.00
2 ASh(c),JSm,O:Phantom Bullet A:Zephyr Jones & K4,Laughing Mask Mr.E,B:Trojak 6,500.00
3 ASh(c),JSm,A:Phantom Reporter,Marvex,Breeze Barton, B:Purple Mask . . . 4,000.00
4 ASh(c),A:G-Man Ace,K4, Monako,Marvex,E:Purple Mask,B:Whirlwind Carter . . 2,500.00
5 JSm,B:Falcon,A:Fiery Mask,K4, Little Hercules, Bondage(c) 2,500.00
6 S&K,O:Marvel Boy,A:Fiery Mask, Flying Fame,Dynaman, Stuporman,E:Trojak 3,500.00
7 S&K,O:Blue Diamond,A:The Fin, Challenger,Captain Daring, Silver Scorpion,Thunderer . 2,700.00
8 S&K,O:Citizen V,A:Thunderer, Fin Silver Scorpion,Captain Daring Blue Diamond. 2,200.00

Becomes:

DARING COMICS

9 ASh(c),B:Human Torch,Toro, Sub Mariner 900.00
10 ASh(c),A;The Angel 800.00
11 ASh(c),A:The Destroyer 800.00
12 E:Human Torch,Toro,Sub-Mariner, Fall, 1945 . . . . 800.00

Becomes:

JEANIE COMICS

13 B:Jeanie,Queen of the Teens Mitzi,Willie 125.00
14 Baseball(c) 100.00
15 Schoolbus(c) 90.00
16 Swimsuit(c) 125.00
17 HK,Fancy dress party(c), Hey Look 75.00
18 HK,Jeanie'sDate(c),Hey Look . 75.00
19 Ice-Boat(c),Hey Look 75.00
20 Jukebox(c). 60.00
21 . . . . 60.00
22 HK,Hey Look 75.00
23 . . . . 60.00
24. . . . . 60.00
25. . . . . 60.00
26. . . . . 60.00
27 E:Jeanie,Queen of Teens. 60.00

Becomes:

COWGIRL ROMANCES

28 Ph(c),Mona Freeman/MacDonald Carey,Copper Canyon 150.00

DARK ANGEL

See: HELL'S ANGEL

DARK CRYSTAL

April, 1983

1 movie adaption. 2.00
2 movie adaption,May 1983. . . . . . 2.00

Dark Guard #3
© Marvel Entertainment Group

DARK GUARD

1993–94

1 A:All UK Heroes 3.00
2 A:All UK Heroes 2.00
3 V:Leader,MyS-Tech 2.00
4 V:MyS-Tech 2.00
5 . . . . 2.00
6 and 7 . . . . @2.00

DARKHAWK

March, 1991

1 MM,I&O:Darkhawk, A:Hobgoblin 3.00
2 MM,A:Spider-Man,V:Hobgoblin . . 2.50
3 MM,A:Spider-Man,V:Hobgoblin . . 2.50
4 MM,I:Savage Steel 2.50
5 MM,I:Portal. 2.50
6 MM,A:Cap.Am,D.D.,Portal, V:U-Foes 2.50
7 MM,I:Lodestone 2.00
8 MM,V:Lodestone 2.00
9 MM,A:Punisher,V:Savage Steel . 2.00
10 MM,A&N:Tombstone 2.00
11 MM,V:Tombstone. 2.00
12 MM,V:Tombstone,R:Dark Hawks'Father. 2.00
13 MM,V:Venom. 3.00
14 MM,V:Venom,D:Dark Hawks Father. 3.00
15 MM,Heart of the Hawk,concl . . . 2.00
16 MM,V:Terrorists 2.00
17 MM,I:Peristrike Force. 2.00

Darkhawk #20
© Marvel Entertainment Group

18 MM,V:Mindwolf 2.00
19 MM,R:Portal,A:Spider-Man,V:The Brotherhood of Evil Mutants . . . 2.00
20 MM,A:Spider-Man,Sleepwalker, V:Brotherhood of Evil Mutants . 2.00
21 MM,B:Return to Forever 2.00
22 MM,A:Ghost Rider 2.00
23 MM,I:Evilhawk 2.00
24 V:Evilhawk 2.00
25 MM,O:Darkhawk,V:Evilhawk, Holo-graphx(c) 3.50
26 A:New Warriors 2.00
27 A:New Warriors,V:Zarrko 2.00
28 A:New Warriors,Zarrko 2.00
29 A:New Warriors 2.00
30 I:Purity 2.00
31 Infinity Crusade 2.00
32 R:Savage Steel 2.00
33 I:Cuda 2.00
34 V:Cuda 2.00
35 DFr(s),V:Venom 2.00
36 DFr(s),V:Scokers,A:Venom 2.00
37 DFr(s),V:Venom 2.00
38 DFr(s),N:Darkhawk 2.00
39 DFr(s) 2.00
40 DFr(s) 2.00
41 DFr(s) 2.00
42 DFr(s), V:Portal,I:Shaper 2.00
43 DFr(s) 2.00
44 DFr(s) 2.00
45 DFr(s),A:Portal 2.00
46 DFr(s) 2.00
47 . . . . . 2.00
48 R:Darkhawk,V:Mahari 2.00
49 V:Overhawk 2.00
50 V:Overhawk 2.50
Ann.#1 MM,Assault on ArmorCity . . 3.00
Ann.#2 GC,AW,I:Dreamkiller, w/Trading card 3.00
Ann.#3 I:Damek 3.00

DARKHOLD
1992–94

1 RCa,I:Redeemers,Polybagged w/poster,A:Gh.Rider,Blaze 3.00
2 RCa,R:Modred 2.50
3 A:Modred,Scarlet Witch 2.00
4 V:Sabretooth,N'Garai 2.00
5 A:Punisher, Ghost Rider 2.00
6 RCa,V:Dr.Strange 2.00
7 A:Dr.Strange,V:Japanese Army. . 2.00
8 Betrayal #1 . . . . . 2.00
9 Diabolique 2.00
10 V:Darkholders 2.00
11 Midnight Massacre#3,D:Modred, Vicki 2.50
12 V:Chthon 2.00
13 V:Missing Link 2.00
14 Vicki's Secret revealed 2.00
15 Siege of Darkness,pt.#4 . . . . . 2.00
16 Siege of Darkness,pt.#12 . . . . . 2.00

DARK MAN
MOVIE ADAPTION
Sept., 1990

1 BH/MT/TD 2.00
2 BH/TD 2.00
3 BH/TD,final issue 2.00

DARKMAN
Sept., 1990

1 JS,R:Darkman 3.50
2 JS,V:Witchfinder 3.00
3 JS,Witchfinder 3.00
4 JS,V:Dr.West 3.00
5 JS,Durant 3.00
6 JS,V:Durant 3.00

DATE WITH MILLIE
Atlas Oct., 1956
[1st Series]

1 . . . . . 150.00
2 . . . . . 75.00
3 thru 7 . . . . . @50.00

[2nd Series] Oct., 1959

1 . . . . . 75.00
2 thru 7 . . . . . @50.00
Becomes:

LIFE WITH MILLIE

8 . . . . . 50.00
9 & 10 . . . . . @35.00
11 thru 20 . . . . . @30.00
Becomes:

MODELING WITH MILLIE

21 . . . . . 40.00
22 thru 54 June, 1967 . . . . . @30.00

DATE WITH PATSY
Sept., 1957

1 A:Patsy Walker 60.00

DAYDREAMERS
Aug., 1997

1 (of 3) JMD,MEg,HSm 2.50
2 JMD,MEg,HSm, ... 2.50
3 JMD,TDz,MEg,HSm,concl. 2.50

DAZZLER
March, 1981

1 AA,JR2,A:X-Men,Spm, O:Dazzler 2.50
2 WS,JR2,AA,X-Men,A:SpM 2.00
3 JR2,Dr.Doom 2.00
4 FS,Dr.Doom 2.00
5 FS,I:Blue Shield 2.00
6 FS,Hulk 2.00
7 FS,Hulk 2.00
8 FS,Quasar 2.00
9 FS,D:Klaw 2.00
10 FS,Galactus 2.00
11 FS,Galactus 2.00
12 FS,The Light That Failed 2.00
13 FS,V:Grapplers 2.00
14 FS,She Hulk 2.00
15 FS,BSz,Spider Women 2.00
16 FS,BSz,Enchantress 2.00

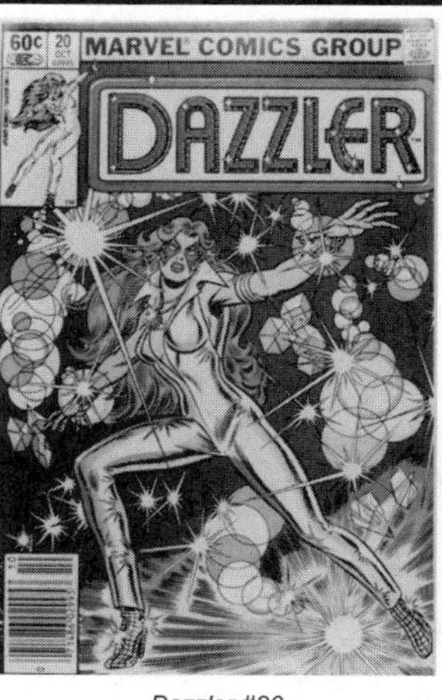

Dazzler #20
© Marvel Entertainment Group

17 FS,Angel,V:Doc Octopus 2.00
18 FS,BSz,A:Fantastic Four,Angel, V:Absorbing Man 2.00
19 FS,Blue Bolt,V:Absorbing Man . . 2.00
20 FS,V:Jazz and Horn 2.00
21 FS,A:Avengers,F.F.,C:X-Men, (double size) 2.00
22 FS,V:Rogue,Mystique 3.50
23 FS,V:Rogue,A:Powerman, Iron Fist 2.00
24 FS,V:Rogue,A:Powerman, Iron Fist 3.00
25 FS,`The Jagged Edge' 2.00
26 FS,Lois London 2.00
27 FS,Fugitive 2.50
28 FS,V:Rogue 3.00
29 FS,Roman Nekoboh 2.00
30 FS,Moves to California 2.00
31 FS,The Last Wave 2.00
32 FS,A:Inhumans 2.00
33 Chiller 2.50
34 FS,Disappearance 2.00
35 FS,V:Racine Ramjets 2.00
36 JBy(c),FS,V:Tatterdemalion 2.00
37 JBy(c),FS 2.00
38 PC,JG,X-Men 5.00
39 PC,JG,Caught in the grip of death 1.50
40 PC,JG,Secret Wars II 2.50
41 PC,JG,A:Beast 2.50
42 PC,JG,A:Beast,last issue 2.50

DEADLIEST HEROES OF KUNG FU
Summer, 1975

1 Magazine size 7.00

DEADLY FOES OF SPIDER-MAN
May, 1991

1 AM,KGa,V:Sinister Syndicate . . . 4.00
2 AM,Boomerang on Trial 3.00
3 AM,Deadly Foes Split 3.00
4 AM,Conclusion 3.00
TPB rep. #1–#4 . . . . . 12.95

MARVEL

MARVEL

DEADLY HANDS OF KUNG FU

April, 1974

1 NA(c),JSa,JSon,O:Sons of the Tiger, B:Shang-Chi, Bruce Lee Pin-up 30.00
2 NA(c),JSa 25.00
3 NA(c),JSon,A:Sons of the Tiger 20.00
4 NA(Bruce Lee)(c),JSon,Bruce Lee biography 20.00
5 BWS,PG. 15.00
6 GP,JSon,A:Sons of the Tiger . . 15.00
7 GP,JSon,A:Sons of the Tiger . . 20.00
8 GP,JSon,A:Sons of the Tiger. . . 12.00
9 GP,JSon,A:Sons of the Tiger . . 12.00
10 GP,JSon,A:Sons of the Tiger . . 20.00
11 NA(c),GP,JSon,A:Sons of the Tiger. 12.00
12 NA(c),GP,JSon,A:Sons of the Tiger. 10.00
13 GP,JSon,A:Sons of the Tiger . . 10.00
14 NA(c),GP,HC,JSon,A:Sons of the Tiger. 35.00
15 JS.PG,JSn,,Annual #1 . . . . . . 15.00
16 JSn,A:Sons of the Tiger 10.00
17 NA(c),JSn,KG,A:Sons of the Tiger. 10.00
18 JSn,A:Sons of the Tiger 10.00
19 JSn,I:White Tiger 15.00
20 GP,O:White Tiger 10.00
21 . . . . 10.00
22 KG,C:Jack of Hearts 10.00
23 GK,Jack of Hearts 15.00
24 KG,Ironfist 15.00
25 I:Shimaru. 15.00
26 . . . . 15.00
27 . . . . 9.00
28 Bruce Lee Special 40.00
29 Ironfist vs. Shang Chi. 15.00
30 Swordquest 10.00
31 JSon, Jack of Hearts 10.00
32 MR,JSon,Daughters of the Dragon. 10.00
33 MR,Feb., 1977. . . . . 12.00
Spec. Album Ed.,NA, Sum.1974 . . 15.00

DEAD OF NIGHT

Dec., 1973–Aug. 1975

1 JSt,Horror reprints,A Haunted House is not a Home 15.00
2 BEv(c),House that Fear Built . . 10.00
3 They Lurk Below. 10.00
4 Warewolf Beware 10.00
5 Deep Down 10.00
6 Jack the Ripper 10.00
7 SD,The Thirteenth Floor 10.00
8 Midnight Brings Dark Madness 10.00
9 Deathride 10.00
10 SD,I Dream of Doom 10.00
11 GK/BWr(c),I:Scarecrow, Fires of Rebirth,Fires of Death. 18.00

DEADPOOL

1993

1 B:FaN(s),JMd,MFm(i), V:Slayback,Nyko 4.00
2 JMd,MFm(i),V:Black Tom Cassidy,Juggernaut 3.00
3 JMd,MFm(i),I:Comcast, Makeshift,Rive,A:Slayback 2.50
4 E:FaN(s),JMd,MFm(i), A:Slayback,Kane 2.50

[2nd Limited Series] 1994

1 A:Banshee,Syrin,Juggernaut Black Tom 2.00
2 A:Banshee,Syrin,V:Juggernaut . . 2.00
3 A:Syrin,Juggernaut. 2.00
4 Final issue 2.00

DEADPOOL

1996

1 NMa,V:Sasquatch,48pg, ... 3.50
2 NMa,A:Copycat 3.00
3 NMa,A:Siryn. 2.50
4 NMa,Will Hulk cure him? 2.00
5 NMa,A:Siryn,T-Ray. 2.00
6 NMa,I: 2.00
7 AaL,A:Typhoid Mary 2.00
8 NMa, cont. from Daredevil/ Deadpool '97,A:Gerry. 2.00
9 NMa, new villain 2.00
10 NMa,A:Great Lake Avengers . . . 2.00
11 NMa,Fall through time, A:Alfred . 5.00
12 NMa,Typhoid Mary, Zoe Cullodon & Siryn return 2.00
13 NMa,V:T-Ray. 2.00
14 WMc,Deal of a Lifetime 2.00
15 WMc,A:Landau, Luckman & Lake 2.00
16 WMc, in middle east 2.00
17 WMc, Landau, Luckman & Lake's plan 2.00
18 WMc,V:Ajax. 2.00
19 WMc,more secrets of blind Al . . 2.00
20 Cosmic Messiah 2.00
21 . . . . 2.00
22 WMc,A:Cable 2.00
23 WMc,Dead Reckoning,pt.1 48-page 3.00
24 WMc,Dead Reckoning,pt.2. . . . . 2.00
25 WMc,Dead Reckoning,pt.3. . . . . 2.00
26 Dead Reckoning,aftermath. 2.00
27 V:A.I.M. concl. 2.00
28 R:Weasel. 2.00
29 V:Bullseye 2.00
30 A:Mercedes,T-Ray. 2.00
31 V:T-Ray. 2.00
32 V:T-Ray,A:Mercedes 2.00
33 V:T-Ray. 2.00
34 CPr,Chapter Pt.1 . . . . 2.00
35 CPr 2.00
36 CPr 2.00
37 CPr,Chapter X,Addendum 2.00
38 CPr,F:Taskmaster 2.00
39 CPr,F:Taskmaster 2.00
40 CPr,space station 2.00
41 CPr,V:Dirty Wolf. 2.25
42 V:Humbug 2.25
43 CPr,JCf,V:Rasputin 2.25
44 CPr,JCf,CatTrap,pt.1,x-over 2.25
45 CPr,JCf,Constrictor 2.25
46 JJu,JP,PC,CruelSummer,pt.1 . . . 2.25

Deadpool #5
© Marvel Entertainment Group

47 JP,PC,CruelSummer,pt.2 . . . . . . 2.25
Ann. '98 BCh(c) F:Deadpool & Death, 48-pg. 3.00
Minus 1 Spec., ALo, flashback, O:Deadpool 2.00
Spec. Deadpool Team-Up,2 Deadpools F:Widdle Wade. 3.00
Spec. Baby's First Deadpool Book . 3.00
Spec. Encyclopedia Deadpoolica . . 3.00
TPB Circle Chase,FaN,JMd, MFm 12.95
TPB Mission Improbable. 14.95
TPB MWa,IaC,Sins of the Past, rep. limited series 6.00

DEATH3

1993

1 I:Death Metal,Death Wreck 3.00
2 V:Ghost Rider. 2.00
3 A:Hulk,Cable,Storm,Thing. 2.00
4 Last issue. 2.00

DEATHLOK

[Limited Series] July, 1990

1 JC,SW,I:Michael Colins (2nd Deathlok) 4.00
2 JC,SW,V:Wajler 3.00
3 DCw,SW,V:Cyberants 3.00
4 DCw,SW,V:Sunfire,final issue . . . 3.00

[Regular Series] 1991–94

1 DCw,MM,V:Warwolf 2.50
2 DCw,MM,A:Dr.Doom,Machine Man, Forge 2.50
3 DCw,MM,V:Dr.Doom, A:Mr.Fantastic 2.50
4 DCw,MM,A:X-Men,F.F.,Vision, O:Mechadoom 2.50
5 DCw,MM,V:Mechadoom, A:X-Men,Fantastic Four 2.50
6 DCw,MM,A:Punisher, V:Silvermane 2.50
7 DCw,MM,A:Punisher, V:Silvermane 2.50
8 A:Main Frame,Ben Jacobs 2.00
9 DCw,MM,A:Ghost Rider, V:Nightmare 2.50
10 DCw,MM,A:GhR,V:Nightmare . . 2.50
11 DCw,MM,V:Moses Magnum 2.00
12 DCw,MM,Biohazard Agenda . . . 2.00
13 DCw,MM,Biohazard Agenda . . . 2.00
14 DCw,MM,Biohazard Agenda . . . 2.00
15 DCw,MM,Biohazard Agenda . . . 2.00
16 DCw,MM,Inf.War,V:Evilok. 2.00
17 WMc,MM,B:Cyberwar 2.00
18 WMc,A:Silver Sable. 2.00
18a Newstand Ed. 2.00
19 SMc,Cyberwar#3 . . . . 2.00
20 SMc,Cyberwar#4 . . . . 2.00
21 E:Cyberwar,A:Cold Blood Nick Fury 2.00
22 V:MosesMagnum,A:Bl.Panther. . 2.00
23 A:Bl.Panther,V:Phreak,Stroke. . . 2.00
24 V:MosesMagnum,A:Bl.Panther. . 2.00
25 WMc,V:MosesMagnum,A:Black Panther,holo-grafx(c) 2.50
26 V:Hobogoblin 2.00
27 R:Siege 2.00
28 Infinty Crusade 2.00
29 Inner Fears 2.00
30 KHd,V:Hydra 2.00
31 GWt(s),KoK,B:Cyberstrike, R:1st Deathlok 2.00
32 GWt(s),KoK,A:Siege 2.00
33 GWt(s),KoK,V:Justice Peace . . . 2.00
34 GWt(s),KoK,E:Cyberstrike,V:Justice Peace,final issue 2.00
Ann.#1 JG,I:Timestream. 2.75
Ann.#2 I:Tracer,w/card 2.95

DEATHLOK
July, 1999
1 JoC,JQ&JaL(c),Marvel Tech 2.00
2 JoC,A:Nick Fury 2.00
2a variant cover. 2.00
3 JoC,I:Billy Bailey. 2.00
4 JoC,R:Clown 2.00
5 JoC,I:Jack Truman 2.00
6 JoC, ... 2.00
7 JoC,V:Serpent Society 2.00
8 JoC,Nick Fury. 2.50
9 JoC,V:Ringmaster. 2.50
10 JoC,V:Clown 2.50
11 JoC,V:Clown 2.50

DEATHLOK SPECIAL
1991
1 Rep.Mini Series 2.50
2 Rep.Mini Series 2.50
3 Rep.Mini Series 2.50
4 Rep.Mini Series, final issue. 2.50

DEATH METAL
Marvel UK 1994
1 JRe,I:Argon,C:Alpha Flight 2.00
2 JRe,V:Alpha Flight 2.00
3 JRe,I:Soulslug 2.00
4 Re,Last Issue 2.00

DEATH METAL VS. GENETIX
Marvel UK 1993–94
1 PaD,w/card. 3.00
2 PaD,w/card. 3.00

DEATH'S HEAD
Marvel UK Dec., 1988
1 V:Backbreaker 5.00
2 A:Dragons Claws 4.00
3 . . . . 4.00
4 V:Plague Dog 3.00
5 V:Big Shot 3.00
6 V:Big Shot 3.00
7 & 8 . . . . @3.00
9 A:Fantastic Four. 3.50
10 A:Iron Man. 3.50
TPB Reprints#1-#10 . . . . 12.95

Death's Head II #10
© Marvel Entertainment Group

DEATH'S HEAD
[Limited Series]
1 A:`Old' Death's Head 2.00

DEATH'S HEAD II
Marvel UK March, 1992
[Limited Series]
1 LSh,I:2nd Death's Head,
D:1st Death's Head 4.00
1a 2nd printing,Silver. 2.50
2 LSh,A:Fantastic Four 3.00
2a 2nd printing,Silver. 3.00
3 LSh,I:Tuck 3.50
4 LSh,A:Wolverine,Spider-Man,
Punisher. 3.50

[Regular Series] 1992
1 LSh,A:X-Men,I:Wraithchilde 3.00
2 LSh,A:X-Men 2.25
3 LSh,A:X-Men,V:Raptors 2.25
4 LSh,A:X-Men,V:Wraithchilde. . . . 2.25
5 V:UnDeath's Head II,
A:Warheads 2.25
6 R:Tuck,V:Major Oak 2.25
7 V:Major Oak 2.25
8 V:Wizard Methinx 2.25
9 BHi,V:Cybernetic Centaurs 2.25
10 DBw,A:Necker 2.25
11 SCy,R:Charnel. 2.25
12 DAn(s),SvL,V:Charnel 2.25
13 SvL,A:Liger 2.25
14 SvL,Brain Dead Cold,Blue
Foil(c). 3.25
15 SvL,V:Duplicates 2.25
16 SvL,DAn 2.25
17 SvL,DAn 2.00
18 SvL,DAn 2.00
Spec. Gold Ed. LSh(a&s) 3.95

DEATH'S HEAD II/DIE CUT
Marvel UK 1993
1 I:Die Cut. 3.25
2 O:Die Cut. 2.00

DEATH'S HEAD II/ KILLPOWER: BATTLETIDE
[1st Limited Series]
1 GSr,A:Wolverine. 2.50
2 thru 4 GSr,A:Wolverine . . . . . . @2.00

[2nd Limited Series]
1 A:Hulk 3.25
2 V:Hulk 2.00
3 A:Hulk 2.00
4 last issue 2.00

DEATH-WRECK
Marvel UK 1994
1 A:Death's Head II 2.00
2 V:Gangsters 2.00
3 A:Dr.Necker 2.00
4 last issue 2.00

DEEP, THE
Nov., 1977
1 CI,Movie Adaption 2.00

DEFENDERS
August, 1972
1 SB,I&D:Necrodames. 65.00
2 SB,V:Calizuma 35.00
3 GK(c),SB,JM,V:UndyingOne . . . 25.00
4 SB,FMc,Bl.Knight,V:Valkyrie . . . 25.00
5 SB,FMc,D:Omegatron. 25.00
6 SB,FMc,V:Cyrus Black 20.00
7 SB,FBe,A:Hawkeye 20.00

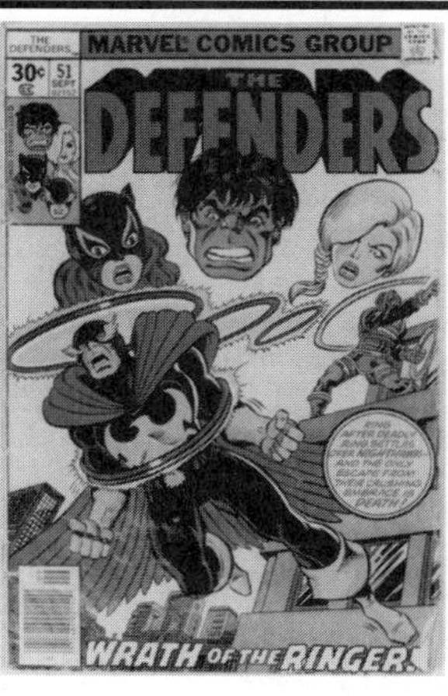

Defenders #51
© Marvel Entertainment Group

8 SB,FBe,Avengers,Silver Surfer . 20.00
9 SB,FMc,Avengers. 20.00
10 SB,FBe,Thor vs. Hulk 22.00
11 SB,FBe,A:Avengers 10.00
12 SB,JA,Xemnu 9.00
13 GK(c),SB,KJ,J:Night Hawk. 9.00
14 SB,DGr,O:Hyperion 9.00
15 SB,KJ,A:Professor X,V:Magneto,
Savage Land Mutates. 12.00
16 GK(c),SB,Professor X,V:Magneto,
Savage Land Mutates. 12.00
17 SB,DGr,Power Man 7.00
18 GK(c),SB,DGr,A:Power Man . . . 7.00
19 GK(c),SB,KJ,A:Power Man 7.00
20 K&R(c),SB,A:Thing 7.00
21 GK(c),SB,O:Valkyrie 6.00
22 GK(c),SB,V:Sons o/t Serpent . . . 6.00
23 GK(c),SB,A:Yellow Jacket 6.00
24 GK(c),SB,BMc,A:Daredevil 6.00
25 GK(c),SB,JA,A:Daredevil 6.00
26 K&R(c),SB,A:Guardians. 8.00
27 K&R(c),SB,A:Guardians
C:Starhawk 8.00
28 K&R(c),SB,A:Guardians
I:Starhawk 7.00
29 K&R(c),SB,A:Guardians. 7.00
30 JA(i),A:Wong 5.00
31 GK(c),SB,JM,Nighthawk 5.00
32 GK(c),SB,JM,O:Nighthawk. 5.00
33 GK(c),SB,JM,V:Headmen 5.00
34 SB,JM,V:Nebulon 5.00
35 GK(c),SB,KJ,I:Red Guardian . . . 5.00
36 GK(c),SB,KJ,A:Red Guardian . 12.00
37 GK(c),SB,KJ,J:Luke Cage 5.00
38 SB,KJ,V:Nebulon 12.00
39 SB,KJ,V:Felicia 4.00
40 SB,KJ,V:Assassin 4.00
41 KG,KJ,Nighthawk. 4.00
42 KG,KJ,V:Rhino 4.00
43 KG,KJ,Cobalt Man,Egghead . . . 4.00
44 KG,KJ,J:Hellcat,V:Red Rajah . . . 4.00
45 KG,KJ,Valkyrie V:Hulk 4.00
46 KG,KJ,L:DrStrange,LukeCage . . 4.00
47 KG,KJ,Moon Knight 4.00
48 KG,A:Wonder Man. 4.00
49 KG,O:Scorpio 4.00
50 KG,Zodiac,D:Scorpio 4.00
51 KG,Moon Knight 4.00
52 KG,Hulk,V:Sub Mariner 4.00
53 KG,DC,MG,TA,C&I:Lunatik 3.00
54 MG,Nigh Fury 3.00
55 CI,O:Red Guardian 3.00
56 CI,KJ,Hellcat,V:Lunatik 3.00

57 DC,Ms.Marvel 3.00
58 Return of Dr.Strange 3.00
59 I:Belathauzer 3.00
60 V:Vera Gemini 3.00
61 Spider-Man,A:Lunatik 2.50
62 Hercules,C:Polaris 2.50
63 Mutli Heroes 2.50
64 Mutli Heroes 2.50
65 Red Guardian 2.50
66 JB,Valkyrie I 2.50
67 Valkryie II 2.50
68 HT,When Falls the Mountain . . . 2.50
69 HT,A:The Anything Man 2.50
70 HT,A:Lunatik 2.50
71 HT,O:Lunatik 2.50
72 HT,V:Lunatik 2.50
73 HT,Foolkiller,V:WizardKing 5.00
74 HT,Foolkiller,L:Nighthawk 5.00
75 HT,Foolkiller. 4.00
76 HT,O:Omega 2.00
77 HT,Moon Dragon 2.00
78 HT,Yellow Jacket 2.00
79 HT,Tunnel World 2.00
80 HT,DGr,Nighthawk 2.00
81 HT,Tunnel World 2.00
82 DP,JSt,Tunnel World 2.00
83 DP,JSt,Tunnel World 2.00
84 DP,JSt,Black Panther. 2.00
85 DP,JSt,Black Panther. 2.00
86 DP,JSt,Black Panther. 2.00
87 DP,JSt,V:Mutant Force. 2.00
88 DP,JSt,Matt Mardock 2.00
89 DP,JSt,D:Hellcat's
Mother, O:Mad-Dog 2.00
90 DP,JSt,Daredevil 2.00
91 DP,JSt,Daredevil 2.00
92 DP,JSt,A:Eternity,
Son of Satan 3.00
93 DP,JSt,Son of Satan 3.00
94 DP,JSt,I:Gargoyle 2.00
95 DP,JSt,V:Dracula,O:Gargoyle. . . 2.00
96 DP,JSt,Ghost Rider 3.00
97 DP,JSt,False Messiah 2.00
98 DP,JSt,A:Man Thing. 2.00
99 DP,JSt,Conflict. 2.00
100 DP,JSt,DoubleSize,V:Satan . . . 3.00
101 DP,JSt,Silver Surfer 2.00
102 DP,JSt,Nighthawk 2.00
103 DP,JSt,I:Null 2.00
104 DP,JSt,Devilslayer,J:Beast 2.00
105 DP,JSt,V:Satan 2.00
106 DP,Daredevil,D:Nighthawk 2.00
107 DP,JSt,Enchantress,A:D.D. . . . 2.00
108 DP,A:Enchantress 2.00
109 DP,A:Spider-Man 2.50
110 DP,A:Devilslayer 2.00
111 DP,A:Hellcat. 2.00
112 DP,A:SquadronSupreme 2.00
113 DP,A:SquadronSupreme 2.00
114 DP,A:SquadronSupreme 2.00
115 DP,A:Submariner 2.00
116 DP,Gargoyle. 2.00
117 DP,Valkyrie. 2.00
118 DP,V:Miracleman 2.00
119 DP,V:Miracleman 2.00
120 DP,V:Miracleman 2.00
121 DP,V:Miracleman 2.00
122 DP,A:Iceman 2.00
123 DP,I:Cloud,V:Secret Empire . . . 2.00
124 DP,V:Elf 2.00
125 DP,New Line-up:Gargoyle,Moon
dragon,Valkyrie,Iceman,Beast,
Angel,W:Son of Satan & Hellcat
I:Mad Dog 3.00
126 DP,A:Nick Fury 2.00
127 DP,V:Professor Power 2.00
128 DP,V:Professor Power 2.00
129 DP,V:Professor Power,New
Mutants X-over. 2.00
130 DP,V:Professor Power 2.00
131 DP,V:Walrus,A:Frogman. 2.00

Defenders #129
© Marvel Entertainment Group

132 DP,V:Spore Monster. 2.00
133 DP,V:Spore Monster. 2.00
134 DP,I:Manslaughter 2.00
135 DP,V:Blowtorch Brand 2.00
136 DP,V:Gargoyle 2.00
137 DP,V:Gargoyle 2.00
138 DP,O:Moondragon 2.00
139 DP,A:Red Wolf,V:Trolls. 2.00
140 DP,V:Asgardian Trolls 2.00
141 DP,All Flesh is Grass 2.00
142 DP,V:M.O.N.S.T.E.R. 2.00
143 DP,I:Andromeda,Runner 2.00
144 DP,V:Moondragon 2.00
145 DP,V:Moondragon 2.00
146 DP,Cloud 2.00
147 DP,A:Andromeda,I:Interloper . . 2.00
148 DP,A:Nick Fury 2.00
149 DP,V:Manslaughter,O:Cloud . . . 2.00
150 DP,O:Cloud,double-size 3.00
151 DP,A:Interloper 2.00
152 DP,Secret Wars II,D:Moon-
dragon,Valkyrie,Gargoyle 3.00
G-Size#1 GK(c),JSn,AM,O:Hulk . . 12.00
G-Size#2 GK,KJ,Son of Satan 8.00
G-Size#3 JSn,DA,JM,DN,A:D.D.. . . 6.00
G-Size#4 GK(c),DH,A:YellowJack . . 6.00
G-Size#5 K&R(c),DH,A:Guardians . 6.00
Ann.#1 SB,KJ. 6.00

DEFENDERS OF DYNATRON CITY

1992

1 FC,I:Defenders of Dynatron City
(from video game & TV ser.). . . 2.00
2 FC,O:Defender of D.City. 2.00
3 FC,A:Dr Mayhem 2.00
4 FC 2.00
5 FC,V:Intelligent Fleas 2.00
6 FC,V:Dr.Mayhem 2.00

DEFENDERS OF THE EARTH

Jan., 1987—Sept., 1984

1 AS,Flash Gordon & Mandrake . . 3.00
2 AS,Flash Gordon & Mandrake . . 2.50
3 AS,O:Phantom 2.50
4 AS,O:Mandrake 2.50

DELLA VISION

Atlas April, 1955

1 The Television Queen. 125.00
2 . . . . 75.00
3 . . . . 75.00
Becomes:

PATTY POWERS

4 . . . . 35.00
5 . . . . 22.00
6 . . . . 22.00
7 Oct., 1956 . . . . 22.00

DENNIS THE MENACE

Nov., 1981–Nov., 1982

1 . . . . 2.00
2 thru 13 . . . . @2.00

DESTROYER, THE

Nov., 1989

1 Black & White Mag. 3.50
2 thru 9 . . . . @2.25
10 June 1990 . . . . 2.25
TPB rep. B/w mag(color) 9.95

THE DESTROYER: TERROR

Dec., 1991

1 V:Nuihc 2.00
2 V:Nuihc 2.00
3 GM,V:Nuihc 2.00
4 DC,`The Last Dinosaur' 2.00

DEVIL DINOSAUR

April, 1978—Dec., 1978

1 JK,I:Devil Dinosaur,Moon Boy . 10.00
2 JK,War With the Spider God. . . . 7.00
3 JK,Giant 7.00
4 JK,Objects From the Sky 7.00
5 JK,The Kingdom of the Ants . . . 7.00
6 JK.The Fall 7.00
7 JK,Prisoner of the Demon Tree . 7.00
8 JK,V:Dino Riders 7.00
9 JK,Lizards That Stand 7.00

DEVIL DINOSAUR SPRING FLING

1997

Spec. F:Devil Dinosaur,
Moon-Boy, 48pg 3.00

DEVIL-DOG DUGAN

Atlas July, 1956

1 War Stories 90.00
2 . . . . 50.00
3 . . . . 40.00
Becomes:

TALE OF THE MARINES

4 BP,War Stories 45.00
Becomes:

MARINES AT WAR

5 War Stories 40.00
6 . . . . 40.00
7 The Big Push,August, 1957 . . . 40.00

DEXTER THE DEMON

See: MELVIN THE MONSTER

All comics prices listed are for *Near Mint* condition.

DIE-CUT
Marvel UK 1993–94
1 A:Beast . . . 2.50
2 V:X-Beast . . . 2.00
3 A:Beast,Prof.X . . . 2.00
4 V:Red Skull . . . 2.00

DIE-CUT VS. G-FORCE
Marvel UK 1993
1 SFr(s),LSh(c),I:G-Force . . . 2.75
2 SFr(s),LSh(c),Last issue . . . 2.75

DIGITEK
Marvel UK 1992–93
1 DPw,I:Digitek,C:Deathlok . . . 2.25
2 DPw,A:Deathlok,V:Bacillicons . . . 2.25
3 DPw,A:Deathlok,V:Bacillicons . . . 2.25
4 DPw,V:Bacillicons . . . 2.25

DINO RIDERS
Feb., 1989
1 Based on Toys . . . 2.00
2 . . . 2.00
3 May, 1989 . . . 2.00

DINOSAURS: A CELEBRATION
Epic 1992
Horns and Heavy Armor . . . 5.00
Bone-Heads and Duck-Bills . . . 5.00
Terrible Claws and Tyrants . . . 5.00
Egg Stealers and Earth Shakers . . . 5.00
TPB 192pg . . . 12.95

DISNEY AFTERNOON
1994–95
1 DarkwingDuck vs.FearsomeFive . 2.00
2 . . . 2.50
3 . . . 2.50
4 DarkwingDuck:Gum w/t Wind . . . 2.50
5 F:Baloo, Mrs. Cunningham . . . 2.50
6 . . . 2.50
7 F:Darkwing Duck . . . 2.50
8 . . . 2.50
9 DarkwingDuck:Borsht to Death . . 2.50
10 F:Scrooge & Mrs. Beakley . . . 2.50

Disney Afternoon #4
© Marvel Entertainment Group

DISNEY COMIC HITS
1995
1 . . . 5.00
2 F:Lion King . . . 4.00
3 F:Pocahontas . . . 4.00
4 F:Toy Story . . . 4.00
5 Holiday . . . 4.00
6 Aladdin . . . 4.00
7 . . . 4.00
8 Lion King story . . . 4.00
9 . . . 4.00
10 Hunchback of Notre Dame . . . 5.00
11 thru 13 . . . @4.00
14 F:Toy Story characters . . . 4.00
15 101 Dalmations . . . 4.00
16 101 Dalmatians . . . 4.00
17 final issue . . . 4.00

DISNEY PRESENTS
1 F:Aladdin . . . 2.50
2 F:Timon & Pummba . . . 2.50
3 . . . 2.50

DOC SAMSON
1996
1 From The Incredible Hulk . . . 2.00
2 A:She-Hulk . . . 2.00
3 . . . 2.00
4 . . . 2.00

DOC SAVAGE
Oct., 1972
1 JM,Pulp Adapts,Death Eighty Stories High . . . 15.00
2 JSo(c),The Feathered Serpent Strikes . . . 10.00
3 JSo(c),Silver Death's Head . . . 10.00
4 JSo(c),The Hell Diver . . . 9.00
5 GK(c),Night of the Monsters . . . 9.00
6 JSo(c),Where Giants Walk . . . 9.00
7 JSo(c),Brand of the Werewolfs . . 9.00
8 In the Lair of the Werewolf Jan., 1974 . . . 9.00
G-Size#1 thru #2 Reprints . . . 8.00

DOC SAVAGE
August, 1975
(Black & White Magazine)
1 JB,Ph(c),Ron Ely . . . 9.00
2 JB . . . 6.00
3 JB . . . 6.00
4 . . . 6.00
5 thru 7 . . . @6.00
8 Spring 1977 . . . 6.00

DR. STRANGE
[1st Series] June, 1968
Prev: Strange Tales

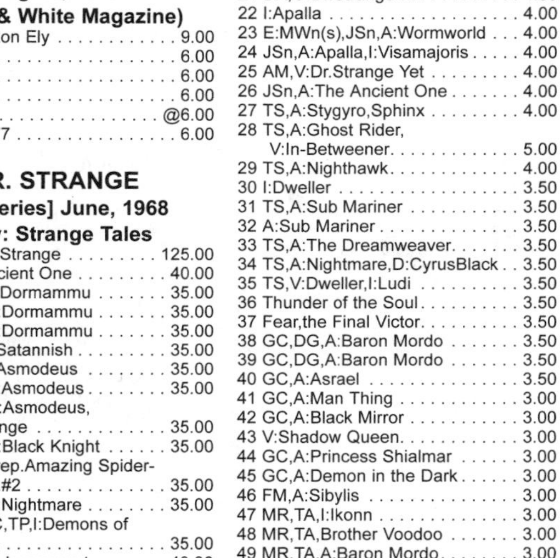

169 DA,O:Dr.Strange . . . 125.00
170 DA,A:Ancient One . . . 40.00
171 TP,DA,V:Dormammu . . . 35.00
172 GC,TP,V:Dormammu . . . 35.00
173 GC,TP,V:Dormammu . . . 35.00
174 GC,TP,I:Satannish . . . 35.00
175 GC,TP,I:Asmodeus . . . 35.00
176 GC,TP,V:Asmodeus . . . 35.00
177 GC,TP,D:Asmodeus, N:Dr.Strange . . . 35.00
178 GC,TP,A:Black Knight . . . 35.00
179 BWS(c),rep.Amazing Spider-Man Ann.#2 . . . 35.00
180 GC,TP,V:Nightmare . . . 35.00
181 FB(c),GC,TP,I:Demons of Despair . . . 35.00
182 GC,TP,V:Juggernaut . . . 40.00
183 BEv(c),GC,TP,

Doctor Strange, 2nd Series, #34
© Marvel Entertainment Group

I:Undying Ones . . . 40.00

[2nd Regular Series] 1974–87
1 FB,DG,I:Silver Dagger . . . 35.00
2 FB,DG,I:Soul Eater . . . 15.00
3 FB,A:Dormammu . . . 9.00
4 FB,DG,V:Death . . . 9.00
5 FB,DG,A:Silver Dagger . . . 9.00
6 FB(c),GC,KJ,A:Umar,I:Gaea . . . 6.00
7 GC,JR,A:Dormammu . . . 6.00
8 GK(c),GC,TP,O:Clea . . . 6.00
9 GK(c),GC,A:Dormammu,O:Clea . 6.00
10 B:MWn(s),GK(c),GC,A:Eternity . 6.00
11 JR(c),GC,TP,A:Eternity . . . 4.50
12 GC,TP,A:Eternity . . . 4.50
13 GC,TP,A:Eternity . . . 4.50
14 GC,TP,A:Dracula . . . 4.50
15 GC,TP,A:Devil . . . 4.50
16 GC,TP,A:Devil . . . 4.50
17 GC,TP,A:Styggro . . . 4.50
18 GC,A:Styggro . . . 4.50
19 GC,AA,I:Xander . . . 4.50
20 A:Xander . . . 4.50
21 DA,O:Dr.Strange . . . 4.00
22 I:Apalla . . . 4.00
23 E:MWn(s),JSn,A:Wormworld . . . 4.00
24 JSn,A:Apalla,I:Visamajoris . . . 4.00
25 AM,V:Dr.Strange Yet . . . 4.00
26 JSn,A:The Ancient One . . . 4.00
27 TS,A:Stygyro,Sphinx . . . 4.00
28 TS,A:Ghost Rider, V:In-Betweener . . . 5.00
29 TS,A:Nighthawk . . . 4.00
30 I:Dweller . . . 3.50
31 TS,A:Sub Mariner . . . 3.50
32 A:Sub Mariner . . . 3.50
33 TS,A:The Dreamweaver . . . 3.50
34 TS,A:Nightmare,D:CyrusBlack . . 3.50
35 TS,V:Dweller,I:Ludi . . . 3.50
36 Thunder of the Soul . . . 3.50
37 Fear,the Final Victor . . . 3.50
38 GC,DG,A:Baron Mordo . . . 3.50
39 GC,DG,A:Baron Mordo . . . 3.50
40 GC,A:Asrael . . . 3.50
41 GC,A:Man Thing . . . 3.00
42 GC,A:Black Mirror . . . 3.00
43 V:Shadow Queen . . . 3.00
44 GC,A:Princess Shialmar . . . 3.00
45 GC,A:Demon in the Dark . . . 3.00
46 FM,A:Sibylis . . . 3.00
47 MR,TA,I:Ikonn . . . 3.00
48 MR,TA,Brother Voodoo . . . 3.00
49 MR,TA,A:Baron Mordo . . . 3.00
50 MR,TA,A:Baron Mordo . . . 3.00

MARVEL

51 MR,TA,A:Sgt. Fury,
V:Baron Mordo . . . 3.00
52 MR,TA,A:Nightmare . . . 2.50
53 MR,TA,A:Nightmare,Fantastic
Four,V:Rama-Tut . . . 2.50
54 PS,V:Tiboro . . . 2.50
55 MGo,TA,V:Madness . . . 2.50
56 PS,TA,O:Dr.Strange . . . 4.00
57 KN,TA,A:Dr.Doom . . . 2.50
58 DGr,TA,V:Dracula . . . 2.50
59 DGr,TA,V:Dracula . . . 3.50
60 DGr,TA,Scarlet Witch . . . 3.50
61 DGr,TA,V:Dracula . . . 3.50
62 SL,V:Dracula . . . 3.50
63 CP,V:Topaz . . . 2.50
64 TSa,`Art Rage' . . . 2.50
65 PS,Charlatan . . . 2.50
66 PS,`The Cosen One' . . . 2.50
67 SL,A:Jessica Drew,Shroud . . . 2.50
68 PS,A:Black Knight . . . 2.25
69 PS,A:Black Knight . . . 2.25
70 BBl,V:Umar . . . 2.25
71 DGr,O:Dormammu . . . 2.25
72 PS,V:Umar . . . 2.25
73 PS,V:Umar . . . 2.25
74 MBg,Secret Wars II . . . 2.25
75 A:Fantastic Four . . . 2.25
76 A:Fantastic Four . . . 2.25
77 A:Topaz . . . 2.25
78 A:Cloak,I:Ecstacy . . . 3.00
79 A:Morganna . . . 2.00
80 A:Morganna,C:Rintah . . . 2.00
81 V:Urthona,I:Rintah . . . 2.00
Ann.#1 CR,`Doomworld' . . . 4.50
G-Size#1 K&R(c),reps Strange
Tales#164-#168 . . . 6.00
GN Dr.Strange: What is it that
Distrubs you, Stephen?, CR,
revised from Dr.Strange Ann.#1,
48pg bookshelf (Aug. 1997) . . . 6.00

[3rd Regular Series] 1988–96

1 V:Dorammu . . . 4.00
2 V:Dorammu . . . 3.00
3 I:Dragon Force . . . 3.00
4 EL(c),A:Dragon Force . . . 3.00
5 JG,V:Baron Mordo . . . 3.50
6 JG,I:Mephista . . . 3.00
7 JG,V:Agamotto,Mephisto . . . 3.00
8 JG,V:Mephisto & Satanish . . . 3.00
9 JG,O:Dr.Strange . . . 3.00
10 JG,V:Morbius . . . 3.50
11 JG,A of V,V:Hobgoblin,
C:Morbius . . . 4.00
12 JG,A of V,V:Enchantress . . . 2.75
13 JG,A of V,V:Arkon . . . 2.75
14 JG,B:Vampiric Verses,
A:Morbius . . . 3.50
15 JG,A:Morbius,Amy Grant(C) . . . 5.00
16 JG,A:Morbius,Brother Voodoo . . . 3.50
17 JV,TD,A:Morbius,Br.Voodoo . . . 3.50
18 JG,E:Vampiric Verses,A:Morbius,
Brother Voodoo,R:Varnae . . . 3.50
19 GC,A:Azrael . . . 2.50
20 JG,TD,A:Morbius,V:Zom . . . 3.50
21 JG,TD,B:Dark Wars,
R:Dormammu . . . 2.50
22 JG,TD,LW,V:Dormammu . . . 2.50
23 JG,LW,V:Dormammu . . . 2.50
24 JG,E:Dark Wars,V:Dormammu . . . 2.50
25 RLm,A:Red Wolf, Black Crow . . . 2.50
26 GI,V:Werewolf By Night . . . 2.50
27 GI,V:Werewolf By Night . . . 2.50
28 X-over Ghost Rider #12,
V:Zodiac . . . 3.00
29 A:Baron Blood . . . 2.50
30 Topaz' Fate . . . 2.50
31 TD,Inf.Gauntlet,A:Silver Surfer . . . 3.00
32 Inf.Gauntlet,A:Warlock,Silver
Surfer,V:Silver Dagger . . . 2.50
33 Inf.Gauntlet,V:Thanos,
Zota,A:Pip . . . 2.50
34 Inf.Gauntlet,V:Dr.Doom,
A:Pip,Scartlet Witch . . . 2.50
35 Inf.Gauntlet,A:Thor,Pip,
Scarlet Witch . . . 2.50
36 Inf.Gauntlet,A:Warlock(leads
into Warlock&Inf.Watch#1) . . . 3.00
37 GI,V:Frankensurfer . . . 2.00
38 GI,Great Fear #1 . . . 2.00
39 GI,Great Fear #2 . . . 2.00
40 GI,Great Fear #3,A:Daredevil . . . 2.00
41 GI,A:Wolverine . . . 3.00
42 GI,Infinity War,V:Galactus,A:
Silver Surfer . . . 2.25
43 GI,Infinity War,Galactus Vs.
Agamotto,A:Silver Surfer . . . 2.00
44 GI,Infinity War,V:Juggernaut . . . 2.00
45 GI,Inf.War,O:Doctor Strange . . . 2.00
46 GI,Inf.War,R:old costume . . . 2.00
47 GI,Inf.War,V:doppleganger . . . 2.00
48 GI,V:The Vishanti . . . 2.00
49 GI,R:Dormammu . . . 2.00
50 GI,A:Hulk,Ghost Rider,Silver
Surfer,V:Dormammu(leads into
Secret Defenders)holo-grafx(c) . 3.50
51 GI,V:Religious Cult . . . 2.00
52 GI,A:Morbius . . . 2.00
53 GI,Closes Mansion,L:Wong . . . 2.00
54 GI,Infinity Crusade . . . 2.00
55 GI,Inf.Crusade . . . 2.00
56 GI,Inf.Crusade . . . 2.00
57 A:Kyllian,Urthona . . . 2.00
58 V:Urthona . . . 2.00
59 GI,V:Iskelior . . . 2.00
60 B:DQ(s),Siege of
Darkness,pt.#7 . . . 4.00
61 Siege of Darkness,pt.#15 . . . 3.25
62 V:Dr.Doom . . . 2.25
63 JJ(c),V:Morbius . . . 2.00
64 MvR,V:Namor . . . 2.00
65 MvR,V:Namor,Vengeance . . . 2.25
66 A:Wong . . . 2.25
67 R:Clea . . . 2.25
68 MvR . . . 2.00
69 MvR . . . 2.00
70 A:Hulk . . . 2.00
71 V:Hulk . . . 2.00
72 Metallic(c),Last Rites,pt.1 . . . 2.00
73 Last Rites,pt.2 . . . 2.00
74 SY,DQ,Last Rites,pt.3 . . . 2.00
75 Prismatic cover . . . 4.00
76 I:New Costume . . . 2.00
77 Mob Clean-up . . . 2.00
78 R:Chton . . . 2.00
79 Doc's new Asylum . . . 2.00
80 Missing for four months? . . . 2.00
81 A:Nick Fury . . . 2.00
82 A:Hellstorm . . . 2.00
83 V:Tempo Mob,Dormammu . . . 2.00
84 The Homecoming,pt.1 . . . 2.00
85 The Homecoming,pt.2 . . . 2.00
86 The Homecoming,pt.3 . . . 2.00
87 The Homecoming,pt.4 . . . 2.00
88 The Fall of the Tempo,pt.1 . . . 2.00
89 The Fall of the Tempo,pt.2 . . . 2.00
90 final issue . . . 2.00
Ann #2 Return of Defenders,Pt4 . . . 5.00
Ann #3 GI,I:Killiam,w/card . . . 3.25
Ann.#4 V:Salome . . . 3.00
Spec. Dr. Strange/Ghost Rider#1
Newsstand vers. of Dr.
Strange #28 (1991) . . . 6.00
Spec.#1 Dr. Strange vs. Dracula
rep. MWn(s),GC (1994) . . . 2.00
GNv Triumph and Torment MBg,
F:Dr. Strange & Dr.Doom . . . 9.95
HC . . . 14.95
Ashcan 75

DOCTOR STRANGE

Dec., 1998

1 (of 4) TyH,killer pursued . . . 3.00
2 TyH,secrets in Topaz . . . 3.00
3 TyH,magic in Manhattan . . . 3.00
4 TyH,PC,conclusion . . . 3.00

DR. STRANGE CLASSICS

March, 1984

1 SD,Reprints . . . 2.00
2 . . . 2.00
3 . . . 2.00
4 June, 1984 . . . 2.00

Doctor Who #20
© Marvel Entertainment Group

DOCTOR WHO

1984–86

1 BBC TV Series,UK reprints,
Return of the Daleks . . . 4.50
2 Star Beast . . . 3.00
3 Transformation . . . 3.00
4 A:K-9,Daleks . . . 3.00
5 V:Time Witch,Colin Baker
interview . . . 3.00
6 B:Ancient Claw saga . . . 3.00
7 . . . 3.00
8 The Collector . . . 3.00
9 The Life Bringer . . . 3.00
10 This is your Life . . . 3.00
11 The Deal . . . 3.00
12 End of the Line . . . 3.00
13 V:The Cybermen . . . 3.00
14 Clash of the Neutron Knight . . . 3.00
15 B:Peter Davison-Dr. Who . . . 3.00
16 Into the Realm of Satan, . . . 3.00
17 Peter Davison Interview . . . 3.00
18 A:Four Dr.Who's . . . 3.00
19 A:The Sontarans . . . 3.00
20 The Stockbridge Horror . . . 3.00
21 The Stockbridge Horror . . . 3.00
22 The Stockbridge Horror . . . 3.00
23 The Unearthly Child . . . 3.00

DR. ZERO

Epic April, 1988

1 BSz,DCw,I:Dr.Zero . . . 2.50
2 BSz,DCw . . . 2.00
3 BSz,DCw . . . 2.00
4 thru 6 . . . @2.00
7 DSp . . . 2.00
8 End series, August, 1989 . . . 2.00

DOLLY DILL

1945

1 Newsstand 80.00

DOMINATION FACTOR

Sept., 1999

1.1 Fantastic Four (of 4) DJu, JOy,BMc,x-over 2.50
1.2 Avengers, DJu,JO, DJa, x-over 2.50
2.3 Fantastic Four, DJu,BMc. 2.50
2.4 Avengers, DJu,JOy,DJa 2.50
3.5 Fantastic Four, DJu,BMc. 2.50
3.6 Avengers, JOy,DJa 2.50
4.7 Fantastic Four, DJu,BMc. 2.50
4.8 Avengers, DJa,JOy,concl 2.50

DOMINO

1996

1 thru 3 . . . . @2.00

DOOM 2099

1993–96

1 PB,I:Doom 2099,V:Tiger Wylde, foil(c) 3.00
2 I:Rook Seven 2.00
3 PB,V:Tiger Wylde 2.00
4 PB,V:Tiger Wylde 2.00
5 PB,I:Fever 2.00
6 I:Duke Stratosphear 2.00
7 PB,I:Paloma,V:Duke,Fever Haze 2.00
8 PB,C:Ravage 2.00
9 EC,V:Jack the Ripper 2.00
10 PB,w/Poster. 2.00
11 PB,I:Thandaza. 2.00
12 PB,V:Thandaza. 2.00
13 PB(c),JFm(s),V:Necrotek 2.00
14 RLm(c),PB,Fall o/t Hammer#4 . . 2.00
15 PB,I:Radian. 2.00
16 EC(a&s), ... 2.00
17 PB,V:Radian,w/card. 2.00
18 PB, ... 2.00
19 PB,C:Bloodhawk 2.00
20 PB,A:Bloodhawk 2.00
21 PB,Shadow King 2.00
22 PB,R:Duke Stratosphere 2.00
23 PB,R:Tyger Wylde 2.00
24 PB. 2.00
25 PB. 2.50
25a foil cover 3.25

Doom 2099 #25
© Marvel Entertainment Group

26 . . . . 2.00
27 Revolution 2.00
28 Prologue to D-Day. 2.00
Becomes:

DOOM 2099 A.D.

29 Doom Invades America 2.25
29a Chromium Cover 4.00
30 D:Corporate Head 2.25
31 PB,One Nation Under Doom . . . 2.25
32 Ravage Aftermath 2.25
33 . . . . 2.25
34 I:Anthony Herod. 2.25
35 E:One Nation Under Doom 2.25
36 . . . . 2.25
37 . . . . 2.25
38 . . . . 2.25
39 . . . . 2.25
40 Rage Against Time,pt.1 . . . . 2.25
41 Rage Against Time,pt.2 . . . . 2.25
TPB Villainy of Doctor Doom. 17.95

DOOM

Aug., 2000

1 (of 3) CDi,F:Dr.Doom 3.00
2 CDi,Al Khalad. 3.00
3 CDi,concl.. . . . . 3.00

DOPEY DUCK COMICS

Timely Fall, 1945

1 A:Casper Cat,Krazy Krow . . . 125.00
2 A:Casper Cat,Krazy Krow . . . 100.00
Becomes:

WACKY DUCK

3 Paperchase(c) 80.00
4 Wacky Duck(c) 110.00
5 Duck & Devil(c) 65.00
6 Cliffhanger(c) 65.00
1 Baketball(c) 50.00
2 Traffic Light(c). 50.00
Becomes:

JUSTICE COMICS

DOUBLE DRAGON

July, 1991

1 I:Billy&Jimmy Lee. 2.00
2 Dragon Statue Stolen,V:Stelth . . 2.00
3 Billy Vs. Jimmy. 2.00
4 Dragon Force out of control 2.00
5 V:Stealth 2.00
6 V:Nightfall, final issue 2.00

DOUBLE EDGE

1995

Alpha Punisher vs. Nick Fury 5.00
Omega D:Major Character 5.00

D.P. 7

Nov., 1986

1 O:DP7 . . . . 2.00
2 V:Headhunter 2.00
3 RT,Headhunters 2.00
4 RT,V:Wompus. 2.00
5 RT,Exorcist. 2.00
6 RT,I:The Sweat Shop 2.00
7 RT,V:Clinic 2.00
8 RT,V:Clinic 2.00
9 RT,AW,I:New Paranormals 2.00
10 RT,I:Mysterious People 2.00
11 AW(i)V:Regulator 2.00
12 O:Randy 2.00
13 O:Charly 2.00
14 AW 2.00
15 . . . . 2.00
16 V:BlackPower 2.00
17 . . . . 2.00

D.P. 7 #1
© Marvel Entertainment Group

18 Pitt tie-in 2.00
19 . . . . 2.00
20 Spitfire. 2.00
21 . . . . 2.00
22 . . . . 2.00
23 A:PsiForce. 2.00
24 A:Mastodon 2.00
25 V:Famileech 2.00
26 V:Famileech 2.00
27 The Pitt 2.00
28 V:The Candidate 2.00
29 Deadweight 2.00
30 V:Para-troop 2.00
31 A:Chrome 2.00
32 I:The Cure,last issue, June 1989 . . . . 2.00
Ann.#1,I:Witness 2.00

DRACULA LIVES

B&W Magazine, 1973—75

1 GC 45.00
2 NA,GC,JSn,O:Dracula 35.00
3 NA,JB, ... 30.00
4 MP 22.00
5 GC 22.00
6 JB,GC 22.00
7 GE 22.00
8 GC 22.00
9 AA,RG 22.00
10 . . . . 27.00
11 thru 13 . . . . @22.00

DRACULA: LORD OF THE UNDEAD

Oct., 1998

1 (of 3) PO,TP,R:Dracula 3.00
2 PO,TP,V:Seward. 3.00
3 PO,TP,conclusion 3.00

DRAFT, THE

1988

1 Sequel to The Pit 3.75

DRAGON LINES

Epic *Heavy Hitters* 1993

[1st Limited Series]

1 RLm,V:Terrorist on Moon, Embossed(c) 3.00
2 RLm,V:Kuei Emperor 2.25

3 RLm,V:Spirit Boxer 2.25
4 RLm,K:Kuei Emperor 2.25

[Regular Series]

1 B:PQ(s),RLm,I:Tao 2.50
2 RLm, ... 2.50

DRAGONSLAYER

Oct.–Nov., 1981

1 Movie adapt.. . . . . 2.50
2 Movie adapt.. . . . . 2.50

DRAGON STRIKE

1 Based on TSR Game 2.00

DRAGON'S TEETH/ DRAGON'S CLAWS

July, 1988

1 GSr,I:Mercy Dragon,
Scavenger,Digit Steel 2.00
2 GSr,V:Evil Dead 2.00
3 GSr,Go Home. 2.00
4 GSr 2.00
5 GSr,I:Death's Head. 18.00
6 thru 10 GSr. . . . . @2.00

DREADLANDS

Epic

@WP Listing: 1 Post-Apocalyptic Mini-series 4.00
2 Trapped in Prehistoric Past. 4.00
3 V:Alien Time Travelers 4.00
4 Final Issue 4.00

DREADSTAR

Epic Nov., 1982

1 JSn,I:Lord Papal. 4.00
2 JSn,O:Willow 2.50
3 JSn,V:Lord Papal 2.25
4 JSn,I:Z 2.25
5 JSn,V:Teutun 2.25
6 JSn,BWr,Interstellar Toybox 2.25
7 JSn,BWr,V:Dr.Mezlo 2.25
8 JSn,V:Z 2.25
9 JSn,V:Z 2.25
10 JSn,V:Z 2.25
11 JSn,O:Lord Papal 2.00
12 JSn,I:Dr.Delphi. 2.00
13 JSn,V:Infra Red & Ultra Violet . . 2.00
14 JSn,V:Lord Papal. 2.00
15 JSn,new powers 2.00
16 JSn,V:Lord Papal. 2.00
17 JSn,V:Willows father 2.00
18 JSn,V:Dr.Mezlo 2.00
19 JSn,V:Dr Mezlo 2.00
20 JSn,D:Oedi 2.00
21 JSn,D:Dr.Delphi 2.00
22 JSn,V:Lord Papal. 2.00
23 JSn,V:Lord Papal. 2.00
24 JSn,JS,V:Lord Papal 2.00
25 JSn,V:Lord Papal. 2.00
26 JSn,R:Oedi 2.00
Ann.#1 JSn,The Price. 2.50

See COLOR COMICS section

DREADSTAR & COMPANY

July, 1985

1 JSo,reprint 2.00
2 JSo,rep. 2.00
3 JSo,rep. 2.00
4 JSo,rep. 2.00
5 JSo,rep,Dec., 1985. . . . . 2.00

DROIDS

Star April, 1986

1 JR 3.00
2 AW. 3.00
3 JR/AW 3.00
4 AW. 3.00
5 AW. 3.00
6 EC/AW,A:Luke Skywalker. 3.00
7 EC/AW,A:Luke Skywalker. 3.00
8 EC/AW,A:Luke Skywalker. 3.00

DRUID

1995

1 R:Dr. Druid Surprise!!!. 2.50
2 F:Nekra 2.25
3 deranged canibal wisemen 2.25
4 Why Must He Die? 2.25

DUNE

April–June, 1985

1 Movie Adapt,Rep. Marvel
Super Spec,BSz. 2.00
2 Movie Adapt,BSz 2.00
3 Movie Adapt,BSz, ... 2.00

DYNOMUTT

Nov., 1977

1 Based on TV series 10.00
2 thru 5 . . . . @8.00
6 Sept., 1978 . . . . 8.00

EARTHWORM JIM

1995–96

1 I:Earthworm Jim 2.25
2 Cow tipping 2.25
3 V:Lawyers,conclusion 2.25

EARTH X

Jan., 1999

0 (of 14) AxR,JPL,Machine Man
& Watcher 4.00
0a signed 30.00
1 AxR,JPL,V:Inhumans,32-page . . 3.00
1a signed 30.00
2 AxR,JPL,fate of Fant.Four 3.00
3 AxR,JPL,World Super Powers . . 3.00
4 JPL,AxR(c),A:new Hulk. 3.00
5 JPL,AxR(c),V:Doombots 3.00

Ectokid #4
© Marvel Entertainment Group

6 JPL,AxR(c),different X-Men 3.00
7 JPL,AxR(c),A:Hulk 3.00
8 JPL,AxR(c),A:Venom 3.00
9 JPL,AxR(c),Revelations 3.00
10 JPL,AxR(c) 3.00
11 JPL,AxR(c),V:Skull. 3.00
12 JPL,AxR(c),concl 3.00
Spec.X AxR(c) concl.,48-pg 4.00
Sketchbook 4.00

ECTOKID

Razorline 1993–94

1 I:Dex Mungo,BU:Hokum & Hex. . 2.75
2 O:Dex. 2.00
3 I:Ectosphere. 2.00
4 I:Brothers Augustine 2.00
5 A:Saint Sinner 2.00
6 Highway 61 Revisited. 2.00
7 . . . . 2.00
8 V:Ice Augustine 2.00
9 Love is like a Bullet. 2.00
10 . . . . 2.00
Ectokid Unleashed 2.95

ELECTRIC UNDERTOW

Dec., 1989

1 MBa,Strike Force 4.00
2 MBa, Will Deguchis 4.00
3 MBa, Alien Invaders 4.00
4 MBa,Attack on Beijing 4.00
5 MBa, Morituri defeated,March,
1990 . . . . 4.00

ELEKTRA

Nov., 1996

1 PrM,MD2,. 3.00
1A variant (c). 4.00
2 PrM,MD2,V:Bullseye, round two . 2.00
3 PrM,MD2,. 2.00
4 PrM,MD2 . . . . 2.00
5 PrM,MD2,. 2.00
6 PrM,MD2 . . . . 2.00
7 PrM,MD2,A:Konrad,The
Architect. 2.00
8 PrM,MD2,V:The Architect 2.00
9 PrM,MD2,V:The Four Winds 2.00
10 PrM,MD2,V:Daredevil,"American
Samurai," pt.1 . . . . 2.00
11 PrM,MD2,F:Daredevil. 2.00
12 PrM,MD2,F:Daredevil,V:American
Samuri 2.00
13 PrM,MD2,F:Daredevil, concl. . . . 2.00
14 LHa,MD2,A:Wolverine 2.00
15 LHa,MD2,A:Silver Samurai 2.00
16 LHa,MD2,A Hole in the Soul . . . 2.00
17 LHa,MD2,V:The Hand 2.00
18 LHa,MD2,A:Shang-Chi&Kingpin. 2.00
19 LHa,MD2,last issue 2.00
Minus 1 Spec.,PMg,MD2,flashback. 2.00

ELEKTRA: ASSASSIN

August, 1986

1 FM,BSz,V:Shield 6.00
2 FM,BSz,I:Garrett. 5.00
3 FM,BSz,V:Shield,A:Garrett 5.00
4 FM,BSz,V:Shield,A:Garrett 5.00
5 FM,BSz,I:Chastity,A:Garrett 5.00
6 FM,BSz,A:Nick Fury,Garrett 5.00
7 FM,BSz,V:Ken Wind,A:Garrett . . 5.00
8 FM,BSz,V:Ken Wind,A:Garrett . . 6.00
TPB Rep #1-8 . . . . 13.00

ELEKTRA LIVES AGAIN

Graphic Novel FM,R:Elektra,A:Matt
Murdock,V:The Hand 30.00
TPB FM, rep. of HC, 80pg. 7.00

 All comics prices listed are for *Near Mint* condition.

ELEKTRA: ROOT OF EVIL

1 V:Snakeroot 3.00
2 V:Snakeroot 3.00
3 Elektra's Brother. 3.00
4 V:The Hand 3.00

ELEKTRA: SAGA

Feb., 1984

1 FM,rep.Daredevil 7.00
2 FM,rep.Daredevil 7.00
3 FM,rep.Daredevil 7.00
4 FM,rep.Daredevil 7.00
TPB Reprints#1-#4 . . . . 17.00
GN Book One FM,KJ, rep. fr00 Daredevil, 96pg 3.95
GN Book Two FM,KJ, rep. from Daredevil, 96pg 3.95

ELEKTRA/WITCHBLADE

1-shot "Devil's Reign," pt.6, x-over. 3.00

Elfquest #1
© Marvel Entertainment Group

ELFQUEST

August, 1985

1 WP,reprints. 4.00
2 WP. 2.50
3 WP. 2.50
4 WP. 2.50
5 WP. 2.50
6 WP,Young Cutter V:Mad Coil . . . 2.50
7 WP,Young Cutter V:Mad Coil . . . 2.25
8 WP. 2.25
9 WP. 2.25
10 WP,A:Cutter, Skywise 2.25
11 WP,I:Two Edge 2.25
12 WP,The Mysterious Forest 2.25
13 WP,The Forest, A:Leetah 2.25
14 WP,A:The Bone Woman 2.25
15 WP,The Forest, continued 2.25
16 WP,Forbidden Grove 2.00
17 WP,Blue Mountain 2.00
18 WP,Secrets 2.00
19 WP,Twisted Gifts 2.00
20 WP,Twisted Gifts 2.00
21 WP 2.00
22 WP,A:Winnowill 2.00
23 WP,Blue Mountain,A:Winnowill. . 2.00
24 WP,The Quest Usurped 2.00
25 WP,Northern Wastelands 2.00
26 WP,Rayeks Story. 2.00
27 WP,Battle Preparations 2.00
28 WP,Elves vs. Trolls 2.00
29 WP,Battle Beneath Blue Mountain 2.00
30 and 31 WP. . . . . @2.00
32 WP,Conclusion, March 1988 . . . 2.00

ELSEWHERE PRINCE

Epic May–Oct., 1990

1 thru 6 . . . . @2.00

ELVIRA

Oct., 1988

Spec.B&W, Movie Adapt. 2.00

EPIC

1992

1 Wildcards,Hellraiser 5.00
2 Nightbreed,Wildcards 5.00
3 DBw,MFm,Alien Legion, ... 5.00
4 Stalkers,Metropol,Wildcards 5.00

EPIC GRAPHIC NOVEL

Moebius 1: Upon a Star 10.00
Moebius 2: Arzach 10.00
Moebius 3: Airtight Garage 10.00
Moebius 4: Long Tomorrow. 10.00
Moebius 5: 10.00
Moebius 6: Pharadonesia 10.00
Last of Dragons 7.00
The Incal 1 Moebius 11.00
The Incal 2 Moebius 11.00
The Incal 3 Moebius 11.00
JBo,Someplace Strange 7.00
MZ,Punisher. 16.95

EPIC ILLUSTRATED

Spring, 1980

1 Black and White/Color Mag. . . . 6.00
2 thru 10 . . . . @4.50
11 thru 15 . . . . @3.50
16 . . . . 4.00
17 thru 20 . . . . @3.00
21 thru 25 . . . . @3.00
26 thru 34, March, 1986 . . . . @5.50

EPIC LITE

Epic Nov., 1991

One-shot short stories 4.00

ESSENTIAL SPIDER-MAN

1997

Vol. 1 StL,SD, rep. Amaz. Fant. #15, Amaz Sp.-M #1–#20, Ann. #1. 13.00
Vol. 2 StL,SD, rep. Amaz. Sp.-M #21–#43, Ann.#2 . . . . 13.00
Vol. 3 StL,JR,Lizard,Vulture, Kraven 13.00

ESSENTIAL WOLVERINE

May, 1998

Vol 3 TPB. 13.00

ESSENTIAL X-MEN

Vol. 2 rep. Uncanny X-Men #120-#145. . . . . 15.00
Vol. 3 rep. Uncanny X-Men #145-#161, Annuals #3-#5 . . . . 15.00

ETERNALS

[1st Series] July, 1976

1 JK,I:Ikaris,25 cent edition 6.00
2 JK,I:Ajak,25 cent edition 5.00

Eternals #6
© Marvel Entertainment Group

3 JK,I:Sersi 5.00
4 JK,Night of the Demons 4.00
5 JK,I:Makarri,Zuras Thena,Domo . 4.00
6 JK,Gods & Men at City College. . 4.00
7 JK,V:Celestials 4.00
8 JK,I:Karkas, Reject 4.00
9 JK,I:Sprite,Reject vs. Karkas. . . . 4.00
10 JK,V:Celestials 4.00
11 JK,I:Kingo Sunen 4.00
12 JK,I:Uni-Mind. 4.00
13 JK,I:FOrgottenOne(Gilgamesh) . 4.00
14 JK,V:Hulk 4.00
15 JK,V:Hulk 4.00
16 JK,I:Dromedan. 4.00
17 JK,I:Sigmar 4.00
18 JK,I:Nerve Beast 4.00
19 JK,Secret o/t Pyramid 4.00
Ann.#1 JK,V:Timekillers 3.00

[2nd Series] Oct., 1985

1 SB,I:Cybele 2.00
2 SB,V:Deviants 2.00
3 SB,V:Deviants 2.00
4 SB,V:Deviants 2.00
5 SB,V:Deviants 2.00
6 SB,V:Deviants 2.00
7 SB,V:Deviants 2.00
8 WS,SB,V:Deviants 2.00
9 WS,SB,V:Deviants 2.00
10 WS,SB,V:Deviants. 2.00
11 WS,KP,V:Deviants 2.00
12 WS,KP,V:Deviants 2.00

ETERNALS: HEROD FACTOR

Nov., 1991

1 MT/BMc,A:Sersi (giant size) 2.50

EVERYMAN

Epic 1991

1-shot Supernatural Story (Animated Cel Artwork) 4.50

EWOKS

Star June, 1985—Sept., 1987

1 Based on TV Series 3.00
2 . . . . 2.50
3 . . . . 2.50
4 A:Foonars 2.50
5 Wicket vs. Ice Demon. 2.50
6 Mount Sorrow, A:Teebo 2.50

MARVEL

7 A:Logray,V:Morag 2.50
8 . . . . 2.50
9 Lost in Time 2.50
10 Lost in Time. 2.00
11 Kneesaa Shrunk,A:Fleebogs . . . 2.00
12 . . . . 2.00
13 . . . . 2.00
14 Teebo- King for a Day 2.00
15 . . . . 2.00

EXCALIBUR

April, 1988

1 AD,Special,O:Excalibur, V:Technet. 5.00
1a 2nd Printing 2.50
1b 3rd Printing. 2.00
2 AAd,Mojo Mayhem,A:X-Babies . . 2.50
3 Air Apparent Spec.RLm,KJ,JG,TP, RL,EL,JRu,A:Coldblood 3.00

[Regular Series]

1 B:CCl(s),AD,V:Warwolves, I:Widget 5.00
2 AD,V:Warwolves,I:Kylun 4.00
3 AD,V:Juggernaut 3.50
4 AD,V:Arcade,Crazy Gang 3.00
5 AD,V:Arcade. 3.00
6 AD,Inferno,I:Alistaire Stuart. 3.00
7 AD,Inferno 3.00
8 RLm,JRu,A:New Mutants 3.00
9 AD,I:Nazi-Excalibur. 3.00
10 MR,V:Nazi-Excalibur 3.00
11 MR,V:Nazi-Excalibur 3.00
12 AD,Fairy Tale Dimension 3.00
13 AD,The Prince,N:Capt.Britian. . . 3.00
14 AD,Too Many Heroes. 2.50
15 AD,I:US James Braddock 2.50
16 AD,V:Anjulie 2.50
17 AD,C:Prof.X,Starjammers 2.50
18 DJ,DA,V:Jamie Braddock. 2.50
19 RL,TA,AM,V:Jamie Braddock . . . 2.50
20 RLm,JRu,V:Demon Druid. 2.50
21 I:Crusader X 2.50
22 V:Crusader X. 2.50
23 AD,V:Magik 2.50
24 AD,Return Home,C:Galactus . . . 2.50
25 E:CCl(s),AM,A:Galactus,Death, Watcher 2.50
26 RLm,JRu,V:Mastermind 2.50
27 BWS,BSz,A:Nth Man 3.00
28 BBl,Night at Bar. 2.50
29 JRu,V:Nightmare,A:PowerPack . 2.50
30 DR,AM,A:Doctor Strange 2.50
31 DR,AM,V:Son of Krakoa 2.50
32 V:Mesmero 2.50
33 V:Mesmero 2.50
34 V:Mesmero 2.50
35 AM,Missing Child. 2.50
36 AM,V:Silv.Sable,Sandman 2.50
37 A:Avengers W.C.,Dr.Doom. 2.50
38 A:Avengers W.C.,Dr.Doom. 2.50
39 A:Avengers W.C.,Dr.Doom. 2.50
40 O:Excalibur,Trial-Lockheed 2.50
41 V:Warwolves,C:Cable 3.00
42 AD,Team Broken Up 3.50
43 AD,Nightcrawler,V:Capt.Brit 3.00
44 AD,Capt.Britain On Trial. 3.00
45 AD,I:N-Men,. 3.00
46 AD,Return of Kylun,C:Cerise . . . 3.00
47 AD,I:Cerise 3.00
48 AD,A:Anti-Phoenix. 3.00
49 AD,MFm,V:Necrom,R:Merlyn . . . 3.00
50 AD,Phoenix,V:Necrom,Merlyn . . 4.00
51 V:Giant Dinosaurs 2.00
52 O:Phoenix,A:Prof X,MarvGirl . . . 2.00
53 A:Spider-Man,V:The Litter 2.00
54 AD,MFm,V:Crazy Gang 2.50
55 AD,MFm,A:Psylocke 2.50
56 AD,MFm,A:Psylocke, V:Saturyne,Jamie Braddock . . . 2.50
57 A:X-Men,Alchemy,V:Trolls 2.75
58 A:X-Men,Alchemy,V:Trolls 2.75
59 A:Avengers 2.25
60 A:Avengers 2.25
61 AD,MFm,Phoenix Vs.Galactus . . 2.25
62 AD,MFm,A:Galactus 2.25
63 AD,MFm,V:Warpies 2.25
64 AD,MFm,V:RCX,R:Rachel 2.25
65 AD,MFm,R:Dark Phoenix. 2.25
66 AD,MFm,V:Ahab,Sentinels, O:Widget 2.25
67 AD,MFm,V:Ahab,Sentinels. 2.25
68 V:Starjammers. 2.00
69 A:Starjammers. 2.00
70 A:Starjammers. 2.00
71 DaR,Hologram(c),N:Excalibur . . 4.00
72 KeL,V:Siena Blaze. 2.00
73 TSr,V:Siena Blaze 2.00
74 InC,A:Mr.Sinster,Siena Blaze . . . 2.00
75 SLo(s),KeL,I:Daytripper(Amanda Sefton),Britannic(Capt.Britain), BU:Nightcrawler 3.50
75a Newsstand Ed. 2.25
76 KeL,V:D'spayre 2.00
77 KeL,R:Doug Ramsey 2.00
78 A:Zero,Doug Ramsey 2.25
79 A:Zero,Doug Ramsey 2.25
80 A:Zero,Doug Ramsey 2.25
81 Doug Ramsey 2.25
82 . . . . 2.50
82a foil(c) 3.50
83 regular ed. 2.00
83a Deluxe ed. Kitty,Nightcrawler . . 2.25
84 regular ed. 2.00
84a Deluxe ed. 2.25
85 regular ed. 2.00
85a Deluxe ed. 2.25
86 regular ed. 2.00
86a Deluxe ed. 2.25
87 KeL,Secrets of the Genoshan Mutate Technology 2.00
88 Dream Nails,pt.1 . . . . 2.00
89 Dream Nails,pt.2 . . . . 2.00
90 Between Uncreated,Phalanx . . . 3.00
91 F:Colossus 2.00
92 F:Colossus 2.00
93 F:Wolfsbane 2.00
94 A:Karma & Psylocke 2.00
95 . . . . 2.00
96 . . . . 2.00
97 BWi,B.Braddock's secrets told . . 2.00
98 . . . . 2.00
99 European Hellfire Club, Onslaught 2.00

Excalibur #99
© Marvel Entertainment Group

100 Onslaught saga, double size . . 3.00
101 . . . . 2.00
102 . . . . 2.00
103 WEI,F:Colossus,Kitty & Nichtcrawler 2.00
104 JAr,BHi,PNe,Douglock's dark side 2.00
105 JAr,BHi,PNe,V:Moonstar, ... 2.00
106 . . . . 2.00
107 SvL,New direction 2.00
108 Dragons of the Crimson Dawn . 2.00
109 V:Spiral,A:Captain Britain. 2.00
110 V:The Dragons of the Crimson Dawn 2.00
111 F:Shadowcat,R:Rory Cambell (Ahab?) 2.00
112 Quicksilver tie-in 2.00
113 BRa,Colossus & Meggan 2.00
114 BRa,Vanisher. 2.00
115 BRa,Quarantine,F:GenerationX 2.00
116 BRa,Legacy Virus, cont. 2.00
117 BRa,F:Kitty Pryde, Colossus & Nightcrawler. 2.00
118 BRa,V:Creatures from the Shadows 2.00
119 BRa,V:Nightmare 2.00
120 BRa,F:Kitty Pryde & Pete Wisdom 2.00
121 BRa,to Egypt 2.00
122 BRa,V:Original X-Men? 2.00
123 BRa,V:Mimic 2.00
124 BBr,Captain Britain's bachelor party 2.00
125 TvS,SHa, W:Captain Britain & Meggan, final issue 3.00
Minus 1 Spec., flashback, F:Nightcrawler 2.00
Ann.#1 I:Khaos,w/card 3.25
Spec #1 The Possession 4.00
Spec #2 RLm,DT,JG,RL, A:Original X-Men 2.75
PF Cold Blood 4.95
GN Weird War III 9.95
TPB Wild, Wild Life. 5.95

FACTOR X

1995

1 After Xavier 4.00
2 Scott vs. Alex Summers 3.00
3 Cyclops vs. Havok 2.50
4 Jean & Scott. 2.50
TPB Rep. #1-#4 . . . . 8.95

FAFHRD AND THE GRAY MOUSER

Epic Oct., 1990

1 MMi,Fritz Leiber adapt. 5.00
2 & 3 MMi . . . . @5.00
4 MMi, Feb. 1991 . . . . 5.00

FAITHFUL

Nov., 1949

1 Ph(c),I Take This Man. 75.00
2 Ph(c),Love Thief,Feb.,1950. . . . 60.00

FALCON

Nov., 1983

1 PS,V:Nemesis 2.00
2 V:Sentinels. 2.00
3 V:Electro 2.00
4 A:Capt.America, Feb., 1984 . . . . 2.00

FALLEN ANGELS

April, 1987

1 KGa,TP,A:Sunspot,Warlock. 3.00
2 KGa,TP,I:Gomi,Fallen Angels . . . 2.50

 All comics prices listed are for *Near Mint* condition.

3 KGa,TP,A:X-Factor 2.50
4 KGa,TP,A:Moon Boy, Devil Dinosaur 2.50
5 JSon,D:Angel,Don 2.50
6 JSon,Coconut Grove 2.50
7 KGa,Captured in Coconut Grove. 2.50
8 KGa,L:Sunspot,Warlock 2.50

FANTASTIC FIVE

Aug., 1999

1 TDF,PR,AM,New Team:Human Torch Thing,Ms.Fantastic,Psilord & Big Brain. 2.00
2A TDF,PR,AM,Bloody Reunions x-over. 2.00
2B variant MSh(c) 2.00
3 TDF,PR,AM,A:Spider-Girl 2.00
4 TDF,PR,AM 2.00
5 TDF,PR,AM,A:Kristoff 2.00

FANTASTIC FORCE

1994–96

1 Foil stamped cover. 2.50
2 Moses 2.25
3 . . . . 2.25
4 A:Captain America 2.25
5 I:Dreadface. 2.25
6 F:Vibraxis. 2.00
7 V:Doom 2.00
8 V:Crimson Cadre 2.00
9 Atlantis Rising 2.00
10 A:Human Torch 2.00
11 A:Black Panther. 2.00
12 V:Vanguard 2.00
13 J:She-Hulk. 2.00
14 V:Wakanda 2.00
15 End of the Fantastic Force?. . . . 2.00
16 End of the Fantastic Force?. . . . 2.00
17 . . . . 2.00
18 . . . . 2.00

FANTASTIC FOUR

Nov., 1961

1 JK,I&O:Mr.Fantastic,Thing Invisible Girl,Human Torch Mole Man 20,000.00
2 JK,I:Skrulls 3,800.00
3 JK,I:Miracleman. 2,500.00
4 JK,R:Submariner 3,000.00
5 JK,JSt,I&O:Doctor Doom . . . 3,300.00

Fantastic Four #12
© Marvel Entertainment Group

6 JK,V:Doctor Doom 1,700.00
7 JK,I:Kurrgo 875.00
8 JK,I:Alicia Masters,I&O: Puppet Master 875.00
9 JK,V:Submariner. 850.00
10 JK,V:Doctor Doom,I:Ovoids . . 850.00
11 JK,I:Impossible Man. 700.00
12 JK,V:Hulk 1,200.00
13 JK,SD,I&O:Red Ghost, I:Watcher 500.00
14 JK,SD,V:Submariner 300.00
15 JK,I:Mad Thinker 300.00
16 JK,V:Doctor Doom 300.00
17 JK,V:Doctor Doom 300.00
18 JK,I:Super Skrull 300.00
19 JK,I&O:Rama Tut. 300.00
20 JK,I:Molecule Man 325.00
21 JK,I:Hate Monger. 250.00
22 JK,V:Mole Man 250.00
23 JK,V:Doctor Doom 250.00
24 JK,I:Infant Terrible 250.00
25 JK,Thing vs.Hulk 450.00
26 JK,V:Hulk,A:Avengers 375.00
27 JK,A:Doctor Strange 175.00
28 JK,1st X-Men x-over 250.00
29 JK,V:Red Ghost. 150.00
30 JK,I&O:Diablo 150.00
31 JK,V:Mole Man 125.00
32 JK,V:Superskrull 125.00
33 JK,I:Attuma 125.00
34 JK,I:Gideon 125.00
35 JK,I:Dragon Man,A:Diablo . . . 125.00
36 JK,I:Medusa,Frightful Four . . . 125.00
37 JK,V:Skrulls 100.00
38 JK,V:Frightful Four,I:Trapster . 100.00
39 JK,WW,A:Daredevil 100.00
40 JK,A:Daredevil,Dr.Doom 100.00
41 JK,V:Fright.Four,A:Medusa . . . 75.00
42 JK,V:Frightful Four 75.00
43 JK,V:Frightful Four. 75.00
44 JK,JSt,I:Gorgon, V:Dragon Man 100.00
45 JK,JSt,I:Inhumans(Black Bolt, Triton,Lockjaw,Crystal, Karnak) 100.00
46 JK,JSt,V:Seeker. 100.00
47 JK,JSt,I:Maximus,Attilan, Alpha Primitives 100.00
48 JK,JSt,I:Silver Surfer, C:Galactus 900.00
49 JK,JSt,A:Silver Surfer, V:Galactus 250.00
50 JK,JSt,V:Galactus,Silver Surfer,I:Wyatt Wingfoot. 275.00
51 JK,JSt,I:Negative Zone 65.00
52 JK,JSt,I:Black Panther 125.00
53 JK,JSt,I:Klaw,Vibranium 100.00
54 JK,JSt,I:Prester John 60.00
55 JK,JSt,A:Silver Surfer 90.00
56 JK,JSt,O:Klaw,A:Inhumans, C:Silver Surfer 65.00
57 JK,JSt,V:Doc Doom, A:Silver Surfer. 65.00
58 JK,JSt,V:Doc Doom, A:Silver Surfer. 65.00
59 JK,JSt,V:Doc Doom, A:Silver Surfer. 65.00
60 JK,JSt,V:Doc Doom, A:Silver Surfer. 65.00
61 JK,JSt,V:Sandman, A:Silver Surfer 65.00
62 JK,JSt,I:Blastaar 45.00
63 JK,JSt,V:Blastaar. 50.00
64 JK,JSt,I:The Kree,Sentry 50.00
65 JK,JSt,I:Ronan,Supreme Intelligence. 50.00
66 JK,JSt,O:Him,A:Crystal 100.00
67 JK,JSt,I:Him. 125.00
68 JK,JSt,V:Mad Thinker 60.00
69 JK,JSt,V:Mad Thinker 50.00
70 JK,JSt,V:Mad Thinker 50.00

Fantastic Four #113
© Marvel Entertainment Group

71 JK,JSt,V:Mad Thinker 50.00
72 JK,JSt,A:Watcher,S.Surfer 50.00
73 JK,JSt,A:SpM,DD,Thor 40.00
74 JK,JSt,A:Silver Surfer 45.00
75 JK,JSt,A:Silver Surfer 45.00
76 JK,JSt,V:Psycho Man,S.Surf . . 45.00
77 JK,JSt,V:Galactus,S.Surfer . . . 45.00
78 JK,JSt,V:Wizard. 40.00
79 JK,JSt,A:Crystall,V:Mad Thinker. 40.00
80 JK,JSt,A:Crystal. 40.00
81 JK,JSt,J:Crystal,V:Wizard. 40.00
82 JK,JSt,V:Maximus 40.00
83 JK,JSt,V:Maximus 40.00
84 JK,JSt,V:Doctor Doom 30.00
85 JK,JSt,V:Doctor Doom 30.00
86 JK,JSt,V:Doctor Doom 30.00
87 JK,JSt,V:Doctor Doom 30.00
88 JK,JSt,V:Mole Man 30.00
89 JK,JSt,V:Mole Man 30.00
90 JK,JSt,V:Skrulls 27.00
91 JK,JSt,V:Skrulls,I:Torgo 27.00
92 JK,JSt,V:Torgo,Skrulls 27.00
93 JK,V:Torgo,Skrulls 27.00
94 JK,JSt,I:Agatha Harkness 27.00
95 JK,JSt,I:Monocle 27.00
96 JK,JSt,V:Mad Thinker 27.00
97 JK,JSt,V:Monster from Lost Lagoon 27.00
98 JK,JSt,V:Kree Sentry 27.00
99 JK,JSt,A:Inhumans 27.00
100 JK,JSt,V:Puppetmaster 100.00
101 JK,JSt,V:Maggia 25.00
102 JK,JSt,V:Magneto 25.00
103 JR,V:Magneto 25.00
104 JR,V:Magneto 22.00
105 JR,L:Crystal. 20.00
106 JR,JSt,'Monster's Secret'. . . . 20.00
107 JB,JSt,V:Annihilus 20.00
108 JK,JB,JR,JSt, V:Annihilus. . . . 20.00
109 JB,JSt,V:Annihilus 20.00
110 JB,JSt,V:Annihilus 20.00
111 JB,JSt,A:Hulk 20.00
112 JB,JSt,Thing vs. Hulk 60.00
113 JB,JSt,I:Overmind 15.00
114 JR(c),JB,V:Overmind 15.00
115 JR(c),JB,JSt,I:Eternals 15.00
116 JB,JSt,O:Stranger 15.00
117 JB,JSt,V:Diablo 11.00
118 JR(c),JB,JM,V:Diablo 11.00
119 JB,JSt,V:Klaw. 11.00
120 JB,JSt,I:Gabriel(Airwalker) (Robot). 11.00

MARVEL

121 JB,JSt,V:Silver Surfer,D: Gabriel Destroyer 15.00
122 JR(c),JB,JSt,V:Galactus, A:Silver Surfer 15.00
123 JB,JSt,V:Galactus, A:Silver Surfer 14.00
124 JB,JSt,V:Monster 10.00
125 E:StL(s),JB,JSt,V:Monster . . . 10.00
126 B:RTs(s),JB,JSt, O:FF,MoleMan 10.00
127 JB,JSt,V:Mole Man 10.00
128 JB,JSt,V:Mole Man. 11.00
129 JB,JSt,I:Thundra, V:Frightful Four. 10.00
130 JSo(c),JB,JSt,V:Frightful Four. 10.00
131 JSo(c),JB,JSt,V:Quicksilver . . 10.00
132 JB,JSt,J:Medusa 10.00
133 JSt(i),V:Thundra. 10.00
134 JB,JSt,V:Dragon Man. 10.00
135 JB,JSt,V:Gideon. 10.00
136 JB,JSt,A:Shaper 10.00
137 JB,JSt,A:Shaper 10.00
138 JB,JSt,O:Miracle Man 10.00
139 JB,V:Miracle Man. 10.00
140 JB,JSt,O:Annihilus 10.00
141 JR(c),JB,JSt,V:Annihilus. 10.00
142 RB,JSt,A:Doc Doom 10.00
143 GK(c),RB,V:Doc Doom. 10.00
144 RB,JSt,V:Doc Doom. 10.00
145 JSt&GK(c),RA,I:Ternak. 10.00
146 RA,JSt,V:Ternak. 10.00
147 RB,JSt,V:Subby 10.00
148 RB,JSt,V:Frightful Four 10.00
149 RB,JSt,V:Sub-Mariner. 10.00
150 GK(c),RB,JSt,W:Crystal & Quicksilver,V:Ultron 9.00
151 RB,JSt,O:Thundra 8.00
152 JR(c),RB,JM,A:Thundra 8.00
153 GK(c),RB,JSt,A:Thundra 8.00
154 GK(c),rep.Str.Tales #127 . . . . . 8.00
155 RB,JSt,A:Surfer 9.00
156 RB,JSt,A:Surfer,V:Doom 9.00
157 RB,JSt,A:Surfer 9.00
158 RB,JSt,V:Xemu 7.00
159 RB,JSt,V:Xemu 7.00
160 K&R(c),JB,V:Arkon 7.00
161 RB,JSt,V:Arkon 5.00
162 RB,DA,JSt,V:Arkon 5.00
163 RB,JSt,V:Arkon 5.00
164 JK(c),GP,JSt,V:Crusader,R: Marvel Boy,I:Frankie Raye 5.00
165 GP,JSt,O:Crusader, O&D:Marvel Boy 5.00
166 GP,V:Hulk 6.00
167 JK(c),GP,JSt,V:Hulk 6.00
168 RB,JSt,J:Luke Cage. 5.00
169 RB,JSt,V:Puppetmaster 5.00
170 GP,JSt,L:Luke Cage. 5.00
171 JK(c),RB,GP,JSt,I:Gor 4.50
172 JK(c),GP,JSt,V:Destroyer 5.00
173 JB,JSt,V:Galactus,O:Heralds . . 5.00
174 JB,V:Galactus 5.00
175 JB,A:High Evolutionary 4.50
176 GP,JSt,V:Impossible Man. 4.50
177 JP,JS,A:Frightful Four I:Texas Twister,Capt.Ultra 4.50
178 GP,V:Frightful Four,Brute 4.50
179 JSt,V:Annihilus. 4.50
180 reprint #101 . . . . 4.50
181 E:RTs(s),JSt,V:Brute, Annihilus 4.50
182 SB,JSt,V:Brute,Annihilus 4.50
183 SB,JSt,V:Brute,Annihilus 4.50
184 GP,JSt,V:Eliminator 4.50
185 GP,JSt,V:Nich.Scratch 4.50
186 GP,JSi,I:Salem's Seven 4.50
187 GP,JSt,V:Klaw,Molecule Man . . 4.50
188 GP,JSt,V:Molecule Man 4.50
189 reprint FF Annual #4 . . . . 4.50
190 SB,O:Fantastic Four 5.00
191 GP,JSt,V:Plunderer, Team Breaks Up. 4.00
192 GP,JSt,V:Texas Twister 4.00
193 KP,JSt,V:Darkoth,Diablo. 4.00
194 KP,V:Darkoth,Diablo. 4.00
195 KP,A:Sub-Mariner 4.00
196 KP,V:Invincible Man (Reed), A:Dr.Doom,Team Reunited 4.00
197 KP,JSt,Red Ghost 4.00
198 KP,JSt,V:Doc Doom 4.00
199 KP,JSt,V:Doc Doom 4.00
200 KP,JSt,V:Doc Doom 5.00
201 KP,JSt,FF's Machinery 4.00
202 KP,JSt,V:Quasimodo 4.00
203 KP,JSt,V:Mutant 4.00
204 KP,JSt,V:Skrulls 4.00
205 KP,JSt,V:Skrulls 4.00
206 KP,JSt,V:Skrulls,A:Nova 4.00
207 SB,JSt,V:Monocle,A:SpM. 4.00
208 SB,V:Sphinx,A:Nova 4.00
209 JBy,JSt,I:Herbie,A:Nova 5.00
210 JBy,JS,A:Galactus 4.00
211 JBy,JS,I:Terrax,A:Galactus 5.00
212 JBy,JSt,V:Galactus,Sphinx 4.00
213 JBy,JSt,V:Terrax,Galactus Sphinx 4.00
214 JBy,JSt,V:Skrull 4.00
215 JBy,JSt,V:Blastaar 4.00
216 JBy,V:Blastaar 4.00
217 JBy,JSt,A:Dazzler 4.00
218 JBy,JSt,V:FrightfulFour, A:Spider-Man 5.00
219 BSz,JSt,A:Sub-Mariner 4.00
220 JBy,JSt,A:Vindicator. 4.00
221 JBy,JSt,V:Vindicator. 4.00
222 BSz,JSt,V:Nicholas Scratch . . . 4.00
223 BSz,JSt,V:Salem's Seven 4.00
224 BSz,A:Thor 4.00
225 BSz,A:Thor 4.00
226 BSz,A:Shogun 4.00
227 BSz,JSt,V:Ego-Spawn 4.00
228 BSz,JSt,V:Ego-Spawn 4.00
229 BSz,JSt,I:Firefrost,Ebon Seeker 4.00
230 BSz,JSt,A:Avengers, O:Firefrost & Ebon Seeker 4.00
231 BSz,JSt,V:Stygorr 4.00
232 JBy,New Direction,V:Diablo . . . 6.00
233 JBy,V:Hammerhead 4.50
234 JBy,V:Ego 4.50
235 JBy,O:Ego 4.50
236 JBy,V:Dr.Doom,A:Puppet Master, 20th Anniv.. . . . . 4.50
237 JBy,V:Solons 4.00

Fantastic Four #249
© Marvel Entertainment Group

238 JBy,O:Frankie Raye, new Torch 4.00
239 JBy,I:Aunt Petunia, Uncle Jake 4.50
240 JBy,A:Inhumans,b:Luna 4.00
241 JBy,A:Black Panther 4.00
242 JBy,A:Daredevil,Thor,Iron Man Spider-Man,V:Terrax. 4.00
243 JBy,A:Daredevil,Dr.Strange, Spider-Man,Avengers,V:Galactus, Terrax. 4.00
244 JBy,A:Avengers,Dr.Strange, Galactus, Frankie Raye Becomes Nova. 4.00
245 JBy,V:Franklin Richards 4.00
246 JBy,V:Dr.Doom, A:Puppet Master 4.00
247 JBy,A:Dr.Doom,I:Kristoff, D:Zorba 4.00
248 JBy,A:Inhumans. 4.00
249 JBy,V:Gladiator 4.00
250 JBy,A:Capt.America,SpM V:Gladiator 4.00
251 JBy,A:Annihilus 4.00
252 JBy,1st sideways issue,V: Ootah,A:Annihilus,w/tattoo 4.00
252a w/o tattoo. 4.00
253 JBy,V:Kestorans,A:Annihilus . . 4.00
254 JBy,V:Mantracora, A:She-Hulk,Wasp 4.00
255 JBy,A:Daredevil,Annihilus, V:Mantracora 4.00
256 JBy,A:Avengers,Galactus, V:Annihilus,New Costumes. . . . 4.00
257 JBy,A:Galactus,Death,Nova, Scarlet Witch 3.50
258 JBy,A:Dr.Doom,D:Hauptmann . 3.50
259 JBy,V:Terrax,Dr.Doom, C:Silver Silver 3.50
260 JBy,V:Terrax, Dr.Doom, A:Silver Surfer,Sub-Mariner . . . 4.00
261 JBy,A:Sub-Mariner,Marrina, Silver Surfer,Sc.Witch,Lilandra . 4.00
262 JBy,O:Galactus,A:Odin, (J.Byrne in story) 3.00
263 JBy,V:Messiah,A:Mole Man . . . 3.00
264 JBy,V:Messiah,A:Mole Man . . . 3.00
265 JBy,A:Trapster,Avengers, J:She-Hulk,Secret Wars 3.00
266 KGa,JBy,A:Hulk,Sasquatch, V:Karisma 3.00
267 JBy,A:Hulk,Sasquatch,Morbius, V:Dr.Octopus,Sue miscarries . . 3.00
268 JBy,V:Doom's Mask 3.00
269 JBy,R:Wyatt Wingfoot, I:Terminus 3.00
270 JBy,V:Terminus 3.00
271 JBy,V:Gormuu 3.00
272 JBy,I:Warlord (Nathaniel Richards) 3.00
273 JBy,V:Warlord 3.00
274 JBy,AG,cont.from Thing#19, A:Spider-Man's Black Costume. 3.00
275 JBy,AG,V:T.J.Vance 3.00
276 JBy,JOy,V:Mephisto, A:Dr.Strange 3.00
277 JBy,JOy,V:Mephisto, A:Dr.Strange,R:Thing 3.00
278 JBy,JOy,O:Dr.Doom,A:Kristoff (as Doom) 3.00
279 JBy,JOy,V:Dr.Doom(Kristoff), I:New Hate-Monger 3.00
280 JBy,JOy,I:Malice, V:Hate-Monger. 3.00
281 JBy,JOy,A:Daredevil,V:Hate Monger,Malice 3.00
282 JBy,JOy,A:Power Pack,Psycho Man,Secret Wars II. 3.00
283 JBy,JOy,V:Psycho-Man 3.00
284 JBy,JOy,V:Psycho-Man 3.00
285 JBy,JOy,Secret Wars II

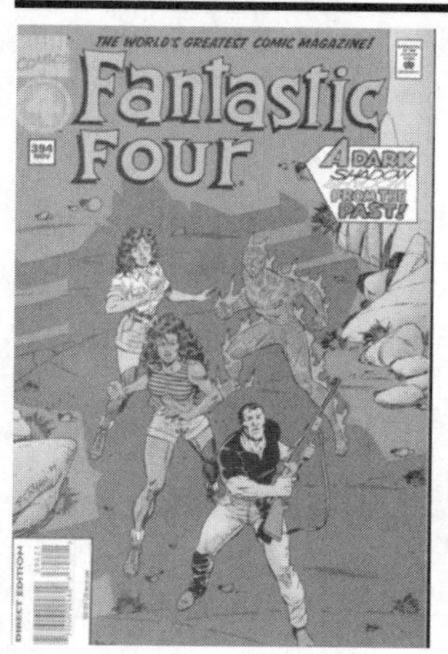

Fantastic Four #394
© Marvel Entertainment Group

A:Beyonder 3.00
286 JBy,TA,R:Jean Grey, A:Hercules Capt.America 3.50
287 JBy,JSt,A:Wasp,V:Dr.Doom . . . 3.00
288 JBy,JSt,V:Dr.Doom,Secret Wars II 3.50
289 JBy,AG,D:Basilisk,V:Blastaar, R:Annihilus. 3.00
290 JBy,AG,V:Annihilus 3.00
291 JBy,CR,A:Nick Fury 3.00
292 JBy,AG,A:Nick Fury,V:Hitler . . . 3.00
293 JBy,AG,A:Avengers.W.C. 3.00
294 JOy,AG,V:FutureCentralCity . . . 2.50
295 JOy,AG,V:Fut.Central City 2.50
296 BWS,KGa,RF,BWi,AM,KJ,JB, SL,MS,JRu,JOy,JSt,25th Anniv.,V:MoleMan. 3.00
297 JB,SB,V:Umbra-Sprite 2.50
298 JB,SB,V:Umbra-Sprite 2.50
299 JB,SB,She-Hulk,V:Thing, A:Spider-Man,L:She-Hulk 2.50
300 JB,SB,W:Torch & Fake Alicia (Lyja),A:Puppet-Master,Wizard, Mad Thinker,Dr.Doom. 3.00
301 JB,SB,V:Wizard,MadThinker . . 2.25
302 JB,SB,V:Project Survival 2.25
303 JB,RT,A:Thundra,V:Machus . . . 2.25
304 JB,JSt,V:Quicksilver, A:Kristoff 2.25
305 JB,JSt,V:Quicksilver, J:Crystal,A:Dr.Doom 2.25
306 JB,JSt,A:Capt.America, J:Ms.Marvel,V:Diablo 2.25
307 JB,JSt,L:Reed&Sue,V:Diablo . . 2.25
308 JB,JSt,I:Fasaud 2.25
309 JB,JSt,V:Fasaud 2.25
310 KP,JSt,V:Fasaud,N:Thing & Ms.Marvel. 2.25
311 KP,JSt,A:Black Panther, Dr.Doom,V:THRob 2.25
312 KP,JSt,A:Black Panther, Dr.Doom,X-Factor 2.25
313 SB,JSt,V:Lava Men, A:Moleman. 2.00
314 KP,JSt,V:Belasco 2.00
315 KP,JSt,V:Mast.Pandem. 2.00
316 KP,JSt,A:CometMan 2.00
317 KP,JSt,L:Crystal 2.00
318 KP,JSt,V:Dr.Doom 2.00
319 KP,JSt,G-Size,O:Beyonder. . . . 2.25
320 KP,JSt,Hulk vs Thing 2.50
321 RLm,RT,A:She-Hulk. 2.00
322 KP,JSt,Inferno,V:Graviton. 2.00
323 KP,JSt,RT,Inferno A:Mantis . . . 2.00
324 KP,JSt,RT,A:Mantis 2.00
325 RB,RT,A:Silver Surfer, D:Mantis. 2.50
326 KP,RT,I:New Frightful Four. . . . 2.00
327 KP,RT,V:Frightful Four 2.00
328 KP,RT,V:Frightful Four 2.00
329 RB,RT,V:Mole Man 2.00
330 RB,RT,V:Dr.Doom 2.00
331 RB,RT,V:Ultron 2.00
332 RB,RT,V:Aron 2.00
333 RB,RT,V:Aron,Frightful Four. . . 2.00
334 RB,Acts of Vengeance. 2.00
335 RB,RT,Acts of Vengeance 2.00
336 RLm,Acts of Vengeance, ... 2.00
337 WS,A:Thor,Iron Man, B:Timestream saga 4.00
338 WS,V:Deathshead,A:Thor, Iron Man 2.50
339 WS,V:Gladiator 2.50
340 WS,V:Black Celestial 2.50
341 WS,A:Thor,Iron Man 2.50
342 A:Rusty,C:Spider-Man 2.50
343 WS,V:Stalin 2.50
344 WS,V:Stalin 2.50
345 WS,V:Dinosaurs 2.50
346 WS,V:Dinosaurs 2.50
347 AAd,ATi(i)A:Spider-Man, GhostRider,Wolverine,Hulk. . . . 4.00
347a 2nd printing 2.00
348 AAd,ATi(i)A:Spider-Man, GhostRider,Wolverine,Hulk. . . . 4.00
348a 2nd printing 2.00
349 AAd,ATi(i),AM(i)A:Spider-Man, Wolverine,GhostRider,Hulk, C:Punisher. 3.50
350 WS,Am(i),R:Ben Grimm as Thing,(48p). 3.00
351 MBa,Kubic. 2.50
352 WS,Reed Vs.Dr.Doom 2.50
353 WS,E:Timestream Saga, A:Avengers, ... 2.50
354 WS,Secrets of the Time Variance Authority 2.50
355 AM,V:Wrecking Crew 2.00
356 B:TDF(s),PR,A:New Warriors, V:Puppet Master. 2.00
357 PR,V:Mad Thinker, Puppetmaster, ... 2.00
358 PR,AAd,30th Anniv.,1st Marv. Die Cut(c),D:Lyja,V:Paibok,BU: Dr.Doom. 3.00
359 PR,I:Devos the Devastator. . . . 2.00
360 PR,V:Dreadface 2.00
361 PR,V:Dr.Doom,X-masIssue . . . 2.00
362 PR,A:Spider-Man, I:WildBlood. 2.00
363 PR,I:Occulus,A:Devos 2.00
364 PR,V:Occulus 2.00
365 PR,V:Occulus 2.00
366 PR,Infinity War,R:Lyja 2.00
367 PR,Inf.War,A:Wolverine 2.00
368 PR,V:Infinity War X-Men 2.00
369 PR,Inf.War,R:Malice, A:Thanos 2.00
370 PR,Inf.War,V:Mr.Fantastic Doppleganger. 2.00
371 PR,V:Lyja,foil(c) 4.00
371a 2nd Printing 3.00
372 PR,A:Spider-Man,Silver Sable 2.00
373 PR,V:Aron,Silver sable. 2.00
374 PR,V:Secret Defenders 2.00
375 V:Dr.Doom,A:Inhumans,Lyja, Holo-Grafix(c). 3.00
376 PR,A:Nathan Richards,V:Paibok, Devos,w/Dirt Magazine. 2.75
376a w/out Dirt Magazine 2.00
377 PR,V:Paibok,Devos,Klaw, I:Huntara 2.00
378 PR,A:Sandman,SpM,DD 2.00
379 PR,V:Ms.Marvel. 2.00
380 PR,A:Dr.Doom,V:Hunger 2.00
381 PR,D:Dr.Doom,Mr.Fantastic, V:Hunger 5.00
382 PR,V:Paibok,Devos,Huntara . . 3.00
383 PR,V:Paibok,Devos,Huntara . . 2.00
384 PR,A:Ant-Man,V:Franklin Richards. 2.00
385 PR,A:Triton,Tiger Shark, Starblast#7. . . . . 2.00
386 PR,Starblast#11,A:Namor,Triton, b:Johnny & Lyja child 2.00
387 Die-Cut & Foil (c),PR,N:Invisible Woman,J:Ant-Man,A:Namor . . . 3.25
387a Newsstand Ed. 2.00
388 PR,I:Dark Raider,V:FF, Avengers,w/cards. 2.00
389 PR,I:Raphael Suarez,A:Watcher, V:Collector 2.00
390 PR,A:Galactus 2.00
391 PR,I:Vibraxas. 2.00
392 Dark Raider 2.00
393 . . . . 2.00
394 Neon(c) w/insert print. 3.00
394a Newsstand ed.,no bag/inserts 2.00
395 Thing V:Wolverine 2.00
396 . . . . 2.00
397 Resurrection,pt.1 . . . . 2.00
398 regular edition 2.00
398a Enhanced cover. 2.75
399 Watcher's Lie. 2.00
399a Foil stamped cover 2.50
400 Watcher's Lie,pt.3 . . . . 3.95
401 V:Tantalus 2.00
402 Atlantis Rising,Namor vs. Black Bolt 2.00
403 TDF,PR,DBi,F:Thing,Medusa . . 2.00
404 R:Namor,I:New Villian 2.00
405 J:Namor. 2.00
406 TDF,PR,DBI,R:Dr. Doom, I:Hyperstorm 2.00
407 TDF,PR,DBi,Return of Reed Richards 2.00
408 TDF,PR,DBi,Original FF unite. . 2.00
409 TDF,PR,DBi,All new line-up . . . 2.00
410 . . . . 2.00
411 . . . . 2.00
412 TDF,PR,DBi,Mr.Fantastic vs. Sub-Mariner 2.00
413 . . . . 2.00
414 Galactus vs. Hyperstorm 2.00
415 Onslaught saga, A:X-Men 2.50
416 Onslaught saga, A:Dr. Doom,

Fantastic Four #414
© Marvel Entertainment Group

MARVEL

double size, finale 2.50
Ann.#1 JK,SD,I:Atlantis,Dorma, Krang,V:Namor,O:FF 700.00
Ann.#2 JK,JSt,O:Dr.Doom. 375.00
Ann.#3 JK,W:Reed and Sue 145.00
Ann.#4 JK,JSt,I:Quasimodo 75.00
Ann.#5 JK,JSt,A:Inhumans,Silver Surfer,Black Panther, I:Psycho Man 120.00
Ann.#6 JK,JSt,I:Annihilus, Franklin Richards 50.00
Ann.#7 JK(c),reprints 25.00
Ann.#8 JR(c),reprints 20.00
Ann.#9 JK(c),reprints. 20.00
Ann.#10 reprints Ann.#3 . . . . 20.00
Ann.#11 JK(c),JB,A:The Invaders . . 7.00
Ann.#12 A:The Invaders 7.00
Ann.#13 V:The Mole Man 7.00
Ann.#14 GP,V:Salem's Seven 7.00
Ann.#15 GP,V:Dr.Doom,Skrulls 5.00
Ann.#16 V:Dragonlord 5.00
Ann.#17 JBy,V:Skrulls. 5.00
Ann.#18 KGa,V:Skrulls,W:Black Bolt and Medusa,A:Inhumans. . 5.00
Ann.#19 JBy,V:Skrulls. 5.00
Ann.#20 TD(i),V:Dr.Doom 4.00
Ann.#21 JG,JSt,Evol.Wars 4.00
Ann.#22 RB,Atlantis Attacks, A:Avengers 4.00
Ann.#23 JG,GCa,Days of Future Present #1 . . . . 5.00
Ann.#24 JG,AM,Korvac Quest #1, A:Guardians of the Galaxy 3.00
Ann.#25 Citizen Kang #3 . . . . 2.50
Ann.#26 HT,I:Wildstreak, V:Dreadface,w/card 3.25
Ann.#27 MGu,V:Justice Peace 3.25
G-Size#1 RB,Thing/Hulk. 15.00
G-Size#2 K&R(c),JB,Time to Kill. . . 9.00
G-Size#3 RB,JSt,Four Horseman . . 9.00
G-Size#4 JB,JSt,I:Madrox. 10.00
G-Size#5 JK(c),V:Psycho Man, Molecule Man. 7.00
G-Size#6 V:Annihilus 7.00
Spec.#1 Rep.Ann.#1 JBy(c) 2.00
TPB Rep.#347-349. . . . . 5.95
TPB Nobody Gets Out Alive, rep. Fant.Four #387–#392 + new. . 15.95
TPB Trial of Galactus,reprints #242-244,#257-262 . . . . 9.95
Marvel Milestone rep. #1 (1991) . . . 2.95
Marvel Milestone rep. #5 (1992) . . . 2.95
Ashcan. 75

Fantastic Four, 2nd Series #1
© Marvel Entertainment Group

Spec. The Origin of Galactus 2.50

[2nd Series] Nov., 1996

1 JLe,BCi,SW, 48pg 5.00
1A Mole Man cover 12.00
1B Gold signature, bagged, limited 25.00
2 JLe,BCi,V:Namor 4.00
3 JLe,BCi,SW,A:Avengers 3.00
4 JLe,BCi,SW,I:Black Panther 3.00
4A x-mas cover 3.50
5 JLe,BCi,SW,V:Dr. Doom 3.50
6 JLe,BCi,SW,Industrial Revolution prologue. 3.00
7 JLe,BCi,BBh,V:Blastaar 3.00
8 JLe,BCi,BBh,V:Inhumans 3.00
9 JLe,BCi,BBh,V:Inhumans 3.00
10 JLe,BCi,BBh,A:Silver Surfer, Tyrax 3.00
11 JLe,BCi,BBh,A:Silver Surfer, Firelord, Terrax. 3.00
12 JLe,BCi,BBh,GalactusSaga,pt.1, reunited 3.00
13 JeR,Wildstorm x-over. 3.00
Ashcan, signed, numbered 10.00

[3rd Series] Nov., 1997

1 SLo,AD,MFm, The Ruined, 48pg debut 5.00
2 SLo,AD,MFm,A:Iconoclast 4.00
3 SLo,AD,MFm,V:Red Ghost 4.00
4 SLo,SvL,ATi,A:Silver Surfer, double size. 4.00
4 signed by SLo, (500 copies) . . . 20.00
5 SLo,SvL,ATi,V:The Crucible 3.00
6 CCl,SvL, new villains 3.00
7 CCl,SvL,ATi,V:Technet 3.00
8 CCl,SvL,V:Captain Britain corp. . 3.00
9 CCl,SvL,A:Spider-Man 3.00
10 CCl,SvL,ATi 3.00
11 CCl,SvL,ATi,Crucible—unleashed in Genosha 3.00
12 CCl,SvL,ATi,V:Fantastic Four double-size. 4.50
13 CCl,SvL,A:Ronan the Accuser . . 2.50
14 CCl,SvL,V:Ronan. 2.00
15 CCl,SvL,ATi,Iron Man x-over . . . 2.00
16 CCl,SvL,ATi,V:Kree Avengers . . 2.00
17 CCl,SvL,ATi,I:Lockdown. 2.00
18 CCl,SvL,ATi,Jail Break. 2.00
19 CCl,SvL,ATi,V:Annihilus 2.00
20 CCl,SvL,ATi,V:Ruined 2.00
21 CCl,SvL,ATi,V:Hades 2.00
22 CCl,SvL,ATi,V:Valeria Von Doom 2.00
23 CCl,SvL,ATi,A:She-Hulk. 2.00
24 CCl,SvL,ATi,F:FranklinRichards . 2.00
25 CCl,SvL,ATi,V:Dr.Doom 2.00
26 CCl,SvL,ATi,F:ValeriaVonDoom . 2.00
27 CCl,SvL,F:Invisible Woman 2.00
28 CCl,SvL,ATi,Planet Doom 2.00
29 CCl,SvL,ATi,Frightful Four 2.00
30 CCl,SvL,ATi,Castle Doom 2.25
31 CCl,SvL,ATi,InvisibleWoman . . . 2.25
32 CCl,SvL,ATi,InvisibleWoman . . . 2.25
33 JFM,SvL,ATi,Kid Colt. 2.25
34 JFM,SvL,ATi,aliens 2.25
35A CPa,Diablo,foil (c) 3.25
35B painted (c). 2.25
36 CPa,Diablo triumphant. 2.25
Ann.1998 Fant.Four & Fant.Four . . 3.50
Ann. 1999 CCl,I:Mechamage 3.50
Ann. 2000 LSi,SvL,48-pg. 3.50
Spec.#1 KIK FantasticFour (2000) . 2.25
TPB Heroes Return, 96-page 10.95
TPB Essential Fantastic Four 14.95
TPB Essential Fant.Four, Vol.2 . . . 14.95
TPB Heroes Reborn, 176-pg. 17.95

FANTASTIC FOUR: ATLANTIS RISING

1995

1 B:Atlantis Rising 4.00
2 TDF,MCW,finale, acetate(c) 4.00

FANTASTIC FOUR INDEX

See: OFFICIAL MARVEL INDEX TO THE FANTASTIC FOUR

FANTASTIC FOUR ROAST

1 FH/MG/FM/JB/MA/TA,May,1982 . 5.00

FANTASTIC FOUR 2099

1996

1 Cont. from 2099 Genesis 4.00
2 V:Stark/Fujikawa elite guard 2.00
3 . . . . 2.00
4 . . . . 2.00
5 A:Spider-Man 2099. . . . . 2.00

FANTASTIC FOUR UNLIMITED

1993–96

1 HT,A:Bl.Panther,V:Klaw. 4.50
2 HT,JQ(c),A:Inhumans 4.25
3 HT,V:Blastaar,Annihilus. 4.25
4 RTs(s),HT,V:Mole Man,A:Hulk. . . 4.25
5 RTs(s),HT,V:Frightful Four. 4.25
6 RTs(s),HT,V:Namor 4.00
7 HT,V:Monsters 4.00
8 . . . . 4.00
9 A:Antman 4.00
10 RTs,HT,V:Maelstrom,A:Eternals . 4.00
11 RTs,HT,Atlantis Rising fallout . . . 4.00
12 RTs,TDF,V:Hyperstorm. 4.00
13 . . . . 4.00

FANTASTIC FOUR UNPLUGGED

1995–96

1 comic for a buck. 2.00
2 Reed Richard's Will 2.00
3 F:Mr. Fantastic 2.00
4 . . . . 2.00
5 Back in NY,V:Blastaar. 2.00

FANTASTIC FOUR VS. X-MEN

Feb., 1987

1 JBg,TA,V:Dr.Doom 4.00
2 JBg,TA,V:Dr.Doom 3.00
3 JBg,TA,V:Dr.Doom 3.00
4 JBg,TA,V:Dr.Doom, June 1987 . . 3.00
TPB Reprints Mini-series 12.95

FANTASTIC WORLD OF HANNA-BARBERA

Dec., 1977

1 . . . . 2.00
2 . . . . 2.00
3 June, 1978 . . . . 2.00

FANTASY MASTERPIECES

Feb., 1966

1 JK/DH/SD,reprints 75.00
2 JK,SD,DH,Fin Fang Foom 35.00
3 GC,DH,JK,SD,Capt.A rep. 30.00
4 JK,Capt.America rep. 30.00

 All comics prices listed are for *Near Mint* condition.

5 JK,Capt.America rep. 30.00
6 JK,Capt.America rep. 30.00
7 SD,Sub Mariner rep. 30.00
8 H.Torch & Sub M.rep. 35.00
9 SD,MF,O:Human Torch Rep . . . 30.00
10 rep.All Winners #19 . . . . 30.00
11 JK,(rep),O:Toro 30.00
Becomes:

MARVEL SUPER-HEROES

FANTASY MASTERPIECES

[Volume 2], Dec., 1979

1 JB,JSt,Silver Surfer rep. 5.00
2 JB,JSt,Silver Surfer rep. 5.00
3 JB,JSt,Silver Surfer rep. 5.00
4 JB,JSt,Silver Surfer rep. 5.00
5 JB,JSt,Silver Surfer rep. 5.00
6 JB,JSt,Silver Surfer rep. 5.00
7 JB,JSt,Silver Surfer rep. 5.00
8 JB/JSn,Warlock rep.Strange Tales #178 . . . . 4.00
9 JB,JSn,rep.StrangeTales#179. . . 4.00
10 JB,JSn,rep.StrangeTales#180 . . 4.00
11 JB,JSn,rep.StrangeTales#181 . . 4.00
12 JB,JSn,rep.Warlock #9. . . . . 4.00
13 JB,JSn,rep.Warlock #10. . . . . . . 4.00
14 JB,JSn,rep.Warlock #11. . . . . . . 4.00

FAREWELL TO WEAPONS

1 DirtBag,W/Nirvana Tape 3.50

FEAR

Nov., 1970

1 1950's Monster rep. B:I Found Monstrum;The Dweller in the Black Swamp 35.00
2 X The Thing That Lived 20.00
3 Zzutak, The Thing That Shouldn't Exist 20.00
4 I Turned Into a Martian 20.00
5 I Am the Gorilla Man. 20.00
6 The Midnight Monster. 20.00
7 I Dream of Doom 12.00
8 It Crawls By Night! 12.00
9 Dead Man's Escape 12.00
Becomes:

ADVENTURE INTO FEAR

1972

10 GM,B:Man-Thing 25.00

Fear #25
© Marvel Entertainment Group

11 RB,I:Jennifer Kale,Thog 10.00
12 JSn,RB 10.00
13 VM,Where World's Collide 8.00
14 VM,Plague o/t Demon Cult. 8.00
15 VM,Lord o/t Dark Domain 8.00
16 VM,ManThing in Everglades . . . 8.00
17 VM,I:Wundarr(Aquarian) 8.00
18 VM 8.00
19 VM,FMc,I:Howard the Duck, E:Man-Thing 25.00
20 PG,B:Morbius 28.00
21 GK,V:Uncanny Caretaker. 8.00
22 RB,V:Cat-Demond 8.00
23 1st CR art,A World He Never Made 8.00
24 CR,V:Blade, The Vampire Slayer 20.00
25 You Always Kill the One You Love 7.00
26 V:Uncanny Caretaker. 7.00
27 V:Simon Stroud 7.00
28 Doorway Down into Hell. 7.00
29 Death has a Thousand Eyes . . . 7.00
30 Bloody Sacrifice. 7.00
31 last issue,Dec. 1975 . . . . 7.00

FEUD

Epic 1993

1 I:Skids,Stokes,Kite 2.50
2 V:Grunts,Skide,Stockers 2.25
3 . . . . 2.25
4 . . . . 2.25

FIGHT MAN

1993

1 I:Fight Man 2.00

FIRESTAR

March, 1986

1 MW,SL,O:Firestar,A:X-Men, New Mutants 4.00
2 MW,BWI,A:New Mutants. 4.00
3 AAd&BSz(c),MW,SL, A:White Queen. 3.00
4 MW,SL,V:White Queen 3.00

FISH POLICE

1992–93

1 V:S.Q.U.I.D,Hook 2.00
2 V:Hook 2.00
3 V:Hook 2.00
4 V:Hook 2.00
5 V:Goldie Prawn 2.00
6 Shark Bait #1 . . . . 2.00

FLASH GORDON

1995

1 R:Flash Gordon 2.00
2 AW,V:Ming, final issue 2.95

FLINTSTONE KIDS

Star Comics August, 1987

1 thru 10 . . . . @2.00
11 April, 1989 . . . . 2.00

FLINTSTONES

Oct., 1977–Feb., 1979

1 From TV Series 2.00
2 . . . . 2.00
3 . . . . 2.00
4 A:Jetsons 2.00
5 thru 7 . . . . @2.00

FLYING HERO BARBIE

1 Super Hero Barbie 2.00

Foolkiller #4
© Marvel Entertainment Group

FOOLKILLER

Oct., 1990

1 I:Kurt Gerhardt (Foolkiller III) 3.50
2 O:Foolkiller I & II 3.00
3 Old Costume 3.00
4 N:Foolkiller. 2.50
5 Body Count 2.50
6 Fools Paradise 2.00
7 Who the Fools Are 2.00
8 Sane Must Inherit Earth,A:SpM. . 2.00
9 D:Darren Waite. 2.00
10 New Identity, July 1991 . . . . 2.00

FOORFUR

Star Comics August, 1987

1 thru 6 . . . . @2.00

FORCE WORKS

1994–96

1 TmT,Pop-up(c),I:Century,V:Kree, N:US Agent 4.00
2 TmT,V:Scatter. 2.00
3 TmT,V:Scatter. 2.00
4 Civil War. 2.00
5 regular cover 2.00
5a Neon(c),bagged w/print. 2.95
6 Hands of the Mandarin,pt.1. . . . . 2.00
7 Hands of the Mandarin,pt.2. . . . . 2.00
8 DAn,ALa,Christmas Party 2.00
9 I:Dream Guard 2.00
10 V:Dream Guard 2.00
11 F:War Machine 2.00
12 V:Recorder 2.50
13 DAn,ALa,A:Avengers 2.00
14 . . . . 2.00
15 DAn,ALa,O:Century 2.00
16 . . . . 2.00
17 DAn,ALa,The Crossing 2.00
18 DAn,ALa,The Crossing 2.00
19 DAn,ALa,The Crossing 2.00
20 DAn,cont.Avengers:Timeslide . . 2.00

FOR YOUR EYES ONLY

1 HC,James Bond rep. 2.00
2 HC,James Bond rep. 2.00

FRAGGLE ROCK
1985

1 thru 8 . . . . @2.00

[Volume 2] April, 1988

1 thru 5 rep. . . . . @2.00
6 Sept., 1988 . . . . 2.00

FRANCIS, BROTHER OF THE UNIVERSE
1980

1-shot SB 2.50

FRANKENSTEIN
See: MONSTER OF FRANKENSTEIN

FRED HEMBECK

1-shot Destroys the Marvel Universe, parody (1989) 2.00
1-shot Sells the Marvel Universe parody (1990). 2.00

FRIGHT
June, 1975

1 Son of Dracula 15.00

FRONTIER WESTERN
Feb., 1956

1 RH,. 125.00
2 AW,GT 75.00
3 MD. 75.00
4 MD. 50.00
5 RC 60.00
6 AW, ... 75.00
7 JR 50.00
8 RC 50.00
9 . . . . 50.00
10 August, 1957 . . . . 50.00

FUNNY FROLICS
Summer, 1945

1 (fa) 135.00
2 . . . . 75.00
3 . . . . 60.00
4 . . . . 60.00
5 HK 75.00

FURTHER ADVENTURES OF CYCLOPS AND PHOENIX
1996

1 thru 4 . . . . 2.00
TPB PrM,JPL, O:Mr. Sinister, ... 12.00

FURY
1994

1 MCW,O:Fury,A:S.A. Heroes 3.25

FURY/AGENT 13
March, 1998

1 (of 2) TKa,is Nick Fury alive? . . . 3.00
2 TKa,MZ(c),Sharon Carter's searches for Nick 3.00

FURY OF S.H.I.E.L.D.
1995

1 Foil etched cover 2.50
2 A:Iron Man 2.00
3 J:Hydra 2.00
4 w/decoder card. 2.50

GALACTIC GUARDIANS
1994

1 KWe,C:Woden 2.00
2 KWe,I:Hazmat,Savant,Ganglia . . 2.00
3 KWe. 2.00
4 KWe,final issue. 2.00

GALACTUS THE DEVOURER
April, 1999

1 (of 6) JMu,LSi,A:Silver Surfer, Fant.Four & Avengers,48-page. 3.50
2 LSi,JB,BSz 2.50
3 LSi,JB,BSz 2.50
4 LSi,JB,BSz,A:Silver Surfer 2.50
5 LSi,JB,BSz 2.50
6 LSi,JB,BSz,concl 3.50

GAMBIT
1997

1 HMe(c),LW,KJ,V:Assassin'sGuild, D:Henri LeBeau,Embossed(c) . 5.00
1a Gold Ed. 15.00
2 LW,KJ,C:Gideon,A:Rogue 3.00
3 LW,KJ,A:Candra,Rogue, D:Gambit's Father 3.00
4 LW,KJ,A:Candra,Rogue,D:Tithe Collector. 3.00
TPB Rep.#1-#4. . . . . 8.95

GAMBIT
1997

1 (of 4) HMe,KJ,In Miami. 2.50
2 HMe,KJ, ... 2.50
3 HMe,KJ,in the Vatican 2.50
4 HMe V:Stoker, concl. 2.50

GAMBIT
Dec., 1998

1 FaN,SSr,O:Gambit,48-page 3.00
1a signed 24.95
2 FaN,SSr,V:Storm 3.00
2a variant cover. 3.00
3 FaN,SSr,V:Mengo Brothers. 2.00
4 FaN,SSr,A:Blade 2.00
5 FaN,SSr,R:Rogue. 2.00

Gambit #6
© Marvel Entertainment Group

6 FaN,SSr,I:The Pig. 2.00
7 FaN,SSr, ... 2.00
8 FaN,A:Sinister,Sabretooth. 2.00
9 FaN,The Shattering,x-over 2.00
10 FaN,V:Candra & Fenris 2.00
11 FaN,A:Daredevil 2.00
12 FaN. 2.00
13 FaN,Black Womb. 2.00
14 FaN,ALa,A:Mr. Sinister 2.00
15 FaN,F:Rogue. 2.00
16 FaN,X-Men: Revolution 2.00
16a variant (c) 2.00
17 FaN,AssassinationGame,pt.1. . . 2.25
18 FaN,AssassinationGame,pt.2. . . 2.25
19 FaN,AssassinationGame,pt.3. . . 2.25
20 FaN,Fontanelle 2.25
21 FaN,Remy LeBeau 2.25
22 FaN,Neo,Remy LeBeau,Rax . . . 2.25
23 FaN,X-Cutioner 2.25
Ann.1999 48-page 3.50
Ann.2000 FaN,F:X-Men 3.50
Giant Sized Gambit, 96-page, rep. . 4.00

GAMBIT AND THE X-TERNALS
1995

1 X-Force after Xavier 3.50
2 V:Deathbird,Starjammers 2.50
3 V:Imperial Guard 2.25
4 Charles Kidnapped 2.25

GARGOYLE
June, 1985

1 BWr(c),from `Defenders'. 4.00
2 thru 4 . . . . @3.00

GARGOYLES
1995–96

1 TV Series. 2.50
2 TV Series. 2.00
3 F:Broadway 2.00
4 V:Statues 2.00
5 Humanoid Gargoyles 2.00
6 Medusa Project concl. 2.00
7 Demona & Triad 2.00
8 I:The Pack 2.00
9 V:Demonia,Triad. 2.00
10 Demonia gains magical powers . 2.00
11 Elisa turns to Xanatos 2.00
12 Sorceress traps Gargoyles. 2.00
13 Behind Enemy Lines 2.00
14 . . . . 2.00
15 . . . . 2.00
16 Hammer of Fear 2.00

GENE DOGS
Marvel UK 1993–94

1 I:Gene DOGS,w/cards 2.75
2 V:Genetix 2.00
3 V:Hurricane 2.00
4 last issue 2.00

GENERATION NEXT
1995

1 Generation X AX 3.50
2 Genetic Slave Pens 2.50
3 V:Sugar Man 2.25
4 V:Sugar Man 2.25

GENERATION X
Oct., 1994

1 CBa,Banshee & White Queen. . . 7.00
2 CBa,SLo. 3.00
2a Deluxe edition. 4.00
3 CBa 2.50

3a Deluxe edition. 4.00
4 CBa,V:Nanny,Orphanmaker 2.50
4a Deluxe edition. 4.00
5 SLo,CBa,MBu,two new young mutants at the Academy. 3.50
6 A:Wolverine 3.50
7 SLo,F:Banshee,A:White Queen . 3.50
8 F:Banshee 3.50
9 SLo,TG,Chamber in a kilt 3.50
10 SLo,TG,MBu,Banshee vs. OmegaRed. 3.50
11 SLo,TG,V:Omega Red 3.00
12 SLo,TG,V:Emplate. 3.00
13 . . . . 3.00
14 . . . . 3.00
15 SLo,MBu,Synch goes psycho . . 3.00
16 . . . . 3.00
17 SLo,CBa,Onslaught saga, X-Cutioner vs. Skin. 3.00
18 SLo,CBa,Onslaught saga. 3.00
19 SLo,CBa,. 3.00
20 SLo,CBa,. 3.00
21 SLo,CBa,MBu,F:Skin & Chamber, A:Beverly Switzer, Howard the Duck 3.00
22 SLo,CBa,. 3.00
23 SLo,CBa,V:Black Tom Cassidy . 3.00
24 SLo,MBy,F:Monet,Emplate. 3.00
25 SLo,CBa,double size 4.00
26 SLo,CBa,Shot down over the Atlantic. 3.00
27 SLo,CBa,on nuclear sub. 3.00
28 SLo,CBa,No Exit prelude 3.00
29 JeR,CBa, V:Sentinels 3.00
30 JeR,CBa, V:Zero Tolerance 3.00
31 JeR,CBa, ... 2.50
32 TDF,MBu,F:Banshee, Moira McTaggert 2.50
33 LHa,MBu,new direction 2.50
34 LHa,Truth behind M 2.50
35 LHa,Jubilee,V:Emplate. 2.50
36 LHa,Final Fate of M. 2.50
37 LHa,Final Fate of M. 2.50
38 LHa,TyD,kids save universe. . . . 2.50
39 LHa,TyD, multi-dimensional trip . 2.50
40 LHa,TyD,Penance mystery revealed. 2.50
41 LHa,TyD,Jubilee,V:Bastion, Omega Red, Sabretooth. 2.50
42 LHa,TyD,results of EMP wave . . 2.50
43 LHa,TyD,V:Bianca LaNiege 2.50
44 LHa,TyD,V:White Queen 2.50
45 LHa,TyD,F:Banshee. 2.50
46 LHa,TyD,F:Forge 2.50
47 LHa,TyD,Danger Room 2.50
48 TyD,Jubilee vs. M 2.50
49 TyD,V:Maggott. 2.50
50 TyD,War of the Mutants,pt.1. . . . 3.50
50a signed 20.00
51 V:Hunter Brawn 2.00
52 TyD,blackmail 2.00
53 TyD,V:Rising Sons,A:Paladin . . . 2.00
54 TyD,A:Paladin 2.00
55 TyD,in bodies of Hellions 2.00
56 TyD,A:X-Men of past 2.00
57 TyD, double sized 3.00
58 TyD, new Penance 2.00
59 TyD, ... 2.00
60 TyD,F:Siryn 2.00
61 TyD,ATi,R:Mondo. 2.00
62 TyD,F:Monet St. Croix 2.00
63 WEI,X-Men Revolution. 2.00
63a variant (c) 2.00
64 WEI,Correction,pt.2 . . . . 2.25
65 WEI,Correction,pt.3 . . . . 2.25
66 WEI,Correction,pt.4 . . . . 2.25
67 WEI,Come On Die Young,pt.1 . . 2.25
68 WEI,Come On Die Young,pt.2 . . 2.25
69 WEI,Come On Die Young,pt.3 . . 2.25
70 WEI,Come On Die Young,pt.4 . . 2.25
Minus 1 Spec., JeR,CBa, flashback, F:Banshee 2.00
Ann. '95 SLo,J:Mondo, V:Hellfire Club 4.00
Ann. '96 GN MGo,JJ,DPs,V:Fenris . 3.00
Ann. '97, Haunted by Ghosts of Hellions 2.00
Ann.1998 Generation X/Dracula . . . 3.50
Ann.1999 48-pg.. . . . . 3.50
Holliday Spec. 48-page 1-shot 3.50

Generation X/Gen 13 #1
© Marvel Entertainment Group

GENERATION X/GEN 13
Dec., 1997

1-shot JeR,SvL,V:Mr. Pretorious . . . 4.00
1a variant cover CBa (1:4) 4.00

GENERATION X: UNDERGROUND
March, 1998

1-shot by Jim Mahfood, b&w. 2.50

GENERIC COMIC

1 . . . . 2.00

GENETIX
Marvel UK 1993–94

1 B:ALa(s),w/cards 2.75
2 I:Tektos 2.00
3 V:Tektos 2.00
4 PGa,V:MyS-Tech 2.00
5 PGa,V:MyS-Tech 2.00
6 V:Tektos 2.00

GEORGIE COMICS
Spring, 1945

1 Georgie stories begin 150.00
2 Pet Shop (c) 65.00
3 Georgie/Judy(c) 50.00
4 Wedding Dress(c) 50.00
5 Monty/Policeman(c) 50.00
6 Classroom(c) 50.00
7 Fishing(c) 55.00
8 Soda Jerk(c) 40.00
9 Georgie/Judy(c),HK,Hey Look . 50.00
10 Georgie/Girls(c),HK,Hey Look . 50.00
11 Table Tennis(c),A:Margie,Millie . 30.00
12 Camping(c) 30.00
13 Life Guard(c),HK,Hey Look . . . 45.00
14 Classroom(c),HK,Hey Look . . . 50.00
15 Winter Sports(c). 30.00
16 . . . . 30.00
17 HK,Hey Look 30.00
18 . . . . 30.00
19 Baseball(c) 30.00
20 Title change to Georgie & Judy Comics 30.00
21 Title change to Georgie & Judy Comics 25.00
22 Georgie comics 25.00
23 . . . . 25.00
24 . . . . 25.00
25 . . . . 40.00
26 . . . . 20.00
27 . . . . 20.00
28. . . . . 20.00
29 . . . . 35.00
30 thru 38 . . . . @20.00
39 Oct., 1952 . . . . 20.00

GETALONG GANG
May, 1985—March, 1986

1 thru 6 . . . . @2.00

GHOST RIDER
[1st Regular Series] Sept., 1973

1 GK,JSt,C:Son of Satan 60.00
2 GK,I:Son of Satan,A:Witch Woman 25.00
3 JR,D:Big Daddy Dawson, new Cycle 15.00
4 GK,A:Dude Jensen 15.00
5 GK,JR,I:Roulette. 15.00
6 JR,O:Ghost Rider 11.00
7 JR,A:Stunt Master. 11.00
8 GK,A:Satan,I:Inferno. 10.00
9 GK,TP,O:Johnny Blaze 11.00
10 JSt,A:Hulk 11.00
11 GK,KJ,SB,A:Hulk 10.00
12 GK,KJ,FR,A:Phantom Eagle . . . 8.00
13 GK,JS,GT,A:Trapster 8.00
14 GT,A:The Orb 8.00
15 SB,O:The Orb 8.00
16 DC,GT,Blood in the Water 8.00
17 RB,FR,I:Challenger 8.00
18 RB,FR,A:Challenger, Spider-Man 9.00
19 GK,FR,A:Challenger 8.00
20 GK,KJ,JBy,A:Daredevil 10.00
21 A:Gladiator,D:Eel 5.00
22 AM,DH,KP,JR,A:Enforcer. 5.00

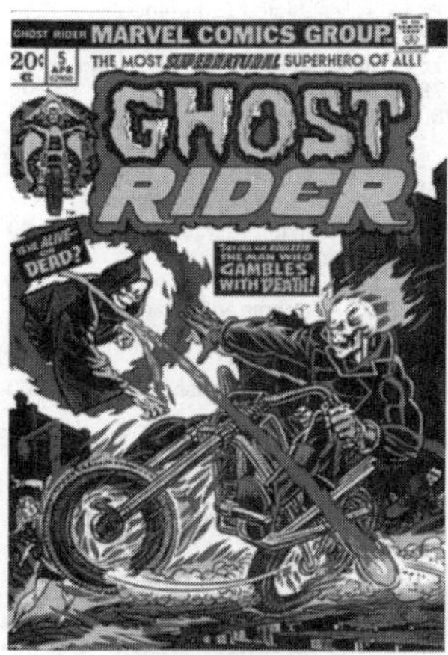

Ghost Rider #5
© Marvel Entertainment Group

23 JK,DH,DN,I:Water Wiz. 5.00
24 GK,DC,DH,A:Enforcer 5.00
25 GK,DH,A:Stunt Master. 5.00
26 GK,DP,A:Dr. Druid 5.00
27 SB,DP,A:Hawkeye 5.00
28 DP,A:The Orb 5.00
29 RB,DP,A:Dormammu 5.00
30 DP,A:Dr.Strange 5.00
31 FR,DP,BL,A:Bounty Hunt. 5.00
32 KP,BL,DP,A:Bounty Hunt. 5.00
33 DP,I:Dark Riders 5.00
34 DP,C:Cyclops 5.00
35 JSn,AM,A:Death 6.00
36 DP,Drug Mention 5.00
37 DP,I:Dick Varden 5.00
38 DP,A:Death Cult. 5.00
39 DP,A:Death Cult. 5.00
40 DP,I:Nuclear Man. 5.00
41 DP,A:Jackal Gang 5.00
42 DP,A:Jackal Gang 5.00
43 CI:Crimson Mage. 5.00
44 JAb,CI,A:Crimson Mage. 5.00
45 DP,I:Flagg Fargo 5.00
46 DP,A:Flagg Fargo 5.00
47 AM,DP. 5.00
48 BMc,DP. 5.00
49 DP,I:The Manitou 5.00
50 DP,A:Night Rider 6.00
51 AM,PD,A:Cycle Gang 4.00
52 AM,DP. 4.00
53 DP,I:Lord Asmodeus 4.00
54 DP,A:The Orb 4.00
55 DP,A:Werewolf By Night. 4.00
56 DP,A:Moondark,I:Night Rider . . . 4.00
57 AM,DP,I:The Apparition 4.00
58 DP,FM,A:Water Wizard 4.00
59 V:Water Wizard,Moon Dark 4.00
60 DP,HT,A:Black Juju 4.00
61 A:Arabian Knight 4.00
62 KJ,A:Arabian Knight. 4.00
63 LMc,A:The Orb 4.00
64 BA,V:Azmodeus. 4.00
65 A:Fowler 4.00
66 BL,A:Clothilde 4.00
67 DP,A:Sally Stantop. 4.00
68 O:Ghost Rider 4.00
69 . . . . 4.00
70 I:Jeremy 4.00
71 DP,I:Adam Henderson 4.00
72 A:Circus of Crime 4.00
73 A:Circus of Crime 4.00
74 A:Centurions 4.00
75 I:Steel Wind 4.00
76 DP,A:Mephisto,I:Saturnine 4.00
77 O:Ghost Rider's Dream 4.00
78 A:Nightmare 4.00
79 A:Man Cycles 4.00
80 A:Centurions 4.00
81 D:Ghost Rider 9.00

[2nd Regular Series] 1990–98

1 JS,MT,I:2nd Ghost Rider, Deathwatch 4.00
1a 2nd printing 2.00
2 JS,MT,I:Blackout. 3.00
3 JS,MT,A:Kingpin,V:Blackout, Deathwatch 3.00
4 JS,MT,V:Mr.Hyde 3.00
5 JLe(c),JS,MT,A:Punisher. 3.00
5a rep.Gold 2.50
6 JS,MT,A:Punisher 3.00
7 MT,V:Scarecrow 3.00
8 JS,MT,V:H.E.A.R.T 3.00
9 JS,MT,A:Morlocks,X-Factor. 2.50
10 JS,MT,V:Zodiac 2.50
11 LSn,MT,V:Nightmare, A:Dr.Strange 2.50
12 JS,MT,A:Dr.Strange 2.50
13 MT,V:Snow Blind,R:J.Blaze 2.50
14 MT,Blaze Vs.Ghost Rider. 2.50
15 MT,A:Blaze,V:Blackout Glow in Dark(c) 3.00
15a 2nd printing (gold) 2.50
16 MT,A:Blaze,Spider-Man, V:Hobgoblin 2.50
17 MT,A:Spider-Man,Blaze, V:Hobgoblin 2.50
18 MT,V:Reverend Styge 2.25
19 MT,A:Mephisto. 2.25
20 MT(i),O:Zodiac. 2.25
21 MT(i),V:Snowblind, A:Deathwatch. 2.25
22 MT,A:Deathwatch,Ninjas 2.25
23 MT,I:Hag & Troll,A:Deathwatch . 2.25
24 MT,V:Deathwatch,D:Snowblind, C:Johnny Blaze 2.25
25 V:Blackout (w/Center spread pop-up) 2.50
26 A:X-Men,V:The Brood 2.50
27 A:X-Men,V:The Brood 2.50
28 NKu,JKu,Rise of the Midnight Sons#1,V:Lilith,w/poster 2.50
29 NKu,JKu,A:Wolverine,Beast. . . . 2.50
30 NKu,JKu,V:Nightmare 2.25
31 NKu,JKu,Rise o/t Midnight Sons#6, A:Dr.Strange,Morbius, Nightstalkers,Redeemers, V:Lilith,w/poster 2.25
32 BBi,A:Dr.Strange 2.00
33 BBl,AW,V:Madcap (inc.Superman tribute on letters page) 2.00
34 BBl,V:Deathwatchs' ninja 2.00
35 BBl,AW,A:Heart Attack. 2.00
36 BBl,V:Mr.Hyde,A:Daredevil. 2.00
37 BBl,A:Archangel,V:HeartAttack . 2.00
38 MM,V:Scarecrow 2.00
39 V:Vengeance 2.00
40 Midnight Massacre#2, D:Demogblin 2.50
41 Road to Vengeance#1 . . . . 2.00
42 Road to Vengeance#2 . . . . 2.00
43 Road to Vengeance#3 . . . . 2.00
44 Siege of Darkness,pt.#2. . . . . . . 2.00
45 Siege of Darkness,pt.#10. . . . . . 2.00
46 HMe(s),New Beginning 2.00
47 HMe(s),RG, ... 2.00
48 HMe(s),RG,A:Spider-Man 2.00
49 HMe(s),RG,A:Hulk,w/card 2.25
50 Red Foil(c),AKu,SMc,A:Blaze, R:2nd Ghost Rider 3.25
50a Newsstand Ed. 2.75
51 SvL 2.25
52 SvL 2.00
53 SvL,V:Blackout 2.00
54 SvL,V:Blackout 2.00
55 V:Mr. Hyde 2.00

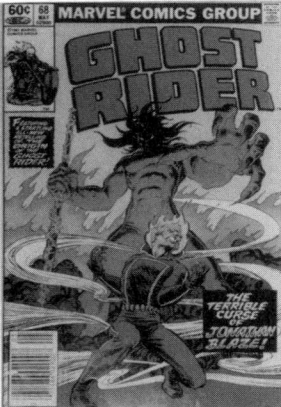

Ghost Rider #68
© Marvel Entertainment Group

56 The Next Wave 2.00
57 A:Wolverine. 2.00
58 HMe,SvL,Betrayal,pt.1 . . . . 2.00
59 Betrayal,pt.2 . . . . 2.00
60 Betrayal,pt.3 . . . . 2.00
61 Betrayal,pt.4 . . . . 2.00
62 EventInChains,pt.1,A:Fury 2.00
63 EventInChains,pt.2 . . . . 2.00
64 EventInChains,pt.3 . . . . 2.00
65 EventInChains,pt.4,R:Blackout . . 2.00
66 V:Blackout 2.00
67 A:Gambit,V:Brood 2.00
68 A:Gambit,Wolverine,V:Brood . . . 2.00
69 Domestic Violence. 2.00
70 New Home in Bronx. 2.00
71 . . . . 2.00
72 . . . . 2.00
73 John Blaze is back. 2.00
74 A:Blaze, Vengeance 2.00
75 . . . . 2.00
76 V:Vengeance 2.00
77 A:Dr. Strange. 2.00
78 new costume, A:Dr. Strange . . . 2.00
79 IV,New costume, A:Valkyrie, . . . 2.00
80 IV,V:Furies,Valkyrie, A:Black Rose 2.00
81 IV,A:Howard the Duck, Devil Dinosaur 2.00
82 IV,A:Devil Dinosaur, ... 2.00
83 IV,A:Scarecrow,Lilith 2.00
84 IV,A:Scarecrow, Lilith 2.00
85 IV,V:Lilith, Scarecrow 2.00
86 IV,rampage through the Bronx . . 2.00
87 IV,KIK,AM, ... 2.00
88 IV, V:Pao Fu,Blackheart 2.00
89 IV,JS, ... 2.00
90 IV,JS,Last Temptation, pt.1. . . . . 2.00
91 IV,JS,A:Blackheart 2.00
92 IV,JS,Journey into the past 2.00
93 IV,JS,MT,Last Temptation concl., double sized. 3.00
94 IV,JS,MT,Becomes Lord of the Underworld, last issue 2.00
Ann.#1 I:Night Terror,w/card 3.25
Ann.#2 F:Scarecrow 2.95
GN Ghost Rider/Captain America: Fear, AW, V:Scarecrow (1992) . 6.25
TPB Midnight Sons,rep.GhR#28,31, Morbius#1,Darkhold#1,Spirirts of Vengeance#1,Nightstalkers#1. 19.95
TPB Resurrected rep.#1-#7 . . . . . 12.95
TPB Ghost Rider/Wolverine/Punisher: Dark Design (1994) 5.95
TPB Ghost Rider/Wolverine/Punisher: Hearts of Darkness, JR2/KJ,V: Blackheart, double gatefold cover (1991) 5.50
Poster Book 4.95
Spec. Crossroads. 3.95
Minus 1 Spec., IV,JS, flashback . . . 2.00

GHOST RIDER/BALLISTIC

Marvel/Top Cow 1996

1-shot WEl,BTn,"Devil's Reign," pt.3, x-over. 3.00

GHOST RIDER/BLAZE SPIRITS OF VENGEANCE

1992–94

1 AKu,polybagged w/poster,V:Lilith, Rise of the Midnight Sons#2. . . 3.50
2 AKu,V:Steel Wind 2.50
3 AKu,CW,V:The Lilin 2.00
4 AKu,V:Hag & Troll,C:Venom 3.00
5 AKu,BR,Spirits of Venom#2, A:Venom,Spidey,Hobgoblin. . . . 5.00
6 AKu,Spirits of Venom#4,A:Venom, Spider-Man,Hobgoblin 3.50
7 AKu,V:Steel Vengeance 2.00

8 V:Mephisto 2.00
9 I:Brimstone 2.00
10 AKu,V:Vengeance 2.00
11 V:Human Spider Creature 2.00
12 AKu,BR,Vengeance,glow in the dark(c) 3.25
13 AKu,Midnight Massacre#5 . . . . . 2.50
14 Missing Link#2. . . . . 2.00
15 Missing Link#3. . . . . 2.00
16 V:Zarathos,Lilith. 2.00
17 HMe(s),Siege/Darkness,pt.8 . . . 2.00
18 HMe(s),Siege/Darkness,pt.13 . . 2.00
19 HMe(s),HMz,V;Vampire 2.00
20 HMe(s),A:Steel Wind 2.00
21 HMe(s),HMz,V:Werewolves 2.00
22 HMe(s),HMz,V:Cardiac 2.25
23 HMe(s),HMz,A:Steel Wind 2.25

GHOST RIDER/CYBLADE
Marvel/Top Cow 1996

1-shot IV,ACh,"Devil's Reign," pt.2, x-over. 2.95

GHOST RIDER 2099
1994–96

1 Holografx(c),LKa,CBa,MBu,I:Ghost Rider 2099,w/card 2.75
1a Newsstand Ed. 2.00
2 LKa,CBa,MBu, ... 2.00
3 LKa,CBa,MBu,I:Warewolf 2.00
4 LKa,CBa,MBu,V:Warewolf 2.00
5 LKa,CBa,MBu. 2.00
6 LKa,CBa,MBu. 2.00
7 LKa,CBa,MBu. 2.00
8 LKa,CBa,MBu. 2.00
9 . . . . 2.00
10 . . . . 2.00
11 V:Bloodsport Society 2.00
12 I:Coda 2.00

Becomes:

GHOST RIDER 2099 A.D.

13 F:Doom 2.00
14 Deputized by Doom 2.00
15 One Nation Under Doom 2.00
16 V:Max Synergy 2.00
17 . . . . 2.00
18 V:L-Cipher 2.00
19 V:L-Cipher 2.00
20 . . . . 2.00
21 V:Vengeance 2099 . . . . 2.00
22 V:Vengeance 2099 . . . . 2.00

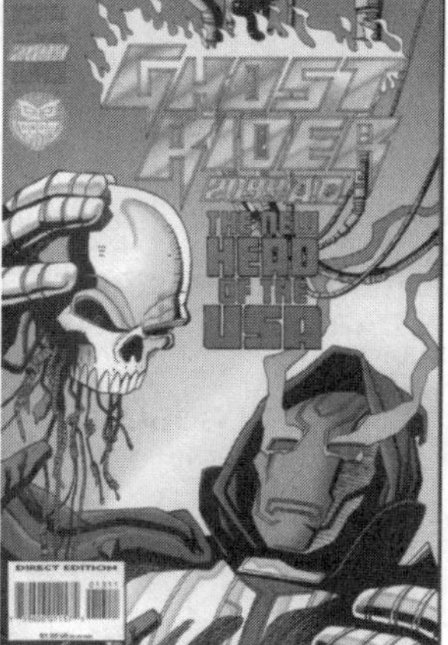

Ghost Rider 2099 #13
© Marvel Entertainment Group

23 . . . . 2.00
24 . . . . 2.00
25 Double size final issue. 3.00

GIANT-SIZE CHILLERS
1975

1 AA,. 20.00
2 . . . . 12.00
3 BWr,Night of the Gargoyle 20.00

GIANT-SIZE CHILLERS
1974

1 I&O:Lilith,F:Curse of Dracula. . . 30.00

Becomes:

GIANT-SIZE DRACULA

2 Vengeance of the Elder Gods . . 15.00
3 rep. Uncanny Tales #6 . . . . 12.00
4 SD,Demon of Devil's Lake 12.00
5 JBy, 1st Marvel art 20.00

G.I. JOE: A REAL AMERICAN HERO
June, 1982

1 HT,BMc,Baxter paper 5.00
2 DP,JAb,North Pole 4.00
3 HT,JAb,Trojan Robot 4.00
4 HT,JAb,Wingfield 4.00
5 DP,Central Park 4.00
6 HT,V:Cobra. 4.00
7 HT,Walls of Death. 4.00
8 HT,Sea Strike 4.00
9 The Diplomat 4.00
10 Springfield 4.00
11 Alaska Pipeline 4.00
12 V:Snake Eyes 5.00
13 Rio Lindo. 3.50
14 V:Destro 3.50
15 A:Red Eye 3.50
16 V:Cobra 3.50
17 Loose Ends 3.50
18 V:Destro 5.00
19 D:General Kwinn 3.50
20 JBy(c),GI,Clutch 3.50
21 SL(i),Silent Interlude 3.50
22 V:Destro 3.50
23 I:Duke 3.50
24 RH,I:Storm Shadow 3.50
25 FS,I:Zartan 3.50
26 SL(i),O:Snake Eyes 5.00
27 FS,O:Snake Eyes 5.00
28 Swampfire 3.50
29 FS,V:Destro. 3.50
30 JBy(c),FS,V:Dreddnoks 3.50
31 V:Destro 2.50
32 FS,V:Dreddnoks 2.50
33 FS,Celebration. 2.50
34 Shakedown 2.50
35 JBy(c),MBr,V:Dreddnoks 2.50
36 MBr,Shipwar 2.50
2a to 36a 2nd printings . . . . @2.00
37 FS,Twin Brothers,I:Flint 2.25
38 V:Destro 2.25
39 Jungle 2.25
40 Hydrofoil 2.25
41 . . . . 2.25
42 A:Stormshadow 2.25
43 Death Issue,New Joe. 2.25
44 V:Cobra. 2.25
45 V:Cobra. 2.25
46 V:Cobra. 2.25
47 V:Cobra,D:Stormshadow 2.25
48 V:Cobra. 2.25
49 V:Cobra,I:Serpentor 2.25
50 I:G.I.Joe Missions,R:S'shadow . . 2.50
51 V:Cobra Emperor. 2.25
52 V:Stormshadow 2.25
53 Hawk V:Cobra 2.25

G. I. Joe #38
© Marvel Entertainment Group

54 V:Destro 2.25
55 The Pit 2.25
56 V:Serpentor 2.25
57 V:Destro 2.25
58 V:Cobra. 2.25
59 Armor 2.25
60 TM,I:Zanzibar 4.50
61 MR,D:Cobra Commander 2.25
62 Trial. 2.25
63 A:GI Joe Snow Job 2.25
64 V:Baroness 2.25
65 V:Cobra. 2.25
66 Stalker Rescued 2.25
67 . . . . 2.25
68 I:Battleforce 2000 . . . . 2.25
69 TSa. 2.25
70 V:Destro 2.25
71 . . . . 2.25
72 . . . . 2.25
73 . . . . 2.25
74 . . . . 2.25
75 MR 2.25
76 D:Serpentor. 2.25
77 MR,V:Cobra. 2.25
78 V:Cobra. 2.25
79 MR,V:Dreadnoks 2.25
80 V:Cobra. 2.25
81 MR,V:Dreadnoks 2.25
82 MR,V:Cobra. 2.25
83 I:RoadPig 2.25
84 MR,O:Zartan 2.25
85 Storm Shadow,Vs.Zartan 2.25
86 MR,25th Anniv. 2.25
87 TSa,V:Cobra 2.25
88 TSa,V:Python Patrol 2.25
89 MBr,V:Road Pig 2.25
90 MBr,R:Red Ninjas 2.25
91 TSa,V:Red Ninjas,D:Blind Masters 2.25
92 MBr,V:Cobra Condor 2.25
93 MBr,V:Baroness. 15.00
94 MBr,A:Snake Eyes. 5.00
95 MBr,A:Snake Eyes. 5.00
96 MBr,A:Snake Eyes. 5.00
97 . . . . 2.25
98 MBr,R:Cobra Commander 2.25
99 HT. 2.25
100 MBr 2.25
101 MBr 2.25
102 MBr 2.25
103 MBr,A:Snake Eyes. 2.25
104 MBr,A:Snake Eyes. 2.25
105 MBr,A:Snake Eyes. 2.25

106 MBr,StormShadowStalker 2.25
107 . . . . 2.25
108 I:G.I.Joe Dossiers 2.25
109 Death Issue 2.25
110 Mid-East Crisis. 4.00
111 A:Team Ninjas 4.00
112 A:Team Ninjas 4.00
113 V:Cobra 4.00
114 V:Cobra 2.25
115 Story Concl.Dusty Dossier 2.25
116 Destro:Search&Destroy #1. . . . 2.25
117 Destro:Search&Destroy #2. . . . 2.25
118 Destro:Search&Destroy #3. . . . 2.25
119 HT,Android Dopplegangers . . . 2.25
120 V:Red Ninjas,Slice & Dice 5.00
121 V:Slice & Dice 2.25
122 V:Slice & Dice 2.25
123 I:Eco-Warriors,A:Big Man. 2.25
124 V:Headman 2.25
125 V:Headhunters. 2.25
126 R:Firefly. 2.25
127 R:Original G.I.Joe 2.25
128 V:Firefly. 2.25
129 V:Cobra Commander. 2.25
130 V:Cobra Commander. 2.25
131 V:Cobra Commander. 2.25
132 V:Cobra. 2.25
133 V:Cobra. 2.25
134 V:Red Ninjas, Firefly,
Hostilities 2.25
135 V:Cobra Ninja w/card. 2.25
136 w/Trading Card 2.25
137 V:Night Creepers,w/card 2.25
138 V:Night Creepers,w/card 2.25
139 R:Transformers,V:Cobra 2.25
140 A:Transformers 2.25
141 A:Transformers 2.25
142 A:Transformers 2.25
143 F:Scarlet 2.25
144 O:Snake Eyes 2.25
145 V:Cobra. 2.25
146 F:Star Brigade 2.25
147 F:Star Brigade 2.25
148 F:Star Brigade 2.25
149. . . . . 2.25
150 Cobra Commander vs.
Snake Eyes 2.50
151 V:Cobra. 5.00
152 First G.I. Joe 5.00
153 V:Cobra. 5.00
154 . . . . 15.00
155 final issue 20.00
SC GI Joe and the Transformers . . 4.95
Spec. TM rep.#61. . . . . 3.00
Ann.#1 . . . . 3.00
Ann.#2 . . . . 3.00
Ann.#3 . . . . 3.00
Ann.#4 . . . . 3.00
Ann.#5 . . . . 3.00
Yearbook #1 (1985) 2.50
Yearbook #2 (1986) 2.50
Yearbook #3 (1987) 2.50
Yearbook #4 (1988) 2.50

G.I. JOE EUROPEAN MISSIONS

June, 1988

1 British rep. 2.50
2 . . . . 2.50
3 . . . . 2.50
4 . . . . 2.50
5 thru 15 . . . . @2.50

G.I. JOE SPECIAL MISSIONS

Oct., 1986

1 HT,New G.I. Joe 2.00
2 HT 2.00
3 HT 2.00
4 HT 2.00
5 HT 2.00
6 HT,Iron Curtain 2.00
7 HT 2.00
8 HT 2.00
9 HT 2.00
10 thru 21 HT . . . . @2.00
22 . . . . 2.00
23 HT. 2.00
24 . . . . 2.00
25 HT. 2.00
26 HT. 2.00
27 . . . . 2.00
28 HT,final 2.00

G.I. JOE AND THE TRANSFORMERS

1987

1 HT,mini-series. 2.00
2 HT,Cobra 2.00
3 HT,Cobra,Deceptions 2.00
4 HT,Cobra,Deceptions 2.00

G.I. JOE UNIVERSE

1 Biographies rep.#1 . . . . 2.50
2 . . . . 2.00
3 MZ(c) 2.00
4 . . . . 2.00

G.I. TALES

See: SERGEANT BARNEY BARKER

GIRL COMICS

Atlas Nov., 1949

1 Ph(c),True love stories,I Could
Escape From Love 125.00
2 Ph(c),JKu,Blind Date 75.00
3 BEv,Ph(c),Liz Taylor 100.00
4 PH(c),Borrowed Love 50.00
5 Love stories 50.00
6 same 50.00
7 same 50.00
8 same 50.00
9 same 50.00
10 The Deadly Double-Cross 50.00
11 Love stories. 50.00
12 BK,The Dark Hallway. 60.00

Becomes:

GIRL CONFESSIONS

13 . . . . 60.00
14 . . . . 35.00
15 . . . . 35.00
16 BEv. 45.00
17 BEv. 45.00
18 BEv. 45.00
19 . . . . 30.00
20 . . . . 30.00
21 thru 34 . . . . @25.00
35 August, 1954 . . . . 25.00

GIRLS' LIFE

Atlas Jan., 1954

1 . . . . 50.00
2 . . . . 25.00
3 . . . . 20.00
4 . . . . 20.00
5 . . . . 20.00
6 November, 1954 . . . . 20.00

GLADIATOR/SUPREME

1997

1 KG,ASm,x-over 5.00

Godzilla #1
© Marvel Entertainment Group

GODZILLA

August, 1977

1 HT,JM,Based on Movie Series . 10.00
2 HT,FrG,GT,Seattle Under Seige . 7.00
3 HT,TD,A;Champions 10.00
4 TS,TD,V;Batragon 7.00
5 TS,KJ,Isle of the Living
Demons 7.00
6 HT,A Monster Enslaved 7.00
7 V:Red Ronin 7.00
8 V:Red Ronin 7.00
9 Las Gamble in Las Vegas 7.00
10 V:Yetrigar. 7.00
11 V;Red Ronin,Yetrigar 5.00
12 Star Sinister. 5.00
13 V:Mega-Monster 5.00
14 V:Super-Beasts 5.00
15 Stampede 5.00
16 Jaws of Fear 5.00
17 Godzilla Shrunk. 5.00
18 Battle Beneath Eighth Avenue . . 5.00
19 Panic on the Pier. 5.00
20 A;Fantastic Four 6.00
21 V;Devil Dinosaur 5.00
22 V:Devil Dinosaur 5.00
23 A;Avengers 6.00
24 July, 1979 . . . . 5.00

GOLDEN AGE OF MARVEL

TPB RyL. 10.00
Vol.1, 176-page 20.00
Vol.2, 176-page 20.00

GREATEST SPIDER-MAN & DAREDEVIL TEAM-UPS

TPB 175pg 10.00

GREEN GOBLIN

1995–96

1 I:New Green Goblin 3.00
2 TDF,SMc,V:Rhino 2.00
3 TDF,SMc,CyberWar tie-in 2.00
4 TDF,SMc,V:Hobgoblin. 2.00
5 TDF,V:Hobgoblin 2.00
6 . . . . 2.00
7 . . . . 2.00
8 TDF,SMc,I:Angelface 2.00
9 . . . . 2.00
10 . . . . 2.00

11 . . . 2.00
12 Onslaught saga . . . 2.00
13 Onslaught saga . . . 2.00

GROO CHRONICLES
Epic 1989

1 SA . . . 5.00
2 SA . . . 4.00
3 SA . . . 4.00
4 SA . . . 4.00
5 SA . . . 4.00
6 SA . . . 3.50

Groo, The Wanderer #1
© Marvel Entertainment Group

[SERGIO ARAGONE'S] GROO, THE WANDERER
(see Pacific, Eclipse)
Epic 1985–95

1 SA,I:Minstrel . . . 9.00
2 SA,A:Minstrel . . . 6.00
3 SA,Medallions . . . 5.00
4 SA,Airship . . . 4.00
5 SA,Slavers . . . 4.00
6 SA,The Eye of the Kabala . . . 4.00
7 SA,A:Sage . . . 4.00
8 SA,A:Taranto . . . 4.00
9 SA,A:Sage . . . 4.00
10 SA,I:Arcadio . . . 4.00
11 SA,A:Arcadio . . . 4.00
12 SA,Groo Meets the Thespians . . 4.00
13 SA,A:Sage . . . 4.00
14 SA . . . 4.00
15 SA,Monks . . . 4.00
16 SA,A:Taranto . . . 4.00
17 SA,Pirannas . . . 4.00
18 SA,I:Groo Ella . . . 4.00
19 SA,A:Groo Ella . . . 3.00
20 SA,A:Groo Ella . . . 3.00
21 SA,I:Arba,Dakarba . . . 3.00
22 SA,Ambassador . . . 3.00
23 SA,I:Pal,Drumm . . . 3.00
24 SA,Arcadio's . . . 3.00
25 SA,Taranto . . . 3.00
26 SA,A:Arba,Taranto . . . 3.00
27 SA,A:Minstrel,Sage . . . 3.00
28 SA . . . 3.00
29 SA,I:Ruferto . . . 4.00
30 SA,A:Ruferto . . . 3.00
31 SA,A:Pal,Drumm . . . 3.00
32 SA,C:Sage . . . 3.00
33 SA,Pirates . . . 3.00
34 SA,Wizard's amulet . . . 3.00
35 SA,A:Everybody . . . 3.00
36 SA,A:Everybody . . . 3.00
37 SA,A:Ruferto . . . 3.00
38 SA,Dognappers . . . 3.00
39 SA,A:Pal,Drumm . . . 3.00
40 SA . . . 3.00
41 SA,I:Granny Groo . . . 3.00
42 SA,A:Granny Groo . . . 3.00
43 SA,A:Granny Groo . . . 3.00
44 SA,A:Ruferto . . . 3.00
45 SA . . . 3.00
46 SA,New Clothes . . . 3.00
47 SA,A:Everybody . . . 3.00
48 SA,A:Ruferto . . . 3.00
49 SA,C:Chakaal . . . 3.00
50 SA,double size . . . 4.00
51 SA,A:Chakaal . . . 2.50
52 SA,A:Chakaal . . . 2.50
53 SA,A:Chakaal . . . 2.50
54 SA,A:Ahak . . . 2.50
55 SA,A:Ruferto . . . 2.50
56 SA,A:Minstrael . . . 2.50
57 SA,A:Ruferto . . . 2.50
58 SA,A:Idol . . . 2.50
59 SA . . . 2.50
60 SA,A:Ruferto . . . 2.50
61 SA,A:Horse . . . 2.50
62 SA,A:Horse . . . 2.50
63 SA,A:Drumm . . . 2.50
64 SA,A:Artist . . . 2.50
65 SA . . . 2.50
66 SA . . . 2.50
67 SA . . . 2.50
68 SA . . . 2.50
69 SA . . . 2.50
70 SA . . . 2.50
71 SA . . . 2.50
72 SA . . . 2.50
73 SA,Amnesia,pt1 . . . 2.50
74 SA,Amnesia,pt2 . . . 2.50
75 SA,Memory Returns . . . 2.50
76 SA . . . 2.50
77 SA . . . 2.50
78 SA,R:Weaver,Scribe . . . 2.50
79 SA,Groo the Assassin . . . 2.50
80 SA,I:Thaiis,pt.1 . . . 2.50
81 SA,Thaiis,pt.2 . . . 2.50
82 SA,Thaiis,pt.3 . . . 2.50
83 SA,Thaiis,pt.4 . . . 2.50
84 SA,Thaiis Conclusion . . . 2.50
85 SA,Groo turns invisible . . . 2.50
86 SA,Invisible Groo . . . 2.50
87 SA,Groo's Army . . . 2.50
88 SA,V:Cattlemen,B.U. Sage . . . 3.00
89 SA,New Deluxe Format . . . 2.50
90 SA,Worlds 1st Lawyers . . . 2.50
91 SA,Bonus Pages . . . 2.50
92 SA,Groo Becomes Kid Groo . . . 2.50
93 SA,Groo destroys glacier . . . 2.50
94 SA . . . 2.50
95 SA,Endangered Species . . . 2.50
96 SA,Wager of the Gods#1 . . . 2.50
97 SA,Wager of the Gods#2 . . . 2.50
98 SA,Wager of the Gods#3 . . . 2.50
99 SA,E:Wager of the Gods . . . 2.50
100 SA,Groo gets extra IQ points . 13.00
101 SA,Groo loses intelligence . . . 2.50
102 SA,F:Newly literate Groo . . . 2.50
103 SA,General Monk . . . 2.50
104 SA,F:Oso,Ruferto . . . 2.50
105 SA,V:Minotaurs . . . 2.50
106 SA,B:Man of the People . . . 2.50
107 SA,Man of the People#2 . . . 2.50
108 SA,Man of the People#3 . . . 2.50
109 SA,E:Man of the People . . . 2.50
110 SA,Mummies . . . 2.50
111 SA,The Man who Killed Groo . . 2.50
112 SA,Rufferto Avenged . . . 2.50
113 SA . . . 2.50
114 SA,V:Vultures . . . 2.50
115 SA . . . 2.50
116 SA,Early unto Morning . . . 2.50
117 SA . . . 2.50
118 SA . . . 2.50
119 SA . . . 2.50
120 Groo hangs up swords . . . 2.50
GNv Death of Groo . . . 15.00
GNv 2nd print . . . 8.00
TPB Groo Adventures . . . 8.95
TPB Groo Carnival . . . 8.95
TPB Groo Expose . . . 8.95
TPB GRoo Festival . . . 8.95
TPB Groo Garden . . . 10.95

GROOVY
March, 1968—July, 1968

1 Monkeys,Ringo Starr,Photos . . . 65.00
2 Cartoons,Gags,Jokes . . . 50.00
3 . . . 50.00

GUARDIANS OF THE GALAXY
June, 1990

1 B:JV(a&s),I:Taserface,R:Aleta . . . 3.00
2 MZ(c),JV,V:Stark,C:Firelord . . . 2.50
3 JV,V:Stark,I:Force,C:Firelord . . . 2.50
4 JV,V:Stark,A:Force,Firelord . . . 2.50
5 JV,TM(c),V:Force,I:Mainframe (Vision) . . . 2.50
6 JV,V:Force,Vance Possesses Capt.America Shield . . . 2.50
7 GP(c),JV,I:Malevolence, O:Starhawk . . . 3.00
8 SLi(c),JV,V:Yondu,C:Rancor . . . 3.00
9 RLd(c),JV,I:Replica,Rancor . . . 3.00
10 JLe(c),JV,V:Rancor,The Nine I&C:Overkill(Taserface) . . . 3.00
11 BWi(c),JV,V:Rancor,I:Phoenix . . . 3.00
12 ATb(c),JV,V:Overkill A:Firelord . . . 2.50
13 JV,A:Ghost Rider,Force, Malevolence . . . 3.00
14 JS(c),JV,A:Ghost Rider,Force, Malevolence . . . 3.00
15 JSn(c),JV,I:Protege,V:Force . . . 2.50
16 JV,V:Force,A:Protege, Malevolence,L:Vance Astro . . . 2.50
17 JV,V:Punishers(Street Army), L:Martinex,N:Charlie-27, . . . 2.50
18 JV,V:Punishers,I&C:Talon,A: Crazy Nate . . . 3.00

Guardians of the Galaxy #8
© Marvel Entertainment Group

19 JV,V:Punishers,A:Talon 2.50
20 JV,I:Major Victory (Vance Astro) J:Talon & Krugarr 2.50
21 JV,V:Rancor. 2.50
22 JV,V:Rancor. 2.50
23 MT,V:Rancor,C:Silver Surfer. . . . 2.50
24 JV,A:Silver Surfer. 3.00
25 JV, Prismatic Foil(c) V:Galactus,A:SilverSurfer 3.50
25a 2nd printing,Silver 2.50
26 JV,O:Guardians(retold) 2.00
27 JV,Infinity War,O:Talon, A:Inhumans 2.00
28 JV,Inf.War,V:Various Villians. . . . 2.00
29 HT,Inf.War,V:Various Villians . . . 2.00
30 KWe,A:Captain America 2.00
31 KWe,V:Badoon,A:Capt.A.. . . . . . 2.00
32 KWe,V:Badoon Gladiator 2.00
33 KWe,A:Dr.Strange,R:Aleta 2.00
34 KWe,J:Yellowjacket II. 2.00
35 KWe,A:Galatic Guardians, V:Bubonicus 2.00
36 KWe,A:Galatic Guardians, V:Dormammu 2.00
37 KWe,V:Dormammu,A:Galatic Guardians 2.00
38 KWe,N:Y.jacket,A:Beyonder 2.00
39 KWe,Rancor Vs. Dr.Doom,Holo-grafx(c) 3.25
40 KWe,V:Loki,Composite 2.00
41 KWe,V:Loki,A:Thor 2.00
42 KWe,I:Woden 2.00
43 KWe,A:Woden,V:Loki. 2.00
44 KWe,R:Yondu 2.00
45 KWe,O:Starhawk 2.00
46 KWe,N:Major Victory 2.00
47 KWe,A:Beyonder,Protoge, Overkill. 2.00
48 KWe,V:Overkill. 2.00
49 KWe,A:Celestial. 2.00
50 Foil(c),R:Yondu,Starhawk separated,BU:O:Guardians 3.25
51 KWe,A:Irish Wolfhound 2.00
52 KWe,A:Drax. 2.00
53 KWe,V:Drax. 2.00
54 KWe,V:Sentinels 2.00
55 KWe,Ripjack 2.00
56 Ripjack 2.00
57 R:Keeper. 2.00
58 . . . . 2.00
59 A:Keeper. 2.00
60 F:Starhawk 2.00
61 F:Starhawk 2.00
62 Guardians Stop War of the Worlds last issue 2.00
Ann.#1 Korvac Quest #4,I:Krugarr . 3.00
Ann.#2 HT,I:Galactic Guardians, System Bytes #4 . . . . 3.00
Ann.#3 CDo,I:Irish Wolfhound, w/Trading card 3.25
Ann.#4 V:Nine 3.25
TPB rep #1 thru #6. . . . . 12.95

GUNHAWK, THE
See: BLAZE CARSON

GUNHAWKS
Oct., 1972

1 SSh,B:Reno Jones & Kid Cassidy Two Rode Together. . 15.00
2 Ride out for Revenge 12.00
3 Indian Massacre. 12.00
4 Trial by Ordeal 12.00
5 The Reverend Mr. Graves. 12.00
6 E:Reno Jones & Kid Cassidy D:Kid Cassidy. 12.00
7 A Gunhawks Last Stand A;Reno Jones, Oct., 1973 . . . 12.00

Gunhawks #1
© Marvel Entertainment Group

GUNRUNNER
Marvel UK 1993–94

1 I:Gunrunner,w/trading cards 2.95
2 A:Ghost Rider. 2.00
3 V:Cynodd 2.00
4 . . . . 2.00
5 A:Enhanced 2.00
6 final issue. 2.00

GUNSLINGERS
Dec., 1999

1-shot 64-pg. 3.00

GUNSLINGER
See: TEX DAWSON, GUNSLINGER

GUNSMOKE WESTERN
See: ALL WINNERS COMICS

HARROWERS
1993–94

1 MSt(s),GC,F:Pinhead 3.25
2 GC,AW(i),. 2.75
3 GC,AW(i),. 2.75
4 GC,AW(i),. 2.75
5 GC,AW(i),Devil's Pawn#1 . . . . . . 2.75
6 GC,AW(i),Devil's Pawn#2 . . . . . . 2.75

HARVEY
Oct., 1970–Dec., 1972

1 . . . . 60.00
2 thru 6 . . . . @40.00

HARVEY PRESENTS: CASPER

1 . . . . 2.00

HAVOK & WOLVERINE
Epic March, 1988

1 JMu,KW,V:KGB,Dr.Neutron. 5.00
2 JMu,KW,V:KGB,Dr.Neutron. 4.00
3 JMu,KW,V:Meltdown. 4.00
4 JMu,KW,V:Meltdown,Oct.1989 . . 4.00

TPB rep.#1-4 . . . . 16.95

HAWKEYE
[1st Limited Series] Sept., 1983

1 A:Mockingbird. 3.00
2 I:Silencer 2.50
3 I:Bombshell,Oddball 2.00
4 V:Crossfire,W:Hawkeye & Mockingbird, (Dec. 1983) 2.00

[2nd Limited Series] 1994

1 B:CDi(s),ScK,V:Trickshot, I:Javelynn,Rover. 2.00
2 ScK,V:Viper 2.00
3 ScK,A:War Machine,N:Hawkeye, V:Secret Empire 2.00
4 E:CDi(s),ScK,V:Trickshot,Viper, Javelynn. 2.00

HAWKEYE: EARTH'S MIGHTIEST MARKSMAN
Aug., 1998

1-shot TDF,MBa,JJ,DR,AM 48pg . . 3.00

HEADMASTERS
Star July, 1987

1 FS,Transformers. 2.00
2 and 3 . . . . @2.00
4 Jan., 1988 . . . . 2.00

HEATHCLIFF
Star April, 1985

1 thru 16 . . . . @2.00
17 Masked Moocher. 2.00
18 thru 49 . . . . @2.00
50 Double-size 2.00
51 thru 55 . . . . @2.00

HEATHCLIFF'S FUNHOUSE
Star May, 1987

1 thru 9 . . . . @2.00
10 1988 . . . . 2.00

HEAVY HITTERS

Ann.#1 (1993) 4.00

HEDY DEVINE COMICS
Aug., 1947—Sept., 1952

22 I:Hedy Devine 100.00
23 BW,Beauty and the Beach, HK,Hey Look 125.00
24 High Jinx in Hollywood, HK, Hey Look. 125.00
25 Hedy/Bull(c),HK,Hey Look . . . 125.00
26 Skating(c),HK,Giggles&Grins . . 70.00
27 Hedy at Show(c),HK,Hey Look. 80.00
28 Hedy/Charlie(c),HK,Hey Look . 80.00
29 Tennis(c),HK,Hey Look 80.00
30 . . . . 80.00
31 thru 50. . . . . @50.00

HEDY WOLFE
Atlas August, 1957

1 Patsy Walker's Rival. 70.00

HELLCAT
July, 2000

1 (of 3) SEt,NBy,F:PatsyWalker . . . 3.00
2 SEt,NBy,. 3.00
3 SEt,NBy,Concl. 3.00

HELLHOUND
1993–94
1 Hellhound on my Trial. 2.50
2 Love in Vain 2.50
3 Last Fair Deal Gone Down 2.25

HELLRAISER
See: CLIVE BARKER'S HELLRAISER

HELLRAISER III HELL ON EARTH
1 Movie Adaptation,(prestige) 5.00
1a Movie Adapt.(magazine). 3.00

HELLSTORM, PRINCE OF LIES
1993
1 R:Daimon Hellstrom,
Parchment(c) 3.50
2 A:Dr.Strange,Gargoyle 3.00
3 O:Hellstorm. 2.75
4 V:Ghost Rider 2.75
5 MB, ... 2.50
6 MB,V:Dead Daughter 2.50
7 A:Armaziel 2.50
8 Hell is where the heart is 2.25
9 LKa(s),Highway to Heaven 2.25
10 LKa(s),Heaven's Gate 2.25
11 LKa(s),PrG,Life in Hell 2.25
12 Red Miracles 2.25
13 Red Miracles Sidewalking 2.25
14 Red Miracles Murder is Easy . . . 2.25
15 Cigarette Dawn 2.75
16 Down Here 2.25
17 The Saint of the Pit 2.00
18 . . . . 2.00
19 . . . . 2.00
20 . . . . 2.00
21 final issue 2.00

HELL'S ANGEL
1992
1 GSr,A:X-Men,O:Hell's Angel 3.00
2 GSr,A:X-Men,V:Psycho Warriors. 2.50
3 GSr,A:X-Men,V:MyS-Tech. 2.00
4 GSr,A:X-Men,V:MyS-Tech. 2.00

Dark Angel #7
© Marvel Entertainment Group

5 GSr,A:X-Men,V:MyS-Tech. 2.00
6 Gfr,A:X-Men,V:MyS-Tech 2.00
Becomes:

DARK ANGEL
7 DMn,A:Psylocke,V:MyS-Tech . . . 2.00
8 DMn,A:Psylocke 2.00
9 A:Punisher 2.00
10 MyS-Tech Wars tie-in 2.00
11 A:X-Men,MyS-Tech wars tie-in . . 2.00
12 A:X-Men 2.00
13 A:X-Men,Death's Head II 2.00
14 Afthermath#2. . . . . 2.00
15 Afthermath#3. . . . . 2.00
16 SvL,E:Afthermath,last issue 2.00

HERCULES AND THE HEART OF CHAOS
[Limited Series] Aug., 1997
1 (of 3) TDF,RF,PO,. 2.50
2 TDF,RF,PO, ... 2.50
3 TDF,RF,PO,V:Ares, concl. 2.50

HERCULES PRINCE OF POWER
Sept., 1982
1 BL,I:Recorder 5.00
2 BL,I:Layana Sweetwater 3.00
3 BL,V:The Brothers,C:Galactus . . 3.00
4 BL,A:Galactus 3.00
[2nd Series] March, 1984
1 BL,I:Skyypi 3.00
2 BL,A:Red Wolf 2.00
3 BL,A:Starfox. 2.00
4 BL,D:Zeus, June, 1984. . . . . 2.00
TPB BL rep. Vol.1 #1–#4 and
Vol.2 #1–#4 . . . . 6.00

HERO
May, 1990
1 . . . . 2.50
2 . . . . 2.00
3 . . . . 2.00
4 RH 2.00
5 RH 2.00
6 Oct., 1990 . . . . 2.00

HERO FOR HIRE
June, 1972
1 GT,JR,I&O:Power Man 35.00
2 GT,A:Diamond Back 12.00
3 GT,I:Mace. 10.00
4 V:Phantom of 42nd St. 10.00
5 GT,A:Black Mariah 10.00
6 V:Assassin 7.00
7 GT,Nuclear Bomb issue 7.00
8 GT,A:Dr.Doom 7.00
9 GT,A:Dr.Doom,Fant.Four 7.00
10 GT,A:Dr.Death,Fant.Four 7.00
11 GT,A:Dr.Death 5.00
12 GT,C:Spider-Man. 5.00
13 A:Lion Fang. 5.00
14 V:Big Ben 5.00
15 Cage Goes Wild 5.00
16 O:Stilletto,D:Rackham 5.00
Becomes:

POWER MAN

HEROES FOR HIRE
July, 1997
1 JOs,PFe,F:Iron Fist 4.00
2 JOs,PFe,V:Nitro 3.00
2A Variant PFe cover. 3.00
3 JOs,PFe,V:Nitro 3.00
4 JOs,Power Man vs. Iron Fist. . . . 3.00

Hero For Hire #1
© Marvel Entertainment Group

5 JOs,V:Sersi, Diabolical Deviants . 3.00
6 JOs,PFe, Deviants 3.00
7 JOs V:Thunderbolts 3.00
8 JOs,Iron Fist's agenda revealed . 3.00
9 JOs,Search for Punisher. 3.00
10 JOs,Deadpool hired 3.00
11 JOs,PFe,A:Deadpool, V:Silver
Sable and Wild Pack 3.00
12 JOs,PFe,Traitor revealed, 48pg . 3.50
13 JOs,PFe,V:Master 3.00
14 JOs,F:Black Knight 3.00
15 JOs,PFe,Siege of Wundagore,
pt.1 (of 5) 3.00
16 JOs,PFe,Siege of Wundagore,
pt.3 . . . . 2.00
17 JOs,DBw,F:Luke Cage
& She-Hulk. 2.00
18 JOs,PFe,A:Wolverine. 2.00
19 JOs,PFe,F:Wolverine. 2.00
Ann.'98 JOs,BWi,PFe,Heroes For
Hire/Quicksilver, The Siege of
Wundagore, pt.5 (of 5) 48pg. . . 3.00

HEROES FOR HOPE
1 TA/JBy/HC/RCo/BWr,A:XMen . . . 7.00

HEROES REBORN: THE RETURN
Oct., 1997
½ Heroes Reborn prequel, (Marvel/
Wizard 1996) 7.50
1 (of 4) PDd,ATi,SvL,F:Franklin
Richards. 2.50
2 PDd,ATi,SvL, F:Spider-Man,
Thunderbolts & Doctor Strange. 2.50
3 PDd,SvL,ATi,A Universe May
Die 2.50
4 PDd,SvL,ATi, crossover to Marvel
Universe?. 2.50
TPB Return of the Heroes. 14.95

HOKUM & HEX
Razorline 1993–94
1 BU:Saint Sinner 2.75
2 I:Analyzer. 2.00
3 I:Wrath 2.00
4 I:Z-Man 2.00
5 V:Hyperkind 2.00
6 B:Bloodshed. 2.00
7 V:Bloodshed. 2.00
8 V:Bloodshed. 2.00
9 E:Bloodshed,final issue. 2.25

HOLIDAY COMICS

Jan., 1951

1 LbC(c),Christmas(c) 250.00
2 LbC(c),Easter Parade(c) 275.00
3 LbC(c),4th of July(c) 175.00
4 LbC(c),Summer Vacation 150.00
5 LbC(c),Christmas(c) 150.00
6 LbC(c),Birthday(c). 150.00
7 LbC(c),Rodeo (c) 150.00
8 LbC(c),Christmas(c)
Oct., 1952 . . . . 150.00

HOLLYWOOD SUPERSTARS

Epic Nov., 1990

1 DSp 2.00
2 thru 5 DSp, March, 1991 . . . . . @2.25

HOMER, THE HAPPY GHOST

March, 1955

1 . . . . 100.00
2 . . . . 50.00
3 . . . . 40.00
4 thru 15 . . . . @35.00
16 thru 22 . . . . @30.00

[2nd Series] Nov., 1969

1 . . . . 60.00
2 thru 5 . . . . @30.00

HOOK

1992

1 JRy,GM,movie adaption 2.00
2 JRy,Return to Never Land. 2.00
3 Peter Pans Magic. 2.00
4 conclusion 2.00
Hook Super Spec.#1 . . . . 3.00

HORRORS, THE

Jan., 1953—April, 1954

11 LbC(c),The Spirit of War. 225.00
12 LbC(c),Under Fire 200.00
13 LbC(c),Terror Castle. 200.00
14 LbC(c),Underworld Terror. . . . 200.00
15 LbC(c),The Mad Bandit 200.00

HOT SHOTS:

Avengers

1 Painted Pin-ups (1995). 2.95

Spider-Man

1 Painted pin-ups 2.95

X-Men

1 Painted pin-ups 2.95

HOUSE II

1 1987, Movie Adapt.. . . . . 2.00

HOWARD THE DUCK

Jan., 1976

1 FB,SL,A:Spider-Man,I:Beverly. . 10.00
2 FB,V:TurnipMan&Kidney Lady . . 4.00
3 JB,Learns Quack Fu. 3.00
4 GC,V:Winky Man 3.00
5 GC,Becomes Wrestler 3.00
6 GC,V:Gingerbread Man 3.00
7 GC,V:Gingerbread Man 3.00
8 GC,A:Dr.Strange,ran for Pres.. . . 3.00
9 GC,V:Le Beaver 3.00
10 GC,A:Spider-Man 3.00
11 GC,V:Kidney Lady 3.00
12 GC,I:Kiss. 8.00
13 GC,A:Kiss 12.00

Howard the Duck #27
© Marvel Entertainment Group

14 GC,Howard as Son of Satan . . . 3.00
15 GC,A:Dr.Strange,A:Dr.Bong 3.00
16 GC,DC,JB,DG,TA,
V:Incredible Creator 3.00
17 GC,D:Dr.Bong 3.00
18 GC,Howard the Human #1. . . . . 3.00
19 GC,Howard the Human #2. . . . . 3.00
20 GC,V:Sudd 3.00
21 GC,V:Soofi 3.00
22 A:ManThing,StarWars Parody . . 3.00
23 A:ManThing,StarWars Parody . . 3.00
24 GC,NightAfter..SavedUniverse . . 3.00
25 GC,V:Circus of Crime 3.00
26 GC,V:Circus of Crime 3.00
27 GC,V:Circus of Crime 3.00
28 GC,Cooking With Gas 3.00
29 Duck-Itis Poster Child 1978 . . . . 3.00
30 Iron Duck,V:Dr. Bong 3.00
31 Iron Duck,V:Dr. Bong 3.00
32 V:Gopher. 3.00
33 BB(c),The Material Duck 3.00
Ann.#1, V:Caliph of Bagmom 3.00
Holiday Spec. LHa,ATi,PFe (1996) . 3.50

HOWARD THE DUCK MAGAZINE

(B&W) Oct., 1979–March 1981

1 . . . . 5.00
2 & 3 . . . . @3.00
4 Beatles,Elvis,Kiss 5.00
5 thru 9 . . . . @3.00

HUGGA BUNCH

Star Oct., 1986—Aug., 1987

1 . . . . 2.00
2 thru 6 . . . . @2.00

HULK, THE

Feb., 1999

1 JBy,RG,DGr,48-page 3.00
1a signed 20.00
1b gold foil cover 10.00
2 JBy,RG,DGr,Hulk unleashed 2.00
2a variant AdP cover 2.00
3 JBy,RG,DGr,Hulk berserk 2.00
4 JBy,RG,DGr,old foe 2.00
5 JBy,RG,DGr,V:Man-Thing 2.00
6 JBy,RG,DGr,V:Man-Thing 2.00
7 JBy,RG,DGr,A:Avengers. 2.00
8 JBy,RG,DGr,V:Wolverine 2.00
9 RG,V:Thing 2.00
10 RG 2.00
11 PJe,RG,SB,A:DocSamson 2.00

Becomes:

INCREDIBLE HULK

12 PJe,RG,SB,48-pg 3.00
13 PJe,RG,SB,new Hulk. 2.00
14 PJe,RG,SB,V:Ryker 2.00
15 PJe,RG,SB,Dogs of War,pt.2 . . . 2.25
16 PJe,RG,SB,Dogs of War,pt.3 . . . 2.25
17 PJe,RG,SB,Dogs of War,pt.4 . . . 2.25
18 PJe,RG,SB,Dogs of War,pt.5 . . . 2.25
19 PJe,RG,SB,Dogs of War,pt.6 . . . 2.25
20 PJe,RG,SB,Dogs of War,pt.7 . . . 2.25
21 PJe,Maximum Security 2.25
Ann. 1999 JBy,DGr,48-page 3.50

HULK 2099

1994–95

1 GJ,Foil(c),V:Draco 2.50
2 GJ,V:Draco. 2.00
3 I:Golden Boy 2.00
4 . . . . 2.00
5 Ultra Hulk 2.00

Becomes:

HULK 2099 A.D.

6 Gamma Ray Scientist. 2.00
7 A:Doom,Dr.Apollo 2.00
8 One Nation Under Doom 2.00
9 California Quake. 2.00

HUMAN FLY

July, 1987

1 I&O:Human Fly,A:Spider-Man . . 5.00
2 A:Ghost Rider. 7.50
3 DC,JSt(c),DP,`Fortress of Fear'. . 2.00
4 JB/TA(c),`David Drier' 2.00
5 V:Makik 2.00
6 Fear in Funland 2.00
7 ME,Fury in the Wind 2.00
8 V:White Tiger 2.00
9 JB/TA(c),ME,V:Copperhead,A:
White Tiger,Daredevil 2.00
10 ME,Dark as a Dungeon 2.00
11 ME,A:Daredevil 2.00
12 ME,Suicide Sky-Dive 2.00
13 BLb/BMc(c),FS,V:Carl Braden . . 2.00
14 BLb/BMc(c),SL,Fear Over
Fifth Avenue. 2.00
15 BLb/BMc(c),War in the
Washington Monument. 2.00
16 BLb/BMc(c),V:Blaze Kendall . . . 2.00
17 BLb,DP,Murder on the Midway. . 2.00
18 V:Harmony Whyte 2.00
19 BL(c),V:Jacopo Belbo
March, 1979. . . . . 2.00

RED RAVEN COMICS

Timely Comics August, 1940

1 JK,O:Red Raven,I:Magar,A:Comet
Pierce & Mercury,Human Top,
Eternal Brain 11,000.00

Becomes:

HUMAN TORCH

Fall, 1940–Aug., 1954

2 (#1)ASh(c),BEv,B:Sub-Mariner
A:Fiery Mask,Falcon,Mantor,
Microman 22,000.00
3 (#2)Ash(c),BEv,V:Sub-
Mariner,Bondage(c) 4,500.00
4 (#3)ASh(c),BEv,O:Patriot . . . 3,500.00
5 (#4)V:Nazis,A:Patriot,Angel
crossover 2,500.00
5a(#5)ASh(c),V:Sub-Mariner. . 4,000.00
6 ASh(c),Doom Dungeon 1,500.00
7 ASh(c),V:Japanese 1,600.00
8 ASh(c),BW,V:Sub-Mariner . . 2,800.00

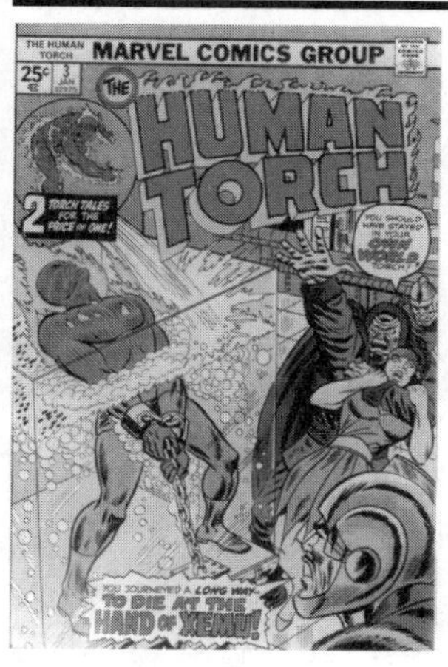

Human Torch #3
© Marvel Entertainment Group

9 ASh(c),V:General Rommel . . 1,500.00
10 ASh(c),BW,V:Sub-Mariner . . 2,100.00
11 ASh(c),Nazi Oil Refinery . . . 1,300.00
12 ASh(c),V:Japanese, Bondage(c) 2,000.00
13 ASh(c),V:Japanese, Bondage(c) 1,300.00
14 ASh(c),V:Nazis 1,300.00
15 ASh(c),Toro Trapped 1,300.00
16 ASh(c),V:Japanese 900.00
17 ASh(c),V:Japanese 900.00
18 ASh(c),V:Japanese, MacArthurs HQ. 900.00
19 ASh(c),Bondage(c) 900.00
20 ASh(c),Last War Issue 900.00
21 ASh(c),V:Organized Crime . . . 900.00
22 ASh(c),V:Smugglers. 900.00
23 ASh(c),V:Giant Robot 1,000.00
24 V:Mobsters 900.00
25 The Masked Monster 900.00
26 Her Diary of Terror 900.00
27 SSh(c),BEv,V:The Asbestos Lady 900.00
28 BEv,The Twins Who Weren't . 900.00
29 You'll Die Laughing 900.00
30 BEv,The Stranger,A:Namora . 800.00
31 A:Namora 700.00
32 A:Sungirl,Namora. 700.00
33 Capt.America crossover 750.00
34 The Flat of the Land. 700.00
35 A;Captain America,Sungirl . . . 750.00
36 A:Submariner. 700.00
37 BEv,A:Submariner 700.00
38 BEv,A:Submariner 700.00

HUMAN TORCH
Sept., 1974

1 JK,rep.StrangeTales #101 . . . . . 15.00
2 rep.Strange Tales #102. . . . . . . 10.00
3 rep.Strange Tales #103. . . . . . . 10.00
4 rep.Strange Tales #104. . . . . . . 10.00
5 rep.Strange Tales #105. . . . . . . 10.00
6 rep.Strange Tales #106. . . . . . . 10.00
7 rep.Strange Tales #107. . . . . . . 10.00
8 rep.Strange Tales #108. . . . . . . 10.00

HUMAN TORCH COMICS
Feb., 1999

1-shot V:Sub-Mariner, 48-page 4.00

HYPERKIND
Razorline

1 I:Hyperkind,BU:EctoKid 2.75
2 I:Bliss. 2.00
3 V:Living Void 2.00
4 FBk(s),I:Paragon John 2.00
5 V:Paragon John 2.00
6 Vetus Unleashed 2.00
7 Ambertrance. 2.00
8 I:Tempest 2.00
9 I:Lazurex,w/card 2.25

HYPERKIND UNLEASHED
1994

1 BU,V:Thermakk 2.95

ICEMAN
Dec., 1984

1 DP,mini-series 2.50
2 DP,V:Kali 2.00
3 DP,A;Original X-Men,Defenders Champions. 2.00
4 DP,Oblivion,June, 1985. . . . . 2.00

IDEAL
Timely July, 1948

1 Antony and Cleopatra 250.00
2 The Corpses of Dr.Sacotti . . . 225.00
3 Joan of Arc 200.00
4 Richard the Lionhearted A:The Witness 325.00
5 Phc,Love and Romance 125.00

Becomes:

LOVE ROMANCES

6 Ph(c),I Loved a Scoundrel . . . 100.00
7 Ph(c) 60.00
8 Ph(c) 65.00
9 thru 12 Ph(c). . . . . @40.00
13 thru 20 . . . . @40.00
21 BK. 50.00
22 . . . . 30.00
23 . . . . 30.00
24 BK. 45.00
25 . . . . 45.00
26 thru 35 . . . . @30.00
36 BK. 45.00
37 . . . . 30.00
38 BK. 45.00
39 thru 44 . . . . @30.00
45 MB 40.00
46 . . . . 30.00
47 . . . . 30.00
48 . . . . 25.00
49 ATh 45.00
50 . . . . 25.00
51 . . . . 25.00
52 . . . . 25.00
53 ATh 45.00
54 . . . . 25.00
55 . . . . 25.00
56 . . . . 25.00
57 MB 40.00
58 thru 74 . . . . @25.00
75 MB 35.00
76 . . . . 25.00
77 MB 35.00
78 . . . . 25.00
79 . . . . 25.00
80 RH(c). 30.00
81 . . . . 25.00
82 MB,JK(c) 30.00
83 JSe,JK(c). 40.00
84 JK 30.00
85 JK 30.00
86 thru 95 . . . . @20.00
96 JK 45.00
97 . . . . 25.00
98 JK 45.00
99 JK 45.00
100 thru 104 . . . . @25.00
105 JK 40.00
106 JK,July, 1963. . . . . 40.00

IDEAL COMICS
Timely Fall, 1944

1 B:Super Rabbit,Giant Super Rabbit V:Axis(c) 125.00
2 Super Rabbit at Fair(c) 85.00
3 Beach Party(c) 75.00
4 How to Catch Robbers 75.00

Becomes:

WILLIE COMICS

5 B:Willie,George,Margie,Nellie Football(c) 100.00
6 Record Player(c) 60.00
7 Soda Fountain(c),HK,Hey Look 65.00
8 Fancy Dress(c) 60.00
9 . . . . 60.00
10 HK,Hey Look 60.00
11 HK,Hey Look 60.00
12 . . . . 50.00
13 . . . . 50.00
14 thru 18 . . . . @40.00
19 . . . . 60.00
20 Li'L Willie Comics 40.00
21 Li'L Willie Comics 40.00
22 . . . . 40.00
23 May, 1950 . . . . 40.00

IDOL
Epic 1992

1 I:Idol. 2.95
2 Phantom o/t Set 2.95
3 Conclusion 2.95

Illuminator #3
© Marvel Entertainment Group

ILLUMINATOR
1993

1 . . . . 5.00
2 . . . . 5.00
3 & 4 . . . . @3.00

IMMORTALIS

1 A:Dr.Strange. 2.00
2 A:Dr.Strange. 2.00
3 A:Dr.Strange,V:Vampires 2.00
4 Mephisto, final issue 2.00

MARVEL

IMPERIAL GUARD

[Limited Series] 1997

1 (of 3) BAu,Woj, ... 2.00
2 and 3 BAu,Woj . . . . @2.00

IMPOSSIBLE MAN SUMMER VACATION

1990–91

1 GCa,DP 2.50
2 . . . . 2.00
Summer Fun Spec. TPe, Vacation on Earth 2.50

INCAL, THE

Epic Nov., 1988

1 Moebius,Adult 2.50
2 Moebius,Adult 2.00
3 Moebius,Adult, Jan., 1989 . . . . . 2.00

INCOMPLETE DEATH'S HEAD

1993

1 thru 10 rep.Death's Head #1 thru #10 . . . . @2.00
11 rep.Death's Head #11 . . . . 2.00

INCREDIBLE HULK

May, 1962

1 JK,I:Hulk(Grey Skin),Rick Jones, Thunderbolt Ross,Betty Ross, Gremlin,Gamma Base . . . 13,000.00
2 JK,SD,O:Hulk,(Green skin). . 2,500.00
3 JK,O:rtd.,I:Ring Master, Circus of Crime 1,600.00
4 JK,V:Mongu 1,400.00
5 JK,I:General Fang 1,400.00
6 SD,I:Metal Master 2,000.00

See: Tales to Astonish #59-#101

April, 1968

102 MSe,GT,O:Retold. 175.00
103 MSe,I:Space Parasite 75.00
104 MSe,O&N:Rhino 65.00
105 MSe,GT,I:Missing Link 60.00
106 MSe,HT,GT 55.00
107 HT,V:Mandarin. 55.00
108 HT,JMe,A:Nick Fury 55.00
109 HT,JMe,A:Ka-Zar 55.00
110 HT,JMe,A:Ka-Zar 55.00
111 HT,DA,I:Galaxy Master 35.00
112 HT,DA,O:Galaxy Master 35.00
113 HT,DA,V:Sandman 35.00
114 HT,DA 35.00
115 HT,DA,A:Leader. 35.00
116 HT,DA,V:Super Humanoid . . . 35.00
117 HT,DA,A:Leader. 35.00
118 HT,V:Sub-Mariner. 35.00
119 HT,V:Maximus 25.00
120 HT,V:Maximus 25.00
121 HT,I:The Glob 25.00
122 HT,V:Thing. 45.00
123 HT,V:Leader. 22.00
124 HT,SB,V:Rhino,Leader 22.00
125 HT,V:Absorbing Man 22.00
126 HT,A:Dr.Strange. 22.00
127 HT,Moleman vs.Tyrannus I:Mogol. 15.00
128 HT,A:Avengers. 15.00
129 HT,V:Glob 15.00
130 HT,Banner Vs Hulk 15.00
131 HT,A:Iron Man 12.00
132 HT,JSe,V:Hydra 12.00
133 HT,JSe,I:Draxon. 12.00
134 HT,SB,I:Golem 12.00
135 HT,SB,V:Kang 12.00
136 HT,SB,I:Xeron 12.00
137 HT,V:Abomination 12.00
138 HT,V:Sandman. 12.00
139 HT,V:Leader. 12.00
140 HT,V:Psyklop 12.00
141 HT,JSe,I&O:Doc Samson 14.00
142 HT,JSe,V:Valkyrie,A:Doc Samson 10.00
143 DA,JSe,V:Dr.Doom 10.00
144 DA,JSe,V:Dr.Doom 10.00
145 HT,JSe,O:Retold 11.00
146 HT,JSe,Leader. 10.00
147 HT,JSe,Doc Samson loses Powers. 9.00
148 HT,JSe,I:Fialan 9.00
149 HT,JSe,I:Inheritor. 9.00
150 HT,JSe,I:Viking,A:Havoc. 11.00
151 HT,JSe,C:Ant Man 9.00
152 HT,DA,Many Cameos 9.00
153 HT,JSe,C:Capt.America 9.00
154 HT,JSe,A:Ant Man, V:Chameleon 9.00
155 HT,JSe,I:Shaper of Worlds. . . . 9.00
156 HT,V:Hulk 9.00
157 HT,I:Omnivac,Rhino. 9.00
158 HT,C:Warlock,V:Rhino 9.00
159 HT,V:Abomination,Rhino 9.00
160 HT,V:Tiger Shark 8.00
161 HT,V:Beast. 10.00
162 HT,I:Wendigo I 11.00
163 HT,I:Gremlin 8.00
164 HT,I:Capt.Omen. 8.00
165 HT,I:Aquon. 8.00
166 HT,I:Zzzax 8.00
167 HT,JAb,V:Modok 8.00
168 HT,JAb,I:Harpy 8.00
169 HT,JAb,I:Bi-Beast. 8.00
170 HT,JAb,V:Volcano 8.00
171 HT,JAb,A:Abomination,Rhino . . 8.00
172 HT,JAb,X:X-Men 12.00
173 HT,V:Cobolt Man 8.00
174 HT,V:Cobolt Man 8.00
175 JAb,V:Inhumans 8.00
176 HT,JAb,A:Man-Beast,C:Warlock Crisis on Counter-Earth 14.00
177 HT,JAb,D:Warlock 15.00
178 HT,JAb,Warlock Lives 15.00
179 HT,JAb, ... 8.00
180 HT,JAb,I:Wolverine V:Wendigo I 100.00
181 HT,JAb,A:Wolverine (1st Full Story),V:Wendigo II 525.00
182 HT,JAb,I&D:Crackajack Jackson,C:Wolverine 65.00
183 HT,V:Zzzaz 7.00

Incredible Hulk #116
© Marvel Entertainment Group

184 HT,V:Living Shadow. 7.00
185 HT,V:General Ross 7.00
186 HT,I:Devastator 7.00
187 HT,JSt,V:Gremlin 7.00
188 HT,JSt,I:Droog 7.00
189 HT,JSt,I:Datrine 7.00
190 HT,MSe,Toadman 7.00
191 HT,JSt,Toadman,I:Glorian 7.00
192 HT,V:The Lurker. 7.00
193 HT,JSt,Doc.Samson regains Powers. 7.00
194 SB,JSt,V:Locust. 7.00
195 SB,JSt,V:Abomination 7.00
196 SB,JSt,V:Army. 7.00
197 BWr(c),SB,JSt,A:Man-Thing. . . 7.00
198 SB,JSt,A:Man-Thing 7.00
199 SB,JSt,V:Shield,Doc Samson. . 7.00
200 SB,JSt,Multi,Hulk in Glenn Talbots Brain 30.00
201 SB,JSt,V:Fake Conan 5.00
202 SB,JSt,A:Jarella. 5.00
203 SB,JSt,A:Jarella. 5.00
204 SB,JStI:Kronus 5.00
205 SB,JSt,D:Jarella. 5.00
206 SB,JSt,C:Dr.Strange 5.00
207 SB,JSt,A:Dr.Strange 5.00
208 SB,JSt,V:Absorbing Man 5.00
209 SB,JSt,V:Absorbing Man 5.00
210 SB,A:Dr.Druid,O:Merlin II 5.00
211 SB,A:Dr.Druid 5.00
212 SB,I:Constrictor 6.00
213 SB,TP,I:Quintronic Man 5.00
214 SB,Jack of Hearts 5.00
215 SB,V:Bi-Beast 4.50
216 SB,Gen.Ross. 4.50
217 SB,I:Stilts,A:Ringmaster. 4.50
218 SB,KP,Doc Samson versus Rhino 4.50
219 SB,V:Capt.Barravuda. 4.50
220 SB,Robinson Crusoe 4.50
221 SB,AA,A:Sting Ray 4.50
222 JSn,AA,Cavern of Bones 4.50
223 SB,V:Leader 4.50
224 SB,V:The Leader 4.50
225 SB,V:Leader,A:Doc Samson . . 4.50
226 SB,JSt,A:Doc Samson 4.50
227 SB,JK,A:Doc Samson 4.50
228 SB,BMc,I:Moonstone,V:Doc Samson 7.00
229 SB,O:Moonstone,V:Doc Samson 4.50
230 JM,BL,A:Bug Thing 4.50
231 SB,I:Fred Sloan 4.50
232 SB,A:Capt.America 4.50
233 SB,A:Marvel Man. 4.50
234 SB,Marvel Man Changes name to Quasar. 4.50
235 SB,A:Machine Man 4.50
236 SB,A:Machine Man 4.50
237 SB,A:Machine Man 4.50
238 SB,JAb,Jimmy Carter. 4.50
239 SB,I:Gold Bug 4.50
240 SB,Eldorado 4.50
241 SB,A:Tyrannus. 4.00
242 SB,Eldorado 4.00
243 SB,A:Gammernon 4.00
244 SB,A:It. 4.00
245 SB,A:Super Mandroid 4.00
246 SB,V:Capt.Marvel 4.00
247 SB,A:Bat Dragon 4.00
248 SB,V:Gardener 4.00
249 SD,R:Jack Frost 4.00
250 SB,A:Silver Surfer 10.00
251 MG,A:3-D Man. 4.00
252 SB,A:Woodgod 4.00
253 SB,A:Woodgod 4.00
254 SB,I:U-Foes. 4.00
255 SB,V:Thor 4.00
256 SB,I&O:Sabra 4.00
257 SB,I&O:Arabian Knight. 4.00
258 I:Soviet Super Soldiers 4.00

All comics prices listed are for *Near Mint* condition.

Incredible Hulk #212
© Marvel Entertainment Group

259 SB,A:Soviet Super-Soldiers O:Darkstar . . . 4.00
260 SB,Sugata . . . 4.00
261 SB,V:Absorbing Man . . . 4.00
262 SB,I:Glazer . . . 4.00
263 SB,Avalanche . . . 4.00
264 SB,A:Corruptor . . . 4.00
265 SB,I:Rangers . . . 3.75
266 SB,V:High Evolutionary . . . 3.75
267 SB,V:Rainbow,O:Glorian . . . 3.75
268 SB,I:Pariah . . . 3.75
269 SB,I:Bereet . . . 3.75
270 SB,A:Abomination . . . 3.75
271 SB,I:Rocket Raccoon, 20th Anniv. . . . 3.75
272 SB,C:X-Men,I:Wendigo III . . . 5.00
273 SB,A:Alpha Flight. . . . 4.00
274 SB,Beroct . . . 3.75
275 SB,JSt,I:Megalith . . . 3.75
276 SB,JSt,V:U-Foes . . . 3.75
277 SB,JSt,U-Foes. . . . 3.75
278 SB,JSt,C:X-Men, Avengers,Fantastic Four. . . . 3.75
279 SB,JSt,C:X-Men, Avengers,Fantastic Four. . . . 3.75
280 SB,JSt,Jack Daw . . . 3.75
281 SB,JSt,Trapped in Space . . . 3.75
282 SB,JSt,A:She Hulk. . . . 3.75
283 SB,JSt,A:Avengers . . . 3.75
284 SB,JSt,A:Avengers . . . 3.75
285 SB,JSt,Northwind,V:Zzzax . . . 3.75
286 SB,JSt,V:Soldier . . . 3.75
287 SB,JSt,V:Soldier . . . 3.75
288 SB,JSt,V:Abomination . . . 3.75
289 SB,JSt,V:Modok. . . . 3.75
290 SB,JSt,V:Modok. . . . 3.75
291 SB,JSt,V:Thunderbolt Ross . . . 3.75
292 SB,JSt,V:Dragon Man . . . 3.75
293 SB,V:Nightmare. . . . 3.75
294 SB,V:Boomerang. . . . 3.75
295 SB,V:Boomerang. . . . 3.75
296 SB,A:Rom . . . 3.75
297 SB,V:Nightmare. . . . 3.75
298 KN(c),SB,V:Nightmare . . . 3.75
299 SB,A:Shield . . . 3.75
300 SB,A:Spider-Man,Avengers Doctor Strange. . . . 6.00
301 SB,Crossroads . . . 3.00
302 SB,Crossroads . . . 3.00
303 SB,V:The Knights . . . 3.00
304 SB,V:U-Foes . . . 3.00
305 SB,V:U-Foes . . . 3.00
306 SB,V:Klaatu. . . . 3.00
307 SB,V:Klaatu. . . . 3.00
308 SB,V:Puffball Collective . . . 3.00
309 SB,V:Goblin & Glow. . . . 3.00
310 Crossroads . . . 3.00
311 Crossroads . . . 3.00
312 Secret Wars II,O:Bruce . . . 3.50
313 A:Alpha Flight . . . 3.00
314 JBy,V:Doc Samson . . . 5.00
315 JBy,A:Doc Samson,Banner & Hulk Separated. . . . 3.00
316 JBy,A:Avengers,N:Doc Samson . . . 3.00
317 JBy,I:Hulkbusters,A:Doc Samson . . . 3.00
318 JBy,A:Doc Samson . . . 3.00
319 JBy,W:Bruce & Betty . . . 5.00
320 AM,A:Doc Samson . . . 2.50
321 AM,A:Avengers . . . 2.50
322 AM,A:Avengers . . . 2.50
323 AM,A:Avengers . . . 2.50
324 AM,R:Grey Hulk(1st since #1), A:Doc Samson. . . . 10.00
325 AM,Rick Jones as Hulk . . . 3.50
326 A:Rick Jones,New Hulk . . . 6.00
327 AM,F:General Ross . . . 2.50
328 AM,1st PDd(s),Outcasts. . . . 7.00
329 AM,V:Enigma. . . . 5.00
330 1st TM Hulk,D:T-bolt Ross . . . 15.00
331 TM,V:Leader . . . 11.00
332 TM,V:Leader . . . 7.00
333 TM,V:Leader . . . 7.00
334 TM,I:Half-life . . . 7.00
335 HorrorIssue . . . 4.00
336 TM,A:X-Factor . . . 5.00
337 TM,A:X-Factor, A:Doc Samson. . . . 5.00
338 TM,I:Mercy,V:Shield . . . 5.00
339 TM,A:RickJones. . . . 5.00
340 TM,Hulk vs Wolverine . . . 25.00
341 TM,V:Man Bull. . . . 4.00
342 TM,V:Leader . . . 4.00
343 TM,V:Leader . . . 4.00
344 TM,V:Leader . . . 4.00
345 TM,V:Leader,Double-Size . . . 7.00
346 TM,EL,L:Rick Jones. . . . 6.00
347 In Las Vegas,I:Marlo Chandler, V:Absorbing Man . . . 4.00
348 V:Absorbing Man . . . 3.00
349 A:Spider-Man. . . . 3.50
350 Hulk vs Thing,A:Beast V:Dr.Doom . . . 4.00
351 R:Jarella's World . . . 3.00
352 V:Inquisitor . . . 3.00
353 R:Bruce Banner. . . . 3.00
354 V:Maggia . . . 3.00
355 V:Glorian . . . 3.00
356 V:Glorian,Cloot . . . 3.00
357 V:Glorian,Cloot . . . 3.00
358 V:Glorian,Cloot . . . 3.00
359 JBy(c),C:Wolverine(illusion) . . . 4.00
360 V:Nightmare & Dyspare . . . 3.00
361 A:Iron Man,V:Maggia . . . 3.00
362 V:Werewolf By Night . . . 3.00
363 Acts of Vengeance. . . . 3.00
364 A:Abomination,B:Countdown . . . 3.00
365 A:Fantastic Four . . . 3.00
366 A:Leader,I:Riot Squad . . . 3.00
367 1st DK Hulk,I:Madman(Leader's brother),E:Countdown. . . . 8.00
368 SK,V:Mr.Hyde . . . 4.00
369 DK,V:Freedom Force. . . . 3.00
370 DK,R:Original Defenders . . . 3.00
371 DK,BMc,A:Orig.Defenders . . . 3.00
372 DK,R:Green Hulk. . . . 9.00
373 DK,Green Hulk & Grey Hulk. . . 4.00
374 DK,BMc,Skrulls, R:Rick Jones . . . 4.00
375 DK,BMc,V:Super Skrull . . . 4.00
376 DK,BMc,Green Hulk,Grey Hulk & Banner fight . . . 5.00
377 DK,BMc,New Green Hulk,

Incredible Hulk #447
© Marvel Entertainment Group

combination of green,grey, and Bruce Banner,A:Ringmaster . . . 9.00
377a 2nd printing (gold) . . . 5.00
378 V:Rhino,Christmas Issue . . . 3.00
379 DK,MFm,I:Pantheon . . . 4.00
380 A:Nick Fury,D:Crazy-8 . . . 3.00
381 DK,MFm,Hulk J:Pantheon . . . 4.00
382 DK,MFm,A:Pantheon. . . . 4.00
383 DK,MFm,Infinity Gauntlet. . . . 4.00
384 DK,MFm,Infinity Gauntlet. . . . 4.00
385 DK,MFm,Infinity Gauntlet. . . . 4.00
386 DK,MFm,V:Sabra,A:Achilles. . . 4.00
387 DK,MFm,V:Sabra,A:Achilles. . . 4.00
388 DK,MFm,I:Speed Freak,Jim Wilson,revealed to have AIDS . 5.00
389 1st Comic art By Gary Barker (Garfield),A:Man-Thing,Glob . . . 4.00
390 DK,MFm,B:War & Pieces, C:X-Factor . . . 4.00
391 DK,MFm,V:X-Factor. . . . 4.00
392 DK,MFm,E:War & Pieces, A:X:Factor . . . 4.00
393 DK,MFm,R:Igor,A:Soviet Super Soldiers,30th Anniv.,Green foil(c). . 5.00
393a 2nd printing,Silver . . . 2.50
394 MFm(i),F:Atalanta,I:Trauma . . . 3.00
395 DK,MFm,A:Punisher, I:Mr.Frost . . . 3.00
396 DK,MFm,A:Punisher, V:Mr.Frost . . . 3.00
397 DK,MFm,B:Ghost of the Past,V:U-Foes,A:Leader. . . . 3.00
398 DK,MFm,D:Marlo,V:Leader . . . 3.00
399 JD,A:FF,Dr.Strange . . . 3.00
400 JD,MFm,E:Ghost of the Past, V:Leader,1st Holo-grafx(c),1st GFr Hulk(pin-up) . . . 3.50
400a 2nd Printing . . . 2.50
401 JDu,O:Agememnon . . . 2.00
402 JDu,V:Juggernaut . . . 2.00
403 GFr,V:Red Skull,A:Avengers . . 3.00
404 GFr,V:Red Skull,Juggernaut, A:Avengers . . . 3.50
405 GFr,Ajax Vs. Achilles . . . 2.75
406 GFr,V:Captain America . . . 2.00
407 GFr,I:Piecemeal,A:Madman, B:O:Ulysses . . . 2.00
408 GFr,V:Madman,Piecemeal, D:Perseus,A:Motormouth, Killpower . . . 2.00
409 GFr,A:Motormouth,Killpower, V:Madman . . . 2.00
410 GFr,A:Nick Fury,S.H.I.E.L.D.,

Margo agrees to marry Rick . . . 2.00
411 GFr,V:Nick Fury,S.H.I.E.L.D.. . . 2.00
412 PaP,V:Bi-Beast,A:She-Hulk . . . 2.00
413 GFr,CaS,B:Troyjan War, I:Cassiopea,Armageddon, V:Trauma 2.00
414 GFr,CaS,V:Trauma,C:S.Surfer . 2.00
415 GFr,CaS,V:Trauma,A:Silver Surfer,Starjammers. 2.00
416 GFr,CaS,E:Troyjan War,D:Trauma, A:S.Surfer,Starjammers 2.00
417 GFr,CaS,Rick's/Marlo's Bachelor/ Bachelorette Party 2.00
418 GFr,CaS,W:Rick & Marlo, A:Various Marvel persons, Die Cut(c). 2.75
418a Newsstand Ed. 2.00
419 CaS,V:Talos. 2.00
420 GFr,CaS,AIDS Story, D: Jim Wilson. 2.00
421 CaS,B:Myth Conceptions 2.00
422 GFr,Myth Conceptions,pt.2. . . . 2.00
423 GFr,CaS,MythConcept.,pt.3 . . . 2.00
424 B:Fall of the Hammer. 2.00
425 Regular Edition 2.00
425a Enhanced cover. 3.50
426 PDa,LSh,R:Mercy 2.00
426a Deluxe edition 2.00
427 A:Man-Thing 2.00
427a Deluxe edition 2.00
428 Suffer The Children 2.00
429 Abortion Issue 2.00
430 A:Speed Freak. 2.00
431 PDa,LSh R:Abomination 2.00
432 V:Abomination 2.00
433 PDd,V:Abomination 2.00
434 Funeral of the Year 2.00
435 Hulk Vs. Rhino baseball. 2.50
436 PDd,Ame,Ghosts of the Future,pt.1 . . . . 2.00
437 PDd,AMe,Ghosts of the Future,pt.2 . . . . 2.00
438 PDd,AMe,Ghosts of the Future,pt.3 . . . . 2.00
439 PDd,AMe,Ghosts of the Future,pt.4 . . . . 2.00
440 PDd,AMe, ... 2.00
441 PDd,AMe,A:She-Hulk. 2.00
442 A:Molecule Man, She-Hulk. . . . 2.00
443 Janis 2.00
444 Onslaught saga, V:Cable 2.00
445 Onslaught saga 2.00
446 blamed for loss of Fantastic Four and Avengers. 2.00
447 PDd,MD2,F:The Unleashed Hulk 2.00
447a Variant Tank Smashing cover. 5.00
448 PDd,MD2,V:The Pantheon. . . . 2.00
449 PDd,MD2,I:Thunderbolts 2.00
450 PDd,MD2,F:Doctor Strange, 56pg. 3.00
451 PDd,MD2, ... 2.00
452 PDd,MD2, ... 2.00
453 PDd,MD2,V:Future Hulk. 2.00
454 PDd,AKu,MFm,A God, in Savage Land 2.00
455 PDd,AKu,MFm,in X-Mansion . . 2.00
456 PDd,AKu,MFm,A:Apocalypse. . 2.00
457 PDd,Hulk vs. Juggernaut 2.00
458 PDd,AKu,MFm,V:Mercy 2.00
459 PDd,AKu,MFm,V:Abomination . 2.00
460 PDa,AKu,MFm, Return of Bruce Banner. 2.00
461 PDa,V:Thunderbolt Ross 2.00
462 PDa,AKu,MFm,V:Thunderbolt Ross 2.00
463 PDa,AKu,MFm,V:Thunderbolt Ross 2.00
464 PDa,AKu,MFm,V:Troygens & Silver Surfer. 2.00
465 PDa,MFm,Poker game. 2.00
466 PDa,AKu,MFm,tragic loss 2.00
467 PDa,AKu,MFm,Hulk attempts suicide 2.00
468 JoC,new direction, ... 2.00
469 JoC,LMa,F:Super-Adaptoid . . . 2.00
470 JoC,NMa,V:Ringmaster & Circus of Crime. 2.00
471 JoC,NMa,Circus of Crime,concl. 2.00
472 JoC,Great Astonishment,pt.1 . . 2.00
473 JoC,Great Astonishment,pt.2 . . 2.00
474 JoC,Great Astonishment,pt.3 . . 2.00
Spec.#1,A:Inhumans (1968) 75.00
Spec.#2 rep.O:Hulk,A:Leader (1969) 50.00
Spec.#3 rep.A:Leader (1971) 18.00
Spec.#4 IR:Hulk/Banner (1972). . . 15.00
Ann.#5 V:Xemnu,Diablo (1976). . . 10.00
Ann.#6 HT,A:Dr.Strange,I:Paragon (Her) (1977) 6.00
Ann.#7 JBy,BL,A:Angel,Iceman A:Doc Samson (1978) 7.00
Ann.#8 Alpha Flight (1979). 6.00
Ann.#9 Checkmate (1980) 3.00
Ann.#10,A:CaptainUniverse(1981) . 3.00
Ann.#11 RB,JSt,A:Spider-Man, Avengers,V:Unis (1982) 4.00
Ann.#12 (1983). 3.00
Ann.#13 (1984). 3.00
Ann.#14 JBy,SB (1985) 3.00
Ann.#15 V:Abomitation (1986) 3.00
Ann.#16 HT,Life Form #3, A:Mercy (1990). 3.00
Ann.#17 Subterran.Odyssey #2 (1991) 3.00
Ann #18 KM,TA,TC(1st Work),Return of the Defenders,Pt.1 (1992). . . 7.00
Ann.#19 I:Lazarus,w/card (1993) . . 3.25
Ann.#20 SvL,SI (1994) 2.00
Ann.'98 F:Hulk&Sub-Mariner, 48-pg. 3.00
Ann. Hulk 1999. . . . . 3.50
Marvel Milestone rep. #1 (1991) . . . 2.95
G-Size#1 rep.Greatest Foes 10.00
Minus 1 Spec., PDd,AKu,MFm, flashback 2.00
Spec. '97 Onslaught aftermath 3.00
Spec. Incredible Hulk vs. Superman, 48-page 6.00
Spec. Hulk vs. Superman, signed . 20.00
Milestone #181, F:Wolverine. 3.00
Hulk vs. Thing, rep. 4.00
TPB Ground Zero rep.#340-345 . . 12.95
TPB Future Imperfect, PDd,GP, 96-pg. 12.00

Incredible Hulk King Size Special #1
© Marvel Entertainment Group

TPB Ghosts of the Past, Rep. #396–#400. . . . . 12.00
TPB Transformations, 176-pg. . . . 12.00
TPB Beauty and the Beast, ... 17.00
TPB Essential Incredible Hulk. . . . 14.95

INCREDIBLE HULK: FUTURE IMPERFECT

1 GP,V:Maestro 10.00
2 GP,V:Maestro 8.00
TPB Rep. 12.95

INCREDIBLE HULK MEGAZINE

TPB six stories, 96-pg. 4.00

INCREDIBLE HULK/PITT

1997

Spec. PDd,DK,x-over 6.00

INCREDIBLE HULK VS. WOLVERINE

Oct., 1986

1 HT,rep #181 B:,V:Wolverine. . . . 12.00

INDEPENDENCE DAY

1996

0 . . . . 2.00
1 . . . . 2.00
2 . . . . 2.00
TPB rep. #0–#2, 96-pg. 6.95

[Further Adventures of] INDIANA JONES

Jan., 1983

1 JBy/TA 3.00
2 JBy/TA 2.50
3 . . . . 2.50
4 KGa 2.50
5 KGa 2.50
6 HC/TA 2.50
7 thru 24 KGa . . . . @2.50
25 SD,What Lurks Within the Tomb 2.50
26 SD. 2.50
27 SD. 2.50
28 SD. 2.50
29 SD. 2.50
30 SD. 2.50
31 SD,The Summit Meeting 2.50
32 SD,Fly the Friendly Skies. 2.50
33 SD. 2.50
34 SD, March, 1986 . . . . 2.50

INDIANA JONES AND THE LAST CRUSADE

1 B&W,Mag.,movie adapt, 1989. . . 2.95

[Mini-Series] 1989

1 Rep,Movie adapt, 1989. . . . . 2.50
2 Rep,Movie adapt. 2.50
3 Rep,Movie adapt 2.50
4 Rep,Movie adapt. 2.50

INDIANA JONES AND THE TEMPLE OF DOOM

1984

1 Movie adapt 2.50
2 Movie adapt.. . . . . 2.50
3 Movie adapt.. . . . . 2.50

INFINITY CRUSADE

1993

1 RLm,AM,I:Goddess,A:Marvel

Heroes,foil(c) 4.00
2 RLm,AM,V:Goddess 3.00
3 RLm,AM,V:Goddess,Mephisto . . 3.00
4 RLm,AM,V:Goddess,A:Magnus . . 3.00
5 RLm,AM,V:Goddess 3.00
6 RLm,AM,V:Goddess 3.00

INFINITY GAUNTLET

July, 1991

1 GP,O:Infinity Gauntlet 5.00
2 GP,JRu,2ndRebirth:Warlock 4.00
3 GP,JRu,I:Terraxia 4.00
4 GP,JRu,RLm,V:Thanos 4.00
5 JRu,RLm,V:Thanos,D:Terraxia . . 4.00
6 RLm,JRu,V:Nebula 4.00
TPB rep. #1 thru 6 . . . . 24.95

INFINITY WAR

1992

1 RLm,AM,R:Magus,Thanos 5.00
2 RLm,AM,V:Magus,A:Everyone . . 3.00
3 RLm,AM,V:Magus,A:Everyone . . 2.50
4 RLm,AM,Magus gets Gauntlet . . 2.50
5 RLm,AM,V:Magus 2.50
6 RLm,AM,V:Magus 2.50

INHUMANOIDS

Star Jan.–July, 1987

1 Hasbro Toy 2.00
2 O:Inhumanoids 2.00
3 V:D'Compose 2.00
4 A:Sandra Shore 2.00

INHUMANS

Oct., 1975

1 GP,V:Blastaar 10.00
2 GP,V:Blastaar 5.00
3 GP,I:Kree S 4.00
4 GK,Maximus 4.00
5 GK,V:Maximus 4.00
6 GK,Maximus 4.00
7 GK,DP,I:Skornn 4.00
8 GP,DP,Skornn 4.00
9 reprint,V:Mor-Tog 4.00
10 KP,D:Warkon 4.00
11 KP,JM,I:Pursuer 4.00
12 KP,Hulk 4.00
Spec.#1(The Untold Saga), O:Inhumans 4.00
Spec. Atlantis Rising story 2.95

INHUMANS

Sept., 1998

1 (of 12) PJe,JaL,F:Black Bolt, Medusa, Karnak, Triton, Gorgon, Crystal, Lockjaw 3.00
2 PJe,JaL,F:Tonaje 3.00
2a variant cover 3.00
3 PJe,JaL,Attilan's dark side 3.00
4 PJe,JaL,War against Attilan 3.00
5 PJe,JaL,Earth vs. Attilan 3.00
6 PJe,JaL,V:Maximus 3.00
7 PJe,JaL,F:Black Bolt 3.00
8 PJe,JaL,F:Lockjaw 3.00
9 PJe,JaL,F:Triton 3.00
10 PJe,JaL,F:Woz & Medusa 3.00
11 JaL,PJe,F:Black Bolt 3.00
12 JaL,PJe,concl. 3.00
TPB 264pg. 24.95

INHUMANS

Apr., 2000

1 (of 4) V:Ronan the Accuser 3.00
2 A:Kree 3.00
3 Maximus the Mad 3.00
4 concl. 3.00

INTERFACE

Epic Dec., 1989

1 ESP 2.50
2 thru 7 . . . . @2.00
8 . . . . 2.25

INVADERS

August, 1975

1 FR,JR(c),A:Invaders, A:Mastermind 20.00
2 FR,JR(c)I:Brain Drain 7.00
3 FR,JR(c),I:U-Man 6.00
4 FR,O&V:U-Man 5.00
5 RB,JM,V:Red Skull 5.00
6 FR,V:Liberty Legion 5.00
7 FR,I:Baron Blood, 1st Union Jack 5.00
8 FR,FS,J:Union Jack 5.00
9 FR,FS,O:Baron Blood 5.00
10 FR,FS,rep.Captain America Comics#22 . . . . 5.00
11 FR,FS,I:Blue Bullet 4.00
12 FR,FS,I:Spitfire 4.00
13 FR,FS,GK(c),I:Golem, Half Face 4.00
14 FR,FS,JK(c),I:Crusaders 4.00
15 FR,FS,JK(c),V:Crusaders 4.00
16 FR,JK(c),V:Master Man 4.00
17 FR,FS,GK(c),I:Warrior Woman . . 4.00
18 FR,FS,GK(c),R:1st Destroyer . . . 4.00
19 FR,FS,V:Adolph Hitler 4.00
20 FR,FS,GK(c),I&J:2nd Union Jack BU:rep.Marvel Comics #1 . . . . 7.50
21 FR,FS,GK(c),BU:rep.Marvel Mystery #10 . . . . 5.50
22 FR,FS,GK(c),O:Toro 3.00
23 FR,FS,GK(c),I:Scarlet Scarab . . 3.00
24 FR,FS,GK(c),rep.Marvel Mystery #17 . . . . 4.00
25 FR,FS,GK(c),V:Scarlet Scarab . . 3.00
26 FR,FS,GK(c),V:Axis Agent 3.00
27 FR,FS,GK(c),V:Axis Agent 3.00
28 FR,FS,I:2nd Human Top, Golden Girl,Kid Commandos . . 3.00
29 FR,FS,I:Teutonic Knight 3.00
30 FR,FS,V:Teutonic Knight 3.00
31 FR,FS,V:Frankenstein 3.00
32 FR,FS,JK(c),A:Thor 4.50
33 FR,FS,JK(c),A:Thor 4.50
34 FR,FS,V:Master Man 3.00
35 FR,FS,I:Iron Cross 3.00
36 FR,FS,O:Iron Cross 3.00

Invaders #38
© Marvel Entertainment Group

37 FR,FS,V:Iron Cross 3.00
38 FR,FS,V:Lady Lotus 3.00
39 FR,FS,O:Lady Lotus 3.00
40 FR,FS,V:Baron Blood 3.00
41 E:RTs(s)FR,FS,V:Super Axis, double-size 5.00
Ann.#1 A:Avengers,R:Shark 5.00
G-Size#1 FR,rep.Submariner#1 . . . 5.00

[Limited Series] 1993

1 R:Invaders 2.00
2 V:Battle Axis 2.00
3 R:Original Vison (1950's) 2.00
4 V:The Axis 2.00

IRON FIST

Nov., 1975

1 JBy,A:Iron Man 35.00
2 JBy,V:H'rythl 17.00
3 JBy,KP,KJ,V:Ravager 12.00
4 JBy,V:Radion 14.00
5 JBy,V:Scimitar 12.00
6 JBy,O:Misty Knight 10.00
7 JBy,V:Khimbala Bey 10.00
8 JBy,V:Chaka 10.00
9 JBy,V:Chaka 10.00
10 JBy,DGr,A:Chaka 10.00
11 JBy,V:Wrecking Crew 10.00
12 JBy,DGr,V:Captain America . . . 10.00
13 JBy,A:Boomerang 10.00
14 JBy,I:Sabretooth 125.00
15 JBy,A&N:Wolverine,A:X-Men Sept. 1977 . . . . 35.00
Marvel Milestone rep. #14 (1992) . . 4.00

IRON FIST

May, 1998

1 (of 3) DJu,JG, from Heroes For Hire 2.50
2 DJu,JG,search for Scorpio Key, V:S.H.I.E.L.D. 2.50
3 DJu,JG,concl. 2.50

IRON FIST/WOLVERINE

Sept., 2000

1 (of 4) F:DannyRand,JunzoMoto . 3.00
2 K'un L'un 3.00

IRON MAN

May, 1968

1 B:StL,AGw(s),JCr,GC, I:Mordius 350.00
2 JCr,I:Demolisher 125.00
3 JCr,V:The Freak 75.00
4 JCr,A:Unicorn 65.00
5 JCr,GT,I:Cerebos 55.00
6 JCr,GT,V:Crusher 60.00
7 JCr,GT,V:Gladiator 45.00
8 JCr,GT,O:Whitney Frost 45.00
9 JCr,GT,A:Mandarin 45.00
10 JCr,GT,V:Mandarin 45.00
11 JCr,GT,V:Mandarin 28.00
12 JCr,GT,I:Controller 28.00
13 JCr,GT,A:Nick Fury 28.00
14 JCr,V:Night Phantom 28.00
15 JCr,GT,A:Red Ghost 28.00
16 JCr,GT,V:Unicorn 20.00
17 JCr,GT,I:Madam Masque, Midas 22.00
18 JCr,GT,V:Madame Masque . . . 20.00
19 JCr,GT,V:Madame Masque . . . 20.00
20 JCr,I:Charlie Gray 20.00
21 JCr,I:Eddie 15.00
22 JCr,D:Janice Cord 15.00
23 JCr,I:Mercenary 17.00
24 JCr,GT,V:Madame Masque . . . 15.00
25 JCr,A:Sub-Mariner 17.00
26 JCr,DH,J:Val-Larr 15.00

27 JCr,DH,I:Firebrand 15.00
28 E:AGw(s),JCr,DH,
V:Controller 15.00
29 B:StL,AyB(s),DH,V:Myrmidon . . 15.00
30 DH,I:Monster Master 15.00
31 DH,I:Mastermind 15.00
32 GT,I:Mechanoid 15.00
33 DH,I:Spy Master 15.00
34 DH,A:Spy Master 15.00
35 DH,A:Daredevil,Spymaster. . . . 15.00
36 E:AyB(s),DH,I:RamRod 15.00
37 DH,A:Ramrod 15.00
38 GT,Jonah. 15.00
39 HT,I:White Dragon 14.00
40 GT,A:White Dragon 14.00
41 GT,JM,I:Slasher 14.00
42 GT,I:Mikas 14.00
43 GT,JM,A:Mikas,I:Guardsmen . . 15.00
44 GT,A:Capt.America 14.00
45 GT,A:Guardsman 14.00
46 GT,D:Guardsman 14.00
47 BS,JM,O:Iron Man 15.00
48 GT,V:Firebrand 12.00
49 GT,V:Adaptoid 12.00
50 B:RTs(s),GT,V:Prin.Python 12.00
51 GT,C:Capt.America 12.00
52 GT,I:Raga 12.00
53 GT,JSn,I:BlackLama 12.00
54 GT,BEv,Sub-Mariner,I:Madame
MacEvil (Moondragon) 20.00
55 JSn,I:Destroyer,Thanos,Mentor
Starfox(Eros),Blood Bros. 85.00
56 JSn,I:Fangor 18.00
57 GT,R:Mandarin 10.00
58 GT,V:Mandarin 10.00
59 GT,A:Firebrand 10.00
60 GT,C:Daredevil 10.00
61 GT,Marauder 10.00
62 whiplash 10.00
63 GT,A:Dr.Spectrum 10.00
64 GT,I:Rokk 10.00
65 GT,O:Dr.Spectrum 10.00
66 GT,V:Thor 10.00
67 GT,V:Freak 10.00
68 GT,O:Iron Man 12.00
69 GT,V:Mandarin 9.00
70 GT,A:Sunfire 9.00
71 GT,V:Yellow Claw 7.50
72 E:RTs(s),GT,V:Black Lama 7.50
73 B:LWn(s),KP,JM,V:Titanic
Three 7.50
74 KP,V:Modok 7.50
75 V:Black Lama 7.50

Iron Man #5
© Marvel Entertainment Group

76 Rep,A:Hulk 7.50
77 V:Thinker 7.50
78 GT,V:Viet Cong 7.50
79 GT,I:Quasar(not Current one). . . 7.50
80 JK(c),O:Black Lama 7.50
81 A:Black Lama 6.00
82 MSe,A:Red Ghost 6.00
83 E:LWn(s),HT,MSe,Red Ghost. . . 6.00
84 HT,A:Dr.Ritter 6.00
85 HT,MSe,A:Freak 6.00
86 B:MWn(s),GT,I:Blizzard 7.00
87 GT,V:Blizzard 6.00
88 E:MWn(s),GT,
V:Blood Brothers 6.00
89 GT,A:D.D.,Blood Bros. 6.00
90 JK(c),GT,Controller,A:Thanos . . . 7.50
91 GT,BL,A:Controller 6.00
92 JK(c),GT,V:Melter 6.00
93 JK(c),HT,V:Kraken 6.00
94 JK(c),HT,V:Kraken 6.00
95 JK(c),GT,PP,V:Ultimo 6.00
96 GT,DP,V:Ultimo 6.00
97 GT,DP,I:Guardsman II 6.00
98 GT,DP,A:Sunfire 6.00
99 GT,V:Mandarin. 6.00
100 JSn(c),GT,V:Mandarin 16.00
101 GT,I:Dread Knight 5.00
102 GT,O:Dread Knight 5.00
103 GT,V:Jack of Hearts 5.00
104 GT,V:Midas 5.00
105 GT,V:Midas 5.00
106 GT,V:Midas 5.00
107 KP,V:Midas 5.00
108 CI,A:Growing Man 5.00
109 JBy(c),CI,V:Van Guard 5.00
110 KP,I:C.Arcturus. 5.00
111 KP,O:Rigellians 5.00
112 AA,KP,V:Punisher from
Beyond 5.00
113 KP,HT,V:Unicorn,Spymaster . . . 5.50
114 KG,I:Arsenal 5.00
115 JR2,O:Unicorn,V:Ani-men 5.00
116 JR2,BL,V:MadameMasque. . . . 5.00
117 BL,JR2,1st Romita Jr 6.00
118 JBy,BL,A:Nick Fury 8.00
119 BL,JR2,Alcholic Plot. 6.00
120 JR2,BL,A:Sub-Mariner,
I:Rhodey(becomes War Machine),
Justin Hammer. 6.00
121 BL,JR2,A:Submariner 5.00
122 DC,CI,BL,O:Iron Man. 5.00
123 BL,JR2,V:Blizzard 5.00
124 BL,JR2,A:Capt.America 4.00
125 BL,JR2,A:Ant-Man 4.00
126 BL,JR2,V:Hammer. 4.00
127 BL,JR2,Battlefield 4.00
128 BL,JR2,Alcohol 6.00
129 SB,A:Dread Night 3.50
130 BL,V:Digital Devil. 3.50
131 BL,V:Hulk 3.50
132 BL,V:Hulk 3.50
133 BL,A:Hulk,Ant-Man 3.50
134 BL,V:Titanium Man 3.50
135 BL,V:Titanium Man 3.50
136 V:Endotherm 3.50
137 BL,Fights oil rig fire 3.50
138 BL,Dreadnought,Spymaster . . . 3.50
139 BL,Dreadnought,Spymaster . . . 3.50
140 BL,V:Force 3.50
141 BL,JR2,V:Force 3.50
142 BL,JR2,Space Armor 3.50
143 BL,JR2,V:Sunturion 3.50
144 BL,JR2,Sunturion,O:Rhodey . . 3.50
145 BL,JR2,A:Raiders 3.50
146 BL,JR2,I:Black Lash. 3.50
147 BL,JR2,V:Black Lash 3.00
148 BL,JR2,V:Terrorists 3.00
149 BL,JR2,V:Dr.Doom. 3.00
150 BL,JR2,V:Dr.Doom,Dble. 5.00
151 TA,BL,A:Antman 3.00
152 BL,JR2,New Armor 3.00

153 BL,JR2,V:Living Laser 3.00
154 BL,JR2,V:Unicorn 3.00
155 JR2,V:Back-Getters 3.00
156 JR2,I:Mauler 3.25
157 V:Spores 3.00
158 CI,AM,Iron Man Drowning 3.00
159 PS,V:Diablo 3.00
160 SD,V:Serpent'sSquad 3.00
161 A:Moon Knight. 3.00
162 V:Space Ships 3.00
163 V:Chessmen 3.00
164 LMc,A:Bishop 3.00
165 LMc,Meltdown 3.00
166 LMc,V:Melter 2.50
167 LMc,Alcholic Issue. 2.50
168 LMc,A:Machine Man 2.50
169 LMc,B:Rhodey as 2nd
Ironman 13.00
170 LMc,2nd Ironman. 12.00
171 LMc,2nd Ironman. 3.00
172 LMc,V:Firebrand 3.00
173 LMc,Stane International 3.00
174 LMc,Alcoholism 3.50
175 LMc,Alcoholism 3.50
176 LMc,Alcoholism 3.50
177 LMc,Alcoholism 3.00
178 LMc,V:Wizard 3.00
179 LMc,V:Mandarin. 3.00
180 LMc,V:Mandarin. 3.00
181 LMc,V:Mandarin. 3.00
182 LMc,Secret Wars 3.00
183 LMc,Turning Point 3.00
184 LMc,Moves to California. 3.00
185 LMc,V:Zodiac Field 3.00
186 LMc,I:Vibro 3.00
187 LMc,V:Vibro. 3.00
188 LMc,I:New Brother's Grimm . . . 3.00
189 LMc,I:Termite. 3.00
190 LMc,O:Termite,A:Scar.Witch. . . 3.00
191 LMc,New Grey Armor 5.00
192 LMc,V:Iron Man(Tony Stark). . . 5.00
193 LMc,V:Dr.Demonicus 3.00
194 LMc,I:Scourge,A:West Coast
Avengers 3.00
195 LMc,A:Shaman 3.00
196 LMc,V:Dr.Demonicus 3.00
197 LMc,Secret Wars II 3.00
198 SB,V:Circuit Breaker 3.00
199 LMc,E:Rhodey as 2nd Ironman,
V:Obadiah Stone 3.00
200 LMc,D:Obadiah Stone 6.00
201 MBr,V:Madam Masque. 2.00
202 A:Kazar 2.00

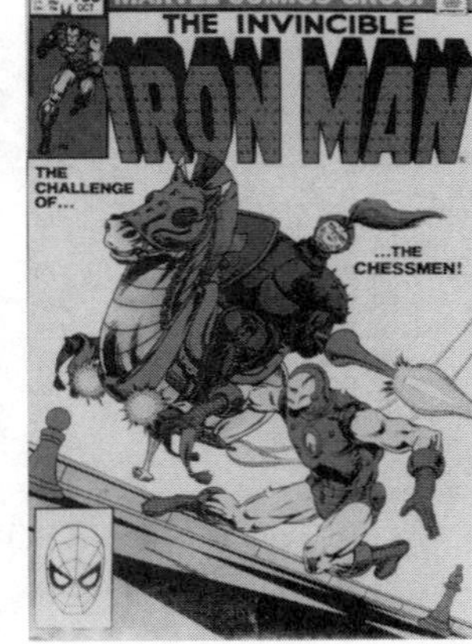

Iron Man #163
© Marvel Entertainment Group

All comics prices listed are for *Near Mint* condition.

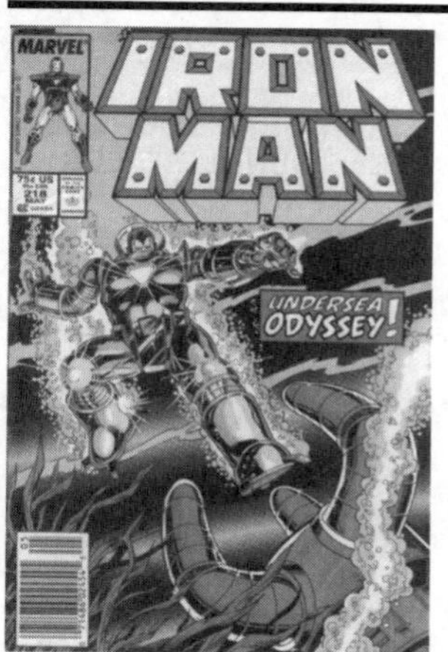

Iron Man #218
© Marvel Entertainment Group

203 MBr,A:Hank Pym 2.00
204 MBr,V:Madame Masque. 2.00
205 MBr,V:A.I.M. 2.00
206 MBr,V:Goliath 2.00
207 MBr,When t/Sky Rains Fire . . . 2.00
208 MBr,V:A.I.M. 2.00
209 V:Living Laser 2.00
210 MBr,V:Morgan Le Fey 2.00
211 AS,V:Living Laser. 2.00
212 DT,V:Iron Monger. 2.00
213 A:Dominic Fortune 2.00
214 A:Spider-Woman 2.00
215 BL,AIM 2.00
216 BL,MBr,D:Clymenstra. 2.00
217 BL,MRr,V:Hammer. 2.00
218 BL,MBr,Titanic 2.00
219 BL,V:The Ghost 2.00
220 BL,MBr,V:The Ghost,
D:Spymaster 2.00
221 BL,MBr,V:The Ghost 2.00
222 BL,MBr,R:Abrogast 2.00
223 BL,MBr,V:Blizzard,Beetle 2.00
224 BL,V:Justin Hammer,Force. . . . 2.00
225 BL,MBr,B:Armor Wars 5.00
226 BL,MBr,V:Stingray 4.50
227 BL,MBr,V:Mandroids, ... 4.00
228 BL,MBr,V:Guardsmen 4.00
229 BL,D:Titanium Man 4.00
230 V:Firepower, ... 4.00
231 V:Firepower,N:Iron Man 4.00
232 BWS,Nightmares,E:Armor
Wars 4.50
233 JG,BL,A:AntMan 2.00
234 JG,BL,A:Spider-Man 3.00
235 JG,BL,V:Grey Gargoyle 2.00
236 JG,BL,V:Grey Gargoyle 2.00
237 JG,BL,V:SDI Monster. 2.00
238 JG,BL,V:Rhino,D:M.Masque. . . 2.00
239 JG,BL,R:Ghost 2.00
240 JG,BL,V:Ghost. 2.00
241 BL,V:Mandarin. 2.00
242 BL,BWS,V:Mandarin 3.00
243 BL,BWS,Stark Paralyzed 3.00
244 BL,V:Fixer,A:Force(D.Size) . . . 5.00
245 BL(c),V:Dreadnaughts 2.00
246 BL,HT,V:A.I.M.,Maggia. 2.00
247 BL,A:Hulk 2.25
248 BL,Tony Stark Cured 2.25
249 BL,V:Dr.Doom 2.00
250 BL,V:Dr.Doom,A of V 2.00
251 HT,AM,V:Wrecker,A of V 2.00
252 HT,AM,V:Chemistro,A of V. . . . 2.00
253 BL,V:Slagmire 2.00
254 BL,V:Spymaster. 2.00
255 HT,V:Devestator
I:2nd Spymaster. 2.00
256 JR2,V:Space Station 2.00
257 V:Samurai Steel. 2.00
258 JR2,BWi,B:Armor Wars II,V:
Titanium Man 2.25
259 JR2,BWi,V:Titanium Man 2.00
260 JR2,BWi,V:Living Laser 2.00
261 JR2,BWi,A:Mandarin 2.00
262 JR2,BWi,A:Mandarin 2.00
263 JR2,BWi,A:Wonderman,
V:Living Laser 2.00
264 JR2,BWi,A:Mandarin 2.00
265 JR2,BWi,V:Dewitt. 2.00
266 JR2,BWi,E:Armor Wars II. 2.00
267 PR,BWi,B:New O:Iron Man,
Mandarin,V:Vibro 2.00
268 PR,BWi,E:New O:Iron Man. . . . 2.00
269 PR,BWi,A:Black Widow 2.00
270 PR,BWi,V:Fin Fang Foom 2.00
271 PR,BWi,V:Fin Fang Foom 2.00
272 PR,BWi,O:Mandarin. 2.00
273 PR,BWi,V:Mandarin 2.00
274 MBr,BWi,V:Mandarin 2.00
275 PR,BWi,A:Mandarin,Fin Fang
Foom (Double size) 4.00
276 PR,BWi,A:Black Widow 2.00
277 PR,BWi,A:Black Widow 2.00
278 BWi,Galactic Storm,pt.6
A:Capt.America,V:Shatterax . . . 2.00
279 BWi,Galactic Storm,pt.13,
V:Ronan,A:Avengers 2.00
280 KHd,V:The Stark 2.00
281 KHd,I&V:Masters of Silence,
C:War Machine Armor 3.50
282 KHd,I:War Machine Armor,
V:Masters of Silence. 3.50
283 KHd,V:Masters of Silence 2.50
284 KHd,Stark put under Cryogenic
Freeze,B:Rhodey as Iron Man . 3.50
285 KHd,BWi(i),Tony's Funeral 2.00
286 KHd,V:Avengers West Coast . . 2.00
287 KHd,I:New Atom Smasher 2.00
288 KHd,30th Anniv.,V:Atom
Smasher,foil(c) 4.50
289 KHd,V:Living Laser,
R:Tony Stark 2.00
290 KHd,30th Anniv.,N:Iron Man,
Gold foil(c) 4.50
291 KHd,E:Rhodey as Iron Man,
Becomes War Machine. 2.00
292 KHd,Tony reveals he is alive . . 2.00
293 KHd,V:Controller 2.00
294 KHd,Infinity Crusade 2.00
295 KHd,Infinity Crusade 2.00
296 KHd,V:Modam,A:Omega Red. . 2.00
297 KHd,V:Modam,Omega Red . . . 2.00
298 KHd(c),I:Earth Mover 2.00
299 KHd(c),R:Ultimo. 2.00
300 KHd,TMo,N:Iron Man,I:Iron
Legion,A:War Machine,V:Ultimo
Foil(c). 5.00
300a Newstand Ed. 2.75
301 KHd,B:Crash and Burn,
A:Deathlok,C:Venom 2.00
302 KHd,V:Venom 2.00
303 KHd,V:New Warriors,
C:Thundrstrike 2.00
304 KHd,C:Hulk,V:New Warriors,
Thundrstrike,N:Iron Man 2.00
305 KHd,V:Hulk, ... 2.00
306 KHd,E:Stark Enterprise 2.00
307 TMo,I:Vor/Tex,R:Mandarin 2.00
308 TMo,Vor/Tex 2.00
309 TMo,Vor/Tex 2.00
310 regular. 2.00
310a Neon(c),with insert print 3.50
311 V:Mandarin 2.00
312 double size 3.00
313 LKa,TMo,AA Meeting. 2.00

Iron Man #328
© Marvel Entertainment Group

314 LKa,TMo,new villain. 2.00
315 A:Black Widow. 2.00
316 I:Slag,A:Crimson Dynamo 2.00
317 In Dynamos Armor. 3.00
318 LKa,TMo,V:Slag. 2.00
319 LKa,TMo,New Space Armor. . . 2.00
320 F:Hawkeye 2.00
321 Cont. From Avg. Crossing 2.00
322 TKa,TheCrossing,V:JackFrost . 2.00
323 TKa,V:Avengers. 2.00
324 TKa,The Crossing 2.00
325 TKa,Avengers:Timeslide after . 3.50
326 . . . . 2.00
327 . . . . 2.00
328 TKa,Tony Stark at ColumbiaU . 2.00
329 thru 332 final issue 2.00
Ann.#1 rep.Iron Man #25 . . . . 25.00
Ann.#2 rep.Iron Man #6 . . . . 10.00
Ann.#3 SB,Manthing. 6.00
Ann.#4 DP,GT,V:Modok,
A:Champions 4.00
Ann.#5 JBr,A:Black Panther 2.50
Ann.#6 A:Eternals,V:Brother
Tode. 2.50
Ann.#7 LMc,A:West Coast
Avengers, I:New Goliath 2.50
Ann.#8 A:X-Factor 3.00
Ann.#9 V:Stratosfire,A:Sunturion. . . 2.50
Ann.#10 PS,BL,Atlantis Attacks #2
A:Sub-Mariner 3.00
Ann.#11 SD,Terminus Factor #2 . . . 2.00
Ann.#12 Subterran.Odyssey #4 . . . 2.00
Ann.#13 GC,AW,Assault on Armor
City,A:Darkhawk. 2.50
Ann.#14 TMo,I:Face Theif,w/card,
BU:War Machine 3.25
Ann.#15 GC,V:Controller 3.25
Spec.#1 rep.Sub-Mariner x-over . . 20.00
Spec.#2 rep.(1971). 8.00
Marvel Milestone rep. #55 (1992) . . 2.95
G-Size#1 Reprints 8.00
1-shot Iron Man/Force Works Collectors' Preview, Neon wrap-around cover, double size, X-over 2.00
1-shot Iron Manual, BSz(c),Guide to Iron Man's technology. 2.00
GN Iron Man 2020 . . . . 5.95
TPB Armor Wars rep.#225-#232. . 12.95
TPB Many Armors of Iron Man . . . 15.95
TPB Power of Iron Man 9.95
TPB JR2,BL,Iron Man vs. Dr. Doom
rep. #149-#150,#249-#250 . . . 12.95
Iron Manual BSz(c),guide to Iron

Man's technology 2.00

[2nd Series] Nov. 1996

1 JLe,SLo,WPo,SW,A:Bruce Banner, New O:Hulk,48pg., . . . 4.00
1A variant Hulk showing cover. . . . 5.00
1 gold signature edition, bagged . 25.00
2 JLe,SLo,WPo,SW. 3.00
3 JLe,SLo,WPo,SW,Heroes brawl . 2.50
4 JLe,SLo,WPo,SW,V:Laser 2.25
4A Xmas cover 4.00
5 JLe,SLo,WPo,SW, Whirlwind . . . 2.00
6 JLe,SLo,WPo,SW,"Industrial Revolution," pt.2 x-over 2.00
7 JLe,SLo,WPo,SW,A:Pepper Potts,Villain revealed 2.00
8 JLe,SLo,RBn,fate of Rebel 2.00
9 JLe,SLo,RBn,V:Mandarin 2.00
10 JLe,SLo,RBn,F:The Hulk 2.00
11 JLb,RBn,V:Dr. Doom,A:Hydra. . . 2.00
12 WPo,JLe,JLb,F:Dr. Doom, Galactus. 2.00
13 JeR,LSn,Wildstorm x-over 2.00

[3rd Series] 1997

1 SCh,KBk,V:Mastermind,48 pg. . . 3.00
2 KBk,SCh,in Switzerland 2.00
3 KBk,SCh,V:Hydra Dreadnought Robot. 2.00
4 KBk,SCh,R:Firebrand 2.00
5 KBk,SCh,V:Firebrand 2.00
6 KBk,F:Black Widow 2.00
7 KBk,SCh,Live Kree or Die, pt.1 x-over. 2.00
8 KBk,SCh,secret identity out 2.00
9 KBk,SCh,A:Black Widow 2.00
10 KBk,SCh,A:Avengers. 2.00
11 KBk,SCh,A:Warbird & War Machine 2.00
12 KBk,V:War Machine. 2.00
13 KBk,SCh,V:Controller,48-page . . 3.00
13a signed 20.00
14 KBk,SCh,Fant.Four x-over 2.00
15 KBk,SCh,V:Nitro 2.00
16 KBk,RSt,V:Dragon Lord 2.00
17 KBk,RSt,SCh,V:Fin Fang Foom . 2.00
18 KBk,RSt,SCh,V:War Machine. . . 2.00
19 KBk,RSt,SCh,V:War Machine. . . 2.00
20 KBk,RSt,SCh,V:War Machine. . . 2.00
21 KBk,RSt,TGu,MBa, Eighth Day prologue. 2.00
22 KBk,RSt,Eighth Day,pt.2, I:Carnivore 2.00
23 KBk,RSt,UltimateDanger,pt.1 . . . 2.00
24 KBk,RSt,UltimateDanger,pt.2 . . . 2.00
25 KBk,RSt,Ultimate Danger,pt.3, 48-pg.. . . . . 3.00
26 JQ,Mask of Iron Man,pt.1. . . . . . 2.00
27 JQ,Mask of Iron Man,pt.2. . . . . . 2.00
28 JQ,Mask of Iron Man,pt.3. . . . . . 2.00
29 JQ,Mask of Iron Man,pt.4. . . . . . 2.25
30 JQ,Mask of Iron Man,pt.5. . . . . . 2.25
31 JQ,Sons of Yinsen,pt.1 . . . . 2.25
32 JQ,Sons of Yinsen,pt.2 . . . . 2.25
33 JQ,Sons of Yinsen,pt.3 . . . . 2.25
34 JQ,Dr. Power. 2.25
35 JQ,Maximum Security 2.25
Ann. 1998 Iron Man/Captain America, KBk,MWa, 48-page . . 3.50
Ann.1999 KBk,JoC,48-page 3.50
Ann.2000 Sons of Yin-Sen,pt.3 . . . . 3.50
TPB Essential Iron Man 14.95

IRON MAN: AGE OF INNOCENCE

1-shot Avengers:Timeslide. 2.50

IRON MAN & SUB-MARINER

April, 1968

1 GC, 2 stories 125.00

IRON MAN: BAD BLOOD

July, 2000

1 (of 4) BL,DvM,V:JustinHammer. . 3.00
2 BL,DvM,Spymaster. 3.00
3 BL,DvM,James Rhodes 3.00
4 BL,DvM,Justin Hammer 3.00

IRON MAN: THE IRON AGE

June, 1998

1 (of 2) KBk,48pg bookshelf. 6.00
2 KBk,48pg bookshelf, concl.. . . . . 6.00

ISLAND OF DR. MOREAU

Oct., 1977

1 GK(c),movie adapt.. . . . . 2.00

IT'S A DUCK'S LIFE

Feb., 1950

1 F;Buck Duck,Super Rabbit 75.00
2 . . . . 35.00
3 thru 10 . . . . @25.00
11 Feb., 1952 . . . . 25.00

Jack of Hearts #2
© Marvel Entertainment Group

JACK OF HEARTS

Jan., 1984

1 Mini series 2.00
2 O:Jack of Hearts. 2.00
3 . . . . 2.00
4 Final issue,April 1984 . . . . 2.00

JAMES BOND JR.

1992

1 I&O:JamesBondJr.(TVseries) . . . 3.00
2 Adventures Contd. 2.00
3 V:Goldfinger,Odd Job 2.00
4 thru 6 . . . . @2.00
V:Scumlord 2.00
8 V:Goldfinger,Walter D.Plank 2.00
9 V:Dr.No in Switzerland 2.00
10 V:Robot,Dr.DeRange 2.00
11 V:S.C.U.M.. . . . . 2.00
12 V:Goldfinger,Jaws 2.00

JANN OF THE JUNGLE

See: JUNGLE TALES

JEANIE COMICS

See: DARING MYSTERY

JIHAD

Epic

1 Cenobites vs. Nightbreed 4.50
2 E:Cenobites vs. Nightbreed 4.50

JOHN CARTER, WARLORD OF MARS

June, 1977

1 GK,DC,O:John Carter,Created by Edgar Rice Burroughs 5.00
2 GK/DC(c),GK,RN, White Apes of Mars. 3.00
3 GK,RN,Requiem for a Warlord . . 3.00
4 GK,RN, Raiding Party. 3.00
5 GK,RN,Giant Battle Issue 3.00
6 GK/DC(c),GK,Alone Against a World 3.00
7 GK,TS,Showdown 3.00
8 GK,RN,Beast With Touch of Stone 3.00
9 GK,RN,Giant Battle Issue 3.00
10 GK,The Death of Barsoom?. . . . 3.00
11 RN,O:Dejah Thoris. 2.50
12 RN,City of the Dead. 2.50
13 RN,March of the Dead 2.50
14 RN,The Day Helium Died. 2.50
15 RN,GK,Prince of Helium Returns 2.50
16 RN,John Carters Dilemna 2.50
17 BL,What Price Victory 5.00
18 FM,Tars Tarkas Battles Alone. . . 2.50
19 RN(c),War With the Wing Men . . 2.50
20 RN(c),Battle at the Bottom of the World 2.50
21 RN(c),The Claws of the Banth . 2.50
22 RN(c),The Canyon of Death. . . . 2.50
23 Murder on Mars 2.50
24 GP/TA(c),Betrayal 2.50
25 Inferno. 2.50
26 Death Cries the Guild of Assassins 2.50
27 Death Marathon. 2.50
28 Guardians of the Lost City Oct., 1979 . . . . 2.50
Ann.#1 RN(c),GK,Battle story 3.00
Ann.#2 RN(c),GK,Outnumbered . . . 2.50
Ann.#3 RN(c),GK,Battle story 2.50

JOKER COMICS

Timely April, 1942

1 BW,I&B:Powerhouse Pepper, A:Stuporman 2,000.00
2 BW,I:Tessie the Typist 700.00
3 BW,A:Tessie the Typist, Squat Car Squad 450.00
4 BW,Squat Car (c) 450.00
5 BW,same 450.00
6 BW, ... 300.00
7 BW 300.00
8 BW 300.00
9 BW 300.00
10 BW,Shooting Gallery (c). 300.00
11 BW 250.00
12 BW 250.00
13 BW 250.00
14 BW 250.00

15 BW 250.00
16 BW 250.00
17 BW 250.00
18 BW 250.00
19 BW 250.00
20 BW 250.00
21 BW 200.00
22 BW 200.00
23 BW,HK,`Hey Look' 200.00
24 BW,HK,`Laff Favorites' 200.00
25 BW,HK,same 200.00
26 BW,HK,same 200.00
27 BW 200.00
28 . . . . 60.00
29 BW 200.00
30 BW 200.00
31 BW 150.00
32 B:Millie,Hedy 60.00
33 HK. 60.00
34 . . . . 50.00
35 HK. 60.00
36 HK. 60.00
37 . . . . 50.00
38 . . . . 50.00
39 . . . . 50.00
40 . . . . 50.00
41 A:Nellie the Nurse 50.00
42 I:Patty Pin-up 60.00
Becomes:

ADVENTURES INTO TERROR

43(1)AH,B:Horror Stories 500.00
44(2)AH,`Won't You Step Into
My Parlor' 350.00
3 GC,`I Stalk By Night' 200.00
4 DR,`The Torture Room' 200.00
5 GC,DR,`The Hitchhicker' 225.00
6 RH,`The Dark Room' 200.00
7 GT(c),BW,`Where Monsters
Dwell' 450.00
8 JSt,`Enter... the Lizard' 175.00
9 RH(c),JSt,`The Dark
Dungeon' 190.00
10 `When the Vampire Calls' 190.00
11 JSt,`Dead Man's Escape' 135.00
12 BK,`The Man Who Cried
Ghost' 175.00
13 BEv(c),`The Hands of Death' . 175.00
14 GC,`The Hands' 135.00
15 `Trapped by the Tarantula' . . . 135.00
16 RH(c),`Her Name Is Death' . . 135.00
17 `I Die Too Often',Bondage(c) . 135.00
18 `He's Trying To Kill Me' 135.00

Adventures Into Terror #2
© Marvel Entertainment Group

19 `The Girl Who Couldn't Die' . . 150.00
20 . . . . 150.00
21 GC 125.00
22 . . . . 125.00
23. . . . . 125.00
24 MF,GC 125.00
25 MF. 150.00
26 GC 125.00
27 . . . . 125.00
28 GC 125.00
29 GC 125.00
30 . . . . 125.00
31 May, 1954 . . . . 125.00

JOURNEY INTO MYSTERY

June, 1952

1 RH(c),B:Mystery/Horror
stories 3,000.00
2 `Don't Look' 900.00
3 `I Didn't See Anything' 700.00
4 RH,BEv(c),`I'm Drowning,'
severed hand (c) 700.00
5 RH,BEv(c),`Fright' 450.00
6 BEv(c),`Till Death Do
Us Part' 450.00

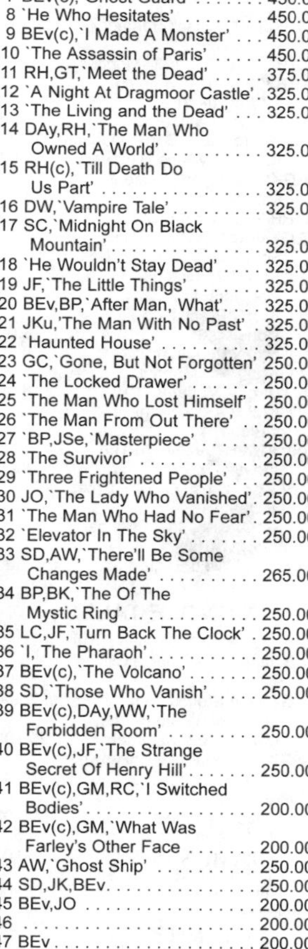

7 BEv(c),`Ghost Guard' 450.00
8 `He Who Hesitates' 450.00
9 BEv(c),`I Made A Monster' . . . 450.00
10 `The Assassin of Paris' 450.00
11 RH,GT,`Meet the Dead' 375.00
12 `A Night At Dragmoor Castle' . 325.00
13 `The Living and the Dead' . . . 325.00
14 DAy,RH,`The Man Who
Owned A World' 325.00
15 RH(c),`Till Death Do
Us Part' 325.00
16 DW,`Vampire Tale' 325.00
17 SC,`Midnight On Black
Mountain' 325.00
18 `He Wouldn't Stay Dead' 325.00
19 JF,`The Little Things' 325.00
20 BEv,BP,`After Man, What' 325.00
21 JKu,'The Man With No Past' . 325.00
22 `Haunted House' 325.00
23 GC,`Gone, But Not Forgotten' 250.00
24 `The Locked Drawer' 250.00
25 `The Man Who Lost Himself' . 250.00
26 `The Man From Out There' . . 250.00
27 `BP,JSe,`Masterpiece' 250.00
28 `The Survivor' 250.00
29 `Three Frightened People' . . . 250.00
30 JO,`The Lady Who Vanished' . 250.00
31 `The Man Who Had No Fear' . 250.00
32 `Elevator In The Sky' 250.00
33 SD,AW,`There'll Be Some
Changes Made' 265.00
34 BP,BK,`The Of The
Mystic Ring' 250.00
35 LC,JF,`Turn Back The Clock' . 250.00
36 `I, The Pharaoh' 250.00
37 BEv(c),`The Volcano' 250.00
38 SD,`Those Who Vanish' 250.00
39 BEv(c),DAy,WW,`The
Forbidden Room' 250.00
40 BEv(c),JF,`The Strange
Secret Of Henry Hill' 250.00
41 BEv(c),GM,RC,`I Switched
Bodies' 200.00
42 BEv(c),GM,`What Was
Farley's Other Face 200.00
43 AW,`Ghost Ship' 250.00
44 SD,JK,BEv. 250.00
45 BEv,JO 200.00
46 . . . . 200.00
47 BEv 200.00
48 . . . . 200.00
49 . . . . 200.00
50 SD 200.00
51 SD,JK 250.00
52 JK 200.00

Journey Into Mystery #96
© Marvel Entertainment Group

53 DH. 200.00
54 AW 225.00
55 . . . . 200.00
56 thru 61 SD,JK. . . . . @200.00
62 SD,JK,I:Xemnu 250.00
63 thru 68 SD,JK. . . . . @200.00
69 thru 82 . . . . @225.00
83 JK,SD,I&O:Thor 4,700.00
84 JK,SD,DH,I:Executioner . . . 1,000.00
85 JK,SD,I:Loki,Heimdall,Balder,
Tyr,Odin,Asgard 600.00
86 JK,SD,DH,V:Tomorrow Man . . 400.00
87 JK,SD,V:Communists 300.00
88 JK,SD,V:Loki 300.00
89 JK,SD,O:Thor(rep) 300.00
90 SD,I:Carbon Copy 175.00
91 JSt,SD,I:Sandu 175.00
92 JSt,SD,V:Loki,I:Frigga 175.00
93 DAy,JK,SD,I:Radioactive
Man 175.00
94 JSt,SD,V:Loki. 135.00
95 JSt,SD,I:Duplicator. 135.00
96 JSt,SD,I:Merlin II 125.00
97 JK,I:Lava Man,O:Odin 150.00
98 DH,JK,I&O:Cobra. 125.00
99 DH,JK,I:Mr.Hyde,Surtur 125.00
100 DH,JK,V:Mr.Hyde 125.00
101 JK,V:Tomorrow Man 100.00
102 JK,I:Sif,Hela. 100.00
103 JK,I:Enchantress,
Executioner 100.00
104 JK,Giants. 100.00
105 JK,V:Hyde,Cobra 100.00
106 JK,O:Balder 100.00
107 JK,I:Grey Gargoyle,Karnilla . 100.00
108 JK,A:Dr.Strange 100.00
109 JK,V:Magneto 135.00
110 JK,V:Hyde,Cobra,Loki 90.00
111 JK,V:Hyde,Cobra,Loki 90.00
112 JK,V:Hulk,O:Loki 200.00
113 JK,V:Grey Gargoyle 90.00
114 JK,I&O:Absorbing Man. 90.00
115 JK,O:Loki,V:Absorbing Man . 100.00
116 JK,V:Loki,C:Daredevil. 90.00
117 JK,V:Loki 90.00
118 JK,I:Destroyer 90.00
119 JK,V:Destroyer,I:Hogun,
Fandrall,Volstagg 90.00
120 JK,A:Avengers,Absorbing
Man 90.00
121 JK,V:Absorbing Man 90.00
122 JK,V:Absorbing Man 90.00
123 JK,V:Absorbing Man 90.00

MARVEL

124 JK,A:Hercules 90.00
125 JK,A;Hercules 90.00
Annual #1, JK,I:Hercules. 160.00
Becomes:

THOR

JOURNEY INTO MYSTERY
[2nd series] Oct., 1972

1 GK,TP,MP,`Dig Me No Grave' . 15.00
2 GK,`Jack the Ripper' 8.00
3 JSn,TP,`Shambler From the Stars' 8.00
4 GC,DA,`Haunter of the Dark', H.P. Lovecraft adaptation. 8.00
5 RB,FrG,`Shadow From the Steeple',R. Bloch adaptation . . 8.00
6 Mystery Stories 7.00
7 thru 19 . . . . @7.00

JOURNEY INTO UNKNOWN WORLDS See: ALL WINNERS COMICS

J-2
Aug., 1998

1 TDF,RLm,AM,F:J2 with the powers of Juggernaut 2.00
2 TDF,RLm,AM,V:Buffer Zone, Enthralla & Uncanny X-People . 2.00
2a variant cover. 2.00
3 TDF,RLm,AM,V:Hulk. 2.00
4 TDF,RLm,AM,turning points 2.00
5 TDF,RLm,AM,Ghosts of the Past 2.00
6 TDF,RLm,AM,Majority Rules. . . . 2.00
7 TDF,RLm,AM,Last Days of the Original Juggernaut 2.00
8 TDF,RLm,AM,Uneasy Allies 2.00
9 TDF,RLm,AM,Critical Choices. . . 2.00
10 TDF,RLm,AM,Incredible Journeys 2.00
11 TDF,RLm,AM,Master of Jug-Fu . 2.00
12 TDF,RLm,AM,A:Juggernaut, last issue 2.00

JUGGERNAUT
1997

1-shot 48pg. 3.00

JUGGERNAUT: THE EIGHTH DAY
Sept., 1999

1-shot JoC,TSr,AKu(c),x-over,pt.4. . 3.00

JUNGLE ACTION
Atlas Oct., 1954

1 JMn,JMn(c),B:Leopard Girl . . 275.00
2 JMn,JMn(c) 300.00
3 JMn,JMn(c) 200.00
4 JMn,JMn(c) 200.00
5 JMn,JMn(c) 200.00
6 JMn,JMn(c),August, 1955 . . . 200.00

JUNGLE ACTION
Oct., 1972—Nov., 1976

1 JB(c),Lorna,Tharn,Jann reprints 15.00
2 GK(c),same 10.00
3 JSn(c),same 10.00
4 GK(c),same 10.00

Jungle Action #1
© Marvel Entertainment Group

5 JR(c),JB,B:Black Panther, V:Man-Ape 15.00
6 RB/FrG(c),RB,V:Kill-Monger . . . 10.00
7 RB/KJ(c),RB,V:Venomn 10.00
8 RB/KJ(c),RB,GK, O:Black Panther 10.00
9 GK/KJ(c),RB,V:Baron Macabre 10.00
10 GK/FrG(c),V:King Cadaver. . . . 10.00
11 GK(c),V:Baron Macabre,Lord Karnaj 10.00
12 RB/KJ(c),V:Kill Monger 8.00
13 GK/JK(c),V:White Gorilla, Sombre 8.00
14 GK(c),V:Prehistoric Monsters. 8.00
15 GK(c),V:Prehistoric Monsters 8.00
16 GK(c),V:Venomm. 8.00
17 GK(c),V:Kill Monger. 8.00
18 JKu(c),V:Madame Slay 8.00
19 GK(c),V:KKK,`Sacrifice of Blood'. 8.00
20 V:KKK,`Slaughter In The Streets' 8.00
21 V:KKK,`Cross Of Fire, Cross Of Death' 7.00
22 JB(c),V:KKK,Soul Stranger 7.00
23 JBy(c),V:KKK. 7.00
24 GK(c),I:Wind Eagle 7.00

JUNGLE TALES
Atlas Sept., 1954

1 B:Jann of the Jungle,Cliff Mason,Waku 275.00
2 GT,Jann Stories cont. 225.00
3 Cliff Mason,White Hunter, Waku Unknown Jungle 200.00
4 Cliff Mason,Waku,Unknown Jungle 200.00
5 RH(c),SSh,Cliff Mason,Waku, Unknown Jungle 200.00
6 DH,SSh,Cliff Mason,Waku, Unknown Jungle 200.00
7 DH,SSh,Cliff Mason,Waku, Unknown Jungle. 200.00
Becomes:

JANN OF THE JUNGLE

8 SH,SSh,`The Jungle Outlaw' . 225.00
9 `With Fang and Talons'. 150.00
10 AW,`The Jackal's Lair' 125.00
11 `Bottomless Pit' 125.00
12 `The Lost Safari' 125.00
13 `When the Trap Closed' 125.00
14 V:Hunters 125.00
15 BEv(c),DH,V:Hunters 125.00
16 BEv(c),AW,`Jungle Vengeance' 150.00
17 BEv(c),DH,AW,June, 1957 . . . 150.00

JUSTICE
Nov., 1986

1 I:Justice 2.00
2 . . . . 2.00
3 Yakuza Assassin 2.00
4 thru 8 . . . . @2.00
9 KG 2.00
10 thru 18. . . . . @2.00
19 thru 31. . . . . @2.00
32 Last issue,A:Joker 2.00

JUSTICE COMICS
Atlas Fall, 1947

7(1) B:FBI in Action,`Mystery of White Death'. 200.00
8(2),HK,`Crime is For Suckers' . 150.00
9(3),FBI Raid 125.00
4 Bank Robbery 125.00
5 Subway(c) 100.00
6 E:FBI In Action 100.00
7 Symbolic(c) 100.00
8 Funeral(c) 100.00
9 B:`True Cases Proving Crime Can't Win'. 100.00
10 Ph(c),Bank Hold Up 100.00
11 Ph(c),Behind Bars 100.00
12 Ph(c),The Crime of Martin Blaine 75.00
13 Ph(c),The Cautiouc Crook 75.00
14 Ph(c) 75.00
15 Ph(c) 75.00
16 F:"Ears"Karpik-Mobster 60.00
17 `The Ragged Stranger' 60.00
18 `Criss-Cross' 60.00
19 `Death Of A Spy' 60.00
20 `Miami Mob'. 60.00
21 `Trap'. 60.00
22 `The Big Break' 60.00
23 thru 40 . . . . @50.00
41 Electrocution cover 100.00
42 thru 51 . . . . @50.00
52 `Flare Up' 50.00
Becomes:

TALES OF JUSTICE
May, 1955—Aug., 1957

53 BEv,`Keeper Of The Keys' . . . 125.00
54 thru 57 . . . . @85.00
58 BK. 100.00
59 BK. 100.00
60 thru 63 . . . . @50.00
64 RC,DW,JSe 75.00
65 RC. 75.00
66 JO,AT 75.00
67 DW 75.00

JUSTICE: FOUR BALANCE

1 A:Thing, Yancy Street Gang 2.00
2 V:Hate Monger 2.00
3 the story continues... . . . . 2.00
4 ...to its conclusion. 2.00

KATHY
Atlas Oct., 1959—Feb., 1964

1 `Teenage Tornado' 50.00
2 . . . . 25.00
3 thru 15 . . . . @20.00
16 thru 27 . . . . @15.00

KA-ZAR

[Reprint Series] Aug., 1970

1 X-Men ID 20.00
2 Daredevil 12, 13. . . . . 15.00
3 DDH,Spider-Man,March, 1971 . 15.00

[1st Series] Jan., 1974

1 O:Savage Land 10.00
2 DH,JA,A:Shanna The She-Devil . 7.00
3 DH,V:Man-God,A:El Tigre 7.00
4 DH,V:Man-God. 7.00
5 DH,D:El-Tigre. 5.00
6 JB/AA,V:Behemoth 5.00
7 JB/BMc`Revenge of the
River-Gods' 5.00
8 JB/AA,`Volcano of
Molten Death'. 5.00
9 JB,`Man Who Hunted Dinosaur' . 5.00
10 JB,`Dark City of Death' 5.00
11 DH/FS,`Devil-God of Sylitha' . . . 4.00
12 RH,`Wizard of Forgotten
Death' 4.00
13 V:Lizard Men 4.00
14 JAb,V:Klaw 4.00
15 VM,V:Klaw,`Hellbird' 3.00
16 VM,V:Klaw. 3.00
17 VM,V:Klaw. 3.00
18 VM,V:Klaw,Makrum 3.00
19 VM,V:Klaw,Raknor the Slayer . . 3.00
20 VM,V:Klaw,`Fortress of Fear' . . . 3.00

[2nd Series] Apr., 1981

1 BA,O:Ka-Zar. 3.50
2 thru 7 BA . . . . @3.00
8 BA,Kazar Father. 2.00
9 BA 2.00
10 BA,Direct D 2.00
11 BA/GK,Zabu 2.00
12 BA,Panel Missing 2.00
12a Scarce Reprint. 2.00
13 BA. 2.00
14 BA/GK,Zabu 2.00
15 BA. 2.00
16 . . . . 2.00
17 Detective 2.00
18 . . . . 2.00
19 . . . . 2.00
20 A:Spider-Man 2.00
21 . . . . 2.00
22 A:Spider-Man 2.00
23 A:Spider-Man 2.00
24 A:Spider-Man 2.00
25 A:Spider-Man 2.00
26 A:Spider-Man 2.00

Kazar, 2nd Series, #25
© Marvel Entertainment Group

27 A:Buth 2.00
28 Pangea 2.00
29 W:Kazar & Shanna, Doub.Size . 2.00
30 V:Pterons 2.00
31 PangeaWarII 2.00
32 V:Plunderer 2.00
33 V:Plunderer 2.00
34 Last Issue Doub.Size. 2.00

[3rd Series] 1997

1 MWa,NKu,Ka-Zar, Shanna, Zabu,
V:Gregor, 40pg. 5.00
1a 2nd printing 2.50
2 MWa,NKu,V:Gregor 4.00
2A NKu variant cover. 3.00
3 MWa,NKu,Ka-Zar's son dead? . . 3.00
4 MWa,NKu,in New York City 3.00
5 MWa,NKu, ... 2.50
6 MWa,V:Rampaging Rhino. 2.00
7 MWa,NKu,F:Shanna the
She-Devil 2.00
8 MWa,NKu, Urban Jungle, pt.1. . . 2.00
9 MWa,NKu, Urban Jungle, pt.2. . . 2.00
10 MWa,NKu, Urban Jungle, pt.3 . . 2.00
11 MWa,NKu, Urban Jungle, pt.4,
concl. 2.00
12 MWa,A:High Evolutionary 2.00
13 MWa,A:High Evolutionary 2.00
14 MWa,NKu,end old & begin new
storyline, double size 3.00
15 A:Punisher. 3.00
16 A:Punisher. 2.00
17 Ka-Zar clears his name,
A:Jameka. 2.00
18 People of the Savage Land
revolt 2.00
19 V:Gregor 2.00
20 A:Gregor,Zira, final issue 2.00
Ann. '97 V:Garrok, the Petrified
Man 2.50
Ann. '98 Kazar/Daredevil heroes
unite. 3.00

KA-ZAR OF THE SAVAGE LAND

1996

1-shot CDi,V:Sauron, 48pg.
prelude to series. 3.00

KA-ZAR: SIBLING RIVALRY

1997

1 MWa,TDz, Flashback 2.00

KELLYS, THE

See: KID KOMICS

KENT BLAKE OF THE SECRET SERVICE

May, 1951—July, 1953

1 U.S. Govt. Secret Agent
stories,Bondage cover 150.00
2 JSt,Drug issue,`Man with-
out A Face 100.00
3 `Trapped By The Chinese
Reds' 50.00
4 Secret Service Stories 50.00
5 RH(c),`Condemned To Death' . 50.00
6 Cases from Kent Blake files . . . 50.00
7 RH(c),Behind Enemy Lines . . . 50.00
8 V:Communists 50.00
9 thru 14 . . . . @50.00

KICKERS INC.

Nov., 1986

1 SB,O:Kickers 2.00
2 SB 2.00
3 RF,Witches. 2.00
4 RF,FIST 2.00
5 RF,A:D.P.7 . . . . 2.00
6 thru 8 RF . . . . @2.00
9 . . . . 2.00
10 TD. 2.00
11 . . . . 2.00
12 Oct., 1987 . . . . 2.00

KID & PLAY

1 Based on Rap Group 2.00
2 Drug Issue 2.00
3 At your Friends Expense 2.00
4 . . . . 2.00
5 . . . . 2.00
6 Record Contract 2.00
7 Fraternity Pledging 2.00
8 Kid and Cindy become an item . . 2.00
9 C:Marvel Heroes 2.00

Kid Colt Outlaw #103
© Marvel Entertainment Group

KID COLT OUTLAW

Atlas Aug., 1948

1 B:Kid Colt,A:Two-Gun Kid . . . 800.00
2 `Gun-Fighter and the Girl' 350.00
3 `Colt-Quick Killers
For Hire'. 275.00
4 `Wanted',A:Tex Taylor 275.00
5 `Mystery of the Misssing
Mine',A:Blaze Carson 275.00
6 A:Tex Taylor,`Valley of
the Warewolf' 185.00
7 B:Nimo the Lion 185.00
8 . . . . 185.00
9 . . . . 185.00
10 `The Whip Strikes',E:Nimo
the Lion' 185.00
11 O:Kid Colt 225.00
12 . . . . 150.00
13 DRi 150.00
14 . . . . 150.00
15 `Gun Whipped in Shotgun
City' 150.00
16 . . . . 150.00
17 . . . . 150.00
18 DRi 150.00
19 . . . . 125.00
20 `The Outlaw' 125.00

21 thru 30 . . . . @125.00
31 . . . . 125.00
32 . . . . 125.00
33 thru 45 A:Black Rider . . . . . @80.00
46 RH(c). 75.00
47 DW 75.00
48 RH(c),JKu 75.00
49 . . . . 75.00
50 . . . . 75.00
51 thru 56 . . . . @55.00
57 AW 60.00
58 AW 60.00
59 AW 60.00
60 AW 60.00
61 . . . . 40.00
62 . . . . 40.00
63 . . . . 40.00
64 . . . . 45.00
65 . . . . 45.00
66 thru 78 . . . . @40.00
79 Origin Retold 45.00
80 thru 86 . . . . @40.00
87 JDa(reprint) 45.00
88 AW 50.00
89 AW,Matt Slade. 50.00
90 thru 99 . . . . @30.00
100 . . . . 40.00
101 . . . . 35.00
102 . . . . 30.00
103 'The Great Train Robbery' . . . 30.00
104 JKu(c),DH,'Trail of
Kid Colt' 30.00
105 DH,V:Dakota Dixon 30.00
106 JKu(c),'The Circus
of Crime' 30.00
107 . . . . 30.00
108 BEv 30.00
109 DAy,V:The Barracuda. 30.00
110 GC,V:Iron Mask 30.00
111 JKu(c),V:Sam Hawk, The
Man Hunter 30.00
112 JKu(c),V:Mr. Brown 30.00
113 JKu(c),GC,V:Bull Barton. 30.00
114 JKu(c),Return of Iron Mask. . . 30.00
115 JKu(c),V:The Scorpion 30.00
116 JKu(c),GC,V:Dr. Danger &
Invisible Gunman. 30.00
117 JKu(c),GC,V:The Fatman &
His Boomerang 30.00
118 V:Scorpion,Bull Barton,
Dr. Danger 30.00
119 DAy(c),JK,V:Bassett The
Badman 30.00
120 'Cragsons Ride Again' 30.00
121 A:Rawhide Kid,Iron Mask. . . . 25.00
122 V:Rattler Ruxton 25.00
123 V:Ringo Barker 25.00
124 A:Phantom Raider 25.00
125 A:Two-Gun Kid 25.00
126 V:Wes Hardin. 15.00
127 thru 129 . . . . @15.00
130 O:Kid Colt 15.00
131 thru 150 . . . . @15.00
151 thru 200 reprints . . . . @12.00
201 thru 228 reprints . . . . @10.00
229 April, 1979. . . . . 10.00

KID FROM DODGE CITY

Atlas July, 1957—Sept., 1957

1 . . . . 60.00
2 . . . . 35.00

KID FROM TEXAS

Atlas June, 1957—Aug., 1957

1 . . . . 60.00
2 . . . . 35.00

KID KOMICS

Timely Feb., 1943

1 SSh(c),BW,O:Captain Wonder
& Tim Mulrooney I:Whitewash,
Knuckles,Trixie Trouble,
Pinto Pete Subbie 3,300.00
2 AsH(c),F:Captain Wonder
Subbie, B:Young Allies,B:Red
Hawk,Tommy Tyme 1,400.00
3 ASh(c),A:The Vision &
Daredevils 1,000.00
4 ASh(c),B:Destroyer,A:Sub-Mariner,
E:Red Hawk,Tommy Tyme . . 900.00
5 ASh(c),V:Nazis 650.00
6 ASh(c),V:Japanese 650.00
7 ASh(c),B;Whizzer 625.00
8 ASh(c),V:Train Robbers 625.00
9 ASh(c),V:Elves 625.00
10 ASh(c),E:Young Allies,
The Destoyer,The Whizzer . 625.00

Becomes:

KID MOVIE KOMICS

11 F:Silly Seal,Ziggy Pig
HK,Hey Look. 200.00

Becomes:

RUSTY COMICS

12 F:Rusty,A:Mitzi. 150.00
13 Do not Disturb(c) 75.00
14 Beach(c),BW,HK,Hey Look . . 100.00
15 Picnic(c),HK,Hey Look 75.00
16 Juniors Grades,HK,HeyLook . . 75.00
17 John in Trouble,HK,HeyLook . . 75.00
18 John Fired 50.00
19 Fridge raid(c),HK 50.00
20 And Her Family,HK 75.00
21 And Her Family,HK 125.00
22 . . . . 125.00

Becomes:

KELLYS, THE

23 F:The Kelly Family(Pop,
Mom,Mike,Pat & Goliath) 75.00
24 Mike's Date,A;Margie. 50.00
25 Wrestling(c) 50.00

Becomes:

SPY CASES

26(#1) Spy stories 165.00
27(#2) BEv,Bondage(c). 100.00
28(#3) Sabotage,A:Douglas
Grant Secret Agent 100.00
4 The Secret Invasion 90.00
5 The Vengeance of Comrade
de Casto 90.00
6 A:Secret Agent Doug Grant . . . 90.00
7 GT,A:Doug Grant 90.00
8 Atom Bomb(c),Frozen
Horror 75.00
9 Undeclared War 70.00
10 Battlefield Adventures 65.00
11 Battlefield Adventures 60.00
12 Battlefield Adventures 60.00
13 Battlefield Adventures 60.00
14 Battlefield Adventures 60.00
15 Doug Grant 60.00
16 Doug Grant 60.00
17 Doug Grant 60.00
18 Contact in Ankara 60.00
19 Final Issue,Oct., 1953 . . . . 60.00

KID SLADE GUNFIGHTER

See: MATT SLADE

KILLFRENZY

1 . . . . 2.00
2 Castle Madspike. 2.00

KILLPOWER: THE EARLY YEARS

1993

1 B:MiB,Goes on Rampage 3.25
2 thru 3 O:Killpower. 2.00
4 E:MiB,last issue 2.00

KING ARTHUR & THE KNIGHTS OF JUSTICE

1993–94

1 Based on Cartoon 2.00
2 Based on Cartoon 2.00
3 Based on Cartoon 2.00

KING CONAN:

See: CONAN THE KING

KINGPIN

Nov., 1997

1-shot StL,JR, bookshelf 48pg 6.00

KISSNATION

1997

1 Rock & Roll, A:X-Men. 10.00

KITTY PRYDE: AGENT OF S.H.I.E.L.D.

Oct., 1997

1 (of 3) LHa,V:Ogun 2.50
2 LHa,V:Ogun 2.50
3 LHa,Ogun's Slave?. 2.50

Kitty Pryde & Wolverine #1
© Marvel Entertainment Group

KITTY PRYDE & WOLVERINE

Nov., 1984

1 AM,V:Ogun. 6.00
2 AM,V:Ogun. 4.00
3 thru 5 AM,V:Ogun . . . . @4.00
6 AM,D:Ogun, April, 1985 . . . . 3.00

KNIGHTS OF PENDRAGON

[1st Regular Series] July, 1990

1 GEr 2.75

Knights of Pendragon #6
© Marvel Entertainment Group

2 thru 7 . . . . @2.25
8 inc.SBi Poster. 2.25
9 V:Bane Fisherman 2.25
10 Cap.Britain/Union Jack 2.25
11 A:Iron Man. 2.25
12 A:Iron Man,Union Jack. 2.25
13 O:Pendragon 2.25
14 A:Mr.Fantastic,Invisible Woman
Black Panther. 2.25
15 BlackPanther/Union Jack T.U. . . 2.25
16 A:Black Panther. 2.25
17 D:Albion, Union Jack,
A:Black Panther 2.25
18 A:Iron Man,Black Panther 2.25

[2nd Regular Series]

1 GEr,A:Iron Man,R:Knights of
Pendragon,V:MyS-TECH 2.25
2 A:Iron Man,Black Knight 2.00
3 PGa,A:Iron Man,Black Knight . . . 2.00
4 Gawain Vs. Bane 2.00
5 JRe,V:Magpie. 2.00
6 A:Spider-Man 2.00
7 A:Spider-Man,V:Warheads 2.00
8 JRe,A:Spider-Man 2.00
9 A:Spider-Man,Warheads. 2.00
10 V:Baron Blood 2.00
11. . . . . 2.00
12 MyS-TECH Wars,V:Skire 2.00
13 A:Death's Head II 2.00
14 A:Death's Head II 2.00
15 D:Adam,A:Death's Head II 2.00

KRAZY KOMICS

Timely July, 1942

1 B:Ziggy Pig,Silly Seal 450.00
2 Toughy Tomcat(c) 200.00
3 Toughy Tomcat/Bunny(c) 150.00
4 Toughy Tomcat/Ziggy(c) 150.00
5 Ziggy/Buzz Saw(c) 150.00
6 Toughy/Cannon(c) 150.00
7 Cigar Store Indian(c) 150.00
8 Toughy/Hammock(c) 150.00
9 Hitler(c) 150.00
10 Newspaper(c) 150.00
11 Canoe(c) 150.00
12 Circus(c) 200.00
13 Pirate Treasure(c) 100.00
14 Fishing(c). 100.00
15 Ski-Jump(c) 100.00
16 Airplane(c). 75.00
17 Street corner(c) 75.00
18 Mallet/Bell(c) 75.00

19 Bicycle(c). 75.00
20 Ziggy(c) 75.00
21 Toughy's date(c) 75.00
22 Crystal Ball(c) 75.00
23 Sharks in bathtub(c). 75.00
24 Baseball(c) 75.00
25 HK,Krazy Krow(c) 100.00
26 Super Rabbit(c) 75.00
Becomes:

CINDY COMICS

27 HK,B:Margie,Oscar 135.00
28 HK,Snow sled(c) 75.00
29 . . . . 75.00
30 . . . . 75.00
31 HK. 75.00
32 . . . . 50.00
33 A;Georgie 50.00
34 thru 40 . . . . @50.00
Becomes:

CRIME CAN'T WIN

41 Crime stories 175.00
42 . . . . 100.00
43 GT,Horror story 125.00
4 thru 11 . . . . @75.00
12 Sept., 1953 . . . . 75.00

KRAZY KOMICS

Timely

[2nd Series] Aug., 1948

1 BW,HK,B:Eustice Hayseed . . 300.00
2 BW,O:Powerhouse Pepper
November, 1948 . . . . 225.00

KRAZY KROW

Summer, 1945

1 B:Krazy Krow 125.00
2 . . . . 75.00
3 Winter, 1945-46 . . . . 75.00

KREE/SKRULL WAR

Sept.–Oct., 1983

1 & 2 JB,NA,reprints . . . . @5.00

KRULL

Nov.–Dec., 1983

1 Ph(c),BBI,movie adapt 2.00
2 BBI,rep.,Marvel Super Spec.. . . . 2.00

KULL THE CONQUEROR

[1st Series] June, 1971

1 MSe,RA,WW,A King Comes
Riding,O:Kull 20.00
2 MSe,JSe,Shadow Kingdom 9.00
3 MSe,JSe,Death Dance of
Thulsa Doom 9.00
4 MSe,JSe,Night o/t Red Slayers. . 6.00
5 MSe,JSe,Kingdom By the Sea . . 4.00
6 MSe,JSe,Lurker Beneath
the Sea 3.00
7 MSe,JSe,Delcardes'Cat,
A:Thulsa Doom 3.00
8 MSe,JSe,Wolfshead 3.00
9 MSe,JSe,The Scorpion God 3.00
10 MSe,Swords o/t White Queen . . 3.00
11 MP,King Kull Must Die, O:Kull
cont.,A:Thulsa Doom 3.00
12 MP,SB,Moon of Blood,V:Thulsa
Doom,B:SD,B.U.stories 3.00
13 MP,AM,Torches From Hell,
V:Thulsa Doom 3.00
14 MP,JA,The Black Belfry,
A:Thulsa Doom 3.00
15 MP,Wings o/t Night-Beast,
E:SD,B.U.stories 3.00
16 EH,Tiger in the Moon,

Kull The Conqueror #5
© Marvel Entertainment Group

A:Thulsa Doom 3.00
17 AA,EH,Thing from Emerald
Darkness 3.00
18 EH,AA,Keeper of Flame
& Frost. 3.00
19 EH,AA,The Crystal Menace 3.00
20 EH,AA,Hell Beneath Atlantis . . . 3.00
21 City of the Crawling Dead 2.00
22 Talons of the Devil-Birds 2.00
23 Demon Shade 2.00
24 Screams in the Dark 2.00
25 A Lizard's Throne 2.00
26 Into Death's Dimension 2.00
27 The World Within 2.00
28 Creature and the Crown,
A:Thulsa Doom 2.00
29 To Sit the Topaz Throne,
V:Thulsa Doom, final issue 2.00

[2nd Series] 1982

1 JB,Brule 2.50
2 Misareenia 2.00

[3rd Series] 1983–85

1 JB,BWi,DG,Iraina 2.00
2 JB,Battle to the Death. 2.00
3 JB 2.00
4 JB 2.00
5 JB 2.00
6 JB 2.00
7 JB,Masquerade Death 2.00
8 JB 2.00
9 JB 2.00
10 JB 2.00

KULL AND THE BARBARIANS

May, 1975

1 NA,GK,reprint Kull #1 . . . . 10.00
2 BBI,reprint,Dec., 1983 . . . . 7.00
3 NA,HC,O:Red Sonja. 8.00

LABRYNTH

1986–87

1 Movie adapt 2.00
2 and 3 . . . . @2.00

LAFF-A-LYMPICS

1978–79

1 F;Hanna Barbera 15.00
2 thru 5 . . . . @10.00
6 thru 13 . . . . @10.00

LANA
August, 1948

1 F:Lana Lane The Show Girl, A:Rusty,B:Millie 100.00
2 HK,Hey Look,A:Rusty 60.00
3 Show(c),B:Nellie 40.00
4 Ship(c) 40.00
5 Audition(c) 40.00
6 Stop sign(c) 40.00
7 Beach(c) 40.00
Becomes:

LITTLE LANA
8 Little Lana(c) 26.00
9 Final Issue,March, 1950 . . . . . . 26.00

LANCE BARNES: POST NUKE DICK
Epic 1993

1 I:Lance Barnes 2.50
2 Cigarettes. 2.50
3 Warring Mall Tribe 2.50
4 V:Ex-bankers,last issue 2.50

LAST AMERICAN
Epic 1990–91

1 . . . . 3.50
2 . . . . 3.00
3 . . . . 2.50
4 Final issue. 2.25

THE LAST AVENGERS STORY
1 PDd, Alterverse,Future world . . . 6.00
2 PDd, Final fate,fully painted 6.00
TPB PDd,AOI, rep. Alterniverse story, 96pg. 12.95

LAST STARFIGHTER, THE
Oct.–Dec., 1984

1 JG(c),BBI,Movie adapt. 2.00
2 Movie adapt 2.00
3 BBI 2.00

LAWBREAKERS ALWAYS LOSE!
Spring, 1948–Oct., 1949

1 Partial Ph(c),Adam and Eve, HK,Giggles and Grins 250.00
2 FBI V:Fur Thieves 125.00
3 . . . . 100.00
4 Asylum(c) 125.00
5 . . . . 125.00
6 Pawnbroker(c) 125.00
7 Crime at Midnight 175.00
8 Prison Break 100.00
9 Ph(c),He Prowled at Night . . . 100.00
10 Phc(c),I Met My Murderer . . . 100.00

LAWDOG
1 B:CDi(s),FH,I:Lawdog 2.50
2 FH,V:Vocal-yokel Cultist 2.25
3 FH,Manical Nazis 2.25
4 FH,V:Zombies 2.25
5 FH 2.25
6 FH 2.25
7 FH,V:Zombies 2.25
8 FH,w/card. 2.25
9 FH,w/card. 2.25
10 last issue, w/card. 2.25

LAWDOG & GRIMROD: TERROR AT THE CROSSROADS
1993

1 . . . . 3.50

LEGION OF MONSTERS
Sept., 1975
(black & white magazine)

1 NA(c),GM,I&O:Legion of Monsters,O:Manphibian 30.00

LEGION OF NIGHT
Oct., 1991

1 WPo/SW,A:Fin Fang Foom. 5.50
2 WPo,V:Fin Fang Foom 5.50

LETHAL FOES OF SPIDER-MAN
1993

1 B:DFr(s),SMc,R:Stegron 2.00
2 SMc,A:Stegron 2.00
3 SMc,V:Spider-Man 2.00
4 E:DFr(s),SMc,Last Issue. 2.00

LIFE OF CAPTAIN MARVEL
August, 1985

1 rep.Iron Man #55, Capt.Marvel #25,26 . . . . 9.00
2 rep.Capt.Marvel#26-28 . . . . 6.50
3 rep.Capt.Marvel#28-30 Marvel Feature #12 . . . . 6.00
4 rep.Marvel Feature #12,Capt. Marvel #31,32,Daredevil#105 . . 6.00
5 rep.Capt.Marvel #32-#34 . . . . . . 6.00

LIFE OF CHRIST
1993

1 Birth of Christ 3.00
2 MW,The Easter Story 3.00

LIFE OF POPE JOHN-PAUL II
1983

1 JSt, Jan., 1983 . . . . 5.00
1a Special reprint 3.00

LIFE WITH MILLIE
See: DATE WITH MILLIE

LIGHT AND DARKNESS WAR
Epic Oct., 1988

1 . . . . 4.00
2 . . . . 3.00
3 thru 6 Dec., 1989 . . . . @2.50

LINDA CARTER, STUDENT NURSE
Atlas Sept., 1961

1 . . . . 40.00
2 thru 9, Jan., 1963 . . . . @30.00

LION KING
1 based on Movie 2.75

Li'l Kids #1
© Marvel Entertainment Group

LI'L KIDS
Aug., 1970–June, 1973

1 . . . . 30.00
2 thru 12 . . . . @15.00

LI'L PALS
Sept., 1972

1 . . . . 20.00
2 thru 5, May, 1973 . . . . @18.00

LITTLE ASPRIN
July, 1949

1 HK,A;Oscar 125.00
2 HK 65.00
3 Dec., 1949 . . . . 45.00

LITTLE LANA
See: LANA

LITTLE LENNY
June, 1949

1 . . . . 50.00
2 . . . . 35.00
3 November, 1949 . . . . 35.00

LITTLE LIZZIE
June, 1949

1 Roller Skating(c) 60.00
2 Soda(c) 40.00
3 Movies(c) 40.00
4 Lizzie(c) 40.00
5 Lizzie/Swing(c) April,1950 . . . . 40.00
[2nd Series] Sept., 1953
1 . . . . 40.00
2 . . . . 30.00
3 Jan., 1954 . . . . 30.00

LITTLE MERMAID, THE
1993

1 . . . . 2.00
2 Reception for Pacifica royalty . . . 2.00
3 TrR,Ariel joins fish club. 2.00
4 . . . . 2.00
5 . . . . 2.00
6 TrR,Ariel decorates coral"tree" . . 2.00
7 TrR,Flogglefish banished 2.00
8 . . . . 2.00

9 Annual Sea Horse Tournament . . 2.00
10 TrR,AnnualBlowfishTournament . 2.00
11 TrR,Sharkeena,King Triton 2.00
12 . . . . 2.00
13 Lobster Monster. 2.00

LOGAN

1-shot HMe,48pg 6.00
1-shot Logan: Path of the Warrior (1996) 5.00
1-shot Logan: Shadow Society, HMe,TCk Early life of Wolverine (1996) 5.00

Logan's Run #4
© Marvel Entertainment Group

LOGAN'S RUN
Jan., 1977

1 GP,From Movie. 6.00
2 GP,Cathedral Kill 5.00
3 GP,Lair of Laser Death 5.00
4 GP,Dread Sanctuary. 5.00
5 GP,End Run 5.00
6 MZ,B.U.Thanos/Drax 10.00
7 TS,Cathedral Prime 5.00

LONGSHOT
Sept., 1985

1 AAd,WPo(i),BA,I:Longshot 8.00
2 AAd,WPo(i),I:RicoshetRita 6.00
3 AAd,WPo(i),I:Mojo,Spiral 6.00
4 AAd,WPo(i),A:Spider-Man 6.00
5 AAd,WPo(i),A:Dr. Strange. 6.00
6 AAd,WPo(i),A:Dr. Strange. 6.00
TPB Reprints #1-#6 . . . . 16.95
1-shot, JMD,MZi,AW, 48pg (Dec. 1997) 4.00

LOOSE CANNONS

1 and 2 DAn . . . . @2.50
3 DAn 2.75

LORNA, THE JUNGLE GIRL
Atlas 1953–57

1 Terrors of the Jungle,O:Lorna . 275.00
2 Headhunter's Strike I:Greg Knight 150.00
3 . . . . 125.00
4 . . . . 125.00
5 . . . . 125.00
6 RH(c),GT 90.00
7 RH(c) 90.00
8 Jungle Queen Strikes Again . . . 90.00
9 . . . . 90.00
10 White Fang 90.00
11 Death From the Skies 90.00
12 Day of Doom 75.00
13 thru 17 . . . . @75.00
18 AW(c) 85.00
19 thru 26 . . . . @60.00

LOVE ADVENTURES
Atlas Oct., 1949

1 Ph(c) 100.00
2 Ph(c),Tyrone Power/Gene Tierney 100.00
3 thru 12 . . . . @50.00
Becomes:

ACTUAL CONFESSIONS

13 . . . . 16.00
14 Dec., 1952. . . . . 16.00

LOVE DRAMAS
Oct., 1949

1 Ph(c),JKa 125.00
2 Jan., 1950 . . . . 90.00

LOVE ROMANCES
See: IDEAL

LOVERS
See: ALL-SELECT COMICS

LOVE SECRETS
Oct., 1949

1 . . . . 100.00
2 Jan., 1950 . . . . 60.00

LUNATIK
1995

1 KG 2.00
2 V:The Avengers 2.00
3 conclusion 2.00

MACHINE MAN
April, 1978

1 JK,From 2001. . . . . 3.00
2 JK 2.50
3 JK,V:Ten-For,The Mean Machine 2.50
4 JK,V;Ten-For,Battle on A Busy Street 2.50
5 JK,V;Ten-For,Day of the Non-Hero 2.50
6 JK,V;Ten-For 2.50
7 JK,With A Nation Against Him. . . 2.50
8 JK,Escape:Impossible. 2.50
9 JK,In Final Battle 2.50
10 SD,Birth of A Super-Hero. 2.50
11 SD,V;Binary Bug 2.50
12 SD,"Where walk the Gods" 2.50
13 SD,Xanadu 2.50
14 SD,V:Machine Man 2.50
15 SD,A:Thing,Human Torch 2.50
16 SD,I:Baron Brimstone And the Satan Squad 2.50
17 SD,Madam Menace. 2.50
18 A:Alpha Flight 3.50
19 I:Jack o'Lantern 15.00

Machine Man, Limited Series, #4
© Marvel Entertainment Group

MACHINE MAN
[Limited-Series]
Oct., 1984

1 HT,BWS,V:Baintronics 3.00
2 HT,BWS,C:Iron Man of 2020. . . . 3.00
3 HT,BWS,I:Iron Man of 2020 . . . . 3.50
4 HT,BWS,V:Iron Man of 2020. . . . 3.00
TPB rep.#1-4 . . . . 5.95

MACHINE MAN 2020
1994

1 rep. limited series #1–#2. . . . . . . 2.00
2 rep. limited series #3–#4. . . . . . . 2.00

MAD ABOUT MILLIE
April, 1969

1 . . . . 35.00
2 thru 16 . . . . @15.00
17 Dec., 1970. . . . . 15.00
Ann.#1 . . . . 12.00

MADBALLS
Star Sept., 1986

1 Based on Toys 3.00
2 thru 9 . . . . @3.00
10 June, 1988 . . . . 3.00

MAD DOG

1 from Bob TV Show 2.00
2 V:Trans World Trust Corp. 2.00
3 V:Cigarette Criminals 2.00
4 V:Dogs of War 2.00
5 thru 6 . . . . @2.00

MADE MEN
May, 1998

1-shot HMe gangster epic. 6.00

MAGIK
Dec., 1983

1 JB,TP,F:Storm and Illyana 4.00
2 JB,TP,A:Belasco,Sym 3.00
3 TP,A:New Mutants,Belasco. 3.00
4 TP,V:Belasco,A:Sym 3.00

MARVEL

MAGNETO
1993
0 JD,JBo,rep. origin stories. 6.00
0a Gold ed. 8.00
0b Platinum ed. 10.00

MAGNETO
1996
1 (of 4) PrM,KJo,JhB, Joseph 2.00
2 PrM,KJo,JhB, Joseph's search for his past life 2.00
3 PrM,KJo,JhB 2.00
4 PrM,KJo,JhB, concl. 2.00

MAGNETO: DARK SEDUCTION
April, 2000
1 (of 4) FaN,X-Men: Revolution . . . 3.00
2 FaN,Scarlet Witch. 3.00
3 FaN,RCz,V:Scarlet Witch 3.00
4 FaN,RCz,concl 3.00

MAGNETO REX
March, 1999
1 (of 3) BPe,takes over Genosha. . 2.50
1a signed 19.95
2 BPe,V:Rogue 2.50
3 BPe,A:Rogue,Quicksilver 2.50
GN Magneto Ascendant, 96-page rep.. . . . . 4.00

MAN COMICS
Atlas 1949–53
1 GT, Revenge 150.00
2 GT, Fury in his Fists 85.00
3 Mantrap 75.00
4 The Fallen Hero 75.00
5 Laugh,Fool,Laugh 75.00
6 Black Hate 60.00
7 The Killer 60.00
8 BEv,An Eye For an Eye 75.00
9 B:War Issues,Here Comes Sergeant Smith 40.00
10 Korean Communism 40.00
11 RH,Cannon Fodder 40.00
12 The Black Hate 40.00
13 GC,RH,Beach Head. 40.00
14 GT,No Prisoners 50.00
15 . . . . 40.00
16 . . . . 35.00
17 RH. 35.00
18 thru 20 . . . . @35.00
21 GC 35.00
22 BEv,BK,JSt 60.00
23 thru 26 . . . . @35.00
27 E:War Issues 35.00
28 Where Mummies Prowl 35.00

MANDRAKE
1995
1 fully painted series 2.95
2 V:Octon 2.95
3 final issue. 2.95

MAN FROM ATLANTIS
Feb., 1978–Aug., 1978
1 TS,From TV Series,O:Mark Harris 5.00
2 FR,FS,The Bermuda Triangle Trap 3.00
3 FR,FS,Undersea Shadow 3.00
4 FR,FS,Beware the Killer Spores 3.00
5 FR,FS,The Ray of the Red Death 3.00
6 FR,FS,Bait for the Behemoth . . . 3.00
7 FR,FS,Behold the Lan Forgotten 3.00

Man-Thing #19
© Marvel Entertainment Group

MAN-THING
[1st Series] Jan., 1974
1 FB,JM,A:Howard the Duck 20.00
2 VM,ST,Hell Hath No Fury 11.00
3 VM,JA,I:Original Foolkiller. 9.00
4 VM,JA,O&D:Foolkiller. 7.00
5 MP,Night o/t Laughing Dead 6.00
6 MP,V:Soul-Slayers,Drug Issue . . 6.00
7 MP,A Monster Stalks Swamp . . . 6.00
8 MP,Man Into Monster 6.00
9 MP,Deathwatch 6.00
10 MP,Nobody Dies Forever 6.00
11 MP,Dance to the Murder 4.00
12 KJ,Death-Cry of a Dead Man. . . 4.00
13 TS,V:Captain Fate 4.00
14 AA,V:Captain Fate 4.00
15 A Candle for Saint Cloud 4.00
16 JB,TP,Death of a Legend 4.00
17 JM,Book Burns in Citrusville . . . 4.00
18 JM,Chaos on the Campus 4.00
19 JM,FS,I:Scavenger 4.00
20 JM,A:Spider-Man,Daredevil, Shang-Chi,Thing 4.50
21 JM,O:Scavenger,Man Thing. . . . 4.00
22 JM,C:Howard the Duck 4.00
G-Size #1 MP,SD,JK,rep.TheGlob . 5.00
G-Size #2 JB,KJ,The Monster Runs Wild. 4.00
G-Size #3 AA,A World He Never Made 4.00
G-Size #4 FS,EH,inc.Howard the Duck vs.Gorko 4.00
G-Size #5 DA,EH,inc.Howard the Duck vs.Vampire 6.00

[2nd Series] 1979—1981
1 JM,BWi 2.00
2 BWi,JM,Himalayan Nightmare . . 2.00
3 BWi.JM,V:Snowman 2.00
4 BWi,DP,V:Mordo,A:Dr Strange . . 2.00
5 DP,BWi,This Girl is Terrified 2.00
6 DP,BWi,Fraternity Rites 2.00
7 BWi,DP Return of Captain Fate . 2.00
8 BWi,DP,V:Captain Fate. 2.00
9 BWi(c),Save the Life of My Own Child 2.00
10 BWi,DP,Swampfire. 2.00
11 Final issue 2.00

[3rd Series] Oct., 1997
1 JMD,LSh, non-code 3.00
2 JMD,LSh, reunion with ex-wife, A:Dr. Strange 3.00
3 JMD,LSh, visit to Devil Slayer. . . 3.00
4 JMD,LSh, V:Devil-Slayer. 3.00
5 JMD,LSh, new abilities revealed . 3.00
6 JMD,LSh, V:Cult of Entropy 3.00
7 JMD,LSh, Muck Monster, Namor 3.00
8 JMD,LSh, Muck Monster turned back into Ted Sallis. 3.00

Storyline continues in Strange Tales

MARINES AT WAR
See: DEVIL-DOG DUGAN

MARINES IN ACTION
Atlas June, 1955
1 B:Rock Murdock,Boot Camp Brady 75.00
2 thru 13 . . . . @50.00
14 Sept., 1957 . . . . 50.00

MARINES IN BATTLE
Atlas Aug., 1954
1 RH,B:Iron Mike McGraw 150.00
2 . . . . 75.00
3 thru 6 . . . . @50.00
7 . . . . 55.00
8 . . . . 50.00
9 . . . . 50.00
10 . . . . 50.00
11 thru 16 . . . . @45.00
17 . . . . 70.00
18 thru 22 . . . . @45.00
23 . . . . 70.00
24 . . . . 50.00
25 Sept., 1958 . . . . 60.00

MARK HAZZARD: MERC
Nov., 1986–Oct. 1987
1 GM,O:Mark Hazzard. 2.00
2 GM. 2.00
3 M,Arab Terrorists 2.00
4 GM 2.00
5 GM 2.00
6 GM 2.00
7 GM 2.00
8 GM 2.00
9 NKu/AKu 2.00
10 thru 12. . . . . @2.00
Ann.#1 D:Merc 2.00

MARSHALL LAW
Epic 1987–89
1 . . . . 4.50
2 . . . . 3.00
3 thru 6 . . . . @2.50

MARVEL ACTION HOUR: FANTASTIC FOUR
1994–95
1 regular 2.00
1a bagged with insert print from animated series 3.00
2 V:Puppet Master. 2.00
3 . . . . 2.00
4 V:Sub-Mariner 2.00
5 . . . . 2.00
6 R:Skrulls. 2.00
7 V:Doctor Doom. 2.00
8 Wanted by the Law. 2.00

 All comics prices listed are for *Near Mint* condition.

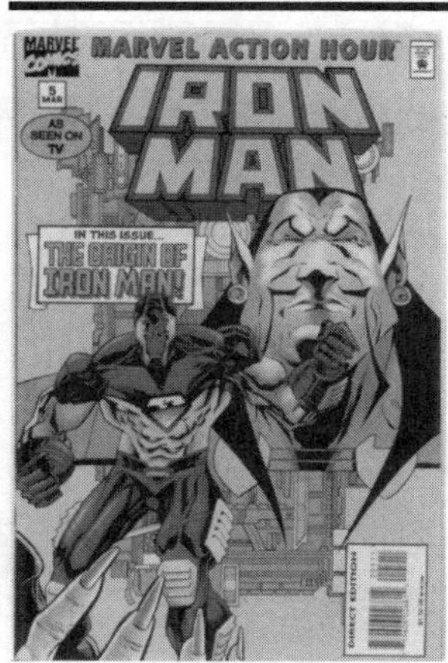

Marvel Action Hour: Iron Man #5
© Marvel Entertainment Group

MARVEL ACTION HOUR: IRON MAN

1994–95

1 regular 2.00
1a bagged with insert print from animated series 3.25
2 V:War Machine. 2.00
3 V:Ultimo 2.00
4 A:Force Works, Hawkeye, War Machine 2.00
5 O:Iron Man. 2.00
6 V:Fing Fang Foom 2.00
7 V:Mandarin. 2.00
8 V:Robots 2.00

MARVEL ACTION UNIVERSE

TV Tie-in, Jan., 1989

1 Rep.Spider-Man & Friends 2.50

MARVEL ADVENTURES STARRING DAREDEVIL

Dec., 1975–Oct., 1976

1 Rep,Daredevil #22 . . . . 5.00
2 thru 5, Rep,Daredevil #23-26 . @3.00
6 DD #27. 3.00

MARVEL ADVENTURES

Feb., 1997

1 RMc,F:The Hulk 2.00
2 RMc,F:Spider-Man 2.00
3 RMc,F:Quicksilver & Scarlet Witch 2.00
4 RMc,BHr,F:Hulk,V:Brotherhood of Evil Mutants 2.00
5 RMc,BHr,F:Spider-Man, The X-Men 2.00
6 RMc,BHr,A:Spider-Man,Invisible Woman, Human Torch 2.00
7 RMc,F:Hulk,V:Tyrannus 2.00
8 RMc,V:Molto. 2.00
9 RMc,F:Fantastic Four, Subterranean War, concl. 2.00
10 RMc,Sky-Rider vs. Gladiator . . . 2.00
11 RMc,F:Spider-Man,Sandman . . . 2.00
12 RMc,F:Fantastic Four,V:Frightful Four. 2.00
13 AM,F:Spider-Man, Silver Surfer . 2.00
14 RMc,F:The Hulk,A:Dr. Strange, Juggernaut. 2.00
15 RMc,F:X-Men,V:Beast's army . . 2.00
16 RMc,F:Silver Surfer 2.00
17 RMc,F:Spider-Man, Iron Man . . . 2.00
18 RMc,F:Sentinel of Liberty. 2.00
19 RMc,F:The Avengers 2.00
20 RMc,F:Iron Man. 2.00

MARVEL & DC PRESENTS

Nov., 1982

1 WS,TA,X-Men & Titans,A:Darkseid, Deathstroke(3rd App.), ... 18.00

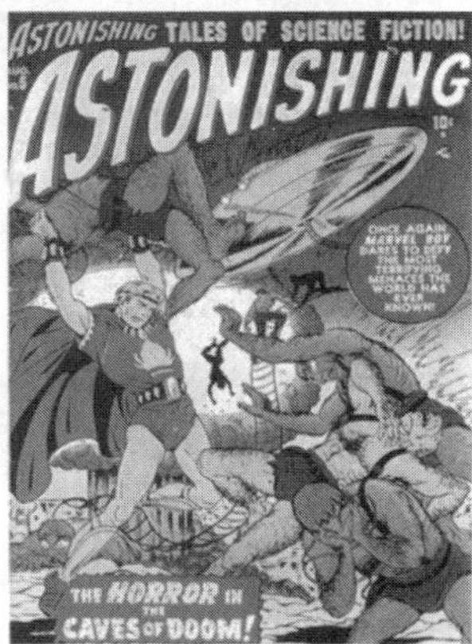

Astonishing #5
© Marvel Entertainment Group

MARVEL BOY

Dec., 1950

1 RH,O:Marvel Boy,Lost World . 750.00
2 BEv,The Zero Hour 600.00

Becomes:

ASTONISHING

3 BEv,Marvel Boy,V:Mr Death . . 700.00
4 BEv,Stan Lee,The Screaming Tomb 500.00
5 BEv,Horro in the Caves of Doom 500.00
6 BEv,My Coffin is Waiting E:Marvel Boy 500.00
7 JR,Nightmare 200.00
8 RH,Behind the Wall 200.00
9 RH(c),The Little Black Box . . . 200.00
10 BEv,Walking Dead 200.00
11 BF,JSt.Mr Mordeau 175.00
12 GC,BEv,Horror Show 175.00
13 BK,MSy,Ghouls Gold 200.00
14 BK,The Long Jump Down . . . 200.00
15 BEv(c),Grounds for Death . . . 175.00
16 BEv(c),DAy,SSh,Don't Make a Ghoul of Yourself. 200.00
17 Who Was the Wilmach Werewolf? 175.00
18 BEv(c),JR,Vampire at my Window 200.00
19 BK,Back From the Grave 200.00
20 GC,Mystery at Midnight 175.00
21 Manhunter 150.00
22 RH(c),Man Against Werewolf . 150.00
23 The Woman in Black 175.00
24 JR,The Stone Face 150.00
25 RC,I Married a Zombie. 175.00
26 RH(c),I Died Too Often. 150.00
27 . . . . 150.00
28 No Evidence 150.00
29 BEv(c),GC,Decapitation(c) . . . 150.00
30 Tentacled eyeball story 200.00
31 . . . . 125.00
32 A Vampire Takes a Wife. 125.00
33 SMo. 125.00
34 Transformation. 125.00
35 . . . . 125.00
36 Pithecanthrope Giant 125.00
37 BEv,Poor Pierre 125.00
38 The Man Who Didn't Belong . 100.00
39 . . . . 100.00
40 . . . . 100.00
41 . . . . 100.00
42 . . . . 100.00
43 . . . . 100.00
44 RC. 110.00
45 BK 110.00
46 . . . . 100.00
47 BK. 110.00
48 . . . . 100.00
49 . . . . 100.00
50 . . . . 100.00
51 . . . . 100.00
52 . . . . 100.00
53 . . . . 110.00
54 . . . . 110.00
55 . . . . 125.00
56 . . . . 100.00
57 . . . . 150.00
58 . . . . 100.00
59 . . . . 100.00
60 . . . . 100.00
61 . . . . 100.00
62 . . . . 100.00
63 August, 1957 . . . . 100.00

MARVEL BOY

June, 2000

1 (of 6) GMo,F:Noh-Varr 3.00
2 GMo,V:Human Race. 3.00
3 GMo,Hexus 3.00
4 GMo,Exterminatrix 3.00
5 GMo,Oubliette 3.00

MARVEL CHILLERS

Oct., 1975

1 GK(c),I:Mordred the Mystic . . . 10.00
2 E:Mordred 6.00
3 HC/BWr(c),B:Tigra,The Were Woman 6.00
4 V:Kraven The Hunter 6.00
5 V:Rat Pack,A:Red Wolf 6.00
6 RB(c),JBy,V:Red Wolf 6.00
7 JK(c),GT,V:Super Skrull E:Tigra,Oct., 1976 . . . . 6.00
GN MGu(s),LSh,F:The Hulk 5.00
GN LHa(s) F:Wolverine 5.00

MARVEL CHRISTMAS SPECIAL

1 DC/AAd/KJ/SB/RLm,A:Ghost Rider X-Men,Spider-Man 2.25

MARVEL CLASSICS COMICS

1976–78

1 GK/DA(c),B:Reprints from Pendulum Illustrated Comics Dr.Jekyll & Mr. Hyde 15.00
2 GK(c),AN,Time Machine 10.00
3 GK/KJ(c) The Hunchback of Notre Dame 10.00
4 GK/DA(c),20,000 Leagues– Beneath the Sea by Verne. . . 10.00
5 GK(c),RN,Black Beauty 10.00
6 GK(c),Gulliver's Travels 10.00

MARVEL

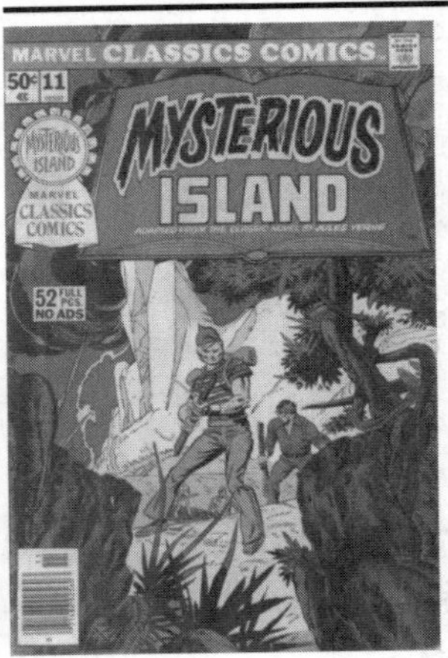

Marvel Classics Comics #11
© Marvel Entertainment Group

7 GK(c),Tom Sawyer 10.00
8 GK(c),AN,Moby Dick 10.00
9 GK(c),NR,Dracula. 10.00
10 GK(c),Red Badge of Courage . 10.00
11 GK(c),Mysterious Island 10.00
12 GK/DA(c),AN,3 Musketeers . . . 10.00
13 GK(c),Last of the Mohicans . . . 10.00
14 GK(c),War of the Worlds 10.00
15 GK(c),Treasure Island 10.00
16 GK(c),Ivanhoe 9.00
17 JB/ECh(c),The Count of Monte Cristo 9.00
18 ECh(c),The Odsyssey 9.00
19 JB(c),Robinson Crusoe 9.00
20 Frankenstein 9.00
21 GK(c),Master of the World 9.00
22 GK(c),Food of the Gods. 9.00
23 Moonstone by Wilkie Collins . . . 9.00
24 GK/RN(c),She 9.00
25 The Invisible Man by H.G.Wells . 9.00
26 JB(c),The Illiad by Homer 9.00
27 Kidnapped 9.00
28 MGo(1st art) The Pit and the Pendulum. 12.00
29 The Prisoner of Zenda 9.00
30 The Arabian Nights 9.00
31 The First Men in the Moon. 9.00
32 GK(c),White Fang 9.00
33 The Prince and the Pauper 9.00
34 AA,Robin Hood 9.00
35 FBe,Alice in Wonderland 9.00
36 A Christmas Carol 9.00

MARVEL COLLECTORS ITEM CLASSICS

Feb., 1965

1 SD,JK,reprint FF #2 . . . . 80.00
2 SD,JK,reprint FF #3 . . . . 40.00
3 SD,JK,reprint FF #4 . . . . 40.00
4 SD,JK,reprint FF #7 . . . . 40.00
5 SD,JK,reprint FF #8 . . . . 35.00
6 SD,JK,reprint FF #9 . . . . 35.00
7 SD,JK,reprint FF #13 . . . . 35.00
8 SD,JK,reprint FF #10 . . . . 35.00
9 SD,JK,reprint FF #14 . . . . 35.00
10 SD,JK,reprint FF #15 . . . . 35.00
11 SD,JK,reprint FF #16 . . . . 25.00
12 SD,JK,reprint FF #17. . . . . 25.00
13 SD,JK,reprint FF #18. . . . . 25.00
14 SD,JK,reprint FF #20. . . . . 25.00
15 SD,JK,reprint FF #21. . . . . 25.00
16 SD,JK,reprint FF #22. . . . . 25.00
17 SD,JK,reprint FF #23. . . . . 25.00
18 SD,JK,reprint FF #24. . . . . 25.00
19 SD,JK,reprint FF #27. . . . . 25.00
20 SD,JK,reprint FF #28. . . . . 25.00
21 SD,JK,reprint FF #29 . . . . 25.00
22 SD,JK,reprint FF #30. . . . . 25.00
Becomes:

MARVEL'S GREATEST COMICS

23 SD,JK,reprint FF#31 . . . . 15.00
24 SD,JK,reprint FF#32 . . . . 15.00
25 SD,JK,reprint FF#33 . . . . 15.00
26 SD,JK,reprint FF#34 . . . . 15.00
27 SD,JK,reprint FF#35 . . . . 15.00
28 SD,JK,reprint FF#36 . . . . 15.00
29 JK,reprint FF#37 . . . . 15.00
30 JK,reprint FF#38 . . . . 15.00
31 JK,reprint FF#40 . . . . 15.00
32 JK,reprint FF#42 . . . . 15.00
33 JK,reprint FF#44 . . . . 15.00
34 JK,reprint FF#47 . . . . 15.00
35 JK,reprint FF#48 . . . . 8.50
36 JK,reprint FF#49 . . . . 8.50
37 JK,reprint FF#50 . . . . 8.50
38 JK,reprint FF#51 . . . . 6.00
39 JK,reprint FF#52 . . . . 6.00
40 JK,reprint FF#53 . . . . 6.00
41 JK,reprint FF#54 . . . . 6.00
42 JK,reprint FF#55 . . . . 6.00
43 JK,reprint FF#56 . . . . 6.00
44 JK,reprint FF#61 . . . . 6.00
45 JK,reprint FF#62 . . . . 6.00
46 JK,reprint FF#63 . . . . 6.00
47 JK,reprint FF#64 . . . . 6.00
48 JK,reprint FF#65 . . . . 6.00
49 JK,reprint FF#66 . . . . 6.00
50 JK,reprint FF#67 . . . . 6.00
51 thru 75 JK,reprint FF . . . . . . @3.50
76 thru 82 JK,reprint FF . . . . . . @3.00
83 thru 95 Reprint FF . . . . @3.00
96 Reprint FF#, Jan., 1981 . . . . . . 3.00

MARVEL COMICS

Oct.–Nov., 1939

1 FP(c),BEv,CBu,O:Sub-Mariner I&B:The Angel,A:Human Torch, Kazar,Jungle Terror, B:The Masked Raider . . 130,000.00
Becomes:

MARVEL MYSTERY COMICS

2 CSM(c),BEv,CBu,PGn, B:American, Ace,Human Torch,Sub-Mariner,Kazar . 21,000.00
3 ASh(c),BEv,CBu,PGn, E:American Ace 9,000.00
4 ASh(c),BEv,CBu,PGn, I&B:Electro,The Ferret, Mystery Detective 7,500.00
5 ASh(c),BEv,CBu,PGn, Human Torch(c) 16,000.00
6 ASh(c),BEv,CBu,PGn, Anglel(c) 5,000.00
7 ASh(c),BEv,CBu,PGn, Bondage(c) 5,000.00
8 ASh(c),BEv,CBu,PGn,Human TorchV:Sub-Mariner 7,700.00
9 ASh(c),BEv,CBu,PGn,Human Torch V:Sub-Mariner(c) . . 20,000.00
10 ASh(c),BEv,CBu,PGn,B:Terry Vance Boy Detective 5,500.00
11 ASh(c),BEv,CBu,PGn, Human Torch V:Nazis(c) . . 2,800.00
12 ASh(c),BEv,CBu, PGn,Angel(c). 3,400.00
13 ASh(c),BEv,CBu,PGn,S&K, I&B:The Vision. 4,000.00
14 ASh(c),BEv,CBu,PGn,S&K, Sub-Mariner V:Nazis 2,000.00

Marvel Collectors' Item Classics #20
© Marvel Entertainment Group

15 ASh(c),BEv,CBu,PGn,S&K, Sub-Mariner(c). 2,000.00
16 ASh(c),BEv,CBu,PGn,S&K, HumanTorch/NaziAirbase. . 2,000.00
17 ASh(c),BEv,CBu,PGn,S&K Human Torch/Sub-Mariner 2,200.00
18 ASh(c),BEv,CBu,PGn,S&K, Human Torch & Toro(c) . . . 1,700.00
19 ASh(c),BEv,CBu,PGn,S&K, O:Toro,E:Electro 1,800.00
20 ASh(c),BEv,CBu,PGn,S&K, O:The Angel 1,800.00
21 ASh(c),BEv,CBu,PGn,S&K, I&B:The Patriot 1,700.00
22 ASh(c),BEv,CBu,PGn,S&K, Toro/Bomb(c). 1,500.00
23 ASh(c),BEv,CBu,PGn,S&K, O:Vision,E:The Angel. 1,500.00
24 ASh(c),BEv,CBu,S&K, Human Torch(c). 1,500.00
25 BEv,CBu,S&K,ASh Nazi(c) . 1,500.00
26 ASh(c),BEv,CBu,S&K, Sub-Mariner(c). 1,400.00
27 ASh(c),BEv,CBu, S&K,E:Kazar 1,400.00
28 ASh(c),BEv,CBu,S&K,Bondage (c),B:Jimmy Jupiter. 1,400.00
29 ASh(c),BEv,CBu,Bondage(c) 1,400.00
30 BEv,CBu,Pearl Harbor(c) . . 1,400.00
31 BEv,CBu,HUman Torch(c). . 1,200.00
32 CBu,I:The Boboes. 1,200.00
33 ASHc(c),CBu,Japanese(c). . 1,200.00
34 ASh(c),CBu,V:Hitler. 1,400.00
35 ASh(c),Beach Assault(c) . . . 1,200.00
36 ASh(c),Nazi Invasion of New York(c). 1,200.00
37 SSh(c),Nazi(c) 1,200.00
38 SSh(c),Battlefield(c) 1,200.00
39 ASh(c),Nazis/U.S(c) 1,200.00
40 ASh(c),Zeppelin(c) 1,200.00
41 ASh(c),Japn. Command(c) . 1,100.00
42 ASh(c),Japanese Sub(c) . . . 1,100.00
43 ASh(c),Destroyed Bridge(c). 1,100.00
44 ASh(c),Nazi Super Plane(c) 1,100.00
45 ASh(c),Nazi(c) 1,100.00
46 ASh(c),Hitler Bondage(c). . . 1,100.00
47 ASh(c),Ruhr Valley Dam(c) . 1,100.00
48 ASh(c),E:Jimmy Jupiter, Vision,Allied Invasion(c). . . 1,100.00
49 SSh(c),O:Miss America, Bondage(c). 1,400.00
50 ASh(c),Bondage(c),Miss

Patriot . . . 1,200.00
51 ASh(c),Nazi Torture(c). . . . 1,000.00
52 ASh(c),Bondage(c) . . . 1,000.00
53 ASh(c),Bondage(c) . . . 1,000.00
54 ASh(c),Bondage(c) . . . 1,000.00
55 ASh(c),Bondage(c) . . . 1,000.00
56 ASh(c),Bondage(c) . . . 1,000.00
57 ASh(c),Torture/Bondage(c) . 1,000.00
58 ASH(c),Torture(c) . . . 1,000.00
59 ASh(c),Testing Room(c) . . . 1,000.00
60 ASh(c),Japanese Gun(c) . . 1,000.00
61 Torturer Chamber(c) . . . 1,000.00
62 ASh(c),Violent(c). . . . 1,000.00
63 ASh(c),NaziHigh
Command(c) . . . 1,000.00
64 ASh(c),Last Nazi(c). . . . 1,000.00
65 ASh(c),Bondage(c) . . . 1,000.00
66 ASh(c),Last Japanese(c). . . 1,000.00
67 ASh(c),Treasury raid(c) . . . 800.00
68 ASh(c),Torture Chamber(c) . . 800.00
69 ASh(c),Torture Chamber(c) . . 800.00
70 Cops & Robbers(c) . . . 800.00
71 ASh(c),Egyptian(c). . . . 800.00
72 Police(c) . . . 800.00
73 Werewolf Headlines(c). . . . 800.00
74 ASh(c),Robbery(c),E:The
Patriot . . . 800.00
75 Tavern(c),B:Young Allies . . . 800.00
76 ASh(c),Shoot-out(c),B:Miss
America . . . 800.00
77 Human Torch/Sub-Mariner(c) . 800.00
78 Safe Robbery(c). . . . 800.00
79 Super Villians(c),E:The
Angel . . . 800.00
80 I:Capt.America(in Marvel) . . 1,000.00
81 Mystery o/t Crimson Terror. . . 850.00
82 I:Sub-Mariner/Namora Team-up
O:Namora,A:Capt.America. 2,000.00
83 The Photo Phantom,E;Young
Allies . . . 750.00
84 BEv,B:The Blonde Phantom 1,000.00
85 BEv,A:Blonde Phantom,
E;Miss America . . . 750.00
86 BEv,Blonde Phantom ID
Revealed,E:Bucky . . . 850.00
87 BEv,I:Capt.America/Golden
Girl Team-up. . . . 900.00
88 BEv,E:Toro. . . . 800.00
89 BEv,I:Human Torch/Sun Girl
Team-up. . . . 850.00
90 BEv,Giant of the Mountains . . 850.00
91 BEv,I:Venus,E:Blonde
Phantom,Sub-Mariner. . . . 850.00
92 BEv,How the Human Torch was
Born,D:Professor Horton,I:The
Witness,A:Capt.America . . 2,000.00
92a Marvel #33(c)rare,reprints 10,000.00
Becomes:

MARVEL TALES

August, 1949

93 The Ghoul Strikes. . . . 1,100.00
94 BEv,The Haunted Love . . . 750.00
95 The Living Death . . . 500.00
96 MSy,The Monster Returns . . . 500.00
97 DRi,MSy,The Wooden Horror. 600.00
98 BEv,BK,MSy,The Curse of
the Black Cat . . . 500.00
99 DRi,The Secret of the Wax
Museum. . . . 500.00
100 The Eyes of Doom. . . . 500.00
101 The Man Who Died Twice . . 500.00
102 BW,A Witch Among Us . . . 650.00
103 RA,A Touch of Death . . . 550.00
104 RH(c),BW,BEv,The Thing
in the Mirror . . . 700.00
105 RH(c),GC,JSt,The Spider. . . 500.00
106 RH(c),BK,BEv,In The Dead of
the Night . . . 400.00
107 GC,OW,BK,The Thing in the
Sewer. . . . 400.00
108 RH(c),BEv,JR,Horror in the
Moonlight . . . 300.00
109 BEv(c),Sight for Sore Eyes. . 300.00
110 RH,SSh,A Coffin for Carlos . 300.00
111 BEv,Horror Under the Earth . 300.00
112 The House That Death Built. 300.00
113 RH,Terror Tale . . . 300.00
114 BEv(c),GT,JM,2 for Zombie . 300.00
115 The Man With No Face . . . 300.00
116 JSt. . . . 300.00
117 BEv(c),GK,Terror in the
North. . . . 300.00
118 RH,DBr,GC,A World
Goes Mad . . . 300.00
119 RH,They Gave Him A Grave 300.00
120 GC,Graveyard(c) . . . 300.00
121 GC,Graveyard(c) . . . 250.00
122 JKu,Missing One Body. . . . 250.00
123 No Way Out. . . . 250.00
124 He Waits at the Tombstone . 250.00
125 JF,Horror House. . . . 250.00
126 DW,It Came From Nowhere . 200.00
127 BEv(c),GC,MD,Gone is the
Gargoyle . . . 200.00
128 Emily,Flying Saucer(c) . . . 200.00
129 You Can't Touch Bottom . . . 200.00
130 RH(c),JF,The Giant Killer . . . 200.00
131 GC,BEv,Five Fingers . . . 200.00
132 . . . 150.00
133 . . . 150.00
134 BK,JKu,Flying Saucer(c) . . . 150.00
135 thru 141 . . . @125.00
142 . . . 125.00
143 . . . 125.00
144 . . . 135.00
145 . . . 125.00
146 . . . 100.00
147 . . . 125.00
148 . . . 100.00
149 . . . 100.00
150 . . . 100.00
151 . . . 100.00
152 . . . 125.00
153 . . . 135.00
154 . . . 100.00
155 . . . 100.00
156 . . . 100.00
157 . . . 125.00
158 . . . 100.00
159 August, 1957 . . . 125.00

MARVEL COMICS PRESENTS

Sept., 1988

1 WS(c),B:Wolverine(JB,KJ),Master
of Kung Fu(TS),Man-Thing(TGr,DC)
F:Silver Surfer(AM). . . . 10.00
2 F:The Captain(AM). . . . 5.00
3 JR2(c),F:The Thing(AM) . . . 4.00
4 F:Thor(AM). . . . 4.00
5 F:Daredevil(DT,MG) . . . 4.00
6 F:Hulk . . . 4.00
7 F:Sub-Mariner(SD) . . . 4.00
8 CV(c),E:Master of Kung Fu,F:
Iron Man(JS) . . . 4.00
9 F:Cloak,El Aquila . . . 4.00
10 E:Wolverine,B:Colossus(RL,CR),
F:Machine Man(SD,DC) . . . 4.00
11 F:Ant-Man(BL),Slag(RWi). . . . 3.00
12 E:Man-Thing,F:Hercules(DH),
Namorita(FS) . . . 3.00
13 B:Black Panther(GC,TP),F:
Shanna,Mr.Fantastic &
Invisible Woman. . . . 3.00
14 F:Nomad(CP),Speedball(SD). . . 3.00
15 F:Marvel Girl(DT,MG),Red
Wolf(JS). . . . 3.00
16 F:Kazar(JM),Longshot(AA). . . . 3.00
17 E:Colossus,B:Cyclops(RLm),
F:Watcher(TS) . . . 4.00

Marvel Comics Presents #149
© Marvel Entertainment Group

18 F:She-Hulk(JBy,BWi),Willie
Lumpkin(JSt) . . . 3.00
19 RLd(c)B:Dr.Strange(MBg),
I:Damage Control(EC,AW) . . . 3.00
20 E:Dr.Strange,F:Clea(RLm) . . . 3.00
21 F:Thing,Paladin(RWi,DA). . . . 3.00
22 F:Starfox(DC),Wolfsbane &
Mirage . . . 3.00
23 F:Falcon(DC),Wheels(RWi) . . . 3.00
24 E:Cyclops,B:Havok(RB,JRu),
F:Shamrock(DJ,DA) . . . 3.00
25 F:Ursa Major,I:Nth Man . . . 4.00
26 B&I:Coldblood(PG),F:Hulk . . . 2.50
27 F:American Eagle(RWi) . . . 2.50
28 F:Triton(JS) . . . 2.50
29 F:Quasar(PR) . . . 2.50
30 F:Leir(TMo) . . . 2.50
31 EL,E:Havok,B:Excalibur
(EL,TA). . . . 4.00
32 TM(c),F:Sunfire(DH,DC) . . . 3.00
33 F:Namor(JLe) . . . 4.00
34 F:Captain America(JsP). . . . 3.00
35 E:Coldblood,F:Her(EL,AG). . . . 4.00
36 BSz(c),F:Hellcat(JBr) . . . 4.00
37 E:Bl.Panther,F:Devil-Slayer . . . 3.00
38 E:Excalibur,B:Wonderman(JS),
Wolverine(JB),F:Hulk(MR,DA) . 4.00
39 F:Hercules(BL),Spider-Man . . . 3.50
40 F:Hercules(BL),Overmind(DH) . . 3.50
41 F:Daughters of the Dragon(DA),
Union Jack(KD) . . . 3.50
42 F:Iron Man(MBa),Siryn(LSn) . . . 3.50
43 F:Iron Man(MBa),Siryn(LSn) . . . 3.50
44 F:Puma(BWi),Dr.Strange . . . 3.50
45 E:Wonderman,F:Hulk(HT),
Shooting Star . . . 3.50
46 RLd(c),B:Devil-Slayer,F:Namor,
Aquarian . . . 3.50
47 JBy(c),E:Wolverine,F:Captain
America,Arabian Knight(DP). . . 3.50
48 B:Wolverine&Spider-Man(EL),
F:Wasp,Storm&Dr.Doom . . . 5.00
49 E:Devil-Slayer,F:Daredevil(RWi),
Gladiator(DH). . . . 4.50
50 E:Wolverine&Spider-Man,B:Comet
Man(KJo),F:Captain Ultra(DJ),
Silver Surfer(JkS). . . . 4.50
51 B:Wolverine(RLd),F:Iron Man
(MBr,DH),Le Peregrine. . . . 4.00
52 F:Rick Jones,Hulk(RWi,TMo). . . 4.00
53 E:Wolverine,Comet Man,F:
Silver Sable&Black Widow
(RLd,BWi),B:Stingray . . . 4.00

54 B:Wolverine&Hulk(DR), Werewolf,F:Shroud(SD,BWi). . . 6.00
55 F:Collective Man(GLa). 6.00
56 E:Stingray,F:Speedball(SD) 6.00
57 DK(c),B:Sub-Mariner(MC,MFm), Black Cat(JRu). 6.00
58 F:Iron Man(SD) 6.00
59 E:Sub-Mariner,Werewolf, F:Punisher 6.00
60 B:Poison,Scarlet Witch, F:Captain America(TL) 6.00
61 E:Wolverine&Hulk, F:Dr.Strange. 6.00
62 F:Wolverine(PR),Deathlok(JG) . . 6.00
63 F:Wolverine(PR),E:Scarlet Witch,Thor(DH) 4.00
64 B:Wolverine&Ghost Rider(MT), Fantastic Four(TMo),F:Blade . . 4.00
65 F:Starfox(ECh). 3.50
66 F:Volstagg 3.50
67 E:Poison,F:Spider-Man(MG) . . . 3.50
68 B:Shanna(PG),E:Fantastic Four F:Lockjaw(JA,AM) 3.50
69 B:Daredevil(DT),F:Silver Surfer . 3.50
70 F:BlackWidow&Darkstar(AM) . . . 3.50
71 E:Wolverine&Ghost Rider,F: Warlock(New Mutants)(SMc) . . 3.50
72 B:Weapon X(BWS),E:Daredevil, F:Red Wolf(JS). 7.00
73 F:Black Knight(DC), Namor(JM). 5.00
74 F:Constrictor(SMc),Iceman & Human Torch(JSon,DA) 5.00
75 F:Meggan & Shadowcat, Dr.Doom(DC) 5.00
76 F:Death's Head(BHi,MFm), A:Woodgod(DC). 5.00
77 E:Shanna,B:Sgt.Fury&Dracula (TL,JRu),F:Namor 4.50
78 F:Iron Man(KSy),Hulk&Selene . . 4.50
79 E:Sgt.Fury&Dracula,F:Dr.Strange, Sunspot(JBy) 4.50
80 F:Daughters of the Dragon,Mister Fantastic(DJ),Captain America (SD,TA) 4.50
81 F:Captain America(SD,TA), Daredevil(MR,AW),Ant-Man . . . 4.00
82 B:Firestar(DT),F:Iron Man(SL), Power Man. 4.00
83 F:Hawkeye,Hum.Torch(SD,EL) . 4.00
84 E:Weapon X 4.00
85 B:Wolverine(SK),Beast(RLd,JaL-1st Work),F:Speedball(RWi), I:Cyber 7.00
86 F:PaladinE:RLd on Beast. 5.00
87 E:Firestar,F:Shroud(RWi) 5.00
88 F:Solo,Volcana(BWi) 5.00
89 F:Spitfire(JSn),Mojo(JMa) 5.00
90 B:Ghost Rider & Cable,F: Nightmare 4.50
91 F:Impossible Man 3.50
92 E:Wolverine,Beast, F:Northstar(JMa) 3.50
93 SK(c),B:Wolverine,Nova, F:Daredevil. 3.00
94 F:Gabriel 3.00
95 SK(c),E:Wolverine,F:Hulk. 3.00
96 B:Wolverine(TT),E:Nova, F:Speedball 3.00
97 F:Chameleon,Two-Gun Kid, E:Ghost Rider/Cable. 3.00
98 E:Wolverine,F:Ghost Rider, Werewolf by Night 2.50
99 F:Wolverine,Ghost Rider, Mary Jane,Captain America. . . 2.50
100 SK,F:Ghost Rider,Wolverine, Dr.Doom,Nightmare 3.00
101 SK(c),B:Ghost Rider&Doctor Strange,Young Gods,Wolverine &Nightcrawler,F:Bar With No Name 2.00
102 RL,GC,AW,F:Speedball 2.00
103 RL,GC,AW,F:Puck 2.00
104 RL,GC,AW,F:Lockheed 2.00
105 RL,GC,AW,F:Nightmare. 2.00
106 RL,GC,AW,F:Gabriel,E:Ghost Rider&Dr.Strange 2.00
107 GC,AW,TS,B:Ghost Rider& Werewolf 2.00
108 GC,AW,TS,SMc,E:Wolverine& Nightcrawler,B:Thanos 2.00
109 SLi,TS,SMc,B:Wolverine& Typhoid Mary,E:Young Gods. . . 2.00
110 SLi,SMc,F:Nightcrawler 2.00
111 SK(c),SLi,RWi,F:Dr.Strange, E:Thanos 2.00
112 SK(c),SLi,F:Pip,Wonder Man, E:Ghost Rider&Werewolf 2.00
113 SK(c),SLi,B:Giant Man, Ghost Rider&Iron Fist. 2.00
114 SK(c),SLi,F:Arabian Knight. . . . 2.00
115 SK(c),SLi,F:Cloak&Dagger. . . . 2.00
116 SK(c),SLi,E:Wolverine & Typhoid Mary 2.00
117 SK,PR,B:Wolverine&Venom, I:Ravage 2099 . . . . 4.00
118 SK,PB,RWi,E:Giant Man, I:Doom 2099 . . . . 3.00
119 SK,GC,B:Constrictor,E:Ghost Rider&Iron Fist,F:Wonder Man . 3.00
120 SK,GC,E:Constrictor,B:Ghost Rider/Cloak & Dagger, F:Spider-Man 2.50
121 SK,GC,F:Mirage,Andromeda . . 2.50
122 SK(c),GK,E:Wolverine&Venom, Ghost Rider&Cloak&Dagger,F: Speedball&Rage,Two-Gun Kid . 2.50
123 SK(c),DJ,SLi,B:Wolverine&Lynx, Ghost Rider&Typhoid Mary, She-Hulk,F:Master Man 2.00
124 SK(c),DJ,MBa,SLi,F:Solo 2.00
125 SLi,SMc,DJ,B:Iron Fist. 2.00
126 SLi,DJ,E:She-Hulk. 2.00
127 SLi,DJ,DP,F:Speedball. 2.00
128 SLi,DJ,RWi,F:American Eagle . 2.00
129 SLi,DJ,F:Ant Man. 2.00
130 DJ.SLi,RWi,E:Wolverine&Lynx, Ghost Rider&Typhoid Mary,Iron Fist,F:American Eagle 2.00
131 MFm,B:Wolverine,Ghost Rider& Cage,Iron Fist&Sabretooth, F:Shadowcat 2.00
132 KM(c),F:Iron Man. 2.00
133 F:Cloak & Dagger 2.00

Marvel Comics Presents #163
© Marvel Entertainment Group

134 SLi,F:Vance Astro 2.00
135 SLi,F:Daredevil 2.00
136 B:Gh.Rider&Masters of Silence, F:Iron Fist,Daredevil. 2.00
137 F:Ant Man 2.00
138 B:Wolverine,Spellbound. 2.00
139 F:Foreigner 2.00
140 F:Captain Universe 2.00
141 BCe(s),F:Iron Fist 2.00
142 E:Gh.Rider&Masters of Silence, F:Mr.Fantastic 2.00
143 Siege of Darkness,pt.#3, B:Werewolf,Scarlet Witch, E:Spellbound 2.00
144 Siege of Darkness,pt.#6, B:Morbius. 2.00
145 Siege of Darkness,pt.#11 . . . . . 2.00
146 Siege of Darkness,pt.#14. . . . . 2.00
147 B:Vengeance,F:Falcon,Masters of Silence,American Eagle 2.00
148 E:Vengeance,F:Capt.Universe, Black Panther. 2.00
149 F:Daughter o/t Dragon,Namor, Vengeance,Starjammers. 2.00
150 ANo(s),SLi,F:Typhoid Mary,DD, Vengeance,Wolverine. 2.00
151 ANo(s),F:Typhoid Mary,DD, Vengeance. 2.00
152 CDi(s),PR,B:Vengeance,Wolverine, War Machine,Moon Knight 2.00
153 CDi(s),A:Vengeance,Wolverine, War Machine,Moon Knight 2.00
154 CDi(s),E:Vengeance,Wolverine, War Machine,Moon Knight 2.00
155 CDi(s),B:Vengeance,Wolverine, War Machine,Kymaera 2.00
156 B:Shang Chi,F:Destroyer 2.00
157 F:Nick Fury 2.00
158 AD,I:Clan Destine,E:Kymaera, Shang Chi,Vengeance 2.00
159 B:Hawkeye, New Warriors, F:Fun,E:Vengeance 2.00
160 B:Vengeance,Mace 2.00
161 E:Hawkeye 2.00
162 B:Tigra,E:Mace 2.00
163 E:New Warriors 2.00
164 Tigra, Vengeance. 2.00
165 Tigra, Vengeance. 2.00
166 Turbo, Vengeance 2.00
167 Turbo, Vengeance 2.00
168 Thing, Vengeance 2.00
169 Mandarin, Vengeance 2.00
170 Force, Vengeance 2.00
171 Nick Fury. 2.00
172 Lunatik 2.00
173 . . . . 2.00
174 . . . . 2.00
175 . . . . 2.00
TPB Ghost Rider & Cable,rep #90-97 . . . . 3.95
TPB Save the Tyger,rep.Wolverine story from #1-10. . . . . 3.95

MARVEL COMICS SUPER SPECIAL

[Magazine, 1977]

1 JB,WS,Kiss,Features &Photos . 80.00
2 JB,Conan(1978) 15.00
3 WS,Close Encounters 8.00
4 GP,KJ,Beatles story 30.00
Becomes:

MARVEL SUPER SPECIAL

5 Kiss 1978 . . . . 80.00
6 GC,Jaws II 7.00
7 Does Not Exist
8 Battlestar Galactica(Tabloid) . . . 7.00
9 Conan 9.00
10 GC,Starlord 7.00
11 JB,RN,Weirdworld,. 7.00

12 JB,Weirdworld, ... 7.00
13 JB,Weirdworld, ... 7.00
14 GC,Meteor,adapt 7.00
15 Star Trek 6.00
15a Star Trek 9.00
16 AW,B:Movie Adapts,Empire Strikes Back 7.00
17 Xanadu 2.00
18 HC(c),JB,Raiders of the Lost Ark 2.00
19 HC,For Your Eyes Only 5.00
20 Dragonslayer 2.50
21 JB,Conan 2.00
22 JSo(c),AW,Bladerunner 2.00
23 Annie 2.00
24 Dark Crystal 2.00
25 Rock and Rule 2.00
26 Octopussy 2.50
27 AW,Return of the Jedi 6.00
28 PH(c),Krull 2.00
29 DSp,Tarzan of the Apes 2.00
30 Indiana Jones and the Temple of Doom 2.50
31 The Last Star Fighter 2.00
32 Muppets Take Manhattan 2.00
33 Buckaroo Banzai 2.00
34 GM,Sheena 2.00
35 JB,Conan The Destroyer 2.00
36 Dune 2.00
37 2010 . . . . 2.00
38 Red Sonja 2.00
39 Santa Claus 2.00
40 JB,Labrynth 2.00
41 Howard the Duck,Nov.,1986 . . . . 2.00

MARVEL DOUBLE FEATURE

Dec., 1973

1 JK,GC,B:Tales of Suspense Reprints,Capt.America, Iron-Man 9.00
2 JK,GC ,A:Nick Fury 5.00
3 JK,GC 5.00
4 JK,GC,Cosmic Cube 5.00
5 JK,GC,V:Red Skull 5.00
6 JK,GC,V:Adaptoid 5.00
7 JK,GC,V:Tumbler 5.00
8 JK,GC,V:Super Adaptoid 5.00
9 GC,V:Batroc 5.00
10 GC 5.00
11 GC,Capt.America Wanted 4.00
12 GC,V:Powerman,Swordsman . . . 4.00
13 GC,A:Bucky 4.00
14 GC,V:Red Skull 4.00
15 GK,GC,V:Red Skull 4.00
16 GC,V;Assassin 4.00
17 JK,GC,V:Aim,Iron Man & Sub-Mariner #1 . . . . 4.00
18 JK,GC,V:Modok,Iron Man #1 . . . 6.00
19 JK,GC,E:Capt.America 6.00
20 JK(c) 4.00
21 Capt.America,Black Panther March, 1977 . . . . 4.00

MARVEL FANFARE

March, 1972

1 MG,TA,PS,F:Spider-Man, Daredevil,Angel 7.00
2 MG,SM,FF,TVe,F:SpM,Ka-Zar . . 5.00
3 DC,F:X-Men 5.00
4 PS,TA,MG,F:X-Men,Deathlok . . . 5.00
5 MR,F:Dr.Strange 4.00
6 F:Spider-Man,Scarlet Witch 4.50
7 F:Hulk/Daredevil 3.00
8 CI,TA,GK,F:Dr.Strange 3.00
9 GM,F:Man Thing 3.00
10 GP,B:Black Widow 3.50
11 GP,D:M.Corcoran 3.50
12 GP,V:Snapdragon 3.50

Marvel Fanfare #24
© Marvel Entertainment Group

13 GP,E:B.Widow,V:Snapdragon . . . 3.50
14 F:Fantastic Four,Vision 2.75
15 BWS,F:Thing,Human Torch 3.00
16 DC,JSt,F:Skywolf 2.50
17 DC,JSt,F:Skywolf 2.50
18 FM,JRu,F:Captain America 3.00
19 RL,F:Cloak and Dagger 2.50
20 JSn,F:Thing&Dr.Strange 3.00
21 JSn,F:Thing And Hulk 3.00
22 KSy,F:Iron Man 2.50
23 KSy,F:Iron Man 2.50
24 F:Weird World 3.00
25 F:Weird World 2.50
26 F:Weird World 2.50
27 F:Daredevil 2.50
28 KSy,F:Alpha Flight 2.50
29 JBy,F:Hulk 3.00
30 BA,AW,F:Moon Knight 2.50
31 KGa,F:Capt.America, Yellow Claw 2.50
32 KGa,PS,F:Capt.America, Yellow Claw 2.50
33 JBr,F:X-Men 5.00
34 CV,F:Warriors Three 2.50
35 CV,F:Warriors Three 2.50
36 CV,F:Warriors Three 2.50
37 CV,F:Warriors Three 2.50
38 F:Captain America 2.50
39 JSon,F:Hawkeye,Moon Knight . . 2.50
40 DM,F:Angel,Storm,Mystique 3.00
41 DGb,F:Dr.Strange 2.50
42 F:Spider-Man 3.00
43 F:Sub-Mariner,Human Torch . . . 2.50
44 KSy,F:Iron Man vs.Dr.Doom 2.50
45 All Pin-up Issue,WS,AAd,MZ, JOy,BSz,KJ,HC,PS,JBy 3.00
46 F:Fantastic Four 2.50
47 MG,F:Spider-Man,Hulk 3.00
48 KGa,F:She-Hulk 2.50
49 F:Dr.Strange 2.50
50 JSon,JRu,F:Angel 3.00
51 JB,JA,GC,AW,F:Silver Surfer . . . 4.00
52 F:Fantastic Four 2.50
53 GC,AW,F:Bl.Knight,Dr.Strange . . 2.50
54 F:Black Knight,Wolverine 3.50
55 F:Powerpack,Wolverine 3.50
56 CI,DH,F:Shanna t/She-Devil . . . 2.50
57 BBl,AM,F:Shanna,Cap.Marvel . . 2.50
58 BBl,F:Shanna,Vision/Sc.Witch . . 2.50
59 BBl,F:Shanna,Hellcat 2.50
60 PS,F:Daredevil,Capt.Marvel 2.50

MARVEL FANFARE

Second Series 1996

1 Captain America, Falcon 2.00
2 New Fantastic Four 2.00
3 BbB,F:Spider-Man, Ghost Rider, . 2.00
4 F:Longshot 2.00
5 F:Longshot 2.00
6 F:Power Man & Iron Fist V. Sabretooth 2.00

Marvel Feature #5
© Marvel Entertainment Group

MARVEL FEATURE

[1st Regular Series]

Dec., 1971

1 RA,BE,NA,I&O:Defenders & Omegatron 120.00
2 BEv,F:The Defenders 60.00
3 BEv,F:The Defenders 50.00
4 F:Ant-Man 20.00
5 F:Ant-Man 11.00
6 F:Ant-Man 10.00
7 CR,F:Ant-Man 10.00
8 JSc,CR,F:Ant-Man,O:Wasp 10.00
9 CR,F:Ant-Man 10.00
10 CR,F:Ant-Man 10.00
11 JSn,JSt,F:Thing & Hulk 15.00
12 JSn,JSt,F:Thing,Iron Man, Thanos,Blood Brothers 12.00

[2nd Regular Series]

(All issues feature Red Sonja)

1 DG,The Temple of Abomination . 5.00
2 FT,Blood of the Hunter 3.00
3 FT,Balek Lives 3.00
4 FT,Eyes of the Gorgon 3.00
5 FT,The Bear God Walks 3.00
6 FT,C:Conan,Belit 3.00
7 FT,V:Conan,A:Belit,Conan#68 . . . 3.00

MARVEL FRONTIER COMICS SPECIAL

1 All Frontier Characters 3.25
1994 . . . . 2.95

MARVEL FUMETTI BOOK

April, 1984

1 NA(c),Stan Lee, All photos 2.00

MARVEL

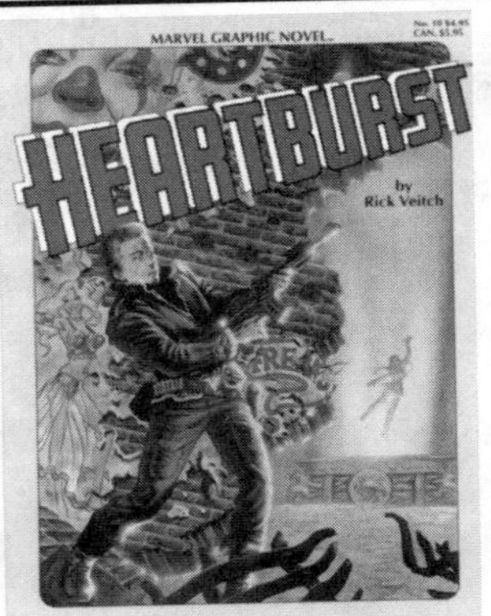

Marvel Graphic Novel #10
© Marvel Entertainment Group

MARVEL GRAPHIC NOVEL
1982

1 JSn,D:Captain Marvel,A:Most Marvel Characters 30.00
1a 2nd printing 10.00
1b 3rd-5th printing 7.00
2 F:Elric,Dreaming City 12.00
2a 2nd printing 7.00
3 JSn,F:Dreadstar 12.00
3a 2nd-3rd printing 7.00
4 BMc,I:New Mutants,Cannonball Sunspot,Psyche,Wolfsbane . . 22.00
4a 2nd printing 10.00
4b 3rd-4th printing 8.00
5 BA,F:X-Men 17.00
5a 2nd printing 9.00
5b 3rd-5th printing 7.00
6 WS,F:Starslammers 10.00
6a 2nd printing 7.00
7 CR,F:Killraven 7.00
8 RWi,AG,F:Super Boxers 8.00
8a 2nd printing 7.00
9 DC,F:Futurians 12.00
9a 2nd printing 7.00
10 RV,F:Heartburst 8.00
10a 2nd printing 6.00
11 VM,F:Void Indigo 12.00
12 F:Dazzler the Movie 10.00
12a 2nd printing 6.00
13 MK,F:Starstruck 7.00
14 JG,F:SwordsofSwashbucklers . . 6.00
15 CV,F:Raven Banner 6.00
16 GLa,F:Alladin Effect 6.00
17 MS,F:Living Monolith 7.00
18 JBy,F:She-Hulk 9.00
18 later printings 8.00
19 F:Conan 6.00
20 F:Greenberg the Vampire 6.00
21 JBo,F:Marada the She-wolf 6.00
22 BWr,Hooky,F:Spider-Man 12.00
23 DGr,F:Dr.Strange 6.00
24 FM,BSz,F:Daredevil 10.00
25 F:Dracula 8.00
26 FC,TA,F:Alien Legion 6.00
27 BH,F:Avengers 6.00
28 JSe,F:Conan the Reaver 6.50
29 BWr,F:Thing & Hulk 8.00
30 F:A Sailor's Story 6.00
31 F:Wolf Pack 6.00
32 SA,F:Death of Groo 15.00
33 F:Thor 6.00
34 AW,F:Cloak & Dagger 6.00
35 MK/RH,F:The Shadow 12.00
36 F:Willow movie adaption 7.00
37 BL,F:Hercules 7.00
38 JB,F:Silver Surfer 15.00
39 F:Iron Man,Crash 14.50
40 JZ,F:The Punisher 12.00
41 F:Roger Rabbit 7.00
42 F:Conan of the Isles 9.00
43 EC,F:Ax 6.00
44 BJ,F:Arena 6.00
45 JRy,F:Dr.Who 9.00
46 TD,F:Kull 7.00
47 GM,F:Dreamwalker 7.00
48 F:Sailor's Storm II 7.00
49 MBd,F:Dr.Strange&Dr.Doom . . 16.00
50 F:Spider-Man,Parallel Lives 9.00
51 F:Punisher,Intruder 10.00
52 DSp,F:Roger Rabbit 9.00
53 PG,F:Conan 6.95
54 HC,F:Wolverine & Nick Fury . . 17.00

MARVEL HALLOWEEN: THE SUPERNATURALS TOUR BOOK
Sept., 1999

1-shot, 16-page, cardstock cov 3.00

MARVEL HEROES

1 StL,FaN,Mega-Jam,48pg 3.00

MARVEL: HEROES AND LEGENDS 1997
Aug., 1997

1-shot, Stan Lee, JR(c) 6.00

MARVEL HOLIDAY SPECIAL

1 StG(s),PDd(s),SLo(s),RLm,PB, . . 3.25
1-shot MWa,KK 2.95

MARVEL KIDS
1999

Fantastic Four: Franklins Adventures 3.50
Incredible Hulk: Project Hide 3.50
Spider-Man Mysteries 3.50
X-Men: Mutant Search R.U.1 . . . . . 3.50

MARVEL KNIGHTS TOUR BOOK
Aug., 1998

1-shot, cardstock cover 3.00

MARVEL KNIGHTS
May, 2000

1 JQ,JP,KJ 3.00
2A JQ,KJ,CDi,EB,V:Ulik 3.00
2B variant EB(c) 3.00
3 JQ,KJ,CDi,EB,V:Ulik 3.00
4 JQ,KJ,CDi,EB,Zaran 3.00
5 JQ,KJ,CDi,EB,DaddyWronglegs . 3.00
6 JQ,KJ,CDi,EB,MaximumSecurity . 3.00

MARVEL: THE LOST GENERATION
Jan., 2000

12 (of 12) JBy,AM,Fireball, Flatiron, Cassandra, Oxbow, etx. 3.00
11 JBy,AM,F:Justice 3.00
10 JBy,AM,O:Walkabout 3.00
9 JBy,AM,Effigy,Black Fox 3.00
8 JBy,AM,Nocturne 3.00
7 JBy,AM,Knight Templar 3.00
6 JBy,AM,First Line 3.00
5 JBy,AM,F:Thor 3.00
4 JBy,AM,Yankee Clipper 3.00
3 JBy,AM,Liberty Girl 3.00

MARVEL MASTERPIECES COLLECTION
1993

1 Joe Jusko Masterpiece Cards . . . 3.25
2 F:Wolverine,Thanos,Apocalypse . 3.00
3 F:Gambit,Venom,Hulk 3.00
4 F:Wolverine Vs. Sabretooth 3.00

MARVEL MASTERPIECES II COLLECTION
1994

1 thru 3 w/cards . . . . @3.00

MARVEL MILESTONE EDITIONS 1991–95
See: ORIGINAL TITLES

MARVEL MINI-BOOKS
1966
(black & white)

1 F:Capt.America,Spider-Man,Hulk Thor,Sgt.Fury 15.00
2 F:Capt.America,Spider-Man,Hulk Thor,Sgt.Fury 15.00
3 F:Capt.America,Spider-Man,Hulk Thor,Sgt.Fury 15.00
4 thru 6 F:Capt.America,Spider-Man, Hulk,Thor,Sgt.Fury . . . . @15.00

MARVEL MOVIE PREMIERE
B&W Magazine, 1975

1 Land That Time Forgot, Burroughs adapt. 5.00

MARVEL MOVIE SHOWCASE FEATURING STAR WARS
Nov., 1982

1 Rep,Stars Wars #1-6 . . . . 4.00
2 Dec., 1982 . . . . 4.00

MARVEL MOVIE SPOTLIGHT FEATURING RAIDERS OF THE LOST ARK
Nov., 1982

1 Rep,Raiders of Lost Ark#1-3 . . . 3.00

MARVEL MYSTERY COMICS
See: MARVEL COMICS

MARVEL MYSTERY COMICS
Oct., 1999

Spec. 80-pg. 4.00

MARVEL NO-PRIZE BOOK
Jan., 1983

1 MGo(c),Stan Lee as Dr Doom(c) 3.00

 All comics prices listed are for *Near Mint* condition.

MARVEL: PORTRAITS OF A UNIVERSE

1 Fully painted moments 3.00
2 Fully painted moments 3.00
3 F:Death of Elektra 3.00
4 final issue 3.00

MARVEL PREMIERE

April, 1972

1 GK,O:Warlock,Receives Soul Gem, Creation of Counter Earth 40.00
2 GK,JK,F:Warlock 25.00
3 BWS,F:Dr.Strange 28.00
4 FB,BWS,F:Dr.Strange 14.00
5 MP,CR,F:Dr.Strange,I:Sligguth . 10.00
6 MP,FB,F:Dr.Strange 10.00
7 MP,CR,F:Dr.Strange,I:Dagoth . . 10.00
8 JSn,F:Dr.Strange 10.00
9 NA,FB,F:Dr.Strange 10.00
10 FB,F:Dr.Strange, D:Ancient One 10.00
11 NA,FB,F:Dr.Strange,I:Shuma . . 10.00
12 NA,FB,F:Dr.Strange 10.00
13 NA,FB,F:Dr.Strange 10.00
14 NA,FB,F:Dr.Strange 10.00
15 GK,DG,I&O:Iron Fist,pt.1 . . . . . 50.00
16 DG,O:Iron Fist,pt.2,V:Scythe . . 25.00
17 DG,`Citadel on the Edge of Vengeance' 15.00
18 DG,V:Triple Irons 15.00
19 DG,A:Ninja 13.00
20 I:Misty Knight 13.00
21 V:Living Goddess 13.00
22 V:Ninja 13.00
23 PB,V:Warhawk 13.00
24 PB,V:Monstroid 13.00
25 1st JBy,AMc,E:Iron Fist 18.00
26 JK,GT,F:Hercules 7.00
27 F:Satana 7.00
28 F:Legion Of Monsters,A:Ghost Rider,Morbius,Werewolf 15.00
29 JK,I:Liberty Legion, O:Red Raven 5.00
30 JK,F:Liberty Legion 5.00
31 JK,I:Woodgod 5.00
32 HC,F:Monark 5.00
33 HC,F:Solomon Kane 5.00
34 HC,F:Solomon Kane 5.00
35 I&O:Silver Age 3-D Man 5.00
36 F:3-D Man 5.00
37 F:3-D Man 5.00
38 AN,MP,I:Weird World 5.00

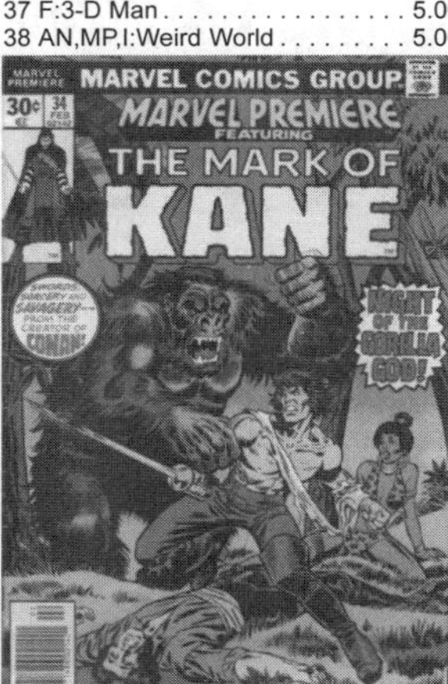

Marvel Premiere #34
© Marvel Entertainment Group

39 AM,I:Torpedo(1st solo) 5.00
40 AM,F:Torpedo 5.00
41 TS,F:Seeker 3000 . . . . 5.00
42 F:Tigra 5.00
43 F:Paladin 5.00
44 KG,F:Jack of Hearts(1stSolo) . . . 5.00
45 GP,F:Manwolf 5.00
46 GP,F:Manwolf 5.00
47 JBy,I:2nd Antman(Scott Lang) . . 5.00
48 JBy,F:2nd Antman 4.00
49 F:The Falcon 4.00
50 TS,TA,F:Alice Cooper 7.00
51 JBi,F:Black Panther,V:Klan 3.00
52 JBi,F:B.Panther,V:Klan 3.00
53 JBi,F:B.Panther,V:Klan 3.00
54 GD,TD,I:Hammer 3.00
55 JSt,F:Wonderman(1st solo) 4.00
56 HC,TA,F:Dominic Fortune 2.50
57 WS(c),I:Dr.Who 3.50
58 TA(c),FM,F:Dr.Who 3.00
59 F:Dr.Who 3.00
60 WS(c),DGb,F:Dr.Who 3.00
61 TS,F:Starlord 3.00

MARVEL PRESENTS

Oct., 1975

1 BMc,F:Bloodstone 10.00
2 BMc,O:Bloodstone 9.00
3 AM,B:Guardians/Galaxy 16.00
4 AM,I:Nikki 12.00
5 AM,`Planet o/t Absurd' 12.00
6 AM,V:Karanada 12.00
7 AM,`Embrace the Void' 12.00
8 AM,JB,JSt,reprint.S.Surfer#2 . . 15.00
9 AM,O:Starhawk 12.00
10 AM,O:Starhawk 12.00
11 AM,D:Starhawk's Children 12.00
12 AM,E:Guardians o/t Galaxy . . . 12.00

MARVEL PREVIEW

Feb., 1975

(black & white magazine)

1 NA,AN,Man Gods From Beyond the Stars 8.00
2 GM(c),O:Punisher 80.00
3 GM(c),Blade the Vampire Slayer . 9.00
4 GM(c),I&O:Starlord 9.00
5 Sherlock Holmes 9.00
6 Sherlock Holmes 9.00
7 KG,Satana,A:Sword in the Star . 9.00
8 GM,MP,Legion of Monsters . . . 11.00
9 Man-God,O:Starhawk 10.00
10 JSn,Thor the Mighty 6.00
11 JBy,I:Starlord 6.00
12 MK,Haunt of Horror 3.50
13 JSn(c),Starhawk 5.00
14 JSn(c),Starhawk 5.00
15 MK(c),Starhawk 3.50
16 GC,Detectives 3.00
17 GK,Black Mask 3.00
18 GC,Starlord 3.00
19 Kull 3.00
20 HC,NA,GP,Bizarre Adventures . . 4.00
21 SD,Moonlight 4.00
22 JB,King Arthur 3.00
23 JB,GC,FM,Bizarre Adventures . . 5.00
24 Debut Paradox 3.00

Becomes:

BIZARRE ADVENTURES

25 MG,TA,MR,Lethal Ladies 3.00
26 JB(c),King Kull 3.00
27 JB,AA,GP,Phoenix,A:Ice-Man . . 6.00
28 MG,TA,FM,NA,The Unlikely Heroes,Elektra 4.00
29 JB,WS,Horror 3.50
30 JB,Tomorrow 3.00
31 JBy,After the Violence Stops . . . 3.50
32 Gods 3.00
33 Ph(c),Horror 3.00

Bizarre Adventures #34
© Marvel Entertainment Group

34 PS,Christmas Spec,Son of Santa Howard the Duck,Feb.,1983 . . . 3.50

MARVEL PREVIEW

1993

Preview of 1993 . . . . 4.00

MARVEL REMIX

Nov., 1998

1 (of 3) Fantastic Four 3.00
1a signed 20.00
2 Fantastic Four:Fireworks 3.00
3 Fantastic Four:Fireworks 3.00

MARVELS

1 B:KBk(s),AxR,I:Phil Sheldon, A:G.A.Heroes,Human Torch Vs Namor 8.00
2 AxR,A:S.A.Avengers,FF,X-Men . . 6.00
3 AxR,FF vs Galactus 5.00
4 AxR,Final issue 5.00
HC rep.#1-#4 . . . . 34.95

MARVEL SAGA

Dec., 1985

1 JBy,Fantastic Four,Wolv. 2.50
2 Hulk 2.00
3 Spider-Man 2.50
4 X-Men 2.50
5 Thor 2.00
6 Fantastic Four 2.00
7 Avengers 2.00
8 X-Men 2.00
9 Angel 2.00
10 X-Men 2.00
11 X-Men 2.00
12 O:Capt. America 2.00
13 O:Daredevil,Elektra 2.00
14 O:Green Goblin 2.00
15 Avengers 2.00
16 Daredevil,X-Men 2.00
17 Kazar,X-Men 2.00
18 Hawkeye-Quicksilver 2.00
19 SpM,Thor,Daredevil 2.00
20 Daredevil,Giant Man 2.00
21 FF,V:Frightful Four 2.00
22 Wedding 2.00
23 . . . . 2.00
24 . . . . 2.00
25 O:Silver Surfer,Dec.,1987 . . . . . 2.25

MARVEL

MARVEL SELECTS: FANTASTIC FOUR
Nov., 1999

1 (of 12) 2.75
2 rep. Vol. 1, #108, AD(c) 2.75
3 rep. Vol. 1, #109, AD(c) 2.75
4 rep. Vol. 1, #110, AD(c) 2.75
5 rep. Vol. 1, #111, AD(c). . . . 2.75
6 rep. Vol. 1, #112, AD(c) 2.75

MARVEL SELECTS: SPIDER-MAN
Nov., 1999

1 (of 12) 2.75
2 rep. Amaz.Sp-M #101. . . . . 2.75
3 rep. Amaz.Sp-M #102. . . . . 2.75
4 rep. Amaz.Sp-M #103. . . . . 2.75
5 rep. Amaz.Sp-M #104. . . . . 2.75
6 rep. Amaz.Sp-M #105. . . . . 2.75

MARVEL: SHADOWS & LIGHT
B&W 1996

1-shot MGo,JPL,KJ,48pg. 3.00

MARVEL SPECTACULAR
August, 1973

1 JK,rep Thor #128 . . . . . . 8.00
2 JK,rep Thor #129 . . . . . . 5.00
3 JK,rep Thor #130 . . . . . . 5.00
4 JK,rep Thor #133 . . . . . . 5.00
5 JK,rep Thor #134 . . . . . . 5.00
6 JK,rep Thor #135 . . . . . . 5.00
7 JK,rep Thor #136 . . . . . . 5.00
8 JK,rep Thor #137 . . . . . . 5.00
9 JK,rep Thor #138 . . . . . . 5.00
10 JK,rep Thor #139 . . . . . 5.00
11 JK,rep Thor #140. . . . . . 4.00
12 JK,rep Thor #141. . . . . . 4.00
13 JK,rep Thor #142. . . . . . 4.00
14 JK,rep Thor #143. . . . . . 4.00
15 JK,rep Thor #144. . . . . . 4.00
16 JK,rep Thor #145. . . . . . 4.00
17 JK,rep Thor #146. . . . . . 4.00
18 JK,rep Thor #147. . . . . . 4.00
19 JK,rep Thor#148,Nov.,1975 . . . 4.00

MARVEL SPOTLIGHT
[1st Regular Series] Nov., 1971

1 NA(c)WW,F:Red Wolf 25.00
2 MP,BEv,NA,I&O:Werewolf. . . . 100.00
3 MP,F:Werewolf 37.00
4 SD,MP,F:Werewolf 37.00
5 SD,MP,I&O:Ghost Rider 85.00
6 MP,TS,F:Ghost Rider 35.00
7 MP,TS,F:Ghost Rider 35.00
8 JM,MB,F:Ghost Rider. 35.00
9 TA,F:Ghost Rider 25.00
10 SD,JM,F:Ghost Rider. 25.00
11 SD,F:Ghost Rider. 25.00
12 SD,2nd A:Son of Satan 25.00
13 F:Son of Satan 10.00
14 JM,F:Son of Satan,I:Ikthalon . . 10.00
15 JM, F:Son of Satan, I:Baphomet. 7.00
16 JM,F:Son of Satan. 7.00
17 JM,F:Son of Satan. 7.00
18 F:Son of Satan, I:Allatou 7.00
19 F:Son of Satan 7.00
20 F:Son of Satan 7.00
21 F:Son of Satan 7.00
22 F:Son of Satan, Ghost Rider . . . 8.00
23 F:Son of Satan 7.00
24 JM,F:Son of Satan. 7.00
25 GT,F:Sinbad 4.00
26 F:The Scarecrow 4.00
27 F:The Sub-Mariner. 4.00
28 F:Moon Knight (1st full solo). . . 11.00
29 F:Moon Knight 10.00
30 JSt,JB,F:Warriors Three. 6.00
31 HC,JSn,F:Nick Fury 6.00
32 I:Spiderwoman, Jessica Drew . . 9.00
33 F:Deathlok, I:Devilslayer 6.00

[2nd Regular Series] 1979

1 PB,F:Captain Marvel. 2.50
1a No`1' on Cover 4.00
2 FM(c),F:Captain Marvel,A:Eon . . 2.00
3 PB,F:Captain Marvel. 2.00
4 PB,F:Captain Marvel. 2.00
5 FM(c),SD,F:Dragon Lord 2.00
6 F:Star Lord 2.00
7 FM(c),F:StarLord 2.00
8 FM,F:Captain Marvel 2.50
9 FM(c),SD,F:Captain Universe . . . 2.00
10 SD,F:Captain Universe 2.00
11 SD,F:Captain Universe 2.00

MARVEL SPOTLIGHT ON CAPTAIN AMERICA

1 thru 4, Captain America rep. . . @2.95

MARVEL SPOTLIGHT ON DR. STRANGE

1 thru 4, Dr. Strange, rep.. . . . . @2.95

MARVEL SPOTLIGHT ON SILVER SURFER

1 thru 4, Silver Surfer, rep. . . . . @2.95

MARVEL SUPER ACTION
Jan., 1976

1-shot TD,GE,FS,MP,HC,F:Punisher, Weirdworld,Dominic Fortune, I:Huntress(Mockingbird) 50.00

MARVEL SUPER ACTION
May, 1977–Nov., 1981

1 JK,reprint,Capt.America #100 . . . 8.00
2 JK,reprint,Capt.America #101 . . . 6.00
3 JK,reprint,Capt.America #102 . . . 6.00
4 BEv,RH,reprint,Marvel Boy #1. . . 6.00
5 JK,reprint,Capt.America #103 . . . 6.00
6 JK,reprint,Capt.America #104 . . . 5.00
7 JK,reprint,Capt.America #105 . . . 5.00
8 JK,reprint,Capt.America #106 . . . 5.00
9 JK,reprint,Capt.America #107 . . . 5.00
10 JK,reprint,Capt.America #108 . . 5.00
11 JK,reprint,Capt.America #109. . . 5.00
12 JSo,reprint,Capt.America #110. . 5.00
13 JSo,reprint,Capt.America #111 . . 5.00
14 JB,reprint,Avengers #55. . . . . 5.00
15 JB,reprint,Avengers #56. . . . . 5.00
16 Reprint,Avengers,annual #2 . . . 4.00
17 Reprint,Avengers # 4.00
18 JB(c),reprint,Avengers #57. . . . 4.00
19 JB(c),reprint,Avengers #58. . . . 4.00
20 JB(c),reprint,Avengers #59 . . . 4.00
21 Reprint,Avengers #60 . . . . . 3.00
22 JB(c),reprint,Avengers #61. . . . 3.00
23 Reprint,Avengers #63 . . . . . 3.00
24 Reprint,Avengers #64 . . . . . 3.00
25 Reprint,Avengers #65 . . . . . 3.00
26 Reprint,Avengers #66 . . . . . 3.00
27 BWS,Reprint,Avengers #67 . . . 3.00
28 BWS,Reprint,Avengers #68 . . . 3.00
29 Reprint,Avengers #69 . . . . . 3.00
30 Reprint,Avengers #70 . . . . . 3.00
31 Reprint,Avengers #71 . . . . . 3.00
32 Reprint,Avengers #72 . . . . . 3.00
33 Reprint,Avengers #73 . . . . . 3.00
34 Reprint,Avengers #74 . . . . . 3.00
35 JB(c),Reprint,Avengers #75 . . . 3.00
36 JB(c),Reprint,Avengers #75 . . . 3.00
37 JB(c),Reprint,Avengers #76 . . . 3.00

Marvel Super Action #24
© Marvel Entertainment Group

MARVEL SUPERHEROES
Oct., 1966

1-shot Rep. D.D. #1, Avengers #2, Marvel Mystery #8 . . . . . . 75.00

Marvel Super Heroes #15
© Marvel Entertainment Group

MARVEL SUPER-HEROES
[1st Regular Series] 1967–71
(Prev.: Fantasy Masterpieces)

12 GC,I&O:Captain Marvel 100.00
13 GC,2nd A:Captain Marvel 65.00
14 F:Spider-Man. 90.00
15 GC,F:Medusa 30.00
16 I:Phantom Eagle 30.00
17 O:Black Knight. 30.00
18 GC,I:Guardians o/t Galaxy. . . . 50.00
19 F:Kazar 15.00
20 F:Dr.Doom,Diablo 15.00
21 thru 31 reprints. . . . . . @12.00
32 thru 55 rep. Hulk/Submariner from Tales to Astonish. . . . . @5.00

56 reprints Hulk #102 . . . . 3.50
57 thru 105 reps.Hulk issues . . . . @3.00

MARVEL SUPERHEROES
[2nd Regular Series] May, 1990

1 RLm,F:Hercules,Moon Knight, Magik,Bl.Panther,Speedball . . . 4.00
2 . . . . 3.50
3 F:Captain America,Hulk,Wasp . . 4.00
4 AD,F:SpM,N.Fury,D.D.,Speedball Wond.Man,Spitfire,Bl.Knight . . . 3.50
5 F:Thor,Thing,Speedball, Dr.Strange 3.50
6 RB,SD,F:X-Men,Power Pack, Speedball,Sabra. 3.00
7 RB,F:X-Men,Cloak & Dagger . . . 2.75
8 F:X-Men,Iron Man,Namor 2.50
9 F:Avengers W.C,Thor,Iron Man . . 3.00
10 DH,F:Namor,Fantastic Four, Ms.Marvel#24. . . . . 3.50
11 F:Namor,Ms.Marvel#25 . . . . 3.00
12 F:Dr.Strange,Falcon,Iron Man . . 3.00
13 F:Iron Man. 2.75
14 BMc,RWi,F:Iron Man, Speedball, Dr.Strange 2.75
15 KP,DH,F:Thor,Iron Man,Hulk . . . 2.75
Holiday Spec.#1 AAd,DC,JRu,F:FF, X-Men,Spider-Man,Punisher. . . 3.25
Holiday Spec.#2 AAd(c),SK,MGo, RLm,SLi,F:Hulk,Wolverine, Thanos,Spider-Man 3.25
Fall Spec.RB,A:X-Men,Shroud, Marvel Boy,Cloak & Dagger . . . 2.25

MARVEL SUPERHEROES MEGAZINE

1 thru 6 rep. . . . . @3.00

MARVEL SUPER SPECIAL
See: MARVEL COMICS

MARVEL SWIMSUIT
1992

1 Schwing Break 5.00

MARVEL TAILS
Nov., 1983

1 ST,Peter Porker 2.00

MARVEL TALES
1964

1 All reprints,O:Spider-Man 275.00
2 rep.Avengers #1,X-Men #1, Hulk #3. . . . . 100.00
3 rep.Amaz.SpM.#6. . . . . 45.00
4 rep.Amaz.SpM.#7. . . . . 30.00
5 rep.Amaz.SpM.#8. . . . . 30.00
6 rep.Amaz.SpM.#9. . . . . 30.00
7 rep.Amaz.SpM.#10. . . . . 30.00
8 rep.Amaz.SpM.#13. . . . . 20.00
9 rep.Amaz.SpM.#14. . . . . 24.00
10 rep.Amaz.SpM.#15 . . . . 24.00
11 rep.Amaz.SpM.#16 . . . . 24.00
12 rep.Amaz.SpM.#17 . . . . 24.00
13 rep.Amaz.SpM.#18 rep.1950's Marvel Boy 20.00
14 rep.Amaz.SpM.#19, reps.Marvel Boy 19.00
15 rep.Amaz.SpM.#20, reps.Marvel Boy 19.00
16 rep.Amaz.SpM.#21, reps.Marvel Boy 19.00
17 thru 22 rep.Amaz.SpM. #22-#27 . . . . @17.00
23 thru 27 rep.Amaz.SpM. #30-#34 . . . . @17.00

Marvel Tales #39
© Marvel Entertainment Group

28 rep.Amaz.SpM.#35&36 . . . . . . 17.00
29 rep.Amaz.SpM.#39&40 . . . . . . 17.00
30 rep.Amaz.SpM.#58&41 . . . . . . 17.00
31 rep.Amaz.SpM.#42 . . . . 17.00
32 rep.Amaz.SpM.#43&44 . . . . . . 17.00
33 rep.Amaz.SpM.#45&47 . . . . . . 17.00
34 rep.Amaz.SpM.#48 . . . . 6.00
35 rep.Amaz.SpM.#49 . . . . 6.00
36 thru 41 rep. Amaz.SpM#51-#56 . . . . @6.00
42 thru 53 rep. Amaz.SpM#59-#70 . . . . @6.00
54 thru 80 rep. Amaz.SpM#73-#99 . . . . @6.00
81 rep.Amaz.SpM.#103 . . . . 6.00
82 rep.Amaz.SpM.#103-4 . . . . 6.00
83 thru 97 rep. Amaz.SpM#104-#118 . . . . . . @6.00
98 rep.Amaz.SpM.#121 . . . . 6.00
99 rep.Amaz.SpM.#122 . . . . 6.00
100 rep.Amaz.SpM.#123,BU:Two Gun Kid,Giant-Size. 3.50
101 thru 105 rep.Amaz. SpM.#124-#128 . . . . @3.00
106 rep.Amaz.SpM.#129, (I:Punisher) 4.00
107 thur 110 rep.Amaz. SpM.#130-133 . . . . @2.50
111 Amaz.SpM#134,A:Punisher . . . 4.00
112 Amaz.SpM#135,A:Punisher . . . 3.00
113 thru 125 rep.Amaz.Spider Man #136-#148 . . . . @2.50
126 rep.Amaz.Spider-Man#149. . . . 4.00
127 rep.Amaz.Spider-Man#150. . . . 3.00
128 rep.Amaz.Spider-Man#151. . . . 4.00
129 thru 136 rep.Amaz.Spider Man #152-#159 . . . . @3.00
137 rep.Amaz.Fantasy#15 . . . . 7.00
138 rep.Amaz.SpM.#1 . . . . 7.00
139 thru 149 rep. AmazSpM#2-#12 . . . . @3.00
150 rep.AmazSpM Ann#1. . . . . 2.50
151 rep.AmazSpM#13 . . . . 2.50
152 rep.AmazSpM#14 . . . . 4.00
153 thru 190 rep.AmazSpM#15-52 . . . . . . @2.00
191 rep. #96-98 . . . . 2.25
192 rep. #121-122 . . . . 2.25
193 thru 198 rep.Marv.Team Up#59-64 . . . . @2.00
199 . . . . 2.00
200 rep. SpM Annual 14. . . . . 2.00
201 thru 206 rep.Marv. Team Up#65-70 . . . . @2.00
207 . . . . 2.00
208 . . . . 2.00
209 MZ(c),rep.SpM#129,Punisher. . 3.00
210 MZ(c),rep.SpM#134. . . . . 4.00
211 MZ(c),rep.SpM#135 . . . . 4.00
212 MZ(c),rep.Giant-Size#4 . . . . . . 4.00
213 MZ(c),rep.Giant-Size#4 . . . . . . 4.00
214 MZ(c),rep.SpM#161 . . . . 4.00
215 MZ(c),rep.SpM#162 . . . . 3.00
216 MZ(c),rep.SpM#174 . . . . 3.00
217 MZ(c),rep.SpM#175 . . . . 3.00
218 MZ(c),rep.SpM#201 . . . . 3.00
219 MZ(c),rep.SpM#202 . . . . 3.00
220 MZ(c),rep.Spec.SpM #81 . . . . . 3.00
221 MZ(c),rep.Spec.SpM #82 . . . . . 3.00
222 MZ(c),rep.Spec.SpM #83 . . . . . 2.00
223 thru 227 TM(c),rep. SpM #88-92 . . . . @2.25
228 TM(c),rep.Spec.SpM.#17 . . . . . 2.00
229 TM(c),rep.Spec.SpM.#18 . . . . . 2.00
230 TM(c),rep.SpM #203 . . . . 2.00
231 TM(c),rep.Team-Up#108 . . . . . 2.00
232 TM(c),rep. 2.00
233 TM(c),rep. X-Men. 2.00
234 TM(c),rep. X-Men. 2.00
235 TM(c),rep. X-Men. 2.00
236 TM(c),rep. X-Men. 2.00
237 TM(c),rep. 2.00
238 TM(c),rep. 2.00
239 TM(c),rep.SpM,Beast. 2.00
240 rep.SpM,Beast,MTU#90. . . . . . 2.00
241 rep.MTU#124. . . . . 2.00
242 rep.MTU#89,Nightcrawler 2.00
243 rep.MTU#117,SpM,Wolverine. . 2.00
244 MR(c),rep. 2.00
245 MR(c),rep. 2.00
246 MR(c),rep. 2.00
247 MR(c),rep.MTU Annual #6 . . . . 2.00
248 MR(c),rep. 2.00
249 MR(c),rep.MTU #14 . . . . 2.00
250 MR(c),rep.MTU #100 . . . . 2.00
251 rep.Amaz.SpM.#100 . . . . 2.00
252 rep.Amaz.SpM.#101 . . . . 3.50
253 rep.Amaz.SpM.#102 . . . . 3.00
254 rep.MTU #15,inc.2 Ghost Rider pin-ups by JaL 3.00
255 SK(c),rep.MTU #58, BU:Ghost Rider 2.00
256 rep. MTU 2.00
257 rep.Amaz.SpM.#238 . . . . 2.00
258 rep.Amaz.SpM.#239 . . . . 2.00
259 thru 261 rep.Amaz.SpM.#249 thru 251 . . . . 2.00
262 rep Marvel Team-Up #53 . . . . . 2.00
263 rep Marvel Team-Up #54 . . . . . 2.00
264 rep.B:Amaz.SpM.Ann.#5 . . . . . 2.00
265 rep.E:Amaz.SpM.Ann.#5 . . . . . 2.00
266 thru 274 rep.Amaz.SpM#252 thru #260. . . . . @2.00
275 rep.Amaz.SpM#261 . . . . 2.00
276 rep.Amaz.SpM#263 . . . . 2.00
277 rep.Amaz.SpM#265 . . . . 2.00
278 thru 282 rep.Amaz.SpM#268 thru 272 . . . . 2.00
283 rep.Amaz.SpM#273 . . . . 2.00
284 rep.Amaz.SpM#275 . . . . 2.00
285 rep.Amaz.SpM#276 . . . . 2.00
286 rep.Amaz.SpM#277 . . . . 2.00
287 rep.Amaz.SpM#278 . . . . 2.00
288 rep.Amaz.SpM#280 . . . . 2.00
289 rep.Amaz.SpM#281 . . . . 2.00
290 & 291 rep.Amaz.SpM. 2.00

MARVEL TALES
See: MARVEL COMICS

MARVEL TEAM-UP
March, 1972

(Spider-Man in all,unless *)

1 RA,F:Hum.Torch,V:Sandman . 120.00
2 RA,F:Hum.Torch,V:Sandman . . 35.00
3 F:Human Torch,V:Morbius. 50.00
4 GK,F:X-Men,A:Morbius 50.00
5 GK,F:Vision 20.00
6 GK,F:Thing,O:Puppet Master,
V:Mad Thinker 20.00
7 RA,F:Thor. 20.00
8 JM,F:The Cat 20.00
9 RA,F:Iron Man 20.00
10 JM,F:Human Torch 20.00
11 JM,F:The Inhumans 18.00
12 RA,F:Werewolf 20.00
13 GK,F:Captain America 25.00
14 GK,F:Sub-Mariner 15.00
15 RA,F:Ghostrider. 15.00
16 GK,JM,F:Captain Marvel 14.00
17 GK,F:Mr.Fantastic,
A:Capt.Marvel 14.00
18 *F:Hulk,Human Torch. 14.00
19 SB,F:Ka-Zar 14.00
20 SB,F:Black Panther 17.00
21 SB,F:Dr.Strange 7.00
22 SB,F:Hawkeye. 7.00
23 *F:Human Torch,Iceman,
C:Spider-Man,X-Men 8.00
24 JM,F:Brother Voodoo. 7.00
25 JM,F:Daredevil 7.00
26 *F:H.Torch,Thor,V:Lavamen 7.00
27 JM,F:The Hulk. 7.00
28 JM,F:Hercules 7.00
29 *F:Human Torch,Iron Man 7.00
30 JM,F:The Falcon 7.00
31 JM,F:Iron Fist 7.00
32 *F:Hum.Torch,Son of Satan 7.00
33 SB,F:Nighthawk. 7.00
34 SB,F:Valkyrie. 7.00
35 SB,*F:H.Torch,Dr.Strange 7.00
36 SB,F:Frankenstein 6.00
37 SB,F:Man-Wolf 6.00
38 SB,F:Beast 5.00
39 SB,F:H.Torch,I:Jean Dewolff . . . 5.00
40 SB,F:Sons of the Tiger. 5.00
41 SB,F:Scarlet Witch. 5.00
42 SB,F:Scarlet Witch,Vision 5.00
43 SB,F:Dr.Doom 5.00
44 SB,F:Moon Dragon 5.00
45 SB,F:Killraven 5.00
46 SB,F:Deathlok 6.00
47 F:The Thing. 5.00
48 SB,F:Iron Man,I:Wraith 5.00
49 SB,F:Iron Man 5.00
50 SB,F:Dr.Strange 5.00
51 SB,F:Iron Man 4.00
52 SB,F:Captain America 4.00
53 1st JBy New X-Men,F:Hulk . . . 25.00
54 JBy,F:Hulk,V:Woodgod 6.00
55 JBy,F:Warlock,I:Gardener 8.00
56 SB,F:Daredevil 5.00
57 SB,F:Black Widow 5.00
58 SB,F:Ghost Rider,V:Trapster . . . 5.00
59 JBy,F:Yellowjacket,V:Equinox. . . 5.00
60 JBy,F:Wasp,V:Equinox. 5.00
61 JBy,F:Human Torch 5.00
62 JBy,F:Ms.Marvel 5.00
63 JBy,F:Iron Fist 5.50
64 JBy,F:Daughters o/t Dragon. . . . 5.00
65 JBy,I:Captain Britain(U.S.)
I:Arcade 7.50
66 JBy,F:Captain Britain 6.00
67 JBy,F:Tigra,V:Kraven 5.00
68 JBy,F:Man-Thing,I:D'Spayre. . . . 5.00
69 JBy,F:Havok 6.00
70 JBy,F:Thor. 5.00
71 F:The Falcon,V:Plantman. 4.00
72 F:Iron Man. 4.00
73 F:Daredevil 4.00
74 BH,F:Not ready for prime time
players(Saturday Night Live). . . 5.00
75 JBy,F:Power Man 4.00
76 HC,F:Dr.Strange 4.00
77 HC,F:Ms.Marvel. 4.00
78 DP,F:Wonderman 4.00
79 JBy,TA,F:Red Sonja. 5.00
80 SpM,F:Dr.Strange,Clea 4.00
81 F:Satana 4.00
82 SB,F:Black Widow 5.00
83 SB,F:Nick Fury 5.00
84 SB,F:Master of Kung Fu 5.00
85 SB,F:Bl.Widow,Nick Fury 5.00
86 BMc,F:Guardians o/t Galaxy . . . 4.00
87 GC,F:Black Panther. 4.00
88 SB,F:Invisible Girl 4.00
89 RB,F:Nightcrawler 4.50
90 BMc,F:The Beast. 4.00
91 F:Ghost Rider 4.00
92 CI,F:Hawkeye,I:Mr.Fear IV 3.50
93 CI,F:Werewolf
I:Tatterdemalion (named) 4.00
94 MZ,F:Shroud 3.50
95 I:Mockingbird(Huntress) 4.00
96 F:Howard the Duck 3.50
97 *F:Hulk,Spiderwoman 3.50
98 F:Black Widow. 3.50
99 F:Machine Man 3.50
100 FM,JBy,F:F.F.,I:Karma,
BU:Storm & Bl.Panther. 8.00
101 F:Nighthawk 3.00
102 F:Doc Samson,Rhino. 3.00
103 F:Antman. 3.00
104 *F:Hulk,Ka-zar 3.00
105 *F:Powerman,Iron Fist,Hulk . . . 3.00
106 HT,F:Captain America 3.00
107 HT,F:She-Hulk 3.00
108 HT,F:Paladin 3.00
109 HT,F:Dazzler 3.00
110 HT,F:Iron Man 3.00
111 HT,F:Devil Slayer 3.00
112 HT,F:King Kull 3.00
113 HT,F:Quasar,V:Lightmaster. . . . 3.00
114 HT,F:Falcon 3.00
115 HT,F:Thor 3.00
116 HT,F:Valkyrie 3.00
117 HT,F:Wolv,V:Prof Power 12.00
118 HT,F:Professor X 4.00
119 KGa,F:Gargoyle. 3.00
120 KGa,F:Dominic Fortune 3.00
121 KGa,F:Human Torch,I:Leap
Frog(Frog Man) 3.00
122 KGa,F:Man-Thing 3.00
123 KGa,F:Daredevil 3.00

Marvel Team-Up #1
© Marvel Entertainment Group

124 KGa,F:Beast 3.50
125 KGa,F:Tigra. 3.00
126 BH,F:Hulk 3.00
127 KGa,F:Watcher,X-mas issue . . 3.00
128 Ph(c)KGa,F:Capt.America. . . . 3.00
129 KGa,F:The Vision 3.00
130 KGa,F:The Scarlet Witch 3.00
131 KGa,F:Leap Frog. 3.00
132 KGa,F:Mr.Fantastic 3.00
133 KGa,F:Fantastic Four. 3.00
134 F:Jack of Hearts 3.00
135 F:Kitty Pryde 3.00
136 F:Wonder Man. 3.00
137 *F:Aunt May & F.Richards 3.00
138 F:Sandman,I:New Enforcers . . 3.00
139 F:Sandman,Nick Fury 3.00
140 F:Black Widow. 3.00
141 SpM(2nd App Black Costume)
F:Daredevil. 4.00
142 F:Captain Marvel(2nd one). . . . 3.00
143 F:Starfox 3.00
144 F:M.Knight,V:WhiteDragon. . . . 3.00
145 F:Iron Man. 3.00
146 F:Nomad 3.50
147 F:Human Torch 3.00
148 F:Thor 3.00
149 F:Cannonball 3.50
150 F:X-Men,V:Juggernaut 5.50
Ann.#1 SB,F:New X-Men 16.00
Ann.#2 F:The Hulk 5.00
Ann.#3 F:Hulk,PowerMan 4.00
Ann.#4 F:Daredevil,Moon Knight. . . 3.00
Ann.#5 F:Thing,Scarlet Witch,
Quasar,Dr.Strange 3.00
Ann.#6 F:New Mutants,Cloak &
Dagger(cont.New Mutants#22) . 4.00
Ann.#7 F:Alpha Flight. 3.00

MARVEL TEAM-UP INDEX
See: OFFICIAL MARVEL INDEX TO MARVEL TEAM-UP

MARVEL TEAM-UP
1997

1 TPe,PO,AW, F:Spider-Man,
Generation X 2.00
2 TPe,PO,AW, F:Spider-Man &
Hercules. 2.00
3 TPe,DaR,AW, F:Spider-Man &
Sandman 2.00
4 TPe,DaR,F:Spider-Man &
Man-Thing 2.00
5 TPe,DaR,F:Spider-Man &
Mystery guest. 2.00
6 TPe,F:Spider-Man & Sub-Mariner 2.00
7 MWn,TPe,F:Spider-Man & Blade 2.00
8 TPe,F:Sub-Mariner & Doctor
Strange 2.00
9 TPe,F:Sub-Mariner & Captain
America 2.00
10 TPe,AW,F:Sub Mariner & Thing . 2.00
11 TPe,AW,PO,F:Sub-Mariner & Iron
Man, final issue 2.00

MARVEL
Treasury Edition
Sept., 1974

1 SD,Spider-Man,I:Contemplator . 45.00
2 JK,F:Fant.Four,Silver Surfer . . . 20.00
3 F:Thor 18.00
4 BWS,F:Conan 15.00
5 O:Hulk 15.00
6 GC,FB,SD,F:Dr.Strange 15.00
7 JB,JK,F:The Avengers 15.00
8 F:X-Mas stories 18.00
9 F:Super-Hero Team-Up. 15.00

Marvel Treasury Edition #12
© Marvel Entertainment Group

10 F:Thor 15.00
11 F:Fantastic Four. 12.00
12 F:Howard the Duck 12.00
13 F:X-Mas stories 12.00
14 F:Spider-Man. 12.00
15 BWS,F:Conan,Red Sonja. 15.00
16 F:Defenders. 12.00
17 F:The Hulk. 12.00
18 F:Spider Man,X-Men 15.00
19 F:Conan 15.00
20 F:Hulk 15.00
21 F:Fantastic Four 15.00
22 F:Spider-Man. 15.00
23 F:Conan 15.00
24 F:The Hulk. 15.00
25 F:Spider-Man,Hulk. 15.00
26 GP,F:Hulk,Wolverine,Hercules . 17.00
27 HT,F:Hulk,Spider-Man 15.00
28 JB,JSt,F:SpM/Superman 25.00

MARVEL TREASURY OF OZ

(oversized) 1975

1 JB,movie adapt. 4.00

MARVEL TREASURY SPECIAL

Vol. I Spider-Man, 1974 . . . . 4.00
Vol. II Capt. America, 1976 . . . . . . 3.50

MARVEL TRIPLE ACTION

Feb., 1972

1 Rep. 4.00
2 thru 47 rep. . . . . @2.00
G-Size#1 F:Avengers 3.00
G-Size#2 F:Avengers 3.00

MARVEL TWO-IN-ONE

Jan., 1974

(Thing in all, unless *)

1 GK,F:Man-Thing. 45.00
2 GK,JSt,F:Namor,Namorita. 14.00
3 F:Daredevil. 14.00
4 F:Capt.America,Namorita 14.00
5 F:Guardians of the Galaxy 15.00
6 F:Dr.Strange. 15.00
7 F:Valkyrie 6.00
8 F:Ghost Rider. 7.00
9 F:Thor 5.00
10 KJ,F:Black Widow 5.00
11 F:Golem 4.00
12 F:Iron Man. 4.00
13 F:Power Man. 4.00
14 F:Son of Satan 5.00
15 F:Morbius 5.00
16 F:Ka-zar 4.00
17 F:Spider-Man. 4.50
18 F:Spider-Man. 4.50
19 F:Tigra. 4.00
20 F:The Liberty Legion 4.00
21 F:Doc Savage 3.50
22 F:Thor,Human Torch 3.50
23 F:Thor,Human Torch 3.50
24 SB,F:Black Goliath. 3.50
25 F:Iron Fist 4.00
26 F:Nick Fury 3.00
27 F:Deathlok. 4.00
28 F:Sub-Mariner 3.00
29 F:Master of Kung Fu 3.00
30 JB,F:Spiderwoman 4.00
31 F:Spiderwoman 3.00
32 F:Invisible girl 3.00
33 F:Modred the Mystic 3.00
34 F:Nighthawk,C:Deathlok 3.50
35 F:Skull the Slayer 3.00
36 F:Mr.Fantastic 3.00
37 F:Matt Murdock 3.00
38 F:Daredevil 3.00
39 F:The Vision 3.00
40 F:Black Panther. 3.00
41 F:Brother Voodoo 3.00
42 F:Captain America. 3.00
43 JBy,F:Man-Thing 5.00
44 GD,F:Hercules. 3.00
45 GD,F:Captain Marvel. 4.50
46 F:The Hulk. 5.00
47 GD,F:Yancy Street Gang,
I:Machinesmith. 3.00
48 F:Jack of Hearts 3.00
49 GD,F:Dr.Strange 3.00
50 JBy,JS,F:Thing & Thing 3.50
51 FM,BMc,F:Wonderman,Nick
Fury, Ms.Marvel 4.00
52 F:Moon Knight,I:Crossfire 3.00
53 JBy,JS,F:Quasar,C:Deathlok . . . 3.50
54 JBy,JS,D:Deathlok,
I:Grapplers 6.00
55 JBy,JS,I:New Giant Man 3.00
56 GP,GD,F:Thundra 2.50
57 GP,GD,F:Wundarr 2.50
58 GP,GD,I:Aquarian,A:Quasar. . . . 2.50
59 F:Human Torch 2.50
60 GP,GD,F:Impossible Man,
I:Impossible Woman 2.50
61 GD,F:Starhawk,I&O:Her. 3.00
62 GD,F:Moondragon 3.00
63 GD,F:Warlock 3.00
64 DP,GD,F:Stingray,
I:Serpent Squad 2.50
65 GP,GD,F:Triton 2.50
66 GD,F:Scarlet Witch,
V:Arcade 2.50
67 F:Hyperion,Thundra 2.50
68 F:Angel,V:Arcade. 2.50
69 GD,F:Guardians o/t Galaxy 2.50
70 F:The Inhumans 2.50
71 F:Mr.Fantastic,I:Deathurge,
Maelstrom 2.50
72 F:Stingray 2.50
73 F:Quasar 2.50
74 F:Puppet Master,Modred 2.50
75 F:The Avengers,O:Blastaar 2.50
76 F:Iceman,O:Ringmaster 2.50
77 F:Man-Thing 2.50
78 F:Wonder Man. 2.50
79 F:Blue Diamond,I:Star Dancer . . 2.50
80 F:Ghost Rider 2.00
81 F:Sub-Mariner 2.00
82 F:Captain America. 2.00
83 F:Sasquatch 3.00
84 F:Alpha Flight 3.00

Marvel Two In One #95
© Marvel Entertainment Group

85 F:Giant-Man 2.00
86 O:Sandman 2.25
87 F:Ant-Man 2.00
88 F:She-Hulk 2.00
89 F:Human Torch 2.00
90 F:Spider-Man. 2.25
91 V:Sphinx 2.00
92 F:Jocasta,V:Ultron 2.00
93 F:Machine Man,D:Jocasta 2.25
94 F:Power Man,Iron Fist 2.00
95 F:Living Mummy 2.00
96 F:Sandman,C:Marvel Heroes. . . 2.00
97 F:Iron Man. 2.00
98 F:Franklin Richards 2.00
99 JBy(c),F:Rom 2.00
100 F:Ben Grimm 2.50
Ann.#1 SB,F:Liberty Legion 5.00
Ann.#2 JSn,2nd D:Thanos,A:Spider
Man,Avengers,Capt.Marvel,
I:Lord Chaos,Master Order . . . 12.00
Ann.#3 F:Nova 4.00
Ann.#4 F:Black Bolt 3.50
Ann.#5 F:Hulk,V:Pluto. 3.00
Ann.#6 I:American Eagle 3.00
Ann.#7 I:Champion,A:Hulk,Thor,
DocSamson,Colossus,Sasquatch,
WonderMan 3.50

OFFICIAL HANDBOOK OF THE MARVEL UNIVERSE

Jan., 1983

1 Abomination-Avengers'
Quintet. 7.50
2 BaronMordo-Collect.Man 6.00
3 Collector-Dracula 5.00
4 Dragon Man-Gypsy Moth 5.00
5 Hangman-Juggernaut. 5.00
6 K-L. 4.00
7 Mandarin-Mystique 4.00
8 Na,oria-Pyro 4.00
9 Quasar to She-Hulk 4.00
10 Shiar-Sub-Mariner 4.00
11 Subteraneans-Ursa Major 4.00
12 Valkyrie-Zzzax 4.00
13 Book of the Dead. 4.00
14 Book of the Dead. 4.00
15 Weaponry 4.00

[2nd Series]

1 Abomination-Batroc 5.00
2 Beast-Clea 4.00
3 Cloak & D.-Dr.Strange 4.00
4 Dr.Strange-Galactus 4.00

5 Gardener-Hulk 4.00
6 Human Torch-Ka-Zar 3.25
7 Kraven-Magneto 3.25
8 Magneto-Moleman 3.25
9 Moleman-Owl 3.25
10 . . . . 3.25
11 . . . . 2.50
12 S-T 2.50
13 . . . . 2.50
14 V-Z 2.50
15 . . . . 2.50
16 Book of the Dead. 2.50
17 Handbook of the Dead,inc. JLe illus. 2.50
18 . . . . 2.50
19 . . . . 2.50
20 Inc.RLd illus. 2.50

Marvel Universe Update

1 thru 8 . . . . @2.00

Marvel Universe Packet

1 inc. Spider-Man 5.50
2 inc. Captain America 4.50
3 inc. Ghost Rider 5.00
4 inc. Wolverine. 4.50
5 inc. Punisher 4.25
6 inc. She-Hulk 4.00
7 inc. Daredevil 4.00
8 inc. Hulk. 4.00
9 inc. Moon Knight. 4.00
10 inc. Captain Britain 4.00
11 inc. Storm 4.00
12 inc. Silver Surfer 4.00
13 inc. Ice Man. 4.50
14 inc. Thor 4.50
15 thru 22 . . . . @4.50
23 inc. Cage. 4.50
24 inc. Iron Fist. 4.50
25 inc.Deadpool,Night Thrasher . . . 4.50
26 inc. Wonderman 5.00
27 inc.Beta Ray Bill,Pip 5.00
28 inc.X-Men 5.00
29 inc.Carnage. 5.00
30 thru 36 . . . . @5.00

MARVEL UNIVERSE 1996

1 Post Onslaught. 2.95

MARVEL UNIVERSE April 1998

1 CPa(c),RSt,SEp,AW,F:Human Torch,Capt.Am.,Namor,48pg . . . 3.00
2A JBy(c),RSt,SEp,AW,V:Hydra, Baron Strucker 2.00
2B DGb(c). 2.00
3 RSt,SEp,AW,V:Hydra 2.00
4 RSt,MM, all-star jam cover, F:Monster Hunters 2.00
5 MM,RSt,F:The Monster Hunters . 2.00
6 MM,RSt,F:Monster Hunters,pt.3 . 2.00
7 MM,RSt,F:Monster Hunters,pt.4 . 2.00

MARVEL VALENTINE'S SPECIAL 1997

1-shot MWa,TDF, 48pg 3.00

MARVEL X-MEN COLLECTION 1994

1 thru 3 JL from the 1st series X-Men Cards 3.25

MARVIN MOUSE Atlas Sept., 1957

1 BEv,F:Marvin Mouse 30.00

MASTER OF KUNG FU, SPECIAL MARVEL ED. April, 1974

Prev: Special Marvel Edition

17 JSn,I:Black Jack Tarr 20.00
18 PG,1st Gulacy Art 14.00
19 PG,A:Man-Thing 10.00
20 GK(c),PG,AM,V:Samurai 10.00
21 AM,Season of Vengeance.. Moment of Death 8.00
22 PG,DA,Death. 8.00
23 AM,KJ,River of Death 8.00
24 JSn,WS,AM,ST,Night of the Assassin 8.00
25 JSt(c),PG,ST,Fists Fury... Rites of Death 8.00
26 KP,ST,A:Daughter of Fu Manchu. 7.00
27 SB,FS,A:Fu Manchu 7.00
28 EH,ST,Death of a Spirit 7.00
29 PG,V:Razor-Fist. 7.00
30 PG,DA,Pit of Lions. 7.00
31 GK&DA(c),PG,DA,Snowbuster. . 7.00
32 GK&ME(c),SB,ME,Assault on an Angry Sea 7.00
33 PG,Messenger of Madness, I:Leiko Wu 7.00
34 PG,Captive in A Madman's Crown 7.00
35 PG,V:Death Hand 7.00
36 The Night of the Ninja's 7.00
37 V:Darkstrider & Warlords of the Web 5.00
38 GK(c),PG,A:The Cat 5.00
39 GK(c),PG,A:The Cat 5.00
40 PG,The Murder Agency 5.00
41 . . . . 5.00
42 GK(c),PG,TS,V:Shockwave 5.00
43 PG,V:Shockwave. 5.00
44 SB(c),PG,V:Fu Manchu 5.00
45 GK(c),PG,Death Seed 5.00
46 PG,V:Sumo 5.00
47 PG,The Cold White Mantle of Death 5.00
48 PG,Bridge of a 1,000 Dooms . . . 5.00
49 PG,V:Shaka Kharn,The Demon Warrior. 5.00

Master of Kung Fu #47
© Marvel Entertainment Group

50 PG,V:Fu Manchu 5.00
51 PG(c),To End...To Begin 5.00
52 Mayhem in Morocco 4.00
53 . . . . 4.00
54 JSn(c),Death Wears Three Faces. 4.00
55 PG(c),The Ages of Death. 4.00
56 V:The Black Ninja 4.00
57 V:Red Baron 4.00
58 Behold the Final Mask 4.00
59 GK(c),B:Phoenix Gambit, Behold the Angel of Doom 4.00
60 A:Dr.Doom,Doom Came 4.00
61 V:Skull Crusher 3.50
62 Coast of Death 3.50
63 GK&TA(c),Doom Wears Three Faces. 3.50
64 PG(c),To Challenge a Dragon . . 3.50
65 V:Pavane. 3.50
66 V:Kogar 3.50
67 PG(c),Dark Encounters 3.50
68 Final Combats,V:The Cat. 3.50
69 . . . . 3.50
70 A:Black Jack Tarr,Murder Mansion 3.50
71 PG(c),Ying & Yang (c) 3.50
72 V:Shockwave. 3.50
73 RN(c),V:Behemoths 3.50
74 TA(c),A:Shockwave 3.50
75 Where Monsters Dwell. 3.50
76 GD,Battle on the Waterfront. . . . 3.75
77 GD,I:Zaran 3.75
78 GD,Moving Targets 3.75
79 GD,This Side of Death. 3.75
80 GD,V:Leopard Men 3.75
81 GD,V:Leopard Men 3.75
82 GD,Flight into Fear 3.75
83 GD, ... 3.75
84 GD,V:Fu Manchu. 3.75
85 GD,V:Fu Manchu. 3.75
86 GD,V:Fu Manchu. 3.75
87 GD,V:Zaran, ... 3.75
88 GD,V:Fu Manchu. 3.75
89 GD,D:Fu Manchu. 3.75
90 MZ,Death in Chinatown 3.75
91 GD,Gang War,drugs 4.00
92 GD,Shadows of the Past 3.75
93 GD,Cult of Death 3.75
94 GD,V:Agent Synergon 3.75
95 GD,Raid 3.75
96 GD,I:Rufus Carter 3.75
97 GD,V:Kung Fu's Dark Side. 3.75
98 GD,Fight to the Finish 3.75
99 GD,Death Boat 3.75
100 GD,Doublesize 5.00
101 GD,Not Smoke,Nor Beads, Nor Blood. 3.75
102 GD,Assassins,1st GD(p) 4.00
103 GD,V:Assassins. 3.75
104 GD,Fight without Reason, C:Cerberus. 3.75
105 GD,I:Razor Fist 3.75
106 GD,C:Velcro 3.75
107 GD,A:Sata 3.75
108 GD 3.75
109 GD,Death is a Dark Agent 3.75
110 GD,Perilous Reign 3.75
111 GD. 3.75
112 GD(c),Commit and Destroy . . . 3.75
113 GD(c),V:Panthers. 3.75
114 Fantasy o/t Autumn Moon 3.75
115 GD. 3.75
116 GD. 3.75
117 GD,Devil Deeds Done in Darkness 3.75
118 GD,D:Fu Manchu,double 4.50
119 GD. 3.75
120 GD,Dweller o/t Dark Stream. . . 3.75
121 Death in the City of Lights'. . . . 3.00
122 . . . . 3.00
123 V:Ninjas. 3.00

124 . . . 3.00
125 . . . 4.00
G-Size#1,CR,PG . . . 3.00
G-Size#2 PG,V:Yellow Claw . . . 2.00
G-Size#3 . . . 2.00
G-Size#4 JK,V:Yellow Claw . . . 2.00
Spec.#1 Bleeding Black . . . 3.25

MASTER OF KUNG FU: BLEEDING BLACK

1 V:ShadowHand, 1991 . . . 3.00

MASTERS OF TERROR

July–Sept., 1975

1 GM(c),FB,BWS,JSn,NA . . . 3.00
2 JSn(c),GK,VM, . . . 2.00

MASTERS OF THE UNIVERSE

Star May, 1986—March, 1988

1 I:Hordak . . . 2.00
2 thru 12 . . . @1.00
Movie #1 GT . . . 2.00

MATT SLADE, GUNFIGHTER

Atlas May, 1956

1 AW,AT,F:Matt Slade,Crimson Avenger . . . 150.00
2 AW,A:Crimson Avenger . . . 100.00
3 A:Crimson Avenger . . . 90.00
4 A:Crimson Avenger . . . 75.00
Becomes:

KID SLADE GUNFIGHTER

5 F:Kid Slade . . . 75.00
6 . . . 50.00
7 AW,Duel in the Night . . . 65.00
8 July, 1957 . . . 50.00

MAVERICK

1997

1 JGz,F:Christopher Nord/David North/Maverick, 48pg . . . 3.00
2 JGz,A:Victor Creed and Logan . . 2.00
2a variant cover . . . 2.00
3 JGz,V:Puck & Vindicator . . . 2.00
4 JGz,A:Wolverine . . . 2.00
5 JGz,A:The Blob . . . 2.00
6 JGz,V:Sabretooth . . . 2.00
7 JGz,V:Sabretooth . . . 2.00
8 JGz,V:The Confessor . . . 2.00
9 JGz,Maverick's secrets . . . 2.00
10 JGz,V:Ivan the Terrible, Chris Bradley becomes Bolt . . . 2.00
11 JGz,A:Darkstar,Vanguard, Ursa Major . . . 2.00
12 JGz, double sized last issue . . . 3.00
1-shot LHa, V:Sabretooth,48pg . . . 2.95

Maverick #3
© Marvel Entertainment Group

MAXIMUM SECURITY

October 2000

1 (of 3) KBk,JOy,x-over . . . 3.00
2 KBk,JOy,x-over . . . 3.00
Spec. Thor vs. Ego, 64pg,SL,JK . . . 3.00
Spec. Dangerous Planet . . . 3.00

MELVIN THE MONSTER

Atlas July, 1956

1 . . . 100.00
2 thru 6 . . . @60.00
Becomes:

DEXTER THE DEMON

Sept., 1957

7 . . . 35.00

MEMORIES

Epic

1 Space Adventures . . . 2.50

MENACE

Atlas May, 1953

1 RH,BEv,GT,One Head Too Many . . . 500.00
2 RH,BEv,GT,JSt,Burton'sBlood . 350.00
3 BEv,RH,JR,The Werewolf . . . 250.00
4 BEv,RH,The Four Armed Man. 250.00
5 BEv,RH,GC,GT,I&O:Zombie . . 400.00
6 BEv,RH,JR,The Graymoor Ghost . . . 250.00
7 JSt,RH,Fresh out of Flesh . . . 200.00
8 RH,The Lizard Man . . . 200.00
9 BEv,The Walking Dead . . . 225.00
10 RH(c),Half Man,Half... . . . 200.00
11 JKz,JR,Locked In,May, 1954 . 200.00

MEN IN ACTION

Atlas April, 1952

1 Sweating it Out . . . 60.00
2 US Infantry stories . . . 35.00
3 RH . . . 25.00
4 War stories . . . 25.00
5 Squad Charge . . . 25.00
6 War stories . . . 25.00
7 RH(c),BK,No Risk Too Great . . 45.00
8 JRo(c),They Strike By Night . . . 25.00
9 SSh(c),Rangers Strike Back . . 25.00
Becomes:

BATTLE BRADY

10 SSh(c),F:Battle Brady . . . 100.00
11 SSh(c) . . . 75.00
12 SSh(c),Death to the Reds . . . 50.00
13 . . . 50.00
14 Final Issue,June, 1953 . . . 50.00

MEN IN BLACK

1 ANi, prequel to movie (1997) . . . 4.00
Spec. Movie Adaptation (1997) . . . 4.00

MEN IN BLACK: RETRIBUTION

Aug., 1997

1 continuation from movie . . . 2.50

MEN'S ADVENTURES

See: TRUE WESTERN

MEPHISTO vs. FOUR HEROES

April–July, 1987

1 JB,BWi,A:Fantastic Four . . . 2.50
2 JB,BWi,A:X-Factor . . . 2.25
3 JB,AM,A:X-Men . . . 2.25
4 JB,BWi,A:Avengers . . . 2.00

METEOR MAN

1993–94

1 R:Meteor Man . . . 2.00
2 V:GhostStrike,Malefactor,Simon . 2.00
3 A:Spider-Man . . . 2.00
4 A:Night Thrasher . . . 2.00
5 Exocet . . . 2.00
6 final issue . . . 2.00

[TED McKEEVER'S} METROPOL

Epic 1991–92

1 Ted McKeever . . . 3.00
2 . . . 3.00
3 . . . 3.00
4 . . . 3.00
5 . . . 3.00
6 . . . 3.00
7 . . . 3.00
8 Return of Eddy Current . . . 3.00
9 `Wings of Silence' . . . 3.00
10 `Rotting Metal,Rusted Flesh' . . . 3.00
11 `Diagram of the Heart' . . . 3.00
12 . . . 3.00

METROPOL A.D.

Epic 1992

1 R:The Angels . . . 3.50
2 V:Demons . . . 3.50
3 V:Nuclear Arsenal . . . 3.50

MICRONAUTS

[1st Series] Jan., 1979

1 MGo,JRu,O:Micronauts . . . 3.00
2 MGo,JRu,Earth . . . 2.50
3 MGo,JRu . . . 2.50
4 MGo . . . 2.50
5 MGo,V:Prometheus . . . 2.50
6 MGo . . . 2.00
7 MGo,A:Man Thing . . . 2.00
8 MGo,BMc,I:Capt. Univ. . . . 2.50
9 MGo,I:Cilicia . . . 2.00
10 MGo . . . 2.00
11 MGo . . . 2.00
12 MGo . . . 2.00
13 HC,F:Bug . . . 2.00
14 HC,V:Wartstaff . . . 2.00
15 HC,AM,A:Fantastic Four . . . 2.00
16 HC,AM,A:Fantastic Four . . . 2.00
17 HC,AM,A:Fantastic Four . . . 2.00
18 HC,Haunted House Issue . . . 2.00
19 PB,V:Odd John . . . 2.00
20 PB,A:Antman . . . 2.00
21 PB,I:Microverse . . . 2.00
22 PB . . . 2.00
23 PB,V:Molecule Man . . . 2.00
24 MGo,V:Computrex . . . 2.00

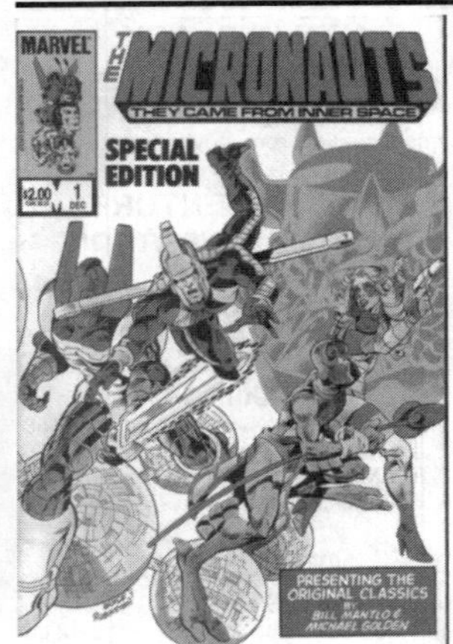

Micronauts, 2nd. Series #1
© Marvel Entertainment Group

25 PB,A:Mentallo 2.00
26 PB,A:Baronkarza 2.00
27 PB,V:Hydra,A:Shield 2.00
28 PB,V:Hydra,A:Shield 2.00
29 PB,Doc Samson 2.00
30 PB,A:Shield 2.00
31 PB,A:Dr.Strange 2.00
32 PB,A:Dr.Strange 2.00
33 PB,A:Devil of Tropica 2.00
34 PB,A:Dr.Strange 2.00
35 O:Microverse 2.00
36 KG,Dr.Strange 2.00
37 KG,Nightcrawler 3.50
38 GK,1st direct 2.50
39 SD 2.00
40 GK,A:FF 2.00
41 GK,Dr.Doom 2.00
42 GK 2.00
43 . . . . 2.00
44 . . . . 2.00
45 Arcade 2.00
46 . . . . 2.00
47 . . . . 2.00
48 JG 2.50
49 JG,V:BaronKarza 2.00
50 JG,V:BaronKarza 2.00
51 JG 2.00
52 JG 2.00
53 JG,V:Untouchables 2.00
54 JG,V:Tribunal 2.00
55 JG,V:KarzaWorld 2.00
56 JG,Kaliklak 2.00
57 JG,V:BaronKarza 2.00
58 JG,V:BaronKarza 2.00
59 JG,V:TheMakers 2.00
Ann.#1,SD 2.50
#2 SD 2.00

[2nd Series]

1 V:The Makers 2.00
2 AAd(c),V:The Makers 2.00
3 Huntarr'sEgg 2.00
4 V:The Makers 2.00
5 The Spiral Path 2.00
6 L:Bug 2.00
7 Acroyear 2.00
8 V:Scion 2.00
9 R:Devil 2.00
10 V:Enigma Force 2.00
11 V:Scion 2.00
12 V:Scion 2.00
13 V:Dark Armada 2.00
14 V:Keys of the Zodiac 2.00
15 O:Marionette 2.00
16 Secret Wars II 2.50
17 V:Scion 2.00
18 Acroyear 2.00
19 R:Baron Karza 2.00
20 Last Issue 2.00

MICRONAUTS
(Special Edition) Dec., 1983

1 MGo/JRu,rep. 2.00
2 MGo/JRu,rep. 2.00
3 Rep.MG/JRu 2.00
4 Rep.MG/JRu 2.00
5 Rep.MG/JRu,April, 1984 . . . . 2.00

MIDNIGHT MEN
Epic *Heavy Hitters* 1993

1 HC,I:Midnight Men 2.75
2 HC,J:Barnett 2.25
3 HC,Pasternak is Midnight Man . . 2.25
4 HC,Last issue 2.25

Midnight Suns Unlimited #3
© Marvel Entertainment Group

MIDNIGHT SONS UNLIMITED
1993–95

1 JQ,JBi,MT(c),A:Midnight Sons . . 4.25
2 BSz(c),F:Midnight Sons 4.25
3 JR2(c),JS,A:Spider-Man 4.25
4 Siege of Darkness #17, D:2nd Ghost Rider 4.25
5 DQ(s),F:Mordred,Vengeance, Morbius,Werewolf,Blaze, I:Wildpride 4.25
6 DQ(s),F:Dr.Strange 3.95
7 DQ(s),F:Man-Thing 3.95
8 . . . . 3.95
9 J:Mighty Destroyer 3.95

MIGHTY MARVEL WESTERN
Oct., 1968

1 JK,All reprints,B:Rawhide Kid Kid Colt,Two-Gun Kids 40.00
2 JK,DAy,Beware of the Barker Brothers 25.00
3 HT(c),JK,DAy,Walking Death . . 25.00
4 HT(c),DAy 25.00
5 HT(c),DAy,Ambush 25.00
6 HT(c),DAy Doom in the Desert . 25.00
7 DAy,V:MurderousMasquerader 25.00
8 HT(c),DAy,Rustler's on the Range 25.00
9 JSe(c),JK,DAy,V:Dr Danger . . . 25.00
10 OW,DH,Cougar 25.00
11 V:The Enforcers 20.00
12 JK,V:Blackjack Bordon 20.00
13 V:Grizzly 20.00
14 JK.V:The Enforcers 20.00
15 Massacre at Medicine Bend . . . 20.00
16 JK,Mine of Death 20.00
17 Ambush at Blacksnake Mesa . . 15.00
18 Six-Gun Thunderer 15.00
19 Reprints cont 15.00
20 same 15.00
21 same 12.00
22 . . . . 12.00
23 same 12.00
24 JDa,E:Kid Colt 12.00
25 B:Matt Slade 12.00
26 thru 31 Reprints . . . . @12.00
32 JK,AW,Ringo Kid #23 . . . . 10.00
33 thru 36 Reprints . . . . @10.00
37 JK,AW Two-Gun #51 . . . . 10.00
38 thru 45 Reprints . . . . @10.00
46 same,Sept., 1976 . . . . 10.00

MIGHTY HEROES
Nov., 1997

1-shot SLo, Diaper Man, Rope Man, Cuckoo Man, Tornado Man, Strong Man, etc. 3.00

SABAN'S MIGHTY MORPHIN POWER RANGERS

1 SLo,FaN,New ongoing series . . . 2.25
2 FaN,RLm,JP,more 2.00
3 FaN,RLm,JP,more adventures . . 2.00
4 LSn,JP,V:Glob monster 2.00
5 . . . . 2.00
6 . . . . 2.00
7 Close Encounter with Alien 2.00
Photo Adaptation 2.95

SABAN'S MIGHTY MORPHIN POWER RANGERS: NINJA RANGERS/ VR TROOPERS

1 FaN,RLm,JP,flip book 2.00
2 JP,flip book 2.00
3 New outfits 2.00
4 . . . . 2.00
5 . . . . 2.00
6 . . . . 2.00

MIGHTY MOUSE
[1st Series] Fall, 1946

1 Terytoons Presents 1,000.00
2 . . . . 450.00
3 . . . . 300.00
4 Summer, 1947 . . . . 300.00

MIGHTY MOUSE
Oct., 1990

1 EC,Dark Mite Returns 3.00
2 EC,V:The Glove 2.00
3 EC/JBr(c)Prince Say More 2.00
4 EC/GP(c)Alt.Universe #1 . . . . . . 2.00
5 EC,Alt.Universe #2 . . . . 2.00
6 `Ferment',A:MacFurline' 2.00
7 EC,V:Viral Worm 2.00
8 EC,BAT-BAT:Year One,

Mighty Mouse #3
© Marvel Entertainment Group

O:Bug Wonder 2.00
9 EC,BAT-BAT:Year One,
V:Smoker 2.00
10 `Night o/t Rating Lunatics' 2.00

MILLIE THE MODEL
Winter, 1945
1 O:Millie the Model,
Bowling(c) 550.00
2 Totem Pole(c) 300.00
3 Anti-Noise(c) 200.00
4 Bathing Suit(c) 200.00
5 Blame it on Fame 200.00
6 Beauty and the Beast 200.00
7 Bathing Suit(c) 200.00
8 Fancy Dress(c),HK,Hey Look . 200.00
9 Paris(c),BW 225.00
10 Jewelry(c),HK,Hey Look. 175.00
11 HK,Giggles and Grins 125.00
12 A;Rusty,Hedy Devine 100.00
13 A;Hedy Devine,HK,Hey Look . 125.00
14 HK,Hey Look 125.00
15 HK,Hey Look 100.00
16 HK,Hey Look 100.00
17 thru 20 . . . . @80.00
21 thru 30 . . . . @60.00
31 thru 75 . . . . @50.00
76 thru 99 . . . . @35.00
100 . . . . 40.00
101 thru 126 . . . . @30.00
127 Millie/Clicker 35.00
128 A:Scarlet Mayfair 30.00
129 The Truth about Agnes 30.00
130 thru 153 . . . . @30.00
154 B:New Millie. 30.00
155 thru 206 . . . . @30.00
207 Dec., 1973. . . . . 30.00
Ann.#1 How Millie Became
a Model 160.00
Ann.#2 Millies Guide to
the world of Modeling 125.00
Ann.#3 Many Lives of Millie 75.00
Ann.#4 Many Lives of Millie 30.00

MISS AMERICA COMICS
1944
1 Miss America(c),pin-ups . . . 1,200.00

MISS AMERICA MAGAZINE
Nov., 1944—Nov., 1958
2 Ph(c),Miss America costume
I;Patsy Walker,Buzz Baxter,
Hedy Wolfe 1,000.00
3 Ph(c),A:Patsy Walker,Miss
America. 400.00
4 Ph(c),Betty Page,A:Patsy
Walker,Miss America 400.00
5 Ph(c),A:Patsy Walker,Miss
America 400.00
6 Ph(c),A:Patsy Walker 85.00
7 Patsy Walker stories 50.00
8 same 50.00
9 same 50.00
10 same 50.00
11 same 50.00
12 same 50.00
13 thru 18 . . . . @50.00
21 . . . . 55.00
22 thru 45 . . . . @35.00
46 thru 93 . . . . @30.00

MISS FURY COMICS
Timely Winter, 1942-43
1 Newspaper strip reprints,
ASh(c) O:Miss Fury 3,000.00
2 V:Nazis(c) 1,400.00
3 Hitler/Nazi Flag(c) 1,100.00
4 ASh(c),Japanese(c) 850.00
5 ASh(c),Gangster(c) 800.00
6 Gangster(c) 750.00
7 Gangster(c) 700.00
8 Atom-Bomb Secrets(c)
Winter, 1946 . . . . 650.00

MISTY
Star Dec., 1985
1 F:Millie the Models Niece 2.00
2 thru 5 . . . . @2.00
6 May, 1986 . . . . 2.00

MITZI COMICS
Timely Spring, 1948
1 HK:Hey Look,Giggles
and Grins 150.00
Becomes:

MITZI'S BOYFRIEND
2 F:Chip,Mitzi/Chip(c) 75.00
3 Chips adventures 50.00
4 thru 7 same . . . . @50.00
Becomes:

MITZI'S ROMANCES
8 Mitzi/Chip(c) 75.00
9 . . . . 50.00
10 Dec., 1949. . . . . 50.00

MODELING WITH MILLIE
See: DATE WITH MILLIE

MOEBIUS
Epic Oct., 1987
1 . . . . 12.00
2 . . . . 12.00
3 . . . . 15.00
4 . . . . 12.00
5 . . . . 12.00
6 1988 . . . . 12.00

MOEBIUS: FUSION
1 128pg Sketchbook 19.95

MOLLY MANTON'S ROMANCES
Sept., 1949
1 Ph(c),Dare Not Marry 100.00
2 Ph(c),Romances of 75.00
Becomes:

ROMANTIC AFFAIRS
3 Ph(c) 50.00

MONSTER MENACE
1 thru 4 SD,rep. . . . . @2.00

Frankenstein #13
© Marvel Entertainment Group

MONSTER OF FRANKENSTEIN
Jan., 1973
1 MP,Frankenstein's Monster 40.00
2 MP,Bride of the Monster 25.00
3 MP,Revenge. 25.00
4 MP,Monster's Death 25.00
5 MP,The Monster Walks
Among Us. 25.00
Becomes:

FRANKENSTEIN
1973–75
6 MP,Last of the Frankensteins . . 18.00
7 JB,The Fiend and the Fury . . . 18.00
8 JB,A:Dracula 30.00
9 JB,A:Dracula 30.00
10 JB,Death Strikes Frankenstein . 15.00
11 Carnage at CastleFrankenstein 10.00
12 Frankenstein's Monster today . 10.00
13 Undying Fiend 10.00
14 Fury of the Night Creature 10.00
15 Trapped in a Nightmare 10.00
16 The Brute and the Berserker . . 10.00
17 Phoenix Aflame 10.00
18 Children of the Damned
Sept., 1975. . . . . 10.00

MONSTERS ON THE PROWL
See: CHAMBER OF DARKNESS

MONSTERS UNLEASHED
July, 1973
1 GM(c),GC,DW,B&W Mag 30.00

MARVEL

2 JB,FB,BEv,B:Frankenstein 25.00
3 NA(c),GK,GM,GT,B:Man-Thing 25.00
4 JB,GC,BK,I:Satana 25.00
5 JB 15.00
6 MP 15.00
7 AW 15.00
8 GP,NA 20.00
9 A:Wendigo 20.00
10 O:Tigra 20.00
11 FB(C),April, 1975 . . . . 20.00
Ann.#1 GK 20.00

MOON KNIGHT

[1st Regular Series] Nov., 1980

1 BSz,O:Moon Knight 5.00
2 BSz,V:Slasher 3.50
3 BSz,V:Midnight Man 3.50
4 BSz,V:Committee of 5 . . . . 3.50
5 BSz,V:Red Hunter 3.50
6 BSz,V:White Angels 3.50
7 BSz,V:Moon Kings 3.50
8 BSz,V:Moon Kings, Drug 3.00
9 BSz,V:Midnight Man 3.00
10 BSz,V:Midnight Man 3.00
11 BSz,V:Creed (Angel Dust) 3.00
12 BSz,V:Morpheus 3.00
13 BSz,A:Daredevil & Jester. 3.00
14 BSz,V:Stained Glass Scarlet . . . 3.00
15 FM(c),BSz,1st Direct 3.50
16 V:Blacksmith 3.00
17 BSz,V:Master Sniper 3.00
18 BSz,V:Slayers Elite 3.00
19 BSz,V:Arsenal 3.00
20 BSz,V:Arsenal 3.00
21 A:Bother Voodoo 2.25
22 BSz,V:Morpheus 2.50
23 BSz,V:Morpheus 2.50
24 BSz,V:Stained Glass Scarlet . . . 2.50
25 BSz,Black Specter. 2.50
26 KP,V:Cabbie Killer 2.00
27 A:Kingpin. 2.00
28 BSz,"Spirits in the Sands" 2.00
29 BSz,V:Werewolf. 2.50
30 BSz,V:Werewolf. 2.50
31 TA,V:Savage Studs 2.00
32 KN,Druid Walsh 2.00
33 KN,V:Druid Walsh 2.00
34 KN,Marc Spector 2.00
35 KN,X-Men,FF,V:The Fly
DoubleSized. 3.00
36 A:Dr.Strange 2.00
37 V:Zohar 2.00

Moon Knight #36
© Marvel Entertainment Group

38 V:Zohar 2.00

[2nd Regular Series] 1985

1 O:Moon Knight,DoubleSize. 2.00
2 Yucatan 2.00
3 V:Morpheus 2.00
4 A:Countess. 2.00
5 V:Lt.Flint. 2.00
6 GI,LastIssue 2.00

[3rd Regular Series] 1989–94

1 V:Bushmaster. 4.00
2 A:Spider-Man 3.00
3 V:Bushmaster. 2.50
4 RH,A:Midnight,Black Cat 2.50
5 V:Midnight,BlackCat 2.50
6 A:BrotherVoodoo 2.50
7 A:BrotherVoodoo 2.50
8 TP,A:Punisher,A of V 3.00
9 TP,A:Punisher,A of V 3.00
10 V:Killer Shrike,A of V 2.00
11 TP,V:Arsenal 2.00
12 TP,V:Bushman,A:Arsenal 2.00
13 TP,V:Bushman. 2.00
14 TP,V:Bushman. 2.00
15 TP,Trial o/Marc Spector #1,A:
Silv.Sable,Sandman,Paladin . . . 3.00
16 TP,Trial o/Marc Spector #2,A:
Silv.Sable,Sandman,Paladin . . . 3.00
17 TP,Trial o/Marc Spector #3. . . . . 3.00
18 TP,Trial o/Marc Spector #4. . . . . 3.00
19 RLd(c),TP,SpM,Punisher 3.00
20 TP,A:Spider-Man,Punisher 3.00
21 TP,Spider-Man,Punisher 3.00
22 I:Harbinger 2.00
23 Confrontation. 2.00
24 A:Midnight 2.00
25 MBa,TP,A:Ghost Rider. 3.00
26 BSz(c),TP,B:Scarlet Redemption
V:Stained Glass Scarlet 2.00
27 TP,V:Stained Glass Scarlet 2.00
28 TP,V:Stained Glass Scarlet 2.00
29 TP,V:Stained Glass Scarlet 2.00
30 TP,V:Stained Glass Scarlet 2.00
31 TP,E:Scarlet Redemption,
A:Hobgoblin 2.50
32 TP,V:Hobgoblin,SpM(in Black) . . 3.00
33 TP,V:Hobgoblin,A:Spider-Man . . 3.00
34 V:Killer Shrike 2.00
35 TP,Return of Randall Spector
Pt.1,A:Punisher 2.00
36 TP,A:Punisher,Randall 2.00
37 TP,A:Punisher,Randall 2.00
38 TP,A:Punisher,Randall 2.00
39 TP,N:Moon Knight,A:Dr.Doom . . 2.00
40 TP,V:Dr.Doom 2.00
41 TP,Infinity War,I:Moonshade. . . . 2.00
42 TP,Infinity War,V:Moonshade . . . 2.00
43 TP(i),Infinity War 2.00
44 Inf.War,A:Dr.Strange.FF 2.00
45 V:Demogoblin 2.00
46 V:Demogoblin 2.00
47 Legacy Quest Scenario 2.00
48 I:Deadzone 2.00
49 V:Deadzone. 2.00
50 A:Avengers,I:Hellbent,
Die-cut(c) 3.50
51 A:Gambit,V:Hellbent 2.00
52 A:Gambit,Werewolf 2.00
53 "Pang" 2.00
54 . . . . 2.00
55 SPa,V:Sunstreak 6.00
56 SPa,V:Seth 6.00
57 SPa,Inf.Crusade 4.00
58 SPa(c),A:Hellbent 3.00
59 SPa(c), ... 3.00
60 E:TKa(s),SPa,D:Moonknight . . . 4.00
Spec.#1 ANi,A:Shang-Chi. 2.50
1-shot Moon Knight: Divided We Fall
DCw,V:Bushman (1992) 4.95

MOON KNIGHT

(Special Edition) Nov., 1983

1 BSz,reprints 2.00
2 BSz,reprints 2.00
3 BSz,reprints,Jan., 1984. . . . . 2.00

MOON KNIGHT

Nov. 1997–Feb., 1998

1 (of 4) DgM, Moon Knight returns. 2.50
1 signed by Tommy Lee Edwards
(250 copies) 20.00
2 DgM,A:Scarlet 2.50
3 DgM,Resurrection War,V:Black
Spectre 2.50
4 DgM,Resurrecton War, concl. . . . 2.50

MOON KNIGHT

Dec., 1998

1 (of 4) DgM,MT,A:Marlene 3.00
2 DgM,MT. 3.00
3 DgM,MT 3.00
4 DgM,MT,concl. 3.00

MOONSHADOW

Epic May, 1985

1 JMu,O:Moonshadow. 5.50
2 JMu,Into Space 3.50
3 JMu,The Looney Bin. 3.50
4 JMu,Fights Ira 3.50
5 JMu,Prisoner 3.50
6 JMu,Hero of War 3.50
7 JMu,UnkshussFamily 3.50
8 JMu,Social Outcast. 3.50
9 JMu,Search For Ira. 3.50
10 JMu,Internat.House of T 3.50
11 JMu,UnkshussFamily. 3.50
12 JMu,UnkshussFamily,Feb.1987 . 3.50

MORBIUS

1992–95

1 V:Lilith,Lilin,A:Blaze,Gh.Rider,
Rise o/t Midnight Sons #3,
polybagged w/poster 3.00
2 V:Simon Stroud 2.50
3 A:Spider-Man 2.00
4 I:Dr.Paine,C:Spider-Man 2.00
5 V:Basilisk,(inc Superman tribute
on letters page) 2.00
6 V:Basilisk 2.00
7 V:Vic Slaughter. 2.00
8 V:Nightmare 2.00
9 V:Nightmare 2.00
10 Two Tales 2.00
11 A:Nightstalkers. 2.00
12 Midnight Massacre#4. . . . . 2.50
13 R:Martine,A:Lilith 2.00
14 RoW,V:Nightmare,A:Werewolf . . 2.00
15 A:Ghost Rider,Werewolf. 2.00
16 GWt(s),Siege of Darkness#5 . . . 2.00
17 GWt(s),Siege of Darkness#17 . . 2.00
18 GWt(s),A:Deathlok. 2.00
19 GWt(s),A:Deathlok. 2.00
20 GWt(s),I:Bloodthirst 2.00
21 B:Dance of the Hunter,A:SpM . . 2.25
22 A:Spider-Man 2.25
23 E:Dance of the Hunter,A:SpM . . 2.25
24 Return of the Dragon. 2.25
25 RoW 2.50
26 . . . . 2.00
27 . . . . 2.00
28 A:Werewolf 2.00
29 . . . . 2.00
30 New Morbius 2.00
31 A:Mortine. 2.00
32 Another Kill 2.00

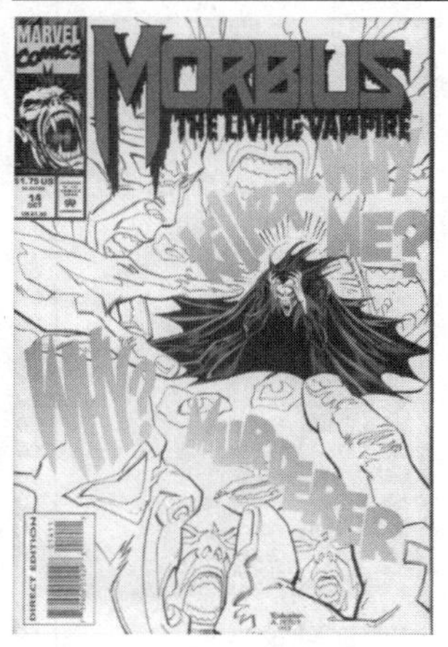

Morbius #14
© Marvel Entertainment Group

MORBIUS REVISITED

1993

1 WMc,rep.Fear #20 . . . . 2.00
2 WMc,rep.Fear #28 . . . . 2.00
3 WMc,rep.Fear #29 . . . . 2.00
4 WMc,rep.Fear #30 . . . . 2.00
5 WMc,rep.Fear #31 . . . . 2.00

MORT THE DEAD TEENAGER

1993–94

1 LHa(s),I:Mort 2.00
2 thru 4 LHa(s), ... 2.00

MOTHER TERESA

1984

1 Mother Teresa Story 2.00

MOTOR MOUTH & KILLPOWER

Marvel UK 1992–93

1 GFr,A:Nick Fury,I:Motor Mouth,Killpower 2.50
2 GFr,A:Nick Fury, ... 2.00
3 GFr,V:Killpower,A:Punisher 2.00
4 GFr,A:Nick Fury,Warheads, Hell's Angel,O:Killpower 2.00
5 GFr,A:Excalibur,Archangel 2.00
6 GFr,A:Cable,Punisher 2.00
7 EP,A:Cable,Nick Fury 2.00
8 JFr,A:Cable,Nick Fury 2.00
9 JFr,A:Cable,N.Fury,V:Harpies . . . 2.00
10 V:Red Sonja 2.00
11 V:Zachary Sorrow 2.00
12 A:Death's Head II 2.00
13 A:Death's Head II 2.00

MS. MARVEL

Jan., 1977

1 JB,O:Ms Marvel 7.00
2 JB,JSt,V:Scorpion 5.00
3 JB,JSt,V:Doomsday Man 3.00
4 JM,JSt,V:Destructor 3.00
5 JM,JSt,A:V:Vision 3.00
6 JM,JSt,V:Grotesk 3.00
7 JM,JSt,V:Modok 3.00
8 JM,JSt,V:Grotesk 3.00
9 KP,JSt,I:Deathbird 5.00
10 JB,TP,V:Deathbird,Modok 3.00
11 V:Elementals 3.00
12 V:Hecate 3.00
13 Bedlam in Boston 2.00
14 V:Steeplejack. 2.00
15 V:Tigershark 2.00
16 V:Tigershark,A:Beast 14.00
17 . . . . 6.00
18 I:Mystique,A;Avengers 17.00
19 A:Captain Marvel. 3.00
20 V:Lethal Lizards,N:Ms.Marvel . . 2.00
21 V:Lethal Lizards. 2.00
22 V:Deathbirds 2.00
23 The Woman who Fell to Earth April, 1979 . . . . 2.00

MUPPET BABIES

Star August, 1984

1 thru 10 . . . . @2.00
11 thru 20 . . . . @2.00
21 thru 25 July, 1989 . . . . @2.00

MUPPETS TAKE MANHATTAN

1 movie adapt,November, 1984 . . . 2.00
2 movie adapt 2.00
3 movie adapt,Jan., 1985 . . . . 2.00

MUTANTS: THE AMAZING X-MEN

1 X-Men After Xavier 3.50
2 Exodus, Dazzler,V:Abyss 2.25
3 F:Bishop. 2.00
4 V:Apocalypse 2.00

MUTANTS: THE ASTONISHING X-MEN

1 Uncanny X-Men 3.50
2 V:Holocaust 2.25
3 V:Abyss 2.00
4 V:Beast,Infinities. 2.00

MUTANTS: GENERATION NEXT

1 Generation X Ax. 3.50
2 Genetic Slave Pens 2.25
3 V:Sugar Man 2.00
4 V:Sugar Man 2.00

MUTANT X

Aug., 1998

1 HMe,TR,F:Havok, 48pg 3.00
2 HMe,TR,F:Havok 2.00
2a variant cover. 2.00
3 HMe,TR,V:Pack 2.00
4 HMe,TR,V:Goblin Queen 2.00
5 HMe,F:Brute, Fallen 2.00
6 HMe,A:Mutant-X Spider-Man . . . 2.00
7 HMe,Trial of the Brute. 2.00
8 HMe,V:Goblin Queen 2.00
9 HMe,V:Sentinels. 2.00
10 HMe,V:The Six 2.00
11 HMe,Bloodstorm vs. Havok 2.00
12 HMe,O:Goblin Queen,Havok, 48-page 3.00
13 O:Bloodstorm 2.00
14 HMe,CNr,I:Cyclops 2.00
15 HMe,F:Havok 2.00
16 HMe 2.00
17 HMe,CNr,V:Cyclops 2.00
18 HMe,CNr,A:Punisher 2.00
19 HMe,A:Professor X 2.00
20 HMe,A:Havok 2.25
21 HMe,BS,Prof.X & Apocalypse . . 2.25
22 HMe,BS,Galactus 2.25

Mutant X #4
© Marvel Entertainment Group

23 HMe,TL,Apocalypse. 2.25
24 HMe,TL,Master Planner. 2.25
25 HMe,TL,The Six,48-pg. 3.00
26 HMe,TL,The Six,Bloodstorm . . . 2.25
GN Mutant X, rep.#1 & #2 . . . . . . 6.00
Ann. 1999, 48-page 3.50
Ann.2000 HMe,secrets 3.50

MUTATIS

Epic

1 I:Mutatis 2.25
2 O:Mutatis 2.25
3 A:Mutatis 2.25

MY DIARY

Dec., 1949–March, 1950

1 Ph(c),The Man I Love 100.00
2 Ph(c),I Was Anybody's Girl 75.00

MY LOVE

July, 1949

1 Ph(c),One Heart to Give 100.00
2 Ph(c),Hate in My Heart 50.00
3 Ph(c), ... 50.00
4 Ph(c),Betty Page, April,1950. . 225.00

MY LOVE

Sept., 1969

1 Love story reprints 40.00
2 thru 9 . . . . @20.00
10 . . . . 30.00
11 thru 38 . . . . @15.00
39 March, 1976 . . . . 15.00

MY ROMANCE

Sept., 1948

1 Romance Stories 100.00
2 . . . . 55.00
3 . . . . 55.00

Becomes:

MY OWN ROMANCE

4 Romance Stories Continue . . . 100.00
5 thru 10 . . . . @50.00
11 thru 20 . . . . @40.00
21 thru 50 . . . . @35.00
51 thru 54 . . . . @30.00
55 ATh 40.00
56 thru 60 . . . . @30.00

61 thru 70 . . . . @25.00
71 AW 55.00
72 thru 76 . . . . @25.00
Becomes:

TEENAGE ROMANCE

77 Romance Stories Continue . . . 25.00
78 thru 85 . . . . @25.00
86 March, 1962 . . . . 25.00

MYS-TECH WARS
Marvel UK 1993

1 BHi,A:FF,X-Men,Avengers 2.00
2 A:FF,X-Men,X-Force 2.00
3 BHi,A:X-Men,X-Force 2.00
4 A:Death's Head II 2.00

MYSTERY TALES
Atlas March, 1952

1 GC,Horror Strikes at Midnight . 650.00
2 BK,BEv,OW,The Corpse is Mine 350.00
3 RH,GC,JM, The Vampire Strikes 250.00
4 Funeral of Horror 250.00
5 Blackout at Midnight 250.00
6 . . . . 250.00
7 JRo,The Ghost Hunter 250.00
8 BEv 250.00
9 BEv(c),the Man in the Morgue 250.00
10 BEV(c),GT,What Happened to Harry 250.00
11 BEv(c) 200.00
12 GT,MF 225.00
13 . . . . 200.00
14 BEv(c),GT 200.00
15 RH(c),EK 200.00
16 . . . . 200.00
17 RH(c) 200.00
18 AW,DAy,GC 210.00
19 . . . . 185.00
20 Electric Chair 185.00
21 JF,MF,BP,Decapitation 200.00
22 JF,MF 200.00
23 thru 27 . . . . @150.00
28 . . . . 125.00
29 thru 32 . . . . @135.00
33 BEv 125.00
34 . . . . 125.00
35 BEv,GC 125.00
36 . . . . 135.00
37 DW,BP,JR 125.00
38 BP 125.00
39 BK 135.00
40 . . . . 135.00
41 MD,BEv 125.00
42 . . . . 125.00
41 GC 125.00
44 AW 150.00
45 SD 135.00
46 RC,SD,JP 150.00
47 DAy,BP 150.00
48 . . . . 125.00
49 GM,AT,DAy 125.00
50 JO,AW,GM 150.00
51 DAy,JO 150.00
52 . . . . 125.00
53 . . . . 125.00
54 RC,August, 1957 . . . . 150.00

MYSTICAL TALES
Atlas June, 1956

1 BEv,BP,JO,Say the Magical Words 350.00
2 BEv(c),JO,Black Blob 200.00
3 BEv(c),RC,Four Doors To . . . 175.00
4 BEv(c).The Condemned 175.00
5 AW,Meeting at Midnight 175.00
6 BK,AT,He Hides in the Tower . 150.00
7 BEv,JF,JO,AT,FBe,The Haunted Tower 150.00
8 BK,SC, Stone Walls Can't Stop Him,August, 1957 . . . . 150.00

MYSTIC COMICS
Timely March, 1940
[1st Series]

1 ASh(c),O;The Blue Blaze,Dynamic Man,Flexo,B:Dakor the Magician A:Zephyr Jones,3X's,Deep Sea Demon,Bondage(c) 13,000.00
2 ASh(c),B:The Invisible Man Mastermind, ... 3,500.00
3 ASh(c),O:Hercules 2,500.00
4 ASh(c),O:Thin Man,Black Widow E:Hercules,Blue Blazes,Dynamic Man,Flexo,Invisible Man . . 2,800.00
5 ASh(c)O:The Black Marvel, Blazing Skull,Super Slave Terror,Sub-Earth Man 2,500.00
6 ASh(c),O:The Challenger, B:The Destroyer 2,800.00
7 S&K(c),B:The Witness,O:Davey and the Demon,E;The Black Widow,Hitler(c) 3,000.00
8 Bondage(c) 1,500.00
9 MSy,DRi,Hitler/Bondage(c) . 1,500.00
10 E:Challenger,Terror 1,500.00

[2nd Series] Oct., 1944

1 B:The Angel,Human Torch, Destroyer,Terry Vance, Tommy Tyme,Bondage(c) . 1,800.00
2 E:Human Torch,Terry Vance,Bondage(c) 1,000.00
3 E:The Angel,Tommy Tyme Bondage(c) 900.00
4 ASh(c),A:Young Allies Winter, 1944-45 . . . . 800.00

MYSTIC
[3rd Series] March, 1951

1 MSy,Strange Tree 700.00
2 MSy,Dark Dungeon 400.00
3 GC,Jaws of Creeping Death . 300.00
4 BW,MSy,The Den of the Devil Bird 600.00
5 MSy,Face 225.00
6 BW,She Wouldn't Stay Dead . 600.00
7 GC,Untold Horror waits in the Tomb 225.00
8 DAy(c),BEv,GK,A Monster Among Us 225.00
9 BEv 225.00
10 GC 225.00
11 JR,The Black Gloves 200.00
12 GC 200.00
13 In the Dark 200.00
14 The Corpse and I 200.00
15 GT,JR,House of Horror 200.00
16 A Scream in the Dark 200.00
17 BEv,Behold the Vampire 200.00
18 BEv(c),The Russian Devil . . . 200.00
19 Swamp Girl 200.00
20 RH(c) 200.00
21 BEv(c),GC 150.00
22 RH(c) 150.00
23 RH(c),RA,Chilling Tales 150.00
24 GK,How Many Times Can You Die 150.00
25 RH(c),RA,E.C.Swipe 150.00
26 Severed Head(c) 150.00
27 Who Walks with a Zombie . . . 135.00
28 DW,Not Enough Dead 135.00
29 SMo,The Unseen 135.00
30 RH(c),DW 135.00
31 SC,JKz 135.00
32 The Survivor 135.00
33 thru 36 . . . . @135.00
37 thru 51 . . . . @125.00
52 WW 150.00
53 thru 57 . . . . @125.00
58 thru 60 . . . . @140.00
61 . . . . 125.00

'NAM, THE
Dec., 1986

1 MGo,Vietnam War 3.00
1a 2nd printing 2.00
2 MGo,Dust Off 2.50
3 MGo,Three Day Pass 2.00
4 MGo,TV newscrew 2.00
5 MGo,Top Sgt. 2.00
6 MGo,Monsoon 2.00
7 MGo,Cedar Falls 2.00
8 MGo,5th to the 1st 2.00
9 MGo,ActionIssue 2.00
10 MGo,Saigon 2.00
11 MGo,Christmas 2.00
12 MGo,AgentOrange 2.00
13 MGo 2.00
14 . . . . 2.00
15 ReturningVets 2.00
16 . . . . 2.00
17 Vietcong 2.00
18 . . . . 2.00
19 . . . . 2.00
20 . . . . 2.00
21 . . . . 2.00
22 Thanksgiving 2.00
23 XmasTruce of'67 . . . . 2.00
24 TetOffensive 2.00
25 TetOffensive-KheSanh 2.00
26 HomefrontIssue 2.00
27 Candle in the Wind 2.00
28 Borderline 2.00
29 PeaceTalks 2.00
30 TheBunker 2.00
31 Fire and Ice 2.00
32 Nam in America 2.00
33 SpecialistDaniels 2.00
34 OperationPhoenix 2.00
35 Xmas-BobHope 2.00
36 RacialTension 2.00
37 Colorblind 2.00
38 Minefields 2.00
39 . . . . 2.00
40 . . . . 2.00
41 ,A:Thor,Iron Man, Cap.Am 2.00
42 . . . . 2.00
43 . . . . 2.00

'Nam #15
© Marvel Entertainment Group

44 SDr 2.00
45 . . . . 2.00
46 . . . . 2.00
47 TD. 2.00
48 TD. 2.00
49 Donut Dolly #1. . . . . 2.00
50 HT,Donut Dolly #2 DoubSz 2.50
51 HT,Donut Dolly #3 . . . . 2.00
52 Frank Castle(Punisher)#1 . . . . . 3.00
52a 2nd printing 2.00
53 Punisher #2. . . . . 2.50
54 Death of Joe Hallen #1 . . . . 2.00
55 TD,Death of Joe Hallen #2. . . . . 2.00
56 TD,Death of Joe Hallen #3. . . . . 2.00
57 TD,Death of Joe Hallen #4. . . . . 2.00
58 TD,Death of Joe Hallen #5. . . . . 2.00
59 P.O.W. Story #1 . . . . 2.00
60 P.O.W. Story #2. . . . . 2.00
61 P.O.W. Story #3. . . . . 2.00
62 Speed & Ice,pt.1 . . . . 2.00
63 Speed & Ice,pt.2 . . . . 2.00
64 Speed & Ice,pt.3 . . . . 2.00
65 Speed & Ice,pt.4 . . . . 2.00
66 RH,Speed & Ice,pt.5 . . . . 2.00
67 A:Punisher. 2.25
68 A:Punisher. 2.25
69 A:Punisher. 2.25
70 Don Lomax writes 2.00
71 Vietnamese Point of View 2.00
72 The trials of war. 2.00
73 War on the Homefront 2.00
74 Seige at An Loc. 2.00
75 My Lai Massacre 2.25
76 R:Rob Little 2.00
77 Stateside 2.00
78 . . . . 2.00
79 Beginning of the End#1 . . . . 2.00
80 MGo(c),'68 Tet Offensive 2.00
81 MGo(c),TET Offensive ends. . . . 2.00
82 TET Offensive 2.00
83 thru 84 Last issue 2.00
TPB rep. #1–#4 (1999) 14.95

'NAM MAGAZINE, THE

(B&W) Aug., 1988–May, 1989

1 Reprints 3.00
2 thru 10 . . . . @2.50

NAMORA

Fall, 1948

1 BEv,DR 1,800.00
2 BEv,A:Sub-Mariner,Blonde
Phantom 1,100.00
3 BEv,A:Sub-Mariner,
Dec.,1948 . . . . 1,000.00

NAMOR THE SUB-MARINER

April, 1990

1 JBy,BWi,I:Desmond
& Phoebe Marrs 3.50
2 JBy,BWi,V:Griffin 2.50
3 JBy,BWi,V:Griffin 2.50
4 JBy,A:Reed & Sue Richards,
Tony Stark 2.50
5 JBy,A:FF,IronMan,C:Speedball . . 2.50
6 JBy,V:Sluj 2.50
7 JBy,V:Sluj 2:50
8 JBy,V:Headhunter,R:D.Rand. . . . 2.50
9 JBy,V:Headhunter. 2.50
10 JBy,V:Master Man,Warrior
Woman 2.00
11 JBy,V:Mast.Man,War.Woman . . . 2.00
12 JBy,R:Invaders,Spitfire. 2.00
13 JBy,Namor on Trial,A:Fantastic
Four,Captain America,Thor. . . . 2.00
14 JBy,R:Lady Dorma,A:Kazar
Griffin 2.00

Namor The Sub Mariner #57
© Marvel Entertainment Group

15 JBy,A:Iron Fist 2.00
16 JBy,A:Punisher,V:Iron Fist 2.00
17 JBy,V:Super Skrull(Iron Fist) . . . 2.00
18 JBy,V:SuperSkrull,A:Punisher . . 2.00
19 JBy,V:Super Skrull,D:D.Marrs. . . 2.00
20 JBy,Search for Iron Fist,
O:Namorita. 2.00
21 JBy,Visit to K'un Lun 2.00
22 JBy,Fate of Iron Fist,
C:Wolverine 2.00
23 JBy,BWi,Iron Fist Contd.,
C:Wolverine 2.00
24 JBy,BWi,V:Wolverine 2.50
25 JBy,BWi,V:Master Khan 2.00
26 JaL,BWi,Search For Namor 5.00
27 JaL,BWi,V:Namorita. 4.00
28 JaL,BWi,A:Iron Fist 3.00
29 JaL,BWi,After explosion. 2.50
30 JaL,A:Doctor Doom 2.50
31 JaL,V:Doctor Doom 2.50
32 JaL,V:Doctor Doom,
Namor regains memory 2.50
33 JaL,V:Master Khan 2.00
34 JaL,R:Atlantis 2.00
35 JaL,V:Tiger Shark 2.00
36 JaL,I:Suma-Ket,A:Tiger Shark . . 2.00
37 JaL,Blue Holo-Grafix,Altantean
Civil War,N:Namor 2.50
38 JaL,O:Suma-Ket 2.00
39 A:Tigershark,V:Suma-Ket. 2.00
40 V:Suma-Ket. 2.00
41 V:War Machine 2.00
42 MCW,A:Stingray,V:Dorcas 2.00
43 MCW,V:Orka,Dorcas 2.00
44 I:Albatross 2.00
45 GI,A:Sunfire,V:Attuma 2.00
46 GI,. 2.00
47 GI,Starblast #2 . . . . 2.00
48 GI,Starblast #9,A:FF 2.00
49 GI,A:Ms. Marrs 2.00
50 GI,Holo-grafx(c),A:FF. 3.00
50a Newsstand Ed. 2.00
51 AaL, ... 2.00
52 GI,I:Sea Leopard 2.00
53 GI,V:Sea Leopard 2.00
54 GI,I:Llyron 2.00
55 GI,V:Llyron 2.00
56 GI,V:Llyron 2.00
57 A:Capt. America, V:Llyron 2.00
58 . . . . 2.00
59 GI,V:Abomination. 2.00
60 A:Morgan Le Fay. 2.00
61 Atlantis Rising 2.00
62 V:Triton 2.00
Ann.#1 Subterran.Odyssey #3 . . . . 2.00
Ann.#2 Return o/Defenders,pt.3 . . . 4.00
Ann.#3 I:Assassin,A:Iron Fist,
w/Trading card 3.25
Ann.#4 V:Hydra 3.25

NAVY ACTION

August, 1954

1 US Navy War Stories 125.00
2 Navy(c) 75.00
3 thru 17 . . . . @50.00
18 August, 1957. . . . . 50.00

NAVY COMBAT

Atlas June, 1955

1 DH,B;Torpedo Taylor. 125.00
2 DH 75.00
3 DH 50.00
4 DH 50.00
5 DH 50.00
6 A:Battleship Burke 50.00
7 thru 10 . . . . @50.00
11 MD 40.00
12 RC. 75.00
13 . . . . 45.00
14 . . . . 50.00
15 . . . . 45.00
16 . . . . 45.00
17 AW 65.00
18 . . . . 45.00
19 . . . . 45.00
20 Oct., 1958 . . . . 45.00

NAVY TALES

Atlas Jan., 1957

1 BEv(c),BP,Torpedoes 125.00
2 AW,RC,One Hour to Live 100.00
3 JSe(c) 75.00
4 JSe(c),GC,JSt,RC,July, 1957 . . 75.00

NELLIE THE NURSE

Atlas 1945

1 Beach(c) 300.00
2 Nellie's Date(c) 150.00
3 Swimming Pool(c) 100.00
4 Roller Coaster(c) 100.00
5 Hospital(c),HK,Hey Look. 100.00
6 Bedside Manner(c) 100.00
7 Comic book(c)A:Georgie 100.00
8 Hospital(c),A:Georgie 100.00
9 BW,Nellie/Swing(c)A:Millie . . . 100.00
10 Bathing Suit(c),A:Millie. 100.00
11 HK,Hey Look 125.00
12 HK,Giggles `n' Grins 100.00
13 HK. 75.00
14 HK. 100.00
15 HK. 100.00
16 HK. 100.00
17 HK.A:Annie Oakley 100.00
18 HK. 100.00
19 . . . . 75.00
20 . . . . 75.00
21 . . . . 60.00
22 . . . . 60.00
23 . . . . 60.00
24 . . . . 60.00
25 . . . . 60.00
26 . . . . 60.00
27 . . . . 60.00
28 HK,Rusty Reprint. 60.00
29 thru 35 . . . . @50.00
36 Oct., 1952 . . . . 50.00

NEW ADVENTURES OF CHOLLY & FLYTRAP

Epic

1 . . . . . 4.95
2 . . . . . 3.95
3 . . . . . 3.95

NEW ETERNALS: APOCALYPSE NOW

Dec., 1999

1-shot JoB,SHa,64-pg. 4.00

NEW MUTANTS, THE

March, 1983

1 BMc,MG,O:New Mutants 5.00
2 BMc,MG,V:Sentinels. 4.00
3 BMc,MG,V:Brood Alien 3.00
4 SB,BMc,A:Peter Bristow 3.00
5 SB,BMc,A:Dark Rider 3.00
6 SB,AG,V:Viper 3.00
7 SB,BMc,V:Axe 3.00
8 SB,BMc,I:Amara Aquilla 3.00
9 SB,TMd,I:Selene 3.00
10 SB,BMc,C:Magma 3.00
11 SB,TMd,I:Magma 3.00
12 SB,TMd,J:Magma 3.00
13 SB,TMd,I:Cypher(Doug Ramsey) A:Kitty Pryde,Lilandra 4.00
14 SB,TMd,J:Magik,A:X-Men 3.00
15 SB,TMd,Mass.Academy. 3.00
16 SB,TMd,V:Hellions,I:Warpath I:Jetstream 4.00
17 SB,TMd,V:Hellions,A:Warpath . . 4.00
18 BSz,V:Demon Bear,I:New Warlock,Magus. 5.00
19 BSz,V:Demon Bear 3.00
20 BSz,V:Demon Bear 3.00
21 BSz,O&J:Warlock,doub.sz 5.00
22 BSz,A:X-Men. 3.50
23 BSz,Sunspot,Cloak & Dagger . . 3.00
24 BSz,A:Cloak & Dagger. 3.00
25 BSz,A:Cloak & Dagger. 6.00
26 BSz,I:Legion(Prof.X's son) 7.00
27 BSz,V:Legion. 4.00
28 BSz,O:Legion 4.00
29 BSz,V:Gladiators,I:Guido (Strong Guy) 3.00
30 BSz,A:Dazzler 3.00
31 BSz,A:Shadowcat 3.00
32 SL,V:Karma. 3.00
33 SL,V:Karma. 3.00
34 SL,V:Amahl Farouk 3.00
35 BSz,J:Magneto 3.00
36 BSz,A:Beyonder 3.00
37 BSz,D:New Mutants. 3.00
38 BSz,A:Hellions. 3.00
39 BSz,A:White Queen. 3.00
40 JG,KB,V:Avengers 3.00
41 JG,TA,Mirage 3.00
42 JG,KB,A:Dazzler 3.00
43 SP,V:Empath,A:Warpath 3.00
44 JG,V:Legion. 5.00
45 JG,A:Larry Bodine 3.00
46 JG,KB,Mutant Massacre 3.50
47 JG,KB,V:Magnus 3.00
48 JG,CR,Future 3.00
49 VM,Future 3.00
50 JG,V:Magus,R:Prof.X. 4.00
51 KN,A:Star Jammers 3.00
52 RL,DGr,Limbo 3.00
53 RL,TA,V:Hellions 3.00
54 SB,TA,N:New Mutants 3.00
55 BBl,TA,V:Aliens 3.00
56 JBr,TA,V:Hellions,A:Warpath . . . 3.00
57 BBl,TA,I&J:Bird-Boy. 3.00
58 BBl,TA,Bird-Boy. 3.00
59 BBl,TA,Fall of Mutants, V:Dr.Animus 3.00
60 BBl,TA,F.of M.,D:Cypher 2.50
61 BBl,TA,Fall of Mutants 2.50
62 JMu,A:Magma,Hellions 2.50
63 BHa,JRu,Magik 2.50
64 BBl,TA,R:Cypher 2.50
65 BBl,TA,V:FreedomForce 2.50
66 BBl,TA,V:Forge 2.50
67 BBl,I:Gosamyr 2.50
68 BBl,V:Gosamyr 2.50
69 BBl,AW,I:Spyder 2.50
70 TSh,AM,V:Spyder 2.50
71 BBl,AW,V:N'Astirh 2.50
72 BBl,A,Inferno 2.50
73 BBl,W,A:Colossus 3.00
74 BBl,W,A:X-Terminators. 2.50
75 JBy,Mc,Black King,V:Magneto . . 3.50
76 RB,TP,J:X-Terminators. 2.50
77 RB,V:Mirage 2.50
78 RL,AW,V:FreedomForce 2.50
79 BBl,AW,V:Hela. 2.50
80 BBl,AW,Asgard 2.50
81 LW,TSh,JRu,A:Hercules. 2.50
82 BBl,AW,Asgard 2.50
83 BBl,Asgard 2.50
84 TSh,AM,A:QueenUla 2.50
85 RLd&TMc(c),BBl,V:Mirage 5.00
86 RLd,BWi,V:Vulture,C:Cable 6.00
87 RLd,BWi,I:Mutant Liberation Front,Cable 15.00
87a 2nd Printing 2.00
88 RLd,2nd Cable,V:Freedom Force 7.00
89 RLd,V:Freedom Force 6.00
90 RLd,A:Caliban,V:Sabretooth . . . 6.00
91 RLd,A:Caliban,Masque, V:Sabretooth 6.00
92 RLd(c),BH,V:Skrulls 4.00
93 RLd,A:Wolverine,Sunfire, V:Mutant Liberation Front 6.00
94 RLd,A:Wolverine,Sunfire, V:Mutant Liberation Front 5.00
95 RLd,Extinction Agenda,V:Hodge A:X-Men,X-Factor,D:Warlock . . 5.00
95a 2nd printing(gold) 5.00
96 RLd,ATb,JRu,Extinction Agenda V:Hodge,A:X-Men,X-Factor . . . 5.00
97 E:LSi(s),RLd(c),JRu,Extinction Agenda,V:Hodge 5.00
98 FaN(s),RLd,I:Deadpool,Domino, Gideon,L:Rictor 9.00
99 FaN(s),RLd,I:Feral,Shatterstar, L:Sunspot,J:Warpath 5.00
100 FaN(s),RLd,J:Feral,Shatterstar, I:X-Force,V:Masque,Imperial Protectorate,A:MLF 6.00

New Mutants #2
© Marvel Entertainment Group

100a 2nd Printing(Gold) 4.00
100b 3rd Printing(Silver) 3.50
Ann.#1 BMc,TP,L.Cheney 7.00
Ann.#2 AD,V:Mojo,I:Psylocke,Meggan (American App.) 9.00
Ann.#3 AD,PN,V:Impossible Man . . 4.00
Ann.#4 JBr,BMc,Evol.Wars 6.00
Ann.#5 RLd,JBg,MBa,KWi,Atlantis Attacks,A:Namorita,I:Surf 8.00
Ann.#6 RLd(c),Days o/Future Present V:FranklinRichards,(Pin-ups) . . 6.00
Ann.#7 JRu,RLd,Kings of Pain, I:Piecemeal & Harness, Pin-ups X-Force 5.00
Spec #1,AAd,TA,Asgard War 6.00
Summer Spec.#1 BBl,Megapolis. . . 3.50
TPB New Mutants: Demon Bear, CCl/BSz,Rep #18–#21 . . . . . 8.95

NEW MUTANTS

Sept., 1997

1 (of 3) BRa,BCh,F:Cannonball, Moonstar, Wolfsbane,Karma & Sunspot 2.50
2 BRa,BCh,meeting with mutants of the past 2.50
3 BRa,BCh, will Magik return for good? 2.50

NEW WARRIORS

July, 1990

1 B:FaN(s),MBa,AW,V:Terrax, O:New Warriors 4.00
1a Gold rep. 2.50
2 FaN(s),MBa,AW,I:Midnight's Fire, Silhouette. 3.50
3 MBa,LMa(i),V:Mad Thinker 3.50
4 MBa,LMa(i),I:Psionex 3.50
5 MBa,LMa(i),V:Star Thief, C:White Queen. 3.50
6 MBa,LMa(i),V:StarThief, A:Inhumans 3.50
7 MBa,LMa(i),V:Bengal, C:Punisher 3.50
8 MBa,LMa(i),V:Punisher, I:Force of Nature 3.50
9 MBa,LMa(i),V:Punisher,Bengal, Force of Nature 3.50
10 MBa,LMa(i),V:Hellions,White Queen,I:New Sphinx. 3.50
11 MBa,LMa(i),V:Sphinx, B:Forever Yesterday. 2.50
12 MBa,LMa(i),V:Sphinx 2.50
13 MBa,LMa(i),V:Sphinx, E:Forever Yesterday. 2.50
14 MBa,LMa(i),A:Namor, Darkhawk. 2.50
15 MBa,LMa(i),V:Psionex, R:Terrax,N:Nova. 2.50
16 MBa,LMa(i),A:Psionex, V:Terrax 2.50
17 MBa,LMa(i),A:Silver Surfer,Fant. Four,V:Terrax,I:Left Hand 2.50
18 MBa,LMa(i),O:Night Thrasher . . 2.00
19 MBa,LMa(i),V:Gideon. 2.00
20 MBa,LMa(i),V:Clan Yashida, Marvel Boy kills his father. 2.00
21 MBa,LMa(i),I:Folding Circle 2.00
22 MBa,LMa(i),A:Darkhawk,Rage . . 2.00
23 MBa,LMa(i),V:Folding Circle. . . . 2.00
24 LMa(i),V:Folding Circle. 2.00
25 MBa,LMa(i),Die-Cut(c),Marvel Boy found guilty of murder,D:Tai, O:Folding Circle 2.50
26 DaR,LMa(i),V:Guardsmen 2.00
27 DaR,LMa(i),Inf.War,Speedball Vs. his doppelganger,N:Rage 2.00
28 DaR,LMa(i),I:Turbo,Cardinal . . . 2.00

 All comics prices listed are for *Near Mint* condition.

New Warriors #11
© Marvel Entertainment Group

29 DaR,LMa(i),V:Trans-Sabal 2.00
30 DaR,LMa(i),V:Trans Sabal 2.00
31 DaR,LMa(i)A:Cannonball,Warpath, Magma,O&N:Firestar 2.00
32 DaR,LMa(i),B:Forces of Darkness, Forces of Light,A:Spider-Man, Archangel,Dr.Strange 2.00
33 DaR,LMa(i),A:Cloak & Dagger, Turbo,Darkhawk 2.00
34 DaR,LMa(i),A:Avengers,SpM, Thing,Torch,Darkhawk, C:Darkling 2.00
35 DaR,LMa(i),A:Turbo 2.00
36 DaR,LMa(i),A:Turbo 2.00
37 F:Marvel Boy,V:Wizard 2.00
38 DaR,LMa(i),D:Rage's granny, V:Poison Memories 2.00
39 DaR,LMa(i),L:Namorita 2.00
40 DaR,LMa(i),B:Starlost, V:Supernova 2.50
40a Newsstand Ed. 2.00
41 DaR,LMa(i),V:Supernova 2.00
42 DaR,LMa(i),E:Starlost,N:Nova, V:Supernova 2.00
43 DaR,LMa(i),N&I:Justice (Marvel Boy). 2.00
44 Ph(c),DaR,LMa(i),N&I:Kymaera (Namorita) 2.00
45 DaR,LMa(i),Child's Play#2, N:Silhouette,Speedball, V:Upstarts 2.00
46 DaR,LMa(i),Child's Play#4, V:Upstarts 2.00
47 DaR,LMa(i),Time&TimeAgain,pt.1, A:Sphinx,I:Powerpax 2.00
48 DaR,LMa(i),Time&TimeAgain,pt.4, J:Cloak&Dagger,Darkhawk,Turbo, Powerpax,Bandit 2.00
49 DaR,LMa(i),Time&TimeAgain,pt.8 V:Sphinx 2.00
50 reg. (c) 2.25
50a Glow-in-the-dark(c),V:Sphinx . . 3.25
51 revamp 2.00
52 R:Psionex 2.00
53 V:Psionex 2.00
54 V:Speedball 2.00
55 V:Soldiers of Misfortune 2.00
56 V:Soldiers 2.00
57 A:Namor 2.00
58 F:Sabra 2.00
59 F:Speedball 2.00
60 Nova Omega,pt.2 . . . . 2.50
61 J:Scarlet Spider,Maximum Clonage prologue 2.00
62 F:Scarlet Spider,Maximum Clonage tie-in 2.00
63 F:Firestar 2.00
64 I:Psionix 2.00
65 F:Scarlet Spider,V:Kymaera 2.00
66 F:Speedball 2.00
67 Nightmare in Scarlet,pt.2 . . . . . . 2.00
68 Future Shock,pt.1 . . . . 2.00
69 . . . . 2.00
70 . . . . 2.00
71 Future Shock,pt.4 . . . . 2.00
Ann.#1 MBa,A:X-Force,V:Harness, Piecemeal,Kings of Pain #2 . . . 4.00
Ann.#2 Hero Killers #4,V:Sphinx . . . 2.75
Ann.#3 LMa(i),E:Forces of Light, Forces of Darkness,I:Darkling w/card 3.25
Ann.#4 DaR(s),V:Psionex 3.25
TPB New Beginnings rep.Thor #411, 412,New Warriors #1-#4 . . . . . 12.95

NEW WARRIORS
Aug., 1999

1 F:Speedball,48-page 3.00
2A DaR 2.50
2B variant Steve Scott (c) 2.50
3 . . . . 2.50
4 . . . . 2.50
5 F:Generation X 2.50
6 F:Night Thrasher, Nova 2.50
7 F:Turbo 2.50
8 A:Iron Fist & Night Thrasher 2.50
9 Iron Man #29 x-over 2.50
10 A:Hercules 2.50

NFL SUPERPRO

1 . . . . 7.00
Spec.#1 reprints 2.00

[Regular Series] Oct., 1991

1 A:Spider-Man,I:Sanzionaire 2.50
2 V:Quickkick 2.00
3 I:Instant Replay 2.00
4 V:Sanction 2.00
5 A:Real NFL Player 2.00
6 Racism Iss.,recalled by Marvel . . 6.00
7 thru 11 . . . . @2.00
12 V:Nefarious forces of evil 2.00

NICK FURY, AGENT OF S.H.I.E.L.D.

[1st Regular Series] June, 1968

1 JSo/JSt,I:Scorpio 75.00
2 JSo,A:Centaurius 40.00
3 JSo,DA,V:Hell Hounds 35.00
4 FS,O:Nick Fury 30.00
5 JSo,V:Scorpio 30.00
6 FS,"Doom must Fall" 15.00
7 FS,V:S.H.I.E.L.D. 15.00
8 FS,Hate Monger 8.00
9 FS,Hate Monger 8.00
10 FS,JCr,Hate Monger 8.00
11 BS(c),FS,Hate Monger 8.00
12 BS 10.00
13 . . . . 6.00
14 . . . . 6.00
15 I:Bullseye 28.00
16 JK,rep. 4.00
17 JK,rep. 4.00
18 JK,rep. 4.00

[Limited Series] 1983–94

1 JSo,rep. 3.00
2 JSo,rep. 2.00

[2nd Regular Series] 1989–93

1 BH,I:New Shield,V:Death's Head(not British hero) 3.00
2 KP,V:Death's Head 2.00

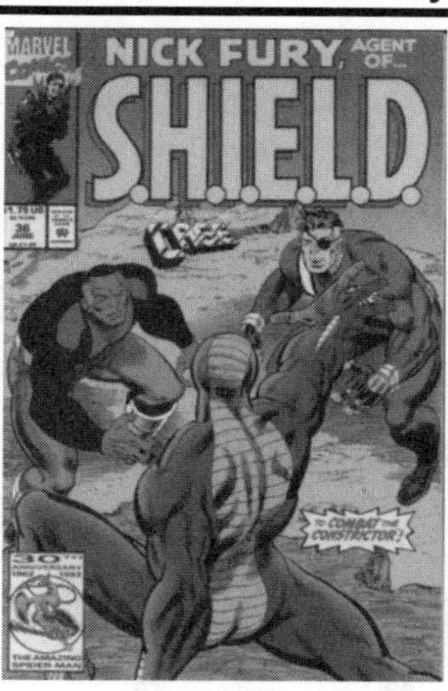

Nick Fury, Agent of S.H.I.E.L.D. #36
© Marvel Entertainment Group

3 KP,V:Death's Head 2.00
4 KP,V:Death's Head 2.00
5 KP,V:Death's Head 2.00
6 KP,V:Death's Head 2.00
7 KP,Chaos Serpent #1 . . . . 2.00
8 KP,Chaos Serpent #2 . . . . 2.00
9 KP,Chaos Serpent #3 . . . . 2.00
10 KP,Chaos Serpent ends, A:Capt.America 2.00
11 D:Murdo MacKay 2.00
12 Hydra Affair #1 . . . . 2.00
13 Hydra Affair #2 . . . . 2.00
14 Hydra Affair #3 . . . . 2.00
15 Apogee of Disaster #1 . . . . 2.00
16 Apogee of Disaster #2 . . . . 2.00
17 Apogee of Disaster #3 . . . . 2.00
18 Apogee of Disaster #4 . . . . 2.00
19 Apogee of Disaster #5 . . . . 2.00
20 JG,A:Red Skull 2.50
21 JG,R:Baron Strucker 2.00
22 JG,A:Baron Strucker,R:Hydra . . . 2.00
23 JG,V:Hydra 2.00
24 A:Capt.Am,Thing,V:Mandarin . . . 2.00
25 JG,Shield Vs. Hydra 2.00
26 JG,A:Baron Strucker, C:Wolverine 2.50
27 JG,V:Hydra,A:Wolverine 2.50
28 V:Hydra,A:Wolverine 2.50
29 V:Hydra,A:Wolverine 2.50
30 R:Leviathan,A:Deathlok 2.00
31 A:Deathlok,V:Leviathan 2.00
32 V:Leviathan 2.00
33 Super-Powered Agents 2.00
34 A:Bridge(X-Force),V:Balance of Terror 2.00
35 A:Cage,V:Constrictor 2.00
36 . . . . 2.00
37 . . . . 2.00
38 Cold War of Nick Fury #1 . . . . . . 2.00
39 Cold War of Nick Fury #2 . . . . . . 2.00
40 Cold War of Nick Fury #3 . . . . . . 2.00
41 Cold War of Nick Fury #4 . . . . . . 2.00
42 I:Strike Force Shield 2.00
43 R:Clay Quatermain 2.00
44 A:Captain America 2.00
45 A:Bridge 2.00
46 V:Gideon,Hydra 2.00
47 V:Baron Strucker,last issue 2.00
TPB Death Duty V:Night Raven . . . 5.95
TPB Captain America 5.95
TPB Scorpion Connection 7.95
TPB JSo, 248-pg 19.95
TPB Scorpio 14.95

MARVEL

Ashcan 75

NICK FURY, VERSUS S.H.I.E.L.D.

June, 1988

1 JSo(c),D:Quartermail 6.00
2 BSz(c),Into The Depths 5.00
3 Uneasy Allies 4.00
4 V:Hydra 4.00
5 V:Hydra 4.00
6 V:Hydra, Dec., 1988 . . . . 4.00
TPB Reprints #1-#6 . . . . 15.95

NIGHTBREED

Epic April, 1990

1 . . . . 4.00
2 . . . . 3.00
3 . . . . 2.50
4 . . . . 2.50
5 JG 2.50
6 BBl,Blasphemers,pt.1 . . . . 2.50
7 JG,Blasphemers,pt.2 . . . . 2.50
8 BBl,MM,Blasphemers,pt.3. . . . . . 2.50
9 BBl,Blasphemers,pt.4 . . . . 2.50
10 BBl,Blasphemers,pt.5 . . . . 2.50
11 South America,pt.1 . . . . 2.25
12 South America,pt.2 . . . . 2.25
13 Emissaries o/Algernon Kinder . . 2.25
14 Rawhead Rex Story. 2.25
15 Rawhead Rex 2.25
16 Rawhead Rex 2.25
17 KN(i),V:Werewolves. 2.25
18 V:Werewolves 2.25
19 V:Werewolves 2.25
20 Trapped in the Forest 2.25
21 V:Ozymandias 2.50
22 V:Ozymandias 2.50
23 F:Peloquin 2.50
24 Search for New Midian 2.50
25 Search for New Midian 2.50
Nightbreed:Genesis, Rep.#1-#4 . . . 9.95

NIGHTCAT

1 DCw,I&O:Night Cat. 4.50

NIGHTCRAWLER

Nov., 1985

1 DC,A;Bamfs 4.00
2 DC 3.00
3 DC,A:Other Dimensional X-Men . 3.00
4 DC,A:Lockheed,V:Dark Bamf
Feb., 1986 . . . . 3.00

NIGHTHAWK

July, 1998

1 (of 3) RCa,BWi,Nighthawk shake
off coma. 2.50
2 (of 3) RCa,BWi,V:Mephisto. 2.50
3 RCa,BWi,conclusion. 2.50

NIGHTMARE

1994

1 ANo 2.00
2 ANo 2.00
3 ANo 2.00

NIGHTMARE CIRCUS

1 video-game tie-in 2.50
2 video-game tie-in 2.50

NIGHTMARE ON ELM STREET

Oct., 1989

1 RB/TD/AA.,Movie adapt 3.00
2 AA,Movie adapt,Dec., 1989 . . . . 2.25

NIGHTMASK

Nov., 1986

1 O:Night Mask 2.00
2 V:Gnome 2.00
3 V:Mistress Twilight 2.00
4 EC,D:Mistress Twilight 2.00
5 EC,Nightmare. 2.00
6 EC 2.00
7 EC 2.00
8 EC 2.00
9 . . . . 2.00
10 Lucian 2.00
11 . . . . 2.00
12 Oct. 1987 . . . . 2.00

NIGHT NURSE

Nov., 1972

1 The Making of a Nurse 100.00
2 Moment of Truth 75.00
3 . . . . 75.00
4 Final Issue,May, 1973 . . . . 75.00

NIGHT RIDER

Oct., 1974

1 Reprint Ghost Rider #1. . . . . . . 15.00
2 Reprint Ghost Rider #2. . . . . . . 10.00
3 Reprint Ghost Rider #3. . . . . . . 10.00
4 Reprint Ghost Rider #4. . . . . . . 10.00
5 Reprint Ghost Rider #5. . . . . . . 10.00
6 Reprint Ghost Rider #6
August, 1975 . . . . 10.00

NIGHTSTALKERS

1992–94

1 TP(i),Rise o/t Midnight Sons#5
A:GR,J.Blaze,I:Meatmarket,
polybagged w/poster 3.00
2 TP(i),V:Hydra 2.50
3 TP(i),V:Dead on Arrival. 2.00
4 TP(i),V:Hydra 2.00
5 TP(i),A:Punisher. 2.00
6 TP(i),A:Punisher. 2.00
7 TP(i),A:Ghost Rider 2.00
8 Hannibal King vs Morbius 2.00
9 MPa,A:Morbius. 2.00
10 Midnight Massacre#1,D:Johnny
Blaze,Hannibal King 2.50
11 O:Blade 2.00
12 V:Vampires 2.00
13 V:Vampires 2.00
14 Wld,Siege of Darkness#1. . . . . . 2.00
15 Wld,Siege of Darkness#9. . . . . . 2.00
16 V:Dreadnought 2.00
17 F:Blade 2.00
18 D:Hannibal King,Frank Drake,
last issue 2.00

NIGHT THRASHER

[Limited Series] 1992–93

1 B:FaN(s),DHv,N:Night Thrasher,
V:Bengal 2.50
2 DHv,I:Tantrium 2.25
3 DHv,V:Gideon. 2.25
4 E:FaN(s),DHv,A:Silhoutte 2.25

[Regular Series] 1993–95

1 B:FaN(s),MBa,JS,V:Poison
Memories. 3.25
2 JS,V:Concrete Dragons 2.00
3 JS(c),I:Aardwolf,A:Folding Circle. 2.00
4 JS(c),V:Aardwolf,I:Air Force 2.00
5 JS,V:Air Force 2.00
6 Face Value,A:Rage. 2.00
7 DdB,V:Bandit 2.00
8 DdB,V:Bandit 2.00

Night Thrasher #2
© Marvel Entertainment Group

9 DdB,A:Tantrum. 2.00
10 DdB,A:Iron Man,w/card 2.25
11 DdB,Time & Time Again,pt.2 . . . 2.25
12 DdB,Time & Time Again,pt.5 . . . 2.25
13 Lost in the Shadows,pt.1 . . . . . . 2.00
14 Lost in the Shadows,pt.2 . . . . . . 2.00
15 Money Don't Buy,pt.1. . . . . 2.00
16 A:Prowler. 2.00
17 . . . . 2.00
18 . . . . 2.00
19 V:Tantrum 2.00
20 . . . . 2.00
21 Rage vs. Grind 2.00

NIGHTWATCH

1994–95

1 RLm,I:Salvo,Warforce Holo(c). . . 3.00
1a Newsstand ed. 2.00
2 RLm,AM,I:Flashpoint 2.00
3 RLm,AM,V:Flashpoint. 2.00
4 RLm,A:Warrent,V:Gauntlet 2.00
5 I:Sunstreak,A:Venom 2.00
6 V:Venom 2.00
7 I:Cardiaxe. 2.00
8 V:Cardiaxe 2.00
9 origins 2.00
10 . . . . 2.00
11 . . . . 2.00
12 . . . . 2.00

NOCTURNE

1995

1 DAn, in London 2.00
2 DAn,O:Nocturne. 2.00
3 Interview with Amy 2.00
4 V:Dragon 2.00

NO ESCAPE

1994

1 & 2 Movie adaptation . . . . @2.00

NOMAD

[Limited Series] Nov., 1990

1 B:FaN(s),A:Capt.America 3.00
2 A:Capt.America 2.50
3 A:Capt.America 2.50
4 A:Capt.America, final issue,
Feb. 1989. . . . . 2.50

 All comics prices listed are for *Near Mint* condition.

Nomad #2
© Marvel Entertainment Group

[Regular Series] 1992–94

1 B:FaN(s),R:Nomad,[Gatetfold(c), map] 3.00
2 V:Road Kill Club 2.50
3 V:U.S.Agent 2.00
4 DeadMan's Hand#2,V:Deadpool . 2.00
5 DeadMan's Hand#4,V:Punisher . 2.00
6 DeadMan's Hand#8,A:Punisher, Daredevil 2.00
7 Infinity War,V:Gambit, Doppleganger. . . . 2.00
8 L.A.Riots 2.00
9 I:Ebbtide. . . . 2.00
10 A:Red Wolf 2.00
11 in Albuquerque 2.00
12 In Texas. . . . 2.00
13 AIDS issue 2.00
14 Hidden in View 2.00
15 Hidden in View 2.00
16 A:Gambit. . . . 2.00
17 Bucky Kidnapped. . . . 2.00
18 A:Captain America,Slug. . . . 2.00
19 FaN(s),Faustus Affair. . . . 2.00
20 A:Six Pack. . . . 2.00
21 A:Man-Thing 2.00
22 American Dreamers#1,V:Zaran . 2.00
23 American Dreamers#2. . . . 2.00
24 American Dreamers#3. . . . 2.00
25 American Dreamers#4, finale. . . 2.00

NORTHSTAR
1994

1 SFr,DoC,V:Weapon:P.R.I.M.E. . . 2.00
2 SFr,DoC,V:Arcade 2.00
3 SFr,DoC,V:Arcade 2.00
4 SFr,DoC,final issue. . . . 2.00
N Presents James O'Barr. . . . 2.50

NOT BRAND ECHH
August, 1967

1 JK(c),BEv,Forbush Man(c) 35.00
2 MSe,FrG,Spidey-Man,Gnat-Man & Rotten 25.00
3 MSe(C),TS,JK,FrG,O:Charlie America 25.00
4 GC,JTg,TS,Scaredevil, ECHHs-Men 25.00
5 JK,TS,GC,I&O:Forbush Man . . 25.00
6 MSe(c),GC,TS,W:Human Torch 25.00
7 MSe(c),JK,GC,TS,O:Fantastical Four,Stupor Man 25.00
8 MSe(c),GC,TS,C:Beatles 28.00
9 MSe,GC,TS,Bulk V:Sunk-Mariner 30.00
10 JK,TS,MSe,The Worst of.... . . 30.00
11 King Konk 30.00
12 MSe,Frankenstein,A:Revengers 30.00
13 GC,MSe,Stamp Out Trading Cards(c). . . . 30.00

NOTHING CAN STOP THE JUGGERNAUT
1989

1 JR2,rep.SpM#229æ. . . . 4.00

NOVA
[1st Regular Series] Sept., 1976

1 B:MWn(s),JB,JSt,I&O:Nova 7.00
2 JB,JSt,I:Condor,Powerhouse . . . 4.00
3 JB,JSt,I:Diamondhead 4.00
4 SB,TP,A:Thor,I:Corruptor 4.00
5 SB,V:Earthshaker. . . . 3.50
6 SB,V:Condor,Powerhouse, Diamondhead,I:Sphinx 3.50
7 SB,War in Space,O:Sphinx. . . . 3.50
8 V:Megaman 3.50
9 V:Megaman 3.50
10 V:Condor,Powerhouse, Diamond-head Sphinx 3.50
11 V:Sphinx 2.00
12 A:Spider-Man 2.50
13 I:Crimebuster,A:Sandman 2.50
14 A:Sandman 2.00
15 CI,C:Spider-Man, Hulk. . . . 2.00
16 CI,A:Yellow Claw 2.00
17 A:Yellow Claw 2.00
18 A:Yellow Claw, Nick Fury 2.00
19 CI,TP,I:Blackout. . . . 2.00
20 What is Project X?. . . . 2.00
21 JB,BMc,JRu. . . . 2.00
22 CI,I:Comet. . . . 2.00
23 CI,V:Dr.Sun 2.00
24 CI,I:New Champions,V:Sphinx . . 2.00
25 E:MWn(s),CI,A:Champions, V:Sphinx 2.00

[2nd Regular Series] 1994–95

1 B:FaN(s),ChM,V:Gladiator,Foil Embossed(c) 3.00
2 ChM,V:Tail Hook Rape 2.00
3 ChM,A:Spider-Man,Corruptor . . . 2.00
4 ChM,I:NovaO:O 2.00
5 ChM,R:Condor,w/card. . . . 2.25
6 ChM,Time & Time Again,pt.3 . . . 2.25
7 ChM,Time & Time Again,pt.6 . . . 2.25
8 ChM,I:Shatterforce 2.25
9 ChM,V:Shatterforce 2.00
10 ChM,V:Diamondhead. . . . 2.00
11 ChM,V:Diamondhead. . . . 2.00
12 ChM,A:Inhumans. . . . 2.00
13 ChM,A:Inhumans. . . . 2.00
14 A:Condor. . . . 2.00
15 V:Brethern of Zorr 2.00
16 Countdown Conclusion 2.00
17 Nova Loses Powers. . . . 2.00
18 Nova Omega,pt.1 . . . . 2.00

NOVA
March, 1999

1 EL,JoB,F:Rich Rider,48-page . . . 3.00
2 EL,JoB,A:Capt.America 2.00
2a variant JoB cover 2.00
3 EL,JoB,A:Capt.America & Hulk . . 2.00
4 EL,JoB,A:Mr.Fantastic 2.00
5 EL,JoB,A:Spider-Man 2.00
6 EL,JoB,V:Sphinx. . . . 2.00
7 EL,JoB, final issue 2.00

Nth MAN
August, 1989

1 . . . . 2.00
2 . . . . 2.00
3 . . . . 2.00
4 . . . . 2.00
5 thru 7 . . . . @2.00
8 DK 2.00
9 thru 16, finale, Sept., 1990 . . . @2.00

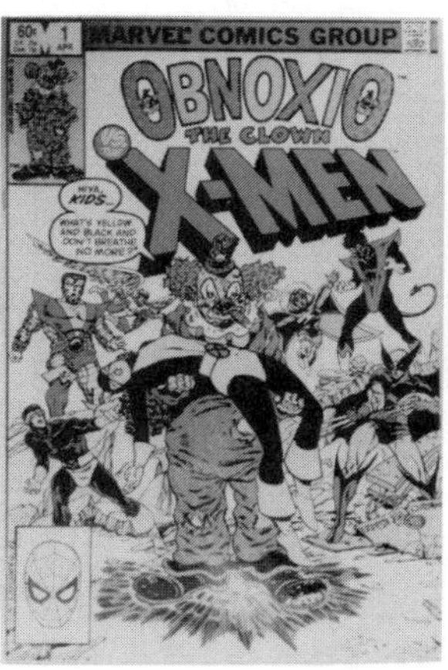

Obnoxio The Clown 31
© Marvel Entertainment Group

OBNOXIO THE CLOWN
April, 1983

1 X-Men 2.00

OFFCASTES
Epic *Heavy Hitters* 1993

1 MV,I:Offcastes 2.50
2 MV,V:Kaoro 2.00
3 MV,Last Issue. . . . 2.00

OFFICIAL MARVEL INDEX: 1985–88
TO THE AMAZING SPIDER-MAN

Index 1 . . . . 3.00
Index 2 thru 9 . . . . @2.50

TO THE AVENGERS

Index 1 thru 7 . . . . @2.50

TO THE FANTASTIC FOUR

Index 1 thru 12 . . . . @2.25

TO MARVEL TEAM-UP

Index 1 thru 6 . . . . @2.00

TO THE X-MEN

Index 1 thru 7 . . . . @2.95

[Vol. 2] 1994

Index 1 thru 5 . . . . @2.00

OFFICIAL MARVEL TIMELINE

1-shot, 48pg 5.95

MARVEL

OFFICIAL TRUE CRIME CASES

Fall, 1947

24 (1)SSh(c),The Grinning Killer . 175.00
25 (2)She Made Me a Killer,HK. . 125.00
Becomes:

ALL-TRUE CRIME

26 SSh(c),The True Story of Wilbur Underhill. 225.00
27 Electric Chair(c),Robert Mais . 150.00
28 Cops V:Gangsters(c) 75.00
29 Cops V:Gangsters(c) 75.00
30 He Picked a Murderous Mind . 75.00
31 Hitchiking Thugs(c) 75.00
32 Jewel Thieves(c) 75.00
33 The True Story of Dinton Phillips 75.00
34 Case of the Killers Revenge. . . 75.00
35 Ph(c),Date with Danger 75.00
36 Ph(c) 75.00
37 Ph(c),Story of Robert Marone . 75.00
38 Murder Weapon,Nick Maxim . . 75.00
39 Story of Vince Vanderee 75.00
40 . . . . 75.00
41 Lou "Lucky" Raven. 75.00
42 BK,Baby Face Nelson 85.00
43 Doc Channing Paulson 70.00
44 Murder in the Big House 70.00
45 While the City Sleeps. 70.00
46 . . . . 70.00
47 Gangster Terry Craig 70.00
48 GT,They Vanish By Night 70.00
49 BK,Squeeze Play. 75.00
50 Shoot to Kill. 70.00
51 Panic in the Big House 70.00
52 Prison Break, Sept., 1952 . . . . 70.00

OLYMPIANS

Epic July, 1991

1 Spoof Series. 3.95
2 Conclusion 3.95

OMEGA THE UNKNOWN

March, 1976

1 JM,I:Omega 4.00
2 JM,A:Hulk. 2.50
3 JM,A:Electro. 2.00
4 JM,V:Yellow Claw 2.00
5 JM,V:The Wrench. 2.00
6 JM,V:Blockbuster 2.00
7 JM,V:Blockbuster 2.00
8 JM,C:New Foolkiller,V:Nitro. 5.00
9 JM,A:New Foolkiller, D:Blockbuster. 7.00
10 JM,D:Omega the Unknown 2.00

ONE, THE

Epic July, 1985

1 thru 5 . . . . @2.00
6 Feb., 1986 . . . . 2.00

101 WAYS TO END THE CLONE SAGA

1-shot (1997). 2.50

ONSLAUGHT

1996–97

Marvel Universe: AKu,SLo,MWd, Marvel Heroes vs. Onslaught . . 7.00
Marvel Universe: Gold edition 15.00
X-Men: AKu,SLo,MWd (1996). 6.00
X-Men: Gold editon. 15.00
Onslaught: Epilogue (1997) 3.00
TPB Book 1, rep. X-Men #53 & #54, Uncanny X-Men 322 & 334 and Onslaught X-Men. 12.95
TPB Book 2, rep. X-Man #18 & #19 and X-Force #57 & 58 . . . . 9.95
TPB Book 3, rep. Uncanny X-Men #335, Avengers #401, FF #415, X-Men #55 . . . . 9.95
TPB Book 4, rep. Inc.Hulk #444 & #445, Cable #34 & #35 . . . . . 9.95
TPB Book 5, rep. X-Factor #125, Punisher #11, Green Goblin #12, Amaz. Sp.-M. #415, Sp.-M. #72 9.95
TPB Book 6, rep. Uncanny X-Men #336, X-Men #56, Avengers #402, FF #416 & Onslaught: Marvel Universe. 12.95

ONYX OVERLORD

Epic 1992–93

1 JBi,Sequel to Airtight Garage . . . 3.00
2 JBi,The Joule 2.75
3 JBi,V:Overlord 2.75
4 V:Starbilliard. 2.75

OPEN SPACE

Dec., 1989–Aug., 1990

1 . . . . 6.00
2 thru 4 . . . . @5.25

ORIGINAL GHOST RIDER

1992–94

1 MT(c),rep Marvel Spotlight#5 . . . 2.25
2 rep.Marvel Spotlight#6 . . . . 2.00
3 rep.Marvel Spotlight#7 . . . . 2.00
4 JQ(c),rep.Marvel Spotlight#8. . . . 2.00
5 KM(c),rep.Marvel spotlight#9 . . . 2.00
6 rep.Marvel Spotlight#10 . . . . 2.00
7 rep.Marvel Spotlight#11 . . . . 2.00
8 rep.Ghost Rider#1 . . . . 2.00
9 rep.Ghost Rider#2 . . . . 2.00
10 rep.Marvel Spotlight#12. . . . . . . 2.00
11 rep.Ghost Rider#3 . . . . 2.00
12 rep.Ghost Rider#4 . . . . 2.00
13 rep.Ghost Rider#38 . . . . 2.00
14 rep.Ghost Rider#6 . . . . 2.00
15 rep.Ghost Rider#7 . . . . 2.00
15 rep.Ghost Rider#8 . . . . 2.00
18 rep.Ghost Rider#9 . . . . 2.00
18 rep.Ghost Rider#10 . . . . 2.00
19 rep.Ghost Rider#11 . . . . 2.00
20 rep.Ghost Rider#12 . . . . 2.00
21 rep.Ghost Rider#13 . . . . 2.00
22 rep.Ghost Rider#14 . . . . 2.00
23 rep.Ghost Rider#15 . . . . 2.00

Original Ghost Rider #6
© Marvel Entertainment Group

ORIGINAL GHOST RIDER RIDES AGAIN

July, 1991

1 rep.GR#68+#69(O:JohnnyBlaze) 3.00
2 rep.G.R. #70,#71 . . . . 2.00
3 rep.G.R. #72,#73 . . . . 2.00
4 rep.G.R. #74,#75 . . . . 2.00
5 rep.G.R. #76,#77 . . . . 2.00
6 rep.G.R. #78,#79 . . . . 2.00
7 rep.G.R. #80,#81 . . . . 2.00

ORIGINS OF MARVEL COMICS

TPB StL,JK,SD reprinting, 260pg . 25.00

OSBORN JOURNALS, THE

1997

1-shot KHt,F:Norman Osborn 3.00

OUR LOVE

Sept., 1949

1 Ph(c),Guilt of Nancy Crane . . 100.00
2 Ph(c),My Kisses Were Cheap . 50.00
Becomes:

TRUE SECRETS

3 Love Stories,continued 90.00
4 . . . . 50.00
5 . . . . 50.00
6 BEv 60.00
7 . . . . 50.00
8 . . . . 50.00
9 . . . . 50.00
10 . . . . 50.00
11 thru 21 . . . . @35.00
22 BEv 50.00
23 thru 39 . . . . @30.00
40 Sept., 1956 . . . . 30.00

OUR LOVE STORY

Oct., 1969

1 . . . . 40.00
2 . . . . 20.00
3 . . . . 20.00
4 . . . . 20.00
5 JSo 75.00
6 thru 13 . . . . @20.00
14 Gary Friedrich &Tarpe Mills . . . 25.00
15 thru 37 . . . . @15.00
38 Feb., 1976. . . . . 15.00

OUTLAW FIGHTERS

Atlas August, 1954

1 GT,Western Tales 100.00
2 GT 60.00
3 . . . . 60.00
4 A;Patch Hawk 60.00
5 RH, Final Issue,April, 1955 . . . 60.00

OUTLAW KID

Atlas Sept., 1954

1 SSh,DW,B&O:Outlaw Kid,A;Black Rider 200.00
2 DW,A:Black Rider 100.00
3 DW,AW,GWb 100.00
4 DW(c),Death Rattle 90.00
5 . . . . 90.00
6 . . . . 90.00
7 . . . . 90.00
8 AW,DW 100.00
9 . . . . 90.00
10 . . . . 90.00

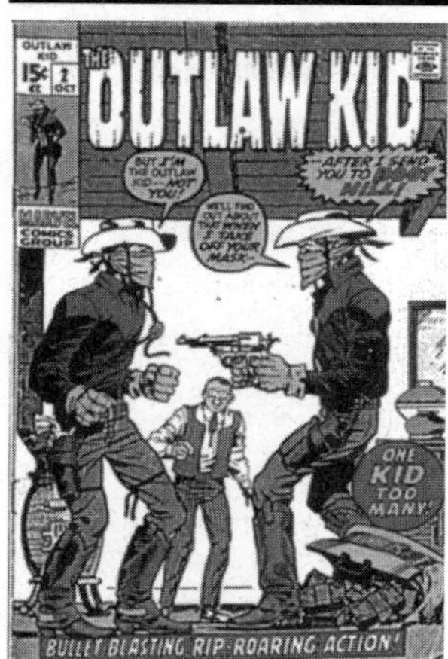

Outlaw Kid #2
© Marvel Entertainment Group

11 thru 17 . . . . @60.00
18 AW 75.00
19 Sept., 1957 . . . . 60.00

[2nd series] August, 1970

1 JSe(c),DW,Jo,Showdown,rep . . 22.00
2 DW,One Kid Too Many 18.00
3 HT(c),DW,Six Gun Double Cross 18.00
4 DW 15.00
5 DW 15.00
6 DW 15.00
7 HT(c),DW,Treachery on the Trail 15.00
8 HT(c),DW,RC,Six Gun Pay Off . 15.00
9 JSe(c),DW,GWb,The Kids Last Stand 12.00
10 GK(c),DAy,NewO:Outlaw Kid . . 22.00
11 GK(c),Thunder Along the Big Iron 10.00
12 The Man Called Bounty Hawk . 10.00
13 The Last Rebel 10.00
14 The Kid Gunslingers of Calibre City 10.00
15 GK(c),V:Madman of Monster Mountain 10.00
16 The End of the Trail 10.00
17 thru 29 . . . . @10.00
30 Oct., 1975 . . . . 10.00

OVER THE EDGE AND UNDER A BUCK

1995–96

1 F:Daredevil vs. Mr. Fear 2.00
2 F:Doctor Strange 2.00
3 F:Hulk 2.00
4 in Cypress Hills 2.00
5 . . . . 2.00
6 F:Daredevil. 2.00
7 Doc & Nightmare 2.00

PARAGON

1 I:Paragon,Nightfire 5.00

PATSY & HEDY

Atlas Feb., 1952

1 B:Patsy Walker&Hedy Wolfe . 150.00
2 Skating(c) 90.00
3 Boyfriend Trouble 75.00
4 Swimsuit(c) 75.00
5 Patsy's Date(c). 75.00
6 Swimsuit/Picnic(c) 75.00
7 Double-Date(c) 75.00
8 The Dance 75.00
9 . . . . 75.00
10 . . . . 75.00
11 thru 25 . . . . @45.00
26 thru 50. . . . . @35.00
51 thru 60 . . . . @30.00
61 thru 109 . . . . @25.00
110 Feb., 1967 . . . . 25.00

PATSY & HER PALS

May, 1953

1 MWs(c),F:Patsay Walker 125.00
2 MWs(c),Swimsuit(c) 75.00
3 MWs(c),Classroom(c) 60.00
4 MWs(c),Golfcourse(c) 60.00
5 MWs(c).Patsy/Buzz(c) 60.00
6 thru 10 . . . . @60.00
11 thru 28 . . . . @40.00
29 August, 1957 . . . . 40.00

PATSY WALKER

1945–Dec., 1965

1 F:Patsy Walker Adventures . . 375.00
2 Patsy/Car(c) 175.00
3 Skating(c) 140.00
4 Perfume(c) 140.00
5 Archery Lesson(c) 140.00
6 Bus(c) 140.00
7 Charity Drive(c) 140.00
8 Organ Driver Monkey(c) 140.00
9 Date(c) 140.00
10 Skating(c),Wedding Bells 140.00
11 Date with a Dream 100.00
12 Love in Bloom,Artist(c). 100.00
13 Swimsuit(c),There Goes My Heart;HK,Hey Look. 100.00
14 An Affair of the Heart, HK,Hey Look 100.00
15 Dance(c) 90.00
16 Skating(c) 90.00
17 Patsy's Diary(c),HK,Hey Look 100.00
18 Autograph(c) 90.00
19 HK,Hey Look 100.00
20 HK,Hey Look 100.00
21 HK,Hey Look 100.00
22 HK,Hey Look 100.00
23 . . . . 65.00
24 . . . . 65.00
25 HK,Rusty 100.00
26 . . . . 50.00
27 . . . . 50.00
28 . . . . 50.00
29 . . . . 50.00
30 HK,Egghead Double 75.00
31 . . . . 50.00
32 thru 57 . . . . @30.00
58 thru 99 . . . . @25.00
100 . . . . 25.00
101 thru 124 . . . . @20.00
Fashion Parade #1 . . . . 75.00

PETER PARKER, THE SPECTACULAR SPIDER-MAN

Dec., 1976

1 SB,V:Tarantula 35.00
2 SB,V:Kraven,Tarantula 15.00
3 SB,I:Lightmaster. 10.00
4 SB,V:Vulture,Hitman 10.00
5 SB,V:Hitman,Vulture 10.00
6 SB,V:Morbius,rep.M.T.U.#3 . . . . 12.00
7 SB,V:Morbius,A:Human Torch. . 15.00
8 SB,V:Morbius 12.00
9 SB,I:White Tiger 6.00
10 SB,A:White Tiger 6.00

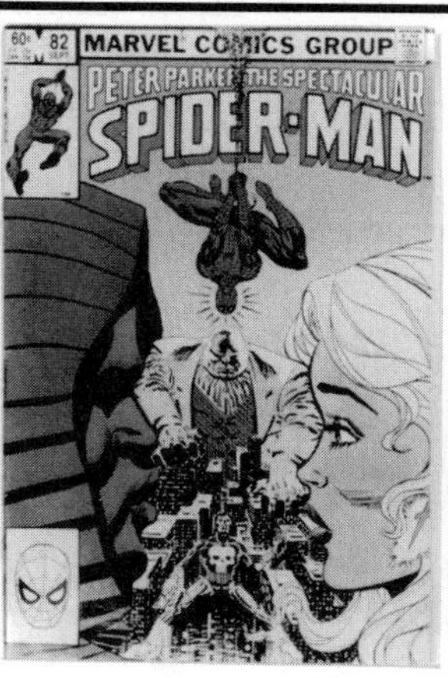

Peter Parker #82
© Marvel Entertainment Group

11 JM,V:Medusa. 5.00
12 SB,V:Brother Power. 5.00
13 SB,V:Brother Power. 5.00
14 SB,V:Brother Power. 5.00
15 SB,V:Brother Power. 5.00
16 SB,V:The Beetle 5.00
17 SB,A:Angel & Iceman Champions disbanded 6.00
18 SB,A:Angel & Iceman 6.00
19 SB,V:The Enforcers 5.00
20 SB,V:Lightmaster. 5.00
21 JM,V:Scorpion 5.00
22 MZ,A:Moon Knight,V:Cyclone . . 5.00
23 A:Moon Knight,V:Cyclone 5.00
24 FS,A:Hypno-Hustler. 4.00
25 JM,FS,I:Carrion 5.00
26 JM,A:Daredevil,V:Carrion 4.00
27 DC,FM,I:Miller Daredevil, V:Carrion 18.00
28 FM,A:Daredevil,V:Carrion 15.00
29 JM,FS,V:Carrion 5.00
30 JM,FS,V:Carrion 5.00
31 JM,FS,D:Carrion 5.00
32 BL,JM,FS,V:Iguana 5.00
33 JM,FS,O:Iguana 5.00
34 JM,FS,V:Iguana,Lizard. 5.00
35 V:Mutant Mindworm. 5.00
36 JM,V:Swarm 5.00
37 DC,MN,V:Swarm 5.00
38 SB,V:Morbius. 5.00
39 JM,JR2,V:Schizoid Man 5.50
40 FS,V:Schizoid Man 5.50
41 JM,V:Meteor Man,A:GiantMan . . 5.00
42 JM,A:Fant.Four,V:Frightful 4. . . . 5.00
43 JBy(c),MZ,V:The Ringer, V:Belladonna 5.00
44 JM,V:The Vulture. 5.00
45 MSe,V:The Vulture. 5.00
46 FM(c),MZ,V:Cobra 5.00
47 MSe,A:Prowler II 5.00
48 MSe,A:Prowler II 5.00
49 MSe,I:Smuggler. 5.00
50 JR2,JM,V:Mysterio. 5.00
51 MSe&FM(c),V:Mysterio 5.00
52 FM(c),D:White Tiger. 5.00
53 JM,FS,V:Terrible Tinkerer. 5.00
54 FM,WS,MSe,V:Silver Samurai . . 5.00
55 LMc,JM,V:Nitro 5.00
56 FM,JM,V:Jack-o-lantern 12.00
57 JM,V:Will-o-the Wisp 5.00
58 JBy,V:Ringer,A:Beetle 6.00
59 JM,V:Beetle. 5.00
60 JM&FM(c),O:Spider-Man,

MARVEL

V:Beetle 5.50
61 JM,V:Moonstone 4.50
62 JM,V:Goldbug 4.50
63 JM,V:Molten Man. 4.50
64 JM,I:Cloak&Dagger 8.00
65 BH,JM,V:Kraven,Calypso. 4.50
66 JM,V:Electro 4.00
67 AMb,V:Boomerang. 4.00
68 LMc,JM,V:Robot of Mendell Stromm 4.00
69 AM,A:Cloak & Dagger 5.00
70 A:Cloak & Dagger 5.00
71 JM,Gun Control issue 4.00
72 AM,V:Dr.Octopus. 4.00
73 AM,JM,V:Dr.Octopus,A:Owl 4.00
74 AM,JM,V:Dr.Octopus,R:Bl.Cat . . 4.00
75 AM,JM,V:Owl,Dr.Octopus. 5.00
76 AM,Black Cat on deathbed 4.00
77 AM,V:Gladiator,Dr.Octopus 4.00
78 AM,V:Dr.Octopus,C:Punisher . . . 4.00
79 AM,V:Dr.Octopus,A:Punisher . . . 4.00
80 AM,F:J.Jonah Jameson 3.50
81 A:Punisher. 6.00
82 A:Punisher. 6.00
83 A:Punisher. 6.00
84 AM,F:Black Cat 3.50
85 AM,O:Hobgoblin powers (Ned Leeds) 12.00
86 FH,V:Fly 3.50
87 AM,Reveals I.D.to Black Cat . . . 3.50
88 AM,V:Cobra,Mr.Hyde 3.50
89 AM,Secret Wars,A:Kingpin. 4.00
90 AM,Secret Wars 5.00
91 AM,V:Blob 3.50
92 AM,I:Answer 3.50
93 AM,V:Answer. 3.50
94 AM,A:Cloak & Dagger,V: Silver Mane 3.50
95 AM,A:Cloak & Dagger,V: Silvermane. 3.50
96 AM,A:Cloak & Dagger,V: Silvermane. 3.50
97 HT,JM,A:Black Cat. 3.50
98 HT,JM,I:Spot 3.50
99 HT,JM,V:Spot. 3.50
100 AM,V:Kingpin,C:Bl.Costume. . . 6.00
101 JBy(c),AM,V:Killer Shrike 3.00
102 JBy(c),AM,V:Backlash 3.00
103 AM,V:Blaze;Not John Blaze . . . 3.00
104 JBy(c),AM,V:Rocket Racer. . . . 3.00
105 AM,A:Wasp 3.00
106 AM,A:Wasp 3.00
107 RB,D:Jean DeWolf,I:SinEater. . 4.00
108 RB,A:Daredevil,V:Sin-Eater . . . 3.00
109 RB,A:Daredevil,V:Sin-Eater . . . 3.00
110 RB,A:Daredevil,V:Sin-Eater . . . 3.00
111 RB,Secret Wars II 3.00
112 RB,A:Santa Claus,Black Cat . . 3.00
113 RB,Burglars,A:Black Cat 3.00
114 BMc,V:Lock Picker. 3.00
115 BMc,A:Black Cat,Dr.Strange, I:Foreigner 3.50
116 A:Dr.Strange, Foreigner, Black Cat, Sabretooth. 5.00
117 DT,C:Sabretooth,A:Foreigner, Black Cat,Dr.Strange 4.00
118 MZ,D:Alexander,V:SHIELD. . . . 3.00
119 RB,BMc,V:Sabretooth, A:Foreigner,Black Cat. 5.00
120 KG. 3.00
121 RB,BMc,V:Mauler 3.00
122 V:Mauler 3.00
123 V:Foreigner,Black Cat 3.00
124 V:Dr.Octopus. 3.00
125 V:Wr.Crew,A:Spiderwoman . . . 3.00
126 JM,A:Sp.woman,V:Wrecker . . . 3.00
127 AM,V:Lizard 3.00
128 C:DDevil,A:Bl.Cat,Foreigner. . . 3.50
129 A:Black Cat,V:Foreigner. 3.00
130 A:Hobgoblin. 6.00
131 MZ,BMc,V:Kraven 7.00

Peter Parker, King Size Annual #3
© Marvel Entertainment Group

132 MZ,BMc,V:Kraven 7.00
133 BSz(c),Mad Dog,pt.3 . . . . 5.00
Ann.#1 RB,JM,V:Dr.Octopus. 5.00
Ann.#2 JM,I&O:Rapier 4.50
Ann.#3 JM,V:Manwolf. 4.50
Ann.#4 AM,O:Aunt May,A:Bl.Cat. . . 5.00
Ann.#5 I:Ace,Joy Mercado 4.50
Ann.#6 V:Ace 4.50
Ann.#7 Honeymoon iss,A:Puma . . . 4.50
Becomes:

SPECTACULAR SPIDER-MAN

PETER PARKER: SPIDER-MAN

Nov., 1998

1 JR2,HMe,SHa,A:new Spider-Man, V:Ranger,48-page 3.00
1a signed 35.00
2 JR2,HMe,SHa,A:Thor 2.00
2a variant cover. 2.00
3 HMe,JR2,SHa,A:Iceman, V:Shadrac 2.00
4 HMe,JR2,SHa,V:Marrow. 2.00
5 HMe,SHa,BS,JBy(c),F:Spider-Woman,Aunt May, Black Cat . . 2.00
6 HMe,SHa,RJ2,JBy(c),V:Kingpin . 2.00
7 JR2,HMe,SHa,Reality Bent. 2.00
8 JR2,HMe,SHa,V:Bullseye 2.00
9 JR2,HMe,SHa,R:Venom 2.00
10 JR2,HMe,SHa,R:Carnage 2.00
11 JR2,HMe,SHa,Eighth Day,pt.3 x-over. 2.00
12 JR2,HMe,SHa, 48-pg. 3.00
13 JR2,HMe 2.00
14 JR2,HMe,A:Hulk 2.00
15 JR2,HMe,x-over. 2.00
16 JR2,HMe,V:Sinister Six 2.00
17 JR2,HMe,SHa,V:Kraven. 2.00
18 HMe,JR2,SHa,V:Green Goblin . . 2.25
19 HMe,JR2,SHa,Mary Jane dies . . 2.25
20 PJe,MBu,DGr,Mary Jane dead. . 2.25
21 PJe,MBu,DGr,HumanTorch 2.25
22 PJe,MBu,DGr,FlintMarko 2.25
23 PJe,MBu,DGr,Type Face 2.25
24 PJe,MBu,DGr,Max.Security 2.25
Ann.1999,CCs, 48-page 3.50
Ann.2000 CCl,JoB,80-pg. 3.50
Spec. Peter Parker, Spider-Man 2000. . . . . 3.50

PETER PORKER

Star May, 1985

1 Parody 2.50
2 . . . . 2.00
3 . . . . 2.00
4 . . . . 2.00
5 V:Senior Simians 2.00
6 A Blitz in Time 2.00
7 . . . . 2.00
8 Kimono My House 2.00
9 Uncouth my Tooth 2.00
10 Lost Temple of the Golden Retriever 2.00
11 Dog Dame Afternoon 2.00
12 The Gouda,Bad & Ugly 2.00
13 Halloween issue 2.00
14 Heavy Metal Issue. 2.00
15 . . . . 2.00
16 Porker Fried Rice,Final Issue . . 2.00
17 Sept., 1987 . . . . 2.00

PETER, THE LITTLE PEST

Nov., 1969

1 F:Peter 35.00
2 Rep,Dexter & Melvin 25.00
3 Rep,Dexter & Melvin 25.00
4 Rep,Dexter & Melvin, May, 1970 . . . . 25.00

PHANTOM

1 Lee Falk's Phantom 4.00
2 V:General Babalar 4.00
3 final issue. 4.00

PHANTOM 2040

1 Based on cartoon 2.50
2 V:Alloy 2.50
3 MPa,V:Crime Syndicate 2.50
4 Vision Quest. 2.50

PHOENIX (UNTOLD STORY)

April, 1984

1 JBy,O:Phoenix (R.Summers) . . 12.00

PILGRIM'S PROGRESS

1 adapts John Bunyans novel . . . 10.00

PINHEAD

1993–94

1 Red Foil(c),from Hellraiser 3.00
2 DGC(s),V:Cenobites 2.50
3 DGC(s),V:Cenobites 2.50
4 DGC(s),V:Cenobites 2.50
5 DGC(s),Devil in Disguise 2.50
6 DGC(s), ... 2.50

PINHEAD VS. MARSHALL LAW

1993

1 KON,In Hell 3.00
2 KON. 3.00

PINOCC

HIO & THE EMPEROR OF THE NIGHT

March, 1988

1 Movie adapt.. . . . . 2.00

 All comics prices listed are for *Near Mint* condition.

PINT-SIZED X-BABIES: MURDERAMA

June, 1998

1-shot, Mojo, Arcade, 48pg, ... 3.00

PIRATES OF DARK WATERS

Nov., 1991

1 based on T.V. series 2.00
2 Search for 13 Treasures 2.00
3 V:Albino Warriors,Konk 2.00
4 A:Monkey Birds 2.00
5 Tula Steals 1st Treasuer 2.00
6 thru 9 . . . . @2.00

PITT, THE

March, 1988

1 SB,SDr,A:Spitfire 4.00

PLANET OF THE APES

Aug., 1974–Feb. 1977
(black & white magazine)

1 MP 30.00
2 MP 20.00
3 . . . . 10.00
4 . . . . 10.00
5 . . . . 10.00
6 thru 10 . . . . @10.00
11 thru 20 . . . . @10.00
21 thru 29 . . . . @15.00

PLANET TERRY

Star April, 1985

1 thru 11 . . . . @2.00
12 March, 1986 . . . . 2.00

PLASMER

Marvel UK 1993–94

1 A:Captain America 3.50
2 A:Captain Britain,Black Knight . . 2.25
3 A:Captain Britain 2.25
4 A:Captain Britain 2.25
5 thru 7 . . . . 2.00

Plasmer #1
© Marvel Entertainment Group

PLASTIC FORKS

Epic 1990

1 . . . . 5.50
2 thru 5 . . . . @5.25

POLICE ACADEMY

Nov., 1989

1 Based on TV Cartoon 2.00
2 . . . . 2.00
3 . . . . 2.00
4 and 5 . . . . @2.00
6 Feb., 1990 . . . . 2.00

POLICE ACTION

Jan., 1954

1 JF,GC,Riot Squad 150.00
2 JF,Over the Wall 100.00
3 . . . . 75.00
4 DAy 75.00
5 DAy 75.00
6 . . . . 75.00
7 BPNov., 1954 . . . . 75.00

POLICE BADGE
See: SPY THRILLERS

POPPLES

Star Dec., 1986

1 Based on Toys 2.00
2 . . . . 2.00
3 . . . . 2.00
4 . . . . 2.00
5 August, 1987 . . . . 2.00

POWDERED TOAST-MAN

Spec. F:Powder Toast-Man 3.25

POWERHOUSE PEPPER COMICS

1943—Nov., 1948

1 BW,Movie Auditions(c) 1,300.00
2 BW,Dinner(c) 750.00
3 BW,Boxing Ring(c) 650.00
4 BW,Subway(c) 650.00
5 BW,Bankrobbers(c) 750.00

POWER LINE

Epic May, 1988

1 BMc(i) 2.25
2 Aw(i) 2.00
3 A:Dr Zero 2.00
4 . . . . 2.00
5 thru 7 GM . . . . @2.00
8 GM Sept., 1989 . . . . 2.00

POWER MAN

Prev: Hero for Hire
Feb., 1974

17 GT,A:Iron Man 9.00
18 GT,V:Steeplejack 6.00
19 GT,V:Cottonmouth 6.00
20 GT,Heroin Story 6.00
21 V:Original Power Man 5.00
22 V:Stiletto & Discus 5.00
23 V:Security City 5.00
24 GT,I:BlackGoliath(BillFoster) . . . 5.00
25 A:Circus of Crime 5.00
26 GT,V:Night Shocker 5.00
27 GP,AMc,V:Man Called X 5.00
28 V:Cockroach 5.00
29 V:Mr.Fish 5.00
30 RB,KJ,KP,I:Piranha 5.00
31 SB,NA(i),V:Piranha 5.00
32 JSt,FR,A:Wildfire 3.50
33 FR,A:Spear 3.50
34 FR,A:Spear,Mangler 3.50
35 DA,A:Spear,Mangler 3.50
36 V:Chemistro 3.50
37 V:Chemistro 3.50
38 V:Chemistro 3.50
39 KJ,V:Chemistro,Baron 3.50
40 V:Baron 3.50
41 TP,V:Thunderbolt,Goldbug 3.50
42 V:Thunderbolt,Goldbug 3.50
43 AN,V:Mace 3.50
44 TP,A:Mace 3.50
45 JSn,A:Mace 4.00
46 GT,I:Zzzax(recreated) 3.50
47 BS,A:Zzzax 4.00
48 JBy,A:Iron Fist 4.00
49 JBy,A:Iron Fist 4.00
Becomes:

POWER MAN & IRON FIST

50 JBy,I:Team-up with Iron Fist 2.50
51 MZ,Night on the Town 2.50
52 MZ,V:Death Machines 2.50
53 SB,O:Nightshade 2.50
54 TR,O:Iron Fist 2.50
55 Chaos at the Coliseum 2.50
56 Mayhem in the Museum 2.50
57 X-Men,V:Living Monolith 6.00
58 1st El Aguila(Drug) 2.00
59 BL(c),TVE,V:Big Apple
Bomber 2.00
60 BL(c),V:Terrorists 2.00
61 BL(c),V:The Maggia 2.00
62 BL(c),KGa,V:Man Mountain
D:Thunerbolt 2.00
63 BL(c),Cage Fights Fire 2.00
64 DGr&BL(c),V:Suetre,Muertre . . . 2.00
65 BL(c),A:El Aquila, ... 2.00
66 FM(c),Sabretooth(2nd App.) . . . 30.00
67 V:Bushmaster 2.00
68 FM(c),V:Athur Nagan 2.00
69 V:Soldier 2.00
70 FM(c)V:El Supremo 2.00
71 FM(c),I:Montenegro 2.00
72 FM(c),V:Chako 2.00
73 FM(c),V:Rom 2.00
74 FM(c),V:Ninja 2.00
75 KGa,O:IronFist 2.50
76 KGa,V:Warhawk 2.50
77 KGa,A:Daredevil 2.50
78 KGa,A:El Aguila,Sabretooth
(Slasher)(3rd App.) 20.00
79 V:Dredlox 2.00
80 KJ(c),V:Montenegro 2.00
81 V:Black Tiger 2.00
82 V:Black Tiger 2.00
83 V:Warhawk 2.00
84 V:Constrictor,A:Sabertooth
(4th App.) 18.00
85 KP,V:Mole Man 2.00
86 A:Moon Knight 2.00
87 A:Moon Kinght 2.00
88 V:Scimtar 2.00
89 V:Terrorists 2.00
90 V:Unus BS(c) 2.00
91 “Paths and Angles” 2.00
92 V:Hammeread,I:New Eel 2.00
93 A:Chemistro 2.00
94 V:Chemistro 2.00
95 Danny Rand 2.00
96 V,Chemistro 2.00
97 K'unlun,A:Fera 2.00
98 V:Shades & Commanche 2.00
99 R:Daught.of Dragon 2.00
100 O:K'unlun,DoubleSize 2.00
101 A:Karnak 2.00
102 V:Doombringer 2.00
103 O:Doombringer 2.00
104 V:Dr.Octopus,Lizard 2.00
105 F:Crime Buster 2.00

106 Luke Gets Shot 2.00
107 JBy(c),Terror issue. 2.00
108 V:Inhuman Monster 2.00
109 V:The Reaper 2.00
110 V:Nightshade,Eel 2.00
111 I:Captain Hero 2.00
112 JBy(c),V:Control7. . . . . 2.00
113 JBy(c),A:Capt.Hero 2.00
114 JBy(c),V:Control7. . . . . 2.00
115 JBy(c),V:Stanley. 2.00
116 JBy(c),V:Stanley. 2.00
117 R:K'unlun. 2.00
118 A:Colleen Wing 2.00
119 A:Daught.of Dragon 2.00
120 V:Chiantang. 2.00
121 Secret Wars II 2.00
122 V:Dragonkin. 2.00
123 V:Race Killer 2.00
124 V:Yellowclaw 2.00
125 MBr,LastIssue;D:Iron Fist. 3.00
G-Size#1 reprints 4.00
Ann.#1 Earth Shock 5.00

POWER PACHYDERMS
Sept., 1989

1 Elephant Superheroes 1.50

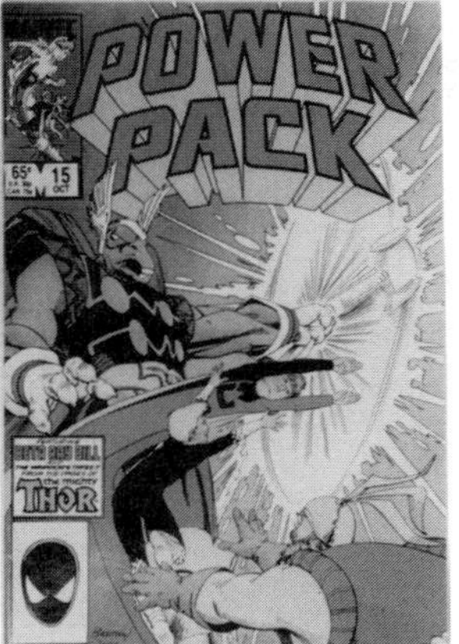

Power Pack #15
© Marvel Entertainment Group

POWER PACK
August, 1984

1 JBr,BWi,I&O:Power Pack,
I:Snarks 2.50
2 JBr,BWi,V:Snarks 2.00
3 JBr,BWi,V:Snarks 2.00
4 JBr,BWi,V:Snarks 2.00
5 JBr,BWi,V:Bogeyman 2.00
6 JBr,BWi,A:Spider-Man 2.00
7 JBr,BWi,A:Cloak & Dagger 2.00
8 JBr,BWi,A:Cloak & Dagger 2.00
9 BA,BWi,A:Marrina. 2.00
10 BA,BWi,A:Marrina 2.00
11 JBr,BWi,V:Morlocks 2.00
12 JBr,BWi,A:X-Men,V:Morlocks . . . 3.00
13 BA,BWi,Baseball issue 2.00
14 JBr,BWi,V:Bogeyman. 2.00
15 JBr,BWi,A:Beta Ray Bill 2.00
16 JBr,BWi,I&O:Kofi,J:Tattletale
(Franklin Richards). 2.00
17 JBr,BWi,V:Snarks 2.00
18 BA,SW,Secret Wars II,
V:Kurse 2.00
19 BA,SW,Doub.size,Wolverine . . . 4.00
20 BMc,A:NewMutants 2.00
21 BA,TA,C:Spider-Man 2.00
22 JBg,BWi,V:Snarks 2.00
23 JBg,BWi,V:Snarks,C:FF 2.00
24 JBg,BWi,V:Snarks,C:Cloak 2.00
25 JBg,BWi,A:FF,V:Snarks 2.00
26 JBg,BWi,A:Cloak & Dagger 2.00
27 JBg,AG,A:Wolverine,X-Factor,
V:Sabretooth 3.50
28 A:Fantastic Four,Hercules 2.00
29 JBg,DGr,A:SpM,V:Hobgoblin . . . 2.00
30 VM,Crack 2.00
31 JBg,I:Trash 2.00
32 JBg,V:Trash. 2.00
33 JBg,A:Sunspot,Warlock,
C:Spider-Man. 2.00
34 TD,V:Madcap. 2.00
35 JBg,A:X-Factor,D:Plague 2.00
36 JBg,V:Master Mold 2.00
37 SDr(i),I:Light-Tracker 2.00
38 SDr(i),V:Molecula. 2.00
39 V:Bogeyman 2.00
40 A:New Mutants,V:Bogeyman . . . 2.00
41 SDr(i),V:The Gunrunners 2.00
42 JBg,SDr,Inferno,V:Bogeyman. . . 2.00
43 JBg,SDr,AW,Inferno,
V:Bogeyman. 2.00
44 JBr,Inferno,A:New Mutants. 2.25
45 JBr,End battle w/Bogeyman 2.00
46 WPo,A:Punisher,Dakota North . . 2.00
47 JBg,I:Bossko 2.00
48 JBg,Toxic Waste #1 . . . . 2.00
49 JBg,JSh,Toxic Waste #2 . . . . . . 2.00
50 AW(i),V:Snarks 2.00
51 GM,I:Numinus 2.00
52 AW(i),V:Snarks,A:Numinus 2.00
53 EC,A of V,A:Typhoid Mary 2.00
54 JBg,V:Mad Thinker 2.00
55 DSp,V:Mysterio 2.00
56 TMo,A:Fant.Four,Nova. 2.00
57 TMo,A:Nova,V:Star Stalker 2.00
58 TMo,A:Galactus,Mr.Fantastic . . . 2.00
59 TMo,V:Ringmaster. 2.00
60 TMo,V:Puppetmaster 2.00
61 TMo,V:Red Ghost & Apes 2.00
62 V:Red Ghost & Apes
(last issue) 2.00
Holiday Spec.JBr,Small Changes . . 2.25

POWER PACK: PEER PRESSURE
June, 2000

1 (of 4) TA,CDo 3.00
2 TA,CDo,V:Snarks 3.00
3 TA,CDo, ... 3.00
4 Ta,CDo,concl 3.00

PRINCE NAMOR, THE SUB-MARINER
Sept., 1984

1 I:Dragonrider, Dara. 2.50
2 I:Proteus. 2.00
3 . . . . 2.00
4 Dec., 1984 . . . . 2.00

PRINCE VALIANT
1994–95

1 JRy,CV,Thule, Camelot
and the Misty Isles 4.00
2 JRy,CV. 4.00
3 JRy,CV. 4.00
4 JRy,CV, final issue 4.00

PRIVATE EYE
Atlas Jan., 1951

1 . . . . 150.00
2 . . . . 100.00
3 GT 100.00
4 . . . . 75.00
5 . . . . 75.00
6 JSt 75.00
7 . . . . 75.00
8 March, 1952 . . . . 75.00

PROFESSOR XAVIER AND THE X-MEN
1995

1 1st Year Together 2.00
2 V:The Vanisher. 2.00
3 FaN,F:The Blob 2.00
4 V:Magneto & Brotherhood. 2.00
5 . . . . 2.00
6 . . . . 2.00
7 FdS,Sub-Mariner 2.00
8 thru 12 . . . . 2.00
13 AHo,F:Juggernaut 2.00
14 JGz,V:Juggernaut, ... 2.00
15 JGz,F:Quicksilver & Scarlet
Witch 2.00
16 . . . . 2.00
17 JGz,V:Sentinels,F:Beast 2.00
18 JGz,X-Men vs. Sentinels,
final issue. 2.00

PROWLER, THE
1994

1 Creatures of the Night, pt.1. . . . . 2.00
2 V:Nightcreeper, Creatures, pt.2. . 2.00
3 Creatures of the Night, pt.3. . . . . 2.00
4 V:Vulture, Creatures, pt.4 . . . . . . 2.00

PSI FORCE
Nov., 1986

1 MT,O:PSI Force 2.00
2 MT 2.00
3 MT,CIA. 2.00
4 MT,J:Network 2.00
5 MT 2.00
6 MT(c) 2.00
7 MT(c) 2.00
8 MT 2.00
9 MT(c) 2.00
10 PSI Hawk 2.00
11 . . . . 2.00
12 MT(c) 2.00
13 . . . . 2.00

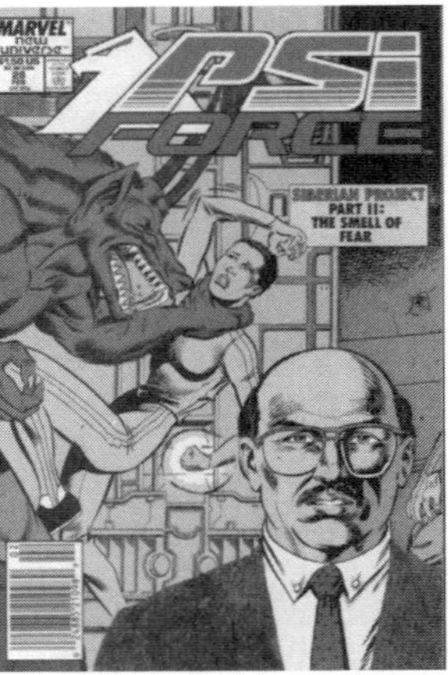

Psi Force #28
© Marvel Entertainment Group

14 AW 2.00
15 . . . . 2.00
16 RLm 2.00
17 RLm 2.00
18 RLm 2.00
19 RLm 2.00
20 RLm,V:Medusa Web;Rodstvow . 2.00
21 RLm 2.00
22 RLm,A:Nightmask 2.00
23 A:D.P.7 . . . . 2.00
24 . . . . 2.00
25 . . . . 2.00
26 . . . . 2.00
27 thru 31 . . . . @2.00
32 June, 1989 . . . . 2.00
Ann.#1 . . . . 2.00

PSYCHONAUTS

Epic 1993–94

1 thru 4 War in the Future 4.95

PSYLOCKE & ANGEL: CRIMSON DAWN

1997

1 SvL,ATi,V:Obsideon 3.00
2 SvL,ATi, ... 3.00
3 BRa,SvL,ATi 3.00
4 (of 4) BRa,SvL,ATi 3.00

PUNISHER

[Limited Series] Jan., 1986

1 MZ,Circle of Blood,double size . . 6.00
2 MZ,Back to the War 5.00
3 MZ,V:The Right 4.00
4 MZ,V:The Right 4.00
5 V:Jigsaw,end Mini-Series 4.00

[Regular Series] 1987–95

1 KJ,V:Wilfred Sobel,Drugs 5.00
2 KJ,V:General Trahn,Bolivia 3.50
3 KJ,V:Colonel Fryer 3.25
4 KJ,I:The Rev,Microchip Jr. 3.25
5 KJ,V:The Rev 3.25
6 DR,KN,V:The Rosettis 3.25
7 DR,V:Ahmad,D:Rose 3.25
8 WPo,SW(1st Punisher), V:Sigo & Roky 3.50
9 WPo,SW,D:MicrochipJr,V:Sigo . . 3.00
10 WPo,SW,A:Daredevil (x-over w/Daredevil #257) 3.00

Punisher #25
© Marvel Entertainment Group

11 WPo,SW,O:Punisher 2.00
12 WPo,SW,V:Gary Saunders 2.00
13 WPo,SW,V:Lydia Spoto 2.00
14 WPo,SW,I:McDowell,Brooks . . . 2.00
15 WPo,SW,V:Kingpin 2.00
16 WPo,SW,V:Kingpin 2.00
17 WPo,SW,V:Kingpin 2.00
18 WPo,SW,V:Kingpin,C:X-Men . . . 2.00
19 LSn,In Australia 2.00
20 WPo(c),In Las Vegas 2.00
21 EL,SW,Boxing Issue 2.00
22 EL,SW,I:Saracen 2.00
23 EL,SW,V:Scully 2.00
24 EL,SW,A:Shadowmasters 2.00
25 EL,AW,A:Shadowmasters 2.00
26 RH,Oper.Whistle Blower#1. . . . . 2.00
27 RH,Oper.Whistle Blower#2. . . . . 2.00
28 BR,A:Dr.Doom,A of Veng. 2.00
29 BR,A:Dr.Doom,A of Veng. 2.00
30 BR,V:Geltrate 2.00
31 BR,V:Bikers #1 . . . . 2.00
32 BR,V:Bikers #2 . . . . 2.00
33 BR,V:The Reavers. 2.00
34 BR,V:The Reavers. 2.00
35 BR,MF,Jigsaw Puzzle #1 . . . . . . 2.00
36 MT,MF,Jigsaw Puzzle #2 . . . . . . 2.00
37 MT,Jigsaw Puzzle #3 . . . . 2.00
38 BR,MF,Jigsaw Puzzle #4 . . . . . . 2.00
39 JSh,Jigsaw Puzzle #5 . . . . 2.00
40 BR,JSh,Jigsaw Puzzle #6 . . . . . 2.00
41 BR,TD,V:Terrorists. 2.00
42 MT,V:Corrupt Mili. School. 2.00
43 BR,Border Run 2.00
44 Flag Burner 2.00
45 One Way Fare 2.00
46 HH,Cold Cache 2.00
47 HH,Middle East #1. . . . . 2.00
48 HH,Mid.East #2,V:Saracen 2.00
49 HH,Punisher Hunted 2.00
50 HH,MGo(c),I:Yo Yo Ng. 2.00
51 Chinese Mafia 2.00
52 Baby Snatchers. 2.00
53 HH,in Prison 2.00
54 HH,in Prison 2.00
55 HH,in Prison 2.00
56 HH,in Prison 2.00
57 HH,in Prison 2.00
58 V:Kingpin's Gang,A:Micro 2.50
59 MT(c),V:Kingpin. 2.00
60 VM,AW,Black Punisher, A:Luke Cage 2.00
61 VM,A:Luke Cage 2.00
62 VM,AW,A:Luke Cage 2.00
63 MT(c),VM,V:Thieves 2.00
64 Eurohit #1 . . . . 2.00
65 thru 70 Eurohit . . . . @2.00
71 AW(i). 2.00
72 AW(i). 2.00
73 AW(i),Police Action #1 . . . . 2.00
74 AW(i),Police Action #2 . . . . 2.00
75 AW(i),Police Action #3,foil(c), double size. 2.50
76 LSn,in Hawaii 2.00
77 VM,Survive#1 . . . . 2.00
78 VM,Survive#2 . . . . 2.00
79 VM,Survive#3 . . . . 2.00
80 Goes to Church 2.00
81 V:Crooked Cops 2.00
82 B:Firefight 2.00
83 Firefight#2 . . . . 2.00
84 E:Firefight 2.00
85 Suicide Run. 2.25
86 Suicide Run#3,Foil(c), ... 2.25
87 Suicide Run#6. . . . . 2.00
88 LSh(c),Suicide Run#9 . . . . 2.00
89 . . . . 2.00
90 Hammered 2.00
91 Silk Noose. 2.00
92 Razor's Edge. 2.00
93 Killing Streets 2.00
94 B:No Rules 2.00
95 No Rules 2.00
96 . . . . 2.00
97 CDi 2.00
98 . . . . 2.00
99 . . . . 2.00
100 New Punisher 3.00
100a Enhanced ed. 4.00
101 CC,Raid's Franks Tomb 2.00
102 A:Bullseye 2.00
103 Countdown 4 . . . . 2.00
104 CDi,Countdown 1, V:Kingpin, final issue. 2.00
Ann.#1 MT,A:Eliminators, Evolutionary War. 4.00
Ann.#2 JLe,Atlantis Attacks #5, A:Moon Knight 3.50
Ann.#3 LS,MT,Lifeform #1 . . . . 3.00
Ann.#4 Baron Strucker,pt.2 (see D.D.Annual #7). 3.00
Ann.#5 System Bytes #1 . . . . 2.50
Ann.#6 I:Eradikator,w/card 3.25
GNv 5.00
Summer Spec.#1 VM,MT 3.50
Summer Spec.#2 SBs(c) 2.50
Summer Spec.#3 V:Carjackers 2.50
Summer Spec.#4 . . . . 3.25
Spec. Punisher/Batman,CDi,JR2, 48pg (1994) 5.00
Spec.#1 Punisher/Daredevil, rep. Daredevil 6.00
Punisher:No Escape A:USAgent, Paladin (1990) 5.50
Punisher Movie Spec.BA (1989) . . . 5.95
GNv Punisher: The Prize (1990) . . 5.50
Punisher:Bloodlines DC 6.25
Punisher:Blood on the Moors 16.95
Punisher:G-Force 5.25
Punisher:Origin of Mirco Chip #1, O:Mirco Chip 2.00
Punisher:Origin of Mirco Chip #2 V:The Professor 2.00
Classic Punisher rep early B&W magazines. 7.00
Punisher:Back To School Spec.
#1 JRy,short stories 3.25
#2 BSz. 2.95
Punisher:Die Hard in the Big Easy Mardi Gras 5.25
Holiday Spec.#1 V:Young Mob Capo 3.25
Holiday Spec #2. . . . . 2.95
Punisher:Ghosts of the Innocent#1 TGr, V:Kingpin's Dead Men . . . 5.95

Punisher, Volume 2, #4
© Marvel Entertainment Group

MARVEL

Punisher:Ghosts of the Innocent#2
TGr, V:Kingpin,Snake 5.95
TPB Punisher: Eye For An Eye. . . . 9.95

[2nd Regular Series] 1995

1 JOs,TL,Clv,Punisher sent to the Electric Chair, foil(c) 2.95
2 JOs,TL,Clv,Crime family boss . . . 2.00
3 JOs,TL,Clv,V:Hatchetman. 2.00
4 JOs,TL,Clv,A:Daredevil,Jigsaw . . 2.00
5 . . . . 2.00
6 . . . . 2.00
7 JOs,TL,Clv,V:Son of Nick Fury . . 2.00
8 . . . . 2.00
9 . . . . 2.00
10 . . . . 2.00
11 Onslaught saga 2.00
12 A:X-Cutioner 3.00
13 JOs,TL, Working for S.H.I.E.L.D.?, A:X-Cutioner 2.00
14 . . . . 2.00
15 JOs,TL, X-Cutioner 2.00
16 JOS,TL, concl.? 2.00
17 JOS,TL,A:Daredevil,Doc Samson, Spider-Man 2.00
18 JOS,TL,Frank Castle amnesia? . 2.00
19 JOS,TL,V:Taskmaster 2.00
20 JOS,TL, fugitive Punisher 2.00

PUNISHER
Sept., 1998

1 (of 4) BWr,JP,TSg,F:Frank Castle 3.00
2 BWr,JJu,JP,A:Hellstrom 3.00
3 BWr,JJu,TSg,JP,A:Gadriel. 3.00
4 BWr,JJu,TSg,JP,Hell on Earth. . . 3.00

PUNISHER
Jan., 2000

1 (of 12) JP,GEn,SDi,R:Punisher . . 3.00
2A JP,GEn,SDi,V:Ma Gnucci 3.00
2B variant SDi(c) 3.00
3 GEn,JP,SDi,polybaged 4.00
4 GEn,JP,SDi,Gnuccis 3.00
5 GEn,JP,SDi,Mr.Payback 3.00
6 GEn,JP,SDi,Elite. 3.00
7 GEn,JP,SDi,Mr.Payback 3.00
8 GEn,JP,SDi,Gnuccis 3.00
9 GEn,JP,SDi,Russian 3.00
Spec. Punisher/Painkiller Jane 3.50
GN Punisher Kills the Marvel Universe, 48-pg. GEn,DBw. . . . 5.95

PUNISHER ARMORY
July, 1990

1 JLe(c). 3.00
2 JLe(c). 2.00
3 . . . . 2.00
4 thru 6 . . . . @2.00
7 thru 10 . . . . @2.00

PUNISHER/ CAPTAIN AMERICA: BLOOD AND GLORY

1 thru 3 KJ,V:Drug Dealers. . . . . @6.25

CLASSIC PUNISHER

1 TDz 4.95

PUNISHER KILLS THE MARVEL UNIVERSE
1995

1-shot Alterniverse. 5.95

PUNISHER MAGAZINE
Oct., 1989

1 MZ,rep.,Punisher #1 . . . . 2.50
2 MZ,rep 2.25
3 thru 13 KJ,rep. . . . . @2.25
14 rep. PWJ #1 . . . . 2.25
15 rep. PWJ 2.25
16 rep.,1990. . . . . 2.25

PUNISHER MEETS ARCHIE
1994

1 JB 4.25
1a newsstand ed. 3.25

PUNISHER MOVIE COMIC
Nov., 1989

1 Movie adapt.. . . . . 2.00
2 Movie adapt.. . . . . 2.00
3 Movie adapt,Dec., 1989 . . . . 2.00

PUNISHER P.O.V.
July, 1991

1 BWr,Punisher/Nick Fury 5.50
2 BWr,A:Nick Fury,Kingpin. 5.50
3 BWr,V:Mutant Monster, A:Vampire Slayer 5.50
4 BWr,A:Nick Fury. 5.25

PUNISHER 2099
1993–95

1 TMo,Jake Gallows family Killed, foil(c) 2.50
2 TMo,I:Fearmaster,Kron,Multi Factor 2.25
3 TMo,V:Frightening Cult. 2.25
4 TMo,V:Cyber Nostra 2.00
5 TMo,V:Cyber Nostra,Fearmaster. 2.00
6 TMo,V:Multi-Factor 2.00
7 TMo,Love and Bullets#1 . . . . 2.00
8 TMo,Love and Bullets#2 . . . . 2.00
9 TMo,Love and Bullets#3 . . . . 2.00
10 TMo,I:Jigsaw 2.00
11 TMo,V:Jigsaw 2.00
12 TMo,A:Spider-Man 2099 . . . . . . 2.00
13 TMo,Fall of the Hammer#5 . . . . 2.00
14 WSm, ... 2.00
15 TMo,V:Fearmaster, I:Public Enemy 2.00

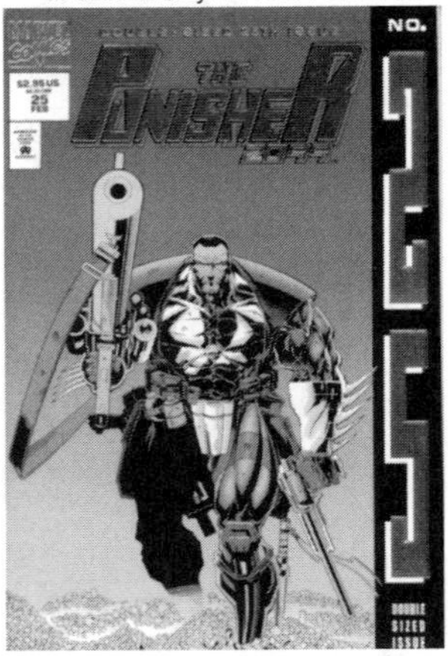

Punisher 2099 #25
© Marvel Entertainment Group

16 TMo,V:Fearmaster, Public Enemy 2.00
17 TMo,V:Public Enemy 2.00
18 TMo,I:Goldheart. 2.00
19 TMo,I:Vendetta 2.00
20 . . . . 2.00
21 . . . . 2.00
22 V:Hotwire. 2.00
23 I:Synchron,V:Hotwire 2.00
24 V:Synchron 2.00
25 Enhanced cover. 2.95
25a newsstand ed. 2.25
26 V:Techno-Shaman 1.50
27 R:Blue Max 1.50
Becomes:

PUNISHER 2099 A.D.

28 Minister of Punishment 2.00
29 Minister of Punishment 2.00
30 One Nation Under Doom 2.00
31 . . . . 2.00
32 Out of Ammo. 2.00
33 Counddown to final issue. 2.00
34 final issue 2.00

PUNISHER WAR JOURNAL
Nov., 1988

1 CP,JLe,O:Punisher 3.00
2 CP,JLe,A:Daredevil. 2.50
3 CP,JLe,A:Daredevil. 2.50
4 CP,JLeV:The Sniper 2.50
5 CP,JLe,V:The Sniper. 2.50
6 CP,JLe,A:Wolverine 2.50
7 CP,JLe,A:Wolverine 2.50
8 JLe,I:Shadowmasters 2.50
9 JLe,A:Black Widow. 2.50
10 JLe,V:Sniper 2.50
11 JLe,Shock Treatment 2.00
12 JLe,AM,V:Bushwacker 2.00
13 JLe(c),V:Bushwacker 2.00
14 JLe(c),DR,RH,A:Spider-Man . . . 2.00
15 JLe(c),DR,RH,A:Spider-Man . . . 2.00
16 MT(i),Texas Massacre 2.00
17 JLe,AM,Hawaii. 2.00
18 JLe,AM,Kahuna,Hawaii 2.00
19 JLe,AM,Traume in Paradise. . . . 2.00
20 AM 2.00
21 TSm,AM 2.00
22 TSm,AM,Ruins #1 . . . . 2.00
23 TSm,AM,Ruins #2 . . . . 2.00
24 . . . . 2.00
25 MT 2.00
26 MT,A:Saracen 2.00
27 MT,A:Saracen 2.00
28 MT 2.00
29 MT,A:Ghostrider. 2.00
30 MT,A:Ghostrider. 2.00
31 NKu,Kamchatkan Konspiracy#1 . . . . 2.00
32 Kamchatkan Konspiracy #2 . . . . 2.00
33 Kamchatkan Konspiracy #3 . . . . 2.00
34 V:Psycho 2.00
35 Movie Stuntman. 2.00
36 Radio Talk Show #1. . . . . 2.00
37 Radio Talk Show #2. . . . . 2.00
38 . . . . 2.00
39 DGr,V:Serial Killer 2.00
40 MWg 2.00
41 Armageddon Express 2.00
42 Mob run-out. 2.00
43 JR2(c) 2.00
44 Organ Donor Crimes 2.00
45 Dead Man's Hand #3,V:Viper. . . 2.00
46 Dead Man's Hand #6,V:Chainsaw and the Praetorians 2.00
47 Dead Man's Hand #7,A:Nomad, D.D,V:Hydra,Secret Empire . . . 2.00
48 B:Payback. 2.00
49 JR2(c),V:Corrupt Cop 2.00

Punisher War Journal #2
© Marvel Entertainment Group

50 MT,V:Highjackers,I:Punisher 2099 . . . . 2.00
51 E:Payback 2.00
52 A:Ice(from The'Nam) 2.00
53 A:Ice(from the Nam) 2.00
54 Hyper#1 . . . . 2.00
55 Hyper#2 . . . . 2.00
56 Hyper#3 . . . . 2.00
57 A:Ghost Rider,Daredevil. 2.00
58 A:Ghost Rider,Daredevil. 2.00
59 F:Max the Dog. 2.00
60 CDi(s),F:Max the Dog 2.00
61 CDi(s),Suicide Run#1,Foil(c) . . . 3.00
62 CDi(s),Suicide Run#4 . . . . 2.00
63 CDi(s),Suicide Run#7 . . . . 2.00
64 CDi(s),Suicide Run#10 . . . . 3.00
64a Newsstand Ed. 2.50
65 B:Pariah 2.00
66 A:Captain America. 2.25
67 Pariah#3 . . . . 2.25
68 A:Spider-Man 2.25
69 E:Pariah 2.00
70 . . . . 2.00
71 . . . . 2.00
72 V:Fake Punisher 2.00
73 E:Frank Castle. 2.00
74 . . . . 2.00
75 MT(c) 2.50
76 First Entry 2.00
77 R:Stone COld 2.00
78 V:Payback,Heathen 2.00
79 Countdown 3 . . . . 2.00
80 Countdown 0, A:Nick Fury, V:Bullseye, final issue. 2.00
TPB reprints #6,7 . . . . 4.95

PUNISHER WAR ZONE
1992

1 JR2,KJ,Punisher As Johnny Tower Die-Cut Bullet Hole(c). 3.00
2 JR2,KJ,Mafia Career 2.00
3 JR2,KJ,Punisher/Mafia,contd . . . 2.00
4 JR2,KJ,Cover gets Blown 2.00
5 JR2,KJ,A:Shotgun 2.00
6 JR2,KJ,A:Shotgun 2.00
7 JR2,V:Rapist in Central Park . . . 2.00
8 JR2,V:Rapist in Central Park . . . 2.00
9 JR2,V:Magnificent Seven 2.00
10 JR2,V:Magnificent Seven. 2.00
11 JR2,MM,V:Magnificent Seven. . . 2.00
12 Punisher Married 2.00
13 Self-Realization 2.00
14 Psychoville#3 . . . . 2.00
15 Psychoville#4 . . . . 2.00
16 Psychoville#5 . . . . 2.00
17 Industrial Esponiage 2.00
18 Jerico Syndrome#2 . . . . 2.00
19 Jerico Syndrome#3 . . . . 2.00
20 B:2 Mean 2 Die 2.00
21 2 Mean 2 Die#2. . . . . 2.00
22 A:Tyger Tyger 2.00
23 Suicide Run#2,Foil(c). 3.25
24 Suicide Run#5, ... 2.00
25 Suicide Run#8, ... 2.50
26 CDi(s),JB,Pirates 2.00
27 CDi(s),JB, ... 2.25
28 CDi(s),JB,Sweet Revenge 2.25
29 CDi(s),JB,The Swine 2.25
30 CDi(s),JB. 2.00
31 CDi(s),JB,River of Blood,pt.1 . . . 2.00
32 CDi(s),JB,River of Blood,pt.2 . . . 2.00
33 CDi(s),JB,River of Blood,pt.3 . . . 2.00
34 CDi(s),JB,River of Blood,pt.4 . . . 2.00
35 River of Blood,pt.5. . . . . 2.00
36 River of Blood,pt.6. . . . . 2.00
37 O:Max. 2.00
38 Dark Judgment,pt.1 . . . . 2.00
39 Dark Judgment,pt.2 . . . . 2.00
40 In Court 2.00
41 CDi,Countdown 2, final issue . . . 2.00
Ann.#1 Jb,MGo,(c),I:Phalanx, w/Trading card 3.25
Ann.#2 CDi(s),DR. 2.95

PUNISHER: YEAR ONE
1994

1 O:Punisher. 2.50
2 O:Punisher. 2.50
3 O:Punisher. 2.50
4 finale 2.50

PUSSYCAT
(B&W Magazine) Oct., 1968

1 BEv,BWa,WW 175.00

QUASAR
Oct., 1989

1 O:Quasar 2.50
2 V:Deathurge,A:Eon. 2.00
3 A:Human Torch,V:The Angler . . . 2.00
4 Acts of Vengeance,A:Aquarian . . 2.00
5 A of Veng,V:Absorbing Man 2.00
6 V:Klaw,Living Laser,Venom, Red Ghost 3.00
7 MM,A:Cosmic SpM,V:Terminus. . 2.50
8 MM,A:New Mutants,BlueShield. . 2.00
9 MM,A:Modam 2.00
10 MM,A:Dr.Minerva 2.00
11 MM,A:Excalibur,A:Modred 2.00
12 MM,A:Makhari,Blood Bros.. . . . . 2.00
13 JLe(c)MM,J.into Mystery #1 . . . . 2.00
14 TM(c)MM,J.into Mystery #2 . . . . 2.00
15 MM,Journey into Mystery #3 . . . 2.00
16 MM,Double sized. 2.00
17 MM,Race,A:Makkari,Whizzer, Quicksilver,Capt.Marv,Super Sabre,Barry Allen Spoof 2.25
18 GCa,N:Quasar. 2.00
19 GCa,B:Cosmos in Collision, C:Thanos 2.00
20 GCa,A:Fantastic Four 2.00
21 GCa,V:Jack of Hearts 2.00
22 GCa,D:Quasar,A:Ghost Rider . . 2.00
23 GCa,A:Ghost Rider 2.00
24 GCa,A:Thanos,Galactus, D:Maelstrom. 2.00
25 GCa,A:Eternity & Infinity,N:Quasar, E:Cosmos Collision 2.00
26 GCa,Inf.Gauntlet,A:Thanos 2.50
27 GCa,Infinity Gauntlet,I:Epoch. . . 2.00

Quasar #41
© Marvel Entertainment Group

28 GCa,A:Moondragon,Her, X-Men 2.00
29 GCa,A:Moondragon,Her 2.00
30 GCa,What If? tie-in 2.00
31 GCa,R:New Universe. 2.00
32 GCa,Op.GalacticStorm,pt.3 . . . . 2.00
33 GCa,Op.GalacticStorm,pt.10 . . . 2.00
34 GCa,Op.GalacticStorm,pt.17 . . . 2.00
35 GCa,Binary V:Her 2.00
36 GCa,V:Soul Eater 2.00
37 GCa,V:Soul Eater 2.00
38 GCa,Inf.War,V:Warlock 2.00
39 SLi,Inf.War,V:Deathurge. 2.00
40 SLi,Inf.War,V:Deathurge. 2.00
41 R:Marvel Boy. 2.00
42 V:Blue Marvel 2.00
43 V:Blue Marvel 2.00
44 V:Quagmire 2.00
45 V:Quagmire,Antibody. 2.00
46 Neutron,Presence 2.00
47 1st Full Thunderstrike Story 2.00
48 A:Thunderstrike 2.00
49 Kalya Vs. Kismet 2.00
50 A:Man-Thing,Prism(c) 3.25
51 V:Angler,A:S.Supreme 2.00
52 V:Geometer. 2.00
53 . . . . 2.00
54 MGu(s),Starblast #2. . . . . 2.00
55 MGu(s),A:Stranger. 2.00
56 MGu(s),Starblast #10. . . . . 2.00
57 MGu(s),A:Kismet 2.00
58 . . . . 2.00
59 A:Thanos,Starfox. 2.00
60 final issue 2.00

QUESTPROBE
August, 1984

1 JR,A:Hulk,I:Chief Examiner. 2.00
2 AM,JM,A:Spider-Man 2.00
3 JSt,A:Thing & Torch 2.00

QUICKSILVER
Sept., 1997

1 CJ,TPe, V:Exodus, cont. from Excalibur #113 . . . . 3.00
2 TPe,CJ,A:Knights of Wundagore. 2.00
3 TPe,CJ,V:Arkon 2.00
4 TPe, Crystal returns 2.00
5 TPe,V:Inhumans. 2.00
6 TPe,Inhumands trilogy concl. . . . 2.00
7 JOs,F:The Black Knight 2.00
8 JOs,F:Pietro,V:Pyro 2.00

9 JOs,Savage Land concl.,A:High Evolutionary . . . 2.00
10 JOS,Live Kree or Die, pt.3, x-over . . . 2.00
11 JOs,The Seige of Wundagore, pt.2 (of 5) . . . 2.00
12 JOs,The Seige of Wundagore, pt.4 (of 5) 48pg. . . . 3.00
13 JOs,Seige of Wundagore,pt.5, final issue . . . 2.00

QUICK-TRIGGER WESTERN

See: WESTERN THRILLERS

RAIDERS OF THE LOST ARK

Sept., 1981

1 JB/KJ,movie adaption . . . 2.00
2 JB/KJ, . . . 2.00
3 JB/KJ,Nov.,1981 . . . 2.00

RAMPAGING HULK, THE

May, 1998

1 RL,double size, savage Hulk era. 3.00
2A RL,DGr,I:Ravage . . . 2.00
2B JQ,JP,variant cover . . . 2.00
3 RL,DGr,V:Ravage, concl. . . . 2.00
4 DR,Trapped by an Avalanche . . . 2.00
5 RL,F:Fantastic Four . . . 2.00
6 RL,DGr,V:Puma . . . 2.00

RAVAGE 2099

1992–95

1 PR,I:Ravage . . . 2.50
2 PR,V:Deathstryk . . . 2.00
3 PR,V:Mutroids . . . 2.00
4 PR,V:Mutroids . . . 2.00
5 PR,Hellrock . . . 2.00
6 PR,N:Ravage . . . 2.00
7 PR,new Powers . . . 2.00
8 V:Deathstryke . . . 2.00
9 PR,N:Ravage . . . 2.00
10 V:Alchemax . . . 2.00
11 A:Avatarr . . . 2.00
12 Ravage Transforms . . . 2.00
13 V:Fearmaster . . . 2.00
14 V:Punisher 2099 . . . 2.00
15 Fall of the Hammer #2 . . . 2.00
16 I:Throwback . . . 2.00
17 GtM,V:Throwback,O:X-11. . . . 2.00
18 GtM,w/card . . . 2.00
19 GtM, . . . 2.00
20 GtM,V:Hunter . . . 2.00
21 Savage on the Loose . . . 2.00
22 Exodus . . . 2.00
23 Blind Justice . . . 2.00
24 Unleashed . . . 2.00
25 Flame Bearer . . . 2.25
25a Deluxe ed. . . . 2.95
26 V:Megastruck . . . 2.00
27 V:Deathstryke . . . 2.00
28 R:Hela . . . 2.00
29 V:Deathstryke . . . 2.00
30 King Ravage . . . 2.00

Becomes:

RAVAGE 2099 A.D.

31 V:Doom . . . 2.00
32 One Nation Under Doom . . . 2.00
33 Final issue . . . 2.00

RAWHIDE KID

Atlas March, 1955—May, 1979

1 B:Rawhide Kid & Randy, A:Wyatt Earp . . . 700.00
2 Shoot-out(c) . . . 275.00
3 V:Hustler . . . 200.00
4 Rh(c) . . . 200.00
5 GC . . . 200.00
6 Six-Gun Lesson . . . 150.00
7 AW . . . 150.00
8 . . . 150.00
9 . . . 150.00
10 thru 16 . . . @125.00
17 JK,O:Rawhide Kid . . . 125.00
18 thru 20 . . . @125.00
21 . . . 125.00
22 . . . 125.00
23 JK,O:Rawhide Kid Retold . . . 175.00
24 thru 30 . . . @100.00
31 JK,DAy,No Law in Mesa . . . 100.00
32 JK,DAy,Beware of the Parker Brothers . . . 100.00
33 JK(c),JDa,V:Jesse James . . . 100.00
34 JDa,JK,V:Mister Lightning . . . 100.00
35 JK(c),GC,JDa,I&D:The Raven 100.00
36 DAy,A Prisoner in Outlaw Town . . . 80.00
37 JK(c),DAy,GC,V:The Rattler . . . 80.00
38 DAy.V:The Red Raven . . . 80.00
39 DAy . . . 80.00
40 JK(c),DAy,A:Two Gun Kid . . . 80.00
41 JK(c),The Tyrant of Tombstone Valley . . . 80.00
42 JK . . . 80.00
43 JK . . . 80.00
44 JK(c),V:The Masked Maverick . 80.00
45 JK(c),O:Rawhide Kid Retold . . 100.00
46 JK(c),ATh . . . 75.00
47 JK(c),The Riverboat Raiders . . 50.00
48 GC,V:Marko the Manhunter . . . 40.00
49 The Masquerader . . . 45.00
50 A;Kid Colt,V:Masquerader . . . 45.00
51 DAy,Trapped in the Valley of Doom . . . 45.00
52 DAy,Revenge at Rustler's Roost . . . 45.00
53 Guns of the Wild North . . . 45.00
54 DH,BEv,The Last Showdown . . 45.00
55 . . . 45.00
56 DH,JTgV:The Peacemaker . . . 45.00
57 V:The Scorpion . . . 45.00
58 DAy . . . 45.00
59 V:Drako . . . 45.00

Rawhide Kid, new series #2
© Marvel Entertainment Group

60 DAy,HT,Massacre at Medicine Bend . . . 45.00
61 DAy,TS,A:Wild Bill Hickok . . . 35.00
62 Gun Town,V:Drako . . . 35.00
63 Shootout at Mesa City . . . 35.00
64 HT,Duel of the Desparadoes . . 35.00
65 JTg,HT,BE . . . 35.00
66 JTg,BEv,Death of a Gunfighter. 35.00
67 Hostage of Hungry Hills . . . 35.00
68 JB,V:The Cougar . . . 35.00
69 JTg,The Executioner . . . 35.00
70 JTg,The Night of the Betrayers 30.00
71 JTg,The Last Warrior . . . 30.00
72 JTg,The Menace of Mystery Valley . . . 30.00
73 JTg,The Manhunt . . . 30.00
74 JTg,The Apaches Attack . . . 30.00
75 JTg,The Man Who Killed The Kid . . . 30.00
76 JTg,V:The Lynx . . . 30.00
77 JTg,The Reckoning . . . 30.00
78 JTg . . . 30.00
79 JTg,AW,The Legion of the Lost 30.00
80 Fall of a Hero . . . 30.00
81 thru 85 . . . @30.00
86 JK,O:Rawhide Kid retold . . . 30.00
87 thru 99 . . . @15.00
100 O:Rawhide Kid retold . . . 25.00
101 thru 135 . . . @15.00
126 thru 151 . . . @10.00

RAWHIDE KID

August, 1985

1 JSe,mini-series . . . 2.00
2 thru 4 . . . @2.00

RAZORLINE FIRST CUT

1993

1 Intro Razorline . . . 2.00

REAL EXPERIENCES

See: TESSIE THE TYPIST

RED RAVEN

See: HUMAN TORCH

RED SONJA

[1st Series] Jan., 1977

1 FT,O:Red Sonja,`Blood of the Unicorn' . . . 3.50
2 FT,`Demon of the Maze' . . . 2.50
3 FT,`The Games of Gita' . . . 2.00
4 FT,`The Lake of the Unknown' . . 2.00
5 FT,`Master of the Bells' . . . 2.00
6 FT,`The Singing Tower' . . . 2.00
7 FT,`Throne of Blood' . . . 2.00
8 FT,Vengeance o/t Golden Circle . 2.00
9 FT,`Chariot o/t Fire-Stallions' . . . 2.00
10 FT,Red Lace,pt.1 . . . 2.00
11 FT,Red Lace,pt.2 . . . 2.00
12 JB/JRu,`Ashes & Emblems' . . . 2.00
13 JB/AM,`Shall Skranos Fall' . . . 2.00
14 SB/AM,`Evening on the Border' . 2.00
15 JB/TD,`Tomb of 3 Dead Kings' May, 1979 . . . 2.00

[2nd Series] Feb., 1983

1 TD,GC, The Blood That Binds . . 2.00
2 GC, March,1983 . . . 2.00

[3rd Series] August, 1983

1 . . . 2.00
2 thru 13 . . . @2.00
1 movie adaption, 1985 . . . 2.00
2 movie adaption, 1985 . . . 2.00

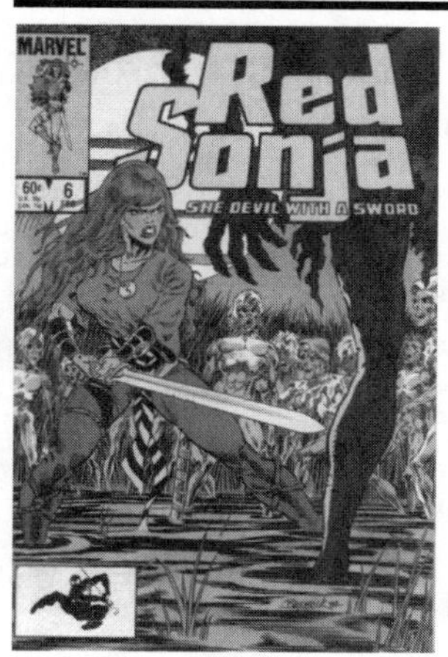

Red Sonja, Vol. 3, #6
© Marvel Entertainment Group

RED SONJA

1-shot Bros.Hildebrandt(c),48pg . . . 2.95

RED WARRIOR

Atlas Jan.–Dec., 1951

1 GT,Indian Tales 100.00
2 GT(c),The Trail of the Outcast . 65.00
3 The Great Spirit Speaks 50.00
4 O:White Wing 50.00
5 . . . . 50.00
6 Final Issue 50.00

RED WOLF

May, 1972–Sept., 1973

1 SSh(c),GK,JSe,F:Red Wolf & Lobo 18.00
2 GK(c),SSh,Day of the Dynamite Doom 10.00
3 SSh,War of the Wolf Brothers . 10.00
4 SSh,V:Man-Bear 10.00
5 GK(c),SSh 10.00
6 SSh,JA,V;Devil Rider 10.00
7 SSh,JA,Echoes from a Golden Grave 10.00
8 SSh,Hell on Wheels 10.00
9 DAy,To Die Again,O:Lobo 10.00

REN AND STIMPY SHOW

1992–96

1 Polybagged w/Air Fowlers, Ren(c) 5.00
1a Stimpy(c) 4.00
1b 2nd Printing 3.00
1c 3rd Printing 2.00
2 Frankenstimpy 3.00
2a 2nd Printing 2.00
3 Christmas issue 3.00
3a 2nd Printing 2.00
4 Where's Stimpy? 3.00
5 Teacher Bingo 3.00
6 A:SpM,V:Powdered Toast Man . . 3.00
7 F:Offical Yak Shaving Day 3.00
8 F:Bun Boy Burger Bunny 3.00
9 Untamed World 3.00
10 Bug Out. 3.00
11 Ren's Peaceful Place. 3.00
12 Teacher Bingo 3.00
13 Halloween issue 2.50
14 Mars needs Vecro 2.50
15 Christmas Spec. 2.25
16 . . . . 2.25
17 This Year's Model 2.25
18 U.S. Ohhhhh No! 2.25
19 Minimalist issue 2.25
20 F:Muddy Mudskipper 2.25
21 I'm The Cat 2.25
22 Badtime Stories 2.00
23 Athletics 2.00
24 Halloween 2.00
25 regular (c) 2.00
25a die-cut(c),A new addition 3.00
26 . . . . 2.00
27 . . . . 2.00
28 Filthy the Monkey 2.00
29 Loch Ness Mess 2.00
30 Pinata game 2.00
31 Sausage Castle 2.00
32 Join Circus, UFO Abduction 2.00
33 Bowling 2.00
34 lottery ticket 2.00
35 Pasta Monster 2.00
36 Ren Cabby Driver 2.00
37 Medical experiment 2.00
38 Cat who Knew too Much 2.00
39 Mad Computer. 2.00
40 . . . . 2.00
41 . . . . 2.00
42 at Cap'n Salty Wet World. 2.00
Spec.#1 . . . . 3.25
Spec.#2 . . . . 3.25
Spec.#3 Powder Toast Man 3.00
Spec.#4 . . . . 3.00
Spec.#5 Virtual Stupidity. 3.00
Spec.#6 History of Music 3.00
Holiday Special. 3.00
Spec. Radio Dazed & Confused . . . 2.00
Spec. Around the World in a Daze . 3.00
TPB Running Joke,rep.#1-4,w/new material 13.25
TPB Pick of the Litter 13.25
TPB Tastes Like Chicken 13.25
TPB Your Pals 12.95
TPB Seech Little Monkeys 12.95

RETURN OF THE JEDI

1 AW,movie adapt 3.00
2 AW,movie adapt 3.00
3 AW,movie adapt 3.00
4 AW,movie adapt 3.00

REX HART

See: BLAZE CARSON

RICHIE RICH

1 Movie Adaptation 2.95

RINGO KID

[2nd Series] Jan., 1970

1 AW,Reprints 20.00
2 JSe,Man Trap 10.00
3 JR,Man from the Panhandle . . 10.00
4 HT(c),The Golden Spur 10.00
5 JMn,Ambush 10.00
6 Capture or Death 10.00
7 HT(c),JSe,JA,Terrible Treasure of Vista Del Oro 10.00
8 The End of the Trail 10.00
9 JSe,Mystery of the Black Sunset 10.00
10 Bad day at Black Creek 10.00
11 Bullet for a Bandit 10.00
12 A Badge to Die For 15.00
13 DW,Hostage at Fort Cheyenne . 7.50
14 Showdown in the Silver Cartwheel. 7.50
15 Fang,Claw, and Six-Gun 7.50
16 Battle of Cattleman's Bank. 7.50
17 Gundown at the Hacienda 7.50
18 . . . . 7.50
19 Thunder From the West. 7.50
20 AW 7.50
21 thru 29 . . . . @7.50
30 Nov., 1973. . . . . 7.50

RINGO KID WESTERN

Atlas August, 1954

1 JSt,O:Ringo Kid,B:Ringo Kid . 225.00
2 I&O:Arab,A:Black Rider 125.00
3 . . . . 75.00
4 . . . . 75.00
5 . . . . 75.00
6 . . . . 75.00
7 . . . . 75.00
8 JSe 75.00
9 . . . . 50.00
10 JSe(c),AW 60.00
11 JSe(c) 50.00
12 JO 50.00
13 AW 60.00
14 thru 20 . . . . @50.00
21 Sept., 1957 . . . . 50.00

ROBOCOP

March, 1990

1 LS,I:Nixcops 6.00
2 LS,V:Nixcops 4.00
3 LS 3.00
4 LS 3.00
5 LS,WarzonePt1 . . . . 3.00
6 LS,WarzonePt2 . . . . 3.00
7 LS 2.50
8 LS,V:Gang-5. . . . . 2.50
9 LS,V:Vigilantes 2.50
10 LS 2.50
11 HT 2.50
12 LS,Robocop Army #1. . . . . 2.00
13 LS,Robocop Army #2. . . . . 2.00
14 LS,Robocop Army #3. . . . . 2.00
15 LS,Robocop Army #4. . . . . 2.00
16 TV take over 2.00
17 LS,V:The Wraith 2.00
18 LS,Mindbomb #1 . . . . 2.00
19 LS,Mindbomb #2 . . . . 2.00
20 In Detroit 2.00
21 LS,Beyond the Law,pt.1 . . . . 2.00
22 LS,Beyond the Law,pt.2 . . . . 2.00
23 LS,Beyond the Law,pt.3,final . . . 2.00
Robocop Movie Adapt 4.95
Robocop II Movie Adapt 4.95

Rocko's Modern Life #1
© Marvel Entertainment Group

ROBOCOP II
August, 1990

1 MBa,rep.Movie Adapt 2.00
2 and 3 MBa,rep.Movie adapt . . @2.00

ROBOTIX
Feb., 1986

1 Based on toys 2.00

ROCKET RACCOON
May, 1985—Aug., 1985

1 thru 4 MM . . . . @2.00

ROCKO'S MODERN LIFE
1994

1 and 2 . . . . @2.25
3 and 4 . . . . @2.00

ROGUE
1995

1 Enhanced cover 4.50
2 A:Gambit 4.00
3 Gamtit or Rogue? 3.00
4 final issue 3.00

ROM
Dec., 1979

1 SB,I&O:Rom 3.00
2 FM(c),SB,V:Dire Wraiths 2.50
3 FM(c),SB,I:Firefall 2.50
4 SB,A:Firefall 2.00
5 SB,A:Dr.Strange 2.00
6 SB,V:Black Nebula 2.00
7 SB,V:Dark Nebula 2.00
8 SB,V:Dire Wraiths 2.00
9 SB,V:Serpentyne 2.00
10 SB,V:U.S.Air Force 2.00
11 SB,V:Dire Wraiths 2.00
12 SB,A:Jack O' Hearts 2.00
13 SB,V:Plunderer 2.00
14 SB,V:Mad Thinker 2.00
15 SB,W:Brandy and Dire Wraith . . 2.00
16 SB,V:Watchwraith 2.00
17 SB,A:X-Men 3.00
18 SB,A:X-Men 3.00
19 SB,JSt,C:X-Men 2.00
20 SB,JSt,A:Starshine 2.00
21 SB,JSt,A:Torpedo 2.00
22 SB,JSt,A:Torpedo 2.00
23 SB,JSt,A:Powerman,Iron Fist . . . 2.00
24 SB,JSt,A:Nova 2.00
25 SB,JSt,Double-Sized 2.00
26 SB,JSt,V:Galactus 2.00
27 SB,JSt,V:Galactus 2.00
28 SB,JSt,D:Starshine 2.00
29 SB,Down in the Mines 2.00
30 SB,JSt,A:Torpedo 2.00
31 SB,JSt,V:Evil Mutants,Rogue . . . 2.00
32 SB,JSt,V:Evil Mutants 2.00
33 SB,V:Sybil 2.00
34 SB,A:Sub-Mariner 2.00
35 SB,A:Sub-Mariner 2.00
36 SB,V:Scarecrow 2.00
37 SB,A:Starshine 2.00
38 SB,A:Master of Kung Fu 2.00
39 SB,A:Master of Kung Fu 2.00
40 SB,A:Torpedo 2.00
41 SB,A:Dr.Strange 2.00
42 SB,A:Dr.Strange 2.00
43 SB,Rom Becomes Human 2.00
44 SB,A:Starshine,O:Gremlin 2.00
45 SB,V:Soviet Super Soldiers 2.00
46 SB,V:Direwraiths 2.00
47 SB,New Look for Wraiths 2.00
48 SB,V:Dire Wraiths 2.00
49 SB,V:Dire Wraiths 2.00

Rom #57
© Marvel Entertainment Group

50 SB,D:Torpedo,V:Skrulls 2.00
51 SB,F:Starshine 2.00
52 BSz(c),SB,V:Dire Wraiths 2.00
53 SB,BSz,V:Dire Wraiths 2.00
54 V:Dire Wraiths 2.00
55 V:Dire Wraihs 2.00
56 A:Alpha Flight 2.25
57 A:Alpha Flight 2.25
58 JG(c),A:Antman 2.00
59 SD,BL,V:Microbe Menace 2.00
60 SD,TP,V:Dire Wraiths 2.00
61 SD,V:Wraith-Realm 2.00
62 SD,A:Forge 2.00
63 SD,V:Dire Wraiths 2.00
64 SD,V:Dire Wraiths 2.00
65 SD,A:X-Men,Avengers 2.00
66 SD,Rom leaves Earth 2.00
67 SD,V:Scorpion 2.00
68 BSz(c)SD,Man & Machine 2.00
69 SD,V:Ego 2.00
70 SD 2.00
71 SD,V:Raak 2.00
72 SD,Secret Wars II 2.00
73 SD,JSt 2.00
74 SD,JBy,Code of Honor 2.00
75 SD,CR,Doublesize,last issue . . . 2.00
Ann.#1 PB,A:Stardust 2.00
Ann.#2 I:Knights of Galador 2.00
Ann.#3 A:New Mutants 2.25
Ann.#4 V:Gladiator 2.00

ROMANCE DIARY
Dec., 1949

1 . . . . 80.00
2 March, 1950 . . . . 75.00

ROMANCES OF THE WEST
Nov., 1949

1 Ph(c),Calamity Jane,
Sam Bass 160.00
2 March, 1950 . . . . 120.00

ROMANCE TALES
Oct., 1949
(no #1 thru 6)

7 . . . . 80.00
8 . . . . 50.00
9 March, 1950 . . . . 50.00

ROMANTIC AFFAIRS
See: MOLLY MANTON'S ROMANCES

ROYAL ROY
Star May, 1985

1 thru 5 . . . . @2.00
6 March, 1986 . . . . 2.00

RUGGED ACTION
Atlas Dec., 1954

1 Man-Eater 120.00
2 JSe,DAy.Manta-Ray 70.00
3 DAy 70.00
4 . . . . 70.00
Becomes:

STRANGE STORIES OF SUSPENSE

5 RH,The Little Black Box 300.00
6 BEv,The Illusion 175.00
7 JSe(c),BEv,Old John's House 185.00
8 AW,BP,TYhumbs Down 185.00
9 BEv(c),Nightmare 175.00
10 RC,MME,AT 165.00
11 BEv(c) 135.00
12 AT 135.00
13 BEv,GM 125.00
14 AW 160.00
15 BK 150.00
16 MF,BP, August, 1957 . . . . 150.00

RUINS
1995

1 Marvel's Alterverse 4.95
2 Fully painted, 32pg 4.95

RUSTY COMICS
See: KID KOMICS

SABRETOOTH
[Limited Series] 1993

1 B:LHa(s),MT,A:Wolverine 5.00
2 MT,A:Mystique,C:Wolverine 4.00
3 MT,A:Mystique,Wolverine 3.50
4 E:LHa(s),MT,D:Birdy 3.00
TPB rep. #1-#4 . . . . 12.95

SABRETOOTH CLASSICS
1994–95

1 rep. Power Man/Iron Fist #66 . . . 2.00
2 rep. Power Man/Iron Fist #78 . . . 2.00
3 rep. Power Man/Iron Fist #84 . . . 2.00
4 rep. Spider-Man #116 . . . . 2.00
5 rep. Spider-Man #119 . . . . 2.00
6 reprints 2.00
7 reprints 2.00
8 reprints 2.00
9 reprints 2.00
10 Morlock Massacre 2.00
11 rep. Daredevil #238 . . . . 2.00
12 rep. V:Wolverine 2.00
13 rep. 2.00
14 A:Mauraders 2.00
15 Mutant Massacre, rep.
Uncanny X-Men #221 . . . . 2.00

SABRETOOTH

Spec.#1 FaN, cont.from X-Men#48 . 4.95

 All comics prices listed are for *Near Mint* condition.

Savage Sword of Conan #1
© Marvel Entertainment Group

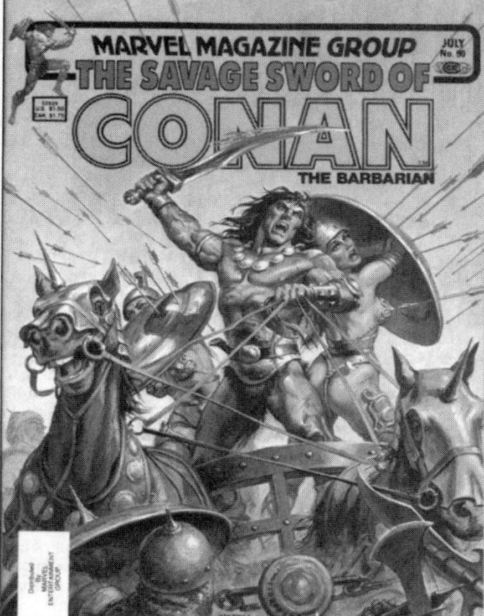

Savage Sword of Conan #90
© Marvel Entertainment Group

SABRETOOTH
Oct., 1997
1-shot,F:Wildchild 2.50

SABRETOOTH & MYSTIQUE
1 JGz,AOI,. 2.00
2 thru 4 JGz,AOI . . . . @2.00

SACHS & VIOLENS
Epic 1993–94
1 GP,PDd(s) 3.00
2 GP,PDd(s),V:Killer 2.50
3 GP,PDd(s),V:White Slavers. 2.50
4 GP,PDd(s),D:Moloch. 2.25

SAGA OF CRYSTAR
May, 1983
1 O:Crystar 2.25
2 A:Ika 2.00
3 A:Dr.Strange. 2.00
4 . . . . 2.00
5 . . . . 2.00
6 A:Nightcrawler 2.25
7 I:Malachon 2.00
8 . . . . 2.00
9 . . . . 2.00
10 Chaos 2.00
11 Alpha Flight,Feb., 1985 . . . . 2.00

SAGA OF ORIGINAL HUMAN TORCH
1 RB,O:Original Human Torch 3.00
2 RB,A:Toro. 2.50
3 RB,V:Adolph Hitler 2.50
4 RB,Torch vs. Toro. 2.50

ST. GEORGE
Epic June, 1988
1 KJ,Shadow Line 2.00
2 KJ,I:Shrek 2.00
3 KJ 2.00
4 KJ 2.00
5 . . . . 2.00
6 . . . . 2.00
7 DSp 2.00
8 Oct., 1989 . . . . 2.00

SAINT SINNER
Razorline 1993–94
1 I:Phillip Fetter. 2.75
2 F:Phillip Fetter 2.00
3 in Vertesque. 2.00
4 . . . . 2.00
5 Arcadia. 2.00
6 . . . . 2.00
7 The Child Stealer 2.00
8 . . . . 2.00

SAM & MAX GO TO THE MOON
1 Dirtbag Special,w/Nirvana Tape . 4.00

[Regular Series]
1 MMi,AAd,F:Skull Boy 3.25
2 AAd,MMi 2.95
3 . . . . 2.95

SAMURAI CAT
Epic 1991
1 I:MiaowaraTomokato. 2.25
2 I:Con-Ed,V:Thpaghetti-Thoth. . . . 2.25
3 EmpireStateStrikesBack 2.25

SATANA
Nov., 1997
1 JaL,WEI,AOI,V:Doctor Strange, non-code series 3.00
2 WEI,AOI,to the gates of Hell 3.00

SAVAGE SWORD OF CONAN
August, 1974
(black & white magazine)
1 BWS,JB,NA,GK,O:Blackmark, 3rdA:Red Sonja,Boris(c). 75.00
2 NA(c),HC,GK,`Black Colossus,' B.U.King Kull;B.U.Blackmark . 35.00
3 JB,BWS,GK,`At The Mountain of the Moon God;B.U.s: Kull;Blackmark 30.00
4 JB,RCo,GKIron Shadows in the Moon B.U.Blackmark,Boris(c) . 15.00
5 JB,A WitchShall beBorn,Boris(c) 15.00
6 AN,`Sleeper `Neath the Sands'. 12.50
7 JB,Citadel at the Center of Time Boris(c) 12.50
8 inc.GK,`Corsairs against Stygia. 12.50
9 Curse of the Cat-Goddess, Boris(c),B.U.King Kull 12.50
10 JB,`Sacred Serpent of Set' Boris(c) 10.00
11 JB,`The Abode of the Damned' 10.00
12 JB,Haunters of Castle Crimson Boris(c) 10.00
13 GK,The Thing in the Temple, B.U. Solomon Kane 10.00
14 NA,Shadow of Zamboula, B.U.Solomon Kane. 10.00
15 JB,Boris(c),`Devil in Iron' 10.00
16 JB,BWS,People of the Black Circle,B.U.Bran Mak Morn . . . 10.00
17 JB,`On to Yimsha!, B.U.Bran Mak Morn 10.00
18 JB,`The Battle of the Towers' B.U. Solomon Kane 10.00
19 JB,`Vengeance in Vendhya' B.U. Solomon Kane 10.00
20 JB,`The Slithering Shadow' B.U. Solomon Kane 10.00
21 JB,`Horror in the Red Tower' . . 10.00
22 JB,`Pool o/t Black One' B.U. Solomon Kane 10.00
23 JB,FT,`Torrent of Doom'

MARVEL

B.U. Solomon Kane 10.00
24 JB,BWS,`Tower of the Elephant'B.U.Cimmeria. 10.00
25 DG,SG,Jewels of Gwahlur, B.U.Solomon Kane. 10.00
26 JB/TD,Beyond the Black River, B.U.Solomon Kane. 8.00
27 JB/TD,Children of Jhebbal Sag . 8.00
28 JB/AA,Blood of the Gods 8.00
29 ECh,FT,Child of Sorcery, B.U. Red Sonja 8.00
30 FB,The Scarlet Citadel. 8.00
31 JB/TD,The Flaming Knife,pt.1 . . 8.00
32 JB/TD,Ghouls of Yanaldar,pt.2 . . 8.00
33 GC,Curse of the Monolith, B.U.Solomon Kane. 8.00
34 CI/AA,MP,Lair o/t Ice Worm;B.U. Solomon Kane,B.U.King Kull . . 8.00
35 ECh,Black Tears 8.00
36 JB,AA,Hawks over Shem. 8.00
37 SB,Sons of the White Wolf B.U. Solomon Kane 8.00
38 JB/TD,The Road of the Eagles. . 8.00
39 SB/TD,The Legions of the Dead, B.U.Solomon Kane concl. 8.00
40 JB/TD,A Dream of Blood 8.00
41 JB/TD,Quest for the Cobra Crown A:Thoth-Amon,B.U.Sol.Kane . . 8.00
42 JB/TD,Devil-Tree of Gamburu, A:Thoth-Amon,B.U.Sol.Kane . . 8.00
43 JB/TD,King Thoth-Amon, B.U.King Kull 8.00
44 SB/TD,The Star of Khorala 8.00
45 JB/TD,The Gem in the Tower, B.U. Red Sonja 8.00
46 EC/TD,Moon of Blood, B.U. Hyborian Tale 8.00
47 GK/JB/JRu,Treasure of Tranicos C:Thoth-Amon 8.00
48 JB/KJ,A Wind Blows from Stygia C:Thoth-Amon 8.00
49 JB/TD,When Madness Wears the Crown, B.U.Hyborian Tale 6.00
50 JB/TD,Swords Across the Alimane 6.00
51 JB/TD,Satyrs' Blood. 6.00
52 JB/TD,Conan the Liberator 6.00
53 JB,The Sorcerer and the Soul, B.U. Solomon Kane 6.00
54 JB,The Stalker Amid the Sands, B.U. Solomon Kane 6.00
55 JB,Black Lotus & Yellow Death B.U. King Kull. 6.00
56 JB/TD,The Sword of Skelos. . . . 6.00
57 JB/TD,Zamboula 6.00
58 JB/TD,KGa,For the Throne of Zamboula,B.U.OlgerdVladislav . 6.00
59 AA,ECh,City ofSkulls,B.U.Gault . 6.00
60 JB,The Ivory Goddess 6.00
61 JB,Wizard Fiend of Zingara 6.00
62 JB/ECh,Temple of the Tiger, B.U. Solomon Kane 6.00
63 JB/ECh,TP/BMc,GK,Moat of Blood I:Chane of the Elder Earth 6.00
64 JB/ECh,GK,Children of Rhan, B.U. Chane 6.00
65 GK,JB,Fangs of the Serpent, B.U. Bront 6.00
66 thru 75 . . . . @6.00
76 thru 80 . . . . @5.00
81 JB/ECh,Palace of Pleasure, B.U. Bront 5.00
82 AA,BWS,Devil in the Dark.Pt.1 B.U.repConan#24,Swamp Gas. 5.00
83 AA,MW,NA,ECh,Devil in the Dark Pt.2,B.U. Red Sonja,Sol.Kane . 5.00
84 VM,Darksome Demon of Rabba Than. 5.00
85 GK,Daughter of the God King . . 5.00
86 GK,Revenge of the Sorcerer . . . 5.00
87 . . . . 5.00
88 JB,Isle of the Hunter 5.00
89 AA,MW,Gamesman of Asgalun, B.U. Rite of Blood. 5.00
90 JB,Devourer of Souls. 5.00
91 JB,VM,Forest of Friends, B.U. The Beast,The Chain 5.00
92 JB,The Jeweled Bird 5.00
93 JB/ECh,WorldBeyond the Mists . 5.00
94 thru 101 . . . . @5.00
102 GD,B.U.Bran Mac Morn 4.00
103 GD,White Tiger of Vendhya, B.U. Bran Mac Morn. 4.00
104 . . . . 4.00
105 . . . . 4.00
106 Feud of Blood 4.00
107 thru 118 . . . . @4.00
119 ECh,A:Conan's Sister. 4.00
120 Star of Thama-Zhu. 4.00
121 . . . . 4.00
122 . . . . 4.00
123 ECh,Secret of the GreatStone . 4.00
124 ECh,Secret of the Stone 4.00
125 Altar of the Goat God. 4.00
126 The Mercenary 4.00
127 Reunion in Scarlet,Return of Valeria 4.00
128 . . . . 4.00
129 . . . . 4.00
130 Reavers of the Steppes 4.00
131 GI,Autumn of the Witch 4.00
132 ECh,Masters o/t Broadsword . . 4.00
133 . . . . 4.00
134 Conan the Pirate 4.00
135 Conan the Pirate 4.00
136 NKu,Stranded on DesertIsland. 4.00
137 ECh,The Lost Legion 4.00
138 ECh,Clan o/t Lizard God 4.00
139 ECh,A:Valeria 4.00
140 ECh,The Ghost's Revenge. . . . 4.00
141 ECh. 4.00
142 ECh,V:Warlord. 4.00
143 ECh. 4.00
144 ECh. 4.00
145 ECh. 4.00
146 ECh. 4.00
147 ECh. 4.00
148 BMc. 4.00
149 TGr,BMc,Conan Enslaved 4.00
150 ECh. 4.00
151 ECh. 4.00
152 ECh,Valley Beyond the Stars . . 4.00
153 Blood on the Sand,Pt.1 . . . . . . 4.00
154 Blood on the Sand,Pt.2 . . . . . . 4.00
155 ECh,V:Vampires. 4.00
156 V:Corinthian Army 4.00
157 V:Hyborians. 4.00

Savage Sword of Conan, Ann. #1
© Marvel Entertainment Group

158 ECh,The Talisman-Gem. 4.00
159 Conan Enslaved 4.00
160 . . . . 4.00
161 V:Magician/Monsters 4.00
162 AW,Horned God,B.U.Sol.Kane. 3.50
163 V:Picts 3.50
164 Conan's Revenge 3.50
165 B.U. King Kull 3.50
166 ECh,Conan in New World,Pt.1 . 3.50
167 ECh,Conan in New World,Pt.2 . 3.50
168 ECh,Conan in New World,concl 3.50
169 . . . . 3.50
170 AW,A:Red Sonja,Valeria B.U. Solomon Kane 3.50
171 TD,Conan Youth Story 3.50
172 JS,JRu,Haunted Swamp, B.U.King Kull,Valeria, Red Sonja 3.00
173 ECh,Under Siege. 3.00
174 AA,Red Stones of Rantha Karn. 3.00
175 The Demonslayer Sword 3.00
176 FH,TT,V:Wizard,B.U. Witch Queen,Dagon,Ghouls 3.00
177 LMc,TD,ECh,Conan the Prey, B.U.King Conan,Red Sonja . . . 3.00
178 AA,The Dinosaur God 3.00
179 ECh,A:Red Sonja,Valeria, B.U.Conan 3.00
180 ECh,Sky-God Bardisattva, B.U. King Kull. 3.00
181 TD,Conan the Pagan God?, B.U. Voodoo Tribe 3.00
182 RB/RT,V:Killer Ants 3.00
183 ECh,V:Kah-Tah-Dhen, B.U.King Kull 3.00
184 AA,Return of Sennan. 3.00
185 The Ring of Molub 3.00
186 AW,A:Thulsa Doom 3.00
187 ECh,A:Conan's Brother? 3.00
188 V:Kharban the Sorcerer 3.00
189 A:Search Zukala for Gem. 3.00
190 JB/TD,Skull on the Seas,pt.1 . . 2.50
191 JB/ECh,Skull on the Seas,pt.2 Thulsa Doom Vs.Thoth-Amon. . 2.50
192 JB/ECh,Skull on the Seas,pt.3 B.U. King Kull. 2.50
193 JB/ECh,Skull on the Seas concl. V:Thulsa Doom & Thoth-Amon . 2.50
194 JB/ECh,Wanted for Murder, B.U. Li-Zya. 2.50
195 JB/ECh,V:Yamatains, Giant Tortoise. 2.50
196 JB/ECh,Treasure of the Stygian Prince-Toth-Mekri,A:Valeria. . . . 2.50
197 RTs,JB,EC,Red Hand 2.50
198 RTs,JB,EC,Red Hand 2.50
199 RTs,JB,EC,V:Black Zarona. . . . 2.50
200 RTs,JB,ECh,JJu(c),The Barbarian from Cross Plains. 2.50
201 RTs,MCW,return to Tarantia . . . 2.50
202 RTs,JB,ECh,Conan in the City City of Magicians,pt.1 . . . . 2.50
203 RTs,JB,ECh,Conan in the City City of Magicians,pt.2 . . . . 2.50
204 RTs,JB,ECh,Conan in the City City of Magicians,pt.3 . . . . 2.50
205 RTs,JB,ECh,Conan in the City City of Magicians,pt.4 . . . . 2.50
206 RTs,JB,ECh,BLr(c),Conan in the City of Magicians,concl. 2.50
207 RTs,JB,ECh,MK(c), Conan and the Spider God, pt.1 . . . . 2.50
208 RTs,JB,ECh, Conan and the Spider God, pt.2. . . . . 2.50
209 RTs,JB,Conan and the Spider God,pt.3 . . . . 2.50
210 RTs,Conan and the Spider God,pt.4 . . . . 2.50
211 RTs,Conan and the Gods of

the Mountain,pt.1 . . . . 2.50
212 RTs,Conand and the Gos of the Mountain,pt.2 . . . . 2.50
213 RTs,Conan and the Gods of the Mountain,pt.3 . . . . 2.50
214 RTs,Conan and the Gods of the Mountain,pt.4 . . . . 2.50
215 RTs,JuB(c),Conan and the Gods of the Mountain,concl.. . . . . 2.50
216 RTs,AA,Vengeance of Nitocris . 2.50
217 RTs,Conan theMercenary,pt.1 . 2.50
218 RTs,Conan theMercenary,pt.2 . 2.50
219 RTs,A:Solomon Kane. 2.50
220 RTs,V:Skull Out of Time 2.50
221 RTs,C.L.Moore story adapt. . . . 2.50
222 RTs,The Haunter of the Towers B.U.JB,Conan Barbarian #1 . . . 2.50
223 RTs,A:Tuzune Thune 2.50
224 RTs,JWk,The Dwellers Under the Tombs,adapt. B.U.V:Dinosaurs . 2.50
225 . . . . 2.50
226 RTs,EN(c),The Four Ages of Conan, A:Red Sonja. 2.50
227 RTs,JBu, besieged in a lost city, B.U. Kull,Red Sonja. 2.50
228 RTs,AN,Conan in chains! 2.50
229 RTs 2.50
230 RTs, Acheron falls, Ring of Tkrubu,pt.2, R:Kull 2.50
231 RTs, V:Tuzoun Thune, B.U. EM,Red Sonja 2.50
232 RTs 2.50
233 A:Juma the Black, Kull. 2.50
234 RTs,JBu, A:Nefartari; A:Red Sonja, Zula 2.50
235 RTs,JBu,The Daughter of Raktauanishi, final issue. 2.50
Ann.#1 SB,BWS,inc.`Beware the Wrath of Anu',B.U. King Kull Vs.Thulsa Doom 2.50

SAVAGE TALES
May, 1971
(black & white magazine)

1 GM,BWS,JR,I&O:Man-Thing, B:Conan,Femizons,A:Kazar . 150.00
2 GM,FB,BWS,AW,BWr,A:King Kull rep,Creatures on the Loose #10 . . . . 50.00
3 FB,BWS,AW,JSo 35.00
4 NA(c),E:Conan 20.00
5 JSn,JB,B:Brak the Barbarian . . 20.00
6 NA(c),JB,AW,B:Kazar 8.00
7 GM,NA 6.00
8 JB,A:Shanna,E:Brak 5.00

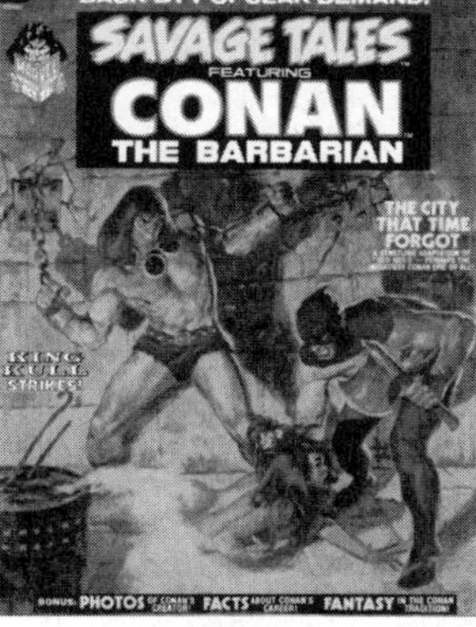

Savage Tales #2
© Marvel Entertainment Group

9 MK,A:Shanna 5.00
10 RH,NA,AW,A:Shanna. 5.00
11 RH. 5.00
12 Summer, 1975. . . . . 5.00
Ann.#1 GM,GK,BWS,O:Kazar. 6.00

SAVAGE TALES
Nov., 1985
(black & white magazine)

1 MGo,I:The `Nam 3.00
2 MGo 2.00
3 MGo 2.00
4 MGo 2.00
5 MGo 2.00
6 MGo 2.00
7 MGo 2.00
8 MGo 2.00
9 MGo,March, 1987 . . . . 2.00

SCARLET SPIDER
1995–96

1 HMe,GK,TP,VirtualMortality,pt.3 . 2.00
2 HMe,JR2,AW,CyberWar,pt.3. . . . 2.00
3 and 4 HMe . . . . @2.00

SCARLET SPIDER UNLIMITED
1995

1 True Origin,64pg. 3.95

SCARLET WITCH
1994

1 ALa(s),DAn(s),JH,I:Gargan, C:Master Pandemonium 2.00
2 C:Avengers West Coast 2.00
3 A:Avengers West Coast 2.00
4 V:Lore,last issue 2.00

SCOOBY-DOO
Oct., 1977

1 B:DynoMutt 9.00
2 thru 8 . . . . @8.00
9 Feb., 1979 . . . . 8.00

SECRET DEFENDERS
1993–95

1 F:Dr.Strange(in all),Spider Woman,Nomad,Darkhawk, Wolverine,V:Macabre 3.25
2 F:Spider Woman,Nomad,Darkhawk, Wolverine,V:Macabre 2.50
3 F:Spider Woman,Nomad,Darkhawk, Wolverine,V:Macabre 2.00
4 F:Namorita,Punisher, Sleepwalker,V:Roadkill 2.00
5 F:Naromita,Punisher, Sleepwalker, V:Roadkill 2.00
6 F:Spider-Man,Scarlet Witch,Captain America,V:Suicide Pack 2.00
7 F:Captain America,Scarlet Witch, Spider-Man 2.00
8 F:Captain America,Scarlet Witch, Spider-Man 2.00
9 F:War Machine,Thunderstrike, Silver Surfer. 2.00
10 F:War Machine,Thunderstrike, Silver Surfer. 2.00
11 TGb,F:Hulk,Nova,Northstar 2.00
12 RMz(s),TGb,F:Thanos 2.75
13 RMz(s),TGb,F:Thanos,Super Skrull, Rhino,Nitro,Titanium Man 2.00
14 RMz(s),TGb,F:Thanos,Super Skrull, Rhino,Nitro,Titanium Man, A:Silver Surfer 2.00
15 F:Dr.Druid,Cage,Deadpool 2.25

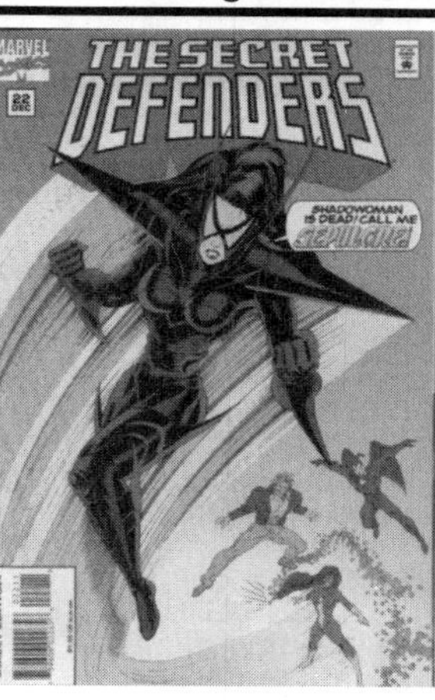

Secret Defenders #22
© Marvel Entertainment Group

16 F:Dr.Druid,Cage,Deadpool 2.25
17 F:Dr.Druid,Cage,Deadpool 2.25
18 F:Iron Fist,Giant Man 2.25
19 F:Dr.Druid,Cadaver, Shadowoman 2.00
20 V:Venom 2.00
21 V:Slaymaker 2.00
22 Final Defense,pt.1 . . . . 2.00
23 Final Defense,pt.2 . . . . 2.00
24 Final Defense,pt.3 . . . . 2.00
25 V:Dr.Druid 2.00

SECRET WARS
May, 1984

1 MZ,A:X-Men,Fant.Four,Avengers, Hulk,SpM in All,I:Beyonder. . . . 4.00
2 MZ,V:Magneto 3.00
3 MZ,I:Titania & Volcana 3.00
4 BL,V:Molecule Man. 3.00
5 BL,F:X-Men 3.00
6 MZ,V:Doctor Doom. 3.00
7 MZ,I:New Spiderwoman 3.50
8 MZ,I:Alien Black Costume (for Spider-Man). 12.00
9 MZ,V:Galactus 2.00
10 MZ,V:Dr.Doom. 2.00
11 MZ,V:Dr.Doom. 2.00
12 MZ,Beyonder Vs. Dr.Doom 2.50
TPB rep #1-#12 . . . . 19.95
TPB rep. 12 issues, 336-pg. 24.95

SECRET WARS II
July, 1985

1 AM,SL,A:X-Men,New Mutants. . . 2.00
2 AM,SL,A:Fantastic Four 2.00
3 AM,SL,A:Daredevil 2.00
4 AM,I:Kurse 2.00
5 AM,SL,I:Boom Boom 2.50
6 AM,SL,A:Mephisto 2.00
7 AM,SL,A:Thing 2.00
8 AM,SL,A:Hulk. 2.00
9 AM,SL,A:Everyone,double-size. . 2.00

SECTAURS
June, 1985

1 Based on toys 2.00
2 . . . . 2.00
3 . . . . 2.00
4 . . . . 2.00
5 thru 10 1986 . . . . @2.00

SEEKER 3000
April, 1998

1 (of 4) DAn,IEd,sci-fi adventure, 48pg 3.00
2 DAn,IEd,encounter with aliens . . 3.00
3 DAn,IEd,V:Hkkkt, ... 2.50
4 DAn,IEd,V:Hkkkt, concl. 2.50

SEMPER FI
Dec., 1988

1 JSe 2.00
2 JSe 2.00
3 JSe 2.00
4 JSe 2.00
5 JSe 2.00
6 . . . . 2.00
7 and 8 . . . . @2.00
9 August, 1989,final issue 2.00

SENSATIONAL SPIDER-MAN

1 KM/TP/KJ,rep. (1989). 6.00

SENSATIONAL SPIDER-MAN
Jan., 1996

0 DJu,KJ,Return of Spider-Man,pt.1 Lenticular cover 5.00
1 DJu,KJ,Media Blizzard,pt.1, V:New Mysterio 4.00
2 DJu,KJ,Return of Kaine,pt.2 . . . . 2.50
3 DJu,KJ,Web of Carnage,pt.1 . . . 2.50
4 DJu,KJ,Blood Brothers,pt.1. . . . . 2.50
5 DJu 2.50
6 DJu 2.50
7 TDz,A:Onslaught 2.50
8 TDz,The Looter 2.50
9 TDz,Onslaught tie-in. 2.50
10 TDz,RCa,V:Swarm. 2.50
11 TDz,Revelations, pt.2. . . . . 2.50
11A bagged with card, etc. 5.00
12 TDz,SwM, V:Trapster. 2.00
13 TDz,RCa,A:Ka-zar, Shanna 2.00
14 TDz,RCa,Savage Land saga . . . 2.00
15 TDz,RCa,Savage Land saga . . . 2.00
16 TDz,RCa,R:Black Cat, V:Prowler,Vulture 2.00
17 TDz,RCa,V:Black Cat, Prowler,Vulture. 2.00
18 TDz,RCa,V:Vulture 2.00
19 TDz,RCa,R:Living Monolith 2.00
20 TDz,RCa,Living Pharoah, concl. 2.00
21 TDz,RCa,Techomancers 2.00
22 TDz,RCa,A:Doctor Strange 2.00
23 TDz,RCa,A:Doctor Strange 2.00
24 TDz,RCa,A:S.H.I.E.L.D., Looter . 2.50
25 TDz,RCa,Spider-Hunt,pt1 x-over 3.00
26 TDz,RCa,JoB,Identity Crisis prelude. 2.00
27 TDz,RCa,MeW,Identity Crisis, as Hornet V:Phaeton 2.00
28 TDz,RCa,as Hornet, V:Vulture . . 2.00
29 TDz,RCa,V:Arcade, Black Cat . . 2.00
30 TDz,A:Black Cat,V:Arcade 2.00
31 TDz,MeW,RCa,V:Rhino 2.00
32 TDz,JoB,The Gathering of the Five, pt.1 (of 5). 2.00
33 TDz,JoB,Gathering of the Five,pt.5 . . . . 2.00
Minus 1 Spec.,TDz,RCa, flashback. 2.00
TPB In the Savage Land rep.#13-#15 . . . . 6.00
Wizard mini-comic 1.00
TPB Sensational Spider-Man '96 JMD,SwM, seq. to Kraven's Last Hunt, 64pg.. . . . . 2.95

Sensational Spider-Man #33
© Marvel Entertainment Group

SENTRY
July, 2000

1 (of 5) PJe,JaL. 3.00
2 PJe,JaL,Unicorn 3.00
3 PJe,JaL,Hulk,Spider-Man 3.00
4 PJe,JaL,Prof.X 3.00

SERGEANT BARNEY BARKER
August, 1956

1 JSe,Comedy 100.00
2 JSe,Army Inspection(c) 75.00
3 JSe,Tank(c) 75.00
Becomes:

G.I. TALES

4 JSe,At Grips with the Enemy . . 45.00
5 . . . . 30.00
6 JO,BP,GWb, July, 1957 . . . . . . 35.00

SGT. FURY & HIS HOWLING COMMANDOS
May, 1963–Dec., 1981

1 Seven Against the Nazis . . . 1,200.00
2 JK,Seven Doomed Men 350.00
3 JK,Midnight on Massacre Mountain 200.00
4 JK,V:Lord Ha-Ha,D:Junior Juniper 200.00
5 JK,V:Baron Strucker 200.00
6 JK,The Fangs of the Fox 125.00
7 JK,Fury Court Martial 125.00
8 JK,V:Dr Zemo,I:Percival Pinkerton 125.00
9 DAy,V:Hitler 125.00
10 DAy,On to Okinwawa,I:Capt. Savage. 125.00
11 DAy,V:Capt.Flint. 75.00
12 DAy,Howler deserts 75.00
13 DAy,JK,A;Capt.America 300.00
14 DAy,V:Baron Strucker 75.00
15 DAy,SD,Too Small to Fight Too Young to Die 75.00
16 DAy,In The Desert a Fortress Stands 75.00
17 DAy,While the Jungle Sleeps . . 75.00
18 DAy,Killed in Action 75.00
19 DAy,An Eye for an Eye 75.00
20 DAy,V:the Blitz Squad 75.00
21 DAy,To Free a Hostage 50.00
22 DAy,V:Bull McGiveney 50.00
23 DAy,The Man who Failed 50.00
24 DAy,When the Howlers Hit the Home Front 50.00
25 DAy,Every Man my Enemy. . . . 50.00
26 DAy,Dum Dum Does it the Hard Way. 50.00
27 DAy,O:Fury's Eyepatch 50.00
28 DAy,Not a Man Shall Remain Alive. 50.00
29 DAy,V:Baron Strucker 50.00
30 DAy,Incident in Italy 50.00
31 Day,Into the Jaws of Death . . . 25.00
32 DAy,A Traitor in Our Midst 25.00
33 DAy,The Grandeur That was Greece. 25.00
34 DAy,O:Howling Commandoes . 25.00
35 DAy,Berlin Breakout,J:Eric Koenig 25.00
36 DAy,My Brother My Enemy . . . 25.00
37 DAy,In the Desert to Die 25.00
38 This Ones For Dino 25.00
39 Into the Fortress of Fear 25.00
40 That France Might be Free . . . 25.00
41 V:The Blitzers 25.00
42 Three Were AWOL 25.00
43 Scourge of the Sahara,A:Bob Hope,Glen Miller. 25.00
44 JSe,The Howlers First Mission. 25.00
45 JSe,I:The War Lover 25.00
46 JSe,They Also Serve 25.00
47 Tea and Sabotage 25.00
48 A:Blitz Squad. 25.00
49 On to Tarawa. 25.00
50 The Invasion Begins 25.00
51 The Assassin. 25.00
52 Triumph at Treblinka 25.00
53 To the Bastions of Bavaria 25.00
54 Izzy Shoots the Works 25.00
55 Cry of Battle, Kiss of Death . . . 20.00
56 Gabriel Blow Your Horn 20.00
57 TS,The Informer 20.00
58 Second Front. 20.00
59 D-Day for Dum Dum 20.00
60 Authorised Personnel Only . . . 20.00
61 The Big Breakout. 20.00
62 The Basic Training of Fury. . . . 20.00
63 V:Nazi Tanks 20.00
64 The Peacemonger,A:Capt Savage. 20.00
65 Eric Koenig,Traitor 20.00
66 Liberty Rides the Underground. 20.00
67 With a Little Help From My Friends. 20.00
68 Welcome Home Soldier 20.00
69 While the City Sleeps. 20.00
70 The Missouri Marauders 20.00
71 Burn,Bridge,Burn 20.00
72 Battle in the Sahara 20.00
73 Rampage on the Russian Front. 20.00
74 Each Man Alone 20.00
75 The Deserter 15.00
76 He Fought the Red Baron 15.00
77 A Traitor's Trap,A:Eric Koenig . 15.00
78 Escape or Die 15.00
79 Death in the High Castle 15.00
80 To Free a Hostage 15.00
81 The All American 15.00
82 Howlers Hit The Home Front,rep 15.00
83 Dum DumV:Man-Mountain McCoy 15.00
84 The Devil's Disciple 15.00
85 Fury V:The Howlers. 15.00
86 Germ Warfare 15.00
87 Dum Dum does it...rep 15.00
88 Save General Patton 15.00
89 O:Fury's eyepatch,rep 15.00
90 The Chain That Binds 15.00
91 Not A Man...rep 12.00

Sgt. Fury and His Howling Commandos #18 © Marvel Entertainment Group

92 Some Die Slowly 12.00
93 A Traitor...rep 12.00
94 GK(c),Who'll Stop the Bombs. . 12.00
95 7 Doomed Men, rep. 12.00
96 GK(c),Dum-Dum Sees it Through 12.00
97 Till the Last Man Shall Fail. . . . 12.00
98 A:Deadly Dozen. 12.00
99 Guerillas in Greece 12.00
100 When a Howler Falls 12.00
101 Pearl Harbor 9.00
102 Death For A Dollar. 9.00
103 Berlin Breakout 9.00
104 The Tanks Are Coming 9.00
105 My Brother,My Enemy 9.00
106 Death on the Rhine 9.00
107 Death-Duel in the Desert 9.00
108 Slaughter From the Skies. 9.00
109 This Ones For Dino,rep 9.00
110 JSe(c),The Reserve 9.00
111 V:Colonel Klaw 9.00
112 V:Baron Strucker 9.00
113 That France Might Be Free,rep 9.00
114 Jungle Bust Out 9.00
115 V:Baron Strucker 9.00
116 End of the Road. 9.00
117 Blitz Over Britain 9.00
118 War Machine 9.00
118 War Machine 9.00
119 They Strike by Machine 9.00
120 Trapped in the Compound of Death 9.00
121 An Eye for an Eye 8.00
122 A;The Blitz Squad 8.00
123 To Free a Hostage. 8.00
124 A:Bull McGiveney 8.00
125 The Man Who Failed 8.00
126 When the Howlers Hit Home.. . 8.00
127 Everyman My Enemy,rep 8.00
128 Dum Dum does it...rep. 8.00
129 O:Fury's Eyepatch 8.00
130 A:Baron Strucker 8.00
131 Armageddon 8.00
132 Incident in Italy 8.00
133 thru 140 . . . . @8.00
141 thru 150 . . . . @8.00
151 thru 160 . . . . @7.00
161 thru 167 . . . . @7.00
Ann.#1 Korea #4,#5 . . . . 150.00
Ann.#2 This was D-Day 50.00
Ann.#3 Vietnam 30.00
Ann.#4 Battle of the Bulge 20.00
Ann.#5 Desert Fox 15.00
Ann.#6 Blaze of Battle 15.00
Ann.#7 Armageddon. 15.00

SERGIO ARAGONES MASSACRES MARVEL

1996

1-shot Parody. 5.00

SEVEN BLOCK

Epic 1990

1 . . . . 2.50

SHADOWMASTERS

Oct., 1989–Jan., 1990

1 RH 7.00
2 . . . . 5.00
3 . . . . 4.00
4 . . . . 4.00

SHADOWRIDERS

1993

1 I:Shadowriders,A:Cable, Ghost Rider 2.00
2 A:Ghost Rider. 2.00
3 A:Cable 2.00
4 A:Cable 2.00

SHADOWS & LIGHT

Dec., 1997

1 BSf,RMz,LWn,BWr,GeH,SD,B&W anthology series. 3.00
2 JSn,LW,LSh,GK 3.00
3 BL,JSn 3.00
4 three new tales. 3.00

SHANNA, THE SHE-DEVIL

Dec., 1972–Aug., 1973

1 GT,F:Shanna 15.00
2 RA,The Dungeon of Doom 12.00
3 RA,The Hour of the Bull 10.00
4 RA,Mandrill. 10.00
5 JR(c),RA,V:Nekra 10.00

SHEENA

Dec., 1984–Feb., 1985

1 and 2 Movie adapt . . . . @2.00

SHE-HULK

[1st Regular Series]Feb., 1980

1 JB,BWi,I&O:She-Hulk 6.00
2 BWi,D:She-Hulk's best friend . . . 3.00
3 BWi,Wanted for Murder 3.00
4 BWi,V:Her Father 3.00
5 BWi,V:Silver Serpent 3.00
6 A:Iron Man 2.50
7 BWi,A:Manthing 2.50
8 BWi,A:Manthing 2.50
9 BWi,Identity Crisis 2.50
10 V:The Word 2.50
11 BWi,V:Dr.Morbius. 2.50
12 V:Gemini 2.50
13 V:Man-Wolf 2.00
14 V:Hellcat 2.00
15 V:Lady Kills 2.00
16 She Hulk Goes Berserk 2.00
17 V:Man-Elephant. 2.00
18 V:Grappler. 2.00
19 V:Her Father 2.00
20 A:Zapper 2.00
21 V:Seeker 2.00
22 V:Radius 2.00
23 V:Radius 2.00

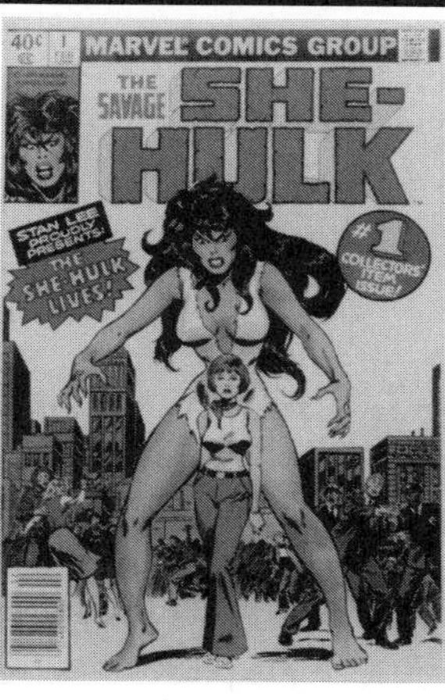

She-Hulk #1 © Marvel Entertainment Group

24 V:Zapper 2.00
25 Double-sized,last issue 2.50

[2nd Regular Series] 1989–94

1 JBy,V:Ringmaster 3.00
2 JBy. 2.25
3 JBy,A:Spider-Man. 2.25
4 JBy,I:Blond Phantom 2.25
5 JBy. 2.25
6 JBy,A:U.S.1,Razorback. 2.25
7 JBy,A:U.S.1,Razarback. 2.25
8 JBy,A:Saint Nicholas. 2.25
9 AM(i) 2.00
10 AM(i) 2.00
11 . . . . 2.00
12 . . . . 2.00
13 SK(c). 2.00
14 MT(c),A:Howard the Duck 2.00
15 SK(c). 2.00
16 SK(c). 2.00
17 SK(c),V:Dr.Angst 2.00
18 SK(c). 2.00
19 SK(c),V:Nosferata 2.00
20 SK(c),Darkham Asylum 2.00
21 SK(c),V:Blonde Phantom 2.00
22 SK(c),V:Blonde Phantom,A:All Winners Squad. 2.00
23 V:Blonde Phantom. 2.00
24 V:Deaths'Head 4.00
25 A:Hercules,Thor. 2.00
26 A:Excalibur 2.00
27 Cartoons in N.Y. 2.00
28 Game Hunter Stalks She-Hulk . . 2.00
29 A:Wolv.,Hulk,SpM,Venom 2.50
30 MZ(c),A:Silver Surfer,Thor Human Torch 2.25
31 JBy,V:Spragg the Living Hill 2.50
32 JBy,A:Moleman,V:Spragg. 2.00
33 JBy,A:Moleman,V:Spragg. 2.00
34 JBy,Returns to New York 2.00
35 JBy,V:X-Humed Men 2.00
36 JBy,X-mas issue (#8 tie-in) 2.00
37 JBy,V:Living Eraser 2.00
38 JBy,V:Mahkizmo 2.00
39 JBy,V:Mahkizmo 2.00
40 JBy,V:Spraggs,Xemnu 2.00
41 JBy,V:Xemnu. 2.00
42 JBy,V:USArcher. 2.00
43 JBy,V:Xemnu. 2.00
44 JBy,R:Rocket Raccoon 2.00
45 JBy,A:Razorback 2.00
46 JBy,A:Rocket Raccoon 2.00
47 V:D'Bari. 2.00
48 JBy,A:Rocket Raccoon 2.00

MARVEL

49 V:Skrulls,D'Bari 2.00
50 JBy,WS,TA,DGb,AH,HC, D:She-Hulk. 4.00
51 TMo,V:Savage She-Hulk 2.00
52 D:She-Hulk,A:Thing,Mr.Fantastic, I:Rumbler,V:Titania 2.00
53 AH(c),A:Zapper 2.00
54 MGo(c),A:Wonder Man 2.00
55 V:Rumbler 2.00
56 A:War Zone 2.00
57 A:Hulk 2.00
58 V:Electro 2.00
59 V:Various Villains 2.00
60 last issue 2.00
TPB rep. #1-#8. . . . . 12.95

SHE HULK: CEREMONY

1989

1 JBr/SDr 4.00
2 JBr/FS 4.00

SHIELD

Feb., 1973

1 . . . . 9.00
2 . . . . 5.00
3 . . . . 5.00
4 . . . . 5.00
5 Oct., 1973 . . . . 5.00

SHOGUN WARRIORS

Feb., 1979

1 HT,DGr,F:Raydeen, Combatra, Dangard Ace 4.00
2 HT,DGr,V:Elementals of Evil 2.50
3 AM(c),HT,DGr,V:Elementals of Evil 2.50
4 HT,DGr,`Menace of the Mech Monsters' 2.50
5 HT,DGr,`Into The Lair of Demons' 2.50
6 HT,ME 2.00
7 HT,ME 2.00
8 HT,ME 2.00
9 `War Beneath The Waves' 2.00
10 `Five Heads of Doom' 2.00
11 TA(c) 2.00
12 WS(c) 2.00
13 `Demons on the Moon' 2.00
14 V:Dr. Demonicus 2.00
15 . . . . 2.00
16 . . . . 2.00
17 . . . . 2.00
18 . . . . 2.00
19 A:Fantastic Four 2.50
20 Sept., 1980 . . . . 2.00

SHROUD

Limited Series 1994

1 B:MiB(s),MCW,A:Spider-Man, V:Scorpion 2.00
2 MCW,A:Spider-Man,V:Scorpion . 2.00
3 MCW,I:Kali 2.00
4 MCW,Final Issue 2.00

SILVERHAWKS

August, 1987

1 thru 5 . . . . @2.00
6 June, 1988 . . . . 2.00

SILVER SABLE

1992–95

1 Foil stamped(c),A:Sandman, Spider-Man 3.00
2 I:Gattling. 2.00
3 V:Gattling,Foreigner 2.00
4 Infinity War,V:Doctor Doom 2.00
5 Infinity War,V:Doctor Doom 2.00
6 A:Deathlok 2.00
7 A:Deathlok 2.00
8 V:Hydra 2.00
9 O:Silver Sable 2.00
10 A:Punisher,Leviathan 2.00
11 Cyber Warriors,Hydra. 2.00
12 V:Cyberwarriorss,R:Sandman . . 2.00
13 For Love Nor Money#3, A:Cage,Terror. 2.00
14 For Love Nor Money#6, A:Cage,Terror. 2.00
15 V:Viper,A:Captain America 2.00
16 SBt,Infinty Crusade 2.00
17 Infinity Crusade 2.00
18 A:Venom 2.00
19 Siege of Darkness x-over. 2.00
20 GWt(s),StB,BU:Sandman,Fin . . . 2.00
21 Gang War 2.00
22 . . . . 2.00
23 GWt(s),A:Deadpool,Daredevil, BU:Sandman 2.00
24 GWt(s),BU:Crippler,w/card 2.00
25 V:Hydra 2.25
26 F:Sandman 2.00
27 A:Code Blue 2.00
28 F:Chen 2.00
29 A:Wild Pack. 2.00
30 problems with law 2.00
31 V:terrorists. 2.00
32 A:The Foreigner. 2.00
33 V:Hammerhead 2.00
34 . . . . 2.00
35 Li'l Silvie Tale. 2.00

SILVER SURFER

[1st Series] August, 1968

1 B:StL(s),JB,JSr,GC,O:Silver Surfer, O:Watcher,I:Shala Bal. 450.00
2 JB,JSr,GC,A:Watcher 200.00
3 JB,JSr,GC,I:Mephisto 150.00
4 JB,A:Thor,low distribution scarce 425.00
5 JB,A:Fant.Four,V:Stranger . . . 100.00
6 JB,FB,A:Watcher 125.00
7 JB,A:Watcher,I:Frankenstein's Monster 100.00
8 JB,DA,A:Mephisto,I:Ghost. 75.00
9 JB,DA,A:Mephisto,A:Ghost 75.00
10 JB,DA,South America 75.00
11 JB,DA 60.00
12 JB,DA,V:The Abomination 60.00

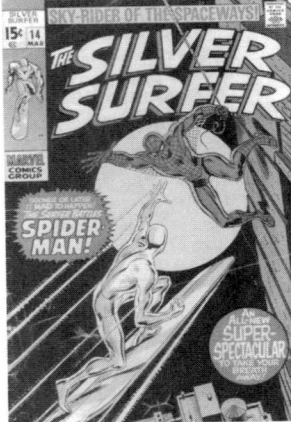

Silver Surfer #14
© Marvel Entertainment Group

13 JB,DA,V:Doomsday Man 60.00
14 JB,DA,A:Spider-Man 75.00
15 JB,DA,A:Human Torch 60.00
16 JB,V:Mephisto 60.00
17 JB,V:Mephisto 60.00
18 E:StL(s),JK,V:Inhumans. 60.00

[2nd Regular Series] 1982

1 JBy,TP,Direct Only,V:Mephisto . 10.00

[3rd Regular Series] July, 1987

1 MR,JRu,A:Fantastic Four, Galactus,V:Champion 9.00
2 MR,A:Shalla Bal,V:Skrulls. 6.00
3 MR,V:Collector & Runner 5.00
4 MR,JRu,A:Elders,I:Obliterator . . . 5.00
5 MR,JRu,V:Obliterator 5.00
6 MR,JRu,O:Obliterator,A:Kree, Skrulls 5.00
7 MR,JRu,V:Supremor,Elders/ Soul Gems. 5.00
8 MR,JRu,V:Supremor. 5.00
9 MR,Elders Vs.Galactus. 5.00
10 MR,A:Galactus,Eternity 5.00
11 JSon,JRu,V:Reptyl 4.50
12 MR,JRu,V:Reptyl,A:Nova 4.50
13 JSon,DC,V:Ronan 4.50
14 JSon,JRu,V:Skrull Surfer 4.50
15 RLm,JRu,A:Fantastic Four. 6.00
16 RLm,Inbetweener possesses Soul Gem,A:Fantastic Four. . . . 4.00
17 RLm,A:Inbetweener,Galactus, Fantastic Four,D:Trader, Possessor,Astronomer 4.00
18 RLm,Galactus V:Inbetweener. . . 4.00
19 RLm,MR,V:Firelord 4.00
20 RLm,A:Superskrull,Galactus . . . 4.00
21 MR,DC,V:Obliterator 4.00
22 RLm,V:Ego 4.00
23 RLm,V:Dragon. 4.00
24 RLm,V:G.I.G.O. 4.00
25 RLm,V:Ronan,Kree Skrull War . . 4.00
26 RLm,V:Nenora. 4.00
27 RLm,V:Stranger. 4.00
28 RLm,D:Super Skrull,V:Reptyl . . . 4.00
29 RLm,V:Midnight Sun 4.00
30 RLm,V:Midnight Sun 4.00
31 RLm,O:Living Tribunal & Stranger (double size) 4.50
32 RF,JSt,A:Mephisto 4.00
33 Rlm,V:Impossible Man. 4.00
34 RLm,(1stJSn),2nd R:Thanos . . . 5.00
35 RLm,A:Thanos,R:Drax. 4.00
36 RLm,V:Impossible Man,A:Warlock Capt.Marvel,C:Thanos 4.00
37 RLm,V:Drax,A:Mentor 4.00
38 RLm,V:Thanos(continued in Thanos Quest) 4.00
39 JSh,V:Algol 3.00
40 RLm,V:Dynamo City 3.00
41 RLm,V:Dynamo City,A:Thanos . . 3.00
42 RLm,V:Dynamo City,A:Drax 3.00
43 RLm,V:DynamoCity 3.00
44 RLm,R:Thanos,Drax, O:Inf.Gems. 3.00
45 RLm,Thanos vs. Mephisto 3.00
46 RLm,R:Warlock,A:Thanos 3.00
47 RLm,Warlock V:Drax, A:Thanos 3.00
48 RLm,A:Galactus,Thanos 3.00
49 RLm,V:Thanos Monster 3.00
50 RLm,Silver Stamp(D.size), V:Thanos Monster 8.00
50a 2nd printing 2.50
50b 3rd printing 2.00
51 RLm,Infinity Gauntlet x-over. . . . 2.50
52 RLm,Infinity Gauntlet x-over. . . . 2.50
53 RLm,Infinity Gauntlet x-over. . . . 2.50
54 RLm,I.Gauntlet x-over,V:Rhino. . 2.50
55 RLm,I.Gauntlet x-over,Universe According to Thanos,pt.1 . . . . . 2.50
56 RLm,I.Gauntlet x-over,Universe

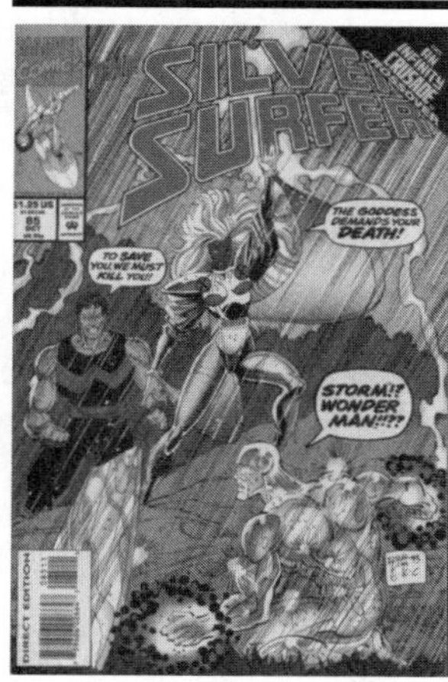

Silver Surfer, 3rd Series, #85
© Marvel Entertainment Group

According to Thanos,pt.2 . . . . . 2.50
57 RLm,Infinity Gauntlet x-over. . . . 2.50
58 RLm(c),Infinity Gauntlet x-over, A:Hulk,Namor,Dr.Strange 2.50
59 RLm(c),TR,Infinity Gauntlet, Thanos V:Silver Surfer 2.50
60 RLm,V:Midnight Sun, A:Inhumans 2.00
61 RLm,I:Collection.Agency 2.00
62 RLm,O:Collection Agency 2.00
63 RLm,A:Captain Marvel. 2.00
64 RLm,V:Dark Silver Surfer. 2.00
65 RLm,R:Reptyl,I:Princess Alaisa. 2.00
66 RLm,I:Avatar,Love & Hate 2.00
67 RLm(c),KWe,Inf.War,V:Galactus A:DrStrange 2.00
68 RLm(c),KWe,Inf.War,O:Nova . . . 2.00
69 RLm(c),KWe,Infinity War, A:Galactus 2.00
70 RLm(c),Herald War#1,I:Morg . . . 2.00
71 RLm(c),Herald War#2,V:Morg . . 2.00
72 RLm(c),Herald War#3,R:Nova . . 2.00
73 RLm,R:Airwalker 2.00
74 RLm,V:Terrax. 2.00
75 RLm,E:Herald Ordeal,V:Morg, D:Nova. 3.00
76 RLm,A:Jack of Hearts 2.00
77 RLm,A:Jack of Hearts 2.00
78 RLm,R:Morg,V:Nebula 2.00
79 RLm,V:Captain Atlas 2.00
80 RLm,I:Ganymede,Terrax Vs.Morg 2.00
81 RLm,O:GanymedeI:Tyrant 2.00
82 RLm,V:Tyrant,double sized 2.00
83 Infinity Crusade 2.00
84 RLm(c),Infinity Crusade 2.00
85 RLm(c),Infinity Crusade 2.25
86 RLm(c), Blood & Thunder,pt.2 V:Thor,A:Beta Ray Bill 2.00
87 RLm(c),Blood & Thunder,pt.7. . . 2.00
88 RLm(c),Blood & Thunder,pt.10. . 2.00
89 RLm(c),CDo,C:Legacy. 2.00
90 RLm(c),A:Legacy,C:Avatar. 2.00
91 RLm 2.00
92 RLm,V:Avatar 2.00
93 V:Human Torch 2.00
94 A:Fantastic Four, Warlock 2.00
95 SEa,A:Fantastic Four. 2.00
96 A:Fantastic Four,Hulk. 2.00
97 A:Fantastic Four,R:Nova 2.00
98 R:Champion 2.00
99 A:Nova 2.00
100 V:Mephisto 2.50
100a enhanced ed.. . . . . 4.50
101 RMz,JoP,A:Shalla Bal 2.00
102 V:Galactus. 2.00
103 I:Death quad 2.00
104 Surfer Rampage 2.00
105 V:Super Skrull 2.00
106 A:Legacy,Morg. 2.00
107 TGb,BAn,A:Galactus,Morg, Tyrant. 2.00
108 Galactus Vs. Tyrant 2.00
109 Morg has Ultimate Nulifier 2.00
110 JB,F:Nebula. 2.00
111 GP,TGb,BAn,to Other Side of Galaxy 2.00
112 GP,TGb,BAn,. 2.00
113 GP,TGb,BAn,V:Blackbody 2.00
114 . . . . 2.00
115 GP,TGb,BAn,Surfer in pieces . . 2.00
116 GP,TGb,BAn,Pieces cause trouble 2.00
117 . . . . 2.00
118 . . . . 2.00
119 . . . . 2.00
120 . . . . 2.00
121 A:Quasar, Beta Ray Bill 2.00
122 GP,SEa, returns to Marvel Universe. 2.00
123 GP,RG. 2.00
124 GP,RG. 2.00
125 RG,V:Hulk, double size 3.00
126 JMD,RG,BWi,A:Dr. Strange . . . 2.00
127 JMD,RG,BWi,A:Alicia Masters . 2.00
128 JMD,RG,BWi,V:Puppet Master. 2.00
129 JMD,RG,BWi,back in time, late 1940s 2.00
130 JMD,CNr,BWi, trapped in past . 2.00
131 JMD,RG,BWi, ... 2.00
132 JMD,PaP,Puppet Master missing 2.00
133 JMD,MRy,PaP,V:PuppetMaster 2.00
134 JMD,TGm,MRy,Regains his memories, pt.1 (of 4) 2.00
135 JMD,TGm,MRy,Alicia summons Scrier. 2.00
136 JMD,TGm,MRy, ... 2.00
137 JMD,TGm,MRy,Mephisto v. Scrier. 2.00
138 JMD,RCz,MRy,A:The Thing, tie-in. 2.00
139 JMD,RCz,MRy,V:Gargoyle 2.00
140 JMD,JMu,on Zenn-La untouched by Galactus 2.00
141 JMD,JMu,A:Sama-D,Alicia Masters 2.00
142 JMD,JMu,Tenebrae,The Union, Cipher 2.00
143 JMD,DCw,Tenebrae,V:Psycho Man 2.00

Bi-Weekly Issues

144 JMD,JMu,V:Psycho-Man, A:Tenebrae. 2.00
145 JMD,JMu,A:Psycho-Man, Tenebrae,Cypphyrr. 2.00
146 TDF,DCw,V:Firelord 2.00
Minus 1 Spec., JMD,RG,BWi, flashback, first human contact . 2.00
Spec. Silver Surfer: Dangerous Artifacts,RMz, Galactus,T hanos (1996) 4.00
Spec. Silver Surfer: Inner Demons, rep. JMD,RGa,BWi (1998) 3.00
Ann.#1 RLm,JSon,Evolution War . . 7.00
Ann.#2 RLm,Atlantis Attacks. 5.00
Ann.#3 RLm,Lifeform #4. . . . . 4.00
Ann.#4 RLm,Korvac Quest #3,A: Guardians of Galaxy. 3.00
Ann.#5 RLm,Ret.o/Defenders #3 . . 2.50
Ann.#6 RLm(c),I:Legacy,w/card . . . 3.75
Ann.'97 1 JMD,VS,KJ,V:Scrier, 48pg 2.00

Silver Surfer, 3rd Series, #140
© Marvel Entertainment Group

Ann.'98 MPe,RBe,TDF,F:Thor, 48pg 3.00
TPB Silver Surger, The Enslavers, KP 16.95
TPB Homecoming,A:Moondragon . 12.95
TPB Silver Surfer: Parable, StL,Moe, rep. of hc, 64pg (1998) 6.00
TPB Rebirth of Thanos,reprints #34-38 . . . . 12.95
TPB StL,JK, new origin. 13.00
Ashcan. 75

SILVER SURFER

Epic Dec., 1988

1 Moebius,V:Galactus 3.00
2 Moebius,V:Galactus 3.00
Graphic Novel. 14.95

SILVER SURFER: LOFTIER THAN MORTALS

Aug., 1999

1 MFr,V:Dr. Doom 2.50
2 MFr,V:Dr. Doom, concl.. . . . . 2.50

SILVER SURFER/ SUPERMAN

Marvel/DC 1996

Spec. GP,RLm,TA, x-over 6.00

SILVER SURFER VS. DRACULA

1994

1 rep,MWn(s),GC,TP 2.00

SILVER SURFER/ WARLOCK: RESURRECTION

1993

1 JSn,V:Mephisto,Death 3.50
2 JSn,TA,V:Death 3.00
3 JSn,TA,V:Mephisto 3.00
4 JSn,TA,V:Mephisto 3.00

MARVEL

SILVER SURFER/ WEAPON ZERO
Marvel/Top Cow 1997

1-shot Devil's Reign, pt.8 . . . . 4.00

SISTERHOOD OF STEEL
Epic Dec., 1984

1 I:Sisterhood 2.00
2 . . . . 2.00
3 . . . . 2.00
4 thru 8 . . . . @2.00

SIX FROM SIRIUS
Epic July, 1984

1 PG,limited series 3.00
2 PG 2.00
3 PG 2.00
4 PG 2.00

SIX FROM SIRIUS II
Epic Feb., 1986

1 PG 2.00

SIX-GUN WESTERN
Atlas Jan., 1957

1 JSe(c),RC,JR,'Kid Yukon Gunslinger' 150.00
2 SSh,AW,DAy,JO,`His Guns Hang Low' 125.00
3 AW,BP,DAy 125.00
4 JSe(c),JR,GWb 100.00

SKELETON WARRIORS
1995

1 based on cartoon 2.00
2 Legion of Light 2.00
3 V:Grimstar 2.00
4 Grimskull abandons Legion of Light 2.00

SKRULL KILL CREW
1995

1 I:Kill Crew 3.00
2 V:Hydra 3.00
3 V:Captain America 3.00
4 V:Fantastic Four 3.00
5 Conclusion 3.00

SKULL, THE SLAYER
August, 1975

1 GK(c),O:Skull the Slayer 2.50
2 GK(c),`Man Against Gods' 2.00
3 `Trapped in the Tower of Time' 2.00
4 `Peril of the Pyramids', A:Black Knight 2.00
5 A:Black Knight 2.00
6 `The Savage Sea' 2.00
7 `Dungeon of Blood' 2.00
8 JK(c),Nov., 1976 . . . . 2.00

SLAPSTICK
1992–93

1 TA(i),I:Slapstick 2.00
2 TA(i),A:Spider-Man,V:Overkill . . . 2.00
3 V:Dr.Denton 2.00
4 A:GR,DD,FF,Cap.America 2.00

SLEDGE HAMMER
Feb., 1988

1 . . . . 2.00
2 March, 1988 . . . . 2.00

Sleepwalker #31
© Marvel Entertainment Group

SLEEPWALKER
June, 1991

1 BBI,I:Rick Sheridan,C:8-Ball 3.00
2 BBI,V:8-Ball 2.00
3 BBI,A:Avengers,X-Men,X-Factor, FF,I:Cobweb,O:Sleepwalker . . . 2.00
4 RL,I:Bookworm 2.00
5 BBI,A:SpM,K.Pin,V:Ringleader . . 2.00
6 BBI,A:SpM,Inf.Gauntlet x-over . . 2.00
7 BBI,Infinity Gauntlet x-over, V:Chain Gang 2.00
8 BBI,A:Deathlok 2.00
9 BBI,I:Lullabye 2.00
10 BBI,MM,I:Dream-Team 2.00
11 BBI,V:Ghost Rider 2.00
12 JQ,A:Nightmare 2.50
13 BBI,MM,I:Spectra 2.00
14 BBI,MM,V:Spectra 2.00
15 BBI,MM,I:Thought Police 2.00
16 BBI,MM,A:Mr.Fantastic,Thing . . . 2.00
17 BBI,A:Spider-Man,Darkhawk, V:Brotherhood o/Evil Mutants . . 2.00
18 JQ(c),Inf.War,A:Prof.X 2.00
19 V:Cobweb,w/pop out Halloween Mask 2.25
20 V:Chain Gang,Cobweb 2.00
21 V:Hobgoblin 2.00
22 V:Hobgoblin,8-Ball 2.00
23 V:Cobweb,Chain Gang 2.00
24 Mindfield#6 . . . . 2.00
25 O:Sleepwalker,Holo-grafx(c) 3.50
26 V:Mindspawn 2.00
27 A:Avengers 2.00
28 I:Psyko 2.00
29 DG,V:Psyko 2.00
30 V:Psyko 2.00
31 DG(ci),A:Spectra 2.00
32 V:Psyko 2.00
33 V:Mindspawn,Last issue 2.00
Holiday Spec.#1 JQ(c) 2.25

SLEEZE BROTHERS
August, 1989

1 Private Eyes 2.00
2 . . . . 2.00
3 . . . . 2.00
4 . . . . 2.00
5 . . . . 2.00
6 . . . . 2.00

SLINGERS
Oct. 1998

1 Ccs,F:Ricochet, Hornet, Prodigy & Dusk, 48-page:
1a Ricochet edition 3.00
1b Hornet edition 3.00
1c Prodigy edition 3.00
1d Dusk edition 3.00
2 CCs,V:Maggia 2.00
2a variant cover 2.00
3 CCs,F:Prodigy 2.00
4 CCs,F:Prodigy 2.00
5 CCs,F:Black Marvel 2.00
6 CCs,Truth or Dare 2.00
7 CCs,V:The Griz 2.00
8 CCs,V:The Griz 2.00
9 CCs,A:Ricochet 2.00
10 CCs,Raising Hell'sChildren,pt.1 . 2.00
11 CCs,Raising Hell'sChildren,pt.2 . 2.00
12 CCs,Hell's Children,pt.3 final . . . 2.00

SMURFS
Dec., 1982

1 . . . . 3.00
2 . . . . 3.00
3 . . . . 3.00
Treasury Edition 15.00

SOLARMAN
Jan., 1989

1 JM 2.00
2 MZ/NR,A:Dr.Doom, May, 1990 . . 2.00

SOLO
[Limited Series] 1994

1 RoR,I:Cygnus 2.00
2 RoR,V:A.R.E.S. 2.00
3 RoR,V:Spidey 2.00
4 final issue 2.00

SOLO AVENGERS
Dec., 1987

1 MBr,JRu,JLe,AW,Hawkeye; Mockingbird 4.00
2 MBr,JRu,KD,BMc,Hawkeye; Capt.Marvel 2.00
3 MBr,JRu,BH,SDr,Hawkeye; Moon Knight 2.00
4 RLm,JRu,PR,BL,Hawkeye; Black Knight 2.00
5 MBr,JRu,JRy,Hawkeye; Scarlet Witch 2.00
6 MBr,JRu,TGr,Hawkeye;Falcon . . 2.00
7 MBr,JG,BL,Hawkeye;Bl.Widow . . 2.00
8 MBr,Hawkeye;Dr.Pym 2.00
9 MBr,JBr,SDr,Hawkeye;Hellcat . . . 2.00
10 MBr,LW,Hawkeye;Dr.Druid 2.00
11 MBr,JG,BL,Hawkeye;Hercules . . 2.00
12 RLm,SDr,Hawkeye; New Yellow Jacket 2.00
13 RLm,JG,Hawkeye;WonderMan . 2.00
14 AM,AD,JRu,Hawkeye;She-Hulk . 2.00
15 AM,Hawkeye;Wasp 2.00
16 AM,DP,JA,Hawkeye; Moondragon 2.00
17 AM,DH,DC,Hawkeye; Sub-Mariner 2.00
18 RW,DH,Hawkeye;Moondragon . . 2.00
19 RW,DH,Hawkeye,BlackPanther . 2.00
20 RW,DH,Hawkeye;Moondragon . . 2.00
Becomes:

AVENGERS SPOTLIGHT

Solomon Kane #1
© Marvel Entertainment Group

SOLOMON KANE
Sept., 1985

1 F:Solomon Kane 2.00
2 . . . . 2.00
3 BBl,`Blades of the Brotherhood' . 2.00
4 MMi 2.00
5 `Hills of the Dead' 2.00
6 . . . . 2.00

SON OF SATAN
Dec., 1975–Feb., 1977

1 GK(c),JM,F:Daimon Hellstrom. . 20.00
2 Demon War,O:Possessor 12.00
3 . . . . 12.00
4 The Faces of Fear 11.00
5 V:Mind Star. 11.00
6 A World Gone Mad 11.00
7 Mirror of Judgement 11.00
8 RH,To End in Nightmare 11.00

SOVIET SUPER SOLDIERS

1 AMe,JS,I:Redmont 4. . . . . 2.00

SPACEKNIGHTS
Aug., 2000

1 (of 5) JSn,R:Spaceknights 3.00
2 JSn,Terminator 3.00
3 JSn,Deathwings 3.00

SPACEMAN
Atlas Sept., 1953

1 BEv(c),F:Speed Carter and
the Space Sentinals 500.00
2 JMn,`Trapped in Space' 325.00
3 BEv(c),JMn,V:Ice Monster. . . . 300.00
4 JMn 300.00
5 GT 300.00
6 JMn,`The Thing From Outer
Space',Oct., 1954 . . . . 300.00

SPACE SQUADRON
Atlas June, 1951

1 F:Capt. Jet Dixon,Blast,Dawn,
Revere,Rusty Blake 500.00
2 GT(c),. 450.00
3 `Planet of Madness',GT 350.00
4 . . . . 350.00
5 . . . . 350.00

Becomes:

SPACE WORLDS
April, 1952

6 `Midnight Horror'. 325.00

SPECIAL COLLECTOR'S EDITION
Dec., 1975

1 Kung-Fu,Iron Fist 6.00

SPECIAL MARVEL EDITION
Jan., 1971

1 JK,B:Thor,B:Reprints 25.00
2 JK,V:Absorbing Man 15.00
3 JK,'While a Universe
Trembles' 15.00
4 JK,`Hammer and the Holocaust',
E:Thor 15.00
5 JSe(c),JK,DAy,B:Sgt. Fury 15.00
6 HT(c),DAy,`Death Ray of
Dr. Zemo' 9.00
7 DAy,V:Baron Strucker 9.00
8 JSe(c),DAy`On To Okinawa' . . . 9.00
9 DAy,`Crackdown of
Captain Flint 9.00
10 DAy. 9.00
11 JK,DAy,A:Captaim
America & Bucky 9.00
12 DAy,V:Baron Strucker 9.00
13 JK/DAy(c),DAy,SD,`Too Small
to Fight, Too Young To Die'. . . . 9.00
14 DAy,E:Reprints,Sgt. Fury 9.00
15 JSn,AM,I:Shang-Chi & Master of
Kung Fu,I&O:Nayland Smith,
Dr. Petrie 50.00
16 JSn,AM,I&O:Midnight. 20.00
KingSz.Ann.#1 A:Iron Fist. 18.00

Becomes:

MASTER OF KUNG FU

SPECTACULAR SCARLET SPIDER
1995

1 SB,BSz,Virtual Morality,pt.4 . . . . 2.00
2 SB,BSz,CyberWar,pt.4 . . . . 2.00

SPECTACULAR SPIDER-MAN
(Magazine) July, 1968

1 . . . . 65.00
2 V:Green Goblin,Nov.1968 . . . . 110.00

SPECTACULAR SPIDER-MAN
Dec., 1976
Prev: Peter Parker

134 SB,A:Sin-Eater,V:Electro 4.00
135 SB,A:Sin-Eater,V:Electro 3.00
136 SB,D:Sin-Eater,V:Electro 3.00
137 SB,I:Tarantula II. 3.00
138 SB,A:Capt.A.,V:TarantulaII 3.00
139 SB,O:Tombstone 4.00
140 SB,A:Punisher,V:Tombstone. . . 3.00
141 SB,A:Punisher,V:Tombstone. . . 3.00
142 SB,A:Punisher,V:Tombstone. . . 3.00
143 SB,A:Punisher,D:Persuader,
I:Lobo Brothers. 3.00
144 SB,V:Boomerang 3.00
145 SB,A:Boomerang 3.00
146 SB,R:Green Goblin 5.00
147 SB,V:Hobgoblin (Demonic
Power) 15.00

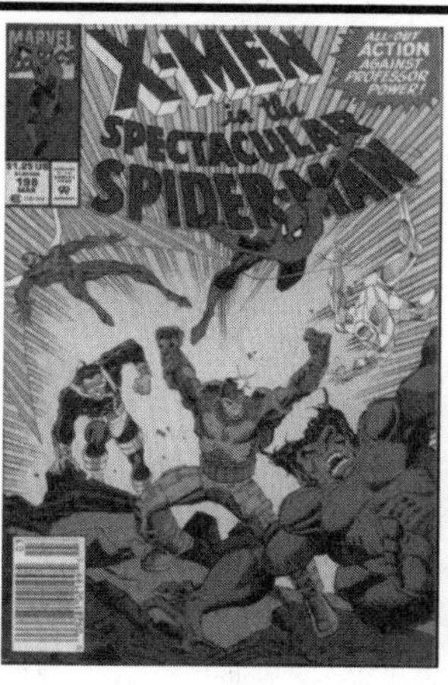

Spectacular Spider-Man #198
© Marvel Entertainment Group

148 SB,Inferno 3.00
149 SB,V:Carrion II. 5.00
150 SB,A:Tombstone,Trial
J.Robertson. 3.00
151 SB,V:Tombstone 3.00
152 SB,O:Lobo Bros.,A:Punisher,
Tombstone 4.00
153 SB,V:Hammerhead,A:
Tombstone 3.00
154 SB,V:Lobo Bros.,Puma 3.00
155 SB,V,Tombstone 3.00
156 SB,V:Banjo,A:Tombstone 3.00
157 SB,V:Shocker,Electro,
A:Tombstone 3.00
158 SB,Super Spider Spec.,
I:Cosmic Spider-Man. 7.00
159 Cosmic Powers,V:Brothers
Grimm 5.00
160 SB,A:Hydro Man,Shocker,
Rhino,Dr.Doom. 4.00
161 SB,V:Hobgoblin,Hammerhead,
Tombstone 3.00
162 SB,V:Hobgoblin,Carrion II 3.00
163 SB,V:Hobgoblin,D:Carrion II. . . 3.00
164 SB,V:Beetle 2.50
165 SB,SDr,D:Arranger,I:Knight
& Fogg. 2.50
166 SB,O:Knight & Fogg 2.50
167 SB,D:Knight & Fogg. 2.50
168 SB,A:Kingpin,Puma,
Avengers 2.50
169 SB,I:Outlaws,A:R.Racer,
Prowler,Puma,Sandman 2.50
170 SB,A:Avengers,Outlaws 2.50
171 SB,V:Puma 2.50
172 SB,V:Puma 2.50
173 SB,V:Puma 2.50
174 SB,A:Dr.Octopus 2.50
175 SB,A:Dr.Octopus 2.50
176 SB,I:Karona 2.50
177 SB,V:Karona,A:Mr.Fantastic. . . 2.50
178 SB,B:Child Within,V:Green
Goblin, A:Vermin 2.50
179 SB,V:Green Goblin,Vermin. . . . 2.50
180 SB,V:Green Goblin,Vermin. . . . 2.50
181 SB,V:Green Goblin 2.50
182 SB,V:Green Goblin 2.50
183 SB,V:Green Goblin 2.50
184 SB,E:Child Within,V:Green
Goblin 2.50
185 SB,A:Frogman,White Rabbit . . 2.00
186 SB,B:FuneralArrangements
V:Vulture 2.00

MARVEL

187 SB,V:Vulture 2.00
188 SB,E:Funeral Arrangements
V:Vulture 2.00
189 SB,30th Ann.,Hologram(c),
V:Green Goblin 6.00
189a Gold 2nd printing 3.00
190 SB,V:Rhino,Harry Osborn 2.00
191 SB,Eye of the Puma 2.00
192 SB,Eye of the Puma 2.00
193 SB,Eye of the Puma 2.00
194 SB,Death of Vermin#1 . . . . 2.00
195 SB,Death of Vermin#2 . . . . 2.00
195a Dirtbag Spec,w/Dirt#2 tape . . 2.50
196 SB,Death of Vermin#3 . . . . 2.00
197 SB,A:X-Men,V:Prof.Power 2.00
198 SB,A:X-Men,V:Prof.Power 2.00
199 SB,A:X-Men,Green Goblin 2.00
200 SB,V:Green Goblin,D:Harry
Osborn,Holografx(c) 4.00
201 SB,Total Carnage,V:Carnage,
Shriek,A:Black Cat,Venom 2.00
202 SB,Total Carnage#9,A:Venom,
V:Carnage 2.00
203 SB,Maximum Carnage#13 . . . . 2.00
204 SB,A:Tombstone 2.00
205 StG(s),SB,V:Tombstone,
A:Black Cat 2.00
206 SB,V:Tombstone 2.00
207 SB,A:The Shroud. 2.00
208 SB,A:The Shroud. 2.00
209 StB,SB,I:Dead Aim,
BU:Black Cat 2.00
210 StB,SB,V:Dead Aim,
BU:Black Cat 2.00
211 Pursuit#2,V:Tracer 2.00
212 . . . . 2.00
213 ANo(s),V:Typhiod Mary,w/cel . . 3.50
213a Newsstand Ed. 2.00
214 V:Bloody Mary 2.00
215 V:Scorpion. 2.00
216 V:Scorpion. 2.00
217 V:Judas Traveller,clone 2.00
217a Foil(c),bonus stuff 5.00
218 V:Puma 2.00
219 Back from the Edge,pt.2 . . . . . 2.00
220 Web of Death,pt.3 . . . . 2.50
221 Web of Death,finale 3.00
222 The Price of Truth 2.00
223 Aftershocks,pt.4. . . . . 3.00
223a enhanced cover 2.00
224 The Mark of Kaine,pt.4. . . . . . . 2.50
225 SB,TDF,BSz,I:New Green
Goblin, 48pg.s 3.00
225a 3-D HoloDisk Cover 5.00
226 SB,BSz,The Trial of Peter
Parker,pt.4, identity revealed . . 3.00
227 TDF,SB,BSz,Maximum
Clonage,pt.5. . . . . 2.00
228 Timebomb,pt.1. . . . . 2.00
229 Greatest Responsibility,pt.3 . . . 2.50
229a Special cover. 4.00
230 SB,Return of Spider-Man,pt.4 . 2.00
231 SB,Return of Kaine,pt.1 . . . . . . 2.00
232 . . . . 2.00
233 SB,JP,Web of Carnage,pt.4 . . . 2.00
234 SB,Blood Brothers,pt.4. . . . . . . 2.00
235 . . . . 2.00
236 . . . . 2.00
237 V:Lizard 2.00
238 V:Lizard 2.00
239 V:Lizard 2.00
240 TDz,LRs,"Book of Revelations,"
pt.1 (of 4) 2.00
241 Revelations epilogue 2.00
242 JMD,LRs,R:Chameleon,
A:Kangaroo 2.00
243 JMD,LRs,R:Chameleon 2.00
244 JMD,LRs,V:Chameleon 2.00
245 JMD,LRs,V:Chameleon,
A:Kangaroo 2.00
246 JMD,LRs,V:Kangaroo,Grizzly . . 2.00

Spectacular Spider-Man #263
© Marvel Entertainment Group

247 JMD,LRs,F:JackO'Lantern,pt.1. 2.00
248 JMD,LRs,DGr,F:Jack O'
Lantern, pt.2. . . . . 2.00
249 JMD,LRs,DGr, Last Temptation
of Flash Thompson. 2.00
250 JR, V:Original Green Goblin,
double gatefold cover 3.50
251 JMD,LRs,DGr,V:Kraven the
Hunter 2.00
252 JMD,LRs,DGr,V:Norman
Osborn. 2.00
253 JMD,LRs,DGr,V:Norman Osborn,
Gibbon, Grizzly. 2.00
254 JMD,LRs,DGr,V:Prof.Angst . . . 2.00
255 JMD,LRs,DGr,Spider-Hunt,pt.4
x-over, double size 3.00
256 JMD,LRs,DGr,Identity Crisis
prelude, A:Prodigy 2.00
257 JMD,LRs,DGr,Identity Crisis,
as Prodigy, V:Conundrum 2.00
258 JMD,LRs,DGa,as Prodigy 2.00
259 RSt,LRs,DGa,V:Hobgoblin 2.00
260 JR,RSt,LRs,DGa,Green Goblin
vs. Hobgoblin 2.00
261 RSt,LRs,AM,Goblins at the
Gate,pt.3 . . . . 2.00
262 JBy, AM, LRs, The Gathering of
the Five, pt.4 (of 5) x-over 2.00
263 JBy,AM,LRs,The Final
Chapter,pt.3 x-over. 2.00
Ann.#8 MBa,RLm,TD,Evolutionary
Wars,O:Gwen Stacy Clone 5.00
Ann.#9 DR,MG,DJu,MBa,Atlantis
Attacks. 4.00
Ann.#10 SLi(c),RB,MM,TM,RA 6.00
Ann.#11 EL(c),RWi,Vib.Vendetta. . . 2.50
Ann.#12 Hero Killers#2,A:New
Warriors,BU:Venom 4.50
Ann.#13 I:Noctune,w/Card 3.25
Ann.#14 V:Green Goblin. 2.95
Super-Size Spec.#1 Planet of the
Symbiotes,pt.4,64pg flip-book. . 3.95
Minus 1 Spec., JMD,LRs,DGr,
flashback, F:Flash Thompson. . 2.00

SPEEDBALL

Sept., 1988

1 SD,JG,O:Speedball 2.00
2 SD,JG,V:Sticker,GraffitiGorillas . . 2.00
3 SD,V:Leaper Logan 2.00
4 SD,DA,Ghost Springdale High . . 2.00
5 SD,V:Basher. 2.00
6 SD,V:Bug-Eyed Voice. 2.00
7 SD,V:Harlequin Hit Man 2.00
8 SD,V:Bonehead Gang 2.00
9 SD,V:Nathan Boder 2.00
10 SD,V:Mutated Pigs,Killer
Chickens, last issue 2.00

SPELLBOUND

Atlas March, 1952

1 'Step into my Coffin' 500.00
2 BEv,RH,'Horror Story',
A:Edgar A. Poe 275.00
3 RH(c),OW 225.00
4 RH,Decapitation story 225.00
5 BEv,JM,'Its in the Bag' 225.00
6 BK,'The Man Who Couldn't
be Killed' 225.00
7 BEv,JMn,'Don't Close
the Door' 200.00
8 BEv(c),RH,JSt,DAy,
'The Operation' 200.00
9 BEv(c),RH,'The Death of
Agatha Slurl' 200.00
10 JMn(c),BEv,RH,'The Living
Mummy' 200.00
11 'The Empty Coffin' 150.00
12 RH,'My Friend the Ghost' . . . 150.00
13 JM,'The Dead Men' 150.00
14 BEv(c),RH,JMn,'Close Shave' 150.00
15 'Get Out of my Graveyard' . . . 150.00
16 RH,BEv,JF,JSt,'Behind
the Door' 150.00
17 BEv(c),GC,BK,'Goodbye
Forever' 150.00
18 BEv(c),JM 150.00
19 BEv(c),BP,'Witch Doctor' 150.00
20 RH(c),BP 150.00
21 RH(c). 135.00
22 . . . . 135.00
23 . . . . 135.00
24 JMn(c),JR 125.00
25 JO,'Look into my Eyes' 125.00
26 JR,'The Things in the Box'. . . 125.00
27 JMn,JR,'Trap in the Mirage' . . 125.00
28 BEv. 125.00
29 JSe(c),SD 150.00
30 BEv(c) 125.00
31 . . . . 125.00
32 BP,'Almost Human' 125.00
33 AT 125.00
34 June, 1957. . . . . 125.00

SPELLBOUND

Jan., 1988

1 thru 3 . . . . @2.00
4 A:New Mutants. 2.00
5 . . . . 2.00
6 double-size. 2.25

SPIDER-GIRL

August, 1998

0 TDF,RF,BSz, cont. from What-If?
#105, Peter & Mary Jane's
daughter. 3.00
1 TDF,PO,AW, F:Mayday Parker,
V:Mr. Nobody 2.00
2 TDF,PO,AW,V:Crazy Eight
& Darkdevil 2.00
2a variant cover. 2.00
3 TDF,PO,AW,A:Fantastic Five . . . 2.00
4 TDF,PO,AW,turning points 2.00
5 TDF,PO.AW,Ghosts of the Past . 2.00
6 TDF,PO,AW,Majority Rules. 2.00
7 TDF,PO.AW,Last Days of
Spider-Man 2.00
8 TDF,PO,AW,A:Spider-Man,
Uneasy Allies 2.00
8a autographed 20.00

9 TDF,PO,AW,Critical Choices 2.00
10 TDF,PO,AW,Incredible Journeys 2.00
11 TDF,PO.AW,V:Spider-Man 2.00
12 TDF,PO,AW,A:Darkdevil. 2.00
13 TDF,Po,AW,Joins A-Next 2.00
14 TDF,PO,AW,Bloody Reunions x-over. 2.00
15 TDF,PO,AW,A:Speedball 2.00
16 TDF,PO,AW. 2.00
17 TDF,PO,AW,48-pg 3.00
18 TDF,SB,RF,A:Buzz. 2.00
19 TDF,AW,PO,V:A-Next foes 2.00
20 TDF,AW,PO,R:Green Goblin . . . 2.00
21 TDF,AW,PO,V:Earthshaker 2.25
22 TDF,AW,PO,Darkdevil 2.25
23 TDF,AW,PO,Basketball 2.25
24 TDF,AW,PO,Dragonfist 2.25
25 TDF,AW,PO,Savage Six. 2.25
26 TDF,AW,PO,Phil Urich 2.25
27 TDF,AW,PO,Parker/Osborn war concl.. . . . . 2.25
Ann.#1 TDF,PO,AW,A:Green Goblin 4.00
TPB rep. #1 & #2 . . . . 9.95

SPIDER-GIRL PRESENTS: THE BUZZ

May, 2000

1 (of 3) TDF,RF,SB 3.00
2 TDF,RF,SB,A:Spider-Girl. 3.00
3 TDF,RF,SB,Dr.Jade. 3.00

SPIDER-GIRL PRESENTS: DARKDEVIL

Sept., 2000

1 (of 3) TDF,RF,AM,Kingpin 3.00
2 TDF,RF,AM,O:Darkdevil 3.00

SPIDER-MAN

August, 1990

1 TM Purple Web(c),V:Lizard, A:Calypso,B:Torment 5.00
1a Silver Web(c) 6.00
1b Bag,Purple Web 8.00
1c Bag,Silver Web 12.00
1d 2nd print,Gold(c). 5.00
1e 2nd print Gold UPC(rare) 15.00
1f Platinum Ed. 135.00
2 TM,V:Lizard,A:Calypso 4.00
3 TM,V:Lizard,A:Calypso 4.00

Spider-Man #57
© Marvel Entertainment Group

4 TM,V:Lizard,A:Calypso 4.00
5 TM,V:Lizard,A:Calypso, E:Torment 4.00
6 TM,A:Ghost Rider,V:Hobgoblin . . 4.00
7 TM,A:Ghost Rider,V:Hobgoblin . . 4.00
8 TM,B:Perceptions,A:Wolverine I:Wendigo IV 4.00
9 TM,A:Wolverine,Wendigo 4.00
10 TM,RLd,SW,JLe(i),A:Wolv. 4.00
11 TM,A:Wolverine,Wendigo. 4.00
12 TM,E:Perceptions,A:Wolv.. . . . . . 4.00
13 TM,V:Morbius,R:Black Cost. . . . 4.00
14 TM,V:Morbius,A:Black Cost.. . . . 4.00
15 EL,A:Beast 4.00
16 TM,RLd,A:X-Force,V:Juggernaut, Black Tom,cont.in X-Force#4 . . 4.00
17 RL,AW,A:Thanos,Death 4.00
18 EL,B:Return of the Sinister Six, A:Hulk 4.00
19 EL,A:Hulk,Deathlok 4.00
20 EL,A:Nova 4.00
21 EL,A:Hulk,Deathlok,Solo 4.00
22 EL,A:Ghost Rider,Hulk 2.50
23 EL,E:Return of the Sinister Six, A:Hulk,G.Rider,Deathlok,FF . . . 4.00
24 Infinity War,V:Hobgoblin, Demogoblin 4.00
25 CMa,A:Excalibur,V:Arcade 4.00
26 RF,MBa,Hologram(c),30th Anniv. I:New Burglar 5.00
27 MR,Handgun issue 2.25
28 MR,Handgun issue 2.25
29 CMa,Ret.to Mad Dog Ward#1 . . 2.25
30 CMa,Ret.to Mad Dog Ward#2 . . 2.25
31 CMa,Ret.to Mad Dog Ward#3 . . 2.25
32 BMc,A:Punisher,V:Master of Vengeance. 2.25
33 BMc,A:Punisher,V:Master of Vengeance. 2.25
34 BMc,A:Punisher,V:Master of Vengeance. 2.25
35 TL,Total Carnage#4,V:Carnage, Shriek,A:Venom,Black Cat 2.25
36 TL,Total Carnage#8,V:Carnage, A:Venom,Morbius 2.25
37 TL,Total Carnage#12, V:Carnage 2.25
38 thru 40 KJ,V:Electro. 2.25
41 TKa(s),JaL,I:Platoon, A:Iron Fist 2.25
42 TKa(s),JaL,V:Platoon, A:Iron Fist 2.25
43 TKa(s),JaL,V:Platoon, A:Iron Fist 2.25
44 HMe(s),TL,V:Hobgoblin 2.25
45 HMe(s),TL,SHa,Pursuit#1, V:Chameleon 2.25
46 HMe(s),TL,V:Hobgoblin,w/cel . . . 3.25
46a Newsstand Ed. 2.00
47 TL,SHa,V:Demogoblin 2.25
48 TL,SHa,V:Hobgoblin, D:Demogoblin 2.25
49 TL,SHa,I:Coldheart 2.25
50 TL,SHa,I:Grim Hunter,foil(c). . . . 5.00
50a newsstand ed. 2.50
51 TL,SHa,Power,pt.3,foil(c) 4.00
51a newsstand ed. 2.25
52 TL,SHa,Spide-clone,V:Venom . . 2.25
53 TL,SHa,Clone,V:Venom 2.25
54 Web of Life,pt.3 . . . . 2.25
55 Web of Life,finale. 2.25
56 Smoke and Mirrors 2.00
57 Aftershocks,pt.1. . . . . 2.50
57a enhanced cover. 3.00
58 The Mark of Kaine,pt.3 . . . . 2.00
59 F:Travellor,Host 2.00
60 TL,SHa,HMa,The Trial of Peter Parker,pt.3 . . . . 2.00
61 TL,Maximum Clonage,pt.4 . . . . . 2.00
62 HMe,TL,Exiled,pt.3 . . . . 2.00
63 HMe,TL,Greatest

Spider-Man #96
© Marvel Entertainment Group

Responsibility,pt.2. . . . . 2.00
64 HMe,JR2,Return of Spider-Man,pt.3 . . . . 2.00
65 HMe,JR2,AW,Media Blizzard,pt.3 . . . . 2.00
66 HMe,JR2,Return of Kaine,pt.4 . . 2.00
67 HMe,JR2,Web of Carnage,pt.3 . 2.00
68 HMe,JR2,AW,Blood Brothers,pt.3 . . . . 2.00
69 HMe,JR2,Blood Brothers aftermath 2.00
70 HMe,JR2,A:Onslaught 3.00
71 HMe,JR2, ... 2.00
72 HMe,JR2,Onslaught saga 2.00
73 HMe,JR2 . . . . 2.00
74 HMe,JR2,AW,A:Daredevil, V:Fortunato 2.00
75 HMe,JR2,Revelations, pt.4. . . . . 3.00
76 HMe,JR2,SHa,Post-Onslaught world,I:Shoc 2.00
77 HMe,JR2,SHa,V:Morbius 2.00
Becomes:

PETER PARKER, SPIDER-MAN

78 HMe,JR2,SHa,F:Mary Jane Parker 2.00
79 HMe,JR2,SHa,V:Hydra,A:Captain Arthur Stacy 2.00
80 HMe,JR2,SHa,V:S.H.O.C. 2.00
81 HMe,JR2,SHa,V:Shang-Chi,pt.1. 2.00
82 HMe,JR2,SHa,Anti-Mutant Movement 2.00
83 HMe,JR2,SHa,V:Morbius 2.00
85 HMe,JR2,SHa,V:Friends of Humanity 2.00
86 HMe,JR2,SHa,F:Jimmy Six, Hammerhead 2.00
87 HMe,JR2,SHa,A:Trapster & Shocker 2.00
88 HMe,JR2,SHa,Spider-Man is Public Enemy #1 . . . . 2.00
89 HMe,JR2,SHa,Spider-Hunt,pt.3 x-over. 2.00
90 HMe,JR2,SHa,Identity Crisis prelude. 2.00
91 HMe,JR2,SHa,Identity Crisis, as Dusk 2.00
92 HMe,JR2,as Dusk, V:Trapster . . 2.00
93 HMe,JS,R:Ghost Rider 2.00
94 HMe,JR2,SHa,Who wasJoeyZ? . 2.00
95 HMe,JR2,SHa,Trapped in elevator shaft 2.00
96 HMe,JR2,SHa,The Gathering of

the Five (pt. 3 (of 5)x-over 2.00
97 HMe,JR2,SHa,JBy(c),The Final Chapter,pt.2 x-over 2.00
98 HMe,JR2,SHa,JBy(c),The Final Chapter,pt.4 x-over 2.00
98a alternate JBy(c) (1:2) 2.00
Minus 1 Spec., HMe,JR2,SHa, flashback, A:Stacys 2.00
Ann.'97 Simon Garth—Zombie 2.95
Ann. '98 HMe, Spider-Man/Elektra, V:The Silencer, 48pg. 3.00
GN Fear Itself. 12.95
GN Nothing Stops Juggernaut 3.95
GN Parallel Lives 8.95
GN JMD,MZ,Soul of the Hunter . . . 5.95
HC Kraven's Last Hunt 19.95
HC CV,Spirits of the Earth 18.95
Spec. Chaos in Calgary 2.00
Spec. Double Trouble 2.00
Spec. Hit and Run, Canadian 2.00
Spec. Skating on Thin Ice. 2.00
Spec. Trial of Venom,UNICEF. . . . 15.00
Spec.#1 Spider-Man (2000) 2.25
Spec.Spider-Man vs. Punisher 3.00
Spec. Year in Review(1999)48-pg. . 3.00
Sup.Sz.Spec#1 Planet of the Symbiotes, pt.2; flipbook F:Scarlet Spider. 3.95
Giant-Sized CCl,JBy. 4.00
TPB Assasination Plot 14.95
TPB Carnage 6.95
TPB Cosmic Adventures. 19.95
TPB Death of Gwen Stacy 14.95
TPB Hooky. 6.95
TPB Identity Crisis 19.95
TPB Maximum Carnage 24.95
TPB Origin of the Hobgoblin 14.95
TPB Return of the Sinister Six . . . 15.95
TPB Spider-Man: Revelations,JR2, rep. +14 new pages (1997). . . 12.00
TPB Round Robin. 15.95
TPB Saga of the Alien Costume . . 14.00
2nd printing 12.95
TPB Spider-Man vs. Venom 9.95
TPB Torment Rep.#1-#5 . . . . 12.95
TPB Venom Returns. 12.95
TPB Very Best of Spider-Man 15.95
TPB The Wedding 12.95
TPB Invasion Spider Slayers 15.95
TPB Clone Genesis 16.95
TPB V:Green Goblin. 15.95
TPB Spider-Man'sGreatestVillains. 15.95
TPB Spider-Man vs.DocOc, 176-pg.. . . . . 17.95
Holiday Spec.'95 . . . . 2.95

SPIDER-MAN ADVENTURES
1994–96

1 From animated series. 2.00
1a foil (c). 3.00
2 Animated Adventures 2.00
3 V:Spider-Slayer 2.00
4 Animated Adventures 2.00
5 V:Mysterio 2.00
6 V:Kraven 2.00
7 V:Doctor Octopus 2.00
8 O:Venom,pt.1 . . . . 2.00
9 O:Venom,pt.2 . . . . 2.00
10 V:Venom 2.00
11 V:Hobgoblin. 2.00
12 V:Hobgoblin. 2.00
13 V:Chameleon. 2.00
14 V:Doc Octopus 2.00
15 Doc Conners 2.00
TPB Rep.#1-#5, 112pg 8.95

Spider-Man Adventures #1
© Marvel Entertainment Group

SPIDER-MAN & AMAZING FRIENDS
Dec., 1981

1 DSp,A:Iceman,I:Firestar 5.50

SPIDER-MAN/BADROCK
Marvel/Maximum Press 1997

1 x-over, pt.1 . . . . 3.00
2 x-over, pt. 2 . . . . 3.00

SPIDER-MAN/BATMAN
1995

1 JMD,MBa,MFm,V:Carnage,Joker 6.00

SPIDER-MAN, CHAPTER 1
Oct., 1998

1 (of 13) JBy,formative years 2.50
1a signed 19.63
2 JBy,A:Fantastic Four. 2.50
2a variant JBy cover 5.00
2b signed, both covers. 30.00
3 JBy,V:J.Jonah Jameson 2.50
4 JBy,V:Dr.Octopus & Dr.Doom . . . 2.50
5 JBy,V:Lizard 2.50
6 JBy,V:Electro 2.50
7 JBy,V:Mysterio 2.50
8 JBy,V:Green Goblin 2.50
9 JBy,V:Circus of Crime. 2.50
10 JBy,V:Green Goblin 2.50
11 JBy,V:Giant-Man 2.50
12 JBy,V:Sandman, double size final issue. 3.50
Spec.#0 JBy,O:Sandman,Vulture & Lizard 2.50

SPIDER-MAN CLASSICS
1993–94

1 rep.Amazing Fantasy#15 . . . . . . 2.00
2 thru 11 rep.Amaz.SpM#1-#10 . @2.00
12 rep.Amaz.SpM#11 . . . . 2.00
13 rep.Amaz.SpM#12. . . . . 2.00
14 rep.Amaz.SpM#13. . . . . 2.00
15 rep.Amaz.SpM#14,w/cel 3.25
15a Newsstand Ed. 2.00

SPIDER-MAN COMICS MAGAZINE
Jan., 1987

1 . . . . 2.50
2 thru 13 . . . . @2.00

SPIDER-MAN: DEAD MAN'S HAND
1997

1-shot, RSt,DaR,JeM,V:Carrion . . . 3.00

SPIDER-MAN: DEATH & DESTINY
June, 2000

1 (of 3) LW,RCa,F:Gwen Stacy . . . 3.00
2 LW,RCa,Doctor Octopus. 3.00
3 LW,RCa,concl. 3.00
Spec.Death of Gwen Stacy,64-pg. rep. of Amaz.Sp-M #88–#90. . . 3.50

SPIDER-MAN: THE FINAL ADVENTURE
1995–96

1 FaN,DaR,Clv,I:Tendril 3.00
2 FaN,DaR,JAl,V:Tendril 3.00
3 FaN,DaR,JAl,V:Tendril 3.00
4 FaN,DaR,JAl,V:Tendril,concl. . . . 3.00

SPIDER-MAN: FRIENDS AND ENEMIES
1995

1 V:Metahumes 2.00
2 A:Nova,Darkhawk,Speedball. . . . 2.00
3 V:Metahumes 2.00
4 F:Metahumes 2.00

SPIDER-MEN: FUNERAL FOR AN OCTOPUS
1995

1 Doc Oc Dead 2.50
2 A:Sinister Six 2.00
3 Final Issue 2.00

SPIDER-MAN/GEN13
Marvel/Wildstorm 1996

1-shot PDd,SI,CaS x-over 5.00

SPIDER-MAN: HOBGOBLIN LIVES
1997

1 (of 3) RSt,RF,GP 2.50
2 RSt,RF,GP,Who was the original Hobgoblin?. 2.50
3 RSt,RF,GP,Original identity revealed. 2.50
TPB RF(c), series rep. 15.00

SPIDER-MAN: MADE MEN
June, 1998

GN HMe,gangster epic 6.00

SPIDER-MAN: THE MANGA
Black & White, Oct., 1997
Bi-weekly

1 imported, translated 4.00
2 . . . . 3.00
3 V:Elektro 3.00

Spider-Man The Manga #20
© Marvel Entertainment Group

4 V:Lizard 3.00
5 V:Lizard 3.00
6 V:Lizard, concl. 3.00
7 V:Kangaroo 3.00
8 V:Kangaroo 3.00
9 V:Kangaroo 3.00
10 Imposter Spider-Man 3.00
11 Real Spider-Man returns 3.00
12 name dragged through the mud . 3.00
13 V:Mysterio 3.00
14 V:Mysterio 3.00
15 V:Mysterio, double size 4.00
16 Human side of Japanese Spider-Man 3.00
17 Human side cont.. . . . . 3.00
18 Human side concl.. . . . . 3.00
19 Spidey's vacation. 3.00
20 and 21 . . . . @3.00
22 woman who creates blizzards . . 3.00
23 secrets of the Ice Woman 3.00
24 blood donated 3.00
25 V:Mitsuo Kitano 3.00
26 Mitsuo Kitano insane 3.00
27 Yu refuses costume 3.00
28 JMd(c), Yu puts on costume. . . . 3.00
29 JMd(c), Yu vs. Kitano. 3.00
30 Yu vs. Kitano 3.00
31 . . . . 3.00
32 Yu escapes 3.00
33 V:Motorcyclists 3.00
34 thru 37 . . . . @3.00

SPIDER-MAN: MAXIMUM CLONAGE

1995

Alpha Maximum Clonage,pt.1 . . . . . 5.50
Omega TL,Maximum Clonage,pt.6 . 4.95

SPIDER-MAN MEGAZINE

1994–95

1 thru 4 rep. . . . . @3.00
5 Vision rep. 3.00
6 V:Thing & Torch, rep. 3.00

SPIDER-MAN: MUTANT AGENDA

0 thru 2 Paste in Book . . . . @2.00
3 Paste in Book. 2.00

SPIDER-MAN: POWER OF TERROR

1995

1 R:Silvermane,A:Deathlok 2.00
2 V:Silvermane 2.00
3 New Scorpion. 2.00
4 V:Silvermane 2.00

SPIDER-MAN/PUNISHER

Part 1 TL,A:Tombstone. 3.00
Part 2 TL,A:Tombstone. 3.00

SPIDER-MAN/PUNISHER/ SABERTOOTH: DESIGNER GENES

1 SMc,Foil(c). 9.50

SPIDER-MAN: REDEMPTION

1996

1 thru 4 JMD,MZ,BMc, Mary Jane arrested for Murder . . . . @2.00

SPIDER-MAN: REVENGE OF THE GREEN GOBLIN

Aug. 2000

1 (of 3) RCa,LW,RSt,R:Norman Osborn. 3.00
2 LW,RSt,F:NormanOsborn 3.00
3 RSt,RF,PO, concl 3.00

SPIDER-MAN SAGA

Nov., 1991

1 SLi(c),History from Amazing Fantasy #15-Amaz.SpM#100 . . 3.25
2 SLi(c),Amaz.SpM#101-#175. . . . 3.25
3 Amaz.SpM#176-#238 . . . . 3.25
4 Amaz.SpM #239-#300 . . . . 3.25

SPIDER-MAN SUPER SIZE SPECIAL

1 Planet of the Symbiotes,pt.2 . . . . 3.95

SPIDER-MAN TEAM-UP

1995–96

1 MWa,KeL,V:Hellfire Club 3.00
2 thru 4 . . . . 3.00
5 SvG,DaR,JFr,F:Gambit, Howard the Duck 3.00
6 JMD,LHa,F:Hulk & Doctor Strange 3.00
7 KBk,SB,F:Thunderbolts 3.00

SPIDER-MAN: THE ARACHNIS PROJECT

1984–95

1 Wld, beginnings 2.00
2 Wld,V:Diggers 2.00
3 Wld,V:Jury 2.00
4 Wld,V:Life Foundation. 2.00
5 Wld,V:Jury 2.00

SPIDER-MAN: THE CLONE JOURNALS

1-shot (1995) 2.00

SPIDER-MAN: THE JACKAL FILES

1 Files of the Jackal (1995) 2.00

SPIDER-MAN: THE LOST YEARS

1995

0 JMD,JR2,LSh,64pg,rep. 4.00
1 History of Kaine,Ben. 3.00
2 JMD,JR2,KJ,Kaine & Ben. 3.00
3 Ben vs. Kaine. 3.00

SPIDER-MAN: THE PARKER YEARS

1995

1 JR2,JPi,F:The real Clone 2.50

SPIDER-MAN 2099

1992–96

1 RL,AW,I:Spider-Man 2099 . . . . . 4.00
2 RL,AW,O:Spider-Man 2099. . . . . 3.00
3 RL,AW,V:Venture 2.50
4 RL,AW,I:Specialist, A:Doom 2099. . . . . 2.00
5 RL,AW,V:Specialist. 2.00
6 RL,AW,I:New Vulture 2.00
7 RL,AW,Vulture of 2099 . . . . 2.00
8 RL,AW,V:New Vulture. 2.00
9 KJo,V:Alchemax 2.00
10 RL,AW,O:Wellvale Home 2.00
11 RL,AW,V:S.I.E.G.E. 2.00
12 RL,AW,w/poster. 2.00
13 RL,AW,V:Thanatos 2.00
14 PDd(s),RL(c),TGb,Downtown. . . 2.00
15 PDd(s),RL,I:Thor 2099, Heimdall 2099 . . . . 2.00
16 PDd(s),RL,Fall of the Hammer#1 . . . . 2.00
17 PDd(s),RL,V:Bloodsword 2.00
18 PDd(s),RLm,V:Lyla 2.00
19 PDd(s),RL,w/card 2.00
20 PDd(s),RL,Crash & Burn 2.00
21 V:Gangs 2.00
22 V:Gangs 2.00
23 RL,I:Risque 3.00
24 Kasey 2.00
25 A:Hulk 2099, dbl-size,foil(c) 3.25
25a Newsstand ed.. . . . . 2.25
26 V:Headhunter, Travesty 2.00
27 V:Travesty 2.00
28 V:Travesty 2.00
29 V:Foragers. 2.00
30 V:Flipside 2.00
31 I:Dash 2.00

Spider-Man 2099 #25
© Marvel Entertainment Group

Becomes:

SPIDER-MAN 2099 A.D.

32 I:Morgue 2.00
33 One Nation Under Doom 2.00
34 V:Alchemex 2.00
35 . . . . 2.00
36a Spider-Man 2099(c). 2.00
36b Venom 2099(c) 2.00
37a Venom 2099 . . . . 2.00
37b variant cover 2.00
38 . . . . 2.00
39 A:Venom 2099. . . . . 2.00
40 V:Goblin 2099 . . . . 2.00
41 and 42 . . . . @2.00
43 V:Sub-Mariner 2099. . . . . 2.00
Ann.#1 PDd(s),RL 3.00
Spec.#1 I:3 new villains 4.00

SPIDER-MAN UNLIMITED

1993

1 RLm,Maximun Carnage#1,I:Shriek, R:Carnage 5.00
2 RLm,Maximum Carnage#14 . . . . 4.50
3 RLm,O:Doctor Octopus. 4.50
4 RLm,V:Mystrerio,Rhino 4.25
5 RLm,A:Human Torch, I:Steel Spider 4.25
6 RLm,A:Thunderstrike 4.00
7 RLm,A:Clone 4.00
8 Tom Lyle. 4.00
9 The Mark of Kaine,pt.5 . . . . 4.00
10 SwM,Exiled,pt.4. . . . . 4.00
11 FaN,V:Black Cat 4.00
12 Blood Brother tie-in 4.00
13 . . . . 3.00
14 JoB, an ally dies 3.00
15 TDF,JoB,F:Puma 3.00
16 cont. from X-Force #64 . . . . 3.00
17 JoB, Revelations, sequel 3.00
18 TDF,JoB,F:Doctor Octopus 3.00
19 JoB,F:Lizard 3.00
20 JoB,A:Hannibal King, V:Lilith . . . 3.00
21 MD2,Frankenstein Monster lives 3.00
22 MD2,V:The Scorpion 3.00

SPIDER-MAN UNIVERSE

Jan., 2000

1 rep. 3 stories, 80-pg.. . . . . 5.00
2 rep. 3 stories, 80-pg.. . . . . 5.00
3 rep. 3 stories, 80-pg.. . . . . 5.00
4 rep. 3 stories, 80-pg.. . . . . 5.00
5 rep. 3 stories, 80-pg 5.00
6 rep. 3 stories, 80-pg 5.00
7 rep. 3 stories, 80-pg 4.00
8 rep. 3 stories, 80-pg 4.00
9 rep. 3 stories, 80-pg 4.00

SPIDER-MAN UNLIMITED

Nov., 1999

1 cartoon, tie-in 2.00
2 cartoon, tie-in 2.00
3 cartoon, tie-in 2.00
4 Counter-Earth. 2.00
5 F:Wolverine 2.00

SPIDER-MAN UNMASKED

1996

1-shot 64pg information source . . . 6.00

SPIDER-MAN VS. DRACULA

1994

1 rep. 2.00

SPIDER-MAN vs. VENOM

1990

1 TM(c) 8.95

SPIDER-MAN: THE VENOM AGENDA

Nov., 1997

1-shot LHa,TL, J. Jonah Jameson, V:Venom 3.00

SPIDER-MAN vs. WOLVERINE

1990

1 MBr,AW,D:Ned Leeds(the original Hobgoblin),V:Charlie. 22.00
1a reprint. 5.00

SPIDER-MAN: WEB OF DOOM

1994

1 3-part series. 2.00
2 Spidey falsely accused 2.00
3 conclusion 2.00

SPIDER-MAN & X-FACTOR: SHADOW GAMES

1 PB,I:Shadowforce. 2.25
2 PB,V:Shadowforce 2.25
3 PB,V:Shadowforce, final issue . . 2.25

SPIDER-WOMAN

April, 1978

1 CI,TD,O:Spiderwoman 6.00
2 CI,TD,I:Morgan Le Fey 2.00
3 CI,TD,I:Brother's Grimm 2.00
4 CI,TD,V:Hangman 2.00
5 CI,TD,Nightmares. 2.00
6 CI,A:Werewolf By Night 2.00
7 CI,SL,AG,V:Magnus 2.00
8 CI,AG,"Man who would not die" . 2.00
9 CI,AG,A:Needle,Magnus. 2.00
10 CI,AG,I:Gypsy Moth 2.00
11 CI,AG,V:Brothers Grimm 2.00
12 CI,AG,V:Brothers Grimm 2.00
13 CI,AG,A:Shroud. 2.00

Spider-Woman #48
© Marvel Entertainment Group

14 BSz(c),CI,AG,A:Shroud 2.00
15 BSz(c),CI,AG,A:Shroud 2.00
16 BSz(c),CI,AG,V:Nekra 2.00
17 CI,Deathplunge 2.00
18 CI,A:Flesh 2.00
19 CI,A:Werewolf By Night, V:Enforcer 2.00
20 FS,A:Spider-Man 2.00
21 FS,A:Bounty Hunter. 2.00
22 FS,A:Killer Clown. 2.00
23 TVE,V:The Gamesmen 2.00
24 TVE,V:The Gamesmen 2.00
25 SL,Two Spiderwomen 2.00
26 JBy(c),SL,V:White Gardenia. . . . 2.00
27 BSz(c),JBi,A:Enforcer 2.00
28 BSz(c),SL,A:Enforcer,Spidey . . . 2.00
29 JR2(c),ECh,FS,A:Enforcer, Spider-Man 2.00
30 FM(c),SL,JM,I:Dr.Karl Malus . . . 2.00
31 FM(c),SL,JM,A:Hornet 2.00
32 FM(c),SL,JM,A:Werewolf 2.00
33 SL,V:Yesterday's Villian 2.00
34 SL,AM,V:Hammer and Anvil. . . . 2.00
35 SL,AG,V:Angar the Screamer . . 2.00
36 SL,Spiderwoman Shot 2.00
37 SL,TA,BWi,AM,FS,A:X-Men,I: Siryn,V:Black Tom 4.00
38 SL,BWi,A:X-Men,Siryn. 5.00
39 SL,BWi,Shadows. 2.00
40 SL,BWi,V:The Flying Tiger 2.00
41 SL,BWi,V:Morgan LeFay 2.00
42 SL,BWi,V:Silver Samurai 2.00
43 SL,V:Silver Samurai. 2.00
44 SL,V:Morgan LeFay. 2.00
45 SL,Spider-Man Thief Cover 2.00
46 SL,V:Mandroids,A:Kingpin 2.00
47 V:Daddy Longlegs 2.00
48 O:Gypsy Moth 2.00
49 A:Tigra 2.00
50 PH(c),D:Spiderwoman 3.50

[Limited Series] 1993–94

1 V:Therak 2.00
2 O:Spider-Woman 2.00
3 V:Deathweb 2.00
4 V:Deathweb,Last issue 2.00

SPIDER-WOMAN

May, 1999

1 JBy,BS,48-page 3.00
1a signed 20.00
2 BS,JBy,A:Dr. Octopus. 2.00
2a variant JR2 cover 2.00
3 BS,JBy,V:Flesh & Bones. 2.00
4 BS,JBy,V:Flesh & Bones. 2.00
5 BS,JBy,I:Shadowcaster. 2.00
6 BS,JBy,V:Shadowcaster 2.00
7 BS,JBy. 2.00
8 BS,JBy,A:Cluster,x-over 2.00
9 BS,JBy,A:Mattie 2.00
10 BS,JBy,A:Rhino 2.00
11 BS,JBy,V:Exomorph. 2.00
12 BS,JBy,F:J.Jonah Jameson 2.25
13 BS,JBy,V:Werewolf 2.25
14 JBy,GN,BS(c),V:Nighteyes. 2.25
15 JBy,BS,Itch&Scratch 2.25
16 JBy,BS,Flesh. 2.25
17 JBy,BS,Flesh & Bones. 2.25
18 JBy,BS,final issue 2.25

SPIDEY SUPER STORIES

Oct., 1974

1 Younger reader's series in association with the Electric Company,O:Spider-Man 12.00
2 A:Kraven 8.00
3 A:Ringleader 8.00
4 A:Medusa 8.00

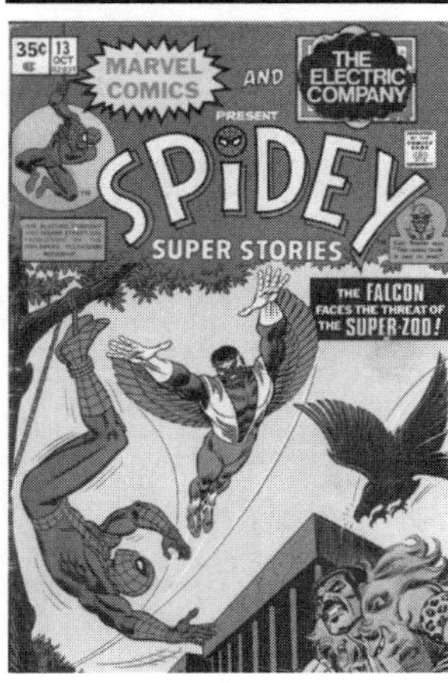

Spidey Super Stories #13
© Marvel Entertainment Group

5 A:Shocker 8.00
6 A:Iceman 8.00
7 A:Lizard, Vanisher 8.00
8 A:Dr. Octopus 8.00
9 A:Dr. Doom 8.00
10 A:Green Goblin 7.00
11 A:Dr. Octopus 7.00
12 A:The Cat,V:The Owl 7.00
13 A:Falcon 7.00
14 A:Shanna 7.00
15 A:Storm 8.00
16 . . . . . 6.00
17 A:Captain America 6.00
18 A:Kingpin 6.00
19 A:Silver Surfer,Dr. Doom 6.00
20 A;Human Torch,Invisible Girl . . . 6.00
21 A:Dr. Octopus 5.00
22 A:Ms. Marvel,The Beetle 5.00
23 A:Green Goblin 5.00
24 A:Thundra 5.00
25 A:Dr. Doom 5.00
26 A:Sandman 5.00
27 A:Thor,Loki 5.00
28 A:Medusa 5.00
29 A:Kingpin 5.00
30 A:Kang 5.00
31 A:Moondragon,Dr. Doom 4.00
32 A:Spider-Woman,Dr. Octopus . . 4.00
33 . . . . . 4.00
34 A:Sub-Mariner 4.00
35 . . . . . 4.00
36 A:Lizard 4.00
37 A:White Tiger 4.00
38 A:Fantastic Four 4.00
39 A:Hellcat,Thanos 6.00
40 A:Hawkeye 4.00
41 A:Nova,Dr. Octopus 4.00
42 A:Kingpin 4.00
43 A:Daredevil,Ringmaster 4.00
44 A:Vision 4.00
45 A:Silver Surfer,Dr. Doom 6.00
46 A:Mysterio 4.00
47 A:Spider-Woman,Stilt-Man 4.00
48 A:Green Goblin 4.00
49 Spidey for President 4.00
50 A:She-Hulk 4.00
51 and 52 . . . . . @4.00
53 A:Dr. Doom 4.00
54 `Attack of the Bird-Man' 4.00
55 A:Kingpin 4.00
56 A:Captain Britain,
Jack O'Lantern 4.00
57 March, 1982 . . . . . 4.00

SPITFIRE AND THE TROUBLESHOOTERS

Oct., 1986

1 HT/JSt 2.00
2 HT 2.00
3 HT,Macs Armor 2.00
4 TM/BMc(Early TM work) 3.00
5 HT/TD,A:StarBrand 2.00
6 HT,Trial 2.00
7 HT 2.00
8 HT,New Armor 2.00
9 . . . . . 2.00
Becomes:

CODE NAME: SPITFIRE

10 MR/TD 2.00
11 thru 13 . . . . . @2.00

SPOOF

Oct., 1970

1 MSe 12.00
2 MSe,`Brawl in the Family' 10.00
3 MSe,Richard Nixon cover 10.00
4 MSe,`Blechhula' 10.00
5 MSe,May, 1973 . . . . . 11.00

SPORT STARS

Nov., 1949

1 The Life of Knute Rockne . . . 250.00
Becomes:

SPORTS ACTION

2 BP(c),Life of George Gipp 250.00
3 BEv,Hack Wilson 165.00
4 Art Houtteman 150.00
5 Nile Kinnick 150.00
6 Warren Gun 150.00
7 Jim Konstanty 150.00
8 Ralph Kiner 175.00
9 Ed "Strangler" Lewis 150.00
10 JMn,'The Yella-Belly' 150.00
11 `The Killers' 150.00
12 BEv,`Man Behind the Mask' . . 150.00
13 BEv,Lew Andrews 150.00
14 MWs,Ken Roper,Sept.,1952 . . 150.00

SPOTLIGHT

Sept., 1978

1 F:Huckleberry Hound,YogiBear . 20.00
2 Quick Draw McDraw 15.00
3 The Jetsons 20.00
4 Magilla Gorilla, March, 1979 . . 15.00

SPUMCO COMIC BOOK

1 I:Jimmy the Hapless Boy 7.00
2 . . . . . 7.00
3 64pgs of sick humor 7.00
4 More sick humor 7.00
TPB 24.95

SPY CASES
See: KID KOMICS

SPY FIGHTERS

March, 1951

1 GT 175.00
2 GT 100.00
3 . . . . . 75.00
4 thru 13 . . . . . @75.00
14 thru 15 July, 1953 . . . . . @85.00

SPYKE

Epic *Heavy Hitters* 1993

1 MBn,BR,I:Spyke 2.75
2 MBn,BR,V:Conita 2.75
3 thru 4 MBn,BR . . . . . @2.00

SPY THRILLERS

Atlas Nov., 1954

1 `The Tickling Death' 150.00
2 V:Communists 100.00
3 . . . . . 75.00
4 . . . . . 75.00
Becomes:

POLICE BADGE

5 Sept., 1955 . . . . . 75.00

Squadron Supreme #4
© Marvel Entertainment Group

SQUADRON SUPREME

Sept., 1985

1 BH,L:Nighthawk 3.00
2 BH,F:Nuke,A:Scarlet Centurion . . 2.50
3 BH,D:Nuke 2.50
4 BH,L:Archer 2.00
5 BH,L:Amphibian 2.00
6 PR,J:Institute of Evil 2.00
7 JB,JG,V:Hyperion 2.00
8 BH,V:Hyperion 2.00
9 BSz(c),PR,D:Tom Thumb 2.00
10 PR,V:Quagmire 2.00
11 PR,V:Redeemers 2.00
12 PR,D:Nighthawk,Foxfire,
Black Archer 2.50
GN Death of a Universe 9.95
TPB 352 pages 15.00

STALKERS

Epic 1990–91

1 MT 2.00
2 MT 2.00
3 MT 2.00
4 MT 2.00
5 MT 2.00
6 VM,MT 2.00
7 VM,MT 2.00
8 VM,MT 2.00
9 thru 12 VM . . . . . @2.00

STARBLAST

1994

1 MGu(s),HT,After the Starbrand . . 2.25
2 MGu(s),HT,After the Starbrand . . 2.00
3 MGu(s),HT,After the Starbrand . . 2.00
4 MGu(s),HT,Final Issue 2.00

MARVEL

STARBRAND

Oct., 1986

1 JR2,O:Starbrand. 2.00
2 JR2/AW 2.00
3 JR2/AW 2.00
4 JR2/AW 2.00
5 JR2/AW 2.00
6 JR2/AW 2.00
7 JR2/AW 2.00
8 JR2/AW 2.00
9 KG/BWi,A:Nightmask 2.00
10 . . . . 2.00
11 JR2,TP 2.00
12 JR2,TP,X-Men X-over 2.00
13 JR2,TP 2.00
14 JR2,TP 2.00
15 . . . . 2.00
16 . . . . 2.00
17 JBy,TP,New Starbrand 2.00
18 JBy/TP 2.00
19 JBy/TP 2.00
Ann.#1 . . . . 2.00

STAR COMICS MAGAZINE

Dec., 1986 (digest size)

1 F:Heathcliff,Muppet Babies, Ewoks 2.00
2 thru 13 1988 . . . . @2.00

STARJAMMERS

1995–96

1 I:The Uncreated 3.00
2 War For the Shi'ar 3.00
3 stuck in deep space 3.00
4 conclusion 3.00

STAR-LORD, SPECIAL EDITION

Feb., 1982

1 JBy reprints 6.00

STARLORD

Mini-Series 1996

1 (of 3) DLw, ... 2.50
2 DLw 2.50
3 DLw,V:Damyish 2.50

STARLORD MEGAZINE

TPB CCI,JBy,TA, rep., 64pg 2.95

STAR MASTER

1 MGu,Cosmic Avengers assemble 2.00
2 MGu,Worldengine saga 2.00
3 MGu,Cauldron of Conversion . . . 2.00

STARRIORS

August, 1984

1 . . . . 2.00
2 . . . . 2.00
3 . . . . 2.00
4 Feb., 1982 . . . . 2.00

STARSTRUCK

March, 1985

1 MK. 2.00
2 MK. 2.00
3 thru 8 MK, Feb. 1986 . . . . @2.00

STAR TREK

April, 1980

1 DC,KJ,rep.1st movie Adapt. 8.00
2 DC,KJ,rep.1st movie Adapt. 6.00
3 DC,KJ,rep.1st movie Adapt. 5.00
4 DC,KJ,The Weirdest Voyage . . . 5.00
5 DC,KJ,Dr.McCoy..Killer 5.00
6 DC,KJ,A:Ambassador Phlu 5.00
7 MN,KJ,Kirk/Spock(c). 5.00
8 DC(p),F:Spock 5.00
9 DC,FS,Trapped in a Web of Ghostly Vengeance 5.00
10 KJ(i),Spock the Barbarian 5.00
11 TP(i),Like A Woman Scorned . . . 5.00
12 TP(i),Trapped in a Starship Gone Mad 5.00
13 TP(i),A:Barbara McCoy 5.00
14 LM,GD,We Are Dying, Egypt,Dying 5.00
15 GK,The Quality of Mercy 5.00
16 LM,There's no Space like Gnomes 5.00
17 EH,TP,The Long Nights Dawn . . 7.00
18 A Thousand Deaths,last issue . 15.00

Star Trek: Deep Space Nine #9
© Marvel Entertainment Group

STAR TREK: DEEP SPACE NINE

1996

1 HWe(s),TGb,AM,DS9 in the Gamma Quadrant,pt.1 (of 2). . . 2.00
2 DS9 in Gamma Quadrant,pt.2. . . 2.00
3 TGb,AM,pt.1 (of 2) 2.00
4 TGb,AM,pt.2. . . . . 2.00
5 AM,terrorist attack 2.00
6 HWe(s),TGb,AM,Shirn sentence Sisko to Death, "Risk," pt.1 . . . . 2.00
7 HWe(s),TGb,"Risk," pt.2 . . . . 2.00
8 TGb,AM,V:Maquis & Romulans. . 2.00
9 TGb,AM,V:Maquis & Romulans, pt.2 . . . . 2.00
10 HWe,TGb, trapped in the holosuite 2.00
11 HWe,TGb, ... 2.00
12 Telepathy War x-over. 2.00
13 Jem'Hadar battle 2.00
14 Why do Klingons hate tribbles? . 2.00
15 The Tailor's deeds 2.00

STAR TREK: EARLY VOYAGES

Dec., 1996

1 DAn,IEd,Captain Pike's crew, double size premier 3.00
2 DAn,IEd,distress signal. 2.00
3 DAn,IEd,on Rigel 7, prologue to "The Cage". 2.00
4 DAn,IEd, prologue to "The Cage" 2.00
5 DAn,IEd, V:Vulcans 2.00
6 DAn,IEd, Cloak & Dagger concl. . 2.00
7 DAn,IEd, The wrath of Kaaj 2.00
8 DAn,IEd,F:Dr. Boyce. 2.00
9 DAn,IEd,F:Nano 2.00
10 DAn,V:Chakuun, Tholians 2.00
11 DAn,IEd,The Fallen, pt. 2. . . . . . 2.00
12 DAn,IEd, ... 2.00
13 DAn,IEd,F:Yeoman Colt. 2.00
14 DAn,IEd,Pike vs. Kirk. 2.00
15 DAn,IEd,F:Yeoman Colt. 2.00
16 . . . . 2.00
17 DAn,IEd, Pike & Kaaj. 2.00

STAR TREK: FIRST CONTACT

GN Movie Adapt. 6.00

STAR TREK: MIRROR, MIRROR

1996

1-shot continuation of famous classic episode. 4.00

STAR TREK: THE NEXT GENERATION— RIKER SPECIAL

May, 1998

1-shot, DAn,IEd,Riker photo cover . 3.50

STAR TREK: THE NEXT GENERATION/X-MEN: SECOND CONTACT

March, 1998

1-shot, DAn,IEd,64pg 5.00
1-shot, variant CNr cover (1:5) 5.00

STAR TREK: OPERATION ASSIMILATION

1-shot Borg story. 3.00

STAR TREK: STARFLEET ACADEMY

1996

1 Cadets vs. Gorns 2.00
2 ALa, R&R in Australia. 2.00
3 F:Decker 2.00
4 V:Klingon Bird-of-prey. 2.00
5 V:Klingons 2.00
6 Funeral of Kamilah Goldstein,I:Edam Astrun. 2.00
7 ALa,F:Edam Astrun,Nog 2.00
8 ALa, Return of Charlie X. 2.00
9 ALa, on Talos, V:Jem'Hadar 2.00
10 ALa,F:Captain Pike, Jem'Hadar . 2.00
11 F:Christopher Pike 2.00
12 ALa, Telepathy War x-over. 2.00
13 Parent's Day 2.00
14 T'Priell revealed, pt.1 (of 3) 2.00
15 T'Priell dead?, pt.2. . . . . 2.00
16 T'Priell Revealed, pt3. . . . . 2.00
17 Battle for T'Priell's mind 2.00
18 Entirely in Klingon language. . . . 2.00
19 Pava vs. Kovold. 2.00

All comics prices listed are for *Near Mint* condition.

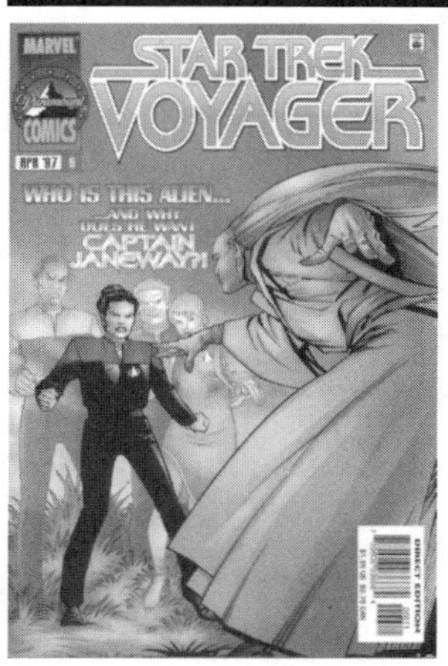

Star Trek Voyager #6
© Marvel Entertainment Group

STAR TREK: TELEPATHY WAR
Sept., 1997

1-shot Telepathy War, pt.4 x-over, 48pg 3.00

STAR TREK: UNLIMITED
1996

1 DAn,IEd,MBu,JeM,AW, Classic series & TNG 3.00
2 DAn,IEd,MBu,. 3.00
3 DAn,IEd,MBu,. 3.00
4 DAn,IEd,MBu,AW, 2 tales 3.00
5 DAn,IEd,TMo,RoR,AW,ANi,48pg. 3.00
6 DAn, Telepathy War x-over 2.00
7 DAn,IEd,F:Q & Trelane 2.00
8 DAn,IEd,Day of Honor tie-in 2.00
9 DAn,IEd,V:Klingons 2.00
10 A Piece of the Action, conclusion of series 2.00

STAR TREK: THE UNTOLD VOYAGES
Jan., 1998

1 (of 5) Star Trek 2nd Five Year Mission 2.50
2 Spock, Savik, Dr. McCoy 2.50
3 F:McCoy, McCoy's Daughter. . . . 2.50
4 F:Sulu 2.50
5 48pg finale 3.50

STAR TREK: VOYAGER
1996

1 F:Neelix & Talaxians, pt.1 . . . . . 2.00
2 F:Neelix & Talaxians, pt.2 . . . . . 2.00
3 F:Neelix & Talaxians, pt.3 . . . . . 2.00
4 HWe(s),"Homeostasis," pt.1 . . . . 2.00
5 HWe(s),"Homeostasis," pt.2 . . . . 2.00
6 HWe(s),"Homeostasis," pt.3 . . . . 2.00
7 Ancient Relic 2.00
8 Mysterious Relic encountered . . . 2.00
9 DAn,IEd,AM, rescue mission . . . 2.00
10 The Borg are back 2.00
11 Zoological Experiment 2.00
12 Zoological Experiment 2.00
13 Crew loses a member 2.00
14 Distress Call 2.00
15 Tuvok Trapped 2.00

STAR TREK: VOYAGER: SPLASHDOWN
Jan., 1998

1 (of 4) AM,Crash landing on water planet 2.00
2 AM,The ship may sink 2.00
3 AM,adventure undersea 2.00
4 AM,escape from sea creatures . . 2.00

STAR TREK/X-MEN

1-shot SLo,MS, 64pg. 5.00
1a rep. of STAR TREK/X-MEN . . . 4.95

STAR WARS
July, 1977

1 HC,30 Cent,movie adaption. . . . 65.00
1a HC,35 Cent(square Box). . . . 400.00
1b "Reprint" 7.50
2 HC,movie adaptation 25.00
2b "Reprint" 4.00
3 HC,movie adaptation 25.00
3b "Reprint" 4.00
4 HC,SL,movie adapt.(low dist.). . 22.00
4b "Reprint" 4.00
5 HC,SL,movie adaptation 22.00
5b "Reprint" 3.00
6 HC,DSt,E:movie adaption 22.00
6b "Reprint" 3.00
7 HC,FS,F:Luke&Chewbacca . . . 20.00
7b "Reprint" 2.50
8 HC,TD,Eight against a World . . 20.00
8b "Reprint" 2.50
9 HC,TP,V:Cloud Riders. 20.00
9b "Reprint" 2.50
10 HC,TP,Behemoth fr.Below 20.00
11 CI,TP,Fate o/Luke Skywalker . . 18.00
12 TA,CI,Doomworld. 18.00
13 TA,JBy,CI,Deadly Reunion 18.00
14 TA,CI 18.00
15 CI,V:Crimson Jack 18.00
16 WS,V:The Hunter. 18.00
17 Crucible, Low Dist.. . . . . 18.00
18 CI,Empire Strikes(Low Dist). . . 18.00
19 CI,Ultimate Gamble(Low Dist) . 18.00
20 CI,Death Game(Scarce). 18.00
21 TA,CI,Shadow of a Dark Lord(Scarce) 18.00
22 CI,Han Solo vs.Chewbacca . . . 15.00
23 CI,Flight Into Fury 15.00
24 CI,Ben Kenobi Story 15.00
25 CI,Siege at Yavin 15.00
26 CI,Doom Mission 15.00
27 CI,V:The Hunter. 15.00
28 CI,Cavern o/t Crawling Death. . 15.00
29 CI,Dark Encounter 15.00
30 CI,A Princess Alone. 15.00
31 CI,Return to Tatooine. 15.00
32 CI,The Jawa Express. 15.00
33 CI,GD,V:Baron Tagge 15.00
34 CI,Thunder in the Stars 15.00
35 CI,V:Darth Vader 15.00
36 CI,V:Darth Vader 15.00
37 CI,V:Darth Vader 15.00
38 TA,MG,Riders in the Void. . . . 15.00
39 AW,B:Empire Strikes Back 25.00
40 AW,Battleground Hoth 25.00
41 AW,Imperial Pursuit 25.00
42 AW,Bounty Hunters 25.00
43 AW,Betrayal at Bespin 25.00
44 AW,E:Empire Strikes Back 25.00
45 CI,GD,Death Probe 20.00
46 DI,TP,V:Dreamnaut Devourer . . 20.00
47 CI,GD,Droid World. 20.00
48 CI,Leia vs.Darth Vader. 20.00
49 SW,TP,The Last Jedi 20.00
50 WS,AW,TP,G-Size issue 20.00
51 WS,TP,Resurrection of Evil . . . 15.00
52 WS,TP. 15.00
53 CI,WS 15.00

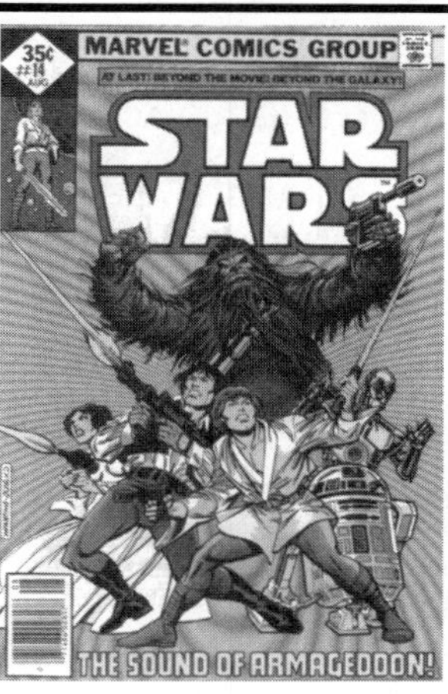

Star Wars #14
© Marvel Entertainment Group

54 CI,WS 15.00
55 thru 66 WS,TP . . . . . @15.00
67 TP 15.00
68 GD,TP. 20.00
69 GD,TP. 20.00
70 A:Han Solo 20.00
71 A:Han Solo 20.00
72 . . . . . 20.00
73 Secret of Planet Lansbane. . . . 20.00
74 thru 91 . . . . . @20.00
92 BSz(c) 20.00
93 thru 97 . . . . . @20.00
98 AW 20.00
99 . . . . . 20.00
100 Painted(c),double-size 20.00
101 BSz 15.00
102 KRo's Back 15.00
103 thru 106 . . . . . @15.00
107 WPo(i),last issue 50.00
Ann.#1 WS(c),V:Winged Warlords. 10.00
Ann.#2 RN 8.00
Ann.#3 RN,Darth Vader(c) 8.00

STEELGRIP STARKEY
Epic July, 1986

1 . . . . . 2.00
2 . . . . . 2.00
3 . . . . . 2.00
4 . . . . . 2.00
5 . . . . . 2.00
6 June, 1987 . . . . . 2.00

STEELTOWN ROCKERS
April, 1990—Sept., 1990

1 SL 2.00
2 thru 6 SL. . . . . @2.00

STORM

1 TyD,KIS,V:Candra. 3.00
2 . . . . . 3.00
3 . . . . . 3.00
4 TyD,KIS, conclusion,foil cover. . . 3.00

STRANGE COMBAT TALES

1 thru 2 . . . . . 2.75
3 Tiger by the Tail 2.50
4 Midnight Crusade 2.50

STRANGE STORIES OF SUSPENSE
See: RUGGED ACTION

STRANGE TALES
[1st Regular Series]June, 1951

1 `The Room' . . . 2,800.00
2 `Trapped In A Tomb' . . . 950.00
3 JMn,`Man Who Never Was' . . 650.00
4 BEv,`Terror in the Morgue' . . . 725.00
5 `A Room Without A Door' . . . 650.00
6 RH(c),`The Ugly Man' . . . 500.00
7 `Who Stands Alone' . . . 500.00
8 BEv(c),`Something in the Fog' 500.00
9 `Drink Deep Vampire' . . . 500.00
10 BK,`Hidden Head' . . . 550.00
11 BEv(c),GC,'O'Malley's Friend' 325.00
12 `Graveyard At Midnight' . . . 325.00
13 BEv(c),`Death Makes A Deal'. 325.00
14 GT,`Horrible Herman' . . . 325.00
15 BK,`Don't Look Down' . . . 350.00
16 Decapitation cover . . . 325.00
17 DBr,JRo,`Death Feud' . . . 325.00
18 `Witch Hunt' . . . 325.00
19 RH(c),`The Rag Doll' . . . 325.00
20 RH(c),GC,SMo,`Lost World' . . 325.00
21 BEv . . . 275.00
22 BK,JF . . . 275.00
23 `The Strangest Tale in the World' . . . 275.00
24 `The Thing in the Coffin' . . . 275.00
25 . . . 275.00
26 . . . 275.00
27 JF,`The Garden of Death' . . . 275.00
28 `Come into my Coffin' . . . 275.00
29 `Witch-Craft' . . . 250.00
30 `The Thing in the Box' . . . 250.00
31 `The Man Who Played with Blocks' . . . 250.00
32 . . . 250.00
33 JMn(c),`Step Lively Please' . . 250.00
34 `Flesh and Blood' . . . 200.00
35 `The Man in the Bottle' . . . 200.00
36 . . . 200.00
37 `Out of the Storm' . . . 200.00
38 . . . 200.00
39 `Karnoff's Plan' . . . 200.00
40 BEv,`The Man Who Caught a Mermaid' . . . 200.00
41 BEv,`Riddle of the Skull' . . . 225.00
42 DW,BEv,JMn,`Faceless One' . 225.00
43 JF,`The Mysterious Machine' . 200.00
44 . . . 200.00
45 JKa,`Land of the Vanishing Men' . . . 225.00
46 thru 57 . . . @200.00
58 AW . . . 200.00
59 BK . . . 200.00
60 . . . 175.00
61 BK . . . 200.00
62 . . . 175.00
63 . . . 200.00
64 AW . . . 200.00
65 . . . 175.00
66 . . . 175.00
67 thru 78 . . . @250.00
79 SD,JK,Dr.Strange Prototype . . 250.00
80 thru 83 SD,JK . . . @175.00
84 SD,JK,Magneto Prototype . . . 175.00
85 SD,JK . . . 160.00
86 SD,JK,`I Who Created Mechano' . . . 160.00
87 SD,JK,`Return of Grogg' . . . 160.00
88 SD,JK,`Zzutak' . . . 160.00
89 SD,JK,`Fin Fang Foom' . . . 450.00
90 SD,JK,`Orrgo the Unconquerable' . . . 160.00
91 SD,JK,`The Sacrifice' . . . 160.00
92 SD,JK,`The Thing That Waits For Me' . . . 160.00
93 SD,JK,`The Wax People' . . . 160.00
94 SD,JK,`Pildorr the Plunderer' . 160.00
95 SD,JK,`Two-Headed Thing' . . 160.00
96 SD,JK,`I Dream of Doom' . . . 160.00
97 SD,JK,`When A Planet Dies' . 350.00
98 SD,JK,`No Human Can Beat Me' . . . 150.00
99 SD,JK,`Mister Morgan's Monster' . . . 150.00
100 SD,JK,`I Was Trapped in the Crazy Maze' . . . 150.00
101 B:StL(s),SD,JK, B:Human Torch . . . 900.00
102 SD,JK,I:Wizard . . . 300.00
103 SD,JK,I:Zemu . . . 250.00
104 SD,JK,I:The Trapster . . . 250.00
105 SD,JK,V:Wizard . . . 250.00
106 SD,A:Fantastic Four . . . 175.00
107 SD,V:Sub-Mariner . . . 200.00
108 SD,JK,A:FF,I:The Painter . . . 175.00
109 SD,JK,I:Sorcerer . . . 175.00
110 SD,I&B:Dr.Strange, Nightmare . . . 1,200.00
111 SD,I:Asbestos, Baron Mordo . . . 350.00
112 SD,I:The Eel . . . 125.00
113 SD,I:Plant Man . . . 125.00
114 SD,JK,A:Captain America . . . 400.00
115 SD,O:Dr.Strange . . . 500.00
116 SD,V:Thing . . . 125.00
117 SD,V:The Eel . . . 100.00
118 SD,V:The Wizard . . . 125.00
119 SD,C:Spider-Man . . . 125.00
120 SD,1st Iceman/Torch T.U. . . 135.00
121 SD,V:Plantman . . . 75.00
122 SD,V:Dr.Doom . . . 65.00
123 SD,A:Thor,I:Beetle . . . 65.00
124 SD,I:Zota . . . 65.00
125 SD,V:Sub-Mariner . . . 65.00
126 SD,I:Dormammu,Clea . . . 65.00
127 SD,V:Dormammu . . . 60.00
128 SD,I:Demon . . . 60.00
129 SD,I:Tiboro . . . 60.00
130 SD,C:Beatles . . . 65.00
131 SD,I:Dr.Vega . . . 55.00
132 SD,I:Orini . . . 55.00
133 SD,I:Shazana . . . 55.00
134 SD,E:Torch,I:Merlin . . . 55.00
135 SD,JK:I:Shield & Hydra B:Nick Fury . . . 125.00
136 SD,JK,V:Dormammu . . . 50.00
137 SD,JK,A:Ancient One . . . 60.00
138 SD,JK,I:Eternity . . . 45.00

Strange Tales #72
© Marvel Entertainment Group

139 SD,JK,V:Dormammu . . . 45.00
140 SD,JK,V:Dormammu . . . 45.00
141 SD,JK,I:Fixer,Mentallo . . . 45.00
142 SD,JK,I:THEM,V:Hydra . . . 45.00
143 SD,JK,V:Hydra . . . 45.00
144 SD,JK,V:Druid,I:Jasper Sitwell . . . 45.00
145 SD,JK,I:Mr.Rasputin . . . 45.00
146 SD,JK,V:Dormammu,I:AIM . . . 45.00
147 BEv,JK,F:Wong . . . 45.00
148 BEv,JK,O:Ancient One . . . 75.00
149 BEv,JK,V:Kaluu . . . 45.00
150 BEv,JK,JB(1st Marvel Art) I:Baron Strucker,Umar . . . 45.00
151 JK,JSo(1st Marvel Art), I:Umar . . . 60.00
152 BEv,JK,JSo,V:Umar . . . 40.00
153 JK,JSo,MSe,V:Hydra . . . 40.00
154 JSo,MSe,I:Dreadnought . . . 40.00
155 JSo,MSe,A:L.B.Johnson . . . 40.00
156 JSo,MSe,I:Zom . . . 40.00
157 JSo,MSe,A:Zom,C:Living Tribunal . . . 40.00
158 JSo,MSe,A:Zom,I:Living Tribunal(full story) . . . 45.00
159 JSo,MSe,O:Nick Fury,A:Capt. America,I:Val Fontaine . . . 50.00
160 JSo,MSe,A:Captain America I:Jimmy Woo . . . 40.00
161 JSo,I:Yellow Claw . . . 40.00
162 JSo,DA,A:Captain America . . . 40.00
163 JSo,DA,V:Yellow Claw . . . 40.00
164 JSo,DA,V:Yellow Claw . . . 40.00
165 JSo,DA,V:Yellow Claw . . . 40.00
166 DA,GT,JSo,A:AncientOne . . . 40.00
167 JSo,DA,V:Doctor Doom . . . 50.00
168 JSo,DA,E:Doctor Strange,Nick Fury,V:Yandroth . . . 40.00
169 JSo,I&O:Brother Voodoo . . . 15.00
170 JSo,O:Brother Voodoo . . . 12.00
171 GC,V:Baron Samed . . . 12.00
172 GC,DG,V:Dark Lord . . . 12.00
173 GC,DG,I:Black Talon . . . 12.00
174 JB,JM,O:Golem . . . 10.00
175 SD,R:Torr . . . 10.00
176 F:Golem . . . 10.00
177 FB,F:Golem . . . 10.00
178 JSn,B&O:Warlock,I:Magus . . . 27.00
179 JSn,I:Pip,I&D:Capt.Autolycus . 15.00
180 JSn,I:Gamora,Kray-tor . . . 15.00
181 JSn,E:Warlock . . . 15.00
182 SD,GK,rep Str.Tales #123,124 . . . 10.00
183 SD,rep Str.Tales #130,131 . . . 10.00
184 SD,rep Str.Tales #132,133 . . . 10.00
185 SD,rep Str.Tales #134,135 . . . 10.00
186 SD,rep Str.Tales #136,137 . . . 10.00
187 SD,rep Str.Tales #138,139 . . . 10.00
188 SD,rep Str.Tales #140,141 . . . 10.00
Ann.#1 V:Grottu,Diablo . . . 475.00
Ann.#2 A:Spider-Man . . . 500.00
Marvel Milestone rep. stories from #110–#111, #114–#115 (1995) . 2.95

[2nd Regular Series] 1987–88

1 BBl,CW,B:Cloak&Dagger,Dr. Strange,V:Lord of Light . . . 2.00
2 BBl,CW,V:Lord of Light,Demon . . 2.00
3 BBl,AW,CW,A:Nightmare,Khat . . 2.00
4 BBl,CW,V:Nightmare . . . 2.00
5 BBl,V:Rodent,A:Defenders . . . 2.00
6 BBl,BWi,V:Erlik Khan, A:Defenders . . . 2.00
7 V:Nightmare,A:Defenders . . . 2.00
8 BBl,BWi,V:Kaluu . . . 2.00
9 BBl,BWi,A:Dazzler,I:Mr.Jip, V:Kaluu . . . 2.00
10 BBl,BWi,RCa,A:Black Cat, V:Mr.Jip,Kaluu . . . 2.00
11 RCa,BWi,V:Mr.Jip,Kaluu . . . 2.00
12 WPo,BWi,A:Punisher,V:Mr.Jip . . 2.25
13 JBr,BWi,RCa,Punisher,

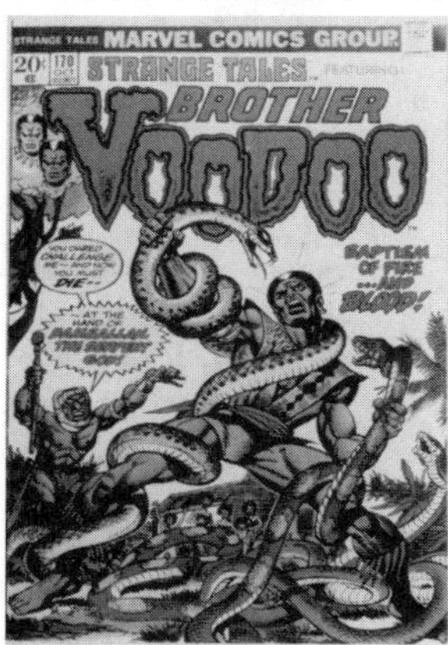

Strange Tales #170
© Marvel Entertainment Group

Power Pack 2.25
14 JBr,BWi,RCa,Punisher,P.Pack . . 2.25
15 RCa,BMc,A:Mayhem 2.00
16 RCa,BWi,V:Mr.Jip 2.00
17 RCa,BWi,V:Night 2.00
18 RCa,KN,A:X-Factor`,V:Night . . . 2.00
19 MMi(c),EL,TA,RCa,A:Thing 2.00
TPB Fully painted 6.95

STRANGE TALES
June, 1998

1 JMD,PJe,LSh,Man-Thing, 64pg. . 5.00
2A JMD,PJe,LSh,Man-Thing, Werewolf, 64pg 5.00
2B variant cover 5.00
3 JMD,PJe,NA(c),Man-Thing, Werewolf, 64pg 5.00
4 JMD,PJe,LSh,F:Man-Thing final issue. 5.00

STRANGE TALES: DARK CORNERS
March, 1998

1-shot JEs, three stories, 48pg. . . . 4.00

STRANGE TALES OF THE UNUSUAL
Dec., 1955—Aug., 1957

1 JMn(c),BP,DH,JR,`Man Lost' . 350.00
2 BEv,`Man Afraid' 200.00
3 AW,`The Invaders' 200.00
4 `The Long Wait' 135.00
5 RC,SD,`The Threat' 175.00
6 BEv 150.00
7 JK,JO 150.00
8 . . . . 125.00
9 BEv(c),BK 150.00
10 GM,AT 125.00
11 BEv(c),August, 1957 . . . . 125.00

STRANGE WORLDS
Dec., 1958

1 JK,SD 675.00
2 SD 400.00
3 JK 300.00
4 AW 275.00
5 SD 225.00

STRAWBERRY SHORTCAKE
Star June, 1985—April, 1986

1 . . . . 2.00
2 thru 7 . . . . @2.00

STRAY TOASTERS
Epic Jan., 1988

1 BSz 5.00
2 BSz 4.50
3 and 4 BSz. . . . . @4.00

STRIKEFORCE MORITURI
Dec., 1986

1 BA,SW,WPo(1st pencils-3 pages),I:Blackwatch 3.00
2 BA,SW,V:The Horde 2.50
3 BA,SW,V:The Horde. 2.50
4 BA,SW,WPo,V:The Horde. 2.00
5 BA,SW,V:The Horde. 2.00
6 BA,SW,V:The Horde. 2.00
7 BA,SW,V:The Horde. 2.00
8 BA,SW,V:The Horde. 2.00
9 BA,SW,V:THe Horde 2.00
10 WPo,(1st pencils-full story), SW,R:Black Watch,O:Horde . . . 3.00
11 BA,SW,V:The Horde 2.00
12 BA,SW,D:Jelene 2.00
13 BA,SW,Old V:NewTeam. 2.00
14 BA,AW,V:The Horde 2.00
15 BA,AW,V:The Horde 2.00
16 WPo,SW,V:The Horde 2.50
17 WPo(c),SW,V:The Horde 2.00
18 BA,SW,V:Hammersmith 2.00
19 BA,SW,V:THe Horde,D:Pilar . . . 2.00
20 BA,SW,V:The Horde 2.00
21 MMi(c),TD(i),V:The Horde 2.00
22 TD(i),V:The Horde 2.00
23 MBa,VM,V:The Horde 2.00
24 VM(i),I:Vax,V:The Horde 2.00
25 TD(i),V:The Horde 2.00
26 MBa,VM,V:The Horde 2.00
27 MBa,VM,O:MorituriMaster 2.00
28 MBa,V:The Tiger 2.00
29 MBa,V:Zakir Shastri. 2.00
30 MBa,V:Andre Lamont,The Wind . 2.00
31 MBa(c),V:The Wind,last issue . . 2.00

STRONG GUY REBORN

Spec. TDz,ASm,ATi, (1997) 3.00

STRYFE'S STRIKE FILE

1 LSn,NKu,GCa,BP,C:Siena Blaze,Holocaust (1993) 4.00
1a 2nd Printing 2.00

SUB-MARINER
May, 1968

1 JB,O:Sub-Mariner. 125.00
2 JB,A:Triton 45.00
3 JB,A:Triton 30.00
4 JB,V:Attuma 30.00
5 JB,I&O:Tiger Shark. 30.00
6 JB,DA,V:Tiger Shark. 30.00
7 JB,I:Ikthon 30.00
8 JB,V:Thing 30.00
9 MSe,DA,A:Lady Dorma. 30.00
10 GC,DA,O:Lemuria 30.00
11 GC,V:Capt.Barracuda. 20.00
12 MSe,I:Lyna 20.00
13 MSe,JS,A:Lady Dorma. 20.00
14 MSe,V:Fake Human Torch 25.00
15 MSe,V:Dragon Man 20.00
16 MSe,I:Nekaret,Thakos 12.00
17 MSe,I:Stalker,Kormok 12.00

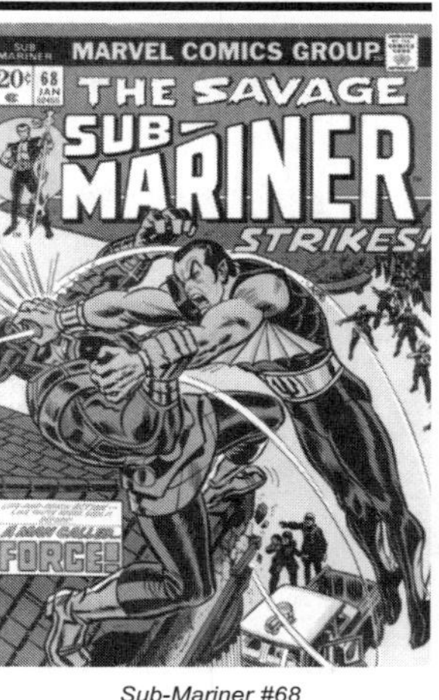

Sub-Mariner #68
© Marvel Entertainment Group

18 MSe,A:Triton 12.00
19 MSe,I:Stingray. 15.00
20 JB,V:Dr.Doom 12.00
21 MSe,D:Lord Seth 12.00
22 MSe,A:Dr.Strange 12.00
23 MSe,I:Orka 10.00
24 JB,JM,V:Tiger Shark 10.00
25 SB,JM,O:Atlantis 10.00
26 SB,A:Red Raven 10.00
27 SB,I:Commander Kraken 11.00
28 SB,V:Brutivae 10.00
29 SB,V:Hercules 9.00
30 SB,A:Captain Marvel 10.00
31 SB,A:Triton 9.00
32 SB,JM,I&O:Llyra 9.00
33 SB,JM,I:Namora 10.00
34 SB,JM,AK,1st Defenders 20.00
35 SB,JM,A:Silver Surfer 20.00
36 BWr,SB,W:Lady Dorma 10.00
37 RA,D:Lady Dorma 10.00
38 RA,JSe,O:Rec,I:Thakorr,Fen . . 10.00
39 RA,JM,V:Llyra 10.00
40 GC,I:Turalla,A:Spidey 12.00
41 GT,V:Rock 10.00
42 GT,JM,V:House Named Death . 10.00
43 GC,V:Tunal 8.00
44 MSe,JM,V:Human Torch 7.00
45 MSe,JM,V:Tiger Shark. 6.00
46 GC,D:Namor's Father 6.00
47 GC,A:Stingray,V:Dr.Doom 6.00
48 GC,V:Dr.Doom. 6.00
49 GC,V:Dr.Doom. 6.00
50 BEv,I:Namorita. 9.00
51 BEv,O:Namorita,C:Namora 7.00
52 GK,V:Sunfire 6.00
53 BEv,V:Sunfire 6.00
54 BEv,AW,V:Sunfire,I:Lorvex. 6.00
55 BEv,V:Torg. 6.00
56 DA,I:Coral 6.00
57 BEv,I:Venus. 6.00
58 BEv,I:Tamara. 6.00
59 BEv,V:Tamara 6.00
60 BEv,V:Tamara 6.00
61 BEv,JM,V:Dr.Hydro 6.00
62 HC,JSt,I:Tales of Atlantis.. . . . . 6.00
63 HC,JSt,V:Dr.Hydro,I:Arkus 6.00
64 HC,JSe,I:Maddox. 6.00
65 DH,DP,V:She-Devil,inc.BEv Eulogy Pin-up. 6.00
66 DH,V:Orka,I:Raman 6.00
67 DH,A:FF,V:Triton,N:Namor I&O:Force 6.00
68 DH,O:Force. 6.00

69 GT,V:Spider-Man 7.00
70 GT,I:Piranha 6.00
71 GT,V:Piranha. 6.00
72 DA,V:Slime/Thing 6.00
Spec.#1 Rep. Tales to Astonish #70-#73 . . . . 8.25
Spec.#2 Rep. Tales to Astonish #74-#76 . . . . 8.25

[Limited Series]

1 RB,BMc,Namor's Birth 2.50
2 RB,BMc,Namor Kills Humans . . . 2.00
3 RB,BMc,V:Surface Dwellers 2.00
4 RB,BMc,V:Human Torch 2.00
5 RB,BMc,A:Invaders 2.00
6 RB,BMc,V:Destiny 2.00
7 RB,BMc,A:Fantastic Four 2.00
8 RB,BMc,A:Hulk,Avengers 2.00
9 RB,BMc,A:X-Men,Magneto 2.00
10 RB,BMc,V:Thing 2.00
11 RB,BMc,A:Namorita,Defenders . 2.00
12 RB,BMc,A:Dr.Doom, AlphaFlight 2.00

(SAGA OF THE) SUB-MARINER

[Mini-Series] Nov., 1988

1 RB,BMc,Namor's Birth 2.50
2 RB,BMc,Namor Kills Humans . . . 2.00
3 RB,BMc,V:Surface Dwellers 2.00
4 RB,BMc,V:Human Torch 2.00
5 RB,BMc,A:Invaders 2.00
6 RB,BMc,V:Destiny 2.00
7 RB,BMc,A:Fantastic Four 2.00
8 RB,BMc,A:Hulk,Avengers 2.00
9 RB,BMc,A:X-Men,Magneto 2.25
10 RB,BMc,V:Thing 2.00
11 RB,BMc,A:Namorita,Defenders . 2.00
12 RB,BMc,A:Dr.Doom,Alp.Flight . . 2.00

SUB-MARINER COMICS

Timely Spring, 1941

1 ASh(c),BEv,PGn,B:Sub-Mariner, The Angel 22,000.00
2 ASh(c),BEv,Nazi Submarine (c) 4,800.00
3 ASh(c),BEv 3,500.00
4 ASh(c),BEv,BW 2,700.00
5 . . . . 2,000.00
6 ASh(c) 1,700.00
7 . . . . 1,700.00
8 ASh(c) 1,700.00
9 ASh(c),BW 1,700.00
10 ASh(c) 1,700.00
11 ASh(c) 1,500.00
12 ASh(c) 1,500.00
13 ASh(c) 1,500.00
14 ASh(c) 1,500.00
15 ASh(c) 1,500.00
16 ASh(c) 1,500.00
17 ASh(c) 1,500.00
18 ASh(c) 1,500.00
19 . . . . 1,500.00
20 ASh(c) 1,500.00
21 SSh(c),BEv 800.00
22 SSh(c),BEv 800.00
23 SSh(c),BEv 800.00
24 MSy(c),BEv,A:Namora, bondage cover 800.00
25 MSy(c),HK,B:The Blonde Phantom, A:Namora, bondage(c) 1,000.00
26 BEv,A:Namora 800.00
27 DRi(c),BEv,A:Namora 800.00
28 DRi(c),BEv,A:Namora 800.00
29 BEv,A:Namora,Human Torch . 800.00
30 DRi(c),BEv,`Slaves Under the Sea' 800.00
31 BEv,`The Man Who Grew', A:Capt. America,E:Blonde Phantom. 800.00
32 BEv,O:Sub-Mariner 1,300.00
33 BEv,O:Sub-Mariner,A:Human Torch,B:Namora 700.00
34 BEv,A:Human Torch,bondage cover 600.00
35 BEv,A:Human Torch. 600.00
36 BEv 600.00
37 JMn(c),BEv 600.00
38 SSh(c),BEv,JMn. 650.00
39 JMn(c),BEv 575.00
40 JMn(c),BEv 575.00
41 JMn(c),BEv 575.00
42 BEv,Oct., 1955. . . . . 700.00

SUBURBAN JERSEY NINJA SHE-DEVILS

1 I:Ninja She-Devils. 2.00

SUNFIRE & BIG HERO 6

July, 1998

1 (of 3) SLo,from Alpha Flight 2.50
2 SLo,V:Everwraith 2.50
3 SLO,conclusion 2.50

SUPERNATURALS

Oct., 1998

1 (of 4) BnP,JBa(c),F:Brother Voodoo, V:Jack O'Lantern, with mask 4.00
1a signed 30.00
2 BnP,JBa(c), with mask 4.00
3 BnP,JBa(c), with mask 4.00
4 BnP,JBa(c), with mask, concl. . . . 4.00

SUPERNATURAL THRILLERS

Dec., 1972

1 JSo(c),JSe,FrG,IT! 20.00
2 VM,DA,The Invisible Man 15.00
3 GK,The Valley of the Worm . . . 15.00
4 Dr. Jekyll and Mr. Hyde 15.00
5 RB,The Living Mummy 35.00
6 GT,JA,The Headless Horseman 10.00
7 VM,B:The Living Mummy,` Back From The Tomb' 10.00
8 VM,`He Stalks Two Worlds' . . . 10.00
9 GK/AM(c),VM,DA,`Pyramid of the Watery Doom' 10.00
10 VM,`A Choice of Dooms' 10.00
11 VM,`When Strikes the ASP' . . . 10.00
12 VM,KJ,`The War That Shook the World'. 10.00
13 VM,DGr,`The Tomb of the Stalking Dead' 10.00
14 VM,AMc,`All These Deadly Pawns'. 10.00
15 TS, E:The Living Mummy,`Night of Armageddon',Oct., 1975 . . . 10.00

Supernatural Thrillers #1
© Marvel Entertainment Group

SUPER SOLDIERS

Marvel UK 1993

1 I:Super Soldier,A:USAgent 2.75
2 A:USAgent 2.00
3 A:USAgent 2.00
4 A:USAgent,Avengers 2.00
5 A:Captain America,AWC. 2.00
6 O:Super Soldiers 2.00
7 in Savage Land 2.00

SUPER-VILLAIN CLASSICS

May, 1983

1 O:Galactus 5.00

SUPER-VILLAIN TEAM-UP

August, 1975

1 GT/BEv(c),B:Dr.Doom/Sub-Mariner,A:Attuma,Tiger Shark 15.00
2 SB,A:Tiger Shark, Attuma 10.00
3 EH(c),JA,V:Attuma 7.00
4 HT,JM,Dr.Doom vs. Namor 7.00
5 RB/JSt(c),HT,DP,A:Fantastic Four,I:Shroud 7.00
6 HT,JA,A:Shroud,Fantastic Four . . 6.00
7 RB/KJ(c),HT,O:Shroud 6.00
8 KG,V:Ringmaster 6.00
9 ST,A:Avengers,Iron Man 6.00
10 BH,DP,A:Capt.America, V:Attuma,Red Skull 6.00
11 DC/JSt(c),BH,DP,B:Dr. Doom, Red Skull,A:Capt. America 6.00
12 DC/AM(c),BH,DP,Dr.Doom vs. Red Skull 6.00
13 KG,DP,Namor vs. Krang 6.00
14 JBy/TA(c),BH,DP,V:Magneto, X-over with Champions #15 . . . 6.00
15 GT,ME,A:Red Skull 6.00
16 CI,A:Dr. Doom 6.00
17 KP(c),Red Skull Vs.Hatemonger June 1976 . . . . 6.00
G-Size#1 F:Namor, Dr.Doom 6.00
G-Size#2 F:Namor, Dr.Doom 6.00

SUSPENSE

Atlas Dec., 1949

1 BP,Ph(c),Sidney Greenstreet/ Peter Lorne (Maltese Falcon) 450.00
2 Ph(c),Dennis O'Keefe/Gale Storm (Abandoned) 225.00
3 B:Horror stories,`The Black Pit' 225.00
4 `Thing In Black' 200.00
5 BEv,GT,RH,BK,DBr, `Hangman's House' 200.00
6 BEv,GT,PAM,RH,`Madness of Scott Mannion' 200.00
7 DBr,GT,DR,`Murder' 200.00
8 GC,DRi,RH,`Don't Open the Door' 200.00
9 GC,DRi,Back From The Dead. 200.00
10 JMn(c),WIP,RH,`Trapped In Time' 200.00
11 MSy,`The Suitcase' 150.00

 All comics prices listed are for *Near Mint* condition.

12 GT,`Dark Road' 150.00
13 JMn(c),`Strange Man',
bondage cover 150.00
14 RH,Death And Doctor Parker . 200.00
15 JMn(c),OW,`The Machine' . . . 150.00
16 OW,`Horror Backstage' 150.00
17 `Night Of Terror' 150.00
18 BK,`The Cozy Coffin' 175.00
19 BEv,RH 150.00
20 . . . . 150.00
21 BEv(c) 150.00
22 BEv(c),BK,OW 150.00
23 BEv 150.00
24 RH,GT 175.00
25 `I Died At Midnight' 200.00
26 BEv(c) 135.00
27 DBr 150.00
28 BEv 150.00
29 JMn,BF,JRo,April, 1953 . . . . . 150.00

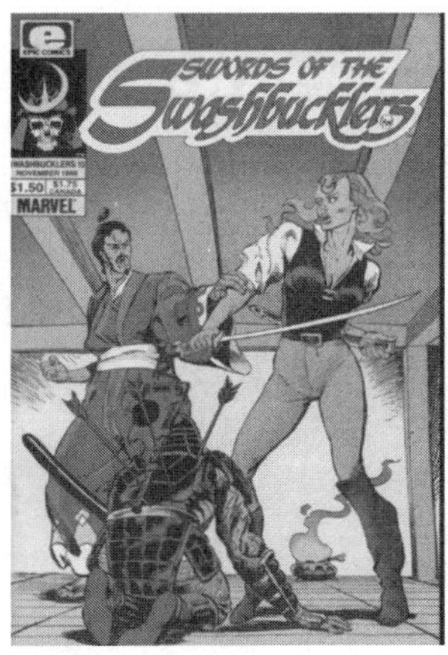

Swords of the Swashbucklers #10
© Marvel Entertainment Group

SWORDS OF THE SWASHBUCKLERS
Epic 1985–87

1 JG,Adult theme. 2.25
2 JG 2.00
3 JG 2.00
4 JG 2.00
5 JG 2.00
6 JG 2.00
7 JG 2.00
8 thru 12, June 1987 . . . . @2.00

TALE OF THE MARINES
See: DEVIL-DOG DUGAN

TALES OF ASGARD
Oct., 1968

1 . . . . 35.00
Vol.2 #1 Feb,1984 . . . . 2.00

TALES OF G.I. JOE
Jan., 1988

1 reprints,#1 . . . . 2.00
2 #2 . . . . 2.00
3 #3 . . . . 2.00
4 #4 . . . . 2.00
5 #5 . . . . 2.00
6 #6 . . . . 2.00

7 rep. #7 - #16. . . . . 2.00

TALES OF JUSTICE
See: JUSTICE COMICS

TALES OF THE AGE OF APOCALYPSE
1996

1-shot SLo,JoB,Age of Apocalypse
stories 5.00
GN, rep. 6.00

TALES OF THE AGE OF APOCALYPSE: SINISTER BLOODLINE
Dec., 1997

GN JFM,SEp, 48pg bookshelf. 6.00

TALES OF THE MARVELS: BLOCKBUSTER

Fully Painted (1995) 6.00

TALES OF THE MARVELS: INNER DEMONS

Fully painted, 48pg. (1996) 6.00

TALES OF THE MARVELS: WONDER YEARS

1 & 2 DAb (1995 . . . . @5.00

TALES OF SUSPENSE
Jan., 1959

1 DH(c),AW,`The Unknown
Emptiness' 1,700.00
2 SK,JH,`Robot in Hiding' 600.00
3 SD,JK,`The Aliens Who
Captured Earth' 500.00
4 JK,AW,`One Of Us
Is A Martian' 550.00
5 JF,`Trapped in the Tunnel
To Nowhere' 350.00
6 JK(c),`Howl in the Swamp' . . . 350.00
7 SD,JK,Molten Man-Thing 400.00
8 BEv,`Monstro' 325.00
9 JK(c),JF,`Diablo' 425.00
10 RH,`I Bought Cyclops Back
To Life' 325.00
11 JK(c),`I Created Sporr' 275.00
12 RC,`Gorkill The Living Demon' 275.00
13 `Elektro' 275.00
14 JK(c),`I Created Colossus' . . . 275.00
15 JK/DAy(c),`Behold...Goom' . . 275.00
16 JK/DAy(c),`The Thing Called
Metallo' 325.00
17 JK/DAy(c),`Goo Gam, Son
of Goom' 275.00
18 JK/DAy(c),`Kraa the Inhuman' 275.00
19 JK,DAy,SD,`The Green Thing' 275.00
20 JK,DAy,SD,`Colossus Lives
Again'. 275.00
21 JK/DAy(c),SD,`This Is Klagg' . 225.00
22 JK/DAy(c),SD,`Beware
Of Bruttu' 225.00
23 JK,DAy,SD,`The Creature
in the Black Bog' 225.00
24 JK,DAy,SD,`Insect Man'. 225.00
25 JK,DAy,SD,`The Death of
Monstrollo' 225.00
26 JK,DAy,SD,`The Thing That
Crawled By Night'. 200.00
27 JK,DAy,SD,`When Oog Lives
Again'. 200.00

Tales of Suspense #58
© Marvel Entertainment Group

28 JK,DAy,SD,`Back From
the Dead' 200.00
29 JK,DAy,SD,DH,`The Martian
Who Stole A City' 175.00
30 JK,DAy,SD,DH,`The Haunted
Roller Coaster' 200.00
31 JK,DAy,SD,DH,`The Monster
in the Iron Mask'. 225.00
32 JK,DAy,SD,DH,`The Man in
the Bee-Hive' 350.00
33 JK,DAy,SD,DH,`Chamber of
Fear' 175.00
34 JK,DAy,SD,DH,`Inside The
Blue Glass Bottle'. 175.00
35 JK,DAy,SD,DH,`The Challenge
of Zarkorr' 225.00
36 SD,`Meet Mr. Meek'. 175.00
37 DH,SD,`Hagg' 175.00
38 JDa,`The Teenager who ruled
the World 175.00
39 JK,O&I:Iron Man 4,500.00
40 JK,C:Iron Man. 1,400.00
41 JK,A:Iron Man,V:Dr. Strange . 700.00
42 DH,SD,I:Red Pharoah 325.00
43 JK,DH,I:Kala,A:Iron Man 325.00
44 DH,SD,V:Mad Pharoah 325.00
45 DH,V:Jack Frost. 325.00
46 DH,CR,I:Crimson Dynamo . . . 250.00
47 SD,V:Melter 200.00
48 SD,N:Iron Man. 250.00
49 SD,A:Angel 200.00
50 DH,I:Manderin 150.00
51 DH,I:Scarecrow 125.00
52 DH,I:Black Widow 150.00
53 DH,O:Watcher 135.00
54 DH,V:Mandarin 85.00
55 DH,V:Mandarin 85.00
56 DH,I:Unicorn 85.00
57 DH,I&O:Hawkeye. 175.00
58 DH,GT,B:Captain America . . . 300.00
59 DH,1st S.A. Solo Captain
America,I:Jarvis 300.00
60 DH,JK,V:Assassins 125.00
61 DH,JK,V:Mandarin 75.00
62 DH,JK,O:Mandarin. 75.00
63 JK,O:Captain America 225.00
64 DH,JK,A:Black Widow,
Hawkeye 85.00
65 DH,JK,I:Red Skull 150.00
66 DH,JK,O:Red Skull 150.00
67 DH,JK,V:Adolph Hitler 50.00
68 DH,JK,V:Red Skull. 50.00
69 DH,JK,I:Titanium Man 50.00

70 DH,JK,GT,V:Titanium Man 45.00
71 DH,JK,WW,GT,V:Titanium Man 55.00
72 DH,JK,GT,V:The Sleeper 45.00
73 JA,JK,GT,A:Black Knight 45.00
74 JA,JK,GT,V:The Sleeper 45.00
75 JA,JK,I:Batroc,Sharon Carter . . 45.00
76 JA,JR,V:Mandarin 50.00
77 JA,JK,JR,V:Ultimo,I:Peggy Carter. 45.00
78 JA,GC,JK,V:Ultimo. 45.00
79 JA,GC,JK,V:Red Skull, I:Cosmic Cube 75.00
80 JA,GC,JK,V:Red Skull 80.00
81 JA,GC,JK,V:Red Skull 50.00
82 GC,JK,V:The Adaptoid. 50.00
83 GC,JK,V:The Adaptoid. 50.00
84 GC,JK,V:Mandarin. 50.00
85 GC,JK,V:Batroc 50.00
86 GC,JK,V:Mandarin. 50.00
87 GC,V:Mole Man 50.00
88 GK,JK,GC,V:Power Man 50.00
89 GK,JK,GC,V:Red Skull. 50.00
90 GK,JK,GC,V:Red Skull. 50.00
91 GK,GC,JK,V:Crusher 50.00
92 GC,JK,A:Nick Fury. 50.00
93 GC,JK,V:Titanium Man. 50.00
94 GC,JK,I:Modok 50.00
95 GC,JK,V:Grey Gargoyle, IR:Captain America 50.00
96 GC,JK,V:Grey Gargoyle. 50.00
97 GC,JK,I:Whiplash, A:Black Panther 50.00
98 GC,JK,I:Whitney Frost A:Black Panther 75.00
99 GC,JK,A:Black Panther 85.00
Marvel Milestone rep. #39 (1993) . . 2.95
Becomes:

CAPTAIN AMERICA

TALES OF THE ZOMBIE

August, 1973

(black & white magazine)

1 Reprint Menace #5,O:Zombie . 25.00
2 GC,GT 15.00
3 . . . . 15.00
4 `Live and Let Die' 15.00
5 BH 15.00
6 . . . . 15.00
7 thru 9 AA . . . . @15.00
10 March, 1975 . . . . 15.00

TALES TO ASTONISH

[1st Series] Jan., 1959

1 JDa,`Ninth Wonder of the World' 1,600.00
2 SD,`Capture A Martian' 650.00
3 SD,JK,`The Giant From Outer Space' 450.00
4 SD,JK,`The Day The Martians Struck' 450.00
5 SD,AW,`The Things on Easter Island' 475.00
6 SD,JK,`Invasion of the Stone Men' 400.00
7 SD,JK,`The Thing on Bald Mountain' 400.00
8 DAy,SD,JK,`Mummex, King of the Mummies'. 400.00
9 DAy,JK(c),SD,`Droom, the Living Lizard' 400.00
10 DAy,JK,SD,`Titano' 400.00
11 DAy,JK,SD,`Monstrom, the Dweller in the Black Swamp'. 250.00
12 JK/DAy(c),SD,`Gorgilla' 250.00
13 JK,SD,`Groot, the Monster From Planet X' 250.00
14 JK,SD,`Krang' 250.00
15 JK/DAy,`The Blip'. 400.00
16 DAy,JK,SD,`Thorr' 300.00
17 JK,SD,`Vandoom'. 250.00
18 DAy,JK,SD,`Gorgilla Strikes Again'. 250.00
19 DAy,JK,SD,`Rommbu' 250.00
20 JK,SD,`X, The Thing That Lived' 250.00
21 JK,SD,`Trull the Inhuman' . . . 250.00
22 JK,SD,`The Crawling Creature' 200.00
23 JK,SD,`Moomba is Here' 200.00
24 JK,SD,`The Abominable Snowman' 200.00
25 JK,SD,`The Creature From Krogarr' 200.00
26 JK,SD,`Four-Armed Things' . . 200.00
27 StL(s),SD,JK,I:Antman 3,400.00
28 JK,SD,I Am the Gorilla Man . . 200.00
29 JK,SD,When the Space Beasts Attack 200.00
30 JK,SD,Thing From the Hidden Swamp. 200.00
31 JK,SD,The Mummy's Secret . 200.00
32 JK,SD,Quicksand. 200.00
33 JK,SD,Dead Storage 200.00
34 JK,SD,Monster at Window . . . 200.00
35 StL(s),JK,SD, B:Ant Man (2nd App.) 1,500.00
36 JK,SD,V:Comrade X 600.00
37 JK,SD,V:The Protector. 375.00
38 JK,SD,Betrayed By the Ants . 375.00
39 JK,DH,V:Scarlet Beetle 375.00
40 JK,SD,DH,The Day Ant-Man Failed. 375.00
41 DH,St,SD,V:Kulla 300.00
42 DH,JSe,SD,Voice of Doom. . . 300.00
43 DH,SD,Master of Time. 300.00
44 JK,SD,I&O:Wasp 300.00
45 DH,SD,V:Egghead 175.00
46 DH,SD,I:Cyclops(robot) 175.00
47 DH,SD,V:Trago 175.00
48 DH,SD,I:Porcupine. 175.00
49 JK,DH,AM,Ant-Man Becomes Giant-Man 200.00
50 JK,SD,I&O:Human Top 125.00
51 JK,V:Human Top 125.00
52 I&O:Black Knight 125.00
53 DH,V:Porcupine 125.00
54 DH,I:El Toro 125.00
55 V:Human Top. 125.00
56 V:The Magician 125.00
57 A:Spider-Man. 150.00
58 V:Colossus(not X-Men one) . . 125.00
59 V:Hulk,Black Knight 175.00
60 SD,B:Hulk,Giant Man. 200.00
61 SD,I:Glenn Talbot, V:Egghead 75.00
62 I:Leader,N:Wasp 75.00
63 SD,O:Leader(1st full story). . . . 75.00
64 SD,V:Leader 75.00
65 BP,DH,SD,N:Giant-Man,. 75.00
66 BP,JK,SD,V:Leader,Chameleon 75.00
67 BP,JK,SD,I:Kanga Khan. 75.00
68 BP,JK,N:Human Top,V:Leader . 75.00
69 BP,JK,V:Human Top,Leader, E:Giant-Man. 75.00
70 GC,JK,B:Sub-Mariner/Hulk,I: Neptune 100.00
71 GC,JK,V:Leader,I:Vashti. 60.00
72 GC,JK,V:Leader. 60.00
73 GC,JK,V:Leader,A:Watcher . . . 60.00
74 GC,JK,V:Leader,A:Watcher . . . 60.00
75 GC,JK,A:Watcher. 60.00
76 GC,GK,JK,Atlantis 60.00
77 JK,V:Executioner 60.00
78 BEv,GC,JK,Prince and the Puppet 60.00
79 BEv,GC,JK,Hulk vs.Hercules . . 60.00
80 BEv,GC,JK,Moleman vs Tyrannus 60.00
81 BEv,GC,JK,I:Boomerang,Secret Empire,Moleman vs Tyrannus. 60.00
82 BEv,GC,JK,V:Iron Man. 75.00
83 BEv,JK,V:Boomerang. 50.00
84 BEv,GC,JK,Like a Beast at Bay 50.00
85 BEv,GC,JB,Missile & the Monster 50.00
86 BEv,JB,V:Warlord Krang 50.00
87 BEv,JB,IR:Hulk 50.00
88 BEv,GK,V:Boomerang 50.00
89 BEv,GK,V:Stranger 50.00
90 JK,GK,BEv,I:Abomination. 50.00
91 GK,BEv,DA,V:Abomination. . . . 50.00
92 MSe,C:Silver Surfer x-over . . . 62.00
93 MSe,Silver Surver x-over 60.00
94 BEv,MSe,V:Dragorr,High Evolutionary.. . . . . 50.00
95 BEv,MSe,V:High Evolutionary . 50.00
96 MSe,Skull Island,High Evol. . . . 50.00
97 MSe,C:Kazar,X-Men 55.00
98 DA,MSe,I:Legion of the Living Lightning,I:Seth 50.00
99 DA,MSe,V:Legion of the Living Lighting 50.00
100 MSe,DA,Hulk v.SubMariner . . 60.00
101 MSe,GC,V:Loki 85.00
Becomes:

INCREDIBLE HULK

Tales to Astonish, 2nd Series, #1
© Marvel Entertainment Group

TALES TO ASTONISH

[2nd Series] Dec., 1979

1 JB,rep.Sub-Mariner#1. . . . . 5.00
2 JB,rep.Sub-Mariner#2. . . . . 3.00
3 JB,rep.Sub-Mariner#3. . . . . 3.00
4 JB,rep.Sub-Mariner#4. . . . . 3.00
5 JB,rep.Sub-Mariner#5. . . . . 3.00
6 JB,rep.Sub-Mariner#6. . . . . 3.00
7 JB,rep.Sub-Mariner#7. . . . . 3.00
8 JB,rep.Sub-Mariner#8. . . . . 3.00
9 JB,rep.Sub-Mariner#9. . . . . 3.00
10 JB,rep.Sub-Mariner#10 . . . . 3.00
11 JB,rep.Sub-Mariner#11 . . . . 3.00
12 JB,rep.Sub-Mariner#12 . . . . 3.00
13 JB,rep.Sub-Mariner#13 . . . . 3.00
14 JB,rep.Sub-Mariner#14 . . . . 3.00

TARZAN

June, 1977

1 JB,Edgar Rice Burroughs Adapt. 5.00
2 JB,O:Tarzan 4.00
3 JB,`The Alter of the Flaming God',I:LA 2.00

All comics prices listed are for *Near Mint* condition.

Tarzan #21
© Marvel Entertainment Group

4 JB,TD,V:Leopards 2.00
5 JB,TD,`Vengeance',A:LA 2.00
6 JB,TD,`Rage of Tantor,A:LA 2.00
7 JB,TD,`Tarzan Rescues The Moon' 2.00
8 JB,`Battle For The Jewel Of Opar' 2.00
9 JB,`Histah, the Serpent' 2.00
10 JB,`The Deadly Peril of Jane Clayton' 2.00
11 JB 2.00
12 JB,`Fangs of Death' 2.00
13 JB,`Lion-God' 2.00
14 JB,`The Fury of Fang and Claw'. 2.00
15 JB,`Sword of the Slaver' 2.00
16 JB,`Death Rides the Jungle Winds' 2.00
17 JB,`The Entrance to the Earths Core' 2.00
18 JB,`Corsairs of the Earths Core'. 2.00
19 `Pursuit' 2.00
20 `Blood Bond' 2.00
21 `Dark and Bloody Sky' 2.00
22 JM,RN,`War In Pellucidar' 2.00
23 `To the Death' 2.00
24 `The Jungle Lord Returns' 2.00
25 RB(c),V:Poachers 2.00
26 RB(c),`Caged' 2.00
27 RB(c),`Chaos in the Caberet' . . . 2.00
28 `A Savage Against A City' 2.00
29 Oct., 1979 . . . . 2.00
Ann.#1 JB 2.50
Ann.#2 `Drums of the Death-Dancers' 2.00
Ann.#3 `Ant-Men and the She-Devils 2.00

TARZAN OF THE APES
July, 1984

1 (movie adapt.) 2.00
2 . . . . 2.00

TEAM AMERICA
June, 1982

1 O:Team America. 2.00
2 V:Marauder 2.00
3 LMc,V:Mr.Mayhem 2.00
4 Lmc,V:Arcade Assassins 2.00
5 A:Marauder 2.00
6 A:R.U. Ready 2.00
7 LMc,V:Emperor of Texas. 2.00
8 DP,V:Hydra. 2.00
9 A:Iron Man 2.00
10 V:Minister Ashe 2.00
11 A:Marauder,V:GhostRider. 3.00
12 DP,Marauder unmasked, May, 1983 . . . . 2.50

TEAM HELIX
1993

1 A:Wolverine 2.00
2 A:Wolverine 2.00

TEAM X/TEAM 7
1996

1-shot LHa,SEp,MRy 4.95

TEAM X 2000
Dec., 1998

1-shot, 48-page. 3.50

TEEN COMICS
See: ALL WINNERS COMICS

TEENAGE ROMANCE
See: MY ROMANCE

TEK WORLD
See: WILLIAM SHATNER'S TEK WORLD

TERMINATOR 2
Sept., 1991

1 KJ,movie adaption 2.00
2 KJ,movie adaption 2.00
3 KJ,movie adaption 2.00
Terminator II (bookshelf format) . . . 5.00
Terminator II (B&W mag. size) 2.25

TERRARISTS
Epic 1993–94

1 thru 4 w/card. . . . . @2.50
5 thru 7 . . . . @2.50

Terrarists #3
© Marvel Entertainment Group

TERROR INC.
1992–93

1 JZ,I:Hellfire. 3.00
2 JZ,I:Bezeel,Hellfire 2.50
3 JZ,A:Hellfire 2.00
4 JZ,A:Hellfire,V:Barbatos 2.00
5 JZ,V:Hellfire,A:Dr Strange. 2.00
6 JZ,MT,A:Punisher 2.00
7 JZ,V:Punisher. 2.00
8 Christmas issue 2.00
9 JZ,V:Wolverine 2.25
10 V:Wolverine 2.25
11 A:Silver Sable,Cage. 2.00
12 For Love Nor Money#4,A:Cage, Silver Sable 2.00
13 Inf.Crusade,A:Gh.Rider 2.00

TESSIE THE TYPIST
Timely Summer, 1944

1 BW,`Doc Rockblock' 400.00
2 BW,`Powerhouse Pepper' . . . 225.00
3 Football cover 75.00
4 BW 125.00
5 BW 125.00
6 BW,HK,`Hey Look' 125.00
7 BW 125.00
8 BW 125.00
9 BW,HK,`Powerhouse Pepper' 150.00
10 BW,A:Rusty 150.00
11 BW,A:Rusty 150.00
12 BW,HK. 150.00
13 BW,A:Millie The Model,Rusty . 110.00
14 BW 100.00
15 HK,A:Millie,Rusty 100.00
16 HK. 75.00
17 HK,A:Millie, Rusty 75.00
18 HK. 75.00
19 Annie Oakley story. 50.00
20 . . . . 50.00
21 A:Lana, Millie 50.00
22 . . . . 50.00
23 . . . . 50.00

Becomes:

TINY TESSIE

24 . . . . 50.00

Becomes:

REAL EXPERIENCES

25 Ph(c),Jan., 1950 . . . . 50.00

TEXAS KID
Atlas Jan., 1951

1 GT,JMn,O:Texas Kid 150.00
2 JMn 75.00
3 JMn,`Man Who Didn't Exist' . . . 60.00
4 JMn 60.00
5 JMn 60.00
6 JMn 60.00
7 JMn 60.00
8 JMn 60.00
9 JMn 60.00
10 JMn,July, 1952. . . . . 60.00

TEX DAWSON, GUNSLINGER
Jan., 1973

1 JSo(c) 15.00

Becomes:

GUNSLINGER

2 . . . . 10.00
3 June, 1973 . . . . 10.00

TEX MORGAN
August, 1948

1 . . . . 200.00
2 `Boot Hill Welcome For A

MARVEL

Bad Man' . . . 135.00
3 . . . 100.00
4 `Trapped in the Outlaws Den',
A:Arizona Annie . . . 90.00
5 `Valley of Missing Cowboys' . . . 90.00
6 `Never Say Murder',
A:Tex Taylor . . . 90.00
7 CCB,Ph(c),`Captain Tootsie',
A:Tex Taylor . . . 135.00
8 Ph(c),`Terror Of Rimrock
Valley', A:Diablo . . . 135.00
9 Ph(c),`Death to Tex Taylor'
Feb., 1950 . . . 135.00

TEX TAYLOR
Sept., 1948

1 `Boot Hill Showdown' . . . 225.00
2 `When Two-Gun Terror Rides
the Range' . . . 125.00
3 `Thundering Hooves and
Blazing Guns' . . . 125.00
4 Ph(c),`Draw or Die Cowpoke' . 125.00
5 Ph(c),`The Juggler of Yellow
Valley',A:Blaze Carson . . . 125.00
6 Ph(c),`Mystery of HowlingGap' 100.00
7 Ph(c),`Trapped in Times' Lost
Land',A:Diablo . . . 150.00
8 Ph(c),`The Mystery of Devil-
Tree Plateau',A:Diablo . . . 150.00
9 Ph(c),`Guns Along the Border',
A:Nimo,March, 1950 . . . 150.00

THANOS QUEST
1990

1 JSn,RLm,V:Elders,
for Soul Gems . . . 7.00
1a 2nd printing . . . 3.00
2 JSn,RLm,O:SoulGems,I:
Infinity Gauntlet (story
cont.in SilverSurfer #44) . . . 6.00
2a 2nd printing . . . 3.00

THANOS QUEST
Jan., 2000

GN JSn,RLm,96-pg. . . . 4.00

THING, THE
July, 1983

1 JBy,O:Thing . . . 3.50
2 JBy,Woman from past. . . . 2.50
3 JBy,A:Inhumans . . . 2.50
4 JBy,A:Lockjaw . . . 2.50
5 JBy,A:Spider-Man,She-Hulk . . . 2.50
6 JBy,V:Puppet Master . . . 2.50
7 JBy,V:Goody Two Shoes. . . . 2.50
8 JBy,V:Egyptian Curse . . . 2.50
9 JBy,F:Alicia Masters . . . 2.50
10 JBy,Secret Wars . . . 2.50
11 JBy,B:Rocky Grimm . . . 2.50
12 JBy,F:Rocky Grimm . . . 2.50
13 JBy,F:Rocky Grimm . . . 2.50
14 F:Rocky Grimm . . . 2.50
15 F:Rocky Grimm . . . 2.50
16 F:Rocky Grimm . . . 2.50
17 F:Rocky Grimm . . . 2.50
18 F:Rocky Grimm . . . 2.50
19 F:Rocky Grimm . . . 2.50
20 F:Rocky Grimm . . . 2.50
21 V:Ultron . . . 2.50
22 V:Ultron . . . 2.50
23 R:Thing to Earth,A:Fant.Four . . . 2.50
24 V:Rhino,A:Miracle Man . . . 2.50
25 V:Shamrock. . . . 2.50
26 A:Vance Astro . . . 2.50
27 I:Sharon Ventura . . . 2.50
28 A:Vance Astro . . . 2.50
29 A:Vance Astro . . . 2.50
30 Secret Wars II,A:Vance Astro . . . 2.50
31 A:Vance Astro . . . 2.50
32 A:Vance Astro . . . 2.50
33 A:Vance Astro,I:NewGrapplers . . 2.50
34 V:Titania,Sphinx. . . . 2.50
35 I:New Ms.Marvel,PowerBroker . . 2.50
36 Last Issue,A:She-Hulk . . . 2.50

[Mini-Series]

1 rep.Marvel Two-in-One #50. . . . 2.50
2 rep Marvel Two-in-One,V:GR . . . 2.50
3 rep Marvel Two-in-One #51 . . . 2.00
4 rep Marvel Two-in-One #43 . . . 2.00

THING/SHE-HULK
March, 1998

1-shot TDz,V:Dragon Man, 48pg. . . 3.00

THOR, THE MIGHTY
Prev: Journey Into Mystery
March, 1966

126 JK,V:Hercules . . . 135.00
127 JK,I:Pluto,Volla . . . 55.00
128 JK,V:Pluto,A:Hercules . . . 55.00
129 JK,V:Pluto,I:Ares . . . 55.00
130 JK,V:Pluto,A:Hercules . . . 55.00
131 JK,I:Colonizers. . . . 55.00
132 JK,A:Colonizers,I:Ego . . . 55.00
133 JK,A:Colonizers,A:Ego. . . . 55.00
134 JK,I:High Evolutionary,
Man-Beast . . . 60.00
135 JK,O:High Evolutionary . . . 50.00
136 JK,F:Odin . . . 45.00
137 JK,I:Ulik. . . . 45.00
138 JK,V:Ulik,A:Sif . . . 45.00
139 JK,V:Ulik . . . 45.00
140 JK,V:Growing Man. . . . 45.00
141 JK,V:Replicus . . . 35.00
142 JK,V:Super Skrull. . . . 35.00
143 JK,BEv,V:Talisman. . . . 35.00
144 JK,V:Talisman . . . 35.00
145 JK,V:Ringmaster . . . 35.00
146 JK,O:Inhumans Part 1 . . . 45.00
147 JK,O:Inhumans Part 2 . . . 40.00
148 JK,I:Wrecker,O:Black Bolt . . . 40.00
149 JK,O:Black Bolt,Medusa. . . . 40.00
150 JK,A:Triton. . . . 35.00
151 JK,V:Destroyer. . . . 35.00
152 JK,V:Destroyer. . . . 35.00
153 JK,F:Dr.Blake. . . . 35.00
154 JK,I:Mangog . . . 35.00
155 JK,V:Mangog. . . . 35.00

Thor #233
© Marvel Entertainment Group

156 JK,V:Mangog. . . . 35.00
157 JK,D:Mangog. . . . 35.00
158 JK,O:Don Blake Part 1. . . . 75.00
159 JK,O:Don Blake Part 2. . . . 35.00
160 JK,I:Travrians. . . . 32.00
161 JK,Shall a God Prevail. . . . 32.00
162 JK,O:Galactus . . . 45.00
163 JK,I:Mutates,A:Pluto. . . . 25.00
164 JK,A:Pluto,V:Greek Gods. . . . 25.00
165 JK,V:Him/Warlock . . . 60.00
166 JK,V:Him/Warlock . . . 50.00
167 JK,F:Sif . . . 23.00
168 JK,O:Galactus . . . 42.00
169 JK,O:Galactus . . . 42.00
170 JK,BEv,V:Thermal Man . . . 25.00
171 JK,BEv,V:Wrecker . . . 25.00
172 JK,BEv,V:Ulik. . . . 25.00
173 JK,BEv,V:Ulik,Ringmaster . . . 25.00
174 JK,BEv,V:Crypto-Man. . . . 25.00
175 JK,Fall of Asgard,V:Surtur . . . 25.00
176 JK,V:Surtur . . . 25.00
177 JK,I:Igon,V:Surtur. . . . 25.00
178 JK,C:Silver Surfer . . . 26.00
179 JK,MSe,C:Galactus . . . 25.00
180 NA,JSi,V:Loki. . . . 20.00
181 NA,JSi,V:Loki. . . . 20.00
182 JB,V:Dr.Doom . . . 10.00
183 JB,V:Dr.Doom . . . 10.00
184 JB,I:The Guardian . . . 10.00
185 JB,JSt,V:Silent One . . . 10.00
186 JB,JSt,V:Hela. . . . 10.00
187 JB,JSt,V:Odin . . . 10.00
188 JB,JM,F:Odin. . . . 10.00
189 JB,JSt,V:Hela. . . . 10.00
190 JB,I:Durok . . . 10.00
191 JB,JSt,V:Loki . . . 10.00
192 JB . . . 10.00
193 JB,SB,V:Silver Surfer. . . . 40.00
194 JB,SB,V:Loki . . . 10.00
195 JB,JR,V:Mangog . . . 10.00
196 JB,NR,V:Kartag . . . 10.00
197 JB,V:Mangog. . . . 10.00
198 JB,V:Pluto . . . 10.00
199 JB,V:Pluto,Hela . . . 10.00
200 JB,Ragnarok . . . 12.00
201 JB,JM,Odin resurrected. . . . 8.00
202 JB,V:Ego-Prime . . . 8.00
203 JB,V:Ego-Prime . . . 8.00
204 JB,JM,Demon from t/Depths . . 8.00
205 JB,V:Mephisto . . . 8.00
206 JB,V:Absorbing Man . . . 7.00
207 JB,V:Absorbing Man . . . 7.00
208 JB,V:Mercurio . . . 7.00
209 JB,I:Druid . . . 7.00
210 JB,DP,I:Ulla,V:Ulik . . . 7.00
211 JB,DP,V:Ulik. . . . 7.00
212 JB,JSt,V:Sssthgar . . . 7.00
213 JB,DP,I:Gregor. . . . 7.00
214 SB,JM,V:Dark Nebula . . . 7.00
215 JB,JM,J:Xorr . . . 7.00
216 JB,JM,V:4D-Man . . . 7.00
217 JB,SB,I:Krista,V:Odin . . . 7.00
218 JB,JM,A:Colonizers . . . 7.00
219 JB,I:Protector. . . . 7.00
220 JB,V:Avalon. . . . 7.00
221 JB,V:Olympus . . . 7.00
222 JB,JSe,A:Hercules,V:Pluto. . . . 7.00
223 JB,A:Hercules,V:Pluto . . . 7.00
224 JB,V:Destroyer. . . . 7.00
225 JB,JSi,I:Fire Lord . . . 10.00
226 JB,A:Watcher,Galactus . . . 7.00
227 JB,JSi,V:Ego . . . 7.00
228 JB,JSi,A:Galactus,D:Ego . . . 7.00
229 JB,JSi,A:Hercules,I:Dweller . . . 7.00
230 JB,A:Hercules . . . 7.00
231 JB,DG,V:Armak . . . 7.00
232 JB,JSi,A:Firelord . . . 7.00
233 JB,Asgard Invades Earth . . . 7.00
234 JB,V:Loki . . . 7.00
235 JB,JSi,I:Possessor
(Kamo Tharnn). . . . 7.00

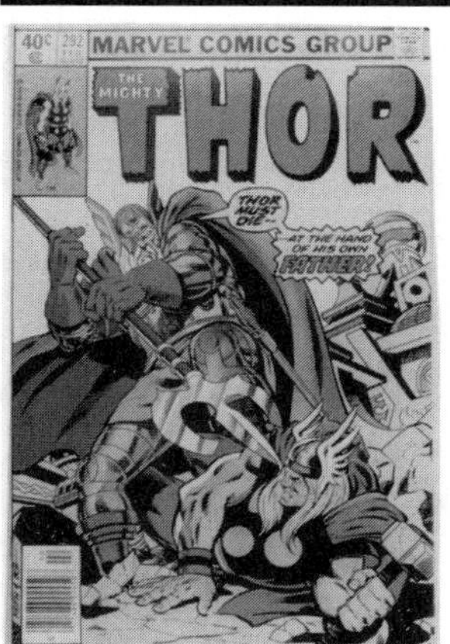

Thor #292
© Marvel Entertainment Group

236 JB,JSi,V:Absorbing Man. 7.00
237 JB,JSi,V:Ulik 7.00
238 JB,JSi,V:Ulik 7.00
239 JB,JSi,V:Ulik 7.00
240 SB,KJ,V:Seth. 7.00
241 JB,JGi,I:Geb 7.00
242 JB,JSi,V:Servitor 7.00
243 JB,JSt,V:Servitor 7.00
244 JB,JSt,V:Servitor 7.00
245 JB,JSt,V:Servitor 7.00
246 JB,JSt,A:Firelord 7.00
247 JB,JSt,A:Firelord 7.00
248 JB,V:Storm Giant. 7.00
249 JB,V:Odin 7.00
250 JB,D:Igron,V:Mangog. 7.00
251 JB,A:Sif. 5.00
252 JB,V:Ulik 5.00
253 JB,I:Trogg 5.00
254 JK,O:Dr.Blake rep 5.00
255 Stone Men of Saturn Rep. 5.00
256 JB,I:Sporr 5.00
257 JK,JB,I:Fee-Lon. 5.00
258 JK,JB,V:Grey Gargoyle 5.00
259 JB,A:Spider-Man 4.00
260 WS,I:Doomsday Star 4.00
261 WS,I:Soul Survivors. 4.00
262 WS,Odin Found,I:Odin Force . . 4.00
263 WS,V:Loki 4.00
264 WS,V:Loki 4.00
265 WS,V:Destroyer. 4.00
266 WS,Odin Quest 4.00
267 WS,F:Odin. 4.00
268 WS,V:Damocles. 4.00
269 WS,V:Stilt-Man 4.00
270 WS,V:Blastaar 4.00
271 Avengers,Iron Man x-over 4.00
272 JB,Day the Thunder Failed . . . 4.00
273 JB,V:Midgard Serpent 4.00
274 JB,D:Balder,I:Hermod,Hoder . . 4.00
275 JB,V:Loki,I:Sigyn 4.00
276 JB,Trial of Loki. 4.00
277 JB,V:Fake Thor 4.00
278 JB,V:Fake Thor 4.00
279 A:Pluto,V:Ulik. 4.00
280 V:Hyperion. 4.00
281 O:Space Phantom 3.50
282 V:Immortus,I:Tempus 3.50
283 JB,V:Celestials. 3.50
284 JB,V:Gammenon 3.50
285 JB,R:Karkas 3.50
286 KP,KRo,D:Kro,I:Dragona 3.50
287 KP,2nd App & O:Forgotten
One(Hero) 3.50
288 KP,V:Forgotten One 3.50
289 KP,V:Destroyer 3.50
290 I:Red Bull(Toro Rojo) 3.50
291 KP,A:Eternals,Zeus 3.50
292 KP,V:Odin 3.50
293 KP,Door to Minds Eye 3.50
294 KP,O:Odin & Asgard,I:Frey. . . . 3.50
295 KP,I:Fafnir,V:Storm Giants 3.50
296 KP,D:Siegmund 3.50
297 KP,V:Sword of Siegfried 3.50
298 KP,V:Dragon(Fafnir). 3.50
299 KP,A:Valkyrie,I:Hagen 3.50
300 KP,giant,O:Odin & Destroyer,
Rindgold Ring Quest ends,D:Uni-
Mind,I:Mother Earth 7.00
301 KP,O:Mother Earth,V:Apollo . . . 3.00
302 KP,V:Locus 3.00
303 Whatever Gods There Be 3.00
304 KP,V:Wrecker. 3.00
305 KP,R:Gabriel(Air Walker) 3.00
306 KP,O&V:Firelord,O:AirWalker . . 3.00
307 KP,I:Dream Demon 3.00
308 KP,V:Snow Giants 3.00
309 V:Bomnardiers. 3.00
310 KP,V:Mephisto 3.00
311 KP,GD,A:Valkyrie 3.00
312 KP,V:Tyr. 3.00
313 KP,Thor Trial 3.00
314 KP,A:Drax,Moondragon 3.00
315 KP,O:Bi-Beast 3.00
316 KP,A:Iron Man,Man Thing,
V:Man-Beast 3.00
317 KP,V:Man-Beast. 3.00
318 GK,V:Fafnir 3.00
319 KP,I&D:Zaniac 3.00
320 KP,V:Rimthursar. 3.00
321 I:Menagerie 3.00
322 V:Heimdall 3.00
323 V:Death 3.00
324 V:Graviton 3.00
325 JM,O:Darkoth,V:Mephisto 3.00
326 I:New Scarlet Scarab. 3.00
327 V:Loki & Tyr. 3.00
328 I:Megatak 3.00
329 HT,V:Hrungnir 3.00
330 BH,I:Crusader 3.00
331 Threshold of Death 3.00
332 V:Dracula. 3.00
333 BH,V:Dracula. 3.00
334 Quest For Rune Staff. 3.00
335 V:Possessor 3.00
336 A:Captain Ultra 3.00
337 WS,I:Beta Ray Bill,A:Surtur . . . 7.50
338 WS,O:Beta Ray Bill,I:Lorelei . . 5.00
339 WS,V:Beta Ray Bill 3.50
340 WS,A:Beta Ray Bill 3.00
341 WS,V:Fafnir 3.00
342 WS,V:Fafnir,I:Eilif. 3.00
343 WS,V:Fafnir 3.00
344 WS,Balder Vs.Loki,I:Malekith . . 3.00
345 WS,V:Malekith 3.00
346 WS,V:Malekith 3.00
347 WS,V:Malekith,I:Algrim
(Kurse). 3.00
348 WS,V:Malekith 3.00
349 WS,R:Beta Ray Bill,O:Odin,
I&O:Vili & Ve(Odin's brothers). . 3.00
350 WS,V:Surtur. 3.00
351 WS,V:Surtur. 3.00
352 WS,V:Surtur. 3.00
353 WS,V:Surtur,D:Odin 3.00
354 WS,V:Hela. 3.00
355 WS,SB,A:Thor's Great
Grandfather 3.00
356 BL,BG,V:Hercules 3.00
357 WS,A:Beta Ray Bill 3.00
358 WS,A:Beta Ray Bill 3.00
359 WS,V:Loki 3.00
360 WS,V:Hela. 3.00
361 WS,V:Hela. 3.00
362 WS,V:Hela. 3.00
363 WS,Secret Wars II,V:Kurse . . . 3.00

Thor #501
© Marvel Entertainment Group

364 WS,I:Thunder Frog 3.00
365 WS,A:Thunder Frog. 3.00
366 WS,A:Thunder Frog. 3.00
367 WS,D:Malekith,A:Kurse 3.00
368 WS,F:Balder t/Brave,Kurse . . . 3.00
369 WS,F:Balder the Brave 3.00
370 JB,V:Loki 3.00
371 SB,I:Justice Peace,V:Zaniac . . 3.00
372 SB,V:Justice Peace 3.00
373 SB,A:X-Factor,(Mut.Mass) 5.00
374 WS,SB,A:X-Factor,(Mut.Mass)
A:Sabretooth 7.00
375 WS,SB,N:Thor(Exoskeleton) . . 3.00
376 WS,SB,V:Absorbing Man 3.00
377 WS,SB,N:Thor,A:Ice Man. 3.00
378 WS,SB,V:Frost Giants 3.00
379 WS,V:Midgard Serpent 3.00
380 WS,V:Midgard Serpent 3.00
381 WE,SB,A:Avengers 3.00
382 WS,SB,V:Frost Giants,Loki . . . 3.00
383 BBr,Secret Wars story 3.00
384 RF,BBr,I:Future Thor(Dargo) . . 5.00
385 EL,V:Hulk 2.50
386 RF,BBr,I:Leir 2.50
387 RF,BBr,V:Celestials 2.50
388 RF,BBr,V:Celestials 2.50
389 RF,BBr,V:Celestials 2.50
390 RF,BBr,A:Avengers,V:Seth 2.50
391 RF,BBr,I:Mongoose,Eric
Masterson,A:Spider-Man 5.00
392 RF,I:Quicksand 4.00
393 RF,BBr,V:Quicksand,A:DD 4.00
394 RF,BBr,V:Earth Force. 4.00
395 RF,V:Earth Force 4.00
396 RF,A:Black Knight 4.00
397 RF,A:Loki. 4.00
398 RF,DH,R:Odin,V:Seth. 4.00
399 RF,RT,R:Surtur,V:Seth 4.00
400 RF,JSt,CV,V:Surtur,Seth. 5.00
401 V:Loki 2.50
402 RF,JSt,V:Quicksand 2.50
403 RF,JSt,V:Executioner 2.50
404 RF,JSt,TD,V:Annihilus 2.50
405 RF,JSt,TD,V:Annihilus 2.50
406 RF,JSt,TD,V:Wundagore 2.50
407 RF,JSt,R:Hercules,High Evol. . . 2.50
408 RF,JSt,I:Eric Masterson/Thor
V:Mongoose. 3.50
409 RF,JSt,V:Dr.Doom 2.50
410 RF,JSt,V:Dr.Doom,She-Hulk. . . 2.50
411 RF,JSt,C:New Warriors
V:Juggernaut,A of V 3.00
412 RF,JSt,I:New Warriors

V:Juggernaut,A of V 4.00
413 RF,JSt,A:Dr.Strange. 2.50
414 RF,JSt,V:Ulik 2.50
415 HT,O:Thor 2.50
416 RF,JSt,A:Hercules 2.50
417 RF,JSt,A:High Evolutionary . . . 2.50
418 RF,JSt,V:Wrecking Crew 2.50
419 RF,JSt,B:Black Galaxy
Saga,I:Stellaris. 2.50
420 RF,JSt,A:Avengers,V:Stellaris. . 2.50
421 RF,JSt,V:Stellaris 2.50
422 RF,JSt,V:High Evol.,Nobilus . . . 2.50
423 RF,JSt,A:High Evol.,Celestials
Count Tagar 2.00
424 RF,JSt,V:Celestials,E:Black
Galaxy Saga 2.00
425 RF,AM,V:Surtur,Ymir 2.00
426 RF,JSt,HT,O:Earth Force 2.00
427 RF,JSt,A:Excalibur 2.00
428 RF,JSt,A:Excalibur 2.00
429 RF,JSt,A:Ghost Rider. 2.25
430 RF,AM,A:Mephisto,Gh.Rider . . 2.25
431 HT,AM,V:Ulik,Loki 2.00
432 RF,D:Loki,Thor Banished,Eric
Masterson becomes 2nd Thor . 4.00
433 RF,V:Ulik 5.00
434 RF,AM,V:Warriors Three 2.50
435 RF,AM,V:Annihilus 2.50
436 RF,AM,V:Titania,Absorbing
Man,A:Hercules 2.00
437 RF,AM,V:Quasar 2.00
438 RF,JSt,A:Future Thor(Dargo) . . 2.00
439 RF,JSt,A:Drago 2.00
440 RF,AM,I:Thor Corps 2.50
441 RF,AM,Celestials vs.Ego 2.50
442 RF,AM,Don Blake,Beta Ray
Bill,Mephisto. 2.00
443 RF,AM,A:Dr.Strange,Silver
Surfer,V:Mephisto 2.00
444 RF,AM,Special X-mas tale 2.00
445 AM,Galactic Storm,pt.7
V:Gladiator 2.00
446 AM,Galactic Storm,pt.14
A:Avengers 2.00
447 RF,AM,V:Absorbing Man
A:Spider-Man 2.00
448 RF,AM,V:Titania,A:SpM 2.00
449 RF,AM,V:Ulik 2.00
450 RF,AM,V:Heimdall,A:Code Blue
Double-Sized,Gatefold(c),rep.
Journey Into Mystery#87 . . . . . 3.00
451 RF,AM,I:Bloodaxe 2.00
452 RF,AM,V:Bloodaxe. 2.00
453 RF,AM,V:Mephisto 2.00
454 RF,AM,V:Mephisto,Loki,
Karnilla. 2.00
455 AM(i),V:Loki,Karnilla,R:Odin,
A:Dr.Strange 2.00
456 RF,AM,V:Bloodaxe. 2.00
457 RF,AM,R:1st Thor 2.00
458 RF,AM,Thor vs Eric 2.00
459 RF,AM,C&I:Thunderstrike(Eric
Masterson). 2.25
460 I:New Valkyrie 2.00
461 V:Beta Ray Bill. 2.00
462 A:New Valkyrie 2.00
463 Infinity Crusade 2.00
464 Inf.Crusade,V:Loki 2.00
465 Infinity Crusade 2.00
466 Infinity Crusade 2.00
467 Infinity Crusade 2.00
468 RMz(s),Blood & Thunder#1 . . . 3.00
469 RMz(s),Blood & Thunder#5 . . . 2.00
470 MCW,Blood & Thunder#9 . . . . 2.00
471 MCW,E:Blood & Thunder. 2.00
472 B:RTs(s),MCW,I:Godling,C:High
Evolutionary 2.00
473 MCW,V:Godling,High Evolutionary
I&C:Karnivore(Man-Beast) 2.00
474 MCW,C:High Evolutionary 2.00
475 MCW,Foil(c),A:Donald Blake,
N:Thor 3.00
475a Newsstand Ed. 2.00
476 V:Destroyer 2.00
477 V:Destroyer,A:Thunderstrike. . . 2.00
478 V:Norvell Thor 2.00
479 V:Norvell Thor 2.00
480 V:High Evolutionary 2.00
481 V:Grotesk 2.00
482 Don Blake construct. 2.00
483 RTs,MCW,V:Loki 2.00
484 Badoy and Soul 2.00
485 V:The Thing. 2.00
486 High Evolutionary,Godpack . . . 2.00
487 V:Kurse 2.00
488 RTs,MCW,Kurse Saga concl. . . 2.00
489 RTs,V:Kurse,A:Hulk 2.00
490 TDF,after Thunderstrike 2.00
491 N:Thor. 7.50
492 Worldengine's Secrets 5.00
493 Worldengine trigers Ragnarok . 3.00
494 Worldengine saga conclusion. . 3.00
495 BML,Avengers:Timeslide 2.50
496 MD2,BML 2.50
497 MD2,BML 2.50
498 BML,V:Absorbing Man 2.00
499 MD2,BML,. 2.00
500 MD2,BML,double size,A:Dr.
Strange 3.00
501 MD2,BML,I:Red Norvell 2.00
502 MD2,BML,Onslaught tie-in, A:Red
Norvell, Jane Foster, Hela 2.00

Becomes:

JOURNEY INTO MYSTERY

Third Series Nov. 1996

503 TDF,MD2, The Lost Gods, New
Norse gods?. 2.00
504 TDF,Golden Realm in ruins,
V:Ulik the Troll 2.00
505 TDF,MD2, V:Wrecker,
A:Spider-Man 2.00
506 TDF,MD2, R:Heimdall 2.00
507 TDF,Odin kidnapped 2.00
508 TDF, ... 2.00
509 TDF,Battle for the Future
of Asgard 2.00
510 TDF,Return of Loki,A:Seth 2.00
511 TDF,EBe,Lost Gods reunited
with Odin 2.00
512 EBe, Odin vs. Seth 2.00
513 TDF,SB,AM, Odin vs. Seth, concl.
514 BRa,VRu,F:Shang Chi, Master
of Kung Fu 2.00
515 BRa,VRu,F:Shang Chi, Master

Journey Into Mystery #510
© Marvel Entertainment Group

of Kung Fu, pt.2 . . . . 2.00
516 BRa,VRu,F:Shang Chi, Master
of Kung Fu, pt.3 . . . . 2.00
517 SLo,RGr,F:Black Widow. 2.00
518 SLo,RGr,F:Black Widow. 2.00
519 SLo,RGr,F:Black Widow, concl. 2.00
520 MWn,F:Hannibal King pt.1 . . . . 2.00
521 MWn,F:Hannibal King, pt.2 . . . 2.00
Ann.#2 JK,V:Destroyer 50.00
Ann.#3 JK,rep,Grey Gargoyle. . . . 13.00
Ann.#4 JK,rep,TheLivingPlanet. . . 11.00
Ann.#5 JK,JB,Hercules,O:Odin . . . 10.00
Ann.#6 JK,JB,A:Guardians of the
Galaxy,V:Korvac. 10.00
Ann.#7 WS,Eternals 9.00
Ann.#8 JB,V:Zeus. 8.00
Ann.#9 LMc,Dormammu 7.00
Ann.#10 O:Chthon,Gaea,A:Pluto . . 6.00
Ann.#11 O:Odin 6.00
Ann.#12 BH,I:Vidar(Odin's son) . . . 6.00
Ann.#13 JB,V:Mephisto 6.00
Ann.#14 AM,DH,Atlantis Attacks. . . 5.00
Ann.#15 HT,Terminus Factor #3 . . . 4.00
Ann.#16 Korvac Quest,pt.2,
Guardians of Galaxy. 2.50
Ann.#17 Citizen Kang#2 . . . . 2.50
Ann.#18 TGr,I:The Flame,w/card . . 3.25
Ann.#19 V:Flame 3.25
G-Size.#1 Battles,A:Hercules 14.00
TPB Alone Against the Celestials,
rep.Thor#387-389. . . . . 5.95
TPB Ballad of Beta Ray Bill,rep.
Thor#337-340. . . . . 8.95
Minus 1 Spec., TDF,EBe,flashback . 2.00
1-shot, Rough Cut, DJu,JR,original
pencils, b&w 48pg 3.00

THOR

May, 1998

1 JR2,KJ,DJu,The hero returns,
48pg 5.00
2A JR2,KJ,DJu,V:Destroyer,A:Hela,
Marnot 3.00
2B JR2,KJ variant cover 3.00
3 DJu,JR2,KJ,A:Marnot,V:Sedna . . 2.00
4 DJu,JR2,KJ,A:Namor,Sedna. . . . 2.00
5 DJu,JR2,KJ,V:Charles Diamond . 2.00
6 DJu,JR2,KJ,V:Hercules. 2.00
7 DJu,JR2,KJ,V:Zeus 2.00
8 DJu,JR2,KJ,PeterParker x-over . 2.00
9 DJu,JB,JOy,War on
Asgard,prelude. 2.00
10 DJu,JR2,KJ,War on Asgard,pt.1. 2.00
11 DJu,JR2,KJ,War on Asgard,pt.2. 2.00
12 DJu,JR2,KJ,War on
Asgard,concl. 48-page 3.00
12a signed 20.00
13 DJu,JR2,KJ,A:Marnot 2.00
14 DJu,Hammer secret. 2.00
15 DJu,KJ,JR2(c),A:Warriors 3 . . . . 2.00
16 DJu,KJ,JR2,A:Warriors 3 . . . . . . 2.00
17 DJu,KJ,JR2,Eighth
Day,pt.1, x-over 2.00
18 DJu,KJ,JR2,V:Enrakt 2.00
19 DJu, ... 2.00
20 DJu,V:Loki. 2.00
21 DJu,JR2,KJ,R:Thanos 2.00
22 DJu,JR2,KJ,V:Thanos 2.00
23 DJu,JR2,DG,V:Thanos. 2.00
24 DJu,JR2,DG,V:Thanos. 2.25
25A DJu,JR2,DG,48-pg.,foil(c) 4.00
25B variant (c) 3.00
26 DJu,EL,KJ,V:AbsorbingMan 2.25
27 DJu,EL,KJ,Dr.Jane Foster 2.25
28 DJu,EL,KJ,WarriorsThree 2.25
29 DJu,NKu,SHa,Jagrfelm 2.25
30 DJu,NKu,SHa,MaxSecurity 2.25
Ann.1999 DJu,KJ, 48-page. 3.50
Ann.1999 signed. 20.00
Ann.2000, 48-pg. 3.50

Spec.#1 Thor (2000). 2.25
Spec. rep.#1 & #2. . . . . 6.00
HC Marvel Masterworks, 272-pg. . 34.95
TPB The Dark Gods, 128-pg. 15.95

THOR CORPS
[Limited Series]

1 TDF(s),PO,V:Demonstaff 2.00
2 TDF(s),PO,A:Invaders 2.00
3 TDF(s),PO,A:Spider-Man 2099 . . 2.00
4 TDF(s),PO,Last Issue 2.00

THREE MUSKETEERS

1 thru 2 movie adapt.. . . . . 2.00

THUNDERBOLTS
Feb., 1997

1 KBk,MBa,VRu,Post-onslaught new team:Citizen V, Meteroite, Techno, Songbird, Atlas & Mach-1, ... 3.00
1 rep. 2.50
2 KBk,MBa,VRu,V:Mad Thinker . . . 2.00
2a variant cover by MBa&VRu 2.00
2 rep. 2.00
3 KBk,MBa,VRu,Headquarters at Freedom's Plaza 2.00
4 KBk,MBa,VRu,I:Jolt 2.00
5 KBk,MBa,VRu,V:Elements of Doom. 2.00
6 KBk,MBa,VRu,V:Elements of Doom. 2.00
7 KBk,MBa,VRu,F:Citizen V. 2.00
8 KBk,MBa,VRu,Songbird fights alone 2.00
9 KBk,MBa,VRu,Black Widow 2.00
10 KBk,MBa,VRu,Secret Identities discovered 2.00
11 KBk,MBa,VRu,V:Citizen V 2.00
12 KBk,MBa,VRu,A:Fantastic Four, Avengers 2.00
13 KBk,MBa,SHa,on trial 3.00
14 KBk,MBa,VRu,V:Citizen V, Meteorite 2.00
15 KBk,MBa,VRu,V:S.H.I.E.L.D. . . . 2.00
16 KBk,MBa,SHa,V:Lightningrods. . 2.00
17 KBk,MBa,SHa,V:Graviton 2.00
18 KBk,MBa,SHa,villains once again? 2.00
19 KBk,MBa,SHa,. 2.00
20 KBk,MBa,SHa,V:Masters of Evil. 2.00
21 KBk,MBa,SHa,F:Songbird 2.00

Thunderbolts #28
© Marvel Entertainment Group

22 KBk,MBa,SHa,A:Hercules 2.00
23 KBk,MBa,SHa,V:U.S.Agent 2.00
24 KBk,MBa,SHa,R:Citizen V 2.00
25 KBk,MBa,SHa,48-page 3.00
25a signed 20.00
26 KBk,MBa,SHa,JoC,A:Mach-1. . . 2.00
27 KBk,MBa,SHa,A:Archangel 2.00
28 KBk,MBa,SHa,V:Graviton 2.00
29 KBk,MBa,SHa,V:Graviton 2.00
30 KBk,MBa,SHa,V:Graviton 2.00
31 KBk,MBa,SHa,R:Citizen V 2.00
32 KBk,MBa,SHa,V:Citizen V 2.00
33 KBk,MBa,SHa,F:Jolt 2.00
34 MBa,SHa. 2.00
35 FaN,MBa,SHa 2.00
36 FaN,MBa,SHa,V:Beetle 2.00
37 FaN,MBa,SHa,A:Hawkeye 2.00
38 FaN,MBa,SHa,V:Citizen V 2.00
39 FaN,MBa,SHa,100-pg.. . . . . 3.00
40 FaN,MBa,SHa,V:Citizen V 2.25
41 FaN,MBa,Sandman 2.25
42 FaN,MBa,Avengers x-over 2.25
43 FaN,MBa,Avengers x-over. 2.25
44 FaN,MBa,Avengers x-over. 2.25
45 FAn,MBa,Maximum Security . . . 2.25
Ann. '97 KBk,MBa,TGu,GP, O:Thunderbolts, 48pg. 2.95
Ann.2000 FaN,NBy, 48-pg. 3.50
Spec.#0 Wizard Nov. 1998 . . . . 5.00
Spec.First Strikes, rep.#1 & #2 . . . . 5.00
TPB 176pg, secret history. 12.00

THUNDERBOLTS: DISTANT RUMBLINGS
1997

1 KBk,SEp,Flashback,F:Citizen V . 2.50

THUNDERCATS
Star Dec., 1985

1 JM,TV tie-in 6.00
1a 2nd printing 3.00
2 JM,A:Berbils,V:Mumm-Ra 3.00
3 . . . . 3.00
4 JM,I:Lynxana 3.00
5 JM 3.00
6 JM 3.00
7 Return to Thundera 3.00
8 V:Monkiang 3.00
9 V:Pekmen. 3.00
10 . . . . 3.00
11 I:The Molemen. 3.00
12 `The Protectors'. 3.00
13 EC/AW,V:Safari Joe. 3.00
14 V:Snaf 3.00
15 JM,A:Spidera. 3.00
16 `Time Capsula' 3.00
17 . . . . 3.00
18 EC/AW,`Doom Gaze' 3.00
19 . . . . 3.00
20 EC/AW 3.00
21 JM,A:Hercules Baby 3.00
22 I:Devious Duploids. 3.00
23 V:Devious Duploids 3.00
24 June, 1988 . . . . 3.00

THUNDERSTRIKE
1993–95

1 B:TDF(s),RF,Holografx(c), V:Bloodaxe,I:Car Jack 3.25
2 RF,V:Juggernaut. 2.00
3 RF,I:Sangre 2.00
4 RF,A:Spider-Man,I:Pandora 2.00
5 RF,A:Spider-Man,V:Pandora 2.00
6 RF,I:Blackwulf,Bristle,Schizo,Lord Lucian,A:SpM,Code:Blue,Stellaris, V:SHIELD,Pandora,C:Tantalus . 2.00
7 KP,V:Tantalus,D:Jackson 2.00
8 RF,I&V:Officer ZERO 2.00

Thunderstrike #1
© Marvel Entertainment Group

9 RF,V:Bloodaxe 2.00
10 RF,A:Thor 2.00
11 RF,A:Wildstreak 2.00
12 RF,A:Whyte Out. 2.00
13 RF,Inferno 42. . . . . 2.00
13a Double Feature flip book with Code Blue #1 . . . . 2.50
14 RF, Inferno 42 . . . . 2.00
14a Double Feature flip book with Code Blue #2 . . . . 2.50
15 RF,V:Methisto 2.00
15a Double Feature flip book with Code Blue #3 . . . . 2.50
16 . . . . 2.00
17 V:Bloodaxe 2.00
18 V:New Villain 2.00
19 Shopping Network 2.00
20 A: Black Panther 2.00
21 A:War Machine,V:Loki 2.00
22 TDF,AM,RF,Mystery of Bloodaxe blows open. 2.00
23 TDF,A:Avengers 2.00
24 TDF,V:Bloodaxe, final issue 2.00

TIMELY PRESENTS: HUMAN TORCH COMICS
Aug., 1998

1-shot GN. 6.00

TIMESLIP COLLECTION
Sept., 1998

1-shot, 48-page 3.00

TIMESLIP: THE COMING OF THE AVENGERS
Aug., 1998

1-shot GN. 6.00

TIMESPIRITS
Epic Jan., 1985

1 TY 3.00
2 . . . . 2.00
3 . . . . 2.00
4 AW 2.00
5 . . . . 2.00
6 . . . . 2.00
7 . . . . 2.00
8 March, 1986. . . . . 2.00

TIMESTRYKE

1 . . . . 2.00
2 . . . . 2.00

TINY TESSIE
See: TESSIE THE TYPIST

TOMB OF DARKNESS
See: BEWARE

TOMB OF DRACULA
April, 1972

1 GC,Night of the Vampire 100.00
2 GC,Who Stole My Coffin? 50.00
3 GC,TP,I:Rachel Van Helsing . . . 35.00
4 GC,TP,Bride of Dracula! 35.00
5 GC,TP,To Slay A Vampire 35.00
6 GC,TP,Monster of the Moors. . . 30.00
7 GC,TP,Child is Slayer of the Man 30.00
8 GC(p),The Hell-Crawlers. 30.00
9 The Fire Cross 30.00
10 GC,I:Blade Vampire Slayer . . . 45.00
11 GC,TP,Master of the Undead Strikes Again! 18.00
12 GC,TP,House that Screams . . . 18.00
13 GC,TP,O:Blade 25.00
14 GC,TP,Vampire has Risen from the Grave 18.00
15 GC,TP,Stay Dead 18.00
16 GC,TP,Back from the Grave. . . 18.00
17 GC,TP,A Vampire Rides This Train! 18.00
18 GC,TP,A:Werewolf By Night. . . 20.00
19 GC,TP,Snowbound in Hell 18.00
20 GC,TP,ManhuntForAVampire . . 18.00
21 GC,TP,A:Blade 15.00
22 GC,TP,V:Gorna 15.00
23 GC,TP,Shadow over Haunted Castle 15.00
24 GC,TP,I am your Death 15.00
25 GC,TP,Blood Stalkers of Count Dracula 15.00
26 GC,TP,A Vampire Stalks the Night 15.00
27 GC,TP,..And the Moon Spews Death! 15.00
28 GC,TP,Five came to Kill a Vampire' 15.00
29 GC,TP,Vampire goes Mad? . . . 15.00
30 GC,TP,A:Blade 15.00
31 GC,TP,Child of Blood 15.00
32 GC,TP,The Vampire Walks Among Us 15.00
33 GC,TP,Blood on My Hands . . . 15.00
34 GC,TP,Bloody Showdown 15.00
35 GC,TP,A:Brother Voodoo 15.00
36 GC,TP,Dracula in America 15.00
37 GC,TP,The Vampire Walks Among Us 12.00
38 GC,TP,Bloodlust for a Dying Vampire. 15.00
39 GC,TP,Final Death of Dracula . 15.00
40 GC,TP,Triumph of Dr.Sun. 15.00
41 GC,TP,A:Blade 10.00
42 GC,TP,V:Dr.Sun. 10.00
43 GC,TP,A:NewYear'sNightmare . 10.00
44 GC,TP,A:Dr.Strange. 10.00
45 GC,TP,A:Hannibal King 10.00
46 GC,TP,W:Dracula & Domini . . . 10.00
47 GC,TP,Death-Bites. 10.00
48 GC,TP,A:Hannibal King 10.00
49 GC,TP,A:Robin Hood, Frankenstein's Monster. 10.00
50 GC,TP,A:Silver Surfer 15.00
51 GC,TP,A:Blade 10.00
52 GC,TP,V:Demon 10.00

Tomb of Dracula #23
© Marvel Entertainment Group

53 GC,TP,A:Hannibal King,Blade . 10.00
54 GC,TP,Twas the Night Before Christmas. 10.00
55 GC,TP,Requiem for a Vampire . 10.00
56 GC,TP,A:Harold H. Harold 10.00
57 GC,TP,The Forever Man 10.00
58 GC,TP,A:Blade 10.00
59 GC,TP,The Last Traitor 10.00
60 GC,TP,The Wrath of Dracula . . 10.00
61 GC,TP,Resurrection 10.00
62 GC,TP,What Lurks Beneath . . . 10.00
63 GC,TP,A:Janus 10.00
64 GC,TP,A:Satan 10.00
65 GC,TP,Where No Vampire Has Gone Before 10.00
66 GC,TP,Marked for Death 10.00
67 GC,TP,A:Lilith 10.00
68 GC,TP,Dracula turns Human . . 10.00
69 GC,TP,Cross of Fire. 10.00
70 GC,TP,double size,last issue . . 12.00
Savage Return of Dracula. rep. Tomb of Dracula #1,#2 . . . . 2.00
Wedding of Dracula. rep.Tomb of Dracula #30,#45,#46 . . . . . . 2.00
Requiem for Dracula. rep.Tomb of Dracula #69,70. . . . . 2.00

TOMB OF DRACULA
[Mini-Series] Nov., 1991

1 GC,AW,Day of Blood 6.00
2 GC,AW,Dracula in DC 5.50
3 GC,AW,A:Blade 5.50
4 GC,AW,D:Dracula. 5.50

TOMB OF DRACULA
(B&W Mag.) Nov., 1979

1 . . . . 6.50
2 SD 7.00
3 FM 7.00
4 . . . . 6.00
5 . . . . 6.00
6 Sept., 1980 . . . . 6.00

TOMB OF DRACULA MEGAZINE

TPB Halloween, MWn,GC,TP 3.95

TOMORROW KNIGHTS
Epic June, 1990

1 . . . . 2.00
2 . . . . 2.00
3 . . . . 2.00
4 Origin 2.00
5 . . . . 2.25
6 . . . . 2.25

TOP DOG
Star Comics April, 1985

1 . . . . 2.00
2 thru 14, June 1987 . . . . @2.00

TOR
Epic *Heavy Hitters* 1993

1 JKu,R:Tor,Magazine Format 6.25
2 JKu 6.25
3 JKu,V:The Iduard Ring 6.25

TOUGH KID SQUAD COMICS
Timely March, 1942

1 O:The Human Top,Tough Kid Squad,A:The Flying Flame, V:Doctor Klutch 8,500.00

TOWER OF SHADOWS
Sept., 1969

1 JR(c),JSo,JCr,`At The Stroke of Midnight' 50.00
2 JR(c),DH,DA,NA,`The Hungry One' 30.00
3 GC,BWs,GT,`Midnight in the Wax Museum' 30.00
4 DH,Within The Witching Circle . 20.00
5 DA,BWS,WW,`Demon That Stalks Hollywood' 35.00
6 WW,SD,`Pray For the Man in the Rat-Hole 35.00
7 BWS,WW,`Titano' 35.00
8 WW,SD,`Demons of Dragon-Henge' 35.00
9 BWr(c),TP,Lovecraft story 35.00

Becomes:

CREATURES ON THE LOOSE
March, 1971

10 BWr,A:King Kull 50.00
11 DAy,rep Moomba is Here 15.00
12 JK,`I Was Captured By Korilla'. 15.00
13 RC,`The Creature From Krogarr'. 15.00
14 MSe,`Dead Storage' 15.00
15 SD,Spragg the Living Mountain 15.00
16 GK,BEv,GK,B&O:Gullivar Jones, Warrior of Mars 10.00
17 GK,`Slaves o/t Spider Swarm' . 10.00
18 RA,`The Fury of Phra' 10.00
19 WB,JM,GK,`Red Barbarian of Mars' 10.00
20 GK(c),GM,SD,`The Monster... And the Maiden 10.00
21 JSo(c),GM,`Two Worlds To Win',E:Guilliver. 10.00
22 JSo(c),SD,VM,B:Thongor, Warrior of Lost Lemuria 12.00
23 VM,`The Man-Monster Strikes'. . 8.00
24 VM,`Attack of the Lizard-Hawks' 8.00
25 VM,GK(c),`Wizard of Lemuria' . . 8.00
26 VM,`Doom of the Serpent Gods' 8.00
27 VM,SD,`Demons Dwell in the Crypts of Yamath'. 8.00
28 SD,`The Hordes of Hell'. 8.00
29 GK(c),`Day of the Dragon Wings', E:Thongor,Warrior of Lost Lemuria 8.00
30 B:Man-Wolf,`Full Moon, Dark Fear' 15.00
31 GT,`The Beast Within' 10.00

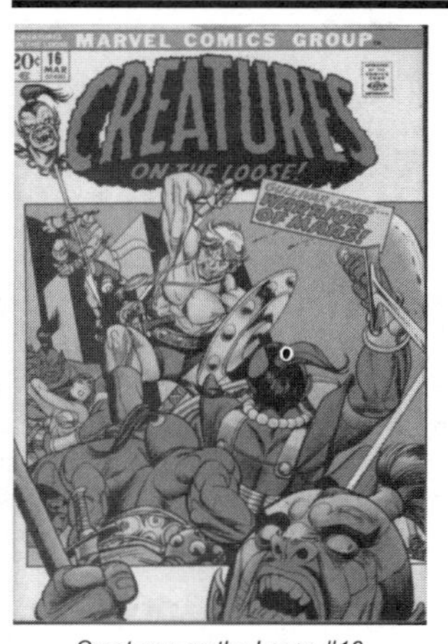

Creatures on the Loose #16
© Marvel Entertainment Group

32 GT,V:Kraven the Hunter 10.00
33 GK(c),GP,`The Name of the Game is Death' 10.00
34 GP,`Nightflight to Fear' 8.00
35 GK(c),GP 8.00
36 GK(c),GP,`Murder by Moonlight'. 8.00
37 GP,Sept., 1975 . . . . 8.00

TOXIC AVENGER
March, 1991

1 VM(i)I&O:Toxic Avenger. 2.00
2 VM(i) 2.00
3 VM(i)`Night of LivingH.bodies . . . 2.00
4 Legend of Sludgeface. 2.00
5 I:Biohazard 2.00
6 V:Biohazard 2.00
7 `Sewer of Souviaki'. 2.00
8 `Sewer of Souviaki' conc. 2.00
9 Abducted by Aliens. 2.00
10 `Die,Yuppie Scum',pt.1 . . . . 2.00

TOXIC CRUSADERS
1992

1 F:Toxic Avengers & Crusaders . . 2.00
2 SK(c),V:Custard-Thing 2.00
3 SK(c),V:Custard-Thing 2.00
4 V:Giant Mutant Rats 2.00
5 V:Dr.Killemoff 2.00
6 V:Dr.Killemoff 2.00
7 F:Yvonne 2.00
8 V:Psycho 2.00

[2nd Series]

1 . . . . 2.00
2 . . . . 2.00

TRANSFORMERS
[1st Regular Series] Sept., 1984

1 FS,Toy Comic 11.00
2 FS,OptimusPrime V:Megatron. . . 7.00
3 FS.A:Spider-Man 7.00
4 MT(c),FS 3.00
5 Transformers Dead? 3.00
6 Autobots vs.Decepticons 3.00
7 KB,V:Megatron 3.00
8 KB,A:Dinobots 3.00
9 MM,A:Circuit Breaker 3.00
10 Dawn of the Devastator 3.00
11 HT 3.00
12 HT,V:Shockwave 3.00
13 DP,Return of Megatron 3.00
14 DP,V:Decepticons 3.00
15 DP 3.00
16 KN,A:Bumblebee 3.00
17 DP,I:New Transformers,pt.1 . . . . 3.00
18 DP,I:New Transformers,pt.2 . . . . 3.00
19 DP,I:Omega Supreme 3.00
20 HT,Skid vs.Ravage 3.00
21 DP,I:Aerialbots 3.00
22 DP,I:Stuntacons(Menasor) 3.00
23 DP,Return of Circuit Breaker . . . 3.00
24 DP,D:Optimus Prime 3.00
25 DP,Decpticons (full story) 3.00
26 DP 3.00
27 DP,V:Head Hunter 3.00
28 DP 3.00
29 DP,I:Scraplets, Triplechangers . . 3.00
30 DP,V:Scraplets 3.00
31 DP,Humans vs. Decepticons . . . 3.00
32 DP,`Autobots for Sale' 3.00
33 DP,Autobots vs.Decepticons . . . 3.00
34 V:Sky Lynx 3.00
35 JRy,I:UK.version Transformers. . 3.00
36 . . . . 3.00
37 . . . . 3.00
38 . . . . 3.00
39 . . . . 3.00
40 Autobots' New Leader 3.00
41 . . . . 3.00
42 Return of Optimus Prime 3.00
43 Optimus Prime,Goldbug. 3.00
44 FF,Return of Circuit Breaker. . . . 3.00
45 V:The Jammers 3.00
46 I:New Transformers 3.00
47 B:Underbase saga,I:Seacons. . . 3.00
48 Optimus Prime/Megatron (past story). 3.00
49 Underbase saga Contd. 3.00
50 E:Underbase saga,I:New Characters 3.00
51 I:Pretender Decepticon Beasts. . 3.00
52 I:Mecannibles,pt.1 . . . . 3.00
53 Mecannibles,pt.2 . . . . 3.00
54 I:Micromasters 3.00
55 MG 3.00
56 Return of Megatron 3.00
57 Optimus Prime vs.Scraponok. . . 3.00
58 V:Megatron 3.00
59 A:Megatron,D:Ratchet 3.00
60 Battle on Cybertron 3.00
61 O:Transformers 3.00
62 B:Matrix Quest,pt.1 . . . . 3.00
63 . . . . 3.00
64 I:The Klud 3.00
65 GSr 3.00
66 E:Matrix Quest,pt.5 . . . . 3.00
67 V:Unicorn,Also Alternative World 3.00
68 I:Neoknights 3.00
69 Fate of Ratchet & Megatron revealed 3.00
70 Megatron/Ratchet fused together 3.00
71 Autobots Surrender to Decepticons 3.00
72 Decepticon Civil War, I:Gravitron 3.00
73 I:Unicron,A:Neoknights 3.00
74 A:Unicron&Brothers of Chaos . . 3.00
75 V:Thunderwing & Dark Matrix . . 4.00
76 Aftermath of War 3.00
77 Unholy Alliance 3.00
78 Galvatron vs.Megatron. 3.00
79 Decepticons Invade Earth 3.00
80 Return of Optimus Prime,final . . 3.00

[2nd Regular Series]

1 Split Foil(c),A:Dinobots 3.00
2 A:G.I.Joe,Cobra 2.00
3 . . . . 2.00
4 MaG,V:Jhiaxus 2.00
5 . . . . 2.00
6 V:Megatron. 2.00
7 V:Darkwing 2.00
8 V:Darkwing 2.00
9 . . . . 2.00
10 Total War 2.00
11 . . . . 2.00

TRANSFORMERS COMICS MAGAZINE
1986–88

1 Digest Size 2.00
2 thru 11 . . . . @2.00

TRANSFORMERS, THE MOVIE
Dec., 1986–Feb., 1987

1 thru 3 Animated Movie adapt. . @2.00

TRANSFORMERS UNIVERSE
Dec., 1986

1 . . . . 3.00
2 . . . . 3.00
3 . . . . 3.00
4 March, 1987 . . . . 3.00

TRANSMUTATION OF IKE GARAUDA
Epic 1991

1 JSh,I:IkeGaruda 3.95
2 JSh,conclusion 3.95

TROUBLE WITH GIRLS: NIGHT OF THE LIZARD
Epic *Heavy Hitters* 1993

1 BBI,AW,R:Lester Girls. 2.75
2 BBI,AW,V:Lizard Lady. 2.25
3 BBI,AW,V:Lizard Lady. 2.25
4 BBI,AW,last issue 2.25

TRUE COMPLETE MYSTERY
See: COMPLETE MYSTERY

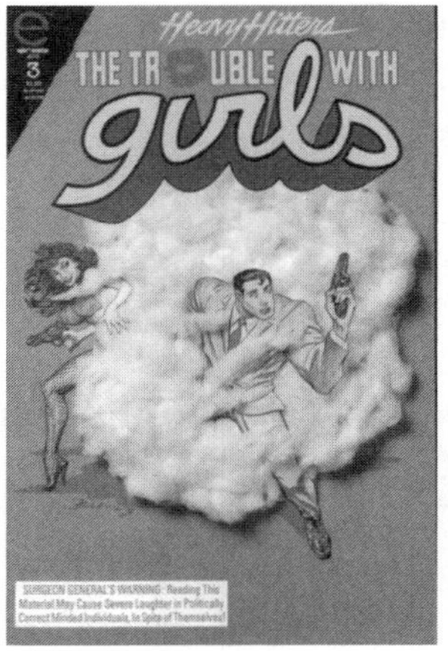

Trouble With Girls #3
© Marvel Entertainment Group

MARVEL

TRUE SECRETS
See: OUR LOVE

TRUE WESTERN
Dec., 1949

1 Ph(c),Billy the Kid 125.00
2 Ph(c),Alan Ladd,Badmen vs. Lawmen 150.00

Becomes:

TRUE ADVENTURES
3 BP,MSy,Boss of Black Devil . . 125.00

Becomes:

MEN'S ADVENTURES
4 He Called me a Coward 225.00
5 Brother Act 150.00
6 Heat of Battle 125.00
7 The Walking Death 125.00
8 RH,Journey Into Death 125.00
9 Bullets,Blades and Death 100.00
10 BEv,The Education of Thomas Dillon 100.00
11 Death of A Soldier 100.00
12 Firing Squad 100.00
13 RH(c),The Three Stripes 100.00
14 GC,BEv,Steel Coffin. 100.00
15 JMn(c). 100.00
16 . . . . 100.00
17 . . . . 100.00
18 . . . . 100.00
19 JRo 100.00
20 RH(c) 100.00
21 BEv(c),JSt,The Eye of Man . . 125.00
22 BEv,JR,Mark of the Witch . . . 125.00
23 BEv(c),RC,The Wrong Body. . 125.00
24 RH,JMn,GT,Torture Master. . . 125.00
25 SSh(c),Who Shrinks My Head 125.00
26 Midnight in the Morgue 125.00
27 CBu(c),A:Capt.America,Human Torch,Sub-Mariner 800.00
28 BEv,A:Capt.America,Human Torch, Sub-Mariner,July, 1954 . . . . . 750.00

TRY-OUT WINNER BOOK
March, 1988

1 Spider-Man vs. Doc Octopus . . 15.00

TV STARS
August, 1978

1 A:Great Grape Ape 12.00
2 . . . . 10.00
3 . . . . 10.00
4 A:Top Cat,Feb., 1979 . . . . 10.00

2099: MANIFEST DESTINY
March 1998

GN LKa,MMK,F:MiguelO'Hara,48pg 6.00

2-GUN KID
See: BILLY BUCKSKIN

TWO-GUN KID
Atlas March, 1948—April, 1977

1 B:Two-Gun Kid,The Sheriff . . 800.00
2 Killers of Outlaw City 325.00
3 RH,A:Annie Oakley 250.00
4 RH,A:Black Rider 250.00
5 . . . . 300.00
6 . . . . 200.00
7 RH,Brand of a Killer 200.00
8 The Secret of the Castle of Slaves 200.00
9 JSe,Trapped in Hidden Valley A:Black Rider 200.00

Two-Gun Kid #91
© Marvel Entertainment Group

10 JK(c),The Horrible Hermit of Hidden Mesa 200.00
11 JMn(c),GT,A:Black Rider 150.00
12 JMn(c),GT,A:Black Rider 150.00
13 thru 24 . . . . @125.00
25 AW 125.00
26 . . . . 100.00
27 . . . . 100.00
28 . . . . 100.00
29 . . . . 100.00
30 AW 100.00
31 thru 44. . . . . 75.00
45 . . . . 55.00
46 . . . . 55.00
47 . . . . 50.00
48 . . . . 50.00
49 . . . . 50.00
50 . . . . 45.00
51 AW 45.00
52 thru 59 . . . . @45.00
60 DAy,New O:Two Gun Kid 40.00
61 JK,DAy,The Killer and The Kid . 40.00
62 JK,DAy,At the Mercy of Moose Morgan. 40.00
63 DAy,The Guns of Wild Bill Taggert. 25.00
64 DAy,Trapped by Grizzly Gordon. 25.00
65 DAy,Nothing Can Save Fort Henry. 25.00
66 DAy,Ringo's Raiders 25.00
67 DAy,The Fangs of the Fox 25.00
68 DAy,The Purple Phantom. 25.00
69 DAy,Badman Called Goliath. . . 25.00
70 DAy,Hurricane 25.00
71 DAy,V:Jesse James 25.00
72 DAy,V:Geronimo 25.00
73 Guns of the Galloway Gang . . . 25.00
74 Dakota Thompson 25.00
75 JK,Remember the Alamo 25.00
76 JK,Trapped on the Doom. 25.00
77 JK,V:The Panther 25.00
78 V:Jesse James 25.00
79 The River Rats 25.00
80 V:The Billy Kid 25.00
81 The Hidden Gun 20.00
82 BEv,Here Comes the Conchos. 20.00
83 Durango,Two-Gun Kid Unmasked 20.00
84 Gunslammer 20.00
85 Fury at Falcon Flats, A:Rawhide Kids 20.00
86 V:Cole Younger 20.00
87 OW,The Sidewinder and the Stallion. 20.00
88 thru 100 . . . . @20.00
101 . . . . 20.00
102 thru 136 . . . . @10.00

TWO-GUN KID: SUNSET RIDERS
1995

1 FaN,R:Two-Gun Kid,64pgs 6.95
2 FaN,concl. 64pgs.. . . . . 6.95

TWO GUN WESTERN
See: CASEY–CRIME PHOTOGRAPHER

TWO-GUN WESTERN
See: BILLY BUCKSKIN

2001: A SPACE ODYSSEY
Oct., 1976

1 JK,FRg,Based on Movie 3.00

2001: A SPACE ODYSSEY
Dec., 1976—Sept., 1977

1 JK,Based on Movie 7.00
2 JK,Vira the She-Demon 5.00
3 JK,Marak the Merciless 5.00
4 JK,Wheels of Death 5.00
5 JK,Norton of New York 5.00
6 JK,Immortality ...Death 5.00
7 JK,The New Seed 5.00
8 JK,Capture of X-51,I&O:Mr. Machine(Machine-Man) 6.00
9 JK,A:Mr Machine 5.00
10 Hotline to Hades,A:Mr Machine . 5.00

2010
April, 1985

1 TP,movie adapt. 2.00
2 TP,movie adapt,May, 1985 . . . . . 2.00

2099 A.D.
1995

1 Chromium cover. 4.00

2099 APOCALYPSE
1995

1 . . . . 5.00

2099 GENESIS
1996

1 Chromium Cover 4.00

2099 SPECIAL: THE WORLD OF DOOM
1995

1 The World of Doom 2.25

2099 UNLIMITED
1993–96

1 DT,I:Hulk 2099,A:Spider-Man 2099, I:Mutagen. 4.50
2 DT,F:Hulk 2099,Spider-Man 2099, I:R-Gang 4.25
3 GJ(s),JJB,F:Hulk & SpM 2099 . . 4.25
4 PR(c),GJ(s),JJB,I:Metalscream 2099,Lachryma 2099 . . . . 4.25
5 GJ(s),I:Vulx,F:Hazarrd 2099 . . . . 3.95
6 . . . . 3.95

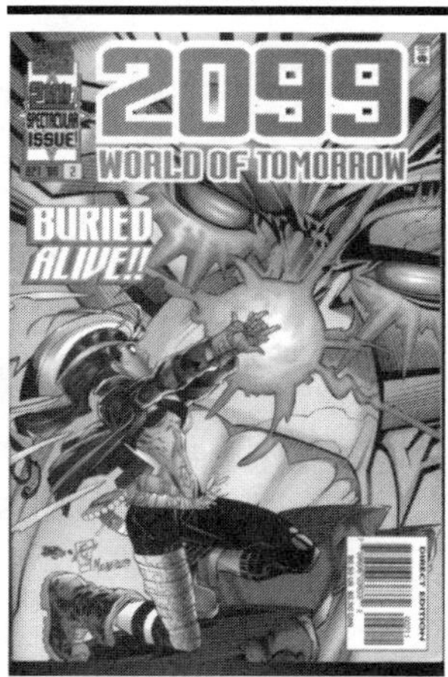

2099 World of Tomorrow #2
© Marvel Entertainment Group

Becomes:

2099 A.D. UNLIMITED

7 . . . . 3.95
8 F:Public Enemy 3.95
9 One Nation Under Doom 3.95
10 V:Chameleon 2099 . . . . . . 3.95
Spec. #1 The World of Doom 2.25

2099: WORLD OF TOMORROW

1996–97

1 . . . . 2.50
2 . . . . 2.50
3 MMk,MsM,ATi,F:Spider-Man, X-Men 2.50
4 ATi,X-Men 2099 discover secret . 2.50
5 ATi 2.50
6 PFe&ATi(c),Phalanx's final assault 2.50
7 Spider-Man 2099 searches for his brother: Green Goblin 2.50
8 Phalanx invasion aftermath 2.50
9 Humanity vs. Lunatika 2.50

TYPHOID

1995–96

1 ANo,JVF,Painted series 3.95
2 ANo,JVF,Hunt for serial killer . . . 3.95
3 ANo,JVF,sex,blood & videotapes 3.95
4 ANo,JVF,conclusion 3.95

ULTIMATE AGE OF APOCALYPSE

Rep. #1-#4 Age of Apocalypse stories:
Ultimate Amazing X-Men 8.95
Ultimate Astonishing X-Men 8.95
Ultimate Factor X 8.95
Ultimate Gambit and the X-Ternals . 8.95
Ultimate Generation Next 8.95
Ultimate Weapon X 8.95
Ultimate X-Calibre 8.95
Ultimate X-Man 8.95

ULTIMATE SPIDER-MAN

Sept., 2000

1 JQ,MBa,ATi,48-pg 3.00
2A MBa,ATi, Dr. Otto Octopus 2.50
2B variant JaL(c) 2.50

ULTRAFORCE/AVENGERS

1 V:Loki,A:Malibu's Ultraforce 3.95

ULTRA GIRL

Mini-Series 1996

1 BKs,I&O:Ultra Girl 2.00
2 BKs, ... 2.00
3 BKs,R:New Warriors 2.00

ULTRA X-MEN COLLECTION

1 Metallic(c), art from cards 3.00
2 thru 5 art from cards . . . . @3.00

ULTRA X-MEN III

Preview 3.00

ULTRON

June 1999

1-shot Ultron Unleashed, rep. 3.50

Uncanny Origins #2
© Marvel Entertainment Group

UNCANNY ORIGINS

Sept. 1996

1 F:Cyclops 2.00
2 F:Quicksilver 2.00
3 DHv,BAn,F:Archangel 2.00
4 F:Firelord 2.00
5 MHi,F:Hulk 2.00
6 F:Beast 2.00
7 F:Venom 2.00
8 F:Nightcrawler 2.00
9 F:Storm 2.00
10 F:Black Cat 2.00
11 F:Luke Cage 2.00
12 F:Black Knight 2.00
13 LWn,MCa,F:Doctor Strange 2.00
14 LWn,MCW,F:Iron Fist 2.00

UNCANNY TALES

Atlas June, 1952

1 RH,While the City Sleeps 650.00
2 JMn,BEv 350.00
3 Escape to What 300.00
4 JMn,Nobody's Fool 300.00
5 Fear 300.00
6 He Lurks in the Shadows 300.00
7 BEv,Kill,Clown,Kill 250.00
8 JMn,Bring Back My Face 250.00
9 BEv,RC,The Executioner 250.00
10 RH(c),JR,The Man Who Came Back To Life 250.00
11 GC,The Man Who Changed . . 200.00
12 BP,BEv,Bertha Gets Buried . . 200.00
13 RH,Scared Out of His Skin . . . 200.00
14 RH,The Victims of Vonntor . . . 200.00
15 RA,JSt,The Man Who Saw Death 200.00
16 JMn,GC,Zombie at Large 200.00
17 GC,I Live With Corpses 200.00
18 JF,BP,Clock Face(c) 200.00
19 DBr,RKr,The Man Who Died Again 200.00
20 DBr,Ted's Head 200.00
21 . . . . 175.00
22 DAy 175.00
23 . . . . 175.00
24 . . . . 175.00
25 MSy 175.00
26 . . . . 175.00
27 RA 175.00
28 . . . . 175.00
29 . . . . 100.00
30 . . . . 100.00
31 . . . . 100.00
32 BEv 100.00
33 . . . . 100.00
34 BP 100.00
35 . . . . 100.00
36 BP,BEv 100.00
37 MD 100.00
38 BP 100.00
39 BEv 100.00
40 . . . . 100.00
41 . . . . 100.00
42 MD 125.00
43 . . . . 100.00
44 . . . . 100.00
45 MD 100.00
46 GM 100.00
47 TSe 100.00
48 BEv 100.00
49 JO 100.00
50 JO 100.00
51 GM 125.00
52 GC 100.00
53 JO,AT 100.00
54 . . . . 120.00
55 . . . . 100.00
56 Sept., 1957 . . . . 125.00

UNCANNY TALES FROM THE GRAVE

Dec., 1973—Oct., 1975

1 RC,Room of no Return 20.00
2 DAy,Out of the Swamp 10.00
3 No Way Out 10.00
4 JR,SD,Vampire 10.00
5 GK,GT,Don't Go in the Cellar . . 10.00
6 JR,SD,The Last Kkrul 10.00
7 RH,SD,Never Dance With a Vampire 10.00
8 SD,Escape Into Hell 10.00
9 JA,The Nightmare Men 10.00
10 SD,DH,Beware the Power of Khan 10.00
11 SD,JF,RH,Dead Don't Sleep . . . 10.00
12 SD,Final Issue 10.00

UNCANNY X-MEN

See: X-MEN

MARVEL

UNKNOWN WORLDS OF SCIENCE FICTION

Jan., 1975

(black & white magazine)

1 AW,RKr,AT,FF,GC 4.00
2 FB,GP 3.25
3 GM,AN,GP,GC 3.25
4 . . . . 3.25
5 GM,NC,GC 3.25
6 FB,AN,GC,Nov., 1975 . . . . 3.25
Spec.#1 AN,NR,JB 3.50

UNION JACK

Oct., 1998

1 (of 3) BRa,F:Joey Chapman 3.00
2 BRa,V:Baroness 3.00
3 BRa,conclusion 3.00

U.S.A. COMICS

Timely Aug., 1941

1 S&K(c),BW,Bondage(c),The Defender(c) 11,000.00
2 S&K(c),BW,Capt.Terror(c) . . 3,000.00
3 S&K(c),Capt.Terror(c). 2,200.00
4 . . . . 1,600.00
5 Hitler(c),O:AmericanAvenger 1,800.00
6 ASh(c),Capt.America(c) 2,200.00
7 BW,O:Marvel Boy 1,900.00
8 Capt.America (c) 1,500.00
9 Bondage(c), Capt.America . . 1,500.00
10 SSh(c),Bondage(c), Capt. America 1,500.00
11 SSh(c),Bondage(c), Capt. America 1,200.00
12 ASh(c),Capt.America. 1,200.00
13 ASh(c),Capt.America. 1,200.00
14 Capt.America. 900.00
15 Capt.America. 900.00
16 ASh(c),Bondage(c), Capt.America 900.00
17 Bondage(c),Capt.America . . . 900.00

U.S. 1

May, 1983–Oct., 1984

1 AM(c),HT,Trucking Down the Highway 2.00
2 HT,Midnight 2.00
3 FS,ME,Rhyme of the Ancient Highwayman 2.00
4 FS,ME 2.00
5 FS,ME,Facing The Maze 2.00
6 FS,ME 2.00
7 FS,ME 2.00
8 FS,ME 2.00
9 FS,ME,Iron Mike-King of the Bike 2.00
10 thru 12 FS,ME . . . . @2.00

U.S. AGENT

June – Dec. 1993

1 V:Scourge,O:U.S.Agent 2.00
2 V:Scourge 2.00
3 V:Scourge 2.00
4 last issue 2.00

UNIVERSE X

July, 2000

0 AxR,DBw,48-pg. 4.00
1 (of 12) AxR,DBw,Capt.MarVell . . 3.50
2 AxR,DBw,. 3.50
3 AxR,DBw,. 3.50
Spec."4",F:Fantastic Four 4.00

UNTAMED

Epic *Heavy Hitters* 1993

1 I:Griffen Palmer 2.75
2 V:Kosansui 2.25
3 V:Kosansui 2.25

Untold Legend of Captain Marvel #2
© Marvel Entertainment Group

UNTOLD LEGEND OF CAPTAIN MARVEL, THE

1997

1 (of 3) Early days of Captain Marvel 2.50
2 Early days of Captain Marvel . . . 2.50
3 V:Kree 2.50

UNTOLD TALES OF SPIDER-MAN

Sept., 1995–Sept., 1997

1 F:Young Spider-Man. 3.00
2 V:Batwing. 2.00
3 V:Sandman 2.00
4 V:J.Jonah Jameson 2.00
5 V:Vulture 2.00
6 A:Human Torch. 2.00
7 . . . . 2.00
8 . . . . 2.00
9 A:Batwing,Lizard. 2.00
10 KBk,PO,I:Commanda. 2.00
11 KBk,PO, ... 2.00
12 KBk,PO, ... 2.00
13 KBk,PO, ... 2.00
14 KBk,PO, ... 2.00
15 KBk,PO,AV,Gordon's plan to control the Bugle 2.00
16 Re-I:Mary Jane Watson 2.00
17 KBk,PO,AV,V:Hawkeye 2.00
18 KBk,PO,AV,A:Green Goblin, Headsman 2.00
19 KBk,PO,AW,F:Doctor Octopus . . 2.00
20 KBk,PO,AW,V:Vulture 2.00
21 KBk,PO,AW,V:Menace,A:Original X-Men 2.00
22 KBk,PO,AW,V:Scarecrow, ... 2.00
23 KBk,PO,AW,V:Crime Master, A:Green Goblin 2.00
24 KBk,PO,BMc, Fate of Batwing . . 2.00
25 LBl,PO,BMc, V:Green Goblin, final issue. 2.00
Minus 1 Spec., RSt,JR, flashback, Peter's parents. 2.00
Ann.'96 1 KBk,MiA,JSt,A date with Invisible Girl? 2.00
Ann.'97 KBk,TL,A:everyone, 48pg . 2.95
TPB rep. #1–#8 . . . . 17.00
one-shot GN KBk,SL,Encounter, A:Dr. Strange 48pg. 6.00

VALKYRIE

1996

1-shot JMD,. 2.50

VAMPIRE TALES

August, 1973

(black & white magazine)

1 BEv,B:Morbius the Living Vampire. 50.00
2 JSo,I:Satana 40.00
3 A:Satana 20.00
4 GK 30.00
5 GK,O:Morbius The Living Vampire 35.00
6 AA,I:Lilith 30.00
7 HC,PG 30.00
8 AA,A:Blade The Vampire Slayer 30.00
9 RH,AA 30.00
10 . . . . 30.00
11 June, 1975. . . . . 30.00
Ann.#1 . . . . 15.00

Vault of Evil #14
© Marvel Entertainment Group

VAULT OF EVIL

Feb., 1973—Nov., 1975

1 B:1950's reps,Come Midnight, Come Monster 17.00
2 The Hour of the Witch 11.00
3 The Woman Who Wasn't 11.00
4 Face that Follows 11.00
5 Ghost 11.00
6 The Thing at the Window 11.00
7 Monsters 11.00
8 The Vampire is my Brother 11.00
9 Giant Killer 11.00
10 The Lurkers in the Caves 11.00
11 Two Feasts For a Vampire 11.00
12 Midnight in the Haunted Mansion 11.00
13 Hot as the Devil 11.00
14 Midnight in the Haunted Manor 11.00
15 Don't Shake Hands with the Devil. 11.00
16 A Grave Honeymoon 11.00
17 Grave Undertaking. 11.00

18 The Deadly Edge 11.00
19 Vengeance of Ahman Ra 11.00
20 . . . . 11.00
21 Victim of Valotorr 11.00
22 . . . . 11.00
23 Black Magician Lives Again . . . 11.00

VENOM: ALONG CAME A SPIDER

1996

1 LHA,GLz,V:New Spider-Man. . . . 3.00
2 LHa,JPi,V:New Spider-Man. 3.00
3 . . . . 3.00
4 conclusion, 48pg 3.00

VENOM: CARNAGE UNLEASHED

1995

1 Venom vs. Carnage 3.00
2 Venom vs. Carnage 3.00
3 No Spider-Help. 3.00
4 JRu,Wld,LHa,cardstock(c) 3.00

VENOM: THE ENEMY WITHIN

1994

1 BMc,Glow-in-the-dark(C),
A:Demogoblin,Morbius 3.25
2 BMc,A:Demogoblin,Morbius 3.25
3 BMc,V:Demogoblin,A:Morbius. . . 3.25

VENOM: FINALE

1997–98

1 (of 3) LHa, ... 3.00
2 LJa, ... 3.00
3 LHa, finale 3.00

VENOM: FUNERAL PYRE

1993

1 TL,JRu,A:Punisher 3.50
2 TL,JRu,AM,V:Gangs. 3.50
3 TL,JRu,Last issue. 3.50

VENOM: THE HUNGER

1996

1 thru 4 LKa,TeH,V:Dr. Paine . . . @2.00

VENOM: THE HUNTED

1996

1 LHa,3 part mini-series. 3.00

VENOM: LETHAL PROTECTOR

1993

1 MBa,A:Spider-Man.holo-grafx(c). 5.00
1a Gold Ed.. . . . . 15.00
2 MBa,A:Spider-Man 3.50
3 MBa,Families of Venom's
victims 3.50
4 RLm,A:Spider-Man,V:Life
Foundation. 3.50
5 RLm,V:Five Symbiotes,A:SpM . . 3.50
6 RLm,V:Spider-Man 3.50
Super Size Spec.#1 Planet of
the Symbiotes,pt.3 . . . . 3.95
Venom:Deathtrap:The Vault,RLm,
A:Avengers,Freedom Force . . . 6.95
TPB Lethal Protector RLm,DvM . . 15.95

VENOM: LICENSE TO KILL

1997

1 (of 3) LHa,KHt, sequel to Venom
on trial 2.00
2 LHa,V:Dr. Yes. 2.00
3 LHa,V:Dr. Yes. 2.00

VENOM: THE MACE

1994

1 Embossed(c),CP(s),LSh,I:Mace . 3.25
2 CP(s),LSh,V:Mace 3.25
3 CP(s),LSh,V:Mace,final issue . . . 3.25

VENOM: THE MADNESS

1993–94

1 B:ANi(s),KJo,V:Juggernaut 3.50
2 KJo,V:Juggernaut. 3.25
3 E:ANi(s),KJo,V:Juggernaut 3.25

VENOM: NIGHTS OF VENGEANCE

1994

1 RLm,I:Stalkers,A:Vengeance . . . 3.25
2 RLm,A:Vengeance,V:Stalkers . . . 3.25
3 RLm,V:Stalkers. 3.25
4 RLm,final issue. 3.25

VENOM: ON TRIAL

Jan.–May, 1997

1 LHa,Tries to break out 2.00
2 LHa,Defended by Matt Murdock
(Daredevil),A:Spider-Man 2.00
3 LHa,A:Spider-Man, Carnage,
Daredevil 2.00

VENOM: SEED OF DARKNESS

1997

1 LKa,JFy,Flashback, early Eddie
Brock 2.00

VENOM: SEPARATION ANXIETY

1994–95

1 Embossed(c) 3.00
2 V:Symbiotes 3.00
3 . . . . 3.00
4 . . . . 3.00
TPB Rep.#1-#4 HMe,RoR,SDR . . . 9.95

VENOM: SIGN OF THE BOSS

1997

1 (of 2) IV,TDr,V:Ghost Rider 2.00
2 (of 2) IV,TDr,conclusion. 2.00

VENOM: SINNER TAKES ALL

1995

1 LHa,GLz,I:New Sin-Eater 3.00
2 V:Sineater 3.00
3 Wrong Man 3.00
4 LHa,GLz,V:Sin-Eater 3.00
5 LHa, finale 3.00

VENOM: TOOTH AND CLAW

1996–97

1 (of 3) LHa,JPi,AM, Dirtnap usurps
Venom's body. 2.00
2 LHa,JPi,AM,V:Wolverine. 2.00
3 LHa,JPi,AM,V:Wolverine,
Chimera 2.00

VENUS

Atlas August, 1948

1 B:Venus,Hedy Devine,HK,Hey
Look 1,000.00
2 Venus(c) 550.00
3 Carnival(c) 475.00
4 Cupid(c).HK,Hey Look 475.00
5 Serenade(c) 450.00
6 Wrath of a Goddess,A:Loki . . . 425.00
7 The Romance That Could
Not Be 425.00
8 The Love Trap 425.00
9 Whom the Gods Destroy 425.00
10 B:Scince Fiction/Horror,
Trapped On the Moon. 600.00
11 The End of the World 700.00
12 GC,The Lost World 400.00
13 BEv,King of the Living Dead. . 600.00
14 BEv,The Fountain of Death . . 600.00
15 BEv,The Empty Grave 600.00
16 BEv,Where Gargoyles Dwell . 600.00
17 BEv,Tower of Death,
Bondage(c). 600.00
18 BEv,Terror in the Tunnel. 600.00
19 BEv,THe Kiss Of Death 600.00

VERY BEST OF MARVEL COMICS

1-shot reps Marvel Artists
Favorite Stories 12.95

VIDEO JACK

Nov., 1987

1 KGi,O:Video Jack 2.50
2 KGi. 2.00
3 KGi. 2.00
4 KGi. 2.00
5 KGi. 2.00
6 KGi,NA,BWr,AW. 2.00

VISION, THE

1994–95

1 BHs,mini-series 2.00
2 BHs 2.00

Vision and Scarlet Witch #2
© Marvel Entertainment Group

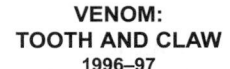

MARVEL

3 BHs 2.00
4 BHs 2.00

VISION & SCARLET WITCH

[1st Series] Nov., 1982

1 RL,V:Halloween 2.00
2 RL,V:Isbisa,D:Whizzer 2.00
3 RL,A:Wonderman,V:GrimReaper 2.00
4 RL,A:Magneto,Inhumans 2.00

[2nd Series] 1985–86

1 V:Grim Reaper 2.00
2 V:Lethal Legion,D:Grim Reaper . 2.00
3 V:Salem's Seven 2.00
4 I:Glamor & Illusion 2.00
5 A:Glamor & Illusion. 2.00
6 A:Magneto 2.00
7 V:Toad 2.00
8 A:Powerman. 2.00
9 V:Enchantress 2.00
10 A:Inhumans 2.00
11 A:Spider-Man. 2.00
12 Birth of V&S's Child 2.00

VISIONARIES

Star Nov., 1987

1 thru 5 . . . . @2.00
6 Sept., 1988 . . . . 2.00

VOID INDIGO

Epic Nov., 1984

1 VM,Epic Comics. 2.00
2 VM,Epic Comics,March, 1985. . . 2.00

WACKY DUCK

See: DOPEY DUCK

WALLY THE WIZARD

Star April, 1985

1 . . . . 2.00
2 thru 11 . . . . @2.00
12 March, 1986. . . . . 2.00

WAR, THE

1989

1 Sequel to The Draft & The Pit . . 3.50
2 . . . . 3.50
3 . . . . 3.50
4 1990. . . . . 3.50

WAR ACTION

Atlas April, 1952

1 JMn,RH,War Stories, Six Dead Men 150.00
2 . . . . 75.00
3 Invasion in Korea 50.00
4 thru 10 . . . . @50.00
11 . . . . 65.00
12 . . . . 65.00
13 BK. 65.00
14 Rangers Strike,June, 1953. . . . 55.00

WAR ADVENTURES

Atlas Jan., 1952

1 GT,Battle Fatigue 125.00
2 The Story of a Slaughter 65.00
3 JRo 45.00
4 RH(c) 45.00
5 RH,Violent(c) 45.00
6 Stand or Die 45.00
7 JMn(c) 45.00
8 BK 75.00
9 RH(c) 45.00
10 JRo(c),Attack at Dawn 45.00
11 Red Trap 45.00
12 . . . . 45.00
13 RH(c),The Commies Strike Feb., 1953 . . . . 45.00

WAR COMBAT

Atlas March, 1952

1 JMn,Death of Platoon Leader . 100.00
2 . . . . 50.00
3 JMn(c) 35.00
4 JMn(c) 35.00
5 The Red Hordes 35.00
Becomes:

COMBAT CASEY

6 BEv,Combat Casey cont 100.00
7 . . . . 75.00
8 JMn(c) 50.00
9 . . . . 45.00
10 RH(c). 75.00
11 . . . . 40.00
12 . . . . 40.00
13 thru 19 . . . . @75.00
20 . . . . 40.00
21 thru 33 . . . . @35.00
34 July, 1957 . . . . 35.00

WAR COMICS

Atlas Dec., 1950

1 You Only Die Twice 175.00
2 Infantry's War 100.00
3 . . . . 75.00
4 GC,The General Said Nuts . . . 75.00
5 . . . . 75.00
6 The Deadly Decision of General Kwang 75.00
7 RH 75.00
8 RH,No Survivors 75.00
9 RH 75.00
10 . . . . 75.00
11 thru 21 . . . . @65.00
22. . . . . 70.00
23 thru 37 . . . . @45.00
38 JKu 50.00
39 . . . . 45.00
40 . . . . 45.00
41 . . . . 45.00
42 . . . . 45.00
43 AT 50.00
44 . . . . 45.00
45 . . . . 45.00
46 RC. 55.00
47 . . . . 45.00
48 . . . . 45.00
49 Sept., 1957 . . . . 55.00

WARHEADS

Marvel UK 1992–93

1 GEr,I:Warheads,A:Wolverine, . . . 2.25
2 GEr,V:Nick Fury 2.00
3 DTy,A:Iron Man. 2.00
4 SCy,A:X-Force 2.00
5 A:X-Force,C:Deaths'Head II 2.00
6 SCy,A:Death's Head II 2.00
7 SCy,A:Death's Head II,S.Surfer. . 2.00
8 SCy,V:Mephisto 2.00
9 SCy,V:Mephisto 2.00
10 JCz,V:Mephisto 2.00
11 A:Death's Head II. 2.00
12 V:Mechanix 2.00
13 Xenophiles Reptiles. 2.00
14 last issue. 2.00

WARHEADS: BLACK DAWN

1 A:Gh.Rider,Morbius 3.25
2 V:Dracula 2.00

WAR IS HELL

Jan., 1973—Oct., 1975

1 B:Reprints,Decision at Dawn . . 15.00
2 Anytime,Anyplace,War is Hell . . 9.00
3 Retreat or Die 9.00
4 Live Grenade 9.00
5 Trapped Platoon 9.00
6 We Die at Dawn 9.00
7 While the Jungle Sleeps,A:Sgt Fury 9.00
8 Killed in Action,A;Sgt Fury 9.00
9 B:Supernatural,War Stories . . . 20.00
10 Death is a 30 Ton Tank 10.00
11 thru 15 . . . . @10.00

Warlock #5
© Marvel Entertainment Group

WARLOCK

[1st Regular Series] Aug., 1972

1 GK,I:Counter Earth,A:High Evolutionary 18.00
2 JB,TS,V:Man Beast 10.00
3 GK,TS,V:Apollo 7.00
4 JK,TS,V:Triax 6.00
5 GK,TS,V:Dr.Doom 6.00
6 TS(i),O:Brute 6.00
7 TS(i),V:Brute,D:Dr.Doom. 6.00
8 TS(i),R:Man-Beast(cont in Hulk #176) 6.00
9 JSn,1st`Rebirth'Thanos,O:Magnus, N:Warlock,I:In-Betweener 10.00
10 JSn,SL,O:Thanos,V:Magus, A:In-Betweener. 16.00
11 JSn,SL,D:Magus,A:Thanos, In-Betweener. 10.00
12 JSn,SL,O:Pip,V:Pro-Boscis A:Starfox 9.00
13 JSn,SL,I&O:Star-Thief 9.00
14 JSn,SL,V:Star-Thief 9.00
15 JSn,A:Thanos,V:Soul-Gem . . . 15.00

[2nd Regular Series] 1992

1 JSn,rep.Strange Tales #178-180 Baxter Paper 4.00
2 JSn,rep.Strange Tales #180 & Warlock #9 . . . . 3.00
3 JSn,rep.Warlock #10-#12 . . . . . . 3.00
4 JSn,rep.Warlock #13-#15 . . . . . . 3.00
5 JSn,rep.Warlock #15 . . . . 3.00
6 JSn,rep. 3.00

WARLOCK
[Limited Series]

1 Rep.Warlock Series 3.50
2 Rep.Warlock Series 3.00
3 Rep.Warlock Series 3.00
4 Rep.Warlock Series 3.00
5 Rep.Warlock Series 3.00
6 Rep.Warlock Series 3.00

WARLOCK
Sept., 1998

1 (of 4) TL,RJn,R:Adam Warlock . . 3.00
2 TL,murderer revealed 3.00
3 TL,V:Drax 3.00
4 TL,Concl. 3.00

WARLOCK
Aug., 1999

1 LSi,PFe,Marvel Tech. 2.00
2 LSi,PFe,A:Iron Man 2.00
2a variant PFe cover 2.00
3 LSi,PFe,MMo,F:Psiren 2.00
4 LSi,PFe,MMo,V:Mole Man 2.00
5 LSi,PFe,MMo 2.00
6 LSi,PFe,MMo,A:Kitty Pryde. 2.00
7 LSi,PFe,MMo,R:Wolfsbane, Magus 2.50
8 LSi,PFe,MMo,V:Bastion 2.50
9 LSi,PFe,MMo,F:Bastion 2.50

WARLOCK AND THE INFINITY WATCH
1992–95

1 AMe,Trial of the Gods(from Infinity Gauntlet). 3.00
2 AMe,I:Infinity Watch(Gamora,Pip, Moondragon,Drax & 1 other) . . 2.75
3 RL,TA,A:High Evolutionary, Nobilus,I:Omega. 2.75
4 RL,TA,V:Omega 2.50
5 AMe,TA,V:Omega. 2.50
6 AMe,V:Omega(Man-Beast) 2.50
7 TR,TA,V:Mole Man,A:Thanos . . . 2.50
8 TR,TA,Infinity War,A:Thanos 2.25
9 AMe,TA,Inf.War,O:Gamora 2.00
10 AMe,Inf.War,Thanos vs Doppleganger. 2.50
11 O:Pip,Gamora,Drax,M'dragon . . 2.00
12 TR,Drax Vs.Hulk 2.00

Warlock and the Infinity Watch #5
© Marvel Entertainment Group

13 TR,Drax vs Hulk 2.00
14 AMe,V:United Nations 2.00
15 AMe,Magnus,Him 2.00
16 TGr,I:Count Abyss 2.00
17 TGr,I:Maxam 2.00
18 AMe,Inf.Crusade,N:Pip 2.00
19 TGr,A:Hulk,Wolverine,Infinity Crusade 2.00
20 AMe,Inf.Crusade 2.00
21 V:Thor 2.00
22 AMe,Infinity Crusade 2.00
23 JSn(s),TGb,Blood & Thunder#4 . . . . 2.00
24 JSn(s),TGb,V:Geirrodur 2.00
25 JSn(s),AMe,Die-Cut(c),Blood & Thunder #12. . . . . 3.25
26 A:Avengers 2.00
27 TGb,V:Avengers 2.00
28 TGb,V:Man-Beast 2.00
29 A:Maya 2.25
30 PO 2.25
31 . . . . 2.00
32 Heart & Soul 2.00
33 V:Count Abyss. 2.00
34 V:Count Abyss. 2.00
35 V:Tyrannus 2.00
36 . . . . 2.00
37 A:Zaharius. 2.00
38 . . . . 2.00
39 V:Domitron 2.00
40 A:Thanos. 2.00
41 Monster Island. 2.00
42 Warlock vs. Maxam, Atlantis Rising, final issue 2.00

WARLOCK CHRONICLES
1993–94

1 TR,F:Adam Warlock,holo-grafx(c), I:Darklore,Meer'lyn 3.25
2 TR,Infinity Crusade,Thanos revealed to have the Reality Gem. 2.25
3 TR,A:Mephisto 2.25
4 TR,A:Magnus 2.25
5 TR(c),Inf.Crusade. 2.25
6 TR,Blood & Thunder,pt.#3 . . . . . 2.25
7 TR,Blood & Thunder,pt.#7 . . . . . 2.25
8 TR,Blood & Thunder,pt.#11. . . . . 2.25
9 TR 2.00
10 TR. 2.00
11 TR. 2.00

WAR MACHINE
1994–96

1 GG,Foil Embossed(c),B:LKa&StB, O:War Machine,V:Cable, C:Deathlok 3.25
1a Newstand Ed. 2.25
2 GG,V:Cable,Deathlok,w/card . . . 2.00
3 GG,V:Cable,Deathlok 2.00
4 GG,C:Force Works 2.00
5 GG,I:Deachtoll 2.00
6 GG,V:Deathtoll 2.00
7 GG,A:Hawkeye. 2.00
8 reg ed. 2.00
8a neon(c),w/insert print 3.00
9 Hands of Mandarin,pt.2 . . . . 2.00
10 Hands of Mandarin,pt.5 . . . . 2.00
11 X-Mas Party. 2.00
12 V:Terror Device 2.00
13 V:The Rush Team 2.00
14 A:Force Works. 2.00
15 In The Past of WWII 2.00
16 DAn,A:Rick Fury,Cap.America . . 2.00
17 The Man Who Won WWII 2.00
18 DAn,N:War Machine 2.00
19 DAn,A:Hawkeye 2.00
20 DAn,The Crossing 2.00
21 DAn,The Crossing 2.00
22 DAn,V:Iron Man. 2.00
23 DAn,Avengers:Timeslide 2.00

WAR MAN
Epic 1993

1 thru 2 CDi(s). 2.50

WEAPON X
1995

1 Wolverine After Xavier 4.00
2 Full Scale War 2.25
3 Jean Leaves. 2.00
4 F:Gateway 2.00
TPB Rep.#1-#4. . . . . 8.95

WEAVEWORLD
Epic 1991–92

1 MM, Clive Barker adaptation. . . . 5.00
2 MM,`Into the Weave' 5.00
3 MM. 5.00

WEB OF SCARLET SPIDER
1995–96

1 TDF,Virtual Mortality,pt.1 . . . . 2.00
2 TDF,CyberWar,pt.2 . . . . 2.00
3 Nightmare in Scarlet,pt.1 . . . . . . 2.00
4 Nightmare in Scarlet,pt.3 . . . . . . 2.00

WEB OF SPIDER-MAN
April, 1985

1 JM,V:New Costume 15.00
2 JM,V:Vulture. 8.00
3 JM,V:Vulture. 6.00
4 JM,JBy,V:Dr.Octopus 5.00
5 JM,JBy,V:Dr.Octopus 5.00
6 MZ,BL,JM,Secret Wars II 5.00
7 SB,A:Hulk,V:Nightmare, C:Wolverine 5.00
8 V:Smithville Thunder. 5.00
9 V:Smithville Thunder. 5.00
10 JM,A:Dominic Fortune, V:Shocker 5.00
11 BMc,V:Thugs 5.00
12 BMc,SB,V:Thugs 5.00
13 BMc,V:J.JonahJameson. 5.00
14 KB,V:Black Fox 5.00
15 V:Black Fox,I:Chance 4.00
16 MS,KB,V:Magma 4.00

MARVEL

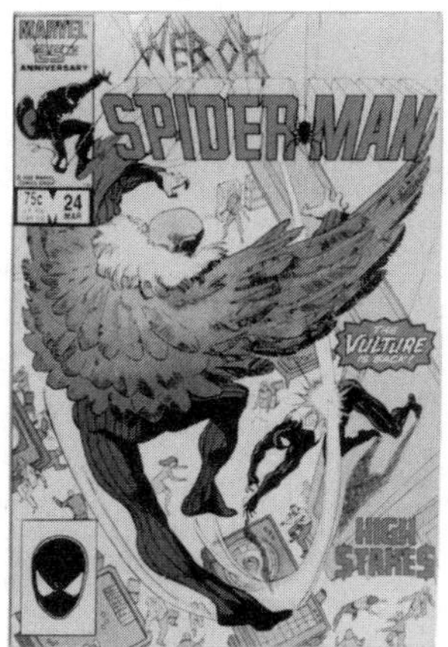

Web of Spider-Man #24
© Marvel Entertainment Group

17 MS,V:Magma 4.00
18 MS,KB,Where is Spider-Man? . . 4.00
19 MS,BMc,I:Solo,Humbug 4.00
20 MS,V:Terrorists 4.00
21 V:Fake Spider-Man 4.00
22 MS,V:Terrorists 4.00
23 V:Slyde 4.00
24 SB,V:Vulture,Hobgoblin 4.00
25 V:Aliens 4.00
26 V:Thugs 4.00
27 V:Headhunter 4.00
28 BL,V:Thugs 4.00
29 A:Wolverine,2nd App:New Hobgoblin 9.00
30 KB,O:Rose,C:Daredevil,Capt. America,Wolverine,Punisher . . . 7.00
31 MZ,BMc,V:Kraven 6.00
32 MZ,BMc,V:Kraven 6.00
33 BSz(c),SL,V:Kingpin,Mad Dog Ward,pt.#1 . . . . 4.00
34 SB,A:Watcher 4.00
35 AS,V:Living Brain 4.00
36 AS,V:Phreak Out,I:Tombstone . . 5.00
37 V:Slasher 5.00
38 AS,A:Tombstone,V:Hobgoblin . . 5.00
39 AS,V:Looter(Meteor Man) 4.00
40 AS,V:Cult of Love 4.00
41 AS,V:Cult of Love 4.00
42 AS,V:Cult of Love 4.00
43 AS,V:Cult of Love 4.00
44 AS,V:Warzone,A:Hulk 3.00
45 AS,V:Vulture 3.00
46 A:Dr.Pym,V:Nekra 3.00
47 AS,V:Hobgoblin 4.00
48 AS,O:New Hobgoblin's Demonic Power 11.00
49 VM,V:Drugs 3.00
50 AS,V:Chameleon(double size) . . 5.00
51 MBa,V:Chameleon,Lobo Bros. . . 3.00
52 FS,JR,O:J.Jonah Jameson V:Chameleon 3.00
53 MBa,V:Lobo Bros.,C:Punisher A:Chameleon 3.00
54 AS,V:Chameleon,V:Lobo Bros. . 3.00
55 AS,V:Chameleon,Hammerhead, V:Lobo Bros. 3.00
56 AS,I&O:Skin Head, A:Rocket Racer 3.00
57 AS,D:SkinHead, A:Rocket Racer 3.00
58 AS,V:Grizzly 3.00
59 AS,Acts of Vengeance,V:Titania A:Puma,Cosmic Spider-Man . . . 5.00
60 AS,A of V,V:Goliath 3.00
61 AS,A of V,V:Dragon Man 3.00
62 AS,V:Molten Man 2.00
63 AS,V:Mister Fear 2.00
64 AS,V:Graviton,Titania,Trapster . . 2.00
65 AS,V:Goliath,Trapster,Graviton . . 2.00
66 AS,V:Tombstone,A:G.Goblin . . . 2.50
67 AS,A:GreenGoblin, V:Tombstone 2.50
68 AS,A:GreenGoblin, V:Tombstone 2.50
69 AS,V:Hulk 2.50
70 AS,I:The Spider/Hulk 2.50
71 A:Silver Sable 2.00
72 AM,A:Silver Sable 2.00
73 AS,A:Human Torch, Colossus,Namor 2.00
74 AS,I:Spark,V:Bora 2.00
75 AS,C:New Warriors 2.00
76 AS,Spidey in Ice 2.00
77 AS,V:Firebrand,Inheritor 2.00
78 AS,A:Firebrand,Cloak&Dagger . . 2.00
79 AS,V:Silvermane 2.00
80 AS,V:Silvermane 2.00
81 I:Bloodshed 2.00
82 V:Man Mountain Marko 2.00
83 V:A.I.M. Supersuit 2.00
84 AS,B:Name of the Rose 2.50
85 AS,Name of the Rose 2.00
86 AS,I:Demogoblin 2.50
87 AS,I:Praetorian Guard 2.00
88 AS,Name of the Rose 2.00
89 AS,E:Name of the Rose, I:Bloodrose 2.00
90 AS,30th Ann.,w/hologram, polybagged,V:Mysterio 3.00
90a Gold 2nd printing 2.50
91 AS,V:Whisper And Pulse 2.00
92 AS,V:Foreigner 2.00
93 AS,BMc,V:Hobgoblin,A:Moon Knight,Foreigner 2.00
94 AS,V:Hobgoblin,A:MoonKnight . . 2.00
95 AS,Spirits of Venom#1,A:Venom, J.Blaze,GR,V:Hag & Troll 2.50
96 AS,Spirits of Venom#3, A:G.R, J.Blaze,Venom,Hobgoblin 2.00
97 AS,I:Dr.Trench,V:Bloodrose 2.00
98 AS,V:Bloodrose,Foreigner 2.00
99 I:Night Watch,V:New Enforcer . . 2.00
100 AS,JRu,V:Enforcers,Bloodrose, Kingpin(Alfredo),I:Spider Armor, O:Night Watch,Holografx(c) . . . 4.00
101 AS,Total Carnage,V:Carnage, Shriek,A:Cloak and Dagger, Venom 2.00
102 Total Carnage#6,V:Carnage, A:Venom,Morbius 2.00
103 AS,Maximum Carnage#10, V:Carnage 2.00
104 AS,Infinity Crusade 2.00
105 AS,Infinity Crusade 2.00
106 AS,Infinity Crusade 2.00
107 AS,A:Sandman,Quicksand 2.00
108 B:TKa(s),AS,I:Sandstorm, BU:Cardiac 2.00
109 AS,V:Shocker,A:Night Thrasher, BU:D:Calypso 2.00
110 AS,I:Warrant,A:Lizard 2.00
111 AS,V:Warrant,Lizard 2.00
112 AS,Pursuit#3,V:Chameleon, w/card 2.00
113 AS,A:Gambit,Black Cat,w/cel . . 3.50
113a Newsstand Ed. 2.00
114 AS 2.00
115 AS,V:Facade 2.00
116 AS,V:Facade 2.00
117 Foil(c), flip book with Power & Responsibility #1 . . . . 5.00
117a Newsstand ed. 2.00
118 Spider-clone, V:Venom 3.00
119 Clone,V:Venom 2.50
119a bagged with Milestone rep. Amazing Sp-Man #150,checklist 6.50
120 Web of Life,pt.1 . . . . 2.50
121 Web of Life,pt.3 . . . . 2.50
122 Smoke and Mirrors,pt.1 . . . . 2.50
123 The Price of Truth,pt.2 . . . . 1.50
124 The Mark of Kaine,pt.1 . . . . 1.50
125 R:Gwen Stacy 3.00
125a 3-D Holodisk cover 4.25
126 The Trial of Peter Parker,pt.1 . . 2.00
127 Maximum Clonage,pt.2 . . . . 2.00
128 TDF,Exiled,pt.1 . . . . 2.00
129 Timebomb,pt.2 . . . . 2.00
Ann.#1 V:Future Max 6.00
Ann.#2 AAd,MMi,A:Warlock 8.00
Ann.#3 AS,DP,JRu,JM,BL 4.50
Ann.#4 AS,TM,RLm,Evolutionary Wars,A:Man Thing,V:Slug 5.00
Ann.#5 AS,SD,JS,Atlantis Attacks,A:Fantastic Four 3.50
Ann.#6 SD,JBr,SB,A:Punisher 4.50
Ann.#7 Vibranium Vendetta #3 . . . . 2.50
Ann.#8 Hero Killers#3,A:New Warriors,BU:Venom,Black Cat . 3.00
Ann.#9 CMa,I:Cadre,w/card 3.25
Ann.#10 V:Shriek 3.75
Super Size Spec.#1 Planet of the Symbiotes,pt.5 . . . . 3.95

WEBSPINNERS: TALES OF SPIDER-MAN

Nov., 1998

1 JMD,JR,MZi,A:Mysterio,seq.to Amaz.Sp-M#38, 48-page 3.00
1a signed 19.63
2 JMD,JR,V:J.Jonah Jameson 2.50
2a variant SR cover 2.50
3 JMD,V:Mysterio, concl. 2.50
4 KG,ErS,seq.to Silver Surfer#18 . . 2.50
5 KG,ErS,A:Silver Surfer 2.50
6 KG,ErS,F:Silver Surfer, Psycho-Man & Annihilus 2.50
7 BS,MPn,V:Sandman 2.50
8 BS,MPn,V:Sandman 2.50
9 V:Sandman 2.50
10 V:Chameleon, pt.1 . . . . 2.50
11 V:Chameleon, pt.2 . . . . 2.50
12 conclusion, 48-pg 3.50
13 . . . . 2.50
14 HMe,BS,A:Carnage 2.50
15 V:Vulture 2.50
16 V:Vulture 2.50
17 TDF, black costume 2.50
18 TDF, Silversable 2.50

Weird Wondertales #20
© Marvel Entertainment Group

WEIRD WONDERTALES

Dec., 1973

1 B:Reprints 18.00
2 I Was Kidnapped by a Flying Saucer 12.00
3 The Thing in the Bog 12.00
4 It Lurks Behind the Wall 12.00
5 . . . . 12.00
6 The Man Who Owned a Ghost . 12.00
7 The Apes That Walked like Men 12.00
8 Reap A Deadly Harvest 12.00
9 The Murder Mirror 12.00
10 Mister Morgans Monster 12.00
11 Slaughter in Shrangri-La 10.00
12 The Stars Scream Murder 10.00
13 The Totem Strikes 10.00
14 Witching Circle 10.00
15 . . . . 10.00
16 The Shark 10.00
17 Creature From Krogarr 10.00
18 Krang 10.00
19 A:Dr Druid 10.00
20 The Madness 10.00
21 A:Dr Druid 10.00
22 The World Below,May, 1975. . . 10.00

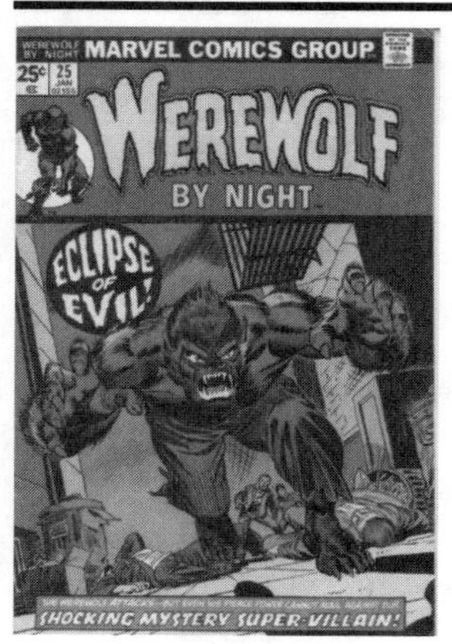

Werewolf by Night #25
© Marvel Entertainment Group

WEREWOLF BY NIGHT
Sept., 1972

1 MP(cont from Marvel Spotlight) FullMoonRise..WerewolfKill. . . 65.00
2 MP,Like a Wild Beast at Bay . . . 30.00
3 MP,Mystery of the Mad Monk . . 20.00
4 MP,The Danger Game 20.00
5 MP,A Life for a Death 20.00
6 MP,Carnival of Fear 15.00
7 MP,JM,Ritual of Blood. 15.00
8 MP,Krogg,Lurker from Beyond . 15.00
9 TS,V:Tatterdemalion 15.00
10 TS,bondage cover 15.00
11 GK,TS,Full Moon..Fear Moon. . 12.00
12 GK,Cry Monster. 12.00
13 MP,ManMonsterCalledTaboo . . 10.00
14 MP,Lo,the Monster Strikes 10.00
15 MP,(new)O:Werewolf, V:Dracula 14.00
16 MP,TS,A:Hunchback of Notre Dame. 10.00
17 Behold the Behemoth 10.00
18 War of the Werewolves 10.00
19 V:Dracula. 11.00
20 The Monster Breaks Free 10.00
21 GK(c),To Cure a Werewolf 7.00
22 GK(c),Face of a Friend 7.00
23 Silver Bullet for a Werewolf 7.00
24 GK(c),V:The Brute 7.00
25 GK(c),Eclipse of Evil 7.00
26 GK(c),A Crusade of Murder 7.00
27 GK(c),Scourge o/t Soul-Beast . . 7.00
28 GK(c),V:Dr.Glitternight 7.00
29 GK(c),V:Dr.Glitternight 7.00
30 GK(c),Red Slash across Midnight 7.00
31 Death in White. 7.00
32 I&O:Moon Knight 75.00
33 Were-Beast..Moon Knight A:Moon Knight(2nd App) 35.00
34 GK(c),TS,House of Evil..House of Death 9.00
35 TS,JS,BWi,Jack Russell vs. Werewolf 9.00
36 Images of Death 9.00
37 BWr(c),BW,A:Moon Knight, Hangman,Dr.Glitternight 10.00
38 . . . . 8.00
39 V:Brother Voodoo 8.00
40 A:Brother Voodoo,V:Dr. Glitternight 8.00
41 V:Fire Eyes 8.00
42 A:IronMan,Birth of a Monster . . . 8.00
43 Tri-Animal Lives,A:Iron Man 8.00
G-Size#2,SD,A:Frankenstein Monster (reprint). 8.00
G-Size#3 GK(c),Transylvania 8.00
G-Size#4 GK(c),A:Morbius 12.00
G-Size#5 GK(c),Peril of Paingloss 7.00

WEREWOLF BY NIGHT
Dec., 1997

1 PJe,F:Jack Russell returns 3.00
2 PJe,Search for wolf Amulet. 3.00
3 PJe,Stuck between man & wolf. . 3.00
4 PJe,to the depths of hell 3.00
5 PJe, confronts demon. 3.00
6 PJe, visit Underworld nightclub . . 3.00
Storyline continues in Strange Tales

WEST COAST AVENGERS
[Limited Series] Sept., 1984

1 BH,A:Shroud,J:Hawkeye,IronMan, WonderMan,Mockingbird,Tigra . 4.00
2 BH,V:Blank. 3.00
3 BH,V:Graviton 2.00
4 BH,V:Graviton 2.00

[Regular Series] 1985–89

1 AM,JSt,V:Lethal Legion 4.00
2 AM,JSt,V:Lethal Legion 3.00
3 AM,JSt,V:Kraven 3.00
4 AM,JSt,A:Firebird,Thing,I:Master Pandemonium 3.00
5 AM,JSt,A:Werewolf,Thing 3.00
6 AM,KB,A:Thing. 3.00
7 AM,JSt,V:Ultron 3.00
8 AM,JSt,V:Rangers,A:Thing 3.00
9 AM,JSt,V:Master Pandemonium . 3.00
10 AM,JSt,V:Headlok,Griffen. 3.00
11 AM,JSt,A:Nick Fury 2.50
12 AM,JSt,V:Graviton 2.50
13 AM,JSt,V:Graviton 2.50
14 AM,JSt,V:Pandemonium 2.50
15 AM,JSt,A:Hellcat 2.50
16 AM,JSt,V:Tiger Shark, Whirlwind 2.50
17 AM,JSt,V:Dominus' Minions 2.50
18 AM,JSt,V:The Wild West 2.50
19 AM,JSt,A:Two Gun Kid 2.50
20 AM,JSt,A:Rawhide Kid. 2.50
21 AM,JSt,A:Dr.Pym,Moon Knight. . 2.50
22 AM,JSt,A:Fant.Four,Dr.Strange, Night Rider. 2.00
23 AM,RT,A:Phantom Rider 2.00
24 AM,V:Dominus. 2.00
25 AM,V:Abomination 2.00
26 AM,V:Zodiac 2.00
27 AM,V:Zodiac 2.00
28 AM,V:Zodiac 2.00
29 AM,V:Taurus,A:Shroud. 2.00
30 AM,C:Composite Avenger 2.00
31 AM,V:Arkon 2.00
32 AM,TD,V:Yetrigar,J:Wasp 2.00
33 AM,O:Ant-Man,Wasp; V:Madam X,El Toro 2.00
34 AM,V:Quicksilver,J:Vision & Scarlet Witch 2.00
35 AM,V:Dr.Doom,Quicksilver. 2.00
36 AM,V:The Voice. 2.00
37 V:The Voice,A:Mantis. 2.00
38 AM,TMo,V:Defiler 2.00
39 AM,V:Swordsman 2.00
40 AM,MGu,V:NightShift, A:Shroud 2.00
41 TMo,I:New Phantom Rider, L:Moon Knight 2.00
42 JBy,Visionquest#1,V:Ultron 2.50
43 JBy,Visionquest#2,. 2.25
44 JBy,Visionquest#3,J:USAgent . . 2.00
45 JBy,Visionquest#4, I:New Vision. 2.25
46 JBy,I:Great Lakes Avengers. . . . 2.00

West Coast Avengers #1
© Marvel Entertainment Group

Ann. #1 MBr,GI,V:Zodiak 2.25
Ann. #2 AM,A:SilverSurfer,V:Death, Collector,R:Grandmaster 2.00
Ann. #3 AM,RLm,TD,Evolutionary Wars,R:Giant Man 3.50
Becomes:

AVENGERS WEST COAST

WESTERN GUNFIGHTERS
[2nd series] August, 1970

1 JK,JB,DAy,B:Ghost Rider A:Fort Rango,The Renegades Gunhawk 30.00
2 HT(c),DAy,JMn,O:Nightwind, V:Tarantula 22.00
3 DAy,V:Hurricane(reprint) 22.00
4 HT(c),DAy,TS,B:Gunhawk, Apache Kid,A;Renegades . . . 22.00
5 DAy,FrG,A:Renegades 22.00
6 HT(c),DAy,SSh,Death of Ghost Rider. 20.00
7 HT(c),DAy,SSh,O:Ghost Rider retold,E:Ghost Rider,Gunhawk 20.00
8 DAy,SSh,B:Black Rider,Outlaw Kid(rep) 15.00
9 DW,Revenge rides the Range. . 15.00
10 JK,JMn,O:Black Rider,B:Matt Slade,E:Outlaw Kid. 15.00
11 JK,Duel at Dawn 15.00
12 JMn,O:Matt Slade 16.00
13 Save the Gold Coast Expires . . 15.00
14 JSo(c),Outlaw Town. 15.00
15 E:Matt Slade,Showdown in Outlaw Canyon. 15.00
16 B:Kid Colt,Shoot-out in Silver City 15.00
17 thru 20. . . . . @15.00
21 thru 24 . . . . @10.00
25 . . . . 10.00
26 F:Kid Colt,Gun-Slinger, Apache Kid. 10.00
27 thru 32. . . . . @10.00
33 Nov., 1975. . . . . 10.00

WESTERN KID
[1st Series] Dec., 1954

1 JR,B:Western Kid,O:Western Kid (Tex Dawson) 150.00
2 JMn,JR,Western Adventure . . . 75.00
3 JMn(c),JR,Gunfight(c) 60.00
4 JMn(c),JR,The Badlands 60.00

5 JR 60.00
6 JR 60.00
7 JR 60.00
8 JR 60.00
9 JR,AW 75.00
10 JR,AW,Man in the Middle. 75.00
11 thru 16 . . . . @50.00
17 August, 1957 . . . . 50.00

[2nd Series] Dec., 1971–Aug., 1972

1 Reprints 20.00
2 . . . . 15.00
3 AW. 20.00
4 . . . . 15.00
5 . . . . 15.00

WESTERN OUTLAWS

Atlas Feb., 1954—Aug., 1957

1 JMn(c),RH,BP,The Greenville Gallows,Hanging(c) 150.00
2 . . . . 90.00
3 thru 10 . . . . @60.00
11 AW 60.00
12 . . . . 55.00
13 MB 60.00
14 AW 65.00
15 AT,GT 60.00
16 BP. 50.00
17 . . . . 55.00
18 . . . . 50.00
19 . . . . 60.00
20 and 21 . . . . @55.00

WESTERN OUTLAWS & SHERIFFS See: BEST WESTERN

WESTERN TALES OF BLACK RIDER See: ALL WINNERS COMICS

WESTERN TEAM-UP

Nov., 1973

1 Rawhide Kid/Dakota Kid 2.00

WESTERN THRILLERS

Nov., 1954

1 JMn,Western tales 125.00
2 . . . . 75.00
3 . . . . 75.00
4 . . . . 75.00

Becomes:

COWBOY ACTION

5 JMn(c),The Prairie Kid 75.00
6 . . . . 50.00
7 . . . . 50.00
9 . . . . 50.00
10 . . . . 50.00
11 MN,AW,Ther Manhunter March, 1956. . . . . 75.00

Becomes:

QUICK-TRIGGER WESTERN

12 Bill Larson Strikes 75.00
13 The Man From Cheyenne 85.00
14 BEv,RH(c) 60.00
15 AT 50.00
16 JK 45.00
17 GT. 45.00
18 GM 45.00
19 JSe 40.00

WESTERN WINNERS See: ALL WINNERS COMICS

WHAT IF?

[1st Regular Series] Feb., 1977

1 Spider-Man joined Fant.Four. . . 18.00
2 GK(c),Hulk had Banner brain . . . 9.00
3 GK,KJ,F:Avengers 6.00
4 GK(c),F:Invaders 6.00
5 F:Captain America 6.00
6 F:Fantastic Four 6.00
7 GK(c),F:Spider-Man 6.00
8 GK(c),F:Daredevil. 5.50
9 JK(c),F:Avengers of the '50s. . . . 6.00
10 JB,F:Thor 5.00
11 JK,F:FantasticFour. 5.00
12 F:Hulk 5.00
13 JB,Conan Alive Today 6.00
14 F:Sgt. Fury 5.00
15 CI,F:Nova 5.00
16 F:Master of Kung Fu 5.00
17 CI,F:Ghost Rider 5.00
18 TS,F:Dr.Strange. 4.00
19 PB,F:Spider-Man 5.00
20 F:Avengers 4.00
21 GC,F:Sub-Mariner 4.00
22 F:Dr.Doom. 4.00
23 JB,F:Hulk. 4.00
24 GK,RB,Gwen Stacy had lived . . 5.00
25 F:Thor,Avengers,O:Mentor. 4.00
26 JBy(c),F:Captain America 4.00
27 FM(c),Phoenix hadn't died 10.00
28 FM,F:Daredevil,Ghost Rider. . . 10.00
29 MG(c),F:Avengers 4.00
30 RB,F:Spider-Man. 10.00
31 Wolverine killed the Hulk 15.00
32 Avengers lost to Korvac. 3.50
33 BL,Dazzler herald of Galactus . . 3.50
34 FH,FM,JBy,BSz:Humor issue. . . 3.50
35 FM,Elektra had lived 6.00
36 JBy,Fant.Four had no powers . . 3.00
37 F:Thing,Beast,Silver Surfer 3.50
38 F:Daredevil,Captain America . . . 3.00
39 Thor had fought Conan 3.00
40 F:Dr.Strange 3.00
41 F:Sub-Mariner 3.50
42 F:Fantastic Four 3.00
43 F:Conan 3.00
44 F:Captain America. 3.00
45 F:Hulk,Berserk. 3.50

What If #35
© Marvel Entertainment Group

46 Uncle Ben had lived. 5.00
47 F:Thor,Loki 3.00
Spec.#1 F:Iron Man,Avengers. 4.00
Best of What IF? rep.#1,#24, #27,#28 . . . . 12.95

[2nd Regular Series]

1 RWi,MG,The Avengers had lost the Evolutionary War 5.00
2 GCa,Daredevil Killed Kingpin, A:Hobgoblin, The Rose 4.00
3 Capt.America Hadn't Given Up Costume,A:Avengers 3.50
4 MBa,Spider-Man kept Black Costume,A:Avengers,Hulk 4.50
5 Vision Destroyed Avengers, A:Wonder Man 3.50
6 RLm,X-Men Lost Inferno, A:Dr.Strange 6.00
7 RLd,Wolverine Joined Shield, A:Nick Fury,Black Widow 7.00
8 Iron Man Lost The Armor Wars, A:Ant Man 3.50
9 RB,New X-Men Died 6.00
10 MZ(c),BMc,Punisher's Family Didn't Die,A:Kingpin 3.00
11 TM(c),JV,SM,Fant.Four had the Same Powers,A:Nick Fury 3.50
12 JV,X-Men Stayed in Asgard, A:Thor,Hela 3.00
13 JLe(c),Prof.X Became Juggernaut,A:X-Men. 3.50
14 RLm(c),Capt.Marvel didn't die A:Silver Surfer 3.00
15 GCa,Fant.Four Lost Trial of Galactus,A:Gladiator 3.00
16 Wolverine Battled Conan, A:X-Men,Red Sonja 5.00
17 Kraven Killed Spider-Man, A:Daredevil,Captain America . . 3.00
18 LMc,Fant.Four fought Dr.Doom before they gained powers 2.50
19 RW,Vision took over Earth, A:Avengers,Dr.Doom 2.50
20 Spider-Man didn't marry Mary Jane,A:Venom,Kraven 3.00
21 Spider-Man married Black Cat, A:Vulture,Silver Sable. 2.50
22 RLm,Silver Surfer didn't escape Earth,A:F.F,Mephisto,Thanos . . 4.00
23 New X-Men never existed, A:Eric the Red,Lilandra. 2.50
24 Wolverine Became Lord of Vampires,A:Punisher 3.00
25 Marvel Heroes lost Atlantis Attacks,double size 3.25
26 LMc,Punisher Killed Daredevil, A:Spider-Man. 2.50
27 Submariner Joined Fantastic Four,A:Dr. Doom 2.00
28 RW,Capt.America led Army of Super-Soldiers,A:Submariner . . 2.00
29 RW,Capt.America formed the Avengers 2.00
30 Inv.Woman's 2nd Child had lived,A:Fantastic Four. 2.00
31 Spider-Man/Captain Universe Powers. 2.00
32 Phoenix Rose Again,pt.1 . . . . . . 2.00
33 Phoenix Rose Again,pt.2 . . . . . . 2.00
34 Humor Issue 2.00
35 B:Time Quake,F.F. vs.Dr. Doom & Annihilus. 2.00
36 Cosmic Avengers,V:Guardians of the Galaxy 2.00
37 X-Vampires,V:Dormammu 2.00
38 Thor was prisoner of Set 2.00
39 E:Time Quake,Watcher saved the Universe. 2.00
40 Storm remained A thief? 2.00
41 JV,Avengers fought Galactus . . . 2.25
42 KWe,Spidey kept extra arms . . . 2.00

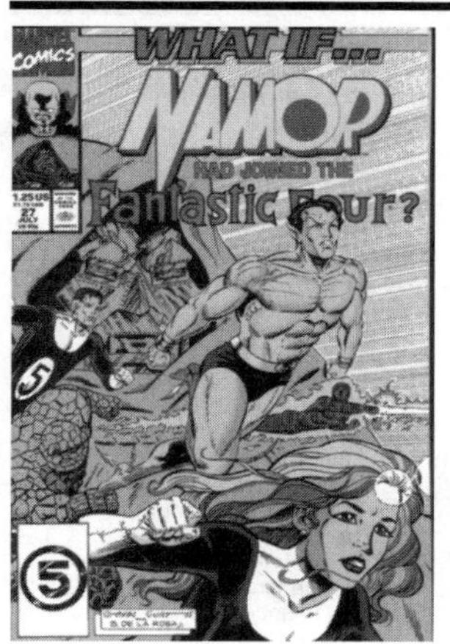

What If, Vol. 2, #27
© Marvel Entertainment Group

43 Wolverine married Mariko 2.00
44 Punisher possessedby Venom . . 2.00
45 Barbara Ketch became G.R. . . . 2.00
46 Cable Killed Prof.X,Cyclops & Jean Grey 2.00
47 Magneto took over USA. 2.00
48 Daredevil Saved Nuke 2.00
49 Silver Surfer had Inf.Gauntlet? . . 2.00
50 Hulk killed Wolverine 4.00
51 PCu,Punisher is Capt.America. . 2.00
52 BHi,Wolverine led Alpha Flight. . 2.25
53 F:Iron Man,Hulk. 2.00
54 F:Death's Head 2.00
55 LKa(s),Avengers lose G.Storm. . 2.00
56 Avengers lose G.Storm#2 . . . . 2.00
57 Punisher a member of SHIELD . 2.00
58 Punisher kills SpM. 2.00
59 Wolverine lead Alpha Flight 2.00
60 RoR,Scott & Jean's Wedding . . . 2.00
61 Spider-Man's Parents 2.00
62 Woverine vs Weapon X 2.25
63 F:War Machine,Iron Man 2.00
64 Iron Man sold out. 2.25
65 Archangel fell from Grace 2.00
66 Rogue and Thor 2.00
67 Cap.America returns 2.00
68 Captain America story 2.00
69 Stryfe Killed X-Men 2.00
70 Silver Surfer 2.00
71 The Hulk 2.00
72 Parker Killed Burglar 2.00
73 Daredevil,Kingpin. 2.00
74 Sinister Formed X-Men 2.00
75 Gen-X's Blink had lived 2.00
76 Flash Thompson Spider-Man. . . 2.00
77 Legion had killed Magneto 2.00
78 FF had stayed together 2.00
79 Storm had Phoenix's Power. . . . 2.00
80 KGa,Hulk was Cured 2.00
81 Age of Apocalypse didn't end. . . 2.00
82 WML,J.JonahJameson adopted Spider-Man. 2.00
83 . . . . . . 2.00
84 . . . . . . 2.00
85 Magneto Ruled all mutants 2.00
86 . . . . . . 2.00
87 . . . . . . 2.00
88 . . . . . . 2.00
89 . . . . . . 2.00
90 . . . . . . 2.00
91 F:Hulk, nice guy, Banner violent. 2.00
92 F:Cannonball,Husk 2.00
93 F:Wolverine. 2.00
94 JGz,F:Juggernaut 2.00
95 IV,F:Ghost Rider 2.00
96 CWo,F:Quicksilver, ... 2.00
97 F:Black Knight. 2.00
98 F:Nightcrawler & Rogue. 2.00
99 F:Black Cat 2.00
100 IV,KJ,F:Gambit & Rogue, 48pg 3.00
101 ATi,F:Archangel 2.00
102 F:Daredevil's Dad 2.00
103 DaF,F:Captain America 2.00
104 F:Silver Surver,ImpossibleMan. 2.00
105 TDF,RF,F:Spider-Man and Mary Jane's Daughter. 25.00
106 TDF,F:X-Men,Gambit sentenced to death. 2.00
107 TDF,RF,BSz,F:Thor 2.00
108 TDF,F:The Avengers 2.00
109 TA,F:Fantastic Four 2.00
110 TDF,F:Wolverine 2.00
111 TDF,F:Wolverine. 2.00
112 F:Ka-Zar 2.00
113 F:Iron Man, Dr. Strange, ... 2.00
114 F:Secret Wars, 32-page, final issue. 2.50
Minus 1 Spec., AOI, flashback, F:Bishop. 2.00
TPB Best of What If? 12.95

WHAT THE -?!
[Parodies]
August, 1988

1 . . . . . . 5.00
2 JBy,JOy,AW, ... 4.00
3 TM, ... 5.00
4 . . . . . . 3.00
5 EL,JLe,WPo,Wolverine 5.00
6 Wolverine,Punisher. 3.00
7 . . . . . . 2.50
8 DK 2.50
9 . . . . . . 2.00
10 JBy,X-Men,Dr.Doom, Cap. America 2.00
11 DK,RLd(part) 2.00
12 Conan, F.F.,Wolverine. 2.00
13 Silver Burper,F.F.,Wolverine. . . . 2.00
14 Spittle-Man 2.00
15 Capt.Ultra,Wolverina 2.00
16 Ant Man,Watcher 2.00
17 Wulverean/Pulverizer,Hoagg/ Spider-Ham,SleepGawker,F.F. . 2.00
18 . . . . . . 2.00
19 . . . . . . 2.00
20 Infinity Wart Crossover. 2.00
21 Weapon XX,Toast Rider. 2.00
22 F:Echs Farce. 2.00
23 . . . . . . 2.00
24 Halloween issue 2.00
25 . . . . . . 2.00
26 Spider-Ham 2099 . . . . . . 2.00
Summer Spec. 2.50
Fall Spec. 2.50

WHERE CREATURES ROAM
July, 1970—Sept., 1971

1 JK,SD,DAy,B:Reprints The Brute That Walks. 25.00
2 JK,SD,Midnight/Monster 15.00
3 JK,SD,DAy,Thorg 15.00
4 JK,SD,Vandoom 15.00
5 JK,SD,Gorgilla 15.00
6 JK,SD,Zog 15.00
7 SD 15.00
8 The Mummy's Secret,E:Reprints 15.00

Where Monsters Dwell #31
© Marvel Entertainment Group

WHERE MONSTERS DWELL
Jan., 1970

1 B:Reprints,Cyclops 30.00
2 Sporr 20.00
3 Grottu 20.00
4 . . . . . . 20.00
5 Taboo 20.00
6 Groot 20.00
7 Rommbu 20.00
8 The Four-Armed Men 20.00
9 Bumbu 20.00
10 Monster That Walks Like A Man. 20.00
11 Gruto 15.00
12 Orogo 15.00
13 The Thing That Crawl 15.00
14 The Green Thing 15.00
15 Kraa- The Inhuman 15.00
16 Beware the Son Of Goom 15.00
17 The Hidden Vampires 15.00
18 The Mask of Morghum. 15.00
19 The Insect Man 15.00
20 Klagg 15.00
21 Fin Fang Foom 15.00
22 Elektro. 15.00
23 The Monster Waits For Me. . . . 15.00
24 The Things on Easter Island . . 15.00
25 The Ruler of the Earth 15.00
26 . . . . . . 15.00
27 . . . . . . 15.00
28 Droom,The Living Lizard 15.00
29 thru 37 Reprints . . . . . . @15.00
38 Reprints,Oct., 1975 . . . . . . 15.00

WHIP WILSON
See: BLAZE CARSON

WILD
Atlas Feb., 1954

1 BEv,JMn,Charlie Chan Parody 200.00
2 BEv,RH,JMn,Witches(c) 125.00
3 CBu(c),BEv,RH,JMn, ... 100.00
4 GC,Didja Ever See a Cannon Brawl. 100.00
5 RH,JMn,August, 1954 . . . . . . 100.00

MARVEL

MARVEL

WILD CARDS
Epic Sept., 1990
1 JG 5.50
2 JG,V:Jokers 4.50
3 A:Turtle 4.50

WILDC.A.T.S/X-MEN: THE DARK AGE
Dec., 1997
1-shot MtB,WEI,V:Daemonites & Sentinels, 48pg 4.50
1a variant cover MGo 4.50

WILD THING
Marvel UK 1993
1 A:Virtual Reality Venom and Carnage 3.00
2 A:VR Venom and Carnage 2.00
3 A:Shield 2.00
4 . . . . 2.00
5 Virtual Reality Gangs 2.00
6 Virtual Reality Villians 2.00
7 V:Trask. 2.00
8 . . . . 2.00
9 . . . . 2.00
10 . . . . 2.00
11 . . . . 2.00
12 . . . . 2.00
13 . . . . 2.00

WILD THING
Aug., 1999
1 RLm,AM,LHa,F:Wolverine's daughter Rina 2.00
2A RLm,AM,LHa,Bloody Reunions 2.00
2B variant AW (c) 2.00
3 RLm,AM,LHa,A:Rina 2.00
4 RLm,AM,LHa 2.00
5 RLm,AM,LHa,V:Robot monster. . 2.00

WILD WEST
Spring, 1948
1 SSh(c),B:Two Gun Kids,Tex Taylor,Arizona Annie 250.00
2 SSh(c),CCb, Captain Tootsie . 200.00

Becomes:

WILD WESTERN
3 SSh(c),B:Tex Morgan,Two Gun Kid,Tex Taylor,Arizona Annie 200.00
4 Rh,SSh,CCB,Capt. Tootsie. A:Kid Colt,E:Arizona Annie . . 150.00
5 RH,CCB,Captain Tootsie A;Black Rider,Blaze Carson . 150.00
6 A:Blaze Carson,Kid Colt 100.00
7 . . . . 100.00
8 RH 100.00
9 Ph(c),B:Black Rider 150.00
10 Ph(c) 175.00
11 . . . . 100.00
12 . . . . 100.00
13 . . . . 100.00
14 . . . . 100.00
15 . . . . 125.00
16 thru 20 . . . . @100.00
21 thru 29 . . . . @85.00
30 JKa 85.00
31 thru 40 . . . . @55.00
41 thru 47 . . . . @50.00
48 AW 75.00
49 thru 53 . . . . @50.00
54 AW 75.00
55 AW 75.00
56 and 57 Sept. 1957 . . . . @45.00

William Shatner's Tek World #12
© Marvel Entertainment Group

WILLIAM SHATNER'S TEK WORLD
1992–94
1 LS,Novel adapt. 2.25
2 LS,Novel adapt.cont. 2.00
3 LS,Novel adapt.cont. 2.00
4 LS,Novel adapt.cont. 2.00
5 LS,Novel adapt.concludes 2.00
6 LS,V:TekLords 2.00
7 E:The Angel 2.00
8 . . . . 2.00
9 . . . . 2.00
10 . . . . 2.00
11 thru 17. . . . . 2.00
18 . . . . 2.00
19 Sims of the Father#1 . . . . 2.00
20 Sims of the Father#2 . . . . 2.00
21 Who aren't in Heaven 2.00
22 Father and Guns 2.00
23 We'll be Right Back 2.00
24 . . . . 2.00

WILLIE COMICS
See: IDEAL COMICS

WILLOW
August, 1988
1 Movie adapt.. . . . . 2.00
2 Movie adapt.. . . . . 2.00
3 Movie adapt,Oct., 1988. . . . . 2.00

WITNESS, THE
Sept., 1948
1 . . . . 1,400.00

WOLFPACK
August, 1988
1 I:Wolfpack 2.00
2 thru 11 . . . . @2.00
12 July, 1988 . . . . 2.00

WOLVERINE
[Limited Series] Sept., 1982
1 B:CCl(s),FM,JRu,A:Mariko, I:Shingen 42.00
2 FM,JRu,A:Mariko,I:Yukio. 30.00
3 FM,JRu,A:Mariko,Yukio. 30.00
4 B:CCl(s),FM,JRu,A:Mariko, D:Shingen 32.00

[Regular Series] 1988
1 JB,AW,V:Banipur 25.00
2 JB,KJ,V:Silver Samurai. 12.00
3 JB,AW,V:Silver Samurai 10.00
4 JB,AW,I:Roughouse, Bloodsport 10.00
5 JB,AW,V:Roughouse, Bloodsport 10.00
6 JB,AW,V:Roughouse, Bloodsport 9.00
7 JB,A:Hulk 8.00
8 JB,A:Hulk 8.00
9 GC,Old Wolverine Story 8.00
10 JB,BSz,V:Sabretooth (1st battle) 24.00
11 JB,BSz,B:Gehenna Stone 7.00
12 JB,BSz,Gehenna Stone. 7.00
13 JB,BSz,Gehenna Stone. 7.00
14 JB,BSz,Gehenna Stone. 7.00
15 JB,BSz,Gehenna Stone. 7.00
16 JB,BSz,E:Gehenna Stone 7.00
17 JBy,KJ,V:Roughouse 6.00
18 JBy,KJ,V:Roughouse 6.00
19 JBy,KJ,A of V,I:La Bandera 6.00
20 JBy,KJ,A of V,V:Tigershark. 5.00
21 JBy,KJ,V:Geist. 5.00
22 JBy,KJ,V:Geist,Spore 5.00
23 JBy,KJ,V:Geist,Spore. 5.00
24 GC,`Snow Blind' 4.00
25 JB,O:Wolverine(part) 4.00
26 KJ,Return to Japan 4.00
27 thru 30 Lazarus Project 4.00
31 MS,DGr,A:Prince o'Mandripoor . 4.00
32 MS,DGr,V:Ninjas 4.00
33 MS,Wolverine in Japan 4.00
34 MS,DGr,Wolverine in Canada . . 4.00
35 MS,DGr,A:Puck 4.00
36 MS,DGr,A:Puck,Lady D'strike. . . 4.00
37 MS,DGr,V:Lady Deathstrike 4.00
38 MS,DGr,A:Storm,I:Elsie Dee . . . 4.00
39 MS,DGr,Wolverine Vs. Clone. . . 4.00
40 MS,DGr,Wolverine Vs. Clone. . . 4.00
41 MS,DGr,R:Sabretooth, A:Cable 7.00
41a 2nd printing 2.25
42 MS,DGr,A:Sabretooth,Cable . . . 5.00
42a 2nd printing 2.00
43 MS,DGr,A:Sabretooth,C:Cable. . 4.00
44 LSn,DGr 3.50
45 MS,DGr,A:Sabretooth 4.00
46 MS,DGr,A:Sabretooth 4.00
47 V:Tracy 3.50
48 LHa(s),MS,DGr,B:Shiva Scenario. 3.50
49 LHa(s),MS,DGr,. 3.50
50 LHa(s),MS,DGr,A:X-Men,Nick Fury, I:Shiva,Slash-Die Cut(c) 5.50
51 MS,DGr,A:Mystique,X-Men 3.00
52 MS,DGr,A:Mystique,V:Spiral . . . 3.00
53 MS,A:Mystique,V:Spiral,Mojo . . . 3.00
54 A:Shatterstar 3.00
55 MS,V:Cylla,A:Gambit,Sunfire . . . 3.00
56 MS,A:Gambit,Sunfire,V:Hand, Hydra. 3.00
57 MS,D:Lady Mariko,A:Gambit . . . 3.50
58 A:Terror 3.00
59 A:Terror 3.00
60 Sabretooth vs.Shiva, I:John Wraith 3.00
61 MT,History of Wolverine and Sabretooth,A:John Wraith. 3.00
62 MT,A:Sabretooth,Silver Fox 3.00
63 MT,V:Ferro,D:Silver Fox. 3.00
64 MPa,V:Ferro,Sabretooth 3.00
65 MT,A:Professor X. 3.00
66 MT,A:X-Men. 3.00
67 MT,A:X-Men. 3.00
68 MT,V:Epsilon Red 3.00
69 DT,A:Rogue,V:Sauron,tie-in to

X-Men#300 . . . . 3.00
70 DT,Sauron,A:Rogue,Jubilee 3.00
71 DT,V:Sauron,Brain Child, A:Rogue, Jubilee 3.00
72 DT,Sentinels 3.00
73 DT,V:Sentinels 3.00
74 ANi,V:Sentinels 3.00
75 AKu,Hologram(c),Wolv.has Bone Claws,leaves X-Men 6.00
76 DT(c),B:LHa(s),A:Deathstrike, Vindicator,C:Puck 3.00
77 AKu,A:Vindicator,Puck,V:Lady Deathstrike. 3.00
78 AKu,V:Cylla,Bloodscream 3.00
79 AKu,V:Cyber,I:Zoe Culloden. . . . 3.00
80 IaC,V:Cyber, ... 3.00
81 IaC,V:Cyber,A:Excalibur. 3.00
82 AKu,BMc,A:Yukio,Silver Samurai 3.00
83 AKu,A:Alpha Flight. 3.00
84 A:Alpha Flight 3.00
85 Phalanx Covenant, Final Sanction, V:Phalanx,holografx(c) 4.00
85a newsstand ed. 5.00
86 AKu,V:Bloodscream. 3.00
87 AKu,deluxe,V:Juggernaut. 3.00
87a newsstand ed. 3.00
88 AKu,deluxe ed. 3.00
88a newsstand ed. 3.00
89 deluxe ed. 3.00
89a newsstand ed. 2.00
90 V:Sabretooth, deluxe ed. 4.00
90a newsstand ed. 2.00
91 LHa,Logan's future unravels . . . 3.00
92 LHa,AKu,DGr,A:Sabretooth 3.00
93 R:Cyber. 3.00
94 Feral Wolverine 3.00
95 LHa,AKu,DGr,V:Dark Riders . . . 3.00
96 LHa,Aku,DGr,Death of Cyber. . . 3.00
97 LHa,AKu,DGr,A:Genesis 3.00
98 LHa,AKu,F:Genesis 3.00
99 . . . . 3.00
100 LHa,AKu,DG,A:Elektra;double-size, Foil Hologram cover 10.00
100a regular edition 4.00
101 LHa,AKu,A:Elektra. 3.00
102 LHa 3.00
103 LHa,Elektra,A:Onslaught 3.00
104 LHa,Gateway, Onslaught 3.00
105 LHa,Gateway, Elektra 3.00
106 LHa 3.00
107 LHa,VS,prologue to Elektra#1 . 3.00
108 LHa,back to Tokyo,A:Yukio. . . . 3.00
109 LHa,DG, ... 3.00
110 LHa,DG,Who's spying on Logan. 3.00
111 LHa,DG,Logan moves to NYC . 3.00
112 LHa,DG,Logan in NYC. 3.00
113 LHa,R:Ogun,A:Lady Deathstrike & Spiral 3.00
114 LHa,back in costume,V:Cyborg Donald Pierce 3.00
115 LHa,Zero Tolerance,V:Bastion . 3.00
116 LHa,Zero Tolerance, ... 3.00
117 LHa,Zero Tolerance, V:Prime Sentinels 3.00
118 LHa,Zero Tolerance aftermath . 3.00
119 WEl,Pt.1 (of 4) 3.00
120 WEl,The White Ghost 3.00
121 WEl,Not Yet Dead, pt.3 . . . . . . 3.00
122 WEl,Not Yet Dead, pt.4 . . . . . . 3.00
123 TDF,DCw,R:Roughouse, Bloodscream 3.00
124 TDF,DCw,A:Captain America, V:Rascal 3.00
125 CCl,V:Viper,48pg 8.00
126 CCl,V:Sabretooth. 3.00
127 CCl,Sabretooth takes over 3.00
128 CCl,V:Hydra, The Hand 3.00
129 TDz,A:Wendigo 3.00
130 TDz,V:Viper 3.00

Wolverine #125
© Marvel Entertainment Group

131 TDz,V:Viper 3.00
132 TDz,Halloween in SalemCenter 3.00
133 EL,JMs,F:Warbird 3.00
133a variant EL cover (1:4). 3.00
134 EL,JMs,V:Big Apple heroes . . . 3.00
135 EL,JMs,Joins Starjammers. . . . 3.00
136 EL,JMs,on prison planet. 3.00
137 EL,JMs,V:The Collector 3.00
138 EL,JMs,Great Escape concl. . . 3.00
139 EL,A:Cable 3.00
140 EL,Xavier paranoid 3.00
141 EL,Wolverine paranoid. 3.00
142 EL,R:Alpha Flight. 3.00
143 EL,A:Alpha Flight. 3.00
144 EL,A:Hercules,V:Leader. 3.00
145 EL,25th Anniv. 48-pg.. . . . . 3.00
145A Foil Stamped (c) 4.00
146 EL 2.50
147 FaN. 2.50
148 EL,Ages of Apocalypse,pt.3 . . . 2.50
149 EL,mutant no more? 2.50
150 X-Men: Revolution 3.00
150a variant (c) 3.00
151 SSr,V:Lord Haan 2.25
152 SSr,Lord Haan, Gom 2.25
153 SSr,Kia 2.25
154 RLd,ErS,Deadpool. 2.25
155 RLd,Watchtower,Siryn 2.25
156 RLd,IaC,F:Spider-Man 2.25
157 RLd,IaC,F:Spider-Man 2.25
Ann. '97 JOs,V:Volk 3.00
Ann.1999 F:Deadpool, 48-pg. 3.50
Spec. '95 LHa,F:Nightcrawler 3.95
Minus 1 Spec., LHa,CNn, flashback, F:Weapon X. 2.25
Global Jeapordy,PDd(s) 2.95
Save the Tiger,rep. 2.95
Winter Spec. MWa B&W. 3.00
Jungle Adventure MMi,(Deluxe) . . . 5.50
SC Acts of Vengeance, rep. 6.95
Bloodlust (one shot),AD V:Siberian Were-Creatures. . . . 6.00
Killing, KSW,JNR 5.95
Rahne of Terror, C:Cable 8.00
GNv Bloody ChoicesJB,A:N.Fury . 12.95
Typhoid's Kiss,rep. 6.95
Inner Fury,BSz,V:Nanotech Machines 6.25
GN Scorpio Rising, T.U.Fury. 5.95
GN Black Rio, 48-page. 6.00
HC Weapon X 19.95
TPB Wolverine rep Marvel Comics Presents #1-#10. . . . . 12.95
TPB Triumphs & Tragedies. 16.95
TPB Not Dead Yet 14.95
TPB Essential Wolverine, vol.1 . . . 14.95

WOLVERINE & PUNISHER: DAMAGING EVIDENCE

1993

1 B:CP(s),GEr,A:Kingpin 2.25
2 GEr,A:Kingpin,Sniper 2.25
3 GEr,Last issue 2.25

WOLVERINE: DAYS OF FUTURE PAST

Oct., 1997

1 (of 3) JFM,JoB,JHo, Logan & Magneto in far future 2.50
2 JFM,JoB,JHo,with Jubilee. 2.50
3 JFM,JoB,JHo,V:Council of the Chosen, concl. 2.50

WOLVERINE: DOOMBRINGER

Nov., 1997

1-shot DgM,JP,F:Silver Samurai . . . 3.00

WOLVERINE ENCYCLOPEDIA

Vol. 1 AKu(c) 48pg. 5.95
Vol. 2 48pg 5.95
Vol. 3 48pg 5.95

WOLVERINE/GAMBIT: VICTIMS

1995

1 Takes Place in London 3.00
2 Is Wolverine the Killer?. 3.00
3 V:Mastermind 3.00
4 conclusion 3.00

WOLVERINE/PUNISHER: REVELATION

Apr., 1999

1 (of 4) TSg,PtL,Revelation 3.00
1a signed 30.00
2 TSg,PtL,V:Revelation 3.00
3 TSg,PtL,V:Revelation 3.00
4 TsG,PtL,V:Revelation,concl. 3.00
TPB rep.. . . . . 14.95

WOLVERINE SAGA

Sept., 1989

1 RLd(c), ... 6.50
2 . . . . 5.00
3 . . . . 5.00
4 Dec., 1989 . . . . 5.00

WONDER DUCK

Sept., 1949

1 Whale(c) 50.00
2 . . . . 33.00
3 March, 1950 . . . . 33.00

WONDERMAN

March, 1986

1 KGa,one-shot special 3.00

WONDER MAN

Sept., 1991

1 B:GJ(s),JJ,V:Goliath 2.50

MARVEL

2 JJ,A:West Coast Avengers 2.00
3 JJ,V:Abominatrix,I:Spider 2.00
4 JJ,I:Splice,A:Spider. 2.00
5 JJ,A:Beast,V:Rampage. 2.00
6 JJ,A:Beast,V:Rampage. 2.00
7 JJ,Galactic Storm,pt.4,
A:Hulk & Rich Jones. 2.00
8 JJ,GalacticStorm,pt.11,A:Vision. . 2.00
9 JJ,GalacticStorm,pt.18,A:Vision . 2.00
10 JJ,V:Khmer Rouge. 2.00
11 V:Angkor 2.00
12 V:Angkor 2.00
13 Infinity War 2.00
14 Infinity War,V:Warlock 2.00
15 Inf.War,V:Doppleganger 2.00
16 JJ,I:Armed Response,
A:Avengers West Coast 2.00
17 JJ,A:Avengers West Coast. 2.00
18 V:Avengers West Coast. 2.00
19 . . . . 2.00
20 V:Splice,Rampage. 2.00
21 V:Splice,Rampage. 2.00
22 JJ,V:Realm of Death 2.00
23 JJ,A:Grim Reaper,Mephisto 2.00
24 JJ,V:Grim Reaper,Goliath. 2.00
25 JJ,N:Wonder Man,D:Grim Reaper,
V:Mephisto 3.25
26 A:Hulk,C:Furor,Plan Master 2.00
27 A:Hulk 2.00
28 RoR,A:Spider-Man. 2.00
29 RoR,A:Spider-Man. 2.00
30 V:Hate Monger 2.00
31 . . . . 2.00
32 . . . . 2.00
33 . . . . 2.00
Spec.#1 (1985),KGa. 3.00
Ann.#1 System Bytes #3 . . . . 2.25
Ann.#2 I:Hit-Maker,w/card. 2.95

WORLD CHAMPIONSHIP WRESTLING

1 F:Lex Luger,Sting 2.00
2 . . . . 2.00
3 . . . . 2.00
4 Luger Vs El Gigante 2.00
5 Rick Rude Vs. Sting 2.00
6 F:Dangerous Alliance,R.Rude. . . 2.00
7 F:Steiner Brothers 2.00
8 F:Sting,Dangerous Alliance. 2.00
9 Bunkhouse Brawl 2.00
10 Halloween Havoc. 2.00
11 Sting vs Grapplers 2.00
12 F:Ron Simmons. 2.00

WORLD OF FANTASY

Atlas May, 1956

1 The Secret of the Mountain. . . 350.00
2 AW,Inside the Tunnel 225.00
3 DAy,SC, The Man in the Cave 175.00
4 BEv(c),BP,JF,Back to the
Lost City. 150.00
5 BEv(c),BP,In the Swamp. 150.00
6 BEv(c),BP,The Strange Wife
of Henry Johnson 150.00
7 BEv(c),GM,Man in Grey 150.00
8 GM,JO,MF,The Secret of the
Black Cloud 165.00
9 BEv,BK. 150.00
10 . . . . 125.00
11 AT 125.00
12 BEv(c) 125.00
13 BEv,JO 125.00
14 JMn(c),GM,JO,CI,JM 125.00
15 JK(c) 125.00
16 AW,SD,JK 175.00
17 JK(c),SD 165.00
18 JK(c) 165.00
19 JK(c),SD,August, 1959. . . . . . 165.00

World of Fantasy #8
© Marvel Entertainment Group

WORLD OF MYSTERY

Atlas June, 1956

1 BEv(c),AT,JO,The Long Wait . 350.00
2 BEv(c),The Man From
Nowhere 125.00
3 SD,AT,JDa, The Bugs 150.00
4 SD(c),BP,What Happened in
the Basement 150.00
5 JO,She Stands in Shadows . . 125.00
6 AW,SD,GC,Sinking Man 150.00
7 Pick A Door July, 1957 . . . . . . 125.00

WORLD OF SUSPENSE

Atlas April, 1956

1 JO,BEv,MO,A Stranger
Among Us 275.00
2 SD,LC,When Walks
the Scarecrow 150.00
3 AW,The Man Who Couldn't
Be Touched 150.00
4 Something is in This House . . 125.00
5 BEv,DH,JO 125.00
6 BEv(c),BP. 125.00
7 AW,The Face 150.00
8 Prisoner of the Ghost Ship . . . 125.00

WORLDS UNKNOWN

May, 1973

1 GK,AT,The Coming of the
Martians,Reprints 15.00
2 GK,TS,A Gun For A Dinosaur . . 10.00
3 The Day the Earth Stood
Still. 10.00
4 JB,Arena 10.00
5 DA,JM,Black Destroyer. 10.00
6 GK(c),The Thing Called It 10.00
7 GT,The Golden Voyage of
Sinbad,Part 1 . . . . 10.00
8 The Golden Voyage of
Sinbad,Part 2, August, 1974 . 10.00

WYATT EARP

Atlas Nov., 1955

1 JMn,F:Wyatt Earp 150.00
2 AW,Saloon(c) 90.00
3 JMn(c),The Showdown,
A:Black Bart 75.00
4 Ph(c),Hugh O'Brian,JSe,
India Sundown 75.00
5 Ph(c),Hugh O'Brian,DW,
Gun Wild Fever 75.00
6 . . . . 75.00
7 AW 75.00
8 . . . . 75.00
9 and 10 . . . . @75.00
11 . . . . 75.00
12 AW 75.00
13 thru 20 . . . . @60.00
21 JDa(c) 50.00
22 thru 29 . . . . @35.00
30 Reprints 15.00
31 thru 33 Reprints . . . . @10.00
34 June, 1973 . . . . 10.00

XAVIER INSTITUTE ALUMNI YEARBOOK

GN 48pg (1996) 5.95

X-CALIBRE

1995

1 Excaliber After Xavier 4.00
2 V:Callisto & Morlock Crew 3.00
3 D:Juggernaut 3.00
4 Secret Weapon. 3.00
TPB Rep.#1-#4. . . . . 8.95

X-FACTOR

Feb., 1986

1 WS(c),JG,BL,JRu,I:X-Factor,
Rusty 8.00
2 JG,BL,I:Tower. 5.00
3 JG,BL,V:Tower 4.00
4 KP,JRu,V:Frenzy. 4.00
5 JG,JRu,I:Alliance of Evil,
C:Apocalypse. 5.00
6 JG,BMc,I:Apocalypse 12.00
7 JG,JRu,V:Morlocks,I:Skids 4.00
8 MS,JRu,V:Freedom Force 4.00
9 JRu(i),V:Freedom Force
(Mutant Massacre) 5.00
10 WS,BWi,V:Marauders(Mut.Mass),
A:Sabretooth 6.00
11 WS,BWi,A:Thor(Mutant Mass) . . 5.00
12 MS,BWi,V:Vanisher 4.00
13 WS,DGr,V:Mastermold. 4.00
14 WS,BWi,V:Mastermold. 4.00
15 WS,BWi,D:Angel 5.00
16 DM,JRu,V:Masque. 4.00
17 WS,BWi,I:Rictor. 5.00
18 WS,BWi,V:Apocalypse. 4.00
19 WS,BWi,V:Horsemen of
Apocalypse 3.00
20 JBr,A:X-Terminators. 2.50
21 WS,BWi,V:The Right 2.50
22 SB,BWi,V:The Right. 2.50
23 WS,BWi,C:Archangel. 9.00
24 WS,BWi,Fall of Mutants,
I:Archangel. 12.00
25 WS,BWi,Fall of Mutants. 3.00
26 WS,BWi,Fall of Mutants,
N:X-Factor 3.00
27 WS,BWi,Christmas Issue 2.50
28 WS,BWi,V:Ship 2.00
29 WS,BWi,V:Infectia 2.00
30 WS,BWi,V:Infectia,Free.Force . . 2.00
31 WS,BWi,V:Infectia,Free.Force . . 2.00
32 SLi,A:Avengers 2.00
33 WS,BWi,V:Tower & Frenzy,
R:Furry Beast. 2.00
34 WS,BWi,I:Nanny,
Orphan Maker 2.00
35 JRu(i),WS(c),V:Nanny,
Orphan Maker 2.00
36 WS,BWi,Inferno,V:Nastirh 2.50
37 WS,BWi,Inferno,V:Gob.Queen . . 2.50
38 WS,AM,Inferno,A:X-Men,D:
MadelynePryor(GoblinQueen). . 2.50
39 WS,AM,Inferno,A:X-Men,
V:Mr.Sinister. 2.50

 All comics prices listed are for *Near Mint* condition.

40 RLd,AM,O:Nanny,Orphan Maker
1st Liefeld Marvel work 6.00
41 AAd,AM,I:Alchemy 2.50
42 AAd,AM,A:Alchemy 2.50
43 PS,AM,V:Celestials 2.00
44 PS,AM,V:Rejects 2.00
45 PS,AM,V:Rask 2.00
46 PS,AM,V:Rejects 2.00
47 KD,AM,V:Father 2.00
48 thru 49 PS,AM,V:Rejects 2.00
50 RLd&TM(c),RB,AM,A:Prof.X
(double sized),BU:Apocalypse . 3.00
51 AM,V:Sabretooth,Caliban 4.00
52 RLd(c),AM,V:Sabretooth,
Caliban 3.00
53 AM,V:Sabretooth,Caliban 3.00
54 MS,AM,A:Colossus,I:Crimson . . 2.00
55 MMi(c),CDo,AM,V:Mesmero 2.00
56 AM,V:Crimson 2.00
57 NKu,V:Crimson 2.00
58 JBg,AM,V:Crimson 2.00
59 AM,V:Press Gang 2.00
60 JBg,AM,X-Tinction Agenda#3 . . 3.00
60a 2nd printing(gold) 2.00
61 JBg,AM,X-Tinction Agenda#6 . . 3.00
62 JBg,AM,JLe(c),E:X-Agenda 3.00
63 WPo,I:Cyberpunks 3.00
64 WPo,ATb,V:Cyberpunks 3.00
65 WPo,ATb,V:Apocalypse 3.00
66 WPo,ATb,I:Askani,
V:Apocalypse 3.00
67 WPo,ATb,V:Apocalypse,I:Shinobi
Shaw,D:Sebastian Shaw 2.00
68 WPo,ATb,JLe(c),V:Apocalypse,
L:Nathan,(taken into future) . . . 3.00
69 WPo,V:Shadow King 2.00
70 MMi(c),JRu,Last old team 2.00
71 LSn,AM,New Team 4.00
71a 2nd printing 2.00
72 LSn,AM,Who shot Madrox
revealed 2.00
73 LSn,AM,Mob Chaos in D.C.. . . . 2.00
74 LSn,AM,I:Slab 2.00
75 LSn,AM,I:Nasty Boys(doub.sz) . . 3.00
76 LSn,AM,A:Hulk,Pantheon 2.00
77 LSn,AM,V:Mutant Lib. Front. . . . 2.00
78 LSn,AM,V:Mutant Lib. Front 2.00
79 LSn,AM,V:Helle's Belles 2.00
80 LSn,AM,V:Helle's Belles,
C:Cyber 2.00
81 LSn,AM,V:Helle's Belles,Cyber . 2.00
82 JQ(c),LSn,V:Brotherhood of Evil
Mutants,I:X-iles 2.00
83 MPa,A:X-Force,X-iles 2.00
84 JaL,X-Cutioners Song #2,
V:X-Force,A:X-Men 2.50
85 JaL,X-Cutioners Song #6,
Wolv.& Bishop,V:Cable 2.50
86 JaL,AM,X-Cutioner's Song#10,
A:X-Men,X-Force,V:Stryfe 2.50
87 JQ,X-Cutioners Song
Aftermath 2.50
88 JQ,AM,V:2nd Genegineer,
I:Random 4.00
89 JQ,V:Mutates,Genosha 2.00
90 JQ,AM,Genosha vs. Aznia 2.00
91 AM,V:Armageddon 2.00
92 JQ,AM,V:Fabian Cortez,
Acolytes,hologram(c) 5.00
93 Magneto Protocols 3.00
94 PR,J:Forge 3.00
95 B:JMD(s),AM,Polaris
Vs. Random 2.00
96 A:Random 2.00
97 JD,I:Haven,A:Random 2.00
98 GLz,A:Haven,A:Random 2.00
99 JD,A:Haven,Wolfsbane returns
to human 2.00
100 JD,Red Foil(c),V:Haven,
D:Madrox 3.25
100a Newstand Ed. 2.00

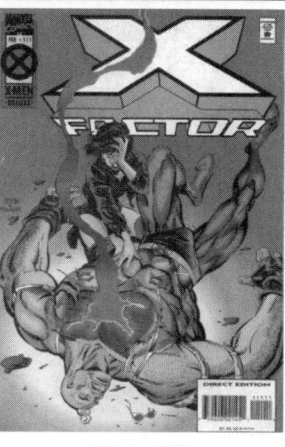

X-Factor #111
© Marvel Entertainment Group

101 JD,AM,Aftermath 2.00
102 JD,AM,V:Crimson Commando,
Avalanche 2.00
103 JD,AM,A:Malice 2.00
104 JD,AM,V:Malice,
C:Mr. Sinister 2.00
105 JD,AM,V:Malice 2.00
106 Phalanx Covenant,Life Signs
Holografx(c) 3.25
106a newsstand ed 2.00
107 A:Strong Guy 2.00
108 A:Mystique, deluxe ed.. . . . . . . 2.50
108a newsstand ed. 2.00
109 A:Mystique,V:Legion, deluxe . . 2.00
109a newsstand ed. 2.00
110 Invasion 2.00
110a deluxe ed. 2.00
111 Invasion 2.00
111a deluxe ed. 2.00
112 AM,JFM,SEp,F:Guido,Havok . . 2.00
113 A:Mystique 2.00
114 AM,Wild Child & Mystique 2.00
115 F:Wild Child,Havok 2.00
116 F:Wild Child 2.00
117 HMe,AM,F:Cyclops 2.00
118 HMe,AM,A:Random,Shard 2.00
119 HMe,AM,F:Sabretooth 2.00
120 . . . . 2.00
121 . . . . 2.00
122 HMe,SEp,AM,J:Sabretooth . . . 2.00
123 . . . . 2.00
124 A:Onslaught 3.00
125 Onslaught saga, double size . . 3.00
126 Beast vs. Dark Beast 2.00
127 Mystique 2.00
128 HMe,JMs,AM,Hound Program . 2.00
129 HMe,JMs,AM,Graydon Creed's
campaign 2.00
130 HMe,JMs,AM,Assassination of
Graydon Creed 2.50
131 HMe,JMs,ATi,Havok strikes
back 2.00
132 HMe,JMs,ATi,Break away from
government 2.00
133 HMe,JMs,ATi,A:Multiple Man &
Strong Guy 2.00
134 HMe,JMs,Ati,"Operation X-Factor
Underground," cont. 2.00
135 HMe,JMs,Strong Guy awakes . 2.00
136 HMe,JMs,ATi, A:Sabretooth . . . 2.00
137 HMe,JMs,ATi, Final fate of
Shard and Polaris 2.00
138 HMe,JMs,ATi,Sabertooth,
V:Maberick 2.00
139 HMe,ATi,Who killed Graydon
Creed 2.00
140 HMe,ATi,Who killed Graydon
Creed, A:Mystique 2.00
141 HMe,ATi,Shard's Plan 2.00
142 ATi,F:Wild Child 2.00
143 HMe,ATi,Havok vs.DarkBeast . 2.00
144 HMe,ATi,V:Brotherhood,
Dark Beast 2.00
145 HMe,ATi,Havok vs. X.U.E. 2.00
146 HMe,ATi,Havok, Multiple
Man,V:Polaris 2.00
147 HMe,Havok v. Mandroids 2.00
148 F:Shard 2.00
149 HMe,Polaris & Madrox rejoin . . 2.00
Spec #1 JG,Prisoner of Love 5.00
Ann.#1 BL,BBr,V:CrimsonDynamo . 5.00
Ann.#2 TGr,JRu,A:Inhumans 4.00
Ann.#3 WS(c),AM,JRu,PC,TD,
Evolutionary War 3.50
Ann.#4 JBy,WS,JRu,MBa,Atlantis
Attacks,BU:Doom & Magneto . . 3.50
Ann.#5 JBg,AM,DR,GI,Days of Future
Present,A:Fant.Four,V:Ahab . . 4.00
Ann.#6 Flesh Tears Saga,pt.4,
A:X-Force, New Warriors 4.00
Ann #7 JQ,JRu,Shattershot,pt.3 . . . 4.00
Ann.#8 I:Charon,w/card 3.25
Ann.#9 JMD(s),MtB,V:Prof.Power,
A:Prof.X,O:Haven 3.25
Minus 1 Spec., HMe,JMs,ATi,
flashback,F:Havok 2.00
GN X-Men: Wrath of Apocalypse,
rep.X-Factor#65-#68 . . . . 4.95

X-51
July, 1999

1 JQ&JP(c) Marvel Tech 2.00
2 JoB,V:Brotherhood of Mutants . . 2.00
2a variant cover 2.00
3 JoB,A:X.E.R.O. 2.00
4 JoB,A:Avengers 2.00
5 JoB,V:Vision 2.00
6 JoB 2.00
7 JoB,A:Sebastian Shaw 2.00
8 JoB,F:X-Men 2.50
9 JoB, ... 2.50
10 JoB,F:Machine Man 2.50
11 JoB,F:Celestial 2.50
12 JoB,final issue 2.50

X-FORCE
August, 1991

1 RLd,V:Stryfe,Mutant Liberation
Front,bagged, white on black
graphics with X-Force Card . . . 3.00
1a with Shatterstar Card 2.00
1b with Deadpool Card 2.00
1c with Sunspot & Gideon Card . . . 2.00
1d with Cable Card 3.00
1e Unbagged Copy 2.00
1f 2nd Printing 2.00
2 RLd,I:New Weapon X,V:
Deadpool 3.00
3 RLd,C:Spider-Man,
V:Juggernaut,Black Tom 3.00
4 RLd,SpM/X-Force team-up,
V:Juggernaut(cont.from SpM#16)
Sideways format 3.00
5 RLd,A:Brotherhood Evil Mutants . 2.50
6 RLd,V:Bro'hood Evil Mutants . . . 2.50
7 RLd,V:Bro'hood Evil Mutants . . . 2.50
8 MMi,O:Cable(Part) 2.50
9 RLd,D:Sauron,Masque 2.50
10 MPa,V:Mutant Liberation Front. . 2.00
11 MPa,Deadpool Vs Domino 2.00
12 MPa,A:Weapon Prime,Gideon . . 2.00
13 MPa,V:Weapon Prime 2.00

14 TSr,V:Weapon Prime,Krule 2.00
15 GCa,V:Krule,Deadpool. 2.00
16 GCa,X-Cutioners Song #4, X-Factor V:X-Force. 2.00
17 GCa,X-Cutioners Song#8, Apocalypse V:Stryfe 2.00
18 GCa,X-Cutioners Song#12, Cable vs Stryfe. 2.00
19 GCa,X-Cutioners Song Aftermath,N:X-Force. 2.00
20 GCa,O:Graymalkin 2.00
21 GCa,V:War Machine,SHIELD. . . 2.00
22 GCa,V:Externals 2.00
23 GCa,V:Saul,Gigeon,A:Six Pack . 2.00
24 GCa,A:Six Pack,A:Deadpool . . . 2.00
25 GCa,A:Mageneto,Exodus, R:Cable 5.00
26 GCa(c),MtB,I:Reignfire. 2.00
27 GCa(c),MtB,V:Reignfire,MLF, I:Moonstar,Locus 2.00
28 MtB,V:Reignfire,MLF 2.00
29 MtB,V:Arcade,C:X-Treme. 2.00
30 TnD,V:Arcade,A:X-Treme. 2.00
31 F:Siryn. 2.00
32 Child's Play#1,A:New Warriors. . 2.00
33 Child's Play#3,A:New Warriors, V:Upstarts 2.00
34 F:Rictor,Domino,Cable. 2.00
35 TnD,R:Nimrod 2.00
36 TnD,V:Nimrod 2.00
37 PaP,I&D:Absalom 2.00
38 TaD,Life Signs,pt.2, I:Generation X, foil(c) 5.00
38a newsstand ed. 2.00
39 TaD 2.00
40 TaD, deluxe 2.00
40a newsstand ed. 2.00
41 TaD,O:feral,deluxe 2.00
41a newsstand ed. 2.00
42 Emma Frost, deluxe. 2.00
42a newsstand ed. 2.00
43 Home is Where Heart 2.00
43a deluxe ed. 2.00
44 AdP,Prof.X,X-Mansion 2.00
45 AdP,Caliban vs. Sabretooth 2.00
46 R:The Mimic 2.00
47 A:Deadpool 2.00
48 AdP,Siryn Takes Charge 2.00
49 ADp,MBu,Holocaust is here 2.00
50 AdP,MPn,F:Sebastian Shaw . . . 2.00
50a prismatic foil cover. 4.00
50b variant RLd(c) 6.00
51 AdP,MPn,V:Risque. 2.00
52 A:Onslaught. 3.50
53 . . . . 2.00
54 AdP, Can X-Force protect X-Ternals? 2.00
55 . . . . 2.00
56 Deadpool, A:Onslaught 3.50
57 Onslaught saga 2.00
58 Onslaught saga 2.00
59 . . . . 2.00
60 JLb,,F:Shatterstar,A:Long Shot . 2.00
61 JLb,R:Longshot,O:Shatterstar . . 2.00
62 JLb,F:Sunspot 2.00
63 JFM,AdP,F:Risque,Cannonball. . 2.00
64 JFM,AdP,In Latveria, searching for Doctor Doom's weapons . . . 2.00
65 JFM,AdP,Warpath follows Risque to Florida 2.00
66 JFM,AdP,A:Risque,James Proudstar 2.00
67 JFM,AdP,F:Warpath, Risque . . . 2.00
68 JFM,AdP,Zero Tolerance 2.00
69 JFM,AdP,Zero Tolerance aftermath 2.00
70 JFM,AdP,new direction starts . . . 2.00
71 JFM,AdP,new direction 2.00
72 JFM,AdP,on the road 2.00
73 JFM,AdP,in New Orleans 2.00
74 JFM,ASm,Skids is back 2.00

X-Force #1
© Marvel Entertainment Group

75 JFM,AdP,A:Reignfire, double size. 3.00
76 JFM,AdP,F:Shatterstar 2.00
77 JFM,AdP,F:Sunfire & Meltdown . 2.00
78 JFM,AdP,Reignfire makes his move 2.00
79 JFM,AdP,O:Reignfire 2.00
80 JFM,AdP,V:Reignfire 2.00
81 JFM,AdP,trip to Hawaii, V:Lava Men, AdP Poster 2.00
82 JFM,V:Griffin, Damocles Foundation 2.00
83 JFM,F:Cannonball 2.00
84 JFM,V:Deviants 2.00
85 JFM,Return of Skids 2.00
86 JFM,A:Hulk 2.00
87 JFM,V:new Hellions 2.00
88 JFM,V:new Hellions 2.00
89 JFM,prisoners of the Hellions. . . 2.00
90 JFM,Hellion War,concl. 2.00
91 JFM,home to San Francisco . . . 2.00
92 JFM,F:Domino. 2.00
93 JFM,Domino returns 2.00
94 JFM,destination Genosha 2.00
95 JFM,F:Magneto 2.00
96 JFM,A:Selene 2.00
97 JFM,V:Reignfire. 2.00
98 . . . . 2.00
99 JFM,F:Dani Moonstar 2.00
100 JFM,Four Personas,48-pg.. . . . 3.00
101 new members,some gone 2.00
102 WPo,X-Men: Revolution. 2.00
102a variant (c) 2.00
103 WPo,WEl,Games Without Frontiers,pt.2 . . . . 2.25
104 WPo,WEl,Games,pt.3 . . . . 2.25
105 WPo,WEl,Games,pt.4 . . . . 2.25
106 WEl,IEd,WPo,Murder Ballads,pt.1 . . . . 2.25
107 WEl,IEd,MurderBallads,pt.2 . . . 2.25
108 WEl,IEd,Ballads,pt.3 . . . . 2.25
109 WEl,IEd,Ballads,pt.4 . . . . 2.25
Ann.#1 Shattershot,pt1 . . . . 2.75
Ann.#2 JaL,LSn,I:X-Treme,w/card. . 3.25
Ann.#3 . . . . 2.95
Annual 1998 X-Force/Champions . . 6.00
Ann.1999 R:Shatterstar & Rictor. . . 3.50
Spec.#102 Rough cut edition 3.00
Minus 1 Spec., JFM,AdP, flashback, F:John Proudstar 2.00
TPB X-Force & Spider-Man: Sabotage, rep.X-Force #3 & #4 and Spider-Man #16 . . . . 6.95

X-FORCE MEGAZINE

TPB LSi,RLd, rep. New Mutants #99–#100. . . . . 3.95

X-MAN

March, 1995

1 Cable after Xavier. 5.00
2 Sinister's Plan 4.00
3 V:Domino 2.50
4 V:Sinister 2.50
5 Into this World 2.50
6 V:X-Men 2.50
7 Evil from Age of Apocalypse 2.25
8 Crossover Adventure 2.00
9 F:Nate's Past 2.00
10 Nate's Past 2.00
11 Young Nate seeks out X-Men. . . 2.00
12 F:Excalibur 2.00
13 . . . . 2.00
14 . . . . 2.00
15 JOs,X-Men/Cable war aftermath 3.00
16 Holocaust,A:Onslaught 2.50
17 Holocaust,Quicksilver,Scarlet Witch, A:Onslaught. 2.50
18 Onslaught saga 2.50
19 Onslaught saga 2.50
20 . . . . 2.50
21 TKa,RCz,F:Nate 2.50
22 TKa,RCz,F:Threnody,A:Madelyne Pryor 2.50
23 TKa,RCz,F:Bishop. 2.50
24 TKa,RCz,Spider-Man vs. Nate . . 2.50
25 TKa,RCz,Madelyne Pryor, double size. 4.00
26 TKa,RCz,Nate limps to Muir Isle,A:Moira Mactaggert 2.50
27 TKa,RCz,Hellfire Club, concl.. . . 2.50
28 TKa,RCz,Dark Beast's offer 2.50
29 TKa,RCz,Back in New York,. . . . 2.50
30 TKa,RCz,F:Nate Grey 2.50
31 RL,DGr,F:Nate Grey 2.00
32 TKa,V:Jacknife 2.00
33 TKa,V:Jacknife 2.00
34 TKa,Secret of Nate's popularity . 2.00
35 TKa,Terrorists Strike 2.00
36 TKa,V:Purple Man 2.00
37 TKa,Nate leaves N.Y., A:Spider-Man 2.00
38 TKa,A:Spider-Man, Gwen Stacy. 2.00
39 TKa,AOl,Nate & Madeline Pryor. 2.00
40 TKa,RPc,V:Great Beasts 2.00
41 TKa,RCz,Madelyne Pryor 2.00
42 TKa,RCz,hunted by leprechauns 2.00
43 TKa,RCz,Nate Grey–murderer?! 2.00
44 TKa,RCz,F:Nate Grey,Gauntlet . 2.00
45 TKa,prelude to X-Man/Cable x-over. 2.00
46 TKa,Cable x-over. 2.00
47 TKa,Blood Brothers,pt.3. . . . . . . 2.00
48 LRs,V:Crusader 2.00
49 LRs,TKa,F:Nate. 2.00
50 TKa,LRs,War of the Mutants,pt.2, 48-page. 2.00
51 TKa,LRs,V:Psi-Ops 2.00
52 TKa,LRs,V:Psi-Ops 2.00
53 TKa,Strange Relations,pt.1 . . . . 2.00
54 TKa,Strange Relations,pt.2 . . . . 2.00
55 TKa,M'Kraan Crystal 2.00
56 TKa,Nate in Greyville. 2.00
57 TKa,V:Mysterio 2.00
58 TKa,V:Threnody. 2.00
59 TKa 2.00
60 TKa, ... 2.00
61 TKa, ... 2.00
62 TKa,trapped. 2.00
63 WEl,X-Men: Revolution 2.00
63a variant(c) 2.00
64 WEl,No Direction Home,pt.2 . . . 2.25
65 WEl,No Direction Home,pt.3 . . . 2.25
66 WEl,No Direction Home,pt.4 . . . 2.25

MARVEL

X-Man #53
© Marvel Entertainment Group

67 WEI,Down the Spiral,pt.1 . . . . . . 2.25
68 WEI,Down the Spiral,pt.2 . . . . . . 2.25
69 WEI,Down the Spiral,pt.3 . . . . . . 2.25
70 WEI,Down the Spiral,pt.4 . . . . . . 2.25
Minus 1 Spec., TKa,RCz, flashback,O:Nate Grey 2.00
Spec.#1 X-Man '96 . . . . 2.95
Ann. '97 RBe, Nate, Sugar Man, Dark Beast, Holocaust 3.00
Ann. '98 X-Man, The Hulk, Thanos, 48pg 3.00
GNv X-Man,BRa,TyD, 48pg 6.00

X-MEN
Sept., 1963

1 JK,O:X-Men,I:Professor X,Beast Cyclops,Marvel Girl,Iceman Angel,Magneto 6,500.00
2 JK,I:Vanisher 1,800.00
3 JK,I:Blob. 800.00
4 JK,I:Quicksilver,Scarlet Witch Mastermind,Toad 650.00
5 JK,V:Broth. of Evil Mutants . . . 500.00
6 JK,V:Sub-Mariner 350.00
7 JK,V:Broth. of Evil Mutants, Blob 325.00
8 JK,I:Unus,1st Ice covered Iceman 325.00
9 JK,A:Avengers,I:Lucifer. 325.00
10 JK,I:Modern Kazar 325.00
11 JK,I:Stranger 275.00
12 JK,O:Prof.X,I:Juggernaut 350.00
13 JK,JSt,V:Juggernaut 250.00
14 JK,I:Sentinels. 250.00
15 JK,O:Beast,V:Sentinels 250.00
16 JK,V:Mastermold,Sentinels. . . 250.00
17 JK,V:Magneto 150.00
18 V:Magneto 150.00
19 I:Mimic. 150.00
20 V:Lucifer 150.00
21 V:Lucifer,Dominus 135.00
22 V:Maggia 135.00
23 V:Maggia 135.00
24 I:Locust(Prof.Hopper). 135.00
25 JK,I:El Tigre. 135.00
26 V:El Tigre. 125.00
27 C:Fant.Four,V:Puppet Master . 125.00
28 I:Banshee 175.00
29 V:Super-Apaptoid. 125.00
30 JK,I:The Warlock 125.00
31 JK,I:Cobalt Man 85.00
32 V:Juggernaut 85.00
33 GK,A:Dr.Strange,Juggernaut . . 85.00
34 V:Tyrannus,Mole Man 85.00
35 JK,A:Spider-Man,Banshee . . . 125.00
36 V:Mekano 85.00
37 DH,V:Blob,Unus. 85.00
38 DH,A:Banshee,O:Cyclops . . . 125.00
39 DH,GT,A:Banshee,V:Mutant Master,O:Cyclops 85.00
40 DH,GT,V:Frankenstein, O:Cyclops 85.00
41 DH,GT,I:Grotesk,O:Cyclops . . . 75.00
42 DH,GT,JB,V:Grotesk, O:Cyclops,D:Prof.X 75.00
43 GT,JB,V:Magneto,Quicksilver, Scarlet Witch,C:Avengers 85.00
44 V:Magneto,Quicksilver,Sc.Witch, R:Red Raven,O:Iceman 85.00
45 PH,JB,V:Magneto,Quicksilver, Scarlet Witch,O:Iceman 85.00
46 DH,V:Juggernaut,O:Iceman . . . 75.00
47 DH,I:Maha Yogi 75.00
48 DH,JR,V:Quasimodo 75.00
49 JSo,DH,C:Magneto,I:Polaris, Mesmero,O:Beast. 75.00
50 JSo,V:Magneto,O:Beast. 85.00
51 JSo,V:Magneto,Polaris, Erik the Red,O:Beast 75.00
52 DH,MSe,JSt,O:Lorna Dane V:Magneto,O:Beast 55.00
53 1st BWS,O:Beast. 85.00
54 BWS,DH,I:Havok,O:Angel 80.00
55 BWS,DH,O:Havok,Angel 75.00
56 NA,V:LivingMonolith,O:Angel . . 75.00
57 NA,V:Sentinels,A:Havok. 75.00
58 NA,A:Havoc,V:Sentinels. 100.00
59 NA,V:Sentinels,A:Havoc. 75.00
60 NA,I:Sauron. 75.00
61 NA,V:Sauron 75.00
62 NA,A:Kazar,Sauron,Magneto . . 75.00
63 A:Ka-Zar,V:Magneto. 65.00
64 DH,A:Havok,I:Sunfire. 55.00
65 NA,MSe,A:Havok,Shield, Return of Prof.X 65.00
66 SB,MSe,V:Hulk,A:Havok 65.00
67 rep.X-Men #12,#13 . . . . 35.00
68 rep.X-Men #14,#15 . . . . 35.00
69 rep.X-Men #16,#19 . . . . 35.00
70 rep.X-Men #17,#18 . . . . 35.00
71 rep.X-Men #20. . . . . 35.00
72 rep.X-Men #21,#24 . . . . 35.00
73 thru 93 rep.X-Men #25-45 . . @35.00
94 GK(c),B:CCl(s),DC,BMc,B:2nd X-Men,V:Count Nefaria. 525.00
95 GK(c),DC,V:Count Nefaria, Ani-Men,D:Thunderbird. 125.00
96 DC,I:Moira McTaggert, Kierrok 100.00
97 DC,V:Havok,Polaris,Eric the Red,I:Lilandra 85.00
98 DC,V:Sentinels,Stephen Lang . 90.00
99 DC,V:Sentinels,S.Lang. 90.00
100 DC,V:Stephen Lang 100.00
101 DC,I:Phoenix,Black Tom, A:Juggernaut 75.00
102 DC,O:Storm,V:Juggernaut, Black Tom 40.00
103 DC,V:Juggernaut,Bl.Tom 40.00
104 DC,V:Magneto,I:Star Jammers,A:Lilandra 35.00
105 DC,BL,V:Firelord 35.00
106 DC,TS,V:Firelord 35.00
107 DC,DGr,I:Imperial Guard,Star Jammers,Gladiator,Corsair . . . 40.00
108 JBy,TA,A:Star Jammers, C:Fantastic Four,Avengers. . . 80.00
109 JBy,TA,I:Vindicator. 55.00
110 TD,DC,V:Warhawk 35.00
111 JBy,TA,V:Mesmero,A:Beast, Magneto. 35.00
112 GP(c),JBy,TA,V:Magneto, A:Beast 32.00

X-Men #73
© Marvel Entertainment Group

113 JBy,TA,V:Magneto,A:Beast. . . 32.00
114 JBy,TA,A:Beast,R:Sauron. . . . 32.00
115 JBy,TA,V:Sauron,Garokk, A:Kazar,I:Zaladane 30.00
116 JBy,TA,V:Sauron,Garokk, A:Kazar 30.00
117 JBy,TA,O:Prof.X,I:Amahl Farouk (Shadow King) 35.00
118 JBy,I:Moses Magnum,A:Sunfire C:Iron Fist,I:Mariko 32.00
119 JBy,TA,V:Moses Magnum, A:Sunfire 32.00
120 JBy,TA,I:AlphaFlight (Shaman, Sasquatch,Northstar,Snowbird, Aurora). 55.00
121 JBy,TA,V:Alpha Flight. 65.00
122 JBy,TA,A:Juggernaut,Black Tom,Arcade,Power Man 30.00
123 JBy,TA,V:Arcade,A:SpM. 28.00
124 JBy,TA,V:Arcade 28.00
125 JBy,TA,A:Beast,Madrox the Multiple Man,Havok,Polaris. . . 28.00
126 JBy,TA,I:Proteus, A:Havok,Madrox. 28.00
127 JBy,TA,V:Proteus,A:Havok, Madrox. 28.00
128 GP(c),JBy,TA,V:Proteus, A:Havok,Madrox. 28.00
129 JBy,TA,I:Shadow Cat,White Queen,C:Hellfire Club. 35.00
130 JR2(c),JBy,TA,I:Dazzler V:White Queen 30.00
131 JBy,TA,V:White Queen, A:Dazzler 25.00
132 JBy,TA,I:Hellfire Club, V:Mastermind 25.00
133 JBy,TA,V:Hellfire Club, Mastermind,F:Wolverine 25.00
134 JBy,TA,V:Hellfire Club,Master mind,I:Dark Phoenix,A:Beast . 25.00
135 JBy,TA,V:Dark Phoenix,C:SpM, Fant.Four,Silver Surfer 25.00
136 JBy,TA,V:Dark Phoenix, A:Beast 25.00
137 JBy,TA,D:Phoenix,V:Imperial Guard,A:Beast 28.00
138 JBy,TA,History of X-Men, L:Cyclops,C:Shadow Cat 25.00
139 JBy,TA,A:Alpha Flight,R:Wendigo, N:Wolverine,J:Shadowcat. . . . 35.00
140 JBy,TA,V:Wendigo,A:Alpha Flight 35.00
141 JBy,TA,I:2nd Brotherhood of Evil Mutants,I:Rachel (Phoenix II) . 35.00

Becomes:

MARVEL

UNCANNY X-MEN

142 JBy,TA,V:Evil Mutants, A:Rachel (Phoenix II) 30.00
143 JBy,TA,V:N'Garai,I:Lee Forrester 15.00
144 BA,JRu,A:Man-Thing, O:Havok, V:D'Spayre 9.00
145 DC,JRu,V:Arcade,A:DrDoom . . 9.00
146 DC,JRu,V:Dr.Doom,Arcade . . . 9.00
147 DC,JRu,V:Dr.Doom,Arcade . . . 9.00
148 DC,JRu,I:Caliban,A:Dazzler Spiderwoman 9.00
149 DC,JRu,A:Magneto 9.00
150 DC,JRu,BWi,V:Magneto 10.00
151 JSh,BMc,JRu,V:Sentinels. 6.00
152 BMc,JRu,V:White Queen 6.00
153 DC,JRu,I:Bamf. 6.00
154 DC,JRu,BWi,I:Sidrian Hunters A:Corsair,O:Cyclops(part) 6.00
155 DC,BWi,V:Deathbird,I:Brood . . 6.00
156 DC,BWi,V:Death Bird, A:Tigra, Star Jammers 6.00
157 DC,BWi,V:Deathbird 6.00
158 DC,BWi,2nd A:Rogue, Mystique 9.00
159 BSz,BWi,V:Dracula 6.00
160 BA,BWi,V:Belasco,I:Magik 6.00
161 DC,BWi,I:Gabrielle Haller, O:Magneto,Professor X 8.00
162 DC,BWi,V:Brood 9.00
163 DC,BWi,V:Brood 6.00
164 DC,BWi,V:Brood,I:Binary 6.00
165 PS,BWi,V:Brood 7.00
166 PS,BWi,V:Brood,A:Binary, I:Lockheed 7.00
167 PS,BWi,V:Brood,A:N.Mutants. . 7.00
168 PS,BWi,I:Madelyne Pryor. 5.00
169 PS,BWi,I:Morlocks 5.00
170 PS,BWi,A:Angel,V:Morlocks . . . 5.00
171 WS,BWi,J:Rogue,V:Binary . . . 10.00
172 PS,BWi,V:Viper,Silver Samurai, ... 7.00
173 PS,BWi,V:Viper,Silver Samurai, ... 5.00
174 PS,BWi,A:Mastermind 5.00
175 PS,JR2,BWi,W:Cyclops and Madelyne,V:Mastermind 8.00
176 JR2,BWi,I:Val Cooper 5.00
177 JR2,JR,V:Brotherhood of Evil Mutants 5.00
178 JR2,BWi,BBr,V:Brotherhood of Evil Mutants 5.00
179 JR2,DGr,V:Morlocks. 5.00
180 JR2,DGr,BWi,Secret Wars 5.00
181 JR2,DGr,A:Sunfire 5.00
182 JR2,DGr,V:S.H.I.E.L.D. 5.00
183 JR2,DGr,V:Juggernaut 5.00
184 JR2,DGr,V:Selene,I:Forge 7.00
185 JR2,DGr,V:Shield,U.S. Govt.,Storm loses powers. 5.00
186 BWS,TA,Lifedeath, V:Dire Wraiths 6.00
187 JR2,DGr,V:Dire Wraiths 5.00
188 JR2,DGr,V:Dire Wraiths 5.00
189 JR2,SL,V:Selene,A:Magma . . . 5.00
190 JR2,DGr,V:Kulan Gath,A:SpM, Avengers,New Mutants. 5.00
191 JR2,DGr,A:Avengers,Spider-Man, New Mutants,I:Nimrod 5.00
192 JR2,DGr,V:Magus 5.00
193 JR2,DGr,V:Hellions,I:Firestar Warpath,20th Anniv. 8.00
194 JR2,DGr,SL,V:Nimrod 5.00
195 BSz(c),JR2,DGr,A:Power Pack,V:Morlocks. 5.00
196 JR2,DGr,J:Magneto 6.00
197 JR2,DGr,V:Arcade 5.00
198 BWS,F:Storm,'Lifedeath II' 5.00
199 JR2,DGr,I:Freedom Force, Rachel becomes 2nd Phoenix . 5.00
200 JR2,DGr,A:Magneto,I:Fenris . . 8.00
201 RL,WPo(i),I:Nathan Christopher (Cyclops son) 9.00
202 JR2,AW,Secret Wars II 5.00
203 JR2,AW,Secret Wars II 5.00
204 JBr,WPo,V:Arcade 5.00
205 BWS,A:Lady Deathstrike 11.00
206 JR2,DGr,V:Freedom Force. . . . 4.00
207 JR2,DGr,V:Selene 4.00
208 JR2,DGr,V:Nimrod, A:Hellfire Club 4.00
209 JR2,CR,V:Nimrod,A:Spiral 4.00
210 JR2,DGr,I:Marauders, (Mutant Massacre) 10.00
211 JR2,BBl,AW,V:Marauders, (Mutant Massacre) 10.00
212 RL,DGr,V:Sabretooth, (Mutant Massacre) 12.00
213 AD,V:Sabretooth (Mut.Mass) . 12.00
214 BWS,BWi,V:Malice,A:Dazzler. . 4.00
215 AD,DGr,I:Stonewall,Super Sabre,Crimson Commando . . . 4.00
216 BWS(c),JG,DGr,V:Stonewall . . 4.00
217 WS(c),JG,SL,V:Juggernaut . . . 4.00
218 AAD(c),MS,DGr,V:Juggernaut . 4.00
219 BBl,DGr,V:Marauders,Polaris becomes Malice,A:Sabertooth . 5.00
220 MS,DGr,A:Naze 4.00
221 MS,DGr,I:Mr.Sinister, V:Maruaders. 8.00
222 MS,DGr,V:Marauders,Eye Killers,A:Sabertooth 9.00
223 KGa,DGr,A:Freedom Force . . . 4.00
224 MS,DGr,V:Adversary 4.00
225 MS,DGr,Fall of Mutants I:1st US App Roma 6.00
226 MS,DGr,Fall of Mutants 6.00
227 MS,DGr,Fall of Mutants 6.00
228 RL,TA,A:OZ Chase 4.00
229 MS,DGr,I:Reavers,Gateway . . . 4.00
230 RL,DGr,Xmas Issue 4.00
231 RL,DGr,V:Limbo. 4.00
232 MS,DGr,V:Brood 4.00
233 MS,DGr,V:Brood 4.00
234 MS,JRu,V:Brood 4.00
235 RL,CR,V:Magistrates 4.00
236 MS,DGr,V:Magistrates 4.00
237 RL,TA,V:Magistrates 4.00
238 MS,DGr,V:Magistrates 4.00
239 MS,DGr,Inferno,A:Mr.Sinister . . 4.00
240 MS,DGr,Inferno,V:Marauders . . 4.00
241 MS,DGr,Inferno,O:Madeline Pryor,V:Marauders 4.00
242 MS,DGr,Inferno,D:N'Astirh,

Uncanny X-Men #195
© Marvel Entertainment Group

A:X-Factor,Double-sized 4.00
243 MS,Inferno,A:X-Factor. 4.00
244 MS,DGr,I:Jubilee 15.00
245 RLd,DGr,Invasion Parody. 4.00
246 MS,DGr,V:Mastermold, A:Nimrod 4.00
247 MS,DGr,V:Mastermold 3.00
248 JLe(1st X-Men Art),DGr, V:Nanny & Orphan Maker. . . . 16.00
248a 2nd printing 2.00
249 MS,DGr,C:Zaladane, V:Savage Land Mutates. 4.00
250 MS,SL,I:Zaladane. 4.00
251 MS,DGr,V:Reavers 4.00
252 JLe,BSz(c),RL,SW,V:Reavers . 4.00
253 MS,SL,V:Amahl Farouk 4.00
254 JLe(c),MS,DGr,V:Reavers 4.00
255 MS,DGr,V:Reavers,D:Destiny. . 4.00
256 JLe,SW,Acts of Vengeance, V:Manderin,A:Psylocke. 8.00
257 JLe,JRu,AofV,V:Manderin 6.00
258 JLe,SW,AofV,V:Manderin 7.00
259 MS,DGr,V:Magistrates,. 5.00
260 JLe(c),MS,DGr,A:Dazzler. 4.00
261 JLe(c),MS,DGr,V:Hardcase & Harriers 4.00
262 KD,JRu,V:Masque,Morlocks. . . 4.00
263 JRu(i),O:Forge,V:Morlocks 4.00
264 JLe(c),MC,JRu,V:Magistrate. . . 4.00
265 JRu(i),V:Shadowking 4.00
266 NKu(c),MC,JRu,I:Gambit 30.00
267 JLe,WPo,SW,V:Shadowking. . 15.00
268 JLe,SW,A:Captain America, Black Widow,V:The Hand, Baron Strucker 17.00
269 JLe,ATi,Rogue V:Ms.Marvel . . . 4.00
270 JLe,ATi,SW,X-Tinction Agenda #1, A:Cable,New Mutants 10.00
270a 2nd printing(Gold) 4.00
271 JLe,SW,X-Tinction Agenda #4,A:Cable,New Mutants 5.00
272 JLe,SW,X-Tinction Agenda #7,A:Cable,New Mutants 5.00
273 JLe,WPo,JBy,KJ,RL,MS,MGo, LSn,SW,A:Cable,N.Mutants . . . 5.00
274 JLe,SW,V:Zaladane,A:Magneto, Nick Fury,Kazar 4.00
275 JLe,SW,R:Professor X,A:Star Jammers,Imperial Guard 6.00
275a 2nd Printing (Gold). 3.00
276 JLe,SW,V:Skrulls,Shi'ar 3.00
277 JLe,SW,V:Skrulls,Shi'ar 3.00
278 PS,Professor X Returns to Earth,V:Shadowking 3.00
279 NKu,SW,V:Shadowking 3.00
280 E:CCl(s),NKu,A:X-Factor, D:Shadowking,Prof.X Crippled . 3.00
281 WPo,ATi,new team (From X-Men #1),D:Pierce,Hellions,V:Sentinels, I:Trevor Fitzroy,Upstarts 5.00
281a 2nd printing,red(c) 2.00
282 WPo,ATi,V:Fitzroy,C:Bishop . . . 9.00
282a 2nd printing,gold(c) of #281 inside 2.00
283 WPo,ATi,I:Bishop,Malcolm, Randall. 10.00
284 WPo,ATi,SOS from USSR. 3.00
285 WPo,I:Mikhail(Colossus' brother from Russia) 3.00
286 JLe,WPo,ATi,A:Mikhail. 3.00
287 JR2,O:Bishop, D:Malcolm,Randall 3.00
288 NKu,BSz,A:Bishop. 3.00
289 WPo,ATi,Forge proposes to Storm. 3.00
290 WPo,SW,V:Cyberpunks, L:Forge 3.00
291 TR,V:Morlocks 3.00
292 TR,V:Morlocks 3.00
293 TR,D:Morlocks,Mikhail 3.00
294 BP,TA,X-Cutioner's Song#1,

 All comics prices listed are for *Near Mint* condition.

Stryfe shoots Prof X,A:X-Force, X-Factor,polybag.w/ProfX card . 3.00
295 BP,TA,X-Cutioners Song #5, V:Apocalypse 3.00
296 BP,TA,X-Cutioners Song #9, A:X-Force,X-Factor,V:Stryfe . . . 3.00
297 BP,X-Cutioners Song Aftermath 3.00
298 BP,TA,V:Acolytes 3.00
299 BP,A:Forge,Acolytes,I:Graydon Creed (Sabretooth's son) 3.00
300 JR2,DGr,BP,V:Acolytes,A:Forge, Nightcrawler,Holografx(c) 5.00
301 JR2,DGr,I:Sienna Blaze, V:Fitzroy. 2.50
302 JR2,V:Fitzroy. 2.50
303 JR2,V:Upstarts,D:Illyana 6.00
304 JR2,JaL,PS,L:Colossus, V:Magneto,Holo-grafx(c) 5.00
305 JD,F:Rogue,Bishop 2.50
306 JR2,V:Hodge 2.50
307 JR2,Bloodties#4,A:Avengers, V:Exodus,Cortez 6.00
308 JR2,Scott & Jean announce impending marriage 2.50
309 JR2,O:Professor X & Amelia . . 2.50
310 JR2,DG,A:Cable,V:X-Cutioner, w/card 4.00
311 JR2,DG,AV,V:Sabretooth, C:Phalanx 2.50
312 JMd,DG,A:Yukio,I:Phalanx, w/card 4.00
313 JMd,DG,V:Phalanx 2.50
314 LW,BSz,R:White Quen 2.50
315 F:Acolytes 2.50
316 V:Phalanx,I:M,Phalanx Covenant Generation Next,pt.1, holo(c) . . 5.00
316a newsstand ed. 2.00
317 JMd,V:Phalanx,prism(c) 5.00
317a newsstand ed. 2.00
318 JMd,L:Jubilee, deluxe 2.25
318a newsstand ed. 2.00
319 R:Legion, deluxe 2.25
319a newsstand ed. 2.00
320 deluxe ed. 4.00
320 newsstand ed. 2.00
321 R:Lilandra, deluxe ed. 2.25
321 newsstand ed. 2.00
322 SLo,TGu,Rogue,Iceman run from Gambit's Secret 6.00
323 I:Onslaught 2.25
324 SLo,F:Cannonball 2.25
325 R:Colossus 4.50
326 SLo,JMd,F:Gambit,Sabretooth . 2.50
327 SLo,JMd,Magneto's Fate 2.50
328 SLo,JMd,Sabretooth freed 2.50
329 SLo,JMd,A:Doctor Strange. . . . 2.50
330. . . . . 2.50
331 . . . . 2.50
332 SLo,JMd, cont from Wolverine #100 . . . . 2.50
333 SLo,JMd, Operation: Zero Tolerance, Onslaught saga 3.00
334 SLo,JMd, Onslaught saga 3.00
335 SLo,JMd, Onslaught saga 3.00
336 Apocalypse vs. Onslaught 2.50
337 Operation: Zero Tolerance 2.50
338 SLo,JMd,R:Angel. 2.50
339 SLo,JMd,F:Cyclops, J.J. Jameson, Havok 2.50
340 SLo,JMd,F:Iceman. 2.50
341 SLo,JMd,Rogue gets gift 2.50
342 SLo,JMd, Shi'ar Empire, pt.1 . . 4.00
342a Rogue cover 17.00
343 SLo,JMd, Shi'ar Empire, pt.2 . . 2.50
344 SLo,JMd, Shi'ar Empire, pt.3 . . 2.50
345 SLo,JMd, trip home, A:Akron . . 5.00
346 SLo,JMd,Zero Tolerance, A:Spider-Man 4.00
347 SLo,JMd,Zero Tolerance 2.50
348 SLo,JMd,at Magneto's base. . . 2.50
349 SLo,JMd,Maggot vs. Psylocke & Archangel 2.50
350 SSe,JMd,Trial of Gambit, double-sized. 4.00
350a Gambit (c) 15.00
351 SSe,JMd,Dr. Cecilia Reyes . . . 3.00
352 SSe,EBe,Cyclops & Phoenix leave, Facade arrives 3.00
353 SSe,CBa,Rogues Anguish 2.50
354 SSe,CBa,F:Rogue 2.50
354a Jean Gray (c). 6.00
355 SSe,CBa, North & South pt.2 x-over 5.00
356 SSe,CBa, originals V:Phoenix . 2.50
357 SSe,Cyclops & Phoenix 2.50
358 SSe,CBa,Phoenix collapses. . . 2.50
359 SSe,CBa,Rogue 2.50
360A SSe,CBa, I:New X-Men, foil etched cover 5.00
360B regular cover 4.00
361 SSe,SSr,R:Gambit 2.50
362 SSe,CBa,Hunt for Xavier,pt.1 . . 2.50
363 SSe,CBa,Hunt for Xavier,pt.3. . 2.50
364 SSe,Hunt for Xavier,pt.5. . . . . . 2.50
365 SSe,CBa,A:Professor X 2.50
366 AD,BPe,Magneto War,pt.1 . . . . 2.50
367 AD,Magneto War,pt.3. . . . . 2.50
368 AD,AKu,Requiem for an X-Man 2.50
368a signed 19.95
369 AD,AKu,V:Juggernaut 2.50
370 AD,AKu,in the past 2.50
371 AD,AKu(c),Rage Against the Machine, pt.1 x-over. 2.50
371a signed 20.00
372 AKu,AD,The Shattering,pt.1 . . . 2.50
373 AKu,AD,The Shattering,pt.2 . . . 2.50
374 AKu,AD,The Shattering 2.50
375 AKu,AD,48-pg.. . . . . 3.50
376 AKu,AD 2.50
377 AKu,AD,Apocalypse12,pt.5 . . . 2.50
378 AKu,AD,TTn,Ages of Apocalypse,pt.1,x-over 2.50
379 AKu,AD,TTn,mutants no more . 2.50
380 AD,TR,poly-bagged w/Genesis 3.50
381 CCl,AKu,TTn,X-Men:Revolution 2.25
382 CCl,TTn,Shockwave Riders . . . 2.25
383 CCl,AKu,TTn,48-pg.. . . . . 3.00
384 CCl,AKu,TTn,I:Killion 2.25
385 CCl,TR,Red Pirates 2.25
386 CCl,TR,Phoenix. 2.25
387 CCl,TTn,Maximum Security . . . 2.25
Ann.#1 rep.#9,#11 . . . . 75.00
Ann.#2 rep.#22,#23 . . . . 65.00
Ann.#3 GK(c),GP,TA,A:Arkon 20.00
Ann.#4 JR2,BMc,A:Dr.Strange . . . 15.00
Ann.#5 BA,BMc,A:F.F.. . . . . 12.00
Ann.#6 BSz,BWi,Dracula 13.00
Ann.#7 MGo,TMd,BWi,TA,BBr, BA,JRu,BBl,SL,AM, V:Impossible Man 10.00
Ann.#8 SL,Kitty's story 10.00
Ann.#9 AAd,AG,MMi,Asgard,V:Loki, Enchantress,A:New Mutants. . 15.00
Ann.#10 AAd,TA,V:Mojo, J:Longshot,A:New Mutants . . . 13.00
Ann.#11 AD,V:Horde,A:CaptBrit . . . 6.00
Ann.#12 AAd,BWi,RLm,TD,Evol. War,V:Terminus,Savage Land . . 6.00
Ann.#13 MBa,JRu,Atlantis Attacks . 5.00
Ann.#14 AAd,DGr,BWi,AM,ATi, V:Ahab,A:X-Factor, ... 8.00
Ann.#15,TR,JRu,MMi(c),Flesh Tears, Pt.3,A:X-Force,New Warriors . . 5.00
Ann.#16 JaL,JRu,Shattershot Part.2. . . . . 4.00
Ann.#17 JPe,MFm,I:X-Cutioner, D:Mastermind,w/card 4.00
Ann.#18 JR2,V:Caliban, BU:Bishop 3.25
Ann.1999 AD 3.50
Marvel Milestone rep. #1 (1991) . . . 2.95

Uncanny X-Men #374
© Marvel Entertainment Group

Marvel Milestone rep. #9 (1993) . . . 2.95
Marvel Milestone rep. #28 (1994) . . 2.95
G-Size #1,GK,DC,I:New X-Men (Colossus,Storm,Nightcrawler, Thunderbird,3rd A:Wolv.) . . . 575.00
G-Size #2,rep.#57-59 . . . . 55.00
Marvel Milestone rep. Giant Size #1 (1991) 3.95
Spec.#1 X-Men: Earth Fall, rep. #232–#234 (1996) 2.95
Spec.#1 X-Men vs. Dracula, rep. X-Men Ann.#6 (1993). 2.00
GNv X-Men: Days of Future Past rep. X-Men #141-142 . . . . 5.00
GNv Pryde of the X-Men. 10.95
GNv God Loves,Man Kills, (1994) prestige. 6.95
GN X-Men Firsts, I:Wolverine,Rogue, Gambit & Mr. Sinister, rep. Avengers Ann.#10, Uncanny X-Men #221,#266 & Incredible Hulk #181 (1996) . 5.00
GNv X-Men Rarities,F:Classic Stories (1995) 5.95
TPB Asgardian Wars 15.95
TPB Bloodties V:Exodus. 15.95
TPB The Coming of Bishop, rep. #282–#285,#287–#288 (1995) 12.95
TPB Dark Phoenix Saga 12.95
TPB X-Men: Days of Future Present, MMi(c),Rep.F.F.Ann.#23,X-Men Ann.#14,X-Factor Ann.#5, New Mutant Ann.#10 . . . . 14.95
TPB Essential X-Men collection, rep. 12.95
TPB Fatal Attractions (1994). 17.95
TPB From the Ashes 16.95
TPB Greatest Battles 15.95
TPB X-Men: Inferno, 352pg 19.95
TPB X-Men Megazine, CCl,JLe, rep. Uncanny X-Men #273–#275 . . . 3.95
TPB X-Men: Mutant Massacre, rep. 256pg.. . . . . 24.95
TPB Savage Land 9.95
TPB X-Cutioner's Song. 24.95
TPB X-Tinction Agenda, rep.X-Men #270-272,X-Factor #60-62, New Mutants #95-97 . . . . 19.95
X-Men Survival Guide to the Mansion, NKu(c) (1993) 6.95

MARVEL

X-MEN

[2nd Regular Series] Oct., 1991

1A(c);Storm,Beast,B:CCl(s),JLe,SW I:Fabian Cortez,Acolytes, V:Magneto 3.00
1B(c);Colossus,Psylocke 3.00
1C(c);Cyclops,Wolverine 3.00
1D(c);Magneto. 3.00
1E(c);Gatefold w/pin-ups 6.50
2 JLe,SW,V:Magneto Contd. 4.00
3 E:CCl(s),JLe,SW,V:Magneto . . . 4.00
4 JBy(s),JLe,SW,I:Omega Red, V:Hand. 4.00
5 B:SLo(s),JLe,SW,V:Hand, Omega Red,I:Maverick. 4.00
6 JLe,SW,V:Omega Red, Hand, Sabretooth 4.00
7 JLe,SW,V:Omega Red,Hand, Sabretooth 3.00
8 JLe,SW,Bishop vs. Gambit 3.00
9 JLe,SW,A:Ghost Rider,V:Brood. . 3.00
10 JLe,SW,MT,Longshot Vs. Mojo, BU:Maverick. 3.00
11 E:SLo(s)JLe,MT,V:Mojo, BU:Maverick. 2.50
12 B:FaN(s),ATb,BWi,I:Hazard 2.50
13 ATb,BWi,V:Hazard. 2.50
14 NKu,X-Cutioners Song#3,A:X-Fact. X-Force,V:Four Horsemen 2.50
15 NKu,X-Cutioners Song #7, V:Mutant Liberation Front 2.50
16 NKu,MPn,X-Cutioners Song #11, A:X-Force,X-Factor,V:Dark Riders, Apocalypse Vs.Archangel,IR:Stryfe is Nathan Summers 2.50
17 NKu,MPn,R:Illyana,A:Darkstar . . 2.50
18 NKu,MPn,R:Omega Red,V:Soul Skinner 2.50
19 NKu,MPn,V:Soul Skinner, Omega Red 2.50
20 NKu,MPn,J.Grey vs Psylocke . . 2.50
21 NKu,V:Silver Samurai,Shinobi . . 2.50
22 BPe,V:Silver Samurai,Shinobi . . 2.50
23 NKu,MPn,V:Dark Riders, Mr.Sinister 2.50
24 NKu,BSz,A Day in the Life. 2.50
25 NKu,Hologram(c),V:Magneto, Wolverine's Adamantium skeleton pulled out 14.00
25a Gold Edition. 38.00
25b B&W cover 30.00
26 NKu,Bloodties#2,A:Avengers, I:Unforgiven 2.50
27 RiB,I:Threnody. 2.50
28 NKu,MRy,F:Sabretooth 2.50
29 NKu,MRy,V:Shinobi 2.50
30 NKu,MRy,W:Cyclops&Jean Grey, w/card 5.00
31 NKu,MRy,A:Spiral,Matsuo, D:Kwannon 2.50
32 NKu,MRy,A:Spiral,Matsuo 2.25
33 NKu,MRy,F:Gambit & Sabretooth 2.25
34 NKu,MRy,A:Riptide 2.25
35 LSh,A:Nick Fury. 2.25
36 NKu,MRy,I:Synch,PhalanxCovenant Generation Next,pt.2, deluxe . . 5.00
36a Newsstand ed.. . . . . 2.00
37 NKu,MRy,Generation Next,pt.3 foil(c) 5.00
37a newsstand ed. 2.00
38 NKu,MRy,F:Psylocke 2.50
38a newsstand ed. 2.00
39 X-Treme, deluxe 2.50
39a newsstand ed. 2.00
40 deluxe 3.00
40a newsstand ed. 2.00
41 V:Legion, deluxe 2.50
41a newsstand ed. 2.00
42 PS,PaN,Mysterious Visitor 2.50
43 Rogue and Iceman 2.50
44 FaN,Mystery of Magneto 2.50
45 20th Anniv.pt.2. . . . . 5.00
46 FaN,Aku,V:Comcast 3.00
47 SLo,AKu,CaS,F:Dazzler. 3.00
48 SLo,AKu,CaS,F:Sabretooth 3.00
49 SLo,AKu,Bishop wanted 3.00
50 Onslaught(c) 6.00
50a regular edition 5.00
51 MWa,Onslaught. 3.00
52 MWa,AKu,CaS,V:Sinister. 3.00
53 Onslaught saga 6.00
54 Onslaught saga 5.00
55 Onslaught saga 3.00
56 Onslaught saga 3.00
57 Operation: Zero Tolerence 3.00
58 SLo,NKu 3.00
59 . . . . 3.00
60 SLo,NKu,F:Ororo, V:Candra. . . . 3.00
61 SLo,CNn,F:Storm, V:Candra . . . 3.00
62 SLo,CPa,F:Sebastian Shaw, Shang Chi 3.00
62A variant Storm/Wolverine(c). . . 13.00
63 SLo,CPa,ATi,A:Sebastian Shaw, Inner Circle 3.00
64 SLo,CPa,ATi,V:Hellfire Club 3.00
65 SLo,CPa,ATi, No Exit prelude . . 3.00
66 SLo,CPa,ATi, Zero Tolerance, A:Bastion 3.00
67 SLo,CPa,ATi, Zero Tolerance, F:Iceman, Cecilia Reyes. 3.00
68 SLo,CPa,ATi, Operation: Zero Tolerance 3.00
69 SLo,CPa, Operation: Zero Tolerance, concl. 3.00
70 ATi,Who will join X-Men?, double-sized. 5.00
71 ATi,Cyclops banished. 4.00
72 ATi,Professor Logan's School of Hard Knocks 2.50
73 ATi,Marrow visits Callisto 2.50
74 ATi,Terror in Morlock Tunnels. . . 2.50
75 ATi,V:N'Garai, double size 3.00
76 CCl,V:Sabretooth, 35th anniv kickoff 2.50
77 ATi,A:Black Panther,Maggott . . . 2.50
78 Return of Professor X 2.50
79 ATi,Cannonball must leave team 2.50
80A BPe, ATi, cont. from Uncanny X-Men #360, etched foil (c) 7.50
80B regular cover. 4.00
81 AKu,MFm,Search for Prof.X. . . . 2.50
82 AKu,MFm,Hunt for Xavier 2.50
83 AKu,MFm,Hunt for Xavier,pt.4 . . 2.50

X-Men, 2nd Series, #24
© Marvel Entertainment Group

84 AJu,Hunt for Xavier,concl. 2.50
85 AD,MFm,R:Magneto 2.50
85a signed 30.00
86 AD,MFm,Magneto War,pt.2, O:Joseph 2.50
87 AD,MFm,Magneto War,pt.4 . . . . 2.50
88 AD,MFm,R:Juggernaut 2.50
89 AD,MFm,In the past. 2.50
90 AD,MFm,In the past,concl.. . . . . 2.50
91 AD,AKu,Rage Against the Machine, pt.2 x-over. 2.50
91a signed 30.00
92 AD,MFm,The Shattering x-over . 2.50
93 AD,MFm,The Shattering x-over . 2.50
94 AD,MFm,Shattering,x-over. 4.00
95 AD,TR,A:Death,. 2.50
96 AD. 2.50
97 AD,MFm,Apocalypse12,pt.7. . . . 2.50
97a variant (c) 3.00
98 AD,MFm,Ages of Apocalypse,pt.5 . . . . 2.50
99 AD,BBh,mutants no more? 2.50
100 CCl,X-Men:Revolution,48-pg. . . 3.00
100a variant covers 5.00
101 CCl,X-Men:Revolution 2.25
102 CCl,R:Wolverine 2.25
103 CCl,Wolverine v. Rogue 2.25
104 CCl,V:Killion. 2.25
105 CCl,Archangel,Psylocke. 2.25
106 CCl,Neo,Cecelia Reyes 2.25
107 CCl,Cadre K 2.25
Ann.#1 JLe,Shattershot,pt.1, I:Mojo II 3.50
Ann.#2 I:Empyrean,w/card 3.25
Ann.#3 F:Storm 3.50
Ann. Uncanny X-Men '97, V:Brotherhood, 48pg. 3.50
Ann. '98 RMz, F:X-Men & Doctor Doom. 3.50
Ann. '98 X-Men/Fantastic Four, JoC, PaP, 48pg 3.50
Ann.1999 Rage Against the Machine, pt.3 x-over, 48-page . 3.50
Ann.2000 CCl,SHa,SEa,48-pg.. . . . 3.50
Uncanny X-Men'95 Spec. F:Husk . . 3.95
Spec.X-Men '95, F:Mr.Sinister. 3.95
Spec.X-Men'96 LHa, 64pg., F:Gambit, Rogue, Magneto, Jubilee & Wolverine 3.00
Spec. X-Men'97,JFM,SEp,F:Gambit, Joesph & Phoenix 3.00
Minus 1 Spec., SLo,JMd,, flashback, discovery of mutants 2.00
Spec.#1 X-Men: Road to Onslaught (1996) 2.50
Spec. X-Men Universe: Past, Present and Future. 3.00
Spec. X-Men:Year in Review 3.00
Spec.#1 X-Men (2000) 2.25
Spec. Millennial Visions 4.00
Spec. X-Men:Declassified,48-pg . . . 3.50
Spec. Unearthed Archives Sketchbook 3.00
Chrom.Classics, Vol.2,#1,signed. . 30.00
GN TKa,AD,MFm, Age of Apocalypse 2.95
TPB Dark Phoenix Saga. 15.95
TPB Dawn of the Age of Apocalypse, gold foil cover. . . . 8.95
TPB Legion Quest 8.95
TPB Magneto Returns 15.95
TPB Rise of Apocalypse. 9.00
TPB Twilight of the Age of Apocalypse, gold foil cover. . . . 8.95
TPB Crossroads. 15.95
TPB Phoenix Rising 14.95
TPB Road Trippin. 20.00
TPB Zero Tolerance, 336pg. 24.95
TPB Visionaries Joe Madureira. . . 17.95

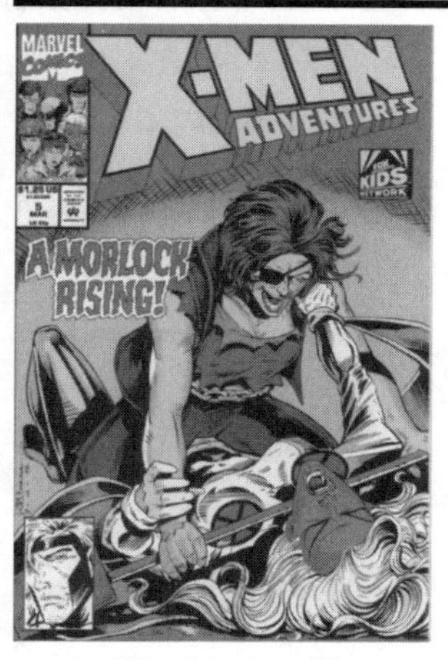

X-Men Adventures #5
© Marvel Entertainment Group

X-MEN ADVENTURES

[1st Season] 1992–94

1 V:Sentinals, Based on TV Cartoon 6.00
2 V:Sentinals,D:Morph 5.00
3 V:Magneto,A:Sabretooth 4.00
4 V:Magneto 4.00
5 V:Morlocks 4.00
6 V:Sabretooth 3.50
7 V:Cable,Genosha,Sentinels 3.00
8 A:Colossus,A:Juggernaut 3.00
9 I:Colussus(on cartoon), V:Juggernaut 3.00
10 A:Angel,V:Mystique 3.00
11 I:Archangel(on cartoon) 2.00
12 V:Horsemen of Apocalypse 2.00
13 RMc(s),I:Bishop(on cartoon) . . . 2.00
14 V:Brotherhood of Evil Mutants . . 2.00
15 . . . . 2.00
TPB Vol.1 . . . . 4.95
TPB Vol.2 . . . . 4.95
TPB Vol.3 . . . . 5.95
TPB Vol.4 rep. Days of Future Past and Final Conflict 6.95

[2nd Season] 1994–95

1 R:Morph,I:Mr. Sinister (on cartoon) 3.00
2 I:Nasty Boys (on cartoon) 2.00
3 I:Shadow King (on cartoon) 2.00
4 I:Omega Red (on cartoon) 2.00
5 I:Alpha Flight (on cartoon). 2.00
6 F:Gambit 2.00
7 A:Cable,Bishop,Apocalypse 2.00
8 A:Cable,Biship,Apocalypse 2.00
9 O:Rogue. 2.00
10 . . . . 2.00
11 F:Mojo,Longshot 2.00
12 Reunions,pt.1 . . . . 2.00
13 Reunions,pt.1 . . . . 2.00

[3rd Season] 1995–96

1 Out of the Past,pt.1 . . . . 3.00
2 V:Spirit Drinker 2.00
3 Phoenix Saga,pt.1 . . . . 2.00
4 Phoenix Saga,pt.2 . . . . 2.00
5 Phoenix Saga,pt.3 . . . . 2.00
6 Phoenix Saga,pt.4 . . . . 2.00
7 Phoenix Saga,pt.5 . . . . 2.00
8 War in The Savage Land 2.00
9 F:Ka-Zar. 2.00
10 Dark Phoenix,Saga,pt.1 . . . . 2.00
11 Dark Phoenix Saga,pt.2 . . . . 2.00
12 Dark Phoenix Saga,pt.3 . . . . 2.00
13 Dark Phoenix Saga,pt.4 . . . . 2.00

X-MEN: ALPHA

1994

1 Age of Apocalypse, double size . 7.00
1a gold edition, 48pp 45.00

X-MEN/ALPHA FLIGHT

Jan., 1986

1 PS,BWi,V:Loki 5.00
2 PS,BWi,V:Loki 4.00

X-MEN/ALPHA FLIGHT: THE GIFT

Jan., 1998

1-shot CCl,PS, rep. of limited series 6.00

X-MEN/ ANIMATION SPECIAL

TV Screenplay Adapt 10.95

X-MEN ARCHIVES: CAPTAIN BRITAIN

1995

1 AMo,AD,Secret History. 3.00
2 AMo,AD,F:Captain Britain. 3.00
3 AMo,AD,Trial of Captain Britain . 3.00
4 AMo,AD,Trial cont. 3.00
5 AD,AMo,F:Captain Britain. 3.00
6 AMo,AD,Final Apocalypse? 3.00
7 AMo,AD,conclusion 3.00

X-MEN: ASKANI'SON

1 SLo,GeH,sequel to Adventures of Cyclops & Phoenix 3.00
2 SLo,GeH,A:Stryfe 3.00
3 SLo,GeH 3.00
4 SLo,GeH,conclusion 3.00
Books of Askani, portraits (1995) . . 3.00

X-MEN AT STATE FAIR

1 KGa,Dallas Times Herald 40.00

X-MEN: BLACK SUN

Sept., 2000

1 (of 5) CCl,New X-Men 3.00
2 CCl,Storm 3.00
3 CCl,RT,Banshee & Sunfire 3.00
4 CCl,LSi,Colossus&Nightcrawler . 3.00
5 CCl,Wolverine & Thunderbird . . . 3.00

X-MEN: CHILDREN OF THE ATOM

Jan. 2000

1 (of 6) JoC,SR,O:X-Men. 3.00
2 JoC,SR,F:Professor X 3.00
3 JoC,SR 3.00
4 JoC,SR 3.00
5 JoC,SR, ... 3.00
6 JoC,SR,concl.. . . . . 3.00

X-MEN CHRONICLES

1995

1 X-Men Unlimited AX. 4.00
2 V:Abbatoir 4.00

X-MEN/CLANDESTINE

1996

1 & 2 AD,MFm,48pg . . . . @3.00

X-MEN CLASSICS

Dec., 1983

1 NA,rep.. . . . . 3.50
2 NA,rep.. . . . . 3.50
3 NA,rep.. . . . . 3.50

CLASSIC X-MEN

Sept., 1986

1 AAd(c),JBo,New stories, rep. giant size X-Men 1 . . . . 9.00
2 rep.#94,JBo/AAd(c),BU: Storm & Marvel Girl 6.00
3 rep.#95,JBo/AAd(c),BU: I:Thunderbird II. 4.00
4 rep.#96,JBo/AAd(c),BU: Wolverine & N.Crawler 3.50
5 rep.#97,JBo/AAd(c),BU: Colossus 3.00
6 rep.#98,JBo/AAd(c),BU: JeanGrey,I:Seb.Shaw 3.00
7 rep.#99,JBo/AAd(c),BU: HellfireClub,W.Queen 3.00
8 rep.#100,JBo/AAd(c),BU: O:Jean Grey/Phoenix 3.00
9 rep.#101,JBo/AAd(c),BU: Nightcrawler 3.00
10 rep.#102,JBo/AAd(c),BU: Wolverine,A:Sabretooth 8.00
11 rep.#103,JBo/BL(c),BU:Storm . . 3.00
12 rep.#104,JBo/AAd(c),BU: O:Magneto 7.00
13 rep.#105,JBo/AAd(c),BU: JeanGrey & Misty Knight 3.00
14 rep.#107,JBo/AAd(c),BU: Lilandra 3.00
15 rep.#108,JBo/AAd(c),BU: O:Starjammers 3.00
16 rep.#109,JBo/AAd(c),BU: Banshee. 3.00
17 rep.#111,JBo/TA(c),BU: Mesmero 5.00
18 rep.#112,JBo/AAd(c),BU: Phoenix 4.00
19 rep.#113,JBo/AAd(c),BU: Magnetoo. 4.00
20 rep.#114,JBo/AAd(c), BU:Storm 3.00
21 rep.#115,JBo/AAd(c), BU:Colossus. 3.00
22 rep.#116,JBo/AAd(c), BU:Storm 3.00
23 rep.#117,JBo/KGa(c),BU: Nightcrawler. 3.00
24 rep.#118,JBo/KGa(c),BU: Phoenix 3.00
25 rep.#119,JBo/KGa(c),BU:Wolv.. . 3.00
26 rep.#120,JBo/KGa(c),BU:Wolv. . 4.00
27 rep.#121,JBo/KD(c),BU: Wolverine & Phoenix 3.00
28 rep.#122,JBo/KD(c),BU:X-Men. . 3.00
29 rep.#123,JBo/KD(c),BU: Colossus 3.00
30 rep.#124,JBo/SLi(c),BU: O:Arcade 3.00
31 rep.#125,JBo/SLi(c),BU: Professor.X 3.00
32 rep.#126,JBo/SLi(c),BU: Wolverine. 3.00
33 rep.#127,JBo/SLi(c),BU: Havok 3.00
34 rep.#128,JBo/SLi(c),BU: W.Queen,M.Mind 3.00
35 rep.#129,JBo/SLi(c),BU: K.Pryde 3.00
36 rep.#130,MBr/SLi(c),BU: Banshee & Moira 3.00
37 rep.#131,RL/SLi(c),BU: Dazzler 3.00
38 rep.#132,KB/SLi(c),BU: Dazzler 3.00

MARVEL

Classic X-Men #9
© Marvel Entertainment Group

39 rep.#133,2nd JLe X-Men/SLi(c), BU:Storm 11.00
40 rep.#134,SLi(c),BU:N.Crawler . . 2.00
41 rep.#135,SLi(c),BU: Mr. Sinister,Cyclops 2.00
42 rep.#136,SLi(c),BU: Mr. Sinister,Cyclops 2.00
43 rep.#137,JBy(c),BU: Phoenix,Death 2.50

Becomes:

X-MEN CLASSICS
1990

44 rep.#138,KD/SLi(c) 2.00
45 thru 49 rep.#139-#145,SLi(c) . @2.00
50 thru 69 rep.#146-#165 . . . . . . @2.00
70 rep.#166 . . . . 2.00
71 thru 99 rep.#167-#195 . . . . . . @2.00
100 thru 105 rep. #196–#201 . . . @2.00
106 Phoenix vs. Beyonder 2.00
107 F:Rogue 2.00
108 F:Nightcrawler 2.00
109 Rep. Uncanny X-Men #205 . . . 2.00
110 Rep. Uncanny X-Men #206 . . . 2.00

X-MEN: EARLY YEARS

1 rep. X-Men (first series) #1 . . . . 2.00
2 rep. X-Men (first series) #2 . . . . 2.00
3 rep. X-Men (first series) #3 . . . . 2.00
4 thru 16 rep. X-Men (first series) #4 to #16 . . . . @2.00
17 Rep. X-Men #17 & #18 . . . . 2.50

X-MEN: HELLFIRE CLUB
Nov., 1999

1 (of 4) AKu,BRa,CAd 2.50
2 AKu,BRa,CAd,O:Inner Circle . . . 2.50
3 AKu,BRa,CAd,O:cont.. . . . . 2.50
4 AKu,BRa,O:Concl. 2.50

X-MEN: THE HIDDEN YEARS
Oct., 1999

1 JBy,TP,Original team,48-pg. 3.50
2 JBy,TP 2.50
3 JBy,TP,. 2.50
4 JBy,TP,Savage Land concl.. . . . . 2.50
5 JBy,TP,A:Candy Southern 2.50
6 JBy,TP,F:Storm. 2.50
7 JBy,TP,V:Deluge 2.50
8 JBy,TP,Fant.Four 2.50
9 JBy,TP,Phoenix. 2.50
10 JBy,TP,Candy Southern 2.50
11 JBy,TP,Beast 2.50
12 JBy,TP,48-pg. 3.00
13 JBy,TP,Beast 2.50

X-MEN INDEX
See: OFFICIAL MARVEL INDEX TO THE X-MEN

X-MEN: LIBERATORS
Sept. 1999

1 (of 4) PJ,F:Wolverine,Nightcrawler & Colossus. 3.00
2 PJ,V:Russian army 3.00
3 PJ,V:Nikolas. 3.00
4 PJ,V:Omega Red 3.00

X-MEN: LOST TALES
1997

1 CCl,JBo,rep. from Classic X-Men 3.00
2 CCl,JBo,rep. from Classic X-Men 3.00

X-MEN: MAGIK
Oct., 2000

1 (of 4) DAn,ALa,LSh 3.00

X-MEN/MICRONAUTS
Jan., 1984

1 JG,BWi,Limited Series 3.50
2 JG,BWi,KJo,V:Baron Karza. 2.50
3 JG,BWi,V:Baron Karza 2.50
4 JG,BWi,V:Baron Karza,Apr.1984. 2.50

X-MEN: THE MANGA
Jan. 1998

1 b&w,translated,F:Jubilee. 3.00
2 Jubilee joins, V:Sentinels 3.00
3 Agent Gyrich strikes 3.00
4 Beast captured, morph dead. . . . 3.00
5 Magneto attempts to rescue Beast 3.00
6 Beast on trial, A:Sabretooth 3.00
7 V:Magneto 3.00
8 V:Magneto 3.00
9 V:Morlocks 3.00
10 V:Morlocks, 40pg finale 3.00
11 Wolverine vs. Sabretooth 3.00
12 Wolverine vs. Sabretooth 3.00
13 F:Storm, Jubilee & Gambit. 3.00
14 . . . . 3.00
15 . . . . 3.00
16 A:Colossus,V:Juggernaut, double-size. 4.00
17 F:Cable & Angel 3.00
18 Angel becomes Archangel 3.00
19 Angel becomes Death 3.00
20 Rogue vs. Apocalypse 3.00
21 V:Four Horsemen 3.00
22 V:Sentinels 3.00
23 RGr(c),F:Bishop. 3.00
24 RGr(c),V:Nimrod 3.00
25 Bishop vs. Gambit 3.00
26 V:Brotherhood of Evil Mutants . . 3.00
27 Magneto Returns 3.00
28 V:Master Mold,A:Magneto 3.00
29 thru 32 . . . . @3.00

X-MEN: THE MOVIE
June, 2000

Magneto, photo(c) 5.95
Rogue, photo(c) 5.95
Wolverine, photo(c) 5.95
X-Men The Movie, photo(c) 5.95
TPB Beginnings, 144-pg. 14.95
TPB X-Men The Movie, 4 diff. photo(c)s . . . . @14.95

X-MEN OMEGA
1995

1 FaN,Slo,After Xavier, concl. . . . 10.00
1a Gold ed. Chromium(c) 48pg. . . 45.00

X-MEN: PHOENIX
Oct., 1999

1 (of 3) JFM,F:Rachel Summers . . 2.50
2 JFM 2.50
3 JFM,concl. 2.50

X-MEN PRIME
1995

1 SLo,FaN,BHi,major plotlines for all X books begin, chromium(c)10.00

X-MEN: PRYDE & WISDOM

1 WEl,TyD,KIS. 2.00
2 & 3 WEl,TyD,KIS. . . . . @2.00

X-MEN: THE MAGNETO WAR
Jan., 1999

1-shot AD, Joseph vs. Magneto . . . 3.00
1a signed 20.00

X-MEN: THE RISE OF APOCALYPSE

1 TKa,AdP, ancient history of X-Men 2.00
2 thru 4 TKa,AdP,. . . . . @2.00
TPB 10.00

X-MEN: THE SEARCH FOR CYCLOPS
Oct., 2000

1A (of 4) TR,SHa, ... 3.00
1B variant AdP (c). 3.00

X-MEN SPOTLIGHT ON STARJAMMERS
1990

1 DC,F:Starjammers,A:Prof.X 5.00
2 DC,F:Starjammers,A:Prof.X 5.00

X-MEN: TRUE FRIENDS
July 1999

1 (of 3) CCl,RL,JP,F:Shadowcat. . . 2.00
2 CCl,RL,JP,A:Kitty Pryde 2.00
3 CCl,RL,JP,A:Wolverine,concl. . . . 3.00

X-MEN 2099
1993–96

1 B:JFM(s),RLm,JP,I:X-Men 2099 . 3.00
1a Gold Ed.. . . . . 5.00
2 RLm,JP,V:Rat Pack 2.50
3 RLm,JP,D:Serpentina 2.50
4 RLm,JP,I:Theatre of Pain 2.00
5 RLm,JP,Fall of the Hammer#3 . . 2.00
6 RLm,JP,I:Freakshow. 2.00
7 RLm,JP,V:Freakshow 2.00
8 RLm(c),JS3,JP,N;Metalhead, I:2nd X-Men 2099. . . . . 2.00
9 RLm,JP,V:2nd X-Men 2099. . . . . 2.00
10 RLm,JP,A:La Lunatica 2.00
11 RLm,JP,V:2nd X-Men 2099 . . . . 2.00
12 RLm,JP,A:Junkpile. 2.00
13 RLm,JP 2.00

14 RLm,JP,R:Loki 2.00
15 RLm,JP,F:Loki,I:Haloween Jack . 1.50
16 . . . . 1.50
17 X'ian 1.50
18 Haloween Jack 1.50
19 Conclusion Halloween Jack 1.50
Becomes:

X-MEN 2099 A.D.

20 F:Bloodhawk 2.00
21 Doom Factor 2.00
22 One Nation Under Doom 2.00
23 V:Junkpile 2.00
24 . . . . 2.00
25 X-Men Reunited. 2.50
25a variant cover 4.25
26 V:Graverobber. 2.00
27 . . . . 2.00
28 X-Nation x-over 2.00
29 X-Nation x-over 2.00
30 . . . . 2.00
31 . . . . 2.00
32 V:Foolkiller. 2.00
Spec.#1 Bros.Hildebrandt(c) 3.95
GN X-Men 2099: Oasis, rep., Greg Hildebrandt(c) 64pg, (1998) . . . 6.00

X-MEN UNIVERSE
Oct., 1999

1 rep. July 99 stories,80-pg.. . . . . . 5.00
2 rep. Aug.99 stories,80-pg.. . . . . . 5.00
3 rep. Sept.99 stories,80-pg. 5.00
4 rep. Oct.99 stories,80-pg. 5.00
5 rep. Nov.99 stories,80-pg.. . . . . . 5.00
6 rep. Dec.99 stories,80-pg.. . . . . . 5.00
7 rep. Jan.00 stories,80-pg. 5.00
8 rep. Feb.00 stories,80-pg 5.00
9 rep. Mar.00 stories,80-pg 5.00
10 rep. Apr.00 stories,80-pg 5.00
11 rep. May 00 stories,80-pg 5.00
12 rep. June 00 stories,80-pg 4.00
13 rep. July 00 stories,80-pg. 4.00

X-MEN UNLIMITED
1993

1 CBa,BP,O:Siena Blaze 7.00
2 JD,O:Magneto 6.00
3 FaN(s),BSz(c),MMK,Sabretooth joins X-Men,A:Maverick 7.00
4 SLo(s),RiB,O:Nightcrawler,Rogue, Mystique,IR:Mystique is Nightcrawler's mother. 5.00
5 JFM(s),LSh,After Shi'ar/ Kree War 4.00
6 JFM(s),PS,Sauron 4.00
7 JR2,HMe,O:Storm 4.00
8 Legacy Virus Victim 4.00
9 LHa,Wolverine & Psylocke 4.00
10 MWa,Dark Beast,Beast, double-size. 8.00
11 Rogue & Magneto, double-size . 8.00
12 Onslaught x-over,A:Juggernaut . 3.00
13 GP,Binary gone berserk 3.00
14 TKa, Onslaught fallout 3.00
15 HMe,F:Wolverine, Iceman & Maverick 3.00
16 MvR,F:Banshee, White Queen, I:Primal 3.00
17 TKa,Wolverine vs. Sabretooth, minds are switched. 3.00
18 TDF,V:Hydro Man 3.00
19 BRa,Nightcrawler v. Belasco . . . 3.00
20 F:Generation X 3.00
21 TDz,Strong Guy returns. 3.00
22 into Marrow's World 3.00
23 F:Professor X 3.00
24 F:Wolverine & Cecilia Reyes . . . 3.00
25 BBh,48-pg. 3.00
26 BBh,Ages of Apocalypse,pt.4. . . 3.00
27 BBh,X-Men: Revolution 3.00
28 BBh,Russia 3.00
29 BBh,Maximum Security 3.00

X-MEN VS. AVENGERS
April, 1987

1 MS,JRu,V:Soviet SuperSoldiers . 4.50
2 MS,JRu,V:Sov.Super Soldiers . . 3.50
3 MS,JRu,V:Sov.Super Soldiers . . 3.50
4 KP,JRu,BMc,AW,AM,V:Magneto July 1987 . . . . 3.00
TPB 12.95

X-MEN VS. THE BROOD
1996

1 and 2 Day of Wrath . . . . @3.00
TPB rep. #1,#2 and Unc.X-Men #232–#234 . . . . 17.00

X-NATION 2099
1996

1 . . . . 2.00
2 . . . . 2.00
3 At Herod's Themepark 2.00

X.S.E.
Mini-Series 1996

1 (of 4) JOs,Bishop & Shard's secrets 2.00
2 JOs, How did Shard die 2.00
3 JOs, How Shard died 2.00
4 JOs, conclusion 2.00

X-TERMINATORS
Oct., 1988—Jan., 1989

1 JBg,AW,AM,I:N'astirh 4.00
2 JBg,AM,V:N'astirh. 3.50
3 JBg,AM,V:N'astirh. 3.00
4 JBg,AM,A:New Mutants 3.00

X-UNIVERSE
1995

1 The Other Heroes. 3.50
2 F:Ben Grimm,Tony Stark. 3.50

YOGI BEAR
Nov., 1977

1 A:Flintstones 15.00
2 . . . . 10.00
3 . . . . 10.00
4 . . . . 10.00
5 . . . . 10.00
6 . . . . 10.00
7 . . . . 10.00
8 . . . . 10.00
9 March, 1979 . . . . 10.00

YOUNG ALLIES COMICS
Timely Summer, 1941—Oct., 1946

1 S&K,Hitler(c),I&O:Young Allies 1st meeting Capt. America & Human Torch,A:Red Skull 11,000.00
2 S&K,A;Capt.America,Human Torch. 2,700.00

Young Allies Comics #14
© Marvel Entertainment Group

3 Remember Pearl Harbor(c) . 2,000.00
4 A;Capt. America,Torch,Red Skull ASh(c),Horror In Hollywood A:Capt.America,Torch 3,200.00
5 ASh(c). 1,300.00
6 ASh(c) 850.00
7 ASh(c) 850.00
8 ASh(c) 850.00
9 ASh(c),Axis leaders(c), B:Tommy Type 900.00
10 ASh(c). 850.00
11 ASh(c). 700.00
12 ASh(c). 700.00
13 ASh(c). 700.00
14 . . . . 700.00
15 ASh(c). 700.00
16 ASh(c). 700.00
17 ASh(c). 700.00
18 ASh(c). 700.00
19 ASh(c),E:Tommy Type 700.00
20 . . . . 700.00

YOUNG HEARTS
Nov., 1949—Feb., 1950

1 . . . . 75.00
2 Feb., 1950 . . . . 50.00

YOUNG MEN
See: COWBOY ROMANCES

YUPPIES FROM HELL
1989

1 Satire 3.00
2 . . . . 3.00
3 . . . . 3.00

ZORRO
Marvel UK 1990

1 Don Diego 2.00
2 thru 12 . . . . @2.00

GOLDEN AGE

A-1 COMICS

Magazine Enterprises, 1944

N# F:Kerry Drake,BU:Johnny Devildog & Streamer Kelly . . 200.00
1 A:Dotty Driple,Mr. EX,Bush Berry and Lew Loyal 90.00
2 A:Texas Slim & Dirty Dalton, The Corsair,Teddy Rich, Dotty Dripple,Inca Dinca,Tommy Tinker Little Mexico and Tugboat. . . . 50.00
3 same 35.00
4 same 35.00
5 same 35.00
6 same 30.00
7 same 30.00
8 same 30.00
9 Texas Slim Issue 40.00
10 Same characters as issues #2–#8 . . . . 30.00
11 Teena 50.00
12 Teena 35.00
13 JCr,Guns of Fact and Fiction, narcotics & junkies featured . 225.00
14 Tim Holt WesternAdventures . 500.00
15 Teena 35.00
16 Vacation Comics 30.00
17 Tim Holt #2, E:A-1 on cover . . 275.00
18 Jimmy Durante, Ph(c) 350.00
19 Tim Holt #3 . . . . 200.00
20 Jimmy Durante Ph(c) 300.00
21 OW,Joan of Arc movie adapt.. 200.00
22 Dick Powell (1949). 175.00
23 Cowboys N' Indians #6 . . . . . . 35.00
24 FF(c),LbC,Trail Colt #2. . . . . . 275.00
25 Fibber McGee & Molly (1949) . 50.00
26 LbC, Trail Colt #2. . . . . 200.00
27 Ghost Rider#1,O:GhostRider . 550.00
28 Christmas (Koko & Kola) 20.00
29 FF(c), Ghost Rider #2 . . . . . . 500.00
30 BP, Jet Powers #1 . . . . 250.00
31 FF,Ghost Rider#3,O:Ghost Rider 475.00
32 AW,GE,Jet Powers #2 . . . . . . 200.00
33 Muggsy Mouse #2 . . . . 45.00
34 FF(c),Ghost Rider #4 . . . . 475.00
35 AW,Jet Powers 275.00
36 Muggsy Mouse 35.00
37 FF(c),Ghost Rider 475.00
38 AW,WW,Jet Powers 275.00
39 Muggsy Mouse 20.00
40 Dogface Dooley. 35.00
41 Cowboys N' Indians 22.00
42 BP,Best of the West 325.00
43 Dogface Dooley. 25.00
44 Ghost Rider 200.00
45 American Air Forces 35.00
46 Best of the West 175.00
47 FF,Thunda 900.00
48 Cowboys N' Indians 22.00
49 Dogface Dooley. 15.00
50 BP,Danger Is Their Busines . . 100.00
51 Ghost Rider 200.00
52 Best of the West 150.00
53 Dogface Dooley. 15.00
54 BP,American Air Forces 35.00
55 BP,U.S. Marines 25.00
56 BP,Thunda. 150.00
57 Ghost Rider 175.00
58 American Air Forces 35.00
59 Best of the West 100.00
60 The U.S. Marines. 35.00
61 Space Ace. 375.00
62 Starr Flagg. 300.00
63 FF,Manhunt 275.00
64 Dogface Dooley. 15.00
65 BP,American Air Forces 35.00
66 Best of the West 100.00
67 American Air Forces 35.00
68 U.S. Marines 35.00
69 Ghost Rider 175.00
70 Best of the West 100.00
71 Ghost Rider 175.00
72 U.S. Marines 35.00
73 BP,Thunda. 125.00
74 BP,American Air Forces 30.00
75 Ghost Rider 150.00
76 Best of the West 100.00
77 LbC,Grl,Manhunt 225.00
78 BP,Thunda. 100.00
79 American Air Forces 35.00
80 Ghost Rider 150.00
81 Best of the West 100.00
82 BP,Cave Girl 325.00
83 BP,Thunda. 100.00
84 Ghost Rider 150.00
85 Best of the West 100.00
86 BP,Thunda. 100.00
87 Best of the West 100.00
88 Bobby Benson's B-Bar-B 50.00
89 BP,Home Run,Stan Musial . . . 175.00
90 Red Hawk 70.00
91 BP,American Air Forces 30.00
92 Dream Book of Romance. 35.00
93 BP,Great Western 150.00
94 FF,White Indian 175.00
95 BP,Muggsy Mouse. 15.00
96 BP,Cave Girl 250.00
97 Best of the West 100.00
98 Undercover Girl 275.00
99 Muggsy Mouse 12.00
100 Badmen of the West 175.00
101 FF,White Indian 150.00
101(a) FG, Dream Book of Romance, Marlon Brando . . . 125.00
103 BP,Best of the West 100.00
104 FF,White Indian 150.00
105 Great Western 100.00
106 BP,Dream Book of Love 75.00
107 Hot Dog. 25.00
108 BP,BC,Red Fox 125.00
109 BP,Dream Book of Romance . 40.00
110 Dream Book of Romance 40.00

A-1 Comics #23
© Magazine Enterprises

111 BP,I'm a Cop 125.00
112 Ghost Rider 110.00
113 BP,Great Western. 100.00
114 Dream Book of Love 55.00
115 Hot Dog. 18.00
116 BP,Cave Girl 200.00
117 White Indian. 75.00
118 BP(c),Undercover Girl 250.00
119 Straight Arrow's Fury 100.00
120 Badmen of the West 125.00
121 Mysteries of the Scotland Yard. 125.00
122 Black Phantom. 275.00
123 Dream Book of Love 40.00
124 Hot Dog. 18.00
125 BP,Cave Girl 200.00
126 BP,I'm a Cop. 55.00
127 BP,Great Western 100.00
128 BP,I'm a Cop 55.00
129 The Avenger 275.00
130 BP,Strongman 150.00
131 BP,The Avenger. 200.00
132 Strongman. 125.00
133 BP,The Avenger. 200.00
134 Strongman. 125.00
135 White Indian 75.00
136 Hot Dog. 15.00
137 BP,Africa 135.00
138 BP,Avenger 200.00
139 BP,Strongman, 1955 . . . . . . 100.00

ABBIE AN' SLATS

United Features Syndicate
March–Aug., 1948

1 RvB(c) 200.00
2 RvB(c) 175.00
3 RvB(c) 100.00
4 Aug., 1948 . . . . 100.00
N# 1940,Earlier Issue 275.00
N#. 225.00

ABBOTT AND COSTELLO

St. John Publishing Co.
Feb., 1948

1 PP(c), Waltz Time. 425.00
2 Jungle Girl and Snake(c) 200.00
3 Outer Space cover 150.00
4 MD, Circus cover 125.00
5 MD,Bull Fighting cover 125.00
6 MD,Harem cover 125.00
7 MD,Opera cover. 125.00
8 MD,Pirates cover 125.00
9 MD,Polar Bear cover 125.00
10 MD,PP(c),Son of Sinbad tale . 170.00
11 MD 100.00
12 PP(c), Movie issue. 100.00
13 Fire fighters cover 100.00
14 Bomb cover. 100.00
15 Bubble Bath cover 100.00
16 thru 29 MD. . . . . @75.00
30 thru 39 MD. . . . . @50.00
40 MD,Sept., 1956 . . . . 50.00
3-D #1, Nov. 1953. . . . . 250.00

ACE COMICS

David McKay Publications
April, 1937

1 JM, F:Katzenjammer Kids . . 2,800.00
2 JM, A:Blondie 800.00
3 JM, A:Believe It Or Not 525.00
4 JM, F:Katzenjammer Kids 500.00

All comics prices listed are for *Near Mint* condition.

5 JM, A:Believe It Or Not 500.00
6 JM, A:Blondie 375.00
7 JM, A:Believe It Or Not 375.00
8 JM, A:Jungle Jim 375.00
9 JM, A:Blondie 375.00
10 JM, F:Katzenjammer Kids 350.00
11 I:The Phantom series 600.00
12 A:Blondie, Jungle Jim 325.00
13 A:Ripley's Believe It Or Not 300.00
14 A:Blondie, Jungle Jim 300.00
15 A:Blondie 275.00
16 F:Katzenjammer Kids 275.00
17 A:Blondie 275.00
18 A:Ripley's Believe It Or Not 275.00
19 F:Katzenjammer Kids 275.00
20 A:Jungle Jim 275.00
21 A:Blondie 250.00
22 A:Jungle Jim 250.00
23 F:Katzenjammer Kids 250.00
24 A:Blondie 250.00
25 250.00
26 O:Prince Valiant 750.00
27 thru 36 @250.00
37 Krazy Kat Ends 175.00
38 thru 49 @150.00
50 thru 59 @125.00
60 thru 69 @120.00
70 thru 79 @110.00
80 thru 89 @100.00
90 thru 99 @85.00
100 100.00
101 thru 109 @75.00
110 thru 119 @65.00
120 thru 143 @60.00
144 Phantom covers begin 100.00
145 thru 150 @75.00
151 Oct.–Nov., 1949 100.00

ACES HIGH

E.C. Comics, March–April, 1955

1 GE(c),JDa,WW,GE,BK 200.00
2 GE(c),JDa,WW,GE,BK 125.00
3 GE(c),JDa,WW,GE,BK 100.00
4 GE(c),JDa,WW,GE,BK 100.00
5 GE(c),JDa,WW,BK, Nov.–Dec., 1955 100.00

ADVENTURES INTO DARKNESS

Standard Publications
Aug., 1952

5 JK(c), ATh 250.00

Adventures Into Darkness #11
© Standard Publications

6 GT, JK 150.00
7 JK(c) 150.00
8 ATh 160.00
9 JK,ATh 175.00
10 JK,ATh,MSy 125.00
11 JK,ATh,MSy 125.00
12 JK,ATh,MYs 125.00
13 Cannibalism feature 150.00
14 100.00

Adventures Into the Unknown #14
© American Comics Group

ADVENTURES INTO THE UNKNOWN!

American Comics Group
Fall, 1948

1 FG, Haunted House cover 1,500.00
2 Haunted Island cover 600.00
3 AF, Sarcophagus cover 625.00
4 Monsters cover 275.00
5 Monsters cover 275.00
6 Giant Hands cover 225.00
7 Skeleton Pirate cover 225.00
8 Horror 225.00
9 Snow Monster 225.00
10 Red Bats 225.00
11 Death Shadow 225.00
12 OW(c) 225.00
13 OW(c),Dinosaur 175.00
14 OW(c),Cave 175.00
15 Red Demons 175.00
16 175.00
17 OW(c),The Thing Type 225.00
18 OW(c),Wolves 175.00
19 OW(c),Graveyard 150.00
20 OW(c),Graveyard 150.00
21 Bats and Dracula 150.00
22 Death 150.00
23 Bats 150.00
24 150.00
25 150.00
26 150.00
27 AW 200.00
28 thru 39 @125.00
40 thru 49 @110.00
50 125.00
51 Lazarus 250.00
52 Lazarus 235.00
53 225.00
54 225.00
55 225.00
56 Lazarus 225.00
57 225.00
58 Lazurus 225.00
59 200.00
60 85.00
61 85.00
62 thru 69 @60.00
70 thru 79 @45.00
80 thru 89 @35.00
90 thru 99 @50.00
100 45.00
101 thru 115 @40.00
116 AW,AT 45.00
117 thru 127 @40.00
128 AW,Forbidden Worlds 45.00
129 thru 152 @35.00
153 A:Magic Agent 35.00
154 O:Nemesis 45.00
155 35.00
156 A:Magic Agent 35.00
157 thru 174, Aug. 1967 @35.00

ADVENTURES IN WONDERLAND

Lev Gleason Publications
April, 1955

1 75.00
2 40.00
3 35.00
4 35.00
5 50.00

ADVENTURES OF MIGHTY MOUSE

St. John Publishing Co.
Nov., 1951

1 Mighty Mouse Adventures 175.00
2 Menace of the Deep 135.00
3 Storm Clouds of Mystery 100.00
4 Thought Control Machine 85.00
5 Jungle Peril 75.00
6 `The Vine of Destruction' 70.00
7 Space Ship(c) 70.00
8 Charging Alien(c) 70.00
9 Meteor(c) 65.00
10 Revolt at the Zoo" 65.00
11 Jungle(c) 65.00
12 A:Freezing Terror 65.00
13 A:Visitor from Outer Space 65.00
14 V:Cat 55.00
15 60.00
16 60.00
17 60.00
18 May, 1955 60.00

AGGIE MACK

Four Star Comics/
Superior Comics, Jan., 1948

1 AF,HR(c) 225.00
2 JK(c) 125.00
3 AF,JK(c) 100.00
4 AF 150.00
5 AF,JK(c) 125.00
6 AF,JK(c) 110.00
7 AF,Burt Lancaster on cover 125.00
8 AF,JK(c), Aug. 1949 110.00

BILL BARNES, AMERICA'S AIR ACE

Street and Smith Publications
July, 1940

1 (Bill Barnes Comics) 650.00
2 Second Battle Valley Forge 350.00
3 A:Aviation Cadets 300.00
4 Shotdown(c) 275.00
5 A:Air Warden, Danny Hawk 250.00
6 A:Danny Hawk,RocketRodney 225.00
7 How to defeat the Japanese 225.00
8 Ghost Ship 225.00

9 Flying Tigers, John Wayne . . . 235.00
10 I:Roane Waring 225.00
11 Flying Tigers 225.00
12 War Workers 225.00
Becomes:

AIR ACE

2-1 Invades Germany 200.00
2-2 Jungle Warfare 125.00
2-3 A:The Four Musketeers 100.00
2-4 A:Russell Swann 100.00
2-5 A:The Four Musketeers 100.00
2-6 Raft(c). 75.00
2-7 BP, What's New In Science . . 75.00
2-8 XP-59 . . . . 75.00
2-9 The Northrop P-61. . . . . 75.00
2-10 NCG-14. . . . . 75.00
2-11 Whip Lanch 75.00
2-12 PP(c). 75.00
3-1 . . . . 65.00
3-2 Atom and It's Future 65.00
3-3 Flying in the Future 65.00
3-4 How Fast Can We Fly 65.00
3-5 REv(c). 65.00
3-6 V:Wolves. 65.00
3-7 BP(c), Vortex of Atom Bomb 150.00
3-8 Feb.–March, 1947 . . . . 90.00

AIRBOY (see AIR FIGHTERS COMICS)

AIR FIGHTERS COMICS

Hillman Periodicals, Nov., 1941

1 I:Black Commander
(only App) 1,700.00
2 O:Airboy A:Sky Wolf 2,700.00
3 O:Sky Wolf and Heap 1,400.00
4 A:Black Angel, Iron Ace 900.00
5 A:Sky Wolf and Iron Ace. 675.00
6 Airboy's Bird Plane 650.00
7 Airboy battles Kultur 575.00
8 A:Skinny McGinty 550.00
9 A:Black Prince, Hatchet Man. . 550.00
10 I:The Stinger 550.00
11 Kida(c). 550.00
12 A:Misery 550.00
2-1 A:Flying Dutchman 500.00
2-2 I:Valkyrie. 800.00
2-3 Story Panels cover 500.00
2-4 V:Japanese 500.00
2-5 Air Boy in Tokyo 500.00
2-6 `Dance of Death'. 500.00
2-7 A:Valkyrie. 500.00
2-8 Airboy Battles Japanese 500.00
2-9 Airboy Battles Japanese 500.00
2-10 O:Skywolf. 600.00
Becomes:

AIRBOY

2-11. . . . . 550.00
2-12 A:Valykrie 350.00
3-1 . . . . 300.00
3-2 . . . . 275.00
3-3 Never published
3-4 I:The Heap 250.00
3-5 Airboy 225.00
3-6 A:Valykrie 225.00
3-7 AMc,Witch Hunt. 225.00
3-8 A:Condor. 235.00
3-9 O:The Heap. 250.00
3-10 . . . . 200.00
3-11 . . . . 200.00
3-12 Airboy missing. 250.00
4-1 Elephant in chains cover . . . 235.00
4-2 I:Rackman. 150.00
4-3 Airboy profits on name. 150.00
4-4 S&K. 180.00
4-5 S&K,The American Miracle . 180.00

Airfighters #5
© Hillman Periodicals

4-6 S&K,A:Heap and
Flying Fool 180.00
4-7 S&K. 180.00
4-8 S&K,Girlfriend captured 180.00
4-9 S&K,Airboy in quick sand. . . 180.00
4-10 S&K,A:Valkyrie 180.00
4-11 S&K,A:Frenchy 180.00
4-12 FBe. 200.00
5-1 LSt 125.00
5-2 I:Wild Horse of Calabra 125.00
5-3 . . . . 125.00
5-4 Cl 125.00
5-5 Skull on cover 125.00
5-6 . . . . 125.00
5-7 . . . . 125.00
5-8 Bondage Cover 150.00
5-9 Zoi,Row. 125.00
5-10 A:Valykrie,O:The Heap. . . . 135.00
5-11 Airboy vs. The Rats 125.00
5-12 BK,Rat Army captures
Airboy. 125.00
6-1 . . . . 125.00
6-2 . . . . 125.00
6-3 . . . . 125.00
6-4 Airboy boxes 135.00
6-5 A:The Ice People. 125.00
6-6 . . . . 125.00
6-7 Airboy vs. Chemical Giant . . 125.00
6-8 O:The Heap. 150.00
6-9 . . . . 125.00
6-10 . . . . 125.00
6-11 . . . . 125.00
6-12 . . . . 125.00
7-1 . . . . 120.00
7-2 BP. 120.00
7-3 BP. 120.00
7-4 I:Monsters of the Ice 120.00
7-5 V:Monsters of the Ice. 120.00
7-6 . . . . 120.00
7-7 Mystery of the Sargasso
Sea 120.00
7-8 A:Centaur 120.00
7-9 I:Men of the StarlightRobot . 120.00
7-10 O:The Heap. 120.00
7-11 . . . . 120.00
7-12 Airboy visits India. 120.00
8-1 BP,A:Outcast and Polo
Bandits. 100.00
8-2 BP,Suicide Dive cover 100.00
8-3 I:The Living Fuse. 100.00
8-4 A:Death Merchants o/t Air . . 120.00
8-5 A:Great Plane from Nowhere 100.00
8-6 . . . . 100.00
8-7 . . . . 100.00
8-8 . . . . 100.00
8-9 . . . . 100.00
8-10 A:Mystery Walkers. 100.00
8-11 . . . . 100.00
8-12 . . . . 120.00
9-1 . . . . 100.00
9-2 A:Valykrie 90.00
9-3 A:Heap (cover) 90.00
9-4 A:Water Beast, Frog Headed
Riders 100.00
9-5 A:Heap vs.Man of Moonlight . 90.00
9-6 Heap cover 90.00
9-7 Heap cover 90.00
9-8 Heap cover 100.00
9-9 . . . . 100.00
9-10 Space cover 100.00
9-11 . . . . 90.00
9-12 Heap cover 90.00
10-1 Heap cover 90.00
10-2 Ships on Space 90.00
10-3 . . . . 90.00
10-4 May, 1953 . . . . 90.00

AL CAPP'S DOG PATCH COMICS

Toby Press, June, 1949

1 . . . . 175.00
2 A:Daisy. 150.00
3 . . . . 125.00
4 Dec., 1949 . . . . 125.00

AL CAPP'S SHMOO

Toby Press, July, 1949

1 100 Trillion Schmoos 300.00
2 Super Shmoo(c) 175.00
3 . . . . 175.00
4 . . . . 150.00
5 April, 1950 . . . . 150.00

AL CAPP'S WOLF GAL

Toby Press, 1951

1 Pin-Up 250.00
2 1952. . . . . 225.00

ALL-FAMOUS CRIME

Star Publications, May, 1951

8 LbC(c) 125.00
9 LbC(c) 200.00
10 LbC(c). 100.00
4 LbC(c) 125.00
5 LbC(c) 125.00
Becomes:

ALL-FAMOUS POLICE CASES

6 LbC(c) 125.00
7 LbC(c) 100.00
8 LbC(c) 100.00
9 LbC(c) 90.00
10 thru 15 LbC(c) . . . . @90.00
16 Sept., 1954 . . . . 90.00

ALL GOOD COMICS

R. W. Voight/Fox Publ./ St. John Publ.

1 1944. . . . . 175.00
1 1946. . . . . 150.00
N# 1949 . . . . 500.00

ALL GREAT COMICS (see DAGGER, DESERT HAWK)

ALL HERO COMICS
Fawcett Publications
March, 1943

1 A:Capt. Marvel Jr.,Capt. Midnight,Ibis, Golden Arrow and Spy Smasher 1,400.00

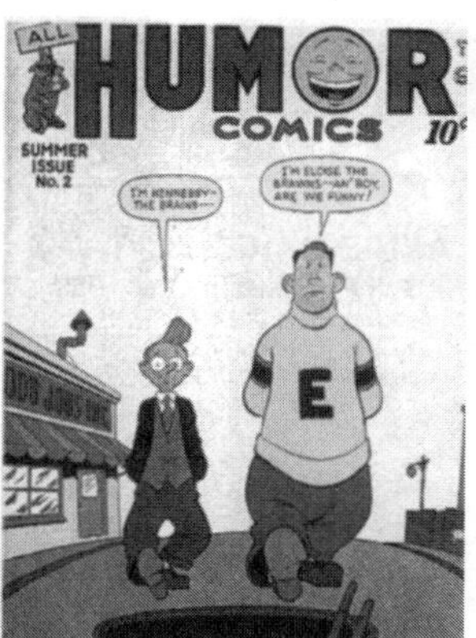

All-Humor Comics #2
© Quality Comics

ALL HUMOR COMICS
Comic Favorites, Inc.
(Quality Comics), Spring, 1946

1 . . . . 150.00
2 PG 75.00
3 I:Kelly Poole 45.00
4 thru 7 . . . . @40.00
8 PG 45.00
9 . . . . 45.00
10 . . . . 45.00
11 thru 17 . . . . @30.00

ALL LOVE ROMANCES (see SCREAM COMICS)

ALL NEGRO COMICS
June, 1947

1 . . . . 2,900.00

ALL-NEW COMICS
Family Comics
(Harvey Publ.), Jan., 1943

1 A:Steve Case, Johnny Rebel I:Detective Shane 2,300.00
2 JKu,O:Scarlet Phantom. 800.00
3 . . . . 550.00
4 AdH 600.00
5 Flash Gordon 550.00
6 I:Boy Heroes and Red Blazer . 550.00
7 JKu,AS(c),A:Black Cat & Zebra 550.00
8 JKu,A:Shock Gibson 550.00
9 JKu,A:Black Cat 550.00
10 JKu,A:Zebra. 500.00
11 BP,A:Man in Black, Girl Commandos. 500.00
12 JKu 500.00
13 Stuntman by S&K, A:Green Hornet&cover 475.00
14 BP,A:Green Hornet 450.00
15 Smaller size, Distributed by Mail, March–April, 1947 . . 425.00

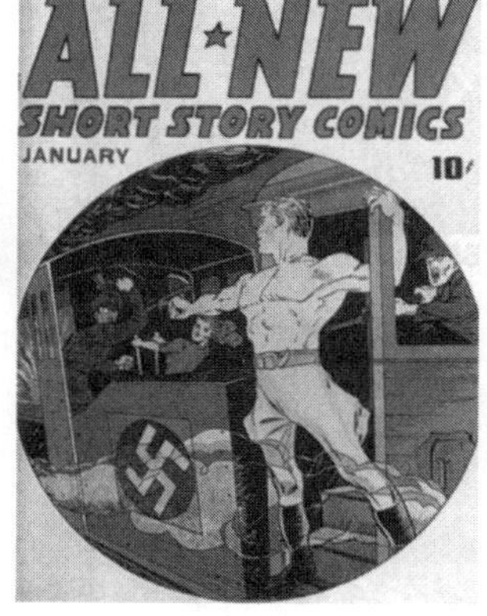

All-New Comics #1
© Family Comics/Harvey Publications

ALL TOP COMICS
William H. Wise Co., 1944

N# 132pgs.,A:Capt. V,Red Robbins 225.00

ALL TOP COMICS
Fox Features Syndicate
Spring, 1946

1 A:Cosmo Cat, Flash Rabbit. . . 175.00
2 . . . . 75.00
3 . . . . 60.00
4 . . . . 60.00
5 . . . . 60.00
6 . . . . 60.00
7 . . . . 60.00
7a 85.00
8 JKa(c),I:Blue Beetle 1,800.00
9 JKa(c),A:Rulah 900.00
10 JKa(c),A:Rulah 1,000.00
11 A:Rulah,Blue Beetle 800.00
12 A:Rulah,Jo Jo,Blue Beetle . . . 800.00
13 A:Rulah 800.00
14 A:Rulah,Blue Beetle 1,000.00
15 A:Rulah 800.00
16 A:Rulah,Blue Beetle. 800.00
17 A:Rulah,Blue Beetle. 800.00
18 A:Dagar,Jo Jo 500.00

Green Publ.

6 1957 . . . . 20.00
6 1958 . . . . 20.00
6 1959 . . . . 20.00
6 1959 . . . . 20.00
6 Supermouse cover. 20.00

ALLEY OOP
Argo Publications Nov., 1955

1 . . . . 125.00
2 . . . . 100.00
3 March, 1956 . . . . 100.00

AMAZING ADVENTURES
Ziff-Davis Publ. Co., 1950

1 WW, Asteroid Witch 550.00
2 Masters of Living Flame 225.00
3 The Evil Men Do. 225.00
4 Invasion of the Love Robots . . 225.00
5 Secret of the Crater-Men 225.00
6 Man Who Killed a World 250.00

AMAZING GHOST STORIES (See: WEIRD HORRORS)

AMAZING-MAN COMICS
Centaur Publications
Sept., 1939–Feb., 1942

5 BEv,O:Amazing Man 15,000.00
6 BEv,B:The Shark 2,700.00
7 BEv,I:Magician From Mars . . 1,600.00
8 BEv 1,200.00
9 BEv 1,200.00
10 BEv 1,100.00
11 BEv,I:Zardi 1,000.00
12 SG(c). 900.00
13 SG(c). 900.00
14 B:Reef Kinkaid, Dr. Hypo 750.00
15 A:Zardi. 600.00
16 Mighty Man's powers revealed 650.00
17 A:Dr. Hypo 600.00
18 BLb(a),SG(c) 600.00
19 BLb(a),SG(c) 600.00
20 BLb(a),SG(c) 600.00
21 O:Dash Dartwell. 625.00
22 A:Silver Streak, The Voice . . . 600.00
23 I&O:Tommy the Amazing Kid . 600.00
24 B:King of Darkness,Blue Lady 550.00
25 A:Meteor Marvin 950.00
26 A:Meteor Marvin,ElectricRay . 900.00

AMAZING MYSTERY FUNNIES
Centaur Publications, 1938

1 Skyrocket Steele in the Year X 2,800.00
2 WE,Skyrocket Steele 1,500.00
3 . . . . 700.00
(#4) WE,bondage (c) 700.00
2-1(#5) 650.00
2-2(#6) Drug use 550.00
2-3(#7) Air Sub DX 550.00
2-4(#8) 550.00
2-5(#9) 700.00
2-6(#10) 550.00
2-7(#11) scarce 2,700.00
2-8(#12) Speed Centaur 1,000.00
2-9(#13) 600.00
2-10(#14) 600.00
2-11(#15) 600.00
2-12(#16) BW,I:Space Patrol . . 1,500.00
3-1(#17) I:Bullet 600.00
18 . . . . 600.00
19 BW,Space Patrol 750.00
20 . . . . 600.00
21 BW,Space Patrol 750.00
22 BW,Space Patrol 750.00
23 BW,Space Patrol 750.00
24 BW,Space Patrol 750.00

AMAZING WILLIE MAYS
Famous Funnies, 1954

1 Willie Mays(c). 600.00

AMERICAN LIBRARY
David McKay Publ., 1943

(#1) Thirty Seconds Over Tokyo, movie adapt. 250.00
(#2) Guadalcanal Diary. 175.00
3 Look to the Mountain 100.00
4 The Case of the Crooked Candle (Perry Mason). 100.00
5 Duel in the Sun. 100.00
6 Wingate's Raiders. 110.00

America's Best Comics #24
© Better Publications

AMERICA'S BEST COMICS
Nedor/Better/Standard Publications, Feb., 1942

1 B:Black Terror, Captain Future, The Liberator,Doc Strange . 1,900.00
2 O:American Eagle. 750.00
3 B:Pyroman 550.00
4 A:Doc Strange, Jimmy Cole . . 450.00
5 A:Lone Eagle, Capt. Future. . . 425.00
6 A:American Crusader 400.00
7 A:Hitler,Hirohito. 600.00
8 The Liberator ends 400.00
9 ASh(c) 450.00
10 ASh(c). 365.00
11 ASh(c). 365.00
12 Red Cross cover 365.00
13 . . . . 365.00
14 Last American Eagle app. . . . 365.00
15 ASh(c). 350.00
16 ASh(c). 360.00
17 Doc Strange carries football. . 350.00
18 Bondage cover 350.00
19 ASh(c). 350.00
20 vs. the Black Market 350.00
21 Infinity cover 350.00
22 A:Captain Future 325.00
23 B:Miss Masque 400.00
24 Bondage cover 375.00
25 A:Sea Eagle 300.00
26 A:The Phantom Detective . . . 300.00
27 ASh(c). 300.00
28 A:Commando Cubs, Black Terror 300.00
29 A:Doc Strange 300.00
30 ASh(c). 300.00
31 July, 1949 . . . . 300.00

AMERICA'S BIGGEST COMICS BOOK
William H. Wise, 1944

1 196 pgs. A:Grim Reaper, Zudo, Silver Knight, Thunderhoof, Jocko and Socko,Barnaby Beep,Commando Cubs. 350.00

AMERICA'S GREATEST COMICS
Fawcett Publications, Fall 1941

1 MRa(c),A:Capt. Marvel, Bulletman,Spy Smasher and Minute Man 2,300.00
2 F:Capt. Marvel. 1,200.00
3 F:Capt. Marvel 800.00
4 B:Commando Yank. 600.00
5 Capt.Marvel in "Lost Lighting" . 600.00
6 Capt.Marvel fires Machine Gun 550.00
7 A:Balbo the Boy Magician. . . . 550.00
8 A:Capt.Marvel Jr.,Golden Arrow, Summer 1943 . . . . . . 550.00

AMERICA IN ACTION
Dell Publishing Co., 1942

1 . . . . 150.00

ANDY COMICS (see SCREAM COMICS)

ANGEL
Dell Publishing Co., Aug., 1954

(1) *see Dell Four Color #576*
2 . . . . 30.00
3 thru 16 . . . . @20.00

ANIMAL ANTICS
Dell Publishing Co., 1946

1 B:Racoon Kids 350.00
2 . . . . 200.00
3 thru 10 . . . . @125.00
11 thru 23 . . . . @75.00

ANIMAL COMICS
Dell Publishing Co., 1942

1 WK,Pogo. 1,000.00
2 Uncle Wiggily(c),A:Pogo 450.00
3 Muggin's Mouse(c),A:Pogo . . . 325.00
4 Uncle Wiggily(c) 250.00
5 Uncle Wiggily(c) 325.00
6 Uncle Wiggily 200.00
7 Uncle Wiggily 200.00
8 Pogo 250.00
9 War Bonds(c),A:Pogo 250.00
10 Pogo 250.00
11 Pogo 175.00
12 Pogo 175.00
13 Pogo 175.00
14 Pogo 175.00
15 Pogo 175.00
16 Uncle Wiggily. 100.00
17 Pogo(c) 125.00
18 Pogo(c) 125.00
19 Pogo(c) 125.00
20 Pogo 100.00
21 Pogo(c) 125.00
22 Pogo 75.00
23 Pogo 75.00
24 Pogo(c) 85.00
25 Pogo(c) 85.00
26 Pogo(c) 85.00
27 Pogo(c) 75.00
28 Pogo(c) 75.00
29 Pogo(c) 75.00
30 Pogo(c) 75.00

ANIMAL FABLES
E.C. Comics, July–Aug., 1946

1 B:Korky Kangaroo,Freddy Firefly Petey Pig and Danny Demon 275.00
2 B:Aesop Fables 200.00
3 . . . . 150.00
4 . . . . 150.00
5 Firefly vs. Red Ants 150.00
6 . . . . 150.00
7 O:Moon Girls,Nov.–Dec.1947 . 450.00

ANIMAL FAIR
Fawcett Publications, March, 1946

1 B:Captain Marvel Bunny, Sir Spot 175.00
2 A:Droopy, Colonel Walrus . . . 100.00
3 . . . . 60.00
4 A:Kid Gloves, Cub Reporter . . . 60.00
5 thru 7 . . . . 60.00
8 . . . . 50.00
9 . . . . 50.00
10 . . . . 50.00
11 Feb. 1947 . . . . 50.00

ANNIE OAKLEY & TAGG
Dell Publishing Co., 1953

(1) *see Dell Four Color #438*
(2) *see Dell Four Color #481*
(3) *see Dell Four Color #575*
4 . . . . 125.00
5 . . . . 90.00
6 thru 10 . . . . @75.00
11 thru 18 . . . . @50.00

ARCHIE COMICS
MLJ Magazines Winter, 1942-43

1 I:Jughead & Veronica. 13,000.00
2 . . . . 2,700.00
3 . . . . 2,000.00
4 . . . . 1,000.00
5 . . . . 900.00
6 . . . . 750.00
7 thru 11 . . . . @700.00
12 thru 15 . . . . @500.00
16 thru 19 . . . . @450.00

Archie Publications

20 . . . . 450.00
21 . . . . 300.00
22 thru 31 . . . . @275.00
32 thru 42 . . . . @150.00
43 thru 50 . . . . @100.00
51 thru 60 . . . . @75.00
61 thru 70 . . . . @50.00
71 thru 80 . . . . @40.00
81 thru 99 . . . . @30.00
100 . . . . 50.00
101 . . . . 25.00
102 thru 115 . . . . @15.00
116 thru 130 . . . . @12.00
131 thru 145 . . . . @10.00
146 thru 160 . . . . @7.50
161 thru 180 . . . . @5.00
181 thru 200 . . . . @4.00
201 thru 250 . . . . @3.00
251 thru 280 . . . . @3.00
281 thru 389 . . . . @3.00

ARCHIE'S GIANT SERIES MAGAZINE
Archie Publications, 1954

1 . . . . 1,000.00
2 . . . . 600.00
3 . . . . 400.00
4 . . . . 350.00
5 . . . . 350.00
6 thru 10 . . . . @250.00
11 thru 20 . . . . @200.00
21 thru 29 . . . . @125.00
30 thru 35 . . . . @60.00
136 thru 141 . . . . @60.00
142 . . . . 50.00
143 thru 160 . . . . @25.00
161 thru 199 . . . . @20.00
200 . . . . 12.00
201 thru 250 . . . . @10.00

251 thru 299 . . . . @10.00
300 thru 500 . . . . @10.00

ARCHIE'S GIRLS BETTY AND VERONICA
Archie Publications, 1950

1 . . . . 1,300.00
2 . . . . 600.00
3 . . . . 400.00
4 . . . . 375.00
5 . . . . 375.00
6 thru 10 . . . . @300.00
11 thru 15 . . . . @225.00
16 thru 20 . . . . @200.00
21 . . . . 150.00
22 thru 29 . . . . @140.00
30 thru 40 . . . . @100.00
41 thru 50 . . . . @90.00
51 thru 60 . . . . @75.00
61 thru 70 . . . . @50.00
71 thru 80 . . . . @40.00
81 thru 90 . . . . @40.00
91 thru 99 . . . . @40.00
100. . . . . 50.00
101 thru 120 . . . . @35.00
121 thru 140 . . . . @20.00
141 thru 160 . . . . @15.00
161 thru 180 . . . . @10.00
181 thru 199 . . . . @10.00
200 . . . . 12.00
201 thru 220 . . . . @10.00
221 thru 240 . . . . @9.00
241 thru 347 . . . . @7.00

ARCHIE'S JOKE BOOK MAGAZINE
Archie Publications, 1953

1 . . . . 675.00
2 . . . . 375.00
3 . . . . 275.00
15 thru 19 . . . . @165.00
20 thru 25 . . . . @120.00
26 thru 35 . . . . @90.00
36 thru 40 . . . . @75.00
41 1st NA art 150.00
42 & 43 . . . . 75.00
44 thru 48 NA . . . . @100.00
49 thru 60 . . . . @30.00
61 thru 70 . . . . @20.00
71 thru 80 . . . . @15.00
81 thru 100 . . . . @15.00
101 thru 200 . . . . @10.00
201 thru 288 . . . . @7.00

ARCHIE'S MECHANICS
Archie Publications, Sept., 1954

1 . . . . 650.00
2 . . . . 400.00
3 . . . . 300.00

ARCHIE'S PAL, JUGHEAD
Archie Publications, 1949

1 . . . . 1,100.00
2 . . . . 500.00
3 . . . . 300.00
4 . . . . 275.00
5 . . . . 275.00
6 . . . . 200.00
7 thru 10 . . . . @175.00
11 thru 15 . . . . @150.00
16 thru 20 . . . . @125.00
21 thru 30 . . . . @100.00
31 thru 39 . . . . @60.00
40 thru 50 . . . . @50.00
51 thru 60 . . . . @40.00
61 thru 70 . . . . @35.00
71 thru 80 . . . . @30.00
81 thru 99 . . . . @25.00
100 . . . . 27.00
101 thru 126 . . . . @15.00

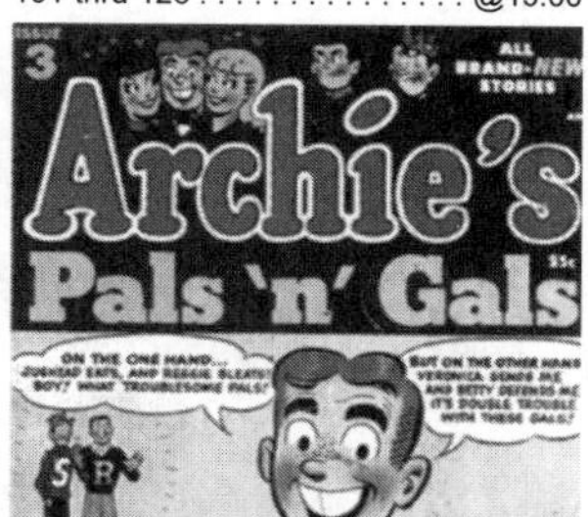

Archie's Pals 'N' Gals #3
© Archie Publications

ARCHIE'S PALS `N' GALS
Archie Publications 1952–53

1 . . . . 600.00
2 . . . . 300.00
3 . . . . 225.00
4 . . . . 135.00
5 . . . . 135.00
6 . . . . 80.00
7 . . . . 80.00
8 thru 10 . . . . @75.00
11 thru 15 . . . . @60.00
16 thru 20 . . . . @50.00
21 thru 30 . . . . @30.00
31 thru 40 . . . . @30.00
41 thru 50 . . . . @30.00
51 thru 60 . . . . @18.00
61 thru 70 . . . . @15.00
71 thru 80 . . . . @15.00
81 thru 99 . . . . @15.00
100 . . . . 10.00
101 thru 120 . . . . @8.00
121 thru 160 . . . . @8.00
161 thru 224 . . . . @8.00

ARCHIE'S RIVAL REGGIE
Archie Publications, 1950

1 . . . . 600.00
2 . . . . 300.00
3 . . . . 225.00
4 . . . . 200.00
5 . . . . 200.00
6 . . . . 175.00
7 thru 10 . . . . @150.00
11 thru 13 . . . . @125.00
14 thru 15 . . . . @100.00
16 Aug., 1954. . . . . 120.00

ARMY & NAVY COMICS
(see SUPERSNIPE COMICS)

ARROW, THE
Centaur Publications Oct., 1940–Oct., 1941

1 B:Arrow 2,400.00
2 BLB(c) 1,000.00
3 O:Dash Dartwell,Human Meteor, Rainbow, Bondage(c) 900.00

ATOMAN
Spark Publications, Feb., 1946

1 JRo,MMe,O:Atoman,A:Kid Crusaders 500.00
2 JRo,MMe 350.00

ATOMIC COMICS
Green Publishing Co. Jan., 1946

1 S&S,A:Radio Squad, Barry O'Neal. 1,100.00
2 MB,A:Inspector Dayton, Kid Kane 500.00
3 MB,A:Zero Ghost Detective . . 350.00
4 JKa(c), July–Aug., 1946 . . . . . 325.00

ATOMIC COMICS
Daniels Publications 1946 (Reprints)

1 A:Rocketman,Yankee Boy, Bondage cover,rep. 250.00

ATOMIC MOUSE
Capital Stories/ Charlton Comics, March, 1953

1 AFa,O:Atomic Mouse 200.00
2 AFa,Ice Cream cover 75.00
3 AFa,Genie and Magic Carpet cover 60.00
4 AFa 60.00
5 AFa,A:Timmy the Timid Ghost . 60.00
6 thru 10 Funny Animal . . . . . . @50.00
11 thru 14 Funny Animal . . . . . . @35.00
15 A:Happy the Marvel Bunny . . . 40.00
16 Funny Animal,Giant 32.00
17 thru 30 Funny Animal . . . . . . @25.00
31 thru 36 Funny Animal . . . . . . @20.00
37 A:Atom the Cat 20.00
38 thru 40 Funny Animal . . . . . . @15.00
41 thru 53 Funny Animal . . . . . . @10.00
54 June, 1963 . . . . 10.00

ATOMIC THUNDER BOLT, THE
Regor Company, Feb., 1946

1 I:Atomic Thunderbolt, Mr. Murdo 500.00

AUTHENTIC POLICE CASES
St. John Publ. Co., 1948

1 Hale the Magician. 275.00
2 Lady Satan, Johnny Rebel . . . 200.00
3 A:Avenger 350.00
4 Masked Black Jack. 175.00
5 JCo 175.00
6 JCo,MB(c) 400.00
7 thru 10 . . . . @150.00
11 thru 15 . . . . @150.00

16 thru 23 . . . . @100.00
24 thru 28 . . . . @175.00
29 thru 38 . . . . @75.00

AVIATION AND MODEL BUILDING (see TRUE AVIATION PICTURE STORIES)

AVON ONE-SHOTS
Avon Periodicals
1949-1953
{Listed in Alphabetical Order}

1 Atomic Spy Cases 225.00
N# WW,Attack on Planet Mars . . 600.00
1 Batchelor's Diary. 250.00
1 Badmen of the West. 250.00
N# Badmen of Tombstone. 100.00
1 Behind Prison Bars. 200.00
2 Betty and Her Steady 55.00
N# Blackhawk Indian
Tomahawk War. 125.00
1 Blazing Sixguns 125.00
1 Butch Cassidy 150.00
N# Chief Crazy Horse. 150.00
N# FF,Chief Victorio's
Apache Massacre. 350.00
N# City of the Living Dead 350.00
1 Complete Romance 200.00
N# Custer's Last Fight 100.00
1 Dalton Boys 110.00
N# Davy Crockett 110.00
N# The Dead Who Walk 400.00
1 Diary of Horror,Bondage(c) . . . 275.00
N# WW,An Earth Man on Venus 1000.00
1 Eerie, bondage (c) 675.00
1 Escape from Devil's Island . . . 300.00
N# Fighting Daniel Boone 100.00
N# For a Night of Love 150.00
1 WW,Flying Saucers 650.00
N# Flying Saucers. 450.00
1 Going Steady with Betty 75.00
N# Hooded Menace 400.00
N# King of the Badmen
of Deadwood 125.00
1 King Solomon's Mines 225.00
N# Kit Carson & the
Blackfeet Warriors 60.00
N# Last of the Comanches 90.00
N# Masked Bandit 125.00

Avon One-Shot: Out of the World
© Avon Periodicals

1 WW,Mask of Dr. Fu Manchu . . 750.00
N# Night of Mystery 350.00
1 Outlaws of the Wild West 200.00
1 Out of this World. 500.00
N# Pancho Villa 175.00
1 Phantom Witch Doctor 350.00
1 Pixie Puzzle Rocket
to Adventureland 75.00
1 Prison Riot,drugs 200.00
N# Red Mountain Featuring
Quantrell's Raiders 200.00
N# Reform School Girl. 1,200.00
1 Robotmen of the Lost Planet. . 800.00
N# WW(c),Rocket to the Moon . . 850.00
N# JKu,Secret Diary of
Eerie Adventures 1,300.00
1 Sheriff Bob Dixon's
Chuck Wagon. 100.00
1 Sideshow 225.00
1 JKu,Sparkling Love. 150.00
N# Speedy Rabbit 50.00
1 Teddy Roosevelt &
His Rough Riders 125.00
N# The Underworld Story 200.00
N# The Unknown Man 200.00
1 War Dogs of the U.S. Army. . . 100.00
N# White Chief of the
Pawnee Indians 90.00
N# Women to Love. 300.00

BABE
Prize/Headline Feature
June–July, 1948

1 BRo,A;Boddy Rogers 150.00
2 BRo,same 100.00
3 Bro,same 75.00
4 thru 9 BRo,same. . . . . @65.00

BABE RUTH SPORTS COMICS
Harvey Publications,
April, 1949

1 BP 350.00
2 BP 250.00
3 BP,Joe Dimaggio(c) 300.00
4 BP,Bob Feller(c) 200.00
5 BP,Football(c). 200.00
6 BP,Basketball(c) 200.00
7 BP 200.00
8 BP 200.00
9 BP, Stan Musial(c) 175.00
11 Feb., 1951 . . . . 175.00

BANNER COMICS
Ace Magazines, Sept., 1941

3 B:Captain Courageous,
Lone Warrior 850.00
4 JM(c),Flag(c) 650.00
5 . . . . 500.00

Becomes:

CAPTAIN COURAGEOUS COMICS

6 I:The Sword 650.00

BARNYARD COMICS
Animated Cartoons
June, 1944

1 (fa). 125.00
2 (fa). 50.00
3 (fa). 35.00
4 (fa). 35.00
5 (fa). 35.00
6 thru 12 (fa) . . . . @30.00
13 FF(ti). 35.00
14 FF(ti). 35.00
15 FF(ti). 35.00
16 . . . . 40.00
17 FF(ti). 35.00
18 FF,FF(ti). 75.00
19 FF,FF(ti). 75.00
20 FF,FF(ti) 75.00
21 FF(ti) 30.00
22 FF,FF(ti). 75.00
23 FF(ti) 30.00
24 FF,FF(ti). 75.00
25 FF,FF(ti). 75.00
26 FF(ti) 30.00
27 FF(ti) 30.00
28 . . . . 20.00
29 FF(ti). 30.00
30 and 31 . . . . @20.00

Becomes:

DIZZY DUCK

32 thru 39. . . . . @15.00

BASEBALL COMICS
Will Eisner Productions
Spring, 1949

1 A:Rube Rocky 600.00

BASEBALL HEROS
Fawcett Publications, 1952

N# Babe Ruth cover 650.00

BASEBALL THRILLS
Ziff-Davis Publ. Co.
Summer, 1951

10 Bob Feller Predicts Pennant
Winners 350.00
2 BP, Yogi Berra story 250.00
3 EK, Joe DiMaggio story,
Summer 1952. . . . . 350.00

BATTLEFIELD ACTION (see DYNAMITE)

BEANY & CECIL
Dell Publishing Co., Jan., 1952

1 . . . . 175.00
2 . . . . 125.00
3 . . . . 125.00
4 . . . . 125.00
5 . . . . 125.00

BEN BOWIE & HIS MOUNTAIN MEN
Dell Publishing Co., 1952

(1) *see Dell Four Color #443*
(2 thru 6) *see Dell Four Color*
7 . . . . 35.00
8 thru 10 . . . . @30.00
11 I:Yellow Hair. 35.00
12 . . . . 25.00
13 . . . . 25.00
14 . . . . 25.00
15 . . . . 25.00
16 . . . . 25.00
17 . . . . 25.00

BEST COMICS
Better Publications, Nov., 1939

1 B:Red Mask 650.00
2 A:Red Mask, Silly Willie 400.00
3 A:Red Mask 400.00
4 Cannibalism story,
Feb., 1940 . . . . 425.00

 All comics prices listed are for *Near Mint* condition.

BEWARE
(see CAPTAIN SCIENCE)

BIG CHIEF WAHOO
Eastern Color Printing
July, 1942

1 . . . . 325.00
2 BWa(c),Three Ring Circus . . . 175.00
3 BWa(c) 125.00
4 BWa(c) 125.00
5 BWa(c),Wild West Rodeo 125.00
6 A:Minnie-Ha-Cha 100.00
7 . . . . 75.00
8 . . . . 75.00
9 . . . . 75.00
10 . . . . 85.00
11 thru 22 . . . . @35.00
23 1943 . . . . 35.00

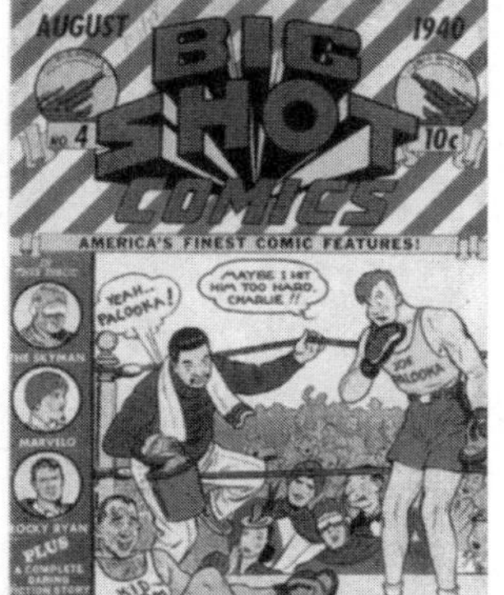

Big Shot Comics #4
© Columbia Comics

BIG SHOT COMICS
Columbia Comics Group
May, 1940

1 MBI,OW,Skyman,B:The Face,
Joe Palooka, Rocky Ryan . 1,700.00
2 MBi,OW,Marvelo cover 700.00
3 MBi,Skyman cover 600.00
4 MBi,OW,Joe Palooka cover . . 500.00
5 MBi,Joe Palooka cover 450.00
6 MBi,Joe Palooka cover 375.00
7 MBi,Elect Joe Palooka
and Skyman 350.00
8 MBi,Joe Palooka and Skyman
dress as Santa 350.00
9 MBi,Skyman 350.00
10 MBi,Skyman 350.00
11 MBi 300.00
12 MBi,OW. 300.00
13 MBi,OW. 300.00
14 MBi,OW,O:Sparky Watts 300.00
15 MBi,OW,O:The Cloak. 350.00
16 MBi,OW. 225.00
17 MBi(c),OW. 225.00
18 MBi,OW. 225.00
19 MBi,OW,The Face cover 235.00
20 MBi,OW,OW(c),Skyman cov. . 235.00
21 MBi,OW,A:Raja the Arabian
Knight. 200.00
22 MBi,OW,Joe Palooka cover . . 200.00
23 MBi,OW,Sparky Watts cover . 175.00
24 MBi,OW,Uncle Sam cover . . . 200.00
25 MBi,OW,Sparky Watts cover . 175.00
26 MBi,OW,Devildog cover 200.00
27 MBi,OW,Skyman cover 200.00
28 MBi,OW,Hitler cover. 250.00
29 MBi,OW,I:Captain Yank 200.00
30 MBi,OW,Santa cover 165.00
31 MBi,OW,Sparky Watts cover . 135.00
32 MBi,OW,B:Vic Jordan
newspaper reps 175.00
33 MBi,OW,Sparky Watts cover . 135.00
34 MBi,OW. 150.00
35 MBi,OW. 150.00
36 MBi,OW,Sparky Watts cover . 135.00
37 MBi,OW. 130.00
38 MBi,Uncle Slap Happy cover . 135.00
39 MBi,Uncle Slap Happy cover . 135.00
40 MBi,Joe Palooka Happy (c) . . 135.00
41 MBi,Joe Palooka 125.00
42 MBi,Joe Palooka parachutes . 125.00
43 MBi,V:Hitler 135.00
44 MBi,Slap Happy cover 125.00
45 MBi,Slap Happy cover 125.00
46 MBi,Uncle Sam cover,V:Hitler. 135.00
47 MBi,Uncle Slap Happy cover . 125.00
48 MBi 125.00
49 MBi 100.00
50 MBi,O:The Face 100.00
51 MBi 100.00
52 MBi,E:Vic Jordan (Hitler cov)
newspaper reps 125.00
53 MBi,Uncle Slap Happy cover . 100.00
54 MBi,Uncle Slap Happy cover . 100.00
55 MBi,Happy Easter cover 100.00
56 MBi 100.00
57 MBi 100.00
58 MBi 100.00
59 MBi,Slap Happy. 100.00
60 MBi,Joe Palooka 90.00
61 MBi 75.00
62 MBi 75.00
63 MBi 75.00
64 MBi,Slap Happy. 75.00
65 MBi,Slap Happy. 75.00
66 MBi,Slap Happy. 75.00
67 MBi 75.00
68 MBi,Joe Palooka 75.00
69 MBi 75.00
70 MBi,OW,Joe Palooka cover . . . 75.00
71 MBi,OW. 80.00
72 MBi,OW. 80.00
73 MBi,OW,The Face cover 80.00
74 MBi,OW. 80.00
75 MBi,OW,Polar Bear swim
club cover 80.00
76 thru 80 MBi,OW . . . . @65.00
81 thru 84 MBi,OW . . . . @55.00
85 MBi,OW,Dixie Dugan cover . . . 60.00
86 thru 95 MBi,OW . . . . @55.00
96 MBi,OW,X-Mas cover. 55.00
97 thru 99 MBi,OW . . . . @55.00
100 MBi,OW,Special issue 60.00
101 thru 103 MBi,OW . . . . @55.00
104 MBi, Aug., 1949 . . . . 60.00

BIG-3
Fox Features Syndicate
Fall, 1940

1 B:BlueBeetle,Flame,Samson 1,700.00
2 A:BlueBeetle,Flame,Samson. . 725.00
3 same 550.00
4 same 500.00
5 same 500.00
6 E:Samson, bondage cover . . . 450.00
7 A:V-Man, Jan., 1942 . . . . 425.00

BILL BARNES, AMERICA'S AIR ACE
(see AIR ACE)

BILL BOYD WESTERN
Fawcett Publications
Feb., 1950

1 B:Bill Boyd, Midnite,Ph(c) 400.00
2 P(c) 200.00
3 B:Ph(c). 150.00
4 . . . . 125.00
5 . . . . 125.00
6 . . . . 125.00
7 . . . . 100.00
8 . . . . 100.00
9 . . . . 100.00
10 . . . . 100.00
11 . . . . 100.00
12 . . . . 90.00
13 . . . . 90.00
14 . . . . 90.00
15 thru 21 . . . . @90.00
22 E:Ph(c) 90.00
23 June, 1952. . . . . 100.00

BILL STERN'S SPORTS BOOK
Approved Comics
Spring–Summer, 1951

1 Ewell Blackwell. 175.00
2 . . . . 125.00
2-2 EK Giant 150.00

BILLY THE KID ADVENTURE MAGAZINE
Toby Press, Oct., 1950

1 AW,FF,AW(c),FF(c) 250.00
2 Photo cover 75.00
3 AW,FF 250.00
4 . . . . 50.00
5 . . . . 50.00
6 FF,Photo cover 60.00
7 Photo cover 50.00
8 . . . . 50.00
9 HK Pot-Shot Pete 60.00
10 . . . . 50.00
11 . . . . 50.00
12 . . . . 50.00
13 HK. 50.00
14 AW,FF 60.00
15 thru 21 . . . . @35.00
22 AW,FF 50.00
23 thru 29 . . . . @30.00
30 1955 . . . . 35.00

BINGO COMICS
Howard Publications, 1945

1 . . . . 225.00

BLACK CAT COMICS
Harvey Publications
(Home Comics),
June–July, 1946

1 JKu 550.00
2 JKu,JSm(c) 275.00
3 JSm(c) 225.00
4 B:Red Demon 200.00
5 S&K 250.00
6 S&K,A:Scarlet Arrow,
O:Red Demon 250.00
7 S&K 250.00
8 S&K,B:Kerry Drake 225.00
9 S&K,O:Stuntman 275.00
10 JK,JSm 175.00
11 . . . . 175.00
12 "Ghost Town Terror". 175.00
13 thru 16 LEI . . . . @150.00
17 A:Mary Worth, Invisible
Scarlet 150.00

GOLDEN AGE

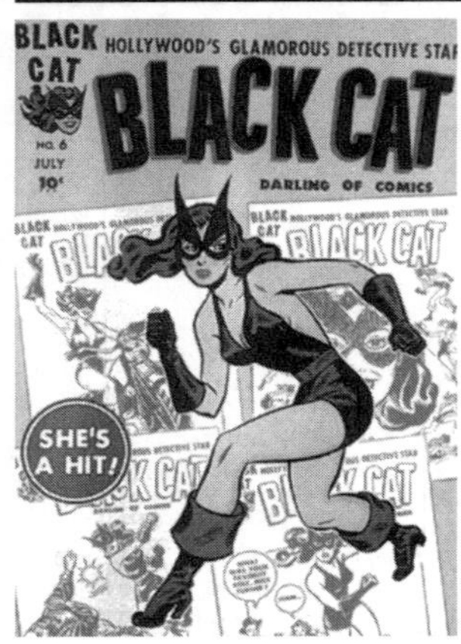

Black Cat #6
© Harvey Publications

18 LEI. 150.00
19 LEI. 150.00
20 A:Invisible Scarlet 150.00
21 LEI. 150.00
22 LEI thru 26 . . . . . . @150.00
27 X-Mas issue. 150.00
28 I:Kit,A:Crimson Raider 150.00
29 Black Cat bondage cover 150.00
Becomes:

BLACK CAT MYSTERY

30 RP,Black Cat(c) 200.00
31 RP. 135.00
32 BP,RP,Bondage cover 150.00
33 BP,RP,Electrocution cover . . . 175.00
34 BP,RP 135.00
35 BP,RP,OK, Atomic Storm 175.00
36 RP. 200.00
37 RP. 150.00
38 RP. 150.00
39 RP. 175.00
40 RP. 150.00
41 . . . . 150.00
42 . . . . 150.00
43 BP. 150.00
44 BP,HN,JkS,Oil Burning cover . 175.00
45 BP,HN,Classic cover 200.00
46 BP,HN 150.00
47 BP,HN 150.00
48 BP,HN 150.00
49 BP,HN 150.00
50 BP,Rotting Face. 375.00
51 BP,HN,MMe. 150.00
52 BP 100.00
53 BP 100.00
Becomes:

BLACK CAT WESTERN

54 A:Black Cat & Story 125.00
55 A:Black Cat 100.00
56 same 100.00
Becomes:

BLACK CAT MYSTIC

58 JK,Starts Comic Code 135.00
59 KB. 125.00
60 JK 135.00
61 HN. 125.00
62 . . . . 100.00
63 JK 100.00
64 JK 125.00
65 April, 1963 . . . . 125.00

BLACK DIAMOND WESTERN (see DESPERADO)

UNCLE SAM QUARTERLY
Quality Comics Group
Fall, 1941

1 BE,LF(c),JCo. 3,000.00
2 LG(c),BE 1,100.00
3 GT,GT(c) 800.00
4 GT,GF(c) 700.00
5 RC,GT 700.00
6 GT 550.00
7 Hitler, Tojo, Mussolini 750.00
8 . . . . 550.00
Becomes:

BLACKHAWK
Comic Magazines, Winter, 1944

9 Bait for a Death Trap 2,800.00
10 RC. 900.00
11 RC. 600.00
12 Flies to thrilling adventure . . . 550.00
13 Blackhawk Stalks Danger. . . . 550.00
14 BWa 525.00
15 Patrols the Universe. 525.00
16 RC,BWa,Huddles for Action . . 450.00
17 BWa,Prepares for Action 450.00
18 RC,RC(c),BWa,One for All and All for One. 425.00
19 RC,RC(c),BWa,Calls for Action 425.00
20 RC,RC(c),BWa,Smashes Rugoth the ruthless God. . . . 425.00
21 BWa,Battles Destiny Written n Blood. 350.00
22 RC,RC(c),BWa,Fear battles Death and Destruction 350.00
23 RC,RC(c),BWa,Batters Down Oppression. 350.00
24 RC,RC(c),BWa 350.00
25 RC,RC(c),BWa,V:The Evil of Mung 350.00
26 RC,RC(c),V:Menace of a Sunken World. 325.00
27 BWa,Destroys a War-Mad Munitions Magnate 325.00
28 BWa,Defies Destruction in the Battle of the Test Tube 325.00
29 BWa,Tale of the Basilisk Supreme Chief 325.00
30 BWa,RC,RC(c),The Menace of the Meteors 325.00
31 BWa,RC,RC(c),JCo,Treachery among the Blackhawks. . . . 250.00
32 BWa,RC,RC(c),A:Delya, Flying Fish 250.00
33 RC,RC(c),BWa, A:The Mockers 250.00
34 BWa,A:Tana,Mavis. 250.00
35 BWa,I:Atlo,Strongest Man on Earth 250.00
36 RC,RC(c),BWa,V:Tarya 225.00
37 RC,RC(c),BWa,V:Sari,The Rajah of Ramastan. 225.00
38 BWa 225.00
39 RC,RC(c),BWa,V:Lilith 225.00
40 RC,RC(c),BWa,Valley of Yesterday. 225.00
41 RC,RC(c),BWa 200.00
42 RC,RC(c),BWa, V:Iron Emperor. 200.00
43 RC,RC(c),BWa,Terror from the Catacombs 200.00
44 RC,RC(c),BWa,The King of Winds. 200.00
45 BWa,The Island of Death 200.00
46 RC,RC(c),BWa,V:DeathPatrol 200.00
47 RC,RC(c),BWa,War! 200.00
48 RC,RC(c),BWa,A:Hawks of Horror,Port of Missing Ships . 200.00
49 RC,RC(c),BWa,A:Valkyrie, Waters of Terrible Peace. . . . 200.00
50 RC,RC(c),BWa,I:Killer Shark, Flying Octopus 225.00
51 BWa,V:The Whip, Whip of Nontelon. 200.00
52 RC,RC(c),BWa,Traitor in the Ranks. 200.00
53 RC,RC(c),BWa,V:Golden Mummy 200.00
54 RC,RC(c),BWa,V:Dr. Deroski, Circles of Suicide 200.00
55 RC,RC(c),BWa,V:Rocketmen . 200.00
56 RC,RC(c),BWa,V:The Instructor, School for Sabotage 200.00
57 RC,RC(c),BWa,Paralyzed City of Armored Men 200.00
58 RC,RC(c),BWa,V:King Cobra, The Spider of Delanza 200.00
59 BWa,V:Sea Devil 200.00
60 RC,RC(c),BWa,V:Dr. Mole and His Devils Squadron. 200.00
61 V:John Smith, Stalin's Ambassador of Murder 180.00
62 V:General X, Return of Genghis Kahn 180.00
63 RC,RC(c),The Flying Buzz-Saws. 180.00
64 RC,RC(c),V:Zoltan Korvas, Legion of the Damned 180.00
65 Olaf as a Prisoner in Dungeon of Fear 180.00
66 RC,RC(c),V:The Red Executioner, Crawler. 180.00
67 RC,RC(c),V:Future Fuehrer . . 180.00
68 V:Killers of the Kremlin. 170.00
69 V:King of the Iron Men, Conference of the Dictators . 170.00
70 V:Killer Shark. 170.00
71 V:Von Tepp, The Man Who could Defeat Blackhawk O:Blackhawk 200.00
72 V:Death Legion 170.00
73 V:Hangman,The Tyrannical Freaks 150.00
74 Plan of Death. 150.00
75 V:The Mad Doctor Baroc, The Z Bomb Menace 150.00
76 The King of Blackhawk Island 150.00
77 V:The Fiendish Electronic Brain 150.00

Blackhawk #12
© Comic Magazines

78 V:The Killer Vulture, Phantom Raider 150.00
79 V:Herman Goering, The Human Bomb 150.00
80 V:Fang, the Merciless, Dr. Death 150.00
81 A:Killer Shark, The Sea Monsters of Killer Shark 150.00
82 V:Sabo Teur, the Ruthless Commie Agent 150.00
83 I:Hammmer & Sickle, V:Madam Double Cross 150.00
84 V:Death Eye,Dr. Genius, The Dreaded Brain Beam . . . 150.00
85 V:The Fiendish Impersonator . 150.00
86 V:The Human Torpedoes 150.00
87 A:Red Agent Sovietta,V:Sea Wolf, Le Sabre,Comics Code 125.00
88 V:Thunder the Indestructible, The Phantom Sniper. 125.00
89 V:The Super Communists . . . 135.00
90 V:The Storm King, Villainess who smashed the Blackhawk team. 135.00
91 Treason in the Underground. . 135.00
92 V:The World Traitor 135.00
93 V:Garg the Destroyer, O:Blackhawk 150.00
94 V:Black Widow, Darkk the Destroyer 135.00
95 V:Madam Fury, Queen of the Pirates 135.00
96 Doom in the Deep 135.00
97 Revolt of the Slave Workers. . 135.00
98 Temple of Doom 135.00
99 The War That Never Ended . . 135.00
100 The Delphian Machine 150.00
101 Satan's Paymaster 125.00
102 The Doom Cloud 125.00
103 The Super Race 125.00
104 The Jet Menace 125.00
105 The Red Kamikaze Terror . . 125.00
106 The Flying Tank Platoon . . . 125.00
107 The Winged Menace 125.00

(Please see DC Listings)

BLACK HOOD (see LAUGH COMICS)

BLACK TERROR

Better Publications/ Standard, Winter, 1942-43

1 Bombing cover 2,400.00
2 V:Arabs,Bondage(c) 850.00
3 V:Nazis,Bondage(c) 600.00
4 V:Sub Nazis 500.00
5 V:Japanese 500.00
6 Air Battle 450.00
7 Air Battle,V:Japanese, A:Ghost 450.00
8 V:Nazis 450.00
9 V:Japanese,Bondage(c) 460.00
10 V:Nazis 425.00
11 thru 16 . . . . @350.00
17 Bondage(c) 350.00
18 ASh. 325.00
19 ASh. 325.00
20 ASh. 325.00
21 ASh 350.00
22 FF,ASh 325.00
23 ASh 325.00
24 Bondgae(c) 350.00
25 ASh. 325.00
26 GT,ASh 325.00
27 MME,GT,ASh 325.00

BLAZING COMICS

Enwil Associates/Rural Home June, 1944

1 B:Green Turtle, Red Hawk, Black Buccaneer 400.00
2 Green Turtle cover 250.00
3 Green Turtle cover 225.00
4 Green Turtle cover 225.00
5 March, 1945 . . . . 225.00
5a Black Buccaneer(c),1955 . . . 100.00
6 Indian-Japanese(c), 1955 . . . . 100.00

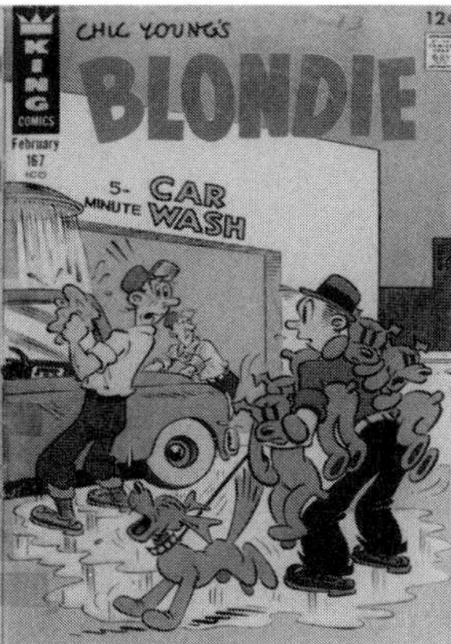

Blondie #167
© King Comics

BLONDIE COMICS

David McKay, Spring, 1947

1 . . . . 200.00
2 . . . . 100.00
3 . . . . 75.00
4 . . . . 75.00
5 . . . . 75.00
6 thru 10 . . . . @50.00
11 thru 15 . . . . @35.00

Harvey Publications

16 . . . . 45.00
17 thru 20 . . . . @35.00
21 thru 30 . . . . @25.00
31 thru 50 . . . . @20.00
51 thru 80 . . . . @15.00
81 thru 99 . . . . @10.00
100 . . . . 15.00
101 thru 124 . . . . @10.00
125 Giant 15.00
126 thru 135 . . . . @10.00
136 thru 140 . . . . @10.00
141 thru 163 . . . . @15.00

King Publications

164 thru 167 . . . . @15.00
168 thru 174 . . . . @7.00

Charlton Comics

175 thru 200 . . . . @7.00
201 thru 220 . . . . @7.00

BLUE BEETLE, THE

Fox Features Syndicate/ Holyoke Publ., Winter, 1939

1 O:Blue Beetle,A:Master Magician 3,700.00
2 . . . . 1,200.00
3 JSm(c) 850.00
4 Mentions marijuana 600.00
5 A:Zanzibar the Magician 500.00
6 B:Dynamite Thor, O:Blue Beetle 500.00
7 A:Dynamo 450.00
8 E:Thor,A:Dynamo 450.00
9 A:Black Bird,Gorilla 450.00
10 A:Black Bird, bondage cover . 450.00
11 A:Gladiator. 400.00
12 A:Black Fury 400.00
13 B:V-Man 500.00
14 JKu,I:Sparky 450.00
15 JKu 450.00
16 . . . . 325.00
17 A:Mimic 300.00
18 E:V-Man,A:Red Knight. 300.00
19 JKu,A:Dascomb Dinsmore . . . 325.00
20 I&O:The Flying Tiger Squadron 350.00
21 . . . . 225.00
22 A:Ali-Baba 225.00
23 A:Jimmy DooLittle 225.00
24 I:The Halo 225.00
25 . . . . 225.00
26 General Patton story 235.00
27 A:Tamoa 225.00
28 . . . . 200.00
29 . . . . 200.00
30 L:Holyoke 200.00
31 F:Fox. 175.00
32 Hitler cover 225.00
33 Fight for Freedom 175.00
34 A:Black Terror,Menace of K-4. 175.00
35 . . . . 175.00
36 The Runaway House 175.00
37 Inside the House 175.00
38 Revolt of the Zombies 175.00
39 . . . . 175.00
40 . . . . 175.00
41 A:O'Brine Twins 150.00
42 thru 45 . . . . @150.00
46 A:Puppeteer. 175.00
47 JKa,V:Junior Crime Club 900.00
48 JKa,A:Black Lace. 700.00
49 JKa 700.00
50 JKa,The Ambitious Bride 650.00
51 JKa, Shady Lady 575.00
52 JKa(c),Bondage cover 900.00
53 JKa,A:Jack "Legs" Diamond,Bondage(c) 600.00
54 JKa,The Vanishing Nude. . . 1,000.00
55 JKa 550.00
56 JKa,Tri-State Terror 550.00
57 JKa,The Feagle Bros. 550.00
58 . . . . 125.00
59 . . . . 100.00
60 Aug., 1960 . . . . 125.00

Blue Beetle #54
© Fox Features Syndicate

GOLDEN AGE

BLUE BEETLE
(see THING!, THE)

BLUE BOLT
Funnies, Inc./Novelty Press/ Premium Service Co, June, 1940

1 JSm,PG,O:Blue Bolt 2,700.00
2 JSm 1,300.00
3 S&K,A:Space Hawk 1,100.00
4 PG 1,000.00
5 BEv,B:Sub Zero 900.00
6 JK,JSm 875.00
7 S&K,BEv 900.00
8 S&K(c) 875.00
9 . . . . 825.00
10 S&K(c). 825.00
11 BEv(c) 875.00
12 . . . . 875.00
2-1 BEv(c),PG,O:Dick Cole & V:Simba 250.00
2-2 BEv(c),PG 200.00
2-3 PG,Cole vs Simba 175.00
2-4 BD 175.00
2-5 I:Freezum. 175.00
2-6 O:Sgt.Spook, Dick Cole 150.00
2-7 BD 125.00
2-8 BD 125.00
2-9 JW 125.00
2-10 JW 125.00
2-11 JW 125.00
2-12 E:Twister 125.00
3-1 A:115th Infantry 100.00
3-2 A:Phantom Sub 100.00
3-3 . . . . 100.00
3-4 JW(c) 75.00
3-5 Jor 75.00
3-6 Jor 75.00
3-7 X-Mas cover 75.00
3-8 . . . . 75.00
3-9 A:Phantom Sub 75.00
3-10 DBa 75.00
3-11 April Fools cover. 75.00
3-12 . . . . 75.00
4-1 Hitler,Tojo,Mussolini cover. . . 135.00
4-2 Liberty Bell cover 75.00
4-3 What are You Doing for Your Country 75.00
4-4 I Fly for Vengence 75.00
4-5 TFH(c) 75.00
4-6 HcK 75.00
4-7 JWi(c). 75.00
4-8 E:Sub Zero. 75.00

Blue Bolt 20
© Novelty Press

4-9 . . . . 75.00
4-10 . . . . 75.00
4-11 . . . . 75.00
4-12 . . . . 75.00
5-1 thru 5-12. . . . . @75.00
6-1 . . . . 75.00
6-2 War Bonds (c) 60.00
6-3 . . . . 60.00
6-4 Racist(c). 85.00
6-5 Soccer cover 60.00
6-6 thru 6-12. . . . . @60.00
7-1 thru 7-12. . . . . @60.00
8-1 Baseball cover 60.00
8-2 JHa 60.00
8-3 JHe 60.00
8-4 JHa 60.00
8-5 JHe 60.00
8-6 JDo 60.00
8-7 LbC(c). 125.00
8-8 . . . . 60.00
8-9 AMc(c) 60.00
8-10 . . . . 60.00
8-11 Basketball cover 65.00
8-12 . . . . 60.00
9-1 AMc,Baseball cover 60.00
9-2 AMc 50.00
9-3 . . . . 50.00
9-4 JHe 50.00
9-5 JHe 50.00
9-6 LbC(c),Football cover 70.00
9-7 JHe 50.00
9-8 Hockey cover 60.00
9-9 LbC(c),3-D effect 90.00
9-10 . . . . 50.00
9-11 . . . . 50.00
9-12 . . . . 50.00
10-1 Baseball cover,3-D effect . . . 60.00
10-2 3-D effect 55.00

Star Publications

102 LbC(c),Chameleon. 250.00
103 LbC(c),same 225.00
104 LbC(c),same 225.00
105 LbC(c),O:Blue Bolt Space, Drug Story 375.00
106 S&K,LbC(c),A;Space Hawk . 350.00
107 S&K,LbC(c),A;Space Hawk . 350.00
108 S&K,LbC(c),A:Blue Bolt 350.00
109 BW,LbC(c) 350.00
110 B:Horror covers,A:Target . . . 350.00
111 Weird Tales of Horror, A:Red Rocket. 350.00
112 JyD,WiP. 300.00
113 BW,JyD,A:Space Hawk 300.00
114 LbC(c),JyD. 300.00
115 LbC(c),JyD,A:Sgt.Spook. . . . 350.00
116 LbC(c),JyD,A:Jungle Joe . . . 350.00
117 LbC(c),A:Blue Bolt,Jo-Jo . . . 350.00
118 WW,LbC(c),A:White Spirit. . . 350.00
119 LbC(c) 350.00

Becomes:

GHOSTLY WEIRD STORIES
Star Publications, Sept., 1953

120 LbC,A:Jo-Jo 275.00
121 LbC,A:Jo-Jo. 225.00
122 LbC,A:The Mask 225.00
123 LbC,A:Jo-Jo. 225.00
124 LbC, Sept., 1954 . . . . 225.00

BLUE CIRCLE COMICS
Enwil Associates/ Rural Home, June, 1944

1 B:Blue Circle,O:Steel Fist 200.00
2 . . . . 150.00
3 Hitler parody cover 175.00
4 . . . . 75.00
5 E:Steel Fist,A:Driftwood Davey . 75.00
6 . . . . 75.00

BLUE RIBBON COMICS
MLJ Magazines, Nov., 1939

1 JCo,B:Dan Hastings, Richy-Amazing Boy 2,700.00
2 JCo,B:Bob Phantom, Silver Fox 1,000.00
3 JCo,A:Phantom,Silver Fox . . . 700.00
4 O:Fox,Ty Gor,B:Doc Strong, Hercules. 750.00
5 Gattling Gun cover 550.00
6 Amazing Boy Richy cover . . . 500.00
7 A:Fox cover,Corporal Collins V:Nazis. 500.00
8 E:Hercules 500.00
9 O&I:Mr. Justice 2,200.00
10 Mr. Justice cover 800.00
11 SCp(c) 800.00
12 E:Doc Strong 800.00
13 B:Inferno 800.00
14 A:Inferno 700.00
15 A:Inferno,E:Green Falcon. . . . 700.00
16 O:Captain Flag 1,400.00
17 Captain Flag V:Black Hand . . 725.00
18 Captain Flag-Black Hand 700.00
19 Captain Flag cover. 700.00
20 Captain Flag V:Nazis cover . . 750.00
21 Captain Flag V:Death. 700.00
22 Circus Cover, March, 1942. . . 700.00

BLUE RIBBON COMICS
St. John Publications Feb., 1949

1 Heckle & Jeckle 75.00
2 MB(c),Diary Secrets 150.00
3 MB,MB(c),Heckle & Jeckle 75.00
4 Teen-age Diary Secrets 150.00
5 MB,Teen-age Diary Secrets . . 200.00
6 Dinky Duck 30.00

BO
Charlton Comics, June, 1955

1 . . . . 45.00
2 . . . . 40.00
3 Oct., 1955 . . . . 40.00

BOB COLT
Fawcett Publications Nov., 1950

1 B:Bob Colt,Buck Skin 350.00
2 Death Round Train 225.00
3 Mysterious Black Knight of the Prairie 175.00
4 Death Goes Downstream 175.00
5 The Mesa of Mystery 175.00
6 The Mysterious Visitors. 175.00
7 Dragon of Disaster 150.00
8 Redman's Revenge 150.00
9 Hidden Hacienda 150.00
10 Fiend from Vulture Mountain 150.00

BOLD STORIES
Kirby Publishing Co. March, 1950

1 WW,Near nudity cover 1,000.00
2 GI,Cobra's Kiss 850.00
3 WW,Orge of Paris,July, 1950 . 750.00
4 Case of the Winking Buddha. . 300.00
5 It Rhymes with Lust 300.00
6 Candid Tales, April 1950. . . . . 300.00

BOMBER COMICS
Elliot Publishing Co. March, 1944

1 B:Wonder Boy,Kismet,

All comics prices listed are for *Near Mint* condition.

Eagle Evans 550.00
2 Wonder Boy cover 350.00
3 Wonder Boy-Kismet cover . . . 300.00
4 Hitler,Tojo, Mussolini cover . . . 400.00

BOOK OF ALL COMICS

William H. Wise, 1945

1 A:Green Mask,Puppeteer 300.00

BOOK OF COMICS, THE

William H. Wise, 1945

N# A:Captain V 300.00

Boy Comics #11
© Lev Gleason Publications

BOY COMICS

Comic House, Inc.
(Lev Gleason Publ.), April, 1942

3 O:Crimebuster,Bombshell,Young Robin, B:Yankee Longago, Swoop Storm 2,500.00
4 Hitler,Tojo,Mussolini cover . . 1,000.00
5 Crimebuster saves day cover . 750.00
6 O:Iron Jaw & Death of Son, B:Little Dynamite 2,200.00
7 Hitler,Tojo,Mussolini cover . . . 650.00
8 D:Iron Jaw 700.00
9 I:He-She 600.00
10 Iron Jaw returns 1,000.00
11 Iron Jaw falls in love. 600.00
12 Crimebuster V:Japanese 500.00
13 V:New,more terrible Iron Jaw 500.00
14 V:Iron Jaw 500.00
15 I:Rodent,D:Iron Jaw 550.00
16 Crimebuster V:Knight 250.00
17 Flag cover,Crimebuster V:Moth 275.00
18 Smashed car cover 250.00
19 Express train cover 250.00
20 Coffin cover 250.00
21 Boxing cover 175.00
22 Under Sea cover 175.00
23 Golf cover 175.00
24 County insane asylum cover . 175.00
25 52 pgs 175.00
26 68 pgs 175.00
27 Express train cover 200.00
28 E:Yankee Longago. 200.00
29 Prison break cover 200.00
30 O:Crimebuster,Murder cover . 250.00
31 68 pgs 175.00
32 E:Young Robin Hood 175.00
33 . . . . 175.00
34 Suicide cover & story 135.00
35 . . . . 125.00
36 . . . . 125.00
37 . . . . 125.00
38 . . . . 125.00
39 E:Little Dynamite 125.00
40 . . . . 125.00
41 thru 50 . . . . @110.00
51 thru 56 . . . . @100.00
57 B:Dilly Duncan 125.00
58 . . . . 100.00
59 . . . . 100.00
60 Iron Jaw returns 125.00
61 O:Iron Jaw,Crimebuster 135.00
62 A:Iron Jaw 125.00
63 thru 70 . . . . @75.00
71 E:Dilly Duncan 75.00
72 . . . . 75.00
73 . . . . 75.00
74 thru 79 . . . . @75.00
80 I:Rocky X 60.00
81 thru 88 . . . . @60.00
89 A:The Claw 65.00
90 same 65.00
91 same 65.00
92 same 65.00
93 The Claw(c),A:Rocky X 65.00
94 . . . . 55.00
95 . . . . 55.00
96 . . . . 55.00
97 . . . . 55.00
98 A:Rocky X 65.00
99 . . . . 55.00
100 . . . . 65.00
101 . . . . 65.00
102 . . . . 65.00
103 thru 118 . . . . @65.00
119 March, 1956. . . . . 65.00

BOY EXPLORERS (see TERRY AND THE PIRATES)

BRENDA STARR

Four Star Comics Corp./ Superior Comics Ltd., Sept., 1947

13(1) 650.00
14(2) JKa,Bondage cover 700.00

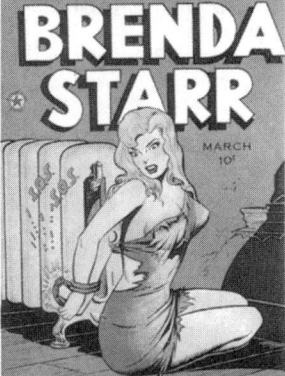

Brenda Starr #14
© Superior Comics

2-3 . . . . 525.00
2-4 JKa,Operating table cover. . . 650.00
2-5 Swimsuit cover 500.00
2-6 . . . . 500.00
2-7 . . . . 500.00
2-8 Cosmetic cover 500.00
2-9 Giant Starr cover 500.00
2-10 Wedding cover 500.00
2-11 . . . . 500.00
2-12 . . . . 500.00

BRICK BRADFORD

Best Books
(Standard Comics), July, 1949

5 . . . . 150.00
6 Robot cover 175.00
7 AS 100.00
8 . . . . 100.00

BROADWAY ROMANCES

Quality Comics Group
Jan., 1950

1 PG,BWa&(c). 250.00
2 BWa,Glittering Desire 200.00
3 BL,Stole My Love 85.00
4 Enslaved by My Past 100.00
5 Flame of Passion,Sept.,1950 . 100.00

BRONCHO BILL

Visual Editions
(Standard Comics), Jan., 1948

5 . . . . 100.00
6 AS(c) 50.00
7 AS(c) 40.00
8 ASh 40.00
9 AS(c) 40.00
10 AS(c). 40.00
11 AS(c). 35.00
12 AS(c). 35.00
13 AS(c). 35.00
14 ASh. 35.00
15 ASh. 35.00
16 AS(c). 35.00

BRUCE GENTRY

Four Star Publ./ Visual Editions/ Superior, Jan., 1948

1 B:Ray Bailey reprints 350.00
2 Plane crash cover 250.00
3 E:Ray Bailey reprints 225.00
4 Tiger attack cover 175.00
5 . . . . 175.00
6 Help message cover. 175.00
7 . . . . 175.00
8 End of Marriage cover, July, 1949. . . . . 175.00

BUCCANEERS (see KID ETERNITY)

BUCK JONES

Dell Publishing Co., Oct.., 1950

1 . . . . 150.00
2 . . . . 75.00
3 . . . . 60.00
4 . . . . 60.00
5 . . . . 60.00
6 . . . . 60.00
7 . . . . 60.00
8 . . . . 60.00

BUCK ROGERS
Eastern Color Printing
Winter, 1940

1 Partial Painted(c) ... 2,900.00
2 ... 1,100.00
3 Living Corpse from Crimson Coffin ... 900.00
4 One man army of greased lightning ... 850.00
5 Sky Roads ... 800.00
6 Sept., 1943 ... 800.00

Toby Press

100 Flying Saucers ... 200.00
101 ... 175.00
9 ... 175.00

BUG MOVIES
Dell Publishing Co., 1931

1 ... 100.00

BUGS BUNNY
DELL GIANT EDITIONS
Dell Publishing Co.
Christmas

1 Christmas Funnies (1950) ... 300.00
2 Christmas Funnies (1951) ... 250.00
3 Christmas Funnies (1952) ... 200.00
4 Christmas Funnies (1953) ... 200.00
5 Christmas Funnies (1954) ... 200.00
6 Christmas Party (1955) ... 175.00
7 Christmas Party (1956) ... 185.00
8 Christmas Funnies (1957) ... 185.00
9 Christmas Funnies (1958) ... 185.00
1 County Fair (1957) ... 200.00

Halloween

1 Halloween Parade (1953) ... 200.00
2 Halloween Parade (1954) ... 175.00
3 Trick 'N' Treat Halloween Fun (1955) ... 185.00
4 Trick 'N' Treat Halloween Fun (1956) ... 185.00

Vacation

1 Vacation Funnies (1951) ... 300.00
2 Vacation Funnies (1952) ... 275.00
3 Vacation Funnies (1953) ... 250.00
4 Vacation Funnies (1954) ... 200.00
5 Vacation Funnies (1955) ... 200.00
6 Vacation Funnies (1956) ... 175.00
7 Vacation Funnies (1957) ... 175.00
8 Vacation Funnies (1958) ... 175.00
9 Vacation Funnies (1959) ... 175.00

BUGS BUNNY
Dell Publishing Co., 1942
see Four Color for early years

28 thru 30 ... @40.00
31 thru 50 ... @30.00
51 thru 70 ... @25.00
71 thru 85 ... @20.00
86 Giant-Show Time ... 75.00
87 thru 100 ... @15.00
101 thru 120 ... @10.00
121 thru 140 ... @7.00
141 thru 190 ... @6.00
191 thru 245 ... @5.00

BULLETMAN
Fawcett Publications
Summer, 1941

1 I:Bulletman & Bulletgirl ... 3,000.00
2 MRa(c) ... 1,200.00
3 MRa(c) ... 900.00
4 V:Headless Horror, Guillotine cover ... 850.00
5 Riddle of Dr. Riddle ... 800.00
6 V:Japanese ... 650.00
7 V:Revenge Syndicate ... 625.00
8 V:Mr. Ego ... 600.00
9 V:Canine Criminals ... 600.00
10 I:Bullet Dog ... 625.00
11 V:Fiendish Fiddler ... 550.00
12 ... 500.00
13 ... 500.00
14 V:Death the Comedian ... 500.00
15 V:Professor D ... 500.00
16 VanishingElephant,Fall 1946 ... 500.00

Buster Crabbe #7
© Famous Funnies

BUSTER CRABBE
Famous Funnies, Nov., 1951

1 The Arrow of Death ... 250.00
2 AW&GE(c) ... 275.00
3 AW&GE(c) ... 300.00
4 FF(c) ... 400.00
5 AW,FF,FF,(c) ... 900.00
6 Sharks cover ... 125.00
7 FF ... 150.00
8 Gorilla cover ... 125.00
9 FF ... 150.00
10 ... 125.00
11 Snakes cover ... 75.00
12 Sept., 1953 ... 75.00

BUSTER CRABBE
Lev Gleason Pub., 1953

1 Ph(c) ... 150.00
2 ATh ... 150.00
3 ATh ... 150.00
4 F. Gordon(c) ... 125.00

BUZ SAWYER
Standard Comics, June, 1948

1 ... 150.00
2 I:Sweeney ... 100.00
3 ... 75.00
4 ... 75.00
5 June, 1949 ... 75.00

CALLING ALL BOYS
Parents Magazine Institute
Jan., 1946

1 Skiing ... 75.00
2 ... 30.00
3 Peril Out Post ... 25.00
4 Model Airplane ... 25.00
5 Fishing ... 25.00
6 Swimming ... 25.00
7 Baseball ... 30.00
8 School ... 25.00
9 The Miracle Quarterback ... 25.00
10 Gary Cooper cover ... 35.00
11 Rin-Tin-Tin cover ... 25.00
12 Bob Hope cover ... 70.00
13 Bing Cosby cover ... 50.00
14 J. Edgar Hoover cover ... 25.00
15 Tex Granger cover ... 20.00
16 ... 20.00
17 Tex Granger cover, May, 1948 ... 20.00

Becomes:

TEX GRANGER

18 Bandits of the Badlands ... 55.00
19 The Seven Secret Cities ... 45.00
20 Davey Crockett's Last Fight ... 35.00
21 Canyon Ambush ... 35.00
22 V:Hooded Terror ... 35.00
23 V:Billy the Kid ... 35.00
24 A:Hector, Sept., 1949 ... 40.00

CALLING ALL GIRLS
Parent Magazine Press, Inc.
Sept., 1941

1 ... 100.00
2 Virginia Weidler cover ... 50.00
3 Shirley Temple cover ... 65.00
4 Darla Hood cover ... 35.00
5 Gloria Hood cover ... 35.00
6 ... 30.00
7 ... 30.00
8 ... 30.00
9 Flag cover ... 35.00
10 ... 30.00
11 thru 20 ... @30.00
21 thru 39 ... @20.00
40 Liz Taylor ... 75.00
41 ... 20.00
42 ... 20.00
43 Oct., 1945 ... 20.00

CALLING ALL KIDS
Quality Comics, Inc.
Dec./Jan., 1946

1 Funny Animal stories ... 75.00
2 ... 25.00
3 ... 20.00
4 ... 15.00
5 ... 15.00
6 ... 15.00
7 ... 15.00
8 ... 15.00
9 ... 15.00
10 ... 15.00
11 thru 25 ... @12.00
26 Aug., 1949 ... 12.00

CAMERA COMICS
U.S. Camera Publishing Corp.
July–Sept., 1944

1 Airfighter,Grey Comet ... 150.00
2 How to Set Up a Darkroom ... 125.00
3 Linda Lens V:Nazi cover ... 100.00
4 Linda Lens cover ... 75.00
5 Diving cover ... 75.00
6 Jim Lane cover ... 75.00
7 Linda Lens cover ... 75.00
8 Linda Lens cover ... 75.00
9 Summer, 1946 ... 75.00

CAMP COMICS
Dell Publishing Co., 1942

1 Ph(c),WK,A:Bugs Bunny ... 450.00
2 Ph(c),WK,A:Bugs Bunny ... 350.00

Captain Aero #6
© Holyoke Publishing Co.

3 Ph(c),Wk 450.00

CAPTAIN AERO COMICS
Holyoke Publishing Co.
Dec., 1941

1 B:Flag-Man&Solar,Master of Magic Captain Aero, Captain Stone 1,300.00
2 A:Pals of Freedom 600.00
3 JKu,B:Alias X,A:Pals of Freedom 600.00
4 JKu,O:Gargoyle, Parachute jump 600.00
5 JKu 500.00
6 JKu,Flagman,A:Miss Victory . . 450.00
7 Alias X 300.00
8 O:Red Cross,A:Miss Victory . . 300.00
9 A:Miss Victory,Alias X 225.00
10 A:Miss Victory,Red Cross. . . . 200.00
11 A:Miss Victory 160.00
12 same 160.00
13 same 160.00
14 same 160.00
15 AS(c),A:Miss Liberty 160.00
16 AS(c),Leather Face 150.00
17 LbC(c) 250.00
21 LbC(c) 250.00
22 LbC(c),I:Mighty Mite. 250.00
23 LbC(c) 250.00
24 LbC(c) American Planes Dive Bomb Japan. 375.00
25 LbC(c),Science Fiction(c). . . . 275.00
26 LbC(c) 250.00

CAPTAIN BATTLE
New Friday Publ./
Magazine Press, Summer, 1941

1 B:Captain Battle,O:Blackout 1,000.00
2 Pirate Ship cover 650.00
3 Dungeon cover 550.00
4. . . . . 400.00
5 V:Japanese, Summer, 1943 . . 400.00

CAPTAIN BATTLE, Jr.
Comic House, Fall, 1943

1 Claw V:Ghost, A:Sniffer 850.00
2 Man who didn't believe in Ghosts 650.00

CAPTAIN COURAGEOUS
(see BANNER COMICS)

CAPTAIN EASY
Standard Comics, 1939

N# Swash Buckler 750.00
10 . . . . 80.00
11 . . . . 60.00
12 . . . . 60.00
13 ASh(c). 60.00
14 . . . . 60.00
15 . . . . 60.00
16 ASh(c). 60.00
17 Sept., 1949 . . . . 60.00

CAPTAIN FEARLESS COMICS
Helnit Publishing Co.
Aug., 1941

1 O:Mr. Miracle,Alias X,Captain Fearless Citizen Smith, A:Miss Victory 700.00
2 A:Border Patrol, Sept.,1941 . . 450.00

CAPTAIN FLASH
Sterling Comics, Nov., 1954

1 O:Captain Flash 300.00
2 V:Black Knight 175.00
3 Beasts from 1,000,000 BC . . . 175.00
4 Flying Saucer Invasion 175.00

CAPTAIN FLEET
Approved Comics, Fall, 1952

1 Storm and Mutiny ...Typhoon . 125.00

CAPTAIN FLIGHT COMICS
Four Star Publications
March, 1944

N# B:Captain Flight,Ace Reynolds Dashthe Avenger,Professor X 325.00
2 . . . . 175.00
3 . . . . 150.00
4 B:Rock Raymond Salutes America's Wartime Heroines. 175.00
5 Bondage cover,B:Red Rocket A:The Grenade 650.00
6 Girl tied at the stake 175.00
7 Dog Fight cover 350.00
8 B:Yankee Girl,A:Torpedoman . 350.00
9 Dog Fight cover 350.00
10 Bondage cover 350.00
11 LBc(c),Future(c), Feb-March, 1947 . . . . 650.00

CAPTAIN GALLANT
Charlton Comics, 1955

1 Ph(c),Buster Crabbe. 65.00
2 . . . . 55.00
3 . . . . 55.00
4 Sept., 1956 . . . . 55.00

CAPTAIN JET
Four Star Publ., May, 1952

1 Factory bombing cover 150.00
2 Parachute jump cover 90.00
3 Tank bombing cover 75.00
4 Parachute cover 75.00
5 . . . . 50.00

CAPTAIN KIDD
(see ALL GREAT COMICS)

CAPTAIN MARVEL ADVENTURES
Fawcett Publications
Spring, 1941

N# JK, B:Captain Marvel & Sivana 29,000.00
2 GT,JK(c),Billy Batson (c) . . . 3,700.00
3 JK(c),Thunderbolt (c) 2,200.00
4 Shazam(c). 1,500.00
5 V:Nazis 1,200.00
6 Solomon, Hercules, Atlas, Zeus, Achilles & Mercury cover . . . 900.00
7 Ghost of the White Room 900.00
8 Forward America 900.00
9 A:Ibac the Monster, Nippo the Nipponese, Relm of the Subconscious 900.00
10 V:Japanese 900.00
11 V:Japanese and Nazis 700.00
12 Joins the Army 700.00
13 V:Diamond-Eyed Idol of Doom 700.00
14 Nippo meets his Nemesis . . . 700.00
15 Big "Paste the Axis" contest. . 700.00
16 Uncle Sam cover, Paste the Axis 700.00
17 P(c), Paste the Axis 650.00
18 P(c), O:Mary Marvel 1,700.00
19 Mary Marvel & Santa cover . . 550.00
20 Mark of the Black Swastika 3,400.00
21 Hitler cover 700.00
22 B:Mr. Mind serial, Shipyard Sabotage. 750.00
23 A:Steamboat 500.00
24 Minneapolis Mystery 500.00
25 Sinister Faces cover 500.00
26 Flag cover 500.00
27 Joins Navy. 425.00
28 Uncle Sam cover 425.00
29 Battle at the China Wall 425.00
30 Modern Robinson Crusoe . . . 425.00
31 Fights his own Conscience. . . 425.00
32 V:Mole Men, Dallas 425.00
33 Mt. Rushmore parody cover, Omaha. 400.00
34 Oklahoma City 400.00
35 O:Radar the International Policeman, Indianapolis 350.00

Captain Marvel #22
© Fawcett Publications

GOLDEN AGE

36 Missing face contest, St. Louis 350.00
37 V:Block Busting Bubbles, Cincinnati 350.00
38 V:Chattanooga Ghost, Rock Garden City 350.00
39 V:Mr. Mind's Death Ray, Pittsburgh 350.00
40 V:Ghost of the Tower,Boston . 350.00
41 Runs for President, Dayton . . 250.00
42 Christmas special, St. Paul . . 250.00
43 V:Mr. Mind,I:Uncle Marvel, Chicago 250.00
44 OtherWorlds,Washington,D.C. 250.00
45 V:Blood Bank Robbers 250.00
46 E: Mr. Mind Serial, Tall Stories of Jonah Joggins . . . 250.00
47 . . . . 240.00
48 Signs Autographs cover 235.00
49 V: An Unknown Killer 235.00
50 Twisted Powers 235.00
51 Last of the Batsons 200.00
52 O&I:Sivana Jr.,V:Giant Earth Dreamer 225.00
53 Gets promoted 200.00
54 Marooned in the Future, Kansas City 225.00
55 Endless String, Columbus . . . 200.00
56 Goes Crazy, Mobile 200.00
57 A:Haunted Girl, Rochester . . . 200.00
58 V:Sivana 200.00
59 . . . . 200.00
60 Man who made Earthquakes . 200.00
61 I&V: Oggar, the Worlds Mightiest Immortal 250.00
62 The Great Harness Race 200.00
63 Stuntman 200.00
64 . . . . 200.00
65 V:Invaders from Outer Space . 200.00
66 Atomic War cover 225.00
67 Hartford 200.00
68 Scenes from the Past, Baltimore 200.00
69 Gets Knighted 200.00
70 Horror in the Box 200.00
71 Wheel of Death 200.00
72 . . . . 200.00
73 Becomes a Petrophile 200.00
74 Who is the 13th Guest 200.00
75 V:Astonishing Yeast Menace . 200.00
76 A:Atom Ambassador 200.00
77 The Secret Life 200.00
78 O:Mr. Tawny 225.00
79 O:Atom,A:World's Worst Actor 250.00
80 Twice told story 450.00
81 A:Mr. Atom 175.00
82 A:Mr. Tawny 175.00
83 Indian Chief 175.00
84 V:Surrealist Imp 175.00
85 Freedom Train 225.00
86 A:Mr. Tawny 175.00
87 V:Electron Thief 175.00
88 Billy Batson's Boyhood 175.00
89 V:Sivana 175.00
90 A:Mr. Tawny 175.00
91 A:Chameleon Stone 175.00
92 The Land of Limbo 175.00
93 Book of all Knowledge 175.00
94 Battle of Electricity 175.00
95 The Great Ice Cap 175.00
96 V:Automatic Weapon 175.00
97 Wiped Out 175.00
98 United Worlds 175.00
99 Rain of Terror 175.00
100 V:Sivana,Plot against the Universe 350.00
101 Invisibility Trap 175.00
102 Magic Mix-up 175.00
103 Ice Covered World of 1,000,000 AD 175.00
104 Mr. Tawny's Masquerade . . . 175.00
105 The Dog Catcher 175.00
106 V:Menace of the Moon 175.00
107 V:Space Hunter 175.00
108 V:Terrible Termites 175.00
109 The Invention Inventor 175.00
110 V:Sivana 175.00
111 The Eighth Sea 175.00
112 . . . . 175.00
113 Captain Marvel's Feud 175.00
114 V:The Ogre 175.00
115 . . . . 175.00
116 Flying Saucer 200.00
117 . . . . 175.00
118 V:Weird Water Man 175.00
119 . . . . 175.00
120 . . . . 175.00
121 . . . . 175.00
122 . . . . 175.00
123 . . . . 175.00
124 V:Discarded Instincts 175.00
125 V:Ancient Villain 175.00
126 thru 130 . . . . @175.00
131 . . . . 175.00
132 V:Flood 175.00
133 . . . . 175.00
134 . . . . 175.00
135 Perplexing Past Puzzle 175.00
136 . . . . 175.00
137 . . . . 175.00
138 V:Haunted Horror 175.00
139 . . . . 175.00
140 Hand of Horror 175.00
141 Horror 175.00
142 . . . . 175.00
143 Great Stone Face on the Moon 175.00
144 thru 147 . . . . @175.00
148 V:The World 175.00
149 . . . . 175.00
150 Captains Marvel's Wedding, Nov., 1953 . . . . 300.00

CAPTAIN MARVEL JR.
Fawcett Publications
Nov., 1952

1 O:Captain Marvel, Jr., A:Capt. Nazi 4,800.00
2 O:Capt.Nippon,V:Capt. Nazi 1,700.00
3 Parade to Excitement 850.00
4 V:Invisible Nazi 900.00
5 V:Capt. Nazi 800.00
6 Adventure of Sabbac 600.00
7 City under the Sea 600.00

Captain Marvel Jr. #3
© Fawcett Publications

8 Dangerous Double 575.00
9 Independence cover 625.00
10 Hitler cover 650.00
11 . . . . 500.00
12 Scuttles the Axis Isle in the Sky 525.00
13 V:The Axis,Hitler,cover 475.00
14 X-Mas cover, Santa wears Capt. Marvel uniform 450.00
15 . . . . 500.00
16 A:Capt. Marvel, Sivana, Pogo 450.00
17 Meets his Future self 450.00
18 V:Birds of Doom 450.00
19 A:Capt. Nazi & Capt. Nippon . 450.00
20 Goes on the Warpath 425.00
21 Buy War Stamps 350.00
22 Rides World's oldest steamboat 350.00
23 . . . . 350.00
24 V:Weather Man 350.00
25 Flag cover 350.00
26 Happy New Year 350.00
27 Jungle Thrills 350.00
28 V:Sivana's Crumbling Crimes . 350.00
29 Blazes a Wilderness Trail 350.00
30 . . . . 350.00
31 . . . . 225.00
32 Keeper of the Lonely Rock . . . 225.00
33 . . . . 225.00
34/35 I&O:Sivana Jr. 225.00
36 Underworld Tournament 225.00
37 FreddyFreeman'sNews-stand . 225.00
38 A:Arabian Knight 225.00
39 V:Sivana Jr., Headline Stealer 225.00
40 Faces Grave Situation 225.00
41 I:The Acrobat 175.00
42 V:Sivana Jr. 175.00
43 V:Beasts on Broadway 175.00
44 Key to the Mystery 175.00
45 A:Icy Fingers 175.00
46 . . . . 175.00
47 V:Giant of the Beanstalk 175.00
48 Whale of a Fish Story 175.00
49 V:Dream Recorder 175.00
50 Wanted: Freddy Freeman . . . 175.00
51 The Island Riddle 150.00
52 A:Flying Postman 150.00
53 Atomic Bomb on the Loose . . 200.00
54 V:Man with 100 Heads 175.00
55 Pyramid of Eternity 175.00
56 Blue Boy's Black Eye 175.00
57 Magic Ladder 175.00
58 Amazing Mirror Maze 175.00
59 . . . . 175.00
60 V:Space Menace 175.00
61 V:Himself 150.00
62 . . . . 150.00
63 V:Witch of Winter 150.00
64 thru 70 . . . . @150.00
71 thru 74 . . . . @150.00
75 V:Outlaw of Crooked Creek . . 150.00
76 thru 85 . . . . @150.00
86 Defenders of time 150.00
87 thru 89 . . . . @150.00
90 The Magic Trunk 125.00
91 thru 99 . . . . @125.00
100 V:Sivana Jr 150.00
101 thru 106 . . . . @125.00
107 The Horror Dimension 125.00
108 thru 118 . . . . @125.00
119 Condemned to Die, June, 1953 . . . . 125.00

CAPTAIN MIDNIGHT
Fawcett Publications
Sept., 1942

1 O:Captain Midnight, Capt. Marvel cover 2,500.00
2 Smashes Jap Juggernaut . . . 1,100.00

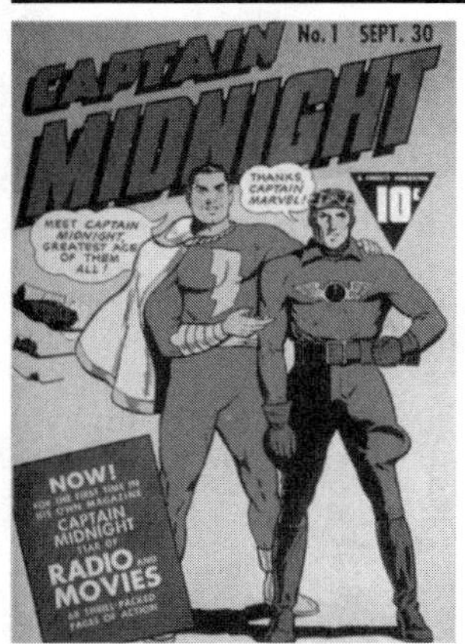

Captain Midnight #1
© Fawcett Publications

3 Battles the Phantom Bomber . 800.00
4 Grapples the Gremlins 750.00
5 Double Trouble in Tokyo 750.00
6 Blasts the Black Mikado 600.00
7 Newspaper headline cover . . . 600.00
8 Flying Torpedoes Berlin-Bound 575.00
9 MRa(c), Subs in Mississippi . . 575.00
10 MRa(c), Flag cover 575.00
11 MRa(c), Murder in Mexico . . . 425.00
12 V:Sinister Angels 425.00
13 Non-stop Flight around the World 425.00
14 V:King of the Villains 425.00
15 V:Kimberley Killer. 425.00
16 Hitler's Fortress Breached . . . 425.00
17 MRa(c), Hello Adolf 400.00
18 Death from the Skies 400.00
19 Hour of Doom for the Axis . . . 400.00
20 Brain and Brawn against Axis 400.00
21 Trades with Japanese 325.00
22 Plea for War Stamps 325.00
23 Japanese Prison cover. 325.00
24 Rising Sun Flag cover 325.00
25 Amusement Park Murder 325.00
26 Hotel of Horror. 325.00
27 Death Knell for Tyranny 325.00
28 Gliderchuting to Glory 325.00
29 Bomb over Nippon. 325.00
30 . . . . 325.00
31 . . . . 225.00
32 . . . . 225.00
33 V:Shark 225.00
34 . . . . 225.00
35 thru 40 . . . . @225.00
41 thru 50 . . . . @175.00
51 thru 63 . . . . @175.00
64 V:XOG, Ruler of Saturn 175.00
65 . . . . 175.00
66 V:XOG. 175.00
67 Fall, 1948 . . . . 175.00
Becomes:

SWEET HEART

68 Robert Mitchum 100.00
69 thru 118 . . . . @35.00
111 Ronald Reagan story 40.00
119 Marilyn Monroe 175.00
120 Atomic Bomb story . . . . @45.00
121 . . . . 25.00
122 1954 . . . . 20.00

CAPTAIN SCIENCE
Youthful Magazines
Nov., 1950

1 WW,O:Captain Science, V:Monster God of Rogor 650.00
2 WW,V:Cat Men of Phoebus, Space Pirates. 350.00
3 Ghosts from the Underworld . 350.00
4 WW,Vampires 625.00
5 WW,V:Shark Pirates of Pisces 625.00
6 WW,V:Invisible Tyrants, bondage cover 500.00
7 WW,Bondage(c) Dec., 1951 . . 500.00
Becomes:

FANTASTIC

8 Isle of Madness 300.00
9 Octopus cover 225.00
Becomes:

BEWARE

10 SHn,Doll of Death 350.00
11 SHn,Horror Head 250.00
12 SHn,Body Snatchers 225.00
Becomes:

CHILLING TALES

13 MF,Screaming Skull 400.00
14 SHn,Smell of Death 250.00
15 SHn,Curse of the Tomb 300.00
16 HcK,Mark of the Beast Bondage(c) 225.00
17 MFc(c),Wandering Willie, Oct.,1953 . . . . 300.00

CAPTAIN STEVE SAVAGE
Avon Periodicals
[1st Series] 1950

N# WW 300.00
2 EK(c),The Death Gamble 125.00
3 EK(c),Crash Landing in Manchuria 75.00
4 EK(c),V:Red Raiders from Siang-Po 50.00
5 EK(c),Rockets of Death 50.00
6 Operation Destruction 50.00
7 EK(c),Flight to Kill 50.00
8 EK(c),V:Red Mystery Jet 50.00
9 EK(c) 50.00
10 . . . . 50.00
11 EK(c). 55.00
12 WW. 75.00
13 . . . . 65.00

[2nd Series] Sept./Oct., 1954

5 . . . . 50.00
6 WW 75.00
7 thru 13 . . . . @30.00

CAPTAIN VIDEO
Fawcett Publications
Feb., 1951

1 GE,Ph(c) 900.00
2 Time when Men could not Walk. 600.00
3 GE,Indestructible Antagonist . 500.00
4 GE,School of Spies 500.00
5 GE,Missiles of Doom, photo cover 500.00
6 GE,Island of Conquerors, Photo cover; Dec. 1951 . . . . 500.00

CASPER, THE FRIENDLY GHOST
St. John Publishing
Sept., 1949

1 O:Baby Huey 1,300.00
2 . . . . 600.00
3 . . . . 550.00
4 . . . . 450.00
5 . . . . 425.00

Harvey Publications

7 . . . . 325.00
8 thru 9 . . . . @200.00
10 I:Spooky 225.00
11 A:Spooky 125.00
12 thru 18 . . . . @100.00
19 I:Nightmare 150.00
20 I:Wendy the Witch 175.00
21 thru 30 . . . . @100.00
31 thru 40 . . . . @75.00
41 thru 50 . . . . @50.00
51 thru 60 . . . . @50.00
61 thru 69 . . . . @50.00
70 July, 1958 . . . . 50.00

CAT MAN COMICS
Helnit Publ. Co./ Holyoke Publ. Co./ Continental Magazine
May, 1941

1 O:Deacon&Sidekick Mickey, Dr. Diamond & Ragman,A:Black Widow, B:Blaze Baylor. . . . 3,000.00
2 Ragman. 1,000.00
3 B:Pied Piper 800.00
4 CQ 700.00
5 I&O: The Kitten 600.00
6 CQ 575.00
7 CQ 575.00
8 JKa, I:Volton 700.00
9 JKa 500.00
10 JKa,O:Blackout, B:Phantom Falcon 500.00
11 JKa,DRi,BF 500.00
12 . . . . 450.00
13 . . . . 450.00
14 CQ 450.00
15 Rajah of Destruction 450.00
16 Bye-Bye Axis. 550.00
17 Buy Bonds and Stamps 425.00
18 Buy Bonds and Stamps 425.00
19 CQ,Hitler,Tojo and Mussolini cover. 525.00
20 CQ,Hitler,Tojo and Mussolini cover. 525.00
21 CQ 400.00
22 CQ 400.00
23 CQ 400.00
N# V:Japanese,Bondage(c) 425.00

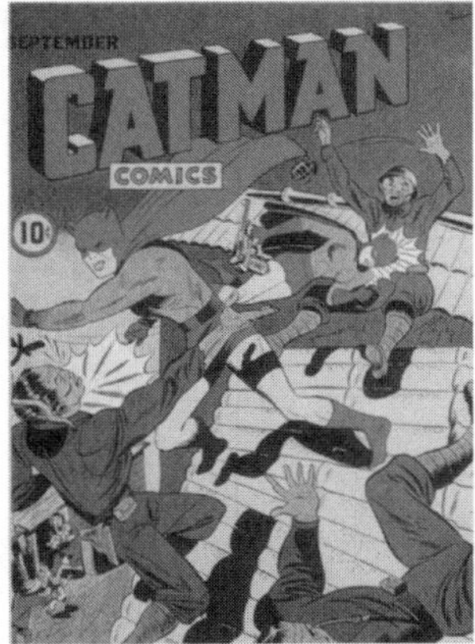

Cat Man Comics Vol. 3 #1
© Continental Magazine

GOLDEN AGE

N# V:Demon 400.00
N# A:Leather Face 400.00
27 LbC(c),Flag cover,O:Kitten . . . 650.00
28 LbC(c),Horror cover 700.00
29 LbC(c),BF 600.00
30 LbC(c),Bondage(c) 625.00
31 LbC(c) 600.00
32 Aug., 1946 . . . . 600.00

CHALLENGER, THE
Interfaith Publications, 1945

N# O:The Challenger Club 275.00
2 JKa 225.00
3 JKa 225.00
4 JKa,BF 225.00

Chamber of Chills #28
© Harvey Publications

CHAMBER OF CHILLS
Harvey Publications/
Witches Tales, June, 1951

21 . . . . 350.00
22 . . . . 200.00
23 Eyes Ripped Out 200.00
24 Bondage cover 225.00
5 Shrunken Skull,
Operation Monster 225.00
6 Seven Skulls of Magondi 200.00
7 Pit of the Damned 175.00
8 Formula for Death 200.00
9 Bondage cover 150.00
10 Cave of Death 150.00
11 Curse of Morgan Kilgane 125.00
12 Swamp Monster 125.00
13 The Lost Race 150.00
14 Down to Death 125.00
15 Nightmare of Doom 150.00
16 Cycle of Horror 150.00
17 Amnesia 150.00
18 Hair cut-Atom Bomb 175.00
19 Happy Anniversary 150.00
20 Shock is Struck 150.00
21 BP,Nose for News 160.00
22 Is Death the End? 125.00
23 BP,Heartline 125.00
24 BP,Bondage(c) 175.00
25 . . . . 100.00
26 HN,Captains Return 100.00

Becomes:

CHAMBER OF CLUES

27 BP,A:Kerry Drake 100.00
28 A:Kerry Drake 50.00

CHAMPION COMICS
Worth Publishing Co.
Dec., 1939

2 B:Champ, Blazing Scarab, Neptina, Liberty Lads, Jingleman . . . 1,300.00
3 . . . . 600.00
4 Bailout(c) 625.00
5 Jungleman(c) 625.00
6 MNe 625.00
7 MNe,Human Meteor 650.00
8 . . . . 1,000.00
9 . . . . 1,000.00
10 Bondage cover 1,100.00

Becomes:

CHAMP COMICS

11 Human Meteor 700.00
12 Human Heteor 550.00
13 Dragon's Teeth 500.00
14 Liberty Lads 500.00
15 Liberty Lads 500.00
16 Liberty Lads 500.00
17 Liberty Lads 500.00
18 Liberty Lads 650.00
19 A:The Wasp 675.00
20 A:The Green Ghost 500.00
21 . . . . 425.00
22 A:White Mask 450.00
23 Flag cover 450.00
24 . . . . 400.00
25 . . . . 400.00
26 thru 29 . . . . 400.00

CHARLIE McCARTHY
Dell Publishing Co.
Nov., 1947

1 . . . . 150.00
2 . . . . 75.00
3 . . . . 75.00
1 . . . . 75.00
2 . . . . 75.00
3 . . . . 75.00
4 . . . . 75.00
5 . . . . 75.00
6 . . . . 75.00
7 . . . . 75.00
8 . . . . 75.00
9 . . . . 75.00

CHIEF, THE
Dell Publishing Co.
Aug., 1950

(1) *see Dell Four Color #290*
2 . . . . 55.00

CHILLING TALES (see CAPTAIN SCIENCE)

CHUCKLE THE GIGGLY BOOK OF COMIC ANIMALS
R. B. Leffing Well Co., 1944

1 . . . . 135.00

CINEMA COMICS HERALD
Paramount/Universal/RKO/
20th Century Fox
Giveaways 1941–43

N# Mr. Bug Goes to Town 90.00
N# Bedtime Story 75.00
N# Lady for a Night,J.Wayne . . . 150.00
N# Reap the Wild Wind 90.00
N# Thunderbirds 75.00
N# They All Kissed Me 75.00
N# Bombardier 90.00
N# Crash Dive 90.00
N# Arabian Nights 75.00

CIRCUS THE COMIC RIOT
Globe Syndicate, June, 1938

1 BKa,WE,BW 6,000.00
2 BKa,WE,BW 2,800.00
3 BKa,WE,BW, Aug., 1938 . . . 2,800.00

CISCO KID, THE
Dell Publishing Co.

(1) *See Dell Four Color #292*
2 Jan., 1951 . . . . 125.00
3 thru 5 . . . . @100.00
6 thru 10 . . . . @90.00
11 thru 20 . . . . @75.00
21 thru 36 . . . . @60.00
37 thru 41 Ph(c)'s . . . . @100.00

CLAIRE VOYANT
Leader Publ./Visual Ed./
Pentagon Publ., 1946-47

N# 500.00
2 JKa(c) 450.00
3 Case of the Kidnapped Bride . 400.00
4 Bondage cover 425.00

CLOAK AND DAGGER
Approved Comics
(Ziff-Davis), Fall, 1952

1 NS(c),Al Kennedy of the Secret Service 175.00

CLUE COMICS
Hillman Periodicals
Jan., 1943

1 O:Boy King,Nightmare,Micro-Face, Twilight,Zippo 850.00
2 . . . . 400.00
3 Boy King V:The Crane 400.00
4 V:The Crane 300.00
5 V:The Crane 300.00
6 Hells Kitchen 200.00
7 V:Dr. Plasma,Torture(c) 225.00
8 RP,A:The Gold Mummy King . 250.00
9 I:Paris 200.00
10 O:Gun Master 200.00
11 A:Gun Master 150.00
12 O:Rackman 200.00
2-1 S&K,O:Nightro,A:Iron Lady . . 350.00
2-2 S&K,Bondage(c) 375.00
2-3 S&K 325.00

Becomes:

REAL CLUE CRIME STORIES

2-4 DBw,S&K,True Story of Ma Barker 375.00
2-5 S&K, Newface surgery cover 275.00
2-6 S&K, Breakout cover 250.00
2-7 S&K, Stick up cover 250.00
2-8 Kidnapping cover 75.00
2-9 DBa,Boxing fix cover 75.00
2-10 DBa,Murder cover 75.00
2-11 Attempted bank robbery cover 75.00
2-12 Murder cover 75.00
3-1 thru 3-12 . . . . @50.00
4-1 thru 4-12 . . . . @75.00
5-1 thru 5-12 . . . . @50.00
6-1 thru 6-12 . . . . @50.00

6-10 Bondage(c) 75.00
7-1 thru 7-12 . . . . @40.00
8-1 thru 8-4 . . . . @40.00
8-5 May, 1953 . . . . 40.00

C-M-O COMICS
Comic Corp. of America (Centaur), May, 1942

1 Invisible Terror 800.00
2 Super Ann 600.00

COCOMALT BIG BOOK OF COMICS
Harry A. Chesler, 1938

1 BoW,PGn,FG,JCo,(Give away) Little Nemo 2,000.00

COLOSSUS COMICS
Sun Publications March, 1940

1 A:Colossus 3,500.00

COLUMBIA COMICS
William H. Wise Co., 1944

1 Joe Palooka,Charlie Chan . . . 200.00

COMICS, THE
Dell Publishing Co. March, 1937

1 I:Tom Mix & Arizona Kid. . . . 1,500.00
2 A:Tom Mix & Tom Beaty 700.00
3 A:Alley Oop 550.00
4 same 550.00
5 same 550.00
6 thru 11 same. . . . . @550.00

COMICS ON PARADE
United Features Syndicate April, 1938–Feb., 1955

1 B:Tarzan,Captain and the Kids, Little Mary, Mixup,Abbie & Slats, Broncho Bill,Li'l Abner 3,200.00
2 Circus Parade of all 1,100.00
3 . . . . 850.00
4 On Rocket 750.00
5 All at the Store 750.00
6 All at Picnic. 450.00
7 Li'l Abner(c) 450.00
8 same 450.00
9 same 450.00
10 same 450.00
11 same 350.00
12 same 350.00
13 same 350.00
14 Abbie n' Slats (c) 350.00
15 Li'l Abner(c) 350.00
16 Abbie n' Slats(c). 350.00
17 Tarzan,Abbie n' Slats(c) 375.00
18 Li'l Abner(c) 350.00
19 same 350.00
20 same 300.00
21 Li'l Abner(c) 300.00
22 Tail Spin Tommy(c) 300.00
23 Abbie n' Slats(c). 300.00
24 Tail Spin Tommy(c) 300.00
25 Li'l Abner(c) 300.00
26 Abbie n' Slats(c). 300.00
27 Li'l Abner(c) 300.00
28 Tail Spin Tommy(c) 300.00
29 Abbie n' Slats(c). 300.00
30 Li'l Abner(c) 200.00
31 The Captain & the Kids(c) . . . 175.00
32 Nancy and Fritzi Ritz(c) 125.00
33 Li'l Abner(c) 150.00

Comics on Parade #10
© United Features Syndicate

34 The Captain & the Kids(c) . . . 125.00
35 Nancy and Fritzi Ritz(c) 125.00
36 Li'l Abner(c) 145.00
37 The Captain & the Kids(c) . . . 125.00
38 Nancy and Fritzi Ritz(c) 110.00
39 Li'l Abner(c) 135.00
40 The Captain & the Kids(c) . . . 125.00
41 Nancy and Fritzi Ritz(c) 75.00
42 Li'l Abner(c) 125.00
43 The Captain & the Kids(c) . . . 125.00
44 Nancy and Fritzi Ritz(c) 75.00
45 Li'l Abner(c) 125.00
46 The Captain & the Kids(c) 90.00
47 Nancy and Fritzi Ritz(c) 75.00
48 Li'l Abner(c) 125.00
49 The Captain & the Kids(c) 90.00
50 Nancy and Fritzi Ritz(c) 75.00
51 Li'l Abner(c) 125.00
52 The Captain & the Kids(c) 75.00
53 Nancy and Fritzi Ritz(c) 75.00
54 Li'l Abner(c) 125.00
55 Nancy and Fritzi Ritz(c) 75.00
56 The Captain & the Kids(c) 75.00
57 Nancy and Fritzi Ritz(c) 70.00
58 Li'l Abner(c) 125.00
59 The Captain & the Kids(c) 70.00
60 Nancy and Fritzi Ritz(c) 55.00
61 thru 76 same . . . . @55.00
77 Nancy & Sluggo(c). 50.00
78 thru 104 same . . . . @50.00

COMPLETE BOOK OF COMICS AND FUNNIES
William H. Wise & Co., 1945

1 Wonderman-Magnet 300.00

CONFESSIONS OF LOVE
Artful Publications April, 1950

1 . . . . 200.00
2 July, 1950. . . . . 125.00

CONFESSIONS OF LOVE
Star Publications, July, 1952

11 AW,LbC(c)Intimate Secrets of Daring Romance 100.00
12 AW,LbC(c),I Couldn't Say No 100.00
13 AW,LbC(c),Heart Break 100.00
14 AW,LbC(c),My Fateful Love . . 75.00
4 JyD,AW,LbC(c),The Longing Heart 75.00
5 AW,LbC(c),I Wanted Love. 75.00
6 AW,LbC(c),My Jealous Heart . . 75.00

Becomes:

CONFESSIONS OF ROMANCE

7 LbC(c)Too Good 100.00
8 AW,LbC(c),I Lied About Love . . 75.00
9 WW,AW,LbC(c),I Paid Love's Price 100.00
10 JyD,AW,LbC(c),My Heart Cries for Love 75.00
11 JyD,AW,LbC(c),Intimate Confessions, Nov., 1954. . . . . 75.00

CONFESSIONS OF LOVELORN (see LOVELORN)

CONQUEROR COMICS
Albrecht Publications Winter, 1945

1 . . . . 150.00

CONTACT COMICS
Aviation Press, July, 1944

N# LbC(c),B:Black Venus, Golden Eagle 400.00
2 LbC(c),Peace Jet 300.00
3 LbC(c),LbC,E:Flamingo 275.00
4 LbC(c),LbC 275.00
5 LbC(c),A:Phantom Flyer 300.00
6 LbC(c),HK 350.00
7 LbC(c),Flying Tigers 250.00
8 LbC(c),Peace Jet 250.00
9 LbC(c),LbC,A:Marine Flyers . . 250.00
10 LbC(c),A:Bombers of the AAF 250.00
11 LbC(c),HK,AF,Salutes Naval Aviation 350.00
12 LbC(c),A:Sky Rangers, Air Kids, May, 1946 . . . . 350.00

COO COO COMICS
Nedor/Animated Cartoons (Standard), Oct., 1942

1 O&I:Super Mouse 225.00
2 . . . . 100.00
3 . . . . 50.00
4 . . . . 50.00
5 . . . . 50.00
6 . . . . 40.00
7 thru 10 . . . . @35.00
11 thru 33 . . . . @35.00
34 thru 40 FF illustration . . . . . . @50.00
41 FF 125.00
42 FF 125.00
43 FF illustration. 75.00
44 FF illustration. 75.00
45 FF illustration. 75.00
46 FF illustration. 45.00
47 FF 75.00
48 FF illustration. 50.00
49 FF illustration. 60.00
50 FF illustration 60.00
51 thru 61 . . . . @25.00
62 April, 1952. . . . . 25.00

"COOKIE"
Michel Publ./Regis Publ. (American Comics Group) April, 1946

1 . . . . 135.00
2 . . . . 60.00
3 . . . . 40.00

4 ... 40.00
5 ... 40.00
6 thru 20 ... @35.00
21 thru 30 ... @30.00
31 thru 54 ... @25.00
55 Aug., 1955 ... 25.00

COSMO CAT
Fox Features Syndicate
July/Aug., 1946

1 ... 200.00
2 ... 100.00
3 O:Cosmo Cat ... 100.00
4 thru 10 ... @35.00

COURAGE COMICS
J. Edward Slavin, 1945

1 ... 75.00
2 Boxing cover ... 80.00
77 Naval rescue, PT99 cover ... 80.00

COWBOY COMICS
(see STAR RANGER)

COWBOYS `N' INJUNS
Compix
(M.E. Enterprises), 1946-47

1 Funny Animal Western ... 50.00
2 thru 8 ... @30.00

COWBOY WESTERN COMICS/HEROES
(see YELLOWJACKET COMICS)

COWGIRL ROMANCES
Fiction House Magazine, 1952

1 The Range of Singing Guns ... 225.00
2 The Lady of Lawless Range ... 125.00
3 Daughter of the Devil's Band ... 100.00
4 Bride Wore Buckskin ... 90.00
5 Taming of Lone-Star Lou ... 90.00
6 Rose of Mustang Mesa ... 85.00
7 Nobody Loves a Gun Man ... 85.00
8 Wild Beauty ... 85.00
9 Gun-Feud Sweethearts ... 85.00
10 JKa,AW,No Girl of Stampede Valley ... 90.00
11 Love is Where You Find It ... 85.00
12 Dec., 1952 ... 85.00

COW PUNCHER
Avon Periodicals/
Realistic Publ., Jan., 1947

1 JKu ... 325.00
2 JKu,JKa(c),Bondage cover ... 250.00
3 AU(c) ... 200.00
4 ... 200.00
5 ... 200.00
6 WJo(c),Drug story ... 225.00
7 ... 175.00
1 JKu ... 175.00

CRACK COMICS
Comic Magazines
(Quality Comics Group)
May, 1940

1 LF,O:Black Condor,Madame Fatal, Red Torpedo, Rock Bradden, Space Legion, B:The Clock,Wizard Wells ... 4,500.00
2 Black Condor cover ... 2,000.00
3 The Clock cover ... 1,300.00
4 Black Condor cover ... 1,100.00
5 LF,The Clock cover ... 850.00
6 PG,Black Condor cover ... 800.00
7 Clock cover ... 800.00
8 Black Condor cover ... 800.00
9 Clock cover ... 800.00
10 Black Condor cover ... 800.00
11 LF,PG,Clock cover ... 750.00
12 LF,PG,Black Condor cover ... 750.00
13 LF,PG,Clock cover ... 750.00
14 AMc,LF,PG,Clack Condor(c) ... 750.00
15 AMc,LF,PG,Clock cover ... 750.00
16 AMc,LF,PG,Black Condor(c) ... 750.00
17 FG,AMc,LF,PG,Clock cover ... 750.00
18 AMc,LF,PG,Black Condor(c) ... 750.00
19 AMc,LF,PG,Clock cover ... 750.00
20 AMc,LF,PG,Black Condor(c) ... 750.00
21 AMc,LF,PG,same ... 600.00
22 LF,PG,same ... 600.00
23 AMc,LF,PG,same ... 600.00
24 AMc,LF,PG,same ... 600.00
25 AMc,same ... 500.00
26 AMc,same ... 500.00
27 AMc,I&O:Captain Triumph ... 800.00
28 Captain Triumph cover ... 500.00
29 A:Spade the Ruthless ... 500.00
30 I:Biff ... 400.00
31 Helps Spade Dig His Own Grave ... 200.00
32 Newspaper cover ... 200.00
33 V:Men of Darkness ... 200.00
34 ... 200.00
35 V:The Man Who Conquered Flame ... 200.00
36 Good Neighbor Tour ... 200.00
37 V:The Tyrant of Toar Valley ... 200.00
38 Castle of Shadows ... 200.00
39 V:Crime over the City ... 200.00
40 Thrilling Murder Mystery ... 150.00
41 ... 150.00
42 All that Glitters is Not Gold ... 150.00
43 Smashes the Evil Spell of Silent ... 150.00
44 V:Silver Tip ... 150.00
45 V:King-The Jack of all Trades ... 150.00
46 V:Mr. Weary ... 150.00
47 V:Hypnotic Eyes Khor ... 165.00
48 Murder in the Sky ... 165.00
49 ... 165.00
50 A Key to Trouble ... 165.00

Crack Comics #5
© Quality Comics Group

51 V:Werewolf ... 165.00
52 V:Porcupine ... 165.00
53 V:Man Who Robbed the Dead ... 165.00
54 Shoulders the Troubles of the World ... 165.00
55 Brain against Brawn ... 165.00
56 Gossip leads to Murder ... 165.00
57 V:Sitok–Green God of Evil ... 165.00
58 V:Targets ... 125.00
59 A Cargo of Mystery ... 125.00
60 Trouble is no Picnic ... 125.00
61 V:Mr. Pointer-Finger of Fear ... 125.00
62 V:The Vanishing Vandals ... 125.00

Becomes:

CRACK WESTERN

63 PG, I&O:Two-Gun Lil, B:Frontier Marshal,Arizona Ames, ... 175.00
64 RC,Arizona AmesV:Two-Legged Coyote ... 125.00
65 RC,Ames Tramples on Trouble ... 125.00
66 Arizona Ames Arizona Raines, Tim Holt,Ph(c) ... 100.00
67 RC, Ph(c) ... 125.00
68 ... 100.00
69 RC ... 100.00
70 O&I:Whip and Diablo ... 110.00
71 RC(c) ... 125.00
72 RC,Tim Holt,Ph(c) ... 90.00
73 Tim Holt,Ph(c) ... 60.00
74 RC(c) ... 75.00
75 RC(c) ... 75.00
76 RC(c),Stage Coach to Oblivion 75.00
77 RC(c),Comanche Terror ... 75.00
78 RC(c),Killers of Laurel Ridge ... 75.00
79 RC(c),Fires of Revenge ... 75.00
80 RC(c),Mexican Massacre ... 75.00
81 RC(c),Secrets of Terror Canyon ... 75.00
82 The Killer with a Thousand Faces ... 50.00
83 Rattlesnake Pete's Revenge ... 50.00
84 PG(c),Revolt at Broke Creek May,1951 ... 50.00

CRACKAJACK FUNNIES
Dell Publishing Co.
June, 1938

1 AMc,A:Dan Dunn,The Nebbs, Don Winslow ... 2,000.00
2 AMc,same ... 800.00
3 AMc,same ... 600.00
4 AMc,same ... 450.00
5 AMc,Naked Women(c) ... 500.00
6 AMc,same ... 350.00
7 AMc,same ... 350.00
8 AMc,same ... 350.00
9 AMc,A:Red Ryder ... 1,000.00
10 AMc,A:Red Ryder ... 350.00
11 AMc,A:Red Ryder ... 300.00
12 AMc,A:Red Ryder ... 300.00
13 AMc,A:Red Ryder ... 300.00
14 AMc,A:Red Ryder ... 300.00
15 AMc,A:Tarzan ... 350.00
16 AMc ... 250.00
17 AMc ... 250.00
18 AMc ... 250.00
19 AMc ... 250.00
20 AMc ... 250.00
21 AMc ... 250.00
22 AMc ... 250.00
23 AMc ... 250.00
24 AMc ... 250.00
25 AMc,I:The Owl ... 600.00
26 AMc ... 425.00
27 AMc ... 425.00
28 AMc,A:The Owl ... 425.00
29 AMc,A:Ellery Queen ... 425.00
30 AMc,A:Tarzan ... 425.00

Crackajack #42
© Dell Publishing Co.

31 AMc,A:Tarzan 425.00
32 AMc,O:Owl Girl 475.00
33 AMc,A:Tarzan 375.00
34 AMc,same 375.00
35 AMc,same 375.00
36 AMc,same 375.00
37 AMc. 375.00
38 AMc. 375.00
39 AMc,I:Andy Panada 450.00
40 AMc,A:Owl(c). 325.00
41 AMc. 325.00
42 AMc. 325.00
43 AMc,A:Owl(c). 300.00

CRASH COMICS
Tem Publishing Co.
May, 1940

1 S&K,O:Strongman, B:Blue Streak, Perfect Human, Shangra . . 2,500.00
2 S&K 1,200.00
3 S&K 1,000.00
4 S&K,O&I:Catman 2,400.00
5 S&K, Nov., 1940 . . . . 1,000.00

CRIME AND PUNISHMENT
Lev Gleason Publications
April, 1948

1 CBi(c),Mr.Crime(c) 250.00
2 CBi(c). 125.00
3 CBi(c),BF 150.00
4 CBi(c),BF 100.00
5 CBi(c). 100.00
6 thru 10 CBi(c) . . . . @75.00
11 thru 15 CBi(c). . . . . @50.00
16 thru 27 CBi(c). . . . . @40.00
28 thru 38 . . . . @35.00
39 Drug issue 60.00
40 thru 44 . . . . @35.00
45 Drug issue 60.00
46 thru 73 . . . . @35.00
66 ATh 250.00
67 Drug Storm 200.00
68 ATh(c) 200.00
69 Drug issue 70.00
74 Aug., 1955 . . . . 40.00

CRIME DETECTIVE COMICS
Hillman Publications
March–April, 1948

1 BFc(c),A:Invisible 6 . . . . 200.00
2 Jewel Robbery cover 75.00
3 Stolen cash cover. 65.00
4 Crime Boss Murder cover 65.00
5 BK,Maestro cover 65.00
6 AMc,Gorilla cover 60.00
7 GMc,Wedding cover 60.00
8 . . . . 55.00
9 Safe Robbery cover (a classic). 250.00
10 . . . . 60.00
11 BP 60.00
12 BK 60.00
2-1 Bluebird captured 75.00
2-2 . . . . 40.00
2-3 . . . . 40.00
2-4 BK. 45.00
2-5 . . . . 40.00
2-6 . . . . 40.00
2-7 BK,GMc. 45.00
2-8 . . . . 40.00
2-9 . . . . 40.00
2-10 . . . . 40.00
2-11 . . . . 40.00
2-12 . . . . 40.00
3-1 Drug Story. 40.00
3-2 thru 3-7 . . . . @40.00
3-8 May/June, 1953 . . . . 35.00

CRIME DOES NOT PAY
(see SILVER STREAK COMICS)

CRIME ILLUSTRATED
E.C. Comics, Nov.–Dec., 1955

1 Grl,RC,GE,JO. 125.00
2 Grl,RC,JCr,JDa,JO 100.00

CRIME MUST STOP
Hillman Periodicals, Oct., 1952

1 BK 500.00

CRIME MYSTERIES
Ribage Publishing Corp.
May, 1952

1 Transvestism,Bondage(c) 400.00
2 A:Manhunter, Lance Storm, Drug. 275.00
3 FF-one page, A:Dr. Foo 225.00
4 A:Queenie Star, Bondage Star 400.00
5 Claws of the Green Girl 200.00
6 . . . . 200.00
7 Sons of Satan 200.00
8 Death Stalks the Crown, Bondage(c) 200.00
9 You are the Murderer 175.00
10 The Hoax of the Death. 175.00
11 The Strangler. 175.00
12 Bondage(c) 190.00
13 AT,6 lives for one 225.00
14 Painted in Blood 175.00
15 Feast of the Dead,Acid Face . 275.00

Becomes:

SECRET MYSTERIES

16 Hiding Place,Horror 200.00
17 The Deadly Diamond,Horror. . 125.00
18 Horror 135.00
19 Horror,July, 1955 . . . . 135.00

CRIMES ON THE WATERFRONT
(see FAMOUS GANGSTERS)

INTERNATIONAL COMICS
E.C. Publ. Co., Spring, 1947

1 KS,I:Manhattan's Files 650.00
2 KS,A: Van Manhattan & Madelon 500.00
3 KS,same 300.00
4 KS,same 300.00
5 I:International Crime-Busting Patrol 300.00

Becomes:

INTERNATIONAL CRIME PATROL

6 A:Moon Girl & The Prince . . . 550.00

Becomes:

CRIME PATROL

7 SMo,A:Capt. Crime Jr.,Field Marshall of Murder 475.00
8 JCr,State Prison cover 400.00
9 AF,JCr,Bank Robbery 400.00
10 AF,JCr,Wanted:James Dore . . 400.00
11 AF,JCr 400.00
12 AF,Grl,JCr,Interrogation(c) . . . 400.00
13 AF,JCr 400.00
14 AF,JCr,Smugglers cover. 400.00
15 AF,JCr,Crypt of Terror 2,200.00
16 AF,JCr,Crypt of Terror 1,400.00

Becomes:

CRYPT OF TERROR
E.C. Comics, April, 1950

17 JCr&(c),AF,`Werewolf Strikes Again' 2,400.00
18 JCr&(c),AF,WW,HK `The Living Corpse' 1,400.00
19 JCr&(c),AF,Grl, `Voodoo Drums'. 1,400.00

Becomes:

TALES FROM THE CRYPT
Oct.., 1950

20 JCr&(c),AF,GI,JKa `Day of Death' 1,100.00
21 AF&(c),WW,HK,GI,`Cooper Dies in the Electric Chair . . . 800.00

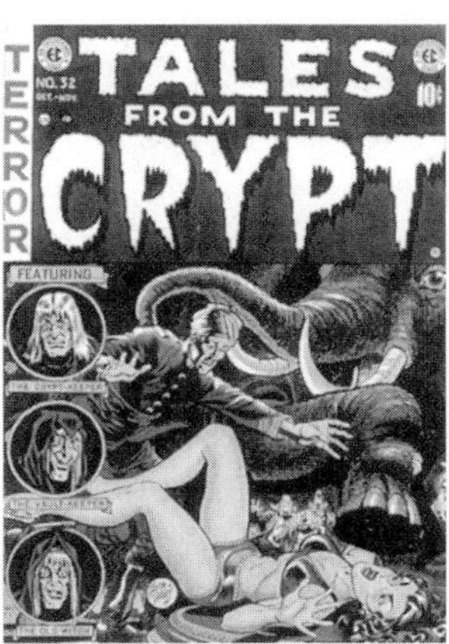

Tales From the Crypt #32
© E.C. Comics

22 AF, JCr(c) 750.00
23 AF&(c),JCr,JDa,Grl
`Locked in a Mauseleum' . . . 500.00
24 AF(c),WW,JDa,JCr,Grl
`Danger...Quicksand' 500.00
25 AF(c),WW,JDa,JKa,Grl
`Mataud Waxworks' 500.00
26 WW(c),JDa,Grl,
`Scared Graveyard'. 350.00
27 JKa, WW(c), Guillotine cover . 350.00
28 AF(c),JDa,JKa,Grl,JO
`Buried Alive' 350.00
29 JDa&(c),JKa,Grl,JO
`Coffin Burier' 350.00
30 JDa&(c),JO,JKa,Grl
`Underwater Death' 350.00
31 JDa&(c),JKa,Grl,AW
`Hand Chopper' 400.00
32 JDa&(c),GE,Grl,`Woman
Crushed by Elephant' 300.00
33 JDa&(c),GE,JKa,Grl,`Lower
Berth',O:Crypt Keeper. 550.00
34 JDa&(c),JKa,GE,Grl,`Jack the
Ripper,'Ray Bradbury adapt. . 300.00
35 JDa&(c),JKa,JO,Grl,
`Werewolf' 300.00
36 JDa&(c),JKa,GE,Grl, Ray
Bradbury adaptation 300.00
37 JDa(c),JO,BE. 300.00
38 JDa(c),BE,RC,Grl,`Axe Man' . 300.00
39 JDa&(c),JKa,JO,Grl,`Children
in the Graveyard' 300.00
40 JDa&(c),GE,BK,Grl,
`Underwater Monster' 300.00
41 JDa&(c),JKa,GE,Grl,
`Knife Thrower'. 275.00
42 JDa(c),JO,Vampire cover 275.00
43 JDa(c),JO,GE 275.00
44 JO,RC,Guillotine cover. 275.00
45 JDa&(c),JKa,BK,Gl,`Rat
Takes Over His Life' 275.00
46 JDa&(c),GE,JO,Gl,`Werewolf
man being hunted,Feb.1955 . 350.00

CRIME REPORTER
St. John Publishing Co.
Aug., 1948

1 Death Makes a Deadline 375.00
2 GT,MB(c),Matinee Murders . . 550.00
3 GT,MB(c),Dec., 1948 . . . . 275.00

CRIMES BY WOMEN
Fox Features Syndicate
June, 1948

1 Bonnie Parker 1,000.00
2 Vicious Female 550.00
3 Prison break cover 450.00
4 Murder cover 450.00
5 . . . . 450.00
6 Girl Fight cover. 500.00
7 . . . . 450.00
8 . . . . 450.00
9 . . . . 450.00
10 . . . . 450.00
11 . . . . 450.00
12 . . . . 450.00
13 ACME jewelry robbery cover . 450.00
14 Prison break cover. 450.00
15 Aug., 1951. . . . . 450.00

CRIME SMASHER
Fawcett Publications
Summer, 1948

1 The Unlucky Rabbit's Foot . . . 325.00

CRIME SMASHERS
Ribage Publishing Corp.
Oct., 1950

1 Girl Rape 650.00
2 JKu,A:Sally the Sleuth, Dan
Turner, Girl Friday, Rat Hale . 300.00
3 MFa 200.00
4 Zak(c) 200.00
5 WW 250.00
6 . . . . 175.00
7 Bondage cover,Drugs 200.00
8 . . . . 175.00
9 Bondage cover 200.00
10 . . . . 175.00
11 . . . . 175.00
12 FF 200.00
13 . . . . 200.00
14 . . . . 165.00
15 . . . . 165.00

CRIME SUSPENSTORIES
L.L. Publishing Co.
(E.C. Comics), Oct.–Nov., 1950

1a JCr,Grl 1,200.00
1 JCr,WW,Grl 1,000.00
2 JCr,JKa,Grl 500.00
3 JCr,WW,Grl 375.00
4 JCr,Gln,Grl,JDa 350.00
5 JCr,JKa,Grl,JDa 325.00
6 JCr,JDa,Grl 300.00
7 JCr,Grl 300.00
8 JCr,Grl 300.00
9 JCr,Grl 300.00
10 JCr,Grl. 300.00
11 JCr,Grl. 200.00
12 JCr,Grl. 200.00
13 JCr,AW 225.00
14 JCr 200.00
15 JCr 200.00
16 JCr,AW 225.00
17 JCr,FF,AW, Ray Bradbury . . . 275.00
18 JCr,RC,BE. 200.00
19 JCr,RC,GE,AF(c) 200.00
20 RC,JCr, Hanging cover 250.00
21 JCr 150.00
22 RC,JO,JCr(c),
Severed head cover 175.00
23 JKa,RC,GE 175.00
24 BK,RC,JO 150.00
25 JKa,(c),RC. 150.00
26 JKa,(c),RC,JO 150.00
27 JKa,(c),GE,Grl,March, 1955. . 150.00

Crime SuspenStories #22
© E.C. Comics

CRIMINALS ON THE RUN
Premium Group of Comics
Aug., 1948

4-1 LbC(c) 200.00
4-2 LbC(c), A:Young King Cole . 175.00
4-3 LbC(c), Rip Roaring Action
in Alps 175.00
4-4 LbC(c), Shark cover 175.00
4-5 AMc 175.00
4-6 LbC 150.00
4-7 LbC 400.00
5-1 LbC 150.00
5-2 LbC 150.00
10 LbC 150.00

Becomes:

CRIME-FIGHTING DETECTIVE

11 LbC, Brodie Gang Captured . . 125.00
12 LbC(c), Jail Break Genius . . . 125.00
13 . . . . 100.00
14 LbC(c), A Night of Horror 100.00
15 LbC(c) 100.00
16 LbC(c), Wanton Murder 100.00
17 LbC(c), The Framer
was Framed 100.00
18 LbC(c), A Web of Evil 100.00
19 LbC(c), Lesson of the Law . . . 100.00

Becomes:

SHOCK DETECTIVE CASES

20 LbC(c), The Strangler 150.00
21 LbC(c), Death Ride 150.00

Becomes:

SPOOK DETECTIVE CASES

22 Headless Horror. 225.00

Becomes:

SPOOK SUSPENSE AND MYSTERY

23 LbC,Weird Picture of Murder . 150.00
24 LbC(c),Mummy's Case. 175.00
25 LbC(c),Horror Beyond Door . . 150.00
26 LbC(c),JyD,Face of Death . . . 150.00
27 LbC(c),Ship of the Dead. 150.00
28 LbC(c),JyD,Creeping Death . . 150.00
29 LbC(c),Solo for Death 150.00
30 LbC(c),JyD,Nightmare,
Oct.,1954 . . . . 150.00

CROWN COMICS
Golfing/McCombs Publ.
Winter, 1944

1 Edgar Allen Poe adapt.. . . . . . 275.00
2 MB,I:Mickey Magic 200.00
3 MB,Jungle adventure cover . . 200.00
4 MB(c) 200.00
5 MB(c),Jungle adventure cover 200.00
6 MB(c),Jungle adventure cover 200.00
7 JKa,AF,MB(c),Race Car driving
cover 200.00
8 MB 135.00
9 . . . . 125.00
10 Plane crash cover 125.00
11 LSt. 100.00
12 LSt 100.00
13 LSt 100.00
14 . . . . 125.00
15 FBe 100.00
16 FBe,Jungle adventure(c) 100.00
17 FBe 100.00
18 FBe 100.00
19 BP,July, 1949. . . . . 100.00

CRUSADER FROM MARS
Approved Publ.
(Ziff-Davis), Jan.–March, 1952

1 Mission Thru Space, Death in the Sai 600.00
2 Beachhead on Saturn's Ring, Bondage(c),Fall, 1952 . . . . . 450.00

CRYIN' LION, THE
William H. Wise Co.
Fall, 1944

1 . . . . 100.00
2 . . . . 75.00
3 Spring, 1945 . . . . 75.00

CRYPT OF TERROR (see CRIME PATROL)

CYCLONE COMICS
Bibara Publ. Co., June, 1940

1 O:Tornado Tom 1,200.00
2 . . . . 600.00
3 . . . . 575.00
4 Voltron 450.00
5 A:Mr. Q,Oct., 1940 . . . . 450.00

ALL GREAT COMICS
Fox Features Syndicate
Oct., 1947

12 A:Brenda Starr. 450.00
13 JKa,O:Dagger, Desert Hawk . 400.00
Becomes:

DAGAR, DESERT HAWK

14 JKa,Monster of Mura 650.00
15 JKa,Curse of the Lost Pharaoh 400.00
16 JKa,Wretched Antmen 350.00
19 Pyramid of Doom. 325.00
20 . . . . 325.00
21 JKa(c),The Ghost of Fate. . . . 350.00
22 . . . . 300.00
23 Bondage cover 350.00
Becomes:

CAPTAIN KIDD

24 Blackbeard the Pirate. 100.00
25 Sorceress of the Deep 100.00
Becomes:

Dagar Desert Hawk #21
© Fox Features Syndicate

MY SECRET STORY

26 He Wanted More Than Love . . 85.00
27 My Husband Hated Me 50.00
28 I Become a Marked Women. . . 50.00
29 My Forbidden Rapture, April, 1950 . . . . 50.00

DAFFY
Dell Publishing Co.,
March, 1953

(1) *see Dell Four Color #457*
(2) *see Dell Four Color #536*
(3) *see Dell Four Color #615*
4 thru 7 . . . . @30.00
8 thru 11 . . . . @25.00
12 thru 17. . . . . @20.00
Becomes:

DAFFY DUCK

18 . . . . 20.00
19 . . . . 20.00
20 . . . . 20.00
21 thru 30. . . . . @15.00

Gold Key

31 thru 40. . . . . @10.00
41 thru 59. . . . . @7.00
60 B&A:Road Runner 4.00
61 thru 90 same . . . . @4.00
91 thru 127 . . . . @3.00

Whitman

128 thru 145 . . . . @3.00

DAGWOOD
Harvey Publications
Sept., 1950

1 . . . . 135.00
2 . . . . 75.00
3 thru 10 . . . . @55.00
11 thru 20 . . . . @50.00
21 thru 30. . . . . @40.00
31 thru 50. . . . . @30.00
51 thru 70. . . . . @20.00
71 thru 109 . . . . @15.00
110 thru 140 . . . . @15.00

DANGER AND ADVENTURE (see THIS MAGAZINE IS HAUNTED)

DANGER IS OUR BUSINESS
Toby Press/
I.W. Enterprises, 1953

1 AW,FF,Men who Defy Death for a Living 350.00
2 Death Crowds the Cockpit . . . 100.00
3 Killer Mountain 75.00
4 . . . . 75.00
5 thru 9 . . . . @60.00
10 June, 1955 . . . . 75.00

DAREDEVIL COMICS
Lev Gleason Publications
July, 1941

1 Daredevil Battles Hitler, A:Silver Streak, Lance Hale, Dickey Dean, Cloud Curtis,V:The Claw, O:Hitler 11,000.00
2 I:The Pioneer, Champion of American,B:London,Pat Patriot,Pirate Prince. 2,800.00
3 CBi(c),O:Thirteen 1,500.00

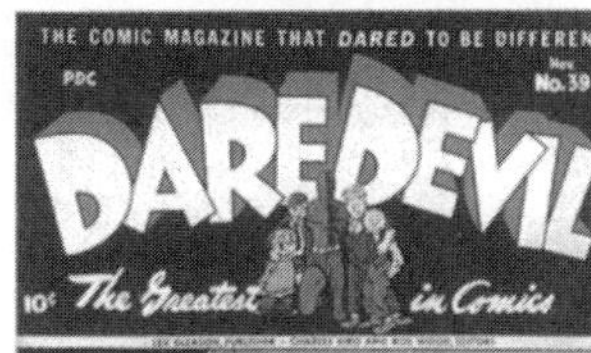

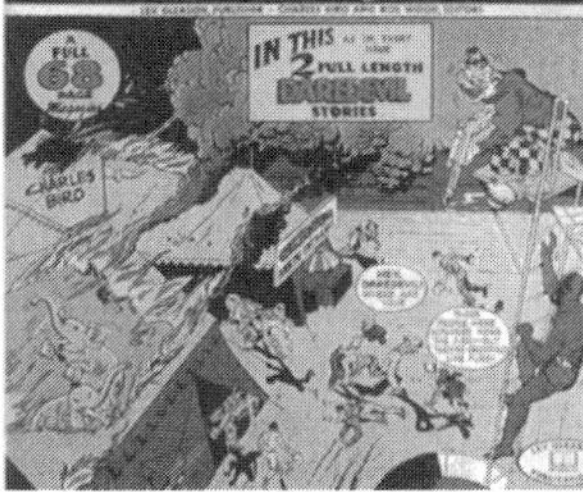

Daredevil #39
© Lev Gleason

4 CBi(c),Death is the Refere . . 1,300.00
5 CBi(c),I:Sniffer&Jinx, Claw V:Ghost,Lottery of Doom . . 1,100.00
6 CBi(c) 850.00
7 CBi(c), What Ghastly Sight Lies within the Mysterious Trunk . 775.00
8 V:Nazis cover, E:Nightro 725.00
9 V:Double 725.00
10 America will Remember Pearl Harbor. 725.00
11 Bondage cover, E:Pat Patriot, London. 825.00
12 BW,CBi(c), O:The Law 1,200.00
13 BW,I:Little Wise Guys 1,000.00
14 BW,CBi(c) 550.00
15 BW,CBi(c), D:Meatball 750.00
16 BW,CBi(c) 500.00
17 BW,CBi(c), Into the Valley of Death 475.00
18 BW,CBi(c), O:Daredevil, double length story 1,000.00
19 BW,CBi(c), Buried Alive 400.00
20 BW,CBi(c), Boxing cover 400.00
21 CBi(c), Can Little Wise Guys Survive Blast of Dynamite?. . 700.00
22 CBi(c) 325.00
23 CBi(c), I:Pshyco. 325.00
24 CBi(c), Punch and Judy Murders 325.00
25 CBi(c), baseball cover 325.00
26 CBi(c) 300.00
27 CBi(c), Bondage cover. 325.00
28 CBi(c) 300.00
29 CBi(c) 300.00
30 CBi(c), Ann Hubbard White 1922-1943 . . . . 300.00
31 CBi(c), D:The Claw 650.00
32 V:Blackmarketeers. 225.00
33 CBi(c) 225.00
34 CBi(c) 225.00
35 B:Two Daredevil stories every issue. 200.00
36 CBi(c) 200.00
37 CBi(c) 200.00
38 CBi(c), O:Daredevil 350.00
39 CBi(c) 200.00
40 CBi(c) 200.00
41 . . . . 175.00
42 thru 50 CBi(c). . . . . @175.00
51 CBi(c) 125.00
52 CBi(c),Football cover 150.00
53 thru 57 . . . . @125.00
58 Football cover 150.00
59 . . . . 125.00
60 . . . . 125.00

61 thru 68 . . . . @125.00
69 E:Daredevil 125.00
70 . . . . 100.00
71 thru 78 . . . . @75.00
79 B:Daredevil 85.00
80 . . . . 80.00
81 . . . . 65.00
82 . . . . 65.00
83 thru 99 . . . . @65.00
100 . . . . 75.00
101 thru 133 . . . . @60.00
134 Sept., 1956 . . . . 60.00

DARING CONFESSIONS (see YOUTHFUL HEART)

DARING LOVE (see YOUTHFUL ROMANCES)

DARK MYSTERIES
Merit Publications
June–July, 1951

1 WW, WW(c), Curse of the Sea Witch. 750.00
2 WW, WW(c), Vampire Fangs of Doom 550.00
3 Terror of the Unwilling Witch 275.00
4 Corpse that Came Alive 275.00
5 Horror of the Ghostly Crew . . 250.00
6 If the Noose Fits Wear It! 250.00
7 Terror of the Cards of Death . 250.00
8 Terror of the Ghostly Trail . . . 250.00
9 Witch's Feast at Dawn 250.00
10 Terror of the Burning Witch . . 275.00
11 The River of Blood 200.00
12 Horror of the Talking Dead . . . 200.00
13 Terror of the Hungry Cats. . . . 200.00
14 Horror of the Fingers of Doom 250.00
15 Terror of the Vampires Teeth . 200.00
16 Horror of the Walking Dead . . 200.00
17 Terror of the Mask of Death . . 200.00
18 Terror of the Burning Corpse . 200.00
19 The Rack of Terror. 250.00
20 Burning Executioner 235.00
21 The Sinister Secret 150.00
22 The Hand of Destiny 150.00
23 The Mardenburg Curse 125.00
24 Give A Man enough Rope, July, 1955. . . . . 125.00

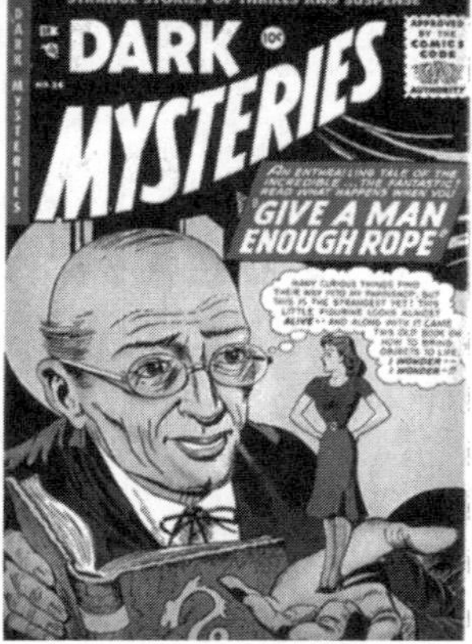

Dark Mysteries #24
© Merit Publications

DAVY CROCKETT
Avon Periodicals, 1951

1 . . . . 125.00

DEAD END CRIME STORIES
Kirby Publishing Co.
April, 1949

N# BP 400.00

DEAD-EYE WESTERN COMICS
Hillman Periodicals
Nov.–Dec., 1948

1 BK 125.00
2 . . . . 75.00
3 . . . . 50.00
4 thru 12 . . . . @35.00
2-1 . . . . 30.00
2-2 . . . . 30.00
2-3 . . . . 45.00
2-4 . . . . 45.00
2-5 thru 2-12 . . . . @25.00
3-1 . . . . 25.00

DEADWOOD GULCH
Dell Publishing Co., 1931

1 . . . . 125.00

DEAR BEATRICE FAIRFAX
Best Books
(Standard Comics), Nov., 1950

5 . . . . 50.00
6 thru 9 . . . . @35.00

DEAR LONELY HEART
Artful Publications
March, 1951

1 . . . . 125.00
2 . . . . 50.00
3 MB,Jungle Girl 125.00
4 . . . . 50.00
5 thru 8 . . . . @40.00

DEAR LONELY HEARTS
Comic Media, Aug., 1953

1 Six Months to Live 60.00
2 Date Hungry, Price of Passion . 40.00
3 thru 8 . . . . @40.00

DEARLY BELOVED
Approved Comics
(Ziff-Davis), Fall, 1952

1 Ph(c) 125.00

DEBBIE DEAN, CAREER GIRL
Civil Service Publishing
April, 1945

1 . . . . 100.00
2 . . . . 90.00

DELL GIANT EDITIONS
Dell Publishing Co.
1953-58

Abe Lincoln Life Story. 125.00
Cadet Gray of West Point 100.00
Golden West Rodeo Treasury . . . 150.00
Life Stories of American Presidents 90.00
Lone Ranger Golden West 300.00
Lone Ranger Movie Story 500.00
Lone Ranger Western Treasury('53) 300.00
Lone Ranger Western Treasury('54) 200.00
Moses & Ten Commandments . . . 75.00
Nancy & Sluggo Travel Time. . . . 100.00
Pogo Parade 450.00
Raggedy Ann & Andy 275.00
Santa Claus Funnies 150.00
Tarzan's Jungle Annual #1 . . . . . 225.00
Tarzan's Jungle Annual #2 . . . . . 175.00
Tarzan's Jungle Annual #3 . . . . . 150.00
Tarzan's Jungle Annual #4 . . . . . 150.00
Tarzan's Jungle Annual #5 . . . . . 150.00
Tarzan's Jungle Annual #6 . . . . . 150.00
Tarzan's Jungle Annual #7 . . . . . 150.00
Treasury of Dogs 100.00
Treasury of Horses 100.00
Universal Presents-Dracula-The Mummy & Other Stories 350.00
Western Roundup #1 . . . . 375.00
Western Roundup #2 . . . . 200.00
Western Roundup #3 . . . . 175.00
Western Roundup #4 thru #5. . @150.00
Western Roundup #6 thru #10. @140.00
Western Roundup #11 thru #17 @135.00
Western Roundup #18 . . . . 125.00
Western Roundup #19 thru #25 . 125.00
Woody Woodpecker Back to School #1. . . . . 165.00
Woody Woodpecker Back to School #2. . . . . 120.00
Woody Woodpecker Back to School #3. . . . . 100.00
Woody Woodpecker Back to School #4. . . . . 100.00
Woody Woodpecker County Fair #5 . . . . 100.00
Woody Woodpecker Back to School #6. . . . . 135.00
Woody Woodpecker County Fair #2 . . . . 100.00

Also See: Bugs Bunny; Marge's Little Lulu; Tom and Jerry, and Walt Disney Dell Giant Editions

DELL GIANT COMICS
Dell Publishing Co.
Sept., 1959

21 M.G.M. Tom & Jerry Picnic Time. 200.00
22 W.Disney's Huey, Dewey & Louie Back to School (Oct 1959) . . 135.00
23 Marge's Little Lulu & Tubby Halloween Fun. 200.00
24 Woody Woodpeckers Family Fun 125.00
25 Tarzan's Jungle World 175.00
26 W.Disney's Christmas Parade,CB 375.00
27 W.Disney's Man in Space (1960) 200.00
28 Bugs Bunny's Winter Fun. . . . 175.00
29 Marge's Little Lulu & Tubby in Hawaii 200.00
30 W.Disney's DisneylandU.S.A.. 175.00
31 Huckleberry Hound Summer Fun 225.00
32 Bugs Bunny Beach Party 100.00

33 W.Disney's Daisy Duck &
Uncle Scrooge Picnic Time . . 175.00
34 Nancy&SluggoSummerCamp. 120.00
35 W.Disney's Huey, Dewey &
Louie Back to School 175.00
36 Marge's Little Lulu & Witch
Hazel Halloween Fun 200.00
37 Tarzan, King of the Jungle . . . 165.00
38 W.Disney's Uncle Donald and
his Nephews Family Fun . . . 200.00
39 W.Disney's Merry Christmas . 200.00
40 Woody Woodpecker
Christmas Parade. 100.00
41 Yogi Bear's Winter Sports . . . 225.00
42 Marge's Little Lulu &
Tubby in Australia. 150.00
43 Mighty Mouse in OuterSpace . 400.00
44 Around the World with
Huckleberry & His Friends . . 225.00
45 Nancy&SluggoSummerCamp. 100.00
46 Bugs Bunny Beach Party 100.00
47 W.Disney's Mickey and
Donald in Vacationland 175.00
48 The Flintstones #1
(Bedrock Bedlam). 300.00
49 W.Disney's Huey, Dewey &
Louie Back to School 150.00
50 Marge's Little Lulu &
Witch Hazel Trick 'N' Treat . . 225.00
51 Tarzan, King of the Jungle . . . 150.00
52 W.Disney's Uncle Donald &
his Nephews Dude Ranch . . 150.00
53 W.Disney's Donald Duck
Merry Christmas. 135.00
54 Woody Woodpecker
Christmas Party 120.00
55 W.Disney's Daisy Duck & Uncle
Scrooge Show Boat (1961). . 130.00

DELL JUNIOR TREASURY
Dell Publishing Co.
June, 1955

1 Alice in Wonderland 125.00
2 Aladdin. 75.00
3 Gulliver's Travels 65.00
4 Adventures of Mr. Frog 70.00
5 Wizard of Oz 70.00
6 Heidi. 75.00
7 Santa & the Angel 75.00
8 Raggedy Ann 75.00
9 Clementina the Flying Pig. 70.00
10 Adventures of Tom Sawyer . . . 70.00

DENNIS THE MENACE
Visual Editions/Literary Ent.
(Standard, Pines)
Aug., 1953

1 . . . . 425.00
2 . . . . 200.00
3 . . . . 125.00
4 . . . . 125.00
5 thru 10 . . . . @100.00
11 thru 20 . . . . @90.00
21 thru 31 . . . . @65.00

Hallden (Fawcett)

32 thru 40 . . . . @35.00
41 thru 50 . . . . @30.00
51 thru 60 . . . . @25.00
61 thru 70 . . . . @20.00
71 thru 90 . . . . @15.00
91 thru 140 . . . . @7.00
141 thru 166 . . . . @5.00

DESPERADO
Lev Gleason Publications
June, 1948

1 CBi(c) 100.00

Black Diamond Western #38
© Lev Gleason

2 CBi(c) 50.00
3 CBi(c) 50.00
4 CBi(c) 40.00
5 CBi(c) 40.00
6 CBi(c) 40.00
7 CBi(c) 40.00
8 CBi(c) 40.00
Becomes:

BLACK DIAMOND WESTERN

9 CBi(c) 150.00
10 CBi(c) 75.00
11 CBi(c) 50.00
12 CBi(c) 50.00
13 CBi(c) 50.00
14 CBi(c) 50.00
15 CBi(c) 50.00
16 thru 28 BW,Big Bang Buster. @75.00
29 thru 40 . . . . @30.00
41 thru 52 . . . . @25.00
53 3-D 60.00
54 3-D 50.00
55 thru 60 . . . . @35.00

DETECTIVE EYE
Centaur Publications
Nov., 1940

1 B:Air Man, The Eye Sees,
A:Masked Marvel 1,700.00
2 O:Don Rance, Mysticape,
Dec., 1940 . . . . 1,200.00

DETECTIVE PICTURE STORIES
Comics Magazine Co.
Dec., 1936

1 The Phantom Killer 4,000.00
2 . . . . 1,700.00
3 . . . . 1,100.00
4 WE, Muss Em Up 1,000.00
5 Trouble, April, 1937 . . . . 1,200.00

DEXTER COMICS
Dearfield Publications
Summer, 1948–July, 1949

1 . . . . 50.00
2 . . . . 40.00
3 thru 5 . . . . 30.00

DIARY CONFESSIONS
(see TENDER ROMANCE)

DIARY LOVES
Comic Magazines
(Quality Comics Group)
Sept., 1949

1 BWa Love Diary 150.00
2 BWa 125.00
3 . . . . 40.00
4 RC 50.00
5 . . . . 35.00
6 . . . . 35.00
7 . . . . 35.00
8 BWa 75.00
9 BWa 75.00
10 BWa 75.00
11 . . . . 30.00
12 . . . . 30.00
13 . . . . 30.00
14 . . . . 30.00
15 BWa 75.00
16 BWa 75.00
17 . . . . 30.00
18 . . . . 30.00
19 . . . . 30.00
20 . . . . 30.00
21 BWa 55.00
22 thru 31 . . . . @20.00
Becomes:

G.I. SWEETHEARTS

32 Love Under Fire. 45.00
33 . . . . 30.00
34 . . . . 30.00
35 . . . . 30.00
36 Lend Lease Love Affair 30.00
37 thru 45 . . . . @30.00
Becomes:

GIRLS IN LOVE

46 Somewhere I'll Find You 35.00
47 thru 56 . . . . @25.00
57 MB,MB(c), Can Love Really
Change Him, Dec., 1956 . . . . 45.00

DIARY SECRETS
(see TEEN-AGE DIARY SECRETS)

DICK COLE
Curtis Publ./
Star Publications
Dec.–Jan., 1949

1 LbC,LbC(c),CS,All sports(c) . . 225.00
2 LbC 100.00
3 LbC, LbC(c) 150.00
4 LbC, LbC(c),Rowing cover . . . 150.00
5 LbC,LbC(c) 150.00
6 LbC,LbC(c), Rodeo cover . . . 150.00
7 LbC,LbC(c) 150.00
8 LbC,LbC(c), Football cover . . . 150.00
9 LbC,LbC(c), Basketball cover . 150.00
10 Joe Louis. 150.00
Becomes:

SPORTS THRILLS

11 Ted Williams & Ty Cobb 275.00
12 LbC, Joe Dimaggio & Phil
Rizzuto, Boxing cover. 225.00
13 LbC(c),Basketball cover. 175.00
14 LbC(c),Baseball cover 175.00
15 LbC(c),Baseball cover,
Nov., 1951 . . . . 175.00

DICKIE DARE
Eastern Color Printing Co.
1941

1 BEv(c) 325.00
2 . . . . 200.00
3 . . . . 200.00
4 1942. . . . . 225.00

DICK TRACY MONTHLY
Dell Publishing Co.
Jan., 1948

1 ChG,Dick Tracy & the Mad Doctor' 450.00
2 ChG,A:MarySteele,BorisArson 250.00
3 ChG,A:Spaldoni,Big Boy 250.00
4 ChG,A:Alderman Zeld 200.00
5 ChG,A:Spaldoni,Mrs.Spaldoni 200.00
6 ChG,A:Steve the Tramp 200.00
7 ChG,A:Boris Arson,Mary Steele 200.00
8 ChG,A:Boris & Zora Arson . . . 200.00
9 ChG,A:Chief Yellowpony 200.00
10 ChG,A:Cutie Diamond 200.00
11 ChG,A:Toby Townly, Bookie Joe 150.00
12 ChG,A:Toby Townly, Bookie Joe 150.00
13 ChG,A:Toby Townly, Blake . . . 160.00
14 ChG,A:Mayor Waite Wright . . 150.00
15 ChG,A:Bowman Basil. 150.00
16 ChG,A:Maw,`Muscle' & `Cut' Famon 150.00
17 ChG,A:Jim Trailer, Mary Steele 150.00
18 ChG,A:Lips Manlis, Anthel Jones 150.00
19 `Golden Heart Mystery' 200.00
20 `Black Cat Mystery' 200.00
21 `Tracy Meets Number One' . . 200.00
22 `Tracy and the Alibi Maker'. . . 150.00
23 `Dick Tracy Meets Jukebox' . . 150.00
24 `Dick Tracy and Bubbles' 150.00

Becomes:

DICK TRACY COMICS MONTHLY
Harvey

25 ChG,A:Flattop 175.00
26 ChG,A:Vitamin Flintheart 150.00
27 ChG,`Flattop Escapes Prision' 150.00
28 ChG,`Case o/t Torture Chamber' 160.00
29 ChG,A:Brow,Gravel Gertie . . . 200.00
30 ChG,`Blackmail Racket' 150.00
31 ChG,A:Snowflake Falls 125.00
32 ChG,A:Shaky,Snowflake Falls 125.00
33 ChG,`Strange Case of Measles'. 150.00
34 ChG,A:Measles,Paprika 125.00
35 ChG,`Case of Stolen $50,000' 125.00
36 ChG,`Case of the Runaway Blonde' 150.00
37 ChG,`Case of Stolen Money' . 125.00
38 ChG,A:Breathless Mahoney . . 125.00
39 ChG,A:Itchy,B.O.Pleanty 125.00
40 ChG,`Case of Atomic Killer' . . 125.00
41 ChG,Pt.1`Murder by Mail'. . . . 100.00
42 ChG,Pt.2`Murder by Mail'. . . . 100.00
43 ChG,`Case of the Underworld Brat'. 100.00
44 ChG,`Case of the Mouthwash Murder'. 100.00
45 ChG,`Case of the Evil Eyes'. . 100.00
46 ChG,`Case of the Camera Killers'. 100.00
47 ChG,`Case of the Bloodthirsty Blonde' 100.00

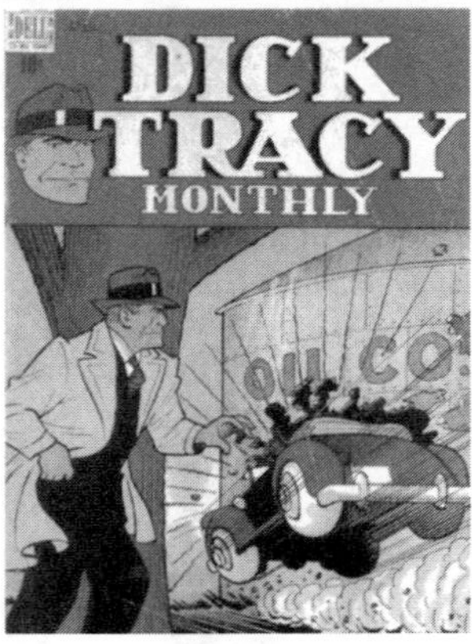

Dick Tracy Monthly #4
© Dell Publishing Co.

48 ChG,`Case of the Murderous Minstrel' 100.00
49 ChG,Pt.1`Killer Who Returned From the Dead 100.00
50 ChG,Pt.2`Killer Who Returned From the Dead' . . . 100.00
51 ChG,`Case of the High Tension Hijackers' 90.00
52 ChG,`Case of the Pipe-Stem Killer 90.00
53 ChG,Pt.1`Dick Tracy Meets the Murderous Midget' 90.00
54 ChG,Pt.2`Dick Tracy Meets the Murderous Midget' 90.00
55 ChG,Pt.3`Dick Tracy Meets the Murderous Midget' 90.00
56 ChG,`Case of the Teleguard Terror' 90.00
57 ChG,Pt.1`Case of the Ice Cold Killer' 100.00
58 ChG,Pt.2`Case of the Ice Cold Killer' 90.00
59 ChG,Pt.1`Case of the Million Dollar Murder' 90.00
60 ChG,Pt.2`Case of the Million Dollar Murder' 75.00
61 ChG,`Case of the Murderers Mask'. 75.00
62 ChG,Pt.1`Case of the White Rat Robbers' 75.00
63 ChG,Pt.2`Case of the White Rat Robbers' 75.00
64 ChG,Pt.1`Case of the Interrupted Honeymoon' 75.00
65 ChG,Pt.2`Case of the Interrupted Honeymoon' 75.00
66 ChG,Pt.1`Case of the Killer's Revenge'. 75.00
67 ChG,Pt.2`Case of the Killer's Revenge'. 75.00
68 ChG,Pt.1`Case of the TV Terror'. 75.00
69 ChG,Pt.2`Case of the TV Terror'. 75.00
70 ChG,Pt.3`Case of the TV Terror'. 75.00
71 ChG,A:Mrs. Forchune,Opal . . . 75.00
72 ChG,A:Empty Wiliams,Bonny. . 75.00
73 ChG,A:Bonny Braids 75.00
74 ChG,A:Mr. & Mrs. Fortson Knox 75.00
75 ChG,A:Crewy Lou, Sphinx 75.00
76 ChG,A:Diet Smith,Brainerd . . . 75.00
77 ChG,A:Crewy Lou, Bonny Braids 75.00
78 ChG,A:Spinner Records. 75.00
79 ChG,A:Model Jones, Larry Jones 75.00
80 ChG,A:Tonsils,Dot View 75.00
81 ChG,A:Edward Moppet,Tonsils. 75.00
82 ChG,A:Dot View,Mr. Crime. . . . 75.00
83 ChG,A:Rifle Ruby,Newsuit Nan 75.00
84 ChG,A:Mr. Crime,Newsuit Nan. 75.00
85 ChG,A:Newsuit Nan, Mrs.Lava. 75.00
86 ChG,A:Mr. Crime, Odds Zonn . 75.00
87 ChG,A:Odds Zonn,Wingy. 75.00
88 ChG,A:Odds Zonn,Wingy. 75.00
89 ChG,Pt.1`Canhead' 75.00
90 ChG,Pt.2`Canhead' 75.00
91 ChG,Pt.3`Canhead' 75.00
92 ChG,Pt.4`Canhead' 75.00
93 ChG,Pt.5`Canhead' 75.00
94 ChG,Pt.6`Canhead' 75.00
95 ChG,A:Mrs. Green,Dewdrop . . 75.00
96 ChG,A:Dewdrop,Sticks 75.00
97 ChG,A:Dewdrop,Sticks 75.00
98 ChG,A:Open-Mind Monty, Sticks. 75.00
99 ChG,A:Open-Mind Monty, Sticks. 80.00
100 ChG,A:Half-Pint,Dewdrop. . . 100.00
101 ChG,A:Open-Mind Monty. . . . 75.00
102 ChG,A:Rainbow Reiley,Wingy 75.00
103 ChG,A:Happy,Rughead 75.00
104 ChG,A:Rainbow Reiley,Happy 75.00
105 ChG,A:Happy,Rughead 75.00
106 ChG,A:Fence,Corny,Happy . . 75.00
107 ChG,A:Rainbow Reiley 75.00
108 ChG,A:Rughead,Corny,Fence 75.00
109 ChG,A:Rughead,Mimi,Herky . 75.00
110 ChG,A:Vitamin Flintheart 75.00
111 ChG,A:Shoulders,Roach. 75.00
112 ChG,A:Brilliant,Diet Smith . . . 75.00
113 ChG,A:Snowflake Falls 75.00
114 ChG,A:`Sketch'Paree, ... 75.00
115 ChG,A:Rod & Nylon Hoze . . . 75.00
116 ChG,A:Empty Williams 75.00
117 ChG,A:Spinner Records. 75.00
118 ChG,A:Sleet. 75.00
119 ChG,A:Coffyhead 75.00
120 ChG,`Case Against Mumbles Quartet'. 70.00
121 ChG,`Case of the Wild Boys' . 70.00
122 ChG,`Case of the Poisoned Pellet' 70.00
123 ChG,`Case of the Deadly Treasure Hunt' 70.00
124 ChG,`Case of Oodles Hears Only Evil 70.00
125 ChG,`Case of the Desparate Widow' 70.00
126 ChG,`Case of Oodles' Hideout' 70.00
127 ChG,`Case Against Joe Period'. 70.00
128 ChG,`Case Against Juvenile Delinquent'. 70.00
129 ChG,`Case of Son of Flattop' . 70.00
130 ChG,`Case of Great Gang Roundup' 70.00
131 ChG,`Strange Case of Flattop's Conscience' 70.00
132 ChG,`Case of Flattop's Big Show'. 70.00
133 ChG,`Dick Tracy Follows Trail of Jewel Thief Gang'. 70.00
134 ChG,`Last Stand of Jewel Thieves' 70.00
135 ChG,`Case of the Rooftop Sniper'. 70.00
136 ChG,`Mystery of the Iron Room' 70.00
137 ChG,`Law Versus Dick Tracy'. 70.00
138 ChG,`Mystery of Mary X' 70.00
139 ChG,`Yogee the Merciless'. . . 70.00
140 ChG,`The Tunnel Trap' 70.00

GOLDEN AGE

141 ChG,`Case of Wormy & His Deadly Wagon 70.00
142 ChG,`Case of the Killer's Revenge'. 70.00
143 ChG,`Strange Case of Measles'. 70.00
144 ChG,`Strange Case of Shoulders' 70.00
145 ChG,`Case of the Feindish Photo-graphers';April, 1961 . . 70.00

DIME COMICS
Newsbook Publ. Corp., 1945

1 LbC,A:Silver Streak 500.00

DING DONG
Compix
(Magazine Enterprises), 1947

1 (fa). 135.00
2 (fa). 60.00
3 thru 5 (fa) . . . . @50.00

DINKY DUCK
St. John Publ. Co./Pines
Nov., 1951

1 . . . . 60.00
2 . . . . 35.00
3 thru 10 . . . . @25.00
11 thru 15 . . . . @20.00
16 thru 18. . . . . @15.00
19 Summer, 1958. . . . . 15.00

DIXIE DUGAN
Columbia Publ./
Publication Enterprises
July, 1942

1 Boxing cover,Joe Palooka. . . . 225.00
2 . . . . 125.00
3 . . . . 85.00
4 & 5. @60.00
6 thru 12 . . . . @45.00
13 1949 . . . . 45.00

DIZZY DAMES
B&M Distribution Co.
(American Comics)
Sept.–Oct., 1952

1 . . . . 100.00
2 . . . . 50.00
3 thru 6 July–Aug., 1953 . . . . . @40.00

DIZZY DON COMICS
Howard Publications/
Dizzy Dean Ent., 1943

1 B&W interior. 60.00
2 B&W Interior. 40.00
3 B&W Interior. 30.00
4 B&W Interior. 30.00
5 thru 21 . . . . @30.00
22 Oct., 1946 . . . . 60.00
1a thru 3a . . . . @50.00

DIZZY DUCK
(see BARNYARD COMICS)

DOC CARTER V.D. COMICS
Health Publ. Inst., 1949

N# 150.00
N# 100.00

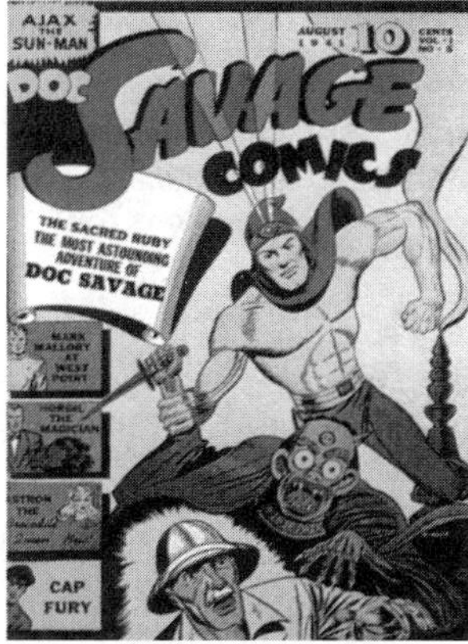

Doc Savage #5
© Street & Smith

DOC SAVAGE COMICS
Street & Smith, May, 1940

1 B:Doc Savage, Capt. Fury, Danny Garrett, Mark Mallory, Whisperer, Capt. Death, Treasure Island, A: The Magician . . . 4,500.00
2 O:Ajax,The Sun Man,E:The Whisperer 1,300.00
3 Artic Ice Wastes 1,100.00
4 E:Treasure Island, Saves U.S. Navy. 800.00
5 O:Astron, the Crocodile Queen, Sacred Ruby 600.00
6 E: Capt. Fury, O:Red Falcon, Murderous Peace Clan 500.00
7 V:Zoombas 500.00
8 Finds the Long Lost Treasure . 500.00
9 Smashes Japan's Secret Oil Supply 500.00
10 O:Thunder Bolt, The Living Dead A:Lord Manhattan 500.00
11 V:Giants of Destruction. 450.00
12 Saves Merchant Fleet from Complete Destruction 450.00
2-1 The Living Evil 450.00
2-2 V:Beggar King 450.00
2-3 . . . . 450.00
2-4 Fight to Death. 450.00
2-5 Saves Panama Canal from Blood Raider 450.00
2-6 . . . . 450.00
2-7 V:Black Knight 450.00
2-8 Oct., 1943 . . . . 450.00

DR. ANTHONY KING HOLLYWOOD LOVE DOCTOR
Harvey, Publ., 1952

1 . . . . 75.00
2 . . . . 40.00
3 . . . . 40.00
4 BP,May, 1954 . . . . 40.00

DOLL MAN
Comic Favorites
(Quality Comics Group)
Fall, 1941

1 RC,B:Doll Man & Justine Wright 3,000.00
2 B:Dragon 1,100.00

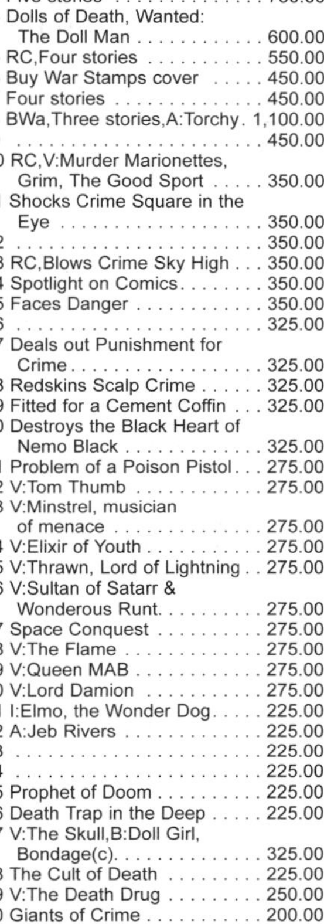

3 Five stories 750.00
4 Dolls of Death, Wanted: The Doll Man 600.00
5 RC,Four stories 550.00
6 Buy War Stamps cover 450.00
7 Four stories 450.00
8 BWa,Three stories,A:Torchy. 1,100.00
9 . . . . 450.00
10 RC,V:Murder Marionettes, Grim, The Good Sport 350.00
11 Shocks Crime Square in the Eye 350.00
12 . . . . 350.00
13 RC,Blows Crime Sky High . . . 350.00
14 Spotlight on Comics. 350.00
15 Faces Danger 350.00
16 . . . . 325.00
17 Deals out Punishment for Crime 325.00
18 Redskins Scalp Crime 325.00
19 Fitted for a Cement Coffin . . . 325.00
20 Destroys the Black Heart of Nemo Black 325.00
21 Problem of a Poison Pistol. . . 275.00
22 V:Tom Thumb 275.00
23 V:Minstrel, musician of menace 275.00
24 V:Elixir of Youth 275.00
25 V:Thrawn, Lord of Lightning . . 275.00
26 V:Sultan of Satarr & Wonderous Runt. 275.00
27 Space Conquest 275.00
28 V:The Flame 275.00
29 V:Queen MAB 275.00
30 V:Lord Damion 275.00
31 I:Elmo, the Wonder Dog. 225.00
32 A:Jeb Rivers 225.00
33 . . . . 225.00
34 . . . . 225.00
35 Prophet of Doom 225.00
36 Death Trap in the Deep 225.00
37 V:The Skull,B:Doll Girl, Bondage(c). 325.00
38 The Cult of Death 225.00
39 V:The Death Drug 250.00
40 Giants of Crime 200.00
41 The Headless Horseman 200.00
42 Tale of the Mind Monster 200.00
43 The Thing that Kills 200.00
44 V:Radioactive Man. 200.00
45 What was in the Doom Box? . 200.00
46 Monster from Tomorrow 200.00
47 V:Mad Hypnotist, Oct., 1953 . . . . 200.00

Doll Man #32
© Quality Comics Group

FAMOUS GANG, BOOK OF COMICS
Firestone Tire & Rubber Co.
1942

N# 800.00
Becomes:

DONALD AND MICKEY MERRY CHRISTMAS

N# (2),CB, 1943 . . . . 750.00
N# (3),CB, 1944 . . . . 700.00
N# (4),CB, 1945 . . . . 1,000.00
N# (5),CB, 1946 . . . . 750.00
N# (6),CB, 1947 . . . . 650.00
N# (7),CB, 1948 . . . . 650.00
N# (8),CB, 1949 . . . . 675.00

DONALD DUCK
Whitman

W.Disney's Donald Duck ('35) . 2,500.00
W.Disney's Donald Duck ('36) . 2,500.00
W.Disney's Donald Duck ('38) . 2,500.00

DONALD DUCK GIVEAWAYS

Donald Duck Surprise Party (Icy Frost Ice Cream 1948)WK . . 900.00
Donald Duck (Xmas Giveaway 1944) 600.00
Donald Duck Tells About Kites (P.G.&E., Florida 1954) . . . 2,000.00
Donald Duck Tells About Kites (S.C.Edison 1954) 1,800.00
Donald Duck and the Boys (Whitman 1948) 550.00
Donald Ducks Atom Bomb (Cherrios 1947) 600.00

(WALT DISNEY'S) DONALD DUCK
Dell Publishing Co.
Nov., 1952

(#1-#25) See Dell Four Color
26 CB;"Trick or Treat" (1952) . . . 350.00
27 CB(c);"Flying Horse"('53) 150.00
28 CB(c); Robert the Robot. 125.00
29 CB(c). 125.00
30 CB(c). 125.00
31 thru 39 . . . . @65.00
40 thru 44 . . . . @60.00
45 CB. 160.00
46 CB; "Secret of Hondorica" . . . 250.00
47 thru 51 . . . . @60.00
52 CB; "Lost Peg-Leg Mine" 150.00
53 . . . . 50.00
54 CB; "Forbidden Valley" 150.00
55 thru 59 . . . . @50.00
60 CB; "Donald Duck & the Titanic Ants" 150.00
61 thru 67 . . . . @40.00
68 CB. 125.00
69 thru 78 . . . . @35.00
79 CB (1 page). 45.00
80 . . . . 30.00
81 CB (1 page). 35.00
82 . . . . 30.00
83 . . . . 30.00
84 . . . . 30.00
See: Independent Color Listings

DON FORTUNE MAGAZINE
Don Fortune Publ. Co.
Aug., 1946

1 CCB 175.00
2 CCB 125.00
3 CCB,Bondage(c) 100.00
4 CCB 100.00
5 CCB 100.00
6 CCB, Jan., 1947 . . . . 100.00

DON NEWCOMBE
Fawcett Publications, 1950

1 Baseball Star 400.00

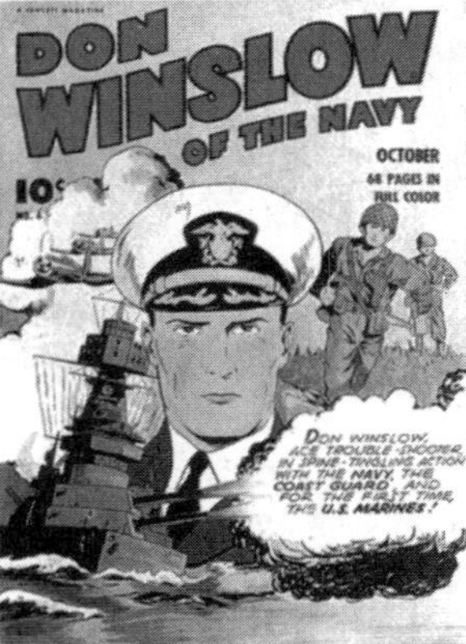

Don Winslow of the Navy #8
© Fawcett Publications

DON WINSLOW OF THE NAVY
Fawcett Publ./
Charlton Comics, Feb., 1943

1 Captain Marvel cover 900.00
2 Nips the Nipponese in the Solomons 450.00
3 Single-Handed invasion of the Philippines 300.00
4 Undermines the Nazis! 250.00
5 Stolen Battleship Mystery 250.00
6 War Stamps for Victory cover . 250.00
7 Coast Guard 175.00
8 U.S. Marines 175.00
9 Fighting Marines 175.00
10 Fighting Seabees. 175.00
11 . . . . 150.00
12 Tuned for Death. 150.00
13 Hirohito's Hospitality. 150.00
14 Catapults against the Axis . . . 150.00
15 Fighting Merchant Marine. . . . 135.00
16 V:The Most Diabolical Villain of all Time 135.00
17 Buy War Stamps cover 135.00
18 The First Underwater Convoy. 125.00
19 Bonape Excersion 125.00
20 The Nazi Prison Ship 125.00
21 Prisoner of the Nazis 100.00
22 Suicide Football 100.00
23 Peril on the High Seas 100.00
24 Adventures on the High Seas. 100.00
25 Shanghaied Red Cross Ship . 100.00
26 V:The Scorpion 100.00
27 Buy War Stamps 100.00
28 . . . . 100.00
29 Invitation to Trouble 100.00
30 . . . . 100.00
31 Man or Myth? 90.00
32 Return of the Renegade. 90.00
33 Service Ribbons 90.00
34 Log Book. 90.00
35 . . . . 90.00
36 . . . . 90.00
37 V: Sea Serpent 90.00
38 Climbs Mt. Everest. 90.00
39 Scorpion's Death Ledger 90.00
40 Kick Off! 90.00
41 Rides the Skis! 75.00
42 Amazon Island. 75.00
43 Ghastly Doll Murder Case 75.00
44 The Scorpions Web 75.00
45 V:Highwaymen of the Seas . . . 75.00
46 Renegades Jailbreak 75.00
47 The Artic Expedition. 75.00
48 Maelstrom of the Deep. 75.00
49 The Vanishing Ship!. 75.00
50 V:The Snake 75.00
51 A:Singapore Sal. 70.00
52 Ghost of the Fishing Ships. . . . 70.00
53 . . . . 70.00
54 . . . . 70.00
55 . . . . 70.00
56 Far East 70.00
57 A:Singapore Sal. 70.00
58 . . . . 70.00
59 . . . . 70.00
60 thru 63 . . . . @70.00
64 MB 80.00
65 Ph(c) 100.00
66 Ph(c) 100.00
67 Ph(c) 100.00
68 Ph(c) 100.00
69 Ph(c), Jaws of Destruction . . . 100.00
70 . . . . 60.00
71 . . . . 60.00
72 . . . . 60.00
73 Sept., 1955 . . . . 60.00

DOPEY DUCK
Non-Pareil Publ. Corp.
Fall, 1945

1 A:Krazy Krow,Casper Cat 125.00
2 same 100.00
Becomes:

WACKY DUCK

3 . . . . 65.00
4 . . . . 50.00
5 . . . . 50.00
6 Summer, 1947 . . . . 50.00

DOROTHY LAMOUR (see JUNGLE LIL)

DOTTY DRIPPLE
Magazine Enterprises/
Harvey Publications, 1946

1 . . . . 70.00
2 . . . . 40.00
3 thru 10 . . . . @25.00
11 thru 20 . . . . @15.00
21 thru 23 . . . . @10.00
24 June, 1952 . . . . 10.00
Becomes:

HORACE & DOTTY DRIPPLE

25 thru 42 . . . . @7.00
43 Oct., 1955 . . . . 7.00

DOUBLE COMICS
Elliot Publications

1 ('40),Masked Marvel. 1,800.00
2 ('41),Tornado Tim. 1,300.00
3 ('42) 1,000.00
4 ('43) 750.00
5 ('44) 750.00

DOUBLE UP
Elliot Publications, 1941

1 . . . . 650.00

DOWN WITH CRIME
Fawcett Publications
Nov., 1951

1 A:Desarro 250.00
2 BP, A:Scanlon Gang 150.00
3 H-is for Heroin 125.00
4 BP, A:Desarro 100.00
5 No Jail Can Hold Me 125.00
6 The Puncture-Proof Assassin . 100.00
7 The Payoff, Nov., 1952 . . . . . 100.00

DUDLEY
Prize Publications
Nov.–Dec., 1952

1 . . . . 100.00
2 . . . . 75.00
3 March–April, 1950 . . . . 65.00

DUMBO WEEKLY
The Walt Disney Co., 1942

1 Gas giveaways 500.00
2 . . . . 200.00
3 . . . . 200.00
4 . . . . 200.00
5 thru 16 . . . . @200.00

DURANGO KID
Magazine Enterprises
Oct.–Nov., 1949

1 FF, Charles Starrett photo cover B:Durango Kid & Raider . . . 600.00
2 FF, Charles Starrett Ph(c) 300.00
3 FF, Charles Starrett Ph(c) . . . 275.00
4 FF, Charles Starrett Ph(c), Two-Timing Guns 250.00
5 FF, Charles Starrett Ph(c), Tracks Across the Trail 250.00
6 FF 150.00
7 FF,Atomic(c) 165.00
8 FF thru 10 . . . . @150.00
11 FF 125.00
12 FF 125.00
13 FF 125.00
14 thru 16 FF . . . . @125.00
17 O:Durango Kid 150.00
18 FMe,DAy(c) 85.00
19 FMe,FG 75.00
20 FMe,FG 75.00
21 FMe,FG 75.00
22 FMe,FG 80.00
23 FMe,FG,I:Red Scorpion 80.00
24 thru 30 FMe,FG . . . . @80.00
31 FMe,FG 80.00
32 thru 40 FG . . . . @70.00
41 FG,Oct., 1941 . . . . 75.00

DYNAMIC COMICS
Dynamic Publications
(Harry 'A' Chesler)
Oct., 1941

1 EK,O:Major Victory, Dynamic Man, Hale the Magician, A:Black Cobra 1,400.00
2 O:Dynamic Boy & Lady Satan,I:Green Knight, Lance Cooper 650.00
3 GT 550.00
8 Horror cover 550.00
9 MRa,GT,B:Mr.E 550.00
10 . . . . 450.00

Dynamic Comics #13
© Harry A Chesler

11 GT 350.00
12 GT 325.00
13 GT 350.00
14 . . . . 325.00
15 . . . . 325.00
16 GT,Bondage(c),Marijuana. . . . 350.00
17 . . . . 500.00
18 Ric. 275.00
19 A:Dynamic Man 250.00
20 same,Nude Woman 375.00
21 same 250.00
22 same 250.00
23 A:Yankee Girl,1.0948 . . . . 250.00

DYNAMITE
Comic Media/Allen Hardy Publ.
May, 1953

1 DH(c),A:Danger#6 . . . . 150.00
2 . . . . 100.00
3 PAM,PAM(c),B:Johnny Dynamite,Drug 100.00
4 PAM,PAM(c),Prostitution 125.00
5 PAM,PAM(c) 100.00
6 PAM,PAM(c) 100.00
7 PAM,PAM(c) 100.00
8 PAM,PAM(c) 100.00
9 PAM,PAM(c) 100.00

Becomes:

JOHNNY DYNAMITE
Charlton Comics

10 PAM(c) 70.00
11 . . . . 50.00
12 . . . . 55.00

Becomes:

FOREIGN INTRIGUES

13 A:Johnny Dynamite 50.00
14 same 40.00
15 same 40.00

Becomes:

BATTLEFIELD ACTION

16 . . . . 35.00
17 . . . . 20.00
18 . . . . 20.00
19 . . . . 20.00
20 . . . . 20.00
21 thru 30 . . . . @15.00
31 thru 70 . . . . @7.00
71 thru 84 Oct. 1984 . . . . @5.00

EAGLE, THE
Fox Features Syndicate
July, 1941

1 B:The Eagle,A:Rex Dexter of Mars 1,500.00
2 B:Spider Queen 700.00
3 B:Joe Spook 550.00
4 Jan., 1942 . . . . 500.00

EAGLE
Rural Home Publ.
Feb.–March, 1945

1 LbC 275.00
2 LbC,April–May, 1945 . . . . 175.00

EAT RIGHT TO WORK AND WIN
Swift Co., 1942

N# Flash Gordon,Popeye 350.00

EDDIE STANKY
Fawcett Publications, 1951

N# New York Giants 250.00

EERIE
Avon Periodicals
May–June, 1951–
Aug.–Sept., 1954

1 JKa,Horror from the Pit, Bondage(c) 2,800.00
2 WW,WW(c), Chamber of Death 500.00
3 WW,WW(c),JKa,JO Monster of the Storm 550.00
4 WW(c),Phantom of Reality . . . 450.00
5 WW(c), Operation Horror 400.00
6 Devil Keeps a Date 200.00
7 WW(c),JKa,JO,Blood for the Vampire 350.00
8 EK, Song of the Undead 200.00
9 JKa, Hands of Death 200.00
10 Castle of Terror 200.00
11 Anatomical Monster 200.00
12 Dracula 250.00
13 . . . . 200.00
14 Master of the Dead 200.00
15 . . . . 175.00
16 WW, Chamber of Death 175.00
17 WW(c),JO,JKa, ... 200.00

Eerie #17
© Avon Periodicals

GOLDEN AGE

EERIE ADVENTURES
Approved Comics (Ziff-Davis), Winter, 1951

1 BP,JKa,Bondage 300.00

EGBERT
Arnold Publications/ Comic Magazine Spring, 1946

1 I:Egbert & The Count 150.00
2 . . . . 75.00
3 . . . . 40.00
4 . . . . 40.00
5 . . . . 40.00
6 . . . . 50.00
7 . . . . 40.00
8 . . . . 40.00
9 . . . . 40.00
10 . . . . 40.00
11 thru 17 . . . . @25.00
18 1950 . . . . 25.00

EH!
Charlton Comics Dec., 1953

1 DAy(c),DG 230.00
2 DAy(c) 150.00
3 DAy(c) 125.00
4 DAy(c) 125.00
5 DAy(c) 125.00
6 DAy(c) 125.00
7 DAy(c),Nov., 1954 . . . . 125.00

EL BOMBO COMICS
Frances M. McQueeny, 1945

1 . . . . 75.00

ELLERY QUEEN
Superior Comics May–Nov., 1949

1 LbC(c),JKa,Horror. 400.00
2 . . . . 300.00
3 Drug issue 275.00
4 The Crooked Mile 375.00

ELLERY QUEEN
Approved Comics (Ziff-Davis) Jan.–March, 1952

1 NS(c),The Corpse the Killed . . 350.00
2 NS,Killer's Revenge,
Summer, 1952 . . . . 275.00

ELSIE THE COW
D.S. Publishing Co. Oct.–Nov., 1949

1 P(c) 175.00
2 Bondage(c). 200.00
3 July–Aug., 1950 . . . . 175.00

ENCHANTING LOVE
Kirby Publishing Co. Oct., 1949

1 Branded Guilty, Ph(c) 100.00
2 Ph(c),BP. 50.00
3 Ph(c),Utter Defeat was our
Victory; Jan.–Feb., 1950 . . . . 40.00

ETTA KETT
Best Books, Inc. (Standard Comics) Dec., 1948

11 . . . . 75.00
12 . . . . 40.00
13 . . . . 40.00
14 Sept., 1949 . . . . 40.00

ERNIE COMICS (see SCREAM COMICS)

Exciting Comics #3
© Standard Comics

EXCITING COMICS
Better Publ./Visual Editions (Standard Comics) April, 1940

1 O:Mask, Jim Hatfield,
Dan Williams 3,400.00
2 B:Sphinx 1,400.00
3 V;Robot 900.00
4 V:Sea Monster 600.00
5 V:Gargoyle 600.00
6 . . . . 650.00
7 AS(c) 450.00
8 . . . . 450.00
9 O:Black Terror & Tim,
Bondage(c) 7,500.00
10 A:Black Terror 2,400.00
11 same. 1,200.00
12 Bondage(c) 750.00
13 Bondage(c) 750.00
14 O:Sphinx 500.00
15 O:Liberator 525.00
16 Black Terror 400.00
17 same 400.00
18 same 400.00
19 same 400.00
20 E:Mask,Bondage(c) 375.00
21 A:Liberator. 350.00
22 O:The Eaglet,B:American
Eagle 400.00
23 Black Terror. 325.00
24 Black Terror 325.00
25 Bondage(c) 350.00
26 ASh(c). 325.00
27 ASh(c). 325.00
28 ASh(c),B:Crime Crusader. . . . 525.00
29 ASh(c). 425.00
30 ASh(c),Bondage(c) 450.00
31 ASh(c). 400.00
32 ASh(c). 400.00
33 ASh(c). 400.00
34 ASh(c). 400.00
35 ASh(c),E:Liberator 400.00
36 ASh(c). 400.00
37 ASh(c). 400.00
38 ASh(c). 400.00
39 ASh(c)O:Kara, Jungle
Princess. 450.00
40 ASh(c) 425.00
41 ASh(c). 425.00
42 ASh(c),B:Scarab 450.00
43 ASh(c). 425.00
44 ASh(c). 425.00
45 ASh(c),V:Robot 425.00
46 ASh(c). 425.00
47 ASh(c). 425.00
48 ASh(c). 425.00
49 ASh(c),E:Kara &
American Eagle 425.00
50 ASh(c),E:American Eagle . . . 425.00
51 ASh(c),B:Miss Masque. 500.00
52 ASh(c),Miss Masque 375.00
53 ASh(c),Miss Masque 375.00
54 ASh(c),E:Miss Masque. 375.00
55 ASh(c),O&B:Judy o/t Jungle. . 425.00
56 ASh(c). 375.00
57 ASh(c). 375.00
58 ASh(c). 375.00
59 ASh(c),FF,Bondage(c) 425.00
60 ASh(c),The Mystery Rider . . . 375.00
61 ASh(c). 375.00
62 ASh(c). 375.00
63 thru 65 ASh(c) . . . . @375.00
66 . . . . 375.00
67 GT. 375.00
68 . . . . 375.00
69 Sept., 1949 . . . . 375.00

EXCITING ROMANCES
Fawcett Publications, 1949

1 Ph(c) 100.00
2 thru 3 . . . . @50.00
4 Ph(c) 50.00
5 thru 14 . . . . @45.00

EXOTIC ROMANCE (see TRUE WAR ROMANCES)

EXPLORER JOE
Approved Comics (Ziff-Davis) Winter, 1951

1 NS,The Fire Opal
of Madagscar 100.00
2 BK, Oct.–Nov., 1952 . . . . 120.00

EXPOSED
D.S. Publishing Co. March–April, 1948

1 Corpses Cash and Carry 175.00
2 Giggling Killer 200.00
3 One Bloody Night 75.00
4 JO,Deadly Dummy 75.00
5 Body on the Beach 75.00
6 Grl,The Secret in the Snow . . 300.00
7 The Gypsy Baron,
July–Aug., 1949 . . . . 320.00

EXTRA
Magazine Enterprises, 1947

1 . . . . 400.00

EXTRA!
E.C. Comics, March–April, 1955

1 JCr,RC,JSe . . . 150.00
2 JCr,RC,JSe . . . 100.00
3 JCr,RC,JSe . . . 100.00
4 JCr,RC,JSe . . . 100.00
5 Nov.–Dec., 1955 . . . 100.00

FACE, THE
Publication Enterprises (Columbia Comics), 1942

1 MBi(c),The Face . . . 750.00
2 MBi(c) . . . 500.00

Becomes:

TONY TRENT

3 MBi,A:The Face . . . 100.00
4 1949 . . . 75.00

FAIRY TALE PARADE
Dell Publishing Co., 1942

1 WK,Giant . . . 1,400.00
2 WK,Flying Horse . . . 600.00
3 WK . . . 425.00
4 WK . . . 400.00
5 WK . . . 400.00
6 WK . . . 300.00
7 WK . . . 300.00
8 WK . . . 300.00
9 WK . . . 300.00

FAMOUS COMICS
Zain-Eppy Publ.

N# Joe Palooka . . . 400.00

FAMOUS CRIMES
Fox Features Syndicate June, 1948

1 Cold Blooded Killer . . . 400.00
2 Near Nudity cover . . . 300.00
3 Crime Never Pays . . . 375.00
4 . . . 150.00
5 . . . 150.00
6 . . . 150.00
7 Drug issue . . . 300.00
8 thru 19 . . . @125.00
20 Aug., 1951 . . . 125.00
51 1952 . . . 65.00

FAMOUS FAIRY TALES
K.K. Publication Co., 1942

N# WK, Giveaway . . . 350.00
N# WK, Giveaway . . . 250.00
N# WK, Giveaway . . . 250.00

FAMOUS FEATURE STORIES
Dell Publishing Co., 1938

1A:Tarzan, Terry and the Pirates
Dick Tracy,Smilin' Jack . . . 550.00

FAMOUS FUNNIES
Eastern Color Printing Co. 1933

N# A Carnival of Comics . . . 9,000.00
N# Feb., 1934,
1st 10¢ comic . . . 24,000.00
1 July, 1934 . . . 17,000.00
2 . . . 3,500.00
3 B:Buck Rogers . . . 4,500.00
4 Football cover . . . 1,400.00
5 . . . 1,200.00

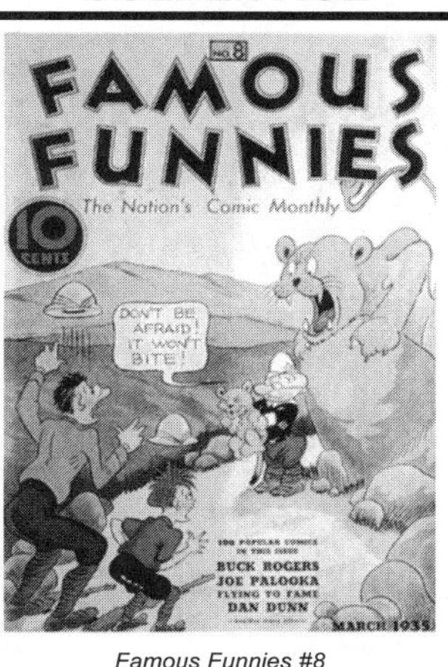

Famous Funnies #8
© Eastern Color Printing

6 . . . 750.00
7 . . . 750.00
8 . . . 750.00
9 . . . 750.00
10 . . . 750.00
11 Four pages of Buck Rogers . . 700.00
12 Four pages of Buck Rogers . . 700.00
13 . . . 550.00
14 . . . 550.00
15 Football cover . . . 550.00
16 . . . 550.00
17 Christmas cover . . . 550.00
18 Four pages of Buck Rogers . . 700.00
19 . . . 550.00
20 . . . 550.00
21 Baseball . . . 400.00
22 Buck Rogers . . . 400.00
23 . . . 375.00
24 B: War on Crime . . . 375.00
25 . . . 375.00
26 . . . 375.00
27 G-Men cover . . . 375.00
28 . . . 375.00
29 . . . 375.00
30 . . . 375.00
31 . . . 300.00
32 . . . 300.00
33 A:Baby Face Nelson &
John Dillinger . . . 300.00
34 . . . 300.00
35 Buck Rogers . . . 325.00
36 . . . 275.00
37 . . . 275.00
38 Portrait,Buck Rogers . . . 300.00
39 . . . 275.00
40 . . . 275.00
41 thru 50 . . . @250.00
51 thru 57 . . . @200.00
58 Baseball cover . . . 200.00
59 . . . 200.00
60 . . . 200.00
61 . . . 175.00
62 . . . 175.00
63 . . . 175.00
64 . . . 175.00
65 JK . . . 175.00
66 . . . 175.00
67 . . . 175.00
68 JK . . . 175.00
69 . . . 175.00
70 . . . 175.00
71 BEv . . . 125.00
72 BEv,B:Speed Spaulding . . . 125.00
73 BEv . . . 125.00
74 BEv . . . 125.00
75 BEv . . . 125.00
76 BEv . . . 125.00
77 BEv,Merry Christmas cover . . 125.00
78 BEv . . . 125.00
79 BEv . . . 125.00
80 BEv,Buck Rogers . . . 125.00
81 O:Invisible Scarlet O'Neil . . . 100.00
82 Buck Rogers cover . . . 125.00
83 Dickie Dare . . . 100.00
84 Scotty Smith . . . 100.00
85 Eagle Scout,Roy Rogers . . . 100.00
86 Moon Monsters . . . 100.00
87 Scarlet O'Neil . . . 100.00
88 . . . 100.00
89 O:Fearless Flint . . . 100.00
90 Bondage cover . . . 110.00
91 . . . 100.00
92 . . . 100.00
93 . . . 100.00
94 War Bonds . . . 120.00
95 Invisible Scarlet O'Neil . . . 100.00
96 . . . 100.00
97 War Bonds Promo . . . 100.00
98 . . . 100.00
99 . . . 100.00
100 Anniversary issue . . . 100.00
101 thru 110 . . . @100.00
111 thru 130 . . . @60.00
131 thru 150 . . . @50.00
151 thru 162 . . . @50.00
163 Valentine's Day cover . . . 45.00
164 . . . 40.00
165 . . . 40.00
166 . . . 40.00
167 . . . 40.00
168 . . . 40.00
169 AW . . . 75.00
170 AW . . . 75.00
171 thru 190 . . . @40.00
191 thru 203 . . . @35.00
204 War cover . . . 32.00
205 thru 208 . . . @30.00
209 FF(c),Buck Rogers . . . 800.00
210 FF(c),Buck Rogers . . . 800.00
211 FF(c),Buck Rogers . . . 800.00
212 FF(c),Buck Rogers . . . 800.00
213 FF(c),Buck Rogers . . . 800.00
214 FF(c),Buck Rogers . . . 800.00
215 FF(c),Buck Rogers . . . 800.00
216 FF(c),Buck Rogers . . . 800.00
217 . . . 40.00
218 July, 1955 . . . 40.00

FAMOUS GANG, BOOK OF COMICS
(see DONALD AND MICKEY MERRY CHRISTMAS)

FAMOUS GANGSTERS
Avon Periodicals April, 1951

1 Al Capone, Dillinger,
Luciano & Shultz . . . 250.00
2 WW(c),Dillinger Machine-
Gun Killer . . . 250.00
3 Lucky Luciano & Murder Inc.. . 250.00

Becomes:

CRIME ON THE WATERFRONT

4 Underworld Gangsters who
Control the Shipment of Drugs!,
May, 1952 . . . 225.00

GOLDEN AGE

FAMOUS STARS
Ziff-Davis Publ. Co.
Aug., 1950

1 OW,Shelley Winter,Susan Peters & Shirley Temple 225.00
2 BEv,Betty Hutton, Bing Crosby 175.00
3 OW,Judy Garland, Alan Ladd . 200.00
4 RC,Jolson, Bob Mitchum 150.00
5 BK,Elizabeth Taylor, Esther Williams. 200.00
6 Gene Kelly, Spring, 1952 . . . . 150.00

FAMOUS STORIES
Dell Publishing Co., 1942

1 Treasure Island 250.00
2 Tom Sawyer 225.00

FAMOUS WESTERN BADMEN
(see REDSKIN)

FANTASTIC
(see CAPTAIN SCIENCE)

Fantastic Comics #10
© Fox Features Syndicate

FANTASTIC COMICS
Fox Features Syndicate
Dec., 1939

1 LF(c),I&O:Samson,B:Star Dust, Super Wizard, Space Smith & Capt. Kid 4,500.00
2 BP,LF(c),Samson destroyed the Battery and Routed the Foe 2,000.00
3 BP,LF(c),Slays the Iron Monster. 5,500.00
4 GT,LF(c),Demolishes the Closing Torture Walls. 1,500.00
5 GT,LF(c),Crumbles the Mighty War Machine 1,400.00
6 JSm(c),Bondage(c) 1,100.00
7 JSm(c) 1,100.00
8 GT,Destroys the Mask of Fire,Bondage(c) 750.00
9 Mighty Muscles saved the Drowning Girl 750.00
10 I&O:David 750.00
11 Wrecks the Torture Machine to save his fellow American . 650.00
12 Heaved the Huge Ship high into the Air 650.00
13 . . . . 650.00
14 . . . . 650.00
15 . . . . 650.00
16 E:Stardust 650.00
17 . . . . 650.00
18 I:Black Fury & Chuck 650.00
19 . . . . 625.00
20 . . . . 625.00
21 B&I: The Banshee,Hitler(c). . . 650.00
22 . . . . 625.00
23 O:The Gladiator, Nov., 1941 . . 650.00

FARGO KID
(see JUSTICE TRAPS OF THE GUILTY)

FAST FICTION
Seaboard Publ./ Famous Author Illustrated
Oct., 1949

1 Scarlet Pimpernel 275.00
2 HcK,Captain Blood 250.00
3 She 350.00
4 The 39 Steps 200.00
5 HcK,Beau Geste 200.00

Becomes:

STORIES BY FAMOUS AUTHORS ILLUSTRATED

1a Scarlet Pimpernel 250.00
2a Captain Blood. 250.00
3a She 300.00
4a The 39 Steps 200.00
5a Beau Geste 175.00
6 HcK,MacBeth 200.00
7 HcK,Window. 165.00
8 HcK,Hamlet 175.00
9 Nicholas Nickleby 150.00
10 HcK,Romeo & Juliet. 150.00
11 GS,Ben Hur 165.00
12 GS,La Svengali 165.00
13 HcK,Scaramouche. 165.00

FAWCETT FUNNY ANIMALS
Fawcett Publications
Dec., 1942

1 I:Hoppy the Marvel, Captain Marvel cover 450.00
2 X-Mas Issue 225.00
3 Spirit of '43 . . . . 150.00
4 and 5 . . . . @150.00
6 Buy War Bonds and Stamps . 100.00
7 . . . . 100.00
8 Flag cover 100.00
9 and 10 . . . . @100.00
11 thru 20 . . . . @75.00
21 thru 30 . . . . @50.00
31 thru 40 . . . . @35.00
41 thru 83 . . . . @30.00

Charlton Comics

84 . . . . 30.00
85 thru 91 Feb. 1956. . . . . @25.00

FAWCETT MOVIE COMICS
Fawcett Publications, 1949

N# Dakota Lil 250.00
N#a Copper Canyon 200.00
N# Destination the Moon 650.00
N# Montana 175.00
N# Pioneer Marshal 175.00
N# Powder River Rustlers 200.00
N# Singing Guns 160.00
7 Gunmen of Abilene 175.00
8 King of the Bull Whip 275.00
9 BP,The Old Frontier 160.00
10 The Missourians 160.00
11 The Thundering Trail 225.00
12 Rustlers on Horseback. 165.00
13 Warpath. 125.00
14 Last Outpost,RonaldReagan . 300.00
15 The Man from Planet-X. . . . 1,800.00
16 10 Tall Men 125.00
17 Rose Cimarron 65.00
18 The Brigand. 75.00
19 Carbine Williams 100.00
20 Ivanhoe, Dec., 1952 . . . . 150.00

FEATURE BOOKS
David McKay Publications
May, 1937

N# Dick Tracy 7,000.00
N# Popeye 7,000.00
1 Zane Grey's King of the Royal Mounted 650.00
2 Popeye 750.00
3 Popeye and the "Jeep" 700.00
4 Dick Tracy 1,200.00
5 Popeye and his Poppa 650.00
6 Dick Tracy 900.00
7 Little Orphan Annie 900.00
8 Secret Agent X-9 . . . . 550.00
9 Tracy & the Famon Boys 900.00
10 Popeye & Susan 650.00
11 Annie Rooney 275.00

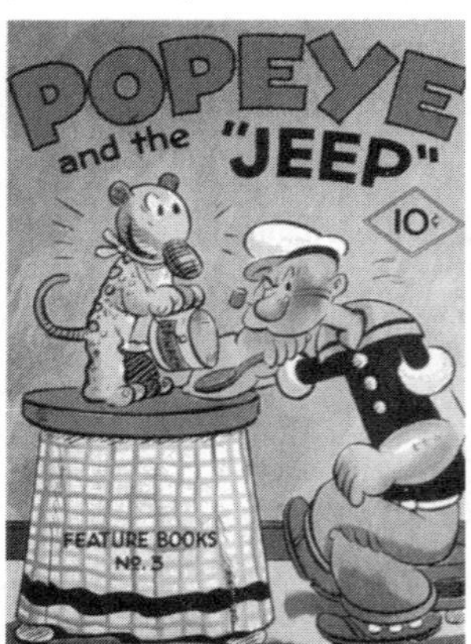

Feature Books #3
© David McKay Publications

12 Blondie 650.00
13 Inspector Wade 225.00
14 Popeye in Wild Oats 750.00
15 Barney Baxter in the Air. 300.00
16 Red Eagle 300.00
17 Gang Busters. 600.00
18 Mandrake the Magician 500.00
19 Mandrake 500.00
20 The Phantom 750.00
21 Lone Ranger 750.00
22 The Phantom. 600.00
23 Mandrake in Teibe Castle. . . . 500.00
24 Lone Ranger 750.00
25 Flash Gordon on the Planet Mongo. 900.00
26 Prince Valiant. 800.00
27 Blondie 150.00
28 Blondie and Dagwood 150.00
29 Blondie at the Home Sweet Home. 150.00
30 Katzenjammer Kids 150.00

31 Blondie Keeps the Home Fires Burning 150.00
32 Katzenjammer Kids 125.00
33 Romance of Flying. 100.00
34 Blondie Home is Our Castle. . 150.00
35 Katzenjammer Kids 125.00
36 Blondie on the Home Front . . 125.00
37 Katzenjammer Kids 125.00
38 Blondie the Model Homemaker 80.00
39 The Phantom. 400.00
40 Blondie 125.00
41 Katzenjammer Kids 125.00
42 Blondie in Home-Spun Yarns . 125.00
43 Blondie Home-Cooked Scraps 125.00
44 Katzenjammer Kids in Monkey Business 125.00
45 Blondie in Home of the Free and the Brave. 125.00
46 Mandrake in Fire World 350.00
47 Blondie in Eaten out of House and Home 125.00
48 The Maltese Falcon 600.00
49 Perry Mason - The Case of the Lucky Legs 200.00
50 The Shoplifters Shoe, P. Mason 200.00
51 Rip Kirby - Mystery of the Mangler 250.00
52 Mandrake in the Land of X. . . 275.00
53 Phantom in Safari Suspense . 350.00
54 Rip Kirby - Case of the Master Menace. 250.00
55 Mandrake in 5-numbers Treasue Hunt 275.00
56 Phantom Destroys the Sky Band 325.00
57 Phantom in the Blue Gang, 1948. . . . . 325.00

FEATURE FUNNIES
Harry A. Chesler Publ./ Comic Favorites
Oct.., 1937–May 1950

1 RuG,RuG(c),A:Joe Palooka, Mickey Finn, Bungles, Dixie Dugan, Big Top, Strange as It Seems, Off the Record . . 2,400.00
2 A: The Hawk 1,000.00
3 WE,Joe Palooka,The Clock. . . 800.00
4 RuG,WE,RuG(c),Joe Palooka . 600.00
5 WE, Joe Palooka drawing . . . 600.00
6 WE, Joe Palooka cover 600.00
7 WE,LLe, Gallant Knight story by Vernon Henkel 475.00
8 WE 450.00
9 WE, Joe Palooka story 450.00
10 WE,Micky Finn(c). 425.00
11 WE,LLe,The Bungles(c) 425.00
12 WE, Joe Palooka(c). 450.00
13 WE,LLe, World Series(c) 500.00
14 WE,Ned Brant(c) 350.00
15 WE,Joe Palooka(c) 375.00
16 Mickey Finn(c). 350.00
17 WE 350.00
18 Joe Palooka cover 375.00
19 WE,LLe,Mickey Finn(c) 350.00
20 WE,LLe 350.00
Becomes:

FEATURE COMICS
Quality Comics Group

21 Joe Palooka(c). 475.00
22 LLe(c),Mickey Finn(c). 350.00
23 B:Charlie Chan 375.00
24 AAr,Joe Palooka(c) 325.00
25 AAr,The Clock(c) 325.00
26 AAr,The Bundles(c) 325.00
27 WE,AAr,I:Doll Man 3,400.00
28 LF,AAr,The Clock(c) 1,400.00
29 LF,AAr,The Clock(c). 750.00
30 LF,AAr,Doll Man(c) 750.00
31 LF,AAr,Mickey Finn(c) 600.00
32 PGv,LF,GFx,Doll Man(c). 450.00
33 PGv,LF,GFx,Bundles(c) 425.00
34 PGv,LF,GFx,Doll Man(c). 450.00
35 PGv,LF,GFx,Bundles(c) 425.00
36 PGv,LF,GFx,Doll Man(c). 450.00
37 PGv,LF,GFx,Bundles(c) 425.00
38 PGv,GFx,Doll Man(c) 325.00
39 PGv,GFx,Bundles(c) 350.00
40 PGv,GFx,WE(c),Doll Man(c) . 325.00
41 PGv,GFx,WE(c),Bundles(c) . . 350.00
42 GFx,Doll Man(c). 250.00
43 RC,GFx,Bundles(c) 225.00
44 RC,GFx,Doll Man(c). 325.00
45 RC,GFx,Bundles(c) 225.00
46 RC,PGv,GFx,Doll Man(c) 250.00
47 RC,GFx,Bundles(c) 225.00
48 RC,GFx,Doll Man(c). 250.00
49 RC,GFx,Bundles(c) 225.00
50 RC,GFx,Doll Man(c) 250.00
51 RC,GFx,Bundles(c) 225.00
52 RC,GFx,Doll Man(c). 225.00
53 RC,GFx,Bundles(c) 200.00
54 RC,GFx,Doll Man(c). 225.00
55 RC,GFx,Bundles(c) 200.00
56 RC,GFx,Doll Man(c). 250.00
57 RC,GFx,Bundles(c) 200.00
58 RC,GFx,Doll Man cover 225.00
59 RC,GFx,Mickey Finn(c) 200.00
60 RC,GFx,Doll Man(c) 225.00
61 RC,GFx,Bundles(c) 185.00
62 RC,GFx,Doll Man(c). 190.00
63 RC,GFx,Bundles(c) 175.00
64 BP,GFx,Doll Man(c) 185.00
65 BP,GFx(c),Bundles(c). 175.00
66 BP,GFx,Doll Man(c) 175.00
67 BP 165.00
68 BP,Doll Man vs.BeardedLady . 175.00
69 BP,GFx(c),Devil cover 165.00
70 BP,Doll Man(c) 175.00
71 BP,GFx(c) 135.00
72 BP,Doll Man(c). 135.00
73 BP,GFx(c),Bundles(c). 125.00
74 Doll Man(c) 135.00
75 GFx(c). 125.00
76 GFx(c). 125.00
77 Doll Man cover until #140. . . . 125.00
78 Knows no Fear but the Knife Does 125.00
79 Little Luck God. 125.00
80 . . . . 125.00
81 Wanted for Murder. 100.00
82 V:Shawunkas the Shaman . . . 100.00
83 V:Mechanical Man 100.00
84 V:Masked Rider, Death Goes to the Rodeo 100.00
85 V:King of Beasts 100.00
86 Is He A Killer? 100.00
87 The Maze of Murder 100.00
88 V:The Phantom Killer 100.00
89 Crook's Goose. 100.00
90 V:Whispering Corpse 100.00
91 V:The Undertaker. 100.00
92 V:The Image 100.00
93 . . . . 100.00
94 V:The Undertaker. 100.00
95 Flatten's the Peacock's Pride . 100.00
96 Doll Man Proves Justice is Blind 100.00
97 V:Peacock 100.00
98 V:Master Diablo 100.00
99 On the Warpath Again!. 100.00
100 Crushes the City of Crime . . 135.00
101 Land of the Midget Men! 90.00
102 The Angle 90.00
103 V:The Queen of Ants 90.00
104 V:The Botanist 90.00
105 Dream of Death 90.00
106 V:The Sword Fish 90.00
107 Hand of Horror! 90.00
108 V:Cateye 90.00
109 V:The Brain 90.00
110 V:Fat Cat 90.00
111 V:The Undertaker 90.00
112 I:Mr. Curio & His Miniatures . . 90.00
113 V:Highwayman. 90.00
114 V:Tom Thumb. 90.00
115 V:The Sphinx 90.00
116 V:Elbows 90.00
117 Polka Dot on the Spot 90.00
118 thru 144 . . . . @90.00

FEDERAL MEN COMICS
Gerard Publ. Co., 1942

2 S&S,Spanking 275.00

FELIX THE CAT
Dell Publishing Co.
Feb.–March 1948

1 . . . . 300.00
2 . . . . 200.00
3 . . . . 125.00
4 . . . . 125.00
5 . . . . 125.00
6 . . . . 100.00
7 . . . . 100.00

Feature Comics #34
© Quality Comics Group

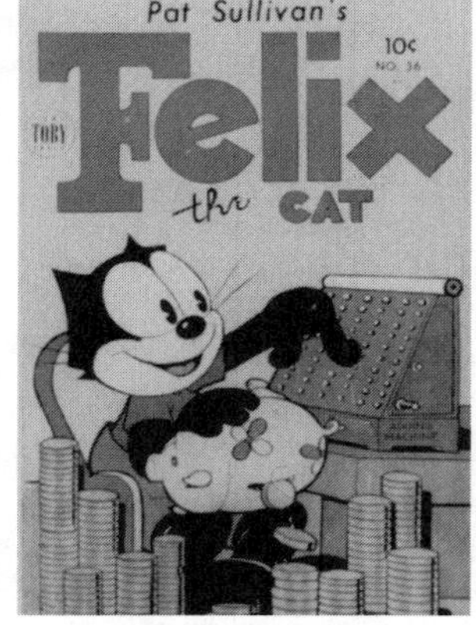

Felix the Cat #36
© Dell Publishing Co./Toby Press

GOLDEN AGE

8 . . . . . 100.00
9 . . . . . 100.00
10 . . . . . 100.00
11 thru 19 . . . . . @90.00

Toby Press

20 thru 30 . . . . . @250.00
31 . . . . . 100.00
32 . . . . . 250.00
33 . . . . . 250.00
34 . . . . . 100.00
35 . . . . . 100.00
36 thru 59 . . . . . @250.00
60 . . . . . 225.00
61 . . . . . 225.00

Harvey

62 thru 80 . . . . . @45.00
81 thru 99 . . . . . @35.00
100 . . . . . 40.00
101 thru 118 . . . . . @25.00
Spec., 100 pgs, 1952 . . . . . 300.00
Summer Ann., 100 pgs. 1953 . . . 400.00
Winter Ann.,#2 100 pgs, 1954. . . 400.00

FERDINAND THE BULL

Dell Publishing Co., 1938

1 . . . . . 140.00

FIGHT AGAINST CRIME

Story Comics May, 1951

1 Scorpion of Crime Inspector "Brains" Carroway 250.00
2 Ganglands Double Cross 150.00
3 Killer Dolan's Double Cross . . 100.00
4 Hopped Up Killers - The Con's Slaughter,Drug issue . 100.00
5 Horror of the Avenging Corpse 100.00
6 Terror of the Crazy Killer 100.00
7 . . . . . 100.00
8 Killer with the Two-bladed Knife 90.00
9 Rats Die by Gas,Horror. 225.00
10 Horror of the Con's Revenge . 225.00
11 Case of the Crazy Killer 225.00
12 Horror,Drug issue. 250.00
13 The Bloodless Killer 225.00
14 Electric Chair cover 250.00
15 . . . . . 225.00
16 RA,Bondage(c) 250.00
17 Knife in Neck(c) 250.00
18 Attempted hanging cover 250.00
19 Bondage(c) 250.00
20 Severed Head cover 400.00
21 . . . . . 200.00

Becomes:

FIGHT AGAINST THE GUILTY

22 RA,Electric Chair 225.00
23 March, 1955 . . . . . 150.00

FIGHT COMICS

Fight Comics Inc. (Fiction House Magazines) Jan., 1940

1 LF,GT,WE(c),O:Spy Fighter . 2,400.00
2 GT,WE(c),Joe Lewis 900.00
3 WE(c),GT,B:Rip Regan, The Powerman 650.00
4 GT,LF(c). 550.00
5 WE(c) 550.00
6 GT,BP(c) 400.00
7 GT,BP(c),Powerman-Blood Money 400.00
8 GT,Chip Collins-Lair of the Vulture 400.00
9 GT,Chip Collins-Prey of the War Eagle 400.00
10 GT,Wolves of the Yukon. 400.00
11 . . . . . 350.00
12 RA,Powerman-Monster of Madness 350.00
13 Shark Broodie-Legion of Satan 350.00
14 Shark Broodie-Lagoon of Death 350.00
15 Super-American-Hordes of the Secret Dicator. 500.00
16 B:Capt.Fight,SwastikaPlague . 500.00
17 Super-American-Blaster of the Pig-Boat Pirates 400.00
18 Shark Broodie-Plague of the Yellow Devils 400.00
19 E:Capt. Fight 400.00
20 . . . . . 300.00
21 Rip Carson-Hell's Sky-Riders . 250.00
22 Rip Carson-Sky Devil's Mission. 250.00
23 Rip Carson-Angels of Vengeance 250.00
24 Baynonets for the Banzai Breed! Bondage(c) 235.00
25 Rip Carson-Samurai Showdown 225.00
26 Rip Carson-Fury of the Sky-Brigade 225.00
27 War-Loot for the Mikado Bondage(c). 225.00
28 Rip Carson 225.00
29 Rip Carson-Charge of the Lost Region 225.00
30 Rip Carson-Jeep-Raiders of the Torture Jungle 225.00
31 Gangway for the Gyrenes, Decapitation cover 235.00
32 Vengeance of the Hun-Hunters,Bondage(c) 235.00
33 B:Tiger Girl 175.00
34 Bondage(c) 175.00
35 MB 175.00
36 MB 175.00
37 MB 175.00
38 MB,Bondage(c) 200.00
39 MB,Senorita Rio-Slave Brand of the Spider Cult 175.00
40 MB,Bondage cover 200.00
41 MB,Bondage cover 200.00
42 MB 175.00
43 MB,Senorita Rio-The Fire-Brides of the Lost Atlantis, Bondage(c). 200.00
44 MB,R:Capt. Fight 175.00
45 MB,Tonight Don Diablo Rides. 175.00

Fight Comics #13
© Fiction House Magazines

46 MB 175.00
47 MB,SenoritaRio-Horror's Hacienda 175.00
48 MB 175.00
49 MB,JKa,B:Tiger Girl(c) 175.00
50 MB 175.00
51 MB,O:Tiger Girl 300.00
52 MB,Winged Demons of Doom 150.00
53 MB,Shadowland Shrine 150.00
54 MB,Flee the Cobra Fury. 150.00
55 MB,Jungle Juggernaut 150.00
56 MB 150.00
57 MB,Jewels of Jeopardy 150.00
58 MB 150.00
59 MB,Vampires of Crystal Cavern 150.00
60 MB,Kraal of DeadlyDiamonds 150.00
61 MB,Seekers of the Sphinx, O:Tiger Girl. 175.00
62 MB,Graveyard if the Tree Tribe. 150.00
63 MB 150.00
64 MB,DawnBeast from Karama-Zan! 150.00
65 Beware the Congo Girl. 150.00
66 Man or Ape!. 125.00
67 Head-Hunters of Taboo Trek . 125.00
68 Fangs of Dr. Voodoo 125.00
69 Cage of the Congo Fury. 125.00
70 Kraal of Traitor Tusks 125.00
71 Captives for the Golden Crocodile 125.00
72 Land of the Lost Safaris. 125.00
73 War-Gods of the Jungle 125.00
74 Advengers of the Jungle 125.00
75 Perils of Momba-Kzar 125.00
76 Kraal of Zombi-Zaro. 125.00
77 Slave-Queen of the Ape Man. 125.00
78 Great Congo Diamond Robbery 135.00
79 A:Space Rangers. 135.00
80 . . . . . 125.00
81 E:Tiger Girl(c) 125.00
82 RipCarson-CommandoStrike . 125.00
83 NobodyLoves a Minesweeper 125.00
84 Rip Carson-Suicide Patrol . . . 125.00
85 . . . . . 125.00
86 GE,Tigerman,Summer,1954. . 135.00

FIGHTING AMERICAN

Headline Publications (Prize), April–May, 1954

1 S&K,O:Fighting American & Speedboy 1,400.00
2 S&K,S&K(c) 650.00
3 S&K,S&K(c) 500.00
4 S&K,S&K(c) 500.00
5 S&K,S&K(c) 500.00
6 S&K,S&K(c),O:Fighting American 475.00
7 S&K,S&K(c), April–May, 1955 425.00

FIGHTING DAVY CROCKETT

(see KIT CARSON)

FIGHTING INDIANS OF THE WILD WEST

Avon Periodicals March, 1952

1 EK,EL,Geronimo, Crazy Horse, Chief Victorio 100.00
2 EK,Same, Nov., 1952 . . . . . 75.00

FIGHTING LEATHERNECKS
Toby Press, Feb., 1952

1 JkS,Duke's Diary 100.00
2 . . . . 75.00
3 . . . . 60.00
4 . . . . 60.00
5 . . . . 50.00
6 Dec., 1952 . . . . 50.00

FIGHTIN' TEXAN (see TEXAN, THE)

FIGHTING YANK
Nedor Publ./Better Publ. (Standard Comics) Sept., 1942

1 B:Fighting Yank, A:Wonder Man, Mystico, Bondage cover. . . 1,800.00
2 JaB 800.00
3 . . . . 600.00
4 AS(c) 550.00
5 AS(c) 475.00
6 AS(c) 475.00
7 AS(c),A:Fighting Yank 425.00
8 AS(c) 425.00
9 AS(c) 425.00
10 AS(c). 425.00
11 AS(c), A:Grim Reaper, Nazis bomb Washington cover 375.00
12 AS(c), Hirohito bondage cover 375.00
13 AS(c). 350.00
14 AS(c). 350.00
15 AS(c). 350.00
16 AS(c). 350.00
17 AS(c). 350.00
18 AS(c), A:American Eagle 350.00
19 AS(c). 350.00
20 AS(c) 350.00
21 AS(c) A:Kara,Jungle Princess 365.00
22 AS(c) A:Miss Masque-cover story 400.00
23 AS(c) Klu Klux Klan parody cover 350.00
24 A:Miss Masque 335.00
25 JRo,MMe,A:Cavalier 400.00
26 JRo,MMe,A:Cavalier 350.00
27 JRo,MMe,A:Cavalier 350.00
28 JRo,MMe,AW,A:Cavalier 375.00
29 JRo,MMe,Aug., 1949 . . . . 375.00

FILM STAR ROMANCES
Star Publications, 1950

1 LbC(c), Rudy Valentino story . 350.00
2 Liz Taylor & Robert Taylor, photo cover 275.00
3 May–June, 1950, photo(c) . . . 175.00

FIREHAIR COMICS
Flying Stories, Inc. (Fiction House Magazine) Winter, 1948

1 I:Firehair, Riders on the Pony Express 450.00
2 Bride of the Outlaw Guns 200.00
3 Kiss of the Six-Gun Siren! . . . 175.00
4 & 5 . . . . @175.00
6 . . . . 150.00
7 War Drums at Buffalo Bend . . 150.00
8 Raid on the Red Arrows 150.00
9 French Flags and Tomahawks 150.00
10 Slave Maiden of the Crees. . . 150.00
11 Wolves of the Overland Trail,Spring, 1952 . . . . 150.00

Flame #1
© Fox Feature Syndicate

FLAME, THE
Fox Feature Syndicate Summer, 1940

1 LF,O:The Flame 2,800.00
2 GT,LF 1,200.00
3 BP 800.00
4 . . . . 750.00
5 GT 750.00
6 GT 750.00
7 A:The Yank 750.00
8 The Finger of the Frozen Death!, Jan., 1942 . . . . 750.00

FLAMING LOVE
Comic Magazines (Quality Comics Group) Dec., 1949

1 BWa,BWa(c),The Temptress I Feared in His Arms 275.00
2 Torrid Tales of Turbulent Passion 125.00
3 BWa,RC,My Heart's at Sea . . 200.00
4 One Women who made a Mockery of Love, Ph(c). 100.00
5 Bridge of Longing, Ph(c) 100.00
6 Men both Loved & Feared Me, Oct., 1950 . . . . 100.00

FLASH GORDON
Harvey Publications Oct., 1950

1 AR,Bondage(c) 250.00
2 AR 175.00
3 AR Bondage(c). 165.00
4 AR, April, 1951 . . . . 150.00

FLIP
Harvey Publications April, 1954

1 HN 175.00
2 HN,BP,June, 1954 . . . . 175.00

FLY BOY
Approved Comics (Ziff-Davis) Spring, 1952

1 NS(c),Angels without Wings . . 150.00
2 NS(c),Flyboy's Flame-Out, Oct.–Nov., 1952 . . . . 100.00

THE FLYING A'S RANGE RIDER
Dell Publishing Co. June–Aug., 1953

(1) = *Dell Four Color #404*
2 Ph(c) all 125.00
3 . . . . 75.00
4 . . . . 60.00
5 . . . . 60.00
6 . . . . 60.00
7 . . . . 60.00
8 . . . . 60.00
9 . . . . 60.00
10 . . . . 60.00
11 . . . . 50.00
12 . . . . 50.00
13 . . . . 50.00
14 . . . . 50.00
15 . . . . 50.00
16 . . . . 50.00
17 ATh 75.00
19 . . . . 50.00
20 . . . . 50.00
21 . . . . 50.00
22 . . . . 50.00
23 . . . . 50.00
24. . . . . 50.00

FOODINI
Continental Publications March, 1950

1 . . . . 150.00
2 . . . . 75.00
3 . . . . 50.00
4 Aug., 1950 . . . . 50.00

FOOTBALL THRILLS
Approved Comics (Ziff-Davis) Fall-Winter, 1952

1 BP,NS(c),Red Grange story . . 200.00
2 NS(c),Bronko Nagurski, Spring,1952 . . . . 150.00

FORBIDDEN LOVE
Comic Magazine (Quality Comics Group) March, 1950

1 RC,Ph(c),Heartbreak Road . . 600.00
2 Ph(c),I loved a Gigolo 350.00
3 Kissless Bride 275.00
4 BWa,Brimstone Kisses, Sept., 1950 . . . . 300.00

FORBIDDEN WORLDS
American Comics Group July–Aug., 1951

1 AW,FF 1,200.00
2 . . . . 550.00
3 AW,WW,JD. 550.00
4 Werewolf cover 275.00
5 AW 450.00
6 AW,King Kong cover 350.00
7 . . . . 250.00
8 . . . . 250.00
9 Atomic Bomb 275.00
10 JyD 200.00
11 The Mummy's Treasure 150.00
12 Chest of Death. 150.00
13 Invasion from Hades 150.00
14 Million-Year Monster 150.00
15 The Vampire Cat 150.00
16 The Doll. 150.00
17 . . . . 150.00

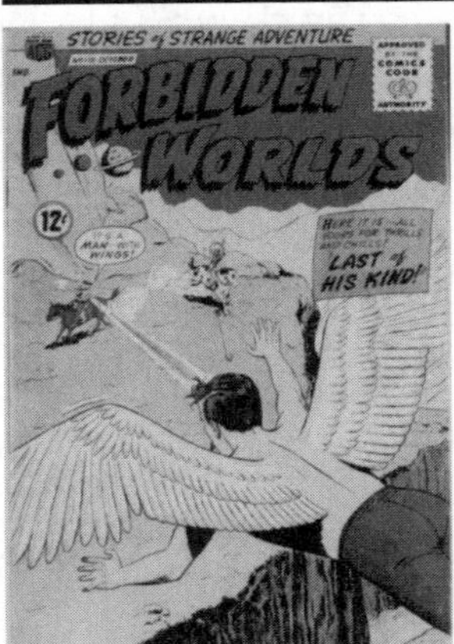

Forbidden Worlds #115
© American Comics Group

18 The Mummy 150.00
19 Pirate and the Voodoo Queen 150.00
20 Terror Island 150.00
21 The Ant Master 100.00
22 The Cursed Casket 100.00
23 Nightmare for Two 100.00
24 . . . . . 100.00
25 Hallahan's Head 100.00
26 The Champ 100.00
27 SMo,The Thing with the Golden Hair 100.00
28 Portrait of Carlotta 100.00
29 The Frogman 100.00
30 The Things on the Beach . . . 100.00
31 SMo,The Circle of the Doomed 90.00
32 The Invasion of the Dead Things 90.00
33 . . . . . 90.00
34 Atomic Bomb 125.00
35 Comics Code 100.00
36 thru 62 . . . . . @65.00
63 AW 75.00
64 . . . . . 50.00
65 . . . . . 50.00
66 . . . . . 50.00
67 . . . . . 50.00
68 OW(c) 50.00
69 AW 75.00
70 . . . . . 50.00
71 . . . . . 50.00
72 . . . . . 50.00
73 OW,I:Herbie 250.00
74 . . . . . 50.00
75 JB 50.00
76 AW 75.00
77 . . . . . 50.00
78 AW,OW(c) 75.00
79 thru 85 JB . . . . . @50.00
86 Flying Saucer 60.00
87 . . . . . 50.00
88 . . . . . 50.00
89 . . . . . 50.00
90 . . . . . 50.00
91 . . . . . 50.00
92 . . . . . 50.00
93 . . . . . 50.00
94 OW(c),A:Herbie 75.00
95 . . . . . 35.00
96 AW 50.00
97 thru 115 . . . . . @35.00
116 OW(c)A:Herbie 40.00
117 . . . . . 35.00
118 . . . . . 35.00
119 . . . . . 35.00
120 thru 124 . . . . . @35.00
125 I:O:Magic Man 40.00
126 A:Magic Man 30.00
127 same 30.00
128 same 30.00
129 same 30.00
130 same 30.00
131 same 30.00
132 same 30.00
133 I:O:Dragona 30.00
134 A:Magic Man 30.00
135 A:Magic Man 30.00
136 A:Nemesis 30.00
137 A:Magic Man 30.00
138 A:Magic Man 30.00
139 A:Magic Man 30.00
140 SD,A:Mark Midnight 30.00
141 thru 145 . . . . . @25.00

FOREIGN INTRIGUES
(see DYNAMITE)

FOUR COLOR
Dell Publishing Co., 1939

N# Dick Tracy 7,000.00
N# Don Winslow of the Navy . 1,500.00
N# Myra North 850.00
4 Disney'sDonaldDuck(1940) 12,000.00
5 Smilin' Jack 650.00
6 Dick Tracy 1,700.00
7 Gang Busters 400.00
8 Dick Tracy 850.00
9 Terry and the Pirates 650.00
10 Smilin' Jack 600.00
11 Smitty 400.00
12 Little Orphan Annie 550.00
13 Walt Disney's Reluctant Dragon (1941) 1,800.00
14 Moon Mullins 400.00
15 Tillie the Toiler 400.00
16 W.Disney's Mickey Mouse Outwits the Phantom Blob (1941) . 11,000.00
17 W.Disney's Dumbo the Flying Elephant (1941) 2,000.00
18 Jiggs and Maggie 450.00
19 Barney Google and Snuffy Smith 450.00
20 Tiny Tim 350.00
21 Dick Tracy 675.00
22 Don Winslow 350.00
23 Gang Busters 300.00
24 Captain Easy 500.00
25 Popeye 800.00

[Second Series]

1 Little Joe 500.00
2 Harold Teen 300.00
3 Alley Oop 550.00
4 Smilin' Jack 475.00
5 Raggedy Ann and Andy 550.00
6 Smitty 250.00
7 Smokey Stover 350.00
8 Tillie the Toiler 250.00
9 Donald Duck finds Pirate Gold! 8,500.00
10 Flash Gordon 90 0.00
11 Wash Tubs 350.00
12 Bambi 600.00
13 Mr. District Attorney 350.00
14 Smilin' Jack 400.00
15 Felix the Cat 750.00
16 Porky Pig 850.00
17 Popeye 600.00
18 Little Orphan Annie's Junior Commandos 450.00
19 W.Disney's Thumper meets the Seven Dwarfs 600.00
20 Barney Baxter 275.00
21 Oswald the Rabbit 550.00
22 Tillie the Toiler 225.00
23 Raggedy Ann and Andy 400.00
24 Gang Busters 300.00
25 Andy Panda 500.00
26 Popeye 600.00
27 Mickey Mouse and the Seven Colored Terror 1,000.00
28 Wash Tubbs 250.00
29 CB,Donald Duck and the Mummy's Ring 7,000.00
30 Bambi's Children 600.00
31 Moon Mullins 200.00
32 Smitty 175.00
33 Bugs Bunny 1,200.00
34 Dick Tracy 475.00
35 Smokey Stover 175.00
36 Smilin' Jack 250.00
37 Bringing Up Father 200.00
38 Roy Rogers 2,200.00
39 Oswald the Rabbit 400.00
40 Barney Google and Snuffy Smith 250.00
41 WK,Mother Goose 250.00
42 Tiny Tim 175.00
43 Popeye 350.00
44 Terry and the Pirates 450.00
45 Raggedy Ann 350.00
46 Felix the Cat and the Haunted House 450.00
47 Gene Autry 450.00
48 CB,Porky Pig o/t Mounties . 1,100.00
49 W.Disney's Snow White and the Seven Dwarfs 700.00
50 WK,Fairy Tale Parade 325.00
51 Bugs Bunny Finds the Lost Treasure 400.00
52 Little Orphan Annie 350.00
53 Wash Tubbs 150.00
54 Andy Panda 300.00
55 Tillie the Toiler 125.00
56 Dick Tracy 350.00
57 Gene Autry 375.00
58 Smilin' Jack 250.00
59 WK,Mother Goose 200.00
60 Tiny Folks Funnies 150.00
61 Santa Claus Funnies 250.00
62 CB,Donald Duck in Frozen Gold 2,300.00
63 Roy Rogers-photo cover 600.00
64 Smokey Stover 150.00
65 Smitty 125.00
66 Gene Autry 450.00
67 Oswald the Rabbit 200.00
68 WK,Mother Goose 225.00
69 WK,Fairy Tale Parade 275.00

Four Color #9
© Dell Publishing Co.

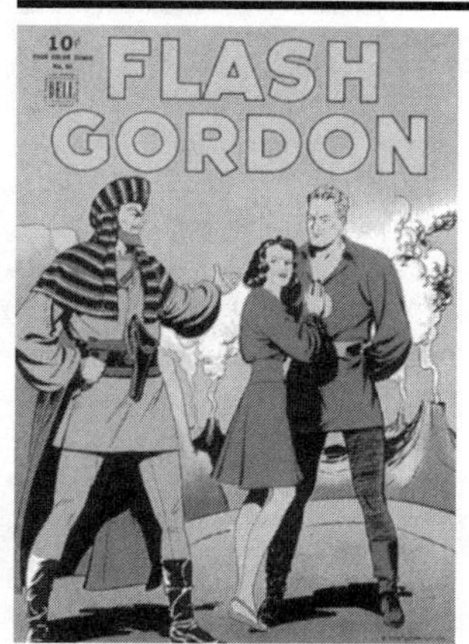

Four Color #84
© Dell Publishing Co.

70 Popeye and Wimpy 300.00
71 WK,Walt Disney's
Three Caballeros 900.00
72 Raggedy Ann. 300.00
73 The Grumps 125.00
74 Marge's Little Lulu. 1,100.00
75 Gene Autry and the Wildcat . . 300.00
76 Little Orphan Annie 275.00
77 Felix the Cat 450.00
78 Porky Pig & the Bandit Twins . 275.00
79 Mickey Mouse in the Riddle
of the Red Hat. 1,200.00
80 Smilin' Jack 175.00
81 Moon Mullins 125.00
82 Lone Ranger 450.00
83 Gene Autry in Outlaw Trail . . . 325.00
84 Flash Gordon. 450.00
85 Andy Panda and the
Mad Dog Mystery 175.00
86 Roy Rogers-photo cover 400.00
87 WK,Fairy Tale Parade 300.00
88 Bugs Bunny. 250.00
89 Tillie the Toiler 150.00
90 WK,Christmas with
Mother Goose 200.00
91 WK,Santa Claus Funnies 200.00
92 WK,W.Disney's Pinocchio . . . 700.00
93 Gene Autry 300.00
94 Winnie Winkle 125.00
95 Roy Rogers,Ph(c) 400.00
96 Dick Tracy 275.00
97 Marge's Little Lulu 500.00
98 Lone Ranger 325.00
99 Smitty 100.00
100 Gene Autry Comics-photo
cover 300.00
101 Terry and the Pirates 300.00
102 WK,Oswald the Rabbit. 175.00
103 WK,Easter with
Mother Goose 200.00
104 WK,Fairy Tale Parade 225.00
105 WK,Albert the Aligator 750.00
106 Tillie the Toiler 100.00
107 Little Orphan Annie 250.00
108 Donald Duck in the
Terror of the River 1,600.00
109 Roy Rogers Comics. 300.00
110 Marge's Little Lulu 350.00
111 Captain Easy 150.00
112 Porky Pig's Adventure in
Gopher Gulch. 150.00
113 Popeye 150.00
114 WK,Fairy Tale Parade 200.00
115 Marge's Little Lulu 350.00
116 Mickey Mouse and the
House of Many Mysteries . . . 275.00
117 Roy Rogers Comics,
Ph(c) 250.00
118 Lone Ranger 325.00
119 Felix the Cat 300.00
120 Marge's Little Lulu 300.00
121 Fairy Tale Parade. 125.00
122 Henry. 150.00
123 Bugs Bunny's Dangerous
Venture 165.00
124 Roy Rogers Comics,Ph(c) . . 250.00
125 Lone Ranger 250.00
126 WK,Christmas with
Mother Goose 175.00
127 Popeye 150.00
128 WK,Santa Claus Funnies . . . 150.00
129 W.Disney's Uncle Remus
& his tales of Brer Rabbit . . . 325.00
130 Andy Panda 125.00
131 Marge's Little Lulu 325.00
132 Tillie the Toiler 100.00
133 Dick Tracy 250.00
134 Tarzan and the Devil Ogre . . 700.00
135 Felix the Cat 250.00
136 Lone Ranger 225.00
137 Roy Rogers Comics. 250.00
138 Smitty 100.00
139 Marge's Little Lulu 275.00
140 WK,Easter with
Mother Goose 175.00
141 Mickey Mouse and the
Submarine Pirates 250.00
142 Bugs Bunny and the
Haunted Mountain 175.00
143 Oswald the Rabbit & the
Prehistoric Egg. 100.00
144 Poy Rogers Comics,Ph(c) . . 250.00
145 Popeye 150.00
146 Marge's Little Lulu 300.00
147 W.Disney's Donald Duck
in Volcano Valley 1,100.00
148 WK,Albert the Aligator
and Pogo Possum 650.00
149 Smilin' Jack 125.00
150 Tillie the Toiler 100.00
151 Lone Ranger 200.00
152 Little Orphan Annie 150.00
153 Roy Rogers Comics. 200.00
154 Andy Panda. 125.00
155 Henry. 100.00
156 Porky Pig and the Phantom . 125.00
157 W.Disney's Mickey Mouse
and the Beanstalk. 250.00
158 Marge's Little Lulu 300.00
159 CB,W.Disney's Donald Duck
in the Ghost of the Grotto . . . 900.00
160 Roy Rogers Comics,Ph(c) . . 175.00
161 Tarzan & the Fires of Tohr . . 600.00
162 Felix the Cat 200.00
163 Dick Tracy 175.00
164 Bugs Bunny Finds the
Frozen Kingdom. 175.00
165 Marge's Little Lulu 300.00
166 Roy Rogers Comics,Ph(c) . . 200.00
167 Lone Ranger 175.00
168 Popeye 150.00
169 Woody Woodpecker,Drug. . . 165.00
170 W.Disney's Mickey Mouse
on Spook's Island. 200.00
171 Charlie McCarthy. 275.00
172 WK,Christmas with
Mother Goose 150.00
173 Flash Gordon. 150.00
174 Winnie Winkle 100.00
175 WK,Santa Claus Funnies . . . 150.00
176 Tillie the Toiler 75.00
177 Roy Rogers Comics,Ph(c) . . 175.00
178 CB,W.Disney's Donald
Duck Christmas on Bear
Mountain 1,400.00

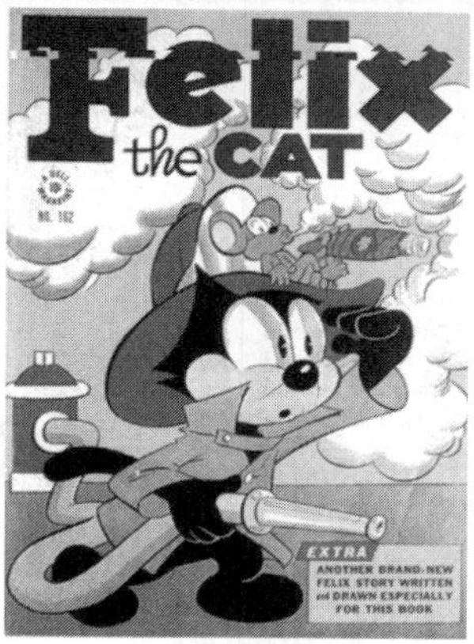

Four Color #162
© Dell Publishing Co.

179 WK,Uncle Wiggily 175.00
180 Ozark the Ike 100.00
181 W.Disney's Mickey Mouse
in Jungle Magic 200.00
182 Porky Pig in Never-
Never Land 125.00
183 Oswald the Rabbit 100.00
184 Tillie the Toiler 100.00
185 WK,Easter with
Mother Goose 175.00
186 W.Disney's Bambi 200.00
187 Bugs Bunny and the
Dreadful Bunny 125.00
188 Woody Woodpecker. 125.00
189 W.Disney's Donald Duck in
The Old Castle's Secret 800.00
190 Flash Gordon 175.00
191 Porky Pig to the Rescue. . . . 125.00
192 WK,The Brownies 135.00
193 Tom and Jerry 150.00
194 W.Disney's Mickey Mouse
in the World Under the Sea. . 200.00
195 Tillie the Toiler 75.00
196 Charlie McCarthy in The
Haunted Hide-Out. 175.00
197 Spirit of the Border. 125.00
198 Andy Panda. 125.00
199 W.Disney's Donald Duck in
Sheriff of Bullet Valley. 900.00
200 Bugs Bunny, Super Sleuth . 125.00
201 WK,Christmas with
Mother Goose 125.00
202 Woody Woodpecker. 75.00
203 CB,W.Disney's Donald Duck in
The Golden Christmas Tree . 650.00
204 Flash Gordon. 125.00
205 WK,Santa Claus Funnies . . . 150.00
206 Little Orphan Funnies. 125.00
207 King of the Royal Mounted. . 175.00
208 W.Disney's Brer Rabbit
Does It Again 125.00
209 Harold Teen. 50.00
210 Tippe and Cap Stubbs 45.00
211 Little Beaver. 60.00
212 Dr. Bobbs 40.00
213 Tillie the Toiler 50.00
214 W.Disney's Mickey Mouse
and his Sky Adventure 175.00
215 Sparkle Plenty 100.00
216 Andy Panda and the
Police Pup 75.00
217 Bugs Bunny in Court Jester . 125.00
218 W.Disney's 3 Little Pigs 150.00
219 Swee'pea. 120.00
220 WK,Easter with

GOLDEN AGE

Mother Goose 150.00
221 WK,Uncle Wiggly 125.00
222 West of the Pecos 75.00
223 CB,W.Disney's Donald Duck in Lost in the Andes 850.00
224 Little Iodine 75.00
225 Oswald the Rabbit 60.00
226 Porky Pig and Spoofy 75.00
227 W.Disney's Seven Dwarfs . . 125.00
228 The Mark of Zorro 250.00
229 Smokey Stover 50.00
230 Sunset Press 60.00
231 W.Disney's Mickey Mouse and the Rajah's Treasure . . . 150.00
232 Woody Woodpecker 75.00
233 Bugs Bunny 125.00
234 W.Disney's Dumbo in Sky Voyage 125.00
235 Tiny Tim 45.00
236 Heritage of the Desert 75.00
237 Tillie the Toiler 50.00
238 CB,W.Disney's Donald Duck in Voodoo Hoodoo 600.00
239 Adventure Bound 50.00
240 Andy Panda 60.00
241 Porky Pig 75.00
242 Tippie and Cap Stubbs 35.00
243 W.Disney's Thumper Follows His Nose 125.00
244 WK,The Brownies 125.00
245 Dick's Adventures in Dreamland 40.00
246 Thunder Mountain 45.00
247 Flash Gordon 125.00
248 W.Disney's Mickey Mouse and the Black Sorcerer 150.00
249 Woody Woodpecker 65.00
250 Bugs Bunny in Diamond Daze 135.00
251 Hubert at Camp Moonbeam . . 50.00
252 W.Disney's Pinocchio 125.00
253 WK,Christmas with Mother Goose 140.00
254 WK,Santa Claus Funnies, A:Pogo 140.00
255 The Ranger 45.00
256 CB,W.Disney's Donald Duck in Luck of the North 450.00
257 Little Iodine 50.00
258 Andy Panda and the Ballon Race 75.00
259 Santa and the Angel 50.00
260 Porky Pig, Hero of the Wild West 75.00
261 W.Disney's Mickey Mouse and the Missing Key 150.00
262 Raggedy Ann and Andy 60.00
263 CB,W.Disney's Donald Duck in Land of the Totem Poles 450.00
264 Woody Woodpecker in the Magic Lantern 60.00
265 King of the Royal Mountain . . 85.00
266 Bugs Bunny on the Isle of Hercules 125.00
267 Little Beaver 40.00
268 W.Disney's Mickey Mouse's Surprise Visitor 150.00
269 Johnny Mack Brown,Ph(c) . . 250.00
270 Drift Fence 40.00
271 Porky Pig 75.00
272 W.Disney's Cinderella 125.00
273 Oswald the Rabbit 60.00
274 Bugs Bunny 125.00
275 CB,W.Disney's Donald Duck in Ancient Persia 425.00
276 Uncle Wiggly 75.00
277 Porky Pig in Desert Adventure 75.00
278 Bill Elliot Comics,Ph(c) 150.00
279 W.Disney's Mickey Mouse & Pluto Battle the Giant Ants . . 125.00
280 Andy Panda in the Isle of the Mechanical Men 60.00
281 Bugs Bunny in The Great Circus Mystery 125.00
282 CB,W.Disney's Donald Duck in The Pixilated Parrot 450.00
283 King of the Royal Mounted . . 100.00
284 Porky Pig in the Kingdom of Nowhere 75.00
285 Bozo the Clown 200.00
286 W.Disney's Mickey Mouse and the Uninvited Guest 125.00
287 Gene Autry's Champion in the Ghost of BlackMountain,Ph(c)100.00
288 Woody Woodpecker 75.00
289 BugsBunny in IndianTrouble. 120.00
290 The Chief 50.00
291 CB,W.Disney's Donald Duck in The Magic Hourglass 450.00
292 The Cisco Kid Comics 225.00
293 WK,The Brownies 125.00
294 Little Beaver 45.00
295 Porky Pig in President Pig . . . 75.00
296 W.Disney's Mickey Mouse Private Eye for Hire 125.00
297 Andy Panda in The Haunted Inn 50.00
298 Bugs Bunny in Sheik for a Day 125.00
299 Buck Jones & the Iron Trail . 175.00
300 CB,W.Disney's Donald Duck in Big-Top Bedlam 450.00
301 The Mysterious Rider 40.00
302 Santa Claus Funnies 40.00
303 Porky Pig in The Land of the Monstrous Flies 65.00
304 W.Disney's Mickey Mouse in Tom-Tom Island 100.00
305 Woody Woodpecker 35.00
306 Raggedy Ann 40.00
307 Bugs Bunny in Lumber Jack Rabbit 100.00
308 CB,W.Disney's Donald Duck in Dangerous Disguise 375.00
309 Dollface and Her Gang 50.00
310 King of the Rotal Mounted . . . 55.00
311 Porky Pig in Midget Horses of Hidden Valley 55.00
312 Tonto 150.00
313 W.Disney's Mickey Mouse in the Mystery of the Double-Cross Ranch 125.00
314 Ambush 40.00
315 Oswald Rabbit 50.00
316 Rex Allen,Ph(c) 150.00

Four Color #295
© Dell Publishing Co.

317 Bugs Bunny in Hare Today Gone Tomorrow 85.00
318 CB,W.Disney's Donald Duck in No Such Varmint 375.00
319 Gene Autry's Champion 40.00
320 Uncle Wiggly 60.00
321 Little Scouts 35.00
322 Porky Pig in Roaring Rockies. 50.00
323 Susie Q. Smith 35.00
324 I Met a Handsome Cowboy . . 75.00
325 W.Disney's Mickey Mouse in the Haunted Castle 125.00
326 Andy Panda 35.00
327 Bugs Bunny and the Rajah's Treasure 100.00
328 CB,W.Disney's Donald Duck in Old California 400.00
329 Roy Roger's Trigger,Ph(c) . . 150.00
330 Porky Pig meets the Bristled Bruiser 50.00
331 Disney's Alice in Wonderland 150.00
332 Little Beaver 40.00
333 Wilderness Trek 40.00
334 W.Disney's Mickey Mouse and Yukon Gold 120.00
335 Francis the Famous Talking Mule 75.00
336 Woody Woodpecker 35.00
337 The Brownies 35.00
338 Bugs Bunny and the Rocking Horse Thieves 90.00
339 W.Disney's Donald Duck and the Magic Fountain 100.00
340 King of the Royal Mountain . . 65.00
341 W.Disney's Unbirthday Party with Alice in Wonderland 150.00
342 Porky Pig the Lucky Peppermint Mine 45.00
343 W.Disney's Mickey Mouse in Ruby Eye of Homar-Guy-Am 100.00
344 Sergeant Preston from Challenge of the Yukon 125.00
345 Andy Panda in Scotland Yard. 40.00
346 Hideout 40.00
347 Bugs Bunny the Frigid Hare . . 75.00
348 CB,W.Disney's Donald Duck The Crocodile Collector 250.00
349 Uncle Wiggly 60.00
350 Woody Woodpecker 40.00
351 Porky Pig and the Grand Canyon Giant 50.00
352 W.Disney's Mickey Mouse Mystery of Painted Valley 85.00
353 CB(c),W.Disney'sDuckAlbum 100.00
354 Raggedy Ann & Andy 45.00
355 Bugs Bunny Hot-Rod Hair . . . 75.00
356 CB(c),W.Disney's Donald Duck in Rags to Riches 250.00
357 Comeback 40.00
358 Andy Panada 40.00
359 Frosty the Snowman 70.00
360 Porky Pig in Tree Fortune . . . 45.00
361 Santa Claus Funnies 40.00
362 W.Disney's Mickey Mouse & the Smuggled Diamonds 100.00
363 King of the Royal Mounted . . . 60.00
364 Woody Woodpecker 40.00
365 The Brownies 35.00
366 Bugs Bunny Uncle Buckskin Comes to Town 85.00
367 CB,W.Disney's Donald Duck in A Christmas for Shacktown . . 375.00
368 Bob Clampett's Beany and Cecil 300.00
369 Lone Ranger's Famous Horse Hi-Yo Silver 100.00
370 Porky Pig in Trouble in the Big Trees 65.00
371 W.Disney's Mickey Mouse the Inca Idol Case 85.00

GOLDEN AGE

372 Riders of the Purple Sage . . . 30.00
373 Sergeant Preston. 75.00
374 Woody Woodpecker. 30.00
375 John Carter of Mars 275.00
376 Bugs Bunny. 75.00
377 Susie Q. Smith. 35.00
378 Tom Corbett, Space Cadet. . 200.00
379 W.Disney's Donald Duck in Southern Hospitality 100.00
380 Raggedy Ann & Andy 40.00
381 Marge's Tubby 200.00
382 W.Disney's Show White and the Seven Dwarfs. 150.00
383 Andy Panda. 25.00
384 King of the Royal Mounted. . . 50.00
385 Porky Pig. 45.00
386 CB,W.Disney's Uncle Scrooge in Only A Poor Old Man. . . 1,000.00
387 W.Disney's Mickey Mouse in High Tibet. 85.00
388 Oswald the Rabbit 45.00
389 Andy Hardy Comics 35.00
390 Woody Woodpecker 40.00
391 Uncle Wiggly 60.00
392 Hi-Yo Silver 50.00
393 Bugs Bunny. 75.00
394 CB(c),W.Disney's Donald Duck in Malayalaya 250.00
395 Forlorn River 35.00
396 Tales of the Texas Rangers, Ph(c) 125.00
397 Sergeant Preston o/t Yukon . . 75.00
398 The Brownies. 35.00
399 Porky Pig in the Lost Gold Mine 45.00
400 AMc,Tom Corbett 125.00
401 W.Disney's Mickey Mouse & Goofy's Mechanical Wizard. . . 75.00
402 Mary Jane and Sniffles 75.00
403 W.Disney's Li'l Bad Wolf. . . . 125.00
404 The Ranger Rider,Ph(c) 100.00
405 Woody Woodpecker 30.00
406 Tweety and Sylvester. 75.00
407 Bugs Bunny, Foreign-Legion Hare 65.00
408 CB,W.Disney's Donald Duck and the Golden Helmet. 400.00
409 Andy Panda. 35.00
410 Porky Pig in the Water Wizard 40.00
411 W.Disney's Mickey Mouse and the Old Sea Dog 75.00
412 Nevada 35.00
413 Disney's Robin Hood(movie), Ph(c) 125.00
414 Bob Clampett's Beany and Cecil 175.00
415 Rootie Kazootie 125.00
416 Woody Woodpecker. 40.00
417 Double Trouble with Goober. . 25.00
418 Rusty Riley 40.00
419 Sergeant Preston. 75.00
420 Bugs Bunny 65.00
421 AMc,Tom Corbett. 125.00
422 CB,W.Disney's Donald Duck and the Gilded Man 375.00
423 Rhubarb 35.00
424 Flash Gordon. 150.00
425 Zorro 140.00
426 Porky Pig. 40.00
427 W.Disney's Mickey Mouse & the Wonderful Whizzix 65.00
428 Uncle Wiggily. 40.00
429 W.Disney's Pluto in Why Dogs Leave Home 100.00
430 Marge's Tubby 100.00
431 Woody Woodpecker. 40.00
432 Bugs Bunny and the Rabbit Olympics. 60.00
433 Wildfire 35.00
434 Rin Tin Tin,Ph(c) 165.00
435 Frosty the Snowman 40.00
436 The Brownies. 35.00
437 John Carter of Mars 175.00
438 W.Disney's Annie Oakley (TV) 150.00
439 Little Hiawatha. 50.00
440 Black Beauty 35.00
441 Fearless Fagan 30.00
442 W.Disney's Peter Pan 100.00
443 Ben Bowie and His Mountain Men 50.00
444 Marge's Tubby. 75.00
445 Charlie McCarthy. 40.00
446 Captain Hook and Peter Pan 100.00
447 Andy Hardy Comics 30.00
448 Beany and Cecil. 175.00
449 Tappan's Burro. 35.00
450 CB(c),W.Disney's DuckAlbum 75.00
451 Rusty Riley 30.00
452 Raggedy Ann and Andy 50.00
453 Susie Q. Smith. 30.00
454 Krazy Kat Comics 35.00
455 Johnny Mack Brown Comics, Ph(c) 60.00
456 W.Disney's Uncle Scrooge Back to the Klondike. 650.00
457 Daffy 100.00
458 Oswald the Rabbit 35.00
459 Rootie Kazootie 75.00
460 Buck Jones 100.00
461 Marge's Tubby. 90.00
462 Little Scouts. 15.00
463 Petunia 30.00
464 Bozo 100.00
465 Francis the Talking Mule 50.00
466 Rhubarb, the Millionaire Cat. . 35.00
467 Desert Gold 30.00
468 W.Disney's Goofy. 125.00
469 Beettle Bailey. 110.00
470 Elmer Fudd 35.00
471 Double Trouble with Goober. . 20.00
472 Wild Bill Elliot,Ph(c) 55.00
473 W.Disney's Li'l Bad Wolf. 65.00
474 Mary Jane and Sniffles 75.00
475 M.G.M.'s the Two Mouseketeers. 75.00
476 Rin Tin Tin,Ph(c) 60.00
477 Bob Clampett's Beany and Cecil. 175.00
478 Charlie McCarthy. 40.00
479 Queen o/t West Dale Evans . 200.00
480 Andy Hardy Comics 25.00
481 Annie Oakley and Tagg 100.00
482 Brownies 35.00
483 Little Beaver 35.00
484 River Feud. 35.00
485 The Little People 55.00
486 Rusty Riley 35.00
487 Mowgli, the Jungle Book 35.00
488 John Carter of Mars 175.00
489 Tweety and Sylvester. 35.00
490 Jungle Jim 60.00
491 EK,Silvertip 100.00
492 W.Disney's Duck Album 65.00
493 Johnny Mack Brown,Ph(c) . . . 60.00
494 The Little King 125.00
495 CB, W.Disney's Uncle Scrooge 500.00
496 The Green Hornet 275.00
497 Zorro, (Sword of) 150.00
498 Bugs Bunny's Album 55.00
499 M.G.M.'s Spike and Tyke 35.00
500 Buck Jones 65.00
501 Francis the Famous Talking Mule 40.00
502 Rootie Kazootie 75.00
503 Uncle Wiggily 40.00
504 Krazy Kat 40.00
505 W.Disney's the Sword and the Rose (TV),Ph(c) 100.00
506 The Little Scouts 20.00

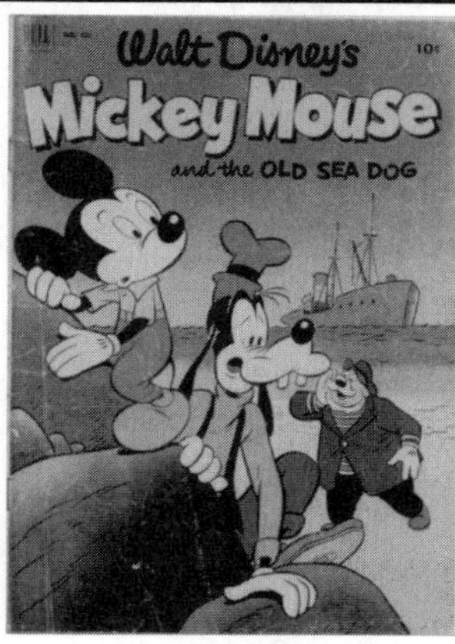

Four Color #411
© Dell Publishing Co.

507 Oswald the Rabbit 35.00
508 Bozo 100.00
509 W.Disney's Pluto 65.00
510 Son of Black Beauty 35.00
511 EK,Outlaw Trail 40.00
512 Flash Gordon. 60.00
513 Ben Bowie and His Mountain Men 30.00
514 Frosty the Snowman 30.00
515 Andy Hardy 25.00
516 Double Trouble With Goober . 20.00
517 Walt Disney's Chip 'N' Dale . 100.00
518 Rivets 25.00
519 Steve Canyon 100.00
520 Wild Bill Elliot,Ph(c) 50.00
521 Beetle Bailey 40.00
522 The Brownies. 25.00
523 Rin Tin Tin,Ph(c) 100.00
524 Tweety and Sylvester. 25.00
525 Santa Claus Funnies 40.00
526 Napoleon. 20.00
527 Charlie McCarthy. 35.00
528 Queen o/t West Dale Evans, Ph(c) 100.00
529 Little Beaver 30.00
530 Bob Clampett's Beany and Cecil 175.00
531 W.Disney's Duck Album 55.00
532 The Rustlers 35.00
533 Raggedy Ann and Andy 40.00
534 EK,Western Marshal 40.00
535 I Love Lucy,Ph(c). 550.00
536 Daffy 50.00
537 Stormy, the Thoroughbred . . . 30.00
538 EK,The Mask of Zorro 165.00
539 Ben and Me. 25.00
540 Knights of the Round Table, Ph(c) 75.00
541 Johnny Mack Brown,Ph(c) . . . 50.00
542 Super Circus Featuring Mary Hartline 50.00
543 Uncle Wiggly 35.00
544 W.Disney's Rob Roy(Movie), Ph(c) 100.00
545 The Wonderful Adventures of Pinocchio 100.00
546 Buck Jones 75.00
547 Francis the Famous Talking Mule. 40.00
548 Krazy Kat. 30.00
549 Oswald the Rabbit 25.00
550 The Little Scouts 15.00
551 Bozo 100.00
552 Beetle Bailey 45.00
553 Susie Q. Smith. 30.00

554 Rusty Riley 30.00
555 Range War 30.00
556 Double Trouble with Goober. . 20.00
557 Ben Bowie and His
Mountain Men 30.00
558 Elmer Fudd 30.00
559 I Love Lucy,Ph(c). 400.00
560 W.Disney's Duck Album 60.00
561 Mr. Magoo 125.00
562 W.Disney's Goofy. 85.00
563 Rhubarb, the Millionaire Cat. . 30.00
564 W.Disney's Li'l Bad Wolf. 60.00
565 Jungle Jim. 30.00
566 Son of Black Beauty 30.00
567 BF,Prince Valiant,Ph(c). 125.00
568 Gypsy Cat 40.00
569 Priscilla's Pop 25.00
570 Bob Clampett's Beany
and Cecil 175.00
571 Charlie McCarthy. 50.00
572 EK,Silvertip 40.00
573 The Little People 30.00
574 The Hand of Zorro 150.00
575 Annie and Oakley and Tagg,
Ph(c) 100.00
576 Angel. 25.00
577 M.G.M.'s Spike and Tyke 25.00
578 Steve Canyon 55.00
579 Francis the Talking Mule 40.00
580 Six Gun Ranch 30.00
581 Chip 'N' Dale 55.00
582 Mowgli, the Jungle Book 30.00
583 The Lost Wagon Train 35.00
584 Johnny Mack Brown,Ph(c) . . . 40.00
585 Bugs Bunny's Album 50.00
586 W.Disney's Duck Album 110.00
587 The Little Scouts 15.00
588 MB,King Richard and the
Crusaders,Ph(c) 125.00
589 Buck Jones 60.00
590 Hansel and Gretel 50.00
591 EK,Western Marshal 50.00
592 Super Circus 45.00
593 Oswald the Rabbit 25.00
594 Bozo 100.00
595 Pluto 50.00
596 Turok, Son of Stone. 625.00
597 The Little King 75.00
598 Captain Davy Jones. 30.00
599 Ben Bowie and His
Mountain Men 25.00
600 Daisy Duck's Diary. 70.00
601 Frosty the Snowman 30.00
602 Mr. Magoo and the Gerald
McBoing-Boing 125.00
603 M.G.M.'s The Two
Mouseketeers. 30.00
604 Shadow on the Trail 35.00
605 The Brownies. 25.00
606 Sir Lancelot 100.00
607 Santa Claus Funnies 30.00
608 EK,Silver Tip 40.00
609 The Littlest Outlaw,Ph(c) 60.00
610 Drum Beat,Ph(c) 120.00
611 W.Disney's Duck Album 60.00
612 Little Beaver 30.00
613 EK,Western Marshal 50.00
614 W.Disney's 20,000 Leagues
Under the Sea (Movie) 100.00
615 Daffy 40.00
616 To The Last Man 30.00
617 The Quest of Zorro 135.00
618 Johnny Mack Brown,Ph(c) . . . 50.00
619 Krazy Kat. 30.00
620 Mowgli, Jungle Book 30.00
621 Francis the Famous
Talking Mule. 35.00
622 Beetle Bailey 40.00
623 Oswald the Rabbit 20.00
624 Treasure Island,Ph(c). 100.00
625 Beaver Valley. 75.00
626 Ben Bowie and His
Mountain Men 30.00
627 Goofy. 100.00
628 Elmer Fudd 25.00
629 Lady & The Tramp with Jock . 75.00
630 Priscilla's Pop 30.00
631 W.Disney's Davy Crockett
Indian Fighter (TV),Ph(c) . . . 175.00
632 Fighting Caravans 35.00
633 The Little People 30.00
634 Lady and the Tramp Album . . 60.00
635 Bob Clampett's Beany
and Cecil 175.00
636 Chip 'N' Dale 55.00
637 EK,Silvertip 45.00
638 M.G.M.'s Spike and Tyke 20.00
639 W.Disney's Davy Crockett
at the Alamo (TV),Ph(c) 150.00
640 EK,Western Marshal 50.00
641 Steve Canyon 75.00
642 M.G.M.'s The Two
Mouseketeers. 30.00
643 Wild Bill Elliott,Ph(c). 35.00
644 Sir Walter Raleigh,Ph(c). 75.00
645 Johnny Mack Brown,Ph(c) . . . 50.00
646 Dotty Dripple and Taffy. 30.00
647 Bugs Bunny's Album 50.00
648 Jace Pearson of the
Texas Rangers,Ph(c) 50.00
649 Duck Album. 60.00
650 BF,Prince Valiant 75.00
651 EK,King Colt 35.00
652 Buck Jones 45.00
653 Smokey the Bear 120.00
654 Pluto 50.00
655 Francis the Famous
Talking Mule. 35.00
656 Turok, Son of Stone. 375.00
657 Ben Bowie and His
Mountain Men 30.00
658 Goofy 75.00
659 Daisy Duck's Diary. 60.00
660 Little Beaver 30.00
661 Frosty the Snowman 30.00
662 Zoo Parade 50.00
663 Winky Dink 75.00
664 W.Disney's Davy Crockett in
the Great Keelboat
Race (TV),Ph(c) 150.00
665 The African Lion 60.00
666 Santa Claus Funnies 35.00
667 EK,Silvertip and the Stolen
Stallion. 40.00
668 W.Disney's Dumbo. 100.00

Four Color #666
© Dell Publishing Co.

668a W.Disney's Dumbo. 90.00
669 W.Disney's Robin Hood
(Movie),Ph(c) 60.00
670 M.G.M.'s Mouse Musketeers . 25.00
671 W.Disney's Davey Crockett &
the River Pirates(TV),Ph(c). . 150.00
672 Quentin Durward,Ph(c) 70.00
673 Buffalo Bill Jr.,Ph(c) 70.00
674 The Little Rascals 75.00
675 EK,Steve Donovan,Ph(c) 90.00
676 Will-Yum! 30.00
677 Little King 75.00
678 The Last Hunt,Ph(c). 60.00
679 Gunsmoke 175.00
680 Out Our Way with the
Worry Wart 25.00
681 Forever, Darling,Lucile
Ball Ph(c) 125.00
682 When Knighthood Was
in Flower,Ph(c) 75.00
683 Hi and Lois 25.00
684 SB,Helen of Troy,Ph(c). 125.00
685 Johnny Mack Brown,Ph(c) . . . 60.00
686 Duck Album 50.00
687 The Indian Fighter,Ph(c). 50.00
688 SB,Alexander the Great,
Ph(c) 75.00
689 Elmer Fudd 25.00
690 The Conqueror,
John Wayne Ph(c) 175.00
691 Dotty Dripple and Taffy. 25.00
692 The Little People 30.00
693 W.Disney's Brer Rabbit
Song of the South. 125.00
694 Super Circus,Ph(c). 50.00
695 Little Beaver 25.00
696 Krazy Kat. 30.00
697 Oswald the Rabbit 20.00
698 Francis the Famous
Talking Mule. 30.00
699 BA,Prince Valiant. 75.00
700 Water Birds and the
Olympic Elk 60.00
701 Jimmy Cricket 100.00
702 The Goofy Success Story. . . 100.00
703 Scamp. 100.00
704 Priscilla's Pop 30.00
705 Brave Eagle,Ph(c) 50.00
706 Bongo and Lumpjaw 40.00
707 Corky and White Shadow,
Ph(c) 60.00
708 Smokey the Bear. 60.00
709 The Searchers,John
Wayne Ph(c) 275.00
710 Francis the Famous
Talking Mule 30.00
711 M.G.M.'s Mouse Musketeers . 25.00
712 The Great Locomotive
Chase, Ph(c) 75.00
713 The Animal World 40.00
714 W.Disney's Spin
& Marty (TV). 125.00
715 Timmy 30.00
716 Man in Space. 100.00
717 Moby Dick,Ph(c) 100.00
718 Dotty Dripple and Taffy. 25.00
719 BF,Prince Valiant 75.00
720 Gunsmoke,Ph(c) 100.00
721 Captain Kangaroo,Ph(c). . . . 150.00
722 Johnny Mack Brown,Ph(c) . . . 40.00
723 EK,Santiago. 100.00
724 Bugs Bunny's Album 45.00
725 Elmer Fudd 20.00
726 Duck Album. 45.00
727 The Nature of Things. 65.00
728 M.G.M.'s Mouse Musketeers . 20.00
729 Bob Son of Battle. 30.00
730 Smokey Stover 30.00
731 EK,Silvertip and The
Fighting Four 40.00
732 Zorro, (the Challenge of) . . . 150.00

733 Buck Rogers 35.00
734 Cheyenne,C.Walker Ph(c) . . 175.00
735 Crusader Rabbit. 350.00
736 Pluto 45.00
737 Steve Canyon 55.00
738 Westward Ho, the Wagons, Ph(c) 90.00
739 MD,Bounty Guns 30.00
740 Chilly Willy 30.00
741 The Fastest Gun Alive,Ph(c) . 75.00
742 Buffalo Bill Jr.,Ph(c) 55.00
743 Daisy Duck's Diary. 45.00
744 Little Beaver 25.00
745 Francis the Famous Talking Mule. 30.00
746 Dotty Dripple and Taffy. 25.00
747 Goofy 90.00
748 Frosty the Snowman 30.00
749 Secrets of Life,Ph(c) 50.00
750 The Great Cat 50.00
751 Our Miss Brooks,Ph(c). 75.00
752 Mandrake, the Magician. . . . 125.00
753 Walt Scott's Little People 30.00
754 Smokey the Bear. 60.00
755 The Littlest Snowman 30.00
756 Santa Claus Funnies 30.00
757 The True Story of Jesse James,Ph(c) 110.00
758 Bear Country 45.00
759 Circus Boy,Ph(c) 125.00
760 W.Disney's Hardy Boys(TV) . 125.00
761 Howdy Doody 125.00
762 SB,The Sharkfighters,Ph(c) . 100.00
763 GrandmaDuck'sFarmFriends . 75.00
764 M.G.M.'s Mouse Musketeers . 20.00
765 Will-Yum! 20.00
766 Buffalo Bill,Ph(c) 35.00
767 Spin and Marty 75.00
768 EK,Steve Donovan, Western Marshal,Ph(c). 45.00
769 Gunsmoke. 75.00
770 Brave Eagle,Ph(c) 30.00
771 MD,Brand of Empire 30.00
772 Cheyenne,C.Walker Ph(c) . . . 65.00
773 The Brave One,Ph(c). 35.00
774 Hi and Lois 25.00
775 SB,Sir Lancelot and Brian,Ph(c). 85.00
776 Johnny Mack Brown,Ph(c) . . . 40.00
777 Scamp. 75.00
778 The Little Rascals 50.00
779 Lee Hunter, Indian Fighter . . . 40.00
780 Captain Kangaroo,Ph(c). . . . 150.00
781 Fury,Ph(c) 75.00
782 Duck Album. 50.00
783 Elmer Fudd 20.00
784 Around the World in 80 Days,Ph(c). 75.00
785 Circus Boys,Ph(c) 125.00
786 Cinderella 50.00
787 Little Hiawatha. 40.00
788 BF,Prince Valiant 75.00
789 EK,Silvertip-Valley Thieves. . . 45.00
790 ATh,The Wings of Eagles, J.Wayne Ph(c) 175.00
791 The 77th Bengal Lancers, Ph(c) 75.00
792 Oswald the Rabbit 20.00
793 Morty Meekle. 25.00
794 SB,The Count of Monte Cristo 100.00
795 Jiminy Cricket 65.00
796 Ludwig Bemelman's Madeleine and Genevieve . . . 35.00
797 Gunsmoke,Ph(c) 85.00
798 Buffalo Bill,Ph(c) 40.00
799 Priscilla's Pop 30.00
800 The Buccaneers,Ph(c) 50.00
801 Dotty Dripple and Taffy 25.00
802 Goofy 75.00
803 Cheyenne,C.Walker Ph(c) . . . 85.00

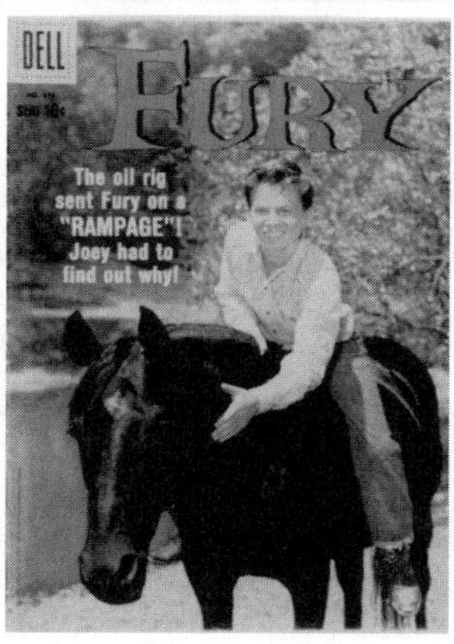

Four Color #975
© Dell Publishing Co.

804 Steve Canyon 50.00
805 Crusader Rabbit. 275.00
806 Scamp. 65.00
807 MB,Savage Range. 30.00
808 Spin and Marty,Ph(c) 110.00
809 The Little People 30.00
810 Francis the Famous Talking Mule 25.00
811 Howdy Doody 120.00
812 The Big Land,A.Ladd Ph(c) . 120.00
813 Circus Boy,Ph(c) 120.00
814 Covered Wagon,A:Mickey Mouse 80.00
815 Dragoon Wells Massacre 75.00
816 Brave Eagle,Ph(c) 30.00
817 Little Beaver 25.00
818 Smokey the Bear. 60.00
819 Mickey Mouse in Magicland . . 45.00
820 The Oklahoman,Ph(c) 120.00
821 Wringle Wrangle,Ph(c). 90.00
822 ATh,W.Disney's Paul Revere's Ride (TV) 125.00
823 Timmy 25.00
824 The Pride and the Passion, Ph(c) 100.00
825 The Little Rascals 50.00
826 Spin and Marty and Annette, Ph(c) 235.00
827 Smokey Stover 30.00
828 Buffalo Bill, Jr,Ph(c).. . . . . 35.00
829 Tales of the Pony Express, Ph(c) 40.00
830 The Hardy Boys,Ph(c) 120.00
831 No Sleep 'Til Dawn,Ph(c) 65.00
832 Lolly and Pepper 30.00
833 Scamp. 75.00
834 Johnny Mack Brown,Ph(c) . . . 50.00
835 Silvertip- The Fake Rider 40.00
836 Man in Fight. 75.00
837 All-American Athlete Cotton Woods 40.00
838 Bugs Bunny's Life Story Album 60.00
839 The Vigilantes 75.00
840 Duck Album 55.00
841 Elmer Fudd 20.00
842 The Nature of Things 70.00
843 The First Americans. 100.00
844 Gunsmoke,Ph(c) 100.00
845 ATh,The Land Unknown. . . . 150.00
846 ATh,Gun Glory. 125.00
847 Perri 65.00
848 Marauder's Moon. 40.00
849 BF,Prince Valiant 75.00
850 Buck Jones 30.00
851 The Story of Mankind, V.Price Ph(c) 60.00
852 Chilly Willy. 30.00
853 Pluto 50.00
854 Hunchback of Notre Dame, Ph(c) 150.00
855 Broken Arrow,Ph(c) 45.00
856 Buffalo Bill, Jr.,Ph(c). 40.00
857 The Goofy Adventure Story . . 75.00
858 Daisy Duck's Diary. 50.00
859 Topper and Neil 30.00
860 Wyatt Earp,Ph(c) 125.00
861 Frosty the Snowman 30.00
862 Truth About Mother Goose. . . 75.00
863 Francis the Famous Talking Mule. 30.00
864 The Littlest Snowman 30.00
865 Andy Burnett,Ph(c). 100.00
866 Mars and Beyond. 100.00
867 Santa Claus Funnies 30.00
868 The Little People 30.00
869 Old Yeller,Ph(c) 75.00
870 Little Beaver 25.00
871 Curly Kayoe. 25.00
872 Captain Kangaroo,Ph(c). . . . 150.00
873 Grandma Duck's Farm Friends 55.00
874 Old Ironsides 70.00
875 Trumpets West 30.00
876 Tales of Wells Fargo,Ph(c) . . 110.00
877 ATh,Frontier Doctor,Ph(c). . . 120.00
878 Peanuts. 165.00
879 Brave Eagle,Ph(c) 30.00
880 MD,Steve Donovan,Ph(c). . . . 40.00
881 The Captain and the Kids. . . . 25.00
882 ATh,W.DisneyPresentsZorro 200.00
883 The Little Rascals 50.00
884 Hawkeye and the Last of the Mohicans,Ph(c). 75.00
885 Fury,Ph(c) 65.00
886 Bongo and Lumpjaw 35.00
887 The Hardy Boys,Ph(c) 100.00
888 Elmer Fudd 20.00
889 ATh,W.Disney's Clint & Mac(TV),Ph(c). 150.00
890 Wyatt Earp,Ph(c) 80.00
891 Light in the Forest, C.Parker Ph(c) 75.00
892 Maverick,J.Garner Ph(c) . . . 300.00
893 Jim Bowie,Ph(c). 50.00
894 Oswald the Rabbit 20.00
895 Wagon Train,Ph(c). 150.00
896 Adventures of Tinker Bell . . . 100.00
897 Jiminy Cricket 65.00
898 EK,Silvertip 45.00
899 Goofy 60.00
900 BF,Prince Valiant 75.00
901 Little Hiawatha 60.00
902 Will-Yum! 25.00
903 Dotty Dripple and Taffy. 25.00
904 Lee Hunter, Indian Fighter . . . 30.00
905 W.Disney's Annette (TV), Ph(c) 300.00
906 Francis the Famous Talking Mule. 30.00
907 Ath,Sugarfoot,Ph(c) 150.00
908 The Little People and the Giant 40.00
909 Smitty 25.00
910 ATh,The Vikings, K.Douglas Ph(c) 100.00
911 The Gray Ghost,Ph(c) 100.00
912 Leave it to Beaver,Ph(c). . . . 200.00
913 The Left-Handed Gun, Paul Newman Ph(c) 125.00
914 ATh,No Time for Sergeants, Ph(c) 125.00
915 Casey Jones,Ph(c). 50.00
916 Red Ryder Ranch Comics . . . 25.00
917 The Life of Riley,Ph(c) 125.00
918 Beep Beep, the Roadrunner. 100.00

919 Boots and Saddles,Ph(c) 75.00
920 Ath,Zorro,Ph(c) 150.00
921 Wyatt Earp.Ph(c) 75.00
922 Johnny Mack Brown,Ph(c) . . . 50.00
923 Timmy 20.00
924 Colt .45,Ph(c). 100.00
925 Last of the Fast Guns,Ph(c) . . 75.00
926 Peter Pan 35.00
927 SB,Top Gun 30.00
928 Sea Hunt,L.Bridges Ph(c). . . 125.00
929 Brave Eagle,Ph(c) 30.00
930 Maverick,J. Garner Ph(c) . . 125.00
931 Have Gun, Will Travel,Ph(c). 165.00
932 Smokey the Bear. 60.00
933 ATh,W.Disney's Zorro. 150.00
934 Restless Gun 125.00
935 King of the Royal Mounted. . . 30.00
936 The Little Rascals 50.00
937 Ruff and Ready 125.00
938 Elmer Fudd 20.00
939 Steve Canyon 60.00
940 Lolly and Pepper 25.00
941 Pluto 40.00
942 Pony Express 40.00
943 White Wilderness. 65.00
944 SB,7th Voyage of Sinbad . . . 150.00
945 Maverick,J.Garner Ph(c) . . . 125.00
946 The Big Country,Ph(c) 75.00
947 Broken Arrow,Ph(c) 50.00
948 Daisy Duck's Diary. 55.00
949 High Adventure,Ph(c). 50.00
950 Frosty the Snowman 30.00
951 ATh,Lennon Sisters
Life Story,Ph(c). 150.00
952 Goofy 60.00
953 Francis the Famous
Talking Mule 30.00
954 Man in Space 75.00
955 Hi and Lois 25.00
956 Ricky Nelson,Ph(c) 225.00
957 Buffalo Bee 90.00
958 Santa Claus Funnies 30.00
959 Christmas Stories 30.00
960 ATh,W.Disney's Zorro. 150.00
961 Jace Pearson's Tales of
Texas Rangers,Ph(c) 60.00
962 Maverick,J.Garner Ph(c) . . . 125.00
963 Johnny Mack Brown,Ph(c) . . . 40.00
964 The Hardy Boys,Ph(c) 110.00
965 GrandmaDuck'sFarmFriends . 55.00
966 Tonka,Ph(c) 90.00
967 Chilly Willy. 25.00
968 Tales of Wells Fargo,Ph(c) . . . 75.00
969 Peanuts 125.00
970 Lawman,Ph(c) 150.00
971 Wagon Train,Ph(c). 75.00
972 Tom Thumb 100.00
973 SleepingBeauty & the Prince 150.00
974 The Little Rascals 75.00
975 Fury,Ph(c) 65.00
976 ATh,W.Disney's Zorro,Ph(c) . 150.00
977 Elmer Fudd 25.00
978 Lolly and Pepper 20.00
979 Oswald the Rabbit 20.00
980 Maverick,J.Garner Ph(c) . . . 125.00
981 Ruff and Ready 100.00
982 The New Adventures of
Tinker Bell 100.00
983 Have Gun, Will Travel,Ph(c). 125.00
984 Sleeping Beauty's Fairy
Godmothers 100.00
985 Shaggy Dog,Ph(c) 75.00
986 Restless Gun,Ph(c) 100.00
987 Goofy 60.00
988 Little Hiawatha 30.00
989 Jimmy Cricket 50.00
990 Huckleberry Hound 125.00
991 Francis the Famous
Talking Mule 30.00
992 ATh,Sugarfoot,Ph(c) 140.00
993 Jim Bowie,Ph(c). 50.00
994 Sea HuntL.Bridges Ph(c) . . . 100.00
995 Donald Duck Album 60.00
996 Nevada 30.00
997 Walt Disney Presents,Ph(c) . . 75.00
998 Ricky Nelson,Ph(c) 225.00
999 Leave It To Beaver,Ph(c) . . . 175.00
1000 The Gray Ghost,Ph(c) 100.00
1001 Lowell Thomas' High
Adventure,Ph(c) 55.00
1002 Buffalo Bee 60.00
1003 ATh,W.Disney's Zorro,Ph(c) 150.00
1004 Colt .45,Ph(c). 80.00
1005 Maverick,J.Garner Ph(c). . . 135.00
1006 SB,Hercules 100.00
1007 John Paul Jones,Ph(c) 45.00
1008 Beep, Beep, the
Road Runner 50.00
1009 CB,The Rifleman,Ph(c) . . . 250.00
1010 Grandma Duck's Farm
Friends. 150.00
1011 Buckskin,Ph(c). 75.00
1012 Last Train from Gun
Hill,Ph(c) 100.00
1013 Bat Masterson,Ph(c) 135.00
1014 ATh,The Lennon Sisters,
Ph(c) 150.00
1015 Peanuts 125.00
1016 Smokey the Bear. 50.00
1017 Chilly Willy. 25.00
1018 Rio Bravo,J.Wayne Ph(c) . . 225.00
1019 Wagoon Train,Ph(c) 75.00
1020 Jungle 25.00
1021 Jace Pearson's Tales of
the Texas Rangers,Ph(c) 50.00
1022 Timmy 25.00
1023 Tales of Wells Fargo,Ph(c) . . 75.00
1024 ATh,Darby O'Gill and
the Little People,Ph(c) 100.00
1025 CB,W.Disney's Vacation in
Disneyland 225.00
1026 Spin and Marty,Ph(c) 100.00
1027 The Texan,Ph(c). 100.00
1028 Rawhide,
Clint Eastwood Ph(c) 250.00
1029 Boots and Saddles,Ph(c) . . . 50.00
1030 Spanky and Alfalfa, the
Little Rascals 50.00
1031 Fury,Ph(c) 60.00
1032 Elmer Fudd 20.00
1033 Steve Canyon,Ph(c). 60.00
1034 Nancy and Sluggo
Summer Camp 25.00
1035 Lawman,Ph(c) 75.00
1036 The Big Circus,Ph(c) 60.00
1037 Zorro,Ph(c) 175.00
1038 Ruff and Ready 100.00

Four Color #1013
© Dell Publishing Co.

1039 Pluto 40.00
1040 Quick Draw McGraw 150.00
1041 ATh,Sea Hunt,
L.Bridges Ph(c). 100.00
1042 The Three Chipmunks 50.00
1043 The Three Stooges,Ph(c) . . 225.00
1044 Have Gun,Will Travel,Ph(c) 100.00
1045 Restless Gun,Ph(c) 100.00
1046 Beep Beep, the
Road Runner 50.00
1047 CB,W.Disney's
GyroGearloose 220.00
1048 The Horse Soldiers
J.Wayne Ph(c) 165.00
1049 Don't Give Up the Ship
J.Lewis Ph(c) 75.00
1050 Huckleberry Hound 100.00
1051 Donald in Mathmagic Land. 100.00
1052 RsM,Ben-Hur 125.00
1053 Goofy. 60.00
1054 Huckleberry Hound
Winter Fun 75.00
1055 CB,Daisy Duck's Diary 125.00
1056 Yellowstone Kelly,
C.Walker Ph(c). 55.00
1057 Mickey Mouse Album 40.00
1058 Colt .45,Ph(c). 75.00
1059 Sugarfoot. 100.00
1060 Journey to the Center of the
Earth, P.Boone Ph(c) 125.00
1061 Buffalo Bill 50.00
1062 Christmas Stories. 35.00
1063 Santa Claus Funnies 35.00
1064 Bugs Bunny's Merry
Christmas. 55.00
1065 Frosty the Snowman 30.00
1066 ATh,77 Sunset Strip,Ph(c) . 150.00
1067 Yogi Bear. 120.00
1068 Francis the Famous
Talking Mule. 30.00
1069 ATh,The FBI Story,Ph(c). . . 125.00
1070 Soloman and Sheba,Ph(c) . 110.00
1071 ATh,TheRealMcCoys,Ph(c) 125.00
1072 Blythe 40.00
1073 CB,Grandma Duck's Farm
Friends. 150.00
1074 Chilly Willy. 25.00
1075 Tales of Wells Fargo,Ph(c) . 100.00
1076 MSy,The Rebel,Ph(c). 125.00
1077 SB,The Deputy,
H.Fonda Ph(c) 150.00
1078 The Three Stooges,Ph(c) . . 125.00
1079 The Little Rascals 50.00
1080 Fury,Ph(c) 60.00
1081 Elmer Fudd 20.00
1082 Spin and Marty 90.00
1083 Men into Space,Ph(c). 100.00
1084 Speedy Gonzales. 45.00
1085 ATh,The Time Machine . . . 175.00
1086 Lolly and Pepper 25.00
1087 Peter Gunn,Ph(c) 110.00
1088 A Dog of Flanders,Ph(c). . . . 45.00
1089 Restless Gun,Ph(c) 100.00
1090 Francis the Famous
Talking Mule 30.00
1091 Jacky's Diary 40.00
1092 Toby Tyler,Ph(c). 50.00
1093 MacKenzie's Raiders,Ph(c) . 75.00
1094 Goofy. 55.00
1095 CB,W.Disney's
GyroGearloose 125.00
1096 The Texan,Ph(c). 100.00
1097 Rawhide,C.Eastwood Ph(c) 175.00
1098 Sugarfoot,Ph(c) 75.00
1099 CB(c),Donald Duck Album . . 75.00
1100 W.Disney's Annette's
Life Story (TV),Ph(c). 250.00
1101 Robert Louis Stevenson's
Kidnapped,Ph(c). 70.00
1102 Wanted: Dead or Alive,
Ph(c) 150.00

Four Color #1120
© Dell Publishing Co.

1103 Leave It To Beaver,Ph(c) . . 175.00
1104 Yogi Bear Goes to College . . 85.00
1105 ATh,Gale Storm,Ph(c) 125.00
1106 ATh,77 Sunset Strip,Ph(c) . 125.00
1107 Buckskin,Ph(c) 60.00
1108 The Troubleshooters,Ph(c) . . 50.00
1109 This Is Your Life, Donald Duck,O:Donald Duck 175.00
1110 Bonanza,Ph(c) 400.00
1111 Shotgun Slade 65.00
1112 Pixie and Dixie and Mr. Jinks 70.00
1113 Tales of Wells Fargo,Ph(c) . 100.00
1114 Huckleberry Finn,Ph(c). 55.00
1115 Ricky Nelson,Ph(c). 165.00
1116 Boots and Saddles,Ph(c) . . . 50.00
1117 Boy and the Pirate,Ph(c). . . . 50.00
1118 Sword and the Dragon,Ph(c)100.00
1119 Smokey and the Bear Nature Stories 50.00
1120 Dinosaurus,Ph(c) 75.00
1121 RC,GE,HerculesUnchained 120.00
1122 Chilly Willy 25.00
1123 Tombstone Territory,Ph(c). . 100.00
1124 Whirlybirds,Ph(c) 100.00
1125 GK,RH,Laramie,Ph(c). 125.00
1126 Sundance,Ph(c) 75.00
1127 The Three Stooges,Ph(c) . . 125.00
1128 Rocky and His Friends 425.00
1129 Pollyanna,H.Mills Ph(c) 85.00
1130 SB,The Deputy, H.Fonda Ph(c) 125.00
1131 Elmer Fudd 20.00
1132 Space Mouse. 30.00
1133 Fury,Ph(c) 50.00
1134 ATh,Real McCoys,Ph(c) . . . 110.00
1135 M.G.M.'s Mouse Musketeers 60.00
1136 Jungle Cat,Ph(c) 45.00
1137 The Little Rascals 50.00
1138 The Rebel,Ph(c). 100.00
1139 SB,Spartacus,Ph(c) 150.00
1140 Donald Duck Album 65.00
1141 Huckleberry Hound for President 75.00
1142 Johnny Ringo,Ph(c) 65.00
1143 Pluto 40.00
1144 The Story of Ruth,Ph(c) . . . 110.00
1145 GK,The Lost World,Ph(c) . . 125.00
1146 Restless Gun,Ph(c) 100.00
1147 Sugarfoot,Ph(c) 100.00
1148 I aim at the Stars,Ph(c) 75.00
1149 Goofy. 55.00
1150 CB,Daisy Duck's Diary . . . 125.00
1151 Mickey Mouse Album 40.00
1152 Rocky and His Friends 275.00
1153 Frosty the Snowman 30.00
1154 Santa Claus Funnies 30.00
1155 North to Alaska 175.00
1156 Walt Disney Swiss Family Robinson. 65.00
1157 Master of the World 60.00
1158 Three Worlds of Gulliver. . . . 60.00
1159 ATh,77 Sunset Strip 125.00
1160 Rawhide 175.00
1161 CB,Grandma Duck's Farm Friends 150.00
1162 Yogi Bera joins the Marines . 85.00
1163 Daniel Boone 55.00
1164 Wanted: Dead or Alive 125.00
1165 Ellery Queen 125.00
1166 Rocky and His Friends 275.00
1167 Tales of Wells Fargo,Ph(c) . 100.00
1168 The Detectives, R.Taylor Ph(c) 125.00
1169 New Adventures of Sherlock Holmes 175.00
1170 The Three Stooges,Ph(c) . 125.00
1171 Elmer Fudd 25.00
1172 Fury,Ph(c) 70.00
1173 The Twilight Zone. 235.00
1174 The Little Rascals 40.00
1175 M.G.M.'s Mouse Musketeers 25.00
1176 Dondi,Ph(c) 45.00
1177 Chilly Willy 25.00
1178 Ten Who Dared 75.00
1179 The Swamp Fox, L.Nielson Ph(c). 100.00
1180 The Danny Thomas Show . 165.00
1181 Texas John Slaughter,Ph(c) . 75.00
1182 Donald Duck Album 45.00
1183 101 Dalmatians 125.00
1184 CB,W.Disney's Gyro Gearloose 125.00
1185 Sweetie Pie 30.00
1186 JDa,Yak Yak. 100.00
1187 The Three Stooges,Ph(c) . . 125.00
1188 Atlantis the Lost Continent,Ph(c) 110.00
1189 Greyfriars Bobby,Ph(c) 75.00
1190 CB(c),Donald and the Wheel 75.00
1191 Leave It to Beaver,Ph(c). . . 175.00
1192 Rocky Nelson,Ph(c) 175.00
1193 The Real McCoys,Ph(c) . . . 100.00
1194 Pepe,Ph(c). 45.00
1195 National Velvet,Ph(c) 65.00
1196 Pixie and Dixie and Mr. Jinks 60.00
1197 The Aquanauts,Ph(c) 75.00
1198 Donald in Mathmagic Land. . 75.00
1199 Absent-Minded Professor, Ph(c) 75.00
1200 Hennessey,Ph(c) 60.00
1201 Goofy 55.00
1202 Rawhide,C.Eastwood Ph(c) 175.00
1203 Pinocchio. 60.00
1204 Scamp 40.00
1205 David & Goliath,Ph(c). 50.00
1206 Lolly and Pepper 25.00
1207 MSy,The Rebel,Ph(c) 100.00
1208 Rocky and His Friends 275.00
1209 Sugarfoot,Ph(c) 100.00
1210 The Parent Trap, H.Mills Ph(c) 100.00
1211 RsM,77 Sunset Strip,Ph(c) . 100.00
1212 Chilly Willy 25.00
1213 Mysterious Island,Ph(c) . . . 100.00
1214 Smokey the Bear 50.00
1215 Tales of Wells Fargo,Ph(c) . . 90.00
1216 Whirlybirds,Ph(c) 100.00
1218 Fury,Ph(c) 65.00
1219 The Detectives, Robert Taylor Ph(c) 85.00
1220 Gunslinger,Ph(c) 100.00
1221 Bonanza,Ph(c). 200.00
1222 Elmer Fudd 25.00
1223 GK,Laramie,Ph(c) 75.00
1224 The Little Rascals 40.00
1225 The Deputy,H.Fonda Ph(c). 100.00
1226 Nikki, Wild Dog of the North . 50.00
1227 Morgan the Pirate,Ph(c) 90.00
1229 Thief of Bagdad,Ph(c) 70.00
1230 Voyage to the Bottom of the Sea,Ph(c) 125.00
1231 Danger Man,Ph(c) 125.00
1232 On the Double 40.00
1233 Tammy Tell Me True. 60.00
1234 The Phantom Planet 75.00
1235 Mister Magoo 125.00
1236 King of Kings,Ph(c) 100.00
1237 ATh,The Untouchables, Ph(c) 250.00
1238 Deputy Dawg 125.00
1239 CB(c),Donald Duck Album . . 65.00
1240 The Detectives, R.Taylor Ph(c) 85.00
1241 Sweetie Pies 30.00
1242 King Leonardo and His Short Subjects 150.00
1243 Ellery Queen 100.00
1244 Space Mouse. 30.00
1245 New Adventures of Sherlock Holmes 175.00
1246 Mickey Mouse Album. 40.00
1247 Daisy Duck's Diary. 45.00
1248 Pluto 40.00
1249 The Danny Thomas Show, Ph(c) 175.00
1250 Four Horseman of the Apocalypse,Ph(c) 75.00
1251 Everything's Ducky. 60.00
1252 The Andy Griffith Show, Ph(c) 375.00
1253 Spaceman 100.00
1254 "Diver Dan" 60.00
1255 The Wonders of Aladdin. . . . 65.00
1256 Kona, Monarch of Monster Isle 65.00
1257 Car 54, Where Are You?, Ph(c) 100.00
1258 GE,The Frogmen 75.00
1259 El Cid,Ph(c) 75.00
1260 The Horsemasters,Ph(c) . . 125.00
1261 Rawhide,C.Eastwood Ph(c) 175.00
1262 The Rebel,Ph(c). 100.00
1263 RsM,77 Sinset Strip,Ph(c) . 100.00
1264 Pixie & Dixie & Mr.Jinks 50.00
1265 The Real McCoys,Ph(c) . . . 100.00
1266 M.G.M.'s Spike and Tyke . . . 20.00
1267 CB,GyroGearloose. 90.00
1268 Oswald the Rabbit 20.00
1269 Rawhide,C.Eastwood Ph(c) 175.00
1270 Bullwinkle and Rocky 225.00
1271 Yogi Bear Birthday Party . . . 60.00
1272 Frosty the Snowman 30.00
1273 Hans Brinker,Ph(c). 65.00
1274 Santa Claus Funnies 30.00
1275 Rocky and His Friends 260.00
1276 Dondi. 30.00
1278 King Leonardo and His Short Subjects 150.00
1279 Grandma Duck's Farm Friends. 55.00
1280 Hennessey,Ph(c) 65.00
1281 Chilly Willy. 25.00
1282 Babes in Toyland,Ph(c) . . . 135.00
1283 Bonanza,Ph(c). 200.00
1284 RH,Laramie,Ph(c) 75.00
1285 Leave It to Beaver,Ph(c). . . 175.00
1286 The Untouchables,Ph(c). . . 175.00
1287 Man from Wells Fargo,Ph(c). 50.00
1288 RC,GE,The Twilight Zone. . 150.00
1289 Ellery Queen 100.00
1290 M.G.M.'s Mouse Musketeers 25.00
1291 RsM,77 Sunset Strip,Ph(c). 100.00
1293 Elmer Fudd 25.00
1294 Ripcord 75.00

1295 Mr. Ed, the Talking Horse, Ph(c) 150.00
1296 Fury,Ph(c) 75.00
1297 Spanky, Alfalfa and the Little Rascals 40.00
1298 The Hathaways,Ph(c). 35.00
1299 Deputy Dawg 125.00
1300 The Comancheros 175.00
1301 Adventures in Paradise 40.00
1302 JohnnyJason,TeenReporter . 30.00
1303 Lad: A Dog,Ph(c) 35.00
1304 Nellie the Nurse 75.00
1305 Mister Magoo 125.00
1306 Target: The Corruptors, Ph(c) 55.00
1307 Margie 45.00
1308 Tales of the Wizard of Oz . . 100.00
1309 BK,87th Precinct,Ph(c) 125.00
1310 Huck and Yogi Winter Sports 100.00
1311 Rocky and His Friends 275.00
1312 National Velvet,Ph(c) 35.00
1313 Moon Pilot.Ph(c) 75.00
1328 GE,The Underwater City,Ph(c) 75.00
1330 GK,Brain Boy 150.00
1332 Bachelor Father 100.00
1333 Short Ribs 45.00
1335 Aggie Mack 30.00
1336 On Stage 40.00
1337 Dr. Kildare,Ph(c). 100.00
1341 The Andy Griffith Show, Ph(c) 375.00
1348 JDa,Yak Yak 125.00
1349 Yogi Berra Visits the U.N. . . 125.00
1350 Commanche,Ph(c) 60.00
1354 Calvin and the Colonel 75.00

FOUR FAVORITES
Ace Magazines
Sept., 1941

1 B:Vulcan, Lash Lighting, Magno the Magnetic Man, Raven, Flag cover,Hitler. 1,200.00
2 A: Black Ace 450.00
3 E:Vulcan 375.00
4 E:Raven,B:Unknown Soldiers 350.00
5 B:Captain Courageous 325.00
6 A: The Flag, B: Mr. Risk 325.00
7 JM 300.00
8 . . . . 300.00
9 RP,HK 350.00
10 HK. 400.00
11 HK,LbC,UnKnown Soldier . . . 400.00
12 LbC 250.00
13 LbC 200.00
14 Fer 200.00
15 Fer 200.00
16 Bondage(c) 225.00
17 Magno Lighting 200.00
18 Magno Lighting 200.00
19 RP,RP(c) 200.00
20 RP,RP(c) 200.00
21 RP,RP(c) 150.00
22 RP(c). 150.00
23 RP(c). 150.00
24 RP(c). 150.00
25 RP(c). 150.00
26 RP(c). 150.00
27 RP(c). 110.00
28 thru 32 . . . . @100.00

FRANKENSTEIN COMICS
Crestwood Publications
(Prize Publ.)
Summer, 1945

1 B:Frankenstein,DBr,DBr(c) . . . 900.00
2 DBr,DBr(c) 450.00

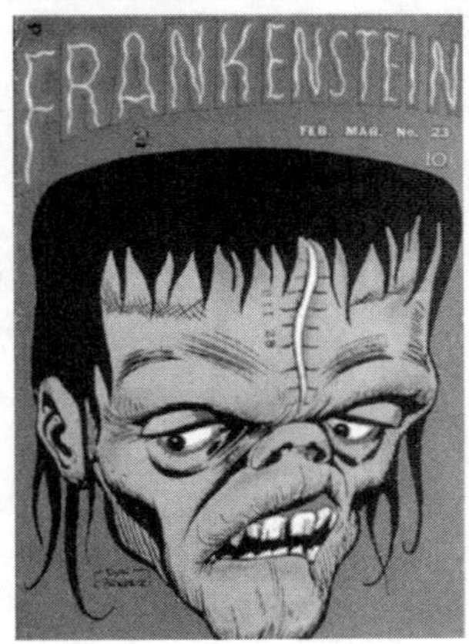

Frankenstein #24
© Crestwood Publications

3 DBr,DBr(c) 300.00
4 DBr,DBr(c) 300.00
5 DBr,DBr(c) 300.00
6 DBr,DBr(c),S&K 250.00
7 DBr,DBr(c),S&K 250.00
8 DBr,DBr(c),S&K 250.00
9 DBr,DBr(c),S&K 250.00
10 DBr,DBr(c),S&K 250.00
11 DBr,DBr(c)A:Boris Karloff 225.00
12 DBr,DBr(c). 225.00
13 DBr,DBr(c). 225.00
14 DBr,DBr(c). 225.00
15 DBr,DBr(c). 225.00
16 DBr,DBr(c). 225.00
17 DBr,DBr(c). 225.00
18 B:Horror 300.00
19 . . . . 200.00
3-4 . . . . 175.00
3-5 . . . . 175.00
3-6 . . . . 175.00
4-1 thru 4-6. . . . . @175.00
5-1 thru 5-4. . . . . @175.00
5-5 Oct.–Nov., 1954 . . . . 175.00

FRISKY FABLES
Novelty Press/Premium Group
Spring, 1945

1 AFa 125.00
2 AFa 60.00
3 AFa 40.00
4 AFa 30.00
5 AFa 30.00
6 AFa 30.00
7 AFa,Flag (c) 35.00
2-1 AFa,Rainbow(c) 40.00
2-2 AFa 35.00
2-3 AFa 35.00
2-4 AFa 35.00
2-5 AFa 35.00
2-6 AFa 35.00
2-7 AFa 35.00
2-8 AFa,Halloween (c) 35.00
2-9 AFa,Thanksgiving(c). 30.00
2-10 AFa,Christman cover 35.00
2-11 AFa 35.00
2-12 AFa,Valentines Day cover. . . 30.00
3-1 AFa 30.00
3-2 AFa 30.00
3-3 AFa 33.00
3-4 AFa 30.00
3-5 AFa 30.00
3-6 AFa 30.00
3-7 AFa 30.00
3-8 AFa,Turkey (c) 30.00
3-9 AFa 30.00
3-10 AFa 30.00
3-11 AFa,1948(c) 30.00
3-12 AFa 30.00
4-1 thru 4-7 AFa . . . . @30.00
5-1 AFa 30.00
5-2 AFa 30.00
5-3 . . . . 30.00
5-4 Star Publications. 30.00
39 LbC(c) 100.00
40 LbC(c) 100.00
41 LbC(c) 100.00
42 LbC(c) 100.00
43 LbC(c) 30.00

Becomes:

FRISKY ANIMALS
Star Publications

44 LbC 150.00
45 LbC 200.00
46 LbC,Baseball 100.00
47 LbC 100.00
48 LbC 100.00
49 LbC 100.00
50 LbC 100.00
51 LbC(c) 100.00
52 LbC(c) 125.00
53 LbC(c) 100.00
54 LbC(c),Supercat(c). 100.00
55 LbC(c),same 100.00
56 LbC(c),same 100.00
57 LbC(c),same 100.00
58 LbC(c),same,July, 1954 . . . . . 100.00

FRITZI RITZ
United Features Syndicate/
St. John Publications
Fall, 1948

N# Special issue 100.00
2 . . . . 50.00
3 . . . . 40.00
4 thru 7 . . . . @30.00
6 A:Abbie & Slats 35.00
8 thru 10 . . . . @25.00
11 1958 . . . . 25.00

FROGMAN COMICS
Hillman Periodicals
Jan.–Feb., 1952–May, 1953

1 . . . . 100.00
2 . . . . 50.00
3 . . . . 50.00
4 MMe. 30.00
5 BK,AT. 40.00
6 . . . . 25.00
7 . . . . 25.00
8 thru 11 . . . . @25.00

FRONTIER ROMANCES
Avon Periodicals
Nov.–Dec., 1949

1 She Learned to Ride and Shoot, and Kissing Came Natural . . 400.00
2 Bronc-Busters Sweetheart, Jan.–Feb., 1950 . . . . 250.00

FRONTLINE COMBAT
Tiny Tot Publications
(E.C. Comics),
July–Aug., 1951

1 HK(c),WW, JSe,JDa,Hanhung Changjn cover 550.00
2 HK(c),WW,Tank Battle cover . 300.00
3 HK(c),WW,Naval Battleship fire cover 275.00

4 HK(c),WW, Bazooka cover . . . 225.00
5 HK(c),JSe. 200.00
6 HK(c),WW,JSe 175.00
7 HK(c),WW,JSe,Document of the
Action at Iwo Jima 175.00
8 HK(c),WW,ATh 175.00
9 HK(c),WW,JSe,Civil War iss. . 175.00
10 GE,HK(c),WW,
Crying Child cover 225.00
11 GE. 150.00
12 GE,Air Force issue. 150.00
13 JSe,GE,WW(c),
Bi-Planes cover 150.00
14 JKu,GE,WW(c) 150.00
15 JSe,GE,WW(c), Jan., 1954 . . 150.00

FRONT PAGE COMIC BOOK

Front Page Comics, 1945

1 JKu,BP,BF(c),I:Man in Black . 275.00

FUGITIVES FROM JUSTICE

St. John Publishing Co. Feb., 1952

1 . . . . 150.00
2 MB, Killer Boomerang 160.00
3 GT 150.00
4 . . . . 60.00
5 Bondage cover, Oct., 1952 . . . 75.00

FUNNIES, THE (1ST SERIES)

Dell Publishing Co. 1929-30

1 B:Foxy Grandpa, Sniffy. 600.00
2 thru 21 . . . . @250.00
N#(22) 225.00
N#(23) thru (36) . . . . @200.00

FUNNIES, THE (2ND SERIES)

Dell Publishing Co. Oct., 1936

1 Tailspin Tommy,Mutt & Jeff,
Capt. Easy,D.Dixon 2,500.00
2 Scribbly 1,000.00
3 . . . . 8000.00
4 Christmas issue 650.00
5 . . . . 650.00
6 thru 22 . . . . @500.00
23 thru 29 . . . . @325.00
30 B:John Carter of Mars. 1,000.00
31 inc. Dick Tracy. 600.00
32 . . . . 600.00
33 . . . . 600.00
34 . . . . 600.00
35 John Carter (c). 600.00
36 John Carter (c). 600.00
37 John Carter (c). 600.00
38 Rex King of the Deep (c) 600.00
39 Rex King (c). 600.00
40 John Carter (c). 600.00
41 Sky Ranger (c). 600.00
42 Rex King (c). 600.00
43 Rex King (c). 600.00
44 Rex King (c). 600.00
45 I&O:Phantasmo:Master of
the World 550.00
46 Phantasmo (c). 550.00
47 Phantasmo (c). 425.00
48 Phantasmo (c). 400.00
49 Phantasmo (c). 400.00
50 Phantasmo (c). 400.00
51 Phantasmo (c) 400.00
52 Phantasmo (c) 375.00
53 Phantasmo (c) 375.00
54 Phantasmo (c) 375.00
55 Phantasmo (c) 375.00
56 Phantasmo (c) E:John Carter 375.00
57 I&O:Captain Midnight 2,000.00
58 Captain Midnight (c). 700.00
59 Captain Midnight (c). 700.00
60 Captain Midnight (c). 700.00
61 Captain Midnight (c). 550.00
62 Captain Midnight (c). 550.00
63 Captain Midnight (c). 550.00
64 B: Woody Woodpecker 900.00
Becomes:

NEW FUNNIES

Dell Publishing Co. July, 1942

65 Andy Panda, Ragady Ann &
Andy, Peter Rabbit 750.00
66 same 350.00
67 Felix the Cat 350.00
68 . . . . 350.00
69 WK, The Brownies 350.00
70 . . . . 350.00
71 . . . . 225.00
72 WK 225.00
73 . . . . 225.00
74 . . . . 225.00
75 WK,Brownies. 225.00
76 CB,Andy Panda, Woody
Woodpecker 1,100.00
77 same 225.00
78 Andy Panda. 225.00
79 . . . . 150.00
80 . . . . 150.00
81 . . . . 150.00
82 WK,Brownies. 175.00
83 WK,Brownies. 175.00
84 WK,Brownies. 150.00
85 WK,Brownies. 175.00
86 . . . . 125.00
87 Woody Woodpecker. 100.00
88 same 100.00
89 same 100.00
90 same 100.00
91 thru 99 . . . . @75.00
100 . . . . 85.00
101 thru 110 . . . . @60.00
111 thru 118 . . . . @50.00
119 Christmas 40.00
120 thru 142 . . . . @40.00
143 Christmas cover. 45.00
144 thru 149 . . . . @40.00
150 thru 154 . . . . @30.00

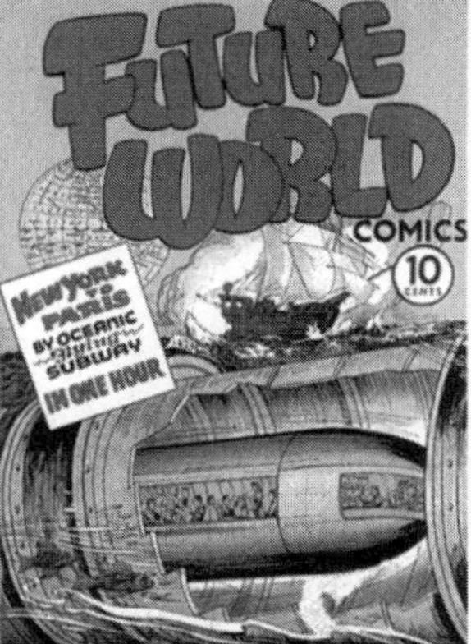

Future World Comics #2
© George W. Dougherty

155 Christmas cover. 32.00
156 thru 167 . . . . @30.00
168 Christmas cover. 32.00
169 thru 181 . . . . @30.00
182 I&O:Knothead & Splinter 30.00
183 thru 200 . . . . @30.00
201 thru 240 . . . . @20.00
241 thru 288 . . . . @15.00

FUNNY BOOK

Funny Book Publ. Corp. (Parents Magazine) Dec., 1952

1 Alec, the Funny Bunny,
Alice in Wonderland 100.00
2 Gulliver in Giant-Land 50.00
3 . . . . 45.00
4 Adventures of Robin Hood 40.00
5 . . . . 40.00
6 . . . . 40.00
7 . . . . 40.00
8 . . . . 40.00
9 . . . . 40.00

FUNNY FILMS

Best Syndicated Features (American Comics Group) Sept.–Oct., 1949

1 B:Puss An' Boots,
Blunderbunny 150.00
2 . . . . 75.00
3 . . . . 50.00
4 . . . . 45.00
5 . . . . 45.00
6 . . . . 45.00
7 . . . . 45.00
8 . . . . 45.00
9 . . . . 45.00
10 . . . . 45.00
11 thru 20 . . . . @35.00
21 thru 28 . . . . @30.00
29 May–June, 1954 . . . . 30.00

FUNNY FUNNIES

Nedor Publ. Co. April, 1943

1 Funny Animals 135.00

FUNNYMAN

Magazine Enterprises of Canada Dec., 1947

1 S&K,S&K(c) 350.00
2 S&K,S&K(c) 200.00
3 S&K,S&K(c) 175.00
4 S&K,S&K(c) 175.00
5 S&K,S&K(c) 175.00
6 S&K,S&K(c), Aug., 1948 . . . . 175.00

FUTURE COMICS

David McKay Publications June, 1940

1 Lone Ranger,Phantom 2,200.00
2 Lone Ranger 1,000.00
3 Lone Ranger. 850.00
4 Lone Ranger,Sept., 1940 . . . . 800.00

FUTURE WORLD COMICS

George W. Dougherty Summer, 1946

1 . . . . 225.00
2 Fall, 1946 . . . . 200.00

GOLDEN AGE

GABBY HAYES WESTERN

Fawcett Publ./Charlton Comics

Nov., 1948

1 Ph(c) 450.00
2 Ph(c) 200.00
3 The Rage of the Purple Sage, Ph(c) 125.00
4 Ph(c) 125.00
5 Ph(c) 100.00
6 Ph(c) 100.00
7 Ph(c) 90.00
8 Ph(c) 90.00
9 Ph(c),V:The Kangaroo Crook . . 90.00
10 Ph(c) 90.00
11 Ph(c), Chariot Race 90.00
12 V:Beaver Ben, The Biting Bandit, Ph(c) 75.00
13 thru 15 . . . . @75.00
16 . . . . 65.00
17 . . . . 65.00
18 thru 20 . . . . @65.00
21 thru 51 . . . . @50.00
51 thru 59 Dec., 1954 . . . . @35.00

GANGSTERS AND GUN MOLLS

Realistic Comics (Avon)

Sept., 1951

1 WW,A:Big Jim Colosimo, Evelyn Ellis 350.00
2 JKa, A:Bonnie Parker, The Kissing Bandit 300.00
3 EK, A:Juanita Perez, Crimes Homicide Squad 250.00
4 A:Mara Hite, Elkins Boys, June, 1952 . . . . 200.00

GANGSTERS CAN'T WIN

D.S. Publishing Co.

Feb.–March, 1948

1 Shot Cop cover 250.00
2 A:Eddie Bentz 125.00
3 Twin Trouble Trigger Man . . . 100.00
4 Suicide on SoundStageSeven 100.00
5 Trail of Terror 100.00
6 Mystery at the Circus 100.00
7 Talisman Trail 75.00
8 . . . . 75.00
9 Suprise at Buoy 13, June–July, 1949 . . . . 75.00

GANG WORLD

Literary Enterprises (Standard Comics)

Oct., 1952

5 Bondage cover 150.00
6 Mob Payoff, Jan., 1953 . . . . . 100.00

GASOLINE ALLEY

Star Publications

Oct., 1950

1 . . . . 150.00
2 LBc 175.00
3 LBc(c), April, 1950 . . . . 175.00

GEM COMICS

Spotlight Publ.

April, 1945

1 A:Steve Strong,Bondage(c) . . 250.00

GENE AUTRY COMICS

Fawcett Publications

Jan., 1942

1 The Mark of Cloven Hoof . . 7,500.00
2 . . . . 1,200.00
3 Secret of the Aztec Treasure 1,000.00
4 . . . . 800.00
5 Mystery of PaintRockCanyon . 850.00
6 Outlaw Round-up 700.00
7 Border Bullets 700.00
8 Blazing Guns 650.00
9 Range Robbers 650.00
10 Fightin' Buckaroo, Danger's Trail, Sept., 1943 . . . . 650.00
11 . . . . 675.00
12 . . . . 650.00

GENE AUTRY COMICS

Dell Publishing Co.

May/June, 1946

1 . . . . 450.00
2 Ph(c) 250.00
3 Ph(c) 175.00
4 Ph(c),I:Flap Jack. 175.00
5 Ph(c), all. 150.00
6 thru 10 . . . . @135.00
11 thru 19 . . . . @125.00
20 . . . . 135.00
21 thru 29 . . . . @100.00
30 thru 40, B:Giants . . . . @75.00
41 thru 56 E:Giants. . . . . @60.00
57 . . . . 35.00
58 Christmas cover. 40.00
59 thru 66 . . . . @35.00
67 thru 80, B:Giant . . . . @40.00
81 thru 90, E:Giant . . . . @30.00
91 thru 93 . . . . @25.00
94 Christmas cover. 28.00
95 thru 99 . . . . @25.00
100 . . . . 30.00
101 thru 111 . . . . @25.00
112 thru 121 . . . . @20.00

GENE AUTRY'S CHAMPION

Dell Publishing Co.

Aug., 1950

(1) *see Dell Four Color #287*
(2) *see Dell Four Color #319*
3 . . . . 50.00
4 . . . . 35.00
5 thru 19 . . . . @35.00

GEORGE PAL'S PUPPETOON'S

Fawcett Publications

Dec., 1945

1 Captain Marvel (c) 350.00
2 . . . . 175.00
3 . . . . 100.00
4 thru 17 . . . . @90.00
18 Dec., 1947. . . . . 90.00

GERALD McBOING-BOING AND THE NEARSIGHTED MR. MAGOO

Dell Publishing Co.

Aug.–Oct., 1952

1 . . . . 100.00
2 . . . . 75.00
3 . . . . 75.00
4 . . . . 75.00
5 . . . . 75.00

GERONIMO

Avon Periodicals, 1950

1 Massacre at San Pedro Pass . 125.00
2 EK(c), Murderous Battle at Kiskayah 75.00
3 EK(c) 75.00
4 EK(c),Apache Death Trap, Feb., 1952 . . . . 75.00

GET LOST

Mikeross Publications

Feb.–March, 1954

1 . . . . 225.00
2 . . . . 150.00
3 June–July, 1954 . . . . 125.00

Ghost #4
© Fiction House

GHOST

Fiction House Magazine

Winter, 1951

1 The Banshee Bells 550.00
2 I Woke In Terror 250.00
3 The Haunted Hand of X 225.00
4 Flee the Mad Furies 225.00
5 The Hex of Ruby Eye 225.00
6 The Sleepers in the Crypt . . . 225.00
7 When Dead Rogues Ride . . . 225.00
8 Curse of the Mist-Thing 225.00
9 It Crawls by Night,Bondage(c). 250.00
10 Halfway to Hades. 225.00
11 GE, The Witch's Doll, Summer, 1954 . . . . 225.00

GHOST BREAKERS

Street & Smith, Sept., 1948

1 BP,BP(c), A:Dr. Neff 325.00
2 BP,BP(c), Breaks the Voodoo Hoodoo,Dec., 1948. . . . . 250.00

GHOSTLY WEIRD STORIES (see BLUE BOLT)

GIANT BOY BOOK OF COMICS

Newsbook Publ. (Lev Gleason), 1945

1 A:Crime Buster & Young Robin Hood 750.00

GIANT COMICS EDITION
St. John Publ., 1948

1 Mighty Mouse . . . 450.00
2 Abbie and Slats . . . 200.00
3 Terry Toons . . . 350.00
4 Crime Comics . . . 500.00
5 MB, Police Case Book . . . 500.00
6 MB,MB(c), Western Picture Story. . . . 475.00
7 May not exist
8 The Adventures of Mighty Mouse . . . 300.00
9 JKu,MB,Romance & Confession Stories,Ph(c) . . . 450.00
10 Terry Toons . . . 300.00
11 MB,MB(c),JKu,Western Picture Stories . . . 450.00
12 MB,MB(c),Diary Secrets, Prostitute . . . 750.00
13 MB,JKu, Romances . . . 425.00
14 Mighty Mouse Album . . . 350.00
15 MB(c),Romance. . . . 425.00
16 Little Audrey . . . 300.00
N#, Mighty Mouse Album . . . 300.00

GIANT COMICS EDITION
United Features Syndicate 1945

1 A:Abbie & Slats, Jim Hardy, Ella Cinders,Iron Vic . . . 275.00
2 Elmo, Jim Hardy, Abbie & Slats, 1945. . . . 200.00

G.I. COMBAT
Quality Comics Group Oct., 1952

1 RC(c), Beyond the Call of Duty . . . 500.00
2 RC(c), Operation Massacre . . 225.00
3 An Indestructible Marine . . . 200.00
4 Bridge to Blood Hill . . . 200.00
5 Hell Breaks loose on Suicide Hill. . . . 200.00
6 Beachhead Inferno . . . 175.00
7 Fire Power Assault . . . 150.00
8 RC(c),Death-trap Hill . . . 150.00
9 Devil Riders . . . 150.00
10 RC(c), Two-Ton Booby Trap. . 175.00
11 Hell's Heroes . . . 125.00
12 Hand Grenade Hero. . . . 125.00
13 Commando Assault . . . 125.00
14 Spear Head Assault. . . . 125.00
15 Vengeance Assault . . . 125.00
16 Trapped Under Fire . . . 110.00
17 Attack on Death Mountain . . . 110.00
18 Red Battle Ground . . . 110.00
19 Death on Helicopter Hill . . . 110.00
20 Doomed Legion-Death Trap . 110.00
21 Red Sneak Attack . . . 100.00
22 Vengeance Raid . . . 100.00
23 No Grandstand in Hell . . . 100.00
24 Operation Steel Trap,Comics Code . . . 100.00
25 Charge of the CommieBrigade 100.00
26 Red Guerrilla Trap . . . 100.00
27 Trapped Behind Commie Lines . . . 100.00
28 Atomic Battleground. . . . 100.00
29 Patrol Ambush. . . . 100.00
30 Operation Booby Trap . . . 100.00
31 Human Fly on Heartbreak Hill 100.00
32 Atomic Rocket Assault. . . . 125.00
33 Bridge to Oblivion . . . 100.00
34 RC,Desperate Mission . . . 125.00
35 Doom Patrol . . . 100.00
36 Fire Power Assault. . . . 100.00
37 Attack at Dawn . . . 100.00
38 Get That Tank . . . 100.00
39 Mystery of No Man's Land . . . 100.00
40 Maneuver Battleground . . . 100.00
41 Trumpet of Doom. . . . 100.00
42 March of Doom . . . 100.00
43 Operation Showdown. . . . 100.00
See DC Comics for 44-120

G.I. Combat #2
© Quality Comics Group

GIFT COMICS
Fawcett Publications March, 1942

1 A:Captain Marvel, Bulletman, Golden Arrow,Ibis, the Invincible, Spy Smasher . . 2,400.00
2 . . . 1,650.00
3 . . . 1,100.00
4 A:Marvel Family, 1949 . . . 650.00

GIGGLE COMICS
Creston Publ./ American Comics Group Oct., 1943

1 (fa)same. . . . 200.00
2 KHu . . . 100.00
3 KHu . . . 70.00
4 KHu . . . 60.00
5 KHu . . . 60.00
6 KHu . . . 50.00
7 KHu . . . 50.00
8 KHu . . . 50.00
9 I:Super Katt . . . 60.00
10 KHu. . . . 40.00
11 thru 20 KHu . . . @35.00
21 thru 30 KHu . . . @30.00
31 thru 40 KHu . . . @25.00
41 thru 94 KHu . . . @30.00
95 A:Spencer Spook. . . . 25.00
96 KHu. . . . 25.00
97 KHu. . . . 25.00
98 KHu. . . . 25.00
99 KHu. . . . 25.00
100 and 101 March–April,1955 . @25.00

G.I. JANE
Stanhall Publ. May, 1953

1 . . . 100.00
2 thru 6 . . . @50.00
7 thru 9 . . . @25.00
10 Dec., 1954. . . . 20.00

G.I. Joe #15
© Ziff-Davis Publication Co.

G.I. JOE
Ziff-Davis Publication Co. 1950

10 NS(c),Red Devils of Korea, V:Seoul City Lou. . . . 100.00
11 NS(c),The Guerrilla's Lair. . . . 75.00
12 NS(c). . . . 75.00
13 NS(c),Attack at Dawn. . . . 75.00
14 NS(c),Temple of Terror, A:Peanuts the Great. . . . 50.00
2-6 It's a Foot Soldiers Job, I:Frankie of the Pump . . . 50.00
2-7 BP,NS(c),The Rout at Sugar Creek . . . 50.00
8 BP,NS(c),Waldo'sSqueezeBox . 50.00
9 NS(c),Dear John. . . . 50.00
10 NS(c),Joe Flies the Payroll . . . 50.00
11 NS(c),For the Love of Benny . . 50.00
12 NS(c),Patch work Quilt. . . . 50.00
13 NS(c). . . . 50.00
14 NS(c),The Wedding Ring . . . 50.00
15 The Lacrosse Whoopee. . . . 50.00
16 Mamie's Mortar . . . 50.00
17 A Time for Waiting . . . 50.00
18 Giant . . . 150.00
19 Old Army Game..Buck Passer . 45.00
20 General Confusion . . . 45.00
21 Save 'Im for Brooklyn. . . . 45.00
22 Portrait of a Lady. . . . 45.00
23 Take Care of My Little Wagon . 45.00
24 Operation 'Operation'. . . . 45.00
25 The Two-Leaf Clover . . . 45.00
26 NS(c),Nobody Flies Alone Mud & Wings . . . 45.00
27 "Dear Son...Come Home" . . . 45.00
28 They Alway's Come Back Bondage cover. . . . 45.00
29 What a Picnic . . . 40.00
30 NS(c),The One-Sleeved Kimono . . . 40.00
31 NS(c),Get a Horse. . . . 35.00
32 thru 47. . . . @35.00
48 Atom Bomb . . . 40.00
49 thru 51 June, 1957. . . . @35.00

GINGER
Close-Up Publ. (Archie Publications) Jan., 1951

1 GFs . . . 100.00
2 . . . 60.00
3 . . . 45.00

4 . . . . 45.00
5 . . . . 35.00
6 . . . . 35.00
7 thru 9 . . . . @50.00
10 A:Katy Keene,Summer,1954 . . 50.00

GIRLS IN LOVE
Fawcett Publications
May, 1950

1 . . . . 75.00
2 Ph(c),July, 1950 . . . . 70.00

GIRLS IN LOVE
(see DIARY LOVES)

G.I. SWEETHEARTS
(see DIARY LOVES)

G.I. WAR BRIDES
Superior Publ. Ltd.
April, 1954

1 . . . . 50.00
2 . . . . 35.00
3 thru 7 . . . . @25.00
8 June, 1955 . . . . 25.00

GOING STEADY
(see TEEN-AGE TEMPTATIONS)

GOLDEN ARROW
Fawcett Publications
Spring, 1942

1 B:Golden Arrow 750.00
2 . . . . 350.00
3 . . . . 275.00
4 . . . . 250.00
5 Spring, 1947 . . . . 250.00
6 BK 275.00
6a 1944 Well Known Comics (Giveaway) 300.00

GOLDEN LAD
Spark Publications
July, 1945

1 MMe,MMe(c),A:Kid Wizards, Swift Arrow,B:Golden Ladd . . 600.00
2 MMe,MMe(c) 275.00
3 MMe,MMe(c) 275.00
4 MMe,MMe(c), The Menace of the Minstrel 275.00
5 MMe,MMe(c),O:Golden Girl, June, 1946 . . . . 275.00

GOLDEN WEST LOVE
Kirby Publishing Co.
Sept.–Oct., 1949

1 BP,I Rode Heartbreak Hill, Ph(c) 150.00
2 BP 100.00
3 BP,Ph(c) 100.00
4 BP,April, 1950 . . . . 100.00

GOLD MEDAL COMICS
Cambridge House, 1945

N# Captain Truth 200.00

GOOFY COMICS
Nedor Publ. Co./
Animated Cartoons
(Standard Comics)
June, 1943

1 (fa) 175.00
2 . . . . 100.00
3 VP 60.00
4 VP 50.00
5 VP 50.00
6 thru 10 VP . . . . @50.00
11 thru 15 . . . . @40.00
15 thru 19 . . . . @35.00
20 thru 35 FF . . . . @50.00
36 thru 48 . . . . @35.00

GREAT AMERICAN COMICS PRESENTS– THE SECRET VOICE
4 Star Publ., 1944

1 Hitler,Secret Weapon 225.00

GREAT COMICS
Novak Publ. Co., 1945

1 LbC(c) 275.00

GREAT COMICS
Great Comics Publications
Nov., 1941

1 I:The Great Zorro 1,100.00
2 Buck Johnson 600.00
3 The Lost City, Jan., 1942 . . 1,500.00

GREAT LOVER ROMANCES
Toby Press, March, 1951

1 Jon Juan,A:Dr. King 125.00
2 Hollywood Girl 65.00
3 Love in a Taxi 35.00
4 The Experimental Kiss 35.00
5 After the Honeymoon 35.00
6 HK,The Kid Sister Falls in Love 60.00
7 Man Crazy 30.00
8 Stand-in Boyfriend 30.00
9 The Cheat 30.00
10 Heart Breaker 30.00
11 . . . . 30.00
12 . . . . 30.00
13 Powerhouse of Deciet 30.00
14 . . . . 30.00
15 Ph(c),Still Undecided, Liz Taylor 75.00
16 thru 21 . . . . @30.00
22 May, 1955 . . . . 30.00

GREEN GIANT COMICS
Pelican Publications, 1941

1 Black Arrow, Dr. Nerod O:Colossus 9,000.00

GREEN HORNET COMICS
Helnit Publ. Co./
Family Comics
(Harvey Publ.), Dec., 1940

1 B:Green Hornet,P(c) 4,400.00
2 . . . . 1,400.00
3 BWh(c) 1,200.00
4 BWh(c) 800.00
5 BWh(c) 800.00

Green Hornet #10
© Harvey Publications

6 . . . . 800.00
7 BP, O:Zebra, B:Robin Hood & Spirit of 76 . . . . 700.00
8 BP,Bondage cover 600.00
9 BP, Behind the Cover 600.00
10 BP 600.00
11 Who is Mr. Q? 600.00
12 BP,A:Mr.Q 600.00
13 Hitler cover 650.00
14 BP,Spirit of 76-Twinkle Twins, Bondage(c) 475.00
15 ASh(c),Nazi Ghost Ship 450.00
16 BP,Prisoner of War. 450.00
17 BP,ASh(c),Nazis' Last Stand . 450.00
18 BP,ASh(c),Jap's Treacherous Plot,Bondage cover 475.00
19 BP,ASh(c),Clash with the Rampaging Japs 450.00
20 BP,ASh(c),Tojo's Propaganda Hoax 475.00
21 BP,ASh(c),Unwelcome Cargo. 375.00
22 ASh(c),Rendezvous with Jap Saboteurs 375.00
23 BF,ASh(c),Jap's Diabolical Plot #B2978 . . . . 375.00
24 BF,Science Fiction cover 400.00
25 thru 29 . . . . @375.00
30 BP,JKu 375.00
31 BP,JKu. 400.00
32 BP,JKu. 325.00
33 BP,JKu. 325.00
34 BP,JKu. 325.00
35 BP,JKu. 325.00
36 BP,JKu,Bondage cover 350.00
37 BP,JKu. 325.00
38 BP,JKu. 325.00
39 S&K. 400.00
40 thru 45 . . . . @250.00
46 Drug 275.00
47 Sept., 1949 . . . . 250.00

GREEN LAMA
Spark Publications/Prize Publ.
Dec., 1944

1 I:Green Lama, Lt. Hercules & Boy Champions 1,200.00
2 MRa,Forward to Victory in 1945 . . . . 600.00
3 MRa,The Riddles of Toys 500.00
4 MRa,Dive Bombs Japan 475.00
5 MRa,MRa(c),Fights for the Four Freedoms 475.00
6 MRa,Smashes a Plot against America 475.00

GOLDEN AGE

All comics prices listed are for *Near Mint* condition.

7 MRa,Merry X-Mas 400.00
8 MRa,Smashes Toy Master of Crime, March, 1946 . . . . . 400.00

Green Mask #11
© Fox Features Syndicate

GREEN MASK, THE
Fox Features Syndicate
Summer, 1940

1 O:Green Mask & Domino . . 3,500.00
2 A:Zanzibar 1,100.00
3 BP 700.00
4 B:Navy Jones 550.00
5 . . . . 450.00
6 B:Nightbird,E:Navy Jones, Bondage cover 350.00
7 B:Timothy Smith & The Tumbler 300.00
8 JSs 250.00
9 E:Nightbird, Death Wields a Scalpel! 275.00
10 . . . . 225.00
11 The Banshee of Dead Man's Hill 225.00
2-1 Election of Skulls 175.00
2-2 Pigeons of Death 175.00
2-3 Wandering Gold Brick 150.00
2-4 Time on His Hands 150.00
2-5 JFe,SFd 175.00
2-6 Adventure of the Disappearing Trains, Oct.–Nov., 1946 . . . . 175.00

GUMPS, THE
Dell Publishing Co., 1945

1 . . . . 150.00
2 . . . . 125.00
3 . . . . 100.00
4 . . . . 100.00
5 . . . . 100.00

GUNS AGAINST GANGSTERS
Curtis Publ./Novelty Press
Sept.–Oct., 1948

1 LbC,LbC(c),B:Toni Gayle 250.00
2 LbC,LbC(c) 200.00
3 LbC,LbC(c) 175.00
4 LbC,LbC(c) 175.00
5 LbC,LbC(c) 175.00
6 LbC,LbC(c),Shark. 175.00
2-1 LbC,LbC(c), Sept.–Oct., 1949 . . . . 175.00

GUNSMOKE
Western Comics, Inc.
April–May, 1949

1 GRi,GRi(c),Gunsmoke & Masked Marvel,Bondage cover 350.00
2 GRi,GRi(c) 200.00
3 GRi,GRi(c) 175.00
4 GRi(c),Bondage(c) 150.00
5 GRi(c) 150.00
6 . . . . 75.00
7 . . . . 75.00
8 . . . . 75.00
9 . . . . 75.00
10. . . . . 75.00
11 thru 15 . . . . @60.00
16 Jan., 1952 . . . . 60.00

HA HA COMICS
Creston Publ.
(American Comics Group)
Oct., 1943

1 Funny Animal, all 225.00
2 . . . . 125.00
3 . . . . 80.00
4 . . . . 80.00
5 . . . . 80.00
6 thru 10 . . . . @60.00
11 . . . . 40.00
12 thru 15 KHu . . . . @40.00
16 thru 20 KHu . . . . @35.00
21 thru 30 KHu . . . . @30.00
31 thru 101 . . . . @25.00
102 Feb.–March, 1955 . . . . 25.00

MISTER RISK
Humor Publ.
(Ace Magazines)
Oct., 1950

1 (7) B:Mr. Risk 50.00
2 . . . . 35.00
Becomes:

MEN AGAINST CRIME

3 A:Mr. Risk, Case of the Carnival Killer 75.00
4 Murder-And the Crowd Roars . 40.00
5 . . . . 40.00
6 . . . . 40.00
7 Get Them! 40.00
Becomes:

HAND OF FATE
Ace Magazines

8 . . . . 275.00
9 LC 175.00
10 LC 150.00
11 Genie(c). 125.00
12 . . . . 125.00
13 Hanging(c). 150.00
14 . . . . 135.00
15 . . . . 135.00
16 . . . . 125.00
17 . . . . 125.00
18 . . . . 125.00
19 Drug issue,Quicksand(c) 135.00
20 . . . . 125.00
21 Drug issue 135.00
22 . . . . 125.00
23 Graveyard(c) 125.00
24 LC,Electric Chair 200.00
25 Nov., 1954 . . . . 100.00
25a Dec., 1954 . . . . 125.00

HANGMAN COMICS
(see LAUGH COMICS)

HAP HAZARD COMICS
A.A. Wyn/Red Seal Publ./
Readers Research
Summer, 1944

1 Funny Teen 75.00
2 Dog Show 40.00
3 Sgr, ... 35.00
4 Sgr, ... 35.00
5 thru 10 Sgr, ... @25.00
11 thru 13 Sgr, ... @20.00
14 AF(c). 40.00
15 . . . . 20.00
16 thru 24 . . . . @20.00
Becomes:

REAL LOVE

25 Dangerous Dates. 60.00
26 . . . . 30.00
27 LbC(c), Revenge Conquest . . . 40.00
28 thru 40 . . . . @25.00
41 thru 66 . . . . @20.00
67 Comics code 15.00
68 thru 76, Nov. 1956 . . . . @15.00

HAPPY COMICS
Nedor Publications/
Animated Cartoons
(Standard Comics)
Aug., 1943

1 Funny Animal in all 150.00
2 . . . . 100.00
3 . . . . 50.00
4 . . . . 45.00
5 thru 10 . . . . @45.00
11 thru 20 . . . . @40.00
21 thru 30 . . . . @35.00
31 and 32 . . . . @60.00
33 FF 135.00
34 thru 37 FF . . . . @60.00
38 thru 40 . . . . @25.00
Becomes:

HAPPY RABBIT

41 Funny Animal in all 30.00
42 thru 50 . . . . @20.00
Becomes:

HARVEY COMIC HITS

51 Phantom 225.00
52 Steve Canyon's Air Power . . . 100.00
53 Mandrake 150.00
54 Tim Tyler's Tales of Jungle Terror 75.00
55 Love Stories of Mary Worth . . . 40.00
56 Phantom, Bondage cover. . . . 175.00
57 AR,Kidnap Racket 110.00
58 Girls in White. 40.00
59 Tales of the Invisible 75.00
60 Paramount Animated Comics 275.00
61 Casper the Friendly Ghost . . . 300.00
62 Paramount Animated Comics, April, 1953 . . . . 100.00

HAPPY HOULIHANS
(see SADDLE JUSTICE)

HAUNTED THRILLS
Four Star Publ.
(Ajax/Farrell)
June, 1952

1 Ellery Queen 350.00
2 LbC,Ellery Queen 225.00

GOLDEN AGE

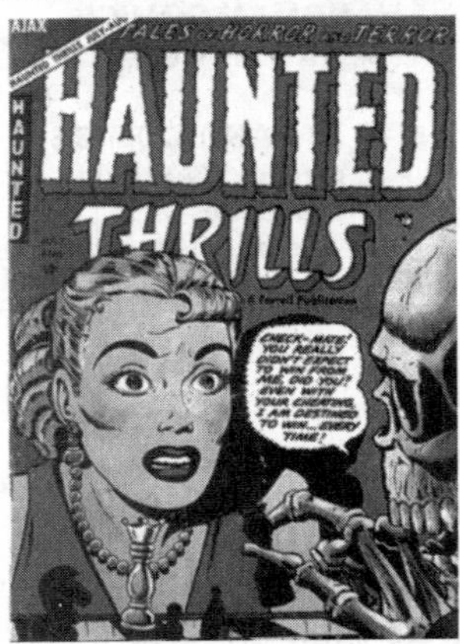

Haunted Thrills #16
© Four Star Publications

3 Drug Story 200.00
4 Ghouls Castle 175.00
5 Fatal Scapel 175.00
6 Pit of Horror 150.00
7 Trail to a Tomb 150.00
8 Vanishing Skull 150.00
9 Madness of Terror 150.00
10 . . . . 150.00
11 Nazi Concentration Camp . . . 175.00
12 RWb 125.00
13 . . . . 125.00
14 RWb 150.00
15 The Devil Collects 125.00
16 . . . . 125.00
17 Mirror of Madness 125.00
18 No Place to Go,
Nov.–Dec., 1954 . . . . 135.00

HAUNT OF FEAR
Fables Publ.
(E.C. Comics)
May–June, 1950

15 JCr,JCr(c),AF,WW 2,500.00
16 JCr,JCr(c),AF,WW 1,000.00
17 JCr,JCr(c),AF,WW,O:Crypt
of Terror,Vault of Horror
& Haunt of Fear 950.00
4 AF(c),WW,JDa 650.00
5 JCr,JCr(c),WW,JDa,Eye Injury 500.00
6 JCr,JCr(c),WW,JDa. 350.00
7 JCr,JCr(c),WW,JDa. 350.00
8 AF(c),JKa,JDa,
Shrunken Head 350.00
9 AF(c),JCr,JDa 350.00
10 AF(c),Grl,JDa 325.00
11 JKa,Grl,JDa 275.00
12 JCr,Grl,JDa 275.00
13 Grl,JDa 275.00
14 Grl,Grl(c),JDa,O:Old Witch. . . 350.00
15 JDa 275.00
16 GRi(c),JDa,Ray Bradbury
adaptation 275.00
17 JDa,Grl(c),Classic
Ghastly (c) 275.00
18 JDa,Grl(c),JKa,Ray Bradbury
adaptation 300.00
19 JDa,Guillotine (c),
Bondage cover 300.00
20 RC,JDa,Grl,Grl(c) 250.00
21 JDa,Grl,Grl(c) 200.00
22 same 200.00
23 same 200.00
22 same 200.00
23 same 200.00
24 same 200.00
25 same 200.00
26 RC,same 250.00
27 same, Cannibalism 225.00
28 Dec., 1954. . . . . 225.00

HAWK, THE
Approved Comics
(Ziff-Davis)
Winter, 1951

1 MA,The Law of the Colt,P(c) . 150.00
2 JKu,Iron Caravan of the
Mojave, P(c) 100.00
3 Leverett's Last Stand,P(c) 90.00
4 Killer's Town,P(c) 75.00
5 . . . . 75.00
6 . . . . 75.00
7 . . . . 75.00
8 MB(c),Dry River Rampage . . . 100.00
9 MB,MB(c),JKu 100.00
10 MB(c) 100.00
11 MB(c). 100.00
12 MB,MB(c), May, 1955 . . . . . . 100.00

HEADLINE COMICS
American Boys Comics/
Headline Publ. (Prize Publ.)
Feb., 1943

1 B:Jr. Rangers 350.00
2 JaB,JaB(c) 175.00
3 JaB,JaB(c) 125.00
4 . . . . 125.00
5 HcK 125.00
6 HcK 125.00
7 HcK,Jr. Rangers 125.00
8 HcK,Hitler cover 300.00
9 HcK 125.00
10 HcK,Hitler story,Wizard(c) . . . 150.00
11 . . . . 100.00
12 HcK,Heroes of Yesterday. . . . 100.00
13 HcK,A:Blue Streak. 100.00
14 HcK,A:Blue Streak. 100.00
15 HcK,A:Blue Streak. 100.00
16 HcK,O:Atomic Man 200.00
17 Atomic Man(c) 100.00
18 Atomic Man(c) 100.00
19 S&K,Atomic Man(c) 200.00
20 Atomic Man(c) 100.00
21 E:Atomic Man 100.00
22 HcK. 75.00
23 S&K,S&K(c),Valentines Day
Massacre 200.00
24 S&K,S&K(c),You can't Forget
a Killer 200.00
25 S&K,S&K(c),CrimeNeverPays 200.00
26 S&K,S&K(c),CrimeNeverPays 200.00
27 S&K,S&K(c),CrimeNeverPays 200.00
28 S&K,S&K(c),CrimeNeverPays 200.00
29 S&K,S&K(c),CrimeNeverPays 200.00
30 S&K,S&K(c),CrimeNeverPays 200.00
31 S&K,S&K(c),CrimeNeverPays 200.00
32 S&K,S&K(c),CrimeNeverPays 200.00
33 S&K,S&K(c),Police and FBI
heroes 200.00
34 S&K,S&K(c),same 200.00
35 S&K,S&K(c),same 200.00
36 S&K,S&K(c),same,Ph(c) 135.00
37 S&K,S&K(c),MvS,same,Ph(c). 150.00
38 S&K,S&K(c),same,Ph(c) 50.00
39 S&K,S&K(c),same,Ph(c) 50.00
40 S&K,S&K(c),Ph(c)Violent
Crime 50.00
41 Ph(c),J.Edgar Hoover(c) 50.00
42 Ph(c) 40.00
43 Ph(c) 40.00
44 MMe,MvS,WE,S&K 60.00
45 JK 35.00
46 . . . . 35.00
47 . . . . 35.00
48 . . . . 35.00
49 MMe 35.00
50 . . . . 35.00
51 JK 38.00
52 . . . . 35.00
53 . . . . 35.00
54 . . . . 35.00
55 . . . . 35.00
56 S&K. 75.00
57 . . . . 30.00
58 . . . . 30.00
59 . . . . 30.00
60 MvS(c). 30.00
61 MMe,MvS(c) 30.00
62 MMe,MMe(c) 30.00
63 MMe,MMe(c) 30.00
64 MMe,MMe(c) 30.00
65 MMe,MMe(c) 30.00
66 MMe,MMe(c) 30.00
67 MMe,MMe(c) 30.00
68 MMe,MMe(c) 30.00
69 MMe,MMe(c) 30.00
70 MMe,MMe(c) 30.00
71 MMe,MMe(c) 30.00
72 MMe,MMe(c) 30.00
73 MMe,MMe(c) 30.00
74 MMe,MMe(c) 30.00
75 MMe,MMe(c) 30.00
76 MMe,MMe(c) 30.00
77 MMe,MMe(c),Oct., 1956 . . . . . 30.00

HEART THROBS
Comics Magazines
(Quality)
Aug., 1949

1 BWa(c),PG,Spoiled Brat 300.00
2 BWa(c),PG,Siren of
the Tropics 175.00
3 PG 60.00
4 BWa(c),Greed Turned Me into
a Scheming Vixen,Ph(c) 100.00
5 Ph(c) 40.00
6 BWa 100.00
7 . . . . 40.00
8 BWa 100.00
9 I Hated Men,Ph(c) 50.00
10 BWa,My Secret Fears 60.00
11 . . . . 25.00
12 . . . . 25.00
13 . . . . 25.00
14 BWa 25.00
15 My Right to Happiness,Ph(c) . . 75.00
16 . . . . 25.00
17 . . . . 25.00
18 . . . . 25.00
19 . . . . 25.00
20 . . . . 25.00
21 BWa 55.00
22 BWa 50.00
23 BWa 50.00
24 thru 30 . . . . @25.00
31 thru 33 . . . . @25.00
34 thru 39 . . . . @25.00
40 BWa 35.00
41 . . . . 25.00
42 . . . . 25.00
43 thru 45 . . . . @25.00
(Please see DC listings)

HECKLE AND JECKLE
St. John Publ./Pines
Nov., 1951

1 Blue Ribbon Comics 200.00
2 Blue Ribbon Comics 125.00
3 . . . . 85.00
4 . . . . 75.00

5 . . . . 75.00
6 . . . . 75.00
7 . . . . 55.00
8 . . . . 50.00
9 . . . . 50.00
10 . . . . 50.00
11 thru 15 . . . . @40.00
16 thru 20 . . . . @35.00
21 thru 33 . . . . @30.00
34 June, 1959 . . . . 32.00

HELLO PAL COMICS
Harvey Publications
Jan., 1943

1 B:Rocketman & Rocket Girl, Mickey Rooney cover, Ph(c) all 500.00
2 Charlie McCarthy cover 450.00
3 Bob Hope cover, May, 1943 . . 400.00

HENRY
Dell Publishing Co.
Oct., 1946

1 . . . . 100.00
2 . . . . 50.00
3 thru 10 . . . . @35.00
11 thru 20 . . . . @25.00
21 thru 30 . . . . @20.00
31 thru 40 . . . . @15.00
41 thru 50 . . . . @12.00
51 thru 65 . . . . @10.00

Henry Aldrich Comics #3
© Dell Publishing Co.

HENRY ALDRICH COMICS
Dell Publishing Co.
Aug.–Sept., 1950

1 . . . . 90.00
2 . . . . 45.00
3 . . . . 35.00
4 . . . . 35.00
5 . . . . 35.00
6 thru 10 . . . . @30.00
11 thru 22 . . . . @25.00

HEROIC COMICS
Eastern Color Printing Co./ Famous Funnies
Aug., 1940

1 BEv,BEv(c),O:Hydroman,Purple Zombie, B:Man of India . . . 1,300.00
2 BEv,BEv(c),B:Hydroman covers 600.00
3 BEv,BEv(c) 375.00
4 BEv,BEv(c) 350.00
5 BEv,BEv(c) 325.00
6 BEv,BEv(c) 300.00
7 BEv,BEv(c),O:Man O'Metal . . 350.00
8 BEv,BEv(c) 225.00
9 BEv 225.00
10 BEv 225.00
11 BEv,E:Hydroman covers. . . . 225.00
12 BEv,B&0:Music Master. . . . 250.00
13 BEv,RC,LF. . . . 225.00
14 BEv 250.00
15 BEv,I:Downbeat 250.00
16 BEv,CCB(c),A:Lieut Nininger, Major Heidger,Lieut Welch,B:P(c) 175.00
17 BEv,A:JohnJames Powers,Hewitt T.Wheless, Irving Strobing . . 175.00
18 HcK,BEv,Pass the Ammunition 175.00
19 HcK,BEv,A:Barney Ross 175.00
20 HcK,BEv 150.00
21 HcK,BEv 125.00
22 HcK,BEv,Howard Gilmore . . . 125.00
23 HcK,BEv 125.00
24 HcK,BEv 125.00
25 HcK,BEv 125.00
26 HcK,BEv 125.00
27 HcK,BEv 125.00
28 HcK,BEv,E:Man O'Metal. . . . 125.00
29 HcK,BEv,E:Hydroman 125.00
30 BEv 125.00
31 BEv,CCB,Capt. Tootsie 30.00
32 ATh,CCB,WWII(c), Capt. Tootsie 50.00
33 ATh, ... 50.00
34 WWII(c). 30.00
35 Ath,B:Rescue(c). 50.00
36 HcK,ATh 50.00
37 same 50.00
38 ATh 50.00
39 HcK,ATh 50.00
40 ATh,Boxing 50.00
41 Grl(c),ATh 50.00
42 ATh 50.00
43 ATh 40.00
44 HcK,ATh 40.00
45 HcK 40.00
46 HcK 40.00
47 HcK 40.00
48 HcK 40.00
49 HcK 40.00
50 HcK 40.00
51 HcK,ATh,AW 50.00
52 HcK,AW. 50.00
53 HcK 45.00
54 . . . . 30.00
55 ATh 30.00
56 ATh(c) 35.00
57 ATh(c) 30.00
58 ATh(c) 30.00
59 ATh(c) 30.00
60 ATh(c) 30.00
61 BEv(c) 25.00
62 BEv(c) 25.00
63 BEv(c) 25.00
64 GE,BEv(c) 28.00
65 HcK(c),FF,ATh,AW,GE 65.00
66 HcK(c),FF 50.00
67 HcK(c),FF,Korean War(c) 50.00
68 HcK(c),Korean War(c) 50.00
69 HcK(c),FF 65.00
70 HcK(c),FF,B:Korean War(c) . . . 50.00
71 HcK(c),FF 50.00
72 HcK(c),FF 65.00
73 HcK(c),FF 50.00
74 HcK(c) 50.00
75 HcK(c),FF 50.00
76 HcK,HcK(c) 25.00

Heroic Comics #4
© Eastern Color Printing

77 same 25.00
78 same 25.00
79 same 25.00
80 same 25.00
81 FF,HcK(c) 30.00
82 FF,HcK(c) 30.00
83 FF,HcK(c) 30.00
84 HcK(c) 30.00
85 HcK(c) 30.00
86 FF,HcK(c) 35.00
87 FF,HcK(c) 35.00
88 HcK(c),E:Korean War covers . . 25.00
89 HcK(c) 25.00
90 HcK(c) 25.00
91 HcK(c) 25.00
92 HcK(c) 25.00
93 HcK(c) 25.00
94 HcK(c) 25.00
95 HcK(c) 25.00
96 HcK(c) 25.00
97 HcK(c),E:P(c),June, 1955. . . . 25.00

HICKORY
Comic Magazine
(Quality Comics Group)
Oct.., 1949

1 ASa, ... 100.00
2 ASa, ... 50.00
3 ASa, ... 45.00
4 ASa, ... 45.00
5 ASa, ... 45.00
6 ASa,Aug., 1950 . . . . 45.00

HI-HO COMICS
Four Star Publications, 1946

1 LbC(c) 225.00
2 LbC(c) 130.00
3 1946 . . . . 130.00

HI-JINX
B & I Publ. Co.
(American Comics Group)
July–Aug., 1947

1 (fa) all. 125.00
2 . . . . 75.00
3 . . . . 60.00
4 thru 7 . . . . @50.00
N# 85.00

GOLDEN AGE

HI-LITE COMICS
E.R. Ross Publ.
Fall, 1945

1 . . . . 100.00

Hit Comics #38
© Quality Comics Group

HIT COMICS
Comics Magazine
(Quality Comics Group)
July, 1940

1 LF(c),O:Neon,Hercules,I:The Red Bee, B:Bob & Swab, Blaze Barton Strange Twins,X-5 Super Agent Casey Jones,Jack & Jill . . . 5,500.00
2 GT,LF(c),B:Old Witch 2,200.00
3 GT,LF(c),E:Casey Jones . . . 2,000.00
4 GT,LF(c),B:Super Agent & Betty Bates,E:X-5 . . . . 1,700.00
5 GT,LF(c),B:Red Bee cover . . 4,800.00
6 GT,LF(c) 1,500.00
7 GT,LF(c),E:Red Bee cover . . 1,550.00
8 GT,LF(c),B:Neon cover 1,500.00
9 JCo,LF(c),E:Neon cover. . . . 1,500.00
10 JCo,RC,LF(c),B:Hercules(c) 1,500.00
11 JCo,RC,LF(c),A:Hercules . . 1,300.00
12 JCo,RC,LF(c),A:Hercules . . 1,300.00
13 JCo,RC,LF(c),A:Hercules . . 1,300.00
14 JCo,RC,LF(c),A:Hercules . . 1,300.00
15 JCo,RC,A:Hercules. 1,000.00
16 JCo,RC,LF(c),A:Hercules . . 1,000.00
17 JCo,RC,LF(c),E:Hercules(c) 1,000.00
18 JCo,RC,RC(c),O:Stormy Foster,B:Ghost of Flanders 1,000.00
19 JCo,RC(c),B:StormyFoster(c). 800.00
20 JCo,RC(c),A:Stormy Foster . . 850.00
21 JCo,RC(c) 825.00
22 JCo 825.00
23 JCo,RC,RC(c) 800.00
24 JCo,E:Stormy Foster cover . . 800.00
25 JCo,RP,O:Kid Eternity 1,500.00
26 JCo,RP,A:Black Hawk 900.00
27 JCo,RP,B:Kid Eternity covers . 400.00
28 JCo,RP,A:Her Highness 400.00
29 JCo,RP 400.00
30 JCo,RP,HK,V:Julius Caesar and his Legion of Warriors . . 350.00
31 JCo,RP 350.00
32 JCo,RP,V:Merlin the Wizard . . 225.00
33 JCo,RP 200.00
34 JCo,RP,E:Stormy Foster 200.00
35 JCo,Kid Eternity accused of Murder 200.00
36 JCo,The Witch's Curse 200.00
37 JCo,V:Mr. Silence 200.00
38 JCo 200.00
39 JCo,Runaway River Boat 200.00
40 PG,V:Monster from the Past . 200.00
41 PG,Did Kid Eternity Lose His Power?. 150.00
42 PG,Kid Eternity Loses Killer Cronson 150.00
43 JCo,PG,V:Modern Bluebeard . 150.00
44 JCo,PG,Trips up the Shoe . . . 150.00
45 JCo,PG,Pancho Villa against Don Pablo 150.00
46 JCo,V:Mr. Hardeel 150.00
47 A Polished Diamond can be Rough on Rats 150.00
48 EhH,A Treasure Chest of Trouble. 150.00
49 EhH,V:Monsters from the Mirror 150.00
50 EhH,Heads for Trouble 150.00
51 EhH,Enters the Forgotten World 125.00
52 EhH,Heroes out of the Past . . 125.00
53 EhH,V:Mr. Puny 125.00
54 V:Ghost Town Killer 125.00
55 V:The Brute 125.00
56 V:Big Odds 125.00
57 Solves the Picture in a Frame 125.00
58 Destroys Oppression!. 125.00
59 Battles Tomorrow's Crimes Today! 125.00
60 E:Kid Eternity covers, V:The Mummy 125.00
61 RC,RC(c),I:Jeb Rivers 150.00
62 RC(c). 125.00
63 RC(c),A:Jeb Rivers 150.00
64 RC,A:Jeb Rivers 150.00
65 Bondage cover,RC,July, 1950 165.00

HOLIDAY COMICS
Fawcett Publ.
Nov., 1942

1 Captain Marvel (c) 1,500.00

HOLIDAY COMICS
Star Publ.
Jan., 1951

1 LbC(c),(fa),Christmas cover . . 250.00
2 LbC(c),Parade(c) 275.00
3 LbC(c),July 4th(c) 175.00
4 LbC(c),Vacation(c) 175.00
5 LbC(c),Christmas(c) 175.00
6 LbC(c),Birthday(c). 175.00
7 LbC(c) 150.00
8 LbC(c),Christmas(c) 175.00

HOLLYWOOD COMICS
New Age Publishers
Winter, 1944

1 (fa). 125.00

HOLLYWOOD CONFESSIONS
St. John Publ. Co.
Oct., 1949

1 JKu,JKu(c) 200.00
2 JKu,JKu(c), Dec., 1949 . . . . . 250.00

HOLLYWOOD DIARY
Comics Magazine
(Quality Comics), Dec., 1949

1 . . . . 135.00
2 Photo cover 100.00
3 Photo cover 75.00
4 . . . . 75.00
5 Photo cover, Aug., 1950 . . . . . 75.00

HOLLYWOOD FILM STORIES
Feature Publications
(Prize)
April, 1950

1 June Allison,Ph(c). 150.00
2 Lizabeth Scott,Ph(c) 100.00
3 Barbara Stanwick,Ph(c) 100.00
4 Beth Hutton, Aug., 1950 . . . . . 100.00

HOLLYWOOD SECRETS
Comics Magazine
(Quality Comics Group)
Nov., 1949

1 BWa,BWa(c) 250.00
2 BWa,BWa(c),RC 175.00
3 Ph(c) 100.00
4 Ph(c),May, 1950 . . . . 100.00
5 Ph(c) 100.00
6 Ph(c) 100.00

HOLYOKE ONE-SHOT
Tem Publ.
(Holyoke Publ. Co.), 1944

1 Grit Grady 85.00
2 Rusty Dugan 75.00
3 JK,Miss Victory,O:Cat Woman. 175.00
4 Mr. Miracle 65.00
5 U.S. Border Patrol 60.00
6 Capt. Fearless 60.00
7 Strong Man 65.00
8 Blue Streak 60.00
9 S&K, Citizen Smith 120.00
10 S&K, Capt. Stone. 135.00

HONEYMOON ROMANCE
Artful Publications
(Digest Size)
April, 1950

1 . . . . 275.00
2 July, 1950 . . . . 250.00

HOODED HORSEMAN
(see OUT OF THE NIGHT)

HOPALONG CASSIDY
Fawcett Publications
Feb., 1943

1 B:Hopalong Cassidy & Topper, Captain Marvel cover 5,000.00
2 . . . . 700.00
3 Blazing Trails 350.00
4 5-full length story 275.00
5 Death in the Saddle, Ph(c) . . . 250.00
6 . . . . 225.00
7 . . . . 225.00
8 Phantom Stage Coach 225.00
9 The Last Stockade 225.00
10 4-spine tingling adventures . . 225.00
11 Desperate Jetters! Ph(c) 175.00
12 The Mysterious Message 175.00
13 The Human Target, Ph(c). . . . 175.00
14 Land of the Lawless, Ph(c). . . 175.00
15 Death holds the Reins, Ph(c) . 175.00
16 Webfoot's Revenge, Ph(c) . . . 175.00
17 The Hangman's Noose, Ph(c) 175.00

18 The Ghost of Dude Ranch, Ph(c) 175.00
19 A:William Boyd,Ph(c) 175.00
20 The Notorious Nellie Blaine!, B:P(c) 150.00
21 V:Arizona Kid 150.00
22 V:Arizona Kid 150.00
23 Hayride Horror 150.00
24 Twin River Giant 150.00
25 On the Trails of the Wild and Wooly West 150.00
26 thru 30 . . . . @125.00
31 52 pages 90.00
32 36 pages 90.00
33 thru 35, 52 pages . . . . @90.00
36 36 pages 75.00
37 thru 40, 52 pages . . . . @90.00
40 36 pages 75.00
41 E:P(c) 40.00
42 B:Ph(c) 75.00
43 . . . . 75.00
44 . . . . 50.00
45 . . . . 60.00
46 thru 51 . . . . @50.00
52 . . . . 45.00
53 . . . . 50.00
54 . . . . 50.00
55 . . . . 45.00
56 . . . . 50.00
57 . . . . 50.00
58 thru 70 . . . . @50.00
71 thru 84 . . . . @40.00
85 E:Ph(c),Jan., 1954 . . . . 50.00
(Please see DC listings)

HOPPY THE MARVEL BUNNY
Fawcett Publications
Dec., 1945

1 A:Marvel Bunny 175.00
2 . . . . 100.00
3 . . . . 75.00
4 . . . . 75.00
5 . . . . 75.00
6 thru 14 . . . . @50.00
15 Sept., 1947 . . . . 50.00

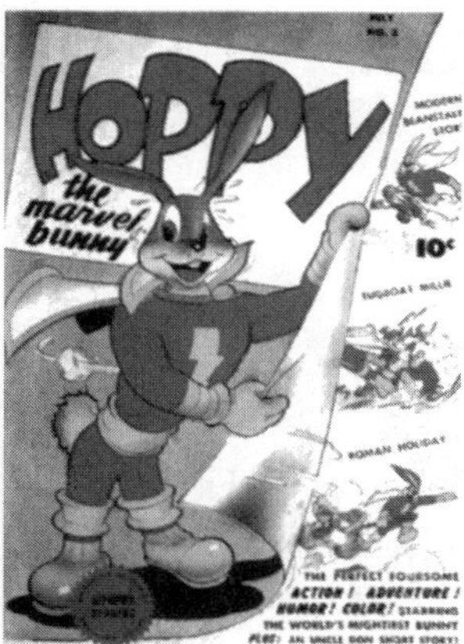

Hoppy The Marvel Bunney #3
© Fawcett Publications

HORRIFIC
Artful/Comic Media/
Harwell Publ./Mystery
Sept., 1952

1 Conductor in Flames(c) 300.00
2 Human Puppets(c) 175.00
3 DH(c),Bullet hole in head(c) 300.00
4 DH(c),head on a stick (c) 125.00
5 DH(c) 150.00
6 DH(c),Jack the Ripper 125.00
7 DH(c),Shrunken Skulls 125.00
8 DH(c),I:The Teller 150.00
9 DH(c),Claws of Horror, Wolves of Midnight 125.00
10 DH(c),The Teller-four eerie tales of Horror 125.00
11 DH(c),A:Gary Ghoul,Freddie, Demon,Victor Vampire Walter Werewolf 100.00
12 DH(c),A:Gary Ghoul,Freddie Demon,Victor Vampire, Walter Werewolf 100.00
13 DH(c),A:Gary Ghoul,Freddie Demom,Victor Vampire, Walter Werewolf 100.00

Becomes:

TERRIFIC COMICS

14 . . . . 225.00
15 . . . . 150.00
16 B:Wonderboy 150.00

Becomes:

WONDERBOY

17 The Enemy's Enemy 350.00
18 Success is No Accident, July, 1955 . . . . 300.00

HORROR FROM THE TOMB (see MYSTERIOUS STORIES)

HORRORS, THE
Star Publications
Jan., 1953

11 LbC(c),JyD,of War 225.00
12 LbC(c),of War 200.00
13 LbC(c),of Mystery 175.00
14 LbC(c),of the Underworld 200.00
15 LbC(c),of the Underworld, April, 1954 . . . . 200.00

HORSE FEATHER COMICS
Lev Gleason Publications
Nov., 1947

1 BW 135.00
2 . . . . 75.00
3 . . . . 50.00
4 Summer, 1948 . . . . 50.00

HOT ROD AND SPEEDWAY COMICS
Hillman Periodicals
Feb.–March, 1952

1 . . . . 225.00
2 BK 150.00
3 . . . . 75.00
4 . . . . 75.00
5 April–May, 1953 . . . . 75.00

HOT ROD COMICS
Fawcett Publications
Feb., 1952–53

N# BP,BP(c),F:Clint Curtis 225.00
2 BP,BP(c),Safety comes First . . 150.00
3 BP,BP(c),The Racing Game . . 100.00
4 BP,BP(c),Bonneville National Championships 100.00
5 BP,BP(c), ... 100.00
6 BP,BP(c),Race to Death 100.00

HOT ROD KING
Approved Comics
(Ziff-Davis), Fall, 1952

1 P(c) 200.00

HOWDY DOODY
Dell Publishing Co.
Jan., 1950

1 Ph(c) 950.00
2 Ph(c) 400.00
3 Ph(c) 225.00
4 Ph(c) 225.00
5 Ph(c) 225.00
6 P(c) 200.00
7 . . . . 175.00
8 . . . . 175.00
9 . . . . 175.00
10 . . . . 175.00
11 . . . . 150.00
12 . . . . 150.00
13 Christmas (c) 150.00
14 thru 20 . . . . @150.00
21 thru 38 . . . . @125.00

HOW STALIN HOPES WE WILL DESTROY AMERICA
Pictorial News, 1951

N# (Giveaway) 450.00

HUMBUG
Harvey Kurtzman, 1957

1 JDa,WW,WE,End of the World 225.00
2 JDa,WE,Radiator 125.00
3 JDa,WE 100.00
4 JDa,WE,Queen Victoria(c) . . . 100.00
5 JDa,WE 100.00
6 JDa,WE 100.00
7 JDa,WE,Sputnik(c) 110.00
8 JDa,WE,Elvis/George Washington(c) 100.00
9 JDa,WE 100.00
10 JDa,Magazine 125.00
11 JDw,WE,HK,Magazine 125.00

HUMDINGER
Novelty Press/
Premium Service
May–June, 1946

1 B:Jerkwater Line,Dink, Mickey Starlight 250.00
2 . . . . 125.00
3 . . . . 100.00
4 . . . . 100.00
5 . . . . 100.00
6 . . . . 100.00
2-1 . . . . 75.00
2-2 July–Aug., 1947 . . . . 75.00

HUMPHREY COMICS
Harvey Publications
Oct., 1948

1 BP,Joe Palooka 80.00
2 BP 50.00
3 BP 40.00
4 BP,A:Boy Heroes 50.00
5 BP 35.00
6 BP 35.00
7 BP,A:Little Dot 35.00
8 BP,O:Humphrey 40.00
9 BP 25.00
10 BP. 25.00
11 thru 21 . . . . @25.00
22 April, 1952. . . . . 25.00

HYPER MYSTERY COMICS
Hyper Publications
May, 1940

1 B:Hyper 1,600.00
2 June, 1940 . . . . 900.00

IBIS, THE INVINCIBLE
Fawcett Publications
Jan., 1942

1 MRa(c),O:Ibis 1,500.00
2 Bondage cover 800.00
3 BW 600.00
4 BW,A:Mystic Snake People . . 400.00
5 BW,Bondage cover,The Devil's Ibistick 425.00
6 BW, The Book of Evil, Spring, 1948 . . . . 425.00

IDEAL ROMANCE
(see TENDER ROMANCE)

IF THE DEVIL WOULD TALK
Catechetical Guild, 1950

N# Rare. 700.00
N#, 1958 Very Rare. 450.00

ILLUSTRATED STORIES OF THE OPERA
B. Bailey Publ. Co., 1943

N# Faust 500.00
N# Aida 450.00
N# Carman 450.00
N# Rigoletto 450.00

I LOVED
(see ZOOT COMICS)

I LOVE LUCY COMICS
Dell Publishing Co.
Feb., 1954

(1) *see Dell Four Color #535*
(2) *see Dell Four Color #559*
3 Lucile Ball Ph(c) all. 225.00
4 . . . . 200.00
5 . . . . 200.00
6 thru 10 . . . . @175.00
11 thru 20. . . . . 125.00
21 thru 35. . . . . 100.00

IMPACT
E.C. Comics
March–April, 1955

1 RC,GE,BK,Grl 150.00
2 RC,JDu,Grl,BK,JO 100.00
3 JO,RC,JDU,Grl,JKa,BK 80.00
4 RC,JO,JDa,GE,Grl,BK 80.00
5 Nov.–Dec., 1955 . . . . 80.00

INCREDIBLE SCIENCE FANTASY
(see WEIRD SCIENCE)

INCREDIBLE SCIENCE FICTION
E.C. Comics
July–Aug., 1955

30 . . . . 300.00
31 . . . . 325.00
32 Jan.–Feb., 1956. . . . . 325.00
33. . . . . 300.00

INDIAN CHIEF
Dell Publishing Co.
July–Sept., 1951

3 P(c) all 40.00
4 . . . . 25.00
5 . . . . 25.00
6 A:White Eagle. 25.00
7 . . . . 25.00
8 . . . . 25.00
9 . . . . 25.00
10 . . . . 25.00
11 . . . . 25.00
12 I:White Eagle. 35.00
13 thru 29. . . . . @15.00
30 SB. 20.00
31 thru 33 SB . . . . @20.00

INDIAN FIGHTER
Youthful Magazines
May, 1950

1 Revenge of Chief Crazy Horse 100.00
2 Bondage cover 50.00
3 . . . . 35.00
4 Cheyenne Warpath 35.00
5 . . . . 35.00
6 Davy Crockett in Death Stalks the Alamo 35.00
7 Tom Horn-Bloodshed at Massacre Valley 35.00
8 Tales of Wild Bill Hickory, Jan., 1952 . . . . 35.00

INDIANS
Wings Publ. Co.
(Fiction House)
Spring, 1950

1 B:Long Bow, Manzar, White Indian & Orphan 200.00
2 B:Starlight 100.00
3 Longbow(c) 75.00
4 Longbow(c) 60.00
5 Manzar(c). 75.00
6 Captive of the Semecas 60.00
7 Longbow(c) 60.00
8 A:Long Bow 60.00
9 A:Long Bow 60.00
10 Manzar(c) 60.00
11 thru 16 . . . . @50.00
17 Spring, 1953,Longbow(c). 50.00

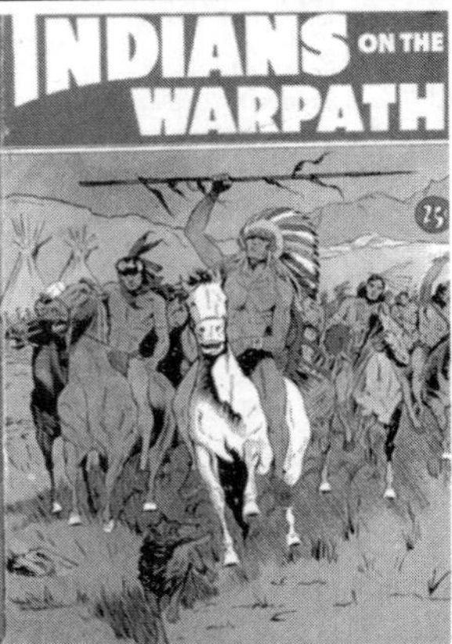

Indians on the Warpath
© St. John Publ. Co.

INDIANS ON THE WARPATH
St. John Publ. Co., 1950

N# MB(c). 225.00

INFORMER, THE
Feature Television Productions
April, 1954

1 MSy,The Greatest Social Menace of our Time! 75.00
2 MSy 50.00
3 MSy 45.00
4 MSy 45.00
5 Dec., 1954 . . . . 45.00

IN LOVE
Mainline/Charlton Comics
Aug., 1954

1 S&K,Bride of the Star 250.00
2 S&K,Marilyn's Men 150.00
3 S&K 125.00
4 S&K,Comics Code 75.00
5 S&K(c) 75.00
6 . . . . 40.00

Becomes:

I LOVE YOU

7 JK(c),BP 100.00
8 . . . . 35.00
9 . . . . 35.00
10 . . . . 35.00
11 thru 16 . . . . @30.00
17 . . . . 25.00
18 . . . . 15.00
19 . . . . 15.00
20. . . . . 15.00
21 thru 50 . . . . @10.00
51 thru 59 . . . . @7.00
60 Elvis 100.00
61 thru 100 . . . . @6.00
101 thru 130 . . . . @5.00

INTERNATIONAL COMICS
(see CRIME PATROL)

INTERNATIONAL CRIME PATROL
(see CRIME PATROL)

GOLDEN AGE

INTIMATE CONFESSIONS
Fawcett Publ./ Realistic Comics, 1951

1a P(c) all, Unmarried Bride . . . 600.00
1 EK,EK(c),Days of Temptation... Nights of Desire . . . 175.00
2 Doomed to Silence . . . 150.00
3 EK(c), The Only Man For Me . 175.00
3a Robert Briffault . . . 150.00
4 EK(c),Tormented Love . . . 150.00
5 Her Secret Sin . . . 150.00
6 Reckless Pick-up . . . 150.00
7 A Love Like Ours,Spanking. . . 175.00
8 Fatal Woman, March, 1953 . . 150.00

INTIMATE LOVE
Standard Magazines Jan., 1950

5 Wings on My Heart,Ph(c) . . . 60.00
6 WE,JSe,Ph(c). . . . 75.00
7 WE,JSe,Ph(c),I Toyed with Love . . . 75.00
8 WE,JSe,Ph(c). . . . 75.00
9 Ph(c) . . . 35.00
10 Ph(c),My Hopeless Heart. . . . 50.00
11 . . . 25.00
12 . . . 25.00
13 thru 18. . . . @25.00
19 ATh . . . 50.00
20 . . . 20.00
21 ATh . . . 50.00
22 ATh . . . 50.00
23 ATh . . . 20.00
24 ATh . . . 50.00
25 ATh . . . 20.00
26 ATh . . . 50.00
27 ATh . . . 20.00
28 ATh,Aug., 1954 . . . 20.00

INTIMATE SECRETS OF ROMANCE
Star Publications Sept., 1953

1 LbC(c) . . . 125.00
2 LbC(c) . . . 100.00

INVISIBLE SCARLET O'NEIL
Harvey Publications Dec., 1950

1 . . . 100.00
2 . . . 75.00
3 April, 1951 . . . 75.00

IT REALLY HAPPENED
William H. Wise/ Visual Editions, 1945

1 Benjamin Franklin, Kit Carson 150.00
2 The Terrible Tiddlers . . . 75.00
3 Maid of the Margiris . . . 60.00
4 Chaplain Albert J. Hoffman . . . 60.00
5 AS(c),Monarchs of the Sea,Lou Gehrig, Amelia Earhart . . . 125.00
6 AS(c),Ernie Pyle . . . 60.00
7 FG,Teddy Roosevelt,Jefferson Davis, Story of the Helicopter 60.00
8 FG,Man O' War,Roy Rogers . . 125.00
9 AS(c),The Story of Old Ironsides . . . 60.00
10 AS(c),Honus Wagner, The Story of Mark Twain . . . 100.00
11 AS(c),MB,Queen of the Spanish Main, Oct., 1947. . . 75.00

JACK ARMSTRONG
Parents' Institute Nov., 1947

1 Artic Mystery . . . 350.00
2 Den of the Golden Dragon . . . 150.00
3 Lost Valley of Ice . . . 125.00
4 Land of the Leopard Men . . . 125.00
5 Fight against Racketeers of the Ring . . . 125.00
6 . . . 100.00
7 Baffling Mystery on the Diamond . . . 100.00
8 . . . 100.00
9 Mystery of the Midgets . . . 100.00
10 Secret Cargo . . . 100.00
11 . . . 100.00
12 Madman's Island, rare . . . 125.00
13 Sept., 1949 . . . 100.00

JACE PEARSON OF THE TEXAS RANGERS
Dell Publishing Co. May, 1952

(1) *see Dell Four Color #396*
2 Ph(c),Joel McRae . . . 50.00
3 Ph(c),Joel McRae . . . 50.00
4 Ph(c),Joel McRae . . . 50.00
5 Ph(c),Joel McRae . . . 50.00
6 Ph(c),Joel McRae . . . 50.00
7 Ph(c),Joel McRae . . . 50.00
8 Ph(c),Joel McRae . . . 50.00
9 Ph(c),Joel McRae . . . 50.00
(10) *see Dell Four Color #648*
Becomes:

TALES OF JACE PEARSON OF THE TEXAS RANGERS

11 . . . 30.00
12 . . . 30.00
13 . . . 30.00
14 . . . 30.00
15 ATh . . . 40.00
16 ATh . . . 40.00
17 thru 20 . . . @30.00

JACKIE GLEASON
St. John Publishing Co. Sept., 1955

1 Ph(c) . . . 700.00
2 . . . 500.00
3 . . . 400.00
4 Dec., 1955 . . . 375.00

Jackie Gleason #4
© St. John Publishing Co.

JACKIE ROBINSON
Fawcett Publications May, 1950

N# Ph(c) all issues. . . . 800.00
2 . . . 500.00
3 thru 5 . . . @400.00
6 May, 1952 . . . 375.00

JACK IN THE BOX
(see YELLOW JACKET COMICS)

JACKPOT COMICS
MLJ Magazines Spring, 1941

1 CBi(c),B:Black Hood,Mr.Justice, Steel Sterling,Sgt.Boyle . . 2,400.00
2 SCp(c), . . . 1,100.00
3 Bondage cover . . . 800.00
4 First Archie . . . 3,500.00
5 Hitler(c) . . . 1,200.00
6 Son of the Skull v:Black Hood, Bondage(c) . . . 900.00
7 Bondage (c) . . . 900.00
8 Sal(c), . . . 900.00
9 Sal(c), . . . 900.00
Becomes:

JOLLY JINGLES

10 Super Duck,(fa) . . . 300.00
11 Super Duck . . . 150.00
12 Hitler parody cover,A:Woody Woodpecker . . . 100.00
13 Super Duck . . . 65.00
14 Super Duck . . . 65.00
15 Super Duck . . . 65.00
16 Dec., 1944. . . . 65.00

JACK THE GIANT KILLER
Bimfort & Co. Aug.–Sept., 1953

1 HcK,HcK(c). . . . 165.00

JAMBOREE
Round Publishing Co. Feb., 1946

1 . . . 200.00
2 March, 1946 . . . 100.00

JANE ARDEN
St. John Publ. Co. March, 1948

1 . . . 120.00
2 June, 1948 . . . 70.00

JEEP COMICS
R.B. Leffingwell & Co. Winter, 1944

1 B;Captain Power. . . . 350.00
2 . . . 250.00
3 LbC(c),March–April, 1948 . . . 350.00

JEFF JORDAN, U.S. AGENT
D.S. Publ. Co., Dec., 1947

1 . . . 100.00

GOLDEN AGE

JESSE JAMES
Avon Periodicals/ Realistic Publ.
Aug., 1950

1 JKu,The San Antonio Stage Robbery 125.00
2 JKu,The Daring Liberty Bank Robbery 110.00
3 JKu,The California Stagecoach Robberies 100.00
4 EK(c),Deadliest Deed! 35.00
5 JKu,WW,Great Prison Break . 100.00
6 JKu,Wanted Dead or Alive . . . 100.00
7 JKu,Six-Gun Slaughter at San Romano! 75.00
8 EK,Daring Train Robbery! 50.00
9 EK 30.00
10 thru 14 {Do not exist}
15 . . . . 40.00
16 . . . . 35.00
17 . . . . 25.00
18 JKu 25.00
19 JKu 25.00
20 AW,FF,A:Chief Vic,Kit West . . 100.00
21 . . . . 25.00
22 . . . . 25.00
23 . . . . 25.00
24 EK,B:New McCarty 25.00
25 EK. 25.00
26 EK. 25.00
27 EK,E:New McCarty 25.00
28 . . . . 25.00
29 Aug., 1956. . . . . 25.00

JEST
Harry 'A' Chesler, 1944

10 J. Rebel,Yankee Boy 125.00
11 1944,Little Nemo 150.00

JET ACES
Real Adventure Publ. Co. (Fiction House), 1952

1 Set 'em up in MIG Alley 100.00
2 Kiss-Off for Moscow Molly 60.00
3 Red Task Force Sighted 60.00
4 Death-Date at 40,000, 1953 . . . 60.00

JET FIGHTERS
Standard Magazines
Nov., 1953

5 ATh,Korean War Stories 85.00
6 Circus Pilot 35.00
7 ATh, Iron Curtains for Ivan, March, 1953 . . . . 50.00

JETTA OF THE 21st CENTURY
Standard Comics
Dec., 1952

5 Teen Stories 175.00
6 . . . . 100.00
7 April, 1953 . . . . 100.00

JIGGS AND MAGGIE
Best Books (Standard)/ Harvey Publ.
June, 1949

11 . . . . 75.00
12 thru 21 . . . . @50.00
22 thru 26 . . . . @30.00
27 Feb.–March, 1954 . . . . 30.00

JIM HARDY
Spotlight Publ., 1944

N# Dynamite Jim,Mirror Man . . . 300.00

JIM RAY'S AVIATION SKETCH BOOK
Vital Publishers
Feb., 1946

1 Radar, the Invisible eye 200.00
2 Gen.Hap Arnold, May, 1946 . . 175.00

JINGLE JANGLE COMICS
Eastern Color Printing Co.
Feb., 1942

1 B:Benny Bear,Pie Face Prince, Jingle Jangle Tales,Hortense 350.00
2 GCn 175.00
3 GCn 150.00
4 GCn,Pie Face cover 150.00
5 GCn,B:Pie Face 150.00
6 GCn, ... 135.00
7 . . . . 135.00
8 . . . . 135.00
9 . . . . 135.00
10 . . . . 135.00
11 thru 15 E:Pie Face . . . . @125.00
16 thru 20 . . . . @100.00
21 thru 25 . . . . @75.00
26 thru 30 . . . . @75.00
31 thru 41 . . . . @60.00
42 Dec., 1949. . . . . 60.00

JING PALS
Victory Publ. Corp.
Feb., 1946

1 Johnny Rabbit 75.00
2 . . . . 40.00
3 . . . . 40.00
4 Aug., 1948 . . . . 40.00

JOE COLLEGE
Hillman Periodicals
Fall, 1949

1 BP,DPr 75.00
2 BP, Winter, 1949 . . . . 60.00

JOE LOUIS
Fawcett Periodicals
Sept., 1950

1 Ph(c),Life Story. 500.00
2 Ph(c),Nov., 1950 . . . . 300.00

JOE PALOOKA
Publication Enterprises (Columbia Comics Group)
1943

1 Lost in the Desert 650.00
2 Hitler cover 400.00
3 KO's the Nazis! 275.00
4 Eiffel tower cover, 1944 . . . . . 250.00

JOE PALOOKA
Harvey Publications
Nov., 1954–March, 1961

1 Joe Tells How he became World Champ 400.00
2 Skiing cover 175.00
3 . . . . 100.00
4 Welcome Home Pals! 100.00

Joe Palooka #1
© Harvey Publications

5 S&K,The Great Carnival Murder Mystery 150.00
6 Classic Joe Palooka (c) 100.00
7 BP,V:Grumpopski 100.00
8 BP,Mystery of the Ghost Ship . 75.00
9 Drooten Island Mystery 75.00
10 BP. 75.00
11 . . . . 65.00
12 BP,Boxing Course 65.00
13 . . . . 60.00
14 BP,Palooka's Toughest Fight . . 60.00
15 BP,O:Humphrey. 100.00
16 BP,A:Humphrey 60.00
17 BP,A:Humphrey 60.00
18 . . . . 60.00
19 BP,Freedom Train(c) 75.00
20 Punch Out(c). 60.00
21 . . . . 50.00
22 V:Assassin. 50.00
23 Big Bathing Beauty Issue. 50.00
24 . . . . 50.00
25 . . . . 50.00
26 BP,Big Prize Fight Robberies . . 50.00
27 BP,Mystery of Bal Eagle Cabin 50.00
28 BP,Fights out West 50.00
29 BP,Joe Busts Crime Wide Open. 50.00
30 BP,V:Hoodlums 40.00
31 BP. 40.00
32 BP,Fight Palooka was sure to Lose. 40.00
33 BP,Joe finds Ann 40.00
34 BP,How to Box like a Champ . . 40.00
35 BP,More Adventures of Little Max 40.00
36 BP. 40.00
37 BP,Joe as a Boy 40.00
38 BP. 40.00
39 BP,Original Hillbillies with Big Leviticus. 40.00
40 BP,Joe's Toughest Fight 40.00
41 BP,Humphrey's Grudge Fight. . 40.00
42 BP. 40.00
43 BP. 40.00
44 BP,M:Ann Howe. 50.00
45 BP. 35.00
46 Champ of Champs. 35.00
47 BreathtakingUnderwaterBattle . 35.00
48 BP,Exciting Indian Adventure . . 35.00
49 BP. 35.00
50 BP,Bondage(c) 35.00
51 BP. 35.00
52 BP,V:Balonki 35.00
53 BP. 35.00

54 V:Bad Man Trigger McGehee . . 35.00
55 . . . 35.00
56 Foul Play on the High Seas . . . 35.00
57 Curtains for the Champ 35.00
58 V:The Man-Eating Swamp Terror . . . 35.00
59 The Enemy Attacks 35.00
60 Joe Fights Escaped Convict . . 35.00
61 . . . 30.00
62 S&K. . . . 45.00
63 . . . 30.00
64 . . . 30.00
65 . . . 30.00
66 . . . 30.00
67 . . . 30.00
68. . . . 30.00
69 A Package from Home. 30.00
70 BP. . . . 30.00
71 . . . 30.00
72 . . . 30.00
73 BP. . . . 30.00
74 thru 118 . . . @30.00
Giant 1 Body Building. 65.00
Giant 2 Fights His Way Back . . . 125.00
Giant 3 Visits Lost City 60.00
Giant 4 All in Family 65.00

JOE YANK

Visual Editions
(Standard Comics)
March, 1952

5 ATh,WE,Korean Jackpot! 60.00
6 Bacon and Bullets, G.I.Renegade . . . 40.00
7 Two-Man War,A:Sgt. Glamour . 30.00
8 ATh(c),Miss Foxhole of 1952, . 30.00
9 G.I.'s and Dolls,Colonel Blood . 25.00
10 A Good Way to Die, A:General Joe . . . 25.00
11 . . . 25.00
12 RA. . . . 25.00
13 . . . 25.00
14 . . . 25.00
15 . . . 25.00
16 July, 1954 . . . 25.00

JOHN HIX SCRAPBOOK

Eastern Color Printing Co.
1937

1 Strange as It Seems 250.00
2 Strange as It Seems 200.00

JOHNNY DANGER

Toby Press, Aug., 1954

1 Ph(c),Private Detective 125.00

JOHNNY DYNAMITE

(see DYNAMITE)

JOHNNY HAZARD

Best Books
(Standard Comics)
Aug., 1948

5 FR . . . 150.00
6 FR,FR(c) . . . 100.00
7 FR(c) . . . 75.00
8 FR,FR(c), May, 1949 . . . . 75.00

JOHNNY LAW, SKY RANGER

Good Comics (Lev Gleason)
April, 1955

1 . . . 65.00
2 . . . 40.00
3 . . . 40.00
4 Nov., 1955 . . . 40.00

JOHN WAYNE ADVENTURE COMICS

Toby Press, Winter, 1949

1 Ph(c),The Mysterious Valley of Violence . . . 1,200.00
2 AW,FF,Ph(c) . . . 500.00
3 AW,FF,Flying Sheriff 500.00
4 AW,FF,Double-Danger,Ph(c) . 500.00
5 Volcano of Death,Ph(c) 450.00
6 AW,FF,Caravan of Doom, Ph(c) . . . 450.00
7 AW,FF,Ph(c) . . . 400.00
8 AW,FF,Duel of Death,Ph(c) . . 500.00
9 Ghost Guns,Ph(c) 300.00
10 Dangerous Journey,Ph(c). . . . 275.00
11 Manhunt!,Ph(c) 275.00
12 HK,Joins the Marines,Ph(c) . . 275.00
13 V:Frank Stacy 250.00
14 Operation Peeping John 250.00
15 Bridge Head 250.00
16 AW,FF,Golden Double-Cross . 250.00
17 Murderer's Music 250.00
18 AW,FF,Larson's Folly 300.00
19 . . . 225.00
20 Whale Cover 225.00
21 . . . 225.00
22 Flash Flood!. 225.00
23 Death on Two Wheels 225.00
24 Desert . . . 225.00
25 AW,FF,Hondo!,Ph(c) 300.00
26 Ph(c) . . . 275.00
27 Ph(c) . . . 275.00
28 Dead Man's Boots!. 275.00
29 AW,FF,Ph(c),Crash in California Desert. 300.00
30 The Wild One, Ph(c) 275.00
31 AW,FF,May, 1955. . . . . 300.00

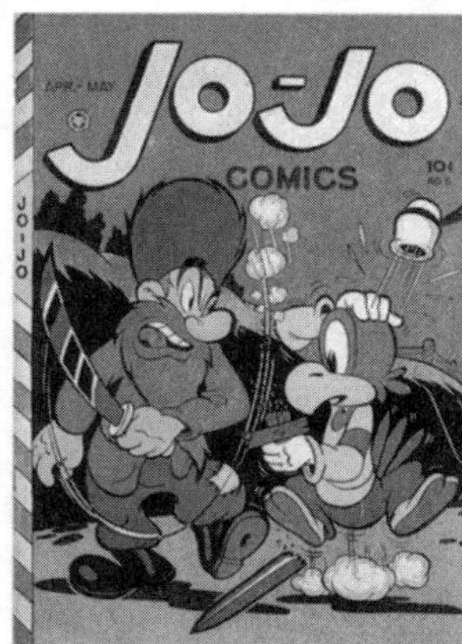

Jo-Jo #6
© Fox Features Syndicate

JO-JO COMICS

Fox Features Syndicate
Spring, 1946

N# (fa) . . . 60.00
2 (fa). . . . 50.00
3 (fa). . . . 50.00
4 (fa). . . . 50.00
5 (fa). . . . 50.00
6 (fa). . . . 50.00
7 B:Jo-Jo Congo King 700.00
8 (7)B:Tanee,V:The Giant Queen. 500.00
9 (8)The Mountain of Skulls 425.00
10 (9)Death of the Fanged Lady . 400.00
11 (10) . . . 400.00
12 (11)Bondage(c), Water Warriors 375.00
13 (12) Jade Juggernaut. 350.00
14 The Leopards of Learda. 350.00
15 The Flaming Fiend. 350.00
16 Golden Gorilla,bondage(c) . . . 350.00
17 Stark-Mad Thespian, bondage(c). 375.00
18 The Death Traveler 350.00
19 Gladiator of Gore 350.00
20 . . . 350.00
21 . . . 350.00
22 . . . 350.00
23 . . . 350.00
24 . . . 350.00
25 Bondage(c) . . . 375.00
26 . . . 350.00
27 . . . 350.00
28 . . . 350.00
29 July, 1949 . . . 400.00

JOURNEY INTO FEAR

Superior Publications
May, 1951

1 MB,Preview of Chaos 500.00
2 Debt to the Devil. 300.00
3 Midnight Prowler 250.00
4 Invisible Terror 250.00
5 Devil Cat . . . 200.00
6 Partners in Blood 200.00
7 The Werewolf Lurks 200.00
8 Bells of the Damned 200.00
9 Masked Death 200.00
10 Gallery of the Dead 200.00
11 Beast of Bedlam 175.00
12 No Rest for the Dead. 175.00
13 Cult of the Dead. 175.00
14 Jury of the Undead 175.00
15 Corpse in Make-up 200.00
16 Death by Invitation. 175.00
17 Deadline for Death. 175.00
18 Here's to Horror 175.00
19 This Body is Mine! 175.00
20 Masters of the Dead 175.00
21 Horror in the Clock, Sept., 1954. . . . . 175.00

JUDO JOE

Jay-Jay Corp.
Aug., 1952

1 Drug. . . . 75.00
2 . . . 50.00
3 Drug, Dec., 1953 . . . . 50.00

JUDY CANOVA

Fox Features Syndicate
May, 1950

23 (1)WW,WW(c) 150.00
24 (2)WW,WW(c) 140.00
3 JO,WW,WW(c) Sept., 1950 . . . . 175.00

JUKE BOX

Famous Funnies
March, 1948

1 ATh(c),Spike Jones. 350.00
2 Dinah Shore,Transvestitism . . 250.00
3 Vic Damone 175.00
4 Jimmy Durante 175.00
5 . . . 150.00
6 Jan., 1949,Desi Arnaz 200.00

GOLDEN AGE

JUMBO COMICS
Real Adventure Publ. Co. (Fiction House)
Sept., 1938

1 LF,BKa,JK,WE,WE(c),B:Sheena Queen of the Jungle,The Hawk The Hunchback 18,000.00
2 LF,JK,WE,BKa,BP, O:Sheena 6,600.00
3 JK,WE,WE(c),BP,LF,BKa . . 4,000.00
4 WE,WE(c),MMe,LF,BKa, O:The Hawk 3,800.00
5 WE,WE(c),BP,BKa 3,200.00
6 WE,WE(c),BP,BKa 2,900.00
7 WE,BKa,BP 2,800.00
8 LF(c),BP,BKa,World of Tommorow. 2,800.00
9 LF(c),BP 2,500.00
10 WE,LF(c),BKa,Regular size issues begin 1,500.00
11 LF(c),WE&BP,War of the Emerald Gas 1,000.00
12 WE(c),WE&BP,Hawk in Buccaneer Vengeance,Bondage(c) . . . 1,100.00
13 WE(c),BP,Sheena in The Thundering Herds 1,000.00
14 WE(c),LF,BP,Hawk in Siege of Thunder Isle,B:Lightning 1,200.00
15 BP(c),BP,Sheena(c). 650.00
16 BP(c),BP,The Lightning Strikes Twice 800.00
17 BP(c), all Sheena covers and lead stories 675.00
18 BP. 650.00
19 BP(c),BKa,Warriors of the Bush. 650.00
20 BP,BKa,Spoilers of the Wild 650.00
21 BP,BKa,Prey of the Giant Killers 500.00
22 BP,BKa,Victims of the Super-Ape,O:Hawk. 550.00
23 BP,BKa,Swamp of the Green Terror. 550.00
24 BP,BKa,Curse of the Black Venom 550.00
25 BP,BKa,Bait for the Beast . . . 500.00
26 BP,BKa,Tiger-Man Terror 500.00
27 BP,BKa,Sabre-Tooth Terror . . 500.00
28 BKa,RWd,The Devil of the Congo 500.00
29 BKa,RWd,Elephant-Scourge . 500.00
30 BKa,RWd,Slashing Fangs . . . 500.00
31 BKa,RWd,Voodoo Treasure of Black Slave Lake 450.00
32 BKa,RWd,AB,Captives of the Gorilla-Men. 450.00
33 BKa,RWd,AB,Stampede Tusks 450.00
34 BKa,RWd,AB,Claws of the Devil-Cat 450.00
35 BKa,RWd,AB,Hostage of the Devil Apes 450.00
36 BKa,RWd,AB,Voodoo Flames 450.00
37 BKa,RWd,AB,Congo Terror . . 450.00
38 BKa,RWd,ABDeath-Trap of the River Demons. 450.00
39 BKa,RWd,AB,Cannibal Bait . . 450.00
40 BKa,RWd,AB, Assagai Poison 450.00
41 BKa,RWd,AB,Killer's Kraal, Bondage(c). 350.00
42 BKa,RWd,AB,Plague of Spotted Killers 350.00
43 BKa,RWd,AB,Beasts of the Devil Queen 350.00
44 BKa,RWd,AB,Blood-Cult of K'Douma 350.00
45 BKa,RWd,AB,Fanged Keeper of the Fire-Gem 350.00

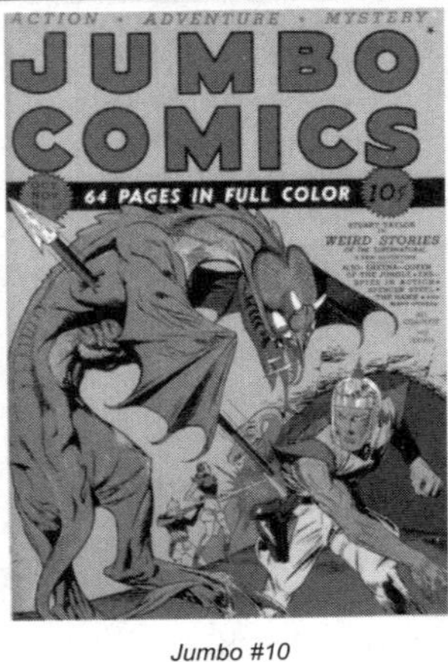

Jumbo #10
© Fiction House

46 BKa,RWd,AB,Lair of the Armored Monsters 350.00
47 BKa,RWd,AB,The Bantu Blood-Monster 350.00
48 BKa,RWd,AB,Red Meat for the Cat-Pack 350.00
49 BKa,RWd,AB,Empire of the Hairy Ones. 350.00
50 BKa,RWd,AB,Eyrie of the Leopard Birds 350.00
51 BKa,RWd.AB,Monsters with Wings. 275.00
52 BKa,RWd,AB,Man-Eaters Paradise. 275.00
53 RWd,AB,Slaves of the Blood Moon 275.00
54 RWd,AB,Congo Kill 275.00
55 RWd,AB,Bait for the Silver King Cat 275.00
56 RWd,AB,Sabre Monsters of the Aba-Zanzi,Bondage(c) . . 275.00
57 RWd,AB,Arena of Beasts. . . . 275.00
58 RWd,AB,Sky-Atlas of the Thunder-Birds. 275.00
59 RWd,AB,Kraal of Shrunken Heads 275.00
60 RWd,AB,Land of the Stalking Death 200.00
61 RWd,AB,King-Beast of the Masai 200.00
62 RWd,AB,Valley of Golden Death 200.00
63 RWd,AB,The Dwarf Makers . . 200.00
64 RWd,The Slave-Brand of Ibn Ben Satan,Male Bondage . . . 200.00
65 RWd,The Man-Eaters of Linpopo 200.00
66 RWd,Valley of Monsters. 200.00
67 RWd,Land of Feathered Evil . 200.00
68 RWd,Spear of Blood Ju-Ju. . . 200.00
69 RWd,AB,MB,Slaves for the White Sheik 200.00
70 RWd,AB,MB,The Rogue Beast's Prey. 200.00
71 RWd,AB,MB,The Serpent-God Speaks 175.00
72 RWd,AB,MB,Curse of the Half-Dead. 175.00
73 RWd,AB,MB,War Apes of the T'Kanis. 175.00
74 RWd,AB,MB,Drums of the Voodoo God 175.00
75 RWd,AB,MB,Terror Trail of the Devil's Horn 175.00
76 RWd,AB,MB,Fire Gems of Skull Valley. 175.00
77 RWd,AB,MB,Blood Dragons from Fire Valley 175.00
78 RWd,AB,MB,Veldt of the Vampire Apes. 175.00
79 RWd,AB,MB,Dancing Skeletons 175.00
80 RWd,AB,MB,Banshee Cats . . 175.00
81 RWd,MB,AB,JKa,Heads for King' Hondo's Harem 160.00
82 RWd,MB,AB,JKa,Ghost Riders of the Golden Tuskers 160.00
83 RWd,MB,AB,JKa,Charge of the Condo Juggernauts 160.00
84 RWd,MB,AB,JKa,Valley of the Whispering Fangs. 160.00
85 RWd,MB,AB,JKa,Red Tusks of Zulu-Za'an 160.00
86 RWd,MB,AB,JKa,Witch-Maiden of the Burning Blade. 160.00
87 RWd,AB,MB,JKa,Sargasso of Lost Safaris 160.00
88 RWd,AB,MB,JKa,Kill-Quest of the Ju-Ju Tusks 160.00
89 RWd,AB,MB,JKa,Ghost Slaves of Bwana Rojo 160.00
90 RWd,AB,MB,JKa,Death Kraal of the Mastadons 160.00
91 RWd,AB,MB,JKa,Spoor of the Sabre-Horn Tiger 150.00
92 RWd,MB,JKa,Pied Piper of the Congo 150.00
93 RWd,MB,JKa,The Beasts that Dawn Begot. 150.00
94 RWd,MB,JKa,Wheel of a Thousand Deaths. 150.00
95 RWd,MB,JKa,Flame Dance of the Ju-Ju Witch. 150.00
96 RWd,MB,JKa,Ghost Safari. . . 150.00
97 RWd,MB,JKa,Banshee Wail of the Undead,Bondage(c) . . 150.00
98 RWd,MB,JKa,Seekers of the Terror Fangs. 150.00
99 RWd,MB,JKa,Shrine of the Seven Souls. 150.00
100 RWd,MB,Slave Brand of Hassan Bey 175.00
101 RWd,MB,Quest of the Two-Face Ju Ju 135.00
102 RWd,MB,Viper Gods of Vengeance Veldt 135.00
103 RWd,MB,Blood for the Idol of Blades 135.00
104 RWd,MB,Valley of Eternal Sleep 135.00
105 RWd,MB,Man Cubs from Momba-Zu 200.00
106 RWd,MB,The River of No-Return 200.00
107 RWd,MB,Vandals of the Veldt. 135.00
108 RWd,MB,The Orphan of Vengeance Vale 135.00
109 RWd,MB,The Pygmy's Hiss is Poison 135.00
110 RWd,MB,Death Guards the Congo Keep 135.00
111 RWd,MB,Beware of the Witch-Man's Brew. 135.00
112 RWd,MB,The Blood-Mask from G'Shinis Grave 125.00
113 RWd,MB,The Mask's of Zombi-Zan 125.00
114 RWd,MB 125.00
115 RWd,MB,Svengali of the Apes. 125.00
116 RWd,MB,The Vessel of Marbel Monsters. 125.00
117 RWd,MB,Lair of the Half-Man King 125.00
118 RWd,MB,Quest of the

GOLDEN AGE

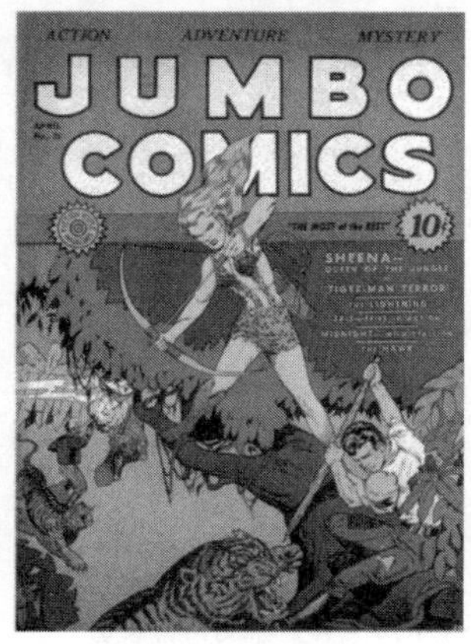

Jumbo Comics #26
© Fiction House

Congo Dwarflings 125.00
119 RWd,MB,King Crocodile's Domain 125.00
120 RWd,MB,The Beast-Pack Howls the Moon 125.00
121 RWd,MB,The Kraal of Evil Ivory 125.00
122 RWd,MB,Castaways of the Congo 125.00
123 RWd,MB, ... 125.00
124 RWd,MB,The Voodoo Beasts of Changra-Lo 125.00
125 RWd,MB,JKa(c),The Beast-Pack Strikes at Dawn 125.00
126 RWd,MB,JKa(c),Lair of the Swamp Beast 125.00
127 RWd,MB,JKa(c),The Phantom of Lost Lagoon 125.00
128 RWd,MB,JKa(c),Mad Mistress of the Congo-Tuskers 125.00
129 RWd,MB,JKa(c),Slaves of King Simbas Kraal 125.00
130 RWd,MB,JKa(c),Quest of the Pharaoh's Idol 125.00
131 RWd,JKa(c),Congo Giants at Bay 125.00
132 RWd,JKa(c),The Doom of the Devil's Gorge 125.00
133 RWd,JKa(c),Blaze the Pitfall Trail 125.00
134 RWd,JKa(c),Catacombs of the Jackal-Men 125.00
135 RWd,JKa(c),The 40 Thieves of Ankar-Lo 125.00
136 RWd,JKa(c),The Perils of Paradise Lost 125.00
137 RWd,JKa(c),The Kraal of Missing Men 125.00
138 RWd,JKa(c),The Panthers of Kajo-Kazar 125.00
139 RWd,JKa(c),Stampede of the Congo Lancers 125.00
140 RWd,JKa(c),The Moon Beasts from Vulture Valley . . 125.00
141 RWd,JKa(c),B:Long Bow . . . 135.00
142 RWd,JKa(c),Man-Eaters of N'Gamba 135.00
143 RWd,JKa(c),The Curse of the Cannibal Drum 135.00
144 RWd,JKa(c),The Secrets of Killers Cave 135.00
145 RWd,JKa(c),Killers of the Crypt 135.00
146 RWd,JKa(c),Sinbad of the Lost Lagoon 135.00
147 RWd,JKa(c),The Wizard of Gorilla Glade 135.00
148 RWd,JKa(c),Derelict of the Slave King 135.00
149 RWd,JKa(c),Lash Lord of the Elephants 135.00
150 RWd,JKa(c),Queen of the Pharaoh's Idol 125.00
151 RWd,The Voodoo Claws of Doomsday Trek 125.00
152 RWd,Red Blades of Africa . . 125.00
153 RWd,Lost Legions of the Nile 125.00
154 RWd,The Track of the Black Devil 125.00
155 RWd,The Ghosts of Blow- Gun Trail. 125.00
156 RWd,The Slave-Runners of Bambaru 125.00
157 RWd,Cave of the Golden Skull. 125.00
158 RWd,Gun Trek to Panther Valley 125.00
159 RWd,A:Space Scout. 110.00
160 RWd,Savage Cargo, E:Sheena covers 110.00
161 RWd,Dawns of the Pit 110.00
162 RWd,Hangman's Haunt 110.00
163 RWd,Cagliostro Cursed Thee. 110.00
164 RWd,Death Bars the Door . . 110.00
165 RWd,Day off from a Corpse . 110.00
166 RWd,The Gallows Bird 110.00
167 RWd,Cult of the Clawmen, March, 1953 . . . . 110.00

JUNGLE COMICS
Glen Kel Publ./Fiction House
Jan., 1940

1 HcK,DBr,LF(c),O:The White Panther,Kaanga,Tabu, B:The Jungle Boy,Camilla, all Kaanga covers & stories . . 3,800.00
2 HcK,DBr,WE(c),B:Fantomah 1,200.00
3 HcK,DBr,GT,The Crocodiles of Death River 1,100.00
4 HcK,DBr,Wambi in Thundering Herds 1,000.00
5 WE(c),GT,HcK,DBr,Empire of the Ape Men 1,100.00
6 WE(c),GT,DBr,HcK,Tigress of the Deep Jungle Swamp. . 600.00
7 BP(c),DBr,GT,HcK,Live Sacrifice,Bondage(c) 550.00
8 BP(c),GT,HcK,Safari into Shadowland 550.00
9 GT,HcK,Captive of the Voodoo Master 550.00
10 GT,HcK,BP,Lair of the Renegade Killer 550.00
11 GT,HcK,V:Beasts of Africa's Ancient Primieval Swamp Land 400.00
12 GT,HcK,The Devil's Death-Trap 400.00
13 GT(c),GT,HcK,Stalker of the Beasts 425.00
14 HcK,Vengeance of the Gorilla Hordes 400.00
15 HcK,Terror of the Voodoo Cauldron 400.00
16 HcK,Caveman Killers 400.00
17 HcK,Valley of the Killer-Birds . 400.00
18 HcK,Trap of the Tawny Killer, Bondage(c) 425.00
19 HcK,Revolt of the Man-Apes . 400.00
20 HcK,One-offering to Ju-Ju Demon 400.00
21 HcK,Monster of the Dismal Swamp, Bondage(c) 375.00
22 HcK,Lair o/t Winged Fiend . . . 350.00
23 HcK,Man-Eater Jaws 350.00
24 HcK,Battle of the Beasts 350.00
25 HcK,Kaghis the Blood God, Bondage(c). 375.00
26 HcK,Gorillas of the Witch-Queen 350.00
27 HcK,Spore o/t Gold-Raiders . . 350.00
28 HcK,Vengeance of the Flame God, Bondage(c) 375.00
29 HcK,Juggernaut of Doom. . . . 350.00
30 HcK,Claws o/t Black Terror . . 350.00
31 HcK,Land of Shrunken Skulls. 350.00
32 HcK,Curse of the King-Beast . 350.00
33 HcK,Scaly Guardians of Massacre Pool,Bondage(c). . 350.00
34 HcK,Bait of the Spotted Fury,Bondage(c). 350.00
35 HcK,Stampede of the Slave-Masters 350.00
36 HcK,GT,The Flame-Death of Ju Ju Mountain. 350.00
37 HcK,GT,Scaly Sentinel of Taboo Swamp 350.00
38 HcK,GT,Duel of the Congo Destroyers 350.00
39 HcK,Land of Laughing Bones. 350.00
40 HcK,Killer Plague 350.00
41 Hck,The King Ape Feeds at Dawn. 250.00
42 Hck,RC,Master of the Moon-Beasts 250.00
43 HcK,The White Shiek. 250.00
44 HcK,Monster of the Boiling Pool 255.00
45 HcK,The Bone-Grinders of B'Zambi, Bondage(c) 250.00
46 HcK,Blood Raiders of Tree Trail 250.00
47 HcK,GT,Monsters of the Man Pool, Bondage(c) 250.00
48 HcK,GT,Strangest Congo Adventure. 225.00
49 HcK,GT,Lair of the King -Serpent. 225.00
50 HcK,GT,Juggernaut of the Bush. 225.00
51 HcK,GT,The Golden Lion of Genghis Kahn 225.00
52 HcK,Feast for the River Devils, Bondage(c) 235.00
53 HcK,GT,Slaves for Horrors Harem 235.00
54 HcK,GT,Blood Bride of the Crocodile 225.00
55 HcK,GT,The Tree Devil 225.00

Jungle Comics #1
© Fiction House

56 HcK,Bride for the Rainmaker Raj 225.00
57 HcK,Fire Gems of T'ulaki 225.00
58 HcK,Land of the Cannibal God 225.00
59 HcK,Dwellers of the Mist Bondage(c). 235.00
60 HcK,Bush Devil's Spoor 225.00
61 HcK,Curse of the Blood Madness 225.00
62 Bondage(c) 235.00
63 HcK,Fire-Birds for the Cliff Dwellers 175.00
64 Valley of the Ju-Ju Idols 175.00
65 Shrine of the Seven Ju Jus, Bondage(c). 185.00
66 Spoor of the Purple Skulls . . . 175.00
67 Devil Beasts of the Golden Temple 175.00
68 Satan's Safari 175.00
69 Brides for the Serpent King . . 175.00
70 Brides for the King Beast, Bondage(c) 185.00
71 Congo Prey,Bondage(c). 185.00
72 Blood-Brand o/t Veldt Cats. . . 150.00
73 The Killer of M'omba Raj, Bondage(c). 175.00
74 AgF,GoldenJaws,Bondage(c) . 175.00
75 AgF,Congo Kill. 150.00
76 AgF,Blood Thrist of the Golden Tusk. 150.00
77 AgF,The Golden Gourds Shriek Blood,Bondage(c) . . . 175.00
78 AgF,Bondage(c). 175.00
79 AgF,Death has a Thousand Fangs 150.00
80 AgF,Salome of the Devil-Cats Bondage(c) 175.00
81 AgF,Colossus of the Congo . . 150.00
82 AgF,Blood Jewels of the Fire-Bird 150.00
83 AgF,Vampire Veldt, Bondage(c). 175.00
84 AgF,Blood Spoor of the Faceless Monster 150.00
85 AgF,Brides for the Man-Apes Bondage(c). 175.00
86 AgF,Firegems of L'hama Lost, Bondage(c) 175.00
87 AgF,Horror Kraal of the Legless One,Bondage(c) . . . 150.00
88 AgF,Beyond the Ju-Ju Mists. . 165.00
89 AgF,Blood-Moon over the Whispering Veldt 150.00
90 AgF,The Skulls for the Altar of Doom,Bondage(c) . . 165.00
91 AgF,Monsters from the Mist Lands, Bondage(c) 165.00
92 AgF,Vendetta of the Tree Tribes. 150.00
93 AgF,Witch Queen of the Hairy Ones 150.00
94 AgF,Terror Raid of the Congo Caesar 150.00
95 Agf,Flame-Tongues of the Sky Gods 150.00
96 Agf,Phantom Guardians of the Enchanted Lake,Bondage(c). 135.00
97 AgF,Wizard of the Whirling Doom,Bondage(c) 165.00
98 AgF,Ten Tusks of Zulu Ivory . . 200.00
99 AgF,Cannibal Caravan, Bondage(c). 150.00
100 AgF,Hate has a Thousand Claws. 150.00
101 AgF,The Blade of Buddha, Bondage(c). 150.00
102 AgF,Queen of the Amazon Lancers 135.00
103 AgF,The Phantoms of Lost Lagoon 135.00

Jungle Comics #34
© Fiction House

104 AgF 135.00
105 AgF,The Red Witch of Ubangi-Shan 135.00
106 AgF,Bondage(c). 150.00
107 Banshee Valley 150.00
108 HcK,Merchants of Murder . . 150.00
109 HcK,Caravan of the Golden Bones 135.00
110 HcK,Raid of the Fire-Fangs . 135.00
111 HcK,The Trek of the Terror-Paws 135.00
112 HcK,Morass of the Mammoths 135.00
113 HcK,Two-Tusked Terror 135.00
114 HcK,Mad Jackals Hunt by Night 135.00
115 HcK,Treasure Trove in Vulture Sky. 135.00
116 HcK,The Banshees of Voodoo Veldt 135.00
117 HcK,The Fangs of the Hooded Scorpion 135.00
118 HcK,The Muffled Drums of Doom 135.00
119 HcK,Fury of the Golden Doom 135.00
120 HcK,Killer King Domain 135.00
121 HcK,Wolves of the Desert Night 135.00
122 HcK,The Veldt of Phantom Fangs 135.00
123 HcK,The Ark of the Mist-Maids 135.00
124 HcK,The Trail of the Pharaoh's Eye 135.00
125 HcK,Skulls for Sale on Dismal River. 135.00
126 HcK,Safari Sinister. 150.00
127 Hck,Bondage(c). 125.00
128 HcK,Dawn-Men of the Congo 125.00
129 Hck,The Captives of Crocodile Swamp 125.00
130 Hck,Phantoms of the Congo 125.00
131 HcK,Treasure-Tomb of the Ape-King 125.00
132 HcK,Bondage(c). 150.00
133 HcK,Scourge of the Sudan Bondage(c). 150.00
134 HcK,The Black Avengers of Kaffir Pass 125.00
135 Hck 125.00
136 HcK,The Death Kraals of Kongola 125.00
137 BWg(c),HcK,The Safari of Golden Ghosts 125.00
138 BWg(c),HcK,Track of the Black Terror Bondage(c) 125.00
139 BWg(c),HcK,Captain Kidd of the Congo 125.00
140 BWg(c),HcK,The Monsters of Kilmanjaro 125.00
141 BWg(c)HcK,The Death Hunt of the Man Cubs. 125.00
142 BWg(c),Hck,Sheba of the Terror Claws,Bondage(c) . . . 150.00
143 BWg(c)Hck,The Moon of Devil Drums 150.00
144 BWg(c)Hck,Quest of the Dragon's Claw 150.00
145 BWg(c)Hck,Spawn of the Devil's Moon. 150.00
146 BWg(c),HcK,Orphans of the Congo 150.00
147 BWG(c),HcK,The Treasure of Tembo Wanculu 150.00
148 BWg(c),HcK,Caged Beasts of Plunder-Men,Bondage(c) . 150.00
149 BWg(c),HcK. 125.00
150 BWg(c),HcK,Rhino Rampage, Bondage(c) 150.00
151 BWg(c),HcK. 125.00
152 BWg(c),HcK,The Rogue of Kopje Kull. 125.00
153 BWg(c),HcK,The Wild Men of N'Gara 125.00
154 BWg(c),HcK,The Fire Wizard 125.00
155 BWg(c),HcK,Swamp of the Shrieking Dead. 125.00
156 BWg(c),HcK. 125.00
157 BWg(c),HcK. 125.00
158 BWg(c),HcK,A:Sheena. 125.00
159 BWg(c),HcK,The Blow-Gun Kill 125.00
160 BWg,HcK,King Fang 125.00
161 BWg(c),HcK,The Barbarizi Man-Eaters 125.00
162 BWg(c) 125.00
163 BWg(c),Jackals at the Kill, Summer,1954 . . . . 125.00

JUNGLE JIM
Best Books
(Standard Comics)
Jan., 1949

11 . . . . 40.00
12 Mystery Island 30.00
13 Flowers of Peril 30.00
14 . . . . 30.00
15 . . . . 30.00
16 . . . . 30.00
17 . . . . 30.00
18 . . . . 30.00
19 . . . . 30.00
20 1951 . . . . 30.00

JUNGLE JIM
Dell Publishing Co.
Aug., 1953

(1) *see Dell Four Color #490*
(1) *see Dell Four Color #565*
3 P(c) all 30.00
4 . . . . 30.00
5 . . . . 30.00
6 . . . . 25.00
7 . . . . 25.00
8 . . . . 25.00
9 . . . . 25.00
10 . . . . 25.00
11 . . . . 25.00
12 . . . . 25.00
13 `Mystery Island' 25.00
14 `Flowers of Peril' 25.00
15 thru 20 . . . . @25.00

JUNGLE JO
Hero Books
(Fox Features Syndicate)
March, 1950

N# 300.00
1 Mystery of Doc Jungle 350.00
2 . . . . 275.00
3 The Secret of Youth,
Sept., 1950 . . . . 250.00

JUNGLE LIL
Hero Books
(Fox Features Syndicate)
April, 1950

1 Betrayer of the Kombe Dead. . 275.00
Becomes:

DOROTHY LAMOUR

2 WW,Ph(c)The Lost Safari 200.00
3 WW,Ph(c), Aug., 1950 . . . . . . 150.00

JUNGLE THRILLS (see TERRORS OF THE JUNGLE)

JUNIE PROM
Dearfield Publishing Co.
Winter, 1947

1 Teenage Stories 75.00
2 . . . . 50.00
3 thru 5 . . . . @40.00
6 June, 1949 . . . . 40.00

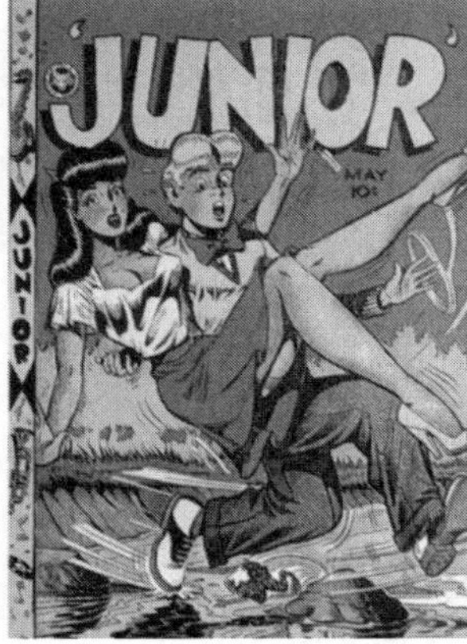

Junior #14
© Fox Features Syndicated

JUNIOR COMICS
Fox Features Syndicate
Sept., 1947

9 AF,AF(c) ,Teenage Stories . . . 650.00
10 AF,AF(c) 550.00
11 AF,AF(c) 550.00
12 AF,AF(c) 550.00
13 AF,AF(c) 550.00
14 AF,AF(c) 550.00
15 AF,AF(c) 550.00
16 AF,AF(c),July,1948. . . . . 550.00

JUNIOR HOOP COMICS
Stanmor Publications
Jan., 1952

1 . . . . 60.00
2 . . . . 40.00
3 July, 1952 . . . . 40.00

JUSTICE TRAPS THE GUILTY
Headline Publications
(Prize)
Oct.–Nov., 1947

2-1 S&K,S&K(c),Electric chair
cover 450.00
2 S&K,S&K(c) 250.00
3 S&K,S&K(c) 225.00
4 S&K,S&K(c),True Confession
of a Girl Gangleader 225.00
5 S&K,S&K(c) 225.00
6 S&K,S&K(c) 225.00
7 S&K,S&K(c) 225.00
8 S&K,S&K(c) 225.00
9 S&K,S&K(c) 225.00
10 S&K,S&K(c). 225.00
11 S&K,S&K(c). 100.00
12 . . . . 50.00
13 . . . . 60.00
14 . . . . 50.00
15 . . . . 50.00
16 . . . . 50.00
17 . . . . 50.00
18 S&K,S&K(c). 50.00
19 S&K,S&K(c). 50.00
20 . . . . 45.00
21 S&K. 80.00
22 S&K(c). 80.00
23 S&K(c). 80.00
24 . . . . 35.00
25 . . . . 35.00
26 . . . . 35.00
27 S&K(c). 50.00
28 . . . . 35.00
29 . . . . 35.00
30 S&K. 75.00
31 thru 50 . . . . @35.00
51 . . . . 30.00
52 . . . . 30.00
53 . . . . 30.00
54 . . . . 30.00
55 . . . . 30.00
56 . . . . 30.00
57 . . . . 30.00
58 Drug 200.00
59 thru 92 . . . . @30.00
Becomes:

FARGO KID
Headline Publications
(Prize)

93 AW,JSe,O:Kid Fargo 120.00
94 JSe 75.00
95 June–July, 1958,JSe 75.00

KA'A'NGA COMICS
Glen-Kel Publ.
(Fiction House)
Spring, 1949

1 Phantoms of the Congo 450.00
2 V:The Jungle Octopus 250.00
3 . . . . 150.00
4 The Wizard Apes of
Inkosi-Khan 135.00
5 . . . . 125.00
6 Captive of the Devil Apes 100.00
7 GT,Beast-Men of Mombassa . 110.00
8 The Congo Kill-Cry 100.00

Ka'a'nga #9
© Fiction House

9 . . . . 100.00
10 Stampede for Congo Gold . . . 100.00
11 Claws of the Roaring Congo . . 85.00
12 Bondage(c) 100.00
13 Death Web of the Amazons . . . 85.00
14 Slave Galley of the Lost
Nile Bondage(c) 100.00
15 Crocodile Moon,Bondage(c). . 100.00
16 Valley of Devil-Dwarfs 100.00
17 Tembu of the Elephants 75.00
18 The Red Claw of Vengeance . . 75.00
19 The Devil-Devil Trail. 75.00
20 The Cult of the Killer Claws,
Summer, 1954 . . . . 75.00

KASCO COMICS
Kasco Grainfeed
(Giveaway), 1945

1 BWo 125.00
2 1949,BWo 100.00

KATHY
Standard Comics
Sept., 1949

1 Teen-Age Stories 40.00
2 ASh 22.00
3 thru 6 . . . . @15.00
7 thru 17 . . . . @12.00

KATY KEENE
Archie Publications/Close-Up
Radio Comics, 1949

1 BWo 800.00
2 BWo 400.00
3 BWo 300.00
4 BWo 300.00
5 BWo 275.00
6 BWo 250.00
7 BWo 250.00
8 thru 12 BWo . . . . @225.00
13 thru 20 BWo. . . . . @200.00
21 thru 29 BWo. . . . . @150.00
30 thru 38 BWo. . . . . @135.00
39 thru 62 BWo. . . . . @125.00
Ann.#1 . . . . 375.00
Ann.#2 thru #6 . . . . 225.00

Keen Detective Funnies #13
© Centaur Publications

KEEN DETECTIVE FUNNIES
Centaur Publications
July, 1938

1-8 B:The Clock, ... 1,700.00
1-9 WE 700.00
1-10 . . . . 600.00
1-11 Dean Denton 600.00
2-1 The Eye Sees 550.00
2-2 JCo 550.00
2-3 TNT. 550.00
2-4 Gabby Flynn 550.00
5 . . . . 575.00
6 . . . . 550.00
7 Masked Marvel 2,000.00
8 PGn,Gabby Flynn,Nudity
Expanded 16 pages 700.00
9 Dean Denton 600.00
10 . . . . 600.00
11 BEv,Sidekick 575.00
12 Masked Marvel(c) 750.00
3-1 Masked Marvel(c). 600.00
3-2 Masked Marvel(c). 600.00
3-3 BEv 600.00
16 BEv. 600.00
17 JSm. 600.00
18 The Eye Sees,Bondage(c) . . . 550.00
19 LFe 550.00
20 BEv,The Eye Sees. 550.00
21 Masked Marvel(c) 550.00
22 Masked Marvel(c) 550.00
23 B:Airman 750.00
24 Airman. 800.00

KEEN KOMICS
Centaur Publications
May, 1939

1 Teenage Stories 800.00
2 PGn,JaB,CBu 500.00
3 JCo 500.00

KEEN TEENS
Life's Romances Publ./Leader/ Magazine Enterprises, 1945

N# P(c) 200.00
N# Ph(c),Van Johnson. 200.00
3 Ph(c), ... 60.00
4 Ph(c),Glenn Ford 60.00
5 Ph(c),Perry Como 60.00
6 . . . . 60.00

KEN MAYNARD WESTERN
Fawcett Publications
Sept., 1950

1 B:Ken Maynard & Tarzan
(horse) The Outlaw
Treasure Trail 500.00
2 Invasion of the Badmen 275.00
3 Pied Piper of the West 225.00
4 Outlaw Hoax 225.00
5 Mystery of Badman City 225.00
6 Redwood Robbery 225.00
7 Seven Wonders of the West . 225.00
8 Mighty Mountain Menace,
Feb.,1952. . . . . 225.00

KEN SHANNON
Quality Comics Group
Oct., 1951

1 RC, Evil Eye of Count Ducrie . 250.00
2 RC, Cut Rate Corpses 200.00
3 RC, Corpse that Wouldn't
Sleep 150.00
4 RC, Stone Hatchet Murder . . . 125.00
5 RC, Case of the Carney Killer 125.00
6 Weird Vampire Mob 150.00
7 RC,Ugliest Man in the World . 125.00
8 Chinatown Murders,Drug 150.00
9 RC, Necklace of Blood 100.00
10 RC, Shadow of the Chair,
Apr. 1953 . . . . 100.00

KERRY DRAKE DETECTIVE CASES
Life's Romances/M.E./, 1944

(1) *see N# A-1 Comics 200.00*
2 A:The Faceless Horror 125.00
3 . . . . 100.00
4 A:Squirrel, Dr. Zero, Caresse . 100.00
5 Bondage cover 110.00

Harvey Publ.

6 A:Stitches 75.00
7 A:Shuteye 80.00
8 Bondage cover 90.00
9 Drug 125.00
10 BP,A:Meatball,Drug 125.00
11 BP,I:Kid Gloves 60.00
12 BP. 60.00
13 BP,A:Torso. 50.00
14 BP,Bullseye Murder Syndicate . 50.00
15 BP,Fake Mystic Racket 50.00
16 BP,A:Vixen. 45.00
17 BP,Case of the $50,000
Robbery 45.00
18 BP,A:Vixen. 45.00
19 BP,Case of the Dope
Smugglers 50.00
20 BP,Secret Treasury Agent 45.00
21 BP,Murder on Record. 35.00
22 BP,Death Rides the Air Waves. 35.00
23 BP,Blackmailer's Secret
Weapon 35.00
24 Blackmailer's Trap 35.00
25 Pretty Boy Killer. 35.00
26 . . . . 35.00
27 . . . . 35.00
28 BP. 35.00
29 BP. 35.00
30 Mystery Mine,Bondage(c) 35.00
31 . . . . 35.00
32 . . . . 35.00
33 Aug., 1952. . . . . 35.00

KEWPIES
Will Eisner Publications
Spring, 1949

1 . . . . 350.00

KEY COMICS
Consolidated Magazines
Jan., 1944

1 B:The Key, Will-O-The-Wisp . 300.00
2 . . . . 175.00
3 . . . . 125.00
4 O:John Quincy,B:The Atom . . 150.00
5 HoK,Aug., 1946 . . . . 125.00

KID COWBOY
Approved Comics/ St. John Publ. Co., 1950

1 B:Lucy Belle & Red Feather . . 125.00
2 Six-Gun Justice 75.00
3 Shadow on Hangman's Bridge . 60.00
4 Red Feather V:Eagle of Doom . 50.00
5 Killers on the Rampage 50.00
6 The Stovepipe Hat 50.00
7 Ghost Town of Twin Buttes . . . 50.00
8 Thundering Hoofs 50.00
9 Terror on the Salt Flats 50.00
10 Valley of Death 50.00
11 Vanished Herds,Bondage(c). . . 60.00
12 . . . . 50.00
13 . . . . 50.00
14 1954 . . . . 50.00

KIDDIE KARNIVAL
Approved Comics, 1952

N# 275.00

KID ETERNITY
Comics Magazine (Quality Comics Group)
Spring, 1946

1 . . . . 700.00
2 . . . . 300.00
3 Follow Him Out of This World 325.00
4 Great Heroes of the Past 200.00
5 Don't Kid with Crime 175.00
6 Busy Battling Crime 175.00
7 Protects the World 175.00
8 Fly to the Rescue 175.00
9 Swoop Down on Crime 175.00
10 Golden Touch from Mr. Midas 175.00
11 Aid the Living by Calling
the Dead 150.00
12 Finds Death 150.00
13 Invades General Poschka . . . 150.00
14 Battles Double 150.00
15 A: Master Man 150.00
16 Balance Scales of Justice . . . 125.00
17 A:Baron Roxx 125.00
18 A:Man with Two Faces. 125.00

Becomes:

BUCCANEERS

19 RC,Sword Fight(c) 400.00
20 RC,Treasure Chest 275.00
21 RC,Death Trap. 325.00
22 A:Lady Dolores,Snuff,
Bondage(c). 225.00
23 RC,V:Treasure Hungry
Plunderers of the Sea. 250.00
24 A:Adam Peril,Black Roger,
Eric Falcon. 175.00
25 V:Clews 175.00
26 V:Admiral Blood. 175.00
27 RC,RC(c)May, 1951. . . . . 275.00

KID ZOO COMICS
Street & Smith, July, 1948
1 (fa) 200.00

KILLERS, THE
Magazine Enterprises, 1947
1 LbC(c),Thou Shall Not Kill. . . . 800.00
2 Grl,OW,Assassins Mad Slayers of the East,Hanging(c),Drug . 700.00

KILROYS, THE
B&L Publishing Co./ American Comics June–July, 1947
1 Three Girls in Love(c) 165.00
2 Flat Tire(c) 75.00
3 Right to Swear(c) 55.00
4 Kissing Booth(c) 55.00
5 Skiing(c) 55.00
6 Prom(c) 40.00
7 To School 40.00
8 . . . . 40.00
9 . . . . 40.00
10 B:Solid Jackson solo 40.00
11 . . . . 35.00
12 Life Guard(c) 35.00
13 thru 21 . . . . @35.00
22 thru 30 . . . . @30.00
31 thru 40 . . . . @25.00
41 thru 47 . . . . @20.00
48 3-D effect 120.00
49 3-D effect. 120.00
50 thru 54, July 1954 . . . . @20.00

KING COMICS
David McKay Publications April, 1936 (all have Popeye covers)
1 AR,EC,B:Popeye,Flash Gordon,B: Henry,Mandrake 8,000.00
2 AR,EC,Flash Gordon 2,500.00
3 AR,EC,Flash Gordon 1,600.00
4 AR,EC,Flash Gordon 1,300.00
5 AR,EC,Flash Gordon 1,000.00
6 AR,EC,Flash Gordon 700.00
7 AR,EC,King Royal Mounties . 675.00
8 AR,EC,Thanksgiving(c) 650.00
9 AR,EC,Christmas(c) 650.00
10 AR,EC,Flash Gordon 650.00
11 AR,EC,Flash Gordon 525.00
12 AR,EC,Flash Gordon 525.00
13 AR,EC,Flash Gordon 525.00
14 AR,EC,Flash Gordon 525.00
15 AR,EC,Flash Gordon 525.00
16 AR,EC,Flash Gordon 525.00
17 AR,EC,Flash Gordon 500.00
18 AR,EC,Flash Gordon 500.00
Covers say: "Starring Popeye"
19 AR,EC,Flash Gordon 500.00
20 AR,EC,Football(c) 500.00
21 AR,EC,Flash Gordon 400.00
22 AR,EC,Flash Gordon 400.00
23 AR,EC,Flash Gordon 400.00
24 AR,EC,Flash Gordon 400.00
25 AR,EC,Flash Gordon 400.00
26 AR,EC,Flash Gordon 350.00
27 AR,EC,Flash Gordon 350.00
28 AR,EC,Flash Gordon 350.00
29 AR,EC,Flash Gordon 350.00
30 AR,EC,Flash Gordon 350.00
31 AR,EC,Flash Gordon 350.00
32 AR,EC,Flash Gordon 350.00
33 AR,EC,Skiing(c). 350.00
34 AR,Ping Pong(c) 300.00
35 AR,Flash Gordon. 300.00
36 AR,Flash Gordon. 300.00

King Comics #15
© David McKay

37 AR,Flash Gordon. 300.00
38 AR,Flash Gordon. 300.00
39 AR,Baseball(c). 300.00
40 AR,Flash Gordon. 300.00
41 AR,Flash Gordon. 275.00
42 AR,Flash Gordon. 275.00
43 AR,Flash Gordon. 275.00
44 AR,Popeye golf(c) 275.00
45 AR,Flash Gordon. 275.00
46 AR,B:Little Lulu 275.00
47 AR,Flash Gordon. 275.00
48 AR,Flash Gordon. 275.00
49 AR,Weather Vane 275.00
50 AR,B:Love Ranger. 275.00
51 AR,Flash Gordon. 275.00
52 AR,Flash Gordon. 175.00
53 AR,Flash Gordon. 175.00
54 AR,Flash Gordon. 175.00
55 AR,Magic Carpet 175.00
56 AR,Flash Gordon. 175.00
57 AR,Cows Over Moon(c) 175.00
58 AR,Flash Gordon. 175.00
59 AR,Flash Gordon. 175.00
60 AR,Flash Gordon. 175.00
61 AR,B:Phantom,Baseball(c). . . 175.00
62 AR,Flash Gordon. 175.00
63 AR,Flash Gordon. 150.00
64 AR,Flash Gordon. 150.00
65 AR,Flash Gordon. 150.00
66 AR,Flash Gordon. 150.00
67 AR,Sweet Pea 150.00
68 AR,Flash Gordon. 150.00
69 AR,Flash Gordon. 150.00
70 AR,Flash Gordon. 150.00
71 AR,Flash Gordon. 150.00
72 AR,Flash Gordon. 125.00
73 AR,Flash Gordon. 125.00
74 AR,Flash Gordon. 125.00
75 AR,Flash Godron. 125.00
76 AR,Flag(c) 135.00
77 AR,Flash Gordon. 125.00
78 AR,Popeye,Olive Oil(c) 125.00
79 AR,Sweet Pea 125.00
80 AR,Wimpy(c) 125.00
81 AR,B:Blondie(c) 125.00
82 thru 91 AR . . . . @100.00
92 thru 98 AR . . . . @100.00
99 AR,Olive Oil(c). 100.00
100 . . . . 125.00
101 thru 116 AR . . . . @110.00
117 O:Phantom. 100.00
118 Flash Gordon 110.00
119 Flash Gordon 100.00
120 Wimpy(c). 75.00
121 thru 140 . . . . @75.00
141 Flash Gordon. 75.00
142 Flash Gordon. 75.00
143 Flash Gordon. 75.00
144 Flash Gordon. 75.00
145 Prince Valiant. 55.00
146 Prince Valiant. 55.00
147 Prince Valiant. 55.00
148 thru 154 . . . . @50.00
155 E:Flash Gordon 50.00
156 Baseball(c) 50.00
157 thru 159 . . . . @45.00

KING OF THE ROYAL MOUNTED
Dell Publishing Co. Dec., 1948–1958
(1) *see Dell Four Color #207*
(2) *see Dell Four Color #265*
(3) *see Dell Four Color #283*
(4) *see Dell Four Color #310*
(5) *see Dell Four Color #340*
(6) *see Dell Four Color #363*
(7) *see Dell Four Color #384*
8 Zane Grey adapt. 40.00
9 . . . . 40.00
10 . . . . 40.00
11 thru 28 . . . . @30.00

KIT CARSON
Avon Periodicals, 1950
N# EK(c) Indian Scout 100.00
2 EK(c),Kit Carson's Revenge, Doom Trail 60.00
3 EK(c),V:Comanche Raiders . . . 50.00
4 . . . . 50.00
5 EK(c),Trail of Doom 50.00
6 EK(c) 50.00
7 EK(c) 50.00
8 EK(c) 50.00
Becomes:

FIGHTING DAVY CROCKETT
9 EK(c),Oct./Nov., 1955 . . . . 45.00

KOKO AND KOLA
Compix/Magazine Enterprises Fall, 1946
1 (fa) 75.00
2 X-Mas Issue 40.00
3 . . . . 35.00
4 . . . . 35.00
5 . . . . 35.00
6 May, 1947 . . . . 35.00

KO KOMICS
Gerona Publications Oct., 1945
1 . . . . 550.00

KOMIK PAGES
Harry 'A' Chestler April, 1945
1 JK,Duke of Darkness 300.00

KRAZY KAT COMICS
Dell Publishing Co. May–June, 1951
1 . . . . 75.00
2 . . . . 50.00
3 . . . . 50.00
4 . . . . 50.00
5 . . . . 50.00

KRAZY LIFE
(See PHANTOM LADY)

LABOR IS A PARTNER
Catechetical Guild Educational Society, 1949
1 . . . . 175.00

LAFFY-DAFFY COMICS
Rural Home Publ. Co. Feb., 1945
1 (fa) 60.00
2 . . . . 60.00

LANCE O'CASEY
Fawcett, 1946–47
1 High Seas Adventure from Whiz comics 250.00
2 thru 4 . . . . @175.00

LAND OF THE LOST
EC Comics
July–Aug., 1946–Spring 1948
1 Radio show adapt. 250.00
2 . . . . 175.00
3 thru 9 . . . . @125.00

LARGE FEATURE COMICS
Dell Publishing Co., 1939
1 Dick Tracy vs. the Blank. . . . 1,500.00
2 Terry and the Pirates. 700.00
3 Heigh-Yo Silver! the Lone Ranger. 900.00
4 Dick Tracy gets his man 700.00
5 Tarzan of the Apes. 1,300.00
6 Terry and the Pirates. 650.00
7 Lone Ranger to the rescue . . . 800.00
8 Dick Tracy, Racket Buster. . . . 700.00
9 King of the Royal Mounted . . . 450.00
10 Gang Busters. 600.00
11 Dick Tracy, Mad Doc Hump . . 850.00
12 Smilin' Jack 550.00
13 Dick Tracy and Scottie of Scotland Yard. 850.00
14 Smilin' Jack helps G-Men. . . . 575.00
15 Dick Tracy and the kidnapped princes. 850.00
16 Donald Duck, 1st Daisy. . . . 5,500.00
17 Gang Busters. 425.00
18 Phantasmo The Master of the World 325.00
19 Walt Disney's Dumbo 2,400.00
20 Donald Duck. 5,500.00
21 Private Buck 100.00
22 Nuts and Jolts 100.00
23 The Nebbs. 125.00
24 Popeye in `Thimble Theatre' . 450.00
25 Smilin'Jack. 500.00
26 Smitty 225.00
27 Terry and the Pirates 550.00
28 Grin and Bear It. 75.00
29 Moon Mullins 200.00
30 Tillie the Toiler 175.00

[Series 2]
1 Peter Rabbit 350.00
2 Winnie Winkle. 150.00
3 Dick Tracy 600.00
4 Tiny Tim 250.00
5 Toots and Casper 100.00
6 Terry and the Pirates. 550.00
7 Pluto saves the Ship 1,200.00
8 Bugs Bunny 750.00
9 Bringing Up Father 150.00

Large Feature Comics #13
© Dell Publishing Co.

10 Popeye 400.00
11 Barney Google&SnuffySmith . 200.00
12 Private Buck 100.00
13 1001 Hours of Fun. 150.00

LARRY DOBY, BASEBALL HERO
Fawcett Publications, 1950
1 Ph(c),BW 650.00

LARS OF MARS
Ziff-Davis Publishing Co.
April–May, 1951
10 MA,`Terror from the Sky' 650.00
11 GC, The Terror Weapon. 550.00

LASH LARUE WESTERN
Fawcett Publications
Summer, 1949
1 Ph(c),The Fatal Roundups . . . 850.00
2 Ph(c),Perfect Hide Out 350.00
3 Ph(c),The Suspect 300.00
4 Ph(c),Death on Stage 300.00
5 Ph(c),Rustler's Haven 300.00
6 Ph(c) 250.00
7 Ph(c),Shadow of the Noose . . 225.00
8 Ph(c),Double Deadline 225.00
9 Ph(c),Generals Last Stand . . . 225.00
10 Ph(c) 225.00
11 Ph(c) 175.00
12 thru 20 Ph(c) . . . . @150.00
21 thru 29 Ph(c) . . . . @125.00
30 thru 46 Ph(c) . . . . @100.00
46 Ph(c),Lost Chance 100.00

LASSIE
(& SEVERAL SPECIAL ISSUES)
Dell Publishing Co.
Oct.–Dec., 1950
1 Ph(c) all 150.00
2 . . . . 75.00
3 . . . . 50.00
4 . . . . 50.00
5 . . . . 50.00
6 . . . . 50.00
7 . . . . 50.00
8 . . . . 50.00
9 . . . . 50.00
10 . . . . 50.00
11 . . . . 35.00
12 Rocky Langford 38.00
13 . . . . 35.00
14 . . . . 35.00
15 I:Timbu 38.00
16 . . . . 35.00
17 . . . . 35.00
18 . . . . 35.00
19 . . . . 35.00
20 MB 40.00
21 MB 40.00
22 MB 40.00
23 thru 38. . . . . @30.00
39 I:Timmy 35.00
40 thru 62 . . . . @25.00
63 E:Timmy 20.00
64 thru 70 . . . . @15.00

LATEST COMICS
Spotlight Publ./ Palace Promotions
March, 1945
1 Funny Animal-Super Duper. . . 100.00
2 . . . . 50.00

SPECIAL COMICS
MLJ Magazines (Archie Publ.)
Winter, 1941
1 O:Boy Buddies & Hangman, D:The Comet 2,200.00

Becomes:

HANGMAN COMICS
2 B:Hangman & Boy Buddies . 1,500.00
3 V:Nazis cover,Bondage(c) . . 1,000.00
4 V:Nazis cover 850.00
5 Bondage cover 850.00
6 . . . . 850.00
7 BF,Graveyard cover 850.00
8 BF 850.00

Becomes:

BLACK HOOD
9 BF 850.00
10 BF,A:Dusty, the Boy Detective. 500.00
11 Here lies the Black Hood 350.00
12 . . . . 325.00
13 EK(c). 325.00
14 EK(c). 325.00
15 EK. 325.00
16 EK(c). 325.00
17 Bondage cover 350.00
18 . . . . 325.00
19 I.D. Revealed. 450.00

Becomes:

LAUGH COMICS
20 BWo,B:Archie,Katy Keene . . . 500.00
21 BWo 250.00
22 BWo 250.00
23 Bwo. 250.00
24 BWo,JK,Pipsy 275.00
25 BWo 250.00
26 BWo 125.00
27 BWo 125.00
28 BWo 125.00
29 BWo 125.00
30 BWo 125.00
31 thru 40 BWo. . . . . @100.00
41 thru 50 BWo. . . . . @65.00
51 thru 60 BWo. . . . . @60.00
61 thru 80 BWo. . . . . @40.00
81 thru 99 BWo. . . . . @30.00
100 BWo 45.00
101 thru 126 BWo . . . . @25.00
127 A:Jaguar 30.00
128 A:The Fly. 30.00

 All comics prices listed are for *Near Mint* condition.

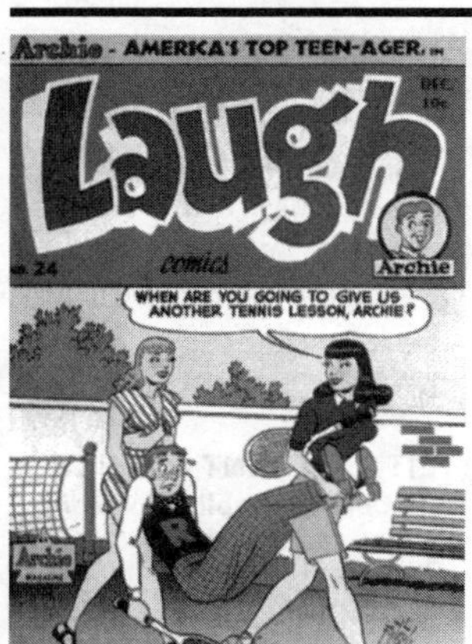

Laugh #24
© Archie Publications

129 A:The Fly 30.00
130 A:Jaguar 30.00
131 A:Jaguar 30.00
132 A:The Fly 30.00
133 A:Jaguar 30.00
134 A:The Fly 30.00
135 A:Jaguar 30.00
136 A:Fly Girl 30.00
137 A:Fly Girl 30.00
138 A:The Fly 30.00
139 A:The Fly 30.00
140 A:Jaguar 30.00
141 A:Jaguar 30.00
142 thru 144 . . . . . @30.00
145 A:Josie 20.00
146 thru 165 . . . . . @15.00
166 Beatles cover 20.00
167 thru 220 . . . . . @7.00
221 thru 250 . . . . . @5.00
251 thru 300 . . . . . @5.00
301 thru 400 . . . . . @3.00

LAUGH COMIX
(see TOP-NOTCH COMICS)

LAUREL AND HARDY
St. John Publishing Co.
March, 1949

1 . . . . . 550.00
2 . . . . . 350.00
3 . . . . . 250.00
26 Rep #1 . . . . . 125.00
27 Rep #2 . . . . . 125.00
28 Rep #3 . . . . . 125.00

LAWBREAKERS
Law & Order Magazines
(Charlton)
March, 1951

1 . . . . . 250.00
2 . . . . . 150.00
3 . . . . . 100.00
4 Drug 125.00
5 . . . . . 100.00
6 LM(c) 125.00
7 Drug 125.00
8 . . . . . 100.00
9 StC(c) 100.00
Becomes:

LAWBREAKERS SUSPENSE STORIES
Jan., 1953

10 StC(c) 250.00
11 LM(c),Negligee(c) 650.00
12 LM(c) 125.00
13 DG(c) 125.00
14 DG(c),Sharks 125.00
15 DG(c),Acid in Face(c) 350.00
Becomes:

STRANGE SUSPENSE STORIES

16 DG(c); Jan., 1954 . . . . . 200.00
17 DG(c) 175.00
18 SD,SD(c) 250.00
19 SD,SD(c),Electric Chair 400.00
20 SD,SD(c) 275.00
21 SD,SD(c) 175.00
22 SD,SD(c) 225.00
Becomes:

THIS IS SUSPENSE

23 WW; Feb., 1955Comics Code 165.00
24 GE,DG(c) 80.00
25 DG(c) 60.00
26 DG(c) 60.00
Becomes:

STRANGE SUSPENSE STORIES

27 Oct., 1955 . . . . . 100.00
28 . . . . . 60.00
29 . . . . . 60.00
30 . . . . . 60.00
31 SD 150.00
32 SD 150.00
33 SD 150.00
34 SD 150.00
35 SD 150.00
36 SD 150.00
37 SD 150.00
38 . . . . . 60.00
39 SD 150.00
40 SD 150.00
41 SD 150.00
42 . . . . . 40.00
43 . . . . . 40.00
44 . . . . . 40.00
45 . . . . . 40.00
46 . . . . . 40.00
47 SD 100.00
48 SD 100.00
49 . . . . . 40.00
50 SD 100.00
51 SD 100.00
52 SD 100.00
53 SD 100.00
54 thru 60 . . . . . @35.00
61 thru 74 . . . . . @20.00
75 SD,SD(c) 150.00
77 Oct 1965 . . . . . 50.00

LAWBREAKERS ALWAYS LOSE
Crime Bureau Stories
Spring, 1948

1 HK; FBI Reward Poster Photo. 225.00
2 . . . . . 150.00
3 . . . . . 125.00
4 Vampire 125.00
5 . . . . . 100.00
6 Anti Wertham Edition 100.00
7 Drug 225.00
8 . . . . . 100.00
9 Ph(c) 100.00
10 Ph(c), Oct. 1949 . . . . . 100.00

LAW-CRIME
Essenkay Publications
April, 1948

1 LbC,LbC-(c);Raymond Hamilton Dies In The Chair 550.00
2 LbC,LbC-(c);Strangled Beauty Puzzles Police 450.00
3 LbC,LbC-(c);Lipstick Slayer Sought; Aug. 1943 . . . . . 550.00

LEROY
Visual Editions
(Standard Comics)
Nov., 1949

1 FunniestTeenager of them All . 50.00
2 . . . . . 35.00
3 thru 6 . . . . . @25.00

LET'S PRETEND
D.S. Publishing Company
May–June, 1950

1 From Radio Nursery Tales . . . 125.00
2 . . . . . 100.00
3 Nov., 1950 . . . . . 100.00

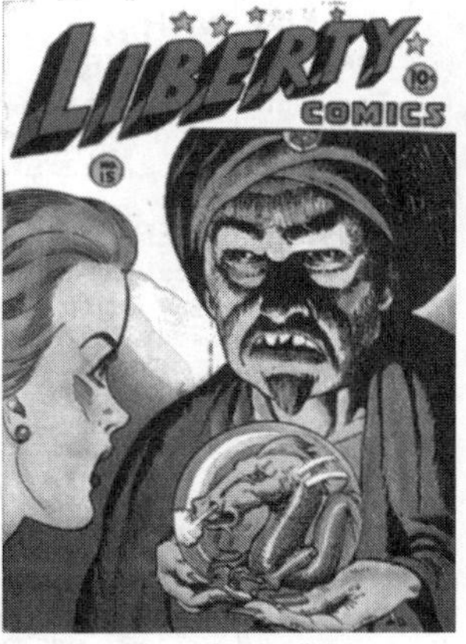

Liberty Comics #15
© Green Publishing

MISS LIBERTY
Burten/Green Publishing
Circa 1944

1 Reprints-Shield,Wizard 300.00
Becomes:

LIBERTY COMICS

10 Reprints,Hangman 135.00
11 . . . . . 100.00
12 Black Hood 100.00
14 . . . . . 100.00
15 . . . . . 75.00

LIBERTY GUARDS
Chicago Mail Order
(Comic Corp of America)
Circa 1942

1 PG(c),Liberty Scouts 275.00
Becomes:

LIBERTY SCOUTS
June, 1941

PG,PG(c)O:Fireman,Liberty Scouts 1,000.00
3 PG,PG(c) Aug.,1941

GOLDEN AGE

O:Sentinel 750.00

LIFE STORY
Fawcett Publications
April, 1949

1 Ph(c) 100.00
2 Ph(c) 40.00
3 Ph(c) 35.00
4 Ph(c) 35.00
5 Ph(c) 35.00
6 Ph(c) 35.00
7 Ph(c) 30.00
8 Ph(c) 30.00
9 Ph(c) 30.00
10 Ph(c) 30.00
11 25.00
12 25.00
13 WW,Drug 100.00
14 thru 21 @20.00
22 Drug 35.00
23 thru 35 @20.00
36 Drug 25.00
37 thru 42 @18.00
43 GE 25.00
44 18.00
45 1952 18.00

LIFE WITH SNARKY PARKER
Fox Feature Syndicate
Aug., 1950

1 200.00

LI'L ABNER
Harvey Publications
Dec., 1947

61 BP,BW,Sadie Hawkins Day 250.00
62 150.00
63 150.00
64 150.00
65 BP 150.00
66 135.00
67 135.00
68 FearlessFosdick V:Any Face 150.00
69 150.00
70 125.00

Toby Press

71 125.00
72 125.00
73 125.00
74 125.00
75 HK 135.00
76 125.00
77 HK 135.00
78 HK 135.00
79 HK 135.00
80 125.00
81 100.00
82 100.00
83 Baseball 110.00
84 100.00
85 100.00
86 HK 150.00
87 100.00
88 100.00
89 100.00
90 100.00
91 Rep. #77 110.00
92 100.00
93 Rep. #71 110.00
94 100.00
95 Fearless Fosdick 125.00
96 100.00
97 Jan., 1955 100.00

LI'L GENIUS
Charlton Comics, 1955

1 70.00
2 25.00
3 thru 15 @20.00
16 Giants 35.00
17 Giants 35.00
18 Giants,100 pages 40.00
19 thru 40 @15.00
41 thru 54 @10.00
55 1965 10.00

LI'L PAN
Fox Features Syndicate
Dec.–Jan., 1946-47

6 35.00
7 25.00
8 April–May, 1947 25.00

LINDA
(see PHANTOM LADY)

LITTLE AUDREY
St. John Publ. Co./
Harvey Comics
April, 1948

1 350.00
2 150.00
3 thru 6 @100.00
7 thru 10 @60.00
11 thru 20 @35.00
21 thru 24 @25.00
25 B:Harvey Comics 85.00
26 A: Casper 50.00
27 A: Casper 50.00
28 A: Casper 50.00
29 thru 31 @30.00
32 A: Casper 35.00
33 A: Casper 35.00
34 A: Casper 35.00
35 A: Casper 35.00
36 thru 53 @20.00

LITTLE BIT
Jubilee Publishing Company
March, 1949

1 35.00
2 June, 1949 35.00

LITTLE DOT
Harvey Publications
Sept., 1953

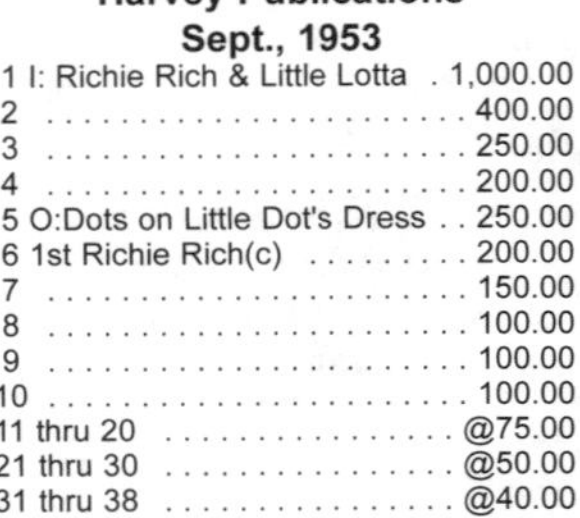

1 I: Richie Rich & Little Lotta 1,000.00
2 400.00
3 250.00
4 200.00
5 O:Dots on Little Dot's Dress 250.00
6 1st Richie Rich(c) 200.00
7 150.00
8 100.00
9 100.00
10 100.00
11 thru 20 @75.00
21 thru 30 @50.00
31 thru 38 @40.00
39 65.00
40 thru 50 @30.00
51 thru 60 @25.00
61 thru 70 @22.00
71 thru 80 @20.00
81 thru 100 @15.00
101 thru 130 @15.00
131 thru 140 @15.00
141 thru 145, 52 pages @15.00
146 thru 163 @5.00

LITTLE EVA
St. John Publishing Co.
May, 1952

1 100.00
2 50.00
3 30.00
4 30.00
5 thru 10 @25.00
11 thru 30 @25.00
31 Nov., 1956 25.00

LITTLE GIANT COMICS
Centaur Publications
July, 1938

1 PG, B&W with Color(c) 500.00
2 B&W with Color(c) 450.00
3 B&W with Color(c) 425.00
4 B&W with Color(c) 425.00

LITTLE GIANT DETECTIVE FUNNIES
Centaur Publications
Oct., 1938

1 B&W 600.00
2 B&W 450.00
3 B&W 450.00
4 Jan. 1939 450.00

LITTLE GIANT MOVIE FUNNIES
Centaur Publications
Aug., 1938

1 Ed Wheelan-a 600.00
2 Ed Wheelan-a, Oct., 1938 450.00

LITTLE IKE
St. John Publishing Co.
April, 1953

1 50.00
2 25.00
3 20.00
4 Oct., 1953 20.00

Lone Ranger #4
© Dell Publishing Co.

LITTLE IODINE
Dell Publishing Co.
April, 1949

1 ... 100.00
2 ... 50.00
3 ... 50.00
4 ... 50.00
5 ... 50.00
6 thru 10 ... @25.00
11 thru 30 ... @20.00
31 thru 50 ... @15.00
51 thru 56 ... @15.00

LITTLE JACK FROST
Avon Periodicals, 1951

1 ... 60.00

LITTLE LULU (see MARGE'S LITTLE LULU)

LITTLE MAX COMICS
Harvey Publications
Oct., 1949

1 I: Little Dot,Joe Palooka ... 150.00
2 A: Little Dot ... 75.00
3 A: Little Dot,Joe Palooka(c) ... 50.00
4 ... 35.00
5 C: Little Dot ... 35.00
6 thru 10 ... @25.00
11 thru 22 ... @25.00
23 A: Little Dot ... 20.00
24 thru 37 ... @15.00
38 Rep. #20 ... 15.00
39 thru 72 ... @15.00
73 A: Richie Rich; Nov.'61 ... 15.00

LITTLE MISS MUFFET
Best Books
(Standard Comics)
Dec., 1948

11 Strip Reprints ... 50.00
12 Strip Reprints ... 30.00
13 Strip Reprints; Mar.'49 ... 30.00

LITTLE MISS SUNBEAM COMICS
Magazine Enterprises
June–July, 1950

1 ... 125.00
2 ... 60.00
3 ... 60.00
4 Dec.–Jan., 1951 ... 60.00

LITTLE ORPHAN ANNIE
Dell Publishing Co., 1941

1 ... 150.00
2 Orphan Annie and the Rescue 100.00
3 ... 100.00

LITTLE ROQUEFORT
St. John Publishing Co.
June,1952

1 ... 75.00
2 ... 50.00
3 thru 9 ... @35.00

Pines

10 Summer 1958 ... 35.00

LITTLE SCOUTS
Dell Publishing Co.
March, 1951

(1) *see Dell Four Color #321*
2 ... 20.00
3 ... 20.00
4 ... 20.00
5 ... 20.00
6 ... 20.00

LITTLEST SNOWMAN
Dell Publishing Co.
Dec., 1956

1 ... 40.00

LIVING BIBLE, THE
Living Bible Corp.
Autumn, 1945

1 LbC-(c) Life of Paul ... 325.00
2 LbC-(c) Joseph &His Brethern 200.00
3 LbC-(c) Chaplains At War ... 300.00

LONE EAGLE
Ajax/Farrell
April–May, 1954

1 ... 100.00
2 ... 50.00
3 Bondage(c) ... 65.00
4 Oct.–Nov., 1954 ... 50.00

LONE RANGER
Dell Publishing Co.
Jan.–Feb., 1948

1 B:Lone Ranger & Tonto
B:Strip Reprint ... 700.00
2 ... 350.00
3 ... 250.00
4 ... 250.00
5 ... 250.00
6 ... 200.00
7 ... 200.00
8 O:Retold ... 250.00
9 ... 200.00
10 ... 200.00
11 B:Young Hawk ... 125.00
12 thru 20 ... @125.00
21 ... 100.00
22 ... 100.00
23 O:Retold ... 125.00
24 thru 30 ... @100.00
31 (1st Mask Logo) ... 110.00
32 thru 36 ... @90.00
37 (E:Strip reprints) ... 90.00
38 thru 50 ... @75.00
51 thru 75 ... @60.00
76 thru 99 ... @55.00
100 ... 75.00
101 thru 111 ... @60.00
112 B:Clayton Moore Ph(c) ... 200.00
113 thru 117 ... @100.00
118 O:Lone Ranger & Tonto
retold, Anniv. issue ... 250.00
119 thru 144 ... @100.00
145 final issue,May/July 1962 ... 100.00

THE LONE RANGER'S COMPANION TONTO
Dell Publishing Co.
Jan., 1951

(1) *see Dell Four Color #312*
2 P(c) all ... 125.00
3 ... 60.00
4 ... 50.00
5 ... 50.00
6 thru 10 ... @50.00
11 thru 20 ... @40.00
21 thru 25 ... @30.00
26 thru 33 ... @25.00

THE LONE RANGER'S FAMOUS HORSE HI-YO SILVER
Dell Publishing Co.
Jan., 1952

(1) *see Dell Four Color #369*
(1) *see Dell Four Color #392*
3 P(c) all ... 35.00
4 ... 35.00
5 ... 35.00
6 thru 10 ... @35.00
11 thru 36 ... @30.00

The Lone Rider #1
© Superior Comics

LONE RIDER
Farrell (Superior Comics) April, 1951

1 ... 150.00
2 I&O: Golden Arrow; 52 pgs. ... 75.00
3 ... 65.00
4 ... 65.00
5 ... 65.00
6 E: Golden Arrow ... 70.00
7 G. Arrow Becomes Swift Arrow 75.00
8 O: Swift Arrow ... 100.00
9 thru 14 ... @50.00
15 O: Golden Arrow Rep. #2 ... 55.00
16 thru 19 ... @40.00
20 ... 35.00
21 3-D (c) ... 100.00
22 ... 35.00
23 A: Apache Kid ... 35.00
24 ... 35.00
25 ... 35.00
26 July, 1955 ... 35.00

LONG BOW
Real Adventures Publ.
(Fiction House)
Winter, 1950

1 ... 125.00
2 ... 75.00
3 "Red Arrows Means War" ... 60.00
4 "Trial of Tomahawk" ... 60.00
5 ... 60.00
6 "Rattlesnake Raiders" ... 50.00

7 . . . . 50.00
8 . . . . 50.00
9 Spring, 1953 . . . . 50.00

LOONEY TUNES AND MERRIE MELODIES

Dell Publishing Co., 1941

1 B:&1st Comic App. Bugs Bunny Daffy Duck,Elmer Fudd . . 11,000.00
2 Bugs/Porky(c) 1,500.00
3 Bugs/Porky(c) B:WK, Kandi the Cave 1,300.00
4 Bugs/Porky(c),WK 1,000.00
5 Bugs/Porky(c),WK, A:Super Rabbit 1,000.00
6 Bugs/Porky/Elmer(c),E:WK, Kandi the Cave. 700.00
7 Bugs/Porky(c). 600.00
8 Bugs/Porky swimming(c),F:WK, Kandi the Cave. 700.00
9 Porky/Elmer car painted(c) . . . 550.00
10 Porky/Bugs/Elmer Parade(c) . 550.00
11 Bugs/Porky(c),F:WK, Kandi the Cave. 550.00
12 Bugs/Porky rollerskating(c). . . 400.00
13 Bugs/Porky(c) 400.00
14 Bugs/Porky(c) 400.00
15 Bugs/Porky X-Mas(c),F:WK Kandi the Cave. 350.00
16 Bugs/Porky ice-skating(c). . . . 350.00
17 Bugs/Petunia Valentines(c) . . 350.00
18 Sgt.Bugs Marine(c) 350.00
19 Bugs/Painting(c) 350.00
20 Bugs/Porky/ElmerWarBonds(c), B:WK,Pat,Patsy&Pete. 350.00
21 Bugs/Porky 4th July(c). 325.00
22 Porky(c). 325.00
23 Bugs/Porky Fishing(c) 325.00
24 Bugs/Porky Football(c). 325.00
25 Bugs/Porky/Petunia Halloween (c),E:WK,Pat, Patsy & Pete . 325.00
26 Bugs Thanksgiving(c). 250.00
27 Bugs/Porky New Years(c) . . . 250.00
28 Bugs/Porky Ice-Skating(c) . . . 250.00
29 Bugs Valentine(c). 250.00
30 Bugs(c) 250.00
31 Bugs(c) 200.00
32 Bugs/Porky Hot Dogs(c). 200.00
33 Bugs/Porky War Bonds(c) . . . 210.00
34 Bugs/Porky Fishing(c) 200.00
35 Bugs/Porky Swimming(c). . . . 200.00
36 Bugs/Porky(c) 200.00
37 Bugs Hallowean(c). 200.00

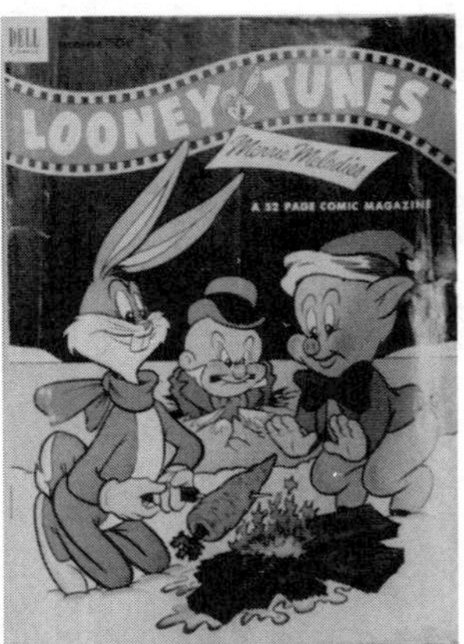

Looney Tunes and Merrie Melodies © Dell PublishingCo.

Looney Tunes and Merrie Melodies © Dell Publishing Co.

38 Bugs Thanksgiving(c). 200.00
39 Bugs X-Mas(c). 200.00
40 Bugs(c) 200.00
41 Bugs Washington's Birthday(c) 175.00
42 Bugs Magician(c). 175.00
43 Bugs Dream(c) 175.00
44 Bugs/Porky(c) 175.00
45 Bugs War Bonds(c) 175.00
46 Bugs/Porky(c) 150.00
47 Bugs Beach(c). 150.00
48 Bugs/Porky Picnic(c) 150.00
49 Bugs(c) 150.00
50 Bugs(c) 150.00
51 thru 60 . . . . @125.00
61 thru 80 . . . . @100.00
81 thru 86 . . . . @75.00
87 Bugs X-Mas(c). 80.00
88 thru 99 . . . . @75.00
100. . . . . 80.00
101 thru 110 . . . . @40.00
111 thru 125 . . . . @35.00
126 thru 150 . . . . @30.00
151 thru 165 . . . . @25.00

Becomes:

LOONEY TUNES

Aug., 1955

166 thru 200 . . . . @20.00
201 thru 245 . . . . @15.00
246 final issue,Sept.1962 . . . . 15.00

LOST WORLD

Literacy Enterprises (Standard Comics) Oct., 1952

5 ATh, Alice in Terrorland 300.00
6 ATh 250.00

LOVE AND MARRIAGE

Superior Comics Ltd. March, 1952

1 . . . . 100.00
2 . . . . 50.00
3 . . . . 30.00
4 . . . . 30.00
5 . . . . 30.00
6 . . . . 30.00
7 . . . . 30.00
8 thru 15 . . . . @30.00
16 Sept., 1954 . . . . 30.00

LOVE AT FIRST SIGHT

Periodical House (Ace Magazines) Oct., 1949

1 P(c) 100.00
2 P(c) 50.00
3 . . . . 30.00
4 P(c) 30.00
5 thru 10 . . . . @30.00
11 thru 33 . . . . @15.00
34 1st Edition Under Code 10.00
35 thru 41 . . . . @10.00
42 1956 . . . . 10.00

LOVE CONFESSIONS

Comics Magazine (Quality Comics Group) Oct., 1949

1 PG,BWa(c)& Some-a 250.00
2 PG 100.00
3 . . . . 50.00
4 RC 75.00
5 BWa 85.00
6 Ph(c) 25.00
7 Ph(c) Van Johnson 25.00
8 BWa 75.00
9 Ph(c)Jane Russell/Robert Mitchum 20.00
10 BWa 75.00
11 thru 18 Ph(c) . . . . @35.00
19 . . . . 75.00
20 BWa 75.00
21 . . . . 25.00
22 BWa 60.00
23 thru 28 . . . . @20.00
29 BWa 75.00
30 thru 38 . . . . @15.00
39 MB 25.00
40 . . . . 20.00
41 . . . . 20.00
42 . . . . 20.00
43 1st Edition Under Code 20.00
44 thru 46 . . . . @20.00
47 BWa(c) 60.00
48 thru 54 Dec., 1956 . . . . @20.00

LOVE DIARY

Our Publishing Co./Toytown July, 1949

1 BK,Ph(c) 125.00
2 BK,Ph(c) 75.00
3 BK,Ph(c) 75.00
4 thru 9 Ph(c) . . . . @35.00
10 BEv, Ph(c). 30.00
11 thru 24 Ph(c) . . . . @28.00
25 . . . . 25.00
26 . . . . 25.00
27 Ph(c). 28.00
28 . . . . 25.00
29 Ph(c). 25.00
30 . . . . 25.00
31 JB(c). 25.00
32 thru 41 . . . . @25.00
42 MB(c) 25.00
43 thru 47 . . . . @25.00
48 1st Edition Under Code, Oct.'55 . . . . 25.00

LOVE DIARY

Quality Comics Group Sept., 1949

1 BWa(c) 225.00

LOVE LESSONS
Harvey Publications
Oct., 1949

1 . . . . . . 100.00
2 . . . . . . 40.00
3 Ph(c) 30.00
4 . . . . . . 30.00
5 June, 1950 . . . . . . 30.00

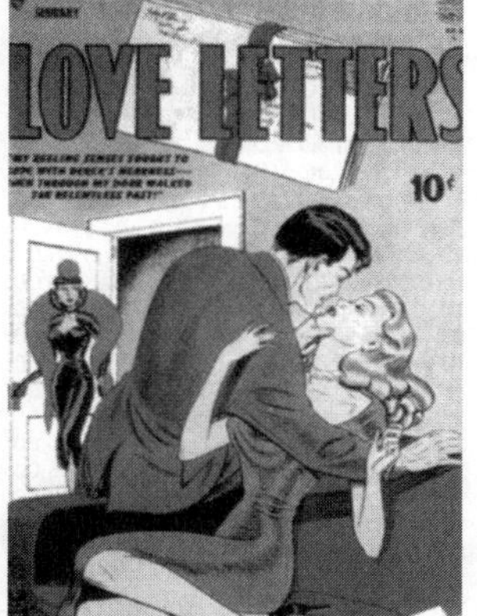

Love Letters #2
© Quality Comics Group

LOVE LETTERS
Comic Magazines
(Quality Comics Group)
Nov., 1949

1 PG,BWa(c) 175.00
2 PG,BWa(c) 150.00
3 PG 100.00
4 BWa 125.00
5 . . . . . . 35.00
6 . . . . . . 35.00
7 . . . . . . 35.00
8 . . . . . . 35.00
9 Ph(c) of Robert Mitchum 50.00
10 . . . . . . 35.00
11 BWa 60.00
12 . . . . . . 30.00
13 . . . . . . 30.00
14 . . . . . . 30.00
15 . . . . . . 30.00
16 Ph(c) of Anthony Quinn 35.00
17 BWa, Ph(c) of Jane Russell . . . 35.00
18 thru 30 . . . . . . @20.00
31 BWa 25.00
Becomes:

LOVE SECRETS

32 . . . . . . 60.00
33 . . . . . . 30.00
34 BWa 60.00
35 thru 39 . . . . . . @30.00
40 MB(c)1st Edition Under Code . 50.00
41 thru 50 . . . . . . @30.00
50 MB 30.00
51 MB(c) 30.00
52 thru 56 . . . . . . @25.00

LOVELORN
Best Syndicated/Michel Publ.
(American Comics Group)
Aug.–Sept., 1949

1 . . . . . . 100.00
2 . . . . . . 50.00
3 thru 10 . . . . . . @35.00
11 thru 17 . . . . . . @30.00
18 2pgs. MD-a 25.00
19 . . . . . . 25.00
20 . . . . . . 25.00
21 Prostitution Story 45.00
22 thru 50 . . . . . . @12.00
51 July, 1954 3-D 100.00
Becomes:

CONFESSIONS OF LOVELORN

52 3-D 125.00
53 . . . . . . 35.00
54 3-D 125.00
55 . . . . . . 25.00
56 Communist Story 40.00
57 Comics Code 15.00
58 thru 90 . . . . . . @15.00
91 AW 35.00
92 thru 105 . . . . . . @10.00
106 P(c) 10.00
107 P(c) 10.00
108 thru 114 . . . . . . @10.00

LOVE MEMORIES
Fawcett Publications
Autumn, 1949

1 Ph(c) 100.00
2 Ph(c) 50.00
3 Ph(c) 50.00
4 Ph(c) 50.00

LOVE MYSTERY
Fawcett Publications
June, 1950

1 GE, Ph(c) 150.00
2 GE, Ph(c) 125.00
3 GE & BP, Ph(c); Oct., 1950 . . . 125.00

LOVE PROBLEMS AND ADVICE ILLUSTRATED
McCombs/Harvey Publications
Home Comics, June, 1949

1 BP 125.00
2 BP 60.00
3 . . . . . . 40.00
4 . . . . . . 40.00
5 L. Elias(c) 35.00
6 . . . . . . 35.00
7 BP 35.00
8 BP 35.00
9 BP 35.00
10 BP 35.00
11 BP 25.00
12 BP 25.00
13 BP 25.00
14 BP 25.00
15 . . . . . . 20.00
16 . . . . . . 20.00
17 thru 23 BP . . . . . . @20.00
24 BP, Rape Scene 25.00
25 BP 15.00
26 . . . . . . 15.00
27 . . . . . . 15.00
28 BP 15.00
29 BP 15.00
30 . . . . . . 15.00
31 . . . . . . 15.00
32 Comics Code 10.00
33 BP 10.00
34 . . . . . . 10.00
35 . . . . . . 10.00
36 . . . . . . 10.00
37 . . . . . . 10.00
38 S&K (c) 10.00
39 . . . . . . 10.00
40 BP 10.00
41 BP 10.00
42 . . . . . . 10.00
43 . . . . . . 10.00
44 March, 1957 . . . . . . 10.00

LOVERS LANE
Lev Gleason Publications
Oct., 1949

1 CBi (c),FG-a 75.00
2 P(c) 35.00
3 P(c) 25.00
4 P(c) 25.00
5 P(c) 25.00
6 GT,P(c), ... 25.00
7 P(c), ... 25.00
8 P(c), ... 25.00
9 P(c), ... 25.00
10 P(c) 25.00
11 thru 19 P(c) . . . . . . @20.00
20 Ph(c); FF 1 page Ad, ... 25.00
21 Ph(c) 15.00
22 Ph(c) 15.00
23 . . . . . . 15.00
24 . . . . . . 15.00
25 . . . . . . 15.00
26 Ph(c) 15.00
27 Ph(c) 15.00
28 Ph(c) 15.00
29 thru 38 . . . . . . @15.00
39 Story Narrated by
Frank Sinatra 35.00
40 . . . . . . 15.00
41 June, 1954 . . . . . . 15.00

LOVE SCANDALS
Comic Magazines
(Quality Comics Group)
Feb., 1950

1 BW(c)&a 200.00
2 PG-a, Ph(c) 75.00
3 PG-a, Ph(c) 75.00
4 BWa(c)&a 18Pgs.; GFx-a 150.00
5 Ph(c), Oct., 1950 . . . . . . 65.00

LOVE STORIES OF MARY WORTH
Harvey Publications
Sept., 1949

1 Newspaper Reprints 50.00
2 Newspaper Reprints 35.00
3 Newspaper Reprints 25.00
4 Newspaper Reprints, ... 25.00
5 May, 1950 . . . . . . 25.00

LUCKY COMICS
Consolidated Magazines
Jan., 1944

1 Lucky Star 150.00
2 Henry C. Kiefer(c) 100.00
3 . . . . . . 100.00
4 . . . . . . 100.00
5 Summer, 1946,Devil(c) 100.00

LUCKY DUCK
Standard Comics
(Literary Enterprises)
Jan., 1953

5 IS (c)&a 65.00
6 IS (c)&a 40.00
7 IS (c)&a 40.00
8 IS (c)&a, Sept., 1953 . . . . . . 40.00

GOLDEN AGE

LUCKY FIGHTS IT THROUGH
Educational Comics, 1949

N# HK-a, V.D. Prevention . . . 1,300.00

LUCKY "7" COMICS
Howard Publications, 1944

1 Bondage(c) Pioneer 250.00

LUCKY STAR
Nationwide Publications
1950

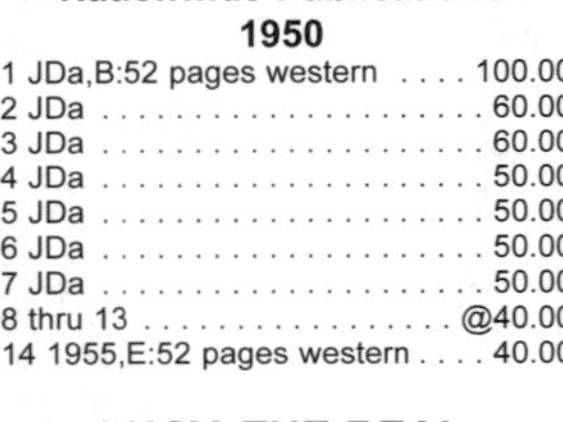

1 JDa,B:52 pages western 100.00
2 JDa 60.00
3 JDa 60.00
4 JDa 50.00
5 JDa 50.00
6 JDa 50.00
7 JDa 50.00
8 thru 13 . . . . @40.00
14 1955,E:52 pages western 40.00

LUCY, THE REAL GONE GAL
St. John Publishing Co.
June, 1953

1 Negligee Panels,Teenage 80.00
2 . . . . 50.00
3 MD-a 40.00
4 Feb., 1954 . . . . 40.00

Becomes:

MEET MISS PEPPER
St. John Publishing Co.
April, 1954

5 JKu-a 120.00
6 JKu (c)&a, June,1954 . . . . . . 100.00

MAD
E.C. Comics
Oct.–Nov., 1952

1 JSe,HK(c),JDa,WW 6,200.00
2 JSe,JDa(c),JDa,WW 1,400.00
3 JSe,HK(c),JDa,WW 850.00
4 JSe,HK(c),JDa-Flob Was A Slob,JDa,WW 800.00
5 JSe,BE(c).JDa,WW 1,400.00
6 JSe,HK(c),Jda,WW. 575.00
7 HK(c),JDa,WW 575.00
8 HK(c),JDa,WW 575.00
9 JSe,HK(c),JDa,WW 575.00
10 JSe,HK(c),JDa,WW 575.00
11 BW,BW(c),JDa,WW,Life(c) . . . 575.00
12 BK,JDa,WW. 475.00
13 HK(c),JDa,WW,Red(c) 475.00
14 RH,HK(c),JDa,WW, Mona Lisa(c) 475.00
15 JDa,WW,Alice in Wonderland(c) 475.00
16 HK(c),JDa,WW,Newspaper(c) 475.00
17 BK,BW,JDa,WW 475.00
18 HK(c),JDa,WW 475.00
19 JDa,WW,Racing Form(c) 350.00
20 JDa,WW,Composition(c) 350.00
21 JDa,WW,1st A.E.Neuman(c) . 350.00
22 BE,JDa,WW,Picasso(c) 350.00
23 Last Comic Format Edition, JDa,WW Think(c) 350.00
24 BK,WW, HK Logo & Border; 1st Magazine Format 850.00
25 WW, Al Jaffee Sterts As Reg.. 350.00
26 BK,WW,WW(c) 300.00
27 WWa,RH,JDa(c) 275.00
28 WW,BE(c),RH Back(c) 275.00
29 JKa,BW,WW,WW(c); 1st Don Martin Artwork 275.00

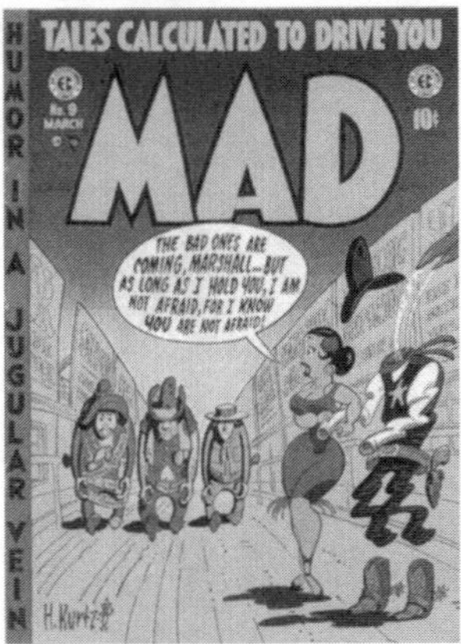

Mad #9
© E.C. Comics

30 BE,WW,RC; 1st A.E. Neuman(c) By Mingo 400.00
31 JDa,WW,BW,Mingo(c) 225.00
32 MD,JO 1st as reg.;Mingo(c); WW-Back(c) 200.00
33 WWa,Mingo(c);JO-Back(c) . . . 200.00
34 WWa,Mingo(c);1st Berg as Reg. 175.00
35 WW,RC,Mingo Wraparound(c) 175.00
36 WW,BW,Mingo(c),JO,MD 125.00
37 WW,Mingo(c)JO,MD 125.00
38 WW,JO,MD 125.00
39 WW,JO,MD 125.00
40 WW,BW,JO,MD 125.00
41 WW,JO,MD 100.00
42 WW,JO,MD 100.00
43 WW,JO,MD 100.00
44 WW,JO,MD 100.00
45 WW,JO,MD 100.00
46 JO,MD. 100.00
47 JO,MD. 100.00
48 JO,MD. 100.00
49 JO,MD. 100.00
50 JO,MD. 100.00
51 JO,MD. 80.00
52 JO,MD. 80.00
53 JO,MD. 80.00
54 JO,MD. 80.00
55 JO,MD. 80.00
56 JO,MD. 75.00
57 JO,MD. 75.00
58 JO,MD. 75.00
59 WW,JO,MD 85.00
60 JO,MD. 75.00
61 JO,MD. 65.00
62 JO,MD. 65.00
63 JO,MD. 65.00
64 JO,MD. 65.00
65 JO,MD. 65.00
66 JO,MD. 60.00
67 JO,MD. 60.00
68 Don Martin(c),JO,MD. 60.00
69 JO,MD. 60.00
70 JO,MD. 60.00
71 JO,MD. 60.00
72 JO,MD. 60.00
73 JO,MD. 60.00
74 JO,MD. 60.00
75 Mingo(c),JO,MD. 55.00
76 Mingo(c),SA,JO,MD 70.00
77 Mingo(c),SA,JO,MD 55.00
78 Mingo(c),SA,JO,MD 55.00
79 Mingo(c),SA,JO,MD 55.00
80 Mingo(c),SA,JO,MD 55.00
81 Mingo(c),SA,JO,MD 55.00
82 BW,Mingo(c),SA,JO,MD. 55.00
83 Mingo(c),SA,JO,MD 55.00
84 Mingo(c),SA,JO,MD 55.00
85 Mingo(c)SA,JO,MD 55.00
86 Mingo(c);1st Fold-in Back(c), SA,JO,MD 55.00
87 Mingo(c),JO,MD. 45.00
88 Mingo(c),JO,MD. 45.00
89 WK,Mingo(c),JO,MD 50.00
90 Mingo(c); FF-Back(c),JO,MD . . 45.00
91 Mingo(c),JO,MD. 40.00
92 Mingo(c),JO,MD. 40.00
93 Mingo(c),JO,MD. 40.00
94 Mingo(c),JO,MD. 40.00
95 Mingo(c),JO,MD. 40.00
96 Mingo(c),JO,MD. 40.00
97 Mingo(c),JO,MD. 40.00
98 Mingo(c),JO,MD. 40.00
99 JDa,Mingo(c),JO,MD 50.00
100 Mingo(c),JO,MD. 40.00
101 Infinity(c) by Mingo,JO,MD . . . 30.00
102 Mingo(c)JO,MD 30.00
103 Mingo(c)JO,MD 30.00
104 Mingo(c)JO,MD 30.00
105 Mingo(c);Batman TV Spoof ,JO,MD. 35.00
106 Mingo(c);FF-Back(c),JO,MD. . 35.00
107 Mingo(c),JO,MD. 30.00
108 Mingo(c),JO,MD. 30.00
109 Mingo(c),JO,MD. 30.00
110 Mingo(c),JO,MD. 30.00
111 Mingo(c),JO,MD 30.00
112 JO,MD 30.00
113 JO,MD 30.00
114 JO,MD 30.00
115 JO,MD 30.00
116 JO,MD 30.00
117 JO,MD 30.00
118 JO,MD 30.00
119 JO,MD 30.00
120 JO,MD. 30.00
121 Beatles,JO,MD. 30.00
122 MD & Mingo(c),JO,MD, Reagan 25.00
123 JO,MD. 20.00
124 JO,MD. 20.00
125 JO,MD. 20.00
126 JO,MD. 20.00
127 JO,MD. 20.00
128 Last JO;MD. 20.00
129 MD 20.00
130 MD 20.00
131 MD 20.00
132 MD 20.00
133 MD 20.00
134 MD 20.00
135 JDa(c),MD 25.00
136 MD 20.00
137 BW,MD 20.00
138 MD 20.00
139 JDa(c),MD 20.00
140 thru 153 MD . . . . @20.00
154 Mineo(c),MD 20.00
155 . . . . 20.00
156 . . . . 20.00
157 . . . . 20.00
158 . . . . 20.00
159 . . . . 20.00
160 Mingo(c),JDa,AT 20.00
161 . . . . 18.00
162 Mingo(c),MD,AT. 18.00
163 . . . . 18.00
164 Mingo,PaperMoon(c),AT, MD,SA 18.00
165 Don Martin(c),At,MD 18.00
166 . . . . 18.00
167 . . . . 18.00
168 Mingo(c),AT,MD 18.00
169 MD(c) 18.00
170 . . . . 18.00

171 Mingo(c) 15.00
172 Mingo(c) 15.00
173 JDa(c) 15.00
174 . . . . 15.00
175 . . . . 15.00
176 MD(c) 15.00
177 . . . . 15.00
178 JDa(c) 15.00
179 . . . . 15.00
180 Jaws(c),SA,MD,JDA,AT 15.00
181 G.Washington(c),JDa 15.00
182 . . . . 15.00
183 Mingo(c),AT,SA,MD 15.00
184 Mingo(c),Md,AT 15.00
185 . . . . 15.00
186 Star Trek Spoof 20.00
187 . . . . 15.00
188 . . . . 20.00
189 . . . . 15.00
190 . . . . 15.00
191 Clark(c),JDa,MD,AT 15.00
192 . . . . 15.00
193 Charlies Angels(c), Rickart,JDa,SA,MD. 15.00
194 Rocky(c),Rickart,AT,MD 15.00
195 . . . . 15.00
196 Star Wars Spoof, Rickart,AT,JDa 25.00
197 . . . . 20.00
198 UPC(c),AT,MD 15.00
199 Jaffee(c),AT,JDa,SA,MD. 15.00
200 Rickart(c),Close Encounters . 20.00
201 Rickart(c),Sat.Night Fever . . . 15.00
202 . . . . 15.00
203 Star Wars Spoof,Rickart(c). . . 10.00
204 Hulk TV Spoof,JawsII(c). 10.00
205 Rickart(c),Grease. 10.00
206 Mingo,(c),AT,JDa,Md 10.00
207 Jones(c),Animal House(c) . . . 10.00
208 Superman Movie Spoof, Rickart(c) 15.00
209 Mingo(c),AT,MD 10.00
210 Mingo,Lawn Mower,AT, JDa,MD 10.00
211 Mingo(c) 10.00
212 Jda(c),AT,MD 11.00
213 JDa(c),SA,AT,JDa 11.00
214 . . . . 10.00
215 Jones(c),MD,AT,JDa 10.00
216 . . . . 10.00
217 Jaffee(c),For Pres,AT,MD 10.00
218 Martin(c),AT,MD 10.00
219 thru 250 . . . . @10.00
251 thru 260 . . . . @8.00
261 thru 299 . . . . @6.00
300 thru 303 . . . . @8.00
304 thru 330 . . . . @5.00
331 thru 350 . . . . @4.00
350 thru 390 . . . . @3.00

MAGIC COMICS

David McKay Publications

Aug., 1939

1 Mandrake the Magician, Henry,Popeye,Blondie, Barney Baxter,Secret Agent X-9, Bunky,Henry on(c) . . . 2,300.00
2 Henry on(c) 800.00
3 Henry on(c) 600.00
4 Henry on(c),Mandrake-Logo . 500.00
5 Henry on(c),Mandrake-Logo . 375.00
6 Henry on(c),Mandrake-Logo . 350.00
7 Henry on(c),Mandrake-Logo . 350.00
8 B:Inspector Wade,Tippie 325.00
9 Henry-Mandrake Interact(c) . . 325.00
10 Henry-Mandrake Interact(c) . . 325.00
11 Henry-Mandrake Interact(c) . . 300.00
12 Mandrake on(c) 300.00
13 Mandrake on(c) 300.00
14 Mandrake on(c) 300.00
15 Mandrake on(c) 300.00
16 Mandrake on(c) 300.00
17 B:Lone Ranger 300.00
18 Mandrake/Robot on(c) 275.00
19 Mandrake on(c) 275.00
20 Mandrake on(c) 275.00
21 Mandrake on(c) 200.00
22 Mandrake on(c) 200.00
23 Mandrake on(c) 200.00
24 Mandrake on(c) 200.00
25 B:Blondie; Mandrake in Logo for Duration 200.00
26 Blondie (c) 175.00
27 Blondie (c); High School Heroes 175.00
28 Blondie (c); High School Heroes 175.00
29 Blondie (c); High School Heroes 175.00
30 Blondie (c) 175.00
31 Blondie(c);High School Sports Page 125.00
32 Blondie (c);Secret Agent X-9 . 125.00
33 C.Knight's-Romance of Flying 125.00
34 ClaytonKnight's-War in the Air 125.00
35 Blondie (c) 125.00
36 July'42; Patriotic-(c) 125.00
37 Blondie (c) 125.00
38 ClaytonKnight's-Flying Tigers . 125.00
39 Blondie (c) 125.00
40 Jimmie Doolittle bombs Tokyo 125.00
41 How German Became British Censor 100.00
42 Joe Musial's-Dollar-a-Dither . . 100.00
43 Clay Knight's-War in the Air . . 100.00
44 Flying Fortress in Action. 100.00
45 Clayton Knight's-Gremlins . . . 100.00
46 Adventures of Aladdin Jr. 100.00
47 Secret Agent X-9 . . . . 100.00
48 General Arnold U.S.A.F. 100.00
49 Joe Musial's-Dollar-a-Dither . . 100.00
50 The Lone Ranger 100.00
51 Joe Musial's-Dollar-a-Dither . . 75.00
52 C. Knights-Heroes on Wings . . 75.00
53 C. Knights-Heroes on Wings . . 75.00
54 High School Heroes. 75.00
55 Blondie (c) 80.00
56 High School Heroes. 75.00
57 Joe Musial's-Dollar-a-Dither . . . 75.00
58 Private Breger Abroad 75.00
59 . . . . 75.00
60 . . . . 75.00
61 Joe Musial's-Dollar-a-Dither . . . 60.00
62 . . . . 60.00
63 B:Buz Sawyer, Naval Pilot 60.00

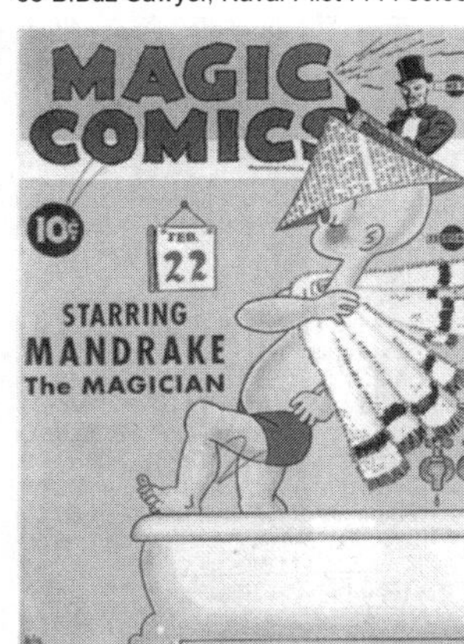

Magic Comics #7
© David McKay Publications

64 thru 70 . . . . @60.00
71 thru 80 . . . . @50.00
80 thru 90 . . . . @45.00
91 thru 99 . . . . @45.00
100 . . . . 60.00
101 thru 108 . . . . @40.00
108 Flash Gordon. 45.00
109 Flash Gordon. 45.00
110 thru 113 . . . . @45.00
114 The Lone Ranger. 45.00
115 thru 119 . . . . @45.00
120 Secret Agent X-9 . . . . 50.00
121 Secret Agent X-9 . . . . 50.00
122 Secret Agent X-9 . . . . 50.00
123 Sec. Agent X-9;Nov-Dec.'49. . 50.00

MAJOR HOOPLE COMICS

Nedor Publications, 1942

1 Mary Worth,Phantom Soldier; Buy War Bonds On(c) 300.00

MAJOR VICTORY COMICS

H. Clay Glover Svcs./ Harry A. Chestler, 1944

1 O:Major Victory,I:Spider Woman 475.00
2 A: Dynamic Boy 300.00
3 A: Rocket Boy 275.00

MAN HUNT!

Magazine Enterprises

Oct., 1953

1 LbC,FG,OW(c);B:Red Fox, Undercover Girl, Space Ace 375.00
2 LbC,FG,OW(c); Electrocution(c) 300.00
3 LbC,FG,OW,OW(c) 275.00
4 LbC,FG,OW,OW(c) 275.00
5 LbC,FG,OW,OW(c) 275.00
6 LbC,OW,OW(c) 250.00
7 LbC,OW; E:Space Ace 250.00
8 LbC,OW,FG(c);B:Trail Colt . . . 250.00
9 LbC,OW 250.00
10 LbC,OW,OW(c),Gwl. 250.00
11 LbC,FF,OW;B:The Duke, Scotland Yard. 300.00
12 LbC,OW 175.00
13 LbC,FF,OW;Rep.Trail Colt #1 . 250.00
14 LbC,OW;Bondage, Hypo-(c);1953. . . . . 225.00

MAN OF WAR

Comic Corp. of America (Centaur Publ.), Nov., 1941

1 PG,PG(c);Flag(c);B:The Fire-Man,Man of War,The Sentinel, Liberty Guards,Vapoman . . 1,300.00
2 PG,PG(c);I: The Ferret 1,000.00

MAN O'MARS

Fiction House/ I.W. Enterprises, 1953

1 MA, Space Rangers 300.00
1 MA, Rep. Space Rangers 50.00

MARCH OF COMICS

K.K. Publications/ Western Publ., 1946 (All were Giveaways)

N# WK back(c),Goldilocks 300.00
N# WK,How Santa got His

GOLDEN AGE

Red Suit 300.00
N# WK,Our Gang 400.00
N# CB,Donald Duck; "Maharajah Donald" 7,500.00
5 Andy Panda 150.00
6 WK,Fairy Tales 200.00
7 Oswald the Lucky Rabbit 150.00
8 Mickey Mouse 550.00
9 Gloomey Bunny 75.00
10 Santa Claus. 65.00
11 Santa Claus. 50.00
12 Santa's Toys 50.00
13 Santa's Suprise 50.00
14 Santa's Kitchen 50.00
15 Hip-It-Ty Hop 75.00
16 Woody Woodpecker. 150.00
17 Roy Rogers 225.00
18 Fairy Tales. 90.00
19 Uncle Wiggily. 75.00
20 CB,Donald Duck 4,500.00
21 Tom and Jerry 100.00
22 Andy Panda. 70.00
23 Raggedy Ann and Andy 125.00
24 Felix the Cat; By Otto Messmer. 200.00
25 Gene Autrey 200.00
26 Our Gang 200.00
27 Mickey Mouse 400.00
28 Gene Autry 200.00
29 Easter 30.00
30 Santa 30.00
31 Santa. 30.00
32 Does Not Exist
33 A Christmas Carol 30.00
34 Woody Woodpecker. 75.00
35 Roy Rogers 225.00
36 Felix the Cat 175.00
37 Popeye 150.00
38 Oswald the Lucky Rabbit 50.00
39 Gene Autry 200.00
40 Andy and Woody 50.00
41 CB,DonaldDuck,SouthSeas. 3,600.00
42 Porky Pig. 70.00
43 Henry 40.00
44 Bugs Bunny. 75.00
45 Mickey Mouse 300.00
46 Tom and Jerry 70.00
47 Roy Rogers 175.00
48 Santa. 20.00
49 Santa. 20.00
50 Santa 20.00
51 Felix the Cat 150.00
52 Popeye 125.00
53 Oswald the Lucky Rabbit 50.00
54 Gene Autrey 175.00
55 Andy and Woody 45.00
56 CB back(c),Donald Duck 275.00
57 Porky Pig. 55.00
58 Henry 30.00
59 Bugs Bunny. 70.00
60 Mickey Mouse 275.00
61 Tom and Jerry 50.00
62 Roy Rogers 175.00
63 Santa. 20.00
64 Santa. 20.00
65 Jingle Bells 20.00
66 Popeye 100.00
67 Oswald the Lucky Rabbit 30.00
68 Roy Rogers 175.00
69 Donald Duck 250.00
70 Tom and Jerry 40.00
71 Porky Pig. 55.00
72 Krazy Kat. 50.00
73 Roy Rogers 150.00
74 Mickey Mouse 250.00
75 Bugs Bunny. 65.00
76 Andy and Woody 35.00
77 Roy Rogers 150.00
78 Gene Autrey; last regular sized issue 150.00
79 Andy Panda,5"x7" format. 25.00

March of Comics #41
© Walt Disney

80 Popeye 65.00
81 Oswald the Lucky Rabbit 35.00
82 Tarzan 150.00
83 Bugs Bunny. 50.00
84 Henry 25.00
85 Woody Woodpecker. 25.00
86 Roy Rogers 125.00
87 Krazy Kat. 25.00
88 Tom and Jerry 30.00
89 Porky Pig. 25.00
90 Gene Autrey 100.00
91 Roy Rogers and Santa. 125.00
92 Christmas w/Santa. 15.00
93 Woody Woodpecker. 25.00
94 Indian Chief 70.00
95 Oswald the Lucky Rabbit 20.00
96 Popeye 60.00
97 Bugs Bunny. 40.00
98 Tarzan,Lex Barker Ph(c) 150.00
99 Porky Pig. 25.00
100 Roy Rogers 100.00
101 Henry 20.00
102 Tom Corbet,P(c). 135.00
103 Tom and Jerry 25.00
104 Gene Autrey 75.00
105 Roy Rogers 100.00
106 Santa's Helpers 15.00
107 *Not Published*
108 Fun with Santa. 15.00
109 Woody Woodpecker. 20.00
110 Indian Chief 35.00
111 Oswald the Lucky Rabbit 25.00
112 Henry. 20.00
113 Porky Pig 25.00
114 Tarzan,RsM 150.00
115 Bugs Bunny 40.00
116 Roy Rogers 100.00
117 Popeye 60.00
118 Flash Gordon, P(c). 120.00
119 Tom and Jerry 20.00
120 Gene Autrey 90.00
121 Roy Rogers 100.00
122 Santa's Suprise 15.00
123 Santa's Christmas Book. 15.00
124 Woody Woodpecker. 20.00
125 Tarzan, Lex Barker Ph(c) . . . 150.00
126 Oswald the Lucky Rabbit 25.00
127 Indian Chief. 30.00
128 Tom and Jerry 25.00
129 Henry 20.00
130 Porky Pig 25.00
131 Roy Rogers 100.00
132 Bugs Bunny. 30.00
133 Flash Gordon,Ph(c) 100.00
134 Popeye 45.00
135 Gene Autrey 60.00
136 Roy Rogers 75.00
137 Gifts from Santa. 10.00
138 Fun at Christmas 10.00
139 Woody Woodpecker. 20.00
140 Indian Chief 30.00
141 Oswald the Lucky Rabbit 20.00
142 Flash Gordon. 80.00
143 Porky Pig. 20.00
144 RsM,Ph(c),Tarzan 135.00
145 Tom and Jerry 20.00
146 Roy Rogers,Ph(c) 100.00
147 Henry 15.00
148 Popeye 35.00
149 Bugs Bunny. 25.00
150 Gene Autrey 75.00
151 Roy Rogers 75.00
152 The Night Before Christmas. . 12.00
153 Merry Christmas 12.00
154 Tom and Jerry 20.00
155 Tarzan,Ph(c) 135.00
156 Oswald the Lucky Rabbit 15.00
157 Popeye 30.00
158 Woody Woodpecker. 20.00
159 Indian Chief. 20.00
160 Bugs Bunny 20.00
161 Roy Rogers 75.00
162 Henry 15.00
163 Rin Tin Tin. 32.00
164 Porky Pig. 20.00
165 The Lone Ranger. 75.00
166 Santa & His Reindeer 12.00
167 Roy Rogers and Santa. 75.00
168 Santa Claus' Workshop 12.00
169 Popeye 30.00
170 Indian Chief 25.00
171 Oswald the Lucky Rabbit 20.00
172 Tarzan 125.00
173 Tom and Jerry 15.00
174 The Lone Ranger. 75.00
175 Porky Pig. 20.00
176 Roy Rogers 60.00
177 Woody Woodpecker. 15.00
178 Henry 15.00
179 Bugs Bunny. 20.00
180 Rin Tin Tin 50.00
181 Happy Holiday 10.00
182 Happi Tim 10.00
183 Welcome Santa 10.00
184 Woody Woodpecker. 15.00
185 Tarzan, Ph(c) 100.00
186 Oswald the Lucky Rabbit 12.00
187 Indian Chief. 30.00
188 Bugs Bunny. 25.00
189 Henry 15.00
190 Tom and Jerry 18.00
191 Roy Rogers 60.00
192 Porky Pig. 20.00
193 The Lone Ranger. 75.00
194 Popeye 25.00
195 Rin Tin Tin. 50.00
196 *Not Published*
197 Santa is Coming 10.00
198 Santa's Helper. 10.00
199 Huckleberry Hound 65.00
200 Fury 30.00
201 Bugs Bunny 25.00
202 Space Explorer 65.00
203 Woody Woodpecker. 15.00
204 Tarzan 75.00
205 Mighty Mouse 35.00
206 Roy Rogers,Ph(c) 60.00
207 Tom and Jerry 15.00
208 The Lone Ranger,Ph(c) 100.00
209 Porky Pig. 15.00
210 Lassie 30.00
211 *Not Published*
212 Christmas Eve 10.00
213 Here Comes Santa 10.00
214 Huckleberry Hound 50.00
215 Hi Yo Silver 35.00

216 Rocky & His Friends 75.00
217 Lassie 20.00
218 Porky Pig. 20.00
219 Journey to the Sun. 35.00
220 Bugs Bunny 20.00
221 Roy and Dale,Ph(c) 60.00
222 Woody Woodpecker. 15.00
223 Tarzan 75.00
224 Tom and Jerry 15.00
225 The Lone Ranger. 50.00
226 Christmas Treasury 10.00
227 *Not Published*
228 Letters to Santa 10.00
229 The Flintstones 100.00
230 Lassie 20.00
231 Bugs Bunny. 20.00
232 The Three Stooges 75.00
233 Bullwinkle 75.00
234 Smokey the Bear. 20.00
235 Huckleberry Hound 40.00
236 Roy and Dale. 50.00
237 Mighty Mouse 20.00
238 The Lone Ranger. 50.00
239 Woody Woodpecker. 15.00
240 Tarzan 75.00
241 Santa Around the World. 10.00
242 Santa Toyland 10.00
243 The Flintstones 100.00
244 Mr.Ed,Ph(c) 35.00
245 Bugs Bunny. 20.00
246 Popeye 20.00
247 Mighty Mouse 20.00
248 The Three Stooges 75.00
249 Woody Woodpecker. 10.00
250 Roy and Dale 50.00
251 Little Lulu & Witch Hazel . . . 120.00
252 P(c),Tarzan 65.00
253 Yogi Bear. 25.00
254 Lassie 35.00
255 Santa's Christmas List 10.00
256 Christmas Party 10.00
257 Mighty Mouse 20.00
258 The Sword in the Stone
(Disney Version). 75.00
259 Bugs Bunny. 20.00
260 Mr. Ed 30.00
261 Woody Woodpecker. 15.00
262 Tarzan 55.00
263 Donald Duck 75.00
264 Popeye 25.00
265 Yogi Bear. 30.00
266 Lassie 30.00
267 Little Lulu. 90.00
268 The Three Stooges 75.00
269 A Jolly Christmas. 10.00
270 Santa's Little Helpers 10.00
271 The Flintstones 75.00
272 Tarzan 55.00
273 Bugs Bunny. 20.00
274 Popeye 20.00
275 Little Lulu. 75.00
276 The Jetsons. 125.00
277 Daffy Duck. 15.00
278 Lassie 20.00
279 Yogi Bear. 30.00
280 Ph(c),The Three Stooges. . . . 75.00
281 Tom & Jerry 15.00
282 Mr. Ed 20.00
283 Santa's Visit. 10.00
284 Christmas Parade 10.00
285 Astro Boy. 325.00
286 Tarzan 40.00
287 Bugs Bunny. 20.00
288 Daffy Duck. 15.00
289 The Flintstones 65.00
290 Ph(c), Mr. Ed. 18.00
291 Yogi Bear. 25.00
292 Ph(c), The Three Stooges . . . 70.00
293 Little Lulu. 55.00
294 Popeye 20.00
295 Tom & Jerry. 15.00

296 Lassie 20.00
297 Christmas Bells 10.00
298 Santa's Sleigh 10.00
299 The Flintstones 60.00
300 Tarzan 50.00
301 Bugs Bunny. 15.00
302 Ph(c), Laurel & Hardy 30.00
303 Daffy Duck. 10.00
304 Ph(c), The Three Stooges . . . 70.00
305 Tom & Jerry 10.00
306 Ph(c), Daniel Boone. 50.00
307 Little Lulu. 45.00
308 Ph(c), Lassie 15.00
309 Yogi Bear. 25.00
310 Ph(c) of Clayton Moore;
The Lone Ranger 75.00
311 Santa's Show. 10.00
312 Christmas Album 10.00
313 Daffy Duck. 12.00
314 Laurel & Hardy. 30.00
315 Bugs Bunny. 15.00
316 The Three Stooges 60.00
317 The Flinstones. 30.00
318 Tarzan 45.00
319 Yogi Bear. 20.00
320 Space Family Robinson 125.00
321 Tom & Jerry. 12.00
322 The Lone Ranger. 50.00
323 Little Lulu. 30.00
324 Ph(c), Lassie 12.00
325 Fun With Santa 10.00
326 Christmas Story 10.00
327 The Flintstones 55.00
328 Space Family Robinson 80.00
329 Bugs Bunny. 15.00
330 The Jetsons. 75.00
331 Daffy Duck. 12.00
332 Tarzan 50.00
333 Tom & Jerry. 12.00
334 Lassie 15.00
335 Little Lulu. 25.00
336 The Three Stooges 55.00
337 Yogi Bear. 20.00
338 The Lone Ranger. 50.00
339 *Not Published*
340 Here Comes Santa 9.00
341 The Flintstones 55.00
342 Tarzan 35.00
343 Bugs Bunny. 20.00
344 Yogi Bear. 23.00
345 Tom & Jerry. 12.00
346 Lassie 15.00
347 Daffy Duck. 12.00
348 The Jetsons. 75.00
349 Little Lulu. 25.00

March of Comics #70
© M. G. M.

350 The Lone Ranger. 35.00
351 Beep-Beep, The
Road Runner 20.00
352 Space Family Robinson 100.00
353 Beep-Beep, The Road
Runner. 20.00
354 Tarzan 30.00
355 Little Lulu. 25.00
356 Scooby Doo, Where Are You . 55.00
357 Daffy Duck & Porky Pig 12.00
358 Lassie 15.00
359 Baby Snoots 12.00
360 Ph(c), H.R. Pufnstuf. 60.00
361 Tom & Jerry. 12.00
362 Smokey the Bear. 15.00
363 Bugs Bunny & Yosemite Sam. 15.00
364 Ph(c), The Banana Splits 50.00
365 Tom & Jerry. 12.00
366 Tarzan 30.00
367 Bugs Bunny & Porky Pig 15.00
368 Scooby Doo. 50.00
369 Little Lulu. 20.00
370 Ph(c), Lassie 12.00
371 Baby Snoots 10.00
372 Smokey The Bear 15.00
373 The Three Stooges 50.00
374 Wacky Witch 10.00
375 Beep-Beep & Daffy Duck 12.00
376 The Pink Panther. 20.00
377 Baby Snoots 10.00
378 Turok, Son of Stone. 125.00
379 Heckle & Jeckle. 10.00
380 Bugs Bunny & Yosemite Sam. 15.00
381 Lassie 12.00
382 Scooby Doo. 18.00
383 Smokey the Bear. 12.00
384 The Pink Panther. 20.00
385 Little Lulu. 15.00
386 Wacky Witch 16.00
387 Beep-Beep & Daffy Duck 10.00
388 Tom & Jerry 10.00
389 Little Lulu. 15.00
390 The Pink Panther. 20.00
391 Scooby Doo. 18.00
392 Bugs Bunny & Yosemite Sam. 15.00
393 Heckle & Jeckle. 10.00
394 Lassie 10.00
395 Woodsy the Owl 10.00
396 Baby Snoots 10.00
397 Beep-Beep & Daffy Duck 10.00
398 Wacky Witch 10.00
399 Turok, Son of Stone. 100.00
400 Tom & Jerry. 10.00
401 Baby Snoots 10.00
402 Daffy Duck. 10.00
403 Bugs Bunny. 10.00
404 Space Family Robinson 40.00
405 Cracky. 7.00
406 Little Lulu. 15.00
407 Smokey the Bear. 7.00
408 Turok, Son of Stone. 45.00
409 The Pink Panther. 15.00
410 Wacky Witch 7.00
411 Lassie 10.00
412 New Terrytoons 6.00
413 Daffy Duck. 6.00
414 Space Family Robinson 35.00
415 Bugs Bunny. 10.00
416 The Road Runner 15.00
417 Little Lulu. 15.00
418 The Pink Panther. 15.00
419 Baby Snoots 6.00
420 Woody Woodpecker. 6.00
421 Tweety & Sylvester 6.00
422 Wacky Witch 6.00
423 Little Monsters 6.00
424 Cracky. 6.00
425 Daffy Duck. 6.00
426 Underdog. 35.00
427 Little Lulu. 10.00
428 Bugs Bunny. 8.00

429 The Pink Panther. 10.00
430 The Road Runner 10.00
431 Baby Snoots 6.00
432 Lassie 7.00
433 Tweety & Sylvester 6.00
434 Wacky Witch 6.00
435 New Terrytoons 6.00
436 Cracky. 6.00
437 Daffy Duck. 6.00
438 Underdog. 20.00
439 Little Lulu. 10.00
440 Bugs Bunny. 7.00
441 The Pink Panther. 10.00
442 The Road Runner 5.00
443 Baby Snoots 4.00
444 Tom & Jerry. 4.00
445 Tweety & Sylvester 4.00
446 Wacky Witch 4.00
447 Mighty Mouse 5.00
448 Cracky. 4.00
449 The Pink Panther. 5.00
450 Baby Snoots 4.00
451 Tom & Jerry. 4.00
452 Bugs Bunny. 4.00
453 Popeye 3.00
454 Woody Woodpecker. 4.00
455 The Road Runner 5.00
456 Little Lulu. 3.00
457 Tweety & Sylvester 3.00
458 Wacky Witch 2.00
459 Mighty Mouse 5.00
460 Daffy Duck. 3.00
461 The Pink Panther. 7.00
462 Baby Snoots 2.00
463 Tom & Jerry. 4.00
464 Bugs Bunny. 5.00
465 Popeye 4.00
466 Woody Woodpecker. 4.00
467 Underdog. 15.00
468 Little Lulu. 4.00
469 Tweety & Sylvester 3.00
470 Wacky Witch 3.00
471 Mighty Mouse 5.00
472 Heckle & Jeckle. 4.00
473 The Pink Panther. 7.00
474 Baby Snoots 2.00
475 Little Lulu. 3.00
476 Bugs Bunny. 5.00
477 Popeye 3.00
478 Woody Woodpecker. 5.00
479 Underdog. 15.00
480 Tom & Jerry. 8.00
481 Tweety & Sylvster 3.00
482 Wacky Witch 3.00
483 Mighty Mouse 5.00
484 Heckle & Jeckle. 3.00
485 Baby Snoots 3.00
486 The Pink Panther. 7.00
487 Bugs Bunny. 5.00
488 April, 1982; Little Lulu 3.00

MARGE'S LITTLE LULU

Dell Publishing Co.

1 B:Lulu's Diary 650.00
2 I:Gloria,Miss Feeny. 300.00
3 . . . . 275.00
4 . . . . 275.00
5 . . . . 275.00
6 . . . . 225.00
7 I:Annie,X-Mas Cover. 225.00
8 . . . . 225.00
9 . . . . 225.00
10 . . . . 225.00
11 thru 18 . . . . @200.00
19 I:Wilbur 200.00
20 I:Mr.McNabbem 200.00
21 thru 25 . . . . @150.00
26 rep.Four Color#110 . . . . 150.00
27 thru 29 . . . . @150.00
30 Christmas cover. 150.00
31 thru 34 . . . . @135.00
35 B:Mumday Story 140.00
36 thru 38 . . . . @135.00
39 I:Witch Hazel. 150.00
40 Halloween Cover 125.00
41 . . . . 125.00
42 Christmas Cover 125.00
43 Skiing Cover 125.00
44 Valentines Day Cover 125.00
45 2nd A:Witch Hazel. 125.00
46 thru 60 . . . . @125.00
61 . . . . 100.00
62 . . . . 100.00
63 I:Chubby 100.00
64 thru 67 . . . . @100.00
68 I:Professor Cleff. 100.00
69 thru 77 . . . . @100.00
78 Christmas Cover 100.00
79 . . . . 100.00
80 . . . . 100.00
81 thru 89 . . . . @75.00
90 Christmas Cover 75.00
91 thru 99 . . . . @75.00
100 . . . . 100.00
101 thru 122 . . . . @75.00
123 I:Fifi 60.00
124 thru 164 . . . . @50.00
165 giant sized 150.00
166 giant sized 150.00
167 thru 169 . . . . @40.00
170 . . . . 20.00
171 . . . . 20.00
172 . . . . 25.00
173 . . . . 20.00
174 . . . . 20.00
175 . . . . 25.00
176 . . . . 25.00
177 . . . . 20.00
178 thru 196 . . . . @20.00
197 . . . . 20.00
198 thru 200 . . . . @25.00
201 . . . . 10.00
202 . . . . 15.00
203 . . . . 10.00
204 . . . . 15.00
205 . . . . 15.00
206 . . . . 10.00

MARMADUKE MOUSE

Quality Comics Group (Arnold Publications)

Spring, 1946

1 Funny Animal 125.00
2 Funny Animal 75.00
3 thru 8 Funny Animal . . . . @50.00
9 Funny Animal 40.00
10 Funny Animal 40.00
11 thru 20 Funny Animal . . . . . . @35.00
21 thru 30 Funny Animal . . . . . . @25.00
31 thru 40 Funny Animal . . . . . . @25.00
41 thru 50 Funny Animal . . . . . . @25.00
51 thru 65 Funny Animal . . . . . . @25.00

MARTIN KANE

Hero Books (Fox Features syndicate)

June, 1950

1 WW,WW-(c) 250.00
2 WW,JO, Auguat, 1950 . . . . . . 200.00

MARVEL FAMILY, THE

Fawcett Publications

Dec., 1945

1 O:Captain Marvel,Captain Marvel Jr., Mary Marvel,Uncle Marvel; V:Black Adam 1,300.00
2 . . . . 600.00

Marvel Family #7
© Fawcett Publications

3 . . . . 400.00
4 The Witch's Tale 350.00
5 Civilization of a Prehistoric Race 325.00
6 . . . . 300.00
7 The Rock of Eternity 275.00
8 The Marvel Family Round Table 275.00
9 V: The Last Vikings 275.00
10 V: The Sivana Family. 275.00
11 V: The Well of Evil 250.00
12 V: The Iron Horseman 250.00
13 . . . . 250.00
14 Captain Marvel Invalid 250.00
15 V: Mr. Triangle 200.00
16 World's Mightiest Quarrell . . . 200.00
17 . . . . 200.00
18 . . . . 200.00
19 V: The Monster Menace. 200.00
20 The Marvel Family Feud 200.00
21 V: The Trio of Terror. 160.00
22 V: The Triple Threat. 160.00
23 March of Independence (c) . . 175.00
24 V: The Fighting Xergos 160.00
25 Trial of the Marvel Family. . . . 160.00
26 V: Mr. Power 150.00
27 V: The Amoeba Men 150.00
28 . . . . 150.00
29 V: The Monarch of Money . . . 150.00
30 A:World's Greatest Magician . 150.00
31 V:Sivana & The Great Hunger 125.00
32 The Marvel Family Goes Into Buisness 125.00
33 I: The Hermit Family 125.00
34 V: Sivana's Miniature Menace 125.00
35 V: The Berzerk Machines. . . . 125.00
36 V: The Invaders From Infinity . 125.00
37 V: The Earth Changer 125.00
38 V: Sivana's Instinct Exterminator Gun 125.00
39 The Legend of Atlantis. 125.00
40 Seven Wonders of the Modern World 125.00
41 The Great Oxygen Theft 125.00
42 V: The Endless Menace 110.00
43 . . . . 110.00
44 V: The Rust That Menaced the World 110.00
45 The Hoax City 110.00
46 The Day Civilization Vanished 110.00
47 V: The Interplanetary Thieves 150.00
48 V: The Four Horsemen. 110.00
49 ...Proves Human Hardness . . 110.00
50 The Speech Scrambler Machine 110.00

GOLDEN AGE

51 The Living Statues 120.00
52 The School of Witches 100.00
53 V: The Man Who Changed the World 100.00
54 . . . . 100.00
55 . . . . 100.00
56 The World's Mightiest Project. 100.00
57 . . . . 100.00
58 The Triple Time Plot. 100.00
59 . . . . 100.00
60 . . . . 100.00
61 . . . . 100.00
62 . . . . 100.00
63 V: The Pirate Planet. 100.00
64 . . . . 100.00
65 . . . . 100.00
66 The Miracle Stone 100.00
67 . . . . 100.00
68 . . . . 100.00
69 V: The Menace of Old Age. . . 100.00
70 V: The Crusade of Evil 100.00
71 . . . . 100.00
72 . . . . 100.00
73 . . . . 100.00
74 . . . . 100.00
75 The Great Space Struggle . . . 100.00
76 . . . . 125.00
77 Anti-Communist. 150.00
78 V: The Red Vulture 125.00
79 . . . . 100.00
80 . . . . 100.00
81 . . . . 100.00
82 . . . . 100.00
83 V: The Flying Skull. 100.00
84 thru 87 . . . . @100.00
88 Jokes of Jeopardy 100.00
89 And Then There Were None; Jan., 1954 . . . . 100.00

MARVELS OF SCIENCE
Charlton Comics
March, 1946

1 1st Charlton Book; Atomic Bomb Story 175.00
2 . . . . 100.00
3 . . . . 100.00
4 President Truman(c); Jun.`6 . . 100.00

MARY MARVEL COMICS
Fawcett Publications/ Charlton Comics
Dec., 1945

1 Intro: Mary Marvel 1,500.00
2 . . . . 600.00
3 . . . . 400.00
4 On a Leave of Absence 375.00
5 Butterfly (c). 275.00
6 A:Freckles,Teenager of Mischief 275.00
7 The Kingdom Undersea 275.00
8 Holiday Special Issue 275.00
9 Air Race (c) 250.00
10 A: Freckles 250.00
11 A: The Sad Dryads. 175.00
12 Red Cross Appeal on(c). 175.00
13 Keep the Homefires Burning . 175.00
14 Meets Ghosts (c) 175.00
15 A: Freckles 175.00
16 The Jukebox Menace. 165.00
17 Aunt Agatha's Adventures . . . 165.00
18 . . . . 165.00
19 Witch (c) 165.00
20 . . . . 165.00
21 V: Dice Head 150.00
22 The Silver Slippers. 150.00
23 The Pendulum Strikes 150.00
24 V: The Nightowl 150.00
25 A: Freckles 150.00

Mary Marvel #4
© Fawcett Publications

26 A:Freckles dressed as Clown. 150.00
27 The Floating Oceanliner. 150.00
28 Sept., 1948 . . . . 150.00
Becomes:

MONTE HALE WESTERN

29 Ph(c),B:Monte Hale & His Horse Pardner 400.00
30 Ph(c),B:Big Bow-Little Arrow; CCB,Captain Tootsie 225.00
31 Ph(c),Giant 175.00
32 Ph(c),Giant 175.00
33 Ph(c),Giant 175.00
34 Ph(c),E:Big Bow-Little Arrow;B:Gabby Hayes,Giant . 175.00
35 Ph(c),Gabby Hayes, Giant . . . 175.00
36 Ph(c),Gabby Hayes, Giant . . . 175.00
37 Ph(c),Gabby Hayes 125.00
38 Ph(c),Gabby Hayes, Giant . . . 150.00
39 Ph(c);CCB, Captain Tootsie; Gabby Hayes, Giant 150.00
40 Ph(c),Gabby Hayes, Giant . . . 150.00
41 Ph(c),Gabby Hayes 100.00
42 Ph(c),Gabby Hayes, Giant . . . 125.00
43 Ph(c),Gabby Hayes, Giant . . . 125.00
44 Ph(c),Gabby Hayes, Giant . . . 125.00
45 Ph(c),Gabby Hayes 100.00
46 Ph(c),Gabby Hayes, Giant . . . 100.00
47 Ph(c),A:Big Bow-Little Arrow; Gabby Hayes, Giant 100.00
48 Ph(c),Gabby Hayes, Giant . . . 100.00
49 Ph(c),Gabby Hayes 100.00
50 Ph(c),Gabby Hayes, Giant . . . 100.00
51 Ph(c),Gabby Hayes, Giant 90.00
52 Ph(c),Gabby Hayes, Giant 90.00
53 Ph(c),A:Slim Pickens; Gabby Hayes 75.00
54 Ph(c),Gabby Hayes, Giant 85.00
55 Ph(c),Gabby Hayes, Giant 85.00
56 Ph(c),Gabby Hayes, Giant 85.00
57 Ph(c),Gabby Hayes 60.00
58 Ph(c),Gabby Hayes, Giant 75.00
59 Ph(c),Gabby Hayes, Giant 75.00
60 thru 79 Ph(c),Gabby Hayes . @65.00
80 Ph(c),E: Gabby Hayes 65.00
81 Ph(c) 65.00
82 Final Ph(c), Last Fawcett Edition 55.00
83 1st Charlton Edition, R:G. Hayes Back B&W Ph(c) 55.00
84 . . . . 55.00
85 . . . . 50.00
86 E: Gabby Hayes 50.00
87 . . . . 50.00
88 Jan., 1956 . . . . 50.00

MASK COMICS
Rural Home Publications
Feb.–March, 1945

1 LbC,LbC-(c), Evil (c) 2,200.00
2 LbC-(c),A:Black Rider,The Collector The Boy Magician; Apr-May'45, Devil (c) 1,400.00

MASKED MARVEL
Centaur Publications
Sept., 1940

1 I: The Masked Marvel 1,300.00
2 PG, ... 900.00
3 Dec., 1940 . . . . 850.00

MASKED RANGER
Premier Magazines
April, 1954

1 FF,O&B:The Masked Ranger, Streak the Horse,The Crimson Avenger 300.00
2 . . . . 100.00
3 . . . . 100.00
4 B: Jessie James,Billy the Kid, Wild Bill Hickock, Jim Bowie's Life Story 125.00
5 . . . . 125.00
6 . . . . 125.00
7 . . . . 125.00
8 . . . . 125.00
9 AT,E:All Features; A:Wyatt Earp Aug., 1955 . . . . 135.00

MASTER COMICS
Fawcett Publications
March, 1940

1-6 Oversized,7-Normal Format
1 O:Master Man; B:The Devil's Dagger, El Carin-Master of Magic, Rick O'Say, Morton Murch, White Rajah, Shipwreck Roberts, Frontier Marshall, Mr. Clue, Streak Sloan. . . . 7,400.00
2 Master Man (c) 1,800.00
3 Master Man (c) Bondage . . . 1,500.00
4 Master Man (c) 1,400.00
5 Master Man (c) 1,400.00
6 E: All Above Features 1,500.00
7 B:Bulletman,Zorro,The Mystery Man, Lee Granger, Jungle King,Buck Jones 2,500.00
8 B:The Red Gaucho,Captain Venture, Planet Princess . . 1,200.00
9 Bulletman & Steam Roller . . 1,000.00
10 E: Lee Granger. 1,000.00
11 O: Minute Man 2,200.00
12 Minute Man (c) 1,100.00
13 O:Bulletgirl; E:Red Gaucho . 1,600.00
14 B: The Companions Three . . . 850.00
15 MRa, Bulletman & Girl (c) . . . 850.00
16 MRa, Minute Man (c) 850.00
17 B:MRa on Bulletman 800.00
18 MRa, ... 800.00
19 MRa, Bulletman & Girl (c) . . . 800.00
20 MRa,C:Cap.Marvel-Bulletman 800.00
21 MRa-(c),Capt. Marvel in Bulletman,I&O:CaptainNazi 4,500.00
22 MRa-(c),E:Mystery Man,Captain Venture; Bondage(c);Capt. Marvel Jr. X-Over In Bulletman; A:Capt. Nazi. . . 4,200.00
23 MRa,MRa(c),B:Capt. Marvel Jr. V:Capt. Nazi . . . 2,500.00
24 MRa,MRa(c),Death By Radio. 775.00
25 MRa,MRa(c),The Jap Invasion 775.00

GOLDEN AGE

26 MRa,MRa(c),Capt. Marvel Jr. Avenges Pearl Harbor 700.00
27 MRa.MRa(c),V For Victory(c) . 700.00
28 MRa,MRa(c)Liberty Bell(c) . . . 700.00
29 MRa,MRa(c),Hitler & Hirohito(c) 700.00
30 MRa,MRa(c),Flag (c);Capt. Marvel Jr, V: Capt. Nazi 700.00
31 MRa,MRa(c),E:Companions Three,Capt.Marvel Jr, V:Mad Dr. Macabre. 550.00
32 MRa,MRa(c),E: Buck Jones; CMJr Strikes Terror Castle . . 550.00
33 MRa,MRa(c),B:Balbo the Boy Magician, Hopalong Cassidy. 550.00
34 MRa,MRa(c),Capt.Marvel Jr V: Capt.Nazi 550.00
35 MRa,MRa(c),CMJr Defies the Flame 550.00
36 MRa,MRa(c),Statue Of Liberty(c) 550.00
37 MRa,MRa(c),CMJr Blasts the Nazi Raiders. 500.00
38 MRa,MRa(c),CMJr V: the Japs 500.00
39 MRa,MRa(c),CMJr Blasts Nazi Slave Ship 500.00
40 MRa,MRa(c),Flag (c) 500.00
41 MRa,MRa(c),Bulletman,Bulletgirl, CMJr X-Over In Minuteman . 550.00
42 MRa,MRa(c),CMJr V: Hitler's Dream Soldier 300.00
43 MRa(c),CMJr Battles For Stalingrad. 300.00
44 MRa(c),CMJr In Crystal City of the Peculiar Penguins. . . . 300.00
45 MRa(c), ... 300.00
46 MRa(c) 300.00
47 MRa(c),A:Hitler; E: Balbo 325.00
48 MRa(c),I:Bulletboy;Capt. Marvel A: in Minuteman 350.00
49 MRa(c),E: Hopalong Cassidy, Minuteman 300.00
50 I&O: Radar,A:Capt. Marvel, B:Nyoka the Jungle Girl 300.00
51 MRa(c),CMJr V: Japanese . . . 175.00
52 MRa(c),CMJr & Radar Pitch War Stamps on (c) 175.00
53 CMJR V: Dr. Sivana 175.00
54 MRa(c),Capt.Marvel Jr Your Pin-Up Buddy 175.00
55 . . . . 175.00
56 MRa(c) 150.00
57 CMJr V: Dr. Sivana 150.00
58 MRA,MRa(c), ... 150.00

Master Comics #7
© Fawcett Publications

59 MRa(c),A:The Upside Downies 175.00
60 MRa(c) 175.00
61 CMJr Meets Uncle Marvel . . . 175.00
62 Uncle Sam on (c). 175.00
63 W/ Radar (c) 150.00
64 W/ Radar (c) 150.00
65 . . . . 150.00
66 CMJr & Secret Of the Sphinx . 150.00
67 Knight (c). 150.00
68 CMJr in the Range of the Beasts 150.00
69 . . . . 150.00
70 . . . . 150.00
71 CMJr,V:Man in Metal Mask . . 125.00
72 CMJr V: Sivana & The Whistle That Wouldn't Stop 125.00
73 CMJr V: The Ghost of Evil . . . 125.00
74 CMJr & The Fountain of Age . 125.00
75 CMJr V: The Zombie Master . 125.00
76 . . . . 125.00
77 Pirate Treasure (c). 125.00
78 CMJr in Death on the Scenic Railway 125.00
79 CMJr V: The Black Shroud. . . 125.00
80 CMJr-The Land of Backwards 125.00
81 CMJr & The Voyage 'Round the Horn 110.00
82 CMJr,IN,Death at the Launching. 110.00
83 . . . . 110.00
84 CMJr V: The Human Magnet . 110.00
85 CMJr-Crime on the Campus . 110.00
86 CMJr & The City of Machines. 110.00
87 CMJr & The Root of Evil. 110.00
88 CMJr V: The Wreckers; B: Hopalong Cassidy 110.00
89 . . . . 110.00
90 CMJr V: The Caveman 110.00
91 CMJr V: The Blockmen 110.00
92 CMJr V: The Space Slavers . . 110.00
93 BK,CMJr,V:TheGrowingGiant . 125.00
94 E: Hopalong Cassidy 100.00
95 B: Tom Mix; CMJr Meets the Skyhawk. 100.00
96 CMJr Meets the Worlds Mightiest Horse 100.00
97 CMJr Faces the Doubting Thomas 100.00
98 KKK Type 100.00
99 Witch (c) 100.00
100 CMJr V: The Ghost Ship . . . 120.00
101 thru 105 . . . . @100.00
106 E: Bulletman 100.00
107 CMJr Faces the Disappearance of the Statue of Liberty 100.00
108 . . . . 100.00
109 . . . . 100.00
110 CMJr & The Hidden Death . 100.00
111 thru 122 . . . . @100.00
123 CMJr V: The Flying Desperado 100.00
124 . . . . 100.00
125 CMJr & The Bed of Mystery . 100.00
126 thru 131 . . . . @100.00
132 V: Migs. 110.00
133 E: Tom Mix; April, 1953 . . . . 120.00

MD

E.C. Comics
April 1955–Jan., 1956

1 RC,GE,Grl,JO,JCr(c) 125.00
2 thru 5 RC,GE,Grl,JO,JCr(c). @100.00

MD #4
© E.C. Publications

MEDAL OF HONOR COMICS

Stafford Publication
Spring, 1947

1 True Stories of Medal of Honor Recipants 80.00

MEET CORLISS ARCHER

Fox Features Syndicate
March, 1948

1 AF,AF(c), Teenage 550.00
2 AF(c) 450.00
3 . . . . 400.00

Becomes:

MY LIFE

4 JKa,AF, ... 300.00
5 JKa, ... 150.00
6 JKa,AF, ... 150.00
7 Watercolor&Ink Drawing on(c) 100.00
8 . . . . 75.00
9 . . . . 75.00
10 WW, July, 1950 . . . . 125.00

MEET MERTON

Toby Press, Dec., 1953

1 Dave Berg-a,Teen Stories. 50.00
2 Dave Berg-a 25.00
3 Dave Berg-a 25.00
4 Dave Berg-a; June, 1954 . . . . . 25.00

MEET THE NEW POST GAZETTE SUNDAY FUNNIES

Pitsberg Post Gazette

N# One Shot Insert F: Several Syndicated Characters in Stories Exclusive to This Edition. . . . 850.00

MEL ALLEN SPORTS COMICS

Visual Editions, 1949

1 GT 175.00
2 Lou Gehrig 125.00

GOLDEN AGE

MEN AGAINST CRIME (see HAND OF FATE)

MERRY-GO-ROUND COMICS
LaSalle/Croyden/ Rotary Litho., 1944

1 LaSalle Publications Edition . . 125.00
1a 1946, Croyden Edition 50.00
1b Sept-Oct.'47,Rotary Litho Ed. . 75.00
2 . . . . 75.00

MERRY MOUSE
Avon Periodicals
June, 1953

1 (fa),F. Carin (c)&a 50.00
2 (fa),F. Carin (c)&a 30.00
3 (fa),F. Carin (c)&a 30.00
4 (fa),F. Carin (c)&a;Jan.'54 . . . . 30.00

METEOR COMICS
Croyden Publications
Nov., 1945

1 Captain Wizard & Baldy Bean. 300.00

MICKEY FINN
Eastern Color/ Columbia Comics Group, 1942

1 . . . . 225.00
2 . . . . 125.00
3 A: Charlie Chan 75.00
4 . . . . 60.00
5 thru 9 . . . . @40.00
10 thru 15 . . . . @30.00

(WALT DISNEY'S) MICKEY MOUSE
Dell Publishing Co.
Dec., 1952

#1-#27 Dell Four Color
28 . . . . 40.00
29 . . . . 35.00
30 . . . . 35.00
31 . . . . 35.00
32 thru 34 . . . . @35.00
35 thru 50 . . . . @25.00
51 thru 73 . . . . @20.00
74 . . . . 25.00
75 thru 99 . . . . @20.00
100 thru 105 rep. . . . . @25.00
106 thru 120 . . . . @20.00
121 thru 130 . . . . @15.00
131 thru 146 . . . . @15.00
147 rep,Phantom Fires 20.00
148 rep. 20.00
149 thru 158 . . . . @8.00
159 rep. 12.00
160 thru 170 . . . . @7.00
171 thru 199 . . . . @3.00
200 rep. 5.00
201 thru 218 . . . . @3.00
See: Independent Color Comics

MICKEY MOUSE MAGAZINE
Kay Kamen

1 (1933) scarce. 4,500.00
2 . . . . 1,200.00
3 thru 8 . . . . @1,100.00
9 . . . . 1,100.00

Mickey Mouse Magazine #c
© Walt Disney

MICKEY MOUSE MAGAZINE
Kay Kamen

1 digest size (1933) 1,800.00
2 dairy give-away promo(1933) . 550.00
3 dairy give-away promo(1934) . 400.00
4 dairy give-away promo(1934) . 400.00
5 dairy give-away promo(1934) . 400.00
6 dairy give-away promo(1934) . 400.00
7 dairy give-away promo(1934) . 400.00
8 dairy give-away promo(1934) . 400.00
9 dairy give-away promo(1934) . 400.00
10 dairy give-awaypromo(1934) . 400.00
11 dairy give-awaypromo(1934) . 400.00
12 dairy give-awaypromo(1934) . 400.00

Volume II

1 dairy give-away promo(1934) . 400.00
2 dairy give-away promo(1934) . 400.00
3 dairy give-away promo(1935) . 400.00
4 dairy give-away promo(1935) . 400.00
5 dairy give-away promo(1935) . 400.00
6 dairy give-away promo(1935) . 400.00
7 dairy give-away promo(1935) . 400.00
8 dairy give-away promo(1935) . 400.00
9 dairy give-away promo(1935) . 400.00
10 dairy give-awaypromo(1935) . 400.00
11 dairy give-awaypromo(1935) . 400.00
12 dairy give-awaypromo(1935) . 400.00

MICKEY MOUSE MAGAZINE
K.K. Pub./Westen Pub

1 (1935) 13¼"x10¼" 12,000.00
2 . . . . 1,200.00
3 . . . . 600.00
4 . . . . 600.00
5 (1936) Donald Duck solo 700.00
6 Donald Duck editor. 600.00
7 . . . . 600.00
8 Donald Duck solo 600.00
9 . . . . 600.00
10 . . . . 600.00
11 Mickey Mouse, editor 550.00
12 . . . . 550.00

Volume II

1 . . . . 550.00
2 . . . . 550.00
3 Christmas issue, 100pg 2,500.00
4 (1937) Roy Ranger adv.strip . . 500.00
5 Ted True strip 450.00
6 Mickey Mouse cut-outs 375.00
7 Mickey Mouse cut-outs 375.00
8 Mickey Mouse cut-outs 375.00
9 Mickey Mouse cut-outs 375.00
10 Full color 600.00
11. . . . . 400.00
12 Hiawatha 400.00
13 . . . . 400.00

Volume III

2 Big Bad Wolf (c) 450.00
3 First Snow White 750.00
4 (1938) Snow White. 600.00
5 Snow White (c). 700.00
6 Snow White ends 500.00
7 7 Dwarfs Easter (c). 375.00
8 . . . . 350.00
9 Dopey(c). 350.00
10 Goofy(c) 350.00
11 Mickey Mouse Sheriff. 350.00
12 A:Snow White 350.00

Volume IV

1 Practile Pig. 350.00
2 I:Huey,Louis & Dewey(c). 400.00
3 Ferdinand the Bull 350.00
4 (1939),B:Spotty. 325.00
5 Pluto solo 350.00
7 Ugly Duckling 325.00
7a Goofy & Wilber 350.00
8 Big Bad Wolf(c) 350.00
9 The Pointer. 350.00
10 July 4th 450.00
11 . . . . 325.00
12 Donald's Penguin. 400.00

Volume V

1 Black Pete 400.00
2 Goofy(c) 600.00
3 Pinochio 600.00
4 (1940). 400.00
5 Jimmy Crickett(c) 400.00
6 Tugboat Mickey 400.00
7 Huey, Louis & Dewey(c) 400.00
8 Figaro & Cleo 400.00
9 Donald(c),J.Crickett 450.00
10 July 4th 425.00
11 Mickey's Tailor 450.00
12 Change of format 4,000.00
becomes:

WALT DISNEY COMICS & STORIES

MICKEY MOUSE
Whitman

904 W.Disney's Mickey Mouse
and his friends (1934) 1,100.00
948 Disney'sMickeyMouse('34) 1,100.00

MIDGET COMICS
St. John Publishing Co.
Feb., 1950

1 MB(c),Fighting Indian Stories . 150.00
2 April, 1950;Tex West-Cowboy
Marshall 75.00

MIGHTY ATOM, THE (see PIXIES)

MIGHTY MIDGET COMICS
Samuel E. Lowe & Co., 1942-43
4"x5" Format

1 Bulletman 150.00
2 Captain Marvel 150.00
3 Captain Marvel Jr. 135.00
4 Golden Arrow 135.00
5 Ibis the Invincible 135.00
6 Spy Smasher 135.00
7 Balbo, The Boy magician 60.00
8 Bulletman 100.00
9 Commando Yank 75.00

GOLDEN AGE

10 Dr. Voltz, The Human
Generator 60.00
11 Lance O'Casey 60.00
12 Leatherneck the Marine 60.00
13 Minute Man 100.00
14 Mister Q 75.00
15 Mr. Scarlet & Pinky 100.00
16 Pat Wilson & His
Flying Fortress 60.00
17 Phantom Eagle 65.00
18 State Trooper Stops Crime. . . . 60.00
19 Tornado Tom 60.00

MIGHTY MOUSE
Fall, 1946
[1st Series]

1 Terytoons Presents 1,000.00
2 . . . . 500.00
3 . . . . 300.00
4 Summer, 1947 . . . . 300.00

MIGHTY MOUSE
St. John Publishing
Aug., 1947

5 . . . . 275.00
6 thru 10 . . . . @150.00
11 thru 20 . . . . @100.00
21 thru 25 . . . . @75.00
26 thru 30 . . . . @60.00
31 thru 34 . . . . @50.00
35 Flying Saucer 65.00
36 . . . . 50.00
37 . . . . 50.00
38 thru 45 Giant 100 pgs. . . . . @150.00
46 thru 66 . . . . @50.00
67 P(c),. 50.00

Pines

68 thru 81 Funny Animal . . . . . . @40.00
82 Infinity (c). 40.00
83 June, 1959 . . . . 40.00

MIGHTY MOUSE ADVENTURE STORIES
St. John Publishing Co., 1953

N# 384 Pages,Rebound. 350.00

MIKE BARNETT, MAN AGAINST CRIME
Fawcett Publications
Dec., 1951

1 The Mint of Dionysosi 150.00
2 Mystery of the Blue Madonna 100.00
3 Revenge Holds the Torch 75.00
4 Special Delivery 75.00
5 Market For Morphine 100.00
6 Oct., 1952 . . . . 75.00

MILITARY COMICS
Comics Magazines
(Quality Comics Group)
Aug., 1941

1 JCo,CCu,FG,BP,WE(c),O:Blackhawk,
Miss America, Death Patrol,
Blue Tracer; B:X of the Under-
ground, Yankee Eagle,Q-Boat,
Shot & Shell, Archie Atkins,
Loops & Banks 8,500.00
2 JCo,FG,BP,CCu,CCu(c),B:
Secret War News 2,200.00
3 JCo,FG,BP,AMc,CCu,CCu(c),
I&O:Chop Chop 1,800.00
4 FG,BP,AMc,CCu,CCu(c), . . 1,400.00
5 FG,BP,AMc,CCu,CCu(c),

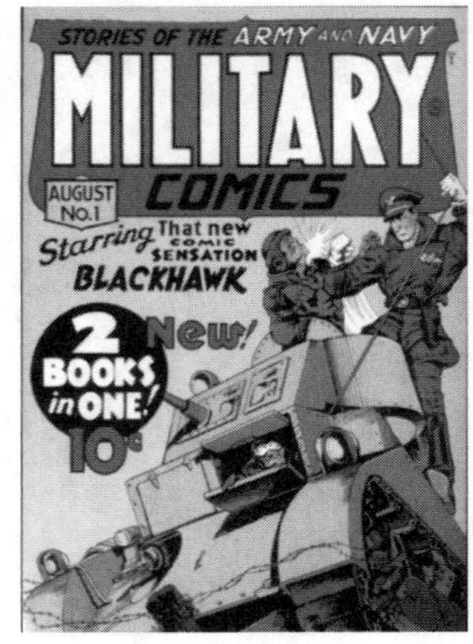

Military Comics #1
© Quality Comics Group

B: The Sniper 1,200.00
6 FG,BP,AMc,CCu,CCu(c) 900.00
7 FG,BP,AMc,CCu,CCu(c)
E:Death Patrol 900.00
8 FG,BP,AMc,CCu,CCu(c) 900.00
9 FG,BP,AMc,CCu,CCu(c),
B: The Phantom Clipper . . . 900.00
10 FG,BP,CCu,AMc,WE(c). . . . 1,000.00
11 FG,BP,CCu,AMc,
WE(c),Flag(c) 750.00
12 FG,BP,AMc,RC,RC(c) 900.00
13 FG,BP,AMc,RC,RC(c),E:X of
the Underground 700.00
14 FG,AMc,RC,RC(c),B:Private
Dogtag 700.00
15 FG,AMc,RC,RC(c), ... 700.00
16 FG,AMc,RC,RC(c),E:The
Phantom Clipper,Blue Tracer 600.00
17 FG,AMc,RC,RC(c),
B:P.T. Boat 600.00
18 FG,AMc,RC,RC(c), V:
The Thunderer 600.00
19 FG,RC,RC(c), V:King Cobra. . 600.00
20 GFx,RC,RC(c), Death Patrol . 600.00
21 FG,GFx 550.00
22 FG,GFx 550.00
23 FG,GFx 550.00
24 FG,GFx,V: Man-Heavy
Glasses 550.00
25 FG,GFx,V: Wang The Tiger . . 550.00
26 FG,GFx,V: Skull. 500.00
27 FG,JCo,R:The Death Patrol . . 500.00
28 FG,JCo, Dungeon of Doom . . 500.00
29 FG,JCo,V: Xanukhara 500.00
30 FG,JCo,BWa,BWa(c),B.Hwk
V: Dr. Koro 500.00
31 FG,JCo,BWa,E:Death
Patrol; I: Captain Hitsu 500.00
32 JCo,A: Captain Hitsu 450.00
33 W/ Civil War Veteran 450.00
34 A: Eve Rice 450.00
35 Shipwreck Island 450.00
36 Cult of the Wailing Tiger. 450.00
37 Pass of Bloody Peace 450.00
38 B.Hwk Faces Bloody Death . . 450.00
39 A: Kwan Yin. 450.00
40 V: Ratru 425.00
41 W/ Chop Chop (c) 425.00
42 V: Jap Mata Hari 425.00
43 . . . . 425.00
Becomes:

MODERN COMICS

44 Duel of Honor 450.00
45 V: Sakyo the Madman 350.00
46 RC, Soldiers of Fortune 350.00
47 RC,PG,V:Count Hokoy. 350.00
48 RC,PG,V:Pirates of Perool . . . 350.00
49 RC,PG,I:Fear,Lady
Adventuress 350.00
50 RC,PG 350.00
51 RC,PG, Ancient City of Evil . . 300.00
52 PG,BWa,V: The Vulture 300.00
53 PG,BWa,B: Torchy. 350.00
54 PG,RC,RC/CCu,BWa. 275.00
55 PG,RC,RC/CCu,BWa. 275.00
56 PG,RC/CCu,BWa. 275.00
57 PG,RC/CCu,BWa. 275.00
58 PG,RC,RC/CCu,BWa,
V:The Grabber 275.00
59 PG,RC,RC/CCu,BWa. 275.00
60 PG,RC/CCu,BWa,RC(c),
V:Green Plague 275.00
61 PG,RC/CCu,BWa,RC(c). 275.00
62 PG,RC/CCu,BWa,RC(c). 275.00
63 PG,RC/CCu,BWa,RC(c). 250.00
64 PG,RC/CCu,BWa,RC(c). 250.00
65 PG,RC/CCu,BWa,RC(c). 250.00
66 PG,RC/CCu,BWa. 250.00
67 PG,RC/CCu,BWa,RC(c). 250.00
68 PG,RC/CCu,BWa,RC(c);
I:Madame Butterfly 250.00
69 PG,RC/CCu,BWa,RC(c). 250.00
70 PG,RC/CCu,BWa,RC(c) 250.00
71 PG,RC/CCu,BWa,RC(c). 250.00
72 PG,RC/CCu,BWa,RC(c). 225.00
73 PG,RC/CCu,BWa,RC(c). 225.00
74 PG,RC/CCu,BWa,RC(c). 225.00
75 PG,RC/CCu,BWa,RC(c). 225.00
76 PG,RC/CCu,BWa,RC(c). 225.00
77 PG,RC/CCu,BWa,RC(c). 225.00
78 PG,RC/CCu,BWa,JCo,RC(c) . 250.00
79 PG,RC/CCu,BWa,JCo,RC(c) . 225.00
80 PG,RC/CCu,BWa,JCo,RC(c) . 225.00
81 PG,RC/CCu,BWa,JCo,RC(c) . 225.00
82 PG,RC/CCu,BWa,JCo,RC(c) . 225.00
83 PG,RC/CCu.BWa,JCo,RC(c);
E: Private Dogtag 225.00
84 PG,RC/CCu,BWa,RC(c). 225.00
85 PG,RC/CCu,BWa,RC(c). 225.00
86 PG,RC/CCu,BWa,RC(c). 225.00
87 PG,RC/CCu,BWa,RC(c). 225.00
88 PG,RC/CCu,BWa,RC(c). 225.00
89 PG,RC/CCu,BWa,RC(c). 225.00
90 PG,RC/CCu,GFx,RC(c) 225.00
91 RC/CCu,GFx,RC(c) 225.00
92 RC/CCu,GFx,RC(c) 225.00
93 RC/CCu,GFx,RC(c) 225.00
94 RC/CCu,GFx,RC(c) 225.00
95 RC/CCu,GFx,RC(c) 225.00
96 RC/CCu,GFx,RC/CCu(c) 225.00
97 RC/CCu,GFx,RC/CCu(c) 225.00
98 RC/CCu,GFx,RC/CCu(c) 225.00
99 RC/CCu,GFx,JCo,RC/CCu(c). 225.00
100 GFx,JCo,RC/CCu(c) 225.00
101 GFx,JCo,RC/CCu(c) 225.00
102 GFx,JCo,WE,BWa,
RC/CCu(c) 275.00

MILT GROSS FUNNIES
Milt Gross, Inc.
Aug., 1947

1 Gag Oriented Caricature. 50.00
2 Gag Oriented Caricature 45.00

MINUTE MAN
Fawcett Publications
Summer, 1941

1 V: The Nazis 1,500.00
2 V: The Mongol Horde 900.00
3 V: The Black Poet;Spr'42 . . . . 850.00

MIRACLE COMICS
E.C. Comics
Feb.,1940

1 B:Sky Wizard,Master of Space, Dash Dixon,Man of Might,Dusty Doyle,Pinkie Parker, The Kid Cop,K-7 Secret Agent,Scorpion & Blandu,Jungle Queen . . 1,500.00
2 . . . . 750.00
3 B:Bill Colt,The Ghost Rider . . 800.00
4 A:The Veiled Prophet, Bullet Bob; Mar'41 . . . . 750.00

MISS CAIRO JONES
Croyden Publishers, 1944

1 BO,Rep. Newspaper Strip . . . 150.00

MR. ANTHONY'S LOVE CLINIC
Hillman Periodicals, 1945

1 Ph(c) 100.00
2 . . . . 65.00
3 . . . . 50.00
4 . . . . 50.00
5 Ph(c),Apr/May'50 . . . . 50.00

MR. MUSCLES (see THING, THE)

MISTER MYSTERY
Media Publ./SPM Publ./ Aragon Publ.
Sept., 1951

1 HK,RA,Horror 650.00
2 RA,RA(c) 450.00
3 RA(c) 450.00
4 Bondage(c) 465.00
5 Lingerie(c) 425.00
6 Bondage(c) 450.00
7 BW,Bondage(c);The Brain Bats of Venus 850.00
8 Lingerie(c) 400.00
9 HN 375.00
10 . . . . 375.00
11 BW,Robot Woman 600.00
12 Flaming Object to Eye (c). . . . 850.00
13 . . . . 250.00
14 . . . . 250.00
15 The Coffin & Medusa's Head . 275.00
16 Bondage(c) 275.00
17 . . . . 250.00
18 BW,Bondage(c) 450.00

MISTER RISK (see HAND OF FATE)

MISTER UNIVERSE
Mr. Publ./Media Publ./ Stanmore
July, 1951

1 . . . . 150.00
2 RA(c);Jungle That time Forgot 125.00
3 Marijuana Story 100.00
4 Mr. Universe Goes to War. 75.00
5 Mr. Universe Goes to War; April, 1952 . . . . 75.00

MODERN COMICS (see MILITARY COMICS)

Modern Love #6
© Hillman Periodicals

MODERN LOVE
Tiny Tot Comics (E.C. Comics)
June–July, 1949

1 Stolen Romance 500.00
2 JcR,AF(c),I Craved Excitement 350.00
3 AF(c);Our Families Clashed . . 300.00
4 AF(c);I Was a B Girl 450.00
5 AF(c);Saved From Shame . . . 450.00
6 AF(c);The Love That Might Have Been 450.00
7 AF(c);They Won't Let Me Love Him 325.00
8 AF(c);Aug-Sept'50 . . . . 325.00

MOE & SHMOE COMICS
O.S. Publishing Co.
Spring, 1948

1 Gag Oriented Caricature 50.00
2 Gag Oriented Caricature 35.00

MOLLY O'DAY
Avon Periodicals
Feb., 1945

1 GT;The Enchanted Dagger . . 400.00

MONKEYSHINES COMICS
Publ. Specialists/Ace/
Summer, 1944

1 (fa),Several Short Features . . . 75.00
2 (fa),Same Format Throughout Entire Run 40.00
3 thru 16 Funny Animal . . . . . . @25.00

Ace

17 Funny Animal 35.00
18 thru 21 . . . . @25.00

Unity Publ.

22 (fa) 25.00
23 (fa) 25.00
24 (fa),AFa,AFa(c) 25.00
25 (fa) 25.00
26 (fa) 25.00
27 (fa),July, 1949 . . . . 25.00

MONSTER
Fiction House Magazines, 1953

1 Dr. Drew. 400.00
2 . . . . 275.00

MONSTER CRIME COMICS
Hillman Periodicals
Oct., 1952

1 52 Pgs,15 Cent Cover Price . . 800.00

MONTE HALL WESTERN (see MARY MARVEL COMICS)

MONTY HALL OF THE U.S. MARINES
Toby Press, Aug., 1951

1 B:Monty Hall,Pin-Up Pete; (All Issues) 75.00
2 . . . . 40.00
3 thru 5 . . . . @35.00
6 . . . . 35.00
7 The Fireball Express 35.00
8 . . . . 35.00
9 . . . . 35.00
10 The Vial of Death. 35.00
11 Monju Island Prison Break 35.00

MOON GIRL AND THE PRINCE
E.C. Comics, Autumn, 1947

1 JCr(c),O:Moon Girl 800.00
2 JCr(c),Battle of the Congo . . . 400.00
3 . . . . 350.00
4 V: A Vampire 350.00
5 1st E.C. Horror-Zombie Terror. 850.00
6 . . . . 450.00
7 O:Star;The Fient Who Fights With Fire 450.00
8 True Crime Feature 450.00

Becomes:

A MOON, A GIRL ...ROMANCE

9 AF,Grl,AF(c),C:Moon Girl; Spanking Panels 550.00
10 AF,Grl,WW,AF(c),Suspicious of His Intentions 500.00
11 AF,Grl,WW,AF(c),Hearts Along the Ski Trail 500.00
12 AF,Grl,AF(c), March–April, 1950 . . . . 600.00

MOPSY
St. John Publishing Co.
Feb., 1948

1 Paper Dolls Enclosed 125.00
2 . . . . 75.00
3 . . . . 70.00
4 Paper Dolls Enclosed 70.00
5 Paper Dolls Enclosed 70.00
6 Paper Dolls Enclosed 70.00
7 . . . . 50.00
8 Paper Dolls Enclosed; Lingerie Panels 55.00
9 . . . . 50.00
10 . . . . 50.00
11 . . . . 40.00
12 . . . . 40.00
13 Paper Dolls Enclosed. 45.00
14 thru 18 . . . . @40.00
19 Lingerie(c);Paper Dolls Enclosed 45.00

MORTIE
Magazine Publishers
Dec., 1952

1 ...Mazie's Friend 40.00
2 . . . . 25.00
3 . . . . 20.00

MOTION PICTURE COMICS
Fawcett Publications
Nov., 1950

101 Ph(c),Monte Hale's-
Vanishing Westerner. 225.00
102 Ph(c),Rocky Lane's-Code
of the Silver Sage. 200.00
103 Ph(c),Rocky Lane's-Covered
Wagon Raid 200.00
104 BP,Ph(c),Rocky Lane's-
Vigilante Hideout 200.00
105 BP,Ph(c),Audie Murphy's-
Red Badge of Courage. 250.00
106 Ph(c),George Montgomery's-
The Texas Rangers 225.00
107 Ph(c),Rocky Lane's-Frisco
Tornado 200.00
108 Ph(c),John Derek's-Mask
of the Avenger 150.00
109 Ph(c),Rocky Lane's-Rough
Rider of Durango 200.00
110 GE,Ph(c), When Worlds
Collide 700.00
111 Ph(c),Lash LaRue's-The
Vanishing Outpost 225.00
112 Ph(c),Jay Silverheels'-
Brave Warrior. 125.00
113 KS,Ph(c),George Murphy's-
Walk East on Beacon 100.00
114 Ph(c),George Montgomery's-
Cripple Creek;Jan, 1953. . . . 100.00

MOTION PICTURES FUNNIES WEEKLY
1st Funnies Incorporated, 1939

1 BEv,1st Sub-Mariner 21,000.00
2 Cover Only 600.00
3 Cover Only 600.00
4 Cover Only 600.00

MOVIE CLASSICS
(NO #S)
Dell Publishing Co.
Jan., 1953

1 Around the World Under
the Sea 30.00
2 Bambi 35.00
3 Battle of the Buldge 25.00
4 Ph(c),Beach Blanket Bingo . . . 50.00
5 Ph(c),Bon Voyage 25.00
6 Castilian 30.00
7 Cat 20.00
8 Cheyenne Autumn 45.00
9 Ph(c),Circus World,
John Wayne (c) 100.00
10 Ph(c),Countdown,J.Caan(c). . . 30.00
11 Creature 75.00
12 Ph(c),David Ladd's Life Story. . 75.00
13 Ph(c),Die Monster Die 50.00
14 Dirty Dozen 40.00
15 Ph(c),Dr. Who & the Daleks . . 125.00
16 Dracula 40.00
17 El Dorado,J.WaynePh(c) 125.00
18 Ensign Pulver 25.00
19 Frankenstein 40.00
20 Ph(c),Great Race. 40.00
21 B.LancasterPh(c). 40.00
22 Hatari 75.00
23 Horizontal Lieutenant. 25.00
24 Ph(c) Mr. Limpet 25.00
25 Jack the Giant Killer. 80.00
26 Ph(c),Jason & the Argonauts . 100.00
27 Lancelot & Guinevere 55.00
28 Lawrence. 55.00
29 Lion of Sparta 25.00
30 Mad Monster Party 55.00
31 Magic Sword 45.00
32 Ph(c),Masque of Red Death. . . 40.00
33 Maya 35.00
34 McHale's Navy. 40.00
35 Ph(c) Merrills' Marauders 25.00
36 Ph(c),Mouse on the Moon 20.00
37 Mummy 40.00
38 Music Man. 30.00
39 Ph(c),Naked Prey 50.00
40 Ph(c),Night of the Grizzly. 35.00
41 None but the Brave 55.00
42 Ph(c),Operation Bikini 30.00
43 Operation Cross Bold. 30.00
44 Prince & the Pauper. 30.00
45 Raven,V.Price(c) 45.00
46 Ring of Bright Water 35.00
47 Runaway 20.00
48 Ph(c),Santa Claus Conquers
the Martians 65.00
49 Ph(c),Six Black Horses 30.00
50 Sky Party. 35.00
51 Smoky. 25.00
52 Ph(c),Sons of Katie Elder. . . . 125.00
53 GE,Tales of Terror 30.00
54 Ph(c),3 Stooges meet
Hercules. 85.00
55 Tomb of Legeia 25.00
56 Treasure Island 25.00
57 Twice Told Tales(V.Price) 40.00
58 Two on a Guillotine 25.00
59 Valley of Gwangi 45.00
60 War Gods of the Deep 20.00
61 War Wagon (John Wayne) 85.00
62 Who's Minding the Mint 25.00
63 Wolfman 35.00
64 Ph(c),Zulu 75.00
65 . . . . 25.00

MOVIE COMICS
Fiction House Magazines
Dec., 1946

1 Big Town on(c) 450.00
2 MB,White Tie & Tails 325.00
3 MB,Andy Hardy Laugh Hit . . . 325.00
4 MB,Slave Girl 400.00

MOVIE LOVE
Famous Funnies Publications
Feb., 1950

1 Ph(c),Dick Powell(c) 100.00
2 Ph(c),Myrna Loy(c) 50.00
3 Ph(c),Cornell Wilde(c) 40.00
4 Ph(c),Paulette Goddard(c) 40.00
5 Ph(c),Joan Fontaine(c) 40.00
6 Ph(c),Ricardo Montalban(c) . . . 40.00
7 Ph(c),Fred Astaire(c) 40.00
8 AW,FF,Ph(c),Corinne
Calvert(c) 300.00
9 Ph(c),John Lund(c) 40.00
10 Ph(c),Mona Freeman(c). 300.00
11 Ph(c),James Mason(c). 45.00
12 Ph(c),Jerry Lewis &
Dean Martin(c) 50.00
13 Ph(c),Ronald Reagan(c). 150.00
14 Ph(c),Janet Leigh,Gene Kelly. . 40.00
15 Ph(c), ... 35.00
16 Ph(c),Angela Lansbury. 60.00
17 FF,Ph(c),Leslie Caron 30.00
18 Ph(c),Cornel Wilde. 30.00
19 Ph(c),John Derek. 30.00
20 Ph(c),Debbie Reynolds 35.00
21 Ph(c),Patricia Medina. 30.00
22 Ph(c),John Payne 30.00

MOVIE THRILLERS
Magazine Enterprises 1949

1 Ph(c),Burt Lancaster's-
Rope of Sand 225.00

MR. MUSCLES (see THING!, THE)

MUGGY-DOO, BOY CAT
Stanhall Publications
July, 1953

1 . . . . 35.00
2 and 3 . . . . @25.00
4 Jan., 1954 . . . . 25.00

Murder Incorporated #4
© Fox Features Incorporated

MURDER, INCORPORATED
Fox Features Incorporated
Jan., 1948

1 For Adults Only-on(c) 400.00
2 For Adults Only-on(c);Male
Bondage(c),Electrocution sty 300.00
3 Dutch Schultz-Beast of Evil . . 175.00
4 The Ray Hamilton Case,
Lingerie(c) 175.00
5 thru 8 . . . . @175.00
9 Bathrobe (c) 165.00
9a Lingerie (c) 175.00
10 . . . . 150.00
11 . . . . 150.00
12 . . . . 150.00
13 . . . . 175.00
14 Bill Hale-King o/t Murderers . . 150.00
15 . . . . 150.00
16(5),Second Series 100.00
17(2) 100.00
18(3), Bondage(c) w/Lingerie,
Aug., 1951 . . . . 125.00

MURDEROUS GANGSTERS
Avon Periodicals/Realistic
July, 1951

1 WW,Pretty Boy Floyd,
Leggs Diamond 350.00

2 WW,Baby Face Nelson,Mad Dog Esposito 225.00
3 P(c),Tony & Bud Fenner, Jed Hawkins 200.00
4 EK(c),Murder By Needle-Drug Story, June, 1952. . . . . 200.00

MUTINY
Aragon Magazines
Oct., 1954

1 AH(c),Stormy Tales of the Seven Seas 125.00
2 AH(c) 100.00
3 Bondage(c),Feb., '55 . . . . 100.00

MY CONFESSIONS (see WESTERN TRUE CRIME)

MY DATE COMICS
Hillman Periodicals
July, 1944

1 S&K,S&K (c), Teenage 250.00
2 S&K,DB,S&K(c) 175.00
3 S&K,DB,S&K(c) 175.00
4 S&K,DB,S&K(c) 175.00

MY DESIRE
Fox Features Syndicate
Oct., 1949

1 Intimate Confessions 100.00
2 WW,They Called Me Wayward . 75.00
3 I Hid My Lover 40.00
4 WW, April, 1950 . . . . 125.00

MY GREAT LOVE
Fox Features Syndicate
Oct., 1949

1 Reunion In a Shack 100.00
2 My Crazy Dreams 50.00
3 He Was Ashamed of Me 45.00
4 My Two Wedding Rings;Apr'50 50.00

MY INTIMATE AFFAIR
Fox Features Syndicate
March, 1950

1 I Sold My Love 100.00
2 I Married a Jailbird;May'50 . . . . 50.00

MY LIFE (see MEET CORLISS ARCHER)

MY LOVE AFFAIR
Fox Features Syndicate
July, 1949

1 Truck Driver's Sweetheart . . . 100.00
2 My Dreadful Secret 65.00
3 WW,I'll Make Him Marry Me . . 125.00
4 WW,They Called Me Wild . . . 125.00
5 WW,Beauty Was My Bait 125.00
6 WW,The Man Downstairs 125.00

MY LOVE MEMORIES (see WOMEN OUTLAWS)

MY LOVE LIFE (see TEGRA, JUNGLE EMPRESS)

MY LOVE STORY
Fox Features Syndicate
Sept., 1949

1 Men Gave Me Jewels 100.00
2 He Dared Me 60.00
3 WW,I Made Love a Plaything . 125.00
4 WW,I Tried to Be Good 125.00

MY PAST CONFESSIONS (see WESTERN THRILLERS)

MY PRIVATE LIFE
Fox Features Syndicate
Feb., 1950

16 My Friendship Club Affair. . . . 90.00
17 My Guilty Kisses;April'50 . . . . 75.00

MY SECRET
Superior Comics
Aug., 1949

1 True Love Stories 100.00
2 I Was Guilty of Being a Cheating Wife 75.00
3 Was I His Second Love?; 75.00

Becomes:

OUR SECRET

4 JKa,She Loves Me,She Loves Me Not; Nov., 1949. . . . 75.00
5 . . . . 50.00
6 . . . . 50.00
7 How Do You Fall In Love? 60.00
8 His Kiss Tore At My Heart; June, 1950. . . . 50.00

MY SECRET AFFAIR
Hero Books
(Fox Features Syndicate)
Dec., 1949

1 WW,SHn,My Stormy Love Affair 150.00
2 WW,I Loved a Weakling 100.00
3 WW, April, 1950 . . . . 125.00

MY SECRET LIFE
Fox Features Syndicate
July, 1949

22 I Loved More Than Once 75.00
23 WW. . . . 125.00
24 Love Was a Habit 50.00
25 . . . . 50.00

Becomes:

ROMEO TUBBS

26 WW,That Lovable Teen-ager . 140.00

MY SECRET LOVE (see PHANTOM LADY)

MY SECRET MARRIAGE
Superior Comics
May, 1953

1 I Was a Cheat 75.00
2 . . . . 35.00
3 We Couldn't Wait 25.00
4 . . . . 25.00
5 . . . . 25.00
6 . . . . 25.00
7 thru 23 . . . . @25.00
24 1956 . . . . 25.00

MY SECRET ROMANCE
Hero Books
(Fox Features Syndicate)
Jan., 1950

1 WW,They Called Me 'That' Woman 100.00
2 WW,They Called Me Cheap . . 125.00

MYSTERIES WEIRD AND STRANGE
Superior Comics/ Dynamic Publ.
May, 1953

1 The Stolen Brain 250.00
2 The Screaming Room, Atomic Bomb 150.00
3 The Avenging Corpse 125.00
4 Ghost on the Gallows 125.00
5 Horror a la Mode 125.00
6 Howling Horror 125.00
7 Demon in Disguise 125.00
8 The Devil's Birthmark 125.00
9 . . . . 125.00
10 . . . . 135.00
11 . . . . 125.00

MYSTERIOUS ADVENTURES
Story Comics
March, 1951

1 Wild Terror of the Vampire Flag 375.00
2 Terror of the Ghoul's Corpse . 200.00
3 Terror of the Witche's Curse . . 175.00
4 The Little Coffin That Grew . . 175.00
5 LC,Curse of the Jungle, Bondage(c). . . . 220.00
6 LC,Ghostly Terror in the Cave 150.00
7 LC,Terror of the Ghostly Castle 275.00
8 Terror of the Flowers of Deat. . 300.00

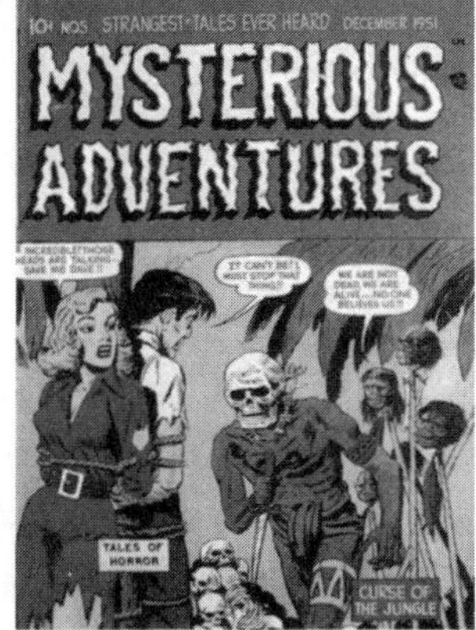

Mysterious Adventures #5
© Story Comics

9 The Ghostly Ghouls-
Extreme Violence 225.00
10 Extreme Violence. 200.00
11 The Trap of Terror 225.00
12 SHn,Vultures of Death-
Extreme Violence 225.00
13 Extreme Violence. 225.00
14 Horror of the Flame Thrower
Extreme Violence 225.00
15 DW,Ghoul Crazy 275.00
16 Chilling Tales of Horror. 275.00
17 DW,Bride of the Dead 275.00
18 Extreme Violence. 275.00
19 The Coffin 275.00
20 Horror o/t Avenging Corpse . . 275.00
21 Mother Ghoul's Nursery
Tales, Bondage (c) 275.00
22 RA,Insane 200.00
23 RA,Extreme Violence. 200.00
24 KS, ... 150.00
25 KS,Aug., 1955 . . . . 150.00

HORROR FROM THE TOMB

Premier Magazines

Sept., 1954

1 AT,GWb,The Corpse Returns . 300.00

Becomes:

MYSTERIOUS STORIES

2 GWb(c),Eternal Life 300.00
3 GWb,The Witch Doctor 200.00
4 That's the Spirit 175.00
5 King Barbarossa 175.00
6 GWb,Strangers in the Night . . 200.00
7 KS,The Pipes of Pan;Dec'55. . 175.00

MYSTERIOUS TRAVELER COMICS

Trans-World Publications

Nov., 1948

1 BP,BP(c),Five Miles Down . . . 450.00

MYSTERY COMICS

William H. Wise & Co., 1944

1 AS(c),B:Brad Spencer-Wonderman,
King of Futeria,The Magnet, Zudo-
Jungle Boy,The Silver Knight 900.00
2 AS(c),Bondage (c) 550.00
3 AS(c),Robot(c),LanceLewis,B . 500.00
4 AS(c),E:All Features,
KKK Type(c). 500.00

MYSTERY MEN COMICS

Fox Features Syndicate

Aug., 1939

1 GT,DBr,LF(c),Bondage(c);I:Blue
Beetle,Green Mask,Rex Dexter
of Mars,Zanzibar,Lt.Drake,D-13
Secret Agent,Chen Chang,
Wing Turner,Capt. Denny 10,000.00
2 GT,BP,DBr,LF(c),
Rex Dexter (c). 2,800.00
3 LF(c) 3,500.00
4 LF(c),B:Captain Savage. . . . 2,000.00
5 GT,BP,LF(c),Green Mask (c) 2,000.00
6 GT,BP 1,800.00
7 GT,BP,Bondage(c),
Blue Beetle(c) 2,000.00
8 GT,BP,LF(c),Bondage(c),
Blue Beetle 1,800.00
9 GT,BP,DBr(c),B:The Moth 900.00
10 GT,BP,JSm(c),A:Wing
Turner; Bondage(c). 800.00
11 GT,BP,JSm(c),I:The Domino. . 800.00
12 GT,BP,JSm(c),BlueBeetle(c). . 800.00

Mystery Men Comics #8
© Fox Features Syndicate

13 GT,I:The Lynx & Blackie. 525.00
14 GT,Male Bondage (c). 500.00
15 GT,Blue Beetle (c) 475.00
16 GT,Hypo(c),MaleBondage(c) . 500.00
17 GT,BP,Blue Beetle (c) 475.00
18 GT,Blue Beetle (c) 475.00
19 GT,I&B:Miss X 550.00
20 GT,DBr,Blue Beetle (c). 450.00
21 GT,E:Miss X. 450.00
22 GT,CCu(c),Blue Beetle (c) . . . 450.00
23 GT,Blue Beetle (c) 450.00
24 GT,BP,DBr, Blue Beetle (c). . . 450.00
25 GT,Bondage(c);
A:Private O'Hara. 475.00
26 GT,Bondage(c);B:The Wraith . 475.00
27 GT,Bondage(c),BlueBeetle(c). 475.00
28 GT,Bondage(c);Satan's
Private Needlewoman. 475.00
29 GT,Bondage(c),Blue
Beetle (c) 475.00
30 Holiday of Death 450.00
31 Bondage(c);Feb'42. . . . . 475.00

MY STORY (see ZAGO, JUNGLE PRINCE)

NATIONAL COMICS

Comics Magazines

(Quality Comics Group)

July, 1940

1 GT,HcK,LF(c),B:Uncle Sam,Wonder
Boy,Merlin the Magician,Cyclone,
Kid Patrol,Sally O'Neil-Police-
woman, Pen Miller,Prop
Powers, Paul Bunyan 5,000.00
2 WE,GT,HcK,LF&RC(c) 2,000.00
3 GT,HcK,WE&RC(c) 1,300.00
4 GT,HcK,LF&RC(c),E:Cyclone;
Torpedo Islands of Death. . 1,200.00
5 GT,LF&RC(c),B:Quicksilver;
O:Uncle Sam 1,200.00
6 GT,LF&RC(c) 1,100.00
7 GT,LF&RC(c) 1,200.00
8 GT,LF&RC(c) 1,100.00
9 JCo,LF&RC(c) 1,100.00
10 RC,JCo,LF&RC(c). 1,100.00
11 RC,JCo,LF&RC(c). 1,100.00
12 RC,JCo,LF&RC(c) 800.00
13 RC,JCo,LF,LF&RC(c). 750.00
14 RC,JCo,LF,PG,LF&RC(c). . . . 750.00
15 RC,JCo,LF,PG,LF&RC(c). . . . 750.00
16 RC,JCo,LF,PG,LF&RC(c). . . . 750.00
17 RC,JCo,LF,PG,LF&RC(c). . . . 550.00
18 JCo,LF,PG,LF&RC(c),
Pearl Harbor 1,000.00
19 JCo,LF,PG,RC(c),The Black
Fog Mystery 550.00
20 JCo,LF,PG,LF&RC(c) 550.00
21 LF,JCo,PG,LF(c) 550.00
22 JCo,LF,PG,FG,GFx,LF(c),
E:Jack & Jill,Pen Miller,
Paul Bunyan. 550.00
23 JCo,PG,FG,GFx,AMc,LF
& GFx(c),B:The Unknown,
Destroyer 171. . . . . 550.00
24 JCo,PG,RC,AMc,FG,
GFx,RC(c) 525.00
25 AMc,RC,JCo,PG,FG,
GFx,RC(c) 400.00
26 AMc,Jco,RC,PG,RC(c),
E:Prop Powers,WonderBoy. . 400.00
27 JCo,AMc 400.00
28 JCo,AMc 400.00
29 JCo,O:The Unknown;U.Sam
V:Dr. Dirge 425.00
30 JCo,RC(c) 375.00
31 JCo,RC(c) 375.00
32 JCo,RC(c) 375.00
33 JCo,GFx,RC(c),B:Chic Carter;
U.Sam V:Boss Spring 375.00
34 JCo,GFx,U.Sam V:Big John
Fales 375.00
35 JCo,GFx,E:Kid Patrol. 300.00
36 JCo 300.00
37 JCo,FG,A:The Vagabond 300.00
38 JCo,FG,Boat of the Dead. . . . 300.00
39 JCo,FG,Hitler(c);U.Sam
V:The Black Market 300.00
40 JCo,FG,U.Sam V:The
Syndicate of Crime 200.00
41 JCo,FG 200.00
42 JCo,FG,JCo(c),B:The Barker . 175.00
43 JCo,FG,JCo(c). 175.00
44 JCo,FG 175.00
45 JCo,FG,E:Merlin the Magician 175.00
46 JCo,JCo(c),Murder is no Joke 175.00
47 JCo,JCo(c),E:Chic Carter. . . . 175.00
48 JCo,O:The Whistler 175.00
49 JCo,JCo(c),A Corpse
for a Cannonball. 175.00
50 JCo,JCo(c),V:Rocks Myzer . . 175.00
51 JCo,BWa,JCo(c),
A:Sally O'Neil 225.00
52 JCo,A Carnival of Laughs . . . 150.00
53 PG,V:Scramolo 150.00
54 PG,V:Raz-Ma-Taz 150.00
55 JCo,AMc,V:The Hawk 150.00

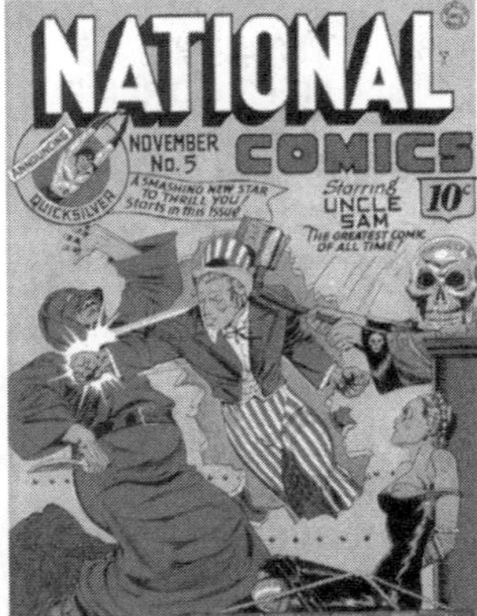

National Comics #5
© Quality Comics Group

56 GFx,JCo,AMc,V:The Grifter . . 150.00
57 GFX,JCo,AMc,V:Witch Doctor 150.00
58 GFz,JCo,AMc,Talking Animals 150.00
59 GFx,JCo,AMc,V:The Birdman 150.00
60 GFx,JCo,AMc,V:Big Ed Grew 150.00
61 GFx,AMc,Trouble Comes in Small Packages 100.00
62 GFx,AMc,V:Crocodile Man . . . 100.00
63 GFx,AMc,V:Bearded Lady . . . 100.00
64 GFx,V:The Human Fly 100.00
65 GFx,GFx(c)V:The King. 100.00
66 GFx,GFx(c)V:THe Man Who Hates the Circus. 100.00
67 GFx,Gfx(c),A:Quicksilver; V:Ali Ben Riff Raff. 100.00
68 GFx,GFx(c),V:Leo theLionMan 100.00
69 GFx,Gfx(c),A:Percy the Powerful. 100.00
70 GFx,GFx(c),Barker Tires of the Big Top 100.00
71 PG,GFx(c),V:SpellbinderSmith 100.00
72 PG,GFx(c),The Oldest Man in the World 100.00
73 PG,GFx(c),V:A CountrySlicker 100.00
74 PG,GFx(c),V:Snake Oil Sam . 100.00
75 PG,GFx(c),Barker Breakes the Bank at Monte Marlo;Nov'49. 100.00

NEBBS, THE

Dell Publishing Co., 1941

1 rep. 150.00

NEGRO ROMANCE

Fawcett Publications

June, 1950

1 GE,Ph(c), Love's Decoy 900.00
2 GE,Ph(c), A Tragic Vow 700.00
3 GE,Ph(c), My Love Betrayed Me 700.00

Charlton Comics

4 Rep.FawcettEd.#2;May,1955 . 550.00

NEW ROMANCES

Standard Comics

May, 1951

5 Ph(c), The Blame I Bore 90.00
6 Ph(c), No Wife Was I 50.00
7 Ph(c), My Runaway Heart, Ray Miland. 40.00
8 Ph(c) 40.00
9 Ph(c) 40.00
10 ATh,Ph(c) 60.00
11 ATh,Ph(c) of Elizabeth Taylor . 100.00
12 Ph(c). 30.00
13 Ph(c). 30.00
14 ATh,Ph(c) 50.00
15 Ph(c). 30.00
16 ATh,Ph(c) 50.00
17 Ath, ... 50.00
18 and 19 . . . . @30.00
20 GT, ... 40.00
21 April, 1954. . . . . 30.00

NICKEL COMICS

Dell Publishing Co., 1938

1 Bobby & Chip 550.00

NICKEL COMICS

Fawcett Publications

May, 1940

1 JaB(c),O&I: Bulletman 3,500.00
2 JaB(c), ... 1,000.00
3 JaB(c), ... 750.00
4 JaB(c), B: Red Gaucho 650.00
5 CCB(c),Bondage(c) 650.00
6 and 7 CCB(c) . . . . @600.00
8 CCB(c),Aug. 23, 1940, World's Fair 650.00

NIGHTMARE (see WEIRD HORRORS)

NIGHTMARE

Ziff-Davis Publishing Co.

1 EK,GT,P(c),The Corpse That Wouldn't Stay Dead 450.00
2 EK,P(c),Vampire Mermaid . . . 325.00

St. John Publishing Co.

3 EK,P(c),The Quivering Brain . 250.00
4 P(c),1953 . . . . 200.00

NORTHWEST MOUNTIES

Jubilee Publications/ St. John Publ. Co.

Oct., 1948

1 MB,BLb(c),Rose of the Yukon 400.00
2 MB,BLb(c),A:Ventrilo. 300.00
3 MB, Bondage(c) 275.00
4 MB(c),A:Blue Monk,July'49 . . 275.00

NURSERY RHYMES

Ziff-Davis Publishing Co., 1950

1 How John Came Clean 125.00
2 The Old Woman Who Lived in a Shoe 100.00

NUTS!

Premere Comics Group

March, 1954

1 . . . . 225.00
2 . . . . 150.00
3 Mention of "Reefers". 165.00
4 . . . . 150.00
5 Captain Marvel Spoof;Nov.'54 150.00

NUTTY COMICS

Fawcett Publications

Winter, 1946

1 (fa),F:Capt. Kid,Richard Richard, Joe Miller...Among others . . 100.00

NUTTY LIFE (see PHANTOM LADY)

NYOKA THE JUNGLE GIRL

Fawcett Publications

Winter, 1945

1 Bondage(c);Partial Ph(c) of Kay Aldridge as Nyoka 450.00
2 . . . . 225.00
3 . . . . 225.00
4 Bondage(c) 225.00
5 Barbacosi Madness; Bondage(c) 225.00
6 . . . . 175.00
7 North Pole Jungle;Bondage(c) 165.00
8 Bondage(c) 165.00
9 . . . . 150.00
10 . . . . 150.00
11 Danger! Death! in an Unexplored Jungle 125.00
12 . . . . 90.00
13 The Human Leopards 125.00
14 The Mad Witch Doctor; Bondage(c). 125.00

Nyoka The Jungle Girl #3
© Fawcett Publications

15 Sacred Goat of Kristan. 125.00
16 BK,The Vultures of Kalahari . . 150.00
17 BK 150.00
18 BK,The Art of Murder 150.00
19 The Elephant Battle 150.00
20 Explosive Volcano Action . . . 150.00
21 . . . . 75.00
22 The Weird Monsters 75.00
23 Danger in Duplicate 75.00
24 The Human Jaguar; Bondage(c) 80.00
25 Hand Colored Ph(c). 60.00
26 A Jungle Stampede 60.00
27 Adventure Laden 60.00
28 The Human Statues of the Jungle 60.00
29 Ph(c). 60.00
30 Ph(c) 60.00
31 thru 40 Ph(c) . . . . @50.00
41 thru 50 Ph(c) . . . . @45.00
51 thru 59 Ph(c) . . . . @40.00
60 Ph(c) 35.00
61 Ph(c),The Sacred Sword of the Jungle 35.00
62 & 63 Ph(c) . . . . @35.00
64 Ph(c), The Jungle Idol 35.00
65 Ph(c). 35.00
66 Ph(c). 35.00
67 Ph(c), The Sky Man. 35.00
68 thru 74 Ph(c) . . . . @35.00
75 Ph(c), The Jungle Myth of Terror 35.00
76 Ph(c). 35.00
77 Ph(c),The Phantoms of the Elephant Graveyard;Jun'53. . . 35.00

OAKY DOAKS

Eastern Color Printing Co.

July, 1942

1 Humor Oriented 250.00

OH, BROTHER!

Stanhall Publications

Jan., 1953

1 Bill Williams-a 40.00
2 thru 5 . . . . @25.00

OK COMICS
United Features Syndicate
July, 1940

1 B:Pal Peyton,Little Giant, Phantom Knight,Sunset Smith,Teller Twins, Don Ramon, Jerrry Sly,Kip Jaxon, Leatherneck,Ulysses 650.00
2 Oct., 1940 . . . . 625.00

100 PAGES OF COMICS
Dell Publishing Co., 1937

101 Alley Oop,OG,Wash Tubbs, Tom Mix,Dan Dunn 1,300.00

ON THE AIR
NBC Network Comics, 1947

1 Giveaway, no cover 175.00

ON THE SPOT
Fawcett Publications
Autumn, 1948

N# Bondage(c),PrettyBoyFloyd . . 250.00

Operation Peril #1
© American Comics Group

OPERATION PERIL
American Comics Group
(Michel Publ.)
Oct.–Nov., 1950

1 LSt,OW,OW(c),B:TyphoonTyler, DannyDanger,TimeTravellers 275.00
2 OW,OW(c) 175.00
3 OW,OW(c),Horror 150.00
4 OW,OW(c), Flying Saucers . . . 150.00
5 OW,OW(c), Science Fiction. . . 150.00
6 OW, Tyr. Rex 150.00
7 OW,OW(c) 125.00
8 OW,OW(c) 125.00
9 OW,OW(c) 125.00
10 OW,OW(c). 125.00
11 OW,OW(c), War 125.00
12 OW,OW(c),E:Time Travellers . 125.00
13 OW,OW(c),War Stories 65.00
14 OW,OW(c),War Stories 65.00
15 OW,OW(c),War Stories 65.00
16 OW,OW(c),April–May,1953, War Stories 65.00

OUR FLAG COMICS
Ace Magazines
Aug., 1941

1 MA,JM,B:Capt.Victory,Unknown Soldier,The Three Cheers . 2,200.00
2 JM,JM(c),O:The Flag 1,000.00
3 Tank Battle (c) 750.00
4 MA 750.00
5 I:Mr. Risk;April, 1942, Male Bondage 775.00

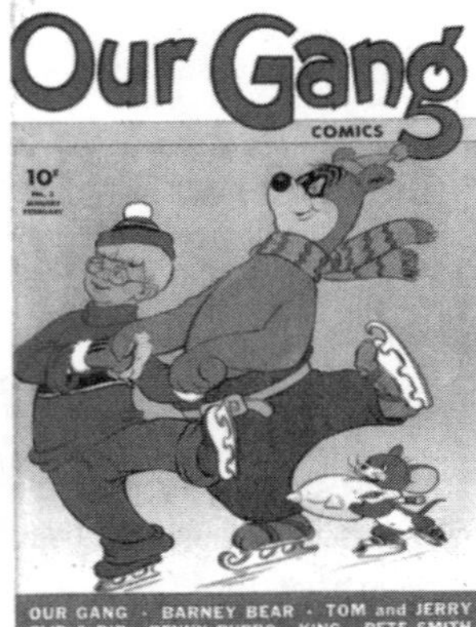

Our Gang #3
© Dell Publishing Co.

OUR GANG COMICS
Dell Publishing Co.
Sept.–Oct., 1942

1 WK,Barney Bear, Tom & Jerry 1,000.00
2 WK. 500.00
3 WK,Benny Burro. 350.00
4 WK. 350.00
5 WK. 350.00
6 WK. 500.00
7 WK. 250.00
8 WK,CB,Benny Burro 600.00
9 WK,CB,Benny Burro 550.00
10 WK,CB,Benny Burro 400.00
11 WK,I:Benny Bear 550.00
12 thru 20 WK. . . . . @250.00
21 thru 29 WK. . . . . @175.00
30 WK,Christmas(c) 150.00
31 thru 34 WK. . . . . @125.00
35 WK,CB 125.00
36 WK,CB 125.00
37 thru 40 WK. . . . . @75.00
41 thru 50 WK. . . . . @50.00
51 thru 56 WK. . . . . @40.00
57 . . . . 35.00
58 Our Gang 35.00
59 Our Gang 35.00

Becomes:

TOM AND JERRY
July, 1949

60 . . . . 100.00
61 . . . . 75.00
62 . . . . 50.00
63 . . . . 50.00
64 . . . . 50.00
65 . . . . 50.00
66 Christmas (c). 60.00
67 thru 70 . . . . @50.00
71 thru 76 . . . . @45.00
77 Christmas (c). 50.00
78 thru 80 . . . . @45.00
81 thru 89 . . . . @40.00
90 Christmas (c). 45.00
91 thru 99 . . . . @40.00
100 . . . . 45.00
101 thru 120 . . . . @30.00
121 thru 150 . . . . @25.00
151 thru 212 . . . . @20.00

OUR SECRET
(see MY SECRET)

OUTLAWS
D.S. Publishing Co.
Feb.–March, 1948

1 HcK,Western Crime Stories . . 250.00
2 Grl,Doc Dawson's Dilema . . . 225.00
3 Cougar City Cleanup 100.00
4 JO,Death Stakes A Claim . . . 125.00
5 RJ,RJ(c),Man Who Wanted Mexico 100.00
6 AMc,RJ,RJ(c),The Ghosts of Crackerbox Hill 100.00
7 Grl,Dynamite For Boss Cavitt . 175.00
8 Grl,The Gun & the Pen 175.00
9 FF,Shoot to Kill;June– July, 1949 . . . . 375.00

WHITE RIDER AND SUPER HORSE
Star Publications
Sept., 1950

1 LbC(c) 100.00
2 LbC(c) 50.00
3 LbC(c) 50.00
4 LbC(c) 55.00
5 LbC(c),Stampede of Hard Riding Thrills 55.00
6 LbC(c),Drums of the Sioux 55.00

Becomes:

INDIAN WARRIORS

7 LbC(c),Winter on the Great Plains 75.00
8 LbC(c) 50.00

Becomes:

WESTERN CRIME CASES

9 LbC(c),The Card Sharp Killer . . 80.00

Becomes:

OUTLAWS, THE

10 LbC(c),Federated Express . . 150.00
11 LbC(c),Frontier Terror!!! 125.00
12 LbC(c),Ruthless Killer!!! 125.00
13 LbC(c),The Grim Avengers . . 125.00
14 AF,JKa,LbC(c),Trouble in Dark Canyon,April'54 . . . . . . 125.00

OUT OF THE NIGHT
American Comics Group/
Best Synd. Feature
Feb.–March, 1952

1 AW 500.00
2 AW 400.00
3 . . . . 200.00
4 AW 325.00
5 . . . . 200.00
6 The Ghoul's Revenge 200.00
7 . . . . 200.00
8 The Frozen Ghost 200.00
9 Death Has Wings, Science Fiction. 200.00
10 Ship of Death. 200.00

11 . . . . 175.00
12 Music for the Dead. 175.00
13 HN,From the Bottom of
the Well 175.00
14 Out of the Screen 175.00
15 The Little Furry Thing. 150.00
16 Nightmare From the Past. . . . 150.00
17 The Terror of the Labyrinth. . . 150.00
Becomes:

HOODED HORSEMAN

18 B: The Hooded Horseman . . . 75.00
19 The Horseman's Strangest
Adventure 100.00
20 OW,O:Johnny Injun 65.00
21 OW,OW(c). 100.00
22 OW 75.00
23 . . . . 75.00
24 . . . . 75.00
25 . . . . 60.00
26 O&I:Cowboy Sahib 75.00
27 Jan.–Feb., 1953. . . . . 65.00

OUT OF THE SHADOWS

Visual Editions
(Standard Comics)
July, 1952

5 ATh,GT,The Shoremouth
Horror 400.00
6 ATh,JKz,Salesman of Death . 275.00
7 JK,Plant of Death 200.00
8 Mask of Death 250.00
9 RC,Till Death Do Us Part 200.00
10 MS,We Vowed,Till Death
Do Us Part 175.00
11 ATh,Fountain of Fear 200.00
12 ATh,Hand of Death 250.00
13 MS,The Cannibal. 225.00
14 ATh,The Werewolf,
Aug., 1954 . . . . 225.00

OXYDOL-DREFT

Giveaways, 1950
The Set is More Valuable if the Original Envelope is Present

1 L'il Abner 100.00
2 Daisy Mae 100.00
3 Shmoo 125.00
4 AW&FF(c),John Wayne 135.00
5 Archie 100.00
6 Terry Toons Comics 100.00

OZZIE AND BABS

Fawcett Publications
Winter, 1946

1 Humor Oriented, Teenage. 60.00
2 Humor Oriented 25.00
3 Humor Oriented 22.00
4 Humor Oriented 22.00
5 Humor Oriented 22.00
6 Humor Oriented 22.00
7 Humor Oriented 22.00
8 Humor Oriented 22.00
9 Humor Oriented 22.00
10 Humor Oriented. 22.00
11 Humor Oriented. 22.00
12 Humor Oriented. 22.00
13 Humor Oriented;1949 . . . . 22.00

PAGEANT OF COMICS

St. John Publishing Co.
Sept., 1947

1 Rep. Mopsy 75.00
2 Rep. Jane Arden,Crime
Reporter. 75.00

PANHANDLE PETE AND JENNIFER

J. Charles Lave Publishing Co.
July, 1951

1 (fa) 40.00
2 (fa) 30.00
3 (fa),Nov.'51 . . . . 30.00

PANIC

Tiny Tot Publications
(E.C. Comics), March, 1954
"Humor in a Jugular Vein"

1 BE,JKa,JO,JDa,AF(c) 250.00
2 BE,JO,WW,JDa,A:Bomb 125.00
3 BE,JO,BW,WW,JDa,AF(c) . . . 110.00
4 BE,JO,WW,JDa,BW(c),
Infinity(c) 110.00
5 BE,JO,WW,JDa,AF(c) 100.00
6 BE,JO,WW,JDa,Blank (c) 100.00
7 BE,JO,WW,JDa 100.00
8 BE,JO,WW,JDa,Eye Chart (c). 100.00
9 BE,JO,WW,JDa,Ph(c),
Confidential(c) 100.00
10 BE,JDa, Postal Package(c) . . 100.00
11 BE,WW,JDa,Wheaties parody
as Weedies (c) 100.00
12 BE,WW,JDa,JDa(c);
Dec.–Jan. 1955–56 . . . . 125.00

PARAMOUNT ANIMATED COMICS

Family Publications
(Harvey Publ.) June, 1953

1 (fa),B:Baby Herman & Katnip,
Baby Huey,Buzzy the Crow . 150.00
2 (fa) 75.00
3 (fa) 60.00
4 (fa) 60.00
5 (fa) 60.00
6 (fa) 60.00
7 (fa), Baby Huey (c) 125.00
8 (fa), Baby Huey (c) 50.00
9 (fa), Infinity(c),Baby Huey (c) . . 50.00
10 thru 21 (fa),Baby Huey(c) . . . @30.00
22 (fa), July, 1956, Baby Huey (c). 30.00

PAROLE BREAKERS

Avon Periodicals/Realistic
Dec., 1951

1 P(c),Hellen Willis,Gun
Crazed Gun Moll 325.00
2 JKu,P(c),Vinnie Sherwood,
The Racket King 250.00
3 EK(c),John "Slicer" Berry,
Hatchetman of Crime;
July,1952 . . . . 200.00

PATCHES

Rural Home Publ./
Patches Publ.
March–April, 1945

1 LbC(c),Imagination In Bed(c) . 250.00
2 Dance (c) 125.00
3 Rocking Horse (c). 100.00
4 Music Band (c) 100.00
5 LbC(c),A:Danny Kaye,Football 150.00
6 A: Jackie Kelk 100.00
7 A: Hopalong Cassidy 150.00
8 A: Smiley Burnettte 100.00
9 BK,A: Senator Claghorn 100.00
10 A: Jack Carson 100.00
11 A: Red Skeleton; Dec'47 . . . . 125.00

PAWNEE BILL

Story Comics
Feb.–July, 1951

1 A:Bat Masterson,Wyatt Earp,
Indian Massacre
at Devil's Gulch 100.00
2 Blood in Coffin Canyon 50.00
3 LC,O:Golden Warrior,Fiery
Arrows at Apache Pass; 50.00

PAY-OFF

D.S. Publishing Co.
July–Aug., 1948–
March–April, 1949

1 . . . . 175.00
2 The Pennsylvania Blue-Beard 125.00
3 The Forgetful Forger 100.00
4 RJ(c),Lady and the Jewels . . . 100.00
5 The Beautiful Embezzeler. . . . 100.00

PEDRO

Fox Features Syndicate
Jan., 1950

1 WW,WW(c),Humor Oriented . 165.00
2 Aug., 1950 . . . . 110.00

PENNY

Avon Publications, 1947

1 The Slickest Chick of 'em All . . 85.00
2 . . . . 50.00
3 America's Teen-age
Sweetheart 50.00
4 . . . . 50.00
5 . . . . 50.00
6 Perry Como Ph(c),Sept.–
Oct., 1949 . . . . 55.00

PEP COMICS

MJL Magazines/
Archie Publications
Jan., 1940

1 IN,JCo,MMe,IN(c),I:Shield,
O:Comet,Queen of Diamonds,
B:The Rocket,Press Guardian,
Sergeant Boyle Chang,Bently
of Scotland Yard 7,500.00
2 CBi,JCo,IN,IN(c),O:Rocket. . 1,800.00
3 JCo,IN,IN(c),Shield (c) 1,300.00

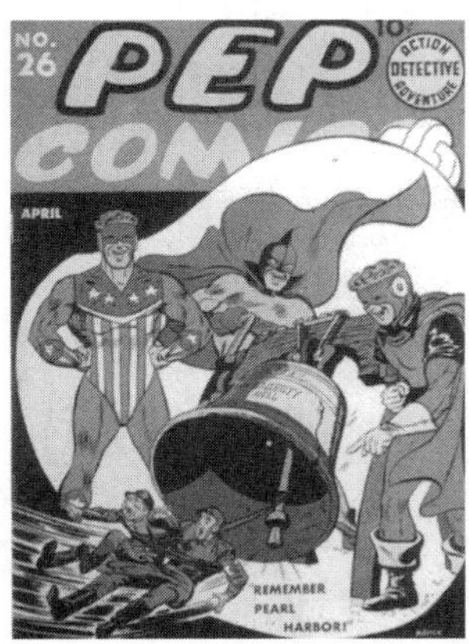

Pep #26
© Archie Publications

GOLDEN AGE

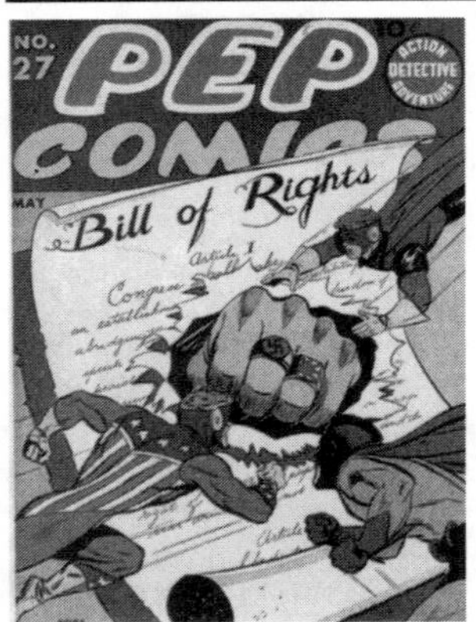

Pep Comics #27
© Archie Publications

4 Cbi,JCo,MMe,IN,IN(c), C:Wizard(not Gareb) 1,100.00
5 Cbi,JCo,MMe,IN,IN(c), C:Wizard 1,100.00
6 IN,IN(c), Shield (c) 800.00
7 IN,IN(c),Bondage(c),Shield(c) . 800.00
8 JCo,IN, Shield (c) 800.00
9 IN, Shield (c) 800.00
10 IN,IN(c), Shield (c) 800.00
11 MMe,IN,IN(c),I:Dusty, Boy Detective 850.00
12 IN,IN(c),O:Fireball Bondage(c), E:Rocket, Queen of Diamonds. 1,100.00
13 IN,IN(c),Bondage(c) 650.00
14 IN,IN(c) 650.00
15 IN,Bondage(c) 650.00
16 IN,O:Madam Satan 1,100.00
17 IN,IN(c),O:Hangman, D:Comet 3,000.00
18 IN,IN(c),Bondage(c) 650.00
19 IN 625.00
20 IN,IN(c),E:Fireball 625.00
21 IN,IN(c),Bondage(c), E: Madam Satan. 650.00
22 IN,IN(c)I:Archie, Jughead, Betty. 12,000.00
23 IN,IN(c). 1,200.00
24 IN,IN(c) 900.00
25 IN,IN(c) 900.00
26 IN,IN(c),I:Veronica. 1,300.00
27 IN,IN(c),Bill of Rights (c). 700.00
28 IN,IN(c), V:Capt. Swastika . . . 700.00
29 ASH (c) 700.00
30 B:Capt.Commando 700.00
31 Bondage(c) 700.00
32 Bondage(c) 600.00
33 . . . . 600.00
34 Bondage(c) 600.00
35 . . . . 600.00
36 1st Archie(c) 1,400.00
37 Bondage(c) 450.00
38 ASH(c). 425.00
39 ASH(c), Human Shield. 425.00
40 . . . . 425.00
41 2nd Archie; I:Jughead 300.00
42 F:Archie & Jughead 275.00
43 F:Archie & Jughead 275.00
44 . . . . 275.00
45 . . . . 275.00
46 . . . . 275.00
47 E:Hangman,Infinity(c). 275.00
48 B:Black Hood. 275.00
49 . . . . 275.00
50 . . . . 275.00
51 . . . . 200.00
52 B:Suzie 200.00
53 . . . . 200.00
54 E:Captain Commando 200.00
55 . . . . 200.00
56 thru 58 . . . . @180.00
59 E:Suzie 180.00
60 B:Katy Keene. 180.00
61 . . . . 150.00
62 I L'il Jinx 150.00
63 . . . . 150.00
64 . . . . 150.00
65 E:Shield. 150.00
66 thru 71 . . . . @100.00
72 thru 80 . . . . @85.00
81 thru 90 . . . . @65.00
91 thru 99 . . . . @50.00
100. . . . . 85.00
101 thru 110 . . . . @50.00
111 thru 120 . . . . @40.00
121 thru 130 . . . . @35.00
131 thru 140 . . . . @30.00
141 thru 150 . . . . @25.00
151 thru 160,A:Super Heroes . . @25.00
161 thru 200 . . . . @15.00
201 thru 250 . . . . @12.00
251 thru 300 . . . . @12.00
301 thru 350 . . . . @10.00
351 thru 411 . . . . @5.00

PERFECT CRIME, THE
Cross Publications
Oct., 1949

1 BP,DW 225.00
2 BP 125.00
3 . . . . 100.00
4 BP 100.00
5 DW 100.00
6 . . . . 100.00
7 B:Steve Duncan 100.00
8 Drug Story 125.00
9 . . . . 100.00
10 . . . . 100.00
11 Bondage (c). 125.00
12 . . . . 100.00
13 . . . . 100.00
14 Poisoning (c) 100.00
15 "The Most Terrible Menace", Drug. 125.00
16 . . . . 100.00
17 . . . . 100.00
18 Drug (c). 150.00
19 . . . . 100.00
20 thru 25 . . . . @75.00
26 Drug w/ Hypodermic (c) 165.00
27 . . . . 100.00
28 . . . . 100.00
29 . . . . 100.00
30 E:Steve Duncan, Rope Strangulation (c). 165.00
31 . . . . 75.00
32 . . . . 75.00
33 . . . . 75.00

PERFECT LOVE
Approved Comics(Ziff-Davis)/ St. John Publ. Co.
Aug.–Sept., 1951

1 (10),P(c),Our Kiss was a Prelude to Love Adrift. 135.00
2 . . . . 100.00
3 P(c) 75.00
4 . . . . 75.00
5 . . . . 75.00
6 . . . . 75.00
7 . . . . 75.00
8 EK 80.00
9 EK,P(c) 50.00
10 Ph(c), Dec '53 . . . . 50.00

PERSONAL LOVE
Famous Funnies, Jan., 1950

1 Ph(c) Are You in Love 125.00
2 Ph(c) Serenade for Suzette Mario Lanzo 75.00
3 Ph(c) 50.00
4 Ph(c) 50.00
5 Ph(c) 50.00
6 Ph(c) Be Mine Forever 60.00
7 Ph(c) You'll Always Be Mine, Robert Walker. 60.00
8 EK,Ph(c),Esther Williams & Howard Keel 70.00
9 EK,Ph(c),Debra Paget & Louis Jordan 70.00
10 Ph(c),Loretta Young Joseph Cotton 50.00
11 ATh, Ph(c),Gene Tierney & Glenn Ford. 100.00
12 Ph(c) Jane Greer & William Lundigan 50.00
13 Ph(c) Debra Paget & Louis Jordan 45.00
14 Ph(c) Kirk Douglas & Patrice Wymore 60.00
15 Ph(c) Dale Robertson & Joanne Dru 40.00
16 Ph(c) Take Back Your Love . . . 40.00
17 Ph(c) My Cruel Deception 40.00
18 Ph(c) Gregory Peck & Susan Hayward 50.00
19 Ph(c) Anthony Quinn 50.00
20 Ph(c) The Couple in the Next Apartment, Bob Wagner . 45.00
21 Ph(c) I'll Make You Care 40.00
22 Ph(c) Doorway To Heartbreak . 40.00
23 Ph(c) SaveMe from that Man . . 40.00
24 FF, Ph(c) Tyrone Power 300.00
25 FF, Ph(c) The Dark Light 300.00
26 Ph(c) Love Needs A Break. . . . 40.00
27 FF, Ph(c) Champ or Chump? . 300.00
28 FF, Ph(c) A Past to Forget . . . 300.00
29 Ph(c) Charlton Heston 50.00
30 Ph(c) The Lady is Lost. 40.00
31 Ph(c) Marlon Brando 70.00
32 FF, Ph(c) The Torment, Kirk Douglas. 400.00
33 Ph(c) June ,1955. . . . . 40.00

PETER COTTONTAIL
Key Publications
Jan., 1954

1 No 3-D (fa). 50.00
1 Feb '54 3-D (fa) 150.00
2 Rep of 3-D #1,not in 3-D. 40.00

PETER PAUL'S 4 IN 1 JUMBO COMIC BOOK
Capitol Stories, 1953

1 F: Racket Squad in Action, Space Adventures,Crime & Justice,Space Western 325.00

PETER PENNY AND HIS MAGIC DOLLAR
American Bakers Assn., 1947

1 History from Colonial America to the 1950's. 150.00
2 . . . . 75.00

PETER RABBIT
Avon Periodicals, 1947

1 H. Cady art. 250.00
2 H. Cady art. 200.00
3 H. Cady art. 175.00
4 H. Cady art. 175.00

5 H. Cady art. 175.00
6 H. Cady art. 175.00
7 thru 10 . . . . @30.00
11. . . . . 15.00

KRAZY LIFE

Fox Features Syndicate, 1945

1 (fa) 60.00

Becomes:

NUTTY LIFE

2 (fa). 50.00

Becomes:

WOTALIFE

Fox Features Synd./ Green Publ., Aug.–Sept., 1946

3 (fa)B:L'il Pan,Cosmo Cat 40.00
4 . . . . 30.00
5 thru 11 . . . . @25.00
12 July, 1947 . . . . 25.00

Becomes:

PHANTOM LADY

Fox Features Syndicate Aug., 1947

13(#1) MB,MB(c) Knights of the Crooked Cross 3,400.00
14(#2) MB,MB(c) Scoundrels and Scandals. 2,000.00
15 MB,MB(c) The Meanest Crook In the World. 1,900.00
16 MB,MB(c) Claa Peete The Beautiful Beast, Negligee. . 1,900.00
17 MB.MB(c) The Soda Mint Killer, Bondage (c) 4,500.00
18 MB,MB(c) The Case of Irene Shroeder 1,400.00
19 MB,MB(c) The Case of the Murderous Model 1,400.00
20 MB,MB(c) Ace of Spades . . 1,100.00
21 MB,MB(c). 1,100.00
22 MB,JKa. 1,100.00
23 MB,JKa Bondage (c). 1,200.00

Becomes:

MY LOVE SECRET

24 JKa, My Love Was For Sale. . 100.00
25 Second Hand Love 50.00
26 WW I Wanted Both Men. 125.00
27 I Was a Love Cheat. 40.00
28 WW, I Gave Him Love 125.00
29. . . . . 40.00
30 Ph(c). 40.00

LINDA

Ajax/Farrell, April–May, 1954

1 . . . . 75.00
2 Lingerie section 55.00
3 . . . . 40.00
4 Oct.–Nov.,1954 . . . . 40.00

Becomes:

PHANTOM LADY

5(1) MB,Dec-Jan'54-55 . . . . 900.00
2 Last Pre-Code Edition 700.00
3 Comics Code 550.00
4 Red Rocket,June, 1955 . . . . . 550.00

PHIL RIZZUTO

Fawcett Publications, 1951

Ph(c) The Sensational Story of The American Leagues MVP 600.00

Phantom Lady #17
© Fox Feature Syndicate

PICTORIAL CONFESSIONS

St. John Publishing Co. Sept., 1949

1 MB,MB(c),I Threw Away My Reputation on a Worthless Love . 200.00
2 MB,Ph(c) I Tried to be a Hollywood Glamour Girl 150.00
3 JKY,MB,MB(c),They Caught Me Cheating. 150.00

Becomes:

PICTORIAL ROMANCES

4 Ph(c) MB, Trapped By Kisses I Couldn't Resist 200.00
5 MB,MB(c). 150.00
6 MB,MB(c) I Was Too Free With Boys 125.00
7 MB,MB(c) 125.00
8 MB,MB(c) I Made a Sinful Bargain. 125.00
9 MB,MB(c) Dishonest Love . . . 125.00
10 MB,MB(c) I Was The Other Woman. 100.00
11 MB,MB(c) The Worst Mistake A Wife Can Make. . . 110.00
12 MB,MB(c) Love Urchin 100.00
13 MB,MB(c) Temptations of a Hatcheck Girl 100.00
14 MB,MB(c) I Was A Gamblers Wife 100.00
15 MB,MB(c) Wife Without Pride or Principles 100.00
16 MB,MB(c) The Truth of My Affair With a Farm Boy 100.00
17 MB,MB(c) True Confessions of a Girl in Love 200.00
18 MB,MB(c) 200.00
20 MB,MB(c) 200.00
21 MB,MB(c) 100.00
22 MB,MB(c) 100.00
23 MB,MB(c) 100.00
24 MB,MB(c) March,1954 . . . . . . 100.00

PICTORIAL LOVE STORIES

St. John Publishing Co. Oct., 1952

1 MB,MB(c) I Lost My Head, My Heart and My Resistance . . . 200.00

PICTURE NEWS

299 Lafayette Street Corp. Jan., 1946

1 Will The Atom Blow The World Apart 300.00
2 Meet America's 1st Girl Boxing Expert,Atomic Bomb. 150.00
3 Hollywood's June Allison Shows You How to be Beautiful, Atomic Bomb 125.00
4 Amazing Marine Who Became King of 10,000 Voodoos, Atomic Bomb 135.00
5 G.I.Babies,Hank Greenberg . . 125.00
6 Joe Louis(c) 135.00
7 Lovely Lady, Englands Future Queen. 100.00
8 Champion of them All 100.00
9 Bikini Atom Bomb, Joe DiMaggio 125.00
10 Dick Quick, Ace Reporter, Atomic Bomb Jan./Feb. 1947 . . . . 125.00

PICTURE STORIES FROM SCIENCE

Educational Comics Spring, 1947

1 Understanding Air and Water . 225.00
2 Fall '47 Amazing Discoveries About Food & Health 200.00

PICTURE STORIES FROM WORLD HISTORY

E.C. Comics, Spring, 1947

1 Ancient World to the Fall of Rome. 250.00
2 Europes Struggle for Civilization 200.00

PINHEAD AND FOODINI

Fawcett Publications July, 1951–Jan., 1952

1 Ph(c) 250.00
2 Ph(c) 125.00
3 Ph(c) Too Many Pinheads. . . . 100.00
4 Foodini's Talking Camel 100.00

PIN-UP PETE

Minoan Magazine Publishers 1952

1 Loves of a GI Casanova 150.00

PIONEER PICTURE STORIES

Street & Smith, Dec., 1941

1 Red Warriors in Blackface. . . . 225.00
2 Life Story Of Errol Flynn 125.00
3 Success Stories of Brain Muscle in Action 100.00
4 Legless Ace & Boy Commando Raid Occupied France 100.00
5 How to Tell Uniform and Rank of Any Navy Man. 100.00
6 General Jimmy Doolittle 110.00
7 Life Story of Admiral Halsey . . 110.00
8 Life Story of Timoshenko 100.00
9 Dec. '43,Man Who Conquered The Wild Frozen North 100.00

PIRACY

E.C. Comics, Oct.–Nov., 1954

1 WW,JDa,AW,WW(c),RC,AT . . 225.00
2 RC,JDa(c),WW,AW,AT 175.00
3 RC,GE, RC(c),Grl 150.00
4 RC,GE,RC(c),Grl 125.00
5 RC,GE,BK(c),Grl 125.00
6 JDa,RC,GE,BK(c),Grl 125.00
7 Oct Nov GE(c),RC,GE,Grl . . . 125.00

PIRATE COMICS

Hillman Periodicals, Feb., 1950

1 . . . . 175.00
2 . . . . 150.00
3 . . . . 125.00
4 Aug–Sept., 1950. . . . . 125.00

PIXIES, THE

Magazine Enterprises Winter, 1946

1 Mighty Atom 50.00
2 . . . . 30.00
3 . . . . 25.00
4 . . . . 25.00
5 . . . . 30.00
Becomes:

MIGHTY ATOM, THE

6 . . . . 30.00

PLANET COMICS

Love Romance Publ. (Fiction House Magazines) Jan., 1940

1 AB,DBR,HCk, Planet Comics, WE&LF,O:Aura,B:Flint Baker, Red Comet,Spurt Hammond, Capt. Nelson Cole 10,000.00
2 HcK,LF(c) 3,800.00
3 WE(c),HcK. 2,800.00
4 HcK,B:Gale Allan and the Girl Squad 2,200.00
5 BP,HcK 2,000.00
6 BP,HcK,BP(c),The Ray Pirates of Venus 2,100.00
7 BP,AB,HcK,BP(c) B:Buzz Crandall Planet Payson . . 1,800.00
8 BP,AB HcK 1,700.00
9 BP,AB,GT,HcK,B:Don Granville Cosmo Corrigan . 1,700.00
10 BP,AB,GT HcK 1,700.00
11 HcK, B:Crash Parker 1,700.00
12 Dri,B:Star Fighter 1,700.00
13 Dri,B:Reef Ryan 1,300.00
14 Dri B:Norge Benson 1,200.00
15 B: Mars,God of War 2,500.00
16 Invasion From The Void . . . 1,100.00
17 Warrior Maid of Mercury . . . 1,100.00
18 Bondage(c). 1,200.00
19 Monsters of the Inner World 1,100.00
20 RP, Winged Man Eaters of the Exile Star. 1,100.00
21 RP,B:Lost World Hunt Bowman 1,200.00
22 Inferno on the Fifth Moon . . 1,100.00
23 GT,Lizard Tyrant of the Twilight World 1,000.00
24 GT,Grl Raiders From The Red Moon. 1,000.00
25 Grl,B:Norge Benson 1,000.00
26 Grl,B:The Space Rangers Bondage(c) 1,100.00
27 Grl, The Fire Eaters of Asteroid Z. 900.00
28 Grl, Bondage (c) 1,000.00
29 Grl,Dragon Raiders of Aztla . . 900.00
30 GT,Grl City of Lost Souls 900.00

Planet Comics #31
© Fiction House Magazines

31 Grl,Fire Priests of Orbit6X . . . 725.00
32 Slaver's Planetoid 800.00
33 MA 725.00
34 MA,Bondage 850.00
35 MA B:Mysta of The Moon. . . . 700.00
36 MA Collosus of the Blood Moon 700.00
37 MA, Behemoths of the Purple Void. 700.00
38 MA 650.00
39 MA. Death Webs Of Zenith 3 . 650.00
40 Chameleon Men from Galaxy 9. . . . . 650.00
41 MA,Aaf,New O: Auro Bondage (c) 675.00
42 MA,AaF,E:Gale Allan 650.00
43 MA,AaF Death Rays From the Sun. 650.00
44 MA,Bbl,B:Futura 650.00
45 Ma,Bbl,Her Evilness from Xanado. 650.00
46 MA,Bbl,GE The Mecho-Men From Mars 650.00
47 MA,Bbl,GE,The Great Green Spawn 550.00
48 MA,GE. 550.00
49 MA,GE, Werewolves From Hydra Hell 550.00
50 MA,GE,The Things of Xeves . 550.00
51 MA,GE, Mad Mute X-Adapts . 500.00
52 GE,Mystery of the Time Chamber 500.00
53 MB,GE,Bondage(c) Dwarflings From Oceania . . . 500.00
54 MB,GE,Robots From Inferno . 500.00
55 MB,GE,Giants of the Golden Atom 500.00
56 MB,GE,Grl. 475.00
57 MB,GE,Grl. 475.00
58 MB,GE,Grl. 475.00
59 MB,GE,Grl,LSe 475.00
60 GE,Grl,Vassals of Volta 475.00
61 GE,Grl, The Brute in the Bubble 400.00
62 GE,Musta,Moon Goddess . . . 400.00
63 GE,Paradise or Inferno 400.00
64 GE,Monkeys From the Blue . . 400.00
65 The Lost World 400.00
66 The Plague of the Locust Men 400.00
67 The Nymphs of Neptune 400.00
68 Synthoids of the 9th Moon . . . 400.00
69 The Mentalists of Mars. 400.00
70 Cargo For Amazonia 400.00
71 Sandhogs of Mars 275.00
72 Last Ship to Paradise. 275.00
73 The Martian Plague, Winter 1953 . . . . 275.00

PLASTIC MAN

Comics Magazines (Quality Comics Group) Summer, 1943

1 JCo,JCo(c)Game of Death. . 3,500.00
2 JCo,JCo(c)The Gay Nineties Nightmare 1,500.00
3 JCo,JCo(c) 900.00
4 JCo,JCo(c) 700.00
5 JCo,JCo(c) 600.00
6 JCo,JCo(c) 500.00
7 JCo,JCo(c) 500.00
8 JCo,JCo(c) 500.00
9 JCo,JCo(c) 500.00
10 JCo,JCo(c) 500.00
11 JCo,JCo(c). 450.00
12 JCo,JCo(c),V:Spadehead. . . . 450.00
13 JCo,JCo(c),V:Mr.Hazard. 450.00
14 JCo,JCo(c),Words,Symbol of Crime 450.00
15 JCo,JCo(c),V:BeauBrummel. . 450.00
16 JCo,JCo(c),Money Means Trouble 450.00
17 JCo,JCo(c),A:The Last Man on Earth 450.00
18 JCo,JCo(c),Goes Back to the Farm. 450.00
19 JCo,JCo(c),V;Prehistoric Plunder 450.00
20 JCo,JCo(c),A:Sadly,Sadly . . . 450.00
21 JCo,JCo(c),V:Crime Minded Mind Reader. 350.00
22 JCo,JCo(c), Which Twin is the Phony 350.00
23 JCo,JCo(c),The Fountain of Age 350.00
24 JCo,JCo(c),The Black Box of Terror 350.00
25 JCo,JCo(c),A:Angus MacWhangus 350.00
26 JCo,JCo(c),On the Wrong Side of the Law? 350.00
27 JCo,JCo(c),V:The Leader. . . . 350.00
28 JCo,JCo(c),V:Shasta 350.00
29 JCo,JCo(c),V:Tricky Toledo . . 350.00
30 JCo,JCo(c),V:Weightless Wiggins 350.00
31 JCo,JCo(c),V:Raka the Witch Doctor. 250.00
32 JCo,JCo(c),V:Mr.Fission. 250.00
33 JCo,JCo(c),V:The Mad Professor 250.00
34 JCo,JCo(c),Smuggler'sHaven. 250.00
35 JCo,JCo(c),V:The Hypnotist . . 250.00
36 JCo,JCo(c),The Uranium Underground 250.00
37 JCo,JCo(c),V:Gigantic Ants . . 250.00
38 JCo,JCo(c),The Curse of Monk Mauley 250.00
39 JCo,JCo(c),The Stairway to Madness 250.00
40 JCo,JCo(c),The Ghoul of Ghost Swamp. 250.00
41 JCo,JCo(c),The Beast with the Bloody Claws 225.00
42 JCo,JCo(c),The King of Thunderbolts 225.00
43 JCo,JCo(c),The Evil Terror. . . 225.00
44 JCo,JCo(c),The Magic Cup . . 225.00
45 The Invisible Raiders 225.00
46 V:The Spider 225.00
47 The Fiend of a Thousand Faces. 225.00
48 Killer Crossbones. 225.00
49 JCo,The Weapon for Evil 225.00
50 V:Iron Fist 225.00

GOLDEN AGE

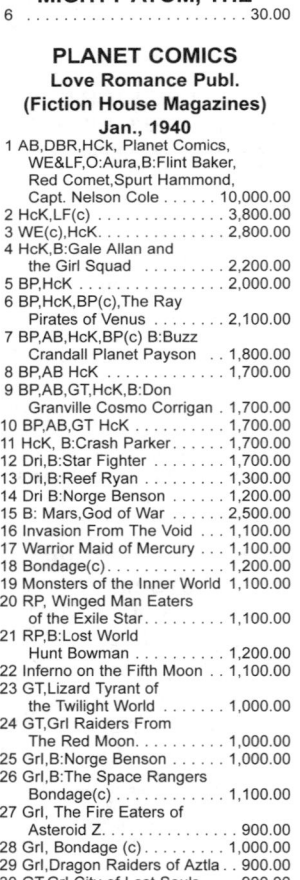

 All comics prices listed are for *Near Mint* condition.

Plastic Man #18
© Quality Comics Group

51 Incredible Sleep Weapon 200.00
52 V:Indestructible Wizard 225.00
53 V:Dazzia,Daughter of Darkness 225.00
54 V:Dr.Quomquat 225.00
55 The Man Below Zero 225.00
56 JCo, The Man Who Broke the Law of Gravity 225.00
57 The Chemist's Cauldron 225.00
58 JCo,The Amazing Duplicating Machine 225.00
59 JCo,V:The Super Spy 225.00
60 The Man in the Fiery Disguise 200.00
61 V:King of the Thunderbolts . . . 200.00
62 V:The Smokeweapon 200.00
63 V:Reflecto 200.00
64 Nov'56 The Invisible Raiders 200.00

POCAHONTAS
Pocahontas Fuel Co.
Oct., 1941

N# 150.00
2 . . . . 125.00

POCKET COMICS
Harvey Publications,
Aug., 1941

1 100 pages,O:Black Cat,Spirit of '76,Red Blazer Phantom Sphinx & Zebra,B:Phantom Ranger,British Agent #99, Spin Hawkins,Satan 800.00
2 . . . . 550.00
3 . . . . 400.00
4 Jan.'42,All Features End 375.00

POGO POSSUM
Dell Publishing Co.

1 WK,A:Swamp Land Band 550.00
2 WK 450.00
3 WK 375.00
4 WK 375.00
5 WK 375.00
6 thru 10 WK . . . . @250.00
11 WK, Christmas cover . . . . . @300.00
12 thru 16 WK . . . . @200.00

POLICE COMICS
Comic Magazines
(Quality Comics Group)
Aug., 1941

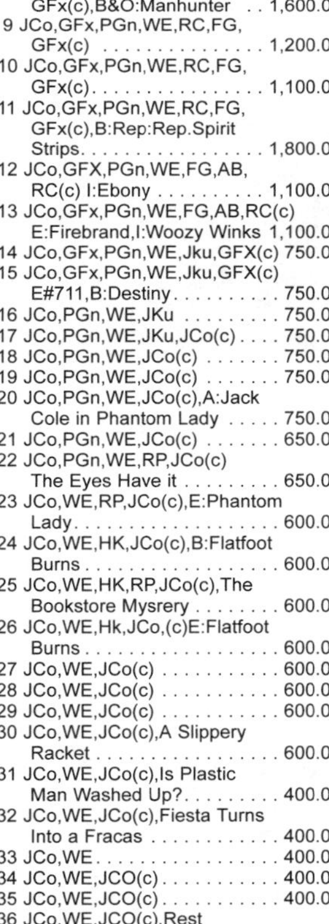
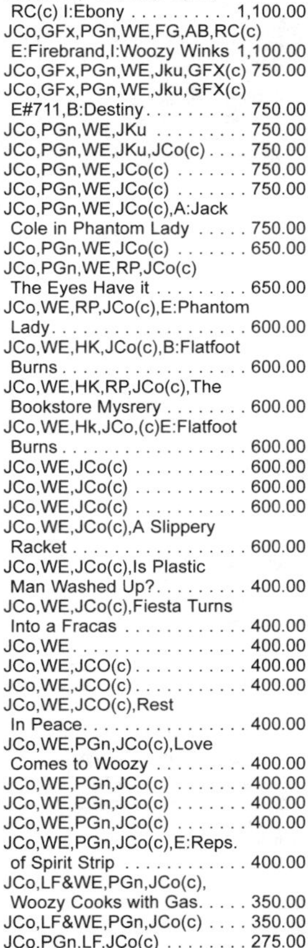

1 GFx,JCo,WE.PGn,RC,FG,AB, GFx(c),B&O:Plastic Man The Human Bomb,#711,I&B, Chic Canter,The Firebrand Mouthpiece,Phantom Lady The Sword 7,000.00
2 JCo,GFx,PGn,WE,RC,FG, GFx(c) 2,500.00
3 JCo,GFx,PGn,WE,RC,FG, GFx(c) 1,700.00
4 JCo,GFx,PGn,WE,RC,FG, GFx&WEC(c) 1,600.00
5 JCo,GFx,PGn,WE,RC,FG, GFx(c) 1,500.00
6 JCo,GFx,PGn,WE,RC,FG, GFx(c) 1,400.00
7 JCo,GFx,PGn,WE,RC,FG, GFx(c) 1,300.00
8 JCo,GFx,PGn,WE,RC,FG, GFx(c),B&O:Manhunter . . 1,600.00
9 JCo,GFx,PGn,WE,RC,FG, GFx(c) 1,200.00
10 JCo,GFx,PGn,WE,RC,FG, GFx(c) 1,100.00
11 JCo,GFx,PGn,WE,RC,FG, GFx(c),B:Rep:Rep.Spirit Strips 1,800.00
12 JCo,GFX,PGn,WE,FG,AB, RC(c) I:Ebony 1,100.00
13 JCo,GFx,PGn,WE,FG,AB,RC(c) E:Firebrand,I:Woozy Winks 1,100.00
14 JCo,GFx,PGn,WE,Jku,GFX(c) 750.00
15 JCo,GFx,PGn,WE,Jku,GFX(c) E#711,B:Destiny 750.00
16 JCo,PGn,WE,JKu 750.00
17 JCo,PGn,WE,JKu,JCo(c) 750.00
18 JCo,PGn,WE,JCo(c) 750.00
19 JCo,PGn,WE,JCo(c) 750.00
20 JCo,PGn,WE,JCo(c),A:Jack Cole in Phantom Lady 750.00
21 JCo,PGn,WE,JCo(c) 650.00
22 JCo,PGn,WE,RP,JCo(c) The Eyes Have it 650.00
23 JCo,WE,RP,JCo(c),E:Phantom Lady 600.00
24 JCo,WE,HK,JCo(c),B:Flatfoot Burns 600.00
25 JCo,WE,HK,RP,JCo(c),The Bookstore Mysrery 600.00
26 JCo,WE,Hk,JCo,(c)E:Flatfoot Burns 600.00
27 JCo,WE,JCo(c) 600.00
28 JCo,WE,JCo(c) 600.00
29 JCo,WE,JCo(c) 600.00
30 JCo,WE,JCo(c),A Slippery Racket 600.00
31 JCo,WE,JCo(c),Is Plastic Man Washed Up? 400.00
32 JCo,WE,JCo(c),Fiesta Turns Into a Fracas 400.00
33 JCo,WE 400.00
34 JCo,WE,JCO(c) 400.00
35 JCo,WE,JCO(c) 400.00
36 JCo,WE,JCO(c),Rest In Peace 400.00
37 JCo,WE,PGn,JCo(c),Love Comes to Woozy 400.00
38 JCo,WE,PGn,JCo(c) 400.00
39 JCo,WE,PGn,JCo(c) 400.00
40 JCo,WE,PGn,JCo(c) 400.00
41 JCo,WE,PGn,JCo(c),E:Reps. of Spirit Strip 400.00
42 JCo,LF&WE,PGn,JCo(c), Woozy Cooks with Gas 350.00
43 JCo,LF&WE,PGn,JCo(c) 350.00
44 JCo,PGn,LF,JCo(c) 275.00

Police Comics #13
© Quality Comics Group

45 JCo,PGn,LF,JCo(c) 275.00
46 JCo,PGn,LF,JCo(c) 275.00
47 JCo,PGn,LF,JCo(c), V:Dr.Slicer 275.00
48 JCo,PGn,LF,JCo(c),V:Big Beaver 275.00
49 JCo,PGn,LF,JCo(c),V:Thelma Twittle 275.00
50 JCo,PGn,LF,JCo(c) 275.00
51 JCo,PGn,LF,JCo(c),V:The Granite Lady 250.00
52 JCo,PGn,LF,JCo(c) 250.00
53 JCo,PGn,LF,JCo(c), V:Dr.Erudite 250.00
54 JCo,PGn,LF,JCo(c) 250.00
55 JCo,PGn,LF,JCo(c),V:The Sleepy Eyes 250.00
56 JCo,PGn,LF,JCo(c),V:The Yes Man 250.00
57 JCo,PGn,LF,JCo(c), V:Mr.Misfit 250.00
58 JCo,PGn,LF,JCo(c),E:The Human Bomb 250.00
59 JCo,PGn,LF,JCo(c),A:Mr. Happiness 250.00
60 JCo,PGn,LF,JCo(c) 200.00
61 JCo,PGn,LF,JCo(c) 200.00
62 JCo,PGn,LF,JCo(c) 200.00
63 JCo,PGn,LF,JCo(c), V:The Crab 200.00
64 JCo,PGn,LF,HK,JCo(c) 200.00
65 JCo,PGn,LF,JCo(c) 200.00
66 JCo,PGn,LF,JCo(c) Love Can Mean Trouble 200.00
67 JCo,LF,JCo(c), V:The Gag Man 200.00
68 JCo,LF,JCo(c) 200.00
69 JCo,LF,JCo(c),V:Strecho 200.00
70 JCo,LF,JCo(c) 200.00
71 JCo,LF,JCo(c) 175.00
72 JCo,LF,JCo(c),V:Mr.Cat 175.00
73 JCo,LF,JCo(c) 175.00
74 JCo,LF,JCo(c),V:Prof.Dimwit . 175.00
75 JCo,LF,JCo(c) 175.00
76 JCo,LF,JCo(c),V:Mr.Morbid. . . 175.00
77 JCo,LF,JCo(c),V:Skull Face & Eloc 175.00
78 JCo,LF,JCo(c),A Hot Time In Dreamland 175.00
79 JCo,LF,JCo(c),V:Eaglebeak . . 175.00
80 JCo,LF,JCo(c),V:Penetro 175.00
81 JCo,LF,JCo(c),V:A Gorilla. . . . 175.00
82 JCo,LF,JCo(c) 175.00
83 JCo,LF,JCo(c) 175.00
84 JCo,LF,JCo(c) 175.00

GOLDEN AGE

85 JCo,LF,JCo(c),V:Lucky 7 . . . . 175.00
86 JCo,LF,JCo(c),V:The Baker . . 175.00
87 JCo,LF,JCo(c) 175.00
88 JCo,LF,JCo(c),V:The Seen. . . 175.00
89 JCo,JCo(c),V:The Vanishers . 150.00
90 JCo,LF,JCo(c),V:Capt.Rivers . 150.00
91 JCo,JCo(c),The Forest Primeval 200.00
92 JCo,LF,JCo(c),V:Closets Kennedy. 200.00
93 JCo,JCo(c),V:The Twinning Terror 160.00
94 JCo,JCo(c),WE 250.00
95 JCo,JCo(c),WE,V:Scowls 250.00
96 JCo,JCo(c),WE,V:Black Widow 250.00
97 JCo,JCo(c),WE,V:The Mime. . 250.00
98 JCo,JCo(c),WE 250.00
99 JCo,JCo(c),WE 250.00
100 JCo,JCo(c). 300.00
101 JCo,JCo(c). 300.00
102 JCo,JCo(c),E:Plastic Man. . . 300.00
103 JCo,LF,B&I:Ken Shannon; Bondage(c). 200.00
104 The Handsome of Homocide 150.00
105 Invisible Hands of Murder. . . 150.00
106 Museum of Murder. 150.00
107 Man with the ShrunkenHead 150.00
108 The Headless Horse Player . 150.00
109 LF,Bondage(c),Blood on the Chinese Fan. 150.00
110 Murder with a Bang 150.00
111 Diana, Homocidal Huntress . 150.00
112 RC,The Corpse on the Sidewalk. 165.00
113 RC,RC(c), The Dead Man with the Size 13 Shoe. 165.00
114 The Terrifying Secret of the Black Bear 150.00
115 Don't Let Them Kill Me 150.00
116 Stage Was Set For Murder . . 150.00
117 Bullet Riddled Bookkeeper . . 150.00
118 Case of the Absent Corpse . 150.00
119 A Fast & Bloody Buck 150.00
120 Death & The Derelict 150.00
121 Curse of the Clawed Killer . . 150.00
122 The Lonely Hearts Killer. . . . 150.00
123 Death Came Screaming. . . . 150.00
124 Masin Murder. 150.00
125 Bondage(c),The Killer of King Arthur's Court 165.00
126 Hit & Run Murders 150.00
127 Oct'53,Death Drivers 150.00

POLICE LINE-UP

Avon Periodicals/ Realistic Comics, Aug., 1951

1 WW,P(c). 300.00
2 P(c),Drugs 200.00
3 JKu,EK,P(c) 150.00
4 July '52;EK 150.00

POLICE TRAP

Mainline Sept., 1954

1 S&K(c) 225.00
2 S&K(c) 125.00
3 S&K(c) 125.00
4 S&K(c) 125.00

Charlton Comics

5 S&K,S&K(c) 175.00
6 S&K,S&K(c) 175.00

Becomes:

PUBLIC DEFENDER IN ACTION

7 . . . . 60.00
8 thru 12, Oct. 1957 . . . . @50.00

POLLY PIGTAILS

Parents' Magazine Institute Jan., 1946

1 Ph(c) 75.00
2 Ph(c) 40.00
3 Ph(c) 30.00
4 Ph(c) 30.00
5 Ph(c) 30.00
6 Ph(c) 30.00
7 Ph(c) 25.00
8 . . . . 25.00
9 . . . . 25.00
10 . . . . 25.00
11 thru 22 . . . . @20.00
22 Ph(c) 20.00
23 Ph(c) 20.00
34 thru 43 . . . . @20.00

Popeye #3
© Dell Publishing Co.

POPEYE

Dell Publishing Co., 1948

1 . . . . 325.00
2 . . . . 150.00
3 `Welcome to Ghost Island' . . . 125.00
4 . . . . 125.00
5 . . . . 125.00
6 . . . . 125.00
7 . . . . 125.00
8 . . . . 125.00
9 . . . . 125.00
10 . . . . 125.00
11 . . . . 100.00
12 . . . . 100.00
13 . . . . 100.00
14 thru 20 . . . . @100.00
21 thru 30 . . . . @75.00
31 thru 40 . . . . @65.00
41 thru 45 . . . . @50.00
46 O:Sweat Pea 65.00
47 thru 50 . . . . @45.00
51 thru 60 . . . . @35.00
61 thru 65 . . . . @25.00

POPULAR COMICS

Dell Publishing Co. Feb., 1936

1 Dick Tracy, Little Orphan Annie. 4,000.00
2 Terry Pirates 1,300.00
3 Terry,Annie,Dick Tracy 1,000.00
4 . . . . 850.00
5 B:Tom Mix 850.00
6 . . . . 750.00
7 . . . . 650.00
8 . . . . 650.00
9 . . . . 650.00
10 Terry,Annie,Tracy 650.00
11 Terry,Annie,Tracy 550.00
12 Christmas(c) 550.00
13 Terry,Annie,Tracy 550.00
14 Terry,Annie,Tracy 550.00
15 same 550.00
16 same 550.00
17 same 550.00
18 same 550.00
19 same 550.00
20 same 550.00
21 same 400.00
22 same 400.00
23 same 400.00
24 same 400.00
25 same 400.00
26 same 400.00
27 E:Terry,Annie,Tracy 400.00
28 A:Gene Autry 350.00
29 . . . . 350.00
30 . . . . 350.00
31 A:Jim McCoy 350.00
32 A:Jim McCoy 350.00
33 . . . . 350.00
34 . . . . 350.00
35 Christmas(c),Tex Ritter. 350.00
36 . . . . 350.00
37 . . . . 350.00
38 B:Gang Busters 375.00
39 . . . . 350.00
40 . . . . 350.00
41 . . . . 350.00
42 . . . . 350.00
43 F:Gang Busters 375.00
44 . . . . 250.00
45 Tarzan(c) 250.00
46 O:Martan the Marvel Man . . . 350.00
47 F:Martan the Marvel Man 225.00
48 F:Martan the Marvel Man 225.00
49 F:Martan the Marvel Man 225.00
50 . . . . 225.00
51 B&O:Voice 225.00
52 A:Voice 200.00
53 F:The Voice 200.00
54 F:Gang Busters,A:Voice 200.00
55 F:Gang Busters 210.00
56 F:Gang Busters 200.00
57 F:The Marvel Man 200.00
58 F:The Marvel Man 200.00
59 F:The Marvel Man 200.00
60 O:Prof. Supermind 210.00
61 Prof. Supermind & Son 150.00
62 Supermind & Son. 150.00
63 B:Smilin' Jack 150.00
64 Smilin'Jack,Supermind 150.00
65 Professor Supermind 150.00
66 . . . . 150.00
67 Gasoline Alley 150.00
68 F:Smilin' Jack 150.00
69 F:Smilin' Jack 150.00
70 F:Smilin' Jack 150.00
71 F:Smilin' Jack 150.00
72 B:Owl,Terry & the Pirates 325.00
73 F:Terry and the Pirates. 200.00
74 F:Smilin' Jack 200.00
75 F:Smilin'Jack,A:Owl 200.00
76 Captain Midnight 275.00
77 Captain Midnight 275.00
78 Captain Midnight 275.00
79 A:Owl 200.00
80 F:Smilin' Jack,A:Owl 200.00
81 F: Terry&thePirates,A:Owl . . . 200.00
82 F:Smilin' Jack,A:Owl 200.00
83 F:Smilin' Jack,A:Owl 200.00
84 F:Smilin' Jack,A:Owl 200.00
85 F:ThreeLittleGremlins,A:Owl. . 200.00
86 F:Three Little Gremlins. 125.00
87 F:Smilin' Jack 125.00
88 F:Smilin' Jack 125.00

89 F:Smokey Stover 125.00
90 F:Terry and the Pirates. 125.00
91 F:Smokey Stover 125.00
92 F:Terry and the Pirates. 125.00
93 F:Smilin' Jack 125.00
94 F:Terry and the Pirates. 125.00
95 F:Smilin' Jack 125.00
96 F:Gang Busters 125.00
97 F:Smilin' Jack 125.00
98 B:Felix Cat. 135.00
99 F:Bang Busters 125.00
100 . . . . 150.00
101 thru 141. . . . . 75.00
142 E:Terry & the Pirates 70.00
143 . . . . 70.00
144 . . . . 70.00
145 F:Harold Teen 70.00

POPULAR ROMANCES

Better Publications (Standard Comics), Dec., 1949

5 B:Ph(c) 75.00
6 Ph(c) 40.00
7 RP 40.00
8 Ph(c) 40.00
9 Ph(c) 40.00
10 WW. 50.00
11 thru 16 . . . . @30.00
17 WE 35.00
18 thru 21 . . . . @35.00
22 thru 27 ATh,Ph(c). . . . . @60.00

SCHOOL DAY ROMANCES

Star Publications Nov.–Dec., 1949

1 LbC(c),Teen-Age 150.00
2 LbC(c) 100.00
3 LbC(c),Ph(c). 100.00
4 LbC(c),JyD,RonaldReagan . . 160.00
Becomes:

POPULAR TEEN-AGERS

5 LbC(c),Toni Gay, Eve Adams 250.00
6 LbC(c),Ginger Bunny, Midge Martin 225.00
7 LbC(c) 225.00
8 LbC(c) 225.00
9 LbC(c) 100.00
10 LbC(c). 100.00
11 LbC(c). 100.00
12 LbC(c). 100.00
13 LbC(c),JyD 100.00
14 LbC,WW,Spanking. 150.00
15 LbC(c),JyD 125.00
16 . . . . 100.00
17 LbC(c),JyD 100.00
18 LbC(c). 100.00
19 LbC(c). 100.00
20 LbC(c),JyD. 110.00
21 LbC(c),JyD. 110.00
22 LbC(c). 100.00
23 LbC(c). 100.00

POWER COMICS

Holyoke/Narrative Publ., 1944

1 LbC(c) 1,200.00
2 B:Dr.Mephisto,Hitler(c). 1,300.00
3 LbC(c) 1,300.00
4 LbC(c) 1,200.00

PRIDE OF THE YANKEES

Magazine Enterprises, 1949

1 N#,OW,Ph(c),The Life of Lou Gehrig 700.00

PRISON BREAK

Avon Periodicals/Realistic Sept., 1951

1 WW(c),WW 350.00
2 WW(c),WW,JKu 250.00
3 JD,JO. 200.00
4 EK 165.00
5 EK,CI 165.00

Prize Comics #44
© Prize Publications

PRIZE COMICS

Feature Publications (Prize Publ.), March, 1940

1 O&B:Power Nelson,Jupiter. B:Ted O'Neil,Jaxon of the Jungle,Bucky Brady, Storm Curtis, Rocket(c) . . . 2,000.00
2 B:The Owl 900.00
3 Power Nelson(c). 800.00
4 Power Nelson(c). 800.00
5 A:Dr.Dekkar 700.00
6 A:Dr.Dekkar 700.00
7 S&K,DBr,JK(c),O&B DR Frost, Frankenstein,B:GreenLama, Capt Gallant,Voodini Twist Turner. 1,500.00
8 S&K,DBr. 775.00
9 S&K,DBr,Black Owl(c). 750.00
10 DBr,Black Owl(c) 600.00
11 DBr,O:Bulldog Denny 550.00
12 DBr 550.00
13 DBR,O&B:Yank and Doodle,Bondage(c). 600.00
14 DBr,Black Owl(c) 550.00
15 DBr,Black Owl(c) 550.00
16 DBr,JaB,B:Spike Mason. 550.00
17 DBr,Black Owl(c) 550.00
18 DBr,Black Owl(c) 550.00
19 DBr,Yank&Doodle(c) 550.00
20 DBr,Yank&Doodle(c) 550.00
21 DBr,JaB(c),Yank&Doodle(c) . . 400.00
22 DBr,Yank&Doodle(c) 400.00
23 DBr,Uncle Sam(c) 400.00
24 DBr,Abe Lincoln(c). 400.00
25 DBr,JaB,Yank&Doodle(c) 400.00
26 DBr,JaB,JaB(c),Liberty Bell(c). 400.00
27 DBr,Yank&Doodle(c) 250.00
28 DBr,Yank&Doodle(c) 225.00
29 DBr,JaB(c)Yank&Doodle(c) . . 225.00
30 DBr,Yank&Doodle(c) 250.00
31 DBr,Yank&Doodle(c) 225.00
32 DBr,Yank&Doodle(c) 225.00
33 DBr,Bondage(c),Yank & Doodle 250.00
34 DBr,O:Airmale;New Black Owl. 250.00
35 DBr,B:Flying Fist & Bingo. . . . 150.00
36 DBr,Yank&Doodle(c) 150.00
37 DBr,I:Stampy,Hitler(c). 225.00
38 DBr,B.Owl,Yank&Doodle(c) . . 150.00
39 DBr,B.Owl,Yank&Doodle(c) . . 150.00
40 DBr,B.Owl,Yank&Doodle(c) . . 150.00
41 DBr,B.Owl,Yank&Doodle(c) . . 150.00
42 DBr,B.Owl,Yank&Doodle(c) . . 125.00
43 DBr,B.Owl,Yank&Doodle(c) . . 125.00
44 DBr, B&I:Boom Boom Brannigan. 125.00
45 DBr 125.00
46 DBr 125.00
47 DBr 125.00
48 DBr,B:Prince Ra;Bondage(c) . 150.00
49 DBr,Boom Boom(c) 125.00
50 DBr,Farnkenstein(c). 125.00
51 DBr 125.00
52 DBr, B:Sir Prize 125.00
53 DBr, The Man Who Could Read Features 125.00
54 DBr 125.00
55 DBr,Yank&Doodle(c) 125.00
56 DBr,Boom Boom (c). 125.00
57 DBr,Santa Claus(c) 125.00
58 DBr,The Poisoned Punch. . . . 125.00
59 DBr,Boom Boom(c) 125.00
60 DBr,Sir Prise(c) 125.00
61 DBr,The Man wih the Fighting Feet 125.00
62 DBr,Hck(c),Yank&Doodle(c) . . 125.00
63 DBr,S&K,S&K(c),Boom Boom(c) 135.00
64 DBr,Blackowl Retires 100.00
65 DBr,DBr(c),Frankenstein 100.00
66 DBr,DBr(c),Frankenstein 100.00
67 DBr,B:Brothers in Crime. 100.00
68 DBr,RP(c) 100.00
Becomes:

PRIZE COMICS WESTERN

69 ACa(c),B:Dusty Ballew 100.00
70 ACa(c). 75.00
71 ACa(c). 75.00
72 ACa(c),JSe 75.00
73 ACa(c). 75.00
74 ACa(c). 75.00
75 JSe,S&K(c),6-Gun Showdown at Rattlesnake Gulch 80.00
76 Ph(c),Randolph Scott. 125.00
77 Ph(c),JSe,Streets of Laredo,movie 75.00
78 Ph(c),JSe,HK,Bullet Code, movie. 135.00
79 Ph(c),JSe,Stage to China, movie 135.00
80 Ph(c),Gunsmoke Justice 90.00
81 Ph(c),The Man Who Shot Billy The Kid. 90.00
82 Ph(c),MBi,JSe&BE,Death Draws a Circle 90.00
83 JSe,S&K(c) 70.00
84 JSe 50.00
85 JSe,B:American Eagle 175.00
86 JSe 60.00
87 JSe&BE. 65.00
88 JSe&BE. 65.00
89 JSe&BE. 65.00
90 JSe&Be 65.00
91 JSe&BE,JSe&BE(c). 65.00
92 JSe,JSe&BE(c) 65.00
93 JSe,JSe&BE(c),. 65.00
94 JSe&BE,JSe&BE(c). 65.00
95 JSe,JSe&BE(c) 65.00
96 JSe,JSe&BE,JSe&BE(c) 65.00
97 JSe,JSe&BE,JSeBE(c) 65.00

GOLDEN AGE

98 JSe&BE,JSe&BE(c) 65.00
99 JSe&BE,JSe&BE(c) 65.00
100 JSe,JSe(c) 85.00
101 JSe 65.00
102 JSe 65.00
103 JSe 65.00
104 JSe 65.00
105 JSe 65.00
106 JSe 50.00
107 JSe 50.00
108 JSe 70.00
109 JSe&AW 80.00
110 JSe&BE 75.00
111 JSe&BE 75.00
112 . . . . 50.00
113 AW&JSe 75.00
114 MMe,B:The Drifter 35.00
115 MMe 35.00
116 MMe 35.00
117 MMe 35.00
118 MMe,E:The Drifter 35.00
119 Nov/Dec'56 . . . . 35.00

PSYCHOANALYSIS
E.C. Comics
March–April, 1955

1 JKa,JKa(c) 150.00
2 JKa,JKa(c) 125.00
3 JKa,JKa(c) 125.00
4 JKa,JKa(c) Sept.–Oct. 1955 . . 125.00

PUBLIC ENEMIES
D.S. Publishing Co., 1948

1 AMc 175.00
2 AMc 150.00
3 AMc 100.00
4 AMc 100.00
5 AMc 100.00
6 AMc 100.00
7 AMc,Eye Injury 120.00
8 . . . . 100.00
9 . . . . 100.00

PUNCH AND JUDY COMICS
Hillman Periodicals, 1944

1 (fa) 150.00
2 . . . . 100.00
3 . . . . 65.00
4 thru 12 . . . . @35.00
2-1 . . . . 50.00
2-2 JK 150.00
2-3 . . . . 40.00
2-4 . . . . 40.00
2-5 . . . . 40.00
2-6 . . . . 40.00
2-7 . . . . 40.00
2-8 . . . . 40.00
2-9 . . . . 40.00
2-10 JK 150.00
2-11 JK 150.00
2-12 JK 150.00
3-1 JK 150.00
3-2 . . . . 135.00
3-3 . . . . 40.00
3-4 . . . . 40.00
3-5 . . . . 40.00
3-6 . . . . 40.00
3-7 . . . . 40.00
3-8 . . . . 40.00
3-9 . . . . 40.00

PUNCH COMICS
Harry 'A' Chesler, Dec., 1941

1 B:Mr.E,The Sky Chief,Hale the Magician,Kitty Kelly . . . 1,100.00
2 A:Capt.Glory 700.00

Punch Comics #16
© Harry A Chesler

3-8 Do Not Exist
9 B:Rocket Man & Rocket girl,Master Ken 650.00
10 JCo,A:Sky Chief 500.00
11 JCo,O:Master Key,A:Little Nemo 500.00
12 A:Rocket Boy,Capt.Glory . . . 1,000.00
13 Ric(c) 500.00
14 GT 425.00
15 FSm(c) 425.00
16 . . . . 425.00
17 . . . . 425.00
18 FSm(c),Bondage(c),Drug 550.00
19 FSm(c) 550.00
20 Women semi-nude(c) 750.00
21 Drug 450.00
22 I:Baxter,Little Nemo 200.00
23 A:Little Nemo 200.00

PUPPET COMICS
Dougherty, Co., Spring, 1946

1 Funny Animal 65.00
2 . . . . 65.00

PURPLE CLAW, THE
Minoan Publishing Co./ Toby Press, Jan., 1953

1 O:Purple Claw 250.00
2 and 3 . . . . @175.00

PUZZLE FUN COMICS
George W. Dougherty Co. Spring, 1946

1 PGn 175.00
2 . . . . 125.00

QUEEN OF THE WEST, DALE EVANS
Dell Publishing Co.
July, 1953

(1) *see Dell Four Color #479*
(1) *see Dell Four Color #528*
3 ATh, Ph(c) all 100.00
4 ATh,RsM 90.00
5 RsM 75.00
6 RsM 75.00
7 RsM 75.00
8 RsM 75.00
9 RsM 75.00
10 RsM 75.00
11 . . . . 50.00
12 RsM 60.00
13 RsM 60.00
14 RsM 60.00
15 RsM 60.00
16 RsM 60.00
17 RsM 60.00
18 RsM 60.00
19 . . . . 50.00
20 RsM 60.00
21 . . . . 50.00
22 RsM 60.00

RACKET SQUAD IN ACTION
Capitol Stories/ Charlton Comics
May–June, 1952

1 Carnival(c) 200.00
2 . . . . 100.00
3 Roulette 100.00
4 FFr(c) 100.00
5 Just off the Boat 165.00
6 The Kidnap Racket 125.00
7 . . . . 100.00
8 . . . . 100.00
9 2 Fisted fix 100.00
10 . . . . 100.00
11 SD,SD(c),Racing(c) 225.00
12 JoS,SD(c),Explosion(c) 375.00
13 JoS(c),The Notorious Modelling Agency Racket,Acid 75.00
14 DG(c),Drug 100.00
15 Photo Extortion Racket 60.00
16 thru 28 . . . . @60.00
29,March, 1958 . . . . 75.00

RAGGEDY ANN AND ANDY
Dell Publishing Co., 1942

1 Billy & Bonnie Bee 300.00
2 . . . . 150.00
3 DNo,B:Egbert Elephant 150.00
4 DNo,WK 175.00
5 DNo 125.00
6 DNo 125.00
7 Little Black Sambo 125.00
8 . . . . 125.00
9 . . . . 125.00
10 . . . . 125.00
11 . . . . 100.00
12 . . . . 100.00
13 . . . . 100.00
14 . . . . 100.00
15 . . . . 100.00
16 thru 20 . . . . @100.00
21 Alice in Wonderland 90.00
22 thru 27 . . . . @65.00
28 WK 75.00
29 thru 39 . . . . @65.00

RALPH KINER HOME RUN KING
Fawcett Publications, 1950

1 N#, Life Story of the Famous Pittsburgh Slugger . . 500.00

RAMAR OF THE JUNGLE
Toby Press/ Charlton Comics, 1954

1 Ph(c),TV Show 150.00
2 Ph(c) 100.00
3 . . . . 100.00

All comics prices listed are for *Near Mint* condition.

4 . . . . 100.00
5 Sept '56 . . . . 100.00

RANGE ROMANCES
Comics Magazines
(Quality Comics), Dec., 1949

1 PGn(c),PGn 200.00
2 RC(c),RC 225.00
3 RC,Ph(c) 150.00
4 RC,Ph(c) 150.00
5 RC,PGn,Ph(c) 150.00

RANGERS OF FREEDOM
Flying Stories, Inc.
(Fiction House), Oct., 1941

1 I:Ranger Girl & Rangers of Freedom;V:Super-Brain . 1,700.00
2 V:Super -Brain 700.00
3 Bondage(c) The Headsman of Hate 600.00
4 Hawaiian Inferno. 500.00
5 RP,V:Super-Brain 500.00
6 RP,Bondage(c);Bugles of the Damned 500.00
7 RP,Death to Tojo's Butchers. 400.00

Becomes:

Rangers of Freedom #3
© Fiction House

RANGERS COMICS

8 RP,B:US Rangers 400.00
9 GT,BLb,Commando Steel for Slant Eyes. 400.00
10 BLb,Bondage (c) 425.00
11 Raiders of the Purple Death 350.00
12 A:Commando Rangers. 350.00
13 Grl,B:Commando Ranger. . . . 350.00
14 Grl,Bondage(c) 350.00
15 GT,Grl,Bondage(c). 350.00
16 Grl,GT;Burma Raid 375.00
17 GT,GT,Bondage(c),Raiders of the Red Dawn 375.00
18 GT. 375.00
19 GE,Blb,GT,Bondage(c). 300.00
20 GT. 275.00
21 GT,Bondage(c). 300.00
22 GT,B&O:Firehair 225.00
23 GT,BLb,B:Kazanda 200.00
24 Bondage(c) 225.00
25 Bondage(c) 225.00
26 Angels From Hell 200.00
27 Bondage(c) 225.00
28 BLb,E:Kazanda;B&O Tiger Man 225.00
29 Bondage(c) 225.00
30 BLb,B:Crusoe Island 235.00
31 BLb,Bondage(c). 200.00
32 BLb 175.00
33 BLb,Drug 175.00
34 BLb 175.00
35 BLB,Bondage(c) 200.00
36 BLb,MB 175.00
37 BLb,Mb 175.00
38 BLb,MB,GE,Bondage(c). 200.00
39 BLb,GE 175.00
40 BLb,GE,BLb(c). 175.00
41 BLb,GE 150.00
42 BLb,GE 150.00
43 BLb,GE 150.00
44 BLb,GE 150.00
45 BLb,GEl. 150.00
46 BLb,GE 135.00
47 BLb,JGr. 135.00
48 BLb,JGr. 135.00
49 BLb,JGr. 135.00
50 BLb,JGr,Bondage(c). 150.00
51 BLb,JGr. 135.00
52 BLb,JGr,Bondage(c). 150.00
53 BLb,JGr,Prisoners of Devil Pass 135.00
54 JGr,When The Wild Commanches Ride. 135.00
55 JGr,Massacre Guns at Pawnee Pass 135.00
56 JGr, Gun Smuggler of Apache Mesa 135.00
57 JGr,Redskins to the Rescue. 135.00
58 JGr,Brides of the Buffalo Men 135.00
59 JGr,Plunder Portage 135.00
60 JGr, Buzzards of Bushwack Trail 135.00
61 BWh(c)Devil Smoke at Apache Basin. 100.00
62 BWh(c)B:Cowboy Bob 100.00
63 BWh(c) 100.00
64 BWh(c)B:Suicide Smith 100.00
65 BWh(c):Wolves of the Overland Trail,Bondage(c) . . 110.00
66 BWh(c) 100.00
67 BWh(c)B:Space Rangers 100.00
68 BWh(c);Cargo for Coje. 100.00
69 BWh(c);Great Red Death Ray 100.00

REAL CLUE CRIME STORIES (see CLUE COMICS)

REAL FUNNIES
Nedor Publishing Co.
Jan., 1943

1 (fa) 200.00
2 and 3 (fa) . . . . @100.00

REAL HEROES COMICS
Parents' Magazine Institiute
Sept., 1941

1 HcK,Franklin Roosevelt. 250.00
2 J, Edgar Hoover 125.00
3 General Wavell. 100.00
4 Chiang Kai Shek. 100.00
5 Stonewall Jackson 100.00
6 Lou Gehrig 150.00
7 Chennault and his Flying Tigers. 75.00
8 Admiral Nimitz 75.00
9 The Panda Man 60.00
10 Carl Akeley-Jungle Adventurer 60.00
11 Wild Jack Howard 55.00
12 General Robert L Eichelberger 50.00
13 HcK,Victory at Climback. 50.00
14 Pete Gray 50.00
15 Alexander Mackenzie. 50.00
16 Balto of Nome Oct '46 . . . . 50.00

REAL LIFE STORY OF FESS PARKER
Dell Publishing Co., 1955

1 . . . . 100.00

REALISTIC ROMANCES
Avon Periodicals/ Realistic Comics
July–Aug., 1951

1 Ph(c) 150.00
2 Ph(c) 75.00
3 P(c) 60.00
4 P(c) 60.00
5 thru 14 . . . . @60.00
15 . . . . 50.00
16 Drug 75.00
17 . . . . 50.00

REAL LIFE COMICS
Visual Editions/Better/ Standard/Nedor, Sept., 1941

1 ASh(c),Lawrence of Arabia,Uncle Sam(c). 400.00
2 ASh(c),Liberty(c) 175.00
3 Adolph Hitler(c). 500.00
4 ASh(c)Robert Fulton, Charles DeGaulle 125.00
5 ASh(c)Alexander the Great . . . 125.00
6 ASh(c)John Paul Jones,CDR . 100.00
7 ASh(c)Thomas Jefferson 100.00
8 Leonardo Da Vinci 100.00
9 US Coast Guard Issue 100.00
10 Sir Hubert Wilkens. 100.00
11 Odyssey on a Raft. 90.00
12 ImpossibleLeatherneck 90.00
13 ASh(c)The Eternal Yank. 90.00
14 Sir Isaac Newton 90.00
15 William Tell 90.00
16 Marco Polo 90.00
17 Albert Einstein 100.00
18 Ponce De Leon 90.00
19 The Fighting Seabees 90.00
20 Joseph Pulitzer 90.00
21 Admiral Farragut 75.00
22 Thomas Paine 75.00
23 Pedro Menendez 75.00
24 Babe Ruth 125.00
25 Marcus Whitman 75.00
26 Benvenuto Cellini. 75.00
27 A Bomb Story 125.00
28 Robert Blake 75.00
29 Daniel DeFoe 75.00
30 Baron Robert Clive 75.00
31 Anthony Wayne 75.00
32 Frank Sinatra. 100.00
33 Frederick Douglas 75.00
34 Paul Revere,Jimmy Stewart. . . 80.00
35 Rudyard Kipling 75.00
36 Story of the Automobile 75.00
37 Francis Manion 75.00
38 Richard Henry Dana 60.00
39 Samuel FB Morse 55.00
40 FG,ASh(c),Hans Christian Anderson 60.00
41 Abraham Lincoln,Jimmy Foxx . 75.00
42 Joseph Conrad,Fred Allen 60.00
43 Louis Braille,O.W.Holmes. 55.00
44 Citizens of Tomorrow 55.00

GOLDEN AGE

Real Life Comics #30
© Standard Comics

45 ASh(c),Francois Villon 80.00
46 The Pony Express 80.00
47 ASh(c),Montezuma 50.00
48 . . . . 50.00
49 ASh(c),Gene Bearden,
Baseball 60.00
50 FF,ASh(c),Lewis & Clark 200.00
51 GE,ASh(c),Sam Houston 150.00
52 GE,FF,ASh(c),JSe&BE
Leif Erickson. 200.00
53 JSe&BE,Henry Wells &
William Fargo 75.00
54 GT,Alexander Graham Bell. . . . 75.00
55 ASh(c),JSe&BE, The James
Brothers 75.00
56 JSe&BE. 75.00
57 JSe&BE. 75.00
58 JSe&BE,Jim Reaves 90.00
59 FF,JSe&BE,Battle Orphan
Sept '52 . . . . 75.00

REAL LOVE (see HAP HAZARD COMICS)

REAL WEST ROMANCES
Crestwood Publishing Co./ Prize Publ., April–May, 1949

1 S&K,Ph(c) 175.00
2 Ph(c),Spanking 100.00
3 JSe,BE,Ph(c) 100.00
4 S&K,JSe,BE,Ph(c) 150.00
5 S&K,MMe,JSe,Audie
Murphy Ph(c) 125.00
6 S&K,JSe,BE,Ph(c) 75.00

RECORD BOOK OF FAMOUS POLICE CASES
St. John Publishing Co., 1949

1 N#,JKu,MB(c). 275.00

RED ARROW
P.L. Publishing Co.
May, 1951

1 Bondage(c). 75.00
2 . . . . 50.00
3 P(c) 50.00

RED BAND COMICS
Enwil Associates
Nov., 1944

1 The Bogeyman 275.00
2 O:Bogeyman,same(c)as#1 . . . 200.00
3 A:Captain Wizard 175.00
4 May '45,Repof#3,Same(c). . . . 175.00

RED CIRCLE COMICS
Enwil Associates
(Rural Home Public)
Jan., 1945

1 B:Red Riot,The Prankster 250.00
2 LSt,A:The Judge. 200.00
3 LSt,LSt(c) 150.00
4 LSt,LSt(c) covers of #4
stapled over other comics. . . 150.00

TRAIL BLAZERS
Street & Smith, Jan., 1942

1 Wright Brothers. 175.00
2 Benjamin Franklin,Dodgers . . . 200.00
3 Red Barber,Yankees. 275.00
4 Famous War song 150.00

Becomes:

RED DRAGON COMICS

5 JaB(c),B&O:Red Rover:
B:Capt.Jack Comkmando
Rex King&Jet,Minute Man . . 900.00
6 O:Red Dragon 1,700.00
7 The Curse of the
Boneless Men 1,200.00
8 China V:Japan 600.00
9 The Reducing Ray,Jan '44 . . . 600.00

(2nd Series) Nov., 1947

1 B:Red Dragon. 750.00
2 BP 600.00
3 BP,BP(c),I:Dr Neff. 450.00
4 BP,BP(c). 600.00
5 BP,BP(c). 400.00
6 BP,BP(c). 400.00
7 BP,BP(c),May 49 . . . . 400.00

RED MASK (see TIM HOLT)

RED RABBIT
Dearfield/
J. Charles Lave Publ. Co.
Jan., 1941

1 (fa). 75.00
2 . . . . 40.00
3 thru 10 . . . . @30.00
11 thru 22 . . . . @25.00

RED SEAL COMICS
Harry 'A' Chesler, Jr./Superior
Oct., 1945

14 GT,Bondage(c),Black Dwarf . . 600.00
15 GT,Torture 375.00
16 GT. 500.00
17 GT,Lady Satan,Sky Chief. . . . 400.00
18 Lady Satan,Sky Chief 400.00
19 Lady Satan,Sky Chief 325.00
20 Lady Satan,Sky Chief 325.00
21 Lady Satan,Sky Chief 300.00
22 Rocketman 250.00

REDSKIN
Youthful Magazines
Sept., 1950

1 Redskin,Bondage(c) 125.00
2 Apache Dance of Death 75.00
3 Daniel Boone 60.00
4 Sitting Bull- Red Devil
of the Black Hills. 60.00
5 . . . . 60.00
6 Geronimo- Terror of the
Desert,Bondage 75.00
7 Firebrand of the Sioux 60.00
8 . . . . 60.00
9 . . . . 60.00
10 Dead Man's Magic. 60.00
11 . . . . 60.00
12 Quanah Parker,Bondage(c) . . . 75.00

Becomes:

FAMOUS WESTERN BADMEN

13 Redskin- Last of the
Comanches 50.00
14 . . . . 35.00
15 The Dalton Boys Apr '52 . . . . . 35.00

REMEMBER PEARL HARBOR
Street & Smith, 1942

1 N# JaB,Battle of the
Pacific,Uncle Sam(c) 350.00

RETURN OF THE OUTLAW
Minoan Publishing Co.
Feb., 1953

1 Billy The Kid 70.00
2 . . . . 50.00
3 thru 11 . . . . @30.00

REVEALING ROMANCES
A.A. Wyn
(Ace Magazines), Sept., 1949

1 . . . . 65.00
2 . . . . 50.00
3 thru 6 . . . . @25.00

REX ALLEN COMICS
Dell Publishing Co.
Feb., 1951

(1) *see Dell Four Color #316*
2 Ph(c) all 150.00
3 thru 10 . . . . @100.00
11 thru 23 . . . . @70.00
24 ATh 80.00
25 thru 31 . . . . @70.00

REX DEXTER OF MARS
Fox Features Syndicate
Autumn, 1940

1 DBr,DBr(c) Battle ofKooba . . 1,700.00

RIBTICKLER
Fox Features Syndicate, 1945

1 . . . . 110.00
2 . . . . 50.00
3 Cosmo Cat. 35.00
4 thru 6 . . . . @30.00
7 Cosmo Cat. 30.00
8 thru 9 . . . . @30.00

RIN TIN TIN
Dell Publishing Co.
Nov., 1952

(1) *see Dell Four Color #434*
(1) *see Dell Four Color #476*
(1) *see Dell Four Color #523*
4 thru 10 Ph(c) all . . . . @65.00
11 thru 20 . . . . @80.00

Rocket Comics #1
© Hillman Periodicals

ROCKET COMICS
Hillman Periodicals
March, 1940

1 O:Red Roberts;B:Rocket Riley,Phantom Ranger,Steel Shank,Buzzard Baynes,Lefty Larson,The Defender,Man with 1,000 Faces 2,000.00
2 . . . . 1,000.00
3 May '40 E:All Features 1,100.00

ROCKET KELLY
Fox Features Syndicate
Autumn, 1945–Oct. Nov., 1946

N#. 225.00
1 . . . . 200.00
2 A:The Puppeteer 175.00
3 thru 6 . . . . @150.00

ROCKETMAN
Ajax/Farrell Publications
June, 1952

1 Space Stories of the Future . . 350.00

ROCKET SHIP X
Fox Features Syndicate
Sept., 1951

1 . . . . 500.00
2 N# Variant of Original 325.00

ROCKY LANE WESTERN
Fawcett/Charlton Comics
May, 1949

1 Ph(c)B:Rocky Lane,Slim Pickins 800.00
2 Ph(c) 350.00
3 Ph(c) 225.00
4 Ph(c)CCB,Rail Riders Rampage,F Capt Tootsie . . . 225.00
5 Ph(c)The Missing Stagecoaches. 200.00
6 Ph(c)Ghost Town Showdown . 150.00
7 Ph(c)The Border Revolt 175.00
8 Ph(c)The Sunset Feud 175.00
9 Ph(c)Hermit of the Hills. 175.00
10 Ph(c)Badman's Reward 150.00
11 Ph(c)Fool's Gold Fiasco 125.00
12 Ph(c),CCB,Coyote Breed F:Capt Tootsie,Giant. 125.00
13 Ph(c),Giant 125.00
14 Ph(c) 100.00
15 Ph(c)B:Black Jacks Hitching Post,Giant. 110.00
16 Ph(c),Giant 100.00
17 Ph(c),Giant 100.00
18 Ph(c) 110.00
19 Ph(c),Giant 115.00
20 Ph(c)The Rodeo Rustler E:Slim Pickens 115.00
21 Ph(c)B: Dee Dickens 100.00
22 Ph(c). 90.00
23 thru 30 . . . . @100.00
31 thru 40 . . . . @90.00
41 thru 55 . . . . @90.00
56 thru 60 . . . . @75.00
61 thru 70 . . . . @70.00
71 thru 87 . . . . @60.00

ROD CAMERON WESTERN
Fawcett Publications
Feb., 1950

1 Ph(c) 450.00
2 Ph(c) 200.00
3 Ph(c),Seven Cities of Cipiola . 175.00
4 Ph(c),Rip-Roaring Wild West . 150.00
5 Ph(c),Six Gun Sabotage 150.00
6 Ph(c),Medicine Bead Murders 150.00
7 Ph(c),Wagon Train Of Death . 150.00
8 Ph(c),Bayou Badman 150.00
9 Ph(c),Rustlers Ruse 150.00
10 Ph(c),White Buffalo Trail 150.00
11 Ph(c),Lead Poison 125.00
12 thru 19 Ph(c) . . . . @125.00
20 Phc(c),Great Army Hoax 125.00

ROLY-POLY COMICS
Green Publishing Co., 1945

1 B:Red Rube&Steel Sterling . . 225.00
6 A:Blue Cycle 125.00
10 A:Red Rube. 125.00
11 . . . . 125.00
12 . . . . 125.00
13 . . . . 125.00
14 A:Black Hood. 125.00
15 A:Steel Fist;1946 . . . . 250.00

ROMANCE AND CONFESSION STORIES
St. John Publishing Co., 1949

1 MB(c),MB 300.00

ROMANTIC LOVE
Avon Periodicals/Realistic
Sept.–Oct., 1949

1 P(c) 175.00
2 P(c) 100.00
3 P(c) 100.00
4 Ph(c) 100.00
5 P(c) 100.00
6 Ph(c),Drug,Thrill Crazy 125.00
7 P(c) 100.00
8 P(c) 100.00
9 EK,P(c). 110.00
10 thru 11 P(c). . . . . @110.00
12 EK 110.00
20 . . . . 100.00
21 . . . . 100.00
22 EK 100.00
23 EK 100.00

ROMANTIC MARRIAGE
Ziff-Davis/
St. John Publishing Co.
Nov.–Dec., 1950

1 Ph(c),Selfish wife 150.00
2 P(c),Mother's Boy 100.00
3 P(c),Hen Peck House 75.00
4 P(c) 75.00
5 Ph(c) 75.00
6 Ph(c) 50.00
7 Ph(c) 50.00
8 P(c) 50.00
9 P(c) 50.00
10 P/PH(c) 125.00
11 . . . . 50.00
12 . . . . 50.00
13 Ph(c) 50.00
14 thru 20 . . . . @50.00
20 Ph(c) 50.00
21 . . . . 50.00
22 . . . . 50.00
23 MB 60.00
24 . . . . 50.00

ROMANTIC PICTURE NOVELETTES
Magazine Enterprises, 1946

1 Mary Wothr adventure 125.00

ROMANTIC SECRETS
Fawcett Publ./Charlton Comics
Sept., 1949

1 Ph(c) 125.00
2 MSy(c) 60.00
3 MSy(c) 60.00
4 GE 75.00
5 BP 55.00
6 . . . . 40.00
7 BP 40.00
8 . . . . 40.00
9 GE 45.00
10 BP 40.00
11 . . . . 35.00
12 BP 40.00
13 . . . . 35.00
14 . . . . 35.00
15 . . . . 35.00
16 BP,MSy 40.00
17 BP 40.00
18 . . . . 35.00
19 . . . . 35.00
20 BP.MBi 40.00
21 . . . . 25.00
22 . . . . 25.00
23 . . . . 25.00
24 GE. 45.00
25 MSy. 25.00
26 BP,MSy 25.00
27 MSy. 25.00
28 . . . . 25.00
29 BP 20.00
30 thru 32 . . . . @18.00
33 MSy. 20.00
34 BP 20.00
35 . . . . 18.00
36 BP 20.00
37 BP 20.00
38 thru 52 . . . . @18.00

GOLDEN AGE

ROMANTIC STORY
Fawcett Publ./Charlton Comics
Nov., 1949

1 Ph(c) 125.00
2 Ph(c) 60.00
3 Ph(c) 50.00
4 Ph(c) 50.00
5 Ph(c) 50.00
6 Ph(c) 50.00
7 BP,Ph(c). 40.00
8 BP,Ph(c). 30.00
9 Ph(c) 30.00
10 Ph(c). 30.00
11 Ph(c). 30.00
12 Ph(c). 30.00
13 Ph(c). 30.00
14 Ph(c). 30.00
15 GE,Ph(c) 45.00
16 BP,Ph(c) 35.00
17 Ph(c). 30.00
18 Ph(c). 30.00
19 Ph(c). 30.00
20 BP,Ph(c) 30.00
22 ATh,Ph(c) 30.00

Charlton Comics

23. . . . . 15.00
24 Ph(c). 15.00
25 thru 29 . . . . @15.00
30 BP. 20.00
31 thru 39 . . . . @15.00

ROMANTIC WESTERN
Fawcett Publications
Winter, 1949

1 Ph(c) 150.00
2 Ph(c),AW,AMc 160.00
3 Ph(c) 125.00

ROMEO TUBBS (see MY SECRET LIFE)

ROUNDUP
D.S. Publishing Co.
July–Aug., 1948

1 HcK 150.00
2 Drug. 125.00
3 . . . . 100.00
4 . . . . 100.00
5 Male Bondage 110.00

ROY CAMPANELLA, BASEBALL HERO
Fawcett Publications, 1950

N# Ph(c),Life Story of the
Battling Dodgers Catcher . . . 500.00

ROY ROGERS
Dell Publishing Co.

1 photo (c). 850.00
2 . . . . 300.00
3 . . . . 200.00
4 . . . . 200.00
5 . . . . 200.00
6 thru 10 . . . . @150.00
11 thru 20 . . . . @125.00
21 thru 30 . . . . @100.00
31 thru 46 . . . . @75.00
47 thru 50 . . . . @65.00
51 thru 56 . . . . @60.00
57 Drug 65.00
58 thru 70 . . . . @60.00
71 thru 80 . . . . @50.00
81 thru 91 . . . . @45.00
Becomes:

Roy Rogers and Trigger
© Dell Publishing Co.

ROY ROGERS AND TRIGGER

92 thru 99 . . . . @45.00
100 . . . . 60.00
101 thru 118 . . . . @45.00
119 thru 125 ATn. . . . . @75.00
126 thru 131 . . . . @55.00
132 thru 144 RsM . . . . @60.00
145 . . . . 75.00

ROY ROGER'S TRIGGER
Dell Publishing Co.
May, 1951

(1) *see Dell Four Color #329*
2 Ph(c) 125.00
3 P(c) 50.00
4 P(c) 50.00
5 P(c) 50.00
6 thru 17 P(c). . . . . @35.00

RULAH, JUNGLE GODDESS (see ZOOT COMICS)

SAARI, THE JUNGLE GODDESS
P.L. Publishing Co.
Nov., 1951

1 The Bantu Blood Curse 350.00

SABU, ELEPHANT BOY
Fox Features Syndicate
June, 1950

1(30) WW,Ph(c) 200.00
2 JKa,Ph(c),Aug.'50 . . . . 150.00

HAPPY HOULIHANS
Fables Publications
(E.C. Comics), Autumn, 1947

1 O:Moon Girl 400.00
2 . . . . 250.00
Becomes:

SADDLE JUSTICE

3 HcK,JCr,AF. 350.00
4 AF,JCr 325.00
5 AF,Grl,WI 300.00
6 AF,Grl. 300.00
7 AF,Grl. 300.00
8 AF,Grl,WI 300.00
Becomes:

SADDLE ROMANCES

9 Grl(c),Grl 325.00
10 AF(c),WW 325.00
11 AF(c),Grl 300.00

SAD SACK
Harvey Publications
Sept., 1949

1 I:Little Dot. 400.00
2 . . . . 200.00
3 . . . . 100.00
4 thru 10 . . . . @75.00
11 thru 21. . . . . 50.00
22 Back in the Army Again,
The Specialist. 35.00
23 thru 50 . . . . @20.00
51 thru 100 . . . . @15.00
100 thru 150 . . . . @7.50
151 thru 200 . . . . @5.00
200 thru 287 . . . . @4.00
See also Other Pub. (Color)

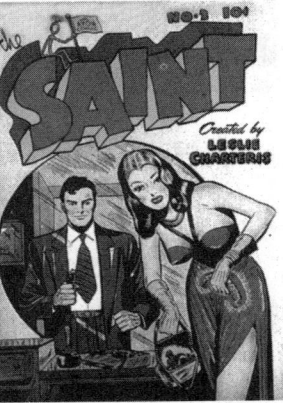

The Saint #2
© Avon Periodicals

SAINT, THE
Avon Periodicals
Aug., 1947

1 JKa,JKa(c),Bondage(c) 600.00
2 . . . . 325.00
3 Rolled Stocking Leg(c) 250.00
4 MB(c) 250.00
5 Spanking Panel 300.00
6 B:Miss Fury 350.00
7 P(c),Detective Cases(c) 200.00
8 P(c),Detective Cases"(c) 175.00
9 EK(c),The Notorious
Murder Mob 175.00
10 WW,P(c),V:The Communist
Menace 200.00
11 P(c),Wanted For Robbery. . . . 125.00
12 P(c),The Blowpipe Murders
March, 1952. . . . . 150.00

SAM HILL PRIVATE EYE
Close-Up Publications, 1950

1 The Double Trouble Caper . . . 125.00
2 . . . . 75.00
3 . . . . 60.00
4 Negligee panels 75.00
5 thru 7 . . . . @50.00

SAMSON
Fox Features Syndicate
Autumn, 1940

1 BP,GT,A:Wing Turner 2,000.00
2 BP,A:Dr. Fung 700.00
3 JSh(c),A:Navy Jones 550.00
4 WE,B:Yarko 500.00
5 WE 450.00
6 WE,O:The Topper;Sept'41 . . . 450.00

SAMSON
Ajax Farrell Publ.
(Four Star)
April, 1955

12 The Electric Curtain 225.00
13 Assignment Danger 200.00
14 The Red Raider;Aug'55 . . . . . 200.00

SANDS OF THE SOUTH PACIFIC
Toby Press, Jan., 1953

1 2-Fisted Romantic Adventure . 150.00

SCHOOL DAY ROMANCES
(see POPULAR TEEN-AGERS)

Science Comics #8
© Fox Features Syndicate

SCIENCE COMICS
Fox Features Syndicate
Feb., 1940

1 GT,LF(c),O&B:Electro,Perisphere Payne,The Eagle,Navy Jones; B:Marga,Cosmic Carson, Dr. Doom; Bondage(c) . . . 3,800.00
2 GT,LF(c) 1,750.00
3 GT,LF(c),Dynamo. 1,500.00
4 JK,Cosmic Carson 1,300.00
5 Giant Comiscope Offer Eagle(c) 750.00
6 Dynamop(c) 750.00
7 Bondage(c),Dynamo 750.00
8 Sept., 1940 Eagle(c). 700.00

SCIENCE COMICS
Humor Publications
Jan., 1946

1 RP(c),Story of the A-Bomb . . . 125.00
2 RP(c),How Museum Pieces Are Assembled 60.00
3 AF,RP(c),How Underwater Tunnels Are Made 100.00
4 RP(c),Behind the Scenes at A TV Broadcast 45.00
5 The Story of the World's Bridges; Sept., 1946 . . . . 50.00

SCIENCE COMICS
Ziff-Davis Publ. Co.
May, 1946

N# Used For A Mail Order Test Market 300.00

SCIENCE COMICS
Export Publication Enterprises
March, 1951

1 How to resurrect a dead rat . . . 60.00

SCOOP COMICS
Harry 'A' Chesler Jr.
Nov., 1941

1 I&B:Rocketman&Rocketgirl;B:Dan Hastings;O&B:Master Key . 1,100.00
2 A:Rocketboy,Eye Injury 1,200.00
3 Partial rep. of #2 . . . . 600.00
4 thru 7 do not exist
8 1945 . . . . 350.00

SCREAM COMICS
Humor Publ./Current Books
(Ace Magazines)
Autumn, 1944

1 . . . . 125.00
2 . . . . 60.00
3 . . . . 50.00
4 thru 15 . . . . @50.00
16 I:Lily Belle 55.00
17 . . . . 40.00
18 Drug 50.00
19 . . . . 40.00
Becomes:

ANDY COMICS

20 Teenage 30.00
21 . . . . 30.00
Becomes:

ERNIE COMICS

22 Teenage 35.00
23 thru 25 . . . . @25.00
Becomes:

ALL LOVE ROMANCES

26 Ernie 35.00
27 LbC 40.00
28 thru 32 . . . . @25.00

(Capt. Silvers Log of...) SEA HOUND, THE
Avon Periodicals, 1945

N# The Esmerelda's Treasure . . 125.00
2 Adventures in Brazil 90.00
3 Louie the Llama 90.00
4 In Greed & Vengence; Jan-Feb, 1946 . . . . 90.00

SECRET LOVES
Comics Magazines
(Quality Comics)
Nov., 1949

1 BWa(c). 175.00
2 BWa(c),Lingerie(c) 150.00
3 RC 100.00
4 . . . . 60.00
5 Boom Town Babe 100.00
6 . . . . 60.00

SECRET MYSTERIES
(see CRIME MYSTERIES)

SELECT DETECTIVE
D.S. Publishing Co.
Aug.–Sept., 1948

1 MB,Exciting New Mystery Cases. 175.00
2 MB,AMc,Dead Men.... . . . . . . 125.00
3 Face in theFrame;Dec-Jan'48 . 100.00

SERGEANT PRESTON OF THE YUKON
Dell Publishing Co., Aug., 1951

(1 thru 4) *see Dell Four Color #344; #373, 397, 419*
5 thru 10 P(c). . . . . @65.00
11 P(c) 50.00
12 P(c) 50.00
13 P(c),O:Sergeant Preston 55.00
14 thru 17 P(c) . . . . @50.00
18 P(c) 55.00
19 thru 29 Ph(c) . . . . @55.00

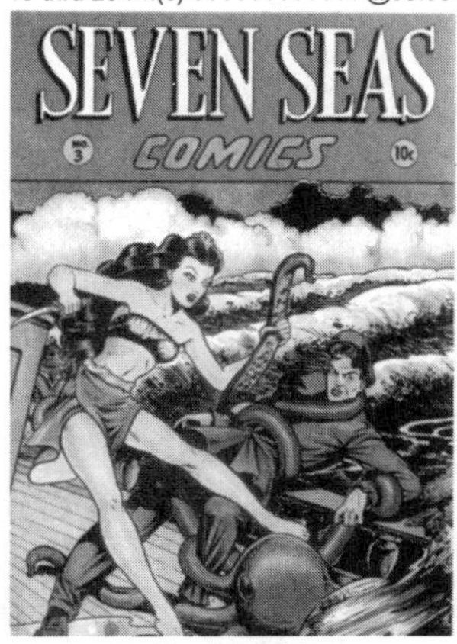

Seven Seas #3
© Universal Phoenix

SEVEN SEAS COMICS
Universal Phoenix Features/
Leader Publ., April, 1946

1 MB,RWb(c),B:South Sea Girl, Captain Cutlass 700.00
2 MB,RWb(c) 600.00
3 MB,AF,MB(c) 500.00
4 MB,MB(c) 550.00
5 MB,MB(c),Hangman's Noose . 500.00
6 MB,MB(c);1947 . . . . 500.00

SHADOW COMICS
Street & Smith, March, 1940

1-1 P(c),B:Shadow,Doc Savage, Bill Barnes,Nick Carter, Frank Merriwell,Iron Munro 4,500.00
1-2 P(c),B: The Avenger 1,500.00
1-3 P(c),A: Norgill the Magician 1,000.00
1-4 P(c),B:The Three Musketeers. 850.00
1-5 P(c),E: Doc Savage 850.00
1-6 A: Captain Fury 700.00
1-7 O&B: The Wasp 750.00
1-8 A:Doc Savage 700.00
1-9 A:Norgill the Magician 700.00
1-10 O:Iron Ghost;B:The Dead End Kids 700.00
1-11 O:Hooded Wasp 700.00
1-12 Crime Does Not pay 550.00
2-1 . . . . 550.00
2-2 Shadow Becomes Invisible . 500.00
2-3 O&B:supersnipe; F:Little Nemo 725.00
2-4 F:Little Nemo 500.00
2-5 V:The Ghost Faker 500.00
2-6 A:Blackstone the Magician . . 400.00
2-7 V:The White Dragon 400.00
2-8 A:Little Nemo 400.00
2-9 The Hand of Death 400.00
2-10 A:Beebo the WonderHorse . 400.00
2-11 V:Devil Kyoti 400.00
2-12 V:Devil Kyoti 375.00
3-1 JaB(c),V:Devil Kyoti 375.00
3-2 Red Skeleton Life Story 375.00
3-3 V:Monstrodamus 375.00
3-4 V:Monstrodamus 375.00
3-5 V:Monstrodamus 375.00
3-6 V:Devil's of the Deep 375.00
3-7 V: Monstrodamus 375.00
3-8 E: The Wasp 375.00
3-9 The Stolen Lighthouse 375.00
3-10 A:Doc Savage. 375.00
3-11 P(c),V: Thade 375.00
3-12 V: Thade. 375.00
4-1 Red Cross Appeal on (c) . . . 350.00
4-2 V:The Brain of Nippon 350.00
4-3 Little Men in Space 350.00
4-4 ...Mystifies Berlin 350.00
4-5 ...Brings Terror to Tokio 350.00
4-6 V:The Tarantula 350.00
4-7 Crypt of the Seven Skulls . . . 350.00
4-8 V:the Indigo Mob 350.00
4-9 Ghost Guarded Treasure of the Haunted Glen 350.00
4-10 V:The Hydra 350.00
4-11 V:The Seven Sinners 350.00
4-12 Club Curio 300.00
5-1 A:Flatty Foote 300.00
5-2 Bells of Doom 300.00
5-3 The Circle of Death. 300.00
5-4 The Empty Safe Riddle. 300.00
5-5 The Mighty Master Nomad . . 300.00
5-6 ...Fights Piracy Among the Golden Isles 300.00
5-7 V:The Talon 300.00
5-8 V:The Talon 300.00
5-9 V:The Talon 300.00
5-10 V:The Crime Master 300.00
5-11 The Clutch of the Talon 300.00
5-12 Most Dangerous Criminal . . 300.00
6-1 Double Z 300.00
6-2 Riddle of Prof.Mentalo 300.00
6-3 V:Judge Lawless 300.00
6-4 V:Dr. Zenith 300.00
6-5 . . . . 300.00
6-6 ...Invades the Crucible of Death 300.00
6-7 Four Panel Cover 300.00
6-8 Crime Among the Aztecs . . . 300.00
6-9 I:Shadow Jr. 350.00
6-10 Devil's Passage 300.00
6-11 The Black Pagoda. 300.00
6-12 BP,BP(c),Atomic Bomb Secrets Stolen 325.00
7-1 The Yellow Band 325.00
7-2 A:Shadow Jr. 325.00
7-3 BP,BP(c),Crime Under the Border 350.00
7-4 BP,BP(c),One Tree Island, Atomic Bomb 375.00
7-5 A:Shadow Jr. 325.00
7-6 BP,BP(c),The Sacred Sword of Sanjorojo 350.00
7-7 Crime K.O. 350.00
7-8 ...Raids Crime Harbor 350.00
7-9 BP.BP(c),Kilroy Was Here . . 350.00
7-10 BP,BP(c),The Riddle of the Flying Saucer 400.00
7-11 BP,BP(c),Crime Doesn't Pay 350.00
7-12 BP,BP(c)Back From the Grave 350.00
8-1 BP,BP(c),Curse of the Cat . . 350.00
8-2 BP,BP(c),Decay,Vermin & Murder in the Bayou 350.00
8-3 BP,BP(c),The Spider Boy . . . 350.00
8-4 BP,BP(c),Death Rises Out of the Sea 350.00
8-5 BP,BP(c),Jekyll-Hyde Murders. 350.00
8-6 Secret of Valhalla Hall 350.00
8-7 BP,BP(c),Shadow in Danger 350.00
8-8 BP,BP(c),...Solves a Twenty Year Old Crime 350.00
8-9 BP,BP(c),3-D Effect(c). 350.00
8-10 BP,BP(c),Up&Down(c) 350.00
8-11 BP,BP(c). 350.00
8-12 BP,BP(c),Arabs,Boat(c). . . . 350.00
9-1 Airport(c) 350.00
9-2 BP,BP(c),Flying Cannon(c) . . 350.00
9-3 BP,BP(c),Shadow's Shadow . 350.00
9-4 BP,BP(c) 350.00
9-5 Death in the Stars;Aug'49 . . 350.00

SHARP COMICS
H.C. Blackerby
Winter, 1945

1 O:Planetarian(c) 300.00
2 O:The Pioneer 250.00

SHEENA, QUEEN OF THE JUNGLE
Real Adventures
(Fiction House)
Spring, 1942

1 Blood Hunger 1,900.00
2 Black Orchid of Death 900.00
3 Harem Shackles 700.00
4 The Zebra Raiders 400.00
5 War of the Golden Apes 375.00
6 . . . . 350.00
7 They Claw By Night 325.00
8 The Congo Colossus 325.00
9 and 10 . . . . @300.00
11 Red Fangs of the Tree Tribe. . 300.00
12 . . . . 225.00
13 Veldt o/t Voo Doo Lions 225.00
14 The Hoo Doo Beasts of Mozambique. 225.00
15 . . . . 225.00
16 Black Ivory. 225.00
17 Great Congo Treasure Trek . . 225.00
18 Doom of the Elephant Drum Winter, 1952. . . . . 225.00

SHIELD-WIZARD COMICS
MLJ Magazines
Summer, 1940

1 IN,EA,O:Shield. 4,000.00
2 O:Shield;I:Roy 1,600.00
3 Roy,Child Bondage(c) 1,000.00
4 Shield,Roy,Wizard 1,000.00
5 B:Dusty-Boy Dectective,Child Bondage. 950.00
6 B:Roy the Super Boy,Child Bondage 850.00
7 Shield(c),Roy Bondage(c) . . . 875.00
8 Bondage(c) 850.00
9 Shield/Roy(c) 700.00
10 Shield/Roy(c). 700.00
11 Shield/Roy(c) 700.00
12 Shield/Roy(c). 700.00
13 Bondage (c);Spring'44 . . . . . 725.00

SHIP AHOY
Spotlight Publishers
Nov., 1944

1 LbC(c) 125.00

SHOCK DETECTIVE CASE(S)
(see CRIMINALS ON THE RUN)

SHOCK SUSPENSTORIES
Tiny Tot Comics
(E.C. Comics)
Feb.–March, 1952

1 JDa,JKa,AF(c),ElectricChair . . 675.00
2 WW,JDa,Grl,JKa,WW(c) 400.00
3 WW,JDa,JKa,WW(c). 300.00
4 WW,JDa,JKa,WW(c). 300.00
5 WW,JDa,JKa,WW(c),Hanging . 275.00
6 WW,AF,JKa,WW(c), Bondage(c). 300.00
7 JKa,WW,GE,AF(c),Face Melting 300.00
8 JKa,AF,AW,GE,WW,AF(c). . . . 300.00
9 JKa,AF,RC,WW,AF(c) 300.00
10 JKa,WW,RC,JKa(c),Drug 300.00
11 JCr,JKa,WW,RC,JCr(c) 275.00
12 AF,JKa,WW,RC,AF(c)Drug(c). 300.00

Shock SuspenStories #13
© E.C. Comics

GOLDEN AGE

13 JKa,WW,FF,JKa(c). 350.00
14 JKa,WW,BK,WW(c) 275.00
15 JKa,WW,RC,JDa(c)
Strangulation 225.00
16 GE,RC,JKa,GE(c),Rape. 225.00
17 GE,RC,JKa,GE(c) 200.00
18 GE,RC,JKa,GE(c);Jan'55. . . . 200.00

SHOCKING MYSTERY CASES (see THRILLING CRIME CASES)

SILVER STREAK COMICS

Your Guide/New Friday/ Comic House/Newsbrook Publications/Lev Gleason Dec., 1939

1 JCo,JCo(c),I&B:The Claw,Red Reeves Capt.Fearless;B:Mr.Midnight,Wasp;A:Spiritman . . 12,000.00
2 JSm,JCo,JSm(c) 4,000.00
3 JaB(c),I&O:Silver Streak; B:Dickie Dean,Lance Hale, Ace Powers,Bill Wayne, Planet Patrol 3,000.00
4 JCo,JaB(c)B:Sky Wolf; N:Silver Streak,I:Lance Hale's Sidekick-Jackie 1,300.00
5 JCo,JCo(c),Dickie Dean V:The Raging Flood. 1,600.00
6 JCo,JaB,JCo(c),O&I:Daredevil [Blue & Yellow Costume]; R:The Claw 13,000.00
7 JCo,N: Daredevil 7,500.00
8 JCo,JCo(c) 2,700.00
9 JCo,BoW(c) 1,600.00
10 BoW,BoW(c). 1,400.00
11 DRi(c) I:Mercury 1,000.00
12 DRi(c) 700.00
13 JaB,JaB(c),O:Thun-Dohr 700.00
14 JaB,JaB(c),A:Nazi Skull Men. 700.00
15 JaB,DBr,JaB(c), B:Bingham Boys. 650.00
16 DBr,BoW(c),Hitler(c). 650.00
17 DBr,JaB(c),E:Daredevil 600.00
18 DBr,JaB(c),B:The Saint 500.00
19 DBr,EA 425.00

Silver Streak Comics #12
© Lev Gleason

20 BW,BEv,EA 425.00
21 BW,BEv. 425.00
Becomes:

CRIME DOES NOT PAY

22(23) CBi(c),The Mad Musician & Tunes of Doom 1,800.00
23 CBi(c),John Dillinger-One Man Underworld 1,000.00
24 CBi(c),The Mystery of the Indian Dick 800.00
25 CBi(c),Dutch Shultz-King of the Underworld. 450.00
26 CBi(c),Lucky Luciano-The Deadliest of Crime Rats 450.00
27 CBi(c),Pretty Boy Floyd 450.00
28 CBi(c),. 450.00
29 CBi(c),Two-Gun Crowley-The Bad Kid with the Itchy Trigger Finger. 350.00
30 CBi(c),"Monk"Eastman V:Thompson's Mob. 350.00
31 CBi(c) The Million Dollar Bank Robbery 275.00
32 CBi(c),Seniorita of Sin 275.00
33 CBi(c),Meat Cleaver Murder. . 275.00
34 CBi(c),Elevator Shaft 275.00
35 CBi(c),Case o/t MissingToe . . 275.00
36 CBi(c) 250.00
37 CBi(c) 225.00
38 CBi(c) 225.00
39 FG,CBi(c) 225.00
40 FG,CBi(c) 250.00
41 FG,RP,CBi(c),The Cocksure Counterfeiter 200.00
42 FG,RP,CBi(c). 225.00
43 FG,RP,CBi(c). 150.00
44 FG,CBi(c),The Most Shot At Gangster 150.00
45 FG,CBi(c) 150.00
46 FG,CBi(c),ChildKidnapping(c) 160.00
47 FG,CBi(c),ElectricChair 225.00
48 FG,CBi(c) 150.00
49 FG,CBi(c) 150.00
50 FG,CBi(c) 150.00
51 FG,GT,CBi(c),1st Monthly Iss. 125.00
52 FG,GT,CBi(c). 125.00
53 FG,CBi(c) 125.00
54 FG,CBi(c) 125.00
55 FG,CBi(c) 125.00
56 FG,GT,CBi(c). 125.00
57 FG,CBi(c) 125.00
58 FG,CBi(c) 125.00
59 FG,Cbi(c). 125.00
60 FG,CBi(c) 125.00
61 FG,GT,CBi(c). 125.00
62 FG,CBi(c),Bondage(c) 125.00
63 FG,GT,CBi(c). 110.00
64 FG,GT,CBi(c). 110.00
65 FG,CBi(c). 110.00
66 FG,GT,CBi(c) 110.00
67 FG,GT,CBi(c) 110.00
68 FG,CBi(c). 110.00
69 FG,CBi(c). 110.00
70 FG,Cbi(c) 110.00
71 FG,CBi(c) 100.00
72 FG,CBi(c) 100.00
73 FG,CBi(c) 100.00
74 FG,CBi(c) 100.00
75 FG,CBi(c) 100.00
76 FG,CBi(c) 100.00
77 FG,CBi(c),Electrified Safe . . . 125.00
78 FG,CBi(c) 100.00
79 FG. 100.00
80 FG. 100.00
81 FG. 100.00
82 FG. 100.00
83 FG. 100.00
84 FG. 100.00
85 FG. 100.00
86 FG. 90.00
87 FG,P(c),The Rock-A-Bye Baby Murder 90.00
88 FG,P(c),Death Carries a Torch. 90.00
89 FG,BF,BF P(c),The Escort Murder Case 90.00
90 FG,BF P(c),The Alhambra Club Murders 90.00
91 FG,AMc,BF P(c),Death Watches The Clock 90.00
92 BF,FG,BF P(c). 90.00
93 BF,FG,AMc,BF P(c) 90.00
94 BF,FG,BF P(c). 90.00
95 FG,AMc,BF P(c) 90.00
96 BF,FG,BF P(c),The Case of the Movie Star's Double 90.00
97 FG,BF P(c) 90.00
98 BF,FG,BF P(c),Bondage(c) . . . 90.00
99 BF,FG,BF P(c). 90.00
100 FG,BF,AMc,P(c),The Case of the Jittery Patient 125.00
101 FG,BF,AMc,P(c). 75.00
102 FG,BF,AMc,BF P(c) 75.00
103 FG,BF,AMc,BF P(c) 75.00
104 thru 110 FG . . . . @75.00
111 thru 120 . . . . @75.00
121 thru 140 . . . . @50.00
141 JKu 45.00
142 JKu,CBi(c) 45.00
143 JKu,Comic Code 45.00
144 I Helped Capture"Fat Face" George Klinerz. 40.00
145 RP,Double Barrelled Menace . 40.00
146 BP,The Con & The Canary. . . 40.00
147 JKu,BP,A Long Shoe On the Highway;July, 1955. . . . . 60.00

SINGLE SERIES

United Features Syndicate 1938

1 Captain & The Kids 750.00
2 Bronco Bill 400.00
3 Ella Cinders 325.00
4 Li'l Abner 600.00
5 Fritzi Ritz 200.00
6 Jim Hardy 325.00
7 Frankie Doodle 200.00
8 Peter Pat 200.00
9 Strange As it Seems 250.00
10 Little Mary Mixup 200.00
11 Mr. & Mrs. Beans 175.00
12 Joe Jinx. 175.00
13 Looy Dot Dope. 175.00
14 Billy Make Believe 175.00
15 How It Began. 200.00
16 Illustrated Gags 150.00
17 Danny Dingle. 150.00
18 Li'l Abner 500.00
19 Broncho Bill 350.00
20 Tarzan 1,200.00
21 Ella Cinders. 250.00
22 Iron Vic 200.00
23 Tailspin Tommy 300.00
24 Alice In Wonderland. 275.00
25 Abbie an' Slats. 250.00
26 Little Mary Mixup 175.00
27 Jim Hardy 250.00
28 Ella Cinders & Abbie AN' Slats 1942 . . . . 200.00

SKELETON HAND

American Comics Group Sept.–Oct., 1952

1 . . . . 325.00
2 The Were-Serpent of Karnak . 225.00
3 Waters of Doom 200.00
4 Black Dust 200.00
5 The Rise & Fall of the Bogey Man. 200.00
6 July–Aug., 1953 . . . . 200.00

SKY BLAZERS
Hawley Publications
Sept., 1940

1 Flying Aces,Sky Pirates 500.00
2 Nov., 1940 . . . . 300.00

Skyman #3
© Columbia Comics Group

SKYMAN
Columbia Comics Group, 1941

1 OW,OW(c),O:Skyman,Face . 1,000.00
2 OW,OW(c),Yankee Doodle . . . 500.00
3 OW,OW(c) 300.00
4 OW,OW(c),Statue of Liberty(c) 1948 . . . . 300.00

SKY PILOT
Ziff-Davis Publishing Co.
1950

10 NS P(c),Lumber Pirates 100.00
11 Ns P(c),The 2,00 Foot Drop; April–May, 1951 . . . . 75.00

SKY ROCKET
Home Guide Publ.
(Harry 'A' Chesler), 1944

1 Alias the Dragon,Skyrocket. . . 250.00

SKY SHERIFF
D.S. Publishing
Summer, 1948

1 I:Breeze Lawson & the Prowl Plane Patrol 100.00

SLAM BANG COMICS
Fawcett Publications
Jan., 1940

1 B:Diamond Jack,Mark Swift, Lee Granger,Jungle King . . 1,700.00
2 F:Jim Dolan Two-Fisted Crime Buster 800.00
3 A: Eric the Talking Lion 1,100.00
4 F: Hurricane Hansen-Sea Adventurer 600.00
5 . . . . 600.00
6 I: Zoro the Mystery Man; Bondage(c) 600.00
7 Bondage(c);Sept., 1940 . . . . . 600.00

SLAPSTICK COMICS
Comic Magazine Distrib., Inc.
1945

N# Humorous Parody 175.00

SLAVE GIRL COMICS
Avon Periodicals
Feb., 1949

1 . . . . 700.00
2 April, 1949 . . . . 500.00

SLICK CHICK COMICS
Leader Enterprises, Inc., 1947

1 Teen-Aged Humor 90.00
2 Teen-Aged Humor 60.00
3 1947. 60.00

SMASH COMICS
Comics Magazine, Inc.
(Quality Comics Group)
Aug., 1939

1 WE,O&B:Hugh Hazard, Bozo the Robot,Black X, Invisible Justice: B:Wings Wendall, Chic Carter 2,500.00
2 WE,A:Lone Star Rider 800.00
3 WE,B:Captain Cook,JohnLaw 550.00
4 WE,PGn,B:Flash Fulton 500.00
5 WE,PGn,Bozo Robot 500.00
6 WE,PGn,GFx,Black X(c). 500.00
7 WE,PGn,GFx,Wings Wendell(c) 400.00
8 WE,PGn,GFx,Bozo Robot. . . . 400.00
9 WE,PGn,GFx,Black X(c). 400.00
10 WE,PGn,GFx,Bozo robot(c) . . 400.00
11 WE,PGn,GFx,BP,Black X(c) . . 400.00
12 WE,PGn,GFx,BP,Bozo(c). . . . 400.00
13 WE,PGn,GFx,AB,BP,B:Mango, Purple Trio,BlackX(c) 400.00
14 BP,LF,AB,PGn,I:The Ray. . . 2,400.00
15 BP,LF,AB,PGn,The Ram(c) . 1,000.00
16 BP,LF,AB,PGn,Bozo(c) 1,000.00
17 BP,LF,AB,PGn,JCo, The Ram(c). 1,000.00
18 BP,LF,AB,JCo,PGn, B&O:Midnight 1,200.00
19 BP,LF,AB,JCo,PGn,Bozo(c) . . 700.00
20 BP,LF,AB,JCo,PGn, The Ram(c) 700.00
21 BP,LF,AB,JCo,PGn 700.00
22 BP,LF,AB,JCo,PGn, B:The Jester. 700.00
23 BP,AB,JCo,RC,PGn, The Ram(c) 525.00
24 BP,AB,JCo,RC,PGn,A:Sword, E:ChicCarter, N:WingsWendall. 525.00
25 AB,JCo,RC,PGn,O:Wildfire . . 525.00
26 AB,JCo,RC,PGn,Bozo(c) 525.00
27 AB,JCo,RC,PGn,The Ram(c) . 525.00
28 AB,JCo,RC,PGn, 1st Midnight (c) 525.00
29 AB,JCo,Rc,PGn,B;Midnight(c) 500.00
30 AB,JCo,PGn 500.00
31 AB,JCo,PGn 400.00
32 AB,JCo,PGn 400.00
33 AB,JCo,PGn,O:Marksman . . . 500.00
34 AB,JCo,PGn 400.00
35 AB,JCo,RC,PGn 400.00
36 AB,JCo,RC,PGn,E:Midnight(c) 400.00
37 AB,JCo,RC,PGn,Doc Wacky becomes Fastest Human on Earth. 400.00
38 JCo,RC,PGn,B:Yankee Eagle 525.00
39 PGn,B:Midnight(c) 375.00
40 PGn,E:Ray 375.00

Smash #38
© Quality Comics Group

41 PGn. 250.00
42 PGn,B:Lady Luck. 275.00
43 PGn. 275.00
44 PGn. 250.00
45 PGn,E:Midnight(c) 250.00
46 RC,Twelve Hours to Live 250.00
47 Wanted Midnight, Dead or Alive 250.00
48 Midnight Meets the Menace from Mars 250.00
49 PGn,FG,Mass of Muscle 250.00
50 I:Hyram the Hermit. 250.00
51 A:Wild Bill Hiccup. 175.00
52 PGn,FG,Did Ancient Rome Fall, or was it Pushed?. 175.00
53 Is ThereHonorAmongThieves. 175.00
54 A:Smear-Faced Schmaltz . . . 175.00
55 Never Trouble Trouble until Trouble Troubles You 175.00
56 The Laughing Killer 175.00
57 A Dummy that Turns Into A Curse 175.00
58 . . . . 175.00
59 A Corpse that Comes Alive . . 175.00
60 The Swooner & the Trush . . . 175.00
61 . . . . 150.00
62 V:The Lorelet. 150.00
63 PGn 150.00
64 PGn,In Search of King Zoris. . 150.00
65 PGn,V:Cyanide Cindy 150.00
66 Under Circle's Spell 150.00
67 A Living Clue. 150.00
68 JCo,Atomic Dice 150.00
69 JCo,V:Sir Nuts. 150.00
70 . . . . 150.00
71 . . . . 125.00
72 JCo,Angela,the Beautiful Bovine 125.00
73 . . . . 125.00
74 . . . . 125.00
75 The Revolution 125.00
76 Bowl Over Crime 125.00
77 Who is Lilli Dilli?. 125.00
78 JCo,Win Over Crime 125.00
79 V:The Men From Mars. 125.00
80 JCo,V:Big Hearted Bosco. . . . 125.00
81 V:Willie the Kid 125.00
82 V:Woodland Boy 125.00
83 JCo,Quizmaster. 125.00
84 A Date With Father Time 125.00
85 JCo,A Singing Swindle. 125.00

SMASH HITS SPORTS COMICS
Essankay Publications
Jan., 1949

1 LbC,LbC(c) ... 225.00

SMILEY BURNETTE WESTERN
Fawcett Publications
March, 1950

1 Ph(c),B:Red Eagle ... 350.00
2 Ph(c) ... 250.00
3 Ph(c) ... 250.00
4 Ph(c) ... 250.00

SMILIN' JACK
Dell Publishing Co., 1940

1 ... 125.00
2 ... 65.00
3 thru 8 ... @40.00

SMITTY
Dell Publishing Co., 1940

1 ... 100.00
2 ... 50.00
3 ... 40.00
4 thru 7 ... @30.00

SNAP
Harry 'A' Chesler Jr. Publications, 1944

N# Humorous ... 100.00

SNAPPY COMICS
Cima Publications (Prize), 1945

1 A:Animale ... 225.00

SNIFFY THE PUP
Animated Cartoons (Standard Comics)
Nov., 1949

5 FF,Funny Animal ... 75.00
6 thru 9 Funny Animal ... @30.00
10 thru 17 Funny Animal ... @20.00
18 Sept., 1953 ... 20.00

SOLDIER COMICS
Fawcett Publications
Jan., 1952

1 Fighting Yanks on Flaming Battlefronts ... 100.00
2 Blazing Battles Exploding with Combat ... 40.00
3 ... 35.00
4 A Blow for Freedom ... 30.00
5 Only The Dead Are Free ... 30.00
6 Blood & Guts ... 25.00
7 The Phantom Sub ... 25.00
8 More Plasma! ... 25.00
9 Red Artillery ... 25.00
10 ... 25.00
11 Sept., 1953 ... 25.00

SOLDIERS OF FORTUNE
Creston Publications (American Comics Group)
Feb.–March, 1952

1 OW(c),B:Ace Carter, Crossbones, Lance Larson ... 175.00
2 OW(c) ... 100.00
3 OW(c) ... 75.00
4 ... 75.00
5 OW(c) ... 75.00
6 OW(c),OW,Bondage(c) ... 85.00
7 ... 75.00
8 OW thru 10 ... @75.00
11 OW,Format Change to War ... 50.00
12 ... 50.00
13 OW,Feb.–March, 1953 ... 50.00

SON OF SINBAD
St. John Publishing Co.
Feb., 1950

1 JKu,JKu(c),The Curse of the Caliph's Dancer ... 300.00

SPACE ACTION
Junior Books (Ace Magazines)
June, 1952

1 Invaders from a Lost Galaxy ... 550.00
2 The Silicon Monster from Galaxy X ... 450.00
3 Attack on Ishtar, Oct., 1952 ... 450.00

Space Adventures #3
© Charlton Comics

SPACE ADVENTURES
Capitol Stories/ Charlton Comics
July, 1952

1 AFa&LM(c) ... 350.00
2 ... 175.00
3 DG(c) ... 150.00
4 DG(c) ... 150.00
5 StC(c) ... 150.00
6 StC(c),Two Worlds ... 125.00
7 DG(c),Transformation ... 150.00
8 DG(c),All For Love ... 125.00
9 DG(c) ... 125.00
10 SD,SD(c) ... 350.00
11 SD,JoS ... 400.00
12 SD(c) ... 400.00
13 A:Blue Beetle ... 150.00
14 A:Blue Beetle ... 150.00
15 Ph(c) of Rocky Jones ... 150.00
16 BKa,A:Rocky Jones ... 150.00
17 A:Rocky Jones ... 125.00
18 A:Rocky Jones ... 125.00
19 ... 100.00
20 First Trip to the Moon ... 200.00
21 ... 100.00
22 Does Not Exist
23 SD,Space Trip to the Moon ... 150.00
24 ... 125.00
25 Brontosaurus ... 125.00
26 SD,Flying Saucers ... 150.00
27 SD,Flying Saucers ... 150.00
28 Moon Trap ... 60.00
29 Captive From Space ... 60.00
30 Peril in the Sky ... 60.00
31 SD,SD(c),Enchanted Planet ... 125.00
32 SD,SD(c),Last Ship from Earth ... 125.00
33 Galactic Scourge, I&O:Captain Atom ... 400.00
34 SD,SD(c),A:Captain Atom ... 150.00
35 thru 40 SD,SD(c), A:Captain Atom ... @150.00
41 ... 35.00
42 SD,A:Captain Atom ... 35.00
43 ... 35.00
44 A:Mercury Man ... 35.00
45 A:Mercury Man ... 35.00
46 thru 58 ... @35.00
59 Nov., 1964 ... 35.00

SPACE BUSTERS
Ziff-Davis Publishing Co.
Spring, 1952

1 BK,NS(c),Ph(c),Charge of the Battle Women ... 650.00
2 EK,BK,MA,NS(c), Bondage(c),Ph(c) ... 500.00
3 Autumn, 1952 ... 475.00

SPACE COMICS
Avon Periodicals
March–April, 1954

4 (fa),F:Space Mouse ... 40.00
5 (fa),F:Space Mouse, May–June, 1954 ... 30.00

SPACE DETECTIVE
Avon Periodicals
July, 1951

1 WW,WW(c),Opium Smugglers of Venus ... 850.00
2 WW,WW(c),Batwomen of Mercury ... 600.00
3 EK(c),SeaNymphs ofNeptune 300.00
4 EK,Flame Women of Vulcan, Bondage(c) ... 325.00

SPACE MOUSE
Avon Periodicals
April, 1953

1 Funny Animal ... 65.00
2 Funny Animal ... 40.00
3 thru 5 Funny Animal ... @25.00

SPACE PATROL
Approved Comics (Ziff-Davis)
Summer, 1952

1 BK,NS,Ph(c), The Lady of Diamonds ... 700.00
2 BK,NS,Ph(c),Slave King of Pluto,Oct.–Nov., 1952 ... 500.00

SPACE THRILLERS
Avon Periodicals, 1954

N# Contents May Vary ... 900.00

GOLDEN AGE

SPACE WESTERN COMICS (see YELLOWJACKET COMICS)

SPARKLER COMICS
United Features Syndicate
July, 1940

1 Jim Handy 300.00
2 Frankie Doodle,Aug., 1940 . . 225.00

SPARKLER COMICS
United Features Syndicate
July, 1941

1 BHg,O:Sparkman;B:Tarzan,Captain & the Kids,Ella Cinders,Danny Dingle,Dynamite Dunn, Nancy, Abbie an' Slats, Frankie Doodle,Broncho Bill 2,000.00
2 BHg, The Case of Poisoned Fruit 650.00
3 BHg 500.00
4 BHg,Case of Sparkman & the Firefly 500.00
5 BHg,Sparkman,Natch 475.00
6 BHg,Case o/t Bronze Bees . . 450.00
7 BHg,Case o/t Green Raiders . 450.00
8 BHg,V:River Fiddler 450.00
9 BHg,N:Sparkman 450.00
10 BHg,B:Hap Hopper, Sparkman's ID revealed 450.00
11 BHg,V:Japanese 375.00
12 BHg,Another N:Sparkman . . . 375.00
13 BHg,Hap Hopper Rides For Freedom 375.00
14 BHg,BHg(c),Tarzan V:Yellow Killer. 400.00
15 BHg. 350.00
16 BHg,Sparkman V:Japanese . . 350.00
17 BHg,Nancy(c) 350.00
18 BHg,Sparkman in Crete 350.00
19 BHg,I&B:Race Riley, Commandos. 350.00
20 BHg,Nancy(c) 350.00
21 BHg,Tarzan(c) 350.00
22 BHg,Nancy(c) 275.00
23 BHg,Capt&Kids(c) 275.00
24 BHg,Nancy(c) 275.00
25 BHg,BHg(c),Tarzan(c) 300.00
26 BHg,Capt&Kids(c) 275.00
27 BHg,Nancy(c) 275.00
28 BHg,BHg(c),Tarzan(c) 300.00
29 BHg,Capt&Kids(c) 275.00
30 BHg,Nancy(c) 275.00
31 BHg,BHg(c),Tarzan(c) 300.00
32 BHg,Capt&Kids(c) 125.00
33 BHg,Nancy(c) 125.00
34 BHg,BHg(c),Tarzan(c) 250.00
35 BHg,Capt&Kids(c) 125.00
36 BHg,Nancy(c) 125.00
37 BHg,BHg(c),Tarzan(c) 250.00
38 BHg,Capt&Kids(c) 125.00
39 BHg,BHg(c),Tarzan(c) 250.00
40 BHg,Nancy(c) 125.00
41 BHg,Capt&Kids(c) 100.00
42 BHg,BHg,Tarzan(c) 200.00
43 BHg,Nancy(c) 100.00
44 BHg,Tarzan(c) 200.00
45 BHg,Capt&Kids(c) 100.00
46 BHg,Nancy(c) 100.00
47 BHg,Tarzan(c) 200.00
48 BHg,Nancy(c) 100.00
49 BHg,Capt&Kids(c) 100.00
50 BHg,BHg(c),Tarzan(c) 165.00
51 BHg,Capt&Kids(c) 100.00
52 BHg,Nancy(c) 100.00
53 BHg,BHg(c),Tarzan(c) 150.00
54 BHg,Capt&Kids(c) 90.00
55 BHg,Nancy(c) 90.00
56 BHg,Capt&Kids(c) 90.00
57 BHg,F:Li'l Abner. 90.00
58 BHg,A:Fearless Fosdick. 100.00
59 BHg,B:Li'l Abner 100.00
60 BHg,Nancy(c) 90.00
61 BHg,Capt&Kids(c) 90.00
62 BHg,Li'L Abner(c) 90.00
63 BHg,Capt&Kids(c) 90.00
64 BHg,Valentines (c). 90.00
65 BHg,Nancy(c) 90.00
66 BHg,Capt&Kids(c) 90.00
67 BHg,Nancy(c) 90.00
68 BHg, ... 90.00
69 BHg,B:Nancy (c) 90.00
70 BHg. 90.00
71 thru 80 BHg . . . . @60.00
81 BHg,E:Nancy(c). 60.00
82 BHg. 60.00
83 BHg,Tarzan(c) 50.00
84 BHg. 50.00
85 BHg,E:Li'l Abner 50.00
86 BHg. 50.00
87 BHg,Nancy(c) 50.00
88 thru 96 BHg . . . . @50.00
97 BHg,O:Lady Ruggles 100.00
98 BHg. 50.00
99 BHg,Nancy(c) 50.00
100 BHg,Nancy(c) 60.00
101 thru 108 BHg . . . . @35.00
109 BHg,ATh 40.00
110 BHg 35.00
111 BHg 35.00
112 BHg 35.00
113 BHg,ATh 60.00
114 thru 120 BHg . . . . @35.00

SPARKLING STARS
Holyoke Publishing Co.
June, 1944

1 B:Hell's Angels,Ali Baba,FBI, Boxie Weaver,Petey & Pop . 125.00
2 . . . . 75.00
3 . . . . 50.00
4 thru 12 . . . . @45.00
13 O&I:Jungo, The Man-Beast . . . 50.00
14 thru 19. . . . . @45.00
20 I:Fangs the Wolfboy. 45.00
21 thru 28. . . . . @45.00
29 Bondage(c) 35.00
30 thru 32. . . . . @30.00
33 March, 1948 . . . . 30.00

SPARKMAN
Frances M. McQueeny, 1944

1 O:Sparkman. 250.00

SPARKY WATTS
Columbia Comics Group, 1942

1 A:Skyman,Hitler(c) 400.00
2 . . . . 200.00
3 . . . . 150.00
4 O:Skyman 150.00
5 A:Skyman 125.00
6 . . . . 75.00
7 . . . . 75.00
8 . . . . 75.00
9 . . . . 75.00
10 1949 . . . . 75.00

[STEVE SAUNDERS] SPECIAL AGENT
Parents Magazine/ Commended Comics,
Dec., 1947

1 J. Edgar Hoover, Ph(c) 90.00
2 . . . . 50.00
3 thru 7 . . . . @30.00
8 Sept., 1949. . . . . 30.00

SPECIAL COMICS (see LAUGH COMICS)

SPECIAL EDITION COMICS
Fawcett Publications
Aug., 1940

1 CCB,CCB(c),F:Captain Marvel 8,500.00

Speed Comics #9
© Harvey Publications

SPEED COMICS
Brookwood/Speed Publ.
Harvey Publications
Oct., 1939

1 BP,B&O:Shock Gibson,B:Spike Marlin,Biff Bannon 2,700.00
2 BP ,B:Shock Gibson(c) 900.00
3 BP,GT 500.00
4 BP 450.00
5 BP,DBr 450.00
6 BP,GT 400.00
7 GT,JKu,B:Mars Mason 400.00
8 JKu 350.00
9 JKu 350.00
10 JKu,E:Shock Gibson(c) 350.00
11 JKu,E:Mars Mason. 350.00
12 B:The Wasp. 425.00
13 I:Captain Freedom;B:Girls Commandos,Pat Parker 475.00
14 Pocket sized format-100pgs. . 475.00
15 Pocket size 475.00
16 JKu,Pocket size. 475.00
17 O:Black Cat 600.00
18 B:Capt.Freedom,Bondage(c) . 450.00
19 . . . . 425.00
20 . . . . 425.00
21 JKu(c) 425.00
22 JKu(c) 425.00
23 JKu(c),O:Girl Commandos . . . 450.00

24 . . . . 325.00
25 . . . . 325.00
26 Flag (c) 325.00
27 . . . . 325.00
28 E:Capt Freedom 325.00
29 Case o/t Black Marketeers . . . 325.00
30 POW Death Chambers 325.00
31 ASh(c),Nazi Thrashing(c). . . . 425.00
32 ASh(c). 375.00
33 ASh(c). 375.00
34 ASh(c). 375.00
35 ASh(c),BlackCat'sDeathTrap . 400.00
36 ASh(c). 375.00
37 RP(c). 375.00
38 RP(c),War Bond Plea with Iwo Jima flag allusion(c) 375.00
39 RP(c),B:Capt Freedom(c). . . . 325.00
40 RP(c). 325.00
41 RP(c). 325.00
42 JKu,RP(c) 325.00
43 JKu,E:Capt Freedom(c) 325.00
44 BP,JKu,Four Kids on a raft, Jan.–Feb., 1947 . . . . 350.00

SPEED SMITH THE HOT ROD KING
Ziff-Davis Publishing Co.
Spring, 1952

1 INS,Ph(c),A:Roscoe the Rascal 175.00

SPIRIT, THE
Will Eisner
(Weekly Coverless Comic Book) June, 1940

WE,O:SPirit 600.00
6/9/40 WE 250.00
6/16/40 WE,Black Queen . . . 175.00
6/23/40 WE,Mr Mystic. 150.00
6/30/40 WE 150.00
7/7/40 WE,Black Queen 150.00
7/14/40 WE 100.00
7/21/40 WE 100.00
7/28/40 WE 100.00
8/4/40 WE 100.00
7/7/40-11/24/40,WE 70.00
12/1/40 WE,Ellen Spanking(c) 125.00
12/8/40-12/29/40 . . . . 60.00
1941 WE Each 50.00
3/16 WE I:Silk Satin 95.00
6/15 WE I Twilight 60.00
6/22 WE Hitler 60.00
1942 WE Each 40.00
2-1 . . . . 60.00
2-15 . . . . 45.00
2-23 . . . . 65.00
1943 WE Each,LF,WE scripts 30.00
1944 JCo,LF. 15.00
1945 LF Each, ... 15.00
1946 WE Each 30.00
1/13 WE,O:The Spirit 50.00
1/20 WE,Satin 50.00
3/17 WE,I:Nylon 50.00
4/21 WE,I:Mr.Carrion 55.00
7/7 WE,I:Dulcet Tone&Skinny . 50.00
10/6 WE,I:F:Gell. 60.00
1947 WE Each 30.00
7/13.,WE,Hansel &Gretel 45.00
7/20,WE,A:Bomb 50.00
9/28,WE,Flying Saucers 65.00
10/5,WE, Cinderella 32.00
12/7,WE,I:Power Puff 32.00
1948 WE Each 30.00
1/11,WE,Sparrow Fallon 35.00
1/25,WE,I:Last A Net 40.00
3/14,WE,A:Kretuama 35.00
4/4,WE,A:Wildrice. 35.00

Spirit #18
© Will Eisner

7/25,The Thing 60.00
8/22,Poe Tale,Horror 65.00
9/18, A:Lorelei 35.00
11/7,WE,A:Plaster of Paris . . . 40.00
1949 WE Each 30.00
1/23 WE,I:Thorne 40.00
8/21 WE,I:Monica Veto 40.00
9/25 WE,A;Ice 40.00
12/4 WE,I:Flaxen 35.00
1950 WE Each 30.00
1/8 WE,I:Sand Saref. 70.00
2/10, Horror Issue. 35.00
1951 WE(Last WE 8/12/51) . . . @30.00
Non-Eisners . . . . @12.00
1952 Non-Eisners . . . . @12.00
7/27 WW,Denny Colt 350.00
8/3 WW,Moon. 350.00
8/10 WW.Moon. 350.00
8/17 WW,WE,Heart 300.00
8/24 WW,Rescue 300.00
8/31 WW,Last Man 300.00
9/7 WW,Man Moon 380.00
9/14 WE. 80.00
9/21 WE Space 250.00
9/28 WE Moon 300.00
10/5 WE Last Story 125.00

SPIRIT, THE
Quality Comics Group/ Vital Publ., 1944

N# Wanted Dead or Alive! 550.00
N# ...in Crime Doesn't Pay. . . . 350.00
N# ...In Murder Runs Wild 250.00
4 ...Flirts with Death. 200.00
5 ...Wanted Dead or Alive 175.00
6 ...Gives You Triple Value. 150.00
7 ...Rocks the Underworld 150.00
8 . . . . 150.00
9 ...Throws Fear Into the Heart of Crime 150.00
10 ...Stalks Crime 150.00
11 ...America's Greatest Crime Buster 150.00
12 WE(c),...The Famous Outlaw Who Smashes Crime 250.00
13 WE(c),...and Ebony Cleans Out the Underworld;Bondage(c) . 250.00
14 WE(c) 250.00
15 WE(c),Bank Robber at Large . 250.00
16 WE(c),The Caase of the Uncanny Cat 250.00
17 WE(c),The Organ Grinding Bank Robber 250.00
18 WE,WE(c),`The Bucket of Blood 300.00
19 WE,WE(c),`The Man Who Murdered the Spirit' 300.00
20 WE,WE(c),`The Vortex' 300.00
21 WE,WE(c),`P'Gell of Paris'. . . 300.00
22 WE(c),TheOctopus,Aug.1950. 450.00

SPIRIT, THE
Fiction House Magazines
1952

1 Curse of Claymore Castle . . . 325.00
2 WE,WE(c),Who Says Crime Doesn't Pay 300.00
3 WE/JGr(c),League of Lions . . 225.00
4 WE,WE&JGr(c),Last Prowl of Mr. Mephisto;Bondage (c) . . 250.00
5 WE,WE(c),Ph(c)1954 . . . . 250.00

SPIRITMAN
Will Eisner, 1944

1 3 Spirit Sections from 1944 Bound Together 150.00
2 LF, 2 Spirit Sections from 1944 Bound Together . 125.00

SPITFIRE COMICS
Harvey Publ., Aug., 1941

1 MKd(c), 100pgs., Pocket size . 600.00
2 100 pgs.,Pocket size, Oct., 1941 . . . . 550.00

SPOOK COMICS
Baily Publications, 1946

1 A:Mr. Lucifer 200.00

SPOOK DETECTIVE CASES
(see CRIMINALS ON THE RUN)

SPOOKY
Harvey Publications
Nov., 1955

1 Funny Apparition 300.00
2 same 175.00
3 thru 10 same . . . . @100.00
11 thru 20 same . . . . @50.00
21 thru 30 same . . . . @40.00
31 thru 40 same . . . . @30.00
41 thru 70 same . . . . @25.00
71 thru 90 same . . . . @20.00
91 thru 120 same . . . . @12.00
121 thru 160 same . . . . @5.00
161 same,Sept., 1980. . . . . 5.00

SPOOKY MYSTERIES
Your Guide Publishing Co.
1946

1 Rib-Tickling Horror 125.00

SPORT COMICS
(see TRUE SPORT PICTURE STORIES)

SPORTS THRILLS
(see DICK COLE)

GOLDEN AGE

SPOTLIGHT COMICS
Harry 'A' Chesler Jr. Publications
Nov., 1944

1 GT,GT(c),B:Veiled Avenger, Black Dwarf,Barry Kuda 500.00
2 . . . . 425.00
3 1945,Eye Injury. 450.00

SPUNKY
Standard Comics
April, 1949

1 FF,Adventures of a Junior Cowboy 50.00
2 FF 35.00
3 . . . . 30.00
4 . . . . 30.00
5 . . . . 30.00
6 . . . . 30.00
7 Nov., 1951 . . . . 30.00

SPY AND COUNTER SPY
Best Syndicated Features (American Comics Group)
Aug.–Sept., 1949

1 I&O:Jonathan Kent 175.00
2 . . . . 100.00

Becomes:

SPY HUNTERS

3 Jonathan Kent 175.00
4 J.Kent. 100.00
5 J.Kent. 100.00
6 J.Kent. 100.00
7 OW(c),J.Kent 100.00
8 OW(c),J.Kent 100.00
9 OW(c),J.Kent 100.00
10 OW(c),J.Kent. 100.00
11 . . . . 75.00
12 OW(c),MD 75.00
13 and 14 . . . . @60.00
15 OW(c) 75.00
16 AW 125.00
17 . . . . 50.00
18 War (c) 60.00
19 and 20 . . . . @60.00
21 B:War Content. 60.00
22 . . . . 60.00
23 Torture. 150.00
24 `BlackmailBrigade',July,1953 . . 60.00

SPY SMASHER
Fawcett Publications
Autumn, 1941

1 B;Spy Smasher 3,200.00
2 Mra(c) 1,500.00
3 Bondage (c) 950.00
4 . . . . 900.00
5 Mra,Mt. Rushmore(c) 900.00
6 Mra,Mra(c),V:The Sharks of Steel 800.00
7 Mra 800.00
8 AB 750.00
9 AB,Hitler,Tojo, Mussolini(c) . . . 750.00
10 AB,Did Spy Smasher Kill Hitler?. 750.00
11 AB,Feb., 1943 . . . . 700.00

SQUEEKS
Lev Gleason Publications
Oct., 1953

1 CBi(c),(fa) 50.00
2 CBi(c),(fa) 25.00
3 CBi(c),(fa) 25.00
4 (fa) 25.00
5 (fa),Jan., 1954 . . . . 25.00

STAMP COMICS
Youthful Magazines/Stamp Comics, Inc.
Oct., 1951

1 HcK,Birth of Liberty 250.00
2 HcK,RP,Battle of White Plains 125.00
3 HcK,DW,RP,Iwo Jima 100.00
4 HcK,DW,RP 100.00
5 HcK,Von Hindenberg disaster . 125.00
6 HcK,The Immortal Chaplains . 100.00
7 HcK,RKr,RP,B&O:Railroad . . . 150.00

Becomes:

THRILLING ADVENTURES IN STAMPS

8 HcK, 100 Pgs.,Jan.,1953 . . . . 550.00

STAR COMICS
Comic Magazines/Ultem Publ./Chesler Centaur Publications
Feb., 1937

1 B:Dan Hastings 1,400.00
2 . . . . 650.00
3 . . . . 550.00
4 WMc(c) 575.00
5 WMc(c),A:Little Nemo 575.00
6 CBi(c),FG 550.00
7 FG 500.00
8 BoW,BoW(c),FG,A:Little Nemo,Horror 525.00
9 FG,CBi(c) 500.00
10 FG,CBi(c),BoW,A:Impyk. 700.00
11 FG,BoW,JCo 500.00
12 FG,BoW,B:Riders of the Golden West 450.00
13 FG,BoW 425.00
14 FG,GFx(c) 425.00
15 CBu,B:The Last Pirate 425.00
16 CBu,B:Phantom Rider 425.00
2-1 CBu,B:Phantom Rider(c) . . . 425.00
2-2 CBu,A:Diana Deane 400.00
2-3 GFx(c),CBu 375.00
2-4 CBu 375.00
2-5 CBu 375.00
2-6 CBu,E:Phanton Rider 375.00
2-7 CBu,Aug., 1939 . . . . 375.00

STARLET O'HARA IN HOLLYWOOD
Standard Comics
Dec., 1948

1 The Terrific Tee-Age Comic. . . 125.00
2 Her Romantic Adventures in Movie land 100.00
3 and 4, Sept., 1949 . . . . @75.00

STAR RANGER
Comics Magazines/Ultem/ Centaur Publ.
Feb., 1937

1 FG,I:Western Comic 1,500.00
2 . . . . 700.00
3 FG 600.00
4 . . . . 600.00
5 . . . . 600.00
6 FG 575.00
7 FG 450.00
8 GFx,FG,PGn,BoW 450.00
9 GFx,FG,PGn,BoW 450.00
10 JCo,GFx,FG,PGn,BoW 700.00
11 . . . . 550.00
12 JCo,JCo(c),FG,PGn. 550.00

Becomes:

COWBOY COMICS

13 FG,PGn. 800.00
14 FG,PGn. 650.00

Becomes:

STAR RANGER FUNNIES

15 WE,PGn 800.00
2-1(16) JCo,JCo(c). 600.00
2-2(17) PGn,JCo,A:Night Hawk. . 500.00
2-3(18) JCo,FG 475.00
2-4(19) A:Kit Carson. 475.00
2-5(20) Oct., 1939 . . . . 475.00

STARS AND STRIPES COMICS
Comic Corp. of America (Centaur Publications)
May, 1941

2 PGn,PGn(c),`Called to Colors', The Shark,The Voice 1,800.00
3 PGn,PGn(c),O:Dr.Synthe . . 1,000.00
4 PGn,PGn(c),I:The Stars & Stripes 900.00
5 . . . . 650.00
6(5), Dec., 1941 . . . . 650.00

STAR STUDDED
Cambridge House, 1945

N# 25 cents (c) price;128 pgs.; 32 F:stories 200.00
N# The Cadet,Hoot Gibson, Blue Beetle. 150.00

STARTLING COMICS
Better Publ./Nedor Publ.
June, 1940

1 WE,LF,B&O:Captain Future, Mystico, Wonder Man; B:Masked Rider 2,000.00
2 Captain Future(c) 750.00
3 same 650.00
4 same 500.00
5 same 400.00
6 same 375.00
7 same 375.00
8 ASh(c) 375.00

Startling Comics #49
© Nedor Publications

9 Bondage(c) 400.00
10 O:Fighting Yank 3,000.00
11 Fighting Yank(c). 850.00
12 Hitler,Mussolini,Tojo cover . . . 650.00
13 JBi. 450.00
14 JBi. 450.00
15 Fighting Yank (c) 450.00
16 Bondage(c),O:FourComrades 500.00
17 Fighting Yank (c),
E:Masked Rider 350.00
18 JBi,B&O:Pyroman 750.00
19 Pyroman(c) 350.00
20 Pyroman(c),B:Oracle 350.00
21 HcK,ASh(c)Bondage(c)O:Ape 375.00
22 HcK,ASh(c),Fighting Yank(c) . 350.00
23 HcK,BEv,ASh(c),Pyroman(c) . 325.00
24 HcK,BEv,ASh(c),Fighting
Yank(c). 325.00
25 HcK,BEv,ASh(c),Pyroman(c) . 325.00
26 BEv,ASh(c),Fighting Yank(c) . 325.00
27 BEv,ASh(c),Pyroman(c) 325.00
28 BEv,ASh(c),Fighting Yank(c) . 325.00
29 BEv,ASh(c),Pyroman(c) 325.00
30 ASh(c),Fighting Yank(c) 325.00
31 ASh(c),Pyroman(c) 325.00
32 ASh(c),Fighting Yank(c) 325.00
33 ASh(c),Pyroman(c) 325.00
34 ASh(c),Fighting Yank(c),
O:Scarab 325.00
35 ASh(c),Pyroman(c) 335.00
36 ASh(c),Fighting Yank(c) 300.00
37 ASh(c),Bondage (c) 300.00
38 ASh(c),Bondage(c) 300.00
39 ASh(c),Pyroman(c) 300.00
40 ASh(c),E:Captain Future 300.00
41 ASh(c),Pyroman(c) 300.00
42 ASh(c),Fighting Yank(c) 300.00
43 ASh(c),Pyroman(c),
E:Pyroman 300.00
44 Grl(c),Lance Lewis(c). 475.00
45 Grl(c),I:Tygra 475.00
46 Grl,Grl(c),Bondage(c) 475.00
47 ASh(c),Bondage(c) 475.00
48 ASh(c),Lance Lewis(c). 450.00
49 ASh(c),Bondage(c),
E:Fighting Yank 2,800.00
50 ASh(c),Lance Lewis(c),
Sea Eagle 450.00
51 ASh(c),Sea Eagle 450.00
52 ASh(c). 450.00
53 ASh(c),Sept., 1948. . . . . 450.00

STARTLING TERROR TALES

Star Publications

May, 1952

10 WW,LbC(c),The Story Starts . 550.00
11 LbC(c),The Ghost Spider
of Death 500.00
12 LbC(c),White Hand Horror . . . 200.00
13 JyD,LbC(c),Love From
a Gorgor. 200.00
14 LbC(c),Trapped by the
Color of Blood 200.00
4 LbC(c),Crime at the Carnival . 175.00
5 LbC(c),The Gruesome
Demon of Terror 175.00
6 LbC(c),Footprints of Death . . . 175.00
7 LbC(c),The Case of the
Strange Murder 175.00
8 RP,LbC(c),Phantom Brigade . . 175.00
9 LbC(c),The Forbidden Tomb . 150.00
10 LbC(c),The Horrible Entity . . . 175.00
11 RP,LbC(c),The Law Will
Win, July, 1954. . . . . 175.00

Steve Canyon #6
© Harvey Publications

STEVE CANYON COMICS

Harvey Publications

Feb., 1948

1 MC,BP,O:Steve Canyon 175.00
2 MC,BP 150.00
3 MC,BP,Canyon's Crew 125.00
4 MC,BP,Chase of Death 125.00
5 MC,BP,A:Happy Easter 125.00
6 MC,BP,A:Madame Lynx,
Dec., 1948 . . . . 135.00

STEVE ROPER

Famous Funnies

April, 1948

1 Reprints newspaper strips 85.00
2 . . . . 35.00
3 . . . . 25.00
4 . . . . 25.00
5 Dec., 1948 . . . . 25.00

STORIES BY FAMOUS AUTHORS ILLUSTRATED

(see FAST FICTION)

STORY OF HARRY S. TRUMAN, THE

Democratic National Committee, 1948

N# Giveaway-The Life of Our
33rd President 125.00

STRAIGHT ARROW

Magazine Enterprises

Feb.–March, 1950

1 OW,B:Straight Arrow & his
Horse Fury 350.00
2 BP,B&O:Red Hawk 175.00
3 BP,FF(c) 250.00
4 BP,Cave(c) 150.00
5 BP,StraightArrow'sGreatLeap . 150.00
6 BP 135.00
7 BP,The Railroad Invades
Comanche Country 135.00
8 BP 135.00
9 BP 135.00
10 BP. 135.00

Straight Arrow #24
© Magazine Enterprises

11 BP,The Valley of Time 150.00
12 thru 19 BP . . . . @100.00
20 BP,Straight Arrow's
Great War Shield 125.00
21 BP,O:Fury 150.00
22 BP,FF(c) 150.00
23 BP. 75.00
24 BP,The Dragons of Doom 75.00
25 BP. 75.00
26 BP. 75.00
27 BP. 75.00
28 BP,Red Hawk 50.00
29 thru 35 BP . . . . @50.00
36 BP Drug 55.00
37 BP. 55.00
38 BP. 55.00
39 BP,The Canyon Beasts 60.00
40 BP,Secret of the
Spanish Specters 60.00
41 BP. 40.00
42 BP. 40.00
43 BP,I:Blaze 55.00
44 BP. 40.00
45 BP. 40.00
46 thru 53 BP . . . . @40.00
54 BP,March, 1956 . . . . 40.00

STRANGE CONFESSIONS

Approved Publications (Ziff-Davis)

Spring, 1952

1 EK,Ph(c). 400.00
2 . . . . 250.00
3 EK,Ph(c),Girls reformatory . . . 250.00
4 Girls reformatory. 250.00

STRANGE FANTASY

Farrell Publications/ Ajax Comics

Aug., 1952

(2)1 . . . . 350.00
2 . . . . 250.00
3 The Dancing Ghost 250.00
4 Demon in the Dungeon,
A:Rocketman 225.00
5 Visiting Corpse 175.00
6 . . . . 175.00
7 A:Madam Satan 225.00
8 A:Black Cat 150.00
9 S&K,SD 175.00
10 . . . . 150.00
11 Fearful Things Can Happen

GOLDEN AGE

in a Lonely Place 150.00
12 The Undying Fiend 150.00
13 Terror in the Attic, Bondage(c) 225.00
14 Monster in the Building, Oct.–Nov., 1954 150.00

UNKNOWN WORLD
Fawcett Publications
June, 1952

1 NS(c),Ph(c),Will You Venture to Meet the Unknown 400.00

Becomes:

STRANGE STORIES FROM ANOTHER WORLD

2 NS(c),Ph(c),Will You? Dare You 375.00
3 NS(c),Ph(c),The Dark Mirror 275.00
4 NS(c),Ph(c),Monsters of the Mind 275.00
5 NS(c),Ph(c),Dance of the Doomed Feb., 1953 275.00

STRANGE SUSPENSE STORIES
Fawcett Publications
June, 1952

1 BP,MSy,MBi 550.00
2 MBi,GE 350.00
3 MBi,GE(c) 300.00
4 BP 300.00
5 MBi(c),Voodoo(c) 300.00
6 BEv 125.00
7 BEv 150.00
8 AW 150.00
9 125.00
10 150.00
11 100.00
12 100.00
13 100.00
14 125.00
15 AW,BEv(c) 125.00

Charlton Comics

16 200.00
17 150.00
18 SD,SD(c) 250.00
19 SD,SD(c) 350.00
20 SD,SD(c) 250.00
21 125.00
22 SD(c) 225.00

Becomes:

THIS IS SUSPENSE!

23 WW 200.00
24 75.00
25 50.00
26 50.00

Becomes:

STRANGE SUSPENSE STORIES

27 100.00
28 75.00
29 75.00
30 75.00
31 SD(c) 150.00
32 SD 150.00
33 SD 150.00
34 SD,SD(c) 300.00
35 SD 150.00
36 SD,SD(c) 150.00
37 SD 175.00
38 150.00
39 SD 200.00
40 SD 150.00
41 SD 150.00
42 45.00
43 45.00
44 45.00
45 SD 125.00
46 45.00
47 SD 125.00
48 SD 125.00
49 45.00
50 SD 125.00
51 thru 53 SD @70.00
54 thru 60 @40.00
61 thru 74 @20.00
75 125.00
76 40.00
77 40.00

STRANGE SUSPENSE STORIES (see LAWBREAKERS)

STRANGE TERRORS
St. John Publishing Co.
June, 1952

1 The Ghost of Castle Karloff, Bondage(c) 375.00
2 UnshackledFlight intoNowhere 225.00
3 JKu,Ph(c),The Ghost Who Ruled Crazy Heights 275.00
4 JKu,Ph(c),Terror from the Tombs 400.00
5 JKu,Ph(c),No Escaping the Pool of Death 275.00
6 LC,PAM,Bondage(c),Giant 350.00
7 JKu,JKu(c),Cat's Death,Giant 375.00

STRANGE WORLD OF YOUR DREAMS
Prize Group
Aug., 1952

1 S&K(c),What Do They Mean– Messages Rec'd in Sleep 500.00
2 MMe,S&K(c),Why did I Dream That I Was Being Married to a Man without a Face? 400.00
3 S&K(c) 350.00
4 MMe,S&K(c),The Story of a Man Who Dreamed a Murder that Happened 325.00

Strange Worlds #5
© Avon Periodicals

STRANGE WORLDS
Avon Periodicals
Nov., 1950

1 JKu,Spider God of Akka 750.00
2 WW,Dara of the Vikings 725.00
3 AW&FF,EK(c),WW,JO 1,500.00
4 JO,WW,WW(c),The Enchanted Dagger 750.00
5 WW,WW(c),JO,Bondage(c); Sirens of Space 500.00
6 EK,WW(c),JO,SC, Maid o/t Mist 350.00
7 EK, Sabotage on Space Station 1 300.00
8 JKu,EK,The Metal Murderer 300.00
9 The Radium Monsters 300.00
18 JKu 300.00
19 Astounding Super Science Fantasies 300.00
20 WW(c),Fighting War Stories 60.00
21 EK(c) 50.00
22 EK(c),Sept.–Oct., 1955 50.00

STRICTLY PRIVATE
Eastern Color Printing
July, 1942

1 You're in theArmyNow-Humor 175.00
2 F:Peter Plink, 1942 160.00

STUNTMAN COMICS
Harvey Publications
April–May, 1946

1 S&K,O:Stuntman 850.00
2 S&K,New Champ of Split-Second Action 550.00
3 S&K,Digest sized,Mail Order Only, B&W interior, Oct.–Nov., 1946 550.00

SUGAR BOWL COMICS
Famous Funnies
May, 1948

1 ATh,ATh(c),The Newest in Teen Age! 100.00
2 30.00
3 ATh 60.00
4 30.00
5 Jan., 1949 30.00

SUN FUN KOMIKS
Sun Publications, 1939

1 F:Spineless Sam the Sweetheart 225.00

SUNNY, AMERICA'S SWEETHEART
Fox Features Syndicate
Dec., 1947

11 AF,AF(c) 575.00
12 AF,AF(c) 450.00
13 AF,AF(c) 450.00
14 AF,AF(c) 450.00

SUNSET CARSON
Charlton Comics
Feb., 1951

1 Painted, Ph(c);Wyoming Mail 700.00
2 Kit Carson-Pioneer 500.00
3 375.00
4 Panhandle Trouble, Aug., 1951 375.00

SUPER BOOK OF COMICS

Western Publishing Co. 1943

N# Dick Tracy . . . 375.00
1 Dick Tracy . . . 375.00
2 Smitty,Magic Morro . . . 150.00
3 Capt. Midnight . . . 275.00
4 Red Ryder,Magic Morro . . . 175.00
5 Don Winslow,Magic Morro . . . 175.00
5 Dom Winslow,Stratosphere Jim175.00
5 Terry & the Pirates . . . 200.00
6 Don Winslow . . . 125.00
7 Little Orphan Annie . . . 125.00
8 Dick Tracy . . . 175.00
9 Terry & the Pirates . . . 175.00
10 Red Ryder, Magic Morro . . . 175.00

SUPER-BOOK OF COMICS

Western Publishing Co., 1944

1 Dick Tracy (Omar) . . . 175.00
1 Dick Tracy (Hancock) . . . 125.00
2 Bugs Bunny (Omar) . . . 40.00
2 Bugs Bunny (Hancock) . . . 30.00
3 Terry & the Pirates (Omar) . . . 100.00
3 Terry & the Pirates (Hancock) . . 75.00
4 Andy Panda (Omar) . . . 35.00
4 Andy Panda (Hancock) . . . 30.00
5 Smokey Stover (Omar) . . . 40.00
5 Smokey Stover (Hancock) . . . 30.00
6 Porky Pig (Omar) . . . 35.00
6 Porky Pig (Hancock) . . . 30.00
7 Smilin' Jack (Omar) . . . 60.00
7 Smilin' Jack (Hancock) . . . 50.00
8 Oswald the Rabbit (Omar) . . . 30.00
8 Oswald the Rabbit (Hancock) . . 20.00
9 Alley Oop (Omar) . . . 120.00
9 Alley Oop (Hancock) . . . 100.00
10 Elmer Fudd (Omar) . . . 30.00
10 Elmer Fudd (Hancock) . . . 20.00
11 Little Orphan Annie (Omar) . . . 50.00
11 Little Orphan Amnie (Hancock). 40.00
12 Woody Woodpecker (Omar). . . 35.00
12 WoodyWoodpecker(Hancock) . 25.00
13 Dick Tracy (Omar) . . . 125.00
13 Dick Tracy (Hancock) . . . 100.00
14 Bugs Bunny (Omar) . . . 30.00
14 Bugs Bunny (Hanock) . . . 25.00
15 Andy Panda (Omar) . . . 20.00
15 Andy Panda (Hancock) . . . 15.00
16 Terry & the Pirates (Omar) . . . 100.00
16 Terry & the Pirates (Hancock) . 75.00
17 Smokey Stover (Omar) . . . 30.00
17 Smokey Stover (Hancock) . . . 30.00
18 Porky Pig (Omar) . . . 25.00
18 Smokey Stover (Hancock) . . . 20.00
19 Smilin' Jack (Omar) . . . 50.00
N# Smilin' Jack (Hancock) . . . 40.00
20 Oswald the Rabbit (Omar) . . . 25.00
N# Oswald the Rabbit (Hancock) . 15.00
21 Gasoline Alley (Omar) . . . 45.00
N# Gasoline Alley (Hancock) . . . 35.00
22 Elmer Fudd (Omar) . . . 25.00
N# Elmer Fudd (Hancock) . . . 30.00
23 Little Orphan Annie (Omar) . . . 60.00
N# Little Orphan Annie (Hancock). 50.00
24 Woody Woodpecker (Omar). . . 22.00
N# WoodyWoodpecker(Hancock) . 18.00
25 Dick Tracy (Omar) . . . 100.00
N# Dick Tracy (Hancock) . . . 75.00
26 Bugs Bunny (Omar) . . . 25.00
N# Bugs Bunny (Hancock) . . . 20.00
27 Andy Panda (Omar) . . . 20.00
27 Andy Panda (Hancock) . . . 15.00
28 Terry & the Pirates (Omar) . . . 100.00
28 Terry & the Pirates (Hancock) . 75.00
29 Smokey Stover (Omar) . . . 25.00
29 Smokey Stover (Hancock) . . . 20.00
30 Porky Pig (Omar) . . . 25.00
30 Porky Pig (Hancock) . . . 20.00
N# Bugs Bunny (Hancock) . . . 20.00

SUPER CIRCUS

Cross Publishing Co.

Jan., 1951

1 Partial Ph(c) . . . 55.00
2 . . . 40.00
3 . . . 30.00
4 . . . 30.00
5 1951 . . . 30.00

Super Comics #33
© Cross Publishing Co.

SUPER COMICS

Dell Publishing Co.

May, 1938

1 Dick Tracy,Terry and the Pirates,Smilin'Jack,Smokey Stover,Orphan Annie,etc. . . 2,200.00
2 . . . 750.00
3 . . . 700.00
4 . . . 600.00
5 Gumps(c) . . . 550.00
6 . . . 450.00
7 Smokey Stover(c) . . . 450.00
8 Dick Tracy(c) . . . 425.00
9 . . . 425.00
10 Dick Tracy(c) . . . 425.00
11 . . . 350.00
12 . . . 350.00
13 . . . 350.00
14 . . . 350.00
15 . . . 350.00
16 Terry & the Pirates . . . 325.00
17 Dick Tracy(c) . . . 325.00
18 . . . 325.00
19 . . . 325.00
20 Smilin'Jack(c) . . . 350.00
21 B:Magic Morro . . . 300.00
22 Magic Morro(c) . . . 325.00
23 all star(c) . . . 300.00
24 Dick Tracy(c) . . . 325.00
25 Magic Morro(c) . . . 300.00
26 . . . 300.00
27 Magic Morro(c) . . . 300.00
28 Jim Ellis(c) . . . 325.00
29 Smilin'Jack(c) . . . 300.00
30 inc.The Sea Hawk . . . 325.00
31 Dick Tracy(c) . . . 225.00
32 Smilin' Jack(c) . . . 235.00
33 Jim Ellis(c) . . . 225.00
34 Magic Morro(c) . . . 225.00
35 thru 40 Dick Tracy(c) . . . @225.00
41 B:Lightning Jim . . . 200.00
42 thru 50 Dick Tracy(c) . . . @200.00
51 thru 54 Dick Tracy(c) . . . @150.00
55 . . . 150.00
56 . . . 150.00
57 Dick Tracy(c) . . . 150.00
58 Smitty(c) . . . 150.00
59 . . . 150.00
60 Dick Tracy(c) . . . 175.00
61 . . . 135.00
62 Flag(c) . . . 135.00
63 Dick Tracy(c) . . . 135.00
64 Smitty(c) . . . 125.00
65 Dick Tracy(c) . . . 135.00
66 Dick Tracy(c) . . . 135.00
67 Christmas(c) . . . 135.00
68 Dick Tracy(c) . . . 135.00
69 Dick Tracy(c) . . . 135.00
70 Dick Tracy(c) . . . 135.00
71 Dick Tracy(c) . . . 100.00
72 Dick Tracy(c) . . . 100.00
73 Smitty(c) . . . 100.00
74 War Bond(c) . . . 100.00
75 Dick Tracy(c) . . . 100.00
76 Dick Tracy(c) . . . 100.00
77 Dick Tracy(c) . . . 100.00
78 Smitty(c) . . . 90.00
79 Dick Tracy(c) . . . 90.00
80 Smitty(c) . . . 90.00
81 Dick Tracy(c) . . . 90.00
82 Dick Tracy(c) . . . 90.00
83 Smitty(c) . . . 85.00
84 Dick Tracy(c) . . . 90.00
85 Smitty(c) . . . 85.00
86 All on cover . . . 90.00
87 All on cover . . . 90.00
88 Dick Tracy(c) . . . 90.00
89 Smitty(c) . . . 75.00
90 Dick Tracy(c) . . . 85.00
91 Smitty(c) . . . 75.00
92 Dick Tracy(c) . . . 85.00
93 Dick Tracy(c) . . . 85.00
94 Dick Tracy(c) . . . 85.00
95 thru 99 . . . @75.00
100 . . . 90.00
101 thru 115 . . . @50.00
116 Smokey Stover(c) . . . 40.00
117 Gasoline Alley(c) . . . 40.00
118 Smokey Stover(c) . . . 40.00
119 Terry and the Pirates(c) . . . 45.00
120 . . . 45.00
121 . . . 45.00

SUPER-DOOPER COMICS

Able Manufacturing Co., 1946

1 A:Gangbuster . . . 125.00
2 . . . 75.00
3 & 4 . . . @50.00
5 A:Captain Freedom,Shock Gibson . . . 50.00
6 & 7 same . . . @50.00
8 A:Shock Gibson, 1946 . . . 50.00

SUPER DUCK COMICS

MLJ Magazines/Close-Up (Archie Publ.)

Autumn, 1944

1 O:Super Duck . . . 350.00
2 . . . 200.00
3 I:Mr. Monster . . . 150.00
4 & 5 . . . @125.00
6 thru 10 . . . @100.00
11 thru 20 . . . @75.00
21 thru 40 . . . @60.00
41 thru 60 . . . @40.00
61 thru 94 . . . @30.00

SUPER FUNNIES
Superior Comics Publishers
March, 1954

1 Dopey Duck 300.00
2 Out of the Booby-Hatch 100.00

Becomes:

SUPER WESTERN FUNNIES

3 F:Phantom Ranger 50.00
4 F:Phantom Ranger,Sept. 1954 50.00

SUPER MAGICIAN COMICS
Street & Smith, May, 1941

1 B:The Mysterious Blackstone 450.00
2 V:Wild Tribes of Africa 275.00
3 V:Oriental Wizard 250.00
4 V:Quetzal Wizard,O:Transo. 225.00
5 A:The Moylan Sisters 225.00
6 JaB,JaB(c),The Eddie Cantor story 225.00
7 In the House of Skulls 250.00
8 A:Abbott & Costello 250.00
9 V:Duneen the Man-Ape 250.00
10 V:Pirates o/t Sargasso Sea 250.00
11 JaB(c),V:Fire Wizards 250.00
12 V:Baal 250.00
2-1 A:The Shadow 250.00
2-2 In the Temple of the 10,00 Idols 150.00
2-3 Optical Illusion on (c)- turn Jap into Monkey 150.00
2-4 V:Cannibal Killers 150.00
2-5 V:The Pygmies of Lemuriai 150.00
2-6 V;Pirates & Indians 150.00
2-7 Can Blackstone Catch the Cannonball? 150.00
2-8 V:Marabout,B:Red Dragon 150.00
2-9 150.00
2-10 Pearl Dives Swallowed By Sea Demons 150.00
2-11 Blackstone Invades Pelican Islands 150.00
2-12 V:Bubbles of Death 150.00
3-1 160.00
3-2 Bondage(c),Midsummers Eve 150.00
3-3 The Enchanted Garden 150.00
3-4 Fabulous Aztec Treasure 150.00
3-5 A:Buffalo Bill 150.00
3-6 Magic Tricks to Mystify 150.00
3-7 V:Guy Fawkes 150.00
3-8 V:Hindu Spook Maker 150.00
3-9 150.00
3-10 V:The Water Wizards 150.00
3-11 V:The Green Goliath 150.00
3-12 Lady in White 150.00
4-1 Cannibal of Crime 125.00
4-2 The Devil's Castle 125.00
4-3 V:Demons of Golden River 125.00
4-4 V:Dr. Zero 125.00
4-5 Bondage(c) 125.00
4-6 V:A Terror Gang 125.00
4-7 125.00
4-8 Mystery of the Disappearing Horse 125.00
4-9 A Floating Light? 125.00
4-10 Levitation 125.00
4-11 Lost, Strange Land of Shangri 125.00
4-12 I:Nigel Elliman 125.00
5-1 V:Voodoo Wizards of the Everglades,Bondage (c) 125.00
5-2 Treasure of the Florida Keys; Bondage (c) 125.00
5-3 Elliman Battles Triple Crime 125.00
5-4 Can A Human Being Really Become Invisible 125.00
5-5 Mystery of the Twin Pools 125.00
5-6 A:Houdini 125.00
5-7 F:Red Dragon 275.00
5-8 F:Red Dragon, Feb.–March, 1947 275.00

SUPERMOUSE
Standard Comics/Pines
Dec., 1948

1 FF,(fa) 175.00
2 FF,(fa) 100.00
3 FF,(fa) 75.00
4 FF,(fa) 75.00
5 FF,(fa) 75.00
6 FF,(fa) 75.00
7 thru 10 (fa) @30.00
11 thru 20 (fa) @25.00
21 thru 44 (fa) @20.00
45 (fa),Autumn, 1958 20.00

SUPER-MYSTERY COMICS
Periodical House (Ace Magazines)
July, 1940

1 B:Magno,Vulcan,Q-13,Flint of the Mountes 1,500.00
2 Bondage (c) 700.00
3 JaB,B:Black Spider 600.00
4 O:Davy;A:Captain Gallant 450.00
5 JaB,JM(c),I&B:The Clown 450.00
6 JM,JM(c),V:The Clown 400.00
2-1 JM,JM(c),O:Buckskin, Bondage(c) 400.00
2-2 JM,JM(c),V:The Clown 350.00
2-3 JM,JM(c),V:The Clown 350.00
2-4 JM,JM(c),V:The Nazis 350.00
2-5 JM,JM(c),Bondage(c) 350.00
2-6 JM,JM(c),Bondage(c), `Foreign Correspondent' 350.00
3-1 B:Black Ace 375.00
3-2 A:Mr, Risk, Bondage(c) 375.00
3-3 HK,HK(c),I:Lancer;B:Dr. Nemesis, The Sword 350.00
3-4 HK 350.00
3-5 HK,LbC,A:Mr. Risk 375.00
3-6 HK,LbC,A:Paul Revere Jr. 375.00
4-1 HK,LbC,A:Twin Must Die 325.00
4-2 A:Mr. Risk 225.00
4-3 Mango out to Kill Davey! 225.00
4-4 Danger Laughs at Mr. Risk 225.00

Super Magician Comics #56
© Street & Smith

4-5 A:Mr. Risk 225.00
4-6 RP,A:Mr. Risk 225.00
5-1 RP 225.00
5-2 RP,RP(c),The Riddle of the Swamp-Land Spirit 225.00
5-3 RP,RP(c),The Case of the Whispering Death 225.00
5-4 RP,RP(c) 225.00
5-5 RP,Harry the Hack 225.00
5-6 225.00
6-1 175.00
6-2 RP,A:Mr. Risk 175.00
6-3 Bondage (c) 175.00
6-4 E:Mango;A:Mr. Risk 175.00
6-5 Bondage(c) 175.00
6-6 A:Mr. Risk 175.00
7-1 175.00
7-2 KBa(c) 175.00
7-3 Bondage(c) 175.00
7-4 175.00
7-5 175.00
7-6 175.00
8-1 The Riddle of the Rowboat 175.00
8-2 Death Meets a Train 175.00
8-3 The Man Who Couldn't Die 175.00
8-4 RP(c) 175.00
8-5 GT,MMe,Staged for Murder 175.00
8-6 Unlucky Seven,July, 1949 175.00

ARMY AND NAVY COMICS
Street & Smith, May, 1941

1 Hawaii is Calling You,Capt. Fury,Nick Carter 400.00
2 Private Rock V;Hitler 250.00
3 The Fighting Fourth 250.00
4 The Fighting Irish 250.00
5 I:Super Snipe 350.00

Becomes:

SUPERSNIPE COMICS

6 A "Comic" With A Sense of Humor 650.00
7 A:Wacky, Rex King 400.00
8 Axis Powers & Satan(c), Hitler(c) 450.00
9 Hitler Voodoo Doll (c) 500.00
10 Lighting (c) 425.00
11 A:Little Nemo 425.00
12 Football(c) 425.00
2-1 B:Huck Finn 275.00
2-2 Battles Shark 275.00
2-3 Battles Dinosaur 275.00
2-4 Baseball(c) 275.00
2-5 Battles Dinosaur 275.00
2-6 A:Pochontas 275.00
2-7 A:Wing Woo Woo 275.00
2-8 A:Huck Finn 275.00
2-9 Dotty Loves Trouble 275.00
2-10 Assists Farm Labor Shortage 275.00
2-11 Dotty & the Jelly Beans 275.00
2-12 Statue of Liberty 275.00
3-1 Ice Skating(c) 250.00
3-2 V:Pirates(c) 250.00
3-3 Baseball(c) 250.00
3-4 Jungle(c) 250.00
3-5 Learn Piglatin 250.00
3-6 Football Hero 250.00
3-7 Saves Girl From Grisley 250.00
3-8 Rides a Wild Horse 250.00
3-9 Powers Santa's Sleigh 250.00
3-10 Plays Basketball 250.00
3-11 Is A Baseball Pitcher 250.00
3-12 Flies with the Birds 250.00
4-1 Catches A Whale 175.00
4-2 Track & Field Athlete 175.00
4-3 Think Machine(c) 175.00
4-4 Alpine Skiier 175.00
4-5 Becomes a Boxer 175.00

4-6 Race Car Driver 175.00
4-7 Bomber(c) 175.00
4-8 Baseball Star 175.00
4-9 Football Hero 175.00
4-10 Christmas(c) 175.00
4-11 Artic Adventure 175.00
4-12 The Ghost Remover 175.00
5-1 Aug.–Sept., 1949 . . . . 175.00

SUPER SPY
Centaur Publications
Oct.–Nov., 1940

1 O:Sparkler 900.00
2 A:Night Hawk, Drew Ghost, Tim Blain, S.S. Swanson the Inner Circle, Duke Collins, Gentlemen of Misfortune 550.00

SUPER WESTERN COMICS
Youthful Magazines Aug., 1950

1 BP,BP,(c),B;Buffalo Bill,Wyatt Earp,CalamityJane,SamSlade100.00
2 thru 4 March, 1951 . . . . @50.00

SUPER WESTERN FUNNIES
(see SUPER FUNNIES)

SUPERWORLD COMICS
Komos Publications
(Hugo Gernsback)
April, 1940

1 FP,FP(c),B:MilitaryPowers,BuzzAllen Smarty Artie, Alibi Alige . . . 5,500.00
2 FP,FP(c),A:Mario 3,200.00
3 FP,FP(c),V:Vest Wearing Giant Grasshoppers 2,200.00

SUSPENSE COMICS
Et Es Go Mag. Inc.
(Continental Magazines)
Dec., 1945

1 LbC, Bondage(c),B:Grey Mask 3,500.00
2 DRi,I:The Mask 2,400.00
3 LbC,ASh(c),Bondage(c) . . 10,000.00

Suspense Comics #9
© Continental Magazines

4 LbC,LbC(c),Bondage(c) . . . 1,900.00
5 LbC,LbC(c) 1,800.00
6 LbC,LbC(c),The End of the Road 1,800.00
7 LbC,LbC(c) 1,500.00
8 LbC,LbC(c) 3,500.00
9 LbC,LbC(c) 1,300.00
10 RP,LbC,LbC(c) 1,300.00
11 RP,LbC,LbC(c),Satan(c) . . . 3,500.00
12 LbC,LbC(c),Dec., 1946 . . . . 1,300.00

SUSPENSE DETECTIVE
Fawcett Publications
June, 1952

1 GE,MBi,MBi(c),Death Poised to Strike 325.00
2 GE,MSy 200.00
3 A Furtive Footstep 175.00
4 MBi,MSy,Bondage(c),A Blood Chilling Scream 150.00
5 MSy,MSy(c),MBi,A Hair-Trigger from Death, March, 1953 . . . 175.00

SUZIE COMICS
(see TOP-NOTCH COMICS)

SWEENEY
Standard Comics
June, 1949

4 Buzz Sawyer's Pal 45.00
5 Sept., 1949 . . . . 40.00

SWEETHEART DIARY
Fawcett
Winter, 1949

1 . . . . 100.00
2 . . . . 50.00
3 and 4 WW. . . . . @100.00
5 thru 10 . . . . @50.00
11 thru 14 . . . . @30.00

SWEETHEART DIARY
Charlton Comics
Jan., 1953

32 . . . . 35.00
33 thru 40 . . . . @25.00
41 thru 65 . . . . @15.00

SWEET HEART
(see CAPTAIN MIDNIGHT)

SWEET LOVE
Harvey Publications
(Home Comics)
Sept., 1949

1 Ph(c) 75.00
2 Ph(c) 30.00
3 BP 25.00
4 Ph(c) 20.00
5 BP,JKa,Ph(c) 50.00

SWEET SIXTEEN
Parents' Magazine Group
Aug.–Sept., 1946

1 Van Johnson story 135.00
2 Alan Ladd story 100.00
3 Rip Taylor. 60.00
4 E:Taylor 85.00
5 Gregory Peck story (c) 60.00
6 Dick Hammes(c). 60.00
7 Ronald Reagan(c). 135.00
8 Shirley Jones(c) 65.00
9 William Holden(c) 65.00
10 James Stewart(c). 75.00
11 . . . . 65.00
12 Bob Cummings(c) 65.00
13 Robert Mitchum(c) 75.00

SWIFT ARROW
Farrell Publications (Ajax)
Feb.–March, 1954

1 Lone Rider's Redskin Brother 100.00
2 . . . . 50.00
3 . . . . 40.00
4 . . . . 40.00
5 Oct.–Nov., 1954 . . . . 40.00

(2nd Series) April, 1957

1 . . . . 45.00
2 B:Lone Rider 30.00
3 Sept., 1957 . . . . 25.00

TAFFY
Orbit Publications/Rural Home/ Taffy Publications
March–April, 1945

1 LbC(c),(fa),Bondage(c) 400.00
2 LbC(c),(fa) 200.00
3 (fa) 100.00
4 (fa) 100.00
5 LbC(c),A:Van Johnson 150.00
6 A:Perry Como 100.00
7 A:Dave Clark 100.00
8 A:Glen Ford 100.00
9 A:Lon McCallister 100.00
10 A:John Hodiak 100.00
11 A:Mickey Rooney 100.00
12 Feb., 1948 . . . . 100.00

TAILSPIN
Spotlight Publications
Nov., 1944

N# LbC(c),A:Firebird 200.00

TALES FROM THE CRYPT
(see CRIME PATROL)

TALES FROM THE TOMB
(see Dell Giants)

TALES OF HORROR
Toby Press/Minoan Publ. Corp.
June, 1952

1 Demons of the Underworld . . . 275.00
2 What was the Thing in the Pool?,Torture 225.00
3 The Big Snake 150.00
4 The Curse of King Kala! 150.00
5 Hand of Fate 150.00
6 The Fiend of Flame 150.00
7 Beast From The Deep 150.00
8 The Snake that Held A City Captive 150.00
9 It Came From the Bottom of the World 175.00
10 The Serpent Strikes 175.00
11 Death Flower? 175.00
12 Guaranteed to Make Your Hair Stand on End 200.00
13 Ghost with a Torch; Oct., 1954 . . . . 150.00

TALES OF TERROR
Toby Press, 1952
1 Just A Bunch of Hokey Hogwash 175.00

Tales of Terror Annual #3
© E.C. Comics

TALES OF TERROR ANNUAL
E.C. 1951
N# AF. 3,500.00
2 AF 1,500.00
3 . . . . 1,200.00

TALLY-HO COMICS
Baily Publishing Co.
Dec., 1944
N# FF,A:Snowman 325.00

TARGET COMICS
Funnnies Inc./Novelty Publ./ Premium Group/Curtis Circulation Co./Star Publications, Feb., 1940
1 BEv,JCo,CBu,JSm;B,O&I:Manowar, White Streak,Bull's-Eye;B:City Editor,High Grass Twins,T-Men, Rip Rory,Fantastic Feature Films, Calling 2-R 4,000.00
2 BEv,JSm,JCo,CBu,White Streak(c) 2,000.00
3 BEv,JSm,JCo,CBu 1,100.00
4 JSm,JCo 1,100.00
5 CBu,BW,O:White Streak . . . 3,700.00
6 CBu,BW,White Streak(c) . . . 1,500.00
7 CBu,BW,BW(c),V:Planetoid Stories,Space Hawk(c) . . . 4,200.00
8 CBu,BW,White Shark(c). . . . 1,100.00
9 CBu,BW,White Shark(c). . . . 1,100.00
10 CBu,BW,JK(c),The Target(c) 1,500.00
11 BW,The Target(c) 1,300.00
12 BW,same 1,100.00
2-1 BW,CBu 700.00
2-2 BW,BoW(c). 600.00
2-3 BW,BoW(c),The Target(c) . . . 475.00
2-4 BW,B:Cadet 475.00
2-5 BW,BoW(c),The Target(c) . . . 450.00
2-6 BW,The Target(c) 450.00
2-7 BW,The Cadet(c) 450.00
2-8 BW,same 450.00

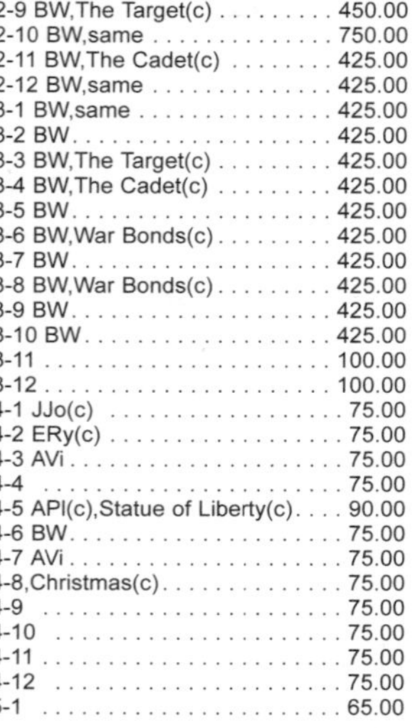

2-9 BW,The Target(c) 450.00
2-10 BW,same 750.00
2-11 BW,The Cadet(c) 425.00
2-12 BW,same 425.00
3-1 BW,same 425.00
3-2 BW. 425.00
3-3 BW,The Target(c) 425.00
3-4 BW,The Cadet(c) 425.00
3-5 BW. 425.00
3-6 BW,War Bonds(c) 425.00
3-7 BW. 425.00
3-8 BW,War Bonds(c) 425.00
3-9 BW. 425.00
3-10 BW. 425.00
3-11 . . . . 100.00
3-12 . . . . 100.00
4-1 JJo(c) 75.00
4-2 ERy(c) 75.00
4-3 AVi 75.00
4-4 . . . . 75.00
4-5 APl(c),Statue of Liberty(c). . . . 90.00
4-6 BW. 75.00
4-7 AVi 75.00
4-8,Christmas(c). 75.00
4-9 . . . . 75.00
4-10 . . . . 75.00
4-11 . . . . 75.00
4-12 . . . . 75.00
5-1 . . . . 65.00

Target Comics #7
© Star Publications

5-2 The Target 65.00
5-3 Savings Checkers(c). 65.00
5-4 War Bonds Ph(c) 65.00
5-5 thru 5-12 . . . . @65.00
6-1 The Target(c) 65.00
6-2 . . . . 65.00
6-3 Red Cross(c) 65.00
6-4 . . . . 65.00
6-5 Savings Bonds(c) 65.00
6-6 The Target(c) 65.00
6-7 The Cadet(c) 65.00
6-8 AFa 65.00
6-9 The Target(c) 65.00
6-10 . . . . 65.00
6-11 . . . . 65.00
6-12 . . . . 65.00
7-1 . . . . 65.00
7-2 Bondage(c). 65.00
7-3 The Target(c) 65.00
7-4 DRi,The Cadet(c) 65.00
7-5 . . . . 65.00
7-6 DRi(c). 65.00
7-7 The Cadet(c) 65.00
7-8 DRi(c). 65.00
7-9 The Cadet(c) 65.00
7-10 DRi,DRi(c) 65.00
7-11 . . . . 65.00
7-12 JH(c) 65.00
8-1 . . . . 60.00
8-2 DRi,DRi(c),BK 60.00
8-3 DRi,The Cadet(c) 60.00
8-4 DRi,DRi(c) 60.00
8-5 DRi,The Cadet(c) 60.00
8-6 DRi,DRi(c) 60.00
8-7 BK,DRi,DRi(c) 60.00
8-8 DRi,The Cadet(c) 60.00
8-9 DRi,The Cadet(c) 60.00
8-10 DRi,KBa,LbC(c) 225.00
8-11 DRi,The Cadet 65.00
8-12 DRi,The Cadet 65.00
9-1 DRi,LbC(c) 225.00
9-2 DRi. 65.00
9-3 DRi,Bondage(c),The Cadet(c). 65.00
9-4 DRi,LbC(c) 225.00
9-5 DRi,Baseball(c). 65.00
9-6 DRi,LbC(c) 225.00
9-7 DRi. 65.00
9-8 DRi,LbC(c) 225.00
9-9 DRi,Football(c) 65.00
9-10 DRi,LbC(c) 225.00
9-11,The Cadet. 65.00
9-12 LbC(c),Gems(c) 225.00
10-1,The Cadet 65.00
10-2 LbC(c) 225.00
10-3 LbC(c) 225.00
Becomes:

TARGET WESTERN ROMANCES
Star Publications
Oct.–Nov., 1949
106 LbC(c),The Beauty Scar. . . . 275.00
107 LbC(c),The Brand Upon His Heart 225.00

TARZAN
Dell Publishing Co.
Jan.–Feb., 1948
1 V:White Savages of Vari. . . . 1,100.00
2 Captives of Thunder Valley . . . 550.00
3 Dwarfs of Didona 400.00
4 The Lone Hunter. 400.00
5 The Men of Greed 400.00
6 Outlwas of Pal-ul-Don. 300.00
7 Valley of the Monsters 300.00
8 The White Pygmies 300.00
9 The Men of A-Lur 300.00
10 Treasure of the Bolgani 300.00

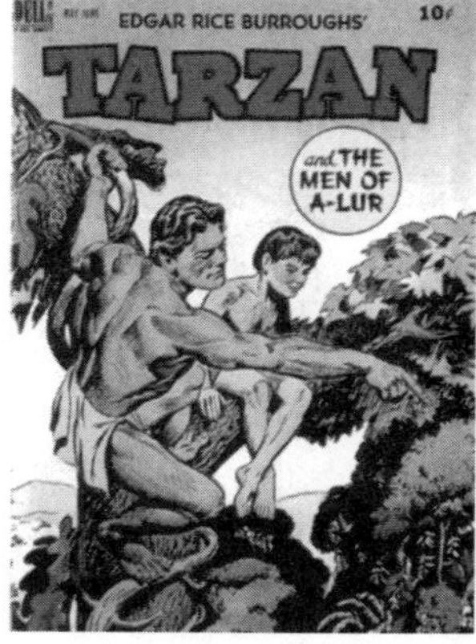

Tarzan #9
© Dell Publishing Co.

11 The Sable Lion. 250.00
12 The Price of Peace 250.00
13 B:Lex Barker photo(c) 225.00
14 . . . . 225.00
15 . . . . 225.00
16 . . . . 200.00
17 . . . . 200.00
18 . . . . 200.00
19 . . . . 200.00
20. . . . . 200.00
21 thru 30 . . . . @150.00
31 thru 54 E:L.Barker Ph(c). . . @100.00
55 thru 70 . . . . @75.00
71 thru 79 . . . . @50.00
80 thru 90 B:ScottGordonPh(c) . @30.00
91 thru 99 . . . . @28.00
100 . . . . 40.00
101 thru 110 E:S.GordonPh(c). . @25.00
111 thru 120 . . . . @20.00
121 thru 131 . . . . @20.00

TEEN-AGE DIARY SECRETS
St. John Publishing Co.
Oct., 1949

6 MB,PH(c) 200.00
7 MB,PH(c) 175.00
8 MB,PH(c) 150.00
9 MB,PH(c) 175.00

Becomes:

DIARY SECRETS

10 MB 125.00
11 MB. 100.00
12 thru 19 MB . . . . @75.00
20 MB,JKu 100.00
21 thru 28 MB . . . . @50.00
29 MB,Comics Code. 40.00
30 MB 40.00

TEEN-AGE ROMANCES
St. John Publishing Co.
Jan., 1949

1 MB(c),MB 275.00
2 MB(c),MB 150.00
3 MB(c),MB 175.00
4 Ph(c) 150.00
5 MB,Ph(c) 150.00
6 MB,Ph(c) 150.00
7 MB,Ph(c) 150.00
8 MB,Ph(c) 150.00
9 MB,MB(c),JKu 160.00
10 thru 27 MB,MB(c),JKu . . . . @125.00
28 thru 30. . . . . @50.00
31 thru 34 MB(c) . . . . @50.00
35 thru 42 MB(c),MB . . . . @60.00
43 MB(c),MB,Comics Code. 40.00
44 MB(c),MB 40.00
45 MB(c),MB 40.00

TEEN-AGE TEMPTATIONS
St. John Publishing Co.
Oct., 1952

1 MB(c),MB 350.00
2 MB(c),MB 125.00
3 MB(c),MB 150.00
4 MB(c),MB 150.00
5 MB(c),MB 150.00
6 MB(c),MB 150.00
7 MB(c),MB 150.00
8 MB(c),MB,Drug. 175.00
9MB(c),MB 150.00

Becomes:

GOING STEADY

10 MB(c),MB 100.00
11 MB(c),MB. 75.00
12 MB(c),MB 75.00

13 MB(c),MB 75.00
14 MB(c),MB 75.00

TEENIE WEENIES, THE
Ziff-Davis Publishing Co.
1951

10 . . . . 125.00
11 . . . . 125.00

TEEN LIFE (see YOUNG LIFE)

TEGRA, JUNGLE EMPRESS (see ZEGRA, JUNGLE EMPRESS)

TELEVISION COMICS
Animated Cartoons
(Standard Comics), Feb., 1950

5 Humorous Format,I:Willie Nilly . 60.00
6 . . . . 40.00
7 . . . . 40.00
8 May, 1950 . . . . 40.00

TELEVISION PUPPET SHOW
Avon Periodicals, 1950

1 F:Sparky Smith,Spotty,
Cheeta, Speedy 100.00
2 Nov., 1950 . . . . 80.00

TELL IT TO THE MARINES
Toby Press, March, 1952

1 I:Spike & Pat 125.00
2 A:Madame Cobra 75.00
3 Spike & Bat on a
Commando Raid! 50.00
4 Veil Dancing(c) 45.00
5 . . . . 45.00
6 To Paris 35.00
7 Ph(c),The Chinese Bugle 30.00
8 Ph(c),V:Communists in
South Korea 30.00
9 Ph(c) 30.00
10 . . . . 30.00
11 . . . . 30.00
12 . . . . 30.00
13 John Wayne Ph(c). 75.00
14 Ph(c). 30.00
15 Ph(c),July, 1955. . . . . 30.00

TENDER ROMANCE
Key Publications
Dec., 1953

1 . . . . 125.00
2 . . . . 65.00

Becomes:

IDEAL ROMANCE

3 . . . . 50.00
4 thru 8 . . . . @30.00

Becomes:

DIARY CONFESSIONS

9 . . . . 35.00
10 . . . . 25.00

TERRIFIC COMICS (see HORRIFIC)

Terrific Comics
© Continental Magazines

TERRIFIC COMICS
Et Es Go Mag. Inc./
Continental Magazines
Jan., 1944

1 LbC,DRi(c),F:Kid
Terrific Drug. 3,000.00
2 LcC,ASh(c),B:Boomerang,
`Comics' McCormic 2,000.00
3 LbC,LbC(c) 2,000.00
4 LbC,RP(c) 3,500.00
5 LbC,BF,ASh(c),Bondage(c) . 4,500.00
6 LbC,LbC(c),BF,Nov.,1944 . . 1,700.00

TERROR ILLUSTRATED
E.C. Comics
Nov.–Dec., 1955

1 JCr,GE,Grl,JO,RC(c) 125.00
2 Spring, 1956 . . . . 100.00

TERRIFYING TALES
Star Publications
Jan., 1953

11 LbC,LbC(c),`TyrantsofTerror'. . 375.00
12 LbC,LbC(c),`Bondage(c),
`Jungle Mystery' 325.00
13 LbC(c),Bondage(c),`The
Death-Fire,Devil Head(c) . . . 400.00
14 LbC(c),Bondage(c),`The
Weird Idol' 325.00
15 LbC(c),`The Grim Secret',
April, 1954 . . . . 325.00

Becomes:

JUNGLE THRILLS
Star Publications Feb., 1952

16 LbC(c),`Kingdom of Unseen
Terror'. 350.00

Becomes:

TERRORS OF THE JUNGLE

17 LbC(c),Bondage(c). 375.00
18 LbC(c),Strange Monsters 250.00
19 JyD,LbC(c),Bondage(c),The
Golden Ghost Gorilla 250.00
20 JyD,LbC(c),The Creeping
Scourge 250.00

GOLDEN AGE

21 LbC(c),Evil Eyes of Death! . . . 275.00
4 JyD,LbC(c),Morass of Death . 225.00
5 JyD,LbC(c),Bondage(c), Savage Train 250.00
6 JyD,LbC(c),Revolt of the Jungle Monsters 250.00
7 JyD,LbC(c) 225.00
8 JyD,LbC(c),Death's Grim Reflection 225.00
9 JyD,LbC(c),Doom to Evil-Doers 225.00
10 JyD,LbC(c),Black Magic, Sept., 1954. . . . . 225.00

BOY EXPLORERS

1 S&K(c),S&K,The Cadet. 650.00
2 S&K(c),S&K 750.00
Becomes:

TERRY AND THE PIRATES

3 S&K,MC(c),MC,Terry and Dragon Lady. 300.00
4 S&K,MC(c),MC 175.00
5 S&K,MC(c),MC,BP, Chop-Chop(c). 100.00
6 S&K,.MC(c),MC 100.00
7 S&K,MC(c),MC,BP 100.00
8 S&K,MC(c),MC,BP 100.00
9 S&K,MC(c),MC,BP 100.00
10 S&K,MC(c),MC,BP. 100.00
11 S&K,MC(c),MC,BP, A:Man in Black 75.00
12 S&K,MC(c),MC,BP. 75.00
13 S&K,MC(c),MC,Belly Dancers . 75.00
14 thru 20 S&K,MC(c),MC. . . . . @60.00
22 thru 26 S&K,MC(c),MC. . . . . @55.00
27 Charlton Comics 50.00
28. . . . . 50.00

TERRY-BEARS COMICS
St. John Publishing Co.
June, 1952

1 . . . . 50.00
2 & 3 . . . . @25.00

TERRY-TOONS COMICS
Select, Timely, Marvel, St. Johns, 1942

1 Paul Terry (fa) 1,300.00
2 . . . . 500.00
3 thru 6 . . . . @350.00
7 Hitler,Hirohito,Mussolini(c) 300.00
8 thru 20. . . . . @225.00
21 thru 37. . . . . @150.00
38 I&(c):Mighty Mouse 850.00
39 Mighty Mouse 250.00
40 thru 49 All Mighty Mouse . . @125.00
50 I:Heckle & Jeckle. 250.00
51 thru 60. . . . . @75.00
61 thru 70. . . . . @65.00
71 thru 86. . . . . @60.00

TEXAN, THE
St. John Publishing Co.
Aug., 1948

1 GT,F:Buckskin Belle,The Gay Buckaroo,Mustang Jack 120.00
2 GT 60.00
3 BLb(c) 50.00
4 MB,MB(c) 75.00
5 MB,MB(c),Mystery Rustlers of the Rio Grande 75.00
6 MB(c),Death Valley Double-Cross 60.00
7 MB,MB(c),Comanche Justice Strikes at Midnight 75.00
8 MB,MB(c),Scalp Hunters Hide their Tracks 75.00
9 MB(c),Ghost Terror of the Blackfeet 75.00
10 MB,MB(c),Treason Rides the Warpath 60.00
11 MB,MB(c),Hawk Knife 75.00
12 MB 75.00
13 MB,Doublecross at Devil'sDen . 75.00
14 MB,Ambush at Buffalo Trail . . . 75.00
15 MB,Twirling Blades Tame Treachery 75.00
Becomes:

FIGHTIN' TEXAN

16 GT,Wanted Dead or Alive 60.00
17 LC,LC(c);Killers Trail, Dec., 1952 . . . . 50.00

TEX FARRELL
D.S. Publishing Co.
March–April, 1948

1 Pride of the Wild West 100.00

TEX GRANGER
(see CALLING ALL BOYS)

TEX RITTER WESTERN
Fawcett Publications/ Charlton Comics
Oct., 1950–May, 1959

1 Ph(c),B:Tex Ritter, his Horse White Flash, his dog Fury, and his mom Nancy 550.00
2 Ph(c),Vanishing Varmints 250.00
3 Ph(c),Blazing Six-Guns 175.00
4 Ph(c),The Jaws of Terror 150.00
5 Ph(c),Bullet Trail 150.00
6 Ph(c),Killer Bait 150.00
7 Ph(c),Gunsmoke Revenge . . . 125.00
8 Ph(c),Lawless Furnace Valley 125.00
9 Ph(c),The Spider's Web 125.00
10 Ph(c),The Ghost Town 125.00
11 Ph(c),Saddle Conquest 125.00
12 Ph(c),Prairie Inferno. 100.00
13 Ph(c). 100.00
14 Ph(c). 100.00
15 Ph(c). 100.00
16 thru 19 Ph(c) . . . . @100.00
20 Ph(c),Stagecoach To Danger . 100.00
21 . . . . 100.00
22 Panic at Diamond B. 75.00
23 A:Young Falcon 60.00
24 A:Young Falcon 60.00
25 A:Young Falcon 60.00
26 thru 38. . . . . @50.00
39 AW,AW(c) 50.00
40 thru 46. . . . . @45.00

THING!, THE
Song Hits/Capitol Stories/ Charlton Comics, Feb., 1952

1 Horror. 650.00
2 Crazy King(c) 450.00
3 . . . . 450.00
4 AFa(c),I Was A Zombie 400.00
5 LM(c),Severed Head(c). 425.00
6 . . . . 400.00
7 Fingenail to Eye(c) 550.00
8 . . . . 400.00
9 Severe 600.00
10 Devil(c) 400.00
11 SC,Cleaver 500.00
12 SD,SD(c),Neck Blood Sucking 650.00
13 SD,SD(c). 650.00
14 SD,SD(c). 650.00

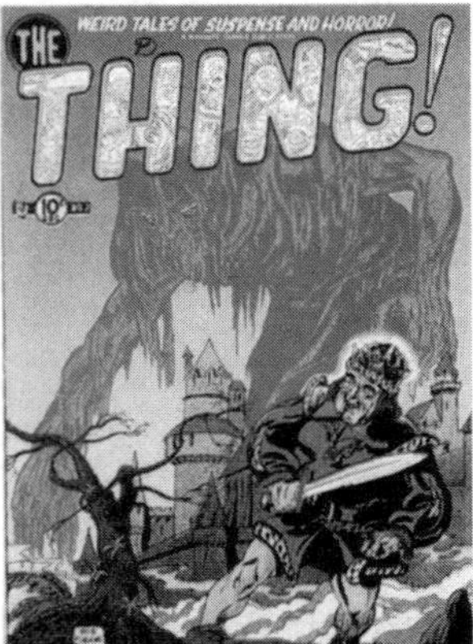

The Thing #2
© Charlton Comics

15 SD,SD(c). 650.00
16 Eye Torture 400.00
17 BP,SD(c) 600.00
Becomes:

BLUE BEETLE

18 America's Fastest Moving Crusader Against Crime 150.00
19 JKa,Lightning Fast. 175.00
20 JKa 175.00
21 The Invincible 125.00
Becomes:

MR. MUSCLES

22 World's Most Perfect Man 50.00
23 Aug., 1956. . . . . 30.00

THIS IS SUSPENSE
(see LAWBREAKERS)

THIS IS WAR
Standard Comics
July, 1952

5 ATh,Show Them How To Die . 100.00
6 ATh,Make Him A Soldier 75.00
7 One Man For Himself 40.00
8 Miracle on Massacre Hill 40.00
9 ATh,May, 1953 . . . . 75.00

THIS IS SUSPENSE!
(see STRANGE SUSPENSE STORIES)

THIS MAGAZINE IS HAUNTED
Fawcett Publications/ Charlton Comics
Oct., 1951

1 MBi,F:Doctor Death 500.00
2 GE 350.00
3 MBi,Quest of the Vampire . . . 250.00
4 BP,The Blind, The Doomed and the Dead 250.00
5 BP,GE,The Slithering Horror of Skontong Swamp! 350.00
6 Secret of the Walking Dead . . 175.00
7 The Man Who Saw Too Much. 175.00
8 The House in the Web 175.00
9 The Witch of Tarlo. 175.00

 All comics prices listed are for *Near Mint* condition.

GOLDEN AGE

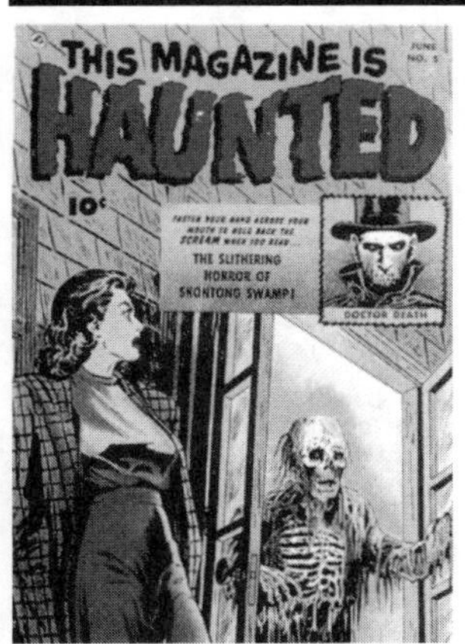

This Magazine is Haunted #5
© Fawcett Publications

10 I Am Dr Death,
Severed Head(c) 250.00
11 BP,Touch of Death 150.00
12 BP 150.00
13 BP,Severed Head(c) 250.00
14 BP,Horrors of the Damned . . . 150.00
15 DG(c) 125.00
16 SD(c). 275.00
17 SD,SD(c). 350.00
18 SD,SD(c). 300.00
19 SD(c). 275.00
20 SMz(c). 135.00
21 SD(c). 250.00
Becomes:

DANGER AND ADVENTURE

22 The Viking King,F:Ibis the
Invincible 75.00
23 F:Nyoka the Jungle Girl
Comics Code 60.00
24 DG&AA(c) 50.00
25 thru 27 . . . . @35.00
Becomes:

ROBIN HOOD AND HIS MERRY MEN

28 . . . . 50.00
29 thru 37 . . . . @40.00
38 SD,Aug., 1958 . . . . 100.00

3-D-ELL
Dell Publishing Co., 1953

1 Rootie Kazootie 300.00
2 Rootie Kazootie 275.00
3 Flunkey Louise 275.00

THREE RING COMICS
Spotlight Publishers
March, 1945

1 Funny Animal 100.00

THREE STOOGES
Jubilee Publ.
Feb., 1949

1 JKu,Infinity(c) 950.00
2 JKu,On the Set of the
`The Gorilla Girl' 650.00

St. John Publishing Co.

1JKu,`Bell Bent for
Treasure, Sept., 1953 . . . . . . 550.00
2 JKu. 400.00
3 JKu,3D 400.00
4 JKu,Medical Mayhem 300.00
5 JKu,Shempador-Matador
Supreme 300.00
6 JKu, ... 300.00
7 JKu,Ocotber, 1954 . . . . 300.00

THRILLING COMICS
Better Publ./Nedor/ Standard Comics
Feb., 1940

1 B&O:Doc Strange,B:Nickie
Norton 2,400.00
2 B:Rio Kid,Woman in Red
Pinocchio 1,100.00
3 B:Lone Eagle,The Ghost 650.00
4 Dr Strange(c) 550.00
5 Bondage(c) 500.00
6 Dr Strange(c) 500.00
7 Dr Strange(c) 500.00
8 V:Pirates 500.00
9 Bondage(c) 500.00
10 V:Nazis 500.00
11 ASh(c),V:Nazis. 425.00
12 ASh(c). 400.00
13 ASh(c),Bondage(c) 450.00
14 ASh(c). 425.00
15 ASh(c),V:Nazis 425.00
16 Bondage(c) 450.00
17 Dr Strange(c). 450.00
18 Dr Strange(c). 450.00
19 I&O:American Crusader 450.00
20 Bondage(c) 450.00
21 American Crusader(c) 350.00
22 Bondage(c) 375.00
23 American Crusader 350.00
24 I:Mike in Doc Strange. 350.00
25 DR Strange(c) 350.00
26 Dr Strange(c). 350.00
27 Bondage(c) 375.00
28 Bondage(c) 375.00
29 E:Rio Kid;Bondage(c). 375.00
30 Bondage(c) 375.00
31 Dr Strange(c). 300.00
32 Dr Strange(c). 275.00
33 Dr Strange(c). 275.00
34 Dr Strange(c). 275.00
35 Dr Strange. 275.00
36 ASh(c),B:Commando 300.00
37 BO,ASh(c). 275.00
38 ASh(c). 275.00
39 ASh(c),E:American Crusader . 275.00
40 ASh(c). 275.00
41 ASh(c),F:American Crusader . 275.00
42 ASh(c). 225.00
43 ASh(c). 225.00
44 ASh(c),Hitler(c) 300.00
45 EK,ASh(c) 235.00
46 ASh(c). 235.00
47 ASh(c). 225.00
48 EK,ASh(c) 225.00
49 ASh(c). 225.00
50 ASh(c). 225.00
51 ASh(c). 225.00
52 ASh(c),E:Th Ghost;
Peto-Bondage(c) 250.00
53 ASh(c),B:Phantom Detective . 225.00
54 ASh(c),Bondage(c) 250.00
55 ASh(c),E:Lone Eagle 250.00
56 ASh(c),B:Princess Pantha . . . 350.00
57 ASh(c). 275.00
58 ASh(c). 275.00
59 ASh(c). 275.00
60 ASh(c). 275.00
61 ASh(c),GRi,A:Lone Eagle. . . . 275.00
62 ASh(c). 275.00
63 ASh(c),GT 275.00
64 ASh(c). 275.00
65 ASh(c),E:Commando Cubs,
Phantom Detective 275.00
66 ASh(c). 275.00
67 FF,ASh(c) 350.00
68 FF,ASh(c) 350.00
69 FF,ASh(c) 350.00
70 FF,ASh(c) 350.00
71 FF,ASh(c) 350.00
72 FF,ASh(c) 350.00
73 FF,ASh(c) 350.00
74 E:Princess Pantha;
B:Buck Ranger 225.00
75 B:Western Front. 125.00
76 . . . . 125.00
77 ASh(c). 125.00
78 Bondage(c) 135.00
79 BK. 125.00
80 JSe,BE,April, 1951. . . . . 135.00

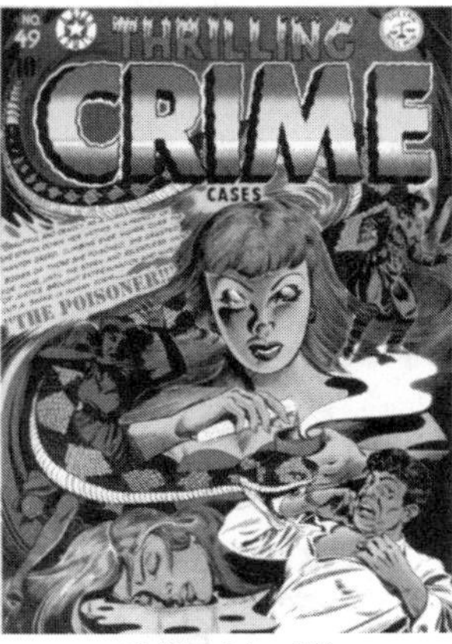

Thrilling Crime #49
© Standard Comics

THRILLING CRIME CASES
Star Publications
June–July, 1950

41 LbC(c),The Unknowns 200.00
42 LbC(c),The Gunmaster 175.00
43 LbC,LbC(c),The Chameleon. . 200.00
44 LbC(c),Sugar Bowl Murder. . . 200.00
45 LbC(c),Maze of Murder 200.00
46 LbC,LbC(c),Modern
Communications. 150.00
47 LbC(c),The Careless Killer . . . 150.00
48 LbC(c),Road Black. 150.00
49 LbC(c),The Poisoner 300.00
Becomes:

SHOCKING MYSTERY CASES

50 JyD,LbC(c),Dead Man's
Revenge. 300.00
51 JyD,LbC(c),A Murderer's
Reward 175.00
52 LbC(c),The Carnival Killer . . . 175.00
53 LbC(c),The Long Shot of Evil . 175.00
54 LbC(c),Double-Cross of Death 175.00
55 LbC(c),Return from Death . . . 175.00
56 LbC(c),The Chase 200.00
57 LbC(c),Thrilling Cases 150.00
58 LbC(c),Killer at Large. 150.00
59 LbC(c),Relentess Huntdown. . 150.00
60 LbC(c),Lesson of the Law,
Oct., 1954 . . . . 150.00

GOLDEN AGE

THRILLING ROMANCES
Standard Comics
Dec., 1949

5 Ph(c) 75.00
6 Ph(c) 40.00
7 Ph(c),JSe,BE 50.00
8 Ph(c) 40.00
9 Ph(c),GT 45.00
10 Ph(c),JSe,BE. 45.00
11 Ph(c),JSe,BE 45.00
12 Ph(c),WW 50.00
13 Ph(c),JSe 40.00
14 Ph(c),Danny Kaye 25.00
15 Ph(c),Tony Martin,Ph(c) 25.00
16 Ph(c). 25.00
17 Ph(c). 25.00
18 Ph(c). 25.00
19 Ph(c). 25.00
20 Ph(c). 25.00
21 Ph(c). 25.00
22 Ph(c),ATn 50.00
23 Ph(c),ATn 50.00
24 Ph(c),ATn3 . . . . 50.00
25 Ph(c),ATn 50.00

THRILLING TRUE STORY OF THE BASEBALL GIANTS
Fawcett Publications, 1952

N# Partial Ph(c),Famous Giants of the Past 550.00
2 Yankees Ph(c),Joe DiMaggio, Yogi Berra,Mickey Mantle, Casey Stengel 550.00

TICK TOCK TALES
Magazine Enterprises
Jan., 1946

1 (fa) Koko & Kola 100.00
2 (fa) Calender 45.00
3 thru 10 (fa) . . . . @35.00
11 thru 18 (fa) . . . . @30.00
19 (fa),Flag(c). 30.00
20 (fa) 30.00
21 (fa) 25.00
22 (fa) 25.00
23 (fa),Mugsy Mouse 25.00
24 thru 33 (fa) . . . . @25.00
34 (fa), 1951. . . . . 25.00

TIM HOLT
Magazine Enterprises
Jan.–Feb., 1949

4 FBe,Ph(c). 350.00
5 FBe,Ph(c). 200.00
6 FBe,Ph(c),I:Calico Kid 225.00
7 FBe,Ph(c),Man-Killer Mustang 175.00
8 FBe,Ph(c) 175.00
9 FBe,DAy(c),TerribleTenderfoot 175.00
10 FBe,DAy(c),The Devil Horse . 175.00
11 FBe,DAy(c),O&I:Ghost Rider . 275.00
12 FBe,DAy(c),Battle at Bullock Gap 80.00
13 FBe,DAy(c),Ph(c). 80.00
14 FBe,DAy(c),Ph(c),The Honest Bandits. 80.00
15 FBe,DAy,Ph(c). 80.00
16 FBe,DAy,Ph(c). 80.00
17 FBe,DAy,Ph(c). 250.00
18 FBe,DAy,Ph(c). 75.00
19 FBe,DAy,They Dig By Night . . . 60.00
20 FBe,DAy,O:Red Mask 90.00
21 FBe,DAy,FF(c). 225.00
22 FBe,DAy 55.00
23 FF,FBe,DAy 175.00
24 FBe,DAy,FBe(c). 55.00
25 FBe,DAy,FBe(c). 100.00
26 FBe,DAy,FBe(c). 50.00
27 FBe,DAy,FBe(c),V:Straw Man . 50.00
28 FBe,DAy,FBe(c),Ph(c) 50.00
29 FBe,DAy,FBe,Ph(c),. 50.00
30 FBe,DAy,FBe(c),Lady Doom & The Death Wheel 45.00
31 FBe,DAy,FBe(c). 45.00
32 FBe,DAy,FBe(c). 45.00
33 FBe,DAy,FBe(c). 45.00
34 FBe,DAy,FBe(c). 60.00
35 FBe,DAy,FBe(c). 60.00
36 FBe,DAy,FBe(c),Drugs. 65.00
37 FBe,DAy,FBe(c). 65.00
38 FBe,DAy,FBe(c). 65.00
39 FBe,DAy,FBe(c),3D Effect 70.00
40 FBe,DAy,FBe(c). 70.00
41 FBe,DAy,FBe(c). 70.00
Becomes:

RED MASK

42 FBe,DAy,FBe(c),3D 150.00
43 FBe,DAy,FBe(c),3D 125.00
44 FBe,DAy,FBe(c),Death at Split Mesa,3D. 125.00
45 FBe,DAy,FBe(c),V:False Red Mask 125.00
46 FBe,DAy,FBe(c). 125.00
47 FBe,DAy,FBe(c). 125.00
48 FBe,DAy,FBe(c),Comics Code 100.00
49 FBe,DAy,FBe(c). 100.00
50 FBe,DAy 100.00
51 FBe,DAy,The Magic of `The Presto Kid' 100.00
52 FBe,DAy,O:Presto Kid 125.00
53 FBe,DAy 75.00
54 FBe,DAy,Sept., 1957 . . . . 125.00

TIM TYLER COWBOY
Standard Comics
Nov., 1948

11 . . . . 50.00
12 . . . . 40.00
13 The Doll Told the Secret. 40.00
14 Danger at Devil's Acres 40.00
15 Secret Treasure. 40.00
16 . . . . 40.00
17 . . . . 40.00
18 1950 . . . . 40.00

TINY TOTS COMICS
Dell Publishing Co., 1943

1 . . . . 300.00

TINY TOTS COMICS
E.C. Comics, March, 1946

N# Your First Comic Book B:Burton Geller(c) and art. . . 225.00
2 . . . . 125.00
3 Celebrate the 4th 100.00
4 Go Back to School 120.00
5 Celebrate the Winter 100.00
6 Do Their Spring Gardening . . . 90.00
7 On a Thrilling Ride 100.00
8 On a Summer Vacation 100.00
9 On a Plane Ride 100.00
10 Merry X-Mas Tiny Tots E:Burton Geller(c)and art . . . 100.00

TIP TOP COMICS
United Features,St. John,Dell
1930

1 HF,Li'l Abner 6,700.00
2 HF. 1,600.00
3 HF,Tarzan(c) 1,500.00
4 HF,Li'l Abner(c). 900.00
5 HF,Capt&Kids(c). 675.00
6 HF 650.00
7 HF 650.00
8 HF,Li'l Abner(c). 650.00
9 HF,Tarzan(c). 800.00
10 HF,Li'L Abner(c). 650.00
11 HF,Tarzan(c) 600.00
12 HF,Li'l Abner 550.00
13 HF,Tarzan(c) 575.00
14 HF,Li'L Abner(c). 550.00
15 HF,Capt&kids(c). 550.00
16 HF,Tarzan(c) 575.00
17 HF,Li'L Abner(c). 550.00
18 HF,Tarzan(c) 575.00
19 HF,Football(c) 450.00
20 HF,Capt&Kids(c) 450.00
21 HF,Tarzan(c) 450.00
22 HF,Li'l Abner(c) 350.00
23 HF,Capt&Kids(c) 350.00
24 HF,Tarzan(c) 450.00
25 HF,Capt&Kids(c) 350.00
26 HF,Li'L Abner(c). 350.00
27 HF,Tarzan(c) 450.00
28 HF,Li'l Abner(c) 350.00
29 HF,Capt&Kids(c) 350.00
30 HF,Tarzan(c) 450.00
31 HFCapt&Kids(c). 350.00
32 HF Tarzan(c) 350.00
33 HF,Tarzan(c) 400.00
34 HF,Capt&Kids(c) 400.00
35 HF. 300.00
36 HF,HK,Tarzan(c) 400.00
37 HF,Tarzan 400.00
38 HF. 300.00
39 HF,Tarzan 400.00
40 HF 300.00
41 Tarzan(c). 450.00
42 . . . . 300.00
43 Tarzan(c). 325.00
44 HF. 300.00
45 HF,Tarzan(c) 325.00
46 HF. 300.00
47 HF,Tarzan(c) 325.00
48 HF. 300.00
49 HF. 300.00
50 HF,Tarzan(c) 325.00
51 . . . . 250.00
52 Tarzan(c). 300.00
53 . . . . 250.00
54 . . . . 325.00
55 . . . . 250.00
56 . . . . 250.00
57 BHg. 250.00
58 . . . . 225.00
59 BHg. 250.00
60 . . . . 200.00

T-Man #21
© Quality Comics Group

61 and 62 BHg . . . . @250.00
63 thru 90 . . . . @125.00
91 thru 99 . . . . @100.00
100. . . . . 125.00
101 thru 150 . . . . @65.00
151 thru 188 . . . . @40.00
189 thru 225 . . . . @40.00

T-MAN
Comics Magazines
(Quality Comics Group)
Sept., 1951

1 JCo,Pete Trask-the Treasury Man 300.00
2 RC(c),The Girl with Death in Her Hands 175.00
3 RC,RC(c),Death Trap in Iran . 150.00
4 RC,RC(c),Panama Peril 150.00
5 RC,RC(c),Violence in Venice . 150.00
6 RC(c),The Man Who Could Be Hitler 150.00
7 RC(c),Mr. Murder & The Black Hand 125.00
8 RC(c),Red Ticket to Hell 125.00
9 RC(c),Trial By Terror 125.00
10 . . . . 125.00
11 The Voice of Russia 100.00
12 Terror in Tokyo 100.00
13 Mind Assassins 100.00
14 Trouble in Bavaria 100.00
15 The Traitor,Bondage(c) 100.00
16 Hunt For a Hatchetman 100.00
17 Red Triggerman. 100.00
18 Death Rides the Rails 100.00
19 Death Ambush 100.00
20 The Fantastic H-Bomb Plot . . 125.00
21 The Return of Mussolini 75.00
22 Propaganda for Doom 90.00
23 Red Intrigue in Parid,H-Bomb . 75.00
24 Red Sabotage 75.00
25 RC,The Ingenious Red Trap . . 75.00
26 . . . . 65.00
27 . . . . 65.00
28 . . . . 65.00
29 . . . . 65.00
30 thru 37 . . . . @65.00
38 Dec., 1956. . . . . 65.00

TNT COMICS
Charles Publishing Co.
Feb., 1946

1 FBI story,YellowJacket 225.00

TODAY'S BRIDES
Ajax/Farrell Publishing Co.
Nov., 1955

1 . . . . 50.00
2 . . . . 35.00
3 . . . . 35.00
4 Nov., 1956 . . . . 35.00

TODAY'S ROMANCE
Standard Comics
March, 1952

5 . . . . 50.00
6 ATh 60.00
7 . . . . 35.00
8 . . . . 35.00

TOM AND JERRY DELL GIANT EDITIONS
Dell Publishing Co.
1952–58

Back to School 200.00

Tom and Jerry Winter Carnival #1
© Dell Publishing Co.

Picnic Time. 150.00
Summer Fun 1 . . . . 250.00
Summer Fun 2 . . . . 100.00
Winter Carnival 1 . . . . 350.00
Winter Carnival 2 . . . . 175.00
Winter Fun 3. . . . . 100.00
Winter Fun 4 . . . . 90.00
Winter Fun 5 . . . . 80.00
Winter Fun 6 . . . . 75.00
Winter Fun 7 . . . . 75.00

TOMB OF TERROR
Harvey Publications
June, 1952

1 BP,The Thing From the Center of the Earth 300.00
2 RP,The Quagmire Beast 175.00
3 BP,RP,Caravan of the Doomed, Bondage(c) 175.00
4 RP,I'm Going to Kill You, Torture 150.00
5 RP 150.00
6 RP,Return From the Grave . . . 150.00
7 RP,Shadow of Death. 150.00
8 HN,The Hive 150.00
9 BP,HN,The Tunnel 150.00
10 BP,HN,The Trial 150.00
11 BP,HN,The Closet 150.00
12 BP,HN,Tale of Cain 165.00
13 BP,What Was Out There 200.00
14 BP,SC,End Result 200.00
15 BP,HN,Break-up. 250.00
16 BP,Going,Going,Gone 200.00

Becomes:

THRILLS OF TOMORROW

17 RP,BP,The World of Mr. Chatt . 50.00
18 RP,BP,The Dead Awaken. 40.00
19 S&K,S&K(c),A:Stuntman 300.00
20 S&K,S&K(c),A:Stuntman 250.00

TOM CORBETT SPACE CADET
Dell Publishing Co.
Jan., 1952

See also Dell Four Color
4 based on TV show 100.00
5 . . . . 85.00
6 . . . . 75.00
7 . . . . 75.00
8 . . . . 75.00
9 . . . . 75.00
10 . . . . 75.00
11. . . . . 75.00

Tom Corbett Space Cadet #2
© Prize Publications

TOM CORBETT SPACE CADET
Prize Publications
May–June, 1955

1 . . . . 225.00
2 . . . . 200.00
3 Sept.–Oct., 1955 . . . . 200.00

TOM MIX
Ralston-Purina Co.
Sept., 1940

1 O:Tom Mix 3,200.00
2 . . . . 1,000.00
3 . . . . 550.00
4 thru 9 . . . . @500.00

Becomes:

TOM MIX COMMANDOS COMICS

10 . . . . 450.00
11 Invisible Invaders 450.00
12 Terrible Talons Of Tokyo. 450.00

TOM MIX WESTERN
Fawcett Publications
Jan., 1948

1 Ph(c),Two-Fisted Adventures. 800.00
2 Ph(c),Hair-Triggered Action . . 350.00
3 Ph(c),Double Barreled Action . 250.00
4 Ph(c),Cowpunching 250.00
5 Ph(c),Two Gun Action 250.00
6 CCB,Most Famous Cowboy . . 225.00
7 CCB,A Tattoo of Thrills 225.00
8 EK,Ph(c),Gallant Guns 200.00
9 CCB,Song o/t Deadly Spurs . . 200.00
10 CCB,Crack Shot Western. . . . 200.00
11 CCB,EK(C),Triple Revenge . . 200.00
12 King of the Cowboys 150.00
13 Ph(c),Leather Burns. 150.00
14 Ph(c),Brand of Death 150.00
15 Ph(c),Masked Treachery 150.00
16 Ph(c),Death Spurting Guns . . 150.00
17 Ph(c),Trail of Doom 150.00
18 Ph(c),Reign of Terror 125.00
19 Hand Colored Ph(c). 150.00
20 Ph(c),CCB,F:Capt Tootsie . . . 125.00
21 Ph(c) 125.00

GOLDEN AGE

22 Ph(c),The Human Beast 125.00
23 Ph(c),Return of the Past 125.00
24 Hand Colored Ph(c), The Lawless City 125.00
25 Hand Colored Ph(c), The Signed Death Warrant 125.00
26 Hand Colored Ph(c), Dangerous Escape 125.00
27 Hand Colored Ph(c), Hero Without Glory 125.00
28 Ph(c),The Storm Kings 125.00
29 Hand Colored Ph(c),The Case of the Rustling Rose 125.00
30 Ph(c),Disappearance in the Hills 125.00
31 Ph(c) 100.00
32 Hand Colored Ph(c), Mystery of Tremble Mountain 100.00
33 100.00
34 75.00
35 Partial Ph(c),The Hanging at Hollow Creek 100.00
36 Ph(c) 100.00
37 Ph(c) 100.00
38 Ph(c),36 pages 75.00
39 Ph(c) 100.00
40 Ph(c) 100.00
41 Ph(c) 100.00
42 Ph(c) 100.00
43 Ph(c) 60.00
44 Ph(c) 60.00
45 Partial Ph(c),The Secret Letter 60.00
46 Ph(c) 60.00
47 Ph(c) 60.00
48 Ph(c) 60.00
49 Partial Ph(c),Blind Date With Death 60.00
50 Ph(c) 60.00
51 Ph(c) 60.00
52 Ph(c) 60.00
53 Ph(c) 60.00
54 Ph(c) 60.00
55 Ph(c) 60.00
56 Partial Ph(c),Deadly Spurs 60.00
57 Ph(c)5 60.00
58 Ph(c) 60.00
59 Ph(c) 60.00
60 Ph(c) 60.00
61 Partial Ph(c),Lost in the Night,May 1953 75.00

TOMMY OF THE BIG TOP

King Features/ Standard Comics, 1948

10 Thrilling Circus Adventures 50.00
11 30.00
12 March, 1949 30.00

TOM-TOM THE JUNGLE BOY

Magazine Enterprises, 1946

1 (fa) 75.00
2 (fa) 50.00
3 Winter 1947,(fa),X-mas issue 20.00
1 20.00

TONTO (See LONE RANGER'S COMPANION TONTO)

TONY TRENT (see FACE, THE)

TOP FLIGHT COMICS

Four Star/St. John Publ. Co. July, 1949

1 100.00
1 Hector the Inspector 50.00

TOP LOVE STORIES

Star Publications May, 1951

3 LbC(c) 175.00
4 LbC(c) 125.00
5 LbC(c) 125.00
6 LbC(c),WW 175.00
7 LbC(c) 125.00
8 LbC(c) 125.00
9 LbC(c) 125.00
10 thru 16 LbC(c) @125.00
17 LbC(c),WW 150.00
18 LbC(c) 125.00
19 LbC(c),JyD 125.00

TOP-NOTCH COMICS

MLJ Magazines Dec., 1939

1 JaB,JCo,B&O:The Wizard, B:Kandak,Swift of the Secret Service,The Westpointer, Mystic, Air Patrol,Scott Rand, Manhunter 5,500.00
2 JaB,JCo,B:Dick Storm, E:Mystic, B:Stacy Knight 2,000.00
3 JaB,JCo,EA(c),E:Swift of the Secret Service,Scott Rand 1,400.00
4 JCo,EA(c),MMe,O&I:Streak, Chandler 1,100.00
5 Ea(c),MMe,O&I:Galahad, B:Shanghai Sheridan 1,100.00
6 Ea(c),MMe,A:The Sheild 1,000.00
7 Ea(c),MMe,N:The Wizard 1,100.00
8 E:Dick Sorm,B&O:Roy The1 Super Boy,The Firefly 1,100.00
9 O&I:Black Hood, B:Fran Frazier 5,000.00
10 1,400.00
11 800.00
12 800.00
13 800.00

Top-Notch Comics #3
© MLJ Magazines

14 Bondage(c) 825.00
15 MMe 800.00
16 750.00
17 Bondage(c) 775.00
18 725.00
19 Bondage(c) 775.00
20 725.00
21 600.00
22 600.00
23 Bondage(c) 625.00
24 Black Hood Smashes Murder Ring 600.00
25 E:Bob Phantom 600.00
26 600.00
27 E:The Firefly 600.00
28 B:Suzie,Pokey Okay, Gag Oriented 600.00
29 E:Kandak 600.00
30 600.00
31 300.00
32 300.00
33 BWo,B:Dotty&Ditto 300.00
34 BWo 300.00
35 BWo 300.00
36 BWo 300.00
37 thru 40 BWo @300.00
41 300.00
42 BWo 300.00
43 300.00
44 EW:Black Hood,I:Suzie 275.00
45 Suzie(c) 275.00
Becomes:

LAUGH COMIX

46 Suzie & Wilbur 125.00
47 Suzie & Wilbur 100.00
48 Suzie & Wilbur 100.00
Becomes:

SUZIE COMICS

49 B:Ginger 175.00
50 AFy(c) 100.00
51 AFy(c) 100.00
52 AFy(c) 100.00
53 AFy(c) 100.00
54 AFy(c) 125.00
55 AFy(c) 125.00
56 BWo,B;Katie Keene 75.00
57 thru 70 BWo @75.00
71 thru 79 BWo @55.00
80 thru 99 BWo @45.00
100 Aug., 1954, BWo 45.00

TOPS

Tops Mag. Inc. (Lev Gleason) July, 1949

1 RC&BLb,GT,DBa,CBi(c),I'll Buy That Girl,Our Explosive Children 900.00
2 FG,BF,CBi(c),RC&BLb 850.00

TOPS COMICS

Consolidated Book Publishers 1944

2000 Don on the Farm 200.00
2001 The Jack of Spades V:The Hawkman 125.00
2002 Rip Raiders 75.00
2003 Red Birch 20.00

TOP SECRET

Hillman Publications Jan., 1952

1 The Tricks of the Secret Agent Revealed 150.00

TOP SECRETS
Street & Smith, Nov., 1947

1 BP,BP(c),Of the Men Who Guard the U.S. Mail 250.00
2 BP,BP(c),True Story of Jim the Penman 200.00
3 BP,BP(c),Crime Solved by Mental Telepathy 175.00
4 Highway Pirates 175.00
5 BP,BP(c),Can Music Kill 175.00
6 BP,BP(c),The Clue of the Forgotten Film 175.00
7 BP,BP(c),Train For Sale 225.00
8 BP,BP(c) 175.00
9 BP,BP(c) 175.00
10 BP,BP(c),July–Aug., 1949 . . . 225.00

TOPS IN ADVENTURE
Approved Comics (Ziff-Davis) Autumn, 1952

1 BP,Crusaders From Mars 350.00

TOP SPOT COMICS
Top Spot Publishing Co. 1945

1 The Duke Of Darkness 250.00

TOPSY-TURVY
R.B. Leffingwell Publ. April, 1945

1 I:Cookie 75.00

TOR
St. John Publishing Co. Sept., 1953

1 JKu,JKu(c),O;Tor,One Million Years Ago 85.00
2 JKu,JKu(c),3-D Issue 75.00
3 JKu,JKu(c),ATh,historic Life . . . 80.00
4 JKu,JKu(c),ATh 80.00
5 JKu,JKu(c),ATh,Oct., 1954 . . . . 80.00

TORCHY
Quality Comics Group Nov., 1949

1 GFx,BWa(c),The Blonde Bombshell 1,100.00
2 GFx,GFx(c),Beauty at its' Best 550.00
3 GFX,GFx(c),You Can't Beat Nature 550.00
4 GFx,GFx(c),The Girl to Keep Your Eye On 650.00
5 BWa,GFx,BWa(c),At the Masquerade Party 850.00
6 Sept., 1950,BWa,GFx, BWa(c),The Libido Driven Boy Scout. 850.00

Torchy #4
© Quality Comics Group

TORMENTED, THE
Sterling Comics July, 1954

1 Buried Alive 175.00
2 Sept., 1954,The Devils Circus 150.00

TOYLAND COMICS
Fiction House Magazines Jan., 1947

1 Wizard of the Moon 200.00
2 Buddy Bruin & Stu Rabbit . . . 125.00
3 GT,The Candy Maker 150.00
4 July, 1947 . . . . 125.00

TOY TOWN COMICS
Toytown Publ./Orbit Publ. Feb., 1945

1 LbC,LbC(c)(fa) 265.00
2 LbC,(fa) 175.00
3 LbC,LbC(c),(fa) 135.00
4 LbC,(fa) 135.00
5 LbC,(fa) 135.00
6 LbC,(fa) 135.00
7 LbC,(fa),May, 1947 . . . . 135.00

TRAIL BLAZERS
(see RED DRAGON COMICS)

TREASURE COMICS
Prize Comics Group, 1943

1 S&K,Reprints of Prize Comics #7 through #11 . . . . 1,700.00

TREASURE COMICS
American Boys Comics (Prize Publications) June–July, 1945

1 HcK,B:PaulBunyan,MarcoPolo 225.00
2 HcK,HcK(c),B:Arabian Knight, Gorilla King,Dr.Styx 125.00
3 HcK 100.00
4 HcK 100.00
5 HcK,JK 150.00
6 HcK,BK,HcK(c) 125.00
7 HcK,FF,HcK(c) 275.00
8 HcK,FF 275.00
9 HcK,DBa 100.00
10 JK,DBa,JK(c). 225.00
11 BK,HcK,DBa,The Weird Adventures of Mr. Bottle 150.00
12 DBa,DBa(c),Autumn, 1947. . . 100.00

TREASURY OF COMICS
St. John Publishing Co., 1947

1 RvB,RvB(c),Abbie an' Slats . . 125.00
2 Jim Hardy 75.00
3 Bill Bimlin 75.00
4 RvB,RvB(c),Abbie an' Slats . . . 75.00
5 Jim Hardy,Jan., 1948 . . . . 70.00

TRIPLE THREAT
Gerona Publications Winter, 1945

1 F:King O'Leary,The Duke of Darkness,Beau Brummell . . 175.00

TRUE AVIATION PICTURE STORIES
Parents' Institute/P.M.I. Aug., 1942

1 How Jimmy Doolittle Bombed Tokyo 100.00
2 Knight of the Air Mail 60.00
3 The Amazing One-Man Air Force 50.00
4 Joe Foss America's No. 1 Air Force 50.00
5 Bombs over Germany 50.00
6 Flight Lt. Richard Hillary R.A.F. 50.00
7 "Fatty" Chow China's Sky Champ 50.00
8 Blitz over Burma 50.00
9 Off the Beam 50.00
10 "Pappy" Boyington 50.00
11 Ph(c) 50.00
12 . . . . 50.00
13 Ph(c),Flying Facts 50.00
14 . . . . 50.00
15 . . . . 50.00

Becomes:

AVIATION AND MODEL BUILDING

16 . . . . 45.00
17 Feb., 1947. . . . . 50.00

TRUE COMICS
True Comics/ Parents' Magazine Press April, 1941

1 My Greatest Adventure-by Lowell Thomas 225.00
2 BEv,The Story of the Red Cross 125.00
3 Baseball Hall of Fame. 135.00
4 Danger in the Artic 100.00
5 Father Duffy-the Fighting Chaplin 120.00
6 The Capture of Aquinaldo . . . 120.00
7 JKa,Wilderness Adventures of George Washington 120.00
8 U.S. Army Wings 75.00
9 A Pig that Made History 75.00
10 Adrift on an Ice Pan. 75.00
11 Gen. Douglas MacArthur 65.00
12 Mackenzie-King of Cananda . . 60.00
13 The Real Robinson Crusoe . . . 65.00
14 Australia war base of the South Pacific 65.00
15 The Story of West Point. 75.00
16 How Jimmy Doolittle Bombed Tokyo 70.00
17 The Ghost of Captain Blig, B.Feller 75.00
18 Battling Bill of the Merchant Marine 80.00
19 Secret Message Codes 50.00
20 The Story of India 45.00
21 Timoshenko the Blitz Buster. . . 50.00
22 Gen, Bernard L. Montgomery. . 45.00
23 The Story of Steel 45.00
24 Gen. Henri Giraud-Master of Escape. 45.00
25 Medicine's Miracle Men 45.00

26 Hero of the Bismarck Sea 45.00
27 Leathernecks have Landed ... 50.00
28 The Story of Radar 40.00
29 The Fighting Seabees 40.00
30 Dr. Norman Bethune-Blood Bank Founder.... 40.00
31 Our Good Neighbor Bolivia, Red Grange 50.00
32 Men against the Desert 35.00
33 Gen. Clark and his Fighting 5th 40.00
34 Angel of the Battlefield.... 35.00
35 Carlson's Marine Raiders.... 35.00
36 Canada's Sub-Busters 35.00
37 Commander of the Crocodile Fleet.... 35.00
38 Oregon Trailblazer.... 35.00
39 Saved by Sub 35.00
40 Sea Furies.... 35.00
41 Cavalcade of England 30.00
42 Gen. Jaques Le Clerc-Hero of Paris 30.00
43 Unsinkable Ship.... 35.00
44 El Senor Goofy 30.00
45 Tokyo Express.... 25.00
46 The Magnificent Runt.... 30.00
47 Atoms Unleashed, Atomic Bomb 75.00
48 Pirate Patriot 30.00
49 Smiking Fists.... 30.00
50 Lumber Pirates 30.00
51 Exercise Musk-Ox 30.00
52 King of the Buckeneers 30.00
53 Baseline Booby 30.00
54 Santa Fe Sailor 30.00
55 Sea Going Santa.... 30.00
56 End of a Terror.... 30.00
57 Newfangled Machines 30.00
58 Leonardo da Vinci-500 years too Soon 30.00
59 Pursuit of the Pirates 35.00
60 Emmett Kelly-The World's Funniest Clown 30.00
61 Peter Le Grand-Bold Buckaneer 30.00
62 Sutter's Gold 30.00
63 Outboard Outcome 30.00
64 Man-Eater at Large 30.00
65 The Story of Scotland Yard ... 30.00
66 Easy Guide to Football Formations.... 35.00
67 The Changing Zebra 30.00
68 Admiral Byrd 25.00
69 FBI Special Agent Steve Saunders 35.00
70 The Case of the Seven Hunted Men 30.00
71 Story of Joe DiMaggio 150.00
72 FBI,Jackie Robinson 60.00
73 The 26 Mile Dash-Story of the Marathon 35.00
74 A Famous Coach's Special Football Tips.... 35.00
75 King of Reporters.... 35.00
76 The Story of a Buried Treasure.... 35.00
77 France's Greatest Detective... 35.00
78 Cagliostro-Master Rogue 50.00
79 Ralph Bunche-Hero of Peace.. 35.00
80 Rocket Trip to the Moon.... 150.00
81 Red Grange.... 150.00
82 Marie Celeste Ship of Mystery 125.00
83 Bullfighter from Brooklyn 125.00
84 King of the Buckaneers, Aug., 1950 .... 125.00

TRUE CONFIDENCES
Fawcett Publications
Autumn, 1949

1 .... 125.00
2 and 3 .... @75.00
4 DP 75.00

True Crime #3
© Magazine Village

TRUE CRIME COMICS
Magazine Village, Inc.
May, 1947

2 JCo(c),JCo(c),James Kent-Crook,Murderer,Escaped Convict; Drug.... 1,100.00
3 JCo,JCo(c),Benny Dickson-Killer;Drug 800.00
4 JCo,JCo(c),Little Jake-Big Shot 750.00
5 JCo(c),The Rat & the Blond Gun Moll;Drug 500.00
6 Joseph Metley-Swindler, Jailbird, Killer 400.00
2-1(7) ATh,WW,Ph(c),Phil Coppolla,Sept., 1949 .... 650.00

TRUE LIFE SECRETS
Romantic Love Stories/ Charlton Comics
March–April, 1951

1 .... 80.00
2 .... 40.00
3 .... 35.00
4 .... 35.00
5 thru 20 .... @35.00
21 thru 25 .... @25.00
26 Comics Code 20.00
27 thru 29 .... @20.00

TRUE LIFE ROMANCES
Ajax/Farrell Publications
Dec., 1955

1 .... 65.00
2 .... 50.00
3 Aug., 1956 .... 55.00

TRUE LOVE PICTORIAL
St. John Publishing Co., 1952

1 Ph(c) 125.00
2 MB 150.00
3 MB(c),MB,JKu 250.00
4 MB(c),MB,JKu 250.00
5 MB(c),MB,JKu 250.00
6 MB(c) 125.00
7 MB(c) 125.00
8 MB(c) 100.00
9 MB(c) 100.00
10 MB(c),MB 100.00
11 MB(c),MB.... 100.00

TRUE MOVIE AND TELEVISION
Toby Press, Aug., 1950

1 Liz Taylor, Ph(c) 350.00
2 FF,Ph(c),John Wayne, L.Taylor 250.00
3 June Allyson,Ph(c) 225.00
4 Jane Powell,Ph(c),Jan.,1951.. 100.00

SPORT COMICS
Street & Smith, Oct., 1940

1 F:Lou Gehrig 500.00
2 F:Gene Tunney 250.00
3 F:Phil Rizzuto 275.00
4 F:Frank Leahy 200.00

Becomes:

TRUE SPORT PICTURE STORIES

5 Joe DiMaggio 300.00
6 Billy Confidence 150.00
7 Mel Ott.... 175.00
8 Lou Ambers 150.00
9 Pete Reiser 150.00
10 Frankie Sinkwich 150.00
11 Marty Serfo 150.00
12 JaB(c),Jack Dempsey 165.00
2-1 JaB(c),Willie Pep 150.00
2-2 JaB(c).... 150.00
2-3 JaB(c),Carl Hubbell.... 165.00
2-4 Advs. in Football & Battle ... 175.00
2-5 Don Hutson 150.00
2-6 Dixie Walker.... 175.00
2-7 Stan Musial 200.00
2-8 Famous Ring Champions of All Time 175.00
2-9 List of War Year Rookies ... 200.00
2-10 Connie Mack 175.00
2-11 Winning Basketball Plays .. 150.00
2-12 Eddie Gottlieb.... 150.00
3-1 Bill Conn 150.00
3-2 Philadelphia Athletics 125.00
3-3 Leo Durocher 150.00
3-4 Rudy Dusek 125.00
3-5 Ernie Pyle 125.00
3-6 Bowling with Ned Day 125.00
3-7 Return of the Mighty (Home from War);Joe DiMaggio(c).. 250.00
3-8 Conn V:Louis 200.00
3-9 Reuben Shark 125.00
3-10 BP,BP(c),Don "Dopey" Dillock 125.00
3-11 BP,BP(c),Death Scores a Touchdown 125.00
3-12 Red Sox V:Senators 125.00
4-1 Spring Training in Full Spring 125.00
4-2 BP,BP(c),How to Pitch 'Em Where They Can't Hit 'Em .. 125.00
4-3 BP,BP(c),1947 Super Stars . 135.00
4-4 BP,BP(c),Get Ready for the Olympics 135.00
4-5 BP,BP,(c),Hugh Casey 125.00
4-6 BP,BP(c),Phantom Phil Hergesheimer 125.00
4-7 BP,BP(c),How to Bowl Better 125.00
4-8 Tips on the Big Fight 135.00
4-9 BP,BP(c),Bill McCahan 125.00
4-10 BP,BP(c),Great Football

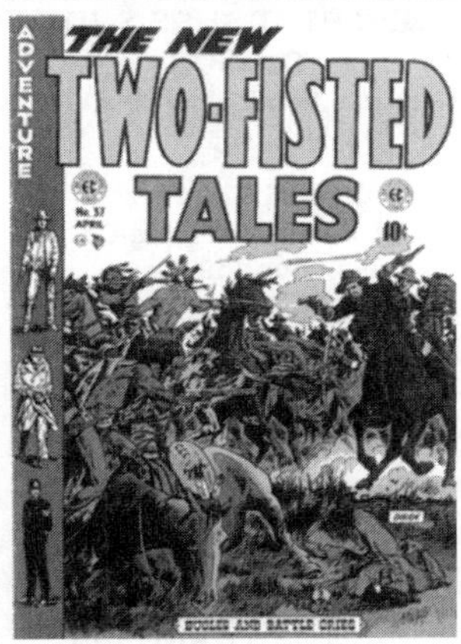

Two-Fisted Tales #37
© E.C. Comics

Plays 125.00
4-11 BP,BP(c),Football 125.00
4-12 BP,BP(c),Basketball 125.00
5-1 Satchel Paige 150.00
5-2 History of Boxing,
July–Aug., 1949 . . . . 125.00

TRUE SWEETHEART SECRETS
Fawcett Publications
May, 1950

1 Ph(c) 100.00
2 WW 125.00
3 BD 75.00
4 BD 75.00
5 BD 75.00
6 thru 11 . . . . @60.00

TRUE-TO-LIFE ROMANCES
Star Publications
Nov.–Dec., 1949

3 LbC(c),GlennFord/JanetLeigh . 175.00
4 LbC(c) 125.00
5 LbC(c) 125.00
6 LbC(c) 125.00
7 LbC(c) 125.00
8 LbC(c) 125.00
9 LbC(c) 125.00
10 LbC(c) 125.00
11 LbC(c) 125.00
12 LbC(c) 125.00
13 LbC(c),JyD 125.00
14 LbC(c),JyD 125.00
15 LbC(c),WW,JyD 150.00
16 LbC(c),WW,JyD 150.00
17 LbC(c),JyD 100.00
18 LbC(c),JyD 100.00
19 LbC(c),JyD 100.00
20 LbC(c),JyD 100.00
21 LbC(c),JyD 100.00
22 LbC(c) 90.00
23 LbC(c) 90.00

TRUE WAR ROMANCES
Comic Magazines, Inc.
(Quality Comics)
Sept., 1952

1 Ph(c) 100.00
2 . . . . 45.00
3 thru 10 . . . . @35.00
11 thru 20 . . . . @30.00
21 Comics Code 30.00
Becomes:

EXOTIC ROMANCES

22 . . . . 40.00
23 thru 26 . . . . @25.00
27 MB 40.00
28 MB 40.00
29 . . . . 25.00
30 MB 40.00
31 MB 40.00

TUROK, SON OF STONE
Dell Publishing Co.
Dec., 1954

(1) *see Dell Four Color #596*
(2) *see Dell Four Color #656*
3 . . . . 250.00
4 and 5 . . . . @225.00
6 thru 10 . . . . @150.00
11 thru 20 . . . . @90.00
21 thru 29 . . . . @60.00
See Other Color section

TWEETY AND SYLVESTER
Dell Publishing Co.
June, 1952

(1) *see Dell Four Color #406*
(2) *see Dell Four Color #489*
(3) *see Dell Four Color #524*
4 thru 20 . . . . @25.00
21 thru 37 . . . . @15.00

TWINKLE COMICS
Spotlight Publications
May, 1945

1 Humor Format 75.00

TWO-FISTED TALES
Fables Publications
(E.C. Comics)
Nov.–Dec., 1950

18 HK,JCr,WW,JSe,HK(c) 800.00
19 HK,JCr,WW,JSe,HK(c) 550.00
20 JDa,HK,WW,JSe,HK(c) 350.00
21 JDa,HK,WW,JSe,HK(c) 300.00
22 JDa,HK,WW,JSe,HK(c) 300.00
23 JDa,HK,WW,JSe,HK(c) 225.00
24 JDa,HK,WW,JSe,HK(c) 200.00
25 JDa,HK,WW,JSe,HK(c) 200.00
26 JDa,JSe,HK(c),Action at
the Changing Reservoir 150.00
27 JDa,JSe,HK(c) 150.00
28 JDa,JSe,HK(c) 150.00
29 JDa,JSe,HK(c) 200.00
30 JDa,JSe,JDa(c) 200.00
31 JDa,JSe,HK(c),Civil
War Story 160.00
32 JDa,JKu,WW(c) 160.00
33 JDa,JKu,WW(c) 175.00
34 JDa,JSe,JDa(c) 160.00
35 JDa,JSe,JDa(c),Civil
War Story 175.00
36 JDa,JSe,JSe(c),A
Difference of Opinion 125.00
37 JSe,JSe(c),Bugles &
Battle Cries 125.00
38 JSe,JSe(c) 125.00
39 JSe,JSe(c) 125.00
40 JDa,JSe,GE,GE(c) 150.00
41 JSe,GE,JDa(c),March, 1955. . 125.00

UNCLE CHARLIE'S FABLES
Lev Gleason Publications
Jan., 1952

1 CBi(c),Ph(c) 100.00
2 BF,CBi(c),Ph(c) 60.00
3 CBi(c),Ph(c) 65.00
4 CBi(c),Ph(c) 65.00
5 CBi,Ph(c),Sept., 1952 . . . . 60.00

UNCLE SAM
(see BLACKHAWK)

UNCLE SCROOGE
Dell Publishing Co.
March, 1952

(1) *see Dell Four Color #386*
(2) *see Dell Four Color #456*
(3) *see Dell Four Color #495*
4 . . . . 400.00
5 . . . . 300.00
6 . . . . 250.00
7 CB 225.00
8 . . . . 200.00
9 . . . . 200.00
10 . . . . 200.00
11 thru 20 . . . . @175.00
21 thru 30 . . . . @150.00
31 thru 39 . . . . @100.00
See Other Pub. section

UNDERWORLD
D.S. Publishing Co.
Feb.–March, 1948

1 SMo(c),Violence 350.00
2 SMo(c),Electrocution. 350.00
3 AMc,AMc(c),The Ancient Club 275.00
4 Grl,The Beer Baron Murder . . 225.00
5 Grl,The Postal Clue 175.00
6 The Polka Dot Gang 125.00
7 Mono-The Master 125.00
8 The Double Tenth 125.00
9 Thrilling Stories of the Fight
against Crime,June, 1953 . . 125.00

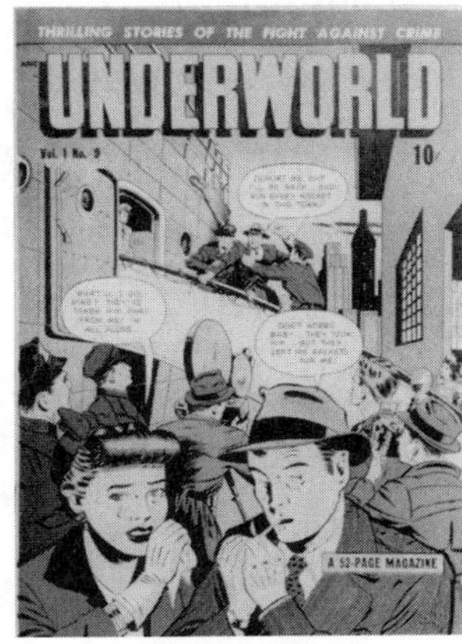

Underworld #9
© DS Publishing

GOLDEN AGE

UNDERWORLD CRIME
Fawcett Publications
June, 1952

1 The Crime Army 225.00
2 Jailbreak 150.00
3 Microscope Murder 125.00
4 Death on the Docks 125.00
5 River of Blood 125.00
6 The Sky Pirates 125.00
7 Bondage & Torture(c) 200.00
8 . . . . 125.00
9 June, 1953 . . . . 125.00

UNITED COMICS
United Features Syndicate
1950

8 thru 26 Bushmiller(c),
Fritzi Ritz . . . . @25.00

UNITED STATES FIGHTING AIR FORCE
Superior Comics, Ltd.
Sept., 1952

1 Coward's Courage 75.00
2 Clouds that Killed 35.00
3 Operation Decoy 20.00
4 thru 28 . . . . @20.00
29 Oct., 1959. . . . . 20.00

UNITED STATES MARINES
Wm. H. Wise/Magazine Ent./
Toby Press, 1943

N# MBi,MBi(c),Hellcat out
of Heaven 100.00
2 MBi,Drama of Wake Island . . 175.00
3 A Leatherneck Flame Thrower 125.00
4 MBi 60.00
5 BP 55.00
6 BP 55.00
7 BP 50.00
8 thru 10 . . . . @50.00
11 1952 . . . . 50.00

UNKEPT PROMISE
Legion of Truth, 1949

1 Anti:Alcoholic Drinking 50.00

UNKNOWN WORLDS (see STRANGE STORIES FROM ANOTHER WORLD)

UNSEEN, THE
Visual Editions
(Standard Comics) 1952

5 ATh,The Hungry Lodger 275.00
6 JKa,MSy,Bayou Vengeance . . 225.00
7 JKz,MSy,Time is the Killer . . . 200.00
8 JKz,MSy,The Vengance Vat . . 200.00
9 JKz,MSy,Your Grave is Ready 200.00
10 JKz,MSy 200.00
11 JKz,MSy 200.00
12 ATh,GT,Till Death Do Us Part. 200.00
13 . . . . 150.00
14 . . . . 150.00
15 ATh,The Curse of the
Undead!, July, 1954 . . . . 200.00

UNTAMED LOVE
Comic Magazines
(Quality Comics Group)
Jan., 1950

1 BWa(c),PGn 200.00
2 Ph(c) 125.00
3 PGn 125.00
4 . . . . 125.00
5 PGn 125.00

USA IS READY
Dell Publishing Co., 1941

1 Propaganda WWII 300.00

U.S. JONES
Fox Features Syndicate
Nov., 1941

1 Death Over the Airways . . . 1,100.00
2 Jan., 1942 . . . . 700.00

U.S. MARINES IN ACTION!
Avon Periodicals
Aug.–Dec., 1952

1 On Land,Sea & in the Air 60.00
2 The Killer Patrol 25.00
3 EK(c),Death Ridge 30.00

U.S. TANK COMMANDOS
Avon Periodicals
June, 1952

1 EK(c),Fighting Daredevils
of the USA 50.00
2 EK(c) 25.00
3 EK,EK(c),Robot Armanda 25.00
4 EK,EK(c),March, 1953 . . . . 25.00

VALOR
E.C. Comics, March, 1955

1 AW,AT,WW,WW(c),Grl,BK. . . . 250.00
2 AW(c),AW,WWGrl,BK 200.00
3 AW,RC,BK,JOc(c). 150.00
4 WW(c),RC,Grl,BK,JO 150.00
5 WW(c),WW,AW,GE,Grl,BK . . . 125.00

VARIETY COMICS
Rural Home Publ./
Croyden Publ. Co., 1944

1 MvS,MvS(c),O:Capt, Valiant . . 175.00
2 MvS,MvS(c) 125.00
3 MvS,MvS(c) 100.00
4 . . . . 85.00
5 1946 . . . . 75.00

VAULT OF HORROR (see WAR AGAINST CRIME)

V...–COMICS
Fox Features Syndicate
Jan., 1942

1 V:V-Man 1,100.00
2 The Horror of the
Dungeons, March, 1942 . . . 750.00

VERI BEST SURE SHOT COMICS
Holyoke Publishing Co., 1945

1 reprint Holyoke One-Shots . . . 275.00

VIC FLINT
St. John Publishing Co.
Aug., 1948

1 ...Crime Buster 100.00
2 . . . . 75.00
3 . . . . 50.00
4 . . . . 50.00
5 April, 1949 . . . . 50.00

VIC JORDAN
Civil Service Publications
April, 1945

1 Escape From a Nazi Prison . . 100.00

VIC TORRY AND HIS FLYING SAUCER
Fawcett Publications, 1950

1 Ph(c),Revealed at Last 475.00

Victory #2
© Hillman Periodicals

VICTORY COMICS
Hillman Periodicals
Aug., 1941

1 BEv,BEv(c),F:TheConqueror 2,500.00
2 BEv,BEv(c) 1,000.00
3 The Conqueror(c) 700.00
4 Dec., 1941 . . . . 650.00

VIC VERITY MAGAZINE
Vic Verity Publications
1945

1 CCB,CCB(c),B:Vic Verity,Hot-
Shot Galvan, Tom Travis . . . 150.00
2 CCB,CCB(c),Annual Classic
Dance Recital 100.00
3 CCB 75.00
4 CCB,I:Boomer Young;The
Bee-U-TiFul Weekend 75.00
5 CCB,Championship Baseball
Game 75.00
6 CCB,High School Hero 75.00
7 CCB,CCB(c),F:Rocket Rex . . . 75.00

VOODOO
Four Star Publ./Farrell/ Ajax Comics, May, 1952

1 MB,South Sea Girl . . . 425.00
2 MB . . . 325.00
3 Face Stabbing . . . 250.00
4 MB,Rendezvous . . . 250.00
5 Ghoul For A Day,Nazi . . . 200.00
6 The Weird Dead, Severed Head . . . 210.00
7 Goodbye World . . . 200.00
8 MB, Revenge . . . 250.00
9 Will this thing Never Stew? . . 200.00
10 Land of Shadows & Screams . 200.00
11 Human Harvest . . . 175.00
12 The Wazen Taper . . . 175.00
13 Bondage(c),Caskets to Fit Everybody . . . 185.00
14 Death Judges the Beauty Contest . . . 175.00
15 Loose their Heads . . . 185.00
16 Fog Was Her Shroud . . . 175.00
17 Apes Laughter,Electric Chair . 185.00
18 Astounding Fantasy . . . 175.00
19 MB,Bondage(c); Destination Congo . . . 225.00
Ann.#1 . . . 650.00
Becomes:

VOODA

20 MB,MB(c),Echoes of an A-Bomb . . . 250.00
21 MB,MB(c),Trek of Danger . . . 225.00
22 MB,MB(c),The Sun Blew Away, Aug., 1955 . . . 225.00

WACKY DUCK (see DOPEY DUCK)

WALT DISNEY'S COMICS & STORIES
Dell Publishing Co.

N# 1943 dpt.store giveway. . . . 450.00
N# 1945 X-mas giveaway . . . 200.00

WALT DISNEY'S COMICS & STORIES
Dell Publishing Co. Oct., 1940

1 (1940)FG,Donald Duck & Mickey Mouse . . . 17,000.00
2 . . . 6,500.00
3 . . . 2,000.00
4 Christmas(c) . . . 1,400.00
4a Promo issue. . . . 1,500.00
5 . . . 1,100.00
6 . . . 900.00
7 . . . 900.00
8 . . . 900.00
9 . . . 900.00
10 . . . 900.00
11 1st Huey,Louie,Dewey . . . 750.00
12 . . . 800.00
13 . . . 750.00
14 . . . 750.00
15 3 Little Kittens . . . 700.00
16 3 Little Pigs . . . 650.00
17 The Ugly Ducklings . . . 700.00
18 . . . 575.00
19 . . . 550.00
20 . . . 550.00
21 . . . 575.00
22 . . . 500.00
23 . . . 475.00
24 . . . 475.00
25 . . . 475.00

Walt Disney's Comics & Stories #114
© Walt Disney

26 . . . 475.00
27 . . . 500.00
28 . . . 475.00
29 . . . 475.00
30 . . . 475.00
31 CB; Donald Duck . . . 3,000.00
32 CB . . . 1,400.00
33 CB . . . 1,000.00
34 CB;WK; Gremlins. . . . 800.00
35 CB;WK; Gremlins. . . . 750.00
36 CB;WK; Gremlins . . . 750.00
37 CB;WK; Gremlins. . . . 375.00
38 CB;WK; Gremlins. . . . 475.00
39 CB;WK; Gremlins. . . . 475.00
40 CB;WK; Gremlins. . . . 475.00
41 CB;WK; Gremlins. . . . 425.00
42 CB. . . . 425.00
43 CB. . . . 400.00
44 CB. . . . 400.00
45 CB. . . . 400.00
46 CB. . . . 400.00
47 CB. . . . 375.00
48 CB. . . . 375.00
49 CB. . . . 375.00
50 CB. . . . 375.00
51 CB. . . . 300.00
52 CB; Li'l Bad Wolf begins. . . . 300.00
53 CB. . . . 300.00
54 CB. . . . 300.00
55 CB. . . . 300.00
56 CB. . . . 300.00
57 CB. . . . 300.00
58 CB. . . . 300.00
59 CB. . . . 300.00
60 CB. . . . 300.00
61 CB; Dumbo . . . 225.00
62 CB. . . . 225.00
63 CB; Pinocchio . . . 225.00
64 CB; Pinocchio . . . 225.00
65 CB; Pluto. . . . 225.00
66 CB. . . . 225.00
67 CB. . . . 225.00
68 CB. . . . 225.00
69 CB. . . . 225.00
70 CB. . . . 225.00
71 CB. . . . 175.00
72 CB. . . . 175.00
73 CB. . . . 175.00
74 CB. . . . 175.00
75 CB; Brer Rabbit . . . 175.00
76 CB; Brer Rabbit . . . 175.00
77 CB; Brer Rabbit . . . 175.00
78 CB. . . . 175.00
79 CB. . . . 175.00
80 CB. . . . 175.00
81 CB. . . . 150.00
82 CB;Bongo . . . 175.00
83 CB;Bongo . . . 175.00
84 CB;Bongo . . . 175.00
85 CB. . . . 175.00
86 CB;Goofy & Agnes. . . . 175.00
87 CB;Goofy & Agnes. . . . 150.00
88 CB;Goofy & Agnes, I:Gladstone Gander . . . 175.00
89 CB;Goofy&Agnes,Chip'n'Dale 150.00
90 CB;Goofy & Agnes. . . . 150.00
91 CB. . . . 125.00
92 CB. . . . 125.00
93 CB. . . . 125.00
94 CB. . . . 125.00
95 . . . 125.00
96 Little Toot. . . . 125.00
97 CB; Little Toot . . . 125.00
98 CB; Uncle Scrooge . . . 275.00
99 CB. . . . 125.00
100 CB. . . . 175.00
101 CB. . . . 125.00
102 CB. . . . 125.00
103 CB . . . 110.00
104 . . . 110.00
105 CB. . . . 125.00
106 CB. . . . 125.00
107 CB. . . . 125.00
108 . . . 110.00
109. . . . 110.00
110 CB . . . 125.00
111 CB . . . 125.00
112 CB; drugs. . . . 125.00
113 CB . . . 125.00
114 CB . . . 125.00
115 . . . 40.00
116 . . . 40.00
117 . . . 40.00
118 . . . 40.00
119 . . . 40.00
120 . . . 40.00
121 Grandma Duck begins . . . 40.00
122 . . . 40.00
123 . . . 40.00
124 CB . . . 110.00
125 CB;I:Junior Woodchucks . . . 125.00
126 CB. . . . 75.00
127 CB. . . . 75.00
128 CB. . . . 75.00
129 CB. . . . 75.00
130 CB. . . . 75.00
131 CB. . . . 75.00
132 CB A:Grandma Duck . . . 75.00
133 CB. . . . 75.00
134 I:The Beagle Boys . . . 175.00
135 CB. . . . 75.00
136 CB. . . . 75.00
137 CB. . . . 75.00
138 CB. . . . 75.00
139 CB. . . . 75.00
140 CB; I:Gyro Gearloose. . . . 175.00
141 CB. . . . 60.00
142 CB. . . . 60.00
143 CB; Little Hiawatha . . . 60.00
144 CB; Little Hiawatha . . . 60.00
145 CB; Little Hiawatha . . . 60.00
146 CB; Little Hiawatha . . . 60.00
147 CB; Little Hiawatha . . . 60.00
148 CB; Little Hiawatha . . . 60.00
149 CB; Little Hiawatha . . . 60.00
150 CB; Little Hiawatha . . . 60.00
151 CB; Little Hiawatha . . . 60.00
152 thru 200 CB . . . @50.00
201 CB. . . . 40.00
202 CB. . . . 40.00
203 CB. . . . 40.00
204 CB, Chip 'n' Dale & Scamp . . 40.00
205 thru 240 CB . . . @40.00
241 CB; Dumbo x-over . . . 30.00
242 CB. . . . 30.00
243 CB. . . . 30.00

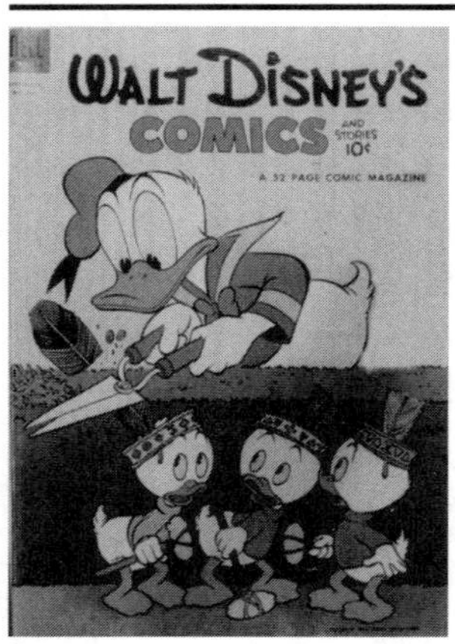

Walt Disney's Comics and Stories #168
© Walt Disney

244 CB. 30.00
245 CB. 30.00
246 CB. 30.00
247 thru 255 CB;GyroGearloose @30.00
256 thru 263 CB;Ludwig Von Drake & Gearloose . . . . @30.00
See: Independent Color Comics

WALT DISNEY ANNUALS

Walt Disney's Autumn Adventure . . 4.00
Walt Disney's Holiday Parade 3.50
Walt Disney's Spring Fever. 3.25
Walt Disney's Summer Fun. 3.25

WALT DISNEY DELL GIANT EDITIONS

Dell Publishing Co.

1 CB,W.Disney'sXmas Parade('49) 900.00
2 CB,W.Disney'sXmas Parade('50) 700.00
3 W.Disney'sXmas Parade('51) . 225.00
4 W.Disney'sXmas Parade('52) . 200.00
5 W.Disney'sXmas Parade('53) . 200.00
6 W.Disney'sXmas Parade('54) . 200.00
7 W.Disney'sXmas Parade('55) . 200.00
8 CB,W.Disney'sXmas Parade('56) 350.00
9 CB,W.Disney'sXmas Parade('57) 300.00
1 CB,W.Disney's Christmas in Disneyland (1957) 400.00
1 CB,W.Disney's Disneyland Birthday Party (1958) 400.00
1 W.Disney's Donald and Mickey in Disneyland (1958). 175.00
1 W.Disney's Donald Duck Beach Party (1954). 225.00
2 W.Disney's Donald Duck Beach Party (1955). 175.00
3 W.Disney's Donald Duck Beach Party (1956). 175.00
4 W.Disney's Donald Duck Beach Party (1957). 175.00
5 W.Disney's Donald Duck Beach Party (1958). 175.00
6 W.Disney's Donald Duck Beach Party (1959). 175.00
1 W.Disney's Donald Duck Fun Book (1954). 600.00
2 W.Disney's Donald Duck Fun Book (1954). 550.00
1 W.Disney's Donald Duck in Disneyland (1955). 200.00
1 W.Disney's Huey, Dewey and Louie (1958) 150.00
1 W.Disney's DavyCrockett('55) . 135.00
1 W.Disney's Lady and the Tramp (1955) 275.00
1 CB,W.Disney's Mickey Mouse Almanac (1957) 400.00
1 W.Disney's Mickey Mouse Birthday Party (1953) 500.00
1 W.Disney's Mickey Mouse Club Parade (1955) 400.00
1 W.Disney's Mickey Mouse in Fantasyland (1957). 200.00
1 W.Disney's Mickey Mouse in Frontierland (1956) 200.00
1 W.Disney's Summer Fun('58) . 200.00
2 CB,W.Disney'sSummer Fun('59) 200.00
1 W.Disney's Peter Pan Treasure Chest (1953). . . . 1,600.00
1 Disney Silly Symphonies('52) . 450.00
2 Disney Silly Symphonies('53) . 400.00
3 Disney Silly Symphonies('54) . 350.00
4 Disney Silly Symphonies('54) . 350.00
5 Disney Silly Symphonies('55) . 300.00
6 Disney Silly Symphonies('56) . 300.00
7 Disney Silly Symphonies('57) . 300.00
8 Disney Silly Symphonies('58) . 300.00
9 Disney Silly Symphonies('59) . 300.00
1 Disney SleepingBeauty('59) . . 450.00
1 CB,W.Disney's Uncle Scrooge Goes to Disneyland (1957) . . 400.00
1 W.Disney's Vacation in Disneyland (1958) 175.00
1 CB,Disney's Vacation Parade('50) 1,300.00
2 Disney'sVacation Parade('51) . 450.00
3 Disney'sVacation Parade('52) . 225.00
4 Disney'sVacation Parade('53) . 225.00
5 Disney'sVacation Parade('54) . 225.00
6 Disney's Picnic Party (1955) . . 175.00
7 Disney's Picnic Party (1956) . . 175.00
8 CB,Disney's Picnic Party (1957) 350.00

DELL JUNIOR TREASURY

1 W.Disney's Alice in Wonderland (1955) 85.00

WALT DISNEY PRESENTS

Dell Publishing Co.
June–Aug., 1952

1 Ph(c), Four Color 75.00
2 Ph(c) 50.00
3 Ph(c) 50.00
4 Ph(c) 50.00
5 and 6 Ph(c). . . . . @50.00

WAMBI JUNGLE BOY

Fiction House Magazines
Spring, 1942

1 HcK,HcK(c),Vengence of the Beasts 750.00
2 HcK,HcK(c),Lair of the Killer Rajah 425.00
3 HcK,HcK(c) 250.00
4 HcK,HcK(c),The Valley of the Whispering Drums 175.00
5 HcK,HcK(c),Swampland Safari 175.00
6 Taming of the Tigress 125.00
7 Duel of the Congo Kings 125.00
8 AB(c),Friend of the Animals . . 125.00
9 Quest of the Devils Juju 125.00
10 Friend of the Animals. 100.00
11 . . . . 100.00
12 Curse of the Jungle Jewels . . 100.00
13 New Adventures of Wambi. . . 100.00
14 . . . . 100.00
15 The Leopard Legions. 100.00
16 . . . . 100.00
17 Beware Bwana! 100.00
18 Ogg the Great Bull Ape, Winter, 1952. . . . . 100.00

WANTED COMICS

Toytown Comics/ Orbit Publications
Sept.–Oct., 1947

9 Victor Everhart 150.00
10 Carlo Banone. 100.00
11 Dwight Band 100.00
12 Ralph Roe 110.00
13 James Spencer;Drug 110.00
14 John "Jiggs" Sullivan;Drug . . . 110.00
15 Harry Dunlap;Drug. 65.00
16 Jack Parisi;Drug 75.00
17 Herber Ayers;Drug. 75.00
18 Satan's Cigarettes;Drug 175.00
19 Jackson Stringer 65.00
20 George Morgan 65.00
21 BK,Paul Wilson 75.00
22. . . . . 75.00
23 George Elmo Wells 50.00
24 BK,Bruce Cornett;Drug 75.00
25 Henry Anger 50.00
26 John Wormly 50.00
27 Death Always Knocks Twice . . 50.00
28 Paul H. Payton 50.00
29 Hangmans Holiday 50.00
30 George Lee 50.00
31 M Consolo 50.00
32 William Davis. 50.00
33 The Web of Davis 50.00
34 Dead End 50.00
35 Glen Roy Wright 65.00
36 SSh,SSh(c),Bernard Lee Thomas 50.00
37 SSh,SSh(c),Joseph M. Moore . 50.00
38 SSh,SSh(c) 50.00
39 The Horror Weed;Drug. 100.00
40. . . . . 50.00
41. . . . . 50.00
42. . . . . 50.00
43. . . . . 50.00
44. . . . . 50.00
45 Killers on the Loose;Drug. 60.00
46 Chalres Edward Crews 50.00
47 . . . . 50.00
48 SSh,SSh(c) 50.00
49 . . . . 50.00
50 JB(c),Make Way for Murder . . 100.00
51 JB(c),Dope Addict on a Holiday of Murder;Drug. 75.00
52 The Cult of Killers; Classic Drug. 75.00
53 April, 1953. . . . . 50.00

WAR AGAINST CRIME

L.L. Publishing Co.
(E.C. Comics) Spring, 1948

1 Grl 600.00
2 Grl,Guilty of Murder 300.00
3 JCr(c) 300.00
4 AF,JCr(c) 275.00
5 JCr(c) 275.00
6 AF,JCr(c) 275.00
7 AF,JCr(c) 275.00
8 AF,JCr(c) 275.00
9 AF,JCr(c),The Kid 275.00
10 JCr(c),I:Vault Keeper 1,700.00
11 JCr(c) 1,000.00

GOLDEN AGE

The Vault of Horror #25
© E.C. Comics

Becomes:

VAULT OF HORROR

12 AF,JCr,JCr(c),Wax Museum 4,500.00
13 AF,WW,JCr(c),Grl,Drug 900.00
14 AF,WW,JCr(c),Grl 750.00
15 AF,JCr,JCr(c),Grl,JKa. 650.00
16 Grl,JKa,JCr,JCr(c) 550.00
17 JDa,Grl,JKa,JCr,JCr(c). 400.00
18 JDa,Grl,JKa,JCr,JCr(c). 400.00
19 JDa,Grl,JKa,JCr,JCr(c). 400.00
20 JDa,Grl,JKa,JCr,JCr(c). 300.00
21 JDa,Grl,JKa,JCr,JCr(c). 300.00
22 JDa,JKa,JCr,JCr(c) 300.00
23 JDa,Grl,JCr,JCr(c). 300.00
24 JDa,Grl,JO,JCr,JCr(c) 300.00
25 JDa,Grl,JKa,JCr,JCr(c). 300.00
26 JDa,Grl,JCr,JCr(c). 300.00
27 JDa,Grl,JCr,GE,JCr(c) 250.00
28 JDa,Grl,JCr,JCr(c). 250.00
29 JDa,Grl,JCr,JKa,JCr(c),
JDa,Grl,JCr,JCr(c)
Bradbury adapt. 250.00
30 JDa,Grl,JCr,JCr(c). 250.00
31 JDa,Grl,JCr,JCr(c),
Bradbury adapt. 225.00
32 JDa,Grl,JCr,JCr(c). 225.00
33 JDa,Grl,RC,JCr(c) 225.00
34 JDa,Grl,JCr,RC,JCr(c) 225.00
35 JDa,Grl,JCr,JCr(c). 225.00
36 JDa,Grl,JCr,BK,JCr(c),Drug . . 225.00
37 JDa,Grl,JCr,AW,JCr(c)
Hanging 225.00
38 JDa,Grl,JCr,BK,JCr(c) 225.00
39 GRi,JCr,BK,RC,JCr(c)
Bondage(c). 225.00
40 Jan., 1955, Grl,JCr,BK,JO
JCr(c). 250.00

WAR BATTLES
Harvey Publications
Feb., 1952

1 BP,Devils of the Deep 100.00
2 BP,A Present From Benny 50.00
3 BP 45.00
4 . . . . 45.00
5 . . . . 45.00
6 HN 45.00
7 BP 50.00
8 . . . . 45.00
9 Dec., 1953 . . . . 45.00

WAR BIRDS
Fiction House Magazines, 1952

1 Willie the Washout 100.00
2 Mystery MIGs of Kwanjamu . . . 60.00
3 thru 6 . . . . @50.00
7 Winter, 1953,Across the
Wild Yalu 50.00

WAR COMICS
Dell Publishing Co.
May, 1940

1 AMc,Sky Hawk 450.00
2 O:Greg Gildam 250.00
3 . . . . 150.00
4 O:Night Devils 200.00

WAR HEROES
Dell Publishing Co.
July–Sept., 1942

1 Gen. Douglas MacArthur (c) . . 175.00
2 . . . . 100.00
3 . . . . 75.00
4 A:Gremlins 125.00
5 . . . . 55.00
6 thru 11 . . . . @50.00

WAR HEROES
Ace Magazines
May, 1952

1 Always Comin' 75.00
2 LC,The Last Red Tank 40.00
3 You Got it 35.00
4 A Red Patrol 35.00
5 Hustle it Up 35.00
6 LC,Hang on Pal 40.00
7 . . . . 40.00
8 LC,April, 1953 . . . . 40.00

WARPATH
Key Publications/ Stanmore
Nov., 1954

1 Red Men Raid 75.00
2 AH(c),Braves Battle 40.00
3 April, 1955 . . . . 40.00

WARRIOR COMICS
H.C. Blackerby, 1944

1 Ironman wing Brady 150.00

WAR SHIPS
Dell Publishing Co., 1942

1 AMc 125.00

WAR STORIES
Dell Publishing Co., 1942

5 O:The Whistler 175.00
6 A:Night Devils. 125.00
7 A:Night Devils 125.00
8 A:Night Devils 125.00

WARTIME ROMANCES
St. John Publishing Co.
July, 1951

1 MB(c),MB 225.00
2 MB(c),MB 175.00
3 MB(c),MB 150.00
4 MB(c),MB 150.00
5 MB(c),MB 125.00
6 MB(c),MB 150.00
7 MB(c),MB 125.00
8 MB(c),MB 125.00
9 MB(c),MB 100.00
10 MB(c),MB 100.00
11 MB(c),MB. 100.00
12 Mb(c),MB. 100.00
13 MB(c) 60.00
14 MB(c) 60.00
15 MB(c) 60.00
16 MB(c),MB 60.00
17 MB(c) 60.00
18 MB(c),MB 60.00

WAR VICTORY COMICS
U.S. Treasury/War Victory/ Harvey Publ.
Summer, 1942

1 Savings Bond Promo with
Top Syndicated Cartoonists,
benefit USO 275.00

Becomes:

WAR VICTORY ADVENTURES

2 BP,2nd Front Comics 150.00
3 BP,F:Capt Cross of the
Red Cross 125.00

WEB OF EVIL
Comic Magazines, Inc.
(Quality Comics Group)
Nov., 1952

1 Custodian of the Dead 450.00
2 JCo,Hangmans Horror 300.00
3 JCo 300.00
4 JCo,JCo(c),Monsters of
the Mist 300.00
5 JCo,JCo(c),The Man who Died
Twice,Electric Chair(c) 350.00
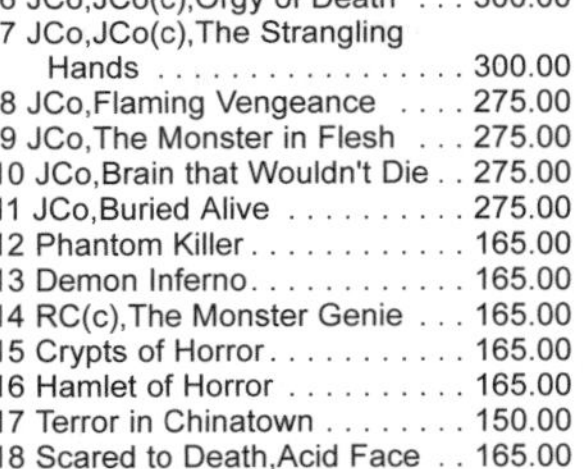
6 JCo,JCo(c),Orgy of Death . . . 300.00
7 JCo,JCo(c),The Strangling
Hands 300.00
8 JCo,Flaming Vengeance 275.00
9 JCo,The Monster in Flesh . . . 275.00
10 JCo,Brain that Wouldn't Die . . 275.00
11 JCo,Buried Alive 275.00
12 Phantom Killer 165.00
13 Demon Inferno 165.00
14 RC(c),The Monster Genie . . . 165.00
15 Crypts of Horror 165.00
16 Hamlet of Horror 165.00
17 Terror in Chinatown 150.00
18 Scared to Death,Acid Face . . 165.00

Web of Evil #4
© Quality Comics Group

19 Demon of the Pit . . . 150.00
20 Man Made Terror . . . 150.00
21 Dec., 1954, Death's Ambush . 150.00

WEB OF MYSTERY
A.A. Wyn Publ.
(Ace Magazines) Feb., 1951

1 MSy,Venom of the Vampires . 400.00
2 MSy,Legacy of the Accursed . 225.00
3 MSy,The Violin Curse . . . 200.00
4 GC . . . 200.00
5 . . . 200.00
6 LC . . . 200.00
7 MSy . . . 200.00
8 LC,LC(c),MSy,The Haunt of
Death Lake . . . 200.00
9 LC,LC(c) . . . 200.00
10 . . . 200.00
11 MSy . . . 200.00
12 LC . . . 175.00
13 LC,LC(c) . . . 175.00
14 MSy . . . 175.00
15 . . . 175.00
16 . . . 175.00
17 LC,LC(c) . . . 175.00
18 LC . . . 175.00
19 LC . . . 175.00
20 LC . . . 175.00
21 MSy . . . 175.00
22 . . . 175.00
23 . . . 175.00
24 LC . . . 175.00
25 LC . . . 175.00
26 . . . 175.00
27 LC . . . 175.00
28 RP,1st Issue under Comics
Code Authority . . . 150.00
29 MSy,Sept., 1955 . . . 150.00

WEDDING BELLS
Quality Comics Group
Feb., 1954

1 OW . . . 100.00
2 . . . 60.00
3 . . . 35.00
4 . . . 35.00
5 . . . 35.00
6 . . . 35.00
7 . . . 35.00
8 . . . 35.00
9 Comics Code . . . 35.00
10 BWa . . . 100.00
11 . . . 30.00
12 . . . 25.00
13 . . . 25.00
14 . . . 25.00
15 MB(c) . . . 30.00
16 MB(c),MB . . . 60.00
17 . . . 25.00
18 MB . . . 30.00
19 MB . . . 30.00

WEEKENDER, THE
Rucker Publishing Co.
Sept., 1945

3 . . . 125.00
4 . . . 100.00
2-1(5)JCo,WMc,Jan., 1946 . . . 145.00

WEIRD ADVENTURES
P.L. Publishing
May, 1951

1 MB,Missing Diamonds . . . 400.00
2 Puppet Peril . . . 325.00
3 Blood Vengeance,
Oct. 1951 . . . 300.00

WEIRD ADVENTURES
Approved Comics
(Ziff-Davis)
July–Aug., 1951

10 P(c),Seeker from Beyond . . . 300.00

WEIRD CHILLS
Key Publications
July, 1954

1 MBi(c),BW . . . 550.00
2 Eye Torture(c) . . . 525.00
3 Bondage(c),Nov., 1954 . . . 325.00

Weird Comics #9
© Fox Features Syndicate

WEIRD COMICS
Fox Features Syndicate
April, 1940

1 LF(c),Bondage(c),B:Birdman,
Thor,Sorceress of Doom,
BlastBennett,Typhon,Voodoo
Man, Dr.Mortal . . . 4,000.00
2 LF(c),Mummy(c) . . . 1,700.00
3 JSm(c) . . . 1,000.00
4 JSm(c) . . . 1,000.00
5 Bondage(c),I:Dart,Ace;
E:Thor . . . 1,000.00
6 Dart & Ace(c) . . . 900.00
7 Battle of Kooba . . . 900.00
8 B:Panther Woman,Dynamo,
The Eagle . . . 900.00
9 V:Pirates . . . 700.00
10 A:Navy Jones . . . 700.00
11 Dart & Ace(c) . . . 500.00
12 Dart & Ace(c) . . . 500.00
13 Dart & Ace(c) . . . 500.00
14 The Rage(c) . . . 500.00
15 Dart & Ace (c) . . . 500.00
16 Flag,The Encore(c) . . . 500.00
17 O:Black Rider . . . 525.00
18 . . . 500.00
19 . . . 500.00
20 Jan., 1941,I'm The Master
of Life and Death . . . 500.00

WEIRD FANTASY
I.C. Publishing Co.
(E.C. Comics)
May–June, 1950

13(1)AF,HK,JKa,WW,AF(c),
Roger Harvey's Brain . . . 1,700.00
14(2)AF,HK,JKa,WW,AF(c),
Cosmic Ray Brain Explosion. 700.00
15(3)AF,HK,JKa,WW,AF(c),Your
Destination is the Moon . . . 550.00
16(4)AF,HK,JKa,WW,AF(c) . . . 525.00
17(5)AF,HK,JKa,WW,AF(c),Not
Made by Human Hands . . . 450.00
6 AF,HK,JKa,WW,AF(c) . . . 325.00
7 AF,JKa,WW,AF(c) . . . 325.00
8 AF,JKa,WW,AF(c) . . . 325.00
9 AF,Jka,WW,JO,AF(c) . . . 325.00
10 AF,Jka,WW,JO,AF(c) . . . 350.00
11 AF,Jka,WW,JO,AF(c) . . . 275.00
12 AF,Jka,WW,JO,AF(c) . . . 275.00
13 AF,Jka,WW,JO,AF(c) . . . 275.00
14 AF,JKa,WW,JO,AW&FF,AF(c) 350.00
15 AF,JKa,JO,AW&RKr,AF(c),
Bondage(c) . . . 275.00
16 AF,JKa,JO,AW&RKr,AF(c) . . . 250.00
17 AF,JOP,JKa,AF(c),Bradbury . 250.00
18 AF,JO,JKa,AF(c),Bradbury . . . 250.00
19 JO,JKa,JO(c),Bradbury . . . 250.00
20 JO,JKa,FF,AF(c) . . . 250.00
21 JO,JKa,AW&FF(c) . . . 400.00
22 JO,JKa,JO(c),Nov.,1953 . . . 200.00

WEIRD HORRORS
St. John Publishing Co.
June, 1952

1 GT,Dungeon of the Doomed . 400.00
2 Strangest Music Ever . . . 300.00
3 PAM,Strange Fakir From
the Orient . . . 300.00
4 Murderers Knoll . . . 200.00
5 Phantom Bowman . . . 200.00
6 Monsters from Outer Space . . 350.00
7 LC,Deadly Double . . . 375.00
8 JKu,JKu(c),Bloody Yesterday . 300.00
9 JKu,JKu(c),Map Of Doom . . . 300.00
Becomes:

NIGHTMARE

10 JKu(c),The Murderer's Mask . 450.00
11 BK,Ph(c),Fangs of Death . . . 300.00
12 JKu(c),The Forgotten Mask . . 275.00
13 BP,Princess of the Sea . . . 250.00
Becomes:

AMAZING GHOST STORIES

14 EK,MB(c), . . . 225.00
15 BP . . . 150.00
16 Feb., 1955, EK,JKu . . . 175.00

WEIRD MYSTERIES
Gilmore Publications
Oct., 1952

1 BW(c) . . . 600.00
2 BWi . . . 850.00
3 Severed Heads(c) . . . 400.00
4 BW,Human headed ants(c) . . . 700.00
5 BW,Brains From Head(c) . . . 700.00
6 Severed Head(c) . . . 400.00
7 Used in "Seduction" . . . 600.00
8 The One That Got Away . . . 400.00
9 Epitaph,Cyclops . . . 400.00
10 The Ruby . . . 325.00
11 Voodoo Dolls . . . 300.00
12 Sept., 1954 . . . 300.00

WEIRD SCIENCE
E.C. Comics, 1950

1 AF(c),AF,JKu,HK,WW . . . 1,700.00
2 AF(c),AF,JKu,HK,WW,Flying
Saucers(c) . . . 800.00
3 AF(c),AF,JKu,HK . . . 750.00
4 AF(c),AF,JKu,HK . . . 750.00
5 AF(c),AF,JKu,HK,WW,
Atomic Bomb(c) . . . 425.00

6 AF(c),AF,JKu,HK 400.00
7 AF(c),AF,JKu,HK,Classic(c). . . 425.00
8 AF(c),AF,JKu 400.00
9 WW(c),JKu,Classic(c) 425.00
10 WW(c),JKu,JO,Classic(c). . . . 425.00
11 AF,JKu,Space war 275.00
12 WW(c),JKu,JO,Classic(c). . . . 275.00
13 WW(c),JKu,JO, ... 300.00
14 WW(c),WW,JO. 300.00
15 WW(c),WW,JO,GRi,AW, RKr,JKa 300.00
16 WW(c),WW,JO,AW,RKr,JKa. . 300.00
17 WW(c),WW,JO,AW,RKr,JKa. . 300.00
18 WW(c),WW,JO,AW,RKr, JKa,Atomic Bomb. 275.00
19 WW(c),WW,JO,AW, FF,Horror(c) 400.00
20 WW(c),WW,JO,AW,FF,JKa. . . 400.00
21 WW(c),WW,JO,AW,FF,JKa. . . 400.00
22 WW(c),WW,JO,AW,FF 400.00

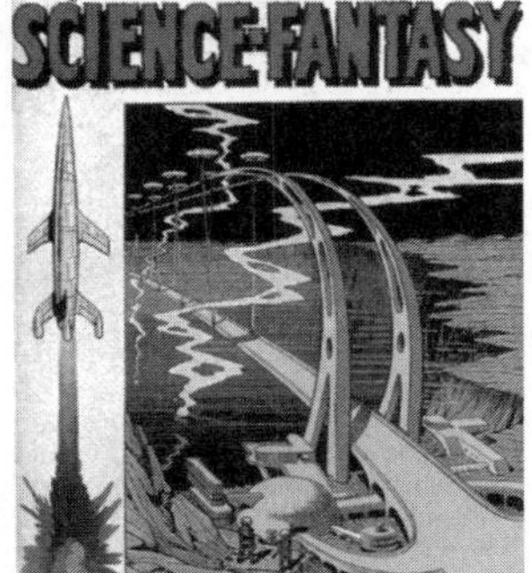

Weird Science Fantasy #28
© E.C. Comics

Becomes:

WEIRD SCIENCE FANTASY

23 WW(c),WW,AW,BK 275.00
24 WW,AW,BK,Classic(c) 250.00
25 WW,AW,BK,Classic(c) 300.00
26 AF(c),WW,RC, Flying Saucer(c). 250.00
27 WW(c),WW,RC 275.00
28 AF(c),WW 300.00
29 AF(c),WW,Classic(c) 500.00

Becomes:

INCREDIBLE SCIENCE FANTASY

30 WW,JDa(c),BK,AW,RKr,JO . . 300.00
31 WW,JDa(c),BK,AW,RKr 325.00
32 JDa(c),BK,WW,JO 325.00
33 WW(c),BK,WW,JO. 325.00

WEIRD TALES OF THE FUTURE

S.P.M. Publ./
Aragon Publications
March, 1952

1 RA 650.00
2 BW,BW(c) 1,000.00
3 BW,BW(c) 950.00
4 BW,BW(c) 700.00
5 BW,BW(c),Jumpin' Jupiter Lingerie(c) 950.00
6 Bondage(c) 400.00
7 BW,Devil(c). 600.00
8 July–Aug. 1953 . . . . 500.00

WEIRD TERROR

Allen Hardy Associates
(Comic Media) Sept., 1952

1 RP,DH,DH(c),Dungeon of the Doomed;Hitler 400.00
2 HcK(c),PAM 275.00
3 PAM,DH,DH(c) 275.00
4 PAM,DH,DH(c) 300.00
5 PAM,DH,RP,DH(c),Hanging(c) 250.00
6 DH,RP,DH(c),Step into My Parlour 275.00
7 DH,PAM,DH(c),Blood o/t Bats . 250.00
8 DH,RP,DH(c),Step into My Parlour 275.00
9 DH,PAM,DH(c),The Fleabite . 250.00
10 DH,BP,RP,DH(c) 250.00
11 DH,DH(c),Satan's Love Call . . 275.00
12 DH,DH(c),King Whitey 250.00
13 DH,DH(c),Sept., 1954, Wings of Death. 250.00

WEIRD THRILLERS

Approved Comics
(Ziff-Davis)
Sept.–Oct., 1951

1 Ph(c),Monsters & The Model. . 600.00
2 AW,P(c),The Last Man 450.00
3 AW,P(c),Princess o/t Sea 600.00
4 AW,P(c),The Widows Lover . . 425.00
5 BP,Oct., 1952,AW,P(c), Wings of Death 450.00

WESTERN ACTION THRILLERS

Dell Publishing Co.
April, 1937

1 . . . . 700.00

WESTERN ADVENTURES COMICS

A.A. Wyn, Inc.
(Ace Magazines) Oct., 1948

N#(1)Injun Gun Bait 175.00
N#(2)Cross-Draw Kid 100.00
N#(3)Outlaw Mesa 100.00
4 Sheriff 75.00
5 . . . . 75.00
6 Rip Roaring Adventure 75.00

Becomes:

WESTERN LOVE TRAILS

7 . . . . 90.00
8 Maverick Love 75.00
9 March, 1950 . . . . 60.00

WESTERN BANDIT TRAILS

St. John Publishing Co.
Jan., 1949

1 GT,MB(c) 200.00
2 GT,MB(c) 150.00
3 GT,MB,MB(c),Gingham Fury . 175.00

WESTERN CRIME-BUSTERS

Trojan Magazines
Sept., 1950

1 Gunslingin' Galoots 250.00
2 K-Bar Kate 125.00
3 Wilma West 125.00
4 Bob Dale 125.00
5 Six-Gun Smith 125.00
6 WW 250.00
7 WW,Wells Fargo Robbery . . . 250.00
8 . . . . 125.00
9 WW,Lariat Lucy 250.00
10 WW,April 1952;Tex Gordon . . 250.00

WESTERN CRIME CASES (see WHITE RIDER)

WESTERNER, THE

Wanted Comics Group/
Toytown Publ.
June, 1948

14 F:Jack McCall 100.00
15 F:Bill Jamett. 50.00
16 F:Tom McLowery 50.00
17 F:Black Bill Desmond. 50.00
18 BK,F:Silver Dollar Dalton 75.00
19 MMe,F:Jess Meeton 45.00
20 . . . . 45.00
21 BK,MMe 75.00
22 BK,MMe 75.00
23 BK,MMe 75.00
24 BK,MMe 75.00
25 O,I,B:Calamity Jane. 75.00
26 BK,F:The Widowmaker 85.00
27 . . . . 100.00
28 thru 31. . . . . @35.00
32 E:Calamity Jane 35.00
33 A:Quest. 35.00
34 . . . . 35.00
35 SSh(c). 35.00
36 . . . . 35.00
37 Lobo-Wolf Boy. 35.00
38 . . . . 35.00
39 . . . . 35.00
40 SSh(c). 35.00
41 Dec., 1951. . . . . 35.00

WESTERN FIGHTERS

Hillman Periodicals
April–May, 1948

1 S&K(c) 250.00
2 BF(c) 75.00
3 BF(c) 65.00
4 BK,BF 75.00
5 . . . . 45.00
6 . . . . 45.00
7 BK 75.00
8 . . . . 45.00
9 . . . . 45.00
10 BK. 75.00
11 AMC&FF 225.00
2-1 BK 75.00
2-2 BP 40.00
2-3 thru 2-12 . . . . @30.00
3-1 thru 3-11 . . . . @30.00
3-12 BK 60.00
4-1 . . . . 30.00
4-2 BK 65.00
4-3 BK 65.00
4-4 BK 65.00
4-5 BK 65.00
4-6 BK 65.00
4-7 March–April 1953 . . . . 30.00

WESTERN FRONTIER

P.L. Publishers
(Approved Comics)
May, 1951

1 Flaming Vengeance 100.00

2 . . . . 50.00
3 Death Rides the Iron Horse . . . 40.00
4 thru 6 . . . . @40.00
7 1952. . . . . 40.00

WESTERN HEARTS
Standard Magazine, Inc.
Dec., 1949

1 Ph(c),JSe 150.00
2 Ph(c),AW,FF. 165.00
3 Ph(c) 85.00
4 Ph(c),JSe,BE 85.00
5 Ph(c),JSe,BE 85.00
6 Ph(c),JSe,BE 85.00
7 Ph(c),JSe,BE 85.00
8 Ph(c) 100.00
9 Ph(c),JSe,BE 100.00
10 Ph(c),JSe,BE. 65.00

WESTERN LOVE
Feature Publications
(Prize Comics Group)
July–Aug., 1949

1 S&K 225.00
2 S&K 175.00
3 JSE,BE. 125.00
4 JSE,BE. 125.00
5 JSE,BE. 125.00

WESTERN PICTURE STORIES
Comics Magazine Co.
Feb., 1937

1 WE,Treachery Trail,
1st Western 1,400.00
2 WE,Weapons of the West . . . 850.00
3 WE,Dragon Pass 650.00
4 June, 1937,CavemanCowboy 650.00

WESTERN THRILLERS
Fox Features Syndicate
Aug., 1948

1 . . . . 400.00
2 . . . . 150.00
3 GT,RH(c) 135.00
4 . . . . 150.00
5 . . . . 150.00
6 June, 1949 . . . . 135.00

Becomes:

MY PAST CONFESSIONS

7 . . . . 100.00
8 . . . . 60.00
9 . . . . 60.00
10 . . . . 60.00
11. . . . . 90.00
12. . . . . 25.00

WESTERN TRUE CRIME
Fox Features Syndicate
Aug., 1948

1 . . . . 225.00
2 . . . . 175.00
3 . . . . 150.00
4 JCr. 175.00
5 . . . . 125.00
6 . . . . 125.00

Becomes:

MY CONFESSION

7 WW 200.00
8 WW,My Tarnished Reputation 150.00
9 I:Tormented Men 75.00
10 Feb., 1950,I Am Damaged
Goods 75.00

WHACK
St. John Publishing Co.
Dec., 1953

1 Steve Crevice,Flush Jordan
V:Bing(Crosby)The Merciful . 225.00
2 . . . . 125.00
3 F:Little Awful Fannie 125.00

WHAM COMICS
Centaur Publications
Nov., 1940

1 PG,The Sparkler & His
Disappearing Suit 1,300.00
2 Dec., 1940,PG,PG(C),
Men Turn into Icicles 1,000.00

Whirlwind Comics #3
© Fox Features Syndicate

WHIRLWIND COMICS
Nita Publications
June, 1940

1 F:The Cyclone 1,400.00
2 A:Scoops Hanlon,Cyclone(c). . 900.00
3 Sept., 1940,A:Magic
Mandarin,Cyclone(c). 850.00

WHITE PRINCESS OF THE JUNGLE
Avon Periodicals
July, 1951

1 EK(c),Terror Fangs 450.00
2 EK,EK(c),Jungle Vengeance . 300.00
3 EK,EK(c),The Blue Gorilla . . . 250.00
4 Fangs of the Swamp Beast . . 225.00
5 EK,Coils of the Tree Snake
Nov., 1952 . . . . 225.00

WHIZ COMICS
Fawcett Publications
Feb., 1940

1 O:Captain Marvel,B:Spy
Smasher,Golden Arrow,Dan
Dare, Scoop Smith,Ibis
the Invincible, Sivana . . . 65,000.00
2 . . . . 4,500.00
3 Make way for
Captain Marvel 4,000.00
4 Captain Marvel
Crashes Through 2,500.00
5 Captain Marvel
Scores Again! 2,000.00
6 Circus of Death 1,800.00
7 B:Dr Voodoo,Squadron
of Death 1,500.00
8 Saved by Captain Marvel! . . 1,400.00
9 MRa,Captain Marvel
on the Job 1,400.00
10 Battles the Winged Death . . 1,400.00
11 Hurray for Captain Marvel . . 1,000.00
12 Captain Marvel rides
the Engine of Doom. 1,000.00
13 Worlds Most Powerful Man! . . 950.00
14 Boomerangs the Torpedo. . . . 950.00
15 O:Sivana. 1,100.00
16 . . . . 1,100.00
17 Knocks out a Tank 1,100.00
18 V:Spy Smasher. 1,100.00
19 Crushes the Tiger Shark 700.00
20 V:Sivana 700.00
21 O:Lt. Marvels. 750.00
22 Mayan Temple 600.00
23 GT,A:Dr. Voodoo 600.00
24 . . . . 600.00
25 O&I:Captain Marvel Jr.,
Stops the Turbine of Death 5,500.00
26 . . . . 500.00
27 V:Death God of the Katonkas. 525.00
28 V:Mad Dervish of Ank-Har . . . 525.00
29 Three Lt. Marvels (c), Pan
American Olympics. 525.00
30 . . . . 500.00
31 Douglass MacArthur&Spy
Smasher(c). 425.00
32 Spy Smasher(c). 425.00
33 Spy Smasher(c). 500.00
34 Three Lt. Marvels (c) 350.00
35 Capt. Marvel and the
Three Fates 400.00
36 Haunted Hallowe'en Hotel . . . 350.00
37 Return of the Trolls 350.00
38 Grand Steeplechase 350.00
39 A Nazi Utopia 350.00
40 A:Three Lt. Marvels, The
Earth's 4 Corners 350.00
41 Captain Marvel 1,000 years
from Now 250.00
42 Returns in Time Chair 250.00
43 V:Sinister Spies,
Spy Smasher(c) 250.00
44 Life Story of Captain Marvel. . 275.00
45 Cures His Critics 250.00
46. . . . . 250.00
47 Captain Marvel needs
a Birthday. 250.00
48 . . . . 250.00
49 Writes a Victory song 250.00
50 Captain Marvel's most
embarrassing moment 250.00
51 Judges the Ugly-
Beauty Contest. 225.00
52 V:Sivana, Chooses
His Birthday 225.00
53 Captain Marvel fights
Billy Batson 225.00
54 Jack of all Trades. 225.00
55 Family Tree 225.00
56 Tells what the Future Will Be . 225.00
57 A:Spy Smasher,Golden Arrow,
Ibis. 225.00
58 . . . . 225.00
59 V:Sivana's Twin 225.00
60 Missing Person's Machine . . . 225.00
61 Gets a first name 200.00
62 Plays in a Band 200.00
63 Great Indian Rope Trick. 200.00
64 Suspected of Murder 200.00
65 Lamp of Diogenes 200.00
66 The Trial of Mr. Morris!. 200.00
67 . . . . 200.00
68 Laugh Lotion, V:Sivana 200.00
69 Mission to Mercury. 200.00

GOLDEN AGE

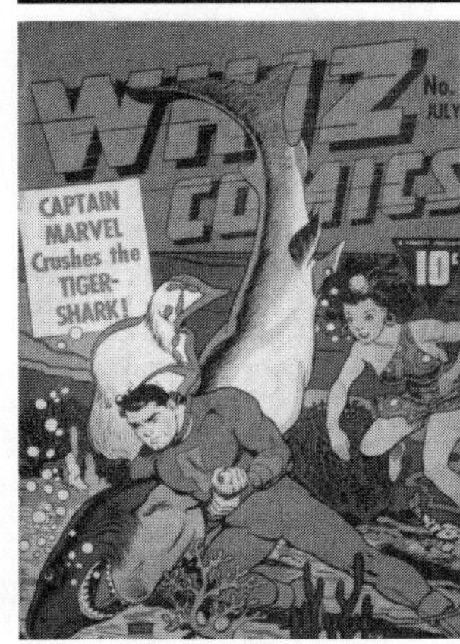

Whiz Comics #19
© Fawcett Publications

70 Climbs the World's Mightiest Mountain 200.00
71 Strange Magician. 175.00
72 V:The Man of the Future 175.00
73 In Ogre Land 175.00
74 Old Man River 175.00
75 The City Olympics 175.00
76 Spy Smasher become Crime Smasher 175.00
77 . . . . 175.00
78 . . . . 175.00
79 . . . . 175.00
80 . . . . 175.00
81. . . . . 175.00
82 The Atomic Ship 175.00
83 Magic Locket 175.00
84 . . . . 175.00
85 The Clock of San Lojardo. . . . 175.00
86 V:Sinister Sivanas 175.00
87 The War on Olympia 175.00
88 The Wonderful Magic Carpet . 175.00
89 Webs of Crime. 175.00
90 . . . . 175.00
91 Infinity (c). 175.00
92 . . . . 175.00
93 Captain America become a Hobo? 175.00
94 V:Sivana 175.00
95 Captain Marvel is grounded . . 175.00
96 The Battle Between Buildings. 175.00
97 Visits Mirage City. 175.00
98 . . . . 175.00
99 V:Menace in the Mountains . . 175.00
100 . . . . 225.00
101 . . . . 165.00
102 A:Commando Yank 165.00
103 . . . . 165.00
104 . . . . 165.00
105 . . . . 165.00
106 A:Bulletman 165.00
107 The Great Experiment 200.00
108 thru 114 . . . . @165.00
115 The Marine Invasion. 165.00
116 . . . . 165.00
117 V:Sivana 165.00
118 . . . . 165.00
119 . . . . 165.00
120 . . . . 165.00
121 . . . . 165.00
122 V:Sivana 165.00
123. . . . . 165.00
124 . . . . 165.00
125 Olympic Games of the Gods 165.00
126 . . . . 165.00
127 . . . . 165.00
128 . . . . 165.00
129 . . . . 165.00
130 . . . . 165.00
131 The Television Trap 165.00
132 thru 142 . . . . @165.00
143 Mystery of the Flying Studio. 165.00
144 V:The Disaster Master 165.00
145 . . . . 165.00
146 . . . . 165.00
147 . . . . 165.00
148 . . . . 165.00
149 . . . . 165.00
150 V:Bug Bombs 165.00
151 . . . . 165.00
152 . . . . 165.00
153 V:The Death Horror 225.00
154 Horror Tale, I:Dr.Death 225.00
155 V:Legend Horror,Dr.Death . . 250.00

WHODUNIT?
D.S. Publishing Co.
Aug.–Sept., 1948

1 MB,Weeping Widow 200.00
2 Diploma For Death 100.00
3 Dec.–Jan., 1949 . . . . 100.00

WHO IS NEXT?
Standard Comics
Jan., 1953

5 ATh,RA,Don't Let Me Kill 150.00

WILD BILL ELLIOT
Dell Publishing Co.
May, 1950

(1) *see Dell Four Color #278*
2 . . . . 65.00
3 thru 5 . . . . @50.00
6 thru 10 . . . . @50.00
(11-12) *see Four Color #472, 520*
13 thru 17 . . . . @45.00

WILD BILL HICKOK AND JINGLES (see YELLOWJACKET COMICS)

WILBUR COMICS
MLJ Magazines
(Archie Publications)
Summer, 1944

1 F:Wilbur Wilkin-America's Song of Fun 400.00
2 . . . . 200.00
3 . . . . 175.00
4 . . . . 150.00
5 I:Katy Keene 600.00
6 . . . . 150.00
7 . . . . 150.00
8 . . . . 150.00
9 . . . . 150.00
10 . . . . 150.00
11 thru 20 . . . . @100.00
21 thru 30 . . . . @50.00
31 thru 40 . . . . @40.00
41 thru 50 . . . . @30.00
51 thru 89 . . . . @25.00
90 Oct., 1965 . . . . 25.00

WILD BILL HICKOK
Avon Periodicals
Sept.–Oct., 1949

1 GRI(c),Frontier Fighter 175.00
2 Ph(c),Gambler's Guns 100.00
3 Ph(c),Great Stage Robbery . . . 50.00
4 Ph(c),Guerilla Gunmen 50.00
5 Ph(c),Return of the Renegade . 50.00
6 EK,EK(c),Along the Apache Trail 50.00
7 EK,EK(c)Outlaws of Hell's Bend 50.00
8 Ph(c),The Border Outlaws 50.00
9 PH(c),Killers From Texas 50.00
10 Ph(c) 50.00
11 EK,EK(c),The Hell Riders. 50.00
12 EK,EK(c),The Lost Gold MIne . 60.00
13 EK,EK(c),Bloody Canyon Massacre 60.00
14 . . . . 60.00
15 . . . . 35.00
16 JKa 50.00
17 thru 23 . . . . @40.00
24 EK,EK(c) 50.00
25 EK,EK(c) 50.00
26 EK,EK(c) 50.00
27 EK,EK(c) 50.00
28 EK,EK(c),May–June, 1956. . . . 50.00

WILD BOY OF THE CONGO
Approved (Ziff-Davis)/
St. John Publ. Co.
Feb.–March, 1951

10(1)NS,PH(c),Bondage(c),The Gorilla God. 175.00
11(2)NS,Ph(c),Star of the Jungle. 100.00
12(3)NS,Ph(c),Ice-Age Men 100.00
4 NS.Ph(c),Tyrant of the Jungle 125.00
5 NS,Ph(c),The White Robe of Courage 75.00
6 NS,Ph(c) 75.00
7 MB,EK.Ph(c) 100.00
8 Ph(c),Man-Eater 75.00
9 Ph(c),Killer Leopard 75.00
10 . . . . 75.00
11 MB(c). 100.00
12 MB(c) 100.00
13 MB(c) 100.00
14 MB(c) 100.00
15 June, 1955 . . . . 60.00

WINGS COMICS
Wings Publ.
(Fiction House Magazines)
Sept., 1940

1 HcK,AB,GT,Ph(c),B:Skull Squad, Clipper Kirk,Suicide Smith, War Nurse,Phantom Falcons, GreasemonkeyGriffin,Parachute Patrol,Powder Burns 2,000.00
2 HCk,AB,GT,Bomber Patrol . . . 750.00
3 HcK,AB,GT. 500.00
4 HcK,AB,GT,B:Spitfire Ace 500.00
5 HcK,AB,GT,Torpedo Patrol . . . 500.00
6 HcK,AB,GT,Bombs for Berlin . 450.00
7 HcK,AB 450.00
8 HcK,AB,The Wings of Doom . 450.00
9 Sky-Wolf 425.00
10 The Upside Down 425.00
11 . . . . 400.00
12 Fury of the fire Boards 400.00
13 Coffin Slugs For The Luftwaffe 400.00
14 Stuka Buster 400.00
15 Boomerang Blitz 400.00
16 O:Capt.Wings 450.00
17 Skyway to Death 300.00
18 Horsemen of the Sky 300.00
19 Nazi Spy Trap 300.00
20 The One Eyed Devil. 300.00

GOLDEN AGE

21 Chute Troop Tornado 275.00
22 TNT for Tokyo 275.00
23 RP,Battling Eagles of Bataan . 275.00
24 RP,The Death of a Hero 275.00
25 RP,Suicide Squeeze 275.00
26 Tojo's Eagle Trap 275.00
27 Blb,Mile High Gauntlet 275.00
28 Blb,Tail Gun Tornado 275.00
29 Blb,Buzzards from Berlin 275.00
30 Blb,Monsters of the Stratosphere 225.00
31 BLb,Sea Hawks away 225.00
32 BLb,Sky Mammoth 225.00
33 BLb,Roll Call of the Yankee Eagles 225.00
34 BLb,So Sorry,Mr Tojo 225.00
35 BLb,RWb,Hell's Lightning 225.00
36 RWb,The Crash-Master 225.00
37 RWb,Sneak Blitz 225.00
38 RWb,Rescue Raid of the Yank Eagle 225.00
39 RWb,Sky Hell/Pigboat Patrol . 225.00
40 RWb,Luftwaffe Gamble 225.00
41 RWb,.50 Caliber Justice 200.00
42 RWb,PanzerMeat forMosquito 200.00
43 RWb,Suicide Sentinels 200.00
44 RWb,Berlin Bombs Away 200.00
45 RWb,Hells Cargo 200.00
46 RWb,Sea-Hawk Patrol 200.00
47 RWb,Tojo's Tin Gibraltar 200.00
48 RWb 200.00
49 RWb,Rockets Away 200.00
50 RWb,Mission For a Madman . 200.00
51 RWb,Toll for a Typhoon 175.00
52 MB,Madam Marauder 175.00
53 MB,Robot Death Over Manhattan 175.00
54 MB,Juggernauts of Death 175.00
55 MB 175.00
56 MB,Sea Raiders Grave 175.00
57 MB,Yankee Warbirds over Tokyo 175.00
58 MB 175.00
59 MB,Prey of the Night Hawks . 175.00
60 MB,E:Skull Squad, Hell's Eyes 175.00
61 MB,Raiders o/t Purple Dawn . 150.00
62 Twilight of the Gods 150.00
63 Hara Kiri Rides the Skyways . 150.00
64 Taps For Tokyo 150.00
65 AB,Warhawk for the Kill 150.00
66 AB,B:Ghost Patrol 150.00
67 AB 150.00
68 AB,ClipperKirkBecomesPhantom Falcon;O:Phantom Falcon . . 150.00
69 AB,O:cont,Phantom Falcon . . 150.00
70 AB,N:Phantom Falcon; O:Final Phantom Falcon 150.00
71 Ghost Patrol becomes Ghost Squadron 150.00
72 V:Capt. Kamikaze 150.00
73 Hell & Stormoviks 150.00
74 BLb(c),Loot is What She Lived For 150.00
75 BLb(c),The Sky Hag 150.00
76 BLb(c),Temple of the Dead . . . 150.00
77 BLb(c),Sky Express to Hell . . . 150.00
78 BLb(c),Loot Queen of Satan's Skyway 150.00
79 BLb(c),Buzzards of Plunder Sky 150.00
80 BLb(c),Port of Missing Pilots . 150.00
81 BLb(c),Sky Trail of the Terror Tong 150.00
82 BLb(c),Bondage(c),Spider & The Fly Guy 160.00
83 BLb(c),GE,Deep Six For Capt. Wings 150.00
84 BLb(c),GE,Sky Sharks to the Kill 150.00
85 BLb(c),GE 150.00

Wings #75
© Fiction House

86 BLb(c),GE,Moon Raiders 150.00
87 BLb(c),GE 150.00
88 BLb(c),GE,Madmans Mission . 150.00
89 BLb(c),GE,Bondage(c), Rockets Away 160.00
90 BLb(c),GE,Bondage(c),The Radar Rocketeers 160.00
91 BLb(c),GE,Bondage(c),V-9 for Vengeance 160.00
92 BLb(c),GE,Death's red Rocket 150.00
93 BLb(c),GE,Kidnap Cargo 150.00
94 BLb(c),GE,Bondage(c),Ace of the A-Bomb Patrol 160.00
95 BLb(c),GE,The Ace of the Assassins 150.00
96 BLb(c),GE 150.00
97 BLb(c),GE,The Sky Octopus . 150.00
98 BLb(c),GE,The Witch Queen of Satan's Skyways 150.00
99 BLb(c),GE,The Spy Circus . . . 150.00
100 BLb(c),GE,King o/t Congo . . 165.00
101 BLb(c),GE,Trator of the Cockpit 150.00
102 BLb(c),GE,Doves of Doom . . 150.00
103 BLb(c),GE 150.00
104 BLb(c),GE,Fireflies of Fury . . 150.00
105 BLb(c),GE 150.00
106 BLb(c),GE,Six Aces & A Firing Squad 150.00
107 BLb(c),GE,Operation Satan . 150.00
108 BLb(c),GE,The Phantom of Berlin 150.00
109 GE,Vultures of Vengeance Sky 150.00
110 GE,The Red Ray Vortex 150.00
111 GE,E:Jane Martin 125.00
112 The Flight of the Silver Saucers 125.00
113 Suicide Skyways 125.00
114 D-Day for Death Rays 125.00
115 Ace of Space 125.00
116 Jet Aces of Korea 125.00
117 Reap the Red Wind 125.00
118 Vengeance Flies Blind 125.00
119 The Whistling Death 125.00
120 Doomsday Mission 125.00
121 Ace of the Spyways 125.00
122 Last Kill Korea 125.00
123 The Cat & the Canaries 125.00
124 Summer, 1954, Death Below Zero 125.00

WINNIE WINKLE

Dell Publishing Co., 1941

1 . . . . 75.00
2 . . . . 40.00
3 . . . . 30.00
4 thru 7 . . . . @30.00

WITCHCRAFT

Avon Periodicals
March–April, 1952

1 SC,JKu,Heritage of Horror . . . 550.00
2 SC,JKu,The Death Tattoo . . . 400.00
3 EK,Better off Dead 275.00
4 Claws of the Cat, Boiling Humans 325.00
5 Ph(c),Where Zombies Walk . . 375.00
6 March, 1953 Mysteries of the Moaning Statue 275.00

WITCHES TALES

Harvey Publications
Jan., 1951

1 RP,Bondage(c),Weird Yarns of Unseen Terror 375.00
2 RP,We Dare You 200.00
3 RP,Bondage(c)Forest of Skeletons 150.00
4 BP 150.00
5 BP,Bondage(c),Share My Coffin 165.00
6 BP,Bondage(c),Servants of the Tomb 165.00
7 BP,Screaming City 165.00
8 Bondage(c) 175.00
9 Fatal Steps 150.00
10 BP,....,IT! 150.00
11 BP,Monster Maker 125.00
12 Bondage(c);The Web of the Spider 135.00
13 The Torture Jar 125.00
14 Transformation 135.00
15 Drooling Zombie 125.00
16 Revenge of a Witch 125.00
17 Dimension IV 150.00
18 HN,Bird of Prey 135.00
19 HN,The Pact 135.00
20 HN,Kiss & Tell 135.00
21 HN,The Invasion 135.00
22 HN,A Day of Panic 135.00
23 HN,The Wig Maker 135.00
24 HN,The Undertaker 135.00
25 What Happens at 8:30 PM? Severed Heads(c) 135.00
26 Up There 125.00
27 The Thing That Grew 125.00
28 Demon Flies 125.00

Becomes:

WITCHES WESTERN TALES

29 S&K,S&K(c),F:Davy Crockett . 150.00
30 S&K.S&K(c) 165.00

Becomes:

WESTERN TALES

31 S&K,S&K(c),F:Davy Crockett . 150.00
32 S&K,S&K(c) 150.00
33 S&K,S&K(c),July–Sept.,1956 . 150.00

WITH THE MARINES ON THE BATTLEFRONTS OF THE WORLD

Toby Press, June, 1953

1 Ph(c),Flaming Soul 250.00
2 Ph(c),March, 1954 . . . . 50.00

GOLDEN AGE

WITTY COMICS
Irwin H. Rubin/Chicago Nite Life News, 1945

1 . . . . 100.00
2 1945. . . . . 50.00
3 thru 7 . . . . @40.00

WOMEN IN LOVE
Fox Features Synd./ Hero Books/ Ziff-Davis, Aug., 1949

1 . . . . 400.00

WOMEN OUTLAWS
Fox Features Syndicate July, 1948

1 . . . . 600.00
2 . . . . 500.00
3 . . . . 500.00
4 . . . . 500.00
5 thru 8 . . . . @400.00
Becomes:

MY LOVE MEMORIES

9 . . . . 100.00
10 . . . . 65.00
11 . . . . 75.00
12 WW. 100.00

WONDERBOY (see HORRIFIC)

WONDER COMICS
Great Publ./Nedor/ Better Publications May, 1944

1 SSh(c),B:Grim Reaper, Spectro Hitler(c) 1,000.00
2 ASh(c),O:Grim Reaper,B:Super Sleuths,Grim Reaper(c) 550.00
3 ASh(c),Grim Reaper(c) 500.00
4 ASh(c),Grim Reaper(c) 475.00
5 ASh(c),Grim Reaper(c) 475.00
6 ASh(c),Grim Reaper(c) 400.00
7 ASh(c),Grim Reaper(c) 400.00
8 ASh(c),E:Super Sleuths, Spectro 400.00
9 ASh(c),B:Wonderman 400.00
10 ASh(c),Wonderman(c) 425.00
11 Grl(c),B:Dick Devins. 425.00
12 Grl(c),Bondage(c) 425.00
13 ASh(c),Bondage(c) 425.00
14 ASh(c),Bondage(c) E:Dick Devins. 425.00
15 ASh(c),Bondage(c),B:Tara . . . 500.00
16 ASh(c),A:Spectro, E:Grim Reaper 450.00
17 FF,ASh(c),A:Super Sleuth . . . 475.00
18 ASh(c),B:Silver Knight 450.00
19 ASh(c),FF 450.00
20 FF,Oct., 1948. . . . . 550.00

WONDERLAND COMICS
Feature Publications (Prize Comics Group) Summer, 1945

1 (fa),B:Alex in Wonderland . . . 100.00
2 . . . . 60.00
3 thru 8 . . . . @50.00
9 1947. . . . . 50.00

Wonder World #6
© Fox Features Syndicate

WONDER COMICS
Fox Features Syndicate May, 1930–Jan., 1942

1 BKa,WE,WE(c),B:Wonderman, DR.Kung,K-51 . . . . 15,000.00
2 WE,BKa,LF(c),B:Yarko the Great,A:Spark Stevens . . . 4,500.00
Becomes:

WONDERWORLD COMICS

3 WE,LF,BP,LF&WE,I:Flame . . 6,500.00
4 WE,LF,BP,LF(c) 3,000.00
5 WE,LF,BP,GT,LF(c),Flame . . 1,600.00
6 WE,LF,BP,GT,LF(c),Flame . . 1,400.00
7 WE,LF,BP,GT,LF(c),Flame . . 2,500.00
8 WE,LF,BP,GT,LF(c),Flame . . 2,000.00
9 WE,LF,BP,GT,LF(c),Flame . . 1,400.00
10 WE,LF,BP,LF(c),Flame 1,400.00
11 WE,LF,BP,LF(c),O:Flame. . . 1,200.00
12 BP,LF(c),Bondage(c),Flame 1,000.00
13 E:Dr Fung,Flame 900.00
14 JoS,Bondage(c),Flame 1,000.00
15 JoS&LF(c),Flame. 900.00
16 Flame(c) 750.00
17 Flame(c) 750.00
18 Flame(c) 750.00
19 Male Bondage(c),Flame. 775.00
20 Flame(c) 750.00
21 O:Black Club &Lion,Flame . . . 625.00
22 Flame(c) 550.00
23 Flame(c) 500.00
24 Flame(c) 500.00
25 A:Dr Fung,Flame 500.00
26 Flame(c) 500.00
27 Flame(c) 500.00
28 Bondage(c)I&O:US Jones, B:Lu-nar,Flame. 700.00
29 Bondage(c),Flame 400.00
30 O:Flame(c),Flame 750.00
31 Bondage(c),Flame 400.00
32 Hitler(c),Flame. 500.00
33 Male Bondage(c) 400.00

WORLD FAMOUS HEROES MAGAZINE
Comic Corp. of America (Centaur) Oct., 1941

1 BLb,Paul Revere 1,000.00
2 BLb,Andrew Jackson,V: Dickinson 450.00
3 BLb,Juarez-Mexican patriot . . 400.00
4 BLb,Canadian Mounties 400.00

WORLD'S GREATEST STORIES
Jubilee Publications Jan., 1949

1 F:Alice in Wonderland. 250.00
2 F:Pinocchio 225.00

WORLD WAR III
Ace Periodicals March–May, 1953

1 Atomic Bomb cover. 500.00
2 The War That Will Never Happen 475.00

WOTALIFE COMICS (see PHANTOM LADY)

WOW COMICS
David McKay/Henle Publ. July, 1936

1 WE,DBr(c),Fu Manchu, Buck Jones 2,200.00
2 WE,Little King 1,700.00

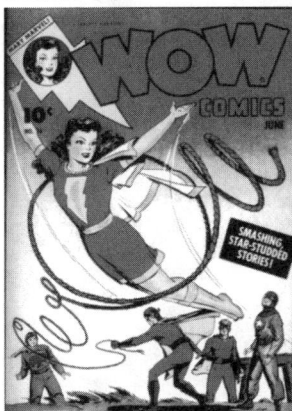

Wow #26
© Fawcett Publications

3 WE,WE(c) 1,500.00
4 WE,BKa,AR,DBr(c),Popeye, Flash Gordon,Nov.,1936 . . 1,800.00

WOW COMICS
Fawcett Publications Winter, 1940

N#(1)S&K,CCB(c),B&O:Mr Scarlett; B:Atom Blake,Jim Dolan,Rick O'Shay,Bondage(c) 14,000.00
2 B:Hunchback 2,000.00
3 V:Mummy Ray Gun 900.00
4 O:Pinky 950.00
5 F:Pinky the Whiz Kid 600.00
6 O:Phantom Eagle; B:Commando Yank 600.00
7 Spearhead of Invasion 500.00
8 All Three Heroes. 500.00
9 A:Capt Marvel,Capt MarvelJr. Shazam,B:Mary Marvel . . . 1,100.00
10 The Sinister Secret of

Hotel Hideaway 500.00
11 . . . . 375.00
12 Rocketing adventures 375.00
13 Thrill Show. 375.00
14 V:Mr Night 375.00
15 The Shazam Girl of America . 350.00
16 Ride to the Moon 350.00
17 V:Mary Batson,Alter Ego Goes Berserk 350.00
18 I:Uncle Marvel,Infinity(c) V is For Victory. 350.00
19 A Whirlwind Fantasy 350.00
20 Mary Marvel's Magic Carpet. . 350.00
21 Word That Shook the World . . 225.00
22 Come on Boys- Everybody Sing 225.00
23 Trapped by the Terror of the Future. 225.00
24 Mary Marvel. 225.00
25 Mary Marvel Crushes Crime. . 225.00
26 Smashing Star- Studded Stories 200.00
27 War Stamp Plea(c). 200.00
28 . . . . 200.00
29 . . . . 200.00
30 In Mirror Land 200.00
31 Stars of Action 150.00
32 The Millinery Marauders. 150.00
33 Mary Marvel(c). 150.00
34 A:Uncle Marvel 150.00
35 I:Freckles Marvel 150.00
36 Secret of the Buried City 150.00
37 7th War loan plea. 150.00
38 Pictures That Came to Life. . . 150.00
39 The Perilous Packages 150.00
40 The Quarrel of the Gnomes . . 150.00
41 Hazardous Adventures. 125.00
42 . . . . 125.00
43 Curtain Time 125.00
44 Volcanic Adventure 125.00
45 . . . . 125.00
46 . . . . 125.00
47 . . . . 125.00
48 . . . . 125.00
49 . . . . 125.00
50 Mary Marvel/Commando Yank 125.00
51 . . . . 100.00
52 . . . . 100.00
53 Murder in the Tall Timbers . . . 100.00
54 Flaming Adventure. 100.00
55 Earthquake! 100.00
56 Sacred Pearls of Comatesh . . 100.00
57 . . . . 100.00
58 E:Mary Marvel;The Curse of the Keys 100.00
59 B:Ozzie the Hilarious Teenager 100.00
60 thru 64 . . . . @100.00
65 A:Tom Mix 100.00
66 A:Tom Mix 100.00
67 A:Tom Mix 100.00
68 A:Tom Mix 100.00
69 A:Tom Mix,Baseball 100.00

Becomes:

REAL WESTERN HERO

70 It's Round-up Time. 250.00
71 CCB,P(c),A Rip Roaring Rodeo 175.00
72 w/Gabby Hayes 175.00
73 thru 75 . . . . @175.00

Becomes:

WESTERN HERO

76 Partial Ph(c)&P(c) 225.00
77 Partial Ph(c)&P(c) 150.00
78 Partial Ph(c)&P(c) 150.00
79 Partial Ph(c)&P(c), Shadow of Death 125.00
80 Partial Ph(c)&P(c) 150.00
81 CCB,Partial Ph(c)&P(c), F:Tootsie 150.00
82 Partial Ph(c)&P(c), A:Hopalong Cassidy 150.00
83 Partial Ph(c)&P(c) 150.00
84 Ph(c) 125.00
85 Ph(c) 125.00
86 Ph(c),The Case of the Extra Buddy, giant 125.00
87 Ph(c),The Strange Lands 125.00
88 Ph(c),A:Senor Diablo 125.00
89 Ph(c),The Hypnotist 125.00
90 Ph(c),The Menace of the Cougar, giant 100.00
91 Ph(c),Song of Death 100.00
92 Ph(c),The Fatal Hide-out, giant. 100.00
93 Ph(c),Treachery at Triple T, giant 100.00
94 Ph(c),Bank Busters,giant 100.00
95 Ph(c),Rampaging River 90.00
96 Ph(c),Range Robbers,giant . . 100.00
97 Ph(c),Death on the Hook,giant 100.00
98 Ph(c),Web of Death,giant. . . . 100.00
99 Ph(c),The Hidden Evidence . . . 90.00
100 Ph(c),A:Red Eagle,Giant . . . 100.00
101 Ph(c) 100.00
102 thru 111 Ph(c). . . . . @90.00
112 Ph(c),March, 1952 . . . . 125.00

Yankee Comics #2
© Harry A. Chesler

YANKEE COMICS
Chesler Publications (Harry A. Chesler) Sept., 1941

1 F:Yankee Doodle Jones . . . 1,300.00
2 The Spirit of `41 . . . . 700.00
3 Yankee Doodle Jones. 500.00
4 JCo,Yankee Doodle Jones March, 1942 . . . . 500.00

YELLOWJACKET COMICS
Levy Publ./Frank Comunale/ Charlton Sept., 1944

1 O&B:Yellowjackets,B:Diana the Huntress 500.00
2 Rosita &The Filipino Kid 300.00
3 . . . . 250.00
4 Fall of the House of Usher . . . 300.00
5 King of Beasts 300.00
6 . . . . 250.00
7 I:Diane Carter;The Lonely Guy 250.00
8 The Buzzing Bee Code 250.00
9 . . . . 250.00
10 Capt Grim V:The Salvage Pirates 250.00

Becomes:

JACK IN THE BOX

11 Funny Animal,Yellow Jacket . . . 75.00
12 Funny Animal 35.00
13 BW,Funny Animal 100.00
14 thru 16 Funny Animal. . . . . . @40.00

Becomes:

COWBOY WESTERN COMICS

17 Annie Oakley,Jesse James . . 135.00
18 JO,JO(c) 85.00
19 JO,JO(c),Legends of Paul Bunyan. 85.00
20 JO(c),Jesse James 50.00
21 Annie Oakley VisitsDryGulch . . 50.00
22 Story of the Texas Rangers . . . 50.00
23 . . . . 50.00
24 Ph(c),F:James Craig 50.00
25 Ph(c),F:Sunset Carson. 50.00
26 Ph(c) 80.00
27 Ph(c),Sunset Carson movie . . 225.00
28 Ph(c),Sunset Carson movie . . 150.00
29 Ph(c),Sunset Carson movie . . 150.00
30 Ph(c),Sunset Carson movie . . 200.00
31 Ph(c) 50.00
32 thru 34 Ph(c) . . . . @45.00
35 thru 37 Sunset Carson . . . @100.00
38 and 39 . . . . @35.00

Becomes:

SPACE WESTERN COMICS

40 Spurs Jackson,V:The Saucer Men 500.00
41 StC(c),Space Vigilantes 350.00
42 StC(c) 400.00
43 StC(c),Battle of Spacemans Gulch 350.00
44 StC(c),The Madman of Mars . 350.00
45 StC(c),The Moon Bat 350.00

Becomes:

COWBOY WESTERN COMICS

46 . . . . 100.00

Becomes:

COWBOY WESTERN HEROES

47 . . . . 35.00
48 . . . . 35.00

Becomes:

COWBOY WESTERN

49 . . . . 35.00
50 F:Jesse James 30.00
51 thru 56 . . . . @30.00
58, giant 35.00
59 thru 66 . . . . @30.00
67 AW&AT 75.00

Becomes:

WILD BILL HICKOK AND JINGLES

68 AW 75.00
69 AW 50.00
70 AW 45.00
71 thru 73 . . . . @35.00
74 1960 . . . . 35.00

YOGI BERRA
Fawcett 1957

1 Ph(c) 550.00

YOUNG BRIDES
Feature Publications
(Prize Comics) Sept.–Oct., 1952

1 S&K,Ph(c) 250.00
2 S&K,Ph(c) 125.00
3 S&K,Ph(c) 100.00
4 S&K 100.00
5 S&K 100.00
6 S&K 100.00
2-1 S&K 75.00
2-2 S&K 50.00
2-3 S&K 60.00
2-4 S&K 60.00
2-5 S&K 60.00
2-6 S&K 60.00
2-7 S&K 60.00
2-8 S&K 40.00
2-9 S&K 40.00
2-10 S&K. 60.00
2-11 S&K. 60.00
2-12 S&K. 60.00
3-1 . . . . 30.00
3-2 . . . . 30.00
3-3 . . . . 30.00
3-4 . . . . 30.00
3-5 . . . . 30.00
3-6 . . . . 30.00
4-1 . . . . 30.00
4-2 S&K 75.00
4-3 . . . . 30.00
4-4 S&K 60.00
4-5 . . . . 30.00

YOUNG EAGLE
Fawcett Publications/ Charlton Comics
Dec., 1950

1 Ph(c) 125.00
2 Ph(c),Mystery of Thunder Canyon 75.00
3 Ph(c),Death at Dawn 60.00
4 Ph(c) 60.00
5 Ph(c),The Golden Flood 60.00
6 Ph(c),The Nightmare Empire. . . 60.00
7 Ph(c),Vigilante Veangeance . . . 60.00
8 Ph(c),The Rogues Rodeo 60.00
9 Ph(c),The Great Railroad Swindle 60.00
10 June, 1952, Ph(c),Thunder Rides the Trail,O:Thunder 50.00

YOUNG KING COLE
Novelty Press/Premium Svcs. Co., Autumn, 1945

1-1 Detective Toni Gayle. 225.00
1-2 . . . . 125.00
1-3 . . . . 100.00
1-4 . . . . 75.00
2-1 . . . . 75.00
2-2 . . . . 75.00
2-3 . . . . 75.00
2-4 . . . . 75.00
2-5 . . . . 75.00
2-6 . . . . 75.00
2-7 . . . . 75.00
3-1 . . . . 60.00
3-2 LbC 60.00
3-3 The Killer With The Hat 60.00
3-4 The Fierce Tiger 60.00
3-5 AMc 60.00
3-6 . . . . 65.00
3-7 LbC(c),Case of the Devil's Twin 150.00
3-8 . . . . 75.00
3-9 The Crime Fighting King 75.00
3-10 LbC(c) 125.00
3-11 LbC(c) 125.00

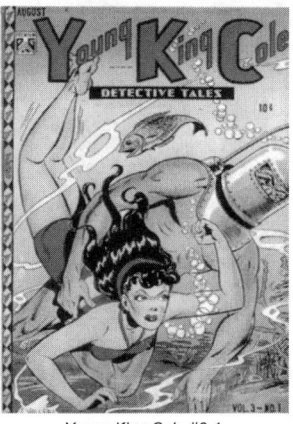

Young King Cole #3-1
© Novelty Press

3-12 July, 1948,AMc(c). 65.00

YOUNG LIFE
New Age Publications
Summer, 1945

1 Partial Ph(c),Louis Prima 100.00
2 Partial Ph(c),Frank Sinatra . . . 125.00
Becomes:

TEEN LIFE

3 Partial Ph(c),Croon without Tricks,June Allyson(c). 85.00
4 Partial Ph(c),Atom Smasher Blueprints,Duke Ellington(c) . . 65.00
5 Partial Ph(c), Build Your Own Pocket Radio, Jackie Robinson(c) 75.00

YOUNG LOVE
Feature Publ.
(Prize Comics Group)
Feb.–March, 1949

1 S&K,S&K(c) 350.00
2 S&K,Ph(c) 200.00
3 S&K,JSe,BE,Ph(c) 150.00
4 S&K,Ph(c) 100.00
5 S&K,Ph(c) 100.00
2-1 S&K,Ph(c) 150.00
2-2 Ph(c) 80.00
2-3 Ph(c) 80.00
2-4 Ph(c) 80.00
2-5 Ph(c) 80.00
2-6 S&K(c) 125.00
2-7 S&K(c),S&K 125.00
2-8 S&K 125.00
2-9 S&K(c),S&K 125.00
2-10 S&K(c),S&K 125.00
2-11 S&K(c),S&K 125.00
2-12 S&K(c),S&K 125.00
3-1 S&K(c),S&K 125.00
3-2 S&K(c),S&K 125.00
3-3 S&K(c),S&K 125.00
3-4 S&K(c),S&K 125.00
3-5 Ph(c) 100.00
3-6 BP,Ph(c) 100.00
3-7 Ph(c) 100.00
3-8 Ph(c) 100.00
3-9 MMe,Ph(c) 100.00
3-10 Ph(c) 100.00
3-11 Ph(c). 100.00
3-12 Ph(c) 100.00
4-1 S&K 100.00
4-2 Ph(c) 65.00
4-3 Ph(c) 65.00
4-4 Ph(c) 65.00
4-5 Ph(c) 65.00
4-6 S&K,Ph(c) 65.00
4-7 thru 4-12 Ph(c) . . . . @60.00
5-1 thru 5-12 Ph(c) . . . . @35.00
6-1 thru 6-9 . . . . @25.00
6-10 thru 6-12 . . . . @25.00
7-1 thru 7-7 . . . . @20.00
7-8 thru 7-11 . . . . @20.00
7-12 thru 8-5 . . . . @20.00
8-6 thru 8-12 . . . . @25.00

YOUNG ROMANCE COMICS
Feature Publ./Headline/ Prize Publ., Sept.–Oct., 1947

1 S&K(c),S&K 375.00
2 S&K(c),S&K 250.00
3 S&K(c),S&K 200.00
4 S&K(c),S&K 200.00
5 S&K(c),S&K 200.00
6 S&K(c),S&K 175.00
2-1 S&K(c),S&K 175.00
2-2 S&K(c),S&K 175.00
2-3 S&K(c),S&K 175.00
2-4 S&K(c),S&K 175.00
2-5 S&K(c),S&K 175.00
2-6 S&K(c),S&K 125.00
3-1 thru 3-12 S&K(c),S&K . . . . @125.00
4-1 thru 4-12 S&K . . . . @125.00
5-1 ATh,S&K. 125.00
2 . . . . 125.00
3 . . . . 125.00
5-4 thru 5-12 S&K . . . . @125.00
6-1 thru 6-3. . . . . @50.00

YOUR UNITED STATES
Lloyd Jacquet Studios, 1946

1N# Teeming nation of Nations . 175.00

YOUTHFUL HEART
Youthful Magazines
May, 1952

1 Frankie Lane(c) 200.00
2 Vic Damone 150.00
3 Johnnie Ray 150.00
Becomes:

DARING CONFESSIONS

4 DW,Tony Curtis. 100.00
5 . . . . 75.00
6 DW. 85.00
7 . . . . 75.00
8 DW. 75.00

YOUTHFUL ROMANCES
Pix Parade/Ribage/ Trojan, Aug.–Sept., 1949

1 . . . . 175.00
2 . . . . 100.00
3 Tex Beneke 75.00
4 . . . . 75.00
5 . . . . 65.00
6 . . . . 65.00
7 Tony Martin(c). 75.00
8 WW(c) 125.00
9 thru 14 . . . . @40.00
Becomes:

DARLING LOVE

15 WD 50.00
16 . . . . 40.00
17 DW,Ph(c). 40.00

ZAGO, JUNGLE PRINCE
Fox Features Syndicate
Sept., 1948

1 A:Blue Beetle 500.00
2 JKa. 350.00
3 JKa. 300.00
4 MB(c) 300.00
Becomes:

MY STORY
5 JKa,Too Young To Fall in Love 150.00
6 I Was A She-Wolf 50.00
7 I Lost My Reputation 50.00
8 My Words Condemned Me . . . 50.00
9 WW,Wayward Bride 100.00
10 WW,March, 1950,Second Rate Girl. 100.00
11 . . . . 50.00
12 . . . . 50.00

TEGRA, JUNGLE EMPRESS
Fox Features Syndicate
Aug., 1948

1 Blue Bettle,Rocket Kelly 450.00
Becomes:

ZEGRA, JUNGLE EMPRESS
2 JKa 500.00
3 . . . . 400.00
4 . . . . 400.00
5 . . . . 400.00
Becomes:

MY LOVE LIFE
6 I Put A Price Tag On Love . . . 125.00
7 An Old Man's Fancy 65.00
8 My Forbidden Affair 65.00
9 I Loved too Often 65.00
10 My Secret Torture 65.00
11 I Broke My Own Heart 65.00
12 I Was An Untamed Filly 65.00
13 I Can Never Marry You, Aug. 1950 . . . . 50.00

ZIP COMICS
MLJ Magazines
Feb., 1940

1 MMe,O&B:Kalathar,The Scarlet Avenger,Steel Sterling,B:Mr Satan,Nevada Jones,War Eagle Captain Valor. 4,000.00
2 MMe,CBi(c)B:Steel Sterling(c) 1,700.00
3 CBi,MMe,CBi(c) 1,200.00
4 CBi,MMe,CBi(c) 1,000.00
5 CBi,MMe,CBi(c) 1,000.00
6 CBi,MMe,CBi(c) 900.00
7 CBi,MMe,CBi(c) 900.00
8 CBi,MMe,CBi(c),Bondage(c) . 900.00
9 CBi,MMe,CBi(c)E:Kalathar, Mr Satan;Bondage(c) 1,000.00
10 CBi,MMe,CBi(c),B:Inferno . . . 900.00
11 CBi,MMe,CBi(c) 800.00
12 CBi,MMe,CBi(c),Bondage(c) . 800.00
13 CBi,MMe,CBi(c)E:Inferno, Bondage(c),Woman in Electric Chair 850.00
14 CBi,MMe,CBi(c),Bondage(c) . 750.00
15 CBi,MMe,CBi(c),Bondage(c) . 750.00
16 CBi,MMe,CBi(c),Bondage(c) . 750.00
17 CBi,CBI(c),E:Scarlet Avenger Bondage(c). 750.00
18 IN(c),B:Wilbur 775.00
19 IN(c),Steel Sterling(c). 750.00
20 IN(c),O&I:Black Jack Hitler(c) 1,200.00
21 IN(c),V:Nazis 675.00
22 IN(c) 675.00
23 IN(c),Flying Fortress 675.00
24 IN(c),China Town Exploit 675.00
25 IN(c),E:Nevada Jones 675.00
26 IN(c),B:Black Witch, E:Capt Valor. 675.00
27 IN(c),I:Web,V:Japanese. . . . 1,100.00
28 IN(C),O:Web,Bondage(c) . . 1,000.00
29 Steel Sterling & Web 500.00
30 V:Nazis 500.00
31 IN(c) 350.00
32 . . . . 350.00
33 Bondage(c) 375.00
34 I:Applejack;Bondage(c) 375.00
35 E:Zambini 350.00
36 I:Senor Banana 350.00
37 . . . . 350.00
38 E:Web 350.00
39 O&B:Red Rule. 350.00
40 . . . . 300.00
41 . . . . 300.00
42 . . . . 300.00
43 . . . . 300.00
44 . . . . 300.00
45 E:Wilbur. 300.00
46 . . . . 300.00
47 Crooks Can't Win, Summer, 1944 . . . . 300.00

Zip Comics #22
© MLJ Magazines

ZIP-JET
St. John Publishing Co.
Feb., 1953

1 Rocketman. 550.00
2 April–May, 1953, Assassin of the Airlanes 400.00

ZOOM COMICS
Carlton Publishing Co.
Dec., 1945

N# O:Captain Milksop 350.00

Zoot #15
© Fox Features Syndicate

ZOOT COMICS
Fox Features Syndicate
Spring, 1946

N#(1)(fa) 150.00
2 A:Jaguar(fa) 125.00
3 (fa) 75.00
4 (fa) 75.00
5 (fa) 50.00
6 (fa) 50.00
7 B:Rulah 800.00
8 JKa(c),Fangs of Stone 600.00
9 JKa(c),Fangs of Black Fury . . 600.00
10 JKa(c),Inferno Land 600.00
11 JKa,The Purple Plague, Bondage(c). 575.00
12 JKa(c),The Thirsty Stone, Bondage(c). 400.00
13 Bloody Moon 400.00
14 Pearls of Pathos,Woman Carried off by Bird 500.00
15 Death Dancers. 400.00
16 . . . . 400.00
Becomes:

RULAH, JUNGLE GODDESS
17 JKa(c),Wolf Doctor. 750.00
18 JKa(c),Vampire Garden 550.00
19 JKa(c) 500.00
20 . . . . 500.00
21 JKa(c) 500.00
22 JKa(c) 500.00
23 . . . . 400.00
24 . . . . 375.00
25 . . . . 375.00
26 . . . . 375.00
27 . . . . 400.00
Becomes:

I LOVED
28 . . . . 75.00
29 thru 31 . . . . @50.00
32 My Poison Love, March, 1950 . 50.00

GOLDEN AGE

ACCLAIM

ACCLAIM ADVENTURE ZONE
Acclaim Young Readers 1997
Digest Size

Ninjak
Spec. "The Boss" 4.50
Turok
Spec. "Extinction" 4.50
Spec. "Dinosaur Rodeo" 4.50
Spec. "Scrounge Rules" 4.50

Archer & Armstrong #12
© Valiant

ARCHER & ARMSTRONG
Valiant 1992
0 JiS(s),BWS,BL,I&O:Archer, I:Armstrong,The Sec. 3.00
0 Gold Ed. 5 . . . . 4.00
1 FM(c),B:JiS(s),BWS,BL,Unity #3, A:Eternal Warrior 2.25
2 WS(c),E:JiS(s),BWS,BL,Unity #11,2nd A:Turok,A:X-O. 2.25
3 B:BWS(a&s), BWi, V:Sect in Rome 2.25
4 BWS,BWi,V:Sect in Rome 2.25
5 BWS,BWi,I:Andromeda. 2.25
6 BWS,BWi, A:Andromeda, V:Medoc. 2.25
7 BWS,ANi,BWi,V:Sect in England 2.25
8 BWS,as Eternal Warrior #8, Three Musketeers,I:Ivan 2.25
9 BCh,BWi,in Britain 2.00
10 BWS,A:Ivar 2.00
11 BWS,A:Solar,Ivar 2.00
12 BWS,V:The Avenger 2.00
13 B:MBn(s),RgM,In Los Angeles . . 2.00
14 In Los Angeles. 2.00
15 E:MBn(s),In LasVegas, I:Duerst . 2.00
16 V:Sect 2.00
17 B:MBn(s),In Florida 2.00
18 MV,in Heaven 2.00
19 MV,V:MircoboticCult,D:Duerst . . 2.00
20 MV,Chrismas Issue 2.00
21 MV,A:Shadowman,Master Darque. 2.00
22 MV,A:Shadowman,Master Darque,w/Valiant Era card 2.00
23 MV, ... 2.00
24 MV, ... 2.00
25 MV,A:Eternal Warrior 2.00
26 Chaos Effect-Gamma #4, A:Ivar, Et. Warrior 2.00

ARMED & DANGEROUS
Valiant (B&W) 1995
1 thru 4 . . . . @2.95
Spec.#1 . . . . 2.95

ARMED & DANGEROUS
Acclaim (B&W) 1996
1 BH,"Hell's Slaughterhouse" Pt.1 . 2.95
2 BH,"Hell's Slaughterhouse" Pt.2 . 2.95
3 BH,"Hell's Slaughterhouse" Pt.3 . 2.95
4 BH,"Hell's Slaughterhouse" Pt.4 . 2.95

ARMED & DANGEROUS No. 2
Acclaim (B&W) Dec., 1996
1 BH,"When Irish Eyes are Dying," pt.1 . . . . 2.95
2 thru 4 BH,"When Irish Eyes," pt.2 thru 4 . . . . @2.95

ARMORINES
Valiant 1994
0 (from X-O #25),Card Stock (c), Diamond Distributors "Fall Fling" Retailer Meeting. 2.50
0a Gold Ed.. . . . . 3.00
1 JGz(s),JCf,B:White Death. 2.25
2 JGz(s),JCf,E:White Death. 2.25
3 JGz(s),JCf,V:Spider Aliens 2.25
4 JCf, V: Spider Aliens. 2.00
5 JCf, Chaos Effect-Delta #2, A:H.A.R.D. Corp. 2.00
6 Spider Alien Mothership 2.00
7 Rescue. 2.00
8 Rescue in Iraq 2.00
9 . . . . 2.00
10 Protect Fidel Castro. 2.00
11 V: Spider Super Suit 2.00
12 F: Sirot 2.00
Yearbook I:Linoff. 3.00

VOLUME 2
1 48-pg.. 3.95
2 . . . . 3.95
3 and 4 . . . . @2.50

BAD EGGS
Acclaim 1996
1 thru 4 BL,DP,"That Dirty Yellow Mustard" . . . . @2.95

BAR SINISTER
Windjammer 1995
1 From Shaman's Tears. 2.50
2 V:SWAT Team 2.50
3 F: Animus Prime. 2.50
4 MGe,RHo,V:Jabbersnatch 2.50

BART SEARS' X-O MANOWAR
Valiant 1995
HC Bart Sears' Artwork. 17.95

BLOODSHOT
Valiant 1992
0 KVH(a&s),DG(i),Chromium (c), O:Bloodshot,A:Eternal Warrior . 3.00
0a Gold Ed.,w/Diamond "Fall Fling" logo 4.00
1 BWS(c),B:KVH(s),DP,BWi, V:Mafia, I:Carboni,1st Chromium(c) 2.50
2 DP,I:Durkins,V:Ax 2.50
3 DP,V:The Mob 2.50
4 DP,A:Eternal Warrior. 2.00
5 DP,A:Eternal Warrior,Rai. 2.00
6 DP,I:Ninjak (Not in Costume) . . . 2.00
7 DP,JDx,A:Ninjak (1st appearance in costume) 2.00
8 DP,JDx,A:Geoff. 2.00
9 DP,JDx,V:Slavery Ring 2.00
10 DP,JDx,V:Tunnel Rat 2.00
11 DP,JDx,V:Iwatsu 2.00
12 DP,JDx,Day Off 2.00
13 DP,JDx,V:Webnet 2.00
14 DP,JDx,V:Carboni 2.00
15 DP,JDx,V:Cinder 2.00
16 DP,JDx,w/Valiant Era Card. 2.00
17 DP,JDx,A:H.A.R.D.Corps 2.00
18 DP,KVH,After the Missile 2.00
19 DP,KVH,I:Uzzi the Clown 2.00
20 DP,KVH, Chaos Effect-Gamma #1, V:Immortal Enemy 2.00
21 DP,V: Immortal Enemy, Ax 2.00
22 Immortal Enemy 2.00
23 Cinder 2.00
24 Geomancer, Immortal Enemy. . . 2.00
25 V:Uzzi the Clown 2.00
26 V:Uzzi the Clown 2.00
27 Rampage Pt. 1 . . . . 2.00
28 Rampage Pt. 3 . . . . 2.00
29 Rampage Conc. A:Ninjak. 2.00
30 V:Shape Shifter 2.00
31 Nanite Killer. 2.00
32 KVH,SCh,V: Vampires 2.00
33 KVH,SCh,V: Vampires 2.00
34 NBy,KVH,new villains spawned . 2.00
35 NBY,KVH,attempts to control . . . 2.00
36 V:Voodoo Drug Dealer. 2.00
37 V:Voodoo Drug Dealer. 2.00
38 V:Rampage 2.00
39 V:Rampage 2.00
40 USA wants Bloodshot 2.00
41 F:Jillian Alcott 2.00
42 Virtual Nightmare. 2.00
43 V:U.S. Troops 2.00
44 I:Deathangel, V:Speedshots. . . . 2.00
45 thru 51 . . . . @2.00
Yearbook #1 KVH,briefcase bomb . 4.25
Yearbook 1995 Villagers 2.95
Spec.GN Last Stand. 5.95

BLOODSHOT Series Two
Acclaim March 1997
1 LKa(s),SaV "Behold, a Pale Horseman" 2.50
1a variant cover. 3.00
2 LKa(s),SaV "Dead Man Walking" 2.50
3 LKa(s),SaV "ChainsawMassacre" 2.50
4 LKa(s),SaV Search for Identity . . 2.50
5 LKa(s),SaV V:Simon Oreck. 2.50
6 LKa(s),SaV "Bloodwhispers" 2.50
7 LKa(s),SaV "To the Bitter End..", pt.1 . . . . 2.50
8 LKa(s),SaV "To the Bitter End..", pt.2 . . . . 2.50
9 LKa(s),SaV "Suicide" 2.50

10 LKa(s),SaV "Dreamland" 2.50
11 LKa(s),SaV 2.50
12 LKa(s),SaV "Cat Scratch Fever". 2.50
13 LKa(s),SaV in Russia. 2.50
14 LKa(s),SaV to the Vatican 2.50
15 LKa(s),SaV DOA Headquarters . 2.50
16 LKa(s),SaV final issue 2.50

CAPTAIN JOHNER & THE ALIENS

Valiant May, 1995

1 Rep. Magnus Robot Fighter #1–7 (Gold Key 1963–64) 2.95

CHAOS EFFECT

Valiant 1994

Alpha DJ(c), BCh, JOy, A:All Valiant Characters 2.25
Alpha Red (c) 3.50
Omega DJ(c), BCh, JOy, A:All Valiant Characters 2.25
Omega Gold(c). 3.50
Epilogue pt.1 . . . . 2.95
Epilogue pt.2 . . . . 2.95

CITY KNIGHTS, THE

Windjammer 1995

1 I:Michael Walker. 2.50
2 I:Herald 2.50
3 & 4 V:Herald . . . . @2.50

CONCRETE JUNGLE: THE LEGEND OF THE BLACK LION

Acclaim 1998

1 (of 6) CPr,JFy,F:Terry Smalls . . . 2.50
2 CPr,JFy,Black Lion Order 2.50
3 CPr,JFy,The Man 2.50
4 CPr,JFy 2.50
5 CPr,JFy 2.50

DARQUE PASSAGES

Acclaim 1997

1 (of 4) sequal to Master Darque . . 2.50
1 signed edition. 4.00
2 . . . . 2.50
3 A:Pere Jean, Voodoo King 2.50

Dark Passages #1
© Acclaim

4 conclusion 2.50

DEADSIDE

Acclaim 1998

1 (of 4) PJe, ... 2.50
2 thru 4 . . . . @2.50

DEATHMATE

Valiant/Image 1993

Preview (Advanced Comics). 2.00
Preview (Previews). 2.00
Preview (Comic Defense Fund) . . . 4.00
Prologue BL,JLe,RLd,Solar meets Void 3.25
Prologue Gold 4.00
Blue SCh, HSn, F:Solar, Magnus, Battlestone, Livewire, Stronghold, Impact, Striker, Harbinger, Brigade, Supreme 3.00
Blue Gold Ed. 4.00
Yellow BCh,MLe,DP,F:Armstrong, H.A.R.D.C.A.T.S.,Ninjak,Zealot, Shadowman,Grifter,Ivar 3.00
Yellow Gold Ed. 4.00
Black JLe,MS,F:Warblade,Ripclaw, Turok,X-O Manowar 4.00
Black Gold Ed. 6.00
Red RLd,JMs, ... 4.00
Red Gold Ed. 3.00
Epilogue. 2.50
Epilogue Gold. 3.00

DESTROYER

Valiant 1994

0 MM 41st Century 2.95

DR. TOMORROW

Acclaim May, 1997

1 (of 12) BL,Bart Simms finds Angel Computer 2.50
2 BL,V:Teutonic Knight 2.50
3 BL,V:Teutonic Knight concl. 2.50
4 BL,V:Joe McCarthy. 2.50
5 BL,V:J. Edgar Hoover 2.50
6 BL,DG,V:Mushroom Cloud 2.50
7 BL,DG,A:Mushroom Cloud 2.50
8 BL,GK,Vietnam. 2.50
9 BL, ... 2.50
10 BL,SMc,on *Oprah* 2.50
11 BL,the time capsule 2.50
12 BL,MBu(c),final issue. 2.50

DISNEY'S ACTION CLUB

Acclaim Young Readers 1997

Digest Size

Aladdin
Spec."An Imp-Perfect Day". 4.50
Spec."Monkey Business" 4.50
Buzz Lightyear
Spec."Antique Attack". 4.50
Hercules
Spec."My Fill of Phil". 4.50
The Lion King
Spec."Lurkers in the Water" 4.50
Mighty Ducks
Spec."Puck Power". 4.50
Spec."Rough Stuff". 4.50

DISNEY'S BEAUTY AND THE BEAST

Acclaim Young Readers 1997

Spec. Holiday Special, digest size . 4.50

DISNEY'S ENCHANTING STORIES

Acclaim Young Readers 1997

Digest Size

Beauty and the Beast
Spec."The Book Crook" 4.50
Hercules
Spec."A Torch for Meg". 4.50
Hunchback of Notre Dame
Spec."Veiled Beauty" 4.50
The Little Mermaid
Spec."Seal of Approval" 4.50
101 Dalmatians
Spec."Star Search". 4.50
Pocahontas
Spec."River of Youth" 4.50
Snow White and the Seven Dwarfs
Spec."Mirror,Mirror,on the Floor" . . . 4.50
Spec."Dopey the Genius" 4.50

DISNEY'S HERCULES

Acclaim Young Readers 1997

1-shot Movie adaptation, 64pg 4.50
Spec. Making of a Hero 6.00

DISNEY'S HERCULES: THE GREATEST BATTLES

Acclaim Young Readers 1997

HC 96pg. 24.00
TPB 13.00

DISNEY'S THE LITTLE MERMAID

Acclaim 1997

Spec. Underwater Engagements flip book, digest size 4.50

DISNEY'S 101 DALMATIANS

Acclaim 1997

HC Bad to the Bone 24.00
TPB Bad to the Bone 13.00

ETERNAL WARRIOR

Valiant 1992

1 FM(c),JDx,Unity #2,O:Eternal Warrior,Armstrong 3.00
1a Gold Ed. 4.00
1b Gold Foil Logo 5.00
2 WS(c),JDx,Unity #10,A:Solar, Harbinger,Eternal Warrior of 4001. . . . . 2.50
3 JDx,V:Armstrong,I:Astrea 2.50
4 JDx(i),I:Caldone, C:Bloodshot. . . 2.50
5 JDx,I:Bloodshot,V:Iwatsu's Men . 2.50
6 BWS,JDx,V:Master Darque. 2.50
7 BWS,V:Master Darque, D:Uncle Buck 2.50
8 BWS,as Archer & Armstrong #8 Three Musketeers,I:Ivar 2.50
9 MMo,JDx,B:Book of the Geomancer 2.50
10 JDx,E:Bk. o/t Geomancer. 2.50
11 B:KVH(s),JDx(i), V:Neo-Nazis . . 2.50
12 JDx(i),V:Caldone 2.50
13 MMo,JDx(i),V:Caldone, A:Bloodshot 2.50
14 E:KVH(s),MMo,V:Caldone, A:Geoff. 2.50
15 YG,A:Bloodshot,V:Tanaka 2.50
16 YG,A:Bloodshot. 2.50
17 A:Master Darque 2.50
18 C:Doctor Mirage 2.50
19 KVH(s),TeH,A:Doctor Mirage . . . 2.50

ACCLAIM

20 KVH(s),Access Denied 2.50
21 KVH(s),TeH,V:Dr. Steiner. 2.50
22 V:Master Darque,w/Valiant Era Card. 2.50
23 KVH(s),TeH,Blind Fate. 2.50
24 KVH(s),TeH,V:Immortal Enemy . 2.50
25 MBn(s),A:Archer,Armstrong 2.50
26 Double(c), Chaos Effect-Gamma #4, A:Archer, Armstrong, Ivar . . 3.00
27 JOs(s) 2.25
28 War on Drugs 2.25
29 Immortal Enemy 2.25
30 Lt. Morgan. 2.25
31 JD,JOs 2.25
32 . . . . 2.25
33 Mortal Kin Pt.1. . . . . 2.25
34 Mortal Kin Pt.2. . . . . 2.25
35 Mortal Kin Finale 2.50
36 Fenris League 2.50
37 Youthful Tale 2.50
38 V:Niala, The Dead Queen 2.50
39 JOs,JG,PG(c),V:body thieves. . . 2.50
40 JOs,JG,PG(c),finds organ farm . 2.50
41 War in Herznia. 2.50
42 I: Brisbane. 2.50
43 V:Neo Nazi 2.50
44 V:Neo Nazi 2.50
45 R:Fenris Society 2.50
46 V:Fenris Society 2.50
47 Jihad 2.50
48 Immortal Life in Danger 2.50
49 JOs,JG,Hallucinations 2.50
50 . . . . 2.50
Yearbook #1 . . . . 4.25
Yearbook #2 . . . . 4.00
Wings of Justice WWI. 2.50
Quarterly
Time and Treachery 3.95
Digital Alchemy. 3.95
Spec. Blackworks AHo, ... 4.00

ETERNAL WARRIORS
Acclaim 1997
Quarterly
Archer & Armstrong AHo 3.95
Mog AHo 3.95
The Immortal Enemy AHo. 3.95

FOX FUNHOUSE
Acclaim Young Readers 1997
Digest Size, Featuring The Tick
Spec. "Spoo-o-o-o-nn" 4.50
Spec. "A World of Pain(t)". 4.50
Spec. "Raw, Uncooked Justice" . . . 4.50
Spec. "Way Out of Tuna" 4.50
Spec. "Tick vs. the Entire Ocean. . . 4.50
Spec. Neato-Keen Holiday Special . 4.50

FOX PRESENTS
Acclaim Young Readers 1997
The Tick "No Time For Sanity" . . . 10.00

GEOMANCER
Valiant 1994
1 RgM, I:Geomancer 3.00
2 RgM, Eternal Warrior 2.00
3 RgM, Darque Elementals 2.00
4 RgM 2.00
5 Riot Gear pt. 1 . . . . 2.00
6 Riot Gear pt. 2 . . . . 2.00
7 F:Zorn 2.00
8 v:Zorn. 2.00

GOAT, THE: H.A.E.D.U.S.
Acclaim 1998
Spec. CPr,KG,F:Vincent Van Goat . 3.95

GRACKLE, THE
Acclaim (B&W) Sept., 1996
1 MBn,PG,"Double Cross" Pt.1 . . . 2.95
2 MBn,PG,"Double Cross" Pt.2 . . . 2.95
3 MBn,PG,"Double Cross" Pt.3 . . . 2.95
4 MBn,PG,"Double Cross" Pt.4 . . . 2.95

GRAVEDIGGERS
Acclaim (B&W) 1996
1 (of 4) 2.95
2 thru 4 . . . . @2.95

Harbinger #25 © Valiant

HARBINGER
Valiant 1992
0 DL,O:Sting,V:Harada, from TPB (Blue Bird Ed.) 2.00
0 from coupons 4.00
1 DL,JDx,I:Sting,Torque, Zeppelin,Flamingo,Kris 3.00
1a w/o coupon. 1.00
2 DL,JDx,V:Harbinger Foundation, I:Dr.Heyward 2.00
2a w/o coupon. 1.00
3 DL,JDx,I:Ax,Rexo, V:Spider Aliens. 2.00
3a w/o coupon. 1.00
4 DL,JDx,V:Ax,I:Fort, Spikeman,Dog,Bazooka 2.00
4a w/o coupon. 1.00
5 DL,JDx,I:Puff,Thumper, A:Solar,V:Harada 2.00
5a w/o coupon. 1.00
6 DL,D:Torque,A:Solar, V:Harada,Eggbreakers 2.00
6a w/o coupon. 1.00
7 DL,Torque's Funeral 2.00
8 FM(c),DL,JDx,Unity#8, A:Magnus,Eternal Warrior. 2.00
9 WS(c),DL,Unity #16, A:Magnus,Armstrong,Rai, Archer,Eternal Warrior 2.00
10 DL,I:H.A.R.D.Corps, Daryl, Shetiqua. 2.00
11 DL,V:H.A.R.D.Corps. 2.00
12 DL,F:Zeppelin,A:Elfquest 2.00
13 Flamingo Vs. Rock 2.00
14 A:Magnus(Dream Sequence), C:Stronghold 2.00
15 I:Livewire,Stronghold 2.00
16 A:Livewire,Stronghold 2.00
17 HSn,I:Simon 2.00
18 HSn,I:Screen. 2.00
19 HSn,I:Caliph 2.00
20 HSn,V:Caliph. 2.00
21 I:Pete's Father. 2.00
22 HSn,A:Archer & Armstrong 2.00
23 HSn,B:Twilight of the Eighth Day 2.00
24 HSn,V:Eggbreakers 2.00
25 HSn,V:Harada,E:Twlight of the Eighth Day 2.50
26 SCh,AdW,I:Jolt,Amazon, Mircowave,Anvil,Sonix 2.00
27 SCh,AdW,Chrismas issue 2.00
28 SCh,AdW,O:Sonix,J:Tyger 2.00
29 SCh,AdW,A:Livewire,Stronghold, w/Valiant Era card 2.00
30 SCh,AdW,A:Livewire,Stronghold 2.00
31 SCh,AdW,V:H.A.R.D.Corps 2.00
32 SCh,AdW,A:Eternal Warrior 2.00
33 SCh, V:Dr. Eclipse 2.00
34 SCh,Chaos Effect-Delta#1, A:X-O, Dr. Eclipse. 2.00
35 Zephyr. 2.00
36 Zephyr, Magnus. 2.00
37 Magnus, Harada 2.00
38 A:Spikeman. 2.00
39 Zepplin vs. Harada 2.00
40 V:Harbinger 2.00
41 V:Harbinger 2.00
TPB w/#0,rep#1-4. . . . . 25.00
TPB 2nd Printing w/o #0. . . . . 9.95
TPB #2, Rep. 6-7,10-11 . . . . 9.95

HARBINGER FILES: HARADA
Valiant 1994
1 BL,DC,O:Harada 2.75
2 Harada's ultimate weapon 2.50

H.A.R.D. CORPS
Valiant 1992
1 JLe(c),DL,BL,V:Harbinger Foundation,I:Flatline,D:Maniac . 2.50
1a Gold Ed. 2.50
2 DL,BL,V:Harb.Foundation 2.50
3 DL,BL,J:Flatline 2.50
4 BL 2.50
5 BCh,BL(i),A:Bloodshot 2.50
5a Comic Defense System Ed. . . . 2.50
6 MLe,A:Spider Aliens 2.50
7 MLe,V:Spider Aliens, I:Hotshot . . 2.50
8 MLe,V:Harada,J:Hotshot. 2.50
9 MLe,V:Harada,A:Turok 2.00
10 MLe,A:Turok,V:Dinosaurs 2.00
11 YG,I:Otherman. 2.00
12 MLe,V:Otherman 2.00
13 YG,D:Superstar 2.50
14 DvM(s),YG,V:Edie Simkus 2.00
15 DvM(s),YG,V:Edie Simkus 2.00
16 DvM(s),YG, ... 2.00
17 DvM(s),RLe,V:Armorines 2.00
18 DvM(s),RLe,V:Armorines, w/Valiant Era card 2.00
19 RLe,A:Harada 2.00
20 RLe,V:Harbingers 2.00
21 RLe,New Direction. 2.00
22 RLe,V:Midnight Earl 2.00
23 RLe,Chaos Effect-Delta #4, A:Armorines, X-O 2.00
24 Ironhead 2.00
25 Midnight Earl 2.00
26 Heydrich, Omen. 2.00
27 Heydrich shows evil. 2.00
28 New Hardcorps 2.00
29 V:New Guard. 2.00
30 Final Issue. 2.00

KILLER INSTINCT
1 thru 3 . . . . @2.50
Spec. Brothers by Art Holcomb. . . . 2.50

KNIGHTHAWK
Windjammer 1995
1 NA(c&a),I:Knighthawk the Protector,V:Nemo 2.75
2 NA(c&a),Birth of Nemo 2.50
3 NA,V:Nemo 2.50
4 NA,V:Nemo 2.50
5 I:Cannon, Brick. 2.50
6 V:Cannon, Brick 2.50

MAGIC THE GATHERING: ANTIQUITIES WAR
Armada 1995
1 Based on the Antiquities Set. . . . 2.75
2 F:Urza, Mishra 2.50
3 I:Tawnos, Ashod 2.50
4 The War Begins 2.50

MAGIC THE GATHERING: ARABIAN KNIGHTS
Armada 1995
1 Based on Rare Card set. 2.75
2 V:Queen Nailah 2.50

MAGIC THE GATHERING: CONVOCATIONS
Armada 1995
1 Gallery of Art from Game 2.50

MAGIC THE GATHERING: FALLEN EMPIRES
[Mini-Series]
Armada
1 with pack of cards. 2.75
2 F:Tymolin 2.50
TPB Rep. #1-#2 . . . . 4.95

MAGIC THE GATHERING: HOMELANDS
Armada 1995
1 I:Feroz, Serra 5.95

MAGIC THE GATHERING: ICE AGE
Armada 1995
1 Dominaia, from card game 3.00
2 Ice Age Adventures 2.50
3 CV(c) Planeswalker battles. 2.50
4 final issue. 2.50
TPB Rep. #1-#2 . . . . 4.95
TPB Rep. #3-#4 . . . . 4.95

MAGIC THE GATHERING: SHADOW MAGE
Armada 1995
1 I:Jared 3.00
2 F:Hurloon the Minotaur. 2.75
3 VMk(c&a),V:Juggernaut 2.50
4 Final issue 2.50
TPB Rep. #1-#2 . . . . 4.95
TPB Rep. #3-#4 . . . . 4.95

MAGIC THE GATHERING: THE URZA-MISHRA WAR
Armada
1 & 2 with Ice Age II card 5.95

MAGIC THE GATHERING: WAYFARER
Armada 1995
1 R:Jared 2.75
2 I:New Land. 2.50
3 R:Liana, Ravidel. 2.50
4 I:Golthonor 2.50
5 . . . . 2.50

MAGIC THE GATHERING: THE LEGENDS OF: THE ELDER DRAGONS
1 & 2. . . . . @2.50
JEDIT OJANEN
1 & 2. . . . . @2.50
SHANDALAR
1 & 2. . . . . @2.50

[ON THE WORLD OF] MAGIC THE GATHERING
GN Serra Angel + card. 5.95
GN Legend of the Fallen Angel + card 5.95
GN Dakkon Blackblade + card 5.95

Magnus Robot Fighter #37
© Valiant

MAGNUS: ROBOT FIGHTER
Valiant 1991
0 PCu,BL,"Emancipator",w/ BWS card 6.00
0a PCu,BL,w/o card. 3.00
1 ANi,BL,B:Steel Nation. 4.00
1a w/o coupon. 1.00
2 ANi,BL,Steel Nation #2. . . . . 3.00
2a w/o coupon. 1.00
3 ANi,BL,Steel Nation #3. . . . . 3.00
3a w/o coupon. 1.00
4 ANi,BL,E:Steel Nation. 3.00
4a w/o coupon. 1.00
5 DL,BL(i),I:Rai(#1),V:Slagger Flipbook format 3.00
5a w/o coupon. 1.00
6 DL,A:Solar,V:Grandmother A:Rai(#2) 2.50
6a w/o coupon. 1.00
7 DL,EC,V:Rai(#3). 2.50
7a w/o coupon. 1.00
8 DL,A:Rai(#4),Solar,X-O Armor.E:Flipbooks 2.50
8a w/o coupon. 1.00
9 EC,V:Xyrkol,E-7 . . . . 2.50
10 V:Xyrkol. 2.50
11 V:Xyrkol. 2.50
12 I:Turok,V:Dr. Noel, I:Asylum,40pgs. 6.00
13 EC,Asylum Pt 1 . . . . 2.50
14 EC,Asylum Pt2 . . . . 2.50
15 FM(c),EC,Unity#4,I:Eternal Warrior of 4001, O:Unity. 2.50
16 WS(c),EC,Unity#12,A:Solar, Archer,Armstrong,Harbinger, X-O,Rai,Eternal Warrior 2.50
17 JaB,V:Talpa 2.50
18 SD,R:Mekman,V:E-7 . . . . 2.50
19 SD,V:Mekmen 2.50
20 EC,Tale of Magnus' past 2.50
21 JaB,R:Malevalents, Grand-mother 3.00
21a Gold Ed. 4.00
22 JaB,D:Felina,V:Malevalents, Grandmother 2.50
23 V:Malevolents 2.50
24 V:Malevolents 2.50
25 N:Magnus,R:1-A,silver-foil(c) . . . 3.00
26 I:Young Wolves 2.50
27 V:Dr.Lazlo Noel 2.50
28 V:The Malevs 2.25
29 JCf,A:Eternal Warrior. 2.25
30 JCf,V:The Malevs 2.25
31 JCf,V:The Malevs 2.25
32 JCf,Battle for South Am 2.25
33 B:JOs(s),JCf,A:Ivar 2.25
34 JCf,Captured 2.25
35 JCf,V:Mekman. 2.25
36 JCf,w/Valiant Era Card. 2.25
37 JCf,A:Starwatchers 2.25
38 JCf, ... 2.25
39 JCf,F:Torque 2.25
40 JCf,F:Torque, A:Rai 2.25
41 JCf,Chaos Effect-Epsilon#4 A:Solar, Psi-Lords,Rai 2.50
42 JCf, F:Torque,A:Takashi. 2.25
43 JCf,F:Torque,Immortal E 2.25
44 JCf,F:Torque,Stagger. 2.25
45 V:Immortal Enemy 2.25
46 V:Immortal Enemy 2.25
47 Cold Blooded,pt.1 . . . . 2.25
48 Cold Blooded,pt.2 . . . . 2.25
49 F:Slagger. 2.25
50 V:Invisible Legion. 2.25
51 KoK,RyR,Return of the Robots,pt.1. . . . . 2.25
52 KoK,RyR,Robots,pt.2. . . . . 2.25
53 KoK,RyR,Robots,pt.3. . . . . 2.25
54 KoK,RyR,Robots,pt.4. . . . . 2.25
55 KG,A:Rai 2.50
56 Magnus in Japan. 2.50
57 . . . . 2.50
58 . . . . 2.50
59 V:Rai 2.50
60 R:The Malevs 2.50
61 Secrets of the Malevs 2.50
62 V:Leeja 2.50
63 R:Destroyer. 2.50
64 Ultimatum, F:Destroyer 2.50
Yearbook #1. . . . . 3.95
TPB 1-4 . . . . 9.95

MAGNUS (ROBOT FIGHTER)
Acclaim Jan., 1997
1 Magnus back from the future . . . 2.50
2 "Tomorrow Never Knows" 2.50
3 "Tomorrow Never Knows" 2.50
4 "Tomorrow Never Knows" 2.50
5 "Tomorrow Never Knows" 2.50
6 A:Janice Whitcraft. 2.50
7 "When Titans Clash". 2.50

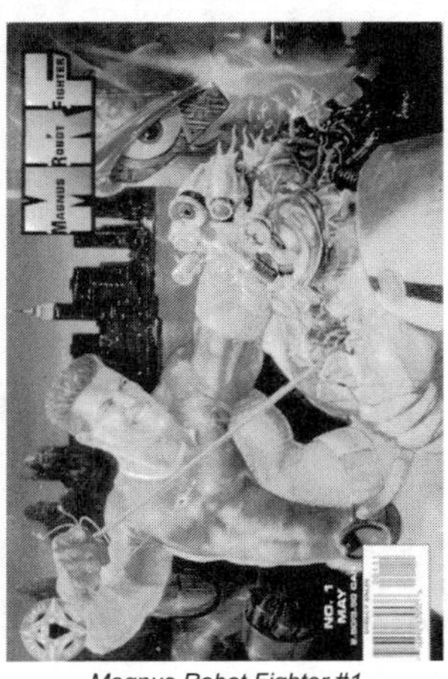

Magnus Robot Fighter #1
© Acclaim

8 TPe,DdB,"When Titans Clash" . . 2.50
9 TPe,"See Tirana and Die" 2.50
10 TPe,"The Memory" 2.50
11 TPe,"Where Angels Fear" 2.50
12 TPe,"Showdown" 2.50
13 TPe, ... 2.50
14 TPe,"Wild in the Streets" 2.50
15 TPe,Magnus stands alone 2.50
16 TPe,"Hart's Home" 2.50
17 TPe,"Invasive Procedures" 2.50
18 TPe,"Welcome to Salvation" 2.50

MAN OF THE ATOM
Valiant Heroes Special Project
Acclaim Jan., 1997

Spec. 3.95
TPB The Rebirth of Solar 8.00

MASTER DARQUE
Acclaim 1997

Spec. F:Brixton Sound, 48pg 4.00

MUTANT CHRONICLES— GOLGOTHA
Valiant

1 thru 4 + game trading card . . . @2.95
TPB, Vol. 1 rep. Pt.#1–#4 . . . . 10.95

NINJAK
Valiant 1994

0: O:Ninjak, Pt. 1 . . . . 2.50
00: O:Ninjak, Pt.2 . . . . 2.50
1 B:MMo(s),JQ,JP,Chromium(c), I:Dr.Silk,Webnet 3.00
1a Gold Ed 4.00
2 JQ,JP,V:Dr.Silk,Webnet 2.50
3 JQ,JP,I:Seventh Dragon 2.25
4 MMo(a&s),V:Seventh Dragon, w/Valiant Era card 2.25
5 MMo(a&s),A:X-O Manowar 2.25
6 MMo(a&s),A:X-O Manowar, V:Dr.Silk,Webnet 2.25
7 MMo(a&s),I:Rhaman 2.25
8 MMo(a&s),Chaos Effect-Gamma #3, A:Madame Noir 2.25
9 Dogs of War 2.00
10 Cantebury Tale #1 . . . . 2.00
11 Cantebury Tale #2 . . . . 2.00
12 . . . . 2.00
13 Mad Dogs and English 2.00
14 Cry Wolf pt. 1 . . . . 2.00
15 Cry Wolf pt. 2 . . . . 2.25
16 Plague Pt. 1 . . . . 2.25
17 Plague Pt. 2 . . . . 2.25
18 Computer Virus 2.25
19 DAn,ALa,MM,Breaking the Web,pt.1 . . . . 2.25
20 DAn,ALa,MM,Breaking the Web,pt.2 . . . . 2.25
21 DAn,ALa,MM,Breaking the Web,pt.3 . . . . 2.25
22 Bitter Wind 2.25
23 w/o arsenal 2.25
24 Unusual sidekick 2.25
25 . . . . 2.25
26 . . . . 2.25
27 Diamond Smugglers 2.25
28 F:Sister Gabriela 2.25
Yearbook #1, Dr. Silk 3.95

Ninjak #6 © Valiant

NINJAK
Acclaim 1996

1 KBk(s), Denny Meechum becomes Ninjak 2.50
2 KBk(s) video game spin-off 2.50
3 KBk(s) video game spin-off 2.50
4 KBk(s) video game spin-off 2.50
5 KBk(s) video game spin-off 2.50
6 KBk(s) "The World's Finest" 2.50
7 KBk(s) video game spin-off 2.50
8 KBk(s) video game spin-off 2.50
9 KBk(s) video game spin-off 2.50
10 KBk(s) F:Maria Barbella 2.50
11 KBk(s) Trial Continues 2.50
12 KBk(s) final issue 2.50

N.I.O.
Acclaim 1998

1 (of 4) by Shon Bury & JPi 2.50
2 . . . . 2.50
3 . . . . 2.50
4 conclusion 2.50

OPERATION: STORMBRINGER
Acclaim Special Event
April, 1997

Spec. F:Teutonic Knight 3.95

ORIGINAL CAPTAIN JOHNAR AND THE ALIENS
Valiant 1995

1 Reprint from Magnus 2.95
2 Russ Manning rep. 2.95

ORIGINAL DR. SOLAR MAN OF THE ATOM
Valiant 1995

1 Reprint 2.95
2 Reprints 2.95
3 Reprints 2.95

ORIGINAL MAGNUS ROBOT FIGHTER
Valiant 1995

1 Reprint 2.95
2 Russ Manning Art 2.95
3 Russ Manning 2.95

ORIGINAL TUROK, SON OF STONE
Valiant 1995

1 Reprint 2.95
2 Alberto Gioletti art 2.95
3 Alberto Gioletti 2.95
4 Reprints 2.95

OUTCAST SPECIAL
Valiant 1995

1 R:The Outcast 2.50

PLANESWALKER WAR
Acclaim Aug., 1996

GN #1 Magic: The Gathering tie-in . 5.95

PSI-LORDS: REIGN OF THE STARWATCHERS
Valiant 1994

1 MLe,DG,Chromium(c),Valiant Vision,V:Spider Aliens 3.00
2 MLe,DG,V:Spider Aliens 2.25
3 MLe,DG,Chaos Effect-Epsilon#2, A:Solar 2.25
Becomes:

PSI-LORDS

4 V:Ravenrok 2.25
5 V:Ravenrok 2.25
6 . . . . 2.25
7 Micro-Invasion 2.25
8 A:Solar the Destroyer 2.25
9 Frozen Harbingers 2.25
10 F:Ravenrok 2.25

PUNX
Windjammer 1995

1 KG,I:Punx 2.50
2 KG,A:Harbinger 2.50
3 KG,F:P.M.S 2.50
4 KG,final issue 2.50
Spec.#1 . . . . 2.50

PUNX REDUX

1 thru 4 . . . . @2.50

PUNX

Acclaim Jan., 1997

One Shot Spec. F:Big Max 2.50

QUANTUM LEAP

Acclaim Jan., 1997

1 BML(s),"Into the Void," pt.1 . . . . . 2.50
2 BML(s),"Into the Void," pt.2 . . . . . 2.50
3 BML(s),"Into the Void," pt.3 . . . . . 2.50
Spec. "The Leaper Before. 3.95

Quantum & Woody #6 © Acclaim

QUANTUM & WOODY

Acclaim Feb., 1997

1 CPr(s),MBr Woodrow Van Chelton & Eric Henderson become unlikely superheros . . . 4.00
1a Variant (c). 5.00
2 CPr(s),MBr,World's worst superhero team 3.00
3 CPr(s),MBr,Woody buys a goat. . 3.00
4 CPr(s),MBr. 3.00
5 CPr(s),MBr 2.75
6 CPr(s),MBr 2.75
7 CPr(s),MBr. 2.75
8 CPr(s),MBr,R:Warrant. 2.75
9 CPr(s),DCw,Woody is dying 2.75
10 CPr(s),MBr,trapped in each other's bodies, Goat month. . . . 2.75
11 CPr(s),MBr,switched body delimma 2.50
12 CPr(s),MBr,switched bodies 2.50
13 CPr(s),MBr,back in own bodies . 2.50
14 CPr(s),MBr,Magnum Force,pt.1 . 2.50
15 CPr(s),MBr,Magnum Force,pt.2 . 2.50
16 CPr(s),MBr,Magnum Force,pt.3 . 2.50
17 CPr(s),MBr,Magnum Force,pt.4 . 2.50
32 Dr. Eclipse, pt.3 . . . . 2.50
18 thru 27 . . . . @2.50
TPB Director's Cut, rep.#1–#4 . . . . 8.00
TPB Kiss Your Ass Goodbye 8.00
TPB Holy S-word We're Cancelled . 8.00
TPB Magnum Force 8.00

RAI

Valiant 1991

0 DL,O:Bloodshot,I:2nd Rai,D:X-O, Archer,Shadowman,F:all Valiant heroes,bridges Valiant Universe 1992-4001 . . . . 3.00
1 V:Grandmother. 5.00
2 V:Icespike. 2.50
3 V:Humanists,Makiko 3.00
4 V:Makiko,rarest Valiant 4.00
5 Rai leaves earth, C:Eternal Warrior. 2.50
6 FM(c),Unity#7,V:Pierce. 2.50
7 WS(c),Unity#15,V:Pierce, D:Rai,A:Magnus 2.50
8 Epilogue of Unity in 4001 . . . . . . 2.50
Becomes:

RAI AND THE FUTURE FORCE

Valiant 1993

9 F:Rai,E.Warrior of 4001,Tekla, X-O Commander,Spylocke 2.50
9a Gold Ed. 3.00
10 Rai vs. Malev Emperor 2.25
11 SCh,V:Malevolents. 2.25
12 V:Cyber Raiders 2.25
13 Spylocke Revealed 2.25
14 SCh,D:M'Ree 2.25
15 SCh,V:X-O. 2.25
16 SCh,V:Malevs 2.25
17 . . . . 2.25
18 JOs(s),Spk,V:Malevs 2.25
19 JCf,V:Malves 2.25
20 JOs(s),DR,V:Malves,Spylocke realed to be Spider Alien 2.25
21 DR,I:Starwatchers,b:Torque, w/Valiant Era card 2.25
22 DR,D:2nd Rai, A:Starwatchers . . 2.25
23 DR,A:Starwatchers, ... 2.25
24 DR,in Tibet 2.00
25 DR,F:Spylocke. 2.00
26 DR,Chaos Effect-Epsilon#3, A:Solar Magnus,Psi-Lords 2.00
Becomes:

RAI

Valiant 1994

27 "Rising Son" 2.00
28 V:Takashi. 2.00
29 A:Rentaro Nakadai 2.00
30 Splocke 2.00
31 Bad Penny pt. 1. . . . . 2.00
32 Bad Penny pt. 2, F:Axscan 2.00
33 F:Spylocke, Rentaro 2.00
TPB #0-#4 . . . . 11.95
TPB Star System ed. 11.95

REVELATIONS

one-shot by Jim Krueger. 3.95

SABAN POWERHOUSE

Acclaim Young Readers 1997
Digest Size,
F: Power Rangers Turbo

Spec. "Simple Simon Says" 4.50
Spec. "Into the Fire" 4.50
Spec. "Mystery of the Phantom Ranger" 4.50

SABAN PRESENTS

Acclaim 1997

Spec. Power Rangers Turbo vs. Big Bad Beetleborgs. 4.50

SAMUREE

Windjammer 1995

1 I:Samuree 2.50
2 V: The Dragon 2.50
3 V: The Dragon 2.50

THE SECOND LIFE OF DR. MIRAGE

Valiant 1993

1 B:BL(s),BCh,V:Mast.Darque 2.50
1a Gold Ed. 3.00
2 BCh,V:Master Darque. 2.50
3 BCh 2.50
4 BCh,V:Bhrama 2.50
5 BCh,A:Shadowman,V:Master Darque. 2.50
6 BCh,V:Dr.Eclipse 2.50
7 BCh,V:Dr.Eclipse,w/card. 2.50
8 BCh,. 2.50
9 BCh,A:Otherman 2.50
10 BCh,V:Otherman 2.50
11 BCh,Chaos Effect-Beta#2, ... 2.50
12 BCh. 2.25
13 BCh. 2.25
14 . . . . 2.25
15 Chaos Effect 2.25
16 & 17. @2.25
18 F:Deathsmith. 2.25
19 R:Walt Wiley 2.25

SECRETS OF THE VALIANT UNIVERSE

Valiant 1994

1 from Wizard 2.50
2 BH,Chaos Effect-Beta#4,A:Master Darque,Dr.Mirage,Max St.James, Dr. Eclipse 2.25

SECRET WEAPONS

Valiant 1993

1 JSP(a&s),BWi(i),I:Dr.Eclipse, A:Master Darque,A:Geoff, Livewire,Stronghold,Solar,X-O, Bloodshot,Shadowman. 2.75
1a Gold Ed. 4.00
2 JSP(a&s),V:Master Darque, Dr.Eclipse. 2.25
3 JSP(a&s),V:Speedshots 2.25
4 JSP(a&s),V:Scatterbrain 2.25
5 JSP(a&s),A:Ninjak 2.25
6 JPS(s),JPh(pl),TeH, V:Spider Aliens. 2.25
7 JPS(s),V:Spider Aliens 2.25
8 JSP(a&pl),V:Harbingers 2.25
9 JSP(a&s),V:Webnet, w/Valiant Era card 2.25
10 JSP(a&s),V:Webnet. 2.25
11 PGr,New Line-up 2.25
12 PGr,A:Bloodshot 2.25
13 PGr,Chaos Effect-Gamma#2 . . . 2.25
14 PGr,F:Bloodshot 2.00
15 . . . . 2.00
16 . . . . 2.00
17 V:Dr. Silk 2.00
18 Gigo 2.00
19 A:Ninjak. 2.00
20 Bloodshot Rampage Pt.2 . . . . . . 2.00
21 Bloodshot Rampage Pt.4 . . . . . . 2.00
22 I:Gestalt, Pyroclast. 2.00
23 A:Bloodshot. 2.00

SECRET WEAPONS: PLAYING WITH FIRE

Valiant

1 & 2 . . . . @2.50

SHADOW MAN

Valiant 1992

0 BH,TmR,Chromium (c),O:Maxim St.James,Shadowman 3.00
0a Newstand ed. 2.50

Shadowman #16 © Valiant

0b Gold Ed. 4.00
1 DL,JRu,I&O:Shadowman 5.00
2 DL,V:Serial Killer 3.00
3 V:Emil Sosa 3.00
4 DL,FM(c),Unity#6,A:Solar 2.50
5 DL,WS(c),Unity#14, A:Archer & Armstrong 2.50
6 SD,L:Lilora 2.50
7 DL,V:Creature 2.50
8 JDx(i),I:Master Darque 3.00
9 JDx(i),V:Darque's Minions. 3.00
10 BH,I:Sandria 2.50
11 BH,N:Shadowman 2.50
12 BH,V:Master Darque 2.50
13 BH,V:Rev.Shadow Man 2.50
14 BH,JDx,V:Bikers 2.50
15 BH,JDx,V:JB,Fake Shadow Man,C:Turok 2.50
16 BH,JDx,I:Dr.Mirage, Carmen . . . 3.00
17 BH,JDx,A:Archer & Armstrong . . 2.25
18 BH,JDx,A:Archer & Armstrong . . 2.25
19 BH,A:Aerosmith. 2.25
20 BH,A:Master Darque, V:Shadowman's Father. 2.25
21 BH,I:Maxim St.James (1895 Shadowman) 2.25
22 V:Master Darque 2.25
23 BH(a&s),A:Doctor Mirage, V:Master Darque 2.25
24 BH(a&s),V:H.A.T.E. 2.25
25 RgM,w/Valiant Era card 2.25
26 w/Valiant Era card 2.50
27 BH,V:Drug Lord 2.25
28 BH,A:Master Darque 2.25
29 Chaos Effect-Beta#1,V:Master Darque. 2.25
30 R:Rotwak. 2.25
31 thru 33. . . . . @2.25
34 Voodoo in Carribean 2.25
35 A:Ishmael 2.25
36 F:Ishmael 2.25
37 A:X-O, V:Blister 2.25
38 V:Ishmael, Blister. 2.25
39 BH,TmR,Explores Powers 2.25
40 BH,TmR,I,Vampire! 2.25
41 A:Steve Massarsky 2.25
42 . . . . 2.25
43 V:Smilin Jack. 2.25
TPB rep.#1-#3,#6 . . . . 9.95

SHADOWMAN

Acclaim Nov., 1996

1 GEn(s),"Deadside," pt.1 . . . . 2.50
2 GEn(s),"Deadside," pt.2 . . . . 2.50
3 GEn(s),"Deadside," pt.3 . . . . 2.50
4 GEn(s),"Deadside," pt.4 . . . . 2.50
5 JaD,CAd,"Nothing is True," pt.1 . 2.50
6 JaD,CAd,"Nothing is True," pt.2 . 2.50
7 JaD,CAd,"Nothing is True," pt.3 . 2.50
8 JaD,CAd,"Nothing is True," pt.4 . 2.50
9 JaD,CAd,"The Buzz," pt.1 . . . . . . 2.50
10 JaD,CAd,"The Buzz," pt.2 . . . . . 2.50
11 JaD,CAd,"ClearBlueSkies,"pt.1. . 2.50
12 JaD,CAd,"ClearBlueSkies,"pt.2 . 2.50
13 JaD,CAd,"Hoodoo Bash,"pt.1 . . . 2.50
14 JaD,CAd,"Hoodoo Bash,"pt.2. . . 2.50
15 JaD,CAd,"Hoodoo Bash,"pt.3. . . 2.50
16 Mask of Shadows ripped out . . . 2.50
17 Mask of Shadows, pt.2 . . . . 2.50
18 Claudine kidnapped? 2.50
19 pursuit of Mah 2.50
20 Deadside vortes. 2.50

VOLUME 3 (1999)

1 DAn,ALa,48-page. 3.95
2 . . . . 2.50
3 Flip-book 2.50
4 Flip-book 2.50
5 thru 7 . . . . @2.50

SLIDERS

Valiant 1996

1 & 2 . . . . @2.50

SLIDERS: DARKEST HOUR

1 DGC,DG. 2.50
2 DGC,DG. 2.50
3 DGC,DG, Concl.. . . . . 2.50
Spec. RgM, Montezuma IV rules the world 3.95
Spec. #2 "Secrets" 3.95
TPB from TV show 9.00

SLIDERS: ULTIMATUM

Valiant 1996

1 & 2 . . . . @2.50

SOLAR: HELL ON EARTH

Acclaim 1997

1 (of 4) CPr,DCw,Seleski twins have power of God. 2.50
2 CPr,Goat Month prelude 2.50
3 CPr,RT,V:Jimmy Six 2.50
4 CPr, ... 2.50

SOLAR: MAN OF THE ATOM

Valiant 1991

1 BWS,DP,BL,B:2nd Death B:Alpha & Omega 4.00
2 BWS,DP,BL,V:Dr Solar 3.00
3 BWS,DP,BL,V:Harada I:Harbinger Foundation. 3.00
4 BWS,DP,BL,E:2nd Death V:Dr Solar 2.50
5 BWS,EC,V:Alien Armada 2.50
6 BWS,DP,SDr, V:Alien Armada X-O Armor. 2.50
7 BWS,DP,SDr, V:Alien Armada X-O Armor. 2.50
8 BWS,V:Dragon of Bangkok. 2.50
9 BWS,DP,SDr, V:Erica's Baby . . . 2.50
10 BWS,DP,SDr,JDx,I:Eternal Warrior,E:Alpha&Omega. 3.00
10a 2nd printing 2.00
11 SDr,A:Eternal Warrior, Prequel to Unity #0 . . . . 3.00
12 SDr,FM(c),Unity#9,O:Pierce, Albert 2.50
13 DP,SDr,WS(c),Unity #17, V:Pierce 2.50
14 DP,SDr,I:Bender (becomes Dr.Eclipse) 3.00
15 SD,V:Bender 3.00
16 Solar moves to California. 2.50
17 SDr(i),V:X-O Manowar 2.50
18 SDr(i),A:X-Manowar. 2.50
19 SDr(i),V:Videogame 2.50
20 SDr(i),Dawn of the Malevolence. 2.50
21 SDr(i),Master Darque. 2.50
22 SDr(i),V:Master Darque,A: Bender(Dr.Eclipse) 2.50
23 SDr(i),JQ(c),V:Master Darque,I:Solar War God 2.50
24 SDr(i),A:Solar War God 2.50
25 V:Dr.Eclpise. 2.25
26 Phil and Gayle on vaction 2.25
27 in Austrialia 2.25
28 A:Solar War God 2.25
29 KVH(s),JP(i),Valiant Vision, A:Solar War God 2.50
30 KVH(s),JP,V:Energy Parasite . . . 2.25
31 KVH(s),JP,Chrismas Issue 2.25
32 KVH(s),JP,Parent's Night 2.25
33 KVH(s),PGr,JP,B:Solar the Destroyer,w/Valiant Era card. . . 2.25
34 KVH(s),PGr,V:Spider Alien. 2.25
35 KVH(s),PGr,JP,E:Solar the Destroyer,Valiant Vision 2.25
36 KVH(s),PGr,JP,B:Revenge times two,V:Doctor Eclipse, Ravenus. 2.25
37 PGr,JP,E:Revenge times two, V:Doctor Eclipse,Ravenus 2.00
38 PGr,JP,Chaos Effect-Epsilon#1 . 2.00
39 . . . . 2.00
40 . . . . 2.00
41 . . . . 2.00
42 Elements of Evil pt.1 . . . . 2.00
43 Elements of Evil pt.2 . . . . 2.00
44 I:New Character. 2.00
45 Explores Powers 2.00
46 I:The Sentry. 2.25
47 DJu,DG,Brave New World,pt.2. . 2.25
48 DJu,DG,Brave New World,pt.3. . 2.25
49 DJu,DG,Brave New World,pt.4. . 2.25
50 DJu,DG,Brave New World,pt.5. . 2.25
51 I:Aliens on the Moon 2.25
52 Solar Saves Earth 2.25
53 I:Marauder. 2.25
54 V:Marauder 2.25
55 I:Black Star 2.25
56 V:Black Star. 2.25

Solar, Man of the Atom #28 © Valiant

57 A:Armorines. 2.25
58 I:Atman, The Inquisitor. 2.25
59 and 60 KG . . . . @2.25
TPB #0 JiS,BWS,BL,Alpha and Omega rep. from Solar #1–#10 9.95
TPB #1 JiS,BWS,GL,V:Doctor Solar rep. from Solar #1–#4. . . . . 9.95

STARSLAYER DIRECTORS CUT

Windjammer 1995

1 R:Starslayer, Mike Grell 2.50
2 I:New Star Slayer 2.50
3 Jolly Rodger 2.50
4 V:Battle Droids 2.50
5 I:Baraka Kuhi 2.50
6 V:Valkyrie 2.50
7 MGr(c&a),Can Torin destroy? . . . 2.50
8 MGr(c&a),JAl, Can Torin live with his deeds?,final issue 2.50

STARWATCHERS

Valiant

1 MLe,DG,Chromium(c),Valiant Vision, ... 3.50

SUPER MARIO BROS.

Valiant 1991

1 thru 6 . . . . @1.95
Spec. #1. . . . . 1.95

TICK, THE

Spec. digest size 4.50

TIMEWALKER

Valiant 1994

0 BH,DP,O:3 Immortals 2.95
1 DP, BH 2.50
2 DP,BH 2.50
3 DP BH 2.50
4 Ten Commandments. 2.50
5 DP,BH 2.50
6 Harbinger Wars Pt.1 . . . . 2.50
7 Harbinger Wars Pt.2 . . . . 2.50
8 Harbinger Wars Pt.3 . . . . 2.50
9 V:Jahk rt. 2.50
10 Last God of Dura-Europus,pt.1 time: 260 A.D. 2.50
11 Last God of Dura-Europus,pt.2. . 2.50
12 3RW,DP,Ashes to Ashes,pt.1 . . . 2.50
13 3RW,DP,Ashes to Ashes,pt.2 . . . 2.50
14 Meets Mozart. 2.50
15 26th Century 2.50
Yearbook F:Harada. 2.95
TPB F:Archer & Armstrong 9.95

TRINITY ANGELS

Acclaim March, 1997

1 KM,DPs, Maria, Gianna & Theresa Barbella become Trinity Angels 2.50
2 KM,DPs, V:The 99 . . . . 2.50
3 KM,DPs, looking for a little head. 2.50
4 KM,DPs, V:Flaming Queen 2.50
5 KM, New costumes. 2.50
6 KM, in Las Vegas 2.50
7 KM, in Las Vegas 2.50
8 KM, "A Woman Scorned" 2.50
9 KM, A:Rumblin' Guys 2.50
10 KM, Mad Cow 2.50
11 KM, ... 2.50
12 KM, Final issue 2.50

Trinity Angels #1 © Acclaim

TROUBLEMAKERS

Acclaim Dec. 1996

1 FaN(s) 2.50
2 FaN(s) go back in time 2.50
3 FaN(s) Jane has a big problem. . 2.50
4 FaN(s) Can Blur prevent parents divorce? 2.50
5 FaN(s) A:Ninjak 2.50
6 FaN(s) in outer space 2.50
7 FaN(s) I:The Rabble Rousers . . . 2.50
8 FaN(s) Rabble Rousers,pt.2 . . . . 2.50
9 FaN(s) F:Christine 2.50
10 FaN(s) F:Zach 2.50
11 FaN(s) F:Calamity Jane 2.50
12 FaN(s) a Troublemaker dead . . . 2.50
13 FaN(s) F:XL. 2.50
14 FaN(s) 2.50
15 FaN(s) Is Parker alive? 2.50
16 FaN(s) Andrew Chase 2.50
17 FaN(s) V:Turnabout 2.50
18 FaN(s) Jacinda Monroe 2.50
19 FaN(s) V:Rabblerousers 2.50

TUROK: CHILD OF BLOOD

Acclaim 1997

1-shot FaN, 48pg 4.00

TUROK: DINOSAUR HUNTER

Valiant 1993

1 BS,Chromium(c),O:Turok retold,V:Monark 3.00
1a Gold Ed. 4.00
2 BS,V:Monark 2.75
3 BCh,V:Monark 2.75
4 TT(s),RgM,O:Turok. 2.75
5 TT(s),RgM,V:Dinosaurs 2.75
6 TT(s),RgM,V:Longhunter 2.75
7 TT(a&s),B:People o/t Spider 2.75
8 TT(a&s),V:T-Rex 2.75
9 TT(a&s),E:People o/t Spider 2.75
10 MBn,RgM,A:Bile 2.75
11 MBn,RgM,V:Chun Yee,w/card . . 2.75
12 MBn,RgM,V:Dinosaur 2.75
13 B:TT(c&s),RgM, ... 2.75
14 V:Dino-Pirate 2.50
15 RgM,V:Dino-Pirate 2.25
16 Chaos Effect-Beta#3, V:Evil Shaman 2.75
17 V:C.I.A. 2.50
18 V:Bionosaurs 2.50
19 A:Manowar 2.50
20 Chichak 2.50
21 Ripsaw 2.50
22 . . . . 2.50
23 A:Longhunter. 2.50
24 R:To The Lost Land 2.50
25 I:Warrior of Mother God 2.50
26 V:Overlord 2.50
27 TT,RgM,Lost Land,pt.4. . . . . 2.50
28 MBn,DEA hunts rogue T-Rex. . . 2.50
29 SFu,Manhunt,pt.1 . . . . 2.50
30 SFu,Manhunt,pt.2 . . . . 2.50
31 F:Darwin Challenger 2.50
32 V:Special Effects 2.50
33 V:Aliens. 2.50
34 V:Alien Ooze 2.50
35 Early Years 2.50
36 Confronts Past. 2.50
37 V:Nazi Women. 2.50
38 V:Bigfoot 2.50
39 TT,Shainer Silver 2.50
40 A:Longhunter. 2.50
41 Church of the Poison Mind. 2.50
42 Church of the Poison Mind. 2.50
43 thru 47 . . . . @2.50
Yearbook #1 MBn(s),DC, N&V:Mon Ark. 4.25
Yearbook 1995 MGr,The Hunted. . . 2.95
Spec. Tales of the Lost Land. 4.00
TPB FaN 112pgs.rep. game 10.00

TUROK

Acclaim 1998

1 FaN 3-D cover 2.50
2 FaN,A:Armorines 2.50
3 FaN,Lazarus Concordance 2.50
4 FaN, real President?. 2.50
TPB Dinosaur Hunter, FaN 9.95

TUROK: COMIC BOOK MAGAZINE

Acclaim 1998

Seeds of Evil 5.00
Adon's Curse 5.00
Turok/Shadowman 5.00

TUROK: THE HUNTED

Valiant

1 & 2. . . . . 2.50

TUROK QUARTERLY—REDPATH

March 1997, FaN(s),"Spring Break in the Lost Land" 3.95
June 1997, FaN(s), Killer loose in Oklahoma City 3.95

TUROK/SHADOWMAN

Acclaim 1999

1-shot 3.95

TUROK 3: SHADOW OF OBLIVION

Acclaim 2000

Spec. 48-page 4.95

TUROK/SHAMAN'S TEARS

Valiant 1995

1 MGr,Ghost Dance Pt. 1. . . . . 2.50
2 MGr,JAl,White Buffalo kidnapped,V:Bar Sinister 2.50
3 V:Supremeists/Circle Sea 2.50

TUROK/TIMEWALKER
Acclaim 1997
1 of 2 FaN(s),"Seventh Sabbath" . . 2.50
2 of 2 FaN(s),"Seventh Sabbath" . . 2.50

UNITY
Valiant 1992
0 BWS,BL,Chapter#1,A:All Valiant Heroes,V:Erica Pierce 3.00
0a Red ed.,w/red logo 4.00
1 BWS,BL,Chapter#18,A:All Valiant Heroes,D:Erica Pierce 3.00
1a Gold logo 4.00
1b Platinum 4.00
TPB Previews Exclusive,Vol.I Chap.#1-9 . . . . 8.00
TPB Previews Exclusive,Vol.II Chap.#10-18 . . . . 3.00
TPB #1 rep Chapters #1-4 . . . . . . 10.95
TPB #2 rep Chapters #5-9 . . . . 9.95
TPB #3 rep Chapters #10-14 . . . . . 9.95

UNITY 2000
Acclaim 1999
1 (of 6) 2.50
2 . . . . 2.50
3 . . . . 2.50
4 . . . . 2.50
5 . . . . 2.50

VALERIA, THE SHE-BAT
Windjammer 1995
1 (of 2) NA,Valeria & 'Rilla 2.50
2 (of 2) NA,BSz, final issue 2.50

VALIANT ERA
Valiant
TPB rep.Magnus #12,Shadowman #8, Solar #10-11,Eternal Warrior#4-5 . . . . 13.95

VALIANT READER: GUIDE TO THE VALIANT

UNIVERSE
1 O:Valiant Universe 1.00

VALIANT VISION STARTER KIT
Valiant
1 w/3-D Glasses 2.95
2 F:Starwatchers 2.95

VINTAGE MAGNUS ROBOT FIGHTER
Valiant
1 rep. Gold Key Magnus #22 (which is #1). 5.00
2 rep. Gold Key Magnus #3 . . . . . . 4.50
3 rep. Gold Key Magnus #13 . . . . . 3.50
4 rep. Gold Key Magnus #15 . . . . . 3.50

VISITOR
Valiant 1994
1 New Series. 2.50
2 F:The Harbinger 2.50
3 The Bomb 2.50
4 V:F/X Specialists 2.50
5 R:Harbinger 2.50
6 KVH,BS(c),V:Men in Black 2.50
7 KVH,BS(c),V:Men in Black,pt.2 . . 2.50
8 KVH,V:Harbinger identity 2.50
9 KVH,A:Harbinger,Flamingo 2.50
10 Weather Problems. 2.50
11 V:Cannibals 2.50
12 V:Harada, Men in Black 2.50
13 Visitor is the Future Harbinger . . 2.50

VISITOR VS. VALIANT
Valiant 1994
1 V:Solar 2.95
2 . . . . 2.95

WATERWORLD
Acclaim 1997
1 of 4 V:Leviathan 2.50
2 of 4 "Children of Leviathan". 2.50
3 of 4 KoK. 2.50
4 of 4 KoK "Children of Leviathan". 2.50

WWF BATTLEMANIA
Valiant
1 WWF Action 2.50
2 thru 5 . . . . @2.50

X-O MANOWAR
Valiant 1992
0 JQ,O:Aric,1st Full Chromium(c) . 3.00
0a Gold Ed.. . . . . 3.50
1 BL,BWS,I:Aric,Ken 4.00
2 BL(i),V:Lydia,Wolf-Class Armor. . 3.00
3 I:X-Caliber,A:Solar 3.00
4 MM,A:Harbinger,C:Shadowman (Jack Boniface) 3.00
5 BWS(c),V:AX 3.00
5a w/Pink logo. 3.00
6 SD,V:Ax(X-O Armor). 3.00
7 FM(c),Unity#5,V:Pierce. 2.75
8 WS(c),Unity#13,V:Pierce 2.75
9 Aric in Italy,408 A.D. 2.75
10 N:X-O Armor 2.75
11 V:Spider Aliens 2.50
12 A:Solar 2.50
13 V:Solar 2.50
14 BS,A:Turok,I:Randy Cartier 3.00
15 BS,A:Turok 2.50
15a Red Ed.. . . . . 3.00
16 V:The Mob. 2.50
17 BL 2.50
18 JCf,V:CIA,A:Randy,I:Paul. 2.50
19 JCf,V:US Government 2.50
20 A:Toyo Harada. 2.50
21 V:Ax 2.50
22 Aria in S.America. 2.50
23 Aria in S.America. 2.50
24 Aria comes back 2.50
25 JCf,JGz,PaK,I:Armories, BU:Armories#0. . . . . 3.00
26 JGz(s),RLv,F:Ken 2.50
27 JGz,RLe,A:Turok,Geomancer, Stronghold,Livewire. 2.50
28 JGz,RLe,D:X-O,V:Spider Aliens,w/Valiant Era card 2.75
29 JGz,RLe,A:Turok,V:SpiderAliens 2.50
30 JGz,RLe,A:Solar 2.50
31 JGz,RLe,. 2.50
32 JGz,RLe,at Orb,Inc.. . . . . 2.25
33 JGz,RLe,Chaos Effect-Delta#3, A:Armorines,H.A.R.D. Corps. . . 2.25
34 thru 36. . . . . @2.25
37 Wolfbridge Affair pt.1 . . . . 2.25
38 Wolfbridge Affair pt.2 . . . . 2.25

X-O Manowar #23 © Valiant

39 Wolfbridge Affair pt.3 . . . . 2.25
40 Wolfbridge Affair pt.4 . . . . 2.25
41 Aftermath. 2.25
42 A:Shadowman Surprise 2.25
43 Chasitty's Boys 2.25
44 Bart Sears New Direction. 2.50
45 RMz,V:Crescendo 2.50
46 RMz,V:Crescendo 2.50
47 RMz,V:Crescendo 2.50
48 RMz,BS,A:Turok 2.50
49 RMz,loses control of armor 2.50
50-X R:Paul, I:Alloy 2.50
50-O V:Alloy. 2.50
51 V:Lummox. 2.50
52 V:A Blast From the Past. 2.50
53 Returns To Space 2.50
54 I:New Aliens 2.50
55 V:Aliens. 2.50
56 V:Aliens. 2.50
57 I:Gamin 2.50
58 I:Volt 2.50
59 thru 67. . . . . @2.50
TPB rep.#1-4,w/X-O Manual 11.00

X-O MANOWAR
Series Two, Acclaim, Oct., 1997
1 Rand Banion v. R.A.G.E. 2.50
2 v. R.A.G.E.. . . . . 2.50
3 . . . . 2.50
4 R.A.G.E. is back. 2.50
5 Donovan Wylie vs. Internaut 2.50
6 Internaut controls X-O suit 2.50
7 SEa, Donovan wears his armor . 2.50
8 SEa, V:Basilisk. 2.50
9 SEa, A: new Hard Corps. 2.50
10 SEa, R:Bravado. 2.50
11 BAu,MWa,SEa,alien creators . . . 2.50
12 BAu,MWa,SEa,O:armor 2.50
13 BAu,SEa,V:Alien creators 2.50
14 BAu,SEa,V:Aliens of Unity 2.50
15 BAu,SEa,out of armor 2.50
16 BAu,SEa,. 2.50
17 DMD,SEa,civil war. 2.50
18 DMD,SEa,Rand Banion 2.50
19 DMD,SEa,V:Master Blaster 2.50
20 DMD,trapped in a sleep-state. . . 2.50
TPB MWa,BAu rep. #1–#4 . . . . . . 10.00

ACCLAIM

DARK HORSE

ABE SAPIEN: DRUMS OF THE DEAD
March, 1998

1-shot Hellboy spin-off 3.00

ABYSS, THE

1 MK,Movie Adaptation pt.1 . . . . . . 2.50
2 MK,Movie Adaptation pt.2 . . . . . . 2.50

ACCIDENT MAN
(B&W)

1 I:Accident Man 2.50
2 and 3 . . . . @2.50

ADVENTURES OF LUTHER ARKWRIGHT
Valkyrie Press/Dark Horse
(B&W) 1987–89

1 thru 9 . . . . @2.00

(B&W) 1990

1 thru 9 Rep. . . . . @1.95
TPB 14.95

ADVENTURES OF THE MASK
1996

1 thru 12 by Michael Eury & Marc Campos, TV cartoon adapt. . @2.50

AGENTS OF LAW
Comics' Greatest World 1995

1 KG, I:Law 2.50
2 A:Barb Wire 2.50
3 KG,DLw,The Judgment Gate . . . 2.50
4 Open Golden City 2.50
5 Who is the Mystery figure 2.50
6 V:Predator 2.50

AGE OF REPTILES
1993–94

1 DRd,Story on Dinosaurs 3.00
2 DRd,Story on Dinosaurs 3.00
3 DRd,Story on Dinosaurs 3.00
4 DRd,Story on Dinosaurs 3.00
TPB Tribal Warfare 14.95

AGE OF REPTILES: THE HUNT
1996

1 thru 5 by Ricardo Delgado. . . . @3.00
TPB The Hunt 17.95

ALIENS
(B&W) 1988

1 Movie Sequel,R:Hicks,Newt . . . 15.00
1a 2nd printing 3.00
1b 3rd printing 2.00
1c 4th printing 1.50
2 Hicks raids Mental Hospital. 8.00
2a 2nd printing 2.50
2a 3rd printing 1.50
3 Realize Queen is on Earth 4.00
3a 2nd printing 1.50
4 Queen is freed, Newton on Aliens World 3.00
5 All out war on Aliens World 3.00
6 Hicks & Newt return to Earth. . . . 3.00
TPB rep.#1–#6 & DHP #24 . . . . . . 11.00
TPB 2nd printing, DvD(c) 11.00
HC rep..#1–#6 & DHP #24 . . . . . . 25.00

ALIENS (II)
[Mini-Series] 1989

1 DB,Hicks,Newt hijack ship 4.00
1a 2nd Printing 3.00
2 DB,Crazed general trains aliens . 3.00
2a 2nd Printing 3.00
3 DB,HicksV:General Spears. 3.00
3a 2nd Printing 2.50
4 DB,Heroes reclaim earth from aliens 3.00
HC, 2,500 made 80.00
HC, 1,000 made 100.00

ALIENS

1-shot Earth Angel, JBy 3.00
HC rep. Earth Angel 15.00
1-shot Glass Corridor, DvL 3.00
1-shot Mondo Heat, I:Herk Mondo . 2.50
1-shot Mondo Pest 3.00
1-shot Purge, IEd,PhH 3.00
1-shot Pig, CDi,FH 3.00
1-shot Sacrifice, rep.Aliens UK 4.95
1-shot Salvation DGb,MMi,KN, F:Selkirk. 4.95
1-shot Special 2.50
1-shot Stalker 2.50
1-shot Wraith 3.00
GN Female War, remastered 16.95
GN Genocide, remastered 16.95
GN Labyrinth, remastered. 17.95
GN Nightmare Asylum, remaster. . 16.95
GN Outbreak, remastered. 17.95
GN Rogue, Remastered 16.95

ALIENS: ALCHEMY
Sept. 1997

1 (of 3) JAr,RCo 3.00
2 thru 3 . . . . @3.00

Aliens: Alchemy #1
© Dark Horse Comics

ALIENS: APOCALYPSE — DESTROYING ANGELS
Jan., 1999

1 (of 4) MSh 3.00
2 thru 4 MSh . . . . @3.00
TPB 10.95

ALIENS: BERSERKER

1 I:Crew of the Nemesis 2.50
2 Terminall 949 . . . . 2.50
3 Traitor 2.50
4 Finale. 2.50

ALIENS: COLONIAL MARINES

1 I: Lt. Joseph Henry. 3.00
2 I: Pvt. Carmen Vasquez 2.75
3 V:Aliens 2.75
4 F:Lt.Henry 2.75
5 V:Aliens 2.75
6 F:Herk Mondo 2.75
7 A:Beliveau 2.75
8 F:Lt.Joseph Henry 2.75
9 F:Lt.Joseph Henry 2.75
10 final issue 2.50

ALIENS: EARTH WAR

1 SK,JBo(c),Alien's War renewed . 4.00
1a 2nd Printing 2.50
2 SK,JBo(c),To trap the Queen . . . 4.00
3 SK,JBo(c) Stranded on Alien's planet 3.00
4 SK,JBo(c),Resolution,final 3.00
HC Earth War, rep. #1–#4, signed and numbered edition 60.00

ALIENS: GENOCIDE

1 Aliens vs. Aliens. 3.50
2 Alien Homeworld 3.00
3 Search for Alien Queen 3.00
4 Conclusion, inc. poster 3.00
TPB Genocide rep. #1–#4 . . . . . . 13.95

ALIENS: HIVE

1 KJo,I:Stanislaw Mayakovsky. . . . 4.00
2 KJo,A:Norbert. 3.50
3 KJo,A:Julie,Gill 3.25
4 KJo,A:Stan,Final. 3.00
TPB Hive rep. #1–#4 . . . . 14.00

ALIENS: HAVOC

1 (of 2) "over 40 creators" 3.00
2 . . . . 3.00

ALIENS: KIDNAPPED
Dec. 1997–Feb., 1998

1 (of 3) 2.50
2 thru 3 . . . . @2.50
TPB Aliens:Kidnapped 9.95

ALIENS: LABYRINTH

1 F:Captured Alien 3.00
2 . . . . 2.50
3 O:Dr.Church 2.50
4 D:Everyone 2.50
TPB rep. #1–#4 . . . . 17.95
TPB remastered 17.95

ALIENS: MUSIC OF THE SPEARS

1 I:Damon Eddington. 3.00
2 TBd(c),A:Damon Eddington 2.75
3 TBd(c),A:Damon Eddington 2.75
4 TBd(c),last issue. 2.75

ALIENS: NEWT'S TALE

1 How Newt Survived 5.50
2 JBo(c),Newt's point of view on how 'Aliens' ended 4.95

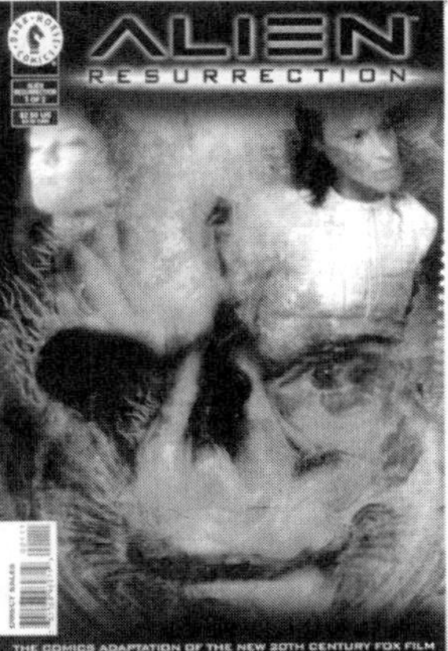

Alien Resurrection #1
© Dark Horse Comics

ALIEN RESURRECTION

Oct., 1997

1 (of 2) movie adaptation. 2.50
2 DMc(c). 2.50

ALIENS: ROGUE

1 F:Mr.Kay. 3.00
2 V:Aliens 3.00
3 V:Aliens 3.00
4 V:Aliens King 3.00
TPB Nel(c),rep.#1–#4 . . . . 14.95

ALIENS: STRONGHOLD

1 DoM,JP 2.50
2 DoM,JP 2.50
3 DoM,JP 2.50
4 DoM,JP 2.50
TPB 16.95

ALIENS: SURVIVAL

Feb.–Apr., 1998

1 (of 3) TyH(c). 3.00
2 thru 3 . . . . @3.00

ALIENS: TRIBES

HC DvD(c) 24.95
TPB 11.95
HC SBi,DvD 24.95

ALIENS/PREDATOR: DEADLIEST OF THE SPECIES

1 B:CCI(s),JG,F:Caryn Delacroix . . 3.75
2 JG,V:Predator. 3.00
3 JG,F:Caryn Delacroix 3.00
4 JG,V:Predator. 3.00
5 JG,Roadtrip 3.00
6 JG,in Space Station 3.00
7 JG,EB 2.50
8 JG,EB 2.50
9 JG,EB 2.50
10 CCI(s), Human Predators. 2.50
11 CCI,EB,JBo(c),Delacroix vs. DeMatier 2.50
12 Caryn's Fate 2.50
TPB 29.95
Lim. Ed. hc. 99.95

ALIENS VS. PREDATOR

0 PN,KS,Rep.DHP#34-36,(B&W). . 5.00
1 Duel to the Death 4.00
1a 2nd Printing 3.00
2 Dr. Revna missing 3.00
3 Predators attack Aliens. 3.00
4 CW,F:Machiko & Predator 3.00
TPB Rep.#1–#4 . . . . 19.95
TPB PN,KS,rep.DHP#34-36 . . . . . 19.95
HC PN,KS,rep.DHP#34-36 . . . . . . 79.95
Ann.#1 (1999) 4.95

ALIENS VS. PREDATOR: BOOTY

1-shot Rep. Diamond Previews . . . 2.50

ALIENS VS. PREDATOR: DUEL

1 Trap, JS 2.50
2 War 2.50

ALIENS VS. PREDATOR: ETERNAL

June, 1998

1 (of 4) IEd,GF(c) 2.50
2 thru 4 IEd,GF(c) . . . . @2.50
TPB 9.95

ALIENS VS. PREDATOR: WAR

0 Prelude to New Series 2.50
1 RSd,MM,RCo(c) F:Machiko 2.50
2 I:Machiko Naguchi 2.50
3 F:Machiko Naguchi. 2.50
4 final issue. 2.50
TPB 19.95

ALIENS VS. PREDATOR: XENOGENESIS

Dec., 1999

1 (of 4) MvR 2.95
2 MvR,trapped. 2.95
3 MvR,trapped. 2.95
4 MvR,battle for survival 2.95

ALIENS VS. PREDATOR VS. THE TERMINATOR

April, 2000

1 (of 4) MSh,MvR 2.95
2 MSh,MvR,V:Terminator-Alien hybrid. 2.95
3 MSh,MvR,on Predator ship. 2.95
4 MSh,MvR,concl. 2.95

ALIENS: XENOGENESIS

Aug., 1999

1 (of 4) 3.00
2 DR 2.95
3 DR 2.95
4 . . . . 2.95

ALIEN 3

1 thru 3 Movie Adaptation . . . . . @2.50

AMERICAN, THE

(B&W)

1 CW,'Chinese Boxes,'D:Gleason . 5.00
2 CW,'Nightmares 4.00
3 CW,Secrets of the American. . . . 4.00
4 CW,American vs.Kid America . . . 4.00
5 A:Kiki the Gorilla. 4.00
6 Rashomon-like plot. 3.50
7 Pornography business issue. . . . 3.50
8 Deals with violence issue 3.50
9 American Falls into a cult 3.50

THE AMERICAN: LOST IN AMERICA

1 CMa, American joins a cult. 2.50
2 CMa, V:"Feel-Good" cult. 2.50
3 CMa, "ApeMask" cult 2.50
4 CMa, Final issue. 2.50
ColorSpec.#1 . . . . 2.95

American Splendor: Music
© Dark Horse Comics

AMERICAN SPLENDOR

1-shot Letterman by Harvey Pekar . 2.95
1-shot A Step Out of the Nest. 2.95
1-shot On the Job. 2.95
1-shot Comics Con, JZe 2.95
1-shot Music Comics 2.95
1-shot Odds & Ends 2.95
1-shot Transatlantic Comics 2.95
1-shot Terminal. 2.95
1-shot Bedtime Stories 3.95

AMERICAN SPLENDOR WINDFALL

(B&W) 1995

1 Windfall Gained,pt.1 . . . . 3.95
2 Windfall Lost. 3.95

ANGEL

Oct., 1999

1 Buffy spin-off 2.95
2 . . . . 2.95
3 . . . . 2.95
4 in Los Angeles 2.95
5 V:Demons, pt.1. . . . . 2.95

6 V:Demons, pt.2. . . . . 2.95
7 V:Demons, pt.3. . . . . 2.95
8 . . . . 2.95
9 . . . . 2.95
10 TSg 2.95
11 TSg, ... 2.95
12 TSg,MMi(c) 3.00
1–12 newsstand photo(c). . . . . . @3.00
TPB The Hollower 9.95

ANOTHER CHANCE TO GET IT RIGHT

1 B&W. 14.95
TPB AVs, GfD(c) 9.95

APPLESEED
(B&W) Manga

TPB Book One: The Promethean Challenge. 14.95
TPB Book Two: Prometheus Unbound 14.95
TPB Book Three: The Scales of Prometheus 14.95
TPB Book Four: The Promethean Balance 14.95

APPLESEED DATABOOK
(B&W) Manga

1 Flip Book, by Masamune Shirow. 5.00
1a 2nd printing 3.50
2 Flip Book 3.50
TPB Rep. #1–#2. . . . . 12.95

ARZACH

TPB by Moebius. 6.95

A SMALL KILLING

GN by Alan Moore & Oscar Zarate 11.95

ATLAS

1 BZ,I:Atlas 2.75
2 BZ,V:Sh'en Chui. 2.75
3 BZ,V:Sh'en Chui. 2.50
4 BZ, final issue. 2.50

BABE
Legend 1994

1 JBy(a&s) 3.00

Babe #1
© Dark Horse Comics

2 thru 4 JBy(a&s). . . . . @2.50

BABE 2
Legend 1995

1 V:Shrewmanoid 2.50
2 A:Abe Sapien 2.50

BACCHUS COLOR SPECIAL

1 A:Thor 2.95
2 A:Abe Sapien 2.50

BADGER: SHATTERED MIRROR

1 R:Badger 2.50
2 R:Badger 2.50
3 Badger 2.50
4 Phantom, final issue 2.50

BADGER: ZEN POP FUNNY ANIMAL VERSION

1 MBn,R:Badger 2.50
2 Ham 2.50

BADLANDS
(B&W)

1 I:Connie Bremen 3.50
2 Anne Peck, C.I.A. 3.00
3 Assassination Rumor 2.50
4 Connie heads South. 2.50
5 November 22, 1963, Dallas 2.25
6 . . . . 2.25

BARB WIRE
Comics' Greatest World

1 Foil(c),I:Deathcard 2.25
2 DLw,I:Hurricane Max 2.25
3 V:Mace Blitzkrieg 2.00
4 Ghost pt.1 . . . . 2.00
5 Ghost pt.2 . . . . 2.00
6 Hardhide, Ignition 2.50
7 A:Motorhead. 2.50
8 V:Ignition 2.50
9 A:Mecha, V:Ignition. 2.50
Movie Spec. 3.95
TPB 8.95

BARB WIRE: ACE OF SPADES

1 thru 4 by CW, TBd & DoM. . . . @2.95

BARRY WINDSOR-SMITH: STORYTELLER
Oct., 1996

TPBs 1 thru 9 9"x12½". . . . . @4.95

BASEBALL GREATS

1 Jimmy Piersall story 3.25

BASIL WOLVERTON'S FANTASIC FABLES
(B&W)

1 BW. 2.50
2 BW. 2.50

BASIL WOLVERTON IN SPACE
Feb., 1999

TPB 240-page 16.95

BATMAN/ALIENS
Dark Horse/DC March, 1997

1 (of 2) RMz,BWr. 4.95
2 conclusion 4.95
TPB RMz,BWr 14.95

BATMAN/TARZAN: CLAWS OF THE CATWOMAN

1 (of 4) RMz,DvD(c),V:Dent,x-over. 2.95
2 RMz,DvD(c) 2.95
3 RMz,DvD(c) 2.95
4 RMz,DvD(c) concl. 2.95
TPB 96-pg.,DvD(c) 10.95

BATTLE GODS: WARRIORS OF THE CHAAK
April, 2000

1 (of 9) by Francisco Ruiz Velasco 2.95
2 the Lucha Libre 2.95
3 F:Takan, El Charro 2.95
4 another tournament 2.95
5 The Chaak begins 2.95
6 Deathmatch: Takan vs. Chilbacan 2.95
7 sleeping god awakens 3.00

BETTIE PAGE

1-shot, some nudity 3.95

BETTIE PAGE COMICS: SPICY ADVENTURE

1-shot by Jim Silke 2.95

BETTIE PAGE: QUEEN OF HEARTS

1 Movie adaptation 2.00
TPB 19.95

BETTIE PAGE: QUEEN OF THE NILE
December 1999

1 (of 3) low-budget time machine. . 2.95
2 . . . . 2.95
3 concl. 2.95

BIG

1 Movie Adaptation 2.00

BIG BLOWN BABY
(B&W) Aug., 1996

1 thru 4 by Bill Wray. . . . . @2.95

BIG GUY AND RUSTY THE ROBOT BOY

1 V:Monster. 4.95
2 V:Monster. 4.95
TPB FM & GfD 14.95
TPB King Size 29.95

BILLI 99
(B&W)

1 `Pray for us Sinners'. 4.50
2 `Trespasses'. 4.00
3 `Daily Bread'. 4.00

DARK HORSE

Black Cross Dirty Work
© Dark Horse Comics

BLACK CROSS: DIRTY WORK
April, 1997

1-shot by Chris Warner. 2.95

BLACK DRAGON, THE
(B&W)

TPB Chris Claremont & John Bolton . . . 17.95

BLACK MAGIC
B&W 1998

TPB 16.95

BLACK PEARL, THE
Sept., 1996

1 by Mark Hamill 2.95
2 thru 5 . . . . @2.95
TPB by Mark Hamill 16.95

BLADE OF THE IMMORTAL
(B&W) Manga

Call of the Worm, April, 1997
9 pt. 1 by Hiroaki Samura 3.95
10 pt. 2 . . . . 3.95
11 pt. 3. 3.95
TPB Cry of the Worm 12.95
Dreamsong, July, 1997
12 pt. 1 (of 7) by Hiroaki Samura . . 2.95
13 pt. 2 F:Makie, Manji. 2.95
14 pt. 3. 2.95
15 pt. 4. 2.95
16 pt. 5. 2.95
17 pt. 6. 2.95
18 pt. 7. 2.95
TPB Dreamsong. 12.95
Rin's Bane, March, 1998
19 pt.1, by Hiroaki Samura 2.95
20 pt.2 . . . . 2.95
On Silent Wings, May, 1998
21 pt. 1 (of 8) 2.95
22 pt. 2. 2.95
23 pt. 3. 2.95
24 pt. 4. 2.95
25 pt. 5. 2.95
26 pt. 6. 2.95
27 pt. 7. 2.95
28 pt. 8. 2.95
TPB Blood of a Thousand. 12.95
TPB On Silent Wings 14.95
Dark Shadows, Jan. 1999
29 pt. 1 (of 5) 2.95
30 pt. 2. 2.95
31 pt. 3. 2.95
32 pt. 4. 2.95
33 pt. 5. 2.95
TPB Dark Shadows 14.95
Food, June 1999
34 . . . . 2.95
Heart of Darkness
35 pt.1 (of 8). 2.95
36 pt.2 . . . . 2.95
37 pt.3 . . . . 2.95
38 pt.4 . . . . 2.95
39 pt.5 . . . . 2.95
40 pt.6 . . . . 2.95
41 pt.7 . . . . 2.95
42 pt.8 . . . . 2.95
The Gathering
43 pt.1 (of 15) by Hiroaki Samura . . 2.95
44 pt.2 . . . . 2.95
45 pt.3 . . . . 2.95
46 pt.4 . . . . 2.95
47 pt.5 . . . . 2.95
48 pt.6 . . . . 2.95
49 pt.7 . . . . 2.95
50 pt.8 . . . . 3.00
TPB On Silent Wings II. 14.95

BLADE OF THE IMMORTAL: CONQUEST
(B&W) Manga

1 by Hiroaki Samura 3.50
2 and 3 . . . . @3.50

BLADE OF THE IMMORTAL: FANATIC
(B&W) Manga

1 by Hiroaki Samura 2.95
2 . . . . 2.95

BLADE OF THE IMMORTAL: GENIUS
(B&W) Manga Oct., 1996

1 by Hiroaki Samura 3.50
2 . . . . 3.50

BLAIR WHICH?
December, 1999

1-shot SA, Scary as heck 2.95

BLANCHE GOES TO NEW YORK

1 Turn of the Century N.Y. 2.95

BLAST CORPS
Sept., 1998

1-shot F:demolition experts 2.50

BLUE LILY

1 thru 3 . . . . @4.00

BODY BAGS
Aug., 1996

1 (of 4) by Jason Pearson and Ken Bruzinak 3.00
2 and 3 . . . . @3.00
TPB 12.95

BOOK OF NIGHT
(B&W)

1 CV 2.50
2 CV 2.00
TPB Children of the Stars 12.95

BOOK OF NIGHT

1 thru 3 . . . . 3.95

BORIS THE BEAR
(B&W)

1 V:Funny Animals 3.00
1a 2nd printing 2.00
2 V:Robots 2.00
3 V:Super Heroes 2.00
4 Bear of Steel 2.00
5 Dump Thing 2.00
6 Bat Bear. 2.00
7 Elves 2.00
8 LargeSize. 2.50
9 Awol. 2.00
10 thru 12 . . . . @2.00
See: B & W Pub. section

BORIS THE BEAR
Color Classics

1 thru 7 . . . . @1.95

BRAVE
March, 1997

1 by Cully Hamner & Jason Martin. 2.95

BUBBLE GUM CRISIS: GRAND MAL
Manga

1 . . . . 2.75
2 and 3 . . . . @2.75
4 final issue. 2.50
TPB Rep.#1–#4 . . . . 14.95

BUFFY THE VAMPIRE SLAYER
Sept., 1998

1 JoB,AAd(c). 3.00
1a 2nd printing 3.00
2 direct market, JoB 3.00
3 direct market, JoB 3.00

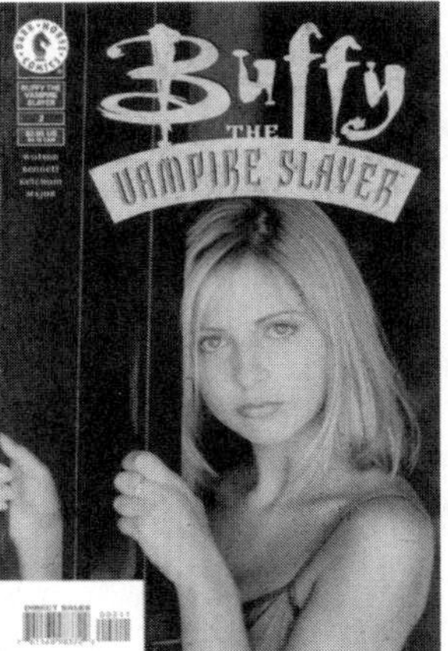

Buffy The Vampire Slayer #2
© Dark Horse Comics

DARK HORSE

4 direct market 3.00
5 direct market 3.00
6 direct market 3.00
7 direct market, JoB 3.00
8 direct market 3.00
9 direct market 3.00
10 direct market 3.00
11 direct market 3.00
12 direct market 3.00
13 F:Cordelia Chase. 2.95
14 . . . . 2.95
15 . . . . 2.95
16 . . . . 2.95
17 . . . . 2.95
18 Mardi Gras 2.95
19 Bad Blood, concl.. . . . . 2.95
20 Angel heads to L.A. 2.95
21 Blood of Carthage, pt.1 . . . . 2.95
22 Blood of Carthage, pt.2 . . . . 2.95
23 Blood of Carthage, pt.3 . . . . 2.95
24 Blood of Carthage, pt.4 . . . . 2.95
25 Blood of Carthage,concl. 2.95
26 Heart of the Slayer,pt.1 . . . . 3.00
2a–26a newsstand photo(c) . . . . @3.00
Ann. 1999, 64-page 4.95
Spec. 1-shot Spike and Dru 3.00
Spec. 1-shot Giles 3.00
Spec. 1-shot Giles, photo(c) 3.00
Spec. 1-shot Spike & Dru—The
Queen of Hearts, photo (c) 2.95
Spec. 1-shot Spike & Dru—All'sFair 3.00
Spec. 1-shot Spike & Dru, photo(c). 3.00
TPB The Dust Waltz 10.00
TPB The Remaining Sunlight 10.00
TPB Uninvited Guests 10.95
TPB The Remaining Sunlight 9.95
TPB The Origin 9.95
TPB Bad Blood. 9.95
TPB Crash Test Demons,
rep.#9–#11 . . . . 9.95
TPB Pale Reflections, rep.#17–#19 9.95
GN Ring of Fire, photo(c) 9.95

BUFFY THE VAMPIRE SLAYER: ANGEL

May, 1999

1 (of 3) 3.00
2 & 3 . . . . @3.00
1a thru 3a newsstand, photo(c) . @3.00

BUFFY THE VAMPIRE SLAYER: THE ORIGIN

Feb., 1999

1 (of 3) DlB,JoB. 3.00
2 & 3 . . . . @3.00
2a & 3a newsstand, photo(c) . . . @3.00
TPB rep. 9.95

BY BIZARRE HANDS

(B&W)

1 JLd(s). 2.50
2 JLd(s). 2.50
3 JLd(s). 2.50

CARAVAN KIDD

(B&W) Manga

1 thru 10 by Johji Manabe . . . . . @2.50

[2nd Series]

1 thru 10 F:Miam . . . . @2.50
TPB Rep. #1–#10. . . . . 19.95
Holiday Spec.. . . . . 2.50
Valentine's Day Spec. 2.50

Caravan Kidd, Part 3, #1
© Dark Horse Comics

[3rd Series]

1 thru 8 . . . . @2.50
Christmas Special. 2.50
TPB Vol. 2 . . . . 19.95
TPB Vol. 3 . . . . 19.95

CATALYST: AGENTS OF CHANGE

Comics' Greatest World

1 JPn(c),V:US Army 2.25
2 JPn(c),I:Grenade 2.25
3 JPn(c),Rebel vs. Titan 2.25
4 JPn(c),Titan vs. Grace 2.00
5 JPn(c),V:Ape 2.00
6 and 7 . . . . @2.00

CHEVAL NOIR

(B&W)

1 DSt(c). 4.00
2 thru 6 . . . . @3.50
7 DSt(c). 3.50
8 . . . . 3.50
9 . . . . 3.50
10 80 page. 4.50
11 80 page. 4.50
12 MM(c) 3.95
13 thru 15. . . . . @3.95
16 thru 19 with 2-card strip . . . . . @3.95
20 Great Power o/t Chninkel. 4.50
21 Great Power o/t Chninkel. 3.95
22 Great Power o/t Chninkel,concl. . 4.50
23 inc.`Rork',`Forever War' concl. . . 3.95
24 In Dreams, Pt.1 . . . . 3.95
25 In Dreams, Pt.2 . . . . 3.95
26 In Dreams, Pt.3 . . . . 3.95
27 I:The Man From Ciguri (Airtight
Garage sequel) Dreams Pt.4 . . 2.95
28 Ciguri cont. 2.95
29 Ciguri cont. 2.95
30 Ciguri,cont. 2.95
31 Angriest Dog in the World 2.95
32 thru 38. . . . . @2.95
39 In Search of Peter Pan 2.95
40 . . . . 2.95
41 F:Demon 2.95
42 F:Demon 2.95
43 F:Demon 2.95
44 F:Demon 2.95
45 . . . . 2.95
46 . . . . 2.95
47 . . . . 2.95
48 SwM(c) 2.95
49 F:Rork. 2.95
50 F:Rork. 2.95

CHRONOWAR

(B&W) Aug., 1996

1 (of 9) by Kazumasa Takayama . . 2.95
2 thru 9 . . . . @2.95

CLASSIC STAR WARS

1 AW,newspaper strip reps. 6.00
2 AW,newspaper strip reps. 4.00
3 AW,newspaper strip reps. 4.00
4 AW,newspaper strip reps. 4.00
5 AW,newspaper strip reps. 4.00
6 AW,newspaper strip reps. 4.00
7 AW,newspaper reps.. . . . . 4.00
8 AW,newspaper reps. w/card 4.00
9 AW,newspaper reps.. . . . . 3.50
10 AW,newspaper reps. 3.50
11 thru 19 AW,newspaper reps. . . @3.00
20 AW,newspaper strip reps., with
trading card, final issue. 4.00
TPB Vol. 1, "In Deadly Pursuit,"
rep.#1–#7. . . . . 15.99
TPB Vol. 1, rep. 2nd edition 16.95
TPB Vol. 2, "Rebel Storm,"
rep. #8–#14 . . . . 16.95
TPB Vol. 3, "Escape to Hoth,"
rep. #15–#20 . . . . 16.95

CLASSIC STAR WARS: A NEW HOPE

1 AAd(c), rep. 4.25
2 AH(c), rep. 3.95
TPB Rep. #1–#2. . . . . 9.95

CLASSIC STAR WARS: DEVILWORLDS

Aug., 1996

1 (of 2) by Alan Moore. 2.50
2 . . . . 2.50

CLASSIC STAR WARS: EARLY ADVENTURES

Aug. 1994–April, 1995

1 MiA(c), Gambler's World. 3.00
2 RHo&MGr(c),Blackhole. 2.50
3 EiS(c),Rebels of Vorzyd-5. . . . . . 2.50
3 bagged with trading card DH2. . . 5.00
4 RHo(c),Tatooine 2.50
5 RHo(c),A:Lady Tarkin 2.50
6 Weather Dominator 2.50
7 RHo(c),V:Darth Vader. 2.50
8 KPl(c),X-Wing Secrets 2.50
9 KPl(c),A:Boba Fett 2.50
TPB RsM & AGw, AW(c). 19.95

CLASSIC STAR WARS: EMPIRE STRIKES BACK

1 Movie Adaptation 4.00
2 Movie Adaptation 4.00
TPB Rep.#1–#2 AW&CG(c) 9.95
TPB reprint, Hildebrandt(c) 9.95

CLASSIC STAR WARS: HAN SOLO AT STAR'S END

March, 1997

1 (of 3) by Alfredo Alcala 3.00
2 thru 3 . . . . @3.00
TPB rep. AW(c) 6.95

CLASSIC STAR WARS: A LONG TIME AGO
(B&W) March, 1999
1 (of 6) rep. Marvel comics 6.00
2 thru 6 . . . . @6.00

CLASSIC STAR WARS: RETURN OF THE JEDI
1 Movie Adaptation 4.00
2 Movie Adaptation 3.50
TPB Rep.#1–#2 . . . . 9.95
TPB rep. Hildebrandt(c) 9.95

Classic Star Wars, Return of the Jedi #1
© Dark Horse Comics

CLASSIC STAR WARS: VANDELHELM MISSION
1995
1-shot F:Han Solo, Lando. 3.95

CLONEZONE
(B&W)
Spec #1 . . . . 2.00

CLOWNS, THE (PAGLIACCI)
April, 1998
1-shot B&W, CR. 2.95

COLORS IN BLACK
Comics From Spike
1 B:Passion Play. 2.95
2 Images. 2.95
3 Back on the Bus. 2.95
4 final issue. 2.95

COMIC BOOK
1 thru 4 9"x12" John Kricfalusi . . @5.95

COMICS AND STORIES
4 (of 4) by Martin & Millionaire 2.95

COMICS' GREATEST WORLD
(Arcadia)
1 B:MRi(s),FM(c),B:LW,B:O:Vortex, F:X,I:Seekers 3.00
1a B&W proof ed. (1,500 made) . . 9.00
1b Hologram(c), with cards 7.00
2 JoP,I:Pit Bulls 1.50
3 AH,I:Ghost 5.00
4 I:Monster 1.50
TPB Arcadia 25.00

(Golden City)
1 B:BKs(s),JOy(c),I:Rebel, Amaz.Grace,V:WarMaker 1.25
1a Gold Ed.. . . . . 5.00
2 I:Mecha 1.25
3 WS(c),I:Titan 1.25
4 E:BKs(s),GP(c),JD,I:Catalyst . . . 1.25
TPB Golden City. 11.00

(Steel Harbor)
1 B:CW(s),PG,I:Barb Wire, V:Ignition 1.25
2 MMi(c),TNa,I:Machine. 1.25
3 CW(a&s),I:Wolf Gang 1.25
4 E:CW(s),VGi,I:Motorhead 1.25
TPB Steel Harbor 11.00

(Vortex)
1 B:RSd(s),LW,DoM,I:Division 13. . 1.25
2 I:Hero Zero. 1.25
3 PC,I:King Tiger 1.25
4 B:RSd(s),E:MRi(s)BMc,E:LW, E:O:Vortex,C:Vortex 1.25
TPB Vortex 11.00
Sourcebook 10.00

CONCRETE
(B&W)
1 PC,R:Concrete, A Stone among Stones 7.00
1a 2nd printing 3.00
2 PC,`Transatlantic Swim' 5.00
3 PC 4.00
4 PC 3.50
5 PC,`An Armchair Stuffed with Dynamite'. 3.50
6 PC,Concrete works on farm 3.50
7 PC,Concrete grows horns. 3.50
8 PC,Climbs Mount Everest. 3.50
9 PC,Mount Everest Pt.2 . . . . 3.50
10 PC,last Issue. 3.50
TPB The Complete Concrete 25.00

CONCRETE
1 PC,ColorSpec. 4.00
EarthDay Spec. PC,Moebius 4.00

Concrete: Strange Armor #1
© Dark Horse Comics

CONCRETE: A NEW LIFE
1 . . . . 3.50
Spec.Land & Sea,rep.. . . . . 3.25

CONCRETE CELEBRATES EARTH DAY 1990
1-shot. 2.50

CONCRETE: ECLECTICA
1 PC,The Ugly Boy 3.25
2 PC 3.25

CONCRETE: FRAGILE CREATURE
1 PC,`Rulers o/t Omniverse'Pt.1 . . 4.00
2 PC,`Rulers o/t Omniverse'Pt.2 . . 3.00
3 PC,`Rulers o/t Omniverse'Pt.3 . . 3.00
4 PC,`Rulers o/t Omniverse'Pt.3 . . 3.00
TPB 15.95

CONCRETE: KILLER SMILE
Dark Horse-Legend 1994
1 PC 3.50
2 PC 3.00
3 PC 3.00
4 PC, final issue 3.00
TPB Rep.#1–#4 . . . . 16.95

CONCRETE: ODD JOBS
(B&W)
1-shot. 3.50

[PAUL CHADWICK'S] CONCRETE: STRANGE ARMOR
Dec. 1997–Apr., 1998
1 (of 5) 3.00
2 thru 5 . . . . @3.00
TPB Strange Armor 17.00

CONCRETE: THINK LIKE A MOUNTAIN
1 thru 6 PC,GfD(c). . . . . @3.00
TPB PC,GfD(c). 17.95

CORMAC MAC ART
1 Robert E. Howard adapt. 2.25
2 . . . . 2.25
3 . . . . 2.25

CORNY'S FETISH
April, 1998
GN by Renee French, 64pg. 4.95

COUTOO
1 Lt. Joe Kraft 3.50

CREEPY
(B&W)
1 KD,TS,GC,SL,Horror 3.95
2 TS,CI,DC,Demonic Baby 3.95
3 JM,TS,JG,V:Killer Clown. 3.95
4 TS,Final issue 3.95

CREATURE FROM THE BLACK LAGOON
1 Movie Adaptation 4.95

CRITICAL ERROR

1 rep.Classic JBy story 2.75

[ANDREW VACHSS'] CROSS

0 GfD(c),I:Cross,Rhino,Princess . . 2.50
1 thru 7 . . . . @2.95

CUD COMICS

(B&W) 1995

1 thru 8 by Terry LaBan . . . . @2.95

THE CURSE OF DRACULA

July, 1998

1 (of 3) MWn,GC 3.00
2 thru 3 . . . . @3.00

CYBERANATICS

HC by Jerry Prosser & Rick Geary 14.95

DANGER UNLIMITED

Dark Horse-Legend

1 JBy(a&s),KD,I:Danger Unlimited, B:BU:Torch of Liberty 2.50
2 JBy(a&s),KD,O:DangerUnlimited. 2.25
3 JBy(a&s),KD,O:Torch of Liberty . 2.25
4 JBy(a&s),KD,Final Issue. 2.25
TPB rep. #1–#4 . . . . 14.95

DARK HORSE CLASSICS

(B&W)

1 Last of the Mohicans 3.95
2 20,000 Leagues Under the Sea . 3.95

DARK HORSE CLASSICS: ALIENS VS. PREDATOR

Feb., 1997

1 thru 6 Rep. . . . . @3.00

DARK HORSE CLASSICS: GODZILLA, KING OF THE MONSTERS

July, 1998

1 RSd,SBi,now color 3.00
2 rep. from 1995 . . . . 3.00
3 rep. from 1995 . . . . 3.00
4 rep. Godzilla #2, from 1995. . . . . 3.00
5 . . . . 3.00
6 V:Bagorah 3.00

DARK HORSE CLASSICS: PREDATOR: JUNGLE TALES

1-shot Rep. 3.00

DARK HORSE CLASSICS: STAR WARS— DARK EMPIRE

1997

1 rep. by Tom Veitch,CK,DvD(c) . . 3.00
2 thru 6 rep., DvD(c) . . . . @3.00

DARK HORSE CLASSICS: TERROR OF GODZILLA

Aug., 1998

1 by Kazuhisa Iwata, AAd(c) 3.00
2 . . . . 3.00

Dark Horse Comics #11
© Dark Horse Comics

3 . . . . 3.00
4 rep. of 1988 B&W. 3.00
5 AAd(c) 3.00
6 AAd(c) 3.00

DARK HORSE COMICS

1 RL,CW,F:Predator,Robocop, I:Renegade,Time Cop,(double gatefold cover) 4.00
2 RL,CW,F:Predator,Robocop, Renegade,Time Cop 3.00
3 CW,F:Robocop,Time Cop,Aliens, Indiana Jones. 3.00
4 F:Predator,Aliens,Ind.Jones 2.75
5 F:Predator,E:Aliens. 2.75
6 F:Robocop,Predator, E:Indiana Jones 2.75
7 F:Robocop,Predator,B:StarWars . 6.00
8 B&I:X,Robocop. 8.00
9 F:Robocop,E:Star Wars 4.00
10 E:X,B:Godzilla,Predator, James Bond 3.50
11 F:Godzilla,Predator,James Bond,B:Aliens. 2.75
12 F:Predator 2.75
13 F:Predator,B:Thing. 2.75
14 MiB(s),B:The Mark. 2.75
15 MiB(s),E:The Mark,B:Aliens 2.75
16 B:Predator,E:Thing,Aliens 2.75
17 B:Aliens,Star Wars:Droids 2.75
18 E:Predator. 2.75
19 RL(c),B:X,E:Star Wars:Droids, Aliens. 2.75
20 B:Predator. 2.75
21 F:Mecha 2.75
22 B:Aliens, E:Mecha 2.75
23 B:The Machine 2.50
24 The Machine 2.50
25 Final issue. 2.50

DARK HORSE DOWNUNDER

(B&W)

1 F:Australian Writers 2.50
2 Australian Writers 2.50
3 Australian Writers, finale. 2.50

DARK HORSE MAVERICK 2000

Ann.#1 48-pg.. . . . . 3.95

DARK HORSE MONSTERS

Feb., 1997

1-shot. 3.00

DARK HORSE PRESENTS

(B&W)

1 PC,I:Concrete. 10.00
1a 2nd printing 2.50
2 PC,Concrete. 6.00
3 Boris theBear,Concrete. 4.00
4 PC,Concrete. 4.00
5 PC,Concrete. 4.00
6 PC,Concrete. 4.00
7 I:MONQ 3.50
8 PC,Concrete. 3.50
9 . . . . 3.50
10 PC,Concrete, I:Masque 6.00
11 Masque 5.00
12 PC,Concrete, Masque 4.00
13 Masque 4.00
14 PC,Concrete, Masque 4.00
15 Masque 4.00
16 PC,Concrete, Masque 4.00
17 . . . . 3.00
18 PC,Concrete, Mask 5.00
19 Masque 5.00
20 double,Flaming Carrot 5.00
21 Masque 5.00
22 . . . . 3.00
23 . . . . 3.00
24 PC,I:Aliens. 10.00
25 thru 31 . . . . @3.00
32 . . . . 4.00
33 . . . . 3.00
34 Aliens 4.00
35 Predator 4.00
36 Aliens vs.Predator 4.00
36a painted cover. 5.00
37 . . . . 2.50
38 . . . . 2.50
39 . . . . 2.50
40 I:The Aerialist 2.50
41 . . . . 2.50
42 Aliens 5.00
43 Aliens 4.00
44 . . . . 2.50
45 . . . . 2.50
46 Predator 4.00
47 . . . . 2.50
48 with 2-card strip. 2.50
49 with 2-card strip. 2.50
50 inc.`Heartbreakers', with 2-card strip. 2.50
51 FM(c),inc.`Sin City' 4.00
52 FM,inc. `Sin City'. 3.00
53 FM,inc. `Sin City'. 3.00
54 FM,Sin City;JBy Preview of Next Men Pt.1 . . . . 5.00
55 FM,Sin City;JBy Preview of Next Men (JBy) Pt.2 . . . . 4.00
56 FM,Sin City,JBy,Next MenPt.3 Aliens Genocide(prologue) 3.00
57 FM,SinCity;JBy Next Men Pt.4 . . 3.00
58 FM,Sin City,Alien Fire 2.50
59 FM,Sin City,Alien Fire 2.50
60 FM,Sin City 2.50
61 FM,Sin City 2.50
62 FM,E:Sin City 2.50
63 Moe,Marie Dakar. 2.50
64 MWg,R:The Aerialist 2.50
65 B:Accidental Death 2.50
66 PC,inc.Dr.Giggles 2.50
67 B:Predator story (lead in to "Race War"),double size. 3.95
68 F:Predator,Swimming Lessons (Nestrobber tie-in) 2.50
69 F:Predator 2.50
70 F:Alec 2.50

DARK HORSE

Dark Horse Presents #100, Cover #4
© Dark Horse Comics

71 F:Madwoman. 2.50
72 F:Eudaemon 2.50
73 F:Eudaemon 2.50
74 . . . . 2.50
75 F:Chairman 2.50
76 F:Hermes Vs.the Eye,Ball Kid . . 2.50
77 F:Hermes Vs.the Eye,Ball Kid . . 2.50
78 F:Hermes Vs.the Eye,Ball Kid . . 2.50
79 B:Shadow Empires Slaves. 2.50
80 AAd,I:Monkey Man & O'Brien. . . 5.00
81 B:Buoy 2.50
82 B:Just Folks. 2.50
83 Last Impression. 2.50
84 MBn,F:Nexus,E:Hermes Vs. the Eye Ball Kid 2.50
85 Winner Circle. 2.50
86 . . . . 2.50
87 F:Concrete 2.50
88 Hellboy 3.00
89 Hellboy 3.00
90 Hellboy 3.00
91 Blackheart, Baden 3.00
92 Too Much Coffee Man 6.00
93 Cud, Blackheart,Coffee Man . . . 8.00
94 A:Eyeball Kid,Coffee Man 6.00
95 Too Much Coffee Man 7.00
96 Kabuli Kid 2.50
97 F:Kabuki Kid 2.50
98 Pot Full of Noodles 2.50
99 Anthology title 2.50
100–#1 Lance Blastoff 2.50
100–#2 Hellboy 2.50
100–#3 Concrete 2.50
100–#4 Black Cross 2.50
100–#5 Pan Fried Girl 2.50
101 BW,F:Aliens. 2.50
102 F:Mr. Painter 2.50
103 F:The Pink Tornado 3.00
104 F:The Pink Tornado 3.00
105 F:The Pink Tornado 3.00
106 F:Godzilla 3.00
107 F:Rusty Razorclam 3.00
108. . . . . 3.00
109. . . . . 3.00
110. . . . . 3.00
111. . . . . 3.00
112 three stories, concl. 3.00
113 . . . . 3.00
114 F:Star Slammers 3.00
115 flip-book. 3.00
116. . . . . 3.00
117 F:Aliens 3.00
118. . . . . 3.00
119. . . . . 3.00
120 "One Last Job". 3.00
121 F: Jack Zero 3.00
122 "Lords of Misrule". 3.00
123 F: Jack Zero 3.00
124 F:Predator 3.00
125 F:Nocturnals 3.00
126 flip book, 48pg. 3.95
127 F:The Nocturnals 3.00
128 . . . . 3.00
129 F:Hammer 3.00
130 F:Zombie Worl. 3.00
131 F:Girl Crazy 3.00
132 flip book. 3.00
133 F:Tarzan 3.00
134 F:The Dirty Pair 3.00
135 F:The Fall, concl. 3.00
136 The Ark 3.00
137 Predator 3.00
138 F:Terminators. 3.00
139 F:Roachmill 3.00
140 F:Aliens 3.00
141 F:Buffy the Vampire Slayer. . . . 3.00
142 F:Lovecraftian tales 3.00
143 F:Tarzan tales 3.00
144 F:Ghost, Burgler Girls, Galactic Jack 3.00
145 F:Ghost. 3.00
146 F:Aliens vs. Predator 2.95
147 F:Ragnok. 2.95
148 . . . . 2.95
149 Wunderkind 2.95
150 F:Buffy, 48-pg. 4.50
151 F:Hellboy 2.95
152 It! The Beast from Twenty Billion Years Beyond Earth 2.95
153 Helm of Harxis. 2.95
154 Iron Reich 3000, flip-book 2.95
155 Angel, flip-book 2.95
156 Witch's Son, flip-book 2.95
157 F:Witch's Son, final issue 2.95
Fifth Anniv. Special DGi,PC, SBi,CW,MW,FM,Sin City, Aliens,Give Me Liberty 8.00
Ann. 1997. . . . . 4.95
Ann. 1998. . . . . 4.95
Ann. 1999. . . . . 4.95
Ann.2000 Girls Rule, 64-pg. 4.95
Milestone Ed.#1,rep.DHP#1 . . . . . . 2.25
TPB rep.Sin City. 6.00
TPB Best of DHP #1–#20. . . . . 9.95
TPB Best of DHP #1–#20 2nd edition 9.95
TPB Best of DHP #21–#30 . . . . 8.95
TPB Best of DHP #31–#50 . . . . 8.95
TPB Best of Dark Horse Presents Two 8.95
TPB Best of Dark Horse Presents Three. 12.95

DARK HORSE PRESENTS: ALIENS

1 Rep. 4.95
1a Platinum Edition 8.00

DEADFACE: DOING ISLANDS WITH BACCHUS

(B&W)

1 rep. Bacchus apps.. . . . . 2.95
2 rep. inc.`Book-Keeper of Atlantis. 2.95

DEADFACE: EARTH, WATER, AIR & FIRE

(B&W)

1 Bacchus & Simpson in Sicily. . . . 2.50
2 A:Don Skylla. 2.50
3 Mafia/Kabeirol-War prep. 2.50
4 Last issue. 2.50

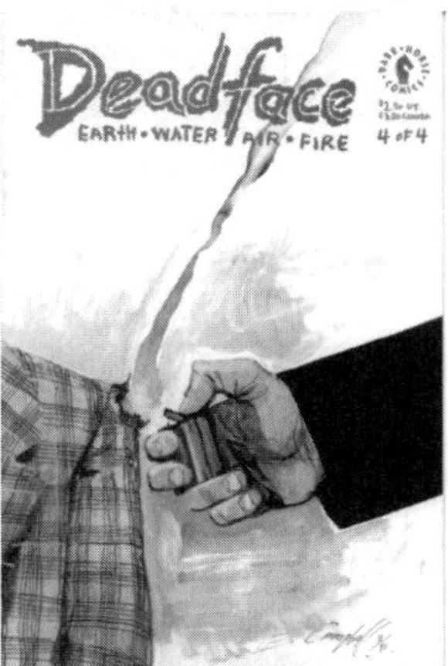

Deadface: Earth, Water, Air & Fire #4
© Dark Horse Comics

DEAD IN THE WEST

(B&W)

1 TT,Joe Landsdale adapt.. . . . . . . 5.00
2 TT,adapt. 5.00

DEAD IN THE WEST

1 TT(c) 3.95

DEAD OR ALIVE— A CYBERPUNK WESTERN

April, 1998

1 (of 4) by Tatjana and Alberto Ponticelli 2.50
2 thru 4 . . . . @2.50

DEADLINE USA

(B&W)

1 rep. Deadline UK,Inc. Tank Girl Johnny Nemo. 9.95
2 inc. Tank Girl,Johnny Nemo 9.95

DECADE OF DARK HORSE, A

1 (of 4) inc. Star Wars, Nexus, Ghost. 2.95
2 thru 4 . . . . @2.95

[RANDY BOWEN'S] DECAPITATOR

June, 1998

1 (of 4) GEr,DoM. 3.00
2 GEr, ... 3.00
3 MMi,KJo,AAl. 3.00
4 MMi, conclusion. 3.00

DEVIL CHIEF

1 I:Devil Chief 2.50

DIGIMON

June, 2000, Bi-weekly

1 . . . . 2.95
2 thru 6 . . . . @2.95
7 thru 9 ND(c) . . . . @2.95
10 ND(c) 3.00
TPB Digital Monsters 10.00

DIRTY PAIR
(B&W) Manga
TPB Book 3 A Plague of Angels . . 12.95
TPB Dangerous Acquaintances . . 12.95
TPB Biohazards 12.95
1-shot Start the Violence, AWa(c) . . 2.95
1-shot Start the Violence, JPn(c). . . 2.95

DIRTY PAIR: FATAL BUT NOT SERIOUS
Manga
1 R:Kei,Yuri. 2.95
2 V:Kevin Sleet,Yuri. 2.95
3 Anti Yuri 2.95
4 V:Terrorists. 2.95
5 conclusion 2.95

DIRTY PAIR: RUN FROM THE FUTURE
January, 2000
1 (of 4) AWa(c) 2.95
1a AH(c) 2.95
2 AWa(c). 2.95
2a BSf(c). 2.95
3 AWa(c). 2.95
3a Bruce Timm(c) 2.95
4 AWa(c). 2.95
4a HuR(c) 2.95

DIRTY PAIR: SIM HELL
(B&W) Manga
1 thru 4 by Adam Warren . . . . . . @3.25
TPB rep. #1–#4 . . . . 13.95

Disney's Tarzan #1
© Dark Horse Comics

DISNEY'S TARZAN
June, 1999
1 (of 2) Animated movie adapt. . . . 2.95
2 conclusion 2.95

DIVISION 13
1 & 2 . . . . @2.50
3 A:Payback 2.50
4 Carnal Genesis. 2.50

DOC SAVAGE: CURSE OF THE FIRE GOD
1 R:Man of Bronze 2.95
2 Exploding Plane 2.95
3 & 4 . . . . @2.95

DR. GIGGLES
1 Horror movie adapt. 2.50
2 Movie adapt.contd. 2.50

DR. ROBOT
April, 2000
1-shot, by Bernie E. Mireault. 2.95

DOMINION
(B&W) Manga
TPB 1 by Masamune Shirow. 15.00
TPB 2nd printing. 14.95
TPB 3rd edition. 16.95

DOMINION: CONFLICT 1 — NO MORE NOISE
(B&W) Manga 1996
1 thru 6 by Masamune Shirow . . @2.95
TPB series rep.. . . . . 14.95

DOMINION SPECIAL: PHANTOM OF THE AUDIENCE
(B&W) Manga
1-shot by Masamune Shirow. 2.50

DOMU: A CHILD'S DREAMS
(B&W) Manga
1 Psychic Warfare 5.95
2 Murders Continue. 5.95
3 Psychic war conclusion. 5.95
TPB by Katsuhiro Otomo 17.95

DRACULA
1 Movie Adaptation 4.95

DRAKUUN
(B&W) Feb., 1997
Rise of the Dragon Princess
1 (of 6) by Johji Manabe 2.95
2 thru 6 . . . . @2.95
TPB rep.. . . . . 12.95
The Revenge of Gustav (Aug., 1997)
7 (1 of 6) by Johji Manabe. 2.95
8 thru 12 pt.2 thru pt.6 . . . . @2.95
TPB, rep. 14.95
Shadow of the Warlock (Feb., 1998)
13 (1 of 6) by Johji Manabe 2.95
14 thru 18 pt.2 thru pt.6. . . . . @2.95
TPB rep.. . . . . 14.95
The Hidden War (Sept., 1998)
19 (1 of 6) by Johji Manabe 2.95
20 thru 24 pt.2 thru pt.6. . . . . @2.95
Flames of Empire (1999)
25 Flames of Empire (1 of 6) 2.95

DYLAN DOG
(B&W) DH/Bonelli Mar. 1999
1 (of 6) by Tiziano Di Sclavi & Angelo Stano, MMi(c), 96-page 4.95
2 thru 6 . . . . @4.95

EDGAR RICE BURROUGHS' RETURN OF TARZAN
April, 1997
1 adapted by Thomas Yeates & John Totleben 3.00
2 thru 3 . . . . @3.00

EDGAR RICE BURROUGHS' TARZAN
Mugambi
1 by Bruce Jones, Christopher Schenck & TY, Betrayed by 3 man-beasts 3.00
2 "Tarzan's Jungle Fury" 3.00
3 "Tarzan's Jungle Fury" 3.00
4 vs. the Tara virus 3.00
5 Cure to the Tara virus 3.00
6 . . . . 3.00
Tarzan and the Legion of Hate
7 by Allan Gross, Christopher Schenck, George Freeman 3.00
8 pt.2. . . . . 3.00
9 pt.3. . . . . 3.00
10 pt.4, concl.. . . . . 3.00
Le Monstre, June, 1997
11 pt.1 . . . . 3.00
12 pt.2 Bernie Wrightson(c) 3.00
Modern Prometheus, Aug., 1997
13 pt.1 MK(c) in New York 3.00
14 pt.2 MK(c) 3.00
Tooth and Nail, Oct., 1997
15 pt.1 MSh(c) 3.00
16 pt.2 . . . . 3.00
TPB adapts #11–#16 . . . . 16.95
Tarzan vs. the Moon Men
17 pt.1 TT,AW,TY 3.00
18 pt.2 TT,AW,TY 3.00
19 pt.3 TT,AW,TY 3.00
20 pt.4 TT,AW,TY 3.00
Primeval
21 pt.1 MGr 3.00
22 pt.2 MGr 3.00
23 pt.3 MGr 3.00
24 pt.4 MGr 3.00
TPB RsM,The Land That Time Forgot 12.95
TPB Tarzan of the Apes 12.95
TPB The Jewls of Opar. 10.95

EDGAR RICE BURROUGHS' TARZAN: CARSON OF VENUS
May, 1998
1 (of 4) by Darko Macan and Igor Kordey, F:Carson Napier . . 3.00
2 thru 4 novels adapt. . . . . @3.00
TPB Carson of Venus 12.95

EDGAR RICE BURROUGHS' TARZAN: THE LOST ADVENTURE
1 Lost Manuscript 3.00
2 V:Gorgo the Buffalo 3.00
3 V:Bandits 3.00
4 V:Bandits 3.00
HC 19.95
HC lim. ed. 100.00

EDGAR RICE BURROUGHS' TARZAN: THE RIVERS OF BLOOD
November, 1999
1 . . . . 2.95
2 . . . . 2.95
3 in Vienna 2.95
4 F:Paul D'Arnot 2.95
5 trouble at the Circus 2.95
6 Freud rescued 2.95
7 & 8 . . . . @2.95

EDGAR RICE BURROUGHS' TARZAN: THE SAVAGE HEART

Apr., 1999

1 (of 4) MGr Jane is dead 3.00
2 thru 4 . . . . @3.00

Egon #2
© Dark Horse Comics

EGON

Jan.–Feb., 1998

1 and 2 . . . . @2.95

EIGHTH WONDER, THE

Nov., 1997

1-shot by Peter Janes & Killian Plunkett 2.95

ELRIC: STORMBRINGER

Dark Horse/Topps 1996

1 by Michael Moorcock & CR. 3.00
2 thru 7 (of 7). . . . . @3.00
TPB rep. series. 17.95

ENEMY

1 MZ(c),StG(s),I:Enemy. 2.75
2 MZ(c),StG(s),F:Heller 2.75
3 MZ(c),StG(s),A:Heller 2.50
4 . . . . 2.50
5 final issue. 2.95
TPB 14.95

ENO AND PLUM

Sept., 1997

TPB 12.95

EUDAEMON, THE

1 Nel,I:New Eudaemon 3.00
2 Nel,V:Mordare 2.75
3 Nel,V:Mordare 2.75

EVIL DEAD III: ARMY OF DARKNESS

1 JBo,Movie adaptation 4.00
2 JBo,Movie adaptation 3.50
3 JBo,Movie adaptation 3.00

EXOTICS, THE

TPB by Moebius. 7.95

EYEBALL KID

(B&W)

1 I:Eyeball Kid. 2.25
2 V:Stygian Leech 2.25
3 V:Telchines Brothers,last iss. . . . 2.25

FAT DOG MENDOZA

(B&W)

1 I&O:Fat Dog Mendoza 2.50

FAX FROM SARAJEVO

Oct., 1996

GN JKu, 224 pg.. . . . . 24.95

FEEDERS

Oct.,1999

1-shot MiA, prequel to Eyes to Heaven 2.95

FLAMING CARROT

(B&W)

18 . . . . 3.50
18a Ash-Can-Limited 4.00
19 . . . . 2.00
20 . . . . 2.00
21 . . . . 2.00
22 . . . . 2.00
23 . . . . 2.00
24 . . . . 3.00
25 F:TMNT,Mysterymen, with 2-card strip. 3.00
26 A:TMNT. 2.50
27 TM(c),A:TMNT conclusion 2.50
28 . . . . 2.50
29 Man in the Moon,Iron City 2.50
30 V:Man in the Moon 2.50
31 A:Fat Fury 2.50
Ann. 1 by Bob Burden 5.00
TPB Man of Mystery, B&W 12.95
TPB The Wild Shall Wild Remain rep. #4–#11 . . . . 17.95
TPB Flaming Carrot's Greatest Hits, rep. #12–#18 . . . . 17.95
TPB Fortune Favors the Bold, rep.#19–#24. . . . . 16.95

FLAXEN

1 Based on Model,w/poster 2.95

FLOATERS

(B&W)

1 thru 6 From Spike Lee 2.50

FOOT SOLDIERS, THE

1 thru 4 by Jim Krueger. 2.95
TPB 14.95
See also Image Comics

FRANKENSTEIN

1 Movie Adaptation 3.95

FREAKSHOW

1 JBo,DMc,KB, "Wanda the Worm Woman," "Lillie" 9.95

GAMERA

Aug., 1996

1 (of 4) by Dave Chipps & Mozart Couto 2.95
2 thru 4 . . . . @2.95

GARY GIANNI'S MONSTERMEN

Aug., 1999

1-shot. 2.95

Ghost #16 © Dark Horse Comics

GHOST

Comics' Greatest World

Spec. AH(c) 3.95

GHOST

1 by Eric Luke, R:Ghost. 2.50
2 AH,MfM,Arcadia Nocturne,pt.2 . . 2.50
3 Arcadia Nocturn,pt.3. . . . . 2.50
4 . . . . 2.50
5 V:Predator 2.50
6 . . . . 2.50
7 Hell Night 2.50
8 thru 20 . . . . @2.50
21 Two heroes, one room 2.50
22 "The key is forever beyond your reach". 2.50
23 I: The Goblins 2.50
24 X is dead. 2.50
25 double size 3.95
26 Fairytale version 2.95
27 . . . . 2.95
28 CW(c),Painful Music, pt.1. . . . . . 2.95
29 CW(c),Painful Music, pt.2. . . . . . 2.95
30 CW(c),Painful Music, pt.3. . . . . . 2.95
31 CW(c),Painful Music, pt.4. . . . . . 2.95
32 A Pathless Land 2.95
33 Jade Cathedral, pt.1 . . . . 2.95
34 Jade Cathedral, pt.2 . . . . 2.95
35 Jade Cathedral, pt.3 . . . . 2.95
36 Jade Cathedral, pt.4 . . . . 2.95
Spec.#2 Immortal Coil 3.95
Spec.#3 Scary Monsters. 3.95
TPB Ghost Stories 8.95
TPB Ghost: Nocturnes 9.95
TPB Exhuming Elisa. 17.95

GHOST

Sept., 1998

1 CW,O:Ghost. 2.95
2 CW,V:Dr.Trouvaille 2.95
3 CW,V:Silhouette 2.95
4 CW,The Devil Inside,O:pt.1. . . . . 2.95
5 CW,Stare at the Sun,O:pt.2 . . . . 2.95

DARK HORSE

6 CW,Stare at the Sun,O:pt.3 . . . . 2.95
7 CW,Shifter,pt.1,F:King Tiger 2.95
8 CW,Shifter,pt.2 . . . . 2.95
9 CW,Shifter,pt.3 . . . . 2.95
10 CW,Shifter,pt.4. . . . . 2.95
11 CW,back in Arcadia 2.95
12 Red Shadows, pt.1 (of 4). 2.95
13 Red Shadows, pt.2 . . . . 2.95
14 Red Shadows, pt.3 . . . . 2.95
15 Red Shadows, pt.4 . . . . 2.95
16 When the Devil Daydreams, pt.1 2.95
17 When the Devil Daydreams, pt.2 2.95
18 rogue agent. 2.95
19 Arcadia in chaos 2.95
20 F:Chris 2.95
21 F:Malcolm Greymater 2.95
22 final issue 2.95
TPB Black October. 14.95
TPB Painful Music 9.95
TPB No World So Dark. 14.95
Spec. Handbook #1 . . . . 2.95

GHOST/BATGIRL
August, 2000

1 (of 4) RBn,A:oracle. 2.95
2 RBn,V:Two-Face 2.95
3 RBn,V:Carver, Greymater 3.00

GHOST/HELLBOY COLLECTION

TPB MMi 4.95

GHOST AND THE SHADOW

Spec. 1-shot. 2.95

GHOST IN THE SHELL
Manga

1 Manga Style. 3.95
2 Wetware Virus 3.95
3 Killer Robots. 3.95
4 Rookie Cop Killed. 3.95
5 F:Major Kusangi 3.95
6 . . . . 3.95
7 Kusanagi in Jail 3.95
8 final issue. 3.95
TPB by Masamune Shirow 24.95

G.I. JOE

1 by Mike Barr & Tatsuya Ishida . . 1.95
2 thru 4 . . . . @2.50

GIRL CRAZY

TPB by GHe, rep.#1–#3 . . . . 9.95

GIVE ME LIBERTY

1 FM/DGb, Homes & Gardens. . . . 6.00
2 FM/DGb 5.00
3 and 4 FM/DGb . . . . @5.00
TPB 16.00

GODZILLA
(B&W) 1988

1 Japanese Manga 3.50
2 thru 6 . . . . @2.25
Spec #1 . . . . 1.50
TPB 2nd printing. 17.95

GODZILLA COLOR SPECIAL

1 AAd,R:Godzilla,V:Gekido-Jin. . . . 3.50
1a rep (1998) 2.95

Godzilla #15 © Dark Horse Comics

GODZILLA
1995

0 RSd,The King of Monsters
is back! 3.00
1 R:Godzill 2.50
2 V:Cybersaur 2.50
3 I:Bagorah the Bat Creature. 2.50
4 V:Bagorah,Cybersaur 2.50
5 V:U.S. Army 2.50
6 thru 14 . . . . @2.50
15 "Thunder Downunder" 2.95
16 "Thunder in the Past". 2.95
TPB Past, Present, Future 17.95
TPB Godzilla: Age of Monsters . . . 17.95

GODZILLA VS. BARKLEY

1 MBn(s),JBt,DvD 3.50

GODZILLA VS. HERO ZERO

1 Tatsuya Ishida 2.50

GREEN LANTERN VS. ALIENS
August, 2000

1 RMz,RL,F:Hal Jordan, x-over . . . 2.95
2 (of 4) RMz,RL,F:Kyle Rayner . . . 3.00

GRENDEL

TPB Past Prime,MWg. 14.95

GRENDEL: BLACK, WHITE, AND RED
B&W&R, Nov., 1998

1 (of 4) MWa, 48-page. 4.00
2 thru 4 MWa, 48-page . . . . @4.00
TPB Black, White & Red, MWg. . . 18.95

GRENDEL CLASSICS

1 Rep.#18–#19 Comico series. . . . 3.95

GRENDEL CYCLE

1 Grendel History 5.95

GRENDEL: DEVIL BY THE DEED
1993

1 MWg,RRa 3.95
1 representation (1997) 3.95
TPB Devil Tales 9.95

GRENDEL: DEVIL CHILD
June, 1999

1 (of 2) MWg, ... 2.95
2 conclusion 2.95

GRENDEL: DEVIL'S LEGACY
Aug., 1996

1 (of 12) by Matt Wagner. 2.75
2 thru 3 . . . . @2.75
TPB Devils and Deaths. 16.95

GRENDEL: DEVIL'S LEGACY
DH/Maverick, March, 2000

1 (of 12) MWg, rep. from 1986. . . . 2.95
2 thru 6 MWg, ... @2.95
7 MWg,V:Tujiro XIV 2.95
8 MWg,back to N.Y.. . . . . 3.00

GRENDEL: HOMECOMING

1 Babylon Crash 2.95
2 Babylon Crash pt. 2 . . . . 2.95
3 Too Dead To Die. 2.95

GRENDEL: WAR CHILD

1 MWg 4.00
2 thru 9 MWg 3.00
10 MWg, final issue, dbl.size 4.00
TPB 18.95
HC signed and numbered. 70.00

GRENDEL TALES: DEVIL'S APPRENTICE
Sept., 1997

1 (of 3) 2.95
2 thru 3 . . . . @2.95

GRENDEL TALES: DEVILS AND DEATHS

1 . . . . 2.95
2 . . . . 2.95
TPB rep. Devils and Deaths plus
Devil's Choices. 16.95

GRENDEL TALES: DEVIL'S CHOICES

1 F:Goran 2.95
2 Marica 2.95
3 Marica vs. Goran 2.95
4 conclusion 2.95

GRENDEL TALES: FOUR DEVILS, ONE HELL

1 MWg(c),F:Four Grendels 3.50
2 MWg(c),F:Four Grendels 3.50
3 MWg(c),F:Four Grendels 3.50
4 MWg(c),F:Four Grendels 3.50
5 MWg(c),F:Four Grendels 3.50
6 MWg(c),last issue. 3.25
TPB Rep. #1–#6. . . . . 17.95

GRENDEL TALES: THE DEVIL IN OUR MIDST

1 MWg(c) 3.50
2 MWg(c) 3.25
3 MWg(c) 2.95
4 & 5 . . . . @2.95
TPB series rep. 15.95

GRENDEL TALES: THE DEVIL MAY CARE

1 thru 6 mini-series 2.95

GRENDEL TALES: THE DEVIL'S HAMMER

1 MWg(a&s),I:Petrus Christus 3.50
2 MWg(a&s),A:P.Christus 3.25
3 MWg(a&s),last issue. 3.25

GRENDEL TALES

TPB Homecoming 7.95

GRIFTER AND THE MASK

Sept. 1996

1 by Seagle, Lima & Pimentel 2.50
2 . . . . 2.50

GUFF

April, 1998

1-shot by Sergio Aragones, flip book, with Meanie Babies card, B&W 1.95

GUNSMITH CATS

(B&W) Manga

1 I:Rally & Mini May. 2.95
2 Revolver Freak. 2.50
3 . . . . 2.95
4 V:Bonnie and Clyde 2.95
5 V:Bonnie and Clyde 2.95
6 Hostage Situation 2.95
7 thru 10 (10 part series) 2.95
TPB Misfire rep. #7–#10 & Return of Gray #1–#3. . . . . . . 12.95

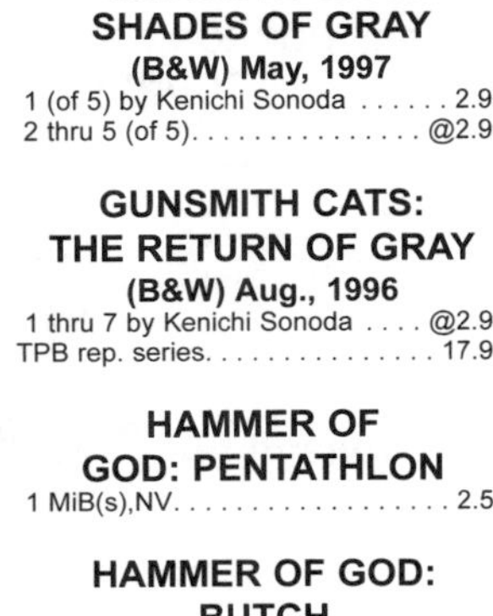

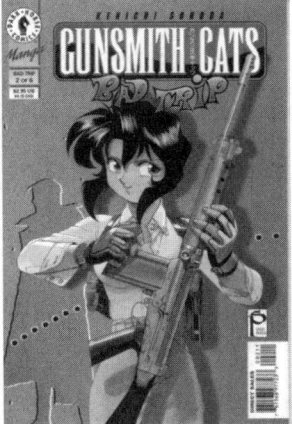

Gunsmith Cats: Bad Trip #2
© Dark Horse Comics

GUNSMITH CATS: BAD TRIP

(B&W) June, 1998

1 (of 6) by Kenichi Sonoda 2.95
2 thru 4 . . . . @2.95
TPB Bad Trip 13.95

GUNSMITH CATS: BEAN BANDIT

(B&W) June, 1998

1 (of 9) by Kenichi Sonoda 2.95
2 thru 9 . . . . @2.95
TPB Bean Bandit, 224-pg. 16.95

GUNSMITH CATS: BONNIE & CLYDE

TPB by Kenichi Sonoda 12.95

GUNSMITH CATS: GOLDIE VS. MISTY

(B&W) Nov. 1997

1 (of 7) by Kenichi Sonoda 2.95
2 thru 7 . . . . @2.95
TPB Goldie vs. Misty 12.95

GUNSMITH CATS: KIDNAPPED

November 1999

1 (of 10) by Kenichi Sonoda 2.95
2 thru 10 . . . . @2.95
TPB Bad Trip 13.95

GUNSMITH CATS: MISTER V

(B&W) October, 2000

1 (of 11) by Kenichi Sonoda. 3.50

GUNSMITH CATS: SHADES OF GRAY

(B&W) May, 1997

1 (of 5) by Kenichi Sonoda 2.95
2 thru 5 (of 5). . . . . @2.95

GUNSMITH CATS: THE RETURN OF GRAY

(B&W) Aug., 1996

1 thru 7 by Kenichi Sonoda . . . . @2.95
TPB rep. series. 17.95

HAMMER OF GOD: PENTATHLON

1 MiB(s),NV. 2.50

HAMMER OF GOD: BUTCH

1 MBn 2.50
2 and 3 MBn . . . . @2.50

THE HAMMER: UNCLE ALEX

Aug., 1998

1-shot KJo. 2.95

HAPPY BIRTHDAY MARTHA WASHINGTON

1 Frank Miller 2.95

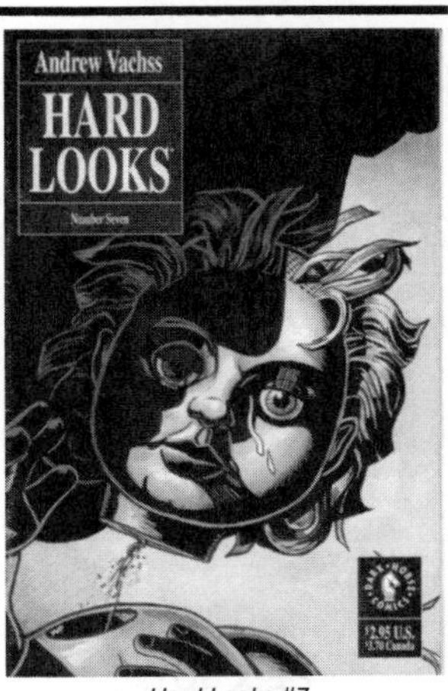

Hard Looks #7
© Dark Horse Comics

HARD BOILED

1 GfD 6.00
2 and 3 . . . . @5.00
TPB 14.95
HC 99.95
TPB Big Damn Hard Boiled 29.95

HARD LOOKS

(B&W)

1 thru 10 AVs Adaptations . . . . . @2.50
Book One. 14.95
TPB AVs. 17.95

HARLAN ELLISON'S DREAM CORRIDOR

1 Various stories 2.95
2 Various stories 2.95
3 JBy, I Have No Mouth and I Must Scream & other stories . . 2.95
4 Catman 2.95
5 . . . . 2.95
6 Opposites Attract 2.95
Spec.#1 Various stories 4.95
TPB 18.95
HC, vol. 1 limited 70.00

HARLAN ELLISON'S DREAM CORRIDOR QUARTERLY

Aug., 1996

1 & 2 . . . . @5.95

HAUNTED MAN, THE

March, 2000

1 (of 3) GJ,MBg. 2.95
2 GJ,MBg 2.95
3 . . . . 2.95

HEARTBREAKERS

1 . . . . 2.95

HEART OF EMPIRE: THE LEGACY OF LUTHER ARKWRIGHT

April, 1999

1 (of 9) BT. 2.95

2 thru 5 . . . . @2.95
6 plot against royal family 3.50
7 countdown to cataclysm 3.50
8 . . . . 3.50
9 conclusion 2.95

HELLBOY

Christmas Special (1997) MMi, 48-pg. 3.95
Hellboy Junior Halloween Special . . 3.95
Hellboy Junior Lurid Easter Special. 3.95
TPB The Lost Army 14.95
TPB The Chained Coffin & Others 17.95
TPB The Right Hand of Doom, MMi 17.95

HELLBOY: ALMOST COLOSSUS

1 (of 2) MMi, sequel to *Wake the Devil* 2.95
2 (of 2) 2.95

HELLBOY: BOX FULL OF EVIL

Aug., 1999

1 (of 2) MMi. 2.95
2 MMi, conclusion 2.95

HELLBOY: SEEDS OF DESTRUCTION

Legend/Dark Horse

1 JBy,MMi,AAd,V:Vampire Frog, BU:Monkeyman & O'Brien 3.50
2 MMi(c),JBy,AAd,BU:Monkeyman & O'Brien 3.00
3 MMi(c),JBy,AAd,BU:Monkeyman & O'Brien 3.00
4 MMi(c),JBy,AAd,BU:Monkeyman & O'Brien 3.00
TPB Seed of Destruction 17.95

DARK HORSE

HELLBOY: WAKE THE DEVIL

Legend

1 (of 5) MMi 2.95
2 thru 5 . . . . @2.95
TPB Wake The Devil 17.95

HELLBOY JR.

October, 1999

1 (of 2) MMi. 2.95
2 . . . . 2.95

HELLHOUNDS

(B&W)

1 I:Hellhounds 2.50
2 thru 6 A:Hellhounds . . . . @2.50

HELLHOUNDS: PANZER CORPS

(B&W) 1994

1 thru 6 . . . . @2.95
TPB 14.95

HERBIE

1 JBy,reps.& new material 2.50
2 Reps.& new material 2.50

HERETIC, THE

Nov., 1996

1 (of 4) by Rich DiLeonardo, Joe Phillips & Dexter Vines 2.95
2 thru 4 . . . . @2.95

Heretic #3 © Dark Horse Comics

HERMES VS. THE EYEBALL KID

1 thru 3 Symphony of Blood 2.95

HERO ZERO

1 First and last issue 2.50

HIEROGLYPH

November, 1999

1 RdD,F:Francisco Chavez 2.95
2 RdD 2.95
3 RdD 2.95
4 RdD, concl. 2.95

THE HORROR OF COLLIER COUNTY

October, 1999

1 (of 5) Halloween special 2.95
2 . . . . 2.95
3 . . . . 2.95
4 . . . . 2.95
5 concl. 2.95

H.P.'S ROCK CITY

TPB by Moebius. 7.95

HYPERSONIC

Nov., 1997

1 (of 4) DAn,GEr 2.95
2 thru 4 . . . . @2.95

INDIANA JONES AND THE ARMS OF GOLD

1 In South America 2.75
2 In South America 2.75
3 V:Incan Gods 2.75
4 . . . . 2.50

INDIANA JONES AND THE FATE OF ATLANTIS

1 DBa,Search for S.Hapgood with 2-card strip. 4.00
1a 2nd printing 3.00
2 DBa,Lost Dialogue of Plato with 2-card strip. 3.00
3 Map Room of Atlantis 3.00
4 Atlantis, Last issue 3.00
TPB 13.95

INDIANA JONES AND THE GOLDEN FLEECE

1 SnW. 2.75
2 SnW. 2.50

INDIANA JONES AND THE IRON PHOENIX

1 . . . . 2.50
2 V:Nazis. 2.50
3 A:Nadia Kirov 2.50
4 V:Undead 2.50

INDIANA JONES AND THE SARGASSO PIRATES

1 thru 4 . . . . @2.50

INDIANA JONES AND THE SHRINE OF THE SEA DEVIL

1 . . . . 2.50

INDIANA JONES AND THE SPEAR OF DESTINY

1 I:Spear T/Pierced Christ 2.50
2 DSp, with Henry Jones 2.50
3 Search for the Shaft 2.50

INDIANA JONES: THUNDER IN THE ORIENT

1 DBa(a&s),in Tripoli 2.75
2 DBa(a&s),Muzzad Ram 2.75
3 DBa(a&s),V:Sgt.Itaki 2.75
4 DBa(a&s),In Hindu Kush. 2.75
5 DBa(a&s),V:Japanese Army 2.75
6 DBa(a&s),last issue 2.75

INSTANT PIANO

1 Offbeat humor 3.95
2 . . . . 3.95
3 Various stories 3.95
4 Devil Puppet. 3.95

INTRON DEPOT

Nov., 1998

TPB Intron Depot 40.00
TPB Intron Depot 2: Blades 37.95

IRON HAND OF ALMURIC

(B&W)

1 Robert E. Howard adaption 2.00
2 A:Cairn,V:Yagas 2.25
3 V:Yasmeena,The Hive Queen. . . 2.00
4 Conclusion 2.25
GN 10.95

JAMES BOND 007: QUASIMODO GAMBIT

1 I:Maximillion Quasimodo. 3.95
2 V:Fanatical Soldiers 3.95
3 V:Steel 3.95

JAMES BOND 007: SERPENT'S TOOTH

1 PG,DgM,V:Indigo 5.50
2 PG,DgM,V:Indigo 5.00
3 PG,DgM 5.25
TPB 15.95

JAMES BOND 007: SHATTERED HELIX

1 V:Cerberus 2.50
2 V:Cerberus 2.50

JAMES BOND 007: A SILENT ARMAGEDDON

1 V:Troy 3.25
2 V:Omega 3.25
3 V:Omega 3.25

JOHN BOLTON'S STRANGE WINK

March, 1998

1 (of 3) 2.95
2 thru 3 . . . . @2.95

JOHNNY DYNAMITE

1 . . . . 2.95
2 . . . . 2.95
3 V:Faust 2.95
4 Last issue 2.95

JOKER/MASK

May, 2000

1 (of 4) Batman x-over 2.95
2 Joker becomes Joker/Mask 2.95
3 A:Harley Quinn, Poison Ivy 2.95
4 three nuclear bombs, concl. 2.95

JONNY DEMON

1 SL(c),KBk,NV 2.75
2 SL(c),KBk,NV 2.75
2 SL(c),KBk,NV, final issue 2.50

JUNIOR CARROT PATROL

(B&W)

1 . . . . 2.00
2 . . . . 2.00

KELLEY JONES' THE HAMMER

Sept., 1997

1 (of 4) KJo, horror series 2.95
2 thru 4 KJo, ... @2.95
TPB 12.95

KELLEY JONES' THE HAMMER: THE OUTSIDER

Feb., 1999

1 (of 3) KJo 2.95
2 & 3 . . . . @2.95

KINGS OF THE NIGHT

1 . . . . 2.25
2 end Mini-Series 2.25

KING TIGER/MOTORHEAD

1 (of 2) by D.G. Chichester, Karl Waller & Eric Shanower 2.95
2 . . . . 2.95

King Tiger & Motorhead #1 © Dark Horse Comics

KLING KLANG KLATCH

GN 11.95

LAND OF NOD

(B&W) July, 1997

1 (of 4) by Jay Stephens 2.95
2 thru 4 . . . . @2.95
TPB Rockabye Book 13.95

LAST DAY IN VIETNAM

GN by Will Eisner 10.95

LAST TEMPTATION, THE

DH/Maverick, November, 2000

TPB NGa,MZi,6"x9" 9.95

THE LEGEND OF MOTHER SARAH

B&W, Manga

1 I:Mother Sarah 2.50
2 Sarah and Tsutsu 2.50
3 Firing Squad 2.50
4 F:Toki 2.50
5 Yunnel Town 2.50
6 Kill or Be Killed 2.95
7 Firing Squad 2.95
8 Conclusion 2.95
TPB The Tunnel Town 18.95

THE LEGEND OF MOTHER SARAH: CITY OF THE ANGELS

(B&W) Oct., 1996

1 (of 9) by Katsuhiro Otomo and Takumi Nagayasu 3.95
1 rep. (1997) 3.95
2 thru 4 . . . . 3.95
2 thru 4 rep. (1997) 3.95
5 Tsue a victim 3.95
6 Mother Teres questioned 3.95
7 put in front trenches 3.95
8 Teres suicide run 3.95
9 . . . . 3.95

THE LEGEND OF MOTHER SARAH: CITY OF THE CHILDREN

(B&W) 1995

1 thru 4 (7 part mini-series) . . . . @3.95

LITTLE ANNIE FANNY 1962–70

October, 2000

TPB cartoons from playboy 25.00

LONE WOLF AND CUB

TPB Vol 1 . . . . 9.95
TPB Vol 2 . . . . 9.95
TPB Vol 3 Flute of the Fallen Tiger . 9.95

LORDS OF MISRULE

(B&W) Jan., 1997

1 by DAn, PSj 2.95
2 thru 6 . . . . @2.95
TPB The Lords of Misrule 17.95

LOST IN SPACE

April, 1998

1 (of 3) sequel to film 2.95
2 thru 3 GEr(c) . . . . @2.95
TPB rep. series, GEr(c) 7.95

THE LUCK IN THE HEAD

TPB 11.95

THE MACHINE

Comics Greatest World 1994

1 (a) The Barb Wire spin 2.50
2 V:Salvage 2.50
3 Freak Show 2.50
4 I:Skion 2.50

MADMAN

Legend 1994

1 MiA(s) 8.00
2 MiA(s) 6.00
3 MiA(s) 5.00
4 MiA(s),Muscleman 5.00
5 MiA(s),I:The Blast 4.00
6 MiA(s),A:Big Guy, Big Brain-

Madman #2 © Dark Horse Comics

o-rama,pt.1. . . . . 12.00
7 MiA(s),FM,A:Big Guy, Big Brain-o-rama,pt.2. . . . . 6.00
8 MiA(s) 4.00
9 Micro Madman 4.00
10 . . . . 4.00
11 . . . . 4.00
12 thru 14. . . . . @5.00
15 . . . . 7.00
Yearbook '95 TPB. 17.95
Yearbook '96 TPB. 17.95
TPB Vol. 1 . . . . 17.95
TPB Vol. 2 . . . . 17.95
HC Vol. 1 & Vol. 2, set 100.00

MADMAN/THE JAM
July, 1998

1 (of 2) MiA. 2.95
2 MiA 2.95

MADMAN COMICS
Apr., 1999

12 MiA 2.95
13 MiA 2.95
14 MiA 2.95
15 MiA 2.95
TPB Boogaloo 8.95
TPB The Exit of Dr. Boiffard 17.95

MADMAN COMICS: THE G-MEN FROM HELL
DH/Maverick, August, 2000

1 (of 4) MiA. 2.95
2 MiA, Is Frank Einstein dead? . . . 2.95
3 MiA,. 3.00

MADWOMAN OF THE SACRED HEART, THE
(B&W)

TPB by Alex Jodorowsky & Moe . . 12.95

MAGIC: THE GATHERING
March, 1998

1 (of 4) MGr,Initiation. 2.95
2 MGr, Legacy. 2.95
3 MGr, Crucible 2.95
4 MGr, Destiny 2.95
TPB Gerrard's Quest 11.95

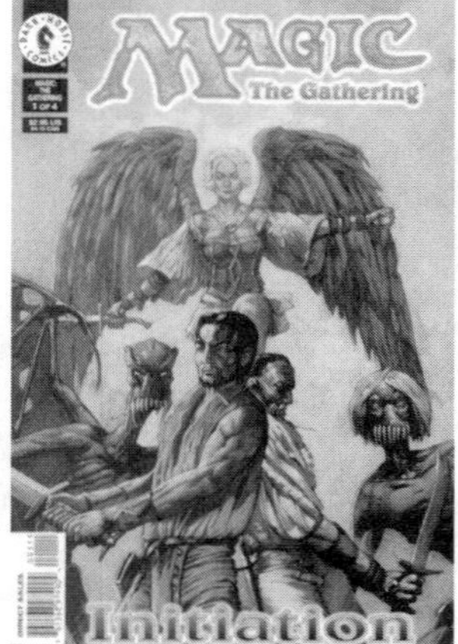

Magic: The Gathering #1
© Dark Horse Comics

MAGNUS/NEXUS
Dark Horse/Valiant

1 MBn(s), SR 3.25
2 MBn(s), SR 3.25

MAN FROM THE CIGUIRI

TPB by Moebius. 7.95

MARK, THE

1 LSn, in America 1.75
2 LSn 1.95
3 LSn 1.95
4 . . . . 1.95

MARK, THE
(B&W)

1 . . . . 1.95
2 thru 7 . . . . @1.75

MARK, THE

1 MiB(s),V:Archon 2.75
2 MiB(s),V:Archon 2.75
3 MiB(s),V:Archon,A:Pierce 2.75
4 MiB(s),last issue 2.75

MARK, THE

1 I:The Mark 2.50
2 V:Child Killer. 2.50

MARSHALL LAW: BLOOD, SWEAT, AND FEARS
Feb., 1998

TPB 15.95

MARSHALL LAW: CAPE FEAR

1 KON. 2.95

MARSHALL LAW: SECRET TRIBUNAL

1 KON. 2.95
2 KON. 2.95

MARSHALL LAW: SUPER BABYLON

1 KON. 4.95

MARTHA WASHINGTON GOES TO WAR
Dark Horse-Legends

1 FM(s),DGb, V:Fat Boys Corp. . . . 3.25
2 FM(s),DGb, V:Fat Boys Corp. . . . 3.25
3 FM(s),DGb, V:Fat Boys Corp. . . . 3.25
4 FM(s),DGb, V:Fat Boys Corp. . . . 3.25
5 FM(s),DBb, final issue 3.25
TPB Rep.#1–#5 . . . . 17.95

MARTHA WASHINGTON SAVES THE WORLD
Dec., 1997

1 (of 3) FM,DGb 2.95
2 thru 3 . . . . @2.95
TPB rep.. 12.95

MARTHA WASHINGTON STRANDED IN SPACE

1 . . . . 2.95

MARTIAN MYSTERY
(B&W) DH/Bonelli Mar., 1999

1 by Alfredo Castelli & Giancarlo Alessandrini, DGb(c) 92-page. . 4.95
2 thru 6 . . . . @4.95

MASAKAZU KATSURA'S SHADOW LADY I— DANGEROUS LOVE
Manga (B&W) Oct., 1998

1 (of 7) Masakazu Katsura. 2.50
2 thru 7 . . . . @2.50
The Eyes of a Stranger, May, 1999
8 thru 12, pt.1–pt.5. . . . . @2.50
The Awakening
13 thru 19,pt.1–pt.7. . . . . @2.50
Sudden Death
20 thru 24, pt.1–pt.5 . . . . @2.50
Spec.48-pg. final issue 4.00
TPB Dangerous Love 17.95
TPB The Awakening. 15.95

MASK, THE

0 . . . . 3.00
1 I:Lt.Kellaway Mask 5.00
2 V:Rapaz & Walter. 4.00
3 O:Mask 4.00
4 final issue. 4.00
TPB 14.95

MASK, THE

1 Movie Adaptation 3.00
2 Movie Adaptation 2.50

MASK, THE
(B&W)

0 `Who's Laughing Now' 5.00

MASK/MARSHALL LAW
Feb., 1998

1 (of 2) by Pat Mills and Kevin O'Neill 2.95
2 concl.. . . . . 2.95

MASK RETURNS, THE

1 inc.cut-out Mask 5.00
2 Mask's crime spree. 4.00
3 . . . . 4.00

Mask: Southern Discomfort
© Dark Horse Comics

4 . . . . 4.00
TPB by John Arcudi & Doug Mahnke 14.95

MASK STRIKES BACK, THE
[Mini-Series]

1 Mask Strikes Back pt.1 . . . . 2.50
2 Mask Strikes Back pt.2 . . . . 2.50
3 Mask Strikes Back pt.3 . . . . 2.50
4 DoM,Mask Strikes Back pt.4 . . . . 2.50
5 Mask Strikes Back,pt.5 . . . . 2.50
TPB by John Arcudi, Doug Mahnke & Keith Williams 14.95

MASK, THE: THE HUNT FOR GREEN OCTOBER

1 . . . . 2.50
2 Kellaway vs. Ray Tuttle 2.50
3 F:Emily Tuttle 2.50
4 final issue 2.50

MASK, THE: SOUTHERN DISCOMFORT

1 Mardi Gras time 2.50

MASK, THE: VIRTUAL SURREALITY

1-shot F: MMi,SA 2.95

MASK, THE: WORLD TOUR

1 thru 4 . . . . @2.50

MASK: TOYS IN THE ATTIC
Aug., 1998

1 (of 4) 2.95
2 thru 4 . . . . @2.95

MAXIMUM OVERLOAD

1 Masque (Mask) 12.00
2 thru 4 Mask . . . . @8.00

MAXIMUM OVERLOAD

1 thru 5 . . . . @3.95

MECHA
Comics Greatest World 1995

1 color 1.75
2 color 1.75
3 thru 6 B&W . . . . @1.75
Spec.(#1) CW(c),color 2.95

MEDAL OF HONOR

1 Ace of Aces 2.50
2 . . . . 2.50
3 Andrew's Raid 2.50
4 Frank Miller(c) 2.50
5 final issue 2.50

MEDAL OF HONOR SPECIAL

1 JKu 2.50

MEZZ GALACTIC TOUR

1 MBn,MV 2.50

THE MINOTAUR'S TALE

TPB by Al Davison 11.95

MR. MONSTER
(B&W)

1 . . . . 3.50
2 . . . . 2.50
3 Alan Moore story 2.50
4 . . . . 2.50
5 I:Monster Boy 2.00
6 . . . . 2.00
7 . . . . 2.00
8 V:Vampires (giant size) 4.95

Monkeyman & O'Brien #2
© Dark Horse Comics

MONKEYMAN & O'BRIEN
Legend

1 by Arthur Adams 2.95
2 and 3 . . . . @2.95
Spec. 2.95
TPB 16.95

MOTORHEAD
Comics Greatest World 1995

1 V:Predator 2.50
2 Laughing Wolf Carnival 2.50
3 V:Jackboot 2.50

MOTORHEAD SPECIAL

1 JLe(c),V:Mace Blitzkrieg 3.95

[BOB BURDEN'S ORIGINAL] MYSTERYMEN
July, 1999

1 . . . . 2.95
2 The Amazing Disc Man 2.95
3 F:Screwball 2.95
4 All Villain Comics #1 . . . . 3.50

MYSTERY MEN
July, 1999

1 (of 2) Movie adapt. 2.95
2 movie adaptation, concl. 2.95

MYST: THE BOOK OF THE BLACK SHIPS
Aug., 1997

1 (of 4) from CD-Rom game 2.95
2 thru 4 . . . . @2.95

NATHAN NEVER
(B&W) DH/Bonelli Mar., 1999

1 (of 6) by Michele Medda & Nicola Mari, AAd(c) 102-page 4.95
2 thru 6 . . . . @4.95

NEVERMEN, THE
May, 2000

1 (of 4) GyD, V:Clockwork 2.95
2 GyD,V:Honshu 2.95
3 GyD,V:Clockwork 2.95
4 GyD,V:League of Crows 2.95

NEW FRONTIER
(B&W)

1 From series in Heavy Metal 2.75
2 Who Killed Ruby Fields? 2.75
3 Conclusion 2.75

NEW TWO-FISTED TALES: VOL. II

1 War stories 4.95

[JOHN BYRNE'S] NEXT MEN

0 Rep Next Men from Dark Horse Presents 3.00
1 JBy,`Breakout'inc.trading card certificate 5.00
1a 2nd Printing Blue 3.00
2 JBy,World View 4.00
3 JBy,A:Sathanis 4.00
4 JBy,A:Sathanis 4.00
5 JBy,A:Sathanis 4.00
6 JBy,O:Senator Hilltop, Sathanis,Project Next Men 3.50
7 JBy,I:M-4,Next Men Powers explained 3.50
8 JBy,I:Omega Project,A:M-4 . . . . . 3.00
9 JBy,A:Omega Project,A:M-4 . . . . 3.00
10 JBy,V:OmegaProject,A:M-4 . . . . 3.00
11 JBy,V:OmegaProject,A:M-4 . . . . 3.00

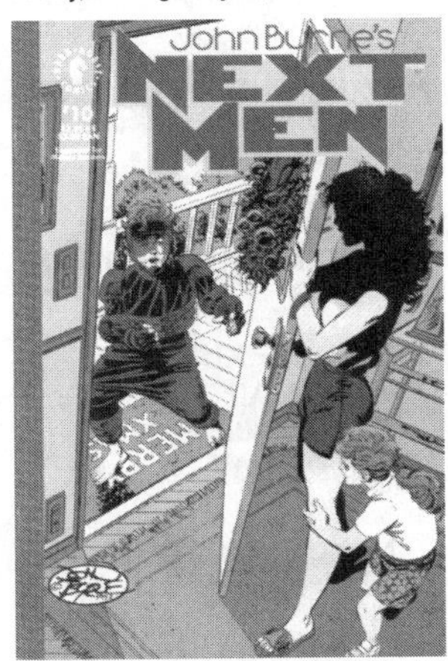

(John Byrne's) Next Men #10
© Dark Horse Comics

DARK HORSE

12 JBy,V:Dr.Jorgenson 3.00
13 JBy,Nathan vs Jack 3.00
14 JBy,I:Speedboy 2.75
15 JBy,in New York. 2.75
16 JBy,Jasmine's Pregnant. 2.75
17 FM(c),JBy,Arrested 2.75
18 JBy,On Trial. 2.75
TPB rep.#1-6 . . . . 16.95
TPB Parallel Collection. 16.95

NEXT MEN: FAITH

Dark Horse-Legend 1993

1 JBy(a&s),V:Dr.Trogg, Blue Dahila 3.25
2 JBy,(a&s),F:Jack. 2.75
3 MMi(c),JBy(a&s),I:Hellboy. 3.50
4 JBy(a&s),Last issue 2.75
TPB Book Four. 14.95

NEXT MEN: LIES

Dark Horse-Legend 1994

1 JBy. 2.50
2 JBy. 2.50
3 JBy. 2.50
4 JBy. 2.50
Book 6 TPB Lies. 16.95

NEXT MEN: POWER

Dark Horse-Legend 1994

1 JBy(a&s) 2.75
2 JBy(a&s) 2.75
3 JBy(a&s) 2.75
4 JBY(a&s), final issue 2.50

NEXUS: ALIEN JUSTICE

1 . . . . 4.25
2 . . . . 4.25
3 . . . . 3.95
TPB 16.95

NEXUS: EXECUTIONER'S SONG

1 (of 4) by Mike Baron, Steve
Rude & Gary Martin 2.95
2 thru 4 . . . . @2.95

NEXUS: GOD CON

April, 1997

1 (of 2) by Mike Baron, Steve
Rude & Gary Martin 2.95
2. . . . . 2.95

NEXUS: THE LIBERATOR

1 "Waking Dreams" 2.75
2 Civil War,D:Gigo. 2.75
3 Civil War contd. 2.75
4 Last issue. 2.75

NEXUS MEETS MADMAN

1-shot. 2.95

NEXUS: NIGHTMARE IN BLUE

(B&W) July, 1997

1 (of 4) MBn,SR,GyM 2.95
2 thru 4 . . . . @2.95

NEXUS: THE ORIGIN

1 SR,O:Nexus 4.95

NEXUS: OUT OF THE VORTEX

1 R:Nexus. 2.50
2 Zolot & Nexus Together 2.50
3 O:Vortex. 2.50

NEXUS: THE WAGES OF SIN

1 The Client. 2.95
2 V:Munson. 2.95
3 SR(c&a) Murders in New Eden. . 2.95

NIGHT BEFORE CHRISTMASK

1 Rick Geary 9.95

NINA'S NEW AND IMPROVED ALL-TIME GREATEST

1 Anthology: Nina Paley 2.50

NINTH GLAND, THE

(B&W) March, 1997

1-shot by Renee French 3.95

NOCTURNALS: WITCHING HOUR

May 1998

1-shot by Dan Brereton. 4.95

NOSFERATU

(B&W)

1 The Last Vampire 3.95
2 . . . . 2.95

OH MY GODDESS!

(B&W) Manga

1 by Kosuke Fujishima 5.00
2 & 3 . . . . @4.00
4 thru 6 . . . . @3.00
TPB 1-555-Goddess. 12.95

Part II, 1995

1 F:Keiichi. 4.00
2 thru 9. . . . . @3.00
TPB Sympathy for the Devil 12.95

Part III, 1996

1 Wishes are Granted 3.00
2 Love Potion Number 9 . . . . 3.00
3 thru 5. 3.00
6 thru 11 Terrible Master Urd,
pt.1 thru pt.6. . . . . @3.00
TPB Love Potion Number 9 . . . . . 12.95
TPB Terrible Master Urd 12.95

Part IV, 1996–97

1 Robot Wars 3.00
2 The Trials of Morisato, pt.1 . . . . . 3.00
3 The Trials of Morisato, pt.2 . . . . . 3.00
4 The Trials of Morisato, pt.3 . . . . . 3.00
5 The Queen of Vengeance. 3.00
6 Mara Strikes Back, pt.1,48-page. 4.00
7 Mara Strikes Back, pt.2. . . . . 3.00
8 Mara Strikes Back, pt.3 . . . . . . @3.00

Part V, 1997–98

1 The Forgotten Promise. 3.00
2 The Lunch Box of Love. 3.00
3 Meet Me by the Seashore, 48pg . 4.00
4 You're So Bad, 48-page 4.00
5 Ninja Master, pt.1 . . . . 3.00
6 Ninja Master, pt.2, 48-page. 4.00
7 Miss Keiichi, pt.1, 48-page 4.00
7 & 8 Miss Keiichi, pt.2 . . . . 3.00
9 It's Lonely at the Top. 3.50
10 Fallen Angel, 48-page 4.00
11 Play the Game, 48-page 4.00
12 Sorrow, Fear Not 4.00

Oh My Goddess! Part 5, #1
© Dark Horse Comics

Part VI, 1998–99

1 Devil in Miss Urd, pt.1, 40pg . . @3.50
2 Devil in Miss Urd, pt.2. . . . . 3.00
3 Devil in Miss Urd, pt.3. . . . . 3.00
4 Devil in Miss Urd, pt.4. . . . . 3.00
5 Devil in Miss Urd, pt.5. . . . . 3.00
6 SuperUrd 3.00

Part VII, 1999

1 (of 8)The Fourth Goddess, pt.1. . 3.00
2 The Fourth Goddess, pt.2. . . . . . 3.00
3 The Fourth Goddess, pt.3. . . . . . 3.00
4 The Fourth Goddess, pt.4,40pg . 3.50
5 The Fourth Goddess, pt.5,40pg . 3.50
TPB The Adventures of the
Mini-Goddesses 9.95

Part VIII, 1999

1 (of 2) Childhood's End,
by Kosuke Fujishima 3.50
2 Childhood's End, pt.2 . . . . 3.50
3 The Queen and the Goddess . . . 3.50
4 Hail to the Chief, pt.1 . . . . 3.50
5 Hail to the Chief, pt.2 . . . . 3.50
6 Hail to the Chief, pt.3 . . . . 3.50

Part IX, 2000

1 Pretty in Scarlet 2.95
2 The Goddess's Apprentice 2.95
3 Queen Sayoko, pt.1 . . . . 2.95
4 Queen Sayoko, pt.2 . . . . 3.50
TPB Ninja Master 13.95
TPB Queen of Vengeance 13.95
TPB Mara Strikes Back. 14.95

OKTANE

1 R:Oktane 2.50
2 V:God Zero. 2.50
3 V:God Zero. 2.50
4 conclusion 2.50

ONE BAD RAT

1 BT 2.95
2 thru 4 . . . . @2.95

ONE-TRICK RIP-OFF

TPB by Paul Pope 12.95

ORION

(B&W) Manga

1 SF by Masamune Shirow 2.50
2 F:Yamata Empire 2.95
3 thru 6 . . . . @2.95

 All comics prices listed are for *Near Mint* condition.

Otis Goes Hollywood #1
© Dark Horse Comics

TPB 15.95

OTIS GOES HOLLYWOOD

(B&W) April 1997

1 (of 2) by Bob Fingerman. 2.95
2 . . . . 2.95

OUT FOR BLOOD

B&W

1 (of 4) GEr,F:Dan Sanger. 2.95
2 The Wings; The Claws 2.95
3 . . . . 2.95
4 concl. 2.95

OUTLANDERS

(B&W) Manga

1 . . . . 3.00
2 . . . . 2.50
3 thru 7 . . . . @2.00
8 thru 20 . . . . @2.25
21 Operation Phoenix. 2.25
22 thru 24 . . . . @2.50
25 thru 29 with 2-card strip . . . . . @2.50
30 . . . . 2.50
31 Tetsua dying 2.50
32 D:The Emperor 2.50
33 Story finale 2.50
#0 The Key of Graciale. 2.75
TPB Vol. 1 by Johji Manabe 13.95
TPB Vol. 1 2nd edition 13.95
TPB Vol. 2 . . . . 13.95
TPB Vol. 2 2nd edition 13.95
TPB Vol. 3 . . . . 13.95
TPB Vol. 4 . . . . 12.95
TPB Vol. 5 . . . . 14.95
TPB Vol. 6 . . . . 14.95
TPB Vol. 7 . . . . 14.95
TPB Vol 8. . . . . 14.95

OUTLANDERS: EPILOGUE

(B&W)

1 . . . . 2.75

OUT OF THE VORTEX

Comics' Greatest World 1993

1 B:JOs(s),V:Seekers 2.25
2 MMi(c),DaW,A:Seekers. 2.25
3 WS(c),E:JOs(s),DaW,A:Seeker,
C:Hero Zero 2.25
4 DaW,A:Catalyst 2.25
5 V:Destroyers,A:Grace 2.25
6 V:Destroyers,A:Hero Zero. 2.25
7 AAd(c),DaW,V:Destroyers,
A:Mecha. 2.25
8 DaW,A:Motorhead 2.25
9 DaW,V:Motorhead 2.25
10 MZ(c), A:Division 13 . . . . 2.25
11 V:Reaver Swarm 2.50
12 Final issue. 2.50

OZ

by Eric Shanower

TPB The Blue Witch of Oz 9.95
TPB The Forgotten Forest of Oz. . . 8.95
TPB The Ice King of Oz 8.95
TPB The Secret Island of Oz 8.95

PETE & MOE VISIT PROFESSOR SWIZZLE'S ROBOTS

HC 14.95

PI: THE BOOK OF ANTS

Artisan Entertainment Sept. 1998

1-shot, movie adapt. 2.95

PREDATOR

1 CW,Mini Series. 6.00
1a 2ndPrinting 3.00
1b 3rdPrinting 2.50
2 CW. 5.00
2a 2ndPrinting 3.00
3 CW. 4.00
3a 2ndPrinting 2.50
4 CW. 3.00
4a 2ndPrinting 2.50

PREDATOR: BAD BLOOD

1 CW,I:John Pulnick 2.75
2 CW,V:Predator 2.75
3 CW,V:Predator,C.I.A. 2.75
4 Last issue. 2.50

PREDATOR: BIG GAME

1 Corp.Nakai Meets Predator. 3.50
2 Army Base Destroyed, with
2-card strip. 3.50
3 Corp.Nakai Arrested, with
2-card strip. 3.50
4 Nakai vs. Predator 3.50
TPB rep. #1–#4 . . . . 13.95
TPB rep. #1–#4, 2nd edition 14.95

PREDATOR: BLOODY SANDS OF TIME

1 DBa,CW,Predator in WWI. 3.50
2 DBa,CW, WWII cont'd. 3.25

PREDATOR: CAPTIVE

April, 1998

1-shot 2.95

PREDATOR: COLD WAR

1 Predator in Siberia 3.50
2 U.S. Elite Squad in Siberia 3.25
3 U.S. vs. USSR commandos 3.25
4 U.S. vs. USSR in Siberia 3.00
TPB 13.95
TPB 2nd printing. 13.95

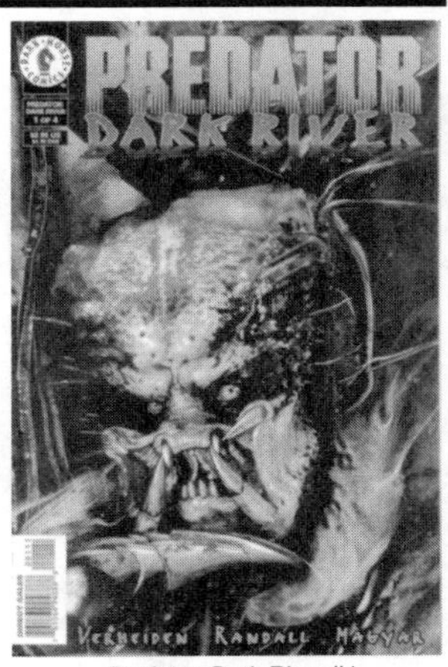

Predator: Dark River #1
© Dark Horse Comics

PREDATOR: CONCRETE JUNGLE

TPB 14.95

PREDATOR: DARK RIVER

1 thru 4 by Verheiden,RoR,RM. . @2.95

PREDATOR: HELL & HOT WATER

1 thru 3 MSh, GC & GWt . . . . . . @2.95
TPB rep.. . . . . 9.95

PREDATOR: HELL COME A WALKIN'

Feb. 1998

1 (of 2) by Nancy C,ollins,
Dean Ormston 2.95
2 concl. 2.95

PREDATOR: HOMEWORLD

Mar., 1999

1 (of 4) 2.95
2 thru 4 . . . . @2.95

PREDATOR: INVADERS FROM THE FOURTH DIMENSION

1 . . . . 3.95

PREDATOR: JUNGLE TALES

1 Rite of Passage 2.95

PREDATOR: KINDRED

1 . . . . 2.50
2 thru 4 . . . . @2.95
TPB Predator: Kindred 14.95

PREDATOR: NEMESIS

Dec., 1997

1 (of 2) TTg(c). 2.95
2 . . . . 2.95

PREDATOR: PRIMAL
1997

1 (of 2) Kevin J. Anderson(s), ScK,Low. 2.95
2 (of 2) 2.95

PREDATOR: RACE WAR

0 F:Serial Killer 2.75
1 V:Serial Killer 2.75
2 D:Serial Killer 2.75
3 in Prison. 2.75
4 Last Issue. 2.75
TPB Race War, serie rep. 17.95

PREDATOR: STRANGE ROUX

1-shot. 2.95

PREDATOR 2

1 DBy, Movie Adapt Pt1. . . . . 3.50
2 MBr, Movie Adapt. Pt2 with 2-card strip. 3.00

PREDATOR VS. JUDGE DREDD
Sept., 1997

1 (of 3) by John Wagner and Enrique Alcatena 2.50
2 thru 3 . . . . @2.50
TPB Predator vs. Judge Dredd 8.95

PREDATOR VS. MAGNUS ROBOT FIGHTER
Valiant/Dark Horse 1992

1 LW,A:Tekla 3.00
1a Platinum Ed. 5.00
1b Gold Ed.. . . . . 3.00
2 LW,Magnus Vs. Predator, with 2-card strip. 3.00
TPB Rep. #1–#2. . . . . 7.95

PREDATOR: XENOGENESIS
Aug., 1999

1 (of 4) 2.95
2 IEd. 2.95
3 IEd. 2.95
4 . . . . 2.95

PRIMAL

1 Contd.from Primal:from the Cradle to the Grave 2.95
2 A:TJ Cyrus 2.50

PRIMAL FROM THE CRADLE TO THE GRAVE

GN 9.95

PROPELLER MAN

1 I:Propeller Man. 2.95
2 O:Propeller Man,w/2 card strip . . 2.95
3 V:Manipulator 2.95
4 V:State Police,w/2 card strip 2.95
5 V:Manipulator 2.95
6 V:Thing, w/2 card strip 2.95
7 . . . . 2.95
8 Last issue,w/2 card strip 2.95

PUMPKINHEAD

1 Based on the movie 2.50

RACE OF SCORPIONS
(B&W)

1 A:Argos,Dito,Alma,Ka 2.25

RACE OF SCORPIONS

Book 1 short stories 5.00
Book 2 . . . . 4.95
Book 3 . . . . 2.50
Book 4 Final issue 2.50

RACK & PAIN

1 GCa(c),I:Rack,Pain. 2.50
2 GCa(c),V:Web 2.50
3 GCa(c),V:Web 2.50
4 GCa(c),Final Issue 2.50

RASCALS IN PARADISE

1 I:Spicy Sanders 3.95
2 . . . . 3.95
3 last issue 3.95
TPB Rep.#1–#3 . . . . 16.95

Real Adventrues of Jonny Quest #1
© Dark Horse Comics

REAL ADVENTURES OF JONNY QUEST, THE
Sept., 1996

1 . . . . 2.95
3 thru 12 . . . . @2.95

REBEL SWORD
(B&W) Manga

1 by Yoshikazu Yashiko 2.50
2 . . . . 2.50
3 . . . . 2.50
4 V:Ruken 2.50
5 Choice of Jiro 2.50
6 R:Ruken. 2.50

REDBLADE

1 V:Demons 2.50
2 V:Tull 2.50
3 Last Issue. 2.50

RED ROCKET 7
Aug., 1997

1 (of 7) MiA 3.95
2 thru 7 . . . . @3.95
TPB rep. series, 208 pg 29.95

RING OF ROSES
(B&W)

1 Alternate world,1991. . . . . 2.50
2 Plague in London 2.50
3 Plague cont.A:Secret Brotherhood of the Rosy Cross 2.50
4 Conclusion 2.50

R.I.P.D.
November, 1999

1 (of 4) F:Rest in Peace Dept. 2.95
2 . . . . 2.95
3 . . . . 2.95
4 concl. 2.95

RING OF THE NIEBELUNG, THE: RHINEGOLD
DH/Maverick, February, 2000

1 (of 4) CR 2.95
2 CR 2.95
3 CR 2.95
4 CR, concl. 2.95

RING OF THE NIEBELUNG, THE: THE VALKYRIE
DH/Maverick, August, 2000

1 (of 3) CR 2.95
2 CR 2.95
3 CR, concl. 3.00

RIO AT BAY

1 F:Doug Wildey art. 2.95
2 F:Doug Wildey art. 2.95
TPB 6.95

ROACHMILL
(B&W)

1 thru 8 . . . . @3.50
9 and 10 . . . . @2.00

ROBOCOP: MORTAL COILS

1 V:Gangs. 2.75
2 V:Gangs. 2.75
3 V:Coffin,V:Gangs 2.75

ROBOCOP VERSUS TERMINATOR

1 FM(s),WS,w/Robocop cut-out . . . 3.50
2 FM(s),WS,w/Terminator cut-out. . 3.00
3 FM(s),WS,w/cut-out 3.00
4 FM(s),WS,Conclusion. 3.00

ROBOCOP: PRIME SUSPECT

1 Robocop framed. 2.75
2 thru 4 V:ZED-309s . . . . @2.50
Collected 13.95

ROBOCOP: ROULETTE

1 V:ED-309s 2.75
2 I:Philo Drut 2.75
3 V:Stealthbot 2.75
4 last issue 2.75

ROBOCOP 3

1 B:StG(s),Movie Adapt. 2.75
2 V:Aliens,OCP 2.75
3 HNg,ANi(i) 2.75

Rocketeer Adventure Magazine #3
© Dark Horse Comics

ROCCO VARGAS

HC by Daniel Torres 30.00

ROCKETEER ADVENTURE MAGAZINE

1988–95

1 and 2 . . . . @4.00
3 . . . . 2.95
TPB Cliff's New York Adventure
by Dave Stevens 9.95

THE SAFEST PLACE

SC, SD. 2.50

SCATTERBRAIN

June 1998

1 (of 4) MMi, ... 2.95
2 thru 4 . . . . @2.95

SECRET OF THE SALAMANDER

(B&W)

1 Jacquestardi, rep 2.95

SERGIO ARAGONES' BOOGEYMAN

(B&W) June, 1998

1 (of 4) 2.95
2 thru 4 . . . . @2.95
TPB, rep. 9.95

SERGIO ARAGONES' DAY OF THE DEAD

Oct., 1998

1-shot. 2.95

SERGIO ARAGONES' GROO

Jan.–April, 1998

1 (of 4) 2.95
2 thru 4 . . . . @2.95
TPB The Most Intelligent Man
in the World 9.95
TPB Houndbook. 9.95
TPB Inferno 9.95
TPB Jamboree 9.95

SERGIO ARAGONES' GROO & RUFFERTO

Dec., 1998

1 (of 4) 2.95
2 thru 4 . . . . @2.95
TPB 9.95

SERGIO ARAGONES' GROO: MIGHTIER THAN THE SWORD

January 2000

1 (of 4) SA. 2.95
2 SA,V:Pipil Khan 2.95
3 SA,V:Relmihio 2.95
4 SA,concl. 2.95

SERGIO ARAGONES' LOUDER THAN WORDS

(B&W) July–Dec., 1997

1 (of 6) SA. 2.95
2 thru 6 . . . . @2.95
TPB rep. series. 12.95

SERGIO STOMPS STAR WARS

1-shot SA, parody 2.95

SEX WARRIORS

1 I:Dakini. 2.50
2 V:Steroids. 2.50

THE SHADOW

1 MK. 2.75
2 MK. 2.50

THE SHADOW AND DOC SAVAGE

1 . . . . 2.95
2 The Shrieking Skeletons. 2.95

THE SHADOW: HELL'S HEAT WAVE

1 Racial War 2.95
2 MK,V:Ghost 2.95
3 Final issue 2.95

THE SHADOW: IN THE COILS OF LEVIATHAN

1 MK,V:Monster. 3.25
2 MK. 3.25
3 MK,w/ GfD poster. 3.25
4 MK,Final issue 3.25
TPB, reprints #1–#4 . . . . 13.95

THE SHADOW AND THE MYSTERIOUS 3

1 Three stories 2.95

SHADOW EMPIRE: FAITH CONQURES

1 CsM 2.95
2 CsM,V:Vaylen. 2.95
3 CsM 2.95
4 CsM, final issue 2.95

SIGNAL TO NOISE

April, 1999

TPB NGa,DMc 14.95

SIN CITY: A DAME TO KILL FOR

Dark Horse-Legend (B&W)

1 FM(a&s),I:Dwight,Ava. 5.00
1a 2nd printing 3.00
2 FM(a&s),A:Ava 4.00
2a 2nd printing 2.50
3 FM(a&s),D:Ava's Husband 4.00
3a 2nd printing 2.95
4 FM(a&s). 4.00
5 FM(a&s). 4.00
6 FM(a&s),Final issue 4.00
TPB rep. #1–#6, new pages 15.00
HC rep. #1–#6, new pages 25.00
HC signed, limited 90.00

SIN CITY: A SMALL KILLING

Dark Horse-Legend

1 GN 14.00

SIN CITY: FAMILY VALUES

(B&W) 1997

GN 128pg by Frank Miller. 10.00

SIN CITY: HELL AND BACK

July, 1999

1 (of 9) FM 2.95
2 . . . . 2.95
3 . . . . 2.95
4 Five Foot Two, Eyes of Blue 2.95
5 . . . . 2.95
6 quest for Esther 2.95
7 & 8 . . . . @2.95
9 56-pg.. . . . . 4.95

SIN CITY: LOST, LONELY, AND LETHAL

Dark Horse–Legend

1-shot, two color. 2.95

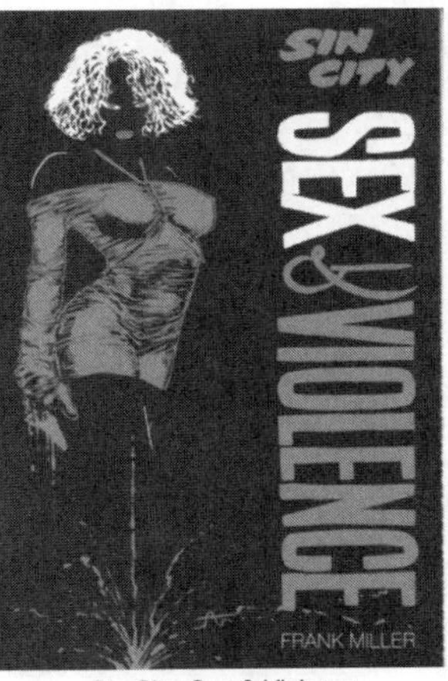

Sin City: Sex & Violence
© Dark Horse Comics

DARK HORSE

SIN CITY: JUST ANOTHER SATURDAY NIGHT
Dark Horse/Wizard

1/2 (Wizard, 24-page) 2.50
1/2 rep., Dark Horse, new (c). 2.50

SIN CITY: SEX AND VIOLENCE
(B&W)

1-shot by Frank Miller. 3.00

SIN CITY: SILENT NIGHT
DH-Legend (B&W) 1995

1-Shot. 2.95

SIN CITY: THAT YELLOW BASTARD
(B&W)

1 F.Miller 4.00
2 . . . . 3.00
3 thru 6 . . . . @3.00
TPB by Frank Miller 15.00
HC 25.00
HC limited 90.00

SIN CITY: THE BABE WORE RED
Dark Horse-Legend 1994

1 PM. 3.50

SIN CITY: THE BABE WORE RED AND OTHER STORIES
(B&W) 1996

1-shot, some nudity. 3.00

SIN CITY: THE BIG FAT KILL
Dark Horse-Legend 1994

1 FM. 4.00
2 FM. 3.50
3 FM, Dump the Stiffs 3.50
4 FM, Town Without Pity 3.50
5 FM, final issue 3.50
TPB 15.00

Sock Monkey #2
© Dark Horse Comics

HC 25.00

SOCK MONKEY
(B&W) Sept., 1998

1 by Tony Millionaire 2.95
2 F:Uncle Gabby 2.95

VOLUME 2

1 (of 2) 2.95
2 . . . . 2.95

SOLO

1 and 2 . . . . @.50

SPACE CIRCUS
DH/Maverick, July, 2000

1 (of 4) SA. 2.95
2 SA 2.95
3 SA 2.95
4 SA 3.00

SPACEHAWK
(B&W)

1 BW reps. 2.25
2 thru 4 BW . . . . @2.00
5 BW. 2.50

SPACE USAGI

1 thru 3 Stan Sakai . . . . @2.95
TPB 16.95

SPECIES

1 Alien Human Hybrid 2.50
2 thru 4 SIL . . . . @2.50

SPECIES: HUMAN RACE

1 PhH 2.95
2 . . . . 2.95
3 SBi. 2.95
4 (of 4) 2.95
TPB 11.95

SPIRIT OF WONDER
(B&W)

1 thru 5 by Kenji Tsuruia . . . . . . @2.95
TPB 12.95

SPYBOY
October 1999

1 PDd,F:Alex Fleming 2.95
2 PDd 2.50
3 PDd,F:Bombshell 2.50
4 PDd,F:Judge and Jury 2.50
5 PDd,V:Judge and Jury 2.50
6 PDd,V:Barbie Q 2.50
7 PDd,V:Madam Imadam. 2.95
8 PDd,V:Madam Imadam. 2.95
9 PDd,V:Madam Imadam
  & Barbie Q 2.95
10 PDd,death-defying action. 2.95
11 PDd,V:Slackjaw 2.95
12 PDd,V:Slackjaw 2.95

STAN SHAW'S BEAUTY & THE BEAST

1 Based on the book 4.95

STARSTRUCK: THE EXPANDING UNIVERSE
(B&W)

1 Pt1. . . . . 2.95
2 Pt2, with 2-card strip. 2.95

STAR WARS
Dec., 1998

1 F:Ki-Adi-Mundi 5.00
2 F:Ki-Adi-Mundi 3.50
3 F:Ki-Adi-Mundi 3.25
4 F:Sylvn. 3.00
5 V:Ephant Mon. 3.00
6 V:Jabba the Hutt. 3.00
7 Outlander 2.50
8 A:Jabba the Hutt. 2.50
9 A:Tusken Raiders. 2.50
10 TT,RL,F:Ki-Adi-Mundi. 2.50
11 TT,RL,F:Aurra Sing 2.50
12 TT. 2.50
13 TT,TL,A'Sharad Hett 2.50
14 TT,TL,on Malastare 2.50
15 TT,TL,Podracing 2.50
16 TT,TL,V:Lannik terrorists 2.50
17 TT,TL,V:Red Iaro terrorists. 2.95
18 TT,TL,Smugglers Moon 2.95
19 JOs,JD,Twilight, pt.1 . . . . 2.95
20 JOs,JD,Twilight, pt.2 . . . . 2.95
21 JOs,JD,Twilight, pt.3 . . . . 2.95
22 JOs,JD,Twilight, pt.4 . . . . 2.95
23 Infinity's End, pt.1 . . . . 3.00

Star Wars: A New Hope, Special Edition #3 © Dark Horse Comics

STAR WARS: A NEW HOPE— SPECIAL EDITION
Jan.–April, 1997

1 EB, AW 6.00
2 thru 4 . . . . @5.00
TPB Rep. #1–#4 Hildebrandt(c) . . . 9.95
Spec. Edition boxed set 30.00

STAR WARS: A NEW HOPE
(B&W) Manga July, 1998

1 (of 4) by Tamaki Hisao, 96pg. . . . 9.95
2 thru 4 . . . . @9.95

STAR WARS: A NEW HOPE—MANGA
November, 1999

1 (of 4) by Kia Asamiya,96-pg.. . . . 9.95
2 thru 4, 88-pg. . . . . @9.95

DARK HORSE

STAR WARS: BATTLE OF THE BOUNTY HUNTERS

July, 1996

Pop-up Comic. 17.95

STAR WARS: BOBA FETT—

1-shot Bounty on Bar-Kooda,48pg 11.00

Star Wars: Boba Fett–Ememy of the Empire #3 © *Dark Horse Comics*

1-shot When the Fat Lady Swings . 7.00
1-shot Murder Most Foul. 7.00
1-shot Twin Engins of Destruction. . 6.00
TPB Death, Lies & Treachery 12.95

STAR WARS: BOBA FETT— ENEMY OF THE EMPIRE

Jan., 1999

1 (of 4) V:Dark Lord of the Sith . . . 3.00
2 thru 4 IG . . . . @3.00
TPB rep., includes #1/2 . . . . 16.95

STAR WARS: BOUNTY HUNTERS

Aug., 1999

1-shot Aurra Sing, TT 3.00
1-shot Kir Kanos, MRi,RSd 3.00
1-shot Scoundrel's Wages,
F:Dengar, 4-LOM & Bossk 3.00
TPB Star Wars: Bounty Hunters. . 12.95

STAR WARS: CHEWBACCA

January, 2000

1 (of 4) various tales 4.00
2 . . . . 3.50
3 . . . . 3.50
4 concl. 3.50

STAR WARS: CRIMSON EMPIRE

Dec. 1997–May, 1998

1 PG,CR,DvD(c) 10.00
3 PG,CR,DvD(c) 8.00
3 thru 5 PG,CR,DvD(c) . . . . @5.00
TPB Crimson Empire 17.95

VOLUME II: COUNCIL OF BLOOD

1 MRi,RSd,PG,DvD(c). 4.00
2 thru 6 RSd,PG,DvD(c). . . . . . . @3.00
TPB Council of Blood 17.95

STAR WARS: DARK EMPIRE

1 CK,Destiny of a Jedi. 15.00
1a 2nd Printing 5.00
1b Gold Ed. 15.00
2 CK,Destroyer of worlds, very
low print run 14.00
2a 2nd Printing 5.00
2b Gold Ed. 15.00
3 CK,V:The Emperor 10.00
3a 2nd printing 4.00
3b Gold Ed. 10.00
4 CK,V:The Emperor 7.00
4a Gold Ed. 7.00
5 CK,V:The Emperor 7.00
5a Gold Ed. 10.00
6 CK,V:Emperor,last issue 5.00
6a Gold Ed. 9.00
Gold editions, foil logo set. 50.00
Platinum editions, embossed set. 100.00
TPB Preview 32pg.. . . . . 1.00
TPB rep.#1–#6 . . . . 19.95
TPB CK & Tom Veitch 2nd ed. . . . 17.95
HC leather bound 125.00

STAR WARS: DARK EMPIRE II

1 2nd chapter 6.00
2 F:Boba Fett 5.00
3 V:Darksiders. 5.00
4 Luke Vs. Darksiders 5.00
5 Creatures 5.00
6 CK,DvD(c), save the twins 5.00
Platinum editions, set 50.00
TPB CK & Tom Veitch rep.#1–#6 . 17.95
HC Leather bound 100.00

STAR WARS: DARK FORCE RISING

May–Oct., 1997

1 thru 6 (of 6) MBn,TyD,KN . . . . @6.00
TPB series rep 17.95

STAR WARS: DARK FORCES

HC Jedi Knight, DvD (Sept. 1998). 24.95
TPB Jedi Knight (Sept. 1998) 14.95
HC Rebel Agent (March 1998) . . . 24.95
TPB Rebel Agent (March 1998) . . 14.95
HC Soldier for the Empire. 24.95
TPB Soldier for the Empire 14.95

STAR WARS: DARTH MAUL

1 (of 4) RMz,JD,Struzan(c) 2.95
1 photo (c). 2.95
2 Struzan(c),V:Black Sun. 3.00
2 photo(c) 3.00

STAR WARS: DROIDS

April–Sept., 1994

1 F:C-3PO,R2-D2 . . . . 4.00
2 V:Thieves 3.00
3 on the Hosk moon 3.00
4 . . . . 3.00
5 A meeting. 2.50
6 final issue. 2.50
Spec.#1 I:Olag Greck 2.50
TPB The Kalarba Adventures, rep. 17.95

2nd Series

1 Deputized Droids 3.00
2 Marooned on Nar Shaddaa. 2.50
3 C-3PO to the Rescue 2.50
4 . . . . 2.50
5 Caretaker virus. 2.50
6 Revolution 2.50
7 & 8 . . . . @2.50
TPB Droids—Rebellion, rep. 17.95

STAR WARS: EMPIRE'S END

Oct.–Nov., 1995

1 R:Emperor Palpatine 3.50
2 conclusion 3.50
TPB rep.. 6.00

STAR WARS: THE EMPIRE STRIKES BACK

TPB Hildebrandt(c). 10.00

STAR WARS: THE EMPIRE STRIKES BACK

(B&W) Manga Dec., 1998

1 (of 4) by Toshiki Dudo, 96pg. . . . 9.95
2 thru 4 . . . . @9.95

STAR WARS: EPISODE I THE PHANTOM MENACE

Apr., 1999

1 RdM,AW. 3.00
1a newsstand edition, photo (c) . . . 3.00
2 RdM,AW. 3.00
2a newsstand edition, photo (c) . . . 3.00
3 RdM,AW. 3.00
3a newsstand edition, photo (c) . . . 3.00
4 RdM,AW. 3.00
4a newsstand edition, photo (c) . . . 3.00
1 RdM,AW. 3.00
1a newsstand edition, photo (c) . . . 3.00
GN Phantom Menace RdM,AW . . 12.95
Spec. Anakin Skywalker 3.00
Spec. Anakin Skywalker, newsstand 3.00
Spec. Obi-Wan Kenobi 3.00
Spec. Obi-Wan Kenobi, newsstand. 3.00
Spec. Queen Amidala. 3.00

Star Wars: The Phantom Menace #4 © *Dark Horse Comics*

Spec. Qui-Gon Jinn 3.00
TPB 12.95
TPB Adventures, rep. 12.95
HC Lim. ed. signed 80.00

STAR WARS: EPISODE I THE PHANTOM MENACE—MANGA

December, 1999

1 (of 2) 88-pg. 9.95

STAR WARS HANDBOOK

July, 1998

1 X-Wing Rogue Squadron 3.50
2 Crimson Empire 3.00
Dark Empire 2.95

STAR WARS: HEIR TO THE EMPIRE

Oct. 1995–April, 1996

1 I:Grand Admiral Thrawn 4.00
2 thru 6 . . . . 3.50
TPB from novel by Timothy Zahn . 19.95
HC signed, slipcase 100.00

STAR WARS: JABBA THE HUTT—

1995–1996

1-shot The Garr Suppoon Hit 3.00
1-shot Hunger of Princess Nampi . . 3.00
1-shot The Dynasty Trap 3.00
1-shot Betrayal 3.00
1-shot The Jabba Tape 3.00

STAR WARS: JEDI ACADEMY LEVIATHAN

Oct., 1998

1 (of 4) by Kevin J. Anderson 3.00
2 thru 4 . . . . @3.00
TPB 11.95

STAR WARS: JEDI COUNCIL — ACTS OF WAR

June, 2000

1 (of 4) RSd, V:Yinchorri 3.00
2 RSd, ... 3.00
3 RSd, ... 3.00
4 concl. 3.00

STAR WARS: THE LAST COMMAND

Nov. 1997–July 1998

1 thru 6 MBn. . . . . @3.50
TPB, rep. 17.95

STAR WARS: MARA JADE— BY THE EMPEROR'S HAND

Aug., 1998

1 (of 6) by Timothy Zahn 5.00
2 thru 6 . . . . @4.00
TPB rep. 15.95

STAR WARS: PRELUDE TO REBELLION

TPB 14.95

Star Wars: Prelude to Rebellion
© Dark Horse Comics

STAR WARS: THE PROTOCOL OFFENSIVE

Sept., 1997

1-shot written by Anthony Daniels. . 4.95

STAR WARS: RETURN OF THE JEDI—SPECIAL EDITION

TPB Hildebrandt(c). 9.95

STAR WARS: THE RETURN OF THE JEDI

(B&W) Manga June, 1999

1 (of 4) by Shin-ichi Hiromoto, 96pg. 9.95
2 thru 4 . . . . @9.95

STAR WARS: RIVER OF CHAOS

May–Nov., 1995

1 LSi,JBr,Emperor sends spies . . . 3.00
2 Imperial in Allies Clothing 3.00
3 . . . . 3.00
4 F:Ranulf 3.00

STAR WARS: SHADOWS OF THE EMPIRE

1 (of 6) by John Wagner, Kilian Plunkett & P. Craig Russell 3.50
2 thru 6 . . . . @3.50
TPB 17.95
HC 80.00

STAR WARS: SHADOWS OF THE EMPIRE — EVOLUTION

Feb.–June, 1998

1 thru 5 . . . . @3.50
TPB Steve Perry(s). 14.95

STAR WARS: SHADOW STALKER

Nov., 1997

1-shot from Star Wars Galaxy Mag. 3.50

STAR WARS: SPLINTER OF THE MIND'S EYE

Dec. 1995–June, 1996

1 thru 4 A.D.Foster novel adapt.. @3.50
TPB 14.95

STAR WARS TALES

Sept., 1999

1 various authors, 64-pg. 4.95
2 64-pg.. . . . . 4.95
3 64-pg.. . . . . 4.95
4 64-pg.. . . . . 4.95
5 F:Lando's Commandos. 5.95
5a photo(c) 5.95

STAR WARS: TALES FROM MOS EISLEY

1-shot, from Star Wars Galaxy Mag. #2–#4 . . . . 3.50

STAR WARS: TALES OF THE JEDI

1 RV,I:Ulic Qel-Droma 6.00
2 RV,A:Ulic Qel-Droma 5.00
3 RV,D:Andur 5.00
4 RV,A:Jabba the Hut 4.00
5 RV,last issue. 4.00
TPB 14.95
TPB 2nd printing. 14.95

STAR WARS: TALES OF THE JEDI: DARK LORDS OF THE SITH

Oct. 1994–March, 1995

1 Bagged with card 3.00
2 . . . . 2.50
3 Krath Attack 2.50
4 F:Exar Kun 2.50
5 V:TehKrath 2.50
6 Final battle 2.50
TPB 17.95

STAR WARS: TALES OF THE JEDI: THE FREEDON NADD UPRISING

Aug.–Sept., 1997

1 and 2 . . . . @2.75
2 . . . . 2.50
TPB series rep. 5.95

STAR WARS: TALES OF THE JEDI: THE SITH WAR

Aug. 1995–Jan., 1996

1 F:Exar Kun 3.00
2 F:Ulic Oel-Droma 2.50
3 F:Exar Kun 2.50
4 thru 6 (6 part mini-series) . . . . @2.50
TPB 17.95

STAR WARS: TALES OF THE JEDI: THE FALL OF THE SITH EMPIRE

June–Oct., 1997

1 (of 5) 3.50
2 thru 5 . . . . @3.00

DARK HORSE

STAR WARS: TALES OF THE JEDI: THE GOLDEN AGE OF THE SITH

Oct. 1996–Feb., 1997

1 thru 5 . . . . @3.50
TPB 16.95

STAR WARS: TALES OF THE JEDI: THE REDEMPTION OF ULIC QEL-DROMA

July, 1998

1 (of 5) by Kevin J. Anderson 3.50
2 thru 5 . . . . @3.50

STAR WARS: UNION

November, 1999

1 (of 4) by Stackpole 2.95
2 the wedding approaches. 2.95
3 almost there 2.95
4 wedding day 2.95
TPB Luke & Mara Jade. 12.95

STAR WARS: VADER'S QUEST

Feb., 1999

1 (of 4) DGb,AMK 3.00
2 thru 4 . . . . @3.00
TPB with poster 11.95

STAR WARS: X-WING ROGUE SQUADRON

July, 1995

The Rebel Opposition
1 F:Wedge Antilles 5.00
2 . . . . 3.50
3 F:Tycho Clehu 3.50
4 F:Tycho Clehu 3.50
½ Wizard limited exclusive 6.00
The Phantom Affair
5 thru 8 . . . . @3.50
TPB rep.. . . . . 12.95
Battleground Tatooine
9 thru 12 . . . . @3.50
TPB rep.. . . . . 12.95
The Warrior Princess
13 thru 16. . . . . @3.50
TPB rep.. . . . . 13.95
Requiem for a Rogue
17 thru 20. . . . . @3.50
TPB rep.. . . . . 12.95
In the Empire's Service
21 thru 24. . . . . @3.50
TPB rep.. . . . . 12.95
Making of Baron Fell
25 . . . . 5.00
Family Ties
26 thru 27. . . . . @3.50
Masquerade
28 thru 31. . . . . @3.50
TPB 12.95
Mandatory Retirement
32 thru 35. . . . . @3.50
TPB Blood and Honor. 12.95

STARSHIP TROOPERS

Sept., 1997

1 (of 2) movie adaptation. 3.00
2 movie adaptation, concl. 3.00
TPB rep., inc. Brute Creations,
Insect Touch, & movie 152 pg. 14.95

Starship Troopers #1
© Dark Horse Comics

STARSHIP TROOPERS: BRUTE CREATIONS

1997

1-shot RbC. 3.00

STARSHIP TROOPERS: DOMINANT SPECIES

Aug., 1998

1 (of 4) 3.00
2 JoB,RyE. 3.00
3 & 4 . . . . @3.00

STARSHIP TROOPERS: INSECT TOUCH

1 by Warren Ellis & Paolo Parente. 3.00
2 and 3 (of 3). . . . . @3.00

SUBHUMAN

Nov., 1998

1 (of 4) MSh 3.00
2 thru 4 MSh . . . . @3.00

SUPERMAN/MADMAN HULLABALOO

June–Aug., 1997

1 (of 3) MiA. 3.00
2 and 3 (of 3). . . . . @3.00

SUPERMAN VS. ALIENS

DC/Dark Horse

1 DJu,KN 6.00
2 V:Queen Alien 5.00
TPB 14.95

SUPERMAN VS. THE TERMINATOR: DEATH TO THE FUTURE

December, 1999

1 (of 4) AlG,StP,x-over. 2.95
2 AlG,StP,into the future 2.95
3 AlG,StP,A:Supergirl. 2.95
4 AlG,StP,concl.. . . . . 2.95
TPB AlG,StP,series rep. 10.95

SUPER MANGA BLAST

March, 2000

1 128-pg.. 4.95
2 128-pg.. 4.95
3 128-pg.. 4.95
4 128-pg.. 4.95
5 128-pg.. 4.95
6 128-pg.. 4.95

TALE OF ONE BAD RAT

1 BT 3.00
2 thru 4 . . . . 3.00
TPB Rep.#1–#4 . . . . 14.95

TALES OF ORDINARY MADNESS

(B&W)

1 JBo(c),Paranoid 3.00
2 JBo(c),Mood. 2.50
3 JBo(c),A Little Bit of Neurosis . . . 2.50

TALES TO OFFEND

July, 1997

1-shot by Frank Miller. 2.95

TANK GIRL

(B&W) 1991

1 Rep. from U.K.Deadline Mag.
with 2-card strip 4.50
2 V:Indiana Potato Jones. 4.00
3 On the Run. 4.00
4 . . . . 4.00
TPB colorized. 14.95

[2nd Series]

1 . . . . 3.50
2 . . . . 3.00
3 and 4 . . . . @3.00

TANK GIRL

1 and 2 . . . . @3.00

TARZAN

HC The Lost Adventure 20.00
TPB The Untamed 11.95

TARZAN/JOHN CARTER: WARLORDS OF MARS

1 thru 4 E.R.Burroughs adapt. . . @2.50

TARZAN VS. PREDATOR AT THE EARTH'S CORE

1 Tarzan vs. Predator 2.50
2 V:Predator 2.50
3 Tarzan on the Hunt. 2.50
4 . . . . 2.50
TPB series rep.. . . . . 12.95

TERMINAL POINT

1 . . . . 2.50
2 . . . . 2.50

TERMINATOR

1 CW,Tempest. 4.00
2 CW,Tempest. 3.00
3 CW. 3.00
4 CW, conclusion. 3.00

TERMINATOR

1-shot MW,3-D const(c2,
pop-up inside 5.00
Spec. AlG,GyD,GeD(1998). 2.95

TERMINATOR, THE
Sept., 1998
1 AlG,StP, ... 2.95
2 F:Sarah Connor 2.95
3 F:Killerman. 2.95
4 F:D-800L & D-810X 2.95
TPB Death Valley 14.95

TERMINATOR, THE: THE DARK YEARS
Sept., 1999
1 (of 4) AlG,MvR,BWi 2.95
2 AlG,MvR,BWi,F:Jon Norden 2.95
3 . . . . 2.95
4 AlG,MvR,concl.. . . . . 2.95

TERMINATOR: END GAME
1 JG,Final *Terminator* series 3.00
2 JG,Cont.last Term.story 2.75
3 JG, Concl. 2.75
TPB Endgame 9.95

TERMINATOR: ENEMY WITHIN
1 cont. from Sec.Objectives 4.00
2 C890.L.threat contd. 3.00
3 Secrets of Cyberdyne 3.00
4 Conclusion 3.00
SC rep #1–#4 . . . . 13.95

TERMINATOR: HUNTERS & KILLERS
1 V:Russians 3.00
2 V:Russians 2.75
3 V:Russians 2.75

TERMINATOR: SECONDARY OBJECTIVES
1 cont. 1st DH mini-series 4.00
2 PG,A:New Female Terminator. . . 3.00
3 PG,Terminators in L.A.&Mexico . 3.00
4 PG,Terminator vs Terminator
concl. 3.00

TERRITORY, THE
Jan., 1999
1 (of 4) JaD,DvL,F:Ishmael 2.95
2 thru 4 . . . . @2.95

TEX AVERY'S DROOPY
1 Dr. Droopenstein 2.50
2 & 3 . . . . @2.50

TEX AVERY'S SCREWBALL SQUIRREL
1 I:Screwball Squirrel. 2.50
2 Cleaning House 2.50
3 School of Hard Rocks. 2.50

THING, THE
1 JHi, Movie adaptation 4.00
2 JHi, Movie adaptation 3.50

THE THING: COLD FEAR
1 R:Thing 3.00
2 . . . . 2.75

THING FROM ANOTHER WORLD: CLIMATE OF FEAR
1 Argentinian Military Base
(Bahiathetis). 2.75
2 Thing on Base 2.75
3 Thing/takeover 2.75
4 Conclusion 2.75
TPB 15.95

THING FROM ANOTHER WORLD: ETERNAL VOWS
1 PG,I:Sgt. Rowan. 2.75
2 PG 2.75
3 PG,in New Zealand 2.75
4 PG,Last issue. 2.75

THIRTEEN O'CLOCK
(B&W)
1 Mr.Murmer,from Deadline USA . . 2.95

3 X 3 EYES
(B&W) Manga
1 I:Pai,Yakumo, (Manga) 2.95
2 & 3 (5-part mini-series) . . . . . . @2.95
TPB Curse of the Gesu, by Yuzo
Takada 12.95
TPB House of Demons 12.95

300
May, 1998
1 (of 5) FM & Lynn Varley 2.95
2 thru 5 F:Spartans . . . . @2.95

TIME COP
1 Movie Adaptation 2.75
2 Movie Adaptation 2.50

TITAN
Spec.#1 BS(c),I:Inhibitors 4.25

TITAN A.E.
May, 2000
1 (of 3) film prequel, pt.1 . . . . 2.95
2 prequel, pt.2. . . . . 2.95
3 prequel, pt.3. . . . . 2.95

Tongue Lash #2
© Dark Horse Comics

TONGUE*LASH
Aug., 1996
1 by Randy and Jean-Marc
Lofficier & Dave Taylor 2.95
2 . . . . 2.95

VOLUME II
1 (of 2) 2.95
2 . . . . 2.95

TONY MILLIONAIRE'S SOCK MONKEY
TPB 9.95

TOO MUCH COFFEE MAN
(B&W) July, 1997
1-shot by Shannon Wheeler 2.95
TPB Guide for the Perplexed 10.95
HC lim. Guide for the Perplexed . . 50.00
TPB Parade of Tirade 12.95

TREKKER
(B&W)
1 thru 4 . . . . @1.50
5 thru 7 . . . . @1.75
8 O:Trekker 1.50
9 . . . . 1.50

TREKKER
1 . . . . 2.95

TRIPLE X
(B&W)
TPB by Arnold & Jacob Pander . . 24.95

TWO FACES OF TOMORROW, THE
(B&W) Manga Aug., 1997
1 (of 13) from James P. Hogan
novel, by Yukinobu Hoshino . . . 2.95
2 thru 4 . . . . @2.95
5 thru 13 . . . . @3.95

TWO-FISTED TALES
Spec. WW,WiS. 4.95

2112
GN JBy,A:Next Men 2.00
2nd Printing 5.00
TPB GNv, JBy,A:Next Men 10.00
2nd & 3rd printing. 9.95

[ANDREW VACHSS'] UNDERGROUND
(B&W)
1 AVs(s) 4.25
2 thru 4 AVs(s). . . . . @3.95

UNIVERSAL MONSTERS
1 AAd,Creature From The
Black Lagoon 5.50
2 The Mummy 5.50

USAGI YOJIMBO
(B&W)
1 by Stan Sakai. 4.00
2 thru 9 . . . . 3.00
10 with Sergio Aragones. 3.00
11 "The Lord of Owls". 3.00

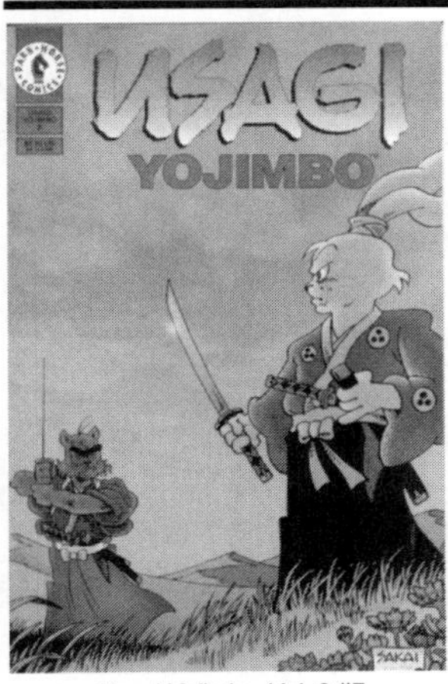

Usagi Yojimbo, Vol. 3 #7
© Dark Horse Comics

12 “Vampire Cat of the Geishu”. . . . 3.00
13 thru 22 “Grasscutter,” pt.1
thru pt. #10. . . . . 3.00
23 My Father’s Sword. 3.00
24 The Demon Flute. 3.00
25 Momo-Usagi-Taro 3.00
26 The Hairpin Murders,pt.1 . . . . . . 3.00
27 The Hairpin Murders,pt.2 . . . . . . 3.00
28 Courtesan conspiracy,pt.1 . . . . . 3.00
29 Courtesan conspiracy,pt.2 . . . . . 3.00
30 Inspector Ishida mystery 3.00
31 The Haunted Inn of Moon
Shadow Hill 3.00
32 Two stories 3.00
33 . . . . 3.00
34 Demon Mask, pt.1 . . . . 3.00
35 Demon Mask, pt.2 . . . . 3.00
36 Demon Mask, pt.3 . . . . 3.00
37 F:Sasuke the Demon Queller . . . 3.00
38 Priest Sanshobo’s temple 3.00
39 Grasscutter II,pt.1 . . . . 3.00
40 V:Captain Quark 3.00
41 V:Neko Ninja 3.00
42 Grasscutter II,pt.4 . . . . 3.00
TPB Shades of Death, rep. of
Mirage series 14.95
HC Shades of Death, lim. 50.00
TPB Daisho, rep. Mirage. 14.95
HC Daisho, 200 pg. signed 50.00
TPB The Brink of Life & Death . . . 14.95
TPB Seasons 14.95
HC Seasons, signed. 55.00
TPB Grasscutter. 16.95
HC Grasscutter. 60.00
TPB Grasscutter. 16.95
TPB Grey Shadows 14.95
HC Lim. Ed. Grey Shadows 55.00

USAGI YOJIMBO
1996
1 SS,color spec. 4.00
2 SS,color spec. 3.00
3 SS,color spec. 3.00
4 thru 6 . . . . @3.00

USAGI YOJIMBO COLOR SPECIAL: GREEN PERSIMMON
1-shot by Stan Sakai 2.95

VAMPIRELLA
(B&W)
1 ‘The Lion and the Lizard’Pt.1 . . . 4.50
2 ‘The Lion and the Lizard’Pt.2 . . . 3.95
3 ‘The Lion and the Lizard’Pt.3 . . . 3.95
4 ‘The Lion and the Lizard’Pt.3 . . . 3.95

VENUS WARS
(B&W) Manga
1 Aphrodia V:Ishtar, with
2-card strip. 3.00
2 I: Ken Seno 2.50
3 Aphrodia V:Ishtar 2.50
4 Seno Joins Hound Corps. 2.50
5 SenoV:Octopus Supertanks 2.50
6 Chaos in Aphrodia 2.50
7 All Out Ground War 2.50
8 Ishtar V:Aphrodia contd. 2.50
9 Ishtar V:Aphrodia contd. 2.50
10 Supertanks of Ishtar Advance . . 2.50
11 Aphrodia Captured. 2.50
12 A:Miranda,48pgs 2.75
13 Hound Brigade-Suicide Assault. 2.25
14 V:Army 2.50
15 . . . . 2.50
TPB Vol. 1 . . . . 13.95

VENUS WARS II
1 V:Security Police 2.75
2 Political Unrest 2.25
3 Conspiracy 2.25
4 A:Lupica. 2.25
5 Love Hotel 2.25
6 Terran Consulate 2.25
7 Doublecross 2.25
8 D:Lupisa. 2.95
9 A:Matthew 2.95
10 A:Mad Scientist 2.95
11 thru 15 V:Troopers . . . . @2.95

VIRUS
1 MP(c),F:The Wan Xuan & the
crew of the Electra 3.00
2 MP(c),V:Captian Powell 3.00
3 MP(c),V:Virus 3.00
4 MP(c),Last issue. 3.00
TPB rep.#1–#4 . . . . 16.95

VERSION
(B&W) Manga
1.1 by Hisashi Sakaguchi 2.50
1.2 thru 1.8 . . . . @2.50

VERSION II
(B&W) Manga
1.1 by Hisashi Sakaguchi 2.50
1.2 thru 1.6 . . . . @2.50

VORTEX, THE
1 . . . . 2.00

WALTER: CAMPAIGN OF TERROR
1 thru 3 . . . . @2.50

WARRIOR OF WAVERLY STREET, THE
Nov., 1996
1 (of 2) by Manny Coto and
John Stokes. 2.95

WARRIOR OF WAVERLY STREET, THE: BROODSTORM
March, 1997
1-shot Manny Coto & John Stokes . 2.95

WARWORLD!
(B&W)
1 . . . . 1.75

WHAT’S MICHAEL?
(B&W) Manga
TPB by Makoto Kobayashi 5.95
TPB Living Together 5.95
TPB Off the Deep End 5.95

WHITE LIKE SHE
(B&W)
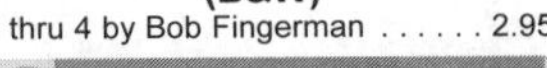
1 thru 4 by Bob Fingerman 2.95

Will to Power #9
© Dark Horse Comics

WILL TO POWER
Comics’ Greatest World 1994
1 BS, A:X 1.25
2 BS, A:X,Monster. 1.25
3 BS, A:X 1.25
4 BS, In Steel Harbor 1.25
5 V:Wolfgang. 1.00
6 V:Motorhead. 1.00
7 JOy(c),V:Amazing Grace 1.00
8 V:Catalyst. 1.00
9 Titan, Grace 1.00
10 Vortex alien, Grace 1.00
11 Vortex alien, King Titan 1.00
12 Vortex alien 1.00

WIZARD OF FOURTH STREET
(B&W)
1 thru 4 . . . . @1.75

WOLF & RED
1 Looney Tunes. 2.50
2 Watchdog Wolf. 2.50
3 Red Hot Riding Hood 2.50

DARK HORSE

WOLVERTON IN SPACE
(B&W) April, 1997

TPB by Basil Wolverton 16.95

WORLD BELOW, THE
Mar., 1999

1 PC 2.50
2 PC 2.50
3 PC 2.50
4 PC 2.50

WORLD BELOW II, THE
December, 1999

1 (of 4) PC 2.95
2 . . . . 2.95
3 PC,Deeper and Stranger 2.95
4 PC,Deeper and Stranger 2.95

X #4 © Dark Horse Comics

X
COMICS' GREATEST WORLD 1994

1 B:StG(s),DoM,JP,I:X-Killer 3.00
2 DoM,JP,V:X-Killer 2.25
3 DoM,JP,A:Pit Bulls 2.25
4 DoM,JP 2.25
5 DoM,JP,V:Chaos Riders 2.00
6 Cyberassassins 2.00
7 Alamout 2.00
8 A:Ghost 2.50
9 War for Arcadia 2.50
10 War for Arcadia 2.50
11 I:Coffin, War. 2.50
12 V:Coffin, A:Monster 2.50
13 D:X 2.50
14 conclusion to War 2.50
15 JS,SiG,war survivors 2.50
16 V:Headhunter 2.50
17 . . . . 2.50
18 V:Predator. 2.50
19 V:Challenge. 2.50
20 thru 24 . . . . @2.50

X: ONE SHOT TO THE HEAD

1 . . . . 2.50

XENA: WARRIOR PRINCESS
Aug., 1999

1 . . . . 2.95
2 . . . . 2.95
3 . . . . 2.95
4 . . . . 2.95
5 . . . . 2.95
6 F:Philomena. 2.95
7 in Rome 2.95
8 chariot race 2.95
9 in Europe 2.95
10 IEd,MD2,wayward viking 2.95
11 IEd,MD2,V:Lamia. 2.95
12 IEd,MD2,Darkness Falls,concl. . 2.95
13 IEd,MD2,F:Legion 2.95
14 conclusion 3.00
1 to 14 newsstand photo(c). . . . . @3.00
TPB Slave 10.00
TPB The Warrior Way of Death. . . 10.00

XXX

1 . . . . 3.95
2 V:Dr. Zemph. 3.95
3 . . . . 3.95
4 V:Rhine Lords. 3.95
5 I:Klaar 3.95
6 Klaar captured 4.95
7 Revolution Consequences 4.95

YOUNG CYNICS CLUB
(B&W)

1 . . . . 2.50

THE YOUNG INDIANA JONES CHRONICLES

1 DBa,FS,TV Movie Adapt. 3.25
2 DBa,TV Movie Adapt 2.75
3 thru 5 DBa,GM . . . . @2.75
6 BBa,GM,WW1,French Army 2.75
7 The Congo 2.75
8 Africa,A:A.Schweitzer 2.50
9 Vienna,Sophie-daughter of Arch-Duke Ferdinand 2.50
10 In Vienna continued. 2.50
11 Far East. 2.50
12 Fever Issue 2.50

YOU'RE UNDER ARREST!
(B&W) Manga 1995–96

1 by Kosuke Fujishima 2.95
2 thru 8 (mini-series) . . . . @2.95

Zombie World: Tree of Death #3
© Dark Horse Comics

TPB rep. 12.95

ZOMBIE WORLD:

1-shot Eat Your Heart Out, KJo. . . . 2.95
1-shot Home for the Holidays 2.95

ZOMBIE WORLD: DEAD END
Jan., 1998

1 (of 2) by Stephen Blue 2.95
2 . . . . 2.95

ZOMBIE WORLD: CHAMPION OF THE WORMS
Sept., 1997

1 (of 3) MMi. 2.95
2 thru 3 . . . . @2.95
Spec. Home for the Holidays 2.95
TPB 8.95

ZOMBIE WORLD: THE TREE OF DEATH
May, 1999

1 (of 4) by Pat Mills & J. Deadstock 2.95
2 thru 4 . . . . @2.95

ZOMBIE WORLD: WINTER'S DREGS
May, 1998

1 (of 4) by Bob Fingerman and Tommy Lee Edwards 2.95
2 thru 4 . . . . @2.95

IMAGE

AARON STRIPS

Image (B&W) April, 1997

1 thru 4 rep. from Sunday comic strips, by Aaron Warner . . . . @2.95

ACTION PLANET

Image (B&W) Sept., 1997

Prev. Action Planet Comics

3 . . . . 3.95

A DISTANT SOIL

Image/Highbrow

(B&W) Prev: Warp Graphics

15 CDo, ... 3.00
16 CDo,A:Bast, Avatar 3.00
17 CDo,D'mer & Bast conflict 3.00
18 CDo,"Ascension" finale 3.00
19 CDo,"Spires of Heaven" pt.1 . . . 3.00
20 CDo,Lord Merai's suicide weakens Hierachy 3.00
21 CDo,"Exile for D'mer?". 3.00
22 CDo,Avatar's secrets,32pg. 3.00
23 CDo,three stories. 3.00
24 CDo,malfunctioning spacesuit . . 3.00
25 CDo,NGa,Troll Bridge,48pg 3.95
26 CDo,B.U.:Red-Cloak by E.Kushner 2.95
27 CDo,B.U.Liaden tale 2.95
28 CDo,B.U.Liaden tale, concl. 2.95
29 CDo,B.U.Delia Sherman story . . 2.95
30 . . . . 3.95
Images of A Distant Soil 3.00
Images of A Distant Soil, signed, limited 34.95
GN The Gathering, rep.#1–#11 . . . 18.95
GN The Gathering, 2nd printing . . 19.95
TPB The Ascendant, rep.#13–#24 18.95
TPB The Gathering. 19.95

ADRENALYNN

Image Aug., 1999

1 F:Sabina Nikoli 2.50
2 TnD,V:Russian monster androids 2.50
3 TnD,V:last 2 Monster-cyborgs. . . 2.50
4 TnD,the real Sabina 2.50

ADVENTURES OF AARON

Image March, 1997

(B&W) by Aaron Warner

1 "Baby-sitter Gone Bad". 2.95
2 "Thunder Thighs of the Terrordome" 2.95
3 Babysitter Gone Bad, concl. 2.95
100 Super Special 2.95
Christmas Spectacular #1. . . . . 2.95

ADVENTURES OF BARRY WEEN, BOY GENIUS, THE

Image (B&W) March, 1999

1 (of 3) by Judd Winick 2.95
2 Growing Pains 2.95
3 School 2.95

ADVENTURE STRIP DIGEST

Image (B&W) April ,1998

1 by Randy Reynaldo 2.95
2 F:Rob Hanes, detective 2.95

AGE OF BRONZE

Image (B&W) Nov., 1998

1 EiS,The Trojan War 2.95
2 EiS,Death of Paris 2.95
3 EiS,F:Herakles, Hektor 2.95
4 EiS,I:Helen 2.95
5 EiS,Achilles disguised. 2.95
6 EiS,Helen gone 3.50
7 EiS,Odysseus mad?. 3.50
8 EiS,Achilles missing 3.50
Spec.#1 EiS, House of Horror. 2.95
Spec.#2 . . . . 2.95

AGE OF HEROES, THE

Image/Halloween 1996

(B&W)

1 JHI & JRy. 2.95
2 JHI & JRy. 2.95
3 JHI & JRy,Luko,Trickster & Aerwyn try to steal treasure of the gods 2.95
4 JHI & JRy,Drake, the blind swordsman returns. 2.95
5 JHI & JRy,O:Conor One-Arm . . . 2.95
Spec. #1 rep. #1 & #2. . . . . 4.95
Spec. #2 rep. #3 & #4. . . . . 6.95

AGE OF HEROES: WEX

Image (B&W) Aug., 1998

1 by JHI,Vurtex 2.95

ALLEGRA

Image/Wildstorm 1996

1 ScC,SSe 2.50
2 . . . . 2.50
3 . . . . 2.50

Allegra #1
© Wildstorm

4 . . . . 2.50

ALLEY CAT

Image July, 1999

1 BNa,MHw,F:Alley Baggett. 2.50
1a variant painted cover (1:4) 2.50
2 BNa,MHw,women murdered 2.50
3 photo (c). 2.50
3a variant JJu cover (1:4) 2.50
4 into darkness 2.50
5 The Martyr,pt.1 . . . . 2.50
6 The Martyr,pt.2 . . . . 2.50
7 . . . . 2.50
Wizard World Spec.#1. . . . .
Lingerie Edition. 4.95

ALLIANCE, THE

Image/Shadowline 1995

1 JV,I:The Alliance, A Call to Arms 2.50
1a variant cover. 2.50
2 JV,Team comes together "Like Pieces of a Puzzle" 2.50
2a variant cover. 2.50
3 I:Slash C 2.50
3a variant cover. 2.50
4 . . . . 2.50
4a variant cover. 2.50

ALLIES, THE

Image/Extreme 1995

1 mini-series 2.50
2 . . . . 2.50
3 . . . . 2.50
4 . . . . 2.50

ALTERED IMAGE

Image April, 1998

1 JV,The Day Reality Went Wild . . 2.50
2 JV,F:Everybody smooshed 2.50
3 JV,Middle Age Crisis, concl. 2.50
TPB F:everybody 9.95

AMANDA AND GUNN

Image (B&W) April, 1997

1 JeR, Montana 2036 . . . . 2.95
2 (of 4) JeR. 2.95
3 (of 4) JeR. 2.95
4 (of 4) JeR, conclusion. 2.95

ANGELA

Image/TMP 1994–95

1 NGa(s),GCa,A:Spawn. 15.00
2 NGa(s),GCa,Angela's trial 14.00
3 NGa(s),GCa,In Hell. 12.00
Spec. Pirate Spawn(c) 32.00
Spec. Pirate Angela(c) (1995). . . . 30.00
TPB Rep.#1–#3 . . . . 9.95

ANGELA/GLORY: RAGE OF ANGELS

Image/TMP/Extreme 1996

1 x-over begins 5.00

APHRODITE IX

Image/Top Cow August, 2000

1 by David Finch 2.50

1a variant JBz (c) 2.50
1b variant Michale Turner (c). 2.50
1c variant MS(c) 2.50
2 amnesia 2.50

ARCANUM
Image/Top Cow March, 1997
Mini-Series

1 BPe, from Medieval Spawn/Witchblade 2.50
1a variant MS(s) (1:4) 2.50
2 BPe, Chi in Asylum. 2.50
3 BPe, Ming Chang captive in Atlantis. 2.50
4 BPe,"The End?" 2.50
5 BPe,Royale's secret journal 2.50
6 BPe,Safe Haven?. 2.50
7 BPe,Egypt 2.50

ARIA
Image/Avalon Nov., 1998

1 by Brian Holguin & Jay Anacleto. 2.50
1a variant cover. 2.50
2 A:Mad Gwynnion 2.50
3 English Countryside 2.50
4 V:Dark One 2.50
4a glow-in-the-dark(c) 6.95
5 London, 1966. . . . . 2.50
6 Subterranean Homesick Blues . . 2.50
7 Mad Gods and Irish Men 2.50
Preview Ed. F:Kildare 2.95
Spec.#1 Blanc & Noir, sketchbook . 2.95
Spec.#1 alternate cover 6.95
Spec.#2 Blanc & Noir 2.50
Sketchbook by Jay Anacleto. 5.95
TPB The Magic of Aria 13.95
HC The Magic of Aria, lim. 49.95
Coll.Ed.#1, rep.#1–#2. . . . . 5.95

ARIA/ANGELA: HEAVENLY CREATURES
Image Feb., 2000

1 (of 2) x-over 2.95
1a variant JQ (c) (1:4) 2.95
1b variant J.G. Jones (c) (1:4) 2.95
1c variant Jay Anacleto (c) (1:4) . . 2.95
1 B&W 2.95
2 x-over concl.. . . . . 2.95
2a variant (c). 2.95
Museum Edition 100.00

ARKAGA
Image Sept., 1997

1 by Arnie Tang Jorgensen 2.95
2 Desire for revenge 2.95

ART OF ERIK LARSEN

1 Sketchbook 4.95

ART OF HOMAGE STUDIOS

1 Various Pin-ups 4.95

ASCENSION
Image/Top Cow Sept. 1997

1 by David Finch, F:Angels 2.50
2 Andromeda fights alone 2.50
3 reunited with Lucien 2.50
4 . . . . 2.50
5 Gregorieff and Dayak Army 2.50
6 Voivodul returns, concl.. . . . . 2.50
7 Andy's problems worsen. 2.50
8 revenge on Dayaks & Mineans . . 2.50
9 Andy exiled 2.50

Ascension #19
© Top Cow

10 A:D. Gavin Taylor. 2.50
11 A:D. Gavin Taylor. 2.50
12 A:turning point 2.50
13 A:Grigorieff, Petra 2.50
14 V:Marcus,A:Andromeda 2.50
15 Rowena's secrets 2.50
16 Petra joins Lucien 2.50
17 a schism 2.50
18 V:new entity. 2.50
19 to Petra's Minean home 2.50
20 Resurrection, pt.1 . . . . 2.50
21 Resurrection, pt.2 . . . . 2.50
22 trapped 2.95
23 Andromeda's new outfit 2.95
Coll.Ed.#1, rep.#1–#2. . . . . 4.95
Coll.Ed.#2 . . . . 4.95

ASTOUNDING SPACE THRILLS
Image April, 2000

1 Ken Kelly (c), Cydonian Contant. 2.95
2 The Criminal Code 2.95
3 Gordo: Earthling Prime, flip-book 2.95

ASTRO CITY
See: KURT BUSIEK'S ASTRO CITY

ATOMIC TOYBOX
Image April, 1999
Odyssey Line

1 AaL, F:Ken Logan 2.50
2 AaL, The Aliens are comming. . . 2.50

AUTOMATION
Image/Flypaper 1998

1 Robots sent to Mars, and back . . 2.95
2 One goes mad 2.95
3 Sherzad vs. Konak 2.95
TPB rep. #1–#3 . . . . 12.95

AVIGON
Image B&W Oct., 2000

Spec. 56-pg. 5.95

THE AWAKENING
Image (B&W) Oct., 1997

1 (of 4) by Stephen Blue 2.95
2 . . . . 2.95
3 . . . . 2.95
4 . . . . 2.95
TPB Rep. #1–#4. . . . . 9.95

BACKLASH
Image/Wildstorm 1994–97

1 Taboo, 2 diff. covers 4.00
1a variant edition, 2 covers 3.00
2 Savage Dragon 2.50
3 V:Savage Dragon 2.50
4 SRf,A:Wetworks 2.50
5 SRf,A:Dane 2.50
6 BBh,SRf,A:Wetworks 2.50
7 BBh,SRf,V:Bounty Hunters 2.50
8 RMz,BBh,BWS(c),WildStorm Rising,pt.8,w/2 cards 2.50
8a Newsstand ed. 1.95
9 F:Taboo,Dingo,V:Chasers 2.50
10 I:Crimson. 2.50
11 R:Bloodmoon. 2.50
12 R:Taboo,Crimson's Costume . . . 3.00
13 Taboo to the Rescue 2.50
14 A:Deathblow 2.50
15 F:Cyberjack. 2.50
16 F:Cole,Marc. 2.50
17 F:Marc,Kink 2.50
18 . . . . 2.50
19 Fire From Heaven,pt.2. . . . . 2.50
20 SRf,BBh,Fire From Heaven,pt.10 . . . . 2.50
21 SRf,BBh 2.50
22 SRf,BBh 2.50
23 SRf,BBh 2.50
24 SRf,BBh,return of Dingo 2.50
25 SRf,BBh,56pg. special. 4.00
26 SRf,BBh,Gramalkin identity revealed. 2.50
27 SRf,BBh, ... 2.50
28 SRf,BBh,Backlash leads PSI team to Europe 2.50
29 SRf,BBh,Haroth raises the remnants of Atlantis 2.50
30 SRf,BBh,Backlash confronts Kherubim lords. 2.50
31 SRf,BBh,team returns to PSI . . . 2.50
32 SRf,BBh,earth-shattering final issue. 2.50
TPB Backlash/Spider-Man, Webs &

Backlash #9
© Wildstorm

IMAGE

Whips, crossover 4.95
TPB The Drahn War, rep.#27–#32 15.00

BACKLASH/SPIDER-MAN
Image/Wildstorm/Marvel 1996

1 x-over,pt.1 . . . . 2.50
1a variant cover. 3.00
2 x-over,pt.2 . . . . 2.50

BADGER
Image (B&W) May, 1997

1 MBn,"Betelgeuse". 2.95
2 MBn,"Beefalo don't like fences". . 2.95
3 MBn,"Loose Eel". 2.95
4 MBn,"Hot House" 2.95
5 MBn,Octopi in the hot tub 2.95
6 MBn,Prime Minister of
Klactoveedesteen. 2.95
7 MBn,Crime Comics. 2.95
8 MBn,Root. 2.95
9 MBn, ... 2.95
10 MBn,Tuesday Ruby 2.95
11 MBn,Watch the Skies. 2.95
12 MBn,The Lady Cobras. 2.95
13 MBn,Horse Police 2.95
14 MBn,Badger Sells Out 2.95

BADROCK
Image/Extreme 1995

1a RLd(p),TM(c), A:Dragon 1.75
1b SPa(ic),A:Savage Dragon. 1.75
1c DF(ic) 1.75
2 RLd,ErS(s),V:Girth,A:Savage
Dragon, flip-book-Grifter/
Badrock #2. . . . . 2.50
3 RLd,ErS,V:The Overlord 2.50
Ann.#1 I:Gunner, 48-page. 2.95
Super-Spec. #1 A:Grifter & The
Dragon. 2.50

BADROCK AND COMPANY
Image/Extreme 1994–95

1 KG(s), ... 2.50
1a San Diego Comic Con Ed. 3.00
2 RLd(c),Fuji 2.50
3 Overtkill,"Overt Operations" 2.50
4 TBm,MBm,TNu,A:Velocity. 2.50
5 A:Grifter 2.50
6 Finale, A:ShadowHawk. 2.50

BALLISTIC
Image/Top Cow 1995

1 F:Wetworks 2.50
2 F:Wetworks,Jesters
Transformation 2.50
3 F:Wetworks,final issue 2.50

BALLISTIC ACTION
Image/Top Cow 1996

1 MSi(c) pin-ups 2.95

BALLISTIC IMAGERY
Image/Top Cow 1995

1 F:Hellcop,Heavy Space,
Cyberforce,anthology 2.50

BALLISTIC/WOLVERINE
Image/Top Cow/Marvel 1996

1 Devil's Reign, pt.4,x-over 4.00

BATTLESTONE
Image/Extreme 1994

1 RLd,ErS,MMy,AV 2.50
1a variant cover. 3.00
2 RLd,ErS,MMy,AV,I&D:Roarke,
finale 2.50

Battle Chasers #3
© Cliffhanger

BATTLE CHASERS
Image/Cliffhanger April, 1998

1 JMd, fantasy, team-up 2.50
1a Chromium edition (5,000 made) 3.00
2 JMd,F:Gully 2.50
3 JMd,new ally 2.50
4 JMd,Red Monika 2.50
4a,b,c JMd variant covers . . . . . @2.50
5 JMd,V:Lord August,with 8-page
Planetary #0. . . . . 2.50
6 JMd,. 2.50
6a variant cover AWa 2.50
7 JMd, Create a Monster. 2.50
TPB Coll.Ed.#1, rep.#1 & #2. . . . . . 5.95
TPB Collected Edition #2 . . . . 6.00
TPB A Gathering of Heroes 14.95
HC A Gathering of Heroes 24.95
Prelude #1, JMd, 16pg 10.00

BEETLEBORGS
Image/Extreme Nov., 1996

1 from TV show. 2.50

BERZERKERS
Image/Extreme 1995

1 F:Greylore,Hatchet,Psi-Storm,
Cross,Wildmane,Youngblood#2 2.50
2 Into the Darkness 2.50
3 Slay Ride 2.50
4 final issue. 2.50

BIG BANG COMICS
Image/Big Bang Studios 1996
(B&W) Prev. Caliber

1 F:Mighty Man 2.00
2 Silver Age Shadowhawk 2.00
3 . . . . 2.00
4 . . . . 2.50
5 Top Secret Origins 2.95
6 Round Table of America and
Knights of Justice meet, orig.
mini-series #3 (color) 2.95
7 . . . . 2.95
8 F:Mister U.S. 2.95
9 I:Peter Chefren. 2.95
10 F:Galahad 2.95
11 Faulty Towers is destroying
Midway City 2.95
12 F:The Savage Dragon 2.95
13 by Jeff Weigel, 40pg spec. 2.95
14 RB,A:The Savage Dragon 2.95
15 SBi(c),F:Dr. Weird 2.95
16 F:Thunder Girl 2.95
17 . . . . 2.95
18 Savage Dragon on Trial. 2.95
19 O:Beacon,Hummingbird. 2.95
20 F:Knight Watchman,Blitz 2.95
21 F:Shadow Lady 2.95
22 The Bird-Man of Midway City. . . 2.95
23 Riddle of the Sphinx, sequel . . . 2.95
24 History of Big Bang,Vol.1 . . . . . . 3.95
25 Anniv. iss. 3.95
26 Murder by Microphone, concl. . . 2.95
27 History of Big Bang, Vol.2 . . . . . 3.95
28 Knight of the Living Dead,pt.1 . . 3.95
29 Knight of the Living Dead,pt.2 . . 3.95
30 F:Knight Watchman 3.95
31 F:Knight-Sprite. 3.95
32 F:Pink Flamingo. 3.95
33 Peril of Parallel Planets 3.95
34 To Save the Gods 3.95
TPB rep. 1994 mini-series. 11.00

BIG BRUISERS
Image/Wildstorm 1996

1 F:Maul,Impact,Badrock. 3.50

BIG HAIR PRODUCTIONS
Image (B&W) Feb., 2000

1 by Andy Suriano,F:Astro-Bug . . . 3.50
2 . . . . 3.50

BLACK AND WHITE
Image/Hack Studios 1996

1 ATi,New heroes,"Beginnings" . . . 1.95
2 ATi(p),apparent death 1.95
3 V:Chang. 1.95
Ashcan. 5.00

BLACK ANVIL
Image/Top Cow 1996

1 & 2. . . . . 2.50

BLACK FLAG
Image/Extreme 1994

1 B&W Preview 3.00

BLACK OPS
Image/Wildstorm 1996

1 . . . . 2.50
2 . . . . 2.50
3 . . . . 2.50
4 . . . . 2.50
5 . . . . 2.50
TPB, rep.#1–#5 . . . . 14.95

BLAIR WITCH: DARK TESTAMENTS
Image Oct., 2000

Spec. IEd,CAd 2.95

BLINDSIDE
Image/Extreme Aug., 1996

1 MMy & AV, F:Nucgaek Jeno 2.50
2 MMy & AV, Origin continues 2.50

BLISS ALLEY

Image (B&W) July, 1997

1 BML 2.95
2 BML,F:Wizard Walker 2.95
3 BML,Inky-Dinks 2.95

BLOODHUNTER

Image/Extreme Nov. 1996

1 RV, Cabbot Stone rises from the slab 2.95

BLOOD LEGACY

Image/Top Cow April, 2000

1 MHw,The Story of Ryan 2.50
1a variant Keu Cha (c). 2.50
1b variant Mike Turner (c) 2.50
2 MHw,F:Dr. Susan Ryerson 2.50
3 MHw 2.50
4 MHw 2.50

BLOODPOOL

Image/Exteme 1995

1 I:Seoul,Rubbe,Wylder, "Discharged" 2.50
1a variant cover. 2.50
2 The Hills Are Alive 2.50
3 Walk Like an Egyptian 2.50
4 final issue. 2.50
TPB Rep. #1-#4 . . . . 12.95

[Regular Series] 1996

1 JDy 2.50
2 JDy 2.50
3 JDy 2.50

BLOODSTRIKE

Image/Extreme 1993

1 A:Brigade,Rub the Blood(c) Blood Brother prelude,x-over . . 3.00
2 I:Lethal,V:Brigade,V:Brigade, BloodBrothers,pt.2,B:BU:Knight 2.50
3 B:ErS(s),ATi(c),V:Coldsnap,Blood Brothers,pt.4,"Turning Point". . . 2.25
4 ErS(s), ... 2.25
5 KG,I:Noble,A:Supreme, ... 2.25
6 KG(s),CAx,C&J:Chapel,"Inside Project:Born Again" 2.25
7 KG,RHe,A:Badrock,"Changing of the Guard" 2.25
8 RHe,A:Spawn,Sleeping & Waking 2.25
9 RHe,Extreme Prejudice,pt.3, I:Extreme Warrior,ATh,BU: Black & White 2.25
10 Extreme Prejudice,pt.7, V:Brigade, B:BU:Knight 1.95
25 I:Cabbot Bloodstrike 2.50
11 ErS(s),ATi(c),V:Coldsnap 1.95
12 ErS(s) 1.95
13 KG,A:Supreme,"BetterOffDead" . 2.50
14 KG(s),CAx,C&J:Chapel 2.50
15 KG,RHe,A:Badrock,War Games,pt.1 Extreme Sacrifice begins 1.95
16 KG,RHe,War Games,pt.3,Extreme Sacrifice ignites 1.95
17 KIA,V:The Horde 2.50
18 ExtremeSacrifice,pt.3,x-over . . . 2.50
19 V:The Horde 2.50
20 R:Deadlock New Order 2.50
21 KA,V:Epiphany New Order. 2.50
22 V:The Horde, last issue 2.50
25 see above, after #10
Ashcan. 5.00

BLOODSTRIKE: ASSASSIN

Image/Extreme 1995

0 R:Battlestone 2.50
1 Debut new series 2.50
1a alternate cover 2.50
2 V:M.D.K. Assassins 2.50
3 V:Persuasion 2.50

Bloodwulf #4
© Image

BLOOD WULF

Image/Extreme 1995

1 RLd,R:Bloodwulf. 2.50
1b Run OJ Run 2.50
1c Alternate cover 2.50
1d Alternate cover 2.50
2 A:Hot Blood 2.50
3 Slippery When Wet. 2.50
4 Darkness Gnaws at my Soul, final issue. 2.50
Summer Spec.#1 V:Supreme Freeferall (1995). 2.50

BLUE

Image Aug., 1999

1 Android teenager 2.50
2 by Greg Aronowitz 2.50
3 rescue mission 2.50

BULLETPROOF MONK

Image/Flypaper Nov., 1998

1 in San Francisco. 2.95
2 N.Y. Chinatown. 2.95
3 conclusion 2.95

BODY COUNT

1 & 2. . . . . @2.50

BOHOS

Image/Flypaper (B&W) 1998

1 by Maggie Whorf & B.Penaranda 2.95
2 F:teenage bohemians. 2.95
3 concl 2.95
TPB Bohos. 12.95

BONE

(B & W)

[Previously by Cartoon Books]

21 . . . . 2.95
22 . . . . 2.95
23 . . . . 2.95
24 . . . . 2.95
25 . . . . 2.95
26 The Turning. 2.95
27 end of dragonslayer storyline . . . 2.95
Bone Sourcebook. 25
HC#1 Out of Boneville, rep. 19.95
HC#2 The Great Cow Race, rep. . 19.95
HC#3 Gran'ma's Story, rep. 19.95

Image reprints with new covers

#1 thru #9 . . . . @2.95
10 rep. "Great Cow Race". 2.95

Image/Cartoon Books

11 Aftermath of the Great Cow Race 2.95
12 . . . . 2.95
13 Thar she blows 2.95
14 . . . . 2.95
15 Double or nothing 2.95
16 hiding from the Rat Creatures . . 2.95
17 with 5 new pages. 2.95
18 Betrayed 2.95
19 three cheers for dragon-slayer Phoney Bone 2.95
20 Phoney Bone vs. Lucius 2.95

BOOF

Image/TMP 1994

1 . . . . 1.95
2 Meathook 1.95
3 Joyride 1.95
4 Beach. 1.95
5 Down on the Farm 1.95
6 V:Gangster Chimps 1.95

BOOF AND THE BRUISE CREW

Image/TMP 1994

1 thru 4 . . . . @1.95
5 Supermarket. 1.95
6 I:Mortar, O:Bruise Crew 1.95

BRASS

Image/Wildstorm 1996

1 Rib,AWa,Folio Edition 3.50
2 Rib,AWa, ... 2.50
3 Rib,AWa,concl. 2.50

Brass #3
© Wildstorm

 All comics prices listed are for *Near Mint* condition.

BRIGADE
Image/Extreme 1993
[1st Series]
1 RLd(s),MMy,I:Brigade,Genocide . 3.50
1a Gold Ed. 4.00
2 RLd(s),V:Genocide,w/coupon#4 . 4.00
2a w/o coupon. 1.00
2b Gold Ed. 4.00
3 I:Birds of Prey,V:Genocide 2.00
4 CyP,Youngblood#5 flip 2.00
[2nd Series]
0 RLd(s),ATi(c),JMs,NRd,I:Warcry, A:Emp,V:Youngblood 2.25
1 I:Boone,Hacker,V:Bloodstrike, Blood Brothers,pt.1. . . . . 2.75
1a Gold Ed. 3.00
2 C:Coldsnap,Blood Brothers,pt.3 . 3.00
3 ErS(s),GP(c),MMy,NRd(i),I:Roman V:Bloodstrike,BloodBrothers,pt.52.25
4 Rip(s),MMy,RHe,Changes BU:Lethal. 2.25
5 Rip(s),MMy,It's A VeryDeepSea . 2.25
6 Rip(s),MMy,I:Coral,Warlok, BU:Hackers Tale 2.25
7 Rip(s),MMy,V:Worlok 2.25
8 ErS(s),MMy,Extreme Prejudice, pt.2,BU:Black & White,pt.5 . . . . 2.25
9 ErS(s),MMy,Extreme Prejudice pt.6,ATh,BU:Black & White 2.25
25 ErS(s),MMy,D:Kayo,Coldsnap, Thermal,. 2.25
26 Images of Tomorrow 2.25
10 Extreme Prejudice 1.95
11 WildC.A.T.S 2.50
12 Battlestone 2.50
13 Thermal. 1.95
14 Teamate deaths. 1.95
15 MWm,R:Roman Birds of Prey . . 1.95
16 ExtremeSacrifice,pt.4,x-over . . . 2.50
17 MWn,I:New Team 2.50
18 I:The Shape New Order. 2.50
19 MWn,F:Troll,Glory 2.50
20 MWn,alien cult saga,concl. 2.50
21 F:ShadowHawk 2.50
22 Supreme Apocalypse, pt.4 . . . . . 2.50
23 & 24. @2.50
25 & 26 see above
27 Extreme Babewatch. 2.50
Sourcebook 2.95

BUGBOY
Image (B&W) June, 1998
1-shot, by Mark Lewis, 48pg 3.95

BUTCHER KNIGHT
Image/Top Cow July, 2000
1 DT,F:Dolgen & Jenelle 2.50
2 DT 2.50
3 DT 2.50

CARVERS
Image/Flypaper Oct., 1998
1 F:five snowboarders 2.95
2 J:Crazy Jack. 2.95
3 V:Evil Yeti 2.95
TPB rep. #1–#3 . . . . 9.95

CASUAL HEROES
Image/Motown 1996
1 . . . . 2.50
2 thru 5 . . . . 2.50

CATHEDRAL CHILD
Image 1998
GN by Lea Hernandez 9.95

Casual Heroes #1
© Motown

GN 2nd printing 9.95

CELESTINE
Image/Extreme 1996
1 . . . . 2.50
2 . . . . 2.50

CHANNEL ZERO
Image (B&W) 1998
1 by Brian Wood 2.95
2 . . . . 2.95
3 gone global 2.95
4 Filter. 2.95
5 Brink of Millennium crash 2.95
6 Sound system 2.95
TPB Collection 11.95

CHAPEL
Image/Extreme 1995
1 BWn,F:Chapel 3.50
2 V:Colonel Black 3.00
2a variant cover. 2.50
[Regular Series]
1 BWn,F:Chapel 2.50
1a variant cover. 2.50
2 V:Giger. 2.50
3 V:Giger. 2.50
4 Extreme Babewatch 2.50
5 Hell on Earth,pt.1 . . . . 2.50
6 Hell on Earth,pt.2 . . . . 2.50
7 Shadowhunt x-over,pt.2 . . . . 2.50

CHASSIS
Image Nov., 1999
1 F:Chassis McBain. 2.95
2 . . . . 2.95
2a variant Matt Busch (c). 2.95
3 Gizmotech Industries 2.95
4 . . . . 2.95
4a Collectors variant (c). 3.95
5 Slic's One Shot, flip-cover. 2.95

CHILDHOOD'S END
Image (B&W) Oct., 1997
1 (of 5) JCf, comunity playground . 2.95

CHILLER
Image Dec., 1998
TPB JHI,F:Brian Marx 17.95

THE C.H.I.X. THAT TIME FORGOT
Image/Studiosaurus Aug., 1998
1 F:Good Girl 2.95

CITY OF SILENCE
Image May, 2000
1 (of 3) WEI,GEr,F:Silencers 2.50
1a variant GEr 3-D (c) (1:4) 2.50
2 WEI,GEr, ... 2.50
3 WEI,GEr, ... 2.50

CLOCKWORK ANGELS
Image (B&W) March, 1999
GN seq. to Cathedral Child. 9.95

CODE BLUE
Image (B&W) April, 1998
1 by Jimmie Robinson 2.95
2 F.I.T.E. creates havoc 2.95

CODENAME: STRYKE FORCE
Image/Top Cow 1994
1A MS(s),BPe,JRu(i), ... 3.50
1B Gold Embossed Cover 6.00
1C Blue Embossed Cover 9.00
2 MS(s),BPe,JRu(i),. 2.50
3 MS(s),BPe,JRu(i),. 2.50
4 MS(s),BPe,JRu(i),. 2.50
5 MS(s),BPe,JRu(i),. 2.50
6 MS(s),BPe,JRu(i),. 2.25
7 MS(s),BPe,JRu(i),. 2.25
8A Cyblade poster (Tucci) 4.00
8B Shi poster (Silvestri) 4.00
8C Tempest poster (Tan) 2.25
9 New Teamate 2.25
10 SvG, B:New Adventure 2.25
11 F:Bloodbow 1.95
12 F:Stryker 1.95
13 SvG(s),F:Strkyer 2.25
14 New Jobs 2.25
Spec.#0 O:Stryke Force 2.50
TPB Rep. Death's Angel Saga 9.95

COMBAT
1 . . . . 2.50

COMPLETE ALEX TOTH ZORRO
Image (B&W) April, 1999
TPB Complete Alex Toth Zorro . . . 18.95

COSMIC RAY
Image June, 1999
1 by Stephen Blue. 2.95
1a alternate cover (1:2) 2.95
2 F:Raymond Mann. 2.95
3 F:Star Marshalls 2.95

COW, THE
Image/Top Cow April, 2000
1 Spring edition 2.95
2 Summer edition 2.95

CREECH, THE

Image/TMP Oct., 1997

1 GCa,DaM,F:Chirs Rafferty 1.95
2 GCa,DaM,F:Dennis Dross 1.95
TPB Race Against Death 9.95

Crimson #1
© Cliffhanger

CRIMSON

Image/Cliffhanger May, 1998

1 BAu,HuR,F:Alex Elder, vampire "Dawn to Dusk" 3.50
1a variant AWa(c) 3.00
1b Chromium Edition 3.00
2 BAu,HuR,V:Jelly-Bats, "Unlife Story" 3.00
2a variant AAd(c). 4.00
3 BAu,HuR,V:Rose,Payment in Blood 3.00
4 BAu,HuR,F:Red Hood,Children of Judas,pt.1 . . . . 2.50
5 BAu,HuR,A:Red Hood,Children of Judas,pt.2 . . . . 2.50
6 BAu,HuR,A:Red Hood,Children of Judas,pt.2 . . . . 2.50
7 BAu,HuR,Christmas day 3.00
½ Dynamic Forces exclusive 4.00

Wildstorm/DC 1999

8 BAu,HuR 2.50
9 BAu,HuR 2.50
10 BAu,HuR 2.50
11 BAu,HuR 2.50
12 BAu,HuR 2.50
13 BAu,HuR 2.50
14 BAu,HuR 2.50
15 BAu,HuR 2.50
16 BAu,HuR 2.50
17 BAu,HuR 2.50
18 BAu,HuR 2.50
19 BAu,HuR 2.50
20 BAu,HuR 2.50
21 BAu,HuR 2.50
22 BAu,HuR, ... 2.50
Spec.#1 Scarlet X: Blood on the Moon BAu,HuR,one-shot 4.00
Spec. Crimson Sourcebook #1 . . . . 2.95
TPB Crimson, rep.#1–#6 . . . . 13.00
TPB Heaven & Earth,rep#7–#12. . 14.95
TPB Loyalty & Loss 12.95

CRIMSON PLAGUE

Image June, 2000

1 GP,64-pg. 3.00
2 GP,Sole Survivor 2.50
3 GP,Blood trail 2.50

CROW, THE

Image/TMP Feb., 1999

1 JMu,F:Eric Draven 3.00
1a variant TP cover (1:4) 3.00
2 JMu,hunt for killers 3.00
3 JMu,justice for killers 3.00
4 JMu,Line Between Devil's Teeth . 3.00
5 JMu,Skin of an Angel,pt.1 . . . . . . 3.00
6 JMu,Skin of an Angel,pt.2 . . . . . . 3.00
7 JMu,Touch of Evil, pt.1 . . . . 3.00
8 JMu,Touch of Evil,pt.2. . . . . 3.00
9 JMu,Wings and Black Feathers. . 3.00
TPB Vol. 1 Vengeance 10.95
TPB Vol. 2 Evil Beyond Reach . . . 10.95
Crow Mag.#1, 56-pg. rep. 4.95
Crow Mag.#2 . . . . 4.95
Crow Mag.#3 . . . . 4.95

CRUSH, THE

Image/Motown Jan., 1996

1 Mini-series 2.50
2 Let Me Light Your Fire 2.50
3 Million Dollar Smile 2.50
4 . . . . 2.50
5 The Hip Hop Slide 2.50

CRYPT

Image/Extreme 1995

1 A:Prophet. 2.50
1a Variant cover 2.50
2 A:Prophet. 2.50

[JIM LEE'S] C-23

Image/Wildstorm April, 1998

1 BCi,JMi,F:Corben Helix. 2.50
2 JMi,TC(c),V:Angelans 2.50
3 JMi,TC(c),with game card 2.50
4 JMi,Corbin, banished 2.50
5 JMi,RCo(c),Queen Mother 2.50
5a variant JLe(c) (1:4) 2.50
6 JMi,RCo(c),V:HyperShock Troopers 2.50
7 JMi,RCo(c),Hail to the Queen . . . 2.50
8 JMi,RCo(c),Long Live the King . . 2.50

CURSE OF THE SPAWN

Image/TMP Sept., 1996

1 DT,DaM,F:Daniel Lianso 9.00
1a B&W Variant. 25.00
2 DT,DaM,Dark Future, Pt. 2: Blood Lust 5.00
3 DT,DaM,Dark Future, Pt. 3: Corpse Candles 5.00
4 DT,DaM, ... 4.00
5 DT,DaM,Sam & Twitch search for Gretchen Culver 3.00
6 DT,DaM,Sam & Twitch pursue Suture 3.00
7 DT,DaM,Suture is captured 3.00
8 DT,DaM,Suture escapes police custody 3.00
9 DT,DaM,Angela's secret origin . . 5.00
10 DT,DaM,Angela, Spawn Slayer . 3.50
11 DT,DaM,Angela's story, concl. . . 3.50
12 DT,DaM,Jessica Priest, movie photo(c) 3.50
13 DT,DaM "Heart of Darkness" . . . 3.50
14 DT,DaM,Jessica, concl. 3.50
15 DT,DaM,Tempt an Angel,pt.1 . . . 3.50
16 DT,DaM,Tempt an Angel,pt.2 . . . 3.50
17 DT,DaM 3.50
18 DT,DaM,F:Tony Twist. 3.50
19 DT,Curse & Tony Twist. 3.50
20 DT,DaM,Monsters & Mythology . 3.50
21 DT,DaM,Zeus Must Die 3.50
22 DT,F:Ryan Hatchett 3.50
23 DT,TM,R:Overtkill. 3.50
24 DT,TM,Pandemic. 3.50
25 DT,TM,"Heart of Hell". 2.00
26 DT.TM,V:The Crocodile 2.00
27 DT,TM,F:Marc Simmons 2.00
28 DT,TM,V:Suture 2.00
29 DT,TM,A:Jonathan Edward Custer 2.00
TPB Vol. 1 Sacrifice the Soul 9.95
TPB Vol. 3 Shades of Gray. 9.95

CYBERFORCE

Image/Top Cow

[Limited Series] 1992–93

0 WS,O:Cyber Force 2.50
1 MS,I:Cyberforce,w/coupon#3 . . . 5.00
1a w/o coupon. 3.00
2 MS,V:C.O.P.S. 3.50
3 MS 2.50
4 MS,V:C.O.P.S,BU:Codename Styke Force.. . . . . 2.50
TPB Rep. mini-series 12.95

[Regular Series] 1993

1 EcS(s),MS,SW,. 2.50
1B Gold Foil Logo 6.00
2 EcS(s),MS,SW,Killer Instinct #2,A:Warblade 2.25
2B Silver Embossed Cover 6.00
3 EcS(s),MS,SW,Killer Instinct #4, A:WildC.A.T.S. 2.25
3B Gold Embossed Cover 6.00
4 EcS(s),MS,Ballistic 2.00
5 EcS(s),MS 2.00
6 EcS(s),MS,Ballistic's Past. 2.00
7 S.H.O.C.s. 2.00
8 . . . . 2.50
9 A:Huntsman 2.00
10 A:Huntsman. 2.00
10a Alternate Cover 4.00
10b Silver Seal Oz-Con 500c 9.00
11 . . . . 2.00
12 T.I.M.M.I.E. goes wild. 2.00
13 EcS,MS,O:Cyberdata. 2.25
14 EcS,MSI,V:T.I.M.M.I.E.. . . . . 2.25
15 New Cyberdata Threat. 2.25
16 O:Ripclaw 2.25
17 Regrouping 2.25
18 . . . . 2.50
19 . . . . 2.50

Cyberforce, Vol. 2, #28
© Top Cow

20 . . . 2.50
21 . . . 2.50
22 . . . 2.50
23 . . . 2.50
24 . . . 2.50
26 KWo . . . 2.50
27 F:Ash . . . 2.50
27a variant cover by JQ&JP (1:4) . . 4.00

Top Cow 1996

28 A:Gabriel . . . 2.50
29 . . . 2.50
30 ScL,"Devil's Reign" tie-in . . . 2.50
31 The team in conflict . . . 2.50
32 Cyblade leads rejuvenated team 2.50
33 KWo, Cheleene in midst of civil war . . . 2.50
34 KWo,Royal Blood, pt.3 . . . 2.50
35 BTn,Royal Blood, concl. . . . 2.50
Ashcan 1 (San Diego) . . . 4.00
Ashcan 1 (signed) . . . 6.00
Sourcebook 1 . . . 2.50
Sourcebook 2 I:W.Zero . . . 2.50
Ann.#1 O:Velocity . . . 2.50
Ann.#2 . . . 2.95
TPB new art . . . 12.95
TPB EcS,MS,SW,Assault with a Deadly Woman . . . 9.95

CYBERFORCE/ CODENAME STRYKEFORCE: OPPOSING FORCES

1 V:Dangerous Threat . . . 2.50
2 Team Vs. Team . . . 2.50

CYBERFORCE ORIGINS

Image/Top Cow 1995

1 O:Cyblade . . . 2.50
1B Gold Seal 1000c . . . 6.00
2 O:Stryker . . . 2.50
3 O:Impact . . . 2.50
4 Misery . . . 3.00

CYBERFORCE UNIVERSE SOURCEBOOK

Image/Top Cow 1994–95

1 and 2 . . . @2.50

CYBERNARY

Image/Wildstorm 1995–96

1 thru 5 mini-series . . . @2.50

CYBERPUNX

Image/Extreme 1996

1 . . . 2.50
2 . . . 2.50
3 RLe & Ching Lau,F:Drake . . . 2.50

CYBLADE/SHI

Image 1995

1 The Battle for Independents . . . 2.95

CY-GOR

Image/TMP July, 1999

1 RV,I:Fatima,Frankie & Zevon . . . 2.50
2 RV,Fire in the Mind,pt.2 . . . 2.50
3 RV,Needles and Pins . . . 2.50
4 RV, Exquisite Corpse . . . 2.50
5 RV . . . 2.50
6 RV, the Terraplane . . . 2.50
7 RV,Young Doctor Acula . . . 2.50

DAMNED

Image/Homage June, 1997

1 (of 4) StG, MZ & DRo . . . 2.50
2 StG, MZ & DRo,F:Mick Thorne . . 2.50
3 StG, MZ & DRo . . . 2.50
4 StG, MZ & DRo . . . 2.50

DANGER GIRL

Wildstorm/Cliffhanger 1998

1 JSC,AGo,"Dangerously Yours," 40-page . . . 2.95
1a chromium edition, 40pg. . . . 5.00
1b Tour Edition . . . 2.95
2 I:Johnny Barracuda,"Dangerous Liaisons" . . . 2.50
3 in Switzerland . . . 2.50
3a variant AH(c) . . . 2.50
3b variant TC(c) . . . 2.50
4 I:Major Maxim . . . 2.50
5 JSC,AGo . . . 2.50

Wildstorm/DC 1999

6 JSC,SW . . . 2.50
6a variant JMd (c) . . . 2.50
6b variant HuR (c) . . . 2.50
7 JSC,SW,concl.,48-pg. . . . 5.95
TPB Dangerous Coll.,Vol.1 . . . 5.95
TPB Dangerous Coll.,Vol.2,rep 2&3 5.95

DARING ESCAPES

Image/TMP 1998

1 ANi,F:Harry Houdini . . . 2.50
2 ANi,search for Mystical Heart . . . 2.50
3 A:Kimiel . . . 2.50
4 conclusion . . . 2.50

DARK ANGEL: PHOENIX RESURRECTION

Image May, 2000

1 by Kia Asamiya, color manga . . . 2.95
1a variant (c) . . . 2.95
2 . . . 2.95
2a variant (c) . . . 2.95
3 . . . 2.95
3a variant (c) . . . 2.95

DARKCHYLDE

Maximum 1996

1 flip-book-Glory/Angel,Angels in Hell,pt.1 . . . 4.00

Darkchylde: Swimsuit Illustrated
© Homage

1a remastered, RLd(c) . . . 6.00
1b American Entertainment . . . 4.00
2 . . . 3.00
2a Variant cover . . . 3.00
2b Remastered, with poster . . . 2.50
3 . . . 3.50
3a Remastered, with poster . . . 2.50

Image 1996

4 RQu,Ariel & Kauldron's past . . . 4.00
5 RQu,No one here gets out alive . 3.00
TPB Rep. #1–#5 . . . 12.95

Series Two:

Image/Homage1998

0 RQu,Ariel's back, Ariel's past . . . 2.50

DARKCHYLDE/GLORY

Image/Extreme

1-shot, four variant covers, by RLd, RQu, JDy & PtL . . . 2.95

DARKCHYLDE: THE DIARY

Image May, 1997

1-shot, RQu et al,diary excerpts . . . 5.00

DARKCHYLDE: THE LEGACY

Image/Wildstorm 1998

1 RQu,F:Ariel . . . 2.50
2 RQu . . . 2.50

Wildstorm/DC 1999

3 RQu,A:Silencer . . . 2.50
4 RQu,Carnival of Fools . . . 2.50
4a RQu,AAd(c) variant cover . . . 2.50
Summer Swimsuit Spectacular #1 . . 4.00
Spec.Dreams of the Darkchylde #0. 2.50
TPB Darkchylde . . . 20.00

DARKCHYLDE/ WITCHBLADE

Image/Top Cow July, 2000

1 RQu,Nightmare City . . . 2.50

DARK CROSSINGS

Image/Top Cow May, 2000

Spec. #1 Dark Cloud Rising . . . 5.95
Spec. #2 Dark Cloud Overhead . . . 5.95

DARKER IMAGE

Image 1993

1 BML,BCi(s),RLd,SK,JLe,I:Blood Wulf,Deathblow,Maxx . . . 4.00
1a Gold logo(c) . . . 8.00
1b White(c) . . . 6.00
Ashcan 1 . . . 4.00

DARKMINDS

Image 1998

1 PtL,cyberpunk,detective . . . 2.50
2 Neon Dragon . . . 2.50
2a variant cover . . . 2.50
3 PtL,A:Neon Dragons . . . 2.50
4 PtL,Paradox killer . . . 2.50
5 PtL,Unlikely friends, enemies . . . 2.95
6 PtL,Aurora Industries . . . 2.95
7 PtL,V:Mamuro Hayabusa . . . 2.95
8 Conclusion, 1st story arc . . . 2.50
½ PtL,Cyborg dreams . . . 2.50
TPB Collection #1 rep. #1–#3 . . . 7.95
TPB Collection #2 rep. #4–#6 . . . 7.95
TPB Collection #3 rep. #7 & #8 . . . 5.95
TPB Vol. I, rep.#1–#8 . . . 18.95

VOL. II Feb., 2000

1 JMd(c) one year later 2.50
1a variant PtL (c). 2.50
1b variant Omar Dogan (c) 2.50
2 Changing Faces 2.50
2a variant PtL (c). 2.50
2b variant Michael Turner (c) 2.50
2c variant (c) 2.50
3 PtL(c),F:Reiko Tetsunori 2.50
3a variant Omar Dogan (c) 2.50
3b variant JQ (c) 2.50
4 PtL,cyborg attack 2.50
5 PtL,The Prize 2.50
6 PtL,9mm Answers 2.50
7 PtL,The Hunger 2.50
8 PtL,Born Again 2.50
#0 The Bullet 2.50
#0a variant(c) 2.50

DARKNESS, THE

Image/Top Cow 1996

0 Preview Edition, B&W. 20.00
½ 15.00
½ variant cover 25.00
1 GEn, MS,Coming of Age 15.00
1a Dark cover 20.00
1b Platinum cover 15.00
2 GEn, MS 9.00
3 GEn,MS,Jackie pursued by many foes 7.00
4 GEn,MS,Jackie explores Darkness power 5.00
5 GEn,MS,New York gangs on verge of all-out war 5.00
6 GEn,MS,F:JackieEstacado,concl. 4.00
7 MS 4.00
7a variant (c) 10.00
8 JBz,retribution 3.00
8a MS(c)(1:4) 5.00
9 Family Ties,pt.2,x-over 5.00
10 Family Ties,pt.3,x-over 6.00
11 GEn,MS,Hearts of Darkness . . . 3.00
11a Chromium (c). 26.00
11b variant (c) 5.00
12 GEn,Hearts of Darkness 3.00
13 GEn,Hearts of Darkness 3.00
14 GEn,JBz,Hearts of Darkness, concl. 3.00
15 JBz,Spear of Destiny,pt.1. . . . . . 3.00
16 JBz,Spear of Destiny,pt.2. . . . . . 3.00
17 JBz,Spear of Destiny,pt.3. . . . . . 3.00
18 JBz,aftermath 3.00
19 JBz,No Mercy,pt.1 . . . . 2.50

Darkness #1
© Top Cow

20 JBz,No Mercy,pt.2 . . . . 2.50
21 JBz,Wynnwood 2.50
22 JBz,Where is Jenny. 2.50
23 JBz,SLo,new characters 2.50
24 JBz,SLo,road trip to Vegas. 2.50
25 JBz,SLo,48-page 3.50
26 JBz,SLo,A:Joey Scarpaggio. . . . 2.50
27 SLo,FBI continues assault 2.50
28 Darkness/Witchblade,pt.4 x-over 2.50
29 SLo,High Noon,pt.1 . . . . 2.50
30 SLo,High Noon,pt.2 . . . . 2.50
31 SLo,High Noon,pt.3 . . . . 2.50
32 SLo,Dark Days Ahead 2.50
33 SLo,Capris Castagliano,pt.1. . . . 2.50
34 SLo,Capris Castagliano,pt.2. . . . 2.50
35 SLo,tour of his life 2.50
GN rep. #1–#2 . . . . 4.95
GN rep. #3–#4, 56 pg. 4.95
GN rep. #5–#6, 56 pg. 4.95
GN rep. #5–#6, with slipcase. 10.00
GN rep. #7–#8 . . . . 4.95
Slipcase and all 3 GNs 25.00
Signed Slipcase and all 3 GNs . . . 50.00
Coll.Ed.#6,rep.#13–#14 . . . . 5.95
Spec. Infinity, SLo. 3.50
Darkness/Witchblade,pt.3 x-over . . 3.95
Spec.#1, Dark Ages 4.95
TPB Coll.Ed.,Vol.V,rep.#11–#12 . . . 5.95
TPB Coll.Ed. deluxe, rep.#1–#6 . . 14.95
TPB Spear of Destiny 12.95

DARKNESS, THE/BATMAN

Image/Top Cow April, 1999

Spec. SLo,MS x-over 5.95

DARK REALM

Image Oct., 2000

1 by Taeson Chang 2.95

DART

Image 1996

1 thru 3 Jozef Szekeres . . . . @2.50

DEADLANDS

Image July 1999

GN 1-shot role-play tie-in 6.95

DEADLY DUO, THE

Image/Highbrow 1994–95

1 A:Kill-Cat 2.50
2 A:Pitt, O:Kid Avenger 2.50
3 A:Roman, O:Kill-Cat 2.50

[Second Series] 1995

1 A:Spawn. 2.50
2 A:Savage Dragon 2.50
3 A:Grunge, Gen13 . . . . 2.50
4 Movie Mayhem 2.50

DEATHBLOW

Image/Wildstorm 1993–96

1 JLe,MN,I:Cybernary 3.00
2 JLe,BU:Cybernary 2.50
3 JLe(a&s),BU:Cybernary 3.00
4 JLe(s),TSe,BU:Cybernary. 2.50
5 JLe(s),TSe,BU:Cybernary. 2.50
5a different cover. 5.00
6 Black Angel 2.00
7 . . . . 2.00
8 Black Angel 2.00
9 The Four Horseman 2.00
10 Michael Cray, Sister Mary 2.00
11 A:Four Horseman 2.00
12 Final Battle 2.50
13 New Story Arc 2.50
14 A:Johnny Savoy. 2.50

Deathblow #7
© Wildstorm

15 F:Michael Cray 2.50
16 TvS,BWS(c),WildStorm Rising,pt.6,w/2 cards 2.50
16a Newsstand ed.. . . . . 2.00
17 V:Gammorran Hunter Killers . . . 2.50
18 F:Cybernary. 2.50
19 F:Cybernary. 2.50
20 A:Gen 13. . . . . 3.50
21 Brothers in Arms,pt.2,A:Gen13. . 3.50
22 Brothers in Arms,pt.3 . . . . 2.50
23 Brothers in Arms,pt.4 . . . . 2.50
24 Brothers in Arms,pt.5 . . . . 3.00
25 Brothers in Arms,pt.6 . . . . 2.50
26 Fire From Heaven prelude 2.50
27 Fire From Heaven,pt.8. . . . . 3.00
28 Fire From Heaven,finale,pt.3 . . . 2.50
29 last issue 2.50
Ashcan 1 . . . . 4.00
TPB Dark Angel Saga,rep.,216pg . 29.95
TPB Sinners and Saints, rep. 19.95

DEATHBLOW/WOLVERINE

Image/Wildstorm

1 RiB, AWs,crossover, set in San Francisco's Chinatown 2.50
2 RiB, AWs,concl. 2.50
TPB rep. series 8.95

DEATHMATE X-OVER
See: Acclaim/Valiant

DECEPTION, THE

Image/Flypaper
(B&W) Jan., 1999

1 (of 3) F:Jordan Risk, magician . . 2.95
2 Framed for murder 2.95
3 V:South American Drug Cartel . . 2.50

DEFCON 4

Image/Wildstorm 1996

1 mini-series 2.50
2 thru 4 . . . . @2.50

DEITY

Image

Collected Ed. Vol. 1 . . . . 9.95
Collected Ed. Vol. 2 . . . . 9.95

DEITY: REVELATIONS
Image June, 1999
1 F:Jamie 2.95
2 F:Joe Tripoli 2.95
3 A legend reborn 2.95
3a variant cover (1:10). 2.95

DEMONSLAYER
Image Nov., 1999
1 MMy. 2.95
2 Jaclyn begins her quest 2.95
3 MMy, Michael & the Demon 2.95
Shadow Edition, Pt.1 B&W 4.95
VOL. II
1 MMy,Into Hell, pt.1 . . . . 2.95
1 variant (c) (1:4). 2.95
2 MMy. 2.95
3 MMy, enter Ebon 2.95

DERRING RISK
Image June, 1999
1 Fantasy Adventure 2.50
1a variant cover AWa 2.50

DESPERADOS
Image/Homage Sept., 1997
1 by JMi & John Cassaday 7.00
2 V:Leander Peik. 3.00
2a 2nd printing 2.50
3 V:Leander Peik. 3.00
4 V:Leander Peik, concl. 3.00
5 V:Gideon Brood, pt.1. . . . . 3.00
TPB A Moment's Sunlight,rep.
#1–#5. . . . . 16.95

DESPERATE TIMES
Image (B&W) June, 1998
1 by Chris Eliopoulos. 2.95
2 Strip joint 2.95
3 EL(c) 2.95
4 Christmas special. 2.95
5 EL(c), sideways 2.95
6 . . . . 2.95
TPB 12.95

DETECTIVES INC.
Image March, 1999
TPB Vol. 1 . . . . 14.95
TPB Vol. 2 A Terror of Dying. 19.95

DEVASTATOR
Image (B&W) April, 1998
1 JHl and Greg Horn 2.95
2 book 1, pt.2 . . . . 2.95
3 concl to book 1. . . . . 2.95

DIVINE RIGHT: THE ADVENTURES OF MAX FARADAY
Image/Wildstorm Sept., 1997
1 JLe,SW,Blaze of Glory 7.00
1a variant cover. 7.50
1b variant, signed 29.95
1c Voyager pollybaged pack 6.00
1d Spanish edition. 5.00
2 JLe,SW,Disco Inferno 4.00
2a variant (c). 5.00
3 JLe,SW,F:Christie Blaze,Enemies
of the State 4.00
4 JLe,SW,F:Lynch,The Love
Connection. 2.50
4a variant (c). 4.00
5 JLe,SW,V:Dominique Faust,Party
Crashers 2.50
6 JLe,SW,Truth or Consequences,
Susanna Chaste located. 2.50
7 JLe,SW,Into the Hollow Realm . . 2.50
8 JLe,SW,Tobru,V:Acheron 2.50
8a variant SW(c) 2.50
Preview edition, JLe(c) (1997) 5.00
TPB Collected Edition #1 . . . . 5.95
TPB Collected Edition #2 . . . . 5.95
Wildstorm/DC 1999
9 JLe,SWi,Final Stand in
Hollow Realm. 2.50
10 JLe,SWi, ... 2.50
11 JLe,SWi,Divine Intervention 2.50
12 JLe,SWi,Divine Intervention 2.50
Collected Ed.#3, rep.#5 & #6 . . . . . 6.00

DOOM'S IV
Image/Extreme 1994
1 I:Doom's IV 2.50
1a Variant(c) 2.50
2 MECH-MAX 2.50
2a variant cover. 2.50
3 Dr. Lychee, Brick 2.50
4 Dr. Lyche, Syber-idol 2.50
Sourcebook 2.50

DRACULA VS. ZORRO
Image (B&W) Sept., 1998
1 DMG,RM 2.95
2 DMG,RM, conclusion 2.95

DRAGON, THE
1 Rep. of Savage Dragon 0.99
2 Rep. of Savage Dragon 0.99

THE DRAGON: BLOOD AND GUTS
Image/Highbrow 1995
1 I:Grip 2.50
2 and 3 JPn,KIS. . . . . @2.50

DUNCAN'S KINGDOM
Image (B&W) October, 1999
1 by Gene Yang & Derek Kirk 2.95
2 . . . . 2.95

DUSTY STAR
Image (B&W) April, 1997
0 sci-fi,western,adventure 2.95
1 . . . . 2.95
2 . . . . 2.95
3 . . . . 2.95

DV8
Image/Wildstorm 1996
1 WEl(s),HuR,"Lust for Life". 4.00
1a JLe(c). 5.00
1b Kevin Nowlan(c) 4.00
2 WEl(s),HuR,Gen-active serial
killers,"Some Weird Sin" 3.00
3 WEl(s), Neighborhood Threat . . 2.50
4 WEl(s),HuR,Miss Drugstore 2.50
5 Ivana sends DV8 to Japan 2.50
6 idle hands are the devil's tools . . 2.50
7 WEl(s),"Shades". 2.50
8 HuR,Sublime, Evo & Frostbite
abandoned,"Three". 2.50
9 MHs,"Evolution" 2.50
10 MHs,"In Service to Nothing". . . . 2.50
11 MHs,F:Copycat,"Facets" 2.50
12 MHs,F:Freestyle,V:Sen.Killory . . 2.50
13 MHs,"The Sad Tales of
Senator Killory". 2.50

DV8 #1
© Wildstorm

14 MHs,TR,New Horizon,TR(c),
"Barely Legal". 2.50
14a TC(c). 2.50
14b Voyager bagged pack 3.50
15 MHs,F:Ivana Baiul,"Settling
Accounts". 2.50
16 MHs,V:Dominique Faust
"Intersection" 2.50
17 MHs,Gen-Passive 2.50
18 MHs,Team 7,A:Grifter,"Same as
It Ever Was" 2.50
19 MHs,First Mision,pt.1,"Larger
Concerns" 2.50
20 MHs,First Mision,pt.2,"Lounging
in the Ammo Dump" 2.50
21 MHs,First Mision,pt.3,V:Arthrax . 2.50
22 MHs,V:Copycat,"Choices" 2.50
22a variant(c) JMd(1:4). 2.50
23 MHs,F:Threshold,"Gone to
Ground" 2.50
24 MHs,F:Sublime,"Slip Stream,"
prologue. 2.50
25 MHs,Slipstream,pt.1. . . . . 2.50
DV8 Rave,preview (1996). 3.00
Ann.#1 "Head Trips" (1998) 3.00
Wildstorm/DC 1999
26 MHs,TVs, ... 2.50
27 MHs,TVs,V:Gen-Actives. 2.50
28 MHs,TVs,F:Evo 2.50
29 MHs,TVs, ... 2.50
30 MHs,TVs,Things Fall Apart,pt.1 . 2.50
31 MHs,TvS,Things Fall Apart,pt.2 . 2.50
32 MHs,TvS,Things Fall Apart,pt.3 . 2.50
Annual'99 Slipstream 3.50
#0 40-pages. 3.00

DV8 VS. BLACK OPS
Image/Wildstorm (Oct., 1997)
1 Techromis Design, pt.1 . . . . 2.50
2 Techromis Design, pt.2 . . . . 2.50
3 Techromis Design, pt.3 . . . . 2.50

ECHO
Image March, 2000
1 A Broken World 2.50
1a variant (c). 2.50
2 Sacrifices 2.50
2a variant PtL (c). 2.50
3 Deadly new echo 2.50
3a variant PtL (c). 2.50
4 PtL,Desperate Times 2.50
5 PtL,Welcoming Party 2.50

6 Conspiracy Theory 2.50
6a variant PtL(c) 2.50
7 Anarchy,pt.1 . . . . 2.50
#0 Thick as Thieves 2.50
#0a variant (c) 2.50
#1 Holochrome edition 6.95

ELEKTRA/CYBLADE
Image/Top Cow/Marvel 1997

1-shot "Devil's Reign" pt.7 (of 8) x-over 2.95

EMPIRE
Image May, 2000

1 MWa,BKi,F:Golgoth 2.50
2 MWa,BKi,F:Xanna 2.50
3 MWa,BKi,F:Lohkyn 2.50

ESPERS
Image April, 1997
(B&W) Vol. 3

1 JHI,A:Brian Marx,V:Architects . . . 2.95
1a 2nd printing 2.95
2 JHI, ... 2.95
3 JHI,Black Magic 2.95
4 JHI,Black Magic, concl. 2.95
5 JHI,two stories 2.95
6 JHI,F:Simon Ashley,Alan Black . . 2.95
7 JHI,Feel the Rapture. 2.95
8 JHI, trip to Hong Kong 2.95
9 JHI, V:Architects 2.95
TPB Undertow, rep.Halloween Comics series. 14.95
TPB Black Magic, rep.Vol.3,#1–4 . 14.95
TPB The Storm, rep.. . . . . 15.95
TPB Interface, rep.2nd series 15.95

E.V.E. PROTOMECHA
Image/Top Cow Feb., 2000

1 . . . . 2.50
1a variant JMd (c) 2.50
1b variant David Finch (c) 2.50
2 Gunner Unleashed 2.50
2a variant Michael Turner (c). 2.50
2b variant SPa (c) 2.50
3 . . . . 2.50
4 . . . . 2.50
5 . . . . 2.50
6 final judgment. 2.50

Exposure #2
© Image

[ADVENTURES OF] EVIL AND MALICE
Image June, 1999

1 by Jimmie Robinson 3.50
2 F:Max 2000 . . . . 3.50
3 V:Cold Heart & Le'Chef 3.50
4 final showdown. 3.50
TPB F:Evelyn & Malinda. 12.95

EXPOSURE
Image July, 1999

1 F:Shawna & Lisa 2.50
2 Mirrors to the Soul 2.50
2a alternate photo(c) (1:2) 2.50
3 . . . . 2.50
3a alternate photo(c) (1:2) 2.50
4 Spark-SpangledSee-ThroughGirl 2.50
4a alternate photo(c) (1:2) 2.50
Prelude 16-pg. 6.95
Prelude holo-foil 14.95

EXTREME ANTHOLOGY

1 . . . . 2.50

EXTREME CHRISTMAS SPECIAL

Various artists, new work 2.95

EXTREME DESTROYER
Image/Extreme 1996

1 prologue, x-over,bagged with card 2.50
2 epilogue, x-over 2.50

EXTREME HERO

1 . . . . 2.95

EXTREME PREJUDICE

0 Prelude to X-over 2.50

EXTREME SACRIFICE
Image/Extreme 1995

Prelude,x-over,pt.1, A:Everyone with trading card. 2.50
Epiloque, x-over,pt.8, conclusion with trading card. 2.50
TPB Rep. whole x-over series. . . . 16.95

EXTREME 3000

Prelude 2.50

EXTREME TOUR BOOK

Tour Book 1992 . . . . 3.00
Tour Book 1994 . . . . 25.00

EXTREMELY YOUNGBLOOD
Image/Extreme Sept., 1997

1 TBm&MBm(s). 3.50

EXTREME ZERO

0 RLd,CYp,ATi(i),I:Cybrid, Law & Order, Risk, Code 9, Lancers, Black Flag 2.75
0a Variant cover 2.75

FALLING MAN
Image (B&W) Dec., 1997

1 (of 3) BMC,PhH 2.95
2 thru 3 Floyd vs. Duncan . . . . . @2.95

Fathom #3
© Top Cow

FATHOM
Image/Top Cow 1998

1 by Michael Turner,F:Aspen 5.00
2 war beneath the waves. 3.50
3 Life changed forever. 3.50
4 Connection to water 3.00
5 Aspen's connection to water 2.50
6 Admiral's plans revealed. 2.50
7 finale, pt.1 . . . . 2.50
8 finale, pt.2 . . . . 2.50
9 finale, conclusion, end 2.50
10 Fathom returns 2.50
11 pt.2 . . . . 2.50
12 Tomb Raider & Witchblade x-over,pt.1 . . . . 2.50
12a variant (c) 2.50
13 x-over,pt.2 . . . . 2.50
13a variant (c) 2.50
14 Aspen & Vana, concl.. . . . . 2.50
14a variant (c) 2.50
#0 rep. new Mike Turner (c) 2.50
Spec. Swimsuit Ed.. . . . . 2.95
Fathom 2000 swimsuit calendar . . . 2.95
Fathom 2000 smimsuit Spec. 2.95
TPB Col.Ed.#1, rep.#1 . . . . 5.95
TPB Col.Ed.#2, rep.#2–#3 . . . . 5.95
TPB Col.Ed.#3, rep.#4–#5 . . . . 5.95
TPB Col.Ed.#4, rep.#6–#7 . . . . 5.95
TPB Col.Ed.#5, rep.#8–#9 . . . . 5.95
HC rep. #1–#9 . . . . 39.95
HC signed 99.95

FEAR EFFECT
Image/Top Cow March, 2000

1-shot MHw, video game tie-in . . . 2.95

F5
Image April, 2000

1 TnD,48-pg. 2.95
2 TnD,life or death. 2.50
3 TnD,. 2.50
4 TnD, betrayed 2.50
Preview Book, TnD,24-pg. 2.50

FIRE
Image (B&W) Dec., 1998

TPB International intelligence 9.95

FIRE FROM HEAVEN
Image/Wildstorm 1996

1 x-over,Chapter 1 . . . 3.50
2 x-over,Finale 2 . . . 2.50

FIRSTMAN
Image April, 1997

1 ASm,LukeHenry becomesApollo. 2.50

FOOT SOLDIERS, THE
Image (B&W) Sept., 1997
Prev. Dark Horse

1 by Jim Krueger, Graveyard of Forgotten Heroes . . . 2.95
2 Tragedy o/t Travesty Tapestry . . . 2.95
3 Arch enemies, pt.3 . . . 2.95
4 It's a Wicker World Afterall . . . 2.95
5 Loose Ends . . . 2.95

FOREVER AMBER
Image (B&W) July, 1999

1 by Don Hudson . . . 2.95
1a variant cover (1:2) . . . 2.95
2 Lady fights back . . . 2.95
3 Amber sent to jail . . . 2.25
4 Amber's revenge, concl. . . . 2.95

FREAK FORCE
Image/Highbrow 1993–95

1 EL(s),KG . . . 2.25
2 EL(s),KG . . . 2.25
3 EL(s),KG . . . 2.25
4 EL(s),KG,A:Vanguard . . . 2.25
5 EL(s),KG . . . 2.25
6 EL(s),KG . . . 2.25
7 EL(s),KG . . . 2.25
8 EL(s),space ants . . . 2.25
9 EL(s),Cyberforce . . . 2.25
10 EL(s),Savage Dragon . . . 2.25
11 EL(s),Invasion pt.1 . . . 2.50
12 EL(s),Invasion pt.2 . . . 2.50
13 EL(s),Invasion pt.3 . . . 2.50
14 EL(s),Team Defeated . . . 2.50
15 EL(s),F:Barbaric . . . 2.50
16 KG,EL(s),V:Chelsea Nirvana . . . 2.50
17 EL,KG,major plots converge . . . 2.50
18 Final Issue . . . 2.50
TPB 448pg . . . 29.95

Series Two
Image March, 1997

1 EL,Star joins team,V:The Frightening Force . . . 2.95
2 EL,Dart quits team . . . 2.95
3 EL,"Lo there shall come..an ending" . . . 2.95

FRIENDS OF MAXX
Image/I Before E

1 WML&SK . . . 2.95
2 MHs&SK . . . 2.95

GAMORRA SWIMSUIT SPECIAL
Image/Wildstorm 1996

Spec.#1 . . . 2.50

GAZILLION
Image Nov.,1998

1 HSm, Mars vs. Xof . . . 2.50
1a variant cover (1:4) . . . 2.50

GEAR STATION, THE
Image March, 2000

1 DaF,Dominion of Souls . . . 2.50
1a variant AxR (c) . . . 2.50
1b variant PtL (c) . . . 2.50
1c variant Michael Turner (c) . . . 2.50
2 DaF,23rd Gear . . . 2.50
2a variant AAd (c) . . . 2.50
3 DaF,Who is Fable . . . 2.50
4 DaF,first showdown . . . 2.50
5 DaF,Gear Station Prime . . . 2.50

GEEKSVILLE
Image (B&W) March, 2000

#0 by Rich Koslowski & Gary Sassaman . . . 2.75
1 Breaking into the Biz,pt.1 . . . 2.95
2 Breaking into the Biz,pt.2 . . . 2.95
3 Back to the Con . . . 2.95

GEMINAR
Image (B&W) June, 2000

1 . . . 3.50
2 F:Captain Champion . . . 3.50

GEN 13
Image/Wildstorm 1994

0 Individual Hero Stories . . . 4.00
1 JLe(s),BCi(s),I:Fairchild,Grunge, Freefall,Burnout . . . 20.00
1a 2nd printing . . . 4.00
2 JLe(s),BCi(s), . . . 16.00
3 JLe(s),BCi(s),A:Pitt,"Payback" . . . 10.00
4 JLe(s),BCi(s),"Free for All" . . . 8.00
5 Final issue . . . 5.00
5a WP variant cover . . . 10.00
TPB Gen13 Collected Edition . . . 12.95
HC 1,000 copies . . . 40.00

Regular Series 1995

1a BCi(s),V:Mercenaries . . . 5.00
1b Common Cover 2 . . . 5.00
1c Heavy Metal Gen . . . 10.00
1d Pulp Fiction Parody . . . 12.00
1e Gen 13 Bunch . . . 10.00
1f Lin-Gen-re . . . 12.00
1g Lil Gen 13 . . . 10.00
1h Friendly Neighbor Grunge . . . 10.00
1i Gen 13 Madison Ave . . . 12.00
1j Gen-Et Jackson . . . 10.00
1k Gen Dress Up cover . . . 10.00

Gen 13 #14 © Wildstorm

1l Verti-Gen . . . 10.00
1m Do It Yourself Cover . . . 10.00
2 BCi,BWS(c),WildStorm Rising, pt.4, w/2 cards . . . 3.00
2a Newstand Edition . . . 2.25
3 BCi,"Magical Mystery Tour" . . . 3.00
4 BCi,"Tourist Trap" . . . 2.50
5 BCi,I:New Member,"Family Feud" 2.50
6 BCi,JLe,I:The Deviants, "Roman Holiday" . . . 3.00
7 BCi,JLe,European Vacation,pt.2 "Veni, Vidi, Vici" . . . 3.00
8 BCi,"Bewitched,Bothered and Bewildered" . . . 2.50
9 . . . 2.50
10 Fire From Heaven, pt.3 . . . 2.50
11 Fire From Heaven, pt.9 . . . 2.50
12 F:Caitlin,her dad . . . 2.50
13 A, B & C, each . . . @1.30
14 "Higher Learning" . . . 2.50
15 Fraternity and Sorority rush . . . 2.50
16 . . . 2.50
17 BCi,JSC,AGo,battle royale in Tower of Luv,"Toy Soldiers" . . . 2.50
18 BCi,JSC,AGo,V:Keepers, "Hello & Good-Byes" . . . 2.50
19 BCi,JSC,AGo,Lynch & kids flee to Antarctica,"Bon Voyage" . . . 2.50
20 BCi,JSC,AGo,"To Boldly Go" . . . 2.50
21 BCi,JSC,AGo,V:D'Rahn,"Lost in Space" . . . 2.50
22 BCi,civil war,"Homecoming" . . . 2.50
23 BCi,21st century . . . 2.50
24 BCi,V:D'Rahn,"Judgment Day" . . 2.50
25 BCi,Homecoming,JsC(c) . . . 3.50
25a TC(c),"Where Angels Fear to Tread" . . . 3.50
25b Voyager bagged pack . . . 3.50
26 JAr,GFr,CaS,"When Worlds Collide" . . . 2.50
27 JAr,GFr,CaS,"Search & Seizure" 2.50
28 JAr,GFr,CaS,"Remote Control" . . 2.50
29 JAr,GFr,CaS,I:Tindalos, "A Firm Grip on Reality" . . . 2.50
30 JAr,GFr,CaS,"Stranger Than Fiction" . . . 2.50
31 JAr,GFr,CaS,Roxy's Big Score, "Paradigm Shift" . . . 2.50
32 JAr,GFr,CaS,"Red Skies at Morning" . . . 2.50
33 JAr,GFr,CaS,aftermaths, "Burning the Candle at Both Ends", with 8-page Planetary #0 . . . 2.50
34 JAr,GFr,CaS,AAd,A:Roxy & Sarah,"Overture" . . . 2.50
35 JAr,GFr,CaS,John Lynch resigns, "But You Can't Hide" . . . 2.50
36 JAr,GFr,CaS,F:John Lynch, "That Was Then" . . . 2.50
College Yearbook 1997, Superheroes at Large . . . 2.50
Ann. #1 WEl,SDi"London'sBrilliant" . 3.00
1-Shot Gen13:Unreal World (1996) . 3.00
Gen13 3-D Special (1997) . . . 5.00
3-D Spec. #1, (1997) . . . 5.00
3-D Spec. #1, variant cover . . . 5.00
3-D Spec. #1, (1998) . . . 5.00
TPB rep.1–#5 of original mini-series, 3rd printing . . . 12.95
TPB Lost in Paradise, rep. #3–#5 . . 6.95
TPB EuropeanVacation,rep.#6–#7 . 6.95
TPB rep. #13 A, B & C . . . 6.95
TPB Ordinary Heroes . . . 12.95
TPB Wildstorm Archives, rep. mini-series, #0–#13, covers, etc. . . 13.00

Wildstorm/DC 1999

37 JAr,GFr,CaS,Reaper . . . 2.50
38 JAr,GFr,CaS,BU:Grunge . . . 2.50
38a variant cover . . . 2.50
39 JAr,GFr,CaS,Genocide . . . 2.50
40 JAr,GFr,CaS,V:Reaper . . . 2.50

Gen 13 #36 © Wildstorm

41 JAr,GFr,CaS, ... 2.50
42 JoC(s),KM,pro wrestlers. 2.50
43 AWa(s&c),F:Fairchild 2.50
44 AWa(s&c),A:Mr.Magestic 2.50
45 SLo,EBe,JSb,fashion show 2.50
46 SLo,EBe,JSb,MightyJoeGrunge . 2.50
47 SLo,EBe,JSb 2.50
48 SLo,EBe,JSb 2.50
49 SLo,EBe,JSb 2.50
50 SLo,EBe,JSb,48-pg. 3.95
50a variant JLe,SW (c) (1:4) 3.95
51 SLo,breather 2.50
52 SLo,F:Caitlin Fairchild 2.50
53 F:all Villains issue 2.50
54 SLo,EBe,SWi,F:Fairchild 2.50
55 EBe,Return to Pod 9,pt.2 . . . . . . 2.50
56 EBe,Fairchild,pt.3 . . . . 2.50
57 BRa,EBe,Tokyo in danger 2.50
58 BRa,EBe,mini-monster massacre 2.50
Annual'99 JAr(s). 3.50
TPB Gen13 . . . . 13.00
Spec. Wired 2.50
GN Grunge Saves the World 6.00
GN Bootleg: Grunge— The Movie. 10.00
Spec. 1-shot Going West 2.50
TPB Interactive Plus 12.00
TPB Starting Over 15.00
Spec.#1 3-D AAd 4.95
Spec.#1a variant (c) 4.95
Spec. Carny Folk 3.50
Ann. 2000 #1, Devil's Night x-over, pt.1 . . . . 3.50
TPB I Love New York 9.95
TPB We'll Take Manhattan 14.95

GEN 13 BOOTLEG
Image/Wildstorm Nov., 1996

1 MFm&AD,lost in the "Linquist Fault," pt.1 . . . . 2.50
1a signed 15.00
2 "Linquist Fault,"pt.2. . . . . 3.50
3 Gen13 Fairy Tale 3.50
4 WS&LSi,F:Valaria,"Little Girl Lost" 3.50
5 F:Fairchild,"Timesick,"pt.1. . . . . . 3.50
6 F:Fairchild,"Timesick,"pt.2. . . . . . 3.50
7 "Renaissance Ruckus" 3.50
8 AWa,"Grunge's Movie,"pt.1 . . . . . 2.50
9 AWa,"Grunge's Movie,"pt.2 . . . . . 2.50
10 AWa,"Grunge's Movie,"pt.3 . . . . 2.50
11 AaL,WS,Chupacabra,pt.1. . . . . . 2.50
12 AaL,WS,Chupacabra,pt.2. . . . . . 2.50
13 F:Grunge,"The Trickster" 2.50
14 JMi,JoP,GL,bad neighbors 2.50
15 KNo,V:Trance,"Hanging,"pt.1 . . . 2.50
16 KNo,V:Trance,"Hanging,"pt.2 . . . 2.50
17 "Virgil Chu's Reality 2.50
18 MFm,"A Day at the Beach" 2.50
19 BKs,JhB,Satyr 2.50
20 CAd,F:John Lynch,"Numbskulls" 2.50
Ann.#1 WEI,SDi, to NYC 2.95
TPB Grunge: The Movie,AWa 9.95
TPB Vol.1, rep.#1–#4 . . . . 11.95

GEN 13: INTERACTIVE
Image/Wildstorm Oct., 1997

1 vote via internet 4.00
2 MHs,vote via internet 3.00
3 MHs,conclusion 3.00
TPB Gen13 Interactive Plus, rep. . 11.95

GEN 13/ GENERATION X
Image/Wildstorm July, 1997

1 BCi&AAd,"Generation Gap" 3.00
1 variant cover by JSC 3.00
3-D Edition, with glasses 4.95
3-Da variant cover, with glasses . . . 4.95

GEN 13: MAGICAL DRAMA QUEEN ROXY
Image/Wildstorm Oct., 1998

1 (of 3) AWa,Mall of Doom. 4.00
2 AWa,V:Caitlin 4.00
3 AWa,dream sequence concl. . . . 4.00

GEN 13/THE MAXX
Image/Wildstorm 1995

Spec.#1 BML,x-over 4.00

GEN 13/MONKEY MAN & O'BRIEN
Image/Wildstorm June, 1998

1 (of 2) AAd. 2.50
1a chromium edition 4.50
2 AAd,alternate universe, concl.. . . 2.50
2a variant AAd(c). 2.50

GEN 13: ORDINARY HEROES
Image/Wildstorm 1996

1 . . . . 2.50
2 . . . . 2.50

GEN 12
Image/Wildstorm Feb., 1998

1 BCi,Team 7 tie-in,"The Legacy". . 2.50
2 BCi,F:Morgan of I.O.. . . . . 2.50
3 BCi,Dominique Faust 2.50
4 BCi,F:Miles Craven. 2.50
5 BCi,Team 7 re-unites 2.50

GLORY
Image/Extreme 1995

0 JDy 2.50
1 JDy,F:Glory 4.00
1a variant cover. 4.00
2 JDy,V:Demon Father. 3.00
3 JDy,A:Rumble & Vandal 2.50
4 Vandal vs. Demon Horde 2.50
4a JDy variant cover 3.00

Glory #3
© Extreme Studios

5 Supreme Apocalypse,pt.3, F:Vandal. 2.50
6 Drug Problem 2.50
7 F:Superpatriot. 2.50
8 Extreme Babewatch 2.50
9 Extreme Destroyer,pt.5 x-over, bagged with card 2.50
10 . . . . 2.50
11 . . . . 2.50
12 JDy, EBe & JSb. 3.50
13 JDy, EBe & JSb. 2.50
14 JDy, EBe & JSb. 2.50
15 JDy, EBe & JSb, Out for vengeance 2.50
continued: see Color Comics section
TPB Rep.#1-#4. . . . . 9.95

GLORY/ANGELA ANGELS IN HELL
Image/Extreme 1996

1 . . . . 4.00

GLORY/AVENGELYNE
Image/Extreme 1996

1 V:B'lial,I:Faith 4.00
1a no chrome (c). 3.00

GLORY/AVENGELYNE: THE GODYSSEY
Image/Extreme

1 RLd & JDy 3.00
1a photo (c). 4.00

GLORY/CELESTINE: DARK ANGEL
Image/Extreme Sept., 1996

1 (of 3) JDy,PtL,sequel to Rage of Angels, A:Maximage. 2.50
2 JDy,PtL,"Doomsday+1". 2.50
3 JDy,PtL, conclusion 2.50

GLORY & FRIENDS
Image/Extreme 1995

Bikini Fest #1 . . . . 2.50
Bikini Fest #2 . . . . 2.50
Lingerie Special #1 (1995) 3.00
Christmas Special #1 (1995). 2.50

IMAGE

GO GIRL!
Image August, 2000

1 TrR,F:Lindsay Goldman 2.50

GOLDFISH
Image (B&W) 1998

TPB by Brian Michael Bendis 16.95

GREASE MONKEY
Image March, 1998

1 TEI. 2.95
2 TEI. 2.95
3 TEI, The Calling; Rewards 2.95

GRIFTER
Image/Wildstorm 1995–96

1 BWS(c), WildStorm Rising,pt.5,w/2 cards 2.50
1a Newsstand Ed. 1.95
2 V:Diabolik,pt.1 . . . . 2.50
3 V:Diabolik,pt.2 . . . . 2.50
4 R:Forgotten Hero 2.50
5 Rampage of a Fallen Hero 2.50
6 V:Poerhouse. 2.50
7 City of Angels,pt.1 . . . . 2.50
8 City of Angels,pt.2 . . . . 2.50
9 City of Angels,pt.3 . . . . 2.50
10 City of Angels,pt.4 . . . . 2.50

GRIFTER/BADROCK
Image/Extreme 1995

1 To Save Badrock's Mom 3.00
1a Variant cover 2.50
2 flip-book-Badrock #2. . . . . 3.00
3 double size. 3.50

GRIFTER ONE-SHOT
Image/Wildstorm 1995

1 SS,DN 4.00

GRIFTER
Image/Wildstorm 1996

1 StG 4.00
2 StG,V:Joe the Dead 3.00
3 StG,captured by MadJackPower. 3.00
4 StG,vs. Condition Red 2.50
5 StG,Grifter meets his dad, F:Molly Ingram 2.50
6 StG,A:Santini 2.50
7 StG,MtB,I:Charlatan 2.50
8 StG,MtB,Zealot disappears,V:Soldier. 2.50
9 StG,Zealot captured?, secret history of Quiet Men 2.50
10 StG,Grifter & Soldier go to rescue Zealot 2.50
11 StG, renegade former agent. . . . 2.50
12 StG,"Who is Tanager?" 2.50
13 StG,F:Condition Red,"Family Feud" 2.50
14 StG,V:Joe the Dead. 2.50

GRIFTER/SHI
Image/Wildstorm 1996

1 BCi,JLe,TC. 3.00
2 BCi,JLe,TC. 3.00
HC 29.95
HC signed & numbered(Lee) 50.00
HC signed & numbered(Tucci) . . . 50.00
HC signed & numbered(Charest) . 35.00
HC signed & numbered(Hubbs) . . 25.00

GROO
Image 1994–95

1 SA 2.25
2 A:Arba, Dakarba. 2.00
3 The Generals Hat. 2.00
4 A Drink of Water. 2.00
5 SA,A Simple Invasion. 2.00
6 SA,A Little Invention 2.00
7 The Plight of the Drazils 2.00
8 . . . . 2.25
9 I:Arfetto 2.25
10 The Sinkes 2.25
11 The Gamblers 2.25
12 . . . . 2.25

HAWKSHAWS
Image March, 2000

1 by Dietrich Smith 2.95
1a variant movie poster (c) 2.95
2 . . . . 2.95
3 . . . . 2.95

Hazard #4 © Wildstorm

HAZARD
Image/Wildstorm 1996

1 JMi,RMr 2.50
2 JMi,RMr 1.75
3 JMi,RMr 1.75
4 JMi,RMr 1.75
5 JMi,RMr,Hazard finds Dr. D'Oro . 1.75
6 JMi,RMr 2.25
7 JMi,RMr,Hazard meets Prism . . . 2.25

HEADHUNTERS
Image (B&W) April, 1997

1 ChM,V:Army of Wrath. 2.95
2 ChM,V:undead militia 2.95
3 ChM,"Slaughterground" 2.95

HEARTBREAKERS
Image July, 1998
Superdigest, 6"x9"

1 B&W and color 104pg. 9.95

HEARTBREAKERS VERSUS BIOVOC
Image

TPB "Bust Out". 9.95

TPB PGn 14.95

HELLCOP
Image/Avalon Oct., 1998

1 JoC,F:Virgil Hilts. 2.50
2 JoC,It's a small underwold after all. 2.50
3 JoC,new circles of Hell 2.50
4 JoC,secrets of Hell revealed. . . . 2.50
5 JoC,Hell & High Water 2.50
5a variant cover. 2.95

HELLHOLE
Image/Top Cow May 1999

1 SLo,AdP,F:Michael Cabrini 2.50
2 SLo,AdP,The Devil's Candy 2.50
3 SLo,AdP,power brokers 2.50

HELLSHOCK
Image 1994

1 I:Hellshock 3.50
2 Powers & Origin 3.50
3 New foe 3.50
4 . . . . 3.50

HELLSHOCK
Image Jan., 1997

1 JaL,Something wrong with Daniel, 48pg. 3.00
2 JaL,Daniel learns to control powers. 2.50
3 JaL,Daniel free of madness 2.50
4 JaL,Daniel searches for his mother, Jonakand plans escape from Hell 2.50
5 JaL,Jonakand and fallen angels tear hell apart. 2.50
6 JaL,"The Milk of Paradise" 2.50
7 JaL,"A Mother's Story", double size. 3.95
8 JaL,House of Torture 2.50

HELLSPAWN
Image/TMP July, 2000

1 The Clown,pt.1 . . . . 2.50
2 The Clown,pt.2 . . . . 2.50
3 Hate Me 2.50

HOMAGE STUDIOS

Swimsuit Spec.#1 JLe,WPo, MS. . . 2.25

HONG ON THE RANGE
Image/Matinee Entertainment/Flypaper

1 (of 3) by William Wu & Jeff Lafferty. 2.50
2 in Washout 2.50
3 Duke Goslin 2.50
TPB Hong on the Range. 12.95

IMAGE ZERO
Image 1993

0 I:Troll,Deathtrap,Pin-ups,rep. Savage Dragon #4,O:Stryker, F:ShadowHawk 15.00

IMAGES OF SHADOWHAWK
Image 1993–94

1 KG,V:Trencher 2.25
2 thru 3 V:Trencher 2.25

IMAGE

Immortal Two #1
© Image

IMMORTAL TWO
Image May, 1997
(B&W) Half-Tone

1 MsM,F:Gaijin & Gabrielle 2.50
2 MsM. 2.50
3 MsM. 2.50
4 MsM,V:Okami Red 2.50
5 MsM,new drug epidemic. 2.50
6 MsM,First Order, cont. 2.50
7 MsM,vs. impossible odds 2.50
7 MsM,flip photo cover 2.50

INTRIGUE
Image Aug., 1999

1 F:Kirk Best 2.50
1a variant cover (1:4). 2.50
2 on the run from the law. 2.50
3 V:NYPD SWAT team 2.50
3a variant HuR cover (1:4). 2.50
4 . . . . 2.50
5 . . . . 2.95
5a variant Mike Wieringo (c) 2.95

INVISIBLE 9
Image/Flypaper

TPB 12.95

IRON WINGS
Image March, 2000

1 Legends of Iron Wings 2.50
1a variant Andy Park (c) 2.50
2 V:Amaxius 2.50
3 Nightmares. 2.50

JACKIE CHAN'S SPARTAN X
Image (B&W) March, 1998

1 MGo,RM,Hell-Bent Hero for Hire. 2.95
2 MGo,to Russia 2.95
3 MGo,V:Kenshi 2.95
4 MGo,RM, in Istanbul. 2.95
5 MGo,RM, Mind of God 2.95
5a MGo,RM, photo cover 2.95
6 MGo,RM, The Armor of Heaven . 2.95
6a MGo,RM, photo cover. 2.95

Jackie Chan's Spartan X #1
© Image

JADE WARRIORS
Image Aug., 1999

1 MD2,Destruction of Japan 2.50
1a variant photo cover (1:2). 2.50
2 MD2,V:Ramthar 2.50
2a photo(c) 2.50
3 MD2,Blood of the Children 2.50
3a photo(c) 2.50
3b movie poster style (c) 2.50

JINN
Image Jan., 2000

1 F:Karen Lane 2.95
1a variant WPo (c) (1:4) 2.95
2 . . . . 2.95
2a variant cover. 2.95
3 . . . . 2.95

JINX
Image (B&W) June, 1997

1 by Brian Michael Bendis 2.95
1a 2nd printing 2.95
2 F:Jinx, female bounty hunter. . . . 2.95
3 thru 5 . . . . @3.95
TPB rep. prev. #1–#4 . . . . 9.95
TPB The Essential Collection 17.95
Spec.#1 Buried Treasure 3.95
Spec.#1 True Crime Confessions . . 3.95

JINX: TORSO
Image (B&W) Aug., 1998

1 by Brian Michael Bendis, 48pg . . 3.95
2 search continues 3.95
3 Torso Killer 3.95
4 breaking the law. 3.95
5 48-page 4.95
6 conclusion, 48-page 4.95
Spec. #@%!! short stories 3.95

JOURNEYMAN
Image Aug., 1999

1 by Brandon McKinney. 2.95
2 enemies become allies 2.95
3 V:Dragon King 2.95

J.U.D.G.E.
Image March, 2000

1 by Greg Horn,F:Victoria Grace . . 2.95
1a variant cover. 2.95

2 V:John Lawson. 2.95
3 Secret Rage,pt.3 . . . . 2.95

KABUKI
Image Sept., 1997

1 DMk,O:Kabuki 6.00
1a variant JSo(c). 7.00
2 DMk,O:Kabuki, pg.2 . . . . 5.00
3 DMk,surprise visitor 5.00
4 DMk,Akemi, romance 4.00
5 DMk,action. 4.00
6 DMk 3.00
7 DMk 3.00
7a DMk variant cover (1:2) 3.00
8 DMk, ... 3.00
9 DMk, finale. 3.00
TPB Circle of Blood,rep. orig. series plus "Fear the Reaper," B&W . 17.95
HC Circle of Blood 29.95
HC Circle of Blood, S&N. 49.95
TPB Dreams. 10.00
TPB Masks of the Noh 10.95
TPB Masks of the Noh, 2nd pr. . . . 12.95
HC Masks of the Noh 39.95
TPB Skin Deep. 9.95
HC Skin Deep 23.95
HC Skin Deep, sign & num. 39.95
TPB 2nd pr. Skin Deep 10.95
TPB Images, part rep. #1, 48pg. . . . 4.95
Reflections #1, 48pg. 4.95
Reflections #2 art & stories. 4.95
Spec. #2 Images, rep. #2 & #3 . . . . 5.95
HC Metamorphosis,rep.#1–#9. . . . 49.95
HC Metamorphosis,lim. ed.,signed 79.95

KABUKI AGENTS
Image (B&W) Aug., 1999

1 DMk,F:Scarab 3.00
2 DMk,F:Scarab, Tiger Lily 3.00
3 DMk,F:Scarab, Tiger Lily 3.00
4 DMk,F:Scarab, Tiger Lily 3.00
Artbook 4.95

KABUKI CLASSICS
Image

1 Fear the Reaper, rep. 3.95
2 Dance of Death 2.95
3 Circle of Blood, act 1, 48-page . . 3.95
4 Circle of Blood, act 2 . . . . 2.95
5 Circle of Blood, act 3 . . . . 2.95
6 Circle of Blood, act 4 . . . . 2.95
7 Circle of Blood, act 5 . . . . 2.95
8 Circle of Blood, conclusion 2.95
9 Masks of the Noh, Act 1 . . . . 3.25
10 Masks of the Noh, Act 2. . . . . . . 3.25
11 Masks of the Noh, Act 3. . . . . . . 3.25
12 Masks of the Noh, concl. 3.25

KID SUPREME
Image/Supreme 1996–97

1 & 2. . . . . 2.50
3 DaF,ErS 2.50
4 DaF,ErS,Party time. 2.50
5 DaF,ErS,"Birds of a Feather". . . . 2.50
6 DaF,ErS,I: The Sensational Spinner 2.50
7 DaF,ErS,Everything falls apart . . 2.50

KID TERRIFIC
Image (B&W) Nov., 1998

1 A:Snedak & Manny Stellar 2.95

KILLER INSTINCT TOUR BOOK

1 All Homage Artist,I:Crusade 5.00

1a signed 45.00

KILLRAZOR SPECIAL

1 O:Killrazor 2.50

KINDRED

Image/Wildstorm 1994

1 JLe,BCi(s),BBh,I:Knidred 5.00
2 JLe,BCi(s),BBh,V:Kindred. 3.50
3 JLe,BCi(s),BBh,V:Kindred. 3.00
3a WPo(c),Alternate(c) 6.00
4 JLe,BCi(s),BBh,V:Kindred. 3.00
TPB rep. #1-#4. . . . . 9.95

KIN

Image/Top Cow Feb. 2000

1 GFr,Neanderthal. 2.95
2 GFr,F:McLoon 2.95
3 GFr,Alaska revenge 2.95
4 GFr, ... 2.95
5 GFr,Born Free 2.95
6 GFr,40-pg.,The End? 3.95
6a variant AAd (c) 3.95

'KINI

Image/Flypaper Feb., 1999

1 KK,BKs,F:Kim Walters 2.50

KISS: THE PSYCHO CIRCUS

Image/TMP July, 1997

1 SvG,AMe 8.00
2 AMe, unearthly origins 6.00
3 AMe, Judgment o/t Elementals . . 5.00
4 AMe,Smoke and Mirrors, pt.1 . . . 4.00
5 AMe,Smoke and Mirrors, pt.2 . . . 3.00
6 AMe,Smoke and Mirrors, concl. . 3.00
7 AMe,Creatures of the Night 3.00
8 AMe,Forever 3.00
9 AMe,Four Sides to Every Story. . 2.50
10 AMe,Destroyer, pt.1. . . . . 2.50
11 AMe,Destroyer, pt.2 . . . . 2.50
12 AMe,Destroyer, pt.3 (of 4) 2.50
13 AMe, Destroyer, pt.4 . . . . 2.50
14 AMe, in Feudal Japan 2.50
15 AMe, in Feudal Japan, choices . 2.25
16 AMe, Ticket for Terror 2.25
17 AMe, World Without Heroes,pt.2 2.25
18 AMe, Sunburst Finish 2.25
19 Fate of the Psycho Circus 2.25
20 Mr. Makebelieve 2.25
21 Don't Talk to Strangers 2.25
22 Twin sisters 2.25
23 Tribunal of souls 2.25
24 Cat's Eye. 2.25
25 . . . . 2.25
26 Nightingale's Song, pt.1 . . . . 2.25
27 Nightingale's Song, pt.2. . . . . . . 2.25
28 Perdition Blues 2.25
29 Shadow of the Moon, pt.1 . . . . . 2.25
30 Shadow of the Moon, pt.2 . . . . . 2.50
31 Sins of Omission 2.50
32 Gallery of God's Mistakes 2.50
33 Gallery of God's Mistakes,pt.2 . . 2.50
34 Far Corners of Night 2.50
TPB Vol. I, rep. #1–#6 . . . . 12.95
TPB Vol. II rep. #10–#13. . . . . 9.95
TPB Vol.3 Whispered Scream. 9.95
Kiss Mag.#5 rep. 4.95

KNIGHTMARE

Image/Extreme 1995

0 O:Knightmare 2.50
1 I:Knightmare MMy 2.50
2 I:Caine 2.50
3 RLd,AV,The New Order,
F:Detective Murtaugh 2.50
4 RLd,AV,MMy,I:Thrillkill. 2.50
5 V:Thrillkill 2.50
6 Extreme Babewatch 2.50
7 . . . . 2.50
8 I:Acid 2.50

KNIGHTSTRIKE

Image/Extreme 1996

1 Extreme Destroyer, pt.6
x-over, bagged with card 2.50

KNIGHT WATCHMAN

Image (B&W) May, 1998

1 by Gary Carlson & Chris Ecker . . 2.95
2 Graveyard Shift, pt.2. . . . . 2.95
3 Graveyard Shift, pt.3. . . . . 2.95
4 Graveyard Shift, concl. 2.95

KOSMIC KAT

Image July, 1999

Activity Book. 2.95

KURT BUSIEK'S ASTRO CITY

Image/Juke Box 1995–96

1 I:Samaritan,"In Dreams" 11.00
1a 2nd printing 2.00
2 I:Silver Agent,V:Shirak
the Devourer 6.00
3 F:Jack in the Box 5.00
4 I:Hanged Man,Safeguards 7.00
5 I:Crackerjack 7.00
6 O:Samaritan,F:Winged Victory . . 7.00
TPB 19.95
HC 39.95

Homage Comics 1996–97 Vol. 2

½ F:Hanged Man (1996) 5.00
1 KBk(s),BA,Welcome to
Astro City 6.00
1a Trunk(c) 8.00
1b 2nd printing 2.50
2 KBk(s),BA,O:First Family,
F:Astra, Everyday Life 6.00
2b 2nd printing 2.50
3 KBk(s),BA,Adventures in
Other Worlds 5.00

Kurt Busiek's Astro City, Vol. 2, #1
© *Homage*

Image/Homage Comics

4 KBk,BA,Teenager seeks to
become teen sidekick,pt.1 (of 6) 5.00
5 Learning the Game. 5.00
6 V: creatures of Shadow Hill. 5.00
7 Aliens invade Astro City 3.00
8 The aliens are out there 2.50
9 Honor Guard vs. Aliens finale . . . 2.50
10 meet the junkman 2.50
11 Serpent's Teeth 2.50
12 F:Jack-In-The-Box 2.50
13 F:Looney Leo 2.50
14 F:Steeljack 2.50
15 F:supervillains 2.50
16 F:El Hombre 2.50
17 F:Steeljack, staying straight 2.50
TPB Confession, rep.#4–#9 . . . . . 19.95
HC Confession 50.00
3-D #1 . . . . 4.95
TPB Life in the Big City. 19.95
HC Life in the Big City 34.95
TPB Family Album 19.95
HC Family Album 49.95

Homage/DC 1999 VOLUME 2

16 KBk(s), El Hombre. 2.50
17 KBk(s), Mock Turtle 2.50
18 KBk(s), F:Steeljack 2.50
19 KBk(s), F:Steeljack 2.50
20 KBk(s). 2.50
21 KBk(s),F:Crackerjack. 2.50
22 KBk(s),F:Samaritan 2.50
Spec.1/2 KBk(s) 2.50
HC Family Album 29.95
HC Life in the Big City 29.95
HC The Tarnished Angel. 29.95

LABMAN

1 . . . . 3.50
1a variant cover. 3.50
2 and 3 . . . . @2.95

LADY PENDRAGON

Image Nov., 1998

1 MHw,Destiny's Embrace 2.50
1a remastered, new cover 2.50
1b Dynamic Forces variant cover. . 6.95
1c JeL (c) glow-in-the-dark 19.95
1d Tour Edition . . . . ??.00
2 MHw,Destiny's Embrace,pt.2 . . . 2.50
3 MHw,Destiny's Embrace,pt.3 . . . 2.50
3a variant cover (1:4). 2.50
0 MHw, Secrets & Origins 2.50
0a Eurosketch cover 10.00
Preview (Wizard, Chicago Comicon)4.95

LADY PENDRAGON: DRAGON BLADE

Image April, 1999

1 MHw,Merlin trains Jennifer 2.50
1a variant cover (1:4). 2.50
1b Chrome Edition. . . . . ??.00
2 MHw,F:Morgana 2.50
2a variant cover (1:4). 2.50
3 MHw,B.U.I:Alley Cat 2.50
4 MHw,Morgana returns 2.50
5 MHw,Spear of Destiny 2.50
6 MHw,Jennifer Drake resigns, . . . 2.50
7 MHw,Future Prophecy, pt.1. . . . . 2.50
8 MHw,Future Prophecy, pt.2. . . . . 2.50
9 MHw,Future Prophecy, pt.3. . . . . 2.50
10 MHw,Messianic Lineage,pt.1 . . . 2.50
11 MHw,Messianic Lineage,pt.2 . . . 2.50
12 MHw,Messianic Lineage,pt.3 . . . 2.50
1a Glow-in-the-dark JaL (c) . . . .
Gallery Ed.#1 . . . . 2.95
Gallery Ed.#1a photo(c) 2.95

IMAGE

LADY PENDRAGON: MORE THAN MORTAL
Image May, 1999

1 MHw,Pendragon vs. Protector. . . 2.50
1a variant cover (1:4). 6.95
1b Gold foil (c). 6.95

Lady Supreme #2
© Extreme

LADY SUPREME
Image/Extreme 1996

1 TMr 2.50
2 TMr,Die & Let Die,pt.2 . . . . 2.50
3 TMr,V:Manassa 2.50
4 TMr,"Lady Supreme goes undercover" 2.50

LEAVE IT TO CHANCE
Homage Comics 1996–98

1 JeR,PS,I:Chance Falconer 2.50
2 JeR,PS,Dragons are a Girl's Best Friend 2.50

Image/Homage Comics

3 JeR,PS,Chance and St. George race against time 2.50
4 JeR,PS, ... 2.50
5 JeR,PS,"Trick or Threat" 2.50
6 JeR,PS,"The Return of Cap'n Hitch". 2.50
7 JeR,PS,"And Not a Drop to Drink". 2.50
8 JeR,PS,"The Phantom of the Mall". 2.50
9 JeR,PS,"Midnite Monster Madness". 2.50
10 JeR,PS,"Destroy All Monsters". . 2.50
11 JeR,PS,"Dead Men Can't Skate" 2.50
12 JeR,PS,visits her friend Dash. . . 2.50
TPB rep. #1–#4 . . . . 9.95
TPB Vol. II, rep. #5–#8 . . . . 12.95
HC Shaman's Rain 24.95
HC Shaman's Rain, signed 34.95

Homage/DC 1999

12 JeR(s),F:Dash 3.00
TPB Trick or Threat 12.95

LEGEND OF SUPREME

1 KG(s),JJ,DPs,Revelations pt.1 . . 2.50
2 Revelations pt.2 . . . . 2.50
3 Conclusion 2.50

LETHAL
Image 1996

1 and 2 . . . . @2.50

LITTLE-GREYMAN
Image (B&W)

TPB by C. Scott Morse 6.95

LITTLE RED HOT: CHANE OF FOOLS
Image (B&W) Feb., 1999

1 (of 3) by Dawn Brown, F:Chane . 2.95
2 stranded in desert. 2.95
3 Heaven vs. Hell 2.95
TPB The Foolish Collection, rep.. . 12.95

LOST ONES, THE
Image March, 2000

1 by Ken Penders 2.95
2 . . . . 2.95

LYNCH
Image/Wildstorm June, 1997

1 TVs,"Terror in the Jungle" 2.50

MAGDALENA
Image/Top Cow March, 2000

1 JBz,Darkness spin-off. 2.50
1a variant MS (c). 2.50
1b variant Michael Turner (c) 2.50
2 JBz,secret revealed 2.50
3 JBz,Blood Divine, pt.3. . . . . 2.50

MAGDALENA/ BLOOD LEGACY
Image/Top Cow June, 2000

Preview 22-pg. . . . .

MAGE: THE HERO DEFINED
Image 1997

1 MWg,F:Kevin Matchstick 5.00
2 MWg,Kirby Hero, V:harpies. 4.00
3 MWg,Isis, Gretch 3.00
4 MWg,Isis, drug 3.00
5 MWg,into Canada. 3.00
6 MWg,V:Dragonslayer 2.50
7 MWg, ... 2.50
8 MWg,V:Red Caps. 2.50
9 MWg,Sibling Trio 2.50
10 MWg,enchanted by a succubus . 2.50
11 MWg,Joe Phat, missing 2.50
12 MWg,Pale Incanter's Lair. 2.50
13 MWg,What color is magic 2.50
14 MWg,Man Mountain of???? 2.50
15 MWg, 48-pg. concl. 5.95
Spec. 3-D #1 (1998). 4.95
TPB Vol. 1 rep.. . . . . 9.95
TPB Vol. II, rep. #5–#8 . . . . 9.95
TPB Vol. 3, rep. #9–#12 . . . . 12.95
Coll.Ed.Vol.1,rep.#1–#2 . . . . 5.95
Coll.Ed.Vol.2,rep.#3–#4 . . . . 5.95
Coll.Ed.Vol.3,rep.#5–#6 . . . . 5.95
Coll.Ed.Vol.4,rep.#7–#8 . . . . 4.95
Coll.Ed.Vol.5,rep.#9–#10 . . . . 4.95
Coll.Ed.Vol.6,rep.#11–#12. . . . . 4.95
Coll.Ed.Vol.7,rep.#13–#14 . . . . 5.50
Coll.Ed.Vol.8,rep.#15–#16 . . . . 4.95

MAN AGAINST TIME
Image/Motown 1996

1 "Every Hero". 2.50

2 . . . . 2.50
3 "Pro Patria Mori". 2.50

MARS ATTACKS
Image 1996

1 KG,BSz(of 4) 2.50
2 . . . . 2.50
3 . . . . 2.50
4 End of their world as they knew it 2.50

MASK OF ZORRO, THE
Image July, 1998

1 (of 4) DMG,RoW,RM,MGo(c), movie adapt. 2.95
2 DMG,RoW,RM,MGo(c) 2.95
3 DMG,RoW,MGo(c) 2.95
4 DMG,RoW,MGo concl. 2.95
4a photo cover 2.95

MAXIMAGE
Image/Extreme 1995–96

1 RLe(c) 2.50
2 Extreme Destroyer,pt.2, x-over, bagged with card 2.50
3 . . . . 2.50
4 A:Angela,Glory 2.50
5 . . . . 2.50
6 . . . . 2.50
7 . . . . 2.50
8 . . . . 2.50
9 BML, Sex Slaves of Bomba Island. 2.50
10 BML, The King of Emotion is back. 2.50

MAXX, THE
Image 1993

1/2 SK,from Wizard 7.00
1 SK,I:The Maxx 4.00
1a glow in the dark(c) 12.00
2 SK,V:Mr.Gone 4.00
3 SK,V:Mr.Gone 4.00
4 SK,. 4.00
5 SK,. 3.00
6 SK,. 3.00
7 SK,A:Pitt. 3.50
8 SK,V:Pitt. 3.50
9 SK 3.00
10 SK. 3.00

The Maxx #22
© Sam Keith

11 SK 2.50
12 SK 2.50
13 Maxx Wanders in Dreams 2.50
14 R:Julie 2.50
15 Julia's Pregnant 2.50
16 SK,Is Maxx in Danger? 2.50
17 SK,Gardener Maxx 2.25
18 SK,"Beware The Hooley" 1.95
19 SK,V:Hooley,"Last Fairy Tale". . . 1.95
20 SK,Questions are answered. . . . 2.25
21 AM(s),SK. 1.95
22 SK,"Other Peoples' Crap" 1.95
23 SK,"Having to Believe". 1.95
24 SK. 1.95
25 SK,"Lost and Found" 1.95
26 SK. 1.95
27 V:Iago the Killer Slug 1.95
28 Sara and Norberg look for Julie . 1.95
29 Sara and Gone defeat Iago the Slug 1.95
30 Lil' Sara faces her fears 1.95
31 F:The Library girl 1.95
32 F:The Library girl,pt.2. . . . . 1.95
33 Sara's back 1.95
34 Mark and Julia. 1.95
35 who knows? 1.95
36 bumfuzzled 1.95
37 Megan's story concl 1.95
38 Mark,Julie,Larry, pt.1 (of 4) 1.95
Spec. Friends of Maxx,F:Dude Japan. 2.95
The Maxx 3-D #1 . . . . 5.00
TPB Rep. #1-#5 . . . . 12.95
TPB Vol. 2 . . . . 12.95

MECHANIC, THE

Image/Homage Aug., 1998

GN JCh,JPe,time travel 5.95

MEDIEVAL SPAWN/ WITCHBLADE

1 . . . . 11.00
2 . . . . 9.00
3 . . . . 7.00
TPB collected 9.95

MEGADRAGON & TIGER

Image March, 1999

1 by Tony Wong, from Hong Kong . 2.95
2 F:Red Tiger 2.95
3 V:Single-Minded Arhat 2.95

Megahurtz #2
© Image

4 V:Fiery Lord 2.95
5 F:Gigi 2.95

MEGAHURTZ

Image (B&W) Aug., 1997

1 JPi,I:Megahurtz 2.95
2 JPi,visit to Wonderland 2.95
3 JPi,V:N-Filtraitors 2.95
4 JPi,Liberaiders 2.95

MEGATON MAN: BOMBSHELL

Image July, 1999

1 DSs,V:Unleash 2.95

MEGATON MAN: HARDCOPY

Image/Fiasco (B&W) Feb., 1999

1 by Don Simpson. 2.95
2 with 6 new pages 2.95

MESSENGER, THE

Image July, 2000

1-shot JOy, 48-pg. 5.95

MIDNIGHT NATION

Image/Top Cow Sept., 2000

1 by J. Michael Straczynski 2.50
1a variant GrF (c) 2.50
2 GrF, on the run. 2.50

MIKE GRELL'S MAGGIE THE CAT

1 thru 4 . . . . @2.50

MISERY SPECIAL

1 Cyberforce Origins 2.95

MONSTER FIGHTERS, INC.

Image April, 1999

1 Who you gonna call 2.95
2 Wake the dead 2.95
1-shot The Black Book 3.50

MONSTER FIGHTERS INC.: THE GHOSTS OF CHRISTMAS

Image Dec., 1999

1 The Fright Before Christmas. . . . 3.95

MONSTERMAN

Image (B&W) Sept., 1997

1 MM,from Action Planet 2.95
2 MM,Inhuman monsters. 2.95
3 MM,King of Monsters 2.95
4 MM, conclusion 2.95

MORE THAN MORTAL/ LADY PENDRAGON

Image June, 1999

1 MHw,x-over 2.50
Prev. Edition 16-page, B&W 4.95

MORE THAN MORTAL: OTHERWORLDS

Image/Liar Comics July, 1999

1 F:Derdre & Morand. 3.00
1a variant cover (1:2) 5.00
2 in Otherworld 3.00
2a variant cover (1:2) 4.00
3 Lady in white 3.00
3a variant Derdre cover (1:2). 3.00
4 Woman in white, concl. 3.00
5 Famine,pt.1 . . . . 3.00
6 Famine,pt.2 . . . . 3.00
7 Famine,pt.3 . . . . 3.00
Art Gallery #1. . . . . 3.50
TPB Vol. 1, rep. #1 & #2. . . . . 6.95
TPB Vol. 2 . . . . 6.95
TPB Vol. 3, Truths & Legends. 5.95

MR. MONSTER VS. GORZILLA

Image (2 Color) July, 1998

1-shot, MGi 2.95

MR. MONSTER'S GAL FRIDAY: KELLY

Image (B&W) Jan., 2000

1 MGi 3.50
2 MGi 2.95
3 MGi,AMo(s) 2.95

M-REX

Image Nov., 1999

1 by Joe Kelly & Duncan Rouleau . 2.95
2 . . . . 2.95
3 . . . . 2.95
4 . . . . 2.95
4a variant cover. 2.95
5 . . . . 2.95
5a variant cover. 2.95
#1 Limited Tour Edition. 5.00
Preview, B&W, 16-pg 5.00

MS. FORTUNE

Image (B&W) 1998

1 by Chris Marrinan. 2.95
2 Carnage in the Caribbean. 2.95
3 Doom at the Dawn of Time 2.95

MYSTERY, INC.

Ashcan 1 . . . . 4.00

NAMELESS, THE

Image (B&W) May, 1997

1 PhH,I:The Nameless, protector of Mexico City's lost children 2.95
2 . . . . 2.95
3 . . . . 2.95
4 . . . . 2.95
5 V:Huitzilopochtili 2.95

NASH

Image July, 1999

1 MMy, by & starring Kevin Nash . . 2.50
1a variant cover (1:2) 2.95
2 MMy, the end of Nash?. 2.50
2a variant cover (1:2). 2.50
#1 Photo-Split edition 2.95
Preview edition MMy,F:Kevin Nash . 2.50
Preview ed.A variant cover (1:2) . . . 2.50

NEON CYBER

Image July, 1999

1 F:Neon Dragons 2.50
1a variant cover (1:2). 2.50
1b glow-in-the-dark edition. 6.95
2 gang alliance 2.50
2a variant cover (1:2). 2.50

IMAGE

3 Neon a suspect 2.50
4 who framed Neon? 2.50
5 . . . . 2.50
6 V:Mohawks. 2.50
7 . . . . 2.50
8 conclusion of Vol. 1 . . . . 2.50

NEW ADVENTURES OF ABRAHAM LINCOLN

Image/Homage Feb., 1998

TPB SMI, 144pg. 19.95

NEWFORCE

Image/Extreme 1996

1 Extreme Destroyer, pt.8
x-over, bagged with card 2.50
2 . . . . 2.50
3 . . . . 2.50
4 Team disbands 2.50

NEWMAN

Image/Extreme 1996

1 Extreme Destroyer,pt.3
x-over, bagged with card 2.50
2 . . . . 2.50
3 . . . . 2.50
4 Shadowhunt x-over,pt.5 . . . . 2.50

NEWMEN

Image/Extreme 1994

1 JMs, ... 3.00
2 JMs,I:Girth 2.25
3 JMs,V:Girth,I:Ikonna 2.25
4 JMs,A:Ripclaw 1.95
5 JMs,Ripclaw,V:Ikonn. 2.50
6 JMs 2.50
7 JMs 2.50
8 JMs,Team Youngblood 2.50
9 ErS(s),JMs,Kodiak Kidnapped . . 2.50
10 ExtremeSacrifice,pt.5,x-over . . . 2.50
11 F:Reign 2.50
12 R:Elemental. 2.50
13 ErS,I:Bootleg 2.50
14 ErS,Dominion's Secret. 2.50
15 I:Time Guild. 2.50
16 . . . . 2.50
16a variant cover 3.00
17 R:Girth. 2.50
18 F:Byrd 2.50
19 I:Bordda Khan,Shepherd 2.50
20 Extreme Babewatch. 2.50
21 ErS,CSp,(1 of 5) 2.50
22 ErS,CSp, Who Needs the
Newmen?. 2.50
23 ErS,CSp,Who are the Newmen? 2.50

THE NEW ORDER HANDBOOK

Various artists. 1.50

NEW SHADOWHAWK, THE

1 I:New ShadowHawk 2.50
2 V:Mutants. 2.50
3 I:Trophy 2.50
4 V:Blowfish 2.50
5 thru 7 . . . . @2.50

NINE RINGS OF WU-TANG, THE

Image Nov., 1999

1 by Brian Haberlin 4.00
2 . . . . 3.00
3 Bringers of Sleep 3.00
4 F:Mza. 3.00
4a variant cover. 3.00
5 . . . . 3.00
#1 limited tour edition 5.00
Preview, B&W, 16-pg 5.00

NINE RINGS OF WU-TANG, THE: FATIMA'S REVENGE

Image May, 2000

1 by Brian Haberlin 2.95

1963 Book Six
© Image

1963

1 Mystery Incorporated, AnM(s),
RV,DGb 2.50
1a Gold Ed. 4.00
1b Bronze Ed. 3.00
2 No One Escapes...The Fury,
RV,SBi,DGb,JV,I:The Fury 2.25
3 Tales of the Uncanny,
RV,SBi,I:U.S.A.. . . . . 2.25
4 Tales From Beyond
JV,SBi,I:N-Man, Johnny Beyond 2.25
5 Horus, Lord of Light,
JV,SBi,I:Horus 2.25
6 Tomorrow Syndicate,
JV,SBi,C:Shaft 2.25
Ashcan #1 . . . . 3.00
Ashcan #2 . . . . 2.50
Ashcan #4 . . . . 2.00

NINE VOLT

Image/Top Cow 1997

1 ACh 3.00
1a Variant (c). 4.00
2 ACh 3.00
3 ACh,V:crazed junkie terrorists. . . 2.50
4 ACh,V:Rev. Cyril Gibson. 2.50

NORMAL MAN/ MEGATON MAN SPECIAL

1 . . . . 2.50

OBJECTIVE FIVE

Image July, 2000

1 biological weapons 2.95
2 F:Lark, Alexis & DJ. 2.50
3 Airborne Virus 2.95

OPERATION KNIGHTSTRIKE

1 RHe,A:Chapel,Bravo,Battlestone 2.50
2 In Afganistan 2.50
3 final issue. 2.50

THE OTHERS

0 JV(s),From ShadowHawk 2.50
1 JV(s)V:Mongrel. 2.50
2 JV,Mongrel takes weapons 2.50
3 War 2.50
4 O:Clone 2.50

OVERKILL

Image/Top Cow October, 2000

1 PJe,x-over,A:Aliens,Predator . . . 5.95

PACT

Image 1994

1 JV(s),WMc,I:Pact, C:Youngblood 2.25
2 JV(s),V:Youngblood 1.95
3 JV(s),V:Atrocity. 1.95

PARTS UNKNOWN: KILLING ATTRACTION

Image (B&W) April, 2000

1 Sci-Fi/UFO adventure. 2.95

PARTS UNKNOWN: HOSTILE TAKEOVER

Image (B&W) June, 2000

1 by Beau SMith & Brad Gorby . . . 2.95
2 . . . . 2.95
3 . . . . 2.95
4 . . . . 2.95

PHANTOM FORCE

1 RLd,JK,w/card 2.75
2 JK,V:Darkfire 1.95
See also Color Comics section

PHANTOM GUARD

Image/Wildstorm Oct., 1997

1 by Sean Ruffner, Ryan Benjamin 2.50
1a variant cover 2.50
1b Voyager bagged pack. 3.50

Phantom Force #1
© Image

IMAGE

All comics prices listed are for *Near Mint* condition.

2 Martian wasteland 2.50
3 Lowell Zerium Mines. 2.50
4 "Target Locked" 2.50
5 V:Vanox, ... 2.50
6 Countdown to Armageddon 2.50

PITT
Image/Top Cow 1993–95
1 DK,I:Pitt,Timmy. 4.00
2 DK,V:Quagg 3.00
3 DK,V:Zoyvod 4.00
4 DK,V:Zoyvod 3.00
5 DK 2.50
6 DK 2.50
7 DK 2.50
8 Ransom 2.50
9 DK,Artic Adventures 2.00
Ashcan 1 . . . . 3.00

POWER OF THE MARK
1 I:Ted Miller 2.50
2 V:The Fuse. 2.50
3 TMB(s), The Mark 2.50
4 TMB,Mark's secrets revealed . . . 2.50

POWER RANGERS ZEO
Image/Extreme Sept., 1997
1 thru 3 TBm&MBm(s),TNu,NRd @2.50

POWER RANGERS ZEO YOUNGBLOOD
Image/Extreme Oct., 1997
1 thru 2 RLd,TBm,MBm . . . . @2.95

POWERS
Image April, 2000
1 Who killed Retro Girl,pt.1 . . . . . . 4.00
2 Who killed Retro Girl,pt.2 . . . . . . 3.00
3 Who killed Retro Girl,pt.3 . . . . . . 3.00
4 . . . . 3.00
5 A murder solved 3.00
6 . . . . 3.00

PRIMAL INSTINCT
Image March 2000
Preview 2.50

PROPHET
Image/Extreme 1993–95
0 San Diego Comic-Con Ed. 4.00
1 RLd(s)DPs,O:Prophet,I:Mary McCormick. 3.00
1a Gold Ed.. . . . . 4.00
2 RLd(s),DPs,C:Bloodstrike 2.50
3 RLd(s),DPs, V:Bloodstrike, I:Judas 2.50
4 RLd(s),DPs,I:Omen,A:Judas 2.50
4a SPa(c),Limited Ed. 3.00
5 SPa,Supreme Apocalypse,pt.2,. . 3.00
6 SPa 2.50
7 SPa War Games pt.1 . . . . 2.25
8 SPa War Games pt.2 . . . . 2.50
9 SPa,Extreme Sacrifice Prelude . . 2.50
10 ExtremeSacrifice,pt.7,x-over . . . 2.50
Sourcebook 2.95
Ashcan #1 . . . . 3.00
Ashcan #2 . . . . 3.00

[Second Series] 1995
1 SPl, New Series 2.75
2 SPl, New Direction 2.50
2a variant cover. 2.50
3 True Nature 2.50
4 The Dying Factor 2.50
5 . . . . 2.50
6 . . . . 2.50
7 CDi,SPa 2.50
8 . . . . 2.50
9 . . . . 2.50
TPB 12.95
Ann.#1 Supreme Apocalypse 2.50
Spec.#1 Babewatch special 2.50

PROPHET/AVENGELYNE
1 . . . . 3.00

Q-UNIT: REVENGE
Image October, 1999
1 KIA,BNa 2.95
1a variant cover (1:2). 2.95
2 KIA,BNa 2.95
2a variant cover (1:2). 2.95

RAGMOP
Image (B&W)
Vol.2 #1 by Rob Walton 2.95
Vol.2 #2 . . . . 2.95

RED STAR, THE
Image June, 2000
1 by Christian Gossett 3.50
2 Project: Antares 3.00
3 Fall of the Red Fleet 3.00

REGULATORS
June, 1995
1 F:Blackjack,"Touch of Scandal" . . 2.50
2 F:Vortex 2.50
3 F:Arson 2.50
4 F:Scandal. 2.50

REPLACEMENT GOD AND OTHER STORIES, THE
Image (B&W) May, 1997
1 Knute vs. King Ursus 2.95
2 by Zander Cannon 2.95
3 thru 4 . . . . @2.95

RESIDENT EVIL
Image/WIldstorm March, 1998
1 comic/game magazine 56pg 4.95
2 thru 4 comic/game mag. 56pg . @4.95

Replacement God and Other Stories #5
© Image

TPB Collection 1, series rep.. . . . . 14.95

RIPCLAW
Image/Top Cow 1995
1/2 Prelude to Series (Wizard). . . . 3.00
1/2a Con versions 7.00
1 A:Killjoy, I:Shadowblade 3.00
2 Cyblade, Heatwave 2.50
3 EcS,BPe,AV,Alliance with S.H.O.C.s. 2.50
4 conclusion 2.50
Spec.#1 I:Ripclaw's Brother 3.00

[1st Regular Series]
1 thru 5 . . . . @2.50

RIPTIDE
Image 1995
1 O:Riptide 2.50
2 O:Riptide 2.50

RISING STARS
Image/Top Cow March, 1999
1 A celestial event. 7.00
1a, b, & c variant covers 5.00
2 life & death of Peter Dawson . . . 4.00
3 new special 3.50
4 . . . . 3.50
5 to the netherworld. 3.00
6 Things Fall Apart,pt.1 . . . . 3.00
7 Things Fall Apart,pt.2 . . . . 2.50
8 Things Fall Apart,pt.3 . . . . 2.50
9 Act Two,pt.1 . . . . 2.50
10 years later 2.50
11 Specials out of control 2.50
#0 rep. from Wizard 2.50
Prelude 2.95
TPB Deluxe,rep.#1–#8 . . . . 19.95
Preview by J. Michael Straczynski, 16-page, B&W 5.00

RUMBLE GIRLS
Image (B&W) April, 2000
1 (of 8) Silky Warrior Tansie. 3.50
2 . . . . 3.50
3 Sugar and Wax. 3.50
4 Sapphire Bullets 3.50

SABRE
Image (B&W) 1998
TPB 20th Anniversary. 12.95

SAFFIRE
Image April, 2000
1 MtB,SRf,F:Melanie,Lyssa, Priscilla 2.95
1a variant JMd (c) 2.95
1b Mat Broome blue foil (c) 11.50
1c Joe Mac blue foil (c) 12.95
2 MtB,SRf,V:The Kraken 2.95
2a randy green (c). 8.95
2b signed & number 10.95
3 MtB,SRf,Hades Gate 2.95

SAINT ANGEL
Image 2000
Preview 2.95
1 KIA,BNa,40-pg.,flip-book. 3.95
1a variant (c). 3.95
2 KIA,BNa,40-pg.,flip-book. 3.95

SAM & TWITCH
Image/TMP Aug., 1999
1 AMe,Spawn tie-in 2.75

2 AMe,The Udaku,pt.2. . . . . 2.50
3 AMe,The Udaku,pt.3. . . . . 2.50
4 AMe,The Udaku,pt.4. . . . . 2.50
5 AMe,The Udaku,pt.5. . . . . 2.50
6 AMe,The Udaku,pt.6. . . . . 2.50
7 AMe,The Udaku,pt.7. . . . . 2.50
8 AMe,The Udaku,pt.8. . . . . 2.50
9 One Really Bad Day. 2.50
10 Witch Hunter,pt.1. . . . . 2.50
11 Witch Hunter,pt.2 . . . . 2.50
12 Witch Hunter,pt.3. . . . . 2.50
13 Witch Hunter,pt.4. . . . . 2.50
14 Dumb Laws and Egg 2.50
15 Bounty Hunter Wars,pt.1 . . . . . . 2.50

SAM STORIES: LEGS

Image Dec., 1999

1-shot SK, 24-pg 2.50

SAVAGE DRAGON

Image/Highbrow

1 EL,I:Savage Dragon 3.00
2 EL,I:Superpatriot. 3.50
3 EL,V:Bedrock,w'coupon#6 . . . . . 3.00
3a EL,w/o coupon 2.50
Spec. Savage Dragon Versus Savage Megaton Man #1 EL,DSm 2.50
Gold Ed. 12.00
TPB 9.95

[2nd Series] 1993

1 EL,I:Freaks. 2.50
2 EL,V:Teen.Mutant Ninja Turtles, Flip book Vanguard #0 . . . . 2.50
3 EL,A:Freaks 2.25
4 EL,A:Freaks 2.25
5 EL,Might Man flip book 2.25
6 EL,A:Freaks 2.25
7 EL,Overlord 2.25
8 EL,V:Cutthroat,Hellrazor 2.25
9 EL 2.25
10 EL 2.25
11 EL,A:Overlord 2.00
12 EL 2.00
13 EL,Mighty Man,Star,I:Widow (appeared after issue #20) 2.50
13a Larsen version of 13 . . . . 2.50
14 Possessed pt.1 . . . . 2.50
15 Possessed pt.2 . . . . 2.50
16 Possessed pt.3,V:Mace 2.50
17 V:Dragonslayer 2.50
18 R:The Fiend 2.50

Savage Dragon #32
© Erik Larsen

19 V:The Fiend. 2.50
20 Rematch with Ovrlord 2.50
21 V:Overlord 2.50
22 A:Teenage Mutant Turtles 2.50
23 Rapture vs. SheDragon 2.50
24 Gang War pt.1 . . . . 2.50
25 Gang War,pt.2 double size. 4.00
26 . . . . 2.50
27 . . . . 2.50
28 . . . . 2.50
29 . . . . 2.50
30 EL,"Overlord Reborn". 2.50
31 "The Dragon is trapped in Hell" . 2.50
32 Kill-Cat vs. Justice 2.50
33 fatherhood 2.50
34 F:Hellboy, pt.1 . . . . 3.00
35 F:Hellboy, pt.2 . . . . 2.50
36 Dragon & Star try to rescue Peter Klaptin 2.50
37 mutants struggle in ruins of Chicago 2.50
38 Dragon vs. Cyberface 2.50
39 Dragon vs. Dung 2.50
40 "G-Man". 2.50
41 Wedding issue. 2.50
42 V:Darklord 2.50
43 Stranded on another world. 2.50
44 in flying saucer, ... 2.50
45 . . . . 2.50
46 She-Dragon vs. Vicious Circle . . 2.50
47 A knight and a mummy 2.50
48 Unfinished Business, pt.1. . . . . . 2.50
49 Unfinished Business, pt.2. . . . . . 2.50
50 Unfinished Business, pt.3, some reps., 96pg 6.00
51 F:She-Dragon 2.50
52 F:She-Dragon,V:Hercules 2.50
53 EL,F:She Dragon. 2.50
54 EL,V:imposter Dragon 2.50
55 EL,Dragon & She-Dragon 2.50
56 EL,Rita Medermade kidnapped . 2.50
57 EL,V:Overlord 2.50
58 EL,Dragon's Resurrection 2.50
59 EL,return of Savage Dragon . . . 2.50
60 EL,R:Devastator 2.50
61 EL,R:Rapture. 2.50
62 EL,Savage Dragon married 2.50
63 EL,Dragon's honeymoon 2.50
64 EL,Overlord's secrets. 2.50
65 EL,Possessed 2.50
66 EL,Dragon shrunk 2.50
67 EL,A:SuperPatriot 2.50
68 EL,V:PowerHouse 2.50
69 EL 2.50
70 EL, Hell on Earth 2.50
71 EL,End of the World,prequel . . . 2.50
72 EL,End of the World,prequel . . . 2.50
73 EL,End of the World,pt.1 . . . . . . 2.95
74 EL,End of the World,pt.2 . . . . . . 2.50
75 EL,End of the World,pt.3 . . . . . . 2.50
76 EL,Hell on Earth begins 2.50
77 EL,Wildstar Returns. 2.50
77a Variant JOy (c). 2.50
78 EL,Mind-slaves of the Brain-Child 2.50
79 EL,Girl Trouble 2.50
80 EL,Lurkers beneath Lake Fear. . 2.50
TPB A Talk With God 17.95
HC A Talk With God, signed 74.95
TPB The Fallen, rep.#7–#11 . . . . . 12.95
HC The Fallen 29.95
TPB Possessed, rep.#12–#16. . . . 12.95
HC Possessed, rep. 89.95
TPB Archives #2, B&W,1982 rep. . . 2.95
TPB Archives #3, B&W,1984 rep. . . 2.95
TPB Archives #4, B&W,1986 rep. . . 2.95
TPB Revenge. 13.95
TPB Greatest Team-ups 19.95
TPB Book 1 Baptism of Fire 14.95
TPB Gang War. 16.95
HC Revenge. 79.95

SAVAGE DRAGON: DESTROYER DUCK

Image Comics

1 SvG,ChM,EL 4.00

SAVAGE DRAGON, THE: RED HORIZON

Image Comics Feb., 1997

1 MsM. 2.50
2 MsM,Dragon in the ER,A:Freak Force 2.50
3 (of 3) MsM,Freak Force beaten. . 2.50

SAVAGE DRAGON: MARSHAL LAW

Image (B&W) July, 1997

1 (of 2) PMs,KON,F:Marshal Law . 3.00
2 PMs,KON, concl. 3.00

SAVAGE DRAGON: SEX & VIOLENCE

Image July, 1997

1 (of 2) TBm,MBm. 2.50
2 TBm,MBm,AH, concl. 2.50

SAVANT GARDE

Image/Wildstorm March, 1997

1 "A team without a rule book". . . . 2.50
2 Between killer & killer cat 2.50
3 V: strange Tapestry. 2.50
4 "Any super-villain can take over the world" 2.50
5 "The Final Showdown" 2.50
6 BKs,Guilty until proven innocent . 2.50
7 BKs,death of John Colt. 2.50
Fan Edition #1, with Fan #22 . . . . . 3.00
Fan Edition #2, with Fan #23 . . . . . 3.00
Fan Edition #3, with Fan #24 . . . . . 3.00

SECTION ZERO

Image June, 2000

1 KK,TG,UFO's etc.. . . . . 2.50
2 KK,TG,Sargasso sea 2.50
3 KK,TG,Curse of Sargasso 2.50
4 KK,TG,Ground Zero revealed . . . 2.50

Savant Garde #2
© Wildstorm

IMAGE

All comics prices listed are for *Near Mint* condition.

SHADOWHAWK
Image/Shadowline
1 JV,I:ShadowHawk,Black Foil(c), Pin-up, with coupon#1 . . . . 3.00
1a w/o coupon. 2.00
2 JV,V:Arsenal,A:Spawn, I:Infiniti . . 3.00
3 JV,V:Arsenal,w/glow-in-the-dark(c) 2.50
4 V:Savage Dragon 2.50
TPB rep.#1-4 . . . . 19.95
Ashcan #1 . . . . 2.00
Ashcan #2 . . . . 2.00
Ashcan #3 . . . . 2.00
Ashcan #4 . . . . 2.00

[2nd Series] 1993
1 JV,Die Cut(c) 2.50
1a Gold Ed. 3.00
2 JV,ShadowHawk I.D. 2.50
2a Gold Ed. 2.50
3 Poster(c),JV,w/Ash Can 2.50
TPB 19.95

[3rd Series] 1993
0 Zero issue 2.25
1 JV,CWf,V:Vortex,Hardedge, Red Foil(c) 2.50
1a Gold Ed. 3.00
1b signed 6.00
2 JV,CWf,MA,I:Deadline, BU&I:US Male 2.50
3 JV(a&s),ShadowHawk has AIDS, V:Hardedge,Blackjak 2.25
4 JV(a&s),V:Hardedge, ... 2.25
Note: #5 to #11 not used; #12 below is the next issue, the 12th overall.
12 Monster Within, pt.1. . . . . 1.95
13 Monster Within, pt.2. . . . . 1.95
14 Monster Within, pt.3. . . . . 2.50
15 Monster Within, pt.4. . . . . 2.50
16 Monster Within, pt.5. . . . . 2.50
17 Monster Within, pt.6. . . . . 2.50
18 JV,D:ShadowHawk 2.50
Spec.#1 . . . . 3.50
Gallery#1 . . . . 1.95

SHADOWHAWK/ VAMPIRELLA
Book 2 V:Kaul 4.95
Book #1: see Vampi/ShadowHawk

SHADOWHUNT SPECIAL
Image/Extreme 1996
1 Shadowhunt x-over, pt.1 . . . . 2.50

SHAMAN'S TEARS
Image/Creative Fire 1993–96
0 MGr,. 2.50
1 MGr,I:Shaman,B:Origin. 3.00
1a Siver Prism Ed.. . . . . 5.00
2 MGr,Poster(c). 2.50
3 MGr,V:Bar Sinister 2.50
4 MGr,V:Bar Sinister,E:Origin. 1.95
5 MGr,R:Jon Sable 1.95
6 MGr,V:Jon Sable 1.95
7 MGr,V:Rabids. 1.95
8 MGr,A:Sable. 1.95
9 MGr,Becoming of Broadarrow. . . 1.95
10 Becoming of Broadarrow,pt.2 . . . 2.50
11 Becoming of Broadarrow,pt.3 . . . 2.50
12 Becoming of Broadarrow,pt.4 . . . 2.50
13 The Offspring,pt.1 . . . . 2.50

SHARKY
Image 1998
1 by Dave Elliott & Alex Horley . . . 2.50
1a variant cover (5,000 made). . . . 2.95
2 coma over 2.50
2a variant cover. 2.95
3 R:Blazin' Glory 2.50
3a variant SBi(c) 2.50
4 tons of guest stars, concl 2.50
4a variant DAy(c) 2.50

SHATTERED IMAGE
Image/Wildstorm 1996
1 KBk,TnD,crossover. 2.50
2 KBk 2.50
3 KBk 2.50
4 KBk,TnD,concl.. . . . . 2.50

SHIP OF FOOLS
Image (B&W) Sept., 1997
0 Bryan J.L. Glass, Michael Avon Oeming 2.95
1 Death & Taxes, pt.1 . . . . 2.95
2 Death & Taxes, pt.2 . . . . 2.95
3 Death & Taxes, pt.3 . . . . 2.95
4 Death & Taxes, pt.4 . . . . 2.95
TPB rep. Caliber series. 14.95

SHOCKROCKETS
Image April, 2000
1 (of 6) KBk,SI. 2.50
2 KBk,SI,Command Decision. 2.50
3 KBk,SI,The Triangle Trade 2.50
4 KBk,SI,Rocket Science. 2.50
5 KBk,SI,sneak attack 2.50
6 KBk,SI,Final Battle,flip-book 2.50

SHUT UP & DIE
Image (B&W) 1998
1 JHI and Kevin Stokes 2.95
2 JHI,Angry White Man 2.95
3 JHI,Wife abducted 2.95
4 JHI 2.95
5 JHI,A:Earl Jackson 2.95

SIEGE
Image/Wildstorm 1997
1 JPe,AV,Nothing you believe is real. 2.50
2 JPe,AV,Omega goes to Hawaii for funeral. 2.50
3 JPe,AV,Zontarian Crab Ships vs. Drop Ship. 2.50
4 JPe,AV,Raid to rescue Omega Squad 2.50

Siege #4
© Wildstorm

SIGMA
Image/Wildstorm 1996
1 BCi,Fire From Heaven prelude . . 2.50
2 BCi,Fire From Heaven, pt.6 . . . . 2.50
3 BCi,Fire From Heaven, pt.14 . . . 2.50

SILENT SCREAMERS
Image Oct., 2000
1 Nosferatu, 40-pg. 4.95

SINKING
Image March, 1999
GN JHI 14.95

SIREN
Image (B&W) May, 1998
1 by J. Torres & Tim Levins 2.95
2 F:Zara Rush, private eye 2.95
3 cpmc;isopm 2.95
TPB rep. Shapes 9.95

SKINNERS
Image/TMP July, 2000
1 MtB,JMd. 3.00
1a variant PtL (c). 3.00
1b variant Andy Park (c) 3.00
1c variant MtB (c) 2-D 3.00
1d limited ed. Broom (c) 8.95
1e limited ed., signed. 10.95
2 MtB,SRf 3.00
2a variant JBz(c) 3.00

SOLAR LORD
Image March, 1999
1 by Khoo Fuk Lung 2.50
2 Nickson is Solar Lord 2.50
3 V:5 enemies 2.50
4 V:5 enemies 2.50
5 V:The Emperor of Darkness 2.50
6 O:Nickson 2.50
7 concl., book one 2.50

SOUL REAVER: LEGACY OF KAIN
Image/Top Cow June, 2000
1-shot MHw,video game tie-in. 2.50

SOUL SAGA
Image/Top Cow 2000
1 SPa,F:Aries, Soulblade. 2.50
1a variant (c) JMd (1:4) 2.50
1b variant Michael Turner (c) (1:4). 2.50
2 SPa,death in the family. 2.50
2a variant David Finch (c) 2.50
2b variant Pat Lee (c) 2.50
3 SPa, Khan Hordes 2.50
4 SPa, Dominion vs. Khan. 2.50
5 SPa, F:Ares 2.50
Coll.Ed.Vol.1. . . . . 5.95

SOULWIND
Image (B&W) March, 1997
1 quest for Soulwind begins. 2.95
2 Nick becomes "Captain Crash" . . 2.95
3 Captain Crash & Poke pursue Soulwind info 2.95
4 concl. of story arc. 2.95
5 The Day I Tried to Live,pt.1. . . . . 2.95
6 The Day I Tried to Live,pt.2. . . . . 2.95
7 The Day I Tried to Live,pt.3. . . . . 2.95

8 The Day I Tried to Live,pt.4. . . . . 2.95
TPB rep #1–#4. . . . . 9.95

SPARTAN: WARRIOR SPIRIT

1 thru 4 . . . . @2.95

SPARTAN X

Image (B&W) Sept., 1998

1 MGo,RM,"Plague Train" 2.95
2 MGo,RM,"Plague Train," pt.2 . . . 2.95
3 MGo,RM,"Plague Train," pt.3 . . . 2.95

SPAWN

Image/TMP May, 1992

1 TM,I:Spawn,w/GP,DK pinups . . 16.00
2 TM,V:The Violator. 12.00
3 TM,V:The Violator 11.00
4 TM,V:The Violator,+coupon #2 . 15.00
4a w/o coupon. 3.00
5 TM,O:Billy Kincaid 10.00
6 TM,I:Overt-Kill 7.00
7 TM,V:Overt-Kill 7.00
8 TM,AMo(s),F:Billy Kincaid. 7.00
9 NGa(s),TM,I:Angela 8.00
10 DS(s),TM,A:Cerebus 5.00
11 FM(s),TM. 5.00
12 TM,Chapel killed Spawn 5.00
13 TM,A:Youngblood 5.00
14 TM,A:The Violator 6.00
15 TM 4.00
16 GCa,I:Anti-Spawn 6.00
17 GCa,V:Anti-Spawn. 8.00
18 GCa,ATi,D:Anti-Spawn. 12.00
19 & 20 see after #25
21 TM,The Hunt,pt.1. . . . . 12.00
22 TM,The Hunt,pt.2. . . . . 4.00
23 TM,The Hunt,pt.3. . . . . 4.00
24 TM,The Hunt,pt.4. . . . . 4.00
25 Image X Book,MS,BTn 6.00
19 I:Houdini 6.00
20 J:Houdini 6.00
26 TM 5.00
27 I:The Curse 5.00
28 Faces Wanda 5.00
29 Returns From Angela. 5.00
30 A:KKK 5.00
31 R:Redeemer 4.00
32 TM,GCa,New Costume 5.00
33 R:Violator 4.00
34 V:Violator. 4.00

Spawn #11
© Todd McFarlane

35 F:Sam & Twitch 4.00
36 Talks to Wanda 4.00
37 I:The Freak 4.00
38 & 39. @4.00
40 & 41 V:Curse . . . . @4.00
42 thru 49. . . . . @4.00
50 48pgs 5.00
51 and 52. . . . . @4.00
53 A:Malebolgia 4.00
54 return to New York, alliance with Terry Fitzgerald 4.00
55 plans to defeat Jason Wynn. . . . 4.00
56 efforts to defeat Jason Wynn . . . 4.00
57 . . . . 3.50
58 sequel to Spawn #29. . . . . 3.50
59 . . . . 3.50
60 battle between Spawn and Clown cont. 3.50
61 battle with Clown concl. 3.50
62 Spawn is Al Simmons for 1 day . 3.50
63 Operation: Wynn fall, pt.1 . . . . . 2.50
64 Wynn falls, bagged with toy catalog 2.50
65 recap issue 2.50
66 TM,GCa,lives of alley bums 2.50
67 TM,GCa,Sam and Twitch. 2.50
68 TM,GCa,R:Freak 2.50
69 TM,GCa,F:Freak 2.50
70 TM,GCa 2.50
71 TM,GCa,Cold Blooded Truth . . . 2.50
72 TM,GCa,Haunting of the Heap. . 2.25
73 TM,GCa,R:The Heap. 2.25
74 TM,GCa,pathway to misery 2.25
75 TM,GCa,Deadly Revelations . . . 2.25
76 TM,GCa,Granny Blake. 2.25
77 TM,GCa,confronts 2.25
78 TM,GCa,DaM,"Sins of Excess" . 2.00
79 TM,GCa,DaM,Killer in N.Y.. . . . . 2.25
80 TM,GCa,DaM,F:Sam & Twitch . . 2.25
81 TM,GCa,DaM,Sins are reborn . . 2.25
82 TM,GCa,DaM,sea of self-doubt . 2.25
83 TM,GCa,V:Jason Wynn 2.25
84 TM,GCa,DaM,Helle's Belles. . . . 2.25
85 TM,GCa,DaM,Legend of Hellspawn 2.25
86 TM,GCa,DaM,V:Al Simmons . . . 2.25
87 TM,GCa,DaM,Al Simmons fate . 2.25
88 TM,GCa,DaM,Seasons of change. 2.25
89 TM,GCa,DaM,secrets revealed . 2.25
90 TM,GCa,DaM,three stories 2.25
91 TM,GCa,DaM,Black Cat Bones,pt.1 . . . . 2.25
92 TM,GCa,DaM,Black Cat Bones,pt.2 . . . . 2.25
93 TM,GCa,DaM,Devil's Banquet . . 2.25
94 TM,GCa,DaM,Children's Hour . . 2.25
95 TM,GCa,DaM,Cracks in the Foundation. 2.25
96 TM,GCa,DaM,Rules of Engagement. 2.25
97 TM,GCa,DaM,Heaven's Folly. . . 2.25
98 TM,GCa,DaM,The Trouble with Angels 2.50
99 TM,GCa,DaM,Edge of Darkness 2.50
100A TM,GCa,DaM,TM(c)She dies. 4.95
100B TM,GCa,DaM,FM(c) 4.95
100C TM,GCa,DaM,GCa(c) 4.95
100D TM,GCa,DaM,Ashley Wood(c)4.95
100E TM,GCa,DaM,MMi(c). 4.95
100F TM,GCa,DaM,AxR(c). 4.95
101 TM,AMe,DaM,The Speed of Night 2.50
102 TM,AMe,DaM,Remains 2.50
103 TM,AMe,DaM,A Town Called Malice 2.50
Ann.#1 Blood & Shadows, 64-page. 4.95
GN Spawn Movie adapt.. . . . . 5.00
TPB Capital Collection rep.#1-3 limited to 1,200 copies 300.00
TPB TM,rep.#1–#5 . . . . 9.95

Spawn #84
© Todd McFarlane

TPB Spawn III rep. #12–#15. . . . . . 9.95
TPB Spawn IV rep. #16–#20 . . . . . 9.95
TPB Spawn V rep.#21–#25 . . . . . . 9.95
TPB Spawn VI, rep.#26–#30. . . . . . 9.95
TPB Vol. VII Deadman's Touch 9.95
TPB Vol. VIII Betrayal of Blood 9.95
TPB Angela's Hunt 9.95
TPB Vol.9 Urban Jungle 9.95
TPB Vol.10 Vengeance of the Dead 9.95
TPB Vol.11 Crossroads. 9.95
GN Spawn: Blood and Salvation. . . 4.95
Fan Edition #1, with Fan #16 . . . . . 3.00
Fan Edition #1a variant cover 4.00
Fan Edition #1b gold logo,retailer . . 5.00
Fan Edition #2, with Fan #17 . . . . . 3.00
Fan Edition #2a variant cover 4.00
Fan Edition #2b gold logo,retailer . . 5.00
Fan Edition #2c platimum Foil logo . 5.00
Fan Edition #2, with Fan #18 . . . . . 3.00
Fan Edition #2a variant cover 4.00
Fan Edition #3b gold logo,retailer . . 5.00

SPAWN/BATMAN

Image/DC

1 FM(s),TM, ... 5.00

SPAWN BLOOD FEUD

1 V:Vampires. 4.00
2 . . . . 4.00
3 Hunted as a Vampire 4.00
4 V:Heartless John 4.00

SPAWN BIBLE

Image/TMP

1 TM,GCa 2.00
2 Book of the Dead, 56-pg. 4.95

SPAWN: THE DARK AGES

Image/TMP March, 1999

1 GF,LSh, from 12th century 2.50
1a variant TM (c) (1:4). 2.50
2 LSh,A:Black Knight. 2.50
3 LSh,A:Black Knight. 2.50
4 LSh,Lord Covenant. 2.50
5 LSh,Lord Covenant. 2.50
6 LSh,Sister Immaculata 2.50
7 LSh,Cogliostro 2.50
8 LSh,Acts of Contrition. 2.50
9 LSh 2.50
10 LSh,F:Lord Covenant. 2.50

11 LSh,Ghost on the Hill 2.50
12 LSh,The Faithful 2.50
13 LSh,Blood and Glory 2.50
14 LSh,The Innocent 2.50
15 LSh,New Beginnings 2.50
16 CWf,Heart of the HellSpawn 2.50
17 CWf,The Circle and the Worm 2.50
18 CWf,Crucified 2.50
19 CWf,Like Any Other Man 2.50
20 Voices in the Dark 2.50

SPAWN THE IMPALER

Image/TMP [Mini-Series]

1 (of 3) MGr, fully painted 5.00
2 and 3 MGr @4.00

SPAWN: THE UNDEAD

Image/TMP May, 1999

1 PJe,DT,CWf,F:Spawn 2.00
2 PJe,DT,CWf,F:Travis Ward 2.00
3 PJe,DT,CWf,Heaven vs. Hell 2.00
4 PJe,DT,CWf,suicide cult 2.00
5 PJe,DT,CWf,The Wind That Shakes the Barley 2.25
6 PJe,DT,CWf 2.25
7 PJe,DT,CWf,Up the Down Stairs 2.25
8 PJe,DT,CWf,One Lunch to Live. 2.25
9 PJe,DT,CWf,Waiting 2.25
10 PJe,DT,CWf,How to Win Friends and Influence People 2.25
11 PJe,DT,CWf,Heaven and Hell and In Between 2.25

SPAWN/WILDC.A.T.S

1 thru 4 mini-series 3.50

SPIRIT OF THE TAO

Image/Top Cow May, 1998

1 BTn,F:Lance & Jasmine 2.50
2 BTn,mission to destroy base. 2.50
3 BTn,V:Jaikap Clan 2.50
4 BTn,F:Jasmine & Lance 2.50
5 BTn, Antidote to virus 2.50
6 BTn, Tao grows stronger. 2.50
7 BTn, V:Menicus 2.50
8 BTn, A:Messiah 2.50
9 BTn, The Dragon is Loose 2.50
10 BTn, Jasmine out of control 2.50
11 BTn, Dragon ash race 2.50
12 BTn, F:Disciple 2.50
13 BTn, friend or foe. 2.50
14 BTn, must one die? 2.50
15 BTn,conclusion, 48-pg. 3.95

SPLITTING IMAGE

1 DsM,A:Marginal Seven 2.25
2 DsM,A:Marginal Seven 2.25

STAR

1 F:Star from Savage Dragon 2.50
2 Buried Alive 2.50
3 A:Savage Dragon,Rapture 2.50
4 A:Savage Dragon,Rapture 2.50

STARCHILD: MYTHOPOLIS

Image (B&W) 1997

0 JOn, "Prologue" 2.95
1 JOn, "Pinehead" 2.95
2 JOn, "Pinehead," pt.2 2.95
3 JOn, "Pinehead," pt.3 2.95
4 JOn, "Fisher King," pt.1. 2.95
5 JOn, "Fisher King," pt.2. 2.95

STONE

Image/Avalon Sept., 1998

2 WPo,V:Rook. 2.50
3 WPo,A:Bann. 2.50
4 WPo, conclusion. 2.50

VOL. II

1 WPo. 2.50
1a Chromium Edition 6.95
2 WPo, search for murderer. 2.50
2 Stonechrome edition. 14.95
3 WPo,Blood from a Stone 2.50
4 WPo,A Rose by Any Other Name 2.50
5 Wpo, series resumes 2.95

STORMWATCH

Image/Wildstorm 1993

0 JSc(c),O:StormWatch, V:Terrorists,w/card 2.50
1 JLe(c&s),ScC,TvS(i), I:StormWatch 2.25
1a Gold Ed. 4.00
2 JLe(c&s),ScC,TvS(i),I:Cannon, Winter,Fahrenheit,Regent 2.25
3 JLe(c&s),ScC,TvS(i),V:Regent, I:Backlash 4.00
4 V:Daemonites. 2.50
5 SRf(s),BBh,V:Daemonites. 2.25
6 BCi,ScC,TC,A:Mercs 2.25
7 BCi,ScC,TC,A:Mercs 2.25
8 BCi,ScC,TC,A:Mercs 2.25
9 BCi,I:Defile 2.25
25 BCi,A:Spartan 2.50
10 V:Talos 2.00
10a variant (c) 3.00
11 RMz(s),the end? 2.00
12 RMz(s),V:Hellstrike,"Visions of Deathtrap" 2.00
13 V:M.A.D.-1. 2.00
14 Despot. 2.00
15 Batallion, Flashpoint 2.00
16 V:Defile 2.00
17 D:Batallion. 2.00
18 R:Argos 2.50
19 R:M.A.D.-1,L:Winter. 2.50
20 F:Cannon,Winter,Bendix 2.50
21 V:Wildcats 2.50
22 RMz,BWS(c),WildStorm Rising,pt.9,w/2 cards 2.50
22a Newsstand ed. 1.95
23 RMz(s),R:Despot,Warguard 2.50
24 V:Despot 2.50
25 SSe,ScC,BCi,A:Spartan. 2.75
25a 2nd printing 2.50

Stormwatch #3 © Jim Lee

26 V:Despot 2.50
27 V:Despot,Rebuilding,"And in the End" 2.50
28 F:Blademaster,Swift,Flint, Comanche,New Adventures 2.50
29 I:Prism,Reorganization. 2.50
30 V:Heaven's Fist 2.50
31 V:Middle Eastern Terrorists 2.50
32 2.50
33 inc. Winters Journey 2.50
34 2.50
35 Fire From Heaven,pt.5. 2.50
36 Fire From Heaven,pt.12. 2.50
37 Double size,F:Weatherman One, I:Rose Tatoo. 4.00
38 WEI(s) 3.00
39 WEI(s) 3.00
40 WEI(s),virus. 3.00
41 WEI(s) 3.00
42 WEI(s),Weatherman discovers a conspiracy 3.00
43 WEI(s) 3.00
44 WEI(s),history of Jenny Sparks 4.00
45 WEI(s),Battalion visits his family 3.00
46 WEI(s),secrets and more secrets, prologue 3.00
47 WEI(s), JLe, SW, dangerous experiment gone awry 3.00
48 WEI(s),"Change or Die" pt.1. 3.00
49 WEI(s),"Change or Die" pt.2. 3.00
50 WEI(s),"Change or Die" concl. large size 5.00
Sourcebok JLe(s),DT 2.75
Spec.#1 RMz(s),DT, 4.25
Spec.#2 F:Fleshpoint 2.50
Ashcan 1 3.00
TPB Change the World. 9.95
TPB A Finer World 14.95
TPB Change or Die 14.95
TPB Force of Nature. 14.95
TPB Lightning Strikes 14.95

STORMWATCH

Image/Wildstorm Oct., 1997

1 WEI,bacterial horror,"Strange Weather,"pt.1,"Hard Rain". 4.00
1a Variant cover 4.00
1b Voyager bagged pack 3.50
2 WEI,Stormwatch Black team, "Strange Weather,"pt.2 3.50
3 WEI,Black team,"Strange Weather,"pt.3,"A Storm Coming" 3.50
4 WEI,A Finer World, pt.1 3.50
5 WEI,A Finer World, pt.2 3.50
6 WEI,A Finer World, pt.3 3.50
7 WEI,Bleed, pt.1. 3.50
8 WEI,Bleed, pt.2. 3.50
9 WEI,Bleed, pt.3. 3.50
10 WEI,"No Reason". 3.50
11 WEI,BHi,PNe,F:Jackson King, "No Direction Home". 3.50
TPB Change or Die 15.00

STRANGERS IN PARADISE VOL. 3

Homage Comics 1996

1 TMr 6.00
2 TMr 4.00

Image/Homage Comics 1996–97

3 TMr,David & Katchoo fight 3.00
4 TMr,Katchoo makes startling discovery 3.00
5 TMr,Francine's college days 3.00
6 TMr,Katchoo searches for David. 3.00
7 TMr, 3.00
8 TMr,demons of the past 3.00

IMAGE

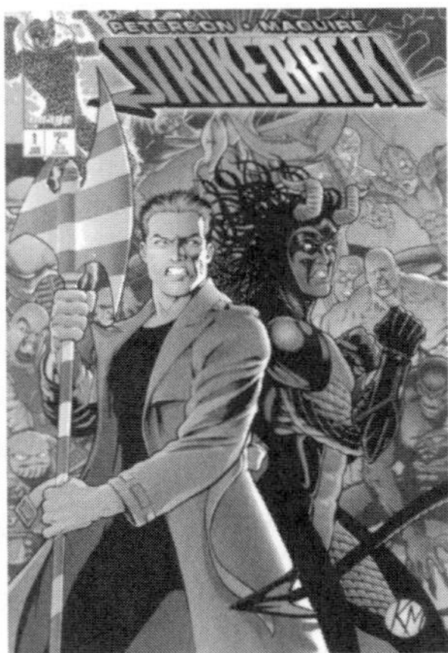

Strikeback #1
© Wildstorm

STREETS
Image April, 1999

TPB Streets 16.95

STRIKEBACK!
Image/Wildstorm 1996

1 thru 5, rep & new art . . . . @2.50

SUPER-PATRIOT

1 N:Super-Patriot. 2.25
2 KN(i),O:Super-Patriot 2.25
3 A:Youngblood. 2.25
4 . . . . 1.95

SUPER-PATRIOT: LIBERTY AND JUSTICE

1 R:Covenant 2.50
2 Tokyo 2.50
3 Tokyo gets Trashed 2.50
4 Final issue 2.50

SUPREME
Image/Supreme 1992

0 O:Supreme. 2.50
1 B:RLd(s&i),BrM, V:Youngblood . . 3.00
1a Gold Ed. 5.00
2 BrM,I:Heavy Mettle,Grizlock 2.50
3 BrM,I:Khrome 2.50
4 BrM 2.50
5 BrM(a&s),Clv(i),I:Thor,V:Chrome. 2.50
6 BrM,Clv(i),I:Starguard,
A:Thor,V:Chrome 2.50
7 Rip,ErS(s),SwM,A:Starguard,
A:Thor, ... 2.50
8 Rip(s),SwM,V:Thor,. 2.50
9 Rip&KtH(s),BrM,Clv(i), V:Thor. . . 2.50
10 KrH(s),BrM,JRu(i), BU:I:Black
& White 2.50
11 Extreme Prejudice,pt.4,
I:Newmen. 2.50
12 SPa(c),RLd(s),SwM, ... 4.00
25 SPa(c),RLd(s),SwM,V:Simple
Simon,Images of Tomorrow . . . 6.00
13 B:Supreme Madness 2.50
14 Supreme Madness, pt.2. . . . . . . 2.50
15 RLd(s)A:Spawn 2.50
16 V:StormWatch 2.50
17 Supreme Madness, pt.5. . . . . . . 2.50
18 E:Supreme Madness 2.50
19 V:The Underworld 2.50
20 V:The Unterworld. 2.50
21 God Wars 2.50
22 RLd,CNn,God Wars, V:Thor. . . . 2.50
23 ExtremeSacrifice,pt.2,x-over . . . 2.50
24 Identity Questions 2.50
#25, see above, after #12
26 F:Kid Supreme 2.50
27 Rising Son,I:Cortex 2.50
28 Supreme Apocalypse:Prelude . . 2.50
29 Supreme Apocalypse,pt.1 . . . . . 2.50
30 Supreme Apocalypse,pt.5 . . . . . 2.50
31 V:Equinox 2.50
32 V:Cortex 2.50
33 Extreme Babewatch. 2.50
34 She-Supreme 2.50
35 Extreme Destroyer, pt.7
x-over, bagged with card 2.50
36 . . . . 2.50
37 . . . . 2.50
38 . . . . 2.50
39 AMo 2.50
40 AMo 2.50
41 AMo 5.00
42 AMo,"Secret Origins" 5.00
43 AMo,"Secrets of the Citadel
Supreme". 2.50
44 See Color Comics section
Ann.#1 TMB,CAd,KG,I:Vergessen. . 2.95
Ashcan #1 . . . . 3.00
Ashcan #2 . . . . 2.00

SUPREME: GLORY DAYS

1 Supreme in WWI 2.95
2 (of 2) BNa&KlA(s),DdW,GyM,
A:Superpatriot 2.95

SWORD OF DAMOCLES
Image/Wildstorm 1996

1 prelude to Fire From Heaven
x-over. 2.50
2 Fire From Heaven,Finale,pt.2 . . . 2.50

TALES OF THE DARKNESS
Image/Top Cow

1 WPo,F:Jackie Estacado 3.00
2 WPo,concl. first story 3.00
3 Dungeon, Fire, and Sword,pt.1 . . 3.00
4 Dungeon, Fire & Sword 3.00
5 in Dark Ages 3.00
6 futuristic story. 3.00

TALES OF THE WITCHBLADE
Image/Top Cow 1996

1 TnD,F:Anne Bonney. 9.00
1a TnD, variant cover (1:4) 12.00
2 TnD,F:Annabella. 6.00
3 WEl,BTn,future. 5.00
4 WEl,BTn,future, pt.2 . . . . 4.00
5 RiB,past 4.00
6 RGr, time of Celts. 3.00
7 in Ancient Egypt 3.00
7a variant cover (1:4). 8.00
1a signed, variant 20.00
8 ancient Egypt,pt.2. . . . . 3.00
Coll.Ed.#1, rep. #1–#2 . . . . 4.95
Coll.Ed.#2, rep.#3–#4 . . . . 5.95

TEAM 1: STORMWATCH

1 I:First StormWatch Team 2.50
2 V:Helspont,D:Think Tank. 2.50

TEAM 1: WILDCATS

1 I:First Wildcats Team 2.50
2 B:Cabal 2.50

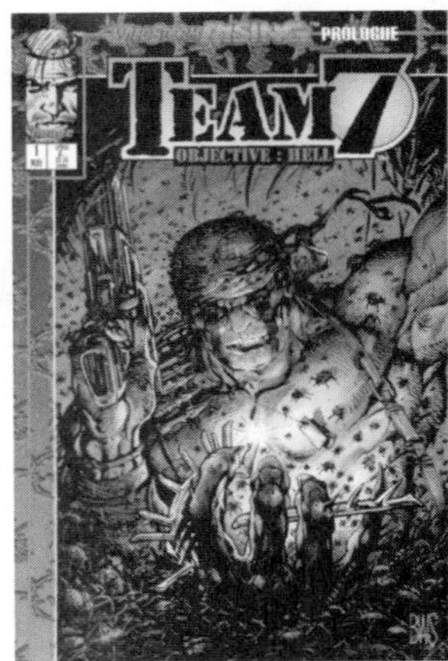

Team 7 Objective: Hell #1
© Image

TEAM 7
Image/Wildstorm 1994–95

1 New team. 4.00
2 New powers 2.50
3 Members go insane 2.50
4 final issue,V:A Nuke 2.50
Ashcan. 2.00
TPB 9.95

TEAM 7 OBJECTIVE: HELL

1 CDi,CW,BWS(c),WildStorm
Rising,Prologue,w/2 cards 2.50
1a Newsstand ed. 1.95
2 Cambodia. 2.50

TEAM 7 III: DEAD REACONING

1 thru 4 . . . . @2.50

TEAM YOUNGBLOOD
Image/Extreme 1993

1 B:ErS(s),ATi(c),CYp,NRD(i),
I:Masada,Dutch,V:Giger 2.50
2 ATi(c),CYp,NRd(i),V:Giger. 2.25
3 RLd(s),CYp,NRd(i),C:Spawn,
V:Giger. 2.25
4 ErS(s), ... 2.25
5 ErS(s),CNn,I:Lynx. 2.25
6 ErS(s),N:Psi-Fire,
BU:Black&White. 2.25
7 ErS(s),CYp,ATh,Extreme
Prejudice,pt.1,I:Quantum,
BU:Black & White. 2.25
8 ErS(s),CYp,ATh,Extreme Prejudice,pt.5, V:Quantum,
BU:Black & White. 2.25
9 RLd 2.50
10 ErS(s),CYp,ATh, ... 2.50
11 RLd,ErS,Cyp 2.00
12 RLd,ErS,Cyp 2.50
13 ErS,Cyp. 2.50
14 RLd,ErS,Cya 2.50
15 New Blood. 2.50
16 RLd,ErS,TNu,I:New Sentinel,
A:Bloodpool 2.50
17 ExtremeSacrifice,pt.6,x-over . . . 2.50
18 MS, membership drive. 2.50
19 R:Brahma 2.50
20 Contact,pt.1 1000 yr Badrock. . . 2.50

21 Contact,pt.2 . . . . 2.50
22 Shadowhunt x-over,pt.4 . . . . 2.50

TEENAGE MUTANT NINJA TURTLES

Image/Highbrow (B&W)

1 thru 3 . . . . @2.00
4 Donatello resurrected 2.00
5 FFo,Warlord Komodo uses Splinter as guinea pig. 2.50
6 FFo 2.50
7 FFo,Raphael joins Foot Clan? . . 2.50
8 FFo,Michelangelo tries to rescue Casey Jones' daughter. 2.95
9 Enter: the Knight Watchman 2.95
10 "Enter: The Dragon". 2.95
11 V:DeathWatch,A:Vanguard 2.95
12 F:Raph, Foot Gang warfare 2.95
13 Shredder is back!. 2.95
14 Shredder vs. Splinter 2.95
15 F:Donatello 2.95
16 reunited with Splinter 2.95
17 F:Leonardo 2.95
18 UFO Sightings 2.95
19 F:Leatherhead 2.95
20 F:Triceraton 2.95
21 A:Pimiko 2.95
22 F:Lady Shredder 2.95
23 F:Lady Shredder 2.95
TPB A New Beginning 9.95

TELLOS

Image May, 1999

1 TDz, The Joining, part 1 . . . . 2.50
2 TDz, The Joining, part 2 . . . . 2.50
3 TDz, The Joining, part 3 . . . . 2.50
4 TDz,Hawke & Rikk 2.50
4a variant JaL cover (1:4) 2.50
4b variant AAd cover (1:4) 2.50
4c variant RGr cover (1:4) 2.50
5 TDz,all-out battle 2.50
6 TDz,Aftermath 2.50
7 TDz,Darkness & Light. 2.50
8 TDz,Tellos Joins Gorilla 2.50
8a variant Kia Asamiya (c). 2.50
8b variant HuR (c) 2.50
9 TDz,Jarek vs. Malesur 2.50
Coll.Ed.#1 The Joining 8.95
Prelude 16-pg. 6.95
Prelude holo-foil 14.95

TENTH, THE

Image Comics

1 BSt,TnD,Last stand against Hell on Earth 6.00
2 BSt,TnD,invasion of Darklon Corp. begins. 5.00
3 BSt,TnD,Tenth & Espy team-up . 4.00
4 BSt,TmD.confrontation with possible Armageddon. 4.00
TPB rep.#1–#4 . . . . 10.95

Regular Series

1 TnD,BSt,V:Blackspell 5.00
2 TnD,BSt,V:Blackspell 4.00
3 TnD,BSt,Gozza,Eve 4.00
4 TnD,BSt,teleported to Japan. . . . 4.00
5 TnD,BSt. 3.50
6 TnD,BSt,CollateralDamage,pt.1 . 3.50
7 TnD,BSt,CollateralDamage,pt.2 . 4.00
8 TnD,BSt,Darkk Wind At Your Back 2.50
9 TnD,BSt,F:Adrenalynn 2.50
10 TnD,pt.1 (of 3) 2.50
10a variant TnD(c) 2.50
11 TnD,Victor retains Tenth. 2.50
11a variant cover 2.50
12 TnD,Black reign begins 2.50
13 TnD,V:Rhazes Darkk 2.50
14 TnD,V:Rhazes Darkk 2.50
Coll.Ed.Vol.1 rep. #1–#2 . . . . 4.95
Spec.Configuration#1, sourcebook . 2.50
TPB rep.#1–#4 . . . . 11.95

TENTH, THE: BLACK EMBRACE

Image Feb., 1999

1 TnD,SLo, V:Gozza 4.00
1a variant cover (1:2). 12.00
2 TnD,SLo, F:Esperanza 2.50
3 TnD,SLo, F:Adrenalynn 2.50
4 TnD,SLo, conclusion. 2.50

TENTH, THE: EVIL'S CHILD

Image Sept., 1999

1 TnD, F:Gozza. 3.00
1a variant cover (1:3). 3.00
1b variant cover (1:3). 3.00
2 TnD, F:Twisted 3 . . . . 2.50
3 TnD 2.50
4 TnD, someone dies 2.50
Spec.Ed.#1, rep.#0 & #1/2 . . . . 2.95

TINCAN MAN

Image Jan., 2000

1 F:Alex Darkstar. 2.95
1a variant GfD (c) (1:4) 2.95
2 no mercy 2.95
3 . . . . 2.95
Preview Book, 24-pg 2.95

TOMB RAIDER

Image/Top Cow Nov., 1999

1 DJu,JSb 3.00
2 DJu,JSb,quest for Medusa Mask 2.50
3 DJu,JSb,secret of Medusa Mask. 2.50
4 DJu,JSb,Medusa Mask found . . . 2.50
5 DJu,JSb,Ancient Futures 2.50
6 DJu,JSb,Death Dance 2.50
7 DJu,JSb,Dead Center,pt.1(of4) . . 2.50
8 DJu,JSb,Dead Center,pt.2 . . . . . 2.50
TPB Saga of the Medusa Mask . . 12.95

TOMB RAIDER/ WITCHBLADE

Image/Top Cow June, 2000

1/2 rep.. . . . . 2.95

TOMB RAIDER/ WITCHBLADE REVISITED

Image/Top Cow Dec., 1998

1 Video game tie-in 00

TOOTH & CLAW

Image Aug., 1999

1 Reborn to rage 2.95
2 MPa 2.95
3 MPa,Retribution,concl. 2.50

TOP COW/BALLISTIC

Swimsuit Spec.#1 MS(c) (1995). . . 4.00

TOP COW CLASSICS

Image/Top Cow 2000

Witchblade #1 B&W 2.95
The Darkness #1 B&W. 2.95
Ascension #1 . . . . 2.95
Fathom #1 . . . . 2.95
Rising Stars #1 B&W 2.95
Cyberforce #1 B&W 2.95

TOP COW SECRETS

Winter Lingerie Spec. (1996) 3.00

A TOUCH OF SILVER

Image (B&W) Jan., 1997

1 JV,"Birthday". 2.95
2 JV,"Dance" 2.95
3 JV,"Bullies" 2.95
4 JV,"Separation". 2.95
5 JV,inc. Tomorrow Syndicate vs. Round Table of America, 12pg. color section. 2.95
6 JV "Choices" Aug. 1963 . . . . 2.95
TPB A Sociopath in Training 12.95

TREKKER

Image May, 1999

1 RoR, in New Gelaph. 00

TRENCHER

1 KG,I:Trencher. 2.25
2 KG, ... 2.25
3 KG,V:Supreme 2.25
4 KG,V:Elvis 2.25

TRIBE

1 TJn(s),LSn,I:The Tribe 2.50
1a Ivory(White) Editon 3.00
2 . . . . 2.25
Ashcan 1 . . . . 3.00

TROLL

Image/Extreme Dec., 1993

1 RLd(s),JMs,I:Evangeliste, V:Katellan Command, ... 2.50
2 . . . . 2.50
Halloween Spec.#1. . . . . 2.50
X-Mas Stocking Stuffer #1 . . . . 2.95

TROLL: ONCE A HERO

1 Troll in WWII. 2.50

TROUBLEMAN

Image/Motown June, 1996

1 and 2 Charles Drost . . . . @2.50

Troll: Once a Hero #1
© Image

IMAGE

TSUNAMI GIRL

Image/Flypaper Jan., 1999

1 F:Michelle Vincent 2.95
2 Sorayama (c), A:Alan Poe 2.95
3 Sorayama(c), Surreal conspiracy 2.95

TUG & BUSTER

Image (B&W) June, 1998

1 MaH, humor, F:Stinkfinger 2.95

"21"

Image/Top Cow

1 thru 3 LWn,MDa, ... @2.50
4 LWn,MDa,"Time Bomb" pt.1 . . . . 2.50
5 LWn,MDa,"Time Bomb" pt.2 . . . . 2.50
6 LWn,MDa,"Time Bomb" pt.3
"Detonation" 2.50

UNBOUND

Image (B&W) Jan., 1998

1 by Joe Pruett & Michael Peters. . 2.95
2 . . . . 2.95
3 F:Marta & Erik 2.95

UNION

Image/Wildstorm

0 O:Union 2.50
0a WPo(c), ... 3.00
1 MT,I:Union,A:StormWatch. 2.75
2 MT 2.75
3 MT 2.75
4 MT,Good Intentions 2.75

Regular Series 1995

1 R:Union, Crusade. 2.50
2 V:Crusade & Mnemo 2.50
3 A:Savage Dragon. 2.50
4 JRo,BWS(c), WildStorm
Rising,pt.3,w/2 cards 2.50
4a Newsstand ed. 1.95
5 V:Necros 2.50
6 V:Necros 2.50
7 Jill's Surprise 2.50
8 Regal Vengeance,pt.1 . . . . 2.50
9 Regal Vengeance,pt.2 . . . . 2.50
10 Regal Vengeance,pt.3 . . . . 2.50
1-shot Final Vengeance, MHs,
V:Regent (1997). 2.50

Union #9
© Wildstorm

UNION

Image/Wildstorm 1996

1 MHs,RBn,"Knight of Faith" 2.50
2 MHs,RBn 2.50
3 MHs,RBn 1.75

VAGABOND

Image August, 2000

1 RBn,SRf,F:Sharon Armstrong . . . 2.95
1a variant (c). 2.95
1b deluxe 8.95
1c signed. 10.95
1d ruby red foil (c) 11.50
2 RBn,SRf. 2.95

VAGRANT STORY

Image/Top Cow Sept., 2000

1 video game tie-in 2.95

VANGUARD

Image/Highbrow 1993–94

1 EL(s),BU:I:Vanguard. 2.25
2 EL(s),Roxann, ... 2.25
3 AMe, ... 2.25
4 AMe, ... 2.25
5 AMe,V:Aliens 2.25
6 V:Bank Robber. 1.95
Spec. B&W 48-pg. 5.95

VANGUARD: STRANGE VISITORS

Image (B&W) 1996

1 (of 4) SEa,BAn,A:Amok,"Strange
Visitors' 2.95
2 SEa,BAn, ... 2.95
3 SEa,BAn, ... 2.95
4 SEa,BAn,finale 2.95

VELOCITY

Image/Top Cow 1995–95

1 V:Morphing Opponent. 2.50
2 V:Charnel 2.50
3 & 4 conclusion . . . . @2.50

VIOLATOR

Image/TMP 1994

1 AMo(s),BS,I:Admonisher. 2.25
2 AMo(s),BS 1.95
3 AMo(s),BS,last issue 1.95

VIOLATOR/BADROCK

Image/Extreme 1995

1 AMo(s),RLe(c),A:Celestine,"Rocks
and Hard Places,"pt.1. . . . . 2.50
2 AMo(s),RLe(c),V:Celestine,"Mondo
Inferno" 2.50
3 RLe(c),F:Dr. McAllister,"Where
Angels Fear to Tread". 2.50
4 RLe(c),"Badrock's Bogus Journey,"
final issue. 2.50
TPB Rep. 9.95

VIOLENT MESSIAHS

Image June, 2000

1 F:Rankor Island 2.95
1a variant AMe (c) (1:4). 2.95
2 . . . . 2.95
2a variant (c). 2.95
3 V:Citizen Pain. 2.95
4 V:Jeremiah Parker 2.95

Vogue #3
© Extreme

VISITATIONS

Image (B&W) 1997

GN by C. Stott Morse 6.95

VOGUE

Image/Extreme 1995–96

1 F:Vogue,I:Redbloods 2.50
2 . . . . 2.50
3 conclusion 2.50

VOODOO

Image/Wildstorm Nov., 1997

1 AMo(s),WildStorm universe 2.50
2 AMo(s),in old New Orleans 2.50
3 AMo(s),Samedi 2.50
4 AMo(s), Christian Charles. 2.50
TPB Voodoo Dancing in the Dark . 10.00

WAHOO MORRIS

Image B&W March, 2000

1 Rock & Roll fantasy 2.75
2 . . . . 2.95

WARBLADE: ENDANGERED SPECIES

Image/Wildstorm 1995

1 I:Pillar. 2.95
2 V:Ripclaw 2.50
3 I:Skinner. 2.50
4 final issue. 2.50

WARLANDS

Image Aug., 1999

1 by Pat Lee 2.50
1a, b & c variant covers. 2.50
1d Armore Chrome edition. 12.95
2 help from the Elves? 2.50
2a variant cover (1:2). 2.50
3 the Dataran invasion. 2.50
3a variant cover (1:2). 2.50
4 . . . . 2.50
5 trapped between enemies. 2.50
6 enemies clash 2.95
7 the Dataran Horde 2.50
8 . . . . 2.50
9 final battle begins 2.50
10 flip-book 2.95
Chronicles Vol.1, rep.#1–#3 . . . . . . 7.95

Chronicles Vol.2, rep.#4–#6 . . . . . . 7.95

WAY OF THE CODA: THE COLLECTED WILDC.A.T.S

TPB VOL.II 12.95

WEAPON ZERO

Image/Top Cow 1995

T-Minus-4 WS 8.00
T-Minus-3 Alien Invasion 5.00
T-Minus-2 Formation of a Team . . . 5.00
T-Minus-1 Alien Invasion 5.00
0 Whole Team Together. 4.00
1 . . . . 5.00
2 . . . . 3.50
3 . . . . 3.50
4 WS,JBz 3.00
5 WS,JBz 3.00
6 WS,JBz 3.00
7 WS,JBz 3.00
8 WS,JBz 3.00
9 WS,JBz 3.00
10 WS,ScL,"Devil's Reign" tie-in . . . 3.00
11 WS,JBz,Weapon Zero & Lilith return to T'srii moonbase 3.00
12 WS,JBz, What's wrong with Jamie 3.00
13 WS,JBz,problems with Jamie . . . 3.00
14 JBz,T'Srrii have returned 3.00
15 JBz,T'Srrii,concl.,48pg 3.50
Weapon Zero/Silver Surfer Spec. x-over (1997) 3.00

WEASEL GUY: ROADTRIP

Image (B&W) Aug., 1999

1 by Steve Buccellato 2.95
1a variant cover (1:4). 2.95
2 Peril in Pennsylvania 2.95
2a variant cover (1:4). 2.95
3 Don't Mess With Texas 2.95
3a variant cover (1:4). 2.95
4 48-pg, guest stars. 4.95
4a variant KIA (c) (1:4). 4.95

WETWORKS

Image/Wildstorm 1994

1 WPo,Rebirth. 4.00
2 WPo,BCi,Brakken,Blood Queen . 3.00

Wetworks #39
© Wildstorm

3 WPo,BCi,V:Vampire 3.00
4 WPo,BCi,Dozer 2.50
5 WPo,BCi,Pilgrim's Turn. 2.50
6 WPo,BCi,Civil War 2.50
7 WPo,BCi,F:Pilgrim 2.50
8 WPo,SW,BWS(c), Wildstorm Rising,pt.7,w/2 cards 2.50
8a Newsstand ed. 2.25
9 F:Jester,Pilgrim Dozer 2.50
10 R:Dozer to Action 2.50
11 Blood Queen Vs. Dane 2.50
12 V:Vampire Nation. 2.50
13 WPo(c) 2.50
14 . . . . 2.50
15 . . . . 2.50
16 Fire From Heaven,pt.4. . . . . 2.50
17 FTa,Fire From Heaven,pt.11. . . . 2.50
18 FTa,. 2.50
19 FTa,. 2.50
20 FTa,. 2.50
21 FTa,. 2.50
22 FTa,Dave vs.Bloodqueen concl. . 2.50
23 FTa,Flattop & Crossbones, V:Lady Feign 2.50
24 FTa,. 2.50
25 FTa,Can Pilgrim withstand the beast that lurks within her, double size. 4.00
26 team parts ways with Armand Waering 2.50
27 V:Craven, no rest for the weary . 2.50
28 Vampire tracked in Pacific Northwest,A:Johnny Savoy. . . . 2.50
29 V:Soulbender,"Power Surge" . . . 2.50
30 "Secret of the Siynn" 2.50
31 "Ashes to shes" 2.50
32 StG,PtL,V:Drakkar,"Sacrements of Damnation,"pt.1 . . . . 2.50
32a Voyager pack, bagged with Phantom Guard preview 3.50
33 StG,PtL,Sacraments, pt.2 . . . . . 2.50
34 StG,PtL,Sacraments, pt.3 . . . . . 2.50
35 StG,PtL,Sacraments, pt.4 . . . . . 2.50
36 StG,"Maximum Security" 2.50
37 StG,V:St.Crispin,"Diversionary Tactics,"pt.1 . . . . 2.50
38 StG,"DiversionaryTactics,"pt.2 . . 2.50
39 StG,"Symbiote Seizure" 2.50
40 StG,"Drawn Swords" 2.50
41 StG,V:Stormwatch,"Drawn Swords," conclusion 2.50
42 StG,"Flash Back,"pt.1. . . . . 2.50
43 StG,"Flash Back,"conclusion . . . 2.50
3-D Spec.#1 (1998) 5.00
Sourcebook #1 (1994) 2.50
Hero Ashcan 3.00
Promo Ashcans #1,#2,#3 . . . . . . @3.00
TPB Rebirth,rep. #1–#3 & preview . 9.95

WETWORKS/VAMPIRELLA

Image/Wildstorm1997

1 JMi & GK, x-over 2.95

WICKED, THE

Image Dec., 1999

1 RMr,FTa,supernatural thriller. . . . 3.00
1a variant Jay Anacleto(c)(1:4) . . . 3.00
2 . . . . 3.00
3 . . . . 3.00
3a variant cover. 3.00
4 . . . . 3.00
4a variant cover. 3.00
5 . . . . 3.00
6 . . . . 3.00
7 . . . . 3.00
Special Medusa's Tale 3.95

WILDC.A.T.S.

Image/Wildstorm 1992

1 B:BCi(s),JLe, SW(i), I:Wild-C.A.T.S. 5.00
1a Gold Ed.. . . . . 5.00
1b Gold and Signed. 10.00
2 JLe,SW(i),V:Master Gnome, I:Wetworks, Prism foil(c), with coupon #5. . . . . 5.00
2a w/o coupon. 2.00
3 RLd(c),JLe,SW(i), V:Youngblood. 4.00
4 E:BCi(s),JLe,LSn,SW(i),w/card, A:Youngblood,BU:Tribe. 4.00
4a w/red card 4.00
5 BCi(s),JLe,SW,I:Misery 3.00
6 BCi(s),JLe,SW,Killer Instinct, A:Misery,C:Ripclaw. 3.00
7 BCi(s),JLe,SW, A:Cyberforce . . . 3.00
8 BCi(s),JLe,SW,. 3.00
9 BCi(s),JLe,SW,. 3.00
10 CCl(s),JLe,SW,I:Huntsman 2.50
11 CCl(s),JLe,SW,V:Triad, A:Huntsman 2.50
11a WPo(c) 4.00
12 JLe,CCl,A:Huntsman 3.00
13 JLe,CCl,A:Huntsman 3.00
14 X book. 3.00
15 F:Black Razors 3.00
16 Black Razors 3.00
17 A:StormWatch 3.00
18 R:Hightower. 3.00
19 V:Hightower. 3.00
20 TC,JeR,BWS(c),WildStorm Rising,pt.2,w/2 cards 2.50
20a Newsstand ed.. . . . . 2.00
21 Into Space Back Home 2.50
22 Space Adventures 2.50
23 F:Mr. Majestic's Team 2.50
24 O:Maul 2.50
25 double sized 5.00
26 . . . . 2.50
27 . . . . 2.50
28 . . . . 2.50
29 Fire From Heaven,pt.7. . . . . 2.50
30 BKs,Fire From Heaven,pt.13 . . . 2.50
31 BKs,"Cats & Dogs" 2.50
32 BKs,"Catharsis" 2.50
33 BKs,"Belling the Cat" 2.50
34 AMo,MtB,New York seconds away from nuclear disaster. . . . 2.50
35 AMo,MtB,BKs,V:Crusade 2.50
36 AMo,MtB,BKs,V:Crusade, A:Union, pt.2 . . . . 2.50
37 BCi,JPe,MtB,WildC.A.T.s team divided. 2.50
38 BCi,JPe,MtB,Puritans debut . . . 2.50
39 BCi,JPe,MtB,"C.A.T. Fight". 2.50
40 BCi,JPe,MtB,MtB(c),"Fight of Flight". 2.50
40a variant cover by TC 3.00
41 BCi,JPe,MtB,backwards in time . 2.50
42 BCi,JPe,MTb,in WWI 2.50
43 BCi,JPe,MTb,in ancient China . . 2.50
44 BCi,JPe,MTb,"Paradise Lost". . . 2.50
45 BCi,JPe,MTb,"Circus Maximus" . 2.50
46 BCi,JPe,MTb,escape from Rome. 2.50
47 BCi,JPe,MTb,time trip concl. . . . 2.50
47a variant JMd(c) 2.50
48 BCi,JPe,trapped in mothership. . 2.50
49 BCi,JPe,return to present. 2.50
50 BCi,JPe,AMo,new costumes,40pg (June 1998) . . . 3.50
TPB A Gathering of Eagles. 9.95
Spec.#1 SrG(s),TC,SW,I:Destine, Pin-ups 3.50
Spec.#2 . . . . 2.50
3-D #1 rep. #1 (1997). 4.95
3-Da variant cover 4.95
TPB rep. #1-4,w/0. . . . . 11.00

IMAGE

WildC.A.T.S. #40
© *Wildstorm*

TPB Homecoming rep.#21–#27 . . 19.95
Ann.#1 JRo,LSn (1998) 2.95
TPB WildC.A.T.S/Cyberforce Killer Instinct. 16.95
TPB Gathering of Eagles 9.95
TPB Gang War,rep.#28–34 . . . . . . 16.95
Volume 2: See COLOR

WILDC.A.T.S ADVENTURES

Image/Wildstorm 1994

1 From animated TV series 2.50
2 Helspont,Troika 2.00
3 Caught in war. 2.00
4 V:The President 2.50
5 I:Lonely 2.50
6 I:Majestics 2.50
7 . . . . 2.50
8 Betrayed. 2.50
9 V:Black Razors. 2.50
10 F:Voodoo. 2.50
Sourcebook (JS(c) 2.95

WILDC.A.T.S/ALIENS

Image/Wildstorm 1998

1-shot WEI,CSp,KN 4.95
1-shotA, variant GK&KN(c)(1:4) . . . 4.95

WILDC.A.T.S. TRILOGY

1 BCi(s),JaL,V:Artemis. 2.50
2 BCi(s),JaL,V:Artemis. 2.25
3 BCi(s),JaL,V:Artemis. 2.25

WILDC.A.T.S/X-MEN

Image/Wildstorm Feb., 1997

1 (of 4) SLo,TC, giant Marvel/ Image x-over 4.50
1a alternate cover by JLe 4.50
2 & 4 see Marvel
TPB WildC.A.T.S/X-Men, rep. 18.50

WILDC.A.T.S/X-MEN

Image/Wildstorm/Marvel 1997

Golden Age #1,SLo,TC. 4.95
Golden Age #1a variant JLe(c) 4.95
3-D Golden Age #1, with glasses . . 4.95
3-D Golden Age #1, variant cover. . 4.95
Silver Age #1 SLo, JLe & SW, x- over 4.50
Silver Age #1a NA&SW(c) 4.50
Silver Age #1b signed. 19.95
Silver Age #1c signed, deluxe. . . . 29.95
3-D Silver Age #1, with glasses . . . 6.50
3-D Silver Age #1, NA(c) variant. . . 6.50
Modern Age #1, JRo,AHu,MFm, V:Hellfire Club 4.50
Modern Age #1a variant cover 4.50
3-D Modern Age #1, with glasses . . 4.95
3-D Modern Age #1, variant cover . 4.95

WILDCORE

Image/Wildstorm 1997–98

1 BBh,SRf,BBh(c), V:Drahn 2.50
1a variant TC(c) 2.50
1b Voyager bagged pack. 3.00
2 BBh,SRf,Brawl joins 2.50
3 BBh,SRf,V:D'rahn. 2.50
4 BBh,SRf,A:Majestic 2.50
5 BBh,SRf,Tapestry 2.50
6 BBh,SRf,Zealot missing 2.50
7 BBh,SRf,caught in fantasy world. 2.50
8 RBn,SRf,V:Tapestry 2.50
9 RBn,SRf,Zealot's soul restored . . 2.50
10 RBn,SRf,Trans-dimensional trauma 2.50
GN Backlash & Taboo's African Vacation. 6.00

WILDSTAR

1 JOy,AG,I:WildStar. 2.25
1a Gold Ed. 3.00
2 JOy,AG 2.25
3 JOy,AG,V:Savage Dragon, D:WildStar 2.25
4 JOy,AG,Last Issue,Pin-ups 2.25
TPB 12.95

[Regular Series]

1 R:WildStar 2.00
2 V:Mighty Man 2.50
3 . . . . 2.50
Ashcan. 1.00
TPB WildStar Sky Zero. 12.95

WILDSTORM!

Image/Wildstorm

1 F:Spartan,Black Razors 2.50
2 F:Deathblow. 2.50
3 F:Taboo,Spartan. 2.50
4 F:Nautika,Sunburst. 2.50
Winter Wonderfest Spec.#1 . . . . . . 3.50
Spec.#1 Chamber of Horrors(1995) 3.50
Spec. Swimsuit Special '97. . . . . . . 2.50
Spec. Ultimate Sports Official Program. 2.50
Sketchbook 2.95
Spec. Halloween '97. . . . . 2.50
GN Thunderbook #1. . . . . 6.95

WILDSTORM ARCHIVES GENESIS

Image/Wildstorm June, 1998

1 The #1 Collection, 238 pg. 7.00

WILDSTORM RISING

Image/Wildstorm

1 JeR,BWS(c&a) WildStorm Rising, pt.1:Tricked by Defile,w/2 cards 2.50
1a Newsstand ed. 1.95
2 RMz,BBo,BWS(c) WildStorm Rising,pt.10,w/2 cards 2.50
2a Newsstand ed. 1.95
Wildstorm Sourcebook #1. . . . . 2.50
TPB Rep. Mini-series 16.95

WILDSTORM SPOTLIGHT

Image/Wildstorm Feb., 1997

1 AMo,F:Majestic, at the end of time 2.50
2 StG,RMr,Loner returns 2.50
3 StG,RMr,Secret past of original Loner 2.50
4 F:Hellstrike,Stormwatch 2.50

WILDSTORM ULTIMATE SPORTS

Image/Wildstorm 1997

Official Program #1 . . . . 2.50

WILDSTORM UNIVERSE '97

Image/Wildstorm Nov., 1997

Sourcebook #1 thru #3 . . . . @2.50

WITCHBLADE

Image/Top Cow 1995–96

1 I:Witchblade 32.00
1A Special retailer edition 40.00
1B Wizard Ace edition,acetate(c). 45.00
2 . . . . 30.00
2 encore edition. 7.00
3 . . . . 25.00
4 . . . . 15.00
5 . . . . 14.00
6 . . . . 8.00
7 . . . . 7.00
8 . . . . 7.00

Top Cow 1996

9 . . . . 8.00
9A variant cover. 11.00
10 I:Darkness (Jackie Estacado). . . 7.00
10a variant Darkness cover (1:4) . 15.00
11 . . . . 6.00
12 Connection between Lisa, Microwave Murderer and Kenneth Irons. 5.00
Witchblade 1/2 mail-in offer from Fan #8 . . . . 4.00

Image/Top Cow 1997

13 Dannette Boucher's secret past. 5.00
14 Sara searches for Microwave Murderer 5.00
15 "There is a war brewing..." 4.00
16 "Will Witchblade come between Sarah and Jake?". 4.00
17 New York City in shambles 4.00
18 Family Ties, pt.1,x-over 4.00
18a variant (c) 7.00
19 Family Ties, pt.4,x-over 3.50
20 Chief Siry, Ian Nottingham 3.00
21 another big surprise. 3.00
22 F:Sara 3.00
23 F:Ian Nottingham. 3.00
24 JPn,Sara learns truth. 3.00
25 Save Jake's Life, 32 pg 3.50
26 "Grey" 2.50
27 A:Kenneth Irons. 2.50
27a variant cover, all villains 2.50
28 A:Jackie Estacado 2.50
29 A:Kenneth Irons. 2.50
30 Siry & Irons 2.50
31 How Sara's father died 2.50
32 answers and questions 2.50
33 F:Eric 2.50
34 F:Tommy Gallo 2.50
35 Sara gets who she wants. 2.50
36 The Darkness, pt.1 x-over 2.50
37 V:wicked creatures 2.50
38 V:Demons of the Underworld . . . 2.50
39 V:Demons of the Underworld . . . 2.50
40 PJe,RV 2.50

41 PJe,RV,arsonist 2.50
42 PJe,pez dispensers 2.50
43 PJe,Impossible Murders. 2.50
44 PJe,Impossible Murders. 2.50
Coll.Ed.Vol.#1. . . . . 4.95
Coll.Ed.Vol.#2. . . . . 4.95
Coll.Ed.Vol.#3. . . . . 4.95
Coll.Ed.Vol.#4, rep. #7 & #8 . . . . . . 4.95
Coll.Ed.Vol.#5, rep. #9 & #10 . . . . . 4.95
Coll.Ed.Vol.#6, rep. #11 & #12 . . . . 4.95
Coll.Ed.Vol.#7, rep. #13 & #14 . . . . 4.95
Coll.Ed.Vol.#8, rep. #15–#17 . . . . . 6.95
Delux Coll.Ed. rep.#1–#8 . . . . 24.95
Spec. Infinity SLo,AdP 3.50
Spec.#40 Preview book, B&W 5.00
Spec.#1 rep.movie photo cover. . . . 2.50
Spec.Witchblade/Darkness, pt.2
x-over, 48-pg. 3.95
Spec. Witchblade/Darkminds x-over 5.95
Gallery Edition #1 . . . . 2.95
TPB Collects Witchblade/Darkness
Family Ties x-over 9.95
TPB Vol.3 Prevailing, deluxe. 14.95
TPB Revelations, deluxe. 24.95
Spec. Tomb Raider. 3.95

WITCHBLADE: DESTINY'S CHILD

Image/Top Cow April, 2000

1 (of 3) O:Witchblade, pt.1. . . . . . . 2.95
2 O:Witchblade, pt.2 . . . . 2.95
3 O:Witchblade, concl.. . . . . 2.95

WITCHFINDER, THE

Image/Liar October, 1999

1 by Robert Lugibihl &
Sharon Scott 2.95
1a variant cover (1:2). 2.95
2 . . . . 2.95
3 Concl.. 2.95

WIZARDS TALE, THE

Image/Homage Comics 1997

TPB KBk,DWe 19.95
TPB 2nd printing. 19.95
HC 29.95
HC, signed, limited 39.95

WOLVERINE/ WITCHBLADE

Image/Top Cow Jan., 1997

1-shot "Devil's Reign" pt.5 (of 8) . . . 4.00

WYNONNA EARP

Image/Wildstorm 1996–97

1 BSt,"Violent Territory" 2.50
2 BSt,The Law comes to San
Diablo 2.50
3 BSt,desperate to stop Hemo
from going nationwide 2.50
4 BSt,goes to New York,
V:ancient evil 2.50
5 BSt,battle with Raduk—Eater
of the Dead concl. 2.50

YOUNGBLOOD

Image/Extreme

0 RLd,O:Youngblood,w/coupon#7 . 3.00
0a without coupon 1.50
0b gold coupon 9.00
1 RLd,I:Youngblood (flipbook) 5.00
1a 2nd print.,gold border 2.50
1b RLD,Silent Edition. 12.95
2 RLd,I:ShadowHawk 5.00
3 RLd,I:Supreme,Showdown 3.00
4 RLd,DK,A:Prophet,BU:Pitt 3.00
5 RLd,Flip book,w/Brigade #4 . . . . 2.50
6 RLd(a&s),J:Troll,Knight Sabre,
2nd Die Hard, Proposal to Girl
friend 3.50
7 Badrock, V:Overtkill 2.50
8 Chapel, V:Spawn 2.50
9 . . . . 2.50
9a variant cover. 5.00
10 Bravo, Badrock, Troll 2.50
Yr.Bk.#1 CYp,I:Tyrax,Kaman. 2.75
Ashcan #1 . . . . 8.00
Ashcan #2 . . . . 4.00
TPB rep. #1-#5. . . . . 16.95

[Volume 2] 1995

1 New Roster 2.50
2 The Program Continues 2.50
3 Extreme Babewatch 2.50
4 Extreme Destroyer,pt.4
x-over, bagged with card 2.50
5 . . . . 2.50
6 . . . . 2.50
7 Shadowhunt x-over,pt.3 . . . . 2.50
8 thru 10, ErS,RCz. . . . . @2.50
TPB Baptism of Fire, F:Spawn . . . .
See Color Pub. section

YOUNGBLOOD BATTLEZONE

1 BrM 2.25
2 . . . . 2.95

YOUNGBLOOD STRIKEFILE

Image/Extreme 1993

1 JaL,RLd,I:Allies,A:Al Simmons
(Spawn)I:Giger,Glory 3.00
1a Gold Ed. 4.00
2 JaL,RLd,V:Super Patriot, Giger. . 2.50
2a Gold Ed. 3.50
3 RLd,JaL,DaM(i), A:Super Partiot. 2.50
4 I:Overtkill 2.25
5 . . . . 3.00
6 flip book 3.00
7 flip book 3.00
8 Shaft 3.00
9 Knight Sabre 3.00
10 RLd,TNu,I:Bloodpool,Task,
Psilence,Wylder,Rubble 3.50
11 ExtremeSacrifice,pt.0,x-over
O:Link Crypt. 2.50
TPB rep.#1-#3,sketchbook 12.95
Ashcan. 3.00

YOUNGBLOOD/X-FORCE

Image/Extreme/Marvel 1996

1-shot Mojo visits Image x-over . . . 5.00
1-shot RLd variant cover 5.00

Zealot #1 © Wildstorm

YOUNGBLOOD YEARBOOK

1 CYp,I:Tyrax. 2.75

YOUNGBLOOD: YEAR ONE

1 KBk(s),RLd, the early years 2.50
2 KBk(s),RLd,V:Giger,Cybernet . . . 2.50

ZEALOT

Image/Wildstorm 1995

1 O:Zealot. 2.50
2 In Japan. 2.50
3 V:Prometheus. 2.50

ZORRO

Image (B&W) 1998

TPB #1 rep. classic Alex Toth 15.95
TPB #2 rep. classic Alex Toth 15.95
TPB The Lady Wears Red 12.95

ZORRO MANTANZAS

Image Sept., 1999

1 (of 4) DMG & Mike Mayhew 2.95
2 DMG,V:Machete. 2.95

ZORRO'S LADY RAWHIDE: OTHER PEOPLE'S BLOOD

Image (B&W) Feb., 1999

1 DMG,EM,JuB(c),cont. from Topps
. . . . 2.95
2 DMG,EM,V:Scarlet Fever 2.95
3 DMG,EM,V:Ansel Plague 2.95
4 DMG,EM,V:Scarlet Fever 2.95
5 DMG,EM,Whiplash 2.95

ZORRO'S RENEGADES

Image

TPB Zorro's Renegades, B&W . . . 14.95
TPB Vol. 2, Lady Rawhide 14.95

IMAGE

MALIBU

Airman #1
© Malibu Comics

AIRMAN
1 I:Thresher. 1.95

ALL NEW EXILES
Ultraverse 1995–96

Infinity F:Juggernaut,Blaze 2.50
1 TKa,KeL,Beginning the Quest. . . 1.50
1a Computer painted cover (1:6) . . 2.50
1b signed edition 4.00
2 I:Hellblade, Phoenix flip issue . . . 1.50
3 TKa,KeL,Phoenix Resurrection . . 1.50
4 . . . . 1.50
5 . . . . 1.50
6 I:Moloch 1.50
7 . . . . 1.50
8 I:Maxis 1.50
9 . . . . 1.50
10 “Aladdin Attacks” 1.50
11 V:Maxis,A:Ripfire 1.50

ANGEL OF DESTRUCTION
Oct., 1996

1 . . . . 2.50

ARROW
1 V:Dr.Sheldon,A:Man O'War. 1.95

BATTLETECH
Feb., 1995

0 . . . . 2.95

BATTLETECH: FALLOUT
Dec. 1994–Mar., 1995

1 3 tales, Based on FASA game . . 2.95
1a gold foil limited edition 3.50
1b limited holographic editon 5.00
2 V:Clan Jade Falcon 2.95
3 R:Lea 2.95
4 Conclusion 2.95

BLACK SEPTEMBER
Ultraverse 1995

Infinity End of Black September . . . 2.95

BRAVURA
1995

0 Preview book, mail-in 5.00

BREAK-THRU
Ultraverse 1993–94

1 GJ(s),GP,AV(i),A:All Ultraverse Heroes 2.75
1a Foil Edition 7.50
2 GJ(s),GP,AV(i),A:All Ultraverse Heroes 2.75

'BREED
Bravura
[Limited Series] 1994

1 JSn(a&s),Black (c),I:Stoner. 3.00
2 JSn(a&s),I:Rachel. 2.75
3 JSn(a&s),V:Rachel 2.75
4 JSn(a&s),I:Stoner's Mom 2.75
5 JSn(a&s),V:Rachel 2.75
6 JSn(a&s),final issue 2.50
TPB Book of Genesis, rep.#1-#6. . 12.95

'BREED II
Bravura
[Limited Series] 1994–95

1 JSn,The Book of Revelation 2.95
1a gold foil edition 4.00
2 JSn,A:Rachel 2.95
3 JSn,V:Actual Demon. 2.95
4 JSn,Language of Demons 2.95
5 JSn,R:Rachael 2.95
6 JSn,final issue 2.95

BRUCE LEE
1994

1 MBn(s), Stories of B.Lee. 2.95
2 MBn(s). 2.95
3 MBn(s). 2.95
4 thru 6 . . . . @2.95

CODENAME: FIREARM
Ultraverse 1995

0 I:New Firearm. 2.95
1 F:Alec Swan. 2.95
2 Dual Identity 2.95
3 F:Hitch and Lopez 2.95
4 F:Hitch and Lopez 2.95
5 Working Together 2.95

CURSE OF RUNE
Ultraverse 1995

1A CU,Rune/Silver Surfer tie-in . . . 2.50
1B CU, alternate cover 2.50
2 COntrol of the Soul Gem 2.50
3 F:Marvel's Adam Warlock 2.50
4 N:Adam Warlock. 2.50

DEAD CLOWN
1 I:Force America 2.50
2 I:Sadistic Six. 2.50
3 TMs(s),last issue 2.50

Dinosaurs for Hire #9
© Malibu Comics

DINOSAURS FOR HIRE
1 3-D rep. B&W . . . . .3.00@
WP Heading 1:[2nd Series] 1993–94
1 B:TMs(s),A:Reese,Archie, Lorenzo 3.00
2 BU:Dinosaurs 2099 . . . . 2.50
3 A:Ex-Mutants 2.50
4 V:Poacher,Revenue 2.50
5 . . . . 2.50
6 V:Samantha 2.50
7 V:Turret 2.50
8 Genesis #2, with Skycap 2.50
9 Genesis #5. . . . . 2.50
10 Flip(c) 2.50
11 V:Tiny Lorenzo. 2.50
12 I:Manhatten Bob 2.50
13 I:Lil' Billy Frankenstein 2.50
14 final issue 2.50

DREADSTAR
Bravura 1994–95

1 JSn(c),PDd(s),EC,I:New Dreadstar (Kalla),w/stamp 2.75
2 JSn(c),PDd(s),EC,w/stamp 2.50
3 JSn(c),PDd(s),EC,w/stamp 2.75
4 PDd,EC,Kalla's origin,w/stamp . . 2.50
5 PDd,F:Vanth,w/stamp 2.50
6 PDd,w/stamp 2.50

EDGE
Bravura 1994–95

1 GK,I:Edge 2.50
2 GK,STg,Gold Stamp. 2.50
3 GK,The Ultimates 2.50
4 GK,V:Mr. Ultimate. 2.50

ELIMINATOR
Ultraverse 1995

0 Man,DJa,MZ,Zothros tries to re-open passage to the Godwheel 2.95
1 MZ,Man,DRo, The Search for the Missing Infinity Gems,I:Siren . . 2.95
1a Black Cover ed. 3.95

 All comics prices listed are for *Near Mint* condition.

2 MZ 2.50
3 MZ, Infinity Gem tie-in,finale 2.50

ELVEN
Ultraverse 1994
0 Rep.,A:Prime, double size 2.95
Mini-Series 1994–95
1 A:Prime, Primevil 2.50
2 AaL,R:Maxi-Man. 2.50
3 AaL,V:Duey, Primevil 2.50
4 AaL,F:Primevil 2.50

ETERNITY TRIPLE ACTION
B&W
1 F:Gazonga 1.95
2 F:Gigantor 2.50

Exiles #1
© Malibu Comics

EXILES
Ultraverse 1993
1 TMs(s),PaP,I:Exiles. 4.00
1a w/out card 2.25
1b Gold hologram ed. 10.00
1c Ultra-limited 12.00
2 V:Kort. 3.00
3 BWS,Mastodon,BU:Rune 4.00
4 V:Kort. 3.00

EX-MUTANTS
Nov. 1992–Apr. 1994
1 I&O:Ex-Mutants 2.25
2 V:El Motho,Beafcake,Brickhouse 2.25
3 A:Sliggo,Zygote 2.25
4 . . . . 2.25
5 Piper Kidnapped. 1.95
6 A:Dr.Kildare 1.95
7 V:Dr.Kildare 1.95
8 O:Gelson 1.95
9 F:Dillion 1.95
10 F:Sluggtown 1.95
11 Man(s),Genesis#1,w/card. 2.25
12 ROM(s),Genesis#4. . . . . 2.25
13 J:Gravestone,Arc. 2.25
14 C:Eye 2.25
15 A:Arrow 2.50
16 A:Arrow,I:KillCorp. 2.50
17 A:Arrow,V:KillCorp 2.50
18 A:Arrow,V:KillCorp 2.50

FERRET
1 (From Protectors),DZ,V:Purple Dragon Tong,A:Iron Skull 2.25
[Regular Series] 1992–93
1 thru 3 . . . . 2.50
4 V:Toxin 2.50
4a Newstand Ed. 2.25
5 SEr,Genesis 2.25
6 SEr,Genesis crossover 2.25
7 V:Airman 2.25
8 I:Posse. 2.25
9 DZ,R:Iron Skull,I:Deathsong 2.25
10 DZ. 2.25
11 . . . . 2.25

FIREARM
Ultraverse 1993–95
0 w/video,I:Duet. 3.00
1 I:Firearm,Alec Swan 2.50
1 silver foil, limited edition 4.00
2 BWS,A:Hardcase,BU:Rune. 2.75
3 V:Sportsmen. 2.25
4 HC,Break-Thru x-over. 2.25
5 O:Prime,I:Ellen 2.25
6 A:Prime 2.25
7 V:Killer 2.25
8 DIB(c). 2.25
9 at the Rose Bowl 1.95
10 The Lodge. 2.25
11 Ultraverse Premier #5,BU:Prime 3.50
12 Rafferty Saga,pt.1 . . . . 1.95
13 Rafferty Saga,pt.2 . . . . 1.95
14 Swan. 1.95
15 Rafferty Saga,pt.3 . . . . 1.95
16 Rafferty Saga,pt.4 . . . . 1.95
17 Rafferty Saga,pt.5 . . . . 1.95
18 JeR,HC(c),Rafferty Saga,finale . 2.50

FLOOD RELIEF
Ultraverse 1994
TPB Ultraverse Heroes. 5.00

FOXFIRE
Ultraverse 1996
1 From Phoenix Resurrection 1.50
2 Fate of Mastodon revealed 1.50
3 & 4 . . . . @1.50

FRANKENSTEIN
1 thru 3 movie promo. . . . . @2.50

FREEX
Ultraverse 1993–95
1 I:Freex w/Ultraverse card 3.00
1a Ultra-Limited. 4.00
1b Full Hologram (c) 5.00
2 L:Valerie,I:Rush 3.00
3 A:Rush 3.00
4 GJ(s),DdW,BWS,BU:Rune 2.75
5 GJ(s),V:Master of the Hunt 2.50
6 GJ(s),BH,Break Thru x-over, A:Night Man 2.25
7 BHr,MZ,O:Hardcase 2.25
8 BHr,V:Lost Angel 2.25
9 BHr,A:Old Man 2.25
10 BHr,V:Ms. Contrary 2.25
11 BHr,E:Origins. 2.25
12 GJ,Ultraforce 1.95
13 New look 1.95
14 R:Boomboy 1.95
15 Death of Teammate 3.50
16 Prelude to Godwheel 1.95
17 A:Rune 2.50
18 GJ,A:Contray, Cayman, Juice . . 2.50
Giant Size#1 A:Prime 2.50

Freex #4
© Malibu Comics

GENESIS
0 GP,w/Pog,F:Widowmaker, A:Arrow 3.50
0a Gold Ed. 5.00

GODWHEEL
Ultraverse 1995
0 R:Argus to Godwheel 2.50
1 I:Primevil 2.50
2 Hardcase new costume 2.50
3 F:Lord Pumpkin 2.50
TPB Wheel of Thunder,rep.#0–#3. . 9.95

GRAVESTONE
July 1993–Feb., 1994
1 D:Gravestone,V:Wisecrack 2.25
1a Newstand Ed. 1.95
2 A:Eternal Man, V:Night Plague . . 2.25
2a Newstand Ed. 1.95
3 Genesis Tie in,w/skycap 2.25
4 Genesis 2.25
5 V:Scythe. 2.25
6 V:Jug 1.95
7 R:Bogg. 2.25
8 & 9 . . . . @2.25

HARDCASE
Ultraverse 1993–95
1 I:Hardcase,D:The Squad 3.00
1a Ultra-Limited, silver foil 4.00
1b Full Hologram (c) 5.00
1c Platinum edition 3.50
2 w/Ultraverse card 3.00
3 Hard decisions 2.75
4 A:Strangers 2.75
5 BWS,V:Hardwire,BU:Rune 2.75
6 V:Hardwire 2.50
7 ScB,Break-Thru x-over, I:Nanotech,A:Solution. 2.25
8 GP,O:Solitare 2.25
9 B:O:Choice,I:Turf 2.25
10 O:Choice. 2.25
11 ScB,V:Aladdin 2.25
12 AV,A:Choice. 1.95
13 A:Choice 2.25
14 A:Choice 2.25
15 Hardwires, NIM-E 1.95
16 NIM-E 3.50
17 Prime,NIM-E 1.95
18 V:Nim-E, Battle Royale 1.95
19 Prelude to Godwheel 1.95

MALIBU

Hardcase #9
© Malibu Comics

20 R:Rex Mundi 2.50
21 Mundiquest prelude 2.50
22 Mundiquest. 2.50
23 A:Loki 2.50
24 Mundiquest,pt.3. . . . . 2.50
25 Mundiquest,concl. 2.95
26 Time Gem Disaster 2.95

HOSTILE TAKEOVER

1 Ashcan Ultraverse x-over 75

LITA FORD
Rock-It Comix

1 JBa 3.95

LORD PUMPKIN
Oct., 1994

0 Sludge 2.50

MAN CALLED A-X
Bravura 1994–95
[Limited Series]

0 1st Puzzle piece. 2.95
1 MWn,SwM 2.95
1a Gold foil Edition 4.00
2 MWn,SwM,VLElectobot 2.95
3 MWn,SwM,Mercy Island 2.95
4 MWn,SwM,One Who Came
Before 2.95
5 MWn,SwM,Climax 2.95

MAN OF WAR
1993–94

1 thru 3 V:Lift. 2.50
1a thru 5a Newsstand Ed. 1.95
4 w/poster 2.50
5 V:Killinger. 2.50
6 KM,Genesis Crossover. 2.50
7 DJu,Genesis Crossover 2.50
8 TMs(s),A:Rocket Ranger 2.25
9 thru 12 . . . . @2.25

MANTRA
Ultraverse 1993–95

1 AV,I:Mantra,w/Ultraverse card . . . 3.00
1a Full Hologram (c) 12.00
1b Silver foil (c). 5.00
2 AV,V:Warstrike 2.50
3 AV,V:Kismet Deadly 2.50
4 BWS,Mantra's marriage,
BU:Rune story 2.50
5 MiB(s),AV(i),V:Wiley Wolf 2.00
6 MiB(s),AV(i),Break Thru x-over . . 2.00
7 DJu,TA,A:Prime, O:Prototype . . . 2.00
8 B:MiB(s),A:Warstrike. 2.00
9 V:Iron Knight,Puppeteer 2.00
10 NBy(c),DaR,B:Archmage Quest,
Flip/UltraversePremiere #2 . . . . 3.00
11 MiB(s),V:Boneyard 2.00
12 MiB(s),A:Strangers 2.00
13 Topaz, Boneyard 2.00
14 Tradesmen, Boneyard 2.00
15 A:Prime,Doc Gross 2.00
16 A:Prime. 2.00
17 A:Necromantra 2.00
18 Pregnancy. 2.25
19 MiB,Pregnancy 2.25
20 Aftermath of Godwheel 2.25
21 TyD,MiB,Mantra goes bad 2.25
22 A:Marvel's Loki 2.25
23 I:Tremblor, A:Prime 2.25
24 V:Topaz 2.25
Giant Sized#1 GP(c),I:Topaz. 2.25
Ashcan #1 . . . . 2.00

MANTRA
Ultraverse 1995–96

Infinity N:Mantra 2.50
1 Mantra in all Female Body 1.50
1a Computer Painted Cover 1.50
2 Phoenix flip issue 1.50
3 Phoenix Resurrection 1.50
4 . . . . 1.50
5 . . . . 1.50
6 TMs,I:Tattoo,A:Rush 1.50
7 . . . . 1.50

MANTRA: SPEAR OF DESTINY
Ultraverse 1995

1 Search for Artifact. 2.50
2 MiB,Eden vs. Aladdin 2.50

MARVEL/ULTRAVERSE BATTLEZONES
Ultraverse 1996

1 DPs(c),The Battle of the Heroes . 3.95

MEGADETH
Rock-it Comix

1 . . . . 4.25

METALLICA
Rock-it Comix

1 . . . . 4.25

METAPHYSIQUE
Bravura 1995

1 NBy,I:Metaphysique 2.95
1a Gold foil edition. 4.00
2 NBy,Mandelbrot malfunctions . . . 2.95
3 I:Harridas 2.95
4 D:Maj.Character,B:Superious . . . 2.95
5 V:Astral Kid 2.95
6 Apocalyptic Armageddon, finale . 2.95
Ashcan NBy,B&W. 1.00

MIGHTY MAGNOR, THE

1 thru 6 SA . . . . @1.95

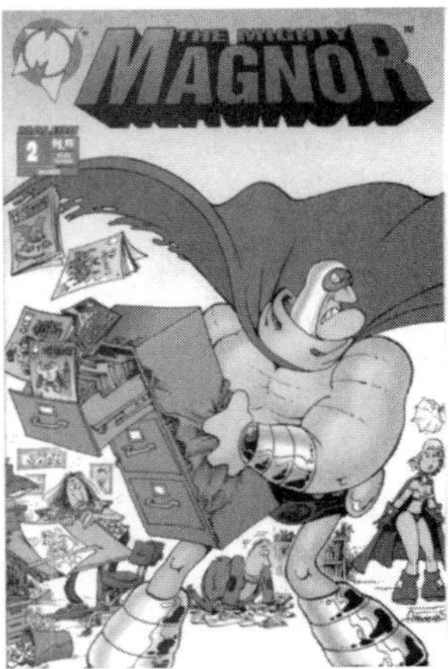

Mighty Mangor #2
© Malibu Comics

MONSTER POSSE
B&W

1 I:Monster Posse 2.50
2 I:P.O.N.E,Wack Mack Dwac's
sister,D-Vicious. 2.50

MORTAL KOMBAT
1994

0 Four stories 2.95
1 Based on the Video Game 2.95
1a Foil Ed 4.00
1b with new material 2.95
2 . . . . 2.95
3 . . . . 2.95
4 . . . . 2.95
5 I:Mortal Kombat II. 2.95
6 Climax 2.95
Spec. #1 Tournament edition 3.95
Spec. #2 Tournament edition II 3.95
TPB rep. #1–#6 . . . . 14.95

MORTAL KOMBAT: BARAKA

1 V:Scorpion 2.95

MORTAL KOMBAT: BATTLEWAVE

1 New series 2.95
2 Action, Action, Action 2.95
3 The Gathering 2.95
4 F:Goro 2.95
5 F:Scorpion 2.95
6 final issue. 2.95

MORTAL KOMBAT: GORO, PRINCE OF PAIN

1 Goro. 2.95
1a Platinum Edition 6.25
2 Goro, V:Kombatant. 2.95
3 Goro, V:God of Pain 2.95

MORTAL KOMBAT: KITANA & MILEENA

1 Secrets of Outworld 2.95

MORTAL KOMBAT: KUNG LAO

1 one-shot Battlewave tie-in. 2.95

MORTAL KOMBAT: RAYDEN AND KANO

1 J:Rayden Kano. 2.95
1a Deluxe Edition 4.95
2 A:Reptile 2.95
3 Kano, conclusion 2.95

MORTAL KOMBAT: U.S. SPECIAL FORCES

1 V:Black Dragon 3.50
2 V:Black Dragon 2.95

NECROMANTRA/ LORD PUMPKIN

Ultraverse 1995

1 A:Loki (from Marvel). 2.95
2 MiB,V:Godwheel, flipbook. 2.95
3 O:Lord Pumpkin 2.95
4 Infinity Gem tie-in 2.95
4a variant cover. 3.50

NECROSCOPE

1 Novel adapt., holo(c) 3.25
1a 2nd printing 2.95
2 thru 4 Adapt. cont. . . . . @2.95

Book II

1 thru 5 . . . . 2.95

NIGHT MAN, THE

Ultraverse 1993–95

1 I:Night Man,Deathmask 2.75
1a Silver foil (c) 4.00
2 GeH,V:Mangle 2.25
3 SEt,GeH,A:Freex,Mangle 2.25
4 HC,I:Scrapyard,O:Firearm 2.25
5 SEt(s). 2.25
6 V:TNTNT 2.25
7 V:Nick 2.25
8 V:Werewolf. 1.95
9 V:Werewolf. 2.25
10 . . . . 1.95
11. . . . . 1.95
12 . . . . 1.95
13 . . . . 1.95
14 V:Rafferty 1.95
15 I:Rigoletto 1.95
16 I:Bloodfly 3.50
17 D:Playland. 2.50
18 DZ,SEt,V:Bloodfly 2.50
19 DZ,SEt,V:Deathmask. 2.50
20 DZ,V:Bloody fly 2.50
21 Identity Revealed. 2.50
22 Infinity Gem tie-in,A:Loki 2.50
23 R:Rhianon 2.50
Ann.#1 V:Pilgrim, 64pg. 3.95

NIGHT MAN, THE

Ultraverse 1995

Infinity Night Man vs. Night Man . . . 2.50
1 Discovers New powers 1.50
1a Computer Painted Cover 1.50
2 Phoenix flip issue 1.50
3 Phoenix Resurrection 1.50
4 final issue. 1.50

NIGHT MAN/GAMBIT

1996

1 thru 3 . . . . @2.50

NOCTURNALS

Bravura 1995

1 DIB,I:Nocturnals 2.95
1a Glow-in-the-Dark 4.00
2 DIB,I:Komodo, Mister Fane. 2.95
3 DIB,F:Raccoon 2.95
4 DIB,I:The Old Wolf 2.95
5 Discovered by Police 2.95
6 DIB, ... 2.95

ORIGINS

Ultraverse

1 O:Ultraverse Heroes. 1.25

OZZY OSBORNE

Rock-It Comix

1 w/guitar pick. 3.95

PANTERA

Rock-it Comix

1 . . . . 3.95
1a Gold Ed. 19.95

PHOENIX RESURRECTION

Ultraverse 1995–96

0 Intro to Phoenix Resurrection . . . 1.95
Genesis, A:X-Men 3.95
Revelations, A:X-Men 3.95
Aftermath, A:X-Men 3.95

PLAN 9 FROM OUTER SPACE

GNv Movie Adapt. 4.95

POWER & GLORY

Bravura 1994

1A HC(a&s),I:American Powerhouse. 3.00
1B alternate cover. 3.00
1c Blue Foil (c) 5.00
1d w/serigraph. 5.00
1e Newsstand 3.00
2 HC(a&s), O:American Powerhouse. 2.75
3 HC(a&s). 2.50
4 HC(a&s). 2.50
Winter Special 2.95
TPB Series reprint, w/stamp 12.95

Prime #12 © Malibu Comics

POWER OF PRIME

Ultraverse 1995

1 O:Prime Powers,Godwheel tie-in 2.50
2 V:Doc Gross, Godwheel tie-in. . . 2.50
3 F:Prime Phade 2.50
4 F:Elven,Turbocharge 2.50

PRIME

Ultraverse 1993–95

1 B:GJ(s),I:Prime. 4.00
1a Ultra-Limited. 5.00
1b Full Hologram (c) 5.00
2 V:Organism 8, with Ultraverse card 3.00
3 NBy,I:Prototype 3.00
4 NBy,V:Prototype 3.00
5 NBy,BWS,I:Maxi-Man, BU:Rune . 3.00
6 NBy,A:Pres. Clinton 2.75
7 NBy,Break-Thru x-over 2.25
8 NBy,A:Mantra 2.25
9 NBy,Atomic Lies 2.25
10 NBy,A:Firearm,N:Prime 2.25
11 NBy 2.25
12 NBy,(Ultraverse Premiere#3) I:Planet Class. 3.50
13 NBy,V:Kutt,Planet Class. 2.95
14 DaR,I:Voodoo Master. 2.25
15 abused kids 2.00
16 I:Turbo. 2.00
17 Atalon 2.00
18 Prime's new partner. 2.00
19 Prime accused. 2.00
20 GJ,LeS,A:Rafferty 2.50
21 GJ,LeS,World without Prime . . . 2.50
22 GJ,LeS,F:Primevil 2.50
23 F:Prime's Mother 2.50
24 F:Prime's Mother 2.50
25 A:Chelsea Clinton 2.50
26 True Powers 2.50
Ashcan (first) 7.00
Ashcan #1 BV(c),B&W 75
Ann.#1 R:Doc Gross. 3.95
TPB Rep. #1-#4 . . . . 9.95

PRIME

Ultraverse 1995–96

Infinty I:Spider-Prime 3.00
1 Spider-Prime vs. Lizard 1.50
1a Computer painted cover 2.00
2 Phoenix flip issue 1.50
3 Phoenix Resurrection 1.50

Prime Vol. 2 #8 © Malibu Comics

MALIBU

4 & 5 . . . . @1.50
6 Prime on Drugs,pt.1,F:Solitaire . . 1.50
7 F:Solitaire, pt.2 . . . . 1.50
8 F:Solitaire, pt.3 . . . . 1.50
9 and 10 . . . . @1.50
11 "Absolute Power Corrupts? Absolutely!" 1.50
12 HuR,KG, pt.3 (of 3) 1.50
13 KG,Prime exposed, V:Colonel Rinaldo 1.50
14 KG, Return of Lord Pumpkin . . . 1.50
15 Return of Lord Pumpkin 1.50

PRIME/CAPTAIN AMERICA
Ultraverse 1996
1 GJ,NBy 3.95

PRIME VS. HULK
0 . . . . 10.00
0a signed premium edition 20.00

PROJECT A-KO
1 thru 4 Based on anime movie . @2.95

PROTECTORS
1992–94
1 I:Protectors, inc. JBi poster (direct) 3.00
1a thru 12a Newsstand . . . . @1.95
2 V:Mr.Monday,w/poster 2.50
3 V:Steel Army,w/poster 2.50
4 V:Steel Army 2.50
5 Die Cut(c),V:Mr.Monday 2.50
6 V:Mr.Monday 2.50
7 A:Thresher 2.50
8 V:Wisecrack 1.95
9 V:Wisecrack 2.50
10 I:Mantoka 2.50
11 A:Ms.Fury,V:Black Fury 2.50
12 A:Arrow 2.50
13 RAJ(s),Genesis#3 . . . . 2.25
14 RB(c),RAJ(s),Genesis#6 . . . . . . 2.25
15 RAJ(s),J:Chalice 2.25
16 So Help Me God 2.25
17 L:Ferret 2.25
18 V:Regulators,BU:Mantako, R:Mr. Monday 2.25
19 A:Gravestone,Arc 2.50
20 V:Nowhere Man 2.50
Protectors Handbook 2.50

Proto bype #9
© Malibu Comics

PROTOTYPE
Ultraverse 1993–95
1 V:Ultra-Tech,w/card 2.50
1a Ultra-lim. silver foil(c) 5.00
1b Hologram 6.00
2 I:Backstabber 2.50
3 LeS(s),DvA,JmP,BWS, V:Ultra-Tech,BU:Rune 2.50
4 TMs(s),V:Wrath 2.25
5 TMs(s),A:Strangers,Break-Thru x-over 2.25
6 TMs(s),Origins Month C:Arena . . 2.25
7 TMs(s),V:Arena 2.25
8 TMs(s),V:Arena 2.25
9 Prototype Unplugged 2.25
10 TMs(s),V:Prototype 1.95
11 TMs(s),R:Glare 2.25
12 V:Ultratech 1.95
13 Ultraverse Premiere #6 . . . . 3.50
14 Jimmy Ruiz, new boss 1.95
15 Techuza, Donovan 1.95
16 New CEO for Terrordy 1.95
17 Ranger Vs. Engine 1.95
18 Turf War 2.50
G-Size, Hostile Takeover 2.50
Spec.#0 LeS,JQ/JP(c) 2.50

PROTOTYPE: TURF WAR
Ultraverse
1 LeS,V:Techuza 2.50
2 LeS,F:Ranger,Arena 2.50
3 . . . . 2.50

RAFFERTY
1 Ashcan 1.00

RAVER
1 Prism cover 3.00
1a Newsstand 2.25
2 . . . . 1.95
3 Walter Koenig(s) 1.95
4 and 5 . . . . @1.95

RIPFIRE
0 Prequel to Ripfire Series 2.50

RUNE
Ultraverse 1994–95
0 BWS(a&s) 4.00
1 BWS(a&s),from Ultraverse 2.50
1a Foil cover 4.00
2 CU(s),BWS,V:Aladdin 2.25
3 DaR,BWS,(Ultraverse Premiere #1), Flip book 3.75
4 BWS,V:Twins 2.25
5 BWS 1.95
6 BWS 1.95
7 CU,JS 1.95
8 Rise of Gods,pt.2 . . . . 1.95
9 Prelude to Godwheel 1.95
G-Size #1 . . . . 2.50
TPB BWS(c&a),CU,The Awakening, rep.#1–#5 . . . . 12.95

RUNE
Ultraverse 1995–96
Infinity V:Annihilus 2.50
1 A:Adam Warlock 1.50
1a Computer painted cover 1.50
2 Phoenix flip issue,A:Adam Warlock 1.50
3 Phoenix Resurrection 1.50
4 . . . . 1.50
5 . . . . 1.50
6 LKa,A:Warlock 1.50
Spec. #1 Rune vs. Venom x-over . . 1.95

RUNE: HEARTS OF DARKNESS
Ultraverse 1996
1 DgM(s),KHt,TBd, flip book 1.50
2 DgM,KHt,TBd, flip book 1.50
3 DgM,KHt,TBd, flip book 1.50

RUNE/SILVER SURFER
Ultravrse 1995
1 BWS(c),A:Adam Warlock 5.95
1a Lim. edition (5,000 made) 8.00
1b Standard ed.newsprint 2.95

RUST
1 O:Rust 2.95
2 V:Marion Labs 2.95
3 I:Ashe Sapphire,5th Anniv. 2.95
4 I:Rustmobile 2.95

SANTANA
Rock-it Comix
1 TT(c&s),TY 3.95

SIREN
Ultraverse 1995
Infinity V:War Machine 2.50
1 V:War Machine 1.50
1a Computer painted cover 1.50
2 Phoenix flip issue 1.50
3 Phoenix Resurrection 1.50
Spec. #1 O:Siren 1.95

SLUDGE
Ultraverse 1993–94
1 BWS,I:Sludge,BU:I:Rune 2.75
1a Ultra-Limited 5.00
2 AaL,I:Bloodstorm 2.25
3 AaL,V:River Men 2.50
4 AaL,Origins Month, V:Alligator . . 2.25
5 AaL,V:Garret Whale 2.25
6 AaL,A:Dragon Fang,Lord Pumpkin 2.25
7 V:Frank Hoag 2.25
8 AaL,V:Monsters 2.25
9 AaL,O:Sludge 2.25
10 AaL,O:Sludge 1.95
11 AaL,V:Bash Brothers 1.95
12 AaL,V:Prime, w/flip book

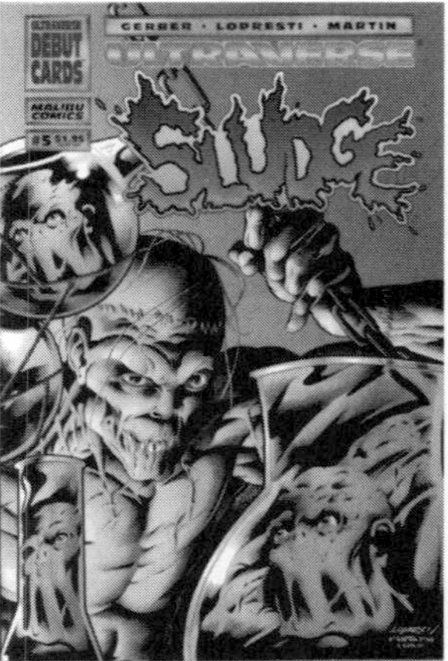

Sludge #5
© Malibu Comics

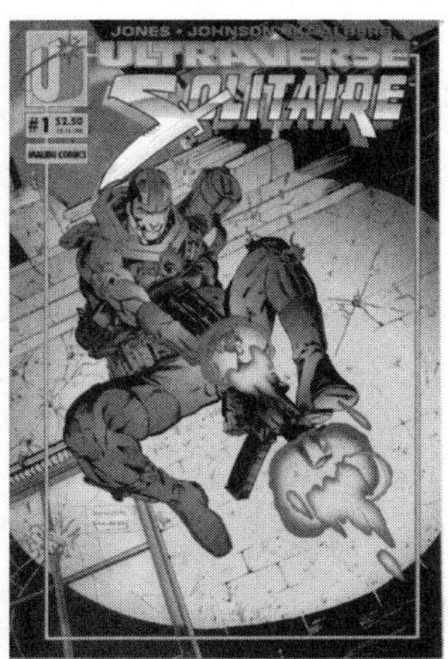

Solitaire #1
© Malibu Comics

w/Ultraverse Premiere #8 . . . . . 3.50
13 . . . . 1.95
Red X-Mas 2.50

SOLITAIRE
Ultraverse 1993–94

1 black bagged edition with playing card: Ace of Clubs, Diamonds, Hearts or Spades 2.75
1d Newsstand edition,no card 2.25
2 GJ(s),JJ,Break-Thru x-over, V:Moon Man. 2.25
3 Origins Month, I:Monkey-Woman 2.25
4 O:Solitaire 2.25
5 JJ,V:Djinn. 2.25
6 JJ,V:Lone 1.95
7 JJ,I:Double Edge 2.25
8 GJ,I:Degenerate. 1.95
9 GJ,Degenerate Rafferty 1.95
10 Hostile Takeover #2. . . . . 1.95
11 V:Djinn. 1.95
12 V:Anton Lowe 1.95

SOLUTION
Ultraverse 1993–95

0 DaR,O:Solution 4.00
1 DaR,I:Solution 2.50
1a foil cover. 4.00
2 DaR,BWS,V:Rex Mundi,Quatro, BU:Rune 2.50
3 DaR,A:Hardcase,Choice. 2.50
4 DaR,Break-Thru x-over, A:Hardcase,Choice. 2.50
5 F:Dropkick 2.25
6 B:O:Solution 2.25
7 KM,O:Solution 2.25
8 KM(c),E:O:Solution. 2.25
9 F:Shadowmage 2.25
10 V:Vyr 2.25
11 V:Vorlexx 2.25
12 JHi 1.95
13 Hostile Takeover pt.3 . . . . 1.95
14 old foes 1.95
15 V:Casino 1.95
16 Flip/UltraverePremiere#10 . . . . . 3.50
17 F:Casino, Dragons Claws 2.50

SQUAD, THE

0-A Hardcase's old team 2.50
0-B 2.50
0-C L.A.Riots. 2.50

STAR SLAMMERS
Bravura 1994

1 WS(a&s). 2.75
2 WS(a&s),F:Meredith 2.75
3 WS(a&s). 2.50
4 WS(a&s). 2.50
5 WS,Rojas Choice 2.50

STAR TREK: DEEP SPACE NINE

1 Direct ed. 3.25
1a Photo(c). 3.00
1b Gold foil 5.00
2 w/skycap 3.50
3 Murder on DS9. . . . . 2.75
4 MiB(s),F:Bashir,Dax 2.75
5 MiB(s),V:Slaves 2.75
6 MiB(s),Three Stories. 2.75
7 F:Kira 2.75
8 B:Requiem 2.75
9 E:Requiem 2.75
10 Descendants 2.50
11 A Short Fuse 2.75
12 Baby on Board. 2.50
13 Problems with Odo 2.75
14 on Bejor. 2.75
15 mythologic dilemma 2.75
16 Shangheid 2.50
17 Voyager preview 2.50
18 V:Gwyn 2.50
19 Wormhole Mystery. 2.50
20 Sisko Injured 2.50
21 Smugglers attack DS9 . . . . 2.50
22 Commander Quark 2.50
23 Secret of the Lost Orb,pt.1. . . . . 2.50
24 Secret of the Lost Orb,pt.2. . . . . 2.50
25 Secret of the Lost Orb,pt.3. . . . . 2.50
26 Mudd's Pets, pt.1. . . . . 2.50
27 Mudd's Pets, pt.2. . . . . 2.50
28 F:Ensign Ro 2.50
29 F:Thomas Riker,Tuvok 2.50
30 F:Thomas Riker 2.50
31 thru 32 . . . . @2.50
Ann.#1 Looking Glass. 3.95
Spec. #1Collision Course 3.50
Spec. #0 Terok Nor. 3.00

STAR TREK: DEEP SPACE NINE CELEBRITY SERIES: BLOOD AND HONOR

1 Mark Lenard(s). 2.95
2 Rules of Diplomacy. 2.95

STAR TREK: DEEP SPACE NINE: LIGHTSTORM

1 Direct ed. 3.50
1a Silver foil 8.00

STAR TREK: DEEP SPACE NINE: HEARTS AND MINDS
[Limited Series]

1 . . . . 3.00
2 . . . . 2.50
3 Into the Abyss,X-over preview . . 2.50
4 final issue 2.50

STAR TREK: DEEP SPACE NINE: THE MAQUIS
[Limited Series]

1 Federation Renegades 2.50
1a Newsstand, photo(c). 2.50
2 Garack 2.50
3 F:Quark, Bashir 2.50

STAR TREK: DEEP SPACE NINE/ THE NEXT GENERATION

1 Prophet & Losses, pt.2 . . . . 2.50
2 Prophet & Losses, pt.4 . . . . 2.50

STAR TREK: VOYAGER

A V:Maquis. 2.75
Aa Newsstand, photo(c) 2.50
B conclusion. 2.75
Ba Newsstand, photo(c) 2.50

STRANGERS, THE
Ultraverse 1993–95

1 I:Strangers 3.00
1a Ultra-Limited. 4.00
1b Full Hologram (c) 5.00
2 A:J.D.Hunt,w/Ultraverse card . . . 3.00
3 I:TNTNT. 2.50
4 A:Hardcase 2.50
5 BWS,BU:Rune 2.50
6 J:Yrial,I:Deathwish 2.25
7 Break-Thru x-over. 2.25
8 RHo,ANi,O:Solution 2.25
9 AV(i),I:Ultra Pirates 2.25
10 AV(i),V:Bastinado. 2.25
11 in Alderson Disk. 2.25
12 O:Yrial. 2.25
13 (Ultraverse Premiere#4). 3.50
14 . . . . 2.25
15 Zip-Zap, Yrail. 1.95
16 Ultras, Teknight 1.95
17 Rafferty 1.95
18 Ultra Pirates 1.95
19 V:Pilgrim 1.95
20 Stranger Destroyed 1.95
21 A:Rex Mundi 2.50
22 SEt,V:Guy Hunt 2.50
23 SEt,RHo,V:Tabboo. 2.50
24 RHo,SEt,V:Taboo. 2.50
25 V:Godwheel Aliens 2.50
26 RHo,SEt,V:Aladdin. 2.50
Ann.#1 Death 3.95
TPB rep. #1-#4. . . . . 9.95
Ashcan 1 (signed) 8.00
Ashcan 1 (unsigned). 8.00

Strangers #5
© Malibu Comics

STREET FIGHTER
1 thru 3 Based on Video Game . @3.00

STRIKEBACK
Bravura 1994–95
1 . . . . 2.95
2 . . . . 2.95
3 V:Doberman 2.95
4 V:Dragonryder Island 2.95
Spec.#1 KM,JRu,V:Dragon 3.50

TARZAN: THE BECKONING
1 TY,I:The Spider Man 2.75
2 TY,Going back to Africa 2.50
3 thru 6 . . . . 2.50

TARZAN THE WARRIOR
1 SBs(c),O:Tarzan 3.50
2 . . . . 2.75
3 . . . . 2.75
4 Wom'cha's Ship 2.75
5 . . . . 2.75

TARZAN: LOVE, LIES, AND THE LOST CITY
1 MWg&WS(s),Short Stories 3.95
2 The lost city of Opar 2.50
3 Final issue 2.50

TERMINATOR 2: CYBERNETIC DAWN
1995–96
1 thru 4 . . . . @2.50
0 flip-book/T2 Nuclear Twilight 2.50

TERMINATOR 2: NUCLEAR TWILIGHT
1995–96
1 thru 4 . . . . @2.50
0 flip-book, see above

ULTRAFORCE
Ultraverse 1994–95
1 Prime, Prototype. 2.50
2 . . . . 1.95
3 . . . . 1.95
4 . . . . 1.95
5 V:Atalon 1.95
6 V:Atalon 2.50
7 CU,GP(c),F:Ghoul 2.50
8 MWn,CV,GP,F:Black Knight 2.50
9 A:Marvel's Black Knight 2.50
10 . . . . 2.50
Spec.#0 . . . . 2.50

Ultraforce #3
© Malibu Comics

ULTRAFORCE
Ultraverse 1995–96
Infinity Fant. Ultraforce Four 2.50
1 George Perez cover 1.50
1a Computer painted cover 1.50
2 Phoenix flip issue,I:Lament 1.50
3 . . . . 1.50
4 . . . . 1.50
5 . . . . 1.50
6 Smoke and Bone,pt.2 . . . . 1.50
7 . . . . 1.50
8 . . . . 1.50
9 . . . . 1.50
10 A:Sersi,Eliminator 1.50
11 . . . . 1.50
12 MD2,LWn, cont. from All-New Exiles #12 . . . . 1.50
13 LWn,MD2,new UltraForce lineup 1.50
14 LWn,MD2,Hardcase returns 1.50
15 LWn,MD2,Hardcase returns 1.50

ULTRAFORCE/AVENGERS
Ultraverse Aug., 1995
1 GP 3.95

ULTRAFORCE/ SPIDER-MAN
Ultraverse 1996
1 . . . . 3.95

ULTRAVERSE DOUBLE FEATURE
Ultraverse
1 F:Prime, Solitaire 3.95

ULTRAVERSE FUTURE SHOCK
Ultraverse 1996
1 one-shot,MPc,alternate futures . . 2.50

ULTRAVERSE ORIGINS
Ultraverse
1 O:Ultraverse Heroes. 1.25
1a Silver foil cover. 12.50

ULTRAVERSE UNLIMITED
Ultraverse 1996
1 F:Warlock. 1.50
2 LWn,KWe, A:All-New Exiles, V:Maxis 1.50

ULTRAVERSE: YEAR ZERO: THE DEATH OF THE SQUAD
Ultraverse 1995
0-A hardcase's old team 2.50
0-B 2.50
0-C L.A. Riots 2.50
1 JHI,A:Squad, Mantra. 2.95
2 JHI,DaR(c) prequel to Prime#1 . . 2.95
3 Cont. Year Zero Story. 2.95
4 I:NM-E 2.95

ULTRAVERSE: YEAR ONE
Ultraverse 1995
1 Handbook, double size. 4.95
2 Prime. 1.95

ULTRAVERSE: YEAR TWO
Ultraverse 1996
1 Marvel/Ultraverse/Info. 4.95

VIRTUA FIGHTER
1 New Video Game Comic 2.95

Warstrike #2
© Malibu Comics

WARSTRIKE
Ultraverse 1994–95
1 HNg,TA,in South America 1.95
2 HNg,TA,Gatefold(c) 1.95
3 in Brazil 1.95
4 HNg,TA,V:Blind Faith 1.95
5 . . . . 1.95
6 Rafferty 1.95
7 Origin 1.95

WARSTRIKE: PRELUDE TO GODWHEEL
Ultraverse 1994
1 Blind Faith/Lord Pumpkin 1.95

WORLD DOMINATION
1 . . . . 3.95
1a 3.95

WRATH
Ultraverse 1994–95
1 B:MiB(s),DvA,JmP,C:Mantra 2.25
1a Silver foil 3.00
2 DvA,JmP,V:Hellion 2.25
3 DvA,JmP,V:Radicals, I:Slayer . . . 2.25
4 DvA,JmP,V:Freex 2.25
5 DvA,JmP,V:Freex 1.95
6 DvA,JmP 2.25
7 DvA,JmP,I:Pierce,Ogre, Doc Virtual 1.95
8 . . . . 1.95
9 A:Prime 2.25
G-Size #1. . . . . 2.50

COLOR COMICS

ABBOTT AND COSTELLO
Charlton Comics 1968–71

1 . . . . 70.00
2 thru 9 . . . . @40.00
10 thru 21 . . . . @25.00
22 . . . . 20.00

ACCIDENT MAN: THE DEATH TOUCH
Apocalypse

One Shot rep.Toxic #10-#16 . . . . @3.95

ACES HIGH
Gemstone 1999

1 (of 5) EC Comics reprint 2.50
2 . . . . 2.50
3 . . . . 2.50
4 . . . . 2.50
5 . . . . 2.50
Annual rep. #1–#5. . . . . @13.50
HC 20.00

ACME NOVELTY LIBRARY
Fantagraphics 1994–98

1 thru 5 . . . . @4.50
6 thru 11 Jimmy Corrigan Meets His Dad, pt. 1 – pt. 6 (of 8) . . @4.50
12 Jimmy & Dad have lunch 4.95
13 Jimmy's Grandfather, 80-page . 10.95
14 F:Jimmy Corrigan 10.95
1 thru 7, 2nd printings . . . . @3.95

A.D.A.M.
Toyman 1998

1 . . . . 2.50
2 . . . . 2.50

ADAM-12
Gold Key 1973–76

1 Photo(c), From TV show. 70.00
2 thru 9 . . . . @30.00
10 . . . . 25.00

ADAPTERS, THE

1 and 2 . . . . @2.00

ADDAMS FAMILY
Gold Key 1974–75

1 TV cartoon adapt. 100.00
2 . . . . 50.00
3 . . . . 35.00

ADLAI STEVENSON
Dell Publishing Co. Dec., 1966

1 Political Life Story 40.00

ADVENTURES OF BARON MUNCHAUSEN
Now Comics 1989

1 thru 4 movie adapt. series. . . . @2.00

ADVENTURES OF CHRISSIE CLAUS, THE
Hero Graphics

1 Trouble in Toyland 2.95

ADVENTURES OF FELIX THE CAT
Harvey 1992

1 Short Stories 2.00

ADVENTURES OF KUNG FU PIG NINJA FLOUNDER AND 4-D MONKEY

1 thru 6 . . . . @1.80
7 thru 10 . . . . @2.00

ADVENTURES OF ROBIN HOOD
Gold Key 1974–75

1 From Disney cartoon 15.00
2 thru 7 . . . . @10.00

Adventures of the Fly #14
© Archie Publications

ADVENTURES OF ROGER WILCO
Adventure

1 Based on Space-Quest Computer games 2.95

ADVENTURES OF THE FLY
Archie Publications/ Radio Comics 1959–65

1 JSm/JK,O:Fly,I:SpiderSpry A:Lancelot Strong/Shield . . . 550.00
2 JSm/JK,DAy,AW 300.00
3 Jack Davis Art, O:Fly 250.00
4 V:Dazzler NA panel 125.00
5 A:Spider Spry 75.00
6 V:Moon Men 75.00
7 A:Black Hood 75.00
8 A:Lancelot Strong/Shield. 75.00
9 A:Lancelot Strong/Shield I:Cat Girl. 75.00
10 A:Spider Spry 75.00
11 V:Rock Men. 50.00
12 V:Brute Invaders 50.00
13 I:Kim Brand 55.00
14 I:Fly-Girl(Kim Brand) 75.00
15 A:Spider 50.00
16 A:Fly-Girl 50.00
17 A:Fly-Girl 50.00
18 A:Fly-Girl 50.00
19 A:Fly-Girl 50.00
20 O:Fly-Girl. 55.00
21 A:Fly-Girl 40.00
22 A:Fly-Girl 40.00
23 A:Fly-Girl,Jaguar 40.00
24 A:Fly-Girl 40.00
25 A:Fly-Girl 40.00
26 A:Fly-Girl,Black Hood. 40.00
27 A:Fly-Girl,Black Hood. 40.00
28 A:Black Hood. 40.00
29 A:Fly-Girl,Black Hood. 40.00
30 A:Fly-Girl,R:Comet. 50.00
31 A:Black Hood, Shield, Comet. . 55.00
Becomes:

FLYMAN

ADVENTURES OF THE JAGUAR
Archie Publications/ Radio Comics 1961–63

1 I:Ralph Hardy/Jaguar 175.00
2 10 cent cover 100.00
3 Last 10 cent cover 75.00
4 A:Cat-Girl 60.00
5 A:Cat-Girl 60.00
6 A:Cat-Girl 50.00
7 . . . . 40.00
8 . . . . 40.00
9 . . . . 40.00
10 . . . . 40.00
11 . . . . 40.00
12 A:Black Hood. 40.00
13 A:Cat-Girl,A:Black Hood. 40.00
14 A:Black Hood. 40.00
15 V:Human Octopus,last issue . . 40.00

ADVENTURES OF YOUNG DR. MASTERS
Archie Comics 1964

1 . . . . 25.00
2 . . . . 15.00

ADVENTUROUS UNCLE SCROOGE McDUCK
Gladstone Oct., 1997

1 . . . . 2.00
2 Don Rosa, A Little Something Special 2.00
3 The Black Widow 2.00

AETERNUS
Brick Comics

1 thru 3 . . . . @2.95

AFTERMATH
Chaos! Comics 2000
1 sequel to Armageddon 2.95
1 premium 9.99
Ashcan, Yellow 10.00
Ashcan, Blue 25.00

AGAINST BLACKSHARD
Sirius Comics Aug., 1986
1 3-D. 2.25

AGENT: AMERICA
Awesome Entertainment 1997
1 RLe 2.50
2 RLe,JSb,JLb,F:Supreme,
V:Smash 2.50

AIR FIGHTERS, SGT. STRIKE SPECIAL
Eclipse 1988
1 A:Airboy,Valkyrie. 2.00

AIR WAR STORIES
Dell Publishing Co. 1964
1 . . . . 50.00
2 . . . . 40.00
3 thru 8 . . . . @30.00

AIRBOY
Eclipse 1986–89
1 TT/TY,D:Golden Age Airboy
O:New Airboy. 3.25
2 TT/TY,I:Marisa,R:SkyWolf 2.25
3 A:The Heap 2.50
4 A:Misery. 2.50
5 DSt(c),R:Valkyrie 4.00
6 R:Iron Ace,I:Marlene. 3.00
7 PG(c), ... 2.50
8 FH/TT(c). 2.50
9 R:Flying Fool, Riot, O'Hara
Cocky, Judge & Turtle 2.00
10 I:Manic,D:Cocky, Judge & Turtle 2.00
11 O:Birdie 2.00
12 R:Flying Fool 2.00
13 I:New Bald Eagle. 2.00
14 A:Sky Wolf, Iron Ace 2.00
15 A:Klu Klux Klan 2.00
16 D:Manic,A:Klu Klux Klan 2.00
17 A:HarryS.Truman,Misery 2.00
18 A:Gold.Age Black Angel. 2.00
19 A:Gold.Age Rats 2.00
20 Rat storyline 2.00
21 I:Lester Mansfield (rel. of
Gold.Age Rackman), Artic
Deathzone #1. . . . . 2.00
22 DSp,Artic Deathzone #2 . . . . . . 2.00
23 A:Gold.Age Black Angle, Artic
Deathzone #3. . . . . 2.00
24 A: Heap. 2.00
25 TY,I:Manure Man,A:Heap. 2.00
26 R:Flying Dutchman 2.00
27 A:Iron Ace, Heap. 2.00
28 A:Heap 2.00
29 . . . . 2.00
30 A:Iron Ace; Sky Wolf story 2.00
31 A:Valkyrie; Sky Wolf story 2.00
32 Hostage Virus, ... 2.00
33 DSp,SkyWolf sty,A:Sgt.Strike . . . 2.00
34 DSp,A:La Lupina 2.00
35 DSp,A:La Lupina, Sky Wolf 2.00
36 . . . . 2.00
37 DSp. 2.00
38 CI, Heap story 2.00
39 CI, Heap story 2.00
40 CI, Heap story 2.00
41 V:Steel Fox, Golden Age rep.
O:Valkyrie. 2.00
42 A:Rackman 2.00
43 Sky Wolf sty, A:Flying Fool. 2.00
44 A:Rackman 2.00
45 . . . . 2.00
46 EC,Airboy Diary #1 . . . . 2.00
47 EC,Airboy Diary #2 . . . . 2.00
48 EC,Airboy Diary #3 . . . . 2.00
49 EC,Airboy Diary #4 . . . . 2.00
50 AKu/NKu,double-size. 3.95
Spec. Meets the Prowler. 2.00
Spec. Mr. Monster 2.00
Spec. Vs Airmaidens 2.00

AIRMAIDENS SPECIAL
Eclipse Comics 1987
1 A:Valkyrie. 2.00

AKEMI
Brainstorm Comics 1997
1 . . . . 2.95

ALADDIN
Walt Disney
Prestige. Movie Adapt. 4.95

ALAN MOORE'S AWESOME ADVENTURES
Awesome Entertainment 1999
1 AMo. 2.50
1a alternate AxR cover 6.95
2 F:Young Guns 2.99
Spec. Awesome Univ. Handbook . . 2.95
Spec.A alternate AxR cover 2.95

ALARMING ADVENTURES
Harvey Publications 1962–63
1 AW,RC,JSe 70.00
2 AW,BP,RC,JSe. 50.00
3 JSe 50.00

ALARMING TALES
Harvey Publications 1957–58
1 JK,JK(c) 175.00
2 JK,JK(c) 125.00
3 JK 100.00
4 JK,BP. 100.00
5 JK,AW 120.00
6 JK 75.00

ALBEDO, VOL. 3
Antartic Press 1994–95
Vol. I and II, See B&W
1 thru 4 Various Artists. . . . . @2.95

ALBINO SPIDER OF DAJETTE
Verotik 1998
0 by Glenn Danzig
& Wayne Robertson 2.95
0a alternate cover 5.00

ALIAS
Now Comics 1990
1 . . . . 2.00
2 thru 5 . . . . @1.75

ALIAS: STORMFRONT
Now Comics
1 . . . . 2.00
2 . . . . 2.00

ALIEN ENCOUNTERS
Eclipse Comics 1985–87
1 . . . . 3.50
2 . . . . 3.00
3 "I Shot the Last Martian". 3.00
4 JBo(c) 2.00
5 RCo,"Night of the Monkey" 2.00
6 "Now You See It,""Freefall" 2.00
7 . . . . 2.00
8 TY,"Take One Capsule Every
Million Years,M.Monroe(c) 2.75
9 The Conquered 2.00
10 . . . . 2.00
11 TT,"Old Soldiers" 2.00
12 "What A Relief,""Eyes of
the Sibyl" 2.00
13 GN,"The Light at the End" 2.00
14 JRy,GN,TL,RT,"Still born" 2.00

ALIEN TERROR
Eclipse 1986
3-D #1 "Standard Procedure" 2.00

Alien Worlds #4
© Pacific Comics

ALIEN WORLDS
Pacific 1982
1 AW,VM,NR 4.00
2 DSt. 3.50
3 . . . . 3.00
4 DSt(i) 3.00
5 thru 7 . . . . @3.00
3-D #1 AAd,DSt. 5.50

Eclipse 1985
8 AW. 2.50
9 . . . . 2.50

[CAPTAIN JOHNER AND] ALIENS, THE
Gold Key 1967
1 Rep. Magnus Robot Fighter . . . 12.50

ALISTER THE SLAYER
Midnight Press 1995
1 I:Alister The Slayer. 2.50
2 V:Lady Hate 2.50
3 JQ&JP(c) V:Subterranean
Vampire Bikers. 2.50

ALL AMERICAN SPORTS
Charlton 1967
1 . . . . 25.00

ALL HALLOWS EVE
Innovation 1991
1 . . . . 4.95

ALLEY OOP
Dell Publishing Co. 1962–63
1 . . . . 60.00
2 . . . . 50.00

ALLEY OOP ADVENTURES
Antarctic Press 1998
1 . . . . 2.95
2 . . . . 2.95
3 I:Granny Green. 2.95
TPB 11.00

ALLIES
Awesome Entertainment 1999
1 RLe,AMo 2.50
1a alternate RLe cover 6.95

ALPHA KORPS
Diversity Comics 1996
1 I:Alpha Korps 3.00
1 signed 4.95
2 "The Price of Freedom," pt.2. . . . 2.50
2 signed 4.95
3 "The Price of Freedom," pt.3. . . . 2.50
3 signed 4.95
4 "The Price of Freedom," pt.4. . . . 2.50

ALPHA WAVE
Darkline 1987
1 . . . . 2.00

ALTER EGO
First 1986
1 RTs, Ron Harris 2.00
2 . . . . 2.00
3 . . . . 2.00
4 . . . . 2.00

ALVIN (& THE CHIPMUNKS)
Dell Publishing Co. 1962–73
1 . . . . 100.00
2 . . . . 65.00
3 . . . . 50.00
4 thru 10 . . . . @45.00
11 thru 20 . . . . @40.00
21 thru 28 . . . . @35.00
1 Alvin for President & his pals in Merry Christmas with Clyde Crashcup & Leonardo. 30.00

AMAZING CHAN & THE CHAN CLAN
Gold Key 1973
1 . . . . 25.00
2 . . . . 15.00
3 and 4 . . . . @12.00

AMAZING HEROES SWIMSUIT ANNUALS
Fantagraphics 1990–93
1990 Spec. A:Dawn 25.00
1990 2nd printing 15.00
1991 A: Dawn. 20.00
1992 A: Dawn. 20.00
1993 A: Dawn. 20.00

AMAZON, THE
Comico 1989
1 . . . . 2.00
2 . . . . 2.00
3 end mini-series. 2.00

AMERICAN FLAGG
First 1983–88
1 HC,I:American Flagg, Hard Times, pt.1 . . . . 3.50
2 HC,Hard Times,pt.2 . . . . 2.75
3 HC,Hard Times,pt.3 . . . . 2.75

American Flagg #5
© First

4 HC,Southern Comfort,pt.1. . . . . . 2.75
5 HC,Southern Comfort,pt.2. . . . . . 2.75
6 HC,Southern Comfort,pt.3. . . . . . 2.75
7 HC,State of the Union,pt.1 . . . . . 2.50
8 HC,State of the Union,pt.2 . . . . . 2.50
9 HC,State of the Union,pt.3 . . . . . 2.50
10 HC,Solidarity-For Now,pt.1 I:Luthor Ironheart 2.50
11 HC,Solidarity-For Now,pt.2. . . . . 2.50
12 HC,Solidarity-For Now,pt.3. . . . . 2.50
13 HC 2.25
14 PB. 2.25
15 HC,American Flagg A Complete story,pt.1 . . . . 2.25
16 HC,Complete Story,pt.2 . . . . 2.00
17 HC,Complete Story,pt.3 . . . . 2.00
18 HC,Complete Story,pt.4 . . . . 2.00
19 HC,Bullets & Ballots, pt.1. . . . . . 2.00
20 HC,LSn,Bullets & Ballots,pt.2. . . 2.00
21 AMo,HC,LSn,Bull&Ballots,pt.3 . 2.00
22 AMo,HC,LSn,Bull&Ballots,pt.4 . . 2.00
23 AMo,HC,LSn,England Swings, pt.1 . . . . 2.00
24 AMo,HC,England Swings,pt.2 . . 2.00
25 AMo,HC,England Swings,pt.3 . . 2.00
26 AMO,HC,England Swings,pt.4 . . 2.00
27 AMo with Raul the Cat. 2.00
28 BWg 2.00
29 JSon 2.00
30 JSon 2.00
31 JSon,O:Bob Violence. 2.00
32 JSon,A:Bob Violence 2.00
33 A:Bob Violence 2.00
34 A:Bob Violence 2.00
35 A:Bob Violence 2.00
36 A:Bob Violence 2.00
37 A:Bob Violence 2.00
38 New Direction 2.00
39 JSon,A:Bob Violence 2.00
40 A:Bob Violence 2.00
41 . . . . 2.00
42 F:Luther Ironheart 2.00
43 . . . . 2.00
44 . . . . 2.00
45 . . . . 2.00
46 PS. 2.00
47 PS. 2.00
48 PS. 2.00
49 . . . . 2.00
50 HC,last issue 2.00
Special #1 HC,I:Time2 . . . . 2.50
See Also: Howard Chaykin's American Flagg

AMERICOMICS
AC Comics 1983
1 GP(c),O:Shade. 3.00
2 . . . . 2.00
3 Blue Beetle. 2.00
4 O:Dragonfly 2.00
5 and 6 . . . . @2.00
Spec.#1 Capt.Atom,BlueBeetle. . . . 2.00

AMERICAN WOMAN
Antarctic Press 1998
1 by Richard Stockton & Brian Denham. 2.95
2 . . . . 2.95
2a deluxe 5.95

ANDROMEDA
Andromeda
1 I:Andromeda. 2.50
2 Andromeda vs. Elite Force 2.50

ANGEL FIRE
Crusade Comics 1997
1 BiT, from Shi #12, BiT(c). 2.95
1a with Roberto Flores cover. 2.95
1b with photo cover 2.95
2 F:Shi 2.95
3 F:Shi, concl. 2.95

ANIMAL MYSTIC: WATER WARS
Sirius 1996
1 (of 6) DOe 4.00
2 thru 6 DOe . . . . @3.00
TPB rep.. . . . . 19.95
TPB Klor 9.95

ANNE McCAFFREY'S THE UNICORN GIRL
Big Entertainment 1997
GN F:Acorna 22.00

ANNE RICE'S THE TALE OF THE BODY THIEF
Sicilian Dragon 1999
1 (of 12) 2.95
2 F:Lestat 2.95
3 thru 6 . . . . @2.95

7 F:Gretchen 2.95
TPB 19.95
TPB Exclusive 19.95

ANYTHING GOES

Fantagraphics 1986

1 GK,FlamingCarot,Savage 3.50
2 S:AnM,JK,JSt,SK 3.50
3 DS,NA(c),A:Cerebus. 3.00
4 . . . . 2.50
5 A:TMNTurtles 5.00
6 . . . . 2.00

APE NATION

Adventure Comics 1991

1 Aliens land on Planet of
the Apes 3.00
2 General Ollo. 3.00
3 V:Gen.Ollo,Danada. 2.50
4 D:Danada. 2.50

APOLLO SMILE

Eagle Wing 1998

1 When the Levee Breaks 2.95
2 When the Levee Breaks, pt.2 . . . 2.95
3 When the Levee Breaks, pt.3 . . . 2.95

ARACHNAPHOBIA

Walt Disney 1990

1 Movie Adapt. 5.95
1a Newsstand 2.95

ARACHNID FOUNDATION

Quantum Comics 1998

1 . . . . 2.95

ARAKNIS

Mushroom Comics 1995–96

1 I:Araknis, Shades of Evil pt.1 . . . 3.50
2 Shades of Evil pt.2 . . . . 3.50
3 with pin-ups 2.50
4 . . . . 2.50

ARAKNIS

Mushroom Comics April, 1996

0 Michael & Mario Ortiz 3.00
0 signed 4.00
1 . . . . 2.50
1 special edition. 10.00

Mystic Comics

2 thru 6 . . . . @2.50

ARAKNIS: RETRIBUTION

Morning Star Productions 1997

1 (of 4) by Michael & Mario Ortiz . . 2.50
1 signed 10.00
2 thru 4 . . . . @2.50

ARAKNIS: SHADES OF EVIL

Morning Star Productions

1 thru 4 . . . . @2.50

ARCHANGELS: THE SAGA

Eternal Studios

1 I:Cameron 2.50
2 V:Demons 2.50
3 and 4 . . . . @2.75
5 and 6 . . . . @2.50
7 . . . . 3.50
8 . . . . 4.50

ARCHIE

Archie Publications

1 thru 300 see Golden Age

301 thru 400 . . . . @3.50
401 thru 449 . . . . @3.00
450 thru 467 . . . . @3.00
468 thru 477 . . . . @2.00
478 thru 489 . . . . @1.75
490 thru 493 . . . . @1.79
494 thru 503 . . . . @1.99
Archie's Christmas Stocking #4. . . . 2.00
Archie's Christmas Stocking #5. . . . 2.00
Archie's Christmas Stocking #6. . . . 2.25
Archie's Christmas Stocking #7. . . . 2.29
Archie's Spring Break Spec.1 . . . . . 2.00
Archie's Spring Break Spec.2 . . . . . 2.00
Archie's Spring Break Spec.3 . . . . . 2.25
Archie's Spring Break Spec.4(1999) 2.25
Archie's Spring Break Spec.5(2000) 2.49
Archie's Vacation Spec.#4 . . . . 2.00
Archie's Vacation Spec.#5 . . . . 2.00
Archie's Vacation Spec.#6 . . . . 2.25

Archie #398
© Archie Publications

Archie's Vacation Spec.#7 . . . . 2.25
Archie's Vacation Spec.#8 . . . . 2.49

ARCHIE AMERICANA SERIES

Archie Comics

TPB Best of the Forties. 10.95
TPB Best of the Fifties 8.95
TPB Best of the Sixties. 9.95
TPB Best of the Seventies 9.95

ARCHIE AND FRIENDS

Archie Publications 1992—98

1 thru 10 . . . . @2.00
11 thru 20 . . . . @2.00
20 thru 26. . . . . @2.00
27 thru 37. . . . . @2.00
38 thru 44. . . . . @1.79

ARCHIE AND ME

Archie Publications 1964–87

1 . . . . 165.00
2 . . . . 90.00
3 . . . . 50.00
4 . . . . 40.00
5 . . . . 40.00
6 thru 10 . . . . @30.00
11 thru 20 . . . . @15.00
21 thru 100. . . . . @7.00
101 thru 162 . . . . @5.00

ARCHIE AS PUREHEART THE POWERFUL

Archie Publications 1966–67

1 superhero parody 80.00
2 . . . . 50.00
3 thru 6 Captain Pureheart. . . . @30.00

ARCHIE AT RIVERDALE HIGH

Archie Publications 1972

1 . . . . 75.00
2 . . . . 40.00
3 . . . . 25.00
4 . . . . 15.00
5 . . . . 15.00
6 thru 10 . . . . @5.00
11 thru 114 . . . . @3.00

ARCHIE COMICS DIGEST

Archie Comics Digest 1973

1 . . . . 80.00
2 . . . . 50.00
3 . . . . 25.00
4 . . . . 10.00
5 thru 10 . . . . @5.00
11 thru 88 . . . . @3.00

ARCHIE MEETS THE PUNISHER

Archie/Marvel 1994

1-shot crossover, same contents
as Punisher meets Archie. 3.00

ARCHIE'S MADHOUSE

Archie Publications 1959–69

1 . . . . 225.00
2 . . . . 135.00
3 thru 5 . . . . @90.00
6 thru 10 . . . . @50.00
11 thru 16 . . . . @40.00
17 thru 21 . . . . @20.00
22 . . . . 50.00
23 thru 30 . . . . @25.00
31 thru 40 . . . . @7.00
41 thru 66 . . . . @4.00

ARCHIE'S PAL JUGHEAD SEE: JUGHEAD

ARCHIE'S SUPERHERO MAGAZINE

Archie Publications

1 JSm/SK,Rept.Double of
Capt.Strong #1,FLy,Black Hood 2.00
2 GM,NA/DG,AMc,I:'70's Black
Hood, Superhero rept. 2.00

ARCHIE'S TV LAUGH-OUT

Archie Publications 1969–86

1 . . . . 75.00
2 . . . . 50.00
3 . . . . 25.00
4 . . . . 25.00
5 . . . . 25.00
6 thru 10 . . . . @10.00
11 thru 106 . . . . @5.00

ARCHIE 3000
Archie Publications
May, 1989–July, 1991
1 thru 16 . . . . @2.00

ARCHIE'S WEIRD MYSTERIES
Archie Comics 1999
1 from animated series 1.79
2 Shriek. 1.79
3 "Return of the Mighty Crusaders" 1.99
4 "Archie Squared" 1.99
5 "Time Space Conundrum". 1.99
6 "A Familiar Old Haunt" 1.99
7 "U.F.O. Uh,Oh" 1.99
8 "Sea Food, Be Food" 1.99
9 "When Your Dreamgirl
is a Nightmare". 1.99
10 "Bigfoot on Campus" 1.99
11 "The Return of Scarlet" 1.99
12 Fear of Frost 1.99

ARENA, THE
Alchemy
1 . . . . 2.00
2 . . . . 2.00

ARIANE & BLUEBEARD
Eclipse 1988
Spec. CR 3.95

ARISTOKITTENS, THE
Gold Key 1971–75
1 Disney 25.00
2 thru 9 . . . . @15.00

ARMAGEDDON
Chaos! Comics 1999
1 (of 4) F:Lady Death, Evil Ernie . . 2.95
1a Premium edition 9.99
2 O:Chaos. 2.95
3 . . . . 2.95
4 concl. 2.95

ARMAGEDDON FACTOR
AC Comics
1 Sentinels of Justice. 2.00
2 . . . . 2.00

ARMOR
Continuity 1985
1 TGr,NA,A:Silver Streak,
silver logo. 5.00
1a 2nd printing,red logo 2.50
2 TGr,NA(c). 2.50
3 TGr,NA(c). 2.50
4 TGr,NA(c). 2.50
5 BS,NA(c) 2.50
6 TVE,NA(c) 2.50
7 NA(c) 2.50
8 FS,NA(c) 2.50
9 FS,NA&KN(c). 2.50
10 FS,NA&KN(c) 2.50
11 SDr(i),KN(c). 2.50
12 KN(c). 2.50
13 NA(c),direct sales 2.50
14 KN(c), newsstand 2.50
[2nd Series]
1 V:Hellbender,Trading Card 2.50
[3rd Series, Deathwatch 2000]
1 Deathwatch 2000 pt.3,w/card . . . 4.00
2 Deathwatch 2000 pt.9,w/card . . . 2.50

Armor #3
© Continuity

3 Deathwatch 2000 pt.15,w/card . . 2.50
4 . . . . 2.50
5 Rise of Magic. 2.50
6 Rise of Magic. 2.50

ARMORED TROOPER VOTOMS
CPM Comics
1 TEI. 2.95
2 TEI. 2.95
3 TEI. 2.95
4 TEI 2.95
GN Supreme Survivor. 16.95

ARMY ATTACK
Charlton 1964
1 SG 35.00
2 SG 20.00
3 SG. 15.00
4 thru 47 . . . . @12.00

ARMY WAR HEROES
Charlton 1963–70
1 . . . . 40.00
2 . . . . 25.00
3 thru 21 . . . . @20.00
22 GS,O&I:Iron Corporal. 25.00
23 thru 38. . . . . @15.00

ART OF ZEN INTER-GALACTIC NINJA
Entity Comics 1994
1 Various artists. 2.95

ARTESIA
Sirius 1999
1 (of 6) by Mark Smylie 2.95
1a limited edition 10.00
2 thru 6 . . . . @2.95
Ann.#1 . . . . 3.50
TPB Vol. 1 . . . . 19.95
HC Vol. 1 . . . . 34.95

ARTESIA AFIELD
Sirius 2000
1 (of 6) by Mark Smylie 2.95
1 Limited Ed. 5.95

2 . . . . 2.95
3 . . . . 2.95

ASH
Event Comics
1 JQ,JP,Fire and Crossfire,pt.1 . . 12.00
1a David Finch/Batt(c). 3.00
1b omnichrome commemorative . 14.95
1c omnichrome signed &
numbered. 29.95
2 JQ,JP,Fire and Crossfire,pt.2 . . . 7.00
2a David Finch/Batt (c) 3.00
3 JQ,JP,Secret of Origin 4.50
4 I:Actor 3.00
5 I:New Character 3.00
6 V:Gabriel 3.00
0 Red Laser ed., Current Ash (c) . 20.00
0 Red Laser ed., Future Ash (c). . 20.00
TPB rep. #1–#5 . . . . 14.95
TPB Vol. 1, JQ,JP,sgn. lim. 34.95

ASH: CINDER AND SMOKE
Event Comics 1997
1 MWa,BAu,HuR,JP 2.95
1a autographed virgin JQ cover. . 19.95
1b signed limited edition 29.95
2 HuR(c) 2.95
2 JQ(c) 2.95
3 (of 6) JQ&JP(c) 2.95
3 variant JP&HuR(c) 2.95
4 (of 6) JQ&JP(c) 2.95
4 variant JP&HuR(c) 2.95
5 (of 6) JQ&JP(c) 2.95
5 variant JP&HuR(c) 2.95
6 (of 6) JQ&JP(c) 2.95
6 variant JP&HuR(c) 2.95

ASH FILES, THE
Event Comics 1997
1 JQ,JP. 2.95
1 signed, limited 19.95

ASH: FIRE AND CROSSFIRE
Event Comics 1998
1 (of 5) JQ,JP 2.95
1a signed & numbered. 24.95
2 . . . . 2.95

ASH: THE FIRE WITHIN
Event Comics
2 JQ,JP. 2.95
3 JQ,JP, Ash Rooftop cover. 2.95
3a JQ,JP, Ash Firefighter cover . . . 2.95

ASH/22 BRIDES
Event Comics 1996
1 FaN,HuR,JP. 2.95

ASSASSIN, INC.
Solson
1 thru 4 . . . . @2.00

ASTER
Entity Comics 1995
0 O:Aster the Celestial Knight 4.50
1 I:Celestial Knight 5.00
1b 2nd printing 3.00
2 . . . . 3.50
3 V:Tolmek 3.25
3a Variant cover 7.00
4 Final Issue 3.00
TPB Rep.#1–#4 + pin-up gallery. . 12.95

COLOR PUB.

ASTER THE LAST CELESTIAL KNIGHT
Entity Comics 1995
1 R:Aster Chromium Cover 2.50
1a Clear Chromium Edition 4.00
1b Holo Chrome Edition. 5.00
2 World Defender 2.50

ASTRO BOY
Gold Key Aug., 1965
1 I:Astro Boy 500.00

ASTRO BOY
Now
Prev. Original Astro Boy
18 . . . . 2.00
19 . . . . 2.00
20 . . . . 2.00

ASYLUM
Pendragon 1995
1 . . . . 2.95
2 . . . . 2.95
3 three stories 2.95

ASYLUM
Maximum Press Dec., 1995
1 Warchild, Beanworld, Avengelyne, Battlestar Galactica 3.00
2 I:Deathkiss 3.00
3 . . . . 3.00
4 RLd,A:Cybrid 3.00
5 I:Black Seed. 3.00
6 R:Steve Austin & Jaime Sommers 3.00
7 RLe,F:Bloodwulf. 3.00
8 RLd 3.00
9 RLd 3.00
10 . . . . 3.00
11 . . . . 3.00
12 MMy,F:Blindside 3.00
13 . . . . 3.00

ATOM ANT
Gold Key Jan., 1966
1 . . . . 350.00

ATOM-AGE COMBAT
Fago Magazines 1958–59
1 . . . . 165.00
2 . . . . 140.00
3 . . . . 120.00

ATOMIC RABBIT
Charlton Comics 1955–58
1 . . . . 200.00
2 . . . . 100.00
3 thru 10 . . . . @50.00
11 . . . . 100.00

Becomes:

ATOMIC BUNNY
12 . . . . 100.00
13 thru 18. . . . . @50.00
19 Dec., 1959. . . . . 50.00

ATOMICS, THE
AAA Pop Comics 1999
1 by Mike Allred. 2.95
2 Zapman 2.95
3 Mutant Street Beatniks 2.95
4 refugees from the Innerverse . . . 2.95
5 The Light 2.95
6 The Physical. 2.95
7 I:The Skunk 2.95
8 F:The Laser 2.95
9 taken hostage. 2.95
10 . . . . 2.95
King Size Giant. 10.00

Atomik Angels #3
© Crusade Entertainment

ATOMIK ANGELS
Crusade Entertainment 1996
1 BiT. 2.95
1 variant cover (1:25). 5.00
2 BiT. 2.95
3 BiT. 2.95
4 BiT, conclusion 2.95

AUTHORITY, THE
Wildstorm/DC 1999
1 WEl(s),BHi,PNe 2.50
2 WEl(s),BHi,PNe,V:Kaizen Gamorra. 2.50
3 WEl(s),BHi,PNe,destruction 2.50
4 WEl(s),BHi,PNe,save L.A.. . . . . . 2.50
5 WEl(s),BHi,PNe,Swiftships,pt.1 . . 2.50
6 WEl(s),BHi,PNe 2.50

AVENGEBLADE
Maximum Press 1996
1 RLe 3.00
2 RLe 3.00

AVENGELYNE
Maximum Press 1995
1 RLd,I:Avengelyne Dir ed. 6.00
1a Newsstand Edition 3.00
1b Holochrome Edition 4.00
1 gold edition. 5.00
2 V:B'Lial. 3.00
3 I:Magogi 3.00
3 variant cover, pin-up 4.00
TPB rep. #1–#3. . . . . @9.95

Regular Series April 1996
0 RLd,O:Avengelyne 3.00
1 RLd,BNa,F:Devlin. 3.00
1 variant photo cover. 3.00
2 I:Darkchylde 7.00
2a variant photo cover. 8.00
3 . . . . 3.00
4 A:Cybrid 3.00
5 A:Cybrid, ... 3.00
6 RLd,F:Divinity. 3.00
7 RLd,F:Divinity. 3.00
8 RLd, ... 3.00
9 RLd, ... 3.00
10 BNa,"The Possession," pt.1 . . . . 3.00
11 BNa,"The Possession," pt.2 . . . . 3.00
12 BNa,"The Possession," pt.3 . . . . 3.00
13 BNa,"The Possession," pt.4 . . . . 3.00
14 A:Bloodwulf 3.00
15 A:Glory, Prophet 3.00
Swimsuit Edition. 3.50
Swimsuit book, American Entertainment exclusive 7.50

AVENGELYNE
Awesome Entertainment 1999
Prelude 2.50
1 RLe,RNa 2.50
1a, b & c variant covers. 2.50
2 RLe,. 2.50
3 . . . . 2.50
Spec. Swimsuit 1999 . . . . 3.00
Spec.#1-shot Demonslayer (2000) . 2.95
Spec.#1a Demonslayer variant (c) . 2.95
Spec.#1b Demonslayer variant (c) . 2.95
Spec.#1c Demonslayer variant (c) . 2.95

AVENGELYNE: ARMAGEDDON
Maximum Press 1996–97
1 (of 3) RLd. 3.00
2 RLd,. 3.00
3 BNa,ScC, finale 3.00

AVENGELYNE: BAD BLOOD
Avatar 2000
1 Matt Haley (c). 3.50
1a Al Rio (c) 3.50
1b Tim Vigil (c) 3.50
1c prism foil (c) previews excl. . . . 12.95
1d Al Rio velvet (c) 19.95
1e leather (c). 25.00
2 . . . . 3.50
2a Haley (c). 3.50
2b Moline (c). 3.50
Prelude Rick Lyon (c) 4.95
Prelude Al Rio (c). 4.95
Prelude Bikini (c) 5.95

AVENGELYNE BIBLE: REVELATIONS
Maximum Press
one-shot RLd,. 3.50

AVENGELYNE: DEADLY SINS
Maximum Press 1996
1 RLd (c). 3.00
1 photo (c). 3.00
2 RLd(c) 3.00

AVENGELYNE/GLORY
Maximum Press 1995
1 V:B'Lial. 3.95
1a variant cover. 5.00
Swimsuit Spec. #1 . . . . 2.95

AVENGELYNE/GLORY: THE GODYSSEY
Maximum Press 1996
1 RLd,BNa 3.00
2 thru 5 RLd. . . . . @3.00

AVENGELYNE/PANDORA
Avatar 2000
Spec. x-over 3.50
Spec.Preview exclusive 3.50
Spec.Preview Bikini ed. 5.95
Spec.McDaniel (c) 5.95
Spec.Previews exlusive Prism ed.. 12.95
Spec.Red Velvet. 25.00
Spec.Ruby Red edition 19.95
Spec.Royal Blue. 75.00

AVENGELYNE/POWER
Maximum Press 1995–96
1 RLd,V:Hollywood 3.00
1 variant cover. 3.50
2 RLd(c) 3.00
3 . . . . 3.00
3a photo (c). 3.00

AVENGELYNE/PROPHET
Maximum Press April, 1996
1 RLd,BNa,MD2 . . . . 3.00
Awesome Entertainment 2000
Rage of Furies #1 RLe(c) 2.99
#1a IaC(c) 2.99
#1b Grant(c). 2.99
#1c Walker Bros.(c) 2.99
#1d Wizard world ed. 5.00
#1e Wizard world, signed 10.00

AVENGELYNE: REVELATION
Avatar 2000
1 Rio (c) 3.50
1a Haley (c). 3.50
1b Wraparound (c) 3.50
1c leather (c). 25.00

AVENGELYNE/SUPREMA
Awesome Entertainment 2000
Rage of Furies #1 (2000). 2.99
1a Wizard world ed. 5.00
1b signed 10.00

AVENGELYNE/ WARRIOR NUN AREALA
Maximum Press 1997
Spec. 3.00
Awesome Entertainment 1997
Spec. #2 The Nazarene Affair. 3.00

AVENGERS, THE
Gold Key Nov., 1968
1 . . . . 250.00

AWESOME
Awesome Entertainment 1997
Holiday Spec. #1 . . . . 2.50
Holiday Spec.'99 . . . . 4.95
Spring '99 Tourbook 4.95

AXA
Eclipse 1987
1 "Axa the Adopted" 2.00
2 . . . . 2.00

AXEL PRESSBUTTON
Eclipse 1984
1 BB(c),Origin 2.00
2 . . . . 2.00
3 thru 4 . . . . @2.00
Becomes:
PRESSBUTTON

AXION
Icon Creations
1 I:Obsidion. 2.50

AXIS ALPHA
Axis Comics
1 LSn,I:BEASTIES,Dethgrip, Shelter,W. 2.75

AZ
Comico
1 . . . . 3.00
2 . . . . 2.25

Aztec Ace #5
© Eclipse

AZTEC ACE
Eclipse 1984
1 NR(i),I:AztecAce. 3.50
2 NR(i) 3.50
3 NR(i) 3.00
4 NR(i) 3.00
5 NR(i) 3.00
6 NR(i) 3.00
7 NR(i) 3.00
8 NR(i) 3.00
9 NR(i) 3.00
10 NR(i) 2.00
11 . . . . 3.50
12 . . . . 2.50
13 . . . . 2.50
14 . . . . 2.50
15 F:Bridget 2.50

BABES OF BROADWAY
Broadway 1996
1 . . . . 2.95

BABY HUEY, THE BABY GIANT
Harvey Publications 1956–80
1 . . . . 350.00
2 . . . . 175.00
3 . . . . 125.00
4 . . . . 100.00
5 . . . . 100.00
6 thru 10 . . . . @50.00
11 thru 20 . . . . @30.00
21 thru 40 . . . . @25.00
41 thru 60 . . . . @15.00
61 thru 79 . . . . @10.00
80 . . . . 10.00
81 thru 95. . . . . @5.00
96 Giant size 6.00
97 Giant size 6.00
98 . . . . 2.50
99 . . . . 2.50

BABY HUEY AND PAPA
Harvey Publications 1962–68
1 . . . . 150.00
2 . . . . 75.00
3 . . . . 50.00
4 . . . . 50.00
5 . . . . 50.00
6 . . . . 20.00
7 . . . . 20.00
8 . . . . 20.00
9 . . . . 20.00
10 . . . . 20.00
11 thru 20 . . . . @5.00
21 thru 33 . . . . @3.50

BABY HUEY DUCKLAND
Harvey Publications 1962–66
1 . . . . 100.00
2 . . . . 50.00
3 . . . . 50.00
4 . . . . 50.00
5 . . . . 50.00
6 thru 14 . . . . @15.00
15 . . . . 15.00

BACHELOR FATHER
Dell Publishing Co. 1962
1 . . . . 85.00
2 . . . . 65.00

BACK TO THE FUTURE
Harvey 1991
1 Chicago 1927. . . . . 2.00
2 Cretaceous Period 2.00
3 World War I 2.00
4 Doc Retires 2.00

BAD BOY
Oni Press 1997
GN Frank Miller & Simon Bisley . . . 4.95

BAD COMPANY
Quality 1988
1 thru 19 . . . . @2.00

BADGER
Capital 1983
1 JBt,I:Badger,Ham,Daisy Yak,Yeti. 3.00
2 JBt,I:Riley,A:YakYeti 3.00
3 JBt,O:Badger,Ham 3.00
4 JBt,A'Ham 3.00
First 1984–91
5 BR,DruidTree Pt1 . . . . 2.50
6 BR,DruidTree Pt2 . . . . 2.50
7 BR,I:Wonktendonk,Lord Weterlackus 2.50
8 BR,V:Demon 2.50
9 BR,I:Connie,WOatesCbra 2.50
10 BR,A:Wonktendonk, I:Hodag Meldrum. 2.50
11 BR,V:Hodag,L.W'lackus 2.50
12 BR,V:Hodag,L.W'lackus. 2.50
13 BR,A:L.W'lakus,Clonezone,

Judah 2.50
14 BR,I:HerbNg 2.50
15 BR,I:Wombat,JMoranlbob 2.50
16 BR,A:Yak,Yeti 2.50
17 JBt,I:Lamont 3.00
18 BR,I:SpudsGroganA:Cbra 2.50
19 BR,I:Senator1,ClZone 2.50
20 BR,Billionaire'sPicnic 2.50
21 BR,I&O:Phantom 2.50
22 BR,I:Dr.Buick Riviera 2.50
23 I:BobDobb,A:Yeti 2.50
24 BR,A:Riley 2.50
25 BR,I:Killdozer 2.50
26 BR,I:RoachWranger 2.50
27 BR,O:RoachWranger 2.50
28 BR,A:Yeti 2.50
29 A:Clonezone,C:GrimJack 2.50
30 BR,I:Dorgan 2.00
31 BR,I:HopLingSung 2.00
32 BR,D:Dorgan,HopLingSng 2.00
33 RLm/AN,I:KidKang 3.00
34 RLm,I:Count Kohler 3.00

Badger #1
© Capital Comics

35 RLm,I:Count Kohler 3.00
36 RLm,V:Dire Wolf 3.00
37 AMe,A:Lamont 2.50
38 Animal Band 2.00
39 I:Buddy McBride 2.00
40 RLm,I:Sister Twyster 3.50
41 RLm,D:Sister Twyster 3.50
42 RLm,A:Paul Bunyan 3.50
43 RLm,V:Vampires 3.50
44 RLm,V:Vampires 3.50
45 RLm,V:Dr.Buick Riviera 3.50
46 RLm,V:Lort Weterlackus 3.50
47 RLm,Hmds.Sacr.BloodI 3.50
48 RLm,Hmds.Sacr.BloodII 3.50
49 RLm,TRoof off SuckerI 3.50
50 RLm,TRoof off SuckerII 5.00
51 RLm,V:Demon 3.00
52 TV,Tinku 4.00
53 TV,I:Shaza,Badass 4.00
54 TV,D:Shaza 4.00
55 I:Morris Myer 2.00
56 I:Dominance 2.00
57 A:KKang,V:L.W'lackus 2.00
58 A:Lamont,W'bat,V:Spuds
Jy,Jessie 3.50
3 JBt/MZ,V:Larry,Jessie 3.00
4 JBt/MZ,V:Larry,Jessie 3.00

BAD GIRLS OF BLACKOUT

Blackout Comics 1995

0 . . . . 3.50
1 I:Ms. Cyanide, Ice 3.50
Ann.#1 Hari Kari, Lady Vampre 3.50
Ann.#1 Commemorative ed 9.95

BADROCK/WOLVERINE

Awesome Entertainment 1997

Spec. #1 JV,CYp,V:Sauron,48pg . . . 4.95

BAKER STREET

1 . . . . 3.00
2 . . . . 2.50

BALLAD OF HALO JONES

Quality 1987

1 IG Alan Moore story 2.00
1a IG rep. 2.00
2 thru 12 . . . . @2.00

BAMM BAMM & PEBBLES FLINTSTONE

Gold Key Oct., 1964

1 . . . . 100.00

BARBARIANS, THE

Atlas June, 1975

1 O: Andrax,F:Iron Jaw 20.00

BARBIE & KEN

Dell Publishing Co. May–July, 1962

1 . . . . 400.00
2 . . . . 300.00
3 . . . . 300.00
4 . . . . 300.00
5 . . . . 325.00

THE BARBIE TWINS ADVENTURES

Topps 1995

1 I:Shane, Sia 2.50

BARBIE TWINS ADVENTURES

Studio Chikara 1998

Color Spec. The Roswell Incident . . 3.95

BARNEY AND BETTY RUBBLE

Charlton Comics 1973–76

1 . . . . 50.00
2 . . . . 20.00
3 . . . . 20.00
4 . . . . 20.00
5 . . . . 20.00
6 thru 10 . . . . @15.00
11 thru 23 . . . . @10.00

BARRY M. GOLDWATER

Dell Publishing Co. March, 1965

1 . . . . 35.00

BARRY WINDSOR-SMITH'S OPUS

Fantagraphics 2000

HC Vol. 1 . . . . 39.95
HC Vol. 2 Time Rise 49.95
HC Vol. 2 limited, signed 69.95

BART-MAN

Bongo 1993

1 Foil(c),I:Bart-Man 4.00
2 I:Penalizer 2.25
3 When Bongos Collide,pt.3,
with card 2.25
4 Crime-Time,pt.1 . . . . 2.25
5 Bad Guys Strike Back 2.25

BART SIMPSONS TREEHOUSE OF HORROR

Bongo Comics 1995

1 Bart People 2.95
2 thru 4 . . . . @2.95
5 48-pg. 3.50
6 64-pg. 4.50

BART SIMPSON'S TREEHOUSE OF TERROR

Bongo Comics 1995

One-shot 2.50

BASEBALL

Kitchen Sink 1991

1 WE (c) reprint of 1949 orig. 3.95
2 Ray Gotto (c), w/4 BB cards 2.95

BAT, THE

Adventure

1 R:The Bat,inspiration for Batman
says Bob Kane 2.50

BATTLEBOOKS

Battlebooks Inc. 1999

all BTi(c)

Bubba-Busters Battlebook 5.00
Captain America Battlebook
Blue print, signed edition 10.00
Colossus Battlebook 4.00
Daredevil Battlebook BTi(c) 4.00
Daredevil Battlebook JQ&JP(c) 4.00
Darkchylde A Battlebook 4.00
Darkchylde B Battlebook 4.00
The Darkness Battlebook 4.00
Dr. Doom Battlebook 4.00
Elektra Battlebook 4.00
Blue print, signed edition 12.95
Elektra Battlebook, revised 4.00
Gambit Battlebook 4.00
Green Goblin Battlebook 4.00
Iron Man Battlebook
Blue print, signed edition 12.95
The Incredible Hulk Battlebook 4.00
Blue print, signed edition 12.95
Magneto Battlebook 4.00
President Clinton Battlebook 5.00
Rogue Battlebook 4.00
Blue print, signed edition 12.95
Sabretooth Battlebook 4.00
Shi: The Spirit of Benkei Battlebook 4.00
Blue print, signed edition 10.00
Spider-Man Battlebook
Blue print, signed edition 12.95
Storm Battlebook 4.00
The Thing Battlebook 4.00

Tomoe: Fan's of Fury Battlebook. . . 4.00
Vampirella Hell on Earth Battlebook 4.00
White Queen Battlebook. 4.00
Witchblade Battlebook 4.00
Wolverine Battlebook 4.00
Wolverine with Bone Claws Battlebook
Blue print, signed edition 12.95

BATTLE FORCE
Blackthorne 1987

1 and 2 . . . . @2.00
3 . . . . 2.00

BATTLE OF THE PLANETS
Gold Key June, 1979

1 TV Cartoon. 25.00
2 . . . . 15.00
3 . . . . 15.00
4 . . . . 15.00
5 . . . . 15.00

Whitman

6 . . . . 10.00
7 thru 10 . . . . @10.00

BATTLESTAR GALACTICA
Maximum Press 1995

1 Finds Earth. 2.50
2 Council of Twelve. 2.50
3 R:Adama 2.50
4 Pyramid Secrets. 2.50
TPB series rep.. . . . . 12.95
Spec. Ed. Painted Book (1997). . . . 3.00
Battlestar Galactica: The Compendium #1 rep. from Asylum. 3.00

Battlestar Galactica #5
© Realm Press

BATTLESTAR GALACTICA
Realm Press 1997

1 by Chris Scalf. 3.00
1a variant cover. 3.00
2 Law of Volhad. 3.00
3 Prison of Souls, pt.1 . . . . 3.00
3a alternate cover 3.00
4 Prison of Souls, pt.2 . . . . 3.00
5 . . . . 3.00
6 A Path of Darkness, pt.1. . . . . . . 3.00
7 A Path of Darkness, pt.2. . . . . . . 3.00
7a photo (c). 3.00
7b signed and numbered 6.00
8 Centurion Prime 3.00
Spec.#1 20 Yahren Reunion 5.00
Spec.#1 No Memory of Earth 3.00
Spec.#1 CenturionPrime,Scott(c) . . 2.99
Spec.#1 CenturionPrime,Parsons(c) 2.99
Spec.#2 Centurion Prime 3.00
Spec. 1999 Tourbook 3.00
Spec. 1999 Tourbook con. ed. 7.00
Spec. 1999 Tourbook sign. 30.00
Spec. Gallery #1. . . . . 3.99
Tech Journal: The Galactica 3.99
Tech Journal: Ships of Fleet 3.99
Spec.No Man's Land 3.99
Spec.No Man's Land, deluxe 4.99
Cylon Dawn Spec. (2000). 3.99
Cylon Dawn Spec. deluxe. 4.99
Darkest Night Spec. (2000). 3.99
Darkest Night Spec. variant (c). . . . 4.99
Dire Prophecy Spec. (2000) 3.99
Dire Prophecy Spec. deluxe 4.99
Eve of Destruction Prelude(1999) . . 3.99
TPB New Beginnings, rep.
#1–#4 . . . . @14.00

BATTLESTAR GALACTICA APOLLO'S JOURNEY
Maximum Press April, 1996

1 story by Richard Hatch 2.95
2 . . . . 2.50
3 . . . . 2.50

BATTLESTAR GALACTICA THE ENEMY WITHIN
Maximum Press Feb., 1996

1 . . . . 3.00
2 . . . . 2.50
3 . . . . 2.50

BATTLESTAR GALACTICA JOURNEY'S END
Maximum Press 1996

1 (of 4) RLd. 3.00
2 RLd 3.00
3 RLd, the end of Galactica? 3.00
4 RLd, conclusion 3.00

BATTLESTAR GALACTICA SEARCH FOR SANCTUARY
Realm Press 1998

1 (of 4) 3.00
2 Path of Darkness 3.00
3 tensions grow. 3.00
4 . . . . 3.00

BATTLESTAR GALACTICA SEASON THREE
Real Press 1999

1 . . . . 3.00
1a alternate JaL(c) 5.00
1b Cylon Attack (c) 5.00
1c Cylon Attack (c) signed 35.00
2 . . . . 3.00
2a alternate cover 5.00
2b pencil sketch cover. 4.99
2c convention edition. 5.00
3 Fire in the Sky 3.00
3a alternate cover 5.00
3b convention edition. 5.00
4 Scott (c) 2.99
4a Parsons (c). 2.99
5 Busch (c) 2.99
5a Parsons (c). 2.99
6 . . . . 2.99
6a 2.99
7 . . . . 2.99
7a deluxe 4.99
8 . . . . 2.99
8a deluxe 4.99
Spec. 80-page Juggernaut 8.99
Tour Book Sketch ed. 25.00

BATTLESTAR GALACTICA STARBUCK
Maximum Press 1997

1 (of 3) RLd. 2.50
2 RLd 2.95
3 RLd, the end of Galactica? 2.95

BATTLETECH
Blackthorne 1987

1 . . . . 2.00
2 . . . . 2.00
3 . . . . 2.00
4 . . . . 2.00
5 . . . . 2.00
6 . . . . 2.00

(Changed to Black & White)

1 3-D. 2.50
2 3-D. 2.50

BEAGLE BOYS, THE
Gold Key 1964–79

1 . . . . 40.00
2 thru 5 . . . . @30.00
6 thru 10 . . . . @20.00
11 thru 20 . . . . @15.00
21 thru 46 . . . . @10.00
47 . . . . 10.00

BEANIE THE MEANIE
Fargo Publications 1958

1 thru 3 . . . . @30.00

B.E.A.S.T.I.E.S.
Axis Comics

1 JS(a&s),I:Beasties 2.25

THE BEATLES, LIFE STORY
Dell Publishing Co. 1964

1 . . . . 600.00

BEAUTY AND THE BEAST
Innovation

1 From TV series. 2.50
1a Deluxe 3.95
2 . . . . 2.50
3 . . . . 2.50
4 Siege 2.50
5 Siege 2.50
6 Halloween 2.50
7 . . . . 2.50

BEAUTY AND THE BEAST PORTRAIT OF LOVE
First 1989–90

1 WP,TV tie in 12.00
2 . . . . 8.00
Book II:Night of Beauty. 5.95

BEAUTY AND THE BEAST
Walt Disney 1992

Movie adapt.(Prestige) 4.95
Movie adapt.(newsstand) 2.50

mini-series

1 Bewitched 2.00

COLOR PUB.

2 Elsewhere 2.00
3 A:Catherine 2.50

BEDLAM!
Eclipse 1985
1 SBi,RV,reprint horror 2.00
2 SBi,RV,reprint horror 2.00

BEETLE BAILEY
Harvey 1992
1 F:Mort Walker's B.Bailey. 2.00
2 Beetle builds a bridge 2.00
3 thru 12 . . . . @2.00

BEETLEJUICE
Harvey 1991
1 EC,"This is your lice" 2.00
Holiday Special #1 . . . . 2.00

BEN CASEY
Dell Publishing Co.
June–July, 1962
1 Ph(c) 65.00
2 Ph(c) 40.00
3 Ph(c) 30.00
4 Drug, Ph(c). 35.00
5 Ph(c) 30.00
6 thru 10 Ph(c). . . . . @30.00

BERNI WRIGHTSON MASTER OF THE MACABRE
Pacific
1 BWr 5.25
2 BWr 3.75
3 BWr 3.50
4 BWr 3.50
Eclipse 1984
5 BWr 3.50

BEST FROM BOY'S LIFE
Gilberton Company Oct., 1957
1 . . . . 80.00
2 . . . . 50.00
3 . . . . 40.00
4 LbC 60.00
5 . . . . 40.00

BEST OF BUGS BUNNY
Gold Key 1966–68
1 Both Giants 50.00
2 . . . . 40.00

BEST OF DENNIS THE MENACE, THE
Hallden/Fawcett Publ.
Summer, 1959
1 . . . . 60.00
2 thru 5 Spring, 1961 . . . . @40.00

BEST OF DONALD DUCK & UNCLE SCROOGE
Gold Key 1964–67
1 . . . . 75.00
2 . . . . 70.00

BEST OF DONALD DUCK
Gold Key Nov., 1965
1 . . . . 75.00

BETTA: TIME WARRIOR
Immortal Comics 1997
1 (of 3)Beginnings's End,pt.1 . . . . . 2.95
2 The Beginnings's End,pt.2 . . . . . 2.95

BETTI COZMO
Antarctic Press 1999
1 (of 3) 3.00
2 . . . . 3.00
3 Raygun For Hire. 3.00

BETTY
Archie Publications 1992
1 thru 39 . . . . @2.00
40 thru 57. . . . . @2.00
58 thru 79. . . . . @2.00
80 thru 83 . . . . @1.79
84 thru 93 . . . . @1.99

BETTY AND ME
Archie Publications 1965–92
1 . . . . 100.00
2 . . . . 50.00
3 . . . . 30.00
4 . . . . 30.00
5 . . . . 30.00
6 thru 10 . . . . @15.00
11 thru 30. . . . . @8.00
31 thru 50. . . . . @5.00
51 thru 55. . . . . @4.00
56 thru 199. . . . . @3.00
200 . . . . 3.00

BETTY AND VERONICA
Archie Publications June, 1987
1 thru 100 . . . . @5.00
101 thru 104 . . . . @4.00
105 thru 119 . . . . @3.00
120 thru 141 . . . . @5.00
142 thru 145 . . . . @2.00
146 thru 155 . . . . @1.99
Summer Fun Special #5 . . . . 2.25
Summer Fun Special #6 . . . . 2.25
Summer Fun Special #7 . . . . 2.49

BETTY & VERONICA SPECTACULAR
1 thru 27 . . . . @2.00
28 thru 38 . . . . @2.00

Betty and Veronica #62
© Archie Publications

39 thru 40 . . . . @1.79
41 thru 45 . . . . @1.99

BETTY BOOP'S SUNDAY BEST
Kitchen Sink 1998
TPB Complete Color Comics, 1934–36, new printing 19.95
HC Complete Color Comics, 1934–36, new printing 34.95

BEVERLY HILLBILLYS
Dell Publishing Co.
April–June, 1963
1 Ph(c) 175.00
2 Ph(c) 100.00
3 Ph(c) 75.00
4 . . . . 40.00
5 . . . . 75.00
6 . . . . 75.00
7 . . . . 75.00
8 Ph(c) 75.00
9 Ph(c) 75.00
10 Ph(c). 75.00
11 Ph(c). 75.00
12 Ph(c). 75.00
13 Ph(c). 75.00
14 Ph(c). 75.00
15 . . . . 50.00
16 . . . . 50.00
17 Ph(c). 50.00
18 Ph(c). 50.00
19 Ph(c). 50.00
20 Ph(c). 50.00
21 Ph(c). 50.00

BEWITCHED
Dell Publishing Co.
April–June, 1965
1 . . . . 165.00
2 . . . . 100.00
3 Ph(c) 75.00
4 Ph(c) 75.00
5 Ph(c) 75.00
6 Ph(c) 75.00
7 Ph(c) 75.00
8 Ph(c) 75.00
9 Ph(c) 75.00
10 Ph(c). 75.00
11 Ph(c). 75.00
12 Ph(c). 75.00
13 Ph(c). 75.00
14 . . . . 50.00

BEYOND THE GRAVE
Charlton Comics 1975–84
1 SD,TS(c),P(c). 30.00
2 thru 5 . . . . @20.00
6 thru 17 . . . . @15.00

BIG BANG
Caliber Press
0 Whole Timeline inc. 2.95
1 . . . . 2.00
2 . . . . 2.00
3 . . . . 2.00
4 25 years after #3 . . . . 2.00

BIG VALLEY, THE
Dell Publishing Co. June, 1966
1 Ph(c) 50.00
2 . . . . 25.00
3 . . . . 25.00
4 . . . . 25.00

5 . . . 25.00
6 . . . 25.00

BILL BLACK'S FUN COMICS
AC Comics
1 Cpt.Paragon,B&W . . . 2.50
2 and 3 B&W . . . @2.25
4 Color . . . 2.25

BILL THE GALACTIC HERO
Topps
1 thru 3 Harry Harrison adapt. . . @4.95

BILLY NGUYEN
Caliber
1 . . . 2.50

Billy the Kid #62
© Charlton

BILLY THE KID
Charlton Publ. Co. 1957–83
9 . . . 75.00
10 . . . 40.00
11 . . . 30.00
12 . . . 25.00
13 AW,AT . . . 35.00
14 . . . 25.00
15 AW,O:Billy the Kid . . . 35.00
16 AW . . . 35.00
17 . . . 25.00
18 . . . 25.00
19 . . . 25.00
20 . . . 35.00
21 . . . 35.00
22 . . . 35.00
23 . . . 15.00
24 . . . 35.00
25 JSe . . . 35.00
26 JSe . . . 35.00
27 . . . 15.00
28 . . . 15.00
29 . . . 15.00
30 . . . 15.00
31 thru 40 . . . @10.00
41 thru 60 . . . @7.00
61 thru 80 . . . @5.00
81 thru 153 . . . @3.00

BIONEERS
Mirage/Next
1 New Heroes . . . 2.75
2 . . . 2.75
3 All-out War . . . 2.75

BIONIC WOMAN, THE
Charlton
1 Oct, 1977, TV show adapt. . . . 10.00
2 . . . 5.00
3 . . . 5.00
4 . . . 5.00
5 . . . 5.00

BIONIX
Maximum Press 1996
1 (of 3) RLd,F:Steve Austin & Jaime Sommers . . . 3.00
2 RLd, . . . 3.00

BIZARRE 3-D ZONE
Blackthorne
1 . . . 2.50

[ORIGINAL] BLACK CAT
1 Reprints . . . 2.00
2 MA(c) rep. . . . 2.00
3 rep. . . . 2.00

BLACK DIAMOND
AC Comics
1 Colt B..U. story . . . 3.00
2 PG(c) . . . 2.00
3 PG(c) . . . 2.00
4 PG(c) . . . 2.00
5 PG(c) . . . 2.00

BLACK ENCHANTRESS
Heroic Publishing
1 and 2 Date Rape issues . . . @2.00

BLACK FLAG
Maximum Press
1 Dan Fraga . . . 3.00
2 I:New Character . . . 2.50
3 V:Network, I:Glitz . . . 2.50
4 V:Glitz, Network . . . 2.50
5 I:Jammers . . . 2.50
6 I:Alphabots . . . 2.50

BLACK FURY
Charlton Comics May, 1955
1 . . . 50.00
2 . . . 20.00
3 thru 15 . . . @15.00
16 SD . . . 50.00
17 SD . . . 50.00
18 SD . . . 50.00
19 and 20 . . . @7.00
21 thru 30 . . . @5.00
31 thru 56 . . . @5.00
57 March-April, 1966 . . . 5.00

BLACK HOLE, THE
Whitman 1980
1 & 2 movie adaptation . . . @2.00
3 & 4 new stories . . . @2.00

BLACK HOOD
Archie Publications
1 ATh,GM,DW . . . 2.00
2 ATh,DSp,A:Fox . . . 2.00
3 ATh,GM . . . 2.00

BLACK JACK
Charlton Comics 1957–59
20 . . . 55.00
21 . . . 25.00
22 . . . 35.00
23 AW,AT . . . 40.00
24 SD . . . 35.00
25 SD . . . 35.00
26 SD . . . 35.00
27 . . . 20.00
28 SD . . . 35.00
29 . . . 20.00
30 . . . 20.00

BLACKJACK: BLOOD & HONOR
Dark Angel 1997
1 by Alex Simmons,JoB, 1930s Adventure, Hildebrandts(c) . . . 2.95
2 KeL, . . . 2.95
3 Tim Cheng disappears . . . 2.95
4 . . . 2.95

BLACK PHANTOM
AC Comics
1 F:Red Mask . . . 2.50
2 F:Red Mask . . . 2.50

BLACK RAVEN
Mad Monkey Press 1996
1 Blueprints pt.1 . . . 2.95
2 Blueprints pt.2 . . . 2.95
3 V:Temple Assassins . . . 2.95
4 Blueprints pt.4 . . . 2.95
GN#1 Blueprints . . . 6.95
GN#2 Blueprints . . . 4.95

BLACK TERROR
Eclipse 1989–90
1 . . . 3.95
2 . . . 3.95
3 . . . 4.95

BLACK WEB
Inks Comics
1 thru 3 V:Seeker . . . @2.50

BLACKBALL COMICS
Blackball Comics
1 KG,A:Trencher . . . 3.25

BLAST-OFF
Harvey Publications Oct., 1965
1 JK,AW . . . 45.00

BLAZING COMBAT
Warren Publishing Co. 1965–66
1 FF(c) . . . 150.00
2 FF(c) . . . 50.00
3 and 4 FF(c) . . . @40.00

BLAZING SIX-GUNS
Skywald Comics 1971
1 F: Red Mask, Sundance Kid . . . 15.00
2 Jesse James . . . 10.00

BLONDIE
See Golden Age Section

BLOOD & ROSES
Sky Comics

1 I:Blood,Rose. 2.75

BLOOD SWORD
Jademan 1988

1 . . . . 3.00
2 . . . . 2.50
3 thru 5 . . . . @2.00
6 thru 9 . . . . @2.00
10 thru 21. . . . . @2.50
22 LW 2.00
23 LW,D:Poisonkiller. 2.00
24 LW,A:Hero 2.00
25 thru 45. . . . . @2.00
46 V:Cannibal. 2.50
47 thru 53. . . . . @2.00

BLOOD SWORD DYNASTY
Jademan 1989

1 . . . . 2.25
2 thru 6 . . . . @2.00
7 thru 14 MB . . . . @2.00
15 thru 18 MB . . . . @2.00
19 Kim & Zeo Escape the Crips . . . 2.00
20 Skeleton Executioners 2.00
21 Kim,Seeto 2.00
22 Infinite Wounded 2.00
23 Kim vs. Ask me not 2.00
24 . . . . 2.00
25 . . . . 2.00
26 V:Fiery Bird 2.00
27 A:Hero, Shou, Fiery Bird 2.00
28 Hero vs. Fiery Bird. 2.00
29 . . . . 2.00
30 . . . . 2.00
31 V:Devil Child 2.00
32 . . . . 2.00
33 . . . . 2.00
34 . . . . 2.00
35 Hero's ancestry 2.00
36 Hero & son in danger. 2.00
37 A:Hell Clan,D:North Pole 2.00
38 Fiery Hawk Vs.Inf.Seeto 2.00
39 Hero vs.Infinite seeto. 2.00
40 Kim Hung vs.Inf.Seeto. 2.00

BLOODBATH
Samson Comics

1 I:Alien,V:Starguile 2.50

BLOODCHILDE
Millennium

0 O:Bloodchilde. 2.95
1 Neil Gaiman, Vampires. 2.95
1 signed (lim. to 500). 4.95
2 Neil Gaiman, Vampires. 2.95
3 Neil Gaiman, Vampires. 2.95
4 . . . . 2.95
5 Talk Show Host 2.95

BLOODFIRE
Lightning Comics

0 O:Bloodfire 3.00
1 JZy(s),JJn, red foil 5.00
1a Platinum foil Ed. 5.00
1b B&W Promo Ed. Silver ink 4.00
1c B&W Promo Ed. Gold ink 6.00
2 JZy(s),JJn,O:Bloodfire 4.00
3 JZy(s),JJn,I:Dreadwolf,
Judgement Day,Overthrow 3.00
4 JZy(s),JJn,A:Dreadwolf, ... 3.00
5 JZy(s),JJn,I:Bloodstorm, w/card . 3.00
6 SZ(s),TLw,V:Storman 3.00
7 SZ(s),TLw,A:Pres.Clinton 3.00
8 SZ(s),TLw,O:Prodigal 3.00
9 SZ(s),TLw,I:Prodigal
(in Costume) 3.00
10 SZ(s),TLw,B:Rampage,I:Thorpe. 3.00
11 . . . . 2.95
12 . . . . 2.95

BLOODFIRE/HELLINA
Lightning Comics

1 V:Slaughterhouse 3.00
1a Nude Version 9.95

BLOODLORE
Brave New Worlds

1 Dreamweavers 2.00
2 A Blow to the Crown. 2.00

BLOODSCENT
Comico

1 GC 2.00

BLUE BEETLE
Charlton Comics June, 1964
(1st S.A. Series)

1 O:Dan Garrett/BlueBeetle 135.00
2 . . . . 75.00
3 V:Mr.Thunderbolt 80.00
4 V:Praying Mantis Man. 50.00
5 V:Red Knight 50.00

(2nd S.A. Series) July, 1965

Previously: UNUSUAL TALES
50 V:Scorpion. 50.00
51 V:Mentor 50.00
52 V:Magno 50.00
53 V:Praying Mantis Man 50.00
54 V:Eye of Horus 50.00
Becomes:

GHOSTLY TALES
(3rd S.A. Series) 1967

1 SD,I:Question. 75.00
2 SD,O:TedKord,D:DanGarrett. . . 35.00
3 SD,I:Madmen,A:Question 25.00
4 SD,A:Question 25.00
5 SD,VicSage(Question) app.
in Blue Beetle Story 25.00

Blue Beetle
© Charlton

BLUE BULLETEER
AC Comics

1 . . . . 2.25

BLUE PHANTOM, THE
Dell Publishing Co.
June–Aug., 1962

1 . . . . 65.00

BLUE RIBBON
Archie Publications

1 JK,AV,O:Fly rep. 2.00
2 TVe,Mr.Justice 2.00
3 EB/TD,O:Steel Sterling 2.00
4 . . . . 2.00
5 S&K,Shield rep. 2.00
6 DAy/TD,Fox 2.00
7 TD,Fox. 2.00
8 NA,GM,Blackhood 2.00
9 thru 11 . . . . @2.00
12 SD,ThunderAgents 2.00
13 Thunderbunny 2.00
14 Web & Jaguar 2.00

BOLD ADVENTURE
Pacific

1 . . . . 2.00
2 . . . . 2.00
3 JSe 2.00

BOLT & STARFORCE
AC Comics

1 . . . . 2.00
Bolt Special #1 . . . . 2.00

BOMBAST
Topps

1 V:Savage Dragon,Trading Card . 3.25

BONANZA
Dell Publishing Co.
June–Aug., 1960

1 . . . . 200.00
2 . . . . 100.00
3 thru 10 . . . . @75.00
11 thru 20 . . . . @60.00
21 thru 37 . . . . @50.00

BORIS KARLOFF TALES OF MYSTERY
Gold Key 1963–80

1 (Thriller) 85.00
2 (Thriller) 60.00
3 thru 8 . . . . @30.00
9 WW 40.00
10 . . . . 25.00
11 AW,JO 35.00
12 AT,AMc,JO. 30.00
13 & 14. . . . . @25.00
15 RC,GE. 25.00
16 thru 20 . . . . @25.00
21 JJ,Screaming Skull 40.00
22 thru 50 . . . . @20.00
51 thru 74 . . . . @15.00
75 thru 97 . . . . @10.00

BOZO
Innovation

1 1950's reprint stories 6.95

BOZO THE CLOWN
Blackthorne
1 3-D. 2.50
2 3-D. 2.50

BRADY BUNCH, THE
Dell Publishing Co. Feb., 1970
1 . . . . 100.00
2 . . . . 75.00

BRAIN BOY
Dell Publishing Co. April–June, 1962
1 . . . . 150.00
2 . . . . 100.00
3 . . . . 75.00
4 . . . . 75.00
5 . . . . 75.00
6 . . . . 75.00

BRAM STOKER'S BURIAL OF THE RATS
Roger Corman's Comics 1995
1 thru 3 film adaptation . . . . @2.50

BREEDING GROUND
Samson Comics
1 I:Mazit, Zero. 2.50

BRENDA LEE STORY, THE
Dell Publishing Co. Sept., 1962
1 . . . . 100.00

BRENDA STARR REPORTER
Dell Publishing Co. Oct., 1963
1 . . . . 175.00

BRIAN BOLLAND'S BLACK BOOK
Eclipse 1985
1 BB 2.50

BRIDES IN LOVE
Charlton Comics 1956–65
1 . . . . 65.00
2 . . . . 40.00
3 thru 10 . . . . @30.00
11 thru 30 . . . . @25.00
31 thru 44 . . . . @20.00
45 . . . . 15.00

BRIGADE
Awesome Entertainment Vol II (2000)
1 A:Badrock 3.00

BRUTE, THE
Atlas Feb.–July, 1975
1 thru 3 . . . . @15.00

BUCK ROGERS
Gold Key 1964
1 P(c) 75.00
2 AMc,FBe,P(c),movie adapt 15.00
3 AMc,FBe,P(c),movie adapt 15.00
4 FBe,P(c). 15.00
5 AMc,P(c) 12.00

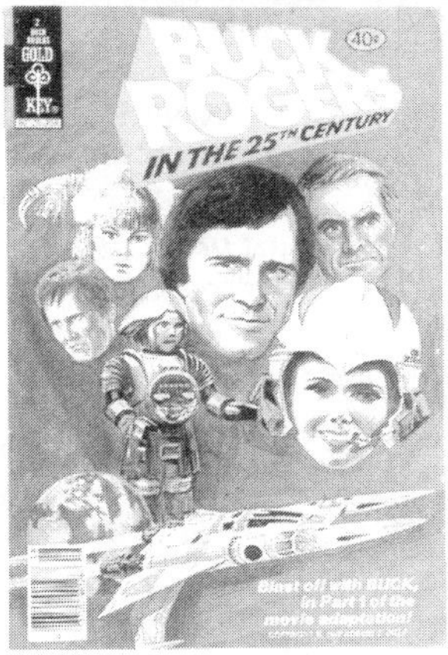

Buck Rogers #2
© Gold Key

6 AMc,P(c) 12.00

Whitman
7 thru 9 AMc,P(c). . . . . @10.00
10 and 11 AMc,P(c) . . . . @8.00
12 and 13 P(c) . . . . @7.00
14 thru 16. . . . . @5.00

BUCK ROGERS
TSR 1990–91
1 thru 3 O:Buck Rogers . . . . @2.95
4 thru 6 Black Barney. . . . . @2.95
7 thru 10 The Martian Wars . . . . @2.95

BUCKY O'HARE
Continuity
1 MGo. 2.75
2 & 3 . . . . @2.00

BUFFALO BILL JR.
Dell Publishing Co. 1956
1 . . . . 75.00
2 . . . . 50.00
3 . . . . 50.00
4 . . . . 50.00
5 . . . . 50.00
6 . . . . 50.00
7 . . . . 40.00
8 . . . . 40.00
9 . . . . 40.00
10 . . . . 40.00
11 thru 13 . . . . @40.00

BUGGED-OUT ADVENTURES OF RALFY ROACH
Bugged Out Comics
1 I: Ralfy Roach. 2.95

BULLWINKLE
Gold Key 1962
1 Bullwinkle & Rocky 200.00
2 . . . . 125.00
3 thru 5 . . . . @60.00
6 and 7, rep. . . . . @50.00
8 thru 11 . . . . @60.00
12 rep. 35.00
13 and 14 . . . . @40.00
15 thru 19. . . . . @35.00
20 thru 24, rep. . . . . @15.00
25. . . . . 25.00

BULLWINKLE
Charlton Comics July, 1970
1 . . . . 60.00

Becomes:

BULLWINKLE AND ROCKY
Charlton Comics 1970–71
2 thru 7 . . . . @50.00

BULLWINKLE & ROCKY
Eclipse
3-D 15.00

BULLWINKLE FOR PRESIDENT
Blackthorne
1 3-D Special 2.50

BURKE'S LAW
Dell Publishing Co. 1964
1 from TV Show 60.00
2 . . . . 40.00
3 . . . . 40.00

BUTCH CASSIDY
Skywald Comics 1971
1 . . . . 15.00
2 & 3 . . . . @12.00

CABBOT: BLOODHUNTER
Maximum Press 1997
1 thru 4 RV . . . . @2.50

CADILLACS & DINOSAURS
Kitchen Sink
1 Rep. from Xenozoic Tales in 3-D. 6.00

Topps
BLOOD & BONES
1 thru 3 rep. Xenozoic Tales, all covers . . . . @2.50

MAN-EATER
1 thru 3, all covers . . . . @2.50

THE WILD ONES
1 thru 3, all covers . . . . @2.50

CAGES
Tundra
1 DMc. 14.00
2 DMc. 11.00
3 DMc. 7.50
4 DMc. 7.50
5 thru 7 DMc . . . . @5.00

CAIN
Harris
1 B:DQ(s),I:Cain,Frenzy. 5.00
2 BSz(c),HBk,V:Mortatira. 3.25

CAIN'S HUNDRED
Dell Publishing Co. May-July, 1962
1 . . . . 25.00
2 . . . . 20.00

COLOR PUB.

CALIFORNIA RAISINS
Blackthorne

1 thru 4 3-D . . . . @2.50
5 3-D,O:Calif.Raisins 2.50
6 thru 8 3-D . . . . @2.50

CALVIN & THE COLONEL
Dell Publishing Co.
April–June, 1962

1 . . . . 100.00
2 . . . . 75.00

CAP'N QUICK & FOOZLE
Eclipse 1984–85

1 . . . . 2.00
2 and 3 . . . . @2.50

CAPT. ELECTRON
Brick Computers Inc.

1 . . . . 2.00
2 . . . . 2.25

CAPTAIN ATOM See: STRANGE SUSPENSE STORIES

CAPTAIN CANUCK
Comely Comix 1975–81

1 I:Blue Fox. 15.00
2 I:Red Coat 10.00
3 I:Heather 10.00
4 thru 14 . . . . @7.00
Summer Spec. #1. . . . . 7.00

CAPTAIN GLORY
Topps

1 A:Bombast,Night Glider, Trading Card 3.25

CAPTAIN GRAVITY
Penny Farthing Press 1998

1 by Steve Vrattos & Keith Martin 2.75
2 No one escapes the Law of Gravity 2.75
3 . . . . 2.75
4 . . . . 2.75

CAPTAIN HARLOCK: FALL OF THE EMPIRE
Eternity

1 R:Captain Harlock 2.50
2 V:Tadashi 2.50
3 Bomb on the Arcadia 2.50
4 Final issue 2.50

CAPTAIN MARVEL
M. F. Enterprises April, 1966

1 . . . . 30.00
2 . . . . 25.00
3 Fights The Bat 20.00
4 . . . . 20.00
5 Captain Marvel Presents the Terrible Five 15.00

CAPTAIN NAUTICUS
Entity 1994

1 V:Fathom 2.95
2 V:Fathom's Henchman 2.95
3 Surf's Up 2.00

CAPTAIN NICE
Gold Key Nov., 1967

1 Ph(c) 75.00

CAPTAIN PARAGON
Americomics

1 thru 4 . . . . @2.00

CAPTAIN POWER
Continuity

1a NA,TVtie-in(direct sale). 2.00
1b NA,TVtie-in(newsstand) 2.00
2 NA 2.00

CAPTAIN STERN
Kitchen Sink Press

1 BWr,R:Captain Stern 5.25
2 BWr,Running Out of Time 4.95

Captain Thunder & Bluebolt #1
© Hero Graphics

CAPTAIN THUNDER AND BLUE BOLT
Hero Graphics

1 I:Capt.Thunder & Paul Fremont . 2.00
2 Paul becomes Blue Bolt 2.00
3 O:Capt.Thunder 2.00
4 V:Iguana Boys 2.00
5 V:Ian Shriver, in Scotland 2.00
6 V:Krakatoa 2.00
7 V:Krakatoa 2.00
8 A:Sparkplug (from League of Champions) 2.00
9 A:Sparkplug 2.00
10 A:Sparkplug. 2.00

CAPTAIN VENTURE & THE LAND BENEATH THE SEA
Gold Key Oct., 1968

1 . . . . 50.00
2 . . . . 40.00

CAPTAIN VICTORY AND THE GALACTIC RANGERS
Pacific 1982

1 JK 2.50
2 JK 2.00
3 JK,BU:NA,I:Ms.Mystic. 2.00
4 JK 2.00
5 JK 2.00
6 JK,SD. 2.00
7 thru 13 JK . . . . @2.00
Spec.#1 JK. 2.00

CAR 54, WHERE ARE YOU?
Dell Publishing Co.
March–May, 1962

1 Ph(c) 75.00
2 thru 7 Ph(c). . . . . @40.00

CARCA JOU RENAISSANCE

1 and 2 . . . . @2.00

CARNOSAUR CARNAGE
Atomeka

TPB 4.95

CAROLINE KENNEDY
Charlton Comics 1961

1 . . . . 125.00

CASEY JONES & RAPHAEL
Mirage

1 Family War. 2.75
2 Johnny Woo Woo 2.75
3 V:Johnny Woo Woo 2.75
4 9mm Raphael. 2.75

CASPER ENCHANTED TALES
Harvey

1 short stories 2.00

CASPER
Harvey

1 thru 7 . . . . @1.00
8 thru 14 . . . . @1.25
15 thru 28 . . . . @1.50

CASPER THE FRIENDLY GHOST
Blackthorne

1 3-D. 2.50

CASPER & FRIENDS
Harvey

1 thru 4 . . . . @2.00
5 short stories, cont. 2.00

CASPER GHOSTLAND
Harvey

1 short stories 2.00

CASPER'S GHOSTLAND
Harvey Publications
Winter, 1958-59
1 . . . . 175.00
2 . . . . 100.00
3 thru 10 . . . . @75.00
11 thru 20 . . . . @50.00
21 thru 40 . . . . @30.00
41 thru 61 . . . . @20.00
62 thru 77 . . . . @15.00
78 thru 97 . . . . @10.00
98 Dec., 1979. . . . . 10.00

CASPER THE FRIENDLY GHOST
Harvey 1990–91
Prev: The Friendly Ghost Casper
254 thru 260 . . . . @2.00
[Second Series] 1991–94
1 thru 14 . . . . @2.00
15 thru 28. . . . . @2.00

CATSEYE
Awesome/Hyperwerks 1999
0 KIA,BNa,O:Catseye 2.95

CAT TALES
Eternity
1 3-D. 2.00

CAULDRON
Real Comics 1995
1 Movie Style Comic 2.95
1a Variant cover 2.95

CAVE GIRL
AC Comics
1 . . . . 2.95

CAVE KIDS
Gold Key 1963
1 . . . . 75.00
2 . . . . 40.00
3 . . . . 40.00
4 . . . . 40.00
5 . . . . 40.00
6 . . . . 25.00
7 A:Pebbles & Bamm Bamm 35.00
8 thru 10 . . . . @20.00
11 thru 16 . . . . @20.00

CAVEWOMAN
Avatar 1999
Color Spec. 3.50
Color Spec. Fauna (c) 3.50
Color Spec. nude (c). 6.00
Color Spec. prism foil (c) 12.95
Color Spec. Royal Blue. 75.00

CENTURY
Awesome Entertainment 2000
1 RLe 2.99
1a Millennium edition. 4.95
2 . . . . 2.99
2a Millennium edition. 4.95
2b signed 12.99
3 . . . . 2.99

CHAINS OF CHAOS
Harris
1 Vampirella, Rook 5.00

2 V:Chaoschild 3.25
3 Final issue 3.25

Champions Vol. 2, #3
© Hero Graphics

CHAMPIONS
Eclipse 1986–87
1 I:Flare,League of Champions Foxbat, Dr.Arcane. 15.00
2 I:Dark Malice 15.00
3 I:Lady Arcane. 10.00
4 O:Dark Malice. 15.00
5 O:Flare. 8.00
6 D:Giant Demonmaster 8.00
[New Series]
Hero Graphics
1 EL,I:Madame Synn,Galloping Galooper 5.00
2 I:Fat Man, Black Enchantress . . . 2.25
3 I:Sparkplug&Icicle,O:Flare 2.25
4 I:Exo-Skeleton Man 2.25
5 A:Foxbat. 2.25
6 I:Mechanon, C:Foxbat 2.00
7 A:Mechanon,J:Sparkplug,Icicle . . 2.00
8 O:Foxbat 2.00
9 Flare #0 (Flare preview) 2.00
10 Olympus Saga #1 . . . . 2.00
11 Olympus Saga #2 . . . . 2.00
12 Olympus Saga #3 . . . . 2.00
Ann.#1 O:Giant & DarkMalice. 2.75
Ann.#2 . . . . 3.95

CHAMPIONS CLASSIC
Hero Graphics
1 GP(c),Rep.1st champions series . 2.00

CHAOS! BIBLE
Chaos! Comics
1 Character Profiles. 3.50

CHAOS! CHRONICLES– THE HISTORY OF A COSMOS
Chaos! Comics 1999
Spec. 3.50
Spec. signed premium 15.00

CHAOS! GALLERY
Chaos! Comics 1997
1 . . . . 2.95

CHAOS! NIGHTMARE THEATER
Chaos! Comics 1997
1 (of 4) BWr(c) 2.50
2 BWr(c) 2.50
3 BWr(c) 2.50
4 BWr(c) 2.50

CHAOS QUARTERLY
Harris Comics 1995
1 F:Lady Death 4.95
1a Premium Edition 10.95
1b Signed,limited edition 20.00

CHAPEL
Awesome Entertainment 1997
1 BNa, from Spawn,Youngblood . . 2.95

CHARLEMAGNE
Defiant
1 JiS(s),From Hero 2.00
2 JiS(s),I:Charles Smith. 2.75
3 JiS(s),A:War Dancer. 2.75
4 DGC(s),V:Dark Powers. 2.75
5 Schism prequel. 2.75
6 V:Wardancer 2.75
7 R:To Vietnam 2.75

CHARLIE CHAN
Dell Publ. Co., Oct.–Dec., 1965
1 . . . . 50.00
2 . . . . 40.00

CHARLTON BULLSEYE
Charlton 1981–82
1 Blue Beetle, I:Rocket Rabbit. . . . 3.50
2 Capt. Catnip; Nell the Horse. . . . 2.50
3 Grundar 2.50
4 Vanguards 2.50
5 Warhound. 2.50
6 Thunder-bunny. 2.50
7 Captain Atom 2.50
8 weird stories. 2.50
9 . . . . 2.50
10 . . . . 2.50
Spec. #1. 2.00
Spec. #2 Atomic Mouse 2.00

CHARLTON SPORT LIBRARY
Charlton 1970
1 Professional Football 35.00

CHASSIS
Millennium/Expand 1995
1 I:Chassis McBain, Aero Run. . . . 2.95
1 2nd printing 2.95
1 chrome cover 9.95
2 . . . . 2.95
2a with racing card 4.95
2b Amanda Conner cover 2.95
2c Amanda Conner cover, signed . 9.95
2d foil cover, signed. 7.95
[Vol. 2] Hurricane Comics 1998
0 by Joshua Dysart & Wm.O'Neill . 2.95
0a variant cover. 2.95
1 . . . . 2.95
2 . . . . 2.95
3 . . . . 2.95

COLOR PUB.

CHASTITY LUST FOR LIFE
Chaos! Comics 1999
1 (of 4) PNu . . . 2.95
1a alternate cover . . . 6.95
1b alternate cover, signed . . . 20.00
1c premium edition . . . 10.00
2 V:Hemlock . . . 2.95
3 . . . 2.95

CHASTITY: REIGN OF TERROR
Chaos! Comics 2000
1 . . . 2.95
1 premium ed. . . . 9.95

CHASTITY ROCKED
Chaos! Comics 1998
1 (of 4) PNu . . . 2.95
1a & 1b variant covers . . . @2.95
2 V:Jade . . . 2.95
3 V:Jade . . . 2.95
4 conclusion . . . 2.95
Chastity/Cremator Preview Book, B&W . . . 5.00

CHASTITY: THEATRE OF PAIN
Chaos! Comics 1997
1 (of 3) BnP, . . . 6.00
1a premium edition . . . 15.00
2 . . . 3.00
3 . . . 3.00
3a premium edition . . . 15.00
TPB rep.#1–#3, Sketchbook . . . @9.95

CHEAP SHODDY ROBOT TOYS
Eclipse
1 A:Ronald Reagan . . . 2.00

CHECKMATE
Gold Key Oct., 1962
1 Ph(c) . . . 60.00
2 Ph(c) . . . 50.00

CHEMICAL MAN
1 . . . 2.00

CHERYL BLOSSOM
Archie Comics April, 1996
1 "Love Showdown" . . . 2.00
2 "Inn Big Trouble" . . . 2.00
3 "Home Um-Improvement" . . . 2.00
4 "Radio Daze" . . . 2.00
5 "Cheryl in the Morning" . . . 2.00
6 "What a Disaster" . . . 2.00
7 "Educating Cheryl" . . . 2.00
8 "Masquerade Madness" . . . 2.00
9 "Tis the Season" . . . 2.00
10 "Who's That Girl", pt.1 . . . 2.00
11 "Who's That Girl", pt.2 . . . 2.00
12 "Stop the Presses" . . . 2.00
13 . . . 2.00
14 "Cheers to You" . . . 2.00
15 "Cheryl's Beach Bash, pt.1" . . . 2.00
16 "Lights, Camera, Action," pt.2. . . 2.00
17 "Cheryl-Mania" . . . 2.00
18 "Strike A Pose!" . . . 2.00
19 "Chill Out" . . . 2.00
20 "Cinderblossom" . . . 2.00
21 "Sugar World" . . . 2.00
22 "Big In Japan" . . . 2.00
23 Cheryl & Betty friends? . . . 2.00
24 . . . 2.00
25 "Creature Feature on Party Beach" . . . 2.00
26 "Take The Mummy and Run" . . . 2.00
27 "It's A Maze Thing" . . . 2.00
28 "Holi-Daze" . . . 2.00
29 . . . 2.00
30 "C'est La Ski" . . . 2.00
31 "In Your Dreams" . . . 2.00
32 "Bug Off" . . . 2.00
33 "Something Fishy" . . . 2.00
34 "Midsummer's Magic" . . . 2.00
35 "Phantom of the Fun House" . . . 2.00
36 thru 37 . . . @2.00

CHERYL BLOSSOM GOES HOLLYWOOD
Archie Comics 1996
1 (of 3) by Dan Parent & Bill Golliher . . . 2.00
2 and 3 . . . @2.00

CHEYENNE
Dell Publishing Co. Oct., 1956
1 Ph(c) all . . . 175.00
2 . . . 100.00
3 . . . 75.00
4 thru 12 . . . @60.00
13 thru 25 . . . @50.00

CHEYENNE KID (see WILD FRONTIER)

CHI-CHIAN
Sirius 1997
1 (of 6) by Voltaire . . . 2.95
2 thru 6 . . . @2.95

CHILD'S PLAY 2
Innovation
1 Movie Adapt Pt. 1 . . . 2.50
2 Adapt Pt. 2 . . . 2.50
3 Adapt Pt. 3 . . . 2.50

CHILD'S PLAY 3
Innovation
1 Movie Adapt Pt. 1 . . . 2.50
2 Movie Adapt Pt. 2 . . . 2.50

CHILD'S PLAY: THE SERIES
Innovation
1 Chucky's Back . . . 2.50
2 Straight Jacket Blues . . . 2.50
3 M.A.R.K.E.D. . . . 2.50
4 Chucky in Toys 4 You . . . 2.50
5 Chucky in Hollywood . . . 2.50

CHILDREN OF FIRE
Fantagor
1 thru 3 RCo . . . @2.00

CHILLING ADVENTURES IN SORCERY AS TOLD BY SABRINA
Archie 1972–74
1 . . . 35.00
2 . . . 25.00
3 thru 5 . . . @20.00

Chilling Adventures in Sorcery #2
© Archie Publications

CHIP 'N DALE
Dell Publishing 1955–66
4 . . . 50.00
5 thru 10 . . . @45.00
11 thru 30 . . . @35.00

Gold Key 1967
1 reprints . . . 20.00
2 thru 10 . . . @10.00
11 thru 20 . . . @5.00
21 thru 83 . . . @2.50

CHIP 'N DALE RESCUE RANGERS
Walt Disney 1990
1 Rescue Rangers to the Rescue, pt.1 . . . 3.50
2 Rescue Rangers to the Rescue, pt.2 . . . 3.00
3 thru 7 . . . @2.50
8 Coast to Coast Pt. 1 . . . 2.00
9 Coast to Coast Pt. 2 . . . 2.00
10 Coast to Coast Pt. 3 . . . 2.00
11 Coast to Coast Pt. 4 . . . 2.00
12 "Showdown at Hoedown" . . . 2.00
13 Raining Cats & Dogs . . . 2.00
14 "Cobra Kadabra" . . . 2.00
15 I:Techno-Rats,WaspPatrol Fearless Frogs Pt.1 . . . 2.00
16 A:Techno-Rats,WaspPatrol, Fearless Frogs Pt.2 . . . 2.00
17 "For the Love of Cheese" . . . 2.00
18 "Ghastly Goat of Quiver Moore," Pt.1 . . . 2.00

CHOO CHOO CHARLIE
Gold Key Dec., 1969
1 . . . 100.00

CHOPPER: EARTH, WIND, AND FIRE
Fleetway
1 F:Chopper . . . 2.95

CHOSEN, THE
Click Comics 1995
1 I:The Chosen . . . 2.50
2 I:Herman Cortez . . . 2.50

CHRISTIAN
Maximum Press 1996

1 and 2 (of 3) RLd . . . . @2.95

CHRISTMAS PARADE
Gladstone

1 GiantEdition 4.00
2 . . . . 3.50

CHRISTMAS SPIRIT, THE
Kitchen Sink

TPB Will Eisner art 15.00

CHROMA-TICK SPECIAL EDITION
New England Press

1 Rep.Tick#1,new stories. 4.00
2 Rep.Tick#2,new stories. 5.00
3 thru 8 Reps.& new stories . . . . @3.50

CHROME
Hot Comics

1 Machine Man 3.50
2 thru 4 . . . . @2.00

CHROME WARRIORS IN A '59 CHEVY
Black Out Comics 1998

0 . . . . 2.95
0a Nude cover. 9.95
0b deluxe nude edition. 14.95
1 Rob Roman & Tommy Castillo . . 2.95
1a nude cover 9.95
1b deluxe nude edition. 14.95

CHROMIUM MAN, THE
Triumphant Comics

0 Blue Logo. 6.00
0 Regular 2.50
1 I:Chromium Man,Mr.Death 3.50
2 I:Prince Vandal 3.00
3 I:Candi,Breaker,Coil 2.50
4 JnR(s),AdP,Unleashed 2.50
5 JnR(s),AdP,Unleashed 2.50
6 JnR(s),Courier,pt.1 . . . . 2.50
7 JnR(s),Courier,pt.2 . . . . 2.50
8 JnR(s),Chromium finds peace. . . 2.50
9 V:Tarsak. 2.50
10 . . . . 2.50
11 Prince Vandal #8 . . . . 2.50
12 Prince Vandal #9 . . . . 2.50
13 V:Realm 2.50
14 A:Light. 2.50
15 . . . . 2.50

CHROMIUM MAN: VIOLENT PAST
Triumphant Comics

1 thru 4 JnR(s). . . . . @2.50

CHRONICLES OF CORUM
First 1987–88

1 Michael Moorcock adapt. 2.25
2 thru 12 . . . . @2.00

CICERO'S CAT
Dell Publishing Co. July–Aug., 1959

1 . . . . 40.00
2 . . . . 35.00

CIMMARON STRIP
Dell Publishing Co. Jan., 1968

1 . . . . 45.00

CITY PERILOUS
Broadway Comics

1 GI,"I Remember the Future," pt. #1 . . . . 2.95
2 GI,"I Remember the Future," pt. #2 . . . . 2.95

Becomes:

KNIGHTS ON BROADWAY

3 GI,"I Remember the Future," pt. #3 . . . . 2.95
4 GI,"I Remember the Future," pt. #4 . . . . 2.95
5 GI,"I Remember the Future," part #5 . . . . 2.95

CLASSICS ILLUSTRATED See Also:CLASSICS ILLUSTRATED SECTION

CLASSICS ILLUSTRATED
First

1 GW,The Raven. 3.75
2 RG,Great Expectations. 3.75
3 KB,Thru the Looking Glass. 3.75
4 BSz,Moby Dick. 3.75
5 SG,TM,KE, Hamlet. 3.75
6 PCr,JT, Scarlet Letter 3.75
7 DSp,Count of Monte Cristo. 3.75
8 Dr.Jekyll & Mr.Hyde 3.75
9 MP,Tom Sawyer 3.75
10 Call of the Wild 3.75
11 Rip Van Winkle 3.75
12 Dr. Moreau 3.75
13 Wuthering Heights 3.75
14 Fall of House of Usher. 3.75
15 Gift of the Magi 3.75
16 A: Christmas Carol 3.75
17 Treasure Island 3.75
18 The Devils Dictionary. 3.95
19 The Secret Agent. 3.95
20 The Invisible Man 3.95
21 Cyrano de Bergerac. 3.95
22 The Jungle Book 3.95
23 Swiss Family Robinson 3.95
24 Rime of Ancient Mariner 3.95
25 Ivanhoe 3.95
26 Aesop's Fables 3.95
27 The Jungle 3.95

CLAUS
Draco 1997

1 by John Kennedy Bowden & Corinne Y. Guichardon 2.95
2 . . . . 3.25
3 . . . . 3.25
4 . . . . 3.25

CLIVE BARKER'S DREAD
Eclipse

Graphic Album 7.95

CLIVE BARKER'S TAPPING THE VEIN
Eclipse

1 . . . . 13.00
2 . . . . 8.50
3 . . . . 8.50
4 . . . . 8.50

5 inc."How Spoilers Breed" 8.50

CLYDE CRASHCUP
Dell Publishing Co. Aug.–Oct., 1963

1 . . . . 150.00
2 . . . . 125.00
3 thru 5 . . . . @125.00

COBALT 60
Innovation

1 reprints. 4.95

COBALT BLUE
Innovation

Spec.#1 . . . . 2.00
Spec.#2 . . . . 2.00
1 and 2 . . . . @2.00

Codename: Danger #2
© Lodestone

CODENAME: DANGER
Lodestone 1985

1 RB/BMc,I:Makor 2.50
2 KB,I:Capt.Energy 2.00
3 PS/RB 2.00
4 PG 2.00

CODE NAME: DOUBLE IMPACT
High Impact 1997

1 RCl. 3.00
1 variant cover. 10.00
1 signed holofoil cover. 14.95

CODENAME: STRIKEFORCE
Spectrum

1 . . . . 2.00

COLLECTOR'S DRACULA
Millennium

1 . . . . 4.25

COLOR PUB.

COLOSSAL SHOW, THE
Gold Key Oct., 1969

1 . . . 50.00

COLOUR OF MAGIC
Innovation

1 Terry Pratchett novel adapt . . . 3.00
2 "The Sending of Eight" . . . 2.50
3 "Lure of the Worm . . . 2.50
4 final issue . . . 2.50

COLT .45
Dell Publishing Co. 1958

1 Ph(c) all . . . 125.00
2 . . . 100.00
3 . . . 75.00
4 . . . 75.00
5 . . . 75.00
6 ATh . . . 90.00
7 . . . 75.00
8 . . . 75.00
9 . . . 75.00

COLT SPECIAL
AC Comics

1 . . . 2.00
2 . . . 2.00
3 . . . 2.00

COMBAT
Dell Publishing Co. 1961

1 SG . . . 50.00
2 SG . . . 25.00
3 SG . . . 25.00
4 JFK cover, Story 2-D . . . 35.00
5 SG . . . 25.00
6 SG . . . 20.00
7 SG . . . 20.00
8 SG . . . 20.00
9 SG . . . 20.00
10 SG . . . 20.00
11 thru 27 SG . . . @15.00
28 thru 40 SG . . . @12.00

COMET
Red Circle/Archie Publications

1 CI,O:Comet . . . 2.00
2 CI,D:Hangman . . . 2.00

COMET, THE
Red Circle 1983

1 Alex Nino . . . 2.00

COMIC ALBUM
Dell Publishing Co. 1958
March–May, 1958

1 Donald Duck . . . 100.00
2 Bugs Bunny . . . 50.00
3 Donald Duck . . . 75.00
4 Tom & Jerry . . . 50.00
5 Woody Woodpecker . . . 50.00
6 Bugs Bunny . . . 50.00
7 Popeye . . . 60.00
8 Tom & Jerry . . . 50.00
9 Woody Woodpecker . . . 50.00
10 Bugs Bunny . . . 50.00
11 Popeye . . . 60.00
12 Tom & Jerry . . . 40.00
13 Woody Woodpecker . . . 40.00
14 Bugs Bunny . . . 40.00
15 Popeye . . . 50.00
16 Flintstones . . . 75.00
17 Space Mouse . . . 50.00
18 3 Stooges,Ph(c) . . . 100.00

COMICO X-MAS SPECIAL
Comico

1 SR/AW/DSt(c) . . . 2.00

COMIX INTERNATIONAL
Warren Magazines July, 1974

1 . . . 100.00
2 WW,BW . . . 35.00
3 . . . 25.00
4 RC . . . 25.00
5 Spring, 1977 . . . 20.00

COMMANDER BATTLE AND HIS ATOMIC SUB

#20 3-D . . . 2.50

COMMANDOSAURS

1 . . . 3.50

CONSTRUCT
Mirage

1 I:Constructs . . . 2.75
2 F:Sect.Eight, Armor . . . 2.75
3 O:Constructs . . . 2.75
4 Fist-O-God . . . 2.75

CORBEN SPECIAL
Pacific

1 RCo . . . 2.00

CORUM: THE BULL & THE SPEAR
First

1 thru 4 Michael Moorcock adapt. @2.00

COSMONEERS SPECIAL

1 . . . 2.00

COUGAR, THE
Atlas Apr.–July, 1975

1 & 2 . . . @15.00

Cougar #1
© Atlas Comics

COUNTER-STRIKE
Infinity Comics 2000

1 (of 4) . . . 2.50
1a premium chroma-foil (c) . . . 12.00
2 thru 4 . . . @2.50

COURTSHIP OF EDDIE'S FATHER
Dell Publishing Co. 1970

1 Ph(c) . . . 50.00
2 Ph(c) . . . 30.00

COVEN
Awesome Entertainment 1997

1 IaC,JLb,JSb,V:The Pentad . . . 15.00
1a variant covers . . . 15.00
2 IaC,JLb,Who is Spellcaster? . . . 8.00
3 IaC,JLb,V:The Pentad . . . 6.00
4 IaC,JLb,Pentad, concl. . . . 4.00
5 IaC,JLb, . . . 4.00
5 gold foil cover . . . 10.00
6 IaC,JLb,Mardi Gras madness . . . 3.00
6 gold foil edition . . . 10.00
7 IaC,JLb,V:Babylon . . . 2.50
8 IaC,JLb,F:Thor, the God of Thunder . . . 2.50
9 IaC,JLb, . . . 2.50
Coll.Ed. #1, rep. #1–#2, new IaC(c) . . . 4.95
Fan Appreciation #1, rep. #1, new cover . . . 2.50
Coven/Menace S.D.Con preview book . . . 5.00
TPB The Gathering . . . 16.99

VOL 2

1 IaC,JLb . . . 2.50
1a, b & c variant covers . . . 2.50
1d chrome edition . . . 15.00
1e gold foil cover . . . 10.00
2 IaC,JLb,V:Supreme . . . 2.50
2a Lionheart (c) . . . 15.00
2b signed . . . 25.00
3 IaC,JLb, Long Flight Home . . . 2.50
4 IaC,JLb . . . 2.50
5 thru 7 . . . @2.99
Coven Sourcebook #1 . . . 2.99

COVEN 13
No Mercy Comics 1997

1 by Rikki Rockett & Matt Busch . . . 2.50
2 . . . 2.50
3 . . . 2.50
4 . . . 2.50

COVEN/RE:GEX
Awesome Entertainment 1999

1 (of 2) RLe,JLb,IaC . . . 2.50
1a alternate IaC cover . . . 6.95
2 JLb, conclusion . . . 2.50

COVEN: DARK ORIGINS
Awesome Entertainment 1999

1 . . . 2.50
1a & b variant covers . . . 2.50

COVER GIRL

1 . . . 2.00

COWBOY IN AFRICA
Gold Key March, 1968

1 Chuck Conners,Ph(c) . . . 50.00

CRACKED
Major Magazines Feb.–Mar., 1958

1 AW 150.00
2 . . . . . 75.00
3 thru 6 . . . . . @50.00
7 thru 10 . . . . . @40.00
11 thru 20 . . . . . @35.00
21 thru 30 . . . . . @30.00
31 thru 60 . . . . . @25.00
61 thru 150 . . . . . @20.00
151 thru 200 . . . . . @7.00
201 thru 252 . . . . . @5.00

[THE INCREDIBLE] CRASH DUMMIES
Harvey 1993

1 thru 3, from the toy series . . . . @2.00

CRAZYMAN
Continuity
[1st Series]

1 Embossed(c),NA/RT(i),
O:Crazyman 6.00
2 NA/BB(c) 2.50
3 DBa,V:Terrorists 2.50

[2nd Series]

1 Die Cut(c) 2.50
2 thru 3 . . . . . 2.50
4 In Demon World 2.50

CREATURE
Antarctic Press Oct. 1997

1 (of 2) by Don Walker & Jason
Maranto 2.95
2 concl. 2.95

CREED: CRANIAL DISORDER
Lightning Comics

1 (of 3) 3.00
1a variant cover, *Previews*
exclusive 3.00
1b Platinum edition 9.00
1c Platinum edition, autographed 16.00
2 . . . . . 3.00
2a variant cover 3.00

Creed: Cranial Disorder #1
© Lightning Comics

CREED/TEENAGE MUTANT NINJA TURTLES
Lightning Comics April, 1996

1 . . . . . 3.00
1 variant cover 3.00
1 platinum edition B&W 9.95

CREMATOR: HELL'S GUARDIAN
Chaos! Comics 1998

1 (of 5) LJi 2.95
2 . . . . . 2.95
3 V:Asteroth 2.95
4 . . . . . 2.95
5 . . . . . 2.95

CRIME MACHINE
Skywald Publications Feb., 1971

1 JK 60.00
2 AT 35.00

CRIME PATROL
Gemstone 2000

1 rep. 2.50
2 rep. Fall 1948 . . . . . 2.50
3 rep. Winter 1948 . . . . . 2.50
4 rep. Feb. 1949 . . . . . 2.50
5 rep. 2.50
6 rep. 2.50
7 rep. 2.50
8 rep. Oct. 1949 . . . . . 2.50
9 rep. Dec. 1949 . . . . . 2.50
"Annuals"
TPB Vol. 1 rep. #1–#5 . . . . . @13.50

CRIME SUSPENSE STORIES
Russ Cochran

1 Rep. C.S.S. #1 (1950) 2.00
2 Rep. C.S.S. 2.00
3 Rep. C.S.S. 2.00
4 thru 6 Rep. C.S.S 2.00
7 Rep. C.S.S. 2.00
8 thru 15 Rep. . . . . . @2.00

Gemstone

16 thru 27 EC comics reprint . . . . @2.50
Ann.#1, rep. #1–#5 . . . . . @8.95
Ann.#2, rep. #6–#10 . . . . . @8.95
Ann.#3, rep. #11–#15 . . . . . @9.95
Ann.#4, rep. #16–#19 . . . . . @10.50
Ann.#5, rep. #20–#23 . . . . . @10.95
Ann.#6 rebinding #24–#27 . . . . @10.95

CRIMSON NUN
Antarctic Press 1997

1 (of 4) 2.95
2 . . . . . 2.95
3 . . . . . 2.95
4 concl 2.95

CRIMSON PLAGUE
Event Comics

1 GP,F:DiNA: Simmons 2.95
2 GP, ... 2.95

CROSSFIRE
Eclipse 1984–86

1 DSp 3.00
2 DSp 2.50
3 DSp 2.00
4 DSp 2.00
5 DSp 2.00
6 DSp 2.00
7 DSp 2.50
8 DSp 2.50
9 DSp 2.00
10 DSp 2.00
11 DSp 2.00
12 DSp,DSt(c),M.Monroe cover
& story 2.50
13 DSp 2.00
14 DSp 2.00
15 DSp,O:Crossfire 2.00
16 DSp,"The Comedy Place" 2.00
17 DSp,"Comedy Place" Pt.2 . . . . . 2.00

CROSSFIRE & RAINBOW
Eclipse 1986

1 DSp,V:Marx Brothers 2.00
2 DSp,PG(c),V:Marx Brothers 2.00
3 DSp,HC(c),A:Witness 2.00
4 DSp,DSt(c),"This Isn't Elvis" 3.50

CROSSROADS
First

1 Sable,Whisper 4.00
2 Sable,Badger 4.00
3 JSon,JAl,Badger/Luther Ironheart 4.00
4 Grimjack/Judah Macabee 4.00
5 LM,Grimjack/Dreadstar/Nexus . . 4.00

CROW, THE: CITY OF ANGELS
Kitchen Sink

1 thru 3 movie adaptation . . . . . @2.95
1 thru 3 movie adaptation,
photo covers . . . . . @2.95
TPB The Crow, The Movie, new
printing 18.95

CRYBABY
Event Comics 1999

1 GrL,SLo 2.95
1a limited, signed 10.00

CRYING FREEMAN III
Viz

1 A:Dark Eyes,Oshu 6.00
2 A:Dark Eyes, V:Oshu 5.25
3 Freeman vs. Oshu 5.25
4 Freeman Defeated 5.25
5 Freeman clones, A:Nitta 5.25
6 V:Nitta 5.25
7 . . . . . 4.95
8 . . . . . 4.95
9 . . . . . 4.95

CRYING FREEMAN IV
Viz

1 B:The Pomegranate 4.95
2 . . . . . 2.75
3 . . . . . 2.75
4 . . . . . 2.75
5 thru 7 . . . . . @2.75
8 E:The Pomegranate 2.75

[2nd Series]

1 The Festival 2.50

CRYPT OF DAWN
Sirius 1996

1 JLi 2.95

COLOR PUB.

CRYPTIC WRITINGS OF MEGADETH
Chaos! Comics 1997
1 BnP 2.95
1a Tour Edition, leather 25.00
1b Tour Edition, deluxe 50.00
2 BnP 2.95
3 BnP 2.95
4 BnP 2.95
TPB 12.95

CYBER CITY: PART ONE
CPM Comics 1995
1 I:Oedo City 2.95
2 Sengoku 2.95

CYBER CITY: PART TWO
CPM Comics 1995
1 Based on Animated Movie 2.95

CYBERCRUSH: ROBOTS IN REVOLT
Fleetway/Quality
1 inc.Robo-Hunter,Ro-Busters . . . 2.00
2 and 3 . . . . . @2.00
4 and 5 V:Terraneks . . . . . @2.00

CYBERFROG
Harris 1995
0 O:Cyberfrog 2.95
0 AAd(c), signed 19.95
0 Alternate AAd(c) 9.95
1 . . . . . 2.00
1a Signed,numbered 24.95
1b Ultra Violent Cover 49.95
2 . . . . . 2.95
3 . . . . . 2.95
4 . . . . . 2.95
4a alternate cover, signed & numbered (#300) 29.95

CYBERFROG: RESERVOIR FROG
Harris
1 Preview Ashcan, signed & numbered 24.95
1 EL(c),V:the Swarm, Mr. Skorpeone 2.95
1 Signed & numbered (#250) 19.95
2 . . . . . 2.95
1 & 2 Signed & numbered, in binder (#250) 39.95

CYBERHOOD
Entity Comics 1995
1 R:Cyberhood 2.50
1a with PC Game 6.95

CYBERPUNK
Innovation
1 . . . . . 2.00
2 . . . . . 2.00
Book 2,#1 . . . . . 2.25
Book 2,#2 . . . . . 2.25

CYBERPUNK: THE SERAPHIM FILES
Innovation 1990
1 . . . . . 2.50
2 . . . . . 2.50

CYBERPUNX
Maximum Press 1997
1 MHw, ... 2.50

CYBERRAD
Continuity
1 NA layouts,I:Cyberran 3.00
2 NA l/o 2.50
3 NA l/o 2.50
4 NA l/o 2.50
5 NA l/o Glow in the Dark cov 5.00
6 NA l/o,Pullout poster 2.50
7 NA l/o,See-thru(c) 2.50

[2nd Series]
1 Hologram cover 2.00
2 NA(c),"The Disassembled Man" . 2.00

[3rd Series]
1 Holo.(c),just say no 3.50

[4th Series, Deathwatch 2000]
1 Deathwatch 2000 pt.8,w/card . . . 2.50
2 Deathwatch 2000 pt. w/card 2.50

CYBRID
Maximum Press 1995
1 F:Cybrid, I:The Clan 2.95

CYBRID
Maximum Press 1997
0 RLd, 48pg 3.50
1 MsM,BNa 3.00
2 MsM,BNa 3.00

CYNDER
Immortelle Studios
1 thru 3: see B&W
Ann. #1 . . . . . 2.95

Series II 1997
1 A:Nira X 2.95

CYNDER/NIRA X
Immortelle Studios 1996
1 x-over 2.95
1 variant cover 3.00
1 gold edition 10.00

DAEMONSTORM
Caliber 1997
1 TM(c),JMt 3.95
1 signed 3.95
1 gold edition 19.95

DAEMONSTORM: DEADWORLD
Caliber
one-shot 3.95

DAEMONSTORM: OZ
Caliber 1997
1 . . . . . 3.95

DAGAR THE INVINCIBLE
Gold Key 1972–82
1 O:Daggar;I:Villians Olstellon & Scorpio 20.00
2 . . . . . 15.00
3 I:Graylon 10.00
4 . . . . . 10.00
5 . . . . . 10.00
6 1st Dark Gods story 5.00
7 . . . . . 5.00
8 . . . . . 5.00
9 . . . . . 5.00
10 . . . . . 5.00
11 thru 19 . . . . . @3.00

Dai Kamikaze #10
© Now

DAI KAMIKAZE
Now 1987–88
1 Speed Racer 7.00
1a 2nd printing 2.00
2 thru 5 . . . . . @2.00
6 thru 12 . . . . . @2.00

DAKTARI
Dell Publishing Co. July, 1967
1 . . . . . 30.00
2 . . . . . 20.00
3 . . . . . 20.00
4 . . . . . 20.00

DALGODA
Fantagraphics
1 . . . . . 3.50
2 KN,I:Grinwood'Daughter 3.00
3 KN 2.50
4 thru 8 . . . . . @2.25

DALKIEL: THE PROPHECY
Verotik 1998
1-shot, prequel to Satanika 3.95

DANGER
Charlton Comics June, 1955
12 . . . . . 60.00
13 . . . . . 50.00
14 . . . . . 50.00
Becomes:

JIM BOWIE
15 . . . . . 30.00
16 . . . . . 20.00
17 . . . . . 20.00
18 . . . . . 20.00
19 April, 1957 . . . . . 20.00

DANGER RANGER
Checker Comics 1998
1 I:Kirby Jackson, BSz(c) 2.00
2 . . . . . 2.00

COLOR PUB.

DANIEL BOONE
Gold Key 1965–69
1 . . . . 100.00
2 thru 5 . . . . @50.00
6 thru 14 . . . . @30.00
15 . . . . 25.00

DANNY BLAZE
Charlton Comics Aug., 1955
1 . . . . 75.00
2 . . . . 50.00
Becomes:

NATURE BOY
3 JB,O:Blue Beetle 135.00
4 . . . . 100.00
5 Feb., 1957 . . . . 85.00

DARE
Fantagraphics
1 F:Dan Dare 2.75
2 F:Dan Dare 2.75
3 F:Dan Dare 2.50
4 F:Dan Dare 2.50

DARE THE IMPOSSIBLE
Fleetway/Quality
1 DGb,rep.Dan Dare from 2000AD 2.00
2 DGb, Dare on Waterworld. 2.00
3 DGb 2.00
4 DGb 2.00
5 DGb,"The Garden of Eden". 2.00
6 DGb 2.00
7 DGb,V:Deadly Primitives. 2.00
8 DGb,The Doomsday Machine . . . 2.00
9 thru 14 DGb . . . . @2.00

The Dark #3
© Continum

DARK, THE
Continum 1992
1 LSn(c),MBr,V:Futura 4.00
2 LSn,Shot by Futura. 3.00
3 MBr,Dark has amnesia 3.00
4 GT(c),MBr,O:The Dark 3.00
Convention Book 1992 MBr,GP, MFm,MMi,VS,LSn,TV. 5.00
Convention Book 1993 MBr,PC, ECh,BS,BWi,GP(c),Foil(c), ... 4.00

Aug. House
1 BS(c),Red Foil(c), ... 3.00
1a BS(c),newsstand ed.. . . . . 3.00
1b BS(c),Blue foil. 3.00
2 . . . . 3.00
3 BS(c),Foil(c), ... 3.00
4 GP(c),Foil(c),w/cards 3.00
5 thru 9 . . . . @2.50

[2nd Series]
1 Dark Regains Memory 3.00
1a Signed, Foil Cover 2.75
2 War on Crime. 2.75
3 Geoffery Stockton. 2.50
4 I:First Monster 2.50

DARK ADVENTURES
1 thru 3 . . . . @2.00

DARK CHYLDE
Maximum Press June, 1996
1 RQu 16.00
1 American Entertainment edition 15.00
1 variant cover. 15.00
2 RQu 12.00
2 variant cover. 14.00
3 RQu 10.00
3 variant cover. 12.00
4 RQu 5.00
5 RQu,"No One Here Gets Out Alive" 12.00
Spec. Dark Chylde/Avengelyne RLd, RQu,I:Witch Tower 3.00
Spec. Dark Chylde/Glory RQu, ... 3.00

DARK DOMINION
Defiant
1 SD,I:Michael Alexander 3.25
2 LWn(s),SLi(i), ... 2.75
3 LWn(s),SLi(i), ... 2.75
4 LWn(s),B:Hoxhunt 3.00
5 LWn(s),I:Puritan,Judah 2.75
6 LWn(s),I:Lurk 2.75
7 LWn(s),V:Glimmer 2.75
8 LWn(s),V:Glimmer 2.50
9 LWn(s)V:Puritan 2.50
10 LWn(s),Schism Prequel 2.50
11 LWn(s), X-Over 2.50
12 LWn(s), V:Chasm. 2.50

DARK ONE'S THIRD EYE
Sirius April,1996
one-shot Vol. 1 DOe. 4.95
Vol. 2 DOe 4.95

DARK SHADOWS
Gold Key March, 1969
1 W/Poster,Ph(c) 275.00
2 Ph(c) 125.00
3 W/Poster,Ph(c) 125.00
4 thru 7,Ph(c). . . . . @75.00
8 thru 10 . . . . @60.00
11 thru 20 . . . . @50.00
21 thru 35 . . . . @40.00

DARK SHADOWS
Innovation
1 Based on 1990's TV series 3.50
2 O:Victoria Winters. 2.50
3 Barnabus Imprisoned 2.50
4 V: Redmond Swann 2.75

[2nd Series]
1 A:Nathan 2.75
2 thru 4 . . . . @2.75
Dark Shadows:Resurrected 15.95

DARK SIDE
Maximum Press 1997
1 RLd,RQu 3.00

DARKSHRINE
Antarctic Press 1999
1 by Shelby Robertson 3.00
1a deluxe 6.00
2 16-page 2.50

DARK TOWN
Mad Monkey Press
1 (of 13) 3.95
2 thru 7 . . . . @3.95

DARKLON THE MYSTIC
Pacific
1 JSn 2.00

DARKWING DUCK
Walt Disney
1 I:Darkwing Duck 2.00
2 V:Taurus Bulba 2.00
3 "Fowl Play" 2.00
4 "End o/t beginning,"final issue. . . 2.00

DARKWOOD
Aircel
1 thru 5 . . . . @2.00

DAUGHTERS OF TIME
3-D
1 I:Kris,Cori,Lhana 3.95

FRONTIER FIGHTER
Charlton Comics Aug., 1955
1 JK 400.00
2 JK 300.00
Becomes:

DAVY CROCKETT
3 thru 7 JK. . . . . @250.00
8 Jan., 1957 JK 225.00
Becomes:

KID MONTANA
9 . . . . 50.00
10 . . . . 40.00
11 . . . . 25.00
12 . . . . 25.00
13 AW 40.00
14 thru 20 . . . . @25.00
21 thru 35 . . . . @20.00
36 thru 49 . . . . @10.00
50 March, 1965 . . . . 10.00

DAWN
Sirius 1995–97
½ Wizard mail-in 15.00
½ variant. 25.00
1 JLi,R:Dawn. 12.00
1a white trash edition. 40.00
1b black light edition 35.00
1c look sharp edition 45.00
2 JLi, Trip to Hell 10.00
2 variant cover. 36.00
3 JLi 9.00
3 limited edition 40.00
4 JLi,"The Gauntlet". 5.00
4a variant cover. 30.00
5 JLi,"Everybody Dies". 4.00
5a variant cover. 20.00
6 (of 6) JLi. 6.00
6a variant cover. 15.00

TPB Lucifer's Halo 20.00
TPB Tears of Dawn. 18.00
10th Anniv. Spec. 2.95
10th Anniv. Spec, sgn,num. 5.00
Portable Dawn, art work 9.95

DAWN: THE RETURN OF THE GODDESS
Sirius 1999

1 (of 4) JLi. 2.95
1a limited, signed 20.00
2 A:Marinen. 2.95
2a limited, signed 20.00
3 . . . . 2.95
3a deluxe 19.95
4 . . . . 2.95
4a deluxe 19.95

DAZEY'S DIARY
Dell Publishing Co. June-Aug., 1962

1 . . . . 40.00

DEAD BOYS: DEATH'S EMBRACE
London Night 1996

1 EHr 3.00
1 platinum edition 6.00

DEADFORCE
Antarctic Press 1999

1 (of 3) by Roy Burdine 3.00
2 . . . . 3.00
3 . . . . 3.00

DEAD KING
Chaos! Comics 1997

1 (of 4) Burnt, pt.1, F:Homicide . . . 2.95
2 Burnt, pt.2 . . . . 2.95
3 Burnt, pt.3 . . . . 2.95
4 Burnt, pt.4, concl. 2.95
TPB Dead King Burnt 12.95

DEAMON DREAMS
Pacific

1 . . . . 2.00
2 . . . . 2.00

DEAR NANCY PARKER
Gold Key 1963

1 P(c) 30.00
2 P(c) 25.00

DEATHDEALER
Verotika 1995

1 FF(c), I:Deathdealer 15.00
2 thru 4 FF(c). . . . . @12.00

DEATH OF HARI KARI
Blackout Comics 1997

0 . . . . 2.95
0 super Sexy Kari Cover 9.95
0 3-D super Sexy Kari Cover 14.95

DEATHRACE 2020
Roger Corman Cosmic Comics

1 Pat Mills, Tony Skinner 2.50
2 V:Spyda, Sawmill Jones 2.50
3 O:Frankenstein. 2.50
4 Deathrace cont. 2.50
5 F:Death Racers, D:Alchoholic . . . 2.50
6 V:Indestructiman. 2.50
7 Smallville Mall 2.50

DEATH OF LADY VAMPIRE
Blackout Comics 1995

1 V:Baraclaw. 2.95
1 Commemorative Issue 9.95

DEATH RATTLE
Kitchen Sink 1985–88

1 thru 7 . . . . @2.00
8 I:Xenozoic Tales 5.00
9 thru 18 . . . . @2.00

DECOY
Penny Farthing Press 1999

1 (of 4) 2.75
2 . . . . 2.75
3 . . . . 2.75
4 . . . . 2.75

DEFENDERS, THE
Dell Publishing Co. Sept.–Nov., 1962

1 . . . . 45.00
2 . . . . 30.00

DEFIANT: ORIGIN OF A UNIVERSE
Defiant

1 Giveaway 2.00

DEITY
Hyperwerks Sept., 1997

0 . . . . 3.00
1 KIA. 5.00
1a Director's Cut 3.00
2 thru 6 KIA . . . . @3.00
TPB rep. #1–#3. . . . . @7.95
TPB rep. #4–#6. . . . . @7.95

VOL II Awesome/Hyperworks 1998

1 KIA,BNa, F:Jamie 2.95
1a Limited edition 7.95
1b Silver Foil edition 12.95
1c Gold Edition 19.95
2 KIA,BNa, A:Diamond Diaz 2.95
3 KIA,BNa, The Soul Crusher 2.95
4 KIA,BNa, A:Ogden 2.95
5 KLa,BNa,V:Ma'Shiva 2.95
6 KIA,BNa 2.95

DEITY II: CATSEYE
Hyperwerks 1998

1 KIA,BNa,F:Digby. 2.95
2 KIA,BNa,A:II 2.95
3 KIA,BNa,F:Catseye. 2.95
4 KIA,BNa,conclusion 2.95

DELIVERER
Zion Comics

1 thru 3 . . . . @2.00
4 F:Gabriel 2.00
5 V:Division 2.00

DEMON HUNTER
Atlas Comics 1975

1 . . . . 15.00

Demon Hunter #1
© Atlas

DEMONIC TOYS
Eternity

1 Based on 1992 movie. 2.50
2 thru 4 . . . . @2.50

DEMONIQUE
London Night 1996

0 Manga 3.00
0a nude cover variant 10.00
0a nude cover variant, signed 8.00
1 EHr 3.00
1a nude cover 6.00
1a nude cover, signed 8.00
2 (of 2) 3.00
2a nude cover 6.00

DEN
Fantagor

1 thru 10 RCo . . . . @2.00

DEN SAGA
Tundra/Fantagor

1 RCo,O:Den begins 4.95

DENNIS THE MENACE
Fawcett 1960-61

Fun Book #1. . . . . 50.00
And his Pal Joey #1 . . . . 30.00
And his Dog Ruff #1 . . . . 30.00
Television Special #1 . . . . 40.00
Triple Feature #1 . . . . 40.00
Television Special #2 . . . . 25.00

DENNIS THE MENACE AND HIS FRIENDS [VARIOUS SUBTITLES]
Fawcett 1969–1980

1 thru 10 rep. . . . . @20.00
11 thru 20 rep.. . . . . @15.00
21 thru 46 rep. . . . . @7.00

DENNIS THE MENACE GIANTS [VARIOUS SUBTITLES]
Fawcett 1955–69

N# Vacation Special 125.00

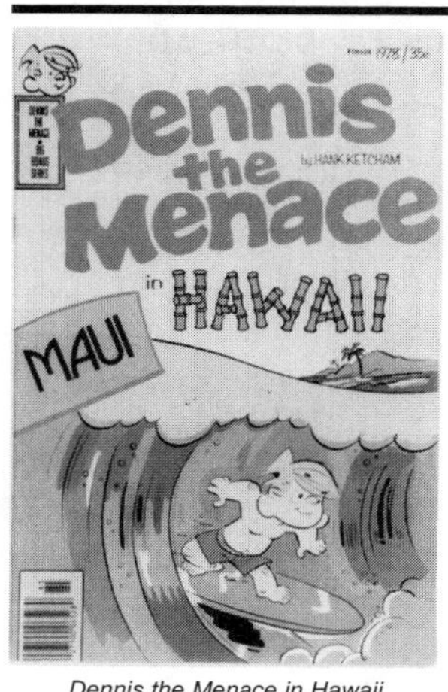

Dennis the Menace in Hawaii
© Fawcett

N# Christmas 100.00
2 thru 10 . . . . @85.00
11 thru 20 . . . . @50.00
21 thru 30 . . . . @35.00
31 thru 40 . . . . @20.00
41 thru 75 . . . . @15.00
Becomes:

DENNIS THE MENACE BONUS MAGAZINE [VARIOUS SUBTITLES]

Fawcett 1970–79

76 thru 100 . . . . @4.00
101 thru 120 . . . . @3.00
121 thru 185 . . . . @2.00
186 thru 196 Big Bonus Series . . @2.00
Becomes:

DENNIS THE MENACE

Fawcett 1979–80

#16 Fun Fest 3.00
#17 Fun Fest 3.00
#10 Big Bonus Series 3.00
#11 Big Bonus Series 3.00

DEPUTY DAWG

Gold Key Aug., 1965

1 . . . . 120.00

DER VANDALE

Innervision 1998

1 (of 3) 2.50
2 (of 3) 2.50
3 (of 3) 2.50
3 variant cover 2.50

DESTROYER DUCK

Eclipse 1982–84

1 JK,AA,SA,I:Groo 12.00
2 JK,AA,Starling 2.00
3 thru 5 JK . . . . @2.00
6 thru 7 JK . . . . @2.00

DESTRUCTOR, THE

Atlas Feb.–Aug., 1975

1 thru 4 . . . . @15.00

DETECTIVES, INC.

Eclipse 1985

1 MR,rep.GraphicNovel 3.00
2 MR 2.25

[2nd Series]

1 GC,"A Terror of Dying Dreams" . . 2.50
2 GC 2.25
3 GC,"Cut to the Bone" 2.00

DETONATOR

Chaos! Comics 1994–95

1 I:Detonator 2.95
2 V:Messiah & Mindbender 2.75

DEVIL KIDS STARRING HOT STUFF

Harvey Publications 1962–81

1 . . . . 150.00
2 . . . . 75.00
3 thru 10 . . . . @50.00
11 thru 20 . . . . @25.00
21 thru 30 . . . . @20.00
31 thru 40 . . . . @15.00
41 thru 50 68 pgs. . . . . @15.00
51 thru 55 62 pgs. . . . . @10.00
56 thru 70 . . . . @7.00
71 thru 100 . . . . @3.00
101 thru 106 . . . . @2.00
107 . . . . 2.00

DEVILMAN

Verotika 1995

1 Go Nagi 2.95
1a San Diego Con Gatefold edition 4.95
2 F:Devilman 2.95
3 Through History 2.95
4 French Revolution 2.95
5 Custer's Last Stand 2.95

DEVLIN

Maximum Press 1996

1 A:Avengelyne,3-part mini-series . 2.50
2 (of 3) RLd,BNa,A:Avengelyne . . . 2.50

DICK TRACY

1 3-D 2.50

DICK TRACY: BIG CITY BLUES

1 Mini Series 3.95
2 Mini Series 5.95
3 Mini Series 5.95

DINO ISLAND

Mirage

1 thru 2 . . . . 2.75

DINOSAUR REX

Upshot/Fantagraphics 1987

1 thru 3 by Jan Strand & Henry Mayo . . . . @2.00

DINOSAURS

Walt Disney

1 Citizen Robbie(From TV) 2.95

DINOSAURS ATTACK

Eclipse

1 HT,Based on Topps cards 3.50
2 and 3 HT,Based on cards . . . . @3.50

DISNEY ADVENTURES

Walt Disney

1 . . . . 2.75
2 . . . . 2.50
3 thru 6 . . . . @2.25
7 Joe Montana 2.25
8 Bronson Pinchot 2.25
9 Hulk Hogan 2.25
10 Mayim Bialik 2.25
11 . . . . 2.25
12 Monsters 2.25
13 A:Darkwing Duck (inc. work by DW) 2.25
14 inc. "Big Top, Big Shot" 2.00
15 . . . . 2.00
16 inc."Turnabout is Fowl Play" 2.00
17 inc."Kitty Kat Kaper" 2.00
18 Kitty Kat Kaper 2.00
19 The Voice of Wisdom 2.00
20 thru 28 . . . . @2.00

DISNEY COLOSSAL COMICS COLLECTION

Walt Disney

1 inc.DuckTales, Chip'n'Dale 2.25
2 inc.Tailspin,Duck Tales 2.00
3 inc.Duck Tales 2.00
4 O:Darkwing Duck 2.00
5 Tailspin,Duck Tales 2.00
6 Darkwing Duck,Goofy 2.00
7 inc.Darkwing Duck.Goofy 2.00
8 inc.Little Mermaid 2.00
9 inc.Duck Tales 2.00

DISNEY COMICS IN 3-D

Walt Disney

1 . . . . 2.95

DISNEY COMICS SPEC: DONALD & SCROOGE

1 inc."Return to Xanadu" 8.95

DISNEYLAND BIRTHDAY PARTY

Gladstone

1 . . . . 6.00

DIVER DAN

Dell Publishing Co. Feb.–April, 1962

1 . . . . 45.00
2 . . . . 30.00

DIVINE INTERVENTION

Wildstorm/DC 1999

1 . . . . 2.50
Wildcats, pt.2, JLe,SLo,RiB 2.50
Gen13, pt.3, JLe,SLo,RiB 2.50

DIVINE MADNESS

Dark Moon

1 Human Flesh Artist 2.50
2 . . . . 2.50
3 Ancient Cult 2.50

DNAGENTS

Eclipse 1983–85

1 O:DNAgents 4.00
2 . . . . 3.00
3 . . . . 2.50
4 . . . . 2.50
5 . . . . 2.50

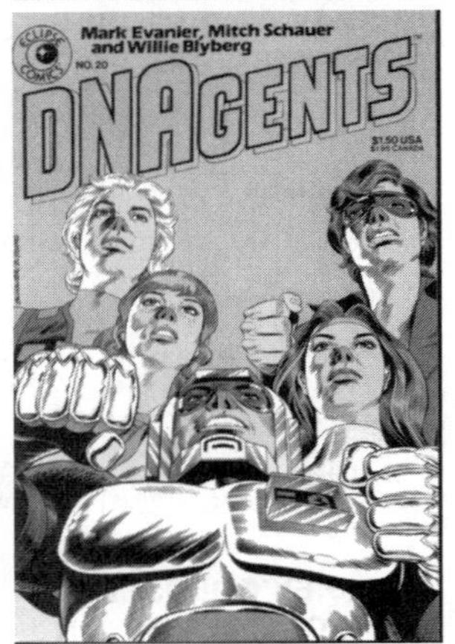

DNAgents #20
© Eclipse

6 . . . . 2.50
7 . . . . 2.50
8 . . . . 2.50
9 DSp 2.50
10 . . . . 2.00
11 . . . . 2.00
12 . . . . 2.50
13 . . . . 2.00
14 . . . . 2.00
15 . . . . 2.50
16 . . . . 2.50
17 thru 21 . . . . @2.00
22 . . . . 2.00
23 . . . . 2.00
24 DSt(c) 2.00
25 . . . . 2.00

See also: NEW DNAGENTS

DO YOU BELIEVE IN NIGHTMARES?
St. John Publishing Co. 1957–58

1 SD 400.00
2 DAy 200.00

DOBER-MAN

1 . . . . 2.50

DOC SAVAGE
Millennium

1 V:Russians 2.50

DOC SAVAGE, THE MAN OF BRONZE
Millennium

1 Monarch of Armageddon,pt.1 . . . 3.00
2 Monarch of Armageddon,pt.2 . . . 2.75
3 Monarch of Armageddon,pt.3 . . . 2.75
4 Monarch of Armageddon,pt.4 . . . 2.75

DOC SAVAGE: THE DEVIL'S THOUGHTS
Millennium

1 V:Hanoi Shan 2.50
2 V:Hanoi Shan 2.50
3 Final issue 2.50

DOC SAVAGE: DOOM DYNASTY
Millennium

1 and 2 . . . . @2.50

DOC SAVAGE: MANUAL OF BRONZE
Millennium

1 Fact File 2.50

DOC SAVAGE: REPEL
Innovation

1 DvD(c) 2.50

DOCTOR BOOGIE
Media Arts

1 and 2 . . . . @2.00

DOCTOR CHAOS
Triumphant Comics 1993

1 JnR(s),I:Doctor Chaos 2.50
2 JnR(s), ... 2.50
3 JnR(s),The Coming of the Cry,pt.1,I:Cry 2.50
4 JnR(s),The Coming of the Cry,pt.2,b:Ky'Li 2.50
5 JnR(s),E:Coming of the Cry,pt.3,V:Cry 2.50
6 Recovery 2.50
7 w/coupon 2.50
8 w/coupon 2.50
9 V:Mirth 2.50
10 Co. X #3 . . . . 2.50
11 Co. X #4 . . . . 2.50
12 A:Charlotte 2.50

DOCTOR SOLAR MAN OF THE ATOM
Gold Key

1 BF,I:Dr. Solar 300.00
2 BF,I:Prof.Harbinger 110.00
3 BF,The Hidden Hands 75.00
4 BF,The Deadly Sea 75.00
5 BF,I:Dr.Solar in costume 75.00
6 FBe,I:Nuro 50.00
7 FBe,Vanishing Oceans 50.00
8 FBe,Thought Controller 50.00
9 FBe,Transivac The Energy Consuming Computer 50.00
10 FBe,The Sun Giant 50.00
11 FBe,V:Nuro 35.00
12 FBe,The Mystery of the Vanishing Silver 35.00
13 FBe,Meteor from 100 Mill.BC . . 35.00
14 FBe,Solar's Midas Touch 35.00
15 FBe O:Dr.Solar 45.00
16 FBe,V:Nuro 35.00
17 FBe,The Fatal Foe 35.00
18 FBe,The Mind Master 35.00
19 FBe,SolarV:Solar 35.00
20 AMc,Atomic Nightmares 35.00
21 AMc,Challenge from Outer Space 25.00
22 AMc,Nuro,I:King Cybernoid . . . 25.00
23 AMc,A:King Cybernoid 25.00
24 EC,The Deadly Trio 25.00
25 EC,The Lost Dimension 25.00
26 EC,When Dimensions Collide . 25.00
27 (1969) The Ladder to Mars . . . 25.00
28 (1981),1 pg AMc,The Dome of Mystery 12.00
29 DSp,FBe,Magnus 12.00
30 DSp,FBe,Magnus 12.00

DOGHEAD
Tundra

1 Al Columbia,"Poster Child" 4.95

DOGS OF WAR
Defiant

1 F:Shooter,Ironhead 2.75
2 . . . . 2.50
3 Mouse Deserts 2.50
4 Schism Prequel 2.50
5 X-over 2.50
6 Aftermath 2.50

DOLLMAN
Eternity

1 Movie adapt. sequel 2.50
2 V:Sprug & Braindead Gang 2.50
3 Toni Costa Kidnapped 2.50
4 . . . . 2.50

DONALD DUCK
Dell/Gold Key Dec., 1962

85 thru 97 . . . . 40.00
98 rep. #46 CB 40.00
99 . . . . 30.00
100 . . . . 25.00
101 . . . . 22.00
102 A:Super Goog 22.00
103 thru 111 . . . . @22.00
112 I:Moby Duck 22.00
113 thru 133 . . . . @22.00
134 CB rep. 22.00
135 CB rep. 22.00
136 thru 156 . . . . @20.00
157 CB rep. 18.00
158 thru 163 . . . . @15.00
164 CB rep. 15.00
165 thru 216 . . . . @10.00

Whitman

217 . . . . 10.00
218 . . . . 10.00
219 CB rep. 10.00
220 thru 245 . . . . @10.00

Gladstone

246 CB,Gilded Man 18.00
247 CB 12.00
248 CB,Forbidden Valley 12.00
249 CB 12.00
250 CB,Pirate Gold 18.00
251 CB,Donald's Best Xmas 5.00
252 CB,Trail o/t Unicorn 5.00
253 CB 3.50
254 CB, in old Calif. 7.00
255 CB 3.50
256 CB,Volcano Valley 3.50
257 CB,Forest Fire 4.00
258 thru 260 CB . . . . @3.00
261 thru 266 CB . . . . @2.50
267 thru 277 CB . . . . @2.00
278 CB 4.00
279 CB 4.00
280 thru 298 CB rep.. . . . . @2.00
299 "Life Guard Daze" 2.00
300 "Donald's 300th Triumph" 48pg 2.25
301 "The Gold Finder" 2.00
302 "Monkey Business" 2.00
303 "The Cantankerous Cat" 2.00
304 "Donald Duck Rants about Ants" 2.00
305 "Mockingbird Ridge" 2.00
306 "Worst Class Mail" 2.00
307 "Going to Sea" 2.00
308 "Worst Class Mail" 2.00

DONALD DUCK ADVENTURES
Gladstone

1 CB,Jungle Hi-Jinks 5.00
2 CB,Dangerous Disquise 4.00
3 CB,Lost in the Andes 5.00
4 CB,Frozen Gold 4.00
5 Rosa Art. 3.50
6 . . . . 2.50
7 . . . . 2.50
8 Rosa 3.50
9 . . . . 2.50
10 . . . . 2.50
11 . . . . 2.50
12 Giant size,Rosa 3.50
13 Rosa(c) 2.50
14 . . . . 3.00
15 CB. 2.00
16 . . . . 2.00
17 . . . . 2.00
18 . . . . 2.00
19 . . . . 4.00
20 Giant size 4.00
21 thru 30. . . . . @2.95
31 thru 40 . . . . @2.00
41 "Bruce McDuck". 2.00
42 "The Saga of Sourdough Sam" . 2.00
43 "The Lost Charts of Columbus" . 2.00
44 "The Kitchy-Kaw Diamond" 2.00
45 "The Red Duck". 2.00
46 . . . . 2.00
47 "Trick or Treat". 2.00
48 "The Saphead Factor" 2.00

DONALD DUCK ADVENTURES
Walt Disney 1990

1 Don Rosa, "The Money Pit" 5.00
2 . . . . 3.00
3 . . . . 2.50
4 . . . . 2.50
5 . . . . 2.50
6 . . . . 2.50
7 . . . . 2.00
8 . . . . 2.00
9 . . . . 2.00
10 "Run-Down Runner". 2.00
11 "Whats for Lunch-Supper" 2.00
12 "Head of Rama Putra" 2.00
13 "JustAHumble,BumblingDuck" . . 2.00
14 "DayGladstonesLuckRanOut". . . 2.00
15 "A Tuft Luck Tale" 2.00
16 "Magica's Missin'Magic". 2.00
17 "Secret of Atlantis". 2.00
18 "Crocodile Donald". 2.00
19 "Not So Silent Service" 2.00
20 "Ghost of Kamikaze Ridge" 2.00
21 "The Golden Christmas Tree". . . 2.00
22 "The Master Landscapist" 2.00
23 "The Lost Peg Leg Mine" 2.00
24 "On Stolen Time" 2.00
25 Sense of Humor 2.00
26 Race to the South Seas. 2.00
27 Nap in Nature 2.00
28 Olympic Tryout 2.00
29 rep.March of Comics#20 . . . . . . 2.00
30 A:The Vikings 2.00
31 The Sobbing Serpent of Loch
McDuck 2.00
32 It Was No Occident 2.00
33 Crazy Christmas on Bear
Mountain 2.00
34 Sup.Snooper Strikes Again 2.00
35 CB rep. 2.00
36 CB rep. 2.00
37 CB rep. 2.00

DONALD DUCK ALBUM
Dell Publishing Co.
May–July, 1959

1 CB(c) 65.00
2 . . . . 50.00

DONATELLO
Mirage

1 . . . . 10.00

DONNA MIA
Dark Fantasy Prod. 1995

1 I:Donna Mia 4.00
1a Deluxe Edition 5.00
1 signed & numbered (100 copies) 8.95
2 . . . . 3.00

DOOMSDAY + 1
Charlton 1975–79

1 JBy,JBy(c) 15.00
2 JBy(c),P(c) 12.00
3 JBy,JBy(c),P(c). 10.00
4 JBy,JBy(c),P(c),I:Lok. 10.00
5 and 6 JBy,JBy(c),P(c) . . . . . . @10.00
7 thru 12 JBy,JBy(c),rep. . . . . . . @3.00

Doomsday Squad #2
© Fantagraphics

DOOMSDAY SQUAD
Fantagraphics

1 rep. JBy 2.00
2 rep. JBy 2.00
3 rep. SS,A:Usagi Yojimbo. 4.00
4 thru 7, rep. JBy . . . . @2.00

DOUBLE DARE ADVENTURES
Harvey Publications

1 I:B-man,Glowing Gladiator,
Magicmaster. 22.00
2 AW/RC rep. A:B-Man,Glowing
Gladiator, Magicmaster. 17.00

DOUBLE IMPACT
High Impact Studios 1995–96

1 RCI,I:China & Jazz, chrome(c) . . 7.00
1 holographic rainbow (c) with
certificate 15.00
1 rainbow (c), no certificate 10.00
1 chromium variant (c). 8.00
2 RCI,V:Castillo 3.00
2a signed, with certificate 4.00
2b nude cover 8.00
2c China Exposed edition 8.00
2d signed by China 10.00
3 China on cover. 5.00
3a Jazzler on cover 3.00
3b Nikki on cover. 3.00
3c "Blondage" 6.00
4 F:Mordred, The Rattler 2.95
4a "Phoenix" variant (c) 6.00
5 RCI. 3.00
5a nude cover 6.00
6 "Buttshots" 4.00
6a Jazz (c) 3.00
6a signed 6.00
7 I:Nikki Blade 3.00
8 . . . . 3.00
8a variant (c). 4.00
Gold edition, Lingerie special 3.00

Volume 2 1996–97

0 RCI 3.00
0a nude cover 8.00
1 RCI. 3.00
1a deluxe edition 4.00
1b prism foil (c) 5.00
1cgold foil (c). 5.00
2 RCI. 3.00
2a Swedish Erotica cover 8.00
2b Swedish Erotica cover, signed 12.00
3 . . . . 2.95
3a special edition RCI(c) 8.00
3b Photo nude cover 12.00

DOUBLE IMPACT: ALIVE
ABC Studios 1999

1 RCI,F:China & Jazz 3.00
1a deluxe 8.00

DOUBLE IMPACT/ HELLINA
High Impact 1996

1-shot RCI. 3.00
1a nude cover 9.95
1b Gold edition, nude cover. 9.95
1c Spec. nude cover, signed 14.95

DOUBLE IMPACT/ LETHAL STRYKE: DOUBLE STRIKE
High Impact/London Night 1996

1-shot RCI. 3.00
1a nude cover 9.95

DOUBLE IMPACT SUICIDE RUN
High Impact

1 RCI. 3.00
1 gold edition. 10.00
1 platinum edition 20.00
2 . . . . 3.00
2a Suicide Cover. 10.00
2b Photo Nude cover. 14.95

DOUBLE IMPACT: 2069
ABC Studios 1999

1 RCI,Independent Day 3.00
1a premium edition 5.00
1b Sexy China ed.. . . . . 5.00
1c Nude cover. 10.00

DOUBLE LIFE OF PRIVATE STRONG
Archie Publications
1 JSm/JK,I:Lancelot Strong/Shield The Fly 600.00
2 JSm/JK,GT A:Fly 350.00

DR. KILDARE
Dell Publishing Co.
April–June, 1962
1 . . . . 100.00
2 . . . . 75.00
3 . . . . 75.00
4 . . . . 75.00
5 . . . . 75.00
6 . . . . 75.00
7 . . . . 75.00
8 . . . . 75.00
9 . . . . 75.00

DRACULA
Dell Publishing Co. Nov., 1966
2 O:Dracula. 35.00
3 . . . . 25.00
4 . . . . 25.00
6 . . . . 20.00
7 . . . . 15.00
8 . . . . 15.00

DRACULA
Topps
1 MMi,Movie adaptation (trading cards in each issue) 5.00
1a Red Foil Logo 12.00
1b 2nd Print. 2.95
2 MMi,Movie adapt.contd. 4.00
3 MMi,Movie adapt.contd. 4.00
4 MMi,Movie adapt.concludes 4.00
TPB Collected Album 13.95

DRACULA CHRONICLES
Topps
1 True Story of Dracula 2.50
2 RTs,rep. Vlad #2. . . . . 2.50
3 RTs,rep. Vlad #3. . . . . 2.50

DRACULA VS. ZORRO
Topps
1 DMg(s),TY,Black(c), ... 3.25
2 DMg(s),TY,w/Zorro #0. . . . . 2.95
TPB 5.95

DRACULA: VLAD THE IMPALER
Topps
1 EM,I:Vlad Dracula, w/cards. 3.25
1a Red Foil 10.00
2 EM, w/cards 3.25

DRAGON CHIANG
Eclipse
1 TT 2.95

DRAGONFLIGHT
Eclipse 1991
1 Anne McCaffrey adapt. 4.95
2 novel adapt 4.95
3 novel adapt 4.95

Dragonflight #3
© Eclipse

DRAGONFLY
AC Comics
1 . . . . 3.50
2 and 3 . . . . @2.00
4 thru 8 . . . . @2.00

DRAGONFORCE
Aircel
1 DK 6.00
2 thru 7 DK . . . . @4.00
8 thru 12 . . . . @4.00
13 . . . . 2.00

DRAGONRING
Aircel 1987–88, Vol. 2
1 . . . . 3.50
2 O:Dragonring 2.50
3 thru 15 . . . . @2.00
See also: B&W

DRAKKON WARS, THE
Realm Press
0 by Richard Hatch & Chris Scalf. . 3.00
1 . . . . 3.00

DREADSTAR
First
27 JSn,from Epic,traitor 2.50
28 JSn 2.25
29 JSn,V:Lord Papal. 2.25
30 JSn,D:Lord Papal 2.25
31 JSn,I:The Power 2.25
32 JSn 2.25
33 . . . . 2.25
34 LM/VM,A:Malchek 2.25
35 LM/VM. 2.25
36 LM/VM. 2.25
37 LM/VM,A:Last Laugh 2.25
38 LM/VM. 2.25
39 AMc,Crossroads tie-in 2.25
40 LM/VM. 2.25
41 AMe 2.25
42 JSn,AMe,B.U.Pawns begins . . . 2.25
43 JSn,AMe,Pawns,pt.2 . . . . 2.25
44 JSn,AMe,Pawns,pt.3 . . . . 2.25
45 JSn,AMe,Pawns,pt.4 . . . . 2.25
46 JSn,AMe,Pawns,pt.5 . . . . 2.25
47 JSn,AMe,Pawns,pt.6 . . . . 2.25
48 JSn,AMe,Pawns,pt.7 . . . . 2.25
49 JSn,AMe,Pawns,pt.8 . . . . 2.25
50 JSn,AMe,Pawns,pt.9 prestige . . 4.25
51 PDd,Woj,Pawns,pt.10, Paladox epic begins. 2.25
52 AMe 2.25
53 AMe,"Messing with Peoples Minds" 2.25
54 JSn,AMe,Pawns ends 2.25
55 AMe,I:Iron Angel 2.25
56 AME,A:Iron Angel 2.25
57 A:Iron Angel 2.25
58 A:Iron Angel 2.25
59 A:Iron Angel 2.25
60 AMe,Paladox epic ends 2.25
61 AME,A:Iron Angel 2.25
62 O:Dreadstar,I:Youngscuz 2.25
63 AMe,A:Youngscuz 2.25
64 AMe,A:Youngscuz 2.25

DREAMS OF THE DARKCHYLDE
Darkchylde Entertainment 2000
1 RQu,BPe 2.95

DREDD RULES
Fleetway/Quality
1 SBs(c),JBy,Prev.unpubl. in USA . 5.00
2 inc."Eldster Ninja Mud Wrestling Vigilantes" 3.50
3 inc."That Sweet Stuff". 3.50
4 Our Man in Hondo City. 3.50
5 . . . . 3.25
6 BKi,DBw. 3.25
7 "Banana City" 3.25
8 "Over the Top" 3.25
9 "Shooting Match" 3.25
10 SBs,inc.Mega-City primer 3.25
11 SBs,Legend/Johnny Biker 3.25
12 SBs,Rock on Tommy Who 3.25
13 BMy,The Ballad of Toad McFarlane 3.25
14 thru 15 . . . . @3.25
16 A:Russians 3.25
17 F:Young Giant 3.25
18 F:Jonny Cool 2.95
19 V:Hunter's Club 2.95

DRIFT MARLO
Dell Publishing Co.
May–July, 1962
1 . . . . 25.00
2 . . . . 20.00

DRUG WARS
Pioneer
1 . . . . 2.00
2 . . . . 2.00
3 . . . . 2.00

DRUNKEN FIST
Jademan
1 . . . . 3.25
2 . . . . 2.50
3 . . . . 2.00
4 . . . . 2.00
5 . . . . 2.00
6 thru 9 . . . . @2.00
10 thru 27 . . . . @2.00
28 D:Mack 2.00
29 . . . . 2.00
30 . . . . 2.00
31 . . . . 2.00
32 Wong Mo-Gei vs.Swordsman. . . 2.00
33 Mo-Gei commits suicide. 2.00
34 . . . . 2.00
35 . . . . 2.00
36 D:Fire Oak. 2.00

37 Iron Law Kills Elephant-Man . . . 2.00
38 A:Wayne Chan 2.00
39 D:Wayne Chan 2.00
40 D:Toro Yamamoto 2.00
41 Lord Algol vs. Ghing Mob. 2.00
42 . . . . 2.00
43 D:Yamamoto,Swordsman in USA 2.00
44 "Cool Hand Wong". 2.00
45 "Black Cult Rising". 2.00
46 . . . . 2.00
47 . . . . 2.00
48 Evil Child 2.00
49 I:Hurricane Child 2.00
50 Lord Algol vs.Diabol.Ent. 2.00
51 F:Flying Thunder 2.00
52 Madcap vs.Yama 2.00
53 Swordsman vs.Catman 2.00

DUCKMAN
Topps

1 USA Cartoon 2.50
2 XXX Files 2.50
3 I:King Chicken 2.50
4 V:Toys 2.50
5 F:Cornfed 2.50
6 Star Trek Parody 2.50
7 rep. 1990 B&W 1st app., now
in color 2.50

DUCKMAN: THE MOB FROG SAGA
Topps

1 I:Mob Frog 2.50
2 D:Mob Frog 2.50
3 In the Name of the Duck. 2.50

DUCK TALES
Gladstone

1 CB(r)I:LaunchpadMcQuck. 6.00
2 CB(r) 4.00
3 . . . . 4.00
4 CB(r) 4.00
5 thru 11 . . . . @4.00
12 . . . . 5.00
13 . . . . 5.00

DUCK TALES
Walt Disney

1 . . . . 4.00
2 . . . . 2.50
3 . . . . 2.25
4 . . . . 2.25
5 Scrooges'Quest 2.25
6 Scrooges'Quest 2.00
7 Return to Duckburg 2.00
8 . . . . 2.00
9 7 Sojourns of Scrooge 2.00
10 Moon of Gold. 2.00
11 Once & Future Warlock 2.00
12 Lost Beyond the MilkyWay. 2.00
13 The Doomed of Sarras 2.00
14 Planet Blues 2.00
15 The Odyssey Ends 2.00
16 The Great Chase. 2.00
17 Duck in Time Pt.1 . . . . 2.00
18 Duck in Time Pt.2 . . . . 2.00
19 Bail Out 2.00

DUDLEY DO-RIGHT
Charlton Comics 1970–71

1 . . . . 100.00
2 thru 7 . . . . @75.00

Dunc and Loo
© Dell Publishing Co.

DUNC & LOO
Dell Publishing Co.
Oct.-Dec., 1961

1 . . . . 90.00
2 . . . . 75.00
3 thru 8 . . . . @50.00

DUNGEONS & DRAGONS: THE LOST CITY
Twenty First Century 1999

1 (of 6) game tie-in 4.95
2 thru 6 . . . . @4.95

DUNGEONS & DRAGONS: AMBER CASTLE
Twenty First Century 2000

1 (of 6) game tie-in 4.95

DWIGHT D. EISENHOWER
Dell Publishing Co. Dec., 1969

1 . . . . 40.00

DYNAMO
Tower Comics Aug., 1966

1 WW,MSy,RC,SD,I:Andor 75.00
2 WW,DA,GT,MSy,Weed solo
story A:Iron Maiden 50.00
3 WW,GT,Weed solo story,
A:Iron Maiden. 50.00
4 WW,DA,A:Iron Maiden, June,
1967. . . . . 50.00

DYNAMO JOE
First 1986–87

1 . . . . 3.00
2 . . . . 2.00
3 thru 14 . . . . @2.00
Spec.#1 . . . . 2.00

EARLY DAYS OF SOUTHERN KNIGHTS

Vol. 2 Graphic Novel. 5.00

EARTH 4
Continuity
[1st Series, Deathwatch 2000]

1 Deathwatch 2000 Pt.6,w/card . . . 2.50
2 Deathwatch 2000 Pt.11,w/card . . 2.50
3 V:Hellbenders, w/card. 2.50

[2nd Series]

1 WMc, ... 2.50
2 . . . . 2.50
3 . . . . 2.50

EAST MEETS WEST
Innovation

1 . . . . 2.50
2 . . . . 2.50
3 . . . . 2.50

EBONY WARRIOR
Africa Rising

1 I:Ebony Warrior 2.00

ECHO OF FUTUREPAST
Continuity

1 NA,MGo,I:Bucky O'Hare,
Frankenstein 4.00
2 NA,MGo,A:Bucky O'Hare, Dracula, . .
Werewolf 3.50
3 NA,MGo,A:Bucky 3.50
4 NA,MGo,A:Bucky 3.50
5 NA,MGo,A:Dracula & Bucky 3.50
6 Ath,B:Torpedo. 3.50
7 ATh 3.50
8 Ath, ... 3.25
9 Ath,Last issue. 3.25

ECLIPSE GRAPHIC NOVELS
Eclipse

1 Axa 7.00
2 MR,I Am Coyote. 7.00
3 DSt,Rocketeer 10.00
3a hard cover 40.00
4 Silver Heels 9.00
4a hard cover 40.00
5 Sisterhood of Steel 10.00
6 Zorro in Old Calif. 8.00

ECLIPSE MONTHLY
Eclipse

1 SD,DW,I:Static&Rio 2.00
2 GC,DW 2.00
3 thru 8 DW . . . . @2.00
9 DW. 2.00
10 DW 2.00

EDGE OF CHAOS
Pacific

1 GM. 2.00
2 GM. 2.00
3 GM. 2.00

87th PRECINCT
Dell Publishing Co.
April-June, 1962

1 BK 125.00
2 . . . . 100.00

ELEMENTALS
Comico 1984–88

1 BWg,I:Destroyers 5.00
2 BWg. 3.00
3 BWg. 3.00

COLOR PUB.

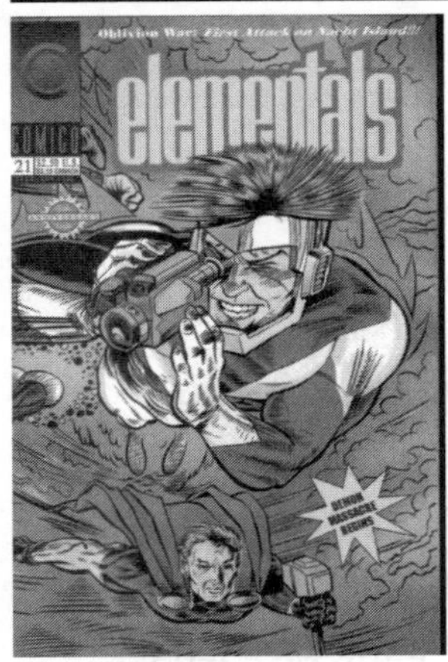

Elementals, Vol. 2, #21
© Comico

4 BWg 2.50
5 BWg 2.50
6 BWg 2.00
7 BWg 2.00
8 BWg 2.00
9 BWg 2.00
10 BWg 2.00
11 BWg 2.00
12 BWg 2.00
13 thru 29 . . . . @2.00
Spec.#1 . . . . 2.00
Spec.#2 . . . . 2.00

[Second Series] 1989–94

1 . . . . 2.25
2 thru 4 . . . . @2.00
5 thru 28 . . . . @2.50
Spec.#1 Lingerie special. 2.95
GN The Natural Order, rep.. . . . . . . 9.95
GN Death & Resurrection 12.95

[Third Series] 1995

1 R:Elementals, polybagged with Chrysalis promo card 2.50
2 R:Original Monolith, polybagged with Chrysalis promo card 2.50
3A Destroy the Shadowspear 2.50
3B variant cover 2.50
4 Memoirs,pt.1 . . . . 2.95
5 Memoirs,pt.2 . . . . 2.95
GN Ghost of a Chance 5.95
Spec. "Babes," photo multimedia bikini special. 3.95
Spec. Hot Bikini Valentine. 3.95
Spec. All New Summer Special . . . 4.95
Spec.#1 Lingerie Metalite 3.95

ELEMENTALS: HOW THE WAR WAS ONE

Comico 1996

1 thru 4 . . . . @2.95

ELEMENTALS: THE VAMPIRE'S REVENGE

Comico 1996–97

1 thru 4 . . . . @2.95

ELEMENTALS VS. THE CHARNEL PRIESTS

Comico 1996

Spec. 1 & 2. . . . . @2.95

ELEVEN OR ONE

Sirius 1995

1 JLi 5.00

ELFLORD

Aircel 1986–88

Volume 1: *See B&W*

Volume II

1 . . . . 3.50
2 . . . . 2.50
3 thru 20 . . . . @2.00
21 double size 4.95
22 thru 24 . . . . @2.00
Spec.#1 . . . . 2.00
25 thru 32, see B&W

ELFQUEST

Warp Graphics 1998

TPB 20th Anniv. Special 8.95
HC Bedtime Stories,RPi, 128pg. . . 19.95
TPB Scores, WPi, best of Elfquest stories 19.95

ELFQUEST: BLOOD OF TEN CHIEFS

Warp Graphics 1993–95

1 WP. 2.50
2 WP. 2.25
3 WP,B:Swift Spear pt. 1 . . . . 2.25
4 WP,B:Swift Spear pt. 2 . . . . 2.25
5 V:Dinosaurs 2.25
6 Snowbeast 2.25
7 . . . . 2.25
8 Spirit Quest 2.25
9 Shadow Shifter. 2.25
10 Spheres pt. 1. . . . . 2.25
11 Spheres pt. 2 . . . . 2.25
12 . . . . 2.25
13 Forest 2.25
14 F:Mantricker 2.25
15 F:Bearclaw 2.25
16 Scar Vs. Bearclaw 2.50
17 F:Eldolil,"Howl for Eldolil" 2.50
18 F:Finder. 2.50
19 F:Cutter & Skywise 2.50
20 final issue 2.50

ELFQUEST: HIDDEN YEARS

Warp Graphics

1 WP 3.00
2 WP, w/coupon promo. 2.75
3 WP, w/coupon promo.Cont.sty. previewed in Harbinger#11 . . . . 3.25
4 WP,w/coupon 2.50
5 WP,O:Skywise 2.50
6 WP,F:Timmain 2.50
7 F:Timmain 2.50
8 Daughter's Day 2.50
9 WP(s),Enemy Face 2.50
9 1/2 WP,JBy,Holiday Spec.. . . . . . 3.50
10 thru 14 WP. . . . . @2.50
15 WP Wolfrider Tribe Splits 3.50
16 thru 18 WP. . . . . @2.25
19 Mousehunt 2.25
20 F:Recognition 2.25
21 F:Teir, Messenger 2.50
22 F:Embu, Making a Point. 2.50
23 Not Wolf And Teir 2.50
24 Magic Menace 2.50
25 *B&W* Wolfrider's Death 2.25
26 thru 29 *B&W* finale . . . . @2.25

ELFQUEST: JINK

Warp Graphics 1994–96

1 Future 3.00
2 Future 2.25
3 Neverending Story 2.25
4 Neverending Story 2.25
5 V:True Sons, Hide and Seek. . . . 2.50
6 V:Truth Holder, Should Auld Acquaintance 2.50
7 F:Black Snakes 2.50
8 *B&W* V:Black Snakes 2.25
9 thru 12 . . . . @2.50

ELFQUEST: NEW BLOOD

Warp Graphics 1992–96

1 JBy,artists try Elfquest 5.00
2 Barry Blair story 3.50
3 thru 5 . . . . @2.50
6 thru 24 . . . . @2.25
25 Forevergreen pt. 13 . . . . 2.25
26 V:Humans 2.25
27 V:Door. 2.25
28 I:Windkin, Triompe and Defeat. . 2.50
29 F:Windkin 2.50
30 V:Door. 2.50
31 F:The Wanderer 2.50
32 *B&W* Sorrow's End 2.25
33 thru 35 *B&W* . . . . @2.25
Summer Spec.1993 . . . . 4.25

ELFQUEST: THE REBELS

Warp Graphics 1994–96

1 Aliens, set several hundred years in future 2.75
2 Escape. 2.50
3 He That Goes. 2.25
4 Reasons. 2.25
5 V:Skyward 2.50
6 F:Shimmer, The Edge. 2.50
7 . . . . 2.50
8 Squatters & Defenders 2.50
9 *B&W* Brother vs. Brother 2.25
10 thru 12 . . . . @2.50

ELFQUEST: SHARDS

Warp Graphics 1994–96

1 Division 2.25
2 thru 5 . . . . @2.25
6 F:Two-Edge 2.25
7 F:Shuma 2.25
8 WP,Turnabout,pt.1 . . . . 2.25
9 WP,Turnabout,pt.2,V:Djun 2.50
10 Revelations,pt.1. . . . . 2.50
11 V:Humans 2.50
12 *B&W* F:High One Timmain. 2.25
13 thru 16 *B&W* finale . . . . @2.25

ELFQUEST: WAVE DANCERS

Warp Graphics 1993–96

1 Foil enhanced. 3.25
2 thru 6 . . . . @2.25
Spec. #1. 3.00

ELIMINATOR COLOR SPECIAL

Eternity 1991

1 DDo(c) set in the future 2.95

ELRIC

Pacific 1983–84

1 CR 4.00
2 CR 3.00

COLOR PUB.

3 thru 6 CR . . . . @2.50

ELRIC
Topps April 1996
0 NGa,CPR, "One Life," based on Michael Moorcock character . . . 2.95

ELRIC, BANE OF THE BLACK SWORD
First 1988–89
1 Michael Moorcock adapt. 2.00
2 . . . . 2.00
3 thru 5 . . . . @2.00

Elric, Sailor on the Seas of Fate #1
© First

ELRIC, SAILOR ON THE SEAS OF FATE
First 1985–86
1 Michael Moorcock adapt. 4.00
2 . . . . 3.00
3 thru 7 . . . . @2.00

ELRIC–VANISHING TOWER
First 1987–88
1 Michael Moorcock adapt. 2.50
2 thru 6 . . . . @2.00

ELRIC, WEIRD OF THE WHITE WOLF
First 1986–87
1 Michael Moorcock adapt. 3.00
2 thru 5 . . . . @2.00
Graphic Novel CR 7.00

E-MAN
Charlton Comics 1973–75
1 JSon,O:E-Man 20.00
2 SD 10.00
3 . . . . 10.00
4 SD 10.00
5 SD,Miss Liberty Belle 10.00
6 JBy,Rog 2000 . . . . 10.00
7 JBy,Rog 2000 . . . . 10.00
8 J:Nova 15.00
9 JBy,Rog 2000 . . . . 10.00
10 JBy,Rog 2000 . . . . 10.00

E-MAN
First
1 JSon,O:E-Man & Nova, A:Rog 2000, 1 pg. JBy 2.00
2 JSon,I:F-Men (X-Men satire) 1-page Mike Mist 2.00
3 JSon, V:F-Men 2.00
4 JSon,Michael Mauser solo 2.00
5 JSon,I:Psychobabbler,A:Omaha, The Cat Dancer 2.00
6 JSon,O:E-Man,V:Feeder. 2.00
7 JSon,V:Feeder 2.00
8 JSon,V:HotWax,A:CuteyBunny . . 2.00
9 JSon,I:Tyger Lili 2.00
10 JSon,O:Nova Kane pt.1 . . . . . . 2.00
11 JSon,O:Nova Kane pt.2 . . . . . . 2.00
12 JSon,A:Tyger Lili 2.00
13 JSon,V:Warp'sPrinceChaos 2.00
14 JSon,V:Randarr. 2.00
15 JSon,V:Samuel Boar 2.00
16 JSon,V:Samuel Boar 2.00
17 JSon,"Smeltquest" satire 2.00
18 JSon,"Rosemary..& Time" 2.00
19 JSon, "Hoodoo Blues" 2.00
20 JSon,A:Donald Duke 2.00
21 JSon,A:B-Team,(satire) 2.00
22 JSon,A:Teddy Q. 2.00
23 JSon,A:TygerLili,B-Team 2.00
24 JSon,O:Michael Mauser. 2.00
25 JSon,last issue 2.00
Spec. #1. 2.75

E-MAN
Comico 1990
1 JSon 2.75
2 and 3 JSon . . . . @2.50

E-MAN
Alpha Productions 1993
1 JSon 2.75

EMERGENCY
Charlton Comics 1976
1 JSon(c),JBy 25.00
2 JSon. 15.00
3 thru 4 . . . . @15.00

ENCHANTED: THE AWAKENING
Sirius 1998
1 by Robert Chang 2.95
2 . . . . 2.95
3 conclusion 2.95

ENGIN
Samson Comics
1 I:The Mesh. 2.50

ENSIGN O'TOOLE
Dell Publishing Co. Aug.-Oct., 1962
1 . . . . 30.00
2 . . . . 25.00

EPSILON WAVE
Independent
1 . . . . 3.00
2 . . . . 2.50
3 . . . . 2.25
4 . . . . 2.00
Elite Comics
5 thru 10 . . . . @2.00

ESC.(ESCAPE)
Comico 1996
1 SPr. 2.95
2 SPr. 2.95
3 SPr. 2.95
4 SPr. 2.95
TPB SPr Rep. #1–#4. . . . . @14.95

ESC: NO EXIT
Comico 1997
1 . . . . 2.95
1 medallion edition 9.95
2 . . . . 2.95

ESPERS
Eclipse
1 I:ESPers. 2.00
2 JBo(c),V:Terrorists 2.00
3 V:Terrorists. 2.00
4 Beirut 2.00
5 "The Liquidators" 2.00
6 V:Benito Giovanetti. 2.00

ESPIONAGE
Dell Publishing Co. May-July, 1964
1 . . . . 30.00
2 . . . . 25.00

ETERNITY SMITH
Hero
1 . . . . 2.00
2 . . . . 2.00
3 . . . . 2.00
4 Knightshade solo 2.00
5 Knightshade solo 2.00
6 . . . . 2.00
7 . . . . 2.00
8 I:Indigo. 2.00
9 A:Walter Koenig 2.00
10 . . . . 2.00
Heroic Publishing
1 Man Vs. Machine 2.00
2 Man Vs. Machine 2.00

EVA THE IMP
Red Top Comic/Decker 1957
1 . . . . 25.00
2 . . . . 20.00

EVANGELINE
Comico 1984
1 Guns of Mars 4.00
2 . . . . 3.00
Lodestone
1 . . . . 2.50
2 . . . . 2.50
First
1 . . . . 3.00
2 thru 9 . . . . @2.00
10 . . . . 2.00
11 . . . . 2.00
12 . . . . 2.00

EVERYTHING'S ARCHIE
Archie Publications May, 1969
1 . . . . 75.00
2 . . . . 50.00
3 thru 5 . . . . @40.00
6 thru 10 . . . . @20.00
11 thru 20 . . . . @10.00
21 thru 40 . . . . @7.00
41 thru 134 . . . . @5.00

COLOR PUB.

EVIL ERNIE
Eternity 1991–92
See: B&W

EVIL ERNIE (THE SERIES)
Chaos! Comics 1998

1 V:Purgatori . . . 3.00
2 Search for Chastity, A:Savior . . . 3.00
3 V:Purgatori . . . 3.00
4 return to New Jersey . . . 3.00
5 two beings . . . 3.00
6 heart of America . . . 3.00
7 Unholy Nights . . . 3.00
8 Trauma,pt.1 . . . 3.00
9 Trauma,pt.2 . . . 3.00
10 Trauma,pt.3 . . . 3.00

EVIL ERNIE: DEPRAVED
Chaos! Comics 1999

1 (of 3) . . . 3.00
1a premium edition . . . 10.00
2 . . . 3.00
3 . . . 3.00

Evil Ernie, Destroyer #6
© Chaos! Comics

EVIL ERNIE: DESTROYER
Chaos! Comics 1997

Prev.#1 . . . 3.00
1 (of 9) BnP . . . 3.00
2 BnP . . . 3.00
3 to Atlanta . . . 3.00
4 siege of Atlanta . . . 3.00
5 . . . 3.00
6 Nuclear launch codes . . . 3.00
7 Nuclear attack . . . 3.00
8 Nuclear attack continues . . . 3.00
9 New forms of living dead, concl. . . 3.00

EVIL ERNIE: REVENGE
Chaos! Comics 1994–95

1 SHu,BnP,A:LadyDeath,glow(c) . 10.00
1a limited, glow-in-the-dark (c) . . . 25.00
1a Commemorative edition . . . 20.00
2 SHu,BnP,Loses Smiley . . . 8.00
3 SHu,BnP,V:Dr. Price . . . 7.00
4 SHu,BnP,Final Issue . . . 7.00
TPB Rep. #1-#4 . . . @12.95
TPB Revenge #2, signed . . . 20.00

EVIL ERNIE: STRAIGHT TO HELL
Chaos! Comics 1995–96

1 Rampage in Hell, coffin(c) . . . 5.00
1 limited, chromium edition . . . 25.00
2 Cremator . . . 4.00
3 . . . 4.00
3a Chastity (c) . . . 22.00
4 and 5 . . . @4.00
Ashcan . . . 1.50
Spec. . . . 25.00

EVIL ERNIE: THE RESURRECTION
Chaos! Comics 1993–94

1 R:Evil Ernie . . . 20.00
1a gold edition . . . 50.00
2 Enhanced Cover . . . 14.00
3 "Massive Mayhem" Lady Death poster . . . 14.00
4 final issue, extra pages . . . 14.00
TPB Rep. #1-#4 . . . @14.95

EVIL ERNIE VS. THE MOVIE MONSTERS
Chaos! Comics

1 one-shot . . . 3.00
1 omega edition . . . 5.00
1 premium edition, signed . . . 20.00

EVIL ERNIE VS. THE SUPER-HEROES
Chaos! Comics 1995

1 one-shot . . . 3.50
1a foil (c) . . . 30.00
1b limited . . . 20.00
Spec. #2 by Hart Fisher & Steve Butler . . . 2.95
Spec. #2, Premium edition . . . 10.00

EVIL ERNIE: WAR OF THE DEAD
Chaos! Comics 1999

1 (of 3) . . . 2.95
1a premium . . . 9.99
2 . . . 2.95
3 concl. . . . 2.95

EVIL ERNIE'S BADDEST BATTLES
Chaos! Comics 1996

1-shot, imaginary battles . . . 2.00

EXECUTIONER
Innovation 1993

1 Don Pendleton(s),F:Mack Bolan . 3.95
1a Collector's Gold Ed. . . . 2.95
1b Tyvek cover . . . 3.95
2 War against Mafia . . . 2.75
3 War against Mafia,pt.3 . . . 2.75

EXEMPLARS

1 and 2 . . . @2.00

EXODUS, THE
Conquest Comics

1 V:Aliens . . . 2.50

EXO-SQUAD
Topps 1994
[Mini-Series]

0 . . . 2.00
1 From Animated Series . . . 2.50
2 F:Nara Burns . . . 2.50
3 V:Neo-Sapiens . . . 2.50

EXPLORERS
Explorer Press 1995

1 I:Explorers . . . 2.95
2 The Cellar . . . 2.95

EXTREME VIOLET
Blackout Comics

0 I:Violet . . . 2.95
1 V:Drug Lords . . . 2.95
Becomes:

EXTREMES OF VIOLET

2 A:Matt Chaney . . . 2.95
Commemorative Issue, 5000c. . . . 9.95

EXTINCTIONERS
Vision Comics 1998

1 by Shawntae Howard & Malcolm Earle . . . 3.95
2 . . . 3.95

EXTRA
Gemstone 1999

1 (of 5) . . . 2.50
2 . . . 2.50
3 . . . 2.50
4 . . . 2.50
5 final issue . . . 2.50
"Annuals"
TPB Vol. 1 . . . 13.50

EYE OF THE STORM
Rival Productions

1 I:Killian, Recon, Finesse, Stray . . 2.95
2 Conspiracy . . . 2.95
3 3-D Comic Background . . . 2.95
4 F:Recon . . . 2.95
5 Sinclair & Rott . . . 2.95

FALCON, THE
Aircel

Spec. #1 . . . 2.00

FAMILY AFFAIR
Gold Key Feb., 1970

1 W/Poster,Ph(c) . . . 65.00
2 . . . 25.00
3 Ph(c) . . . 25.00
4 Ph(c) . . . 25.00

FAMILY MATTER
Kitchen Sink 1998

GN by Will Eisner . . . 15.95
HC . . . 24.95

FAMOUS INDIAN TRIBES
Dell Publishing Co.
July-Sept., 1962

1 . . . 20.00
2 . . . 10.00

COLOR PUB.

FANG
Sirius
1 V:Vampires, I:Fang 4.00
2 5 . . . . 3.25
3 V:The Master 2.95

FANTASTIC VOYAGES OF SINBAD, THE
Gold Key Oct., 1965
1 Ph(c) 65.00
2 June, 1967 . . . . 50.00

FANTASY FEATURES
AC
1 . . . . 2.00
2 . . . . 2.00

FASHION IN ACTION
Eclipse
Summer Special #1 . . . . 2.00
Winter Special #1 . . . . 2.00

FAT ALBERT
Gold Key 1974–79
1 . . . . 30.00
2 . . . . 15.00
3 thru 10 . . . . @15.00
11 thru 29 . . . . @12.00

FATALE
Broadway 1995
1 thru 6 JJo, "Inherit the Earth," pt.5 . . . . @2.95
7 Fatale now Queen of the World . 2.95
8 "Crown of Thorns," pt.2. . . . . 2.95
9 "Crown of Thorns," pt.3. . . . . 2.95
TPB Inherit the Earth 14.95
HC Inherit the Earth 75.00

FATE'S FIVE
Innervision 1998
1 (of 4) 2.50
1 variant cover 2.50
2 (of 4) 2.50
3 (of 4) 2.50

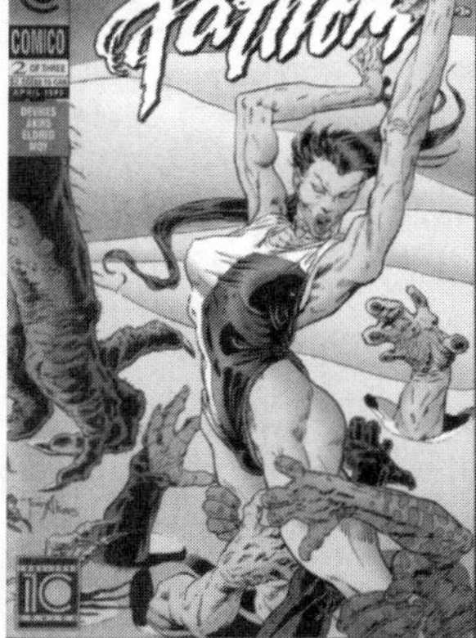

Fathom #2
© Comico

FATHOM
Comico 1987
1 thru 3 From Elementals. . . . . . @2.50

FATMAN, THE HUMAN FLYING SAUCER
Lightning Comics April, 1967
1 CCB,O:Fatman & Tin Man 60.00
2 CCB 50.00
3 CCB,(Scarce). 55.00

FAUST: BOOK OF M
Avatar Press 1999
1 (of 3) DQ,TV. 3.95
1a (of 3) prism foil (c) 12.95
1b signed, leather cover 20.00
1c Royal Blue edition. 75.00
2 . . . . 3.95
3 . . . . 3.95
3a nude (c) 6.00

FAZE ONE
AC Comics
1 . . . . 2.00

FAZE ONE FAZERS
AC Comics
1 . . . . 5.00
2 . . . . 3.00
3 . . . . 2.00
4 thru 6 . . . . @2.00

FEARBOOK
Eclipse
1 SBi,RV,"A Dead Ringer" 2.00

FELIX THE CAT
Harvey
1 thru 4 . . . . @2.00
5 thru 7 . . . . @2.00

FELIX THE CAT: THE MOVIE
Felix Comics 1998
1-shot, issued a mere 10 years after movie 3.95

FELIX'S NEPHEWS INKY & DINKY
Harvey Publications Sept., 1957
1 . . . . 65.00
2 thru 7 . . . . @35.00

FEM 5
Entity 1995
1 thru 4 five-part series . . . . @2.95
1 signed & numbered 12.95

FEMFORCE
AC Comics
1 O:Femforce 7.00
2 A:Captain Paragon 3.50
3 "Skin Game". 3.00
4 "Skin Game". 3.00
5 Back in the Past 3.00
6 EL,Back in the Past 3.00
7 HB,O:Captain Paragon 3.00
8 V:Shade 3.00
9 V:Dr.Rivits 3.00
10 V:Dr.Rivits 3.00
11 D:Haunted Horsemen 3.00
12 V:Dr.Rivits 3.00
13 V:She-Cat 3.00
14 V:Alizarin Crimson 3.00
15 V:Alizarin Crimson 3.00
16 thru 56 See Black & White Pub.
57 V:Goat God 2.75
58 I:New Sentinels 2.75
59 I:Paragon. 2.75
60 V:Sentinels 2.75
61 F:Tara 2.75
62 V:Valkyra 2.75
63 I:Rayda 2.75
64 thru 67 . . . . @2.75
68 "Spellbound" 2.75
69 "She-Cat Possessed". 2.75
70 "Island Out of Time". 2.75
71 . . . . 2.75
72 w/Sentinels of Justice 4.00
72a no extras 3.00
73 w/Compact Comic 4.00
73a Regular edition 3.00
74 Daughter of Darkness 4.00
74a Regular edition 3.00
75 Gorby Poster 5.00
75a Regular edition 3.00
76 Daughters pt. 3, polybagged with Compact Comic 4.00
76a no bag or comic. 3.00
77 V:Sea Monster. 3.00
78 V:Gorgana, bagged with comic . 5.00
78a no bag or comic. 3.00
79 V:Iron Jaw, polybagged with Index. 5.00
79a no bag or index 3.00
80 polybagged with Index. 6.00
80a F:Mr. Brimstone, Rad. 3.00
81 polybagged with Index. 6.00
81a Valentines Day Spec. 3.00
82 polybagged with Index. 6.00
82a F:Ms. Victory 3.00
83 F:Paragon 3.00
84 The Death of Joan Wayne polybagged with index #4B. . . . 6.00
84a no bag or index 3.00
85 Synn vs. Narett, polybagged with card 5.00
85a no bag or card 3.00
86 polybagged with index #5 . . . . . 5.00
86a unbagged, no suplements 3.00
87 Pandemonium in Paradise, polybagged with plate. 10.00
87a unbagged, no plate 3.00
88 F:Garganta, polybagged with index #6. . . . . 6.00
88a unbagged, no index. 3.00
89 polybagged with index 6.00
89a unbagged, no index. 3.00
90 polybagged with index 6.00
90a unbagged, no index. 3.00
91 polybagged with index 6.00
91a unbagged, no index. 3.00
92 polybagged with index 6.00
92a unbagged, no index. 3.00
Spec.#1 . . . . 2.00
Untold Origin Spec #1 . . . . 4.95

FEMFORCE: UP CLOSE
AC Comics
1 F:Stardust 2.75
2 F:Stardust 2.75
3 . . . . 2.75
4 . . . . 2.75
5 with Sticker. 3.95
5a Regular Edition. 2.95
6 with Sticker. 3.95
6a Regular Edition. 2.95
7 with Sticker. 3.95
7a Regular Edition. 2.95
8 with Sticker. 3.95

8a Regular Edition. 2.95
9 thru 11 . . . . @2.95

FENRY
Raven Publications

1 . . . . 6.95
1a Platinum Ed. 15.00

FIGHT THE ENEMY
Tower Comics Aug., 1966

1 BV,Lucky 7 . . . . 40.00
2 AMc 30.00
3 WW,AMc 30.00

FIGHTING AMERICAN
Harvey

1 SK,Rep Fighting American from 1950's 17.50

Fighting American #1a
© Awesome Entertainment

FIGHTING AMERICAN
Awesome Entertainment

1 . . . . 4.00
1a variant (c). 4.00
1b Platinum (c) 15.00
2 . . . . 3.00
Coll.Ed.#1 rep.#1–#2 . . . . 4.95
Spec.#1 Fighting American: Cold War RLe,JLb 2.50

FIGHTING AMERICAN: DOGS OF WAR
Awesome Entertainment 1998

1 JSn,SPa,F:John Flagg 2.50
1a Tour Edition, RLe cover 5.00
1b Tour Edition, signed 14.00
2 JSn,SPa,other super-soldiers . . . 2.50
2a variant cover. 2.50
3 A:Crimson Dragon 2.50
4 Who is No Name? 2.50
Spec.'98 Con preview,b&w,16-page 5.00

FIGHTING AMERICAN: RULES OF THE GAME
Awesome Entertainment 1997

1 JLb. 3.00
2 JLb. 2.50
3 JLb, Baby Buzz Bomber 2.50

FIRST ADVENTURES
First

1 thru 5 . . . . @1.25

FIRST GRAPHIC NOVELS
First

1 JBi,Beowolf 8.00
1a 2nd Printing 7.00
2 TT,Time Beavers 6.00
3 HC,American Flag Hard Times . 12.00
4 Nexus,SR. 8.00
5 Elric,CR 15.00
6 Enchanted Apples of Oz. 6.00
7 Secret Island of Oz. 8.00
8 HC,Time 2 . . . . 28.00
9 TMNT. 20.00
10 TMNT II. 18.00
11 Sailor on the Sea 15.00
12 HC,American Flagg 12.00
13 Ice Ring. 8.00
14 TMNT III 14.00
15 Hex Breaker 8.00
16 Forgotten Forest 9.00
17 Mazinger 9.00
18 TMNT IV 13.00
19 O;Nexus 8.00
20 American Flagg 12.00

1st FOLIO
Pacific

1 Joe Kubert School 2.00

FISH POLICE
Comico

Vol 2 #6 thru #15 rep. . . . . @2.50
Vol 2 #16 rep.. . . . . 3.00
Vol 2 #17 rep.,AuA 3.00
1 Color Special (July 1987) 3.50

FITCH IN TIME

1 and 2 . . . . @2.00

FLAMEHEAD
JNCO Comics 1998

1 I:Flamehead 2.00
2 . . . . 2.00
3 . . . . 2.00
4 . . . . 2.00
5 . . . . 2.00

FLARE
Hero Graphics

1 I:Darkon&Prof.Pomegranite 4.00
2 Blonde Bombshell,A:Galooper . . 3.00
3 I:Sky Marshall. 3.00
Ann.#1 . . . . 4.50

[2nd Series]

1 A:Galloping Galooper 3.00
2 A:Lady Arcane 3.00
3 I:Britannia. 3.00
4 A:Indigo 2.50
5 R:Eternity Smith,O:Die Kriegerin. 3.95
6 I:Tigress 3.50
7 V:The Enemies. 3.95
8 Morrigan Wars#4,A:Icicle Dragon 3.50
9 Morrigan Wars Pt.7 (B&W) 3.50

FLARE ADVENTURES
Hero Graphics

1 rep. 2.95
2 flipbook w/Champions Classics. . 2.95
3 flipbook w/Champions Classics. . 2.95
Becomes: B&W

FLASH GORDON
Gold Key June, 1965

1 . . . . 15.00

FLASH GORDON
King 1966–69

1 AW,DH,A:Mandrake 50.00
1a Comp. Army giveaway 50.00
2 FBe,A:Mandrake,R:Ming. 30.00
3 RE,"Lost in the Land of The Lizardmen" 35.00
4 AW,B:Secret Agent X-9. . . . . . . 38.00
5 AW. 38.00
6 RC,On the Lost Continent of Mongo 35.00
7 MR, rep. "In the Human Forest" 35.00
8 RC,JAp. 35.00
9 AR,rep 40.00
10 AR,rep. 40.00
11 RC. 30.00

Charlton 1969–70

12 RC. 30.00
13 JJ 25.00
14 . . . . 25.00
15 . . . . 25.00
16 . . . . 25.00
17 Brick Bradford story 25.00
18 MK,"Attack of the Locust Men". 25.00

Gold Key Oct.-Nov 1975

19 Flash returns to Mongo 10.00
20 thru 30 . . . . @7.00
31 thru 37 AW movie adapt. . . . . @5.00

FLATLINE COMICS
Flatline Comics

1 Three stories River Prarie. 2.50

FLAXEN: ALTER EGO
Caliber

1 V:Dark Flaxen. 2.95

FLESH AND BONES
Fantagraphics

1 Moore. 2.50
2 thru 4 Moore . . . . @2.00

FLINTSTONES
Harvey

1 . . . . 2.00
2 Romeo and Juliet 2.00

FLINTSTONES
Archie 1995

1 thru 10 . . . . @2.00
11 thru 14 . . . . @2.00
15 "Frankenstone's Monster" 2.00
20 "An Heir-Raising Tale" 2.00
21 "King Fred The Last" 2.00
22 "Something Gruesome This Way Comes" 2.00

FLINTSTONES, THE
Dell Publishing Co. Nov.-Dec., 1961

#1 *see Dell Giant*
2 . . . . 100.00
3 . . . . 75.00
4 . . . . 75.00
5 and 6 . . . . @60.00

Gold Key

7 . . . . 60.00
8 A:Mr.& Mrs J. Evil Scientists . . . 50.00
9 A:Mr.& Mrs.J. Evil Scientists . . . 50.00

10 A:Mr.& Mrs.J. Evil Scientists. . . 50.00
11 I:Pebbles 60.00
12 "The Too-Old Cowhand". 40.00
13 thru 15. . . . . @40.00
16 I:Bamm-Bamm. 50.00
17 thru 20 . . . . @40.00
21 thru 23. . . . . @25.00
24 I:Gruesomes 28.00
25 thru 29. . . . . @22.00
30 "Dude Ranch Roundup". 22.00
31 Christmas(c) 22.00
32 . . . . 20.00
33 A:Dracula & Frankenstein 22.00
34 I:The Great Gazoo. 30.00
35 . . . . 20.00
36 "The Man Called Flintstone". . . 20.00
37 thru 40. . . . . @20.00
41 thru 60. . . . . @16.00

FLINTSTONES, THE
Charlton Comics 1970

1 . . . . 65.00
2 . . . . 40.00
3 thru 7 . . . . @30.00
8 . . . . 35.00
9 . . . . 25.00
10 . . . . 25.00
11 thru 20 . . . . @20.00
21 thru 50 . . . . @15.00

FLINTSTONES IN 3-D
Blackthorne

1 thru 5 . . . . @2.50

FLIPPER
Gold Key April, 1966

1 Ph(c) from TV series. 40.00
2 and 3 Ph(c). . . . . @25.00

FLY IN MY EYE EXPOSED
Eclipse

1 JJo(c),"Our Visitor" 4.95

FLY, THE
Archie Publications

1 JSn,A:Mr.Justice. 2.00
2 thru 9 RB,SD . . . . @2.00

FLYING SAUCERS
Dell April, 1967

1 . . . . 35.00
2 thru 5 . . . . @25.00

FLYMAN
Archie Publications
{Prev: Adventures of the Fly}

31 I:Shield (Bill Higgins), A:Comet, Black Hood. 35.00
32 I:Mighty Crusaders. 30.00
33 A:Mighty Crusaders, R:Hangman Wizard 30.00
34 MSy,A:Black Hood,Shield,Comet Shield back-up story begins 20.00
35 O:Black Hood 20.00
36 O:Web,A:Hangman in Shield strip 20.00
37 A:Shield. 20.00
38 A:Web 18.00
39 A:Steel Sterling 17.00

FOES
Ram Comics

1 TheMaster's Game. 2.00
2 TheMaster's Game #2 . . . . 2.00

FOODANG
Aug. House

1 I:Foodang. 2.00
1a Signed, Foil cover. 2.50
2 I:Maude 2.50
3 V:Undead Clown Man. 2.50
4 V:Executioner. 2.50

FOOTSOLDIERS
Maximum Press 1996

1 KJo,PhH, ... 2.75

FORBIDDEN PLANET
Innovation 1992

1 Movie Adapt. 2.50
2 Movie adapt.contd. 2.50
3 Movie adapt.contd. 2.50
4 Movie adapt.concl. 2.50
GN rep.#1–#4 (1997) 8.95

FORCE OF THE BUDDHA'S PALM
Jademan

1 . . . . 3.00
2 . . . . 2.25
3 thru 10 . . . . @2.00
11 thru 24 . . . . @2.00
25 V:Maskman 2.00
26 V:Maskman 2.00
27 A:SmilingDemon 2.00
28 Maskman v 10 Demons. 2.00
29 Giant Bat. 2.00
30 . . . . 2.00
31 . . . . 2.00
32 "White Crane Villa" 2.00
33 Devilito defeats White Crane & Giant Bat 2.00
34 Samsun vs. Devilito. 2.00
35 Samsun vs. Devilito. 2.00
36 Samsun vs. Devilito. 2.00
37 D:Galacial Moon 2.00
38 Persian Elders, Iron Boy 2.00
39 V:Mad Gen.,White Crane, Iron Boy 2.00

Force of the Buddha's Palm #50
© Jademan

40 D:Heaven & Earth Elders. 2.00
41 thru 43. . . . . @2.00
44 D:White Crane. 2.95
45 V:Iron Boy 2.00
46 thru 48. . . . . @2.00
49 Iron Boy vs Sainted Jade. 2.00
50 Iron Boy & The Holy Blaze. 2.00
51 D:Aquarius 2.00
52 V:Son o/t Gemini Lord 2.00
53 Nine Continent's return to full powers 2.00

4-D MONKEY

1 thru 3 . . . . @2.00

FOREVER WAR, THE
NBM

GN Vol. 1 Joe Haldeman adapt. . . . 8.95
GN Vol. 2 Joe Haldeman adapt. . . . 8.95
GN Vol. 3 Joe Haldeman adapt. . . . 8.95

FRANK
Nemesis

1 thru 4 DGc(s),GgP . . . . @2.50

FRANK FRAZETTA FANTASY ILLUSTRATED
Frank Frazetta 1998

1 . . . . 6.00
1a variant cover 6.00
3 . . . . 6.00
3 Neil Gaiman signed & numbered. 24.95
3 Daniel signed & numbered 19.95
4 thru 9 . . . . @6.00

FRANK FRAZETTA DEATH DEALER
Verotik 1997

1 thru 4 by Glenn Danzig . . . . . @6.95

FRANK IN THE RIVER
Tundra

1 Avery/Jones style cartoons 2.95

FRANK MERRIWELL AT YALE
Charlton Comics 1955–56

1 . . . . 35.00
2 thru 4 . . . . @30.00

FRANKENSTEIN
Dell Publishing Co. 1964

1 . . . . 50.00
2 . . . . 30.00
3 and 4 . . . . @20.00

FRANKENSTEIN
Caliber

Novel Adaptation 2.95

FRANKENSTEIN DRACULA WAR
Topps

1 Frank Vs. Drac. 2.50
2 F:Saint Germaine 2.50
3 Frank Vs. Drac. 2.50

FREDDY
Dell Publishing Co. 1963
1 ... 25.00
2 and 3 ... @15.00

FREDDY'S DEAD
3-D ... 2.50
1 GN, Movie Adapt ... 6.95

FREDDY'S DEAD: THE FINAL NIGHTMARE
Innovation
1 Movie adaption, Pt.1 ... 2.50
2 Movie adaption, Pt.2 ... 2.50

FRIDAY FOSTER
Dell Publishing Co. Oct., 1972
1 ... 25.00

Friendly Ghost Casper #243
© Harvey Publications

FRIENDLY GHOST CASPER, THE
Harvey Publications 1958
1 ... 275.00
2 ... 125.00
3 thru 10 ... @75.00
11 thru 20 ... @50.00
21 thru 30 ... @40.00
31 thru 50 ... @30.00
51 thru 100 ... @20.00
101 thru 159 ... @15.00
160 thru 163 52 pgs. ... @10.00
164 thru 253 ... @5.00
Becomes:

CASPER THE FRIENDLY GHOST

FRIGHT NIGHT
Now
1 thru 22 ... @2.00

FRIGHT NIGHT
Now
1 Dracula,w/3-D Glasses ... 2.95

FRIGHT NIGHT II
Now
Movie Adaptation ... 3.95

FRISKY ANIMALS ON PARADE
Ajax-Farrell Publ. Sept., 1957
1 LbC(c) ... 150.00
2 ... 60.00
3 LbC(c) ... 125.00

FROGMEN, THE
Dell Publishing Co. 1962
1 GE,Ph(c) ... 75.00
2 GE,FF ... 60.00
3 GE,FF ... 60.00
4 ... 35.00
5 ATh ... 40.00
6 thru 11 ... @25.00

FROM HERE TO INSANITY
Charlton Comics Feb., 1955
8 ... 120.00
9 ... 100.00
10 SD(c) ... 150.00
11 JK ... 175.00
12 JK ... 175.00
3-1 ... 250.00

FRONTLINE COMBAT
EC Comics 1995
1 thru 4 rep. ... @2.00
Gemstone
5 thru 13 rep. ... @2.50
14 WW(c) ... 2.50
15 ... 2.50
"Annuals"
TPB Vol. 1 rebinding of #1–#5 ... 10.95
TPB Vol. 2 rebinding of #6–#10 ... 12.95
TPB Vol. 3 rebinding of #11–#15 ... 13.50

F-TROOP
Dell Publishing Co. 1966
1 Ph(c) ... 100.00
2 thru 7 Ph(c) ... @60.00

FUN-IN
Gold Key 1970–74
1 ... 65.00
2 thru 6 ... @35.00
7 thru 10 ... @25.00
11 thru 15 ... @25.00

FUNKY PHANTOM
Gold Key 1972–75
1 ... 50.00
2 thru 5 ... @25.00
6 thru 13 ... @20.00

FUTURIANS
Lodestone
1 DC,I:Dr.Zeus ... 1.00
2 DC,I:MsMercury ... 1.00
3 DC ... 1.00
Eternity Graphic Novel, DC, Rep. +new material ... 9.95

GALACTICA: THE NEW MILLENNIUM
Realm Press 1999
1 Battlestar Galactica ... 2.99
1 convention edition ... 5.00
1a signed ... 15.00
2 Busch (c) ... 2.99
2a Scalf (c) ... 2.99
2b convention edition ... 5.00
3 ... 2.99
3a ... 2.99
4 ... 2.99
4a deluxe ... 4.99
Spec. Fangs of the Beast ... 3.99
Spec. Fangs of the Beast,deluxe ... 4.99
Tour Book, Conv. Ed., signed ... 15.00
Spec.Search for Sanctuary ... 3.99

GALL FORCE: ETERNAL STORY
CPM
1 F:Solnoids ... 2.95
2 V:Paranoid ... 2.95
3 ... 2.95
4 Implant Secrets ... 2.95

GALLANT MEN, THE
Gold Key Oct., 1963
1 RsM ... 25.00

GALLEGHER BOY REPORTER
Gold Key May, 1965
1 ... 22.00

GARRISON
Zion Comics
1 I:Wage, Garrison ... 2.50

GARRISON'S GORRILLAS
Dell Publishing Co. Jan., 1968
1 Ph(c) ... 45.00
2 thru 5 Ph(c) ... @25.00

GASP!
American Comics Group March, 1967
1 ... 35.00
2 thru 4, Aug. 1967 ... @20.00

G-8 & BATTLE ACES
1 based on '40's pulp characters ... 3.00

GENE RODDENBERRY'S LOST UNIVERSE
Teckno-Comics 1994
0 I:Sensua ... 2.50
1 Gene Roddenberry's ... 2.50
2 Grange Discovered ... 2.25
3 Secrets Revealed ... 2.00
4 F:Penultra ... 2.00
5 I:New Alien Race ... 2.00
6 Two Doctor Granges ... 2.00
7 F:Alaa Chi Tskare ... 2.00

GENE RODDENBERRY'S XANDER IN LOST UNIVERSE
Teckno-Comics 1995
1 V:Black Ghost ... 2.25
2 V:Walker ... 2.25
3 V:Lady Sensua ... 2.25
4 thru 7 ... @2.25
8 F:Lady Sensua ... 2.25

[Mini-Series] Teckno-Comics 1995
1 RoR,F:L.Nimoy's Primortals 2.25

GENSAGA: ANCIENT WARRIOR
Entity Comics 1995
1 I:Gensaga 2.50
1a with Computer Games 2.50
2 V:Dinosaurs 2.50
3 V:Lord Abyss 2.50

GENTLE BEN
Dell Publishing Co. Feb., 1968
1 Ph(c) 30.00
2 . . . . 20.00
3 thru 5 . . . . @18.00

GEORGE OF THE JUNGLE
Gold Key Feb., 1969
1 From animated TV show. 135.00
2 . . . . 100.00

GE ROUGE
Verotik 1997
1 by Glenn Danzig & Calvin Irving . 2.95
2 and 3 . . . . @2.95
Biz:GE Rouge #½ SBs 2.95

GET SMART
Dell Publishing Co. June, 1966
1 Ph(c) all 100.00
2 SD 75.00
3 SD 65.00
4 thru 8 . . . . @60.00

[FILMATION'S] GHOSTBUSTERS
First 1987
1 thru 4 . . . . @2.00

GHOST BUSTERS II
Now
1 thru 3 Mini-series . . . . @2.00

GHOST STORIES
Dell Publishing Co. Sept.-Nov., 1962
1 . . . . 55.00
2 . . . . 30.00
3 thru 10 . . . . @25.00
11 . . . . 20.00
12 thru 19 . . . . @15.00
20 . . . . 20.00
21 thru 33 . . . . @15.00
34 rep. 15.00
35 rep. 20.00
36 rep. 15.00
37 rep. 15.00

GHOSTLY TALES
Charlton 1966
Previously: Blue Beetle
55 I&O Dr. Graves 40.00
56 thru 70 . . . . @20.00
71 thru 100 . . . . @10.00
101 thru 169 . . . . @7.00

Ghostly Tales #56
© Charlton

GIANT COMICS
Charlton Comics Summer, 1957
1 A:Atomic Mouse,Hoppy. 150.00
2 A:Atomic Mouse 100.00
3 . . . . 100.00

GIDGET
Dell Publishing Co. April, 1966
1 Ph(c),Sally Field 100.00
2 Ph(c),Sally Field 75.00

GIFT, THE
First
Holiday Special. 6.00

GIGANTOR
Antarctic Press 2000
1 (of 12) BDn. 2.50
2 V:Red Reich. 2.50
3 . . . . 2.50
4 Doppleganger,pt.1 . . . . 2.50
5 Doppleganger,pt.2 . . . . 2.50
6 Doppleganger,pt.3 . . . . 2.50
7 Rulers of the Sea 2.50

G.I. JOE 3-D
Blackthorne
1 . . . . 3.00
2 thru 5 . . . . @2.50
Ann. #1 . . . . 2.50

GIL THORPE
Dell Publishing Co. 1963
1 . . . . 35.00

GINGER FOX
Comico
1 thru 4 . . . . @2.00

GIN-RYU
Believe In Yourself
1 F:Japanese Sword 2.75
2 Identity Revealed 2.75
3 . . . . 2.75
4 Manhunt For Gin-Ryu 2.75

G.I. R.A.M.B.O.T.
Wonder Color 1987
1 thru 3 . . . . @2.00

G.I. ROBOT
Eternity
1 . . . . 2.00

GIRL FROM U.N.C.L.E.
Gold Key, Jan., 1967
1 "The Fatal Accidents Affair". . . 100.00
2 "The Kid Commandos Caper" . . 75.00
3 "The Captain Kidd Affair" 75.00
4 "One-Way Tourist Affair" 75.00
5 "The Harem-Scarem Affair". . . . 75.00

GLOBAL FORCE
Silverline
1 thru 4 . . . . @2.00

GLORY
Maximum Press 1996
1–15 see Image
16 JDy 2.50
17 JDy 2.50
18 JDy 2.50
19 JDy,A:Demeter, Silverfall 2.50
20 JDy,A:Silverfall. 2.50
21 JDy 2.50
22 JDy 2.50
23 A:Prophet 2.50
TPB Vol. 2, rep. 16.95
TPB Glory/Angela RLd,JDy. 16.95
Awesome Entertainment 1999
0 AMo 2.50
0a & b alternate covers 2.50
1 AMo & ATi 3.50
2 AMo & ATi 2.99

GLORY/CELESTINE: DARK ANGEL
Maximum Press 1996
1 & 2 *See: Image*
3 (of 3) JDy. 2.50

GLORY/LIONHEART: RAGE OF FURIES
Awesome Entertainment 2000
1 . . . . 2.99

G-MAN
Conquest Comics
1 I:Richard Glenn 2.50

GOBLIN LORD, THE
Goblin Studios 1996
1 (of 6) sci-fi/fantasy 2.50
2 signed & numbered 9.95
3 . . . . 2.50
3a signed & numbered 9.95
4 thru 6 . . . . @2.50

GO-GO
Charlton Comics June, 1966
1 Miss Bikini Luv 75.00
2 Beatles. 85.00
3 Blooperman 35.00
4 . . . . 35.00
5 . . . . 35.00
6 JAp 35.00
7 . . . . 35.00

8 JAp 35.00
9 Ph(c),Oct., 1965 . . . . 35.00

GODS FOR HIRE
Hot Comics

1 thru 7 . . . . @2.00

GOLDEN COMICS DIGEST
Gold Key 1969–76

1 Tom & Jerry,Woody Woodpecker, Bugs Bunny 40.00
2 Hanna-Barbera, TV Fun Favorites 50.00
3 Tom & Jerry, Woody Woodpecker. 40.00
4 Tarzan 40.00
5 Tom & Jerry, Woody Woodpecker, Bugs Bunny. . . . 20.00
6 Bugs Bunny 20.00
7 Hanna-Barbera, TV Fun Favorites 22.00
8 Tom & Jerry, Woody Woodpecker, Bugs Bunny. . . . 15.00
9 Tarzan 20.00
10 Bugs Bunny. 15.00
11 Hanna-Barbera, TV Fun Favorites 15.00
12 Tom & Jerry,Bugs Bunny 15.00
13 Tom & Jerry. 15.00
14 Bugs Bunny, Fun Packed Funnies 15.00
15 Tom & Jerry, Woody Woodpecker, Bugs Bunny. . . . 15.00
16 Woody Woodpecker. 15.00
17 Bugs Bunny. 15.00
18 Tom & Jerry, ... 15.00
19 Little Lulu. 20.00
20 Woody Woodpecker 15.00
21 Bugs Bunny Showtime. 15.00
22 Tom & Jerry Winter Wingding. . 15.00
23 Little Lulu & Tubby Fun Fling . . 20.00
24 Woody Woodpecker Fun Festival 15.00
25 Tom & Jerry. 15.00
26 Bugs Bunny Halloween Hulla-Boo-Loo,Dr. Spektor article. . . 15.00
27 Little Lulu & Tubby in Hawaii . . 20.00
28 Tom & Jerry. 15.00
29 Little Lulu & Tubby. 20.00
30 Bugs Bunny Vacation Funni . . . 15.00
31 Turk, Son of Stone. 20.00
32 Woody Woodpecker Summer Fun 15.00
33 Little Lulu & Tubby Halloween Fun 20.00
34 Bugs Bunny Winter Funnies. . . 15.00
35 Tom & Jerry Snowtime Funtime 15.00
36 Little Lulu & Her Friends 20.00
37 WoodyWoodpecker County Fair 15.00
38 The Pink Panter. 15.00
39 Bugs Bunny Summer Fun 15.00
40 Little Lulu. 20.00
41 Tom & Jerry Winter Carnival . . 15.00
42 Bugs Bunny. 15.00
43 Little Lulu in Paris 20.00
44 Woody Woodpecker Family Fun Festival 15.00
45 The Pink Panther. 15.00
46 Little Lulu & Tubby. 20.00
47 Bugs Bunny. 15.00
48 The Lone Ranger. 15.00

GOLD DIGGER
Antarctic Press 1999
VOL 2

1 by Fred Perry, F:Gina Diggers . . 2.50
2 . . . . 2.50
3 by Fred Perry 2.50
4 tinted glass is magical 2.50
5 . . . . 2.50
6 ancient cauldrons 2.50
7 Halls of the Extremely Dead 2.50
8 Gone Fishing 2.50
9 Fauntleroy..a God? 2.50
10 Arms Master of Jade 2.50
11 Arms Master of Jade 2.50
12 Arms Master of Jade 2.95
13 Tournament of Arms 2.95
14 Tournament of Arms 2.95
15 . . . . 2.95
Swimsuit Spec. #1 . . . . 4.50
Ann. 2000 b&w. 3.95

GOLD DIGGER BETA
Antarctic Press 1998

Spec. 0 by Ben Dunn, Special Origin Issue, 24pg 2.00
1A bu Fred Perry, John Pound (c) . 2.95
1B Jeff Henderson (c) 2.95
2 and 3 . . . . @2.95

GOLDEN PICTURE STORY BOOK
Racine Press (Western)
Dec., 1961

1 Huckleberry Hound. 250.00
2 Yogi Bear 250.00
3 Babes In Toy Land 275.00
4 Walt Disney 250.00

GOLDEN WARRIOR
Industrial Design

1 by Eric Bansen & RB 2.95
2 and 3 . . . . @2.95

GOMER PYLE
Gold Key July, 1966

1 Ph(c) from TV show 100.00
2 and 3 . . . . @75.00

GOOD GUYS
Defiant

1 JiS(s),I:Good Guys 3.75
2 JiS(s),V:Mulchmorg 3.25
3 V:Chasm 2.75
4 Seduction of the Innocent. 3.25
5 I:Truc 2.75
6 A:Charlemagne 2.75
7 JiS(s),V:Scourge. 2.50
8 thru 11 . . . . @2.50

GOOFY ADVENTURES
Walt Disney 1990

1 "Balboa de Goofy" 2.50
2 . . . . 2.00
3 thru 9 . . . . @2.00
10 Samurai. 2.00
11 Goofis Khan. 2.00
12 "Arizona Goof" Pt. 1. . . . . 2.00
13 "Arizona Goof" Pt. 2. . . . . 2.00
14 "Goofylution" 2.00
15 "Super Goof Vs.Cold Ray" 2.00
16 "Sheerluck Holmes" 2.00
17 GC,TP,"Tomb of Goofula". 2.00

GOOP, THE
JNCO Comics 1998

1 . . . . 2.00
2 . . . . 2.00
3 . . . . 2.00
4 . . . . 2.00

Goofy Adventures #2
© Disney

GORGO
Charlton Comics 1961–65

1 SD 225.00
2 SD,SD(c) 125.00
3 SD,SD(c) 75.00
4 SD(c) 65.00
5 thru 10 . . . . @65.00
11 . . . . 50.00
12 . . . . 40.00
13 thru 15. . . . . @40.00
16 SD. 40.00
17 thru 23. . . . . @35.00

GORGO'S REVENGE
Charlton Comics 1962

1 . . . . 50.00

Becomes:

THE RETURN OF GORGO

2 . . . . 40.00
3 . . . . 40.00

G.O.T.H.
Verotik 1995

1 thru 3 mini-series . . . . @2.95
TPB SBi, rep. of series 9.95

THE GOTHIC SCROLLS, DRAYVEN
Davdez Arts 1997

1 16pg. 2.00
1a limited edition, new cover 2.95
2 and 3 . . . . @2.50
4 V:Lucifer. 2.50
GN 12.95

GRATEFUL DEAD COMIX
Kitchen Sink

1 TT,inc.DireWolf(large format) . . . 5.50
2 TT,inc.Jack Straw 4.95
3 TT,inc. Sugaree 4.95
4 TT,inc. Sugaree 4.95
5 TT,Uncle John's Band. 4.95
6 TT,Eagle Mall #1. . . . . 4.95

COLOR PUB.

 All comics prices listed are for *Near Mint* condition.

GREASE MONKEY
Kitchen Sink 1997

1 by Tim Elred 3.50
2 by Tim Elred 3.50

GREAT AMERICAN WESTERN
AC Comics

1 . . . . 2.00
2 . . . . 2.95
3 . . . . 2.95
4 . . . . 3.50

GREAT EXPLOITS
Decker Publ./Red Top Oct., 1957

91 BK. 65.00

GREEN HORNET, THE
Gold Key Feb., 1967

1 Bruce Lee,Ph(c) 300.00
2 Ph(c) 225.00
3 Ph(c) 175.00

GREEN HORNET
Now

1 O:40's Green Hornet 7.00
1a 2nd Printing 4.00
2 O:60's Green Hornet 5.00
3 thru 5 . . . . @4.00
6 . . . . 3.00
7 BSz(c),I:New Kato 3.00
8 thru 12 . . . . @3.50
13 V:Ecoterrorists 3.50
14 V:Ecoterrorists 3.50
Spec.#1 . . . . 2.50
Spec.#2 . . . . 2.25

[2nd Series]

1 V:Johnny Dollar Pt.1 . . . . 2.25
2 V:Johnny Dollar Pt.2 . . . . 2.25
3 V:Johnny Dollar Pt.3 . . . . 2.25
4 V:Ex-Con/Politician 2.00
5 V:Ex-Con/Politician 2.00
6 Arkansas Vigilante 2.00
7 thru 9 The Beast . . . . @2.00
10 Green Hornet-prey 2.00
11 F:Crimson Wasp 2.00
12 Crimson Wasp/Johnny Dollar Pt.1,polybagged w/Button 2.50
13 TD(i),Wasp/Dollar Pt.2 . . . . 2.50
14 TD(i),Wasp/Dollar Pt.3 . . . . 2.50
15 TD(i),Secondsight 2.00
16 A:Commissioner Hamiliton 2.00
17 V:Gunslinger 2.00
18 V:Sister-Hood 2.00
19 V:Jewel Thief 2.00
20 F:Paul's Friend 2.00
21 V:Brick Arcade 2.00
22 V:Animal Testers, with Hologravure card 2.95
23 with Hologravure card 2.00
24 thru 25 Karate Wars . . . . @2.00
26 B:City under Siege 2.00
27 with Hologravure card 2.00
28 V:Gangs 2.00
29 V:Gangs 2.00
30 thru 37 . . . . @2.00
38 R:Mei Li 2.50
39 Crimson Wasp 2.50
40 . . . . 2.50
41 . . . . 2.50
42 Baby Killer 2.50
43 Wedding Disasters 2.50
44 F:Amy Hamilton 2.50
45 Plane Hijacking 2.50
46 Airport Terrorists 2.50
Ann.#1 The Blue & the Green 2.50
1993 Ann 2.95

Bonus Books

TPB rep. Now comics #1–#12, 296pg. 10.00
TPB deluxe rep. Now comics #1–#12, 296pg. 19.95
HC rep. #1–#12 . . . . 10.00

GREEN HORNET: DARK TOMORROW
Now

1 thru 3 Hornet Vs Kato . . . . @2.50

GREEN HORNET: SOLITARY SENTINAL
Now

1 Strike Force 2.50
2 thru 3 . . . . @2.50

GREENHAVEN
Aircel

1 . . . . 3.00
2 . . . . 2.50
3 . . . . 2.00

GRENDEL
Comico 1986–91

1 . . . . 6.00
1a 2nd printing 2.00
2 . . . . 5.00
3 thru 6 . . . . @4.00
7 MW 4.00
8 thru 12 . . . . @4.00
13 KSy(c) 3.00
14 KSy(c) 3.00
15 KSy(c) 3.00
16 Mage 5.00
17 thru 19 . . . . @4.00
20 thru 32 . . . . @3.00
33 . . . . 3.50
34 thru 36 . . . . @3.00
37 . . . . 5.00
38 . . . . 9.00
39 . . . . 8.00
40 . . . . 15.00

Grim Ghost #2
© Atlas

GREYLORE
Sirius 1985–86

1 thru 5 . . . . @2.00

GRIM GHOST
Atlas 1975

1 thru 3 . . . . @15.00

GRIMJACK
First 1984–91

1 TT Teenage suicide story 3.00
2 TT A:Munden's Bar 2.50
3 TT A:Munden's Bar 2.00
4 TT A:Munden's Bar 2.00
5 TT,JSon,A:Munden's Bar 2.00
6 TT,SR,A:Munden's Bar 2.00
7 TT,A:Munden's Bar 2.00
8 TT,A:Munden's Bar 2.00
9 TT "My Sins Remembered" 2.00
10 TT,Joy,A:Munden's Bar 2.00
11 TT,A:Munden'sBar 2.00
12 TT,A:Munden'sBar 2.00
13 TT,A:Munden'sBar 2.00
14 TT,A:Munden'sBar 2.00
15 TT,A:Munden'sBar 2.00
16 TT,A:Munden'sBar 2.00
17 TT,A:Munden'sBar 2.00
18 TT,A:Munden'sBar 2.00
19 TT,A:Munden'sBar 2.00
20 TT,A:Munden'sBar 2.00
21 TS,A:Munden's Bar 2.00
22 A:Munden's Bar 2.00
23 TS,A:Munden's Bar 2.00
24 PS,TT,rep.Starslayer10-11 . . . . . 2.00
25 TS,A:Munden's Bar 2.00
26 1st color TMNTurtles 10.00
27 TS,A:Munden's Bar 2.00
28 TS,A:Munden's Bar 2.00
29 A:Munden's Bar 2.00
30 A:Munden's Bar 2.00
31 A:Munden's Bar 2.00
32 A:Spook 2.00
33 JSon,Munden'sBar Christmas Tale 2.00
34 V:Spook 2.00
35 A:Munden's Bar 2.00
36 3rd Anniv.IssueD:Grimjack 2.50
37 A:Munden's Bar 2.00
38 A:Munden's Bar 2.00
39 R.Grimjack 2.00
40 . . . . 2.00
41 "Weeping Bride" 2.00
42 "Hardball" 2.00
43 "Beneath the Surface" 2.00
44 Shadow Wars 2.00
45 Shadow Wars 2.00
46 Shadow Wars 2.00
47 Shadow Wars,A:EddyCurrent . . . 2.00
48 Shadow Wars 2.00
49 Shadow Wars 2.00
50 V:Dancer,ShadowWars ends . . . 2.00
51 Crossroads tie-in, A:Judah Macabee 2.00
52 . . . . 2.00
53 Time Story 2.00
54 . . . . 2.50
55 FH 2.00
56 FH 2.00
57 FH 2.00
58 FH 2.00
59 FH 2.00
60 FH,Reunion Pt.1 . . . . 2.00
61 FH,Reunion Pt.2 . . . . 2.00
62 FH,Reunion Pt.3 . . . . 2.00
63 FH,A:Justice Drok 2.00
64 FH,O:Multiverse 2.00
65 FH 2.00
66 FH(c),Demon Wars Pt.1 . . . . 2.00
67 FH(c),Demon Wars Pt.2 . . . . 2.00

COLOR PUB.

68 Demon Wars Pt.3 . . . . 2.00
69 Demon Wars Pt.4 . . . . 2.00
70 FH,I:Youngblood 2.00
71 FH,A:Youngblood. 2.00
72 . . . . 2.00
73 FH(c). 2.00
74 FH(c). 2.00
75 FH,TS,V:The Major 2.00
76 FH,A:Youngblood. 2.00
77 FH,A:Youngblood. 2.25
78 . . . . 2.25
79 FH,Family Business #1 . . . . 2.25
80 FH,Family Business #2 . . . . 2.25
81 FH,Family Business #3 . . . . 2.25

GRIMJACK CASEFILE
First 1990

1 thru 5 rep. . . . . @2.00

GRIMM'S GHOST STORIES
Gold Key/Whitman 1972–82

1 . . . . 25.00
2 . . . . 15.00
3 . . . . 15.00
4 . . . . 15.00
5 AW. 20.00
6 . . . . 8.00
7 . . . . 8.00
8 AW. 12.00
9 . . . . 8.00
10 . . . . 8.00
11 thru 16 . . . . @7.00
17 RC. 10.00
18 thru 60 . . . . @7.00

Groo #4
© Pacific

GROO
Pacific 1983

1 SA,I:Sage,Taranto. 22.00
2 SA,A:Sage 12.00
3 SA,C:Taranto 10.00
4 SA,C:Sage 9.00
5 SA,I:Ahax 9.00
6 SA,I:Gratic 9.00
7 SA,I:Chakaal 9.00
8 SA,A:Chakaal. 9.00

Eclipse 1984

Spec.#1 SA,O:Groo,rep Destroyer Duck #1 . . . . 23.00

GROUND ZERO

1 . . . . 2.00

GROUP LARUE
Innovation

1 . . . . 2.00
2 . . . . 2.00
3 . . . . 2.00

GUILLOTIN
ABC 1997

1 JQ(c) 3.00
1a RCI(c). 6.00
1b gold cover, polybagged with trading card 10.00
2 . . . . 3.00
2a Serpent (c) 6.00
2b Cold Series (c) 6.00

GULLIVER'S TRAVELS
Dell Publishing Co.
Sept.-Nov., 1965

1 . . . . 50.00
2 and 3 . . . . @40.00

GUMBY
Comico

1 AAd,Summer Fun Special. 5.00
2 AAd,Winter Fun Special 3.50

GUMBY IN 3-D

Spec.#1 . . . . 4.00
2 thru 7 . . . . @2.50

GUNSMOKE
Dell Publishing Co. Feb., 1956

1 J.Arness Ph(c) all 175.00
2 . . . . 100.00
3 . . . . 100.00
4 . . . . 100.00
5 . . . . 100.00
6 . . . . 75.00
7 . . . . 75.00
8 . . . . 90.00
9 . . . . 90.00
10 AW,RC 100.00
11 . . . . 90.00
12 AW 100.00
13 thru 27 . . . . @75.00

GUY WITH A GUN: A ZOMBIE NIGHTMARE
Alpha Productions

1 V:Gracel, Zombies 2.75

HALL OF FAME
J.C. Productions

1 WW,GK,ThunderAgents 2.00
2 WW,GK,ThunderAgents 2.00
3 WW,ThunderAgents 2.00

HALLOWEEN
Chaos! Comics 2000

1 premium glow-in-the-dark (c) . . . 12.95
1 chromium edition 15.95

HALLOWEEN: BEHIND THE MASK
Chaos! Comics 2000

1 photo (c). 2.95

HALLOWEEN HORROR
Eclipse 1987

1 . . . . 2.00

HALO: AN ANGEL'S STORY
Sirius April 1996

1 thru 3 by Chris Knowles . . . . . @2.95
TPB rep. #1–#3. . . . . @12.95

HAMMER OF GOD
First

1 thru 4 . . . . @2.00
Deluxe #1"Sword of Justice Bk#1" . 4.95
Deluxe #2"Sword of Justice Bk#2" . 4.95

HAMSTER VICE

10 . . . . 2.00
3-D #1 . . . . 2.50

HAND OF FATE
Eclipse

1 I:Artemus Fate 1.75
2 F:Artemis & Alexis 2.00
3 Mystery & Suspense. 2.00

HANDS OF THE DRAGON
Atlas June 1975

1 . . . . 15.00

HANNA-BARBERA ALL-STARS
Archie 1995

1 thru 5 . . . . @2.00

HANNA-BARBERA BAND WAGON
Gold Key 1962–63

1 . . . . 150.00
2 . . . . 100.00
3 . . . . 75.00

HANNA-BARBERA PARADE
Charlton Comics 1971–72

1 . . . . 75.00
2 thru 10 . . . . @50.00

HANNA-BARBERA PRESENTS
Archie 1995

1 thru 15 . . . . @2.00

HANNA-BARBERA SUPER TV HEROES
Gold Key April, 1968

1 B:Birdman,Herculiods,Moby Dick, Young Samson & Goliath 200.00
2 . . . . 125.00
3 thru 7 Oct. 1969 . . . . @125.00

HARDY BOYS, THE
Gold Key April, 1970

1 . . . . 50.00
2 thru 4 . . . . @30.00

Hari Kari: The Beginning #1
© Blackout

HARI KARI
Blackout Comics 1995
0 I:Hari Kari. 2.95
1 . . . . 2.95
1a commemorative, variant(c) . . . 10.00
Specials & 1-shots
1 The Beginning, O:Kari (1996) . . . 2.95
1a The Beginning, commemorative, signed 9.95
1 Bloodshed (1996). 3.00
1a Bloodshed, deluxe, variant(c) . 10.00
1 Live & Untamed! (1996) 2.95
1 Rebirth (1996) 2.95
0 The Silence of Evil (1996). 2.95
0 The Silence of Evil, limited, foil stamped 12.95
½ The Diary of Kari Sun (1997) . . . 2.95
½ The Diary of Kari Sun, deluxe . . 9.95
0 Life or Death (1997) 2.95
0a Life or Death, super sexy parody edition. 12.95
1 Passion & Death (1997) 2.95
1 Passion & Death, photo(c) 9.95
1 Possessed by Evil (1997) 2.95
1 Resurrection (1997) 2.95
1 Resurrection, nude(c) edition . . . 9.95

HARLEM GLOBETROTTERS
Gold Key April, 1972
1 . . . . 30.00
2 thru 12, Jan. 1975. . . . . @20.00

HARLEY RIDER
1 GM,FS 2.00

HARRIERS
Entity 1995
1 I:Macedon Arsenal, Cardinal. . . . 2.95
1a with Video Game 6.95
2 . . . . 2.50
3 V:Kr'llyn 2.50

HARSH REALM
Harris
1 thru 6 JHi(s),. . . . . @2.95

HARVEY HITS
Harvey Publications 1957–67
1 The Phantom 250.00
2 Rags Rabbit 25.00
3 Richie Rich 825.00
4 Little Dot's Uncles 100.00
5 Stevie Mazie's Boy Friend 15.00
6 JK(c),BP,The Phantom 175.00
7 Wendy the Witch 150.00
8 Sad Sack's Army Life 40.00
9 Richie Rich's Golden Deeds . 350.00
10 Little Lotta 75.00
11 Little Audrey Summer Fun 50.00
12 The Phantom. 150.00
13 Little Dot's Uncles 50.00
14 Herman & Katnip 20.00
15 The Phantom. 135.00
16 Wendy the Witch 60.00
17 Sad Sack's Army Life. 30.00
18 Buzzy & the Crow 20.00
19 Little Audrey 30.00
20 Casper & Spooky 40.00
21 Wendy the Witch 30.00
22 Sad Sack's Army Life. 22.00
23 Wendy the Witch 30.00
24 Little Dot's Uncles 45.00
25 Herman & Katnip 15.00
26 The Phantom. 125.00
27 Wendy the Good Little Witch . . 25.00
28 Sad Sack's Army Life. 15.00
29 Harvey-Toon 20.00
30 Wendy the Witch 20.00
31 Herman & Katnip 10.00
32 Sad Sack's Army Life. 15.00
33 Wendy the Witch 25.00
34 Harvey-Toon 15.00
35 Funday Funnies. 10.00
36 The Phantom. 125.00
37 Casper & Nightmare 14.00
38 Harvey-Toon 12.00
39 Sad Sack's Army Life. 10.00
40 Funday Funnies 10.00
41 Herman & Katnip 10.00
42 Harvey-Toon 10.00
43 Sad Sack's Army Life. 10.00
44 The Phantom. 100.00
45 Casper & Nightmare 12.00
46 Harvey-Toon 10.00
47 Sad Sack's Army Life. 10.00
48 The Phantom. 100.00
49 Stumbo the Giant. 50.00
50 Harvey-Toon 10.00
51 Sad Sack's Army Life. 10.00
52 Casper & Nightmare 15.00
53 Harvey-Toons 10.00
54 Stumbo the Giant. 25.00
55 Sad Sack's Army Life. 10.00
56 Casper & Nightmare 12.00
57 Stumbo the Giant. 25.00
58 Sad Sack's Army Life. 10.00
59 Casper & Nightmare 12.00
60 Stumbo the Giant 25.00
61 Sad Sack's Army Life. 10.00
62 Casper & Nightmare 12.00
63 Stumbo the Giant. 22.00
64 Sad Sack's Army Life. 10.00
65 Casper & Nightmare 10.00
66 Stumbo the Giant. 22.00
67 Sad Sack's Army Life. 10.00
68 Casper & Nightmare 10.00
69 Stumbo the Giant. 22.00
70 Sad Sack's Army Life 10.00
71 Casper & Nightmare 10.00
72 Stumbo the Giant. 22.00
73 Little Sad Sack 10.00
74 Sad Sack's Muttsy 10.00
75 Casper & Nightmare 10.00
76 Little Sad Sack 10.00
77 Sad Sack's Muttsy 10.00
78 Stumbo the Giant. 20.00
79 Little Sad Sack 10.00
80 Sad Sack's Muttsy 10.00
81 Little Sad Sack 10.00
82 Sad Sack's Muttsy 10.00
83 Little Sad Sack 10.00
84 Sad Sack's Muttsy 10.00
85 Gabby Gob 10.00
86 G.I. Juniors 10.00
87 Sad Sack's Muttsy 10.00
88 Stumbo the Giant. 20.00
89 Sad Sack's Muttsy 8.00
90 Gabby Goo 8.00
91 G.I. Juniors 8.00
92 Sad Sack's Muttsy 8.00
93 Sadie Sack 8.00
94 Gabby Goo 8.00
95 G.I. Juniors 8.00
96 Sad Sack's Muttsy 8.00
97 Gabby Goo 8.00
98 G.I. Juniors 8.00
99 Sad Sack's Muttsy 8.00
100 Gabby Goo 8.00
101 G.I. Juniors 6.00
102 Sad Sack's Muttsy 6.00
103 Gabby Goo 6.00
104 G.I. Juniors 6.00
105 Sad Sack's Muttsy 6.00
106 Gabby Goo 6.00
107 G.I. Juniors 6.00
108 Sad Sack's Muttsy 6.00
109 Gabby Goo 6.00
110 G.I. Juniors 6.00
111 Sad Sack's Muttsy 6.00
112 G.I. Juniors 6.00
113 Sad Sack's Muttsy 6.00
114 G.I. Juniors 6.00
115 Sad Sack's Muttsy 6.00
116 G.I. Juniors 6.00
117 Sad Sack's Muttsy 6.00
118 G.I. Juniors 6.00
119 Sad Sack's Muttsy 6.00
120 G.I. Juniors 6.00
121 Sad Sack's Muttsy 6.00
122 G.I. Juniors 6.00

HATE
Fantagraphics
1 thru 15, see B&W
16 thru 29 . . . . @2.95
30 48pg. 3.95
TPB Hey, Buddy, rep. #1–#5 . . . @12.95
TPB Buddy the Dreamer, rep. #6–#10 . . . . @12.95
TPB Fun with Buddy and Lisa. . . . 12.95
TPB Buddy Go Home 16.95
TPB Buddy's Got Three Moms . . . 16.95

HAUNTED
Charlton 1971–75
1 . . . . 25.00
2 . . . . 15.00
3 thru 5 . . . . @15.00
6 thru 10 . . . . @10.00
11 thru 20 . . . . @10.00

HAUNT OF FEAR
Gladstone
1 EC Rep. H of F #17,WS#28 . . . . 3.00
2 EC Rep. H of F #5,WS #29. . . . . 2.50

HAUNT OF FEAR
Russ Cochran 1991
1 EC Rep. H of F #15 . . . . 1.50
2 thru 5 EC Rep. H of F . . . . @1.50
Second Series 1992
1 EC Rep. H of F #14,WS#13 . . . . 2.25
2 EC Rep. H of F #18,WF#14 . . . . 2.00
3 EC Rep. H of F #19,WF#18 . . . . 2.00
4 EC Rep. H of F #16,WF#15 . . . . 2.00
5 EC Rep. H of F #5,WF#22 . . . . . 2.00
6 EC Rep. H of F. 2.00

7 EC Rep. H of F. 2.00
8 thru 15 Rep. . . . . @2.00

Gemstone

16 thru 28 EC comics reprint. . . . @2.50
"Annuals"
TPB Vol. 1 rebinding of #1–#5 . . . . 8.95
TPB Vol. 2 rebinding of #6–#10 . . . 8.95
TPB Vol. 3 rebinding of #11–#15. . . 8.95
TPB Vol. 4 rebinding of #16–#20. . 12.95
TPB Vol. 5 rebinding of #21–#25. . 13.50
TPB Vol. 6 rebinding of #26–#28 . . 8.95

HAVE GUN, WILL TRAVEL

Dell Publishing Co. Aug., 1958

1 Richard Boone Ph(c) all 165.00
2 . . . . 125.00
3 . . . . 125.00
4 thru 14 . . . . @100.00

HAWKMOON, COUNT BRASS

First

1 Michael Moorcock adapt. 2.00
2 . . . . 2.00
3 . . . . 2.00
4 . . . . 2.00

HAWKMOON JEWEL IN THE SKULL

First

1 Michael Moorcock adapt. 3.00
2 . . . . 2.50
3 . . . . 2.00
4 . . . . 2.00

HAWKMOON, MAD GOD'S AMULET

First

1 Michael Moorcock adapt. 2.00
2 . . . . 2.00
3 . . . . 2.00
4 . . . . 2.00

HAWKMOON, SWORD OF THE DAWN

First

1 Michael Moorcock adapt. 2.00
2 thru 4 . . . . @2.00

HAWKMOON, THE RUNESTAFF

First

1 Michael Moorcock adapt. 2.00
2 . . . . 2.00
3 . . . . 2.00
4 . . . . 2.00

HEADMAN

Innovation

1 . . . . 2.50
2 . . . . 2.50

HEARTSTOPPER

Millennium

1 V:Demons 2.95
2 V:Demons 2.95
3 F:Hellfire. 2.95

HEAVY METAL MONSTERS

3-D-Zone

1 w/3-D glasses. 3.95

HECTOR HEATHCOTE

Gold Key March, 1964

1 . . . . 75.00

HELLINA

See Also *B&W*

HELLINA/ DOUBLE IMPACT

Lightning 1996

1-shot JCy(c). 3.00
1-shot variant (c) 3.00
1-shot nude cover 9.95
1-shot platinum edition, nude cover 9.95
1-shot spec. nude cover, signed. . 12.00

Hellina: Heart of Thorns #1
© Lightning Comics

HELLINA: HEART OF THORNS

Lightning Comics 1996

1 . . . . 3.00
1 nude cover editions 10.00
1 autographed edition 10.00
2 . . . . 3.00
2 variant cover. 3.00
2 platinum edition 5.95
2 nude cover editions 10.00

HELLINA: HELLBORN

Lightning 1997

1 . . . . 2.95
1 autographed edition 9.95

HELLINA/NIRA X: ANGEL OF DEATH

Lightning 1996

1A cover A 3.00
1B cover B 3.00
1C Platinum cover. 9.00
1D signed 9.00

HELLINA/NIRA X: CYBERANGEL

Lightning

1 autographed edition 9.95

HERBIE

American Comics Group April-May, 1964

1 . . . . 165.00
2 . . . . 100.00
3 . . . . 100.00
4 . . . . 100.00
5 A:Beatles,Dean Martin, Frank Sinatra 125.00
6 . . . . 75.00
7 . . . . 75.00
8 O:Fat Fury 85.00
9 . . . . 75.00
10 . . . . 75.00
11 thru 13 . . . . @50.00
14 A:Nemesis,Magic Man 50.00
15 thru 22 . . . . @50.00
23 Feb., 1967 . . . . 50.00

HERCULES

Charlton Comics Oct., 1967

1 . . . . 25.00
2 thru 7 . . . . @15.00
8 scarce 25.00
9 thru 13 Sept. 1969 . . . . @15.00

HERCULES: THE LEGENDARY JOURNEYS

Topps 1996

1 & 2 . . . . @3.00
3 RTs,JBt,SeM,The Shaper,pt.1 . . . 5.00
3a Xena Ph(c) 15.00
4 RTs,JBt,SeM,The Shaper,pt.2 . . . 5.00
5 RTs,JBt,SeM,The Shaper,pt.3 . . . 5.00

HERE COMES THE BIG PEOPLE

Event Comics 1997

1 ACo&JP(c) 2.95
1b JfD(c) 2.95
1c JQ&JP alternate (c) 9.95
1d JQ&JP alternate (c) signed . . . 29.95

HERO ALLIANCE

Wonder Color Comics 1987

1 . . . . 2.00

Innovation 1989–91

1 RLm,BS(c),R:HeroAlliance 6.00
2 RLm,BS(c),Victor vs.Rage 5.00
3 RLm,A:Stargrazers 4.00
4 . . . . 3.00
5 RLm(c) 2.50
6 BS(c),RLm pin-up 3.25
7 V:Magnetron 2.50
8 I:Vector 2.50
9 BS(c),V:Apostate 2.50
10 A:Sentry 2.25
11 . . . . 2.25
12 I:Bombshell 2.25
13 V:Bombshell 2.25
14 Kris Solo Story 2.25
15 JLA Parody Issue 2.25
16 V:Sepulchre 2.25
17 O:Victor,I&D:Misty 2.25
Annual #1 PS,BS,RLm 3.00
Spec.#1 Hero Alliance update. 2.50
Spec.Hero Alliance & Justice Machine: Identity Crises 2.50

COLOR PUB.

HERO ALLIANCE: THE END OF THE GOLDEN AGE

Pied Piper 1986

1 Bart Sears/Ron Lim 20.00
1a signed 25.00
1b 2nd printing 2.50
2 . . . . 12.00
3 . . . . 3.00
Graphic Novel 10.00

Innovation 1989

1 RLm. 5.00
1A 2nd printing 2.50
2 RLm. 4.00
3 RLm. 3.00

HERO ALLIANCE QUARTERLY

Innovation

1 Hero Alliance stories. 2.75
2 inc."Girl Happy" 2.75
3 inc."Child Engagement" 2.75
4 . . . . 2.75

HI-SCHOOL ROMANCE DATE BOOK

Harvey Publications Nov., 1962

1 BP 40.00
2 . . . . 25.00
3 March, 1963 . . . . 25.00

HIGH CHAPPARAL

Gold Key Aug., 1968

1 . . . . 50.00

HIGH SCHOOL CONFIDENTIAL DIARY

Charlton Comics June, 1960

1 . . . . 40.00
2 thru 11 . . . . @25.00

Becomes:

CONFIDENTIAL DIARY

12 . . . . 25.00
13 thru 17 March, 1963. . . . . . . @20.00

HIGH VOLTAGE

Blackout 1996

O 2.95

HILLBILLY COMICS

Charlton Comics Aug., 1955

1 . . . . 60.00
2 thru 4 July 1956 . . . . @35.00

HIS NAME IS ROG... ROG 2000

A Plus Comics

1 . . . . 2.00

HOBBIT, THE

Eclipse

1 . . . . 8.00
1a 2ndPrinting. 6.00
2 . . . . 7.00
2a 2ndPrinting. 5.00
3 . . . . 6.00

HOGAN'S HEROES

Dell Publishing Co. June, 1966

1 Ph(c) 90.00
2 Ph(c) 60.00
3 JD,Ph(c). 60.00
4 thru 8 Ph(c) . . . . @35.00
8 and 9 . . . . @35.00

HONEY WEST

Gold Key Sept., 1966

1 . . . . 120.00

HONEYMOONERS

Lodestone

1 . . . . 4.00
5 Mag.. . . . . 2.50

Triad [2nd Series]

1 "They Know What They Like" . . . 3.00
2 "The Life You Save" 2.50
3 X-mas special,inc.Art Carney interview. 3.50
4 "In the Pink" 3.00
5 "Bang, Zoom, To the Moon" 2.00
6 "Everyone Needs a Hero" inc. Will Eisner interview 2.00
7 . . . . 2.00
8 . . . . 2.00
9 Jack Davis(c) 4.50
10 thru 13. . . . . @2.00

HONG KONG

Blackout Comics 1996

0 A:Hari Kari 2.95
0 limited commemorative edition . . 9.95

HOT COMICS PREMIERE

Hot Comics

1 F:Thunderkill, Jacknife 2.00

HOT ROD RACERS

Charlton Comics Dec., 1964

1 . . . . 75.00
2 thru 5 . . . . @50.00
6 thru 15 July 1967 . . . . @30.00

HOT STUFF, THE LITTLE DEVIL

Harvey Publications Oct., 1967

1 . . . . 325.00
2 1st Stumbo the Giant 150.00
3 thru 5 . . . . @125.00
6 thru 10 . . . . @100.00
11 thru 20 . . . . @65.00
21 thru 40 . . . . @35.00
41 thru 60 . . . . @20.00
61 thru 100 . . . . @15.00
101 thru 105 . . . . @12.00
106 thru 112 52 pg Giants. . . . . @15.00
113 thru 172 . . . . @4.00

HOT STUFF SIZZLERS

Harvey Publications July, 1960

1 B:68 pgs. 125.00
2 thru 5 . . . . @60.00
6 thru 10 . . . . @40.00
11 thru 20 . . . . @35.00
21 thru 30 . . . . @25.00
31 thru 44 . . . . @15.00
45 E:68 pgs 10.00
46 thru 50 . . . . @10.00
51 thru 59 . . . . @7.00

HOTSHOTS

1 thru 4 . . . . @2.00

HOTSPUR

Eclipse

1 RT(i),I:Josef Quist 2.00
2 RT(i),Amulet of Kothique Stolen . 2.00
3 RT(i),Curse of the SexGoddess . 2.00

Howard Chaykin's American Flagg #3
© First

HOWARD CHAYKIN'S AMERICAN FLAGG!

First

1 thru 9 . . . . @2.00
10 thru 12. . . . . @2.00

H.P.LOVECRAFT'S CTHULHU

Millenium

1 I:Miskatonic Project,V:Mi-Go 2.50
2 Arkham, trading cards. 2.50

HUCK & YOGI JAMBOREE

Dell Publishing Co. March, 1961

1 . . . . 125.00

HUCKLEBERRY HOUND

Charlton Nov., 1970

1 . . . . 40.00
2 thru 7 . . . . @25.00
3 Jan., 1972 . . . . 30.00

HUCKLEBERRY HOUND

Dell Publishing Co. May-July, 1959

1 . . . . 125.00
2 . . . . 100.00
3 thru 7 . . . . @75.00
8 thru 10 . . . . @60.00
11 thru 17 . . . . @50.00

Gold Key

18 Chuckleberry Tales 100.00
19 Chuckleberry Tales 75.00
20 Chuckleberry Tales 50.00
21 thru 30 . . . . @30.00
31 thru 43 . . . . @20.00

COLOR PUB.

HUEY, DEWEY & LOUIE JUNIOR WOODCHUCKS
Gold Key Aug., 1966
1 . . . . 65.00
2 thru 5 . . . . @40.00
6 thru 17 . . . . @25.00
18 . . . . 20.00
19 thru 25 . . . . @22.00
26 thru 30 . . . . @20.00
31 thru 57 . . . . @20.00
58 . . . . 15.00
59 . . . . 15.00
60 thru 80 . . . . @10.00
81 1984 . . . . 10.00

HYBRIDS
Continuity
1 . . . . 2.50

HYBRIDS
Continuity
0 Deathwatch 2000 prologue 5.00
1 Deathwatch 2000 pt.4,w/card . . . 2.50
2 Deathwatch 2000 pt.13,w/card . . 2.50
3 Deathwatch 2000 w/card 2.50
4 A:Valeria. 2.50
5 O:Valeria 2.50

HYBRIDS: ORIGIN
Continuity
1 thru 5 . . . . @2.50

HYDE-25
Harris
1 New Drug. 2.95

I DREAM OF JEANNIE
Dell Publishing Co. April, 1965
1 Ph(c),B.Eden 175.00
2 Ph(c),B.Eden 150.00

I SPY
Gold Key Aug., 1966
1 Bill Cosby Ph(c) 250.00
2 Ph(c) 175.00
3 thru 4 AMc,Ph(c). . . . . . . @150.00
5 thru 6 Ph(c) Sept.1968 . . . . @150.00

I'M DICKENS – HE'S FENSTER
Dell Publishing Co. May–July, 1963
1 Ph(c) 60.00
2 Ph(c) 50.00

I-BOTS
Big Comics 1996
1 F:Lady Justice 2.25
2 thru 4 . . . . @2.25
5 StG(s),PB. 2.25
6 StG(s),PB. 2.25
7 PB,"Rebirth," pt.1, triptych (c) . . . 2.25
8 PB,"Rebirth," pt.2, triptych (c) . . . 2.25
9 PB,"Rebirth," pt.3, Original I Bots return, triptych (c). 2.25

ICICLE
Hero Graphics
1 A:Flare,Lady Arcane, V:Eraserhead 4.95

Icicle #1
© Hero Graphics

IMP
1 . . . . 2.25

IMPACT
Gemstone 1999
1 EC Comic reprint 2.50
2 thru 5 . . . . @2.50
Annual #1 rep. #1–#5 . . . . 13.50
HC 20.00

INMATES: PRISONERS OF SOCIETY
Delta Comics 1997
1 (of 4) 2.95
2 thru 4 . . . . @2.95

INNER CIRCLE
Mushroom Comics 1995
1.1 I:Point Blank 2.50
1.2 V:Deathcom. 2.50
1.3 V:Deathcom. 2.50
1.4 V:Deathcom. 2.50

INNOCENTS
Radical Comics 1995
1 I:Innocent. 2.50

INNOVATORS
Dark Moon
1 I:Innovator, LeoShan. 2.50
2 O:Mr. Void 2.50
3 I:Quill 2.50

INSANE CLOWN POSSE
Chaos Comics 1999
1 . . . . 2.95
1 premium edition 10.00
1 Jeckel Brothers premium ed. . . 10.00
3 Raze the Desertz of Glass 2.95
3a variant (c). 10.00
Spec. The Amazing Jeckel Brothers 2.95
TPB Vol. 1 . . . . 8.95

INSANE CLOWN POSSE: THE PENDULUM
Chaos! Comics 2000
1 polybagged with CD single 5.95
1a variant (c). 10.00
2 polybagged. 5.95
3 polybagged. 5.95
4 polybagged. 5.95
5 Road Rage, polybagged 5.95
TPB Vol. 1 . . . . 8.95

INTERVIEW WITH A VAMPIRE
Innovation
1 based on novel,preq.to Vampire Chronicles 3.50
2 . . . . 3.00
3 Death & Betrayal 3.00
4 . . . . 3.00
5 D:Lestat 2.50
6 Transylvania Revelation 2.50
7 Louis & Claudia in Paris 2.50
8 thru 10 . . . . @2.50
11. . . . . 2.50

INTERVIEW WITH A VAMPIRE
Innovation
1 based on novel, preq. to Vampire Chronicles 3.50
2 . . . . 3.00
3 Death & Betrayal 3.00
4 . . . . 3.00
5 D:Lestat 2.50
6 Transylvania Revelation 2.50
7 Louis & Claudia in Paris 2.50

INTIMATE
Charlton Comics Dec., 1957
1 thru 3 . . . . @25.00
Becomes:

TEEN-AGE LOVE
4 . . . . 20.00
5 thru 9 . . . . @15.00
10 thru 35 . . . . @10.00
36 thru 96 . . . . @10.00

INTRUDER
TSR 1990–91
1 thru 4 . . . . @2.95
5 thru 8 The Next Dimension . . . @2.95

INVADERS FROM HOME
Piranha Press 1990
1 thru 6 . . . . @2.50

INVADERS, THE
Gold Key Oct., 1967
1 Ph(c),DSp. 125.00
2 Ph(c),DSp. 75.00
3 Ph(c),DSp. 75.00
4 Ph(c),DSp. 75.00

INVINCIBLE FOUR OF KUNG FU & NINJA
Victory
1 . . . . 2.75
2 and 3 . . . . @2.50
4 . . . . 2.00
5 thru 11 . . . . @2.00

IO
Invictus Studios
1 I:IO 2.25
2 . . . . . 2.25
3 V:Major Damage 2.25

IRON HORSE
Dell Publishing Co. March, 1967
1 . . . . . 25.00
2 . . . . . 25.00

Ironjaw #3
© Atlas

IRONJAW
Atlas Jan.–July , 1975
1 NA(c),MSy 10.00
2 NA(c) 8.00
3 . . . . . 8.00
4 O:IronJaw 8.00

IRON MARSHAL
Jademan
1 . . . . . 2.00
2 . . . . . 2.00
3 . . . . . 2.00
4 . . . . . 2.00
5 . . . . . 2.00
6 V:Bloody Duke 2.00
7 . . . . . 2.00
8 . . . . . 2.00
9 The Unicorn Sword 2.00
10 The Great Thor 2.00
11 A:Exterminator 2.00
12 Bloddy Duke vs. Exterminator . . 2.00
13 Secret of Unicorn Supreme 2.00
14 A:The Great Thor 2.00
15 A:The Great Thor 2.00
16 V:Tienway Champ 2.00
17 thru 20 . . . . . @2.00
21 Bloody Duke wounded 2.00
22 A:Great Thor 2.00
23 . . . . . 2.00
24 . . . . . 2.00
25 . . . . . 2.00
26 Iron Marshal Betrayed 2.00
27 thru 30 . . . . . @2.00

IRREGULARS, THE: BATTLETECH Miniseries
Blackthorne
1 . . . . . 2.00
2 . . . . . 2.00
3 B&W 2.00

IRUKASHI
1 . . . . . 2.00

ISAAC ASIMOV'S I-BOTS
Tekno-Comix 1995
1 I:I-Bots 2.00
2 O:I-Bots 2.00
3 V:Black OP 2.25

IT! TERROR FROM BEYOND SPACE
Millennium
1 . . . . . 2.50
2 . . . . . 2.50

IT'S ABOUT TIME
Gold Key Jan., 1967
1 Ph(c) 40.00

ITCHY & SCRATCHY
Bongo Comics
1 DaC(s), ... 2.25
2 DaC(s), ... 2.25

IVANHOE
Dell Publishing Co. July-Sept., 1963
1 . . . . . 30.00

JACK
Med Systems Company
1 Anubis in the 90's 2.95
2 Modern Society 2.95

JACK HUNTER
Blackthorne
1 . . . . . 2.00
2 . . . . . 2.00
3 . . . . . 2.00

JACKIE CHAN'S SPARTAN X
Topps 1997
1 "The Armor of Heaven," pt.1 . . . . 2.95
2 "The Armor of Heaven," pt.2 . . . . 2.95
3 (of 6) 2.95

JADEMAN COLLECTION
1 . . . . . 4.50
2 . . . . . 3.00
3 . . . . . 2.50
4 . . . . . 2.50
5 . . . . . 2.50

JADEMAN KUNG FU SPECIAL
1 I:Oriental Heroes, Blood Sword, Drunken Fist 5.00

JAGUAR GOD
Verotika 1995
1 Frazetta, I:Jaquar God 2.95
2 V:Yi-Cha 2.95
3 V:Yi-Cha 2.95
4 V:Yi-Cha 2.95
5 AOI 2.95
6 LSh,AOI 2.95
7 LSh,AOI 2.95
8 AOI 2.95
Spec.#1 Return to X'ibala,RCo 4.95

JAKE TRASH
Aircel
1 thru 3 . . . . . @2.00

JAMES BOND 007
Eclipse
1 MGr,PerfectBound 5.50
2 MGr 5.00
3 MGr,end series 5.00
GN Licence to Kill, MGr I/o 8.00

JAMES BOND: GOLDENEYE
Topps 1995
1 Movie adaptation 2.95
2 thru 3 Movie adaptation . . . . . @2.95

JAM SPECIAL
Comico
1 . . . . . 2.50

JASON GOES TO HELL
Topps
1 Movie adapt.,w/3 cards 3.25
2 Movie adapt.,w/3 cards 3.25
3 Movie adapt.,w/3 cards 3.25

JASON VS. LEATHERFACE
Topps 1995
1 Jason Meets Leatherface 2.95
2 SBi(c) Leatherface's family 2.95
3 SBi(c),conclusion 2.95

JAVERTZ
Firstlight
1 New Series 2.95
2 thru 5 Pieces of an Icon . . . . . @2.95

JET DREAM
Gold Key June, 1968
1 . . . . . 35.00

JETSONS, THE
Gold Key Jan., 1963
1 . . . . . 250.00
2 . . . . . 125.00
3 thru 10 . . . . . @100.00
11 thru 20 . . . . . @75.00
21 thru 36 Oct. 1970 . . . . . @50.00

JETSONS, THE
Charlton Comics Nov., 1970
1 from Hanna-Barbera TV show. . 75.00
2 . . . . . 40.00
3 thru 10 . . . . . @30.00
11 thru 20 Dec. 1973 . . . . . @25.00

JETSONS, THE
Harvey Comics 1991–92
1 thru 5 . . . . . @2.00

JETSONS, THE
Archie 1995
1 thru 17 . . . . @2.00

JEZEBEL JADE
Comico
1 AKu,A:Race Bannon. 2.00
2 AKu 2.00
3 AKu 2.00

JIGSAW
Harvey Publications Sept., 1966
1 . . . . 6.00
2 . . . . 3.50

JIMBO
Bongo Comics
1 R:Jimbo 2.95
2 thru 4 . . . . @2.95

JIMMY CORRIGAN
Fantagraphics
1 Chris Ware 3.95

J. N. WILLIAMSON'S MASQUES
Innovation
1 TV,From horror anthology 4.95
2 Olivia(c) inc.Better Than One . . . 4.95

JOHN BOLTON, HALLS OF HORROR
Eclipse
1 JBo 2.00
2 JBo 2.00

JOHN F. KENNEDY LIFE STORY (WITH 2 REPRINTS)
Dell Publishing Co. Aug.-Oct., 1964
1 . . . . 50.00
2 . . . . 35.00
3 . . . . 35.00

JOHN JAKES MULLKON EMPIRE
Tekno Comix 1995
1 I:Mulkons 2.25
2 O:Mulkons 2.00
3 D:Company Man 2.00
4 Disposal Problems 2.00
5 F:Granny 2.00
6 Where's Karma. 2.25

JOHN LAW
Eclipse 1983
1 WE. 2.00

JOHNNY GAMBIT
1 . . . . 2.00

JOHNNY JASON TEEN REPORTER
Dell Publishing Co. 1962
1 . . . . 35.00
2 . . . . 30.00

JOHNNY NEMO
Eclipse 1985–86
1 I:Johnny Nemo 2.00
2 . . . . 2.00
3 F:Sindy Shade 2.50

JOHN STEELE SECRET AGENT
Gold Key Dec., 1964
1 . . . . 100.00

JONNY QUEST
Gold Key Dec., 1964
1 TV show. 400.00

JONNY QUEST
Comico June, 1986
1 DW,SR,A:Dr.Zin 4.50
2 WP/JSon,O:RaceBannon 3.50
3 DSt(c). 3.00
4 TY/AW,DSt(i) 2.50
5 DSt(c)A:JezebelJade 2.50
6 AKu 2.00
7 . . . . 2.00
8 KSy 2.00
9 MA 2.00
10 King Richard III 2.00
11 JSon,BSz(c). 2.00
12 DSp. 2.00
12 DSp. 2.00
13 CI 2.00
14 . . . . 2.00
15 thru 31 . . . . @2.00
Spec.#1 . . . . 2.00
Spec.#2 . . . . 2.00

JONNY QUEST CLASSICS
Comico
1 DW. 2.00
2 DW,O:Hadji 2.00
3 DW. 2.00

JON SABLE
First
1 MGr,A:President. 4.50
2 MGr,Alcohol Issue 3.50
3 MGr,O:Jon Sable 3.00
4 MGr,O:Jon Sable 3.00
5 MGr,O:Jon Sable 3.00
6 MGr,O:Jon Sable 3.00
7 MGr,The Target 2.50
8 MGr,Nuclear Energy. 2.50
9 MGr,Nuclear Energy. 2.50
10 MGr,Tripitych 2.50
11 MGr,I:Maggie 2.50
12 MGr,Vietnam 2.50
13 MGr,Vietnam 2.50
14 MGr,East Germany 2.50
15 MGr,Nicaragua 2.50
16 MGr,A:Maggie 2.50
17 MGr,1984 Olympics 2.50
18 MGr,1984 Olympics 2.50
19 MGr,,The Widow 2.50
20 MGr,The Rookie 2.50
21 MGr,Africa 2.25
22 MGr,V:Sparrow 2.25
23 MGr,V:Sparrow 2.25
24 MGr,V:Sparrow 2.25
25 MGr,Shatter. 3.00
26 MGr,Shatter. 3.00
27 MGr,Shatter. 3.00
28 MGr,Shatter. 3.00
29 MGr,Shatter. 3.00
30 MGr,Shatter. 2.25

Jon Sable #30
© First

31 MGr,Nicaragua 2.00
32 MGr,Nicaragua 2.00
33 MGr,SA,Leprechauns. 2.25
34 MGr,Indians. 2.00
35 MGr,Indians. 2.00
36 MGr,Africa 2.00
37 MGr,Africa 2.00
38 MGr,Africa 2.00
39 MGr,Africa 2.00
40 MGr,1st Case 2.00
41 MGr,1st Case 2.00
42 MGr,V:Sparrow 2.00
43 MGr,V:Sparrow 2.00
44 Hard Way 2.00
45 Hard Way II 2.00
46 MM,The Tower pt.1 . . . . 2.00
47 MM,The Tower pt.2 . . . . 2.00
48 MM,Prince Charles 2.00
49 MM,Prince Charles 2.00
50 A:Maggie the Cat. 2.00
51 Jon Sable,babysitter pt.1 . . . . . 2.00
52 Jon Sable,babysitter pt.2 . . . . . 2.00
53 MGr. 2.00
54 Jacklight pt.1 . . . . 2.00
55 Jacklight pt.2 . . . . 2.00
56 Jacklight pt.3 . . . . 2.00

JOSIE
Archie Publications Feb., 1963
1 . . . . 175.00
2 . . . . 100.00
3 . . . . 50.00
4 . . . . 40.00
5 . . . . 50.00
6 thru 10 . . . . @30.00
11 thru 20 . . . . @25.00
21 thru 30 . . . . @15.00
31 thru 40 . . . . @10.00
41 thru 54 . . . . @7.00
55 thru 74 . . . . @5.00
75 thru 105 . . . . @3.00
106 Oct., 1962 . . . . 3.00

JUDGE COLT
Gold Key Oct., 1969
1 . . . . 20.00
2 . . . . 10.00
3 . . . . 10.00
4 Sept., 1980 . . . . 10.00

Judge Dredd #15
© Eagle

JUDGE DREDD
Eagle 1983

1 BB,I:Judge Death(in USA) 15.00
2 BB(c&a),The Oxygen Board . . . 12.00
3 BB(c),Judge Dredd Lives 10.00
4 BB(c),V:Perps. 10.00
5 BB(c),V:Perps. 8.00
6 BB(c),V:Perps. 8.00
7 BB(c),V:Perps. 8.00
8 BB(c),V:Perps. 8.00
9 BB(c),V:Perps. 8.00
10 BB(c),V:Perps 8.00
11 BB(c). 5.00
12 BB(c). 5.00
13 BB(c), The Day the Law Died, pt.5 . . . . 5.00
14 BB(c),Dredd vs. Dredd. 5.00
15 BB(c). 5.00
16 BB(c). 5.00
17 BB(c). 5.00
18 BB(c). 5.00
19 BB(c). 5.00
20 BB(c). 5.00
21 BB(c). 5.00
22 BB(c),V:Perps 4.00
23 BB(c),V:Perps 4.00
24 BB(c),V:Perps 4.00
25 BB(c),V:Perps 4.00
26 BB(c),V:Perps 4.00
27 BB(c),V:Perps 4.00
28 A:Judge Anderson,V:Megaman . 5.00
29 A:Monty, the guinea pig 4.00
30 V:Perps 4.00
31 Destiny's Angel, Pt. 1. . . . . 4.00
32 Destiny's Angel, Pt. 2. . . . . 4.00
33 V:League of Fatties 4.00
34 V:Executioner 4.00

JUDGE DREDD
Quality

1 Cry of the Werewolf Pt.1. . . . . . . 7.00
2 Cry of the Werewolf Pt.2. . . . . . . 5.00
3 Anti-smoking 4.00
4 Wreckers 4.00
5 Highwayman 4.00
6 . . . . 3.00
7 . . . . 3.00
8 . . . . 3.00
9 . . . . 3.00
10 . . . . 3.00
11. . . . . 3.00
12 Starborn Thing, Pt.1. . . . . 3.00
13 Starborn Thing, Pt.2. . . . . 3.00
14 BB, V:50 foot woman 3.00
15 City of the Damned Pt.1. . . . . . . 3.00
16 City of the Damned Pt.2. . . . . . . 3.00
17 City of the Damned conc.. . . . . . 3.00
18 V:Mean Machine Angel 3.00
19 Dredd Angel 3.00
20 V:Perps 3.00
21 V:Perps 3.00
22/23 Booby Trap . . . . @3.00
24 Junk food fiasco 3.00
25/26 V:Perps. . . . . @3.00
27 V:Perps 3.00
28 Dredd Syndrome 3.00
29 V:Perps 3.00
30 V:Perps 3.00
31 Hunt Pudge Dempsey's killer . . . 3.00
32 V:Mutated Sewer Alligator 3.00
33 V:Perps 3.00
34 V:Executioner 3.00
35 V:Shojan 3.00
36 V:Shojan 3.00
37 V:Perps 3.00
38 V:Perps 3.00
39 V:Perps 3.00
40 V:Perps 3.00
41 V:Perps 3.00
42 V:Perps 3.00
43 V:Perps 3.00
44 V:Perps 3.00
45 V:DNA Man 2.50
46 Genie lamp sty 2.50
47 V:Perps 2.50
48 Murder in Mega-City One. 2.50
49 V:Perps 2.50
50 V:Perps 2.50
51 V:Perps 2.50
52 V:Perps 2.50
53 V:Perps 2.50
54 V:Perps 2.50
55 V:Perps 2.50
56 inc.JudgeDredd Postcards 2.50
57 V:Perps 2.50
58 V:370lb Maniac 2.50
59 V:Perps 2.50
60 Social Misfit. 2.50
61 V:Perps 2.50
Becomes:

JUDGE DREDD CLASSICS

62 . . . . 2.50
63 Mutants from the Radlands 2.50
64 . . . . 2.50
65 . . . . 2.50
66 Wit and wisdom of Dredd. 2.50
67 V:Otto Sump 2.50
68 V:Otto Sump 2.50
69 . . . . 2.50
70 Dinosaurs in Mega City 1. . . . . . 2.50
71 . . . . 2.50
72 Pirates o/t Black Atlantic 2.50
73 . . . . 2.50
74 . . . . 2.50
75 . . . . 2.50
76 Diary of a Mad Citizen 3.00
TPB:Democracy Now 10.95
TPB:Rapture. 12.95
Judge Dredd Special #1 . . . . 2.50
GN Bad Science. 7.95
GN Hall of Justice. 7.95
GN Metal Fatigue 7.95

JUDGE DREDD: AMERICA
Fleetway

1 I:America 3.50

JUDGE DREDD: JUDGE CHILD QUEST
Eagle

1 thru 3 . . . . @3.00
4 BB(c) 3.00
5 . . . . 3.00

JUDGE DREDD'S CRIME FILE
Eagle 1984

1 Ron Smith, "The Perp Runners" . 2.50
2 thru 6 . . . . @2.50

Quality (Prestige format)

1 A:Rogue Trooper 6.50
2 IG,V:Fatties, Energy Vampires & Super Fleas 5.95
3 Battles foes from dead A:Judge Anderson 5.95

JUDGE DREDD'S EARLY CASES
Eagle

1 Robot Wars, Pt.1 . . . . 4.00
2 Robot Wars, Pt.2 . . . . 3.00
3 V:Perps 3.00
4 IG, Judge Giant 3.00
5 V:Perps 3.00
6 V:Judge killing car Elvis 3.00

JUDGE DREDD'S HARDCASE PAPERS
Fleetway/Quality

1 V:The Tarantula 7.50
2 Junkies & Psychos 6.50
3 Crime Call Vid. Show 6.50
4 "Real Coffee",A:Johnny Alpha. . . 6.50

JUDGE DREDD: THE MEGAZINE
Fleetway/Quality 1991

1 Midnite's Children Pt.1 A:Chopper, Young Death 5.25
2 Midnite's Children Pt.2 . . . . 4.95
3 . . . . 4.95
23 thru 34. . . . . @3.95
35 thru 43. . . . . @5.25
44 thru 45. . . . . @6.95

Egmont Fleetway Limited

46 thru 71. . . . . @6.95

JUDGE PARKER
Argo Feb., 1956

1 . . . . 25.00
2 . . . . 15.00

JUDGMENT DAY
Lightning Comics

1 B:JZy(s),KIK,V:Razorr,Rift, Nightmare, red prism(c) 5.00
1a Gold Prism(c) 5.00
1b Purple Prism(c). 7.00
1c Misprint,Red Prism(c), Bloodfire Credits inside 8.00
1d Misprint,Gold Prism(c), Bloodfire Credits inside 8.00
1e Misprint,Green Prism(c), Bloodfire Credits inside. 8.00
1f B&W promo ed. Gold ink 5.00
1g B&W promo ed. platinum ed. . . 7.00
2 TLw,I:War Party,BU:Perg, w/Perg card 4.00
3 ErP,O:X-Treme 3.25

COLOR PUB.

4 ErP,In Hell . . . 3.25
5 TLw,In Hell . . . 3.25
6 TLw,I:Red Front,O:Salurio . . . 3.25
7 O:Safeguard . . . 3.25
8 . . . 2.95
9 . . . 2.95
10 . . . 2.95

JUDGMENT DAY
Maximum Press 1997

Alpha AMo(s) . . . 2.50
Alpha variant cover . . . 2.50
Omega AMo(s) . . . 2.50
Omega variant cover . . . 2.50
Final Judgment AMo(s) . . . 2.50
Final Judgment variant cover . . . 2.50

JUDOMASTER
Charlton Comics

(Special War Series #4) I:
Judomaster . . . 15.00
89 FMc,War stories begin . . . 7.00
89 (90) FMc,A:Thunderbolt . . . 6.00
91 FMc,DG,A:Sarge Steel . . . 6.00
92 FMc,DG,A:Sarge Steel . . . 6.00
93 FMc,DG,I:Tiger . . . 6.00
94 FMc,DG,A:Sarge Steel . . . 6.00
95 FMc,DG,A:Sarge Steel . . . 5.00
96 FMc,DG,A:Sarge Steel . . . 5.00
97 FMc,A:Sarge Steel . . . 4.00
98 FMc,A:Sarge Steel . . . 4.00

JUGHEAD
Archie Publications
Dec., 1965–June, 1987

127 thru 130 . . . @25.00
131 thru 150 . . . @20.00
151 thru 160 . . . @12.00
161 thru 200 . . . @10.00
201 thru 250 . . . @7.00
251 thru 300 . . . @5.00
301 thru 352 . . . @3.00

Jughead Vol. 2, #46
© Archie Publications

JUGHEAD
Archie Publications
[2nd Series] Aug., 1987

1 thru 45 . . . @3.00
Becomes:

ARCHIE'S PAL JUGHEAD
June, 1993

46 thru 50 . . . @2.00
51 thru 70 . . . @2.00
71 thru 99 . . . @2.00
100 A Storm Over Uniforms, x-over
(Betty #57, Archie #467) . . . 2.00
101 thru 122 . . . @2.00
123 thru 125 . . . @1.79
126 thru 133 . . . @1.99

JUGHEAD AS CAPTAIN HERO
Archie Publications Oct., 1966

1 . . . 50.00
2 . . . 40.00
3 thru 7 . . . @25.00

JUGHEAD'S FANTASY
Archie Publications Aug., 1960

1 . . . 175.00
2 . . . 125.00
3 . . . 100.00

JUGHEAD'S JOKES
Archie Publications Aug., 1967

1 . . . 75.00
2 . . . 40.00
3 thru 5 . . . @25.00
6 thru 10 . . . @20.00
11 thru 30 . . . @15.00
31 thru 77 . . . @7.00
78 Sept., 1982 . . . 7.00

JUGHEAD WITH ARCHIE DIGEST
Archie Publications March, 1974

1 . . . 50.00
2 . . . 30.00
3 thru 10 . . . @15.00
11 thru 91 . . . @7.00
92 thru 129 . . . @5.00
130 thru 138 . . . @4.00
139 thru 144 . . . @4.00
145 thru 155 . . . @3.00
156 thru 162 . . . @2.19

JUNGLE ADVENTURES
Skywald March–June 1971

1 F:Zangar,Jo-Jo,Blue Gorilla . . . 20.00
2 F:Sheena, Jo-Jo,Zangar . . . 15.00
3 F:Zangar,Jo-Jo,White Princess . 10.00

JUNGLE BOOK, THE
NBM 1997

TPB by P. Craig Russell,
Kipling adapt . . . 16.95

JUNGLE COMICS
Blackthorne

1 DSt(c) . . . 2.00
2 . . . 2.00
3 . . . 2.00

JUNGLE TALES OF TARZAN
Charlton Comics Dec., 1964

1 . . . 50.00
2 . . . 35.00
3 . . . 35.00
4 July, 1965 . . . 35.00

JUNGLE WAR STORIES
Dell Publishing Co.
July-Sept., 1962

1 P(c) all . . . 25.00
2 . . . 20.00
3 . . . 20.00
4 . . . 20.00
5 . . . 20.00
6 . . . 20.00
7 . . . 20.00
8 . . . 20.00
9 . . . 20.00
10 . . . 20.00
11 . . . 20.00
Becomes:

GUERRILLA WAR

12 thru 14 . . . @25.00

JUNIOR WOODCHUCKS
Walt Disney

1 CB,"Bubbleweight Champ" . . . 2.00
2 CB,"Swamp of no Return" . . . 2.00
3 "Rescue Run-Around" . . . 2.00
4 "Cave Caper" . . . 2.00

JURASSIC PARK
Topps

1 Movie Adapt.,w/card . . . 5.00
1a Newsstand Ed. . . . 4.00
2 Movie Adapt.,w/card . . . 3.25
2a Newsstand Ed. . . . 2.75
3 Movie Adapt.,w/card . . . 3.25
3a Newsstand Ed. . . . 2.75
4 Movie Adapt.,w/card . . . 3.25
4a Newsstand Ed. . . . 2.75
Ann.#1 Death Lizards . . . 3.95

JURASSIC PARK: ADVENTURES
Topps

1 thru 10 reprints titles . . . @2.00

JURASSIC PARK: RAPTOR
Topps

1 SE w/Zorro #0 ashcan & cards . . 3.25
2 w/3 cards . . . 2.95

JURASSIC PARK: RAPTORS ATTACK
Topps

1 SEt(s), . . . 2.75
2 SEt(s), . . . 2.75
3 SEt(s), . . . 2.75
4 SEt(s), . . . 2.75

JURASSIC PARK: RAPTOR HIJACK
Topps

1 SEt(s), . . . 2.50
2 SEt(s), . . . 2.50
3 SEt(s), . . . 2.50
4 SEt(s), . . . 2.50

[JURASSIC PARK:] THE LOST WORLD
Topps 1997

1 (of 4) movie adapt . . . 2.95
2 thru 4 . . . @2.95

JUSTICE MACHINE
Noble Comics 1981–85
1 JBy(c) Mag size,B&W. 30.00
2 MGu,Mag size,B&W 16.00
3 MGu,Mag size,B&W 10.00
4 MGu,Bluecobalt 8.00
5 MGu. 7.00
Texas Comics
Ann.#1:BWG,I:Elementals,
A: Thunder Agents 5.00

JUSTICE MACHINE
[Featuring the Elementals]
Comico 1986
1 thru 4 . . . . @2.50

JUSTICE MACHINE
Comico 1987–89
1 MGu. 2.50
2 MGu. 2.00
3 thru 14 MGu . . . . @2.00
15 thru 27 MGu . . . . @2.00
28 MGu 2.00
29 MGu,IW. 2.00
Ann.#1 . . . . 2.50
SummerSpectacular 1 . . . . 2.75
MINI SERIES 1990
1 thru 4 F:Elementals. . . . . @2.00
Innovation 1990
1 . . . . 2.00
2 thru 4 The Ragnarok Portfilio. . @2.00
5 thru 7 Demon trilogy . . . . @2.00

JUSTICE MACHINE: CHIMERA CONSPIRACY
Millennium
1 AH,R&N:Justice Machine,
wraparound cover. 2.50

JUST MARRIED
Charlton Comics Jan., 1958
1 . . . . 60.00
2 . . . . 35.00
3 thru 10 . . . . @25.00
11 thru 30 . . . . @15.00
31 thru 113 . . . . @10.00
114 Dec., 1976. . . . . 8.00

KABOOM
Awesome Entertainment 1997
1 JLb,JMs,. 5.00
1a variant (c)s 6.00
2 JLb,JMs,. 3.00
3 JLb,JMs,. 4.00
4 JLb,JMs,Kaboom the
Barbarian,pt.1 (of 3) 2.50
5 JLb,JMs,Barbarian,pt.2 . . . . 2.50
6 JLb,JMs,Barbarian,pt.3 . . . . 2.50
VOL II
1 (of 3) 2.50
2 JLe,JLb,F:Kyra 2.50
3 JLe,JLb, conclusion 2.50
Collected #1 & #2. . . . . 5.95

KABUKI
Caliber Press
1 Color Gallery,32 paintings. 3.00
1-shot Color Special, inc.
pin-up gallery 3.00
1-shot Fear the Reaper (1994). . . . 7.00

KABUKI: SKIN DEEP
Caliber
1 DMk 2.95
2 DMk(c) 2.95
2 AxR(c) 2.95
3 Origin issue 2.95
4 . . . . 2.95

KATO OF THE GREEN HORNET
Now
1 BA,1st Kato solo story 2.50
2 BA,Kato in China contd. 2.50
3 Kato in China contd 2.50
4 Final Issue 2.50

Kato II, #1
© Now

KATO II
Now
1 VM,JSh,A:Karthage 2.50
2 VM,JSh,V:Karthage 2.50
3 VM,JSh,V:Karthage 2.50

KATY KEENE FASHION BOOK MAGAZINE
Archie Publications
1955
1 . . . . 375.00
2 . . . . 200.00
3 thru 10 not published
11 thru 18 . . . . @150.00
19 . . . . 125.00
20 . . . . 125.00
21 . . . . 125.00
22 . . . . 125.00
23 Winter 1958-59 . . . . 125.00

KATY KEENE PINUP PARADE
Archie Publications
1955
1 . . . . 375.00
2 . . . . 200.00
3 . . . . 175.00
4 . . . . 175.00
5 . . . . 175.00
6 . . . . 150.00
7 . . . . 150.00
8 . . . . 150.00
9 . . . . 150.00
10 . . . . 150.00
11 Story on comics 200.00
12 . . . . 150.00
13 . . . . 150.00
14 . . . . 150.00
15 Sept., 1961 . . . . 300.00

KELLY GREEN
Eclipse
1 SDr,O:Kelly Green 2.50
2 SDr,"One,Two,Three" 2.00
3 SDr,"Million Dollar Hit" 2.00
4 SDr,Rare 4.00

KELVIN MACE
Vortex
1 . . . . 6.50
1a 2nd printing 2.00
2 . . . . 4.00

KID DEATH & FLUFFY
Event Comics 1997
Spec.#1 Halloween Spec. John
Cebollero(c) 2.95
Spec.#1a Halloween Spec. JQ(c) . . 2.95

KILLER TALES
Eclipse 1985
1 Tim Truman 3.00

KING COMICS PRESENTS
King Comics
1 I:Rick Dees, Angel Lopez 2.00

KING LEONARDO AND HIS SHORT SUBJECTS
Dell Publishing Co.
Nov.–Jan., 1961-62
1 . . . . 150.00
2 . . . . 125.00
3 . . . . 125.00
4 . . . . 125.00

KING LOUIE & MOWGLI
Gold Key May, 1968
1 . . . . 30.00

KING OF DIAMONDS
Dell Publishing Co.
July–Sept., 1962
1 Ph(c) 40.00

KIT KARTER
Dell Publishing Co.
May-July, 1962
1 . . . . 25.00

KNIGHTS OF THE ROUND TABLE
Dell Publishing Co.
Nov.–Jan., 1963-4
1 P(c) 35.00

KNUCKLES
Archie Comics
4 Lost Paradise 2.00
5 . . . . 2.00
6 "Lost Paradise". 2.00

7 "Dark Vengeance" 2.00
8 "The Gauntlet" 2.00
9 x-over Sonic #56 . . . . 2.00
10 "The Forgotten Tribe" 2.00
11 Sonic x-over 2.00
12 Sonic x-over 2.00
13 The Chaotix 2.00
14 "A Tenuous Grip on Reality" 2.00
15 "The Chaotix Caper" concl. 2.00
16 "Reunions" 2.00
17 "The Guardian Who Failed" 2.00
18 "Debt of Honor" 2.00
19 "Whatever Happened to Queen Alicia" 2.00
20 "Once Upon A Time In Mobotropolis" 2.00
21 "The Many Facets of the Truth" . 2.00
22 JV,"You Say You Want A Revolution" 2.00
23 JV,HMo, ... 2.00
24 JV,HMo "Primary Night" 2.00
25 "Childhood's End" 2.00
26 "The First Date" 2.00
27 "Who Wrote The Book Of Love, Anyway?" 2.00
28 The First Date, pt.3 . . . . 2.00
29 "My Special Friend" 2.00
30 "King of the Hill," pt.1 . . . . 2.00
31 "Thrill of the Hunt" 2.00
32 "King of the Hill,pt.2" 1.79
33 "Master Emerald" 1.79

KNUCKLES: THE DARK LEGION

Archie Comics 1997

1 . . . . 2.00
2 . . . . 2.00
3 (of 3) 2.00

KOL MANIQUE RENAISSANCE

1 . . . . 2.00
2 . . . . 2.00

KOMAH

Anubis Press

1 Urban Decay Title 2.75

KOMBAT

Random Comics

1 (of 2) by Marcu Marshall & Pablo Villalobos 2.95
2 concl 2.95

KONA

Dell Publishing Co. Feb.–April, 1962

1 P(c) all,SG 70.00
2 SG 30.00
3 SG 30.00
4 SG,B:Anak 30.00
5 SG 30.00
6 SG 30.00
7 SG 30.00
8 SG 30.00
9 SG 30.00
10 SG 30.00
11 SG 20.00
12 SG 20.00
13 SG 20.00
14 SG 20.00
15 SG 20.00
16 SG 20.00
17 SG 20.00
18 SG 20.00
19 SG 20.00
20 SG 20.00
21 SG 20.00

KONGA

Charlton Comics 1960–65

1 SD,DG(c), movie adapt. 250.00
2 DG(c) 125.00
3 SD 100.00
4 SD 100.00
5 SD 100.00
6 thru 15 SD . . . . @70.00
16 thru 23 . . . . @50.00

KONGA'S REVENGE

Charlton Comics

2 Summer, 1962 . . . . 30.00
3 SD,Fall, 1964 . . . . 40.00
1 Dec., 1968 . . . . 17.00

KOOKIE

Dell Publishing Co. Feb.-April, 1962

1 . . . . 75.00
2 . . . . 60.00

Korak, Son of Tarzan #24
© Gold Key

KORAK, SON OF TARZAN

Gold Key Jan., 1964

1 . . . . 75.00
2 thru 11 . . . . @35.00
12 thru 21 . . . . @25.00
22 thru 30 . . . . @15.00
31 thru 40 . . . . @10.00
41 thru 44 . . . . @7.00
45 Jan., 1972 . . . . 7.00
Continued by DC

KRUSTY COMICS

Bongo Comics

1 Rise and Fall of Krustyland 2.25
2 Rise and Fall of Krustyland 2.25
3 Rise and Fall of Krustyland 2.25

KULL IN 3-D

Blackthorne

1 . . . . 2.50
2 . . . . 2.50
3 . . . . 2.50

KUNG FU & NINJA

1 . . . . 2.00
2 . . . . 2.00
3 . . . . 2.00
4 . . . . 2.00

LAD: A DOG

Dell Publishing Co. 1961

1 . . . . 35.00
2 . . . . 30.00

LADY ARCANE

Hero Graphics

1 A: Flare,BU:O:Giant 4.95
2 thru 3 . . . . @2.95

LADY DEATH

Chaos! Comics

1 BnP, A:Evil Ernie 30.00
1a signed gold foil 40.00
2 BnP 30.00
3 BnP 16.00
HC Foil Stamped Rep. #1-#3 . . . . 24.95
TPB Rep. #1-#3 . . . . 6.95
TPB The Reckoning 12.95
TPB The Reckoning, revised, BnP,Shu 12.95
Specials & 1-shots
1 Swimsuit Edition 12.00
1a Velvet Edition 25.00
1 reprint with 8-page pin-up gallery 2.95
1 Lady Death in Lingerie, various artists 5.00
1 Lady Death & the Women of Chaos! Gallery, pin-ups (1996) . 2.25
1-shot Dragon Wars (1998) 2.95
1-shotA Dragon Wars, Premium Ed, Sketchbook cover 15.00
1-shot Retribution (1998) 2.95
1-shotA Retribution (1998) variant cover 2.95
1-shotB Retribution, premium ed. . 10.00

LADY DEATH

Chaos! Comics 1998

½ signed, limited 25.00
1 . . . . 3.00
1a signed, limited 18.00
2 R:Lady Demon 3.00
3 V:Levithia 3.00
4 V:Pagan 3.00
5 The Harrowing, pt.1 . . . . 3.00
6 V:Uriel 3.00
7 V:Moloch 3.00
8 time to sieze Hell 3.00
9 world scythe of the covenant . . . 3.00
10 Goddess War,pt.2 x-over 3.00
11 V:Cremator 3.00
12 Unholy Nights 3.00
13 MD2,DQ,Inferno, pt.1. . . . . 3.00
13a signed 19.95
14 MD2,DQ,Inferno, pt.2. . . . . 2.95
15 MD2,DQ,Inferno, pt.3. . . . . 2.95
15a variant cover 6.00
16 MD2,DQ,Inferno, pt.4. . . . . 2.95
Swimsuit Spec.#1, signed 20.00

LADY DEATH

Chaos! Comics

1/2 Tribute Book 13.95
0 ashcan, yellow 10.00
0 ashcan, yellow, signed 20.00
0 ashcan, blue. 25.00
1 (of 12) by Steve Hughes. 2.95
1a signed 15.00
1b deluxe Steve Hughes (c). 15.95

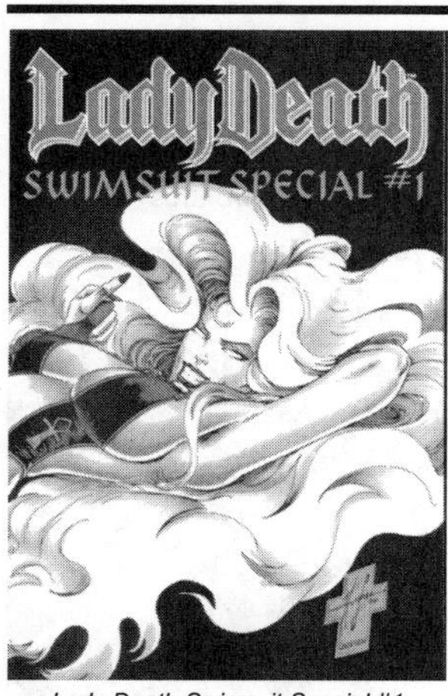

Lady Death Swimsuit Special #1
© Chaos! Comics

LADY DEATH: BETWEEN HEAVEN & HELL
Chaos! Comics
1 V:Purgatori 6.00
1a Limited Edition 5,000c. 25.00
1b premium velvet cover, signed . 30.00
2 Lives As Hope 4.00
3 V:Purgatori 4.00
4 final issue 4.00
TPB 12.95

LADY DEATH: DARK MILLENNIUM
Chaos! Comics 2000
1 (of 3) 2.95
1a premium edition 9.99
1a signed, limited 15.00
2 . . . . 2.95
3 . . . . 2.95
Preview Book B&W 5.00

LADY DEATH: THE CRUCIBLE
Chaos! Comics 1996
1 (of 6) BnP,SHu, ... 3.50
1 leather limited edition 15.00
2 BnP,SHu, ... 3.50
3 BnP,SHu, ... 3.50
4 BnP,SHu, ... 3.50
5 BnP,SHu, ... 3.50
6 BnP,SHu,V:Genocide,concl. 2.95
GN Collected ed. Vol. 1 . . . . 5.95
GN Collected ed. Vol. 2 . . . . 5.95
TPB rep.#1–#6 . . . . 19.95

LADY DEATH: DEATH BECOMES HER
Chaos! Comics 1997
0 follows the *Crucible*, leads to *Wicked Ways* 2.95

LADY DEATH: JUDGMENT WAR
Chaos! Comics 1999
Prelude 2.95
1 (of 3) 2.95
1a premium 9.99
2 . . . . 2.95
3 Hell is vanquished, concl. 2.95
Preview Book B&W 5.00

LADY DEATH: THE ODYSSEY
Chaos! Comics 1996
Sneak Peek Preview 2.00
1 embossed cover 8.00
1 SHu(c) premium edition 22.00
2 . . . . 4.00
3 . . . . 4.00
4 . . . . 4.00
4a variant cover 20.00
Micro Premium Preview Book 15.00
TPB 9.95

LADY DEATH: THE RAPTURE
Chaos! Comics 1999
1 (of 4) BnP,V:Father Orbec. 2.95
1a dynamic forces cover 6.95
1b dynamic forces, signed 15.00
1c premium edition 9.00
2 Heaven vs. Hell 2.95
3 V:Asteroth 2.95
4 BnP 2.95
Preview Book B&W 5.00

LADY DEATH/ VAMPIRELLA: DARK HEARTS
Chaos!/Harris 1999
Spec. x-over, 40-page. 3.50
Spec. Premium Edition 10.00

LADY DEMON
Chaos! Comics 2000
1 (of 3) 2.95
1a premium ed. 9.99
2 . . . . 2.95
3 concl. 2.95
Preview book B&W. 5.00

LADY PENDRAGON
Maximum Press 1996
1 mini-series 2.50
2 . . . . 2.50
3 (of 3) MD2 . . . . 2.50

LADY RAWHIDE
Topps 1995
1 All New Solo series 5.00
2 It Can't Happen Here,pt.2 . . . . . . 3.50
3 . . . . 3.00
4 . . . . 3.00
5 conclusion 3.00
Spec.#1 Rep. Zorro #2-#3 . . . . 6.50

LADY RAWHIDE
Topps
Mini-Series
1 DMG 4.00
1a DMG,signed, numbered 10.00
2 DMG 3.00
3 DMG 3.00
4 DMG, EM, "Intimate Wounds" . . . 3.00
5 DMG, EM 3.00
6 DMG 3.00
7 DMG 3.00
TPB 10.95

LADY RAWHIDE: OTHER PEOPLE'S BLOOD
Topps 1996
Mini-Series
1 DMG,EM,"A Slice of Breast" 3.00

LADY VAMPRE
Blackout 1995
0 B&W 3.50
1 . . . . 3.00

LANCELOT STRONG, THE SHIELD
Red Circle 1983
1 A:Steel Sterling. 3.50
2 A:Steel Sterling. 2.00
3 AN/EB,D:Lancelot Strong 2.00

LAND BEFORE TIME, THE
Kitchen Sink 1998
1-shot 3-D Adventure 3.95

LARS OF MARS
Eclipse 1987
1 3-D MA. 2.50

LASER ERASER & PRESSBUTTON
Eclipse 1985–87
1 GL,R:Laser Eraser 2.00
2 GL 2.00
3 GL,CK,"Tsultrine" 2.00
4 MC,"Death". 2.00
5 MC,JRy,"Gates of Hell" 2.00
6 "Corsairs of Illunium" 2.00
3-D#1 MC,GL(c),"Triple Cross" 2.00

LASH LARUE WESTERN
AC Comics
1 . . . . 3.50
Annual 2.95

LAST OF THE VIKING HEROES
Genesis West
1 JK 4.00
2 JK 3.50
3 . . . . 3.00
4 . . . . 2.50
5A sexy cover 3.00
5B mild cover 2.50
6 . . . . 2.50
7 AA(c) 3.50
8 . . . . 2.25
9 Great Battle of Nidhogger 2.50
10 "Death Among the Heroes" 2.50
Summer Spec.#1 FF,JK 3.50
Summer Spec.#2 . . . . 3.00
Summer Spec.#3,A:TMNT 2.50

LAUGH
Archie 1987–91
1 thru 29 . . . . @2.00

LAUREL AND HARDY
Dell Publishing Co. Oct., 1962
1 . . . . 60.00
2 . . . . 40.00
3 . . . . 40.00
4 . . . . 40.00

COLOR PUB.

LAUREL & HARDY
Gold Key Jan., 1967
1 . . . . 50.00
2 Oct., 1967 . . . . 35.00

LAWMAN
Dell Publishing Co. Feb., 1959
1 Ph(c) all 150.00
2 . . . . 75.00
3 ATh 80.00
4 . . . . 60.00
5 . . . . 60.00
6 . . . . 60.00
7 . . . . 60.00
8 thru 11 . . . . @60.00

LAW AND ORDER
Maximum Press 1995
1 MMy,D:Law,I:New Law, Order . . . 2.50
2 V:Max Spur 2.50
3 V:Law's Murderer 2.50

LAW OF DREDD
Quality
1 V:Perps 5.00
2 BB,Lunar Olympics 4.00
3 BB,V:Judge Death 3.00
4 V:Father Earth 3.00
5 Cursed Earth 3.00
6 V:Perps 3.00
7 V:Perps 3.00
Fleetway
8 Blockmania 3.00
9 BB,DGi,Framed for murders 3.00
10 BB,Day the Law Died Pt.1 . . . . . 2.50
11 BB,Day the Law Died Pt.2 . . . . . 2.50
12 BB,V:Judge Cal 2.50
13 V:Judge Caligula 2.50
14 BB, V:Perps 2.50
15 Under investigation 2.50
16 V:Alien Mercenary 2.50
17 thru 24 . . . . @2.50
25 Ugly Clinic 2.50
26 Judge Dredd & Gavel? 2.50
27 Cycles,Lunatics & Graffiti Guerillas 2.50
28 Cadet Training Mission 2.50
29 "Guinea Pig that changed the world 2.50
30 Meka-City,V:Robot 2.50
31 Iso-Block 666 . . . . 2.50
32 Missing Game Show Hosts 2.50
33 League of Fatties,final issue . . . 3.00

LAZARUS CHURCHYARD
Tundra
1 From UK Blast anthology 4.50
2 Goodnight Ladies 4.50

LEAGUE OF CHAMPIONS
Hero Graphics
{Cont. from Champions #12}
1 Olympus Saga #4 . . . . 2.95
2 Olympus Saga #5,O:Malice 2.95
3 Olympus Saga ends 2.95

LEAGUE OF EXTRA-ORDINARY GENTLEMEN
Wildstorm/DC 1999
America's Best Comics
1 (of 6) AMo(s),KON 3.00
2 AMo(s),KON 3.00
3 AMo(s),KON 3.00
4 AMo(s),KON 3.00
GN Collected Edition 6.00

LEATHERFACE
North Star
1 thru 3 . . . . @2.75

LEGACY
Majestic
0 platinum 12.50
1 I:Legacy 2.25
2 . . . . 2.25

LEGACY
Antarctic Press 1999
1 by Fred Perry 3.00
2 thru 5 . . . . @2.99

LEGEND OF CUSTER, THE
Dell Publishing Co. Jan., 1968
1 Ph(c) 25.00

LEGEND OF SLEEPY HOLLOW
Tundra
One shot.BHa,W.Irving adapt. 6.95

LEGEND OF THE ELFLORD
Davdez Arts 1998
1 by Barry Blair & Colin Chan 2.95
2 . . . . 2.50
3 . . . . 2.95
4 . . . . 2.95
GN Vol. 1 112-page 11.95

LEGENDS OF JESSE JAMES, THE
Gold Key Feb., 1966
1 . . . . 30.00

LEGENDS OF LUXURA
Comic Cavalcade 1998
Commemorative #1 by Kirk Lindo . . 5.95
Commemorative #1a deluxe 14.95

LEGENDS OF NASCAR
Vortex
1 HT,Bill Eliott ($1.50 cover Price) 15,000 copies 25.00
1a ($2.00 cover price) 45,000 copies 8.00
1b 3rd pr., 80,000 copies 5.00
2 Richard Petty 5.00
3 Ken Schroder 3.50
4 Bob Alison 3.00
5 Bill Elliott 2.50
6 Jr. Johnson 2.50
7 Sterling Marlin 2.25
8 Benny Parsons 2.00
9 Rusty Wallace 2.00

LEGENDS OF THE STARGRAZERS
Innovation
1 thru 5 . . . . @2.00

LEJENTIA
1 . . . . 2.00
2 . . . . 2.25

LEMONADE KID
AC Comics
1 . . . . 2.50

Leonard Nimoy's Primortals #13
© Teckno Comics

LEONARD NIMOY'S PRIMORTALS
Teckno-Comics 1994
1 I:Primortals 5.50
2 Zeerus Reveals Himself 4.00
3 Contact 2.50
4 Message Deciphered 2.25
5 Place & Time Announced 2.25
6 Zeerus Arrives on Earth 2.25
7 Zeerus Recieved 2.25
8 Hyperspace Escape 2.25
9 Pristar Lands on Earth 2.00
10 V:U.S. Army 2.00
11 V:U.S. Army 2.00
12 V:Zeerus 2.25
13 thru 15 . . . . @2.25
Big Entertainment April 1996
0 SEa,MKb 2.25
1 . . . . 2.25
2 KWo,ANi 2.25
3 KWo,ANi 2.25
4 KWo,ANi 2.25
5 KWo,ANi 2.25
6 KWo,"Scorched Earth," concl. . . . 2.25
7 PB,KWo&ANi(c),Zeerus & Narab together again 2.25

LEONARDO
Mirage
1 TMNT Character 5.00

LEOPARD
Millenium
1 I:Leopard 2.95
1a Gold Cover 3.95
2 O:Leopard,V:Razor's Edge 2.95

LETHAL STRYKE
London Night Studios 1995
1 F:Stryke 3.00
1a commemorative (1999) 5.95

COLOR PUB.

2 O:Stryke . . . 3.00
Ann. #1 EHr . . . 3.00
Ann. #1 platinum edition . . . 10.00

LETHAL STRIKE/ DOUBLE IMPACT: LETHAL IMPACT

London Night April 1996

1 by Jude Millien . . . 3.00
1 limited . . . 5.00
1 nude edition . . . 6.00

LIBERTY PROJECT, THE

Eclipse 1987–88

1 I:Liberty Project . . . 2.50
2 . . . 2.00
3 V:Silver City Wranglers . . . 2.00
4 . . . 2.00
5 . . . 2.00
6 F:Cimarron,"Misery and Gin" . . . 2.00
7 I:Menace . . . 2.00
8 V:Savage . . . 2.00

LIDSVILLE

Gold Key Oct., 1972

1 . . . 40.00
2 . . . 25.00
3 and 4 . . . @25.00
5 Oct., 1973 . . . 25.00

LIEUTENANT, THE

Dell Publishing Co. April–June, 1962

1 Ph(c) . . . 35.00

LIFE & ADVENTURES OF SANTA CLAUS

Tundra

GN MP,L.Frank Baum adapt. . . . 24.95

LIFE IN HELL

Blackthorne

1 3-D . . . 2.50

LIFE WITH ARCHIE

Archie Publications Sept., 1958

1 . . . 275.00
2 . . . 150.00
3 . . . 100.00
4 . . . 100.00
5 . . . 100.00
6 . . . 50.00
7 . . . 50.00
8 . . . 50.00
9 . . . 50.00
10 . . . 50.00
11 thru 20 . . . @30.00
21 thru 30 . . . @25.00
31 thru 40 . . . @20.00
41 . . . 10.00
42 B:Pureheart . . . 7.00
43 . . . 7.00
44 . . . 7.00
45 . . . 7.00
46 O:Pureheart . . . 25.00
47 thru 59 . . . @20.00
60 thru 100 . . . @10.00
101 thru 200 . . . @4.00
201 thru 285 . . . @3.00

Light Fantastic #2
© Innovation

LIGHT FANTASTIC, THE

Innovation

1 Terry Pratchett adapt. . . . 2.50
2 Adaptation continues . . . 2.50
3 Adaptation continues . . . 2.50
4 Adapt.conclusion . . . 2.50

LIGHTNING COMICS PRESENTS

Lightning Comics

1 B&W Promo Ed. . . . 3.50
1a B&W Promo Ed. Platinum . . . 3.50
1b B&W Promo Ed. Gold . . . 3.50

LILLITH: DEMON PRINCESS

Antarctic Press 1996

1 (of 3) from Warrior Nun Areala . . 2.95
1a Commemorative Edition (1999). 5.95
2 and 3 . . . @2.95

LINCOLN-16

Skarwood Productions

1 GI. . . . 2.95
2 GI. . . . 2.95
3 GI. . . . 2.95

LINDA LARK

Dell Publishing Co. Oct.–Dec., 1961

1 . . . 25.00
2 . . . 15.00
3 . . . 15.00
4 . . . 15.00
5 . . . 15.00
6 . . . 15.00
7 . . . 15.00
8 . . . 15.00

LINUS, THE LIONHEARTED

Gold Key Sept., 1965

1 . . . 100.00

LIONHEART

Awesome Entertainment 1999

1 IaC,JLb, from *The Coven* . . . 2.50
1 Wizard World exclusive . . . 5.50
2 IaC,JLb . . . 2.50
2a variant cover. . . . 2.50
2b variant IaC cover . . . 6.95
3 concl . . . 2.99

LIPPY THE LION AND HARDY HAR HAR

Gold Key March, 1963

1 . . . 100.00

LISA COMICS

Bongo Comics

1 F:Lisa Simpson . . . 2.25

LITTLE AMBROSE

Archie Publications Sept., 1958

1 . . . 125.00

LITTLE ARCHIE

Archie Publications 1956

1 . . . 500.00
2 . . . 225.00
3 . . . 125.00
4 . . . 125.00
5 . . . 125.00
6 thru 10 . . . @100.00
11 thru 20 . . . @75.00
21 thru 30 . . . @50.00
31 thru 40 . . . @30.00
41 thru 60 . . . @20.00
61 thru 80 . . . @10.00
81 thru 100 . . . @7.00
101 thru 180 . . . @5.00

LITTLE ARCHIE MYSTERY

Archie Publications May, 1963

1 . . . 125.00
2 Oct., 1963 . . . 65.00

LITTLE AUDREY & MELVIN

Harvey Publications May, 1962

1 . . . 100.00
2 thru 5 . . . @40.00
6 thru 10 . . . @30.00
11 thru 20 . . . @25.00
21 thru 40 . . . @12.00
41 thru 50 . . . @10.00
51 thru 53 52 pgs Giant size . . . @10.00
54 thru 60 . . . @15.00
61 Dec., 1973. . . . 10.00

LITTLE AUDREY TV FUNTIME

Harvey Publications Sept., 1962

1 A:Richie Rich . . . 85.00
2 same . . . 60.00
3 same . . . 40.00
4 . . . 40.00
5 . . . 40.00
6 thru 10 . . . @25.00
11 thru 20 . . . @15.00
21 thru 32 . . . @10.00
33 Oct., 1971 . . . 10.00

LITTLE DOT DOTLAND

Harvey Publications July, 1962

1 . . . . . 100.00
2 . . . . . 40.00
3 . . . . . 35.00
4 . . . . . 30.00
5 . . . . . 30.00
6 thru 10 . . . . . @25.00
11 thru 20 . . . . . @15.00
21 thru 50 . . . . . @5.00
51 thru 60 . . . . . @3.00
61 Dec., 1973 . . . . . 3.00

LITTLE DOT'S UNCLES & AUNTS

Harvey Enterprises Oct., 1961

1 . . . . . 100.00
2 . . . . . 50.00
3 . . . . . 40.00
4 . . . . . 30.00
5 . . . . . 30.00
6 thru 10 . . . . . @25.00
11 thru 20 . . . . . @22.00
21 thru 40 . . . . . @15.00
41 thru 51 . . . . . @7.00
52 April, 1974 . . . . . 7.00

LITTLE LOTTA

Harvey Publications Nov., 1955

1 B:Richie Rich and Little Lotta . 325.00
2 . . . . . 150.00
3 . . . . . 120.00
4 . . . . . 70.00
5 . . . . . 70.00
6 . . . . . 50.00
7 . . . . . 50.00
8 . . . . . 50.00
9 . . . . . 50.00
10 . . . . . 50.00
11 thru 20 . . . . . @30.00
21 thru 40 . . . . . @20.00
41 thru 60 . . . . . @15.00
61 thru 80 . . . . . @7.00
81 thru 99 . . . . . @5.00
100 thru 103 52 pgs . . . . . @3.00
104 thru 120 . . . . . @2.00
121 May, 1976 . . . . . 2.00

LITTLE LOTTA FOODLAND

Harvey Publications Sept., 1963

1 68 pgs 125.00
2 . . . . . 75.00
3 . . . . . 50.00
4 . . . . . 30.00
5 . . . . . 30.00
6 thru 10 . . . . . @25.00
11 thru 20 . . . . . @15.00
21 thru 26 . . . . . @10.00
27 . . . . . 8.00
28 . . . . . 8.00
29 Oct., 1972 . . . . . 8.00

LITTLE MERMAID

Walt Disney

1 based on movie 2.00
2 "Serpent Teen" 2.00
3 "Guppy Love" 2.00
4 . . . . . 2.00

LITTLE MONSTERS, THE

Gold Key Nov., 1964

1 . . . . . 50.00
2 . . . . . 30.00

Little Monsters
© Gold Key

3 thru 10 . . . . . @25.00
11 thru 20 . . . . . @15.00
21 thru 43 . . . . . @15.00
44 Feb., 1978 . . . . . 15.00

LITTLE MONSTERS

Now

1 thru 6 . . . . . @2.00

LITTLE REDBIRDS

1 . . . . . 2.50
2 . . . . . 2.50
3 . . . . . 2.50
4 . . . . . 2.50

LITTLE SAD SACK

Harvey Publications Oct., 1964

1 Richie Rich(c) 35.00
2 . . . . . 15.00
3 . . . . . 15.00
4 . . . . . 15.00
5 . . . . . 15.00
6 thru 19 Nov. 1967 . . . . . @15.00

LITTLE STOOGES, THE

Gold Key Sept., 1972

1 . . . . . 30.00
2 . . . . . 20.00
3 . . . . . 15.00
4 . . . . . 15.00
5 . . . . . 15.00
6 and 7 March, 1974 . . . . . @15.00

LLOYD LLEWELLYN

1 . . . . . 2.00

LOBO

Dell Publishing Co. Dec., 1965

1 . . . . . 25.00
2 . . . . . 20.00

LOCKE

Blackthorne

1 PO.Jones 2.00
2 TD 2.00
3 . . . . . 2.00
4 . . . . . 2.00
5 . . . . . 2.00

LONE RANGER, THE

Gold Key Sept., 1964

1 . . . . . 60.00
2 . . . . . 30.00
3 . . . . . 25.00
4 . . . . . 25.00
5 . . . . . 25.00
6 thru 10 . . . . . @20.00
11 thru 18 . . . . . @20.00
18 thru 27 . . . . . @15.00
28 March, 1977 . . . . . 15.00

LONE RANGER AND TONTO, THE

Topps 1994

1 JLd,TT,RM,The Last Battle 2.50
2 JLd,TT,RM 2.50
3 JLd,TT,RM, O:Lone Ranger 2.50
4 JLd,TT,RM, It Crawls 2.50
TPB rep. #1–#4 . . . . . 9.95

LOOKERS

Avatar

Combo Spec. 16pg. 3.00
Combo Spec. nude cover, 16pg. 5.00
Combo Spec. Platinum 9.95

LOST HEROES

Davdez Arts 1998

0 by Rob Prior, lost SF heroes 2.95
1 thru 5 . . . . . @2.50
6 . . . . . 2.95
GN 5/6 56-page 7.95

LOST IN SPACE

Innovation

{based on TV series}

1 O:Jupiter II Project 3.00
2 "Cavern of IdyllicSummersLost" . 2.75
2a Special Edition 2.50
3 Do Not Go Gently into that Good Night',Bill Mumy script 2.50
4 "People are Strange" 2.50
5 The Perils of Penelope 2.50
6 Time Warp 2.50
7 thru 9 . . . . . @2.50
10 inc.Afterthought 2.50
11 F:Judy Robinson 2.50
12 . . . . . 2.95
Project Krell 2.50
Ann.#1 (1991) 2.95
Ann.#2 (1992) 2.95
1Spec.#1 & #2 rep. Seduction of the Innocent . . . . . @2.50
GN Strangers among Strangers . . . 6.00
1-shot Project Robinson, follows story in issue #12 (1993) 2.50

Becomes:

LOST IN SPACE: VOYAGE TO THE BOTTOM OF THE SOUL

Innovation 1993–94

13 . . . . . 2.95
14 thru 18 . . . . . @2.50

LOST PLANET

Eclipse 1987–88

1 BHa,I:Tyler FLynn 2.00
2 BHa,R:Amelia Earhart 1.75
3 BHa 1.25
4 BHa,"Devil's Eye" 1.25

COLOR PUB.

5 BHa,A:Amelia Earhart. 2.00
6 . . . . 2.00

LOVECRAFT
Adventure Comics

1 "The Lurking Fear" adapt. 2.95
2 Beyond the Wall of Sleep 2.95
3 . . . . 2.95
4 . . . . 2.95

LOVE DIARY
Charlton Comics July, 1958

1 . . . . 60.00
2 . . . . 40.00
3 . . . . 25.00
4 . . . . 25.00
5 . . . . 20.00
6 . . . . 25.00
7 thru 10 . . . . @20.00
11 thru 15 . . . . @20.00
16 thru 20 . . . . @20.00
21 thru 40 . . . . @10.00
41 thru 101 . . . . @5.00
102 Dec., 1976. . . . . 5.00

LOVE SHOWDOWN COLLECTION
Archie Comics 1997

TPB x-over rep. Archie #429 (pt.1), Betty #19 (pt.2), Betty & Veronica #82, (pt.3), Veronica #39 (pt.4) Return of Cheryl Blossom. 4.95

Lucifer's Hammer #1
© Innovation

LUCIFER'S HAMMER
Innovation 1993–94

1 thru 6 Larry Niven & Jerry Pournelle novel adaptation . . @2.50

LUCY SHOW, THE
Gold Key June, 1963

1 Ph(c) 150.00
2 Ph(c) 75.00
3 thru 5 . . . . @60.00

LUDWIG VON DRAKE
Dell Publishing Co. Nov.–Dec., 1961

1 . . . . 75.00

2 thru 4 . . . . @50.00

LUFTWAFFE 1946
Antarctic Press 1998

1 color special, by Ted Namura . . . 2.95

LUGER
Eclipse 1986–87

1 TY,I:Luger,mini-series 2.00
2 TY 2.00
3 TY,BHa,V:Sharks 2.00

LUNATIC

1 and 2 . . . . @2.00

LUNATIC FRINGE
Innovation

1 . . . . 2.00
2 . . . . 2.00

LUNATIC FRINGE
Innovation

1 . . . . 2.00

LUXURA
Comic Cavalcade 1998

Commemorative #1 by Kirk Lindo . . 5.95
Commemorative #1a deluxe 14.95

LUXURA COLLECTION
Brainstorm

Commemorative edition, red foil cover, 48pg. 10.00

LYNCH MOB
Chaos! Comics

1 GCa(c), I:Mother Mayhem 3.00
2 Lynch Mob Loses 2.50
3 1994 Time Trip 2.50
3a Gold cover 3.00
4 Mother Mayhem at UN 2.50

LYNDON B. JOHNSON
Dell Publishing Co. March, 1965

1 Ph(c) 25.00

M
Eclipse 1990–91

1 thru 4 JMu . . . . @4.95

M.D.
Gemstone 1999

1 (of 5) New Direction 2.50
2 . . . . 2.50
3 . . . . 2.50
4 . . . . 2.50
Annual #1. . . . . 13.50

MACROSS
Comico

1 . . . . 12.00

Becomes:

ROBOTECH, THE MACROSS SAGA

MAD FOLLIES
E.C. Comics
1963

(N#). 275.00
2 1964. . . . . 200.00
3 1965. . . . . 150.00
4 1966. . . . . 165.00
5 1967. . . . . 125.00
6 & 7 1968 and 1969 . . . . @100.00

MAD HOUSE
Red Circle 1974–82

95 thru 97 Horror stories . . . . . . @10.00
98 thru 130 Humor stories. . . . . . @5.00
Annual #8 thru #11 . . . . @6.00

MADMAN
Tundra 1992

1 . . . . 15.00
2 . . . . 15.00
3 . . . . 10.00

MADMAN ADVENTURES
Tundra 1992

1 R & N:Madman. 10.00
2 . . . . 8.00
3 . . . . 8.00

MADRAVEN HALLOWEEN SPECIAL
Hamilton Comics 1995

1 Song of the Silkies 2.95

MAD SPECIAL
E.C. Publications, Inc.
Fall, 1970

1 . . . . 75.00
2 . . . . 50.00
3 . . . . 40.00
4 thru 8 . . . . @40.00
9 thru 13 . . . . @30.00
14 . . . . 20.00
15 . . . . 25.00
16 . . . . 20.00
17 . . . . 20.00
18 . . . . 22.00
19 thru 21 . . . . @22.00
22 thru 31 . . . . @10.00
32 . . . . 12.00
33 thru 58 . . . . @8.00

MAGE
Comico

1 MWg,I:Kevin Matchstick 15.00
2 MWg,I:Edsel. 10.00
3 MWg,V:Umbra Sprite 8.00
4 MWg,V:Umbra Sprite 8.00
5 MWg,I:Sean (Spook) 8.00
6 MWg,Grendel begins 22.00
7 MWg,Grendel. 10.00
8 MWg,Grendel. 6.00
9 MWg,Grendel. 6.00
10 MWg,Grendel,Styx. 6.00
11 MWg,Grendel,Styx. 6.00
12 MWg,D:Sean,Grendel 6.00
13 MWg,D:Edsel,Grendel 6.00
14 MWg,Grendel,O:Kevin 6.00
15 MWg,D:Umbra Sprite. 12.00

MAGEBOOK
Comico

1 rep. Mage #1-4. . . . . 8.95
2 rep. Mage #5-8. . . . . 8.95

COLOR PUB.

MAGIC FLUTE
Eclipse 1989
1 CR 4.95

MAGILLA GORILLA
Gold Key May, 1964
1 . . . . 100.00
2 thru 10 Dec. 1968 . . . . @75.00

MAGILLA GORILLA
Charlton Comics Nov., 1970
1 . . . . 50.00
2 thru 5 . . . . @25.00

MAGNUS: ROBOT FIGHTER
Gold Key Feb., 1963
1 RM,I:Magnus,Teeja,A-1,
I&B:Capt.Johner&aliens 250.00
2 RM,I:Sen.Zeremiah Clane. . . . 125.00
3 RM,I:Xyrkol. 125.00
4 RM,I:Mekamn,Elzy 75.00
5 RM,The Immortal One 75.00
6 RM,I:Talpa 70.00
7 RM,I:Malev-6,ViXyrkol 85.00
8 RM,I:Outsiders(Chet, Horio,
Toun, Malf). 70.00
9 RM, I:Madmot. 70.00
10 RM,Mysterious Octo-Rob. 70.00
11 RM,I:Danae,Neo-Animals. 50.00
12 RM,The Volcano Makers 50.00
13 RM,I:Dr Lazlo Noel 55.00
14 RM,The Monster Robs. 50.00
15 RM,I:Mogul Radur 50.00
16 RM,I:Gophs 50.00
17 RM,I:Zypex 50.00
18 RM,I:V'ril Trent. 50.00
19 RM,Fear Unlimited. 50.00
20 RM,I:Bunda the Great 50.00
21 RM, Space Spectre 50.00
22 Rep. #1 . . . . 35.00
23 DSp,Mission Disaster 35.00
24 Pied Piper of North Am 35.00
25 The Micro Giants 35.00
26 The Venomous Vaper 35.00
27 Panic in Pacifica 35.00
28 Threats from the Depths 35.00
29 Rep. #7 . . . . 16.00
30 Rep. #15 . . . . 16.00
31 Rep. #14 . . . . 16.00
32 Rep. #2 . . . . 16.00
33 Rep. #21 . . . . 16.00
34 Rep. #13 . . . . 16.00
35 Rep. #6 . . . . 16.00
36 Rep. #8 . . . . 16.00
37 Rep. #11 . . . . 16.00
38 Rep. #12 . . . . 16.00
39 Rep. #16 . . . . 16.00
40 Rep. #17 . . . . 16.00
41 Rep. #18 . . . . 16.00
42 Rep. #19 . . . . 16.00
43 Rep. #20 . . . . 16.00
44 Rep. #23 . . . . 16.00
45 Rep. #24 . . . . 16.00
46 Rep. #25 . . . . 16.00

MAJOR DAMAGE
Invictus Studios
1 I:Major Damage 2.25
2 V:Godkin 2.25
3 First Contact Conclusion. 2.25

MAKABRE
Apocalypse
1 Gangsters 3.95

MALICE
Heroic Publishing
1 I:Queen of the Dead 2.00

Mandrake The Magician #5
© King Comics

MANDRAKE THE MAGICIAN
King Comics 1966
1 . . . . 50.00
2 . . . . 30.00
3 . . . . 30.00
4 A:Girl Phantom. 30.00
5 Cape Cod Caper 30.00
6 . . . . 30.00
7 O:Lothar. 30.00
8 . . . . 35.00
9 A:Brick Bradford 30.00
10 A:Rip Kirby 35.00

MAN FROM PLANET X
Planet X Prod.
1 . . . . 3.00

MAN FROM U.N.C.L.E.
Gold Key Feb., 1965
1 "The Explosive Affair" 175.00
2 "The Forthur Cookie Affair" . . . 100.00
3 "The Deadly Devices Affair" . . . 60.00
4 "The Rip Van Solo Affair" 60.00
5 "Ten Little Uncles Affair" 60.00
6 "The Three Blind Mice Affair" . . 60.00
7 "The Pixilated Puzzle Affair"
I:Jet Dream (back-up begins) . 65.00
8 "The Floating People Affair" . . . 60.00
9 "Spirit of St.Louis Affair" 60.00
10 "The Trojan Horse Affair" 60.00
11 "Three-Story Giant Affair" 50.00
12 "Dead Man's Diary Affair". 50.00
13 "The Flying Clowns Affair" 50.00
14 "Great Brain Drain Affair" 50.00
15 "The Animal Agents Affair". . . . 50.00
16 "Instant Disaster Affair" 50.00
17 "The Deadly Visions Affair". . . . 50.00
18 "The Alien Affair" 50.00
19 "Knight in Shining Armor Affair" 50.00
20 "Deep Freeze Affair" 50.00
21 rep. #10 . . . . 45.00
22 rep. #7. . . . . 45.00

MAN FROM U.N.C.L.E.
Entertainment
1 thru 11 . . . . @2.00

MAN FROM U.N.C.L.E.
Millennium
1 The Birds of Prey Affair,pt.1 . . . . 2.95
2 The Birds of Prey Affair,pt.2 . . . . 2.95

MANGA SHI 2000
Crusade Entertainment 1997
1 (of 3) BiT, "Final Jihad" flip-book
Shi: Heaven and Earth 2.95
2 BiT, flip-book Tomoe:
Unforgettable Fire preview 2.95
3 BiT, conclusion 2.95

MANGLE TANGLE TALES
Innovation
1 . . . . 2.95

MANIFEST DESTINY
1 . . . . 2.00

MAN IN BLACK
Harvey Publications Sept., 1957
1 BP 125.00
2 BP 100.00
3 BP 100.00
4 BP, March, 1958 . . . . 100.00

MANIK
Millenium/Expand (1995)
1 I:Macedon, Arsenal,Cardinal. . . . 2.95

MANKIND
Chaos! Comics 1999
1-shot StG. 2.95
1-shotA photo cover 2.95
1-shotB variant cover. 6.95
1-shotC variant cover, signed. . . . 60.00

MAN OF WAR
Eclipse 1987–88
1 thru 3 . . . . @2.00

MARK RAND'S SKY TECHNOLOGIES INC.
Red Mercenary 1995
1 I:Jae,Elliot,Firnn 2.95

MARKSMAN, THE
Hero Graphics
1 O:Marksman, Pt.#1. . . . . 2.00
2 O:Marksman, Pt.#2. . . . . 2.00
3 O:Marksman ends.I:Basilisk 2.00
4 A:Flare 2.00
5 I:Radar,Sonar 2.00
Ann. #1, A:Champions 2.00

MARRIED... WITH CHILDREN
Now
1 . . . . 6.00
1a 2nd printing 2.00
2 . . . . 4.00
3 . . . . 3.00
4 . . . . 2.50
5 . . . . 2.50
6 . . . . 2.00
7 . . . . 2.50

[2nd Series]
1 Peg-Host of Radio Show 2.25

COLOR PUB.

2 The Bundy Invention. 2.00
3 Psychodad,(photo cover) 2.00
4 Mother-In-Law,(photo cover). . . . 2.00
5 Bundy the Crusader 2.00
6 Bundy J: The Order of the
Mighty Warthog 2.00
7 Kelly the VJ 2.00
Spec. 2.00
3-D Spec. 2.50

MARRIED WITH CHILDREN: DYSFUNCTIONAL FAMILY

Now

1 I:The Bundies. 2.50
2 TV Appearance 2.50
3 Morally Pure Bundys 2.50

MARRIED WITH CHILDREN: FLASHBACK SPECIAL

Now

1 Peg and Al's first date. 2.00
2 and 3 . . . . @2.00

MARRIED WITH CHILDREN: KELLY BUNDY SPECIAL

Now

1 with poster 2.00
2 and 3 with poster . . . . @2.00

MARRIED... WITH CHILDREN: QUANTUM QUARTET

Now

1 thru 4 Fantastic Four parody . . @2.00
Fall 1994 Spec., flip book 2.00

MARRIED WITH CHILDREN 2099

Mirage

1 thru 3 Cable Parody. . . . . @2.50

MARS

First

1 thru 12 . . . . @2.00

MARS ATTACKS

Topps

1 KG(s). 6.00
2 . . . . 4.00
3 thru 6 KG(s) 4.00

[Series 2] 1995

1 Counterstrike 3.50
2 Counterstrike,pt.2 . . . . 2.95
3 Counterstrike,pt.3 . . . . 2.95
4 Counterstrike,pt.4 Convictions . . 2.95
5 Counterstrike concl. 2.95
6 "Rescue of Janice Brown,"pt.1 . . 2.95
7 "Rescue of Janice Brown,"pt.2 . . 2.95
8. . . . . 2.95
Spec. Baseball 3.00

MARS ATTACKS HIGH SCHOOL

Topps 1997

Spec. #1 (of 2) BSz(c) 2.95
Spec. #2. . . . . 2.95

Mars Attacks: The Savage Dragon #2
© Topps Comics

MARS ATTACKS THE SAVAGE DRAGON

Topps

1 . . . . 3.00
2 . . . . 3.00
3 . . . . 3.00
4 (of 4) 3.00

MARSHALL LAW: HATEFUL DEAD

Apocalypse

1 "Rise of the Zombies". 5.95

MARTIANS!!! IN 3-D

1 . . . . 2.00

MARY WORTH

ARGO March, 1956

1 . . . . 50.00

MASKED MAN

Eclipse 1985–88

1 . . . . 3.00
2 . . . . 2.00
3 . . . . 2.00
4 . . . . 2.00
5 . . . . 2.00
6 V:Roxie Lamada 2.00
7 . . . . 2.00
8 "Roxy" 2.00
9 W:Dick and Maggie 2.00
10 . . . . 2.00

MASTERWORK SERIES

Seagate DC

1 FFrep.DC,ShiningKnight. 2.00
2 FFrep.DC,ShiningKnight. 2.00
3 BWr,Horror DC rep. 2.00

MAVERICK

Dell Publishing Co. April, 1958

1 Ph(c) all 300.00
2 Ph(c) 125.00
3 Ph(c) 125.00
4 Ph(c) 125.00
5 Ph(c) 125.00
6 thru 15 Ph(c) . . . . @85.00

MAVERICK MARSHALL

Charlton Comics Nov., 1958

1 . . . . 35.00
2 . . . . 25.00
3 . . . . 25.00
4 . . . . 25.00
5 . . . . 25.00
6 . . . . 25.00
7 May, 1960 . . . . 25.00

MAVERICKS

Dagger

1 PuD,RkL, I:Mavericks 2.50
2 PuD,RkL. 2.50

MAXIMORTAL

King Hell/Tundra

1 RV,A:True-Man. 4.50
2 Crack in the New World 4.25
3 RV,Secret of the Manhattan
Project revealed 4.25
4 . . . . 4.25
5 A:True Man 3.25
6 A:El Guano. 3.25

Kitchen Sink 1997

HC Book 1: Cheek, Chin, Knuckle
or Knee 35.00

MAYA

Gold Key March, 1968

1 . . . . 25.00

MAZE AGENCY

Comico

1 O:Maze Agency 3.00
2 thru 6 . . . . @2.50
7 . . . . 2.75
8 thru 11 . . . . @2.00
12 . . . . 2.50
13 thru 15. . . . . @2.00
16 thru 23. . . . . @2.50
Spec. #1. 2.75

McHALE'S NAVY

Dell Publishing Co.
May–July, 1963

1 Ph(c) from TV show 65.00
2 Ph(c) 50.00
3 Ph(c) 50.00

McKEEVER & THE COLONEL

Dell Publishing Co.
Feb.–April, 1963

1 Ph(c) 60.00
2 Ph(c) 40.00
3 Ph(c) 40.00

M.D. GEIST

CPM

1 Cartoon Adaptation. 2.95
2 J:Army 2.95
3 V:Final Terminator 2.95

MECHANICS

Fantagraphics

1 HB,rep.Love & Rockets 3.00
2 HB,rep.Love & Rockets 2.50
3 HB,rep.Love & Rockets 2.50

MEDIA STARR
Innovation
1 thru 3 . . . @2.00

MEGALITH
Continuity
1 MT . . . 6.00
2 MT . . . 4.00
3 MT, Painted issue . . . 2.50
4 NA,TVE . . . 2.50
5 NA,TVE . . . 2.50
6 MN . . . 2.50
7 MN . . . 2.50
8 . . . 2.50
9 SDr(i) . . . 2.50
10 . . . 2.50

[2nd Series, Deathwatch 2000]
0 Deathwatch 2000 prologue . . . 5.00
1 Deathwatch 2000 Pt.5,w/card . . . 2.50
2 Deathwatch 2000 Pt.10,w/card . . . 2.50
3 pt.16,Indestructible(c),w/card . . . 2.50
4 and 5 Rise of Magic . . . @2.50
6 and 7 . . . @2.50

MEGATON
1 . . . 2.00

Entity Comics
Holiday Spec. w/card . . . 2.95

MEGATON EXPLOSION
1 RLd,AMe,I:Youngblood preview 25.00

Megaton Man #6
© Kitchen Sink

MEGATON MAN
Kitchen Sink
1 Don Simpson art, I:Megaton Man 6.00
1a rep. B&W . . . 2.00
2 . . . 4.00
3 and 4 . . . @3.00
5 . . . 2.50
6 Border Worlds . . . 2.50
7 Border Worlds . . . 2.50
8 Border Worlds . . . 2.50
9 Border Worlds . . . 2.50
10 final issue, 1986 . . . 2.50

MELTING POT
Kitchen Sink
1 . . . 4.00
2 and 3 . . . @2.95

4 . . . 3.50
TPB KEa,SBs, rep. . . . 19.95
HC signed, numbered . . . 50.00

MELVIN MONSTER
Dell Publishing Co.
April-June, 1965
1 . . . 125.00
2 thru 10 . . . @75.00

[Katshuiro Otomo's] MEMORIES
Epic 1992
1 . . . 2.50

MEN FROM EARTH
Future Fun
1 based on Matt Mason toy . . . 6.50

MENACE
Awesome Entertainment 1998
1 by Jada Pinkett & Don Fraga . . . 2.50
1a signed . . . 20.00
2 . . . 2.50
3 . . . 2.50

MERCENARY
NBM 1998
TPB The Voyage . . . 10.95
TPB The Black Globe . . . 9.95
TPB The Fortress . . . 9.95
TPB Giants, 48-page . . . 10.95
TPB Year 1000, 48-page . . . 11.95
TPB Lost Civilization . . . 10.95

MERCHANTS OF DEATH
Eclipse 1988
1 King's Castle, The Hero . . . 3.50
2 King's Castle,Soldiers of Fortune 3.50
3 Ransom, Soldier of Fortune . . . 3.50
4 ATh(c),Ransom, Men o/t Legion . 3.50
5 Ransom,New York City Blues . . . 3.50

MERIDIAN
Crossgen Comics 2000
1 BKs . . . 2.95
2 BKs . . . 2.95
3 BKs . . . 2.95
4 BKs . . . 2.95
5 BKs . . . 2.95

MERLIN REALM
Blackthorne
1 3-D . . . 2.50

META 4
First 1990
1 IG . . . 3.95
2 IG . . . 2.25
3 IG/JSon,final monthly . . . 2.25

METAL MILITIA
Entity Comics 1995
1 I:Metal Militia . . . 2.50
1a with Video Game . . . 6.95
2 ICO . . . 2.50
3 F:Detective Calahan . . . 2.50
Ashcan . . . 2.50

MICHAELANGELO
Mirage
1 TMNT Character . . . 15.00

MICKEY & DONALD
Gladstone
1 1449 Firestone . . . 8.00
2 . . . 4.00
3 Man of Tomorrow . . . 3.00
4 thru 15 . . . @2.50
16 giant-size . . . 2.50
17 . . . 3.00
18 . . . 4.00
Becomes:

DONALD AND MICKEY
19 thru 26 . . . @2.00

MICKEY MANTLE COMICS
Magnum
1 JSt,Rise to Big Leagues . . . 2.00

MICKEY MOUSE
Gladstone
219 FG,Seven Ghosts . . . 6.00
220 FG,Seven Ghosts . . . 7.00
221 FG,Seven Ghosts . . . 7.00
222 FG,Editor in Grief . . . 5.00
223 FG,Editor in Grief . . . 4.00
224 FG,Crazy Crime Wave . . . 3.00
225 FG,Crazy Crime Wave . . . 3.00
226 FG,Captive Castaways . . . 3.00
227 FG,Captive Castaways . . . 3.00
228 FG,Captive Castaways . . . 3.00
229 FG,Bat Bandit . . . 3.00
230 FG,Bat Bandit . . . 2.50
231 FG,Bobo the Elephant . . . 2.50
232 FG,Bobo the Elephant . . . 2.50
233 FG,Pirate Submarine . . . 2.50
234 FG,Pirate Submarine . . . 2.50
235 FG,Photo Racer . . . 2.50
236 FG,Photo Racer . . . 2.50
237 FG,Race for Riches . . . 2.50
238 FG,Race for Riches . . . 2.50
239 FG,Race for Riches . . . 2.50
240 FG,March of Comics . . . 2.50
241 FG . . . 4.00
242 FG . . . 2.50
243 FG . . . 2.50
244 FG,60th Anniv . . . 5.00
245 FG . . . 2.25
245 FG . . . 2.25
246 FG . . . 2.25
247 FG . . . 2.25
248 FG . . . 2.25
249 FG . . . 5.00
250 FG . . . 2.25
251 FG . . . 2.25
252 FG . . . 2.25
253 FG . . . 2.25
254 FG . . . 2.25
255 FG . . . 4.00
256 FG . . . 4.00

MICKEY MOUSE
Walt Disney 1990
1 "The Phantom Gondolier" . . . 3.50
2 . . . 3.00
3 . . . 2.50
4 . . . 2.50
5 . . . 2.50
6 . . . 2.00
7 Phantom Blot . . . 2.00
8 Phantom Blot . . . 2.00
9 . . . 2.00
10 Sky Adventure . . . 2.00
11 When Mouston Freezes Over . . . 2.00

12 Hail & Farewell 2.00
13 “What's Shakin'” 2.00
14 Mouseton,Eagle-Landing 2.00
15 “Lost Palace of Kashi” 2.00
16 “Scoundrels in Space” 2.00
17 “Sound of Blunder” Pt.1 . . . . 2.00
18 “Sound of Blunder” Pt.2 . . . . 2.00
19 50th Ann. Fantasia Celebration Sorcerer's Apprentice adapt . . . 2.00

MICKEY SPILLANE'S MIKE DANGER

Tekno Comix 1995

1 I:Mike Danger. 2.25
2 Underside of the City 2.00
3 Judicial System 2.00
4 Mike's First Job 2.00
5 Old New York 2.00
6 Sin Syndicate Leader 2.25
7 thru 11 . . . . @2.25

Big Entertainment 1996

1 . . . . 2.25
2 . . . . 2.25
3 MCn,PGr,TBe,EB 2.25
4 . . . . 2.25
5 “Time Heels”. 2.25
6 TBe,“Paradox Rule” 2.25
7 TBe,“Red Menace,” pt.1 . . . . 2.25
8 TBe,“Red Menace,” pt.2 . . . . 2.25
9 TBe,“Red Menace,” pt.3. . . . . 2.25
10 TBe,“Red Menace,” concl. 2.25

MICROBOTS, THE

Gold Key Dec., 1971

1 . . . . 20.00

MIDNIGHT EYE: GOKU PRIVATE INVESTIGATOR

Viz

1 A.D. 2014: Tokyo city 5.25
2 V:Hakuryu,A:Yoko. 4.95
3 A:Ryoko,Search for Ryu 4.95
4 Goku vs. Ryu 4.95
5 Leilah Abducted 4.95
6 Lisa's I.D. discovered 4.95

MIGHTY COMICS

(Prev: Flyman)

40 A:Web 12.00
41 A:Shield, Black Hood 10.00
42 A:Black Hood. 10.00
43 A:Shield, Black Hood,Web 9.00
44 A:Black Hood, Steel Sterling Shield. 9.00
45 Shield-Black Hood team-up O: Web 9.00
46 A:Steel Sterling, Black Hood, Web. 9.00
47 A:Black Hood & Mr.Justice. 9.00
48 A:Shield & Hangman 9.00
49 Steel Sterling-Black Hood team-up, A:Fox. 9.00

[ALL NEW ADVENTURES OF] THE MIGHTY CRUSADERS

Red Circle

[1st Series] 1983

1 O:Shield (Joe Higgins & Bill Higgins) 25.00
2 MSy,O:Comet. 20.00
3 O:Fly-Man 15.00
4 A:Fireball,Jaguar,Web,Fox, Blackjack Hangman & more Golden Age Archie Heroes . . . 18.00
5 I:Ultra-Men&TerrificThree 15.00

Archie Publications

6 V:Maestro,A:Steel Sterling 12.00
7 O:Fly-Girl,A:Steel Sterling 12.00

[2nd Series]

1 RB,R:Joe Higgins & Lancelot Strong as the SHIELD, Mighty Crusaders, A:Mr.Midnight 2.00
2 RB,V:Brain Emperor & Eterno. . . 2.00
3 RB,I:Darkling 2.00
4 DAy,TD. 2.00
5 . . . . 2.00
6 DAy,TD,Shield 2.00
7 . . . . 2.00
8 . . . . 2.00
9 Trial of the Shield 2.00
10 . . . . 2.00
11 DAy,D:Gold Age Black Hood, I: Riot Squad, series based on toy lines 2.00
12 DAy,I:She-Fox 2.00
13 Last issue 2.00

MIGHTY HERCULES, THE

Gold Key July, 1963

1 . . . . 150.00
2 . . . . 125.00

MIGHTY MORPHIN POWER RANGERS

Hamilton 1994–95

1 From TV Series 2.75
2 Switcheroo 2.50
3 . . . . 2.25
4 F:White Ranger 2.00
5 F:Pink Ranger 2.00
6 V:Garganturon 2.00
TPB Re. #1-#6 photo (c). 9.95

[Series 2] 1995

1 Unstoppable Force 2.00
2 V:Mechanical Octopus 2.00
3 . . . . 2.00
4 Lost Ranger 2.00

[Series 3] 1995

1 O:Green Ranger. 2.00
2 O:Green Ranger. 2.00
3 I:New Megazords 2.00

Mighty Mouse #1
© Spotlight

MIGHTY MOUSE

Spotlight 1987

1 FMc,PC(c) 2.00
2 FMc,CS(c) 2.00
1 Holiday Special. 2.00

MIGHTY MUTANIMALS

Archie Publications

[Mini-Series]

1 Cont.from TMNT Adventures#19, A:Raphael, Man Ray, Leatherhead, Mondo Gecko,Deadman, Wingnut & Screwloose 2.00
2 V:Mr.Null,Malinga,Soul and Bean and the Malignoid Army 2.00
3 Alien Invasion help off, Raphael returns to Earth 2.00
4 “Days of Future Past” 2.00
5 “Into the Sun” 2.00
6 V:Null & 4 Horsemen Pt#2 . . . . . 2.00
7 Jaws of Doom 2.00
Spec.#1 rep. all #1-3 +SBi pin-ups . 2.95

MIGHTY MUTANIMALS

Archie

1 Quest for Jagwar's Mother 2.00
2 V:Snake Eyes. 2.00
3 . . . . 2.00
4 “Days of Future Past” 2.00
5 “Into the Sun” 2.00
6 V:Null & 4 Horsemen Pt#2 . . . . . 2.00
7 Jaws of Doom 2.00

MIGHTY SAMSON

Gold Key 1964–82

1 O:Mighty Samson 100.00
2 . . . . 50.00
3 . . . . 50.00
4 . . . . 50.00
5 . . . . 50.00
6 thru 10 . . . . @30.00
11 thru 20 . . . . @25.00
21 thru 32 . . . . @20.00

MIKE GRELL'S SABLE

First

1 thru 8 rep. . . . . @2.00
9 . . . . 2.00
10 Triptych 2.00

MIKE SHAYNE PRIVATE EYE

Dell Publishing Co. Nov.–Jan., 1961-62

1 . . . . 35.00
2 . . . . 20.00
3 . . . . 20.00

MILLENNIUM INDEX

Independent Comics 1988

1 . . . . 2.00
2 . . . . 2.00

MILTON THE MONSTER & FEARLESS FLY

Gold Key May, 1966

1 . . . . 125.00

MIRACLEMAN

Eclipse 1985–94

1 R:Miracleman 5.00
2 AD,Moore,V:Kid Miracleman. . . . 4.00

COLOR PUB.

3 AD,Moore,V:Big Ben. 4.00
4 AD,Moore,R:Dr.Gargunza 4.00
5 AD,Moore,O:Miracleman. 4.00
6 Moore,V:Miracledog, D:Evelyn Cream 4.00
7 Moore,D:Dr.Gargunza. 4.00
8 Moore. 4.00
9 RV,Moore,Birth of Miraclebaby . . 4.50
10 JRy,RV,Moore 4.00
11 JTo,Moore,Book III, I:Miraclewoman 5.00
12 thru 14 Moore . . . . @5.00
15 Moore 30.00
16 . . . . 5.00
17 thru 23. . . . . @4.00
24 BWS(c),NGa(s),. 4.00
25 thru 28 . . . . @2.95
3-D Special #1 . . . . 2.75

Graphic Albums

HC Book 1 A Dream of Flying. . . . 29.95
TPB Book 1 A Dream of Flying. . . . 9.95
HC Book 2 The Red Kings Syndrome. 30.95
TPB Book 2 The Red Kings Syndrome 9.95
HC Book 3 Olympus. 30.95
TPB Book 3 Olympus 12.00

MIRACLEMAN APOCRYPHA
Eclipse 1991–92

1 inc."Rascal Prince" 2.50
2 Miracleman, Family Stories. 2.50
3 . . . . 2.50

MIRACLEMAN FAMILY
Eclipse 1988

1 British Rep.,A:Kid Miracleman. . . 2.00
2 Alan Moore (s) 2.00

MIRACLE SQUAD, THE
Upshot/Fantagraphics 1986

1 Hollywood 30's. 2.00
2 thru 4 . . . . @2.00

MISS FURY
Adventure Comics

1 O:Cat Suit 2.50
2 Miss Fury impersonator 2.50
3 A:Three Miss Fury's 2.50
4 conclusion 2.50

MISSION IMPOSSIBLE
Dell Publishing Co. May, 1967

1 Ph(c) 125.00
2 Ph(c) 100.00
3 Ph(c) 75.00
4 Ph(c) 75.00
5 Ph(c) 75.00

MISSIONS IN TIBET
Dimension Comics 1995

1 I:New Series. 2.50
2 F:Orlando,Ting,Alex 2.50
3 Two Worlds Collide. 2.50
4 V:Sada 2.50

MISS PEACH (& SPECIAL ISSUES)
Dell Publishing Co. 1963

1 . . . . 75.00

MR. AND MRS. J. EVIL SCIENTIST
Gold Key Nov., 1963

1 . . . . 100.00
2 . . . . 60.00
3 . . . . 60.00
4 . . . . 60.00

MR. JIGSAW

Spec. #1 . . . . 2.00

MR. MAJESTIC
Wildstorm/DC 1999

1 JoC,A:Desmond 2.50
1a variant cover. 3.00
2 JoC,time gone berserk 2.50

MR. MONSTER
Eclipse 1985–87

1 I:Mr. Monster 7.00
2 DSt(c). 5.00
3 V:Dr. NoZone 3.50
4 "Trapped in Dimension X" 3.00
5 V:Flesh-eating Amoebo 3.00
6 KG,SD,reprints 3.00
7 . . . . 3.00
8 V:Monster in the Atomic Telling Machine 3.00
9 V:Giant Clams 3.00
10 R:Dr.No Zone, 3-D. 2.00

MR. MONSTER ATTACKS
Tundra

1 DGb,SK,short stories 4.25
2 SK,short stories cont. 4.25
3 DGb,last issue 4.25

MR. MONSTER SUPERDUPER SPECIAL
Eclipse 1986–87

1 . . . . 2.50
2 . . . . 2.00
3 . . . . 2.00
4 . . . . 2.00
5 . . . . 2.00
6 . . . . 2.00
Hi-Voltage Super Science. 2.00
3-D Spec. Hi-Octane Horror,JKu, "Touch of Death" reprint 2.00
Triple Treat. 3.95

MR. MONSTER TRUE CRIME
Eclipse

1 . . . . 2.00
2 . . . . 2.00
3-D Spec. #1 . . . . 2.00

MR. MUSCLES
Charlton Comics 1956

22 . . . . 50.00
23 . . . . 45.00

MR. MYSTIC
Eclipse

1 . . . . 2.00
2 . . . . 2.00
3 . . . . 2.00

MR. T AND THE T FORCE
Now

1 NA,R:Mr.T,V:Street Gangs 2.50
1a Gold Ed. 10.00
2 NA,V:Demons. 2.25
3 NBy,w/card. 2.25
4 NBy,In Urban America 2.25
5 thru 10, with card . . . . @2.25

MISTER X
Vortex

1 HB 7.00
2 HB 5.00
3 HB 3.50
4 HB 3.00
5 . . . . 3.00
6 thru 10 . . . . @2.50
11 thru 13 . . . . @2.00
14 . . . . 2.25

Mod Squad #7
© Dell Publishing

MOD SQUAD
Dell Publishing Co. 1969–71

1 . . . . 55.00
2 . . . . 40.00
3 . . . . 40.00
4 thru 8 . . . . @40.00

MOD WHEELS
Gold Key 1971–76

1 . . . . 20.00
2 thru 18 . . . . @10.00
19 . . . . 8.00

MONKEE'S, THE
Dell Publishing Co. 1967

1 Ph(c) 100.00
2 Ph(c) 60.00
3 Ph(c) 60.00
4 Ph(c) 60.00
5 . . . . 50.00
6 Ph(c) 60.00
7 Ph(c) 60.00
8 and 9 . . . . @50.00
10 Ph(c). 60.00
11 thru 17. . . . . 40.00

MONOLITH
Comico

1 From Elementals 2.50

2 “Seven Levels of Hell” 2.50
3 “Fugue and Variation” 2.50
4 “Fugue and Variation” 2.50

MONROE'S, THE
Dell Publishing Co. April, 1967
1 Ph(c) 25.00

MONSTER MASSACRE
Atomeka
1 SBs, DBr,DGb 8.50
1a Black Edition. 35.00

MOONWALKER IN 3-D
Blackthorne
1 thru 3 . . . . @2.50

MORBID ANGEL
London Night
½ Angel's Tear, signed. 10.00
1 Commemorative (1999) 5.95

MORBID ANGEL: PENANCE
London Night
Revised Color Spec., double size . . 4.00

More Than Mortal #5
© Liar Comics

MORE THAN MORTAL
Liar Comics 1997
1 . . . . 2.95
1a 2nd printing 2.95
1b convention, sign, num. 9.95
2 Derdre vs. the Host 2.95
2a variant painted cover 5.95
3 MS(c) 2.95
4 concl. 2.95
TPB rep. #1–#4 . . . . 14.95

MORE THAN MORTAL: SAGAS
Liar Comics 1998
1 by Sharon Scott & Romano Molenaar 2.95
1a variant Tim Vigil(c) 2.95
1b variant JLi(c). 9.95
2 . . . . 2.95
3 conclusion 2.95

MORE THAN MORTAL: TRUTHS AND LEGENDS
Liar Comics 1998
1 by Sharon Scott, Steve Firchow, Mark Prudeaux, O:Witchfinder . 3.00
1a signed 9.95
2 . . . . 3.00
3 . . . . 3.00
4 . . . . 3.00
5 . . . . 3.00
5a variant cover (1:4). 3.00
6 . . . . 3.00

MORLOCK 2001
Atlas Feb.–July 1975
1 thru 3 F:Midnight Men . . . . . . @10.00

MORNINGSTAR
Spec. #1 . . . . 2.50

MORRIGAN
Sirius 1997
1 by Lorenzo Bartoli & Saverio Tenuta 2.95
2 and 3 . . . . @2.95
GN rep. #1–#3 . . . . 9.95

MOTORBIKE PUPPIES
Dark Zulu Lies
1 I:Motorbike Puppies 2.50

MOVIE COMICS
Gold Key/Whitman Oct., 1962
Alice in Wonderland 35.00
Aristocats 75.00
Bambi 1 . . . . 35.00
Bambi 2 . . . . 25.00
Beneath the Planet of the Apes. . 100.00
Big Red 25.00
Blackbeard's Ghost. 25.00
Buck Rogers Giant Movie Edition . 22.00
Bullwhip Griffin 35.00
Captain Sinbad. 50.00
Chitty, Chitty Bang Bang 75.00
Cinderella. 30.00
Darby O'Gill & the Little People. . . 50.00
Dumbo 30.00
Emil & the Detectives 30.00
Escapade in Florence 85.00
Fall of the Roman Empire 35.00
Fantastic Voyage 50.00
55 Days at Peking 30.00
Fighting Prince of Donegal 25.00
First Men of the Moon. 30.00
Gay Purr-ee 45.00
Gnome Mobile 30.00
Goodbye, Mr. Chips 30.00
Happiest Millionaire 30.00
Hey There, It's Yogi Bear 60.00
Horse Without a Head 25.00
How the West Was Won 35.00
In Search of the Castaways 75.00
Jungle Book, The 65.00
Kidnapped 30.00
King Kong 30.00
King Kong N#. 25.00
Lady and the Tramp 30.00
Lady and the Tramp 1. . . . . 50.00
Lady and the Tramp 2. . . . . 20.00
Legend of Lobo, The 25.00
Lt. Robin Crusoe 25.00
Lion, The 25.00
Lord Jim. 25.00
Love Bug, The 25.00
Mary Poppins 45.00
Mary Poppins 1 . . . . 65.00
McLintock. 125.00
Merlin Jones as the Monkey's Uncle 45.00
Miracle of the White Stallions 30.00
Misadventures of Merlin Jones . . . 50.00
Moon-Spinners, The 75.00
Mutiny on the Bounty 30.00
Nikki, Wild Dog of the North 25.00
Old Yeller 25.00
One Hundred & One Dalmations. . 25.00
Peter Pan 1 . . . . 30.00
Peter Pan 2 . . . . 25.00
P.T. 109 . . . . 45.00
Rio Conchos. 40.00
Robin Hood 25.00
Shaggy Dog & the Absent-Minded Professor 50.00
Snow White & the Seven Dwarfs . 25.00
Son of Flubber 25.00
Summer Magic 75.00
Swiss Family Robinson. 25.00
Sword in the Stone 60.00
That Darn Cat. 50.00
Those Magnificent Men in Their Flying Machines 30.00
Three Stooges in Orbit 100.00
Tiger Walks, A 40.00
Toby Tyler. 25.00
Treasure Island. 25.00
20,000 Leagues Under the Sea . . 25.00
Wonderful Adventures of Pinocchio 25.00
X, the Man with the X-Ray Eyes . 70.00
Yellow Submarine 250.00

MS. MYSTIC
Pacific
1 NA,Origin 8.00
2 NA,Origin,I:Urth 4 . . . . 6.00

Continuity
1 NA,Origin rep. 2.00
2 NA,Origin,I:Urth 4 rep 2.00
3 NA,New material 2.00
4 TSh 2.00
5 DT 2.00
6 . . . . 2.00
7 . . . . 2.00
8 CH/Sdr,B:Love Story. 2.00
9 DB 2.00
9a Newsstand(c) 2.00

[3rd Series]
1 O:Ms.Mystic 2.50
2 A:Hybrid 2.50
3 . . . . 2.50
4 . . . . 2.50

[4th Series, Deathwatch 2000]
1 Deathwatch 2000 pt.8,w/card . . . 2.50
2 Deathwatch 2000 w/card 2.50
3 Indestructible cover, w/card. 2.50

MS. TREE'S THRILLING DETECTIVE ADVENTURES
Eclipse 1983
1 Miller pin up 4.00
2 . . . . 2.50
3 . . . . 2.00
Becomes:

MS. TREE
1984–89
4 thru 6 . . . . @2.00
7 . . . . 2.50
8 . . . . 8.00
9 . . . . 2.00

COLOR PUB.

Aardvark–Vanaheim
10 . . . . 2.00

Renegade
1 3-D. 2.00

MS. VICTORY GOLDEN ANNIVERSARY
AC Comics
1 Ms.Victory celebration 5.00

MS. VICTORY SPECIAL
AC Comics
1 . . . . 2.00

MUMMY, OR RAMSES THE DAMNED, THE
Millennium 1992
1 Anne Rice Adapt. 5.00
2 JM,"Mummy in Mayfair" 3.75
3 JM 3.25
4 JM, To Egypt 3.00
5 JM"The Mummy's Hand". 2.50
6 JM 20th Century Egypt. 2.50
7 JM,More Ramses Past Revealed 2.50
8 JM,Hunt for Cleopatra. 2.50
9 JM,Cleopatra's Wrath contd. 2.50
10 JM,Subterranian World 2.50
11 JM. 2.50

MUMMY ARCHIVES
Millenium
1.JM,Features,articles. 2.50

MUNDEN'S BAR ANNUAL
First
1 BB,JOy,JSn,SR 2.95

MUNSTERS, THE
Gold Key 1965–68
1 . . . . 225.00
2 . . . . 125.00
3 thru 5 . . . . @100.00
6 thru 16 . . . . @70.00

MUPPET BABIES
Harvey
1 Return of Muppet Babies 2.00

MUTANTS & MISFITS
Silverline
1 thru 4 . . . . @2.00

MY FAVORITE MARTIAN
Gold Key 1964–66
1 . . . . 150.00
2 . . . . 75.00
3 thru 9 . . . . @60.00

MY LITTLE MARGIE
Charlton Comics 1954–65
1 Ph(c) 225.00
2 Ph(c) 125.00
3 . . . . 75.00
4 . . . . 75.00
5 . . . . 75.00
6 . . . . 75.00
7 . . . . 75.00
8 . . . . 75.00
9 . . . . 65.00

My Favorite Martian
© Gold Key

10 . . . . 60.00
11 . . . . 50.00
12 . . . . 50.00
13 . . . . 50.00
14 thru 19. . . . . @40.00
20 . . . . 75.00
21 thru 35. . . . . @35.00
36 thru 53. . . . . @30.00
54 Beatles (c). 150.00

MYSTERIES OF UNEXPLORED WORLDS/ SON OF VULCAN
Charlton Comics 1956
1 . . . . 250.00
2 . . . . 100.00
3 . . . . 200.00
4 SD 225.00
5 SD,SD(c) 200.00
6 SD 200.00
7 . . . . 200.00
8 SD 200.00
9 SD 200.00
10 SD,SD(c). 200.00
11 SD,SD(c). 200.00
12 . . . . 150.00
13 thru 18. . . . . @40.00
19 SD(c). 125.00
20 . . . . 30.00
21 thru 24 SD . . . . @150.00
25 . . . . 20.00
26 SD. 125.00
27 thru 30. . . . . @30.00
31 thru 45. . . . . @20.00
46 I:Son ofVulcan,Dr.Kong(1965) . 40.00
47 V:King Midas. 20.00
48 V:Captain Tuska 20.00
Becomes:

SON OF VULCAN
49 DC redesigns costume. 10.00
50 V:Dr.Kong 10.00

MYSTERIOUS SUSPENSE
Charlton 1968
1 SD,F:Question 65.00

MYSTERY COMICS DIGEST
Gold Key March, 1972–75
1 WW 40.00
2 WW 35.00
3 . . . . 30.00
4 Ripleys Believe It or Not 25.00
5 Boris Karloff 25.00
6 Twilight Zone 25.00
7 thru 20 . . . . @25.00
21 thru 26 . . . . @15.00

MYSTIC
Crosgen Comics 2000
1 RMz,BPe 2.95
2 RMz,BPe 2.95
3 RMz,BPe 2.95
4 RMz,BPe 2.95
5 RMz,BPe 2.95

MYSTIC EDGE
Antarctic Press 1998
1 by Ryan Kinnaird, F:Risa
& Symattra. 2.95

MYSTIC ISLE
1 . . . . 2.00

NANCY & SLUGGO
Dell Publishing Co. 1957
146 B:Peanuts 45.00
147 . . . . 30.00
148 . . . . 30.00
149 . . . . 30.00
150 thru 161. . . . . 30.00
162 thru 165. . . . . 75.00
166 thru 176 A:OONA. 90.00
177 thru 180. . . . . 35.00
181 thru 187. . . . . 30.00

NATIONAL VELVET
Dell Publishing Co.
May–July, 1961
1 Ph(c) 75.00
2 Ph(c) 40.00

NEAT STUFF
Fantagraphics
1 . . . . 4.50
2 . . . . 3.00
3 thru 5 . . . . @2.50
6 . . . . 2.25
7 . . . . 2.25

NECROPOLIS
Fleetway
1 SBs(c),CE,A:Dark Judges/
Sisters Of Death. 2.95
2 . . . . 2.95
3 thru 9 . . . . @2.95

NEIL GAIMAN'S LADY JUSTICE
Tekno Comix (1995)
1 I:Lady Justice 2.50
1a 6.00
2 V:Blood Pirate 2.00
3 V:Blood Pirate 2.00
4 New Story Arc 2.00
5 Street Gang War 2.00
6 Street Gang War 2.25
7 thru 11 . . . . @2.25

Big Entertainment April, 1996
1 thru 4 . . . . @2.25
5 DIB(s). 2.25
6 DIB(s),"Woman About Town," pt.1 2.25
7 DIB(s),"Woman About Town," pt.2 2.25
8 DIB(s),"Woman About Town," pt.3 2.25

 All comics prices listed are for *Near Mint* condition.

NEIL GAIMAN'S MR. HERO THE NEWMATIC MAN

Tekno-Comics 1994

1 I:Mr. Hero, Tecknophage. 2.50
2 A:Tecknophage. 2.25
3 I:Adam Kaine 2.00
4 I:New Body. 2.00
5 Earthquake. 2.00
6 I:New Character 2.00
7 I:Deadbolt, Bloodboil. 2.00
8 V:Avatar 2.00
9 in London 2.00
10 V:Demon 2.00
11 V:Monster 2.00
12 The Great Goward. 2.25
13 thru 17. . . . . @2.25

NEIL GAIMAN'S PHAGE

Tekno-Comics 1996

1 . . . . 2.25

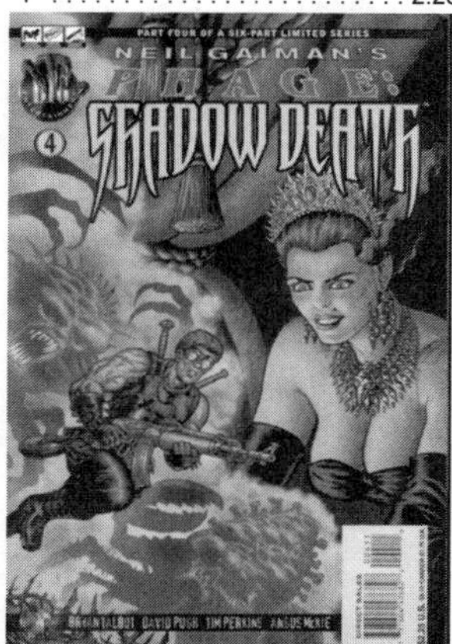

Neil Gaiman's Phange: Shadow Death #4 © Big Entertainment

NEIL GAIMAN'S PHAGE: SHADOW DEATH

Big Entertainment

1 thru 4 . . . . @2.25
5 O:Orlando Holmes,A:Lady Messalina. 2.25
6 conclusion 2.25

NEIL GAIMAN'S TECKNOPHAGE

Teckno-Comics 1995

1 I:Kalighoul, Tom Vietch 2.00
1a Steel Edition. 3.95
2 F:Mayor of New Yorick 2.00
3 Phange Building 2.00
4 Horde eevils. 2.00
5 Middle Management. 2.00
6 Escape from Phange 2.00
7 Mecca 2.25

NEIL GAIMAN'S WHEEL OF WORLDS

Teckno-Comics 1995

0 Deluxe Edition w/Posters 2.95
0a I:Lady Justice 2.00
1 . . . . 3.25

NEMESIS THE WARLOCK

Eagle

1 . . . . 2.00
2 thru 8 . . . . @2.00

NEW ADVENTURES OF FELIX THE CAT

Felix Comics,Inc

1 New stories 2.25
2 "The Magic Paint Brush" 2.25

NEW ADVENTURES OF PINOCCHIO

Dell Publishing Co. 1962

1 . . . . 100.00
2 and 3 . . . . @75.00

NEW ADVENTURES OF SPEED RACER

Now

0 Premiere, 3-D cover 2.00
1 thru 11 . . . . @2.00

NEW AMERICA

Eclipse 1987–88

1 A:Scout 2.00
2 A:Scout 2.00
3 A:Roman Catholic Pope 2.00
4 A:Scout 2.00

NEW BREED

Pied Piper

1 . . . . 2.75
2 . . . . 2.25

NEW CHAMPIONS

1 and 2 . . . . @2.95

NEW DNAGENTS, THE

Eclipse 1985–87

1 R:DNAgents 2.00
2 F:Tank 2.00
3 Repopulating the World 2.00
4 Major Catastrophe for Earth 2.00
5 "Last Place on Earth" 2.00
6 JOy(c),"Postscript" 2.00
7 V:Venimus 2.00
8 DSp,V:Venimus 2.00
9 V:Venimus,I:New Wave. 2.00
10 I:New Airboy 2.00
11 Summer Fun Issue 2.00
12 V:Worm 2.00
13 EL,F:Tank 2.00
14 EL,Nudity,"Grounded" 2.00
15 thru 17. . . . . @2.00
3-D #1 . . . . 2.50

NEW JUSTICE MACHINE

Innovation

1 and 2 . . . . @2.00
2 . . . . 2.00

NEW KABOOM

Awesome Entertainment 1999

1 RLe,JLb 2.50

NEWMEN

Maximum Press

1–22 see Image
23 ErS,CSp,AG,"Anthem," pt.3 . . . . 2.50
24 ErS,CSp,AG,"Anthem," pt.4 . . . . 2.50
25 ErS,CSp,AG,"Anthem," pt.5 . . . . 2.50

NEW ORLEANS SAINTS

1 Playoff season(football team) . . . 6.00

NEW STATESMEN

Fleetway

1 . . . . 4.50
2 thru 5 . . . . @3.95

NEWSTRALIA

Innovation

1 and 2 . . . . @2.00
3 . . . . 2.00

NEW TERRYTOONS

Dell Publishing Co. 1960–61

1 . . . . 55.00
2 thru 8 . . . . @30.00

Gold Key 1962

1 F:Heckle & Jeckle. 75.00
2 . . . . 65.00
3 thru 10 . . . . @25.00
11 thru 20 . . . . @20.00
21 thru 30 . . . . @10.00
31 thru 40 . . . . @7.00
41 thru 54 . . . . @5.00

NEW WAVE, THE

Eclipse 1986–87

1 Error Pages 2.00
1a Correction. 2.00
2 . . . . 2.00
3 "Space Station Called Hell" 2.00
4 Birth of Megabyte 2.00
5 PG(c),O:Avalon 2.00
6 O:Megabyte 2.00
7 Avalon disappears 2.00
8 V:Heap,V:Druids 2.00
9 . . . . 2.00
10 V:Heap Team. 2.00
11 . . . . 2.00
12 . . . . 2.00
13 V:Volunteers 2.00
14 1/3 issue 2.00

NEW WAVE vs. THE VOLUNTEERS

Eclipse

1 3-D,V:Volunteers 2.50
2 3-D,V:Volunteers 2.50

NEXT MAN

Comico 1985

1 I&O:Next Man. 2.50
2 . . . . 2.00
3 . . . . 2.00
4 . . . . 2.00
5 . . . . 2.00

NEXT NEXUS

First

1 SR 2.00
2 SR 2.00
3 SR 2.00
4 SR 2.00

NEXUS
Capital
1 SR,I:Judah Maccabee . . . 5.00
2 SR,Origin,V:Bellows . . . 4.00
3 SR,Sundra Captive . . . 4.00
4 SR,V:Ziggurat . . . 4.00
5 SR,"I'm Bored!" . . . 4.00
6 SR,A:Badger,TrialogueTrilogy#1 . 4.00
First
7 SR,A:Badger,TrialogueTrilogy#2 . 4.00
8 SR,A:Badger,TrialogueTrilogy#3 . 3.00
9 SR,Teen Angel . . . 2.50
10 SR,BWg,Talking Heads . . . 2.00
11 SR,V:Clausius . . . 2.00
12 SR,V:The Old General . . . 2.00
13 SR,Sundra Peale solo . . . 2.00
14 SR,A:Clonezone,Hilariator . . . 2.00
15 SR,A:Clonezone . . . 2.00
16 SR,A:Clonezone . . . 2.00
17 Judah vs. Jacque,the Anvil . . . 2.00
18 SR,A:Clonezone . . . 2.00
19 SR,A:Clonezone . . . 2.00
20 SR,A:Clonezone . . . 2.00
21 SR,A:Clonezone . . . 2.00
22 KG,A:Badger . . . 2.00
23 SR,A:Clonezone . . . 2.00
24 SR,A:Clonezone . . . 2.00
25 SR,A:Clonezone . . . 2.00
26 SR,A:Clonezone . . . 2.00
27 SR,A:Clonezone . . . 2.00
28 MMi . . . 2.00
29 A:Kreed & Sinclair . . . 2.00
30 JL,C:Badger . . . 2.50
31 Judah solo story . . . 2.00
32 JG,Judah solo story . . . 2.00
33 SR,A:Kreed & Sinclair . . . 2.00
34 SR,Judah solo story . . . 2.00
35 SR,Judah solo story . . . 2.00
36 SR . . . 2.00
37 PS . . . 2.00
38 . . . 2.00
39 SR, The Boom Search . . . 2.00
40 SR . . . 2.00
41 SR . . . 2.00
42 SR,Bowl-Shaped world . . . 2.00
43 PS . . . 2.00
44 PS . . . 2.00
45 SR,A:Badger Pt.1 . . . 2.00
46 SR,A:Badger Pt.2 . . . 2.00
47 SR,A:Badger Pt.3 . . . 2.00
48 SR,A:Badger Pt.4 . . . 2.00
49 PS,A:Badger Pt.5 . . . 2.00
50 SF,double size,A:Badger Pt.6
Crossroads tie-in . . . 3.50
51 PS . . . 2.00
52 PS . . . 2.00
53 PS . . . 2.00
54 PS . . . 2.00
55 PS . . . 2.00
56 . . . 2.00
57 AH . . . 2.00
58 Sr,I:Stanislaus Korivitsky
as Nexus . . . 2.00
59 SR . . . 2.00
60 SR . . . 2.00
61 . . . 2.00
62 . . . 2.00
63 V:Elvonic Order . . . 2.00
64 V:Elvonic Order . . . 2.00
65 V:Elvonic Order . . . 2.00
66 V:Elvonic Order . . . 2.00
67 V:Elvonic Order . . . 2.00
68 LM . . . 2.00
69 . . . 2.00
70 . . . 2.00
71 V:Bad Brains . . . 2.00
72 V:Renegade heads . . . 2.00
73 Horatio returns to Ylum . . . 2.00
74 Horatio vs. Stan . . . 2.00
75 Horatio vs. Stan . . . 2.00
76 . . . 2.25
77 . . . 2.25
78 O:Nexus,Nexus Files Pt#1 . . . 2.25
79 Nexus Files Pt#2 . . . 2.25
80 Nexus.Files Pt#3,last iss . . . 2.25

Nexus Legends #5
© First

NEXUS LEGENDS
First
1 thru 13 rep.Nexus . . . @2.00
14 rep.Nexus . . . 2.00
15 rep.Nexus . . . 2.00
16 rep.Nexus . . . 2.00
17 rep.Nexus . . . 2.00
18 rep.Nexus . . . 2.00
19 rep.Nexus . . . 2.00
20 SR,Sanctuary . . . 2.00
21 thru 23 SR . . . @2.00

NICK HOLIDAY
Argo May, 1956
1 Strip reprints . . . 50.00

NICKI SHADOW
Relentless Comics
1 by Eric Burnham & Ted Naifeh . . 2.50
2 Killing Zone, pt.2 . . . 2.50
3 Killing Zone, pt.3 . . . 2.50
4 Killing Zone, concl. . . . 2.50

NIGHT GLIDER
Topps
1 V:Bombast,C:Captain Glory, Trading Card . . . 3.25

NIGHTMARE
Innovation
1 . . . 2.50

NIGHTMARE AND CASPER
Harvey Publications 1963
1 . . . 65.00
2 . . . 40.00
3 . . . 40.00
4 . . . 40.00
5 . . . 40.00
Becomes:
CASPER AND

NIGHTMARE
6 B:68 pgs . . . 20.00
7 . . . 10.00
8 . . . 10.00
9 . . . 10.00
10 . . . 10.00
11 thru 20 . . . @7.00
21 thru 30 . . . @5.00
31 . . . 5.00
32 E:68 pgs . . . 5.00
33 thru 45 . . . @3.00
46 Aug., 1974 . . . 3.00

NIGHTMARE ON ELM STREET
Blackthorne
1 3-D . . . 2.50
2 3-D . . . 2.50
3 3-D . . . 2.50

NIGHTMARES ON ELM STREET
Innovation
1 Yours Truly, Freddy Krueger Pt.1 3.00
2 Yours Truly ,Freddy Krueger Pt.2 2.50
3 Loose Ends Pt.1,Return to
Springwood . . . 2.50
4 Loose Ends Pt 2 . . . 2.50
5 . . . 2.50
6 . . . 2.50

NIGHTMARES
Eclipse 1985
1 . . . 2.50
2 . . . 2.00

NIGHT MUSIC
Eclipse 1984–88
1 . . . 2.50
2 . . . 2.50
3 CR, Jungle Bear . . . 3.00
4 Pelias & Melisande . . . 2.00
5 Pelias . . . 2.00
6 same as Salome #1
7 same as Red Dog #1
Graphic Novel . . . 8.00

NIGHTS INTO DREAMS
Archie Comics 1997
1 based on Sega game . . . 2.00
2 thru 6 . . . 2.00

NIGHTSHADE
No Mercy Comics 1997
1 by Mark Williams . . . 2.50
2 and 3 . . . @2.50

NIGHT TRIBES
Wildstorm/DC 1999
1-shot Night Tribes unite . . . 5.00

NIGHTEVIL
AC Comics
1 . . . 3.50
2 . . . 2.50
3 . . . 2.25
4 . . . 2.25
5 . . . 2.25
6 . . . 2.00
7 . . . 2.00
Spec.#1 . . . 2.00

NIGHT WALKER
Fleetway
1 thru 2 ... @2.95

NIGHTWOLF
1 ... 2.00
2 ... 2.00

9 LIVES OF FELIX
Harvey
1 thru 4 ... @2.00

NINE LIVES TO LIVE
Fantagraphics
HC 9"x12" Felix the Cat strips, by Otto Messmer ... 40.00

NINJA HIGH SCHOOL
Eternity
1 Reps.orig.N.H.S.in color ... 2.00
2 thru 13 reprints ... @2.00

NINJA HIGH SCHOOL VERSION 2
Antarctic Press 1999
1 by Ben Dunn ... 7.00
2 ... 5.00
3 ... 4.00
4 ... 3.00
5 thru 8 ... @2.50
9 Yumei strikes back ... 2.50
10 ... 2.50
11 Time & space distorted ... 2.50
12 When Worlds Colide, last issue . 2.50

Ninja High School #2B
© Eternity

NINJA HIGH SCHOOL FEATURING SPEED RACER
Eternity 1993
1B ... 2.95
2B ... 2.95

NINJA STAR
1 ... 2.00

NIRA X: ANIME
Entity Comics 1997
1 BMs ... 2.95
1a deluxe, foil cover ... 3.50
2 BMs ... 2.95
2a deluxe, foil cover ... 3.50
Swimsuit #0 ... 2.75
Swimsuit #0 Manga (c) ... 2.75

NIRA X: CYBERANGEL
Entity 1994
1 From pages of Zen ... 2.95
1a 2nd printing ... 2.75
2 V:Parradox ... 2.50
3 In Hydro-Dams ... 2.50
4 final issue ... 2.50
4a with computer game ... 6.95
Ashcan ... 2.50
TPB Birth of an Angel ... 12.95

[Series 2] 1995
1 R:Nira X ... 3.75
1a Clear Chromium Edition ... 8.00
1b Holo-Chrome edition ... 10.00
2 Alien Invasion ... 2.50
3 Mecha New York ... 2.50
4 Final Issue ... 2.50

[Series 3] 1996
0 ... 2.75
0a signed & numbered ... 8.00
1 ... 2.50
1a gold edition, signed & numb.... 5.00
2 ... 2.50
3 ... 3.00

NIRA X/CYNDER: ENDANGERED SPECIES
Entity Comics 1996
1 ... 3.00
1a gold ink enhanced, bagged ... 13.00

NOID IN 3-D
Blackthorne
1 thru 3 ... @2.50

NOMAN
Tower Comics 1966
1 GK,OW,WW,AW ... 75.00
2 OW,WW,A:Dynamo ... 50.00

NOOGIE KOOTCH: SECRET AGENT MAN
Hobo Comics
1 I:Noogie Kootch ... 2.75
2 F:Celutron CIty ... 2.75

NOSFERATU: PLAGUE OF TERROR
Millennium
1 I:Orlock ... 2.50
2 19th Century India,A:Sir W. Longsword ... 2.50
3 WWI/WWII to Viet Nam ... 2.50
4 O:Orlock,V:Longsword,conc.... 2.50

NO TIME FOR SERGEANTS
Dell Publishing Co. July, 1958
1 Ph(c) ... 125.00
2 Ph(c) ... 65.00
3 Ph(c) ... 50.00

NOVA HUNTER
Ryal Comics
1 thru 3 ... @2.50
4 Climax ... 2.50
5 Death and Betrayal ... 2.50

NUBIAN KNIGHT
Samson Comics
1 I:Shandai ... 2.50

NURSES, THE
Gold Key April, 1963
1 ... 40.00
2 ... 25.00
3 ... 25.00

NYOKA, JUNGLE GIRL
Charlton Comics 1955–57
14 ... 75.00
15 ... 50.00
16 ... 50.00
17 ... 50.00
18 ... 50.00
19 ... 50.00
20 ... 50.00
21 ... 50.00
22 ... 50.00

NYOKA, THE JUNGLE GIRL
AC Comics
1 and 2 ... @2.00

OBLIVION
Comico 1995
1 R:The Elementals ... 2.50
2 I:Thunderboy, Lilith ... 2.50
3 I:Fen, Ferril ... 2.50
4 War ... 2.95
5 The Unholy Trilogy ... 2.95

OCCULT FILES OF DR. SPEKTOR
Gold Key April, 1973
1 I:Lakot ... 25.00
2 thru 5 ... @12.00
6 thru 10 ... @10.00
11 I:Spertor as Werewolf ... 10.00
12 and 13 ... @8.00
14 A:Dr. Solar ... 25.00
15 thru 24 ... @8.00

Whitman
25 rep ... 3.00

O.G. WHIZ
Gold Key 1971–79
1 ... 60.00
2 ... 35.00
3 ... 30.00
4 ... 30.00
5 ... 30.00
6 ... 30.00
7 ... 15.00
8 ... 15.00
9 ... 15.00
10 ... 15.00
11 ... 15.00

COLOR PUB.

OINK: BLOOD AND CIRCUS
Kitchen Sink 1997
1 (of 4) by John Mueller. 4.95
2 . . . . 4.95
3 . . . . 4.95
4 conclusion 4.95

O'MALLEY AND THE ALLEY CATS
Gold Key 1971–74
1 . . . . 25.00
2 thru 9 . . . . @20.00

OMEGA 7
Omega 7
1 V:Exterminator X 3.95
½ by Alonzo L. Washington 3.95
0 . . . . 3.00

OMEGA ELITE
Blackthorne
1 . . . . 2.00
2 . . . . 2.00

OMEGA SAGA, THE
Southpaw Publishing 1998
0 by Mike Gerardo & Chris Navetta 3.00
1 Episode One, pt.1. . . . . 3.00
2 Episode One, pt.2 . . . . 3.00
Axess Comics
3 by Mike Gerardo, Heroes (c). . . . 3.00
3b Villains (c) 3.00

OMEN, THE
Chaos! Comics
Preview Book, BnP. 2.00
1 by PNu & Justiniano 2.95
2 . . . . 2.95
3 . . . . 2.95
4 . . . . 2.95
5 concl. 2.95
1-shot The Omen Vexed. 2.95
TPB The Omen 12.95

OMNI MEN
Blackthorne
1 . . . . 2.00
2 . . . . 2.00

ON A PALE HORSE
Innovation
1 Piers Anthony adapt 4.95
2 "Magician",I:Kronos. 4.95
3 . . . . 4.95
4 VV, ... 4.95
5 . . . . 4.95
6 . . . . 4.95

ONE-ARM SWORDSMAN
1 . . . . 2.95
2 . . . . 2.95
3 . . . . 2.75
4 . . . . 2.00
5 . . . . 2.00
6 . . . . 2.00
7 . . . . 2.00
8 . . . . 2.00
9 . . . . 2.00
10 . . . . 2.00
11 . . . . 2.00

ORBIT
Eclipse 1990
1 DSt(c). 3.95
2 . . . . 3.95
3 . . . . 4.95

ORIENTAL HEROES
Jademan
1 . . . . 2.50
2 . . . . 2.00
3 thru 13 . . . . @2.00
14 thru 27 . . . . @2.00
28 V:Skeleton Secretary 2.00
29 Barbarian vs.Lone Kwoon 2.00
30 Barbarian vs.Lone Kwoon 2.00
31 SkeletonSecretaryUprisng 2.00
32 Uprising Continues 2.00
33 Jupiter Kills His Brother 2.00
34 Skeleton Sec. Suicide 2.00
35 Red Sect Vs. Global Cult. 2.00
36 A:Tiger 2.00
37 Old Supreme 2.00
38 Tiger vs. 4 Hitmen 2.00
39 D:Infinite White, V:Red Sect. . . . 2.00
40 The Golden Buddhha Temple. . . 2.00
41 thru 43. . . . . 2.00
44 SilverChime rescue 2.00
45 Global Cult Battle. 2.00
46 thru 48 . . . . @2.00
49 F:GoldDragon/SilverChime 2.00
50 Return to Global Cult. 2.00
51 Gang Of Three Vs.White Beau & Lone Kwoon-Tin 2.00
52 Global Cult vs Red Sect. 2.00
53 Global Cult vs.Red Sect. 2.00

ORIGINAL ASTRO BOY
Now
1 KSy 3.00
2 thru 5 KSy. . . . . @2.00
6 thru 17 KSy . . . . @2.00

ORIGINAL DICK TRACY
Gladestone
1 rep.V:Mrs.Pruneface. 2.00
2 rep.V:Influence 2.00
3 rep.V:TheMole 2.00
4 rep.V:ItchyOliver. 2.00
5 rep.V:Shoulders 2.00

ORIGINAL E-MAN
First
{rep. Charlton stories}
1 JSon,O:E-Man & Nova 2.00
2 JSon,V:Battery,SamuelBoar 2.00
3 JSon,"City in the Sand". 2.00
4 JSon,A:Brain from Sirius. 2.00
5 JSon,V:T.V. Man 2.00
6 JSon,I:Teddy Q. 2.00
7 JSon,Vamfire 2.00

ORIGINAL SHIELD
ABC
1 DAy/TD,O:Shield 2.00
2 DAy,O:Dusty. 2.00
3 DAy 2.00
4 DAy 2.00

ORIGIN OF THE DEFIANT UNIVERSE
Defiant
1 O:Defiant Characters 2.00

Original Shield #1
© ABC

OUTBREED 999
Blackout Comics
1 thru 4 . . . . @2.95
5 Search For Daige 2.95

OUTCASTS
1 . . . . 2.00

OUTER LIMITS, THE
Dell Publishing Co.
Jan.–March, 1964
1 P(c) 125.00
2 P(c) 75.00
3 P(c) 60.00
4 P(c) 60.00
5 P(c) 60.00
6 P(c) 60.00
7 P(c) 60.00
8 P(c) 60.00
9 P(c) 60.00
10 P(c). 60.00
11 thru 18 P(c) . . . . @40.00

OUTLAWS OF THE WEST
Charlton Comics 1956–80
11 . . . . 50.00
12 . . . . 30.00
13 . . . . 30.00
14 Giant. 50.00
15 . . . . 30.00
16 . . . . 30.00
17 . . . . 30.00
18 SD. 75.00
19 . . . . 30.00
20 . . . . 30.00
21 thru 30. . . . . @25.00
31 thru 50. . . . . @20.00
51 thru 70. . . . . @15.00
71 thru 88. . . . . @10.00

OUT OF THIS WORLD
Charlton Comics 1956–59
1 . . . . 175.00
2 . . . . 100.00
3 SD 225.00
4 SD 225.00
5 SD 225.00
6 SD 225.00

COLOR PUB.

7 SD,SD(c) 225.00
8 SD 200.00
9 SD 175.00
10 SD. 175.00
11 SD. 200.00
12 SD. 175.00
13 thru 15 . . . . @60.00
16 . . . . 165.00

OUTPOSTS
Blackthorne

1 thru 6 . . . . @2.00

OWL, THE
Gold Key April, 1967

1 . . . . 40.00
2 April, 1968 . . . . 35.00

PACIFIC PRESENTS
Pacific 1992

1 DSt,Rocketeer,(3rd App.) 12.00
2 DSt,Rocketeer,(4th App.) 9.00
3 SD,I:Vanity 2.50
4 and 5 . . . . @2.00

P.A.C.
Artifacts, Inc.

1 I:P.A.C. 2.00

PAINKILLER JANE
Event Comics 1997

1 JQ(c) 2.95
1 RL(c) 2.95
1 Red foil logo, signed 24.95
2 JQ&JP(c) 2.95
2 JP&RL(c) 2.95
3 JQ&JP(c) 2.95
3a JP&RL(c) 2.95
4 JQ&JP(c) A Too Bright Place
For Dying 2.95
4a RL&JP(c) 2.95
5 JQ&JP(c) Purgatory
Station—Next Stop Hell 2.95
5a RL&JP(c) 2.95
6 RL&JP(c) Blood Harvest 2.95
6a BSz&JP(c) 2.95
7 Jane in the Jungle,
pt.1,BiT&JP(c) 2.95
7a RL&JP(c) 2.95
Spec.#0 O:Painkiller Jane,48-page . 3.95
Spec.#0A signed 30.00
Spec. Painkiller Jane/Hellboy
Ancient Laughter (1998) 2.95
Spec. Painkiller Jane/Hellboy,
signed 20.00
Spec. Painkiller Jane/The Darkness,
signed, limited edition, JQ(c). . 29.95

PAINKILLER JANE/ DARKCHYLDE
Event Comics 1998

1 BAu,RQu 2.95
1a signed & numbered. 30.00
1b Omnichrome edition 14.95
1c Omnichrome, signed. 30.00
1d Dynamic Forces cover 6.95

PAINKILLER JANE VS. THE DARKNESS: STRIPPER
Event Comics 1997

1 GEn,JP,x-over, Amanda Connor
cover 2.95

1a Greg & Tim Hildebrandt 2.95
1b MS(c) 2.95
1c JQ(c) 2.95

PALADIN ALPHA
Firstlight

1 I:Paladin Alpha 2.95
2 V:Hellfire Triger. 2.95

PANDEMONIUM: DELIVERANCE
Chaos! Comics 1998

1-shot by Jesse Leon McCann &
Jack Jadson. 2.95

PANIC
Gemstone 1997

1 thru 12 EC Comics reprint. . . . @2.50
"Annuals"
TPB Vol. 1 rebinding #1–#4 . . . . . 10.50
TPB Vol. 2 rebinding #5–#8 . . . . . 10.95

PANTHA
Harris Comics 1997

1 (of 2) MT 3.50
1 Marylin Monroe MT alt.cov. 9.95
2 MT alternate (c) 9.95
2 photo (c). 9.95

PARADAX
Eclipes

1 . . . . 2.25

PARADIGM
Gauntlet

1 A:Predator 2.95

PARADISE
Twenty First Century 2000

1 thru 7 . . . . @2.95

PARAGON DARK APOCALYPSE
AC 1993

1 thru 4, Fem Force crossover. . . . 2.95

Paragon Dark Apocalypse #1
© AC Comics

PARANOIA
Adventure Comics

1 (based on video game)"Clone1" . 3.25
2 King-R-Thr-2 . . . . 2.95
3 R:Happy Jack,V:N3F 2.95
4 V:The Computer 2.95
5 V:The Computer 2.95
6 V:Lance-R-Lot,last issue 2.95

PARTRIDGE FAMILY, THE
Charlton Comics 1971–73

1 . . . . 60.00
2 thru 4 . . . . @25.00
5 Summer Special 75.00
6 thru 21 . . . . @25.00

PASSOVER
Maximum Press

1 (of 2) BNa 3.00
2 BNa,A:Avengelyne 3.00

PATHWAYS TO FANTASY
Pacific

1 BS,JJ art 3.00

PAT SAVAGE: WOMAN OF BRONZE
Millennium

1 F:Doc Savage's cousin 2.50

PEACEMAKER
Charlton

1 A:Fightin' 5 . . . . 5.00
2 A:Fightin' 5 . . . . 3.00
3 A:Fightin' 5 . . . . 3.00
4 O:Peacemaker,A:Fightin' 5 . . . . . 4.00
5 A:Fightin' 5 . . . . 2.50

PEANUTS
Dell Publishing Co. 1958

1 . . . . 175.00
2 . . . . 135.00
3 . . . . 125.00
4 . . . . 100.00
5 . . . . 75.00
6 . . . . 75.00
7 . . . . 75.00
8 . . . . 75.00
9 . . . . 75.00
10 . . . . 75.00
11 . . . . 75.00
12 . . . . 75.00
13 . . . . 75.00

PEANUTS
Gold Key May, 1963

1 . . . . 125.00
2 thru 4 . . . . 100.00

PEBBLES & BAMM-BAMM
Charlton Comics 1972–76

1 . . . . 50.00
2 thru 10 . . . . @25.00
11 thru 36 . . . . @20.00

PEBBLES FLINTSTONE
Gold Key Sept., 1963

1 "A Chip off the old block" 125.00

PELLESTAR

1 . . . . 2.00

PERG

Lightning Comics

1 Glow in the dark(c),JS(c), B:JZy(s),KIK,I:Perg 3.75
1a Platinum Ed. 5.00
1b Gold Ed. 7.00
1 gold edition, glow-in-the-dark flip cover 30.00
2 KIK,O:Perg 3.25
2a Platinum Ed. 5.00
3 Flip Book (c), ... 3.25
3a Platinum Ed 5.00
4 TLw,I:Hellina. 9.00
4a Platinum Ed 5.00
5 A:Hellina. 3.25
6 PIA,A:Hellina 3.25
6 nude cover 9.00
7 . . . . 3.00
8 V:Police 3.00

PERRY MASON MYSTERY MAGAZINE

Dell Publishing Co. 1964

1 . . . . 40.00
2 Ray Burr Ph(c) 30.00

PETER PAN: RETURN TO NEVER NEVER LAND

1 Peter in Mass. 2.50
2 V:Tiger Lily 2.50

PETER POTAMUS

Gold Key Jan., 1965

1 . . . . 100.00

PETTICOAT JUNCTION

Dell Publishing Co. 1964

1 Ph(c) 75.00
2 Ph(c) 50.00
3 Ph(c) 50.00
4 . . . . 50.00
5 Ph(c) 50.00

PHANTOM, THE

Gold Key 1962

1 RsM 165.00
2 B:King, Queen & Jack. 85.00
3 . . . . 65.00
4 . . . . 65.00
5 . . . . 65.00
6 . . . . 65.00
7 "The Super Apes". 65.00
8 . . . . 65.00
9 . . . . 65.00
10 "The Sleeping Giant" 65.00
11 E:King,Queen and Jack 50.00
12 B:Track Hunter 50.00
13 . . . . 50.00
14 "The Historian". 50.00
15 . . . . 50.00
16 . . . . 50.00
17 "Samaris". 50.00

King Comics Sept. 1966

18 "The Treasure of the Skull Cave;"BU:Flash Gordon 65.00
19 "The Astronaut & the Pirates". . 40.00
20 A:GirlPhantom,E:FlashGordon . 40.00
21 BU:Mandrake. 40.00
22 "Secret of Magic Mountain" . . . 40.00
23 . . . . 40.00
24 A:Girl Phantom 40.00
25 . . . . 40.00
26 . . . . 40.00
27 . . . . 40.00
28 . . . . 40.00
29. . . . . 40.00

Charlton Comics 1969–77

30 . . . . 20.00
31 JAp,"Phantom of Shang-Ri-La" 20.00
32 JAp,"The Pharaoh Phantom" . . 20.00
33 . . . . 20.00
34 . . . . 20.00
35 . . . . 20.00
36 . . . . 20.00
37 . . . . 20.00
38 . . . . 20.00
39 . . . . 20.00
40 "The Ritual" 20.00
41 . . . . 15.00
42 . . . . 15.00
43 . . . . 15.00
44 "To Right A Wrong" 15.00
45 . . . . 15.00
46 I:Piranha 20.00
47 "The False Skull Cave" 15.00
48 . . . . 15.00
49 . . . . 15.00
50 . . . . 15.00
51 "A Broken Vow" 15.00
52 . . . . 15.00
53 . . . . 15.00
54 . . . . 15.00
55 . . . . 15.00
56 . . . . 15.00
57 NightmareMedicine in Bengali . 15.00
58 . . . . 15.00
59 . . . . 15.00
60 . . . . 15.00
61 "A Dead Man's Promise" 15.00
62 . . . . 15.00
63 . . . . 15.00
64 "Duel With Death" 15.00
65 . . . . 15.00
66 "Goldbeard the Pirate". 15.00
67 "Triumph of Evil" 20.00
68 . . . . 15.00
69 . . . . 15.00
70 . . . . 15.00
71 . . . . 10.00
72 "Man in the Shadows" 10.00
73 . . . . 10.00
74 . . . . 20.00

PHANTOM

Wolf Publishing 1992

1 Drug Runners. 2.25
2 Mystery Child of the Sea. 2.25
3 inc.feature pages on Phantom/Merchandise 2.25
4 TV Jungle Crime Buster 2.25
5 Castle Vacula-Transylvania. 2.25
6 The Old West 2.25
7 Sercet of Colussus 2.75
8 Temple of the Sun God. 2.75

PHANTOM BOLT, THE

Gold Key 1964–66

1 . . . . 60.00
2 . . . . 40.00
3 . . . . 30.00
4 . . . . 30.00
5 . . . . 30.00
6 . . . . 30.00
7 . . . . 30.00

PHANTOM FORCE

Genesis West 1994

Previously: Image

0 JK/JLe(c) 2.75
3 thru 10 . . . . @2.50

PHAZE

Eclipse 1988

1 BSz(c),Takes place in future 2.25
2 PG(c),V:The Pentagon 2.00
3 Schwieger Vs. Mammoth 2.00

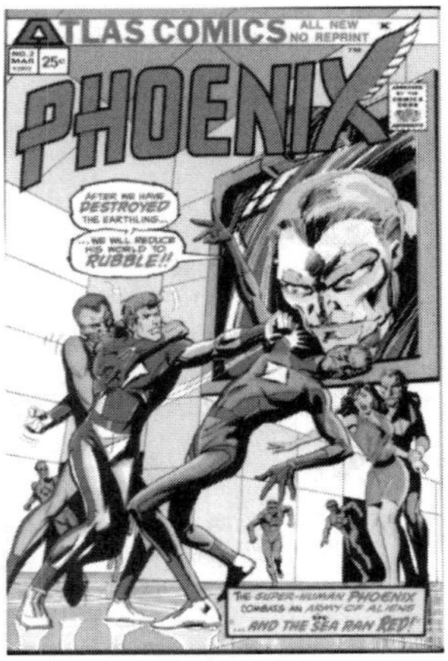

Phoenix #2
© Atlas Comics

PHOENIX

Atlas 1975

1 thru 4 . . . . @5.00

PINK PANTHER, THE

Gold Key April, 1971

1 . . . . 50.00
2 thru 10 . . . . @25.00
11 thru 30 . . . . @15.00
31 thru 60 . . . . @10.00
61. . . . . 10.00

PINOCCHIO

1 . . . . 2.00

PIRACY

Gemstone 1998

1 EC comics reprint. 2.50
2 thru 7 EC comics reprints . . . . @2.50
"Annuals"
TPB Vol. 1 rebinding #1–#4 . . . . . 10.50
TPB Vol. 2 rebinding #5–#7 . . . . . . 7.95

PIRATE CORP.

Eternity

1 thru 5 . . . . @2.00

P.I.'S, THE

First

1 JSon,Ms.Tree,M Mauser. 2.00
2 JSon,Ms.Tree,M Mauser. 2.00
3 JSon,Ms.Tree,M Mauser. 2.00

PITT

Full Bleed Studios

1 thru 9, see Image
10 thru 14 DK . . . . @2.50
14a variant cover 7.00
15 DK. 2.50

COLOR PUB.

16 DK, Ugly Americans, pt.1 . . . . . . 2.50
17 DK, Ugly Americans, pt.2 . . . . . . 2.50
18 DK, Ugly Americans, pt.3, concl. 2.50
19 by Brian Dawson 2.95
20 DK, Urgral Thul 2.50
TPB Vol. 1, rep. ½ –#4 . . . . . . 10.95
TPB Vol. 2, rep. #5–#9 . . . . 11.95
Spec. In the Blood 2.50

PITT CREW

Full Bleed Studios 1998

1 Monster 2.50
2 F:Rai-Kee. 2.50
3 Tyrants 2.50
4 The Slayer 2.50
5 . . . . 2.50

PITT: BIOGENESIS

Full Bleed Studios 2000

1 (of 3) DK 2.50
2 DK. 2.50

PLANETARY

Wildstorm/DC 1999

1 WEI 2.50
2 WEI 2.50
3 WEI 2.50
4 WEI 2.50
5 WEI 2.50
6 WEI 2.50

PLANET COMICS

Blackthorne

1 DSt(c). 2.00
2 thru 4 . . . . @2.00

PLANET OF VAMPIRES

Atlas Feb.–July 1975

1 thru 3 . . . . @10.00

POGZ N SLAMMER

Blackout Comics 1995

1 I:Pogz N Slammer 2.00
2 Contact Other Schools 2.00

POISON ELVES

Sirius Entertainment 1998

Color Special #1 by Drew Hayes . . 2.95
Color Spec.#1 limited 9.95

POIZON

London Night Studios 1995

0 . . . . 3.00
0 signed gothchik edition 9.00
½ O:Poizon 3.00
½a Commemorative (1999) 5.95
1 . . . . 3.00
1a Necro-Nude edition. 5.95
1b Photo Nude Edition signed 9.00
1c signed 7.00
2 EHr 3.00

POIZON: CADILLACS AND GREEN TOMATOES

London Night 1997

2 . . . . 3.00
2a deluxe nude cover 5.00
3 . . . . 3.00
6 deluxe 5.00

POIZON: DEMON HUNTER

London Night 1998

1 . . . . 3.00
1 Green Death edition 14.95

POIZON: LOST CHILD

London Night Studios 1996

0 . . . . 3.00
1 mini series 3.00
1a Necro-Nude variant cover 5.95
1 signed 9.00
1 Green Death edition 14.95
2 thru 3 . . . . @3.00

POKÉMAN TALES:

Viz Communications 1999 (Boardbooks)

1 Charmander Sees a Ghost 4.95
2 Pikachu's Day 4.95
3 Come Out, Squirtle! 4.95
4 Bulbasaur's Trouble 4.95
5 . . . . 4.95
6 . . . . 4.95
7 . . . . 4.95
8 . . . . 4.95
9 Meet Mew 4.95
10 Snorlax's Snack. 4.95
11 Jigglypuff's Magic Lullaby. 4.95
12 Lapras Makes a Friend 4.95
13 Eevee's Weather Report 4.95
14 Diglett's Birthday Party 4.95
15 First Prize for Starmie 4.95
16 Seel to the Rescue 4.95
Gift Set Vol. 1 . . . . 19.95
Gift Set Vol. 2 . . . . 19.95
Movie Spec. 4.95

POKÉMAN THE MOVIE 2000: REVELATION LUGIA

Viz Communications 2000

1 . . . . 3.95
2 . . . . 3.95
3 . . . . 3.95
Spec. Pikachu's Rescue Adventure 3.95
Art of Pokeman The Movie 2000. . . 9.95

POKÉMAN: THE FIRST MOVIE

Viz Communications 1999

1 (of 4) Mewtwo Strikes Back 3.95
2 . . . . 3.95
3 . . . . 3.95
4 conclusion 3.95
Spec. Pikachu's Vacation 3.95
Art of Pokeman: First Movie 8.95
TPB 15.95

POKÉMON TV ANIMATION

Viz Comics 2000

TPB Vol. 1 . . . . 10.95

POPEYE

Gold Key 1962

1-65 See Golden Age Section
66 . . . . 75.00
67 . . . . 50.00
68 thru 80 . . . . @25.00

King Comics 1966

81 thru 92 . . . . @20.00

Charlton 1969

94 thru 99 . . . . @20.00
100 . . . . 25.00
101 thru 138 . . . . @15.00

Popeye #146
© Gold Key

Gold Key 1978

139 thru 143 . . . . @7.00
144 50th Aniv. Spec.. . . . . 10.00
155 . . . . @10.00

Whitman

156 thru 159 . . . . @10.00
162 thru 171 . . . . @10.00

POPEYE

Harvey Comics 1993–94

1 thru 7 . . . . @2.00
Summer Spec.#1 . . . . 2.25

POPEYE SPECIAL

Ocean 1987–88

1 . . . . 2.00
2 . . . . 2.00

POWER FACTOR

Wonder Color Comics 1986

1 . . . . 4.00
2 . . . . 3.00
3 . . . . 3.00

POWER FACTOR

Innovation

1 thru 4 . . . . @2.25

POWERKNIGHTS

Amara 1995

P I:Powerknights 2.00

POWER RANGERS ZEO/YOUNGBLOOD

Maximum Press 1997

1 TNu,NRd 3.00

POWERS THAT BE

Broadway Comics

Preview Editions Sept. 1995

1 thru 3 B&W. . . . . @2.50

Regular Series Nov. 1995

1 JiS,I:Fatale, Star Seed 3.00
2 thru 4 . . . . @2.95
5 "It's the End of the World As We Know It" pt.1. . . . . 2.95

COLOR PUB.

6 "It's the End of the World As We Know It" pt.2. . . . . 2.95
Becomes:

STAR SEED

7 "It's the End of the World As We Know It" pt.3. . . . . 2.95
8 "It's the End of the World As We Know It" pt.4. . . . . 2.95
9 "It's the End of the World As We Know It" pt.5. . . . . 2.95
10 JiS(s),JRs,"It's the End of the World As We Know It" pt6. . . . . 2.95
11 JiS(s),JRs,"It's the End of the World As We Know It" pt7. . . . . 2.95

PRESSBUTTON
Eclipse
(see Axel Pressbutton)
5 and 6 . . . . @2.00

PRIEST
Maximum Press 1996
1 RLd, F:Michael O'Bannon. 3.00
2 RLd,BNa, ... 3.00
3 RLd 3.00

PRIMAL RAGE
Sirius 1996
1 TAr,from video game 2.95
1 foil cover, limited edition 2.95
2 TAr,DOe(c) 2.95

PRIMER
Comico 1982–84
1 . . . . 10.00
2 I:Grendel 85.00
3 . . . . 5.00
4 C:Maxx. 7.00
5 I:Maxx 30.00
6 I:Evangelyne. 14.00
[Volume 2] 1996
1 F:Lady Bathory. 2.95

PRIMUS
Charlton Comics 1972
1 . . . . 15.00
2 thru 5 . . . . @10.00
6 thru 7 . . . . @8.00

Primus #6
© Charlton Comics

PRINCESS SALLY
Archie Comics
1 thru 3 Sonic tie-in . . . . @3.00

PRINCE VANDAL
Triumphant
1 JnR(s), ... 2.50
2 JnR(s), ... 2.50
3 JnR(s),ShG,I:Claire,V:Nicket, Vandal goes to Boviden 2.50
4 JnR(s),ShG,Game's End 2.50
5 JnR(s),ShG,The Sickness, the rat appears. 2.50
6 JnR(s),ShG,B:Gothic 2.50

PRIORITY: WHITE HEAT
AC Comics 1986
1 thru 2 miniseries . . . . @2.00

PRISON SHIP
1 . . . . 2.00

PRIVATEERS
Vanguard Graphics
1 . . . . 2.00
2 . . . . 2.00

PROFESSIONAL: GOGOL 13
Viz
1 . . . . 4.95
2 and 3 . . . . @4.95

PROFESSOR OM
Innovation
1 I:Rock Warrior 2.50
2 Samurai Drama 2.50

PROJECT A-KO 0
Antarctic Press 1994
0 digest size 5.00
Continued by Malibu

PROJECT A-KO 2
CPM 1995
Previously Malibu
1 Space Saga 2.95
2 Space Saga 2.95
3 Queen Margarita 2.95

PROJECT A-KO: VERSUS THE UNIVERSE
CPM 1995
1 Based on Animation 2.95
2 strange magician 3.00
3 . . . . 3.00
4 (of 5) TEI 2.95

PROMETHEA
Wildstorm/DC 1999
America's Best Comics
1 AMo(s),F:Sophie Bangs,40-page 3.50
2 AMo(s),Judgment of Solomon. . . 3.00
3 AMo(s),Misty Magic Land 3.00

PROPHECY
Immortelle Studios 1998
1 by Hawk, Lovalle, & Wong, F:Cynder & War Dragon 2.95
2 . . . . 2.95

PROPHECY OF THE SOUL SORCERER
Arcane Comics 1999
1 (of 4) by Eric Dean Seaton 2.95
2 . . . . 2.95
3 . . . . 2.95
3a variant (c). 2.95
4 . . . . 2.95
4a variant (c). 2.95
5 . . . . 2.95
5a variant (c). 2.95
6 Nighthawk vs. Morbid 2.95
6a variant (c). 2.95
7 . . . . 2.95
TPB Vol. 1 . . . . 10.95

PROPHET II
Awesome Entertainment 1999
1 . . . . 2.99
1a holochrome wraparound (c) . . 15.00
TPB Timetrap 12.99

PROPHET: LEGACY
Awesome Entertainment 1999
1 RLe 2.99
2 . . . . 2.99
2a variant (c). 2.99
3 . . . . 2.99

PROPHET/CABLE
Maximum 1997
1 (of 2) RLd x-over 3.50
2 RLd x-over,A:Domino, Kirby, Blaquesmith 3.50

PROWLER
Eclipse 1987
1 I:Prowler. 2.00
2 GN,A:Original Prowler 2.00
3 GN. 2.00
4 GN. 2.00
5 GN, adaption of "Vampire Bat" . . 2.00
6 w/flexi-disk record. 2.00

PROWLER IN "WHITE ZOMBIE", THE
Eclipse 1988
1 . . . . 2.00

PRUDENCE AND CAUTION
Defiant
1 CCl(s), ... 3.25
1a Spanish Version 3.25
2 CCl(s), ... 2.50
2a Spanish Version 2.50
3 CCl(s), ... 2.50
3a Spanish Version 2.50
4 CCl(s), ... 2.50
4a Spanish Version 2.50
5 CCl(s), ... 2.50
5a Spanish Version 2.50

PSYCHO
Innovation
1 Hitchcock movie adapt 2.50
2 continued 2.50
3 continued 2.50

PSYCHOANALYSIS
Gemstone 1999
1 (of 4) 2.50
2 . . . . 2.50
3 . . . . 2.50
TPB Ann. #1. . . . . 10.95
HC 20.00

PSYCHOBLAST
First
1 thru 9 . . . . @2.00

PUBLIC DEFENDER IN ACTION
Charlton Comics 1957
7 . . . . 75.00
8 and 9 . . . . @40.00
10 thru 12, ... @40.00

PUDGE PIG
Charlton Comics Sept., 1958
1 . . . . 30.00
2 . . . . 25.00

PUPPET MASTER
Eternity
1 Movie Adapt.Andre Toulon 2.50
2 Puppets Protecting Diary 2.50
3 R:Andre Toulon. 2.50
4 . . . . 2.50

PUPPET MASTER: CHILDREN OF THE PUPPET MASTER
Eternity
1 Killer Puppets on the loose 2.50
2 concl. 2.50

PURGATORI
Chaos! Comics
1-shot prelude 3.00
1-shot signed, limited + print 25.00

PURGATORI
Chaos! Comics 1998
1 DQ from slave to Goddess? 2.95
2 Goddess War,pt.1, x-over 2.95
3 Goddess War, epilog 2.95
4 Unholy Nights. 2.95
5 V:Karmilla. 2.95
6 . . . . 2.95
7 V:Dracula 2.95
Coll. Vol. 1 . . . . 5.95
Coll. Vol. 2 . . . . 5.95
Coll. Vol. 3 . . . . 5.95
Coll. Vol. 4 . . . . 5.95

PURGATORI: THE DRACULA GAMBIT
Chaos! Comics 1997
1 DQ & Brian LeBlanc 3.00
1a signed 20.00
Sketchbook, b&w 3.50

PURGATORI: EMPIRE
Chaos! Comics 2000
1 (of 3) 2.95
1a premium 9.95
2 . . . . 2.95
3 concl. 2.95
Preview Book B&W 5.00

PURGATORI: GODDESS RISING
Chaos! Comics 1999
1 (of 4) MD2 . . . . 2.95
1a premium edition 10.00
2 . . . . 2.95
3 . . . . 2.95
4 conclusion 2.95
Preview Book B&W 5.00

PURGATORI: THE VAMPIRE'S MYTH
Chaos! Comics
1 (of 3) 4.00
1-shot limited chromium edition . . 19.95
2 BnP,JBa 3.00
3 BnP,JBa, final issue 3.00
TPB with CD. 25.00
TPB 12.95
Micro Premium Preview Book 15.00

PURGATORI VS. CHASTITY
Chaos! Comics 2000
1 Alpha ending 2.95
1a Omega ending 2.95
1b deluxe 12.00

PURGATORI VS. VAMPIRELLA
Chaos! Comics 2000
1 . . . . 2.95
1 premium. 9.99

QUANTUM LEAP
Innovation
{based on TV series}
1 1968 Memphis 3.50
1a Special Edition 2.50
2 Ohio 1962,"Freedom of the Press" 3.00
3 1958 "The $50,000 Quest" 3.00
4 "Small Miracles" 2.50
5 . . . . 2.50
6 . . . . 2.50
7 Golf Pro,School Bus Driver. 2.50
8 1958,Bank Robber 2.50
9 NY 1969,Gay Rights. 2.50
10 1960s' Stand-up Comic 2.50
11 1959,Dr.(LSD experiments) 2.50
12 . . . . 2.50

QUEEN OF THE DAMNED
Innovation
1 Anne Rice Adapt."On the Road to the Vampire Lestat" 3.50
2 Adapt. continued 2.50
3 The Devils Minion. 2.50
4 Adapt.continued 2.50
5 Adapt.continued 2.50
6 Adapt.continued 2.50
7 Adapt.continued 2.50
8 Adapt.continued 2.50

QUICK-DRAW McGRAW
Charlton Comics 1970–72
1 TV Animated Cartoon 50.00
2 . . . . 30.00
3 . . . . 30.00

Quick Draw McGraw #4
© Charlton Comics

4 thru 8 . . . . @30.00

Q-UNIT
Harris
1 I:Q-Unit,w/card 3.25

RACE FOR THE MOON
Harvey Publications 1958
1 BP 100.00
2 JK,AW,JK/AW(c). 200.00
3 JK,AW,JK/AW(c) 225.00

RACER-X
Now
Premire Special 5.00
1 thru 3 . . . . @2.50
4 thru 11 . . . . @2.00
[2nd Series]
1 thru 10 . . . . @2.00

RACK & PAIN
Chaos! Comics
3 (of 4) BnP,LJi,. 2.95
4 BnP,LJi, final issue 2.95

RACK & PAIN: KILLERS
Chaos! Comics
1 (of 4) JaL(c) 2.95
2 BnP,LJi,JaL(c) 2.95

RADICAL DREAMER
Blackball
0 . . . . 2.00
1 thru 5 V:Jorge Futran . . . . @2.50

RADIOACTIVE MAN
Bongo
1 I:Radioactive Man. 4.00
1 80pg offered again 3.25
88 V:Lava Man 2.00
212 V:Hypno Head 2.00
412 V:Dr. Crab 2.25
679 with card 2.25
1000 Final issue. 2.25

RAEL
Eclipse

Vol 1. . . . . 6.95

RAGAMUFFINS
Eclipse 1985

1 . . . . 3.00

RALPH SNART ADVENTURES
Now

[Volumes 1 & 2]

see B&W

9 and 10, color 2.50

[Volume 3]

1 . . . . 4.00
2 thru 10 . . . . @3.00
11 thru 21 . . . . @2.00
22 thru 26. . . . . @2.00
TPB 9.95

[Volume 4]

1 thru 3, with 1 of 2 trading cards. . 2.50

[Volume 5]

1 thru 5, with 1 of 2 trading cards. . 2.50
3-D Spec.#1 with 3-D glasses and 12 trading cards 3.50

RAMAR OF THE JUNGLE
Toby Press 1954

1 Ph(c), John Hall 150.00

Charlton

2 . . . . 100.00
3 . . . . 100.00
4 . . . . 100.00
5 Sept., 1956. . . . . 100.00

RAMPANT
Manifest Destiny Comics

1/2 Various Artists 2.50

RANDOM 5
Amara Inc. 1995

1 I:Random 5 . . . . 2.00

RANGO
Dell Publishing Co. Aug., 1967

1 Tim Conway Ph(c) 35.00

RANMA 1/2
Viz 1992

1 I:Ranma 40.00
2 I:Upperclassmen Kuno 25.00
3 F:Upperclassmen Kuno 20.00
4 Confusion. 5.00
5 A:Ryoga 5.00
6 Ryoga plots revenge. 9.00
7 Conclusion 5.00

[Part 2]

1 . . . . 8.00
2 . . . . 5.00
3 thru 7 . . . . @4.00
8 . . . . 5.00
9 . . . . 6.00
10 and 11 . . . . @3.00
continued, see Other Pub. B&W

RAPHAEL
Mirage

1 TMNTurtle characters 8.00

RARE BREED
Dark Moon Productions 1995

1 V:Anarchy. 2.50
2 V:Anarchy. 2.50

RAT BASTARD
Crucial Comics 1997

1 by The Huja Brothers 2.00
2 . . . . 2.00
3 . . . . 2.00
4 (of 4) 2.00
5 . . . . 2.00
5 . . . . 2.00
6 . . . . 2.00

RAT PATROL, THE
Dell Publishing Co. March, 1967

1 Ph(c) 75.00
2 . . . . 50.00
3 thru 6 Ph(c). . . . . @40.00

Raven #3
© Renaissance Comics

RAVEN
Renaissance Comics 1994

1 I:Raven 2.50
2 V:Macallister. 2.50
3 thru 5 . . . . @2.50
6 V:Nightmare Creatures 2.75

RAVENING
Avatar 1998

½ Busch (c) F:Ravyn & Glyph 3.00
½a Meadows(c). 3.00
½b nude cover 6.00
½c nude leather cover 25.00
½d Sketched Edition 60.00
½e Blood Red Foil, signed. 9.00

RAVENS AND RAINBOWS
Pacific

1 . . . . 2.00

RAY BRADBURY CHRONICLES
Byron Press

1 short stories 10.00
2 short stories 10.00
3 short stories 10.00

RAY BRADBURY COMICS
Topps 1993–94

1 thru 5 w/Trading Card. 3.25
Spec.#1 The Illustrated Man 3.00
Spec. Trilogy of Terror 2.50
Spec. The Martian Chronicles. 3.00

R.A.Z.E.
Firstlight

1 I:R.A.Z.E., Secret Weapon 2.95
2 V:Exterminators 2.95

RAZOR
London Night Studios

0 . . . . 9.00
0a second printing. 3.00
1 I:Razor 9.00
1a second printing 3.00
2 . . . . 10.00
2a limited ed., red & blue. 19.00
2b platinum ed. 20.00
3 . . . . 7.00
3a with poster 15.00
4 . . . . 4.00
4a with poster 9.00
5 . . . . 7.00
5a platinum ed. 15.00
6 . . . . 5.00
7 . . . . 4.00
8 . . . . 3.00
9 . . . . 3.00
10 . . . . 3.00
11 & 12 B&W . . . . @3.00
Ann.#1 I:Shi 25.00
Ann.#2 O:Razor B&W. 35.00
Becomes:

RAZOR UNCUT see B&W

RAZOR
Volume 2

London Knight 1996

1 DQ, ... 3.00
1a holochrome edition 5.00
2 DQ 3.00
2a holochrome edition 4.00
3 thru 7 . . . . @3.00
Razor Analog Burn 2.50

RAZOR AND SHI SPECIAL
London Night Studios 1994

1 Rep. Razor Ann.#1 + new art . . . 5.00
1a platinum version 9.00

RAZOR ARCHIVES
London Night

1 & 2 see B&W
3 rep. Razor #10–12 . . . . 7.00

RAZOR BURN
London Night Studios 1994

1 V:Styke. 3.00
1a signed 5.00
2 Searching for Styke 3.00
2a Platinum. 7.00
3 Stryke's War. 3.00
4 D:Razor, bagged 3.00
5 Epilogue. 3.00

RAZOR: CRY NO MORE
London Night Studios 1995

1-shot 3.00
1a variant 4.00
1b Commemorative (1999) 5.95

RAZOR: HEX & VIOLENCE
EH! Productions 2000

0 EHr 3.00

RAZOR/MORBID ANGEL: SOUL SEARCH
London Night

1 (of 3) 3.00
1 platinum edition 5.00
1 Chromium edition 7.00
2 . . . . 3.00
3 . . . . 3.00

RAZOR/POISON/ AREALA WARRIOR NUN: LITTLE BAD ANGELS
London Night 1999

Spec. x-over Raxor cover 3.95
Spec.A Poison cover 3.95
Spec.B Areala cover. 3.95

RAZOR THE RAVENING
Avatar

1 . . . . 3.50
1a Previews cover. 3.50
1b Bondage cover 6.00

RAZOR: THE SUFFERING
London Night Studios 1994

1 . . . . 4.00
1a Director's cut 3.00
1b signed, limited 9.00
2 . . . . 3.00
2a Director's cut 2.50
3 final chapter 3.00

RAZOR: TORTURE
London Night Studios 1995

0 Razor back from dead 4.00
0a signed edition 7.00
1 . . . . 3.00
1a Commemorative (1999) 5.95
2 . . . . 3.00
3 EHr 3.00
4 . . . . 3.00
5 alt. cover, signed 4.00
6 alt. cover, signed 4.00
7 . . . . 3.00

Razor Torture #5
© London Night

RAZOR: SWIMSUIT SPECIAL
London Night Studios 1995

1 pin-ups. 3.00
1a platinum version 7.00
1b commemorative edition. 4.00

RAZOR/WARRIOR NUN AREALA: DARK MENACE
London Night 1999

Spec. x-over 3.95
Spec.A x-over, variant cover 3.95

RAZOR/ WARRIOR NUN AREALA: FAITH
London Night

1 by Jude Millien 3.00
1a variant cover. 4.00

REAL GHOSTBUSTERS
Now

1 KSy(c) 4.50
2 thru 7 . . . . @2.50
8 thru 24 . . . . @2.00

[2nd Series]

1 Halloween Special 2.00
Ann. 3-D w/glasses & pinups 2.95

REALITY CHECK
Sirius 1996

1 by Tavicat. 2.95
2 thru 8 . . . . @2.95
9 Nonesuch Nonsense, pt.1. . . . . . 2.95
10 Nonesuch Nonsense, pt.2 . . . . . 2.95
11 Nonesuch Nonsense, pt.3 . . . . . 2.95
12 Nonesuch Nonsense, pt.4 . . . . . 2.95
TPB Vol. 1 . . . . 17.95
TPB Vol. 2, rep.#7–#12. . . . . 17.95

REAL WAR STORIES
Eclipse 1987–91

1 BB 3.00
1a 2nd printing 2.00
2 . . . . 4.95

RE-ANIMATOR
Adventure Comics

1 movie adaption 2.95
2 movie adaption 2.95

RE-ANIMATOR
Adventure

1 Prequel to Orig movie. 2.50

RE-ANIMATOR: DAWN OF THE RE-ANIMATOR
Adventure

1 Prequel to movie 2.50
2 . . . . 2.50
3 . . . . 2.50
4 V:Erich Metler. 2.50

RE-ANIMATOR: TALES OF HERBERT WEST
Adventure Comics

1 H.P.Lovecraft stories. 4.95

RED DOG
Eclipse 1988

1 CR,Mowgli "Jungle Book" story. . 2.00

RED DRAGON
Comico 1995

1 SBs,I:Red Dragon. 2.50
2 How Soon is Nau? 2.95

REDEEMERS
Antarctic Press 1997

1 (of 5) by Herb Mallette
& Patrick Blain 2.95
2 . . . . 2.95

RED HEAT

1 3-D. 2.50

RED SONJA in 3-D
Blackthorne

1 thru 3 . . . . @2.50

RED SONJA
Cross Plains Comics 1999

1 Death in Scarlet,pt.1. . . . . 2.95
1a photo (c). 2.95
2 Death in Scarlet,pt.2. . . . . 2.95
3 Death in Scarlet,pt.3. . . . . 2.95

REESE'S PIECES
Eclipse 1985

1 reprint from Web of Horror 2.00
2 reprint from Web of Horror 2.00

RE: GEX
Awesome Entertainment 1998

0 RLe,. 2.50
0a Red Foil variant 4.00
1 RLe,JLb 2.50
1a Platinum cover 7.00
1b Red Foil cover 12.00
1c Variant RL cover. 4.00
1d prime 2.99
1e prime millennium ed.. . . . . 4.95
2 RLe,JLb 2.50
2a prime 2.99
2b Millennium edition. 4.95
3 RLe,A:The Coven,V:Youngblood. 2.50
Con Spec. '98. . . . . 5.00
Orlando Megacon ashcan. 10.00
Orlando Megacon ashcan, signed. 20.00

REGGIE
Archie Publications 1963–65

15 . . . . 50.00
16 . . . . 40.00
17 . . . . 40.00
18 . . . . 40.00
Becomes:

REGGIE AND ME
Archie Publications 1966–80

19 . . . . 30.00
20 thru 23 . . . . @20.00
24 thru 40 . . . . @15.00

41 thru 50 . . . @10.00
51 thru 99 . . . @7.00
100 . . . 10.00
101 thru 126 . . . @5.00

REGGIE'S WISE GUY JOKES

Archie Publications April, 1968

1 . . . 40.00
2 . . . 20.00
3 . . . 20.00
4 . . . 20.00
5 thru 15 Giants . . . @20.00
16 thru 28 Giants . . . @15.00
29 thru 40 . . . @8.00
41 thru 60 . . . @5.00
11 thru 59 . . . @4.00
60 Jan. 1982 . . . 4.00

REIVERS

Enigma

1 thru 3 Rock 'n' Roll . . . 2.95

REPTILICUS

Charlton Comics Aug., 1961

1 . . . 150.00
2 . . . 100.00

Becomes:

REPTISAURUS

3 . . . 75.00
4 . . . 50.00
5 . . . 50.00
6 . . . 50.00
7 . . . 50.00
8 Summer, 1963 . . . 50.00

RETURN OF KONGA, THE

Charlton Comics 1962

N# . . . 75.00

RETURN OF MEGATON MAN

Kitchen Sink

1 Don Simpson art (1988) . . . 2.00
2 Don Simpson art. . . . 2.00
3 Don Simpson art. . . . 2.00

RETURN TO JURASSIC PARK

Topps 1995

1 R:Jurassic Park . . . 2.50
2 V:Blosyn Team, Army . . . 2.50
3 The Hunted . . . 2.50
4 Army . . . 2.50
5 Heirs to the Thunder,pt.1 . . . 2.95
6 Heirs to the Thunder,pt.2 . . . 2.95
7 Inquiring Minds,pt.1 . . . 2.95
8 Photo Finish, concl. . . . 2.95
9 Jurassic Jam issue . . . 2.95

REVENGE OF THE PROWLER

Eclipse 1988

1 GN,R:Prowler . . . 2.00
2 GN,A:Fighting Devil Dogs with Flexi-Disk . . . 2.50
3 GN,A:Devil Dogs . . . 2.00
4 GN,V:Pirahna . . . 2.00

REVENGERS

Continuity

1 NA,O:Megalith,I:Crazyman . . . 4.00
2 NA,Megalith meets Armor & Silver Streak,Origin Revengers#1 . . . 2.50
3 NA/NR,Origin Revengers #2 . . . 2.50
4 NA,Origin Revengers #3 . . . 2.50
5 NA,Origin Revengers #4 . . . 2.50
6 I:Hybrids . . . 3.00
Spec. #1 F:Hybrids . . . 4.95

RIBIT

Comico

1 FT,Mini-series . . . 2.00
2 FT,Mini-series . . . 2.00
3 FT,Mini-series . . . 2.00
4 FT,Mini-series . . . 2.00

RICHIE RICH

Harvey Publications 1960–91

1 . . . 1,500.00
2 . . . 500.00
3 . . . 300.00
4 . . . 300.00
5 . . . 300.00
6 . . . 175.00
7 . . . 175.00
8 . . . 175.00
9 . . . 175.00
10 . . . 175.00
11 thru 20 . . . @125.00
21 thru 40 . . . @100.00
41 thru 60 . . . @75.00
61 thru 80 . . . @50.00
81 thru 99 . . . @20.00
100 . . . 25.00
101 thru 111 . . . @15.00
112 thru 116 52 pg Giants . . . @20.00
117 thru 120 . . . @15.00
121 thru 140 . . . @10.00
141 thru 160 . . . @7.00
161 thru 180 . . . @5.00
181 thru 254 . . . @3.00

RICHIE RICH

Harvey 1991

1 thru 15 . . . @3.00
16 thru 28 . . . @2.00

RICHIE RICH BANK BOOKS

Harvey 1972–82

1 . . . 45.00
2 thru 5 . . . @30.00
6 thru 10 . . . @20.00
11 thru 20 . . . @15.00
21 thru 30 . . . @10.00
31 thru 40 . . . @7.00
41 thru 59 . . . @5.00

RICHIE RICH BILLIONS

Harvey 1974–82

1 . . . 35.00
2 thru 5 . . . @20.00
6 thru 10 . . . @15.00
11 thru 20 . . . @10.00
21 thru 30 . . . @5.00
31 thru 48 . . . @4.00

RICHIE RICH DIAMONDS

Harvey 1972–82

1 . . . 60.00

Richie Rich Bank Books #24
© Harvey Publications

2 thru 5 . . . @25.00
6 thru 10 . . . @20.00
11 thru 20 . . . @15.00
21 thru 30 . . . @5.00
31 thru 59 . . . @4.00

RICHIE RICH DOLLARS & CENTS

Harvey Publications 1963–82

1 . . . 165.00
2 . . . 75.00
3 thru 5 . . . @50.00
6 thru 10 . . . @30.00
11 thru 20 . . . @25.00
21 thru 30 . . . @15.00
31 thru 43 . . . @10.00
44 thru 60 . . . @7.00
61 thru 70 . . . @4.00
71 thru 109 . . . @3.00

RICHIE RICH FORTUNES

Harvey 1971–82

1 . . . 60.00
2 thru 5 . . . @30.00
6 thru 10 . . . @20.00
11 thru 20 . . . @10.00
21 thru 30 . . . @7.00
31 thru 63 . . . @5.00

RICHIE RICH GEMS

Harvey 1974–82

1 . . . 35.00
2 thru 5 . . . @20.00
6 thru 10 . . . @15.00
11 thru 20 . . . @10.00
21 thru 30 . . . @7.00
31 thru 43 . . . @5.00

RICHIE RICH JACKPOTS

Harvey 1974–82

1 . . . 60.00
2 thru 5 . . . @30.00
6 thru 10 . . . @20.00
11 thru 20 . . . @15.00
21 thru 30 . . . @7.00

31 thru 58 . . . . @4.00

RICHIE RICH MILLIONS
Harvey Publications 1961–82

1 . . . . 200.00
2 . . . . 125.00
3 thru 10 . . . . @100.00
11 thru 20 . . . . @75.00
21 thru 30 . . . . @50.00
31 thru 48 . . . . @25.00
49 thru 60 . . . . @20.00
61 thru 64 . . . . @15.00
65 thru 74 . . . . @12.00
75 thru 94 . . . . @10.00
95 thru 113 . . . . @7.00

RICHIE RICH MONEY WORLD
Harvey 1972–82

1 . . . . 60.00
2 thru 5 . . . . @30.00
6 thru 10 . . . . @25.00
11 thru 20 . . . . @12.00
21 thru 30 . . . . @7.00
31 thru 59 . . . . @5.00

RICHIE RICH PROFITS
Harvey 1974–82

1 . . . . 40.00
2 thru 5 . . . . @20.00
6 thru 10 . . . . @15.00
11 thru 20 . . . . @10.00
21 thru 30 . . . . @7.00
31 thru 47 . . . . @5.00

RICHIE RICH RICHES
Harvey 1972–82

1 . . . . 60.00
2 thru 5 . . . . @30.00
6 thru 10 . . . . @20.00
11 thru 20 . . . . @10.00
21 thru 30 . . . . @7.00
31 thru 59 . . . . @5.00

RICHIE RICH SUCCESS STORIES
Harvey Publications 1964–82

1 . . . . 200.00
2 thru 5 . . . . @100.00
6 thru 10 . . . . @75.00
11 thru 30 . . . . @50.00
31 thru 38 . . . . @35.00
39 thru 55 . . . . @25.00
56 thru 66 . . . . @10.00
67 thru 105 . . . . @7.00

RICHIE RICH VAULT OF MYSTERY
Harvey 1974–82

1 . . . . 30.00
2 thru 5 . . . . @15.00
6 thru 10 . . . . @10.00
11 thru 20 . . . . @5.00
21 thru 30 . . . . @5.00
31 thru 47 . . . . @4.00

RICHIE RICH ZILLIONS
Harvey 1976–82

1 . . . . 25.00
2 thru 5 . . . . @15.00
6 thru 10 . . . . @8.00
11 thru 20 . . . . @4.00
21 thru 33 . . . . @3.00

RIFLEMAN, THE
Dell Publishing Co. 1959

1 Chuck Connors Ph(c) all 250.00
2 . . . . 125.00
3 ATh 100.00
4 . . . . 85.00
5 . . . . 85.00
6 ATh 110.00
7 . . . . 85.00
8 . . . . 85.00
9 . . . . 85.00
10 . . . . 85.00
11 . . . . 75.00
12 . . . . 75.00
13 . . . . 75.00
14 . . . . 75.00
15 . . . . 75.00
16 . . . . 75.00
17 . . . . 75.00
18 . . . . 75.00
19 . . . . 75.00
20 . . . . 75.00

RIOT GEAR
Triumphant

1 JnR(s),I:Riot Gear. 2.50
2 JnR(s),I:Rabin 2.50
3 JnR(s),I:Surzar 2.50
4 JnR(s),D:Captain Tich. 2.50
5 JnR(s),reactions 2.50
6 JnR(s),Tich avenged. 2.50
7 JnR(s),Information Age 2.50
8 JnR(s), ... 2.50

RIOT GEAR: VIOLENT PAST
Triumphant

1 and 2 . . . . @2.50

R.I.P.
TSR 1990–91

1 thru 4 . . . . @2.95
5 thru 8 Brasher, Avenger of the Dead . . . . @2.95

RIPLEY'S BELIEVE IT OR NOT!
Gold Key 1967–80

4 Ph(c),AMc 40.00
5 GE,JJ. 30.00
6 AMc 30.00
7 . . . . 25.00
8 . . . . 30.00
9 . . . . 25.00
10 GE. 30.00
11 . . . . 20.00
12 . . . . 20.00
13 . . . . 20.00
14 . . . . 20.00
15 GE. 22.00
16 . . . . 20.00
17 . . . . 20.00
18 . . . . 20.00
19 . . . . 20.00
20 . . . . 20.00
21 thru 30 . . . . @15.00
31 thru 38 . . . . @10.00
39 RC. 12.00
40 thru 50 . . . . @10.00
51 thru 94 . . . . @8.00

RISK
Maximum Press 1995

1 V:Furious 2.50

ROB
Awesome Entertainment 1999

1 RLe 2.50

ROBERT E. HOWARD'S
Cross Plains Comics 1999

GN Marchers of Valhalla. 6.95
GN Wolfshead 6.95
GN Worms of the Earth 9.95

ROBIN HOOD
Eclipse 1991

1 TT,Historically accurate series. . . 2.75
2 and 3 TT. . . . . @2.75

ROBO HUNTER
Eagle

1 . . . . 2.00
2 thru 5 . . . . @2.00

Robotech #7
© Antarctic Press

ROBOTECH
Antarctic Press 1997

1 by Fred Perry & BDn 2.95
2 . . . . 2.95
3 . . . . 2.95
4 Rolling Thunder, pt.1 . . . . 2.95
5 Rolling Thunder, pt.2 . . . . 2.95
6 Rolling Thunder, pt.3 . . . . 2.95
7 Rolling Thunder, pt.4 . . . . 2.95
8 Variants, pt.1 . . . . 2.95
9 Variants, pt.2 . . . . 2.95
10 Variants, pt.3 . . . . 2.95
11 Variants, pt.4 . . . . 2.95
TPB Megastorm by Fred Perry & Ben Dunn 7.95
Spec.1-shot Robotech: Final Fire . . 2.95
Spec.1-shot Robotech: Class Reunion 2.95

ROBOTECH: GENESIS
The Legend of Zor
Eternity

1 O:Robotech w/cards. 2.95
1a Limited Edition,extra pages with

cards #1 & #2 . . . . 5.95
2 thru 6, each with cards . . . . . . @2.50

ROBOTECH IN 3-D
Comico

1 . . . . 2.50

Robotech, The Macross Saga #4
© Comico

ROBOTECH, THE MACROSS SAGA
Comico 1985–89
(formerly Macross)

2 . . . . 5.00
3 . . . . 4.00
4 . . . . 3.00
5 . . . . 2.50
6 J:Rick Hunter 2.50
7 V:Zentraedi. 2.00
8 A:Rick Hunter. 2.00
9 V:Zentraedi. 2.00
10 "Blind Game" 2.00
11 V:Zentraedi 2.00
12 V:Zentraedi 2.00
13 V:Zentraedi 2.00
14 "Gloval's Reports" 2.00
15 V:Zentraedi 2.00
16 V:Zentraedi 2.00
17 V:Zentraedi 2.00
18 D:Roy Fokker 2.00
19 V:Khyron 2.00
20 V:Zentraedi 2.00
21 "A New Dawn" 2.00
22 V:Zentraedi 2.00
23 "Reckless" 2.00
24 HB,V:Zentraedi 2.00
25 "Wedding Bells" 2.00
26 "The Messenger" 2.00
27 "Force of Arms" 2.00
28 "Reconstruction Blues" 2.00
29 "Robotech Masters" 2.00
30 "Viva Miriya" 2.00
31 "Khyron's Revenge" 2.00
32 "Broken Heart" 2.00
33 "A Rainy Night" 2.00
34 "Private Time" 2.00
35 "Season's Greetings" 2.00
36 last issue 2.00
Graphic Novel #1 . . . . 6.00

ROBOTECH MASTERS
Comico 1985–88

1 . . . . 4.00
2 . . . . 3.00
3 Space Station Liberty 3.00
4 V:Bioroids. 2.50
5 V:Flagship 2.50
6 "Prelude to Battle" 2.50
7 "The Trap" 2.50
8 F:Dana Sterling 2.50
9 "Star Dust" 2.50
10 V:Zor 2.50
11 A:De Ja Vu 2.00
12 2OR 2.00
13 . . . . 2.00
14 "Clone Chamber,"V:Zor 2.00
15 "Love Song" 2.00
16 V:General Emerson 2.00
17 "Mind Games" 2.00
18 "Dana in Wonderland" 2.00
19 . . . . 2.00
20 A:Zor,Musica 2.00
21 "Final Nightmare" 2.00
22 "The Invid Connection" 2.00
23 "Catastrophe," final issue 2.00

ROBOTECH: THE NEW GENERATION
Comico 1985–88

1 . . . . 4.00
2 "The Lost City" 3.00
3 V:Yellow Dancer 3.00
4 A:Yellow Dancer 3.00
5 SK(i),A:Yellow Dancer. 2.50
6 F:Rook Bartley 2.50
7 "Paper Hero" 2.00
8 . . . . 2.00
9 KSy,"The Genesis Pit" 2.00
10 V:The Invid 2.00
11 F:Scott Bernard 2.00
12 V:The Invid 2.00
13 V:The Invid 2.00
14 "Annie"s Wedding" 2.00
15 "Seperate Ways" 2.00
16 "Metamorphosis" 2.00
17 "Midnight Sun" 2.00
18 . . . . 2.00
19 . . . . 2.00
20 "Birthday Blues" 2.00
21 "Hired Gun" 2.00
22 "The Big Apple" 2.00
23 Robotech Wars 2.00
24 Robotech Wars 2.00
25 V:Invid, last issue. 2.00

ROBOTECH SPECIAL DANA"S STORY
Eclipse

1 . . . . 5.00

ROBOTECH II: THE SENTINELS
Eternity

Swimsuit Spec.#1. . . . . 2.95

ROCK & ROLL
Revolutionary
Prev: Black & White

15 Poison. 6.00
16 Van Halen 5.00
17 Madonna 6.00
18 AliceCooper. 5.00
19 Public Enemy, 2 Live Crew 5.00
20 Queensryche 5.00
21 Prince 5.00
22 AC/DC. 5.00
23 Living Color 5.00
24 Anthrax 5.00
25 Z.Z.Top 5.00
26 Doors 3.00
27 Doors 3.00
28 Ozzy Osbourne 3.00
29 The Cure. 3.00
30 . . . . 3.00
31 Vanilla Ice 3.00
32 Frank Zappa 3.00
33 Guns "N" Roses. 3.00
34 The Black Crowes 3.00
35 R.E.M.. . . . . 3.00
36 Michael Jackson 3.00
37 Ice T 3.00
38 Rod Stewart 3.00
39 . . . . 3.00
40 N.W.A./Ice Cube 3.00
41 Paula Abdul. 2.50
42 Metallica II. 3.00
43 Guns "N" Roses. 2.50
44 Scorpions 2.50
45 Greatful Dead 3.50
46 Grateful Dead 3.50
47 Grateful Dead 3.50
48 (now b/w),Queen 2.50
49 Rush 2.50
50 Bob Dylan Pt.1 . . . . 3.00
51 Bob Dylan Pt.2 . . . . 3.00
52 Bob Dylan Pt.3 . . . . 3.00
53 Bruce Springsteen 3.00
54 U2 Pt.1 . . . . 3.00
55 U2 Pt.2 . . . . 3.00
56 thru 72 . . . . @2.50

ROCK 'N' ROLL HIGH SCHOOL
Cosmic Comics 1995

1 Sequel to the movie 2.50

ROCKETEER
Walt Disney

1 DSt(c)RH,MovieAdaptation 7.00
Newsstand Version. 3.25

ROCKETEER ADVENTURE MAGAZINE
Comico

1 DSt,MK,Rocketeer(6thApp.) . . . 10.00
2 DSt,MK,Rocketeer(7thApp.) 8.00

ROCKETEER SPECIAL
Eclipse 1984

1 DSt, Rocketeer(5th App.) 15.00

ROCKET MAN: KING OF THE ROCKET MEN
Innovation

1 thru 4 Adapts movie series . . . @2.50

ROCKET RANGER
Adventure Comics

1 Based on computer game 2.95

ROCKMEEZ
Jzink Comics

1 I:Rockmeez,V:Pyrites 2.50
2 V:Pyrites,Silv.Embos.(c) 2.50

ROCKY HORROR PICTURE SHOW
Calibre/Tome

1 . . . . 6.00
1a 2nd printing 3.25
2 . . . . 3.50

3 "The Conclusion" 3.25
Rocky Horror Collection reps. 4.95

ROG 2000
Pacific
1 One-Shot, JBy 2.00

ROGER RABBIT
Walt Disney 1990
1 I:Rick Flint, "The Trouble with Toons" 5.50
2 . . . . 3.50
3 . . . . 2.50
4 . . . . 2.50
5 . . . . 2.50
6 thru 9 . . . . @2.50
10 "Tuned-in-toons" 2.50
11 "Who Framed Rick Flint" 2.00
12 "Somebunny to Love 2.00
13 "Honey,I Stink with Kids 2.00
14 "Who Fired Jessica Rabbit" 2.00
15 "The Great Toon Detective" 2.00
16 "See you later Aviator" 2.00
17 Flying Saucers over Toontown . . 2.00
18 "I Have Seen the Future" 2.00

ROGER RABBIT'S TOONTOWN
Walt Disney
1 Baby Herman,Jessica stories . . . 2.00
2 "Pre-Hysterical Roger" 2.00
3 "Lumberjack of tomorrow" 2.00
4 "The Longest Daze" 2.00

Rogue Trooper #4
© Fleetway/Quality

ROGUE TROOPER
Fleetway/Quality
1 thru 5 . . . . @2.00
6 . . . . 2.00
7 thru 21 . . . . @2.00
22/23 . . . . 2.00
24 . . . . 2.00
25/26 . . . . 2.00
27 thru 35 . . . . @2.00
36 . . . . 2.00
37 . . . . 2.00
38 thru 40 . . . . @2.00
41 thru 43 . . . . @2.00

ROGUE TROOPER: THE FINAL WARRIOR
Fleetway
1 RS,Golden Rebellion,pt 1 . . . . . . 2.95
2 thru 3 . . . . @2.95
4 "Saharan Ice-Belt War 2.95

ROLAND: DAYS OF WRATH
Terra Major 1999
1 (of 4) 2.95
2 thru 4 . . . . @2.95
TPB 17.95

ROMAN HOLIDAYS, THE
Gold Key 1973
1 . . . . 45.00
2 . . . . 25.00
3 . . . . 25.00
4 . . . . 25.00

ROOK, THE
Harris Comics 1995
0 O:Rook 2.95
1 N:Rook 2.95
2 I:Coffin 2.95
3 The Spider Obsidian 2.95

ROOM 222
Dell Publishing Co. Jan., 1970
1 . . . . 50.00
2 . . . . 30.00
3 Drug 35.00
4 Ph(c) 30.00

ROSWELL
Bongo Comics 1996
1 by Bill Morrison,"The Story of the Century" 2.95
2 "The Untold Story" 2.95
3 "The Untold Story," concl. 2.95
4 V:Mutato 2.95
5 . . . . 2.95
6 time-traveling comic collector . . . 2.95
TPB Roswell Walks Among Us . . . 12.95

ROY ROGERS WESTERN CLASSICS
AC Comics
1 . . . . 2.95
2 . . . . 2.95
3 . . . . 2.95
4 . . . . 3.95

RUFF AND READY
Dell Publishing Co. Sept., 1958
1 . . . . 150.00
2 . . . . 100.00
3 . . . . 100.00
4 . . . . 75.00
5 . . . . 75.00
6 . . . . 75.00
7 . . . . 75.00
8 . . . . 75.00
9 . . . . 75.00
10 thru 12 . . . . @75.00

RUGRATS COMIC ADVENTURES
New England Comics 1999
VOL 1
1 thru 10 . . . . @2.95
VOL 2
1 thru 4 . . . . @2.95

RUN, BUDDY, RUN
Gold Key June, 1967
1 . . . . 25.00

RUST
Now
1 . . . . 4.00
2 . . . . 3.00
3 thru 11 . . . . @2.00
12 I:Terminator 10.00
13 thru 15 . . . . @2.00
[Volume 2]
1 thru 10 . . . . @2.00

SABLE
First 1988–90
1 AIDS story 2.00
2 Sable in Iran 2.00
3 Pentathelon 2.00
4 . . . . 2.00
5 DCw,V:Tong Gangs 2.00
6 In Atlantic City 2.00
7 V:EnvironmentalTerrorists 2.00
8 In Argentina 2.00
9 In Kenya Pt.1 . . . . 2.00
10 In Kenya Pt.2 . . . . 2.00
11 Jon Sable bodyguard 2.00
12 In Cambodia Pt.1 . . . . 2.00
13 In Cambodia Pt.2 . . . . 2.00
14 Christmas story 2.00
15 A:Ted Koppel 2.00
16 Sable as "B.B.Flemm" rev. 2.00
17 Turning point issue 2.00
18 Richard Rockwell(i) 2.00
19 A:Maggie the Cat 2.00
20 A:Gary Adler 2.00
21 Richard Rockwell(i) 2.00
22 A:Eden Kendall 2.00
23 TV cover 2.00
24 TV cover 2.00
25 TV cover 2.00
26 TV cover 2.00
27 . . . . 2.00
28 last issue 2.00

SABRE
Eclipse 1982–85
1 PG 2.50
2 PG 3.00
3 thru 14 . . . . @2.00

SABRINA, THE TEENAGE WITCH
Archie Publications 1971–83
1 . . . . 125.00
2 . . . . 60.00
3 . . . . 40.00
4 . . . . 35.00
5 . . . . 35.00
6 thru 10 . . . . @30.00
11 thru 20 . . . . @15.00
21 thru 77 . . . . @5.00

SABRINA THE TEENAGE WITCH
Archie Comics 1996

one-shot photo cover ... 2.00
1 photo cover ... 2.00
2 "Trouble in Time" ... 2.00
3 photo cover ... 2.00
4 photo cover ... 2.00
5 "Driver's License" ... 2.00
6 "Treasure Troubles" ... 2.00
7 "The Sculpture Switch" ... 2.00
8 "The Cable Girl" photo (c) ... 2.00
9 "Farewell Feline" ... 2.00
10 "No Brain, No Pain" ... 2.00
11 "Mirror, Mirror" ... 2.00
12 "" ... 2.00
13 "Kin You Believe It" ... 2.00
14 "Too Much Magic" ... 2.00
15 "Wedding or Not" ... 2.00
16 How does your garden grow? ... 2.00
17 F:Josie & The Pussycats ... 2.00
18 photo (c) ... 2.00
19 photo (c) ... 2.00
20 thru 27 photo (c) ... @2.00
28 A:Sonic The Hedgehog ... 2.00
29 thru 33 photo (c) ... @2.00

VOLUME 2

1 thru 3 from animated series ... @1.79
4 thru 13 ... @1.99
Halloween Spooktacular #1 ... 2.00
Halloween Spooktacular #2 ... 2.00
Holiday Spectacular #3 ... 2.00

Sad Sack and Sarge #140
© Harvey Publications

SAD SACK AND THE SARGE
Harvey Publications 1957–82

1 ... 135.00
2 ... 60.00
3 thru 10 ... @50.00
11 thru 20 ... @40.00
21 thru 40 ... @25.00
41 thru 50 ... @15.00
51 thru 90 ... @10.00
91 thru 96 52 pg Giants ... @12.00
97 thru 155 ... @5.00

SAD SACK'S ARMY LIFE
Harvey Publications 1963–76

1 ... 60.00
2 thru 10 ... @30.00
11 thru 20 ... @20.00
21 thru 30 ... @15.00
31 thru 50 ... @10.00
51 thru 61 ... @7.00

SAD SACK'S FUNNY FRIENDS
Harvey Publications 1955–69

1 ... 100.00
2 thru 10 ... @50.00
11 thru 20 ... @25.00
21 thru 30 ... @15.00
31 thru 40 ... @12.00
41 thru 75 ... @7.00

SAD SACK in 3-D
Blackthorne

1 and 2 ... @2.50

SAFETY-BELT MAN ALL HELL
Sirius 1996

1 ... 2.95
2 ... 2.95
3 ... 2.95
4 Linsner back (c) ... 4.00
5 ... 2.95

[SAGA OF] THE METABARONS
Humanoids Publishing 1999

1 (of 16) Sci-fi ... 2.95
2 thru 9 ... @2.95

SALOME
Eclipse 1987

1 CR ... 2.00

SAM AND MAX, FREE-LANCE POLICE SPECIAL
Comico 1987–89

1 ... 2.75

SAM SLADE ROBOHUNTER
Quality 1986–89

1 ... 2.00
2 ... 2.00
3 Filby Case ... 2.00
4 ... 2.00
5 ... 2.00
6 Bax the Burner,Moore ... 2.00
7 ... 2.00
8 thru 21 ... @2.00
22/23 ... 2.00
24 ... 2.00
25/26 ... 2.00
27 thru 33 ... @2.00

SAMSONS
Samsons Comics

1/2 Various Artists ... 2.50

SAMURAI
Eclipse

1 thru 5 ... @2.00

SAMUREE
Continuity 1993–94

1 NA,A:Revengers ... 2.00
2 A:Revengers ... 2.00
3 NA,A:Revengers ... 2.00
4 A:Revengers ... 2.00
5 BSz(c),A:Revengers ... 2.00
6 A:Revengers ... 2.00
7 ... 2.00
8 Drug story ... 2.00
9 Drug story ... 2.00

[2nd Series]

1 thru 3 Rise of Magic ... 2.50

SARGE STEEL/ SECRET AGENT
Charlton 1964–66

1 DG,I:SargeSteel & IvanChung ... 30.00
2 DG,I:Werner Von Hess ... 20.00
3 DG,V:Smiling Skull ... 20.00
4 DG,V:Lynx ... 20.00
5 FMc,V:Ivan Chung ... 20.00
6 FMc,A:Judomaster ... 20.00
7 DG ... 20.00
8 V:Talon ... 20.00

Becomes:

SECRET AGENT

9 DG,A:The Lynx ... 15.00
10 DG,JAp,A:Tiffany Sinn ... 15.00

SATANIKA
Verotik 1995

0 ... 5.00
1 New ongoing series ... 6.00
2 Femininity ... 3.50
3 thru 5 ... @3.00
6 thru 10 ... @2.95
10a Wingbird variant cover ... 5.00
11 SBi,final issue ... 3.95
11a Jason Blood variant (c) ... 10.00
11b Superfest 99 limited ... 15.00
1-shot Satanika X (adult) ... 5.00
1-shot Satanika vs.Shilene ... 9.95

SATAN'S SIX
Topps 1993

1 F:Satan's Six,w/3 cards ... 3.25
2 V:Kalazarr,w/3 cards ... 2.95
3 w/3 cards ... 2.95
4 w/3 cards ... 2.95

SATURDAY KNIGHTS
Hot

1 ... 2.00
2 thru 4 ... @2.00

SAURAUS FAMILY
Blackthorne

1 3-D ... 2.00

SAVAGE COMBAT TALES
Atlas Feb.–July, 1975

1 F:Sgt Strykers Death Squad ... 10.00
2 ATh,A:Warhawk ... 8.00
3 final issue ... 8.00

SAVAGE DRAGON/ TEENAGE MUTANT NINJA TURLES CROSSOVER
Mirage

1 EL(s) ... 2.75

SAVED BY THE BELL
Harvey

1 based on TV series 2.00

SCARLET CRUSH
Awesome Entertainment 1998

1 by John Stinsman. 2.50
2 . . . . 2.50
3 Icaria's decision 2.50
4 Nirasawa arrives 2.50

SCARY TALES
Charlton 1975

1 . . . . 20.00
2 thru 11 . . . . @15.00
12 thru 46. . . . . @10.00

SCAVENGERS
Quality 1988–89

1 thru 7 . . . . @2.00
8 thru 14 . . . . @2.00

SCAVENGERS
Triumphant Comics 1993–94

0 Fso(c),JnR(s),. 2.50
0a "Free Copy" 2.50
0b Red Logo. 2.50
1 JnR(s),I:Scavengers,Ximos,
C:Doctor Chaos 2.50
1a 2nd Printing 2.50
2 JnR(s),. 2.50
3 JnR(s),I:Lurok. 2.50
4 JnR(s),. 2.50
5 Fso(c),JnR(s),D:Jack Hanal 2.50
6 JnR(s),. 2.50
7 JnR(s),I:Zion. 2.50
8 JnR(s),Nativity 2.50
9 JnR(s),The Challenge. 2.50
10 JnR(s),Snowblind. 2.50

SCHISM
Defiant

1 thru 4 Defiant's x-over 3.25

SCIENCE COMIC BOOK
Nature Publishing House 1997

TPB Earth Adventures by James
Laurie. 8.95
TPB Car Adventure by James
Laurie. 8.95
TPB Volcano Adventures by Stu
Duval 8.95
TPB World of Dinosaurs, by Paul Xu
and James Passmore. 8.95
TPB Beyond the Star, by James
Passmore. 8.95
TPB Weather Genie, by James
Laurie. 8.95
TPB Rain Forest Adventure
by James Passmore. 8.95
TPB Wildlife Adventure by Stu
Duval 8.95

SCION

1 and 2 . . . . @2.00

SCION
Crossgen Comics 2000

1 thru 5 RMz . . . . @2.95

SCI-TECH
Wildstorm/DC 1999

1 (of 4) BCi,Ebe, ... 2.50
2 BCi,EBe, ... 2.50

SCOOBY DOO
Gold Key 1970–75

1 . . . . 100.00
2 . . . . 75.00
3 . . . . 60.00
4 . . . . 60.00
5 . . . . 60.00
6 . . . . 40.00
7 . . . . 40.00
8 . . . . 40.00
9 . . . . 40.00
10. . . . . 40.00
11 thru 20 . . . . @30.00
21 thru 30 . . . . @25.00

Scooby Doo, Where Are You #1
© Charlton

SCOOBY DOO
Charlton Comics 1975–76

1 . . . . 40.00
2 . . . . 25.00
3 . . . . 25.00
4 . . . . 25.00
5 . . . . 25.00
6 . . . . 20.00
7 . . . . 20.00
8 . . . . 20.00
9 . . . . 20.00
10 . . . . 20.00
11 . . . . 20.00

SCOOBY DOO
Archie 1995

1 thru 10 . . . . @2.00
11 thru 13 . . . . @2.00
14 "The Balloon Busters" 2.00
15 "On the Boardwalk in
Atlantic City". 2.00
16 "The Ghost of Central Park". . . . 2.00
19 "Electric Monster" 2.00
20 "The Legend of Spooky Doo". . . 2.00
21 "Monster Park After Dark" 2.00

SCORCHED EARTH
Tundra 1991

1 Earth 2025,I:Dr.EliotGodwin 3.50
2 Hunt for Eliot 2.95
3 Mystical Transformation 2.95

SCORPION, THE
Atlas 1975

1 HC, bondage cover. 10.00
2 HC,BWi,MK 7.00
3 . . . . 5.00

SCORPION CORP.
Dagger 1993

1 PuD,JRI,CH,. 2.75
2 PuD,JRI,CH,V:Victor Kyner. 2.75
3 PuD,BIH,V:Victor Kyner 2.75

SCORPIO ROSE
Eclipse 1983

1 MR/TP,I:Dr.Orient 2.00
2 MR/TP 2.00

SCOUT
Eclipse 1985–87

1 TT,I:Scout,Fash.In Action 6.00
2 TT,V:Buffalo Monster 3.00
3 TT,V:President Grail 2.50
4 TT,V:President Grail 2.50
5 TT,"Killin' Floor" 2.50
6 TT,V:President Grail 2.50
7 TT,TY,Rosanna's Diary 2.50
8 TT,TY 2.50
9 TT,TY,A:Airboy 2.50
10 TT,TY,I:Proj.Mountain Fire 2.00
11 TT,FH,V:Rangers 2.00
12 TT,FH,"Me and the Devil". 2.00
13 TT,FH,Monday:Eliminator. 2.00
14 TT,FH,Monday:Eliminator. 2.00
15 TT,FH,Monday:Eliminator. 2.00
16 TT,3-D issue,F:Santana 2.00
17 TT,A:Beanworld 2.00
18 TT,FH,V:Lex Lucifer 2.00
19 TT,w/Record,V:Lex Lucifer 3.00
20 TT,A:Monday:Eliminator 2.00
21 TT,A:Monday:Eliminator 2.00
22 TT,A:Swords of Texas 2.00
23 TT,A:Swords of Texas 2.00
24 TT,last Issue 2.00

SCOUT: WAR SHAMAN
Eclipse 1988–89

1 TT,R:Scout (now a father). 2.25
2 TT,I:Redwire 2.00
3 TT,V:Atuma Yuma. 2.00
4 TT,"Rollin' on the River" 2.00
5 TT,Hopi Katchina dieties 2.00
6 TT,Scout vs. Rosa Winter 2.00
7 TT,R:Redwire 2.00
8 TT,R:Beau LaDuke 2.00
9 TT,V:Doodyists 2.00
10 TT,TY,V:Redwire 2.00
11 TT,V:Redwire 2.00
12 TT,V:Snow Leopards 2.00
13 TT,F:Beau LaDuke. 2.00
14 TT,V:Redwire. 2.00
15 TT,V:Redwire. 2.00
16 TT,"Wall of Death,"last issue . . . 2.00

SEADRAGON
Elite 1986–87

1 . . . . 3.00
1a 2nd printing 2.00
2 . . . . 2.00
3 . . . . 2.00
4 . . . . 2.00
5 thru 8 . . . . @2.00

SEA HUNT
Dell Publishing Co. 1958

1 L.BridgesPh(c) all 125.00

2 .... 100.00
3 ATh 110.00
4 RsM 100.00
5 RsM 100.00
6 RsM 100.00
7 .... 90.00
8 RsM 100.00
9 RsM 100.00
10 RsM 100.00
11 RsM 100.00
12 .... 100.00
13 RsM 100.00

SEAQUEST
Nemesis 1994
1 HC(c),DGC,KP,AA,Based on TV Show 2.50

SEBASTIAN
Walt Disney
1 From Little Mermaid 2.00
2 "While da Crab's Away" 2.00

SECRET AGENT
Gold Key Nov., 1966
1 .... 120.00
2 .... 85.00

SECRET CITY SAGA
Topps 1993
0 JK 3.25
0 Gold Ed. 15.00
0 Red 10.00
1 w/3 cards 3.25
2 w/3 cards 3.25
3 w/3 cards 3.25
4 w/3 cards 3.25

SECRET SQUIRREL
Gold Key Oct., 1966
1 .... 125.00

SEDUCTION OF THE INNOCENT
Eclipse 1985–86
1 ATh,"Hanged by the Neck" reps. 2.50
2 .... 2.25
3 ATh,"The Crushed Gardenia" 2.00
4 ATh,NC,"World's Apart" 2.00
5 ATh,"The Phantom Ship" 2.00
6 ATh,RA,"Hands of Don Jose" 2.00
3-D #1 DSt(c) 2.25
3-D #2 ATh,MB,BWr,"Man Who Was Always on Time" 2.00

SEEKER
Sky Comics 1995
1 JMt(s),I:Seeker 2.50

SENSEI
First
1 Mini-Series 2.75
2 .... 2.75
3 .... 2.75
4 .... 2.75

SENTINELS OF JUSTICE
AC Comics
1 Capt.Paragon 2.00
2 .... 2.00
3 .... 2.00
4 .... 2.00
5 .... 2.00
6 .... 2.00
7 .... 2.00

SENTRY: SPECIAL
Innovation 1991
1 .... 2.75

SERAPHIM
Innovation 1990
1 and 2 .... @2.50

SERINA
Antarctic 1996
1 .... 2.95

SERPENTINA
Lightning 1997
1 .... 3.00
1a variant cover 3.00

SEVEN SISTERS
Zephyr Comics 1997
1 by Curley, Cruickshank & Garcia. 2.95
2 .... 2.95
3 .... 2.95
4 .... 2.95

77 SUNSET STRIP
Dell Publishing Co. Jan.-March, 1960
1 Ph(c) 125.00
2 Ph(c),RsM 135.00

SHADE SPECIAL
AC Comics
1 .... 2.00

SHADOW, THE
Archie Comics 1964–65
1 .... 60.00
2 .... 40.00
3 .... 40.00
4 .... 40.00
5 .... 40.00
6 and 8 .... @35.00

SHADOW COMICS
1 Guardians of Justice & The O-Force 2.00

SHADOW OF THE TORTURER, THE
Innovation 1991
1 thru 6 Gene Wolfe adapt. .... @2.00

SHADOW RAVEN
Poc-It Comics
1 I:Shadow Raven 2.95

SHADOW STATE
Preview Editions
1 and 2 B&W .... @2.50
Broadway 1995
1 thru 4 F:BloodS.C.R.E.A.M. .... @2.50
5 JiS, "Image Isn't Everything," concl. 2.50
6 "Anger of Lovers" pt.1 .... 2.50
7 "Anger of Lovers" pt.2 .... 2.95

SHAFT
Maximum Press 1997
1 RLd 2.50

SHAIANA
Entity 1995
1 R:Shaiana from Aster 3.75
1a clear chromium 8.00
1b Holochrome 10.00
2 Guardians of Earth 2.50

SHANGHAI BREEZE
1 .... 2.00

SHAOLIN
Black Tiger Press
1 I:Tiger 2.95
2 I:Crane 2.95

Shatter #3
© First

SHATTER
First 1985–88
1 .... 3.00
2 .... 2.50
3 .... 2.50
4 and 5 .... @2.00
6 thru 14 .... @2.00
Spec. #1 Computer Comic 5.00
#1a 2nd Printing 2.00

SHE-DEVILS ON WHEELS
Aircel
1 V:Man-Eaters 2.95
2 V:Man-Eaters 2.95
3 V:Man-Eaters 2.95

SHEENA: QUEEN OF THE JUNGLE
London Night
0 by Gabriel Cain & Wilson 3.00
0a Zebra Edition 5.00
0b Leopard Edition 5.00
0c Alligator Edition 5.00

SHEENA: QUEEN OF THE JUNGLE: BOUND

London Night

1 (of 4) by Everette Hartsoe & Art Wetherell 3.00
1 ministry ed.. . . . . 5.00
1 Leather retro edition 12.00

SHERIFF OF TOMBSTONE

Charlton Comics 1958–61

1 AW,JSe 50.00
2 . . . . 30.00
3 thru 10 . . . . @20.00
11 thru 17 . . . . @20.00

Shi: Way of the Warrior #2
© Crusade Entertainment

SHI

Crusade Comics

1 BiT,HMo,I:Shi 15.00
2 BiT. 8.00
2 BiT, reissue, new cover. 2.95
3 BiT. 5.00
4 BiT. 4.00
5 V:Arashi 3.00
5a variant cover. 8.00
6 V:Tomoe. 3.00
7 V:Nara Warriors 3.00
8 New costume 3.00
9 thru 11 . . . . @3.00
12 "Way of the Warrior" concl, flip-book Angel Fire. 3.00
TPB Vol. 1 revised rep.JuB(c). . . . 14.95
TPB Vol. 2, rep. Shi #5–#8 . . . . . 14.95
TPB rep. Shi #9–#12 & Shi vs. Tomoe 17.95
TPB Shi:Way of the Warrior 12.95
Shi/Cyblade Spec.#1 Battle of the Independents 4.00
Spec.#1a variant cover. 6.00

SHI: THE SERIES

Crusade Entertainment 1997

1 sequel to *Shi: Heaven and Earth*, F:Tomoe. 2.95
2 Unforgettable Fire, concl. 2.95
3 A Rock and a Hard Place, pt.1 . . 2.95
4 A Rock and a Hard Place, pt.2 . . 2.95
5 A Rock and a Hard Place, pt.3 . . 2.95
6 . . . . 2.95
7 Photographer's lucky picture . . . 2.95
8 V:Gemini Dawn twins 2.95
9 Bad Blood, pt.1 . . . . 2.95
9a variant BTi(c) 2.95
9b variant Ahn (c) 2.95
9c variant Kevin Lau (c) 2.95
10 Bad Blood, pt.2 . . . . 2.95
10a variant BTi(c) 2.95
10b variant Ahn (c) 2.95
10c variant Kevin Lau (c) 2.95
11 Bad Blood, pt.3 . . . . 2.95
12 The Dark Crusade, pt.1 (of 8) . . 2.95
13 The Dark Crusade, pt.2 (of 8) . . 2.95
14 The Dark Crusade, pt.3 (of 8) . . 2.95
15 The Dark Crusade, pt.4 (of 8) . . 2.95
16 The Dark Crusade, pt.5 (of 8) . . 2.95
1-shot The Essential Dark Crusade. 2.95
1-shot Shi:Five Year Celebration. . . 5.00
1-shotA,B,C,&D variant covers 5.00
#0 & Wolverine/Shi flip book 2.99

SHI: ART OF WAR TOUR BOOK

Crusade Entertainment

Wizard Chicago Con (c) 5.95

SHI: BLACK WHITE & RED

Crusade Entertainment

1 Night of the Rat, pt.1 . . . . 2.95
2 Night of the Rat, pt.2 . . . . 2.95
Coll. Ed. rep. #1–#2 . . . . 6.95

SHI/CYBLADE

Crusade

Spec.#1 The Battle for Independents...Endgame 2.95

SHI: EAST WIND RAIN

Crusade Entertainment 1997

1 BiT,MSo, fully painted. 3.50
2 BiT, concl.. . . . . 3.50

SHI: HEAVEN AND EARTH

Crusade Entertainment 1997

1 (of 3) BiT 2.95
1 variant cover. 2.95
2 BiT. 2.95
3 BiT. 2.95
4 BiT. 2.95
TPB rep. #1–#4 . . . . 15.95

SHI: MASQUERADE

Crusade Entertainment 1997

1 by Christopher Golden 3.50

SHI: NIGHTSTALKERS

Crusade Entertainment 1997

1-shot by Christopher Golden & VMk,F:T.C.B. 3.50

SHI: REKISHI

Crusade Entertainment 1997

1 (of 2) BiT 2.95
2 BiT, conclusion 2.95
Coll.Ed. Shi:Reshiki, sourcebook, MS(c). 4.95

SHI/VAMPIRELLA

Crusade 1997

1 WEI,. 2.95

SHI VS. TOMOE

Crusade April, 1996

Spec. #1 BiT, double size 3.95
GN Unforgettable Fire, rep.. . . . . . . 6.99

SHI-SENRYAKU

Crusade 1995

1 BiT,R:Shi 3.00
1a variant cover. 5.00
1 (of 3) 2nd edition 2.50
2 BiT,Arts of Warfare 3.00
2 2nd edition 2.50
3 BiT. 3.00
3 2nd edition 2.50
HC Rep.#1-#2 . . . . 24.95
TPB Rep.#1-#2. . . . . 12.95

SHI – YEAR OF THE DRAGON

Crusade Entertainment 2000

1 (of 3) BiT 2.99
1a variant (c). 2.99
2 Ana Tears (c) BiT 2.99
2a Death Incarnate (c) BiT. 2.99
Coll. Ed. Black,White,Red. 6.95
GN #1 & #2 Black,White,Red 5.99
Poster Book 2.99

SHOCK SUSPENSE STORIES

Russ Cochran Press 1992

1 reps.horror stories 2.00
2 inc.Kickback 2.00
3 thru 4 . . . . @2.00
5 thru 7 reps.horror stories. . . . . @2.00
8 reps.horror stories 2.00

Gemstone

18 EC comics reprint 2.50
TPB Vol. 1 rebinding of #1–#5 . . . . 8.95
TPB Vol. 2 rebinding of #5–#10 . . . 9.95
TPB Vol. 3 rebinding of #11–#15. . . 8.95
TPB Vol. 4 rebinding of #16–#20 . . 9.95

SHOCK THE MONKEY

Millennium/Expand 1995

1 Shock therapy 2.95

SHOGUNAUT

Firstlight

1 I:Shogunaut 2.95
2 V:Teckno Terror 2.95

SHOOTING STARS

1 . . . . 2.50

SHOTGUN MARY

Antarctic Press 1995

1 I:Shotgun Mary. 2.95
1a with CD Soundtrack 8.95
1b Red Foil cover 8.00
2 . . . . 2.95
Spec. Shooting Gallery. 2.95
Spec. Deviltown 2.95
Spec. Deviltown, commem. (1999) . 5.95

SHOTGUN MARY

Antarctic Press

1 by Herb Mallette & Kelsey Shannon 2.95
2 Early Days, pt.2 . . . . 2.95
3 Early Days, pt.3 . . . . 2.95

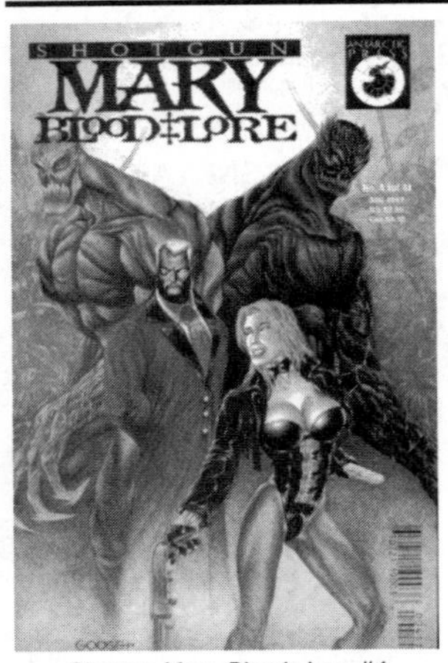

Shotgun Mary, Bloody Lore #4
© Antarctic Press

SHOTGUN MARY: BLOOD LORE
Antarctic Press 1997

1 (of 4) by Herb Mallette & Neil Googe 2.95
2 . . . . 2.95
3 . . . . 2.95
4 concl. 2.95

SHOTGUN MARY: SON OF THE BEAST, DAUGHTER OF LIGHT
Antarctic Press 1997

1 by Miljenko Horvatic & Esad T. Ribic. 2.95

SIEGEL & SHUSTER
Eclipse 1984–85

1 . . . . 2.00
2 . . . . 2.00

SIGIL
Crossgen Comics 2000

1 BKs 2.95
2 BKs 2.95
3 BKs 2.95
4 BKs 2.95
5 BKs 2.95

SILENT MOBIUS
Viz 1991–92

1 Katsumi 5.75
2 Katsumi vs. Spirit 5.25
3 Katsumi trapped within entity . . . 4.95
4 Nami vs. Dragon. 4.95
5 Kiddy vs. Wire 4.95
6 Search for Wire 4.95
GN 14.95

SILENT MOBIUS II
Viz

1 AMP Officers vs. Entities cont. . . 4.95
2 Entities in Amp H.Q. 4.95
3 V:Entity. 4.95
4 The Esper Weapon. 4.95
5 Last issue. 4.95

SILENT MOBIUS III
Viz

1 F:Lebia/computer network. 2.75
2 Lebia/computer link cont. 2.75
3 Lebia in danger 2.75
4 Return to Consciousness 2.75
5 Conclusion 2.75

SILVERBACK
Comico 1989–90

1 thru 3 . . . . @2.50

SILVER CROSS
Antarctic Press 1997

1 (of 3) by Ben Dunn 2.95
2 . . . . 2.95

SILVERHEELS
Pacific 1983–84

1 . . . . 2.00
2 and 3 . . . . @2.00

SILVER STAR
Pacific 1983–84

1 JK 2.00
2 JK 2.00
3 JK 2.00
4 JK 2.00
5 JK 2.00
6 JK 2.00

SILVER STAR
Topps

1 w/Cards 2.95

SILVER STORM

1 . . . . 2.25
2 thru 4 . . . . @2.00

SIMPSONS COMICS
Bongo Comics 1993

1 Colossal Horner 3.00
2 A:Sideshow Bob. 2.00
3 F:Bart. 2.00
4 F:Bart. 2.25
5 A:Itchy & Scratchy 2.25
6 F:Lisa. 2.25
7 Circus in Town 2.25
8 Mr. Burns Voyage. 2.25
9 Autobiographies 2.25
10 Tales of the Kwik-E-Mart 2.25
11 Ned Flanders Public Enemy. . . . 2.25
12 In the Blodome 2.25
13 F:Bart & Millhouse 2.25
14 Homer owns beer company 2.25
15 Waltons parody 2.25
16 thru 18. . . . . @2.25
19 thru 23. . . . . @2.25
24 . . . . 2.25
25 . . . . 2.25
26 Bart: action hero! 2.25
27 . . . . 2.25
28 Krusty the Clown, tax protest . . . 2.25
29 Captain Slamtastic. 2.25
30 Montgomery Burns clones Smithers. 2.25
31 Radioactive Homer 2.25
32 F:Lisa and her sax. 3.00
33 Reality on the blink 2.25
34 C. Montgomery Burns International Games. 2.25
35 20 kids 2.25
36 Three geeks computer company 2.25
37 Grampa Abe Simpson 2.25
38 chemically-engineered donuts . . 2.25
39 People vs. Homer Simpson and the Comic Book Guy 2.25
40 F:Krusty the Clown 2.50
41 Krusty Fun Factory 2.50
42 . . . . 2.50
43 Urban legends. 2.50
44 substitute teachers. 2.50
45 Santa's Little Helper. 2.50
46 Sideshow Bob 2.50
47 30 years in the future. 2.50
48 dating game 2.50
49 Lisa double feature 2.50
50 80-page. 5.95
51 thanksgiving 2.50
TPB Rep.#1-#4. . . . . 10.00
TPB Wing Ding, 120pg 11.95
TPB Simpsons Comics on Parade (1998). 11.95
TPB Simpsons Comics Big Bonanza. 11.95
TPB Comics A Go-Go. 11.95
TPB Comics Extravaganza 10.00
TPB Bartman Best of the Best . . . 10.00
TPB Simpsons Comics Strike Back 10.95
TPB Comics Wing Ding 11.95
Comic Spectacular,Vol.1 Rep.. . . . 10.00
Comic Spectacular,Vol.2 Rep.. . . . 10.00

SIMPSONS COMICS & STORIES
Welsh Publishing 1993

1 with poster 4.00
1a without poster. 2.50

Bongo Comics 1998

1 F:Bartman, Itchy & Scratchy 2.95

SINTHIA
Lightning 1997

1A by Joseph Adam, Daughter of Lucifer 3.00
1B 3.00
1c Platinum Edition 9.95
1d Autographed Edition 9.95
2 Sisters of Darkness 2.95
2a variant cover 2.95
3 Wagner(c) 2.95
3a variant Abrams cover 2.95
3b deluxe variant cover 9.95
4 Wagner(c) 2.95
4a variant John Cleary cover 2.95

SISTERS OF MERCY
No Mercy Comics

TPB rep. #1–#5 . . . . 14.95

Vol 2

1 by Mark Williams & Rikki Rockett 2.50
2 . . . . 2.50
3 . . . . 2.50

SISTERS OF MERCY: PARADISE LOST
London Night

by Ricki Rockett & Mark Williams
2 . . . . 2.50
3 . . . . 2.50
4 . . . . 2.50

SISTERS OF MERCY: WHEN RAZORS CRY CRIMSON TEARS
No Mercy Comics

1 . . . . 2.50

COLOR PUB.

SIX MILLION DOLLAR MAN, THE
Charlton June, 1976
1 JSon,Lee Majors Ph(c) 15.00
2 NA(c),JSon,Ph(c) 12.00
3 Ph(c) 12.00
4 Ph(c) 8.00
5 Ph(c) 8.00
6 Ph(c) 8.00
7 Ph(c) 8.00
8 Ph(c) 8.00
9 Ph(c) 8.00

666: MARK OF THE BEAST
Fleetway/Quality
1 I:Fludd, BU:Wolfie Smith. 2.00
2 thru 18. . . . . @2.00

SIX STRING SAMURAI
Awesome Entertainment 1998
1 RLe 2.95

SKATEMAN
Pacific 1983
1 NA 2.00

SKY WOLF
Eclipse 1988
1 V:Baron Von Tundra 2.00
2 TL,V:Baron Von Tundra 2.00
3 TL,cont. in Airboy #41. . . . . 2.00

SLAINE THE BERSERKER
Quality 1987–89
1 thru 14 . . . . @2.00
15/16 . . . . 2.00
17 . . . . 2.00
18/19 . . . . 2.00
20 thru 28 . . . . @2.00
Becomes:

SLAINE THE KING
26 . . . . 2.00

SLAINE
Fleetway
1 thru 4 SBs,From 2000 AD . . . . @4.95

SLAINE THE HORNED GOD
Egmont Fleetway 1998
1 (of 3) Pat Millagan & SBs, 68pg. . 7.00
2 (of 3) Pat Millagan & SBs, 68pg. . 7.00
3 68-page, conclusion 7.00

SLIMER
Now 1989
1 . . . . 2.50
2 thru 15 . . . . @2.00
Becomes:

SLIMER & REAL GHOSTBUSTERS
16 thru 18. . . . . @2.00

SMILEY
Chaos! Comics 1998
1 the Psychotic Button. 2.95
Spec. Smiley Anti-Holiday Spec.. . . 2.95
Spec. Smiley Psychotic Button's Spring Break Road Trip 2.95
Spec. Whacky Wrestling Spec. 2.95

SNAGGLEPUSS
Gold Key 1962–63
1 . . . . 75.00
2 . . . . 60.00
3 . . . . 60.00
4 . . . . 60.00

SNOOPER AND BLABBER DETECTIVES
Gold Key 1962–63
1 . . . . 75.00
2 . . . . 60.00
3 . . . . 60.00

SNOW WHITE & SEVEN DWARFS GOLDEN ANNIVERSARY
Gladstone
1 w/poster & stickers 24.00

SO DARK THE ROSE
CFD 1995
1 Fully Painted 2.95

SOJOURN
Dreamer Comics 1998
1 by Jim Somerville, Stranger & Stranger, pt.1 . . . . 2.95
2 Stranger & Stranger, pt.2 . . . . . . 2.95
3 Malice in Wonderland. 2.95
4 A Game of Conscience, pt.1 . . . . 2.95
5 A Game of Conscience, pt.2. . . . 2.10
6 A Game of Conscience, pt.3. . . . 3.15
7 A Game of Conscience, pt.4. . . . 3.15
8 The Hunt 3.15
9 The Hunt, pt.2 . . . . 3.15
10 The Hunt, Bloodied 3.15

SOLDIERS OF FREEDOM
Americomics 1987
1 . . . . 2.00
2 . . . . 2.00

SOLOMON KANE
Blackthorne
1 3-D Special 2.50
2 3-D Special 2.50
1 thru 4 . . . . @2.50

SOMERSET HOLMES
Pacific 1983–84
1 BA,AW,I:Cliff Hanger & Somerset Holmes 2.50
2 thru 4 BA,AW . . . . @2.00
Eclipse 1984
5 BA,AW. 2.00
6 BA 2.00

SONG OF THE CID
Calibre/Tome
1 Story of El Cid 2.95
2 Story of El Cid concl. 2.95

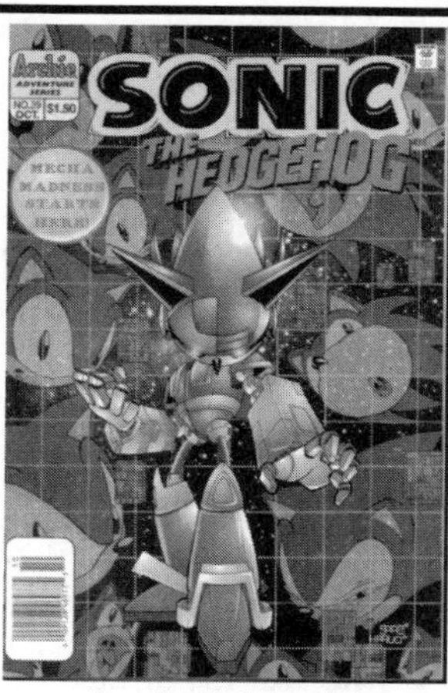

Sonic the Hedgehog #39
© Archie Publications

SONIC THE HEDGEHOG
Archie Publications 1993
1 A:Mobius,V:Robotnik 10.00
2 . . . . 7.00
3 thru 6 . . . . @6.00
7 thru 10 . . . . @5.00
11 thru 30 . . . . @3.00
31 thru 39. . . . . @3.00
40 thru 54. . . . . @3.00
55 . . . . 3.00
56 x-over with Knuckles #9. . . . . . . 3.00
57 . . . . 3.00
58 x-over with Knuckles #11 . . . . . . 2.00
59 R:Horizont-Al and Verti-Cal 2.00
60 Arsenal of the Iron King 2.00
61 Downunda. 2.00
62 in Sand Dalvador. 2.00
63 . . . . 2.00
64 "The Naugus Trilogy" pt.1 . . . . . 2.00
65 "The Naugus Trilogy" pt.2 . . . . . 2.00
66 "The Naugus Trilogy" pt.3 . . . . . 2.00
67 "Tomb Raiders" 2.00
68 "The Year 'O The Hog" 2.00
69 "A Day in the Life" 2.00
70 "Saving Nate Morgan" 2.00
71 All-Backwards Issye. 2.00
72 "I, Robotnik". 2.00
73 "The Truth Is Out There" 2.00
74 "Don't Call It A Comeback" 2.00
75 "A Am The Eggman" 2.00
76 "Business As Usual" 2.00
77 "Rebel Without A Pause" 2.00
78 "Changes" 2.00
79 and 80 . . . . @1.79
81 thru 90. . . . . @1.99
GN Sonic Firsts, rep.#0, #1/4 ashcan,#3,#4,#13. . . . . 4.95
Sonic Live Spec.#1. . . . . 2.00

SONIC QUEST: THE DEATH EGG SAGA
Archie Comics
1 (of 3) by Mike Gallagher & MaG, cont. from Sonic the Hedgehog #41 . . . . 2.00
2 and 3 . . . . @2.00

COLOR PUB.

SONIC THE HEDGEHOG PRESENTS KNUCKLES CHASTIC
Archie Comics 1995

1 I:New Heroes 2.00
Sonic Versus Knuckles Battle Royal
Spec.#1 . . . . 2.00

SONIC THE HEDGEHOG PRESENTS TAILS
Archie Comics 1995

1 F:Tails 2.00
2 F:Tails 2.00

SONIC'S FRIENDLY NEMESIS: KNUCKLES
Archie 1996

1 . . . . 2.00

SONIC SUPER SPECIAL
Archie Comics 1997

1 Brave New World 2.00
3 Sonic Firsts 2.00
4 The Return of the King 2.25
5 Sonic Kids 2.25
6 Expanded Sonic #50, 48pg. 2.25
7 F:Shadowhawk, The Maxx,
Savage Dragon 2.25
8 four stories, 48-page. 2.25
9 R:Sonic Kids. 2.25
10 Some Enchantra Evening 2.25
11 . . . . 2.29
12 48-page. 2.49
13 . . . . 2.49
14 . . . . 2.49

SON OF MUTANT WORLD
Fantagor 1990

1 BA 2.00
2 . . . . 2.00

SOJOURN
Dreamer Comics

1 by Jim Somerville, Stranger &
Stranger, pt.1 . . . . 2.95
2 Stranger & Stranger, pt.2 . . . . . . 2.95
3 Malice in Wonderland 2.95
4 A Game of Conscience, pt.1. . . . 2.95

SOULMAN
Quantum Comics 1998

1 . . . . 2.95
2 . . . . 2.95
3 16-page 2.95
4 16-page 2.95
5 24-page 2.95

SOULQUEST
Innovation 1989

1 BA 3.95

SOUPY SALES COMIC BOOK
Archie Publications 1965

1 . . . . 75.00

SPACE ADVENTURES
Charlton 1967–79, Volume 3

1 (#60) O&I:Paul Mann & The
Saucers From the Future 40.00
2 thru 8 (1968–69) . . . . @20.00
9 thru 13 (1978–79) . . . . @10.00

SPACE: ABOVE AND BEYOND
Topps 1995

1 thru 3 TV pilot adaptation . . . . @2.95

SPACE: ABOVE AND BEYOND— THE GAUNTLET
Topps 1996

1 . . . . 2.95
2 (of 2) 2.95

SPACE ARK
AC Comics 1985–87

1 . . . . 3.00
2 . . . . 2.00

SPACE FAMILY ROBINSON
Gold Key Dec., 1962–69

1 DSp 275.00
2 . . . . 125.00
3 . . . . 75.00
4 . . . . 75.00
5 . . . . 75.00
6 B:Captain Venture 75.00
7 . . . . 75.00
8 . . . . 75.00
9 . . . . 75.00
10 . . . . 75.00
11 thru 20 . . . . @50.00
21 thru 36 . . . . @30.00

SPACE GHOST
Gold Key March, 1967

1 . . . . 375.00

SPACE GHOST
Comico 1987

1 SR,V:Robot Master. 6.00

SPACE GIANTS, THE
Pyramid Comics 1997

0 . . . . 2.00
0a deluxe 2.25
1 . . . . 2.00
3 by Jeff Newman 2.00

SPACE MAN
Dell Publishing Co. 1962–72

1 . . . . 75.00
2 . . . . 40.00
3 . . . . 40.00
4 . . . . 30.00
5 . . . . 30.00
6 . . . . 30.00
7 . . . . 30.00
8 . . . . 30.00
9 . . . . 30.00
10 . . . . 30.00

SPACE: 1999
Charlton 1975–76

1 . . . . 10.00
2 JSon,"Survival". 8.00
3 JBy,"Bring Them Back Alive". . . . 7.00
4 JBy. 7.00
5 JBy. 7.00
6 JBy. 7.00
7 . . . . 7.00
8 B&W 7.00

SPACE: 1999
A Plus Comics

1 GM,JBy 2.50

SPACE USAGI
Mirage 1993

1 thru 3 From TMNT . . . . @2.75

Space War
© Charlton

SPACE WAR
Charlton Comics Oct., 1959

1 . . . . 150.00
2 . . . . 75.00
3 . . . . 70.00
4 SD,SD(c) 150.00
5 SD,SD(c) 150.00
6 SD 150.00
7 . . . . 40.00
8 SD,SD(c) 150.00
9 . . . . 45.00
10 SD,SD(c). 150.00
11 . . . . 40.00
12 . . . . 40.00
13 thru 15 . . . . @40.00
16 thru 27 . . . . @35.00
Becomes:

FIGHTIN' FIVE

28 SD,SD(c). 40.00
29 SD,SD(c). 40.00
30 SD,SD(c). 50.00
31 SD,SD(c). 50.00
32 . . . . 10.00
33 SD,SD(c). 50.00
34 Sd,SD(c) 50.00

SPECTRUM COMICS PRESENTS
Spectrum

1 I:Survivors 3.50

SPEED RACER
Now 1987–90

1 . . . . 3.50
1a 2nd printing 2.00
2 thru 33 . . . . @2.00
34 thru 38 . . . . @2.00
Spec. #1 . . . . 2.50

#1 2nd printing 2.00
Spec. #2. . . . . 3.50
Classics, Vol #2 . . . . 3.95
Classics, Vol #3 . . . . 3.95

[2nd Series]

1 R:Speed Racer. 2.00
2 . . . . 2.00
3 V:Giant Crab 2.00
4 . . . . 2.00
5 Racer-X 2.00
6 . . . . 2.00
7 . . . . 2.00

SPEED RACER

Wildstorm/DC 1999

1 Demon on Wheels 2.50

SPELLBINDERS

Quality 1986–88

1 Nemesis the Warlock 2.00
2 Nemesis the Warlock 2.00
3 Nemesis the Warlock 2.00
4 Nemesis the Warlock 2.00
5 Nemesis the Warlock 2.00
6 Nemesis the Warlock 2.00
7 Nemesis the Warlock 2.00
8 Nemesis the Warlock 2.00
9 Nemesis the Warlock 2.00
10 Nemesis the Warlock. 2.00
11 Nemesis the Warlock. 2.00

S.P.I.C.E.

Awesome Entertainment 1998

1 RLe,JLb,F:Kaboom. 2.50

SPIDER

Eclipse 1991

1 TT,"Blood Dance" 7.00
2 TT,"Blood Mark" 6.00
3 TT,The Spider Unmasked 5.50

SPIDER: REIGN OF THE VAMPIRE KING

Eclipse 1992

1 TT,I:Legion of Vermin 5.25
2 thru 4 TT. . . . . @2.50

SPIDERFEMME

Personality

1 Rep. parody 2.50

SPIDER-MAN/BADROCK

Maximum Press

1 (of 2) DJu,MMy x-over 3.00
2 DJu,DaF x-over 3.00

SPIRAL PATH

Eclipse 1986

1 V:Tairngir 2.00
2 V:King Artuk 2.00

SPIRIT

Harvey 1966

1 WE,O:Spirit 75.00
2 WE,O:The Octopus. 60.00

SPIRIT, THE

Kitchen Sink 1983–92

1 WE(c) (1983) 5.25
2 WE(c). 4.25
3 WE(c) (1984) 4.00

Spirit #1
© Kitchen Sink

4 WE(c) 4.00
5 WE(c) 3.00
6 WE(c) 3.00
7 WE(c) 3.00
8 thru 11 WE(c) (1985) color . . . @3.00
See: B&W section

SPIRIT, THE: THE NEW ADVENTURES

Kitchen Sink 1997

1 AMo,DGb 3.95
2 Eisner/Stout cover 3.50
2a Eisner/Schultz cover. 3.50
3 AMo,Last Night I Dreamed of Dr. Cobra 3.50
4 Dr. Broca von Bitelbaum. 3.50
5 Cursed Beauty 3.50
6 Swami Vashti Bubu. 3.50
7 Central City 3.50
8 by Joe Lansdale 3.50
9 . . . . 3.50
10 CAd,BRa 3.50

SPOOKY HAUNTED HOUSE

Harvey Publications 1972–75

1 . . . . 30.00
2 . . . . 15.00
3 thru 5 . . . . @15.00
6 thru 10 . . . . @10.00
11 thru 15 . . . . @7.00

SPOOKY SPOOKTOWN

Harvey Publications 1966–76

1 B:Casper,Spooky,68 pgs. 165.00
2 . . . . 90.00
3 . . . . 60.00
4 . . . . 60.00
5 . . . . 60.00
6 thru 10 . . . . @40.00
11 thru 20 . . . . @30.00
21 thru 30 . . . . @30.00
31 thru 39 E:68 pgs. . . . . @25.00
40 thru 45 . . . . @10.00
46 thru 66 . . . . @7.00

SPYMAN

1 GT,JSo,1st prof work, I:Spyman 65.00
2 DAy,JSo,V:Cyclops 40.00
3 . . . . 40.00

SQUALOR

First 1989

1 . . . . 2.75
2 . . . . 2.75
3 . . . . 2.75

STAINLESS STEEL RAT

Eagle 1986

1 Harry Harrison adapt. 2.25
2 thru 6 . . . . @2.00

STAR BLAZERS

Comico 1989

1 . . . . 3.00
2 . . . . 2.00
3 . . . . 2.00
4 . . . . 2.00

[2nd Series]

1 . . . . 2.00
2 . . . . 2.00
3 thru 5 . . . . @2.50

STARBLAZERS

Argo Press 1995

0 Battleship Yamato. 2.95
1 F:Dereck Wildstar. 2.95
2 After the Comet War. 2.95
3 . . . . 2.95
4 TEl. 2.95
5 . . . . 2.95
6 . . . . 2.95
7 Icarus, pt.2 . . . . 2.95
8 . . . . 2.95
9 . . . . 2.95
10 . . . . 2.95
11 . . . . 2.95
12 Nova captured. 2.95

STARFORCE SIX SPECIAL

AC Comics

1 . . . . 2.00

STARGATE

Entity Comics 1996

1 . . . . 2.95
2 . . . . 2.95
3 . . . . 2.95
4 (of 4) 2.95
4a deluxe limited edition 3.50

STARGATE: DOOMSDAY WORLD

Entity Comics 1996

1 new crew explores 2nd StarGate 2.95
1 prism-foil edition 3.50
2 . . . . 2.95
3 . . . . 2.95
3 deluxe 3.50

STARGODS

Antarctic Press 1998

1 by Zachary, Clark & Beaty 2.95
1a deluxe 5.95
2 The Golden Bow. 2.95
2a deluxe, with poster 5.95
Spec. Stargods Visions. 2.95

STARLIGHT

1 . . . . 2.00

STAR MASTERS
AC Comics

1 . . . . 2.00

STAR REACH CLASSICS
Eclipse 1984

1 JSn,NA(r) 2.00
2 AN 2.00
3 HC 2.00
4 FB(r) 2.00
5 . . . . 2.00
6 . . . . 2.00

STAR SEED
See: POWERS THAT BE

STARSLAYER
Pacific 1982–83

1 MGr,O:Starslayer 4.00
2 MGr,DSt,I:Rocketeer. 10.00
3 DSt,MGr,A:Rocketeer(2ndApp.) . 6.00
4 MGr,Baraka Kuhr 2.00
5 MGr,SA,A:Groo 7.00
6 MGr.conclusion story 2.00

First

7 MGr layouts 2.00
8 MGr layouts, MG 2.00
9 MGr layouts, MG 2.25
10 TT,MG,I:Grimjack. 4.00
11 TT,MG,A:Grimjack 2.00
12 TT,MG,A:Grimjack 2.00
13 TT,MG,A:Grimjack 2.00
14 TT,A:Grimjack 2.00
15 TT,A:Grimjack 2.00
16 TT,A:Grimjack 2.00
17 TT,A:Grimjack 2.00
18 TT,Grimjack x-over. 2.00
19 TT,TS,A:Black Flame 2.00
20 TT,TS,A:Black Flame 2.00
21 TT,TS,A:Black Flame 2.00
22 TT,TS,A:Black Flame 2.00
23 TT,TS,A:Black Flame 2.00
24 TT,TS,A:Black Flame 2.00
25 TS,A:Black Flame 2.00
26 TS,Black Flame full story 2.00
27 A:Black Flame 2.00
28 A:Black Flame 2.00
29 TS,A:Black Flame 2.00
30 TS,A:Black Flame 2.00
31 2nd Anniversary Issue 2.00
32 TS,A:Black Flame 2.00
33 TS,A:Black Flame 2.00
34 last issue. 2.00
Graphic Novel 9.95

STAR TREK
Gold Key 1967–79

1 Planet of No Return 500.00
2 Devil's Isle of Space 300.00
3 Invasion of City Builders 200.00
4 Peril of Planet Quick Change . 200.00
5 Ghost Planet. 200.00
6 When Planets Collide 165.00
7 Voodoo Planet 175.00
8 Youth Trap 150.00
9 Legacy of Lazarus 150.00
10 Sceptre of the Sun. 100.00
11 Brain Shockers 100.00
12 Flight of the Buccaneer 90.00
13 Dark Traveler. 80.00
14 Enterprise Mutiny. 80.00
15 Museum a/t End of Time 80.00
16 Day of the Inquisitors. 80.00
17 Cosmic Cavemen 80.00
18 The Hijacked Planet. 80.00
19 The Haunted Asteroid 80.00
20 A World Gone Mad 80.00
21 The Mummies of Heitus VII . . . 65.00
22 Siege in Superspace 65.00
23 Child's Play 65.00
24 The Trial of Capt. Kirk 65.00
25 Dwarf Planet 65.00
26 The Perfect Dream 65.00
27 Ice Journey 65.00
28 The Mimicking Menace 65.00
29 rep. Star Trek #1 . . . . 65.00
30 Death of a Star 50.00
31 "The Final Truth". 50.00
32 "The Animal People" 50.00
33 "The Choice" 50.00
34 "The Psychocrystals" 50.00
35 rep. Star Trek #4 . . . . 50.00
36 "A Bomb in Time". 50.00
37 rep. Star Trek #5 . . . . 40.00
38 "One of our Captains
is Missing" 40.00
39 "Prophet of Peace" 40.00
40 AMc,Furlough to Fury, A:
Barbara McCoy 40.00

Star Trek #40
© Whitman

41 AMc,The Evictors. 40.00
42 "World Against Time" 40.00
43 "World Beneath the Waves" . . . 40.00
44 "Prince Traitor" 40.00
45 rep. Star Trek #7 . . . . 40.00
46 "Mr. Oracle" 40.00
47 AMc,"This Tree Bears Bitter
Fruit" 40.00
48 AMc,Murder on Enterprise 40.00
49 AMc,"A Warp in Space" 40.00
50 AMc,"The Planet of No Life". . . 40.00
51 AMc,DestinationAnnihilation6 . . 30.00
52 AMc,"And A Child Shall
Lead Them" 30.00
53 AMc,"What Fools..Mortals Be" . 30.00
54 AMc,"Sport of Knaves". 30.00
55 AMc,A World Against Itself. . . . 30.00
56 AMc,No Time Like The Past,
A:Guardian of Forever 30.00
57 AMc,"Spore of the Devil" 30.00
58 AMc,"Brain Damaged Planet". . 30.00
59 AMc,"To Err is Vulcan" 30.00
60 AMc,"The Empire Man" 30.00
61 AMc,"Operation Con Game". . . 30.00

STAR WARS IN 3-D
Blackthorne

1 thru 7 . . . . @2.50

STARWOLVES: JUPITER RUN

1 . . . . 2.00

S.T.A.T.
Majestic 1993

1 FdS(s),PhH,I:S.T.A.T. 2.50

STEALTH SQUAD
Petra Comics 1993

1 I:Stealth Squad. 2.50

STEED & MRS PEEL
Eclipse 1990

1 IG,The Golden Game 4.95
2 IG,The Golden Game 4.95
3 IG,The Golden Game 4.95

STEEL CLAW
Quality

1 H:Ken Bulmer. 2.00
2 thru 4 . . . . @2.00

STEEL STERLING
Archie Publications 1984
(formerly LANCELOT STRONG)

4 EB 2.00
5 EB 2.00
6 EB 2.00
7 EB 2.00

STEVE CANYON 3-D
Kitchen Sink 1986

Milton Caniff & Peter Poplaski(c),
w/glasses (1985) 2.00

STEVE ZODIAC & THE FIREBALL XL-5
Gold Key Jan., 1964

1 . . . . 100.00

STING OF THE GREEN HORNET
Now 1992

1 Polybagged w/trading card 2.75
2 inc.Full color poster 2.75
3 inc.Full color poster 2.75

STINGER

1 . . . . 2.00

STITCH
Samsons Comics

1 I:Stitch. 2.50

STONE COLD STEVE AUSTIN
Chaos! Comics 1999

1 (of 4) Whoop Ass personified . . . 2.95
1a photo (c). 2.95
1b Premium. 9.99
2 . . . . 2.95
2a photo (c). 2.95
3 . . . . 2.95
3a photo (c). 2.95
4 . . . . 2.95
4a photo (c). 2.95
TPB Vol. 1 . . . . 12.95

STORMQUEST
Caliber 1994
1 I:Stormquest 2.00
2 Time Stone 2.00
3 BU:Seeker 2.00
4 F:Shalimar 2.00
5 Reunion 2.00
6 V:Samuroids 2.00

STRANGE DAYS
Eclipse 1984–85
1 . . . . 3.50
2 . . . . 2.50
3 . . . . 2.00

STRANGE SUSPENSE STORIES/ CAPTAIN ATOM
Charlton Comics
75 SD,O:CaptainAtom,1960Rep.. 125.00
76 SD, Capt.Atom,1960Rep. 75.00
77 SD, Capt.Atom,1960Rep. 75.00
Becomes:

CAPTAIN ATOM
Charlton Comics 1965–67
78 SD, new stories begin 100.00
79 SD,I:Dr.Spectro 65.00
80 SD. 65.00
81 SD,V:Dr.Spectro 65.00
82 SD,I:Nightshade,Ghost 65.00
83 SD,I:Ted Kord/Blue Beetle 45.00
84 SD,N:Captain Atom 40.00
85 SD,A:Blue Beetle,I:Punch & Jewelee 40.00
86 SD,A:Ghost, Blue Beetle 40.00
87 SD,JAp,A:Nightshade 40.00
88 SD/FMc,JAp,A:Nightshade. . . . 40.00
89 SD/FMc,JAp,A:Nightshade, Ghost, last issue Dec.1967 . . . 40.00

STRAW MEN
Innovation
1 & 2 . . . . @2.00

STREET FIGHTER
Ocean 1986–87
1 thru 3 . . . . @2.00

STREET SHARKS
Archie Comics 1995
1 & 2 Based on Cartoons . . . . . . @2.00

STRIKE!
Eclipse 1988
1 TL,RT,I&O:New Strike. 2.00
2 TL,RT. 2.00
3 TL,RT. 2.00
4 TL,RT,V:Renegade CIA Agents. . 2.00
5 TL,RT,V:Alien Bugs. 2.00
6 TL,RT,“Legacy of the Lost” 2.00
Spec. #1 Strike vs. Sgt. Strike TL,RT,“The Man” 2.00

Strike #3
© Eclipse

3 Breakout, pt.2. . . . . 2.95
[Volume 2] 1995
1 ScC,polybagged with Chrysalis promo card. 2.95

STRIKER
Viz
1 thru 2 . . . . @2.75

STRIKEFORCE AMERICA
Comico 1995
1 ScC,SK(c),I:StrikeforceAmerica . 2.50
2 V:Superior-prisoner. 2.95

STRONG MAN
AC Comics
1 . . . . 2.95

STRONTIUM DOG
Eagle 1985
1 . . . . 2.00
2 . . . . 2.00
3 . . . . 2.00
4 . . . . 2.00
5 . . . . 2.00
6 . . . . 2.00
Quality
7 . . . . 2.00
8 . . . . 2.00
9 . . . . 2.00
10 . . . . 2.00
11 . . . . 2.00
12 . . . . 2.00
13 . . . . 2.00
14 . . . . 2.00
15/16 . . . . 2.00
17 . . . . 2.00
18/19 . . . . 2.00
20 thru 29 . . . . @2.00
[2nd Series]
1 . . . . 2.00
Quality
Spec.#1 . . . . 2.00

STRYKE
London Night Studios 1995
0 I:Stryke. 5.00
1 . . . . 4.00

STUMBO THE GIANT
Blackthorne
1 3-D. 2.50

STUMBO TINYTOWN
Harvey Publications 1963–66
1 . . . . 150.00
2 . . . . 100.00
3 . . . . 65.00
4 . . . . 65.00
5 . . . . 65.00
6 thru 13 . . . . @50.00

STUPID HEROES
Next
1 PeL(s),w/ 2 card-strip 2.75
2 . . . . 2.75
3 F:Cinder. 2.75

STURM THE TROOPER
1 . . . . 2.00
2 . . . . 2.00
3 . . . . 2.00

SUBSPECIES
Eternity 1991
1 Movie Adaptation 3.00
2 Movie Adaptation 2.50
3 Movie Adaptation 2.50
4 Movie Adaptation 2.50

SUN GLASSES AFTER DARK
Verotik 1995
1 . . . . 2.95
2 and 3 . . . . @2.95
4 thru 6 . . . . @3.95
½ prequel, San Diego Con ed.. . . . 2.95

SUN-RUNNERS
Pacific 1984
1 . . . . 2.50
2 . . . . 2.00
3 . . . . 2.00
Eclipse 1984–86
4 . . . . 2.00
5 . . . . 2.00
6 “Sins of the Father” 2.00
7 “Dark Side of Mark Dancer” 2.00
Summer Special #1 . . . . 2.00

SUNSET CARSON
AC Comics
1 Based on Cowboy Star. 5.00

SUPERBABES: FEMFORCE
AC Comics
1 Various Artists 5.00

SUPER CAR
Gold Key 1962–63
1 . . . . 250.00
2 . . . . 125.00
3 . . . . 125.00
4 . . . . 175.00

SUPERCOPS
Now 1990
1 thru 4 . . . . @2.00

SUPER COPS, THE
Red Circle 1974
1 . . . . 3.00

SUPER GOOF
Gold Key 1965–82
1 . . . . 30.00

2 thru 10 . . . . @15.00
11 thru 20 . . . . @10.00
21 thru 30 . . . . @8.00
31 thru 74 . . . . @5.00

SUPER HEROES VERSUS SUPERVILLIANS
Archie Publications July, 1966
1 A:Flyman,Black Hood,The Web, The Shield 65.00

SUPERHUMAN SAMURAI SYBER SQUAD
Hamilton Comics 1995
0 Based on TV Show. 2.95

SUPERNAUT
Anarchy 1997
1 (of 3) 3.00
1 gold logo 6.00
2 by Rob Hand, Hand of Doom . . . 3.00
2a gold logo 6.00

SUPREME
Maximum Press
#1–#43 see Image
44 AMo, JoB, A:Glory 3.00
45 AMo, JoB, A:Glory 3.00
46 AMo,Suprema 3.00
47 AMo 3.00
48 AMo 2.50
49 AMo 2.50
50 double size 3.95
51 . . . . 3.50
52A AMo, Book 1 . . . . 3.50
52B AMo, Book 2, continuation. . . . 3.50
53 AMo,CSp,AG,V:Omniman 3.00
54 AMo,CSp,AG,Ballad of Judy Jordan 3.00
55 AMo,CSp,AG,Silence At Gettysburg 3.00
56 AMo,CSp,AG,Reflections,pt.1 . . 3.00
57 AMo,CSp,AG,Reflections,pt.2 . . 3.00
58 AMo,CSp,AG,A World of His Own 3.00
59 AMo,CSp,AG,Professor Night of the Prism World 3.00
60 AMo,CSp,AG,F:Radar in Puppy Love. 3.00
61 AMo,CSp,AG,Meet Mr. Meteor. . 3.00
Coll.Ed.#1, rep.#1–#2. . . . . 4.95
Coll.Ed.#2, rep.. . . . . 4.95
Coll.Ed.#3 rep. #45–#46, AMo 4.95
Classic Col.Ed.#1,rep.#1 . . . . . 5.95
Classic Col.Ed.#2,rep.#43,. . . . 5.95
HC rep.#1–#12. . . . . 49.95
TPB Secret Origins, rep. 16.95
TPB Supreme Madness 14.95
HC Supreme Madness 40.00
TPB rep. #41–#46, AMo 14.95

SUPREME: THE RETURN
Awesome Entertainment 1999
1 AMo,CSp,AG 3.00
1a variant AxR cover 6.95
2 AMo,JSn, ... 3.00
3 . . . . 3.00
4 . . . . 3.00
5 . . . . 2.99
6 New York City. 2.99
7 . . . . 2.99
8 . . . . 2.99

SURGE
Eclipse 1984
1 A:DNAgents 3.00
2 A:DNAgents 2.00
3 A:DNAgents 3.00
4 A:DNAgents 3.00

SURROGATE SAVIOR
Hot Brazer Comic Pub.
1 I:Ralph 2.50
2 Baggage. 2.50

SURVIVORS
Spectrum
1 Mag. size 5.00
2 . . . . 3.50
3 The Old One 2.50
4 . . . . 2.50

SURVIVORS
Fantagraphics
1 thru 3 . . . . @2.50

SUSPIRA: THE GREAT WORKING
Chaos! Comics 1997
1 (of 4) PNa 2.95
2 PNa 2.95
3 PNa 2.95
4 PNa 2.95
HC signed, limited 20.00

Swords of Texas #2
© Eclipse

SWORDS OF TEXAS
Eclipse 1987
1 FH,New America 2.00
2 FH,V:Baja Badlands 2.00
3 FH,TY(c),V:Dogs of Danger 2.00
4 FH,V:Samurai Master 2.00

SYMBOLS OF JUSTICE
High Impact Studios
1 I:Granger,Justice,Rayven 2.95
2 V:Devil's Brigade 2.95

SYPHONS
Now 1994
1 thru 7 . . . . @2.00

SYPHONS: COUNTDOWN
Now
1 F:Brigade 2.95
2 Led By Cross 2.95
3 Blown Cover. 2.95
1995 Ann. Doomsday Device 2.95

SYPHONS: THE STARGATE STRATAGEM
Now
1 thru 3 . . . . @2.95

TALES CALCULATED TO DRIVE YOU BATS
Archie Publications 1961–62
1 . . . . 100.00
2 . . . . 75.00
3 thru 6 . . . . @50.00

TALES FROM THE CRYPT
Gladstone 1990–91
1 E.C.rep.AW/FF,GS 5.00
2 rep. 4.00
3 rep. 3.50
4 rep. 3.00
5 rep.TFTC #45. . . . . 3.00
6 rep.TFTC #42. . . . . 3.00

TALES FROM THE CRYPT
Russ Cochran Publ 1992
1 rep. TFTC #31,CSS#12 . . . . 2.75
2 rep. TFTC #34,CSS#15 . . . . 2.50
3 rep. TFTC, CSS 2.50
4 rep. TFTC #43,CSS#18 . . . . 2.50
5 rep. TFTC,CSS#23. . . . . 2.00

[2nd Series]
1 rep.horror stories 2.00
2 inc.The Maestro's Hand 2.00
3 thru 6 . . . . @2.00
7 thru 8 . . . . @2.00

Gemstone
16 thru 30 EC comics reprint. . . . @2.50
"Annuals"
TPB Vol. 1 rebinding of #1–#5 . . . . 8.95
TPB Vol. 2 rebinding of #5–#10 . . . 8.95
TPB Vol. 3 rebinding of #11–#15. . . 8.95
TPB Vol. 4 rebinding of #16–#20. . 12.95
TPB Vol. 5 rebinding #21–#24 . . . 13.95

TALES OF EVIL
Atlas Comics 1975
1 . . . . 5.00

TALES OF TERROR
Eclipse 1985–87
1 . . . . 3.00
2 "Claustrophobia". 2.00
3 GM,"Eyes in the Darkness". 2.00
4 TT,TY,JBo(c),"The Slasher". 2.00
5 "Back Forty,""Shoe Button Eyes" 2.00
6 "Good Neighbors". 2.00
7 SBi,JBo,SK(i),"Video" 2.00
8 HB,"Revenant,""Food for Thought" 2.00
9 . . . . 2.00
10 . . . . 2.00
11 TT,JBo(c),"Black Cullen". 2.00
12 JBo,FH,"Last of the Vampires" . . 2.00
13 . . . . 2.00

TALES OF THE GREEN BERET
Dell Publishing Co. Jan., 1967
1 SG . . . 30.00
2 thru 4 . . . @20.00
5 . . . 20.00

TALES OF THE GREEN HORNET
Now 1990
1 NA(c),O:Green Hornet Pt.1 . . . 3.00
2 O:Green Hornet Pt.2 . . . 2.50
3 Gun Metal Green . . . 2.50
4 Targets . . . 2.00

TALES OF THE MYSTERIOUS TRAVELER
Charlton Comics Aug., 1956
1 DG . . . 350.00
2 SD . . . 300.00
3 SD,SD(c) . . . 300.00
4 SD,SD(c) . . . 350.00
5 SD,SD(c) . . . 350.00
6 SD,SD(c) . . . 350.00
7 SD . . . 275.00
8 SD . . . 275.00
9 SD . . . 275.00
10 SD,SD(c) . . . 300.00
11 SD,SD(c) . . . 300.00
12 . . . 125.00
13 . . . 125.00
14 (1985) . . . 10.00
15 (1985) . . . 10.00

TALES OF THE SUN RUNNERS
Sirius Comics 1986
1 . . . 2.00
2 and 3 . . . @2.00

TALESPIN
Walt Disney 1991
(Reg.-Series)
1 "Sky-Raker" Pt.1 . . . 2.50
2 "Sky-Raker" Pt.2 . . . 2.00
3 "Idiots Abroad" . . . 2.00
4 "Contractual Desperation" . . . 2.00
5 "The Oldman & the Sea Duck" . . 2.00
6 "F'reeze a Jolly Good Fellow" . . . 2.00

TALESPIN
Walt Disney 1991
[Mini-Series]
1 Take-off Pt.1 . . . 3.00
2 Take-off Pt 2 . . . 3.00
3 Take-off Pt 3,Khan Job . . . 2.00
4 Take-off pt 4 . . . 2.00

TAOLAND
Severe Reality Productions
4 1st full color issue . . . 5.95
5 48pg . . . 5.95

TAOLAND ADVENTURES
Antarctic Press 1999
1 by Jeff Amano . . . 3.00
2 . . . 3.00

TARGET AIRBOY
Eclipse 1988
1 SK,A:Clint . . . 2.00

TARGITT
Atlas March–July 1975
1 thru 3 . . . @5.00

TAROT WITCH OF THE BLACK ROSE
Broadsword Comics 2000
1 (of 4) JBa(c) . . . 2.95
1a deluxe . . . 19.95
2 . . . 2.95
3 . . . 2.95
4 . . . 2.95
4a deluxe . . . 19.95

TARZAN OF THE APES
Gold Key 1962–72
prev. Dell (see Golden Age)
132 . . . 40.00
133 . . . 30.00
134 . . . 30.00
135 . . . 30.00

Tarzan #183
© Gold Key

136 . . . 30.00
137 . . . 30.00
138 . . . 30.00
139 I:Korak . . . 35.00
140 . . . 30.00
141 . . . 30.00
142 . . . 30.00
143 . . . 30.00
144 . . . 30.00
145 . . . 30.00
146 . . . 30.00
147 . . . 30.00
148 . . . 30.00
149 . . . 30.00
150 . . . 30.00
151 . . . 30.00
152 . . . 30.00
153 . . . 30.00
154 . . . 30.00
155 O:Tarzan . . . 40.00
156 . . . 25.00
157 Banlu, Dog o/t Arande, Pt.1 . . 25.00
158 Banlu, Dog o/t Arande, Pt.2 . . 25.00
159 Banlu, Dog o/t Arande, Pt.3 . . 25.00
160 . . . 25.00
161 . . . 25.00
162 TV photo (c) . . . 30.00
163 . . . 25.00
164 . . . 25.00
165 TV photo (c) . . . 35.00
166 . . . 25.00
167 . . . 25.00
168 TV photo (c) . . . 35.00
169 A:Leopard Girl . . . 25.00
170 . . . 25.00
171 TV photo (c) . . . 40.00
172 . . . 20.00
173 . . . 20.00
174 . . . 20.00
175 . . . 20.00
176 . . . 20.00
177 . . . 20.00
178 O:Tarzan, rep. #155 . . . 20.00
179 A:Leopard Girl . . . 20.00
180 . . . 20.00
181 . . . 20.00
182 . . . 20.00
183 Down Trails of Terror . . . 20.00
184 . . . 20.00
185 . . . 20.00
186 . . . 20.00
187 . . . 20.00
188 . . . 20.00
189 . . . 20.00
190 . . . 20.00
191 . . . 20.00
192 Tarzan and the Foreign Legion adaptation . . . 20.00
193 "Escape From Sumatra" . . . 20.00
194 thru 199 . . . @20.00
200 . . . 25.00
201 thru 205 . . . @20.00
206 last issue . . . 20.00
Continued by DC; see also Marvel

TARZAN IN COLOR
NBM 1997
TPB Vol. 1, 1931–1933, by Hal Foster . . . 24.95
TPB Vol. 2, 1933–1935, by Hal Foster . . . 24.95
TPB Vol. 3, 1935–1937, by Hal Foster . . . 24.95

TASK FORCE ALPHA
Alpha Productions
1 Forged in Fire . . . 3.50

TASMANIAN DEVIL & HIS TASTY FRIENDS
Gold Key Nov., 1962
1 . . . 150.00

TASTEE-FREEZ COMICS
Harvey Comics 1957
1 Little Dot . . . 40.00
2 Rags Rabbit . . . 20.00
3 Casper . . . 30.00
4 Sad Sack . . . 20.00
5 Mazie . . . 20.00
6 Dick Tracy . . . 35.00

TEAM ANARCHY
Anarchy 1993
1 I:Team Anarchy . . . 2.75
2 thru 3 . . . @2.75
4 PuD,MaS,I:Primal . . . 2.75

TEAM YANKEE
First 1989
1 Harold Coyle novel adapt. . . . 2.00
2 thru 6 . . . @2.00
Trade Paperback . . . 12.95

T.E.C.H. BOYZ HYPERACTIVE

Dynasty Comics

1 I:T.E.C.H. Boyz 2.95
2 Man vs. Nature 2.95

TEEN-AGE CONFIDENTIAL CONFESSIONS

Charlton Comics 1960–64

1 . . . . 35.00
2 thru 5 . . . . @25.00
6 thru 10 . . . . @20.00
11 thru 22 . . . . @15.00

TEENAGE HOTRODDERS

Charlton Comics April, 1963

1 . . . . 50.00
2 thru 5 . . . . @30.00
6 thru 10 . . . . @25.00
11 thru 23 . . . . @20.00
24 . . . . 20.00

Becomes:

TOP ELIMINATOR

25 thru 29 . . . . @20.00

Becomes:

DRAG 'N' WHEELS

30 . . . . 20.00
31 thru 58 . . . . @4.00
59 May, 1973 . . . . 4.00

TEENAGE MUTANT NINJA TURTLES

First

1 . . . . 6.00
2 . . . . 4.50
Graphic Novel 17.00

TEENAGE MUTANT NINJA TURTLES

Archie

(From T.V. Series)

1 O:TMNT,April O'Neil,Shredder Krang 6.00
2 V:Shredder,O:Bebop & Rocksteady 4.00
3 V:Shredder & Krang 3.00

Teenage Mutant Ninja Turtles Vol. 2, #11 © Mirage

TEENAGE MUTANT NINJA TURTLES

Mirage 1993

1 A:Casey Jones 3.00
2 JmL(a&s) 3.00
3 thru 8 . . . . @2.75
9 V:Baxter Bot 2.75
10 Mr. Braunze 2.75
11 V:Raphael 2.75
12 V:Darpa 2.75
13 J:Triceraton 2.75

TEENAGE MUTANT NINJA TURTLES ADVENTURES

Archie 1988 [2nd Series]

1 Shredder,Bebop,Rocksteady return to earth 5.00
2 I:Baxter Stockman 3.00
3 "Three Fragments" #1 . . . . 3.00
4 "Three Fragments" #2 . . . . 2.50
5 Original adventures begin, I:Man Ray 2.50
6 I:Leatherhead,Mary Bones 2.50
7 I:Cuddley the Cowlick; Inter-Galactic wrestling issue 2.50
8 I:Wingnut & Screwloose 2.00
9 I:Chameleon 2.00
10 I:Scumbug, Wyrm 2.00
11 I:Rat King & Sons of Silence; Krang returns to earth 2.00
12 Final Conflict #1, A:Leatherhead Wingnut,Screwloose,Trap, I:Malinga 2.00
13 Final Conflict #2 . . . . 2.00
14 Turtles go to Brazil;I:Jagwar Dreadman 2.00
15 I:Mr. Null 2.00
16 I&D:Bubbla,the Glubbab 2.00
17 Cap'n Mossback 2.00
18 'Man Who Sold World' 2.00
19 I: Mighty Mutanimals 2.00
20 V:Supersoldier,War.Dragon 2.00
21 V:Vid Vicious 2.00
22 GC,Donatello captured 2.00
23 V:Krang,I:Slash,Belly Bomb 2.00
24 V:Krang 2.00
25 . . . . 2.00
26 I:T'Pau & Keeper 2.00
27 I:Nevermore,Nocturno&Hallocat . 2.00
28 Turtle go to Spain, I:Nindar & Chein Klan 2.00
29 Warrior Dragon captured 2.00
30 TMNT/Fox Mutant Ninjara team-up 2.00
31 TMNT/Ninjara team-up cont. . . . 2.00
32 A:Sumo Wrestler Tatoo 2.00
33 The Karma of Katmandu 2.00
34 Search For Charlie Llama 2.00
35 . . . . 2.00
36 V:Shredder 2.00
37 V:Shredder 2.00
38 V:Null & 4 Horsemen Pt.1 . . . . . 2.00
39 V:Null & 4 Horseman Pt.3 . . . . . 2.00
40 1492,A:The Other 2.00
41 And Deliver us from Evil 2.00
42 Time Tripping Trilogy #1 . . . . 2.00
43 thru 51 . . . . @2.00
52 thru 54 . . . . @2.00
55 thru 57 Terracide . . . . @2.00
58 thru 70 . . . . @2.00
1990 Movie adapt(direct) 5.50
1990 Movie adapt(newsstand) 2.50
1991 TMNT meet Archie 2.50
1991 Movie Adapt II 2.50
Spec.#2 Ghost of 13 Mile Island . . . 2.50
Spec.#3 Night of the Monsterex . . . 2.50
TMNT Mutant Universe Sourcebook 2.00

TEENAGE MUTANT NINJA TURTLES/ FLAMING CARROT

Mirage/Dark Horse

1 JmL 3.00
2 thru 3 JmL 3.00
4 JmL 3.00

TMNT PRESENTS: APRIL O'NEIL

Archie

1 A:Chien Khan,Vid Vicious 2.00
2 V:White Ninja,A:V.Vicious 2.00
3 V:Vhien Khan,concl. 2.00

TMNT: THE MALTESE TURTLE

Mirage

Spec. F:Raphael Detective 2.95

TMNT PRESENTS: DONATELLO AND LEATHERHEAD

1 thru 2 . . . . @2.00

TMNT PRESENTS: MERDUDE VS. RAY FILLET

Archie 1993

1 thru 3 . . . . @2.00

TMNT: APRIL O'NEIL THE MAY EAST SAGA

Archie

1 A:TMNT 2.00

TMNT: YEAR OF THE TURTLE

Archie Comics 1995

1 All New Era 2.00

[JACK KIRBY'S] TEENAGENTS

Topps

[Mini-Series]

1 WS,AH,w/3 cards 2.95
2 NV,w/3 cards 2.95
3 NV,w/3 cards 2.95
4 NV,w/3 leftover? cards 2.95

TEEN CONFESSIONS

Charlton Comics 1959–76

1 . . . . 75.00
2 . . . . 40.00
3 . . . . 25.00
4 . . . . 25.00
5 . . . . 25.00
6 . . . . 25.00
7 . . . . 25.00
8 . . . . 25.00
9 . . . . 25.00
10 . . . . 25.00
11 thru 30 . . . . @20.00
31 Beatles cover 75.00
32 thru 36 . . . . @15.00
37 Beatles cover,Fan Club story . . 75.00
38 thru 97 . . . . @10.00

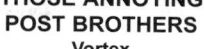

TEEN SECRET DIARY
Charlton Comics 1959–61

1 ... 35.00
2 ... 25.00
3 ... 20.00
4 ... 20.00
5 ... 20.00
6 ... 20.00
7 ... 20.00
8 ... 20.00
9 ... 20.00
10 ... 20.00
11 ... 20.00

TEKKEN 2
Knightstone 1997

1 (of 4) Tekken Saga, pt.3 ... 2.95
2 ... 2.95
2a photo cover ... 2.95
3 ... 2.95
3a photo cover ... 2.95

TEKKEN SAGA
Knightstone 1997

1 (of 8) ... 3.95
2 ... 2.95
3 ... 2.95
4 Paul vs. Kazuya ... 2.95
5 Paul a prisoner ... 2.95
Nightstone Unlimited & Tekken ½ ... 2.95

TENSE SUSPENSE
Fargo Publications 1958–59

1 ... 55.00
2 ... 50.00

TERMINATOR, THE
Now 1988–89

1 ... 10.00
2 ... 5.00
3 ... 4.00
4 ... 3.50
5 ... 3.50
6 ... 3.50
7 ... 3.50
8 ... 3.50
9 ... 3.50
10 ... 3.50
11 ... 3.50
12 I:JohnConnor($1.75,cov,dbl.sz) ... 3.50
13 ... 3.50
14 ... 3.50
15 ... 3.50
16 ... 3.50
17 ... 3.50
Spec. #1 ... 3.50

TERMINATOR: ALL MY FUTURES PAST
Now 1990

1 Painted Art ... 3.00
2 Painted Art ... 3.00

TERMINATOR: THE BURNING EARTH
Now 1990

1 ... 7.00
2 ... 6.00
3 ... 6.00
4 ... 10.00
5 ... 10.00

TERRAFORMERS
Wonder Comics 1987

1 ... 2.00
2 ... 2.00
3 ... 2.00
4 ... 2.00

TERRANAUTS
Fantasy General 1986

1 ... 2.00
2 ... 2.00

TESS

1 ... 2.00

TEXAS RANGERS IN ACTION
Charlton Comics 1956–70

5 ... 50.00
6 ... 30.00
7 ... 30.00
8 ... 30.00
9 ... 30.00
10 ... 30.00
11 ... 50.00
12 ... 20.00
13 ... 45.00
14 thru 20 ... @20.00
21 thru 30 ... @15.00
31 thru 59 ... @10.00
60 B:Riley's Rangers ... 12.00
61 thru 79 ... @5.00

THAT WILKIN BOY
Archie Publications Jan., 1969

1 ... 35.00
2 ... 15.00
3 ... 15.00
4 ... 15.00
5 ... 15.00
6 ... 15.00
7 ... 15.00
8 ... 15.00
9 ... 15.00
10 ... 15.00
11 thru 20 ... @8.00
21 thru 26 E:Giant size ... @7.00
27 thru 52 ... @7.00

THESPIAN
Dark Moon

1 I:Thespian ... 2.50
2 V:Lemming ... 2.50
3 Lord of Manhattan ... 2.50

THING: COLD FEAR

1 R:Thing ... 3.00
2 ... 2.75

THIRD WORLD WAR
Fleetway 1990–91

1 HamburgerLady ... 2.50
2 ... 2.50
3 The Killing Yields ... 2.50
4 ... 2.50
5 ... 2.50
6 ... 2.50

13: ASSASSIN
TSR 1990–91

1 thru 4 from game ... @2.95
5 thru 8 The Search for Maggie Darr ... @2.95

THOSE ANNOYING POST BROTHERS
Vortex

1 ... 2.00
2 ... 2.00
3 ... 2.00
4 ... 2.00
5 ... 2.00
6 ... 2.00

3-D ZONE PRESENTS
Renegade 1987–89

1 L.B.Cole(c) ... 2.00
2 ... 2.00
3 ... 2.00
4 ... 2.00
5 ... 2.00
12 3-D Presidents ... 2.50
13 Flash Gordon ... 2.50
14 Tyranostar ... 2.50
15 Tyranostar ... 2.50
16 SpaceVixen ... 2.50

3-D ZONE - 3 DEMENTIA

15 ... 2.50

THREE FACES OF GNATMAN

1 ... 2.00

THREE STOOGES
Dell Publishing Co.
Oct.–Dec., 1959

6 Ph(c),B:Prof. Putter ... 125.00
7 Ph(c) ... 125.00
8 Ph(c) ... 125.00
9 Ph(c) ... 125.00

Gold Key 1962

10 Ph(c) ... 125.00
11 Ph(c) ... 100.00
12 Ph(c) ... 100.00
13 Ph(c) ... 100.00
14 Ph(c) ... 100.00
15 Ph(c) ... 125.00
16 Ph(c),E:Prof. Putter ... 100.00
17 Ph(c),B:Little Monsters ... 100.00
18 Ph(c) ... 100.00
19 Ph(c) ... 100.00
20 Ph(c) ... 100.00
21 Ph(c) ... 100.00

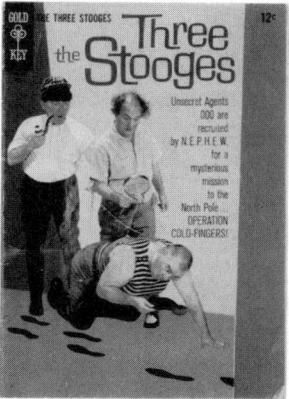

Three Stooges #28
© Gold Key

22 Ph(c),Movie Scenes. 100.00
23 Ph(c) 75.00
24 Ph(c) 75.00
25 Ph(c) 75.00
26 Ph(c) 75.00
27 Ph(c) 75.00
28 Ph(c) 75.00
29 Ph(c) 75.00
30 Ph(c) 75.00
31 Ph(c) 60.00
32 Ph(c) 60.00
33 Ph(c) 60.00
34 Ph(c) 60.00
35 Ph(c) 60.00
36 Ph(c) 60.00
37 Ph(c) 60.00
38 Ph(c) 60.00
39 Ph(c) 60.00
40 Ph(c) 60.00
41 Ph(c) 60.00
42 Ph(c) 60.00
43 Ph(c) 60.00
44 Ph(c) 60.00
45 Ph(c) 60.00
46 Ph(c) 60.00
47 Ph(c) 60.00
48 Ph(c) 60.00
49 Ph(c) 60.00
50 Ph(c) 60.00
51 . . . . 55.00
52 Ph(c) 60.00
53 Ph(c) 60.00
54 Ph(c) 60.00
55 Ph(c) 60.00

THREE STOOGES 3-D

Eclipse 1991

1 thru 3 reprints from 1953. . . . . @2.50
4 reprints from 1953 . . . . 3.50

THRILLING SCIENCE TALES

AC Comics 1989

1 . . . . 3.50

THRILLOGY

Pacific 1984

1 . . . . 2.00

THRILL-O-RAMA

Harvey Publications 1965–66

1 A:Man in Black(Fate),DW,AW . . 40.00
2 AW,A:Pirana,I:Clawfang, The Barbarian 30.00
3 A:Pirana, Fate 20.00

THUNDER AGENTS

Tower 1965–69

1 WW,RC,GK,MSy,GT,I:Thunder Agents,IronMaiden,Warlord. . 175.00
2 WW,MSy,D:Egghead 100.00
3 WW,DA,MSy,V:Warlords 60.00
4 WW,MSy,RC,I:Lightning 60.00
5 WW,RC,GK,MSy 60.00
6 WW,SD,MSy,I:Warp Wizard . . . 50.00
7 WW,MSy,SD,D:Menthor 50.00
8 WW,MSy,GT,DA,I:Raven. 50.00
9 OW,WW,MSy,A:Andor 50.00
10 WW,MSy,OW,A:Andor 50.00
11 WW,DA,MSy 35.00
12 SD,WW,MSy 35.00
13 WW,OW,A:Undersea Agent . . . 35.00
14 SD,WW,GK,N:Raven,A:Andor . 35.00
15 WW,OW,GT,A:Andor 30.00
16 SD,GK,A:Andor 30.00
17 WW,OW,GT. 30.00
18 SD,OW,RC 30.00
19 GT,I:Ghost 30.00
20 WW,RC,MSy,all reprints. 25.00

T.H.U.N.D.E.R. AGENTS

J.C. Productions 1983

1 MA,Centerfold 2.00
2 I:Vulcan 2.00

T.H.U.N.D.E.R. AGENTS

Maximum 1995

1 and 2. . . . . @2.95

THUNDERBOLT

Charlton Comics 1966–67

1 PAM,O:Thuderbolt 25.00

Prev: Son of Vulcan

51 PAM,V:Evila. 15.00
52 PAM,V:Gore the Monster 10.00
53 PAM,V:The Tong 10.00
54 PAM,I:Sentinels 10.00
55 PAM,V:Sentinels 10.00
56 PAM,A:Sentinels 10.00
57 A:Sentinels 10.00
58 PAM,A:Sentinels 10.00
59 PAM,A:Sentinels 10.00
60 PAM,JAp,I:Prankster 15.00

TIGER GIRL

Gold Key Sept., 1968

1 . . . . 35.00

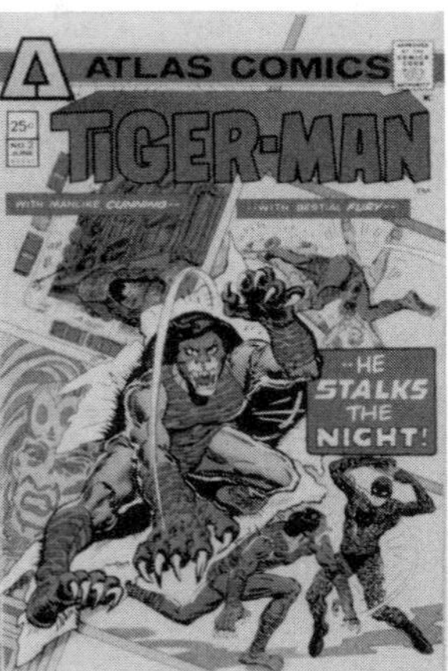

Tiger-Man #2
© Atlas

TIGER-MAN

Atlas April–Sept. 1975

1 thru 3 . . . . @6.00

TIME TUNNEL, THE

Gold Key Feb., 1967

1 from TV show. 60.00
2 . . . . 50.00

TIME TWISTERS

Quality 1987–89

1 Alan Moore ser. 2.00
2 Alan Moore ser. 2.00
3 Alan Moore ser. 2.00
4 Alan Moore ser. 2.00
5 . . . . 2.00
6 Alan Moore ser. 2.00
7 Alan Moore ser. 2.00
8 . . . . 2.00
9 . . . . 2.00
10 . . . . 2.00
11 . . . . 2.00
12 . . . . 2.00
13 thru 21. . . . . @2.00

TIME 2

1 Graphic Novel 8.00

TIPPY'S FRIENDS GO-GO & ANIMAL

Tower Comics 1966–69

1 . . . . 50.00
2 . . . . 35.00
3 . . . . 35.00
4 . . . . 35.00
5 . . . . 35.00
6 . . . . 35.00
7 . . . . 35.00
8 Beatles on cover & back 75.00
9 thru 15 . . . . @20.00

TIPPY TEEN

Tower Comics Nov., 1965–70

1 . . . . 50.00
2 thru 27 . . . . @30.00

TOHUBOHU

New Breed Comics 1999

1 . . . . 3.25
2 thru 5 . . . . @3.00
6 A Serpent in the Garden. 3.25

TO DIE FOR

1 3-D. 2.50

TOM MIX WESTERN

AC Comics 1988

1 . . . . 2.95

TOMMY & THE MONSTERS

1 . . . . 2.00

TOM TERRIFIC!

Pines Comics Summer, 1957

1 . . . . 175.00
2 . . . . 125.00
3 . . . . 125.00
4 . . . . 125.00
5 . . . . 125.00
6 Fall, 1958 . . . . 125.00

TOMMI-GUNN

London Night 1997

0 . . . . 3.00
0 nude cover 6.00
½ 3.00
½a photo nude edition 10.00
1 signed 15.00
1a, chromium, elite edition 19.95
2 . . . . 3.00
2 photo nude edition 6.00
3 . . . . 3.00
3 photo nude edition 6.00

COLOR PUB.

TOMMI-GUNN: KILLER'S LUST
London Night 1997

1 . . . . 3.00
1 Japanese Chromium edition . . . 12.00
2 . . . . 3.00
2 photo nude edition 6.00
2 photo nude edition, signed 15.00

TOMOE
Crusade Entertainment 1996

0 BiT,. 3.00
1 BiT,Fan Appreciation Edition. . . . 3.00
2 . . . . 3.00
TPB rep.. . . . . 13.95

TOMOE/WITCHBLADE: FIRE SERMON
Crusade Entertainment 1996

1 . . . . 5.00
1a Gold foil 10.00

TOMOE: UNFORGETTABLE FIRE
Crusade Entertainment 1997

1 (of 3) 2.95

TOMORROW STORIES
Wildstorm/DC 1999
America's Best Comics

1 AMo,AxR(c) anthology 3.50
1a AxR(c),variant cover 3.50

TOM STRONG
Wildstorm/DC 1999
America's Best Comics

1 AMo(s),CSp,40-page 3.50
2 AMo(s),CSp,Millennium City 3.00
3 AMo(s),CSp,Millennium City 3.00
4 AMo,CSp,AAd,Berlin in WW2 . . . 3.00
5 AMo,JOy,CSp,Memories of Pangea 3.00

TOOL AND DIE
Samson Comics

1 Autographed. 4.95

Top Cat #20
© Charlton

1a Blue Edition 9.95

TOP CAT
Charlton Comics 1970–73

1 . . . . 50.00
2 thru 10 . . . . @25.00
11 thru 20 . . . . @20.00

TOP TEN
Wildstorm/DC 1999
America's Best Comics

1 AMo(s),GeH,40-page 3.50
2 AMo(s),GeH 3.00

TOR IN 3-D
Eclipse 1986

1 JKu 3.00
1a B&W limited 100 sign 5.00
2 JKu 3.00

TORI-SHI-KITA
Relative Burn

1 Hunter Prey 2.50

TORMENTRESS: MISTRESS OF HELL
Blackout Comics 1977

0 . . . . 2.95
0a nude variant 9.95

TOTAL ECLIPSE
Eclipse 1988–89

1 BHa,BSz(c),A:Airboy,Skywolf . . . 3.95
2 BHa,BSz(c),A:New Wave, Liberty Project 3.95
3 BHa,BSz(c),A:Scout,Ms.Tree . . . 3.95
4 BHa,BSz(c),A:Miracleman, Prowler 3.95
5 BHa,BSz(c),A:Miracleman, Aztec Ace 3.95

TOTAL ECLIPSE, THE SERAPHIM OBJECTIVE
Eclipse 1988

1 tie-in Total Eclipse #2 . . . . 2.00

TOTAL WAR
Gold Key July, 1965

1 . . . . 60.00
2 . . . . 60.00
Becomes:

M.A.R.S. PATROL

3 WW 60.00
4 . . . . 35.00
5 . . . . 35.00
6 . . . . 35.00
7 . . . . 35.00
8 . . . . 35.00
9 . . . . 35.00
10 . . . . 35.00

TOY BOY
Continuity 1986–91

1 NA.I&O:Toy Boy,A:Megalith 2.00
2 TVE 2.00
3 TVE 2.00
4 TVE 2.00
5 TVE 2.00
6 TVE 2.00
7 MG. 2.00

TRANCERS: THE ADVENTURES OF JACK DETH
Eternity

1 I:Jack Deth. 2.50
2 A:Whistler, final issue 2.50

TRANSFORMERS

1 Robotics. 2.00
2 . . . . 2.00
3 . . . . 2.50

TRANSFORMERS in 3-D
Blackthorne

1 thru 5 . . . . @2.50

TRAVEL OF JAMIE McPHEETERS, THE
Gold Key Dec., 1963

1 Kurt Russell 35.00

TRAVELLER
Maximum Press 1996

1 (of 3) RLd,MHw,. 3.00

TRIBE
Axis Comics 1993–94

1 see Image Comics section
2 TJn(s),LSn,V:Alex. 2.25
3 TJn(s),LSn,. 2.00

Good Comics 1996

0 TJn,LSn 2.95
1 TJn,LSn,Choice and Responsibility. 2.95
2 TJn,LSn,Choice and Responsibility. 2.95

TROLL LORDS
Comico 1989–90

Spec. #1 . . . . 2.00
1 . . . . 2.00
2 and 3 . . . . @2.00
4 . . . . 2.50

TROUBLE WITH GIRLS
Comico 1987–88

1 . . . . 3.00
2 . . . . 2.50
3 . . . . 2.50
4 . . . . 2.00

TRUE LOVE
Eclipse 1986

1 ATh,NC,DSt(c),reprints 2.00
2 ATh,NC,BA(c),reprints 2.00

TRUE ROMANCE
Pyramid Comics 1997

1 . . . . 2.00
1a deluxe 2.25
2 . . . . 2.00
3 . . . . 2.00
4 . . . . 2.00

TUFF GHOSTS STARRING SPOOKY
Harvey Publications 1962–72

1 . . . . 125.00
2 . . . . 60.00
3 . . . . 60.00
4 . . . . 60.00

5 . . . 60.00
6 . . . 50.00
7 . . . 50.00
8 . . . 50.00
9 . . . 50.00
10 . . . 50.00
11 thru 20 . . . @25.00
21 thru 30 . . . @20.00
31 thru 39 . . . @15.00
40 thru 42 52 pg. Giants . . . @15.00
43 . . . 15.00

TUROK: SON OF STONE

Gold Key 1962

1 thru 29 see Golden Age

30 . . . 75.00
31 thru 40 . . . @60.00
41 thru 50 . . . @50.00
51 thru 60 . . . @40.00
61 thru 75 . . . @35.00
76 thru 91 . . . @25.00

Whitman

92 thru 130 . . . @10.00
Giant #1 . . . 100.00

TURTLE SOUP

Millennium 1991

1 Book 1, short stories . . . 2.50
2 thru 4 . . . @2.50

TV CASPER & COMPANY

Harvey Publications 1963–74

1 B:68 pg. Giants . . . 125.00
2 . . . 60.00
3 . . . 60.00
4 . . . 60.00
5 . . . 60.00
6 . . . 45.00
7 . . . 45.00
8 . . . 45.00
9 . . . 45.00
10 . . . 45.00
11 thru 20 . . . @25.00
21 thru 31 E:68 pg. Giants . . . @20.00
32 thru 46 . . . @15.00

TWEETY AND SYLVESTER

Gold Key 1963–84

1 . . . 35.00
2 thru 10 . . . @20.00
11 thru 30 . . . @15.00
31 thru 121 . . . @6.00

22 BRIDES

Event 1996

1 . . . 3.00
2 . . . 3.00
2a variant (c) . . . 4.00
3 . . . 3.00
3a variant (c) . . . 4.00
4 . . . 3.00

TWILIGHT AVENGER

Elite 1986

1 thru 4 . . . @2.00

TWILIGHT MAN

First 1989

1 Mini-Series . . . 2.75
2 Mini-Series . . . 2.75
3 Mini-Series . . . 2.75
4 Mini-Series . . . 2.75

TWILIGHT X-TRA

Antarctic Press 1999

1 (of 3) by Joe Wright . . . 2.50
2 . . . 2.50
3 conclusion . . . 2.50

TWILIGHT ZONE, THE

Gold Key

March–May, 1961

1 RC,FF,GE,P(c) all . . . 125.00
2 . . . 75.00
3 ATh,MSy . . . 55.00
4 ATh . . . 55.00
5 . . . 50.00
6 . . . 50.00
7 . . . 50.00
8 . . . 50.00
9 ATh . . . 60.00

Twilight Zone #78
© Gold Key

10 . . . 50.00
11 . . . 50.00
12 AW . . . 50.00
13 AW,RC,FBe,AMc . . . 40.00
14 RC,JO,RC,AT . . . 40.00
15 RC,JO . . . 40.00
16 . . . 25.00
17 . . . 25.00
18 . . . 25.00
19 JO . . . 25.00
20 . . . 20.00
21 RC . . . 25.00
22 JO . . . 25.00
23 JO . . . 25.00
24 . . . 20.00
25 GE,RC,ATh . . . 20.00
26 RC,GE . . . 20.00
27 GE . . . 20.00
28 . . . 15.00
29 . . . 15.00
30 . . . 15.00
31 . . . 15.00
32 GE . . . 20.00
33 . . . 15.00
34 . . . 15.00
35 . . . 15.00
36 . . . 15.00
37 . . . 15.00
38 . . . 15.00
39 WMc . . . 15.00
40 . . . 12.00
41 . . . 12.00
42 . . . 12.00
43 RC . . . 15.00
44 . . . 12.00
45 . . . 12.00
46 . . . 12.00
47 . . . 12.00
48 . . . 12.00
49 . . . 12.00
50 FBe,WS . . . 12.00
51 AW . . . 15.00
52 . . . 12.00
53 . . . 12.00
54 . . . 12.00
55 . . . 12.00
56 . . . 12.00
57 FBe . . . 12.00
58 . . . 12.00
59 FBe,AMc . . . 15.00
60 . . . 10.00
61 . . . 10.00
62 . . . 10.00
63 . . . 10.00
64 . . . 10.00
65 . . . 10.00
66 . . . 10.00
67 . . . 10.00
68 . . . 10.00
69 . . . 10.00
70 . . . 10.00
71 rep . . . 8.00
72 . . . 10.00
73 rep . . . 8.00
74 . . . 10.00
75 . . . 10.00
76 . . . 10.00
77 FBe . . . 12.00
78 FBe,AMc,The Missing Mirage . 12.00
79 rep . . . 8.00
80 FBe,AMc . . . 12.00
81 . . . 10.00
82 AMc . . . 12.00
83 FBe,WS . . . 12.00
84 FBe,AMc . . . 12.00
85 . . . 10.00
86 rep . . . 8.00
87 thru 91 . . . @10.00

TWILIGHT ZONE

Now 1990

1 NA,BSz(c) . . . 8.00
1a 2nd printing Prestige +Harlan Ellison sty . . . 6.00

[Volume 2]

#1 "The Big Dry" (direct) . . . 2.50
#1a Newsstand . . . 2.00
2 "Blind Alley" . . . 2.00
3 Extraterrestrial . . . 2.00
4 The Mysterious Biker . . . 2.00
5 Queen of the Void . . . 2.00
6 Insecticide . . . 2.00
7 The Outcasts,Ghost Horse . . . 2.00
8 Colonists on Alcor . . . 2.00
9 Dirty Lyle's House of Fun (3-D Holo) . . . 2.95
10 Stairway to Heaven,Key to Paradise . . . 2.00
11 TD(i),Partial Recall . . . 2.00
3-D Spec . . . 2.50
Ann. #1 . . . 2.75

[Volume 3]

1 thru 2 . . . @2.50

TWISTED TALES

Pacific 1982–84

1 RCo. "Infected" . . . 3.50
2 . . . 2.00
3 . . . 2.00
4 . . . 2.00

 All comics prices listed are for *Near Mint* condition.

5 . . . . 2.00
6 . . . . 2.00
7 . . . . 2.00
8 . . . . 2.00

Eclipse

9 . . . . 2.00
10 GM,BWr 2.00

TWISTED TALES OF BRUCE JONES

Eclipse 1982–84

1 . . . . 2.00
2 . . . . 2.00
3 . . . . 2.00
4 . . . . 2.00

Twister #1
© Harris

TWISTER

Harris

1 inc.Special newspaper/poster, and trading cards 2.95

TWO FISTED TALES

Russ Cochran 1992

1 JSe,HK,WW,JCr,reps 2.00
2 Reps inc.War Story. 2.00
3 rep. 2.00
4 thru 6 rep. . . . . @2.00
7 thru 8 rep. . . . . @2.00

Gemstone

17 thru 24 EC comics reprints . . . @2.50

"Annuals"

TPB Vol.#4 reprint #16–#20 . . . . 12.95
TPB Vol. 2 rebinding of #5–#10 . . . 9.95
TPB Vol. 3 rebinding of #11–#15. . 10.95
TPB Vol. 4 rebinding. 10.95
TPB Vol. 5 rebinding. 10.95

2000 A.D. MONTHLY

Eagle 1985

1 A:JudgeDredd 4.00
2 A:JudgeDredd 30.00
3 A:JudgeDredd 2.00
4 A:JudgeDredd 2.00
5 . . . . 2.00
6 . . . . 2.00

[2nd Series]

1 . . . . 2.00
2 . . . . 2.00
3 . . . . 2.00
4 . . . . 2.00

Quality

5 . . . . 2.00
6 . . . . 2.00
7 thru 27 . . . . @2.00
28/29 . . . . 2.00
30 . . . . 2.00
31/32 . . . . 2.00
33 . . . . 2.00
34 . . . . 2.00
35 . . . . 2.00
36 . . . . 2.00
37 . . . . 2.00

Becomes:

2000 A.D. SHOWCASE

38 . . . . 2.00
39 . . . . 2.00
40 . . . . 2.00
41 . . . . 2.00
42 . . . . 2.00
43 . . . . 2.00
44 . . . . 2.00
45 . . . . 2.00
46 . . . . 2.00
47 . . . . 2.00
48 thru 54. . . . . @2.00
TPB:Killing Time. 12.95

TZU THE REAPER

Murim Studios 1997

1 by Gary Cohn & C.S. Chun. . . . 2.95
2 . . . . 2.95
3 . . . . 2.95
4 . . . . 2.95
5 . . . . 2.95

TZU: SPIRITS OF DEATH

Murim Studios 1997

1 . . . . 2.95

UFO FLYING SAUCERS

Gold Key Oct., 1968

1 . . . . 30.00
2 . . . . 20.00
3 thru 13 . . . . @15.00

Becomes:

UFO & OUTER SPACE

Gold Key June, 1978

14 thru 25. . . . . @10.00

ULTRAMAN

Nemesis 1994

1 EC,O:Ultraman. 2.25
2 . . . . 2.50
3 . . . . 2.50
4 V:Blue Ultraman 2.50

ULTRAMAN

Harvey/Ultracomics 1993

1 with 1 of 3 cards. 2.50
2 with 1 of 3 cards & virgin cover. . 2.50
3 with 1 of 3 cards & virgin cover. . 2.50

UNCLE SCROOGE

Dell/Gold Key Dec., 1962

40 . . . . 125.00
41 . . . . 100.00
42 . . . . 100.00
43 . . . . 100.00
44 . . . . 100.00
45 . . . . 100.00
46 Lost Beneath the Sea 100.00
47 . . . . 100.00
48 . . . . 100.00
49 Loony Lunar Gold Rush. . . . 100.00
50 Rug Riders in the Sky 100.00
51 How Green Was my Lettuce . . 90.00
52 Great Wig Mystery. 90.00
53 Interplanetary Postman 90.00
54 Billion-Dollar Safari! 90.00
55 McDuck of Arabia 90.00
56 Mystery of the Ghost Town Railroad 90.00
57 Swamp of No Return 90.00
58 Giant Robot Robbers. 90.00
59 North of the Yukon. 90.00
60 Phantom of Notre Duck 90.00
61 So Far and No Safari. 75.00
62 Queen of the Wild Dog Pack . . 75.00
63 House of Haunts!. 75.00
64 Treasure of Marco Polo!. . . . 75.00
65 Micro-Ducks from OuterSpace . 75.00
66 Heedless Horseman 75.00
67 CB rep. 75.00
68 Hall of the Mermaid Queen!. . . 75.00
69 Cattle King! 75.00
70 CB,The Doom Diamond! 75.00
71 . . . . 70.00
72 CB rep. 75.00
73 CB rep. 75.00
74 thru 110 . . . . @50.00
111 thru 148 . . . . @30.00
149. . . . . 20.00
150 thru 168 . . . . @15.00
169 thru 173 . . . . @10.00

Whitman

174 thru 182 . . . . @20.00
183 thru 200 . . . . @15.00
201 thru 209 . . . . @20.00

Gladstone

210 CB. 15.00
211 CB,Prize of Pizzaro 15.00
212 CB,city-golden roofs. 15.00
213 CB,city-golden roofs. 15.00
214 CB. 15.00
215 CB, a cold bargain 15.00
216 CB. 15.00
217 CB,7 cities of Cibola 15.00
218 CB. 15.00
219 Don Rosa,Son of Sun 25.00
220 CB,Don Rosa 5.00
221 CB,A:BeagleBoys 3.00
222 CB,Mysterious Island. 3.00
223 CB. 3.00
224 CB,Rosa,Cash Flow. 6.00
225 CB. 3.00
226 CB,Rosa 4.00
227 CB,Rosa 4.00
228 CB. 3.00
229 CB. 3.00
230 CB. 5.00
231 CB,Rosa(c) 3.00
232 CB. 3.00
233 CB. 3.00
234 CB. 3.00
235 Rosa 3.50
236 CB. 3.00
237 CB. 3.00
238 CB. 3.00
239 CB. 3.00
240 CB. 3.00
241 CB,giant 5.00
242 CB,giant 4.00

Walt Disney 1990

243 CB,"Pie in the Sky" 3.50
244 . . . . 2.50
245 . . . . 2.50
246 . . . . 2.50
247 . . . . 2.50
248 . . . . 2.50
249 . . . . 2.50
250 CB. 3.50
251 . . . . 2.50
252 "No Room For Human Error" . . 2.50

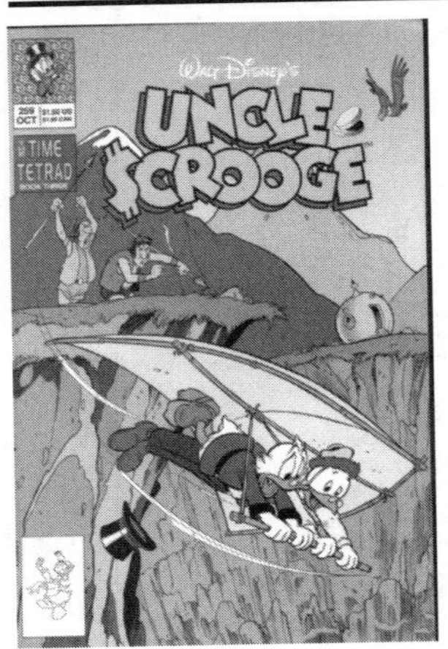

Uncle Scrooge #259
© Walt Disney

253 "Fab.Philosophers Stone 2.50
254 The Filling Station 2.50
255 The Flying Dutchman. 2.50
256 CB,"Status Seeker" 2.50
257 "Coffee,Louie or Me" 2.50
258 CB,"Swamp of no return" 2.50
259 "The only way to Go" 2.50
260 The Waves Above, The Gold Below 2.50
261 Rosa,"Return to Zanadu" Pt.1 . 2.50
262 Rosa,"Return to Zanadu" Pt.2 . 2.50
263 Rosa,"Treasure Under Glass" . 2.50
264 Snobs Club 2.25
265 CB,Ten Cent Valentine. 2.25
266 The Money Ocean,Pt.1 . . . . . . 2.25
267 The Money Ocean,Pt 2 . . . . . . 2.25
268 CB,Rosa,Island in the Sky 2.00
269 The Flowers. 2.25
270 V:Magica DeSpell 2.25
271 The Secret o/t Stone 2.25
272 Canute The Brute's Battle Axe . 2.25
273 CB,Uncle Scrooge-Ghost. 2.00
274 CB,Hall of the Mermaid Queen 2.00
275 CB,Rosa,Christmas Cheers,inc. D.Rosa centerspread 2.50
276 Rosa, thru 277 . . . . @2.25
278 thru 280 . . . . @2.25

Gladstone

281 Rosa 5.00
282 thru 284 . . . . @2.50
285 Rosa, Life & Times 10.00
286 thru 293 Rosa, Life & Times . @5.00
294 thru 299 . . . . @2.00
300 Rosa & Barks 3.00
301 "Statuesque Spendthrifts". 2.00
302. . . . . 2.00
303 "Rocks to Riches" 2.00
304 "My Private Eye" 2.00
305 "The Vigilante of Pizen Bluff" . . 2.00
306. . . . . 2.00
307 "Temper Temper" 2.00
308 "Revenge of the Witch" 2.00

Prestige format, 64pg.

309 "Whadalottajargon" 6.95
310 "The Sign of the Triple Distelfink". 6.95
311 "The Last Lord of Eldorado" . . . 6.95
312 "The Hands of Zeus". 6.95
313 "The Fantastic River Race" . . . 6.95
314 . . . . 6.95
315 "The Flying Scot," pt.1 . . . . 6.95
316 "The Flying Scot," pt.2. . . . . . . 6.95
317 "Pawns of the Lamp Garou" . . . 6.95
318 "Cowboy Captain of Cutty Sark" 6.95
319 "The Horse Radish Story" 6.95
320 "The Mysterious Stone Ray". . . 6.95
321 "The Giant Robot Robbers" . . . 6.95
322 "Secret of the Lost Dutchman's Mine" 6.95

UNCLE SCROOGE ADVENTURES
Gladstone

1 CB,McDuck of Arabia 9.00
2 translated from Danish 5.00
3 translated from Danish 5.00
4 CB 5.00
5 Rosa 5.00
6 CB 3.50
7 CB 3.00
8 CB 3.00
9 Rosa 3.50
10 CB. 3.00
11 CB. 3.00
12 CB. 3.00
13 CB. 3.00
14 Rosa 3.50
15 CB. 3.00
16 CB. 3.00
17 CB. 3.00
18 CB. 3.00
19 CB,Rosa(c) 3.50
20 CB,giant 4.00
21 CB,giant 4.00
22 Rosa(c) 5.00
23 CB,giant 4.00
24 thru 26 . . . . @2.00
27 Rosa,O:Jr. Woodchuck 4.00
28 giant 3.00
29 . . . . 2.00
30 giant 4.00
31 thru 32 . . . . @3.00
33 Barks. 4.00
34 thru 40 . . . . @3.00
41 . . . . 2.00
42 "The Dragon's Amulet". 2.00
43 "Queen of the Wild Dog Pack" . . 2.00
44 . . . . 2.00
45 "The Secret of the Duckburg Triangle". 2.00
46 "The Tides Turn" 2.25
47 "The Menehune Mystery". 2.25
48 "The Tenth Avatar". 2.25
49 "Dead-Eye Duck". 2.25
50 CB,"The Secret of Atlantis" 2.50
51 . . . . 2.00
52 The Black Diamond 2.00
53 Secret of the Incas 2.00
54 Secret of the Incas, pt.2 . . . . . . 2.00

UNCLE SCROOGE ADVENTURES
Gladstone 1997–98
Don Rosa Specials

Spec.#1 (of 4). 10.95
Spec.#2 thru #4 . . . . @9.95
Van Horn Specials
Spec.#1 . . . . 9.95
Spec.#2 . . . . 9.95
Spec.#3 . . . . 9.95
Spec.#4 . . . . 9.95

UNCLE SCROOGE ADVENTURES IN COLOR
Gladstone
Carl Barks reprints

1 thru 32 . . . . @8.95
33 thru 35. . . . . @9.95
36 32pg. 8.95
37 thru 53 . . . . @9.95
54 Hall of the Mermaid Queen 9.95
55 The Doom Diamond. 9.95
56 two adventures 9.95

UNCLE SCROOGE & DONALD DUCK
Gold Key

1 rep. 75.00

UNCLE SCROOGE AND DONALD DUCK
Gladstone Oct., 1997

1 . . . . 2.00
2 Christmas stories 2.00
3 Back to Long Ago. 2.00
TPB Vol. 1 . . . . 9.95
TPB Vol. 2 . . . . 9.95
TPB Vol. 3 . . . . 9.95
TPB Vol. 4 . . . . 9.95

UNCLE SCROOGE GOES TO DISNEYLAND
Gladstone 1985

1 CB,etc. 100pp. 11.00

UNDERDOG
Charlton July, 1970

1 Planet Zot. 75.00
2 Simon Sez/The Molemen 45.00
3 Whisler's Father 45.00
4 The Witch of Pycoon 45.00
5 The Snowmen 45.00
6 The Big Shrink 45.00
7 The Marbleheads 45.00
8 The Phoney Booths 45.00
9 Tin Man Alley 45.00
10 Be My Valentine (Jan. 1972) . . 45.00

UNDERDOG
Gold Key March, 1975

1 The Big Boom 50.00
2 The Sock Singer Caper 25.00
3 The Ice Cream Scream. 25.00
4 . . . . 25.00
5 . . . . 25.00
6 Head in a Cloud 25.00
7 The Cosmic Canine 25.00
8 . . . . 25.00
9 . . . . 25.00
10 Bouble Trouble Gum 25.00
11 The Private Life of Shoeshine Boy. 15.00
12 The Deadly Fist of Fingers. . . . 15.00
13 . . . . 15.00
14 Shrink Shrank Shrunk 15.00
15 Polluter Palooka 15.00
16 The Soda Jerk. 15.00
17 Flee For Your Life 15.00
18 Rain Rain Go Away...Okay. . . . 15.00
19 Journey To the Center of the Earth 15.00
20 The Six Million Dollar Dog 15.00
21 Smell of Success. 15.00
22 Antlers Away 15.00
23 Wedding Bells In Outer Space (Feb.,1979) 15.00

UNDERDOG
Spotlight 1987

1 FMc,PC(c),The Eredicator 2.00
2 FMc,CS(c), Prisoner of Love/ The Return of Fearo. 2.00

COLOR PUB.

UNDERDOG IN 3-D
Blackthorne
1 Wanted Dead or Alive. 2.50

UNDERSEA AGENT
Tower 1966–97
1 F:Davy Jones,UnderseaAgent. . 75.00
2 thru 4 . . . . @50.00
5 O&I:Merman. 60.00
6 GK,WW(c) 60.00

UNDERTAKER
Chaos! Comics 1999
Preview BSt, WWF character. 2.50
Preview, photo (c) 2.50
1 Prophecy of the Dead. 2.95
1a photo cover 2.95
1b premium edition 10.00
1c Death Chrome cover. 14.95
1d Death Chrome cover, signed. . 19.95
2 V:Embalmer & Paul Bearer. 2.95
3 O:Undertaker 2.95
4 Kane 2.95
5 Jezebel 2.95
6 thru 12 . . . . @2.95
2a thru 12a photo covers . . . . . . @2.95
Halloween Spec. 2.95
Halloween Spec. photo(c). 2.95
TPB Prophecy of the Dead,
rep.#1–#4. . . . . 12.95
TPB Vol.2 rep.#5–#8. . . . . 12.95

UNEARTHLY SPECTACULARS
1 DW,AT,I:Tiger Boy 30.00
2 WW,AW,GK,I:Earthman,Miracles,
Inc. A:Clawfang,TigerBoy 40.00
3 RC,AW,JO,A:Miracles,Inc. 35.00

U.N. FORCE
Gauntlet Comics
0 BDC(s). 2.95
1 B:BDC(s),I:U.N.Force 2.95
2 O:Indigo 2.95
3 . . . . 2.95
4 A:Predator 2.95
5 B:Critial Mass. 2.95

U.N. FORCE FILES
Gauntlet Comics
1 KP(c),F:Hunter Seeker, Lotus . . . 2.95

UNION OF JUSTICE
Quantum Comics 1998
1 by David Watkins & Steve Kurth . 2.95
2 . . . . 2.95
3 A:Golden Age Union. 2.95

UNIVERSAL SOLDIER
Now 1992
1 Based on Movie,Holo.(c). 2.75
2 Luc & Ronnie on the run
from UniSols 2.50
2a Photo cover 2.00
3 Photo(c) 2.00

UNKNOWN WORLDS OF FRANK BRUNNER
Eclipse 1985
1 and 2 FB. . . . . @2.50

UNLEASHED!
Triumphant
0 JnR(s),I:Skyfire. 2.50
1 JnR(s), ... 2.50

UNLV
1 Championship season (basketball
based on college team) 3.00

UNTAMED LOVE
1 FF 2.00

UNTOLD TALES OF
Chaos! Comics 2000
Purgatori #1 . . . . 2.95
Purgatori #1 premium ed. 12.95
Chastity #1. . . . . 2.95
Chastity premium #1. . . . . 12.95
Lady Death #1 . . . . 2.95
Lady Death premium #1 . . . . 12.95

UNUSUAL TALES
Charlton Comics 1955–65
1 . . . . 175.00
2 . . . . 100.00
3 thru 5 . . . . @65.00
6 SD,SD(c) 165.00
7 SD,SD(c) 165.00
8 SD,SD(c) 165.00
9 SD,SD(c) 175.00
10 SD,SD(c). 165.00
11 SD 165.00
12 SD. 120.00
13 . . . . 60.00
14 SD. 120.00
15 SD,SD(c). 135.00
16 thru 20. . . . . @50.00
21 . . . . 35.00
22 SD. 90.00
23 . . . . 35.00
24 . . . . 35.00
25 SD. 85.00
26 SD. 85.00
27 SD. 85.00
28 . . . . 35.00
29 SD. 85.00
30 thru 49. . . . . @35.00

URI-ON
1 and 2 . . . . @2.00

URTH 4
Continuity 1990
1 TVE,NA(c) 2.00
2 TVE,NA 2.00
3 TVE,NA 2.00
4 NA,Last issue. 2.00

USAGI YOJIMBO
Mirage 1993
1 A:TMNT 3.00
2 . . . . 3.00
3 . . . . 3.00
4 thru 16 . . . . @3.00
17 . . . . 8.00

VALERIA THE SHE BAT
Continuity 1993
1 NA,I:Valeria 20.00
2 thru 4. . . . . **[NOT RELEASED]**
5 Rise of Magic 2.50

VALHALLA
Antarctic Press 1999
1 BDn set in 1939 . . . . 3.00

VALKYRIE
Eclipse 1988
1 PG,I:Steelfox,C:Airboy, Sky Wolf. 3.00
2 PG,O:New Black Angel. 2.50
3 PG 2.50

[2nd Series]
1 BA,V:Eurasian Slavers 2.00
2 BA,V:Cowgirl 2.00
3 BA,V:Cowgirl 2.00

Valley of the Dinosaurs #7
© Charlton Comics

VALLEY OF THE DINOSAURS
Charlton 1975
1 Hanna-Barbera TV adapt. 3.00
2 thru 11 . . . . @2.00

VALOR
Gemstone 1998
1 EC comics reprint. 2.50
2 . . . . 2.50
3 AW, The Cloak of Command. . . . 2.50
4 WW(c) 2.50
5 final issue. 3.50
HC 20.00
Annual
TPB Vol. 1 rebinding of series. . . . 13.50

VAMPEROTICA
Brainstorm
1–16 see B&W
17 . . . . 3.00
17a signed 5.00
17 Holochrome cover 65.00
18 Blood of the Damned (color) . . . 3.00
18a Blood of the Damned,
nude cover 4.00
18b signed 5.00
18c nude cover, signed. 10.00
19 "Hunter's Blood" 3.00
19a deluxe 3.00
20 "Vampire Quest" 3.00
20a nude edition. 4.00
21 hunting & feeding. 3.00
21a nude edition. 4.00
21b nude luxury edition. 10.00

21c nude deluxe luxury edition . . . 15.00
22 . . . . 3.00
22a nude edition. 4.00
TPB Red Reign, rep. 12.95

VAMPEROTICA LINGERIE

Comic Cavalcade 1998

Commemorative #1 by Kirk Lindo . . 5.95
Commemorative #1a deluxe 14.95

VAMPI

Harris Comics 2000

1 Switchblade Kiss,pt.1 . . . . 2.95
1a deluxe 9.95
1b limited chrome (c). 14.95
1c signed & numbered. 19.95
1d gold foil. 29.95
2 Switchblade Kiss,pt.2 . . . . 2.95
2a deluxe 9.95
3 Switchblade Kiss,pt.3 . . . . 2.95
3a deluxe 9.95
Vampi #1 preview. 2.95

VAMPIRE LESTAT

Innovation 1990–91

1 Anne Rice Adapt. 17.00
1a 2nd printing 4.00
1b 3rd printing 2.50
2 . . . . 7.00
2a 2nd printing 4.00
2b 3rd printing 2.50
3 . . . . 5.00
3a 2nd printing 2.50
4 . . . . 5.00
4a 2nd printing 2.50
5 . . . . 5.00
6 . . . . 5.00
7 . . . . 5.00
8 . . . . 5.00
9 scarce 8.00
9a 2nd Printing 3.00
10 . . . . 5.00
11 "Those Who Must Be Kept" 4.00
12 conclusion 4.00
Vampire Companion #1 . . . . 4.00
Vampire Companion #2 (preview
"Interview With The Vampire" . . 3.00
Vampire Companion #3 . . . . 3.00
GN rep.#1-#12 (Innovation) 24.95
GN rep.#1-#12 (Ballantine) 25.00

VAMPIRELLA

Warren Publishing Co. 1969–83

1 NA,FF(c),I:Vampirella 450.00
2 B:Amazonia 125.00
3 Very scarce 350.00
4 . . . . 100.00
5 FF(c) 100.00
6 . . . . 100.00
7 FF(c) 120.00
8 B:horror 100.00
9 BWS,BV(c),WW 110.00
10 No Vampirella,WW. 40.00
11 TS,FF(c)O&I Pendragon. 60.00
12 WW. 60.00
13 . . . . 50.00
14 . . . . 50.00
15 . . . . 50.00
16 . . . . 50.00
17 B:Tomb of the Gods. 50.00
18 . . . . 50.00
19 WW,1973 Annual. 65.00
20 thru 25 . . . . @45.00
26 . . . . 40.00
27 1974 Annual 45.00
28 thru 30 . . . . @40.00
31 FF(c) 45.00
32 thru 36 . . . . @35.00
37 1975 Annual 45.00
38 . . . . 35.00
39 . . . . 35.00
40 . . . . 35.00
41 thru 45 . . . . @30.00
46 O:Vampirella 35.00
47 thru 99 . . . . @30.00
100 Double Size 40.00
101 thru 110 . . . . @25.00
111 Giant Edition 35.00
112 . . . . 30.00

VAMPIRELLA

Harris 1992

0 Dracula Wars 5.00
0a Blue version 22.00
1 V:Forces of Chaos, w/coupon for
DSt poster 20.00
1a 2nd printing 5.00
2 AH(c) 12.00
3 A:Dracula 7.00

Vampirella #12
© Harris Comics

4 A:Dracula 6.00
5 . . . . 6.00
TPB The Dracula War signed &
numbered. 39.95

Harris Comics 1996

0 gold foil signed & numbered . . . 22.00
1 Commemorative Edition 3.00
1a Commemorative Edition,
sgn & num.. . . . . 10.00
25th Anniv. Spec., FF(c) 5.95
25th Anniv. Spec., lim. 6.95
25th Anniv. Spec., lim., signed, . . . 49.95
Spec. Death of Vampirella,
memorial, chromium cover . . . .
Spec. Death of Vampirella,
memorial, chromium cover,
signed 29.95

VAMPIRELLA

Harris Comics 1997

1 (of 3) Ascending Evil, pt.1. . . . . . 2.95
1 ultra-violent cover. 2.95
1 JaL(c). 9.95
1 signed & numbered 19.95
2 Ascending Evil, pt.2 . . . . 2.95
2a JaL(c). 9.95
3 Ascending Evil, pt.3 . . . . 2.95
3a JaL(c). 9.95
4 Holy War, pt.1. . . . . 2.95
4a Crimson edition, Joe Linsner (c) 2.95
5 Holy War, pt.2. . . . . 2.95
6 Holy War, pt.3. . . . . 2.95
7 Queen's Gambit, pt.1 . . . . 2.95
7a variant cover, signed. 29.95
7b chromium Edition 10.95
8 Queen's Gambit, pt.2 . . . . 2.95
8a San Diego Con variant cover . . 9.95
9 Queen's Gambit, pt.3, concl.. . . . 2.95
10 Hell on Earth, pt.1 (of 3) V:Nyx . 2.95
10a signed and numbered 19.95
10b variant JaL cover 9.95
10c Holoplaid Chromium Ed. 19.95
11 Hell on Earth, pt.2 . . . . 2.95
12 Hell on Earth, pt.3,
New costume 2.95
12a variant cover, new costume . . . 2.95
12b chromium cover. 10.95
13 World's End,pt.1 . . . . 2.95
13a variant cover 2.95
13b Pantha cover. 9.95
14 World's End,pt.2 . . . . 2.95
14a variant cover 2.95
15 World's End,pt.3 . . . . 2.95
15a variant cover 2.95
16 Pantha #1 . . . . 2.95
16a Pantha photo cover 2.95
16b limited photo ed. 9.95
16c Julie Strain photo (c) ed. 9.95
17 Pantha #2 . . . . 2.95
17a Phantha photo cover 2.95
17b Julie Strain photo (c) ed. 9.95
18 Rebirth, pt.1,JaL(c) 2.95
18a alternate cover, signed & num. 29.95
19 Rebirth, pt.2, ... 2.95
20 Rebirth, pt.3. . . . . 2.95
21 Dangerous Games,pt.1 . . . . 2.95
21a Julie Strain photo (c) 9.95
21b Linsner chrome ed 14.95
21c Millennium ed. 19.95
22 Dangerous Games,pt.2 . . . . 2.95
22a Dorian (c) 9.95
22b Julie Strain signed 19.95
22c Julie Strain photo (c) 9.95
22d Linsner chrome (c). 14.95
23 Vampirella/Lady Death:
The Revenge, pt.1 . . . . 2.95
23a limited ed. 9.95
23b limited chrome ed. 14.95
24 Hell's Angels, Vampirella (c). . . . 2.95
24a Pantha (c) 2.95
24b penciled ed. sign & num. 14.95
25 Hells Angels, vol.2 . . . . 2.95
25a alternate (c). 2.95
25b Monte Moore (c) 14.95
26 The End #1 . . . . 2.95
26a alternate (c). 9.95
26b platinum ed.. . . . . 19.95
Ashcan, Ascending Evil, b&w, 16pg. 1.50
Ashcan, Ascending Evil, b&w,
signed, limited 24.95
Ashcan, Queen's Gambit, 16 pg.
b&w 6.00
Ashcan, Queen's Gambit, 16 pg.
b&w, signed & numbered 24.95
Ashcan World's End, b&w 16pg. . . . 6.00
Ashcan Rebirth preview,b&w 16-pg. 6.00
Vampirella, Queen's Gambit #1
special edition, alternate (c) . . . 9.95
Chromium Edition. 10.95
Vampirella/Lady Death Limited
Preview Ashcan B&W. 6.00
TPB Ascending Evil 7.50
Spec.#0 A:Lady Death,B.U.:Pantha 2.95
Spec.#0a Pantha(c) 2.95
Spec.#0b Vampirella(c). 9.95
Spec.#0c Vampirella(c), signed. . . 29.95
Spec.#0d Pantha(c) 9.95
HC Halloween Horror Special 19.95
Ann.Ed.#2 Rebirth 9.95
Ann.Ed.#3 Rebirth,Bruce Timm(c). . 9.95

Julie Strain Special 3.95
Julie Strain Special variant(c) 9.95

VAMPIRELLA/CAIN
Harris 1996
1-shot flipbook, 72-pages. 6.95

VAMPIRELLA/DRACULA: THE CENTENNIAL
Harris 1997
1-shot Vampirella/Dracula & Pantha Showcase, 16pg. 2.00
1 48pg. 4.95

VAMPIRELLA/ LADY DEATH
Harris/Chaos! 1999
1 x-over. 3.50
1a Valentine ed. 9.95
1b signed and numbered 20.00
1c gold edition 29.95
1d penciled edition. 10.00
1e The End, chrome edition. 14.95

VAMPIRELLA/ PAINKILLER JANE
Harris 1998
1 foil JQ(c) 3.50
1a signed & numbered. 39.95
1b alternate RL&JP(c) 9.95
1c alternate RL&JP(c) signed & numbered. 29.95
1d Gold Edition 24.95
Ashcan Preview, signed & numbered. 29.95

VAMPIRELLA/ SHADOWHAWK: CREATURES OF THE NIGHT
Harris/Image 1995
1 Book One. 5.50

VAMPIRELLA/SHI
Harris
Ash-Can #1, limited, 16pg. 3.00
1 . . . . 2.95
1a Chromium Edition. 7.00
1b signed & numbered. 19.95
1c penciled cover 9.95
1c penciled cover, signed and numbered 29.95

VAMPIRELLA/WETWORKS
Harris 1997
1 StG,SSh,image x-over 2.95
1 signed & numbered 17.95
1b Sean Shaw & Kevin Nowlan (c) 9.95

VAMPIRELLA: BLOOD LUST
Harris 1997
1 (of 2) JeR & JJu 3.95
2 JJu(c). 3.95
Book 1, JJu(c) Virgin edition 10.95
Book 2, JJu(c) Virgin edition 10.95
HC leather-bound 95.00
HC 40.00

VAMPIRELLA CLASSIC
Harris Comics 1995
1 Dark Angel 3.50
2 V:Demogorgon 3.25
3 V:Were Beast 3.25
4 R:Papa Voodoo 3.25
5 . . . . 3.00

VAMPIRELLA: CROSSOVER GALLERY
Harris 1997
1 art gallery 2.95
1a signed and numbered 19.95
1b chromium edition 10.00
1c Painkiller Jane JQ(c),signed . . 29.95
1d Holochrome cover. 20.00

VAMPIRELLA: DEATH AND DESTRUCTION
Harris
1 limited preview ash can 4.00

Vampirella: Death and Destruction #1
© Harris Comics

1a limited preview ash can, signed & numbered 20.00
1b "The Dying of the Light" 3.00
1c signed & numbered. 3.00
1d satin edition 25.00
1e satin edition, signed & numb. . 50.00
1f Lim. Ed., Mark Beachum (c) . . . 9.95
2 "The Nature of the Beast" 3.00
3 (of 3) TSg,ACo,JP,JJu(c),Mistress Nyx kills Vampi 2.95
TPB 14.95

VAMPIRELLA LIVES
Harris
1 Linen Edition 7.00
1a Censored Photo cover edition. . 8.00
2 Vengeance edition 3.00
2 Model photo edition 3.00
2 alternate edition, AH(c). 10.00
2 alternate edition, AH(c) signed . 10.00
3 WEI(s),ACo,JP,Graveyard edition, JSC(c) 3.00
3 WEI(s),ACo,JP,Model photo edition 3.00

VAMPIRELLA OF DRAKULON
Harris Comics 1996
1 V:assassin 3.00
1a alternate MiB(c) 9.95
2 Dracula returns. 3.00
2a signed & numbered 8.00
3 thru 5 . . . . @3.00

VAMPIRELLA PINUP SPECIAL
Harris Comics 1995
1 Various Artists 3.50

VAMPIRELLA: SAD WINGS OF DESTINY
Harris
1 DQ(s),JJu(c). 4.00
1 signed & numbered (#1,500). . . . 5.00
Gold Emblem Seal Edition 4.00
Gold Emblem Seal Edition, signed 25.00

VAMPIRELLA STRIKES
Harris Comics 1995
1 The Prize,pt.1 . . . . 3.00
1a limited, signed & numbered. . . 10.00
1b full moon background 3.50
2 V:Dante Corp.,A:Passion 3.00
3 V:subway stalker 3.00
4 IEd,RN "Soul Food" 3.00
5 DQ,RN,F:Eudaemon. 3.00
5 signed & numbered, (200) 10.00
6 . . . . 3.00
6 signed, alternate cover 10.00
6 signed & numbered 12.00
7 silver special flip book. 3.00
Ann. #1 new cover 10.00
Ann. #1 new cover, signed & numbered. 25.00

VAMPIRELLA VS. EUDAEMON
Harris 1996
1 . . . . 10.00
1 signed & numbered 25.00

VAMPIRELLA VS. HEMORRHAGE
Harris 1997
1 IEd,MIB 3.50
1 signed & numbered 12.00
1 Linen edition, signed & numb. . . 25.00
1 MIB alternate cover. 9.95
2 IEd,MIB 3.50
3 (of 3) IEd,MIB 3.50

VAMPIRELLA VS. PANTHA
Harris 1997
Showcase #1 preview. 2.00
1 MMr,MT, MT(c) Vampirella vs. Pantha 3.50
1 MMr,MT, MT(c) Pantha vs. Vampirella 3.50
1 MT(c) Vampirella vs. Pantha, signed 19.95
1 MT(c) Pantha vs. Vampirella, signed 19.95
1a MMr,MT, MT(c). 9.95
1a MMr,MT, MT(c) signed & numbered. 29.95

COLOR PUB.

VAMPRESS LUXURA, THE
Brainstorm 1996

1 . . . 3.00
1a gold edition . . . 10.00
2 . . . 2.95
2a gold foil . . . 10.00

VANGUARD

1 . . . 2.00

VANGUARD ILLUSTRATED
Pacific 1983

1 . . . 2.00
2 DSt(c) . . . 2.00
3 thru 5 SR . . . @2.00
6 GI . . . 2.00
7 GE,I:Mr.Monster . . . 6.00

VANITY
Pacific 1984

1 and 2 . . . @2.00

VARICK: CHRONICLES OF THE DARK PRINCE
Q Comics 1999

1 by Nick Marcari & Major Fareed . 2.00
2 32-page . . . 2.00
3 thru 6 . . . @2.00

VAULT OF HORROR
Gladstone 1990–91

1 Rep.GS,WW . . . 5.00
2 Rep.VoH #27 & HoF #18 . . . 3.00
3 Rep.VoH #13 & HoF #22 . . . 3.00
4 Rep.VoH #23 & HoF #13 . . . 2.50
5 Rep.VoH #19 & HoF #5 . . . 2.50
6 Rep.VoH #32 & WF #6 . . . 2.50
7 Rep.VoH #26 & WS #7 . . . 2.50

Vault of Horror #26
© Gemstone

VAULT OF HORROR
Russ Cochran Publ. 1991–92

1 Rep.VoH #28 & WS #18 . . . 2.25
2 Rep.VoH #33 & WS #20 . . . 2.25
3 Rep.VoH #26 & WS #7 . . . 2.25
4 Rep.VoH #35 & WS #15 . . . 2.00
4 Rep.VoH #18 & WS #11 . . . 2.00
5 Rep.VoH #18 & WS #11 . . . 2.00

2nd Series

1 thru 7 Rep.VoH . . . @2.00
8 . . . 2.00

Gemstone

17 thru 29 EC comics reprints . . . @2.50
"Annuals"
TPB Vol. 1 rebinding of #1–#5 . . . 8.95
TPB Vol. 2 rebinding of #6–#10 . . . 8.95
TPB Vol. 3 rebinding of #11–#15 . . 10.95
TPB Vol. 4 rebinding of #16–#20 . . 12.95
TPB Vol. 5 rebinding #21–#25 . . . 13.50
TPB Vol. 6 reginding #26–#29 . . . 10.95

VECTOR
Now 1986

1 . . . 2.50
2 thru 5 . . . @2.00

VEGAS KNIGHTS
Pioneer 1989

1 . . . 2.00
2 . . . 2.00
3 . . . 2.00

VENGEANCE OF VAMPIRELLA
Harris 1994

1 Hemorrhage . . . 6.00
1a Gold Edition . . . 9.00
1 gold edition, signed, numbered . 20.00
2 Dervish . . . 3.00
3 On the Hunt . . . 3.00
4 Teenage Vampries . . . 3.00
5 Teenage Vampires . . . 3.00
6 . . . 3.00
7 . . . 3.00
8 bagged w/card . . . 3.00
9 . . . 3.00
10 Bad Jack Rising . . . 3.00
11 Pits of Hell, w/card . . . 3.00
12 V:Passion . . . 3.00
13 V:Passion . . . 3.00
14 Prelude to the Walk,pt.2 . . . 3.00
14a Buzz . . . 5.00
15 The Mystery Walk,pt.1 . . . 3.25
15a Buzz . . . 5.00
16 The Mystery Walk,pt.2 . . . 3.25
16a Buzz . . . 5.00
17 The Mystery Walk,pt.3 . . . 3.25
17a Buzz . . . 5.00
18 The Mystery Walk,pt.4 . . . 3.00
18a Buzz . . . 5.00
19 The Mystery Walk,pt.5 . . . 3.00
19a Buzz . . . 5.00
20 Mystery Walk epilog . . . 3.00
21 thru 24 . . . @3.00
25 "The End" . . . 3.00
25 variant cover, signed & numbered . . . 8.00
25 signed & numbered (2,500) . . . 8.00
25 gold edition, signed & numb. . . 20.00
25 alternate cover, signed by Jae Lee & numbered (#1,500) . . . 15.00
Mini-comic gold foil, signed . . . 20.00
TPB 1-3 Bloodshed . . . 6.95

VENTURE
AC Comics 1986

1 . . . 2.00
2 thru 4 . . . @2.00

VERONICA
Archie Publications April, 1989

1 thru 50 . . . @2.00
51 thru 71 . . . @2.00
72 thru 93 . . . @2.00
94 thru 97 . . . @1.79
98 thru 107 . . . @1.99

VEROTIKA
Verotika 1995

1 thru 3 Jae Lee, Frazetta . . . @2.95
4 thru 9 . . . @2.95

VEROTIK ILLUSTRATED
Verotik 1997

1 48pg . . . 6.95
2 . . . 6.95
3 . . . 6.95
3a alternate cover . . . 6.95
3 variant cover . . . 10.00

VEROTIK ROGUES GALLERY OF VILLAINS
Verotik 1998

1-shot . . . 3.95

VESPERS
Mars Media Group

1 Tony Caputo . . . 2.50
2 I:Dark Side . . . 2.50

VIC FLINT
Argo Publ. Feb., 1956

1 . . . 60.00
2 . . . 50.00

VICKI
Atlas Feb.–Aug., 1975

1 Rep . . . 25.00
2 thru 4 . . . @15.00

VICTORIAN
Penny Farthing Press 1999

1 . . . 2.95
2 thru 5 . . . @2.95
6 thru 8 . . . @2.95

VILLAINS & VIGILANTES
Eclipse 1986–87

1 A:Crusaders,Shadowman . . . 2.00
2 A:Condor . . . 2.00
3 V:Crushers . . . 2.00
4 V:Crushers . . . 2.00

VIOLENT CASES
Tundra

1 20's Chicago . . . 11.00

VIRGINIAN, THE
Gold Key June, 1963

1 . . . 50.00

VIRTEX
Oktomica Entertainment 1998

0 16-page . . . 2.00
1 V:Ripnun . . . 2.50
2 V:Ripnun . . . 2.50
3 alternate endings . . . 2.50
4 Night of the Ninjella,pt.1 . . . 2.50
5 Night of the Ninjella,pt.2 . . . 2.95
6 All My Sins Remembered . . . 2.95

VOLTRON
Solson 1985

1 TV tie-in . . . 2.00

2 . . . . 2.00
3 . . . . 2.00

VORTEX

Vortex 1982–88

1 Peter Hsu art 12.00
2 Mister X on cover 7.00
3 . . . . 4.00
4 . . . . 4.00
5 . . . . 3.00
6 thru 8 . . . . @3.00
9 thru 13 . . . . @2.00

VORTEX

Comico 1991

1 SBt,from Elementals 2.50
2 SBt, ... 2.50

VORTEX: THE SECOND COMING

Entity 1996

1 (of 6) 2.95
1a variant cover. 2.95
2 . . . . 2.95

VOYAGE TO THE DEEP

Dell Publishing Co.
Sept.-Nov., 1962

1 P(c) 50.00
2 P(c) 40.00
3 P(c) 40.00
4 P(c) 40.00

WACKY ADVENTURES OF CRACKY

Gold Key 1972–75

1 . . . . 20.00
2 thru 11 . . . . @10.00
12 . . . . 7.00

WACKY WITCH

Gold Key 1971–75

1 . . . . 30.00
2 . . . . 15.00
3 thru 20 . . . . @10.00
21 . . . . 7.00

WAGON TRAIN

Gold Key Jan.–Oct., 1964

1 . . . . 60.00
2 . . . . 40.00
3 . . . . 40.00
4 . . . . 40.00

WALLY

Gold Key 1962–63

1 . . . . 35.00
2 . . . . 25.00
3 . . . . 25.00
4 . . . . 25.00

WALLY WOOD'S THUNDER AGENTS

Delux 1984–86

1 GP,KG,DC,SD,I:New Menth 3.00
2 GP,KG,DC,SD,"The Raven" 2.50
3 KG,DC,SD 2.00
4 GP,KG,RB,DA 2.00
5 JOy,KG,A:CodenamDangr 2.00

WALT DISNEY ANNUALS

Walt Disney's Autumn Adventure . . 4.00
Walt Disney's Holiday Parade #1 . . 3.50
Walt Disney's Spring Fever. 3.25
Walt Disney's Summer Fun. 3.25
Walt Disney's Holiday Parade #2 . . 3.25

WALT DISNEY'S AUTUMN ADVENTURE

1 Rep. CB 4.00

WALT DISNEY'S COMICS AND STORIES

Dell/ Gold Key 1962

264 CB;Von Drake & Gearloose . . 30.00
265 CB; Von Drake & Gearloose. . 30.00
266 CB; Von Drake & Gearloose. . 30.00
267 CB; Von Drake & Gearloose. . 30.00
268 CB; Von Drake & Gearloose. . 30.00
269 CB; Von Drake & Gearloose. . 30.00
270 CB; Von Drake & Gearloose. . 30.00
271 CB; Von Drake & Gearloose. . 30.00
272 CB; Von Drake & Gearloose. . 30.00
273 CB; Von Drake & Gearloose. . 30.00
274 CB; Von Drake & Gearloose. . 30.00
275 CB. 25.00
276 CB. 25.00
277 CB. 25.00
278 CB. 25.00
279 CB. 25.00
280 CB. 25.00
281 CB. 25.00
282 CB. 25.00
283 CB. 25.00
284. . . . . 15.00
285. . . . . 15.00
286 CB. 25.00
287. . . . . 15.00
288 CB. 20.00
289 CB. 20.00
290. . . . . 15.00
291 CB. 20.00
292 CB. 20.00
293 CB; Grandma Duck's Farm
Friends 20.00
294 CB. 20.00
295. . . . . 15.00
296. . . . . 15.00
297 CB; Gyro Gearloose. 20.00
298 CB; Daisy Duck's Dairy 20.00
299 CB rep. 20.00
300 CB rep. 20.00
301 CB rep. 20.00
302 CB rep. 20.00
303 CB rep. 20.00
304 CB rep. 20.00
305 CB rep. Gyro Gearloose. 20.00
306 CB rep. 20.00
307 CB rep. 20.00
308 CB. 20.00
309 CB. 20.00
310 CB. 20.00
311 CB. 20.00
312 CB. 20.00
313 thru 327 . . . . @15.00
328 CB rep. 20.00
329. . . . . 12.00
330. . . . . 12.00
331. . . . . 12.00
332. . . . . 12.00
333. . . . . 12.00
334. . . . . 12.00
335 CB rep. 15.00
336. . . . . 12.00
337. . . . . 12.00
338. . . . . 12.00
339. . . . . 12.00

Walt Disney's Comics and Stories #305
© Gold Key

340. . . . . 12.00
341. . . . . 12.00
342 CB rep. 15.00
343 CB rep. 15.00
344 CB rep. 15.00
345 CB rep. 15.00
346 CB rep. 15.00
347 CB rep. 15.00
348 CB rep. 15.00
349 CB rep. 15.00
350 CB rep. 15.00
351 CB rep. with poster 20.00
351a CB rep. without poster 15.00
352 CB rep. with poster12 . . . . . . 20.00
352a CB rep. without poster 15.00
353 CB rep. with poster 20.00
353a CB rep. without poster 15.00
354 CB rep. with poster 20.00
354a CB rep. without poster 15.00
355 CB rep. with poster 20.00
355a CB rep. without poster 15.00
356 CB rep. with poster 20.00
356a CB rep. without poster 15.00
357 CB rep. with poster 20.00
357a CB rep. without poster 15.00
358 CB rep. with poster 20.00
358a CB rep. without poster 15.00
359 CB rep. with poster 20.00
359a CB rep. without poster 15.00
360 CB rep. with poster 20.00
360a CB rep. without poster 15.00
361 thru 400 CB rep.. . . . . @15.00
401 thru 409 CB rep.. . . . . @12.00
410 CB rep. Annette Funichello . . 12.00
411 thru 429 CB rep.. . . . . @12.00
430. . . . . 8.00
431 CB rep. 10.00
432 CB rep. 10.00
433. . . . . 8.00
434 CB rep. 10.00
435 CB rep. 10.00
436 CB rep. 10.00
437. . . . . 7.00
438. . . . . 7.00
439 CB rep. 8.00
440 CB rep. 8.00
441. . . . . 7.00
442 CB rep. 8.00
443 CB rep. 8.00
444. . . . . 7.00
445. . . . . 7.00
446 thru 465 CB rep.. . . . . @8.00
466 . . . . 8.00
467 thru 473 CB rep.. . . . . @8.00

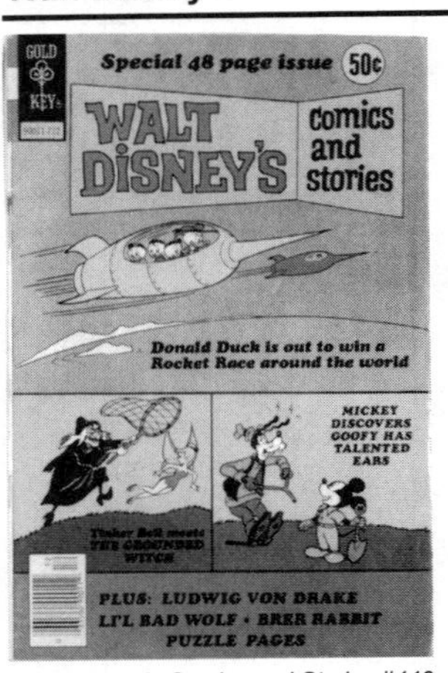

Walt Disney's Comics and Stories #446
© Gold Key

Whitman

474 thru 493 CB rep. . . . . @10.00
494 CB rep.Uncle Scrooge 11.00
495 thru 505 CB rep. . . . . @10.00
506. . . . . 15.00
507 CB rep. 15.00
508 CB rep. 15.00
509 CB rep. 15.00
510 CB rep. 15.00

Gladstone

511 translation of Dutch 22.00
512 translation of Dutch 15.00
513 translation of Dutch 15.00
514 translation of Dutch 8.00
515 translation of Dutch 8.00
516 translation of Dutch 8.00
517 translation of Dutch 3.50
518 translation of Dutch 3.50
519 CB,Donald Duck 3.50
520 translation of Dutch, Rosa 7.00
521 Walt Kelly 3.00
522 CB,WK,nephews 3.00
523 Rosa,Donald Duck. 7.00
524 Rosa,Donald Duck. 7.00
525 translation of Dutch 3.00
526 Rosa,Donald Duck. 7.00
527 CB. 3.00
528 Rosa,Donald Duck. 5.00
529 CB. 3.00
530 Rosa,Donald Duck. 5.00
531 WK(c),Rosa,CB 5.00
532 CB. 2.50
533 CB. 2.50
534 CB. 2.50
535 CB. 2.50
536 CB. 2.50
537 CB. 2.50
538 CB. 2.50
539 CB. 2.50
540 CB new art 3.50
541 double-size,WK(c) 3.00
542 CB. 5.00
543 CB,WK(c) 2.50
544 CB,WK(c) 2.50
545 CB. 2.50
546 CB,WK,giant 4.00
547 CB,WK,Rosa,giant. 4.50

Walt Disney 1990

548 CB,WK,"Home is the Hero" . . . 3.00
549 CB, ... 2.50
550 CB,prev.unpub.story! 3.50
551 . . . . 2.25
552 . . . . 2.25
553 . . . . 2.25
554 . . . . 2.25
555 . . . . 2.25
556 . . . . 2.25
557 . . . . 2.25
558 "Donald's Fix-it Shop" 2.25
559 "Bugs" 2.25
560 CB,April Fools Story 2.00
561 CB,Donald the "Flipist". 2.00
562 CB,"3DirtyLittleDucks" 2.00
563 CB,"Donald Camping" 2.00
564 CB,"Dirk the Dinosaur". 2.00
565 CB,DonaldDuck,TruantOfficer . 2.00
566 CB,"Will O' the Wisp". 2.00
567 CB,"Turkey Shoot" 2.00
568 CB,"AChristmas Eve Story" . . . 2.00
569 CB, New Years Resolutions . . . 2.00
570 CB,Donald the Mailman + Poster 2.00
571 CB,"Atom Bomb" 4.50
572 CB, April Fools 2.00
573 TV Quiz Show 2.00
574 Pinocchio,64pgs 3.50
575 Olympic Torch Bearer, Li'l Bad Wolf,64 pgs. 3.50
576 giant 3.50
577 A:Truant Officers,64 pgs. 3.50
578 CB,Old Quacky Manor 2.00
579 CB,Turkey Hunt 2.00
580 CB,The Wise Little Red Hen, 64 page-Sunday page format . 3.50
581 CB,Duck Lake 2.00
582 giant 3.50
583 giant 3.50
584 . . . . 2.00
585 CB, giant 3.00

Gladstone

586 . . . . 2.00
587 thru 600 . . . . @2.00
601 thru 605 prestige format . . . . @6.00
606 "Winging It" 7.00
607 "Number 401" 7.00
608 "Sleepless in Duckburg". 7.00
609. . . . . 7.00
610 "Treasures Untold". 7.00
611 "Romance at a Glance" 7.00
612 "The Sod Couple" 7.00
613 "Another Fine Mess" 7.00
614 "Airheads" 7.00
615 "Backyard Battlers" 7.00
616. . . . . 7.00
617 "Tree's A Crowd" 7.00
618 "A Dolt from the Blue" 7.00
619 "Queen of the Ant Farm" 7.00
620 "Caught in the Cold Rush" 7.00
621 "Room and Bored" 7.00
622 "" 7.00
623 "All Quacked Up" 7.00
624 "Their Loaded Forebear" 7.00
625 "Mummery's the Word". 7.00
626 "A Real Gone Guy" 7.00
627 "To Bee or Not to Bee". 7.00
628 "Officer for a Day" 7.00
629 "The Ghost Train" 7.00
630 two Donald Duck stories 7.00
631 "Music Hath Charms". 7.00
632 "A Day in a Duck's Life" 7.00
633 All Donald issue. 7.00
634 "The Runaway Train" 7.00
635 "Volcano Valley". 7.00
636 "Mission to Codfish Cove" 7.00
637 "Pizen Springs Dude Ranch" . . 7.00

WALT DISNEY COMICS DIGEST

Gold Key 1968–76

[All done by Carl Barks]

1 Rep,Uncle Scrooge. 40.00
2 . . . . 25.00
3 . . . . 25.00
4 . . . . 25.00
5 . . . . 45.00
6 . . . . 20.00
7 . . . . 20.00
8 . . . . 20.00
9 . . . . 20.00
10 . . . . 20.00
11 . . . . 20.00
12 . . . . 20.00
13 . . . . 20.00
14 . . . . 10.00
15 . . . . 10.00
16 rep.Donald Duck #26 . . . . 20.00
17 . . . . 15.00
18 . . . . 15.00
19 . . . . 15.00
20 . . . . 15.00
21 . . . . 18.00
22 . . . . 18.00
23 . . . . 18.00
24 . . . . 18.00
25 . . . . 18.00
26 . . . . 18.00
27 . . . . 18.00
28 . . . . 18.00
29 . . . . 18.00
30 . . . . 18.00
31 . . . . 18.00
32 . . . . 8.00
33 . . . . 18.00
34 rep.Four Color #318 . . . . 15.00
35 . . . . 15.00
36 . . . . 15.00
37 . . . . 15.00
38 rep.Disneyland#1. . . . . 15.00
39 . . . . 15.00
40 . . . . 10.00
41 . . . . 8.00
42 . . . . 8.00
43 . . . . 8.00
44 Rep. Four Color #29 & others . 25.00
45 . . . . 6.00
46 CB. 8.00
47 . . . . 6.00
48 . . . . 6.00
49 . . . . 6.00
50 CB. 8.00
51 rep.Four Color #71. . . . . 12.00
52 CB. 8.00
53 . . . . 6.00
54 . . . . 6.00
55 . . . . 6.00
56 CB,rep. Uncle Scrooge #32 . . . 10.00
57 CB. 8.00

WALT DISNEY SHOWCASE

Gold Key 1970–80

1 Boatniks (photo cover) 30.00
2 Moby Duck 20.00
3 Bongo & Lumpjaw 15.00
4 Pluto. 15.00
5 $1,000,000 Duck (photo cover). 20.00
6 Bedknobs & Broomsticks 15.00
7 Pluto. 15.00
8 Daisy & Donald. 15.00
9 101 Dalmatians rep. 22.00
10 Napoleon & Samantha. 15.00
11 Moby Duck rep. 12.00
12 Dumbo rep. 15.00
13 Pluto rep.. . . . . 15.00
14 World's Greatest Athlete 20.00
15 3 Little Pigs rep.. . . . . 20.00
16 Aristocats rep. 20.00
17 Mary Poppins rep. 20.00
18 Gyro Gearloose rep. 20.00
19 That Darn Cat rep.. . . . . 20.00
20 Pluto rep.. . . . . 15.00
21 Li'l Bad Wolf & 3 Little Pigs . . . 12.00

COLOR PUB.

22 Unbirthday Party rep. 15.00
23 Pluto rep. 15.00
24 Herbie Rides Again rep. 12.00
25 Old Yeller rep. 12.00
26 Lt. Robin Crusoe USN rep. . . . 12.00
27 Island at the Top of the World . 12.00
28 Brer Rabbit, Bucky Bug rep. . . . 15.00
29 Escape to Witch Mountain 12.00
30 Magica De Spell rep. 20.00
31 Bambi rep. 20.00
32 Spin & Marty rep. 15.00
33 Pluto rep. 15.00
34 Paul Revere's Ride rep. 12.00
35 Goofy rep. 12.00
36 Peter Pan rep. 12.00
37 Tinker Bell & Jiminy Cricket rep. 12.00
38 Mickey & the Sleuth, Pt. 1 . . . . 14.00
39 Mickey & the Sleuth, Pt. 2 . . . . 14.00
40 The Rescuers 14.00
41 Herbie Goes to Monte Carlo . . 15.00
42 Mickey & the Sleuth 10.00
43 Pete's Dragon 15.00
44 Return From Witch Mountain & In Search of the Castaways 20.00
45 The Jungle Book rep. 20.00
46 The Cat From Outer Space . . . 10.00
47 Mickey Mouse Surprise Party . . 11.00
48 The Wonderful Adventures of Pinocchio 10.00
49 North Avenue Irregulars; Zorro. 10.00
50 Bedknobs & Broomsticks rep. . 10.00
51 101 Dalmatians 10.00
52 Unidentified Flying Oddball . . . 10.00
53 The Scarecrow 10.00
54 The Black Hole 10.00

WALT DISNEY COMICS IN COLOR

Gladstone 1998

TPB Vol. 1 . . . . 9.95
TPB Vol. 2 . . . . 9.95
TPB Vol. 3 . . . . 9.95
TPB Vol. 4 . . . . 9.95

WALT KELLY'S CHRISTMAS CLASSICS

Eclipse 1987

1 . . . . 2.00

WALT KELLY'S SPRINGTIME TALES

Eclipse 1988

1 . . . . 2.50

WAR AGAINST CRIME

Gemstone 2000

1 rep. 2.50
2 rep. Summer 1942 . . . . 2.50
3 rep. Fall 1948 . . . . 2.50
4 rep. Winter 1948. . . . . 2.50
5 rep. Feb. 1949 . . . . 2.50
6 rep. June 1949 . . . . 2.50
7 rep. 2.50
8 rep. Aug. 1949 . . . . 2.50
9 rep. Oct. 1949 . . . . 2.50
"Annuals"
TPB Vol. 1 rep. #1–#5 . . . . 13.50

WARCAT SPECIAL

Entity Press 1995

1 I:Warcat 2.95

Warp #3
© First

WARCHILD

Maximum Press 1995

1 I:Sword, Stone 3.50
2 I:Morganna Lefay 3.00
3 V: The Black Knight 2.50
4 Rescue Merlyn 2.50

[2nd Series]

1 . . . . 2.50

WAR DANCER

Defiant 1994

1 B:JiS(s),I:Ahrq Tsolmec. 2.75
2 I:Massakur 2.75
3 V:Massakur 2.75
4 JiS(s),A:Nudge 3.25

WARHAWKS

TSR 1990–91

1 thru 6 from game . . . . @2.95
7 thru 10 The Battle of Britain. . . @2.95

WARHAWKS 2050

TSR

1 Pt.1 . . . . 2.95

WAR HEROES

Charlton Comics 1963–67

1 . . . . 30.00
2 thru 10 . . . . @20.00
11 thru 27 . . . . @15.00

WARLASH

CFD

1 Project Hardfire 2.95

WARMASTER

1 and 2 . . . . @3.95

WARP

First March, 1983

1 FB,JSon,I:Lord Cumulus & Prince Chaos, play adapt pt.1 . . . . 2.00
2 FB,SD,play adapt pt.2. . . . . 2.00
3 FB,SD,play adapt pt.3. . . . . 2.00
4 FB,SD,I:Xander,play pt.4 . . . . . . 2.00
5 FB, play adapt pt.5 . . . . 2.00
6 FB/MG, play adapt pt.6. . . . . 2.00
7 FB/MG, play adapt pt.7. . . . . 2.00
8 FB/MG,BWg,play adapt pt.8 . . . . 2.00
9 FB/MG,BWg,play adapt conc. . . . 2.00
10 JBi/MG,BWg, Second Saga, I:Outrider 2.00
11 JBi/MG,A:Outrider 2.00
12 JBi/MG,A:Outrider 2.00
13 JBi/MG,A:Outrider 2.00
14 JBi/MG,A:Outrider 2.00
15 JBi/MG/BWg 2.00
16 BWg/MG,A:Outrider. 2.00
17 JBi/MG,A:Outrider 2.00
18 JBi/MG,A:Outrider&Sargon 2.00
19 MG,last issue. 2.00
Spec. #1 HC,O:Chaos 2.00
Spec. #2 MS/MG,V:Ylem 2.00
Spec. #3 . . . . 2.00

WARRIOR NUN AREALA

Antartic Press 1995

1 V:Lilith 4.00
1a limited edition 6.00
2 V:Lilith 3.00
3 V:Hellmaster. 3.00
3 silver edition 12.00
TPB Rep.#1-#3. . . . . 9.95

BOOK II: RITUALS 1996

1 Land of Rising Sun 2.95
1 Red edition. 9.00
1 signed 9.95
2 I:Cheetah 2.95
3 Iraq, 1989. . . . . 2.95
4 . . . . 2.95
5 Rituals,pt.5 . . . . 2.95
6 . . . . 2.95
Spec. Warrior Nun Portraits 3.95
Spec. Warrior Nun Portraits Commemorative Edition (1999) 5.95
TPB Rituals 15.95

BOOK III 1997

1 The Hammer & the Holocaust. . . 2.95
2 Hammer & the Holocaust,pt.2. . . 2.95
3 Hammer & the Holocaust,pt.3. . . 2.95
4 Holy Man, Holy Terror,pt.1 . . . . . 2.95
5 Holy Man, Holy Terror,pt.2 . . . . . 2.95
6 by Barry Lyga & Ben Dunn 2.95
TPB Vol. 1 . . . . 9.95
TPB.Vol. 1 reprint 9.95
HC Vol. 2, lim. to 1,000 copies . . . 29.95
Spec. Warrior Nun Areala/Glory by Ben Dunn 2.95
Spec. poster edition 5.95
Spec. Warrior Nun Areala vs. Razor, BDn,JWf x-over 3.95
Spec.Warrior Nun Areala vs. Razor commemorative (1999). 5.95
Spec.Warrior Nun Areala/Avengelyne comm. edition (1999) 5.95

VOL 3

1 F:Sister Shannon Masters 2.50
2 . . . . 2.50
3 . . . . 2.50
4 Antichrist arrives. 2.50
5 . . . . 2.50
6 Crimson Nun 2.50
7 V:Ruprecht Marsh. 2.50
8 V:Mr.Zhu 2.50
9 in the Vatican 2.50
10 V:Nebelhexa 2.50
11 A:Demoness Lillith 2.50
12 F:Lillith. 3.50
13 V:Julius Salvius 2.95
14 Rebirth, pt.2. . . . . 2.95
15 Rebirth, pt.3. . . . . 2.95
Ann.2000 b&W 3.95

COLOR PUB.

WARRIOR NUN AREALA: SCORPIO ROSE
Antarctic Press 1996
1 SEt & BDn 2.95
1a commemorative (1999). 5.95
2 thru 4 (of 4). . . . . @2.95

WARRIOR NUN DEI: AFTERTIME
Antarctic Press 1997
1 (of 3) by Patrick Thornton 2.95
1 Commemorative edition (1999). . 5.95
2 . . . . 2.95
3 . . . . 3.00

WARRIOR NUN: FRENZY
Antarctic Press 1998
1 (of 2) by Miki Horvatic
& Esad T. Ribic. 2.95
2 . . . . 2.95

WARRIOR NUN: RESURRECTION
Antarctic Press 1998
1 by Ben Dunn 2.95
1a deluxe 5.95
2 quest for lost God Armor. 3.00
3 . . . . 3.00

WARRIORS OF PLASM
Defiant 1993–95
1 JiS(s),DL,A:Lorca 3.25
2 JiS(s),DL,Sedition Agenda 3.25
3 JiS(s),DL,Sedition Agenda 3.25
4 JiS(s),DL,Sedition Agenda 3.25
5 JiS(s),B:The Demons of
Darkedge 2.75
6 JiS(s),The Demons of
Darkedge,pt.2. . . . . 2.75
7 JiS(s),DL, ... 2.75
8 JiS(s),DL,40pages 3.00
9 JiS(s),LWn(s),DL,40pages 3.00
10 DL, ... 2.50
GN Home for the Holidays 5.95

Warrior's Way #2B
© Bench Press Studios

WARRIOR'S WAY
Bench Press Studios 1998
1 . . . . 3.00
2 . . . . 3.00
3 . . . . 3.00
4 . . . . 3.00
5 . . . . 3.00
6 V:Technoborgs 3.00
7 . . . . 3.00

WART AND THE WIZARD
Gold Key Feb., 1964
1 . . . . 40.00

WAVE WARRIORS
1 . . . . 2.00
2 . . . . 2.00

WAXWORK in 3-D
Blackthorne
1 . . . . 2.50

WAYFARERS
Eternity
1 . . . . 2.00
2 . . . . 2.00

WEAPON ZERO
See: Image

WEASEL GUY WITCHBLADE
Hyperwerks 1998
1-shot by Steve Succellato 3.00
1a variant Jeff Matsuda(c) 5.00
1b variant Karl Altstoeter(c) 8.00

WEB-MAN
Argosy
1 flip book with Time Warrior 2.50

WEB OF HORROR
Major Magazines Dec., 1969
1 JJ(c),Ph(c),BWr 100.00
2 JJ(c),Ph(c),BWr 75.00
3 BWr,April, 1970 . . . . 75.00

WEDDING OF POPEYE AND OLIVE, THE
Ocean Comics 1999
1 PDa,. 2.75
1a signed, numbered 15.95
Spec. Sketch edition. 40.00

WEIRD FANTASY
Russ Cochran 1992
1 Reps 2.00
2 Reps.inc.The Black Arts 2.00
3 thru 4 rep. . . . . @2.00
5 thru 7 rep. . . . . @2.50
8 . . . . 2.50

Gemstone
9 thru 22 EC comics reprint . . . . @2.50
"Annuals"
TPB Vol. #1 rebinding of #1–#5 . . . 8.95
TPB Vol. #2 rebinding of #6–#10 . . 9.95
TPB Vol. #3 rebinding of #11–#14. . 8.95
TPB Vol. #4 rebinding of #15–#18. . 9.95
TPB Vol. #5 rebinding of #19–#22. 10.50

WEIRD SCIENCE
Gladstone 1990–91
1 Rep. #22 + Fantasy #1. . . . . 4.00
2 Rep. #16 + Fantasy #17 . . . . 3.50
3 Rep. #9 + Fantasy #14 . . . . 3.50
4 Rep. #27 + Fantasy #11 . . . . 2.00

Russ Cochran/Gemstone 1992
1 thru 21 EC comics reprint . . . . @2.50
"Annuals"
TPB Vol. #1 rebinding of #1–#5 . . . 8.95
TPB Vol. #2 rebinding of #6–#10 . . 9.95
TPB Vol. #3 rebinding of #11–#15. . 8.95
TPB Vol. #4 rebinding of #16–#18. . 9.95
TPB Vol. #5 rebinding of #19–#22. 10.50

WEIRD SCIENCE–FANTASY
Russ Cochran/Gemstone 1992
1 Rep. W.S.F. #23 (1954) 2.00
2 Rep. Flying Saucer Invasion 2.00
3 Rep. 2.00
4 thru 6 Rep. . . . . @2.00
7 rep #29. . . . . 2.00
8 . . . . 2.00

Gemstone
"Annuals"
TPB Vol. #1 rebinding of #1–#5 . . . 8.95
TPB Vol. #2 rebinding of #6–#10. . 12.95

WEIRD SUSPENSE
Atlas Feb.–July, 1975
1 thru 3 F:Tarantula . . . . @12.00

WEIRD TALES ILLUSTRATED
Millennium 1992
1 KJo,JBo,PCr,short stories 4.95

WENDY
Blackthorne
1 3-D. 2.50

WENDY, THE GOOD LITTLE WITCH
Harvey Publications 1960–76
1 . . . . 200.00
2 . . . . 75.00
3 . . . . 60.00
4 . . . . 60.00
5 . . . . 60.00
6 . . . . 50.00
7 . . . . 50.00
8 . . . . 50.00
9 . . . . 50.00
10 . . . . 50.00
11 thru 20 . . . . @30.00
21 thru 30 . . . . @20.00
31 thru 50 . . . . @15.00
51 thru 69 . . . . @10.00
70 thru 74 52 pg Giants . . . . @7.00
75 thru 93 . . . . @7.00

WENDY WITCH WORLD
Harvey Publications 1961–74
1 . . . . 125.00
2 . . . . 60.00
3 . . . . 60.00
4 . . . . 60.00
5 . . . . 60.00
6 . . . . 35.00
7 . . . . 35.00
8 . . . . 35.00
9 . . . . 35.00

10 . . . . 35.00
11 thru 20 . . . . @30.00
21 thru 30 . . . . @25.00
31 thru 39 . . . . @15.00
40 thru 50 . . . . @7.00
51 thru 53 . . . . @7.00

WEREWOLF
Blackthorne
1 3-D. 3.50

WESTERN ACTION
Atlas Feb., 1975
1 F:Kid Cody,Comanche Kid 2.00

WESTWYND
Westwynd 1995
1 I:Sable,Shiva,Outcast,Tojo 2.50

WHAM
1 . . . . 2.00

Whisper #2
© Capital

WHISPER
Capital 1983–84
1 MG(c). 9.00
2 . . . . 7.00

First
1 . . . . 2.50
2 . . . . 2.00
3 . . . . 2.00
4 . . . . 2.00
5 . . . . 2.00
6 thru 12 . . . . @2.00
13 thru 19 . . . . @2.00
20 O:Whisper 2.00
21 thru 26 . . . . @2.00
27 Ghost Dance #2 . . . . 2.00
28 Ghost Dance #3 . . . . 2.00
29 thru 37 . . . . @2.00
Spec. #1. 4.00

WHITE FANG
Walt Disney 1990
1 Movie Adapt. 5.95

WHITE LAMA
Humanoids Publishing 1999
HC Vol. 1 . . . . 14.95
HC Vol. 2 Second Sight 14.95
HC Vol. 3 Three Ears 14.95
HC Vol. 4 The Fourth Voice 14.95

WHITE TRASH
Tundra
1 I:Elvis & Dean. 3.95
2 Trip to Las Vegas contd. 3.95
3 V:Purple Heart Brigade. 3.95

WHODUNNIT
Eclipse 1986–87
1 DSp,A:Jay Endicott. 2.00
2 DSp,"Who Slew Kangaroo?". . . . 2.00
3 DSp,"Who Offed Henry Croft" . . . 2.00

WIDOW MADE IN BRITAIN
N Studio
1 I:Widow 2.60
2 F:Widow. 2.60
3 Rampage 2.60
4 In Jail. 2.60

WIDOW METAL GYPSIES
London Night Studios 1995
1 I:Emma Drew 3.00
2 Father Love 3.00
3 Final issue 3.00

WILD ANIMALS
Pacific 1982
1 . . . . 2.00

WILD BILL PECOS
AC Comics 1989
1 . . . . 3.50

WILDCATS
Wildstorm/DC 1999
Previously from Image
VOLUME 2
1 SLo,TC, ... 2.50
1a variant cover. 2.50
1b variant cover. 2.50
1c variant cover. 2.50
1d variant cover. 2.50
1e variant cover. 2.50
2 SLo,TC. 2.50
3 SLo,TC,F:Grifter 2.50
4 SLo,TC, ... 2.50
TPB WildC.A.T.S.: Compendium. . 10.00
TPB WildC.A.T.S.: Homecoming . . 20.00

WILDFIRE
Zion Comics
1 thru 3 V:Mr. Reeves . . . . @2.00
4 Lord D'Rune. 2.00

WILD FRONTIER
Charlton Comics Oct., 1955
1 Davy Crockett. 60.00
2 same 35.00
3 same 35.00
4 same 35.00
5 same 35.00
6 same 35.00
7 O:Cheyenne Kid 35.00
Becomes:

CHEYENNE KID
8 . . . . 30.00
9 . . . . 15.00
10 . . . . 45.00
11 . . . . 45.00
12 . . . . 45.00
13 . . . . 30.00
14 . . . . 30.00
15 . . . . 15.00
16 . . . . 15.00
17 . . . . 15.00
18 . . . . 30.00
19 . . . . 15.00
20 . . . . 18.00
21 . . . . 18.00
22 . . . . 18.00
23 . . . . 8.00
24 . . . . 8.00
25 . . . . 15.00
26 . . . . 10.00
27 thru 29. . . . . @8.00
30 . . . . 10.00
31 thru 59. . . . . @3.00
60 thru 98. . . . . @2.00
99 Nov., 1973. . . . . 2.00

WILD TIMES
Wildstorm/DC 1999
Deathblow 2.50
DV8 . . . . 2.50
Gen13 . . . . 2.50
Grifter. 2.50
Wetworks 2.50

WILD WEST C.O.W.-BOYS OF MOO MESA
Archie 1992–93
1 Based on TV cartoon 2.00
2 Cody kidnapped 2.00
3 Law of the Year Parade,
last issue 2.00

(Regular series)
1 Valley o/t Thunder Lizard 2.00
2 Plains, Trains & Dirty Deals 2.00

WILD WESTERN ACTION
Skywald 1971
1 thru 3 . . . . @10.00

WILD WILD WEST
Gold Key 1966–69
1 TV show tie-in. 135.00
2 . . . . 125.00
3 . . . . 90.00
4 . . . . 90.00
5 . . . . 90.00
6 . . . . 90.00
7 . . . . 90.00

WILD WILD WEST
Millennium 1990–91
1 . . . . 2.95
2 thru 4 . . . . @2.95

WILL EISNER'S 3-D CLASSICS
Kitchen Sink
WE art, w/glasses (1985) 2.00

WIN A PRIZE COMICS
Charlton Comics Feb., 1955
1 S&K,Edgar Allen adapt. 600.00
2 S&K 400.00
Becomes:

TIMMY THE TIMID GHOST
3 . . . . 60.00

4 ... 30.00
5 ... 30.00
6 ... 20.00
7 ... 20.00
8 ... 20.00
9 ... 20.00
10 ... 20.00
11 ... 60.00
12 ... 60.00
13 thru 20 ... @20.00
21 thru 44 ... @15.00
45 1966 ... 15.00

WINDRAGE

1 and 2 ... @2.00

WINTERWORLD

Eclipse 1987–88

1 JZ,I:Scully, Wynn ... 2.00
2 JZ,V:Slave Farmers ... 2.00
3 JZ,V:Slave Farmers ... 2.00

WIREHEADS

Fleetway

1 ... 2.95

WISP

Oktomica Entertainment 1999

1 All Along the Watchtower,pt.1 ... 2.50
2 All Along the Watchtower,pt.2 ... 2.50
3 All Along the Watchtower,pt.3 ... 2.95
4 The Acheron Protocol ... 2.95

WITCHBLADE

See Image

WITCHING HOUR, THE

Millennium/Comico

1 Anne Rice adaptation ... 2.50
2 thru 5 ... @2.50

WOODY WOODPECKER

Harvey 1991–93

1 thru 5 ... @2.00

WORLD OF ARCHIE

Archie 1994

1 thru 21 ... @2.00

WORLD OF WOOD

Eclipse 1986–87

1 WW ... 2.00
2 WW,DSt(i) ... 2.00
3 WW ... 2.00
4 WW ... 2.00

WORLD WAR II: 1946

Antarctic Press 1999

1 by Ted Nomura ... 2.50
2 Born to Die ... 2.50
3 Battle for Moscow ... 2.50
4 Flying Tigers ... 2.50
5 ... 2.50
6 The Hunley vs. the Potsdam ... 2.50
7 The Yamato ... 2.50
8 Tuskegee Airmen ... 2.50
9 Firestorm ... 2.50
10 Destination: Space ... 2.50
11 Night Witches ... 2.50
12 Korea ... 2.50
Ann. 2000 b&w ... 3.95

Wulf The Barbarian #1
© Atlas Comics

WULF THE BARBARIAN

Atlas Feb.–Sept., 1975

1 O:Wulf ... 10.00
2 NA,I:Berithe The Swordsman ... 8.00
3 & 4 ... @5.00

WYATT EARP

Dell Publishing Co. Nov., 1957

1 ... 150.00
2 ... 100.00
3 ... 90.00
4 ... 75.00
5 ... 75.00
6 ... 75.00
7 ... 75.00
8 ... 75.00
9 ... 75.00
10 ... 75.00
11 ... 60.00
12 ... 60.00
13 ... 60.00

XANADU

Eclipse 1988

1 ... 2.00

XENYA

Sanctuary Press 1994

1 Hildebrandt Brothers ... 4.00
2 ... 3.25
3 ... 3.25
4 conclusion, Homecoming ... 2.95

XENA: WARRIOR PRINCESS

Topps 1997

1 RTs,Revenge of the Gorgons, pt.1 ... 5.00
1a photo (c) ... 8.00
2 (of 2) rescue of Gabrielle ... 4.00
TPB ... 9.95

[VOL 2]

0 AaL Temple of the Dragon God ... 3.00
1 (of 3) Joxer, Warrior Prince, pt.1 ... 5.00
1a deluxe ... 8.00
2 Joxer, Warrior Prince, pt.2 ... 4.00
2a photo (c) ... 4.00
TPB rep. #0–#2 ... 9.95

XENA: WARRIOR PRINCESS: BLOOD LINES

Topps 1997

1 (of 3) ALo ... 3.00
1a photo (c) ... 3.00
2 (of 3) ALo ... 3.00
2a photo (c) ... 3.00

XENA: WARRIOR PRINCESS: CALLISTO

Topps 1997

1 (of 3) RTs, ... 3.00
1a photo (c) ... 3.00
2 (of 3) RTs, ... 3.00
2a photo (c) ... 3.00
3 (of 3) RTs, ... 3.00
3a photo (c) ... 3.00

XENA: WARRIOR PRINCESS: ORPHEUS

Topps 1998

1 (of 3) ... 3.00
1a photo (c) ... 3.00
2 (of 3) ... 3.00
2a photo (c) ... 3.00
3 (of 3) ... 3.00
3a photo (c) ... 3.00

XENA: WARRIOR PRINCESS: THE ORIGINAL OLYMPICS

Topps 1998

1 (of 3) ... 3.00
1a photo cover ... 3.00
2 F:Hercules ... 3.00
2a photo cover ... 3.00
3 ... 3.00
3a photo cover ... 3.00

XENA: WARRIOR PRINCESS: THE WEDDING OF XENA & HERCULES

Topps 1998

1-shot ... 3.00
1-shot photo (c) ... 3.00

XENA, WARRIOR PRINCESS: THE WRATH OF HERA

Topps 1998

1 (of 2) ... 3.00
1a photo cover edition ... 3.00
2 conclusion ... 3.00
2a photo cover edition ... 3.00

XENA: WARRIOR PRINCESS: XENA AND THE DRAGON'S TEETH

Topps 1997

1 (of 3) RTs, ... 3.00
1a photo (c) ... 3.00
2 (of 3) RTs, ... 3.00

2a photo (c). 3.00
3 (of 3) RTs, ... 3.00
3a photo (c). 3.00

XENO MAN

1 . . . . 2.00

XENOTECH

Mirage 1993–94

1 I:Xenotech 2.75
2 . . . . 2.75
3 w/2 card strip 2.75

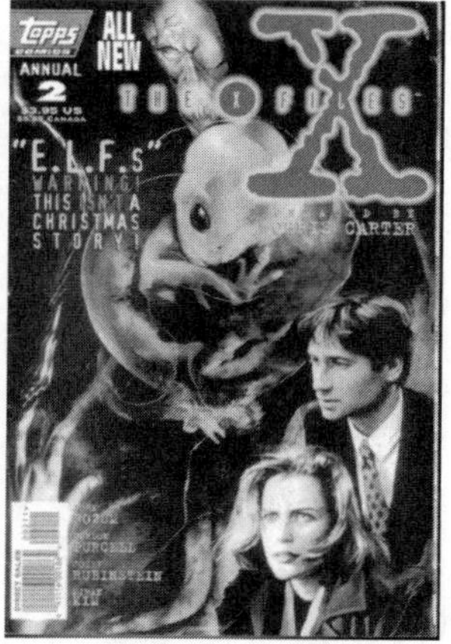

X-Files Annual #2
© Topps Comics

X-FILES

Topps 1994–97

1 From Fox TV Series 40.00
1a Newsstand. 30.00
2 Aliens Killing Witnesses 25.00
3 The Return 22.00
4 Firebird,pt.1 . . . . 15.00
5 Firebird,pt.2 . . . . 10.00
6 Firebird,pt.3 . . . . 8.00
7 Trepanning Opera 7.00
8 Silent Cities of the Mind,pt.1 . . . . 6.00
9 Silent Cities of the Mind,pt.2 . . . . 5.00
10 Feeling of Unreality,pt.1 . . . . . . 5.00
11 Fealing of Unreality,pt.2 . . . . . . 5.00
12 Fealing of Unreality,pt.3 . . . . . . 5.00
13 A Boy and His Saucer 5.00
14 . . . . 4.00
15 Home of the Brave. 4.00
16 Home of the Brave,pt.2 . . . . 3.50
17 DgM,CAd. 3.50
18 thru 21 . . . . @3.50
22 JRz,CAd,"The Kanishibari". 3.00
23 JRz,CAd,"Donor" 3.00
24 JRz,"Silver Lining" 3.00
25 JRz,CAd,"Remote Control,"pt.1 . 3.00
26 JRz,CAd,"Remote Control,"pt.2 . 3.00
27 JRz,CAd,"Remote Control,"pt.3 . 3.00
28 JRz,"Be Prepared," pt.1,
V:Windigo. 3.00
29 JRz,"Be Prepared," pt.2 . . . . 3.00
30 JRz,"Surrounded," pt.1. . . . . 3.00
31 JRz,"Surrounded," pt.2 (of 2) . . . 3.00
32 . . . . 3.00
33 widows on San Francisco 3.00
33 variant photo (c) 3.00
34 Project HAARP 3.00
35 Near Death Experience 3.00
36 Near Death Experience, pt.2 . . . 3.00
37 JRz,The Face of Extinction 3.00
38 JRz,. 3.00
39 JRz, Widow's Peak 3.00
40 Devil's Advocate 3.00
40a photo cover 3.00
41 Severed. 3.00
41a photo cover 3.00
Ann.#1 Hollow Eve 5.00
Ann.#2 E.L.F.S. 4.50
Spec.#1 Rep. #1-#3 . . . . 6.00
Spec.#2 Rep. #4-#6 Firebird 5.00
Spec.#3 Rep. #7-#9 . . . . 5.00
Spec.#4 Rep. 5.00
TPB Vol. 2 . . . . 19.95
GN Afterflight 5.95
GN Official Movie Adapt. (1998) . . . 5.95

X-FILES DIGEST

Topps 1995

1 All New Series, 96pg. 3.50
2 and 3 . . . . 3.50

X-FILES, THE: GROUND ZERO

Topps 1997

1 (of 4) based on novel 2.95
2 . . . . 2.95
3 . . . . 2.95
4 . . . . 2.95

X-FILES, THE: SEASON ONE

Topps

1 RTs,JVF(c) "Deep Throat" 4.95
Deep Throat, variant (c) 7.50
2 RTs,JVF(c) "Squeeze" 3.95
Squeeze, RTs, JVF(c). 4.95
3 RTs,SSc,"Conduit" 3.95
Conduit, RTs. 4.95
4 RTs,"The Jersey Devil" 3.95
5 RTs,"Shadows". 3.95
Shadows JVF(c). 4.95
6 "Fire" 3.95
Fire 4.95
7 RTs,JVF,"Ice" 3.95
Ice 4.95
8 RTs,"Space". 3.95
Space JVF(c) 4.95
Spec. Pilot Episode RTs,JVF
new JVF(c). 4.95
Beyond the Sea JVF(c). 4.95

XIMOS: VIOLENT PAST

Triumphant 1994

1 JnR(s) 2.50
2 JnR(s) 2.50

XL

1 . . . . 2.00

YAKKY DOODLE & CHOPPER

Gold Key Dec., 1962

1 . . . . 75.00

YEAH!

Homage/DC 1999

1 GHe 3.00

YIN FEI

Leung's Publications 1988–90

5 . . . . 2.00
6 thru 11 . . . . @2.00

YOGI BEAR

Dell Feb.-March, 1962

#1 thru #6, See Dell Four Color

7 thru 9 . . . . @75.00

Gold Key

10 . . . . 85.00
11 Jellystone Follies 75.00
12 . . . . 45.00
13 Surprise Party 75.00
14 thru 19 . . . . @40.00
20 thru 29 . . . . @25.00
30 thru 42 . . . . @20.00

YOGI BEAR

Charlton Comics 1970–76

1 . . . . 40.00
2 thru 10 . . . . @25.00
11 thru 35 . . . . @20.00

YOGI BEAR

Archie Comics 1997

1 . . . . 2.00

Yosemite Sam #5
© Gold Key

YOSEMITE SAM

Gold Key/Whitman 1970–84

1 . . . . 35.00
2 thru 10 . . . . @20.00
11 thru 40 . . . . @15.00
41 thru 81 . . . . @10.00

YOUNGBLOOD

Maximum Press/Extreme
Volume 2 1996

Vol. 1 & Vol. 2 #1–#10, see Image

11 RLd,RCz,. 2.50
12 Rle, V:Lord Dredd,A:New
Man,double size 3.50
13 RLd,RCz,F:Die-Hard 2.50
14 RLd,RCz,. 2.50
Super Spec.#1 ErS,CSp,AG 3.00
TPB Youngblood, rep. orig.
Youngblood #1–#5 . . . . 16.95
TPB Baptism of Fire rep.
Youngblood #6–#8, #10 & Team
Youngblood #9–#11 . . . . 16.95

COLOR PUB.

YOUNGBLOOD
Awesome Entertainment 1998

1 AMo,SSr. 2.50
1a variant covers, 7 different 2.50
1+ foil logo 6.00
1+ custom illustration. 72.00
2 AMo,SSr,Baptism of Fire. 2.50
3 AMo,SSr,V:Professor Night. 2.50
4 AMo,SSr,Young Guns. 2.50
5 AMo,SSr,Young Guns. 2.50
TPB rep.#1–#10 orig. series 14.95

YOUNGBLOOD CLASSICS
Image/Extreme Sept. 1996

1 RLd,ErS,rewritten & redrawn, new cover 2.25
2 RLd,ErS,rewritten & redrawn, new cover 2.25
3 RLd,ErS,rewritten & redrawn, new cover 2.25

YOUNGBLOOD GENESIS
Awesome Entertainment 2000

1 . . . . 2.99

YOUNGBLOOD/X-FORCE
Awesome Entertainment 1998

1-shot, 48pg. 4.95

ZAANAN
Mainstream Comics

1 The Collectio,I:Zaanan 2.50

ZEN INTERGALACTIC NINJA
Archie 1992

1 Rumble in the Rain Forest prequel,inc.poster. 2.00
2 Rumble in Rain Forest #1. . . . . . 2.00
3 Rumble in Rain Forest #2. . . . . . 2.00

Entity Comics 1994

0 Chromium (c),JaL(c). 4.00
1 Joe Orbeta 2.50
1a Platinum Edition 20.00
2 Deluxe Edition w/card. 4.95
3 V:Rawhead. 3.00
4 thru 7 . . . . @3.25
GN A Fire Upon The Earth 12.95

[2nd Series]

1 Joe Orbeta 4.95
2 . . . . 4.95
3 thru 5 . . . . @2.50

Zen Comics 1998

Commemorative Ed. #1 . . . . 5.95

ZEN INTERGALACTIC NINJA
Studio Chikara 1999

1 . . . . 3.95
1 variant (c). 9.95
2 . . . . 3.95
3 . . . . 3.95

ZEN/NIRA X: HELLSPACE
Zen Comics

1 . . . . 2.95

ZEN: NOVELLA
Eternity Comics

1 thru 8 . . . . @2.95

ZEN SPECIALS
Eternity

Spring#1 V:Lord Contaminous 2.50
April Fools#1 parody issue 2.50
Color Spec.#0 . . . . 3.50

ZEN: WARRIOR
Eternity Comics 1994

1 vicious video game. 3.00

ZENITH PHASE II
Fleetway

1 thru 2 . . . . @2.00

ZERO PATROL
Continuity 1984–90

1 EM,NA,O&I:Megalith. 2.50
2 EM,NA 2.00
3 EM,NA,I:Shaman 2.00
4 EM,NA 2.00
5 EM 2.00
6 thru 8 EM . . . . @2.00

ZERO TOLERANCE
First 1990–91

1 TV 3.50
2 TV 3.00
3 TV 2.25
4 TV 2.25

ZOONIVERSE
Eclipse 1986–87

1 I:Kren Patrol,wrap-around(c). . . . 2.00
2 . . . . 2.00
3 . . . . 2.00
4 V:Wedge City 2.00
5 Spak vs. Agent Ty-rote 2.00
6 last issue 2.00

ZORRO
Dell Publ. Co. 1959–61

1 thru 8, see Dell 4-Color
8 . . . . 100.00
9 . . . . 85.00
10 . . . . 85.00
11 . . . . 85.00
12 ATh 100.00
13 . . . . 75.00
14 . . . . 75.00
15 . . . . 75.00

ZORRO
Gold Key 1966–68

1 Rep. 75.00
2 Rep. 50.00
3 Rep. 50.00
4 Rep. 50.00
5 Rep. 50.00
6 Rep. 50.00
7 Rep. 50.00
8 Rep. 50.00
9 Rep. 50.00

ZORRO
Topps Nov., 1993

0 BSf(c),DMG(s), came bagged with Jurassic Park Raptor #1 and Teenagents #4 . . . . 4.00
1 DMG(s),V:Machete 3.00
2 DMG(s) 5.00
3 DMG(s) I:Lady Rawhide 15.00
4 MGr(c),DMG(s),V:Moonstalker . . 2.50
5 MGr,DMG(s),V:Moonstalker 2.50
6 A:Lady Rawhide 8.00
7 A:Lady Rawhide 7.00
8 MGr(c),DMG(s). 3.00
9 A:Lady Rawhide 4.00
10 A:Lady Rawhide 4.50
11 A:Lady Rawhide. 8.00

ZOT!
Eclipse 1984–85

1 by Scott McCloud 7.00
2 . . . . 3.00
3 Art and Soul 3.00
4 Assault on Castle Dekko. 3.00
5 Sirius Business. 3.00

Zot #6
© Eclipse

6 It's always darkest 2.00
7 Common Ground 2.50
8 Through the Door 2.00
9 Gorilla Warfare 2.50
10 T.K.O. The Final Round 2.00
10a B&W 6.00
10b 2nd printing 2.50
Original Zot! Book 1 . . . . 9.95
Book One TPB 24.95
(Changed to B & W)

ZOT!
Kitchen Sink

Book One TPB 24.95
Book One HC signed & numbered 55.00

B&W COMICS

A1

Atomeka Press 1989–92

1 BWs,A:Flaming Carrot,Mr.X. . . . 10.00
2 BWs . . . 9.75
3 . . . 9.75
4 . . . 5.95
5 . . . 6.95
6a . . . 4.95

AARDWOLF

Aardwolf 1994

1 DC,GM(c) . . . 2.95
1a Certificate ed. signed . . . 12.00
2 World Toughest Milkman . . . 2.95
3 R.Block(s),O:Aardwolf . . . 2.95

A.B.C. WARRIORS

Fleetway/Quality

1 thru 8 . . . @2.00

ABSOLUTE ZERO

Antarctic Press 1995

1 . . . 2.95
2 Rooftop,Athena . . . 2.95
3 Stan Sakai . . . 3.50
4 3-D Man and Kirby . . . 2.95
5 & 6 Super Powers . . . @2.95

AC ANNUAL

Aircel 1990

1 . . . 3.95
2 Based on 1940's heroes . . . 5.00
3 F:GoldenAge Heroes . . . 3.50
4 F:Sentinels of Justice . . . 3.95

ACE COMICS PRESENTS

Ace 1987

1 thru 7 . . . @2.00

ACE McCOY

ACG Comics 1999

1 FF . . . 2.95
2 FF, SD . . . 2.95
3 FF . . . 2.95
4 FF . . . 2.95

ACES

Eclipse 1988

1 thru 5, mag. size . . . @2.95

ACG'S AMAZING COMICS

ACG Comics 2000

1 (of 4) F:Dragon Lady . . . 2.95
2 thru 5 . . . @2.95

ACHILLES STORM

Brainstorm 1997

1 by Sandra Chang . . . 2.95
1a nude cover . . . 2.95

ACHILLES STORM: DARK SECRET

Brainstorm 1997

1 by Sandra Chang . . . 2.95
1 nude cover edition . . . 3.95
2 . . . 2.95
2a nude cover edition . . . 2.95
2 luxury edition . . . 5.00

ACME

Fandom House

1 thru 9 . . . @2.00

ACOLYTE CHRONICLES

Azure Press 1995

1 I:Korath . . . 2.95
2 V:Korath . . . 2.95

A COP CALLED TRACY

ACG Comics 1998

1 by Chester Gould . . . 2.95
2 thru 8 . . . @2.95
9 . . . 2.95
9a deluxe . . . 2.95
10 thru 18 . . . @2.95
19 64-page . . . 5.95
Ann.#1 . . . 2.95

ACTION FORCE

Lightning 1987

1 . . . 2.00

ACTION GIRL COMICS

Slave Labor Graphics 1994

1 thru 7 . . . @2.75
1 thru 7, later printings . . . @2.75
8 thru 12 . . . @2.95
13 Halloween issue . . . 2.95
14 F:Elizabeth Lavin . . . 2.95
15 . . . 2.95
16 GoGo Gang, pt.1 . . . 2.75
17 GoGo Gang, pt.2 . . . 2.75
18 Blue Monday . . . 2.95
19 Halloween . . . 2.95

ADAM AND EVE A.D.

Bam

1 . . . 3.00
2 thru 10 . . . @2.00

ADDAM OMEGA

Antarctic Press 1997

1 (of 4) by Bill Hughes . . . 2.95
2 thru 4 . . . @2.95

ADOLESCENT RADIOACTIVE BLACK-BELT HAMSTERS

Eclipse

1 I:Bruce,Chuck,Jackie,Clint . . . 2.50
1a 2nd printing . . . 2.00
2 A parody of a parody . . . 2.00
3 I:Bad Gerbil . . . 2.00
4 A:Heap (3-D),Abusement Park . . 2.00
5 Abusement Park #2 . . . 2.00
6 SK,Abusement Park #3 . . . 2.00
7 SK,V:Toe-Jam Monsters . . . 2.00
8 SK . . . 2.00
9 All-Jam last issue . . . 2.00

[2nd Series]

Parody Press

1 . . . 2.50
2 Hamsters Go Hollywood . . . 2.50

Adventures Into the Unknown #1
© A Plus Comics

ADVENTURES INTO THE UNKNOWN

A Plus Comics 1990

1 AW,WW, rep. classic horror . . . 2.95
2 AW . . . 2.95
3 AW . . . 2.95
Halloween Spec. reps. Charlton & American Comics GroupHorror. 2.50

ACG Comics 1997

1 FF,AW, Charlton comics reprint. . 2.95

ADVENTURERS

Aircel/Adventure Publ.

0 Origin Issue . . . 2.50
1 with Skeleton . . . 5.00
1a Revised cover . . . 3.00
1b 2nd printing . . . 2.00
2 Peter Hsu (c) . . . 2.50
3 Peter Hsu (c) . . . 2.50
4 Peter Hsu (c) . . . 2.00
5 Peter Hsu (c) . . . 2.00
6 Peter Hsu (c) . . . 2.00
7 thru 9 . . . @2.00

ADVENTURERS BOOK II

Adventure Publ.

0 O:Man Gods . . . 2.00
1 . . . 2.00
2 thru 9 . . . @2.00

ADVENTURERS BOOK III

1A Lim.(c)Ian McCaig . . . 2.25
1B Reg.(c)Mitch Foust . . . 2.25
2 thru 6 . . . @2.25

ADVENTURES OF BARRY WEEN BOY GENIUS 2.0
Oni Press 2000

1 by Judd Winick 2.95
2 . . . . 2.95
3 . . . . 2.95
TPB 8.95

ADVENTURES OF CHRISSY CLAWS, THE
Heroic 1991

1 thru 2 . . . . @3.25

ADVENTURES OF CHUK THE BARBARIC
White Wolf

1 & 2 . . . . @1.25

ADVENTURES OF LUTHER ARKWRIGHT
Valkyrie Press 1987–89

1 thru 9 . . . . @2.25
See Also: Dark Horse section

ADVENTURES OF MR. PYRIDINE
Fantagraphics

1 . . . . 2.25

ADVENTURES OF THE AEROBIC DUO
Lost Cause Productions

1 thru 3 . . . . @2.25
4 Gopher Quest. 2.25
5 V:Stupid Guy 2.25

ADVENTURES OF THEOWN
Pyramid 1986

1 thru 3, Limited series . . . . @1.75

AESOP'S FABLES
Fantagraphics

1 Selection of Fables. 2.25
2 Selection of Fables. 2.25
3 inc. Boy who cried wolf. 2.25

AETOS
Hall of Heroes Jan., 1997

1 by Dan Parsons 2.50
1 variant cover. 4.00
2 . . . . 2.50

AETOS THE EAGLE
Ground Zero Aug., 1997

1 (of 3) by Dan Parsons. 3.00
2 . . . . 3.00
3 concl. 3.00

AETOS 2: CHILDREN OF THE GRAVES
Orpahn Underground 1995

1 A:Nightmare 2.50

AGENT UNKNOWN
Renegade

1 thru 3 . . . . @2.00

Agent Unknown #2
© Renegade

AGE OF HEROES, THE
Halloween Comics 1996

1 JHI 2.95
1A signed 2.95
2 JHI 2.95
2A signed 2.95

AGONY ACRES
AA2 Entertainment

1 thru 3 . . . . @2.50
4 and 5 . . . . @2.95

AIRCEL

1 Graphic Novel year 1 . . . . 6.95

AIRFIGHTERS CLASSICS
Eclipse

1 O:Airboy,rep.Air Fighters#2. . . . . 3.00
2 rep.Old Airboy appearances 3.00
3 thru 6 . . . . @3.95

AIRMEN
Mansion Comics

1 I:Airmen 2.50

AIRWAVES
Caliber 1990

1 Radio Security 2.50
2 A:Paisley,Ganja 2.50
3 Formation of Rebel Alliance 2.50
4 Big Annie,pt. 1 . . . . 2.50
5 Big Annie,pt 2. . . . . 2.50

AKIKO
Sirius 1996

1 MCi 6.50
2 MCi 4.00
3 thru 17 MCi. . . . . @3.00
18 Alia Rellapor, concl. 3.00
19 new story, pt.1 . . . . 3.00
20 F:Mr. Beeba. 3.00
21 On the Road 3.00
22 . . . . 3.00
23 space station Fognon-6 . . . . 3.00
24 escape spaceship 3.00
25 Done in One, 32pg. 3.00
26 reunited on planet Smoo 2.50
27 MCi,Bornstone's Elixir, pt.2 . . . . 2.50
28 MCi,Bornstone's Elixir, pt.3 . . . . 2.50
29 MCi,Bornstone's Elixir, pt.4 . . . . 2.50
30 MCi,Bornstone's Elixir, pt.5 . . . . 2.50
31 MCi,Bornstone's Elixir, concl. . . . 2.50
32 MCi,On Planet Earth, pt.1 . . . . . 2.50
33 MCi,On Planet Earth, pt.2 . . . . . 2.50
34 MCi,On Planet Earth, pt.3 . . . . . 2.50
35 Moonshopping, pt.1 . . . . 2.50
36 Moonshopping, pt.2 . . . . 2.95
37 Moonshopping, pt.3 . . . . 2.50
38 Moonshopping, pt.4 . . . . 2.50
39 Big Bag of This and That 2.95
40 . . . . 2.95
41 . . . . 2.95
TPB Vol. 1 rep. #1–#6 . . . . 14.95
TPB Vol. 2 rep. #8–#13. . . . . 11.95
TPB Vol. 3 rep. #14–#18. . . . . 11.95
TPB Vol. 4 rep. #19–#24. . . . . 14.95
HC Vol. 1 . . . . 20.00
GN Akiko on the Planet Smoo . . . 14.95
Spec. Akiko on the Planet Smoo. . . 3.50

ALBEDO
Thoughts & Images

0 white cover, yellow drawing table Blade Runner 20.00
0a white(c) 15.00
0b blue(c),1st ptg. 12.00
0c blue(c),2nd ptg 10.00
0d blue(c),3rd ptg 5.00
0e Photo(c),4th ptg.,inc. extra pages. 3.00
1 SS,I:Nilson Groundthumper, dull red cover 7.00
1a bright red cover 6.00
2 SS,I:Usagi Yojimbo 5.00
3 SS,Erma, Usagi 4.00
4 SS,Usagi 6.00
5 Nelson Groundthumper. 5.00
6 Erma, High Orbit. 4.00
7 . . . . 2.00
8 Erna Feldna 2.00
9 High Orbit,Harvest Venture 2.00
10 thru 14 . . . . @2.00

ALBEDO VOL. II
Anarctic Press 1991–93

1 New Erma Story 2.50
2 E.D.F. HQ. 2.50
3 Birth of Erma's Child. 2.50
4 Non action issue. 2.50
5 The Outworlds 2.50
6 War preparations 2.50
7 Ekosiak in Anarchy. 2.50
8 EDF High Command 2.50
Spec. Color 3.00

VOL. III

1 . . . . 3.50

ALIEN ENCOUNTERS
Fantagor

1 . . . . 1.25

ALIEN FIRE
Kitchen Sink Press 1987

1 Eric Vincent art. 3.50
2 Eric Vincent art. 2.50
3 Eric Vincent art. 2.00

ALIEN NATION: A BREED APART
Adventure Comics 1990

1 Friar Kaddish 3.00
2 . . . . 2.50
3 The `Vampires' Busted 2.50
4 Final Issue 2.50

ALIEN NATION: THE FIRSTCOMERS
Adventure Comics 1991

1 New Mini-series 2.50
2 Assassin. 2.50
3 Search for Saucer 2.50
4 Final Issue 2.50

ALIEN NATION: THE PUBLIC ENEMY
Adventure Comics 1991

1 'Before the Fall' 2.50
2 Earth & Wehlnistrata. 2.50
3 Killer on the Loose 2.50

ALIEN NATION: THE SKIN TRADE
Adventure Comics 1991

1 'Case of the Missing Milksop' . . . 2.50
2 'To Live And Die in L.A' 2.50
3 A:Dr. Jekyll. 2.50
4 D.Methoraphan Exposed 2.50

Alien Nation: The Spartans #2
© Adventure Comics

ALIEN NATION: THE SPARTANS
Adventure Comics

1 JT/DPo,Yellow wrap 4.00
1a JT/DPo,Green wrap 4.00
1b JT/DPo,Pink wrap. 4.00
1c JT/DPo,blue wrap 4.00
1d LTD collectors edition 7.00
2 JT,A:Ruth Lawrence 2.50
3 JT/SM,Spartians. 2.50
4 JT/SM,conclusion 2.50

ALL-PRO SPORTS
All Pro Sports

1 Unauthorized Bio-Bo Jackson. . . 2.50
2 Unauthorized Bio-Joe Montana. . 2.50

ALLURA AND THE CYBERANGELS
Avatar Press 1998

Spec.#1 by Bill Maus 3.95
Spec.#1 nude cover 6.00

ALLY
Ally Winsor Productions 1995

1 I&O: Ally. 2.95
2 and 3 . . . . @2.95

ALTERNATE HEROES
Prelude Graphics

1 and 2 . . . . @2.00

AMAZING COMICS PREMIERES

1 thru 9 . . . . @2.00

AMAZING CYNICALMAN
Eclipse

1 . . . . 1.50

AMAZON WOMAN
Fantaco

Christmas Spec. 4.95
Beach Party 5.95
Amazing Colossal Amazon Woman #1 . . . . 7.95
Amazing Colossal Amazon Album 12.95
Jungle Annual #1 . . . . 5.95
Jungle Album 9.95
TPB Amazon Woman: The Art of Tom Simonton 9.95
TPB Amazon Woman, deluxe 19.95
Spec. Invaders of Terror 5.95
TPB Book One by Tom Simonton . 14.95
TPB Book Two The Curse of the Amazon 14.95
HC, limited 50.00
HC, limited, signed, numbered . . . 75.00
1-shot Attack of the Amazon Girls, cont. nudity 4.95

AMAZONS GONZANGAS: BAD GIRLS OF THE JUNGLE
Academy Comics 1995

0 Rites of passage(Jason Waltrip) . 3.50

AMERICAN ANNIHILATOR
Night Realm Publishing

0 V:Synthetic Assassin 1.85

AMERICAN SPLENDOR
Harvey Bekar 1976–90

1 thru 15 . . . . @3.25

Tundra 1991

16 . . . . 3.95

AMERICAN WOMAN
Antarctic Press 1998

1 by Brian Denham & Richard Stockton. 2.95

AMUSING STORIES
Blackthorne

1 thru 3 . . . . @2.00

ANATOMIC BOMBS
Brainstorm 1998

1 Angelissa, by Mike James 2.95
1a Angelissa, nude cover edition . . 3.95
1 Bad Tabitha, by Mike James. . . . 2.95
1a Bad Tabitha, photo cover edition 3.95

ANGEL GIRL
Angel Entertainment 1997

0 by David Campiti & Al Rio. 2.95
1 by David Campiti & Richard Fraga 2.95
1 deluxe 5.95
1 Virgin nude cover 5.00
1 Nude Manga cover. 5.00
1 Nude Platinum cover 8.00
Spec. #1 Angels Illustrated Swimsuit Special. 5.00
Spec. #1 Swimsuit Special, Nude Oily Angels (c) 5.00
1-shot Against All Evil. 2.95
1-shot Against All Evil, nude cover . 2.95
1-shot Before the Wings 2.95
1-shot Before the Wings, nude cover A 2.95
1-shot Before the Wings, nude cover B 2.95
1-shot Demonworld, by Ellis Bell & Mark Kuettner 2.95
1-shot Doomsday, by Ellis Bell & Mark Kuettner 3.00

ANGEL GIRL: HEAVEN SENT
Angel Entertainment 1997

0 by David Campiti & Al Rio. 2.95
0 Virgin nude. 5.00
0 nude platinum cover 12.00
1 . . . . 3.00
1 nude Michelle in Hell cover. 4.00

ANGEL OF DEATH
Innovation

1 thru 4 . . . . @2.25

ANIMAL MYSTIC
Cry For Dawn/Sirus 1993–95

1 DOe 32.00
1a variant, signed 42.00
1b 2nd printing, new (c). 7.00
2 I:Klor 30.00
2a 2nd printing, new (c). 6.00
3 . . . . 12.00
3a 2nd printing 5.00
4 last issue 4.00
4a special 15.00
TPB DOe 14.95

ANIMAL MYSTIC: KLOR
Sirius 1999

1 (of 3) DOe 2.95
2 DOe 2.95
3 DOe, conclusion. 2.95

ANIMERICA
Viz Comics

1 F:Bubble Gum Crisis 2.95
2 F:Bubble Gum Crisis 2.95
3 F:Bubble Gum Crisis 2.95

ANIMERICA EXTRA
Viz Communications 1998

VOL 1

1 & 2. . . . . @4.95

VOL 2, 1998

1 thru 11 . . . . @4.95

VOL 3

1 thru 11 . . . . @4.95

ANTARES CIRCLE
Antarctic Press

1 . . . . 1.75
2 . . . . 1.75

ANUBIS
Unicorn Books

1 I:Anubis 2.50
2 F:Anubis. 2.50
3 . . . . 2.50

Didactic Chocolate Press

3 by Scott Berwanger 2.75
4 thru 6 . . . . @2.75

Adventure Comics

7 "Sandy's Plight" 2.75
8 . . . . 2.95

A-OK #3
© Antarctic Press

A-OK
Antarctic Press

1 Ninja H.S. spin-off series 2.50
2 F:Paul,Moniko,James 2.50
3 Confrontation 2.50
4 . . . . 2.50

APATHY KAT
Entity 1995

1 . . . . 2.75
1 signed, numbered. 9.95
1 2nd printing 2.75
2 . . . . 2.75
2 2nd printing 2.75
3 & 4 . . . . 2.75
TPB Kollection #1. . . . . 7.95

APE CITY
Adventure Comics

1 Monkey Business 3.00
2 thru 4 . . . . @2.50

APPARITION, THE
Caliber

1 thru 4 . . . . @2.95
5 "Black Clouds" 2.95

APPLESEED
Eclipse

1 MSh,rep. Japanese comic 9.00
2 MSh,arrival in Olympus City 6.00
3 MSh,Olympus City politics 5.00
4 MSh,V:Director 5.00
5 MSh,Deunan vs. Chiffon. 5.00

Book Two

1 MSh,AAd(c),Olympus City 4.00
2 MSh,AAd(c),Hitomi vs.EswatUnit 3.50
3 MSh,AAd(c),Deunan vs.Gaia . . . 3.50
4 MSh,AAd(c),V:Robot Spiders . . . 3.50
5 MSh,AAd(c),Hitome vs.Gaia 3.50

Book Three

1 MSh,Brigreos vs.Biodroid 5.00
2 MSh,V:Cuban Navy 3.50
3 MSh,`Benandanti' 3.50
4 MSh,V:Renegade biodroid 3.50
5 MSh 3.50

Book Four 1990

1 MSh,V:Munma Terrorists. 3.50
2 MSh,V:Drug-crazed Munma 3.50
3 Msh,V:Munma Drug Addicts 3.50
4 MSh,Deunan vs. Pani. 3.50

AQUA KNIGHT
Viz Communications 2000

1 (of 6) by Yukito Kishiro 3.50
2 thru 6 . . . . @3.50

PART 2

#1 (of 5). 3.50

AQUARIUM
CPM Manga 2000

1 by Tomoko Taniguchi 2.95
2 thru 6 . . . . @2.95

ARAMIS WEEKLY

1 mini-series 2.00
2 . . . . 2.00
3 . . . . 2.00

AREA 88
Eclipse

1 I:Shin Kazama 3.00
1a 2nd printing 1.50
2 Dangerous Mission. 2.00
2a 2nd printing 1.50
3 O:Shin,Paris '78 . . . . 2.00
4 thru 8 . . . . @2.00
9 thru 39 . . . . @1.50
40 . . . . 1.75
41 . . . . 1.75
42 . . . . 2.00

ARGONAUTS
Eternity

1 thru 5 . . . . @2.00

ARGOSY
Caliber

1 `Walker' vs. Myth Beasts 2.50

ARIK KHAN
A Plus Comics

1 I:Arik Khan 2.50
2 . . . . 2.50

ACG Comics 1998

1 by Frank Reyes, heroic fantasy . 2.95

ARISTOCRATIC EXTRA-TERRESTRIAL TIME-TRAVELING THIEVES
Fictioneer Books

1 V:IRS 3.00
2 V:Realty 1.75
3 V:MDM. 1.75
4 thru 12 . . . . @1.75

ARIZONA: A SIMPLE HORROR
London Night/ EH Productions 1998

1 (of 3) by Joe Kennedy & Jerry Beck 3.00
1a nude cover 6.00
2 double sized 3.00
2a nude cover 6.00
3 . . . . 3.00
3a nude cover 6.00
1-shot Wild at Heart, signed alternate cover 10.00

A.R.M.
Adventure Comics 1990

1 Larry Niven adapt. Death by Ecstasy,pt.1 . . . . 2.50
2 Death by Ecstasy,pt.2. . . . . 2.50
3 Death by Ecstasy,pt.3. . . . . 2.50

ARROW SPOTLIGHT
Arrow Comics 1998–99

Advendures of Simone & Ajax 2.95
Allison Chains 2.95
Descendants of Toshin 2.95
Max Velocity, by Jack Snider 2.95
Red Vengeance, by Chris Kemple . 2.95
Talonback. 2.95

ARSENIC LULLABY
A Silent Comics 1999

Spec. May '99 . . . . 2.50
Spec. July '99. . . . . 2.50
Spec. Sept.'99 . . . . 2.50
Spec. Jan. 2000 . . . . 2.50
8 thru 11 . . . . @2.50
TPB The Devil Your Neighbor 12.99

ASHEN VICTOR
Viz Communications 1998

1 (of 4) by Yukito Kishiro 2.95
2 thru 4 concl. . . . . @2.95
TPB 14.95

ASHES
Caliber 1990–91

1 thru 6 . . . . @2.50

ASHLEY DUST
Knight Press 1995

1 thru 3 . . . . @2.50
4 V:Allister Crowley 2.50
5 Metaphysical Adventure 2.50

ASRIAL VS. CHEETAH
Antarctic Press 1995–96

1 & 2 Ninja High School Gold Digger x-over . . . . @2.95

ASSASSINETTE
Pocket Change Comics

1 thru 3 . . . . @2.50
4 Psychic Realm 2.50
5 V:Nemesis 2.50
6 The Second Coming,pt.2 . . . . . . 2.50
7 The Second Coming,pt.3 . . . . . . 2.50
8 V:Crazy Actor 2.50

9 . . . . 2.50
10 final issue. 2.50
Spec. Assassinette Returns 2.50
Spec. Assassinette Violated 2.50
Deluxe Assassinette Violated 4.25

ASSASSINETTE: HARDCORE

Pocket Change Comics

1 By Shadow Slasher Team. 2.50
2 V:Bolero 2.50

ASTOUNDING SPACE THRILLS

Day One Comics 1998

1 by Steve Conley, The Codex Reckoning, pt.1 . . . . 2.95
2 Bros. Hildebrandt (c). 2.95
3 Aspects of Iron 2.95
4 The Robot Murders. 2.95
5 Gordo returns. 2.95

ASTRONAUTS IN TROUBLE: LIVE FROM THE MOON

Gun Dog Comics 1999

1 (of 5) 2.95
2 thru 5 . . . . @2.95

AIT Comics 1999

Spec.#1 Cool Ed's 2.95
Spec.#1 CAd, One Shot, One Beer. 7.95

ASTRONAUTS IN TROUBLE: SPACE: 1959

AIT/Planetlar 2000

1 (of 3) by Larry Young, CAd 2.95
2 . . . . 2.95
3 . . . . 2.95
TPB 7.95

ATHENA

A.M. Works

7 thru 14 by Dean Hsieh . . . . . . @2.95
TPB Vol. 1 . . . . 14.95
TPB Vol. 2 . . . . 15.95

Atomic Man #1
© Blackthorne

ATOMIC COMICS

1 . . . . 1.50
Becomes:

MARK I

ATOMIC MAN

Blackthrone

1 . . . . 3.00
2 . . . . 2.00
3 . . . . 1.75

ATOMIC MOUSE

A Plus Comics 1990

1 A:Atomic Bunny 2.50

ATOMIC OVERDRIVE

Caliber

1 by Dave Darrigo & PGr. 2.95
2 1950s Sci-Fi,Horror,Humor 2.95
3 . . . . 2.95

A TRAVELLER'S TALE

Antarctic Press

1 I:Goshin the Traveller 2.50
2 . . . . 2.50

ATOMIC CITY TALES

Kitchen Sink

1 thru 4 by Jay Stephens . . . . . . @3.50
TPB Vol. 1 Go Power 12.95
TPB Vol. 1 signed & numbered . . . 20.95

ATTACK OF THE MUTANT MONSTERS

A Plus Comics

1 SD,rep.Gorgo(Kegor) 2.50

AUGUST

Arrow Comics 1998

1 by Scott Rosema 2.95
2 thru 4 . . . . @2.95

AUTUMN

Caliber Press 1995

1 I:James Turell. 2.95
GN 7"x10" 12.95

AVALON

Harrier

1 thru 3 . . . . 1.50

AVANT GUARD

Day 1 Comics

1 thru 4 F:Feedback 2.50

AVATARS

Avatar Press 1998

1 (of 2) by Gregory & Holaso 3.95
1a nude cover 6.00
2 F:Pandora & Atlas 3.50
2a nude cover 6.00

AV IN 3D

Aardvark–Vanaheim

1 Color,A:FlamingCarot 6.00

AVELON

Kenzer & Company 1998

1 . . . . 2.95
2 thru 5 . . . . @2.95
6 thru 11 Legacy of Thrain . . . . . @2.95
11 & 12 Heir to Legend . . . . @2.95

AVENUE X

Innovation

1 Based on NY radio drama 2.50

Purple Spiral

3 signed & numbered 3.00

AWAKENING COMICS

Awakening Comics 1997

1 by Steve Peters 3.50
2 . . . . 3.50
3 . . . . 2.95
4 . . . . 2.95

Awakening Comics 1999

1 by Steve Peters 3.50
Spec. Millennium Bug Fever 2.95

AWESOME COMICS

1 thru 3 . . . . @2.00

AWESOME

Awesome Entertainment

1 anthology, partial color. 2.95

AXED FILES, THE

Entity Comics

1 X-Files Parody 2.50
1 3rd printing, parody. 2.75

B-MOVIE PRESENTS

B-Movie Comics

1 . . . . 1.70
2 . . . . 1.70
3 Tasma, Queen of the Jungle. . . . 1.70
4 . . . . 1.70

BABES OF AREA 51

Blatant Comics 1997

1 . . . . 2.95
1a Nude Alien Autopsy cover 9.95
1b Nude Roswell Crash cover 9.95

BABY ANGEL X

Brainstorm 1996

1 . . . . 2.95
2 . . . . 2.95
3 gold edition. 5.00
3a signed edition 10.00

BABY ANGEL X: SCORCHED EARTH

Brainstorm 1997

1 by Scott Harrison 2.95
1a nude cover 2.95
2 . . . . 2.95
2a nude cover 2.95

BABYLON CRUSH

Boneyard Press

1 I:Babylon Crush 2.95
2 V:A Gang 2.95
3 V:Mafiaso Brothers 2.95
4 & 5 . . . . @2.95

CFD
6 & 7 . . . . @3.95

Boneyard 1998
1-shot Buddha, F:Lesbian dominatrix vigilante 4.95
Spec. Babylon Bondage Christmas. 2.95
Spec. Bondage nude (c). 3.95
Spec. Girlfriends. 2.95
Spec. Girlfriends, nude (c) 3.95
Spec. The Last Shepherd 2.95
Spec. The Last Shepherd, nude(c) . 4.95

BAD APPLES
High Impact Jan. 1997
1 . . . . 2.95
1 Bad Candies cover 9.95
2 . . . . 2.95
2 deluxe 15.00
3 by Billy Patton 2.95
3 deluxe adult cover 10.00

ABC Studios 1999
VOL 2
1 RCI. 3.00
1a deluxe variant. 8.00
1b adult manga 8.00
2 . . . . 3.00
2 nude manga ed. 8.00

VOL 3
1 by Greg Narvasa 3.00
1a manga nude cover 8.00
1b gold manga 10.00

BAD APPLES: HIGH EXPECTATIONS
ABC Studios 1999
1 . . . . 3.00
1a Beach Fun (c). 8.00
2 . . . . 3.00
2a deluxe 8.00

BAKER STREET
(Prev. color)
Caliber
3 . . . . 3.25
4 . . . . 2.00
5 Children of the Night Pt.1 . . . . . . 2.00
6 Children of the Night Pt.2 . . . . . . 2.00
7 thru 10 Children of the Night pt.3–pt.6 . . . . @2.50

BAKER ST.: GRAPHITTI
Caliber
1 `Elemenary, My Dear' 2.50

BALANCE OF POWER
MU Press 1990–91
1 thru 4 . . . . @2.50

BALLAD OF UTOPIA
Black Daze 2000
1 by Barry Buchanan & Mike Hoffman 2.95
2 thru 5 . . . . @2.95

BANDY MAN, THE
Caliber 1996
1 SPr,CAd 2.95
2 SPr,CAd,JIT 2.95
3 SPr,CAd,JIT, conclusion 2.95
HC 96pg. 19.95
HC Deluxe 39.95

Baoh #5
© Viz Communications

BAOH
Viz 1990
1 thru 8 . . . . @2.95
GN V:Juda Laboratory 14.95

BARABBAS
Slave Labor
1 . . . . 4.50
2 thru 4 . . . . @1.50

BARBARIANS
ACG Comics
1 by Jeff Jones, Mike Kaluta, Wayne Howard. 2.95
2 WW 2.95

BARBARIC TALES
Pyramid
1 . . . . 3.00
2 and 3 . . . . @1.70

BASEBALL SUPERSTARS
Revolutionary
1 Nolan Ryan 2.50

BATTLE ANGEL ALITA
Viz 1992
1 I:Daisuka,Alita 8.00
2 Alita becomes warrior 6.00
3 A:Daiuke,V:Cyborg 4.00
4 Alita/Cyborg,A:Makaku 4.00
5 The Bounty Hunters Bar 4.00
6 Confrontation 4.00
7 Underground Sewers,A:Fang . . . 3.00
8 & 9 . . . . @2.75

Part Two 1993
1 V:Zapan 3.00
2 V:Zapan 3.00
3 F:Ido 2.75
4 thru 7 V:Zapan . . . . @2.75
TPB Killing Angel 15.95

Part Three 1993
1 thru 5 . . . . @2.75
6 . . . . 5.00
7 thru 13 . . . . @2.75

Part Four 1994
1 thru 7 . . . . @2.75

Part Five 1995
1 thru 6 . . . . @2.75
7 . . . . 2.95

Part Six 1995–96
1 thru 8 YuK. . . . . @2.95
TPB Angel of Chaos. 15.95

Part Seven Oct., 1996
1 thru 8 YuK. . . . . @2.95

Part Eight 1997
1 thru 9 YuK. . . . . @2.95
TPB Vol. 2 Tears of an Angel 15.95
TPB Vol. 4 Angel of Victory. 15.95
TPB Vol. 5 . . . . 15.95
TPB Vol. 6 Angel of Death 15.95
TPB Vol. 7 Angel of Chaos 15.95
TPB Vol. 8 Fallen Angel 15.95
TPB Vol. 9 Angel's Ascension. . . . 16.95

BATTLE ARMOR
Eternity
1 thru 4 . . . . @2.00

BATTLE BEASTS
Blackthorne
1 thru 4 . . . . @1.50

BATTLEGROUND EARTH
Best Comics 1996
1 . . . . 2.50
2 . . . . 2.50
3 "Destiny Quest: The Vengeance" concl. 2.50
4 V:Conjura 2.50
5 "The Pit of Black Death" 2.50

BATTLETECH
(Prev. Color)
7 thru 12 . . . . @1.75
Ann.#1 . . . . 4.50

BATTRON
NEC
1 WWII story 2.75
2 WWII contd. 2.75

BEAST WARRIOR OF SHAOLIN
1 thru 5 . . . . @2.00

THE BEATLES EXPERIENCE
Revolutionary
1 Beatles 1960's 3.00
2 Beatles 1964-1966 . . . . 2.50
3 . . . . 2.50
4 Abbey Road, Let it be. 2.50
5 The Solo Years. 2.50
6 Paul McCartney & Wings 2.50
7 The Murder of John Lennon 2.50
8 To 1992, final issue. 2.50

BECK AND CAUL
Gauntlet
1 I:Beck and Caul 2.95
2 thru 6 . . . . @2.95
Ann.#1 A Single Step 3.50

BERZERKER
Gauntlet (Caliber)
1 thru 6 . . . . @2.95

BEST OF THE WEST
AC Comics 1998

1 F:Durango Kid 4.95
2 F:The Haunted Horseman 4.95
3 F:The Haunted Horseman 4.95
4 F:Roy Rogers, 44-page 5.95
5 F:Durango Kid 5.95
6 F:Durango Kid 5.95
7 F:Monte Hale 5.95
8 . . . . 5.95
9 F:Sunset Carson 5.95
10 F:Durango Kid 5.95
11 F:Black Diamond 5.95
12 F:Latigo Kid 5.95
13 F:The Durango Kid 5.95
14 F:Haunted Horseman. 5.95
15 F:Roy Rogers 5.95
16 O:The Whip 5.95

BETHANY THE VAMPFIRE
Brainstorm Dec., 1997

0 O:Bethany 2.95
0a nude cover 3.95
1 by Holly Galightly 2.95
1 luxury edition 5.00
2 . . . . 2.95
2a nude cover 3.95
3 . . . . 2.95
3a nude cover 3.95
3b Photo cover 3.95

BEYOND MARS
Blackthorne

1 thru 5 . . . . @2.00

BIG BLACK KISS
Vortex

3 HC some color 3.75

BIG NUMBERS

1 BSz 6.00
2 BSz 5.50

BILL THE BULL
Boneyard Press

1 I:Bill the Bull 2.95
2 & 3 For Hire . . . . @2.95

BILLY DOGMA
Millennium April, 1997

1 by Dean Haspiel. 2.95
1 signed print edition 4.95
2 . . . . 2.95
3 . . . . 2.95
4 They Found A Sawed-Off in
My Afro 2.95

BILLY NGUYEN PRIVATE EYE
Caliber 1990

1 . . . . 2.00
1a 2nd Printing 2.00
2 thru 6 . . . . @2.00

BIO-BOOSTER ARMOR GUYVER
Viz

Part II

1 thru 3 F:Sho . . . . @2.75
4 V:Enzyme II 2.75
5 Sho VS Enzyme II 2.75
6 Final Issue 2.75

Part III

1 Sho Unconscious 2.75
2 V:Zoanoids 2.75
3 F:Murahani 2.75
4 . . . . 2.75
5 . . . . 2.75
6 V:Commando Guyver 2.75
7 Sho to the rescue 2.75

Part Four

1 thru 7 . . . . @2.95

Part Five

1 thru 7 . . . . @2.95

Part Six Dec., 1996

1 thru 6 by Yoshiki Takaya . . . . . @2.95
TPB Vol. 1 . . . . 15.95
TPB Vol. 2 Revenge of Chronos . . 15.95
TPB Vol. 4 Escape From Chronos 15.95
TPB Vol. 5 Guyver Reborn 15.95
TPB Vol. 6 Heart of Chronos. 15.95
TPB Vol. 7 Armageddon 15.95

Bizarre Heroes #1
© Kitchen Sink

BIZARRE HEROES
Kitchen Sink 1990

1 DSs, parody 2.50

Fiasco Comics

1 DSs, reprint 2.95

[Original] BLACK CAT

4 rep.. . . . . 2.00
5 A:Ted Parrish 2.00
6 50th Anniv. Issue 2.00
7 rep. 2.00

BLACK AND WHITE
Viz Communications 1999

1 (of 5) by Taiyo Matsumoto 3.25
2 thru 5 . . . . @3.25
TPB Vol. 1 216-page 15.95
TPB Vol. 2 208-page 15.95
TPB Vol. 3 208-page 15.95

BLACKENED
Enigma

1 V:Killing Machine 2.95
2 V:Killing Machine 2.95
3 Flaming Altar 2.95

BLACK KISS
Vortex

1 HC,Adult. 7.00
1a 2nd printing 4.00
1b 3rd printing 1.25
2 HC 6.00
2a 2nd printing 3.00
3 HC 5.00
4 HC 4.00
5 & 6 HC . . . . @2.00
7 thru 12 HC . . . . @1.50

BLACKMASK
Eastern Comics

1 thru 6 . . . . @1.75

BLACK MIST
Caliber Core 1998

1 by James Pruett & Mike Perkins,
Blood of Kali, pt.1 . . . . 2.95
1a variant MV(c) 2.95
1b variant Jordan Raskin(c) 2.95
1c variant GyD(c) 2.95
1d premium edition, signed 9.95
2 thru 5 Blood of Kali,pt.2–pt.5 . . @2.95
Spec. Dawn of Armageddon, Blood
of Kali, pt.6 & pt.7, 48-page . . . 3.95

BLACK SCORPION
Special Studio 1991

1 Knight of Justice. 2.75
2 A Game for Old Men 2.75
3 Blackmailer's Auction 2.75

BLACKTHORNE 3 in 1

1 and 2 . . . . @2.00

BLACK ZEPPLIN
Renegade

1 . . . . 2.50
2 thru 6 . . . . @2.00

BLADE OF SHURIKEN
Eternity

1 thru 8 . . . . @2.00

BLAIR WITCH PROJECT
Oni Press 1999

Spec. Movie adapt.. . . . . 2.95

BLAIR WITCH CHRONICLES
Oni Press 2000

1 (of 4) by Jen Van Meter
& Guy Davis. 2.95
2 thru 4 . . . . @2.95
TPB Rep. 15.95

BLANDMAN
Eclipse

1 Sandman parody 2.50

BLIND FEAR
Eternity

1 thru 4 . . . . @2.00

BLONDE AVENGER
Blonde Avenger Comics 1998

25 flip-book, Full Metal Corset 3.95
27 Full Metal Corset, pt.2 . . . . 3.95

Spec. Short Blonde Girl with the Two Big Boobs 3.95

BLONDE AVENGER: DANGEROUS CONCLUSIONS

Brainstorm 1997

1 V:Victor Von Fuchs 2.95
1a photo deluxe cover 3.95
2 . . . . 2.95
2a photo deluxe cover 3.95

BLOOD & ROSES ADVENTURES

Knight Press

1 F:Time Agents 2.95
2 F:Time Agents 2.95
3 Search for Time Agents 2.95
4 Time Adventures 2.95

BLOOD 'N' GUTS

Aircel 1990

1 thru 3 . . . . @2.50

BLOODBROTHERS

Eternity

1 thru 4 . . . . @2.00

Blood is the Harvest #2
© Eclipse

BLOOD IS THE HARVEST

Eclipse 1992

1 I:Nikita,Milo. 4.50
2 V:M'Raud D:Nikita? 2.50
3 Milo captured 2.50
4 F:Nikita/Milo 2.50

BLOOD JUNKIES

Eternity

1 Vampires on Capitol Hill 2.50
2 final issue 2.50

BLOODLETTING

Fantaco

1 A Shilling for a Redcoat 2.95
2 . . . . 2.95
3 Flee 2.95
4 thru 10 (of 11) by Chynna Clugston, ... @3.95

BLOOD OF DRACULA

Apple 1987–90

1 thru 7 . . . . @1.75
8 thru 14 . . . . @2.00
15 +Record&Mask 3.50
16 . . . . 2.00
17 thru 20 . . . . @2.25

BLOOD OF INNOCENT

Warp Graphics

1 thru 4 . . . . @2.50

BLOODSHED

Damage

1 Little Brother. 2.95
1a Commemorative issue 4.00
1 Encore edition, gold foil(c) 3.50
2 Little Brother. 2.95
3 O:Bloodshed 2.95
3 "The Wastelands," cont. 3.50
4 The City 3.50
5 the end is near 3.50
6 . . . . 3.50
7 Lies, concl. 3.50
"M" 3.50
"M" deluxe 5.00
Spec. Lunatics Fringe. 3.50
Spec. Lies Epilogue, final issue . . . 3.50
Spec. Chris Mass #1 . . . . 3.50
Spec. Requiem. 3.50

BLOODWING

Eternity

1 thru 5 . . . . @2.00

BLUDGEON

Aardwolf 1997

1 by JPi & David Chylsetk 2.95
2 "Alise in Wonderland" 2.95
3 "Seeing Red" 2.95

BOGIE MAN: CHINATOON

Atomeka

1 I:Francis Claine 2.95
2 F:Bogie Man. 2.95
3 thr 4 F:Bogie Man. 2.95

BOGIE MAN: MANHATTEN PROJECT

Apocalypse

1-Shot. D.Quale Assassination Plot 3.95

BONAFIDE

Bonafide Productions

1 F:Doxie 'th Mutt 3.50
2 F:Doxie 'th Mutt 3.50
3 F:Doxie 'th Mutt 3.50

BONE

Cartoon Books 1991

1 I:Bone 90.00
1a 2nd printing 10.00
1b 3rd Printing. 8.00
1c 4th printing 3.00
1d thru 1f 5th-7th printing . . . . . . @3.00
2 . . . . 50.00
2a 2nd printing 7.00
2b thru 2e 3rd-6th printing . . . . . @3.00
3 . . . . 35.00
3a 2nd printing 5.00
3b thru 3d 3rd-5th printing . . . . . @3.00
4 . . . . 25.00
4a thru 4c 2nd-4th printing . . . . . @3.00
5 . . . . 20.00
5a thru 5c 2nd-4th printing . . . . . @3.00
6 . . . . 15.00
6a thru 6c 2nd-4th printing . . . . . @3.00
7 . . . . 10.00
7a,7b 2nd,3rd printing . . . . @3.00
8 . . . . 9.00
8a,8b 2nd,3rd printing . . . . @3.00
9 . . . . 8.00
9a 2nd printing 3.00
10 . . . . 6.00
11 . . . . 3.00
12 . . . . 3.00
13 . . . . 3.00
14 thru 17. . . . . @3.25
18 V:Bar owner. 3.25
19 F:Phoney Bone 3.25
20 Dragonslayer Phoney Bone 3.25
21 thru 27, *see Image*
21 thru 27 reprints. . . . . @2.95
28 "Rockjaw: Master of the Eastern Border" 3.00
29 . . . . 3.00
30 . . . . 3.00
31 . . . . 3.00
32 Bartleby the Rat Creature Cub saga, concl. 3.00
33 Phoney's fate. 3.00
34 Kingdok Slayer 2.95
35 return of Gran'ma Ben 2.95
36 Return of Rockjaw 2.95
37 Extravaganza Issue 2.95
38 48-page. 4.95
39 Ghost Circles. 2.95
40 wrap-around cover. 2.95
PB rep.#1-4 . . . . 14.00
TPB Vol. 1 Rep.1-#6. . . . . 12.95
TPB Vol. 2 Rep.#7-#12. . . . . 12.95
TPB Vol. 3 Eyes of the Storm 16.95
HC Vol. 3 . . . . 24.95
TPB Vol.4 Dragonslayer 16.95
HC Vol. 4 . . . . 24.95
TPB Vol. 5 Rock Jaw: Master of the Eastern Border. 14.95
HC Vol. 5 . . . . 22.95
TPB Vol. 6 Old Man's Cave 17.95
TPB Bone Reader 9.95

BONESHAKER

Caliber Press

1 Suicidal Wrestler 3.50

BOOK, THE

DreamSmith Studios 1998

1 epic fantasy 72pg. 3.50
2 . . . . 3.50
3 . . . . 3.95
4 . . . . 3.95
5 . . . . 4.00
6 . . . . 4.00
7 . . . . 4.00
Ashcan Preview, 24-page 5.00
Ashcan Preview, GP(c). 10.00
Handbook, 32-page 2.00

BOOK OF BALLADS AND SAGAS

Green Man Press

1 False Knight in the Road 2.95
2 thru 5 . . . . @3.00
5 . . . . 3.50

BOOK OF THE TAROT

Caliber Tome Press 1998

1 History/Development o/t Tarot. . . 3.95
1 64pg. 4.95
1 signed 4.95

BOOKS OF LORE
Peregrine

Spec.#1 fantasy anthology 2.95
Spec.#2 . . . . 2.95
Spec.#3 . . . . 2.95
1-shot Shattered Lives 2.95

BOOKS OF LORE: THE KAYNIN GAMBIT
Peregrine 1998

0 by Kevin Tucker
& David Napoliello 2.95
1 (of 4) 2.95
1a Xavier (c) 2.95
2 thru 4 . . . . @2.95

BOOKS OF LORE: THE SHAPE OF EVIL
Peregrine Entertainment 1999

1 (of 2) 2.95
2 . . . . 2.95

BOOKS OF LORE: THE STORYTELLER
Peregrine Entertainment 2000

1 (of 3) by Kevin Tucker
& Philip Xavier 2.95
2 . . . . 2.95
3 concl. 2.95

Boondoggle 33
© Knight Press

BOONDOGGLE
Knight Press 1995

1 Waffle War 2.95
2 Waffle War 2.95
3 Waffle War 2.95

BOONDOGGLE
Caliber Tapestry 1997

Spec. 2.95
Spec., signed 2.95
1 thru 3 . . . . @2.95
4 At Wo's 2.95

BORDER WORLDS
Kitchen Sink

1 adult. 2.00
2 thru 7 . . . . @2.00
Spec.#1 Border Worlds: Marooned . 2.00

BORIS' ADVENTURE MAGAZINE
Nicotat

1 and 2 . . . . @2.00
3 thru 6 . . . . @2.95

BORIS THE BEAR
Nikotat

1–12: See Dark Horse section
13 thru 29 . . . . @2.00
30 thru 34 . . . . @2.50

BORN TO KILL
Aircel 1991

1 thru 3 . . . . @2.50

BOSTON BOMBERS
Caliber

1 . . . . 2.00
2 . . . . 2.50
Spec.#1 . . . . 3.95
Note: other issues are flipbooks with: Oz #17; The Searchers #5; Raven Chronicles #12; & LegendLore #6

BOUNTY
Caliber 1991

1 `Bounty,'`Navarro' Pt.1 . . . . 2.50
2 `Bounty,'`Navarro' Pt.2 . . . . 2.50
3 `Bounty,'`Navarro' Pt.3 . . . . 2.50

BOX OFFICE POISON
Antarctic Press 1996

1 by Alex Robinson 9.00
2 . . . . 6.00
3 thru 5 . . . . @4.00
6 thru 10 . . . . @3.00
11 thru 21 . . . . @3.00
TPB 160-page 14.95
Big Super Spec.#1 . . . . 4.95

BRAT PACK
King Hell Publications

1 . . . . 6.00
1a 2nd printing 3.00
2 thru 5 . . . . @4.00
Brat Pack Collection 13.00

BRATPACK/MAXIMORTAL
King Hell

Super Spec.#1 RV 3.00
Super Spec.#2 RV 3.00

BREAKNECK BLVD
Slave Labor Graphics 1995–96

1 thru 3 Jhonen Vasques art . . . @2.95
4 by Timothy Markin 2.95
5 . . . . 2.95
6 . . . . 2.95

BRENDA STARR, ACE REPORTER
ACG Comics 1998

1 by Dale Messick, Charlton reprint 3.00
2 . . . . 2.95
Spec.#1 Pin-ups,rep. from 40s
and 50s (1998). 2.95

BRILLIANT BOY
Circus Comics 1997

1 . . . . 2.95
2 Drake, pt.1 (of 5) 2.95
3 Drake, pt.2 . . . . 2.50
4 Drake, pt.3 . . . . 2.50
5 Drake, pt.4 . . . . 2.50
6 Drake, pt.5 . . . . 2.50
7 The Great Thunder, pt. 1 (of 6). . 2.50
8 The Great Thunder, pt. 2 . . . . . . 2.50

BROID
Eternity

1 thru 4. . . . . @2.25

BROKEN HALO: IS THERE NOTHING SACRED
Broken Halos Comics 1998

1 by Donald J. Vigil & Tim Vigil . . . 2.95
1a nude cover 4.95
2 . . . . 2.95
2a nude cover 4.95
3 . . . . 2.95
3a Adult edition, nude cover 5.95
Ashcan, limited ed. 16-page 6.95
TPB Vol. 1 by Joe & Tim Vigil,
limited ed. 9.95

BROKEN HEROES
Sirius 1998

1 by Fillbach Bros 2.50
2 The Neon Graveyard 2.50
3 Rocket Man 2.50
4 thru 12 final issue . . . . @2.50
TPB Captain Freebird rep. #1–#12 19.95

BRONX
Eternity 1991

1 A.Saichann Short Stories 2.50
2 to 3 . . . . @2.50

Aircel

Reprint 2.95

BROTHER MAN
New City Comics

1 . . . . 5.00
1a 2.00
2 thru 7 . . . . @2.00

BRUCE JONES: OUTER EDGE
Innovation

1 All reprints 2.00

BRUCE JONES: RAZORS EDGE
Innovation

1 All reprints 2.50
2 D:Grimm, Gritty 2.50

BRU-HEAD
Schism Comics

1 Blockhead 2.95
1a 2nd printing 2.75
2 Blockhead 2.95
Vol. 1 Bru-Head's Bunnies, Baddies
& Buddies (1998) 2.50
Vol. 1 Bru-Head's Guide to Gettin'
Girls Now 2.50
Vol. 2 Bru-Head's Guide 2.50

BUCE-N-GAR
RAK

1 . . . . . 1.75
2 . . . . . 1.75
3 . . . . . 1.75

BUCK GODOT
Palliard Press

1 I:Buck Godot 2.95

BUCK GODOT: ZAP GUN FOR HIRE
Studio Foglio

1 thru 7 . . . . . @2.95
7 by Phil Foglio & Barb Kaalberg . . 2.95
8 finale 3.50
TPB Gallimaufry Vol. 1 . . . . . 12.50
HC Gallimaufry Vol. 1 . . . . . 29.95
TPB Gallimaufry Vol. 2 . . . . . 14.95
HC Gallimaufry Vol. 2 . . . . . 29.95

BUFFALO WINGS
Antarctic Press

1 and 2 . . . . . @2.50

BUG
Planet X Productions

1 . . . . . 1.50
2 . . . . . 1.50

BULLET CROW
Eclipse

1 & 2 . . . . . @2.00

BULWARK
Millennium 1995

1 I:Bulwark 2.95
2 O:Bulwark 2.95

BUSHIDO
Eternity

1 thru 6 . . . . . @2.00

BUZZ
Kitchen Sink

1 Mark Landman (c) (1990) 2.95
2 Mark Landman (c) 2.95
3 Mark Landman (c) (1991) 2.95

CABLE TV
Parody Press

1 Cable Satire 2.50

CADILLACS AND DINOSAURS
Kitchen Sink

3-D comic 3.95

CALIBER CORE
Caliber 1998

0 48pg 2.95
1 gestalt cover 2.95
1a Rain People cover 2.95
1b Spiral cover 2.95
2 F:Al-Haquat 2.95

CALIBER DOUBLE FEATURE
Caliber 2000

1 48-page 3.95
2 . . . . . 3.95
3 . . . . . 3.95

CALIBER FOCUS
Caliber 2000

1 48-page 3.95
2 thru 4 . . . . . @3.95

CALIBER PRESENTS
(Prev. High Caliber)

1 TV,I:Crow 50.00
2 Deadworld 7.00
3 Realm 3.00
4 Baker Street 3.00
5 TV,Heart of Darkness, Fugitive 2.50
6 TV,Heart of Darkness, Fugitive 2.50
7 TV,Heart of Darkness, Dragonfeast 2.50
8 TV,Cuda,Fugitive 2.50
9 Baker Street,Sting Inc. 2.00
10 Fugitive, The Edge 2.50
11 Ashes,Random Thoughts 2.50
12 Fugitive,Random Thoughts 2.50
13 Random Thoughts,Synergist . . . 2.50
14 Random Thoughts,Fugitive 2.50
15 Fringe, F:The Crow 4.00
16 Fugitive, The Verdict 3.50
17 Deadworld, The Verdict 3.50
18 Orlak,The Verdict 3.50
19 Taken Under,Go-Man 3.50
20 The Verdict,Go-Man 3.50
21 The Verdict,Go-Man 3.50
22 The Verdict,Go-Man 3.50
23 Go-Man,Heat Seeker 3.50
24 Heat Seeker,MacktheKnife 3.50
Christmas Spec A:Crow,Deadworld Realm,Baker Street 10.00
Summer Spec. inc. the Silencers, Swords of Shar-Pei (preludes) . 3.95
1-Shot 2.50
1-shot Hybrid 2.50

CALIBER SPOTLIGHT
Caliber

1 F:Kabuki,Oz 2.95

CALIBRATIONS
Caliber

1 WEI,MCy,"Atmospherics," pt.1. . . 2.95
2 WEI,MCy,"Atmospherics," pt.2. . . 2.95
3 WEI,MCy,"Atmospherics," pt.3. . . 2.95
4 WEI,MCy,"Atmospherics," pt.4. . . 2.95
5 WEI,MCy,"Atmospherics," concl. . 2.95

CALIFORNIA GIRLS
Eclipse

1 thru 8 . . . . . @2.00

CALIGARI 2050

1 Gothic Horror 2.25
2 Gothic Horror 2.25

CALL ME PRINCESS
CPM Manga 1999

1 by Tomoko Taniguchi 2.95
1a variant cover 2.95
2 . . . . . 2.95
3 . . . . . 2.95
4 . . . . . 2.95
5 . . . . . 2.95
6 final issue 2.95
TPB Vol. 1 . . . . . 15.95

CAMELOT ETERNAL
Caliber 1990

1 . . . . . 3.00
2 . . . . . 2.50
3 . . . . . 2.50
4 Launcelot & Guinevere 2.50
5 Mordred Escapes 2.50
6 MorganLeFay returns from dead . 2.50
7 Revenge of Morgan 2.50
8 Launcelot flees Camelot 2.50

Captain Canuck Reborn #3
© Semple Comics

CAPTAIN CANUCK REBORN
Semple Comics 1995–96

1 thru 3 by Richard Comely . . . . @2.50

CAPT. CONFEDERACY
Steel Dragon 1985–88

1 adult 6.00
2 . . . . . 2.50
3 . . . . . 2.00
4 . . . . . 2.00
4a 1.50
5 thru 8 . . . . . @2.00
9 thru 11 . . . . . @1.75
12 . . . . . 2.00

CAPT. ELECTRON
Brick Computers Inc.

1 . . . . . 2.00
2 . . . . . 2.25

CAPTAIN HARLOCK
Eternity

1 . . . . . 3.00
1a 2nd printing 2.50
2 . . . . . 2.50
3 . . . . . 2.50
4 thru 13 . . . . . @2.00
Christmas special 2.50
Spec.#1 The Machine People 2.50

CAPTAIN HARLOCK DEATHSHADOW RISING

Eternity 1991

1 . . . . 2.75
2 . . . . 2.50
3 . . . . 2.25
4 Harlock/Nevich Truce 2.25
5 Reunited with Arcadia Crew 2.25
6 . . . . 2.95

[ADVENTURES OF] CAPTAIN JACK

Fantagraphics

1 . . . . 4.00
2 & 3 . . . . @2.50
4 thru 12 . . . . @2.00

CAPTAIN KOALA

Koala Comics 1997

1 . . . . 2.95
2 thru 7 . . . . @2.50

CAPTAIN STERNN: RUNNING OUT OF TIME

Kitchen Sink

1 BWr(c) (1993). 4.95
2 BWr(c) 4.95
3 BWr(c) (1994). 4.95
4 BWr(c) 4.95

CAPTAIN THUNDER AND BLUE BOLT

Hero Graphics

1 New stories 3.50
2 Hard Targets. 3.50

CARDCAPTOR SAKURA

Mixx Entertainment 1999

1 by Clamp 2.95
2 thru 6 . . . . @2.95
Pocket Vol. 1 . . . . 9.95

Tokyopop.Com 2000

7 . . . . 2.95
8 . . . . 2.95
9 . . . . 2.95
10 . . . . 2.95

CARTOON HISTORY OF THE UNIVERSE

Rip Off Press

1 Gonick art. 2.50
2 Sticks & Stones 2.50
3 River Realms 2.50
4 Old Testament 2.50
5 Brains & Bronze 2.50
6 These Athenians 2.50
7 All about Athens. 2.50

CASES OF SHERLOCK HOLMES

Renegade

1 thru 18 . . . . @2.00
19 . . . . 2.25

CASTLE WAITING

Olio 1997

1 by Linda Medley 10.00
2 . . . . 5.00
1a 2nd printing 3.00
2a 2nd printing 3.00
3 Labors of Love 3.00
4 birth of Lady Jain's baby. 3.00
5 . . . . 3.00
6 City Mouse, Country Mouse, pt.1 3.00
7 City Mouse, Country Mouse, pt.2 3.00
8 . . . . 3.00
Spec. The Curse of Brambly Hedge (1996). 3.00
Spec. Curse of Brambly Hedge, revised 1998, 96-page 9.00
TPB Vol. 1 Lucky Road. 16.95

VOL. 2

1 by Linda Medley. 2.95
2 Solicitine,pt.1 . . . . 2.95

Cat & Mouse #7
© Aircel

CAT & MOUSE

Aircel 1989–92

1 . . . . 4.00
2 . . . . 3.00
3 thru 8 . . . . @2.25
9 Cat Reveals Identity 2.25
10 Tooth & Nail. 2.25
11 Tooth & Nail. 2.25
12 Tooth & Nail, Demon 2.25
13 `Good Times, Bad Times' 2.25
14 Mouse Alone 2.25
15 Champion ID revealed 2.25
16 Jerry Critically Ill 2.25
17 Kunoichi vs. Tooth 2.25
18 Search for Organ Donor. 2.25
Graphic Novel 9.95

CAT CLAW

Eternity 1990

1 O:Cat Claw. 2.75
1a 2nd printing 2.50
2 thru 9 . . . . @2.50

CATFIGHT

Lightning Comics

1 V:Prince Nightmare. 4.00
1a Gold Edition 6.00
Spec.#1 Dream Warrior, V:The Slasher 2.75
Spec.#1 Dream intoAction,A:Creed. 3.00
Spec.#1a signed and numbered . . . 8.00
Spec.#1b nude cover edition. 8.00
Spec.#1 Escape From Limbo 2.75
Spec.#1a variant cover (1996) 2.75
Spec.#1b platinum cover 5.95
Spec.#1c nude cover 8.00
Spec.#1d variant nude cover 8.00
Spec.#1 Sweet Revenge (1997) . . 2.95
Spec.#1a variant cover. 2.95
Spec.#1b nude cover 8.00
Spec.#1c nude variant cover. 8.00

CAT-MAN RETRO COMIC

AC Comics

0 by Bill Black & Mark Heike 5.95
1 thru 3 . . . . @5.95
Ashcan #1 I:Catman & Kitten. . . . 5.95

CAVEWOMAN

Bacement/Caliber 1994–95

1 . . . . 70.00
1 by Budd Root 2nd printing 4.00
1 3rd printing, new cover 3.00
2 . . . . 40.00
2a 2nd printing 3.00
2 3rd printing, new cover 3.00
3 . . . . 35.00
4 . . . . 35.00
5 Cavewoman vs. Klyde, Round Two. 25.00
6 . . . . 25.00

CAVEWOMAN: RAIN

Caliber 1996

1 by Budd Root 7.00
1a 2nd printing 3.00
2 . . . . 5.00
2a 2nd printing 3.00
3 . . . . 4.00
3a 2nd edition, new cover 3.00
4 . . . . 4.00
4a 2nd edition, new cover 3.00
5 . . . . 3.50
5 2nd edition, new cover 3.00
6 thru 8 . . . . @3.00

CAVEWOMAN: MISSING LINK

Basement Comics 1997

1 (of 4) 2.95
2 thru 4 . . . . @2.95
TPB 96-page 19.95
TPB 2nd printing. 9.95

CAVEWOMAN: PANGAEAN SEA

Basement Comics 1999

1 . . . . 4.95
Prologue. 2.95

CAVEWOMAN: ODYSSEY

Caliber 1999

1 (of 5) 2.95
2 . . . . 2.95
3 . . . . 2.95
4 . . . . 2.95

CAVEWOMAN ODYSSEY

Basement Comics 2000

1 front row seat (c) by Budd Root . 8.95
1a foil (c). 12.50
2a variant (c). 5.95
2 jungle green foil (c). 12.50
1-shot spec. 2.95
1-shot spec. variant (c) 8.95
1-shot spec. foil (c). 12.50

CAVEWOMAN: JUNGLE TALES
Basement Comics 2000
1 by Budd Root
1a Frank Cho (c) 10.95
1b Meriem nude (c) 10.95

CAVEWOMAN: PANGAEAN SEA
Basement Comics 1999
1 by Bud Root 4.95
1a variant (c) 8.95
1b Root Sea Blue Foil (c) 12.50
1c Cho Sea Blue Foil (c) 12.50
2 . . . . 2.95
Prologue 2.95

CECIL KUNKLE
Darkline Comics 1987
1 . . . . 1.50

CELESTIAL MECHANICS
Innovation
1 thru 3 . . . . @2.25

CELESTIAL ZONE
Asiapac Books 2000
1 by Wee Tian Beng 8.95
2 thru 8 . . . . @8.95

CEMENT SHOOZ
Horse Feathers 1991
1 with color pin-up 2.50

CEREBUS
Aardvark–Vanaheim 1977
0 . . . . 3.00
0a Gold Ed. 10.00
1 B:DS(s&a),I:Cerebus 275.00
1a Counterfeit 50.00
2 DS,V:Succubus 75.00
3 DS,I:Red Sophia 70.00
4 DS,I:Elrod 50.00
5 DS,A:The Pigts 40.00
6 DS,I:Jaka 40.00
7 DS,R:Elrod 25.00
8 DS,A:Conniptins 25.00
9 DS,I&V:K'cor 25.00
10 DS,R:Red Sophia 25.00
11 DS,I:The Cockroach 25.00
12 DS,R:Elrod 25.00
13 DS,I:Necross 15.00
14 DS,V:Shadow Crawler 15.00
15 DS,V: Shadow Crawler 15.00
16 DS, at the Masque 10.00
17 DS,"Champion" 10.00
18 DS,Fluroc 10.00
19 DS,I:Perce & Greet-a 10.00
20 DS,Mind Game 10.00
21 DS,A:CaptCockroach,rare 35.00
22 DS,D:Elrod 15.00
23 DS,DuFort's school 10.00
24 DS,IR:Prof.Clarmont 10.00
25 DS,A:Woman-thing 10.00
26 DS,High Society 10.00
27 DS,Kidnapping of an Aardvark . 10.00
28 DS,Mind Game!! 10.00
29 DS,Reprocussions 10.00
30 DS,Debts 8.00
31 DS,Chasing Cootie 8.00
32 DS 8.00
33 DS,DS,Friction 5.00
34 DS,Three Days Before 5.00
35 thru 50 DS . . . . @5.00
51 DS,(scarce) 17.00
52 DS 5.00
53 DS,C:Wolveroach 7.00
54 DS,I:Wolveroach 9.00
55 DS,A:Wolveroach 8.00
56 DS,A:Wolveroach 8.00
57 DS 5.00
58 DS 5.00
59 DS,Memories Pt.V 5.00
60 DS,more vignettes 5.00
61 DS,A:Flaming Carrot 6.00
62 DS,A:Flaming Carrot 6.00
63 DS,Mind Game VI 5.00
64 DS,Never Pray for Change 5.00
65 DS,Papal Speech 5.00
66 DS,Thrill of Agony 5.00
67 thru 70 DS . . . . @5.00
71 thru 74 DS . . . . @4.00
75 DS,Terrible Analogies 4.00
76 DS,D:Weisshaupt 4.00
77 DS,Surreal daydream 4.00
78 DS,Surreal daydream 4.00
79 DS,Spinning Straw 4.00
80 DS,V:Stone Tarim 4.00
81 DS,A:Sacred Wars Roach 4.00
82 DS,A:Tarim 3.50
83 DS,A:Michele 3.50
84 DS,Weisshaupt's Letter 3.50

Cerebus #47
© Aardvark Vanaheim

85 DS,A:Mick Jagger 3.50
86 DS,A:Mick Jagger 3.50
87 DS,Tower Climb 3.50
88 DS,D:Stone Tarim 3.50
89 DS,A:Cute Elf 3.50
90 DS,Anti-Apartheid(c) 3.50
91 DS 3.50
92 DS,A:Bill & Seth 3.50
93 DS,Astoria in Prison 3.50
94 DS,Rape of Astoria 3.50
95 DS,Sophia-Astoria Dream 3.50
96 DS,Astoria in Prison 3.50
97 DS,Escape Planned 3.50
98 DS,Astoria's Trial 3.50
99 DS,Sorcery in Court 3.50
100 DS,A:Cirin 3.50
101 DS,The Gold Sphere 3.00
102 DS,The Final Ascension 3.00
103 DS,On the Tower 3.00
104 DS,A:Flaming Carrot 3.00
105 DS,V:Fred & Ethel 3.00
106 DS,D:Fred & Ethel 3.00
107 DS,Judge on the Moon 3.00
108 DS,All History 3.00
109 DS,O:Universe 3.00
110 DS,More Universe 3.00
111 DS,Cerebus' Fate 3.00
112 DS,Memories 3.00
113 DS,Memories 3.00
114 DS,I:Rick nash 3.00
115 DS,I:Pud Withers 3.00
116 DS,Rick Meets Cerebus 3.00
117 DS,Young Jaka Injured 3.00
118 DS,Cerebus Apologizes 3.00
119 DS,Jaka Opens Door 3.00
120 DS,I:Oscar 3.00
121 DS,Women Explained 3.00
122 DS,lest History 3.00
123 DS,Each One's Dream 3.00
124 DS 3.00
125 DS,C:Lord Julius 3.00
126 DS,R:Old Vet'ran 2.50
127 DS,Jaka Dances 2.50
128 DS,L:Cerebus as Fred 2.50
129 DS,Jaka's Story 2.50
130 DS,D:Pud Withers 2.50
131 DS,Jaka Imprisoned 4.00
132 DS,A:Nurse 4.00
133 DS,I:Mrs. Thatcher 4.00
134 DS,Dancing Debate 4.00
135 DS,Jaka Signs 4.00
136 DS,L:Rick 4.00
137 DS,Like-a-Looks 4.00
138 DS,Maids'Gossip 4.00
139 A:Misogynist-roach 4.00
140 I:Old Oscar 4.00
141 A:Cerebus 4.00
142 C:Mick Jagger 4.00
143 DS,Oscars Forboding 4.00
144 DS,I:Doris 4.00
145 thru 146 DS . . . . @4.00
147 Neil Gaiman, DS 7.00
148 thru 150 DS 3.00
151 DS,B:Mothers & Daughters, Book 1: Flight pt.1 . . . . 4.00
151a 2nd printing 2.50
152 DS,Flight pt.2 . . . . 4.00
152a 2nd printing 2.50
153 DS,Flight pt.3 . . . . 4.00
153a 2nd printing 2.50
154 DS,Flight pt.4 . . . . 4.00
155 DS,Flight pt.5 . . . . 4.00
156 DS,Flight pt.6 . . . . 3.00
157 DS,Flight pt.7 . . . . 3.00
158 DS,Flight pt.8 . . . . 3.00
159 DS,Flight pt.9 . . . . 3.00
160 DS,Flight pt.10 . . . . 3.00
161 DS,Flight pt.11, Bone story . . . 8.00
162 DS,E:M&D,Bk.1:Flight pt.12 . . . 3.00
163 DS,B:Mothers & Daughters Book 2: Women pt.1 . . . . 2.75
164 DS,Women pt.2,inc. Tour Momentos 2.50
165 thru 174 Women pt.3–12 . . . @2.50
175 DS,B:Mothers & Daughters, Book 3: Reads pt.1 . . . . 2.50
175 thru 186 Reads pt.1–12 . . . . @2.50
187 DS,B:Mothers & Daughters, Book 4:Minds pt.1 . . . . 2.50
188 thru 199 Minds pt.5–13 . . . . . @2.25
200 . . . . 2.50
201 thru 219 Guys pt.1 to pt.19 . . @2.25
220 thru 231 Rick's Story, pt.1 to pt.12 . . . . @2.25
232 thru 259 Going Home,pt.1–28@2.25
Spec.#1 Cerebus Companion 3.95
TPBs
Vol.1 Cerebus, rep.#1–#25 . . . . . . 25.00
Vol.2 High Society, rep.#26–#50 . . 25.00
Vol.3 Church & State I, rep.#52–#85 . . . . 30.00
Vol.4 Church & State II, rep.#86–#111 . . . . 30.00
Vol.5 Jaka'sStory,rep.#114–#136 . . 25.00
Vol.6 Melmoth, rep.#139–#150 . . . 17.00
Vol.7, Flight, rep.#151–#162 . . . . . 17.00
Vol.8 Women, rep.#163–#174 . . . . 17.00

Vol.9 Reads, rep.#175–#186. . . . . 17.00
Vol.9 Reads, 2nd printing 15.00
Vol.9 Reads, signed & numb. 28.00
Vol.10 Minds, rep.#187-#199 . . . . 16.00
Vol.11 Guys rep.#201–#219 . . . . . 30.00
Vol.11, 2nd printing. 20.00
Vol.12 Rick's Story 17.00
Vol.12 signed 25.00
Vol. 13 Going Home, 420-page. . . 25.00
Vol. 13 deluxe. 37.00

CEREBUS CHURCH & STATE
Aardvark–Vanaheim
1 DS rep #51. . . . . 2.25
2 thru 30 DS rep #52-#80 . . . . . @2.00

CEREBUS HIGH SOCIETY
Aardvark–Vanaheim
1 thru 14 DS (biweekly) . . . . @2.00
15 thru 24 DS rep. . . . . @2.00
25 DS rep. #50, final. 2.00

CEREBUSJAM
Aardvark–Vanaheim
1 MA,BHa,TA,WE,A:Spirit 15.00

CEREBUS REPRINTS
Aardvark–Vanaheim
1A thru 28A DS rep . . . . @1.25

See also: Church & State
See also: Swords of Cerebus

CHAINSAW VIGILANTE
New England Press
1 Tick Spinoff 3.25

CHAMPION, THE
Special Studio 1991
1 . . . . 2.50

CHAMPION OF KITARA: DUM DUM & DRAGONS
MU Press
1 Dragons Secret 2.95
2 Dragons Secret 2.95
3 Dragons Secret 2.95

CHARLIE CHAN
Eternity
1 thru 4 . . . . @2.00
5 and 6 . . . . @2.25

CHASER PLATOON
Aircel 1990–91
1 Interstellar War. 2.25
2 Ambush 2.25
3 New Weapon 2.25
4 Saringer Battle Robot 2.25
5 Behind Enemy Lines. 2.25
6 Operation Youthtest 2.25

CHESTY SANCHEZ
Antarctic Press 1995
1 & 2 . . . . @2.95
Giant Size Spec. #1 (1999). 6.00

CHIBI-POP MANGA
Chibi-Pop (1998)
2 thru 6 64-page . . . . @3.95

VOL 2
1 72-page 3.95
2 thru 6 . . . . @3.95

CHINA & JAZZ
ABC Comics 1999
1 RCI. 3.00
1a nude cover 8.00
1b nude manga ed. 8.00

VOL. 2
1 (of 3) RCI 3.00
1a nude cover 8.00
2 RCI. 3.00
2a nude cover 10.00
Spec. Raising Hell 5.00

CHINA & JAZZ CODE NAME DOUBLE IMPACT
High Impact Oct., 1996
1 . . . . 3.00
1a nude cover 9.95
2 . . . . 2.95
2a nude RCI(c) cover. 9.95

CHINA & JAZZ: TRIGGER HAPPY
ABC Comics 1998
1 (of 4) by Clayton Henry 3.00
1a Jazz Bikini cover. 3.95
1b China Bikini cover. 3.95
1c gold variant cover 5.95
2 . . . . 3.00
2a Playtoy edition 5.95
2b Mercenary edition. 5.95
2c Gold edition 5.95
Spec. Trigger Happy Special 3.00
Spec.A manga cover 8.00
Spec.B nude manga cover 8.00
Spec. China & Jazz 3.00
Spec. Nude cover A or B. . . . . . . @8.00

CHINA & JAZZ: SUPERSTARS
ABC Studios 1999
1 (of 3) 3.00
1a deluxe, manga erotica 8.00
Spec. China Platinum. 3.00
Spec. nude RCI cover. 8.00
Spec. nude manga cover 8.00

CHIRALITY
CPM Manga Comics 1997
6 by Satoshi Urushihara, SS(c) . . . 2.95
7 final battle for Shiori's life 2.95
8 . . . . 2.95
9 Adam transformed into
duplicate Carol 2.95
10 . . . . 2.95
11. . . . . 2.95
12 V:Adam 2.95
13 toward Alaska 2.95
14 reach Gaia. 2.95
15 Carol and Shiori. 2.95
16 . . . . 2.95
17 descend into Gaia 2.95
18 final issue 2.95
Spec. Gallery, pin-up book 3.95
GN Book One rep. #1–#4 . . . . 9.95
GN Book Two rep. #4–#8 . . . . 9.95
TPB Book Three rep. #8–#12 . . . . 15.95
TPB Book Four, rep. #13–#18. . . . 15.95

CHIRALITY: TO THE PROMISED LAND
CPM Comics 1997
1 by Satoshi Urushihara 2.95
2 thru 4 . . . . @2.95

CHIRON
Annurel Studio Graphics
1 . . . . 2.50
1a 2nd printing 2.50
2 Transported to Doran 2.50
3 Transported to Doran 2.50
3a Gold Edition 4.00

CHRONOS CARNIVAL
Fleetway
1 reps. 200 AD stories 7.95

CIRCLE WEAVE, THE
Indigo Bean Productions 1995
1 Apprentice to a God 2.00
2 Apprentice to a God,pt.2. . . . . . . 2.00
3 Apprentice to a God,pt.3. . . . . . . 2.00
4 Apprentice to a God,pt.4. . . . . . . 2.00
5 Apprentice to a God,pt.5. . . . . . . 2.50

CLAN APIS
Active Synapse 1998
1 (of 5) by Jay Hosler, F:Bees 2.95
2 F:Nyuki, Zambur. 2.95
3 & 4 . . . . @2.95
5 conclusion 2.95
TPB 160-page 15.00

CLANDE, INC.
Domain Publishing
1 I:Sam Davidson, Jeremy Clande. 2.95
2 V:Dias 2.95

CLERKS: THE COMIC BOOK
Oni Press 1998
1 by Kevin Smith & Jim Mahfood . . 2.95
Spec. The Lost Scene 2.95
Holiday Special. 2.95
TPB 10.95

Cold Blooded Chameleon Commandos #3 © Blackthorne

CLIFFHANGER COMICS
AC Comics

1 rep. 2.50
2 rep. 2.50

CLINT THE HAMSTER
Eclipse

1 . . . . 2.50
2 . . . . 1.50

COBRA
Viz 1990–91

1 thru 6 . . . . @2.95
7 . . . . 3.25
8 V:SnowHawks 3.25
9 Zados. 3.25
10 thru 12. . . . . @3.25

COLD BLOODED CHAMELEON COMMANDOS
Blackthorne 1986

1 . . . . 2.00
2 . . . . 1.50
3 . . . . 1.50
4 . . . . 1.75
5 . . . . 1.75
6 . . . . 2.00
7 . . . . 2.00

COLD EDEN
Legacy 1995

1 Last City on Earth. 2.35
2 V:Mutant Hunting Pack. 2.35
3 D6 Tower 2.35

COLE BLACK

1 Vol.I 15.00
2 Vol.I 10.00
3 Vol.I 10.00
4 Vol.I 10.00
5 Vol.I 12.00
1 Vol.II. 3.50
2 Vol.II. 2.00
3 Vol.II. 1.50

COLONEL KILGORE
Special Studios

1 WWII stories. 2.50
2 Command Performance 2.50

COLT
K-Z Comics

1 . . . . 4.00
2 pin-up by Laird 6.00
2 pin-up by Henbeck 2.00
3 thru 5 . . . . @1.00

COMICS EXPRESS

1 thru 4 . . . . @2.95
5 thru 11 . . . . @3.95

COMING OF APHRODITE
Hero Graphics

1 Aphrodite/modern day 3.95

COMMAND REVIEW
Thoughts & Images

1 rep. Albedo #1-4. . . . . 6.00
2 rep. Albedo #5-8. . . . . 4.00
3 rep. Albedo #9-13. . . . . 4.00

CONDOM-MAN
Aaaahh!! Comics

1 I:Condom Man 3.50
2 F:Condom Man. 3.50
3 V:Alien Army 3.50
4 Brother bought back to life 3.50
5 O:Condom-Man (Chris Swafford) 3.50

CONQUEROR
Harrier 1984–86

1 . . . . 3.50
2 thru 4 . . . . @2.00
5 thru 9 . . . . @1.75

CONQUEROR UNIVERSE
Harrier

1 . . . . 2.75

CONSPIRACY COMICS
Revolutionary

1 Marilyn Monroe 2.50
2 Who Killed JFK. 2.50
3 Who Killed RFK 2.50

CONSTELLATION GRAPHICS
STG

1 thru 4 . . . . @1.50

CONSTRUCT
Caliber "New Worlds"

1 (of 6) PJe,LDu, sci-fi,48pg 3.95
2 PJe,LDu 2.95
3 PJe,LDu 2.95
4 PJe,LDu 2.95
5 PJe,LDu 2.95
6 PJe,LDu, conclusion. 2.95

CORMAC MAC ART

1 thru 4 R.E.Howard adapt. . . . . @2.00

CORTO MALTESE: BALLAD OF THE SALT SEA
NBM 1997

1 by Hugo Pratt. 2.95
1 a 2nd printing 2.95
2 by Hugo Pratt. 2.95
3 Escondida 2.95
4 . . . . 2.95
5 . . . . 2.95
6 . . . . 2.95
7 final issue 2.95
TPB by Hugo Pratt, "In Siberia". . . 10.95
TPB "Fable of Venice". 10.95
TPB "Banana Conga" 8.95
TPB "Voodoo for the President" . . . 8.95
TPB "Midwinter's Morning" 8.95
TPB "In Africa" 8.95

COSMIC HEROES
Eternity

1 Buck Rogers rep. 2.00
2 thru 6 Buck Rogers rep. . . . . . @2.00
7 thru 9 Buck Rogers rep. . . . . . @2.25
10 . . . . 3.50
11 . . . . 3.95

COUNTER PARTS
Tundra

1 thru 3 . . . . @2.95

COVENTRY
Fantagraphics Oct. 1996

1 BWg, "The Frogs of God" 3.95
2 BWg, "Thirteen Dead Guys Named Bob" 3.95
3 BWg. 3.95
4 . . . . 3.95

Cray-Baby Adventures #4
© TV Comics

CRAY BABY ADVENTURES, THE
Electric Milk 1997

1 by Art Baltazar 3.00

TV Comics 1997

1 2nd printing 3.00
2 . . . . 3.00
4 Captain Camel 3.00
5 . . . . 3.00
Advent.Spec.San Diego Con lim. ed.. 5.00
TPB Vol. 1 rep. #1–#5 . . . . 14.95

CRAY BABY ADVENTURES: WRATH OF THE PEDDIDLERS
TV Comics 1998

1 (of 3) by Art Baltazar 3.00
2 . . . . 3.00
3 concl. 3.00

CREED
Hall of Heroes 1994

1 TKn,I:Mark Farley. 30.00
1A Wizard Ace edition rep. 20.00
2 TKn,Camping 35.00

CREED
Lightning Comics 1995

1-shot TKn retelling of #1 . . . . 2.75
See also: Color

CREED THE VOID

TPB Collected edition. 5.95
TPB Deluxe 9.95

CREED/TEENAGE MUTANT NINJA TURTLES
Lightning Comics 1996

1 TKn(c) ... 3.00
2 TKn(c) ... 3.00
1 Gold Collector's Edition ... 5.95
1 Platinum Edition ... 9.95

CREED: CRANIAL DISORDER
Lightning Comics

1 ... 3.00
1A Previews variant cover ... 3.00
1B Platinum Edition ... 6.00
1C signed platinum edition ... 8.00
2 ... 3.00
2b variant cover ... 2.95
3 ... 2.95
3b variant cover ... 2.95
3c limited edition ... 9.95

CREED: THE GOOD SHIP & THE NEW JOURNEY HOME
Lightning Comics

1 ... 2.95
1a variant cover ... 2.95
1b limited edition ... 9.95

CREED: MECHANICAL EVOLUTION
Gearbox Press 2000

1 (of 2) ... 2.95
1a variant (c) ... 2.95
1b signed ... 9.95
2 ... 2.95

CREED: USE YOUR DELUSION
Avatar Press 1998

1 (of 2) by Trent Kaniuga ... 3.00
1 white leather ... 30.00
2 ... 3.00
2 deluxe ... 4.95
GN rep. #1–#2 ... 3.95

CRIME BUSTER
AC Comics

0 from FemForce ... 2.95
1 Rep. From Boys Illustrated ... 3.95

CRIMEBUSTER
ACG Comics 2000

1 (of 3) F:Dick Tracy ... 2.95
2 & 3 ... @2.95

CRIME CLASSICS
Eternity

1 thru 11 rep Shadow comicstrip @2.00
12 ... 2.25

CRIMSON DREAMS
Crimson

1 thru 11 ... @2.00

CRIMSON NUN
Antarctic Press 1997

1 (of 4) ... 2.95

CRITTERS
Fantagraphics Books 1986–90

1 SS,Usagi Yojimbo,Cutey ... 5.00
2 Captain Jack,Birthright ... 4.00
3 SS,Usagi Yojimbo,Gnuff ... 4.00
4 Gnuff,Birthright ... 3.00
5 Birthright ... 3.00
6 SS,Usagi Yojimbo,Birthright ... 3.00
7 SS,Usagi Yojimbo,Jack Bunny ... 3.00
8 SK,Animal Graffiti,Lizards ... 2.50
9 Animal Graffiti ... 2.50
10 SS,Usagi Yojimbo ... 3.00
11 SS,Usagi Yojimbo, ... 3.00
12 Birthright II ... 2.00
13 Birthright II,Gnuff ... 2.00
14 SS,Usagi Yojimbo,BirthrightII ... 2.50
15 Birthright II,CareBears ... 2.00
16 SS,Groundthumper,Gnuff ... 2.00
17 Birthright II,Lionheart ... 2.00
18 Dragon's ... 2.00
19 Gnuff,Dragon's ... 2.00
20 Gnuff ... 2.00
21 Gnuff ... 2.00
22 Watchdogs,Gnuff ... 2.00
23 Flexi-Disc,X-Mas Issue ... 4.00
24 Angst,Lizards,Gnuff ... 2.00
25 Lionheart,SBi,Gnuff ... 2.00
26 Angst,Gnuff ... 2.00
27 SS,Ground Thumper ... 2.00
28 Blue Beagle,Lionheart ... 2.00
29 Lionheart,Gnuff ... 2.00
30 Radical Dog,Gnuff ... 2.00
31 SBi,Gnuffs,Lizards ... 2.00
32 Lizards,Big Sneeze ... 2.00
33 Gnuff,Angst,Big Sneeze ... 2.00
34 Blue Beagle vs. Robohop ... 2.00
35 Lionheart,Fission Chicken ... 2.00
36 Blue Beagle,Fission Chicken ... 2.00
37 Fission Chicken ... 2.00
38 SS,double size,Usagi Yojimbo ... 2.75
39 Fission Chicken ... 2.00
40 Gnuff ... 2.00
41 Duck'Bill Platypus ... 2.00
42 Glass Onion ... 2.00
43 Lionheart ... 2.00
44 Watchdogs ... 2.00
45 Ambrose the Frog ... 2.00
46 Lionheart ... 2.00
47 Birthright ... 2.00
48 Birthright ... 2.00
49 Birthright ... 2.00
50 SS,Neil the Horse, UsagiYojimbo 5.00
Spec.1 Albedo,rep+new 10pgStory. 2.00

CROSSFIRE
Eclipse

18 thru 26 DSp ... @2.00

CROW, THE
Caliber

1 ... 40.00
1a 2nd Printing ... 4.00
1b 3rd Printing ... 3.00
2 ... 25.00
2a 2nd Printing ... 4.00
2b 3rd Printing ... 3.00
3 ... 20.00
3a 2nd Printing ... 3.00
4 ... 20.00

Tundra

1 reps. Crow #1, #2 ... 15.00
2 ... 8.00
3 ... 10.00
TPB ... 20.00

CROW, THE
Kitchen Sink

TPB Flesh & Blood Collection ... 10.95
TPB The Crow Collection, 7th printing 224pg. ... 15.95
HC Author's Edition 280-page ... 35.00
HC signed and numbered ... 60.00

CROW, THE: DEAD TIME
Kitchen Sink

1 ... 5.00
2 ... 4.00
3 ... 3.00
TPB Collection rep. ... 10.95

CROW, THE: DEMON IN DISGUISE
Kitchen Sink 1997

1 (of 4) by John J. Miller & Dean Ormston ... 2.95
2 ... 2.95
3 ... 2.95

CROW, THE: FLESH AND BLOOD
Kitchen Sink 1996

1 thru 3 ... @2.95
TPB rep. 96-page ... 10.95
HC signed & numbered ... 50.00

CROW, THE: WAKING NIGHTMARES
Kitchen Sink Jan., 1997

1 PhH ... 2.95
2 thru 4 PhH ... @2.95

The Crow, Wild Justice #1
© Kitchen Sink

CROW, THE: WILD JUSTICE
Kitchen Sink

1 thru 3 ... @2.95

CROW/RAZOR: KILL THE PAIN
London Night 1998

1 (of 3) JOb,EHr, ... 3.00
1b EHr & Jerry Beck, Director's

B & W PUB.

Cut, 40pg 5.00
1c black leather, signed & numbered 29.95
1d Ministry of Night (c). 5.00
1e Ministry (c) signed 15.00
1f black leather, red foil logos . . . 20.00
2 . . . . . 3.00
2a Ministry of Night (c). 5.00
2b Leather edition 10.00
3 . . . . . 3.00
3a Ministry of Night (c). 5.00
4 . . . . . 3.00
4a Ministry of Night (c). 6.00
4b Leather edition 15.00
4c Leather edition, signed 15.00
Spec. Finale 3.00
Spec. Finale, Ministry (c). 5.00
0 . . . . . 3.00
0a Ministry (c) 5.00
0b Red Velvet Elite 20.00
1-shotA Tour Book, cover A 5.00
1-shotB Tour Book, cover B 5.00
1-shotC Tour Book, cover C 5.00
1-shotD Tour Book, ministry edition. 5.00
1-shotE Tour Book, limited black leather 15.00
1-shotF Tour Book, signed 18.00
Spec. Nocturnal Masque 48-page . . 5.95
TPB Kill The Pain, 150-page. 15.95
HC Kill The Pain, Sketch limited signed ed. 50.00

EH! Productions 1999

Spec. The Lost Chapter 4.95
Spec. The Lost Chapter, Elite Fan Ed. 6.00

CROW OF THE BEAR CLAN

Blackthorne

1 . . . . . 2.25
2 thru 6 . . . . . @1.75

CRUSADERS

Guild

1 Southern Knights 10.00

CRUSHER JOE

Ironcat 1999

1 by Haruka Takachiho 2.95
2 thru 6 . . . . . @2.95
TPB 15.95

CRY FOR DAWN

Cry For Dawn 1989–90

1 . . . . . 125.00
1a 2nd Printing 50.00
1b 3rd Printing. 40.00
2 . . . . . 60.00
2a 2nd Printing 15.00
3 . . . . . 50.00
4 . . . . . 40.00
5 . . . . . 30.00
6 . . . . . 30.00
7 Corporate Ladder,Rock A Bye Baby 20.00
8 Decay,This is the Enemy 15.00
9 . . . . . 15.00
1-shot Subtle Violents,F:Ryder 3.00

CRYING FREEMAN

Viz 1989

1 . . . . . 4.00
2 . . . . . 3.50
3 thru 5 . . . . . @3.50
6 thru 8 . . . . . @3.00

CRYING FREEMAN II

Viz 1990–91

1 . . . . . 4.00
2 . . . . . 3.50
3 . . . . . 3.50
4 thru 6 . . . . . @3.00
7 V:Bugnug 3.00
8 Emu & The Samurai Sword 3.00
9 Final Issue 3.00

CRYING FREEMAN III

Viz 1991

1 thru 10 . . . . . @4.00

CRYING FREEMAN IV

Viz 1992

1 thru 3 . . . . . @4.00
4 thru 8 . . . . . @2.75

CRY FREEMAN V

Viz 1993

1 Return to Japan 4.00
2 A:Tateoka-assassin. 4.00
3 . . . . . 4.00
4 A:Bagwana. 4.00
5 V:Tsunaike 4.00
6 V:Aido Family 4.00
7 V:Tsunaike 4.00
GN:Taste of Revenge 14.95

Crypt of Dawn #5
© Sirius

CRYPT OF DAWN

Sirius 1996

1 JLi(c) 6.00
1 variant cover. 12.00
2 JLi(c) 3.50
3 . . . . . 3.00
4 JLi(c) 3.00
5 JLi(c) 2.95
6 Vanguard of Comics 2.95

CRYSTAL BREEZE

High Impact 1996

1 thru 3 . . . . . @2.95
1 thru 3a nude covers . . . . . @10.00
Spec.#1 Crystal Breeze Unleashed. 3.00
Spec.#1a nude cover 14.95
Spec.#1 Crystal Breeze Revenge . . 2.95
Spec.#1a adult photo cover 10.00
Spec.#1b gold edition cover 10.00

CUDA

Rebel Studios

1 I:Cuda,Zora,V:Shanga Bai 2.00
CUDA B.C. (Rebel Studios) signed 12.95

Avatar Press 1998

1 (of 4) by Tim & Joe Vigil 3.50
1a Gore cover 3.95
1b Lether cover 20.00
1c nude cover 6.00
1d signed 15.00
1e Royal Blue edition. 60.00
2 . . . . . 3.50
2a Gore cover 3.95
2b nude cover 6.00
3 . . . . . 3.50
3a Gore cover 6.00
3b nude cover 6.00
4 . . . . . 3.50
4a Gore cover 6.00
4b nude cover 6.00
0 80-page 7.95
0a Gore (c) 8.95
0b nude (c) 9.00
0c prism foil (c) 12.95
0d Royal blue 75.00
TPB Vol. 1, 160-pg. 19.95
HC Vol. 1 . . . . . 34.95

CULTURAL JET LAG

Fantagraphics

1 . . . . . 2.50

CUTEY BUNNY

1 . . . . . 8.00
2 thru 4 . . . . . @4.00

Eclipse

5 . . . . . 3.00

CUTIE HONEY

Ironcat 1997

1 crime fighting android 2.95
2 . . . . . 2.95
3 Wonderful Mask 2.95
4 thru 6 . . . . . @2.95

VOL 2 CUTIE HONEY '90 1998

1 Sorayama cover 2.95
2 thru 6 . . . . . @2.95

CYBER 7

Eclipse

1 . . . . . 2.50
2 thru 5 . . . . . @2.00

Book 2: Rockland 1990

1 thru 7 . . . . . @2.00
8 thru 10 . . . . . @2.50

CYBERFROG

Hall of Heroes

1 I:Cyberfrog 5.00
1a 2nd printing 2.50
2 V:Ben Riley 4.00
2a 2nd printing 2.50

CYBERFROG

Harris Jan., 1997

1 3rd Anniv. Special. 3.00
1a Walt Simonson(c) 6.00
1b signed & numbered. 10.00
2 . . . . . 3.50
2a variant cover. 4.00
3 . . . . . 3.50
4 . . . . . 3.50
4a signed 10.00
Ashcan Cyberfrog: Amphibionix . . . 6.00

CYBERFROG VS CREED
Harris 1997

1 . . . 3.50
1 Creed vs. Cyberfrog, alternate edition . . . 9.95

CYBERZONE
Jet Black Graphics

1 thru 5 Never-never Land . . . 2.50

CYCLOPS
Blackthorne

1 Mini-series . . . 2.00
2 . . . 2.00
3 . . . 2.00

CYGNUS X-1
Twisted Pearl Press

1 V:Yag'Nost . . . 2.50
2 F:Rex and Bounty Hunters . . . 2.50

CYNDER
Immortelle Studios

1 I:Cynder . . . 5.00
2 . . . 3.00
3 conclusion . . . 2.50

Second Series

1 thru 3 . . . @3.00

CYNDER/HELLINA
Immortelle Studios

Spec. 1 x-over . . . 3.00

DAIKAZU

1 . . . 5.00
1a 2nd Printing . . . 1.50
2 . . . 3.00
2a 2nd Printing . . . 1.50
3 . . . 3.00
3a 2nd Printing . . . 1.50
4 thru 7 . . . @1.50
8 . . . 1.75

DA'KOTA
Millennium Jan., 1997

1 by Pavlet & Petersen . . . 2.95
1 signed . . . 4.95
1 foil edition . . . 9.95
2 . . . 2.95
2 foil edition . . . 4.95
3 foil deluxe edition . . . 6.95
3 . . . 2.95
3a variant cover . . . 2.95
Spec.#1 Orig.Art Edition . . . 9.95

DAMONSTREIK
Imperial Comics

1 I:Damonstreik . . . 2.00
2 V:Sonix . . . 2.00
3 V:Sonix . . . 2.00
4 J:Ohm . . . 2.00
5 V:Drakkus . . . 2.00

DANGEROUS TIMES

1 MK . . . 2.50
2 MA(c) . . . 2.00
2a 2nd printing . . . 1.75
3 MR(c) . . . 2.00
3a 2nd printing . . . 2.00
4 GP(c) . . . 2.00

DAN TURNER HOLLYWOOD DETECTIVE
Eternity 1991

1 'Darkstar of Death' . . . 2.50
Spec.#1 Dan Turner, Homicide Hunch, Dan Turner Framed . . . 2.50
Spec.#1 Dan Turner, The Star Chamber, Death of Folly Hempstead . . . 2.50

DARK ANGEL
Boneyard 1997

1 by Hart Fisher & James Helkowski . . . 2.00
2 . . . 2.00
3 by Hart Fisher & John Cassaday 2.00
4 The Quiet Demon . . . 2.00
Spec.#1 Dark Angel/Bill the Bull, 48-page (1998) . . . 4.95
Spec. 1999 . . . 4.95
GN Last Decade Dead Century . . . 15.95
GN deluxe . . . 19.95

DARK ANGEL
CPM Manga 1999

1 by Kia Asamiya . . . 2.95
2 thru 5 . . . @2.95
6 thru 18 . . . @2.95
TPB Vol. 1 rep. #1–#5 . . . 15.95
HC Vol. 1 . . . 39.95

DARK ASSASSIN

1 thru 3 . . . @1.50

Vol. 2

1 thru 5 . . . @2.00

DARK CITY ANGEL
Freak Pit Productions

1 I:Lt.Michelle Constello . . . 3.50
2 . . . 3.50
3 Sex Doll is Prime Suspect . . . 3.50

DARK FANTASIES
Dark Fantasy 1994–97

0 Donna Mia foil (c) . . . 8.00
0 Destiny Angel foil (c) . . . 7.50
0 photo or nude (c)s . . . @6.00
1 Jli (c) . . . 9.00
1a test print Jli (c) . . . 12.00
1 2nd printing . . . 3.95
1 signed & numbered . . . 7.95
2 Kevin J. Taylor Girl (c) . . . 3.50
2a foil stamped . . . 3.50
3 JOb Crow (c) . . . 4.00
3a foil stamped . . . 3.50
4 . . . 2.95
4a foil stamped . . . 3.50
5 . . . 2.95
5a foil stamped . . . 3.50
6 Angel Destiny . . . 2.95
6a foil stamped . . . 3.50
7 . . . 2.95
7a foil stamped . . . 3.50
8 . . . 2.95
8 Blue cover . . . 3.50
8 Red cover . . . 3.50
8 deluxe foil-enhanced . . . 3.95
9 Destiny Angel (c) . . . 3.50
9a Destiny Angel, red foil (c) . . . 3.95
9b Horror (c) . . . 3.50
9c Horror, red foil (c) . . . 3.95
10 . . . 3.50
10a red foil (c) . . . 3.95
Spec.#1 Summers Eve Pin-up . . . 2.95
Spec.#1 foil-stamped . . . 3.50

DARK FORCE
Omega 7

1 A:Dark Force . . . 2.00

DARK FRINGE
Brainstorm 1996

1 . . . 2.95

DARK FRINGE: SPIRITS OF THE DEAD
Brainstorm 1997

1 by Eman Torre & John Kisse . . . 2.95
2 concl. . . . 2.95

DARK ISLAND
Davdez Arts 1998

1 by Barry Blair & Colin Chan . . . 2.50
2 thru 4 . . . @2.50

DARK LORD
RAK

1 thru 3 . . . @1.75

DARK MANGA
London Night

1 Featuring Demonique . . . 4.95
1 nude cover . . . 6.00

DARK MUSE
Dark Muse Productions

1 with mini-comic . . . 3.50
1a with mini-comic . . . 5.00
2 . . . 3.95
3 F:Coffin Joe . . . 3.95

Dark Oz #2
© Arrow

DARK OZ
Arrow Comics 1997

1 (of 5) by Griffith, Kerr & Bryan . . . 2.75
2 . . . 2.75
3 . . . 2.75
4 . . . 2.75
5 . . . 2.75
Spec. Bill Bryan's Oz Collection . . . 2.95

DARK REGIONS

1 . . . 2.50

B & W PUB.

2 . . . . 2.50
3 Scarce 3.00
4 and 5 . . . . @1.50

DARK STAR

1 I:Ran 2.25
2 thru 3 . . . . @2.25

DARK VISIONS

Pyramid

1 I:Wasteland Man. 1.70
2 thru 4 . . . . @1.70

DARK WOLF

Eternity

1 and 2 . . . . @2.00

Volume 2

1 thru 14 . . . . @2.00
Ann. #1 . . . . 2.25

DARQUE RAZOR

London Night 1996

½ by Dan Membeila & Albert Holaso,
Dark Birth. 2.25
½ necro-embossed edition. 10.00
1 . . . . 3.00
1a nude cover 10.00
2 . . . . 3.00
3 . . . . 3.00

DAYS OF DARKNESS

Apple

1 From Pearl Harbor
to Midway. 2.75
2 Pearl Harbor Attack,cont. 2.75
3 Japanese Juggernaut 2.75
4 Bataan Peninsula 2.75
GN 14.95

Deadbeats #7
© Claypool

DEADBEATS

Claypool Comics 1993

1 thru 13 . . . . @2.50
14 New Ways to Dream 2.50
15 thru 25. . . . . @2.50
26 by Richard Howell & Ricardo
Villagran, The Southland
Family Saga. 2.50
27 Christine transformed into
Predator. 2.50
28 . . . . 2.50
29 forbidden antiquities. 2.50
30 V:Dracula 2.50
31 Reconstructing Deadbeats 2.50
32 New generation of Deadbeats . . 2.50
33 Quiet Night in Fear City 2.50
34 Dagger of Deliverance 2.50
35 Deadbeats of Danger Street . . . 2.50
36 By His Majesty's Request 2.50
37 Carnival of Goals 2.50
38 HorrorFest begins 2.50
39 HorrorFest 2.50
40 HorrorFest. 2.50
41 Guys Night Out 2.50
42 Dark Dealings 2.50
43 Dodging the Bullet 2.50
44 Town for Sale 2.50
TPB Rep. #1–#6. . . . . 12.95

DEADKILLER

Caliber

1 Rep Deadworld 19 thru 21 . . . . . 2.95

DEADTALES

Caliber

1 'When a Body Meets a Body' . . . 2.95

DEADTIME STORIES

1 AAd,WS 1.75

DEADWORLD

Arrow

1 Arrow Pyb 5.00
2 . . . . 4.00
3 V:King Zombie 3.50
4 V:King Zombie 3.50
5 Team Rests 3.50
6 V:King Zombie 3.50
7 F:KZ & Deake, Graphic(c). 3.50
7a Tame cover. 2.00
8 V:Living Corpse, Graphic(c) 2.50
8a Tame cover. 2.00
9 V:Sadistic Punks, Graphic(c). . . . 2.50
9a Tame cover. 2.00
10 V:King Zombie, Graphic(c). 2.50
10a Tame cover 2.00
11 V:King Zombie, Graphic(c) 3.00
11a Tame cover 2.50
12 I:Percy, Graphic(c). 3.00
12a Tame cover 2.50
13 V:King Zombie, Graphic(c). 3.00
13a Tame cover 2.50
14 V:Voodoo Cult,Graphic(c). 3.00
14a Tame cover 2.50
15 Zombie stories,Graphic(c) 3.00
15a Tame cover 2.50
16 V:'Civilized' Community 2.50
17 V:King Zombie. 2.50
18 V:King Zombie. 2.50
19 V:Grakken 2.50
20 V:King Zombie. 2.50
21 Dead Killer. 2.50
22 L:Dan & Joey. 2.50
23 V:King Zombie. 2.50
24 . . . . 2.50
25 (R:Vince Locke). 2.50
26 . . . . 2.50

Caliber

1 thru 11 . . . . @2.95
12 thru 14 Death Call . . . . @2.95
15 Death Call pt. 6 . . . . 2.95
Spec. Deadworld Archives, rep. . . . 2.50
Spec. Bits & Pieces, rep.
Caliber Presents #2 . . . . . . 1.60
Spec. To Kill A King,R:Deadkiller . . 2.95

DEATH ANGEL

Lightning 1997

1 by J. Cleary & Anderson. 2.95
1 variant cover. 2.95
1 limited edition A 9.95
1 limited edition B 9.95

DEATH OF ANGEL GIRL

Angel Entertainment 1997

1 by Ellis Bell & Cam Forrest,
F:Michelle 2.95
1A Deluxe Erotic Nude cover. 3.95
1B Deluxe Erotic Nude cover. . . . 15.00

DEATH OF BLOODFIRE

Lightning

1 . . . . 3.00
1a variant cover. 3.00

DEATHDREAMS OF DRACULA

Apple

1 Selection of short stories 2.50
2 short stories 2.50
3 Inc. Rep. BWr,'Breathless' 2.50
4 short stories 2.50

DEATH HUNT

Eternity

1 . . . . 2.00
2 . . . . 2.00

DEATHMARK

Lightning Comics

1 O:War Party 2.75

DEATH RATTLE

Kitchen Sink (Prev. Color)

4 . . . . 3.00
5 . . . . 2.50
6 Steve Bissette(c) 2.00
7 Ed Gein 2.00
8 I:Xenozoic Tales 10.00
9 BW,rep. 2.00
10 AW,rep. 2.00
11 thru 15 . . . . @2.00
16 BW,Spacehawk 2.00
17 Rand Holmes(c) 2.00
18 FMc. 2.00

DEATH'S HEAD

Crystal

1 thru 3 . . . . @2.00

DEATHWORLD

Adventure Comics 1990

1 Harry Harrison adapt. 2.50
2 thru 4 . . . . @2.50

BOOK II 1991

1 Harry Harrison adapt. 2.50
2 thru 4 . . . . @2.50

BOOK III 1991

1 H.Harrison adapt.,colonization . . 2.50
2 Attack on the Lowlands. 2.50
3 Attack on the Lowlands contd. . . 2.50
4 last issue 2.50

DEE VEE

Dee Vee Feb., 1997

1 ECa, F:Alex 2.95

B & W PUB.

2 ECa 2.95
3 ECa 2.95
4 thru 14 . . . . @2.95
Spec. #1 Life is Cheap 2.95

DEFENSELESS DEAD
Adventure Comics 1991

1 Larry Niven adapt. A:Gil 2.50
2 A:Organlegger 2.50
3 A:Organlegger 2.50

DELTA TENN

1 thru 11 . . . . @1.50

DEMON BABY
SQP/666 Comics Jan., 1997

1 by Rich Larson, seq. to Hell on Heels 2.95
1a deluxe 9.95
2 . . . . 2.95
2a deluxe 9.95
3 . . . . 2.95
3a deluxe 9.95
GN Hell on Heels 9.95
GN Hell on Heels, deluxe 19.95

DEMON BITCH
Forbidden 1997–98

1-shot 2.95
Nude cover 2.95
Spec.#1 DemonBitch vs.AngelGirl . 2.95
Nude cover 4.00
Spec.#1 Demon Bitch: Devilspawn, by Angela Benoit & Nirut Chaswan 3.00
Nude cover 3.00
Spec.#1 Demon Bitch: Hellslave, Free on Earth cover 3.00
Nude Hellslave cover 3.00
Spec.#1 Demon Bitch: Tales of the Damned 2.95
Nude cover 4.00

Demongate #3
© Sirius

DEMONGATE
Sirius 1996–97

1 thru 12 by Bao Lin Hum & Colin Chan . . . . @2.50

DEMON GUN
Crusade Entertainment

1 thru 3 GCh,KtH . . . . @2.95

DEMON HUNTER
Aircel

1 thru 4 . . . . @2.00

DEMON HUNTER
Davdez Arts 1998

1 by Barry Blair & Colin Chan 2.50
2 F:Hunter Gordon 2.50
3 . . . . 2.50

DEMONIQUE
London Night 1997

½ by SKy Owens, A:Anvil 3.00
½a nude cover 5.00
1 by Membeila & Owens 3.00
1a nude cover variant 6.00
2 F:Viper 3.00
3 Mayhem 3.00
4 Final issue 3.00

DEMONIQUE: ANGEL OF NIGHT
London Night 1997

1 (of 3) by Skylar Owens 3.00
1a nude cover variant 6.00
2 . . . . 3.00
2a nude cover variant 6.00
3 final issue 3.00
3a nude cover variant 6.00

DEMON'S TAILS
Adventure

1 . . . . 2.50
2 A:Champion 2.50
3 V:Champion 2.50
4 V:Champion 2.50

DEMON WARRIOR

1 thru 12 . . . . @1.50
13 and 14 . . . . @1.75

DENIZENS OF DEEP CITY
Jabberwocky

1 thru 8 . . . . @2.00

DERRECK WAYNE'S STRAPPED
Gothic Images

1 Confrontational Factor 2.25
2 Confrontational Factor 2.25

DESCENDING ANGELS
Millennium 1995

1 I:3 Angels 2.00
2 F:Jim Johnson 2.95
3 F:Jim Johnson 2.95

DESERT PEACH
Thoughts & Images

1 thru 4 . . . . @2.00

DESTINY ANGEL
Dark Fantasy Productions 1996

1 (of 3) 3.95

1 2nd printing 3.95
1a deluxe 4.50
2 "Sunless Garden" 3.50
2a foil cover 3.95
2b photo cover 3.95

DESTROY
Eclipse

1 Large Size 4.95
2 Small Size,3-D 4.95

DETECTIVE, THE
Caliber 1998

1 by Gerard Goffaux 2.95
2 . . . . 2.95
3 Clutches of the Past 2.95

DEVIL JACK
Doom Theatre 1995

1 I:Devil Jack 2.95
1a Directors Cut 2.95
2 V:Belegosi 2.95
3 . . . . 3.00

DEVIL'S WORKSHOP
Blue Comet Press 1995

1 Iron Cupcakes 2.95

DIABOLIK
Scorpion Productions 1999

VOL. 1

1 Terror Aboard The Karima 5.95
2 Fight Against Time 5.95
3 Crumbs for the Scum 5.95
4 Family with no morals 5.95
5 . . . . 5.95
6 . . . . 5.95

VOL. 2

1 Target: Diabolik 5.95
2 One Crazy Love 5.95
3 . . . . 5.95
4 Interrupted Game 5.95

DICK DANGER
Olsen Comics 1998

1 by W.W. Olsen 2.95
2 F:Red Olga 2.95
3 The Angel Murder 2.95
4 Is Hitler Still Alive? 2.95
5 Nikita, The Cat Girl 2.95

DICK TRACY CRIMEBUSTER
ACG Comics 1998

1 by Max Allan Collins & Dick Locher 2.95
2 thru 9 . . . . @2.95

DICK TRACY DETECTIVE
ACG Comics 1999

1 (of 4) by Chester Gould 2.95
2 thru 4 . . . . @2.95

DICK TRACY MAGAZINE

1 V:Little Face Finnyo 3.95

DICK TRACY MONTHLY
Blackthorne

1 thru 25 . . . . @2.00

DICK TRACY: THE EARLY YEARS

5 and 6 . . . . @2.95
7 and 8 . . . . @3.50

DICK TRACY WEEKLY

26 thru 108 . . . . @2.00
Unprinted Stories #3. . . . . 2.95
1 3-D Special 3.00
Spec. #1. 2.95
Spec. #2. 2.95
Spec. #3. 2.95

DICKS

Caliber 1997

1 (of 4),GEn,JMC, ... 2.95
2 GEn,JMC 2.95
3 GEn,JMC 2.95
4 concl. 2.95
TPB GEn,JMC 12.95

DIGITAL DRAGON

Peregrine Entertainment 1999

1 by Bryan Heyboer. 2.95
2 . . . . 2.95
3 . . . . 2.95
4 . . . . 2.95

DILLINGER

Rip Off Press

1 Outlaw Dillinger 2.50

DIM-WITTED DARRYL

Slave Labor Graphics 1998

1 by Michael Bresnahan 2.95
2 thru 5 . . . . @2.95

DINOSAURS

Caliber

1 History of Dinosaurs 3.00

DINOSAURS FOR HIRE

Eternity

1 . . . . 3.00
1a Rep. 2.00
2 thru 9 . . . . @2.00
Fall Classic #1 . . . . 2.25

Malibu

#1 3-D special 3.50

DIRECTORY TO A NON-EXISTENT UNIVERSE

Eclipse

1 . . . . 2.00

DIRTY PAIR

1 . . . . 9.00
2 . . . . 7.00
3 . . . . 6.00
4 end mini-series. 6.00

Eclipse

reprint 1-3. . . . . 5.00
Vol 2 #1 thru 5 . . . . @5.00

DIRTY PAIR: PLAGUE OF ANGELS

Eclipse 1990

1 thru 5 . . . . @5.00

DIRTY PAIR: SIM EARTH

Eclipse

1 thru 4 . . . . @4.00

DISCIPLES

Caliber Core 1998

1 Climate of fear 2.95
2 . . . . 2.95

A DISTANT SOIL

Warp Graphics

1 A:Panda Khan 10.00
2 . . . . 5.00
3 . . . . 4.00
4 . . . . 3.00
5 . . . . 3.00
6 thru 9 . . . . @3.00

Aria Press

1 F:Seasons of Spring. 6.00
1a-2nd to 4th printing. 2.50
2 . . . . 5.00
3 . . . . 3.00
4 . . . . 3.00
5 thru 8 . . . . @2.00
9 thru 11 Knights of the Angel . . @2.50
12 thru 14 . . . . @3.00
GN Knights of the Angel, deluxe . . 15.95
GN Immigrant Song rep.#1–#3 . . . . 6.95

Ditko's World Static #1
© Renegade

DITKOS WORLD: STATIC

Renegade

1 thru 3 SD . . . . @1.70

DOCTOR

Ironcat 1997

1 (of 5) by Bang Ippongi 2.95
2 . . . . 2.95
4 . . . . 2.95
5 Pay Back in the City of
Santa La Paz 2.95
6 final issue 2.95

DR. GORPON

Eternity 1991

1 I:Dr.Gorpon,V:Demon 2.25
2 A:Doofus,V:ChocolateBunny. . . . 2.50
3 D:Dr.Gorpon. 2.50

DR. RADIUM

Silverline

1 . . . . 3.00
2 . . . . 2.00
3 and 4 . . . . @1.50

DR. RADIUM: MAN OF SCIENCE

Slave Labor

1 And Baby makes 2, BU: Dr.
Radiums' Grim Future 2.50

DOC WEIRD'S THRILL BOOK

1 AW. 1.75
2 . . . . 1.75
3 . . . . 1.75

DOCTOR WEIRD

Caliber Press

1 V:Charnogg 2.50
2 V:Charnogg 2.50

DODEKAIN

Antartic Press

1 and 2 by Masayuki Fujihara . . @2.95
3 Rampage Vs. Zogerians 2.95
4 V:Zogerians 2.95
5 F:Takuma 2.95
6 Dan vs. Takuma 2.75
7 V:Okizon 2.75
8 V:Okizon 2.95

DOGAROO

Blackthorne 1988

1 . . . . 2.00

DOGS O'WAR, THE

Crusade Entertainment 1996–97

1 thru 3 (of 3). . . . . @2.95

DOLLS

Sirius 1998

1-shot science fiction 2.95

DOMINION

Eclipse

1 . . . . 3.00
2 thru 6 . . . . @2.00

DOMINO CHANCE

Chance

1 1,000 printed 10.00
1a 2nd printing 3.50
2 thru 6 . . . . @3.00
7 I:Gizmo 7.00
8 A:Gizmo 11.00
9 . . . . 2.50

[2nd Series]

1 . . . . 3.00
2 and 3 . . . . @2.00

DONATELLO

Mirage

1 A: Turtles 12.00

Donna Mia #2 variant cover
© Avatar

DONNA MIA
Avatar Press 1997

0 by Tevlin Utz. 3.00
0a nude cover 4.95
0b leather cover. 15.00
0c signed 8.00
1 . . . . 3.95
1a signed 8.00
1b Royal Blue edition. 50.00
2 . . . . 3.95
2a deluxe 4.50
3 (of 3) 3.00
3a deluxe 8.00
Giant Size #1 . . . . 3.00
Giant Size #1 nude. 4.95
Giant Size #1 leather cover. 15.00
Giant Size #1 signed 8.00
Giant Size #2 . . . . 3.95
Giant Size #2 Deluxe 10.00
TPB rep. #0–#3 & Giant
Size #1–#2. . . . . 15.95
HC rep. #0–#3 & Giant
Size #1–#2 deluxe 39.95
HC rep. #0–#3 & Giant Size
#1–#2 with original sketch. . . 150.00
Spec. Infinity. 3.00
Spec. Infinity, nude cover 4.95
Spec. Infinity, Leather cover 25.00
Spec.#1 Pin-up (1997) 3.00
Spec.#1a nude cover 4.95

DON SIMPSON'S BIZARRE HEROES
Fiasco Comics

0 thru 7 . . . . @2.95
8 V:Darkcease. 2.95
9 R:Yan Man 2.95
10 F:Mainstreamers 2.95
11 Search for Megaton Man 2.95
12 . . . . 2.95
13 House of Megaton Man 2.95
14 Cec Vs. Dark Cease 2.95
TPB Apocalypse Affiliation 12.95

DOOMSDAY + 1
ACG Comics 1998

1 by JBn rep. Charlton. 2.95
2 A Faceless Foe 2.95
3 . . . . 2.95
4 The Hidden Enemy. 2.95
5 Rule of Fear. 2.95
6 . . . . 2.95
7 NA(c), final issue 2.95

DORK TOWER
Corsair Publishing 1998

1 by John Kovalic 2.95
2 thru 8 . . . . @2.95

DORK TOWER
Dork Storm 2000

1 by John Kovalic 2.95
2 thru 8 . . . . @2.95
9 Angry Young Fan 2.95
10 Road Rules 2.95
11 World of Dorkness 2.95
TPB Dork Tower. 15.95

DOUBLE EDGE DOUBLE
Double Edge

1 thru 3 . . . . @3.50
4 Heroes Inc. Rep.#1-#2 . . . . 2.95

DOUBLE IMPACT
High Impact Studios 1995–96

1 I: China & Jazz. 5.00
1a Chromium (c) variant, signed . . 6.00
1b Rainbow (c) w/certificate. 15.00
1c Rainbow (c) w/o certificate . . . 10.00
2 Castilo's Crime 3.00
2a nude cover variant 10.00
2b silver version 10.00
2c signed, w/certificate 5.00
3 . . . . 5.00
3a Bondage (c) 15.00
4 . . . . 5.00
4a Phoenix (c). 15.00
5 . . . . 5.00
5a nude cover 15.00
6 China cover 3.00
6a Jazz cover 3.00
6b signed China or Jazz(c) 15.00
6c bondage(c) 10.00
7 & 8 . . . . @3.00
8a variant (c). 8.00

2nd Series 1996–97

0 . . . . 3.00
0a nude (c) 10.00
1 . . . . 3.00
1a chromium (c) 4.00
1b Chromium variant edition 14.95
1c Christmas (c) 10.00
2 . . . . 3.00
2a Sweedish Erotica(c) 10.00
Spec.#1 Double Impact/Lethal Strike:
Double Strike, x-over 3.00
Nude RCI(c) cover 9.95
Spec.#1 Double Impact/Nikki Blade:
Hard Core x-over (1997) 2.95
Platinum variant RCI(c). 10.00
Gold Metal variant RCI(c) 20.00
Spec.#1 Raising Hell, RCI,RkB 2.95
Spec.#1 Raising Hell, nude art(c) . 10.00
Spec.#1 Raising Hell,nude
photo(c) 15.00

ABC Comics 1998

1 encore 3.00
1a encore, Chicago cover 6.00
1b encore, San Diego nude cover . 6.00
Spec. Double Impact/Luxura (1998) 3.00
Spec. nude collectors edition 5.95
Spec. Vampeurotica edition. 5.95
Bikini Spec. 3.00
Bikini Spec. nude covers 6.00
Christmas Spec.. . . . . 3.00
Christmas Spec., gold foil 10.00
Christmas Spec., nude cover 8.00
Coll.#1 . . . . 3.00
Coll.#1a x-mas 8.00
Coll.#1b nude cover 8.00
Coll.#1c nude gold foil 10.00
Spring Spec.#1. . . . . 3.00
Spring Spec.#1a manga cover 8.00
Spring Spec.#1b nude manga cover 8.00
Spring Spec.#1c nude photo cover . 8.00
Summer Bikini Spec. 1999 . . . . 3.00
Summer Bikini Spec. 1999 nude(c). 8.00
Gallery Collection #1 . . . . 5.00
Gallery Collection #1 nude(c) 8.00
Lingerie Special 3.00

DOUBLE IMPACT ALIVE
ABC Comics 1999

1 (of 3) Double Impact Alive 2000 . 3.00
1a Double Impact Alive 2000,
gold foil ed. 8.00
1b Red Leather 15.00
2 RCI. 3.00
2a Manga cover 8.00
2b Nude cover. 8.00
2c silver embossed foil 10.00

DOUBLE IMPACT: ASSASSINS FOR HIRE
High Impact April, 1997

1 RCI,RkB 3.00
1 nude art cover 10.00
1 nude photo cover 15.00
2 . . . . 3.00
2 gold nude cover 10.00
2 signed nude cover 15.00

ABC Comics 1998

1 . . . . 3.00
1a gold nude RCI cover 10.00
1b gold nude RCI cover, signed . . 15.00

DOUBLE IMPACT: FROM THE ASHES
ABC Comics 1998

1 (of 2) RCI 3.00
1B variant Swedish Erotika cover B 5.95
1C variant Swedish Erotika cover C 5.95
2 RCI. 3.00
2A variant cover A. 5.95
2B variant cover B. 5.95

DOUBLE IMPACT: HOT SHOTS
ABC Studios 1999

1 RCI. 3.00
1a adult covers 8.00
1b gold medal edition, nude (c) . . 10.00
2 . . . . 3.00
2a adult covers 8.00

DOUBLE IMPACT MERCS
ABC Comics 1999

1 (of 3) RCI 3.00
1a deluxe 8.00
2 RCI. 3.00
2a deluxe 10.00

DOUBLE IMPACT: ONE STEP BEYOND
ABC Comics 1998

1 (of 2) RCI 3.00
1a Leather cover 20.00
1b nude cover. 6.00

DOUBLE IMPACT RAW
ABC Comics 1997
1 (of 3) RCI, adult 3.00
1a adult variant (c). 8.00
1b Star photo (c) 10.00
1A Wraparound cover A 5.95
1B Wraparound cover B 5.95
2 . . . . 2.95
2a nude cover 5.95
3 concl. 2.95
3A Variant cover A. 5.95
3B Variant live model nude cover B 5.95
VOL. 2
1 (of 3) adult material 3.00
1a silver nude cover 6.00
1b nude platinum cover 6.00

DOUBLE IMPACT/RAZOR
ABC Studios 1999
1 (of 3) 3.25
1a Nude Huerta (c) 8.00
1b Previews exclusive 8.00
1c Manga alt.(c) 8.00
2 . . . . 3.25
2a deluxe nude 8.00

DOUBLE IMPACT SUICIDE RUN
ABC Comics 1998
1 (of 2) RCI 3.00
1a nude variant (c) 6.00
1b Nude live model (c). 8.00
1b Leather cover 15.00
2 adult material 3.00
2a nude cover A 8.00
2b nude cover B 8.00
Collected edition. 3.00
Collected, gold foil 10.00
Collected, Manga nude (c) 8.00

DOUBLE IMPACT 2069
ABC Comics 1999
1 Virgin Encore Edition 3.00
1a Deluxe Erotica edition. 8.00
Christmas Spec. 3.00
Christmas Spec. nude (c) 10.00
Christmas Spec. Previews (c). 8.00

DOUBLE IMPACT X
ABC Comics 2000
1 . . . . 5.95
1a alternate (c) 5.95
1b Adult (c) 8.00
2 . . . . 5.95
2 deluxe, vinyl (c) 20.00
Intro 20.00

DRACULA
1 . . . . 3.75
1a 2nd printing 2.50
2 thru 4 . . . . @2.50

DRACULA IN HELL
Apple
1 O:Dracula. 2.50
2 O:Dracula contd. 2.50

DRACULA: SUICIDE CLUB
Adventure
1 I:Suicide Club in UK 2.50
2 Dracula/Suicide Club cont. 2.50
3 Club raid,A:Insp.Harrison 2.50
4 Vision of Miss Fortune 2.50

DRACULA: THE LADY IN THE TOMB
Eternity
1 . . . . 2.50

DRACULA'S COZY COFFIN
Draculina Publishing 1995
1 thru 4 Halloween issue 2.95

DRAGONBALL
Viz Communications March, 1998
1 (of 12) by Akira Toriyama 5.00
2 thru 4 . . . . @4.00
5 thru 12 . . . . @3.00
PART TWO 1999
1 (of 15) by Akira Toriyama 25.00
2 thru 4 . . . . @4.00
5 thru 15 . . . . @3.00
TPB Vol. 1 . . . . 14.95
TPB Vol. 2 . . . . 14.95
PART THREE (2000)
1 (of 14) by Akira Toriyama 2.95
2 thru 5 . . . . @2.95

Dragonball Z, Part Two, #10
© Viz Communications

DRAGONBALL Z
Viz Communications March, 1998
1 (of 9) by Akira Toriyama 2.95
2 thru 9 . . . . @2.95
TPB Vol. 1 . . . . 14.95
PART TWO 1998
1 (of 14) by Akira Toriyama 2.95
2 thru 9 . . . . @2.95
10 thru 14. . . . . @2.95
PART THREE 2000
1 (of 10) by Akira Toriyama 2.95
2 thru 9 . . . . @2.95

DRAGONFORCE
Aircel
(Prev. Color)
8 thru 13 DK . . . . @2.50

DRAGONFORCE CHRONICLES
Aircel
Vol. 1 thru Vol. 5 rep. . . . . @2.95

DRAGONMIST
Raised Brow Publications
1 I:Dragonmist. 2.75
2 F:Assassin 2.75

DRAGON OF THE VALKYR
1 . . . . 1.75
2 thru 4 . . . . @2.00

DRAGON QUEST
1 TV 15.00
2 TV 7.50
3 TV 6.50

DRAGONRING
[1st Series]
1 B.Blair,rare 110.00
Aircel
1 . . . . 3.50
2 . . . . 2.00
3 thru 6 . . . . @1.75
See Also Color Comics

DRAGON WARS
Ironcat 1998
1 by Ryukihei 2.95
2 thru 11 . . . . @2.95
TPB Vol. 1 . . . . 17.95

DRAGON WEEKLY
1 Southern Knights 1.75
2 and 3 . . . . @1.75

DREAD OF NIGHT
Hamilton
1 Horror story collection. 3.95
2 Json, inc.`Genocide'. 3.95

DREAM ANGEL AND ANGEL GIRL
Angel Entertainment 1998
1 . . . . 2.95
1a nude delicious Dream Angel (c) 4.00
1b nude anxious Angel Girl (c). . . . 4.00

DREAM ANGEL: THE QUANTUM DREAMER
Angel Entertainment 1997
0 Nude Manga cover. 5.00
1 by Mort Castle & Adriana Melo . . 2.95
1 Virgin nude cover 5.00
1 Nude Platinum cover 15.00
2 . . . . 2.95
2 Virgin nude cover 5.00
2 Nude Platinum cover 15.00

DREAM ANGEL: WORLD WITHOUT END
Angel Entertainment 1998
1 Dream world cover 3.00
1 nude nightmare cover. 3.00

DREAMGIRL
Angel Entertainment 1996
0 by David Campitti & Al Rio 2.95
0 Virgin Nude cover. 5.00
0 Lost in Heaven nude cover 7.00
0 platinum edition, nude cover 8.00
1 . . . . 2.95
1 deluxe 5.95
1 Manga cover 5.00
1 Nude Manga cover 5.00

DREAMERY
Eclipse
1 thru 13 . . . . @2.00

DREAMLANDS
Caliber "New Worlds" 1996
1 . . . . 2.95
2 flip book with Boston Bombers #3 2.95

DREAMTIME
Blind Rat
1 Young Deserter 2.95
2 Gypsy Trouble 2.50

DREAMWALKER
Caliber Tapestry 1997
1 thru 4 . . . . @2.95
5 by Jenni Gregory, 2nd story arc. . 2.95
6 2nd story arc, concl. 2.95

DREAMWALKER: CAROUSEL
Avatar 1998
0 . . . . 3.00
1 by Jenni Gregory 3.00
2 conclusion 3.00

DREAMWALKER: SUMMER RAIN
Avatar 1999
1 by Jenni Gregory 3.00

DREAMWALKER: AUTUMN LEAVES
Avatar 1999
1 by Jenni Gregory 3.00
2 conclusion 3.00

DREAMWOLVES
Dramenon Studios
1 . . . . 3.00
2 . . . . 3.00
3 F:Desiree 3.00
4 V:Venefica 3.00
5 V:Venefica 3.00
6 R:Carnifax 3.00
7 . . . . 3.00
8 F:Wendy Bascum 3.00

DRIFTERS
Infinity Graphics 1986
1 . . . . 1.75

DRYWALL AND OSWALD SHOW, THE
Fireman Press 1998
1 by Mandy Carter,Trent Kaniuga . 2.95

DUNGEONEERS
1 thru 8 . . . . @1.50

Eagle #5
© Crystal Publications

EAGLE
Crystal
1 . . . . 3.00
1a signed & limited 5.00
2 thru 5 . . . . @2.75
6 thru 11 . . . . @2.25
12 . . . . 2.50
13 thru 17 . . . . @2.00

Apple
18 thru 26 . . . . @2.00

EAGLE
Viz Communications 2000
1 (of 14) The Candidate,112-pages 6.95
2 Scandal 6.95
3 The Vice-President 6.95
4 New Hampshire 6.95
5 On the Battlefield 6.95
6 King of New York 6.95
7 Pandora's Box 6.95
8 The Debate 6.95
9 Passion 6.95
TPB Book 1 . . . . 19.95
TPB Book 2 . . . . 19.95

EAGLE: DARK MIRROR
Comic Zone
1 A:Eagle, inc reps 2.75
2 In Japan, V:Lord Kagami 2.75
3 . . . . 2.95
4 . . . . 2.95

EAGLES DARE
Aager Comics
1 thru 4 . . . . @2.00
5 V:Dragon 2.00

EARTH LORE: LEGEND OF BEK LARSON
Eternity
1 . . . . 1.80

EARTH LORE: REIGN OF DRAGON LORD
1 . . . . 1.80
2 . . . . 1.75

EARTH WAR
Newcomers Publishing 1995
1 and 2 from Newcomers Illus. . . . 2.95

EARTH: YEAR ZERO
Eclipse
1 thru 4 . . . . @2.00

EAT-MAN
Viz Communications 1997
1 (of 6) by Akihito Yoshitami 2.95
2 thru 6 . . . . @2.95
Vol.1 Full Course Meal,rep.Pt.1. . . 15.95

PART TWO Feb., 1998
1 (of 5) by Akihito Yoshitami 2.95
2 (of 5) 3.50
3 thru 5 . . . . @3.25
TPB Vol. 2 Second Course 15.95

EB'NN THE RAVEN
Now
1 . . . . 5.00
2 . . . . 3.00
3 . . . . 2.50
4 . . . . 2.00
5 thru 9 . . . . @1.50

EBONIX-FILES, THE
Blatant Comics 1998
1A TV parody, cover A. 3.95
1B TV parody, cover B. 3.95
1c Nude Agent Sculky cover 9.95
1d Nude Agents in Bed cover 9.95

EDDIE CAMPELL'S BACCHUS
Eddie Campell Comics 1995
1 V:Telchines. 2.95
1 2nd printing 2.95
2 thru 10 V:Telchines . . . . @2.95
11 thru 26 ECa . . . . @2.95
27 thru 37 ECa . . . . @2.95
38 thru 46 . . . . @2.95
47 thru 56 . . . . @2.95
GN Collected Bacchus, Vol. 1. . . . . 9.95
GN Collected Bacchus, Vol. 2. . . . . 9.95
GN Collected Bacchus, Vol. 3, Doing the Islands 17.95
GN Collected Bacchus, Vol. 4, One Man Show 8.50
GN Collected Bacchus, Vol. 5 Earth, Air Water & Fire 9.95
GN Collected Bacchus, Vol. 6 . . . . 9.95
GN Collected Bacchus, Vol. 9, King Bacchus 12.95

EDDY CURRENT
1 thru 12 . . . . @2.00

EDGAR ALLAN POE
Tell Tale Heart 2.00
Pit & Pendulum 2.00
Masque of the Red Death. 2.00
Murder in the Rue Morgue 2.00

EDGE
1 . . . . 3.00

Vol 2 #1 thru #3 . . . . @3.00
Vol 2 #4 thru #6 . . . . @2.00

Eightball #7
© Fantagraphics

EIGHTBALL
Fantagraphics

1 . . . . 10.00
1a 2nd to 6th printing. 3.00
2 . . . . 7.00
2a 2nd to 5th printing. 3.00
3 . . . . 6.00
3a 2nd to 4th printing. 3.00
4 . . . . 5.00
4a 2nd to 4th printing. 3.00
5 . . . . 5.00
5 3rd printing 3.50
6 thru 10 . . . . @4.00
11 A:Ghost World 3.50
12 F:Ghost World 3.25
13 thru 17 . . . . @3.00
18 . . . . 4.00
19 . . . . 3.95
20 . . . . 3.95
21 48-page. 4.95
TPB Orgy Bound, rep. from #7–#14. . . . . 14.95
TPB Lout Rampage 14.95
TPB Pussey 8.95
HC Caricature. 29.95

ELECTRIC BALLET
Caliber

1 Revisionist History of Industrial Revolution 2.50

ELFLORD
[1st Series]

1 all rare 25.00
2 . . . . 20.00
3 . . . . 15.00
4 . . . . 12.00
5 . . . . 12.00
6 . . . . 20.00
7 . . . . 20.00
8 . . . . 20.00
9 thru 15 . . . . @15.00

ELFLORD
Aircel 1986

1 I:Hawk 5.00
1a 2nd printing 3.50
2 . . . . 3.00
2a 2nd printing 2.00
3 V:Doran 3.00
4 V:Doran 3.00
5 V:Doran 2.00
6 V:Nendo 2.00
Compilation Book 4.95

(Vol 2, #1 to #24, see Color)

25 thru 31 . . . . @2.00
32 . . . . 2.50

ELFLORD
Warp Graphics Jan., 1997

1 (of 4) by Barry Blair & Colin Chan 2.95
2 . . . . 2.95
3 . . . . 2.95
4 . . . . 2.95

ELFLORD: ALL THE LONELY PLACES
Warp Graphics Aug., 1997

1 (of 4)Barry Blair & Colin Chan. . . 2.95
Becomes:

HAWK AND WINDBLADE: ALL THE LONELY PLACES

2 (of 2) 2.95

ELFLORD CHRONICLES
Aircel 1990

1 (of 12) thru 8 rep B.Blair . . . . . @2.50

ELFLORD CUTS LOOSE
Warp Graphics Sept., 1997

1 by Barry Blair and Colin Chan. . . 2.95
2 F:Hawk Erik-san 2.95
3 . . . . 2.95
4 all out attack. 2.95
5 north to safety 2.95
6 Homeward 2.95
7 back to Greenhaven 2.95
8 Greenhaven Siege 2.95
9 Felines, Nothing More Than Felines. 2.95

ELFLORD: HAWK
China Winds 1998

1-shot by Barry Blair and Colin Chan. 3.50

ELFLORE: THE HIGH SEAS
Raw Comics

4 by Barry Blair (500 copies) 4.95

ELFQUEST
Warp Graphics 1979–85

1 WP. 30.00
1a WP,2nd printing 10.00
1b WP,3rd printing. 5.00
1c WP,4th printing (1989) 4.00
2 WP. 15.00
2a WP,2nd printing 4.00
2b WP,3rd printing. 3.00
2c WP,4th printing (1989) 2.50
3 WP. 12.00
3a WP,2nd printing 4.00
3b WP,3rd printing. 3.00
3c WP,4th printing (1989) 2.50
4 WP. 12.00
4a WP,2nd printing 4.00
4b WP,3rd printing. 3.00
4c WP,4th printing (1989) 2.50
5 WP. 12.00
5a WP,2nd printing 4.00
5b WP,3rd printing. 3.00
6 WP. 12.00
6a WP,2nd printing 4.00
6b WP,3rd printing. 3.00
7 WP. 10.00
7a WP,2nd printing 3.00
8 WP. 10.00
8a WP,2nd printing 3.00
9 WP. 10.00
9a WP,2nd printing 3.00
10 thru 15 . . . . @8.00
16 WP,I:DistantSoil. 8.00
17 thru 21 WP. . . . . @8.00
TPB Gatherum 19.95

ELFQUEST
Warp Graphics

4 thru 14 ed. RPi. 4.95
15 . . . . 4.95
16 What if Cutter never became chief 4.95
17 F:Fire-Eye 4.95
18 Dreamtime, concl. 4.95
19 Wolfrider begins. 4.95
20 . . . . 4.95
21 20th anniv.. . . . . 4.95
22 F:Wolfrider. 4.95
23 F:WaveDancers. 4.95
24 F:Wolfrider. 4.95
25 F:Wolfrider. 4.95
26 Wild Hunt 4.95
27 . . . . 4.95
28 F:Ember & Teir 4.95
29 three new stories 4.95
30 new stories 4.95
31 new stories 4.95
32 Wild Hunt, pt.1, 24-page 2.95
33 Wild Hunt, pt.2. . . . . 2.95
34 Wild Hunt, pt.3. . . . . 2.95
35 Wild Hunt, pt.4. . . . . 2.95
Spec.#1 Worldpool,pt.1 (1997) 2.95
Spec.#2 Worldpool,pt.2 (1997) 2.95
READERS COLLECTIONS
TPB Vol.1 Fire & Flight 11.95
TPB Vol.2 The Forbidden Grove . . 11.95
TPB Vol.3 Captives of Blue Mountain 11.95
TPB Vol.4 Quest's End 11.95
TPB Vol.5 Siege at Blue Mountain 11.95
TPB Vol.6 Secret of Two-Edge . . . 11.95
TPB Vol.7 Cry From Beyond 11.95
TPB Vol.8 Kings of the Broken Wheel. 11.95
TPB Vol.8A Dreamtime 11.95
TPB Vol. 9 Rogue's Curse 13.95
TPB Vol. 9A Wolfrider 11.95
TPB Vol. 9B Blood of Ten Chiefs. . 12.95
TPB Vol. 9C Kahvi 13.95
TPB Vol.11A Huntress. 11.95
TPB Vol.11B Ascent 12.95
TPB Vol.11C Shadowstalker 12.95
TPB Vol.12 Ascent 12.95
TPB Vol.12A Reunion 12.95
TPB Vol.13A Rebels 11.95
TPB Vol.13B Junk. 11.95
TPB Vol.14 JINK. 11.95
TPB Vol.14A Skyward Shadow . . . 11.95
TPB Vol.14A Mindcoil 11.95
TPB Vol. 15 Forevergreen 12.95
TPB Vol.16 Wave Dancers 11.95
TPB Vol."?" Worldpool 12.95
HC Vol.1 thru Vol.8 . . . . @19.95
HC Beadtime Stories, 128-page . . 19.95
HC The Big Elfquest Gatherum. . . 19.95
HC New Blood 19.95
TPB The Rebels, 176-page. 11.95
GN Shards 13.95
GN Legacy (Hidden Years

#16–#22) 11.95
GN A Gift of Her Own. 16.95
HC Wolfrider's Guide to the World
of Elfquest 19.95
TPB Wolfrider's Guide, revised . . . 16.95
Spec. Metamorphosis, WP,
RPi (1996) 2.95
Spec. Elfquest: Wolfrider 2.95

ELFQUEST: KAHVI
Warp Graphics 1995
1 thru 6 I:Kahvi . . . . @2.25

ELFQUEST: KINGS OF THE BROKEN WHEEL
Warp Graphics 1990–92
1 WP. 2.25
2 thru 9 WP . . . . @2.25

Elfquest: Seige at Blue Mountain #1
© Warp Graphics

ELFQUEST: SEIGE AT BLUE MOUNTAIN
Warp Graphics/Apple Comics, 1987–88
1 WP,JSo 9.00
1a 2nd printing 3.00
2 WP. 6.00
2a 2nd printing 3.00
3 WP. 5.00
3a 2nd printing 2.00
4 thru 8 WP . . . . @5.00

ELFQUEST: TWO SPEAR
Warp Graphics 1995
1 thru 3 (of 5) Two-Spears past . @2.25

ELFQUEST: WORLDPOOL
Warp Graphics
Spec.#1 (of 2). 2.95
Spec.#2 (of 2). 2.95

ELFTHING
Eclipse
1 . . . . 3.00

ELFTREK
Dimension
1 Elfquest's Star Trek parody. 2.00

2 . . . . 1.75

ELF WARRIOR
1 . . . . 3.00
2 . . . . 2.50
3 thru 5 . . . . @2.00

ELIMINATOR
Eternity
1 'Drugs in the Future' 2.50
2 . . . . 2.50

ELVIRA, MISTRESS OF THE DARK
Claypool Comics
1 thru 35 . . . . @2.50
36 thru 74 photo covers . . . . @2.50
75 Mistress of the Jungle,pt.1 . . . . . 2.50
76 Mistress of the Jungle,pt.2 . . . . . 2.50
77 Rome on the Range 2.50
78 thru 90 photo covers . . . . @2.50
TPB Elvira, Mistress of the Dark . . 12.95
TPB Vol. 2 Double Delights. 12.95

ELVIRA
Eclipse
1 Rosalind Wyck 2.50

EMBRACE
London Night
1 NC17 edition, EHr, signed. 10.00

EMBRACE: HUNGER OF THE FLESH
London Night 1997
1 DQ,last of the original
vampire race 3.00
1a DQ,deluxe 6.00
1b signed by Kevin West 15.00
2 DQ. 3.00
2a DQ,deluxe 6.00
3 by Dan Membiela & Kevin
West, concl. 3.00
3a nude cover edition 6.00

EMERALDAS
Eternity 1990
1 thru 4 . . . . @2.25

EMMA DAVENPORT
Lohamn Hill Press
1 I:Emma Davenport 2.75
2 . . . . 2.75
3 O:Hammerin Jim 2.75
4 Cookie Woofer War 2.75

EMPIRE
Eternity
1 thru 4 . . . . @2.00

EMPTY ZONE
Sirius 1998
1 by Jason Alexander 2.95
1a limited edition 5.00
2 . . . . 2.50
3 . . . . 2.50
4 . . . . 2.50
TPB 11.95

VOL. 2 TRANSMISSIONS 1999
1 by Jason Alexander 2.95
2 thru 7 . . . . @2.95

8 History Lessions, pt.1 . . . . 2.95

ENCHANTED
Sirius 1997
1 (of 3) by Robert Chang. 2.95
2 . . . . 2.95
3 concl. 2.95

ENCHANTED VALLEY
Blackthorne
1 . . . . 1.75
2 . . . . 1.75

ENCHANTER
Eclipse
1 thru 3 . . . . @2.00

ENCHANTER: APOCALYPSE WIND NOVELLA
Entity
1 Foil Enhanced Cover 2.95

ENFORCERS
Dark Visions Publishing 1995
0 From Anthology Title. 2.50

ENTITY
Avatar
½ Nira X cover 5.95
½ Snowman cover. 10.95
½ Nira X silver cover 10.95
½ Snowman silver cover 15.95

ENTROPY TALES
1 . . . . 2.00
2 Domino Chance 1.50
3 thru 5 . . . . @1.50

EPSILON WAVE
Elite
1 . . . . 3.00
2 . . . . 2.00
3 thru 5 . . . . @1.60

EQUINE THE UNCIVILIZED
Graphspress
1 . . . . 4.00
2 . . . . 2.50
3 thru 6 . . . . @2.00

EQUINOX CHRONICLES
Innovation
1 I:Team Equinox, Black Avatar . . . 2.25
2 Black Avatar Plans US conquest. 2.25

ERADICATORS
Greater Mercury 1990–91
1 RLm (1st Work) 5.00
1a 2nd printing 1.50
2 . . . . 2.50
3 Vigil 2.00
4 thru 8 . . . . @1.50

ERIC PRESTON IS THE FLAME
B-Movie Comics
1 Son of G.A.Flame. 95

ESCAPE TO THE STARS
Visionary
1 thru 7 . . . . @1.25
[2nd Series]
1 & 2 . . . . @1.25

ESCAPE VELOCITY
Escape Velocity Press
1 and 2 . . . . @1.50

ESMERALDAS
Eternity
1 thru 4 . . . . @2.25

ESPERS
Halloween Comics April, 1996
1 JHI, R:ESPers 2.95
1 JHI,signed 2.95
2 JHI,signed 2.95
3 JHI, ... 2.95
3 JHI,signed 2.95
4 thru 6 JHI, conclusion . . . . @2.95
Volume 2
1 "Undertow" 2.95
2 . . . . 2.95

EVENT PRESENTS THE ASH UNIVERSE
Event Comics 1998
1-shot JQ,JP, 48pg 2.95

EVERETTE HARTSOE'S RAZOR
EH! Productions 2000
1 . . . . 3.50
1a Ruby Foil 5.00
2 . . . . 3.95

EVIL ERNIE
Eternity 1991–92
1 SHu,BnP,I&O:Evil Ernie, Lady Death. 50.00
1a Spec. 1992 reprint, 16 extra pages. 30.00
2 Death & Revival of Ernie, A:Lady Death, 1st (c) 35.00
3 Psycho Plague, A:Lady Death. . 30.00
4 A:Lady Death 25.00
5 A:Lady Death 25.00
TPB rep #1-5 . . . . 10.95

EVIL ERNIE
Chaos! Comics
1 thru 5 reprints . . . . @2.50
Spec. Youth Gone Wild, die-cut cover, Director's cut 5.00
TPB Youth Gone Wild. 9.95
Chaos! Comics 1996
1 encore presentation 2.50
2 thru 5 encore presentation . . . @2.00
TPB Revenge 12.95
Preview Book Depraved 5.00
Pieces of Me Script 4.95

EXIT
Caliber 1995
1 I:New series 2.95
2 thru 4 "The Traitors," pt.2–pt.4. @2.95
Epilogue 2.95
GN rep. 320 pages 19.95
GN rep. 160 pages 14.95

EX-MUTANTS
Amazing Comics 1986
1 AC/RLm 5.00
1a 2nd printing 2.00
2 and 3 . . . . @3.00
EC
4 and 5 . . . . @2.00
6 PP 2.00
7 . . . . 2.00
8 . . . . 2.00
Ann. #1 . . . . 2.00
Pin-Up Spec. #1 . . . . 2.00

Ex-Mutants #12
© Eternity

EX-MUTANTS: THE SHATTERED EARTH CHRONICLES
Eternity
1 thru 3 . . . . @2.00
4 RLd(c) 2.75
5 RLd(c) 2.75
6 thru 14 . . . . @2.00
Winter Special #1 . . . . 2.00

EXPLORERS
Caliber Tapestry 1997
1 . . . . 2.95
2 . . . . 2.95
3 "Nahuatl" 2.95
4 "The Sky is Falling". 2.95

EXTINCTIONERS
Shanda Fantasy Arts
VOL 2 1999
1 . . . . 2.95
2 thru 7 . . . . @2.95

EXTREMELY SILLY
Antarctic Press
1 . . . . 4.00
1 Vol. II 1.25
2 Vol. II 1.25

EYE OF MONGOMBO
Fantagraphics Books 1990–91
1 . . . . 3.00
2 thru 7 . . . . @2.00

FAITH
Lightning Comics 1997
1 (of 2) 2.95
1a variant cover. 2.95
1b Limited, cover A 9.95
1c Limited, cover B 9.95
1d signed & numbered 9.95
1 encore edition. 2.95
1a encore, cover B 2.95
1b deluxe encore edition, cover A . 9.95
1c deluxe encore edition, cover B . 9.95

FANG: TESTAMENT
Sirius 1997
1 by Kevin J. Taylor 2.50
2 . . . . 2.50
3 . . . . 2.50
4 (of 4) 2.50
TPB 11.95

FANGS OF THE WIDOW
Ground Zero
1 I:Emma 2.50
London Night Studios 1995
1 O:The Widow 3.00
1a platinum edition 5.00
2 Body Count 3.00
3 Emma Revealed. 3.00
Ground Zero
7 thru 9 "Metal Gypsies," pt.#1–#3 . . . . @3.00
10 thru 13 rep. Widow: Bound by Blood #1–#4 + additional material . . . . @3.50
14 "Search and Destroy" pt.1 . . . . . 3.00
15 "Search and Destroy" pt.2 . . . . . 3.00
Ann. #1 Search and Destroy. 5.95

FANTASCI
Warp Graphics-Apple
1 . . . . 2.50
2 and 3 . . . . @2.00
4 . . . . 4.00
5 thru 8 . . . . @1.75
9 `Apple Turnover'. 1.75

FANTASTIC ADVENTURES
1 thru 5 . . . . @1.75

FANTASTIC FABLES
Silver Wolf
1 and 2 . . . . @1.50

FANTASTIC PANIC
Antarctic 1993–94
1 thru 8 Ganbear . . . . @2.75
[Volume 2]
1 thru 4 . . . . @2.75
4 thru 9 . . . . @2.95
10 concl. 3.50

FANTASTIC WORLDS
Flashback Comics
1 Space Opera 2.95
2 F:Attu, Captain Courage 2.95

FANTASY QUARTERLY
1 1978 1st Elfquest 50.00

FART WARS: SPECIAL EDITION
Entity Comics 1997
1 Star Wars trilogy parody,A:Nira X 2.75
1a Empire Attacks Back cover 2.75
1b Return of the One-Eye cover . . 2.75

FAR WEST
Antarctic Press 1998
1 (of 4) by Richard Moore 2.95
2 thru 4 . . . . @3.00
VOL. 2
1 (of 4) 2.99
2 . . . . 2.50

FASTLANE ILLUSTRATED
Fastlane Studios
1 Super Powers & Hot Rods 2.50

FATALIS
Caliber Core 1998
1 by Mark Chadbourn
& Vince Danks 2.95
1a signed & numbered 6.95
2 . . . . 2.95

Fat Ninja #5
© Silver Wolf Comics

FAT NINJA
Silver Wolf Comics 1985–86
1 . . . . 2.50
2 Vigil 2.50
3 thru 8 . . . . @1.50

FAUST
North Star
1 Vigil 30.00
1a Vigil,2nd Printing. 5.00
1b Vigil,3rd Printing 2.00
1c Tour Edition 25.00
2 Vigil 20.00
2a Vigil,2nd Printing. 3.00
2b Vigil,3rd Printing 2.50
3 Vigil 15.00
3a Vigil,2nd Printing. 2.50
4 Vigil 12.00
5 Vigil 8.00
6 Vigil 8.00
Rebel Studios
7 Vigil 5.00
8 TV 3.50
9 TV,Love of the Damned 3.50
10 E:DQ(s),TV,Love o/t Damned. . . 3.50
VOL. II
1 TV,Love of the Damned 2.50

FAUST PREMIERE
North Star
1 Vigil 30.00

FAUST/777: THE WRATH
Avatar Press 1998
0 by David Quinn & Tim Vigil,
Darkness in Collision x-over . . . 3.00
0a wrap. 3.95
0b nude cover 6.00
0c leather cover. 20.00
0d Royal Blue edition. 60.00
0e Platinum edition 15.95
1 (of 4) 3.50
1a nude cover 6.00
2 Darkness in Collision,pt.3 . . . . . 3.50
2a nude cover 6.00
3 . . . . 3.50
3a nude cover 6.00
4 . . . . 3.50
4a nude cover 6.00
Faust Hornbook 4.95
TPB 112-page 16.95
HC 34.95
HC Faust Hornbook 29.95

FAUST: SINGHA'S TALONS
Avatar 2000
1/2 . . . . 3.50
1/2 wraparound (c) 3.95
1/2 Beachum (c). 5.95
1/2 adult (c) 6.00
1/2 prism foil. 12.95
1/2 royal blue edition 75.00
1/2 Blood Curse 5.00
1 (of 4) 3.95
1a wraparound (c) 4.50
1b Adult (c) 6.00
1c red foil leather. 25.00
1d prism foil. 12.95
2 . . . . 3.95
2a previews exclusive 4.50
2b adult (c) 6.00
3 . . . . 3.95
3a previews exclusive 4.50
3b adult (c) 6.00
4 . . . . 3.95
4a previews exclusive 4.50
4b adult (c) 6.00
Preview Book 5.95

FELIX THE CAT B&W
Felix Comics 1997
1 inc. Felix's Cafe 2.00
2 Crusin' for a Brusin' 2.00
3 Ah Choo. 2.00
4 inc. Spaced Out 2.00
5 Holiday/Winter issue. 2.00
6 The Felix Force 2.25
7 A Rash of Trash 2.25
8 Halloween 2.25
Cat-A-Strophic Wrestling Spec.#1. . 2.25
Felix Summer Splash #1. . . . . 2.50

FEM FANTASTIQUE
AC Comics
1 . . . . 2.00

FEMFORCE
AC Comics
1 thru 15 See Color
16 I:Thunder Fox 3.00
17 F:She-Cat,Ms.Victory, giant 3.00
18 double size 3.00
19 . . . . 3.00
20 V:RipJaw, Black Commando . . . 3.00
21 V:Dr.Pretorius 3.00
22 V:Dr.Pretorius 3.00
23 V:Rad 3.00
24 A:Teen Femforce 3.00
25 V:Madame Boa 3.00
26 V:Black Shroud 3.00
27 V:Black Shroud 3.00
28 A:Arsenio Hall 3.00
29 V:Black Shroud 3.00
30 V:Garganta 3.00
31 I:Kronon Captain Paragon 3.00
32 V:Garganta 3.00
33 Personal Lives of team 3.00
34 V:Black Shroud 2.75
35 V:Black Shroud 2.75
36 giant,V:Dragonfly,Shade. 2.75
37 A:Blue Bulleteer,She-Cat 2.75
38 V:Lady Luger. 2.75
39 F:She-Cat 2.75
40 V:Sehkmet. 2.75
41 V:Captain Paragon 2.75
42 V:Alizarin Crimson 2.75
43 V:Glamazons of Galaxy G 2.75
44 V:Lady Luger,F:Garganta. 2.75
45 Nightveil Rescued 2.75
46 V:Lady Luger. 2.75
47 V:Alizarin Crimson 2.75
48 . . . . 2.75
49 I:New Msw.Victory 2.75
50 Ms.Victory Vs.Rad,flexi-disc. . . . 2.95
51 . . . . 2.75
52 V:Claw & Clawites 2.75
53 I:Bulldog Deni,V:(Dick
Briefer's)Frightenstein 2.75
54 The Orb of Bliss. 2.75
55 R:Nightveil. 2.75
56 V:Alizarin Crimson 2.75
57 thru 92 See Color
93 "Shattered Memories," pt.2 . . . . 3.00
93a deluxe 5.90
94 "Shattered Memories," pt.3 . . . . 3.00
94a deluxe 5.90
95 . . . . 3.00
95a deluxe 5.90
96 . . . . 3.00
96a deluxe 5.90
97 . . . . 3.00
98 deluxe 5.90
98 . . . . 3.00
98 deluxe 5.90
99 . . . . 3.00
99 deluxe 5.90
100 Anniv. issue, with poster 6.90
100A signed, with poster. 12.00
100B no poster, not signed 4.00
THE YESTERDAY SYNDROME
101 Pt.1 . . . . 4.95
102 Pt.2 . . . . 4.95
103 Pt.3 . . . . 4.95
RETURN FROM THE ASHES
104 pt.1 Firebeam, 44pg. 4.95
105 pt. 2 . . . . 4.95
106 pt. 3 concl. 4.95
DARKGODS: RAMPAGE
107 Darkgods: Rampage, pt.1 . . . . 4.95
108 Darkgods: Rampage, pt.2 . . . . 4.95
109 Darkgods: Rampage, pt.3 . . . . 5.95
Spec.#1 FemForce Timelines,
O:Femforce (1995). 2.95
Spec.#1 FemForce:Frightbook,
Horror tales by Briefer,

Ayers, Powell 2.95
Untold Origin of FemForce 4.95
GN The Capricorn Chronicles 12.50
GN FemForce: Timestorm 9.95
GN, FemForce: Timestorm, deluxe 14.95
TPB Origins 12.95
TPB Origins, signed 13.95
Secret Files of Femforce, deluxe. . . 4.95

FEMFORCE SPECIAL
AC Comics 1999

1 Femforce Special: Rayda–
The Cyberian Connection 2.95
1a Variant cover 2.95
1b Variant cover, signed 9.95
2 . . . . 2.95
3 conclusion 3.95

FEVER, THE
Dark Vision Publishing

1 O:The Fever 2.50
2 Fever's Father 2.50

FIFTIES TERROR
Eternity

1 thru 6 . . . . @2.00

FINAL CYCLE
Sirius

Graphic Novel 4.00
1 thru 4 . . . . @1.50

FINDER
Lightspeed Comics Nov. 1996

1 thru 5 by Carla Speed McNeil . @2.95
6 thru 19 . . . . @2.95
TPB Vol. 1 Sin Eater. 15.95

FINDER FOOTNOTES
Lightspeed Press

2 thru 4 . . . . @6.00

FIRE TEAM
Aircel 1990

1 thru 3 by Don Lomax. . . . . @2.50
4 V:Vietnamese Gangs. 2.50
5 Cam in Vietnam 2.50
6 . . . . 2.50

FISH POLICE
Fishwrap Productions Dec., 1985

1 1st printing 7.00
1a 2nd printing 3.00
2 . . . . 5.00
3 thru 5 . . . . @4.00

Comico Publ.

6 thru 12 . . . . @3.50
13 thru 17 See Color issues

Apple Publ.

18 thru 24 . . . . @2.50

FISH SHTICKS
Apple

1 and 2 . . . . @2.75
3 and 4 . . . . @2.50

FIST OF GOD
Eternity

1 thru 4 . . . . @2.00

Fist of the North Star #7
© Viz Select

FIST OF THE NORTH STAR
Viz Select

1 thru 3 . . . . @3.25
4 . . . . 2.00
5 . . . . 3.25
6 . . . . 2.95
7 . . . . 2.95
TPB Vol. 2 Night of the Jackal, rep.16.95

Part Three

1 thru 5 by Buronson
& Tetsuo Hara. . . . . @2.95

Part Four Dec. 1996

1 thru 7 . . . . @2.95
TPB Volume 2: Southern Cross . . 16.95

FLAG FIGHTERS
Ironcat 1997

1 by Masaomi Kanzaki 2.95
2 Student Flagger, pt.1 . . . . 2.95
3 Student Flagger, pt.2 . . . . 2.95
4 Student Flagger, pt.3 . . . . 2.95
5 . . . . 2.95
6 Death Window 2.95
7 F:Murasame 2.95

FLAMING CARROT
Aardvark–Vanaheim

1 1981 Killian Barracks 50.00
1a 1984. 25.00
2 . . . . 25.00
3 . . . . 25.00
4 thru 6 . . . . @20.00

Renegade

7 . . . . 15.00
8 . . . . 12.00
9 . . . . 8.00
10 . . . . 8.00
11 . . . . 6.00
12 . . . . 6.00
13 thru 15 . . . . @5.00
15a variant without cover price 8.00
16 and 17 . . . . @5.00
See: Dark Horse

FLARE
Hero Graphics

1 thru 8 . . . . @3.95
9 F:Sparkplug 3.95
10 thru 12 . . . . @2.95

FLARE ADVENTURES
Hero Graphics

1 Rep 1st issue Flare 1.00
Becomes:

FLARE ADVENTURES: CHAMPIONS CLASSICS

2 thru 15 . . . . @3.95

FLARE VS. TIGRESS
Hero Graphics

1 and 2 . . . . @3.50

FORBIDDEN KINGDOM

1 thru 11 . . . . @2.00

FORBIDDEN VAMPIRE TALES
Forbidden 1997

0 . . . . 2.95
0A Erotic nude cover 3.95
0b Erotic nude cover 3.95
1 sexy vampire 2.95
1a nude cover 3.95
1b photo nude cover 3.95
2 . . . . 2.95
2A Dulexe erotic nude cover A . . . 3.95
2b Deluxe erotic nude cover B. . . . 3.95
3 . . . . 2.95
3a nude cover 2.95
4 . . . . 2.95
4a erotic nude cover 2.95
5 . . . . 2.95
5a erotic nude cover 2.95
6 . . . . 3.00
6a Forbidden Embrace nude cover 4.00
7 Bloodlust and Bust cover 3.00
7a Nude Kissing the Countess(c) . 3.00
Spec.#1 Vault of Innocents 2.95
Spec.#1 Vault of Innocents, nude(c) 4.00

FORBIDDEN WORLDS
ACG 1996

1 SD,JAp,rep. 2.50

FORCE 10
Crow Comics

0 Ash Can Preview. 75
1 I:Force 10. . . . . 2.50
2 Children of the Revolution,pt#2. . 2.50
3 Against all Odds 2.50

FORETERNITY
Antarctic Press 1997

1 by Rod Espinoza 2.95
2 . . . . 2.95
3 . . . . 2.95

FOREVER WARRIORS
Aardwolf 1996

1 (of 3) RTs,RB 2.95
2 RTs,RB. 2.95
3 RTs,RB, concl. 2.95

FOREVER WARRIORS
CFD 1997

1 RB,RTs. 2.95
2 RB,RTs,KN 2.95
3 RB,RTs, finale 2.95

FORTY WINKS
Oddjobs Limited 1997
1 (of 4) by Sneed & Peters 2.95
2 Everything Right is Wrong Again. 2.95
3 Where Your Eyes Don't Go. 2.95
4 There Might be Giants 2.95
Peregrine Entertainment 1998
Christmas Spec. 2.95
TV Party Spec. 2.95
Spec.#1 Buzzboy (2000). 2.95

FORTY WINKS: MR. HORRIBLE
Peregrine Entertainment 2000
1 . . . . 2.95
2 . . . . 2.95

FORTY WINKS: THE FABLED PIRATE QUEEN OF THE SOUTH CHINA SEA
Peregrine Entertainment 1999
1 by Vincent Sneed & Martinez . . . 2.95
2 . . . . 2.95
3 . . . . 2.95

FOX COMICS
1 Spec. 2.95
25 . . . . 2.95
26 . . . . 3.50

FRANKENSTEIN
Eternity
1 . . . . 2.00
2 . . . . 2.00
3 . . . . 2.00

FRANKIES FRIGHTMARES
1 Celebrates Frank 60th Anniv. . . . 2.00

FRANK THE UNICORN
Fish Warp
1 thru 7 . . . . @2.00

FREAK-OUT ON INFANT EARTHS
1 Don Chin 1.75
2 Don Chin 1.75

FREAKS
Monster Comics
1 Movie adapt 2.50
2 Movie adapt.cont. 2.50
3 thru 4 Movie adapt.. . . . . 2.50

FRED THE POSSESSED FLOWER
Happy Predator 1998
1 The Plant Behind the Scenes . . . 2.95
2 . . . . 2.95
3 Interview with a Demon 2.95
4 The People vs. Hell 2.95
5 . . . . 2.95
6 The Origin of Fred 2.95

FRENCH ICE
Renegade Press
1 thru 15 . . . . @2.00

FRIENDS
1 thru 5 . . . . @2.00

FRIGHT
Eternity
1 thru 13 . . . . @2.00

FRINGE
Caliber
1 thru 7 . . . . @2.50

FROM BEYOND
Studio Insidio
1 Short stories-horror. 2.25
2 inc.Clara Mutilares 2.50
3 inc.The Experiment. 2.50
4 inc.Positive Feedback. 2.50

FROM HELL
Tundra
1 . . . . 15.00
1a 2nd printing 6.00
2 . . . . 7.00
Kitchen Sink [Volume Three]
1 AMo,ECa 8.00
2 AMo,ECa 5.00
2a 2nd printing 6.00
3 . . . . 5.00
3a 2nd printing 6.00
4 . . . . 6.00
4 new printing 5.00
5 . . . . 6.00
5 new printing 5.00
6 . . . . 5.00
7 . . . . 5.00
8 . . . . 5.00
8 AMo,ECa,new printing 5.00
9 AMo,ECa 5.00
9 new printing 5.00
10 AMo,ECa. 5.00
10 new printing. 5.00
Spec. Dance of the Gull Catchers. . 4.95

FROM THE DARKNESS
Adventure Comics 1990
1 JBa 25.00
2 . . . . 30.00
3 and 4 . . . . @12.00

FROM THE DARKNESS II BLOODVOWS
Cry For Dawn
1 R:Ray Thorn,Desnoires 12.00
2 V:Desnoires 8.00
3 . . . . 8.00

FROM THE VOID
1 1st B.Blair,1982 . . . . 75.00

FROST
1 Heart of Darkness 2.00

FROST: THE DYING BREED
Caliber
1 thru 3 Vietnam Flashbacks . . . @2.95

F–III BANDIT
Antartic Press
1 F:Akira, Yoohoo 2.95
2 F:Yukio. 2.95
3 F:Were-Women 2.95
4 . . . . 2.95
5 Romeo & Juliet story 2.95
6 thru 8 . . . . @2.95

Fugitoid #1
© Mirage

FUGITOID
Mirage
1 TMNT Tie-in. 8.00

FULL METAL FICTION
London Night Feb. 1997
1 EHr 4.00
1a Nun with a Gun edition 10.00
1b dark room edition cover 4.00
2 . . . . 4.00
2a signed 10.00
3 "Hellborne" concl. 4.00
4 . . . . 4.00
5 EHr 4.00
6 . . . . 4.00
7 . . . . 4.00
8 . . . . 4.00

FURRLOUGH
Antarctic Press 1991
1 Funny Animal Military stories . . . 3.00
2 thru 10 . . . . @2.50
11 thru 20 . . . . @2.75
21 thru 33 . . . . @2.75
34 . . . . 2.95
35 48-pg. 4.00
36 thru 40 . . . . @2.95
41 thru 51 . . . . @2.95
Best of Furrlough, Vol.1 . . . . 4.95
Best of Furrlough, Vol.2 . . . . 4.95
Radio Comix
52 "Ninjara," pt.4. . . . . 2.95
53 "Bronze Age". 2.95
54 "Heebas". 2.95
55 "Star Run" cont. 2.95
56 "Tobias Wah: Vampire Hunter". . 2.95
57 "Star Run". 2.95
58 F:Heebas. 2.95
59 Sixth anniv., 48-pg. 3.95
60 F:Tobias Wah: Vampire Hunter" . 2.95
61 "" 2.95
62 F:Tobias Wah 2.95
63 F:Full Knight Gear 2.95
64 F:The Wild. 2.95
65 F:Full Knight Gear 2.95
66 F:Tobias Wah: Vampire Hunter. . 2.95
67 F:Full Knight Gear 2.95
68 inc. "Misty the Mouse" 2.95

B & W PUB.

69 inc. "Full Knight Gear" 2.95
70 inc. "Cross of the Dolls" 2.95
71 inc. "Bronze Age" 2.95
72 inc. "The Judgment" 2.95
73 inc. "Dragon Heaven" 2.95
74 inc. "Chronicles of Athras" 2.95
75 inc. "Dragon Heaven" 2.95
76 inc. "China Kate and
the Frisco Force" 2.95
77 inc. "Gama Duck" 2.95
78 inc. "Siberia" 2.95
79 . . . . 2.95
80 inc. "Siberia" 2.95
81 . . . . 2.95
82 inc. "Tall Tails" 2.95
83 . . . . 2.95
84 inc. "Fission Chicken" 2.95
85 inc. "Fission Chicken" 2.95
86 inc. "The Suit" 2.95
87 inc. "Cross of the Dolls" 2.95
88 inc. "Cross of the Dolls" 2.95
89 inc. "Full Knight Gear" 2.95
90 inc. "Tiger Orange" 2.95
91 inc. "Tiger Orange" 2.95
92 inc. "Ebin & May" 2.95
93 inc. "Dragon Heaven" 2.95
94 Tall Tails 2.95

FURY
Aircel

1 thru 3 . . . . @1.70

FURY OF HELLINA, THE
Lightning Comics 1995

1 V:Luciver 3.50
1a limited & signed 8.00
1b platinum 8.00

FUSION
Eclipse

1 . . . . 2.50
2 thru 17 . . . . @2.00

FUTABA-KUN CHANGE
Ironcat 1998

1 by Hiroshi Aro. 2.95
2 thru 6 . . . . @2.95
GN Vol. 1 . . . . 15.95

VOL. 2

1 . . . . 2.95
2 thru 6 . . . . @2.95

VOL. 3 1999

1 . . . . 2.95
2 thru 6 . . . . @2.95
TPB Vol. 3 . . . . 15.95

VOL. 4 2000

1 . . . . 2.95
2 thru 6 . . . . @2.95

VOL. 5 2000

1 by Hiroshi Aro. 2.95
2 thru 4 . . . . @2.95

FUTURAMA
Slave Labor

1 thru 4 . . . . @1.75

FUTURETECH
Mushroom Comics

1 Automotive Hi-Tech 3.50
2 Cyber Trucks 3.50

Futurians #0
© Aardwolf

FUTURIANS
Aardwolf 1995

0 DC R:Futurians, sequal to
Lodestone color series 2.95
0 second printing, DC 2.95

GAIJIN
Caliber 1990

1-shot, 64-pg. 3.50
1 thru 3 . . . . @2.00

GALAXION
Helikon 1997

1 by Tara Jenkins, science fiction. . 2.75
2 . . . . 2.75
3 . . . . 2.75
4 Choices 2.75
5 . . . . 2.75
6 Communication 2.75
7 Song of Hiawatha 2.75
8 Persuasion 2.75
9 Deal with the Devil 2.75
10 . . . . 2.75
11 . . . . 2.75
Spec. #1, 16-pg. 1.00
GN Vol. 1 . . . . 15.95
Spec. Flip Book Galaxion
& Amy Unbound 2.75

GATEKEEPER
GK Publishing

1 . . . . 2.50
2 and 3 . . . . @2.95

GATES OF THE NIGHT
Jademan

1 thru 4 . . . . @3.50

GATEWAY TO HORROR

1 BW. 1.75

GEAR
Fireman Press 1998

1 (of 6) by Douglas TenNaple 2.95
2 thru 6 . . . . @2.95
TPB 14.95

GEISHA
Oni Press 1998

1 (of 4) by Andi Watson 2.95
2 . . . . 2.95
3 . . . . 2.95
4 . . . . 2.95
TPB by Andi Watson 9.95

GEMS OF THE SAMURAI
Newcomers Publishing

1 I:Master Samurai 2.95

GENOCYBER
Viz

1 I:Genocyber 2.75
2 . . . . 2.75
3 ToT. 2.75
4 ToT. 2.75
5 ToT. 2.75

GEOBREEDERS
CPM Manga 1999

1 by Akhiro Ito 2.95
2 thru 6 . . . . @2.95
7 thru 20 . . . . @2.95
TPB Vol. 1 . . . . 15.95
TPB Vol. 2 rep. #8–#14. . . . . 15.95

GERIATRIC GANGRENE JUJITSU GERBILS
Planet X Productions

1 . . . . 2.50
2 . . . . 1.50

GHOSTS OF DRACULA
Eternity

1 A:Dracula & Houdini 2.50
2 A:Sherlock Holmes 2.50
3 A:Houdini 2.50
4 Count Dracula's Castle 2.50
5 Houdini, Van Helsing, Dracula
team-up 2.50

GI GOVERNMENT ISSUED
Paranoid Press

1 thru 7 F:Mac, Jack . . . . @2.00

GIDEON HAWK
Big Shot Comics

1 I:Gideon Hawk, Max 9471. . . . . . 2.00
2 The Jewel of Shamboli,pt.2. . . . . 2.00
3 The Jewel of Shamboli,pt.3. . . . . 2.00
2 The Jewel of Shamboli,pt.4. . . . . 2.50
3 The Jewel of Shamboli,pt.5. . . . . 2.50

GIGANTOR
Antarctic Press

1 (of 12) by Ben Dunn 2.95
2 thru 8 . . . . @2.95

GIZMO
Chance

1 . . . . 7.50

Mirage

1 . . . . 5.50
2 . . . . 2.50
3 . . . . 2.00
4 thru 7 . . . . @1.50

GIZMO & THE FUGITOID

1 and 2 . . . . @1.75

GLOOM COOKIE
Slave Labor Graphics 1999
1 by Serena Valentino
& Ted Naifeh 2.95
2 . . . . 2.95
3 . . . . 2.95
4 . . . . 2.95
5 . . . . 2.95
6 Sebastian's Search. 2.95

GNATRAT
Prelude
1 . . . . 5.00
2 Early Years. 2.00

GNATRAT: THE MOVIE
1 . . . . 2.25

GOBBLEDYGOOK
Mirage
1 1st series, Rare 200.00
2 1st series, Rare 150.00
1 TMNT series reprint 5.00

GOJIN
Antarctic Press 1995
1 F:Terran Defense Force 2.95
2 F:Terran Defense Force 2.95
3 V:Alien Monster 2.95
4 Aliens Bone 2.95
5 thru 8 . . . . @2.95

GOLD DIGGER
Antarctic Press
[Limited Series]
1 Geena & Cheetah in Peru. 8.00
2 Adventures contd.. . . . . 6.00
3 Adventures contd 6.00
4 Adventures contd 5.00
GN Rep. #1–#4 + new material. . . . 9.95
[Volume 2]
1 by Fred Perry . . . . @10.00
2 Fred Perry 8.00
3 Fred Perry 8.00
4 Fred Perry 6.00
5 misnumbered as #0 . . . . 5.00
6 thru 8 by Fred Perry . . . . @4.00
9 and 10 by Fred Perry . . . . @3.50
11 thru 27 by Fred Perry . . . . @3.00
28 and 29 by Fred Perry . . . . @2.75
30 . . . . 3.00
31 . . . . 3.00
32 Time Warp Part One 3.00
33 . . . . 3.00
34 . . . . 3.00
35 Time Warp Part Seven. 3.00
36 . . . . 3.00
37 . . . . 2.95
38 V:Dynasty of Evil 2.95
39 . . . . 2.95
40 Wedding day 2.95
41 Gold Digger Beta. 2.95
42 . . . . 2.95
43 Beta Phase phenomenon. 2.95
44 Beta tool 2.95
45 F:Priestess Tanya 2.95
46 Agent M. 2.95
47 Old Dirty Bastard. 3.00
48 . . . . 3.00
49 The Library of Time 3.00
50 . . . . 3.00
50a deluxe 6.00
Ann. 1995, 48-pg 3.95
Ann. 1996. . . . . 3.95
Ann. 1997. . . . . 3.95
Ann. 1998. . . . . 3.95
Best of Gold Digger Ann. Vol. 1 . . . 3.00
Collected Gold Digger,Vol.1 . . . . . . 9.95
Collected Gold Digger,Vol.2 . . . . . . 9.95
Collected Gold Digger,Vol.3 . . . . . . 9.95
Collected Gold Digger,Vol.4 . . . . . . 9.95
Collected Gold Digger,Vol.5 . . . . . . 9.95
Collected Gold Digger,Vol.6 . . . . . 10.95
Collected Gold Digger,Vol.7 . . . . . 10.95
Collected Gold Digger,Vol.8 . . . . . 10.95
Coll. Vol. 9 . . . . 12.95
Mangazine Spec. #1. . . . . 3.00

GOLD DIGGER: NINJA HIGH SCHOOL
Antarctic Press 1998
Spec. Asrial vs. Cheetah Compilation,
x-over rep. 4.95
Spec. Science Fair Compilation,
x-over rep. 4.95
TPB Time Warp 15.95

GOLD DIGGER: EDGE GUARD
Radio Comix 2000
1 (of 4) by John Barrett 2.95
2 . . . . 2.95

GOLDEN AGE GREATS
AC Comics 1995
Vol.#1 thru #6 40s and 50s . . . . . @9.95
Vol. 7 Best of the West 9.95
Vol. 8 F:Phantom Lady, Miss Victory 9.95
Vol. 9 Fabulous Femmes of Fiction
House 9.95
Vol. 11 Roy Rogers & The Silver
Screen Cowboys 11.95
Vol. 12 Thrilling Science Fiction . . . 9.95
Vol. 13 . . . . 9.95
Vol. 14 The Comic Book Jungle . . 11.95

GOLDEN-AGE MEN OF MYSTERY
AC Comics
5 . . . . 6.95
7 . . . . 5.95
8 . . . . 5.95
9 . . . . 5.95
10 Masked comic book
heroes, 52-pg. 6.95
11 rep. Cat-Man comics 6.95
12 Espionage, WE 6.95
13 F:Daredevil vs. The Claw. 6.95
14 F:Commando Yank 6.95
15 F:Captain 3-D 6.95
16 F:Mr. Scarlet, Airboy 6.95
17 F:Stuntman 6.95
18 . . . . 6.95
19 Space edition. 6.95
19a spec. ed. 68-page 10.95
20 F:Phantom Lady 6.95
21 Fawcett superheroes 6.95
22 Manhunter. 6.95
23 Skyman. 6.95
24 Captain Flash 6.95
25 . . . . 6.95
26 Emerald. 6.95
27 The Fog Robbers. 6.95

GOLDEN WARRIOR ICZER ONE
Antarctic 1994
1 thru 5 . . . . @2.95

GOLDWYN 3-D
Blackthorne
1 . . . . 2.00

GO-MAN
1 thru 4 . . . . @1.50
Graphic Novel `N'. 9.95

GOOD GIRL COMICS
AC
1 F:Tara Fremont. 3.95

Good Girls #1
© Fantagraphics

GOOD GIRLS
Fantagraphics
1 adult. 2.00
2 thru 4 . . . . @2.00

GOON, THE
Avatar Press 1999
1 by Eric Powell. 3.00
2 . . . . 3.00
3 . . . . 3.00

GORE SHRIEK
Fantagor
1 . . . . 2.50
2 and 3 . . . . @1.50
4 +Mars Attacks 2.95
5 . . . . 2.95
6 . . . . 3.50
Vol. 2 #1. 2.50

GOTHESS: DARK ECSTASY
SCC Entertainment 1997
1 (of 3) 2.95
2 . . . . 2.95
2a nude Kristen edition 9.95
2b nude Gothess edition 9.95
3 . . . . 2.95
3a nude vampire slayer edition . . . 9.95
3b nude halloween edition. 9.95

GRAPHIC STORY MONTHLY
1 thru 5 . . . . @2.95

GRAPHIQUE MUSIQUE
Slave Labor 1989–90

1 . . . . 35.00
2 . . . . 30.00
3 . . . . 25.00

GRAVE TALES
Hamilton

1 JSon,GM, mag. size 3.95
2 JSon,GM,short stories 3.95
3 JSon,GM, inc.`Stake Out' 3.95

GREAT DETECTIVE STARRING SHERLOCK HOLMES
ACG Comics 1999

1 by Otto Lagoni 2.95
2 thru 5 . . . . @2.95

GREEN BERETS
ACG 2000

1 JKu 2.95
2 thru 7 JKu, Robin Moore . . . . @2.95
TPB Limited Signed 24.95

GREMLIN TROUBLE
Anti-Ballistic Pixelation

1 & 2 Airstrike on Gremlin Home @2.95
1 new printing 2.95
3 thru 5 . . . . @2.95
6 "Fun with Electricity" 2.95
7 "Cypher in Fairyland" 2.95
8 . . . . 2.95
9 F:Candy Tsai 2.95
10 The Tuberians are coming 2.95
11 V:X-the-Unmentionable 2.95
12 preemptive strike on Site X 2.95
13 Gremlin-Goblin war 2.95
14 . . . . 2.95
15 Battle of 5 Armies 2.95
16 . . . . 2.95
17 kidnapped to Fairyland. 2.95
18 . . . . 2.95
19 The Sky Stone. 2.95
20 Ring Fortress. 2.95
21 A-Girls. 2.95
22 Gremlin Guild 2.95
23 escape from Mordovania 2.95
24 . . . . 2.95

Grendel #3
© Comico

TPB Vol.1 rep.#1–#6. . . . . 14.95
TPB Vol.2 rep.#7–#12. . . . . 12.95

GRENDEL
Comico

1 MW,Rare 75.00
2 MW,Rare 60.00
3 MW,Rare 55.00

GREY
Viz Select

Book 1 . . . . 5.00
Book 2 scarce 5.50
Book 3 . . . . 3.00
Book 4 . . . . 3.00
Book 5 . . . . 3.00
Book 6 thru Book 9 . . . . @2.50

GREYMATTER
Alaffinity Studios

1 thru 14 by Marcus Harwell . . . @2.95

GRIFFIN, THE
Slave Labor

1 . . . . 1.75
1a 2nd printing 1.75
2 thru 4 . . . . @1.75
5 . . . . 2.00

Amaze Ink 1997

1 by DVa & Phil Allora 2.95
2 by DVa & Paul Way 2.95

GRIPS
Silver Wolf

1 Vigil 15.00
2 Vigil 12.00
3 Vigil 9.00
4 Vigil 8.00
Vol. 1 #1 rep. 2.50

Volume 2

1 . . . . 2.50
2 . . . . 2.50
3 thru 6 . . . . @2.00
7 . . . . 2.25
8 . . . . 2.25
9 thru 12 . . . . @2.50

GROUND POUND

1 John Pound art. 2.00

GROUND ZERO
Eternity

1 Science Fiction mini-series 2.50
2 Alien Invasion Aftermath. 2.50

GRRL SCOUTS
Oni Press 1999

1 (of 4) by Jim Mahfood. 2.95
2 thru 4 . . . . @2.95
TPB 11.95

Amazing Aaron 1999

1 Aaron Warner. 2.95
2 . . . . 2.95

GUERRILA GROUNDHOG
Eclipse

1 . . . . 1.50
2 . . . . 1.50

GUILLOTINE
Silver Wolf

1 and 2 . . . . @1.50

GUILLOTIN
High Impact 1997

Preview JQ,RCl 5.00

ABC Studios 1999

Spec. Ed. 3.00
Spec. Ed. Serpent Ed. 8.00

GUN CRISIS
Ironcat 1998

1 (of 3) by Masoami Kanzaki 2.95
2 . . . . 2.95
3 . . . . 2.95

GUNDAM WING
Mixx Entertainment 2000

1 thru 4 . . . . @2.95
TPB Pocket Vol.1 . . . . 9.95

Tokyopop.Com 2000

5 thru 8 . . . . @2.95
TPB Vol. 1 Blue Destiny Mixx 12.95

GUN FURY
Aircel

1 thru 10 . . . . @2.00

GUN FURY RETURNS
Aircel

1 . . . . 2.95
2 . . . . 2.95
3 V:The Yes Men. 2.25
4 . . . . 2.25

GUNNER
Gun Dog Comics 1999

1 by Eric Yonge. 2.95
2 thru 7 . . . . @2.95

GUNS OF SHAR-PEI
Caliber

1 The Good,the Bad & the Deadly. 2.95

GUTWALLOW
Numbskull Press 1998

1 by Dan Berger 2.95
2 thru 7 The Gingerbread Man . . @2.95

GYRE
Abaculus 1997

1 by Martin Shipp & Marc Laming . 2.95
2 . . . . 2.95
3 Soul Keeper, pt.3 . . . . 2.95
4 . . . . 2.95
5 . . . . 2.95
6 . . . . 2.95
Spec. Edition 56-page 4.50

HADES
Domain Publishing 1995

1 F:Civil War Officer 3.00

HALL OF HEROES
Hall of Heroes 1993

1 I:Dead Bolt 12.00
2 and 3 . . . . @4.50
Ashcan, 8-page 5.95
Halloween Horror Special 2.50

Halloween Horror Special '98 . . . . . 2.50

HALL OF HEROES PRESENTS

Hall of Heroes 1996–97

0 by Doug Brammer & Matt Roach, "Slingers" by Matt Martin 2.50
1 . . . . . 2.50
1a signed & numbered 4.00
2 "The Last Days" 2.50
3 "The Power of the Golem" 2.50
4 F:Turaxx the Trobbit 2.50
5 . . . . . 2.50

HALLOWIENERS

Mirage

1 . . . . . 1.50
2 . . . . . 1.50

HALO BROTHERS

Fantagraphics

Special #1 . . . . . 2.25

HAMMER GIRL

Brainstorm April, 1996

1 dinosaur, sci-fi adventure 2.95
2 . . . . . 2.95
2a deluxe 5.00

HAMSTER VICE

Blackthorne

1 . . . . . 3.50
2 . . . . . 2.50
3 thru 11 . . . . . @2.00

New Series

Eternity

1 and 2 . . . . . @2.00

HANGED MAN

Caliber Feb. 1998

1 (of 2) by AIG & Arthur Ranson . . 2.95
2 (of 2) 2.95
TPB 5.95

HARD ROCK COMICS

Revolutionary

1 Metallica-The Early Years 2.50

HARI KARI

Blackout 1995

1 . . . . . 3.00
1a platinum 8.00
1-shot Possessed by Evil(1997) . . . 2.95
1-shot Hari Kari Goes Hollywood (1997) 2.95
Nude edition 9.95
Deluxe 14.95
Spec #1 Sexy Summer Rampage, gallery issue (1997) 2.95
Deluxe, super sexy cover 9.95
1-shot Cry of Darkness (1998) 2.95
Variant photo ultra sexy ed. . . . 9.95
1-shot The Last Stand (1998) 2.95
Ultra sexy edition 9.95
Deluxe 14.95

HARI KARI MANGA

Blackout Comics 1998

Spec. 0 Sex, Thugs & Rock 'n' Roll 2.95
Nude cover 9.95
1-shot Manga Adventures (1997) . . 2.95

1-shot Deadly Exposure, by Rob Roman & Nigel Tully 2.95
Nude cover 9.95
Deluxe 14.95
1-shot Deadtime Stories, by Rob Roman & Nigel Tully 2.95
Nude cover 9.95
Deluxe edition 14.95
1-shot Manga To Die For 2.95
nude cover 9.95
Deluxe 14.95
1-shot Running From Poison 2.95
nude cover 9.95

HARPY: PRIZE OF THE OVERLORD

Ground Zero

1 (of 6) 3.00
2 thru 6 . . . . . @3.00
1-shot Harpy Preview, prequel 3.00

Peregrine 1998

TPB rep. #1–#6 . . . . . 14.95
Spec. Harpy Pin-up Book 2.95

HARTE OF HARKNESS

Eternity

1 I:Dennis Harte,Vampire private-eye 2.50
2 V:Satan's Blitz St.Gang 2.50
3 Jack Grissom/Vampire 2.50
4 V:Jack Grissom, conc. 2.50

HARVY FLIP BOOK

Blackthorne

1 . . . . . 2.00
2 . . . . . 2.00
3 . . . . . 2.00

HATE

Fantagraphics

1 . . . . . 15.00
2 . . . . . 12.00
3 . . . . . 9.00
4 . . . . . 8.00
5 . . . . . 8.00
6 . . . . . 8.00
7 . . . . . 7.00
8 thru 10 . . . . . @6.00
11 and 12 . . . . . @5.00
1a to 12a reprints . . . . . @2.50
13 thru 15 . . . . . @4.00
Hate Jamboree, 64-page 3.95

HAVOC, INC.

Radio Comix 1998

1 by Mark Barnard & Terrie Smith . 2.95
2 . . . . . 2.95
3 . . . . . 2.95
4 . . . . . 2.95
5 . . . . . 2.95
6 . . . . . 2.95

HEAD, THE

1 Old Airboy (1966) 2.00

HEAVY METAL MONSTERS

Revolutionary

1 'Up in Flames' 2.25

HE IS JUST A RAT

Exclaim Bound Comics

1 & 2 V:Jimmy and Billy Bob 2.75

HELLGIRL

Knight Press

1 I:Jazzmine Grayce 2.95
1-shot Demonseed II, Bob Hickey & Bill Nichols (1997) 2.95
1-shot Demonsong, Bob Hickey & Bill Nichols (1997) 2.95
1-shot Purgatory (1997). 2.95

HELLINA

Lightning Comics 1994

1-shot I&O:Hellina 5.00
Commemorative 10.00
Nude cover 8.00
1996 rep. gold 5.00
1996 rep nude (c). 8.00
Spec. Hellina: Genesis with poster (1996) 3.00
Platinum edition 4.00
Nude cover 5.00
Platinum nude edition. 8.00
Spec. Hellina: In the Flesh (1997)
two diff. mild covers . . . . . @3.00
Nude covers, 2 diff.. . . . . . @5.00
Spec. Hellina: Naked Desire (1997) 2.95
Cover B 2.95
Signed, ... 2.95
Nude cover A. 5.00
Nude cover B. 5.00
Spec. Hellina: Taking Back the Night (1995) V:Michael Naynar 3.00
Nude cover 5.00
Spec. Hellina: Wicket Ways (1995)
A:Perg 2.75
Nude cover 5.00
Encore editions 3.00
Encore variant (c). 3.00
Encore, nude cover 5.00
Encore, nude variant (c) 5.00
Spec. Hellina: X-Mas in Hell (1996)
two different covers 3.00
Platinum edition 5.00
Nude cover 5.00
Nude variant cover 5.00
Nude platinum edition. 15.00
Spec. Hellina: The Relic 3.00
Variant cover. 3.00
Nude cover 5.00
Variant nude cover 5.00
Spec. 1997 Pin-up 3.50
1997 Pin-up, cover B 3.50
1997 Pin-up, cover A, nude . . . 5.00

Hellina 1997 Pin-up Special
© Lightning Comics

1997 Pin-up, cover B, nude . . . 5.00
X-Over Hellina/Catfight (1995)
V:Prince of Sommia 2.75
Gold. 4.00
Nude cover 4.00
Encore edition, mild covers,
2 different. 2.95
Encore, nude covers, 2 diff. . . . 5.00
X-Over Hellina/Cynder (1997) covA 2.95
Cover B 2.95
Nude cover A. 5.00
Nude cover B. 5.00
Spec Hellina #1 Skybolt Toyz
lim. ed. (1997) 1.50
TPB rep. Hellina appearances 8.95
TPB rep. one-shots. 12.95

HELLINA: HEART OF THORNS

Lightning Comics

1 (of 2) 3.00
1a nude cover. 5.00
1b autographed. 5.00
2 . . . . 2.75
2a variant cover. 2.75
2b platimum edition 5.95
2c nude cover 5.00
2d variant nude cover 5.00
2e platimum nude edition. 12.00

HELLINA: HELL'S ANGEL

Lightning Comics Oct., 1996

1 . . . . 2.75
1a platinum edition 8.00
1a platinum edition, signed 10.00
1b nude cover. 5.00
1c nude platinum edition 15.00
2 . . . . 2.75
2a platinum edition 8.00
2b nude cover. 5.00
2c nude platinum edition 15.00
1 encore edition, cover A. 2.95
1a encore edition, cover B. 2.95
1b deluxe encore edition, cover A . 5.00
1c deluxe encore edition, cover B . 5.00

HELLINA: KISS OF DEATH

Lightning Comics 1995

1-shot A:Perg 4.00
1-shot nude cover 5.00
1-shot gold edition 10.00
1-shot Encore editions. 3.00
1-shot Encore, nude cover. 5.00

Lightning Feb., 1997

1A 2.95
1B variant cover 2.95
1A nude cover. 5.00
1B nude cover. 5.00
1 encore, signed & numbered 5.00

HELSING

Caliber Core March, 1998

1W by Gary Reed & Low,
Wozniak(c). 2.95
1L Loudon (c) 2.95
1 variant cover. 8.95
1 premium, signed. 9.95
2 . . . . 2.95
3 . . . . 2.95
4 Secrets and Lies. 2.95
Spec. Dawn of Armageddon, Secrets
& Lies, concl. 48-page 3.95

HELTER SKELTER

Antarctic Press 1997

0 by Mike Harris & Duc Tran 2.95

1 (of 4) 2.95
2 thru 6 . . . . @2.95

HEPCATS

Double Diamond

1 . . . . 15.00
2 . . . . 12.00
3 Snow Blind 12.00
4 thru 9 . . . . @9.00
10 thru 13. . . . . @3.50
14 Chapter 12 . . . . 3.00
15 Snowblind Chp. 13 . . . . 2.75

Antarctic Press

1 by Martin Wagner. 3.00
2 "Trial by Intimacy". 3.00
3 Snowblind, pt.1. . . . . 3.00
4 Snowblind, pt.2. . . . . 3.00
5 Snowblind, pt.3. . . . . 3.00
6 Snowblind, pt.4. . . . . 3.00
7 Snowblind, pt.5 Intrusion. 2.95
8 Snowblind, pt.6 Super Heroes . . 2.95
9 Snowblind, pt.7 Kevin & Kathryn. 2.95
10 Snowblind, pt.8 Exorcism,
Prelude 2.95
11 Snowblind, pt.10 Exorcism(a). . . 2.95
12 Snowblind, pt.10 Exorcism(b). . . 2.95
13 Snowbling, pt.11 It's a Garden
of Eden... . . . . 3.50
TPB Collected Hepcats. 14.95

HERCULES

A Plus Comics

1 Hercules Saga 2.50

Hercules Project #1
© Monster Comics

HERCULES PROJECT

Monster Comics 1991

1 Origin issue,V:Mutants 2.00

HEROES

Blackbird

1 . . . . 5.00
2 . . . . 3.00
3 . . . . 2.25
4 comic size 2.00
5 thru 7 . . . . @2.00

HEROES FROM WORDSMITH

Special Studios

1 WWI,F:Hunter Hawke. 2.50

HEROES INCORPORATED

Double Edge Publishing

1 I:Heroes, Inc. 2.95
2 Betrayal 2.95

HEROIC TALES

Lone Star Press 1997

1 by Robb Phipps & Bill Williams. . 2.50
2 Steel of a Soldier's Heart, pt.2 . . 2.50
3 Steel of a Soldier's Heart, pt.3 . . 2.50
4 . . . . 2.50
5 . . . . 2.50
6 The Belles of Freedom, prequel . 2.50
7 The Children of Atlas, pt.1 . . . . . 2.50
8 by Bill Williams & Jeff Parker,
I:Atlas. 2.50

HEROINES, INC.

1 thru 5 . . . . @1.75

HERO SANDWICH

Slave Labor

1 thru 4 . . . . @1.50
5 thru 8 . . . . @1.75
9 . . . . 2.00
Graphic Novel 7.95

HEY MISTER

Insomnia Comics

1 . . . . 2.50
2 . . . . 2.50

Top Shelf

3 by Pete Sickman-Garner. 2.95
4 . . . . 2.95
Spec. Behind the Green Door. 2.95
Spec. The Trouble With Jesus 2.95
Spec. Eyes on the Prize 2.95
TPB After School Special 4.95
TPB Celebrity Roast 144-page 9.95

HIGH CALIBER

1 . . . . 4.00
2 . . . . 3.00
3 and 4 . . . . @2.50

Becomes:

CALIBER PRESENTS

HIGH CALIBER

Caliber 1997

1 64-pg.. 4.00
1 signed edition. 4.00
2 64-pg.. 4.00
3 48-pg.. 4.00
4 . . . . 4.00

HIGH SCHOOL AGENT

Sun Comics

1 I:Kohsuke Kanamori 2.50
2 Treasure Hunt at North Pole. . . . 2.50
3 and 4 . . . . @2.50

HIGH SHINING BRASS

Apple

1 thru 4 . . . . @2.75

HIGH SOCIETY
Aardvark–Vanaheim
1 DS,Cerebus 25.00

HILLY ROSE'S SPACE ADVENTURES
Astro Comics 1995
1 confronts Steeltrap 6.00
1 2nd & 3rd pr. by B.C. Boyer 3.00
2 . . . . 5.00
2 2nd & 3rd printing 3.00
3 . . . . 3.50
3 2nd printing 3.00
4 thru 9 . . . . @3.00
TPB Vol.1 Rocket Reporter 12.95

HIT THE BEACH
Antarctic 1993
1 . . . . 2.95
1a deluxe edition 5.00
2 & 3 . . . . @2.95

HITOMI AND HER GIRL COMMANDOS
Antarctic Press 1992
1 Shadowhunter,from Ninja HS . . . 2.50
2 Synaptic Transducer 2.50
3 Shadowhunter in S.America 2.50
4 V:Mr.Akuma,last issue 2.50
[Series II]
1 thru 10 . . . . @2.75

HOLLYWOOD'S GOLDEN ERA 1930S
A-List Comics 1999
1 (of 3) 2.95
2 . . . . 2.95
3 . . . . 2.95

HOLO BROTHERS, THE
Monster Comics
1 thru 10 . . . . @2.00
Fantagraphics
Spec.#1 . . . . 2.25
TPB The Curse of the Bloated Toad 4.95

HOLY KNIGHT
Pocket Change Comics
1 thru 3 . . . . @2.50
4 V:His Past 2.50
5 V:Souljoiner 2.50
6 V:Demon Priest 2.50
7 Silent Scream,pt.2 . . . . 2.50
8 "Dragon Quest," pt.1 . . . . 2.50
9 "Dragon Quest," pt.2 . . . . 2.50
10 "Dragon Quest," pt.3 . . . . 2.50
11 "Dragon Quest," pt.4 . . . . 2.50

HONK
Fantagraphics
1 Don Martin 2.75
2 . . . . 2.75
3 . . . . 2.75

HONOR AMONG THIEVES
Gateway Grapnics
1 and 2 . . . . @1.50

HOON
Eenieweenie Comics
1 I:Hoon 2.50
2 Calazone Disaster 2.50
3 Reality Check 2.50
4 thru 8 . . . . @2.50

HOON, THE
Caliber Tapestry 1996
1 . . . . 2.95
2 . . . . 2.95
3 . . . . 2.95

HOROBI
Viz
1 . . . . 4.00
2 thru 8 . . . . @3.75
Book 2 1990–91
1 by Yoshihisa Tagami 3.50
2 D:Okado,Shoko Kidnapped 4.25
3 Madoka Attacks Zen 4.25
4 D:Abbess Mitsuko 4.25
5 Catharsis! 4.25
6 Shuichi Vs. Zen 4.25
7 Shuichi vs. Zen, conc. 4.25

HORROR IN THE DARK
Fantagor
1 RCo,Inc.Blood Birth 2.00
2 RCo,Inc.Bath of Blood 2.00
3 RCo 2.00
4 RCo,Inc.Tales o/tBlackDiamond . 2.00

HORROR SHOW
Caliber
1 GD,1977-80 reprint horror 3.50

HOUSE OF FRIGHTENSTEIN
AC Comics
1 . . . . 2.95

HOUSE OF HORROR
AC Comics
1 . . . . 2.50

HOWL
Eternity
1 & 2 . . . . @2.25

HOW TO DRAW TEENAGE MUTANT NINJA TURTLES
Solson
1 Lighter cover 10.00
1a Dark cover 5.00

H.P. LOVECRAFT'S THE DREAM-QUEST OF UNKNOWN KADATH
Mock Man Press 1997
1 (of 5) by Jason Thompson 2.95
1 2nd printing 2.95
2 thru 5 . . . . @2.95

HUGO
Fantagraphics
1 . . . . 4.00
2 . . . . 2.00
3 . . . . 2.00

H.P. Lovecraft's The Dream-Quest of Unknown Kadath #1 © Mock Man

4 . . . . 2.00

HUMAN GARGOYLES
Eternity
Book one 2.00
Book two 2.00
Book three 2.00
Book four 2.00

HUMAN HEAD
Caliber
1 Alice in Flames 2.50

HUNT AND THE HUNTED, THE
Newcomers Publishing
1 I:Aramis Thiron 2.95
2 V:Werewolves 2.95
3 Rio De Janero 2.95
4 F:Aramis Thiron 2.95

HURRICANE GIRLS
Antarctic Press 1995
1 & 2 Tale of Dinon . . . . @3.50
3 thru 7 seven part series . . . . . . @2.95

HUZZAH
1 I:Albedo'sErmaFelna 50.00

HY-BREED
Division Publishing
1 thru 3 F:Cen Intel . . . . @2.25
4 thru 9 . . . . @2.50

HYPER DOLLS
Ironcat Manga 1998
1 by Shinpei Itoh, F:Miyu & Maika . 2.95
2 thru 6 . . . . @2.95
VOL. 2
1 . . . . 2.95
2 thru 6 . . . . @2.95
VOL. 2
1 . . . . 2.95
2 thru 6 . . . . @2.95
VOL. 4 2000
1 . . . . 2.95
2 thru 6 . . . . @2.95

VOL. 5 2000

1 . . . . 2.95
2 . . . . 2.95
TPB Vol. 1 . . . . 15.95

I.F.S. ZONE

1 thru 6 . . . . @1.25

I Am Legend #1
© Eclipse

I AM LEGEND

Eclipse

1 Novel Adaptation 5.95
2 Novel Adaptation cont'd 5.95
3 Novel Adaptation cont'd 5.95

ICARUS

1 thru 9 . . . . @1.70

ICON DEVIL

1 . . . . 2.00
2 . . . . 2.00

[2nd Series]

1 thru 5 . . . . @1.85

ILIAD

Amaze Ink 1997

1 by Darren Brady & Alex Ogle . . . 2.95
2 . . . . 2.95
3 . . . . 2.95
4 . . . . 2.95
5 . . . . 2.95
6 . . . . 2.95
7 . . . . 2.95

ILIAD II

1 . . . . 3.00
1a 2nd cover variation 3.00
2 . . . . 2.00
3 . . . . 2.00
4 . . . . 1.70

ILLUMINATUS

1 . . . . 2.00
2 . . . . 2.50
3 . . . . 2.50

INFERNO

Caliber Press

1 I:City of Inferno 2.95

2 Search for Identity 2.95
3 V:Malateste 2.95
4 by MCy and Michael Gaydos . . . 2.95
5 . . . . 2.95

INTERZONE

Brainstorm Comics

1 w/4 cards 2.50
2 w/4 cards 2.50

INU YASHA

Viz Communications Jan. 1997

1 thru 5 (of 10) by Rumiko Takahashi . . . . @2.95

PART TWO: A FEUDAL FAIRY TALE

1 (of 9) by Rumiko Takahashi 2.95
2 (of 9) 2.95
6 . . . . 2.95
7 . . . . 2.95
8 . . . . 3.25
11 thru 15 (of 15) . . . . @3.25
TPB 15.95
TPB Vol. 2 . . . . 15.95

PART THREE 1999

1 (of 7) thru 7 . . . . @3.25
TPB Vol. 3 . . . . 15.95

PART FOUR 1999

1 (of 7) by Rumiko Takahashi 3.25
2 thru 7 . . . . @3.25
TPB Vol. 4 . . . . 15.95

PART FIVE 2000

1 (of 11) by Rumiko Takahashi. . . . 2.95
2 thru 5 . . . . @2.95
TPB Vol. 5 . . . . 15.95
TPB Vol. 6 . . . . 15.95

INVADERS FROM MARS

Eternity

1 . . . . 2.50
2 . . . . 2.50
3 . . . . 2.50

BOOK II 1991

1 Sequel to '50's SF classic. 2.50
2 Pact of Tsukus/Humans 2.50
3 Last issue. 2.50

INVASION '55

Apple

1 . . . . 2.25
2 . . . . 2.25
3 . . . . 2.25

INVISIBLE PEOPLE

Kitchen Sink

1 WE,I:Peacus Pleatnik 2.95
2 WE,The Power 2.95
3 WE,Final issue 2.95
HC GN by Will Eisner 24.95

ISMET

1 Cartoon Dog. 8.00
2 . . . . 5.00
3 Rare. 5.00
4 . . . . 5.00

IT'S SCIENCE WITH DR. RADIUM

1 thru 7 . . . . @1.50
8 . . . . 1.75
9 . . . . 2.00
Spec #1 . . . . 2.95

JACKAROO

Eternity

1 GCh 2.25
2 GCh 2.25
3 GCh 2.25

JACK HUNTER

Blackthorne

1 . . . . 3.50
2 . . . . 3.50
3 . . . . 3.50

JACK OF NINES

1 . . . . 1.25
2 thru 4 . . . . @1.50
5 . . . . 2.00

JACK THE RIPPER

1 thru 4 . . . . @2.25

JAM, THE

Slave Labor

1 . . . . 2.00
2 . . . . 2.00
3 thru 5 . . . . @2.25

Dark Horse

6 thru 8 . . . . @2.50

Caliber

9 . . . . 2.95
9 signed edition. 2.95
10 It's a Kafka Thing. 2.95
11 thru 14 . . . . @2.95
15 "The Kinetic," pt.3 . . . . 2.95

JAM SPECIAL, THE

Matrix

1 . . . . 2.50

JAMES O'BARR ORIGINAL SINS

ACG Comics 2000

1 . . . . 2.95
2 . . . . 2.95

JAMES O'BARR TASTY BITES

ACG Comics 1999

1 . . . . 2.95
1a signed 9.95

JASON AND THE ARGONAUTS

Caliber

1 thru 5 . . . . @2.50

JAY & SILENT BOB

Oni Press 1998

1 (of 4) by Kevin Smith & Duncan Fregedo 2.95
2 thru 4 . . . . @2.95
TPB rep. #1–#4 . . . . 11.95

JAZZ

High Impact

1 Gold variant edition RCI(c) 9.95

JAZZ THE SERIES

ABC Comics 1999

1 RCI(c). 3.00

1a DOe(c) 3.00
2 . . . . 3.00
2a deluxe nude (c). 8.00

JAZZ: SOLITAIRE
ABC Comics 1998

1 (of 4) by Jose Varese 3.00
1a photo cover 5.95
1b nude variant (c) 5.95
2 . . . . 3.00
2a Variant Exotika (c) 5.95
2b Variant Naughty (c). 5.95
3 . . . . 3.00
3a Variant Kaspar nude (c) 5.95
3b Variant Jazz nude (c) 5.95
Collectors Ed. 4.95

JAZZ: SUPERSTAR
ABC Comics 1998

1 (of 3) by Jose Varese 3.00
1a JQ cover. 6.00
1b Jazz nude variant (c) 10.00

JAZZ AGE CHRONICLES

1 thru 6 . . . . @1.50
7 . . . . 2.50

JCP FEATURES

1 1st MT;S&K,NA/DG rep.
A:T.H.U.N.D.E.R.Agents,
TheFly, Black Hood Mag.Size. . 4.50

JEREMIAH: BIRDS OF PREY
Adventure Comics

1 I: Jeremiah,A:Kurdy 2.50
2 conclusion 2.50

JEREMIAH: FIST FULL OF SAND
Adventure Comics

1 A:Captain Kenney. 2.50
2 conclusion 2.50

JEREMIAH: THE HEIRS
Adventure Comics 1991

1 Nathanial Bancroft estate 2.50
2 conclusion 2.50

JERRY IGERS FAMOUS FEATURES
Blackthorne

1 . . . . 3.00
2 thru 4 . . . . @2.00

Pacific

5 thru 8 . . . . @2.00

JIM
Fantagraphics 1987–90

1 . . . . 15.00
2 . . . . 12.00
3 and 4 . . . . @8.00

Second Series 1994

1 . . . . 4.00
1a 2nd printing 3.00
2 . . . . 3.50
2a 2nd printing 3.00
3 thru 5 . . . . @3.00

J. O'BARR's THE CROW
Kitchen Sink 1998

0 F:Eric Draven, 48-page. 3.50
1 . . . . 3.50
2 Demon in Disguise 3.50

JOE PSYCHO & MOO FROG
Goblin Studios

1 Fanatics Edition 2.50
1 Fanatics signed and numbered
Edition 9.95
2 . . . . 2.50
2 signed & numbered 9.95
3 . . . . 2.50
4 . . . . 2.50
4B San Diego con cover 4.95
5 . . . . 2.50
Spec. Psychosis Abnormalis. 2.50

JOE SINN
Caliber

1 I:Joe Sinn,Nikki. 2.95
2 . . . . 2.95

JOHNNY ATOMIC
Eternity

1 I:Johnny A.Tomick 2.50
2 Project X-contingency plan 2.50
3 . . . . 2.50

JOHNNY DARK
Double Edge

1 V:Biker Gang 2.95

JOHNNY THE HOMICIDAL MANIAC
Slave Labor 1996

1 by Jhonen Vasquez 30.00
1 3rd printing. 4.00
1 signed, limited 9.00
2 . . . . 15.00
2 3rd printing. 3.00
3 . . . . 10.00
3 3rd printing. 3.00
4 . . . . 5.00
4 2nd & 3rd printing. 3.00
5 . . . . 4.00
5 2nd printing 3.00
6 . . . . 3.00
7 . . . . 3.00
TPB 19.95
HC 29.95
TPB Director's Cut 19.95

JOURNEY
Aardvark–Vanaheim

1 . . . . 10.00
2 . . . . 8.00
3 . . . . 7.00
4 . . . . 4.00
5 thru 7 . . . . @3.00
8 thru 14 . . . . @2.50

Fantagraphics

15 . . . . 2.50
16 thru 28. . . . . @2.00

JR. JACKALOPE

1 orange cover,1981 . . . . 8.00
1a Yellow cover,1981. . . . . 12.00
2 . . . . 8.00

JULIE'S JOURNEY: GRAVITY
Paper Live Studios 1998

1 by David Keye 2.50
2 thru 6 . . . . @2.50

JUNGLE COMICS
Blackthorne

4 thru 6 . . . . @2.00

JUNGLE COMICS
A-List Comics

2 reprint of Golden Age 2.95
3 . . . . 2.95
4 . . . . 2.95
5 . . . . 2.95
6 . . . . 2.95
TPB Book of Jungle Comics
Covers, 1940–54 . . . . 7.95

JUNGLE GIRLS
AC Comics

1 incGold.Age reps. 2.00
2 . . . . 2.00
3 Greed,A:Tara 2.75
4 CaveGirl. 2.75
5 Camilla. 2.75
6 TigerGirl 2.75
7 CaveGirl. 2.75
8 Sheena Queen o/t Jungle. 2.95
9 Wild Girl,Tiger Girl,Sheena 2.95
10 F:Tara,Cave Girl,Nyoka 2.95
11 F:Sheena,Tiger Girl,Nyoka 2.95
12 F:Sheena,Camilla,Tig.Girl 2.95
13 F:Tara, Tiger Girl 2.95

JUNGLE COMICS
A List Comics

1 thru 5 reprint of Golden Age . . @2.95
TPB Book of Jungle Comics Covers,
1940–54. . . . . 7.95

JURASSIC JANE
London Night 1997

1 by Sky Owens, F:Tira, elf
princess of Atlantis 3.00
1 deluxe nude edition 6.00
1 deluxe nude edition, signed . . . 10.00
2 . . . . 3.00
2 deluxe 6.00
3 . . . . 3.00
3 deluxe 6.00
4 EHr, Sky Owens. 3.00
4 nude cover edition 6.00
5 by Preston Owens 3.00
5 nude cover edition 6.00
6 by Sky Owens 3.00
6 nude cover edition 6.00
7 by Sky Owens 3.00
7 nude cover edition 6.00
Coll. Ed. 5.00
Coll. Ed. nude EHr(c) 7.00

JUSTICE
Newcomers Publishing 1995

1 I:Judiciary Urban Strike Team . . . 2.95

JUSTY

1 thru 9 . . . . @1.75

KABUKI: CIRCLE OF BLOOD

Caliber Press

1 R:Kabuki 6.00
2 Kabuki Goes Rogue 5.00
3 V:Noh Agents 5.00
4 V:Noh Agents 3.50
5 V:Kai 3.00
6 . . . . 3.00
TPB Rep.#1-#6. . . . . 16.95
TPB 2nd printing. 16.95
HC DAv,rep.#1–#6 272-pg. 100.00
TPB deluxe, signed, etc. 24.95
TPB Compilation 7.95

KABUKI: DANCE OF DEATH

London Night Studios

1 1st Full series 5.00

KABUKI: MASKS OF THE NOH

Caliber April, 1996

1A JQ(c) 3.00
1B Mays/Mack(c). 3.00
1C Buzz(c) 3.00
2 . . . . 3.00
3 DMk 3.00
4 epilog 3.00

KAFKA

1 thru 5 . . . . @2.00
The Execution Spec. 2.25

KAMUI

Eclipse

1 Sanpei Shirato Art 4.00
1a 2nd printing 2.50
2 Mystery of Hanbie 3.00
2a 2nd printing 1.50
3 V:Ichijiro 2.00
3a 2nd printing 1.50
4 thru 15 . . . . @1.50
16 thru 19 . . . . @2.00
20 thru 37 . . . . @1.50

KANE

Dancing Elephant

14 thru 17 by Paul Grist . . . . @3.50
18 thru 22 . . . . @3.50
23 thru 30 . . . . @2.95
TPB Book 1: rep. #1–#4 . . . . 11.95
TPB Book 2: Rabbit Hunt 12.50
TPB Book 3: Histories. 12.50
TPB Book 4: Thrity Ninth 19.95

KAOS MOON

Caliber 1996

1 by DdB 3.50
1a 2nd edition 3.00
2 . . . . 3.50
2a 2nd edition, new cover 3.00
3 . . . . 3.00
4 Anubian Nights, Chapter 2 . . . . . 3.00
GN Full Circle, rep #1–#2 . . . . 5.95

KAPTAIN KEEN

1 thru 3 . . . . @1.75
4 and 5 . . . . @1.50
6 and 7 . . . . @1.75

KATMANDU

Antarctic Press

1 thru 3 . . . . @2.75
4 & 5 Woman of Honor . . . . @2.75
6 F:Laska 2.75

Med Systems

7 and 8 . . . . @2.00

Vision Comics

9 "When Warriors Die," pt.3(of 3) . . 2.00
10 "The Curse of the Blood," pt.1 . . 2.50
11 "The Curse of the Blood," pt.2 . . 2.50
12 "The Curse of the Blood," concl . 2.95
13 "The Search For Magic," pt.1 . . . 2.95

Shanda Fantasy Arts

14 "The Search For Magic," pt.2 . . . 2.95
15 "The Search For Magic," pt.3 . . . 2.95
16 "Ceremonies," pt.1 (of 3) 2.95
17 "Ceremonies," pt.2. . . . . 2.95
18 "Ceremonies," pt.3. . . . . 2.95
19 "Peace Keeper,"pt.1. . . . . 2.95
20 "Peace Keeper,"pt.2. . . . . 2.95
21 "Peace Keeper,"pt.3. . . . . 2.95
22 . . . . 2.95
Ann. #1 48-page. 4.95

KEIF LLAMA

1 thru 6 . . . . @2.00

KELLEY BELLE, POLICE DETECTIVE

Newcomers Publishing

1 Debut issue 2.95
2 Case of the Jeweled Scarab 2.95
3 Case o/t Jeweled Scarab,pt.2 . . . 2.95
TPB #1. . . . . 8.95

KID CANNIBAL

Eternity

1 I:Kid Cannibal 2.50
2 Hunt for Kid Cannibal 2.50
3 A:Janice 2.50
4 final issue. 2.50

KI-GORR THE KILLER

AC

1 I:Ki-Gorr, Rae 2.95

KIKU SAN

Aircel

1 thru 6 . . . . @2.00

KILLING STROKE

Eternity 1991

1 British horror tales 2.50
2 inc.`Blood calls to Blood'. 2.50
3 and 4 . . . . @2.50

KILROY

Caliber Core 1998

1C by Joe Pruett & Feliciano Zecchin, John Cassaday(c) . . . 2.95
1P JoP (c). 2.95
1a premium edition 9.95
2 . . . . 2.95
3 . . . . 2.95
4 O:Kilroy 2.95
Spec. Dawn of Armageddon, x-over, 48-page 3.95
Spec.#1 The Origin. 4.95
Spec.#2 The Origin, pt.2. . . . . 4.95
TPB Kilroy is Here: Pride, Prejudice & Persecution. 6.95

KILROY IS HERE

Caliber Press 1995

1 Kilroy Rescues Infant 2.95
2 Reflections,pt.2. . . . . 2.95
3 Reflections,pt.3. . . . . 2.95
4 Lincoln Memorial 2.95
5 thru 8 . . . . @2.95
9 and 10 . . . . @2.95
11 WEI,RPc,"Screen" 2.95
12 Khymer Rouge 2.95
Spec. Kilroy: Daemonstorm (1997) . 2.95

KIMBER, PRINCE OF FELONS

Antarctic Press

1 I:Kimber 2.50
2 V:Lord Tyrex. 2.50

KINGDOM OF THE WICKED

Caliber 1996

1 IEd 2.95
2 IEd 2.95
3 IEd 2.95
4 IEd 2.95
HC rep. #1–#4 . . . . 49.95
TPB rep. #1–#4 . . . . 12.95

King Kong #1
© Monster Comics

KING KONG

Monster Comics 1991

1 thru 6 . . . . @2.50

KINGS IN DISGUISE

1 thru 5 . . . . @2.00
6 end Mini-series. 2.00

KING ZOMBIE

Caliber 1998

1L by Tom Sniegoski & Jacen Burroughs, VcL(c) 2.95
1M Meadows (c) 2.95
2 . . . . 2.95
3 . . . . 2.95

B & W PUB.

KIRBY KING OF THE SERIALS
Blackthorne
1 . . . . 2.00
2 . . . . 2.00
3 . . . . 2.00
4 . . . . 2.00

KITZ 'N' KATZ
1 . . . . 3.50
Eclipse
2 . . . . 2.00
3 . . . . 1.50
4 and 5 . . . . @2.00

KLOWN SHOCK
North Star
1 Horror Stories. 2.75

KNEWTS OF THE ROUND TABLE
Pan Entertainment 1998
1 . . . . 2.50
2 thru 6 . . . . @2.50

KNIGHTMARE
Anarctic Press
1 . . . . 2.75
2 . . . . 2.75
3 Wedding Knight pt.1 . . . . . 2.75
4 Wedding Knight pt.2 . . . . . 2.75
5 F:Dream Shadow 2.75
6 V:Razorblast. 2.75

KNIGHT MASTERS
1 thru 7 . . . . @1.50

KNIGHTS OF THE DINNER TABLE
Kenzer & Company
4 Have Dice Will Travel 2.95
5 Master of the Game 2.95
6 on the high seas. 2.95
7 Lord of Steam. 2.95
8 A:magic cow. 2.95
9 To Dice for Sister Sara 2.95
16 thru 18. . . . . @2.95
19 Heroes of the Hack League . . . 2.95
20 Hack in Space 2.95
21 Home is Where You Hang Yer Dice Bag 2.95
22 Opportunity Knocks 2.95
23 Dice Follies 2.95
24 Hackzilla 2.95
25 Secrets of the Hackfiles 2.95
26 The Mask of El Ravager 2.95
27 Hackburger Hill 2.95
28 Hoody Freakin' Hoo 2.95
29 Bad Moon Risin' 2.95
30 No Honor. 2.95
31 Don't Fear the Reaper 2.95
32 Tales From Hawg Wallers 2.95
33 Wild, Wild Hack 2.95
34 Of Dice & Men. 2.95
35 Death Awaits 2.95
36 Hackmaster of Puppets 2.95
37 . . . . 2.95
38 Hack Rogers 2.95
39 The Game Must Go On 2.95
40 Hack in the Saddle Again. . . . 2.95
41 . . . . 2.95
42 A Hack in Time Slays Nine . . . 2.95
43 Wasted Days & Wasted Knights. 2.95
44 . . . . 2.95
45 Buddy Can You Spare A Cure . . 2.95
46 Hack & Roll All Night 2.95
47 Hack & Roll All Night 2.95
48 One Ring to Fool Them All. . . . 2.95
TPB Vol. 1 Bundle of Trouble . . . 9.95
TPB Vol. 2 Bundle of Trouble . . . 9.95
TPB Vol. 3 Bundle of Trouble . . . 9.95
TPB Vol. 4 Bundle of Trouble . . . 9.95
TPB Vol. 5 Bundle of Trouble . . . 9.95
TPB Vol. 6 Bundle of Trouble . . . 9.95
TPB Vol. 7 Bundle of Trouble . . . 9.95
TPB Tales From the Vault. 9.95
TPB Tales From the Vault, Vol.2 . . 9.95
TPB Tales From the Vault, Vol.3 . . 12.95

KNIGHTS OF THE DINNER TABLE: FAANS
Six-Handed Press 1999
X-over Spec. 2.95

KNIGHTS OF THE DINNER TABLE: HACKMASTERS
Kenzer & Company 2000
1 . . . . 2.95
2 . . . . 2.95
3 . . . . 2.95

KNIGHTS OF THE DINNER TABLE ILLUSTRATED
Kenzer & Company 2000
1 . . . . 2.95
2 . . . . 2.95
3 . . . . 2.95

KNIGHT WATCHMAN
Caliber Press
1 Graveyard pt. 1 . . . . 2.95
2 Graveyard pt. 2 . . . . 2.95

KOMODO & THE DEFIANTS
1 thru 6 . . . . @1.50

KORVUS
Human Monster Press 1997
1 by Mick Fernette. 2.95
2 . . . . 2.95
Arrow Comics 1998
3 . . . . 2.95
VOL. 2
1 . . . . 2.95
2 . . . . 2.95

KUNG FU WARRIORS (Prev. ROBOWARRIORS)
CFW
12 . . . . 2.00
13 thru 19. . . . . @2.25

KUNOICHI
Lightning Comics 1996
1 2 diff. mild covers 3.00
1 platimum edition. 5.95
1 autographed edition 9.95

KYRA
Elsewhere 1989
1 thru 5 by Robin Ator . . . . . @1.75
TPB rep #1–#5 + pin-ups 6.95

L.A. RAPTOR
Morbid Graphics
1 Velocaraptor loose 2.95

LABOR FORCE
Blackthorne
1 thru 4 . . . . @1.50
5 thru 8 . . . . @1.75

LA COSA NOSTROID
Fireman Press 1997
1 by Don Harmon & Rob Schrab . 2.95
2 by Don Harmon & Edvis 2.95
3 . . . . 2.95
4 . . . . 2.95
5 . . . . 2.95
6 x-over madness 2.95
7 . . . . 2.95
8 . . . . 2.95
9 . . . . 2.95
10 final issue of Volume 1. . . . 2.95

LACUNAE
CFD Producitons 1995
1 thru 4 F:Monkey Boys . . . . @2.50
5 thru 10 . . . . @2.50
11 HMo 2.50
12 HMo 2.50

LADIES OF LONDON NIGHT
London Night 1997
Fall Special 5.00
Nude Heather Parkhurst (c) . . . 7.00
Nude Gloria Gilbert (c) 7.00
Winter Special 5.00
Winter Wonderland Edition . . . 7.00
Spring '98 Special 5.00
Nude Gloria Ann (c) 7.00
Nude Wendy Leigh (c) 7.00
Spotlight: Devon Michaels 3.95
Devon Michaels nude (c) 6.00

LADY ARCANE
Heroic Publishing
1 thru 3 . . . . @3.50

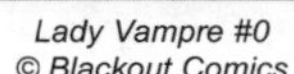
Lady Vampre #0
© Blackout Comics

LADY CRIME
AC Comics
1 Bob Powell reprints. 2.75

LADY VAMPRE
Blackout Comics 1996
0 (1995) 2.75
1 flip-book 2.95
0 Immortal No More (1998) 2.95
0a nude cover 9.95
Spec.#1 In the Flesh (1996) 2.95
Spec.#1a photo sexy cover. 9.95

LADY VAMPRE RETURNS
Blackout Comics 1998
1 by Rob Roman & Kirk Manley. . . 2.95
1a nude cover 9.95
1b Deluxe edition. 14.95

LAFFIN GAS
Blackthorne
1 . . . . 2.50
2 thru 12 . . . . @2.00

LANCE STANTON WAYWARD WARRIOR
1 and 2 . . . . @1.50

LANDER
Mermaid Producions
1 Power of the Dollar,pt.1 . . . . 2.25
2 Power of the Dollar,pt.2 . . . . 2.25
3 Power of the Dollar,pt.3 . . . . 2.25

Vol. 2

1 "By Whose Authority," pt.1 . . . . . 2.75
2 "By Whose Authority," pt.2 . . . . . 2.75

LAND OF OZ
Arrow Comics 1998
1 by Gary Bishop & Bill Bryan 2.95
2 . . . . 2.95
3 . . . . 2.95
4 . . . . 2.95
5 . . . . 2.95
6 . . . . 2.95

LAST DITCH
Edge Press
1 CCa(s),THa, ... 2.50

LAST GENERATION
Black Tie Studios
1 . . . . 5.00
2 . . . . 4.00
3 . . . . 2.25
4 . . . . 2.25
5 . . . . 2.25
Book One Rep.. . . . . 6.95

LAST KISS, THE
Eclipse
Spec. 3.95

LATIGO KID WESTERN
AC Comics
1 . . . . 2.00

LAUREL & HARDY
1 3-D. 2.50

LEAGUE OF CHAMPIONS
Hero Comics
(cont. from Innovation L.of C. #3)

1 GP,F:Sparkplug,Icestar 3.50
2 GP(i),F:Marksman,Flare,Icicle. . . 3.50
3 . . . . 3.50
4 F:Sparkplug,League 3.50
5 Morrigan Wars Pt.#1. . . . . 3.50
6 Morrigan Wars Pt.#3. . . . . 3.50
7 Morrigan Wars Pt.#6. . . . . 3.50
8 Morrigan Wars Conclusion 3.50
9 A:Gargoyle 3.50
10 A:Rose 3.50
11 and 12 . . . . @3.95
13 V:Malice 3.95
14 V:Olympians 3.95
15 V:Olympians 2.95

LE FEMME VAMPRIQUE
Brainstorm 1997
1 . . . . 3.50
1a nude edition 5.00

LEGENDLORE
Caliber "New Worlds"
1 JMt signed 2.95
3 JMt. 2.95
4 JMt 2.95
5 JMt. 2.95
6 flip book w/Boston Bombers #4 . 2.95
7 JMt. 2.95
8 JMt. 2.95
TPB Tainted Soul, rep. #1–#4 . . . . 12.95
TPB In Misery's Shadow, Rep. #5–#7 . . . . 9.95

LEGENDLORE: REALM WARS
Caliber "New Worlds"
1 by Joe Martin & Philip Xavier, Fawn cover by Xavier. 2.95
1a Falla cover by Boller. 2.95
1b signed 2.95
2 . . . . 2.95
3 . . . . 2.95
4 concl. 2.95

LEGENDLORE: WRATH OF THE DRAGON
Caliber Fantasy 1998
1 by JMt & Philip Xavier. 2.95
1 variant Philip Xavier(c) 2.95
2 . . . . 2.95
3 . . . . 2.95
4 . . . . 2.95
5 Prisoner set free. 2.95
Spec. Handbook. 3.95
1-shot Legendlore: Slave of Fate by JMt & Philip Xavier 2.95
1-shot The Wind Spirits, 48-page . . 3.95
Giant Size Spec. 48-page. 3.95

LEGENDS OF CAMELOT
Caliber Fantasy 1999
Excalibur 2.95
Quest For Honor. 2.95
Merlin. 2.95
The Enchanted Lady 2.95
Sir Balin & The Dolorous Stroke . . . 2.95

LEGEND OF LEMNEAR
CPM Manga 1997
1 . . . . 2.95
2 thru 17 . . . . @2.95

18 final issue 2.95
TPB Vol. 1, 160-page 15.95
TPB Vol. 2 . . . . 15.95

LEGENDS OF LUXURA
Brainstorm 1996
1 platinum edition 5.00
2 gold edition. 5.00
3 . . . . 2.95
TPB #1. . . . . 12.95

LEGION ANTHOLOGY
Limelight 1997
1 four stories 2.95
2 . . . . 2.95
3 F:Binary Angel 2.95
4 . . . . 2.95
5 Binary Angel. 2.95

LEGION X-I
1 McKinney 5.00
2 McKinney,rare 15.00

Volume 2

1 thru 4 . . . . @2.00

LEGION X-2
Vol. 2 #1 . . . . 2.00
Vol. 2 #2 . . . . 2.00
Vol. 2 #3 . . . . 2.00
Vol. 2 #4 . . . . 2.00

LENORE
Slave Labor 1998
1 by Roman Dirge 2.95
2 thru 8 . . . . @2.95
TPB 11.95

LENSMAN
Eternity 1990
1 E.E.`Doc' Smith adapt. 2.25
2 . . . . 2.25
3 . . . . 2.25
4 . . . . 2.25
5 On Radelix 2.25
6 . . . . 2.25
Collectors Spec #1, 56-pgs. 3.95
TPB Birth of a Lensman, rep. 5.95
TPB Secret of the Lens, rep.. . . . . . 5.95

Lensman #1
© Eternity

B & W PUB.

LENSMAN: GALACTIC PATROL
Eternity 1990
1 thru 7 E.E. `Doc' Smith adapt. . @2.25

LENSMAN: WAR OF THE GALAXIES
Eternity 1990
1 thru 7 . . . . @2.25

LEONARDO
1 TMNT. 13.00

LETHAL LADIES OF BRAINSTORM
Brainstorm 1997
1 F:Luxura, Vampfire, etc. 2.95
1 nude cover edition 3.95
1 luxury edition 5.00

LETHAL STRIKE ARCHIVES
London Night 1997
1 rep. Razor #7, #10 & Uncut #19–#21. . . . . 3.00
1 nude cover edition 9.00
TPB Lethal Strike (1998). 12.95

LETHAL STRIKE: SHADOW VIPER
London Night 1998
1 (of 2) from Razor: Torture #4. . . . 3.00
1 nude cover. 6.00
1 leather 15.00

LETHARGIC LAD ADVENTURES
Crusade Entertainment 1997
1 by Greg Hyland 2.95
2 . . . . 2.95
Becomes:

LETHARGIC LAD
TV Comics 1997
3 by Greg Hyland 2.95
4 . . . . 2.95
5 . . . . 2.95
TPB Big Book of Lethargic Lad . . . 15.95
Lethargic Comics
6 by Greg Hyland 2.95
7 thru 14 . . . . @2.95

LEVEL X
Caliber 1997
1 . . . . 2.95
2 32-pg.. 2.95
3 48-pg.. 3.95

LEVEL X: THE NEXT REALITY
Caliber 1997
1 (of 2) by Dan Harbison & Randy Buccini, 64-pg. 3.95
2 48-pg.. 3.95

LIBBY ELLIS
1 and 2 . . . . @2.00
Eternity
1 thru 4 . . . . @2.00

LIBERATOR
Eternity
1 thru 6 . . . . @2.00

LIBERTY MEADOWS
Insight Studios 1999
1 by Frank Cho 2.95
2 thru 15 . . . . @2.95

L.I.F.E. BRIGADE
Blue Comet
1 A:Dr. Death 1.50
1a 2nd printing 1.50
2 . . . . 1.50

LIFEQUEST
Caliber Dec. 1997
1 by Matt Vanderpol 2.95
2 . . . . 2.95
3 . . . . 2.95
4 . . . . 2.95
5 . . . . 2.95
6 . . . . 2.95

LIVINGSTONE MOUNTAIN
Adventure Comics 1991
1 I:Scat,Dragon Rax 2.50
2 Scat & Rax Create Monsters . . . 2.50
3 Rax rescue attempt 2.50
4 Final issue 2.50

LLOYD LLEWELLYN
Fantagraphics
1 Mag.Size 4.00
2 Mag. Size. 2.25
3 Mag. Size. 2.25
4 Mag. Size. 2.25
5 Mag. Size. 2.25
6 Mag. Size. 2.25
7 Regular Size. 2.25

LOCO VS. PULVERINE
Eclipse
1 Parody 2.50

LODOSS WAR: CHRONICLES HEROIC KNIGHT
CPM Manga 2000
1 by Ryo Mizuno & Masato Natsumoto 2.95
2 . . . . 2.95

LODOSS WAR: THE GREY WITCH
CPM Manga 1998
1 by Ryo Mizuno & Yoshihiko Ochi 2.95
2 by Ryo Mizuno & Akikiro Yamada 2.95
3 thru 10 . . . . @2.95
11 thru 22 . . . . @2.95
TPB Vol. 2 . . . . 15.95

LODOSS WAR: THE LADY OF PHARIS
CPM Manga 1999
1 by Ryo Mizuno & Akihiro Yamada 2.95
2 thru 7 . . . . @2.95
TPB Vol. 1 208-page 15.95

Logan's Run #2
© Adventure Comics

LOGAN'S RUN
Adventure Comics 1990
1 thru 6 Novel adapt. . . . . @2.50

LOGAN'S WORLD
Adventure Comics 1991
1 Seq. to Logan's Run. 2.50
2 thru 6 . . . . @2.50

LONER
Fleetway
1 Pt. 1 of 7 . . . . 2.00
2 Pt. 2. . . . . 2.00
3 Pt. 3. . . . . 2.00
4 Pt. 4. . . . . 2.00
5 Pt. 5. . . . . 2.00
6 Pt. 6. . . . . 2.00

LONE WOLF & CUB
First
1 FM(c). 7.00
1a 2nd printing 2.50
1b 3rd printing. 1.50
2 . . . . 4.00
2a 2nd printing 2.00
3 . . . . 3.50
4 thru 10 . . . . @3.00
11 thru 17 . . . . @2.75
18 thru 25. . . . . @2.50
26 thru 36. . . . . @2.95
37 and 38 . . . . @3.25
39 120-page. 5.95
40 . . . . 3.25
41 MP(c), 60-page 3.95
42 MP(c) 3.25
43 MP(c) 3.25
44 MP(c) 3.25
45 MP(c) 3.25

LOOKERS
Avatar Press 1997
1 . . . . 3.00
1 deluxe 5.00
1 signed 12.00
2 . . . . 3.00
2 Deluxe cover 8.00
Spec. #1. . . . . 3.00
Spec. #1, nude cover 4.95
Spec. #1 signed 8.00

B & W PUB.

Spec. Allure of the Serpent (1999) . 3.50
Spec. Allure of the Serpent,nude(c) 6.00
Spec. Slaves of Anubis (1998) 3.50
Spec. Slaves of Anubis,nude(c) . . . 6.00

LORD OF THE DEAD
Conquest
1 R.E.Howard adapt. 2.95

LORI LOVECRAFT
Caliber 1997
1 MV, 48pg 3.95
1a signed 3.95
1-shot The Dark Lady (1997). 2.95
1-shot Repression (1998) 2.95
Spec. The Big Comeback (1998) . . 2.95

LOST, THE
Caliber
1 . . . . 3.00
1a special ed. 7.00
1b signed 3.00
2 thru 4 . . . . @3.00

LOST ANGEL
Caliber
1 . . . . 3.50

LOST CONTINENT
Eclipse 1990
1 thru 5, Manga . . . . @3.50

LOST STORIES
Creative Frontiers 1998
1 . . . . 2.95
2 . . . . 2.95
3 . . . . 2.95
4 The Big Horn Bruhaha 2.95
5 Strike Force O'Shea, pt.1 . . . . . . 2.95
6 Strike Force O'Shea, pt.2 . . . . . . 2.95
7 Gnome for a Day 2.95
8 A Vampire Too Far 2.95
9 The Undertroll Saga, pt.1 . . . . . . 2.95

LOST WORLD, THE
Millennium 1996
1 and 2 Arthur Conan Doyle adapt . . . . @2.95

LOTHAR
Powerhouse Graphics
1 I:Lothar,Galactic Bounty Hunter . 2.50
2 I:Nightcap. 2.50

LOVE AND ROCKETS
Fantagraphics Books 1982–96
1 HB,B&W cover, adult 40.00
1a HB,Color cover. 20.00
1b 2nd printing 4.00
2 HB 15.00
3 HB 10.00
4 HB 10.00
5 HB 10.00
6 HB 6.00
7 HB 7.00
8 HB 7.00
9 HB 6.00
10 HB. 6.00
11 HB. 4.00
12 HB. 4.00
13 HB. 4.00
14 HB. 4.00
15 HB. 4.00
16 thru 21 HB . . . . @3.00

Ten Years of Love & Rockets
© Fantagraphics

22 thru 39 HB . . . . @3.00
40 thru 50. . . . . @3.00
Bonanza rep. 3.00
TPB Vol. 9 Flies on the Ceiling, 2nd printing 16.95
HC Vol. 10 Love & Rockets X 35.00
HC Vol. 10 deluxe. 39.95
TPB Vol. 10 . . . . 11.95
HC Vol. 11 Wigwam Bam 35.00
HC Vol. 11 deluxe. 39.95
TPB Vol. 11 . . . . 14.95
HC Vol. 12 Poison River 35.00
HC Vol. 12 deluxe. 39.95
TPB Vol. 12 . . . . 16.95
HC Vol. 13 Chester Square. 34.95
TPB Vol. 14 Luba Conquers the World 14.95
HC Vol. 14 Luba Conquers the World 34.95
HC Vol. 14 , signed. 39.95
TPB Vol. 15 . . . . 14.95
HC Vol. 15 . . . . 34.95
HC Vol. 15 , signed. 39.95

LUFTWAFFE 1946
Antarctic Press
1 (of 4) by Ted Namura & BDn. . . . 2.95
2 Luftsturm, pt.2 thru 4. . . . . @2.95
3 . . . . 2.95
4 . . . . 2.95
5 new weapons 2.95
6 Projekt Saucer, pt.1 . . . . 2.95
7 Projekt Saucer, pt.2 . . . . 2.95
8 Projekt Saucer, pt.3 . . . . 2.95
9 Projekt Saucer, pt.4 . . . . 2.95
10 Projekt Saucer, pt.5 . . . . 2.95
11 Projekt Saucer, epilogue 2.95
12 Richthofen's Flying Circus, pt.1 . 2.95
13 Richthofen's Flying Circus, pt.2 . 2.95
14 Jagdgeschwader,pt.2. . . . . 2.95
15 Jagdeschwader, pt.3 . . . . 3.00
16 Jagdeschwader, pt.4 . . . . 3.00
17 Jagdeschwader, pt.5 . . . . 3.00
18 Schweinfurt 3.00
Tech Manual Vol. 1 . . . . 3.95
Tech Manual Vol. 2 . . . . 4.00
Tech Manual Vol. 3 Rocket Fighters 3.99
Tech Manual Vol. 4 Amerika Bombers 3.99
Tech Manual Vol. 5 Wonder Weapons 3.99
Spec.#1 Triebflugel. 2.95
Spec.#1 World War II: 1946 . . . . . . 3.95

Ann. #1 prototype artwork. 2.95
TPB Vol.1, rep.mini-series #1–#4 . 10.95
TPB Vol.2, rep. #1–#5. . . . . 10.95
TPB Vol. 3, rep. 10.95
TPB Vol. 4, rep. #13–#18 . . . . 14.95

LUM*URUSEI YATSURA
1 Art by Rumiko Takahashi 2.95
2 . . . . 2.95
3 . . . . 2.95
4 . . . . 2.95
5 . . . . 3.25
6 thru 8 . . . . @2.95

LUNAR DONUT
Cosmic Lunchbox Comics
1 thru 4 by Keelan Parham & Ted Tucker . . . . @2.95
Lunar Donut
5 . . . . 2.95
6 Powdered Sugar. 2.95

LUXURA
Brainstorm 1996
Convention Book 2. . . . . 2.95
Ann.#1 48-pg. (1998) 3.95
Ann.#1a nude cover 3.95

LUXURA & VAMPFIRE
Brainstorm 1997
1 by Fauve 2.95
1a nude cover 3.95

LUXURA: BABY ANGEL X
Brainstorm 1996
Spec. x-over. 2.95
Spec. deluxe 5.00
Luxury edition. 8.00
Deluxe luxury edition 12.00

LUXURA: THE GOOD, THE BAD AND THE BEAUTIFUL
Brainstorm 1999
Pin-up magazine 3.95
Pin-up mag. nude (c) 4.95

LUXURA: LEATHER
Brainstorm
Platinum edition 5.00
Signed edition 8.00

LUXURA/WIDOW: BLOOD LUST
Brainstorm
Omega x-over pt.2 concl. 2.95
Omega Fusion cover 5.00
Luxury edition. 8.00
Deluxe luxury edition 12.00
See: Widow/Luxura for pt.1

LYNX: AN ELFLORD TALE
Peregrin 1999
1 by Barry Blair 2.95
2 by Barry Blair & Colin Chan 2.95
3 . . . . 2.95
4 . . . . 2.95

MACH 1
Fleetway
1 I:John Probe-Secret Agent 2.00

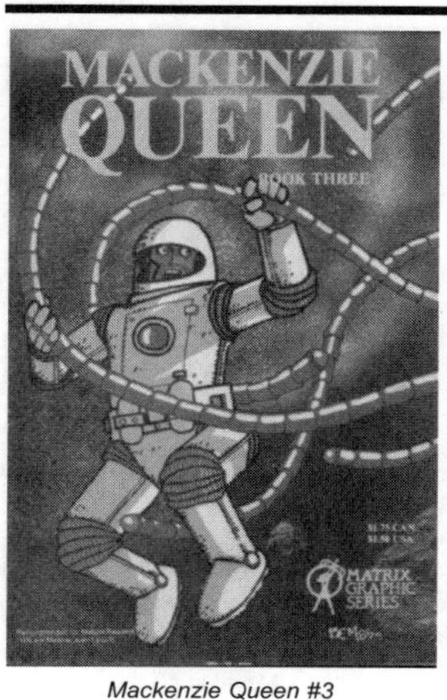

Mackenzie Queen #3
© Matrix

MACKENZIE QUEEN
Matrix 1985
1 thru 5 . . . . @3.75

MACROSS II
Viz
1 Macross Saga sequel 2.75
2 A:Ishtar 2.75
3 F:Reporter Hibiki,Ishtar 2.75
4 V:Feff,The Marduk 2.75
5 . . . . 2.75
6 . . . . 2.75
7 Sylvie Confesses 2.75
8 F:Ishtar 2.75
9 V:Marduk Fleet 2.75
10 . . . . 2.75

MACROSS II: THE MICRON CONSPIRACY
Viz 1994
1 Manga 2.75

MAD DOGS
Eclipse 1992
1 I:Mad Dogs(Cops) 2.50
2 V:Chinatown Hood 2.50
3 . . . . 2.50

MAD RACCOONS
MU Press 1991
1 thru 7 by Cathy Hill, Angst of an Artist . . . . @2.95

MAELSTROM
Aircel
1 thru 5 . . . . @1.70
6 thru 13 . . . . @1.50

MAGGOTS
1 JSon, mag. size 3.95
2 JSon, mag. size 3.95
3 GM/JSon,inc.`Some Kinda Beautiful' 3.95

MAGICAL MATES
Antarctic Press 1995
1 and 2 Manga, by Mio Odagi . . @2.95
3 thru 8 (of 8) . . . . @2.95

MAGICAL POKEMON JOURNEY
Viz Communications 2000
1 How Do You Do, Pikachu 4.95
2 Cooking with Jigglypuff 4.95
3 Pokemon Holiday 4.95
4 Fun at the Beach 4.95
TPB Vol. 1 Party with Pikachu 13.95

PART 2
1 thru 4 . . . . @4.95

MAGUS
Caliber Core May 1998
1L by Gary Reed & Craig Brasfield, VcL(c) 2.95
1D GyD(c) 2.95
1 premium edition, signed 9.95
2 Magus secrets 2.95
3 Lilith & Beezlebub 2.95
1-shot Magus: The Forever King . . . 2.95
Spec. Dawn of Armageddon, x-over, 48-page 2.95

MAI, THE PSYCHIC GIRL
Eclipse
1 I:Mai,Alliance of 13 Sages 3.75
1a 2nd printing 2.00
2 V:Wisdom Alliance 2.00
2a 2nd printing 1.50
3 V:Kaieda,I:Ojii-San 2.00
4 . . . . 2.00
5 thru 19 . . . . @1.75
20 thru 28 . . . . @1.50

MAISON IKKOKU
Viz
1 thru 7 . . . . @2.95

[Part Two]
1 thru 6 . . . . @2.95

[Part Three]
1 thru 6 . . . . @2.95

[Part Four]
1 thru 6 F:Kyoko . . . . @2.95
7 thru 10 . . . . @2.95

[Part Six] Aug. 1996
1 thru 11 by Rumiko Takahashi . @3.50

[Part Seven] July 1997
1 thru 8 by Rumiko Takahashi . . @3.25
9 thru 13 . . . . @3.50

[Part Eight] Aug. 1998
1 (of 8) 3.25
2 . . . . 3.50
3 thru 8 . . . . @3.25

[Part Nine] 1999
1 (of 10) 3.25
2 thru 10 . . . . @3.25
TPB Vol. 4 Good Housekeeping . . 15.95
TPB Vol. 5 Empty Nest 15.95
TPB Vol. 6 Bedside Manners 15.95
TPB Vol. 7 Intensive Care 15.95
TPB Vol. 8 Domestic Dispute 16.95
TPB Vol. 10 Dogged Pursuit 17.95
TPB Vol. 11 Student Affairs 16.95
TPB Vol. 12 The Hounds of War . . 16.95
TPB Vol. 14 Welcome Home 16.95

MAN EATING COW
1 Spin-off from the Tick 3.25

2 O:Mr.Krinkles,A:Lt.Valentine 2.75
3 Final issue 2.75
Bonanza #1, 128-pg. 4.95
Bonanza #2, 100-pg. 4.95

MAN-ELF
3 A:Jerry Cornelius 2.25

MANDRAKE
1 . . . . 3.95
2 . . . . 3.95
3 . . . . 3.95
Ultimate Mandrake 14.95

MANDRAKE MONTHLY
1 . . . . 3.95
2 . . . . 3.95
3 . . . . 4.95
4 . . . . 4.95
5 . . . . 4.95
6 . . . . 6.95
Special #1 . . . . 6.95

MAN FROM U.N.C.L.E.
Entertainment Publ.
1 `Number One with a Bullet Affair. 2.50
2 `Number One with a Bullet Affair. 2.00
3 `The E-I-E-I-O Affair' 1.50
4 `The E-I-E-I-O Affair,' concl. 1.50
5 `The Wasp Affair' 1.50
6 `Lost City of THRUSH Affair' 1.50
7 `The Wildwater Affair' 1.50
8 `The Wilder West Affair' 1.50
9 `The Cahadian Lightning Affair' . . 1.75
10 `The Turncoat Affair' 1.75
11 `Craters of the Moon Affair' 1.75

MANGA MONTHLY
0 . . . . 3.00

MANGA VIZION
Viz
1 thru 8 Ogre Slayer . . . . @4.95

MANGAZINE
Antarctic Press
1 newsprint cover 6.00
1a reprint 3.00
2 . . . . 5.00
3 . . . . 4.00
4 . . . . 2.00
5 . . . . 1.50

New Series
1 . . . . 3.00
2 . . . . 3.00
3 . . . . 1.75
4 . . . . 1.75
5 thru 7 . . . . @2.00
8 thru 13 . . . . @2.25
14 New Format 2.95
15 . . . . 2.95
16 . . . . 2.95
17 . . . . 2.95

MANIMAL
1 EC,rep. 1.70

MAN OF RUST
Blackthorne 1986
1 Cover A 1.50
1 Cover B 1.50

MANSLAUGHTER
Brainstorm 1996

1 . . . . 2.95
1a gold foil edition 5.00

MANTUS FILES
Eternity

1 Sidney Williams novel adapt 2.50
2 Vampiric Figures. 2.50
3 Secarus' Mansion. 2.50
4 A:Secarus 2.50

MARCANE
Eclipse

1 Book 1,JMu 5.95

MARK I
(Prev.: Atomic Comics)

2 . . . . 1.50

MARQUIS, THE
Caliber 1997

1 GyD 3.00
1 spec. double gatefold cover 6.00
2 Marquis cover by Vincent Locke . 3.00
2a Marquis view of world GyD(c) . . 3.00
3 . . . . 3.00
Spec. The Marquis, Gallery of Hell, GyD 3.95
Spec. The Marquis: Les Preludes, GyD prelude edition (1996). 2.95
Spec.A Les Preludes, signed 2.95

MARQUIS, THE: DANSE MACABRE
Oni Press 2000

1 (of 5) by Guy Davis 2.95
2 . . . . 2.95
3 . . . . 2.95
4 . . . . 2.95

MARTIAN SUCCESSOR NADESICO
CPM Manga 1999

1 by Kia Asamiya 2.95
2 . . . . 2.95
3 . . . . 2.95
4 thru 17 . . . . @2.95
TPB Vol. 1 . . . . 15.95

MASKED WARRIOR X
Antarctic Press April 1996

1 (of 6) by Masayuki Fujihara. 3.50
2 . . . . 2.95
3 "The Girls of Olympus," pt.2 . . . . 2.95
4 "Protect the Silver Fortress" 2.95

MASQUERADE
Eclipse

1 . . . . 1.50
2 . . . . 2.00
3 . . . . 2.00

MATAAK
K-Blamm 1995

1 I:Mataak. 2.50
2 Spirit of Peace 2.50

MATT CHAMPION

1 EC 2.00
2 EC 2.00

MAVIS
Exhibit A 1998

1 BLs, F:Wolff & Byrd's secretary. . 2.95
2 . . . . 2.95

MAXION
CPM 1999

1 by Takeshi Takebayashi 2.95
2 thru 11 . . . . @2.95
TPB Book 1 . . . . 15.95

MAX OF REGULATORS

1 . . . . 4.00
2 . . . . 3.50
3 . . . . 3.50
4 . . . . 3.50

MAXWELL MOUSE FOLLIES

1 Large format (1981) 4.00
1a Comic Size(1986). 3.00
2 thru 6 . . . . @2.00

MAYHEM

1 thru 6 . . . . @2.50

MAZE AGENCY
Caliber 1997

1 "The Death of Justice Girl" reprint series 2.95
1a signed 2.95
2 stranded in a monastery, Gene Gonzales(c) 2.95
2a Adam Hughes (c) 2.95
3G The Two Wrong Rhoades, Gonzales(c) 2.95
3H Adam Hughes(c) 2.95

MEASLES
Fantagraphics 1998

1 by Gilbert Hernandez 2.95
2 thru 7 . . . . @2.95

MECHANOIDS
Caliber 1991

1 . . . . 2.50
2 thru 5 . . . . @3.50

MECHARIDER: THE REGULAR SERIES
Castle

1 thru 3 F:Winter 2.95
Spec.#1 Limited Edition 2.95

MEGATON
Megaton

1 JG(c),EL(1stProWork),GD,MG, A:Ultragirl,Vanguard 8.00
2 EL,JG(pin-up),A:Vanguard 8.00
3 MG,AMe,JG,EL,I:Savage Dragon. 13.00
4 AMe,EL,2nd A:Savage Dragon (inc.EL profile) 9.00
5 AMe,RLd(inside front cover) 3.00
6 AMe,JG(inside back cover), EL(Back cover) 3.00
7 AMe 3.00
8 RLd,I:Youngblood(Preview). . . . 18.00

MEGATON MAN

1 . . . . 2.00

Megaton #3
© Megaton

MEGATON MAN MEETS THE UNCATEGORIZABLE X-THEMS
Jabberwocky

1 . . . . 2.00

MEGATON MAN VS. FORBIDDEN FRANKENSTEIN
Fiasco Comics April 1996

1 by Don Simpson & Anton Drek . . 2.95

MELISSA MOORE: BODYGUARD
Draculina Publishing 1995

1 thru 3 V:Machine Gun Eddie . . @2.95

MEN IN BLACK
Aircel 1991

1 by Lowell Cunningham & Sandy Carruthers, basis of Movie . . . 35.00
2 . . . . 20.00
3 F:Jay, Arbiter Doran 15.00

(Book II) 1991

1 . . . . 15.00
2 and 3 . . . . @8.00

MEN IN BLACK: THE ROBORG INCIDENT
Castle

1 thru 3 . . . . @2.95

MEMORY MAN
Emergency Stop Press 1995

1 and 2 Some of the Space Man . . 2.95

MERCEDES
Angus Publishing

8 thru 15 by Mike Friedland & Grant Fuhst. . . . . @2.95
TPB Vol. 2 . . . . 10.95
TPB Vol. 3, rep. The Wicked from #11–#15. . . . . 10.95

VOL. 4

1 thru 4 . . . . @2.95

VOL. 5 1997

1 . . . . 2.95
2 . . . . 2.95
3 . . . . 2.95
Spec. Senseless Acts of
Beauty (1998) 2.95

MERCHANTS OF DEATH

Eclipse

1 thru 5 . . . . @2.00

MERCY

Avatar Press Dec., 1997

0 O:Mercy 3.00
0a nude cover 6.00
0b leather cover. 30.00
1 (of 2) by Bill Maus 3.00
1 nude cover 4.95
1 leather cover 25.00
1 signed 10.00

MERLIN

Adventure Comics Dec,. 1990

1 BMC,Merlin's Visions 2.50
2 V:Warlord Carados 2.50
3 . . . . 2.50
4 Ninevah 2.50
5 D:Hagus 2.50
6 Final Issue 2.50

[2nd Series]

1 Journey of Rhiannon & Tryon . . . 2.50
2 Conclusion 2.50

MERMAID'S GAZE

Viz

1 thru 3 V:Shingo . . . . @2.75
4 final issue 2.75
TPB 15.95

Metacops #2
© Monster Comics

METACOPS

Monster Comics

1 and 2 . . . . @2.00

METAL GUARDIAN FAUST

Viz Communications

March, 1997

1 thru 5 (of 8) by Tetsuo Ueyama @2.95
6 thru 8 . . . . @2.95
TPV Vol. 1 . . . . 16.95

METROPOLIS

Caliber 1997

0 movie adaptation, series
prequel,48-pg. 3.95
1 The Last Fredersen, pt.1 . . . . . . 2.95
2 The Last Fredersen, pt.2 . . . . . . 2.95
3 The Last Fredersen, pt.3 . . . . . . 2.95

METAPHYSIQUE

Eclipse

1 NB,Short Stories. 2.50
2 NB,Short Stories. 2.50

MIAMI MICE

Rip Off Press

1 1st printing 3.00
1a 2nd printing 2.00
3 . . . . 2.00
4 Record,A:TMNT 3.00

MICHELANGELO

Mirage

1 TMNT. 17.00
1a 2nd Printing 4.50

MICRA

Fictioneer

1 . . . . 4.00
2 . . . . 3.00
3 . . . . 3.00
4 . . . . 2.00
5 thru 7 . . . . @1.75
8 . . . . 2.25

MIDNIGHT

Blackthorne

1 thru 4 . . . . @1.75

MIDNIGHT PANTHER

CPM Comics 1997

1 Manga, translated. 2.95
2 . . . . 2.95
3 . . . . 2.95
4 . . . . 2.95
5 . . . . 2.95
6 Den of Scoundrels 2.95
7 The Sleeping Town. 2.95
8 to Reincarnation City 2.95
9 O:Midnight Panthers. 2.95
10 . . . . 2.95
11 . . . . 2.95
12 . . . . 2.95
TPB Sex, Death and Rock 'n' Roll.
rep #1–#6. . . . . 15.95
TPB Book 2: Feline Fanatics,
rep.#7–#12. . . . . 15.95
Spec. Breaking Up is Hard to Do . . 2.95

MIDNIGHT PANTHER: FEUDAL FANTASY

CPM Manga 1998

1 by Yu Asagiri 2.95
2 thru 5 . . . . @2.95
TPB Book 4: Feudal Fantasy 15.95

MIDNIGHT PANTHER: SCHOOL DAZE

CPM Comics 1998

1 (of 5) by Yu Asagiri. 2.95
2 thru 5 . . . . @2.95
TPB Book 3: School Daze 15.95

MIDNITE SKULKER

1 thru 7 . . . . @1.75

MIGHTY GUY

C&T

1 thru 6 . . . . @1.50
Summer Fun Spec. #1 . . . . 2.50

MIGHTY MITES

Continum

1 I:X-Mites. 2.00
2 . . . . 2.00

MIGHTY MOUSE ADVENTURE MAGAZINE

1 . . . . 2.00

MIGHTY TINY

1 thru 4 . . . . @1.75
5 . . . . 2.50
Mouse Marines Collection rep. 7.50

MILK & CHEESE

Slave Labor 1991–97

1 EDo, Milk Products gone bad . . 60.00
1a 2nd thru 7th printing 3.50
2 . . . . 35.00
2a 2nd thru 4th printing 10.00
3 . . . . 25.00
3a 2nd thru 4th printing 10.00
4 . . . . 15.00
4a 2nd & 3rd printing. 3.00
5 . . . . 15.00
5a 2nd & 3rd printing. 3.00
6 . . . . 10.00
6a 2nd printing 2.75
Other #1. 2.75
Third #1 . . . . 2.75
Fourth #1 . . . . 2.75
First #2. . . . . 2.75
Six Six Six #1. . . . . 2.75
Six Six Six 2nd printing, EDo 2.75
Latest Thing 2.95
TPB Fun with Milk & Cheese, rep.
1st 4 issues 11.95

MINIMUM WAGE

Fantagraphics

Vol. 1, new printing. 9.95

Vol. 2

5 by Bob Fingerman 2.95
6 . . . . 2.95
7 . . . . 2.95
8 . . . . 2.95
9 Artsy Fartsy 2.95
10 . . . . 2.95
TPB Vol. 2, rep. #1–#5 . . . . 12.95

MIRACLE SQUAD: BLOOD & DUST

Apple

1 thru 3 . . . . @2.00

MISTER BLANK
Amaze Ink 1997
0 by Chris Hicks 1.75
0a 2nd printing 1.75
1 F:Sam Smith 2.95
2 thru 14 . . . . @2.95
TPB rep. #1–#14, 360-page 29.95

MISTER X
Vortex, Vol. 2
1 thru 11 . . . . @2.00

MITES
1 . . . . 2.50
1a 1.90
2B 1.80
3 and 4 . . . . @1.80

MOBILE POLICE PATLABOR
Viz Communications
1 (of 12) by Masami Yuki. 2.95
PART TWO
1 by Masami Yuki 2.95
2 thru 6 . . . . @2.95
TPB Vol. 1 . . . . 15.95
TPB Vol. 2 Basic Training 15.95

MOBILE SUIT GUNDAM 0079
Viz Communications 1999
1 (of 8) by Kazhisa Kondo . . . . . @2.95
2 thru 7 . . . . @2.95
PART TWO
1 (of 5) 2.95
2 thru 5 . . . . @2.95
TPB Vol. 1 . . . . 15.95
TPB Vol. 2 . . . . 15.95

MOBILE SUIT GUNDAM WING: GROUND ZERO
Viz Communications 2000
1 (of 4) by Reku Fuyynagi 2.95
2 and 3 . . . . @2.95

MODERN PULP
Special Studio
1 Rep.from January Midnight. 2.75

MOEBIUS COMICS
Caliber 1996
1 Moe 2.95
2 Moe 2.95
3 Moe 2.95
4 Moe,MP 2.95
5 Moe,SL 2.95
6 Moe 2.95

MOGOBI DESERT RATS
Midnight Comics
1 I&O:Desert Rats `Waste of the World' 2.25

MONNGA
Daikaiyu Enterprises 1995
1 and 2 Titanic Omega. . . . . @3.95

MONOGRAPHS
Coppervale 1997
1 by James Owen 2.95
2 Bob Phantom 2.95
3 Sidekick Wanted—Benefits Available 2.95
4 thru 6 . . . . @2.95

MONSTER BOY
Monster Comics
1 A:Monster Boy 2.25

MONSTER FRAT HOUSE
Eternity
1 . . . . 2.25

MONSTER POSSE
Adventure
1 thru 3 . . . . @2.50

MONSTERS ATTACK
1 GM,JSe 2.00
2 GC 1.75
3 ATh,GC 1.50

Monsters From Outer Space #2
© Adventure

MONSTERS FROM OUTER SPACE
Adventure 1992
1 thru 3 . . . . @2.50

MORBID ANGEL: DESPERATE ANGELS
London Night 1998
0 EHr, & Jude Millien. 3.00
0A Powell(c) 5.00
0B Powell(c) 5.00

MORBID ANGEL: PENANCE
London Night Studios 1995
1 I:Brandon Watts 4.00

MORBID ANGEL: TO HELL AND BACK
London Night Oct. 1996
1 (of 3) EHr. 4.00
2 and 3 . . . . @3.00

MORNING GLORY
Radio Comix 1998
1 by Loran Gayton & Michael Vega 2.95
2 thru 6 . . . . @2.95

MORTAL COIL
Mermaid
1 thru 3 . . . . @2.25
4 F:Red-Line,Gift. 2.25
5 Pin-Up Issue. 2.25

MORTAR MAN
Marshall Comics
1 I:Mortar Man. 2.00
2 and 3 . . . . @2.00

MOSAIC
Oktober Black Press
1 F:Halo,Daeva 2.25
2 "Gun Metal Gray" 2.50
3 . . . . 2.50
4 Elf(c) 2.50
5 Wisps. 2.50

MOSAIC
Sirius 1999
1 by Kyle Hotz. 2.95
2 thru 5 conclusion. . . . . @2.95
TPB 14.95

MOUNTAIN WORLD
Newcomers Press 1995
1 I:Jeremiah Rainshadow 2.95

MR. BEAT ADVENTURES
Moordam Comics Jan. 1997
1 . . . . 2.95
1 deluxe 5.00
Spec. House of Burning Jazz Love . 2.95
Spec. deluxe 5.00
Two-Fisted Atomic Action Super Spec. 2.95
Two-Fisted Atomic Action Super Spec., deluxe 10.00
Two-Fisted Atomic Action Super Spec., mega deluxe . . . 20.00
Spec. Mr. Beat: Superstar. 3.00
Spec. Mr. Beat: Superstar, deluxe. 10.00
Ann.#1 Babes and Bongos 2.95

MR. FIXITT
Apple
1 and 2 . . . . @2.00

MR. MYSTIC
Eclipse
1 Will Eisner 2.50

MR. NIGHTMARE'S WONDERFUL WORLD
Moonstone 1995
1 thru 3 Dreams So Real, pt.1–pt.3 . . . . @2.95

MS. CHRIST
Draculina Publishing 1995
1 I:Ms. Christ 2.95

MS. TREE
Aardvark–Vanaheim
1-10 see Other Pub. (color)
11 thru 18 . . . . @2.00
Renegade
19 thru 49 . . . . @2.00
50 . . . . 4.50
1 3-D Classic 2.95

MUMMY, THE
Monster Comics
1 A:Dr.Clarke,Prof.Belmore 2.00
2 Mummy's Curse 2.00
3 A:Carloph 2.00
4 V:Carloph, conc. 2.00

MUMMY'S CURSE
Aircel 1990
1 thru 4 B.Blair . . . . @2.25

The Munsters #2
© TV Comics

MUNSTERS, THE
TV Comics 1998
1 photo (c) 3.00
1a variant (c) 8.00
2 Beverly Owen(c) 3.00
2 Pat Priest (c) 3.00
2 Pat Priest (c) signed 19.95
3 . . . . 3.00
3a Celebrity autograph edition . . 22.95
4 . . . . 3.00
4a variant photo (c) 3.00
4b variant (c) celebrity autograph edition 22.95
5 Herman photo (c) 3.00
5 Grandpa photo (c) 3.00
Spec. Comic Con edition 9.95
Celebrity Autograph Edition: Butch Patrick 22.95
TPB Vol. 1, rep. #1–#4 . . . . 10.95
Spec.#1 Herman/Grandpa (c) 3.00
Spec.#1a Grandpa (c) 3.00
Halloween Spec. Munsters 1313 . . . 3.00
Golden Age Adventure Spec.A(c) . . 3.00
Golden Age Adventure Spec.B(c) . . 3.00

MUNSTERS CLASSICS
TV Comics
0 The Fregosi Emerald 3.00
0 variant (c) 7.95

MURCIELAGA: SHE-BAT
Hero Graphics
1 Daerick Gross reps. 1.50
2 Reps. contd 2.95

MURDER
Renegade 1986
1 SD 1.70
2 Cl(c) 1.70
3 SD 1.70

MURDER (2nd series)
1 . . . . 2.00

MURDER CAN BE FUN
Slave Labor
1 thru 6 . . . . @2.95
2 2nd printing 2.95
7 . . . . 2.95
8 . . . . 2.95
9 Seedy Side of Sex 2.95
10 We Love Sports 2.95
11 . . . . 2.95
12 Amusement Park Terror 2.95

MUTANT ZONE
Aircel
1 Future story 2.50
2 F.B.I. Drone Exterminators 2.50
3 conclusion 2.50

MYSTERY MAN
Slave Labor
1 thru 5 . . . . @1.75

MYTH ADVENTURES
Warp Graphics
1 Mag size 1.50
2 thru 4 . . . . @1.50
5 Comic size 1.50
6 thru 11 . . . . @1.50
12 . . . . 1.75

MYTH CONCEPTIONS
Apple
1 . . . . 1.75
2 . . . . 1.75
3 thru 8 . . . . @2.00

MYTHOGRAPHY
Bardic Press 1966
1 F:Poison Elves 3.95
2 fantasy stories 3.95
3 fantasy stories, inc. Elfquest 3.95
4 . . . . 4.25
5 72-pg. 4.25
6 F:Anubis Squadron 72pg. 3.95
7 80-pg. 4.25
8 72-pg. 4.25

MYTHOS
Wonder Comix
1 and 2 . . . . @1.50

NATURE OF THE BEAST
Caliber
1 thru 3 `The Beast' . . . . @2.95

NAUGHTY BITS
Fantagraphics
20 . . . . 2.95
21 I:Bitchy Butch 2.95
22 . . . . 2.95
23 O:Bitchy Butch 2.95
24 . . . . 2.95
25 by Roberta Gregory 2.95
26 thru 32 . . . . @2.95
TPB Vol. 4: Bitchy's School Daze . . 9.95
TPB Vol. 5: Bitchy Butch 9.95

NAUSICAA OF THE VALLEY OF WIND
Viz Select
Book One 4.50
Book Two 5.50
Book Three 4.00
Book Four 3.00
Book Five 2.50
Book Six 2.95
Book Seven 2.95
[Part 2]
#1 thru #4 . . . . @2.95
[Part 3]
#1 thru #3 . . . . @2.95
TPB Vol. 4 . . . . 17.95

NAZRAT
Imperial 1986
1 . . . . 2.50
2 thru 6 . . . . @2.00

NECROSCOPE
Caliber 1997
1 Brian Lumley adapt. 2.95
1 signed 2.95
2 . . . . 2.95
3 . . . . 2.95
4 . . . . 2.95

NEGATIVE BURN
Caliber
1 I:Matrix 7, Flaming Carrot 5.00
2 . . . . 3.50
3 Bone preview 8.00
4 thru 12 various stories . . . . @3.25
13 Strangers in Paradise 7.00
14 thru 18 various stories . . . . . . @3.50
19 Flaming Carrot 5.00
20 In the Park 3.25
21 Trollords 3.00
22 Father the Dryad 3.00
23 I:The Creep 3.00
24 The Factor 3.00
25 The Factor 4.00
26 Very Vicki 3.00
27 Nancy Kate 3.00
28 Favorite Song 4.00
29 thru 33 . . . . @4.00
34 Kaos Moon 6.00
35 thru 38 . . . . @4.00
39 "Iron Empires," pt. 4 . . . . 4.00
40 "Suzi Romaine" 4.00
41 "Iron Empires," cont. 4.00
42 . . . . 4.00
43 "Iron Empires," concl. 4.00
44 "Skeleton Key" 4.00
45 "Divine Winds" 4.00
46 "A Bullet For Me" 4.00
47 . . . . 4.00

48 special 80-page issue 5.00
49 special 80-page issue 5.00
50 96-pg., final issue 6.95
TPB Best of Year One 9.95
TPB Best of Year Two 9.95

NEIL THE HORSE

Aardvark–Vanaheim

1 Art:Arn Sara 5.00
1a 2nd printing 2.00
2 . . . . 3.00
3 . . . . 4.00
4 . . . . 3.00
5 Video Warriors 2.00
6 Video Warriors 2.00
7 Video Warriors 2.00
8 Outer Space 2.00
9 Conan 2.00
10 . . . . 2.00

Renegade

11 Fred Astair 1.70
12 . . . . 1.70
13 . . . . 1.70
14 Special 3.00
15 . . . . 1.70

Nemesis The Warlock #11
© Fleetway

NEMESIS THE WARLOCK

Fleetway

1 thru 16 . . . . @2.00

NEON CITY

Innovation

1 . . . . 2.25

NEON GENESIS EVANGELION

Viz Communication 1997

1 (of 6) by Gainax & Yoshiyuki Sadamoto 3.25
1 special collectors edition 2.95
2 thru 6 . . . . @2.95
2 thru 6 special collectors ed. . . . @2.95
TPB Vol. 1 . . . . 16.50
TPB Vol. 1 special collectors ed. . . 16.50

BOOK TWO March 1998

1 (of 5) by Yoshiyuki Sadamoto . . . 2.95
1 special collectors edition 2.95
2 thru 5 . . . . @2.95
2 thru 5 special collectors ed. . . . @2.95
TPB Book 2 . . . . 15.95
TPB Book 2, collectors ed. 15.95

BOOK THREE

1 thru 6 by Yoshiyuki Sadamoto . @2.95
1a thru 6a Collectors edition. . . . @2.95
GN Vol. 3 Evangelion 15.95
GN Vol. 3 Evangelion, coll. ed. . . . 15.95

BOOK FOUR 1999

1 thru 7 by Yoshiyuki Sadamato . @2.95
1a thru 7a special collectors ed. . @2.95

BOOK FIVE 2000

1 . . . . 2.95
1a collectors ed. 2.95

NERVOUS REX

1 . . . . 3.00
1a 2nd printing 2.00
2 . . . . 3.00
3 . . . . 3.00
4 . . . . 2.50
5 thru 10 . . . . @2.00
GraphicNovel 3.50

NEW ADVENTURES OF TERRY & THE PIRATES

ACG Comics 1998

1 by Bros. Hildebrandt 2.95
2 thru 7 . . . . @2.95

NEW HORIZONS

Shanda Fantasy Arts Jan. 1997

1 . . . . 4.95
2 thru 5 . . . . @4.50
6 thru 9 . . . . @4.95

NEWCOMERS ILLUSTRATED

Newcomers Publishing

1 thru 5 various artists . . . . @2.95
6 Science Fiction 2.95
7 and 8 . . . . @2.95
9 Shocking Machines 2.95
10 . . . . 2.95
11 Hitman 2.95
12 final issue 2.95

NEW ERADICATORS

Vol. 2 #1 NewBeginnings 2.00
Vol. 2 #2 NewBeginnings 2.00
Vol. 2 #3 NewFriends 2.00

NEW FRONTIERS

1 CS(c) 3.00
1a 2nd Printing 1.75

NEW FRONTIERS

Evolution

1 A:Action Master, Green Ghost . . 2.00

NEW HERO COMICS

Pierce

1 and 2 . . . . @1.00

NEW HUMANS

Eternity

1 . . . . 1.80
2 thru 15 . . . . @2.00
Ann. #1 . . . . 2.95

NEW HUMANS

1 Shattered Earth Chronicles 2.00

NEW PULP ADVENTURES SPECIAL

Dunewadd Comics

1 I:Kawala 2.50

NEW REALITY

1 thru 6 . . . . @1.25

NEWSTRALIA

Innovation
(Prev. Color)

4 . . . . 2.25
5 . . . . 2.25

NEW TRIUMPH

Matrix Graphics

1 F:Northguard 3.00
1a 2nd printing 1.75
2 thru 4 . . . . @1.50

NEW VAMPIRE MIYU

Ironcat 1997

1 by Narumi Kakinouchi 2.95
2 thru 6 . . . . @2.95
7 The Past Lies Beyond a Door, finale 2.95
GN rep. #1–#7 . . . . 17.95

VOL. 2 1998

1 by Narumi Kakinouchi 2.95
2 thru 6 . . . . @2.95

VOL. 3 1998

1 . . . . 2.95
2 thru 7 . . . . @2.95

VOL. 4

1 by Narumi Kakinouchi 2.95
2 thru 6 . . . . @2.95

VOL. 5

1 . . . . 2.95
2 thru 7 . . . . @2.95

NEW WORLD DISORDER

Millennium 1995

1 I:King Skin Gang 2.95

NEW WORLD ORDER

Blazer Studios

1 thru 8 . . . . @2.50

NEW YORK CITY OUTLAWS

1 thru 5 . . . . @2.50

NEW YORK, YEAR ZERO

Eclipse

1 thru 4 . . . . @2.00

NEXUS

Capital

1 SR,I:Nexus,large size 12.00
2 SR,Mag.size. 8.00
3 SR,Mag. size 5.00

NIGHT

Amaze Ink 1995

0 V:The Prince 1.50

NIGHT ANGEL
Substance Comics 1995

1 I:Night Angel. 2.95

NIGHT CRY
CFD Productions 1995

1 Evil Ernie & Razor story 8.00
1 signed 9.00
2 . . . . 6.00
3 . . . . 5.00
4 . . . . 4.00
4a platinum (c) 6.00
5 . . . . 4.00
6 . . . . 2.75
6a signed 8.00

NIGHT LIFE
Caliber

1 thru 7 . . . . @1.50

NIGHT MASTER

1 Vigil 5.50
2 Vigil 2.50
3 . . . . 1.50

NIGHT OF THE LIVING DEAD
Fantaco

0 prelude 1.75
1 based on cult classic movie 4.95
2 Movie adapt,continued 4.95
3 Movie adapt,conclusion 4.95
5 . . . . 5.95
TPB Official Complete story, rep. . 24.95
TPB London, Clive Barker's story . 14.95

NIGHT'S CHILDREN
Fantaco

1 . . . . 3.50
2 . . . . 3.50
3 . . . . 3.50

NIGHT'S CHILDREN
Millennium 1995

1 The Ripper, Klaus Wulfe. 3.95
Spec. High Noon (1996) 2.95
Spec. The Churchyard (1997). 3.25

NIGHT'S CHILDREN: THE VAMPIRE
Millennium 1995

1 F:Klaus Wulfe. 2.95
2 F:Klaus Wulfe. 2.95

NIGHT STREETS
Arrow

1 . . . . 2.50
2 thru 4 . . . . @1.50

NIGHTVISION
London Night Nov. 1996

1 DQ,KHt, All About Eve 3.00
1 signed 12.95
1a erotica edition. 10.00

NIGHT WARRIORS: DARKSTALKERS' REVENGE
Viz Communications 1998

1 (of 6) by Run Ishida 2.95
2 . . . . 3.25
3 thru 6 . . . . @2.95
TPB 15.95

NIGHT ZERO
Fleetway

1 thru 4 . . . . @2.00

NIKKI BLADE
High Impact 1997

0 . . . . 2.95
0a deluxe adult cover 10.00
0b gold edition variant cover 14.95
Spec.#0 Nikki Blade: Forever Nikki (1997) MIB(c). 2.95
Deluxe RCI(c). 10.00

ABC Comics 1998

Spec. Nikki Blade: Blades of Death (1998) by RCI & Clayton Henry. 3.00
Puzzle variant A cover 5.95
Puzzle variant B cover 5.95
Puzzle variant C cover 5.95
Spec. Nikki Blade: Revenge 3.00
RCI nude cover 5.95
Clayton Henry nude variant (c) . 5.95

NINJA
Eternity

1 . . . . 3.00
2 thru 6 . . . . @1.80
7 thru 13 . . . . @2.00

NINJA ELITE

1 thru 5 . . . . @1.50
6 thru 8 . . . . @2.00

NINJA FUNNIES
Eternity

1 and 2 . . . . @1.80
3 thru 5 . . . . @2.00

NINJA HIGH SCHOOL
Eternity

1 . . . . 1.75
2 thru 4 . . . . @1.50
5 thru 22 . . . . @2.00
23 Zardon Assassin 2.25
24 . . . . 2.25
25 Return of the Zetramen 2.25
26 Stanley the Demon 2.25
27 Return of the Zetramen 2.25
28 Threat of the super computer. . . 2.25
29 V:Super Computer. 2.25
30 I:Akaru. 2.25
31 Jeremy V:Akaru 2.25
32 thru 34 V:Giant Monsters Pt.1 thru Pt. 3 . . . . @2.50
35 thru 43. . . . . @2.50
44 Combat Cheerleaders 2.75
45 Cheerleader Competition 2.75
46 Monsters From Space 2.75
47 . . . . 2.75
48 F:Jeremy Feeple 2.75
49 thru 51 . . . . @2.95
52 thru 57 Time Warp, pt.4–pt.8 . @2.95
58 Zardon ambassador, BU:BDn . . 2.95
59 Akaru overwhelmed. 2.95
60 to the Himalayas 2.95
61 ancient Himalayan temple 2.95
62 Hillbilly girl. 2.95
63 F:Tetsuo Rivalsan 2.95
64 Jeremy Feeple: Saboteur?. 2.95
65 Quagmire Trial of the Century . . 2.95
66 . . . . 2.95
67 F:Eolata. 3.00
68 F:Akaru & Asrial 3.00
69 Guri-Guri Island. 3.00
70 Mad Bomber in Space. 2.50
71 traitor in secret police. 2.99
72 . . . . 2.50
73 . . . . 2.50
74 Girl Scouts. 2.50
Special #1 . . . . 2.95
Special #2 . . . . 2.95
Special #3 . . . . 2.95
Special #3 1/2 . . . . 2.25
Ann. 1989. . . . . 2.95
Ann.#3 . . . . 3.95
TPB Vol. 1 rep. #1–3 . . . . 12.00
TPB Vol. 1, new edition. 14.95
TPB Vol. 2 rep. #4–7 . . . . 12.00
TPB Vol. 3 rep. #8–11. . . . . 9.00
TPB Vol. 3, rep. #8–#11 . . . . 10.95
TPB Vol. 4 rep. #12–15 . . . . 8.00
TPB Vol. 4, rep. #12–#15 . . . . 10.95
TPB Vol. 5 rep. #16–18 . . . . 7.95
TPB Vol. 6 rep. #19–21 . . . . 7.95
TPB Vol. 7 rep. #22–24 . . . . 7.95
TPB Vol. 7, rep. #22–#24 The Ides of May 10.95
TPB Vol. 8 rep. #25–27 . . . . 7.95
TPB Vol. 9 rep. #28–31. . . . . 10.95
TPB Vol. 9, rep. #28–#31 Long Distance Bottle. 10.95
TPB Vol. 10 rep. #32–35. . . . . 10.95
TPB Vol. 11 rep. #36–39. . . . . 10.95
TPB Vol. 11, rep. #36–#39 Shades of Grey. 10.95
TPB Vol. 12 . . . . 10.95
TPB Vol. 15 three stories 7.95
Yearbook 1994 . . . . 4.00
Yearbook 1995. . . . . 3.95
Yearbook 1996. . . . . 3.95
Yearbook 1997, cover A 3.95
Yearbook 1997, cover B 3.95
Yearbook 1998, cover A 2.95
Yearbook 1998, cover B 2.95
Spec. Girls of Ninja High School (1997) 3.95
Spec. Girls of Ninja High School
1998 cover A 2.95
1998 cover B 2.95
Spec. 1999 . . . . 3.00
Spotlight #4 Rod Espinosa 3.00
Summer Spec.#1 . . . . 3.00

NINJA HIGH SCHOOL GIRLS
Antarctic Press

0 . . . . 2.75
1 and 2 rep. . . . . @2.75
3 thru 5 rep. . . . . @3.95
Yearbook 3.95

NINJA HIGH SCHOOL PERFECT MEMORY
Antarctic Press

1 and 2, 9-pg. . . . . @4.95

NINJA HIGH SCHOOL SMALL BODIES
Antarctic Press

1 "Monopolize" 2.50
2 Omegadon Cannon 2.75
3 Omegadon Cannon 2.75
3a deluxe 4.50
4 Omegadon Cannon 2.75
5 Wrong Order 2.75
6 Chicken Rage. 2.95
7 . . . . 2.95

NIRA X: CYBERANGEL
Entity Comics April, 1996
1 . . . . . 5.00
1a deluxe 8.00
2 BMs 4.00
3 and 4 BMs . . . . . @3.00
4a with PC Game 8.00
Ann.#1 BMs flip-cover. 2.75
2nd Mini Series 1995
1 . . . . . 4.00
1a 2nd printing 2.50
2 thru 4 . . . . . @2.50
3rd Mini Series 1995–96
1 . . . . . 2.50
1a Gold(c) 5.00
2 . . . . . 2.50
3 . . . . . 3.00
Regular Series
1 . . . . . 2.75
1a with game. 7.00
2 thru 4 . . . . . @2.75
4a with game. 7.00
Spec. Nira X:Headwave, encore special toy edition. 2.50
Encore special toy edition, signed & numbered 12.95
Spec. Nira X:Memoirs (1997) BMs . 2.75
Deluxe 3.50

NIRA X/HELLINA: HEAVEN & HELL
Entity Comics
1 San Diego Con edition, BMs 5.00
1a foil. 3.00

NIRA X: EXODUS
Avatar 1997
0 (of 2) BMs 3.00
0a Nude cover. 4.95
0b Leather cover 20.00
0 signed 10.00
1 (of 2) 3.00
1a nude cover 4.95
1b leather cover. 18.00
1 signed 9.00
2 . . . . . 3.00
2 nude cover 4.95
Spec. Shoot First 3.00
Spec. Shoot First, nude cover. 4.95
Spec. Summer Splash 4.95

Nira X: Exodus
© Avatar

Spec. Summer Splash, nude cover. 6.00

NIRA X: HISTORY
Avatar Press 1999
1 (of 2) by Bill Maus 3.50
1a nude cover 6.00
2 . . . . . 3.50
2a nude cover 6.00

NIRA X: SOUL SKURGE
Entity Oct., 1996
1 (of 3) BMs, A:Vortex 2.75
2 BMs, ... 2.75
3 . . . . . 2.75

NO GUTS, NO GLORY
Fantaco
1-shot, K.Eastman's 1st solo work since TMNT 2.95

NOMADS OF ANTIQUITY
1 thru 6 . . . . . @1.50

NO NEED FOR TENCHI
Viz Comics
PART ONE
1 thru 7 (of 7). . . . . @2.95
PART TWO Nov. 1996
1 thru 7 by Hitoshi Okuda. . . . . @2.95
TPB Sword Play 15.95
PART THREE 1997
1 (of 6) by Hitoshi Okuda. 2.95
2 . . . . . 2.95
3 thru 6 . . . . . @2.95
TPB Magical Girl Pretty Sammy . . 15.95
PART FOUR Dec. 1997
1 (of 6) by Hitoshi Okuda. 2.95
2 thru 6 . . . . . @2.95
TPB Vol. 4 Samurai Space Opera. 15.95
PART FIVE 1998
1 (of 6) 2.95
2 thru 6 . . . . . @2.95
TPB Vol. 5 Unreal Genius. 15.95
PART SIX 1998
1 (of 6) 2.95
2 thru 6 . . . . . @2.95
TPB Vol. 6 Dream a Little Scheme 15.95
PART SEVEN 1999
1 (of 6) 2.95
2 thru 6 . . . . . @2.95
TPB Vol. 7 Tenchi in Love. 15.95
PART EIGHT
1 (of 5) by Hitoshi Okuda. 3.25
2 thru 5 . . . . . @2.95
TPB Vol. 8 Chef of Iron. 15.95
PART NINE
1 (of 6) by Hitoshi Okuda. 2.95
2 thru 6 . . . . . @2.95
PART TEN 2000
1 (of 7) 2.95
2 . . . . . 2.95

NORMAL MAN
Aardvark–Vanaheim
1 . . . . . 4.00
2 thru 9 . . . . . @2.50
Renegade
10 thru 19. . . . . @1.70

NOVA GIRLS
MN Design 1998
1 The Immortality Quest, pt.1. . . . . 2.00
1a JJu (c) 2.95
1b photo (c) 3.95
1 variant Starship Discover #0(c). . 3.95
1 variant Phazer #0 cover 3.95
2 The Immortality Quest, pt.2. . . . . 2.00
2a deluxe 2.95
3 The Immortality Quest, pt.3. . . . . 2.00
3a deluxe 2.95
Space 34–24–34 Gold Seal 10th Anniv. Edition 74.95

NOWHERESVILLE
Caliber March 1996
1 thru 3 by MRc. . . . . @2.95
Spec. The History of Cool. 2.95

NYOKA, THE JUNGLE GIRL
AC Comics
3 . . . . . 2.25
4 . . . . . 2.25
5 . . . . . 2.50

OFFERINGS
Cry For Dawn
1 Sword & Sorcery stories 7.00
2 and 3 . . . . . @6.00

OFFICIAL BUZ SAWYER
1 . . . . . 2.00
2 . . . . . 2.00
3 . . . . . 2.00
4 . . . . . 1.50
5 . . . . . 2.00
6 . . . . . 2.00

OFFICIAL HOW TO DRAW G.I. JOE
Blackthorne
1 thru 5 . . . . . @2.00

OFFICIAL HOW TO DRAW ROBOTECH
Blackthorne
1 thru 11 . . . . . @2.00
12 . . . . . 2.95
13 thru 16. . . . . @2.00

OFFICIAL HOW TO DRAW TRANSFORMERS
Blackthorne
1 thru 7 . . . . . @2.00

OFFICIAL JOHNNY HAZARD
1 thru 3 . . . . . @2.00
4 . . . . . 1.50
5 . . . . . 2.00

OFFICIAL JUNGLE JIM
1 thru 5 AR,rep. . . . . . @2.00
6 AR,rep. 1.50
7 thru 10 AR,rep. . . . . . @2.00
11 thru 20 AR,rep. . . . . . @2.50
Ann.#1 . . . . . 2.00
Giant Size 3.95

OFFICIAL MANDRAKE

1 thru 5 . . . . @2.00
6 . . . . 1.50
7 thru 10 . . . . @2.00
11 . . . . 2.50
12 . . . . 2.00
13 thru 17 . . . . @2.50
Ann. #1 . . . . 3.95
King Size #1 . . . . 3.95
Giant Size #1 . . . . 3.95

Official Modesty Blaise #1
© Pioneer

OFFICIAL MODESTY BLAISE

Pioneer 1988

1 thru 4 . . . . @2.00
5 . . . . 1.50
6 thru 14 . . . . @2.00
Ann. #1 . . . . 3.95
King Size #1 . . . . 3.95

OFFICIAL PRINCE VALIANT

1 Hal Foster,rep. 2.00
2 Hal Foster,rep. 2.00
3 Hal Foster,rep. 2.00
4 Hal Foster,rep. 2.00
5 Hal Foster,rep. 2.00
6 Hal Foster,rep. 2.00
7 . . . . 1.50
8 thru 14 . . . . @2.00
15 thru 24 . . . . @2.50
Ann. #1 . . . . 3.95
King Size #1 . . . . 3.95

OFFICIAL RIP KIRBY

1 thru 3 AR . . . . @2.00
4 AR 1.50
5 and 6 AR . . . . @2.00

OFFICIAL SECRET AGENT

Pioneer

1 thru 5 AW rep. . . . . @2.00
6 AW 1.50
7 thru 9 AW . . . . @2.00

OF MIND AND SOUL

Rage Comics 1997

0 . . . . 2.95
0a nude cover edition 6.50
1 . . . . 2.50
1 nude photo cover 6.50
2 . . . . 2.50
2 nude cover 6.50
3 . . . . 1.50
Spec. Standing on a Beach 2.50
Spec. Soul'd Out` 2.95
Spec. A Day in Hell 2.95
Spec. 1-shot 1.50
Spec. 1-shot nude cover 6.00

OHM'S LAW

Imperial Comics

1 and 2 . . . . @2.00
3 V:Men in Black 2.00
4 A:Damonstriek 2.00
5 F:Tryst 2.00

OH MY GOTH!

Sirius/Dog Star 1998

1 by Voltaire 2.95
2 . . . . 2.95
3 . . . . 2.95
4 Goths in Space. 2.95
TPB 13.00

OH MY GOTH: HUMANS SUCK!

Sirius Entertainment 2000

1 (of 3) 2.95
1 deluxe 5.00
2 and 3 . . . . @2.95

OKTOBERFEST

Now & Then

1 (1976) Dave Sim 20.00

OMEGA

North Star

1 1st pr by Rebel,rare 50.00
1a Vigil(Yellow Cov.) 15.00
2 . . . . 2.00

OMEN

North Star

1 . . . . 8.00
1a 2nd printing 2.00
2 thru 4 . . . . @3.50

OMICRON

1 and 2 . . . . @2.25
3 . . . . 2.50

ONE SHOT WESTERN

Calibur

1-shot F:Savage Sisters, Tornpath Outlaw 2.50

ONI DOUBLE FEATURE

Oni Press 1997

1 F:Secret Broadcast. 10.00
1a 2nd printing 3.00
2 F:Car Crash on the 405 . . . . 3.00
3 F:Troy Nixey. 3.00
4 F:A River in Egypt 3.00
5 F:Fan Girl From Hell. 3.00
6 inc. NGa Only the End of the World, pt.1 . . . . 3.00
7 inc. NGa Only the End of the World, pt.2 . . . . 3.00
8 inc. NGa Only the End of the World, pt.3 . . . . 3.00
9 thru 13 . . . . @3.00

ONIGAMI

Antarctic Press 1998

1 (of 3) by Michael Lacombe, sequel to Winter Jade storyline from Warrior Nun: Black and White. . 2.95
2 . . . . 2.95
3 concl. 2.95

OPEN SEASON

Renegade

1 thru 7 . . . . @2.00

OPTIC NERVE

Adrian Tomine 1990

1 thru 5, mini-comic . . . . @12.00
6 . . . . 7.00
7 . . . . 5.00

OPTIC NERVE

Drawn & Quarterly 1995

1 Summer Job. 7.00
1a 2nd printing 3.00
2 . . . . 5.00
3 and 4 . . . . @3.00
5 thru 7 . . . . @2.95
TPB 32 Stories 9.95
HC Sleepwalk and Other Stories, limited 29.95

ORACLE PRESENTS

1 thru 4 . . . . @1.50

ORBIT

Eclipse

1 and 2 . . . . @3.95
3 . . . . 4.95

ORIGINAL TOM CORBETT

Eternity 1990

1 thru 10 rep. newspaper strips . @2.95

ORLAK: FLESH & STEEL

Caliber

1 `1991 A.D.' 2.50

Original Tom Corbett #2
© Eternity

ORLAK REDUX
Caliber 1991
1 rep. Caliber Presents,64-pg. 3.95

OUTLANDER
1 . . . . 4.50
2 . . . . 3.00
3 thru 5 . . . . @2.50
6 and 7 . . . . @2.00
8 . . . . 2.25

OUTLAW OVERDRIVE
Blue Comet Press
1 Red Edition I:Deathrow. 2.95
1a Black Edition 2.95
1b Blue Edition 2.95

OZ
Imperial Comics
1 Land of Oz Gone Mad 9.00
2 Land of Oz Gone Mad 7.00
3 Land of Oz Gone Mad 6.00
4 Tin Woodsmen 6.00
5 F:Pumkinhead 6.00
6 Emerald City. 6.00
7 V:Bane Wolves. 4.00
8 V:Nome Hordes 4.00
9 Freedom Fighters Vs. Heroes. . . 4.00
10 thru 15. . . . . @4.00
16 . . . . 3.50
Spec.#1 . . . . 6.00
Spec. Scarecrow #1 . . . . 3.00
Spec. Lion #1. . . . . 3.00
Spec. Tin Man #1. . . . . 3.00
Spec. Freedom Fighters #1 . . . . . . 3.00
TPB Rep. #1-#4 . . . . 14.95

Caliber "New Worlds"
17 by Ralph Griffith, Stuart Kerr & Tim Holtrop 3.50
18 . . . . 3.00
19 . . . . 3.00
20 . . . . 3.00
21 "Witches War" pt.1 (of 5) 3.00
22 . . . . 2.95
GN Heroes of Oz 14.95

OZ: ROMANCE IN RAGS
Caliber 1996
1 thru 3 Bill Bryan . . . . @2.95

OZ SQUAD
Patchwork Press
1 thru 6 . . . . @2.95
7 Time Train Destroyed 2.95
8 Old West 2.75

OZ: STRAW AND SORCERY
Caliber "New Worlds" 1997
1 thru 3 . . . . @2.95

PAKKINS' LAND
Caliber Tapestry 1996
1 . . . . 6.00
1a signed edition. 3.00
1a second edition, new cover 3.00
2 . . . . 4.00
2a second edition, new cover 3.00
3 . . . . 3.00
3 2nd edition, new cover 3.00
4 thru 6 . . . . @3.00
GN Book One: Paul's Adventure. . . 9.95

PAKKINS' LAND: FORGOTTEN DREAMS
Caliber March 1998
1 by Gary & Rhoda Shipman 2.95
2 thru 5 . . . . @2.95

PAKKINS' LAND: QUEST FOR KINGS
Caliber 1997
1G by Gary & Rhoda Shipman, Shipman(c). 2.95
1J by Gary & Rhoda Shipman, JSi(c) 2.95
2 . . . . 2.95
3 Rahsha's city 2.95
4 . . . . 2.95
5 . . . . 2.95

PALANTINE
Gryphon Rampant 1995
1 thru 5 V:Master of Basilisk. . . . @2.50

PANDA KHAN
1 thru 4 . . . . @2.00

PANDORA
Brainstorm 1996
1 (of 2) 3.00
1a nude cover 5.00

PANDORA
Avatar Press 1997
0 . . . . 3.00
0 nude cover. 4.95
1 signed 12.00
2 (of 2) 3.00
2 deluxe 9.00
X-over Pandora/Ranzor:Devil Inside
(1998) signed 12.00
Rick Lyon nude (c). 6.00
Haley (c) 5.00
X-over Pandora/Razor (1999). 3.50
Nude cover 6.00
Leather cover, signed 15.00
Expanded Edition 5.00
Expanded, nude (c) 6.00
X-over Pandora/Shotgun Mary: Demon Nation (1998). 3.00

Pandora #2
© Avatar Press

Deluxe 4.95
Leather. 20.00
Royal Blue edition 50.00
X-over Pandora/Widow (1997) 3.95
Nude cover 4.95
Leather cover. 15.00
Spec. Arachnophobia 3.50
Nude cover 6.00
Nude Bloodbath cover 6.00
Spec. Pandora Special (1997) 3.00
Nude cover 4.95
Leather cover. 15.00
Avatar convention (c) ed. 15.00
Spec. Pandora Pin-up (1997) 3.00
Nude cover 4.95
Signed 15.00
Spec. Nudes (1997) 3.50
Nude Lyon cover 6.00
Nude Meadows cover. 6.00

PANDORA'S CHEST
Avatar Press 1999
1 (of 3) 2.75
1a nude cover 6.00

PANDORA: DEMONOGRAPHY
Avatar Press 1997
1 . . . . 3.00
1 nude cover. 5.00
2 (of 3) 3.00
2 nude cover. 4.95
3 (of 3) 3.00
3 nude cover. 4.95

PANDORA: DEVILS ADVOCATE
Avatar Press 1999
1 (of 3) 3.50
1a nude cover 6.00
1b Previews exclusive foil (c). . . . 12.95
2 . . . . 3.50
2a nude cover 6.00
3 . . . . 3.50
3a nude cover 6.00

PANDORA: PANDEMONIUM
Avatar Press 1997
1 Pandora goes to Hell 3.00
1 nude cover. 4.95
1 leather cover 25.00
1 signed 10.00
2 (of 3) 3.00
2 nude cover. 4.95

PANTHEON
Lone Star Press 1998
1 (of 12) 2.95
2 Welcome to the Machine 2.95
3 V:Death Boy. 2.95
4 F:Tangeroa. 2.95
5 Under Pressure 2.95
6 All-villain issue 2.95
Spec. Ancient History (1999) 3.50

PAPER CUTS
1 E Starzer-1982. . . . . 15.00
2 and 3 . . . . @2.50

PARTICLE DREAMS
Fantagraphics
1 . . . . 3.00
2 thru 6 . . . . @2.25

B & W PUB.

PARTNERS IN PANDEMONIUM
Caliber
1 `Hell on Earth' 2.50
2 Sheldon&Murphy become mortal 2.50
3 A:Abra Cadaver 2.50

PARTS OF A HOLE
Caliber 1991
1 Short Stories 2.50

PARTS UNKNOWN
Eclipse
1 I:Spurr,V:Aliens. 2.50
2 Aliens on Earth cont. 2.50

PARTS UNKNOWN: DARK INTENTIONS
Knight Press
0 . . . . 2.95
1 I:Prelude to limited Series. 2.95
2 V:Luggnar. 2.95
3 V:Luggnar. 2.95
4 . . . . 2.95
1-shot, Handbook, The Roswell Agenda 2.95
Super-Ann. #1 . . . . 3.95

PATTY CAKE
Caliber Tapestry 1996
1 by Scott Roberts. 2.95
2 . . . . 2.95
3 . . . . 2.95
4 . . . . 2.95
Christmas special 3.95

PATTY-CAKE & FRIENDS
Slave Labor 1997
1 by Scott Roberts 2.95
2 thru 15 . . . . @2.95
Halloween Spec. 3.95

PAUL THE SAMURAI
New England Comics 1991
1 thru 3 . . . . @2.75
Bonanza #2 100-pg. 4.95
GN Collected 8.95

PENDULUM
Adventure
1 Big Hand,Little Hand. 2.50
2 The Immortality Formula. 2.50
3 . . . . 2.50

PENNY CENTURY
Fantagraphics 1997
1 by Jaime Hernandez. 2.95
2 . . . . 2.95
3 . . . . 2.95
4 . . . . 2.95
5 . . . . 2.95
6 The Frog Mouth 2.95
7 . . . . 2.95

PENTACLE: SIGN OF 5
Eternity
1 . . . . 2.25
2 Det.Sandler,H.Smitts 2.25
3 Det.Sandler => New Warlock . . . 2.25
4 5 warlocks Vs. Kaji 2.50

PETE THE P.O.'D POSTAL WORKER
Sharkbait Press 1998
1 by Marcus Pierce & Pete Garcia, Route 666 . . . . 2.95
2 prison mail 2.95
3 To Aliens with Love. 2.95
4 Special Delivery to Conad the Alien 2.95
5 England Vacation 2.95
6 Benedict Postman 2.95
7 Postman on Elm Street. 2.95
8 Postman on Elm Street. 2.95
9 Pete Meets Jerry Ringer. 2.95
10 Y2K Express 2.95
11 Postal Wars 2.95
X-mas Spec.#1. . . . . 3.50

PHANTOM
1 thru 3 . . . . @5.95
4 and 5 . . . . @6.95

PHANTOM, THE
Tony Raiola 2000
TPB Diamond Hunters 9.50
TPB The Little Toma. 9.50
TPB Sea Horse 9.50
TPB Game of Alvar 9.50
TPB Diana Aviatrix 9.50
TPB Phantom's Treasure 9.50

PHANTOM OF FEAR CITY
Claypool 1994–95
1 thru 12 . . . . @2.50

PHANTOM OF THE OPERA
Eternity
1 . . . . 2.00

PHASE ONE
Victory
1 . . . . 3.00
2 . . . . 2.00
3 thru 5 . . . . @1.50

PHIGMENTS
Eternity
1 . . . . 5.00
2 . . . . 2.00
3 . . . . 2.00

PHONEY PAGES
Renegade
1 and 2 . . . . @1.70

PINEAPPLE ARMY
1 thru 10 . . . . @1.75

PINK FLOYD EXPERIENCE
Revolutionary
1 based on rock group 2.50
2 Dark Side of the Moon 2.50
3 Dark Side of the Moon, Wish you were here. 2.50
4 The Wall. 2.50
5 A Momentary lapse of reason . . . 2.50

PIRATE CORPS!
Eternity
6 and 7 . . . . @2.00

Spec. #1 . . . . 2.00

PIRANHA! IS LOOSE
Special Studio
1 Drug Runners,F:Piranha. 2.95
2 Expedition into Terror 2.95

Pixi Junket #6
© Viz Communications

PIXI JUNKET
Viz
1 thru 6 . . . . @2.75

P.J. WARLOCK
Eclipse
1 thru 3 . . . . @2.00

PLANET COMICS
Blackthorne
(Prev. Color)
4 and 5 . . . . @2.00

PLANET COMICS
A-List Comics 1997
1 by Lance Hampton & Ras Leonardo 2.50
2 rep. from 1940 . . . . 2.95
3 . . . . 2.95
5 . . . . 2.95
6 . . . . 2.95
TPB Book of Planet Comics Covers, 1949–54 . . . . 7.95

PLANET OF TERROR
1 BW. 1.75

PLANET OF THE APES
Adventure Comics 1990
1 WD,collect.ed. 6.00
1 2 covers 4.00
1a 2nd printing 2.50
1b 3rd printing 2.25
2 . . . . 3.00
3 . . . . 2.75
4 . . . . 2.75
5 D:Alexander? 2.75
6 Welcome to Ape City 2.75
7 . . . . 2.75
8 Christmas Story 2.50
9 Swamp Ape Village 2.50

10 Swamp Apes in Forbidden City . 2.50
11 Ape War continues. 2.50
12 W.Alexander/Coure 2.50
13 Planet of Apes/Alien Nation/ Ape City x-over 2.50
14 Countdown to Zero Pt.1. . . . . . . 2.50
15 Countdown to Zero Pt.2. . . . . . . 2.50
16 Countdown to Zero Pt.3. . . . . . . 2.50
17 Countdown to Zero Pt.4. . . . . . . 2.50
18 Ape City (after Ape Nation mini-series. 2.50
19 1991 `Conquest..' tie-in 2.50
20 Return of the Ape Riders 2.50
21 The Terror Beneath,Pt.1. . . . . . . 2.50
22 The Terror Beneath,Pt.2. . . . . . . 2.50
23 The Terror Beneath,Pt.3. . . . . . . 2.50
Ann. #1,`Day on Planet o/t Apes' . . 3.50
Lim.Ed. #1 . . . . 5.00

PLANET OF THE APES: BLOOD OF THE APES

Adventure Comics

1 A:Tonus the Butcher. 3.00
2 Valia/Taylorite Connection. 2.50
3 Ape Army in Phis 2.50
4 . . . . 2.50

PLANET OF THE APES: FORBIDDEN ZONE

Adventure

1 Battle for the Planet o/t Apes & Planet o/t Apes tie-in 2.50
2 A:Juilus 2.50

PLANET OF THE APES: SINS OF THE FATHER

Adventure Comics

1 Conquest tie-in. 2.50

PLANET OF THE APES URCHAKS' FOLLY

Adventure Comics

1 . . . . 3.00
2 . . . . 2.50
3 `The Taylorites'. 2.50
4 Conclusion 2.50

PLANET 29

Caliber

1 A Future Snarl Tale 2.50
2 A:Biff,Squakman. 2.50

PLANET-X

Eternity 1991

1 three horror stories. 2.50

PLAN 9 FROM OUTER SPACE

Eternity

1 . . . . 2.50
2 and 3 . . . . @2.25

PLASMA BABY

Caliber

1 `Strange New World' 2.50

PLASTIC LITTLE

CPM Comics 1997

1 (of 5) Manga, by Satoshi Urushihara R:Captain Tita 2.95
2 F:Joshua Balboa 2.95
3 . . . . 2.95
4 . . . . 2.95
5 concl. 2.95
TPB Captain's Log, rep. #1–#5 . . . 15.95

PLASTRON CAFE

Mirage

1 RV,inc.North by Downeast 2.25

POE

Cheese Comics

1 by Jason Asala, reoffer. 2.00
2 . . . . 2.00
3 "The System of Doctor Tarr and Professor Fether" 2.00
4 thru 6 . . . . @2.00

Sirius/Dog Star

10 by Jason Asala, Small Town, pt.3 2.50
TPB Vol. 1 . . . . 14.95

VOL. 2

1 by Jason Asala. 2.50
2 House of Usher, pt.1 (of 4) 2.50
3 House of Usher, pt.2. . . . . 2.50
4 House of Usher, pt.3. . . . . 2.50
5 House of Usher, pt.4. . . . . 2.50
6 . . . . 2.50
7 . . . . 2.50
8 Small Town. 2.50
9 Small Town, pt.2. . . . . 2.50
10 Small Town, pt.3 . . . . 2.50
11 Gold & Lead, pt.1. . . . . 2.50
12 Gold and Lead, pt.2. . . . . 2.50
13 F:Pluto the cat. 2.50
14 A:Mad Meg Mayflower. 2.50
15 Airship. 2.50
16 path of next demon 2.50
17 22 one-page stories. 2.50
18 Airship. 2.50
19 thru 24 Balloon Hoax . . . . @2.95

POINT BLANK

Eclipse

1 thru 5 . . . . @2.95

POISON ELVES

Mulehide Graphics 1993–95

Previously: I, Lusipher

8 DHa(c&a) 20.00
9 DHa 18.00
10 DHa. 12.00
11 DHa, comic size. 12.00
12 DHa. 12.00
13 DHa. 20.00
14 and 15 DHa . . . . @20.00
15a 2nd printing 6.00
16 and 17 DHa . . . . @15.00
17a 2nd printing 6.00
18 DHa. 12.00
19 DHa. 12.00
20 DHa. 12.00

2nd Series, Sirius 1995–97

1 F:Lusipher 10.00
2 V:Assassins Guild. 5.00
3 Sanctuary, pt.3 . . . . 5.00
4 Sanctuary, pt.4 . . . . 6.00
5 Sanctuary, pt.5 . . . . 5.00
6 I:Lester Gran 5.00
7 thru 24 . . . . @4.00
25 DHa. 3.00
26 DHa. 2.50
27 DHa, ... 2.50
28 DHa,F:Lusiphur 2.50
29 DHa, ... 2.50
30 DHa,F:Vido 2.50
31 DHa. 2.50

Poison Elves #11
© Sirius

32 DHa, Cassandra is dead 2.50
33 DHa, temporary truce 2.50
34 DHa, Lusiphur's feminine side . . 2.50
35 DHa, Purple Marauder reappears. 2.50
36 DHa, Lusiphur tracked down . . . 2.50
37 DHa, questionable hlep 2.50
38 DHa. 2.50
39 DHa. 2.50
40 DHa, Sanctuary, concl. 2.50
41 DHa, on to Amrahly'nn. 2.50
42 DHa, Just in Town for the Night,pt.1. . . . . 2.50
43 DHa, Town for the Night, pt.2. . . 2.50
44 DHa, Town for the Night, pt.3. . . 2.50
45 DHa, Petunia. 2.50
46 DHa, High Price of Unemployment. 2.50
47 The Fairy and the Imp 2.50
48 South for the Winter,pt.1 . . . . . . 2.50
49 South for the Winter,pt.2 . . . . . . 2.50
50 South for the Winter,pt.3 . . . . . . 2.95
51 South for the Winter,pt.4 . . . . . . 2.95
52 South for the Winter,pt.5 . . . . . . 2.95
53 South for the Winter,pt.6 . . . . . . 2.95
54 South for the Winter,pt.7 . . . . . . 2.95
55 thru 60 . . . . @2.95
61 by The Fillbach Brothers 2.95
TPB Vol. 1 Requiem for an Elf . . . 14.95
TPB Vol. 2 Traumatic Dogs. 14.95
TPB Vol. 3 Desert of the Third Sin 14.95
TPB Vol. 4 Patrons, 48-pg. 4.95
TPB Vol. 5 rep. 272-page 14.95
TPB Vol. 6 rep. 280-page 14.95

POIZON: DEMON HUNTER

London Night 1998

1 . . . . 3.00
1a nude cover edition 6.00
2 . . . . 3.00
2a deluxe 6.00
3 . . . . 3.00
3a nude cover edition 6.00
4 double sized finale 3.00
4a nude cover edition 6.00

POKEMON ADVENTURES

Viz Communications 1999

1 (of 5) Mysterious Mew 5.95
2 Wanted: Pikachu 5.95
3 The Snorlax Stop 5.95
4 . . . . 5.95

5 The Ghastly Ghosts 5.95

PART TWO

1 (of 6) Team Rocket Returns 2.95
2 The Hunt for Eevee 2.95
3 The Nidoking Safari 2.95
4 Mission: Magmar 2.95
5 The Dangerous Dragonite. 2.95
6 The Mythical Moltres 2.95

PART THREE

1 . . . . 2.95
2 . . . . 2.95
3 . . . . 2.95
TPB Vol. 1 Wanted: Pikachu 14.95

POKEMON: ELECTRIC PIKACHU BOOGALOO

Viz Communications 1999

1 (of 4) by Toshihiro Ono, 48-page. 3.50
2 . . . . 2.95
3 . . . . 2.95
4 finale 2.95
TPB 12.95

POKEMON: THE ELECTRIC TALE OF PIKACHU

Viz Communications 1998

1 (of 4) by Toshiro Ono 16.00
1a 2nd printing 4.00
2 . . . . 8.00
2a 2nd printing 4.00
3 . . . . 5.00
4 . . . . 5.00
GN The Electric Tale of Pikachu . . 12.95

POKEMON: PIKACHU SHOCKS BACK

Viz Communications 1999

1 (of 4) by Toshihiro Ono 3.25
2 thru 4 . . . . @3.25

POKEMON: SURF'S UP PIKACHU

Viz Communications 1999

1 (of 4) thru 3. . . . . @2.95
4 . . . . 3.50
TPB Vol. 3 . . . . 12.95

POKEWOMON: GOTTA SHAG 'EM ALL!

Blatant Comics 1999

1 by Mike Rosenzweig. 2.95
1a nude (c) 9.95

POOT

Fantagraphics 1997

1 by Walt Holcombe 2.95
2 Swollen Holler, pt.2. . . . . 2.95
3 sex issue 2.95
4 final issue, 40-page 3.95

POPCORN

Discovery 1993

1 . . . . 3.95

POP PARODY

Studio Chikara 1999

Big Fat Sci-Fi Spec.:Stawars 2.95
Pokymon–World Domination. 2.95
Dixxi Chix vs. Spice Galz 2.95
The Blair Snitch Project 3.95

PORT

Silver Wolf

1 . . . . 1.50
2 . . . . 1.50

PORTIA PRINZ

Eclipse

1 thru 5 . . . . @2.00

POST BROTHERS

Rip Off Press

15 thru 18. . . . . @2.00
19 and 20 . . . . @2.50

POWER COMICS

1 Smart-Early Ardvaark 12.00
1a 2nd printing 7.00
2 I:Cobalt Blue. 7.00
3 and 4 . . . . @3.00
5 . . . . 4.00

POWER COMICS

Eclipse

1 BB,DGb,Powerbolt 2.00
2 BB,DGb 2.00
3 BB,DGb 2.00

PRACTICE IN PAIN

Dramemon Studios

1 I:Queen of the Dead. 3.00

PREMIERE

Diversity Comics 1995

1 F:Kolmec The Savage 2.75

PRETEEN DIRTY GENE KUNG FU KANGAROOS

Blackthorne 1986

1 and 2 . . . . @1.50

PRETTY CITY ROXX

Mars Press

1 I:Roxx. 3.50

PREY

Monster Comics

1 I:Prey,A:Andrina 2.25
2 V:Andrina 2.25
3 conclusion 2.25

PRICE, THE

1 Dreadstar mag. size 20.00

PRIMITIVES

Spartive Studios 1995

1 thru 3 On the Moon. . . . . @2.50

PRIME CUTS

Fantagraphics

1 adult. 3.50
2 thru 6 . . . . @3.50
7 thru 12 . . . . @3.95

PRIMER

Comico

1 . . . . 10.00

Primer #2
© Comico

2 MW,I:Grendel 90.00
3 . . . . 5.00
4 . . . . 8.00
5 SK(1st work),I:Maxx 25.00
6 IN,Evangeline. 14.00

PRIME SLIME TALES

Mirage

1 . . . . 5.00
2 . . . . 2.50
3 thru 6 . . . . @1.50

PRINCE VALIANT

1 thru 4 . . . . @4.95
Spec. #1. 6.95

PRINCE VALIANT MONTHLY

1 thru 5 . . . . @3.95
6 . . . . 4.95
7 . . . . 4.95
8 . . . . 4.95
9 . . . . 6.95

PRIVATE EYES

Eternity

1 Saint rep. 2.00
2 . . . . 2.00
3 . . . . 2.00
4 . . . . 2.00
5 . . . . 2.00

PSI–JUDGE ANDERSON

1 thru 15 . . . . @2.00

PSYCHOMAN

Revolutionary

1 I:Psychoman 2.50

PULP

Viz Communications 1997

1 Manga anthology magazine 5.95
2 thru 5 . . . . @5.95

VOL. TWO

1 thru 12 . . . . @5.95

VOL. THREE

1 thru 11 . . . . @5.95

Pulp Vol. 2 #4
© Viz Communications

VOL. FOUR
1 . . . 5.95
2 thru 11 . . . @5.95

PULP FICTION
A-List Comics 1997
1 and 2 rep. of Golden Age . . . @2.50
3 . . . 2.95
4 . . . 2.95
5 . . . 2.95
6 . . . 2.95
7 . . . 2.95
Spec. Art of Pulp Fiction . . . 2.95

PUMA BLUES
Aardvark–Vanaheim
1 10,000 printed . . . 4.00
1a 2nd printing . . . 2.00
2 . . . 3.00
3 . . . 2.00
4 thru 19 . . . @1.70
20 Special . . . 2.25
Mirage
21 thru 24 . . . @1.70
25 . . . 2.50
26 thru 28 . . . @1.75

QUACK
Star Reach
1 . . . 2.00
2 . . . 2.00
3 . . . 2.00
4 Dave Sim . . . 3.00
5 Dave Sim . . . 3.00
6 . . . 2.00

QUANTUM MECHANICS
Avatar 1999
1 (of 2) by Barry Gregory & Jacen Burrows . . . 3.50
1a wraparound cover . . . 3.95
2 conclusion . . . 3.50
2a wraparound cover . . . 3.95

QUEST PRESENTS
Quest
1 JD . . . 1.75
2 JD . . . 1.75
3 JD . . . 1.75

QUICKEN FORBIDDEN
Cryptic Press 1998
1 . . . 2.95
2 . . . 2.95
3 . . . 2.95
4 . . . 2.95
5 . . . 2.95
6 Trial Separation,pt.1 . . . 2.95
7 Trial Separation,pt.2 . . . 2.95
8 Trial Separation, concl. . . . 2.95
TPB 152-page . . . 14.95

RABID MONKEY
D.B.I. Comics Jan. 1997
1 thru 4 by Joel Steudler . . . @2.25
5 thru 7 . . . @2.25
8 thru 13 . . . @2.50
#1–#5 Autographed pack . . . 12.00
Dreamriders Workshop 1998
Vol. 2
1 . . . 2.95

RADICAL DREAMER
Mark's Giant Economy Sized Comics
1 thru 3 F:Max Wrighter . . . 3.00
4 is Max the Devil? . . . 3.00
VOL. 2 1998
1 (of 6) by Mark Wheatley, sci-fi . . . 2.95

RADIO BOY
Eclipse
1 . . . 2.00

RAGMOP
Planet Lucy Press
1 by Rob Walton, 3rd. printing . . . 3.00
2 thru 7 reoffer . . . @2.75
8 . . . 2.75
9 . . . 2.75
10 . . . 2.75
VOL. 2 (1997)
3 by Rob Walton . . . 2.95
4 O-ring saga, pt. 2 (of 3) . . . 2.95

RAGNAROK
Sun Comics
1 I:Ragnarok Guy,Honey . . . 2.50
2 The Melder Foundation . . . 2.50
3 Guy/Honey mission contd. . . . 2.50
4 I:Big Gossage . . . 2.50

RAIKA
Sun Comics
1 thru 12 . . . @2.50

RAISING HELL
ABC Comics 1997
1 . . . 2.95
1a gold series, 2 extra pages . . . 3.00
1b nude Jazz gold series . . . 10.00
2 RCI,F:China & Jazz . . . 2.95
2 live nude model cover . . . 14.95
3 conclusion, A:Wild Things . . . 2.95
3 Baby Cheeks edition . . . 10.00
3 Baby Cheeks Gold Edition . . . 14.95

RALPH SNART
Now
1 . . . 5.00
2 . . . 4.00
3 . . . 4.00
[Volume 2]
1 . . . 3.00
2 thru 8 . . . @1.50
Trade Paperback . . . 2.95

RAMBO
Blackthorne
1 thru 5 . . . @2.00

RAMBO III
Blackthorne
1 . . . 2.00

RAMM
Megaton Comics 1987
1 and 2 . . . @1.50

RANMA 1/2
Viz 1993
Parts 1 & 2, see color
[Part Three] 1993–94
1 thru 13 . . . @3.00
[Part Four] 1995
1 thru 11 . . . @3.00
[Part Five] 1996
1 thru 9 . . . @3.00
10 thru 12 . . . @3.00
[Part Six] Dec., 1996
1 thru 8 (of 14) . . . @3.00
9 thru 14 . . . @3.00
TPB Vol. 6 . . . 15.95
TPB Vol. 7 . . . 15.95
TPB Vol. 8 . . . 15.95
TPB Vol. 9 . . . 15.95
TPB Vol. 10 rep. Part Six, 1st half. 15.95
TPB Vol. 11 rep. Part Six, 2nd half 15.95
[Part Seven] Feb., 1998
1 (of 14) . . . 2.95
2 thru 14 . . . @2.95
TPB Vol. 12 . . . 15.95
TPB Vol. 13 . . . 15.95
[Part Eight] 1999
1 (of 13) thru 5 . . . @2.95
6 thru 13 . . . @2.95
TPB Vol. 14 . . . 15.95
TPB Vol. 15 . . . 16.95
[Part Nine] 2000
1 (of 11) . . . 2.95
2 thru 6 . . . @2.95

RAPHAEL
1 TMNT . . . 17.50
1a 2nd printing . . . 7.50

RAPTUS
High Impact
1 . . . 3.00
1 2nd printing, new cover . . . 3.00
2 . . . 3.00
3 . . . 3.00

RAPTUS: DEAD OF NIGHT
High Impact
1 . . . 2.95
2 . . . 2.95
3 . . . 3.00

RAT FINK
World of Fandom

1 . . . . . 2.50
2 . . . . . 2.50

RAVAGER
Kosmic Comic 1997

0 Ashcan 1.50
1 The First Coming 3.55
2 . . . . . 3.55
3 . . . . . 3.55
4 by Kirk Patrick & Babak Homayoun 3.55
5 . . . . . 3.55
6 by Kirk Patrick & Romel Cruz . . . 3.55

RAVEN CHRONICLES
Caliber Press

1 . . . . . 2.95
1a Special Edition 5.95
2 Landing Zone 2.95
3 The Rain People 2.95
4 The Healer 2.95
5 thru 9 . . . . . @2.95

Caliber "New Worlds"

10 by Scott Andrews, Laurence Campbell & Tim Perkins 2.95
11 "The Ghost of Alanzo Mann" . . . 2.95
12 "The Compensators" flip book with Boston Bombers #1 . . . . . 2.95
13 48-pg., bagged with back issue . 3.95
14 . . . . . 2.95
15 . . . . . 2.95
16 inc. Black Mist 2.95
Spec. Heart of the Dragon 2.95
HC 19.95
GN 192-pg. rep. 16.95

The Ravening #0
© Avatar

RAVENING, THE
Avatar Press 1997

0 Trevlin Utz (c) 3.95
0 Matt Martin (c) 3.95
0 Matt Haley (c) 3.95
0 nude cover 6.00
0 leather cover 25.00
0 signed 15.00
1 . . . . . 3.00
1 nude cover 4.95
1 leather cover 25.00
1 Avatar con cover edition 15.00
2 (of 2) 3.00
2 nude cover 4.95
Spec. Secrets of the Ravening 2.75
Spec.A Secrets, nude(c) 6.00

RAW CITY
Dramenon Studios

1 I:Dya,Gino 3.00
2 V:Crucifier 3.00
3 The Siren's Past 3.00

RAW MEDIA MAGS.
Reb

1 TV,SK,short stories 5.00

RAZOR
London Night

6 signed 20.00
10 signed 15.00
TPB The Suffering, rep. #1–#3 . . . 12.95
GN Let Us Prey, rep. of Razor/Wild Child, 80-pg. 5.00
X-over Razor/Embrace: The Spawning (1997) 3.00
Carmen Electra photo (c) 3.00
Carmen Electra photo embossed (c), signed 19.00
Spec. Razor: Switchblade Symphony, Tour Book, limited black leather 15.00

RAZOR ANALOG BURN
London Night Studios 1999

1 by Lee Duhig 2.50
2 . . . . . 2.50

RAZOR: ARCHIVES
London Night 1997

1 EHr, rep #1–#4 . . . . . 5.00
1a signed 12.00
2 EHr, rep #5–#8 . . . . . 5.00
3 EHr, rep #9–#15 . . . . . 5.00
4 EHr, rep #16–#17 . . . . . 5.00

RAZOR/DARK ANGEL: THE FINAL NAIL
Boneyard/London Night

1 X-over (Boneyard Press) 4.00
2 X-over concl.(London Night) 3.00

RAZOR: THE DARKEST NIGHT
London Night 1998

1 . . . . . 4.95
1a white velvet 20.00
2 velvet edition 10.00

EH! Productions 1999

1 . . . . . 4.95
1a Velvet Edition, signed 25.00
2 . . . . . 4.95
3 . . . . . 4.95
3a Fan ed. 6.00

RAZOR: THE FURIES
Avatar 2000

1 48-page 4.95
1a Previews Exclusive 4.95
1b Adult (c) 6.00

RAZOR: GOTHIC
London Night 1998

1 (of 4) by EHr and Scott Wilson . . 3.00
1 nude photo cover 6.00
1 leather 12.00
2 EHr 3.00
2a Graphic/violent cover 6.00
2b Gothic/leather cover 15.00

EH! Productions

3 . . . . . 3.00
3a Elite Fan ed. 5.00
4 . . . . . 3.00
4a Elite Fan ed. 5.00
Spec. Gotherotica 5.00
Spec. Gotherotica nude (c) 5.00

RAZOR: TILL I BLEED DAYLIGHT
Avatar 2000

1 (of 2) Tim Vigil (c) 3.50
1a wraparound (c) 3.95
1b Vampire Razor (c) 5.00
1c adult (c) 6.00
1d prism foil 12.95
2 . . . . . 3.50
2a wraparound (c) 3.95
2b adult (c) 6.00

RAZOR: TORTURE
London Night

0 chromium signed 12.00
1 platinum signed 12.00

RAZOR UNCUT
London Night Studios
Prev. RAZOR (Ind. Color)

13 . . . . . 3.00
14 V:Child Killer 3.00
15 Questions About Father 3.00
16 Nicole's Life,pt.1 . . . . . 3.00
17 Nicole's Life,pt.2 . . . . . 3.00
18 . . . . . 3.00
19 and 20 Kiss from a Rose . . . . @3.00
21 "Kiss From a Rose," pt.3 . . . . . 3.00
22 thru 24 . . . . . @3.00
25 mild cover I:Knyfe 3.00
25a nude photo cover 4.00
25b signed 12.95
26 . . . . . 3.00
27 A:Sade, pt.1 . . . . . 3.00
28 A:Sade, pt.2 . . . . . 3.00
29 . . . . . 3.00
30 . . . . . 3.00
31 "Strength by Numbers" 3.00
32 double sized 3.50
32a signed nude edition 6.00
33 "Let Us Prey," pt.2 . . . . . 3.00
34 "Let Us Prey," pt.4 (of 4) 3.00
35 Let the battle begin 3.00
36 all-out war for Queen City 3.00
37 "After the Fall" pt.1 . . . . . 3.00
38 "After the Fall," pt.2 . . . . . 3.00
39 "Money For Hire" 3.00
40 "Father's Bane," pt.1 . . . . . 3.00
40 nude cover 5.00
41 "Father's Bane," pt.2 . . . . . 3.00
42 "Father's Bane," pt.3 . . . . . 3.00
43 "Father's Bane," pt.4 . . . . . 3.00
44 Razor finds abandoned child . . . 3.00
45 An American Tragedy, pt.1 (of 5) 3.00
45a commemmorative edition, EHr . 5.00
46 An American Tragedy, pt.2 . . . . . 3.00
47 An American Tragedy, pt.3 . . . . . 3.00
48 An American Tragedy, pt.4 . . . . . 3.00
49 An American Tragedy, pt.5 . . . . . 3.00
50 back in Asylum, Tony Daniel (c) . 3.00
50a Michael Bair (c) 5.00
50b Stephen Sandoval (c) 5.00
50c Blood Red Velvet EHr (c) 25.00
Spec. Deep Cuts (1997) 5th Anniv.

rep. #6,#13–#15, 80-pg. 5.00
Nude cover. 10.00

EH! Productions 1999

51 . . . . 3.00
51a Nude cover 5.00

RAZORGUTS

Monster Comics 1992

1 thru 4 . . . . @2.25

RAZOR'S EDGE

London Night 1999

0 Razor/Stryke (c) 4.95
0a Nude Razor photo (c) 6.00
0b Night Vixen (c) 4.95
0c Nude Stryke photo (c). 6.00
1 . . . . 4.95
1a Arizona (c) 4.95
1b Dorian nude (c). 4.95
1c Nude Chrissy Mountjoy (c) 6.00
2 Razorblaze (c) 4.95
2a Battle Girl (c) 6.00
2b Nightvixen (c) 4.95
2c nude cover 6.00
3 . . . . 4.95
3a Nightvixen (c) 4.95
3b Nude Dorian (c) 6.00
3c Nude Razor Photo (c). 6.00
4 . . . . 4.95
4a (c) 4.95
4b Nude (c) 6.00
4c Nude (c) 6.00
5 . . . . 4.95
5a Stryke (c) 4.95
5b Nude Mountjoy (c) 6.00
5c Nude Jordan (c) 6.00

EH! Productions 1999

6 48-page 4.95
7 . . . . 4.95
7a nude (c) 6.00
8 . . . . 4.95
9 . . . . 4.95
9a nude (c) 6.00

REACTOMAN

B-Movie Comics

1 . . . . 1.50
1a signed,numbered 2.75
2 thru 4 . . . . @1.50
collection 4.95

REAGAN'S RAIDERS

1 thru 6 . . . . @2.50

REALM

Arrow

1 Fantasy 6.00
2 . . . . 4.00
3 . . . . 3.00
4 TV,Deadworld. 21.00
5 I:L.Kazan 2.00
6 thru 13 . . . . @1.50
14 thru 18. . . . . @2.00
19 . . . . 2.50

REAL STUFF

Fantagraphic

1 thru 12 . . . . @2.50

REAPER

Newcomers Publishing

1 V:The Chinde 2.95
2 . . . . 2.95
3 conclusion 2.95

REBELLION

Daikaiyu Enterprises 1995

1 I:Rebellion 2.50

RED DIARY

Caliber 1998

1 (of 4) F:Marilyn, JFK, Hoover, CIA 3.95
1a deluxe 6.95
2 . . . . 3.95
3 (of 4) 3.95
4 (signed) 3.95
4 . . . . 3.95
HC Red Diaries 19.95
HC deluxe 39.95

RED FOX

Harrier

1 scarce 6.00
1a 2nd printing 2.50
2 rare 5.00
3 . . . . 3.00
4 I:White Fox. 3.00
5 I:Red Snail 3.00
6 . . . . 1.75
7 Wbolton 1.75
8 . . . . 1.75
9 Demosblurth. 1.75

RED & STUMPY

Parody Press

1 Ren & Stimpy parody 2.95

REDLAW

Caliber

1 Preview Killer of Crows. 2.50

RE:GEX: BLACK & WHITE

Awesome Entertainment 1999

1 RLe,JLb 2.95

REID FLEMING

Blackbird-Eclipse

1 David Boswell,I:Reid Fleming . . . 8.00
1a 2nd printing 5.50
1b 3rd–5th printing. . . . . @2.50

Reid Fleming #2
© Blackbird Eclipse

Volume 2

#1 Rogues to Riches Pt.1 . . . . 6.00
#2 Rogues to Riches Pt.2 . . . . 4.00
#2a Later printings 2.50
#3 Rogues to Riches Pt.3 . . . . 3.00
#3a Later printings 2.50
#4 Rogues to Riches Pt.4 . . . . 3.00
#5 Rogues to Riches Pt.5 . . . . 2.50

REID FLEMING, WORLD'S TOUGHEST MILKMAN

Deep-Sea Comics

3 "Rogue to Riches," pt.2,4th pr. . . 2.95
4 "Rogue to Riches," pt.3,3rd pr. . . 2.95
5 "Rogue to Riches," pt.4,2nd pr . . 2.95
6 "Rogue to Riches," pt.5,2nd pr . . 2.95
7 "Another Dawn,"Pt.1 . . . . 2.95
8 "Another Dawn,"Pt.2 . . . . 2.95
9 "Another Dawn,"Pt.3 . . . . 2.95
TPB Rogue to Riches rep. 13.95
Spec#1 Origins (1998) 3.00

REIVERS

Enigma

1 and 2 Ch'tocc in Space . . . . . . @2.95

RENEGADES OF JUSTICE

Blue Masque

1 I:Monarch,Bloodshadow 2.50
2 Madfire. 2.50
3 Television Chronicles 2.50
4 R:Karen Styles 2.50

RENFIELD

Caliber

GN Conclusion of series. 8.95
HC by Gary Reed & Galen Showman. 19.95
HC Deluxe 39.95

REPENTANCE

Advantage Graphics 1995

1 I:Repentance 2.00

REPLACEMENT GOD

Amaze Ink 1995

1 Child in The Land of Man 6.00
1a 2nd & 3rd printing 3.00
2 Eye of Knute 4.00
3 and 4 "Bravery". . . . . @3.50
5 thru 7 . . . . @3.00
8 Fairie, book one, concl.. . . . . 2.95
TPB rep. #1–#8 . . . . 19.95

REPLACEMENT GOD & OTHER STORIES

Handicraft Guild

Previously published by Image

6 by Zander Cannon, 80-pg. 6.95

RETALIATOR

Eclipse

1 I&O:Retaliator. 2.50
2 O:Retaliator cont. 2.50

RETIEF

Adventure 1990

1 thru 6 Keith Laumer adapt. . . . @2.00

[New Series]

1 thru 6 . . . . @2.25
Spec.#1 Retief:Garbage Invasion . . 2.50

Spec.#1 Retief:The Giant Killer, V:Giant Dinosaur 2.50
Spec.#1 Grime & Punishment, Planet Slunch 2.50

RETIEF OF THE CDT

1 Keith Laumer Novel Adapt. 2.00
2 . . . . 2.00

RETIEF AND THE WARLORDS

Adventure Comics

1 Keith Laumer Novel Adapt. 2.50
2 Haterakans. 2.50
3 Retief Arrested for Treason. 2.50
4 Final Battle (last issue) 2.50

RETIEF: DIPLOMATIC IMMUNITY

Adventure Comics

1 Groaci Invasion. 2.50
2 Groaci story cont. 2.50

RETRO-DEAD

Blazer Unlimited

1 Dimensional Rift 2.95
2 by Dan Reed 2.95

RETROGRADE

Eternity

1 thru 4 . . . . @2.00

RETURN OF HAPPY THE CLOWN

Caliber Press

1 and 2 V:Oni. . . . . @2.95

RETURN OF LUM, THE

Viz Comics

PART THREE

3 thru 11 by Rumiko Takahashi . @2.95
TPB Trouble Times Ten, rep. pt. 2 & Pt.3 #1 . . . . 15.95
TPB Creature Features. 15.95

Return of the Skyman #1
© Ace Comics

PART FOUR*URUSEI YATSURA

1 thru 11 by Rumiko Takahashi . @2.95
TPB Vol. 5 Feudal Furor 15.95
TPB Vol. 6 Creature Features 15.95
TPB Vol. 7 For Better or Curse . . . 15.95
TPB Vol. 8 Ran Attacks 15.95

RETURN OF THE SKYMAN

Ace Comics

1 SD 1.75

REVOLVER

Renegade

1 SD 1.70
2 thru 6 . . . . @1.70
Ann. #1 . . . . 2.00

REVOLVING DOORS

Blackthorne

1 . . . . 1.75
2 . . . . 1.75
3 . . . . 1.75
Graphic Novel 3.95

RHUDIPRRT PRINCE OF FUR

MU Press 1990–91

1 thru 6 . . . . @2.00

RICK RAYGUN

1 . . . . 2.00
2 thru 8 . . . . @1.75

RIO KID

Eternity

1 I:Rio Kid 2.50
2 V:Blow Torch Killer 2.50
3 . . . . 2.50

RION 2990

Rion

1 . . . . 2.75
2 . . . . 1.50

RIOT

Viz 1995

1 F:Riot,Axel 2.75
2 and 3 . . . . @2.75
4 final issue. 2.75
TPB Rep. 15.95

RIOT ACT TWO

Viz Comics

1 thru 7 . . . . @2.95
TPB rep.. . . . . 15.95

RIP IN TIME

Fantagor

1 RCo,Limited series 3.00
2 RCo 2.00
3 RCo 2.00
4 RCo 2.00
5 RCo,Last 2.00

RIPLASH: SWEET VENGEANCE

Pocket Change Comics

1 O:Riplash 2.95

ROACHMILL

1 . . . . 5.00
2 . . . . 3.00
3 . . . . 3.00
4 . . . . 3.00
See: Dark Horse

ROBERT E. HOWARD'S CONAN THE BARBARIAN

Cross Plains Comics 1999

1-shot Horror, 64-page 5.95
TPB Kull. 19.95
1-shot Black Stone 3.95

ROBIN HOOD

1 thru 4 . . . . @2.25

ROBO DEFENSE TEAM MECHA RIDER

Castle Comics

1 I:RDT Mecha Rider. 2.95
2 Identity of Outlaw 2.95

R.O.B.O.T. BATTALION 2050

Eclipse

1 . . . . 2.00

ROBO WARRIORS

CFW

1 thru 11 . . . . @2.00
Becomes:

KUNG FU WARRIORS

ROBOTECH

Eternity

1-shot Untold Stories 2.50

Academy Comics 1995–96

0 Robotech Information 2.50
Spec. Robotech: Macross Tempest F:Roy Fokker, Tempest (1995) . 2.95
Spec. Robotech: Mech Angel, I:Mech Angel (1995) 2.95
Spec. Robotech: The Misfits, from Sothern Cross transferred to Africa 2.95
Spec. #1 and #2 Robotech The Movie, Benny R. Powell & Chi . . . . . @2.95
Spec. Robotech Romance 2.95
Spec. Robotech: Sentinels Star Runners Carpenter's Journey (1996) . . . 2.95
GN The Threadbard Heart 9.95

Antarctic Press 1998

Ann. #1 . . . . 2.95
Spec.#1 Robotech: Escape (1998) . 2.95

ROBOTECH: ACADEMY BLUES

Academy Comics

0 Classroom Blues 3.50
1 F:Lisa. 2.95
2 Bomb at the Academy 2.95
3 Roy's Drinking Buddy 2.95

ROBOTECH: AFTERMATH

Academy Comics

1 thru 10 R:Bruce Lewis. . . . . . . @2.95
11 Zentradi Traitor 2.95
12 and 13 . . . . @2.95

ROBOTECH: CLONE
Academy Comics

1 Dialect of Duality 2.95
2 V:Monte Yarrow 2.95
3 Ressurection 2.95
4 Ressurection 2.95
5 F:Bibi Ava. 2.95

ROBOTECH: COVERT OPS
Antarctic Press 1998

1 (of 2) by Greg Lane 2.95
2 . . . . 2.95

ROBOTECH: INVID WAR
Eternity 1993

1 No Man's Land. 2.50
2 V:Defoliators. 2.50
3 V:The Invid,Reflex Point 2.50
4 V:The Invid. 2.50
5 Moonbase Aluce II 2.50
6 Moonbase-Zentraedi plot 2.50
7 Zentraedi plot contd.. . . . . 2.50
8 A:Lancer. 2.50
9 A:Johnathan Wolfe 2.50
10 . . . . 2.50
11 F:Rand 2.50
12 thru 15. . . . . @2.50

ROBOTECH: INVID WAR AFTERMATH
Eternity

1 thru 6 F:Rand . . . . @2.75

ROBOTECH: MORDECAI
Academy Comics

1 . . . . 2.95
2 Annie meets her clone 2.95

ROBOTECH: RETURN TO MACROSS
Eternity 1993

1 thru 5 . . . . @2.50

Academy Comics

1 thru 17 Roy Fokker . . . . @2.75
18 F:The Faithful 2.75
19 F:Lisa 2.75

Robotech: Return to Macross #20
© Academy Comics

20 F:Lisa 2.75
21 V:Killer Robot 2.95
22 War of the Believers 2.95
23 War of the Believers,pt.2 . . . . . . 2.95
24 War of the Believers,pt.3 . . . . . . 2.95
25 War of the Believers,pt.4 . . . . . . 2.95
26 thru 30. . . . . @2.95
31 What is the Federalist Plan? . . . 2.95
32 thru 34 . . . . @2.95
35 Typhoon threatens Macross Island. 2.95
36 . . . . 2.95
37 round up of Federalist Agents . . 2.95

ROBOTECH: SENTINELS: RUBICON
Antarctic Press 1998

1 (of 7) 2.95
2 Shadows of the Past. 2.95

ROBOTECH II THE SENTINELS
Eternity

1 . . . . 3.00
1a 2nd printing 2.00
2 . . . . 2.50
2a 2nd printing 2.00
3 . . . . 2.00
3a 2nd printing 2.00
4 thru 16 . . . . @2.00

[Book 2]

1 thru 12 . . . . @2.25
13 thru 20. . . . . @2.25
Wedding Special #1 . . . . 2.00
Wedding Special #2 . . . . 2.00
Robotech II Handbook 2.50

[Book Three]

1 thru 8 V:Invid. . . . . @2.50

[Book Four]

Academy Comics Dec. 1995

1 by Jason Waltrip. 2.95
2 thru 4 F:Tesla . . . . @2.75
5 JWp,JWt,interior of Haydon IV . . 2.95
6 thru 8 . . . . @2.95
9 JWp,JWt,Breetai, Wolf & Vince return to Tirol 2.95
10 JWp,JWt,*Ark Angel* attacked by The Black Death Destroyers. . . 2.95
11 JWp,JWt,Tirol, Wolff, Vince & Breetai on trial for treason 2.95
12 JWp,JWt,Dr. Lang exposes General Edwards' evil designs . 2.95
13 F:Tesla 2.75
14 V:Invid. 2.75
15 . . . . 2.75
16 . . . . 2.75
17 V:Invid Mechas 2.75
18 F:"HIN" 2.95
19 V:Invid. 2.95
20 Final Aplp. Invid Regiss 2.95
21 Predator and Prey 2.95
22 A Clockwork Planet 2.95
Halloween Special JWp,JWt, ... 2.95

ROBOTECH II: THE SENTINELS: CYBERPIRATES
Eternity 1991

1 The Hard Wired Coffin 2.25
2 thru 4 . . . . @2.25

ROBOTECH II: THE SENTINELS: THE MALCONTENT UPRISING
Eternity

1 thru 12 . . . . @2.00

ROBOTECH: VERMILION
Antarctic Press 1997

1 (of 4) by Duc Tran 2.95
2 Why did Hiro die?. 2.95
3 . . . . 2.95
4 . . . . 2.95

ROBOTECH: WARRIORS
Academy Comics

1 F:Breetai 2.95
2 F:Mirya. 2.95
3 F:Mirya. 2.95
GN The Terror Maker 9.95

ROBOTECH: WINGS OF GIBRALTAR
Antarctic Press 1998

1 (of 2) by Lee Duhig. 2.95
2 . . . . 2.95

ROCK & ROLL COMICS
Revolutionary

1 Guns N' Roses. 9.00
1a 2nd printing 3.50
1b 3rd printing. 2.00
1c 4th-7th printing 2.00
2 Metallica. 10.00
2a 2nd printing 3.00
2b 3rd-5th printing 2.00
3 Bon Jovi. 9.00
4 Motley Crue 5.00
5 Def Leppard 5.00
6 Rolling Stones 7.00
6a 2nd-4th printing 3.00
7 The Who 5.00
7a 2nd-3rd printing 2.00
9 KISS. 15.00
9a 2nd-3rd Printing 5.00
10 Warrant/Whitesnake 5.00
10a 2nd Printing. 2.00
11 Aerosmith 5.00
12 New Kids on Block. 5.00
12a 2nd Printing. 2.00
13 Led Zeppelin 6.00
14 Sex Pistols 5.00
See Independent Color

ROCKET RANGERS
Adventure

1 . . . . 2.95
2 . . . . 2.95
3 . . . . 2.95

ROCKIN ROLLIN MINER ANTS
Fate Comics

1 As seen in TMNT #40 . . . . 2.25
1a Gold Variant copy. 7.50
2 Elephant Hunting, A:Scorn, Blister 2.25
3 V:Scorn, Inc.,K.Eastman Ant pin-up. 2.25
4 Animal Experiments,V:Loboto . . . 2.25

ROLLING STONES: THE SIXTIES
Personality
1 Regular Version 2.95
1a Deluxe Version,w/cards 6.95

ROSE
Hero Graphics
1 From The Champions. 3.50
2 A:Huntsman 3.50
3 thru 5 . . . . @2.95

ROSE N' GUNN
London Night
1 . . . . 3.00
1a nude cover. 6.00
1b signed 10.00
2 . . . . 3.00
3 . . . . 3.00

ROSE N' GUNN: RECKONING
London Night
1 (of 2) 3.00

ROSE N' GUNN
Bishop Press 1995
1 Deadly Duo 5.00
2 V:Marilyn Monroe 3.00
3 Presidential Affairs 3.00
4 Without Each Other 3.00
5 V:Red. 3.00
6 and 7 . . . . @3.00
Creator's Choice Rep. #1 . . . . 2.95
Creator's Choice Rep. #2 . . . . 2.95
Creator's Choice Rep. #3 . . . . 2.95

ROVERS
Eternity
1 thru 7 . . . . @2.00

RUBES REVIVED
Fishwrap
1 . . . . 2.00
2 and 3 . . . . @2.00

RUK BUD WEBSTER
Fishwrap
1 thru 3 . . . . @1.70

SADE
Bishop Press
0 B:Adventures of Sade. 3.00
1 . . . . 3.00
1a variant 6.00
2 . . . . 3.00

SADE
London Night
1 . . . . 3.00
1a nude cover. 7.00
2 thru 5 . . . . @3.00

SADE SPECIAL
Bishop Press
1 V:Razor 5.00
1a signed 7.00

SADE/ROSE AND GUNN
London Night Nov. 1996
1 Confederate Mist 3.00

SADE: TESTAMENTS OF PAIN
London Night Jan., 1997
1 (of 2) 3.00

SAGA OF THE MAN-ELF
1 thru 5 . . . . @2.25

Sailor Moon #8
© Mixx Entertainment

SAGE
Fantaco 1995
1 O:Sage. 4.95

SAILOR MOON
Mixx Entertainment 1998
1 by Naoko Tekeuchi 2.95
2 thru 11 . . . . @2.95
12 thru 20. . . . . @2.95
Pocket #1 (of 18) 192-page 9.95
Pocket #2 rep. 9.95
Pocket #3 rep. 9.95
Pocket #4 rep. 9.95
Pocket #5 rep. #11–#13 . . . . 9.95
Pocket #6 rep. #14–#17 . . . . 9.95
Scout Guide: Sailor Mars: Fire . . . 12.95
Scout Guide: Sailor Venus: Love. . 12.95
Scout Guide: Sailor Jupiter: Thunder 12.95
Novel A Scout is Born. 5.00
Novel The Power of Love 5.00
Novel 3: Mercury Rising 5.00

Tokyopop.Com 2000
21 thru 25. . . . . @2.95
Pocket Vol. 7 . . . . 9.95
TPB Scout Guide-Meet Sailor Moon: Crystal. 12.95
TPB Scout Guide-Meet Sailor Mercury: Ice 12.95
TPB Scout Guide-Meet Sailor Jupiter: Thunder. 12.95

SAILOR MOON SUPER S
Mixx Entertainment 1999
1 (of 18) 192-page. 9.95
2 Pocket Mixx 9.95
3 Pocket Mixx 9.95
4 Pocket Mixx 9.95

SAINT
Kick Ass Comics
1 and 2 V:Cerran . . . . @2.50

SAINT GERMAINE
Caliber "Core" 1997
0 O:St. Germaine 3.95
1 VcL, two immortals, St. Germain cover 2.95
1 Lilith cover 2.95
2 VcL 2.95
3 VcL 2.95
3a signed 2.95
4 VcL 2.95
5 The Kilroy Mandate, VcL(c) 2.95
5a Meyer (c) 2.95
6 Kilroy Mandate 2.95
7 Ghost Dance 2.95
8 The Man in the Iron Mask. 2.95
10 The Tragedy of Falstaff 2.95
11 by Gary Reed & James Lyle. . . . 2.95
GN Shadows Fall, rep. #1–#4. . . . 14.95
Spec. Casanova's Lament, 48-page 3.95
Spec. Restoration, VcL. 3.95

SAINT GERMAINE: PRIOR ECHOES
Caliber "Core" 1998
1 (of 4) by Gary Reed 2.95
2 . . . . 2.95
3 . . . . 2.95

SALIMBA
Blackthorne
1 . . . . 3.50

SAMURAI (1st series)
1 . . . . 50.00
2 . . . . 25.00
3 . . . . 25.00
4 . . . . 25.00
5 . . . . 25.00

SAMURAI
Aircel
1 rare 6.00
1a 2nd printing 3.00
1b 3rd printing. 2.00
2 . . . . 5.00
2a 2nd printing 2.50
3 . . . . 3.00
4 . . . . 3.00
5 thru 12 . . . . @2.00
13 DK (1st art) 4.00
14 thru 16 DK. . . . . @4.00
17 thru 22. . . . . @2.00

[3rd series]
#1 thru 3 . . . . @1.70
#4 thru 7. . . . . @2.00
Compilation Book 4.95

SAMURAI
Warp Graphics 1997
1 by Barry Blair & Colin Chan 2.95
2 . . . . 2.95
3 . . . . 2.95
4 . . . . 2.95

B & W PUB.

SAMURAI FUNNIES
Solson
1 thru 3 . . . . @2.00

SAMURAI PENGUIN
Solson
1 . . . . 3.00
2 I:Dr.Radium 2.00
3 . . . . 2.00
4 . . . . 1.50
5 FC 1.50
6 color. 2.25
7 . . . . 2.25
8 . . . . 1.75
9 . . . . 1.75

SAMURAI 7
Gauntlet Comics
1 I: Samurai 7 . . . . 2.50

SAMURAI, SON OF DEATH
Eclipse
1 . . . . 3.95
1a 2nd printing 3.95

SANCTUARY
Viz
1 World of Yakuza 5.00
2 thru 4 . . . . @5.00
5 thru 9 . . . . @5.00

[Part Two] 1993–94

1 thru 9 . . . . @5.00

[Part Three] 199–95

1 thru 8 . . . . @3.50

[Part Four] 1995–96

1 thru 7 . . . . @3.50

[Part Five] 1996

7 thru 13 by Sho Fumimura & Ryoichi Ikegami . . . . @3.50
GN rep. ½ of part 4 & ½ part 5 . . . 16.95
GN Vol. 5 . . . . 17.95
GN Vol. 6 . . . . 17.95
GN Vol. 9 . . . . 16.95

SANTA CLAWS
Eternity
1 'Deck the Mall with Blood and Corpses' 2.95

SAVAGE HENRY
Vortex
1 thru 13 . . . . @1.75

Rip Off Press
14 thru 15. . . . . @2.00
16 thru 24. . . . . @2.50

SCARAMOUCH
Innovation
1 . . . . 2.50

SCARLET IN GASLIGHT
1 A:SherlockHolmes 4.00
2 . . . . 3.00
3 and 4 . . . . @2.50

SCARLET SCORPION/ DARKSIDE
AC Comics
1 and 2 Flipbooks . . . . @3.50

SCARLET THUNDER
Amaze Ink
1 thru 3 . . . . @2.50

SCIMIDAR
Eternity
1 . . . . 4.00
1a 2nd Printing 2.50
2 and 3 . . . . @3.00
4 HotCover 3.50
4A MildCover. 3.00

SCORN
SCC Entertainment 1996
Lingerie Spec. 2.95
Lingerie Spec. deluxe 9.95
Super Spec.#1 rep. Deadly Rebellion, Headwave, Fabric of the Mind. 4.95
X-over Scorn/Ardy: Alien Influence (1997) by Rob Potchak & Timothy Johnson 3.95
Bill Maus (c). 3.95
Deluxe gold 9.95
X-over Scorn/Dracula: The Vampire's Blood (1997) 3.95
Dracula cover 3.95
Scorn cover 3.95
Nude cover 9.95
Spec.#1A Scorn; Dead or Alive (1997) Mike Morales(c). 3.95
Andrea Seri(c) 3.95
Spec.# Scorn:Deadly Rebellion. . . . 3.95
Birthday Suit cover 9.95
Celebrity photo cover 9.95
Spec.#1 Scorb: Fractured (1997)
Fear cover 3.95
Rage cover 3.95
Nude cover 9.95
Spec: Scorn: Heatwave (1997) by Chris Crosby & Mike Morales . . 3.95
Nude cover 9.95
Spec. Scorn: Hostage 3.95
Nude cover 9.95
Spec. Scorn: Naked Truth (1997) . . 3.95
Nude cover 9.95

SCOUT HANDBOOK
Eclipse
1 . . . . 1.75

SCRATCH
Outside
1 . . . . 3.00
2 . . . . 2.00
3 . . . . 1.75
4 . . . . 1.75

SCRIMIDAR
CFD Productions 1995
1 I:Bloody Mary 2.75

SCUD: DISPOSABLE ASSASSIN
Fireman Press
1 I:Scud. 14.00
1a 3rd printing 3.50
2 . . . . 8.00
3 . . . . 6.00
4 thru 6 F:Scud . . . . @5.00
7 Lupine Thoughts. 4.00
8 Scud Looks for His Arm 4.00
9 Scud Looks for His Arm 4.00
10 thru 16 by Rob Schrab . . . . . . @3.00
17 . . . . 3.00

Scud The Disposable Assassin #1
© Fireman Press

18 . . . . 3.00
19 . . . . 3.00
20 Horse series, concl. 3.00
TPB Rep.#1-#4. . . . . 12.95
TPB Programmed for Damage, rep.#5–#9. . . . . 14.95
TPB Solid Gold Bomb. 17.95

SCUD: TALES FROM THE VENDING MACHINE
Fireman Press 1998
1 . . . . 2.50
2 . . . . 2.50
3 . . . . 2.50
4 . . . . 2.50
5 . . . . 2.50

SEARCHERS
Caliber "New Worlds"
1A Red cover, signed 3.00
1B Blue cover, signed 3.00
3 . . . . 3.00
4 . . . . 3.00
5 flip book with Boston Bombers . . 3.00

SEARCHERS: APOSTLE OF MERCY
Caliber 1997
1 (of 2) 3.95
2 . . . . 3.95

Vol 2

1 . . . . 2.95
2 . . . . 2.95
3 (of 3) 48-pg 3.95

SECRET FILES
Angel Entertainment 1996
0 gold edition. 7.00
0 nude cover 9.00
0 commemorative edition. 2.95
0 nude commemorative edition . . . 5.00
1 . . . . 2.95
1 spooky silver foil edition 5.95
1 nude signed 9.00
2 . . . . 2.95
2 deluxe 5.95
2 nude cover A 9.00
2 nude cover B 9.00
Spec. Secret Files vs. Vampire Girls:

The Vampire Effece (1997) . . . 2.95
Erotic nude cover 2.95
Pin-up Book Secret Files: Erotic Experiments (1997) 2.95
Erotic nude cover A 2.95
Erotic nude cover B 2.95
Spec.#1 Secret Files: F.B.I. Conspiracy (1997)F:Sabrina & Susanna Sorenson 2.95
Nude cover 2.95

SECRET FILES: THE STRANGE CASE

Angel Entertainment 1996

0 by David Campitti & Al Rio 2.95
0 Virgin nude cover 5.00
0 Slimy Wet Twins nude cover. . . . 7.00
0 nude manga cover 5.00
0 nude platinum cover 12.00
1 by David Campiti & Al Rio. 2.95
1 Virgin nude cover 5.00
1 nude manga cover 5.00
1 nude platinum cover 15.00

SECTION 8

Noir Press 1995

1 Anthology series. 2.50
2 thru 6 . . . . @2.50
7 "Retribution," pt.1 . . . . 2.50
8 "Retribution," pt.2 . . . . 2.50
9 . . . . 2.50
10 "Chance" 2.50

SEEKER

Caliber "Core" 1998

1M by Gary Reed & Chris Massarotto, Meadows(c) 2.95
1W David Williams(c) 2.95
1a variant Greg Louden (c) 2.95
1 premium, signed. 9.95
2 . . . . 2.95
3 . . . . 2.95
4 . . . . 2.95
5 Gestalt vs. LeAnn Heywood 2.95
Spec. Dawn of Armageddon, x-over, 48-page 3.95

SENTINEL

1 . . . . 2.00
2 thru 4 . . . . @2.00

SERAPHIN

Newcomers Press 1995

1 I:Roy Torres 2.95

777: THE WRATH

Avatar Press 1998

1 (of 3) by David Quinn & Tim Vigil 3.00
1a wraparound cover 3.50
1b nude cover 6.00
1c leather cover 6.00
1d royal blue foil logo. 75.00
1e signed 15.00
1f foil platinum edition 16.95
2 . . . . 3.00
2 nude cover 6.00
3 concl. 3.00
3 nude cover 6.00
TPB 777:The Wrath/ Faust Fearbook 15.95

SHADES OF GRAY COMICS AND STORIES

Caliber/Tapestry 1996

1 . . . . 2.95
2 . . . . 2.95
3 . . . . 2.95
4 . . . . 2.95
Super Summer Spec. rep. 3.95

SHADOW CROSS

Darkside Comics 1995

1 I:Shadow Cross 4.95
2 thru 7 . . . . @2.50

SHADOWALKER

Aircel

1 thru 4 . . . . @1.70

SHADOW SLASHER

Pocket Change Comics

1 I:Shadow Slasher 2.50
2 V:Riplash 2.50
3 F:Matt Baker. 2.50
4 Evolution 2.50
5 F:Riplash 2.50
6 Next Victim. 2.50
7 What Can Kill Him 2.50
8 . . . . 2.50
9 final issue. 2.50

SHANDA [THE PANDA]

Antarctic Press

1 thru 11 . . . . @2.75
12 thru 14. . . . . @2.95

Med Systems

15 and 16 . . . . @2.00

Vision Comics

17 by Mike Curtis & Michelle Light . 2.00
18 "Rocky Horror Picture Show" . . . 2.00
19 "Shine on Me, Cajun Moon". . . . 2.50
20 falling in love 2.50
22 Bright Eyes 2.95

Shanda Fantasy

23 Sweet Young Things 2.95
24 graduation night. 2.95
25 48-page. 4.95
26 thru 29. . . . . @2.95

SHANGHAIED

Eternity

1 and 2 . . . . @1.80
3 and 4 . . . . @2.00

SHARDS

Acension Comics

1 I:Silver, Raptor, RIpple 2.50
2 F:Anomoly 2.50

SHATTERED EARTH

Eternity 1988–89

1 thru 9 . . . . @2.00

SHATTERPOINT

Eternity 1990

1 thru 4 Broid miniseries . . . . . . @2.25

SHEBA

Sirius/Dog Star 1997

VOL. 2

1 by Walter S. Crane IV. 2.50

2 . . . . 2.50
3 . . . . 2.50
4 . . . . 2.50

Sick Mind Press

5 . . . . 2.95
6 . . . . 2.95
7 . . . . 2.95

SHE-CAT

AC Comics

1 thru 4 . . . . @2.50

SHE-DEVILS ON WHEELS

Aircel

1 thru 3 . . . . @2.95

She-Devils on Wheels #1
© Aircel

SHERLOCK HOLMES

Eternity

1 thru 22 . . . . @2.00

SHERLOCK HOLMES

Caliber/Tome Press 1997

1-shot Dr. Jekyll and Mr. Holmes by Steve Jones & Seppo Makinen. 2.95
1-shot Return of the Devil. 3.95
1-shot Return of the Devil, signed. . 3.95
GN Adventure of the Opera Ghost . 6.95
TPB Case of Blind Fear 12.95
TPB Scarlet in Gaslight. 12.95
TPB Sussex Vampire 12.95

SHERLOCK HOLMES CASEBOOK

Eternity

1 and 2 . . . . @2.25

SHERLOCK HOLMES: CHRONICLES OF CRIME AND MYSTERY

North Star

1 `The Speckled Band' 2.25

SHERLOCK HOLMES: HOUND OF THE BASKERVILLES

Caliber/Tome Press Dec. 1997

1 (of 3) by Martin Powell & PO . . . 2.95

SHERLOCK HOLMES: MARK OF THE BEAST

Caliber/Tome Press 1997

1 (of 3) by Martin Powell & Seppo Makinen. 2.95
2 . . . . 2.95
GN 12.95

SHERLOCK HOLMES MYSTERIES

Moonstone 1997

1-shot by Joe Gentile & Richard Gulick. 2.95

SHERLOCK HOLMES OF THE '30's

Eternity

1 thru 7 . . . . @2.95

SHERLOCK HOLMES READER

Caliber/Tome Press 1998

1 Curse of the Beast 3.95
2 The Loch Ness Horror 3.95
3 The Loch Ness Horror 3.95
4 The Loch Ness Horror 3.95
5 . . . . 3.95

SHERLOCK HOLMES: RETURN OF THE DEVIL

Adventure

1 V:Moriarty. 2.50
2 V:Moriarty. 2.50

SHERLOCK JUNIOR

Eternity

1 Rep.NewspaperStrips. 2.00
2 Rep.NewspaperStrips. 2.00
3 Rep.NewspaperStrips. 2.00

SHI

Crusade 1999

0 rough cut edition. 4.99
0 ashcan, signed 9.99
Spec.#1 Black,White & Red 2.95
Spec. San Diego (Con) Art of War Tour Book 1998 . . . . 9.95
Spec. Lim. Ed. Shi/Daredevil Banzai 10.00
Spec.#1 Kaidan, macabre. 2.95
Spec.#1 Kaidan, signed & numb. . 19.95
Coll. Ed. Heaven & Earth, Yin & Yang,96-page 5.99
Year of the Dragon preview book . . 2.99
Year of the Dragon tour book 4.99
Year of the Dragon tour Wizard. . . . 4.99
Year of the Dragon tour San Diego . 4.99

SHIELA TRENT VAMPIRE HUNTER

Draculina Publishing

1 O:Sheild Trent 2.50

SHIP OF FOOLS

Caliber 1996

1 signed edition. 3.00
2 "Dante's Compass". 3.00
3 The Great Escape begins 3.00
4 MiA 3.00
5 MiA 3.00
Spec. #1, Bon Voyage, Go to Hell, Mama Hades 3.95
TPB sci-fi action/adventure 11.95
continued: See Image Comics

SHOCK THE MONKEY

Millennium

1 and 2 Entering the Psychotic Mind . . . . @3.95

SHRED

CFW

1 thru 10 . . . . @2.25

SHRIEK

1 . . . . 4.95
2 . . . . 4.95
3 . . . . 7.95

Shuriken #6
© Victory

SHURIKEN

Victory 1986

1 Reggi Byers 5.00
1a 2nd printing 1.50
2 . . . . 3.00
3 . . . . 2.00
4 . . . . 1.75
5 thru 13 . . . . @1.50
Graphic Nov. Reggie Byers. 8.00

SHURIKEN

Eternity 1991

1 Shuriken vs. Slate 2.50
2 Neutralizer, Meguomo. 2.50
3 R:Slate. 2.50
4 Morgan's Bodyguard Serrate . . . 2.50
5 Slate as Shuriken & Megumo . . . 2.50
6 Hunt for Bionauts, final issue . . . 2.50

SHURIKEN: COLD STEEL

1 . . . . 2.00
2 . . . . 2.00
3 thru 6 . . . . @2.00

SHURIKEN TEAM-UP

1 thru 3 . . . . @2.00

SIEGEL & SHUSTER

2 . . . . 1.70

SILBUSTER

Antarctic Press

1 thru 10 . . . . @3.50
11 I:Kizuki Sister. 3.50
12 thru 14 . . . . @3.50
15 . . . . 3.95
16 thru 19 . . . . @3.50
TPB Rep. #1-#4 . . . . 10.95
TPB Vol.2 . . . . 10.95

SILENT INVASION

Renegade

1 . . . . 4.00
2 thru 12, final issue. . . . . @3.00

SILENT INVASION

Caliber

4 Red Shadows, pt.1 . . . . 3.00
5 Red Shadows, pt.2 . . . . 3.00

SILENT INVASION: ABDUCTIONS

Caliber 1998

1 by Larry Hancock & Michael Cherkos 2.95

SILENT MOBIUS

Viz Communications

TPB by Kia Asamiya. 16.95
TPB Vol. 2 . . . . 16.95
TPB Vol. 3 . . . . 16.95
TPB Vol. 4 Into the Labyrinth 16.95
TPB Vol. 5 . . . . 16.95

SILENT MOBIUS: CATASTROPHE

Viz Communications 2000

1 (of 6) by Kia Asamiya 2.95
2 thru 5 . . . . @2.95

SILENT MOBIUS: INTO THE LABYRINTH

Viz Communications 1999

1 (of 6) by Kia Asamiya 2.95
2 thru 4 . . . . @2.95
5 and 6 . . . . @3.25

SILENT MOBIUS: KARMA

Viz Communications 1999

1 (of 7) by Kia Asamiya 3.25
2 thru 7 . . . . @3.25

SILVER STORM

Aircel 1990

1 thru 4 . . . . @2.25

SIMON/KIRBY READER

1 . . . . 1.75

SINBAD

1 . . . . 2.25
2 thru 4 . . . . @2.25

SINBAD: HOUSE OF GOD
Adventure Comics
1 Caliph's Wife Kidnapped. 2.50
2 Magical Genie 2.50
3 Escape From Madhi 2.50
4 A:Genie 2.50

SINNAMON
Catfish Comics 1995
1 remastered. 2.75
1a remastered deluxe 3.75
6 thru 8 . . . . @2.75
Mythic Comics
9 "Ashes to Ashes—The Pyre-Anna Saga," pt.2 . . . . 2.75
10 "Twas Beauty Bashed The Beast" 2.75
11. . . . . 2.75
12 M.G.Delaney (c) 2.75
12 Poliwko (c). 2.75
Archives #1 . . . . 2.75

SISTER ARMAGEDDON
Dramenon Studios
1 and 2 Nun with a Gun . . . . @2.50
3 Mother Superior 2.50
4 V:Apoligon 2.95

SKELETON KEY
Amaze Ink 1995
1 1 I:Skeleton Key. 1.50
1 2nd printing 1.75
2 F:Tansin 1.50
3 V:Japanese Burglar 1.50
4 V:Closet Monster 1.50
5 thru 10 . . . . @1.75
11. . . . . 1.75
12 . . . . 1.75
14 by Andi Watson 1.75
15 "The Celestial Calendar" 1.75
16 thru 30. . . . . @1.75
Spec. 4.95
TPB Vol. 1, Threshold rep.#1–#6 . 11.95
TPB Vol.2 Celestial Calendar, rep.#7–#18. . . . . 19.95
TPB Vol. 3, rep. #19–#24 . . . . 12.95
TPB Vol. 4, Cats & Dogs, rep. #25–#30. . . . . 12.95
Spec.Skeleton Key/Sugar Kat. 2.95
VOL. 2
1 (of 4) 2.95
2 . . . . 2.95
3 . . . . 2.95
4 conclusion 2.95

SKIN 13
Entity/Parody 1995
1/2a Grungie/Spider-Man. 2.50
1/2b Heavy Metal 2.50
1/2c Gen-Et Jackson 2.50

SKUNK, THE
Entity Comics April, 1997
#Uno. 2.75
5 BMs 2.75
6 BMs 2.75
Collection #1 rep. #1–#3. . . . . 4.95
Collection #1a signed & numbered . 9.95
Collection #2 rep. #4–#6. . . . . 4.95

SKUNK/FOODANG
FOODANG/SKUNK
Entity Comics
Spec. 1 BMs, BMs(c) 2.75
Spec. 1a BMs, Mike Duggan(c) . . . 2.75

SKYNN & BONES: DEADLY ANGELS
Brainstorm April, 1996
1 . . . . 2.95

SKYNN & BONES: FLESH FOR FANTASY
Brainstorm 1997
1 erotic missions 2.95
1a nude cover 2.95
2 erotic missions 2.95
2a nude cover 2.95
Spec. #1 Dare to Bare 3.00
Spec. #1 Dare to Bare, nude cover. 4.00

SLACK
Legacy Comics
1 Slacker Anthology. 2.50
2 Loser 2.50

SLAUGHTERHOUSE
Caliber
1 Bizarre medical Operations. 2.95
2 House of Death 2.95
3 House of Death 2.95
4 Dead Killer vs. Mosaic 2.95

SMITH BROWN JONES: ALIEN ACCOUNTANT
Slave Labor 1998
1 by Jon Hastings 2.95
2 . . . . 2.95
3 . . . . 2.95
4 . . . . 2.95
Spec.#1 Halloween Special 2.95
Spec. Convention Mayhem. 5.95

SNAKE, THE
Special Studio 1991
1 . . . . 3.50

SNARF
Kitchen Sink
1 thru 10 . . . . @2.00
10 (c)BE. 2.00
11 thru 13 . . . . @2.00

SNOWMAN
Hall of Heroes 1996
1 . . . . 15.00
1a variant (c). 20.00
1 3rd printing. 2.75
1 San Diego Con. ed. 5.00
2 . . . . 8.00
2a 2nd printing 2.75
2b variant (c). 9.00
3 . . . . 6.00
3a variant (c). 7.00

SNOWMAN
Avatar Press 1997
0 by Matt Martin, O:Snowman 3.00
0a Frozen Fear extra-bloody 4.95
0b Leather cover 25.00
0c signed. 10.00
Spec.#1 Snowman 1944. . . . . 3.95
Spec.#1 Snowman 1944, deluxe. . . 4.95
Spec.#1 Snowman 1944, signed. . 10.00
1-shot Flurries, Glynn (c) 4.95

Snowman #0
© Avatar

1-shotA Flurries, Snowman (c) 4.95
TPB Snowman rep. 128-page. . . . 13.95

SNOWMAN: DEAD & DYING
Avatar Press 1997
1 (of 3) by Matt Martin 3.00
1 deluxe 4.95
1 signed 10.00
2 . . . . 3.00
2 deluxe 4.95
3 by Matt Martin 3.00
3 Frozen Fear 4.95
3 White Velvet. 25.00

SNOWMAN: HORROR SHOW
Avatar Press 1998
1 by Matt Martin 3.00
1a Frozen Fear (c). 4.95
1b Leather cover 25.00
1 deluxe 4.95

SNOWMAN: 1994
Entity Oct. 1996
1 flip cover #0, by Matt Martin, O:Snowman 3.00
1 signed, numbered. 8.00
3 . . . . 2.75
3 deluxe, variant, foil cover 3.50
4 . . . . 2.75
4 deluxe, variant, foil cover 3.50

SNOWMAN 2
Avatar Press 1997
1 (of 2) Snowman vs. Snowman . . 3.00
1a Face-off cover 4.95
1b Leather cover 25.00
1c Royal Blue edition. 50.00
2 concl. 3.00
2a Sudden Death variant cover . . . 4.95

SOB: SPECIAL OPERATIONS BRANCH
Promethean Studios 1994
1 I:SOB 2.50

SOCKETEER
Kardia
Rocketeer parody 2.25

SOLD OUT
Fantagor
1 and 2 . . . . @1.75

SOLO EX-MUTANTS
Eternity
1 thru 6 . . . . @2.00

SONG OF THE SIRENS
Millennium
Earth 2.95
Earth, signed print edition 6.95
Fire 2.95
Fire, signed print edition 9.95
Wind 2.95
Wind collectors edition 4.95
Wind with trading card 4.95
Secrets, Lies, & Videotape Pin-Up Special 2.95
Secrets, Lies, & Videotape Pin-Up Special, foil logo 5.95
Secrets, Lies, & Videotape Pin-Up Special, deluxe 9.95

SOUL
Samson Comics
1 thru 3 F:Sabbeth . . . . @2.50

SOULFIRE
Aircel
1 mini-series 1.70
2 . . . . 1.70
3 . . . . 1.70

Soulsearchers and Co. #6
© Claypool

SOULSEARCHERS AND CO.
Claypool 1993–98
1 thru 10 Peter David(s) . . . . @3.00
11 thru 20 . . . . @2.50
21 thru 24 . . . . @2.50
25 ACo&SL(c) 2.50
26 O:Soulsearchers, pt.1 . . . . 2.50
27 O:Soulsearchers, pt.2 . . . . 2.50
28 O:Soulsearchers, pt.3 . . . . 2.50
29 O:Soulsearchers, pt.4 . . . . 2.50
30 . . . . 2.50
31 The Mystery of the Lighthouse Pirate Treasure 2.50
32 Haunted by Her Past 2.50
33 F:Creature-Feature 2.50
34 And All That Rot 2.50
35 My Mother...Myself. 2.50
36 Bright Lights, Big City, Small Rodent 2.50
37 Hell in a Handbasket 2.50
38 HorrorFest 2.50
39 . . . . 2.50
40 Evil.Com 2.50
41 Titanic Dreams 2.50
42 Kelly the Demon Slayer 2.50
43 It's in the Bag 2.50
TPB 12.95

SOUTHERN KNIGHTS
1 See Crusaders
2 . . . . 7.00
3 and 4 . . . . @5.00
5 thru 7 . . . . @4.00

Fictioneer
8 thru 11 . . . . @2.50
12 thru 33 . . . . @2.00
34 . . . . 2.25
35 The Morrigan Wars Pt.#2 . . . . . . 3.50
36 Morrigan Wars Pt.#5 . . . . 3.50
37 Hell ina Handbasket. 2.50
Ann. #1 . . . . 2.50
DreadHalloweenSpec. #1 . . . . 2.25
Primer #1 . . . . 2.25

SOUTHERN SQUADRON
Aircel
1 thru 4 . . . . @2.25

Eternity
1 I:SQUAD 2.50
2 . . . . 2.25
3 . . . . 2.25
4 . . . . 2.25

SOUTHERN SQUADRON FREEDOM OF INFO. ACT.
Eternity
1 F.F.#1 Parody/Tribute cov. 2.50
2 A:Waitangi Rangers 2.50
3 . . . . 2.50

SPACE ARK
Apple
1 . . . . 2.75
2 . . . . 2.50
3 . . . . 1.75
4 . . . . 1.75
5 . . . . 1.75

SPACE BEAVER
Ten-Buck Comics
1 . . . . 2.50
2 . . . . 1.50
3 O&I:Stinger. 1.50
4 A:Stinger 1.50
5 . . . . 1.50
6 O:Rodent 1.50
7 thru 12 . . . . @1.50

SPACED
1 I:Zip; 800 printed 40.00
2 . . . . 25.00
3 I:Dark Teddy 15.00
4 . . . . 15.00
5 and 6 . . . . @5.00
7 and 8 . . . . @2.00

Eclipse
9 . . . . 1.75
10 . . . . 1.75
11 thru 13 . . . . @1.50

SPACE PATROL
Adventure
1 thru 3 . . . . @2.50

SPACE USAGI
Mirage Studios
1 Stan Sakai,Future Usagi 2.00
2 Stan Sakai,Future Usagi 2.00
3 Stan Sakai.Future Usagi 2.00

SPACE WOLF
Antarctic Press
1 From Albedo,by Dan Flahive. . . . 2.50

SPANDEX TIGHTS
Lost Cause Prod. Jan. 1997 Vol. 2
1 . . . . 2.50
2 prelude to Space Opera 2.95
6 . . . . 2.95
Spec. Vs. Mighty Awful Sour Rangers, signed 2.95

SPANDEX TIGHTS PRESENTS: SPACE OPERA
Lost Cause Productions 1997
Part 1 by Bryan J.L. Glass & Bob Dix, parody. 2.95
Part 1, signed, Star Wars parody . . 2.95
Part 2 "Star Bored," pt.2 . . . . 2.95
Part 3 . . . . 2.95

SPANDEX TIGHTS PRESENTS: THE GIRLS OF '95
Lost Cause Productions
1 The Good, Bad and Deadly, signed (1997). 3.95

SPANDEX TIGHTS PRESENTS: WIN A DREAM DATE WITH SPANDEX-GIRL
Lost Cause Productions
1 (of 3) (1998) 2.95
2 . . . . 2.95
3 . . . . 2.95

SPANDEX TIGHTS: THE LOST ISSUES
Lost Cause Productions
1 (of 4) 2.95
2 . . . . 2.95
3 . . . . 2.95
4 concl. 2.95

SPANK THE MONKEY
Arrow Comics 1999
1 by Randy Zimmerman 2.95
2 thru 6 . . . . @2.95
Skip Month Spec.#1 . . . . 2.95

SPANK THE MONKEY ON THE COMIC MARKET
Arrow Comics 2000
1 (of 3) by Randy Zimmerman 3.25
2 . . . . 3.25

SPARKPLUG
Hero Graphics
1 From League of Champions 2.95

SPARKPLUG SPECIAL
Heroic Publishing
1 V:Overman 2.50

SPARROW
Millennium
1 I:Sparrow 2.95
2 . . . . 2.95
3 Valley of Fire 2.50

SPEED RACER
1 . . . . 3.00
1a 2nd Printing 1.50

SPENCER SPOOK
A.C.E. Comics
1 and 2 . . . . @0.95
3 thru 8 . . . . @1.75

SPICY TALES
1 thru 13 . . . . @2.00
14 thru 20 . . . . @2.25
Special #2 . . . . 2.25

SPIDER KISS
1 Harlan Ellison 3.95

SPINELESS MAN
Parody Press
1 Spider-Man 2099 spoof 2.50

SPIRIT, THE
Kitchen Sink
Note: #1 to #11 are in color
12 thru 86 WE,rep (1986–92) . . . @2.00
GN The Spirit Casebook 16.95
GN The Spirit Jam, 50 artists in 48-page (1998) 5.95

SPIRIT, THE: THE ORIGIN YEARS
Kitchen Sink 1997
1 F:The Origin of the Spirit 3.00
2 F:The Black Queen's Army 3.00
3 F:Palyachi,The Killer Clown 3.00
4 F:The Return of the Orang 3.00
5 WE 3.00
6 WE,Kiss of Death 3.00
7 F:The Kidnapping of Ebony 3.00
8 F:Christmas Spirit of 1940 . . . . . 3.00
9 WE 3.00
10 F:The Substitute Spirits 3.00

SPIRITS
Mindwalker 1995
1 thru 3 Silver City . . . . @2.95
4 Caleb Escapes Zeus 2.95

Spittin' Image
© Eclipse

SPITTIN' IMAGE
Eclipse
1 Marvel & Image parody 2.50

SQUEE
Slave Labor 1997
1 by Jhonen Vasquez 5.00
1a 2nd printing 3.00
2 . . . . 3.00
3 . . . . 3.00
4 . . . . 3.00
TPB 15.95
HC 29.95

STAIN
Fathom Press 1998
1 Byler (c) 3.00
1a Vigil (c) 3.00
1b limited edition 7.95
2 . . . . 3.00
2a Vigil (c) 3.00
3 . . . . 3.00
3a Vigil (c) 3.00
4 . . . . 3.00
4a Vigil (c) 3.00
5 King cover 3.00
5a Ang cover 3.00
6 . . . . 3.00
7 . . . . 3.00
7a nude cover 3.95

STAINLESS STEEL ARMIDILLO
Antarctic Press
1 I:Saisni, Tania Badan 2.95
2 V:Mirage 2.95
3 V:Mirage 2.95
4 Spirit of Gaia 2.95
5 V:Giant 2.95
6 finale 2.95

STAR BLEECH: THE GENERATION GAP
Parody Press
1 Parody 3.95

STARCHILD
Taliesin Press 1992–97
0 . . . . 15.00
1 . . . . 20.00
1a 2nd printing 4.00
2 . . . . 18.00
2a 2nd printing 4.00
3 . . . . 8.00
4 . . . . 6.00
5 . . . . 5.00
6 . . . . 5.00
7 . . . . 5.00
8 . . . . 5.00
9 . . . . 5.00
10 thru 13 . . . . @5.00
14 . . . . 3.00

Coppervale
TPB Coll. Ed. Awakenings, rep. #1–#12 . . . . 5.00
HC 25.00

STARCHILD: CROSSROADS
Coppervale
1 thru 4, reoffer, by James Owen @2.95
TPB Coll. Ed.112-pg. 12.00
HC Coll.Ed. 20.00
Conoisseurs Edition 100.00

STARCHILD MYTHOPOLIS
Coppervale 1997
6 (of 14) Fisher King, concl. 2.95

STARGATE: THE NEW ADVENTURES COLLECTION
Entity 1997
1 rep. Underworld; One Nation Under Ra 5.95
1a photo cover 4.95

STARGATE: ONE NATION UNDER RA
Entity March 1997
1 . . . . 2.75
1a deluxe 3.50

STARGATE: REBELLION
Entity 1997
1 (of 3) from novel, sequel to movie 2.75
1 deluxe 3.50
2 . . . . 2.75
2 deluxe 3.50
3 (of 3) 2.75
3 foil cover 3.50
GN rep. 80-pg. 7.95
GN photo (c) 7.95

STARGATE: UNDERWORLD
Entity April 1997
1 . . . . 2.75
1a deluxe 3.50

STARK FUTURE
Aircel
1 . . . . 2.50
2 thru 7 . . . . @1.75
8 . . . . 2.00
9 thru 14 . . . . @1.70

STAR RANGERS

1 thru 3 . . . . @3.00
4 . . . . 2.00

BOOK II

1 . . . . 2.00
2 . . . . 2.00

STAR REACH

Taliesin Press, 1974

1 HC,I:CodyStarbuck. 8.00
2 DG,JSn,NA(c). 2.00
3 FB 2.00
4 HC,HC(c) 2.00
5 JSon,HC(c). 2.00
6 GD,Elric 2.00
7 DS 2.00
8 CR,KSy 2.00
9 KSy 2.00
10 KSy 2.00
11 GD 2.00
12 MN,SL. 2.00
13 SL,KSy 2.00
14 . . . . 2.00
15 . . . . 2.00
16 . . . . 2.00
17 . . . . 2.00
18 . . . . 2.00

STARLIGHT AGENCY

Antartic Press

1 I:Starlight Agency 2.00
2 Anderson Kidnapped 2.00
3 . . . . 1.50

STATIC

1 SD 1.50
2 SD 1.50
3 SD 1.50

STEALTH FORCE

1 thru 8 . . . . @0.95

STEALTH SQUAD

Petra Comics

0 O:Stealth Squad. 2.50
1 I:Stealth Squad. 2.50
2 I:New Member 2.50

Volume II

1 F:Solar Blade 2.50
2 American Ranger Vs.Jericho . . . 2.50

STEELE DESTINES

Nightscapes

1 and 2 I:One Eyed Stranger . . . @2.95
3 Kidnapped by Aliens. 2.95

STERN WHEELER

Spotlight

1 JA 1.75

STEVE CANYON

Kitchen Sink

1 thru 14 . . . . @5.00
3-D Spec. #1 . . . . 6.00

STEVEN

Kitchen Sink

1 . . . . 4.00
1a 2ndPrinting. 2.95
2 . . . . 4.00
3 . . . . 2.95
4 and 5 . . . . @3.50
TPB The Best of Steven by Doug
Allen (1998) 12.95

STICKBOY

Revolutionary

1 . . . . 2.00
2 thru 5 . . . . @2.50

STIG'S INFERNO

Vortex

1 . . . . 5.00
2 . . . . 3.50
3 . . . . 3.00
4 . . . . 3.00
5 . . . . 2.00

Eclipse

6 . . . . 1.75
7 . . . . 1.75

STINZ

Fantagraphics

1 . . . . 4.00
2 . . . . 4.00
3 . . . . 4.00
4 . . . . 4.00

[2nd series]

Brave New Words

1 thru 3 . . . . @2.50

STORMBRINGER

Taliesin Press

1 thru 3 . . . . @2.00

STORMWATCHER

Eclipse

1 thru 4 . . . . @2.00

STRANGE BEHAVIOR

Twilite Tone Press

1 LSn,MBr,Short Stories 2.95

STRANGE BREW

Aardvark–Vanaheim

1 . . . . 5.00

STRANGEHAVEN

Abiogenesis Press

1 Surrealistic Comic. 2.95
2 Secret Brotherhood 2.95
3 thru 10 by Gary S. Millidge . . . @2.95
11 . . . . 2.95
12 . . . . 2.95
TPB Arcadia, rep. #1–#6. . . . . 14.95
TPB Brotherhood, rep.#7–#12 . . . 14.95

STRANGE SPORTS STORIES

Adventure 1992

1 w/2 card strip 2.50
2 The Pick-Up Game,w/cards 2.50
3 Spinning Wheels,w/cards 2.50
4 thru 6 w/cards. . . . . @2.50

STRANGE WEATHER LATELY

Metaphrog 1997

1 . . . . 3.50
2 thru 4 . . . . @3.50
5 thru 10 . . . . @3.00
TPB Vol. 1 rep. #1–#5 . . . . 9.95
HC Vol. 1 signed & numbered. . . . 40.00

Strange Sports Stories #1
© Adventure

TPB Vol. 2 . . . . 9.95
HC Vol. 2 . . . . 35.95

STRANGE WORLDS

1 . . . . 3.95
2 thru 4 . . . . @3.95

STRANGERS IN PARADISE

Antarctic Press 1993–94

1 by Terry Moore,I:Katchoo 60.00
1a 2nd printing 10.00
1b 3rd printing. 5.00
2 . . . . 40.00
3 . . . . 30.00

Abstract Studio

1 TMr, Gold Logo edition 15.00
1a 2nd printing 5.00
2 and 3, Gold Logo edition. . . . . @8.00
4 . . . . 5.00
5 R:Mrs. Parker. 6.00
6 . . . . 5.00
7 Darcey Uses Francine 5.00
8 thru 13 TMr. . . . . @4.00
HC Complete Strangers In Paradise,
Book One. 29.95

VOL. II

1 TMr, Gold Logo edition, I
Dream of You. 3.00
2 thru 13 Gold Logo . . . . @3.00
TPB I Dream of You 16.95

VOL. III

1 thru 8 See Image
9 TMr,Detective Walsh returns. . . . 2.75
10 . . . . 2.75
11. . . . . 2.75
12 . . . . 2.75
13 High School, pt.1 (of 3) 2.75
14 High School, pt.2. . . . . 2.75
15 High School, pt.3. . . . . 2.75
16A Francine/Katchoo Princess
Warrior (c) 2.75
16B Tambi Princess Warrior (c). . . . 2.75
17 . . . . 2.75
18 Francine & Datchoo. 2.75
19 Lifesize nude of Francine. 2.75
20 Night at the Opera 2.75
21 All not well in paradise. 2.75
22 The Big Rift 2.75
23 Katchoo moves out 2.75
24 steamy affairs 2.75
25 All Beach, All the Time. 2.75

Strangers in Paradise #10
© Abstract

26 . . . 2.75
27 at odds with the Big Six . . . 2.75
28 thru 35 . . . @2.75
TPB Vol.4 Love Me Tender . . . 12.95
TPB Vol.5 Immortal Enemies, rep. #6–#12 . . . 12.95
TPB Vol. 6 High School . . . 8.95
TPB Vol. 8 My Other Life . . . 14.95
HC Complete Strangers in Paradise, Volume #1 . . . 29.95
HC Complete Strangers in Paradise, Volume #2 . . . 49.95
HC Complete Strangers in Paradise Book 3, pt.1 . . . 49.95
HC Complete Strangers in Paradise Book 3, pt.2 . . . 49.95
Spec. #93268 Songs & Lyrics . . . 2.75

STRANGELOVE
Entity Comics 1995

1 I:Strangelove . . . 2.50
2 V:Hyper Bullies . . . 2.50
3 I:Bogie . . . 2.50

STRATA
Renegade 1986

1 . . . 3.00
2 . . . 2.50
3 . . . 1.70
4 . . . 1.70
5 . . . 1.70
6 . . . 2.00

STRAW MEN

1 thru 5 . . . @2.00
6 thru 8 . . . @2.25

STRAY BULLETS
El Capitan

1 . . . 15.00
1a 2nd & 3rd printing . . . 4.00
2 . . . 9.00
2a 2nd printing . . . 3.50
3 . . . 8.00
4 . . . 7.00
5 Dysfunctional Family . . . 5.00
6 F:Amy Racecar . . . 4.50
7 Virginias Freedom . . . 4.50
8 DL,"Lucky to Have Her" . . . 3.00
9 DL,"26 Guys Named Nick" . . . 3.00
10 DL,"Here Comes the Circus" . . . 3.00
11 DL,"How to Cheer Up Your Best Friend" . . . 3.00
12 DL, People Will be Hurt . . . 3.00
13 DL "Selling Candy" . . . 3.00
14 DL,The Killers arrive,4-pg. . . . 3.50
15 Sex and Violence . . . 3.00
16 . . . 3.00
17 While Ricky Fish Was Sleeping . 3.00
18 Sex and Violence, pt.2 . . . 3.00
19 Young and sexy . . . 3.00
20 Motel . . . 3.00
21 . . . 2.95
22 40-page . . . 3.50
TPB Vol. 1 Innocence of Nihilism . 11.95
HC Vol. 1 2nd printing . . . 34.95
TPB Vol. 2 . . . 11.95
HC Vol. 2 Somewhere Out West . . 34.95
TPB Vol. 3 . . . 11.95
TPB Vol. 4 . . . 11.95

STREET FIGHTER
Ocean Comics

1 thru 4 limited series . . . @1.75

STREET HEROES 2005
Eternity

1 thru 3 . . . @2.00

STREET MUSIC
Fantagraphics

1 . . . 2.75
2 . . . 2.75
3 . . . 2.95
4 . . . 2.95
5 . . . 2.50
6 . . . 3.95

STREET POET RAY
Fantagraphics

1 . . . 2.50
2 . . . 2.00
3 . . . 2.95
4 . . . 2.95

STREET WOLF

1 limited series . . . 2.00
2 and 3 . . . @2.00
Graphic Novel . . . 6.95

STRIKER: SECRET OF THE BERSERKER
Viz

1 and 2 V:The Berserker . . . @2.75
3 F:Yu and Maia . . . 2.75

STRIKER: THE ARMORED WARRIOR
Viz

1 Overture . . . 2.75
2 V:Child Esper . . . 2.75
3 Professor taken hostage . . . 2.75
GN Vol.1 The Armored Warrior . . . 16.95
GN Vol.2 Forest of No Return . . . 15.95

STYGMATA YEARBOOK
Entity

1 V:The Rodent . . . 2.95
TPB Dragon Prophet . . . 6.95

SUBTLE VIOLENTS
CFD Productions 1991

1 Linsner (c&a) . . . 25.00
1a San Diego Con . . . 80.00

SUGAR RAY FINHEAD
Wolf Press

1 I&O Sugar Ray Finhead . . . 2.50
2 I:Bessie & Big-Foot Benny the Pit Bull Man . . . 2.95
3 thru 7 Mardi Gras . . . @2.95
9 and 10 . . . @2.95

SULTRY TEENAGE SUPER-FOXES
Solson

1 thru 4 RB,Woj . . . @2.00

SUPERMODELS IN THE RAINFOREST
Sirius 1998

1 (of 3) . . . 2.95
2 and 3 . . . @2.95

SUPERSWINE
Caliber

1 Parody, I:Superswine . . . 2.50

SURVIVALIST CHRONICLES
Survival Art

1 . . . 6.50
2 . . . 6.50
3 I:Bessie & Big Foot Benny . . . 2.00

SWAN
Little Idylls

1 thru 3 Ghost of Lord Kaaren . . @2.95
4 V:Slake . . . 2.95

SWEET CHILDE: BATTLE BOOK
Advantage Graphics 1995

1 I:Tasha Radcliffe . . . 2.50

SWEET CHILDE: LOST CONFESSIONS
Anarchy Bridgeworks 1997

1 F:Tasha Radcliffe . . . 2.95

SWEET LUCY
Brainstorm Comics

1 with 4 cards . . . 2.50
2 . . . 2.50

SWERVE
Amaze Ink Dec. 1995

1 thru 3 by Kyle Hunter . . . @1.75

SWIFTSURE
Harrier Comics

1 . . . 2.00
2 . . . 2.00
3 thru 8 . . . @1.75
9 . . . 9.00
9a 2nd printing . . . 1.75
10 . . . 1.75
11 . . . 2.00

SWITCH B.L.A.Z.E. MANGA
London Night 1999

0 . . . . 3.50
0a nude Japanese cover 6.00
½ Con special 4.95
½ Con special, Japanese (c) 6.00
1 . . . . 3.50
1a Elite fan ed. 6.00
1b Anime cell ed.. . . . . 19.95

SWORD OF VALOR
A Plus Comics

1 JAp,rep.Thane of Bagarth. 2.50
2 JAp/MK rep 2.50

SWORDS AND SCIENCE
Pyramid

1 thru 3 . . . . @1.70

SWORDS OF CEREBUS
Aardvark–Vanaheim

1 rep. Cerebus 1-4 . . . . 15.00
1a reprint editions 10.00
2 rep. Cerebus 5-8 . . . . 12.00
2a reprint editions 8.00
3 rep. Cerebus 9-12. . . . . 12.00
3a reprint editions 8.00
4 rep. Cerebus 13-16. . . . . 12.00
4a reprint editions 8.00
5 rep. Cerebus 17-20. . . . . 12.00
5a reprint editions 8.00
6 rep. Cerebus 21-25. . . . . 12.00
6a reprint editions 8.00

SWORDS OF SHAR-PAI
Caliber 1991

1 Mutant Ninja Dog 2.50
2 Shar-Pei. 2.50
3 Final issue 2.50

SWORDS OF VALORS: ROBIN HOOD
A Plus Comics

1 rep. of Charlton comics. 2.50

SYSTEM SEVEN
Arrow

1 thru 4 . . . . @1.50

TAKEN UNDER COMPENDIUM
Caliber

1 rep. Cal Presents #19-#22 . . . . . 2.95

TALES FROM DIMENSION X
Edge Publishing 1995

1 Dinosaur Mansion. 3.95

TALES FROM THE ANIVERSE
Arrow

1 7,400 printed 9.00
2 . . . . 4.00
3 10,000 printed 2.50
4 . . . . 2.50

[2nd series]
Massive Comics Group

1 thru 3 . . . . @1.50

TALES FROM THE EDGE
Vanguard

5 . . . . 2.95
5 signed 5.95
6 . . . . 2.95
7 . . . . 2.95
7 signed 5.95
8 . . . . 2.95
8 signed 5.95
9 . . . . 2.95
10 . . . . 2.95
10 signed 5.95
11 F:Sacred Monkeys. 2.95
12 spec.F:Steranko 4.00
12 signed, limited 15.00
13 F:Steranko. 2.95
14 . . . . 2.95
15 Sienkiewicz special 4.00
Spec. Nightstand Chillers Benefit Edition 4.95
Spec. Nightstand Chillers, signed . 10.00
Spec. Sienkiewicz Special 10.00

TALES FROM THE HEART

1 thru 5 . . . . @1.75
6 . . . . 2.00
7 . . . . 2.00

TALES OF BEANWORLD
Eclipse

1 . . . . 10.00
2 . . . . 4.00
3 . . . . 2.50
4 I:Beanish 1.50
5 thru 20 . . . . @2.00

TALES OF TEENAGE MUTANT NINJA TURTLES

1 . . . . 8.00
1B 2nd printing 3.00
2 . . . . 8.00
3 . . . . 5.00
4 . . . . 5.00
5 . . . . 5.00
6 thru 9 . . . . @4.00

TALES OF THE FEHNRIK
Antarctic Press

1 I:Lady Zeista. 2.95

TALES OF THE JACKALOPE
BF

1 . . . . 4.00
2 . . . . 3.00
3 and 4 . . . . @2.50
5 thru 9 . . . . @2.00

TALES OF THE NINJA WARRIORS
CFW

1 thru 14 . . . . @2.00
15 thru 19. . . . . @2.25

TALES OF THE PLAGUE
Eclipse

1 RCo 4.00

Tales Too Terrible to Tell #3
© New England Comics

TALES TOO TERRIBLE TO TELL
New England Comics

1 thru 6 Pre-code horror stories . @3.50

TALL TAILS
Vision Comics March 1998

1 Earth Shaking. 2.95
1a Anime Blast cover. 2.95
1b Spell Warrior cover 2.95
1c nude variant cover 3.95
1d signed 4.95
2 Fire Quest, Pt.1 . . . . 2.95
2a nude variant cover 3.95
3 Fire Quest, Pt.2 . . . . 2.95
4 Pain and Compromises,pt.1 . . . . 2.95
5 . . . . 2.95
6 Trail Blazing, pt.1 . . . . 2.95
7 Trail Blazing, pt.2 . . . . 2.95
8 When It Almost Happened 2.95
GN Vol. 1 . . . . 8.95

TANTALIZING STORIES
Tundra

1 F:Frank & Montgomery Wart. . . . 2.25
2 Frank & Mont.stories cont. 2.25

TAOLAND
Sunitek

1 V:The Crocodile Warlord. 1.50
2 and 3 I:New Enemy. . . . . @3.25

TASK FORCE ALPHA
Academy Comics

1 I:Task Force Alpha 3.50

TEAM NIPPON
Aircel

1 thru 7 . . . . @2.00

TECHNOPHILIA
Brainstorm Comics

1 with 4 cards 2.50

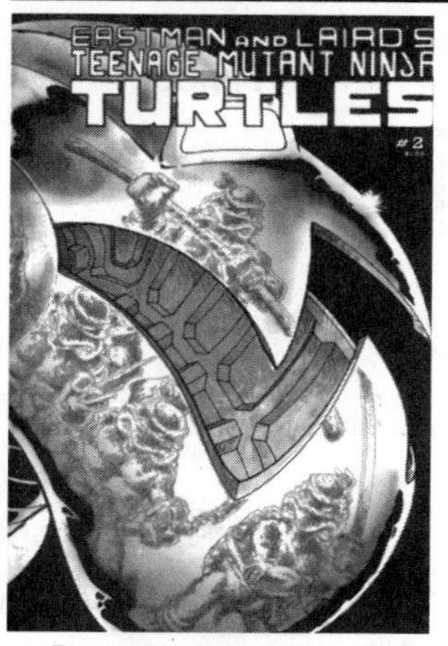

Teenage Mutant Ninja Turtles #2
© Mirage Studios

TEENAGE MUTANT NINJA TURTLES*
Mirage Studios
***Counterfeits Exist - Beware**

1 I:Turtles 150.00
1a 2nd printing 25.00
1b 3rd printing 20.00
1c 4th printing 12.00
1d 5th printing 4.00
2 . . . . 50.00
2a 2nd printing 12.00
2b 3rd printing 4.00
3 . . . . 20.00
3a 2nd printing 3.50
3b Special printing,rare 50.00
4 . . . . 8.00
4a 2nd printing 3.50
5 A:Fugitoid 7.00
5a 2nd printing 3.50
6 A:Fugitoid 7.00
6a 2nd printing 2.50
7 A:Fugitoid 8.00
7a 2nd printing 2.50
8 A:Cerebus 9.00
9 . . . . 7.00
10 V:Shredder 7.00
11 A:Casey Jones 6.00
12 thru 18 . . . . @6.00
19 Return to NY 4.00
20 Return to NY 4.00
21 Return to NY,D:Shredder 4.00
22 thru 32 . . . . @4.00
33 color, Corben 3.50
34 Toytle Anxiety 3.50
35 Souls Withering 3.50
36 Souls Wake 3.50
37 Twilight of the Rings 3.50
38 Spaced Out Pt.1, A:President Bush 3.50
39 Spaced Out Pt.2 . . . . 3.50
40 Spaced Out concl.,I:Rockin' Rollin' Miner Ants (B.U. story) . . 2.00
41 Turtle Dreams issue 2.00
42 Juliets Revenge 2.00
43 Halls of Lost Legends 2.00
44 V:Ninjas 2.00
45 A:Leatherhead 2.00
46 V:Samurai Dinosaur 2.00
47 Space Usagi 2.00
48 Shades of Grey Part 1 . . . . 2.00
49 Shades of Grey Part 2 . . . . 2.00
50 Eastman/Laird,new direction, inc.TM,EL,WS pin-ups 2.00
51 City at War #2 . . . . 2.00
52 City at War #3 . . . . 2.25
53 City at War #4 . . . . 2.25
54 City at War #5 . . . . 2.25
55 thru 65 . . . . @2.25
1990 Movie adaptation 6.50
Spec. The Haunted Pizza 2.25

Volume 2

1 thru 8 . . . . @2.75
9 V:Baxter Bot 2.75
10 Mr. Braunze 2.75
11 F:Raphael 2.75
12 V:DARPA 2.75
13 J:Triceraton 2.75

TMNT TRAINING MANUAL

1 . . . . 5.00
2 thru 5 . . . . @3.00

TEMPEST COMICS PRESENTS
Academy Comics

1 I:Steeple, Nemesis 2.50

TERROR ON THE PLANET OF THE APES
Adventure Comics 1991

1 MP,collectors edition 2.50
2 MP, the Forbidden Zone 2.50
3 . . . . 2.50

TERROR TALES
Eternity

1 Short stories 2.50

TERRY AND THE PIRATES
ACG Comics 1998

1 by Georges Wunder, Charlton reprint 3.00
2 . . . . 2.95
3 . . . . 2.95

TEX BENSON
Metro Comics

1 thru 3 . . . . @2.00

39 SCREAMS

1 thru 6 . . . . @2.00

THEY WERE 11
Viz

1 Galactic University 2.75
2 The Accident 2.75
3 Virus 2.75
4 V:Virus 2.75

THIEVES AND KINGS
I Box 1994–97

1 F:Ruebel The Intrepid 8.00
1a 2nd printing 2.50
2 . . . . 6.00
2a 2nd printing 2.50
3 . . . . 5.00
3a 2nd printing 2.50
4 . . . . 4.00
5 . . . . 4.00
6 V:Shadow Lady 4.00
7 V:Shadow Lady 2.50
8 thru 18 by Mark Oakley . . . . . . @2.50
19 thru 24 . . . . @2.35
25 thru 33 . . . . @2.50
TPB Vol. 1: The Red Book, rep.#1–#6 . . . . 12.00
TPB Vol. 1: 2nd printing 13.50
TPB Vol. 2: The Green Book 14.00
TPB Vol. 2: 2nd printing 16.50
TPB Vol. 3: The Blue Book 16.50

THORR SUERD OR SWORD OF THOR

1 . . . . 3.00
1a 2nd printing 2.00
2 . . . . 1.75
3 . . . . 1.50

THOSE ANNOYING POST BROS.
Aeon

52 thru 56 . . . . @2.95
57 Russ working on chaos wave . . . 2.95
58 Fearsome chaos wave 2.95
59 Recondite Silicates 2.95
60 . . . . 2.95
61 Assassinate JFK's ghost 2.95
62 Post Digestion 64-pg. 5.95
63 . . . . 5.95
GN Distrub the Neighbors 10.00
Ann. #3 Before the Flood, 56-pg. . . 4.95
TPB Das Loot 14.95

THREAT

1 . . . . 5.00
2 . . . . 3.00
3 and 4 . . . . @2.00
5 thru 10 . . . . @2.25

3 X 3 EYES
Innovation

1 Labyrinth o/t DemonsEyePt.1 . . . 2.25
2 Labyrinth o/t DemonsEyePt.2 . . . 2.25
3 Labyrinth o/t DemonsEyePt.3 . . . 2.25
4 Labyrinth o/t DemonsEyePt.4 . . . 2.25
5 Labyrinth o/t DemonsEye conc. . 2.25

THREE GEEKS, THE
3 Finger Prints 1997

1 by Rich Koslowski, Going to the Con, pt.1 . . . . 2.50
2 Going to the Con, pt.2 . . . . 2.50
3 Going to the Con, pt.3 (of 3) 2.50
4 . . . . 2.50
5 five more geeks 2.50
6 F:Allen 2.50
7 . . . . 2.50
8 48-page 3.50
9 24-page 2.50
10 Happy Birthday Allen 2.50
10a variant cover 3.50
11 Happy Birthday Allen, pt.2 . . . . . 2.50
TPB 8.95

THREE MUSKETEERS

1 . . . . 2.00
2 . . . . 2.00
3 . . . . 2.00

THREE ROCKETEERS
Eclipse

1 JK,AW,rep. 2.00
2 JK,AW,rep. 2.00

THRESHOLD
Avatar Press 1998

1 Snowman cover 4.50
1a Tales of the Cyberangels cover . 4.50

1b Tales of the Cyberangels, nude cover 6.00
1c Furies cover 4.50
1d Furies, nude cover 6.00
1e Fuzzie Dice cover 4.50
2 Snowman cover 4.95
2a Tales of the Cyberangels cover. 4.95
2b Tales of the Cyberangels, nude cover 6.00
2c Furies cover 4.95
2d Furies, nude cover 6.00
2e Pandora cover 4.95
3 Ravening (c) 4.95
3a Ravening Nude (c) 6.00
3b Tales of the Cyberangels (c) . . . 4.95
3c Calico (c) 4.95
3d Pandora (c) 4.95
3e Pandora nude (c) 6.00
4 Donna Mia (c) 4.95
4a Dona Mia nude (c) 6.00
4b Lookers (c) 4.95
4c Lookers nude (c) 6.00
4d Black Reign (c) 4.95
4e Journeymen (c) 4.95
5 Black Reign (c) 4.95
5a Journeymen (c) 4.95
5b Midnight Doyle (c) 4.95
5c Midnight Doyle nude (c) 6.00
5d Widow (c) 4.95
5e Widow nude (c) 6.00
6 Luna cover 4.95
6a Pandora (c) 4.95
6b Onyx (c) 4.95
6c Onyx nude (c) 6.00
7 Darkness in Collision, Cavewoman(c) 4.95
7a Ravening (c) 4.95
7b 777 Wrath (c) 4.95
7c 777 Wrath nude (c) 6.00
8 Vigil/Cuda (c) 4.95
8a Lookers (c) 4.95
8b Cyberangels (c) 4.95
8c Cyberangels nude (c) 6.00
9 August (c) 4.95
9a Cyberangels (c) 4.95
9b Donna Mia (c) 4.95
9c Donna Mia nude (c) 6.00
10 Calico (c) 4.95
10a Cyberangels (c) 4.95
10b Pandora (c) 4.95
10c Pandor nude (c) 6.00
11 Scythe (c) 4.95
11a Twilight (c) 4.95
11b Wicked (c) 4.95
11c Maelstrom Nude (c) 6.00
12 Snowman (c) 4.95
12a Pandora (c) 4.95
12b Midnight Doyle (c) 4.95
12c Midnight Doyle nude (c) 6.00
13 Snowman (c) 4.95
13a Pandora (c) 4.95
13b Harpy (c) 4.95
13c Pandor nude (c) 6.00
14 Kaos Moon (c) 4.95
14a Ravening (c) 4.95
14b Calico (c) 4.95
14c Ravening nude (c) 6.00
15 Luna (c) 4.95
15a Avatars (c) 4.95
15b Ravening (c) 4.95
15c Ravening nude (c) 6.00
16 Scythe (c) 4.95
16a Avatars (c) 4.95
16b Cimmerian (c) 4.95
16c Maelstrom nude (c) 6.00
17 Cimmerian (c) 4.95
17a Harpy (c) 4.95
17b Nightvision (c) 4.95
17c Cimmerian nude (c) 6.00
18 Nightvision (c) 4.95
18a Harpy (c) 4.95
18b Furies (c) 4.95
18c Furies nude (c) 6.00
19 Pandora (c) 4.95
19a Wilde Knight (c) 4.95
19b Furies (c) 4.95
19c Furies nude (c) 6.00
20 Kaos Moon (c) 4.95
20a Furies (c) 4.95
20b Ravening (c) 4.95
20c Ravening nude (c) 6.00
21 Jungle Girl (c) 4.95
21a Harpy (c) 4.95
21b Onyx (c) 4.95
21c Jungle Girl nude (c) 6.00
22 . . . . . 4.95
22a 4.95
22b 4.95
22c nude (c) 6.00
23 Ravening (c) 4.95
23a Fauna (c) 4.95
23b Dream Wolves (c) 4.95
23c nude (c) 6.00
24 Faust: Singha's Talons 4.95
24a Fauna (c) 4.95
24b Pandora (c) 4.95
24c Singha's Talons adult (c) 6.00
25 Dark Blue (c) 4.95
25a Pandora (c) 4.95
25b Pandora nude (c) 6.00
25c Fauna nude (c) 6.00
26 Dark Blue (c) 4.95
26a Lookers (c) 4.95
26b Lookers nude (c) 6.00
26c Pandora nude (c) 6.00
27 Dark blue (c) 4.95
27a Lookers (c) 4.95
27b Lookers adult (c) 6.00
27c Dream Wolves nude (c) 6.00
28 Dark blue (c) 4.95
28a Webwitch (c) 4.95
28b Webwitch adult (c) 6.00
28c Ravening nude (c) 6.00
29 Dark Blue (c) 4.95
29a Webwitch (c) 4.95
29b Webwitch adult (c) 6.00
29c Ravening nude (c) 6.00
30 Dark Blue (c) 4.95
30a Luna (c) 4.95
30b Luna nude (c) 6.00
30c Medora nude (c) 6.00
31 Luna (c) 4.95
31a Medora (c) 4.95
31b Tuff Luv nude (c) 6.00
31c Medora nude (c) 6.00
32 Ravening (c) 4.95
32a Tuff Luv (c) 4.95
32b Medora nude (c) 6.00
32c Ravening nude (c) 6.00
33 Pandora (c) 4.95
33a Tundra (c) 4.95
33b Pandora nude (c) 6.00
33c Medora adult (c) 6.00

THRESHOLD OF REALITY

1 5,000 printed 2.50
2 thru 4 . . . . . @2.00

THRILLKILL
Caliber

1 rep. Caliber Presents #1-#4 . . . . 2.50

THUNDERBIRD
Newcomers Publishing

1 and 2 Two Stories . . . . . @2.95
3 . . . . . 2.95
4 I:Mercer 2.95
5 R:Raven 2.95
6 and 7 . . . . . @2.95
8 final issue 3.50
Ann.#1 The Great Escape 3.50

THUNDERBUNNY

1 O:Thunder Bunny 2.50
2 VO:Dr.Fog 2.00
3 I:GoldenMan 1.75
4 V:Keeper 1.75
5 I:Moon Mess 1.75
6 V:Mr.Endall 1.75
7 VI:Dr.Fog 1.75
8 . . . . . 1.75
9 VS:Gen. Agents 1.75
10 thru 12 . . . . . @1.75

THUNDERMICE

1 Proto type-blue & red very rare:1,000 printed 15.00
1a four color cover 3.00
2 thru 5 . . . . . @1.75
6 . . . . . 2.00
7 . . . . . 2.00
Graphic Novel, rep.1-4 . . . . . 5.00

Tick #6
© New England Comics

TICK
New England Comics

1 BEd 45.00
1a 2nd printing 10.00
1b 3rd printing 5.00
1c 4th printing 2.50
2 BEd 45.00
2a 2nd printing 10.00
2b 3rd printing 4.00
2c 4th printing 2.50
3 BEd 12.00
3a 2nd printing 2.50
4 BEd 8.00
4a 2nd printing 2.50
5 BEd 8.00
6 BEd 7.00
7 BEd,A:Chairface Chippendale. . . 7.00
8 BEd 6.00
8a Spec.No Logo edition 12.00
9 BEd,A:Chainsaw Vigilante, Red Eye 5.00
10 BEd 5.00
11 and 12 BEd . . . . . @4.00
9 thru 12, new printings . . . . . @2.95
Spec. Ed. #1, I:Tick 25.00
Spec. Ed. #2, 2nd App. Tick 20.00
Spec. #1 Reprise edition 5.95
TPB Omnibus #1 rep. #1–#6 . . . . . 17.95
TPB Omnibus #2 BEd,fifth printing 14.95
TPB Omnibus #3 BEd 10.95
TPB Omnibus #4 BEd 10.95

The Tick Big Yule Log Special 1998 3.50
The Tick Big Yule Log Special 1999 3.50
Big Giant Summer Special #1, The
Sidekicks are Revolting 3.50
Big Summer Annual #1. . . . . 3.50
TPB Tick Bonanza #3. . . . . 4.95
TPB Tick Bonanza #4. . . . . 4.95
Spec.#1 Back to School 3.50
Big Halloween Special #1 . . . . 3.50
Massive Summer Double Spectacle
Photo-Cover set of 2 . . . . 7.95
13 Pseudo-Tick, not by Edlund 3.50
Big Year 2000 Spectacle. 3.50
Big Romantic Adventure #1, 2nd ed.3.50
Big Tax Time Terror #1 . . . . 3.50
Big Mother's Day Spec. #1 . . . . 3.50
Big Halloween Special 2000 . . . . . . 3.50
Big Father's Day Special 3.50
Big Cruise Ship Vacation Spec.#1. . 3.50
Massive Summer Double Spec.#1 . 3.50
Massive Summer Double Spec.#2 . 3.50

TICK AND ARTHUR, THE
New England Comics 1999

1 by Sean Wang & Mike Baker . . . 3.50
2 Return of the Thorn,pt.2 . . . . 3.50
3 Return of the Thorn,pt.3 . . . . 3.50
4 Tick & Arthur meet Flea & Doyle. 3.50
5 Flea & Doyle superheroes? 3.50
6 Chainsaw Vigilantes 3.50
TPB Bonanza #1 rep. #1–#3. . . . . . 5.50
TPB Bonanza #2 rep. #4–#6. . . . . . 5.50

TICK, THE: BIG BLUE DESTINY
New England Comics 1997

1 by Eli Stone, Keen edition. 3.00
1 Wicked Keen edition. 5.00
2A cover A 3.00
3B cover B 3.00
3 . . . . 3.50
4 . . . . 3.50
5 The Chrysalis Crisis 3.50

TICK CIRCUS MAXIMUS
New England Comics 2000

1 (of 4) by Sean Wang. 3.50
2 . . . . 3.50
3 . . . . 3.50
4 concl. 3.50

Tick: Giant Circus of the Mighty #2
© New England Press

TICK: GIANT CIRCUS OF THE MIGHTY
New England Press

1 A-O 3.00
2 P-Z. 3.00
3 . . . . 3.00

TICK, THE: HEROES OF THE CITY
New England Comics 1999

1 three stories 3.50
2 . . . . 3.50
3 . . . . 3.50
4 . . . . 3.50
5 . . . . 3.50
6 . . . . 3.50
TPB Bonanza #1 rep. #1–#3. . . . . . 5.50
TPB Bonanza #2 rep. #4–#6. . . . . . 5.50

TICK: KARMA TORNADO
New England Press

1 . . . . 4.00
1 2nd printing 3.00
2 . . . . 3.50
2 2nd printing 3.00
3 thru 9 . . . . @3.50
3 thru 9 2nd printings . . . . @3.00
TPB #1 second edition 13.95
TPB Bonanza Edition, Vol.2 . . . . . . 4.95
TPB Bonanza Edition, Vol.3 . . . . . . 4.95

TICK, THE: LUNY BIN
New England Comics 1998

1 (of 3) by Eli Stone, Back to
the Luny Bin. 3.50
2 To the Rescue 3.50
3 Six Eyes in Tears 3.50
Preview Special, 32-pg. 1.50
TPB Luny Bin Trilogy 120-page . . . 4.95

TICK OMNIBUS
New England Press

1 1 to 6 Rep. 14.95

TICK'S BACK, THE
New England Comics

0 by Eli Stone, V:Toy DeForce 3.00

TIGERS OF TERRA
Mind-Visions

1 6,000 printed 4.50
1a Signed & Num. 14.00
2 . . . . 2.00
2a Signed & Num. 11.00
5 thru 7 . . . . @3.50
8 thru 10 . . . . @3.75

Antarctic

11 and 12 . . . . @3.95

[Vol. 2]

0 thru 14 . . . . @2.75
15 Totenkopf Police,pt.2 . . . . 2.75
16 Battleship Arizona,pt.3. . . . . 2.75
17 thru 22. . . . . @2.95
23 "Trouble with Tigers" pt.3 . . . . . 2.95
24 48-pg. 10th Anniv. 3.95
25 "Battle for Terra" pt.1 . . . . 2.95
TPB Book Two 9.95
TPB Book Three. 9.95
TPB Book Four. 9.95

TIGRESS
Hero Graphics

3 A:Lady Arcane 2.95
4 inc. B.U. Mudpie. 2.95

TIGER-X
Eternity

Special #1 . . . . 2.50
Spec. #1a 2nd printing 2.25
1 thru 3 . . . . @2.00

Book II

1 thru 4 . . . . @2.00

TIME DRIFTERS
Innovation

1 . . . . 2.25
2 . . . . 2.25
3 . . . . 2.25

TIME GATES
Double Edge

1 SF series,The Egg #1. . . . . 2.00
2 The Egg #2 . . . . 2.00
3 Spirit of the Dragon #1 . . . . 2.00
4 Spirit of the Dragon #2 . . . . 2.00
4a Var.cover 2.00

TIME JUMP WAR
Apple

1 thru 3 . . . . @2.00

TIME MACHINE

1 thru 3 . . . . @2.50

TIME TRAVELER AI
CPM Manga 1999

1 by Ai Ijima &
Takeshi Takebayashi 2.95
2 thru 13 . . . . @2.95
TPB Book One, rep. 15.95

TIME WARRIORS
Fantasy General

1 rep.Alpha Track #1 . . . . 1.50
1a Bi-Weekly. 0.75
2 . . . . 0.75
3 . . . . 0.75

TITANESS
Draculina Publishing 1995

1 I:Titaness,Tomboy. 2.95

TO BE ANNOUNCED

1 thru 6 . . . . @1.50

TOMB TALES
Cryptic Entertainment

1 . . . . 3.00
2 . . . . 3.00
3 . . . . 3.00
4 A Rare Gem. 3.00
5 . . . . 3.00
6 The Flame Game 3.00
7 Invasion of the Shoddy Snatchers3.00

TOM CORBETT, SPACE CADET
Eternity

1 . . . . 2.00
2 . . . . 2.00

3 . . . . 2.25
4 . . . . 2.25

TOM CORBETT II

1 . . . . 2.25
2 . . . . 2.25
3 . . . . 2.25
4 . . . . 2.25

TOM MIX HOLIDAY ALBUM

Amazing Comics

1 . . . . 3.50

TOM MIX WESTERN

AC Comics

1 . . . . 2.50
2 . . . . 2.50

TOMMI GUNN: KILLERS LUST

London Night Jan. 1997

1 . . . . 3.00
1a nude cover 6.00
1 photo cover 6.00
3 nude cover, signed 12.00
Ann. #1 . . . . 3.00
Ann. #1a nude cover edition 3.00

TOMMY & THE MONSTERS

1 thru 3 . . . . @2.00

TOMORROW MAN

Antarctic

1 R:Tommorrow Man 2.95
Spec.#1 48-page 3.95

TOO MUCH COFFEE MAN

Adhesive Comics 1995

1 F:Too Much Coffee Man 16.00
1a 2nd printing 4.00
2 Wheeler (s&a) 8.00
3 Wheeler (s&a) 5.00
4 In love 5.00
5 thru 7 . . . . @4.00
8 thru 10 . . . . @2.95

TORG

Adventure

1 Based on Role Playing Game . . . 2.50
2 thru 3 Based on Game . . . . . . @2.50

TOR JOHNSON: HOLLYWOOD STAR

Monster Comics

1 Biographical story 2.50

TORRID AFFAIRS

1 . . . . 2.25
2 . . . . 2.25
3 thru 5, 60-page . . . . @2.95

TOTALLY ALIEN

1 . . . . 17.00
2 . . . . 12.00
3 . . . . 8.00

TOUGH GUYS AND WILD WOMEN

Eternity

1 . . . . 2.25
2 . . . . 2.25

TRACKER

Blackthorne

1 . . . . 2.00
2 . . . . 1.75
3 . . . . 2.00
4 . . . . 2.00

TRANSIT

1 . . . . 2.00
2 thru 6 . . . . @1.75

TRICKSTER KING MONKEY

1 thru 5 . . . . @1.75

TRIDENT

1 thru 7 . . . . @3.50
8 . . . . 4.50

TRIMUVERATE

Mermaid Productions

1 I:Trimverate 2.25
2 and 3 Team captured . . . . @2.25
4 V:Ord,Ael 2.25

TROLLORDS

Tru Studios 1986

1 1st printing 5.00
1a 2nd printing 2.00
2 . . . . 3.00
3 . . . . 2.00
4 thru 15 . . . . @1.50
#1 special 1.75

TROLLORDS

Apple Comics 1989–90

1 thru 6 . . . . @2.50

TROLLORDS

Caliber/Tapestry 1996

1 and 2 . . . . @2.95

TROLLORDS: DEATH & KISSES

1 . . . . 2.00
2 thru 5 . . . . @2.25

TROUBLE SHOOTERS

Nightwolf

1 I:Trouble Shooters 2.50
2 V:Ifrit,Djin,Ghul 2.50
3 V:Morgath. 2.50

TROUBLE WITH GIRLS

Eternity 1989–91

1 . . . . 3.00
2 . . . . 2.50
3 thru 14 . . . . @2.00
15 thru 21 . . . . @2.25
22 Lester's Origin 2.25
Ann. #1 . . . . 2.95
Graphic Novel 7.95
Graphic Novel #2 . . . . 7.95
Xmas special `World of Girls' 2.95

The Trouble With Girls #15
© Eternity

NEW SERIES

1 thru 4 see color

5 thru 11 . . . . @2.00

TROUBLE WITH TIGERS

Antarctic Press

1 NinjaHighSchool/Tigers x-over . . 2.00
2 . . . . 2.00

TRUE CRIME

Eclipse

1 and 2 . . . . @2.95

TRUFAN ADVENTURES THEATRE

1 . . . . 7.00
2 3-D issue 5.00

TURTLE SOUP

1 A:TMNT 6.00

TURTLES TEACH KARATE

Solson

1 . . . . 4.00
2 . . . . 3.50

TWILIGHT AVENGER

Eternity

1 thru 18 . . . . @2.00

Miracle Studios

Spec. Twilight Avenger Super Summer Special. 2.75

TWILIGHT X QUARTERLY

Antarctic Press

1 thru 3 by Joseph Wright . . . . . @2.95
4 Celebration. 2.95

TWIST

Kitchen Sink

1 . . . . 2.00
2 and 3 . . . . @2.00

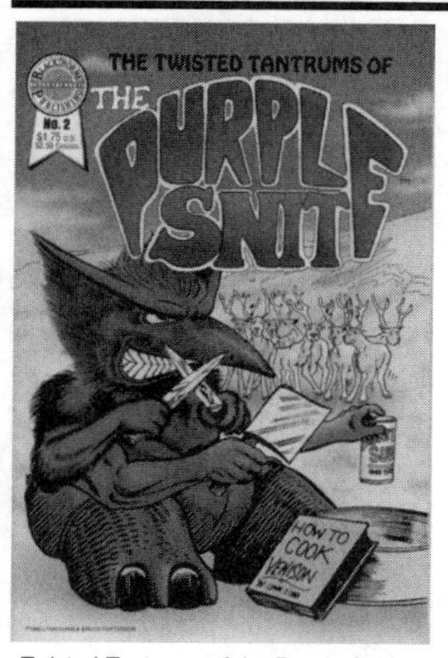

Twisted Tantrums of the Purple Snit #2 © Blackthorne

TWISTED TANTRUMS OF THE PURPLE SNIT

Blackthorne 1986

1 . . . . 2.50
2 . . . . 2.00

2001 NIGHTS

Viz 1990–91

1 by Yukinobu Hoshino 5.00
2 . . . . 4.00
3 thru 5 . . . . @3.75
6 thru 10 . . . . @4.25

TYRANNY REX

Fleetway

GN reps. from 2000A.D. 7.95

ULTIMATE STRIKE

London Night 1996

1 . . . . 2.00
1 holochrome edition 15.00
1a nude commemorative edition . . 5.00
2 . . . . 2.00
3 . . . . 2.00
4 . . . . 2.00
4 Photo nude cover 5.00
5 . . . . 2.00
5 Photo nude cover 5.00
6 sequel to Strike #0 . . . . 2.00
6 limited nude cover 5.00
7 by Kevin Hill, "Stryke: Year One" concl. 2.00
7 limited nude cover 5.00
8 Year One,. 2.00
8a nude cover 5.00
9 Year One, cont. 2.00
9a Nude cover. 5.00
10 . . . . 2.00
10a Nude cover. 5.00
11. . . . . 2.00
11a Nude cover. 5.00
12 . . . . 2.00
12a Nude cover. 5.00

ULTRA KLUTZ

Onward Comics

1 . . . . 2.50
2 thru 18 . . . . @1.50
19 thru 24. . . . . @1.75
25 thru 30. . . . . @2.00

Bad Habit

TBP Book One, rep. #1–#23. . . . . 29.95

UNCANNY MAN-FROG

Mad Dog

1 and 2 . . . . @1.75

UNCENSORED MOUSE

Eternity

1 Mickey Mouse 10.00
2 Mickey Mouse. 11.00

UNFORGIVEN, THE

Trinity Comics Ministries

Mission of Tranquility

1 thru 6 V:Dormian Grath . . . . . . @2.00
7 I:Faith. 2.00

UNICORN ISLE

Genesis West

1 . . . . 2.50
2 . . . . 1.50
3 . . . . 1.50

Apple

4 thru 6 . . . . @1.75

UNLEASHED

Caliber Press

1 F:Carson Davis. 2.95
2 V:North Harbor Crime. 2.95

UNSUPERVISED EXISTENCE

1 . . . . 2.00
2 and 3 . . . . @2.50

UNTOUCHABLES

1 thru 20 . . . . @.75

UNTOUCHABLES

Caliber 1997

1K by Joe Pruett & John Kissee, MK(c). 2.95
1S Showman (c) 2.95
2 . . . . 2.95
3 MK (c) 2.95
4 MK (c) 2.95
HC New Beginning 19.95
Spec. The High Society Killer (1998)3.95

USAGI YOJIMBO

Fantagraphics 1987

1 SS 8.00
1a 2nd printing 5.00
2 SS,Samurai 8.00
3 SS,Samurai,A:Croakers 6.00
4 SS 5.00
5 thru 7 SS . . . . @5.00
8 SS,A Mother's Love 5.00
8a 2nd printing 3.00
9 SS 5.00
10 SS,A:Turtles 5.00
10a 2nd printing 3.00
11 thru 18 SS . . . . @4.00
19 SS,Frost & Fire,A:Nelson Groundthumper 4.00
20 and 21 SS . . . . @4.00
22 SS,A:Panda Khan 4.00
23 SS,V:Ninja Bats 4.00
24 SS. 4.00
25 SS,A:Lionheart 4.00
26 SS,Gambling 4.00
27 SS. 4.00
28 thru 31 SS,Circles pt.1–4 . . . . @4.00
32 . . . . 4.00
33 SS,Ritual Murder 4.00
34 thru 37 . . . . @4.00
Spec.#1 SS,SummerSpec, C:Groo 45.00
TPB Vol. 4, rep. 16.95
TPB Vol. 6, rep., new printing . . . 12.95
TPB Vol. 7, Gen's Story 16.95

Radio Comix

Vol. 1 The Art of Usagi Yojimbo . . . 3.95

VALENTINO

Renegade

1 . . . . 1.70
2 and 3 . . . . @2.00

VALOR THUNDERSTAR

1 and 2 . . . . @1.75

VAMPEROTICA

Brainstorm Comics

1 I:Luxura 8.00
1a 2nd & 3rd printing. 3.00
2 . . . . 6.00
2 2nd printing 3.00
3 . . . . 4.00
4 I:Blood Hunters. 4.00
5 Deadshot 4.00
6 Deadshot 4.00
7 Baptism 4.00
8 Pains,Peepers 4.00
9 thru 11 . . . . @4.00
12 thru 16 . . . . @3.00
17 thru 22 see: color
20 signed 5.00
20 nude cover, signed 5.00
21 nude cover, signed 5.00
23 . . . . 3.00
23a nude edition. 3.00
23 encore edition 2.95
23a encore edition, nude cover . . . 3.95
24 . . . . 3.00
24a nude cover 3.00
25 . . . . 3.00
25a deluxe, nude cover 3.00
26 . . . . 3.00
26a nude cover 3.00
26a nude cover 3.95
27 . . . . 3.00
27 Nude Luxury edition. 5.00
28 A:China & Jazz 3.00
28a nude cover 3.00
28 Nude Luxury edition. 5.00
28 Nude Luxury edition, signed. . . . 5.00
29 mild cover 3.00
30 Legends of Luxura x-over, concl. 2.95
30a nude cover 3.95
31 V:Red Militia 2.95
31a nude cover 3.95
32 . . . . 2.95
32a nude cover 3.95
33 by Kirk Lindo 2.95
33a nude cover 3.95
34 V:Pontius Vanthor 2.95
34a nude cover edition 5.00
34b luxury edition 5.00
35 . . . . 2.95
35a nude cover 5.00
36 I:Countess Vladimira 2.95
36a nude cover edition 3.95
36a photo cover edition 3.95
37 . . . . 2.95
37 nude cover 2.95
37 statue cover. 2.95
38 . . . . 2.95
38 nude cover 3.95

38 nude luxury edition 5.00
39 Death From Above, pt.1 . . . . 2.95
39a nude cover 3.95
39b nude embrace cover 3.95
40 Death From Above, pt.2 . . . . 2.95
40a nude cover 3.95
40a nude embrace cover 3.95
41 . . . . 3.00
41a nude cover 4.00
42 Hostile Seduction 3.00
42a nude cover 4.00
43 Harvest 3.00
43a nude cover 4.00
44 F:Luxura 3.00
44a nude cover 4.00
45 The Kindred Kill 3.00
45a nude cover 4.00
45b photo cover 4.00
46 Murder Most Foul 3.00
46a nude cover 4.00
47 Camelot 3.00
47a nude cover 4.00
48 Reflections Over Blood 3.00
48a nude cover 4.00
49 Love's Story 3.00
49a nude cover 4.00
50 final issue, 48-page 5.00
50a nude cover 5.00
50b commemmorative edition, Julie
Strain photo (c) 7.00
50c commemm. signed 10.00
Commemorative Edition 2.95
Lingerie Special #1 . . . . 2.95
Spec. Lingerie, encore edition 2.95
Spec. Lingerie, deluxe 3.95
Spec. Swimsuit, encore edition 2.95
Spec. Swimsuit, deluxe nude cover. 3.95
Gallery #1 . . . . 4.95
Gallery #1 nude cover 5.95
Gallery #2 . . . . 4.95
Gallery #2 nude cover 5.95
Bondage Spec. #1 . . . . 2.95
Bondage Spec. #1, nude cover 3.95
Bondage Spec. #1, Manga 3.95
Ann. #1 Encore 3.00
Ann. #1 Encore, nude cover 4.00
Spec. #2 Dare to Bare 3.00
Spec. #2 Dare to Bare, nude cover. 4.00
Spec. #4 Encore Edition, new(c) . . . 2.95
Spec. #4a Encore Edition, nude(c) . 2.95
Spec. #5 Encore Edition 2.95
Spec. #5a Encore Edition, nude(c) . 3.95
Spec.#1 Vamperotica Presents:
Countess Vladimira (1998) 3.00
Nude cover edition 4.00
Vamperotica Collector Vol. 1 . . . . . . 3.95
Pin-Up #1 (2000) 2.95
Pin-Up #1a nude (c) 3.95
Pin-Up #1b nude (c) signed 7.00
Spec. Blood of Japan 3.00
Spec. Blood of Japan, nude(c) 4.00
GN Blood of the Impaler 7.95

VAMPEROTICA: DIVIDE & CONQUER

Brainstorm 1999

1 V:The Juicious Edicts 3.00
1a nude cover 4.00
1b Commemorative #1 . . . . 5.00
1c Commemorative #1 deluxe 7.00
2 conclusion 3.00
2a nude cover 4.00

VAMPEROTICA ILLUSTRATED

Brainstorm

1 F:Vampress Luxura 2.95
1a nude (c) 3.95
1b premium ed. 4.95
1c premium signed 5.95
2 . . . . 2.95
2a nude (c) 3.95
3 . . . . 2.95
3a nude photo (c) 3.95
4 . . . . 2.95
4a nude photo (c) 3.95
5 . . . . 2.95
5a nude (c) 3.95
6 . . . . 2.95
6a nude (c) 3.95

VAMPEROTICA MANGA

Brainstorm 1998

1 . . . . 2.95
1a nude cover 3.95
1b nude embrace cover 3.95
2 . . . . 3.00
2a nude cover 4.00

VAMPEROTICA TALES

Brainstorm 1998

1 . . . . 2.95
1a nude cover edition 3.95
1 nude luxury edition 5.00
2 . . . . 2.95
2a nude cover 3.95
2b nude embrace cover 3.95
3 . . . . 3.00
3a nude cover 4.00
4 Veiled Threat 3.00
4a nude cover 4.00
5 A Night of Wine and Roses 3.00
5a nude cover 4.00

VAMPFIRE

Brainstorm 1996

1 . . . . 2.95
1a nude cover 3.95
1 commemorative photo cover . . . 10.00
2 . . . . 2.95
2a nude cover 5.00
2 signed 5.00
2 nude, signed 5.00
Pin-Up Spec. 2.95
Pin-Up Spec. deluxe 3.95
Tour Book #1 . . . . 2.95
Tour Book #1 nude cover 2.95

VAMPFIRE: EROTIC ECHO

Brainstorm 1997

1 by Fauve 2.95
1a nude cover 2.95
1b photo cover 3.00
2 . . . . 2.95
2a nude cover 2.95
2b photo cover 2.95

VAMPFIRE: NECROMANTIQUE

Brainstorm 1997

1 by Holly Golightly 2.95
1a nude edition 3.95
1b luxury edition, virgin cover 5.00
1c luxury edition, signed 15.00
1d regular, signed 8.00
1e nude cover, signed 10.00
2 by Fauve 2.95
2a nude edition 3.95

VAMPIRE BITES

Brainstorm

2 . . . . 2.95
2a nude cover 2.95

VAMPIRE CONFESSIONS

Brainstorm 1998

1 . . . . 3.00
1a nude cover 4.00

VAMPIRE GIRLS: CALIFORNIA 1969

Angel Entertainment 1996

0 nude cover, signed 8.00
1 blood red foil deluxe edition 5.95
2 . . . . 2.95
2 deluxe 5.95
2 nude cover A 10.00
2 nude cover B 10.00
TPB 5.00

VAMPIRE GIRLS: NEW YORK 1979

Angel Entertainment 1996

0 . . . . 2.95
0 virgin nude cover 5.00
0 nude platinum cover 15.00
0 gold edition 8.00
1 . . . . 2.95
1 virgin nude cover 5.00
1 nude platinum cover 15.00

VAMPIRE GIRLS EROTIQUE

Angel Entertainment 1996

1 . . . . 2.95
1 nude cover 2.95
2 . . . . 2.95
2 erotic nude cover A 2.95
2 deluxe nude cover B 2.95
3 . . . . 2.95
3 nude cover 2.95
4 . . . . 2.95
4 erotic nude cover 2.95
5 . . . . 2.95
5 erotic nude kissing Candaze
cover 4.00
6 . . . . 2.95
6 nude cover 2.95
7 Bloodsucker cover 3.00
7 nude gettin lunch cover 3.00
Spec. Gravedigger (1996) by
Alexandra Scott & Bill Wylie . . . 3.00
Nude Alexandra cover 3.00
Nude Candice and Simone cover
. . . . 3.00
Spec. Paris 1968 (1997) by
Alexandra Scott & Dean Burnett 2.95
Nude cover 4.00
Spec. Titanic 1912 (1998) by
Alexandra Scott & Dean Burnett 2.95
Nude cover 4.00

VAMPIRE GIRLS: BUBBLEGUM & BLOOD

Angel Entertainment 1996

1 . . . . 2.95
1 deluxe edition 5.95
1 nude cover 10.00
2 . . . . 2.95
2 deluxe edition 5.95
2 nude cover 10.00

VAMPIRE GIRLS EROTIQUE: GRAVEDIGGER

Angel Entertainment 1996

1 by Alexandra Scott & Bill Wylie . . 3.00

1a Nude Alexandra cover 3.00
1b Nude Candice and Simone(c) . . 3.00

VAMPIRE GIRLS VS. ANGEL GIRL
Angel Entertainment 1997
1 . . . . 2.95
1a erotic nude cover 3.95
1b deluxe nude cover 3.95

VAMPIRELLA
Harris
1 DC,SL,Summer Nights,48-page . 3.95
Pantha Ashcan, 16-page 6.00
Dangerous Games Preview Ashcan 6.00
Hell on Earth, Leather Ashcan . . . 14.95
Hell on Earth, Leather Ashcan, signed 29.95
30th Ann. Spec. Julie Strain photo (c) 9.95
Painkiller Jane preview Ashcan. . . . 6.00
Spec.#1 Vampirella vs. Hemorrhage, Limited Preview Ashcan 5.00
Vampirella/Lady Death Ashcan 16-page, Rematch 6.00
Vampirella/Lady Death Ashcan 16-page, Finale 6.00
Vampirella/Lady Death Ashcan 16-page, Revenge, platinum . . 19.95
Vampirella 2999 A.D. Manga Ashcan 7.95
Vampirella 2999 A.D. Manga Ashcan, leather edition 14.95
Vampirella 3000 A.D. Manga Ashcan 7.95
Vampirella 3000 A.D.Manga Ashcan, leather edition 14.95

VAMPIRELLA
Silver Anniversary Collection
Harris 1996
0 Vampirella of Darkulon, EM 3.00
1 good girl edition 2.50
1a bad girl edition 2.50
2 good girl edition 2.50
2a bad girl edition 2.50
3 good girl edition 2.50
3a bad girl edition. 2.50
4 Silkie(c) 2.50
4a MBc(c) 2.50

Vampirella: Morning in America TPB © Harris/Dark Horse

VAMPIRELLA: MORNING IN AMERICA
Harris/Dark Horse 1991–92
Book 1 . . . . @7.00
Book 2 thru 4 . . . . @5.00
TPB 25.00

VAMPIRELLA RETRO
Harris 1998
1 (of 3) rep. Warren stories 2.50
2 (of 3) rep. Warren stories 2.50
3 (of 3) rep. Warren stories 2.50

VAMPIRELLA: LEGENDARY TALES
Harris Comics 2000
1 . . . . 2.95
1a deluxe 9.95
1b Julie Strain photo (c). 9.95
2 . . . . 2.95
2a variant (c). 9.95
2b Julie Strain photo (c). 9.95

VAMPIRE MIYU
Antarctica Press
1 I:Vampire Princess Miyu 2.95
2 thru 5 . . . . @3.95
6 48-pg.. 4.95

VAMPIRE'S TATTOO
London Night 1997
1 (of 2) by Art Wetherell. 3.00
1 deluxe edition, nude cover 6.00
2 . . . . 3.00
2 deluxe edition, nude cover 6.00
2b nude cover edition, signed . . . 10.00
3 . . . . 3.00
3a nude cover 6.00

VAMPIRE ZONE, THE
Brainstorm 1998
1 . . . . 2.95
1a nude cover 3.95

VAMPORNRELLA
Forbidden 1997
1 parody 2.95
1 erotic nude cover A 2.95
1 erotic nude cover B 2.95

VAMPYRES
Eternity
1 thru 4 . . . . @2.25

VANGUARD: OUTPOST EARTH
1 and 2 . . . . @2.00

VAULT OF DOOMNATION
B-Movie Comics
1 . . . . 1.70

VENGEANCE OF DREADWOLF
Lightning Comics
1 O:Dreadwolf 2.75

VERDICT
Eternity
1 thru 4 . . . . @2.00

VEROTIKA
Verotika 1995–97
1 Magical Times 12.00
2 . . . . 7.00
3 . . . . 5.00
4 thru 6 . . . . @4.00
7 thru 15 . . . . @3.00

VERY VICKY
Meet Danny Ocean
1 . . . . 3.50
1a 2nd printing 3.00

VERY VICKY: CALLING ALL HILLBILLIES
Meet Danny Ocean 1995
1 Pea Pickin Patty. 2.50

VIC & BLOOD
Renegade
1 and 2 RCo,Ellison . . . . @2.00

VICKY VALENTINE
Renegade
1 thru 4 . . . . @1.70

VICTIMS
Silver Wolf
1 and 2 . . . . @1.50

VICTIMS
Eternity
1 thru 5 . . . . @2.00

VIDEO CLASSICS
1 Mighty Mouse. 3.50
2 Mighty Mouse. 3.50

VIETNAM JOURNAL
Apple Comics
1 . . . . 5.00
1a 2nd printing 3.00
2 . . . . 3.00
3 thru 5 . . . . @2.50
6 thru 13 . . . . @2.00
14 thru 16. . . . . @2.25

VIGIL: DESERT FOXES
Millennium
1 and 2 F:Grace Kimble . . . . @3.95

VIGIL: FALL FROM GRACE
Innovation
1 `State of Grace' 2.75
2 The Graceland Hunt 2.50

VINSON WATSON'S RAGE
Trinity Visuals
1 I:Rena Helen 3.00

VINSON WATSON'S SWEET CHILDE
Advantage Graphics
Vol. 2
1 F:Spyder 2.00

VIRGIN: SLUMBER
Entity 1997
1 BMs 2.75
1 deluxe 3.50

VIRGIN: SURROUNDED
Entity 1997
1 BMs 2.75
1 deluxe 3.50

VIRGIN: TILL DEATH DO US PART
Entity April 1997
1 BMs 2.75
1 deluxe 3.50

VISIONS
Vision Publication 1979–83
1 I:Flaming Carrot 50.00
2 Flaming Carrot 30.00
3 Flaming Carrot 15.00
4 Flaming Carrot 25.00

VISUAL ASSAULT OMNIBUS
Visual Assault Comics 1995
1 thru 4 O:Dimensioner 3.00

VIXEN
Meteor Comics
1 and 2 Battle of the Vixens . . . . @2.95

VORTEX
Hall of Heroes
1 . . . . 15.00
1a commemorative 5.00
2 . . . . 10.00
3 thru 5 . . . . @3.50
6 V:The Reverend 3.00

Vox #1
© Apple Comics

VORTEX SPECIAL: CYBERSIN
Avatar Press 1997
1 by Matt Martin & Bil Maus. 3.00
1a nude cover 4.95
1b velvet cover 15.00
1c signed. 10.00
1d Snowman spec. (c). 5.00

VORTEX: DR. KILBOURN
Entity March 1997
1 by Matt Martin 2.75
1a deluxe 3.50

VORTEX: INTO THE DARK
Entity 1997
1 . . . . 2.75
1 deluxe 3.50

VOX
Apple
1 JBy(c). 2.00
2 and 3 . . . . @2.00
4 and 5 . . . . @2.25

WABBIT WAMPAGE
Amazing Comics 1987
1 . . . . 2.00

WACKY SQUIRREL
1 thru 4 . . . . @1.75
Summer Fun Special #1 . . . . 2.00
Christmas Special #1 . . . . 1.75

WAITING PLACE, THE
Slave Labor 1997
5 . . . . 2.95
6 . . . . 2.95
VOL. 2 (2000)
1 . . . . 2.95
2 . . . . 2.95
3 A Sporting Chance 2.95
4 I Care 2.95
5 The Road Home 2.95
6 . . . . 2.95

WALKING DEAD
Aircel
1 thru 4 . . . . @2.25
Zombie Spec. 1 . . . . 2.25

WALK THROUGH OCTOBER
Caliber
1 I:Mr. Balloon 2.95
2 . . . . 2.95
3 All Hallow's Eve 2.95

WALT THE WILDCAT
Motion Comics 1995
1 I:Walt the Wildcat 2.50

WANDERING STAR
Pen & Ink
1 I:Casandra Andrews 15.00
1a 2nd & 3rd printing 3.00
2 . . . . 8.00
3 . . . . 5.00
4 . . . . 4.00
5 . . . . 4.00

Wandering Star #17
© Sirius

6 . . . . 2.50
7 . . . . 2.50
8 and 9 F:Casandra Andrews. . . @2.75
10 R:Mekron. 2.75
11 . . . . 2.75
Sirius 1995–97
12 thru 20 Two . . . . @2.50
21 Two, final issue 2.50
TPB Vol. 1 rep. #1–#7 . . . . 14.95
TPB Vol. 2 . . . . 14.95
TPB Vol. 3 168-page 14.95

WAR
A Plus Comics
1 . . . . 2.50

WARCAT
Alliance Comics
1 thru 7 A:Ebonia 2.50

WARD: A BULLET SERIES
Liar Comics
1 Foresight,pt.1 . . . . 2.50
2 Foresight,pt.2 . . . . 2.50
3 Foresight,pt.3 . . . . 2.50

WARLACE
K-Blamm 1995
1 I:Warlace 2.95

WARLOCK 5
Aircel
1 . . . . 6.00
2 . . . . 5.00
3 . . . . 6.00
4 . . . . 5.00
5 . . . . 5.00
6 thru 11 . . . . @4.00
12 . . . . 3.50
13 . . . . 3.50
14 thru 16. . . . . @2.00
17 . . . . 1.70
18 . . . . 1.75
19 thru 22. . . . . @2.00
Book 2 #1 thru #7. . . . . 2.00

WARLOCK 5
Sirius 1997

1 (of 4) by Barry Blair & Colin Chan 2.50
2 2.50
3 2.50
4 finale 2.50

WARLOCKS
Aircel

1 thru 3 @1.70
4 thru 12 @2.00
Spec #1 Rep. 2.25

WAR OF THE WORLDS
Eternity

1 TV tie-in 2.00
2 thru 6 @2.00

War of the Worlds #4
© Caliber

WAR OF THE WORLDS, THE
Caliber "New Worlds" 1996

1 from H.G. Wells 2.95
1a signed 2.95
2 war for Kansas City 2.95
3 Haven & The Hellweed 2.95
4 2.95
5 2.95
TPB rep. #1–#5 14.95

WAR OF THE WORLDS: THE MEMPHIS FRONT
Arrow Comics 1998

1 (of 5) by Randy Zimmerman & Richard Gulick 2.95
2 thru 5 @2.95
Spec.#1 signed & numbered 2.95

WAR PARTY VS. DEATHMARK
Lightning Comics

1 War Party vs. Deathmark 2.75

WARP WALKING
Caliber

1 'Quick and the Dead' 2.50

WARRIOR NUN AREALA/RAZOR: DARK PROPHECY
London Night 1999

1 16-page 2.50
2 16-page 2.50

Antarctic Press

3 2.50
4 2.50

WARRIOR NUN AREALA: THE MANGA
Antarctic Press 2000

1-shot 2.95

WARRIOR NUN BRIGANTIA
Antarctic Press 2000

1 V:Fata Morgana 2.95
2 Sister Anna 2.95
3 2.95

WARRIOR NUN: BLACK AND WHITE
Antarctic Press 1997

1 3.00
2 3.00
3 3.00
4 Winter Jade, pt.1 F:Ninja Nun 3.00
5 Winter Jade, pt.2 3.00
6 Winter Jade, pt.3 3.00
7 3.00
8 3.00
9 Return of the Redeemers 3.00
10 Return of Lillith 3.00
11 The Redeemers, cont. 3.00
12 The Redeemers, cont. 3.00
13 I:Sister Trinity 2.95
14 Redeemers saga again 2.95
15 F:Sister Trinity 2.95
16 F:Sister Trinity 2.95
17 Showdown 3.00
18 Reaction 3.00
19 Carnivale 3.00
20 Twilight Earth 3.00
21 Lost Souls of Blue Moon Mountain 2.50
Spec. Warrior Nun Areala/Razor: Revenge 3.00
Spec. A Revenge, deluxe 6.00

WARRIORS

1 2.50
2 thru 7 @2.00

WARZONE
Entity

1 I:Bella & Supra 2.95
2 F:Bladeback, Alloy, Granite 2.95
3 F:Bladeback 2.95

WATCHDOG
Hammerhead Comics

1 I:Watchdog 2.95

WEASEL PATROL
Eclipse

Spec. #1 2.00

WEBWITCH
Avatar Press 1997

0 by Raff Ienco 3.00
0 nude cover 5.00
1 (of 2) signed 10.00
1 (of 2) 3.00
1 nude cover 5.00
2 (of 2) 3.00
2 nude cover 4.95
Boxed Set, all rare editions 35.00

WEBWITCH: PRELUDE TO WAR
Avatar Press 1998

1 by Raff Jenco 3.00
1a nude cover 6.00
1b Leather cover 30.00

WEBWITCH: WAR
Avatar Press 1998

1 (of 2) by Bill Maus 3.00
1a nude cover 6.00
1b Leather cover 30.00
2 conclusion 3.00
2a nude cover 6.00

WEIRDFALL
Antarctic Press 1995

1 I:Weirdfall 2.75
2 O:Weirdfall 2.75
3 2.75

WEIRD ROMANCE
Eclipse

1 2.00

WEIRDSVILLE
Blindwolf Studios 1997

1 2.95
1 2nd printing 2.95
2 2.95
2 2nd printing 2.95
3 2.95
3 2nd printing 2.95
4 2.95
5 2.95
6 The Usual Weirdoes, concl. 2.95
7 2.95
8 An American Werewolf in Weirdsville, pt.1 (of 2) 2.95
9 An American Werewolf in Weirdsville, pt.2 2.95
10 2.95

WEIRDSVILLE/CRYBABY: HEY YOU TWO
Blindwolf Studios 1999

1 2.95

WEREWOLF
Blackthorne 1988–89

1 TV tie-in 2.00
2 thru 7 @2.00

WHAT IS THE FACE?
A.C.E. Comics

1 SD/FMc,I:New Face 2.00
2 SD/FMc 2.00
3 SD 1.75

WHISPERS & SHADOWS

1 8 1/2 x 11 . . . . 2.00
1a Regular size 1.50
2 8 1/2 x 11 . . . . 1.50
3 8 1/2 x 11 . . . . 1.50
4 thru 9 . . . . @1.50

WHITE DEVIL
Eternity

1 thru 6 adult 2.50

WHITEOUT
Oni Press 1998

1 (of 4) by Greg Rucka &
Steve Leiber 2.95
2 . . . . 2.95
3 . . . . 2.95
4 conclusion 2.95
TPB 128-page 10.95

WHITEOUT: MELT
Oni Press 1999

1 (of 4) by Greg Rucka
& Steve Lieber 2.95
2 . . . . 2.95
3 . . . . 2.95
4 concl. 2.95
TPB 11.95

WHITE RAVEN
Visionary Publications

1 Government Intrigue 2.95
2 . . . . 2.95
3 Mystery Man Gets Wheels 2.95
4 Facility 2.95
5 V:Douglas 2.95
6 . . . . 2.95
7 . . . . 2.95

WHITLEY STRIEBER'S BEYOND COMMUNION
Caliber Sept. 1997

1 UFO Odyssey 2.95
1 signed 2.95
1 special edition, signed
by Strieber 6.95
1a 2nd printing 2.95
2 . . . . 2.95
3 . . . . 2.95
4 . . . . 2.95

WICKED
Millennium

1 thru 4 . . . . 2.50

WICKED: THE RECKONING
Millennium

1 R:Wicked 2.95
2 F:Rachel Blackstone 2.95

WIDOW
Ground Zero 1996

Cinegraphic Spec. #1: Daughter
of Darkness 4.00

WIDOW/LUXURA: BLOOD LUST
Ground Zero 1996

Alpha x-over, pt.1 . . . . 3.50
see Luxura/Widow for pt. 2

WIDOW: BOUND BY BLOOD
Ground Zero 1996

1 thru 5 by Mike Wolfer . . . . @3.50

WIDOW: PROGENY
Ground Zero April 1997

1 by Mike Wolfer & Karl Moline . . . 3.00
2 (of 3) 3.00
3 concl. 3.00

WIDOW: THE COMPLETE WORKS
Ground Zero 1996

Vol.1 Flesh and Blood 10.95
Vol.1 deluxe 16.95
Vol.2 Kill Me Again 10.95
Vol.2 deluxe 16.95
Vol.3 Metal Gypsies 10.95
Vol.3 deluxe 16.95

WIDOW
Avatar Press 1997

0 by Mike Wolfer 3.95
0a nude cover 6.00
0b Black leather cover 25.00
0 signed 10.00

Widow The Origin #1
© Avatar

WIDOW: THE ORIGIN
Avatar Press 1997

1 (of 3) by Mike Wolfer 3.95
1a nude cover 6.00
1a leather cover 25.00
2 (of 3) 3.00
2 nude cover 4.95

WILD, THE

1 and 2 . . . . @1.50
3 thru 7 . . . . @1.75

WILD KNIGHTS
Eternity

1 thru 10 . . . . @2.00
Shattered Earth Chron. #1 . . . . 2.00

WILDMAN

1 and 2 . . . . @1.50
3 thru 6 . . . . @1.85

WILD THINGZ
ABC Comics 1998

0 RCI & Armando Huerta 3.00
0a painted cover 6.00
0b Fan edition 5.95
0c Summer edition 5.95
0d Leather cover, original art 55.00
1 (of 2) RCI 3.00
1a nude gold (c) 8.00
1b Leather cover 30.00
1c virgin cover 3.00
1d gold cover 5.95
1e Platinum cover 5.95

WILLOW
Angel Entertainment 1996

0 commemorative edition 2.95
0 nude edition 5.00
1 . . . . 2.95
1 black magic foil edition 5.95
1 nude signed 10.00
2 . . . . 2.95
2 gold edition 8.00
2 Virgin nude cover 5.00
2 Virgin Sacrifice nude cover 7.00
2 nude manga cover 5.00
2 nude platinum cover 15.00

WIND BLADE

1 Elford 1st Blair 40.00

WINDRAVEN
Hero Graphics/Blue comet

1 The Healing,(see Rough Raiders)2.95

WINDRAVEN
Heroic

1 . . . . 2.95

WISHMASTER
Pocket Change Comics

1 I:Hell Bore 2.50

WITCH
Eternity

1 . . . . 2.00

WIZARD OF TIME
David House

1 . . . . 1.50
1a 2nd printing(blue) 1.50
2 and 3 . . . . @1.50

WOLFF & BYRD, COUNSELORS OF THE MACABRE
Exhibit A

1 . . . . 6.00
2 thru 4 . . . . @3.50
5 thru 11 . . . . @2.50
12 thru 16 BLs . . . . @2.50
17 thru 23 . . . . @2.50
TPB Casefiles Vol. I rep. #1–#4,
3rd printing 9.95
TPB Casefiles Vol. 2 rep. #5–#8 . . . 9.95
TPB Casefiles Vol. III rep. #9–#12 10.95
TPB Casefiles Vol. IV rep. #13–#16
. . . . 10.95

TPB Supernatural Law 7.95
TPB Supernatural Law rep.. . . . . 7.95
TPB Fright Court rep. 9.95
Spec.#1 Greatest Writs (1997) BLs. 2.95
Becomes:

SUPERNATURAL LAW

24 . . . . 2.50
25 The end of 1999 . . . . 2.50
26 Black Market Souls 2.50
27 Creatures of the Night,
with lawyers 2.50
28 While the City Doesn't Sleep . . . 2.50
TPB Sonofawitch, rep. 14.95

WOLF H

Blackthorne

1 and 2 . . . . @1.75

WORDSMITH

Renegade

1 . . . . 3.00
2 thru 6 . . . . @1.70
7 thru 12 . . . . @2.00

WORLD HARDBALL LEAGUE

Titus Press

1 F:Big Bat 2.95
2 F:Big Bat 2.95
3 Mount Evrest 2.95
4 Juan Hernandez 2.95

WORLD OF ROBOTECH

Academy Comics 1995

GN Tales of Planets 12.95

WORLD OF WOOD

Eclipse

5 Flying Saucers 2.00

WORLDS OF FANTASY

Newcomers Publishing 1995

1 The Jenn Chronicles. 2.95

WORLDS OF H.P. LOVECRAFT

Caliber Tome Press 1997

1-shot The Alchemist. 2.95
1-shot The Tomb 2.95
1-shot The Lurking Fear 2.95
1-shot Beyond the Walls of Sleep . 2.95
HC rep. 14.95

WRAITH

Outlander

1 `Resurrected & the Damned' . . . 1.75

WRETCH, THE

Caliber 1996

1 PhH 2.95
2 PhH 2.95

Amaze Ink 1997

3 PhH 2.95
4 PhH 2.95
5 PhH & Jim Woodyard 2.95
6 PhH & Bruce McCorkindale 2.95
7 PhH 2.95

Worlds of H.P. Lovecraft: Beyond the Laws of Sleep © Caliber

WU WEI

Animus

1 "Debaser" 2.50
2 Blind Whisper 2.50
3 . . . . 2.50
4 . . . . 2.50
5 "Testament" pt.5 . . . . 2.50
6 by Oscar Stern 2.50
7 Explicador 2.95
8 Dead Skin 2.95
9 Apotheosis or Bang You're Dead 2.95

WYRD: THE RELUCTANT WARRIOR

Amaze Ink 1999

1 (of 6) JSn 2.95
2 . . . . 2.95
3 Telemarketing Horrors 2.95
4 Maxi-Man 2.95
5 . . . . 2.95
6 . . . . 2.95
TPB JSn, 132-page 16.95

XANADU

Thoughts & Images

1 thru 5 . . . . @2.00

XENA

Brown Study Comics

1 I:Xena 2.95

XENON

Eclipse

1 . . . . 3.00
2 thru 23 . . . . @1.50

XENO'S ARROW

Cup O' Tea Studios 1999

1 by Greg Beettam 2.50
2 thru 10 . . . . @2.50

XENOZOIC TALES

Kitchen Sink 1986

1 by Mark Schultz 15.00
1a Reprint 2.50
2 . . . . 10.00
2a Reprint 2.50

3 . . . . 8.00
4 . . . . 6.00
5 thru 7 . . . . @4.00
8 thru 13 . . . . @3.00
14 MSh 3.00

X-BABES VS. JUSTICE BABES

Personality

1 Spoof/parody 2.95

X-CONS

Parody Press

1 X-Men satire,flip cover 2.50

X-FARCE

Eclipse

One-Shot X-Force parody. 3.00

X-FLIES BUG HUNT

Twist and Shout 1997

1 Vampires 2.95
2 Monsters 2.95
3 Aliens. 2.95
4 The Truth 2.95
Conspiracy 2.95
Spec. #1 Flies in Black 2.95

XIOLA

Zion Comics

1 thru 3 F:Kantasia . . . . @2.00
4 Visitor. 2.00

XMEN

1 Parody 1.50

X-1999

Viz

1 I:Kamir Shiro 2.75
2 thru 5 F:Princess Hitane 2.75
6 Battle for X-1999 . . . . 2.75

X-THIEVES

1 . . . . 3.00
2 . . . . 1.75
3 . . . . 1.75

YAHOO

Fantagraphics

1 thru 4 . . . . @2.00

YAKUZA

Eternity

1 thru 5 . . . . @2.00

YAWN

Parody Press

1 Spawn parody 2.50

Enigma

1 Spawn parody rep.? 2.75

YOUNG DRACULA: PRAYER OF THE VAMPIRE

Boneyard Press 1997

1 (of 5) sequel to Young Dracula:
Diary of a Vampire 2.95
2 Empire of Madness, pt.2. . . . . . . 2.95
3 Children of Madness. 2.95

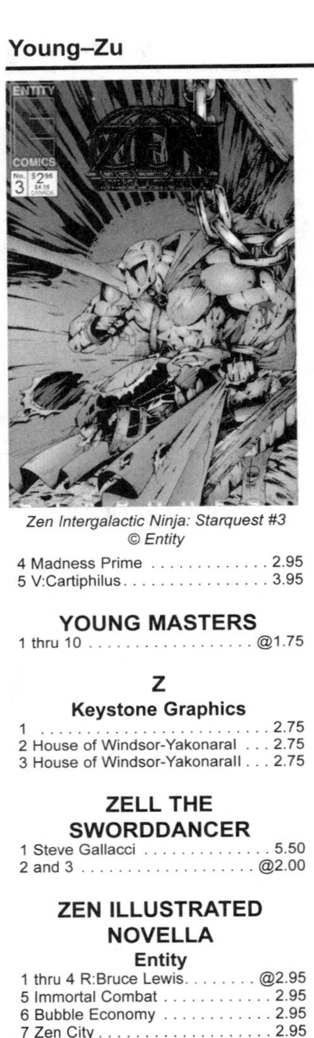

Zen Intergalactic Ninja: Starquest #3
© Entity

4 Madness Prime 2.95
5 V:Cartiphilus 3.95

YOUNG MASTERS

1 thru 10 . . . . @1.75

Z

Keystone Graphics

1 . . . . 2.75
2 House of Windsor-Yakonaral . . . 2.75
3 House of Windsor-Yakonarall . . . 2.75

ZELL THE SWORDDANCER

1 Steve Gallacci 5.50
2 and 3 . . . . @2.00

ZEN ILLUSTRATED NOVELLA

Entity

1 thru 4 R:Bruce Lewis. . . . . @2.95
5 Immortal Combat 2.95
6 Bubble Economy 2.95
7 Zen City 2.95
8 V:Assassins 2.95

ZEN, INTER-GALACTIC NINJA

Entity

1 . . . . 4.00
2 . . . . 3.00
3 thru 9 . . . . @3.00
X-mas Spec #1,V:Black Hole Bob. . 2.95

[2nd Series]

1 `Down to Earth' 2.50
2 RA, A:Jeremy Baker 2.50
2a polybagged, limited. 5.00
3 thru 5 . . . . @2.50

[3rd Series]

0 . . . . 2.95
1 thru 3 A:Niro . . . . @2.95

Sourcebook #1 . . . . 3.50

ZEN INTERGALACTIC NINJA: STARQUEST

Entity

1 thru 6 V:Nolan the Destroyer . . @2.95
7 V:Dimensional 2.95
8 thru 9 I:New Team. . . . . @2.95
10 In Deep Space. 2.95
11 Dimensional Terrorists 2.95
TPB Rep. #1-#4 . . . . @6.95

ZEN INTERGALACTIC NINJA VS. MICHEAL JACK-ZEN

Entity

1 Cameos Galore 2.95

ZENISMS WIT AND WISDOMS

Entity

1 R:Bruce Lewis 2.95

ZEN: MISTRESS OF CHAOS

1 . . . . 2.95

ZENITH: PHASE II

Fleetway

1 GMo(s),SY,Rep.2000 AD 2.00

ZERO ZERO

Fantagraphics 1995

1 thru 10 . . . . @4.00
11 thru 22 . . . . @3.95
23 F:"Tired" 3.95
24 F:Smilin' Ed 3.95
25 . . . . 3.95
26 final issue, 56-page 4.95
27 really final 64-page 4.95

ZETRAMAN

Antarctic

1 thru 3 . . . . @2.00

[Vol. 2]

1 and 2 . . . . @2.75

ZETRAMAN: REVIVAL

Antarctic Press

1 thru 3 . . . . @2.75

ZILLION

Eternity

1 thru 4 . . . . @2.50

ZOLASTRAYA AND THE BARD

1 thru 5 . . . . @1.70

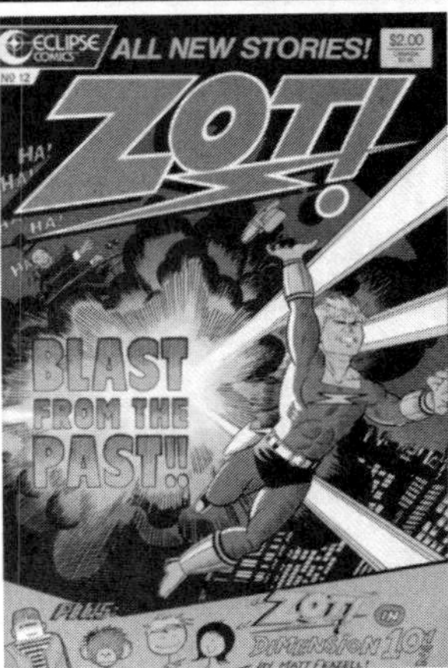

Zot #12
© Eclipse

ZOMBIE WAR: EARTH MUST BE DESTROYED

Fantaco 1993

1 thru 3 Kevin Eastman 3.95

ZONE CONTINUUM

Caliber

1 Master of the Waves. 2.95
2 . . . . 2.95

ZOT!

Eclipse

(#1-#10 See: Color)

11 New Series 3.00
12 thru 15 . . . . @3.00
16 A:De-Evolutionaries 3.00
17 thru 36 . . . . @3.00

Kitchen Sink

Book Two TPB rep. #11–#15, #17–#18. . . . . 19.95
Book Two TPB signed and numbered. 34.95
Book Three TPB rep. #16, #21–#27. . . . . 19.95
Book Three HC, signed & numbered. 34.95
Book Four TPB The Earth Stories 19.95

ZOOT!

Fantagraphics

1 thru 5 . . . . @2.50

ZU

Mu Press

1 thru 11 . . . . @2.95
12 "The Monkey Tales" 2.95
13 . . . . 2.95
14 . . . . 2.95
15 "Curse of the Re-Possessed" . . . 2.95
16 thru 19. . . . . 2.95
20 final issue 2.95

Classics Illustrated

[Issued As Classic Comics]

001-THE THREE MUSKETEERS

By Alexandre Dumas

10/41 **(—-)** MKd,MKd(c), Original,10¢ (c) Price 4,500.00
05/43 **(10)** MKd,MKd(c), No(c)Price; rep 275.00
11/43 **(15)** MKd,MKd(c),Long Island Independent Ed 200.00
6/44 **(18/20)** MKd,MKd(c), Sunrise Times Edition;rep . . . 135.00
7/44 **(21)** MKd,MKd(c),Richmond Courrier Edition;rep 125.00
6/46 **(28)** MKd,MKd(c);rep. 100.00
4/47 **(36)** MKd,MKd(c), New CILogo;rep 50.00
6/49 **(60)** MKd,MKd(c),CI Logo;rep 35.00
10/49 **(64)** MKd,MK(c),CI Logo;rep 35.00
12/50 **(78)** MKd,MKd(c),15¢(c) Price; CI Logo;rep 25.00
03/52 **(93)** MKd,MKd(c), CI Logo;rep 20.00
11/53 **(114)** CI Logo;rep 15.00
09/56 **(134)** MKd,MKd(c),New P(c),CI Logo,64 pgs;rep 15.00
03/58 **(143)** MKd,MKd(c),P(c), CI Logo,64 pgs;rep. 15.00
05/59 **(150)** GE&RC New Art, P(c),CILogo;rep 15.00
03/61 **(149)** GE&RC,P(c), CI Logo;rep 10.00
62-63 **(167)** GE&RC,P(c), CI Logo;rep 10.00
04/64 **(167)** GE&RC,P(c), CI Logo;rep 10.00
01/65 **(167)** GE&RC,P(c), CI Logo;rep 10.00
03/66 **(167)** GE&RC,P(c), CI Logo;rep 10.00
11/67 **(166)** GE&RC,P(c), CI Logo;rep 10.00
Sp/69 **(166)** GE&RC,P(c),25¢(c) Price,CILogo, Rigid(c);rep. . . . 10.00
Sp/71 **(169)** GE&RC,P(c), CI Logo,Rigid(c);rep 10.00

CI #1, The Three Musketeers © Gilberton Publications

002-IVANHOE

By Sir Walter Scott

1941 **(—-)** EA,MKd(c),Original . 1,900.00
05/43 **(1)** EA,MKd(c),word “Presents” Removed From(c);rep. 225.00
11/43 **(15)** EA,MKd(c),Long Island Independent Edition;rep 150.00
06/44 **(18/20)** EA,MKd(c),Sunrise Times Edition;rep 135.00
07/44 **(21)** EA,MKd(c),Richmond Courrier Edition;rep 125.00
06/46 **(28)** EA,MKd(c),rep 100.00
07/47 **(36)** EA,MKd(c),New CI Logo; rep 60.00
06/49 **(60)** EA,MKd(c),CI Logo;rep 35.00
10/49 **(64)** EA,MKd(c),CI Logo;rep 30.00
12/50 **(78)** EA,MKd(c),15¢(c) Price; CI Logo;rep 25.00
11/51 **(89)** EA,MKd(c),CI Logo;rep 20.00
04/53 **(106)** EA,MKd(c),CI Logo;rep. 15.00
07/54 **(121)** EA,MKd(c),CI Logo;rep. 25.00
01/57 **(136)** NN New Art,New P(c),CI Logo;rep. 25.00
01/58 **(142)** NN,P(c),CI Logo;rep. . 10.00
11/59 **(153)** NN,P(c),CI Logo;rep. . 10.00
03/61 **(149)** NN,P(c),CI Logo;rep. . 10.00
62/63 **(167)** NN,P(c),CI Logo;rep . . 9.00
05/64 **(167)** NN,P(c),CI Logo;rep. . 10.00
01/65 **(167)** NN,P(c),CI Logo;rep. . 10.00
03/66 **(167)** NN,P(c),CI Logo;rep. . 10.00
09/67 **(166)** NN,P(c),CI Logo;rep. . 10.00
1968 **(166)** NN,P(c),CI Logo;rep . . 10.00
Wr/69 **(169)** NN,P(c),CI Logo Rigid(c);rep 10.00
Wr/71 **(169)** NN,P(c),CI Logo,Rigid(c);rep 10.00

003-THE COUNT OF MONTE CRISTO

By Alexandre Dumas

03/42 **(—-)** ASm,ASm(c),Orig. . 1,200.00
05/43 **(10)** ASm,ASm(c);rep 200.00
11/43 **(15)** ASm,ASm(c),Long Island Independent Edition;rep 165.00
06/44 **(18/20)** ASm,ASm(c), Sunrise Times Edition;rep . . . 150.00
06/44 **(20)** ASm,ASm(c),Sunrise Times Edition;rep 135.00
07/44 **(21)** ASm,ASm(c),Richmond Courrier Edition;rep 125.00
06/46 **(28)** ASm,ASm(c);rep 100.00
04/47 **(36)** ASm,ASm(c),New CI Logo; rep 50.00
06/49 **(60)** ASm,ASm(c),CI Logo;rep. 40.00
08/49 **(62)** ASm,ASm(c),CI Logo;rep. 50.00
05/50 **(71)** ASm,ASm(c),CI Logo;rep. 30.00
09/51 **(87)** ASm,ASm(c),15¢(c) Price, CI Logo;rep 22.00
11/53 **(113)** ASm,ASm(c), CI Logo; rep 20.00
11/56 **(—-)** LC New Art,New P(c), CI Logo;rep 20.00
03/58 **(135)** LC,P(c),CI Logo;rep . . 10.00
11/59 (153) LC,P(c),CI Logo;rep . . 10.00
03/61 (161) LC,P(c),CI Logo;rep . . 10.00
62/63 **(167)** LC,P(c),CI Logo;rep . . . 9.00
07/64 **(167)** LC,P(c),CI Logo;rep . . . 9.00
07/65 **(167)** LC,P(c),CI Logo;rep . . . 9.00
07/66 **(167)** LC,P(c),CI Logo;rep . . . 9.00
1968 **(166)** LC,P(c),25¢(c) Price, CI Logo;rep 9.00
Wn/69 **(169)** LC,P(c),CI Logo, Rigid(c);rep 9.00

004-THE LAST OF THE MOHICANS

By James Fenimore Cooper

08/42 **(—-)** RR,RR(c),Original . 1,000.00
06/43 **(12)** RR,RR(c),Price Balloon Deleted;rep 200.00
11/43 **(15)** RR,RR(c),Long Island Independent Edition;rep 175.00
06/44 **(20)** RR,RR(c),Long Island Independent Edition;rep 150.00
07/44 **(21)** RR,RR(c),Queens Home News Edition;rep 125.00
06/46 **(28)** RR,RR(c);rep. 100.00
04/47 **(36)** RR,RR(c),New CI Logo; rep 60.00
06/49 **(60)** RR,RR(c),CI Logo;rep . 35.00
10/49 **(64)** RR,RR(c),CI Logo;rep . 25.00
12/50 **(78)** RR,RR(c),15¢(c) Price,CI Logo rep 22.00
11/51 **(89)** RR,RR(c),CI Logo;rep . 20.00
03/54 **(117)** RR,RR(c),CI Logo;rep 18.00
11/56 **(135)** RR,New P(c), CI Logo; rep 18.00
11/57 **(141)** RR,P(c),CI Logo;rep. . 20.00
05/59 **(150)** JSe&StA New Art; P(c), CI Logo;rep 18.00
03/61 **(161)** JSe&StA,P(c),CI Logo; rep 9.00
62/63 **(167)** JSe&StA,P(c),CI Logo; rep 9.00
06/64 **(167)** JSe&StA,P(c),CI Logo; rep 9.00
08/65 **(167)** JSe&StA,P(c),CI Logo; rep 9.00
08/66 **(167)** JSe&StA,P(c),CI Logo; rep 9.00

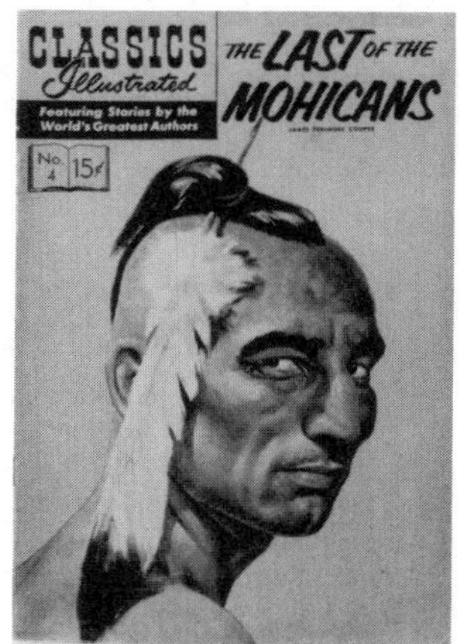

CC #4, The Last of the Mohicans © Gilberton Publications

Classics Illus.

1967 **(166)** JSe&StA,P(c),25¢(c) Price, CI Logo;rep 9.00
Sp/69 **(169)** JSe&StA,P(c),CI Logo, Rigid(c);rep. 9.00

005-MOBY DICK

By Herman Melville

09/42 **(—-)** LZ,LZ(c),Original . . 1,300.00
05/43 **(10)** LZ,LZ(c),Conray Products Edition, No(c)Price;rep 225.00
11/43 **(15)** LZ,LZ(c),Long Island Independent Edition;rep 175.00
06/44 **(18/20)** LZ,LZ(c),Sunrise Times Edition;rep 150.00
07/44 **(20)** LZ,LZ(c),Sunrise Times Edition;rep 135.00
07/44 **(21)** LZ,LZ(c),Sunrise Times Edition;rep 125.00
06/46 **(28)** LZ,LZ(c);rep. 100.00
04/47 **(36)** LZ,LZ(c),New CI Logo;rep. 60.00
06/49 **(60)** LZ,LZ(c),CI Logo;rep . . 35.00
08/49 **(62)** LZ,LZ(c),CI Logo;rep . . 40.00
05/50 **(71)** LZ,LZ(c),CI Logo;rep . . 25.00
09/51 **(87)** LZ,LZ(c),15¢(c) Price, CI Logo;rep 20.00
04/54 **(118)** LZ,LZ(c),CI Logo;rep . 15.00
03/56 **(131)** NN New Art,New P(c), CI Logo;rep 15.00
05/57 **(138)** NN,P(c),CI Logo;rep. . 10.00
01/59 **(148)** NN,P(c),CI Logo;rep. . 10.00
09/60 **(158)** NN,P(c),CI Logo;rep. . 10.00
62/63 **(167)** NN,P(c),CI Logo;rep. . 10.00
06/64 **(167)** NN,P(c),CI Logo;rep. . 10.00
07/65 **(167)** NN,P(c),CI Logo;rep. . 10.00
03/66 **(167)** NN,P(c),CI Logo;rep. . 10.00
09/67 **(166)** NN,P(c),CI Logo;rep. . 10.00
Wn/69 **(166)** NN,P(c),25¢(c) Price, CI Logo, Rigid(c);rep 18.00
Wn/71 **(169)** NN,P(c),CI Logo;rep . 15.00

006-A TALE OF TWO CITIES

By Charles Dickens

11/42 **(—-)** StM,StM(c),Original 1,000.00
09/43 **(14)** StM,StM(c),No(c) Price; rep 200.00
03/44 **(18)** StM,StM(c),Long Island Independent Edition;rep 150.00
06/44 **(20)** StM,StM(c),Sunrise Times Edition;rep 135.00
06/46 **(28)** StM,StM(c);rep. 100.00
09/48 **(51)** StM,StM(c),New CI Logo; rep 50.00
10/49 **(64)** StM,StM(c),CI Logo;rep. 30.00
12/50 **(78)** StM,StM(c),15¢(c) Price, CI Logo; rep 22.00
11/51 **(89)** StM,StM(c),CI Logo;rep 20.00
03/54 **(117)** StM,StM(c),CI Logo;rep. 18.00
05/56 **(132)** JO New Art,New P(c), CI Logo;rep 20.00
09/57 **(140)** JO,P(c),CI Logo;rep. . . 9.00
11/57 **(147)** JO,P(c),CI Logo;rep . . . 9.00
09/59 **(152)** JO,P(c),CI Logo;rep . 150.00
11/59 **(153)** JO,P(c),CI Logo;rep . . 10.00
03/61 **(149)** JO,P(c),CI Logo;rep . . 10.00
62/63 **(167)** JO,P(c),CI Logo;rep. . . 9.00
06/64 **(167)** JO,P(c),CI Logo;rep. . . 9.00
08/65 **(167)** JO,P(c),CI Logo;rep. . . 9.00
05/67 **(166)** JO,P(c),CI Logo;rep. . . 9.00
Fl/68 **(166)** JO,NN New P(c), 25¢(c)Price,CI Logo;rep 20.00
Sr/70 **(169)** JO,NN P(c),CI Logo, Rigid(c);rep. 15.00

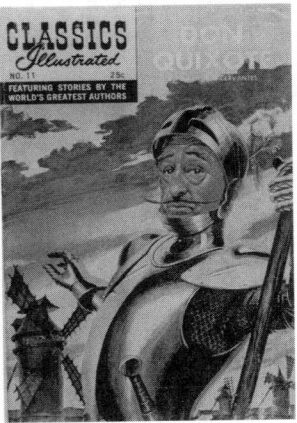

CI #11, Don Quixote
© Gilberton Publications

007-ROBIN HOOD

By Howard Pyle

12/42 **(—-)** LZ,LZ(c),Original 800.00
06/43 **(12)** LZ,LZ(c),P.D.C. on(c) Deleted;rep 200.00
03/44 **(18)** LZ,LZ(c),Long Island Independent Edition;rep 150.00
06/44 **(20)** LZ,LZ(c),Nassau Bulletin Edition;rep 135.00
10/44 **(22)** LZ,LZ(c),Queens City Times Edition;rep. 125.00
06/46 **(28)** LZ,LZ(c),rep. 100.00
09/48 **(51)** LZ,LZ(c),New CI Logo;rep. 50.00
06/49 **(60)** LZ,LZ(c),CI Logo;rep . . 25.00
10/49 **(64)** LZ,LZ(c),CI Logo;rep . . 22.00
12/50 **(78)** LZ,LZ(c),CI Logo;rep . . 22.00
07/52 **(97)** LZ,LZ(c),CI Logo;rep . . 20.00
03/53 **(106)** LZ,LZ(c),CI Logo;rep . 18.00
07/54 **(121)** LZ,LZ(c),CI Logo;rep . 18.00
11/55 **(129)** LZ,New P(c), CI Logo;rep 18.00
01/57 **(136)** JkS New Art,P(c);rep . 10.00
03/58 **(143)** JkS,P(c),CI Logo;rep . 10.00
11/59 **(153)** JkS,P(c),CI Logo;rep . . 9.00
10/61 **(164)** JkS,P(c),CI Logo;rep . . 9.00
62/63 **(167)** JkS,P(c),CI Logo;rep . . 9.00
06/64 **(167)** JkS,P(c),CI Logo;rep . 11.00
05/65 **(167)** JkS,P(c),CI Logo;rep . . 9.00
07/66 **(167)** JkS,P(c),CI Logo;rep . . 9.00
12/67 **(166)** JkS,P(c),CI Logo;rep . 11.00
Sr/69 **(169)** JkS,P(c),CI Logo, Rigid(c);rep. 9.00

008-ARABIAN KNIGHTS

By Antoine Galland

03/43 **(—-)** LCh,LCh(c),Original 1,400.00
09/43 **(14)** LCh,LCh(c);rep 500.00
01/44 **(17)** LCh,LCh(c),Long Island Independent Edition;rep 550.00
06/44 **(20)** LCh,LCh(c),Nassau Bulletin Edition,64 pgs;rep . . 400.00
06/46 **(28)** LCh,LCh(c);rep 250.00
09/48 **(51)** LCh,LCh(c),New CI Logo; rep 250.00
10/49 **(64)** LCh,LCh(c),CI Logo;rep. 200.00
12/50 **(78)** LCh,LCh(c),CI Logo;rep. 160.00
10/61 **(164)** ChB New Art,P(c), CI Logo;rep 135.00

009-LES MISERABLES

By Victor Hugo

03/43 **(—-)** RLv,RLv(c),Original . . 750.00
09/43 **(14)** RLv,RLv(c);rep. 200.00
03/44 **(18)** RLv,RLv(c),Nassau Bulletin Edition;rep. 160.00
06/44 **(20)** RLv,RLv(c),Richmond Courier Edition;rep. 150.00
06/46 **(28)** RLv,RLv(c);rep 125.00
09/48 **(51)** RLv,RLv(c),New CI Logo; rep 60.00
05/50 **(71)** RLv,RLv(c),CI Logo;rep. 50.00
09/51 **(87)** RLv,RLv(c),CI Logo, 15¢(c)Price;rep. 40.00
03/61 **(161)** NN New Art,GMc New P(c), CI Logo;rep 40.00
09/63 **(167)** NN,GMc P(c),CI Logo; rep 25.00
12/65 **(167)** NN,GMc P(c),CI Logo; rep 25.00
1968 **(166)** NN,GMc P(c),25¢(c) Price, CI Logo;rep 25.00

010-ROBINSON CRUSOE

By Daniel Defoe

04/43 **(—-)** StM,StM(c),Original . . 650.00
09/43 **(14)** StM,StM(c);rep. 225.00
03/44 **(18)** StM,StM(c),Nassau Bulletin Ed.,'Bill of Rights'Pge.64;rep. 200.00
06/44 **(20)** StM,StM(c),Queens Home News Edition;rep 150.00
??/45 **(23)** StM,StM(c);rep. 100.00
06/46 **(28)** StM,StM(c);rep. 100.00
09/48 **(51)** StM,StM(c),New CI Logo; rep 50.00
10/49 **(64)** StM,StM(c),CI Logo;rep 35.00
12/50 **(78)** StM,StM(c),15¢(c) Price, CI Logo;rep 25.00
07/52 **(97)** StM,StM(c),CI Logo;rep 22.00
12/53 **(114)** StM,StM(c),CI Logo;rep. 20.00
01/56 **(130)** StM,New P(c),CI Logo; rep 22.00
09/57 **(140)** SmC New Art,P(c), CI Logo; rep 22.00
11/59 **(153)** SmC,P(c),CI Logo;rep . 9.00
10/61 **(164)** SmC,P(c),CI Logo;rep . 9.00
62/63 **(167)** SmC,P(c),CI Logo;rep 10.00
07/64 **(167)** SmC,P(c),CI Logo;rep 12.00
05/65 **(167)** SmC,P(c),CI Logo;rep . 9.00
06/66 **(167)** SmC,P(c),CI Logo;rep 10.00
Fl/68 **(166)** SmC,P(c),CI Logo, 25¢(c)Price;rep. 10.00
1968 **(166)** SmC,P(c),CI Logo,No Twin Circle Ad;rep 9.00
Sr/70 **(169)** SmC,P(c),CI Logo, Rigid(c);rep 9.00

011-DON QUIXOTE

By Miguel de Cervantes Saavedra

05/43 (—-) LZ,LZ(c),Original 700.00
03/44 **(18)** LZ,LZ(c),Nassau Bulletin Edition;rep 200.00
07/44 **(21)** LZ,LZ(c),Queens Home News Edition;rep 150.00
06/46 **(28)** LZ,LZ(c);rep. 100.00
08/53 **(110)** LZ,TO New P(c),New CI Logo;rep 30.00
05/60 **(156)** LZ,TO P(c),Pages Reduced to 48,CI Logo;rep. . . 20.00
1962 **(165)** LZ,TO P(c),CI Logo;rep12.00
01/64 **(167)** LZ,TO P(c),CI Logo;rep. 12.00
11/65 **(167)** LZ,TO P(c),CI Logo;rep. 12.00
1968 **(166)** LZ,TO P(c),CI Logo, 25¢(c)Price;rep. 25.00

012-RIP VAN WINKLE & THE HEADLESS HORSEMAN

By Washington Irving

06/43 **(——)** RLv,RLv(c),Original . 700.00
11/43 **(15)** RLv,RLv(c),Long Island Independent Edition;rep 180.00
06/44 **(20)** RLv,RLv(c),Long Island Independent Edition;rep 150.00
10/44 **(22)** RLv,RLv(c),Queens City Times Edition;rep. 135.00
06/46 **(28)** RLv,RLv(c);rep. 100.00
06/49 **(60)** RLv,RLv(c),New CI Logo;rep. 50.00
08/49 **(62)** RLv,RLv(c),CI Logo;rep. 30.00
05/50 **(71)** RLv,RLv(c),CI Logo;rep. 25.00
11/51 **(89)** RLv,RLv(c),15¢(c) Price, CI Logo;rep 20.00
04/54 **(118)** RLv,RLv(c),CI Logo;rep. 22.00
05/56 **(132)** RLv,New P(c), CI Logo; rep 25.00
05/59 **(150)** NN New Art;P(c), CI Logo; rep 25.00
09/60 **(158)** NN,P(c),CI Logo;rep. . 10.00
62/63 **(167)** NN,P(c),CI Logo;rep. . 10.00
12/63 **(167)** NN,P(c),CI Logo;rep. . 10.00
04/65 **(167)** NN,P(c),CI Logo;rep. . 11.00
04/66 **(167)** NN,P(c),CI Logo;rep. . 10.00
1969 **(166)** NN,P(c),CI Logo, 25¢(c)Price,Rigid(c);rep 16.00
Sr/70 **(169)** NN,P(c),CI Logo, Rigid(c);rep 15.00

013-DR. JEKYLL AND MR. HYDE

By Robert Louis Stevenson

08/43 **(—-)** AdH,AdH(c),Original 1,000.00
11/43 **(15)** AdH,AdH(c),Long Island Independent Edition;rep 250.00
06/44 **(20)** AdH,AdH(c),Long Island Independent Edition;rep 175.00
06/46 **(28)** AdH,AdH(c),No(c) Price; rep 125.00
06/49 **(60)** AdH,HcK New(c),New CI Logo,Pgs.reduced to 48;rep . . 40.00
08/49 **(62)** AdH,HcK(c),CI Logo;rep. 35.00
05/50 **(71)** AdH,HcK(c),CI Logo;rep. 25.00
09/51 **(87)** AdH,HcK(c),Erroneous Return of Original Date, CI Logo;rep 25.00
10/53 **(112)** LC New Art,New P(c), CI Logo;rep 25.00
11/59 **(153)** LC,P(c),CI Logo;rep . . 10.00
03/61 **(161)** LC,P(c),CI Logo;rep . . 10.00
62/63 **(167)** LC,P(c),CI Logo;rep . . 10.00
08/64 **(167)** LC,P(c),CI Logo;rep . . 10.00
11/65 **(167)** LC,P(c),CI Logo;rep . . 10.00
1968 **(166)** LC,P(c),CI Logo, 25¢(c)Price;rep 11.00
Wr/69 **(169)** LC,P(c),CI Logo, Rigid(c);rep 10.00

014-WESTWARD HO!

By Charles Kingsley

09/43 **(—-)** ASm,ASm(c),Orig. . 1,600.00
11/43 **(15)** ASm,ASm(c),Long Island Independent Edition;rep 550.00
07/44 **(21)** ASm,ASm(c);rep 400.00
06/46 **(28)** ASm,ASm(c),No(c) Price; rep 300.00
11/48 **(53)** ASm,ASm(c),Pages reduced to 48, New CI Logo;rep. 275.00

015-UNCLE TOM'S CABIN

By Harriet Beecher Stowe

11/43 **(—-)** RLv,RLv(c),Original . . 650.00
11/43 **(15)** RLv,RLv(c),Blank Price Circle, Long Island Independent Ed.;rep 200.00
07/44 **(21)** RLv,RLv(c),Nassau Bulletin Edition;rep 150.00
06/46 **(28)** RLv,RLv(c),No(c) Price; rep 100.00
11/48 **(53)** RLv,RLv(c),Pages Reduced to 48, New CI Logo;rep. 50.00
05/50 **(71)** RLv,RLv(c),CI Logo;rep 30.00
11/51 **(89)** RLv,RLv(c),15¢(c) Price, CI Logo;rep 30.00
03/54 **(117)** RLv,New P(c),CI Logo, Lettering Changes;rep. . 22.00
09/55 **(128)** RLv,P(c),"Picture Progress"Promotion,CI Logo;rep. 15.00
03/57 **(137)** RLv,P(c),CI Logo;rep . 10.00
09/58 **(146)** RLv,P(c),CI Logo;rep . 10.00
01/60 **(154)** RLv,P(c),CI Logo;rep . 10.00
03/61 **(161)** RLv,P(c),CI Logo;rep . 11.00
62/63 **(167)** RLv,P(c),CI Logo;rep . 10.00
06/64 **(167)** RLv,P(c),CI Logo;rep . 10.00
05/65 **(167)** RLv,P(c),CI Logo;rep . 10.00
05/67 **(166)** RLv,P(c),CI Logo;rep . 10.00
Wr/69 **(166)** RLv,P(c),CI Logo, Rigid(c);rep. 16.00
Sr/70 **(169)** RLv,P(c),CI Logo, Rigid(c);rep. 15.00

016-GULLIVER'S TRAVELS

By Johnathan Swift

12/43 **(——)** LCh,LCh(c),Original 600.00
06/44 **(18/20)** LCh,LCh(c),Queen's Home News Edition,No(c)Price; rep 175.00
10/44 **(22)** LCh,LCh(c),Queen's Home News Editon;rep. 135.00
06/46 **(28)** LCh,LCh(c);rep 100.00
06/49 **(60)** LCh,LCh(c),Pgs. Reduced To 48, New CI Logo;rep 40.00
08/49 **(62)** LCh,LCh(c),CI Logo;rep 30.00
10/49 **(64)** LCh,LCh(c),CI Logo;rep 30.00
12/50 **(78)** LCh,LCh(c),15¢(c) Price, CI Logo;rep 25.00
11/51 **(89)** LCh,LCh(c),CI Logo;rep 20.00
03/60 **(155)** LCh,New P(c),CI Logo; rep 25.00
1962 **(165)** LCh,P(c),CI Logo;rep . 10.00
05/64 **(167)** LCh,P(c),CI Logo;rep . 10.00
11/65 **(167)** LCh,P(c),CI Logo;rep . 10.00
1968 **(166)** LCh,P(c),CI Logo, 25¢(c)Price;rep. 10.00
Wr/69 **(169)** LCh,P(c),CI Logo, Rigid(c);rep. 10.00

017-THE DEERSLAYER

By James Fenimore Cooper

01/44 **(——)** LZ,LZ(c),Original. . . 550.00
03/44 **(18)** LZ,LZ(c),No(c)Price; rep 175.00
10/44 **(22)** LZ,LZ(c),Queen's City Times Edition;rep. 150.00
06/46 **(28)** LZ,LZ(c);rep. 100.00
06/49 **(60)** LZ,LZ(c),Pgs. Reduced to 48,New CI Logo;rep 50.00
10/49 **(64)** LZ,LZ(c),CI Logo;rep . . 25.00
07/51 **(85)** LZ,LZ(c),15¢(c) Price, CI Logo;rep 20.00
04/54 **(118)** LZ,LZ(c),CI Logo;rep . 18.00
05/56 **(132)** LZ,LZ(c),CI Logo;rep . 15.00
11/66 **(167)** LZ,LZ(c),CI Logo;rep . 15.00
1968 **(166)** LZ,StA New P(c),CI Logo, 25¢(c)Price;rep. 25.00
Sg/71 **(169)** LZ,StA P(c),CI Logo,

NO 17
CLASSIC COMICS
FEATURING STORIES BY THE WORLD'S GREATEST AUTHORS
The DEERSLAYER

CI #17, Deerslayer
© Gilberton Publications

Rigid(c), Letters From Parents and Educators;rep 15.00

018-THE HUNCHBACK OF NOTRE DAME

By Victor Hugo

03/44 **(—-)** ASm,ASm(c),Original Gilberton Edition. 700.00
03/44 **(—-)** ASm,ASm(c),Original Island Publications Edition . . 600.00
06/44 **(18/20)** ASm,ASm(c),Queens Home News Edition;rep 200.00
10/44 **(22)** ASm,ASm(c),Queens City Times Edition;rep. 150.00
06/46 **(28)** ASm,ASm(c);rep 125.00
06/49 **(60)** ASm,HcK New(c)8 Pgs. Deleted, New CI Logo;rep . . . 40.00
08/49 **(62)** ASm,HcK(c),CI Logo;rep. 28.00
12/50 **(78)** ASm,HcK(c),15¢(c) Price; CI Logo;rep 25.00
11/51 **(89)** ASm,HcK(c),CI Logo;rep. 22.00
04/54 **(118)** ASm,HcK(c),CI Logo;rep. 25.00
09/57 **(140)** ASm,New P(c),CI Logo; rep 22.00
09/58 **(146)** ASm,P(c),CI Logo;rep 22.00
09/60 **(158)** GE&RC New Art,GMc New P(c),CI Logo;rep. 10.00
1962 **(165)** GE&RC,GMc P(c),CI Logo; rep 10.00
09/63 **(167)** GE&RC,GMc P(c),CI Logo; rep 10.00
10/64 **(167)** GE&RC,GMc P(c),CI Logo; rep 10.00
04/66 **(167)** GE&RC,GMc P(c),CI Logo; rep 10.00
1968 **(166)** GE&RC,GMc P(c),CI Logo, 25¢(c)Price;rep 10.00
Sr/70 **(169)** GE&RC,GMc P(c),CI Logo, Rigid(c);rep. 10.00

019-HUCKLEBERRY FINN

By Mark Twain

04/44 **(—-)** LZ,LZ(c),Original Gilberton Edition. 450.00
04/44 **(—-)** LZ,LZ(c),Original Island Publications Company Edition475.00
03/44 **(18)** LZ,LZ(c),Nassau Bulliten Editon;rep 200.00
10/44 **(22)** LZ,LZ(c),Queens City

Classics Illus.

Times Edition;rep 150.00
06/46 **(28)** LZ,LZ(c);rep. 100.00
06/49 **(60)** LZ,LZ(c),New CI Logo, Pgs.Reduced to 48;rep 40.00
08/49 **(62)** LZ,LZ(c),CI Logo;rep . . 30.00
12/50 **(78)** LZ,LZ(c),CI Logo;rep . . 25.00
11/51 **(89)** LZ,LZ(c),CI Logo;rep . . 20.00
03/54 **(117)** LZ,LZ(c),CI Logo;rep . 20.00
03/56 **(131)** FrG New Art,New P(c), CI Logo; rep. 20.00
09/57 **(140)** FrG,P(c),CI Logo;rep . 10.00
05/59 **(150)** FrG,P(c),CI Logo;rep . 10.00
09/60 **(158)** FrG,P(c),CI Logo;rep . 10.00
1962 **(165)** FrG,P(c),CI Logo;rep. . 10.00
62/63 **(167)** FrG,P(c),CI Logo;rep . 10.00
06/64 **(167)** FrG,P(c),CI Logo;rep . 10.00
06/65 **(167)** FrG,P(c),CI Logo;rep . 10.00
10/65 **(167)** FrG,P(c),CI Logo;rep . 10.00
09/67 **(166)** FrG,P(c),CI Logo;rep . 10.00
Wr/69 **(166)** FrG,P(c),CI Logo, 25¢(c)Price, Rigid(c);rep. 10.00
Sr/70 **(169)** FrG,P(c),CI Logo, Rigid(c);rep 10.00

020-THE CORSICAN BROTHERS

By Alexandre Dumas

06/44 **(—-)** ASm,ASm(c),Original Gilberton Edition. 425.00
06/44 **(—-)** ASm,ASm(c),Original Courier Edition 400.00
06/44 **(—-)** ASm,ASm(c),Original Long Island Independent Edition . . 400.00
10/44 **(22)** ASm,ASm(c),Queens City Times Edition;rep. 175.00
06/46 **(28)** ASm,ASm(c);rep 150.00
06/49 **(60)** ASm,ASm(c),No(c)Price, New CI Logo,Pgs. Reduced to 48;rep. 125.00
08/49 **(62)** ASm,ASm(c),CI Logo;rep. 115.00
12/50 **(78)** ASm,ASm(c),15¢(c) Price, CI Logo;rep 100.00
07/52 **(97)** ASm,ASm(c),CI Logo;rep. 90.00

021-FAMOUS MYSTERIES

By Sir Arthur Conan Doyle Guy de Maupassant & Edgar Allan Poe

07/44 **(—-)** ASm,AdH,LZ,ASm(c), Original Gilberton Edition . . . 800.00
07/44 **(—-)** ASm,AdH,LZ,ASm(c), Original Island Publications Edition; No Date or Indicia . . 825.00
07/44 **(—-)** ASm,AdH,LZ,ASm(c), Original Richmond Courier Edition 700.00
10/44 **(22)** ASm,AdH,LZ,ASm(c), Nassau Bulliten Edition;rep . . 275.00
09/46 **(30)** ASm,AdH,LZ,ASm(c); rep 225.00
08/49 **(62)** ASm,AdH,LZ,ASm(c), New CI Logo;rep 185.00
04/50 **(70)** ASm,AdH,LZ,ASm(c), CI Logo;rep 175.00
07/51 **(85)** ASm,AdH,LZ,ASm(c), 15¢(c) Price,CI Logo;rep. . . . 150.00
12/53 **(114)** ASm,AdH,LZ,New P(c), CI Logo;rep 150.00

022-THE PATHFINDER

By James Fenimore Cooper

10/44 **(—-)** LZ,LZ(c),Original Gilberton Edition. 400.00
10/44 **(—-)** LZ,LZ(c),Original Island Publications Edition . . 300.00
10/44 **(—-)** LZ,LZ(c),Original Queens County Times Edition300.00
09/46 **(30)** LZ,LZ(c),No(c) Price;rep. 100.00
06/49 **(60)** LZ,LZ(c),New CI Logo, Pgs.Reduced To 48;rep 35.00
08/49 **(62)** LZ,LZ(c),CI Logo;rep . . 28.00
04/50 **(70)** LZ,LZ(c),CI Logo;rep . . 25.00
07/51 **(85)** LZ,LZ(c),15¢(c) Price, CI Logo;rep 22.00
04/54 **(118)** LZ,LZ(c),CI Logo;rep . 20.00
05/56 **(132)** LZ,LZ(c),CI Logo;rep . 20.00
09/58 **(146)** LZ,LZ(c),CI Logo;rep . 25.00
11/63 **(167)** LZ,NN New P(c),CI Logo; rep 20.00
12/65 **(167)** LZ,NN P(c),CI Logo;rep. 20.00
08/67 **(166)** LZ,NN P(c),CI Logo;rep. 20.00

023-OLIVER TWIST

By Charles Dickens (First Classic produced by the Iger shop)

07/45 **(—-)** AdH,AdH(c),Original . 350.00
09/46 **(30)** AdH,AdH(c),Price Circle is Blank;rep 250.00
06/49 **(60)** AdH,AdH(c),Pgs. Reduced To 48, New CI Logo;rep 35.00
08/49 **(62)** AdH,AdH(c),CI Logo;rep. 30.00
05/50 **(71)** AdH,AdH(c),CI Logo;rep 25.00
07/51 **(85)** AdH,AdH(c),15¢(c) Price CI Logo;rep 22.00
04/52 **(94)** AdH,AdH(c),CI Logo;rep. 22.00
04/54 **(118)** AdH,AdH(c),CI Logo;rep. 20.00
01/57 **(136)** AdH,New P(c),CI Logo; rep 20.00
05/59 **(150)** AdH,P(c),CI Logo;rep. 15.00
1961 **(164)** AdH,P(c),CI Logo;rep . 15.00
10/61 **(164)** GE&RC New Art,P(c), CI Logo;rep 25.00
62/63 **(167)** GE&RC,P(c),CI Logo; rep 9.00
08/64 **(167)** GE&RC,P(c),CI Logo; rep 9.00
12/65 **(167)** GE&RC,P(c), CI Logo;rep 9.00
1968 **(166)** GE&RC,P(c),CI Logo, 25¢(c)Price;rep. 9.00
Wr/69 **(169)** GE&RC,P(c),CI Logo, Rigid(c);rep. 9.00

024-A CONNECTICUT YANKEE IN KING ARTHUR'S COURT

By Mark Twain

09/45 **(—-)** JH,JH(c),Original. . . . 300.00
09/46 **(30)** JH,JH(c),Price Circle Blank;rep 100.00
06/49 **(60)** JH,JH(c),8 Pages Deleted,New CI Logo;rep 35.00
08/49 **(62)** JH,JH(c),CI Logo;rep . . 30.00
05/50 **(71)** JH,JH(c),CI Logo;rep . . 25.00
09/51 **(87)** JH,JH(c),15¢(c) Price CI Logo;rep 20.00
07/54 **(121)** JH,JH(c),CI Logo;rep . 20.00
09/57 **(140)** JkS New Art,New P(c),CI Logo; rep 25.00
11/59 **(153)** JkS,P(c),CI Logo;rep . 10.00
1961 **(164)** JkS,P(c),CI Logo;rep. . . 9.00
62/63 **(167)** JkS,P(c),CI Logo;rep . . 9.00
07/64 **(167)** JkS,P(c),CI Logo;rep . . 9.00
06/66 **(167)** JkS,P(c),CI Logo;rep . . 9.00
1968 **(166)** JkS,P(c),CI logo, 25¢(c)Price;rep. 9.00
Sg/71 **(169)** JkS,P(c),CI Logo, Rigid(c);rep 9.00

CI #24, A Connecticut Yankee in King Arthur's Court © Gilberton Publications

025-TWO YEARS BEFORE THE MAST

By Richard Henry Dana Jr.

10/45 **(—-)** RWb,DvH,Original; . . 300.00
09/46 **(30)** RWb,DvH,Price Circle Blank;rep 100.00
06/49 **(60)** RWb,DvH,8 Pages Deleted,New CI Logo;rep 35.00
08/49 **(62)** RWb,DvH,CI Logo;rep . 30.00
05/50 **(71)** RWb,DvH,CI Logo;rep . 25.00
07/51 **(85)** RWb,DvH,15¢(c) Price CI Logo;rep 20.00
12/53 **(114)** RWb,DvH,CI Logo;rep 18.00
05/60 **(156)** RWb,DvH,New P(c),CI Logo, 3 Pgs. Replaced By Fillers;rep 22.00
12/63 **(167)** RWb,DvH,P(c),CI Logo; rep 9.00
12/65 **(167)** RWb,DvH,P(c),CI Logo; rep 9.00
09/67 **(166)** RWb,DvH,P(c),CI Logo; rep 9.00
Wr/69 **(169)** RWb,DvH,P(c),25¢(c) Price, CI Logo,Rigid(c);rep 9.00

026-FRANKENSTEIN

By Mary Wollstonecraft Shelley

12/45 **(—-)** RWb&ABr,RWb & ABr(c), Original 800.00
09/46 **(30)** RWb&ABr,RWb &ABr(c), Price Circle Blank;rep 225.00
06/49 **(60)** RWb&ABr,RWb&ABr(c), New CI Logo;rep 125.00
08/49 **(62)** RWb&ABr,RWb & ABr(c), CI Logo;rep 100.00
05/50 **(71)** RWb&ABr,RWb & ABr(c), CI Logo;rep. 45.00
04/51 **(82)** RWb&ABr,RWb &ABr(c), 15¢(c) Price,CI Logo;rep. 40.00
03/54 **(117)** RWb&ABr,RWb & ABr(c),CI Logo;rep 20.00
09/58 **(146)** RWb&ABr,NS New P(c), CI Logo; rep. 25.00
11/59 **(153)** RWb&ABr,NS P(c),CI Logo; rep 35.00
01/61 **(160)** RWb&ABr,NS P(c),CI Logo; rep 8.00

Classics Illus.

165 **(1962)** RWb&ABr,NS P(c), CI Logo; rep 8.00
62/63 **(167)** RWb&ABr,NS P(c), CI Logo; rep 7.00
06/64 **(167)** RWb&ABr,NS P(c), CI logo; rep 7.00
06/65 **(167)** RWb&ABr,NS P(c), CI Logo; rep 7.00
10/65 **(167)** RWb&ABr,NS P(c), CI Logo; rep 7.00
09/67 **(166)** RWb&ABr,NS P(c), CI Logo; rep 7.00
Fl/69 **(169)** RWb&ABr,NS P(c),25¢(c) Price,CI Logo,Rigid(c);rep. 7.00
Sg/71 **(169)** RWb&ABr,NS P(c), CI Logo, Rigid(c);rep 7.00

027-THE ADVENTURES MARCO POLO

By Marco Polo & Donn Byrne

04/46 **(——)** HFl,HFl(c);Original . 350.00
09/46 **(30)** HFl,HFl(c);rep 100.00
04/50 **(70)** HFl,HFl(c),8 Pages Deleted, No(c) Price,New CI Logo;rep . 30.00
09/51 **(87)** HFl,HFl(c),15¢(c) Price,CI Logo;rep 20.00
03/54 **(117)** HFl,HFl(c),CILogo;rep 15.00
01/60 **(154)** HFl,New P(c),CI Logo;rep. 15.00
1962 **(165)** HFl,P(c),CI Logo;rep. . . 9.00
04/64 **(167)** HFl,P(c),CI Logo;rep . . 9.00
06/66 **(167)** HFl,P(c),CI Logo;rep . . 9.00
Sg/69 **(169)** HFl,P(c),CI Logo, 25¢(c)Price,Rigid(c);rep 9.00

028-MICHAEL STROGOFF

By Jules Verne

06/46 **(—-)** AdH,AdH(c),Original . 350.00
09/48 **(51)** AdH,AdH(c),8 Pages Deleted,New CI Logo;rep . . . 100.00
01/54 **(115)** AdH,New P(c),CI Logo; rep 30.00
03/60 **(155)** AdH,P(c),CI Logo;rep. 12.00
11/63 **(167)** AdH,P(c),CI Logo;rep. 12.00
07/66 **(167)** AdH,P(c),CI Logo;rep. 12.00
Sr/69 **(169)**AdH,NN,NewP(c),25¢(c) Price, CI Logo,Rigid(c);rep . . . 18.00

029-THE PRINCE AND THE PAUPER

By Mark Twain

07/46 **(—-)** AdH,AdH(c),Original . 500.00
06/49 **(60)** AdH,New HcK(c),New CI Logo,8 Pages Deleted;rep . . . 40.00
08/49 **(62)** AdH,HcK(c),CILogo;rep 35.00
05/50 **(71)** AdH,HcK(c),CILogo;rep 25.00
03/52 **(93)** AdH,HcK(c),CILogo;rep 22.00
12/53 **(114)** AdH,HcK(c),CI Logo;rep. 20.00
09/55 **(128)** AdH,New P(c),CI Logo; rep 20.00
05/57 **(138)** AdH,P(c),CI Logo;rep. 10.00
05/59 **(150)** AdH,P(c),CI Logo;rep. 10.00
1961 **(164)** AdH,P(c),CI Logo;rep . 10.00
62/63 **(167)** AdH,P(c),CI Logo;rep. 10.00
07/64 **(167)** AdH,P(c),CI Logo;rep. 10.00
11/65 **(167)** AdH,P(c),CI Logo;rep. 10.00
1968 **(166)** AdH,P(c),CI Logo, 25¢(c)Price;rep. 10.00
Sr/70 **(169)** AdH,P(c),CI Logo, Rigid(c);rep 10.00

030-THE MOONSTONE

By William Wilkie Collins

09/46 **(—-)** DRi,DRi(c),Original . . 350.00
06/49 **(60)** DRi,DRi(c),8 Pages Deleted,New CI Logo;rep 50.00
04/50 **(70)** DRi,DRi(c),CI Logo;rep 40.00
03/60 **(155)** DRi,LbC New P(c), CI Logo;rep 50.00
1962 **(165)** DRi,LbC P(c),CI Logo; rep 25.00
01/64 **(167)** DRi,LbC P(c),CI Logo; rep 18.00
09/65 **(167)** DRi,LbC P(c),CI Logo; rep 11.00
1968 **(166)** DRi,LbC P(c),CI Logo, 25¢(c)Price;rep. 10.00

CI #31, The Black Arrow
© Gilberton Publications

031-THE BLACK ARROW

By Robert Louis Stevenson

10/46 **(—-)** AdH,AdH(c),Original . 275.00
09/48 **(51)** AdH,AdH(c),8 Pages Deleted,New CI Logo;rep 35.00
10/49 **(64)** AdH,AdH(c),CI Logo;rep. 25.00
09/51 **(87)** AdH,AdH(c),15¢(c) Price;CI Logo;rep 20.00
06/53 **(108)** AdH,AdH(c),CI Logo;rep. 18.00
03/55 **(125)** AdH,AdH(c),CI Logo;rep. 16.00
03/56 **(131)** AdH,New P(c),CI Logo; rep 12.00
09/57 **(140)** AdH,P(c),CI Logo;rep. 10.00
01/59 **(148)** AdH,P(c),CI Logo;rep. 10.00
03/61 **(161)** AdH,P(c),CI Logo;rep. 10.00
62/63 **(167)** AdH,P(c),CI Logo;rep. 10.00
07/64 **(167)** AdH,P(c),CI logo;rep . 10.00
11/65 **(167)** AdH,P(c),CI Logo;rep . 10.00
1968 **(166)** AdH,P(c),CI Logo, 25¢(c)Price;rep. 10.00

032-LORNA DOONE

By Richard Doddridge Blackmore

12/46 **(—-)** MB,MB(c),Original. . . 300.00
10/49 **(53/64)** MB,MB(c),8 Pages Deleted,New CI Logo;rep 50.00
07/51 **(85)** MB,MB(c),15¢(c) Price, CI Logo;rep 40.00
04/54 **(118)** MB,MB(c),CI Logo;rep 25.00
05/57 **(138)** MB,New P(c); Old(c) Becomes New Splash Pge.,CI Logo;rep. 25.00
05/59 **(150)** MB,P(c),CI Logo;rep . 10.00
1962 **(165)** MB,P(c),CI Logo;rep . . 10.00
01/64 **(167)** MB,P(c),CI Logo;rep . 12.00
11/65 **(167)** MB,P(c),CI Logo;rep. . 12.00
1968 **(166)** MB,New P(c),CI Logo; rep 25.00

033-THE ADVENTURES OF SHERLOCK HOLMES

By Sir Arthur Conan Doyle

01/47 **(—-)** LZ,HcK(c),Original . 1,000.00
11/48 **(53)** LZ,HcK(c),"A Study in Scarlet" Deleted,New CI Logo;rep 350.00
05/50 **(71)** LZ,HcK(c),CI Logo;rep 275.00
11/51 **(89)** LZ,HcK(c),15¢(c) Price,CI Logo;rep 225.00

034-MYSTERIOUS ISLAND

By Jules Verne

Last Classic Comic

02/47 **(—-)** RWb&DvH,Original . . 350.00
06/49 **(60)** RWb&DvH,8 Pages Deleted,New CI Logo;rep 40.00
08/49 **(62)** RWb&DvH,CI Logo;rep 30.00
05/50 **(71)** RWb&DvH,CI Logo;rep 40.00
12/50 **(78)** RWb&DvH,15¢(c) Price, CI Logo;rep 25.00
02/52 **(92)** RWb&DvH,CI Logo;rep 25.00
03/54 **(117)** RWb&DvH,CI Logo; rep 25.00
09/57 **(140)** RWb&DvH,New P(c), CI Logo;rep 25.00
05/60 **(156)** RWb&DvH,P(c),CI Logo;rep. 10.00
10/63 **(167)** RWb&DvH,P(c),CI Logo;rep. 10.00
05/64 **(167)** RWb&DvH,P(c),CI Logo;rep. 10.00
06/66 **(167)** RWb&DvH,P(c),CI logo;rep 10.00
1968 **(166)** RWb&DvH,P(c),CI Logo, 25¢(c)Price;rep. 10.00

035-LAST DAYS OF POMPEII

By Lord Edward Bulwer Lytton

First Classics Illustrated

03/47 **(—-)** HcK,HcK(c),Original . 350.00
03/61 **(161)** JK,New P(c), 15¢(c)Price;rep. 40.00
01/64 **(167)** JK,P(c);rep. 20.00
07/66 **(167)** JK,P(c);rep. 20.00
Sg/70 **(169)** JK,P(c),25¢(c) Price, Rigid(c);rep. 20.00

036-TYPEE

By Herman Melville

04/47 **(—-)** EzW,EzW(c),Original. 175.00
10/49 **(64)** EzW,EzW(c),No(c)price, 8 pages deleted;rep 50.00
03/60 **(155)** EzW,GMc New P(c);rep 25.00
09/63 **(167)** EzW,GMc P(c);rep . . . 15.00
07/65 **(167)** EzW,GMc P(c);rep . . . 15.00
Sr/69 **(169)** EzW,GMc P(c),25¢(c) Price, Rigid(c);rep. 15.00

037-THE PIONEERS

By James Fenimore Cooper

05/47 **(37)** RP,RP(c),Original. . . . 135.00
08/49 **(62)** RP,RP(c),8 Pages Deleted;rep 30.00
04/50 **(70)** RP,RP(c);rep 25.00
02/52 **(92)** RP,RP(c),15¢(c)price; rep 25.00
04/54 **(118)** RP,RP(c);rep 20.00
03/56 **(131)** RP,RP(c);rep 20.00

05/56 **(132)** RP,RP(c);rep 20.00
11/59 **(153)** RP,RP(c);rep 15.00
05/64 **(167)** RP,RP(c);rep 15.00
06/66 **(167)** RP,RP(c);rep 15.00
1968 **(166)** RP,TO New P(c), 25¢(c)Price;rep. 25.00

038-ADVENTURES OF CELLINI

By Benvenuto Cellini

06/47 **(—-)** AgF,AgF(c),Original . . 250.00
1961 **(164)** NN New Art,New P(c); rep 25.00
12/63 **(167)** NN,P(c);rep 15.00
07/66 **(167)** NN,P(c);rep 15.00
Sg/70 **(169)** NN,P(c),25¢(c) Price, Rigid(c);rep. 18.00

039-JANE EYRE

By Charlotte Bronte

07/47 **(—-)** HyG,HyG(c),Original . 225.00
06/49 **(60)** HyG,HyG(c),No(c)Price, 8 pages deleted;rep 35.00
08/49 **(62)** HyG,HyG(c);rep. 30.00
05/50 **(71)** HyG,HyG(c);rep. 25.00
02/52 **(92)** HyG,HyG(c),15¢(c) Price; rep 22.00
04/54 **(118)** HyG,HyG(c);rep 22.00
01/58 **(142)** HyG,New P(c);rep . . . 22.00
01/60 **(154)** HyG,P(c);rep 22.00
1962 **(165)** HjK New Art,P(c);rep. . 22.00
12/63 **(167)** HjK,P(c);rep. 22.00
04/65 **(167)** HjK,P(c);rep. 22.00
08/66 **(167)** HjK,P(c);rep. 22.00
1968 **(166)** HjK,NN New P(c);rep . 50.00

040-MYSTERIES (The Pit & the Pendulum, The Adventures of Hans Pfall, Fall of the House of Usher)

By Edgar Allan Poe

08/47 **(—-)** HcK,AgF,HyG,HcK(c), Original 525.00
08/49 **(62)** HcK,AgF,HyG,HcK(c), 8 Pages deleted;rep 225.00
09/50 **(75)** HcK,AgF,HyG, HcK(c);rep 200.00
02/52 **(92)** HcK,AgF,HyG,HcK(c) 15¢(c) Price;rep 150.00

041-TWENTY YEARS AFTER

By Alexandre Dumas

09/47 **(—-)** RBu,RBu(c),Original . 400.00
08/49 **(62)** RBu,HcK New(c),No(c) Price, 8 Pages Deleted;rep. . . 40.00
12/50 **(78)** RBu,HcK(c),15¢(c) Price; rep 30.00
05/60 **(156)** RBu,DgR New P(c); rep 25.00
12/63 **(167)** RBu,DgR P(c);rep . . . 10.00
11/66 **(167)** RBu,DgR P(c);rep . . . 10.00
Sg/70 **(169)** RBu,DgR P(c),25¢(c) Price, Rigid(c);rep. 10.00

042-SWISS FAMILY ROBINSON

By Johann Wyss

10/47 **(42)** HcK,HcK(c),Original. . 175.00
08/49 **(62)** HcK,HcK(c),No(c)price, 8 Pages Deleted,Not Every Issue Has 'Gift Box' Ad;rep 35.00
09/50 **(75)** HcK,HcK(c);rep 25.00
03/52 **(93)** HcK,HcK(c);rep 22.00
03/54 **(117)** HcK,HcK(c);rep 20.00
03/56 **(131)** HcK,New P(c);rep . . . 18.00
03/57 **(137)** HcK,P(c);rep 18.00
11/57 **(141)** HcK,P(c);rep 18.00
09/59 **(152)** NN New art,P(c);rep. . 18.00
09/60 **(158)** NN,P(c);rep 15.00
12/63 **(165)** NN,P(c);rep 20.00
12/63 **(167)** NN,P(c);rep 9.00
04/65 **(167)** NN,P(c);rep 9.00
05/66 **(167)** NN,P(c);rep 9.00
11/67 **(166)** NN,P(c);rep 9.00
Sg/69 **(169)** NN,P(c);rep. 9.00

043-GREAT EXPECTATIONS

By Charles Dickens

11/47 **(—-)** HcK,HcK(c),Original . 700.00
08/49 **(62)** HcK,HcK(c),No(c)price; 8 pages deleted;rep 450.00

044-MYSTERIES OF PARIS

By Eugene Sue

12/47 **(44)** HcK,HcK(c),Original. . 575.00
08/47 **(62)** HcK,HcK(c),No(c)Price, 8 Pages Deleted,Not Every Issue Has'Gift Box'Ad;rep 225.00
12/50 **(78)** HcK,HcK(c),15¢(c) Price; rep 200.00

045-TOM BROWN'S SCHOOL DAYS

By Thomas Hughes

01/48 **(44)** HFl,HFl(c),Original, 1st 48 Pge. Issue 125.00
10/49 **(64)** HFl,HFl(c),No(c) Price;rep 40.00
03/61 **(161)** JTg New Art,GMc New P(c);rep 20.00
02/64 **(167)** JTg,GMc P(c);rep. . . . 12.00
08/66 **(167)** JTg,GMc P(c);rep. . . . 12.00
1968 **(166)** JTg,GMc P(c), 25¢(c)Price;rep. 12.00

046-KIDNAPPED

By Robert Louis Stevenson

04/48 **(47)** RWb,RWb(c),Original. 100.00
08/49 **(62)** RWb,RWb(c),Red Circle Either Blank or With 10¢;rep. . 62.00
12/50 **(78)** RWb,RWb(c),15¢(c) Price; rep 25.00
09/51 **(87)** RWb,RWb(c);rep 22.00
04/54 **(118)** RWb,RWb(c);rep 20.00
03/56 **(131)** RWb,New P(c);rep. . . 20.00
09/57 **(140)** RWb,P(c);rep. 10.00
05/59 **(150)** RWb,P(c);rep. 10.00
05/60 **(156)** RWb,P(c);rep. 10.00
1961 **(164)** RWb,P(c),Reduced Pge. Wdth;rep 10.00
62/63 **(167)** RWb,P(c);rep. 10.00
03/64 **(167)** RWb,P(c);rep. 10.00
06/65 **(167)** RWb,P(c);rep. 10.00
12/65 **(167)** RWb,P(c);rep. 10.00
09/67 **(167)** RWb,P(c);rep. 10.00
Wr/69 **(166)** RWb,P(c),25¢(c) Price, Rigid(c);rep. 10.00
Sr/70 **(169)** RWb,P(c),Rigid(c);rep. 10.00

047-TWENTY THOUSAND LEAGUES UNDER THE SEA

By Jules Verne

05/58 **(47)** HcK,HcK(c),Original. . 100.00
10/49 **(64)** HcK,HcK(c),No(c) Price; rep 30.00
12/50 **(78)** HcK,HcK(c),15¢(c) Price; rep 25.00
04/52 **(94)** HcK,HcK(c);rep 25.00
04/54 **(118)** HcK,HcK(c);rep 20.00
09/55 **(128)** HcK,New P(c);rep . . . 20.00
07/56 **(133)** HcK,P(c);rep 15.00
09/57 **(140)** HcK,P(c);rep 10.00
01/59 **(148)** HcK,P(c);rep 10.00
05/60 **(156)** HcK,P(c);rep 10.00
62/63 **(165)** HcK,P(c);rep 10.00
05/48 **(167)** HcK,P(c);rep 10.00
03/64 **(167)** HcK,P(c);rep 10.00
08/65 **(167)** HcK,P(c);rep 10.00
10/66 **(167)** HcK,P(c);rep 10.00
1968 **(166)** HcK,NN New P(c), 25¢(c)Price;rep. 15.00
Sg/70 **(169)** HcK,NN P(c), Rigid(c);rep 15.00

048-DAVID COPPERFIELD

By Charles Dickens

06/48 **(47)** HcK,HcK(c),Original. . 100.00
10/49 **(64)** HcK,HcK(c),Price Circle Replaced By Image of Boy Reading;rep 30.00
09/51 **(87)** HcK,HcK(c),15¢(c) Price; rep 25.00
07/54 **(121)** HcK,New P(c);rep . . . 20.00
10/56 **(130)** HcK,P(c);rep 10.00
09/57 **(140)** HcK,P(c);rep 10.00
01/59 **(148)** HcK,P(c);rep 10.00
05/60 **(156)** HcK,P(c);rep 10.00
62/63 **(167)** HcK,P(c);rep 10.00
04/64 **(167)** HcK,P(c);rep 10.00
06/65 **(167)** HcK,P(c);rep 10.00
05/67 **(166)** HcK,P(c);rep 10.00
R/67 **(166)** HcK,P(c);rep 15.00
Sg/69 **(166)** HcK,P(c),25¢(c) Price, Rigid(c);rep. 10.00
Wr/69 **(169)** HcK,P(c),Rigid(c);rep. 10.00

049-ALICE IN WONDERLAND

By Lewis Carroll

07/48 **(47)** AB,AB(c),Original. . . . 150.00
10/49 **(64)** AB,AB(c),No(c)Price; rep 40.00
07/51 **(85)** AB,AB(c),15¢(c)Price; rep 35.00
03/60 **(155)** AB,New P(c);rep 35.00
1962 **(165)** AB,P(c);rep. 25.00
03/64 **(167)** AB,P(c);rep 20.00
06/66 **(167)** AB,P(c);rep 20.00
Fl/68 **(166)** AB,TO New P(c),25¢(c) Price, New Soft(c);rep 35.00
Fl/68 **(166)** AB,P(c),Both Soft & Rigid(c)s;rep. 65.00

050-ADVENTURES OF TOM SAWYER

By Mark Twain

08/48 **(51)** ARu,ARu(c),Original. . 125.00
09/48 **(51)** ARu,ARu(c),Original. . 130.00
10/49 **(64)** ARu,ARu(c),No(c) Price; rep 25.00
12/50 **(78)** ARu,ARu(c),15¢(c) Price; rep 20.00
04/52 **(94)** ARu,ARu(c);rep 20.00
12/53 **(114)** ARu,ARu(c);rep 20.00
03/54 **(117)** ARu,ARu(c);rep 15.00
05/56 **(132)** ARu,ARu(c);rep 15.00
09/57 **(140)** ARu,New P(c);rep . . . 12.00
05/59 **(150)** ARu,P(c);rep 15.00
10/61 **(164)** New Art,P(c);rep 9.00
62/63 **(167)** P(c);rep 9.00

01/65 **(167)** P(c);rep 9.00
05/66 **(167)** P(c);rep 9.00
12/67 **(166)** P(c);rep 9.00
Fl/69 **(169)** P(c),25¢(c) Price, Rigid(c);rep 9.00
Wr/71 **(169)** P(c);rep. 9.00

051-THE SPY

By James Fenimore Cooper

09/48 **(51)** AdH,AdH(c),Original, Maroon(c). 100.00
09/48 **(51)** AdH,AdH(c),Original, Violet(c) 100.00
11/51 **(89)** AdH,AdH(c),15¢(c) Price; rep 25.00
07/54 **(121)** AdH,AdH(c);rep 20.00
07/57 **(139)** AdH,New P(c);rep . . . 20.00
05/60 **(156)** AdH,P(c);rep 10.00
11/63 **(167)** AdH,P(c);rep 10.00
07/66 **(167)** AdH,P(c);rep 10.00
Wr/69 **(166)** AdH,P(c),25¢(c)Price, Both Soft & Rigid(c)s;rep 25.00

052-THE HOUSE OF SEVEN GABLES

By Nathaniel Hawthorne

10/48 **(53)** HyG,HyG(c),Original . 100.00
11/51 **(89)** HyG,HyG(c),15¢(c) Price; rep 25.00
07/54 **(121)** HyG,HyG(c);rep 20.00
01/58 **(142)** GWb New Art,New P(c); rep. 25.00
05/60 **(156)** GWb,P(c);rep. 10.00
1962 **(165)** GWb,P(c);rep 10.00
05/64 **(167)** GWb,P(c);rep. 10.00
03/66 **(167)** GWb,P(c);rep. 10.00
1968 **(166)** GWb,P(c),25¢(c) Price; rep 10.00
Sg/70 **(169)** GWb,P(c),Rigid(c);rep 10.00

053-A CHRISTMAS CAROL

By Charles Dickens

11/48 **(53)** HcK,HcK(c),Original . . 150.00

054-MAN IN THE IRON MASK

By Alexandre Dumas

12/48 **(55)** AgF,HcK(c),Original . . 100.00
03/52 **(93)** AgF,HcK(c),15¢(c) Price; rep 30.00
09/53 **(111)** AgF,HcK(c);rep. 40.00
01/58 **(142)** KBa New Art,New P(c); rep. 25.00
01/60 **(154)** KBa,P(c);rep 10.00
1962 **(165)** KBa,P(c);rep. 10.00
05/64 **(167)** KBa,P(c);rep 10.00
04/66 **(167)** KBa,P(c);rep 10.00
Wr/69 **(166)** KBa,P(c),25¢(c) Price, Rigid(c);rep. 10.00

055-SILAS MARINER

By George Eliot

01/49 **(55)** AdH,HcK(c),Original. . 100.00
09/50 **(75)** AdH,HcK(c),Price Circle Blank,'Coming next'Ad(not usually in reps.);rep 30.00
07/52 **(97)** AdH,HcK(c);rep 22.00
07/54 **(121)** AdH,New P(c);rep . . . 20.00
01/56 **(130)** AdH,P(c);rep 10.00
09/57 **(140)** AdH,P(c);rep 10.00
01/60 **(154)** AdH,P(c);rep 10.00
1962 **(165)** AdH,P(c);rep. 10.00
05/64 **(167)** AdH,P(c);rep 10.00
06/65 **(167)** AdH,P(c);rep 10.00
05/67 **(166)** AdH,P(c);rep 10.00
Wr/69 **(166)** AdH,P(c),25¢(c) Price, Rigid(c);rep,Soft & Stiff 25.00

056-THE TOILERS OF THE SEA

By Victor Hugo

02/49 **(55)** AgF,AgF(c),Original . . 175.00
01/62 **(165)** AT New Art,New P(c); rep. 40.00
03/64 **(167)** AT,P(c);rep. 25.00
10/66 **(167)** AT,P(c);rep. 25.00

057-THE SONG OF HIAWATHA

By Henry Wadsworth Longfellow

03/49 **(55)** AB,AB(c),Original. . . . 100.00
09/50 **(75)** AB,AB(c),No(c)price,' Coming Next'Ad(not usually found in reps.);rep 35.00
04/52 **(94)** AB,AB(c),15¢(c) Price;rep 25.00
04/54 **(118)** AB,AB(c);rep 22.00
09/56 **(134)** AB,New P(c);rep 20.00
07/57 **(139)** AB,P(c);rep 10.00
01/60 **(154)** AB,P(c);rep 10.00
62/63 **(167)** AB,P(c),Erroneosly Has Original Date;rep. 10.00
09/64 **(167)** AB,P(c);rep 10.00
10/65 **(167)** AB,P(c);rep 10.00
Fl/68 **(166)** AB,P(c),25¢(c)Price; rep 10.00

058-THE PRAIRIE

By James Fenimore Cooper

04/49 **(60)** RP,RP(c),Original. . . . 100.00
08/49 **(62)** RP,RP(c);rep 50.00
12/50 **(78)** RP,RP(c),15¢(c) Price In Double Circle;rep 25.00
12/53 **(114)** RP,RP(c);rep 20.00
03/56 **(131)** RP,RP(c);rep 20.00
05/56 **(132)** RP,RP(c);rep 20.00
09/58 **(146)** RP,New P(c);rep 20.00
03/60 **(155)** RP,P(c);rep 11.00
05/64 **(167)** RP,P(c);rep 10.00
04/66 **(167)** RP,P(c);rep 10.00
Sr/69 **(169)** RP,P(c),25¢(c) Price; Rigid(c);rep. 10.00

059-WUTHERING HEIGHTS

By Emily Bronte

05/49 **(60)** HcK,HcK(c),Original. . 125.00
07/51 **(85)** HcK,HcK(c),15¢(c) Price; rep 35.00
05/60 **(156)** HcK,GB New P(c);rep 25.00
01/64 **(167)** HcK,GB P(c);rep 15.00
10/66 **(167)** HcK,GB P(c);rep 15.00
Sr/69 **(169)** HcK,GBP(c),25¢(c) Price, Rigid(c);rep. 12.00

060-BLACK BEAUTY

By Anna Sewell

06/49 **(62)** AgF,AgF(c),Original . . 100.00
08/49 **(62)** AgF,AgF(c);rep. 125.00
07/51 **(85)** AgF,AgF(c),15¢(c) Price; rep 30.00
09/60 **(158)** LbC&NN&StA New Art, LbC New P(c);rep 25.00
02/64 **(167)** LbC&NN&StA,LbC P(c); rep. 20.00
03/66 **(167)** LbC&NN&StA,LbC P(c); rep. 20.00
03/66 **(167)** LbC&NN&StA,LbC P(c), 'Open Book'Blank;rep. . . 20.00
1968 **(166)** LbC&NN&StA,AIM New P(c) 25¢(c) Price;rep 50.00

061-THE WOMAN IN WHITE

By William Wilke Collins

07/49 **(62)** AB,AB(c),Original, Maroon & Violet(c)s 110.00
05/60 **(156)** AB,DgR New P(c);rep 30.00
01/64 **(167)** AB,DgR P(c);rep 20.00
1968 **(166)** AB,DgR P(c), 25¢(c)Price;rep. 20.00

062-WESTERN STORIES (The Luck of Roaring Camp & The Outcasts of Poker Flat)

By Bret Harte

08/49 **(62)** HcK,HcK(c),Original. . 100.00
11/51 **(89)** HcK,HcK(c),15¢(c) Price; rep 30.00
07/54 **(121)** HcK,HcK(c);rep 22.00
03/57 **(137)** HcK,New P(c);rep . . . 20.00
09/59 **(152)** HcK,P(c);rep 11.00
10/63 **(167)** HcK,P(c);rep 11.00
06/64 **(167)** HcK,P(c);rep 10.00
11/66 **(167)** HcK,P(c);rep 10.00
1968 **(166)** HcK,TO New P(c), 25¢ Price;rep 20.00

063-THE MAN WITHOUT A COUNTRY

By Edward Everett Hale

09/49 **(62)** HcK,HcK(c),Original. . 100.00
12/50 **(78)** HcK,HcK(c),15¢(c)Price In Double Circles;rep 30.00
05/60 **(156)** HcK,GMc New P(c); rep 25.00
01/62 **(165)** AT New Art,GMc P(c), Added Text Pages;rep 22.00
03/64 **(167)** AT,GMc P(c);rep 10.00
08/66 **(167)** AT,GMc P(c);rep 10.00
Sr/69 **(169)** AT,GMc P(c),25¢(c) Price, Rigid(c);rep. 10.00

064-TREASURE ISLAND

By Robert Louis Stevenson

10/49 **(62)** AB,AB(c),Original. 90.00
04/51 **(82)** AB,AB(c),15¢(c)

CI #64 Treasure Island
© Gilberton Publications

Classics Illus.

Price;rep 30.00
03/54 **(117)** AB,AB(c);rep 22.00
03/56 **(131)** AB,New P(c);rep 20.00
05/57 **(138)** AB,P(c);rep 10.00
09/58 **(146)** AB,P(c);rep 10.00
09/60 **(158)** AB,P(c);rep 10.00
1962 **(165)** AB,P(c);rep. 10.00
62/63 **(167)** AB,P(c);rep 10.00
06/64 **(167)** AB,P(c);rep 10.00
12/65 **(167)** AB,P(c);rep 10.00
10/67 **(166)** AB,P(c);rep 12.00
10/67 **(166)** AB,P(c),GRIT Ad Stapled In Book;rep 75.00
Sg/69 **(169)** AB,P(c),25¢(c) Price, Rigid(c);rep. 10.00

065-BENJAMIN FRANKLIN

By Benjamin Franklin

11/49 **(64)** AB,RtH,GS(Iger Shop), HcK(c),Original. 100.00
03/56 **(131)** AB,RtH,GS(Iger Shop), New P(c) ;rep. 25.00
01/60 **(154)** AB,RtH,GS(Iger Shop), P(c);rep 12.00
02/64 **(167)** AB,RtH,GS(Iger Shop), P(c);rep 10.00
04/66 **(167)** AB,RtH,GS(Iger Shop), P(c);rep 10.00
Fl/69 **(169)** AB,RtH,GS(Iger Shop), P(c), 25¢(c)Price,Rigid(c);rep . 12.00

066-THE CLOISTER AND THE HEARTH

By Charles Reade

12/49 **(67)** HcK,HcK(c),Original. . 225.00

067-THE SCOTTISH CHIEFS

By Jane Porter

01/50 **(67)** AB,AB(c),Original. . . . 100.00
07/51 **(85)** AB,AB(c),15¢(c) Price;rep 30.00
04/54 **(118)** AB,AB(c);rep 25.00
01/57 **(136)** AB,New P(c);rep 22.00
01/60 **(154)** AB,P(c);rep 12.00
11/63 **(167)** AB,P(c);rep 15.00
08/65 **(167)** AB,P(c);rep 12.00

068-JULIUS CEASAR

By William Shakespeare

02/50 **(70)** HcK,HcK(c),Original. . . 90.00
07/51 **(85)** HcK,HcK(c),15¢(c) Price; rep 28.00
06/53 **(108)** HcK,HcK(c);rep 22.00
05/60 **(156)** HcK,LbC New P(c);rep25.00
1962 **(165)** GE&RC New Art, LbC P(c);rep. 25.00
02/64 **(167)** GE&RC,LbC P(c);rep. 10.00
10/65 **(167)** GE&RC,LbC P(c),Tarzan Books Inside(c);rep. 10.00
1967 **(166)** GE&RC,LbC P(c);rep . 10.00
Wr/69 **(169)** GE&RC,LbC P(c), Rigid(c);rep 10.00

069-AROUND THE WORLD IN 80 DAYS

By Jules Verne

03/50 **(70)** HcK,HcK(c),Original. . . 90.00
09/51 **(87)** HcK,HcK(c),15¢(c) Price; rep 30.00
03/55 **(125)** HcK,HcK(c);rep 22.00
01/57 **(136)** HcK,New P(c);rep . . . 22.00
09/58 **(146)** HcK,P(c);rep 11.00
09/59 **(152)** HcK,P(c);rep 11.00
1961 **(164)** HcK,P(c);rep 11.00
62/63 **(167)** HcK,P(c);rep 10.00
07/64 **(167)** HcK,P(c);rep 10.00
11/65 **(167)** HcK,P(c);rep 10.00
07/67 **(166)** HcK,P(c);rep 10.00
Sg/69 **(169)** HcK,P(c),25¢(c) Price, Rigid(c);rep. 10.00

070-THE PILOT

By James Fenimore Cooper

04/50 **(71)** AB,AB(c),Original. 75.00
10/50 **(75)** AB,AB(c),15¢(c) Price;rep 30.00
02/52 **(92)** AB,AB(c);rep 22.00
03/55 **(125)** AB,AB(c);rep 25.00
05/60 **(156)** AB,GMc New P(c);rep 20.00
02/64 **(167)** AB,GMc P(c);rep 20.00
05/66 **(167)** AB,GMc P(c);rep 16.00

071-THE MAN WHO LAUGHS

By Victor Hugo

05/50 **(71)** AB,AB(c),Original. . . . 125.00
01/62 **(165)** NN,NN New P(c);rep . 75.00
04/64 **(167)** NN,NN P(c);rep 65.00

072-THE OREGON TRAIL

By Francis Parkman

06/50 **(73)** HcK,HcK (c),Original . . 75.00
11/51 **(89)** HcK,HcK (c),15¢(c) Price; rep 30.00
07/54 **(121)** HcK,HcK (c);rep. 22.00
03/56 **(131)** HcK,New P(c);rep . . . 20.00
09/57 **(140)** HcK,P(c);rep 11.00
05/59 **(150)** HcK,P(c);rep 10.00
01/61 **(164)** HcK,P(c);rep 10.00
62/63 **(167)** HcK,P(c);rep 10.00
08/64 **(167)** HcK,P(c);rep 10.00
10/65 **(167)** HcK,P(c);rep 10.00
1968 **(166)** HcK,P(c),25¢(c)Price; rep 10.00

073-THE BLACK TULIP

By Alexandre Dumas

07/50 **(75)** AB,AB(c),Original. . . . 275.00

074-MR. MIDSHIPMAN EASY

By Captain Frederick Marryat

08/50 **(75)** BbL,Original. 275.00

075-THE LADY OF THE LAKE

By Sir Walter Scott

09/50 **(75)** HcK,HcK(c),Original. . . 80.00
07/51 **(85)** HcK,HcK(c),15¢(c) Price; rep 30.00
04/54 **(118)** HcK,HcK(c);rep 25.00
07/57 **(139)** HcK,New P(c);rep . . . 25.00
01/60 **(154)** HcK,P(c);rep 10.00
1962 **(165)** HcK,P(c);rep. 10.00
04/64 **(167)** HcK,P(c);rep 10.00
05/66 **(167)** HcK,P(c);rep 10.00
Sg/69 **(169)** HcK,P(c),25¢(c) Price, Rigid(c);rep. 10.00

076-THE PRISONER OF ZENDA

By Anthony Hope Hawkins

10/50 **(75)** HcK,HcK(c),Original. . . 75.00
07/51 **(85)** HcK,HcK(c),15¢(c) Price; rep 30.00
09/53 **(111)** HcK,HcK(c),rep 25.00
09/55 **(128)** HcK,New P(c);rep . . . 25.00
09/59 **(152)** HcK,P(c);rep 11.00
1962 **(165)** HcK,P(c);rep. 10.00
04/64 **(167)** HcK,P(c);rep 10.00
09/66 **(167)** HcK,P(c);rep 10.00
Fl/69 **(169)** HcK,P(c),25¢(c) Price, Rigid(c);rep 10.00

077-THE ILLIAD

By Homer

11/50 **(78)** AB,AB(c),Original. 80.00
09/51 **(87)** AB,AB(c),15¢(c) Price;rep 30.00
07/54 **(121)** AB,AB(c);rep 25.00
07/57 **(139)** AB,New P(c);rep 25.00
05/59 **(150)** AB,P(c);rep 11.00
1962 **(165)** AB,P(c);rep. 10.00
10/63 **(167)** AB,P(c);rep 10.00
07/64 **(167)** AB,P(c);rep 10.00
05/66 **(167)** AB,P(c);rep 10.00
1968 **(166)** AB,P(c),25¢(c)Price;rep 10.00

078-JOAN OF ARC

By Frederick Schiller

12/50 **(78)** HcK,HcK(c),Original. . . 70.00
09/51 **(87)** HcK,HcK(c),15¢(c) Price; rep 30.00
11/53 **(113)** HcK,HcK(c);rep 25.00
09/55 **(128)** HcK,New P(c);rep . . . 25.00
09/57 **(140)** HcK,P(c);rep 11.00
05/59 **(150)** HcK,P(c);rep 11.00
11/60 **(159)** HcK,P(c);rep 10.00
62/63 **(167)** HcK,P(c);rep 10.00
12/63 **(167)** HcK,P(c);rep 10.00
06/65 **(167)** HcK,P(c);rep 10.00
06/67 **(166)** HcK,P(c);rep 10.00
Wr/69 **(166)** HcK,TO New P(c), 25¢(c)Price, Rigid(c);rep. 25.00

079-CYRANO DE BERGERAC

By Edmond Rostand

01/51 **(78)** AB,AB(c),Original,Movie Promo Inside Front(c). 75.00
07/51 **(85)** AB,AB(c),15¢(c) Price;rep 30.00
04/54 **(118)** AB,AB(c);rep 25.00
07/56 **(133)** AB,New P(c);rep 25.00
05/60 **(156)** AB,P(c);rep 20.00
08/64 **(167)** AB,P(c);rep 20.00

080-WHITE FANG

By Jack London

Last Line Drawn (c)

02/51 **(79)** AB,AB(c),Original. 75.00
09/51 **(87)** AB,AB(c);rep 30.00
03/55 **(125)** AB,AB(c);rep 25.00
05/56 **(132)** AB,New P(c);rep 25.00
09/57 **(140)** AB,P(c);rep 11.00
11/59 **(153)** AB,P(c);rep 11.00
62/63 **(167)** AB,P(c);rep 10.00
09/64 **(167)** AB,P(c);rep 10.00
07/65 **(167)** AB,P(c);rep 10.00
06/67 **(166)** AB,P(c);rep 10.00
Fl/69 **(169)** AB,P(c),25¢(c) Price, Rigid(c);rep. 10.00

081-THE ODYSSEY

By Homer

(P(c)s From Now on)

03/51 **(82)** HyG,AB P(c),Original. . 75.00
08/64 **(167)** HyG,AB P(c);rep 20.00
10/66 **(167)** HyG,AB P(c);rep 20.00
Sg/69 **(169)** HyG,TyT New P(c), Rigid(c);rep 25.00

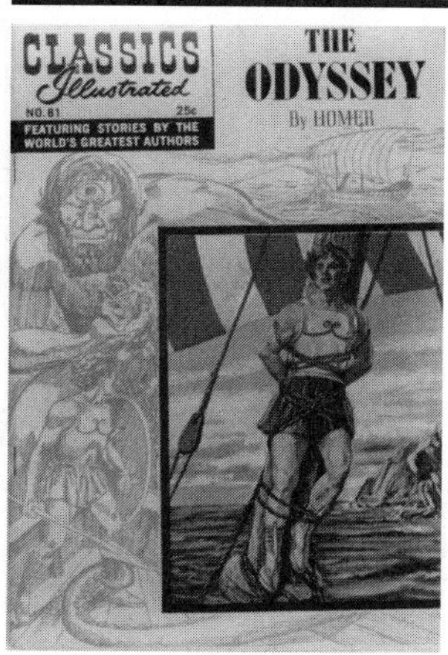

CI #81 The Odyssey
© Gilberton Publications

082-THE MASTER OF BALLANTRAE

By Robert Louis Stevenson

04/51 **(82)** LDr,AB P(c),Original. . . 50.00
08/64 **(167)** LDr,AB P(c);rep 20.00
Fl/68 **(166)** LDr,Syk New P(c), Rigid(c);rep 25.00

083-THE JUNGLE BOOK

By Rudyard Kipling

05/51 **(85)** WmB&AB,AB P(c), Original 40.00
08/53 **(110)** WmB&AB,AB P(c);rep 11.00
03/55 **(125)** WmB&AB,AB P(c);rep 11.00
05/56 **(134)** WmB&AB,AB P(c);rep 11.00
01/58 **(142)** WmB&AB,AB P(c);rep 11.00
05/59 **(150)** WmB&AB,AB P(c);rep 10.00
11/60 **(159)** WmB&AB,AB P(c);rep 10.00
62/63 **(167)** WmB&AB,AB P(c);rep 10.00
03/65 **(167)** WmB&AB,AB P(c);rep 10.00
11/65 **(167)** WmB&AB,AB P(c);rep 10.00
05/66 **(167)** WmB&AB,AB P(c);rep 10.00
1968 **(166)** NN Art,NN New P(c), Rigid(c);rep 25.00

084-THE GOLD BUG & OTHER STORIES

(The Gold Bug-The Telltale Heart The Cask of Amontillado)

By Edgar Allan Poe

06/51 **(85)** AB,RP,JLv,AB P(c), Original 100.00
07/64 **(167)** AB,RP,JLv,AB P(c);rep 75.00

085-THE SEA WOLF

By Jack London

08/51 **(85)** AB,AB P(c),Original . . . 35.00
07/54 **(121)** AB,AB P(c);rep. 11.00
05/56 **(132)** AB,AB P(c);rep. 11.00
11/57 **(141)** AB,AB P(c);rep. 11.00
03/61 **(161)** AB,AB P(c);rep 10.00
02/64 **(167)** AB,AB P(c);rep 10.00
11/65 **(167)** AB,AB P(c);rep. 10.00
Fl/69 **(169)** AB,AB P(c),25¢(c) Price, Rigid(c);rep. 10.00

086-UNDER TWO FLAGS

By Oiuda

08/51 **(87)** MDb,AB P(c),Original. . 30.00
03/54 **(117)** MDb,AB P(c);rep 15.00
07/57 **(139)** MDb,AB P(c);rep 12.00
09/60 **(158)** MDb,AB P(c);rep 12.00
02/64 **(167)** MDb,AB P(c);rep 10.00
08/66 **(167)** MDb,AB P(c);rep 10.00
Sr/69 **(169)** MDb,AB P(c),25¢(c) Price, Rigid(c);rep. 10.00

087-A MIDSUMMER NIGHT'S DREAM

By William Shakespeare

09/51 **(87)** AB,AB P(c),Original . . . 30.00
03/61 **(161)** AB,AB P(c);rep. 11.00
04/64 **(167)** AB,AB P(c);rep 10.00
05/66 **(167)** AB,AB P(c);rep 10.00
Sr/69 **(169)** AB,AB P(c),25¢(c) Price; rep 10.00

088-MEN OF IRON

By Howard Pyle

10/51 **(89)** HD,LDr,GS,Original . . . 35.00
01/60 **(154)** HD,LDr,GS,P(c);rep . . 11.00
01/64 **(167)** HD,LDr,GS,P(c);rep . . 10.00
1968 **(166)** HD,LDr,GS,P(c), 25¢(c)Price;rep. 10.00

089-CRIME AND PUNISHMENT

By Fedor Dostoevsky

11/51 **(89)** RP,AB P(c),Original . . . 40.00
09/59 **(152)** RP,AB P(c);rep. 15.00
04/64 **(167)** RP,AB P(c);rep. 10.00
05/66 **(167)** RP,AB P(c);rep. 10.00
Fl/69 **(169)** RP,AB P(c),25¢(c) Price, Rigid(c);rep. 10.00

090-GREEN MANSIONS

By William Henry Hudson

12/51 **(89)** AB,AB P(c),Original . . . 35.00
01/59 **(148)** AB,New LbC P(c);rep. 20.00
1962 **(165)** AB,LbC P(c);rep 10.00
04/64 **(167)** AB,LbC P(c);rep. 10.00
09/66 **(167)** AB,LbC P(c);rep. 10.00
Sr/69 **(169)** AB,LbC P(c),25¢(c) Price, Rigid(c);rep. 10.00

091-THE CALL OF THE WILD

By Jack London

01/52 **(92)** MDb,P(c),Original 35.00
10/53 **(112)** MDb,P(c);rep 12.00
03/55**(125)**MDb,P(c),'PictureProgress' Onn. Back(c);rep 12.00
09/56 **(134)** MDb,P(c);rep 12.00
03/58 **(143)** MDb,P(c);rep 10.00
1962 **(165)** MDb,P(c);rep 10.00
1962 **(167)** MDb,P(c);rep 10.00
04/65 **(167)** MDb,P(c);rep 10.00
03/66 **(167)** MDb,P(c);rep 10.00
03/66 **(167)** MDb,P(c),Record Edition;rep 10.00
11/67 **(166)** MDb,P(c);rep 10.00
Sg/70 **(169)** MDb,P(c),25¢(c) Price, Rigid(c);rep. 10.00

092-THE COURTSHIP OF MILES STANDISH

By Henry Wadsworth Longfellow

02/52 **(92)** AB,AB P(c),Original . . . 30.00
1962 **(165)** AB,AB P(c);rep 11.00
03/64 **(167)** AB,AB P(c);rep. 11.00
05/67 **(166)** AB,AB P(c);rep. 11.00
Wr/69 **(169)** AB,AB P(c),25¢(c) Price, Rigid(c);rep. 11.00

093-PUDD'NHEAD WILSON

By Mark Twain

03/52 **(94)** HcK,HcK P(c),Original . 35.00
1962 **(165)** HcK,GMc New P(c);rep 15.00
03/64 **(167)** HcK,GMc P(c);rep . . . 12.00
1968 **(166)** HcK,GMc P(c),25¢(c) Price, Soft(c);rep 12.00

094-DAVID BALFOUR

By Robert Louis Stevenson

04/52 **(94)** RP,P(c),Original 35.00
05/64 **(167)** RP,P(c);rep 15.00
1968 **(166)** RP,P(c),25¢(c)Price;rep 15.00

095-ALL QUIET ON THE WESTERN FRONT

By Erich Maria Remarque

05/52 **(96)** MDb,P(c),Original . . . 100.00
05/52 **(99)** MDb,P(c),Original 60.00
10/64 **(167)** MDb,P(c);rep 25.00
11/66 **(167)** MDb,P(c);rep 25.00

096-DANIEL BOONE

By John Bakeless

06/52 **(97)** AB,P(c),Original. 30.00
03/54 **(117)** AB,P(c);rep 11.00
09/55 **(128)** AB,P(c);rep 11.00
05/56 **(132)** AB,P(c);rep 11.00
—— **(134)** AB,P(c),'Story of Jesus'on Back(c);rep 11.00
09/60 **(158)** AB,P(c);rep 11.00
01/64 **(167)** AB,P(c);rep 10.00
05/65 **(167)** AB,P(c);rep 10.00
11/66 **(167)** AB,P(c);rep 10.00
Wr/69 **(166)** AB,P(c),25¢(c) Price, Rigid(c);rep. 15.00

097-KING SOLOMON'S MINES

By H. Rider Haggard

07/52 **(96)** HcK,P(c),Original. 30.00
04/54 **(118)** HcK,P(c);rep 12.00
03/56 **(131)** HcK,P(c);rep 12.00
09/51 **(141)** HcK,P(c);rep 12.00
09/60 **(158)** HcK,P(c);rep 10.00
02/64 **(167)** HcK,P(c);rep 10.00
09/65 **(167)** HcK,P(c);rep 10.00
Sr/69 **(169)** HcK,P(c),25¢(c) Price; Rigid(c);rep. 11.00

098-THE RED BADGE OF COURAGE

By Stephen Crane

08/52 **(98)** MDb,GS,P(c),Original . 32.00
04/54 **(118)** MDb,GS,P(c);rep 12.00
05/56 **(132)** MDb,GS,P(c);rep 12.00
01/58 **(142)** MDb,GS,P(c);rep 12.00
09/59 **(152)** MDb,GS,P(c);rep 11.00
03/61 **(161)** MDb,GS,P(c);rep 11.00
62/63 **(167)** MDb,GS,P(c),Erroneously Has Original Date;rep 11.00
09/64 **(167)** MDb,GS,P(c);rep 11.00
10/65 **(167)** MDb,GS,P(c);rep 11.00
1968 **(166)** MDb,GS,P(c),25¢(c) Price, Rigid(c);rep. 20.00

099-HAMLET

By William Shakespeare

09/52 **(98)** AB,P(c),Original...... 35.00
07/54 **(121)** AB,P(c);rep........ 12.00
11/57 **(141)** AB,P(c);rep........ 12.00
09/60 **(158)** AB,P(c);rep........ 10.00
62/63 **(167)** AB,P(c),Erroneously Has Original Date;rep....... 10.00
07/65 **(167)** AB,P(c);rep........ 10.00
04/67 **(166)** AB,P(c);rep........ 10.00
Sg/69 **(169)** AB,EdM New P(c), 25¢(c)Price, Rigid(c);rep..... 20.00

100-MUTINY ON THE BOUNTY

By Charles Nordhoff

10/52 **(100)** MsW,HcK P(c),Original30.00
03/54 **(117)** MsW,HcK P(c);rep... 12.00
05/56 **(132)** MsW,HcK P(c);rep... 12.00
01/58 **(142)** MsW,HcK P(c);rep... 12.00
03/60 **(155)** MsW,HcK P(c);rep... 10.00
62/63 **(167)** MsW,HcK P(c),Erroneously Has Original Date;rep....... 10.00
05/64 **(167)** MsW,HcK P(c);rep... 10.00
03/66 **(167)** MsW,HcK P(c),N# or Price;rep.............. 12.00
Sg/70 **(169)** MsW,HcK P(c), Rigid(c); rep.............. 10.00

101-WILLIAM TELL

By Frederick Schiller

11/52 **(101)** MDb,HcK P(c),Original 30.00
04/54 **(118)** MDb,HcK P(c);rep... 12.00
11/57 **(141)** MDb,HcK P(c);rep... 12.00
09/60 **(158)** MDb,HcK P(c);rep... 10.00
62/63 **(167)** MDb,HcK P(c),Erroneously Has Original Date;rep....... 10.00
11/64 **(167)** MDb,HcK P(c);rep... 10.00
04/67 **(166)** MDb,HcK P(c);rep... 10.00
Wr/69 **(169)** MDb,HcK P(c)25¢(c) Price, Rigid(c);rep.......... 10.00

102-THE WHITE COMPANY

By Sir Arthur Conan Doyle

12/52 **(101)** AB,P(c),Original..... 65.00
1962 **(165)** AB,P(c);rep......... 25.00
04/64 **(167)** AB,P(c);rep........ 25.00

103-MEN AGAINST THE SEA

By Charles Nordhoff

01/53 **(104)** RP,HcK P(c),Original . 35.00
12/53 **(114)** RP,HcK P(c);rep..... 20.00
03/56 **(131)** RP,New P(c);rep 25.00
03/59 **(149)** RP,P(c);rep........ 20.00
09/60 **(158)** RP,P(c);rep........ 28.00
03/64 **(167)** RP,P(c);rep........ 15.00

104-BRING 'EM BACK ALIVE

By Frank Buck & Edward Anthony

02/53 **(105)** HcK,HcK P(c)Original. 30.00
04/54 **(118)** HcK,HcK P(c);rep.... 12.00
07/56 **(133)** HcK,HcK P(c);rep.... 11.00
05/59 **(150)** HcK,HcK P(c);rep.... 10.00
09/60 **(158)** HcK,HcK P(c);rep.... 10.00
10/63 **(167)** HcK,HcK P(c);rep.... 10.00
09/65 **(167)** HcK,HcK P(c);rep.... 10.00
Wr/69 **(169)** HcK,HcK P(c),25¢(c) Price, Rigid(c);rep.......... 10.00

105-FROM THE EARTH TO THE MOON

By Jules Verne

03/53 **(106)** AB,P(c),Original..... 30.00
04/54 **(118)** AB,P(c);rep........ 11.00
03/56 **(132)** AB,P(c);rep........ 11.00
11/57 **(141)** AB,P(c);rep........ 11.00
09/58 **(146)** AB,P(c);rep........ 11.00
05/60 **(156)** AB,P(c);rep........ 11.00
62/63 **(167)** AB,P(c),Erroneously Has Original Date;rep....... 10.00
05/64 **(167)** AB,P(c);rep........ 10.00
05/65 **(167)** AB,P(c);rep........ 10.00
10/67 **(166)** AB,P(c);rep........ 10.00
Sr/69 **(169)** AB,P(c),25¢(c) Price, Rigid(c);rep.......... 10.00
Sg/71 **(169)** AB,P(c);rep........ 10.00

106-BUFFALO BILL

By William F. Cody

04/53 **(107)** MDb,P(c),Original ... 30.00
04/54 **(118)** MDb,P(c);rep....... 11.00
03/56 **(132)** MDb,P(c);rep....... 11.00
01/58 **(142)** MDb,P(c);rep....... 11.00
03/61 **(161)** MDb,P(c);rep....... 10.00
03/64 **(167)** MDb,P(c);rep....... 10.00
07/67 **(166)** MDb,P(c);rep....... 10.00
Fl/69 **(169)** MDb,P(c),Rigid(c);rep . 10.00

107-KING OF THE KHYBER RIFLES

By Talbot Mundy

05/53 **(108)** SMz,P(c),Original.... 30.00
04/54 **(118)** SMz,P(c);rep....... 11.00
09/58 **(146)** SMz,P(c);rep....... 11.00
09/60 **(158)** SMz,P(c);rep....... 10.00
62/63 **(167)** SMz,P(c),Erroreunsly Has Original Date;rep....... 10.00
62/63 **(167)** SMz,P(c);rep....... 10.00
10/66 **(167)** SMz,P(c);rep....... 10.00

108-KNIGHTS OF THE ROUND TABLE

By Howard Pyle?

06/53 **(108)** AB,P(c),Original..... 35.00
06/53 **(109)** AB,P(c),Original..... 42.00
03/54 **(117)** AB,P(c);rep........ 11.00
11/59 **(153)** AB,P(c);rep........ 10.00
1962 **(165)** AB,P(c);rep......... 10.00
04/64 **(167)** AB,P(c);rep........ 10.00
04/67 **(166)** AB,P(c);rep........ 10.00

109-PITCAIRN'S ISLAND

By Charles Nordhoff

07/53 **(110)** RP,P(c),Original..... 35.00
1962 **(165)** RP,P(c);rep......... 12.00
03/64 **(167)** RP,P(c);rep........ 12.00
06/67 **(166)** RP,P(c);rep........ 12.00

110-A STUDY IN SCARLET

By Sir Arthur Conan Doyle

08/53 **(111)** SMz,P(c),Original... 100.00
1962 **(165)** SMz,P(c);rep........ 75.00

111-THE TALISMAN

By Sir Walter Scott

09/53 **(112)** HcK,HcK P(c),Original 40.00
1962 **(165)** HcK,HcK P(c);rep.... 11.00
05/64 **(167)** HcK,HcK P(c);rep.... 11.00
Fl/68 **(166)** HcK,HcK P(c), 25¢(c)Price;rep............ 11.00

CI #109, Pitcairn's Island
© Gilberton Publications

112-ADVENTURES OF KIT CARSON

By John S. C. Abbott

10/53 **(113)** RP,P(c),Original..... 40.00
11/55 **(129)** RP,P(c);rep......... 11.00
11/57 **(141)** RP,P(c);rep......... 11.00
09/59 **(152)** RP,P(c);rep........ 10.00
03/61 **(161)** RP,P(c);rep........ 10.00
62/63 **(167)** RP,P(c);rep........ 10.00
02/65 **(167)** RP,P(c);rep........ 10.00
05/66 **(167)** RP,P(c);rep........ 10.00
Wr/69 **(166)** RP,EdM New P(c), 25¢(c)Price, Rigid(c);rep..... 15.00

113-THE FORTY-FIVE GUARDSMEN

By Alexandre Dumas

11/53 **(114)** MDb,P(c),Original.... 60.00
07/67 **(166)** MDb,P(c);rep....... 30.00

114-THE RED ROVER

By James Fenimore Cooper

12/53 **(115)** PrC,JP P(c),Original.. 60.00
07/67 **(166)** PrC,JP P(c);rep..... 30.00

115-HOW I FOUND LIVINGSTONE

By Sir Henry Stanley

01/54 **(116)** SF&ST,P(c),Original.. 65.00
01/67 **(167)** SF&ST,P(c);rep..... 40.00

116-THE BOTTLE IMP

By Robert Louis Stevenson

02/54 **(117)** LC,P(c),Original..... 70.00
01/67 **(167)** LC,P(c);rep........ 40.00

117-CAPTAINS COURAGEOUS

By Rudyard Kipling

03/54 **(118)** PrC,P(c),Original.... 60.00
02/67 **(167)** PrC,P(c);rep........ 22.00
Fl/69 **(169)** PrC,P(c),25¢(c) Price, Rigid(c);rep.......... 20.00

Classics Illus.

118-ROB ROY
By Sir Walter Scott
04/54 **(119)** RP,WIP,P(c),Original. . 70.00
02/67 **(167)** RP,WIP,P(c);rep 40.00

119-SOLDERS OF FORTUNE
By Richard Harding Davis
05/54 **(120)** KS,P(c),Original 50.00
03/67 **(166)** KS,P(c);rep 22.00
Sg/70 **(169)** KS,P(c),25¢(c) Price, Rigid(c);rep. 20.00

120-THE HURRICANE
By Charles Nordhoff
1954 **(121)** LC,LC P(c),Original. . . 50.00
03/67 **(166)** LC,LC P(c);rep. 30.00

121-WILD BILL HICKOK
Author Unknown
07/54 **(122)** MI,ST,P(c),Original. . . 25.00
05/56 **(132)** MI,ST,P(c);rep 11.00
11/57 **(141)** MI,ST,P(c);rep 11.00
01/60 **(154)** MI,ST,P(c);rep 11.00
62/63 **(167)** MI,ST,P(c);rep 10.00
08/64 **(167)** MI,ST,P(c);rep 10.00
04/67 **(166)** MI,ST,P(c);rep 10.00
Wr/69 **(169)** MI,ST,P(c),Rigid (c);rep 10.00

122-THE MUTINEERS
By Charles Boardman Hawes
09/54 **(123)** PrC,P(c),Original 35.00
01/57 **(136)** PrC,P(c);rep. 11.00
09/58 **(146)** PrC,P(c);rep. 11.00
09/60 **(158)** PrC,P(c);rep. 10.00
11/63 **(167)** PrC,P(c);rep. 10.00
03/65 **(167)** PrC,P(c);rep. 10.00
08/67 **(166)** PrC,P(c);rep. 10.00

123-FANG AND CLAW
By Frank Buck
11/54 **(124)** LnS,P(c),Original 35.00
07/56 **(133)** LnS,P(c);rep. 11.00
03/58 **(143)** LnS,P(c);rep. 11.00
01/60 **(154)** LnS,P(c);rep 10.00
62/63 **(167)** LnS,P(c),Erroneously Has Original Date;rep 10.00
09/65 **(167)** LnS,P(c);rep 10.00

124-THE WAR OF THE WORLDS
By H. G. Wells
01/55 **(125)** LC,LC P(c),Original . . 50.00
03/56 **(131)** LC,LC P(c);rep. 12.00
11/57 **(141)** LC,LC P(c);rep. 12.00
01/59 **(148)** LC,LC P(c);rep. 12.00
05/60 **(156)** LC,LC P(c);rep. 15.00
1962 **(165)** LC,LC P(c);rep 12.00
62/63 **(167)** LC,LC P(c);rep. 12.00
11/64 **(167)** LC,LC P(c);rep. 12.00
11/65 **(167)** LC,LC P(c);rep. 12.00
1968 **(166)** LC,LC P(c),25¢(c) Price; rep 12.00
Sr/70 **(169)** LC,LC P(c),Rigid (c);rep 12.00

125-THE OX-BOW INCIDENT
By Walter Van Tilberg Clark
03/55 **(—-)** NN,P(c),Original 25.00

CI #125, The Ox-Boy Incident
© Gilberton Publications

03/58 **(143)** NN,P(c);rep 11.00
09/59 **(152)** NN,P(c);rep 11.00
03/61 **(149)** NN,P(c);rep 11.00
62/63 **(167)** NN,P(c);rep 10.00
11/64 **(167)** NN,P(c);rep 10.00
04/67 **(166)** NN,P(c);rep 10.00
r/69 **(169)** NN,P(c),25¢(c) Price, Rigid(c);rep. 10.00

126-THE DOWNFALL
By Emile Zola
05/55 **(—-)** LC,LC P(c),Original, 'Picture Progress'Replaces Reorder List 35.00
08/64 **(167)** LC,LC P(c);rep. 15.00
1968 **(166)** LC,LC P(c),25¢(c) Price;rep 15.00

127-THE KING OF THE MOUNTAINS
By Edmond About
07/55 **(128)** NN,P(c),Original. 35.00
06/64 **(167)** NN,P(c);rep 12.00
Fl/68 **(166)** NN,P(c),25¢(c) Price;rep 12.00

128-MACBETH
By William Shakespeare
09/55 **(128)** AB,P(c),Original. 35.00
03/58 **(143)** AB,P(c);rep 11.00
09/60 **(158)** AB,P(c);rep 11.00
62/63 **(167)** AB,P(c);rep 10.00
06/64 **(167)** AB,P(c);rep 10.00
04/67 **(166)** AB,P(c);rep 10.00
1968 **(166)** AB,P(c),25¢(c) Price;rep 10.00
Sg/70 **(169)** AB,P(c),Rigid(c);rep. . 10.00

129-DAVY CROCKETT
Author Unknown
11/55 **(129)** LC,P(c),Original 100.00
09/66 **(167)** LC,P(c);rep 75.00

130-CAESAR'S CONQUESTS
By Julius Caesar
01/56 **(130)** JO,P(c),Original 40.00
01/58 **(142)** JO,P(c);rep 11.00
09/59 **(152)** JO,P(c);rep 11.00
03/61 **(149)** JO,P(c);rep 11.00
62/63 **(167)** JO,P(c);rep 10.00
10/64 **(167)** JO,P(c);rep 10.00
04/66 **(167)** JO,P(c);rep 10.00

131-THE COVERED WAGON
By Emerson Hough
03/56 **(131)** NN,P(c),Original. 25.00
03/58 **(143)** NN,P(c);rep 11.00
09/59 **(152)** NN,P(c);rep 11.00
09/60 **(158)** NN,P(c);rep 11.00
62/63 **(167)** NN,P(c);rep 10.00
11/64 **(167)** NN,P(c);rep 10.00
04/66 **(167)** NN,P(c);rep 10.00
Wr/69 **(169)** NN,P(c),25¢(c) Price, Rigid(c);rep. 10.00

132-THE DARK FRIGATE
By Charles Boardman Hawes
05/56 **(132)** EW&RWb,P(c),Orig.. . 35.00
05/59 **(150)** EW&RWb,P(c);rep . . . 12.00
01/64 **(167)** EW&RWb,P(c);rep . . . 12.00
05/67 **(166)** EW&RWb,P(c);rep . . . 12.00

133-THE TIME MACHINE
By H. G. Wells
07/56 **(132)** LC,P(c),Original 45.00
01/58 **(142)** LC,P(c);rep 12.00
09/59 **(152)** LC,P(c);rep 12.00
09/60 **(158)** LC,P(c);rep 12.00
62/63 **(167)** LC,P(c);rep 12.00
06/64 **(167)** LC,P(c);rep 15.00
03/66 **(167)** LC,P(c);rep 12.00
03/66 **(167)** LC,P(c),N# Or Price; rep 12.00
12/67 **(166)** LC,P(c);rep 12.00
Wr/71 **(169)** LC,P(c),25¢(c) Price, Rigid(c);rep. 12.00

134-ROMEO AND JULIET
By William Shakespeare
09/56 **(134)** GE,P(c),Original. 30.00
03/61 **(161)** GE,P(c);rep 11.00
09/63 **(167)** GE,P(c);rep 10.00
05/65 **(167)** GE,P(c);rep 10.00
06/67 **(166)** GE,P(c);rep 10.00
Wr/69 **(166)** GE,EdM New P(c), 25¢(c)Price, Rigid(c);rep. 22.00

135-WATERLOO
By Emile Erckmann & Alexandre Chatrian
11/56 (135) GrI,AB P(c),Original . . 35.00
11/59 **(153)** GrI,AB P(c);rep. 11.00
62/63 **(167)** GrI,AB P(c);rep 10.00
09/64 **(167)** GrI,AB P(c);rep 10.00
1968 **(166)** GrI,AB P(c),25¢(c) Price; rep 10.00

136-LORD JIM
By Joseph Conrad
01/57 **(136)** GE,P(c),Original. 35.00
62/63 **(165)** GE,P(c);rep 10.00
03/64 **(167)** GE,P(c);rep 10.00
09/66 **(167)** GE,P(c);rep 10.00
Sr/69 **(169)** GE,P(c),25¢(c) Price, Rigid(c);rep. 10.00

137-THE LITTLE SAVAGE
By Captain Frederick Marryat
03/57 **(136)** GE,P(c),Original. 35.00

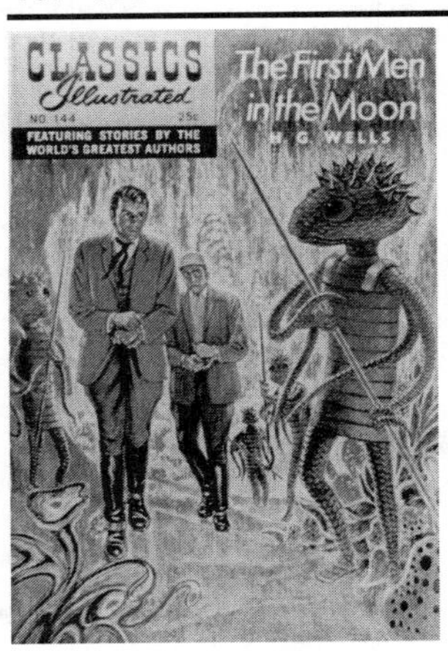

CI #144, First Men in the Moon
© Gilberton Publications

01/59 **(148)** GE,P(c);rep 11.00
05/60 **(156)** GE,P(c);rep 11.00
62/63 **(167)** GE,P(c);rep 10.00
10/64 **(167)** GE,P(c);rep 10.00
08/67 **(166)** GE,P(c);rep 10.00
Sg/70 **(169)** GE,P(c),25¢(c) Price, Rigid(c);rep. 10.00

138-A JOURNEY TO THE CENTER OF THE EARTH
By Jules Verne

05/57 **(136)** NN,P(c),Original. 45.00
09/58 **(146)** NN,P(c);rep 12.00
05/60 **(156)** NN,P(c);rep 12.00
09/60 **(158)** NN,P(c);rep 12.00
62/63 **(167)** NN,P(c);rep 10.00
06/64 **(167)** NN,P(c);rep 11.00
04/66 **(167)** NN,P(c);rep 11.00
1968 **(166)** NN,P(c),25¢(c) Price;rep 10.00

139-IN THE REIGN OF TERROR
By George Alfred Henty

07/57 **(139)** GE,P(c),Original. 25.00
01/60 **(154)** GE,P(c);rep 12.00
62/63 **(167)** GE,P(c),Erroneously Has Original Date;rep. 10.00
07/64 **(167)** GE,P(c);rep 12.00
1968 **(166)** GE,P(c),25¢(c) Price;rep 10.00

140-ON JUNGLE TRAILS
By Frank Buck

09/57 **(140)** NN,P(c),Original. 25.00
05/59 **(150)** NN,P(c);rep 11.00
01/61 **(160)** NN,P(c);rep 11.00
09/63 **(167)** NN,P(c);rep 10.00
09/65 **(167)** NN,P(c);rep 10.00

141-CASTLE DANGEROUS
By Sir Walter Scott

11/57 **(141)** StC,P(c),Original 42.00
09/59 **(152)** STC,P(c);rep 11.00
62/63 **(167)** StC,P(c);rep. 10.00
07/67 **(166)** StC,P(c);rep. 10.00

142-ABRAHAM LINCOLN
By Benjamin Thomas

01/58 **(142)** NN,P(c),Original. 40.00
01/60 **(154)** NN,P(c);rep 11.00
09/60 **(158)** NN,P(c);rep 11.00
10/63 **(167)** NN,P(c);rep 10.00
07/65 **(167)** NN,P(c);rep 10.00
11/67 **(166)** NN,P(c);rep 10.00
Fl/69 **(169)** NN,P(c),25¢(c) Price, Rigid(c);rep 10.00

143-KIM
By Rudyard Kipling

03/58 **(143)** JO,P(c)Original 30.00
62/63 **(165)** JO,P(c);rep 10.00
11/63 **(167)** JO,P(c);rep 10.00
08/65 **(167)** JO,P(c);rep 10.00
Wr/69 **(169)** JO,P(c),25¢(c) Price, Rigid(c);rep 10.00

144-THE FIRST MEN IN THE MOON
By H. G. Wells

05/58 **(143)** GWb,AW,AT,RKr,GMC P(c), Original 35.00
11/59 **(153)** GWb,AW,AT,RKr,GMC P(c); rep 11.00
03/61 **(161)** GWb,AW,AT,RKr,GMC P(c); rep. 10.00
62/63 **(167)** GWb,AW,AT,RKr,GMC P(c); rep. 10.00
12/65 **(167)** GWb,AW,AT,RKr,GMC P(c); rep. 10.00
Fl/68 **(166)** GWb,AW,AT,RKr,GMC P(c),25¢(c) Price,Rigid(c);rep . 10.00
Wr/69 **(169)** GWb,AW,AT,RKr,GMC P(c), Rigid(c);rep 18.00

145-THE CRISIS
by Winston Churchill

07/58 **(143)** GE,P(c),Original. 35.00
05/60 **(156)** GE,P(c);rep 11.00
10/63 **(167)** GE,P(c);rep 10.00
03/65 **(167)** GE,P(c);rep 10.00
1968 **(166)** GE,P(c),25¢(c) Price;rep 10.00

146-WITH FIRE AND SWORD
By Henryk Sienkiewicz

09/58 **(143)** GWb,P(c),Original . . . 40.00
05/60 **(156)** GWb,P(c);rep. 15.00
11/63 **(167)** GWb,P(c);rep. 12.00
03/65 **(167)** GWb,P(c);rep. 12.00

147-BEN-HUR
By Lew Wallace

11/58 **(147)** JO,P(c),Original 35.00
11/59 **(153)** JO,P(c);rep 40.00
09/60 **(158)** JO,P(c);rep 11.00
62/63 **(167)** JO,P(c),Has the Original Date;rep 11.00
—— **(167)** JO,P(c);rep. 10.00
02/65 **(167)** JO,P(c);rep 10.00
09/66 **(167)** JO,P(c);rep 10.00
Fl/68 **(166)** JO,P(c),25¢(c)Price, Both Rigid & Soft (c)s;rep 35.00

148-THE BUCCANEER
By Lyle Saxon

01/59 **(148)** GE&RJ,NS P(c),orig. . 30.00
—— **(568)** GE&RJ,NS P(c),Juniors List Only;rep. 12.00
62/63 **(167)** GE&RJ,NS P(c);rep . . 11.00
09/65 **(167)** GE&RJ,NS P(c);rep . . 11.00
Sr/69 **(169)** GE&RJ,NS P(c),25¢(c) Price, Rigid(c);rep. 11.00

149-OFF ON A COMET
By Jules Verne

03/59 **(149)** GMc,P(c),Original . . . 35.00
03/60 **(155)** GMc,P(c);rep 11.00
03/61 **(149)** GMc,P(c);rep 11.00
12/63 **(167)** GMc,P(c);rep 10.00
02/65 **(167)** GMc,P(c);rep 10.00
10/66 **(167)** GMc,P(c);rep 10.00
Fl/68 **(166)** GMc,EdM New P(c), 25¢(c)Price;rep. 20.00

150-THE VIRGINIAN
By Owen Winster

05/59 **(150)** NN,DrG P(c),Original . 40.00
1961 **(164)** NN,DrG P(c);rep 20.00
62/63 **(167)** NN,DrG P(c);rep 25.00
12/65 **(167)** NN,DrG P(c);rep 20.00

151-WON BY THE SWORD
By George Alfred Henty

07/59 **(150)** JTg,P(c),Original 40.00
1961 **(164)** JTg,P(c);rep 15.00
10/63 **(167)** JTg,P(c);rep. 15.00
1963 **(167)** JTg,P(c);rep 15.00
07/67 **(166)** JTg,P(c);rep. 15.00

152-WILD ANIMALS I HAVE KNOWN
By Ernest Thompson Seton

09/59 **(152)** LbC,LbC P(c),Original 45.00
03/61 **(149)** LbC,LbC P(c),P(c);rep 11.00
09/63 **(167)** LbC,LbC P(c);rep. . . . 10.00
08/65 **(167)** LbC,LbC P(c);rep. . . . 10.00
fl/69 **(169)** LbC,LbC P(c),25¢(c) Price, Rigid(c);rep. 10.00

153-THE INVISIBLE MAN
By H. G. Wells

11/59 **(153)** NN,GB P(c),Original. . 45.00
03/61 **(149)** NN,GB P(c);rep 12.00
62/63 **(167)** NN,GB P(c);rep 10.00
02/65 **(167)** NN,GB P(c);rep 10.00
09/66 **(167)** NN,GB P(c);rep 10.00
Wr/69 **(166)** NN,GB P(c),25¢(c) Price, Rigid(c);rep. 10.00
Sg/71 **(169)** NN,GB P(c),Rigid(c), Words Spelling'Invisible Man' Are' Solid'Not'Invisible';rep . . . 10.00

154-THE CONSPIRACY OF PONTIAC
By Francis Parkman

01/60 **(154)** GMc,GMc P(c), Original 45.00
11/63 **(167)** GMc,GMc P(c);rep . . . 18.00
07/64 **(167)** GMc,GMc P(c);rep. . . 18.00
12/67 **(166)** GMc,GMc P(c);rep. . . 18.00

155-THE LION OF THE NORTH
By George Alfred Henty

03/60 **(154)** NN,GMc P(c),Original 42.00
01/64 **(167)** NN,GMc P(c);rep 15.00
1967 **(166)** NN,GMc P(c),25¢(c) Price; rep 12.00

156-THE CONQUEST OF MEXICO

By Bernal Diaz Del Castillo

05/60 **(156)** BPr,BPr P(c),Original . 40.00
01/64 **(167)** BPr,BPr P(c);rep 12.00
08/67 **(166)** BPr,BPr P(c);rep 12.00
Sg/70 **(169)** BPr,BPr P(c),25¢(c) Price; Rigid(c);rep. 10.00

157-LIVES OF THE HUNTED

By Ernest Thompson Seton

07/60 **(156)** NN,LbC P(c),Original . 45.00
02/64 **(167)** NN,LbC P(c);rep 16.00
10/67 **(166)** NN,LbC P(c);rep 16.00

158-THE CONSPIRATORS

By Alexandre Dumas

09/60 **(156)** GMc,GMc P(c), Original 42.00
07/64 **(167)** GMc,GMc P(c);rep. . . 16.00
10/67 **(166)** GMc,GMc P(c);rep. . . 16.00

159-THE OCTOPUS

By Frank Norris

11/60 **(159)** GM&GE,LbC P(c), Original 42.00
02/64 **(167)** GM&GE,LbC P(c);rep 16.00
166 **(1967)** GM&GE,LbC P(c),25¢(c) Price;rep 16.00

160-THE FOOD OF THE GODS

By H.G. Wells

01/61 **(159)** TyT,GMc P(c),Original 45.00
01/61 **(160)** TyT,GMc P(c),Original; Same Except For the HRN#. . 40.00
01/64 **(167)** TyT,GMc P(c);rep. . . . 16.00
06/67 **(166)** TyT,GMc P(c);rep. . . . 16.00

161-CLEOPATRA

By H. Rider Haggard

03/61 **(161)** NN,Pch P(c),Original . 45.00
01/64 **(167)** NN,Pch P(c);rep. 20.00
08/67 **(166)** NN,Pch P(c);rep. 20.00

162-ROBUR THE CONQUEROR

By Jules Verne

05/61 **(162)** GM&DPn,CJ P(c), Original 45.00
07/64 **(167)** GM&DPn,CJ P(c);rep. 16.00
08/67 **(166)** GM&DPn,CJ P(c);rep. 16.00

163-MASTER OF THE WORLD

By Jules Verne

07/61 **(163)** GM,P(c),Original 40.00
01/65 **(167)** GM,P(c);rep. 16.00
1968 **(166)** GM,P(c),25¢(c) Price;rep 16.00

164-THE COSSACK CHIEF

By Nicolai Gogol

1961 **(164)** SyM,P(c),Original 40.00
04/65 **(167)** SyM,P(c);rep 16.00
Fl/68 **(166)** SyM,P(c),25¢(c) Price;rep 16.00

165-THE QUEEN'S NECKLACE

by Alexandre Dumas

01/62 **(164)** GM,P(c),Original 40.00
04/65 **(167)** GM,P(c);rep. 16.00
Fl/68 **(166)** GM,P(c),25¢(c) Price;rep 16.00

166-TIGERS AND TRAITORS

By Jules Verne

05/62 **(165)** NN,P(c),Original. 80.00
02/64 **(167)** NN,P(c);rep 30.00
11/66 **(167)** NN,P(c);rep 30.00

167-FAUST

By Johann Wolfgang von Goethe

08/62 **(165)** NN,NN P(c),Original. 110.00
02/64 **(167)** NN,NN P(c);rep 50.00
06/67 **(166)** NN,NN P(c);rep 50.00

168-IN FREEDOM'S CAUSE

By George Alfred Henty

Wr/69 **(169)** GE&RC,P(c), Original, Rigid (c) 130.00

169-NEGRO AMERICANS THE EARLY YEARS

AUTHOR UNKNOWN

Sg/69 **(166)** NN,NN P(c), Original, Rigid(c). 100.00
Sg/69 **(169)** NN,NN P(c), Rigid; rep 60.00

See Also:

Independent Color Listings

CLASSICS ILLUSTRATED GIANTS

An Illustrated Library of Great Adventure Stories -(reps. of Issues 6,7,8,10). 1,200.00
An Illustrated Library of Exciting Mystery Stories -(reps. of Issues 30,21,40,13) 1,300.00
An Illustrated Library of Great Indian Stories -(reps. of Issues 4,17,22,37). 1,200.00

CLASSICS ILLUSTRATED JUNIOR

501-Snow White and the Seven Dwarfs. 75.00
502-The Ugly Duckling 50.00
503-Cinderella 30.00
504-The Pied Piper. 25.00
505-The Sleeping Beauty 25.00
506-The Three Little Pigs 25.00
507-Jack and the Beanstalk 25.00
508-Goldilocks and the Three Bears 25.00
509-Beauty and the Beast 25.00
510-Little Red Riding Hood 25.00
511-Puss-N-Boots. 25.00
512-Rumpelstiltskin 25.00
513-Pinocchio. 35.00
514-The Steadfast Tin Soldier. . . . 45.00
515-Johnny Appleseed 25.00
516-Aladdin and His Lamp 25.00
517-The Emperor's New Clothes . 25.00
518-The Golden Goose 25.00
519-Paul Bunyan 25.00
520-Thumbelina 28.00
521-King of the Golden River 25.00
522-The Nightingale 20.00
523-The Gallant Tailor 20.00
524-The Wild Swans. 20.00
525-The Little Mermaid. 27.00
526-The Frog Prince. 25.00
527-The Golden-Haired Giant. . . . 20.00
528-The Penny Prince 20.00
529-The Magic Servants. 20.00
530-The Golden Bird 20.00
531-Rapunzel. 25.00
532-The Dancing Princesses 20.00
533-The Magic Fountain. 20.00
534-The Golden Touch 20.00
535-The Wizard of Oz. 35.00
536-The Chimney Sweep 25.00
537-The Three Fairies 20.00
538-Silly Hans 20.00
539-The Enchanted Fish. 30.00
540-The Tinder-Box 30.00
541-Snow White and Rose Red . . 20.00
542-The Donkey's Tail 20.00
543-The House in the Woods 18.00
544-The Golden Fleece 35.00
545-The Glass Mountain. 22.00
546-The Elves and the Shoemaker 20.00
547-The Wishing Table. 20.00
548-The Magic Pitcher 15.00
549-Simple Kate. 15.00
550-The Singing Donkey 15.00
551-The Queen Bee. 15.00
552-The Three Little Dwarfs 20.00
553-King Thrushbeard 15.00
554-The Enchanted Deer 15.00
555-The Three Golden Apples . . . 15.00
556-The Elf Mound. 15.00
557-Silly Willy. 30.00
558-The Magic Dish 30.00
559-The Japanese Lantern. 35.00
560-The Doll Princess 35.00
561-Hans Humdrum 20.00
562-The Enchanted Pony 35.00
563-The Wishing Well. 20.00
564-The Salt Mountain 20.00
565-The Silly Princess 20.00
566-Clumsy Hans. 20.00
567-The Bearskin Soldier 20.00
568-The Happy Hedgehog 20.00
569-The Three Giants. 20.00
570-The Pearl Princess 20.00
571-How Fire Came to the Indians 30.00
572-The Drummer Boy 30.00
573-The Crystal Ball. 30.00
574-Brightboots 25.00
575-The Fearless Prince. 25.00
576-The Princess Who Saw Everything 32.00
577-The Runaway Dumpling. 40.00

CLASSICS ILLUSTRATED SPECIAL ISSUE

N# United Nations 250.00
129-The Story of Jesus. 65.00
132A-The Story of America. 50.00
135A-The Ten Commandments. . . 50.00
138A-Adventures in Science. 40.00
141A-The Rough Rider. 45.00
144A-Blazing the Trails. 40.00
147A-Crossing the Rockies. 50.00
150A-Royal Canadian Police 45.00
153A-Men, Guns, and Cattle. 45.00
156A-The Atomic Age. 45.00
159A-Rockets, Jets and Missiles. . 45.00
162A-War Between the States . . 100.00
165A-To the Stars. 50.00
166A-World War II 75.00
167A-Prehistoric World 80.00

AMAZING DOPE TALES
Greg Shaw

1 Untrimmed black and white pages, out of order;artist unknown . . 110.00
2 Trimmed and proper pages. . . . 95.00

AMERICAN SPLENDOR
Harvey Pekar May, 1976

1 B:Harvey Pekar Stories, HP,RCr,GDu,GBu 20.00
2 HP,RCr,GDu,GBu 10.00
3 HP,RCr,GDu,GBu 10.00
4 HP,RCr,GDu,GBu 8.00
5 HP,RCr,GDu,GBu 8.00
6 HP,RCr,GDu,GBu,GSh 7.00
7 HP,GSh,GDu,GBu 5.00
8 HP,GSh,GDu,GBu 3.00
9 and 10 HP,GSh,GDu,GBu . . . . @3.00
11 . . . . 3.00
12 . . . . 4.50
13 thru 19. . . . . @3.50
20 E:Harvey Pekar Stories 4.00

ANTHOLOGY OF SLOW DEATH
Wingnut Press/Last Gasp

1 140 pgs, RCr,RCo, GiS, DSh, Harlan Ellison VB,RTu 37.00

APEX TREASURY OF UNDERGROUND COMICS, THE
Links Books Inc. Oct.,1974

1 . . . . 40.00

APEX TREASURY OF UNDERGROUND COMICS –BEST OF BIJOU FUNNIES
Quick Fox 1981

1 Paperback,comix,various artists 21.00

ARCADE THE COMICS REVUE
Print Mint Inc. Spring, 1975

1 ASp,BG,RCr,SRo,SCW. 16.50
2 ASp,BG,RCr,SRo 12.00
3 ASp,BG,RCr,RW,SCW 8.50
4 ASp,BG,RCr,WBu,RW,SCW 8.50
5 thru 7 ASp,BG,SRo,RW,SCW . @7.50

BABYFAT
Comix World/Clay Geerdes 1978

1 B:8pg news parodies, one page comix by various artists 4.50
2 thru 9 same . . . . @3.00
10 thru 26 same . . . . @2.00

BATTLE OF THE TITANS
University of Illinois SF Society 1972

1 Sci-Fi;VB,JGa 50.00

BEST BUY COMICS
Last Gasp Eco-Funnies

1 Rep Whole Earth Review;RCr. . . 3.50

BEST OF BIJOU FUNNIES, THE
Links Books Inc. 1975

1 164 pgs,paperback. 235.00

BEST OF RIP-OFF PRESS
Rip Off Press Inc. 1973

1 132 pgs paperback,SCW, RCr,SRo,RW 25.00
2 100 pgs,GS,FT 27.50
3 100 pgs,FS. 10.75
4 132 pgs,GiS,DSh 13.00

BIG ASS
Rip Off Press 1969–71

1 28 pgs,RCr. 80.00
2 RCr 50.00

BIJOU FUNNIES
Bijou Publishing Empire 1968

1 B:JLy,editor;RCr,GS SW 285.00
2 RCr,GS,SW 110.00
3 RCr,SWi,JsG 60.00
4 SWi,JsG 30.00
5 SWi,JsG. 33.50
6 E:JLy,editor,SWi,RCr,JsG 27.00
7 and 8 . . . . @26.00

BINKY BROWN MEETS THE HOLY VIRGIN MARY
Last Gasp Eco-Funnies March, 1972

N# Autobiography about Growing up w/a Catholic Neurosis,JsG. . . 22.50
2nd Printing:only text in bottom left panel. 12.00

BIZARRE SEX
Kitchen Sink Komix May, 1972

1 B:DKi,editor,various artists 27.00
2 . . . . 22.00
3 . . . . 16.00
4 thru 6 . . . . @11.00
7 . . . . 4.00
8 . . . . 3.50
9 Omaha the Cat Dancer,RW . . . 16.50

Bizarre Sex #9
© Kitchen Sink

10 inc.Omaha the Cat Dancer,RW. 12.50

BLACK LAUGHTER
Black Laughter Pub. Co., Nov., 1972

1 James Dixon art 64.00

BLOOD FROM A STONE (GUIDE TO TAX REFORM)
New York Public Interest Research Group Inc. 1977

1 Tax reform proposals 8.50

BOBBY LONDON RETROSPECTIVE AND ART PORTFOLIO
Cartoonist Representatives

1 . . . . 19.50

BOBMAN AND TEDDY
Parrallax Comic Books Inc. 1966

1 RFK & Ted Kennedy's struggle to control Democratic party. 35.50

BODE'S CARTOON CONCERT
Dell Sept., 1973

1 132 pgs; VB 27.50

BOGEYMAN COMICS
San Fransisco Comic Book Co., 1969

1 Horror,RHa. 55.00
2 Horror,RHa. 42.00

The Company & Sons

3 . . . . 31.00

BUFFALO RAG/THE DEAD CONCERT COMIX
Kenny Laramey Dec. 1973

1 Alice in Wonderland parody . . . 55.00

CAPTAIN GUTS
The Print Mint 1969

1 Super patriotV:Counter culture 26.50
2 V:Black Panthers 19.00
3 V:Dope Smugglers 19.00

CAPTAIN STICKY
Captain Sticky 1974–75

1 Super lawyer V:SocialInjustice . 17.50

CARTOON HISTORY OF THE UNIVERSE
Rip Off Press Sept., 1978

1 Evolution of Everything; B:Larry Gonick 6.50
2 Sticks and Stones 6.50
3 River Realms-Sumer & Egypt . . 6.50
4 Part of the Old Testament 4.50
5 Brains and Bronze 4.50
6 Who are these Athenians 3.75

CASCADE COMIX MONTHLY

Everyman Studios March, 1978

1 Interviews,articles about comix & comix artists 6.50
2 and 3 same. . . . . @6.50
4 thru 11 . . . . @3.00
12 thru 23. . . . . @2.25

CHECKERED DEMON

Last Gasp July, 1977

1 SCW 13.00
2 SCW 8.50
3 SCW 6.50

CHEECH WIZARD

Office of Student Publications, Syracuse U 1967

n/n VB. 120.00

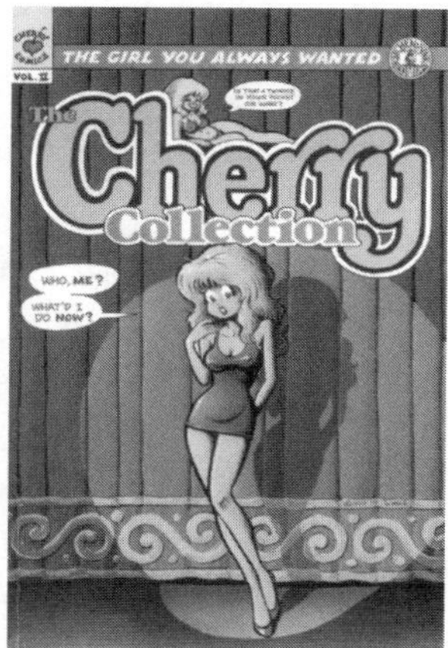

Cherry Collection TPB #2
© Kitchen Sink

CHERRY

Kitchen Sink

1 by Larry Welz 7.50
2 . . . . 6.00
3 thru 5 . . . . @5.00
6 thru 10 . . . . @4.00
11 thru 15 . . . . @3.50
TPB Cherry Collection #1 . . . . 15.00
TPB Cherry Collection #2 . . . . 15.00
TPB Cherry Collection #3 . . . . 12.95
Cherry's Jubilee #1 thru #4 . . . . . @3.00

CHICAGO MIRROR

Jay Lynch/Mirror Publishing Empire Autumn, 1967

1 B:Bijou Funnies 45.00
2 same 35.00
3 same 115.00

COLLECTED CHEECH WIZARD, THE

Company & Sons 1972

n/n VB. 55.00

COLLECTED TRASHMAN #1, THE

Fat City & The Red Mountain Tribe Productions

n/n SRo. 32.50

COMICS & COMIX

October, 1975

1 . . . . 12.00

COMIX BOOK

Magazine Management Co. Oct., 1974

1 Compilation for newsstand distribution 14.50
2 and 3 . . . . @9.00

Kitchen Sink Enterprises

4 . . . . 14.50
5 . . . . 8.50

COMIX COLLECTOR, THE

Archival Press Inc. Dec., 1979

1 Fanzine 5.00
2 & 3 Fanzine . . . . @4.00

COMMIES FROM MARS

Kitchen Sink March, 1973

1 TB 32.50

Last Gasp

2 thru 5 TB . . . . @9.50

COMPLETE FRITZ THE CAT

Belier Press 1978

n/n RCr,SRo,DSh 55.00

CONSPIRACY CAPERS

The Conspiracy 1969

1 Benefit Legal Defense of the Chicago-8. . . . . 79.00

DAN O'NEIL'S COMICS & STORIES

Company & Sons, VOL.1

1 B:Dan O'Neill 45.00
2 & 3 . . . . @30.00

1971 VOL.2

1 . . . . 6.50
2 and E:Dan O'Neill . . . . @4.50

DAS KAMPF

Vaughn Bode May, 1963

N# 100 Loose pgs. 750.00
2nd Printing 52pgs.-produced by Walter Bachner&Bagginer,1977 9.50

DEADBONE EROTICA

Bantam Books Inc. April, 1971

n/n 132 pgs VB 45.00

DEADCENTER CLEAVAGE

April, 1971

1 14 pgs 40.00

DEATH RATTLE

Kitchen Sink June, 1972

1 RCo,TB 25.00
2 TB 20.00
3 TB 16.00

DESPAIR

The Print Mint 1969

1 RCr 33.00

DIRTY DUCK BOOK, THE

Company & Sons March, 1972

1 Bobby London 25.00

DISNEY RAPES THE 1ST AMENDMENT

Dan O'Neil 1974

1 Benefit Air Pirates V:Disney Lawsuit; Dan O'Neill 8.50

DOPE COMIX

Kitchen Sink Feb., 1978

1 Drugs comix;various artists. 7.50
2 same 5.75
3 & 4 LSD issue. . . . . @4.00
5 Omaha the Cat Dancer, RW . . . 10.00

DOPIN DAN

Last Gasp Eco-Funnies April, 1972

1 TR 12.00
2 and 3 TR . . . . @8.50
4 Todays Army,TR. 7.50

DR. ATOMIC

Last Gasp Eco-Funnies Sept., 1972

1 B:Larry S. Todd 12.00
2 and 3 . . . . @10.00
4 . . . . 7.50
5 E:Larry S. Todd 4.75

DR. ATOMIC'S MARIJUANA MULTIPLIER

Kistone Press 1974

1 How to grow great pot 7.50

DRAWINGS BY S. CLAY WILSON

San Francisco Graphics

1 28 pgs 185.00

DYING DOLPHIN

The Print Mint 1970

n/n 14.50

EBON

San Francisco Comic Book Company

1 Comix version; RCr 25.00
1 Tabloid version 18.00

EL PERFECTO COMICS

The Print Mint 1973

N# Benefit Timothy Leary 27.00
2nd Printing-1975 . . . . 4.00

Underground

ETERNAL TRUTH
Sunday Funnies Comic Corp
1 Christian Comix 19.50

EVERMUCH WAVE
Atlantis Distributors
1 Nunzio the Narc; Adventures of God 60.00

The Fabulous Furry Freak Brothers #9
© Rip Off Press

FABULOUS FURRY FREAK BROTHERS, THE
COLLECTED ADVENTURES OF
Rip Off Press #1 Feb., 1971
1 GiS 75.00

FURTHER ADVENTURES OF
Rip Off Press #2
1 GiS,DSh 47.50

A YEAR PASSES LIKE NOTHING WITH
Rip Off Press #3
1 GiS. 17.00

BROTHER CAN YOU SPARE $.75 FOR
Rip Off Press #4
1 GiS,DSh 12.00

FABULOUS FURRY FREAK BROTHERS, THE
Rip Off Press #5
1 GiS,DSh 9.50

SIX SNAPPY SOCKERS FROM THE ARCHIVES OF
Rip Off Press #6
1 GiS 5.25

FANTAGOR
1970
1 (Corben), fanzine 100.00
1a (Last Gasp) 22.00
2 & 3 . . . . @20.00
4 . . . . 30.00

THE ADVENTURES OF FAT FREDDY'S CAT,
Rip Off Press Feb., 1977
1 . . . . 14.00
2 . . . . 4.50
3 . . . . 6.00
4 . . . . 5.00
5 & 6 . . . . @2.50

FEDS 'N' HEADS
Gilbert Shelton/Print Mint 1968
N# I:Fabulous Furry Freak Bros.; Has no `Print Mint' Address 24 pgs. 350.00
2nd printing, 28 pgs. 55.00
3rd printing, May, 1969 . . . . 45.00
4th printing, Says `Forth Printing' 17.50
5th-12th printings . . . . @8.00
13th printing 6.50
14th printing 4.75

FELCH
Keith Green
1 RW,SCW,RCr. 40.00

FEVER PITCH
Kitchen Sink Enterprises July, 1976
1 RCo 20.00

Jabberwocky Graphix
2 250 signed & numbered 14.50
3 400 signed & numbered 13.50
4 . . . . 8.50

50'S FUNNIES
Kitchen Sink Enterprises 1980
1 Larry Shell, editor,various artists 5.00

FLAMING CARROT
Kilian Barracks Free Press 1981
1 Bob Budden,various artists 10.00

FLASH THEATRE
Oogle Productions 1970
1 44 pgs 37.50

FLESHAPOIDS FROM EARTH
Popular Culture Dec., 1974
1 36 pgs 33.00

THE COMPLETE FOO!
Bijou Publishing Sept., 1980
1 RCr, Charles Crumb, r:Crumb brothers fanzines 40.00

FRITZ BUGS OUT
Ballentine Books 1972
n/n RCr 60.50

FRITZ THE CAT
Ballentine Books 1969
n/n RCr. 120.00

FRITZ THE NO-GOOD
Ballentine Books 1972
n/n RCr 50.00

FRITZ: SECRET AGENT FOR THE CIA
Ballentine Books 1972
n/n RCr 45.00

FUNNY AMINALS
Apex Novelties/Don Donahue 1972
1 RCr 60.00

GAY COMIX
Kitchen Sink Sept., 1981
1 36 pgs 7.50
2 36 pgs 5.00

GEN OF HIROSHIMA
Educomics/Leonard Rifas Jan., 1980
1 Antiwar comix by Hiroshima survivor Keiji Nakawaza 9.50
2 same 6.50

GHOST MOTHER COMICS
John "Mad" Peck 1969
1 SCw,JsG 47.50

GIMMEABREAK COMIX
Rhuta Press Feb., 1971
2. . . . . 48 pgs, #0 & #1 were advertised,but . . may not have been printed 95.00

GIRLS & BOYS
Lynda J. Barry 1980
1 B:12 pgs with every other page blank, all Barry art 8.00
2 thru 10 same. . . . . @6.50
11 thru 20 same . . . . @4.50
20 thru 25 same . . . . @3.50

GOD NOSE
Jack Jackson/
Rip Off Press 1964
N# 42 pgs.. . . . . 995.00
2nd printing,Pinkish(c);44p. 60.00
3rd printing,Blue Border(c). 30.00
4th printing,Red Border(c) 15.00

GOTHIC BLIMP WORKS LTD.
East Village Other/
Peter Leggieri 1969
1 VB,Editor,various artists 185.00
2 same 145.00
3 KDe,editor 135.00
4 KDe,editor 130.00
5 thru 7 KDe,editor. . . . . @125.00
8 various artists 185.00

GREASER COMICS
Half-Ass Press Sept. 1971
1 28 pgs, George DiCaprio 17.50

Rip Off Press July 1972
2 George DiCaprio. 10.00

GRIM WIT
Last Gasp 1972
1 RCo 35.00
2 RCo 25.00

HAROLD HEAD, THE COLLECTED ADVENTURES OF
Georgia Straight 1972
1 . . . . 45.00
2 . . . . 10.00

HARRY CHESS THAT MAN FROM A.U.N.T.I.E.
The Uncensored Adventures
Trojan Book Service 1966
N# 1st Comix By & For Gay Community 100.00

HEAR THE SOUND OF MY FEET WALKING....
Glide Urban Center 1969
1 Dan O'Neill, 128 pgs 65.00

HISTORY OF UNDERGROUND COMIX
Straight Arrow Books 1974
1 Book by Mark James Estren about Underground Comix 30.00

HOMEGROWN FUNNIES
Kitchen Sink 1971
1 RCr 45.00

HONKYTONK SUE, THE QUEEN OF COUNTRY SWING
Bob Boze Bell Feb., 1979
1 BBB 7.00
2 & 3 BBB . . . . @5.00

IKE LIVES
Warm Neck Funnies 1973
1 20 pgs,Mark Fisher. 10.00

INSECT FEAR
Last Gasp 1970
1 SRo,GiS,RHa,JsG 75.00
Print Mint 1970–72
2 . . . . 30.00
3 . . . . 20.00

IT AIN'T ME BABE
Last Gasp Eco-Funnies July, 1970
n/n First all women comix Women's Liberation theme . . . 32.50

JAPANESE MONSTER
Carol Lay July, 1979
1 8pgs, Carol Lay 5.00

JESUS LOVES YOU
Zondervan Books/Craig Yoe
1972
1 Christian, RCr 29.50

THE NEW ADVENTURES OF JESUS
Rip Off Press Nov., 1971
1 44 pgs, FSt. 50.00

JIZ
Apex Novelty 1969
1 36 pgs; RCr, SRo, VMo, SCW; hand trimmed and unevenly stapled 45.00

JUNKWAFFEL
The Print Mint 1971
1 VB 30.00
2 and 3 VB . . . . @25.00
4 VB,JJ 18.00

KANNED KORN KOMIX
Canned Heat Fan Club 1969
1 20pgs. 8.00

KAPTAIN AMERIKA KOMIX
Brief Candle Comix March, 1970
1 anti U.S. involvement in Laos. . . 27.50

KING BEE
Apex/Don Donahue & Kerry Clark 1969
1 RCr,SCW 120.00

KURTZMAN COMIX
Kitchen Sink Sept., 1976
1 HK,RCr,GiS,DKi,WE 20.00

LAUGH IN THE DARK
Last Gasp
n/n KDe,RHa,SRo,SCW 14.00

LENNY OF LAVEDO
Sunbury Productions/Print Mint 1965
N# Green(c);1st Joel Beck-a . . . 545.00
2nd printing, Orange(c) 390.00
3rd printing, White(c) 195.00

THE MACHINES
Office of Student Publications Syracuse University 1967
1 VB 125.00

THE MAN
Office of Student Publications Syracuse University 1966
1 VB 155.00

MAGGOTZINE
Charles Schneider May, 1981
1 Various Artists,conceptual maggot stuff 3.50

MANTICORE
Joe Kubert School of Cartooning & Graphic Arts Inc.
Autumn, 1976
1 Fanzine,various artists 7.50

MEAN BITCH THRILLS
The Print Mint 1971
1 SRO. 7.00

MICKEY RAT
Los Angeles Comic Book Co. May, 1972
1 Robert Armstrong 32.50
2 same 29.00
3 same 9.50

MOM'S HOMEMADE COMICS
Kitchen Sink June, 1969
1 DKi, RCr. 125.00
The Print Mint
2 DKi. 35.00
Kitchen Sink Enterprises
3 DKi,RCr 17.00

MONDAY FUNNIES, THE
Monday Funnies 1977
1 8pgs,various artists 6.50
2 16pgs,various artists 9.00
3 16pgs,various artists 6.50
4 16pgs,various artists 5.50

MONDAY FUNNIES, THE
Passtime Publ. July–Aug., 1980
1 thru 8 Marc L.Reed . . . . @4.00

MOUSE LIBERATION FRONT
COMMUNIQUE #2 August, 1979
1 SRo, SCW, VMo,DKi; Disney's sues Dan O'Neil's Air Pirates 9.50

MOONCHILD COMICS
Nicola Cuti 1968
0 Nicola Cuti 27.00
2 Nicola Cuti 27.00
3 Nicola Cuti 75.00

MOONDOG
The Print Mint March, 1970
1 All George Metzer. 11.00
2 same 6.50
3 and 4 same. . . . . @3.75

MORE ADVENTURES OF FAT FREDDY'S CAT
Rip Off Press Jan., 1981
1 GiS. 14.00

MOTOR CITY COMICS
Rip Off Press April, 1969
1 RCr 165.00
2 RCr 125.00

MR. NATURAL
San Fransisco Comic Book Co. August, 1970
1 RCr 100.00
2 RCr 50.00

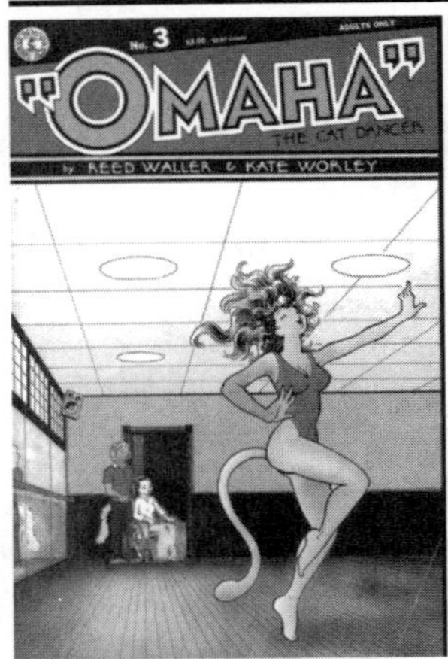

Omaha, The Cat Dancer #3
© Reed Waller

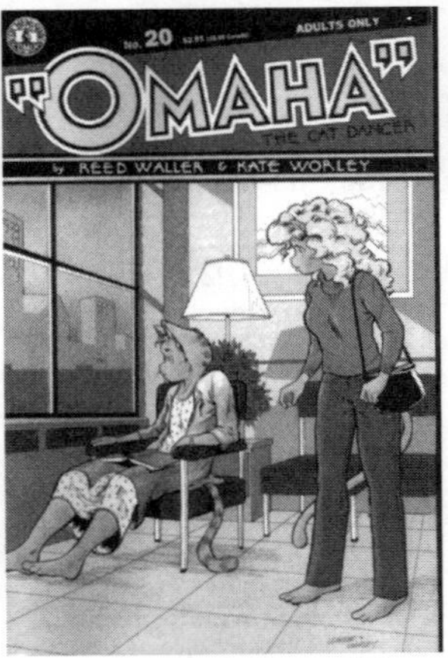

Omaha, The Cat Dancer #20
© Reed Waller

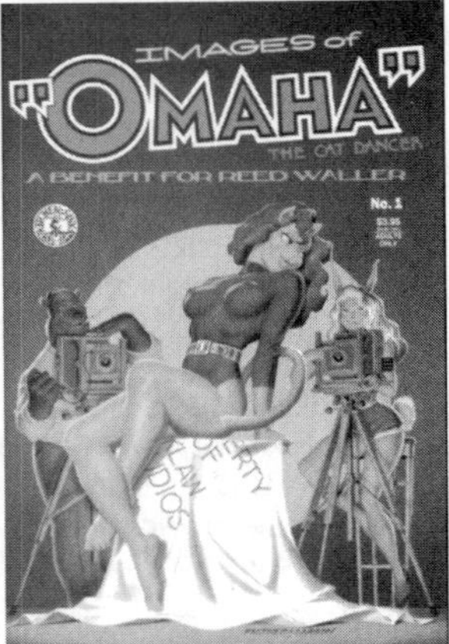

Images of Omaha, Book 1
© Reed Waller

Kitchen Sink
3 RCr, (B&W) 20.00

NARD 'N' PAT, JAYZEY LYNCH'S

Cartoonists Cooperative Press March, 1974
1 Jay Lynch. 7.00
2 Jay Lynch. 4.50

Kitchen Sink Press 1972
3 . . . . 10.00

NEVERWHERE

Ariel Inc. Feb., 1978
1 RCo 17.50

NICKEL LIBRARY

Gary Arlington
1 1 pg heavy stock colored paper, Reed Crandall 5.00
2 Kim Deitch 1.50
3 Harrison Cady 1.50
4 Frank Frazetta 4.00
5 Will Eisner 4.00
6 Justin Green. 1.50
7 C.C. Beck 4.00
8 Wally Wood 4.00
9 Winsor McCay 1.50
10 Jim Osborne 1.50
11 Don Towlley. 1.50
12 Frank Frazetta. 4.00
13 Will Eisner. 4.00
14 Bill Griffith 1.50
15 George Herriman. 1.50
16 Cliff Sterrett 1.50
17 George Herriman. 1.50
18 Rory Hayes & Simon Deitch. . . . 1.50
19 Disney Studios 2.00
20 Alex Toth 2.00
21 Will Eisner. 2.00
22 Jack Davis. 3.00
23 Alex Toth 2.00
24 Michele Brand 1.50
25 Roger Brand 1.50
26 Arnold Roth 1.50
27 Murphy Anderson 2.00
28 Wally Wood 3.00
29 Jack Kirby 4.00
30 Harvey Kurtzman. 3.00
31 Jay Kinney. 1.50
32 Bill Plimpton 1.50
33 . . . . 1.50
34 Charles Dallas. 1.50
35 thru 39. . . . . @1.50
40 Bill Edwards 1.50
41 Larry S. Todd. 1.50
42 Charles Dallas. 1.50
43 Jim Osborne 1.50
43 1/2 Larry S. Todd. 1.50
44 Jack Jackson. 1.50
45 Rick Griffin. 1.50
46 Justin Green 1.50
47 and 48 Larry S. Todd . . . . @1.50
49 Charles Dallas. 1.50
50 Robert Crumb 3.00
51 Wally Wood 3.00
52 Charles Dallas. 3.00
53 and 54 Larry S. Todd . . . . @1.50
55 Charles Dallas. 1.50
56 Jim Chase. 1.50
57 Charles Dallas. 1.50
58 Larry S. Todd. 1.50
59 Dave Geiser 1.50
60 Charles Dallas. 1.50

ODD WORLD OF RICHARD CORBEN

Warren Publishing 1977
1 84pgs paperback 20.00

O.K. COMICS

Kitchen Sink June, 1972
1 and 2 Bruce Walthers . . . . @7.00

O.K. COMICS

O.K. Comic Company 1972
1 Tabloid with comix, articles, reviews, nudie cuties photos. . 27.50
2 thru 18 . . . . @18.75

OMAHA THE CAT DANCER

Steel Dragon Press, 1984
1 RW,F:Omaha, Shelly, Chuck. . . 10.00

Kitchen Sink, 1986
1 RW. 9.00
2 RW 8.00
3 thru 5 . . . . 7.00
6 thru 10 . . . . 6.00
11 thru 20 . . . . 5.00
Spec.#0, 25th Anniv. Classic. 15.00
Images of Omaha, RW benefit 8.00
Images No. 2 . . . . 7.00
TPB Collected Omaha #1, rep. . . . 15.00
TPB Collected Omaha #2, rep. . . . 13.00
TPB Collected Omaha #3, rep. . . . 13.00
TPB Collected Omaha #4, rep. . . . 13.00
TPB Collected Omaha #5, rep. . . . 13.00

Vol. 2, Fantagraphics, 1994
1 . . . . 5.00
2 . . . . 5.00

ORACLE COMIX

Thru Black Holes
Comix Productions Oct., 1980
1 and 2 Michael Roden . . . . @2.50

PENGUINS IN BONDAGE

Sorcerer Studio/ Wayne Gibson July, 1981
1 8pgs,Wayne Gibson 2.75

PHANTOM LADY

Randy Crawford June, 1978
1 Sex funnies 4.50

PHUCKED UP FUNNIES

Suny Binghamton 1969
1 ASp;insert bound in yearbook . 400.00

PINK FLOYD, THE

October, 1974
1 sold at concerts 27.50

PLASTIC MAN

Randy Crawford May, 1977
1 Sex funnies,Randy Crawford . . . 4.00

PORK

Co-op Press May, 1974
1 SCW. 11.00

PORTFOLIO OF UNDERGROUND ART

Schanes & Schanes 1980

1 SRo,SCW,VMo,RW and many others 13 loose sheets in folder, 32-pg book, 1200 signed & numb. . . 75.00

POWERMAN AND POWER MOWER SAFETY

Frank Burgmeir, Co.

Outdoor Power Equipment

1 VB; educational comic about power mower safety 185.00

PROMETHIAN ENTERPRISES

Promethian Enterprises

Memorial Day, 1969

1 B:Jim Vadeboncuor editor 72.00
2 same 60.00
3 thru 5 . . . . @25.00

PURE ART QUARTERLY

John A. Adams July, 1976

1 16pgs, All John A. Adams. 8.50
2 thru 5 same . . . . @8.50
6 thru 10 same. . . . . @5.00
11 thru 14 same . . . . @3.50

QUAGMIRE COMICS

Kitchen Sink Summer, 1970

1 DKi,Peter Poplaski 11.00

RAW

Raw Books 1980

1 36pgs,10pgs insert 310.00
2 36pgs,20pgs insert 185.00
3 52pgs,16pgs insert 155.00
4 44pgs,32pgs insert,Flexi disk record 125.00

R. CRUMB'S COMICS AND STORIES

Rip Off Press 1969

1 RCr. 90.00

RAWARARAWAR

Rip Off Press 1969

1 GSh. 55.00

RED SONJA & CONAN "HOT AND DRY"

Randy Crawford May, 1977

1 Sex funnies,Randy Crawford . . . 3.50

REID FLEMING WORLD'S TOUGHEST MILKMAN

David E. Boswell Dec., 1980

1 . . . . 6.00

RIP OFF COMIX

Rip Off Press April, 1977

1 GiS,FSt,JsG,DSh 17.50
2 thru 5 GiS,FSt. . . . . @6.00
6 thru 10 . . . . @4.25

ROWLF

Rip Off Press July, 1971

1 RCo 55.00

RUBBER DUCK TALES

The Print Mint March, 1971

1 Michael J Becker 12.00
2 Michael J Becker 11.00

S. CLAY WILSON TWENTY DRAWINGS

Abington Book Shop Inc. 1967

N# (a),Cowboy(c) 460.00
(b),Pirate(c). 460.00
(c),Motorcyclist(c) 460.00
(d),Demon(c). 460.00
(e),Deluxe with all 4 variations on same(c) with Gold Embossed Lettering 675.00

SAN FRANCISCO COMIC BOOK

San Francisco Comic Book Co.

Jan.-Feb., 1970

1 . . . . 120.00
2 . . . . 20.00
3 . . . . 17.50
4 thru 6 . . . . @12.00

SAVAGE HUMOR

The Print Mint 1973

1 . . . . 4.00

SAY WHAT?

Loring Park Shelter

Community Cartooning Workshop

April, 1979

1 B:Charles T. Smith,editor, various artists 7.00
2 thru 6 same . . . . @6.50

SCHIZOPHRENIA, CHEECH WIZARD

Last Gasp Eco-Funnies Jan., 1974

1 VB 30.00

SEX AND AFFECTION

C.P. Family Publishers 1974

1 Sex Education for Children 5.50

SHORT ORDER COMIX

Head Press/Family Fun 1973

1 50 cents,36pgs. 8.50
2 75 cents,44pgs. 2.25

SKULL COMICS

Last Gasp March, 1970

1 Horror,RHa 47.00
2 GiS,DSh,RCo 25.50
3 SRo,DSh,RCo 14.00
4 DSh,Lovecraft issue 14.00
5 SRo,RCo,Lovecraft issue 14.00
6 RCo,Herman Hesse 14.00

SLOW DEATH FUNNIES

Last Gasp April 1970

1 Ecological Awareness & Red Border on (c) 47.00
2nd-4th Printings White Border(c) 10.00
2 Silver(c);1st edition, 34 pgs. . . . 85.00
2b Non Silver(c);Says 1st Edition, 34 pgs 20.00
2nd Amorphia Ad on pg 34 . . . . . . 6.75
3rd Yellow Skull on (c). 5.00
4th `Mind Candy For the Masses' Ad on pg. 34 . . . . 5.00
5th $1.00(c) price 3.50
3 thru 5 . . . . @12.00
6 thru 10 . . . . @4.50

SMILE

Kitchen Sink Summer, 1970

1 Jim Mitchell 13.50
2 Jim Mitchell 12.00
3 Jim Mitchell 11.00

SNARF

Kitchen Sink Feb., 1972

1 DKi,editor,various artists 24.50
2 thru 5 same . . . . @15.00
6 thru 9 same . . . . @6.50

SNATCH COMICS

Apex Novelties 1968

1 RCr,SCW 295.00
2 RCr,SCW 150.00
3 RCr,SCW,RW. 75.00

SNATCH SAMPLER

Keith Green 1979

n/n RCr,SCw,RW,RHa 32.00

SPACE INVADERS COMICS, DON CHIN'S

Comix World/Clay Geerdes

April, 1972

1 8pgs 4.00

SPASM!

Last Gasp Eco-Funnies April, 1973

1 JJ 15.00

STONED PICTURE PARADE

San Francisco Comic Book Co., 1975

1 RCr,SRo,SCW,WE 20.00

SUBVERT COMICS

Rip Off Press Nov., 1970

1 SRo 25.00
2 SRo 20.00
3 SRo 12.00

TALES OF SEX & DEATH

Print Mint 1971

1 JsG,KDe.RHa,SRo 32.50
2 JsG,KDe.RHa,SRo 19.50

Zap #1 © Apex Novelties

Zap #3 © Apex Novelties

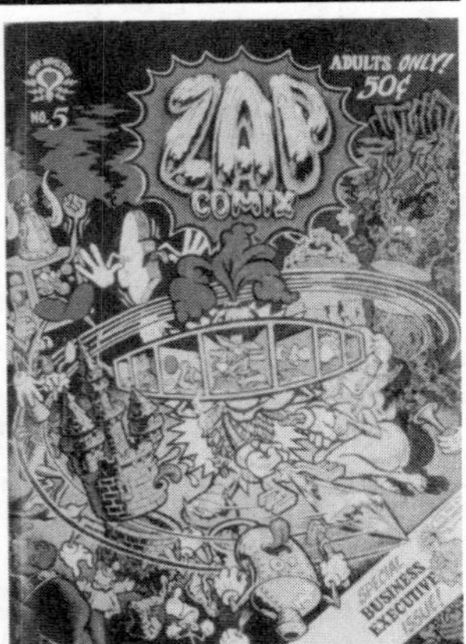

Zap #5 © Apex Novelties

THRILLING MURDER COMICS

San Francisco Comic Book Co., 1971

1 SCW,KDe,RCr,SRo,Jim Arlington,editor 24.50

2 (TWO)

Keith Green Feb., 1975

1 SCW 7.00

VAMPIRELLA

Randy Crawford June, 1978

1 Sex Funnies 3.50

VAUGHN BODE THE PORTFOLIO

Northern Comfort Com. 1976

1 VB,16pgs 125.00

VAUGHN BODE PORTFOLIO #1

Vaughn Bode Productions 1978

1 VB,10 pgs 35.00

VAUGHN BODE'S CHEECH WIZARD, THE COLLECTED ADVENTURES OF THE CARTOON MESSIAH

Northern Comfort Com. 1976

1 VB,88pgs 55.00

VAUGHN BODE'S DEADBONE, THE FIRST TESTAMENT OF CHEECH WIZARD

Northern Comfort Com. 1975

1 VB 65.00

VIETNAM

N# 20pgs. Role of Blacks in the War,TG Lewis 125.00

WEIRDO

Last Gasp Eco-Funnies March, 1981

1 thru 3 RCr. . . . . @10.00

WEIRDO, THE

Rodney Schroeter Oct., 1977

1 B:Rodney Schroezer,1pg 4.50
2 88pgs 4.50
3 44pgs 4.50

WIMMEN'S COMIX

Last Gasp Eco-Funnies Nov., 1972

1 All women artists&comix 10.75
2 thru 3 same . . . . @10.00
4 thru 7 same . . . . @6.75

WONDER WART-HOG AND THE NURDS OF NOVEMBER

Rip Off Press Sept., 1980

1 GiS 15.00

WONDER WART-HOG, CAPTAIN CRUD & OTHER SUPER STUFF

Fawcett Publications 1967

1 GiS,VB 22.00

YELLOW DOG

The Print Mint May, 1968

1 4pgs,RCr 30.00
2 and 3 8pgs,RCr. . . . . @25.00
4 8pgs,RCr,SCW 25.00
5 8pgs,RCr,SCW,KDe 25.00
6 thru 12 . . . . @25.00
13/14 52pgs RCr,Jay Lynch 12.00
15 Don Scheneker,editor 59.00
16. . . . . 55.00
17 thru 24 . . . . @15.00

YOUNG AND LUSTLESS

San Francisco Comic Book Co., 1972

1 BG 15.50

YOUNG LUST

Company & Sons Oct., 1970

1 BG,ASp 27.00
2 BG 15.00
3 BG,JsG,RCr,ASp 12.00
4 KDe,BG,SRo 10.50
5 BG,SRo 7.50
6 SRo,KDe 5.50

YOW

Last Gasp April, 1978

1 BG 5.75
2 BG 4.75
Becomes:

ZIPPY

3 BG 6.50

ZAP COMIX

Apex Novelties Oct., 1967

0 RCr 335.00
1 RCr 325.00
2 RCr,SCW 100.00
3 RCr,SCW,VMo,SRo 55.00
4 VMo,RW,RCr,SCW.SRo,GiS . . . 55.00
5 RW,GiS,RCr,SCW,SRo. 50.00
6 RW,GiS,RCr,SCW,SRo. 25.00
7 RW,GiS,RCr,SCW,SRo. 18.50
8 RW,GiS,RCr,SCW,SRo. 10.00
9 RW,GiS,RCr,SCW,SRo. 12.00

BIBLIOGRAPHY

Daniels, Les. *Comix: A History of Comic Books in America.* New York, NY: Bonanza Books, 1971.

Gerber, Ernst. *The Photo Joumal Guide to Comic Books.* Minden, NV: Gerber Publishing, 1989. Vols. 1 & 2.

Gerber, Ernst. *The Photo Joumal Guide to Marvel Comics.* Minden, NV: Gerber Publishing, 1991. Vols. 3 & 4.

Goulart, Ron. *The Adventurous Decade.* New Rochelle, NY: Arlington House, 1975.

Goulart, Ron. *Comic Book Culture, An Illustrated History.* Portland, OR: Collectors Press, 2000.

Goulart, Ron. *The Encyclopedia of American Comics.* New York, NY: Facts on File Publications, 1990.

Goulart, Ron. *Over 50 Years of American Comic Books.* Lincolnwood, IL: Mallard Press, 1991.

Hegenburger, John. *Collectors Guide to Comic Books.* Radnor, PA: Wallace Homestead Book Company, 1990.

Kennedy, Jay. *The Official Underground and Newave Price Guide.* Cambridge, MA: Boatner Norton Press, 1982.

Malan, Dan. *The Complete Guide to Classics Collectibles.* St. Louis, MO: Malan Classical Enterprises, 1991.

O'Neil, Dennis. *Secret Origins of DC Super Heroes.* New York, NY: Warner Books, 1976.

Overstreet, Robert. *The Overstreet Comic Book Price Guide (28th Edition).* New York, NY: Avon Books, 1998.

Rovin, Jeff. *The Encyclopedia of Super Heroes.* New York, NY: Facts on File Publications, 1985.

Rovin, Jeff. *The Encyclopedia of Super Villains.* New York, NY: Facts on File Publications, 1987.

Thompson, Don & Maggie. The *Golden Age of Comics, Summer 1982.* Tampa, FL: New Media Publishing, 1982.

CVA GRADING GUIDE

Grading comics is an objective art. This grading guide outlines the many conditions you should look for when purchasing comics, from the highest grade and top condition to the lowest collectible grade and condition. Your own comics will fall into one of these categories. A more complete description and our comments on comics grades can be found inside. We would like to point out, however, that no reader or advertiser is required to follow this or any other standard. All prices in Comics Values Annual are for comics in Near Mint condition. Happy collecting!

Mint: Perfect, pristine, devoid of any trace of wear or printing or handling flaws. Covers must be fully lustrous with sharply pointed corners. No color fading. Must be well centered. Many "rack" comics are not "Mint" even when new.

Near Mint: Almost perfect with virtually no wear. No significant printing flaws. Covers must be essentially lustrous with sharp corners. Spine is a tight as new. In older comics, minimal color fading is acceptable, as is slight aging of the paper. Most price guides, including CVA, quote prices in this grade.

Very Fine: Well preserved, still pleasing in appearance. Small signs of wear, most particularly around the staples. Most luster is readily visible. Corners may no longer be sharp, but are not rounded. Typical of a comic read only a few times and then properly stored.

Fine: Clean, presentable, with noticeable signs of wear. Some white may show through enamel around staples, and moderate rounding of corners. No tape or writing damage. Book still lies flat.

Very Good: A well worn reading copy with some minor damage such as creasing, small tears or cover flaking. Some discoloration may be evident, with obvious wear around the staples. Little luster remains, and some rolling of the spine may be seen when comic is laid flat on the table.

Good: A fully intact comic with very heavy wear. Tears, cover creases and flaking, and rolled spine will all be evident. No tape repairs present. Only very scarce or valuable issues are collected in this state.

The adjoining price table shows the prices for the other collectible grades which correspond to any "near mint" price given in this book.

Mint	Near Mint	Very Fine	Fine	Very Good
$6,000	**$5,000**	$3,500	$2,000	$1,000
4,800	**4,000**	2,800	1,600	800
3,600	**3,000**	2,100	1,200	600
2,400	**2,000**	1,400	800	400
1,800	**1,500**	1,050	600	300
1,200	**1,000**	700	400	200
1,080	**900**	630	360	180
960	**800**	560	320	160
900	**750**	525	300	150
840	**700**	490	280	140
780	**650**	455	260	130
720	**600**	420	240	120
660	**550**	385	220	110
600	**500**	350	200	100
570	**475**	332	190	95
540	**450**	315	180	90
510	**425**	297	170	85
480	**400**	280	160	80
450	**375**	262	150	75
420	**350**	245	140	70
390	**325**	227	130	65
360	**300**	210	120	60
330	**275**	192	110	55
300	**250**	175	100	50
270	**225**	157	90	45
240	**200**	140	80	40
210	**175**	122	70	35
180	**150**	105	60	30
150	**125**	87	50	25
120	**100**	70	40	20
114	**95**	66	38	19
108	**90**	63	36	18
102	**85**	59	32	17
96	**80**	56	32	16
90	**75**	52	30	15
84	**70**	49	28	14
78	**65**	45	26	13
72	**60**	42	24	12
66	**55**	38	22	11
60	**50**	35	2	10
54	**45**	31	18	9
48	**40**	28	16	8
42	**35**	24	14	7
36	**30**	21	12	6
30	**25**	17	10	5
24	**20**	14	8	4
22	**18**	12	7	4
21	**17**	11	7	4
18	**15**	10	6	3
17	**14**	9	5	3
16	**13**	9	5	3
15	**12**	8	5	2
14	**11**	7	4	2
12	**10**	7	4	2
11	**9**	6	4	2
10	**8**	5	3	1
9	**7**	5	3	1
7	**6**	4	3	1
6	**5**	4	2	1
5	**4**	3	2	0
4	**3**	2	1	0
3	**2**	2	0	0
2	**1**	0	0	0